Proceedings of the Eighteenth Annual Conference of the Cognitive Science Society

Edited by Garrison W. Cottrell

July 12-15, 1996
University of California, San Diego

Routledge
Taylor & Francis Group

LONDON AND NEW YORK

First published 1996 by Lawrence Erlbaum Associates

Published 2018 by Routledge
2 Park Square, Milton Park, Abingdon, Oxon OX14 4RN
52 Vanderbilt Avenue, New York, NY 10017

Fisrt issued in hardback 2018

Routledge is an imprint of the Taylor & Francis Group, an informa business

Cover art and conference logo by Dan Gruen. Layout by David Noelle.

ISSN 1047-1316
ISBN 13: 978-1-138-87663-7 (hbk)
ISBN 13: 978-0-8058-2541-1 (pbk)

MIX
Paper from responsible sources
FSC
www.fsc.org   FSC™ C013985

Printed in the United Kingdom
by Henry Ling Limited

Table of Contents

The Eighteenth Annual Conference of the
Cognitive Science Society
University of California, San Diego
La Jolla, California
July 12-15, 1996

PAPER PRESENTATIONS

Philosophy

Text Comprehension

Reasoning

Distributed Cognition and Education

Development I

Visual/Spatial Reasoning

Semantics, Phonology, and the Lexicon

Perception

Lexical Ambiguity and Semantic Representation

Problem-Solving and Education

Recurrent Network Models

Cognitive Neuroscience

The Perception of Causality

Categories, Concepts, and Mutability

POSTERS

SOCIETY MEMBER ABSTRACTS

AUTHOR INDEX

Eighteenth Annual Conference of the Cognitive Science Society

Conference Co-Chairs

Edwin Hutchins   Walter Savitch

Program Chair

Garrison W. Cottrell

Local Arrangements Chair

John Batali

Administrative Coordinator: Nancy Santos
Proceedings Coordinator: Marie Kreider
Web Master: David Noelle
Automated Review Processing: Chris Vogt

Officers of the Cognitive Science Society

Paul Smolensky (Chair)	1992-1998
Wendy Lehnert	1990-1996
Philip Johnson-Laird	1990-1996
Janet Kolodner	1991-1997
Kurt VanLehn	1991-1997
Keith Holyoak	1992-1998
Michelene Chi	1993-1999
Gary M. Olson	1993-1999
Colleen Seifert	1994-2000
Jeffrey Elman	1994-2000

Ex-Officio Board Members

James Greeno, Editor of *Cognitive Science*	1995-
Alan Lesgold, Secretary/Treasurer	1988-1997

This conference was supported in part by funds from the UCSD Cognitive Science Department, Computer Science and Engineering Department, the Deans of Social Sciences and Arts and Humanities, and the Vice Chancellor of Academic Affairs. MIT Press contributed to the Reception for the PDP book anniversary.

Electronic Index Information

We have endeavored to make this proceedings volume as easy to use as possible. Papers have been loosely grouped by topic, and an author index is provided in the back. In hopes of facilitating searches of this work, we have also provided an electronic index on the Internet's World Wide Web (WWW). Titles, authors, and summaries of all of the papers published here have been placed in an online database which may be freely searched by anyone. To access this electronic index, direct your favorite WWW browser to open the following URL:

```
http://www.cse.ucsd.edu/events/cogsci96/proceedings/
```

This WWW site includes a complete description of how to search the paper database.

If you are not familiar with the World Wide Web, we encourage you to learn more about this easy to use and free information resource. WWW browsers present information distributed over the Internet in a simple hypertext-like point-and-click manner. Many books have recently become available on using the WWW. Programs which allow you to browse the WWW are widely available, and many cost nothing at all. Some of the more popular browsers include *Netscape*, *Mosaic*, and (for machines with limited graphics capabilities) *Lynx*. These browsers run on a wide variety of hardware platforms, including Unix machines, VMS machines, Apple Macintoshes, NeXT boxes, and IBM PCs. Free browser software may be found at a variety of FTP sites, including:

```
Netscape  –  ftp20.netscape.com
Mosaic    –  ftp.ncsa.uiuc.edu
Lynx      –  ukanaix.cc.ukans.edu
```

If you have questions concerning accessing the conference electronic index, please send electronic mail to "`cogsci96@cs.ucsd.edu`".

Preface

As I sit here composing this, it is May 3, 1996, and I have to pretend the conference is over, and put everything in the past tense. This leads to such turgid prose as: "The Eighteenth Annual Meeting of the Cognitive Science Society was held July 12-15, 1996 at the University of California at San Diego, which turns out to be in La Jolla. The conference featured four plenary sessions, the first one being possibly the start of a trend: A debate-style format pitting Stephen Crain against Mark Seidenberg discussing 'Controversies in Cognitive Science: The case of language'. We also celebrated the tenth anniversary of the publication of the Parallel Distributed Processing books with talks by David Rumelhart, Jay McClelland, and Geoff Hinton. Adele Diamond brought us down to earth with real data about real kids with frontal lobe damage. Paul Churchland discussed how we could be materialists and still think about consciousness. The technical program consisted of research presentations that were rigorously reviewed with respect to originality, quality, significance of research, relevance to a broad audience of cognitive science researchers, and clarity of presentation. Of the 250 paper submissions received, 73 were accepted for presentation in technical sessions and an additional 41 were accepted for poster presentation. All 114 of these are published in the conference proceedings. In addition, as a new feature this year, we accepted one page abstracts from Society members for poster presentation. These appear at the end of the Proceedings. This proved to be a popular option, with 149 abstracts being submitted. The technical sessions covered a wide range of topics, including:

Analogy	Problem-Solving and Education
Categories, Concepts, and Mutability	Reasoning
Cognitive Neuroscience	Recurrent Network Models
Development	Rhythm in Cognition
Distributed Cognition and Education	Semantics, Phonology, and the Lexicon
Lexical Ambiguity and Semantic Representation	Skill Learning and SOAR
Perception	Text Comprehension
The Perception of Causality	Visual/Spatial Reasoning
Philosophy	

The conference also featured four invited and six submitted Symposia:

- Adaptive Behavior and Learning in Complex Environments

- Building a Theory of Problem Solving and Scientific Discovery: How Big is N in N-Space Search?

- Cognitive Linguistics: Mappings in Grammar, Conceptual Systems, and On-Line Meaning Construction

- Computational Models of Development

- Evolution of Language

- Evolution of Mind

- Eye Movements in Cognitive Science

- The Future Of Modularity

- The Role of Rhythm in Cognition

- Update on the Plumbing of Cognition: Brain Imaging Studies of Vision, Attention, and Language

We thank the organizers of these symposia for their efforts in putting together these events. Symposia abstracts and abstracts of the presentations appear in the proceedings.

We are deeply indebted to the authors of all submitted papers for their contribution to the conference, and to the reviewers for their painstaking and constructive reviews of these papers. We would like to thank the Program Committee for their assignments of reviewers to papers under a tight deadline. Helpful suggestions and encouragement regarding the conference format and content were provided by the Society's new Conference

Advisory Board: Jeff Elman, Colleen Seifert and Paul Smolensky. We also wish to thank the members of the Marr Prize committee for their efforts in picking the best student paper from the top 9 student papers, listed below.[1]

We also wish to thank Robert C. Dynes, Senior Vice Chancellor for Academic Affairs, Frantisek Deak, Dean of Arts & Humanities, Paul W. Drake, Dean of Social Sciences, the Cognitive Science and Computer Science and Engineering Departments for their contributions to the conference. Also, we would like to thank Harry and Betty Stanton of MIT Press for their contribution to the reception for the tenth anniversary celebration of the publication of the PDP books.

Finally, it would not have been possible to run this conference without the just-in-time efforts of a large number of volunteers and staff. Thanks for the envelope-stuffing services of Dan Clouse, George Marnellos, Jeanne Milostan, Curt Padgett, and Dimitris Tsioutsias. This proceedings was made possible largely by the efforts of three people: Marie Kreider for her steadfastness in the face of mounting piles of FedEx's, David Noelle for design and organization of the web services, the formatting templates, and last minute formatting of recalcitrant author's abstracts, and Chris Vogt, who learned more than he ever wanted to know about running a conference and programming in Perl, all for the simple mistake of not being a cognitive scientist, when the rest of the Geurons were busy writing their papers. Nancy Santos was instrumental in obtaining funds from the UCSD administration to support the conference, provided much-needed logistical expertise, and coordinated local arrangements; Brian Hazlehurst ably cut deals with the Airlines and the local hotels for our participants; and Mary Hare has organized much of the refreshments and the lovely banquet."

I just can't write prose like that, so instead, I just want to share my excitement at the fact that since I have *some* say in the matter this year, the Unofficial Annual After-Banquet-Dance party, a Cog Sci tradition since 1983, will be *Official* this year! The *Official Blues party*, open to all registrants, promises memorable events such as we have seen in the past: Geoff Hinton betting someone he would eat a cockroach if only one could be found, leading to a mad (unsuccessful) scramble (Ann Arbor, 1989); Zenon Pylyshyn dancing wildly to the Blues (Amherst, 1986); and at the very first one (Rochester, 1983) in my apartment, a whole troop of CMU graduate students singing in unison with Lou Reed, "some people like to go out dancing, other people like us they gotta work...", and then Elvis Costello, "I wanna bite the hand that feeds me, I want bite that hand so badly, I wanna make them wish they never knew me...". I hope that the toils and troubles of graduate school and research will again be exorcised, and a good time will be had by all.

Garrison W. Cottrell
Program Chair

Edwin Hutchins   Walter Savitch
Conference Co-Chairs

Program Committee:

Farrell Ackerman (Linguistics)	Catherine Harris (Psychology)	Kim Plunkett (Psychology)
Tom Albright (Neuroscience)	Ron Langacker (Linguistics)	Martin Sereno (Neuroscience)
Patricia Churchland (Philosophy)	Pat Langley (Computer Science)	Mark St. John (Psychology)
Roy D'Andrade (Anthropology)	Risto Miikkulainen (Computer Science)	Tim van Gelder (Philosophy)
Charles Elkan (Computer Science)	Doug Medin (Psychology)	

Local Arrangements Committee
John Batali (Chair)
Mary Hare
Brian Hazlehurst

net.slaves
David Noelle (Webmaster)
Chris Vogt (Ace Review Parser)
Logo Design: Dan Gruen

---

[1]See, they haven't *really* picked the winner yet, but I have to *pretend* they did.

Marr Prize Committee

Chris Barker
Marlene Behrmann
Charles Elkan
Jeff Elman
Keith Holyoak

Top Nine Student Papers: (alphabetic by first author)

Reviewers

Agnar Aamodt
Farrell Ackerman
Kevin Ashley
Oliva Aude
Timothy Bailey
Chris Barker
Jon Barwise
Miriam Bassok
John Batali
Dorrit Billman
Alan Blair
Phil Blythe
Paul Brna
Andrew Brook
Bruce Burns
Mark Burstein
Ruth Byrne
Tamitha Carpenter
Richard Catrambone
Ramin Charles Nakisa
Nick Chater
Patricia Cheng
Axel Cleeremans
Catherine Clement
Richard Cooper
Gary Cottrell
Richard Cox
Sharon Derry
Eric Dietrich
Charles Dolan
Eric Domeshek
Keith Downing
Renee Elio
Charles Elkan
Jeff Elman
Randi Engle
Julie Epelboim
Nick Flor
Peter Foltz
Ken Forbus
Michael Freed
Robert French
Klaus-Peter Gapp
Gareth Gaskell
Jean Mark Gawron
Jack Gelfand
Dedre Gentner
Fernand Gobet
Ashok Goel
Art Graesser
Barbara Graves
Bill Grundy
Steve Haase
Robert Hadley
Andrea Haessly
Graeme Halford
Catherine Harris

Thomas Haynes
Evan Heit
Barbara Hemforth
Ralph Hertwig
Martin Heydemann
Stephen Hirtle
Cindy Hmelo
Keith Holyoak
Matthew Isaak
Todd Johnson
Randolph Jones
Mark Keane
Smadar Kedar
Cheongtag Kim
David Kirsh
Markus Knauff
John Kolen
Janet Kolodner
John Kruschke
Paul Kube
Jorge Larreamendy-Joerns
David Leake
Adrienne Lee
Jill Fain Lehman
Mihaly Lenart
Alan Lesgold
Joe Levy
Michael Lewis
Vincenzo Lombardo
Bradley Love
Steve Lytinen
Paul Maglio
Kavi Mahesh
Virginia Marchman
Denis Mareschal
Art Markman
W. D. Marslen-Wilson
Joel Martin
Marshall Mayberry
Douglas Medin
Joseph Melcher
Arthur Merin
Craig Miller
Vibhu Mittal
Clayton Morrison
Martin Moser
Hiroshi Motoda
Paul Munro
N. Hari Narayanan
Valeriy Nenov
Tim Norman
Randall O'Reilly
Stellan Ohlsson
Clark Ohnesorge
Takeshi Okada
Tom Ormerod
Ana Pasztor

Andrea Patalano
T. Pattabhiraman
Michael Pazzani
Francis Jeffry Pelletier
Yusuf Pisan
David Plaut
Rolf Ploetzner
Kim Plunkett
Ian Pratt
Ashwin Ram
William Rapaport
Mimi Recker
Robert Rist
Lawrence Roberts
Douglas Rohde
Jenny Saffran
Christian Schunn
Baruch Schwarz
Donia Scott
Julie Sedivy
Sandip Sen
Tom Shultz
Marin Simina
Tony Simon
Steven Sloman
Michael Spivey-Knowlton
Keith Stenning
Suzanne Stevenson
Gerhard Strube
Dan Suthers
Hiroaki Suzuki
Katia Sycara
Whitney Tabor
Michael Tanenhaus
Sheldon Tetewsky
Richmond Thomason
Ryan Tweney
Tim van Gelder
Maarten van Someren
Tony Veale
Shaun Vecera
Alonso Vera
Charles Wharton
Janet Wiles
Margaret Winters
David Wolf
Aaron Yarlas
Jiajie Zhang
Ingrid Zukerman

Plenary Addresses

Controversies in Cognitive Science: The Case of Language
Stephen Crain & Mark Seidenberg

Tenth Anniversary of the PDP Books:

Affect and Neuro-modulators: A Connectionist Account
David E. Rumelhart

Parallel-distributed processing models of normal and disordered cognition
James L. McClelland

Why neural networks need generative models
Geoffrey E. Hinton

Frontal Lobe Development and Dysfunction in Children: Dissociations between Intention and Action
Adele Diamond

Reconstructing Consciousness
Paul Churchland

Invited Symposia

Imaging Studies of Vision, Attention and Language

Helen J. Neville
Department of Psychology
1227 University of Oregon
Eugene, OR 97403-1227
neville@oregon.uoregon.edu

Dr. Marty Sereno
Department of Cognitive Science 0515
University of California-San Diego
9500 Gilman Drive
La Jolla, CA 92093

Visual Cortical Areas in Humans

Over half of the total area of neocortex in non-human primates is occupied by visual areas. Over 25 visual areas beyond primary visual cortex (V1) have been identified in non-human primates using invasive techniques. Recent advances in fMRI, EEG, MEG, stimulus paradigms, and cortical surface reconstruction have finally made it possible to outline the borders of a number of these functionally distinct areas along the complexly folded cortical mantle of humans. These imaging studies are first reviewed. The implications of these studies for how higher level functions (like language comprehension) are implemented in the human cerebral cortex are then explored.

Dr. Steven Hillyard
Department of Cognitive Science 0515
University of California-San Diego
9500 Gilman Drive
La Jolla, CA 92093

Neuroimaging Studies of Attention in Humans

Event-related brain potentials (ERPs) are recorded from the scalp of subjects performing selective attention tasks. By comparing the waveforms and scalp distributions of ERPs elicited by attended and unattended stimuli, inferences can be made about the timing and anatomical localization of stimulus selection processes in the sensory pathways. Topographical mapping of ERPs and associated magnetic (MEG) fields have revealed specific sites of attentional control in extrastriate visual cortex and in supratemporal auditory cortex. These ERP and MEG findings are reinforced by complementary studies of cerebral blood flow patterns during attention
as revealed by positron emission tomography. The implications of these physiological data for psychological theories of attention will be discussed.

Dr. Helen Neville
Department of Psychology
1227 University of Oregon
Eugene, OR 97403-1227

Neuroimaging Studies of Developmental Plasticity Within the Visual and Language Systems of the Human Brain

I will review (a) our ERP and fMRI results during visual processing and language processing from adults who have had different early sensory and/or language experience and (b) ERP results from normally developing infants and children. Taken together these studies suggest that within vision and within language different neural systems display considerable variability in the degree to which they are modified by early experience. Within vision, early auditory deprivation has most marked effects on the organization of systems important in processing motion information. The results raise the hypothesis that the dorsal visual system displays greater developmental plasticity than does the ventral visual pathway. In addition, different subsystems within language display varying degrees of modifiability by experience. The acquisition of lexical semantics appears relatively robust and invariant even in individuals with markedly different timing and modality of language input. By contrast, systems active during grammatical processing display marked effects of alterations in the timing and nature of early language input. These results converge with other lines of evidence that suggest it is important to distinguish these different aspects of language, and they raise hypotheses about the initial development of these different language systems. Different accounts for these differential effects of early experience on subsystems within vision and language will be discussed.

Learning in Complex Environments: Biological and Artificial Adaptive Behavior

Maja J Mataric̀
Volen Center for Complex Systems
Computer Science Department
Brandeis University
Waltham, MA 02254
`maja@cs.brandeis.edu`

In the last decade, the problems being treated in Artificial Intelligence and Robotics have witnessed an increase in complexity as the domains under investigation have transitioned from theoretically clean scenarios to more complex dynamic environments. Agents that must adapt in environments such as the physical world, a factory floor, an active ecology or economy, and the World Wide Web, challenge traditional assumptions and approaches to learning. As a consequence, novel methods for automated adaptation, action selection, and new behavior acquisition have become the focus of much research in the field.

This workshop will focus on situated agent learning in challenging environments that feature noise, uncertainty, and complex dynamics. In all cases we will consider, learning and adaptation occurs during the lifetime of a complete agent situated in a dynamic environment, and must deal with many the following challenges:

- learning from ambiguous perceptual inputs

- learning with noisy/uncertain action/motor outputs

- learning from sparse, irregular, inconsistent, and noisy reinforcement/feedback

- learning in real time

- combining built-in and learned knowledge

- learning in complex environments requiring generalization in state representation

- learning from incremental and delayed feedback

- learning in smoothly or discontinuously changing environments

The goal of this workshop is to bring together four researchers dealing with just those problems. The four speakers of the workshop are Simon Giszter, Maja Mataric̀, Andrew Moore, and Sebastian Thrun. Each has experience with different aspects of adaptive behavior and learning, and will each present their work and insights. All will share a common thread of dealing with complex adaptive agents and domains, but each will introduce a different methodology to dealing with the many challenges of learning and adaptive behavior in complex environments.

- **Simon Giszter** will give a biological perspective, overviewing the complex mechanisms involved in biological motor control and learning.

- **Maja Mataric̀** will overview the issues involved in learning in a complex, multi-robot domain, and present the results of applying a behavior-based approach to control and learning in that domain.

- **Andrew Moore** will describe the issues involved in applying integrated reinforcement learning to a complex factory domain.

- **Sebastian Thrun** will present a framework for life-long learning, an approach to reusing knowledge from what the agent has previously learned.

Primitives as a basis for movement synthesis

Simon F. Giszter

Department of Neurobiology & Anatomy
Medical College of Pennsylvania and Hahnemann University
Philadelphia PA 19129
simon@swampthing.medcolpa.edu

Abstract

Recent data from spinal frogs and mammals suggests that movements may be constructed from a standard set of primitives which represent postures and force patterns around postures. These postural primitives may be combined for movement synthesis and may also interact non-linearly. New data shows that the set of primitives may also contain of a collection of members which encapsulate aspects of movement control and dynamics. The linear interactions, non-linear interactions, and dynamic controls provide a means of bootstrapping motor learning. The non-linear interactions enable a basic pattern generator and a reflex functionality which can be parameterized and modified for elaboration of more complex behaviors.

Postural Primitives

Initial evidence for postural primitives has been obtained in frogs by microstimulation of spinal cord and examination of reflex spinal mechanisms (Bizzi et al. 1991, Giszter et al. 1993). A few types of force-fields were found represented in the frog spinal cord. More recently Tresch and Bizzi (1995) have extended this to the rat spinal cord. The conservation of these organizations through tetrapod phylogeny suggests an important role in the organization of movement. It seems clear that the postural primitives represent elements of reflexes. Microstimulation also showed that the different force-fields represented by primitives could be combined as vector sums. The important role of such a mechanism in movement synthesis was suggested by a theoretical analysis by Mussa-Ivaldi (1992), and simulations of Mussa-Ivaldi and Giszter (1992) which showed arbitrary force-fields could be synthesised by appropriate combination of conservative and circulating basis fields. This analysis suggested that the few primitives obtained in the frog spinal cord could form a substantial underpinning of a large and extensible repertoire of behaviors.

Convergent force-fields and Parallel force-fields

Convergent force-fields and parallel force-fields were observed in the set of primitives located in frog spinal cord but circulating basis fields were absent. It has been pointed out by Hogan, Colgate and others that non-conservative force-fields may cause instability when coupled to some environments. Their work suggests that conservative or parallel fields of the frog will guarantee limb stability in passive environments. The use of such fields for cyclic limit cycle limb motions as for example in swimming, crawling, or human locomotion or bicycling must entail sequencing and dynamic activation of these conservative fields and may use intrinsic dynamics of primitives.

Dynamic controls

We have examined the dynamics of interaction of the primitives with different environments and their control and timing in reflex behaviors. Results remain consistent with the idea of primitive as a basis for movement synthesis but extend the idea beyond static controls.

Reflex synthesis

The reflex behaviors utilize all aspects of primitives including non-linear interactions. In fact the non-linear roles may be essential for synthesis of reflexes. Dynamic pattern generating models based around the models of Maes (1991) for action synthesis and selection can be used to replicate several phenomena of reflex behaviors (Giszter, 1994). The primitives in reflexes and the sequence generating mechanisms utilizing them must be appropriately subsumed by any higher level controls and learning. The models using Maes nets demonstrate the importance of exclusion, and flexible dynamic chaining in flexible adapted reflex responses.

General movement

The scheme suggested by the neurophysiological data and analysis and simulation has ties to both robotic subsumption architectures and basis function approximation. In this scheme a layer of circuitry that represents primitives and encapsulates force-field structure, force-field dynamics and environmental interaction, is played upon both by pattern generator systems and descending controls. These two systems must cooperate through vector summation of primitives and arbitration of access to primitives in order to generate useful purposive movement. Motor learning is likely to involve cooperative learning and adaptation in primitives, generators and higher order controls. The organization of a system based around situated primitives guarantees an adapted initial functionality which may form an important bootstrap for motor learning. This initial functionality is likely to be extensible at each level of organization.

References

Bizzi, E., Mussa-Ivaldi F.A. and Giszter S.F.. (1990). Computations underlying the execution of movement: A biological perspective. *Science* 253:(pp. 287–291).

Colgate E., and Hogan N. (1989) An analysis of contact instability in terms of passive physical equivalents. *IEEE Proc Int Conf Robot Automat* (pp. 404–409).

Giszter S.F., Mussa-Ivaldi F.A. and Bizzi, E.. (1993). Convergent Force-fields organized in the frog's spinal cord. *J. Neurosci* 13(2):(pp. 467–491).

Giszter S.F.(1994). Reinforcement tuning of action synthesis and selection in a virtual frog. In From animals to animats 3: Proc. Third Int'l Conf on Simulation of Adaptive Behavior (pp. 291–301).

Maes P. (1991). Situated agents can have goals. In *Designing Autonomous Agents ed. Maes* (pp. 49–70).

Mussa Ivaldi FA. (1992). From basis functions to basis fields: Using vector primitives to capture vector patterns. *Biol. Cybernetics* 67 (pp.479–489).

Mussa Ivaldi FA. and Giszter S.F. (1992).Vector field approximation: a computational paradigm for motor control and learning. *Biol. Cybernetics* 67 (pp.491–500).

Tresch M. and Bizzi E. (1995). Convergent force-fields in the rat spinal cord. *Soc Neurosci Abstr* 21: Abstr 274.6 (p. 682).

Learning in Multi-Robot Systems

Maja J Matarić

Volen Center for Complex Systems
Computer Science Department
Brandeis University
Waltham, MA 02254
`maja@cs.brandeis.edu`

Learning in Situated Domains

Introduction

Reinforcement learning (RL) has been successfully applied to a variety of domains, and has recently been attempted on situated agents such as mobile robots. While simulation results are encouraging, work on physical robots has been slow to repeated that success. The key challenges of situated domains include: 1) modeling a combination of discrete and continuous state spaces based on multimodal perceptual inputs; 2) modeling real-world events that may neither be caused directly by the agents nor perceived by it, but subsequently affect its behavior; 3) the number of learning trials reasonably available to an agent and the non-uniform exploration of the learning space mandated by the agent's external environment; 4) dealing with multiple concurrent and sequential goals; 5) modeling a combination of discrete and continuous, immediate and delayed, multimodal feedback that may be available to the agent.

Designing Reward Functions

Rather than encode knowledge explicitly, RL methods hide it in the reinforcement function which often employs some *ad hoc* embedding of the domain semantics. One more direct way to utilize implicit domain knowledge is to convert reward functions into error signals, akin to those used in learning control. Immediate reinforcement in RL is a weak version of error signals, using only the sign of the error but not the magnitude. Intermittent reinforcement can be used similarly, by weighting the reward according to the accomplished progress.

We suggest that such reinforcement can be introduced 1) by reinforcing multiple goals, and 2) by using progress estimators. Since situated agents have multiple goals, it is straightforward to reinforce each one individually, with a *heterogeneous reinforcement function*, rather than to attempt to collapse them into a monolithic goal function. However, multiple goals are not sufficient for speeding up situated learning if each of them involves a complex sequence of actions. Such time-delayed goals are aided by progress metrics along the way, in addition to reinforcement upon achievement. We propose *progress estimators*, functions which provide positive or negative

Figure 1: R2 robots used to learn foraging.

reinforcement based on immediate measurable progress relative to specific goals. These "partial internal critics" serve a number of important functions in noisy worlds: they decrease the learner's sensitivity to intermittent errors, they encourage exploration and minimize thrashing, and they decrease the probability of fortuitous rewards for inappropriate behavior that happened, by chance, to achieve the desired goal. For a detailed discussion please see Matarić (1994).

Figure 2: Genghis-II six-legged robots used to learn box-pushing.

Experimental Design

Both of our learning experiments were conducted on fully autonomous mobile robots on-board power, sensing, and computation. The first set of experiments was done with 4 IS Robotics R2 robots equipped with bump and infra-red sensors for detecting collisions and contacts, radio transceivers for positioning, communication, and data gathering, and situated on a differentially steerable wheeled base equipped with a gripper (Figure 1). The second set of experiments was done on 2 IS Robotics Genghis II robots, equipped with two whisker contact sensors, an array of 5 pyro-electric sensor for detecting the location of the goal (the light), and using six-legged alternating tripod gate for propulsion (Figure 2). All of the robots were programmed in the Behavior Language and were controlled by collections of parallel, concurrently active behaviors that gather sensory information, drive effectors, monitor progress, and contribute reinforcement.

The Learning Tasks

The first learning task consisted of finding a mapping between conditions and behaviors into an efficient policy for group foraging. Foraging was chosen because it is a nontrivial and biologically inspired task, and because our previous group behavior work (Matarić 1992) provided the basis behavior repertoire from which to learn behavior selection, consisting of *avoiding, dispersing, searching, homing,* and *resting.* Utility behaviors for grasping and dropping were hard-wired as were their conditions. By considering only the space of conditions necessary and sufficient for triggering the above behaviors, the agents' learning space was reduced to the power set of the following state variables: *have-puck?, at-home?, near-intruder?,* and *night-time?.* The reduced foraging task should, in theory, be easily learnable. In practice, however, quick and uniform exploration is not possible in the noisy multi-agent domain.

The second learning task consisted of finding a policy for each of the robots to cooperatively push a long box to the goal. Unlike the foraging task, box-pushing required careful coordination between the agents, in turn requiring either accurate sensing, or communication, or both. The task is designed so that a single-agent solution, due to the size and shape of the box, is much less efficient than an effective two-agent solution, but the two-agent solution requires intricate cooperation or the box is pushed in the wrong direction or out of reach of one of the robots. The task was decomposed into basic behaviors: *pushing, pausing, turning.* The task required that each agent learn not only its own strategy for keeping the box within reach and moving toward the goal, but also the right behaviors in response to the other agent, as sensed through the state of the box and as communicated between the agents. The details of the experiments and the data are described in Simsarian & Matarić (1995).

Learning Results

The reinforcement learning algorithms we used summed all of the multimodal reinforcement over time. Behaviors were switched based on external events, as well as inputs from internal progress estimators. Reinforcement was based on a collection of internal functions that monitored external events and internal progress estimators. Learning was continuous and incremental over the lifetime of the agent.

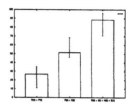

Figure 3: The performance of the three reinforcement strategies on learning to forage. The x-axis shows the three reinforcement strategies. The y-axis maps the percent of the correct policy the agents learned, averaged over twenty trials.

Both learning experiments were evaluated first by comparing the system performance to the control hard-wired behavior for foraging and for box-pushing. Second, the foraging learning performance was also compared to two alternative approaches, one using only multimodal reinforcement but no progress estimators, and the other using traditional Q-learning with positive reinforcement when a puck was dropped in the home region (Figure 3).

Summary

The goal of this work has been to bring to light some of the important properties of situated domains, and their impact on the existing reinforcement learning strategies. We have argued that the noisy and inconsistent properties of complex worlds require the use of domain knowledge. We proposed a principled approach to embedding such knowledge into the reinforcement based on utilizing heterogeneous reward functions and goal-specific progress estimators. We believe that these strategies take advantage of the information readily available to situated agents, make learning possible in complex dynamic worlds, and accelerate it in any domain.

References

Matarić, M. J. (1992), Designing Emergent Behaviors: From Local Interactions to Collective Intelligence, *in* J.-A. Meyer, H. Roitblat & S. Wilson, eds, 'From Animals to Animats: International Conference on Simulation of Adaptive Behavior'.

Matarić, M. J. (1994), Interaction and Intelligent Behavior, Technical Report AI-TR-1495, MIT Artificial Intelligence Lab.

Simsarian, K. T. & Matarić, M. J. (1995), Learning to Cooperate Using Two Six–Legged Mobile Robots, *in* 'Proceedings, Third European Workshop of Learning Robots', Heraklion, Crete, Greece.

Reinforcement learning in Factories: The Auton Project

Andrew W. Moore

Robotics Institute and School of Computer Science
Carnegie Mellon University
Pittsburgh, PA 15213
awm@cs.cmu.edu

Abstract

Factories are fascinating test-beds for integrated learning systems. In recent years their sensory capabilities have, in many cases, been advanced and integrated so that data from all over the plant is available in real time over a LAN. Here we discuss how reinforcement learning, and related machine learning methods, can take advantage of this information to learn to improve performance, to adapt to change, and to exploit databases of historical records or similar processes in different plants.

This research involves very autonomous algorithms which monitor streams of sensory data, spot regularities, and design new control rules accordingly. Autonomous process control can lead to higher quality products, cheaper to manufacture products, and greatly increases flexibility in the running of plants. The modification of old processes and introduction of new processes has reduced reliance on calibration, manual redesign of controllers, and the time of process engineers.

We will talk about memory-based learning, in which the factory builds models of itself with data using nearest neighbor style approximations. We will then describe how these models can be exploited by certain classes of fast reinforcement learning algorithms. We'll outline new investigations into how factories can decide which models are important to learn, and how to actively seek data for those new models.

This arena may provide an important niche for numerical artificial intelligence to become a widespread method of choice throughout manufacturing industries. I will discuss experiences working with departments of two large corporations in putting these systems in place.

I will outline our ongoing project ("Auton") for an integrated autonomous system for robustly learning from process data and subsequently improving the process control. A number of issues arise in such a system, interesting from both a computational and statistical standpoint.

The software systems we have fielded have an unfortunate drawback: they probably have no cognitive or neural plausibility. I will conclude the talk by appealing for help in answering the question "Do these fielded learning systems have anything to say to Cognitive Science?".

The Role of Transfer in Learning (extended abstract)

Sebastian Thrun
Computer Science Department
Carnegie Mellon University
Pittsburgh, PA 15213
http://www.cs.cmu.edu/~thrun/

Introduction

Virtually all of today's approaches to artificial neural network learning generalize considerably well if sufficiently many training examples are available. However, they often work poorly when training data is scarce. Various psychological studies have illustrated that humans are able to generalize accurately even when training data is extremely scarce. Often, we generalize correctly from just a single training instance. In order to do so, we appear to massively re-use knowledge acquired in our previous lifetime.

Lifelong learning is a framework that addresses the issue of knowledge re-use and inductive transfer in learning. In lifelong learning, it is assumed that the learner faces an entire family of learning tasks, not just a single one. When facing a new learning task, the learner may *transfer* knowledge acquired in previous learning tasks to boost generalization. Three questions are of fundamental importance for any approach to lifelong learning: The *what* that is being transfered, the *how* it is being transferred, and the *when* it is that it is being transferred.

Transfer

To successfully transfer knowledge across multiple learning tasks, a learner must identify aspects that its past (and future) learning tasks have in common. Recent research has produced a variety of approaches that are capable of transferring knowledge across multiple inductive learning tasks (see the survey and references in (Thrun, 1996)). Different approaches differ

- in the way they generalize when facing the first learning task, and
- in the way their generalization is affected when previously learned knowledge is transferred.

Using object recognition from color camera images as an example, a recent study compared a variety of lifelong learning with each other, and with the corresponding conventional learning methods (Thrun, 1996). In particular, we examined the generalization accuracy that was obtained after presenting only a single view of the target object (along with a counterexample). The approaches that were capable of transferring knowledge were also provided with views of five additional objects. The idea was that those approaches could learn some of the *invariances* in object recognition, and change the way they generalize to incorporate these invariances.

The results are remarkable. Those approaches capable of transferring knowledge

	error
Back-Propagation with pre-learned invariances	25.2%
nearest neighbor with pre-learned distance metric	24.8%
neighbor neighbor with pre-learned data representation	25.6%

consistently outperformed those that were not:

	error
conventional Back-Propagation	41.3%
conventional nearest neighbor	39.6%
Shepard's interpolation	39.6%

Moreover, the results seem to suggest that the generalization error merely depends on the particular learning method (*e.g.*, neural network vs. nearest neighbor). Instead, the fact that knowledge is transferred from previous object recognition tasks has the strongest impact on the result.

Selective Transfer

Obviously, in real life not every learning task is equally related to every other one. In the study above, we knew that *all* learning tasks were related in the same way (they all were object recognition tasks), so that all approaches could just blindly transfer knowledge among all of them.

In a second study involving a variety of mobile robot perception tasks (involving the recognition of people, landmarks, locations, obstacles), we investigated the robustness of lifelong learning approaches with respect to un-related tasks (Thrun & O'Sullivan, 1996). The results were not surprising: In cases where all tasks were well-related, transferring knowledge improved the generalization accuracy significantly, especially when training data was scarce:

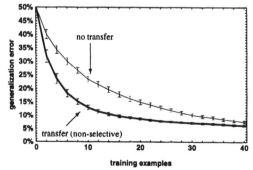

When, however, many tasks were unrelated, transfer did even hurt the overall performance:

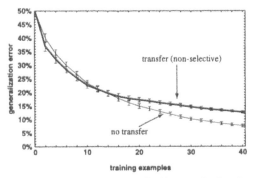

These findings illustrate that blindly transferring knowledge may be problematic in practice.

The TC algorithm transfers knowledge *selectively* (Thrun & O'Sullivan, 1996). It does this by arranging learning tasks into a hierarchy, based on their "relatedness," Relatedness is determined using statistical tests that empirically measure the effectiveness of transfer. The following hierarchy

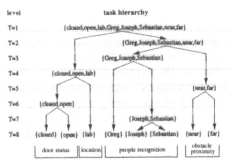

has been obtained in the mobile robot perceptual domain. The most notable result here is that different *types* of learning tasks (namely: tasks involving people, door status, location, obstacles) were grouped into different branches of the hierarchy. In other words, the computer discovered the different *types* of learning tasks.

The task hierarchy enables a learner to transfer knowledge *selectively*, from the most appropriate class of previous learning tasks. The results,

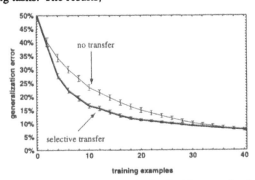

which are superior to those obtained with non-selective transfer, illustrate the role of proper task selection in the transfer of knowledge.

Learning To Act

The ideas presented here are also applicable to reinforcement learning (Sutton, 1991). Reinforcement learning addresses the problem of learning to act from delayed reward. The SKILLS algorithm (Thrun & Schwartz, 1996), a version of reinforcement learning which selectively transfers knowledge across different learning tasks, discovers partial action policies in multiple reinforcement learning tasks based upon a minimum description length argument. These partial policies can be re-used as building blocks in other reinforcement learning tasks.

Initial results, obtained for a simple grid-world scenario, are encouraging:

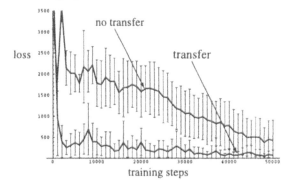

These curves illustrate that reinforcement learning converges faster, if knowledge is transferred from previous learning tasks (in this example: four tasks, two of which are actually related).

These findings are well in tune with results obtained with different learning methods. For example, when training a mobile robot to learn to navigate to a designated target object in an in-door office environment, we also found that reinforcement learning converges significantly faster when knowledge (in this case: neural network action models) acquired in previous learning tasks is being re-used (Thrun, 1996).

Conclusion

We draw three primary conclusions from this research: First, transfer, if applied correctly, is very likely to improve the results of learning, given that more than just a single learning tasks is available. Second, the lifelong learning problem—learning from many related tasks—is easier than the problem of learning from a single task, despite the fact that lifelong learning algorithms tend to be more complex. Third, since we firmly believe that transfer plays an important role in human learning, approaches that transfer knowledge among different learning tasks appear to be cognitively more plausible than approaches that do not.

References

Thrun, S. (1996). Explanation-Based Neural Network Learning: A Lifelong Learning Approach. Kluwer Academic Publishers.

Thrun, S. & O'Sullivan, J. (1996). Discovering structure in multiple learning tasks: The TC algorithm. In *Proceedings of the Thirteenth International Conference on Machine Learning*. San Mateo, CA: Morgan Kaufmann Publishers.

Sutton, R. S. (1991). Integrated Modeling and Control Based on Reinforcement Learning and Dynamic Programming, In *Advances in Neural Information Processing Systems 3*. San Mateo, CA: Morgan Kaufmann Publishers.

Thrun, S. & Schwartz, A. (1996). Finding Structure in Reinforcement Learning. In *Advances in Neural Information Processing Systems 7*. Cambridge, MA: MIT Press.

Cognitive Linguistics Symposium

Gilles Fauconnier
Department of Cognitive Science, UCSD
gfauconnier@ucsd.edu
George Lakoff
Department of Linguistics, UC Berkeley
lakoff@cogsci.berkeley.edu
Ron Langacker
Department of Linguistics, UCSD
rwl@ling.ucsd.edu

Mappings in Conceptual Systems, Grammar, and Meaning Construction

Reflecting basic features of neural organization and mental processing, a central and repeated finding of cognitive linguistics has been the need to posit "mappings" or "correspondences" between different structures or different domains of experience. Included are mappings between the elements of different "mental spaces", as well as correspondences between the "source domain" and the "target domain" of a metaphor. Correspondence is also cited in "cognitive grammar" as being pivotal to grammatical constructions.

In the present symposium, we examine key notions of cognitive linguistics as they relate to cognitive science more generally, focusing in particular on the role of mappings and correspondences in conceptual systems, grammar, and the on-line construction of meaning.

Why should there be such a thing as grammar? It would not exist were lexical units available to symbolize every conception one would want to express. However, lexical units form a limited set, whereas the conceptions we wish to encode linguistically are open-ended and indefinitely varied. We overcome this by resorting to complex expressions comprising multiple lexical elements. Each component element evokes some facet of the overall conception, a facet singled out precisely because it is susceptible to individual lexical encoding. Collectively, these individually symbolized conceptual "chunks" provide enough clues about the intended composite conception intended by the speaker that the addressee (especially in context) is able to reconstruct some approximation to it. But this reconstruction cannot proceed effectively unless information is systematically provided concerning how the conceptual chunks are supposed to fit together. This information is supplied by the manner in which the component lexical elements are combined: a particular means of phonological integration (e.g. linear adjacency) serves to indicate--to symbolize--a particular means of conceptual integration.

Conventional patterns of this sort constitute a grammatical system. Cognitive grammar effects a significant theoretical unification by claiming that grammar consists of patterns of symbolization (thus it forms a gradation with lexicon). Grammar reduces to assemblies of "symbolic structures", each residing in the symbolic association between a conceptual and a phonological structure. In such an assembly--or"construction"--

component symbolic elements are linked by correspondences to one another and also to the composite symbolic structure resulting from their integration. Semantically, these correspondences indicate which substructures of the component conceptions (or "chunks") are to be equated and thus superimposed in forming the composite conception. From another perspective, correspondences represent the distortion engendered by dissociating the integrated composite conception into overlapping chunks for purposes of symbolic encoding. On this account correspondences are inherent and indispensable to grammar--a direct and ineluctable consequence of the very existence of complex expressions and grammatical patterns. Correspondences figure in the characterization of every construction and are the basis for all grammatical dependencies. Adding or adjusting a correspondence can drastically affect an expression's meaning, form, and grammatical behavior. The key to an explicit and revealing grammatical analysis thus lies in elucidating the correspondences linking component and composite structures at multiple levels of organization.

Mapping operations are essential for functional assemblies, and they figure prominently in the constitution of conceptual systems. Metaphorical mappings link domains in multiple and systematic ways that are grounded in human experience and culture. Through projection, they allow some domains to structure the conceptualization of others. Complex metaphorical systems are learned early and they underlie much of semantics, language organization, and category formation. Recent developments in metaphor theory will be discussed.

Finally, correspondences are at the heart of on-line construction of meaning. Multiple mental spaces are set up and dynamically linked as we think and talk. Actual discourse consists in building vast networks of such spaces, shifting viewpoint, focus, and anchoring, as we 'move' through configurations of such spaces.

Very general cognitive operations, like conceptual blending, enter into this process. We will report on recent results concerning blended spaces and conceptual integration, focusing in particular on the 'optimality' principles that constrain integration in context. The research suggests explicit mechanisms of creativity inscribed in everyday thought and language.

Modeling the Evolution of Communication

John Batali
Department of Cognitive Science
University of California, San Diego
batali@cogsci.ucsd.edu

and

David Ackley
Department of Computer Science
The University of New Mexico
ackley@cs.unm.edu

Communication enables animals to coordinate their actions, to express their cognitive and emotional states, to inform, threaten, warn, comfort, deceive, and entertain. Animal communication systems range from apparently simple alarm calls and threats, to honeybee dances, elaborate mating rituals, bird song, and human language. Communication, in one form or another, seems to be a prerequisite for complex social behavior. Furthermore, the processes by which individual animals acquire a communication system involves a complex interplay between innate and learned components

A number of researchers have investigated the evolution of communication by means of computational simulations of simple models of communicative behavior. In some such simulations all behavior is innately specified, usually as the result of a simulation of evolution by natural selection; in some simulations an individual learns from observating the communicative behavior of others, and in some simulations both evolution and learning are combined. Other simulations attempt to model the communicative behavior or the underlying mechanisms of specific animal species, using techniques from behavioral ecology or neuroethology.

Though such models are quite simple, they have begun to prove their value in elucidating aspects of the evolution of communication that are otherwise quite difficult to investigate. For example much attention has been paid to the issue of whether and how various aspects of human language could be innate rather than learned. To some degree such debates rely on intuitions about how certain features of language might or might not be evolutionarily adaptive or learnable or some combination of both. However few such intuitions are trustworthy: The evolution of any complex social behavior involves an environment (the behavior of the other animals) which is changing as the animals learn or evolve new behavioral tendencies, and therefore the system can be highly unstable and unpredictable. Mathematical and computational models, even simple ones, can be used to investigate the consequences of assumptions, and explore proposed scenarios, relevant to the evolution of communication.

In this symposium we will explore these issues and consider how such research ought to proceed. Some specific questions to be addressed are:

- What issues involving communication and language can be usefully explored with computational models?
- How complex and/or realistic do models have to be for their properties to be worth investigating?
- What specific implementation and analysis techniques are available for modeling the evolution of communication?
- What animal species have types of communicative behavior that are worth modeling?
- How much should these models attempt to capture specific aspects of human language?
- How can simulation results be assessed? In particular, how can effects due to arbitrary details of the simulations be separated from the significant results?

The symposium will begin with a presentation of background issues and a survey of the field. This will be followed by short presentations of some recent simulation experiments. A respondent from the field of linguistics will present a critical discussion of the presentations. An open discussion will follow.

References

Ackley, D. H, & Littman, M. L. (1994). Altruism in the evolution of communication. In Rodney Brooks and Pattie Maes, editors, *Proceedings of the Fourth Artificial Life Workshop*, Cambridge, MA, The MIT Press.

Batali, J. (1994). Innate biases and critical periods: combining evolution and learning in the acquisition of syntax. In: *Proceedings of the Fourth Artificial Life Workshop*, R. Brooks and Pattie Maes, (eds.), MIT Press, pp. 160–171.

Hurford, J. R. (1989). Biological evolution of the Saussurean sign as a component of the language acquisition device. *Lingua*, 77:187–222.

Oliphant, M. (1996). The dilemma of Saussurean communication. *BioSystems*, pages 31–38.

Parisi, D. (in press). An artificial life approach to language. *Brain and Language*.

Werner, G. M. & Dyer, M. G. (1991). Evolution of communication in artificial organisms. In C. G. Langton, C. Taylor, J. D. Farmer, and S. Rasmussen, editors, *Artificial Life II: SFI Studies in the Sciences of Complexity, Volume X*, pages 511–547.

Submitted Symposia

Building a theory of problem solving and scientific discovery:

How big is N in N-space search?

Bruce D. Burns
(Symposium Organizer)
Institut für Psychologie
Universität Potsdam
14415 Postdam
Germany
burns@rz.uni-potsdam.de

The framework developed by Newell and Simon (1972) of problem solving as a search of a problem space, provides core concepts (e.g., representations, operators, heuristics, task analyses, etc.) that are used by many researchers studying complex tasks from the point of view of artificial intelligence, psychology, Human-Computer Interaction, and education. However, in recent years some researchers have tried to push beyond seeing tasks as search of a single problem space, and have instead suggested that many tasks can be better treated as a N-space search.

Dual-space search

The idea that there may be more than one type of problem space originated with Simon and Lea (1974), who suggested that problem solving and induction can be unified within a dual-space search framework. They suggested that problem solving was search of a single space, termed "instance space". This space consists of what is normally thought of as problem space, that is, instances of states of a problem (including the goal state). But induction required search of a qualitatively different type of space, "rule space". Search of rule space requires the formulation and testing of rules that may govern the behavior of a system. However, rule-space search is coordinated with search of instance space in that instances allow the testing of rules and provide the raw material for formulating new rules. In this way induction and problem solving, which have often been treated as different phenomena, can be unified into one framework. In fact, the same task could be treated by a solver as either a search of a single space or a dual-space. Even the classic Tower of Hanoi problem can be treated as a single-space search, find a sequence of moves leading to the goal, or a dual-space search, find a rule for transferring disks from one peg to another.

However, the idea of dual-space search received relatively little attention until Klahr and Dunbar (1988) extended it to scientific discovery with their SDDS (Scientific Discovery as Dual Search) model. For scientific discovery they conceptualized searching rule space as searching the space of hypotheses, and searching instance space as searching the space of experiments. Klahr and Dunbar found evidence that problem solvers learned more when they tested hypotheses. Vollmeyer, Burns and Holyoak (1996) found support for dual-spaces search theories by showing that the type of goals subjects have can affect learning.

N-space search

In recent years, both Klahr (Schunn & Klahr, 1995) and Dunbar have for empirical and theoretical reasons suggested that a broad range of tasks can be seen as search of more than two conceptually different spaces. Problem solving and scientific discovery may be better conceptualized as a N-space search, although the size of N is not clear and may not be fixed. Vollmeyer and Burns (1995) have presented evidence from protocols for a three-space search. Critics of the N-space framework have also emerged. Wolf, Beskin and Dietrich (1995) have argued that there is no need to postulate multiple spaces; instead, only the concepts proposed for a single space search need be used.

Given that a number of groups are starting to propose N-space models, now seem to be an opportune time to bring together different proponents and critics of these models so that some basic questions can be addressed. In particular: How strong is the empirical evidence for N-space models? Is there a theoretical need for such models? What distinguishes different N-space models? How can such models be tested, and in particular, what criteria should be used for proposing new spaces? How big is the N in N-space search and can it vary?

If the problem spaces framework can legitimately be extended into N-space search models, this may deepen our understanding of problem solving and scientific discovery. Such extensions may provide a way to unify diverse phenomena.

Speakers

Lisa M. Baker and Kevin Dunbar (McGill University).
Bruce D. Burns and Regina Vollmeyer (Universität Potsdam, Germany).

Chris D. Schunn and David Klahr (Carnegie-Mellon University).

David F. Wolf II (State University of New York at Albany) and Jonathan Beskin (State University of New York at Binghamton).

References

Klahr, D. & Dunbar, K. (1988). Dual space search during scientific reasoning. *Cognitive Science, 12*, 1-55.

Newell, A. & Simon, H.A. (1972). *Human problem solving*. Englewood Cliffs, NJ: Prentice-Hall.

Schunn, C.D. & Klahr, D. (1995). A 4-space model of scientific discovery. In *Proceedings of the 17th Annual Conference of the Cognitive Science Society* (pp. 106-111). Hillsdale, NJ: Erlbaum.

Simon, H.A. & Lea, G. (1974). Problem solving and rule induction: A unified view. In L. W. Gregg (Ed.), *Knowledge and cognition*. Hillsdale, NJ: Erlbaum.

Vollmeyer, R. & Burns, B. D. (1995). *Goal specificity and hypothesis testing in learning a complex system*. Poster presented at the Thirty-sixth Annual Meeting of the Psychonomic Society, Los Angeles, California.

Vollmeyer, R., Burns, B.D., & Holyoak, K.J. (1996). The impact of goal specificity on strategy use and the acquisition of problem structure. *Cognitive Science, 20*, 75-100.

Wolf, D.F., II, Beskin, J., & Dietrich, E. (1995). Does meta-space theory explain insight? In *Proceedings of the 17th Annual Conference of the Cognitive Science Society* (pp. 781-785). Hillsdale, NJ: Erlbaum.

Problem Spaces in Real-World Science:
What are They and How Do Scientists Search Them?

Lisa M. Baker and **Kevin Dunbar**
McGill University Department of Psychology
1205 Dr. Penfield Avenue
Montreal, Quebec H3A 1B1 Canada
lbaker@ego.psych.mcgill.ca or dunbar@ego.psych.mcgill.ca

How do scientists think, reason, and represent their knowledge? We have been investigating these questions in a variety of simulated science and real-world science domains over the last decade (Baker & Dunbar, in preparation; Dunbar, 1993, 1995, 1996; Klahr & Dunbar, 1988). Having explored scientific thinking in a variety of domains, we are now able to address the issue of the types of problem spaces that contemporary experimental scientists use. In this presentation, we will focus on the problem spaces that scientists in immunology and molecular biology use when they reason about their research at laboratory meetings and at the bench. On the basis of our analyses, we propose that real-world scientists represent and conduct their science using three major spaces: a Theory Space, an Experiment Space, and a Data Space. Here we will specify the nature of the three spaces, the criteria for identifying these spaces, and discuss the nature of between- and within-space operations.

The Three Spaces

Theory Space. This space includes specific hypotheses about the scientist's current research, general theories relating to different scientific domains, and theoretical frameworks that guide research.

Experiment Space. This space consists of the knowledge needed to conduct Experiments. The Experiment Space contains a number of different types of knowledge such as experimental approaches, materials, procedures and controls. In a later section on the internal structure of spaces we will specify how these different aspects of experimental knowledge are related.

Data Space. This space contains scientists' representations of the output from experiments. The Data Space consists of the scientists' current representation of their data and other scientists' data. Our conception of the data space is very similar to that of Schunn and Klahr's (1995) "data representation space." Data is represented as having certain sets of features and this representation may change at a later point in time.

Criteria for Identifying Problem Spaces

We used two main criteria to identify the problem spaces that scientists work in. First, when scientists are searching within a space, their search can be represented as a choice among specific features using classic domain-general search heuristics as well as space-specific heuristics. Second, we identified a switch to another space when complex reasoning processes were required to translate from elements of one space into elements of another. When there are no complex translations between conceptual entities, we classify the entities as being in the same space. We will elaborate on these criteria in a later section on within- and between-space operations.

Internal Structure of Problem Spaces

Current-day scientists have complex theories, design and carry out elaborate experiments, and have multifaceted data to interpret. Our analyses indicate that each of the three spaces has a complex, often hierarchically organized internal structure of elements. These elements do not operate at the same "level" but may nevertheless be considered part of the same space. In order to clarify the nature of the internal structure of problem spaces, we will provide an example of search in the Experiment Space.

Our example is taken from immunology where a scientist might be exploring the way in which cells send signals to each other. The scientist may have decided to use a "blocking" approach to investigate the role of cytokines in cell production of growth factors. In this scientist's area of research, there is an accepted structure for blocking experiments. This structure can be said to provide a "frame" with certain "slots." For example, having chosen the blocking approach, the scientist knows that the experiment will involve blocking antibodies mixed with cells in culture. However, the scientist still has choices to make in order to fill in different slots in the design of this experiment. For example, she must specify procedures (how long to incubate the cells?), materials (which antibody will she use?), and control conditions (what antibody and cell controls should she use?).

Within the Experiment Space, experimental approaches or paradigms are situated higher than materials, procedures, and controls in a hierarchy. This is because the paradigm dictates the structure of the experiment. To the extent that experimental paradigms and features of experiments operate at different hierarchical levels, they can be referred to as hierarchically organized "subspaces" of the larger Experiment Space. The subspaces consist of features of the higher space that have been unpacked.

Within- and Between-Space Operations

We distinguish between three classes of operations: between-space, between-subspace, and within-space. Between-space operations involve relating items in different spaces; for example, relating data to theory or theory to experiments. These operations typically involve complex translations, as when a scientist translates a hypothesis about the role of cytokines into a "blocking" experiment. Thus, while there is a relationship between the current hypothesis and the current experiment, the current hypothesis does not fully determine what experiments will be performed (see Baker & Dunbar, 1996). Between-space operations make use of what might be called the scientist's "mental toolkit" of reasoning strategies, such as causal reasoning, induction, deduction, and analogy.

In contrast to between-space operations, between-subspace operations do not involve complex translation processes. Rather, a choice at one level of a within-space hierarchy directly determines features in the subordinate subspace. In our example, the decision to use a "blocking" experimental paradigm determined the structure of the experiment and what slots would need to be filled in.

Within-subspace operations are the types of operations that have been emphasized in models of heuristic search within a problem space. Within-space operations are aimed at searching the current space and making choices among elements in the space. For example, Baker and Dunbar (1996) specify the complex criteria used to search the Experiment Space.

Why N of Spaces is not Constant

Different researchers' multispace models have emphasized the importance of different spaces and have even argued for different numbers of spaces. It is not surprising that different researchers arrive at different values for the N in "N-space search," because researchers are studying different task environments. Newell (1989) has argued that humans construct problem spaces in order to solve particular problems. Further, Newell pointed out that in studying different tasks researchers would be able to identify different spaces. Following this analysis, we argue that at least some of the differences between the different numbers of problem spaces is due to the task demands of the different tasks that researchers have used. Thus, we see the existence of various spaces as arising from the interaction of the human cognitive architecture and the particular task environment under consideration.

In the case of real-world science, we would even go one step further and argue that the three spaces we have identified have been established and stabilized in part through the social interactions that go on in this task environment. Garrod & Doherty (1994) have shown how communication between subjects performing a task can result in task-specific terminology being generated and stabilized. Similarly, we argue that scientists stabilize the Theory Space, Experiment Space, and Data Space by referring among themselves to elements of these spaces as being of different kinds. There are many possible ways science could be and has been done; for instance, science can be observational rather than experimental. The three spaces that we have identified are a product of both the task environment and the representational practices of the general scientific community.

Given that we allow a role for both task demands and the social structure of science, we expect that both the number and types of problem spaces that scientists use can change depending on the task environments and social practices of science. While acknowledging the roles of these two constraints on the generation of problem spaces, we argue that the three-space model of scientific thinking best characterizes "real-world current-day experimental science."

Acknowledgments

This research was supported by a McGill Major Graduate Fellowship to the first author. The second author was funded by grant number OGP0037356 from NSERC and grants from FCAR and SSHRC.

References

Baker, L. M., & Dunbar, K. (in preparation). How scientists deal with unexpected findings: A discovery heuristic.

Baker, L. M., & Dunbar, K. (1996). Constraints on the experimental design process in real-world science. In *Proceedings of the 18th Annual Conference of the Cognitive Science Society.*

Dunbar, K. (1993). Concept discovery in a scientific domain. *Cognitive Science, 17,* 397-434.

Dunbar, K. (1995). How scientists really reason: Scientific reasoning in real-world laboratories. In R.J. Sternberg & J. Davidson (Eds.), *Mechanisms of insight.* Cambridge MA: MIT Press. pp 365-395.

Dunbar, K. (1996). How scientists think: Online creativity and conceptual change in science. In T. B. Ward, S. M. Smith, & J. Vaid, *Conceptual structures and processes: Emergence, discovery, and change.* Washington, DC: American Psychological Association Press.

Garrod, S., & Doherty, G. (1994). Conversation, co-ordination and convention: an empirical investigation of how groups establish linguistic conventions. *Cognition, 53,* 181–215.

Klahr, D., & Dunbar, K. (1988). Dual space search during scientific reasoning. *Cognitive Science, 12,* 1–48.

Newell, A. (1989). Putting it all together. In D. Klahr & K. Kotovsky (Eds.), *Complex information processing: The impact of Herbert A. Simon.* Hillsdale, NJ: Lawrence Erlbaum Associates. pp 399-440.

Schunn, C. D., & Klahr, D. (1995). A 4-space model of scientific discovery. In *Proceedings of the 17th Annual Conference of the Cognitive Science Society.* Hillsdale, NJ: Erlbaum.

Goals and problem solving: Learning as search of three spaces

Bruce D. Burns and **Regina Vollmeyer**
Institut für Psychologie
Universität Potsdam
14415 Postdam
Germany
{burns,vollmeye}@rz.uni-potsdam.de

A recent trend in computer-based learning has been to set up systems that the learner explores, rather than setting very specific goals to reach. Our previous research on complex problem solving has supported this approach (Vollmeyer, Burns, & Holyoak, 1996). When learning how to control a system with a set of inputs linked to a set of outputs, participants learned more about the system when they were given a nonspecific goal rather than a specific goal. These results could be explained using Simon and Lea's (1974) dual-space framework (or that of Klahr & Dunbar, 1988, who extend this framework to scientific discovery) in which induction is seen as a search of instance space (i.e., examining states of the system), integrated with search of rule space (i.e., formulating and testing rules that might govern the system's behavior).

Protocol analysis by Vollmeyer and Burns (1995b) provided evidence that a specific goal increases search of instance space, while a nonspecific goal increases search of rule space in that it increases the amount that problem solvers test and modify hypotheses. The protocol studies also suggest why some problem solvers do very poorly: they test rules that are impossible. Thus a third type of search can be proposed, search of model space. The problem solver's model defines the rule space so if a learner has the wrong model, search of rule space will be ineffectual and they may learn more from search of instance space.

A test of a multispace model

To test if model space is separate from rule space, we manipulated the model participants had as well as their goals. Participants were given an input/output system similar to, though simpler than, that used by Vollmeyer et al. (1996). This task required problem solvers to control a system that consisted of a set of outputs (water quality measures in a tank) that could be manipulated by a set of inputs (catalysts). The inputs had weighted links to the outputs. Presented in Figure 1 are the links, which were not shown to the participants. Similar to Vollmeyer et al., participants were given a specific goal (they were told at the beginning the exact goal values they would later try to reach) or a nonspecific goal (they were not told the goal until they had to reach it). In addition, we manipulated the model that participants had of the task by giving them a good or poor model of the task. Protocol analysis by Vollmeyer and Burns (1995b) found that one type of incorrect hypothesis tested was that inputs interacted, although none did. Accordingly, in this experiment

participants given a poor model of the task were told that inputs may interact. Participants given a good model of the task were told that there was no possibility of interactions between inputs because two catalysts were never put into the tank at the same time. We predicted an interaction between goal specificity and model type.

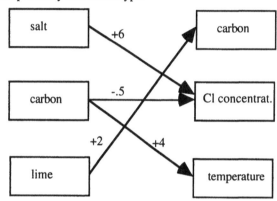

Figure 1: System used in the experiment.

Method

Participants. One hundred and eighty-six students at the University of California, Los Angeles participated in the experiment for course credit.

Procedure. A 2x2 design was used with the factors goal specificity (specific vs. nonspecific) and model (good vs. poor). Participants were given instructions appropriate to their condition; then they had two rounds of six trials each. On each trial participants could manipulate the inputs and observe the resulting outputs. At the end of each round participants completed a diagram on which they indicated what they knew about the structure of the system. From these diagrams a structure score was derived in the same way as described by Vollmeyer et al. (1996).

In the third round, participants tried to reach a goal, one which specific-goal participants had known since the beginning. Then all participants were given a new goal to reach in a fourth round. This goal tested how well participants could transfer what they knew to a new goal. Transfer error was a measure of how close participants got to this goal (see Vollmeyer et al., 1996).

Results and Discussion

As Vollmeyer et al. (1996) found, nonspecific-goal participants ($M = 2.36$) learned more about how the system worked than did specific goal participants ($M = 1.93$), as measured by structure scores, $F(1,182) = 8.83$, $p < .005$. However, there was no effect of model type on structure scores. These finding replicates the results of Vollmeyer et al. and suggests that nonspecific-goal participants searched rule space more, regardless of model type.

There were no significant effects of goal or model on transfer error, nor was there an interaction between these two factors (though the pattern was as predicted). However, there was a significant interaction between model type, goal specificity and output type. Because the Chlorine Concentration output is affected by two inputs, it is harder to control. Vollmeyer and Burns (1995a) found evidence that in a system like the one used in this experiment, Chlorine concentration may show the strongest effects of manipulations. Thus we examined the transfer error for Chlorine concentration (see Figure 2, note that low scores indicate greater accuracy). We found a significant interaction between goal-specificity and model type, $F(1,182) = 4.09$, $p < .05$. If participants were given a good model, they performed better if given a nonspecific-goal, just as in Vollmeyer et al. (1996). However, if given a poor model, participants performed better when given a specific goal.

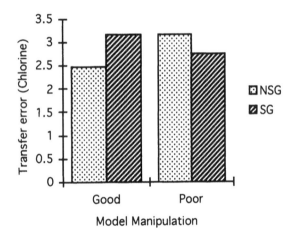

Figure 2: Transfer error for Chlorine concentration.

This experiment supports the theory proposed earlier, that in order to explain problem-solving behavior it is necessary to propose a three-space search. In this model search of model space defines hypothesis space, search of hypothesis space guides search of experiment space, and provides evidence for search of model space. Search of experiment space allows testing of hypotheses, and leads to the goal.

Implications

While we have proposed a three-space search theory, we are not committed to proposing only three spaces. There may be more than three conceptually different spaces, especially for other tasks. What criteria should be used when proposing separate search spaces? Conceptually, new spaces need to make sense, but ultimately empirical support for the existence of multiple search spaces must be found. If conceptually different types of search spaces exist then experimental manipulation at the level of different spaces should lead to different results. The experiment presented here is an example of how empirical evidence can be used to support the idea of separate search spaces, especially when it is possible to predict interactions between factors.

One weakness of the above results is that this experiment could not be used to established that movement is occurring between different models. Thus we did not demonstrate that actual search was occurring at the level of models. Further evidence is required, such as protocol analysis as in Vollmeyer and Burns (1995b), which showed that problem solvers searched different rules, and different instances.

These results, and multispace models in general have implications beyond problem solving and scientific discovery. Most obviously, if they can be generalized they have strong implications for learning. The results suggest that whether a specific or nonspecific goal is beneficial for learning will depend on how good is the learner's model of the task. Furthermore, these types of models suggest ways to understand results in other areas of cognition. For example, implicit learning of artificial grammar may be worse for someone looking for underlying rules, than for someone who does not look for rules (Reber, 1976). However, the result does not hold if the grammar is simple enough. In terms of our three-space model, participants in experiments with difficult grammars have a poor model of the situation. Search of rule space will therefore be ineffectual, so that a specific goal (i.e., focus on instances of letter-strings) leads to better learning.

One challenge for this research is to establish what makes model "poor". The key factor could be the relationship between the true hypothesis space and problem solvers' hypothesis space, but this proposal requires more research.

References

Klahr, D. & Dunbar, K. (1988). Dual space search during scientific reasoning. *Cognitive Science, 12*, 1-55.

Reber, A.S (1976). Implicit learning of synthetic languages: the role of instructional set. *Journal of Experimental Psychology: Human learning and Memory, 2*, 88-94.

Simon, H.A. & Lea, G. (1974). Problem solving and rule induction: A unified view. In L. W. Gregg (Ed.), *Knowledge and cognition*. Hillsdale, NJ: Erlbaum.

Vollmeyer, R. & Burns, B. D. (1995a) Does hypothesis-instruction improve learning? In *Proceedings of the Seventeenth Annual Conference of the Cognitive Science Society* (pp. 711--776). Hillsdale, NJ: Lawrence Erlbaum Associates.

Vollmeyer, R. & Burns, B. D. (1995b). *Goal specificity and hypothesis testing in learning a complex system*. Poster presented at the Thirty-sixth Annual Meeting of the Psychonomic Society, Los Angeles, California.

Vollmeyer, R., Burns, B.D., & Holyoak, K.J. (1996). The impact of goal specificity on strategy use and the acquisition of problem structure. *Cognitive Science, 20*, 75-100.

The problem of problem spaces:
When and how to go beyond a 2-space model of scientific discovery

Christian D. Schunn and David Klahr

Department of Psychology
Carnegie Mellon University
Pittsburgh, PA 15213
{schunn, klahr}@cmu.edu

Adding Problem Spaces — The Issues

The process of scientific discovery has been characterized as a search in two problem spaces: the space of possible experiments and the space of possible hypotheses (Klahr & Dunbar, 1988). More recently, there have been several proposals to include additional problem spaces. In particular, we have proposed the addition of a space of experimental paradigms and a space of data representations (Schunn & Klahr, 1995). These proposals raise meta-theoretical issues: (a) Why these spaces? (b) Why *only* these spaces? Moreover, these issues are not specific to models of scientific discovery—they are general to all problem solving activities.

In our talk, we propose a general set of logical, empirical and implementational criteria for resolving these issues. We illustrate this distinction in the context of distinguishing between the data representation and hypothesis spaces in scientific discovery, focusing on results of psychological labs studies of discovery activities. Before presenting the general criteria, we describe a simple, concrete example which we believe provides an intuitive feel for when distinct problem spaces do and do not occur.

Consider subjects trying to solve simple letter series completion tasks (cf., Simon & Kotovsky, 1963), such as ABMCDM_. Subjects will initially select a representation that involves relations on the English alphabet, and they will seek patterns of sames, differents, nexts, double nexts, priors, etc. In this case, the representation is so obviously immediate and evoked by the stimulus that it makes no sense to view it as involving any search.

Now consider what happens when subjects get a trick problem, such as: OTTFFSS_. Here too, they start with the obvious representation in which the letters are simply letters. But leads subjects to formulate increasingly complex and ad hoc explanations for the O at the beginning of the series. Ultimately, subjects using this straightforward representation hit an impasse. Then they start to consider whether the letters stand for something else (like the first letters of the names of the integers).

At this point, we argue, they are searching a data representation space. That is, they must consider other ways to characterize the items of the list. In the present instance, they might reason that, since the earlier lists are based on the alphabet, and the alphabet is a (the most) familiar ordered list of symbols, then there might be other ordered lists that are relevant: days of the week, names of the Kings of England, Presidents of the US, number names, months, etc. Perhaps the letters in the sequence are related to some feature of these other lists (in this case the first letter of their English names of the integers.)

General Criteria

How does one decide whether to add a new problem space? Below we list three kinds of criteria that 1) we found very useful in making the distinction, and 2) we believe can be applied to understand problem-solving behavior in any task.

Logical Criteria

First, one needs to be able to define the spaces such that they are unambiguously different. Furthermore, the distinction between spaces should be categorical rather than a continuum. There are two important components to the definition of a problem space: the goals used for searching the space, and the entities that are searched. Distinct problem spaces should involve distinct entities and distinct goals. Of course, the problem spaces can be coordinated such that information from one space is used to search the other space—this feature is ubiquitous to the scientific discovery tasks that we have considered.

Empirical Criteria

Second, there should be empirical differences between the spaces. In particular, they should occur (at least occasionally) at different times, they should involve different search heuristics, and there should be different factors that influence behavior in each search space.

Most importantly, there should be activity in each search space. If a subject always stays in the same state with respect to a particular problem space, then that search space is not a useful tool for describing that subject's behavior. This might occur in two ways. First, the subject could know so little about a domain that only one state is available to that subject. Second, subjects might be so knowledgeable about a domain that they are able to pick a good state immediately and need not search any further. Thus, the existence of a particular problem space for a given subject is determined, in part, by their knowledge.

Implementational Criteria

Third, one should be able to represent the problem spaces distinctly in a computational model that is capable of performing the task. In other words, one should be able to map unambiguously from observed behavior to a state in the problem space. Furthermore, search through a specific problem space should be distinct from coordination between problem spaces. This provides an exacting test of the *degree* to which the theoretical distinctions can actually account for the empirical behavior at a precise level.

An Example

Having described the general criteria, we will now describe how we have applied these criteria in proposing our 4-space model. However, in this short abstract, we are only able to explore the addition of the data representation space.

Logical Criteria

First, there are the entities that are searched. The hypothesis space involves propositions about the world, potentially at varying levels of abstraction and of varying levels of generality. For example, one might have the following hypotheses—varying in scope and abstraction—about the results of an experiment on reading comprehension: "there was no effect of manipulating motivation in this experiment (on comprehension of some history text)", "there is generally no effect of monetary manipulations of motivation on comprehension of history texts", or "there is generally no effect of motivation on reading skills".

By contrast, the data representation space involves the objects and object features of the data. For example, one might graph different the relationship between different variables, one might use different kinds of graphs, and one might re-code, collapse, or expand the same data.

The two spaces also differ in terms of their goals. The goal of the hypothesis space is to produce parsimonious explanations/descriptions of objects and relations in the world. By contrast, the goal of the data representation space is to find regularities. A data representation is abandoned if it doesn't lead to regularities or interpretable patterns, whereas it is maintained when it does. In other words, the search in the data representation space seeks to find the regularities, and search in the hypothesis space seeks to explain them.

Note that there are not separate search spaces for hypotheses at different levels of abstraction because 1) this distinction is a continuum; and 2) the goals of the search at different levels is the same. Similarly, there are not different search spaces for tables versus graphs, or internal versus external representations.

Empirical Criteria

The particular data that lead us to propose the data representation space came from a complex discovery microworld called MilkTruck (Schunn & Klahr, 1992, 1995). Subjects in this task were asked to discover the role of a complex, mystery function by conducting experiments in the domain. What is the empirical evidence from this domain for the data representation space?

First, the majority of the subjects radically altered their representation of the task over the course of discovering the correct function. Based on their verbal think-aloud descriptions of the experiments and experiment outcomes, we found that the subjects changed both the kinds of objects they were examining (new objects and new levels of aggregation of the same objects) as well as which features of the objects the described. Interestingly, we found that the

subjects used multiple representations of the same experimental outcome for most experiments. Moreover, we found that, from one experiment to the next, subjects made at least minor changes to the data representation over 90% of the time. This can be contrasted with performance in some simpler tasks, in which people do not need to search the data representation space since there is usually only one way to represent the data.

Second, we found that search in the two spaces did occur at different times. Occasionally, subjects considered several different representations of the data without coming up with a new hypothesis. Similarly, they occasionally considered several different hypotheses all within the same representation of the data.

Third, we found several new heuristics that subjects used in producing data representation change. For example, we found that subjects used a Notice Invariants heuristic (cf., Kaplan & Simon, 1990) in which they recast their representation of the data into the parts of the data that remain constant across experiments and the parts that vary.

Implementational Criteria

While we have not yet completely implemented a running model, in coding the data, we have developed a sense of how easy/difficult it is to unambiguously distinguish between hypothesis and data representation, and it has forced us to revise some previous distinctions that we had initially made only on the basis of logical criteria.

Furthermore, in the symbolic production system schemes that we have constructed, changing data representations is always an important issue that is clearly distinct from selecting among and constructing novel hypotheses.

Conclusions

We have outlined three types of criteria (logical, empirical, and implementational) that we believe are important in determining the number of problems spaces that should be used in describing problem solving behavior in a particular task. In this brief abstract, we could only describe the application of these criteria to justifying the addition of the data representation space in characterizing scientific discovery behavior. However, we have also been able to use these criteria to propose the experimental paradigm space, and we believe these criteria can be applied to resolve these kinds of issues in any problem-solving task.

References

Kaplan, C. A., & Simon, H. A. (1990). In Search of Insight. *Cognitive Psychology*, **22**, 374-419.

Klahr, D., & Dunbar, K. (1988). Dual space search during scientific reasoning. *Cognitive Science*, **12(1)**, 1-55.

Schunn, C. D., & Klahr, D. (1992). Complexity Management in a Discovery Task. In *Proceedings of the 14th Annual Conference of the Cognitive Science Society*. Hillsdale, NJ: Erlbaum.

Schunn, C. D., & Klahr, D. (1995). A 4-space model of scientific discovery. In *Proceedings of the 17th Annual Conference of the Cognitive Science Society*. Hillsdale, NJ: Erlbaum.

Simon, H. A., & Kotovsky, K. (1963). Human acquisition of concepts for sequential patterns. *Psychological Review*, **70**, 534-46.

Task Domains in N-Space Models: Giving Explanation Its Due.

David F Wolf II and Jonathan R. Beskin

Department of Philosophy
SUNY Albany
Albany, NY 12222
dw4570@cnsunix.albany.edu

Reliable Software Technologies Corporation
21515 Ridgetop Circle, Suite 250
Sterling, VA 20166
jrb@rstcorp.com

Our colleagues tacitly agree that N-space models are better at explaining the data on human problem solving than single space models. The primary question of this symposium is how many spaces are necessary to explain the data. We will not be addressing this issue, except to suggest that more 'spaces' are probably needed. This follows from the substantive empirical claims of the three theories presented. These claims, combined with some facts about the computation power of N-spaces, provide strong evidence that the search space paradigm is not needed in theories of problem solving.

Any N-space theory is computationally equivalent to a single search space theory of problem solving. This can be shown by either creating a space that contains the other spaces as branches or by overlapping nodes from different spaces, such that every node has paths leading to nodes in other 'spaces'. By this method, the problem solver can switch from any 'space' to any other 'space', and in fact, several 'spaces' can be traversed in parallel. Thus, an N-space theory is only as powerful as a single space theory. There must be some non-computational reason for distinguishing N-space theories from single space theories. And by extension, all N-space theories are computationally equivalent.

Even if one accepts that N-space theories are computationally equivalent, one need not accept that they are equivalent at providing explanations. As pointed out earlier, N-space theories argue that we need multiple spaces to best understand human problem solving. The evidence supports this claim. N-space models are better explanations than single space models because the bulk of the explanation is in the division of labor between task domains (spaces), and not within the search space theory itself.

A distinction is important here. There is a difference between the mechanisms underlying problem solving, and the explanation of problem solving itself. Chomsky (1965) alluded to this distinction when he differentiated theories of competence from theories of performance. Simon (1981) labeled this distinction as one between substantive and procedural rationality. Similarly, Marr (1982) identifies the level distinctness between computational theories of a device and the theory of its underlying process, i.e., the level of representation and the algorithm. All of these distinctions identify both an abstract specification of behavior and a mechanism for implementing that behavior.

In each case, the abstract specification of a system's behavior, performs an explanatory role. It specifies a method for a system to accomplish its goals, irrespective of how the system will accomplish them. The abstract specification is an idealization of what the system's behavior does and why it does it. This idealization is independent of its underlying process. Consequently, it offers a general description of a broad class of systems and provides information relevant for determining how the system will act as a whole. This allows us to identify significant features of the system from the noise of its lower level implementation.

N-space theorist presuppose that the only way to implement their abstract specifications are by using the low level mechanism of search space. This places an unduly mechanistic constraint on human problem solving research, which is counterproductive. If N-space theories are better theories than single space theory, then the task domains (spaces) the N-space theories define are the source of explanations about problem solving. Consequently, the processes underlying these task domains, the search spaces, become irrelevant noise in light of their specification. The task domain may be implemented in OOS, Prolog, C or even by a Turing machine. Nevertheless, the task domains are providing all the interesting information about the subject by partitioning the problem solving into identifiable high-level processes. Thus, the N-space theorists should be searching for more 'spaces', as every experimentally confirmed task domain contributes to our understanding of human problem solving.

If N-space theories are better than search space theory, then it is in virtue of their task domains' ability to identify significant aspects of the systematic behavior of human problem solving. Search space theory then only specifies one implementation of these task domains. Recognizing this, N-space theories should no longer emphasize the use of search spaces and concentrate more on the task domains to which their 'spaces' refer. Since the division of labor between task domains accounts for the power of the N-space theories, researchers should not restrict themselves to some arbitrary N. Instead, researchers should be open to as many task domains as necessary to explain the significant, observable features of human problem solving.

References

Chomsky, N. (1965). *Aspects of Theory and Syntax*, Cambridge, MA: M.I.T. Press.

Marr, D. (1982). *Vision*. San Francisco, CA: Freemen.

Simon, H. (1981). The Psychology of Thinking: Embedding Artifice in Nature. *The Science of The Artificial*. Cambridge, MA: M.I.T. Press.

A Symposium on the Role of Rhythm in Cognition

Organizer:
J. Devin McAuley
Department of Psychology
University of Queensland
Brisbane, Queensland 4072
Australia
devin@psy.uq.edu.au

Rhythm permeates human experience, such as in listening, performing or dancing to music, in speech communication, or in many other common activities such as walking, running, playing a game of tennis, etc. Although it is easy to agree that many human activities elicit a sense of rhythm, both in the perceiver and the performer, the functional role of rhythm in cognition is less clear. This symposium provides an open forum for psychologists, computer scientists, linguists, philosophers, and neuroscientists to present and discuss research that specifically targets the role of rhythm in cognition. A central question concerns to what extent it is necessary to include rhythm as part of a theory of cognition.

Typically, cognitive scientists have placed a much greater emphasis on how cognitive processing consumes time (e.g., processing load) than on how it is shaped by time. In this symposium, presentations by established cognitive scientists focus on how cognitive processing is shaped by time. Talks by Professor Mari Jones, Dr. Bill Baird, Professor Robert Port, and Professor Elliot Saltzman address the role of rhythm in cognition, targeting the overlapping areas of attention, music perception and performance, speech perception and production, sensorimotor control, and neural dynamics.

Mari Jones has proposed a central role for rhythm in cognitive processing, suggesting that the temporal organization of perception, attention, and memory is inherently rhythmic (Jones, 1976). As part of this theory, it is assumed that the rhythms of music and speech entrain (synchronize) periodic attentional "pulses", forming an attentional rhythm. According to this view, entrainment enhances perception, memory storage and retrieval, and sensorimotor control. This contrasts with theories of cognition that leave out rhythm entirely (Newell, 1990).

Bill Baird reports physiological evidence for attentional entrainment, supporting Jones' theory of a central role for rhythm in cognitive processing. He proposes a neural network model of rhythmic expectancy based on an earlier model of adaptive synchronization of 5-15 Hz and 30-80 Hz oscillations between cortical areas (Baird, Troyer, and Eeckman, 1994). He argues that this model can account for psychological data demonstrating that auditory scene analysis is sensitive to rhythm.

Robert Port targets the role of rhythm in auditory cognition, discussing rhythmic constraints on the types of sound patterns that humans learn. He argues that entrainment is a fundamental tool in our basic toolkit for auditory pattern learning, including language. He reports research from his lab investigating the rhythmic constraints exhibited by subjects repeating a phrase in synchrony with a metronome (Port et al., 1996; Cummins and Port, 1996b). In spite of the substantial timing variability of speech, the results from these studies suggest that speech is easily entrained by an external stimulus and that entrainment is a fundamental tool in speech processing.

Elliot Saltzman reports the results from a series of studies investigating rhythmic pattern generation in speech production. In these studies, speakers repeatedly produce a rhythmic utterance, while systematic mechanical perturbations are delivered to the speakers' articulatory gestures. Perturbations delivered during a critical phase window are found to induce systematic steady-state shifts in the timing of coordinated gestures, suggesting that there is a central "clock" that drives the articulatory periphery and that this clock can be phase-reset by event-specific feedback. Saltzman argues that the phase-resetting results imply that the timing of articulatory gestures are governed by sets of oscillatory units and that during speech production these oscillators behave as non-linear, coupled, limit-cycle oscillators (Saltzman and Munhall, 1989).

In addition to the four presentations at the symposium, several other papers published in the proceedings address the role of rhythm in cognition, providing additional reading and references (see Cummins and Port (1996a), Large (1996), and McAuley (1996)).

References

Baird, B., Troyer, T., and Eeckman, F. H. (1994). Attention as selective synchronization of oscillating cortical sensory and motor associative memories. In Eeckman, F., editor, *Neural Systems Analysis and Modeling*, Norwell, Ma. Kluwer.

Cummins, F. and Port, R. (1996a). Rhythmic commonalities between hand gestures and speech. In *Proceedings of the Eighteenth Annual Conference of the Cognitive Science Society.*

Cummins, F. and Port, R. (1996b). Rhythmic constraints on English stress timing. In *Proceedings of the International Conference on Spoken Language Processing*, Philadelphia, PA.

Jones, M. R. (1976). Time, our lost dimension: Toward a new theory of perception, attention, and memory. *Psychological Review*, 83:323–355.

Large, E. W. (1996). Modeling beat perception with a nonlinear oscillator. In *Proceedings of the Eighteenth Annual Conference of the Cognitive Science Society*.

McAuley, J. D. (1996). On the nature of timing mechanisms in cognition. In *Proceedings of the Eighteenth Annual Conference of the Cognitive Science Society*.

Newell, A. (1990). *Unified Theories of Cognition*. Harvard University Press, Cambridge, Massachusetts.

Port, R., Cummins, F., and Gasser, M. (1996). A dynamic approach to rhythm in language: Toward a temporal phonology. In Luka, B. and Needs, B., editors, *Proceedings of the Chicago Linguistics Society 1995*, pages 375–397. Department of Linguistics, University of Chicago.

Saltzman, E. L. and Munhall, K. G. (1989). A dynamical approach to gestural patterning in speech production. *Ecological Psychology*, 1:333–382.

The Role of Rhythm in Guiding Attending

Mari Riess Jones
Department of Psychology
The Ohio State University
Columbus, Ohio 43210
mrjones@magnus.acs.ohio-state.edu

Much of the environment with which we interact is dynamic in that it changes in meaningfully ways over time. We see this in moving objects, body gestures, conversations, ambient sound patterns and in musical events. How is it that we keep in touch with such things as they unfold in time, monitoring them and anticipating nuances as well as major breakpoints in their structure?

One possibility that has been considered at Ohio State is that the dynamic structure of the events themselves provides a basis for guiding an inherently temporal attending activity (Jones, 1976; Jones & Boltz, 1989). We have assumed that attending is based on the joint activity of many attentional rhythms, or oscillators, of graded periods each of which is capable of locking-into, i.e., entraining to a corresponding periodicity embedded in dynamically patterned events. This entrainment enables real time attentional tracking as well as anticipatory responding; in addition, depending on the task and the particular model, it determines an individual's sensitivity to certain structural changes in the unfolding event. To be more concrete about this it helps to illustrate how we study attending in particular tasks.

Often we use a task where a person is presented with an auditory pattern of some sort in which we embed a structural change i.e, a target. The change might be a spectral alteration to one of the pitches comprising a melody, or it might be a lengthened time interval or a shifted tone within a rhythm. Sometimes the patterns themselves are polyrhythms. Polyrhythms are composed of sequences based on two different tone frequencies (high, low tones) that each trace out an isochronous sequence, but in which the respective rates, related by rational numbers, are dissonant (e.g., 3:2, 4:3, etc.). In other cases, the sequences may consist of rhythms formed by recurrent tones of a single frequency but with different intensities (loud, soft) and also patterned in duration to form rhythms such as short–short–long. A common strategy is to embed a structural change within one of two identical test regions within such sequences thereby permitting the use of a two alternative forced choice (2AFC) procedure. We arrange things so that in all of the events that we study in a given experiment the test regions where a target change occurs are identical. So, for instance, if we insert a time-change into a rhythmical pattern (e.g., a rhythm involving only short–short–short time intervals versus one involving short–short–long), the target time-change will always alter a short interval. In this way, we can study the effect of surrounding rhythmic contexts on listener's abilities to detect a small timing nuance.

In fact, if we focus only upon time-change detection tasks some of the recent work that Ed Large and I have been conducting provides one model that is possible out of this framework (Large & Jones, 1996). In this research, we aimed to address two related problems: 1. How do people who listen to rhythmically patterned sequences of the sort I have just described intuit the form of the rhythm, and hence detect a time deviation? and 2. How do people intuit the underlying rhythmic form even when the tempo or rate of the sequence modulates over time as it does in most dynamic events in our natural environment?

The model is a dynamical systems model, developed by Ed Large, which instantiates many of the assumptions I outlined earlier. It assumes that an oscillator carries a pulse of attentional energy that is maximal for some expected point in time within the period of an attentional oscillator. The oscillator is biased to entrain to time periods within an auditory event sequence that correspond to inter-tone time intervals that are near its stipulated period. Thus, longer or shorter time intervals are noticed as deviant to the extent that they violate these expectancies. A second feature of the model is its adaptability to tempo modulations: the period of any oscillator can adapt, via a phase/period resetting process (short-term learning), to track moderate temporal irregularities within a sequence. Finally, a two oscillator version of the model has the potential to explain how people intuit rhythmic form because each of the two attentional oscillators responds to a different (changing) periodicity within a given rhythmic pattern; nevertheless, together they reveal a coupling bias for a time-ratio of 2:1 (in this model).

We have been able to describe the time discrimination performance of average listeners in 2AFC tasks using a variety of patterns that contain different degrees of tempo (rate) modulations (Large & Jones, 1996). Likewise, in other patterns that vary in their rhythmic complexity we have nicely predicted systematic discrimination responses to simple versus complex rhythmic forms (Jones & Yee, 1996). In summary, the model illustrates how assumptions about the inherent rhythmicity of attending can address the two related problems that come up when we consider how people track dynamic events in their environment. It explains adaptability to tempo change and it explains sensitivity to underlying rhythmic forms.

References

Jones, M. R. (1976). Time, our lost dimension: Toward a new theory of perception, attention, and memory. *Psychological Review*, 83:323–355.

Jones, M. R. and Boltz, M. (1989). Dynamic attending and response to time. *Psychological Review*, 96:459–491.

Jones, M. R. and Yee, W. (1996). Sensitivity to time change: The role of context and skill. *Journal of Experimental Psychology: Human Perception and Performance*. (in press).

Large, E. W. and Jones, M. R. (1996). The dynamics of attending: How we track time-varying events. (manuscript under review).

A Cortical Network Model of Cognitive Attentional Streams, Rhythmic Expectation, and Auditory Stream Segregation

Bill Baird
Dept Mathematics, U.C.Berkeley,
Berkeley, Ca. 94720. baird@math.berkeley.edu

We have developed a neural network architecture that implements a theory of attention, learning, and communication based on adaptive synchronization of 5-15 Hz and 30-80 Hz oscillations between cortical areas[Baird et al., 1994]. Here we present a specific model of rhythmic expectancy and the interaction of higher-order and primary cortical levels of processing which accounts for the results of psychological experiments of Jones [Jones et al., 1981] showing that auditory stream segregation depends on the rhythmic structure of inputs. Further references not cited here may be found in these papers.

Using dynamical systems theory, the architecture is constructed from recurrently interconnected oscillatory associative memory modules that model hypercolumns of associational and higher-order sensory and motor cortical areas. The modules learn interconnection weights that cause the system to evolve under a 10 Hz clocked sensory/motor processing cycle through a sequence of transitions of synchronized 40 Hz oscillatory attractors within the modules. In the brain, we hypothesize these cycles to be adaptively controled by septal and thalamic pacemakers which alter excitability of hippocampal and neocortical tissue through nonspecific biasing currents that appear as the cognitive and sensory evoked potentials of the EEG. The cycles "quantize time" and form the basis of derived rhythms with periods up to 1.5 seconds that entrain to each other in motor coordination and to external rhythms in speech and music perception.

The architecture employs selective "attentional" control of the synchronization of the 30-80 Hz oscillations between modules to direct the flow of communication and computation in learning to recognize and generate sequences. The 30-80 Hz attractor amplitude patterns code the information content of a cortical area, whereas phase and frequency are used to "softwire" the network, since only the synchronized areas communicate by exchanging amplitude information. The system works like a broadcast network where the unavoidable crosstalk to all areas from previous learned connections is overcome by frequency coding to allow the operation of attentional communication only between selected areas relevant to the task of the moment. The behavior of the time traces in different modules of the architecture models the temporary appearance and switching of the synchronization of 5-15 and 30-80 Hz oscillations between cortical areas that is observed during sensory/motor tasks in monkeys and humans.

The model architecture illustrates the notion that synchronization not only preattentively "binds" the features of inputs in primary sensory cortex into "objects", but further binds the activity of an attended object to oscillatory activity in associational and higher-order sensory and motor cortical areas to create an evolving attentional network of intercommunicating cortical areas that directs behavior. This is a model of "attended activity" as that subset which has been included in the selectively attended processing of the moment by synchronization to this network. This involves both a spatial binding of activity and a binding of the last to the next step of a sequence. Only inputs which are synchronized to the internal oscillatory activity of a module can effect the proper learned *transitions* of attractors within it.

The phenomenon of "streaming" in audition most exemplifies this notion of *sequence binding*. There *successive* events of a sound source are bound together into a sequence object or "stream" and segregated from other sources such that one can pay attention only to one sound source at a time - as in the "cocktail party" phenomenon. "Cognitive streams" are in evidence when two stories are told in alternating segments and listeners are unable to recall the relative order of events between them. We view the model attentional network as a stream because the synchronized modules within it are cycling through sequences of attractors at the 10 Hz rate. The feedback from higher-order to primary cortical areas allows top down voluntary control to switch the **primary attention stream** or "searchlight" from one source preattentively bound in primary cortex to another source separately bound at a nearby frequency.

There is evidence from studies of motor and perceptual tasks that motor and perceptual behavior is organized by neural rhythms with periods in the range of 100 - 1500 milliseconds, and that entrainment of these to external rhythms in speech and other forms of communication, and to internal rhythms in motor coordination is essential to effective human performance[Jones et al., 1981]. In this view, just as two cortical areas must synchronize to communicate, so must two nervous systems. Work with slowed film suggests that both speaker and listeners show synchronization of body movements to the beat of the roughly 10 Hz rate of phoneme emission. Steady stimulation at either 10 or 40 Hz in audition, vision, or somatosensation causes entrainment of 10 or 40 Hz activity in those areas. 20 Hz stimulation entrains the 40 Hz activity at a 1:2 resonance ratio and has been used medically as a diagonostic for proper function of cortical areas.

Rhythms related to attentional expectation have been found in the auditory EEG. In experiments where the arrival time of a target stimulus is regular enough to be learned by an experimental subject, it has been shown that the 10 Hz activity *in advance of the stimulus* becomes phase locked to that expected arrival time. The same has been shown for hippocampal theta in rats, which is also found to be entrained to the speed of locomotion of a rat. Rats palpatate an object with their paws at 10 Hz and will entrain this "active touch" to an object vibrating near this rate. The "mismatch negativity" of the auditory evoked potential is a reliable indicator of the action of a physiological expectancy system. Changes in the onset or offset time of a repetitive stimulus produce an increase in the N200 component in primary auditory cortex. This is physiological evidence for Jones' theory postulating a rhythmic expectancy system.

Jones[Jones et al., 1981] replicated and altered a classic streaming experiment of Bregman and Rudnicky, and found that their result depended on a specific choice of the rhythm of presentation. The experiment required human subjects to determine of the order of presentation of a pair of high target tones AB or BA of slightly different frequencies. Also presented before and after the target tones were a series of identical much lower frequency tones called the capture tones CCC and two identical tones of intermediate frequency before and after the target tones called the flanking tones F - CCCFABFCCC.

Target order determination performance deteriorated as the flanking tones were brought near to the target tones in frequency, implying that the flanking tones were captured by that stream and obscured the target tones. Otherwise the flanking tones were captured by the background capture tone stream, leaving the target tones to stand out by themselves in the attended stream. Jones noted that the flanking tones and the capture stream were presented at a stimulus onset rate of one per 240 ms and the targets appeared at 80 ms intervals. In her experiments, when the target tones were given a tempo in common with the captors and flanking tones, no effect of the frequency of flanking tones appeared. This suggested that rhythmic distinction of targets and distractors was paramount over frequency in allowing selective attention to segregate out the target stream.

To implement Jones's theory in the model and account for her data, subsets of the oscillatory modules are dedicated to form a rhythmic temporal coordinate frame or time base of nested periodicites in divisions of the thalamic 10 Hz base clock rate between 10 to .5 Hz. Each periodicity is created by an associative memory module that has been specialized to act stereotypically as a counter or shift register by repeatedly cycling through all its attractors at the rate of one for each time step of the clock. Its overall cycle time is therefore determined by the number of attractors. Only one step of the cycle can send output to primary cortex - the one with the largest weight from receiving the most matches to incomming stimuli. Each clock derived in this manner from the thalamic base clock will therefore phase reset itself to get the best match to incomming rhythms. The match is further refined by phase adjustment of the base clock itself.

The modules of the time base send their internal 30-80 Hz activity to primary auditory cortex in 100msec bursts at their different rhythmic rates through fast adapting connections that continually attempt to match incoming stimulus patterns. These weights effectively compute a rough low frequency discrete Fourier transform over a sliding window of 1.5 seconds. Those temporal stimulus patterns which meet these established rhythmic expectancy signals in time are pulled into synchrony with the 30-80 Hz activity of the time base to form a "stream" of events defined by the common synchrony of each with the time base. Stimuli up to a second apart may thus be bound into the same stream without requiring activity to sit undisturbed in the auditory buffer for that long. Segregation of streams in auditory cortex by frequency, intensity, timbre, and other spatially distributed features is done by frequency segregation of the activity within the 30-80 Hz range. In accordance with Jones' theory, voluntary top-down attention can probe input at different hierarchical levels of periodicity by selectively synchronizing with a particular cortical patch in the time base set at the particular 40 Hz frequency of the primary attention stream. Then the "searchlight" into primary cortex is synchronized with and reading in activity occuring at that rhythm. This is the temporal analog of the body centered spatial coordinate frame and multiscale covert attention window system in vision. Here the body centered temporal coordinates of the internal time base orient by entrainment to the external rhythm, and the window of covert temporal attention can then select a level of the multiscale temporal frame.

Our explanation of Jones' result is that the standard target tones first prime the dynamic attention system, then the slow captor tones establish a background stream with a rhythmic expectancy that is later violated by the fast target tones. These are driven into a separate stream which allows the top down primary attention stream, already primed to look for that rhythm, to synchronize and read in the target tones for order determination. In the absence of a rhythmic distinction for the target tones, their pitch difference alone is insufficient to drive the formation of a separate stream, and the mechanism of dynamic attention cannot help discriminate the targets.

References

[Baird et al., 1994] Baird, B., Troyer, T., and Eeckman, F. H. (1994). Attention as selective synchronization of oscillating cortical sensory and motor associative memories. In Eeckman, F. H., editor, *Neural Systems Analysis and Modeling*, Norwell, Ma. Kluwer. in press.

[Jones et al., 1981] Jones, M., Kidd, G., and Wetzel, R. (1981). Evidence for rhythmic attention. *Journal of Experimental Psychology: Human Perception and Performance*, 7:1059–1073.

Language, Audition and Rhythm

Robert F. Port

Departments of Linguistics, Computer Science, Cognitive Science
Indiana University
Bloomington, IN 47401
port@indiana.edu

Oscillators and entrainment are just as much a part of the Basic Auditory Toolkit of cognition as they are of the Basic Motor Control Toolkit. The kinds of rhythm that are found in human languages may reflect either audition or motor control, or both. And it may be hard to tell which is the primary source. Language is both motor and perceptual, yet, fundamentally, neither. Language is an abstract, medium-independent structure – a system that is shared to varying degrees by members of a speech community. All of this is what is meant by saying that language is a cognitive system (van Gelder and Port, 1995).

What factors constrain the phonetic or phonological form of words and phrases in languages? The standard answer is that the physiology of the speech organs provides constraints (e.g., Hockett, 1955; Chomsky and Halle, 1968). For example, linguists usually describe speech in articulatory terms: 'labials', 'stops', 'high vowels.' Even prosodic patterns (over a longer time scale) may be described as in such articulatory terms as 'breath group'. But traditional articulatory descriptions, such as those of linguists, have typically been completely vague about what, say, a 'labial' gesture really is. Recent developments in the theory of motor control have improved the situation by showing how dynamical systems can model speech gestures as objects that are still flexible and abstract (Kelso et al., 1986; Saltzman, 1995). So articulation still provides the most widespread vocabulary for describing speech. We observe that when producing speech the lips jaw, tongue and larynx move quasi-periodically and exhibit strongly stereotyped behavior. For each language, we find that speakers master quite different yet apparently difficult articulatory skills – as evidenced by the persistence of foreign accent when adults learn a new language.

However, independent of the motor constraints, the perceptual system must also master difficult skills when learning a language. It may take years to learn language to asymptote, and, for an adult, some aspects of the perception (and production) of a second language may be effectively unlearnable (Logan, Lively, and Pisoni, 1991). So what is hearing that it could be so difficult?

But the problem of hearing must set in very general terms. What does the auditory system learn? It learns sound patterns. But what are the requirements for being a learnable pattern? Not every complex sound is an auditory pattern. Patterns must have particular kinds of symmetry - such as being a spatiotemporal event that recurs often in the environment. The frequency space can be modelled as linear summation of independent frequencies. But what kind of structures over time can their be? We think there are 3 basic types: slopes, periods and sequences. One limit is that patterns that are periodic at time scales between about .2 Hz ($T = 5$ sec) and 10 Hz ($T = .1$ sec) can be directly predicted. Some non-speech events exhibit oscillations in this frequency range: cricket chirp patterns, water waves, tree branches and leaves in the wind, animal gaits from mice to elephants, resonance of air-filled tubes (from the size of pen cap to a 10-ft tree trunk).

If perceptual systems are to recognize such time-distributed auditory objects, then they must predict them with oscillatory mechanisms (McAuley, 1995). Thus it is likely that oscillators and entrainment are essential components of the Basic Auditory Toolkit – the inventory of mechanisms that are exploited in learning auditory patterns that occur in time.

Language is permeated with rhythm - both because it involves motor control AND because it involves perceptual processes (Port, Cummins and Gasser, 1996). Both get lots of benefits from oscillation. So it may be difficult to be sure just why speech exhibits any rhythm one observes. One source of complexity in the problem is that languages do not just differ from each other in their rhythmic structure (e.g., Japanese mora timing versus English so-called 'stressed-timing'). Even WITHIN languages there is always great variety in rhythmic style. For example, compare baby-talk with the speech of macho athletes, or prose pronunciation with the sing-song recitation of a limerick; or the speech of an emotional preacher pounding his fist on the Bible. A wide range of speech rhythms are available to skilled speakers of any language.

In fact, in my lab we are studying what speakers do when asked simply to repeat a phrase over and over to a slow metronome that signals when they should start each repetition (Cummins, 1995; Cummins and Port, 1996). Surprisingly, a variety of unexpected constraints on the location of stressed syllable onsets could be observed - such as that a stressed syllable within the phrase must begin at a simple harmonic fraction of the whole sentence repetition (that is, at 1/3 or 1/2 way through the cycle of the whole phrase).

This easily encouraged behavior of subjects reinforces

our sense that *speech is always on the edge of rhythmicity*. It is certainly not highly periodic all the time, but it seems that speech is very susceptible to entrainment by any periodic source that happens to be available – by the beat of a drum, by a melody, by the legs of talking jogger, and by the click of our lab metronome. We do not yet know how to design models that exhibit this kind nearly periodic behavior in a useful way, but it seems important to work on.

Rhythm is widespread in nature. Most often, it results from mechanical constraints (e.g., of wave reflection in a uniform medium like a string or a bar or tube, etc) that result in harmonically related frequencies tending to co-occur. It may be that ultimately, this results in rhythmic, harmonic entrainment being one of the basic auditory mechanisms. The rhythm of speech probably results from some combination of mechanical constraints on the dynamics of the vocal tract combined with perceptual constraints on the oscillatory system that recognizes spoken language.

References

Chomsky, N. and Halle, M. (1968). *The Sound Pattern of English*. Harper Row, New York.

Cummins, F. (1995). Identification of rhythmic forms of speech production. *Journal of the Acoustical Society of America*, 98:2894.

Cummins, F. and Port, R. (1996). Rhythmic constraints on English stress timing. In *Proceedings of the International Conference on Spoken Language Processing*, Philadelphia, PA.

Hockett, C. (1955). *The Manual of Phonology*. Waverly Press, Baltimore, Maryland.

Kelso, J. A., Saltzman, E., and Tuller, B. (1986). The dynamical perspective on speech production: Data and theory. *Journal of Phonetics*, 14:29–60.

Logan, J., Lively, S., and Pisoni, D. (1991). Training japanese listeners to identify English /r/ and /l/. *Journal of the Acoustical Society of America*, 89:874–886.

McAuley, J. D. (1995). Perception of Time as Phase: Toward an Adaptive-Oscillator Model of Rhythmic pattern processing. Ph.D. Thesis, Indiana University.

Port, R., Cummins, F., and Gasser, M. (1996a). A dynamic approach to rhythm in language: Toward a temporal phonology. In Luka, B. and Needs, B., editors, *Proceedings of the Chicago Linguistics Society 1995*, pages 375–397. Department of Linguistics, University of Chicago.

Port, R., McAuley, J. D., and Anderson, S. (1996b). Toward simulated audition in an open environment. In Covey, E., Hawkins, H., and Port, R., editors, *Neural Representation of Temporal Patterns*, pages 77–106. Plenum, New York.

van Gelder, T. and Port, R. (1995). It's about time: Overview of the dynamical approach to cognition. In Port, R. and van Gelder, T., editors, *Mind as Motion: Explorations in the Dynamics of Cognition*, pages 1–43. Bradford Books/MIT Press.

Phase-resetting and rhythmic pattern generation in speech production

Elliot Saltzman

Haskins Laboratories, 270 Crown Street, New Haven, CT;
Department of Psychology, University of Connecticut, Storrs, CT
saltzman@haskins.yale.edu

The postulation of segmental or phonemic units in linguistics implies that there is some degree of cohesion among the articulations that comprise these segments. That is, we expect that the cohesion among *gestures* within segmental units is stronger, in some sense, than the cohesion among gestures of different segmental units. (The term gesture is used here to denote a member of an equivalence class of articulatory movement patterns that are *actively* controlled with reference to a given speech-relevant goal, e.g., coordinated movements of the lips and jaw to produce a bilabial closure for a /p/). However, the nature and origin of this intergestural "glue" are issues that require empirical study. It has been hypothesized from a dynamical systems approach that intergestural cohesion can be accounted for by coupling structures defined among intrasegmental gestural units (Saltzman & Munhall, 1989). If so, evidence of such coupling should be experimentally observable.

We report results from a series of phase-resetting (e.g., Winfree, 1980) studies of speech production indicating that intergestural temporal cohesion is greater within segments than between segments. In our data, the coordinated gestures are a bilabial closing and a laryngeal devoicing gesture for a single /p/, as compared to those for /p/s at the beginnings of successive syllables. In these studies, downward-directed mechanical perturbations are applied to the lower lip during the repetitive, rhythmic utterance /...paepaepae.../ and the nonsense word "puh'saepaepple" (e.g, Saltzman, Löfqvist, K.-Shaw, Kay, & Rubin, 1995).

In the repetitive utterance, the amount of temporal shift introduced by a perturbation is measured relative to the timing pattern that existed prior to the perturbation. This shift is measured after the transient, perturbation-induced distortions to the rhythm have subsided, and the system has returned to its pre-perturbation, steady-state rhythm. The finding of a post-perturbation, steady-state temporal shift using this method supports the hypothesis that there exists a central "clock" that drives the articulatory periphery and whose state is altered (phase-shifted) by feedback specific to events at the periphery. Perturbations that induce transient temporal shifts, but not steady-state shifts, do not indicate resetting of the central clock. A further, crucial aspect of the phase-resetting paradigm is that, across trials, perturbations are delivered so as to sample all phases of the rhythm's cycle in order to examine the variation, over the course of the cycle, in the sensitivity of the central clock to peripheral events.

Using this paradigm, we showed that perturbations delivered during the speech sequence /...paepaepae.../ induce systematic steady-state shifts in the timing between the bilabial closing and laryngeal devoicing gestures for /p/s at the beginnings of successive syllables, and observed smaller steady-state shifts in the *relative* phasing of these gestures within the /p/s. Thus, these results not only demonstrate a resetting of the central "clock" for these utterances, but also demonstrate that intergestural temporal cohesion is greater within segments than between segments. That is, the individual temporal shifts of the bilabial and laryngeal gestures are large compared to the relative temporal shift between these gestures, and the lips and larynx appear to be phase-advanced as a relatively coherent unit. Furthermore, such resetting behavior occurs only when the perturbation is delivered within a "sensitive phase" of the cycle. During this period, the downwardly directed lower lip perturbation opposes the just-initiated, actively controlled bilabial closing gesture for /p/. Thus, the sensitive period corresponds (roughly) to the acceleration portion of the closing gesture (Kawato, personal communication). Additionally, although changes in temporal structure were found for other perturbed phases, these changes were simply transient effects, and do not indicate a resetting of the central "clock." Finally, in conjunction with the repetitive utterance, it is important to analyze a corresponding nonrepetitive utterance that contains the same target sequence. By comparing the transient changes in speech timing induced by perturbations for the repetitive and nonsense word utterances, we conclude that the behaviors observed in the (relatively unnatural) rhythmic sequences and the (more natural) nonsense word sequences are governed by a common set of dynamical principles.

These phase-resetting results imply that each gesture in a rhythmic utterance is governed by a corresponding oscillatory unit (or set of units), and that during the performance of a given sequence these oscillators behave as functionally coupled, nonlinear, limit-cycle oscillators. In unperturbed cases, the observed pattern of gestural activity corresponds to an associated pattern of synchronization (entrainment) and relative phasing among the oscillators that is specific to the utterance. When the system is perturbed in the rhythm's sensitive phase, the entire rhythm is phase-advanced in the steady-state and the relative phasing among gestural units is altered to a smaller degree. Such steady-state shifts of intergestural relative phasing will be seen if either: a) the experimental observation time (approximately 20 syllables) was shorter than the *relaxation time* required to return to the system's pre-perturbation relative phase value; or b) the initially observed relative phasing was simply one value in a *phase window* (Byrd, in press) or interval of allowable relative phases.

This interpretation is also consistent with experiments in which discontinuous transitions of intergestural phasing accompanied continuous increases in speaking rate (e.g., Kelso, Saltzman, & Tuller, 1986a, 1986b; Tuller & Kelso, 1991). Specifically, when subjects spoke the syllable /pi/

repetitively at increasing rates, the relative phasing of the bilabial and laryngeal gestures associated with the /p/ did not change from the pattern observed at a self-selected, comfortable rate. However, when the repeated syllable /ip/ was similarly increased in rate, its relative phasing pattern switched relatively abruptly at a critical speed—from that observed for a self-selected, comfortable rate to the pattern observed for the /pi/ sequences. Such intergestural *phase transitions* may be viewed as behaviors of a system of nonlinearly coupled, limit-cycle oscillators that bifurcate from one modal pattern that becomes unstable with increasing rate to another modal pattern that retains its stability (e.g., Haken, Kelso, & Bunz, 1985).

Acknowledgement

Work described in this paper was supported by NIH Grant DC-00121 (Dynamics of Speech Articulation).

References

Byrd, D. (in press). A phase window framework for articulatory timing. *Phonology*.

Haken, H., Kelso, J. A. S., & Bunz, H. (1985). A theoretical model of phase transitions in human hand movements. *Biological Cybernetics, 51*, 347-356.

Kelso, J. A. S., Saltzman, E. L., & Tuller, B. (1986a). The dynamical perspective on speech production: Data and theory. *Journal of Phonetics, 14*, 29-60.

Kelso, J. A. S., Saltzman, E. L., & Tuller, B. (1986b). Intentional contents, communicative context, and task dynamics: A reply to the commentators. *Journal of Phonetics, 14*, 171-196.

Saltzman, E. L., & Munhall, K. G. (1989). A dynamical approach to gestural patterning in speech production. *Ecological Psychology, 1*, 333-382.

Saltzman, E., Lofqvist, A., Kinsella-Shaw, J., Kay, B., & Rubin, P. (1995). On the dynamics of temporal patterning in speech. In F. Bell-Berti, & L. Raphael, (Eds.). *Studies in speech production: A Festschrift for Katherine Safford Harris*. Woodbury, New York: American Institute of Physics.

Tuller, B. & Kelso, J. A. S. (1991). The production and perception of syllable structure. *Journal of Speech and Hearing Research, 34*, 501-508.

Winfree, A. T. (1980). *The geometry of biological time*. NY: Springer-Verlag.

The Future of Modularity

Symposium Organizers:

Michael Spivey-Knowlton
Department of Psychology
Cornell University
Ithaca, NY 14583
mjsk@cornell.edu

Kathleen Eberhard
Department of Psychology
Notre Dame University
Notre Dame, IN 46556
kathleen.m.eberhard.1@nd.edu

Participants (in order of presentation)

1)**James McClelland**   4)**Dominic Massaro**
2)**Peter Lennie**   5)**Kenneth Forster**
3)**Robert Jacobs**   6)**Gary Dell**

This symposium focused on the role to be played by notions of modularity in the field of cognitive science. Modularity has exhibited several different construals in various areas within the cognitive and neural sciences. It has been applied in language research as a *strict* encapsulation of information (Forster, 1979). It has been employed in defining the initial stages of a fuzzy logical model of information *integration* (Massaro, 1989). It has been split into notions of *representational* versus *processing* modularity (Tanenhaus, Dell & Carlson, 1987). It has been used to partially constrain *interactive* connectionist networks (Jacobs, Jordan & Barto, 1991). It has been loosely accepted in visual neuroscience as a catch-phrase for brain structures that are *mostly* specialized for certain subdomains of information (Lennie, 1996). And, finally, it has been criticized entirely as encouraging oversimplified, and sometimes misleading, "descriptive conveniences" (McClelland, in press).

This symposium brought together proponents of the disparate perspectives on this issue (as well as those who walk the fence between these extremes) in hopes of making progress toward a more unified view of 1) the definition of modularity, and 2) its account of cognitive and perceptual phenomena. To ensure applicability to a wide audience, an emphasis was placed on general theoretical accounts.

Questions Addressed in this Symposium

- How does modularity constrain scientific inquiry?

- What is the difference between encapsulation and specialization?

- Should we think about modularity differently for cognition than for perception?

- Are non-modular systems intractable?

- What aspects of the modularity hypothesis have withstood empirical study?

- Should we, and if so how would we, redefine modularity?

The Continuum of Modularity

In 1983, Fodor offered persuasive (though not demonstrative) arguments that the remarkable speed with which linguistic and perceptual processing occur necessitates their possessing at least three essential properties: domain specificity, mandatoriness, and information encapsulation.

According to Fodor, these properties distinguish the rapid processing in these specialized "modular" systems from the typically slower and rather amorphous processing of general cognition, which integrates the modules' outputs to achieve the individual's goals. In the 1980s, this view of the mind/brain was clearly antithetical to the emerging interactive, connectionist view. Whereas modularity considered the integration of multiple sources of information to be incompatible with rapid processing, the interactive view saw integration as primarily responsible for it.

In recent years, however, the theoretical distinctions between modularity and interactionism have become increasingly vague and indeterminate (cf. Boland & Cutler, 1996; Karmiloff-Smith, 1992). This is because technological advances have provided more precise and informative measures (e.g., eye-movement monitoring, neuroimaging, etc.) for testing the views' contrasting predictions. This has led to both modular and interactive models becoming more explicit in their architectural assumptions, and as a consequence, their differences are now diverse and often subtle. In particular, while a number of different dimensions are considered to instantiate modularity, no single dimension is definitive. Moreover, the particular value on a dimension that is used to typify modularity can differ from one research domain to another. For example, "modular" models of vision tend to process information via *parallel* pathways, whereas "modular" models of language tend to process information in *serial* stages.

At least three other dimensions are relevant for distinguishing between modularity and interactionism (see Figure 1). Like parallel-serial, *bidirectional-unidirectional* relates to processing assumptions. Models that assume strictly feedforward information flow are typically classified as modular, while those that permit bidirectional flow (recurrence) are often classified as interactive. The other two dimensions relate primarily to representational assumptions. Models employing *symbolic* representations are more likely to be considered modular than models employing *distributed* representations. And models that assume *binary* activation values (single representational output) are frequently viewed as modular, whereas those that assume *probabilistic* activations (multiple representational output) are typically viewed as interactive.

Figure 1 depicts these dimensions as a four-dimensional space, and modularity is conceptualized as a continuum (represented by the dashed diagonal) that extends through the center of this space. When a model is specified in enough detail to be associated with a region in this space, that region's projection onto the continuum of modularity

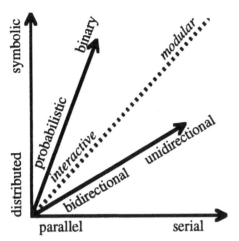

Figure 1: 4-D modularity space, in which various models look more modular or less modular than one another, but in which a true dichotomy of "interactive or modular" does not exist. The dashed line represents the continuum of modularity.

indicates the *degree to which* the model is modular. Thus, according to this conceptualization, modularity is not an all-or-none feature of human information processing systems.

It seems that much of the debate (both within and across domains) over the modularity of the mind/brain stems from differences in which dimensions in this 4-D space are emphasized. For example, one might implicitly accept a model with *serial stages* (e.g., a stage in which representations are <u>accessed</u>, and ambiguity arises, followed by a stage in which one is <u>selected</u>, and ambiguity is resolved) and strictly *feedforward processing* (i.e., constraints that affect a later stage like <u>selection</u> cannot affect an earlier stage like <u>access</u>) (Boland & Cutler, 1996). While these features give the appearance of complete modularity, if the model incorporates an interactive feature (such as probabilistic representations, or multiple-output), then it will not be categorically "modular."

Clearly, both perceptual and linguistic processing are rapid and often mandatory. And, consistent with modularity's requirement of domain specificity, there is evidence that the underlying cortical structures exhibit some degree of independence (e.g., Shallice, 1988). However, contrary to modularity's requirement of information encapsulation, there is compelling evidence for recurrent connections between cortical structures (e.g., Sejnowski & Churchland, 1989) as well as for the computation of vastly distributed representations or "population codes" (e.g., Georgopoulos, Taira, & Lukashin, 1993). Thus, the most accurate view of the mind/brain probably lies on the middle ground of modularity and interactionism.

The Future

Redefining modularity as a continuum radically affects its fundamental tenets. By allowing its characteristics to be graded rather than absolute, its ability to "constrain scientific inquiry" is severely compromised. Moreover, as models become more recurrent and less unidirectional, they blur the distinction between perception and cognition (and action). Conversely, as models approach the extreme in interactionism, incorporating richly distributed representations and nonlinear temporal dynamics, they can become opaque and unfalsifiable. Thus, the challenge for the Continuum view is to construct explicit models that generate testable, coherent predictions.

One important advantage of the Continuum view is that, contrary to Fodor's (1983) claims, general cognition *is* within the realm of scientific investigation. This is important because the vast majority of behavioral measures in cognitive science necessarily reflect the operation of general cognition. Thus, ironically, if modular input systems are viewed as completely encapsulated, *they* are the mental constructs that are less amenable to scientific study (barring the use of neurophysiological techniques). Furthermore, because modularity considers subjects' goals and expectations as contaminating the measurement of modular processes, it encourages studying the processes in highly decontextualized situations. As a result, subjects' goals are often uncontrolled, thus introducing substantial variability in the data. In contrast, the Continuum view considers subjects' goals as crucial factors that affect processing efficiency. Because these effects can, and should, be directly measured, this view encourages highly contextualized experimental situations that create well-defined behavioral goals. Thus, the Continuum view sets a new and, we believe, more fruitful agenda for future research.

References

Boland, J. & Cutler, A. (1996). Interaction with autonomy: Multiple output models and the inadequacy of the Great Divide. *Cognition, 58,* 309-320.

Fodor, J. A. (1983). *The modularity of mind.* Cambridge, MA: MIT Press.

Forster, K. (1979). Levels of processing and the structure of the language processor. In W. Cooper & E. Walker (Eds.), *Sentence processing.* Hillsdale, NJ: Erlbaum.

Georgopoulos, A., Taira, M. & Lukashin, A. (1993). Cognitive neurophysiology of the motor cortex. *Science, 260,* 47-52.

Jacobs, R., Jordan, M., & Barto, A. (1991). Task decomposition through competition in a modular connectionist architecture: The what and where vision tasks. *Cognitive Science, 15,* 219-250.

Karmiloff-Smith, A. (1992). *Beyond modularity: A developmental perspective on cognitive science.* Cambridge, MA: MIT Press.

Lennie, P. (1996). *Single units and visual cortical organization.* Manuscript in preparation.

Massaro, D. (1989). Testing between the TRACE model and the fuzzy logical model of speech perception. *Cognitive Psychology, 21,* 398-421.

McClelland, J. (in press). Integration of information. In T. Inui & J. McClelland (Eds.), *Attention & Performance XVI.* Cambridge, MA: MIT Press.

Sejnowski, T. & Churchland, P. S. (1989). Brain and cognition. In M. Posner (Ed.), *Foundations of cognitive science.* Cambridge, MA: MIT Press.

Shallice, T. (1988). *From neuropsychology to mental structure.* NY, NY: Cambridge U. Press.

Tanenhaus, M., Dell, G., & Carlson, G. (1987). Context effects and lexical processing: A connectionist approach to modularity. In J. Garfield (Ed.), *Modularity in knowledge representation.* Cambridge, MA: MIT Press.

The Basis of Organization in Interactive Processing Systems

James L. McClelland
Department of Psychology and the Center for the Neural Basis of Cognition
Carnegie Mellon University
Pittsburgh, PA 15213
mcclelland+@cmu.edu

The idea that the human cognitive system might consist of a collection of reflexive, autonomous, encapsulated modules serving a general-purpose, open-ended 'central module' was made popular by Fodor in his book, 'The modularity of mind'. The evidence for this view consisted of putative cases of so-called autonomous processing, particularly in lexical access and syntactic parsing. The evidence for this autonomy has not held up, and there is now a wide range of theory and data exploring the ways in which multiple sources of information can be simultaneously exploited for such purposes as segmentation of visual scenes into objects, recognition of phonemes, letters, and words, and assignment of structural relations among constituents of sentences.

Yet it would be absurd to suppose that there is no organization to the cognitive system. The separation of the primary cortices into visual, somatosensory-motor, auditory, and gustatory/olfactory cortices; the further subdivision of the visual system into the dorsal and ventral streams; and the fragmentation of memory, language, and reading following circumscribed lesions to the brain all suggest that the cognitive system is certainly not 'one huge undifferentiated mass of connectoplasm'.

Two of the challenges, then, that face cognitive science and cognitive neuroscience today are the dual challenges of determining (1) how integration occurs within such a highly structured system, and (2) why a system that is so integrative has such a high degree of organization.

The talk will consider what light can be shed on these matters by considering optimal Bayesian approaches to the construction of interpretations of inputs, given the properties that govern their structure. It will turn out that for some cases, at least, optimal organization will imply a certain kind of functional organization; the resulting physical organization can then be understood as reflecting a way of realizing the functional organization with the minimum allocation of hardware (specifically wiring in the form of axonal projections that carry information from one place to another in the brain).

What do Visual Modules do?

Peter Lennie
Department of Brain and Cognitive Sciences and the Center for Visual Science
University of Rochester
Rochester, NY 14627
pl@cvs.rochester.edu

The visual system has a parallel organization, evident at every stage of signal transmission from the retina onwards. The parallel pathways that originate in the retina remain distinct until they reach primary visual cortex, where their separate identities are submerged in a new system of parallel, but interconnected, pathways that contain a hierarchy of modules.

Although the general benefits of parallel and hierarchical organization in the visual system are easily understood, it has not been easy to discern the function of the modules. A widely held view is that in extrastriate cortex the different visual modules analyze different fundamental dimensions of variation in the image (cortical areas V4 and MT being notable examples, associated with the analysis of color and movement, respectively), with the outcomes of these analyses being later brought together to provide a coherent and comprehensive representation of the visual world. This general conception leaves unanswered such questions as why do we need so many visual modules; what is done at each level in the hierarchy; how are the outcomes of the different analyses brought together?

I shall argue that the visual system does not work in the way outlined above. Rather than undertaking multiple relatively independent analyses of the image from which it assembles a unified representation that can be interrogated about the what and where of the world, cortex is organized so that perceptually relevant information can be recovered at every level in the hierarchy, that information used for decisions at one level is not passed on to the next level, and, with one rather special exception, through all stages of analysis all dimensions along which the image is analyzed remain intimately coupled in a retinotopic map.

Modularity and Plasticity are Compatible

Robert A. Jacobs

Department of Brain and Cognitive Sciences
University of Rochester
Rochester, NY 14627
robbie@bcs.rochester.edu

Introduction

Historically, theorists that have highlighted the importance of modular properties of cognitive processing have tended to suggest that the functions, representations, and procedures of cognitive modules are innately specified (e.g., Fodor, 1983). By doing so, these researchers de-emphasize the importance of cognitive development and experience-dependent adaptation. The converse situation also appears to hold; theorists that have stressed the ubiquity of experience-dependent adaptation have tended to ignore or minimize the importance of modular aspects of cognition (e.g., Piaget, 1955). Thus, modularity and experience-dependent plasticity are often seen as incompatible.

Recently, the view that modularity and plasticity are incompatible has been questioned [e.g., Karmiloff-Smith (1992)]. In particular, several researchers have recently proposed computational systems that are modular learning devices. To understand the benefits of incorporating modularity into a learner, it is useful to distinguish between *divergent* computation and *convergent* computation (Jordan and Jacobs, 1992). Divergent computation involves taking data from a single source and performing different computations on it. This is useful whenever an animal has multiple goals and must utilize the data differently depending on the goal. For a learner, it is often advantageous to use different modules to learn different computations because adaptations that occur when learning to satisfy some goal are decoupled from adaptations that are needed to reach other (presumably different) goals. Convergent computation involves taking data in different channels or formats (such as different sensory modalities) and integrating them into a common channel or format. A learner attempting to discover the structure of its environment may benefit from correlating the outputs of distinct sensory modules that each process data from a different modality. In this way, structure can be found that is not present (or not easily detected) in the data from a single modality.

This abstract briefly reviews two recently proposed modular learning devices, one based on divergent computation and the other on convergent computation.

Mixtures-of-Experts Architecture

The first device is referred to as a "mixtures-of-experts" (ME) architecture and it was originally proposed by Jacobs, Jordan, Nowlan, and Hinton (1991). The archi-

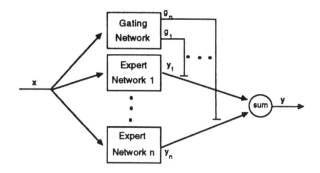

Figure 1: Mixtures-of-Experts Architecture

tecture is intended as an instantiation of the idea that competition can lead to functional specialization. Analogous to Darwinian evolutionary processes, modules of the architecture compete for the right to learn to perform a set of tasks. Due to the competition, modules specialize; that is, modules that are initially functionally undifferentiated learn over time to perform different tasks. More specifically, an ME architecture is a modular system that learns task decompositions in the sense that it uses different connectionist networks to learn input-output training patterns from different regions of the input space (i.e. the space of all possible inputs). As a result of the competition, different networks learn different training patterns and, thus, learn to compute different functions. The architecture consists of two types of networks: *expert networks* and a *gating* network (see Figure 1). The expert networks compete to learn the training patterns. For each training pattern, feedback information is distributed to the experts on the basis of their relative performance; a network whose response most closely matches the desired response (i.e. the winner of the competition) receives lots of feedback information whereas other networks receive no or little feedback. The gating network weights the outputs of the experts so that, for each input pattern, the expert that is most likely to produce the correct response is weighted more heavily than the other experts.

An interesting feature of the mixtures-of-experts framework is the roles it assigns to nature and nurture in the acquisition of functional specializations. The ME architecture tends to allocate to each task an expert network whose structure is well-matched to that task.

Structural properties of a network, such as its topology, receptive field characteristics, or pattern of connectivity, bias a network so as to make it a particularly good learner for some tasks but a poor learner for other tasks. When expert networks with different structural properties compete to learn the training patterns, each network tends to win the competition for those patterns belonging to the task for which its structure makes it a good learner. Consequently, the architecture is capable of discovering structure-function relationships. The performance of the architecture is consistent with the theory that genetic instructions do not necessarily stipulate directly the function to be performed by each brain region. Instead, genetic instructions may assign different structural properties to different regions. These structurally different regions may then, due to their performance characteristics, take on particular functions for which they are well-suited (cf. Bever (1980) and Kosslyn (1987) for related processing accounts of cerebral lateralization). Simulation results using the ME architecture, as well as descriptions of other related architectures, can be found in Jacobs and Jordan (1993), Jordan and Jacobs (1994), Jacobs and Kosslyn (1994), and Peng, Jacobs, and Tanner (1996).

IMAX Learning Architecture

The IMAX learning architecture is a system that uses convergent computation and it was proposed by Becker and Hinton (1992). The modules of this architecture receive data from different modalities (such as vision and touch) or from the same modality at different times (such as consecutive views of a rotating object) or even spatially adjacent parts of the same visual image. It is assumed that different portions of the perceptual input have common causes in the external world. Modules that look at separate but related portions can discover these common causes by striving to produce outputs that agree with each other. In particular, modules adjust their parameters so as to maximize the mutual information among their outputs. This occurs when the output of each module can be used to predict the outputs of the other modules (see Figure 2). An interesting feature of this architecture is that its learning procedure is entirely unsupervised; there is no external teacher that provides the architecture with training information. Instead, each module acts as a teacher for each of the other modules in the sense that each module compares its output with the outputs of the other modules. Becker and Hinton (1992) showed that when two modules view adjacent patches of two-dimensional visual images, an architecture that has no prior knowledge of the third dimension can discover depth in random dot stereograms of curved surfaces.

Acknowledgments

This work was supported by NIH grant R29-MH54770.

References

Becker, S. & Hinton, G.E. (1992) Self-organizing neural network that discovers surfaces in random-dot stereograms. *Nature*, 355, 161-163.

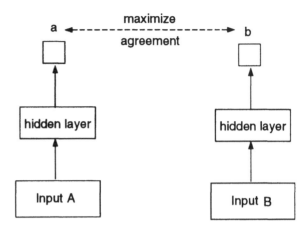

Figure 2: IMAX Learning Architecture (adapted from Becker and Hinton(1992))

Bever, T.G. (1980) Broca and Lashley were right: Cerebral dominance is an accident of growth. In D. Kaplan & N. Chomsky (Eds.), *Biology and Language*. Cambridge, MA: MIT Press.

Fodor, J.A. (1983) *The Modularity of Mind*. Cambridge, MA: MIT Press.

Jacobs, R.A. & Jordan, M.I. (1993) Learning piecewise control strategies in a modular neural network architecture. *IEEE Transactions on Systems, Man, and Cybernetics*, 23, 337-345.

Jacobs, R.A., Jordan, M.I., Nowlan, S.J., & Hinton, G.E. (1991) Adaptive mixtures of local experts. *Neural Computation*, 3, 79-87.

Jacobs, R.A. & Kosslyn, S.M. (1994) Encoding shape and spatial relations: The role of receptive field size in coordinating complementary representations. *Cognitive Science*, 18, 361-386.

Jordan, M.I. & Jacobs, R.A. (1992) Modularity, unsupervised learning, and supervised learning. In S. Davis (Ed.) *Connectionism: Theory and Practice*. Oxford University Press.

Jordan, M.I. & Jacobs, R.A. (1994) Hierarchical mixtures of experts and the EM algorithm. *Neural Computation*, 6, 181-214.

Karmiloff-Smith, A. (1992) *Beyond Modularity: A Developmental Perspective on Cognitive Science*. Cambridge, MA: MIT Press.

Kosslyn, S.M. (1987) Seeing and imagining in the cerebral hemispheres: A computational approach. *Psychological Review*, 94, 148-175.

Piaget, J. (1955) *The Child's Construction of Reality*. Routledge and Kegan Paul.

Peng, F., Jacobs, R.A., & Tanner, M.A. (1996) Bayesian inference in mixtures-of-experts and hierarchical mixtures-of-experts models with an application to speech recognition. *Journal of the American Statistical Association*, in press.

Modularity of Information, not Processing

Dominic W. Massaro
Department of Psychology
University of California, Santa Cruz
Santa Cruz, CA 95064
`massaro@fuzzy.ucsc.edu`

The framework of a Fuzzy Logical Model of Perception (FLMP) has guided our research and also helps clarify the modularity issue. The results from a wide variety of experiments have been described within the framework of the FLMP. Within this framework, pattern recognition is guided by multiple sources of information that the perceiver evaluates and integrates to achieve perceptual recognition. According to the FLMP, well-learned patterns are recognized in accordance with a general algorithm, regardless of the modality or particular nature of the patterns. It is assumed that patterns are processed through a sequence of processing stages: evaluation, integration, and decision. Continuously-valued features are evaluated, integrated, and matched against prototype descriptions in memory, and an identification decision is made on the basis of the relative goodness of match of the stimulus information with the relevant prototype descriptions.

The model allows an important distinction to be made between information and information processing. Information refers to interface between the attributes and characteristics of the stimulus world and the participant's memory, serving as functional inputs to the evaluation operation in the FLMP. Information processing refers to the algorithm describing how this information is processed. Information processing corresponds to the algorithmic nature of the evaluation, integration, and decision operations rather than the actual information that is being operated on. Information is clearly different across different domains such as object recognition and speech perception, but the information processing might follow the same algorithm across these different domains. If we must use the term modularity, there is no question of modularity of information across different domains. On the other hand, there is convincing evidence that information processing is highly similar, if not identical, across the different domains.

Pattern recognition is usually studied in an expanded factorial design. This design has been used to study both speech perception by ear and by eye and affect perception as conveyed by both the face and the voice. As an example, an animated talking head was used to combine each of the four auditory syllables with each of the four visible syllables in a speech identification task (Cohen & Massaro, 1993). In addition, each of the syllables is presented unimodally. Most importantly, we are able to control and manipulate the audible and visible speech independently of one another. This is important because a necessary ingredient of scientific inquiry is to pull apart several variables that are normally confounded in the natural world. The goal of this type of study is to determine how the separate sources of information are processed together to achieve perception. The expanded factorial design also provides a strong test of quantitative models because each candidate model must describe the relationship between unimodal and bimodal performance. More generally, the goal is to determine a theoretical description that can describe or explain the performance on the bimodal conditions as a function of performance on the unimodal conditions.

Our studies of facial affect are exactly parallel to our speech perception studies. In face-to-face communication, perceiving speech does not necessarily correspond to just the sound, but somehow emerges from the sound and sight of the face, respectively. We ask whether the same is true of judgments of affect. In some experiments, our talking head was programmed to say the word "please" under happy, angry, surprise, and fear affects. Using an expanded factorial design, the four affects were presented auditorily, visually, and bimodally.

Fodor's original claim of modularity was that the nature of the information processing would necessarily differ across these different input systems. (Massaro & Cowan, 1993). In contrast, the results of these experiments and a variety of others indicate that speech perception and affect recognition follow the same algorithm. The quantitative judgments are well-described by the FLMP. We take this result as support for the general framework of the FLMP and as evidence against modularity.

In an analogous line of research, we have studied the influence of bottom-up and top-down sources of information in language processing (Massaro, 1994; Massaro & Oden, 1995). Once again, experiments independently manipulating these two sources of information are highly informative. The model tests have established that perceivers integrate top-down and bottom-up information in language processing. This result means that sensory information and context are integrated in the same manner as several sources of bottom-up information.

The nature of this integration process is also accurately described by the FLMP. Many investigators operate as if interactive activation is the only viable alternative to modular or autonomous models. However, the FLMP allows integration while maintaining independence among the sources (at the evaluation stage). Thus, the FLMP and its corresponding theoretical framework offers a viable solution that combines important features of both the modular and interactive activation frameworks.

Acknowledgments

The research reported in this paper and the writing of the paper were supported, in part, by grants from the Public Health Service (PHS R01 NS 20314), the National Science Foundation (BNS 8812728), and the graduate division of the University of California, Santa Cruz. Special thanks to Andrew T. Massaro for expert advise on internet communications.

References

Cohen, M. M., & Massaro, D. W. (1993) Modeling coarticulation in synthetic visual speech. In N. M. Thalmann & D. Thalmann (Eds.), *Computer Animation '93* (pp. 139-156). Tokyo: Springer-Verlag.

Massaro, D. W. (1994). Psychological aspects of speech perception: Implications for research and theory. In M. Gernsbacher (Ed.), *Handbook of Psycholinguistics* (pp. 219-263). New York: Academic Press.

Massaro, D. W., & Cowan, N. (1993). Information processing models: Microscopes of the mind. *Annual Review of Psychology, 44*, 383-425.

Massaro, D. W., & Oden, G. C. (1995). Independence of lexical context and phonological information in speech perception. *Journal of Experimental Psychology: Learning, Memory, and Cognition, 21*, 1053-1064.

Models and Modularity in Language Processing

Gary S. Dell
Department of Psychology and the Beckman Institute
405 N. Mathews St.
University of Illinois
Urbana, IL 61801
gdell@s.psych.uiuc.edu

Ten years ago, everyone in cognitive science had an opinion on modularity. This was particularly true for those working on language, where what Boland and Cutler (1996) call the "Great Divide" in psycholinguistic theory separated autonomous from interactive models. I am sure that most participants in this symposium will agree that this Divide is not as forbidding as it was in the pioneer days of cognitive science. Indeed, many of us now have no idea what side of the debate we are on.

The evolution from a Great Divide to a friendly panel discussion at the Cognitive Science Society Meeting is due, in large part, to the development of explicit models. These models--and here I have particularly in mind connectionist models of word and sentence comprehension and production--have stripped away the rhetoric and allowed us to see the actual operations of "modular" and "interactive" accounts. Sometimes we find out that the differences between such accounts are quite subtle, for example, whether or not there is a hypothesized set of excitatory connections from a word layer to a phoneme layer.

The kinds of models that I have found most useful have the characteristics of being globally modular and locally interactive. There are processing levels, for example, words are associated with a semantics and with phonological forms. Often, there is the need for a processing level simply because of the nature of the required mapping. For example, because the mapping between the semantic representation of a word and its phonological form is not linearly separable, an intermediate "word" level between meaning and form is needed. Processing is interactive in the sense that adjacent levels influence one another through feedback and feedforward. However, this interaction is limited. Only a few levels will participate in an attractor state, the active levels being determined by the task being performed. For example, when we are just about to say a particular word, only levels related to its form are active; there is no interactive influence from meaning at this late stage in processing.

One final point: It isn't too difficult to talk about modularity-related issues in language processing when dealing with lexical processing--word recognition and word production. Sentence processing is another story. It has been my experience as a consumer (and some-time producer) of empirical findings in sentence comprehension that it is hard to get any results that are recognized as definitive. The problem is simply that we don't have sentence processing models that are as explicit as the lexical models. Until we do, we will continue to have trouble relating data to theory.

References

Boland, J. & Cutler, A. (1996). Interaction with autonomy: Multiple output models and the inadequacy of the Great Divide. *Cognition, 58*, 309-320.

The Evolution of Mind

Denise Dellarosa Cummins

Cognitive Science
University of Arizona
Tucson, AZ 85721
dcummins@ccit.arizona.edu

John Tooby

Anthropology
University of California
Santa Barbara, CA
tooby@alishaw.ucsb.edu

Colin Allen

Philosophy
Texas A&M University
College Station, TX
colin-allen@snaefell.tamu.edu

Historically, the psychological investigation of learning and cognition has followed a common pattern. Initially, content-free, domain-general mechanisms are posited to explain a particular phenomenon. Subsequent research then seriously challenges these theories, leading to their modification in order to include species-specific, innate, or other domain specific constraints.

For example, the oft-replicated Garcia effect seriously challenged the notion of equipotentiality of conditionable associations in classical stimulus-response theory in favor of an innate "preparedness" to acquire certain types of associations rather than others (Garcia & Koelling, 1966). Contemporary studies of infant and early childhood cognition have seriously challenged Piagetian (Piaget, 1952 and 1972) and other purely "bottom up" theories of cognitive development in favor of theories that posit innate or early emerging domain-specific constraints on the induction of ontological categories (Carey, 1985; Keil, 1994), causality (Leslie & Keeble, 1987), and the physical properties of objects and object movement (Spelke, 1994). Similarly, decades of research in artificial intelligence seem to be leading to the inexorable conclusion that a reasoner must know something about the domain about which it is to reason if useful inferences are to be made. And in 1982, David Marr exhorted vision researchers to let their research and theories be guided by consideration of the types of problems the visual system must solve in order to allow an organism to negotiate its world successfully.

In recent years, evolutionary psychologists have begun to take this exhortation seriously in their study of cognitive phenomena. The guiding principle of this research is that in order to understand a structure's function, one must consider the problems that the structure evolved to solve. This is not to say that all existing biological structures and their functions were the result of natural selection in the face of evolutionary pressures; sometimes structures or one of a structure's functions can be the by-product of selection for another structure or another of the structure's functions. Nonetheless, allowing this principle to guide one's research is believed to be the most likely way of asking informed questions in our research programs.

Most notable in this regard is research in reasoning and language. In the first two papers, John Tooby and Denise Cummins argue that taking an evolutionary approach in the investigation and explanation of human reasoning can resolve current paradoxes in human reasoning performance. Tooby outlines several evolutionary principles that underlie ecologically rational domain-specific reasoning, reasoning that allows humans to outperform the best artificial systems around today on complex problems such as grammar induction--despite failing on seemingly simple content-free reasoning tasks. Cummins uses evidence from primate field studies, developmental research on early emerging reasoning competence, and neurologically dissociable reasoning competences to posit innate reasoning architecture that is specific to a type of social reasoning called deontic reasoning. Her argument takes seriously the claim made by Cheney and Seyfarth (1985, p. 39) that "...among primates, evolution has acted with particular force in the social domain."

In the symposium's final paper, Colin Allen cites evidence from comparative studies of animal communication to propose an argument concerning the central role of referential signalling in the evolution of language. Allen's argument reaches deep into language's evolutionary roots to shed light on how basic referential signals are used by other species to categorize events in the world. While Universal Grammar appears to be a communicative system that is specific to humans as a species, referential signalling is a fundamental component of natural communicative systems used by other species as well.

References

Carey, 1985 *Conceptual change in childhood*. Cambridge, MA: MIT Press.

Cheney, D.L., & Seyfarth, R.M. 1985: The social and non-social world of non-human primates. In R.A. Hinde, A-N. Perret-Clermont, & J. Stevenson-Hinde (eds.) *Social Relationships And Cognitive Development*. Oxford: Clarendon Press.

Garcia, J., & Koelling, R. (1966) Relation of cue to consequence in avoidance learning. *Psychonomic Science*, 4, 123-124.

Keil, F.C. (1994) Explanation, association, and the acquisition of word meaning. *Lingua*, 92, 169-196.

Leslie, A. M., & Keeble, S. (1987) Do six-month-old infants perceive causality? *Cognition*, 25, 265-288.

Marr, D. (1982) *Vision: a computational investigation into the human representation and processing of visual information*. San Francisco: Freeman.

Piaget, J. (1952) *The origins of intelligence in children*. New York: International University Press.

Piaget, J. (1972) *The child's conception of the world*. Totowa, NJ: Littlefield, Adams.

Spelke, E. (1994) Initial knowledge: six suggestions. *Cognition*, 50, 431-445.

The Evolutionary Principles Underlying Natural Cognitive Competences

John Tooby
Anthropology
University of California
Santa Barbara, CA
tooby@alishaw.ucsb.edu

Modern research into human reasoning and decision-making has produced a formidable paradox. The consensus among many modern reasoning and decision-researchers is that the faculty of human reasoning is governed by crude and error-prone heuristics, bears little or no resemblance to the logician or theorist's ideal, and systemacially departs from normative models of ideal statistical and deductive inference.

Yet despite this apparent human ineptitude on laboratory-administered artificial problems, natural reasoning systems--human and nonhuman minds alike--negotiate the complex natural tasks of their evolutionary world with a level of operational success far surpassing that of the most sophisticated existing artificial intelligence systems. On virtually every natural inferential problem that has been carefully investigated--from grammar induction, semantic induction, and speech perception to vision, object recognition, and color constancy--organisms perform better than the systems that cognitive scientists have been able to construct, even though these scientists have had full access to modern logics, statistical decision theories, and other formal methods of inference.

The paradox can be resolved by considering the evolutionary principles that underlie what we call ecologically rational domain-specific inferential principles. Ecologically rational computational devices can generate effective decisions and reconstruct reliable knowledge that would have been unobtainable by any methods that did not incorporate specializations designed to exploit the evolutionarily stable structure of the world, divided into functionally distinct domains.

Human Reasoning From an Evolutionary Perspective

Denise Dellarosa Cummins

Cognitive Science
University of Arizona
Tucson, AZ 85721
dcummins@ccit.arizona.edu

Contemporary psychological theories of human reasoning are recapitulating the historical pattern observed for theories of other cognitive functions. Initial theories described human reasoning as a content-free, domain-general process (Braine, 1978; Rips, 1983). These theories were seriously challenged by mounting evidence of domain-specific content effects in human reasoning performance (e.g., Cox & Griggs, 1982; Griggs & Cox, 1983; Cheng & Holyoak, 1985; Gigerenzer & Hug, 1992; Thompson, 1994). In order to salvage content-free theories, their proponents have attributed content effects to "bias" (Rumain, Connell, & Braine, 1983; Evans, 1989) or content-specific parameters that modify the inputs to the content-free system (Braine & O'Brien, 1991; Rips, 1994). Other theorists have abandoned the notion of a content-free reasoner, proposing instead collections of domain-specific rules that are induced from life experiences with classes of situations (Cheng & Holyoak, 1985 and 1989).

More recently, however, others have argued that certain reasoning domains are innately specified in the human reasoning architecture, having emerged in response to evolutionary pressures during the Pleistocene (Cosmides, 1989; Cosmides & Tooby, 1994). I argue that the evolutionary origins of some domain-specific effects in human reasoning may predate the origins of the hominid line (Cummins, in press a and b).

The domain I focus on is deontic reasoning, that is, reasoning about what one may, ought, or must not do (Hilpinen, 1981; Manktelow & Over, 1991). This type of reasoning is distinct from indicative reasoning in which the reasoner is required to determine the epistemic status (truth) of a rule or other description of a state of affairs. Reasoners tend to adopt a violation-detection strategy when reasoning deontically and a confirmation-seeking strategy when reasoning about the epistemic status of rules. This indicative-deontic distinction emerges early in human development and colors the reasoning process throughout adulthood (Cummins, in press a). This strongly suggests a fundamental, primitive distinction in our cognitive architecture. Furthermore, the structure of deontic situations is more easily grasped by young children than is the structure of epistemic reasoning tasks (Harris & Nunez, in press). The ease and speed with which young children detect, understand, and reason about deontic situations is consistent with the existence of an innate domain-specific reasoning module that is evoked when a situation with deontic content is encountered.

Deontic reasoning is also apparent in the cognition of non-human primates, suggesting that the capacity for this type of reasoning predates the emergence of the hominid line. Like most avian and mammalian societies, primate social groups are characterized by dominance hierarchies. In functional terms, a dominance hierarchy is simply the statistical observation that particular individuals in social groups have regular priority of access to resources-- particularly reproductive resources--in competitive situations. Rank within the hierarchy is of such importance that non-human primates have been described as consummate tacticians, with much of this tactical reasoning aimed at jockeying for position within the dominance hierarchy (de Waal, 1982; Byrne & Whiten, 1988). Furthermore, there is a direct relation between social reasoning skill and rank within primate hierarchies.

The social reasoning that is required to secure and maintain a high- ranking place within the dominance hierarchy requires the capacity to detect and respond appropriately to a variety of deontic structures, including, most importantly, violations of these structures. For example, those who currently dominate resources determine who may and who may not engage in which activities when, and they punish transgressors. In order to dominate resources, therefore, an individual must have the capacity to recognize violations of permissions and prohibitions. Similarly, in order to avoid agonistic encounters, subordinates must have the capacity to recognize what is permitted and what is forbidden, and to behave accordingly.

It is in the interest of subordinates, on the other hand, to broaden their access to available resources. In other words, it is in their interest to move up in rank. In order to change rank, an individual must have allies who will provide support during a contest of rank. Those who do not have allies can neither move up in rank nor maintain a stable position within the hierarchy, including alpha males (Harcourt & Stewart, 1987; Riss & Goodall, 1977). Primate alliances are formed and maintained on the basis of reciprocal obligations (see Harcourt & de Waal, 1992). For example, Cheney and Seyfarth (1990) report that vervet monkeys are more likely to come to the aid of an individual during an agonistic encounter if that individual has groomed them recently. de Waal (1992) reported observing a subordinate male terminate his long-term alliance with an alpha male in response to the alpha male's increasingly frequent refusals to support him in contests with another male over access to estrus females. Forming and maintaining alliances, therefore, requires effective reasoning about obligations. Taken together, this evidence from primate field studies strongly suggests that deontic reasoning strategies emerged prior to the division of hominids within the primate line.

Finally, there is reason to believe that this type of reasoning may be supported by functionally distinct neural substrates. Damage to the ventro-medial prefrontal cortex in both human and non-human primates has been found to produce a syndrome in which socio-emotional reasoning is impaired while leaving other types of intelligent reasoning untouched (see Damasio, 1994). There is also some evidence that patients suffering from this syndrome do not show the typical deontic reasoning effects observed in normal subjects (Adolphs, Tranel, Bechara, Damasio, & Damasio, 1996). Although far from conclusive, these data suggest that deontic reasoning might be selectively dissociated from other types of reasoning at the neurological level.

In summary, the robustness of the deontic effect in adult reasoning, its early emergence in human development, the central role played by deontic reasoning in primate dominance hierarchies, and the neurological dissociability of socio-emotional reasoning from other types of intelligent reasoning strongly suggest that some aspect of our reasoning architecture is devoted specifically to problems of deontic content.

References

Adolphs, R., Tranel, D., Bechara, A., Damasio, H., & Damasio, A.R. (1996) Neuropsychological approaches to reasoning and decision-making. In A.R. Damasio et al. (eds.), *Neurobiology of decision-making*. Heidelberg: Springer-Verlag.

Braine, M.D.S. (1978). On the relation between the natural logic of reasoning and standard logic. *Psychological Review*, 85, 1-21.

Braine, M.D.S., & O'Brien, D.P. (1991). A theory of *If*: A lexical entry, reasoning program, and pragmatic principles. *Psychological Review*, 98, 182-203.

Byrne, R.W., & Whiten, A. (eds.) (1988)*Machiavellian Intelligence:* Oxford: Oxford University Press.

Cheney, D.L., & Seyfarth, R.M. (1990) *How monkeys see the world.* Chicago: University of Chicago Press.

Cheng, P.W., & Holyoak, K.J. (1985). Pragmatic reasoning schemas. *Cognitive Psychology*, 17, 391-416.

Cheng, P.W., & Holyoak, K.J. (1989) On the natural selection of reasoning theories. *Cognition*, 33, 285-313.

Cosmides, L. (1989). The logic of social exchange: Has natural selection shaped how humans reason? Studies with the Wason selection task. *Cognition*, 3 1, 187-276.

Cosmides, L., & Tooby, J. (1994). Beyond intuition and instinct blindness: Toward an evolutionarily rigorous cognitive science. *Cognition*, 50, 41-77.

Cox, J.R., & Griggs, R.A. (1982). The effects of experience on performance in Wason's selection task. *Memory & Cognition*, 10, 496-502.

Cummins, D.D. in press (a). Evidence on the innateness of deontic reasoning. *Mind & Language*.

Cummins, D.D. in press (b). Evidence of deontic reasoning in 3- and 4-year-olds. *Memory & Cognition*.

Damasio, A.R. *Descartes' Error*. NY: Grosset/Putnam.

de Waal, H. (1982). *Chimpanzee Politics*. Baltimore. Johns-Hopkins University Press.

de Waal, H. 1992: Coalitions as part of reciprocal relations in the Arnhem chimpanzee colony. In Harcourt, A.H., & de Waal, F.B.M (eds.) 1992: *Coalitions And Alliances In Humans And Other Animals*. Oxford: Oxford University.

Evans, J. St. B. T. (1989). *Bias In Human Reasoning*. Hillsdale, N.J.: Lawrence Erlbaum, Inc.

Gigerenzer, G., & Hug, K. (1992). Domain-specific reasoning: Social contracts, cheating, and perspective change. *Cognition*, 43). 127-171.

Griggs, R.A., & Cox, J.R. (1983). The effects of problem content and negation on Wason's selection task. *Quarterly Journal of Experimental Psychology*, 3 5 A. 519-533.

Harcourt, A.H., & de Waal, F.B.M (Eds, 1992). *Coalitions And Alliances In Humans And Other Animals*. Oxford). Oxford University Press.

Harcourt, A.H., & Stewart, K.J. (1987). The influence of help in contests on dominance rank in primates). Hints from gorillas. *Animal Behaviour*, 35, 182-190.

Harris, P.L., & Nuñez, M. (in press). Understanding of permission rules by preschool children. *Child Development*.

Hilpinen, R. (1981). *New Studies In Deontic Logic*. Boston: Reidel/Kluwer.

Manktelow, K.I., & Over, D.E. (1991). Social roles and utilities in reasoning with deontic conditionals. *Cognition*, 39, 85-105.

Rips, L.J. (1983). Cognitive processes in propositional reasoning. *Psychological Review*, 90, 38-71.

Rips, L.J. (1994). *The psychology of proof*. Cambridge, MA: Bradford/MIT Press.

Riss, D.C., & Goodall, J. (1977). The recent rise to the alpha-rank in a population of free-living chimpanzees. *Folia Primatologica*, 27, 134-151.

Rumain, B., Connell, J., & Braine, M.D.S. (1983). Conversational comprehension proceses are responsible for reasoning fallacies in children as well as adults: IF is not the biconditional. *Developmental Psychology*, 19, 471-481.

Thompson, V.A. (1994). Interpretational factors in conditional reasoning. *Memory & Cognition*, 22, 742-758.

Actions and objects: unequal partners in the evolution of communication

Colin Allen

Department of Philosophy
Texas A&M University
College Station, TX 77843-4237
colin-allen@tamu.edu

Some theorists have argued that the evolutionary development of human language lies buried with our hominid ancestors and that the search for precursors of language in nonhuman animals is misguided (Pinker 1994). This view is supported by a common conception of animal communication according to which signal production is an involuntary manifestation of emotional arousal, so that signals convey no independent information about referents external to the signaller. In contrast, human language is thought to be under voluntary control and capable of referring to objects regardless of the emotional state of the speaker.

Recent comparative studies of species including chickens and monkeys provide evidence to support the view that the vocalizations of nonhuman animals are under a greater degree of voluntary control than previously believed (Cheney & Seyfarth 1990; Evans & Marler 1995; Marler & Evans 1996) and that they are "functionally referential" in that they provide specific information about events external to the signaller (Macedonia & Evans 1993). These studies suggest closer similarities between certain aspects of human language and animal communication systems than was previously recognized. It is still unclear whether these similarities reflect common ancestry (homology) or convergent evolutionary processes (analogy) and broader comparative studies are necessary to resolve these issues. Nonetheless, the available data do allow for some interesting comparisons that may allow us to understand some puzzling aspects of human language acquisition.

The concept of a "medium-sized" or "basic-level" category specified in terms of perceived similarity to a morphologically-identified prototype (Rosch et al. 1976) is often appealed to by language learning theorists to account for the ability of human children to identify the correct reference of learned count nouns such as "dog" or "bird" (Hall 1994). But this designation seems suspiciously ad hoc for in some cases the category is at the taxonomic level of species or family (e.g. "dog") and sometimes at the level of a class (e.g. "bird"). The degree of abstraction in these categories does, however, correspond closely to those identified by Cheney & Seyfarth as the referents of vervet monkey alarm calls (e.g., "leopard", "snake", or "eagle") which also correspond to different taxonomic levels. These differentiations are considerably less abstract than the categories identified by Marler & Evans as referents of the alarm calls of chickens (e.g., "avian predator" and "terrestrial predator"). It is possible

that these translational differences reflect nothing more than a lack of knowledge about the vocalizations of chickens and vervets. But if the differences are real, then some available data about the ontogeny of vervet alarm calls suggest an interesting hypothesis about the evolution of communication systems and the ability to conceptualize objects independently of their typical behaviors. The hypothesis would, if correct, have consequences for understanding the acquisition of human language.

Infant vervets begin by giving recognizable "eagle" alarm calls to a variety of birds and even to leaves falling from trees, but as they get older the calls become more specific to those species of eagle that prey on vervets (Seyfarth et al. 1980). Analysis of the ontogeny of eagle alarm calls shows that infants' "mistakes" are most common for nonpredatory species diving rapidly from the sky or closely approaching the vervets, and that such errors not associated merely with morphological similarity (Cheney & Seyfarth 1986). Because these are behaviors that may reasonably be associated with predation, and because moving objects are more easily discriminated from background than static objects, it makes sense that vervets would be innately disposed to react to such events. This suggests the hypothesis that insofar as these calls refer to objects, the objects are initially classified in terms of their behavior or actions. This is consistent with discovery by Evans & Marler (1995) that a moving image of a raccoon shown to a chickens on a video monitor mounted overhead will elicit aerial predator calls at a higher rate than terrestrial predator calls (although such calls were less reliably elicited than by video footage of a raptor on the overhead monitor).

The evidence from chickens suggests that while their signals are referential, the categories referred to are action-oriented (predation from the air versus predation from the ground) although morphological features are also important in affecting call frequency (Evans & Marler 1995). The evolution of functional reference to these categories may have been driven by the different anti-predatory strategies that are appropriate for chickens faced by these different predators (Macedonia & Evans 1993). Similarly, infant vervets seem to begin with an action-oriented classification scheme. In vervets, refinements due to adult reinforcement of infant vocalizations may lead to a classification scheme that is based more on perceptual characteristics abstracted away from behavior. The ability to categorize and refer to objects independently of behavior would be an adaptive trait when the costs of responding to false positives (such as non predators behaving in a predatory fashion) or of failing to respond to false negatives (such as predators behaving in non-typical ways) are relatively high.

If the ontogeny of sophisticated referential skills recapitulates the phylogeny in a transition from action-based categories to feature-based categories, then it may not be necessary to postulate morphologically-specified, innate "middle-sized" or "basic-level" categories to explain how children settle on a reasonable level of interpretation for count nouns. The behavioral differences between dogs and cows (although belonging to the same taxonomic order) may have been evolutionarily salient to humans in ways that differences between behavior in different species of birds was not and thus humans might innately be disposed to categorize initially according to such behaviorally specified categories. An evolutionary and comparative approach to the notion of reference and similarities to various nonhuman communication systems may thus help provide a specification of the basic categories that facilitate the earliest stages of language acquisition.

References

Cheney, D. L. & Seyfarth, R. M. (1986) Vocal development in vervets. *Animal Behavior*, 34, 1640-1658.

Cheney, D. L. & Seyfarth, R. M. (1990) *How monkeys see the world*. Chicago: University of Chicago Press.

Evans, C.S. & Marler, P. (1995) Language and animal communication. In Roitblat, H. & Arcady-Meyer, J. (eds.) *Comparative Approaches to Cognitive Science*. Cambridge, MA: MIT Press.

Hall, D. G. (1994) How children learn common nouns and proper names: a review of the experimental evidence. In Macnamara, J. & Reyes, G. E. (eds.) *The Logical Foundations of Cognition*. New York: Oxford University Press.

Macedonia, J. H. & Evans, C. S. (1993) Variation among mammalian alarm call systems and the problem of meaning in animal signals. *Ethology*, 93, 177-197.

Marler, P. & Evans, C. (1996) Bird calls: just emotional displays or something more? *Ibis*, 138, 26-33

Pinker, S. (1994) The Language Instinct. New York: William Morrow and Company.

Rosch, E., Mervis, C., Gray, W., Johnson, D. & Boyes-Braem, P. (1976) Basic objects in natural categories. *Cognitive Psychology*, 3, 382-439.

Seyfarth, R. M, Cheney, D. L. & Marler, P. Monkey responses to three different alarm calls: Evidence of predator classification and semantic communication. *Science*, 210, 801-803.

Symposium: Eye Movements in Cognitive Science

Organized by:
Julie Epelboim and **Patrick Suppes (Chair)**
Center for the Study of Language and Information
Stanford University
Stanford, CA 94305-4115
yulya@brissun.umd.edu, suppes@ockham.stanford.edu

The field of eye movement research is very versatile. It is of interest to scientists from a broad range of disciplines. A partial list of fields in which eye movements have been studied and lead to useful insights includes Psychology, Neuroscience, Artificial Intelligence, Computer Vision and Human Factors. All of these disciplines are likely to be represented at this Cognitive Science Conference.

Cognitively-oriented research involving eye movements has proceeded in two directions: (i) by finding out how perceptual and cognitive factors influence eye movement patterns, and (ii) by using eye movement data to gain insights about perceptual and cognitive processes. Speakers in this symposium will describe research coming from both directions. Specifically, they will talk about the role that eye movements play in various perceptual and cognitive tasks, and they will also describe eye-movement-based models of how such tasks are performed.

The talks will be ordered in a "bottom-up" manner: starting with sensory and oculomotor processes and moving up to high-level reasoning. The first speaker will talk about cognitive and sensory processes involved in scanning complex visual scenes. The second speaker will focus on a higher-level task, visual search. He will describe model of visual search strategy based on eye movement data. The last speaker will address a very high-level task, solving geometry problems. She will describe the eye movement patterns observed, and a model of mental operations based on these eye movement patterns.

Following the three speakers, Prof. Patrick Suppes, the symposium chair, will comment on the significant insights that eye movement data can provide to the study of cognitive and perceptual processing, and consider theoretical issues involved in modeling eye movement data.

Each speaker will have 17 minutes for the talk and , 3 minutes for questions. There will be a 10 minute period for general discussion, lead by the chair, at the end of the symposium.

The abstracts of the talks of the three main speakers follow.

Scanning of Natural Visual Scenes: How Cognitive and Sensory Mechanisms Work Together to Control Saccades

Eileen Kowler, James McGowan, Dan Bahcall, David Melcher and **Christian Araujo**

Department of Psychology
Rutgers University
New Brunswick, NJ 08903
{kowler,bahcall,caraujo}@psych.rutgers.edu
jamesm@frith.rutgers.edu, melcher@ruccs.rutgers.edu

The ability to use saccadic eye movements to bring the line of sight to targets of choice in natural visual scenes is truly one of the most remarkable motor skills human beings possess. We manage to look precisely where we want while scarcely being aware of making any effort to control the movements. How do we do it? Consider the specific challenges presented by any scanning task:

The natural targets for saccades are spatially-extended objects. At the same time, the line of sight must land at a single spatial position within the object. This single landing position is not determined by deliberate effort: when we scan a scene it's objects we think about looking at – faces, flowers or coffee cups – not tips of noses, petals or rims. Presumably, some involuntary sensory or sensorimotor process operates on the visual information within the chosen target and computes a single saccadic landing position. Yet, computation of the landing position cannot be completely immune to volition because for us to be able to look where we wish, any influence of visual signals from irrelevant backgrounds must be eliminated.

Recent research in our laboratory has shed light on how volitional and involuntary mechanisms work together to direct saccades accurately in natural visual scenes. This work has supported a two-stage model of saccadic control, in which selection of the target object by means of attentional allocation precedes a spatial-pooling process that computes a central location within the attended object. This central location then serves as the target for the saccade. These assertions are supported by the following experimental results:

(1) Saccades are preceded by a shift of spatial attention to the target. Concurrent measurements of saccadic and perceptual performance, analyzed by means of attentional operating characteristics (AOCs), have shown that making a saccade to one location impairs the perceptibility of targets at other locations. The attentional cost of saccades proved to be surprisingly modest: accurate perceptual identification of targets at non-goal locations required only a 10–20% increase in the latency of saccades (Kowler, Anderson, Dosher and Blaser, 1995). Analogous experiments requiring the concurrent perceptual identification of two targets showed comparable interference, which increased the closer the targets were to one another. Such interference would aid saccadic localization because it shows that attending to one target effectively inhibits the processing of nearby targets and reduces their potential for attracting the line of sight (Bahcall and Kowler, 1995).

(2) Saccades land at precise locations within spatially-extended targets. This level of precision has been demonstrated when subjects direct saccades to the "target as a whole" rather than to any specific place within it. Saccadic precision is excellent, with standard deviations of landing positions equal to about 6% of eccentricity, a value only slightly greater than the SDs observed in analogous perceptual localization tasks. The precision of saccades is unaffected by increases in target size (Kowler and Blaser, 1995) and decreases in target contrast.

(3) Saccades directed to spatially-extended targets land close to (but not precisely at) the center-of-gravity. This was observed for different types of targets, i.e., patterns of random dots (McGowan et al., 1996), and outline drawings of a variety of simple shapes. Statistical analyses of landing positions obtained with the random dot patterns show that landing position was determined by pooling information across the form, with no differential weighting of dots according to location (i.e., near vs. far eccentricities; boundary vs. central locations). Differential spatial weighting did not account for the small but reliable departures of landing position from the center-of-gravity.

We conclude that effective, and relatively effortless, saccadic localization of targets in natural scenes is accomplished by allocation of attention to the target object followed by a spatial-pooling process that computes the target's center of gravity. The link between saccades and attention means that no special selection process is needed to determine the saccadic goal. Saccades will be directed to the object you are interested in at the time the movement is triggered, with no additional set of decisions required. The modest attentional costs of saccades means that saccadic localization will interfere only minimally with the concurrent perceptual or cognitive processing of objects at locations other than the saccadic goal. The high level of saccadic precision observed with a wide variety of spatially-extended targets shows that lower-level sensory and sensorimotor mechanisms contribute negligible noise to the localization process. This low level of noise opens the way for cognitive decisions (conveyed, perhaps, by shifts in the distribution of attention) to play the major role in determining landing position. All in all, the mechanisms responsible for directing saccades appear to be remarkably suited to meet the requirements of natural scanning: accurate and precise localization achieved with minimal demand on cognitive resources.

References

Bahcall, D. and Kowler, E. (1995) Attentional interference at close spatial separations. *Investigative Ophthalmology and Visual Sciences Supplement. 36*, S901.

Kowler, E., Anderson, E., Dosher, B. and Blaser, E. (1995) The role of attention in the programming of saccades. *Vision Research, 35*, 1897-1916.

Kowler E. and Blaser, E. (1995) The accuracy and precision of saccades to small and large targets. *Vision Research, 35*, 1741-1754.

McGowan, J., Kowler, E., Sharma, A. and Chubb, C. (1996) Precise saccadic localization of random dot targets. *Investigative Ophthalmology and Visual Sciences Supplement 37*, S524.

Adding Resolution to an Old Problem: Eye Movements as a Measure of Visual Search

Gregory J. Zelinsky[1] **Rajesh P.N. Rao**[2] **Mary M. Hayhoe**[1] and **Dana H. Ballard**[2]

[1]Center for Visual Science and [2]Computer Science Department

University of Rochester

Rochester, NY 14627-0270

gzelinsk@casper.beckman.uiuc.edu, rao@cs.rochester.edu

mary@cvs.rochester.edu, dana@cs.rochester.edu

The process by which we locate a target in a cluttered visual scene has been the topic of fierce debate for the past several decades. While the obvious reason for this debate is that many competing models do an excellent job of describing the basic search phenomenon (an increase in manual reaction time [RT] with the number of objects in the display), a more distal cause may be linked to a limitation of the dependent measures commonly used to study search. For example, one popular class of models liken search behavior to the movements of a fixed-diameter beam or spotlight (Treisman *et al*, 1980, Treisman, 1988). The more items in a display, the more times this spotlight must move, resulting in longer search times. Note however that this very specific theory about the spatial evolution of search over time is being inferred from a RT result without any direct measure of this spotlight or its movements. This failure to directly measure the theoretical construct in question opens the door for other models of search to offer their own explanations for why RTs increase with set size. In this sense a RT measure simply lacks the resolution needed to unambiguously describe the spatiotemporal changes occurring during search.

In response to this resolution problem, three experiments used the sequence of saccades and fixations accompanying search to more directly describe the search process. Stimuli for the first experiment were color images of either 1, 3, or 5 realistic objects arranged on an appropriate surface (*i.e.*, toys on a crib, tools on a workbench, etc.). Each of these objects subtended about 2.5 degrees of visual angle, and appeared initially at 7 degrees eccentricity from a fixation cross. The entire scene subtended 16 degrees. The six subjects participating in this experiment had to indicate the presence or absence of a designated target object in 360 of these scenes by making a speeded keypress response.

Based solely on the RT data, it would be possible to frame a fairly strong argument for a serial search process underlying this task. Increasing the number of objects in the search display yielded a concomitant increase in RT, and the rate of this increase for the target-absent trials was about 1.5 times the slope observed in the target-present data. However, when the pattern of eye movements are considered, evidence for a different search process emerges. Rather than a sequence of saccades directed to individual items in the display, initial saccade landing positions clustered near the center of the image, even though no objects ever appeared at this location. This center-of-gravity averaging behavior (Coren & Hoenig, 1972, Findley, 1982) was most pronounced in the 3 and 5 item displays where the mean distance between the endpoints of these saccades and the target was approximately 5 degrees. In the single item trials, this measure of initial oculomotor error decreased significantly to 3.1 degrees. Targeting accuracy improved markedly by the second saccades, mainly due to gaze shifting to the side of the display containing the target. Second saccade endpoint error at a set size of 1 was 0.8 degrees and increased linearly to 2.7 degrees at the largest set size. The slope of this error function flattened by the third, and typically last, fixations.

Instead of the serial movements of a spotlight, we interpret this eye position data as evidence for a global-to-local search strategy. According to this interpretation, the inaccurate first saccades reflect an initial distribution of the search process over a broad region of the scene, with each subsequent saccade describing a more restricted region until only the target is selected. Recent work in our lab has shown how a simple color and spatial filtering computation also unfolding over time can implement such a search dynamic and parsimoniously account for the eye data results (Rao *et al.*, 1995). Early in the search process there may be many parts of a realistic scene that can be easily confused with the target, thereby forcing the search computation to be distributed over much of the image. Programming an eye movement at this stage in the search process would allow each of these spurious candidates to contribute (weighted by target similarity) to the spatial computation, giving rise to the averaging tendency observed in the initial saccades. Over time, as the decision process converges and less likely candidates drop out of the computation, the search region narrows and gaze moves steadily towards the target.

To test this interpretation, two additional experiments varied the signal-to-noise characteristics of these search displays while again monitoring eye movements. We predicted that a lower signal-to-noise ratio would cause more points in the scene to match the target, yielding increased averaging behavior and a more difficult search task. Likewise, removing background noise from the scene should reduce the number of matching points and attenuate oculomotor averaging. To create stimuli with a lower signal-to-noise ratio, we simply removed chromatic information from the original color scenes. To make stimuli with a more favorable signal-to-noise ratio, the complex backgrounds from the original scenes were replaced with uniform colored fields. As predicted, these manipulations had opposing effects on oculomotor averaging. Initial saccades in the single item grayscale trials landed almost a degree further from the target than in the corresponding color scenes, whereas making the background uniform resulted in a 1.5 degree increase in first saccade accuracy relative to the original single item data. Initial saccade endpoint errors for the 3 and 5 item displays remained essentially unchanged across all three experiments, demonstrating the robustness of this averaging tendency.

To conclude, the greater spatio-temporal resolution of an oculomotor measure allows the search process to be viewed more directly and in finer detail than what is possible from a manual RT. Note also that this direct assessment of search behavior makes it unnecessary to speculate about an ill-defined attentional process. The only assumption being made here is that eye movements are aligned with search during free viewing (Gould, 1973, Jacobs, 1986, Zelinsky & Sheinberg, in press). Based on this oculomotor evidence, search in these realistic tasks can be better described as a global-to-local behavior rather than a serial process. Furthermore, the extent to which search is globally distributed over the display and the timecourse over which this process becomes more local appears to be influenced by the signal-to-noise characteristics of the scene.

References

Treisman, A. & Gelade, G. (1980). A feature-integration theory of attention. *Cognitive Psychology, 12,* 97-136.

Treisman, A. (1988). Features and Objects: The fourteenth Bartlett memorial lecture. *Quarterly Journal of Experimental Psychology, 40A,* 201-237.

Coren, S. & Hoenig, P. (1972). Effect of non-target stimuli upon length of voluntary saccades. *Perceptual and Motor Skills, 34,* 499-508.

Findlay, J. (1982). Global visual processing for saccadic eye movements. *Vision Research, 22,* 1033-1045.

Rao, R., Zelinsky, G., Hayhoe, M. & Ballard, D. (1995). Modeling saccadic targeting in visual search. *Advances in Neural Information Processing.* MIT Press.

Gould, J. (1973). Eye movements during visual search and memory search. *Journal of Experimental Psychology, 98,* 184-195.

Jacobs, A. (1986). Eye-movement control in visual search: How direct is visual span control? *Perception & Psychophysics, 39,* 47-58.

Zelinsky, G. & Sheinberg, D. (in press). Eye movements during parallel/serial visual search tasks. *Journal of Experimental Psychology: Human Perception and Performance.*

Window on the mind? What Eye Movements Reveal about Geometrical Reasoning

Julie Epelboim and **Patrick Suppes**
Center for the Study of Language and Information
Stanford University
Stanford, CA 94305-4115
yulya@brissun.umd.edu, suppes@ockham.stanford.edu

Geometrical concepts involve an intimate mixture of perception and cognition. Most geometry problems are either posed in the form of a diagram, or require construction of a diagram for a successful solution. Yet, unlike the case for reading and arithmetic, a serial algorithm for scanning or constructing diagrams is not taught to students of geometry. Specifically, when learning to read, students are taught to proceed from word to word, from left to right. When learning column arithmetic, they are taught to proceed from right to left through the columns, and from top to bottom within each column. When taught geometry, on the other hand, students are not taught how to look at the diagrams — they must learn an efficient eye movement pattern on their own. Empirical studies of eye movement patterns during reading and arithmetic show that individuals performing these tasks successfully indeed follow an orderly eye movement pattern with very few deviations (Epelboim, Booth & Steinman, 1994; Suppes, 1990). The nature of eye movements performed in order to solve geometry problems is not known. These eye movements and what they can tell us about the underlying mental operations are the topic of our study.

We asked subjects to solve simple geometry problems, each presented to them in the form of a diagram on a computer screen. Their eye movements were recorded, with exceptional precision and accuracy, using the The Maryland Revolving-Field monitor. Three subjects participated. Two of the subjects were skilled at solving geometry problems. They had graduate training in Physics, and encountered problems similar to those used in the experiment in their professional life. The third subject had last solved geometry problems in high school, over 50 years prior to the experiment. He reported that he had "no clue" as to what to do on most of the problems. The subjects were not allowed to write or sketch anything, but the problems were simple enough to solve mentally. The subjects were asked to reason aloud, and their speech was recorded.

Figure 1 shows typical eye movements of one of the skilled subjects. Panel (a) shows the problem as it appeared to the subject. Panels (b-f) show the subject's fixations as he was solving the problem. Each symbol is one fixation. Each panel shows 25 fixations. Each fixation is represented by a circle, a square, or a rhombus, which contains this fixation's sequential number. Circles show brief fixations ($\leq$ 300 msec).

Squares show fixations that lasted longer than 300 msec but less than 800 msec. Rhombi show long fixations that lasted over 800 msec. The subject's reasoning aloud for this problem was as follows (numbers in parenthesis indicate the sequential numbers of fixations that occurred while the phrase was being spoken):

ABCD is a parallelogram.	(1-11)
Ok, so where is the unknown angle?	(12-20)
the unknown angle is AEC	(21-31)
... then since ...	(32-68)
oh, ... it's trivial	(69-80)
the lines AD and BC are parallel	(81-92)
and therefore the angle AEC	(93-105)
is alternate interior to the angle DAE	(106-110)
which is labeled 60 degrees	(110-120)
The answer is 60 degrees	(121-122)

The reader is invited to examine Figure 1 and the protocol above and propose a sequence of mental operations that fit these data.

Quantitative analyses and modeling of the eye movement data and spoken protocols of the 3 subjects are now in progress. The results of these analyses will be presented at the symposium.

References

Epelboim, J., Booth, J. R. & Steinman, R. M. (1994). Reading unspaced text: Implications for theories of reading eye movements. *Vision Research, 34*, 1735–1766.

Suppes, P. (1990). Eye-movement models for arithmetic and reading performance. In: *Eye Movements and their Role in Visual and Cognitive Processes*. Edited by E. Kowler, Elsevier Science (Biomedical Division), Amsterdam. pp. 455–478.

This research was supported by NIMH 1-F32-MH11282-01; AFOSR F49620-94-1-0333

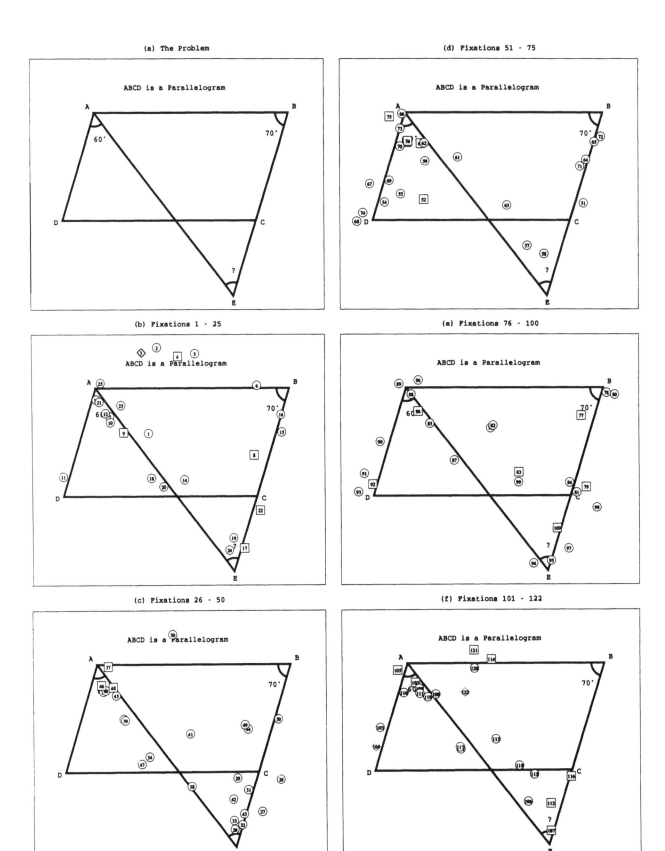

Figure 1: See text.

Computational Models of Development: A Symposium

Kim Plunkett
Department of Experimental Psychology
Oxford University
South Parks Road, Oxford, OX1 3UD
plunkett@psy.ox.ac.uk

Thomas R. Shultz
LNSC, Department of Psychology, McGill University
1205 Penfield Avenue
Montréal, Québec, Canada H3A 1B1
shultz@psych.mcgill.ca

Introduction

Any theory of development must specify its position on three crucial assumptions:

1. The nature of the start state of the organism.
2. The effective learning environment that the organism occupies.
3. The learning procedure that enables the organism to alter its start state via interactions with the learning environment.

Once committed to these assumptions, the developmentalist can make predictions about the trajectory of learning that the organism must follow in order to achieve mature levels of performance. These predictions can be compared to the actual behaviours that the organism produces en route to masterful behaviour. A certain amount of slack is permitted in the fit of the predictions to actual behaviour depending on the manner in which the original assumptions have been stipulated—some theories will permit a greater degree of individual variation than others. In principle, the outcome of the comparison of the predicted developmental trajectory to the organism's actual developmental trajectory will lead to an acceptance or rejection of the theory. In the case of rejection, one or more of the original assumptions may require modification and the process of prediction and comparison reiterated until a successful match can be achieved.

This idealised process of theory building and evaluation is rarely achieved for complex organisms like *homo sapiens* because of the difficulties involved in stipulating the content of the three assumptions outlined above: We still know very little about the genetic code and neural architectures that specify the start state of human development. The nature of the learning environment for young humans may seem self-evident. However, ethology has taught us to be wary of equating environmental input with perceptual uptake. The sensitivities of young humans to features of the environment may vary considerably even from their mature caregivers. Some success has been achieved in discovering neural mechanisms of learning, such as long term potentiation in the mammalian brain. However, it is unlikely that this Hebbian-style learning is the only learning mechanism available to humans. Ignorance as to what gets learning off the ground in humans undermines the constraints necessary for theory building and evaluation.

When there are so many under-specified, free parameters in the theory, the reasons for failure to predict a developmental trajectory become unfathomable.

There are, nevertheless, grounds for optimism for theory building in developmental cognitive science. First, significant progress is being made in decoding the human genome and neuro-physiologists are making dramatic headway in identifying the neural circuitry and constraints on neural plasticity in developing organisms. These advances are likely to have a major impact on developmental psychology over the next decade. Second, developmental psychologists themselves are making enormous headway in understanding the sensory and perceptual sensitivities of human newborns. We know a lot more about the infant's effective learning environment than we did just one decade ago. Thirdly, the advent of computer modelling in developmental psychology permits the rapid evaluation of theories so that a wide range of configurations of start-states, effective learning environments and learning procedures can be explored. In this symposium, we focus on the third of these advances—the application of computational modelling to theory building in developmental cognitive science. We evaluate and compare some of the lessons we have learnt from the study of two particular classes of models—symbolic and neural network simulations of development.

The Role of Modelling

In order to build a computer model of a developmental process, you need a precisely formulated theory—precise enough to specify in a computer programme. This demand for precision forces the theory to be coherent. It may be the wrong theory, but at least it will be internally consistent. If it is not, it won't run properly on the computer. The modelling endeavour forces an elaboration of the fundamental principles underlying the developmental process. The model cannot encompass the whole child, so the modeller must decide which parts of the child are crucial for the problem of interest. This is part of the theory building process itself, but a part that is enforced by the decision to implement the theory on a computer.

Once these parts of the model building process are complete, the next step is to determine whether the programme produces the kind of behaviour produced by developing children. This is not always a straightforward part of the process. Children vary in their behaviour so one must decide whether any observed deviation from the model's performance constitutes a refutation of the model. It is best if the model can vary in its performance too and these variations are caused by factors that might be related to factors underlying variation in children. The theory embodied in the model must be able to make novel predictions that can be tested empirically. In other words, it is not enough for the model to mimic children's behaviour. It must be able to generate testable hypotheses.

Connectionist and Symbolic Modelling

All the papers in this symposium present working models of some aspect of the child's linguistic or cognitive development from a connectionist or symbolic perspective. Both classes of model make their own characteristic assumptions about the nature of the start state, learning algorithms and effective learning environments. All the models assume a set of *patterns* to be processed by some computational architecture. The fundamental difference between the two classes of model is the nature of the processing and inference procedures employed. For connectionist models, patterns are manipulated by a set of adaptable weighted connections that are sensitive to the *content* of the forms encountered. Learning amounts to a process of statistical inference. In symbolic models, patterns are manipulated by a set of *rules* that may be impervious to certain details of the patterns. If a pattern is identified as a certain *type*, then it is handled according to the rules specified for that type, irrespective of any idiosyncrasies concerning the particular token of the type. Learning is often handled by the construction of decision trees that classify the patterns in terms of their symbolic attributes.

Nativism and Empiricism

A common point of contention between connectionist and symbolic models of development concerns the amount of structure that is required to get learning off the ground. From the symbolic perspective, it is sometimes held that stimuli (or training patterns) are too impoverished to account for the richness of human cognition—Plato's well-known "Shadows in the cave" problem. Learning is often seen as a process of triggering innate knowledge bases, where the trigger operates in a domain-specific fashion. Many connectionists maintain that symbolic theorists have underestimated the structural complexity of information available in the environment and the capacity of domain-general learning algorithms to induce domain-specific knowledge bases from this complexity.

The input sensitivity of connectionist systems makes them obvious tools for exploring empiricist accounts of linguistic and cognitive development. However, it should be emphasized that connectionism and empiricism are not necessary bedfellows. In fact, connectionism offers a tool for examining the trade-off between the role of the input and the role of pre-adapted structures and processes in development. Although the representations formed by connectionist systems are indeed highly sensitive to input parameters, it is the architectures and learning algorithms of connectionist systems themselves that afford this sensitivity. Because connectionist architectures differ in terms of their network structures and learning algorithms, they also differ in the manner in which they respond to the same inputs. The potential variety of network architectures thereby contributes to the range of hypotheses that might describe the initial state of the learning device before it is exposed to any input. Consequently, connectionism can also be used to explore interactionist and nativist accounts of linguistic and cognitive development.

Symbolic models also offer considerable flexibility in exploring a range of developmental hypotheses. Although symbolic models necessarily postulate a set of symbolic primitives, the granularity of these atomic building blocks can vary can vary dramatically from one theory to the next. The commitment to the software-hardware distinction that commonly goes hand-in-hand with the symbolic approach, does not preclude the exploration of minimalist programmes of innate structures and processes.

Biological Plausibility and Levels of Explanation

Connectionist models clearly have a neurological appeal. But are connectionist systems constrained to providing models at the neurological level of explanation? Many researchers working within the classical symbolic approach to cognitive science argue that functional accounts of the cognitive level must be couched in terms of discrete, categorical, symbol processing systems. Furthermore, they argue that current connectionist models do not behave in the necessary symbolic fashion. According to this argument, connectionist models will not be able to provide explanations and descriptions at the cognitive level. It is conceded, however, that connectionist models, appropriately hard-wired, may be able to implement the foundations of a cognitive system in much the same way that the hardware of a computer provides the necessary working environment for symbolic programmes. Indeed, it is widely acknowledged that something like a connectionist system must provide the neurological foundations for the apparent symbolic mind. On this view, a symbol processing machine sits on top of a connectionist implementation of the neurological system. It makes sense to talk about a two-level system where the symbolic machine operates according to its own autonomous set of principles.

Many developmental connectionists resist this relegation of their explanations to the implementational level. One of the primary motivations for building connectionist models of cognitive processes is that symbolic approaches seem to lack certain characteristics that are needed at precisely the cognitive level of functioning (parallel processing, graceful degradation, learning).

A compromise solution, in which connectionist mechanisms and symbol manipulating devices work side-by-side in an harmonious cognitive system, is currently fashionable—so-called hybrid systems. Do these offer the way forward or are they merely a confusion in levels of description?

The present symposium features modelling approaches that are either purely symbolic or purely connectionist.

Contrasting Models of Object Permanence

Denis Mareschal
Department of Psychology
Washington Singer Laboratories
Exeter University
Exeter EX4 4QG, UK
dmaresch@singer.exeter.ac.uk

Object Permanence

According to Piaget (e.g., Piaget, 1958) object permanence forms the basis of our understanding of objective space. Through gaining the understanding that objects continue to exist independently of direct perception, infants also begin to understand that they themselves are independent objects within an objective space. While many would agree that having a notion of object permanence is essential for an adult understanding of spatial relations, there is less agreement on what should constitute evidence of object permanence and how it should be measured .

Piaget's now classic studies relied on active retrieval of a hidden object as the measure of knowledge. That is, the infants had to be able to act on the knowledge of hidden objects that they may have. In the last 15 years, a different research paradigm has appeared. These studies have used passive responses such as surprise as a measure of the infants knowledge (see Baillargeon, 1993 for a review). The key idea in these studies is to violate some physical property of a hidden object. If the infants show surprise at the violation, then it is inferred that they remember the hidden object and understand that the object has maintained the physical property that was violated. The new methodology revealed that infants have much greater knowledge of hidden objects than that which they are able to demonstrate in retrieval tasks. This apparent developmental lag between infant's knowledge of hidden objects and their ability to act on that knowledge is a key question of infant cognitive development.

A third research paradigm was pioneered by T. G. R. Bower (1974). This approach relied on observing infant responses to visual tracking events in which an object passed temporarily behind an occluding screen. Knowledge of the hidden object was inferred from the infant's response to surreptitious changes in the object's features and spatial temporal properties while it was behind the screen. Bower argued that visual tracking was an active response with minimal motor task demands. However the reliability of the results obtained through this method is still open to question.

Computational Models

A number of computational models have been built to explore the development of object permanence. These are process models of infants' performance on object permanence tasks. The goal is to describe the nature of the knowledge representations and the mechanisms which operate on these representations during the tasks. As models of development they should not only describe performance, but also provide an account in terms of the mechanisms of development.

Ideally, they might also incorporate general principles which would be extendible to aspects of cognition other than the immediate task being modeled.

In this talk, I will discuss three models. The first two are symbolic rule based models and the third is a connectionist model. The symbolic models (e.g. Prazdny, 1980, Luger, Bower, and Wishart, 1983; Luger, Wishart, and Bower, 1984) were developed to account for the visual pursuit data described by T. G. R. Bower (Bower, 1974). The symbolic models differ in that they base their explanation of the infant behaviors on different underlying theories of information processing.

Prazdny (1980)

Prazdny suggested that there are three levels of representation for objects. The highest level is a conceptual level and the other two are perceptual levels. The conceptual level is the only level to have access to both feature and spatial-temporal information. An Object-Description (OD) is generated by the conceptual level. The OD binds together attributes (e.g., color, size, position, trajectory) into a single structure and labels it with a name. If new perceptual information arrives which is inconsistent with the existing OD, a second OD is generated. Predictions (expectations) based on both ODs are then tested in order to select the best description.

Knowledge is stored in the form of IF-THEN assertions. In particular, IF-ADDED and IF-REMOVED procedures are used to implement expectation behaviors when the state of an object changes (e.g., it disappears after occlusion). Although the perceptual levels are not actually implemented, it is suggested that sensory information enters the system in the form of a snapshot of the visual scene. The lowest perceptual level processes the scene over a single snapshot interval. The next perceptual level abstracts across several snapshots thereby generating trajectory representations. Part of the infant's quirky behavior is explained in terms of competition between this perceptual level representation of trajectory and the conceptual level representation. Finally, although no direct mechanism for development is implemented, it is suggested that development is driven by a streamlining process in which specific rules are combined to produce a single more efficient rule.

Luger et al. (1983, 1984)

Luger's models implements Bower's Identity Theory of object permanence (Luger, Bower, and Wishart, 1983; Luger, Wishart, and Bower, 1984). This theory suggests that young infants understand that objects continue to exist, but that they have difficulty keeping track of objects. Young infants generate a large number of separate object representations for what adults would encode as a single object. The main idea of this model is that infant behaviors can be described by the use of 5 action rules subsumed under 3 conceptual rules. Luger et al. describe the three conceptual rules, but remain non-committal about how the action rules might interact. Hence these authors believe that there is a complete dissociation between the conceptual level and the response level. The conceptual rules are:

Rule 1: An object is a bounded volume of space in a particular place OR on a particular path of movement.

Rule 2: An object is a bounded volume of space of a certain size, shape, and color which can move from place to place among its trajectories. (Note that this rule now integrates feature information with spatial temporal information)

Rule 3: Two or more objects cannot be in the same place OR on the same path of movement simultaneously UNLESS they share a common boundary.

This model is implemented as a PROLOG program. A set of facts is used to make up an object knowledge structure from each temporal snapshot. Each of the conceptual rules is embedded in a separate recursive PROLOG statement. The goal of the statement is to assert the permanence of an object. To do this, the model tests the validity of a number of facts. The last of its conditionals is to move over and test again. The level 1 rule tests for: the location, whether the object has volume, and whether it is occluded. It then moves on to the next position. The level 2 rule adds in a test for the object's features before testing for intact boundaries. Finally the level 3 rule adds another test of features after testing for intact boundaries. As a result, the Level 1 model sets up a new representation of the object every time there is a change in spatial temporal information. The Level 2 model only sets up a new object token when there are changes in the feature representation. Finally the Level 3 models do not set up a new object representation when two objects are contiguous. Again, no specific developmental mechanism is proposed, but it is thought to be driven by the acquisition of procedures that lead to more cost efficient representations.

Mareschal, Plunkett, and Harris (1995)

Mareschal *et al.* describe a connectionist model of the development of object permanence. The model is in the form of a modular network. Units that are shared by modules act as gateways through which information can flow from one module to the other. Information enters the network through a retina that is homogeneously covered with feature detectors. Based loosely on neuropsychological data, the model implements two information pathways: (a) a feature pathway, and (b) a spatial-temporal pathway. The Object Recognition Module uses an unsupervised algorithm to develop a spatially invariant feature representation of the object whose image is projected on the retina. The Trajectory Prediction Module processes the spatial-temporal properties of the object image. This module learns to predict what the next position of the object image will be. Finally, The Response Integration Module recruits and integrates the internal representations developed by the other modules as and when required by an appropriate response task.

Knowledge of past events is stored gradually in the connection weights between the units. A representation of the current object event is stored in the form of a pattern of activation across a band of units. Development occurs thorough the gradual accumulation of knowledge (small changes in connection weights). An implication of the model is that performance on object permanence tasks reflects the ability to internally represent an event, but also the ability to decode successfully that representation into an appropriate action. Both information processing steps need to be learned.

Discussion

The most immediate difference between these models is that the existing symbolic models do not provide a transition mechanism. In contrast, it is the essence of the connectionist model to describe development. Representations in the network emerge through learning. However, it is important to understand that the connectionist networks are not just *tabula rasa* learners. The representations that are developed depend both on the nature of the interactions with the environment, but also on innate knowledge constraints in the form of architectural constraints (determining how information is segregated and recombined) as well as mechanisms (determining the type of information that can be extracted from the environment).

The symbolic models are descriptive models of competence at any one stage. They are not models of the processes of development. Even if a mechanism for rule development was devised, it would have to be more than just a means of passing from one level of description to the next for the model to be a meaningful model of infant development. A connectionist model is a model of the mechanisms involved in changing the knowledge representations. In some sense the knowledge representations are almost secondary to the developmental process.

References

Baillargeon, R. (1993). The object concept revisited: New directions in the investigation of infants' physical knowledge. In C. E. Granrud (Ed.), *Visual Perception and Cognition in Infancy* (pp. 265-318), London: LEA.

Bower, T. G. R. (1974). *Development in Infancy*, San Francisco, CA: Freeman.

Luger, G. F., Bower, T. G. R., & Wishart, J. G. (1983). A model of the development of early object concept. *Perception*, 12, 21-34.

Luger, G. F., Wishart, J. G., & Bower, T. G. R. (1984). Modeling the stages of the identity theory of object concept development in infancy. *Perception*, 13, 97-115.

Mareschal, D., Plunkett, K., & Harris, P. (1995). Developing object permanence: A connectionist model. In J. D. Moore, & J. E. Lehman (Eds.), *Proceedings of the Seventeenth Annual Conference of the Cognitive Science Society* (pp. 170-175). Hillsdale, NJ: Erlbaum.

Piaget, J. (1952). *The Origins of Intelligence in the Child*. New York: International Universities Press.

Prazdny, S. (1980). A computational study of a period of infant object-concept development. *Perception*, 9, 125-150.

A Generative Neural Network Analysis of Conservation

Thomas R. Shultz

LNSC, Department of Psychology, McGill University
1205 Penfield Avenue
Montréal, Québec, Canada H3A 1B1
shultz@psych.mcgill.ca

Conservation

One of the most well studied phenomena in cognitive development is conservation. Conservation involves the belief in the continued equivalence of two physical quantities over a transformation that appears to alter one of them. An example of conservation presents a child with two identical rows of evenly spaced objects. Once the child agrees that the two rows have the same number of objects, the experimenter transforms one of the rows, e.g., by pushing its items closer together. Then the experimenter asks the child whether the two rows still have the same amount or whether one of them now has more. Piaget (1965) and other researchers found that children below about six years of age respond that one of the two rows, usually the longer row, now has more than the other. In contrast, children older than six years respond that the two rows still have equal amounts, i.e., they conserve the equivalence of the two amounts over the compressing transformation.

Despite the many empirical studies of conservation, the cognitive mechanisms underlying conservation acquisition remain obscure. One way to explore such cognitive mechanisms is with computer simulations in which the details of knowledge representations and processing mechanisms must be fully specified.

Cascade-correlation

A successful modeling algorithm for cognitive developmental phenomena is cascade-correlation. This is a generative algorithm for learning in feed-forward neural networks (Fahlman & Lebiere, 1990). It builds its own topology as it learns, by recruiting new hidden units into the network as it needs them. Such networks undergo not only quantitative adjustments in connection weights but also qualitative adjustments in network topology. There have been cascade-correlation models of balance scale phenomena, causal predictions of potency and resistance, seriation, integration of velocity, time, and distance cues, and acquisition of personal pronouns (Shultz, Schmidt, Buckingham, & Mareschal, 1995).

Simulations

Here I report on the simulation of five well known conservation phenomena with neural networks constructed by the cascade-correlation algorithm: (1) shift from nonconservation to conservation beliefs (acquisition effect), (2) emergence of correct conservation judgments for small quantities before larger quantities (problem size effect), (3) conservation of discrete quantities before continuous quantities (discrete advantage effect), (4) nonconservers' choice of the longer row as having more items than the shorter row (length bias effect), and (5) younger children conserving until they see the results of the transformation (screening effect).

Training

Networks were trained in an environment with very few constraints. Inputs described equivalence conservation problems in which rows of objects were described in terms of their perceptual characteristics, namely length and density. Target feedback supplied to the network concerned relative equality judgments comparing the two rows. Transformations included those that alter number (addition and subtraction) and those that preserve number (elongation and compression). Addition and subtraction transformations each altered a row by one item. Elongation and compression transformations decreased or increased the density of the row by one level, respectively. See Table 1 for some example transformations. In the standard rows, there were three levels of length, ranging from 2-6, and two levels of density, ranging from 2-4. Conservation experiments typically present only a few density levels but several levels of length. The quantities for numerical comparisons were computed as number = length x density. In this way, networks could learn about number from the perceptual characteristics of items arranged in rows with a constant within-row density.

Testing

A randomly selected 1/4 of the problems were excluded from training for use as test patterns. Most assessments were performed on test patterns rather than training patterns in order to insulate network performance from the particulars of training.

Acquisition

Networks learned the training problems and generalized well to the test problems, not merely memorizing the problems, but abstracting an underlying function.

Problem Size

Networks showed a problem size effect by performing better on problems in which the number of the smaller row was less than 9 than on problems in which the number of the smaller row was greater than 15. This was evident at all phases of training, except very early, where networks had not learned enough, and very late, where networks had reached a ceiling of performance on all problem sizes. Problem size effects are pervasive in human quantitative judgments; simulations suggest that they result from an analog representation of number.

Discrete Advantage

The discrete advantage effect was captured by adding small amounts of random noise to outputs in the training and test patterns for continuous quantities, which are considered difficult to estimate accurately. It took longer for networks to learn with noisy than with noiseless outputs. Also, except early and late in training, networks performed worse on noisy than on noiseless problems. Thus, the networks were sensitive to noise, but not fatally so. The absence of a noise effect at the beginning of training reflects inability to solve either type of problem. The disappearance of the noise effect at the end of training reflects ceiling levels of performance.

Length Bias

The networks showed biases like those observed in children. They learned to use the dominant dimension of length, and then noticed the compensating dimension of density, before correctly integrating the two dimensions.

The initial length bias was due to learning that longer rows often have more items than shorter rows, particularly in addition and subtraction transformations when density is held constant. This explanation is consistent with the idea that very young children do not show a length bias because they have not yet learned that length is a correlate of number (Miller, Grabowski, & Heldmeyer, 1973). Length bias did not occur in an alternate environment in which length, rather than density, was held constant during transformations. These bias results underscore the tension between perception and cognition in conservation tasks. What the child knows (e.g., that a transformation does not change a quantity) appears to conflict with what she sees (e.g., that one row is longer, and thus seems more numerous than the other).

Screening

The screening effect refers to young children conserving only until they see the results of a transformation (Miller & Heldmeyer, 1975). As long as the effects of the transformation are screened from view, they conserve, but when the screen is removed, they revert to nonconservation. This was simulated by removing information about the appearance of the transformed row after it was transformed, causing more conservation early in training.

Network Analysis

To determine the roles of particular hidden units, information critical to perceptual and cognitive solutions was deleted from the test problems. Missing input critical to a perceptual solution involved the length and density of the post-transformation row, whereas missing input critical to a cognitive solution involved the nature of the transformation. Analysis of errors caused by these deletions indicated that most hidden units played a role in either perceptual or cognitive solutions and a few of them played a role in both solution types.

Conclusions

These simulations captured a variety of effects in the conservation literature and supported the correlation-learning explanation of length bias. They achieved better and more comprehensive coverage of natural conservation phenomena than have previous simulations.

Acknowledgments

This research was supported by a grant from the Natural Sciences and Engineering Research Council of Canada. Adam Waese, Yasser Hashmi, Yuriko Oshima-Takane, and Sylvain Sirois commented on earlier drafts.

References

Fahlman, S. E., & Lebiere, C. (1990). The cascade-correlation learning architecture. In D. S. Touretzky (Ed.), *Advances in Neural Information Processing Systems 2* (pp. 524-532). Los Altos, CA: Morgan Kaufmann.

Miller, P. H., Grabowski, T. L., & Heldmeyer, K. H. (1973). The role of stimulus dimensions in the conservation of substance. *Child Development, 44,* 646-650.

Miller, P. H., & Heldmeyer, K. H. (1975). Perceptual information in conservation: Effects of screening. *Child Development, 46,* 588-592.

Piaget, J. (1965). *The child's conception of number.* New York: Norton.

Shultz, T. R., Schmidt, W. C., Buckingham, D., & Mareschal, D. (1995). Modeling cognitive development with a generative connectionist algorithm. In T. J. Simon & G. S. Halford (Eds.), *Developing cognitive competence: New approaches to process modeling* (pp. 205-261). Hillsdale, NJ: Erlbaum.

Transformation	Length	Density	Row					
Pre-transformation	2	2	o	o	o	o		
Add	2.5	2	o	o	o	o	o	
Subtract	1.5	2	o	o	o			
Elongate	4	1	o		o		o	o
Compress	1.33	3	o o o o					

Table 1: Example transformations.

Can Symbolic Algorithms Model Cognitive Development?

Charles X. Ling

Department of Computer Science
The University of Hong Kong, Hong Kong
ling@cs.hku.hk
(On leave from The University of Western Ontario)

Abstract

Symbolic decision-tree learning algorithms can provide a powerful and accurate transition mechanism for modeling cognitive development. They are valid alternatives to connectionist models.

Symbolic Decision-Tree Learning

In general, a learning algorithm is "symbolic" if it directly operates on a symbolic representation during the learning period, and generates a data processing structure based directly on the symbolic representation. Additionally, one might wish to require that attributes describing training examples should be specified at a symbolic level that corresponds directly to symbolic descriptions in the learning domain. According to this definition, decision-tree learning algorithms, such as ID3 (Quinlan, 1986) and C4.5 (Quinlan, 1993), operating on letters and phonemes in modeling past tense acquisition of English verbs is symbolic (Ling & Marinov, 1993; Ling, 1994). Similarly, decision-tree learning operating on descriptive information based on balance scale problems is symbolic (Schmidt & Ling, 1996a, 1996b). On the other hand, a decision tree which utilizes "subsymbolic" information (i.e., distributed representation) may not be called symbolic. Connectionist models of these same tasks are not either.

Because of continuous weight modification and/or gradual structure change (i.e., generative connectionist algorithms) during learning, connectionist methods are often regarded as a natural approach to modeling developmental process of cognition, and often perceived as superior to their symbolic counterparts. Our work demonstrates that symbolic decision-tree learning algorithms can provide a powerful and accurate transition mechanism for modeling cognitive development. Therefore, symbolic learning methods and models are valid alternatives to connectionist approaches.

Incremental and Developmental

There are two independent dimensions on which we can classify decision-tree learning for modeling development. One is called *incremental*, and the other is *developmental*. These combine to produce four possible classes of model: {incremental, non-incremental} × {developmental, non-developmental}. Note that this classification of model is applicable to other learning algorithms as well.

Incremental learning (a term often used in the machine learning community) requires that the algorithms take training examples one at a time, and only update the decision trees when new examples are received (rather than constructing a new one based on a single expanded set of examples). Although the well-known decision-tree learning algorithms ID3 and C4.5 are non-incremental, there are incremental versions, such as ID5 (Utgoff, 1989), that are guaranteed to produce the same results as the non-incremental versions, if applied to the identical set of examples. Because of this, and because of high computational efficiency (taking just minutes on datasets of thousands of examples), non-incremental decision-tree learning algorithms are often preferred in developmental modeling *for the ease of implementation* (Ling & Marinov, 1993; Schmidt & Ling, 1996a).

Incremental learning is desirable for constructing detailed, internal process of learning and development. However, incrementality plays little role in demonstrating end results and model predictions.

Developmental learning is to construct a series of decision trees in which successors expand upon predecessors, based on a fixed set of training examples (which may have accumulated incrementally). Early decision trees in the series are small, and can only accommodate a relatively small number of examples. The decision trees late in the series are larger, and the overall error rates are generally reduced. There are several possible methods for decision-tree developmental modeling. One obvious approach is to limit the maximum depth of the decision trees constructed, and to increase this limit gradually This method produces trees of uniform depth, but the error rates associated with different leaves are uneven. Another approach is to limit the number (or percent) of errors that leaves can tolerate, and to decrease that limit gradually. In this case, errors at different leaves would be uniform, and parts of trees with higher errors would be expanded more deeply first. A simple way to accomplish this with C4.5 is to manipulate a built-in parameter m, which has the effect of limiting the number of errors allowed in leaves. Note that one can easily combine these strategies. For example, one could gradually decrease the percent of errors allowed on leaves, and if the growth of the next decision tree is abrupt, control the maximum depth of the trees and produce several trees with an increasing depth.

We propose the following hypothesis for modeling cognitive development with developmental decision-tree learning. Early in development, children have limited mental abilities, which include learning capacity and memory capacity: they cannot explain a large number of examples observed, and at the same time, their memory for storing learned hypothesis is limited. Young children's poor performance can be modeled with the small decision trees early in the series by developmental decision-tree learning algorithms. Note that since most decision-tree algorithms (such as C4.5) choose the most discriminant attribute as the root of (sub)trees, such small decision trees are likely the *best* small trees that get as much regularity out of the training examples as possible. This reflects that children maximize learning, even with their limited mental capacity. Late in development, more examples can be accommodated (learning capacity is improved) as more complex regularities are learned (and memory capacity is increased). This can be modeled by large decision trees late in the series generated by the developmental strategies discussed above.

We have successfully used the developmental strategies discussed to model cognitive development on the balance-scale task (Schmidt & Ling, 1996a, 1996b). The set of C4.5 decision-trees demonstrated the major psychological phenomena (orderly stage progression, U-shaped development, and torque difference effect) observed in children, thereby providing evidence that C4.5 can act as a transition mechanism for modeling developmental phenomena.

Competence and performance models

Incremental and developmental decision-tree learning algorithms still lack certain features as development models. For example, decision-tree learning algorithms are deterministic, and they fail to produce individual variations. In the balance scale model, for example, stage skipping, regression, and individual differences, which mark the human developmental data, did not exhibited in C4.5 modeling. It appears too "precise", producing perfect stage progressing each run.

To answer this criticism, we need to first review the difference between *competence* and *performance models* (Chomsky, 1968). Competence is the ability of an idealized subject to execute the task at hand. This ideal is not affected by situational variables, memory span, or perceptual limitations. In reality, competence is revealed only indirectly through a subject's performance, which is always influenced by situational factors. The development model on the balance scale task using C4.5 is intended as a competence model. It is more concerned with characterizing the knowledge structures and the learning process underlying human performance.

Simple measures could be taken to augment the competence model to make it accountable for the intricacies of the human performance data. For example, random sampling can be taken from the entire training set. In addition, one can add probability in building decision trees (by not always choosing the best nodes). This added variability would still clearly be based on the data, and can model human performance (with non-deterministic behavior, ignorance, and individual differences).

Summary

Symbolic decision-tree learning algorithms are incremental and developmental, and are adequate for competence modeling of cognitive development. They can also be augmented to reflect individual human performance.

Acknowledgments

I would like to gratefully thank Billy Schmidt for contributions in the development of the ideas presented here, and for his careful reading and feedbacks on this paper.

Reference

Chomsky, N. (1968). *Language and Mind*. New York: Harcourt, Bruce and World.

Ling, C. X. (1994). Learning the past tense of English verbs: the Symbolic Pattern Associator vs. connectionist models. *Journal of Artificial Intelligence Research*, *1*, 209 – 229.

Ling, C. X., & Marinov, M. (1993). Answering the connectionist challenge: a symbolic model of learning the past tense of English verbs. *Cognition*, *49*(3), 235–290.

Quinlan, J. (1986). Induction of decision trees. *Machine Learning*, *1*(1), 81 – 106.

Quinlan, J. (1993). *C4.5: Programs for Machine Learning*. Morgan Kaufmann: San Mateo, CA.

Schmidt, W. C., & Ling, C. X. (1996a). A decision-tree model of balance scale development. To appear in *Machine Learning*.

Schmidt, W. C., & Ling, C. X. (1996b). A symbolic model of cognitive transition: The balance scale task. In *Proceedings of the Eighteenth Annual Conference of the Cognitive Science Society*. (This volume).

Utgoff, P. E. (1989). Incremental induction of decision trees. *Machine Learning*, *4*, 161 – 186.

Paper Presentations

Beyond Computationalism

Marco Giunti
Dept. of History and Philosophy of Science
Goodbody Hall 130, Indiana University
Bloomington, IN 47405
giunti@dada.it

Abstract

By *computationalism* in cognitive science I mean the view that cognition essentially is a matter of the computations that a cognitive system performs in certain situations. The main thesis I am going to defend is that computationalism is only consistent with symbolic modeling or, more generally, with any other type of computational modeling. In particular, those scientific explanations of cognition which are based on *(i)* an important class of connectionist models or *(ii)* nonconnectionist continuous models cannot be computational, for these models are not the kind of system which can perform computations in the sense of standard computation theory. Arguing for this negative conclusion requires a formal explication of the intuitive notion of computational system. Thus, if my thesis is correct, we are left with the following alternative. Either we construe computationalism by explicitly referring to some nonstandard notion of computation, or we simply abandon the idea that computationalism be a basic hypothesis shared by all current research in cognitive science. I will finally suggest that a different hypothesis, *dynamicism*, may represent a viable alternative to computationalism. According to it, cognition essentially is a matter of the state evolutions that a cognitive system undergoes in certain situations.

Introduction

By *computationalism* in cognitive science I mean the view that cognition essentially is a matter of the computations that a cognitive system performs in certain situations. The main goal of this paper is to assess whether this view may represent a basic hypothesis shared by the three current approaches to cognition: the symbolic (or classic) approach, connectionism, and nonconnectionist dynamics.

If we look at the models actually used in cognitive science, we see that a different type of model corresponds to each approach. The symbolic approach (Newell and Simon, 1972; Newell, 1980; Pylyshyn, 1984; Johnson Laird, 1988) employs symbolic processors as models. As a first approximation, we may take a symbolic processor to be any device that operates effective transformations of appropriately defined symbol structures. The connectionist approach (Rumelhart and McClelland, 1986), on the other hand, employs connectionist networks, while nonconnectionist dynamicists use other kinds of continuous systems specified by differential (or difference) equations. Nonconnectionist researchers favoring a dynamical

perspective are active in many fields. For examples see Port and van Gelder (1995).

The main thesis 1 am going to defend is that computationalism is only consistent with symbolic modeling or, more generally, with any other type of computational modeling. In particular, those scientific explanations of cognition which are based on *(i)* an important class of connectionist models or *(ii)* nonconnectionist continuous models cannot be computational, for these models are not the kind of system which can perform computations in the sense of standard computation theory.

The thesis that computationalism is only consistent with computational modeling is empty unless one gives a sufficiently precise characterization of what a *computational model* of a cognitive system is. By this term, I mean any computational system that describes (or, at least, is intended to describe) some cognitive aspect of the cognitive system. Intuitively, by the term *computational system* I refer to any device of the kind studied by standard computation theory. Thus, for example, Turing machines, register machines, and finite state automata are three different types of computational systems. By contrast, so-called analog computers are not computational systems. I will propose later a formal explication of this intuitive notion of a computational system.

Thus, if my thesis is correct, we are left with the following alternative. Either we construe computationalism by explicitly referring to some nonstandard notion of computation, or we simply abandon the idea that computationalism be a basic hypothesis shared by *all* current research in cognitive science. In the last section of this paper, I will also suggest that a different hypothesis, *dynamicism*, may represent a viable alternative to computationalism. According to it, cognition essentially is a matter of the state evolutions that a cognitive system undergoes in certain situations.

The Argument

The main thesis of this paper is that computationalism is only consistent with symbolic modeling or, more generally, with any other type of computational modeling. The argument I am going to propose is based on two premises. The first one affirms that all models currently employed in cognitive science are *mathematical dynamical systems*. The second premise, on the other hand, affirms that a computation (in the sense of standard computation theory) can only be performed by that special type of mathematical dynamical system which I have called a *computational system*. Having established these two premises, I will then show that *(a)* an important class of connectionist models, and *(b)* nonconnectionist continuous models are not computational systems. Hence, these models cannot perform computations in the standard sense. But then, if our scientific explanations of cognition are based on these models, we cannot maintain that cognition is, essentially, a matter of the computations performed by the cognitive system which these models are intended to describe. On the other hand, *(c)* all symbolic models are computational systems. Therefore, computationalism is only consistent with symbolic modeling or, more generally, with any other approach which employs computational systems as models of cognition.

The First Premise

The first premise of my argument is that all models currently employed in cognitive science are mathematical dynamical systems. A *mathematical* dynamical system is an abstract mathematical structure that can be used to describe the change of a real system as an evolution through a series of states. If the evolution of the real system is deterministic, that is, if the state at any future time is determined by the state at the present time, then the abstract mathematical structure consists of three elements. The first element is a set T that represents time. T may be either the reals, the rationals, the integers, or the nonnegative portions of these structures. Depending on the choice of T, then, time is represented as continuous, dense, or discrete. The second element is a nonempty set M that represents all possible states through which the system can evolve; M is called the *state space* of the system. The third element is a set of functions $\{g^t\}$ that tells us the state of the system at any instant t provided that we know the initial state; each function in $\{g^t\}$ is called a *state transition* of the system. For example, if the initial state is $x \in M$, the state at time t is given by $g^t(x)$, the state at time $u > t$ is given by $g^u(x)$, etc. The functions in the set $\{g^t\}$ must only satisfy two conditions. First, the function g^0 must take each state to itself and, second, the composition of any two functions g^t and g^w must be equal to the function g^{t+w}.

An important subclass of the mathematical dynamical systems is that of all systems with discrete time. Any such system is called a cascade. More precisely, a mathematical dynamical system $<T, M, \{g^t\}>$ is a *cascade* just in case T is equal to the nonnegative integers (or to the integers).

As mentioned, the models currently employed in cognitive science can basically be classified into three different types: *(1)* symbolic processors, *(2)* neural networks, and *(3)* other continuous systems specified by differential (or difference) equations. That a system specified by differential or difference equations is a mathematical dynamical system is obvious, for this concept is expressly designed to describe this class of systems in abstract terms. That a neural network is a mathematical dynamical system is also not difficult to show. A complete

state of the system can in fact be identified with the activation levels of all the units in the network, and the set of state transitions, on the other hand, is determined by the differential (or difference) equations that specify how each unit is updated. To show that all symbolic processors are mathematical dynamical systems is a bit more complicated.

The argumentative strategy I prefer considers first a special class of symbolic processors (such as Turing machines, or monogenic production systems, *etc.*) and it then shows that the systems of this special type are mathematical dynamical systems with discrete time, *i.e.*, cascades. Given the strong similarities between different types of symbolic processors, it is then not difficult to see how the argument given for one type could be modified to fit any other type (Giunti, 1992, 1996). We may thus conclude that all models currently employed in cognitive science are mathematical dynamical systems.

The Second Premise

The second premise of my argument affirms that a computation (in the sense of standard computation theory) can only be performed by a *computational system*. Intuitively, by this term I refer to any device of the kind studied by standard computation theory (*e.g.*, Turing machines, register machines, cellular automata, *etc.*) I call any computation performed by any such device a *standard computation*. According to this terminology, then, my second premise affirms that *a standard computation can only be performed by a computational system*. It is thus clear that I in fact take this premise to be true by definition.

Someone might object that, given my definitions, my second premise is not only true, but also trivial. According to my imaginary critic, the important question is not whether a standard computation can be performed by a noncomputational system but, rather, whether standard computational methods are sufficient to accurately describe the behavior of *all* models employed in cognitive science (be these models computational or not). I will give an answer to this kind of objection later. Before I can proceed with my argument, however, I need to give a formal explication of the intuitive concept of a computational system.

A Formal Definition of a Computational System

To this extent, let us first of all consider the mechanisms studied by standard computation theory and ask *(i)* what type of system they are, and *(ii)* what specific feature distinguishes these mechanisms from other systems of the same type.

As mentioned, standard computation theory studies many different kinds of abstract systems. A basic property that is shared by all these mechanisms is that they are *mathematical dynamical systems with discrete time*, that is *cascades*. However, standard computation theory does not study all cascades. The specific feature that distinguishes computational systems from other mathematical dynamical systems with discrete time is that a computational system *can always be described in an effective way*. Intuitively, this means that the constitution and operations of the system are purely mechanical or that the system can always be identified with an idealized mechanism. However, since we want to arrive at a formal definition of a computational system, we cannot limit ourselves to this intuitive characterization. Rather, we must try to put it in a precise form.

Since I have informally characterized a computational system as a cascade that can be effectively described, let us ask first what a *description* of a cascade is. If we take a structuralist viewpoint, this question has a precise answer. A description (or a representation) of a cascade consists of a second cascade *isomorphic* to it where, by definition, a cascade $MDS_1 = <T, M_1, \{h^t\}>$ is isomorphic to a given cascade $MDS = <T, M, \{g^t\}>$ just in case there is a bijection $f: M \to M_1$ such that, for any $t \in T$ and any $x \in M, f(g^t(x)) = h^t(f(x))$.

In the second place, let us ask what an *effective* description of a cascade is. Since I have identified a description of a cascade $MDS = <T, M, \{g^t\}>$ with a second cascade $MDS_1 = <T, M_1, \{h^t\}>$ isomorphic to MDS, an effective description of MDS will be an *effective cascade* MDS_1 isomorphic to MDS. The problem thus reduces to an analysis of the concept of an effective cascade. Now, it is natural to analyze this concept in terms of two conditions: *(a)* there is an effective procedure for recognizing the states of the system or, in other words, the state space M_1 is a *decidable* set; *(b)* each state transition function h^t is effective or *computable*. As it is well known, these two conditions can be made precise in several ways which turn out to be equivalent. The one I prefer is by means of the concept of Turing computability. If we choose this approach, we will then require that an effective cascade satisfy: *(a')* the state space M_1 is a subset of the set $P(A)$ of all finite strings built out of some finite alphabet A, and there is a Turing machine that decides whether an arbitrary finite string is member of M_1; *(b')* for any state transition function h^t, there is a Turing machine that computes h^t.

Finally, we are in the position to formally define a computational system. The following definition expresses in a precise way the informal characterization of a computational system as a cascade that can be effectively described.

DEFINITION   (computational system)
MDS is a computational system iff $MDS = <T, M, \{g^t\}>$ is a cascade, and there is a second cascade $MDS_1 = <T, M_1, \{h^t\}>$ such that MDS_1 is isomorphic to MDS and
(1) if $P(A)$ is the set of all finite strings built out of some finite alphabet A, $M_1 \subseteq P(A)$ and there is a Turing machine that decides whether an arbitrary finite string is member of M_1;
(2) for any $t \in T$, there is a Turing machine that computes h^t.

It is tedious but not difficult to show that all systems that have been actually studied by standard computation theory (Turing machines, register machines, monogenic production systems, cellular automata, *etc.*) satisfy the definition (Giunti, 1992, 1996).

Two Sufficient Conditions for a System not to Be Computational

The definition of a computational system allows us to deduce two sufficient conditions for a mathematical dynamical system not to be computational. Namely, a mathematical dynamical system $MDS = <T, M, \{g^t\}>$ is not computational if it is continuous in either time or state space or, more precisely, if either *(i)* its time set T is the set of the (nonnegative) real numbers, or *(ii)* its state space M is not denumerable.

An immediate consequence of condition *(ii)* is that *any finite neural network whose units have continuous activation levels is not a computational system*. Also note that *the same conclusion holds for any continuous system specified by differential (or difference) equations*. Since all these systems are continuous (in time or state space), none of them is computational.

Summing up the Argument

We have thus seen that *(I)* all models currently employed in cognitive science are mathematical dynamical systems; *(II)* a standard computation can only be performed by a computational system; *(III)* any finite neural network whose units have continuous activation levels or, more generally, any continuous system specified by differential (or difference) equations is not a computational system. Hence, all connectionist models in this class and all nonconnectionist continuous models cannot perform standard computations. But then, if our scientific explanations of cognition are based on these models, we cannot maintain that cognition is, essentially, a matter of the standard computations performed by the cognitive system which these models are intended to describe. On the other hand, it is obvious that *(IV)* all symbolic models are computational systems. Therefore, computationalism is only consistent with symbolic modeling or, more generally, with any other approach which employs computational systems as models of cognition.

A word of caution is needed here. Somebody might object to this conclusion in the following way. It is well known that the behavior of virtually all continuous systems considered by physics can be simulated, to an arbitrary degree of precision, by a computational system, even though these systems are not computational systems themselves (Kreisel, 1974). Why should the continuous systems considered in cognitive science be different in this respect? As long as the behavior of a continuous model of a cognitive system can be simulated (to an arbitrary degree of precision) by a computational system, there is nothing, in the model, which is beyond the reach of standard computational methods. Therefore, it is false that computationalism is only consistent with computational modeling.

This objection is confused because it blurs the distinction between the standard computations *performed* by a system, and the *simulation* of its behavior by means of standard computations performed by a different system. In the first place, this distinction is essential for the formulation of the computational hypothesis itself. If computationalism is intended as a very general hypothesis that indicates the appropriate style of explanation of cognitive phenomena (namely, a computational style), it is crucial to affirm that cognition depends on the standard computations *performed* by the cognitive system we are studying, for it is precisely by understanding the particular nature of these computations that we can produce a detailed explanation of cognition. But then, in formulating the computational hypothesis, we are in fact implicitly assuming that the cognitive system *is* a computational system, we are not just claiming that its behavior can be simulated by a computational system. In the second place, I have argued that any continuous model is not a computational system, and thus it *cannot perform* standard computations. But then, if our scientific explanations of cognition are based on continuous models, we cannot maintain that cognition is, essentially, a matter of the standard computations performed by the cognitive system which these models are intended to describe. Therefore, computationalism is indeed inconsistent with continuous modeling.

Concluding Remarks

My argument shows that, unless we construe computationalism by explicitly referring to some nonstandard notion of computation, we cannot maintain that computationalism is a basic hypothesis shared by *all* current research in cognitive science. In view of this fact, however, we should consider at least two further questions.

First, what kind of nonstandard notion of computation would be needed for an adequate generalization of the computational hypothesis? And, second, is there some other hypothesis that might play this unifying role as well?

As regards the first question, I will limit myself to just one preliminary remark, for a critical discussion is beyond the scope of this paper. Even within these limits, however, it seems quite reasonable to maintain that a generalized version of the computational hypothesis should be based on a theory of computation that *(i)* applies to continuous systems and standard computational systems as well; *(ii)* in the special case of standard computational systems, this more general theory reduces to the standard one, and thus *(iii)* all the standard computability results should turn out to be special cases of the more general theory. I leave it up for further discussion whether these conditions are indeed well chosen, or whether they are in fact satisfied by some theories which intend to generalize various aspects of standard computation theory (Blum, Shub, and Smale, 1989; Friedman, 1971; Shepherdson, 1975, 1985, 1988; Montague, 1962).

As for the second question, we have seen that all models currently employed in cognitive science are mathematical dynamical systems. Furthermore, in general, a mathematical dynamical system changes its behavior according to the particular state evolution that the system undergoes. But then, if our aim is to model cognition by means of appropriate mathematical dynamical systems, we may very well claim that *cognition is, essentially, a matter of the particular state evolutions that a cognitive system undergoes in certain situations.* I call this hypothesis *dynamicism*. For two, quite different, articulations and defenses of dynamicism see van Gelder and Port (1995) and Giunti (1995, 1996).

It is thus clear that dynamicism, unlike (standard) computationalism, is consistent with symbolic, connectionist, and nonconnectionist continuous modeling as well. Therefore, all research on cognition might end up sharing this new hypothesis, independently of the type of model employed. The question remains, however, whether this possibility will really obtain. I believe that the answer to this question depends on whether the explicit assumption of a dynamical perspective can sharply enhance our understanding of cognition. This issue, however, will ultimately be settled by detailed empirical investigation, not by abstract argument.

On the other hand, it is also quite obvious that the dynamical hypothesis, as stated above, only gives us an extremely general methodological indication. Essentially, it only tells us that cognition can be explained by focusing on the class of the dynamical models of a cognitive system, where a dynamical model is *any* mathematical dynamical system that describes some cognitive aspect of the cognitive system. Now, a standard objection against this version of dynamicism is that this methodological indication is so general as to be virtually empty. Unfortunately, a detailed rebuttal to this charge goes beyond the scope of this paper. Therefore, I must limit myself to briefly outline the three defenses that have been adopted by the proponents of the dynamical approach.

The first line of defense points out that dynamicism, just like computationalism, has in fact two aspects. The first one is the specification of a particular class of models (dynamical *vs.* computational models), while the second is the proposal of a conceptual framework (dynamical systems theory *vs.* computation theory) that should be used in the study of these models. Therefore, if we also consider this second aspect, we see that the mathematical tools of dynamical systems theory provide dynamicism with a rich methodological content, which clearly distinguishes this approach from the computational one (Giunti 1995, 1996; van Gelder and Port 1995; van Gelder 1995).

Second, some proponents of the dynamical approach (van Gelder and Port 1995; van Gelder 1995) have in fact restricted the class of models allowed by the dynamical hypothesis. According to their proposal, dynamical models include most connectionist models and all nonconnectionist continuous models, but they exclude computational models.

Thus, under this interpretation of dynamicism, it is no longer true that the dynamical hypothesis is consistent with symbolic modeling. These authors, however, do not take this to be a drawback, for they maintain that all symbolic models give a grossly distorted picture of real cognition.

Finally, my line of defense (Giunti 1995, 1996) also restricts the class of the dynamical models, but in a different way. The heart of my proposal lies in the distinction between two different kinds of dynamical models: simulation models and Galilean ones. This distinction is an attempt to set apart two, quite different, modeling practices. *Simulation models* are mathematical dynamical systems which, to a certain extent, are able to reproduce available data about certain tasks or domains. Besides this empirical adequacy (which sometimes is itself quite weak) it is very difficult, if not impossible, to find an interpretation which assigns a feature (aspect, property) of the real system to each component of the model. By contrast, *Galilean models* are built in such a way that no component of the model is arbitrary. Rather, each component must correspond to a magnitude of the real system. Galilean modeling is in principle consistent with symbolic, connectionist, and nonconnectionist continuous modeling as well. What I have been arguing for is that we should take the *ideal* of Galilean modeling more seriously for, if we are successful, we are going to build a better science of cognition.

References

Blum, L., Shub, M., and Smale, S. (1989). On a theory of computation and complexity over the real numbers: NP-Completeness, recursive functions and universal machines. *Bulletin of the American Mathematical Society, 21, 1*, 1-46.

Friedman, H. (1971). Algorithmic procedures, generalized Turing algorithms, and elementary recursion theory. In R. O. Gandy and C. M. E. Yates (Eds.), *Logic colloqium '69* (pp. 361-389). Amsterdam: North Holland.

Giunti, M. (1992). *Computers, dynamical systems, phenomena, and the mind.* Doctoral dissertation. Bloomington, IN: Indiana University, Dept. of History and Philosophy of Science.

Giunti, M. (1995). Dynamical models of cognition. In R. F. Port and T. van Gelder (Eds.), *Mind as motion* (pp. 549-571). Cambridge MA: The MIT Press.

Giunti, M. (1996). *Computation, dynamics, and cognition.* New York: Oxford Univ. Press. Forthcoming.

Johnson-Laird, P. N. (1988). *The computer and the mind.* Cambridge MA: Harvard Univ. Press.

Kreisel, G. (1974). A notion of mechanistic theory.*Synthese, 29*, 11-26.

Montague, R. (1962). Toward a general theory of computability. In B. Kazemier and D. Vuysje (Eds.), *Logic and language.* Dordrecht: D. Reidel.

Newell, A. (1980). Physical symbol systems. *Cognitive Science, 4*, 135-183.

Newell, A., and Simon, H. (1972). *Human problem solving.* Englewood Cliffs NJ: Prentice Hall.

Port, R. F., and T. van Gelder (Eds.) (1995). *Mind asmotion: Explorations in the dynamics of cognition.* Cambridge MA: The MIT Press.

Pylyshyn, Z. W. (1984). *Computation and cognition.*Cambridge MA: The Mit Press.

Rumelhart, D. E., and McClelland, J. L. (Eds.) (1986).*Parallel distributed processing.* 2 vols. Cambridge MA: The MIT Press.

Shepherdson, J. C. (1975). Computation over abstract structures: serial and parallel procedures and Friedman's effective definitional schemes. In H. E. Rose and J. C. Shepherdson (Eds.), *Logic colloquium '73* (pp. 445-513). Amsterdam: North Holland.

Shepherdson, J. C. (1985). Algorithmic procedures, generalized Turing algorithms, and elementary recursion theory. In L.A. Harrington, *et al.* (Eds.), *Harvey Friedman's research on the foundations of mathematics* (pp. 285-308). Amsterdam: North Holland.

Shepherdson, J. C. (1988). Mechanisms for computing over abstract structures. In R. Herken (Ed.), *The universal Turing machine: A half century survey* (pp.581-601). Oxford: Oxford Univ. Press.

van Gelder, T. (1995). Connectionism, dynamics, and the philosophy of mind. To appear in the *Proceedings volume of Philosophy and the sciences of mind. The third Pittsburgh-Konstanz colloquium in the philosophy of science. Konstanz, May 1995.*

van Gelder, T., and Port, R. F. (1995). It's about time: an overview of the dynamical approach to cognition. In R. F. Port and T. van Gelder (Eds.), *Mind as motion* (pp. 1-43). Cambridge MA: The MIT Press.

Qualia: The Hard Problem

Todd W. Griffith* and **Michael D. Byrne†**

*College of Computing
Georgia Institute of Technology
Atlanta, Georgia 30332-0280
griffith@cc.gatech.edu

†School of Psychology
Georgia Institute of Technology
Atlanta, GA 30332-0170
byrne@cc.gatech.edu

Abstract

One issue that has been raised time and again in philosophy of mind and more recently in cognitive science is the question of qualia, or "raw feels." What are qualia and how do they fit into the cognitive science conception of mind? We consider some of the classic qualia thought experiments and two proposed solutions to the qualia problem, eliminativism and content-dependence. While neither of these solutions are actually able to dismiss or explain qualia as claimed, the content-based solution does clarify the relation between cognitive science and qualia. Because qualia are precisely the part of our experiences that are not related to informational content (and therefore inter-subjective), and cognitive science is primarily based on information content, qualia are not within the domain of cognitive science.

Introduction

The nature of qualia or "raw feels" has always been a philosophical issue at least implicitly, and recently cognitive science has tried its hand at the problem. In this paper we argue that the real issue of qualia is not an issue for cognitive science as it presently exists, but remains a strictly philosophical issue. Qualia is the term which is applied to indivisible primary feelings such as the feeling of seeing red in an apple or the feeling of pain in one's foot. Traditionally qualia are considered to be purely first-person or subjective in nature. Today, however, with the aid of neuroscience some researchers in cognitive science have claimed to have solved the qualia problem in an objective sense. We disagree.

The problem of qualia is a problem of where. Where do qualia reside? It is the central question of the dualist/materialist debate and a core issue in the philosophy of mind. This question also reduces the question of consciousness to its primitives, e.g. where is my sensation of pain, of red, etc. The problem is best illustrated through an example: Suppose that I take a pin and push it into my finger (OK, so I'm not too bright). This action is objectively observable by normal means. As the pin enters my finger chemicals in the damaged tissue around my finger are released, which cause nerves to fire impulses to my brain. This too is an objectively observable phenomenon, albeit not by normal means. Now let us suppose that we trace these events full circle. We can, in theory at least, objectively observe all the neurons firing throughout my brain in a causal series, eventually ending in a signal from my brain to my hand causing it to move. Break the phenomenon down as you prefer; perhaps to chemical reactions or quantum phenomena. The question is still: where's the pain?

Is the pain reducible to my behavior? Clearly not, given that I can conceive of a situation where I would behave similarly without experiencing the pain (e.g. reflex actions work even on anesthetized patients, and simple robots react to negative stimuli). The problem is that qualia cannot be reduced to a third-person perspective. Searle (1992) attacks materialism by arguing that the first person point of view cannot be ignored, e.g. my pain is clearly mine, and all pain is clearly someone's. Nagel's (1974) idea of "what it is like to be" something also comes to mind. Searle points out that the insistence on objective criteria for truth is misplaced when one is talking about mental activity. Mental activity has a character that is outside the scope of objective observation yet is still clearly true. It is the "terror" of the subjective that has led to many of the current materialist positions in the philosophy of mind.

Two now classic thought experiments have been presented which illustrate some of the difficult issues regarding the nature of qualia: Thomas Nagel's (1974) "What is it like to be a bat?" and the inverted spectrum. Nagel argues that consciousness is an issue of "what it is like to be" something. He presents the argument that given a complete neurophysiological account of the workings of a bat's brain would not in any way enable us to know what it is like to be that bat. So even if we have a complete neurophysiological trace of a bat chasing a fly, we still have no way of knowing what it is like to be that bat observing that fly. Thus objective knowledge can not provide us with access to the bat's qualia. This of course translates to you and I. I cannot know your qualia and you can not know mine. Qualia are in some sense perfectly subjective. The inverted spectrum thought experiment also argues that it is not necessarily the case that my qualia are like yours. The experiment goes something like this: suppose that when I see red I get the same experience as when you see violet. In fact, suppose that for the entire color spectrum my experience is completely inverted with respect to yours. What we both call "red," for example, will be a quale (singular of qualia) of violet for me, and red for you. This experiment shows that there is no logical necessity that our subjective experiences are the same for the same stimulus. It raises the question: is there any way to know that we experience the same things? These thought experiments capture the difficult issues with regard to qualia that cognitive science does not have the tools to address.

Why are cognitive scientists concerned with the issue of qualia? There are at least two important reasons: the first is that qualia are directly tied to consciousness, which many claim is directly related to behavior and action. The second is that in many ways qualia represent the brass ring. If we can scientifically characterize subjective feelings such as pain, fear, or the smell of baking bread, we are very close to understanding a central aspect of human cognition. Unfortunately the current tools of cognitive science are not up to the task. Current solutions either leave the difficult problems totally untouched or discount them as fictitious, both of which are inadequate.

Proposed Solutions to the Qualia Problem

The fact that we lack an adequate account of what qualia actually are does not mean that there have not been approaches from a cognitive science perspective to solving the qualia problem. The two more prominent solutions are eliminativism and the qualia vs. content argument. Each of those will be considered here, beginning with eliminativism. Eliminativism, in particular "eliminative materialism," is most strongly associated with Churchland (e.g. 1988, 1989). The eliminativist perspective on qualia mirrors the eliminativist arguments for essentially all mental phenomena for which eliminativists currently lack a strong neural explanation: qualia do not need to be explained because they do not really exist. The belief that there are qualia is a vestige of the "folk psychological" viewpoint which will ultimately be eliminated when we develop a complete neuroscientific account of mind/brain. The concept of qualia—along with a host of other mind/brain concepts—will simply not be a part of this more mature understanding of neuroscience.

There are (at least) two problems with this proposed solution to the qualia problem. First, there is no guarantee whatsoever that the problem will simply go away if we do the right things in neuroscience. What, exactly, is the basis for the belief that every single extant mind/brain concept will necessarily be eliminated, other than the fact that some concepts in some other fields have been eliminated? This question has never been satisfactorily answered. Furthermore, the eliminativist camp has yet to even approach letting the world know which things and which things will not be eliminated—it has been implied that all current concepts of mind/brain will be eliminated, but this seems unreasonable. Certain concepts in other disciplines have been eliminated by lower-level reductions (e.g. impetus) but others have not (e.g. force, time). Despite what eliminativists (and members of Congress) might believe, problems tend not to simply vanish when vague promises of later solutions are proposed.

Second, this neuroscientific promissory note provides little satisfying information. By what will qualia be eliminated? For that matter, what would a neuroscientific account of whatever will replace qualia even look like?

When will such an account be developed? In the wake of proposing the elimination of qualia and just about everything else in mental life, eliminativism leaves just as many unanswered questions as it started with.

A somewhat more constructive approach to the qualia problem is the content vs. qualia argument offered in slightly different ways by Akins and Tye. Akins's paper is an attempt to rebut the "what is it like to be a bat?" argument. To make the argument, Akins (1994) has the reader consider the following thought experiment: A neuroscientist travels to the future and returns with the authoritative, future-neuroscience-approved "film" of what it's like to be a bat. This film contains:

a kaleidoscopic display of vibrant colour forms. Swirling and pulsating in three dimensions, the colored forms dance across the screen, colliding and dispersing, suddenly appearing or vanishing. That's all. That, I claim, is what it's like. (p. 262)

Obviously, something is amiss here—how can that be all there is? Akins's claim is that the entire qualia enterprise is mistaken just for the same reason that the bat film is nonsensical, because it assumes that "separation of our conscious experience into two parts, the representative and qualitative aspects" is possible. The point of the bat film is that the qualitative aspects of the bat's experience are meaningless to us because we lack the perceptual and representational capacities of the bat. There is no qualia problem because the mere idea of separation of the quality of the experience from the content of the experience is nonsensical. However, the fact that the qualia would be unintelligible hardly constitutes proof that the qualia do not exist.

Tye (1991) presents a similar argument directed at visual qualia. Arguments have been made that the difference between certain visual experiences (e.g. the difference between seeing blue and seeing red) is a difference in the qualia of the two experiences. Tye argues that in all such examples, there is in fact a difference in the information contents of the two experiences and that the experiences feel different not because there are any qualia involved, but because of this difference in content. He maintains that "[t]he 'felt' aspect simply cannot be divorced from the representational aspect" (p. 133). That is, the qualia for seeing red is perfectly correlated with the information that the visual stimulus reflects red light. In essence, this is the same argument as Akins's—qualia do not exist independent of content.

This is a much more clearly elucidated and convincing argument than the eliminativist argument. Rather than ignoring the problem and hoping it will go away, this solution attempts to locate the source of the problem in something familiar to the cognitive/computational perspective: information content. If the qualia issue is a content issue, it lends itself to analysis by the traditional methods of cognitive science. In that case, there is nothing that is in principle unexplainable about qualia and an account, though we may not have it in hand, should certainly be reachable.

While this is a compelling perspective, it still falls short of the goal of eliminating or explaining qualia. While it may be the case that all intra-individual differences in qualia are associated with differences in content, this does not provide a guarantee that the subjective feel of the experiences is the same for different people. Consider again the inverted spectrum problem; that is, persons A and B can both accurately discriminate and name different colors but their subjective experiences are reversed. That is, "seeing red" for A feels like "seeing violet" for B and vice versa. The content perspective does not eliminate this possibility. Both A and B have the same rods and cones (i.e. Akins's perceptual machinery) and both A and B have the same color distinctions and categories (i.e. representational content). As Tye suggests, within an individual, the qualia are perfectly paired with informational content. Person A always has a "red" quale when seeing a red object—the information content determines which quale. Person B also always has a "red" quale when seeing a red object for the same reason. However, there is no way to guarantee that the subjective feel of seeing red is the same for both A and B. Nothing in Tye's account guarantees inter-individual agreement on subjective feel. The inverted spectrum problem clearly remains, even if we assume that a particular quale is tied to particular information content for a given observer. The problem of inter-subjectivity is simply not solved by invoking associations between qualia and contents.

Not a Cognitive Science Problem

While the association between content and qualia does not, as the authors claim, solve the qualia problem in that it does not explain what and where qualia are, the "content solution" has important implications with respect to the nature of qualia and inquiry in cognitive science. The failure of the content solution to actually do away with qualia clearly demarcates the boundaries between what is content and what is quale. That which has informational content is not quale, and, importantly, vice versa: that which is quale has no informational content. Content, specifically informational content, is the objective substance of cognitive science. Conducting experiments without this substance is futile because the experimenter can never know that the "subjective content" of his or her inquiry is remotely similar as the "inverted spectrum" problem clearly illustrates.

Examples may help illustrate. Consider again the inverted spectrum problem. When perceiving light of some wavelength, both person A and person B, there is indeed informational content to the sensation of seeing the color, which would be something like "light of wavelength X." This is the information content of the seeing experience, and both A and B would get this information from the sensation--just as Tye points out. However, in the case of inverted spectra, A and B will **not** have the same subjective feel of the experience. What "feels" red to A may well "feel" blue to B, despite the identical information content of the experience. We define qualia by what they are not: qualia are what is left of sensations after the objective information content is removed. As Tye suggests, there may

be a perfect correspondence between which qualia will be felt when certain information is conveyed, but this does **not** eliminate the qualia.

We do not deny that sensations have informational content--dropping a hammer on one's foot makes this immediately clear.[1] Information about an impact, such as rough estimates of the weight, hardness, and velocity of the object striking the foot, is quit available, and this is indeed information in the objective sense. If one were to hook up sophisticated neuron recording devices, a third-party observer could also likely get much of this information based on which neurons fire and at what rate. But this observer would miss the "feel" of the hammer striking his or her foot. The sensation contains two things: objective information, and something that is **not** objective information. The latter are qualia.

This distinction is of paramount importance to cognitive science. While there are probably few things that all practitioners of cognitive science agree on, the centrality of information processing is almost certainly one of them. Take, for example, the list of keywords for the 1996 Cognitive Science Annual Conference—almost every single one of these research categories implicitly or explicitly relies on information-processing accounts of one form or another. If one were going to select the single identifying characteristic of research in cognitive science, information processing would be an excellent candidate. It is the information in the stimuli that concern the experimental psychologist, it is the information that is handled in the programs of computer scientists, it is the information in language that concerns the linguist. Science in general is an enterprise of explaining the observed and objective information about the natural world. Thus, qualia do not fall under the domain of cognitive science. Qualia are precisely the aspects of our experience that do not have the kind of information content which is at the core of cognitive science. If there is no such objective informational content to study, it is surely impossible to make a science out of the endeavor. How could scientific method be appropriate in domains lacking informational content?

As pointed out earlier, qualia are a problem of inter-subjectivity. Issues regarding qualia fall into the domain of the philosophical phenomenologist, not the cognitive scientist. Cognitive science is materialistic in orientation, and clearly so in scope. Yet phenomenology and "things with no content" seem more along the lines of dualism. However, based on our current knowledge of the material, there may be no other approach, despite the fact that dualism has been rejected even by critics of traditional cognitive science such as Searle.

Even Searle, however, does not adequately answer the dualist. He claims that dualism has been "thoroughly discredited," and therefore should not be considered. We see only three possibilities for his dismissal of the dualist perspective. 1) He is terrified like his peers that there is something beyond the physical. 2) He is making a

[1] We would like to thank an anonymous reviewer for the suggestion that we conduct this particular experiment. However, we conducted it as a thought experiment only.

Lakatosian claim that dualism has ceased to provide interesting scientific problems to work on. 3) He is claiming that dualism has been discredited by the materialist positions which he himself tears down. Of these we believe the answer must be the second. "Dualism in any form is today generally regarded as out of the question because it is assumed to be inconsistent with the scientific world view." (p. 3) Unlike Einstein, however, who eliminated the concept of "aether" from scientific discourse by subsuming those aspects accessible to scientific investigation into the concept of "field," dualism continues to escape subsumption.

It is the subjective aspects of qualia that remain untouched by current attempts to solve the qualia problem. These attempts attack what David Chalmers (1995b) calls the easy problems of consciousness, such as "how can a human subject discriminate sensory stimuli and react to them appropriately?" (p. 81) The hard problem is "the question of how physical processes in the brain give rise to subjective experience" (p.81). The difficulty lies in the fact that normal scientific measures of objective fact fail to have an impact in this domain. In this respect Searle provides us with at least a starting point. He argues that the evidence for the nature of qualia will not be in the realm of the objective but in the equally real realm of the subjective. Thus objective scientific techniques will not suffice. It is for this reason that the qualia problem is a purely philosophical issue and not a cognitive science issue. For until we have the scientific tools to handle subjective evidence, the study of qualia will remain squarely in the realm of phenomenology.

This is not to say that the issues surrounding qualia are unimportant, but simply that they are not issues for cognitive science. We expect reactions to our conclusions to be varied. One of us (MB) believes that this means qualia are really of no concern, while the other (TG) believes this makes dualism and phenomenology attractive alternatives to mainstream cognitive science. We are in agreement, however, that qualia lie outside the domain of inquiry in cognitive science.

Acknowledgments

We would like to thank Nancy Nersessian for getting the two of us interested in this topic at the same time, pointing us to some of these references, and initiating the discussions which ultimately led us to writing this paper.

References

Akins, K. A. (1994). A Bat without Qualities? In M. Davies & G. W. Humphreys, (Eds.) *Consciousness: Psychological and Philosophical Essays.* (pp. 258-273). Cambridge, MA: Blackwell.

Chalmers, D. J. (1995a) The Puzzle of Conscious Experience. *Scientific American*, December, 80-86.

Chalmers, D. J. (1995b) Explaining Consciousness: The "Hard Problem." Special issue of *Journal of Consciousness Studies. Vol. 2. No. 3*; Autumn 1995.

Churchland, P. M. (1988). *Matter and Consciousness* (revised edition). Cambridge, MA: MIT Press.

Churchland, P. M. (1989). *A Neurocomputational Perspective: The Nature of Mind and the Structure of Science.* Cambridge, MA: MIT Press.

Nagel, T. (1974). "What is it like to be a bat?" *Philosophical Review 4 LXXXIII*: 435-450.

Searle, J. R. (1992). *The Rediscovery of the Mind.* Cambridge, MA: MIT Press.

Tye, M. (1991). *The Imagery Debate.* Cambridge, MA: MIT Press.

Connectionism, Systematicity and Nomic Necessity

Robert F. Hadley
School of Computing Science
and Cognitive Science Program
Simon Fraser University
Burnaby, B.C., V5A 1S6
hadley@cs.sfu.ca

Abstract

In their provocative 1988 paper, Fodor and Pylyshyn issued a formidable challenge to connectionists, viz., to provide a *non-classical* explanation of the empirical phenomenon of *systematicity* in cognitive agents. Since the appearance of F&P's challenge, a number of connectionist systems have emerged which *prima facie* meet this challenge. However, Fodor and McLaughlin (1990) advance an argument, based upon a *general* principle of *nomological necessity*, to show that one of these systems (Smolensky's) could not satisfy the Fodor-Pylyshyn challenge. Yet, if Fodor and McLaughlin's analysis is correct, it is doubtful whether any existing connectionist system would fare better than Smolensky's. In the view of Fodor and McLaughlin, humans and classical architectures display systematicity as a matter of nomological necessity (necessity by virtue of natural law), but connectionist architectures do not. However, I argue that the Fodor-Pylyshyn-McLaughlin appeal to nomological necessity is untenable. There is a sense in which neither classical nor connectionist architectures possess nomological (or 'nomic') necessity. However, the sense in which classical architectures *do* possess nomic necessity applies equally well to at least *some* connectionist architectures. Representational constituents can have causal efficacy within both classical and connectionist architectures.

1. Introduction

In their provocative 1988 paper, Fodor and Pylyshyn issued a formidable challenge to connectionists, viz., to provide a non-classical explanation of the empirical phenomenon of *systematicity* in cognitive agents. Fodor and Pylyshyn (F&P) acknowledge that connectionism might provide an implementational foundation for a *classical* explanation of systematicity, but *that*, they observe, would not provide an alternative to the classical account.

Although the precise definition of systematicity is a matter of some dispute (see below), we may, for the moment, ignore subtleties and assume that 'systematicity' refers to the fact that cognitive capacities are systematically related, and come in 'clumps'. As F&P insist, 'you don't find people who can *think the thought* that John loves the girl but can't think the thought that the girl loves John'. F&P maintain that systematicity occurs not only in thought, but in language understanding and production.

Since the appearance of F&P's challenge, a number of connectionist systems have emerged which *prima facie* meet this challenge (cf. Chalmers, 1990; Elman, 1990; Smolensky, 1990; St. John and McClelland, 1990; Niklasson and van Gelder, 1994). However, Fodor and McLaughlin (1990) advance an argument, based upon a *general* principle of *nomological necessity*, to show that Smolensky's methods in particular could not satisfy F&P's challenge. If Fodor and McLaughlin's (F&Mc) analysis is correct, it is doubtful whether any of the connectionist systems just cited would fare better than Smolensky's. In fact, McLaughlin later argues (1993a) that neither the results of Chalmers nor Elman constitute counterexamples to the F&P position (contrary to the explicit claims of Chalmers, 1990).

Now, the crux of F&Mc's argument, and indeed of F&P's original thesis, lies in their appeal to nomological necessity. In their view, humans and classical architectures display systematicity as a matter of nomological necessity (necessity by virtue of natural law), but connectionist architectures do not. In what follows, I argue that the Fodor-Pylyshyn-McLaughlin appeal to nomological necessity is untenable. There is a sense in which neither classical nor connectionist architectures possess nomological (or 'nomic') necessity. However, the sense in which classical architectures *do* possess nomic necessity applies equally well to at least *some* connectionist architectures. Moreover, Fodor, Pylyshyn, and McLaughlin all stress the *causal* efficacy of constituents (atomic elements) in complex *classical* representations. They maintain that complex connectionist representations (such as Smolensky's tensor-product representations) lack atomic constituents, and so, they believe that connectionists cannot appeal to constituent structure to *explain* why systematicity should be nomically necessary. By contrast, I argue (in section 4) that F&Mc ignore the manner in which atomic constituents can causally determine mathematical properties of complex connectionist representations. Yet, those very properties can engender systematicity within the context of some *particular* connectionist architecture. The F&Mc stance seems to arise from the fact that they regard particular connectionist systems as nomically arbitrary, while they regard classical architectures as nomically necessary.

2. Systematicity.

Before proceeding, it would be well to have in mind some more definite notion of systematicity than described above. However, as van Gelder and Niklasson (1994) have observed, F&P do not offer a precise definition of systematicity. Instead, they provide examples to support their contention that certain important cognitive capacities are systematically related. Most of their examples follow the pattern described above; the capacity to think (or understand) aRb is systematically related to the capacity to think (or understand) bRa, where a and b are referential terms, and R is some relation, e.g., 'loves'. However, F&P also include *systematicity of inference* in their discussion of systematicity. They contend, for example, that 'it's a psychological law that thoughts that P & Q tend to cause thoughts that P and thoughts that Q, all else being equal'. F&P's examples of systematicity in inference all involve rather immediate inferences, and it is unclear whether they would agree, for example, that thoughts of the form $P \rightarrow Q$ tend to cause thoughts of the form $\neg Q \rightarrow \neg P$. In any case, van Gelder and Niklasson have taken F&P to task on the question (a) whether humans do in fact exhibit systematicity in inference, and (b) whether F&P have produced a workably clear conception of systematicity. In light of problems raised by van Gelder and Niklasson, and because the issues which here concern us do not obviously involve systematicity in inference, and I shall not address this aspect of F&P's discussion. It is noteworthy that both Fodor and McLaughlin (1990) and McLaughlin (1993a) focus almost entirely upon the aRb, bRa class of mental capacities when presenting their case regarding nomic necessity.

Once we set aside concerns about systematicity in inference, other questions arise. For example, it is not clear whether F&P intend their observations on systematicity to apply to children in the early stages of language learning. At one point, they remark that *grammatically competent* (my emphasis) humans display systematicity in language use, but in a footnote citing Pinker (1984) they seem to suggest that children never lack the combinatorial architecture which engenders systematicity. Given Fodor's repeated stress on the nomic necessity of systematicity, it would seem incumbent upon him, at least, to present a more careful examination of the empirical evidence relevant to these claims. For there is substantial evidence that children do *not* exhibit strong forms of systematicity in very early stages of language learning (see Ingram, 1985).

Now, in Hadley (1992, 1994a) a learning-based hierarchy of *degrees* of systematicity is defined, where levels are distinguished according to the degree of *novelty* of sentences which the learning agent can interpret. Ingram has informed me (personal communication) that children do indeed pass through stages of systematicity which correspond fairly closely to the levels distinguished in those publications. Having noted this, I propose for the present to ignore these complications, and to focus upon F&P's approach to systematicity, since *that* is the basis of F&Mc's claims regarding nomic necessity.

The question we should now consider is whether F&P's conception of systematicity, *vis-a-vis* the ability to represent and process objects of the form aRb and bRa, can be clearly defined. McLaughlin (1993a) provides an analysis of systematicity, which, I believe, provides an affirmative answer. For brevity, I offer the following gloss on McLaughlin's analysis. In doing so, I omit certain details of McLaughlin's presentation which seem to me to go beyond F&P's original conception.

I. Systematicity: A cognitive agent, C, exhibits systematicity just in case its cognitive architecture *causally ensures* that C has the capacity to be in a propositional attitude (A) towards proposition (or sentence) aRb if and only if C has the capacity to be in attitude (A) towards proposition (sentence) bRa.

McLaughlin's examples of propositional attitudes (A) are 'thinks', 'believes', 'prefers that', and 'understands'. By contrast, I propose to restrict the scope of (A) to 'thinks' and 'understands', because these are the attitudes that F&P employ in their examples. Also, to extend (A) to include 'believes', and 'prefers that' would seem to raise unwanted complications. For example, it's far from clear that agents who have the capacity to believe, say, that *Kim sees a tree* also have the capacity to believe that *a tree sees Kim*. Of course, even when we replace 'believes' with 'understands', difficulties may arise. However, it is arguable that anyone who understands *Kim sees the tree* can make *sufficient sense* of *A tree sees Kim* to realize that it describes a factually impossible situation. Also, one can still understand the individual words in the latter sentence and imagine a cartoon that would illustrate the factually problematic situation.

3. Nomic Necessity.

A crucial aspect of F&P's view of systematicity, which is expressed in (I), is the idea that an integrated underlying mechanism *explains* the fact that certain cognitive capacities 'come in pairs'. I have followed McLaughlin (1993a) in building into the *definition* of systematicity a presupposition about the causal genesis of systematically related capacities. In Fodor and McLaughlin (F&Mc, 1990), this presupposition is not a matter of definition, but is described as a separate assumption. However, taken either way, the assumption is crucial to the arguments presented in F&Mc (1990) and McLaughlin (1993a). In F&Mc, the assumption is phrased in terms of nomic necessity (natural law).

The Fodor-McLaughlin stance, which re-emerges in McLaughlin (1993a), is that within *humans* and classical architectures it is a matter of nomic necessity that cognitive capacities are systematically related. By contrast, they hold that in connectionist architectures it is *at best* an accident of nature (i.e., nomically arbitrary) if cognitive capacities are so related. I shall argue, however, that neither F&Mc nor McLaughlin (1993a) succeed in establishing a relevant asymmetry between classical and connectionist architectures. Both architectures can, in principle, exhibit the relevant causal powers, and both architectures depend upon processing mechanisms which (since they might have arisen through evolution) may be viewed as nomically arbitrary to the same degree.

To begin, let us consider *why* F&Mc regard systematicity as a nomically necessary consequence of classical architecture. In (1990) they say:

> Whereas, as we keep on saying, in the Classical architecture, if you meet the conditions for being able to represent aRb, YOU CANNOT BUT MEET THE CONDITIONS FOR BEING ABLE TO REPRESENT bRa; the architecture won't let you do so because (i) the representation of a, R and b are constituents of the repre-

sentation of *aRb*, and (ii) you have to token the constituents of the representations that you token, so Classical constituents can't be just imaginary. So then, it is *built into* the Classical picture that you can't think *aRb* unless you are able to think *bRa*, but the Connectionist picture is *neutral* on whether you can think *aRb* even if you can't think *bRa*. But it is a law of nature that you can't think *aRb* if you can't think *bRa*. So the Classical picture explains systematicity and the Connectionist picture doesn't. So the Classical picture wins.

Now, this passage contains at least two tendentious claims. These are: (a) 'But it is a law of nature that you can't think *aRb* if you can't think *bRa*', and (b) 'it is *built into* the Classical picture that you can't think *aRb* unless you are able to think *bRa*.'

Regarding (a), it is not clear whether F&Mc take this 'law of nature' to be a *fundamental* psychological law about cognitive agents, or to be a derived law of some kind. In either case, (a) is likely to be contested by anyone who believes (i) that language acquisition is a precondition for the capacity to think, or (ii) that children exhibit only partial systematicity in the early stages of language learning. Both (i) and (ii) raise complex and interesting issues, but I propose to focus instead upon what seems to me the more central issue, namely (b). Is it clearly true that, on the Classical picture, 'you can't think *aRb* unless you are able to think *bRa*'? Granted, in a classical symbol system, you cannot token *aRb* without tokening the constituents, 'a', 'R', and 'b'. But, how is this fact supposed to *causally ensure* that you can think *bRa*. F&Mc do not explain in any detail, but they occasionally allude to structure-sensitive processes, which are a topic of emphasis in F&P, 1988.

Now, Smolensky (1994) maintains that classical theorists have no explanation of how the capacity to think *aRb* is supposed to *entail* the capacity to think *bRa*. He says,

> The point here is that *systematicity* is a basic part of the definition of a symbol *system*; the Classical theory gets systematicity by *assuming* it, not by deriving it from more fundamental principles. The necessity of systematicity is not *explained* by the classical theory in any sense, it is simply *described* by it. (original emphasis)

Later, Smolensky says that systematicity 'is achieved by stipulation in the Classical theory, which, on principle, refuses to posit lower-level principles from which systematicity might be derived.' Given the incompleteness of Fodor's, Pylyshyn's and McLaughlin's remarks about how, on the Classical theory, systematicity is supposed to arise, it is not surprising that Smolensky should conclude that systematicity 'is achieved by stipulation in the Classical theory'. However, I believe that Smolensky's analysis is not accurate. For, given F&P's repeated reference to structure-sensitive processes, and tokening of constituents, the outline of a theory can be discerned. In McLaughlin (1993a, p. 170), the theory is succinctly stated, but only in the most general terms. McLaughlin asserts that, 'classical architectures have complex symbols

and algorithmic operations on the constituent structures of such symbols. Even though the symbols do not participate in the algorithmic operations in virtue of their semantic properties, the algorithms will be such that symbol transitions make sense given the meanings of the symbols'.

Now, although details are *not* provided by F&P or McLaughlin about the nature of the relevant algorithmic operations (i.e., the structure-sensitive processes), it is not difficult to imagine the *kind* of algorithms that *might* serve the purpose. The fields of natural language 'comprehension' and generation (in AI) are rife with examples of algorithms that possess the kind of combinatorial properties that could, in principle, explain the *syntactic* requirements of systematicity. To be sure, these algorithms have only been applied to comparatively small languages, and their adequacy for the totality of natural language and mental representation remains uncertain. Nevertheless, it is reasonable to suppose that Fodor, Pylyshyn, and McLaughlin may have had algorithms of this *general type* in mind when they refer to 'algorithmic operations' and 'structure-sensitive' processes. The fact that these authors wish to remain neutral on the details of such algorithms, and upon how such algorithms might be realized in the brain, merely reflects good judgment on their part. It does not, I think, reflect a refusal 'to posit lower-level principles from which systematicity might be derived', as Smolensky suggests. The general nature of the lower-level principles is not hard to surmise. Only the details of such principles remains unspecified.

However, the crucial point I wish to underscore here is that, on the classical account, the systematicity of representations arises *only* in the presence of *assumed* algorithmic processes. Whatever 'causal powers' classical constituents may possess, and whatever nomological necessity may reside in some classical architecture, these exist only against a *background* of algorithms. It follows, then, that when the nomological characteristics of a connectionist architecture are considered, we must permit the connectionist to assume that *correspondingly general* processing mechanisms are in place. (Within connectionism, sets of weighted links between nodes, activation functions, and firing thresholds can all enter into these processing mechanisms.) Yet, F&Mc, and later McLaughlin (1993a) seem unwilling to allow Smolensky the connectionist mechanisms which would permit a network to process his tensor-product representations (activation vectors, for present purposes) in a manner that would engender systematic relations between those representations. For example, F&Mc say,

> No doubt it is possible for Smolensky to wire a network so that it supports a vector that represents *aRb* if and only if it supports a vector that represents *bRa*; and perhaps it is possible for him to do that without making the imaginary units explicit (though there is, so far, no proposal about how to ensure this for *arbitrary a, R and b*). The trouble is that, although the architecture permits this, it equally permits Smolensky to wire a network so that it supports a vector that represents *aRb* if and only if it supports a vector that represents *zSq*; or, for that matter, if and only if it supports a vector that repre-

sents The Last of The Mohicans. The architecture would appear to be absolutely indifferent as among these options.

F&Mc seem willing, for the sake of argument, to grant that Smolensky *could* 'wire a network so that it supports a vector that represents *aRb* if and only if it supports a vector that represents *bRa*', for **arbitrary** *a*, *R*, and *b*. Moreover, results reported in Chalmers (1990), Phillips (1994), and Miyata, Smolensky, Legendre (1993) establish that such *general purpose*, holistic wiring is not merely a theoretical possibility, but is now a reality.[1] Given this, it seems odd that F&Mc should insist upon the *arbitrariness* of the wiring (weighted links) that Smolensky would need to employ. For, it is difficult to see how the algorithmic operations presupposed by classical theorists are any *less* arbitrary than the general purpose processing mechanisms (or *unified* weighted link structures) that Smolensky, Chalmers, and other connectionists have employed. Presumably, both the classical and the connectionist processing mechanisms could (for all Fodor or McLaughlin say to the contrary) be the *products of natural selection*. Moreover, once either of these kinds of mechanisms is integrated within its respective architecture, the causal effects produced by representations via those mechanisms would be nomically necessary in precisely the same sense. The representations (classical or connectionist), together with the processing mechanisms, cause the entire system to behave in a systematic fashion. So, unless F&Mc can provide some reason, beyond natural selection (and beyond verbal stipulation) for saying that classical architectures *must* have the algorithmic mechanisms that they do in fact have, it is difficult to see that they have uncovered any *relevant* asymmetry between classical and connectionist architectures.

Now, F&Mc might rejoin that two relevant asymmetries can yet be found. These are: (1) that the actual physical presence of classical constituents in complex representations makes it possible to *explain* how systematicity arises within classical architectures, whereas no analogous explanation is possible within connectionist architectures; (2) that distributed activation patterns that represent complex meanings in a connectionist system are only *arbitrarily* related to the representations of their constituents, whereas just the opposite is true in classical architectures. Let us consider these two possible rejoinders in turn.

Concerning (1), it may well be true that *classical* constituent structure leads to transparent, obvious explanations of systematicity. The fact that classical algorithmic operations can (among other things) simply recombine atomic constituents in different orderings yields an elegant explanation of systematicity. However, some connectionists (e.g., van Gelder and Niklasson, 1994) have argued that such classical explanations are simplistic and fail to account for the subtle departures from straightforward systematicity that humans exhibit. In any case, the most elegant and obvious explanation of a natural phenomenon may not be the most accurate, and connectionists have argued that it is indeed possible to explain systematicity within connectionist architectures (cf. Chalmers, 1990;

Smolensky, 1994; Niklasson and van Gelder, 1994). At present, the connectionist account may be very abstract and schematic, but, as we have seen, the same is presently true of the classical explanation. As McLaughlin (1993a) observes, 'There are a number of promissory notes in classicism's proposal for explaining systematicity'.

Within connectionism, the explanation appeals to two fundamental truths: (a) it is possible to *generate* distributed representations in such a way that striking *mathematical regularities* exist between those distributed patterns that we would want to describe as systematically related (e.g., the patterns for 'dogs chase cats' and 'cats chase dogs'); (b) it is possible to create holistic (or unified) weight vectors (sets of weighted links) which exploit those mathematical regularities in a way that *causally ensures* that *aRb* is representable if and only if *bRa* is representable. Clear verification of both (a) and (b) can be found in Chalmers (1990), Phillips (1994), and Miyata, Smolensky, Legendre (1993). In addition, cluster analyses of distributed representations reported by Elman (1991) and others dramatically underscore the truth of (a).[2]

I will not attempt to recapitulate arguments already provided by Chalmers, Niklasson and van Gelder, Phillips, and Smolensky. However, the truth of (a) and (b) is implicit in the fact that a single unified weight vector is capable of *transforming* distributed representations of *novel* sentences (both active and passive voice) in the same fashion that it transforms representations of syntactically isomorphic, previously encountered sentences. This point emerges clearly from Chalmers' discussion of his active-passive transformation network. McLaughlin (1993a) disputes Chalmers' claim to systematicity, but he does so, in my view, by raising the hurdle. McLaughlin does *not* dispute the fact that Chalmers' network is capable, in effect, of re-ordering constituents. Rather, his complaint centers upon the fact that Chalmers has not dealt with certain subtle aspects of the active-passive transformation (such as the fact that verbs acquire past tense endings during passivization). However, F&P's examples of systematicity do not involve such subtleties; they focus upon the reordering and decomposition of representations. It is the reordering problem that Chalmers addressed. Whether

---

[1] I am assuming that 'a', 'R', and 'b', though arbitrary, are not entirely novel to the agent.

[2] In a 1991 paper, Elman describes cluster analyses of distributed activation patterns which appear on the hidden layer of the recursive backpropagation networks he employs. These patterns are quite complex, and contain information not only about the most recent input word, but about the syntactic context in which that word occurs. Elman's analyses clearly reveal that distributed patterns, which represent a word in one syntactic context, cluster very close, in vector space, to patterns representing the same word in *other* syntactic contexts. Moreover, Elman discovered that *not only* do nouns form separate clusters from verbs, but subclasses can be discovered within these clusters, corresponding to animate nouns, transitive verbs, etc. This clustering establishes beyond doubt that significant mathematical regularities can exist in distributed connectionist representations. In the case of Smolensky's tensor-product representations, which are *defined by* mathematical formulae, there can be no doubt whatsoever that important mathematical regularities exist. These regularities are exploited both in the active-passive transformations reported in Miyata, Smolensky, Legendre (1993) and in the systematicity results of Phillips (1994).

connectionism can explain *all* linguistic phenomena, including language acquisition, remains unclear, but that is not the point at issue. It is true that McLaughlin also objects to Chalmers' use of *training* to produce an association between active and passive representations. However, even ignoring the empirical likelihood that systematicity is partially a result of learning, Chalmers could very well reply that *certain* weight vectors, which are produced by training in artificial networks, might be innately wired in creatures which have evolved naturally.

Let us now return to the second possible rejoinder (2), introduced above. The rejoinder was: 'that distributed activation patterns that represent complex meanings in a connectionist system are only *arbitrarily* related to the representations of their constituents, whereas just the opposite is true in classical architectures'.

Now, a connectionist might respond to this claim in a number of ways. One approach would be to challenge its relevance. For, as long as distributed connectionist representations can be transformed, via weighted link structures, into *systematically related* new representations, what does it matter whether activation patterns for complex representations are arbitrarily related to representations of constituents? Systematicity and decomposability must be present, but the shapes of the representations involved are not important as long as transformations can be achieved in a holistic (non-piecemeal) fashion.

Perhaps a deeper reply to (2) would be to note that *within the context of the processing mechanisms that could generate* distributed representations of the type employed by Chalmers (1990) and Pollack (1990), complex representations are *not* arbitrarily related to representations of their constituents. For, by means of Recursive Auto-Associative Memories (RAAM), one can generate complex distributed representations that are *functionally related* in a systematic fashion to representations of their constituents (cf. van Gelder, 1990). Indeed, it is for this very reason that complex distributed representations exhibit those mathematical regularities which enable systematic transformations of the activation patterns to occur; witness the transformations described by Chalmers (1990).

The classicist might now object that, although distributed representations can be generated in a systematic fashion, the connectionist networks which *generate* those representations are themselves *nomically arbitrary*. However, the same can be said of classical algorithms which generate complex phrases from atomic constituents. The elegance and simplicity of the rules of formation for well-formed formulae in predicate logic, say, can scarcely be taken as evidence that *natural law* forces our brains to employ these rules. The only argument so far advanced by classicists, to support the claim that our brains (nomically) *must* employ classical rules of formation, is that no other explanation of systematicity is possible. But that, we have seen, is an argument unsupported by the facts.

4. The Causal Power of Constituents.

Both F&P and F&Mc make much of the causal power of constituents in classical representations. In their view, it is because classical constituents are physically present in complex constituents that they can have causal efficacy. Since constituents of distributed representations (including those of Smolensky, Elman, and Chalmers) are *not*

physically present in those representations, they cannot have causal powers (or so it is argued). For this reason, F&Mc have concluded that any connectionist system which does *not* implement a classical architecture cannot create systematicity as a matter of nomic necessity.

In the preceding section, I argued that F&Mc fail to establish any *relevant* asymmetry between classical and connectionist architectures *vis-a-vis* nomic necessity. Both kinds of architectures can achieve such necessity only in the presence of background algorithms or processing mechanisms. In the present section I pursue the Fodor-Pylyshyn-McLaughlin claim that constituents can have causal powers only if they are physically present in complex representations. The issue seems worthy of pursuit for a couple of reasons. First, as suggested above, it appears that confusion on this issue has increased confusion about the alleged lack of nomic necessity in connectionist systems. Second, I believe that Smolensky concedes too much when he says (1988), 'It may be that a good way to characterize the difference [between classical and connectionist architectures] is in terms of whether the constituents in a mental structure are causally efficacious in mental processing'. Although Smolensky's representations can be defined in terms of equations involving the identity of atomic constituents in essential ways, and though he has shown that his composite (tensor-product) representations are *decomposable* into their constituents under certain assumptions, Smolensky views the presence of atomic constituents in the composite representations as *merely imaginary*. F&Mc, of course, welcome this description, for what is merely imaginary cannot have causal efficacy (or so it would seem).

However, consider for a moment the phenomenon of *implicit information*. I have argued elsewhere (Hadley, 1995) that information which is recoverable from complex structures, even when background mechanisms must be assumed, may be regarded as *implicit* in a special sense. One could argue further that information which is implicit in this sense is not *merely* imaginary, since the complex structures in question must possess specific properties that reflect the derivable information. Analogously, Smolensky's tensor-product representations possess special properties that reveal the identity of their (purportedly) 'imaginary' atomic constituents. Thus, some *trace* of the atomic constituents is present even in the complex representations. In this sense those constituents might be regarded as implicitly present. However, I shall not insist upon this view, since I think a stronger, related argument exists. For the crucial point is that certain complex (distributed) connectionist representations can *not only be decomposed* into their atomic constituents, via assumed background processes, but can be *generated* from their atomic constituents in a systematic fashion. That they can be so generated is evident from results reported in Chalmers (1990), Elman (1990), Niklasson and van Gelder (1994), Pollack (1990), and Smolensky (1990) (see previous footnote).

Now, suppose that a given connectionist system employs both atomic representations (for 'cat', 'sees', etc.) and complex distributed representations that are generated from those atomic constituents. We have seen that such complex representations can, if they are *suitably gen-*

erated, exhibit striking mathematical regularities. Also, as argued in the preceding section, these mathematical regularities can engender patterns exhibiting systematicity, provided background processes are in place (and we know that classicists must assume comparable background processes). So, atomic constituents can (in the presence of background structures) cause complex representations to exhibit mathematical regularities. These regularities, in turn, cause systematic relationships to arise in the presence of suitable processing mechanisms. It would seem, therefore, that within *some* connectionist networks, atomic constituents can cause mathematical properties which entail systematicity. In such systems, atomic constituents *do have causal efficacy* because causality is a transitive relation.[3] Moreover, whatever causal efficacy *classical* constituents possess in a classical system, they possess only in the presence of assumed background processes. So, again, there appears to be no relevant asymmetry between classical and connectionist architectures *vis-a-vis* the causal efficacy of constituents. In both cases, much depends upon the nature of the background processing mechanisms that are in place.

It might, perhaps, be objected that connectionist constituents have a less *direct* causal efficacy than classical constituents. However, even if this were true, it is far from obvious that this is a *relevant* difference. Moreover, it's not clear that any appreciable difference in the directness of the causal relationships actually exists. For, a classical constituent in a complex structure may have efficacy only after some algorithm analyses the entire structure and determines both the identity of its constituents and their relationship to one another. It may often happen that neither the connectionist nor the classical constituent will have an immediate causal effect in producing some systematically related effect.

6. Summary.

In the foregoing, I have argued that, contrary to the claims of Fodor, Pylyshyn, and McLaughlin, there is no relevant asymmetry between classical and connectionist architectures with regard to (a) the nomic necessity of the systematicity of cognitive capacities, or (b) the potential for those architectures to *explain* systematicity. We have seen that the mere presence of classical representations within a system does not, by itself, entail systematicity; appropriate processing mechanisms must be in place. Yet, the situation appears to be precisely analogous within connectionism. Provided the *right kinds* of representations are employed, and that appropriate weight vectors (processing mechanisms) are in place, connectionist systems exhibit systematicity as a matter of nomic necessity. Furthermore, an *explanation* of systematicity appears feasible within both architectures. In both cases, the explanation appeals to how the processing mechanisms (whether algorithmic or weight vectors) exploit the structure present within the representations.

References.

➤ Chalmers, D. (1990). Why Fodor and Pylyshyn were wrong: the simplest refutation. *Proceedings of the Twelfth Annual Conference of the Cognitive Science Society*, Cambridge, Mass.

➤ Elman, J.L. (1990). Finding structure in time. *Cognitive Science*, 14, 179-212.

➤ Elman, J.L. (1991). Representation and structure in connectionist models. In G. Altmann (Ed.) *Computational and psycholinguistic approaches to speech processing*. New York: Academic Press.

➤ Fodor, J.A. and McLaughlin, B.P. (1990). Connectionism and the problem of systematicity: Why Smolensky's solution doesn't work. *Cognition*, 35, 183–204.

➤ Fodor, J.A. and Pylyshyn, Z.W. (1988). Connectionism and cognitive architecture: a critical analysis. *Cognition*, 28, 3-71.

➤ Hadley, R.F. (1992). Compositionality and systematicity in connectionist language learning. *Proceedings of the Fourteenth Annual Conference of the Cognitive Science Society*, Bloomington, Indiana, 659-664.

➤ Hadley, R.F. (1994a). Systematicity in connectionist language learning. *Mind and Language*, 9, 247-272.

➤ Hadley, R.F. (1995). The explicit-implicit distinction. *Mind and Machines*, 5, 219-242.

➤ Ingram, D. (1985). The psychological reality of children's grammars and its relation to grammatical theory. *Lingua*, 66, 79-103.

➤ McLaughlin, B.P. (1993a). The connectionism/classicism battle to win souls. *Philosophical Studies*, 71, 163-190.

➤ McLaughlin, B.P. (1993b). Systematicity, Conceptual Truth, and Evolution. In C. Hookway and D. Peterson (Eds.) *Philosophy and Cognitive Science*. Royal Institute of Philosophy, Supplement No. 34.

➤ Miyata, Y., Smolensky, P. and Legendre, G. (1993). Distributed Representation and Parallel Processing of Recursive Structures. *Proceedings of the Fifteenth Annual Conference of the Cognitive Science Society*, Boulder, Colorado, 759-764.

➤ Niklasson, L.F. and van Gelder, T. (1994). On being systematically connectionist. *Mind and Language*, 9, 288-302.

➤ Phillips, S. (1994). Strong systematicity within connectionism: the tensor-recurrent network. *Proceedings of the Sixteenth Annual Conference of the Cognitive Science Society*, Atlanta, GA, 723-727.

➤ Pinker, S. (1984). *Language learnability and language development*. Cambridge, MA: Harvard University Press.

➤ Pollack, J.B. (1990). Recursive distributed representations. *Artificial Intelligence*, 46, 77-105.

➤ Smolensky, P. (1988). Connectionism, constituency, and the language of thought, in Loewer, B. and Rey, G. (Eds.), *Meaning in Mind: Fodor and his critics*. Oxford: Blackwell.

➤ Smolensky, P. (1990). Tensor product variable binding and the representation of symbolic structures in connectionist systems. *Artificial Intelligence*, 46, 159-216.

➤ Smolensky, P. (1994). Constituent structure and explanation in an integrated connectionist/symbolic cognitive architecture. *The Philosophy of Psychology: Debates on Psychological Explanation*, C. Macdonald and G. Macdonald (eds.), Oxford: Basil Blackwell.

➤ St. John, M.F. and McClelland, J.L. (1990). Learning and applying contextual constraints in sentence comprehension. *Artificial Intelligence*, 46, pp. 217-257.

➤ van Gelder, T. (1990). Compositionality: A Connectionist Variation on a Classical Theme. *Cognitive Science*, 14, 355-384.

➤ van Gelder, T. (1991) Classical questions, radical answers: Connectionism and the structure of mental representations. In T. Horgan and J. Tienson (Eds.), Connectionism and the Philosophy of Mind. Dordrecht: Kluwer.

➤ van Gelder, T. and Niklasson, L.F. (1994). Classicism and cognitive architecture. *Proceedings of the Sixteenth Annual Conference of the Cognitive Science Society*, Atlanta, Georgia, 905-909.

---

[3] I have recently learned that the preceding argument, in its essentials, is given by van Gelder in (van Gelder, 1991).

Fodor's New Theory of Content and Computation

Andrew Brook and **Robert J. Stainton**
Interdisciplinary Studies and Philosophy
Carleton University
Ottawa, ON, Canada K1S 5B6
{abrook,stainton}@ccs.carleton.ca

Abstract

In his new book, *The Elm and the Expert*, Fodor attempts to reconcile the computational model of human cognition with information-theoretic semantics, the view that semantic content consists of nothing more than causal or nomic relationships between words and the world, and intentional content of nothing more than causal or nomic relationships between brain states and the world. We do not challenge the project, not in this paper. Nor do we show that Fodor has failed to carry it out. Instead, we urge that his analysis, when made explicit, turns out rather differently than he thinks. In particular, where he sees problems, he sometimes shows that there is no problem. And while he says two conceptions of information come to much the same thing, his analysis shows that they are very different.

1. Introduction

Two old friends show up early in Fodor's new book *The Elm and the Expert* (hereafter *E&E)*. First old friend: psychology must employ intentional concepts such as belief and desire. Second old friend: cognitive processes consist of computations and "computational processes are ones defined over syntactically structured objects" (Fodor, 1994, p. 8). What's new is Fodor's view of intentional content. Narrow content is out; information theoretic semantics is in.[1]

As we read it, *E&E* is about one central problem brought about by this change: whether the old picture of cognition as a computational process can be made to jibe with the new view that content is information, that content consists in a brain-world relationship. Could computational processes correctly 'track' content thus understood? We do not want to challenge the project. Nor do we aim to show that Fodor has failed to carry it out. Instead, we urge that his analysis, when made explicit, turns out rather differently than he thinks. First we will try to get the problem a little clearer, then we will consider peculiarities in Fodor's proposed resolution of it.

2. The Problem: The Argument for Incompatibility

By *computationalism* we mean the view that psychological states and processes are implemented computationally, where a computation is an operation over syntactic objects: a mapping from symbols to symbols, such that the transformations pay attention only to form, never to content. Let *intentionalism* be the view that psychological states are ineliminably content-bearing. Intentionalism can be many different things, depending on how 'intentional' is read. In particular: combining intentionalism with the view that content is information yields what might be called *informational intentionalism*. To avoid such an ugly label, we will speak of 'info-intentionalism'. It's the view that psychological states and processes are ineliminably intentional, *in the sense of being information-bearing*.

With these rough and ready definitions in hand, let us now pose The Question: are computationalism and info-intentionalism compatible? Here's an argument, reconstructed from *E&E,* that they are not. We call it the Argument for Incompatibility.

Premise One: If psychological states and processes are ineliminably intentional and psychological states and processes are implemented computationally then there must be computationally sufficient conditions for the instantiation of intentional properties.

Premise Two: Content, being information, is relational.

Premise Three: If content is relational then there aren't any computationally sufficient conditions for the instantiation of intentional properties.

Now, the antecedent of Premise One follows directly from intentionalism, and therefore from info-intentionalism, when conjoined with computationalism. So, computationalism plus info-intentionalism plus Premise One entail that there *must be* computationally sufficient conditions for the instantiation of intentional properties. Premise Two *also* follows from info-intentionalism. And from Premises Two and Three it follows that there *aren't any* computationally sufficient conditions for the instantiation of intentional properties. Evidently, these two conclusions are inconsistent. It begins to look, then, as though one must give a negative answer to The Question: info-intentionalism and computationalism are not consistent.

---

[1] Incidentally, Fodor underplays the attractions of narrow content. Far from being some unwelcome stepchild to be embraced only in theoreti‹ ‐tremis, narrow content is an intuitively plausible notion. First, it seems that our contents stay with us no matter what causal environment we find ourselves in. Second, we are aware of many of our mental contents in a way that seems inconsistent with mental content being broad. There seems to be an interesting asymmetry here between mental content and semantic content, however. It is easier to think of the latter as relational than the former. Among other reasons, we often do not know the meaning of a word but it is not easy to think of ourselves not knowing the contents of our thoughts, desires, perceptions, etc.

But there may be hope yet for the view that cognition is a matter of computations which track information. Perhaps one could reject one of the Premises. Premise Two, we repeat, is entailed by info-intentionalism. And Premise Three is motivated as follows: computational properties, being syntactic, are internal. But no internal property is such that satisfying it is sufficient for having an external relation. (This is presumably what Fodor has in mind when he remarks that, "It's as though one's having ears should somehow guarantee that one has siblings." [Fodor, 1994, p. 14]) Applying this to the case of computational and intentional states/processes, it seems that computational properties cannot possibly guarantee intentional properties—the former are internal while (ex hypothesi) the latter are relational. Hence Premise Three. Given the solidity of Premises Two and Three, then, Fodor goes after Premise One.

The appeal of Premise One resides in our need for what Fodor calls "a property theory" connecting intentional laws with their computational implementations. As Fodor puts it,

> If the implementing mechanisms for intentional laws are computational, then we need a property theory that provides for *computationally sufficient conditions* for the instantiation of intentional properties. (Fodor, 1994, p. 12; his emphasis)

To this Fodor gives a natural reply: the demand is too strong. In fact, he urges, psychological states and processes could be ineliminably intentional *and* be implemented computationally, even if there were no computationally sufficient conditions for the instantiation of intentional properties. If so, then despite the need for the theory to which Fodor refers, Premise One is too strong; indeed, Not True. In sum: the consequent of Premise One is inconsistent with the consequent of Premise Two, and the antecedents of both are true. But Premise One is not true. So, as far as the foregoing argument shows, the answer to The Question may well be 'yes': computationalism and info-intentionalism are compatible.

3. The Revised Argument for Incompatibility

So far so good. But a still small voice is insistently asking, 'Does the need for a property theory not commit us to *anything*?' Indeed it does. However, Fodor urges, all it commits us to is:

Premise One (Revised): If psychological states and processes are ineliminably intentional and psychological states and processes are implemented computationally, then the co-instantiation of the computational implementer and intentional implemented must be *reliable*.

Here is the argument that Premise One (Revised) is strong enough to allow for intentional psychological laws. One condition sufficient for computations to track content correctly would be supervenience: all differences of content being reflected in a difference within the computational system, across all possible worlds. That something this strong would *suffice* is presumably what motivates premises like our original Premise One. But, argues Fodor, all we *require* for psychology are conditions that reliably link

intentional content to syntactic states. Exceptions are quite all right so long as they *are* (just) exceptions, not counter-examples: that is to say, so long as they are infrequent and unsystematic—particularly unsystematic. (Psychology, goes the mantra, is a *ceteris paribus* science, not a basic one.) Moreover, these conditions need be reliable only in *this* world and worlds nomologically like this one. Psychology is beholden to worlds with the psychological (and related) laws of *our* world; other nomologies need not concern it. In sum: for a property theory to be in the offing, there must be *something* that keeps computation and content in phase, such that computational states/processes track intentional states/processes most of the time—but the tie need not be perfect nor hold in all possible worlds. These conditions can be met far short of sufficient conditions as conceived in classical conceptual analysis.

Unfortunately, the revised Premise One immediately suggests a revised Argument for Incompatibility. Frege cases (such as 'the Morning Star' and 'the Evening Star', 'Mark Twain' and 'Samuel Clemens') appear to be examples of computational type-distinctions to which no content distinction corresponds; Putnam's Twin Earth and Expert ('elm'/'beech') cases appear to be examples of content type-distinctions to which no computational distinction corresponds. (Fodor also discusses what he calls 'Quine cases': 'rabbit' and 'undetached rabbit part', for example. We'll introduce Quine cases later.) Because of Frege, Twin Earth, Expert and other cases, it is tempting to think that:

Premise Three (Revised): If content is relational then the co-instantiation of the computational implementer and intentional implemented will not be reliable.

Premise Two and Premise Three (Revised) entail that co-instantiation *will not be* reliable. Info-intentionalism, computationalism and Premise One (Revised) together entail that co-instantiation *must be* reliable. The ancillary premises seem solid. So it appears, once again, that info-intentionalism and computationalism are not consistent.

In response to this variant of the Argument for Incompatibility, Fodor goes after Premise Three (Revised). Roughly speaking, Fodor argues that—Frege, Twin, Expert and other cases notwithstanding—computational states/processes and intentional states/processes *do* reliably co-instantiate, at least when it matters. So the revised Argument for Incompatibility is also unsound. We turn, at last, to Fodor's defence of this claim.

4. Complications: Tying Content to Computation

When content is construed informationally—that is to say, as a matter of syntactic forms being in relationships to external objects—there are two broad ways in which content and computation could come apart, Fodor suggests.

1. There could be computational distinctions that do not reflect differences of informational content (Frege cases), and,

2. There could be differences of informational content that are not reflected in difference of computational state.

The latter in turn might happen in two ways:

2a. The difference of content is not available to the cognitive system, as in Twin Earth (and also Expert) cases. (In Expert cases it is available to an expert: Fodor cannot tell a beech from an elm but an expert can. In Twin Earth cases, it is not available to anyone.)

2b. The difference is available to the cognitive system, but it cannot be captured in a purely informational theory, as in the case of Quine's rabbit/undetached rabbit part.

For each of these ways in which disconnection might seem possible, 1, 2a, and 2b, Fodor tells us that there is a mechanism tying content and computation together. To explain what he has in mind, he offers an analogy. Why are appearing to be a dollar bill and actually being a dollar bill tied together—not perfectly but very, very reliably? Because of the mechanism of the police stamping out counterfeiting. We would then expect Fodor to say, 'And here are the mechanisms for content and computation for each of the three kinds of case'. But that is not what he does at all. Instead, the analysis goes off in a curious direction, indeed in two curious directions.

i. Instead of identifying three police-like mechanisms, Fodor offers us in effect *a series of explanations of why we do not need one,* at least in two of the three kinds of case. (The problem in his treatment of the third is even bigger, as we will see.)

The second curiosity arises from the fact that Fodor uses at least two variations on the content-as-information theme, which he calls causal and nomic. (We'll untangle these terms shortly.) But,

ii. The explanations mentioned in (i.) go through straightforwardly only for the causal variant.

4(i). Mechanism or Explanation?

The first curiosity is: instead of mechanisms, in two of the three cases Fodor offers us explanations of why we do not need any. These are the Frege and Twin Earth cases. (As we said, the problem with his treatment of Quine cases is different.) Let us begin with Frege cases. Take Oedipus and his unfortunate affair with his mother. Fodor says that, so far as *content* is concerned, the proposition thought by Oedipus to be true—that he was marrying Jocasta—and the proposition thought by Oedipus to be false—that he was (gasp!) marrying his mother—are the same: they have the same reference so carry the same information. Nevertheless, they're computationally distinct and clearly had or would have had different effects on Oedipus. If so, content doesn't map one-to-one with computational state.

But cases like Oedipus are not a problem, says Fodor, because they are *unsystematic accidents*; if it happened regularly that we did not know that co-referring terms referred to the same object, practical reasoning would become useless. Indeed, it takes such complicated circumstances to make a story like Oedipus's plausible that such cases would have to be rare. If these cases are rare accidents, however, all they show is that content and computational state are not perfectly linked. They do not show that the two are not *reliably* linked, and this is all we need. So far so good. But now ask: where's the mechanism? If acci-

dents are allowed, we do not need to block them. So we do not need a content-computation mechanism; there would be nothing for such a mechanism to do. Curious.

'Surely,' it will be protested, 'you have missed Fodor's point. We *also* need something to explain how it is that Oedipus cases *are* unsystematic, that we do generally know that our co-referring terms refer to the same object. *This* is the mechanism Fodor has in mind'. That this is what Fodor has in mind is, at the very least, not obvious. Let us follow his analysis. He starts by saying that,

'Intentional systems' invariably incorporate mechanisms which insure that they generally know the facts upon which the success of their behaviour depends (Fodor, 1994, p. 48)

Is this the mechanism we are looking for? No; for "rational agents" to "reliably make a point of knowing the facts that the success of their behaviour depends upon" (Fodor, 1994, p. 46), the facts have to cooperate. We have to have what poor Oedipus lacked, information adequate to know the truth of the relevant identity-statements. As it happens, we generally do, because "the syntactic structure of a mode of presentation reliably carries information about its causal history" (Fodor, 1994, p. 54). And do they also carry information about other syntactic structures, that they refer to the same object?, we might ask. But that is not the vital question. The vital question is this: Does any *mechanism* guarantee this reliability? Indeed, does anything *guarantee* it? Fodor says nothing to suggest that it is more than a happy accident, though one essential to practical reasoning, indeed probably to life itself.

If there is a mechanism producing the happy covariations that are supposed to allow us to know, most of the time, the identity of reference of our coreferring expressions, the only candidate that we can think of is natural selection. In some contexts, Fodor expresses a distinct lack of enthusiasm for evolutionary arguments (1994, p. 20 for example), but this may be one place where they can do some work. Whatever, it would be peculiar to call anything that could be involved here a *mechanism*, certainly if the police arresting counterfeiters is an example of a mechanism. Compare: 'Why aren't there lots of elephants on Lake Ontario today? Well, you see, there's a mechanism...' .

We discover the same pattern even more clearly in Fodor's treatment of Twin Earth cases. Fodor's response to them is to claim that they do not occur in our world and will not occur in any nomically near one (Fodor, 1994, pp. 38-9). He may well be right; but if he is, we do not need any *mechanism* to deal with them. Once again, instead of identifying a mechanism, Fodor has shown that we do not need one.

That leaves the Quine cases. (We will not consider Expert cases.) They need a word of explanation. The problem that 'rabbit'/'undetached rabbit part' ('urp') cases pose for information semantics Fodor-style is important. The terms 'rabbit' and 'urp' clearly have different contents. Indeed, since a rabbit is more than an urp, if one of them correctly applies, then the other does not. Yet they are always co-instantiated. Given that, the *information* contained in 'rabbit' and 'urp' is the same, on Fodor's stringent notion of information. From this it follows that no semantics based purely on such a notion of information is going to capture the difference of content between the two terms. Fodor's suggestion is that we can capture the difference between 'rabbit' and 'urp' if we add a notion of "inference potential" (shades of conceptual role!). In particular, by checking whether an Informant (Inf) will accept or reject certain conjunction reductions, we can tell whether she uses 'rabbit' to mean *rabbit* or *urp,* 'urp' to mean *urp* or *rabbit*.

Here is how the story goes. (Fodor tells it in terms of triangles and triangle parts but we will tell it in its rabbit and urp version.) In addition to a rabbit and an urp, consider also, say, the front half of a rabbit. An appropriately located urp could be part of both a rabbit and the front half of a rabbit (an undetached ear, eye, or nose would be some examples). Now we ask, does 'rabbit' mean *rabbit* or *urp?* Does 'urp' mean *an undetached rabbit part* or *rabbit?* Being the front half of a rabbit excludes being a rabbit but being an (appropriate) urp is compatible with being part of both a rabbit and the front half of a rabbit. Thus, if 'rabbit' and 'front half of a rabbit' mean *rabbit* and *front half of a rabbit,* Inf will accept 'A is a rabbit' and 'A is a front half of rabbit' in certain circumstances but never, it seems, 'A is a rabbit and a front half of a rabbit'. On the other hand, if 'rabbit' and 'front half of a rabbit' mean *rabbit part* and *part of the front half of a rabbit,* Inf will accept 'A is a rabbit' and 'A is a front half of rabbit' *and also* 'A is a rabbit and a front half of a rabbit' in certain circumstances. So all we have to do is check and see which conjunction reductions Inf accepts and we can determine what she means by 'rabbit' and 'urp' (1994, p. 73). So far so good.

But now a problem appears: What in Inf's *computational structure* could implement the difference of content between 'rabbit' and 'urp'—as the case has been described? It cannot be anything informational because Inf's information about rabbits and about urps is the same; 'rabbit' and 'urp' covary perfectly with both rabbits and urps. So it has to be something syntactic. And the problem is this: what could anything purely syntactic have to do with content here? Notice: here Fodor is not demanding merely that syntax *covary* with content. Here syntax is to be *part* of content.

In the story about 'rabbit', 'urp', and 'front half of a rabbit' we told, most people would be inclined to think that Inf's conjunction reduction predilections are driven by information: she reduces or refuses to refuse in accord with what satisfies these terms and her beliefs about these items. But that cannot be Fodor's story; for him, there is *no difference* in Inf's information about rabbits, front halves of rabbits, and urps. So what drives Inf to reduce or not reduce has to be something purely syntactic, some computational rules for uninterpreted symbol-sets in Mentalese buried in her. This sharpens the problem. What could anything purely syntactic in this way have to do with content?

We think the most probable answer is: nothing. If what governs Inf's reduction predilections is something purely syntactic, rules for the manipulation of uninterpreted symbols, Inf could just as well reduce sentences the *content* of whose predicates are incompatible as compatible, sentences whose subjects are *satisfied* by different objects as by the same one. In short, on a purely syntactic account, conjunction reduction seems to tell us *nothing* about content. And the Quine cases remain, alive and well.

Does Fodor have any escape? If conjunction reduction proclivities are to be part of content, they must at least covary with the relevant differences of content. We can think of two possibilities:

(i) Fodor could simply *define* incompatibility of satisfaction as an Inf's unwillingness to conjunction reduce. This seems a desperate expedient: what does the fact that 'rabbit' is satisfied only when 'urp' is not have to do with some rule for transforming uninterpreted symbols buried deep in the brain? But out of desperation grows an idea. What if,

(ii) we could find a *mechanism* that tied the computational reduction to the semantic difference? This should be the escape Fodor wants, given the rest of *E&E.* Can we think of one?

It does not look promising. Strangely enough, Fodor is no help here; indeed, he does not even mention a mechanism in connection with Quine cases! This gap and the difficulty of bridging it may be an instance of a wider problem. At the beginning of *E&E,* Fodor tells us that if computations are to house content, computations must track truth in the way that our reasonings do. To see the bigger problem first, suppose that Fodor is right about everything and there is no way in which symbol structures and contents might systematically come apart, not in this and near worlds at any rate. Would that be enough to ensure that computation will *track truth* reliably? It is not clear that it would; even if computational and contentful *nodes* line up correctly, the *relationships among them* could still come apart.

Now apply this bigger problem to conjunction reduction and the problem of covarying terms that are not jointly satisfiable. The problem here is to find something to ensure that a purely computational move tracks mutual nonsatisfiability correctly. It's not the same problem, but it is a closely related one. And Fodor says as much about it, namely, nothing.

This problem is far more serious than the problems we identified earlier in connection with Frege and Twin Earth examples. There Fodor promised us mechanisms and instead gave us arguments for why we don't need them—a fairly parochial failing. Here he produces no mechanism *and* no argument that we do not need one. This looks more serious.

The source of the problem seems to be as follows: To discriminate rabbits from urps, we would have to use something that comes to us from these items. Or so it would seem. But Fodor thinks that there is no such information. So he has to go shopping for something purely syntactic, purely internal. Once we see this, a solution to the Quine cases becomes readily apparent. The relationships of rabbits and our syntactic structures and urps and our syntactic structures differ, in lots of relevant ways, in fact, and ways as naturalistic as covariance; all the *causal* relationships are different, as different as the very different causal powers of rabbits and urps. These differences are just as good candidates to ground differences of information in connection with 'rabbit' and 'urp' as co-variance, the one Fodor chooses.

Fodor cannot avail himself of this solution only because he adopts an excessively stringent notion of information. For him, the *only* way in which the information carried by two terms can vary is if there are contexts in which the terms do not co-vary; and the only way they can do that is if they refer to objects that do not always co-vary. In short, Fodor seems to think that the only link between words and the world that counts is covariance. Content is also determined by what *undergirds* the covariance, however: 'dog' has the content it has not simply because it co-varies with dogs, but because tokens of it are *caused* by dogs (see Quine, 1960, p. 30). This is entirely compatible with a naturalistic, externalist account of content. Assuming—as seems plausible—that it is the causal powers of *rabbits* that maintain the co-variance between 'rabbit' and rabbity stuff and that the causal powers of urps are relevantly different, 'rabbit' will mean *rabbit*, not *urp*. In which case, 'rabbit' meaning *urp* is excluded without appeal to conjunction reduction or any other kind of 'inference potential'. And the Quine cases would no longer be a problem. True enough, content so construed will go beyond covariance, but we cannot imagine why this should concern Fodor.

The introduction of 'inference potential' of any kind as an element of content also raises troubling issues all its own. For example, though Fodor argues that this move invites only a benign form of holism, it's surely very hard to help oneself to just a soupçon of conceptual role semantics. Fodor says that he can isolate the "logical syntax" of conjunction reduction from the rest of language, but his treatment of this seems a little blasé. In particular, to make the separation, Fodor would have to be able to separate conjunction-reductions based on syntax from reductions based on evidence, i.e, purely on information. Perhaps he can; but given Quine's worries about the very possibility of doing such things, we'd like to see the argument.

4(ii). Variations on the Notion of Information

Above we urged that, just when Fodor seems poised to describe the police-like 'mechanism' that keeps content and computation reliably in phase, his discussion goes off in peculiar directions. Having explored one of them—no mechanism, just explanation, and in Quine cases no explanation either—, we turn now to the other one. Fodor acknowledges two variations on the content-as-information theme: causal and nomic. Here's what's strange: the explanations Fodor gives in connection with Frege and Twin Earth cases go through straight-forwardly only for the first.

Fodor calls the two conceptions the *causal* informational and the *nomic* informational. Notice first that they are both quite different from the biographical-historical conception propounded by Dretske (1993) and others. Dretske argues that AI systems do not and could not have content, intentionality, etc., simply because they have the wrong kind of history. On this view, even if a system were to be built, to the appropriate fineness of grain, exactly like us in all relevant respects, and even if it behaved exactly like us, the difference in its history would ensure that it does not have content—even though we do. For Fodor, however, history

of the system has little to do with content.

Fodor calls the causal informational notion of content the view that, "the content of mental representations is constituted by their etiology" (Fodor, 1994, p. 82). As we've seen, Fodor goes a long way toward showing that this simple little notion is adequate (though perhaps not quite in the direction he thinks). However, there is also a nomic notion of content-as-information at work in the book.

On the causal story, a computational state comes to carry information by entering a causal relationship with some object: a token of 'dog' comes to carry the information contained in the concept DOG by being in a causal relationship with a dog. On the *nomic* informational story, in contrast, a computational state comes to carry information by satisfying certain counter-factuals: a token of 'dog' as found in me carries the information *dog*, for example, if I *would* say or otherwise token 'dog' *were I* to be in the presence of a dog. It is not necessary that my token of 'dog' was ever *actually* in a causal relationship with a dog.

On the face of it, these seem to be quite different conceptions of content. About all that immediately holds them together is that they are both developed in terms of information. Strangely enough, Fodor seems to think that they are quite similar—similar enough to be roughly substitutable one for the other. Thus, he tells us at one point that he prefers the nomic-informational notion but for the sake of simplicity of exposition has told his story in terms of the causal-informational one (Fodor, 1994, p. 54) and from then on switches back and forth between them pretty much at will, embracing the causal story on pp. 52, 82 and 86, and the nomic story on pp. 72, 90, and 116, for example. (Fodor even makes use of concepts that could only be part of the nomic story before he formally introduces the notion. For example, he speaks of content as dispositions on p. 30 and as specified by counter-factuals on p. 37.)

Contrary to Fodor and anyone else who may suppose that these notions of broad content are quite similar, the two are very different. Consider Davidson's (1987) old friend the Swampman, the molecule for molecule duplicate of Davidson who springs to life ('life'?) one day in a swamp. Intuitively, Swampman seems to have content at the very start of his new life, i.e., prior to entering into causal relationships with objects. Now, this is also what the nomic story would entail, and it's the story Fodor embraces. However, on the *causal* story, we would have to deny that the Swampman had content—and a number of theorists have done so. This is enough by itself to show that the two conceptions are quite different from one another. We so conclude; and turn to the implications for Fodor.

Fodor, as we've seen, argues that—Twin, Frege and Quine cases notwithstanding—the link between content and computational implementation is reliable. However, the nomic story goes quite differently for some of these cases from the causal one. Fodor gives no indication that he see this.

However well his story about why Frege cases are no problem works on the causal informational account, for example, it does not work at all on the nomic informational version. Here is why. If content is a matter of actual causal connection to an object, then it is perfectly possible to locate what is common to Oedipus's two beliefs—it consists in their being linked causally to the same object. Then this becomes the content of both 'Jocasta' and 'Mom'. Because these two are syntactically distinct, we have a case of computation-content disconnection, but that's okay because it's accidental. Treat content as a matter of some kind of disposition, however, and this story utterly collapses. What could be *common* to the disposition activated in Oedipus by the woman presented as Jocasta and the one activated by the woman presented as Mom? Certainly not a disposition to get married! And not, to be more serious, the respective word-tokening dispositions either. Even more seriously, what motive could one have for splitting the dispositions into two elements in the first place, a part common to both and a part distinctive to each? In so far as there is no good answer to this question, Fodor's story about Frege cases does not work on the nomic account of information.

What about Twin Earth cases? Again a problem. Where information derives from *etiology*, the apparent difference in content between (say) Adam and Twadam is that Adam's tokens of 'water' are causally linked to H_2O, Twadam's to XYZ—a substance phenomenally indistinguishable but chemically (or something) distinct from H_2O. Here there is a clear sense in which the two tokens of 'water' have different contents, even though elicited by indistinguishable environments: one is causally linked to H_2O, the other to XYZ. Different contents, same computational state. (And, says Fodor, it doesn't matter because Twin Earth isn't 'nearby'.)

As with Frege cases, however, things turn sour when we go nomic. On the nomic story, the difference in content between Adam and Twadam has to be that Adam would token 'water' in the presence of H_2O while Twadam would token 'water' in the presence of XYZ. The trouble is, Adam's disposition would also lead him to token 'water' in the presence of XYZ and Twadam's to token 'water' in the presence of H_2O. That is to say, on the nomic theory, there is no difference of content between Adam and Twadam in the first place. Which would imply that, for the nomic version of informational content, Twin Earth cases do not pose an even apparent problem for Fodor in the first place.

For Twin Earth cases, then, things are easier for Fodor on the nomic view than the causal one. But if he wants his story of Frege cases to work for the nomic view as well as the causal one, he owes us an argument. Fodor's treatment of Quine cases seems to work equally well, or equally badly, on either view.

In sum: Fodor's strategy in *E&E* is to urge that psychological states and processes can be both ineliminably intentional (information-bearing) and implemented computationally—without there being computationally sufficient conditions for the instantiation of intentional properties. All we need is that computational states/processes reliably co-instantiate with intentional states/processes in our world and worlds nomically near to ours. Which, despite the problems with Fodor's arguments, they may do. But Fodor argues for the thesis in some strange ways and owes us some additional arguments.

Acknowledgements

Andrew Brook would like to thank his fellow participants in a discussion group on *The Elm and the Expert*, The Queen's College, Oxford, Trinity Term 1995, for many important ideas: Alex Rosenberg, Galen Strawson, Michael Lockwood, David Bakhurst, and Frank Jackson. Robert Stainton would like to thank Tracy Isaacs, Daniel Stoljar, and the students in his Mental Representation tutorial at Carleton University for helpful comments. Thanks also to the participants in our workshop on Computationalism and Intentionalism in the Philosophy of Mind, Canadian Philosophical Association, Université du Québec à Montréal, June 3, 1995.

References

Davidson, D. (1987). Knowing One's Own Mind. In *Proceedings and Addresses of the American Philosophical Association* 61:441-458.

Dretske, F. (1993). The Possibility of Artificial Intelligence. Presented to the American Philosophical Association, Eastern Division, December 28, 1993.

Fodor, J.A. (1994). *The Elm and the Expert*. Cambridge, MA: The MIT Press.

Fodor, J.A. (1987). *Psychosemantics*. Cambridge, MA: The MIT Press.

Quine, W.V.O. (1960). *Word and Object*. Cambridge, MA: The MIT Press.

INTEGRATING WORLD KNOWLEDGE WITH COGNITIVE PARSING

Harold Paredes-Frigolett and **Gerhard Strube**
Center for Cognitive Science
Institute for Computer Science and Social Research
University of Freiburg
D-79098 Freiburg i. Brg.
Germany
{paredes,strube}@cognition.iig.uni-freiburg.de

Abstract

The work presented in this article builds on the account of cognitive parsing given by the SOUL system (Konieczny & Strube, 1995), an object-oriented implementation of Parameterized Head Attachment (Konieczny et al., 1991) based on Head-Driven Phrase-Structure Grammar (Pollard & Sag, 1994). We describe how the initial semantic representation proposed by the parser is translated into a logical form suitable for inference, thus making it possible to integrate world knowledge with cognitive parsing. As a semantic and knowledge representation system we use the most expressive implemented logic for natural language understanding, Episodic Logic (Hwang & Schubert, 1993), and its computational implementation, Epilog (Schaeffer et al., 1991).

Introduction

The work reported in this article can be seen as a continuation of psycholinguistic research in sentence parsing (Strube *et al.*, 1990; Konieczny *et al.*; Hemforth *et al.*, 1993) and computational models of human parsing (Konieczny & Strube, 1995). This former work has resulted in a psycholinguistic theory of sentence parsing called Parameterized Head Attachment and in the SOUL parser as a computer model that implements the theory. SOUL makes use of typed feature formalisms to describe the syntax of natural language, especially Head-Driven Phrase-Structure Grammar, HPSG (Pollard & Sag, 1994). SOUL operates in a word-by-word incremental fashion, computing a HPSG structure according to human parsing preferences that have been identified in guiding the first syntactic analysis.

This model of human parsing has to be complemented by processes of semantic interpretation for two reasons. On the one hand, SOUL needs to judge the appropriateness of the analyses given by the parser based on world knowledge in order to trigger reanalysis whenever necessary. On the other hand, the preliminary logical form proposed by SOUL has to be transformed into a logical form that allows for inferences to be drawn in the knowledge base. Our model enables the integration of world knowledge with cognitive parsing and benefits from using Episodic Logic, the most expressive formal computational logic for general natural language understanding. The objective of the present article is to show how the output of the SOUL parser can be semantically interpreted

into an initial representation, which is further transformed removing scope ambiguities and context-dependency. The final result is a logical form in Episodic Logic (Hwang, 1992; Hwang & Schubert, 1993) that is suitable for inference. We also show how this final logical form accounts for semantic biasing of syntactic analyses.

Parameterized Head Attachment

Cognitive parsing in the SOUL system, Semantics-Oriented Unification-Based Language Processing (Konieczny & Strube, 1995), is based on the Parameterized Head Attachment Principle of sentence processing (Konieczny *et al.*, 1991), PHA henceforth. PHA is a theory of sentence processing that originated in recent psycholinguistic investigations of PP-attachment and other phenomena in German, using self-paced reading and eye-movement experiments (Strube *et al.*, 1990; Konieczny *et al.*, 1991; Hemforth *et al.*, 1993; Konieczny *et al.*, 1994). Though a serial model in the tradition of the Garden-Path Theory (Frazier & Fodor, 1978), PHA is a model of sentence processing whose results differ from those predicted by Minimal Attachment and Late Closure, and by the principles put forth with the Construal Theory (Frazier & Clifton, 1996).

PHA consists of the following principles:

- **Head attachment**: Prefer to attach an item to a phrasal unit whose lexical head has already been read.

- **Preferred-role attachment**: Prefer to attach an item to a phrasal unit whose head preferentially subcategorizes for it.

- **Most recent head attachment**: Prefer to attach an item to a head that was read most recently.

- **Parameterized head attachment**: Attempt to apply **Head Attachment** before **Preferred Role Attachment** before **Most Recent Head Attachment**.

SOUL is a cognitive parser that functions complying with the principles described above and has been implemented using HPSG.[1] We will now concentrate on the syntax/semantics

---

[1] The interested reader is referred to Konieczny & Strube (1995) for a description of the SOUL system.

interface used in the system, called the preliminary logical form, and the translation process of this initial representation into a representation suitable for inference using Episodic Logic (Hwang, 1992, Hwang & Schubert, 1993).

Incremental semantic interpretation, scoping, and deindexing

Consider the natural language sentence (1), as presented below:

(1) Marion $_{\uparrow a}$ watched $_{\uparrow b}$ the $_{\uparrow c}$ horse $_{\uparrow d}$ with $_{\uparrow e}$ the $_{\uparrow f}$ white $_{\uparrow g}$ fleck $_{\uparrow h}$. $_{\uparrow i}$

Using this expression, we illustrate the process of incremental semantic interpretation, scoping, and deindexing by virtue of which the preliminary logical form is transformed into a so-called episodic logical form suitable for inference in Epilog (Schaeffer *et al.*, 1991), the computational system for Episodic Logic, EL henceforth.

The extended syntax/semantics interface

We consider the parse obtained by SOUL at point *f*, once the second definite article *the* has been absorbed from the input string. Using subcategorization information for the preferred lexical entry of *watch*, a transitive verb with an instrumental complement, SOUL proposes a parse in which the expected prepositional phrase attaches to the main verb of the sentence. The semantic information is given in HPSG under the feature *content*. Due to its restricted expressiveness we have defined a more expressive syntax/semantics interface in SOUL, which we have termed *preliminary logical form*, $\mathcal{PLF}$ for short, as shown below.

$\mathcal{PLF}_f$:

$$
\begin{bmatrix}
pred & watch \\
arg_{agent} & Marion \\
arg_{theme} & \begin{bmatrix} ind & ind_1 \\ spec & the \\ cond & \begin{bmatrix} pred & horse \\ arg_{inst} & \square_1 \end{bmatrix} \end{bmatrix} \\
arg_{instr} & \begin{bmatrix} ind & ind_2 \\ spec & the \\ cond & \begin{bmatrix} pred & P \\ arg_{inst} & \square_2 \end{bmatrix} \end{bmatrix} \\
a\text{-}mod & \begin{bmatrix} op & adv\text{-}a \\ pred & \begin{bmatrix} pred & with\text{-}instr \\ arg_{theme} & \square_2 \end{bmatrix} \end{bmatrix} \\
e\text{-}mod & \begin{bmatrix} op & past \end{bmatrix} \\
mood & \begin{bmatrix} op & decl \end{bmatrix}
\end{bmatrix}
$$

In $\mathcal{PLF}_f$, the action of Marion watching a horse and being modified so as to be performed with an instrument has been represented. This representation is based on the formalism used to represent the syntax/semantics interface in HPSG (Pollard & Sag, 1994). In $\mathcal{PLF}_f$, the predicate *watch* takes three arguments. The first argument corresponds to the agent of the event described, the second argument corresponds to the theme of the action being described, and the third argument corresponds to an instrument with which the action is performed. The format of the preliminary logical form is borrowed from Fenstad *et al.* (1987). The feature *cond* introduces a well-formed formula and the features *spec* and *ind* introduce the quantificational force of a determiner and the variable quantified over, respectively. In $\mathcal{PLF}_f$, the argument positions are filled with variables, but the scope of the quantifiers is left underspecified, much as in Schubert & Pelletier (1982), Fenstad *et al.* (1987) and Pollard & Sag (1994).

Pollard & Sag (1994) assume a situation-theoretic framework for semantic representation. Unfortunately, Situation Semantics (Barwise, 1987; Devlin, 1991) does not yet offer a framework for representing a variety of semantic phenomena. Note for example that in $\mathcal{PLF}_f$ the expected prepositional phrase is syntactically analyzed as an adverbial. The extension proposed here for the representation of adverbials distinguishes between those that operate on sentences and those that operate on monadic predicates. We take advantage of the representational framework put forth with EL (Hwang, 92; Hwang & Schubert, 1993) and adopt the functions *adv-e* and *adv-a*, which map predicates over episodes/actions into predicate modifiers. In EL, (*adv-e* π), with π a predicate over episodes, is an episode modifier, and (*adv-a* π), with π a monadic predicate over attributes/actions, is an action modifier. *with-instr* is a relational predicate taking in our example the monadic predicate P and mapping it into a monadic predicate over actions. In $\mathcal{PLF}_f$, the tense operator *past* and the mood operator *decl* have also been introduced under the features *e-mod* and *mood*, respectively.

Incremental semantic interpretation

After the parser has generated this initial representation, the preliminary attribute-value representation $\mathcal{PLF}_f$ is translated into a set of fact-schemata using recursive procedures that operate directly on the attribute-value matrices under the feature *cond*. Then, full schemata are constructed for the full sentence. For $\mathcal{PLF}_f$, we obtain the following set of fact schemata:

$$
\begin{aligned}
&\langle C_1 : horse, ind_1, 1 \rangle &(1) \\
&\langle C_2 : P, ind_2, 1 \rangle \\
&\langle C_3 : watch, Marion, ind_1, ind_2, 1 \rangle
\end{aligned}
$$

Incremental scoping

In HPSG the feature *QSTORE* gives the scope disambiguation information. Our approach to scope disambiguation consists in generating a scoped logical form according to psycholinguistically plausible heuristics for scope disambiguation (Kurtzman & MacDonald, 1993). In our example, the surface speech act operator *decl* is assigned scope over the whole sentence, the tense operator *past* is assigned scope within speech act operators and wider scope than all other operators. The two definites are assigned scope through all barriers only if they are salient in the current context, otherwise they are scoped within tense operators.

We obtain the set of scoped fact schemata in (2):

$$(The \ (\langle ind_1 \mid C_1 \rangle) \tag{2}$$
$$(\langle ind_1 \mid The \ (\langle ind_2 \mid C_2 \rangle)(\langle ind_2 \mid C_3 \rangle))))$$

Replacing C_1, C_2, and C_3 in (2) and incorporating the action-modifying operator *((adv-a (with-instr ind_2))*, the tense operator *past*, and the mood operator *decl*, we obtain the parameterized indexical logical form $\mathcal{PILF}_f$.[2]

$\mathcal{PILF}_f$:

(decl (past (The x:[x horse]
        (The y:[y P]
             [Marion ((adv-a (with-instr y))
                 (watch x))])))))

Incremental deindexing

To be suitable for inference in Epilog, the computational system for EL, the final logical form has to be independent of context. Thus, the indexical information conveyed by the tense operator *past* and the mood operator *decl* has to be brought into the final representation. The incremental deindexer applies the compositional deindexing rules for translating the indexical logical forms put forth in Hwang & Schubert (1992). These rules transform the indexical logical form containing tense operators and adverbials into a so-called parameterized episodic logical form, $\mathcal{PELF}$ for short.[3] At point f, the result of this deindexing process is the parameterized episodic logical form $\mathcal{PELF}_f$.

$\mathcal{PELF}_f$:

($\exists u_1$:[[u_1 same-time $Now1$] $\wedge$
  [u_0 immediately-precedes u_1]]
  [[Speaker tell Hearer (That
    ($\exists e_1$:[[e_1 before u_1] $\wedge$ [e_0 orients e_1]]
      [[(The x:[x horse]
         (The y:[y P]
           [[Marion $\mid e_1$]
             ((with-instr y)(watch x))])))]
        ** e_1])))]
  ** u_1])

---

[2]We assume that the definites in question are not salient in the current context.

[3]Due to space limitations, we do not present the deindexing rules here. The interested reader is referred to Hwang (1992) and Hwang & Schubert (1992) for a detailed description.

Expressing knowledge in EL

Knowledge in Epilog takes the form of meaning postulates and world knowledge axioms. These are expressed as probabilistic conditionals of form $\phi \rightarrow_{p,\alpha_1,\ldots,\alpha_n} \psi$, where $\alpha_1, \ldots, \alpha_n$ are controlled variables and p is a statistical probability.

We now introduce the following meaning postulates and world knowledge axioms about people seeing objects.[4]

Meaning postulates about people seeing objects:

If a person watches a thing, then that person sees that thing.[5]

$\mathcal{MP}$ 1: ($\exists x$:[x person]
    ($\exists y$:[y thing]
      ($\exists e_1$:[[[[$x \mid e_1$] P] $\wedge$ [x watch y]] ** e_1])))
  $\rightarrow$ ($\exists e_2$:[$e_1 \preceq e_2$]
      [[[[$x \mid e_2$] P] $\wedge$ [x see y]] ** e_2])

If a person sees something with something, then she/he is seeing it with a viewing instrument.

$\mathcal{MP}$ 2: ($\exists x$:[x person]
    ($\exists y$:[y thing]
      ($\exists z$:[z thing]
        ($\exists e_1$:[[[[$x \mid e_1$] (with-instr z)] $\wedge$
           [x see y]] ** e_1]))))
  $\rightarrow$ [z ((nn viewing) instrument)])

Meaning postulate about unlocated formulas:

$\mathcal{MP}$ 3: ($\forall e_1$:[[[$\phi \wedge \psi$] ** e_1] $\rightarrow$ [$\phi \wedge$ ($\exists e_2$:[$e_2 \preceq e_1$][ψ ** e_2])]])

World knowledge axiom about people seeing things with viewing instruments:

If someone sees something with a viewing instrument, then she/he probably sees it clearly.

$\mathcal{WK}$ 1: ($\exists x$:[x person]
    ($\exists y$:[y thing]
      ($\exists z$:[y ((nn viewing) instrument)]
        ($\exists e_1$:[[[[$x \mid e_1$] (with-instr z)] $\wedge$
           [x see y]] ** e_1]))))
  $\rightarrow_{0.85,e_1,x,y}$ ($\exists e_2$:[$e_1 \preceq e_2$]
      [[[[$x \mid e_2$](in-manner clear)] $\wedge$
        [x see y]] ** e_2])

---

[4]In the meaning postulates above, the operator $\preceq$ is a metalogical operator that corresponds to the operator *coextensive-part-of* in EL. $e_1 \preceq e_2$ indicates that situation e_1 is coextensive with situation e_2, that is, e_1 and e_2 have the same spatiotemporal location. Finally, the modal operators * and ** are introduced with the following intuitive meanings: [ϕ ** η] $\equiv$ ϕ *describes η as a whole* and [ϕ * η] $\equiv$ ϕ *describes some part of η*.

[5]Here, P is a parameter that stand for a monadic predicate over actions/attributes.

Triggering inferences in Epilog

After a formula is asserted in Epilog, a process of input-driven inference triggering via rule instantiation using meaning postulates and world knowledge axioms is started. This process consists of the following six steps: existentially quantified variables are skolemized, top-level conjuncts are split, simplification schemas are applied, the new formulas are checked for their consistency with the previously stored knowledge, the new formulas are classified and stored in the knowledge base, and a process of input-driven inference chaining is started using the meaning postulates and world knowledge axioms in the knowledge base.

For our example above we define the following simplification schema:

SS 1: For P a parameter: $(\forall x:[x\ P] \to [x\ \text{thing}])$

Skolemizing e_1/E_1, x/X, and y/Y in $\mathcal{PELF}_f$, splitting conjunctions, and applying the simplification schema above we obtain:[6]

F_1 $[E_1\ \text{before}\ U_1]$

F_2 $[X\ \text{horse}]$

F_3 $[Y\ \text{thing}]$

F_4 $[[\text{Marion}\ |\ E_1]\ (\text{with-instr}\ Y)]$

F_5 $[[[[\text{Marion}\ |\ E_1]\ (\text{with-instr}\ Y)] \wedge [\text{Marion watch}\ X]] ** E_1]$

The described episode E_1 is characterized by the action of Marion watching a horse and being modified so as to be performed with an instrument. F_5 matches the antecedent of $\mathcal{MP}_3$. We obtain the following additional formulas:

F_6 $[E_2 \preceq E_1]$

F_7 $[[\text{Marion watch}\ X] ** E_2]$

Episode E_2 is coextensive with episode E_1 and is characterized by the action of Marion watching a horse. Let us now assume the following facts:

F_8 $[\text{Marion woman}]$

F_9 $[\text{Marion person}]$

F_{10} $[X\ \text{thing}]$

F_9 and F_{10} are obtained by type-hierarchical knowledge. F_3, F_5, F_9, and F_{10} match the antecedent of $\mathcal{MP}_1$,[7] a meaning postulate connecting watching with seeing events. Thus, the following formulas can be obtained:

F_{11} $[E_3 \preceq E_1]$

F_{12} $[[[[\text{Marion}\ |\ E_3]\ (\text{with-instr}\ Y)] \wedge [\text{Marion see}\ X]] ** E_3]$

F_{12} matches the antecedent of $\mathcal{MP}_3$. This accounts for obtaining the following formulas:

F_{13} $[E_4 \preceq E_3]$

F_{14} $[[\text{Marion see}\ X] ** E_4]$

F_3, F_9, F_{10}, and F_{12} match the antecedent of $\mathcal{MP}_2$, a meaning postulate about seeing things with instruments. Thus, we obtain the following additional formula:

F_{15} $[Y\ ((\text{nn viewing})\ \text{instrument})]$

At point f, we are able to make the prediction that Y is a viewing instrument.[8] Finally, by a process of input-driven inference chaining using $\mathcal{WK}_1$, a world knowledge axiom about seeing things with viewing instruments, we obtain from F_9, F_{10}, F_{12}, and F_{15} the following inferences:[9]

I_1 $[E_5 \preceq E_3]$

I_2 $[[[[\text{Marion}\ |\ E_5]\ (\text{in-manner clear})] \wedge [\text{Marion see}\ X]]_{0.85} ** E_5]$

Incremental interpretation

Although inferences can be triggered at any point by the process described above, we contend that full inferences are not required to be triggered on a word-by-word incremental basis. Our claim is based on the assumption that the number of inferences made during on-line sentence comprehension is to be constrained by computational resources, and on the observation that the inferences drawn during incremental on-line sentence comprehension are a function of the rhetoric aspects used by the writer/speaker. To account for this in our model we introduce the notion of restricted inference.

Restricted inference

We define *restricted inference* as a process of hierarchy climbing, logical form pattern matching, and inference triggering using only meaning postulates in the knowledge base. For semantic biasing the parser uses this restricted form of inferences on a word-by-word incremental basis. We believe that the use of a restricted form of inference based on meaning postulate inference is quite plausible. On the one hand, there

---

[6] We neglect the relation **orients** that may relate the reported episode E_1 to a prior episode E_0.

[7] With $P = (\text{with-instr}\ Y)$ in the antecedent of $\mathcal{MP}_1$.

[8] In formula F_{15}, nn is a function introduced in EL to map 1-place nominal predicates into predicate modifiers.

[9] We write F for inferences drawn by meaning postulates and I for inferences drawn by world knowledge axioms. The probability attached to I_2 tells us that inference I_2, though uncertain, is quite likely. It can be paraphrased as "Marion probably sees the horse clearly."

is enough empirical evidence suggesting that lexical inferences based on both the meaning of open class words[10] and the link between the meaning of a verb and its syntactic characteristics become available to human comprehenders as soon as the open class word or verb in question has been absorbed from the input string. On the other hand, there is a natural, though not ultimate, distinction between knowledge about lexical meanings and knowledge about the world. These observations lead to making the distinction between two modes of inference: (i) restricted inference for semantic biasing via meaning postulates and (ii) full inference for text understanding based on world knowledge axioms and meaning postulates. While the former will be used in a word-by-word incremental fashion, the latter will be used only at certain points, essentially where there is a single parse and the need for full inferential activity arises. This may be the case when resolving anaphoric antecedents, establishing causal and explanatory relations among events, or when a prosodic cue arises during on-line speech comprehension.

Fine-grained, weak interaction

The interface between the parser and the incremental interpreter corresponds to a structure called *analysis* that contains information concerning the analysis currently being pursued by the parser. This structure contains three fields corresponding to the top node of the partial parse tree for the analysis in question, a field that indicates whether or not the analysis has just been repaired by the parser, and a field that indicates whether the set of inferences drawn for the interpretation obtained so far is consistent or not with the previously asserted inferences in the knowledge base. This interface is weak in that the information needed by the parser for semantic biasing corresponds to just one bit, namely, to whether or not the formulas stored in the knowledge base are consistent with the new formulas asserted by the incremental interpreter, or with the inferences derived from them.

Restricted inference for semantic biasing

We now illustrate how the process of incremental interpretation interacts with the parser for purposes of semantic biasing.

After incremental semantic interpretation, scoping, and deindexing of the analysis preferred by SOUL at point h we obtain $\mathcal{ELF}_h$, a shown below:

$\mathcal{ELF}_h$:

$(\exists u_1:[[u_1 \text{ same-time } Now1] \wedge$
$[u_0 \text{ immediately-precedes } u_1]]$
$[[\text{Speaker tell Hearer (That}$
$(\exists e_1:[[e_1 \text{ before } u_1] \wedge [e_0 \text{ orients } e_1]]$
$[[(\text{The } x:[x \text{ horse}]$
$(\text{The } y:[[y \text{ fleck}] \wedge [y \text{ white}]]$
$[[\text{Marion } | e_1]((\text{with-instr } y)$
$(\text{watch } x))])])]$
$** e_1))] ** u_1])$

---

[10]Examples of open class words are adjectives, verbs, nouns, and adverbs. Examples of closed class words are prepositions and determiners.

After asserting $\mathcal{ELF}_h$ we obtain:[11]

F_{16} [Y fleck]

F_{17} [Y white]

By type-hierarchical knowledge, an inconsistency arises between F_{16} and F_{17} and the predicted formula F_{15}. The inconsistency is reported, and the conflicting formula is stored in the knowledge base. The incremental interpreter sets the field *analysis.consistent* to the value *false* and returns the structure *analysis* to SOUL. At point h, SOUL proposes as preferred continuation the analysis in which the prepositional phrase attaches to the noun "the horse," sets the field *analysis.just-repaired* to the value *true* and sends the repaired analysis to the incremental interpreter. The incremental interpreter drops the set of formulas obtained for the first analysis, sets the field *analysis.just-repaired* to the value *false*, obtains the new episodic logical form, and finally asserts it in Epilog.

The resulting episodic logical form for the repaired analysis at point h is shown below:

$\mathcal{ELF}_{h'}$:

$(\exists u_1:[[u_1 \text{ same-time } Now1] \wedge$
$[u_0 \text{ immediately-precedes } u_1]]$
$[[\text{Speaker tell Hearer (That}$
$(\exists e_1:[[e_1 \text{ before } u_1] \wedge [e_0 \text{ orients } e_1]]$
$[[(\text{The } x:[[x \text{ horse}] \wedge (\text{The } y:[[y \text{ fleck}] \wedge [y \text{ white}]]$
$[x \text{ with-part } y])]$
$[\text{Marion watch } x])] ** e_1))] ** u_1])$

Skolemizing e_1/E_1, x/X, and y/Y in $\mathcal{ELF}_{h'}$ and splitting conjunctions we obtain a new set of formulas at point h:

F_1 [E_1 before U_1]

F_2 [X horse]

F_3 [Y fleck]

F_4 [Y white]

F_5 [X with-part Y]

F_6 [[Marion watch X] $** E_1$]

The described episode E_1 is characterized by the action of Marion watching a horse with a white fleck.

---

[11]In Epilog, the skolem constant introduced for an existentially quantified variable is kept on the property list of the variable. Thus, future references to the variable are replaced by the constant within future formulas.

Conclusions

The work reported in this article presents a formal computational framework for integrating world knowledge with cognitive parsing, the center piece of which is a computational model of incremental semantic interpretation, scoping, and deindexing. The model is incremental in that a partial parse tree is transformed into a complete preliminary logical form in which parameters construed as metalogical variables are introduced in the logical form for the missing constituents in the input sentence, thus enabling further semantic processing in a word-by-word incremental fashion. The model is compositional in that each syntactic rule comes equipped with a semantic annotation. Thus, the semantics of a sentence at any point during incremental semantic interpretation is a function of the semantics of the constituents absorbed so far plus the semantics of the parameters introduced for the missing constituents in the corresponding partial parse tree. The psycholinguistic plausibility of the model is not only grounded in SOUL, but also in the use of psycholinguistic well-founded heuristics for scope disambiguation. In our current implementation,[12] we have defined a set of heuristics based on recent empirical results reported in Kurtzman & MacDonald (1993) to transform the preliminary logical form into a single parameterized indexical logical form that is scopally unambiguous, but still context-dependent.

Finally, we have described how our model of incremental semantic interpretation, scoping, and deindexing can be used for fine-grained, weakly interactive incremental interpretation. We think that the distinction between two forms of inference, restricted inference for semantic biasing based on lexical inference through meaning postulates and full inference for text understanding through input-driven inference chaining using both meaning postulates and world knowledge axioms, gives a plausible account of the incremental inference process. In this view of sentence comprehension using a first-analysis parser like SOUL, incremental interpretation is construed as a question answering process (Sanford, 1990). Thus, reanalysis is not triggered on account of whether or not the first analysis reaches a certain plausibility threshold, but rather on whether or not the expectations that arise during incremental interpretation are confirmed or refuted as more information becomes available from the input string.

Acknowledgements

This research was supported by the German National Science Foundation (Deutsche Forschungsgemeinschaft) through the Graduate School of Human and Computational Intelligence at the University of Freiburg. We want to thank our colleagues Barbara Hemforth, Lars Konieczny, and Christoph Scheepers for their helpful comments. Special thanks to Lenhart Schubert for many fruitful discussions on EL.

---

[12] A model of incremental semantic interpretation, scoping, and deindexing has been implemented in Common Lisp for the SOUL system.

References

Barwise, J. (1987). *The Situation in Logic*. Stanford, CA: CSLI.

Devlin, K. (1991). *Logic and Information*. Cambridge, UK: Cambridge University Press.

Fenstad, J.E., Halvorsen, P.K., Langholm, T. & van Benthem, J. (1987). *Situations, Language and Logic*. Reidel.

Frazier, L. & Fodor, J. (1978). The sausage machine: a new two-stage parsing model. *Cognition*, 6, 291–325.

Frazier, L. & Clifton, C. (1996). *Construal*. Cambridge, MA: MIT Press.

Hemforth, B., Konieczny, L. & Strube, G. (1993). Incremental sentence processing and parsing strategies. *Proceedings of the 15th Annual Conference of the Cognitive Science Society*, (pp. 539–545).

Hwang, C.H. (1992). A Logical Approach to Narrative Understanding. Doctoral dissertation. Edmonton, Alberta: University of Alberta, Department of Computing Science.

Hwang, C.H. & Schubert, L.K. (1992). Tense trees as the fine structure of discourse. *Proceedings of the 30th Annual Meeting of the American Association for Computational Linguistics*, (pp. 239–240).

Hwang, C.H. & Schubert, L.K. (1993). Episodic Logic, a comprehensive, natural representation for language understanding. *Minds and Machines*, 3, (pp. 381–419).

Konieczny, L., Hemforth, B. & Strube, G. (1991). Psycholinguistisch fundierte Prinzipien der Satzverarbeitung jenseits von Minimal Attachment. *Kognitionswissenschaft*, 2.

Konieczny, L., Scheepers, C., Hemforth, B. & Strube, G. (1994). Semantikorientierte Syntaxverarbeitung. In C. Felix, C. Habel and G. Rickheit (Eds.), *Kognitive Linguistik: Repräsentationen und Prozesse*. Opladen: Westdeutscher Verlag.

Konieczny, L. & Strube, G. (1995). SOUL: A cognitive parser. *Proceedings of the 17th Annual Conference of the Cognitive Science Society*, (pp. 631–636).

Kurtzman, H. & MacDonald, M. (1993). Resolution of quantifier scope ambiguities. *Cognition*, 48, (pp. 243–279).

Pollard, C. & Sag, I (1994). *Head-Driven Phrase-Structure Grammar*. University of Chicago Press.

Sanford, A. (1990). On the nature of text-driven inference. In D. Balota, G. Flores d'Arcais & K. Rayner (Eds.), *Comprehension Processes in Reading* (pp. 515–535). Hillsdale, NJ: Lawrence Erlbaum Associates.

Schaeffer, S., Hwang, C.H., de Haan, J & Schubert, L.K (1991). EPILOG: The computational system for Episodic Logic. Technical Report, Department of Computing Science, Edmonton, Alberta: University of Alberta.

Schubert, L.K. & Pelletier, J. (1982). From English to Logic: Context-free computation of conventional logical translations. *American Journal of Computational Linguistics*, 10, (pp. 165–176).

Strube, G., Hemforth, B. & Wrobel, H. (1990). Resolution of structural ambiguities in sentence comprehension: On-line analysis of syntactic, lexical, and semantic effects. *Proceedings of the 12th Annual Conference of the Cognitive Science Society* (pp. 558–565).

97

The Role of Ontology in Creative Understanding

Kenneth Moorman and **Ashwin Ram**
Georgia Institute of Technology
College of Computing
Atlanta, GA 30332-0280
{kennethm,ashwin}@cc.gatech.edu

Abstract

Successful creative understanding requires that a reasoner be able to manipulate known concepts in order to understand novel ones. A major problem arises, however, when one considers exactly how these manipulations are to be bounded. If a bound is imposed which is too loose, the reasoner is likely to create bizarre understandings rather than useful creative ones. On the other hand, if the bound is too tight, the reasoner will not have the flexibility needed to deal with a wide range of creative understanding experiences. Our approach is to make use of a principled ontology as one source of reasonable bounding. This allows our creative understanding theory to have good explanatory power about the process while allowing the computer implementation of the theory (the ISAAC system) to be flexible without being bizarre in the task domain of reading science fiction short stories.

Introduction

Over the last several years, we have been developing a functional theory of creative reading (see, e.g., Moorman & Ram, 1994a; Moorman & Ram, 1994b). The theory is being implemented in the ISAAC reading system, which reads short science-fiction stories. An important portion of the theory involves the ability to understand novel concepts, which we call *creative understanding*. The theory has now been developed to a point that we are able to carefully evaluate the precise role that ontology is playing in the process of creative understanding. The questions to answer include: *What are the theory's ontological commitments?*; *Where do they come from?*; *What power do they impart on the theory?*; and *What limitations do they create?*.

The Creative Understanding Process

In order to comprehend texts with novel concepts, we hypothesize the use of a *creative understanding process* (Moorman & Ram, 1994c), made up of four tasks: *memory retrieval*, *analogy*, *base-constructive analogy*, and *problem reformulation*. When a concept is presented to the reasoner, the memory task is used to discover if it is previously known. If it is and if the preexisting knowledge is sufficient to allow the concept to be explained or to make predictions about the concept, then understanding is successful. If there is no existing concept or if existing concepts do not allow explanation and prediction, then the remaining three tasks are called upon to produce a creative understanding of the novel concept. Analogy attempts to find a functionally-consistent mapping between concepts which were retrieved and the one being considered.

Base-constructive analogy is called upon if no concepts exist with which to draw an analogy from; in this case, a new base may be dynamically created for use in an analogy by appealing to known concepts. If the reasoner realizes that the current understanding focus is not the correct one, problem reformulation is invoked; this acts to refocus the reasoner so that successful understanding is more likely to occur. The process iteratively continues until either a successful understanding is achieved or the reasoner is willing to "give up" on understanding.

While performing the creative understanding, the reasoner may need to manipulate existing concepts in order to achieve success. It is here that some constraint must be maintained to avoid the problem of bizarreness. Bizarre understanding occurs when an understanding is reached which is not useful to the reasoner. For example, suppose a reader begins a story which starts with a character, John, slapping another character, Mary. One predictive question which could be generated is why John would do such a thing. One understanding of the event is that it occurred because space aliens from the Vega system has controlled John's mind in an experiment to test human reaction to violent behavior. And, in the scope of a science-fiction story, this might even be the eventual solution. However, assuming this at this point in the story with the information provided is premature and not useful for comprehending the rest of the narrative. Thus, we classify this understanding as bizarre.

There are two primary elements which we use to guide the modification process: satisfaction and ontology. The *satisfaction* solution bounds the creative understanding process by virtue of it existing within a larger cognitive task—in our case, reading. Understanding can be said to be successful as soon as the quality of explanation or prediction provided is high enough to allow the reading process to continue. As an example, consider the world of *Star Trek*. The *warp drive* is an example of a concept which must be understood to comprehend the stories. But, if a particular story has the warp drive functioning normally, then the reader can be satisfied by simply understanding that it provides a way to get from point A to point B really, really quickly. On the other hand, if a story involves the breakdown of the antimatter in the warp core, a reader has to reach a higher level of understanding with respect to the warp drive, or the comprehension of the story will be impaired. In this fashion, the reader will never push a concept to the level at which it becomes bizarre.[1] However,

---

[1]Note that we are not saying that this is the only strategy that a reader may use. Readers with an interest in faster-than-light travel,

the satisfaction solution is only part of the answer. Added to it is the *ontology* solution; that is, it is necessary to create a knowledge organization which reflects the world of the reasoner, allows creative manipulations to occur, and acts to prohibit bizarre ones. This aspect is the focus of the remainder of this paper.

Motivating Examples

Consider the sentence, *John was a bear*, which could be the opening line of a story. Since there is no additional information, at this point, from the text itself, there are numerous interpretations:

- John (a human) acts like a bear.
- John (a human) has been transformed into a bear.
- John (an agent) is a were-bear.
- John (a bear) is a bear.

For comprehension to be successful, a reader must formulate an interpretation which is consistent given other information possessed by the reasoner. Although all of the above interpretations are *possible*, some may be more probable than others in a given context. How is a reasoner to select the "best" interpretation given all other information available?

A reader could simply "skip" this sentence and assume that later sentences will disambiguate the confusion. Unfortunately, this simply pushes the problem back a level—at some point, an interpretation must be created (given the problems of keeping all possible options simultaneously active in memory). Also, human readers *are* able to make a choice between the alternatives if you stop the reading process and query them. Some mechanism must be allowing the selection of a "best" choice at some point in the reading process.

One option is simply to allow an arbitrary choice. On the other end of possibilities, a designer of a reading system could encode a set of rules which would allow the system to select one choice over the other. Unfortunately, the former of these options leads to potentially bizarre results occurring (how often, after all, is a story beginning with the example sentence going to be about were-bears?); the latter option leads to a huge knowledge engineering problem and the potential to overlook possibilities which would then cause less than optimal performance. We follow a more general approach of allowing a basic ontology to constrain the problem. This allows *creative understanding* of concepts to occur, while preventing bizarre interpretations from being formed.

The Ontological Grid

All knowledge within the ISAAC system is organized by a top-level ontological grid, consisting of twenty ontological categories (Figure 1 shows this breakdown and example concepts from each category). One axis of the ontology grid represents the *type* of a concept: *action, agent, state,* and *object* (Domeshek, 1992; Schank & Abelson, 1977). The other dimension represents the *domain* of a concept: *physical, mental, social, emotional,* and *temporal*. A reasoner possesses knowledge concerning the cells of the grid themselves, as well as knowledge about the particular rows and

for instance, may try to extend their understanding of the warp drive even if a more in-depth understanding is not needed for a particular story.

	Physical	Mental	Social	Emotional	Temporal
Agents	person	consciousness	boss	Ares	entropy
Actions	walking	thinking	selling	loving	getting closer to March
Objects	rock	idea	teacher-student relationship	hatred	second
States	young	lack of knowledge	public dishonor	being angry	early

Figure 1: Knowledge grid

columns (e.g., knowledge about physical types in general, or knowledge of objects in general). While performing creative understanding, a concept may need to be *transitioned* from one cell to another. If a principled method can be developed to bound these transitions based on the ontology, then a reasonable bound on the creative understanding process will then exist.

Representation of Concepts

The movements of concepts within the grid is partially dependent on the representation format we make use of in the theory. Concepts must be capable of being combined with other concepts (or parts of concepts), which means a fairly flexible knowledge representation system is required. This aspect of the work draws heavily from research in artificial intelligence concerning exactly what elements should make up a "proper" knowledge representation. Although the ideas of both semantic networks and frame representations go back decades (see, for example, Quillian, 1966 and Minsky, 1975, respectively), the structure of knowledge within many artificial intelligence systems is ad-hoc. A notable exception is that of Wilensky's work (1986) with KODIAK, which motivated much of our current approach.

While a concept is physically created and stored within the system as a frame-like entity, this is more for retrieval ease than anything else. The proper abstraction of the storage used is that a concept is represented as a node in a graph-like structure (Barsalou, 1992; Wilensky, 1986). The traditional role of slots exists in the system as data objects on the node, which contain pointers to other nodes in the memory. These design decisions were driven to allow flexible storage and retrieval of concepts via a spreading activation model of memory (Francis & Ram, 1993).

Consider the robot example in Figure 2. HEIGHT-IS is a pointer to a relationship schema containing general information about *height*. In particular, all such relationships will contain a domain and codomain, represented in the framelike representation as simply the frame-name and the filler for the indicated slot. Furthermore, the role of traditional slot-names, which are assumed to be relationships in our approach, can be described as states. Thus, HEIGHT-IS is part of the state description for an object.

ROBOT-12	
:IS-A	ROBOT
:ROLES	{INDUSTRIAL-TOOL WEAPON TRANSPORT}
:FUNCTION	INDUSTRIAL-TOOL-5
:IS-MADE-OF	TITANIUM-7
:IS-POWERED-BY	ELECTRICITY-6
:CAN-LIFT	WEIGHT-10
:COLOR-IS	GREY-8
:HEIGHT-IS	HEIGHT-11
:P-ATTRIBUTES	{:IS-MADE-OF :IS-POWERED-BY :CAN-LIFT}
:S-ATTRIBUTES	{:COLOR :HEIGHT}
:EXPLANATION	EXPLANATION-9

Figure 2: Represented concept

Additionally, each concept is tagged with the current function it is being viewed as performing, as well as a set of possible functions it is known to be capable of performing. This fact is utilized to achieve flexible memory retrieval—during one search through memory, a car and a horse might be similar; with a different function in mind, a horse and a zebra would be more closely related. The process of function tagging follows the work of Barsalou on *ad hoc categories* (1989); rather than having all categories predefined, a reasoner can create temporary categories by collecting concepts with similar functions. The *primary attributes* of a concept determine how it achieves its function, while the *secondary attributes* represent additional information. If the current function of a concept is changed (for example, a reasoner stops viewing the horse as an animal and starts viewing it as a mode of transportation), it might be necessary to repartition the primary and secondary attributes. And, by considering novel combinations of primary and secondary attributes, it is possible to hypothesize novel functions for a concept.

Manipulations of Concepts

When an existing concept needs to be manipulated during the course of a creative understanding episode, there are three basic outcomes with respect to the grid. The concept can be manipulated, yet remain in the same grid cell as when it started. For example, a reasoner may use a *horse* to understand the concept of a *zebra*. Second, a concept may transition along a row or a column. If a reasoner uses their knowledge of physical concepts in order to understand social ones (a boss blocking your promotion), this is an example of this shift. Finally, a transition may occur which moves the concept in terms of both axes. A reasoner understanding something like *His mind was a steel trap* is making use of this dual transition—a physical object is transitioned to a mental state. These three possibilities represent a simple ordering of the amount of cognitive work required to manipulate any given concept. Finally, a set of high-level heuristics is needed to bound the possible motion within the grid. These are:

- Physical types can become transitioned to other domains more easily than other domain types can be transitioned to physical. This was a recent empirical discovery resulting from experimentation performed on the system. We theorize that since humans are physical entities with a great

deal of experience with other physical entities, it is "easier" to believe in the existence of a novel, non-physical entity formed from a physical analogue than it is to accept the creation of a new type of physical entity. Consider, *John saw the days fly by*. Is this a novel use of *saw* and *fly* created by altering physical concepts into the temporal domain, or is it a novel use of *days* created by considering a temporal object as a physical one?

- An object may transition to an action by creating an action which captures a function of that object and vice versa. English, in particular, tends to have many lexical examples of this. A fax is the thing you send when you fax someone. A (Star Trek) transporter is the device used to transport material from one location to another.

- An object may transition to a state by creating a state which captures a primary attribute for that object, and vice versa. Through this transition, we get many common similes and metaphors, such as *Hungry as a bear* and *As good as gold*.

- Agents and objects can easily transition between each other. This results from two observations. First, agents exist as embodied entities in the world (Johnson, 1987), explaining the agent to object transition. For example, one may treat John as a physical object. Second, it is possible to view objects as though they possess intention (Newell, 1981), enabling the object to agent transition. For instance, a thermostat may be thought of in terms of agency, i.e., it *wants* to keep the house at a constant temperature.

- Make the minimal changes necessary. This is simply a general rule, ala Occam's Razor. It results from the earlier discussed idea of satisfaction ultimately driving the creative understanding process—stop the process once you have a "good enough" understanding to allow the higher cognitive task to continue.

By combining the three basic movement types with the high-level heuristics, we get an ordering of the amount of *cognitive effort* required to manipulate concepts (from easiest to most difficult):

1. Concepts may transition within a single cell.
2. Agents may be treated as objects and objects may be treated as agents.
3. Concepts may vertically transition according to the modification heuristics.
4. Physical types may transition to other domains (horizontal motion).
5. Other domain types may transition to the physical domain (horizontal motion).
6. Combinations of 2–5 may occur.

Within this ordering, however, operations which result in the minimal changes are preferred over those which are more complex.

Implementation Details and Examples

The ISAAC system is the a computer system which instantiates our creative reading theory. ISAAC is written in Common Lisp, using the KR frame package (Giuse, 1990) for knowledge representation, the Garnet package (Myers, 1988) for graphical input and output, and the COMPERE system (Mahesh, 1993) for comprehending individual sentences. While

100

the system is specifically designed to be a testbed for our theory of creative understanding, the complete reading theory is implemented. The theory describes reading as being made up of six *supertasks*, or large collections of functionally related tasks, including *story structure comprehension*, *scenario comprehension*, *memory management*, *sentence processing*, *explanation*, and *metacontrol*. More information on the reading aspects of the model can be found in Moorman and Ram (1994b). ISAAC is currently capable of reading three short, previously published, science fiction stories (one to three pages), as well as several paragraph synopses of *Star Trek: The Original Series* episodes (Asherman, 1989). In addition, several small examples have been studied, outside the context of reading complete stories. We now present several of these to show the extent which the ontology aids the creative understanding process.

First, we return to the original example: *John was a bear*. With all the possibilities, the least movement occurs if we simply allow *John* to be the name of a particular *bear*. Thus, this is the version that ISAAC prefers, if no additional information from the story is provided.[2]

A second example comes from the Meta-AQUA system (Ram & Cox, 1994) which reads a story involving a drug-sniffing dog. Meta-AQUA initially knows only that dogs will bark at agents which threaten them. But, in the story, a dog is barking at a suitcase. In ISAAC, the system is presented with two possibilities—its knowledge of dogs is wrong or its knowledge of suitcases is. The first involves altering an existing physical agent to create a variant of it, an intracellular movement. The second involves shifting a physical object to the physical agent cell, a vertical movement. The intracellular movement is preferred.

In the story *Men Are Different* (Bloch, 1963), a robotic archaeologist is studying the destroyed civilization of mankind. The story is presented as a first-person narrative. ISAAC is aware that narrators, archaeologists, and protagonists are all known to be human; robots are industrial tools; but the narrator, archaeologist, and protagonist of the story is known to be a robot. ISAAC can create a new type of robot which embodies agent-like aspects, or it can change the definitions of narrators, archaeologists, protagonists, and the actions in which they may participate. The new robot concept represents a more minimal change.

The final example involves the story *Zoo* (Hoch, 1978), in which the reader is presented with an intergalactic zoo which travels from planet to planet, giving the inhabitants of those planets a chance to view exotic creatures. At the end of story, however, the reader is shown that the true nature of the intergalactic ship—it is an opportunity for the "creatures" on

the ship to visit exotic planets, protected from the dangerous inhabitants by the cages they are in. To understand the new zoo, the system draws an analogy between the known zoo and the novel one. The result, then, is simply a shift from one physical object to another physical one.

Drawbacks and Limitations

Extra Knowledge Engineering

There are three known problems with the approach which we are currently pursuing. The first is simply the need to correctly mark each concept in memory as belonging to one of the twenty top-level categories. This means some additional work is required when knowledge is being represented for ISAAC initially. However, the level of increased work has not been prohibitive to the project.

Origin of the Categories

There is some concern that the ontological categories being used may be too limited to allow an accurate model of the world. But, we have been driven by functional constraints on the creative understanding process, so we can say that our ontology is sufficient for the cognitive tasks in the theory. Added to this, we have also been motivated by prior psychological research concerning ontology. This has mainly been studied by developmental psychologists who attempt to explain the changes which take place to a child's ontology as they mature, as well as attempting to explain what, if any, ontology may exist from birth.

The first area to consider is that of what ontologies exist. Two important ontological distinctions have been studied by a number of researchers. The *physical–immaterial distinction* is an important one which arises relatively early in the development pattern of normal children, although it continues to be refined and sophisticated as they age (Carey, 1992; Carey & Spelke, 1994). Another major ontological division is the *object–event distinction*—some things in the world are objects (like rocks, people, etc.) while other things are events (such as walking) (Carey, 1992).

The second aspect of the previous research to note is the recognition that shifting basic ontological categories is difficult. Numerous researchers have noticed and theorized about this (e.g., Carey, 1992; Chi, 1993), but one of the best descriptions of the possible range of changes comes from Thagard (1992). In his framework, there are nine degrees to conceptual change, ranging from the simple addition of new instances of known concepts to the complete reorganization of the ontological hierarchy. The lower levels are far easier to perform; it is only with growing ability and sophistication that a reasoner will achieve the reorganization level.

Finally, viewing various ontological experiments over the course of the research has prompted some researchers to claim that certain types of ontological categories are fundamental to human reasoning and would, therefore, need to be accurately modeled. For example, Brewer (1993) suggests that a rich ontology is needed, consisting of (at least) natural kinds, nonexisting natural kinds, artifacts, social entities, psychological entities, and abstract entities. While our approach does not duplicate this exactly, the basic ideas are consistent.

---

[2]This may seem counter-intuitive; to most people, this example would make more "sense" if interpreted as *John is bear-like*, a metaphorical usage. Remember, however, that these ontological constraints have the most effect when no other information is known. This information can be background knowledge or story knowledge, so a reasoner already familiar with the bear metaphor may retrieve that interpretation instead of this default one. It is important to note that our approach handles metaphor as a normal part of the understanding cycle. Since metaphors are pervasive in language (see Carbonell, 1982; Johnson, 1987; Lakoff & Johnson, 1980, for example), we consider this "unified" handling of non-metaphors and metaphors to be an important feature of our overall theory.

Category Membership

Finally, there is potentially the most dangerous problem facing the theory—the problem of deciding category membership for a concept if the system has manipulated it. While it is easy in theory to say that a concept may shift across conceptual grid cell boundaries, it is sometimes difficult in practice to determine where its new location should be.[3] Consider the concept of *time travel*, for a moment. A reasoner with no prior knowledge can utilize information concerning *physical transport actions* and the *temporal column* to transform a physical transport concept into a temporal transport actions; i.e., a horizontal shift from the physical action cell to the temporal action cell. Notice that both actions have physical agents for their initiating actors and physical objects for their transported objects. Now, consider a device capable of performing time travel, namely a *time machine*. Again, a reasoner can start with knowledge of *physical transport machines* and the *temporal domain* and develop the concept of a time machine. But, in this case, a physical object has remained a physical object. Both manipulations used similar knowledge; one resulted in a horizontal shift while the other resulted in an intracellular one. For the moment, the problem is circumvented by appealing to the *minimum change* heuristic, but it is certainly an area of research to be explored.

Conclusion

The knowledge representation and ontological commitments of the ISAAC framework allows us to reasonably bound the creative understanding process without having to resort to a large list of rules and their exceptions. Additionally, there is the added knowledge engineering benefit of not having to worry about the precise placement of concepts within the implemented system—as long as the top-level ontological category is correct, the theory enables the system to function with a great deal of flexibility and robustness. As larger artificial intelligence systems are developed which are expected to be robust, real-world reasoners, it will become important for researchers to be aware of the ontological reality of the world in which their theories exist. Indeed, by taking advantage of the ontology, researchers may discover that the task of engineering large, robust systems is made somewhat easier.

Acknowledgments

This work was supported by a Fannie and John Hertz Foundation fellowship and by the Georgia Institute of Technology. The authors would like to recognize the efforts of Thomas Tiller, a visiting student who worked on aspects of the ISAAC theory, and the time and effort spent by members of the IGOR research group to read and offer useful comments on this work.

References

Asherman, A. (1989). *The Star Trek Compendium*. Pocket Books, New York.

Barsalou, L. W. (1989). Intraconcept similarity and its implications for interconcept similarity. In Vosniadou, S. and Ortony, A., editors, *Similarity and Analogical Reasoning*. Cambridge University Press, Cambridge.

Barsalou, L. W. (1992). Frames, concepts, and conceptual fields. In Lehrer, A. and Kittay, E. F., editors, *Frames, Fields, and Contrasts*. Lawrence Erlbaum Associates, Publishers, Hillsdale, NJ.

Bloch, A. (1963). Men Are Different. In Asimov, I. and Conklin, G., editors, *50 Short Science Fiction Tales*. MacMillan Publishing Co., New York.

Brewer, W. F. (1993). What are concepts? Issues of representation and ontology. In Nakamura, G. V., Taraban, R., and Medin, D. L., editors, *Categorization by Humans and Machines*. Academic Press, Inc., San Diego.

Carbonell, J. G. (1982). Methaphor: An inescapable phenomenon in natural-language comprehension. In Lehnert, W. G. and Ringle, M. H., editors, *Strategies for Natural Language Processing*. Lawrence Erlbaum Associates, Publishers, Hillsdale, NJ.

Carey, S. (1992). The origin and evolution of everyday concepts. In Giere, R. N., editor, *Cognitive Models of Science*. University of Minnesota Press, Minneapolis.

Carey, S. and Spelke, E. (1994). Domain-specific knowledge and conceptual change. In Hirshfeld, L. A. and Gelman, S. A., editors, *Mapping the Mind: Domain specificity in cognition and culture*, pages 169–200. Cambridge University Press, Cambridge, MA.

Chi, M. T. H. (1993). Barriers to conceptual change in learning science concepts: A theoretical conjecture. In *Proceedings of the Fifteenth Annual Conference of the Cognitive Science Society*, pages 312–317.

Domeshek, E. (1992). *Do the Right Thing: A Component Theory of Indexing Stories for Social Advice*. PhD thesis, Yale University, New Haven, CT.

Francis, A. G. and Ram, A. (1993). Conquering the utility problem: Designing a memory module for all seasons. Unpublished draft.

Giuse, D. (1990). Efficient knowledge representation systems. *The Knowledge Engineering Review*, 5(1):35–50.

Hoch, E. D. (1978). Zoo. In Asimov, I., Greenberg, M. H., and Olander, J. D., editors, *100 Great Science Fiction Short Short Stories*. Doubleday, Garden City, NY.

Johnson, M. (1987). *The body in the mind: Bodily basis of meaning, imagination, and reason*. University of Chicago Press, Chicago.

Lakoff, G. and Johnson, M. (1980). *Metaphors We Live By*. University of Chicago Press, Chicago, IL.

Mahesh, K. (1993). A theory of interaction and independence in sentence understanding. Technical Report GIT-CC-93/34, Georgia Institute of Technology.

Minsky, M. L. (1975). A framework for representing knowledge. In Winston, P. H., editor, *The Psychology of Computer Vision*. McGraw-Hill, New York.

Moorman, K. and Ram, A. (1994a). A functional theory of creative reading. Technical Report GIT-CC-94/01, Georgia Institute of Technology.

Moorman, K. and Ram, A. (1994b). Integrating reading and creativity: A functional approach. In *Proceedings of the Sixteenth Annual Cognitive Science Conference*.

---

[3] A similar problem arises in research involved with the formation of novel concepts (see, e.g., Shoben, 1993; Ward, 1995; Wisniewski & Medin, 1994). If a novel concept is formed using existing concepts, what category should the new concept belong to? For example, if *pet* and *fish* are combined, where in a knowledge hierarchy should the resulting concept be placed?

Moorman, K. and Ram, A. (1994c). A model of creative understanding. In *Proceedings of the Twelfth Annual AAAI Conference*.

Myers, B. A. (1988). The garnet user interface development environment: A proposal. Technical Report CMU-CS-88-153, Carnegie-Mellon University.

Newell, A. (1981). The knowledge level. *AI Magazine*, 2:1–20.

Quillian, M. R. (1966). Semantic memory. In Minsky, M., editor, *Semantic Information Processing*, pages 227–270. MIT Press, Cambridge, MA.

Ram, A. and Cox, M. (1994). Introspective reasoning using meta-explanations for multistrategy learning. In Michalski, R. and Tecuci, G., editors, *Machine Learning: A Multistrategy Approach*, volume IV. Morgan Kaufman Publishers, San Mateo, CA.

Schank, R. and Abelson, R. (1977). *Scripts, Plans, Goals, and Understanding*. Lawrence Erlbaum Associates, Hillsdale, NJ.

Shoben, E. J. (1993). Non-predicating conceptual combinations. In Nakamura, G. V. and Medin, D. L., editors, *Categorization by Humans and Machines. The Psychology of Learning and Motivation*, volume 29. Academic Press, San Diego, CA.

Thagard, P. (1992). *Conceptual Revolutions*. Princeton University Press, Princeton, NJ.

Ward, T. B. (1995). What's old about new ideas? In Smith, S. M., Ward, T. B., and Finke, R. A., editors, *The Creative Cognition Approach*. MIT Press, Bradford Books, Cambridge, MA.

Wilensky, R. (1986). Knowledge representation—a critique and a proposal. In Kolodner, J. L. and Riesbeck, C. K., editors, *Experience, Memory and Reasoning*, chapter 2, pages 15–28. Lawrence Erlbaum Associates, Hilldale, NJ.

Wisniewski, E. J. and Medin, D. L. (1994). The fiction and nonfiction of features. In Michalski, R. and Tecuci, G., editors, *Machine Learning: A Multistrategy Approach*, volume IV. Morgan Kaufmann Publishers, San Francisco.

103

Working Memory in Text Comprehension: Interrupting Difficult Text

Danielle S. McNamara
Department of Psychology
Old Dominion University
Norfolk, VA, 23529
dsm200f@oduvm.cc.odu.edu
804-683-4446

Walter Kintsch
Department of Psychology
University of Colorado
Boulder, CO, 80309
wkintsch@clipr.colorado.edu
303-492-8663

Abstract

We compare the effects of interrupting text dealing with familiar or unfamiliar domains with either arithmetic or sentence reading tasks. Readers were interrupted after each of the eight sentences, at the end of each sentence, or in the middle of each sentence. Previous findings of minimal effects of interruptive tasks on comprehension measures (e.g., Glanzer & Nolan, 1986) were replicated in this study. Also, as found by Glanzer and his colleagues, interruptions after each sentence of a familiar text by an unrelated sentence increased reading times by approximately 400 ms per sentence. In contrast, for difficult, unfamiliar texts, mid-sentence interruptions significantly lengthened reading times by 1262 ms for sentence and 1784 ms for arithmetic interruptions. These findings are explained in terms of Ericsson and Kintsch's (1995) memory model which proposes that skilled memory performance relies on the use of long-term memory as an extension of working memory, or long-term working memory.

Introduction

Reading is by its very nature sequential. The glue of memory is needed, therefore, to hold the various elements of the sequence together. The eye moves from word to word, and in general each word is integrated with the previous ones as rapidly as possible (e.g., Just & Carpenter, 1987). According to Kintsch and van Dijk's (1978) model of text comprehension, sentences or phrases also form processing units, which are linked together via a short-term memory buffer. Evidence for the operation of such a buffer has been obtained in various experiments (e.g., Fletcher, 1981; Glanzer & Razel, 1974). However, reading comprehension is still possible when the use of the short-term memory buffer is prevented. For instance, Glanzer and his colleagues (e.g., Fischer & Glanzer, 1986; Glanzer, Dorfman, & Kaplan, 1981; Glanzer, Fischer, & Dorfman, 1984; Glanzer & Nolan, 1986) have used an interruption procedure to interfere with short-term memory processes during reading. They did this by inserting unrelated material (e.g., unrelated sentences or arithmetic problems) after each sentence of a paragraph. The purpose of the intervening material was to interfere with the short-term retention of the just-read sentence. This interruption procedure produced far from dramatic effects. Although reading time for the next sentence in the paragraph was slowed by 300-400 ms, comprehension was totally unaffected.

Since the intervening sentence (or arithmetic problem) certainly must have interfered with integration processes in the short-term memory buffer, Glanzer's subjects must have found some way to continue reading without the use of that buffer. Glanzer and his colleagues interpreted their results as evidence that readers have access to a verbatim memory trace of the text, even after an interruption, that allows them to resume normal processing. An alternative explanation of Glanzer's findings is provided by a recent theory of memory proposed by Ericsson and Kintsch (1995). Accordingly, subjects' ability to successfully read and comprehend interrupted text is attributable to the use of *long-term working memory*. Ericsson and Kintsch assert that skilled memory performance such as reading relies on the use of long-term memory as an extension of working memory (i.e., consciousness or focus of attention). Information in long-term memory that is linked by retrieval structures to cues in working memory forms an extended, long-term working memory. The theory of long-term working memory maintains that all material in long-term memory that is connected via retrieval structures to cues available in working memory is directly accessible via a single retrieval operation.

Retrieval structures are generated during comprehension as an integral part of the comprehension process. Comprehension consists of forming mental representations (textbases and situation models in the theory of van Dijk & Kintsch, 1983) which connect the various elements of the text representation in network-like structures. Thus, generating a text representation in itself creates a retrieval structure. Each successive sentence of a coherent text normally contains retrieval cues, such as related or repeated information (i.e., argument overlap), that provide access to that structure. Hence, the whole previous text structure is but a single retrieval operation away. Retrieval from long-term memory, if the retrieval cues are present in short-term memory, takes about 400 ms (e.g., Anderson, 1990; Yu et al., 1985). Indeed, Glanzer's interruption procedure costs the reader no more than a single retrieval operation, that is, about 400 ms.

A long-term working memory (Ericsson & Kintsch, 1995) explanation of the results obtained with the interruption procedure used by Glanzer (e.g., Glanzer & Nolan, 1986) implies that more serious disruptions of reading should be found (a) if there are no retrieval structures available, or (b) if there are no retrieval cues accessible in short-term memory. In the present experiment, an attempt was made to prevent, or at least interfere with, the formation of retrieval structures during comprehension. For this purpose, the interruption procedure used by Glanzer was elaborated in two ways. First, in one condition, sentences were interrupted in mid-sentence rather than at the end. Since the sentence is incomplete at this point, it is more likely that the partially constructed mental representation would not connect to the earlier portion of the text. Second, for some subjects, difficult texts from unfamiliar domains were used instead of easy, familiar texts. Since the construction of a situation model is strongly dependent on the availability of relevant background knowledge, the use of unfamiliar texts further decreases the likelihood that a workable retrieval structure can be generated. Neither one of these manipulations will completely prevent readers from some understanding -- even difficult half-sentences will be understood to some degree. Nevertheless, a significant deterioration of understanding would be expected. To the degree that this happens: (a) no retrieval structure will be available; (b) the succeeding sentence fragment will not reinstate the previous text in long-term working memory with a single, 400 ms retrieval operation; and (c) more complex, time consuming, retrieval processes (e.g., deliberate search, construction of retrieval cues) will be required. If these retrieval processes are not successful, comprehension difficulties as well as longer reading times will result. If, on the other hand, these retrieval processes are successful, the reading time for the second sentence half will be lengthened by more than 400 ms.

Method

Subjects and Design

The subjects were 72 undergraduate students at the University of Colorado who participated for course credit. A 2 x 2 x (3) mixed factorial design was employed, with two between-subjects factors, text domain (familiar, unfamiliar) and interference task (sentence, arithmetic), and one within-subjects factor, interruption type (control, end, middle). Eighteen subjects were assigned to each of the four between-subjects conditions.

To obtain a more sensitive test of comprehension, a free recall test was used in the present experiment instead of comprehension questions, as in the original work by Glanzer and his collegues.

Apparatus and Materials

Text. The texts were presented either with Zenith Data Systems or IBM/PC computers. The experimental texts included ten paragraphs comprised of eight sentences, as well as 100 unrelated sentences obtained from various sources (e.g., encyclopedias, journals, books). The paragraphs were from domains that according to pilot studies were either highly familiar to undergraduate students (e.g., "body fat") or quite unfamiliar (e.g., "Fourier transformations"). Some of the paragraphs were reworded or altered to improve coherence or reduce length. The mean number of words per sentence for the familiar paragraphs, unfamiliar paragraphs, and unrelated sentences were 18.47, 16.12, and 17.02 words, respectively.

Unrelated sentences were presented in random order, and each sentence was presented only once during an experimental session.

Arithmetic problems. The problems presented to the subjects in the arithmetic condition were presented in three possible randomly chosen formats: addition, subtraction, or multiplication. The integers of the arithmetic problems were randomly chosen with constraints so that all answers to the three types of problems consisted of two or three digits.

Interruption types. There were three interruption types: control, end, and middle. A total of 10 interference tasks (i.e., 10 unrelated sentences or 10 arithmetic problems) were presented in all three conditions. The procedure of the control and end conditions replicated that reported by Glanzer and his colleagues (e.g., Glanzer & Nolan, 1986). In the control condition, the paragraph sentences were presented in immediate succession, followed by a block of 10 interference tasks. In the end interruption condition, each sentence was followed by 1 interference task, except for the last sentence, which was followed by the remaining 3 interference tasks.

In the middle interruption condition, each sentence was interrupted in the middle by an interference task; the remaining 2 interference tasks then followed the last sentence of the paragraph. The interruption was placed between the subject and verb of the sentence, with the constraint that no fewer than three words (and at least two content words) preceded the break in the sentence. Sentences which began with "It is" were interrupted at a point such that there was an equal number of words in each of the two parts. If there were two equally important verbs in the sentence, the interruption was placed before the verb which resulted in the most equal division in the number of content words in the sentence. An example of a text from an unfamiliar domain with the interruption locations indicated with asterisks is presented below in Table 1.

Metamorphic rocks are those that remain in the solid state ** while being changed by heat and/or pressure, with or without overall chemical change.

Most metamorphic rocks crystallize under stress, ** resulting in characteristic foliation or parallelism of the constituent grains, especially micas.

The contact metamorphic rocks, however, more commonly ** form without deformation, resulting in a massive texture.

Their proximity to a heat source and their characteristic spotted appearance resulting from the growth of new minerals ** aid in their recognition.

Table 1: Text example from an unfamiliar domain with asterisks marking the break for the middle interruption condition. Only the first four of the eight text sentences are shown.

Procedure

Subjects were tested individually. All subjects read a series of 10 paragraphs, each consisting of 8 sentences. The first was a practice paragraph, presented in the middle condition. The remaining 9 paragraphs were equally distributed across the three conditions according to a Latin-square design and presented in a random order.

Subjects were instructed to read the texts at their normal reading pace and not to attempt to memorize the sentences. Subjects read aloud both the texts and the interference tasks. Subjects were told that interruptions, either arithmetic problems or unrelated sentences, would occur alternatively after the last sentence in the paragraph, between each sentence in the paragraph, and in the middle of each sentence. They were informed that after they had read all of the sentences in a paragraph, they would be asked to write down as much of the text as they could remember. In the sentence interference task condition they were asked to recall both the sentences from the paragraph and the unrelated sentences.

The subjects in the arithmetic interference condition were allowed to use paper and pencil to solve the problems. As soon as an answer to the problem was entered, the next sentence of the text was presented. If they answered a problem incorrectly in less than 30 seconds, they were instructed on the computer monitor that their solution was incorrect and to try again; after 30 seconds, they were informed that the answer was incorrect and were presented with the next sentence of the text.

Results

Text Recall

For the purpose of scoring recall protocols each text was divided into idea units. For each unit subjects were given 1 point if they recalled the main gist of the unit and half of a point if they recalled only a fraction of the idea unit. An analysis of variance was performed on proportion recall including the two between-subjects factors, text domain (familiar, unfamiliar), and interference task (sentence, arithmetic), and one within-subjects factor, interruption type (control, end, middle). There was a main effect of the familiarity of the text, $F(1,68) = 61.2$, $p < .001$, reflecting greater recall for the familiar text ($\underline{M} = 0.30$) than for the unfamiliar text ($\underline{M} = 0.16$). There was also a main effect of interference task, $F(1,68) = 42.0$, $p < .001$, reflecting greater recall when the texts were interrupted by the math problems ($\underline{M} = 0.29$), than by the sentences ($\underline{M} = 0.18$). The interaction between text and interference task was not statistically significant, $F(1,68) = 2.1$, $p = .157$. There was no effect of interruption type, $F(2,67) < 1$, nor did interruption type interact with either of the between-subjects variables. Thus, subjects recalled the same amount of text regardless of whether the interference tasks occurred at the end of the paragraph ($\underline{M} = 0.23$), at the end of each sentence ($\underline{M} = 0.24$), or in the middle of each sentence ($\underline{M} = 0.24$).

In summary, subjects recalled more from the familiar than the unfamiliar texts, and recalled more when the texts were interrupted by the math problems than by sentences. These results were not affected by interruption types, and interruptions had no effect on text recall.

Sentence reading time

Sentence reading times by text domain (familiar, unfamiliar), interference task (sentence, arithmetic), and interruption type (control, end, middle) are presented in Table 2. An analysis of variance was performed on sentence reading times including the two between-subjects factors, text domain (familiar, unfamiliar), and interference task (sentence, arithmetic), and the two within-subjects factors, interruption type (control, end, middle), and sentence position (sentence 1 - sentence 8). Neither text domain, $F(1,68) < 2$, nor interference task, $F(1,68) = 2.4$, $p = .126$, nor the interaction of the two, $F(1,68) < 1$, had reliable effects on sentence reading times.

	Familiar Text	
	Sentence	Arithmetic
Control	8.700	9.785
End	9.110	10.785
Middle	9.243	10.917
	Unfamiliar Text	
	Sentence	Arithmetic
Control	9.642	10.028
End	9.891	10.887
Middle	10.904	11.812

Table 2: Average sentence reading times in seconds by text (familiar, unfamiliar), interference task (sentence, arithmetic), and interruption condition (control, end, middle).

There was, however, a significant main effect of interruption type, $F(2,67) = 21.2$, $p < .001$. This finding reflects both longer sentence reading times for sentences interrupted in the middle ($\underline{M} = 10.72$ s), compared to both the end and control interruption conditions ($\underline{M} = 9.85$), $F(1,68) = 25.6$, $p < .001$, and longer sentence reading times for those interrupted at the end of each sentence ($\underline{M} = 10.17$) compared to those which were not interrupted at all ($\underline{M} = 9.54$), $F(1,68) = 12.0$, $p < .001$. Thus, the average interruption effect (i.e., the overall increase in reading time compared to the control condition) was 1180 ms when the sentences were interrupted in the middle, versus 630 ms when the sentences were interrupted at the end. Neither text domain, $F(2,67) = 2.5$, $p = .095$, nor interference task, $F(2,67) < 2$, reliably interacted with interruption type. However, a planned-comparison test showed that the contrast between the middle interruption and the two other interruption types (i.e., control and end) interacted significantly with text, F(1,67) = 5.0, p = .030, reflecting the finding that the middle interruption had a greater effect on reading time for the unfamiliar texts than for the familiar texts (see Figure 1). The contrast orthogonal to this comparison, between the end and control interruption conditions, did not reliably interact with text familiarity, F(1,68) < 1.

In summary, for familiar texts interrupted by sentences, we found a 410 ms increase in reading time. This result, in conjunction with our finding little effect of interruptions on recall, replicates Glanzer's earlier findings. We also found that interrupting sentences in the middle had a greater impact on reading times than did interrupting at the end of the sentence. Moreover, this difference depended on the familiarity of the texts -- subjects' reading times were most affected when reading unfamiliar texts with an interruption in the middle of each sentence.

There was also a significant main effect of sentence position, F(7,62) = 34.8, p < .001, reflecting greater sentence reading times for the sentences at the beginning than at the end of the paragraph. Sentence position did not reliably interact with interference task, F(7,62) < 2, nor with interruption type, F(14,55) < 2, but did significantly interact with text familiarity, F(7,62) = 12.8, p < .001. As can be seen in Figure 2, which presents sentence reading times for unfamiliar and familiar texts, it takes longer to read sentences at the beginning of a text dealing with an unfamiliar domain than with an easier, more familiar text domain, whereas these differences diminished towards the end of the paragraph.

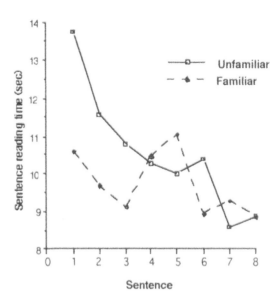

Figure 2: Sentence reading times by text.

For the condition in which sentences were interrupted in the middle, we were interested in whether there were differences in reading time for the two parts of the sentence. The beginning of the sentence was uninterrupted, and thus should take less time to read, than the second, interrupted part of the sentence. We were also interested in whether this difference was augmented by the familiarity of the text or by the type of interference task. A separate analysis of variance was performed for only the middle interruption condition including two between-subjects factors, text domain and interference task, and one within-subjects factor, sentence part (interrupted, uninterrupted). There was neither a main effect of text, F(1,68) = 2.7, p = .110, nor an effect of interference task, F(1,68) = 2.7, p = .106. As predicted, there was an effect of sentence part, F(1,68) = 89.8, p < .001, reflecting shorter reading times for the beginning of the sentence (M = 4770 ms) than for the last interrupted part of the sentence (M = 5949 ms). This difference did not depend on the familiarity of the text, F(1,68) < 1, but did interact with the type of interference task, F(1,68) = 12.7, p < .001. It took longer to read the second part of the sentence following an arithmetic task (M = 6494 ms) than after reading an unrelated sentence (M = 5404 ms). These results indicate that the effect of the middle interruption task is greatest for the clause following the interruption, and that this increase is augmented for the arithmetic task compared to the sentence reading task.

Interference tasks

An analysis of variance was performed on task completion times including the two between-subjects factors, text domain, and interference task, and two within-subjects factors, interruption type, and task order (1-10). The mathematics problems required significantly more time to complete (M = 14.8 s) than the sentences (M = 8.4 s),

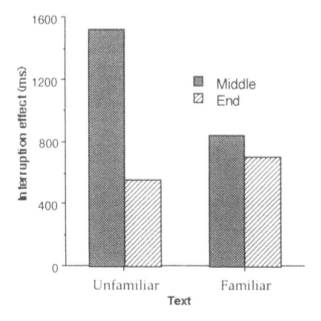

Figure 1: Interruption effects in reading time (i.e., difference from control reading times) for the middle and end interruption conditions by text (averaged over the arithmetic and sentence interference task conditions)

F(1,68) = 153.5, p < .001; and there was an effect of the order of the tasks, F(9,60) = 4.2, p < .001, reflecting a greater amount of time spent on the first task ($\underline{M}$ = 12.9 sec) compared to the remaining nine tasks ($\underline{M}$ = 11.5). No other effects or interactions were significant (all Fs < 2).

General Discussion

The main findings of Glanzer and his collegues (e.g., Glanzer & Nolan, 1986) were replicated in the present study: Interruptions by an unrelated sentence following each sentence of a familiar paragraph had no effect on comprehension (here measured by a free-recall test), but increased reading times by 411 ms per sentence. Placing the interruptions in the middle of each sentence did not greatly change the results, as long as the reading material was familiar. However, for unfamiliar texts, mid-sentence interruptions significantly lengthened reading times by 1262 ms for sentence and 1784 ms for arithmetic interruptions, without affecting free recall.

The pattern of results remained the same when the texts were interrupted by arithmetic operations instead of unrelated sentences, except that considerably larger increases in reading times were obtained. It may be the case that switching from arithmetic to reading requires a constant switching time which is responsible for this increase. Recall was much better in the arithmetic condition than in the sentence condition, in spite of the fact that the arithmetic tasks actually took longer on the average than reading the interpolated sentences. This result has to be expected, in part because reading unrelated sentences produces more verbal interference, and in part because in the sentence task subjects had to recall both the main paragraph and the interpolated sentences.

We also found that it takes longer to read the initial sentences of a text. In terms of theories of text comprehension this result implies that the formation of the initial textbase (Kintsch, 1988; van Dijk and Kintsch, 1983) or the laying of the text structures' foundation (Gernsbacher, 1990) requires more mental processes than does adding on to this structure. More importantly, the reading times at the beginning of the paragraphs were significantly greater for unfamiliar than familiar texts. This result implies that the formation of the initial textbase foundation requires a greater amount of time for unfamiliar texts than it does for texts dealing with more familiar information.

The present study confirms previous results obtained with the interruption procedure of Glanzer. It also extends these results by testing a critical prediction of the long-term working memory theory of Ericsson and Kintsch (1995) against the alternative interpretation of these data offered by Glanzer (e.g., Glanzer & Nolan, 1986). The reading interruption procedure used by Glanzer does not impair comprehension and merely results in a relatively modest increase in reading time. Glanzer explained this finding by assuming that readers have access to a verbatim memory trace (and not thematic information), even after an interruption, that allows them to resume normal processing. This interpretation cannot account for the significant interaction between text familiarity and mid-sentence interruption: If what is reinstated after the interruption were a raw, uninterpreted, verbatim trace of the sentence, this trace would be equally available for familiar and unfamiliar texts. On the other hand, the theory of long-term working memory predicts just such an interaction.

According to models of text and discourse comprehension (e.g., Kintsch, 1988; van Dijk & Kintsch, 1983), as well as other structure-building models (e.g., Gernsbacher, 1990), comprehending a text involves the construction of a coherent mental text representation. Ericsson and Kintsch (1995) postulate that this text representation allows the text to be accessed in long-term working memory via a single retrieval operation. This retrieval operation takes about 400 ms if the appropriate retrieval cues are present in working memory. Ericsson and Kintsch (1995) have reviewed data indicating that retrieval from long-term memory requires 1 to 2 seconds when the appropriate cues are not in the focus of attention (e.g., Charness, 1976; Ericsson & Staszewsky, 1989). In the present experiment, the mid-sentence interruption effect for unfamiliar texts was 1.3 seconds in the sentence condition and 1.8 seconds in the arithmetic condition. Thus, this delay is about what one would expect for long-term memory retrieval -- in contrast to the 400 ms observed for retrieval using long-term working memory. If readers are interrupted in mid-sentence when they are reading an unfamiliar text for which they lack the knowledge to readily access the information needed to construct a situation model, they cannot generate a coherent text representation and hence do not have a retrieval structure to reinstate the previous text after the interruption. They must, therefore, use strategic retrieval operations. One example of such a retrieval operation would be a deliberate search for background knowledge (i.e., situation knowledge) and/or previous sentence fragments to be integrated with the new sentence fragment. Skilled readers are generally quite capable of adopting such strategies, but these mental operations are much more time consuming than the 400 ms retrievals involving long-term working memory.

Interrupting reading with an unrelated sentence or arithmetic problem must interfere with the short-term memory buffer. Nevertheless, as long as readers are able to understand a text (i.e., form a coherent mental representation of the text), interrupting reading merely lengthens reading time for the next sentence by the amount required for a single long-term working memory retrieval operation. This is true even when subjects read unfamiliar texts, or when the interruption occurs in mid-sentence rather than at the end of each sentence. In either case, apparently, readers are still capable of forming mental representations of the sentence (or sentence fragment) that can serve as efficient retrieval structures. Only when readers were given unfamiliar texts combined with mid-sentence interruptions was their comprehension impeded to such an extent that the preconditions for retrieval from long-term working memory were no longer present. In this case, subjects had to rely upon strategic retrieval operations to access information from long-term memory, requiring significantly more time.

Acknowledgements

We are grateful to Anders Ericsson for helpful discussions and to Eileen Kintsch and Timothy Rickard for their comments on this manuscript. This study was partially funded by a Postdoctoral Fellowship (Grant 93-12) and by a Career Development Award (Grant 95-56) to D. McNamara from the J. S. McDonnell Foundation and by NIMH Grant 15872 to W. Kintsch.

References

Anderson, J. R. (1990). Cognitive psychology and its implications. San Francisco: Freeman.

Charness, N. (1976). Memory for chess positions: Resistance to interference. Journal of Experimental Psychology: Human Learning and Memory, 2, 641-653.

Ericsson, K. A., & Kintsch, W. (1995). Long-term working memory. *Psychological Review, 102,* 211-245.

Ericsson, K. A., & Staszewski, J. (1989). Skilled memory and expertise: Mechanisms of exceptional performance. In D. Klahr, & K. Kotovsky (Eds.), Complex information processing: The impact of Herbert A. Simon (pp. 235-268). Hillsdale, N. J.: Erlbaum.

Fischer, B., & Glanzer, M. (1986). Short-term storage and the processing of cohesion during reading. Quarterly Journal of Experimental Psychology, 38, 431-460.

Fletcher, C. (1981). Short-term memory processes in text comprehension. Journal of Verbal Learning and Verbal Behavior, 20, 264-274.

Gernsbacher, M. A. (1990). Language comprehension as structure building. Hillsdale, NJ: Erlbaum.

Glanzer, M., Dorfman, D., & Kaplan, B. (1981). Short-term storage in the processing of text. Journal of Verbal Learning and Verbal Behavior, 20, 656-670.

Glanzer, M., Fischer, B., & Dorfman, D. (1984). Short-term storage in reading. Journal of Verbal Learning and Verbal Behavior, 23, 467-486.

Glanzer, M., & Nolan, S. D. (1986). Memory mechanisms in text comprehension. In G. H. Bower (Ed.), The psychology of learning and motivation (pp. 275-317). New York: Academic Press.

Glanzer, M., & Razel, M. (1974). The size of the unit in short-term storage. Journal of Verbal Learning and Verbal Behavior, 13, 114-131.

Just, M. A., & Carpenter, P. (1987). The psychology of reading and language comprehension. Boston: Allyn and Bacon.

Kintsch, W., & van Dijk, T. A. (1978). Towards a model of text comprehension and production. Psychological Review, 85, 363-394.

van Dijk, T. A., & Kintsch, W. (1983). Strategies of discourse comprehension. New York: Academic Press.

Yu, B., Zhang, W., Jing, Q., Peng, R., Zhang, G., & Simon, H.A. (1985). STM capacity for Chinese and English language material. Memory & Cognition, 13, 202-207.

Reasoning from multiple texts:
An automatic analysis of readers' situation models

Peter W. Foltz
Department of Psychology,
Box 30001, Dept. 3452
New Mexico State University
Las Cruces, NM, 88003
pfoltz@crl.nmsu.edu.

M. Anne Britt
Department of Psychology
226 Vincent Science Hall
Slippery Rock University
Slippery Rock, Pa 16057
meb@sruvm.sru.edu

Charles A. Perfetti
Learning Research and Development
Center
University of Pittsburgh
Pittsburgh, PA, 15260
perfetti@vms.cis.pitt.edu

Abstract

In reading multiple texts, a reader must integrate information from the texts with his or her background knowledge. The resulting situation model represents a rich elaborated structure of events, actions, objects, and people involved in the text organized in a manner consistent with the reader's knowledge. In order to evaluate a reader's situation model, a reader's summary must be analyzed in relation to texts the subject has read as well as to more general knowledge such as an expert's knowledge. However, this analysis can be both time-consuming and difficult. In this paper, we use an automatic approach called Latent Semantic Analysis (LSA) for evaluating the situation model of readers of multiple documents. LSA is a statistical model of word usage that generates a high-dimensional semantic space that models the semantics of the text. This paper describes three experiments. The first two describe methods for analyzing a subject's essay to determine from what text a subject learned the information and for grading the quality of information cited in the essay. The third experiment analyzes the knowledge structures of novice and expert readers and compares them to the knowledge structures generated by the model. The experiments illustrate a general approach to modeling and evaluating readers' situation models.

Introduction

In order to comprehend a text, a reader must integrate the information contained in the text with his or her background knowledge of the world. This integration, or situation model (e.g., van Dijk & Kintsch, 1984), is a rich elaborated structure of events, actions, objects, and people involved in the text organized in a manner consistent with the reader's knowledge of the domain. In the domain of history, a reader will typically read multiple accounts of the same historical event in order to generate an understanding of the event. These texts can include primary sources, participant's and historian's accounts, and textbooks. The task for the reader is to then integrate this information into a coherent cognitive representation.

Studying reasoning from history texts provides a realistic approach to examining learning from texts. In the real world, texts we read will be related to other texts we have read, as well as to experiences and knowledge we have acquired earlier. Nevertheless, the research approach raises a host of discourse processing issues that are not typically found in studies of learning from individual texts. These issues include: Do readers form an integrated situation model of the texts or are texts represented separately? Do certain texts have more influence on the reader's situation model than others? What features of texts are the major sources of influence? How do experts and novice situation models of differ? Although we can not answer these questions decisively in this paper, we demonstrate some approaches to these questions through evaluating readers' situation models.

To evaluate a reader's situation model, it is necessary to derive a representation of the reader's knowledge. Typically, a reader provides written summaries, takes tests assessing their knowledge, or is asked to judge relationships between concepts. The primary theoretical approach has been to develop cognitive models of the reader's representation of the text (e.g., van Dijk & Kintsch, 1983; Kintsch, 1988). In such a model, semantic information from both the text and the reader's summary can be represented as propositions. This permits the experimenter to make a comparison of the semantic content contained in the text to that in the subject's summary. The advantage of making the comparison at the semantic level is that the comparison is not dependent on surface features, such as the choice of words. Nevertheless, propositionalizing texts can be very time consuming and require a lot of effort, often limiting the size of texts that are analyzed.

In this paper, we describe an automatic method that analyzes texts and generates a semantic space that captures many of the semantic associations found in a reader's situation model. The method, Latent Semantic Analysis (LSA) can be applied in the field of text comprehension to evaluate a reader's situation model, providing results similar to propositional analyses. This paper describes some approaches to analyzing the essays of readers of multiple texts as well as demonstrating that the representation of LSA is similar to that generated by readers of the texts.

Latent Semantic Analysis (LSA) is a statistical model of word usage that models semantic relationships between pieces of textual information. A brief technical overview of LSA will be provided here, while more complete descriptions of LSA may be found in Deerwester Dumais, Furnas, Landauer & Harshman (1990) and Foltz (In press). The primary assumption of LSA is that there is some underlying or "latent" structure in the pattern of word usage across documents, and that statistical techniques can be used to estimate this latent structure. The term "documents" in this case, can be thought of as contexts in which words occur and could be considered also to be smaller text segments such as individual paragraphs or sentences. Through an analysis of the associations among words and documents, the method produces a representation in which words that are used in similar contexts will be more semantically associated.

In order to analyze a text, LSA first generates a matrix of occurrences of each word in each document (sentences or paragraphs). LSA then decomposes the matrix using singular-value decomposition (SVD), a technique closely related to eigenvector decomposition and factor analysis. The SVD decomposes the word by document matrix into a set of k, typically 100 to 300, orthogonal factors from which the original matrix can be approximated by linear combination. Instead of representing documents and terms directly as vectors of independent words, LSA represents them as continuous values on each of the k orthogonal indexing dimensions derived from the SVD analysis. Since the number of factors or dimensions is much smaller than the number of unique terms, words will not be independent. For example, if two terms are used in similar contexts (documents), they will have similar vectors in the reduced-dimensional LSA representation. An advantage of the approach is that matching can be performed between two pieces of textual information, even if they have no words in common. To illustrate, if LSA were trained on a large number of documents, including:

1) The U.S.S. Nashville arrived in Colon harbor with 42 marines

2) With the warship in Colon harbor, the Colombian troops withdrew.

The vector for the word "warship" would be similar to that of the word "Nashville" because both words occur in the same context of other words such as "Colon" and "harbor". Thus, LSA automatically captures a deeper associative structure than simple term-term correlations and clusters.

One can interpret the analysis performed by SVD geometrically. The result of the SVD is a k-dimensional vector space containing a vector for each term and each document. The location of term vectors reflects the correlations in their usage across documents. Similarly, the location of document vectors reflects correlations in the terms used in the documents. In this space the cosine or dot product between vectors corresponds to their estimated semantic similarity. Thus, by determining the vectors of two sets of textual information, we can determine the semantic similarity between them.

In recent years, a variety of research approaches to generating high-dimensional semantic spaces have developed models that capture semantic meaning based on analyzing large amounts of textual information (e.g., Landauer & Dumais, 1994; Lund, Burgess & Atchley, 1995; Schutze, 1992). LSA has been used in a variety of applications for representing semantic knowledgebases for modeling results from text and memory experiments. Landauer and Dumais applied LSA for modeling the semantic associations necessary for taking vocabulary tests and for predicting results from studies of semantic priming (See also Lund, Burgess & Atchley for a related approach). Foltz, Kintsch & Landauer (1993) and Foltz (In press) modeled the coherence of texts with LSA to make predictions of reader's comprehension. This paper describes results from three experiments that use LSA to evaluate readers' situation models. The first two experiments analyze subjects' essays to determine from what text a subject learned the information and to grade how much relevant information is cited in the essay. The third experiment analyzes the knowledge structures of subjects and compares them to the knowledge structures generated by LSA.

Predicting the source of the subjects' knowledge

In research on the subject's reasoning after reading multiple documents, it is important to know which documents have the most influence on the subject's recall. Recent studies of learning from history documents have shown that different types of documents have differing amounts of influence on a subjects' reasoning and recall (Britt, Rouet, Georgi & Perfetti, 1994; Perfetti, Britt, Rouet, Georgi, & Mason, 1994). As part of one of the experiments described by Britt et al., 24 college students read 21 texts related to the events leading up to the building of the Panama Canal. The texts included excerpts from textbooks, historians' and participants' accounts, and primary documents such as treaties and telegrams. The total length of text was 6097 words. After reading the texts, subjects wrote an essay on "To what extent was the U.S. intervention in Panama justified?" In the original analysis described by Britt et al., the essays were propositionalized and propositions from the essay were matched against those in the original texts in order to determine which texts showed the most influence in the subjects' essays. In this experiment, we reanalyzed the essays, using LSA to predict which texts influenced the subjects' essays. The goal was to match individual sentences from the subjects' essays against the sentences in the original texts read by the subjects. Sentences in the essays that were highly semantically similar to those in the original texts would likely indicate the source of the subject's knowledge.

To perform the LSA analysis, the texts were first run through the SVD scaling to generate a semantic space on the topic of the Panama canal. The 21 texts the subjects read (6097 words), along with paragraphs from 8 encyclopedia articles on the Panama Canal (~4800 words) and excerpts from 2 books (~17000 words) were included in the scaling. Because the semantic space derived by LSA is dependent on having many examples of the co-occurrences of words, the addition of these other textual materials helped to provide the LSA analysis with additional examples of Panama Canal related words to help better define the semantics of the domain. The LSA analysis resulted in a 100 dimensional space made up of 607 text units by 4829 unique words.

For the analysis of the essays, the vector for each sentence from each subject's essay was compared against the vectors for each of the sentences from the original texts read in the derived semantic space. For each sentence, the analysis returned a rank ordered list of the sentences that best matched along with a cosine indicating the degree of similarity on a scale of 0 to 1. For example, performing an analysis of the sentence from one of the subject's essays: "Only 42 marines were on the U.S.S. Nashville.", the best two matches returned would be the following two sentences:

MF.2.1 Nov. 2, 5:30 P.M.: U.S.S.. Nashville arrives in Colon Harbor with 42 marines. (cosine: 0.640)

P1.2.1. To Hubbard, commander of the U.S.S.. Nashville, from the Secretary of the Navy (Nov. 2, 1903): Maintain free and uninterrupted transit. (cosine: 0.556)

The codes at the beginning of returned sentences (MF.2.1 and P1.2.1) indicate which document and which sentence within the document was matched, while the cosines indicate the degree of semantic similarity. As can be seen, the first document (MF) contains much of the same semantic information as expressed in the sentence from the subject's sentence, and it is highly likely that this document was the source of the subject's knowledge expressed in that sentence.

In order to determine the effectiveness of LSA's predictions about the source of each subject's knowledge, they were compared against the predictions made by two human raters. The raters, who were highly familiar with the topic of the Panama Canal and with the 21 texts, independently read through the essays and for each sentence, they identified which of the 21 texts was the likely source of the information expressed in the sentence. Because sentences in the essays were complex, often expressing multiple pieces of information, the experimenters could identify multiple texts as the sources for any sentence. On average, the raters identified the source of information as coming from 2.1 documents, with a range of 0 to 8. The percent of agreement between the raters was calculated by using a criterion that for each sentence, if any of the documents chosen by one of the raters agreed with any of the documents chosen by the second rater, then it was considered that the two raters agreed on the source. Using this method, the agreement between the raters was 63 percent. The fact that the agreement between two humans was not that high is not surprising. Many of the documents contained similar pieces of information, since all were on the same topic but often just differed on their interpretation of the same historical events.

Since the raters picked on average two documents for each sentence, the best two matches by LSA for each sentence were used for making predictions. The percent agreement between the raters' predictions and LSA's predictions was calculated in the same manner as between the two raters. The agreement between each rater and LSA was 56 percent and 49 percent. While not as high as the inter-rater agreement, the fact that the LSA predictions can get within 7 percent of the agreement between raters indicates that LSA is able to make many of the same predictions as those of the raters.

By analyzing the sentences from subjects' summary of knowledge gained from a set of texts, LSA can predict which documents are reflected in their sentences. These predictions are close to those made by human raters. This permits a characterization of which texts are having the greatest influence on a subject's situation model as reflected in their summary.

Characterizing the quality of essays

Grading can be characterized as a process of determining whether a reader's situation model is appropriate compared to a text that was read or compared to the situation model of a grader. For characterizing the quality of essays, one can think of the degree of semantic similarity between what was read in the texts and what was written in the essay as a measure of how much information was learned from the texts. Thus, subjects who write higher quality essays should have captured more of the semantic information from the texts.

Unlike the first experiment which just used the information on which text was the most similar, this experiment used information on how semantically similar is what a subject wrote in an essay to what the subject read. For grading essays, the cosines between a subject's sentences and sentences in the original texts were used as a characterization of quality of the essay. The more similar sentences in an essay are to the original texts, the higher the score. Thus, this approach can be thought of as a measure of retention of information. It should reflect the degree to which subjects can recall and use the semantic information from the texts they read in their essay.

The same 24 essays as in the previous experiment were used. Four graduate students in history who had all served as instructors and teaching assistants were recruited. After becoming familiarized with the 21 texts that the subjects had read, they graded the essays based on what information was cited and the quality of the information cited, using a 100 point scale. They were instructed to treat the grading of the essays much in the same way as they would for undergraduate classes they had taught. In addition, the graders read through the original 21 texts and choose the ten most important sentences that were in the texts that would be helpful in writing the essay.

Two measures of the quality of the essays were computed using LSA. The first examined the amount of semantic overlap of the essays with the original texts. Each sentence in each essay was compared against all sentences in the original texts and a score was assigned based on the cosine between the essay sentence and the closest sentence in the original texts. Thus, if a subject wrote a sentence that was exactly the same as a sentence in the original text, they would receive a cosine of 1.0, while a sentence that had no semantic overlap with anything in the original texts would receive a cosine of 0.0. A grade was assigned to the subject's essay based on the means of the cosines for all the sentences in the essay. While this measure captures the degree to which the semantic information in the subject's essay is similar to that of the original texts, it can be thought of as a measure of plagiarism or rote recall. If a subject wrote sentences that were exactly the same as the original texts, the assigned grade would be very high.

112

The second measure determined the semantic similarity between what a subject wrote and the ten sentences the expert grader thought were most important. In this way, it captures the degree of overlap with an expert's model of what is important in the original texts. For this analysis, a grade was assigned to each essay based on the mean of the cosines between each sentence in the essay and the closest of the ten sentences chosen by the expert grader.

The grades assigned for the essays by the graders were correlated between the graders and also with the two measures of the quality of the essays. The correlations are shown in Table 1.

	Grader 1	Grader 2	Grader 3	Grader 4
Grader 2	.575 **			
Grader 3	.768 **	.582 **		
Grader 4	.381	.412 *	.367	
LSA overlap with texts	.418 *	.552 **	.317	.117
LSA expert model match	.589 **	.626 **	.384 †	.240

**p<.01   * p<.05   † p<.06

Table 1. Correlation of grades between expert graders and the LSA methods

The correlations between graders ranges from .367 to .768, indicating some variability in the consistency of the grades assigned by the graders. The grades assigned by the first LSA measure, which examined the amount of overlap with texts, correlated significantly with two of the four graders. This indicates that the grades assigned by human graders depend greatly on whether the essay captures a lot of the semantic information of the original texts. The grades assigned by the second LSA measure, which captures the similarity between what a subject wrote and the sentences that the expert grader thought were most important, correlated well with three of the four graders and, overall the correlations were stronger than the first LSA measure. This indicates that the quality of an essay can be characterized as a match between the expert's model of the domain and what was written in the essay. Indeed, the graders' correlations with LSA expert model are well within the range of the correlations between the graders, demonstrating that the automatic grading done by LSA was about as reliable as that of the graders. Additional analyses using a weighted mean grade of the experts can improve LSA's correlation of grades to experts to 0.68, which is as good, if not better than the graders correlation with each other.

The results indicate that the representation generated by LSA is sufficiently similar to the readers' situation model to be able to characterize the quality of their essays. Calculating the amount of similarity between what was read and what was written provides a good measure of the amount of learning by the subject. The results also have implications for understanding what is involved in grading essays. The LSA expert model results indicated that up to about 40 percent of the variance in subjects' essays can be explained by just the amount semantic overlap of sentences in the essays with 10 sentences in the texts that a grader thinks are important. Thus, graders may be looking to see if the essay cites just a few important pieces of information.

While LSA characterizes the degree to which the subjects' situation model matches that of the text of an expert, there still remain questions as to the degree to which other factors such as the quality of the writing and the ability to write a coherent essay are correlated with or are independent of the subjects' situation model.

Comparing reader's knowledge structures to LSA's semantic distances

One of the assumptions of using LSA to model subjects' situation models is that the semantic structures generated by LSA's analysis of the text correspond to the knowledge structures of the readers of the text. The successful results from the first two experiments indicate that these semantic structures do capture useful features of the reader's representation. The third experiment provides a more direct investigation of these knowledge structures by having subjects make explicit ratings of the semantic similarity between concepts mentioned in the texts and comparing them to the semantic similarity predicted by LSA.

Nineteen undergraduates read the same texts on the Panama canal as in the above experiments. After reading the texts, they were presented with a list of 16 concepts mentioned in the texts. The concepts covered a wide range of issues from the text, including people (President Roosevelt, U.S. Marines), events (U.S. recognizes Panama), and key objects and concepts from the story (The right of transit, The Bidlack Treaty). The subjects rated all 120 possible pairs of the concepts as to how related the two concepts were on a 7 point scale. In addition, the two experts from Experiment 1 both performed the rating task. Each expert performed the task twice, separated by a one month interval, in order to characterize how stable their knowledge of the domain was. Predictions of the similarities between concepts were also made by LSA by determining the cosine between each pair of concepts.

To determine the similarity in knowledge structures, the similarity ratings between concepts were correlated between the experts, the novice subjects and LSA. The two experts had correlations with themselves of 0.86 and 0.63, indicating some variability in even the experts' characterization of the relationship between concepts. (For all analyses, any correlation above 0.18 is significant at the .01 level.) The correlations of ratings between the experts ranged from 0.39 to 0.62, while the novices correlated with themselves with an average of 0.26 and a range from -0.12 to 0.48.

Because of the variability in both the experts' and the novices' ratings, two sets of ratings were derived, one representing a general expert's knowledge structures, by averaging the experts' ratings, the other representing a general novices' knowledge structures by averaging the novices' ratings. The correlation of the average expert rating with the average novice rating was 0.75, while the correlation of LSA with the average expert rating was 0.41 and with the average novice rating was 0.36. The fact that the correlation of LSA to the humans is not as high as the correlation between the experts and novices is not surprising. Averaging the human judgments removes a lot of the variability in their data, but since the LSA predictions were based on a single set of judgments, no averaging could be done. Thus, there would likely be more variability in the LSA predictions, resulting in lower correlations with humans than the correlations between the averaged humans. While the LSA correlation is not as strong as the correlation between the experts and novices, LSA manages to capture many of the same semantic relationships as those identified by both the experts and the novices. The above correlations also indicate that LSA's representation is somewhat closer to that of an expert in the domain than that of a novice.

In addition to calculating correlations between the LSA and the expert and novice ratings, Pathfinder analyses (Schvaneveldt, 1990) were performed on the similarity matrices for the experts, novices and LSA. The Pathfinder analyses derives a network structure which represents concepts as nodes and distances between concepts as the number of intervening links between the nodes. Network similarity scores, which indicate the degree to which two networks share similar links on a scale of 0 to 1, were computed. The comparison of pairs of networks indicated that the expert and novice networks were more similar than expected by chance (SIM=0.48, ExpectedSIM=0.14, p<.01) as well as the expert and LSA networks (SIM=0.32, ExpectedSIM=0.14, p<.01). However, the LSA network was not significantly similar to the novice network (SIM=0.21, ExpectedSIM=0.14, p>.1). As in the correlation results, these results indicate that the structures produced by LSA were similar to those produced by the experts.

Since the correlation and network similarity scores between LSA and the experts were lower than those between experts and novices, an analysis of the pairs of concepts was done in order to determine on which pairs LSA was making predictions that differed greatly from the experts. The experts' averaged ratings and the LSA cosines were converted to Z-scores and the differences between Z-scores was computed. This permitted a characterization of overpredictions, where the model predicted that relationship between two concepts was closer than the actual predictions made by the experts, and underpredictions, where the model predicted that relationship between two concepts was not as close as the predictions made by the experts.

The Z-score analyses indicated that LSA tended to overpredict the relationship between pairs of concepts when the two concepts occurred exclusively together in the texts or in cases when the two concepts shared terms (e.g., "U.S. Marines" and "U.S. recognizes Panama"). This indicates that LSA's representation of the texts was sometimes overly contextually based. Given that the LSA scaling was based on only a small sample of text (607 text units), there would be certain words that would occur in only one context and thus would not have as rich a semantic representation. This problem could be alleviated by providing a larger training set for LSA, such as using more encyclopedia articles, which would provide more contexts for words to occur.

The underpredictions made by LSA occurred in cases when the concepts represented more global events and players such as "President Roosevelt" and "U.S. recognizes Panama" as well as "President Roosevelt" and "U.S. Marines". These pairs were never described together in the text, yet their relationships can be inferred if a reader has enough general knowledge about the role of presidents in fomenting revolutions or having command over the Marines. Since LSA was only trained on semantic associations about Panama, it lacked much of this deeper situational knowledge. Thus, in this case, LSA had a somewhat limited situation model in that it was effective at representing semantic relationships about the Panama canal situation, but did not have more domain general history knowledge as do both the experts and novices. Again, this problem could be remedied by providing a larger training set for LSA, such as using more encyclopedia articles covering a wide range of topics in history.

Discussion

When reading multiple texts a reader must integrate the information across the texts as well as combine it with their previous knowledge. LSA captures this integration of information, representing concepts in a semantic space in which vector similarity between concepts represents a characterization of semantic relatedness. The primary properties of LSA that permit this representation is through performing an analysis of co-occurrence of words and then a statistical reduction of the analysis to capture high level associations between terms and documents. Thus, LSA captures a feature inherent in textual information: words that tend to co-occur together or tend to occur in the same contexts will be more semantically related. Based on the results of these studies, the statistical approximation of semantic relatedness generated by LSA corresponds to the knowledge structures generated by readers of multiple texts. In this manner, LSA has similar properties to that of a reader's situation model. It generates a semantic representation of textual information that integrates the information across texts. In addition, it can also integrate that information with outside information (e.g., previous knowledge) as long as the model has been trained on that information. Based on this representation, LSA can be used as a tool for evaluating readers' summaries and as a way of modeling readers' knowledge structures.

The first two experiments demonstrate that LSA provides a representation in which comparisons can be made between readers' summaries of their knowledge and the original texts they have read. These comparisons permit a variety of characterizations of a reader's situation model. By comparing sentences in a reader's summary to sentences from the texts that were read, LSA provides a measure as to which texts had the greatest influence on the reader. In addition, the degree of semantic similarity between the reader's summary and the original texts provides a measure of the amount of information the reader learned from the texts. By comparing the reader's summary to sentences that an expert thought was important, LSA provides a measure of the degree to which the reader's situation model matches that of the expert. Since essays provide a rich source of information about a reader's knowledge, but are often difficult to analyze, this approach permits automatic analyses of the reader's knowledge.

Because the derivation of the semantic space is based on an analyses of multiple texts, LSA generates a rich semantic representation. In the case of the above experiments, the space was derived based on about 23000 words, although the same method has been applied to corpora with millions of words (e.g., Landauer & Dumais, 1994). The third experiment demonstrates that distances between concepts in the semantic space correspond to conceptual distances in the readers' representation of the texts. This indicates that LSA captures a deep associational structure between concepts that is similar to the reader's situation model of the texts. The types of errors that LSA made in its predictions of concept similarities show that both novices and experts are incorporating information in the text with their global knowledge of political roles. Since LSA was not trained with texts that provide this information, it lacked as global a situational representation compared to humans. Thus LSA is dependent on the type of texts provided in order to successfully mimic a human situation model. For the present experiments, the situation model generated was limited only to knowledge about the Panama Canal situation. With a larger corpus, such as that used in the Landauer and Dumais research, LSA would have a more general representation, capturing more global associations that are made by humans when integrating information from the text with their background knowledge. Future research will address these issues as, well as continue to evaluate the boundaries of where the representation generated by LSA successfully captures or differs from the reader's representation.

In summary, LSA can serve both as a tool and as a modeling technique for text researchers. As a tool it can be applied as a method to analyze readers' summaries and characterize both the source and quality of a reader's knowledge. As a model of readers' comprehension, it can be used to generate a semantic representation that captures important features of a reader's situation model.

Acknowledgments

This work has benefited from contributions from Tom Landauer, Walter Kintsch, Susan Dumais, and Mara Georgi. Support for this research was partially funded by a grant to the Learning Research and Development Center from the Office of Educational Research and Improvement, Department of Education.

References

Britt, M. A., Rouet, J. F., Georgi, M. A., & Perfetti, C. A. (1994). Learning from history texts: From causal analysis to argument models. In G. Leinhardt, I. L. Beck & C. Stainton (Eds.), *Teaching and Learning in History.* (pp. 47-84). Hillsdale, NJ: Lawrence Erlbaum Associates.

Deerwester, S., Dumais, S. T., Furnas, G. W., Landauer, T. K., & Harshman, R. (1990). Indexing by latent semantic analysis. *Journal of the American Society for Information Science, 41,* 391-407.

Foltz, P. W. (In Press). Latent Semantic Analysis for text-based research. *Behavior Research Methods, Instruments & Computers.*

Foltz, P. W., Kintsch, W. & Landauer, T. K. (1993, July). An analysis of textual coherence using Latent Semantic Indexing. Paper presented at the Third Annual Conference of the Society for Text and Discourse. Boulder, CO.

Kintsch, W. (1988). The use of knowledge in discourse processing: A construction-integration model. *Psychological Review, 95,* 363-394.

Landauer, T. K. & Dumais, S. T. (1994). Memory model reads encyclopedia, passes vocabulary test. Talk presented at the Psychonomics Society.

Lund, K, Burgess, C. & Atchley, R. A. (1995) Semantic and Associative Priming In High-Dimensional Semantic Space. In *Proceedings of Cognitive Science.* Hillsdale, NJ: Lawrence Erlbaum Associates.

Perfetti, C. A., Britt, M. A., Rouet, J. F., Georgi, M. C., & Mason, R. A. (1994). How students use texts to learn and reason about historical uncertainty. In M. Carretero & J. F. Voss (Eds.) *Cognitive and Instructional Processes in History and the Social Sciences.* Hillsdale, NJ: Lawrence Erlbaum Associates.

Schutze, H. (1992). Dimensions of Meaning. *Proceedings of Supercomputing.*

Schvaneveldt, R. W, (1990) *Pathfinder Associative Networks: Studies in Knowledge Organization.* Norwood, NJ: Ablex Publishing.

van Dijk, T. A., & Kintsch, W. (1983). *Strategies of Discourse Comprehension.* New York: Academic Press.

Lexical Limits on the Influence of Context

Cornelia M. Verspoor
Centre for Cognitive Science
University of Edinburgh
2 Buccleuch Place
Edinburgh EH8 9LW
Scotland, UK
kversp@cogsci.ed.ac.uk

Abstract

This paper introduces an approach to modeling the interpretation of semantically underspecified logical metonymies, such as *John began the book*. A distinctive feature of the theory presented is its emphasis on accounting for their behavior in discourse contexts. The approach depends on the definition of a pragmatic component which interacts in the appropriate manner with lexicosyntactic information to establish the coherence of a discourse. The infelicity of certain logical metonymy constructions in some discourses is shown to stem from the non-default nature of the lexicosyntactically determined interpretation for such constructions. The extent of the influence of contextual information from the discourse on the interpretation of logical metonymies is therefore constrained by the lexical properties of the constituents of the metonymies. Contextually-cued interpretations are shown to be unattainable when indefeasible lexical information conflicts with these interpretations.

Introduction

It is sometimes assumed that with a sufficiently strong context any interpretation of a semantically underspecified sentence can be coerced. If we consider, for example, the sentence (1a) independent of a context we are likely to interpret it as (1b) or possibly (1c). If we then insert the prior context *John is my pet goat; he loves eating things* we suddenly prefer the interpretation in (1d).

(1) a. John enjoyed the book.

    b. John enjoyed reading the book.

    c. John enjoyed writing the book.

    d. John enjoyed eating the book.

This strong influence from context does not, however, operate without limits. There are underspecified constructions which, perhaps surprisingly, appear to disallow any interpretation other than the conventional, context-independent possibilities. These constructions are infelicitous in a context which would seem to require an interpretation at variance with these conventions.

In this paper, I will focus on one such construction, that of *logical metonymies*, for which more meaning than is directly attributable to sentential components arises. Logical metonymies generally occur when a verb has alternate syntactic complement forms, with only a single semantic interpretation for all forms. For example, the sentences in (1a-b) and (2) can be viewed as expressing the same meaning, although in the (a) sentences no reading event is explicitly mentioned.

(2) a. John began the book.

    b. John began reading/to read the book.

The systematic syntactic ambiguity of aspectual verbs and verbs like *enjoy* has been handled in existing approaches to logical metonymy via an operation of *type coercion* (either triggered by constraints on the logical type of the verbal complement, e.g. Pustejovsky (1991, 1995), or internalized in the verb semantics, e.g. Copestake and Briscoe (1995)) such that the logical forms for each verb+complement form will be identical. The coercion which must occur to get the appropriate readings of (1-2a) requires that a missing element of meaning, i.e. the reading event, be introduced. Pustejovsky (1991) has proposed that this element corresponds to one of the roles in the lexical semantic structure of the noun in the complement, the *qualia structure*. Type coercion looks to the qualia structure for an element of meaning with the logical type required by the semantics of the verb.

It could also be argued that the missing element is filled in from context via pragmatic processing rather than from a richly structured lexical representation. There are strong arguments, however, for lexical specification of some aspects of metonymy (see e.g. Copestake (1992) for discussion). An additional argument, which will be provided in this paper, is that a purely pragmatic approach would fail to constrain the possible interpretations of logical metonymies and therefore would fail to account for the full range of data. Consider the discourse in (3), for example. The context clearly cues an interpretation of the sentence (3b) of *John will begin destroying the books tomorrow*. However, this sentence is infelicitous in this discourse. In contrast, (3c) is felicitous in the discourse and has the expected interpretation.

(3) a. John will be audited by the IRS, so he has been destroying things which might incriminate him. He has destroyed the files and the computer disks.

    b.* He will begin the books tomorrow.

    c. He will begin on/with the books tomorrow.

A purely pragmatic approach would fail to constrain the possible interpretations of logical metonymies, while a purely lexical approach fails to accommodate the potential contextual influence on these interpretations (as required to explain the possibility of (1a) being interpreted as (1d)). A combination of the two approaches is necessary to explain the range of logical metonymy data. In this paper, I will show that information derived in the lexicon can be used to constrain the possible interpretations of a phrase in such a way that even a strong context cannot override the lexical specifications. Furthermore, I will argue that these specifications could not be relegated to the pragmatic component without a reduction in the generality of the treatment of logical metonymy phenomena. Thus, lexical specification of conventions are necessary, and the pragmatic component must be able to utilize the information coming from the lexicon in the appropriate ways.

Interpretation of Logical Metonymies

Lexical Approaches

As introduced above, the lexically-based explanations of logical metonymy depend on the representation of core lexical semantic information for nominals in the form of qualia structure. This structure specifies four essential aspects of a word's meaning, described with respect to the denotation of the word (Pustejovsky, 1991, 1995) — CONSTITUTIVE: the relation between the object and its constituent parts; FORMAL: that which distinguishes object within a larger domain; TELIC: the function of the object, what is done with it; and AGENTIVE: how the object came into being.

The roles in qualia structure relevant to logical metonymy are the telic and agentive roles, as these two roles will specify eventualities involving the denotation of the noun in the NP complement. For example, the predicate in the telic role of *book* is *reading*, while the predicate in its agentive role is *writing*. Most existing approaches assume that all concrete nouns always have both the telic and agentive roles specified, and thus the eventualities specified there are always available to the process of type coercion when establishing the interpretation of a logical metonymy structure. No other interpretations will be available, correctly ruling out the specified interpretations of the sentences (4), since the desired eventualities do not fill a role in the qualia structure of the nominal objects.

(4) John began the stone *(*moving)* / the book *(*destroying)* / the desert *(*crossing)*

Type coercion, however, must be constrained in some way, as there are interpretations of metonymies predicted on the basis of the eventualities in qualia structure which are actually ungrammatical, such as those in (5). The constraints which must be added to a qualia structure approach to type coercion to rule out such examples have been discussed by Godard and Jayez (1993) and Pustejovsky and Bouillon (1995).

(5) John began the highway *(*driving on)* / the dictionary *(*consulting)*

The constraint which Godard and Jayez (1993) propose to rule out these cases is that the reconstructed event should be a kind of *modification* (expressing an intuition that the object usually comes into being, is consumed, or undergoes a change of state). Pustejovsky and Bouillon (1995) develop constraints on type coercion in terms of the aspectual properties of the reconstructed event. Their account relies on a structured representation of events, in which subevents are represented and the "focus" of the event is marked as the *head* of the event structure. Left-headed structures correspond to accomplishments, while right-headed structures correspond to achievements. The aspectual constraint on type coercion, then, is that the complement of *begin* must be a left-headed TRANSITION. Sentences like (5) are therefore ruled out because *driving on the highway*, etc. are activities without a definite endpoint, rather than left-headed transitions.

These constraints, however, do not rule out all implausible metonymies, and rule out some plausible ones. The sentences in (6) should be ruled out on the specified interpretations, despite the associated events all being left-headed transitions specified in qualia structure. In contrast, those in (7) would incorrectly be ruled out since the interpretations convey activities.

(6) John began the film *(*watching)* / the nails *(*hammering in)* / the door *(*opening, *walking through)*

(7) John began daycare at his mom's work *(attending)* / the violin when he was five *(playing)* / acupuncture in April and homeopathy in August *(undergoing)*

The solution to this argued for in Verspoor (1996) rejects the assumption that all nouns have telic roles specified in qualia structure and rejects the effectiveness of the proposed aspectual constraints in capturing the range of logical metonymy data, while accepting that the context-independent natural interpretation of logical metonymies does appear to correspond to either the telic or agentive role of the noun in the NP complement. It is therefore proposed in that paper that not all artifacts have a conventionalized telic event in the qualia structure. Those that do not have this conventionalized event are infelicitous in logical metonymic constructions. Examples such as (5) and (6) are ruled out because the relevant eventualities are not specified in the qualia structure, while they are for (7).

Combined Lexical and Pragmatic Approaches

Lascarides and Copestake (1995) (L&C) extend the lexical approaches to logical metonymy to develop a system which takes into account the potential influence of context on the reconstruction of an event in a coercive environment. They utilize the idea that lexical defaults — defaults specified in qualia structure — persist beyond the lexicon into the pragmatic component, and are therefore potentially overridden by default pragmatic information.

L&C formalize their approach in a unification-based framework, with a theory of lexical structure in which the lexical entries are typed default feature structures (TDFSs), and which utilizes persistent default unification (PDU) (Lascarides *et al* 1996). The lexicon is hierarchically ordered (as described in e.g. Copestake (1992)). They adopt Pustejovsky's notion of qualia structure, which provides lexical defaults. For example, the telic role of *book* is *read* by default. Other aspects of lexical representation follow the lexical representation language (LRL) (Copestake, 1993b).

In the pragmatic component DICE (Lascarides and Asher, 1991), L&C propose two axioms, i) `Defaults Survive`: lexical generalisations normally apply in a discourse context and ii) `Discourse Wins`: conflicting discourse information wins over lexical defaults. These axioms together can be used to explain why (8a) has the interpretation (8b) rather than (8c), even though the telic role of *book* is *read*.

(8) a. My goat eats anything. He really enjoyed your book.

    b. The goat enjoyed eating your book.

    c. The goat enjoyed reading your book.

Since L&C build on the Pustejovsky approach to logical metonymy, they adopt the assumption of full representation of qualia structure and rely on constraints applied prior to pragmatic processing to rule out implausible metonymies. The approach therefore suffers from the same over- and under-generation as purely lexical approaches, but it is fully compatible with the Verspoor (1996) view on what information is lexically specified. I now turn to the interaction of that lexical information with the pragmatic component, and show how this can be used to account for incoherent discourses such as that in (3a,b).

Lexical Constraints Interacting with Context

An Example

The discourse in (9) exemplifies a contrast between the behavior of *begin* (or any aspectual verb which may be substituted) and other verbs. The sentence (9c(i)) is infelicitous as a continuation of the discourse (9a,b), while the sentences (9c(ii-iii)) are not. This parallels the distinction in (3). Assuming that default interpretations for *begin (on) your book* and *enjoy your book* are predicted from the lexicon, the example suggests that the default interpretation of *begin+NP* cannot be overridden by contextual cues for its interpretation, while the default interpretations of *begin on+NP* and *enjoy+NP* can be.

(9) a. My goat went nuts last night.
   b. He ate everything in his cage.
   c. i.*He began your book at 9pm.
      ii. He began on your book at 9pm.
      iii. He particularly enjoyed your book.

This contrast was modeled in Verspoor (1996) by having a syntactic rule associated with the structure *aspectual verb+NP* to trigger the operation DefFill (defined in Lascarides *et al* 1996). This operation converts the typed default feature structure (TDFS) representing the lexically specified default interpretation of the *aspectual verb+NP* phrase to a non-default typed feature structure (TFS) prior to pragmatic processing, thus restricting the interpretations which persist into the pragmatic component to those that are lexically specified. This operation is not triggered in the cases of *begin on* or *enjoy* or similar verbs, and thus in these cases the lexically specified default interpretation remains default and can be overridden by contextual information via the axiom `Discourse Wins`.

It was claimed in Verspoor (1996) that the conflict in pragmatics between the non-default information coming from the lexical/grammatical components and the interpretation suggested by context can result in a judgement of the sentence in question as infelicitous, but the process underlying this judgement was not explained. I will outline it here, showing how the judgement crucially depends on the non-default nature of the lexically specified interpretation for *begin the book*, which leads to an inability to connect the sentence coherently to the preceding discourse.

The Analysis

DICE is a theory which allows us to compute rhetorical links between segments of discourse on the basis of the speaker's background semantic and pragmatic knowledge. Discourse representations produced by DICE are in the form of segmented DRSs (SDRSs) (Asher, 1993), in which discourses are represented as DRSs plus discourse relations. These discourse relations act as constraints on discourse coherence by

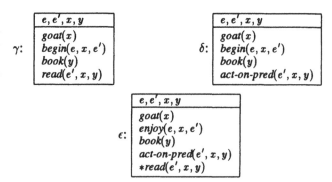

Figure 1: Logical forms associated with the three discourse continuations in (9c).

constraining the semantic content of the DRSs they connect. For example, if the discourse relation *Narration*, which conveys that one constituent of the discourse is a consequent of a previous constituent, is to hold, it must be possible to compute a common topic between the two constituents. This explains the incoherence of the discourse in (10) — there is no topic shared between the two sentences in the discourse.

(10)*Max came in. Mary's hair is black.

For reasons of space, I will not be able to give a formal account of the analysis of the discourses in (9). Rather, I will give an informal description of the analysis. The reader is referred to Lascarides and Asher (1991, 1993), Lascarides and Copestake (1995), and Lascarides *et al* (1995) for details of the formal application of DICE.

I label the DRSs representing (9a,b) as α, β and the DRSs representing (9c(i-iii)) as γ, δ, ϵ respectively in Figure 1. The DRS γ will represent the indefeasible interpretation *He began reading your book at 9pm* for (9c(i)), because the sentence has the form *begin+NP* and so the default telic event *read* is promoted to indefeasible via DefFill in this case. In contrast, δ will represent the interpretation *He began doing something with your book* (there is no default interpretation for what the event done with the book is in the case of *begin on*) and ϵ represents the defeasible interpretation *He enjoyed reading your book*. The * in the DRS ϵ marks the fact that the telic event is a default specification. It has remained default after lexicosyntactic processing due to the nature of *enjoy+NP*. The process by which these interpretations are determined is described in detail in Verspoor (1996).

Let us consider how the rules apply to the discourse (9a,b,c(i)). β must be attached to α. Assuming that DICE calculates that *eating everything in his cage* is a subtype of *going nuts*, we can attach α to β with the discourse relation *Elaboration*, which conveys, as intuitions would dictate, that the event in β is a part of the event in α. Now we must incorporate γ into the SDRS *Elaboration*(α, β). We can attempt to attach γ to either α or β with a discourse relation.

Attaching γ directly to α does not seem to be possible. Intuitively, there is no generalization between α:*going nuts* and γ:*beginning to read your book*, and so there does not seem to be a topic common to the two structures which is consistent with world knowledge about *going nuts*. Attaching γ to α with *Narration* is therefore not possible. Furthermore, the latter

118

event is not a subtype of the former, and so *Elaboration* is not possible either. Indeed, the rules in DICE will compute that no discourse relation can adequately relate them on the basis of semantic and pragmatic knowledge. Attaching γ to β also fails in a similar manner. Thus, there is no way to make sense of (9c(i)) given the preceding context and the indefeasible interpretation resulting from lexicosyntactic processing, as (9a,b,c(i)) is predicted in DICE to be an incoherent discourse.

We can contrast this with the discourses (9a,b,c(ii)) and (9a,b,c(iii)). In both discourses, we have the same first step as above: β is attached to α with the relation *Elaboration*. Subsequently, the DRSs for the continuation of the discourses, δ and ϵ respectively, must be attached. This is done in both cases according to the analysis in L&C (1995) (for details see that paper). Since δ provides only an underspecified interpretation, the context serves to specify *act-on-pred*(e', x, y) to *eat*(e', x, y). This occurs as a result of the constraints imposed by the rhetorical relations; the strongest coherence for the discourse results when δ is in a clear rhetorical relation to the previous discourse. Here, *doing something with your book* has no clear relation to *eating everything in his cage* whereas *eating your book* is a subtype of that event and so the *doing something with your book* event is specified to *eating your book*. Similarly, for ϵ the context overrides the default interpretation *read*(e', x, y) with *eat*(e', x, y), via the axiom `Discourse Wins` combined with the preference for a strongly coherent discourse. In this case, *eating your book* is in a much stronger rhetorical relation to *eating everything in his cage* than *reading your book* is and so the former is preferred. For each of these discourses, then, an interpretation of the continuing sentence is established which would allow DICE to attach the sentence to the discourse via a clear rhetorical relation. This explains the felicity of these discourses in contrast to the discourse (9a,b,c(i)).

Infeasibility of a purely pragmatic explanation

I have shown that lexical specification of defaults combined with syntactic control over the persistence of these defaults into the pragmatic component facilitates interpretation of logical metonymies in a discourse context. A purely pragmatic explanation (e.g. Hobbs *et al*, 1993) of such data, i.e. an explanation not relying on lexicosyntactic factors but only on world knowledge and contextual influences, would fail to account for the incoherence of the discourses (3a,b) and (9a,b,c(i)) in contrast to the coherence of the discourses (3a,c) and (9a,b,c(ii)).

The semantic representations for *begin the book* and *begin on/with the book* in such an approach would be identical — they would both correspond to the logical form δ in Figure 1, as there would be no lexical specification of default interpretations assumed. There would therefore be no basis for distinguishing their behavior with respect to the influence of discourse, even if one wanted to assume that the ability of discourse information to influence the interpretation of a particular construction were specified pragmatically. One probably does not wish to make such an assumption in any case since the primary determining factor of this behavior seems to be syntactic. Furthermore, the specification of default interpretations of logical metonymies in the pragmatic component would result in a great loss of generality, because information such as the relationship between possible default interpreta-

tions and the semantics of the noun in the NP complement (i.e. the fact that default interpretations correspond to the telic or agentive roles) could not be captured in any straightforward way, and also because there are several different types of metonymies (not only *verb+NP* but also *adjective+noun*) which display the same interpretation patterns. A pragmatic approach would be forced to specify the default interpretation of each individual logical metonymy in an *ad hoc* manner.

Conclusions

A lexically-driven approach to logical metonymy allows predictions about the range of interpretations for these constructions and the defeasibility or indefeasibility of those interpretations to be captured in a general way. The definition of a pragmatic component which has access to this lexical information is critical to the modeling of the behavior of logical metonymies in discourse contexts. I have shown that the infelicity of certain logical metonymy constructions in some discourses depends on the non-default nature of the lexicosyntactically determined interpretation for such constructions. When a non-default interpretation for a sentence cannot be coherently tied in to the discourse in which the sentence appears, discourse information cannot override that interpretation with a more coherent one, and so the sentence is judged infelicitous in that discourse — the discourse as a whole is weak. This work emphasizes the complex nature of the interaction between lexicosyntactic and pragmatic processing; discourse-level analysis is often constrained by lexical properties of the constituents of the discourse.

An open issue which remains is why it is that verb phrases differ in the persistence of their default interpretations into the pragmatic component.

Acknowledgements

This research was supported by an award from the Engineering and Physical Sciences Research Council, and by a studentship from the World Bank. The author would also like to thank Alex Lascarides, Bernie Jones, and the CogSci'96 reviewers for valuable feedback on the work.

References

Asher, N. (1993). *Reference to Abstract Objects in Discourse*. Kluwer Academic Pub.

Asher, N. and Lascarides, A. (1995). Lexical disambiguation in a discourse context. *Journal of Semantics*, 12(1):69–108.

Copestake, A. (1992). *The representation of lexical semantic information*. PhD thesis, Sussex University. Cognitive Science Research Paper CSRP 280.

Copestake, A. (1993b). The compleat LKB. ACQUILEX-II Deliverable 3.1.

Copestake, A. and Briscoe, T. (1995). Semi-productive polysemy and sense extension. *Journal of Semantics*, 12(1):15–68.

Godard, D. and Jayez, J. (1993). Towards a proper treatment of coercion phenomena. In *Sixth Conference of the European Chapter of the ACL*, pages 168–177, Utrecht.

Hobbs, J. R., Stickel, M. E., Appelt, D. E., and Martin, P. (1993). Interpretation as abduction. *Artificial Intelligence*, 63:69–142.

Lascarides, A. and Asher, N. (1991). Discourse relations and defeasible knowledge. In *Proceedings of the 29th Annual Meeting of the Association for Computational Linguistics (ACL-91)*, pages 55–63, Berkeley, California.

Lascarides, A. and Asher, N. (1993). Temporal interpretation, discourse relations and common sense entailment. *Linguistics and Philosophy*, 16(5):437–493.

Lascarides, A., Briscoe, E., Asher, N., and Copestake, A. (1996a). Persistent order independent typed default unification. *Linguistics and Philosophy*, 19(1).

Lascarides, A. and Copestake, A. (1995). The pragmatics of word meaning. In *Proceedings of Semantics and Linguistic Theory V*.

Lascarides, A., Copestake, A., and Briscoe, E. (1996b). Ambiguity and coherence. *Journal of Semantics*, 13(2).

Pustejovsky, J. (1991). The generative lexicon. *Computational Linguistics*, 17(4).

Pustejovsky, J. (1995). *The Generative Lexicon*. MIT Press, Cambridge, MA.

Pustejovsky, J. and Bouillon, P. (1995). Aspectual coercion and logical polysemy. *Journal of Semantics*, 12(2):133–162.

Verspoor, C. M. (1996). Conventionality-governed logical metonymy. Unpublished ms.

Dynamics of Rule Induction by Making Queries: Transition Between Strategies

Iris Ginzburg
Terrence J. Sejnowski
Howard Hughes Medical Institute
The Salk Institute
10010 N. Torrey Pines Rd.
La Jolla, CA 92037
e-mail: iris@salk.edu

Abstract

The induction of rules by making queries is a dynamical process based on seeking information. Experimenters typically look for one dominant strategy that is used by subjects, which may or may not agree with normative models of this psychological process. In this study we approach this problem from a different perspective, related to work in learning theory (see for example Baum 1991, Freund et al. 1995). Using information theory in a Bayesian framework, we estimated the information gained by queries when the task is to find a specific rule in a hypothesis space. Assuming that at each point subjects have a preferred working hypothesis, we considered several possible strategies, and determined the best one so that information gain is maximized at each step. We found that when the confidence in the preferred hypothesis is weak, "Confirmation Queries" result in maximum information gain; the information gained by "Investigation Queries" is higher when the confidence in the preferred hypothesis is high. Considering the dynamical process of searching for the rule, starting with low confidence in the preferred hypothesis and gradually raising confidence, there should be a transition from the "Confirmation Strategy" to the "Investigative Strategy", as the search proceeds. If we assume that subjects update their beliefs regarding the task, while performing, we would expect that the "Positive Confirmation Strategy" would yield more information at low confidence levels while the "Negative Confirmation Strategy" (simple elimination) would be more informative at higher confidence levels.

We tested subjects performance in such a task, using a paradigm introduced by Wason (1960). All subjects first assumed a hypothesis and then made positive confirmation queries. Upon receiving confirmation, half the subjects presented negative confirmation queries and later, half switched into investigative queries before attempting to guess the experimenter's rule. Also, the frequency of queries in the more 'advanced' strategies went down as the confidence level required to evoke the strategy went up. We conclude that subjects appear to be using different strategies at different stages of the search, which is theoretically optimal when queries are guided by a paradigm that maximizes information gain at each step.

Introduction

Investigating the induction of rules by making queries is an active area of research. One of the pioneering studies in this field was by Wason (1960) who presented subjects with a rule induction task and found that subjects tended to make queries that conformmed to the rule they have in mind, counter to the 'normative' approach suggesting that subjects should try to disprove their hypotheses. More recent studies (Klayman & Ha, 1987), (Oaksford & Chater, 1994) suggested that under some conditions it may be better to use a confirmation strategy rather than the disproving one.

In general, the information gained at each step of the search depends on the hypothesis space in which the search is conducted and on the apriori beliefs regarding the probability for each hypothesis in this space to be the target hypothesis. An additional factor is how the beliefs are updated given new information. In this study, we present a theoretical framework for a search in a large hypothesis space and study the information gained by several search strategies. Although the space is large, we study strategies that consider explicitly a small number of working hypotheses, while making very general assumptions regarding the rest of the space.

We predict that different strategies will be adopted at different stages of the search, as the confidence in the working hypotheses increases. We compare our theoretical results with behavior of subjects in a modified experiment along the lines of the 'triples guessing game' suggested by Wason (1960).

Theory

Here we present and analyze a theoretical model for the rule induction problem. We suggest an optimal behavior based on maximization of the information gained by individual queries. We define four types of queries and find under which conditions it is best to use which strategy. We begin with definitions. The search is conducted in a hypothesis space $\{H\}$ which we assume contains N independent hypotheses. Each hypothesis, h_n, defines a unique subsets over a data space $\{D\}$. Each hypothesis can be represented by a binary function which has value 1 at data points that lie within the specific subset, and value 0 at other data points in $\{D\}$. One of the hypotheses, h_t, is chosen to be the target hypothesis which an 'optimal seeker' needs to find by making queries. With each query, the seeker chooses a point d

121

in $\{D\}$ and is then informed whether this data point belongs to the target subspace or not. At each point in the search, the knowledge that the seeker has about the solution is represented by assigning each one of the hypotheses a probability that it is the target hypothesis, $p[h_n] \equiv p[h_n = h_t]$. The result is a probability distribution over the hypothesis space which reflects the knowledge or uncertainty of the seeker. The entropy S of the probability distribution over the hypotheses space is a measure of uncertainty:

$$S(P) = -\sum_{n=1}^{N} p[h_n] \log (p[h_n]) \qquad (1)$$

where P is the probability distribution $P \equiv \{p(h_n)\}$. The entropy increases with the uncertainty, which can be easily demonstrated by two extreme cases: (a) When the target hypothesis is known and there is no uncertainty, $p[h_t] = 1$ and all other probabilities are 0. It is easy to see that in this case the entropy is 0. (b) When the uncertainty is at its maximum, all hypotheses are equiprobable, $p[h_n] = 1/N$. The corresponding entropy is $\log(N)$, which is the maximum value the entropy can have in this case. Normally, there is some knowledge regarding the probability distribution and the entropy will have intermediate values. Prior to choosing a query d, there is a prior probability distribution over the hypotheses space, $P^o \equiv \{p^o[h_n]\}$ with a corresponding entropy $S(P^o)$ as defined by (1). Upon receiving the information $h_t(d)$, the seeker updates the probabilities and the result is a set of posterior probabilities $P^p \equiv \{p^p[h_n]\}$. Basically, any hypothesis h_n such that $h_n(d) \neq h_t(d)$ is ruled out, i.e. $p^p[h_{n'}] = 0$. We assume that the probabilities of the remaining (surviving) hypotheses, are updated according to Bayes rule. The uncertainty changes to $S(P^p)$. This change depends on the value that will be obtained in reply to the query, which is not known in advance. Thus, the expected uncertainty after making the query is given by the expected entropy

$$ES(P^p) = p[h_t(d) = 1]S(P^p|h_t(d) = 1) \\ + p[h_t(d) = 0]S(P^p|h_t(d) = 0) \qquad (2)$$

The difference between the prior entropy and the posterior expected entropy is the information gained by the query:

$$EIG = S(P^o) - ES(P^p) \qquad (3)$$

The posterior probabilities may be updated using different rules, but in this study we choose to update the beliefs using Bayes' rule. Therefore,

$$p^p[h_n|h_t(d)] = \frac{p[h_t(d)|h_n]p[h_n]}{p[h_t(d)]} \qquad (4)$$

where $h_t(d)$ can be equal to 1 or 0. Under these conditions it is easy to see that the expected information gain is equal to the entropy of the information source $h_t(d)$, since the hypotheses are deterministic functions over the data set $\{D\}$:

$$EIG = -p[h_t(d) = 1] \log (p[h_t(d) = 1]) \\ -p[h_t(d) = 0] \log (p[h_t(d) = 0]). \qquad (5)$$

In order to compute the expected information gained by any query, one needs to estimate the prior probability of the possible values of $h_t(d)$ and the best strategy would be to choose queries that are expected to yield 0 or 1 with probability of 0.5. In other words choosing the query that is least predictable will yield the maximal information gain. In order to do so, however, one needs to know the values of many hypotheses at each data point, an ability that requires a large memory capacity when dealing with a large space, see (Freund et al. 1995). Since humans have a limited capacity for working memory, the strategies used by subjects will probably not be optimal, leading perhaps to the use of more than one strategy at different times, in a way that approximates the optimal strategy.

We now apply this for the special case of rule induction. One of the main limiting factors is the memory capacity, which translates in this case to the number of hypotheses subjects can consider simultaneously. We consider strategies that involve a small number of explicit working hypotheses; other hypotheses are considered implicitly by assuming that there is some average probability for a 'random' hypothesis to have a value 1 at any specific data point

$$r = p[h_n(d) = 1]. \qquad (6)$$

This is equivalent to assuming that there is a typical size of the subsets corresponding to the hypotheses in the space. We define four different strategies, but our analysis could be easily expanded to more.

The first two types of strategies are the "Confirmation Strategies", which can be positive or negative. When subjects have one working hypothesis, and do not consider any alternatives, they can make two types of queries. The "Positive Confirmation Strategy" (PCS) queries are those data points that conform to the working hypothesis, in other words: theses are the 'classical' confirmation queries (see [Wason 1960]). The "Negative Confirmation Strategy" (NCS) queries are those which yield a negative reply with respect to the working hypothesis. In both cases, subjects consider only THE WORKing hypothesis, and no alternative hypotheses, as a guide to the queries that they make.

Let h_w be the working hypothesis, then this implies that

$$p^o[h_w = h_t] > p^o[h_n = h_t], \qquad n \neq w. \qquad (7)$$

Since we assume that all other hypotheses are equiprobable, the probability of all other hypotheses is

$$p_n = (1 - p_w)/(N - 1), \qquad n \neq w \qquad (8)$$

There are two possible types of queries: the Positive Confirmation query, with a data point d_{pc} for which $h_w(d_{pc}) = 1$ and the Negative Confirmation query, with a point d_{nc} for which $h_w(d_{pc}) = 0$. When choosing a Positive Confirmation query, d_{pc}, we can estimate the prior probability $p[h_t(d_{pc}) = 1]$. If the working hypothesis is correct, $h_w = h_t$, the reply will be 1. There is also a fraction r of the hypotheses for which $h_{n'}(d_{pc}) = 1$ defined in (6). The probability that the reply will be 1 is:

$$p[h_t(d_{pc}) = 1] = p_w + (1 - p_w)r \qquad (9)$$

A similar analysis holds for the negative confirmation query, for which

$$p[h_t(d_{nc}) = 0] = (1 - p_w)r \qquad (10)$$

Two other types of strategies considered here are "Investigative Strategies" in which the seeker considers a working hypothesis and an alternative hypothesis simultaneously. Any query which conforms to one hypothesis but does not conform to the other, will enable the subject to rule out one of these hypotheses. We define the "Positive Investigation Strategy" (PIS) when a query conforms to the working hypothesis and does not conform to he alternative hypothesis. Similarly, define the "Negative Investigation Strategy" (NIS) when a query conforms to the alternative hypothesis and does not conform to the working hypothesis. Note that the only difference between the Confirmation Strategies and the Investigative Strategies is the existance of an alternative hypothesis.

Formally, we define the alternative hypothesis, h_a, as the hypothesis which is less favorable than h_w but is preferable to other hypotheses in the space.

$$p^o[h_w] > p^o[h_a] > p^o[h_n] \qquad n \neq w, a. \qquad (11)$$

The Positive Investigation query d_{pi} is defined by $h_w(d_{pi}) = 1, h_a(d_{pi}) = 0$. The probability that the reply will be 1 is:

$$p[h_t(d_{pi}) = 1] = (1 - p_w - p_a)r + p_w \qquad (12)$$

The Negative Investigation is similar to the Positive Investigation only it has the opposite values with respect to h_w and h_a and the probability that the reply will be 1 is:

$$p[h_t(d_{ni}) = 1] = (1 - p_w - p_a)r + p_a \qquad (13)$$

One can generalize our analysis to the case where there is more than one alternative; the results do not change significantly.

In summary, the strategies are defined by two criteria: First, how many favorable hypotheses are being considered simultaneously? A working hypothesis is always considered, but subjects may or may not consider an alternative hypothesis. Secondly, Is the favorable hypotheses positive or negative at the query point?

The factor that determines the informativeness of the query is the predictability of the reply, which we can estimate for each strategy. The average information gained by the different queries, using eqs. (3) & (5) is:

$$\begin{aligned} EIG &= p[h_t(d) = 1] \log(p[h_t(d) = 1]) \\ &\quad + (1 - p[h_t(d) = 1]) \log(1 - p[h_t(d) = 1]) \end{aligned} \qquad (14)$$

where $p[h_t(d) = 1]$ is the probability of the reply to query d to be 1, and the closer $p[h_t(d) = 1]$ is to 0.5, the more informative the query is. We summarize the results in the following table:

Query Type	Data Point	$p[h_t(d) = 1]$
Pos. Conf.	$d = d_{pc}$	$(1 - p_w)r + p_w$
Neg. Conf.	$d = d_{nc}$	$(1 - p_w)r$
Pos. Inv.	$d = d_{pi}$	$(1 - p_w - p_a)r + p_w$
Neg. Inv.	$d = d_{ni}$	$(1 - p_w - p_a)r + p_a$

Table 1. Predictability of queries: probability of reply equals 1.

These conditions lead to a number of predictions, assuming that the optimal strategy is adopted. Regardless of what r is, the confirmation strategies are always preferable to the investigative strategies at low condifence $p_w < 0.5 + p_a r/2$ and the other way around when the confidence is high. Up to this critical value, $|p[h_t(d_{pc,nc}) = 1] - 0.5| < |p[h_t(d_{pi,ni}) = 1] - 0.5|$, and then the relation is reversed. From a similar comparison of the positive and negative confirmation strategies, when $r < 0.5$ the positive confirmation is always better than the negative confirmation and when $r > 0.5$ the negative confirmation is preferable to the positive confirmation. Although we have no direct measure of the subjective value of r using the current experimental paradigm, we assume that subjects update their subjective estimate of r along the search, from a low value at the start to a higher value after receiving frequent replies of 1, due to the specific design of the Wason test. In summary, we predict:

- Different strategies will be used by subjects according to the following order: positive confirmation, negative confirmation and last, investigation

- The later strategies, corresponding to higher confidence levels, will be less frequent since subjects guess the rule at different subjective confidence levels,

- Confirmation strategies should be correlated with low confidence, and investigative strategies with high confidence.

Experimental Paradigm

Subjects were asked to discover a mathematical rule that applies to triples of numbers by writing down sets of three numbers along with the reasons for the choice. They were also asked to write down their best guess of the unknown rule at this point and their confidence that this may be the correct rule. In addition, they were asked to note their prediction of what will be the experimenter's reply and their confidence in their best guess as well as the predicted reply. The confidence was rated as Low, Medium, High or Very High. Subjects were given one confirming example to begin the process, and all replies were kept on a form (Figure 1). Subjects were given only one chance to explicitly guess the rule, after which the process terminated. We analyzed the data according to the definitions of the strategies given in Table 1. which are demonstrated in Figure 2. We assumed that the best guess at each point was the working hypothesis of subjects.

Results

We analyzed data from 20 subjects, generating a total of 99 queries. We considered the best guess to be the working hypothesis.

Confidence levels were transformed to numbers between 1-4. The most frequent strategy was the positive confirmation: 19/20 subjects used it at some point. The secondary most frequent was the negative confirmation: 10/20 subjects used it. The least frequently used is the investigation strategy: 5/20. This perfectly matched our theoretical predictions, although other explanations can be given for the same data. Since the Investigative strategies were much rarely used, we pooled data from the Positive and Negative Investigation queries together.

We consider each query to be an independent event. The confidence level was found to be correlated with the different types of strategies that are used (Figure 3). However, the two confirmation strategies were not significantly different, probably due to a small sample size. The investigative strategies were found to be used at significantly higher confidence levels with $p < 0.05$.

A similar analysis was performed for the ordering of the different strategies. Each query was given an ordering label within each subject's game, according to its sequential numbering normalized by the number of queries asked by each individual. That is, each query received a label between 0 and 1. There is a correlation between the type of strategy and the ordering (Figure 4). The Positive Confirmation strategy which is more commonly used in the beginning of the game, was found significantly different from the Negative Confirmation which is used at more advanced sequencing, with $p < 0.06$. The investigative strategy was found to be used at higher sequencing, and is significantly distinct from the Confirmation strategies with $p < 0.05$.

It was interesting that 16/20 subjects started their guesses by a positive confirmation query to which they expected a negative reply. This suggests that subjects initially expect that the probability of a random query to yield a positive reply is low, in accordance with our assumption that $r \ll 0.5$. 2/8 subjects who found the correct rule used only positive confirmation queries. These subjects performed a series of spontaneous changes in their working hypothesis.

Summary

We have presented a theoretical analysis of information search in a large hypothesis space. We have shown that subjects used different search strategies at different stages of the search, in a way that was correlated with confidence in their working hypothesis. The confidence level appears as a significant parameter in theoretically determining the best search strategy, as well as in predicting the behavior of subjects.

An important factor in our analysis is the assumption that subjects updated their subjective beliefs regarding the reply to a random query, a direction we intend to explore in the future.

In addition, one can easily show, using the paradigm we have presented, that as the hypothesis space becomes larger, it is less valuable to consider alternative hypotheses. Evidence for this notion was found by (Van Wallendaeland and Hastie, 1990) who showed that when the number of possible alternative hypotheses was large, subjects tended to update their beliefs regarding one working hypothesis only. As the space size was reduced (in that study the space is quite small), subjects began to update their belief in more than one hypothesis.

In our theoretical analysis we assumed that the subjects updated their beliefs about the likelihood of receiving positive (or negative) answers during the task, which is equivalent to the presumed size of the target subset. This correlates with the anchoring effect (Kahneman and Tversky, 1974): information that is explicitly not relevant to the task subjects are required to perform still affects the behavior of subjects.

Acknowldgments

I.G. is grateful to W. Bialek for motivating this study and to C. McKenzie for interesting and helpful discussions.

References

Baum E. (1991). Neural net algorithms that learn in polynomial time from examples and queries. IEEE Trans. Neural Networks, 2:5-19.

Freund Y., Seung H.S., Shamir E. and Tishby N. (1995). Information, prediction, and query by committee. preprint.

Kahneman D. and Tversky A. (1974). Judgment under uncertainty: Heuristics and biases. Science, V185:1124-1131.

Klayman J. and Ha Y-W. (1987). Confirmation, disconfirmation, and information in hypothesis testing. Psychological Review, V94. No 2.211-228.

Oaksford M. and Chater N. (1994). A rational analysis of the selection task as optimal data selection. Psychological Review, V101 (n4):608-631.

Van Wallendaeland L. R. and Hastie R. (1990). Tracing the footsteps of Sherlock Holmes: Cognitive representations of hypothesis testing. Memory & Cognition, V18 (n3):240-250.

Wason P.C. (1960). On the failure to eliminate hypotheses in a conceptual task. Quarterly Journal of Experimental Psychology, V12 129-140.

Three Numbers	Predicted Reply	Confidence in reply: L, M, H, V	Reasons for Choice	Best guess of rule at this point	Confidence in best guess: L, M, H, V	REPLY
example: 2, 4, 6						YES

Figure 1: The form used in the experiment.

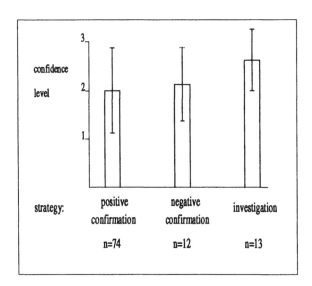

Figure 3: Correlation between strategy and confidence level. n is the number of queries that correspond to each strategy. The error bars represent the standard deviation of the distributions and not the deviations of the means.

Query Type	Three Numbers	Reasons for Choice	Best guess of Rule at this point
1. Positive Confirmation	6, 8, 10	confirm	even numbers increasing by 2
2. Negative Confirmation	1, 3, 5	test	even numbers increasing by 2
3. Positive Investigation	8, 10, 12	rule out possbility that numbers are multiples of the first number	even numbers increasing by 2
4. Negative Investigation	2, 6, 10	perhaps all triples of increasing evens	even numbers increasing by 2

Figure 2: Definition of four different types of queries.

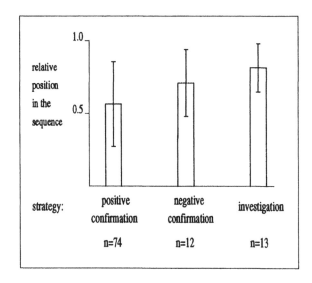

Figure 4: Order of strategies. n is the number of queries that correspond to each strategy. The error bars represent the standard deviation of the distributions and not the deviations of the means.

The Impact of Information Representation on Bayesian Reasoning

Ulrich Hoffrage and **Gerd Gigerenzer**
Center for Adaptive Behavior and Cognition
Max Planck Institute for Psychological Research
Leopoldstrasse 24, 80802 Munich, Germany.
{hoffrage,gigerenzer}@mpipf-muenchen.mpg.de

Abstract

Previous research on Bayesian inference, reporting poor performance by students and experts alike, has often led to the conclusion that the mind lacks the appropriate cognitive algorithm. We argue that this conclusion is unjustified because it does not take into account the information format in which this cognitive algorithm is designed to operate. We demonstrate that a Bayesian algorithm is computationally simpler when the information is represented in a frequency rather than a probability format that has been used in previous research. A frequency format corresponds to the way information is acquired in natural sampling--sequentially and without constraints on which observations will be included in the sample. Based on the assumption that performance will reflect computational complexity, we predict that a frequency format yields more Bayesian solutions than a probability format. We tested this prediction in a study conducted with 48 physicians. Using outcome and process analysis, we categorized their individual solutions as Bayesian or non-Bayesian. When information was presented in the frequency format, 46% of their inferences were obtained by a Bayesian algorithm, as compared to only 10% when the problems were presented in the probability format. We discuss the impact of our results on teaching statistical reasoning.

Is the mind, by design, predisposed against performing Bayesian inference? The classical probabilists of the Enlightenment, including Condorcet, Poisson, and Laplace, who equated probability theory with the common sense of educated people, would have said the answer is no. And when Ward Edwards and his colleagues (Edwards, 1968) started to test experimentally whether human inference follows Bayes' theorem, they gave the same answer: although "conservative," inferences were usually proportional to those calculated from Bayes' theorem. Kahneman and Tversky (1972, p. 450), however, arrived at the opposite conclusion: "In his evaluation of evidence, man is apparently not a conservative Bayesian: he is not a Bayesian at all." In the 1970s and '80s, proponents of their "heuristics-and-biases" program amassed an apparently damning body of evidence that people systematically neglect base rates in Bayesian inference problems. This could be shown not only with students, but also with experts in their fields, for instance, with physicians (Casscells, Schoenberger, & Grayboys, 1978; Eddy, 1982).

Thus, there are two contradictory claims as to whether people naturally reason according to Bayesian inference. In this paper we argue that both views are based on an incomplete analysis: They focus on cognitive processes, Bayesian or otherwise, without making the connection between what we will call a cognitive algorithm and an information format. We (a) provide a theoretical framework (based on Gigerenzer and Hoffrage, 1995) that specifies why a frequency format should improve Bayesian reasoning and (b) present a study that tests this hypothesis.

Algorithms Are Designed for Information Formats

Our argument centers on the intimate relationship between a cognitive algorithm and an information format. This point was made in a more general form by the physicist Richard Feynman. In his classic The Character of Physical Law (1967), Feynman places great emphasis on the importance of deriving different formulations for the same physical law, even if they are mathematically equivalent (e.g., Newton's law, the local field method, and the minimum principle). Different representations of a physical law, Feynman reminds us, can evoke varied mental pictures and thus assist in making new discoveries: "Psychologically they are different because they are completely unequivalent when you are trying to guess new laws" (p. 53). Likewise, Stephen Palmer (1978) points out in his analysis of different modes of representation "that no form of representational equivalence guarantees that performance characteristics will be the same for two representations embedded in process models" (p. 272).

Consider numerical information as one example of an external representation. Numbers can be represented in Roman, Arabic, and binary systems, among others. These representations can be mapped one-to-one onto each other and are in this sense mathematically equivalent. But the form of representation can make a difference for an algorithm that does, say, multiplication. The algorithms of our pocket calculators, for instance, are tuned to Arabic numbers as input data and would fail badly if one entered binary numbers.

Our general argument is that mathematically equivalent representations of information entail algorithms that are not necessarily computationally equivalent. This point has an important corollary for research on inductive reasoning. Suppose we are interested in figuring out what algorithm a system uses. We will not detect the algorithm if the representation of information we provide the system does not match the representation with which the algorithm works. For instance, assume that in an effort to find out whether a system, such as a pocket calculator, has an algorithm for multiplication, we feed that system binary numerals. The observation that the system produces mostly garbage does not entail the conclusion that it lacks an algorithm for multiplication. We will now apply this argument to Bayesian inference.

Probability Format

In this paper we focus on an elementary form of Bayesian inference that has been the subject of almost all experimental studies on Bayesian inference in the last 25 years. The following "mammography problem" (adapted from Eddy, 1982) is one example:

Mammography problem (probability format)
The probability of breast cancer is 1% for a woman at age forty who participates in routine screening. If a woman has breast cancer, the probability is 80% that she will have a positive mammography. If a woman does not have breast cancer, the probability is 10% that she will also have a positive mammography.
A woman in this age group had a positive mammography in a routine screening. What is the probability that she actually has breast cancer? _____%

There are two mutually exclusive and exhaustive hypotheses (H: breast cancer and –H: no breast cancer) and one observation (D: positive test). All information (base rate, hit rate, and false alarm rate) is represented in terms of single-event probabilities attached to a single person. (Here, they are expressed as percentages; alternatively, they can be presented as numbers between zero and one.) The task is to estimate a single-event probability. The algorithm needed to calculate the Bayesian posterior probability p(cancer|positive) from this format can be seen in Figure 1 (left side), where the information is already inserted into Bayes' rule. The result is .075.

We know from several studies that physicians, college students (Eddy, 1982), and staff at Harvard Medical School (Casscells, Schoenberger, & Grayboys, 1978) all have equally great difficulties with this and similar medical disease problems. For instance, Eddy (1982) reported that 95 out of 100 physicians estimated the posterior probability to be between 70% and 80%, rather than 7.5%.

In the last few decades, this probability format has become a common way to communicate information, found everywhere from medical and statistical textbooks to psychological experiments. Not surprisingly, the experimenters who have amassed the evidence that humans fail to meet the norms of Bayesian inference have usually given their subjects information in the probability format (or its variant, in which one or more of the three percentages are relative frequencies). But it is only one of many mathematically equivalent ways of representing information. It is, moreover, a recently invented notation: Percentages became common notation only during the 19th century. How did organisms acquire information before that time?

Probability Format   Frequency Format

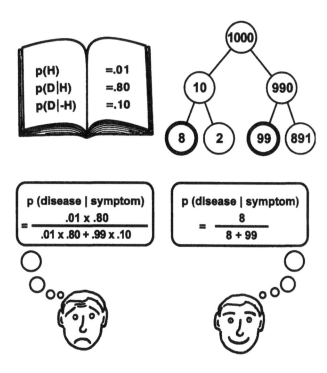

Figure 1: Bayesian inference and information representation (probability format and frequency format with frequencies as obtained by natural sampling).

Natural Sampling of Frequencies

We assume that as humans evolved, the "natural" format was frequency as actually experienced in a series of events, rather than probability or percentage. From animals to neural networks, systems seem to learn about contingencies through sequential encoding and updating of event frequencies. This sequential acquisition of information by updating event frequencies without artificially fixing the marginal frequencies (e.g., of disease and no-disease cases) is what we refer to as natural sampling (Kleiter, 1994). Brunswik's "representative design" is a special case of natural sampling (Brunswik, 1955). In contrast, in experimental research the marginal frequencies are typically fixed a priori. For instance, an experimenter may want to investigate 100 people with disease and a control group of 100 people without disease. This kind of sampling with fixed marginal frequencies is not what we refer to as natural sampling.

The evolutionary argument that cognitive algorithms were designed for frequency information, acquired through natural sampling, has implications for the computations an organism needs to perform when making Bayesian inferences. Imagine an old, experienced physician in an illiterate society. She has no books or statistical surveys and therefore must rely solely on her experience. Her people have been afflicted by a previously unknown and severe disease. Fortunately, the physician has discovered a symptom that signals the disease, although not with certainty. In her lifetime she has seen 1,000 people, 10 of whom had the disease. Of those 10, 8 showed the symptom; of the 990 not afflicted, 95 did. Now a new patient appears. He has the symptom. What is the probability that he actually has the disease?

The physician in the illiterate society does not need a pocket calculator to estimate the Bayesian posterior. All she needs is the number of cases that had both the symptom and the disease (here: 8) and the number of symptom cases (here: 8 + 95). The Bayesian algorithm for computing the posterior probability from the frequency format can be seen in Figure 1 (right side). The physician does not need to keep track of the base rate of the disease. Her modern counterpart, the medical student who struggles with single-event probabilities presented in medical textbooks, may on the other hand have to rely on a calculator and end up with little understanding of the result.

So far, we have seen that Bayesian algorithms are computationally simpler when information is encoded in a frequency format rather than a probability format. By "computationally simpler" we mean that (a) fewer operations (multiplication, addition, or division) need to be performed in the frequency format, and (b) the operations can be performed on natural numbers (absolute frequencies) rather than fractions (such as percentages). From this observation, we derive the prediction that a frequency format elicits a substantially higher proportion of Bayesian algorithms than a probability format. Henceforth, when we use the term "frequency format," we always refer to frequencies as defined by the natural sampling tree in Figure 1.

Study: Frequency Formats Improve Bayesian Reasoning

In a study previously conducted with 60 subjects from the University of Salzburg, Austria (see Gigerenzer & Hoffrage, 1995, Study 1), we demonstrated that the frequency format elicited a substantially higher proportion of Bayesian algorithms than the probability format. In 15 different inferential problems, including the mammography problem, Bayesian reasoning went up from 16% in the probability format to 46% and 50% in two versions of the frequency format. No instruction or feedback was given; the information format by itself improved Bayesian reasoning. Similar results were obtained by Christensen-Szalanski and Beach (1982) and Cosmides and Tooby (1996). Now, remember that both Casscells et al. (1978) and Eddy (1982) reported poor performances from the physicians they investigated. Because Bayesian reasoning is of great importance in medicine, the goal of the current study was to see whether not only students but also physicians could gain from a frequentistic representation of the information. One might suspect that this method only works with students who lack experience in diagnostic inference, but not with physicians who make diagnostic inferences every day. On the other hand, medical textbooks typically present

information about base rates, hit rates, and false alarm rates in a probability format (as in Figure 1, left side). Just as a pocket calculator is unable to process binary numerals adequately, physicians may be unable to process statistical information if it is presented in a format for which their minds were not designed.

Method

Participants. We investigated 48 Munich physicians, 18 from university hospitals, 16 from private or public hospitals, and 14 from private practice. Mean age was 42 years and mean time of professional service was 14 years with a range of one month to 30 years (our sample included beginners as well as directors of clinics). They were studied individually.

Materials. We used four medical problems, including the mammography problem adapted from Eddy (1982). The other three problems concerned (1) colon cancer and positive haemoccult blood test, (2) Bechterew's disease and HL-Antigen B27, and (3) Phenylketonuria and positive Guthrie-test as disease and symptom, respectively. We consulted experts and the literature to determine the best statistical information available for the base rates, hit rates, and false alarm rates.

Design and Procedure. For each problem we constructed two versions: one in the probability format and one in the frequency format. Participants received a booklet containing all four problems, two of them in probability format and two in frequency format. Assignment of problems to formats, as well as order of formats and problems were completely counterbalanced.

The physicians worked on the booklet at their own pace (on average 7 minutes per problem). Each problem was on one sheet, followed by a separate sheet where the physicians were asked to make notes, calculations, or drawings. After filling out the booklet they were interviewed about their mental processes.

Results

We classified an inferential process as a Bayesian algorithm only if (a) the estimated probability or frequency was the same as the value calculated from applying Bayes' theorem to the information given (outcome criterion), and the notes the physicians made while solving the problems and/or the follow-up interviews suggested that the answer was not just a guess but a Bayesian computation as defined by the equations in Figure 1 (process criterion), or if (b) the solution was obtained by a shortcut algorithm that still provided the correct answer plus or minus 5 percentage points.

The results confirmed our prediction: Across all 96 individual problem solutions for the probability format (48 physicians times two problems), 10% were correct, whereas for the frequency format, 46% were correct ($t_{df=190}=5.5$, $p<0.001$). Figure 2 shows the absolute frequencies of Bayesian solutions for the four problems.

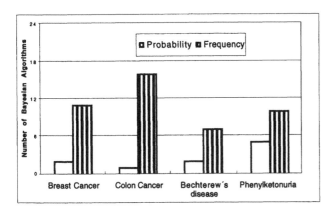

Figure 2: Number of Bayesian algorithms in the four problems. (Maximum number possible: 24.)

This difference in performance is reflected in the remarks the physicians made while working on the problems. For instance, when working on probability-format problems, several made complaints such as "I simply can't do that. Mathematics is not my forte," or "There is a formula, but at the moment I can't derive it." However, with a frequency format, some typical remarks were, "Now it's different. It's quite easy to imagine. There is a frequency; that's more visual," or "Oh, how nice--this is just like the word problems we did in elementary school. A first grader could do this. Wow, if someone can't solve this...!" Like the Bayesian algorithms, the non-Bayesian algorithms were also format-specific: In 18 (5) out of the 96 probability (frequency) versions, our physicians gave the hit rate, $p(D|H)$, as the posterior. For the algorithm that we termed likelihood subtraction, $p(D|H) - p(D|-H)$, the corresponding numbers were 20 (5) out of 96. Two of the algorithms that were dominant in the frequency format were base rate only, $p(H)$, which was applied in 1 (15) out of 96 cases in the probability (frequency) format, and percentage positive, $p(D)$, where frequency of use was 0 (9) out of 96, respectively. (Less frequent algorithms are not reported here). For 28 (12) out of the 96 problem solutions in the probability (frequency) version we were unable to identify any algorithm at all.

The physicians spent about 25% more time on the probability problems, which reflects that they found these more difficult to solve. Many of them reacted -- cognitively, emotionally, and physiologically -- differently to probability and frequency formats. They were more often nervous when information was presented in probabilities, and they were less skeptical of the relevance of statistical information to medical diagnosis when the information was in frequencies. Bayesian responses were age correlated: The older half of the physicians (more than 40 years old) contributed only 37% of the Bayesian solutions, the younger half 63%.

Discussion

We return to our initial question: Is the mind, by design, predisposed against performing Bayesian inference? The conclusion of 25 years of heuristics-and-biases research would suggest as much. This previous research, however, has consistently neglected the insight that mathematically equivalent information formats need not be psychologically equivalent. An evolutionary point of view suggests that the mind is tuned to a frequency format, which is the information format humans encountered long before the advent of probability theory. We have shown that mathematically equivalent representations of information can entail computationally different Bayesian algorithms and we reported a study conducted with physicians that demonstrated how performance can be improved by presenting the information in the frequency rather than the probability format.

This striking result can be useful for teaching statistical reasoning--a field that is still neglected, not only in high school mathematics education but often in research as well. Up until now, only a few studies have attempted to teach Bayesian inference, mainly by outcome feedback, and with little or no success. The present framework suggests an effective way to teach Bayesian inference and statistical reasoning in general: Instead of teaching rules and how to insert probabilities into them, it seems to be more promising to teach representations and how to translate probabilities into frequency representations. Sedlmeier and Gigerenzer (1996) implemented both methods in a computerized tutorial system. And indeed they could show that teaching representations yielded performances more than twice as good as those obtained by rule training. Moreover, the advantage remained stable 5 weeks after training, whereas the effect of the rule-learning program had shown the usual rapid decay.

However, besides teaching statistical reasoning, there is a much more direct impact of our results. Physicians are often reported to become uneasy or even angry when asked for statistical information (Eddy, 1988), and to believe that their patients do not understand, or do not want to understand, the uncertainties inherent in diagnosis and therapy (Katz, 1988). We imagine that a frequency format might help improve the communication between patients and physicians (Bursztajn et al., 1981) and provide a tool for helping the patient to become a more apt decision maker.

Acknowledgments

This work was supported by the Deutsche Forschungsgemeinschaft (Ho 1847/1-1). We thank Maria Zumbeel for collecting the data and Anita Todd for editing the manuscript.

References

Brunswik, E. (1955). Representative design and probabilistic theory in a functional psychology. Psychological Review, 62, 193-217.

Bursztajn, H., Feinbloom, R. I., Hamm, R. H., & Brodsky, A. (1981). Medical choices, medical chances. How patients, families, and physicians can cope with uncertainty. New York: Delta.

Casscells, W., Schoenberger, A., & Grayboys, T. (1978). Interpretation by physicians of clinical laboratory results. New England Journal of Medicine, 299, 999-1000.

Christensen-Szalanski, J. J. J., & Beach, L. R. (1982). Experience and the base-rate fallacy. <u>Organizational Behavior and Human Performance, 29</u>, 270-278.

Cosmides, L., & Tooby, J. (1996). Are humans good intuitive statisticians after all? Rethinking some conclusions from the literature on judgment under uncertainty. <u>Cognition, 58</u>, 1-73.

Eddy, D. M. (1982). Probabilistic reasoning in clinical medicine: Problems and opportunities. In D. Kahneman, P. Slovic, & A. Tversky (Eds.), <u>Judgment under uncertainty: Heuristics and biases</u> (pp. 249-267). Cambridge: Cambridge University Press.

Eddy, D. M. (1988). Variations in physician practice: the role of uncertainty. In J. Dowie & A. S. Elstein (Eds.), <u>Professional judgment. A reader in clinical decision making</u> (pp. 45-59). Cambridge: Cambridge University Press.

Edwards, W. (1968). Conservatism in human information processing. In B. Kleinmuntz (Ed.), <u>Formal representation of human judgment</u> (pp. 17-52). New York: Wiley.

Feynman, R. (1967). <u>The character of physical law</u>. Cambridge, MA: MIT Press.

Gigerenzer, G., & Hoffrage, U. (1995). How to improve Bayesian reasoning without instruction: Frequency formats. <u>Psychological Review, 102</u>, 684-704.

Kahneman, D., & Tversky, A. (1972). Subjective probability: A judgment of representativeness. <u>Cognitive Psychology, 3</u>, 430-454.

Katz, J. (1988). Why doctors don't disclose uncertainty. In J. Dowie & A. S. Elstein (Eds.), <u>Professional judgment. A reader in clinical decision making</u> (pp. 544-565). Cambridge: Cambridge University Press.

Kleiter, G. D. (1994). Natural sampling: Rationality without base rates. In G. H. Fischer & D. Laming (Eds.), <u>Contributions to mathematical psychology, psychometrics, and methodology</u> (pp. 375-388). New York: Springer.

Palmer, S. E. (1978). Fundamental aspects of cognitive representation. In E. Rosch & B. B. Lloyd (Eds.), <u>Cognition and Categorization</u> (pp. 262-303). New York: Lawrence Erlbaum.

Sedlmeier, P., & Gigerenzer, G. (1996). <u>Teaching Bayesian reasoning in less than two hours.</u> Manuscript submitted for publication.

On Reasoning with Default Rules and Exceptions

Renée Elio
Department of Computing Science
University of Alberta
Edmonton, Alberta T6G 2H1
ree@cs.ualberta.ca

Francis Jeffry Pelletier
Departments of Philosophy and Computing Science
University of Alberta
Edmonton, Alberta T6G 2H1
jeffp@cs.ualberta.ca

Abstract

We report empirical results on factors that influence how people reason with default rules of the form "Most x's have property P", in scenarios that specify information about exceptions to these rules and in scenarios that specify default-rule inheritance. These factors include (a) whether the individual, to which the default rule might apply, is similar to a known exception, when that similarity may explain why the exception did not follow the default, and (b) whether the problem involves classes of naturally occurring kinds or classes of artifacts. We consider how these findings might be integrated into formal approaches to default reasoning and also consider the relation of this sort of qualitative default reasoning to statistical reasoning.

Introduction

Default reasoning occurs whenever the evidence available to the reasoner does not guarantee the truth of the conclusion being drawn; that is, does not deductively *force* the reasoner to draw the conclusion under consideration. For example, from the statements 'Most linguists speak more than three languages' and 'Kim is a linguist', one might draw the conclusion, by default, 'Kim speaks more than three languages'. Subsequent information may force the reasoner to withdraw that conclusion; default reasoning is also termed non-monotonic, because the sentences held true at time 1 may not be true at time 2. We will call "Most linguists speak more than three languages" a default rule.

If an artificial agent were to wait for the information necessary to draw an inference sanctioned by classical deductive logic, then no conclusion might ever be drawn. Much of what is considered to true in the world is true only most of the time: there are exceptions and sometimes interacting default assumptions that can lead to conflicting conclusions. A good deal of work has been done in the AI community at formalizing default reasoning, either through qualitative approaches using conditional logics (e.g., Delgrande, 1987), probabilistic approaches (e.g., Bacchus, 1991), or approaches that attempt to capture quantitative notions within a qualitative framework (Gefner, 1992; Pearl, 1989). In the last several years, there has been an increasing attention in the default-reasoning community given to formalizing the notions of relevance and irrelevance, i.e., what information would be (ir)relevant to deciding whether a default rule applies in a particular case (see Greiner & Subramanian, 1994). For example, these frameworks propose ways of assessing the (ir)relevance of Kim's membership in the class of "red-haired people" to the application of the three-languages default rule and similarly, of Kim's membership in the class of "graduates of University X"—about which there may be a conflicting default rule about language skills. In the latter case, default reasoning theories aim to identify general and consistent means of specifying which of possibly several conflicting default rules should apply to an individual.

Generally speaking, the knowledge of *other* exceptions to a default rule has not yet been a factor in whether a particular default rule applies in a given case. As we see below, information about known exceptions to a default rule are not "supposed to" influence the application of that rule in a particular case. The studies we report are a continuation of previous work (Elio & Pelletier, 1993) aimed at understanding how people reason with rules that have exceptions, and what factors influence people's application of those rules. How people reason with default rules and exceptions *per se* has not received much attention within the cognitive psychology community (see, however, Collins & Michalski, 1989). However, there are overlaps between the issues we investigate in this work and those that have been considered in the literatures on statistical and inductive reasoning by people. We highlight some of the relationships we see in the sections that follow.

Benchmark Problems on Default Reasoning

Table 1 presents the a subset of the problem types that we used in this study. These problems were taken from the so-called "Nonmonotonic Benchmark Problems" (Lifschitz, 1989). These benchmarks formalized types of non-monotonic reasoning and specified the answers generally accepted by AI researchers in the area and which any non-monotonic theory was supposed to validate. Put another way, these are the defined "correct answers" for problems that take this form, despite some acknowledged difficulties in deciding just what the correct answers should be (Touretsky, Horty, & Thomason, 1987). Elsewhere, we have argued that, unlike human performance on symbolic deductive logic problems, the kinds of default conclusions people draw actually defines phenomenon of interest to be achieved by artificial agents; and thus empirical data on

1	Blocks X and Y are heavy. Heavy blocks are normally on the table. X is not on the table		2	Blocks X and Y are heavy. Heavy blocks are normally on the table. X is not on the table. Y is red.	
	Q: Where is Block Y?	*A*: on table		*Q*: Where is Block Y?	*A*: on table
3	Blocks X and Y are heavy. Heavy blocks are normally on the table. Most heavy blocks are red. X is not on the table. Y is not red.		4	Blocks X and Y are heavy. Heavy blocks are normally on the table. Block X might be an exception to this rule.	
	Q: What color is Block X? *Q*: Where is Block Y?	*A*: red *A*: on table		*Q*: Where is Block Y?	*A*: on table

Table 1: Four default reasoning problems and benchmark answers

human default reasoning has an important role to play in validating default reasoning theories and in identifying principles by which default answers can be assessed (Pelletier & Elio, 1995). It is this rationale that motivates our interest in understanding factors that influence people's default conclusions on even these simple problems.

We call the four problems in Table 1 the "basic default reasoning problems." They concern two objects governed by one or more default rules. Additional information is given to indicate that one of the objects (at least) does not follow one of the default rules. We refer to this as the *exception object* (for that default rule) or *default violator*. The problems then ask for a conclusion about the remaining object. We refer to this as the *object-in-question*. It is apparent from the sanctioned benchmark answers for these problems that the existence of known default violator, or any additional information about the object-in-question (e.g., Problem 2 in Table 1), should have no bearing on a conclusion drawn about the object-in-question when using that rule.

Experiments on Basic Default Reasoning Problems

In previous studies on these sorts of problems (Elio & Pelletier, 1993), we reported evidence suggesting that people's plausible conclusions about defaults and exceptions are influenced by the apparent similarity between a given default violator and the object-in-question. We were naturally lead to wonder just what kind of similarity mattered to deciding whether or not some object follows a default rule or instead behaves like a known exception. Our conjecture was that the similarity to a default violator may be relevant when the shared features could account for why the exception object violated the default rule in the first place. If the object-in-question also has those features, then it too may behave like the known exception and also violate the default rule. The results we report below are further investigations of those findings.

Design

We defined three conditions in which to present the four canonical default reasoning problems given in Table 1: (a) a

no-shared features condition, (b) a superficial shared-features condition, and (c) an explanatory shared-features condition. In the superficial case, the objects were described as having certain features in common; these features corresponded to those given by subjects in a separate norming study as irrelevant to the conclusion offered by a default rule. Typically, these were physical features for the actual cover stories (example below) that we used for the problems. The explanatory shared-features corresponded to features given by subjects in the norming study as relevant to the conclusion implicated by a default rule; these explanatory features typically concerned an object's use or function. The hypothesis was that subjects would apply the default rule to the object-in-question most often when there was no information about its similarity to the default violator, and least often when the common features between the object-in-question and the default violator could support an explanation of why the default-violator itself did not obey the default rule. The superficial condition should lie somewhere in-between.

Figure 1 illustrates this manipulation for Problem 1. For all problems, the order of information was: the set-up sentences, marked (a) in Figure 1; the sentences corresponding to the similarity information (if any), which are marked (b') and (b'') for the two similarity manipulations; the default rule, marked (c); the sentence marked (d) indicating the rule violator did not follow the default rule; and finally the question (e) asking for a plausible conclusion about the object-in-question. In addition to the medical journals scenario, there were cover stories about membership in university clubs, distribution of student ID cards, and operations of campus parking lots. Similarity was a between-subjects factor and problem type was a within-subjects factor. Subjects saw each of the four benchmark problems under one type of similarity, with each benchmark having one of the four possible cover stories. The assignment of cover-story to each problem type was counterbalanced across subjects.

Subjects and Procedure

Seventy-two subjects were randomly assigned to one of the three similarity conditions. The problems were randomly

132

No Similarity

(a) Cardiac News and Drug Developments are medical journals you need for a research paper.

(c) Medical journals are usually located in the Health Sciences library.

(d) Cardiac News is an exception: It is not in the Health Sciences library—It is kept in the Department of Medicine Reading Room.

Superficial Similarity Additions

(b') Both Cardiac News and Drug Developments are published in Canada. New issues of both journals come out every month. They are bound in light-blue covers.

Explanation Similarity Additions

(b") Both Cardiac News and Drug Developments are among the most expensive journals the university purchases. There have been problems with stolen or missing copies of these journals over the years. Both of them are consulted on a daily basis by graduate students in Medicine.

Question

(e) What would be reasonable to conclude about where Drug Developments is located?

Figure 1: Components of alternative similarity versions for problem type 1

ordered in booklet form. Each problem's question (see Figure 1) was followed by four possible answers, corresponding to these options (tailored to each cover story): (a) the object-in-question followed the default rule, (b) the object-in-question violated the default rule, (c) no conclusion was possible (a "can't tell" option), and (d) "other", for which subjects could write in another conclusion. The instructions emphasized that we were interested in common-sense conclusions, and that there were no right or wrong answers.

Results

The data from three of the 72 subjects had to be discarded, due to a mis-assignment of experimental materials. This left a total of 69 subjects, 23 in each of the three similarity conditions. Table 2 shows the proportions of each answer category as a function of answer category and similarity level.

Because the data we collected are interval data, i.e., answers falling into one of four response categories, they do not necessarily follow a normal distribution. One appropriate treatment of such data is a loglinear analysis of models defined by particular combinations of main effect and interaction terms. Under this approach, we evaluate whether a given model's predicted data is significantly different from the observed data, using a χ^2 likelihood ratio statistic. A model with fewer terms (and more degrees of freedom) is preferred to a model with more terms, provided that the predicted data does not differ significantly from the observed data. The simplest model we identified included a main-effect term for answer category and an answer-category by

similarity interaction term ($\chi^2 = 32.48$, df=38 , p = .722). If the interaction term is removed, the difference between observed and predicted data approaches significance ($\chi^2 = 72.53$, df=56, p = .068).

It is clear from Table 2 that, most of the time, subjects applied the default rule to the object in question (the model's main-effect term for answer category) and it is also apparent that this decision was influenced by the apparent similarity to another object that violated the rule (the model's interaction term). The trend in the frequencies of applying the default rule to the object-in-question was in line with our predictions, occurring least often in the explanatory condition. We note that subjects were conservative in their reluctance to apply the default rule in this case, choosing the "can't tell" (.21) option rather than the explicit rule-violation option. We cannot account for the tendency for subjects in the superficial condition to provide so many "other" conclusions. Although the superficial features were identified from a norming study as being irrelevant to the property implicated in the default rule, it is possible they were not. Hence, a possibility remains that subjects tended to reject the default rule given any information they could use to construct an alternative prediction about the object-in-question. A laboratory manipulation of inter-object similarity may be weaker than tapping into extant knowledge of similarity between object classes; this is a line of investigation we are currently following. Still, these results are consistent with our previous findings that the application of a default rule may be influenced by information about other exceptions to the rule.

		Answer Category			
		Follows Default	Violates Default	Other	Can't Tell
Similarity:	none	.70	.12	.11	.07
	superficial	.54	.18	.25	.03
	causal	.45	.19	.15	.21

Table 2: Proportion of Responses as a Function of Similarity and Response Type

Birds-Fly Context	Birds-&-Bats Fly Context
Animals normally do not fly Birds are animals. Birds normally fly. Ostriches are birds. Ostriches do not fly.	Animals normally do not fly. Birds are animals. Birds normally fly. Bats are animals. Bats normally fly. Ostriches are birds. Ostriches do not fly.
Q: Do birds other than ostriches fly? A: Yes Q: Do animals other than birds fly? A: No	Q: Do birds other than ostriches fly? A: Yes Q: Do animals other than birds & bats fly? A: No

Table 3: Two default inheritance problems

Reasoning about Inherited Default Properties

In Table 3, we present two additional problems from Lifschitz's (1989) nonmonotonic benchmark set. These problems are easily recognized as canonical examples of conflicting default knowledge about classes related in a class-subclass hierarchy. These problems were included in Lifschitz's benchmark set because they capture several essential questions that have been central to reasoning theories about classes, subclasses, and individuals, namely how should properties—some of which are definitional and some of which are prototypical— be "inherited" by the next element down the hierarchy? Other more complex inheritance scenarios are accommodated by different formal default reasoning theories, but these problems present simple cases of conflicting default rules.

In some previous pilot work, we found that subjects generally allowed the default properties to be inherited, as per the "correct" answers given in Table 3. In this study, we examined whether this application of default properties was sensitive to the kind of taxonomic categories being considered, namely *natural kind categories* or *artifact categories*. The notion that "kinds" influences reasoning has been considered in both the inductive inference and the statistical reasoning literatures (Thagard & Nisbett, 1993). People's tendency to reason statistically can also be influenced by perceived variability and homogeneity in the classes they are considering. For example, Nisbett et al. (1983) reports that people expect a lower variability for natural classes than for classes of human behaviors. Hence, it seemed to us that this kind of metaknowledge, implicated in some statistical reasoning studies, may impact upon qualitative judgments concerning the inheritance of default properties.

The second factor we manipulated was whether the problems included class-size information for the classes and subclasses that formed the inheritance hierarchy. Our inclusion of this factor was also motivated by our desire to bridge these qualitative default reasoning decisions with some statistical reasoning results, that have indicated that people are influenced by class size information in making some kinds of inferences (Nisbett et al., 1983). For this initial study, we contrasted a *class size absent* case, in which there was no mention of how large the subclasses were, with a *class size present* case. In this latter condition, the problem mentioned particular figures for class sizes, falling within the 20-80 range. Our contrast of these two cases here was not to assess how particular class-size values would lead to

different conclusions; rather, we wanted first to assess whether framing these qualitative inheritance problems in a somewhat more quantitative guise would influence people's tendency to ascribe the inheritable default properties to particular subclasses.

Design

Each subject received each of the two inheritance problems with both a natural kinds cover story and an artifact cover story. For the natural categories, we used stories about trees and snakes; the artifact categories concerned taxation laws for cigarettes and features of medieval musical instruments. No cover story was repeated in any of the problems that a subject saw, and the assignment of cover stories to problems was counterbalanced across subjects. In addition to these four problems, subjects solved two other inheritance problems that were part of a different study.

Subjects and Procedure

Sixty-four subjects were randomly assigned to receive either the class-size present problems or the class-size absent problems. The problems were presented to subjects as "short paragraphs that were extracted and adapted from newspapers and popular science articles [which presented] some facts but left other information unstated." Subjects were told that their task was to specify the reasonable, common-sense conclusion or inference they would draw, based strictly on the information given to the reader in the excerpts presented. Below is the text of a birds-fly context problem, using natural categories and including class size information:

> ....The kind of trees you plant can also help attract birds year round. Coniferous trees do well in our region. Unfortunately, most of the 63 species of coniferous trees produce a bitter sap. An example is the subclass "cedrus" (cedar): taste the sap from any type of cedar tree and you will be unpleasantly surprised at how bitter it is....
>
> There is, however, a subclass of coniferous trees called "Pinaecea" that any good garden nursery will know about. Most of the 22 Pinaecea species give sweet sap that attract squirrels and certain types of birds.... [however] one Pinaecea tree to be avoided is *picea mariana*: it gives bitter sap. An attractive and

		Class Size Present	Class Size Absent	Mean
		Natural Classes		
Do birds other than ostriches fly?(yes)	birds-fly context	.72	.72	.72
	birds-&-bats-fly context	.69	.69	.69
Do animals other than birds fly?(no)	birds-fly context	.69	.71	.71
	birds-&-bats-fly context	.59	.56	.58
		Artifact Classes		
Do birds other than ostriches fly?(yes)	birds-fly context	.47	.69	.58
	birds-&-bats-fly context	.41	.69	.55
Do animals other than birds fly?(no)	birds-fly context	.59	.63	.61
	birds-&-bats-fly context	.63	.72	.68

Table 4: Proportion of "Correct" Answers Given for Inheritance Problems from Table 3

hardy pine tree, make sure your local garden nursery doesn't try to sell you this one if youraim is to attract local wildlife....

The class-size absent versions of these problems replaced references to statements like "Most of the 63 species" with "Most species". Two questions then followed about subclasses that the alleged article did not mention. For the above example, these questions were:

z(a) "The article mentioned one subclass of conifers—Pinaecea —but did not discuss a second subclass called Juniperous. From the information presented in the article, what is your common-sense conclusion about whether species within the Juniperous subclass produces sweet sap or bitter sap?" [*do animals other than birds fly?*]

(b) "The article failed to mention another Pinaecea tree called *libani chrysolitis*. From the information presented in the article, what is your reasonable conclusion about the kind of sap it produces?" *[do birds other than ostriches fly?]*

Subjects selected their answer to each question from one of three possibilities that corresponded, in essence, to "yes [it can fly]", "no [it can't fly]" and "can't tell."

Results

Even though subjects did not solve problems mentioning birds, bats, and flying, it is easiest to talk about the results by referring to these canonical terms. Table 4 presents the proportion of subjects choosing the prescribed default answer for each of the two possible questions. A loglinear analysis of the data identified a model defined by three interaction

terms: category type X quantifier X question X answer category; category type X context type X answer category, and context type X question X answer category ($\chi^2 = 2.89$, df = 15, p = 1.0). We cannot at this stage propose an account for all these interactions, particularly those involving the birds-fly vs. birds-plus-bats fly context effect. However, the response patterns that give rise to this model are evident in Table 4. First, the proportion of prescribed default-inheritance answers was higher when subjects were reasoning about natural categories and lower when they were reasoning about artificial categories. Second, subjects were less likely to allow the default property to be inherited for artifact classes than for natural classes, particularly when the problems mentioned class size information. This finding is consistent with the notion that people may perceive artifact/artificial classes as inherently more variable than natural kinds and that this impacts their willingness to ascribe default properties. The impact of merely mentioning class sizes may have triggered this consideration of variability. Unfortunately, this sort of conjecture does not seem entirely consistent with the effect of the birds-fly versus birds-&-bats-fly context for the natural classes condition. For those problems, subjects were less likely to apply the default rule to conclude that animals-other-than birds don't fly, when bats were included as a second exception. This did not occur with the non-natural stimuli; whether the number of known (or salient) exceptions influences the application of a default rule needs further study.

Discussion

These results suggest an aspect of plausible reasoning that is missing from current non-monotonic theories, namely that there are certain kinds of information that are relevant to applying default rules. The findings outlined above suggest some considerations about what is relevant in non-monotonic reasoning: inter-object similarity, natural vs. artificial categories, and class-size information. If an unknown case is similar to an understood exception, then a plausible conclusion may not be to apply the default rule, but instead to predict that the unknown case behaves instead like the exception. The influence of the latter two factors border on a meta-knowledge effect: people may work certain assumptions about class variability into their default conclusions, e.g., there is greater regularity to how defaults and exceptions operate in the "natural" world than there is for non-natural classes and subclasses. Other researchers have appealed to this distinction in the realm of inductive reasoning (e.g., Thagard & Nisbett, 1993) and statistical reasoning (Nisbett et al., 1983). Our results in this study are suggestive, though by no means conclusive, that this distinction may come into play in the sort of qualitative default reasoning scenarios we have studied here. Indeed, another interpretation from the inheritance problems is that, in some arenas, human reasoners are much more cautious in their attribution of default properties than we might otherwise believe.

How can our findings, that knowledge about known default-rule exceptions may influence the application of default rules to similar cases, be worked into a specification for non-monotonic reasoning? One idea might be called "explanation-based default reasoning", in the same sense of this notion used in the machine learning literature. That is, a reasoner attempts to explain why some default rule does not apply to the known exception, and then evaluates whether that explanation applies to the object under consideration. This emphasis on reasoning about one known individual case in order to make a decision about another case may sound like there can be no formalized rules for default reasoning. But this account need not be taken as a prescription for a strictly case-based approach to default reasoning. First, the influence of a similar object might be used to direct the selection of an appropriate "reference class," about which some statistical properties could be inherited. Second, some formal theories already appeal to the notions of causality, explanation, or argumentation processes to construct, and then select among, alternative models that are defined by conflicting default rules (e.g., Pollock, 1987; Gefner, 1992). Along these lines, we note that the presence of a known rule violator in the problems we investigated here may be a red herring, insofar as the important aspect for subjects may have been the availability of information that could support an explanation about why a default rule may not apply (quite independent of whether some other known violator was salient). In general, it does not seem plausible that additional information about an individual should necessarily have no impact on determining whether it follows a default rule (e.g., whether a block's color influences whether it is, by default, located on a table). One interpretation of our findings is that such information is relevant to the extent it supports explanations for (or against) a default assumption; a known exception to a default may serve as a touchstone for constructing these explanations.

Acknowledgments

This work was supported by Government of Canada NSERC Research Grants A0089 (RE) and A5525 (FJP). We thank Siobhan Neary for her assistance in conducting these experiments and the University of Alberta Department of Psychology, for their continuing cooperation in allowing us access to their subject pool.

References

Bacchus, F. (1991). *Representing and Reasoning with Probabilistic Knowledge*. Cambridge: The MIT Press.

Collins, A. & Michalski, R. (1989). The logic of plausible reasoning: A core theory. *Cognitive Science, 13*, 1-49.

Delgrande, J. (1987). An approach to default reasoning based on a first order conditional logic. In *Proceedings of AAAI-87*, 340-345, Seattle.

Elio, R. & Pelletier, F. J. (1993) *Human benchmarks on AI's benchmark problems*. In *Proceedings of the Fifteenth Annual Conference of the Cognitive Science Society*. (pp 406-411). Boulder, CO.

Gefner, H. (1992). *Default reasoning: causal and conditional theories*. Cambridge: MIT Press.

Greiner, R. & Subramanian, D. (1994). *Relevance: American Association for Artificial Intelligence 1994 Fall Symposium Series*, November 4-6, New Orleans. Palo Alto: AAAI Press.

Lifschitz, V. (1989). Benchmark problems for formal nonmonotonic reasoning, v. 2.00. In M. Reinfrank, J. de Kleer, & M. Ginsberg (Eds.) *Nonmonotonic Reasoning* 202-219, Berlin: Springer-Verlag.

Nisbett, R. E., Krantz, D. H., Jepson, C., & Kunda, Z. (1983). The use of statistical heuristics in everyday reasoning. *Psychological Review, 90*, 339-363.

Pearl, J. (1989). Probabilistic semantics for nonmonotonic reasoning. *Proceedings of the First International Conference on Principles of Knowledge Representation and Reasoning*, 505-516, Toronto, Canada.

Pelletier, F. J. & Elio, R. What should default reasoning be, by default? (Tech. Rep. 94-13) Edmonton: University of Alberta, Department of Computing Science.

Pollock, J. (1987). Defeasible reasoning. *Cognitive Science, 11*, 481-518.

Thagard, P. & Nisbett, R.E. (1993). Variability and confirmation. In R.E. Nisbett (Ed.) *Rules for Reasoning*. Hillsdale, NJ: Lawrence Erlbaum.

Touretsky, D., Horty, J. & Thomason, R. (1987). A clash of intuitions: The current state of non-monotonic multiple inheritance systems. *Proceedings of IJCAI-87*, 476-482, Milano, Italy.

Satisficing Inference and the Perks of Ignorance

Daniel G. Goldstein and **Gerd Gigerenzer**
Center for Adaptive Behavior and Cognition
Max Planck Institute for Psychological Research
Leopoldstr. 24, 80802 Munich GERMANY
goldstein@mpipf-muenchen.mpg.de

Abstract

Most approaches to modeling rational inference do not take into account that in the real world, organisms make inferences under limited time and knowledge. In this tradition, the mind is treated as a calculating demon equipped with unlimited time, knowledge, and computational might. We propose a family of satisficing algorithms based on a simple psychological mechanism: one-reason decision making. These fast and frugal algorithms violate fundamental tenets of classical rationality, for example, they neither look up nor integrate all information. By computer simulation, we held a competition between the satisficing Take The Best algorithm and various more "optimal" decision procedures. The Take The Best algorithm matched or outperformed all competitors in inferential speed and accuracy. Most interesting was the finding that the best algorithms in the competition, those which used a form of one-reason decision making, exhibited a startling "less-is-more" effect: they performed better with missing knowledge than with complete knowledge. We discuss the less-is-more effect and present evidence of it in human reasoning. This counter-intuitive effect demonstrates that the mind can satisfice and seize upon regularities in the environment to the extent that it can exploit even the absence of knowledge as knowledge.

Toward Satisficing

How does an organism make inferences about unknown aspects of the environment? Three directions have been searched in the hope of an answer. The first, which we might call the computational demon approach, equates reasoning with extensive calculation. It applies to models of mind which describe basic cognitive processes, such as estimation, inference, or categorization, as resulting from sophisticated computations. Examples of this are models of estimation based on multiple regression, or models of foraging behavior based on Bayes' Theorem. How can the mind carry out such tough statistical problems that took millennia of cultural evolution to conquer? This is where the demon comes in. The computational demon, common to all such models, is a consultant to the reasoning agent, capable computing all possible futures based on its extensive and infallible memory of all things past. While this approach is flattering to the organism doing the reasoning, it may posit more computational power than is plausible to assume exists in ordinary minds. Yet, such models abound in human and animal psychology.

Another way to look at reasoning came about in the past few decades and has had a powerful impact on psychology ever since. This is the heuristics-and-biases approach (Kahneman, Slovic & Tversky, 1982), which suggests that reasoning is governed by simple heuristics that generally do the right thing, but that may be systematically and wholly misled. In principle, it is a good idea: do away with computational demons, and replace them with simple principles which may do the job equally well. A problem with the heuristics-and-biases approach comes in practice where most of the research focuses more on biases than heuristics and the heuristics offered are notoriously vague (Gigerenzer & Goldstein, in press).

The third and most promising view comes from Herbert Simon (1956). This view states that good reasoning can come about by simple algorithms that "satisfice". The word satisficing is a blend of the words satisfying and sufficing, and means just that: finding near-optimal solutions to difficult problems under the limited computational constraints of ordinary minds. As with the heuristics-and-biases approach, the computational demon is replaced with something more psychologically plausible, though here the resultant reasoning is quick and clean, as opposed to quick and dirty. Another good feature of Simon's satisficing idea is that it stems from a computational tradition which favors using algorithms as models, instead of just simple heuristics in isolation. Algorithms are easily coded up as computer programs that a researcher can use to put a model through its paces.

What are these simple, intelligent satisficing algorithms capable of making near-optimal inferences? How fast and how accurate are they? In this research, we look at the effectiveness of a satisficing algorithm that operates with simple psychological principles that satisfy the constraints of limited time, knowledge, and computational might. At the same time, it is designed to be fast and frugal without a significant loss of inferential accuracy since it can exploit the structure of environments. For instance, this algorithm uses the "recognition principle", a simple form of one-reason decision making, which seems at first a liability but turns out to an effective and efficient heuristic. In simulating this and other algorithms computationally, we came across a surprising "less-is-more" effect: a certain class of satisficing algorithms made better inferences under conditions of missing knowledge than with complete knowledge. This effect is discussed and its existence is proven to be tied to the recognition principle. We begin with the inference task we used to measure the effectiveness of various algorithms.

The Task

We deal with inferential tasks in which a choice must be made between two alternatives on a quantitative dimension. Consider the following example: Which city has a larger population? (a) Hamburg (b) Cologne. Assume that a subject does not know or cannot deduce the answer to the question, but needs to make an inductive inference from related real-world knowledge. How is this inference derived? How can we predict choice (Hamburg or Cologne) from a person's state of knowledge?

We assume that to make an inference about which of two objects has a higher value, knowledge about a reference class is searched. In our example, knowledge about the reference class "cities in Germany" could be searched. The knowledge could consist of probability cues. For instance, when making inferences about populations of German cities, the fact that a city has a professional soccer team in the major league ("Bundesliga") may come to a person's mind as a potential cue. That is, when considering pairs of German cities, if one city has a soccer team in the major league and the other does not, then the city with the team is likely, but not certain, to have the larger population. It may be useful to think of a knowledge state of a matrix of objects and cues.

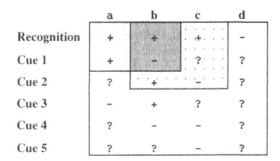

	a	b	c	d
Recognition	+	+	+	–
Cue 1	+	–	?	?
Cue 2	?	+	–	?
Cue 3	–	+	?	?
Cue 4	?	–	–	?
Cue 5	?	?	–	?

Figure 1: Possible knowledge state for 4 objects (a-d), 5 cues, and recognition knowledge.

Figure 1 models a possible limited knowledge state of a person. Limited knowledge means that the matrix of objects by cues has missing entries (that is, objects, cues, or cue values may be unknown). She has heard of three German cities, a, b, and c, but not of d (represented by three positive and one negative "Recognition" values). She knows some facts (cue values) about these cities with respect to five binary cues. For a binary cue, there are two cue values, "positive" (e.g., the city has a soccer team), or "negative" (it does not). "Positive" refers to a cue value that signals a higher value on the target variable (for example, having a

soccer team is correlated with high population). Unknown cue values are shown by a question mark. Since she has never heard of object d, the recognition value of d is negative and all its other cue values are necessarily unknown.

The Environment

We tested the performance of the Take The Best algorithm on how accurately it made inferences about a real-world environment (for a more complete description of these simulations, see Gigerenzer & Goldstein, in press). The environment was the set of all cities in Germany with more than 100,000 inhabitants (83 cities after German reunification), with population as the target variable. The model of the environment consisted of 9 binary ecological cues (such as the soccer team cue), and the actual 9 x 83 cue values.

Each cue had an associated *ecological validity* which is indicative of its predictive power. The ecological validity of a cue is the relative frequency, in a reference class, that objects with positive cue values have higher target variable values than objects with negative cue values (e. g., the relative frequency that cities with soccer teams are more populous than cities without teams in all possible pairs). The ecological validity of the 9 cues we chose ranged over the whole spectrum: from .51 (only slightly better than chance) to 1.0 (certainty).

We simulated subjects with varying degrees of knowledge about this environment. To model limited recognition knowledge, we created subjects who recognized between 0 and 83 German cities. For each of these types of subject, we created 500 simulated individuals, who differed randomly from one another in the particular cities they knew. The simulation needed to be realistic in the sense that people are more likely to recognize large cities than small ones. We performed a survey to get an empirical estimate of the actual covariation between recognition of cities and city populations. In a pilot study of 26 undergraduates at the University of Chicago, we found that the cities they recognized (within the 83 largest in Germany) were larger than the cities they did not recognize in about 80% of all possible comparisons. We refer to this value as the "recognition validity". This value was incorporated into our simulations by choosing sets of cities (for each knowledge state, that is, for each number of cities recognized) where the known cities were larger than the unknown cities in about 80% of all cases. Thus, the cities known by the simulated subjects had the same relationship between recognition and population as did those of the human subjects.

Algorithms

We held a competition in which five decision algorithms, specially designed for two-alternative inference tasks, were matched against each other in a contest. The winner would be the algorithm which made the most correct inferences in the least amount of time. The first competitor is called the *Take The Best* algorithm (Gigerenzer & Goldstein, in press), because its policy is "take the best, ignore the rest".

The Take The Best algorithm assumes a subjective rank order of cues according to their validities. We call the highest ranking cue the "best" cue. Here are the steps of the algorithm:

(1) Recognition principle: The recognition principle is invoked when the mere recognition of an object is a predictor of the target variable (here, population). The recognition principle states: if only one of the two objects is recognized, then choose the recognized object. If neither of the two objects is recognized, then choose randomly between them. If both of the objects are recognized, then proceed to Step 2.

(2) Search for the values of the best cue: For the two objects, retrieve the cue values of the best cue from memory.

(3) Discrimination rule: Decide whether the cue discriminates. The cue is said to discriminate between two objects if one has a positive cue value and the other does not.

(4) Cue substitution principle: If the cue discriminates, then stop searching for cue values. Else, go back to Step 2 and continue with the next best cue until a cue that discriminates is found.

(5) Maximizing rule for choice: Choose the object with the positive cue value. If no cue discriminates, then choose randomly.

One important feature of this algorithm is that search extends through only a portion of the total knowledge in memory (as shown by the shaded parts of Figure 1), and stops immediately when the first discriminating cue is found. Thus, the algorithm is well suited to situations of limited time or knowledge. A seemingly irrational feature of the algorithm is that it does not attempt to integrate information, but uses cue substitution instead. This idea of basing an entire decision on one single cue is what we call one-reason decision making. Note that the recognition principle (Step 1), is a form of one-reason decision making. We shall later see how this satisficing mechanism can actually improve inferential accuracy.

Testing the Algorithms

With the help of some of our colleagues and statistician friends, we created five, more traditional competitors to compare to the Take The Best algorithm. In *Tallying*, the number of positive cue values for each object is tallied across all cues and summed to give a score for each city. The city with the largest number of positive cue values is chosen. *Weighted Tallying* is identical to tallying except that the values added to each city's score are weighted by the respective ecological cue validities. The *Unit-Weight Linear Model* adds one point to a city's score for each positive value, but subtracts one point for each negative cue value, and chooses the city with the best score. Finally, the *Weighted Linear Model* is similar its unit-weighted counterpart, except that it adds and subtracts weighted values (the ecological cue validities) instead of whole points.

We tested how well subjects using the various algorithms did at answering questions of the kind, "Which city has more inhabitants? (a) Heidelberg (b) Bonn." Each of the 500 simulated subjects in each of the 84 types was tested on the exhaustive set of 3403 city pairs resulting in a total of 500 x 84 x 3403 tests, that is, about 143 million for each

algorithm. The number of correct inferences, and the amount of cue values looked up were recorded for each subject and algorithm.

Results

The competition had two quite surprising results. First of all, even though the Take the Best algorithm used far less information than the other algorithms (on average, less than a third of all available cue values), it matched or outperformed all other algorithms in the proportion of correct inferences (Figure 2).

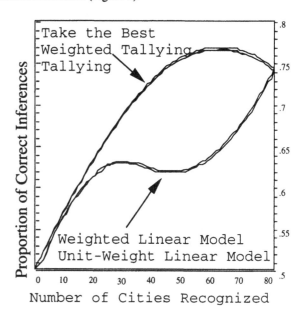

Figure 2: Less-is-more effect appearing for a variety of decision algorithms.

The second, very surprising result was that the best algorithms in the competition performed better with missing knowledge than with complete knowledge, as the non-monotonic upper curves suggest. Notice how for these curves, at any level of limited recognition knowledge of cities, learning more German cities will eventually cause a decrease in proportion correct. We call this intriguing finding the "less-is-more effect".

The Less-is-More Effect

What is behind the less-is-more effect? The most important factor is the recognition principle. All the algorithms which exhibit the less-is-more effect follow the recognition principle. In the case of Take The Best, it is a defining characteristic of the model, in the tallying variants, it arises as a side-effect. The linear models violate the recognition principle regularly; they often predict an unrecognized city to be larger than a recognized one (to understand why, see Gigerenzer & Goldstein, in press). Once this is realized, the reason for the effect can be seen analytically. We will build up to the more complicated analytic result from a simple thought experiment.

Imagine three brothers who sit down to take a quiz on the 100 largest German cities. The youngest brother is ignorant: he has never even heard of Germany before. The middle brother is savvy: he recognizes 25 of the 50 largest cities from what he has overheard from day to day. The eldest brother is quite the scholar: one day he took it upon himself to memorize the names of all the cities on his map of Germany. None of the brothers knows anything significant about the cities other than their names. Now suppose all three brothers adopt the same strategy for taking the test. Each decides that he will use the recognition cue wherever he can: in situations where he is given one city he recognizes and one city he does not, he will always pick the city he recognizes. In all other situations -- two unrecognized or two recognized cities -- he will just guess.

Consider how the brothers will perform. Clearly, the youngest brother will have to guess on every question -- his long-run score will be 50% correct. To the middle brother, the test will look a little different. In 50% of the questions he will be able to use the recognition cue and in the other 50% he will not. As luck would have it, the recognition validity for the middle brother is 80% (a realistic assumption, as our survey showed). By guessing on half the questions and using the 80% successful recognition cue on the other half, a simple calculation shows that the middle brother will end up getting 65% of all questions correct. The eldest and most knowledgeable brother, never being able to activate the recognition cue, will have to guess on every question and thus score 50% correct. Figure 3 shows how the three brothers, and all intermediate knowledge states, would perform in this domain.

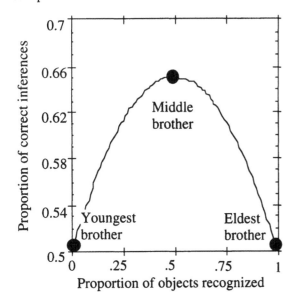

Figure 3: Performance for the three brothers and all intermediate knowledge states.

It becomes clear that the less-is-more effect is brought about by the variable applicability of the recognition principle in various knowledge states. When the recognition cue is not able to be activated, the system is forced to guess. This thought experiment may explain why an elder brother with no real knowledge beyond recognition may perform so poorly, but what about the simulation results, where a less-is-more effect persisted even when the simulated subjects had knowledge in the form of actual cue values? The following proof explains.

Suppose the number of objects (e.g., cities) in the reference class is N. Let n be the number of objects recognized by a subject. These two variables determine the proportions of question types that will appear on a quiz. In $2\left(\frac{n}{N}\right)\left(\frac{N-n}{N-1}\right)$ of all possible questions, one city will be recognized and the other not. In $\left(\frac{N-n}{N}\right)\left(\frac{N-n-1}{N-1}\right)$ of the questions, both cities will be unrecognized, whereas in $\left(\frac{n}{N}\right)\left(\frac{n-1}{N-1}\right)$ of the questions, both cities will be recognized.

When both cities are unrecognized, there is nothing to do but guess, and in the long run, half of these guesses will be correct. If one city is recognized and the other not, the recognition principle says to pick the recognized city. Let α be the probability of choosing the right answer via the recognition principle. If both cities are recognized, the inference has to be made using knowledge other than mere recognition. Let β be the probability of getting the right answer in this case. If α and β are both roughly constant and independent of n, the following function $f(n)$ gives the expected proportion of correct inferences:

$$f(n) = 2\left(\frac{n}{N}\right)\left(\frac{N-n}{N-1}\right)\alpha + \left(\frac{N-n}{N}\right)\left(\frac{N-n-1}{N-1}\right)\frac{1}{2} + \left(\frac{n}{N}\right)\left(\frac{n-1}{N-1}\right)\beta$$

By analyzing the graph of $\phi(n)$, the continuous version of $f(n)$, one sees that the less-is-more effect occurs if this curve has a maximum between $n = 0$ and $n = N - 1/2$. Solving the equation $\phi'(n) = 0$, when $\phi'(n)$ is simply the first derivative of $\phi(n)$, one locates the maximum of $\phi(n)$ at:

$$\frac{-(1 - 2\beta - 2N + 4\alpha N)}{2(1 - 4\alpha + 2\beta)} \qquad (*)$$

A simple calculation shows that when $\alpha = \beta$, the location of the curve's maximum is equal to $N-1/2$. Either increasing α or decreasing β from this point causes the fraction (*) to decrease, which implies the maximum of $\phi(n)$ will be displaced to the left. From this, we can conclude that there will be a less-is-more effect whenever $\alpha > \beta$, that is, whenever the accuracy of mere recognition is greater than the accuracy achievable when both objects are recognized.

Discussion

Two surprising results came out of this competition between algorithms. One is that a non-standard, satisficing algorithm performed as well as or better than all other algorithms in the competition, while looking up only one-third of the knowledge used by the competitors. The second was that the best algorithms in the competition did better with missing knowledge than with complete knowledge. The strong force most accountable for both these results was the simple and bold recognition principle, a form of one-reason decision making. The first result is an existence proof that a satisficing algorithm can do as well computationally-expensive models that use more information. The second suggests that, given the correct environment and an organism that follows the recognition principle, the less-is-more effect ought to emerge in the real world.

How difficult is it to find a less-is-more effect in real human behavior? Doing so depends on finding an environment with the correct structure, and people who apply the recognition principle. It is a relatively simple matter to find a reference class where a less-is-more effect should occur: simply find one where recognition is a better predictor than the environmental cues, and where the ecological validities of recognition and the cues do not change drastically as a more and more objects become recognized. This information about environment structures could be obtained from surveys and interviews about what objects people recognize, and how good they are at making inferences about these objects. Several experimental studies (Goldstein, 1994; Goldstein & Gigerenzer, 1996), show subjects exhibit a high degree of recognition principle adherence, even in cases where they are given information which suggests doing otherwise. The analytic results we have derived allow one to predict when and to what extent the less-is-more effect will occur.

The results of this study paint a new picture of the mind, not a picture where the mind is a computational demon, and not one where it is doomed to follow shoddy heuristics that lead it astray. Rather, it paints the mind as a time-pressed scavenger, one which uses the structures of natural environments to the degree that it can depend on a single, well-chosen cue as opposed to the costly aggregation of many, and one that can exploit any information -- even the very absence of knowledge -- to make accurate inferences about unknown features of the world.

Acknowledgments

Much of this research was completed at The University of Chicago in partial fulfillment of the first author's Master of Arts degree. We would like to thank Jean Czerlinski and Laura Martignon for their assistance on this paper.

References

Gigerenzer, G., & Goldstein, D. G. (in press). Reasoning the fast and frugal way: Models of bounded rationality. *Psychological Review*.

Goldstein, D. G. (1994). The less-is-more effect in inference. M. A. thesis, The University of Chicago.

Goldstein, D. G., & Gigerenzer, G. (1996). The recognition principle and the less-is-more effect. Manuscript submitted for publication.

Kahneman, D., Slovic, P., & Tversky, A. (Eds.). (1982). *Judgment under uncertainty: Heuristics and biases*. Cambridge: Cambridge University Press.

Simon, H. A. (1956). Rational choice and the structure of the environment. *Psychological Review, 63*, 129-138.

A Connectionist Treatment of Negation and Inconsistency

Lokendra Shastri and **Dean J. Grannes**
International Computer Science Institute
1947 Center St., Ste. 600
Berkeley, CA 94704
shastri@icsi.berkeley.edu, grannes@icsi.berkeley.edu

Abstract

A connectionist model capable of encoding positive as well as negated knowledge and using such knowledge during rapid reasoning is described. The model explains how an agent can hold inconsistent beliefs in its long-term memory without being "aware" that its beliefs are inconsistent, but detect a contradiction whenever inconsistent beliefs that are within a certain inferential distance of each other become co-active during an episode of reasoning. Thus the model is not logically omniscient, but detects contradictions whenever it tries to use inconsistent knowledge. The model also explains how limited attentional focus or action under time pressure can lead an agent to produce an erroneous response. A biologically significant feature of the model is that it uses only local inhibition to encode negated knowledge. The model encodes and propagates dynamic bindings using temporal synchrony.

Introduction

The ability to perform inferences in order to establish referential and causal coherence and generate expectations plays a crucial role in understanding language (e.g., McKoon & Ratcliff, 1981). Given that we can understand language at the rate of several hundred words per minute, it is also apparent that we can perform the requisite inferences rapidly — as though they were a *reflex* response of our cognitive apparatus. In view of this, we have described such reasoning as *reflexive* (Shastri, 1991).[1] Certain types of negated knowledge also plays a role in such reasoning. If we were told "John has been to Canada" and "John has not been to Europe", we could readily answer the questions (i) "Has John been to North America?", (ii) "Has John been to France?" and (iii) "Has John been to Australia?" with "yes", "no", and "don't know", respectively. We can also reason reflexively with rules involving certain types of negated conditions. So given "John is a bachelor", we can readily answer "no" to "Is John married to Susan?" Observe that answering this question involves the use of negated knowledge that may be approximated as "A bachelor is not married to anyone" (i.e., $bachelor(x) \Rightarrow \neg married(x,y)$).[2]

Due to the complexity it adds to the inference process, knowledge representation systems often do not deal explicitly with negation. Some models deal partially with negation

by adopting the *closed world assumption* in AI. The intuition behind this assumption is as follows: If an agent knows all the relevant facts about some domain, then it may assume that any fact it does not know is false! In view of this assumption, the agent can treat "don't know" answers as "no" answers. The use of the closed world assumption, however, has limited applicability and cannot be a substitute for the ability to explicitly deal with negated information and distinguish between the epistemic states "don't know" and "no".

The encoding of negated knowledge raises the possibility of inconsistencies in an agent's long-term memory (LTM). We often hold inconsistent beliefs in our LTM without being explicitly aware of such inconsistencies. But at the same time, we often recognize contradictions in our beliefs when we try to bring inconsistent knowledge to bear on a particular task. In view of this, a cognitively plausible model of memory and reasoning should allow inconsistent facts and rules to co-exist in its LTM, but it should be capable of detecting contradictions whenever inconsistent beliefs that are within a certain inferential distance of each other become co-active during an episode of reasoning.

Finally, any agent with limited resources must sometimes act with only limited attentional focus and often under time pressure. This means that an agent may sometimes overlook relevant information and act in an erroneous manner. Extended evaluation or an appropriate cue, however, might make the necessary information available and lead to a correct response. Several interesting aspects of such a situation are captured in the following scenario (which we will refer to as the *Post Office Example*):

> John runs into Mary on the street. "Where are you going?" asks John. "To the post office," replies Mary. "But isn't today Presidents' Day?" remarks John. "Oops! I forgot that today was a federal holiday," says Mary after a momentary pause and heads back.

Clearly, Mary had sufficient knowledge to infer that "today" was a postal holiday. But the fact that she was going to the post office indicates that she had assumed that the post office was open. So in a sense, Mary held inconsistent beliefs. John's question served as a trigger and brought the relevant information to the surface and made Mary realize her mistake. A cognitively plausible model should be capable of modeling such situations.

This paper describes a connectionist model that can encode positive as well as negated rules and facts, rapidly perform a class of inferences, and exhibit the desirable properties discussed above. This work extends our work on SHRUTI, a

---

[1] A formal characterization of reflexive reasoning appears in (Shastri, 1993).

[2] We are using the notation of first-order logic for convenience. This does not mean that we view deduction to be the sole basis of reflexive reasoning. All variables are assumed to be universally quantified.

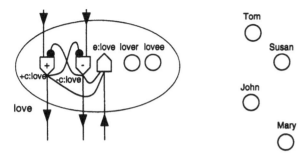

Figure 1: The structure of a predicate cluster.

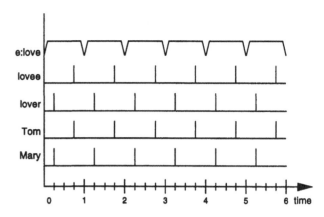

Figure 2: The rhythmic pattern of activation representing the dynamic bindings *love(Mary,Tom)*.

connectionist model of reflexive reasoning (Ajjanagadde & Shastri, 1991; Shastri & Ajjanagadde, 1993; Mani & Shastri 1993) and is partly influenced by (Cottrell, 1985). A detailed description of the extended model appears in (Shastri & Grannes, 1995).

System Overview

This section presents a brief summary of the system. Due to limited space we will not describe the encoding of multiple instantiations, type hierarchy, and context-sensitive rules.

General Representation

Figure 1 illustrates the representation of a predicate and entities. A node such as *John* corresponds to a *focal* node of the representation of the entity "John". Information about the various features of John and the roles he fills in various events is encoded by linking the focal node to appropriate nodes distributed throughout the network (see Shastri & Feldman, 1986; Feldman, 1989).

Encoding of Predicates: Predicate Clusters as Convergence Zones

Consider the encoding of the binary predicate *love* with two roles: *lover* and *lovee*. This predicate is encoded by a cluster of nodes consisting of two role nodes depicted as circular nodes and labeled *lover* and *lovee*; an *enabler* node depicted as a pentagon pointing upwards and labeled *e:love*; and two *collector* nodes depicted as pentagons pointing downwards and labeled *+c:love* and *−c:love* respectively. In general, the cluster for an *n-ary* predicate contains *n* role nodes, one enabler node, and two collector nodes. The circular nodes are ρ-**btu** nodes while the pentagon shaped nodes are τ-**and** nodes. The computational behavior of these nodes will be described shortly.

The cluster of nodes described above act as an anchor for the complete encoding of a predicate. All rules and facts that involve a predicate converge on its cluster, and all rules and facts involving a predicate can be accessed by fanning out from the predicate's cluster. This representation of a predicate is closely related to the notion of "convergence zones" (Damasio, 1989).

Let us examine the semantic import of the *enabler* and *collector* nodes. Assume that the roles of a predicate *P* are dynamically bound to some fillers thereby representing a dynamic instance of *P* (we will see how, shortly). The concomitant activation of the enabler *e:P* means that the system

is trying to explain whether the currently active dynamic instance of *P* is *supported* by the knowledge in the memory. The request for such an explanation might be generated internally by the reasoning system, or be communicated to it by some other subsystem (e.g., the planning module). The semantic import of the two collectors *+c:P* and *−c:P* is the complement of that of the enabler node. The system activates the positive collector *+c:P* when the currently active dynamic instance of *P* is supported by the knowledge encoded in the system. In contrast, the system activates the negative collector *−c:P* when the *negation* of the active instance is supported by the system's knowledge. Neither collector becomes active if the system does not have sufficient information about the currently active dynamic instance. The collectors can also be used by an external process. For example, the language understanding process might activate *c:love* and establish the bindings *(lover=John, lovee=Mary)* upon hearing the utterance "John loves Mary". Since the two collectors encode mutually contradictory information they have mutually inhibitory links. Observe that this inhibition is *local* to the two collectors within a predicate cluster.

Detecting a Contradiction

The levels of activation of the positive and negative collectors of a predicate measure the effective degree of support offered by the system to the currently active predicate instance. These levels of activation are the result of the activation incident on the collectors from the rest of the network and the mutual inhibition between the two collectors. The two activation levels encode a graded belief ranging continuously from "no" on the one extreme — where only the negative predicate is active, to "yes" on the other — where only the positive collector is active, with "don't know" in between — where neither collector is very active. If both the collectors receive comparable and strong activation then both collectors can be in a high state of activity, in spite of the mutual inhibition between them. When this happens, a contradiction is detected. In the current implementation this is done by an additional node within each predicate cluster (not shown in Figure 1) that has a threshold of 1.5 and receives excitatory inputs from both the collectors.

143

Significance of Collector to Enabler Connections

The weighted links between the collectors and the enabler of a predicate convert a dynamic assertion into a query about the assertion. Thus the system can constantly evaluate (or seek an explanation for) incoming knowledge in the context of existing knowledge. The weights on links from collectors to enablers can be viewed as a measure of the system's propensity for seeking such evaluations. A system with a high weight on these links can be viewed as a highly critical and skeptical system, while one with very low weights can be viewed as a credulous system — one which accepts incoming information without actively seeking an explanation or determining how well it coheres with prior knowledge.

The system's ability to evaluate incoming information enables it to detect inconsistencies between incoming information and prior knowledge. This evaluation process is fast and automatic but the scope of inconsistency detection is bounded by the constraint on the maximum depth of reflexive reasoning (Shastri & Ajjanagadde, 1993). Observe that here we are referring to a reflexive process of evaluation and not a deliberate search for inconsistencies.

The links from the collectors of a predicate to its enabler also serve to create positive feedback loops of spreading activation and thereby create stable coalitions of active nodes under appropriate circumstances. Assume that the system is seeking an explanation about the currently active instance of P, and therefore, the enabler of P is active. If the memory supports this instance of P it will activate the positive collector of P. This will create a feedback loop — or a stable coalition — consisting of $e{:}P$, the enablers of other predicates participating in the explanation of P, the appropriate collectors of these predicates, $+c{:}P$, and $e{:}P$.

Computational Behavior of Idealized Nodes

If a ρ-btu node A is connected to another ρ-btu node B then the activity of B synchronizes with the activity of A. In particular, a periodic firing of A leads to a periodic and *in-phase* firing of B.

A τ-and node becomes active on receiving a pulse (or a burst of activity) exceeding a minimum duration, π. Thus a τ-and node behaves like a *temporal and* node. On becoming active, it produces an output pulse similar to the input pulse.

A threshold, n (default value 1), associated with a node indicates that the node will fire upon receiving n or more inputs simultaneously (see Shastri & Ajjanagadde, 1993).

Encoding Dynamic Bindings:

Dynamic bindings are represented by the *synchronous* firing of appropriate role and filler nodes. With reference to Figure 1, the *rhythmic* pattern of activity shown in Figure 2 represents the dynamic bindings *(lover=Mary,lovee=Tom)* (i.e., the dynamic fact *love(Mary,Tom)*). Observe that *Mary* and *lover* are firing in synchrony and *Tom* and *lovee* are firing in synchrony. The absolute phase of firing of nodes is not significant. Also since *e:love* is firing, the system is essentially "asking" whether it believes that Mary loves Tom.

As discussed at length in (Shastri & Ajjanagadde, 1993), there exists substantial neurophysiological evidence to suggest that the propagation of synchronous activity is neurally plausible. A detailed review of synchronous cortical activity appears in (Singer, 1993). The idea that synchronous

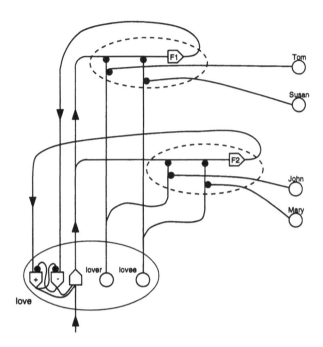

Figure 3: The encoding of facts: *love(John,Mary)* and ¬*love(Tom,Susan)*.

activity can bind features during visual processing had been suggested by von der Malsburg (1986) (also see Bienenstock & Geman, 1995), but SHRUTI is perhaps the first model to demonstrate how synchronous activation can be harnessed to solve complex problems in the representation and processing of conceptual knowledge.

Encoding Long-Term Facts: Memory as a Temporal Pattern Matcher

A long-term fact behaves like a *temporal pattern matcher* that becomes active whenever the static bindings it encodes match the dynamic bindings represented in the system's state of activation. Figure 3 illustrates the encoding of the long-term facts *love(John,Mary)* and ¬*love(Tom,Susan)*. Observe that each long-term fact is encoded using a distinct τ-and node which receives a link from the *enabler* node of the associated predicate and sends a link to the positive or negative collector of the predicate depending on whether the fact encodes a positive or a negative fact. The link from the enabler to the fact node is modified by inhibitory links from role nodes of the associated predicate. If a role is bound to an entity, the modifier input from this role node is in turn modified by an inhibitory link from the appropriate entity. Given the query *love(John,Mary)?* the fact node F2 will become active and activate the collector $+c{:}love$ indicating a "yes" answer. Similarly, given the query *love(Tom,Susan)?*, the fact node F1 will become active and activates the $-c{:}P$ collector indicating a "no" answer. Finally, given the query *love(John,Susan)?*, neither $+c{:}love$ nor $-c{:}love$ would become active, indicating that the system can neither affirm nor deny whether John loves Susan.

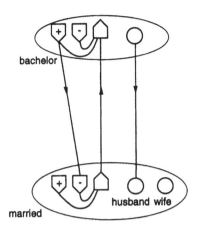

Figure 4: Encoding of the rule: *bachelor(x)* ⇒ ¬*married(x,y)*

Encoding of Rules

A rule is encoded by (i) linking the roles of the antecedent and consequent predicates so as to reflect the correspondence between these roles specified by the rule, (ii) connecting the *enabler* of the consequent predicate to the *enabler* of the antecedent predicate, and (iii) connecting the appropriate collectors of the antecedent predicates to the appropriate collector of the consequent predicate. The collector link originates from the positive (negative) collector of an antecedent predicate if the predicate appears in its positive (negated) form in the antecedent. Similarly, the link terminates at the positive (negative) collector of the consequent predicate if the predicate appears in a positive (negated) form in the consequent. Figure 4 shows the encoding of the rule *bachelor(x)* ⇒ ¬*married(x,y)*. Observe that the system does not encode the contrapositive of a rule by fiat. In our model, a rule and its contrapositive are two *distinct* rules. Thus the contrapositive form of a rule may, or may not, be present in the LTM.

The encoding of rules makes use of weighted links between predicates. These weights distinguish categorical rules from soft (default) rules and also lead to a gradual weakening of activation along a chain of inference. Eventually the chain of inference terminates when activation falls below a threshold.

The solution to the problem of negation and inconsistency proposed above is simpler than the one suggested in (Cottrell, 1993). The latter suggests duplicating the entire predicate bank for each predicate. In this scheme, each predicate P would have two separate banks of role, enabler and collector nodes: one for positive knowledge about P ($+P$), and another for negative knowledge about P ($-P$). Such a scheme would have required a mechanism for comparing bindings across the $+P$ and $-P$ banks in order to detect a contradiction.

Three Examples

In this section we present three examples. These have been greatly simplified in order to focus on the key properties of the model.

First, assume that the system has the following rule and fact in its LTM: *bachelor(x)* ⇒ ¬*married(x,y)* and *bachelor(John)*. Now the system is told "John is married to Susan" by activating +*c:married* and establishing the dynamic bindings

(husband=John,wife=Susan). Activation propagates from +*c:married* to *e:married*, and because of the rule, from *e:married* to *e:bachelor*. The *husband* role of *married* also synchronizes with the role of *bachelor* (refer to Figure 4). At this time, the fact *bachelor(John)* matches the dynamic binding at *bachelor* and activates +*c:bachelor* (the fact is not shown in Figure 4). The activation from +*c:bachelor* propagates down to –*c:married*. Thus both the collectors of *married* become active and signal a contradiction between the agent's existing beliefs and the new information. The system has the option of rejecting the incoming information as spurious or updating its existing beliefs about John. How the system exercises its options is beyond the scope of this work.

Inconsistencies in existing knowledge are also detected in an analogous manner when inconsistent knowledge is activated. This can happen during the processing of a query or during the assimilation of new information. For example, assume that the following (inconsistent) knowledge resides in the LTM:

1. $P(x,y) \Rightarrow R(x,y)$
2. $Q(x,y) \Rightarrow \neg R(x,y)$
3. $P(a,b)$
4. $Q(a,b)$

Now assume that the execution of some cognitive task results in the query $R(a,b)?$ to the memory and reasoning system. As a result of rules (1) and (2), this query leads to the queries $P(a,b)?$ and $Q(a,b)?$. The facts (3) and (4) match the two queries, respectively, and activate +*c:P* and +*c:Q*. These collectors in turn activate +*c:R* and –*c:R* respectively. The activation of the positive and negative collectors of R leads to the detection of a contradiction. Thus the proposed encoding allows inconsistent knowledge to reside in the agent's memory, but detects an inconsistency whenever the agent tries to bring some inconsistent knowledge to bear on a particular task.

Next, we describe a simulation of the Post Office Example introduced earlier to illustrate how an agent may overlook relevant information and act in an erroneous manner. Extended evaluation — or an appropriate cue, however, can make the relevant information accessible and lead to the correct response. We model the agent's knowledge as follows (refer to Figure 5):

(i) *presidents-day(day)* ⇒ *federal-holiday(day)*
(ii) *3rd-Mon-Feb(day)* ⇒ *presidents-day(day)*,
(iii) *3rd-Mon-Feb(20-Feb-95)*
(iv) ¬*3rd-Mon-Feb(21-Feb-95)*
(v) *weekday(day)* ∧ *post-office(x)* ⇒ *open(x,day)* (with a medium weight)
(vi) *weekend(day)* ∧ *post-office(x)* ⇒ ¬*open(x,day)*
(vii) *federal-holiday(day)* ∧ *post-office(x)* ⇒ ¬*open(x,day)*
(viii) *post-office(PO)*

The significance of items (i), (v), (vi), and (vii) is fairly obvious. Item (ii) specifies that third Mondays in February are Presidents' Days. Ideally *3rd-Mon-Feb* would be realized as a mental process. We are indirectly simulating such a procedure by assuming that such a mental process is accessed via the predicate *3rd-Mon-Feb* in order to determine whether the day bound to its role is a third Monday in February. In this example, this mental "calendar" consists of two facts stated in items (iii) and (iv). Item (viii) states that PO is a particular post

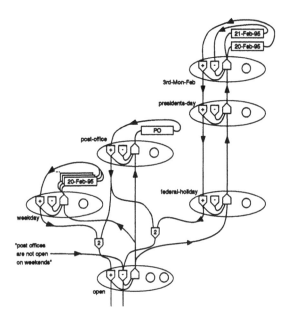

Figure 5: The network representation of the Post Office Example. Links between roles, detailed encoding of facts, the relation *weekend* and the encoding of rule (vi) is not shown. Rules (v) and (vii) are multiple antecedent rules. Thresholds other than 1 are shown inside nodes.

office. Items (i), (ii), (vi), and (vii) are categorical rules about the domain and have a high weight, but item (v) corresponds to default and defeasible information and hence, has a medium weight. In the current implementation, default rules have a weight of 0.70 while categorical rules have a weight of 1. We assume that "Today" is a concept which is bound each day to the appropriate date and to "weekday" or "weekend" depending on the day. These bindings are assumed to be available as facts in the agent's memory.

Imagine it is *20-Feb-95*, which is Presidents' Day, and Mary is planning a trip to the post office (PO). Her "go-to-post-office" schema has the precondition that the post office must be open so it poses the query *open(PO,Today)?* Assume that after posing the query the schema monitors the activity of *+c:open* and *−c:open* and accepts an answer based on the criterion: *Accept a "yes" ("no") answer if the positive (negative) collector stays ahead and exceeds a threshold, θ_{accept}, for some minimum length of time, Δ_t. Once the schema accepts an answer, it terminates the query and proceeds with its execution.

Since "Today" is bound to *20-Feb-95*, the fact *weekday(20-Feb-95)* is present in Mary's memory. When the schema asks the query *open(PO,Today)?*, the default rule about post offices remaining open on weekdays becomes active first and activates the positive collector *+c:open* (refer to Figures 5 and 6). If we assume θ_{accept} to be 0.5, the activation of *+c:open* exceeds θ_{accept} after 12 cycles and stays above threshold for about 20 cycles. During this time, the negative collector does not receive any activation and stays at 0. If we assume that Δ_t is 10 cycles, the schema will accept *+c:open* as an answer and

withdraw the query. So Mary will set off to the post office.[3]

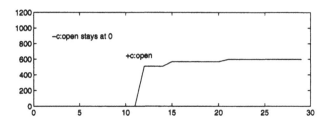

Figure 6: The activation trace for the query *open(PO,Today)?*; where today is 20-Feb-95. The vertical axis denotes activation level and has a scale factor of 1000. The horizontal axis denotes number of simulation steps.

Had the query remained active, the inference process would have eventually inferred that the post office is not open today. The result of the inferential process, if the query *open(PO,Today)?* had not been terminated by the schema, is shown in Figure 7. The dark lines show the activation of the collectors of *open* while the dotted lines show the activation of the collectors of some other relevant predicates. First it is inferred that today is a weekday. Next it is inferred that today is the third Monday in February. As a result, the inference that today is Presidents' Day, and hence, a federal holiday, follows. This in turn leads to the inference that the post office is not open today.

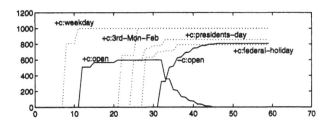

Figure 7: The activation trace for the query *open(PO,Today)?* — today being 20-Feb-95 — allowed to run its full course.

Subsequently, John asks Mary: "Isn't today Presidents' Day?". This causes the language process to activate *e:Presidents-day* and bind the role of Presidents' Day to *20-Feb-95*. This leads to the activation of *e:3rd-Mon-Feb* and then *+c:3rd-Mon-Feb* (via the fact *3rd-Mon-Feb(20-Feb-95)*). The activation from *+c:3rd-Mon-Feb* works its way back and activates *−c:open*. Since this activation is due to categorical rules (rules ii, i, and vii), it is stronger than that arriving at *+c:open* from the default rule (item v). The mutual inhibition between the highly activated *−c:open* and the moderately activated *+c:open* results in the suppression of *+c:open*, making Mary realize that the post office is not open (see Figure 8).

---

[3] The values of θ_{accept} and Δ_t cited above are the ones used in the simulation.

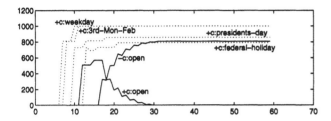

Figure 8: The activation trace for the query "Isn't today Presidents' Day?" posed to Mary on 20-Feb-95 long after her "go-to-post-office" schema has posed the query *open(PO,Today)?* and accepted a yes answer.

Conclusion

This paper describes an extension of the structured connectionist model SHRUTI that can deal with positive as well as negated forms of facts and rules. The model explains how an agent can hold inconsistent beliefs without being "aware" that its beliefs are inconsistent, but detect a contradiction when two contradictory beliefs that are within a small inferential distance of each other become co-active during an episode of reasoning. The model also shows how limited attentional focus or action under time pressure may lead to an erroneous response.

The significance of this work extends beyond reasoning. In essence, SHRUTI demonstrates how connectionist networks can represent relational structures and perform certain types of computations over such structures in an efficient manner. This involves the representation of *static* as well as *dynamic* bindings, interactions between these two types of bindings, and the systematic but context sensitive propagation of dynamic bindings from one relational structure to another. Hence the significance of the representational and inferential mechanisms developed in SHRUTI extends to any cognitive task that involve computations over relational structures such as frames and schemas. For example, Henderson (1994) has shown that the SHRUTI architecture is also appropriate for supporting real-time parsing of English.

In future work we plan a detailed investigation of the interactions between default and categorical rules. In doing so we will draw upon earlier work on connectionist treatment of exceptions, multiple inheritance, and default information (Cottrell, 1985; Shastri, 1988).

Acknowledgment:

This work was partially funded by ONR grants N00014-93-1-1149 and N00014-95-C-0182. Thanks to Jerry Feldman, George Lakoff, D.R. Mani, Srini Narayanan, David Bailey and Dan Jurafsky for intellectual stimulation.

References

Ajjanagadde, V. & Shastri, L. (1991) Rules and variables in neural nets, *Neural Computation*. 3, 121–134.

Bienenstock, E. & Geman, S. (1995) Compositionality in Neural Systems. In M.A. Arbib (Ed.), *The Handbook of Brain Theory and Neural Networks* (pp. 223–226). Cambridge, MA: MIT Press.

Cottrell, G.W. (1985) Parallelism in inheritance hierarchies with exception. In *Proceedings of IJCAI-85* (pp. 194–202). San Mateo, CA: Morgan Kaufmann Publishers.

Cottrell, G.W. (1993) From symbols to neurons: Are we yet there? *Behavioral and Brain Science*, 16:3, 454.

Damasio, A. R. (1989) Time-locked multiregional retroactivation: A systems-level proposal for the neural substrates of recall and recognition. *Cognition*, 33, 25-62.

Feldman, J. A. (1989) Neural Representation of Conceptual Knowledge. In L. Nadel, L.A. Cooper, P. Culicover, & R.M. Harnish (Eds.), *Neural Connections, Mental Computation* (pp. 68–103). Cambridge, MA: MIT Press.

Henderson, J. (1994) Connectionist Syntactic Parsing Using Temporal Variable Binding. *Journal of Psycholinguistic Research*, 23 (5) 353–379.

Mani, D.R. and Shastri, L. (1993) Reflexive Reasoning with Multiple-Instantiation in in a Connectionist Reasoning System with a Typed Hierarchy, *Connection Science*, Vol. 5, No. 3 & 4, 205–242.

McKoon, G., & Ratcliff, R. (1981) The Comprehension Processes and Memory Structures Involved in Instrumental Inference. *Journal of Verbal Learning and Verbal Behavior*, 20, 671-682.

Shastri, L. (1988) *Semantic networks : An evidential formulation and its connectionist realization*. San Mateo, CA: Morgan Kaufmann Publishers.

Shastri, L. (1991) Relevance of Connectionism to AI: A representation and reasoning perspective. In J. Barnden and J. Pollack (Eds.) *Advances in Connectionist and Neural Computation Theory*, vol. 1 (pp. 259–283). Norwood, NJ: Ablex.

Shastri, L. (1993) A Computational Model of Tractable Reasoning – Taking Inspiration from Cognition. In *Proceedings of IJCAI-93* (pp. 202–207). San Mateo, CA: Morgan Kaufmann Publishers.

Shastri, L. & Ajjanagadde, V. (1993) From simple associations to systematic reasoning. *Behavioral and Brain Sciences*, 16:3, 417-494.

Shastri, L. & Feldman, J.A. (1986) Neural Nets, Routines and Semantic Networks. In N. Sharkey (Ed.), *Advances in Cognitive Science* (pp. 158–203). Chichester, UK: Ellis Horwood Publishers.

Shastri, L. & Grannes, D.J. (1995) Dealing with negated knowledge and inconsistency in a neurally motivated model of memory and reflexive reasoning. TR-95-041, ICSI, Berkeley, CA.

Singer, W. (1993) Synchronization of cortical activity and its putative role in information processing and learning. *Annual Review of Physiology* 55: 349-74

von der Malsburg, C. (1986) Am I thinking assemblies? In G. Palm & A. Aertsen (Eds.), *Brain Theory* (pp. 161–176). New York, NY: Springer-Verlag.

Hearing with the eyes: A distributed cognition perspective on guitar song imitation

Nick V. Flor
Graduate School of Industrial Administration
Carnegie Mellon University
Pittsburgh, PA 15213
flor+@cmu.edu

Barbara Holder
Department of Cognitive Science
University of California, San Diego
La Jolla, CA 92093
bholder@cogsci.ucsd.edu

Abstract

Many guitarists learn to play by imitating recordings. This style of learning allows guitarists to master both new songs and new techniques. To imitate a song, a guitarist repeatedly listens to a song recording until the entire song, or the desired portion of that song, can be reproduced by the guitarist. This kind of imitation can be a very difficult process particularly if the recorded guitarist plays fast and other instruments are involved. Besides the difficulty in *hearing* the guitar music, the many different ways to finger and articulate the same notes and chords on a guitar, can also make *playing* the music difficult. In this paper, we describe some of the knowledge guitarists use to minimize these difficulties. We then propose an external representation that guitarists can use to unload some of the cognitive burden imposed by the imitation process. This external representation — the bar chord — transform many of the imitation activities from those requiring both internal computations and memory to those that require the guitarist to merely look and see the desired results. Moreover, bar chords facilitate the social distribution of these individual benefits. This research contributes to the growing field of distributed cognition and to our understanding of both internal and external representations used during music learning and improvisation.

Introduction

There are many ways of learning how to play guitar. Among classical-style guitarists, the most common means of learning is by practicing sheet music — music encoded on paper in a standard notation — under the guidance of an instructor. The typical novice guitarist practices a piece for about a week, then visits the instructor for more fine-grained instruction. The instructor sits to the side of the budding guitarist, correcting mistakes, providing playing tips, offering encouragement, and at times administering a scolding. However, among guitarists, it is well-known that many of the founders of modern rock guitar (such as Jimi Hendrix and Eric Clapton) could not read standard music notation, viz., could not *sight-read*. Even today it is common to find well-known rock guitarists that cannot sight-read. Such musicians learned to play by imitating the guitar players on recorded songs.

This paper is an attempt to understand this unique kind of learning from a distributed cognition perspective. First, we describe the data collection method and the key features of the distributed cognition framework. This is followed by a short tutorial on the guitar and music. We then describe why imitating recorded music can be complex, followed by an analysis of some of the musical regularities and special knowledge that guitarist's possess which minimizes this complexity. Finally, we perform a cognitive analysis of an external representation — the bar chord — which can further reduce the complexity of imitating recorded songs, by transforming many of the imitation related tasks from "in-the-head" conceptual tasks into perceptual or "looking" tasks.

METHOD, BACKGROUND, AND REVIEW

This paper reports on a one and a half year study of rock-and-roll style guitar (hereafter, rock guitar) playing. Both authors are trained in classical guitar, have over five years of playing experience, and are proficient at sight-reading. However, rock guitar is very different from classical, in both training methods, techniques, and terminology. The primary author spent over a year and a half: (a) examining the available printed material; (b) interviewing guitarists from the undergraduate, graduate, and staff populations at Carnegie Mellon University; and (c) sitting in, whenever possible, in informal "jam sessions" with existing bands. Although we did not do a traditional field study, we believe the above activities provided the same end-result — an understanding of the guitar and music from the perspective of a rock guitar player.

The distributed cognition framework (Hutchins, 1995), was used to acquire further insights into the internal and external structures rock-guitarists employ during song imitation. Briefly, this framework views the boundary of cognition as dynamic and flexible; the boundary can expand beyond the individual's skull to include those external structures participating in a task's performance as cognitive structures, and not merely as inputs into a cognitive process inside the skull. Moreover, as Hutchins (1995) demonstrates, these external structures can act as more than just external memory. They can encode complex computations in their surface structure, which can transform certain tasks requiring internal memory and

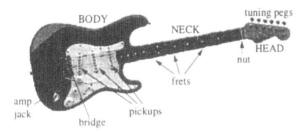

Figure 1. An electric guitar

processing, into tasks which instead use simple physical manipulation of external artifacts and the reading off of results. This framework focused our efforts on characterizing the cognitive consequences of external structures used by guitarists, such as the particular way the guitarists finger chords.

There is a surprising lack of studies on music imitation and improvisation. The key studies, are by Johnson-Laird (1988), Pressing (1988), and Sloboda (1985), who focused on characterizing internal processing capacity constraints on music improvisation. Johnson-Laird and Sloboda argue that the structure of improvised music is constrained (in terms of genres, song forms, and individual styles) so that less internal cognitive processing is required during performance time. However, neither Johnson-Laird (1988) nor Sloboda (1985) offer empirical evidence to support the view that improvised performances are so constrained or that cognitive capacity is limited. Pressing (1988) develops a psychological model of improvisation, but focuses on internal cognitive constraints on the process; external factors are not considered. This study both supports and augments these studies by focusing on how guitarists can *self-impose constraints* over song-form constraints by using external structures. Although this study focuses on external structures used during song imitation, the external structures described can also be used to facilitate guitar improvisation as well.

EXTERNAL STRUCTURES: GUITAR AND MUSIC

From a guitar player's perspective, the typical guitar consists of the following components (see Figure 1): six metal *strings*, attached at one end to *tuning pegs* located on the guitar's *head*, and attached at the other end to a *bridge* on the guitar's *body*. The guitar's head and body are connected via a *neck*; the neck is commonly divided into 19-22 different regions known as *frets*. Collectively, the frets make up the *fretboard*. The guitar body can be hollow, semi-hollow, or solid-body wood. Acoustic, and classical style guitars have hollow or semi-hollow bodies, and one or more *sound holes* which serve to amplify the sound of the vibrating strings. Electric guitars have solid bodies, and generate sound through a complex process: strings vibrating over one or more electromagnetic *pickups,* attached to the body, create an electrical signal which travels over a *cable* to an *amplifier* which finally converts the electrical signal into sound waves (see Figure 3).

Guitarist create music by playing individual notes, or combinations of notes known as chords. Guitarists play notes and chords by using their left hand to depress certain fret regions while their right hand simultaneously plucks or strum the strings along the body of the guitar. The guitarist can play 12 basic sounds (notes) — A, A#, B, C, C#, D, D#, E, F, F#, G, G# —and at least 3 different variations (or octaves) of the basic notes. Each guitar string is tuned to a different note E, A, D, G, B, and E (2 octaves higher than the first-E), so that plucking a string without pressing on the fretboard produces that corresponding note. Other notes are created by depressing strings over different frets, with frets closer to the body producing higher frequency notes than those close to the head (see Figure 2).

INTERNAL STRUCTURES: KNOWLEDGE FOR SONG IMITATION

In the typical imitation process, the guitarist alternates between two activities: playing and listening to a song fragment; and attempting to duplicate that fragment on the guitar (see Figure 3). The activities continue until the guitarist learns the entire song or the desired fragment. However, there are several factors which make the imitation process difficult.

First, on any given song, there are *multiple instruments playing* at the same time, e.g., a drum and a bass. The guitarist needs to learn how to identify the guitar independent of the other instruments. This may seem straightforward, but many modern guitarists attach special-effects instruments to their guitars such as fuzz, wah, and distortion, which can make it even more difficult to pick out the guitar parts in the recording. Even if the guitarist can pick out the guitar parts, a given note can be played on *multiple places* on the fretboard. Furthermore, there are

0	1	2	3	4	5	6	7	8	9	10	11	12	13	14	15	16	17	18	19	20	21	22
e	f	f#	g	g#	a	a#	b	•c	c#	d	•d#	e	f	f#	g	g#	a	a#	b	c	c#	d
B	C	C#	D	D#	e	f	f#	•g	g#	a	•a#	b	c	c#	d	d#	e	f	f#	g	g#	a
G	G#	A	A#	B	C	C#	D	•D	e	•f	f#	g	g#	a	a#	b	c	c#	d	d#	e	f
D	D#	E	F	F#	G	G#	A	•A	B	•C	C#	D	D#	e	f	f#	g	g#	a	a#	b	c
A	A#	B	C	C#	D	D#	E	•F	F#	•G	G#	A	A#	B	C	C#	D	D#	e	f	f#	g
E	F	F#	G	G#	A	A#	B	•C	C#	D	•D	E	F	F#	G	G#	A	A#	B	C	C#	D

Figure 2. Sideways depiction of the first 22 keyboard frets with the 12 different tones superimposed (double vertical lines indicate where the nut is). Column headings denote fret numbers. The top row corresponds to the frets under string 1, with the last row string 6. Different octaves of the same note are depicted with different fonts, e.g., the E note is represented 4 different times (E, *E, e, e*). Note the redundancy; E can be played on the (12th fret, 6th string), (7th fret, 5th string), or (2nd fret, 4th string). Bulleted frets cells depict notes in the C pentatonic scale.

149

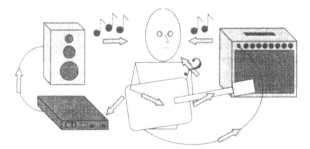

Figure 3. The guitarist's typical setup for imitating a recorded song. The arrows denote trajectories for moving information across different media. The guitarist uses the left-most loop to move a song fragment into memory. The rightmost "loop" is used during the imitation process. The arrow with the question mark denotes a possible visual pathway that can be exploited to assist the imitation process, a central topic of this paper.

multiple ways to play a note. For example, a given note may be played soft, loud, or dampened (palm-muted); or it may be sustained for several beats with or without a tremolo. Moreover, instead of simply depressing a fret location, a guitarist may depress a lower fret location and move the string sideways, an action known as *bending*. Bending simulates playing a higher fret location (for example, instead of playing a "b" by depressing the 7th fret, 1st string; a guitarist can depress the string over the 5th fret, an "a", and bend up to a "b"). Finally, most songs have a complex and *lengthy melody*, and reproducing the melody requires that the guitarist remembers a lengthy sequence of notes (see Table 1). Assuming all the notes and chords are heard and remembered correctly, the guitarist must still get the *timing* right; the notes and chords must be played, in the correct sequence, with a certain temporal spacing, and for a certain length. The following sections look at some of the ways guitarist work around these difficulties during song imitation.

Knowledge 1 & 2: The importance of chord changes and the song's key

Non-musicians think of the changing melody as the defining characteristic for a song. However, guitarists view a song's chord changes as its defining characteristic and thus focus on imitating chord changes instead of melody changes. An analysis of 45 Jimi Hendrix song transcriptions in the Internet guitar archive (ftp.nevada.edu), show that 31 of the songs included chord changes, and no explicit melody transcriptions. Imitating chord changes, instead of melody changes, has important implications for what needs to be remembered. A song can have a fairly complex and changing melody, but the chord changes underlying the melody are less complex. Consider the common nursery song "Twinkle twinkle little star" (hereafter, Twinkle*) by Hayden in the key of C (see Table 1). This song uses only three chords: C, F, and G. However, the melody uses six of the seven notes in the C-major scale. A song in the key of C means that C is the root sound. The root sound gives the song a sense of

completion, and most other chords in the song move towards the root (note that in Twinkle* the C chord more than double the other chords, 11 out of 20). The notion of "sense of completion" is difficult to operationalize, but the analogy is that of the last word in a sentence. If the song does not end with that chord, the song does not seem finished. Most songs in the key of X, start off in X and end in X. Thus, both Hound Dog (see Table 2) and Twinkle* start off with a C chord and end with a C chord.

Table 1. Twinkle Twinkle Little Star by Hayden (in the key of C)

Chords	C			F	C		G		C		G		C
Melody	c	c	g	g	a	a	g		f	f	e	e	d	d	c
Lyrics	Twinkle twinkle little star, How I wonder what you are
Chords	F		C		G		C		F		C		G
Melody	g	gf	f	e		e	d		g	gf	f		e	e	d
Lyrics	Up above the world so high, Like a diamond in the sky
Chords	C			F	C		G		C		G		C
Melody	c	c	g	g	a	a	g		f	f	e	e	d	d	c
Lyrics	Twinkle twinkle little star, How I wonder what you are

Table 2. Hound Dog by Elvis Presley (in the key of C)

Chords	C													
Melody	d#	d#	d#	d#	d#	d#	c		c		d#		g		a	c	c
Lyrics	You aint nothing but a hound dog, Scratching all the time
Chords	F												C	
Melody	d#	d#	d#	d#	d#	d#	c		d#		d#		g		a	c	c
Lyrics	You aint nothing but a hound dog, Scratching all the time
Chords	G								F				C	
Melody	d#	d#	d	d	d			d d d			d d		d#		d d		c	c
Lyrics	You aint never caught a rabbit & you ain't a friend of mine

One may think a rock and roll song is more complex than a common nursery song, but when comparing Hound Dog, by Elvis Presley with Twinkle* by Hayden, the complexity of the nursery song becomes apparent. Like Twinkle*, Hound Dog utilizes only three chords (C, F, G), and five different tones (c, d, d#, g, a). However, the chords change less often six times for Hound Dog (C, F, C, G, F, C) as opposed to twenty times for Twinkle Twinkle Little Star (C, F, C, G, C, G, C, F, C, G, C, F, C, G, C, F, C, G, C, G, C). In either case, the guitarist can reduce the memory requirements for imitating a song, by only imitating chord changes.

Knowledge 3: Many songs conform to standard chord progressions (I-IV-V)

The imitation task is further simplified by the following regularity: many rock and roll songs, and almost all blues style songs, follow a I-IV-V progression. For example, Hound Dog is in the key of C, which means that the root chord is C. Assign C the value one (usually written as the roman numeral, I). Counting up, D would be assigned a two (II), E three (III), F four (IV), G five (V), A six (VI), and B seven (VII). Hound Dog's chord changes only involve C (I), F (IV), and G (V). Thus, it is a I-IV-V progression, even though the actual changes do not go strictly from I to IV to V. Twinkle* is also a I-IV-V progression. Thus a guitarist can classify songs based on chord progressions, further reducing the memory requirements for imitating a song.

Furthermore, during the initial stages of imitating chord progressions, knowing the key and a set of standard chord

150

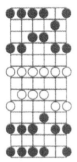 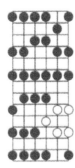

Figure 4. Two commonly used pentatonic scales in the key of A. These scales are represented as lightly-filled circles. The dark-filled circles denote other pentatonic scale members redundantly distributed across the fretboard. Almost all these notes sound "good" when improvised over a I-IV-V progressions.

progressions reduces the space of chords that need to be tried. Given that the guitarist has determined one of the chords, be it the I, IV, or the V, the next possible chord is limited to one of the other two chords. As a final note, space limitations only allow us to describe one of the common chord progressions, I-IV-V. There are also many other progressions such as the ii-V, I-vi-IV-V, and also regularities in changes *between* these chords that reduces the space of chords the guitarist has to consider during the imitation process. However, the basic idea is the same. Given that the guitarist knows: the song's key, has categorized the song as fitting a common progression, and knows at least one of the chords, the next chord is likely to be one of the remaining chords in the chord progression. Thus the decision space for the chords which the guitarist should try is reduced.

Knowledge 4: Pentatonic scales and Improvising

The typical rock song includes a guitar solo, which guitarists often imitate in addition to the chord changes. The guitar solo is usually played over a song's chord changes and substitutes for the melody line. Guitar solos, if imitated at all, are usually learned after the chord changes. When quizzed as to why, one informant explained: "Because you need to know the key the song is in." Recall that the key is usually associated with the last or first chord in a song. Once the key is known the guitarist can usually count on the solo's notes coming from a *pentatonic scale* whose root note is the same as the song's key. In the key of C, those notes are C, D#, F, G, and A# (see Figure 1); in the key of A, they are A, B#, D, E, G (see Figure 4). However, guitarist do not normally think of the pentatonic scale as a particular collection of notes. Instead they view the pentatonic scale as a particular pattern on the fretboard of the guitar starting on a given fret (see Figure 1 for a pentatonic scale in the key of C, starting on fret 8). This same pattern is transposable to other keys as well, thus eliminating the need to remember different scales for different keys. For example, the pentatonic scale in A is the exact same pattern as C, only shifted up 3 frets (starting on fret 5). As another example, the pentatonic scale in the key of D is the exact same pattern but shifted down two

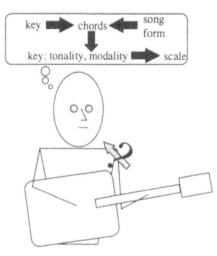

Figure 5. Some of the key pieces of knowledge possessed by rock guitarists. Can these structures be distributed?

frets (starting on fret 10). Another interesting scale property, relevant to improvising, is that most of the notes in the scale sound good over the chord changes. Even a random selection of notes from the correct pentatonic scale sound good. This reduces the spaces of notes that have to be tried during improvisation, and can hide errors which the guitarist makes during improvisation.

Many guitarists do not imitate a song's guitar solo. Instead, the guitarists improvise their own solos by playing notes from a pentatonic scale. In fact, most guitarists think of improvisation as simply playing the correct scale over a sequence of chord changes. For rock and roll and blues songs, knowledge of pentatonic scales and a song's key is usually sufficient for improvising. However, with more complicated songs, a guitarist needs to know: (a) the tonal center of the song; and (b) the modality of the song. Collectively, these two items denote the song's key, which subsequently constrains different kinds of scale patterns.

RE-DISTRIBUTING COGNITION: CHANGING THE SONG IMITATION TASK INTO A LOOKING TASK

A central imitation activity is determining chord changes. The chord changes constrain a key, which in turn constrains a scale, which can then be used for improvising or to help with imitating a guitar solo (see Figure 5). Moreover, the rock guitarist can rely on most songs belonging to a set of common chord progressions, such as the I-IV-V. What was not discussed was how guitarists determine the other chords in a progression once the key (again, usually the first chord in a song) was known. Take for example, a I-IV-V progression in the key of C. By definition, the I-chord is a C-chord, but how does the guitarist determine that the IV chord and V chords are F and G, respectively. One way is for the guitarist to mentally count upwards from C. Alternatively, the guitarist can also memorize all twelve I-IV-V patterns. Both approaches can be difficult, the former requires internal computing effort while the latter requires memory (see Figure 6). However, an alternative approach based on

151

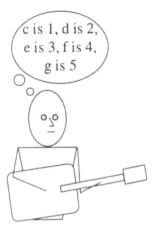

Figure 6. The guitarist using open-chords either has to remember the chords relative to the root, or mentally calculate them.

the distributed cognition framework, is to redistribute the cognition so that instead of relying on internal computations or internal memory, the task is transformed into one where more perceptual mechanisms are employed. Fortunately, the structure of the guitar's fretboard allows such a redistribution of cognition. To understand this redistribution, consider the use of open-chords versus bar chords.

Guitarists typically learn only the open chords when they start playing. Such chords are fingered within the first five frets of the guitar, and they are used by novices because they are easier to form than bar chords (see Figure 7, rows 1 and 2). Note how the root chord in the key of C (Figure 7, row 1, col 1) looks different from the root chord in the key of D (Figure 7, row 2, col 1). If a song does not follow the rule of the "first or last chord being the key," then there is no visual indication of the root. The guitarist must rely on the internal notion of "sense of completion" to determine the key. Moreover, the guitarist must memorize 12 different open-chord fingerings and given a root chord (I), must mentally calculate, or remember what the IV and V chords are for all twelve keys.

Bar-chord benefits 1 and 2: Seeing the root, and looking where the other chords should be

Consider, however, the use of bar-chords. There are two basic types, root-6 bar chords (see Figure 7, rows 3 & 4, col 1), and root-5 bar chords (see Figure 7, rows 3 & 4, col 1 & 2). Bar chords typically use the index finger to depress all the strings on a given fret, while the other fingers depress lower fret regions (see Figure 7, rows 3 and 4). Note how the root chord in the key of C (Figure 7, row 3, col 1) looks the same as the root chord in the key of D (Figure 7, row 4, col 1). Besides a structural regularity for the I-chord, the use of bar chords also introduce a spatial regularity. The four and five chords, however, look the same in both keys (Figure 7, rows 3 & 4, cols 2 & 3). Thus, the guitarist does not need to remember different fingerings for the IV and V chords; only their bar location — the fret where the index finger makes a bar — changes.

Figure 7. Open-chords and bar-chords for a I-IV-V progression in the keys of C and D

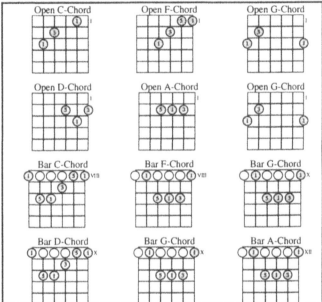

In fact, by moving the root-6 and root-5 bars up and down the frets all 12 different possible chords can be generated, thus the guitarist only needs to remember 2 chord fingerings. Now one may complain that the guitarist still needs to remember the 12 different locations to place the bar for the 12 different chords. However, the fretboard imposes some spatial regularities which reduce the guitarist's need to remember where to place the bar chord. The IV chord is always to the left of the I-chord, and the V chord is always two frets below the IV chord. There are other spatial regularities for the other nine chords. Thus, given a key, the guitarist can rely on these spatial regularities, and just look and see where the other chords should be.

Finally, this spatial regularity means that given that the guitarist knows the key (root-chord), the guitarist can dispense with remembering the labels (C, F, G) for the various chords. The IV chords is just a position to the right of the root-chord, and the V chord is just a position to the right and down several frets from the root chord.

Bar-chord benefit 3: The similarity of external and internal representations

There are other benefits to using bar chords. To see this, consider a song with a I-IV-V chord progression (e.g., "Wild Thing" by the Troggs), played in both the keys of C and D. Most listeners will immediately recognize that the songs are the same, except that one (key of D song) sounds "higher" than the other (key of C song). However, the I-IV-V *open-chords* in the key of C, look very different from the I-IV-V *open-chords* in the key of D (see Figure 7, rows 1 and 2). This difference of open-chord appearance contradicts a person's internal sense that the songs are similar. Moreover, the relationship between the songs — that one sounds "higher" than the other — is not preserved when using the open chords. However, when using bar-chords, the exact same chord fingerings are used except that one (key of D, root at fret 10) starts two frets below the other (key of C, root at fret 8). Thus, using bar chords preserves an individual's sense of similarity between the same song played in two different keys (see Figure 7, rows 3 and 4). Moreover, the relationship that one sounds higher than the other is also depicted visually when using bar chords; in the key of D, the song is played two frets higher than when played in the key of C.

Lastly, there are also social implications from using bar-chords. For example, a guitar teacher that uses bar-chords makes the regularities and benefits described above available to the student. As another example, take a guitarist "sitting in" — a guest musician — during a jam session. If the guitarist sitting in forgets the chord changes to a song, and there is another guitarist in the band using bar chords, then the guitarist sitting in can watch the other guitarist for a while and more easily see what the chord changes are. Both examples illustrate how externally observable representations can provide social benefits as well.

SUMMARY

Guitarists can rely on both internal and external structures to help them imitate songs. The data from our study suggests that guitarists first imitate a song's chord progressions. The chord progressions define a key, which then constrains a scale which can be used either for improvising or to facilitate imitating the song's guitar solo. The imitation process can be difficult, but this difficulty can be alleviated by using the proper external structures. we proposed one such external structure, the bar chord, and showed how the bar chord could transform many of the imitation subtasks from ones which require internal processing and memory, to subtasks which involve merely looking in the world and reading a solution off the guitar's fretboard. Moreover, because bar-chords are visually available to other guitarists, they can facilitate learning and remembering in a social context, such as during a band jam session. We hope our research encourages others to understand naturally occurring cognitive activity as a distributed phenomenon.

ACKNOWLEDGMENTS

Many thanks to the members of the "Cognition in Group Settings" discussion group at the University of Pittsburgh's Learning Research and Development Center, for helpful comments on an earlier draft of this paper.

REFERENCES

Hutchins, E. (1995). *Cognition in the wild*. MA: MIT Press.

Johnson-Laird, P. N. (1988). Freedom and constraint in creativity. In R. J. Sternberg (Ed.), *The nature of creativity*. Cambridge, U.K.: Cambridge University Press.

Pressing, J. (1988). Improvisation: Methods and models. In J. A. Sloboda (Ed.), *Generative processes in music: The psychology of performance, improvisation, and composition*. Oxford, U.K.: Clarendon Press.

Sloboda, J. A. (1985). *The musical mind: The cognitive psychology of music*. Oxford, U.K.: Carendon Press.

Constraints on the experimental design process in real-world science

Lisa M. Baker and **Kevin Dunbar**
McGill University Department of Psychology
1205 Dr. Penfield Avenue
Montreal, Quebec H3A 1B1 Canada
lbaker@ego.psych.mcgill.ca or dunbar@ego.psych.mcgill.ca

Abstract

The goal of the research reported in this paper is to uncover the cognitive processes involved in designing complex experiments in contemporary biology. Models of scientific reasoning often assume that the experimental design process is primarily theoretically constrained. However, designing an experiment is a very complex process in which many steps and decisions must be made even when the theory is fully specified. We uncover a number of crucial cognitive steps in experimental design by analyzing the design of an experiment at a meeting of an immunology laboratory. Based on our analysis, we argue that experimental design involves the following processes: unpacking and specifying slots in possible experimental designs, locally evaluating specific components of proposed designs, and coordinating and globally evaluating possible experimental designs. Four sets of criteria guide local and global evaluation: ensuring a robust internal structure to the experiment, optimizing the likelihood experiments will work, performing costs/benefits analyses on possible design components, and ensuring acceptance of results by the scientific community. Our analyses demonstrate that experimental design is constrained by many non-theoretical factors. In particular, the constant threat of error in experimental results lies behind many of the strategies scientists use.

Introduction

The specification of the cognitive processes underlying scientific thinking has been a central concern of cognitive theories (e.g., Dunbar, 1995, 1996; Klahr & Dunbar, 1988; Langley, Simon, Bradshaw, & Zytkow, 1987; Nersessian, 1992; Thagard, 1992). The main focus of research on scientific thinking has been on inductive reasoning and hypothesis formation; there are now many models of the cognitive processes involved in relating theory to data. However, few models address another important aspect of scientific work, the experimental design process. Most cognitive research that has addressed experimental design has focused on the relationship between theory and experiment (e.g., Klahr & Dunbar, 1988; Klayman & Ha, 1987; Kulkarni & Simon, 1988). However, there is a rich set of reasoning processes that real-world scientists use to design experiments that refers only tangentially to theory. These

cognitive processes "internal" to experimental design exemplify the rich heuristics that reasoners construct amid the constraints of complex, real-world environments. The goal of this research is to present a model of the heuristics used for designing experiments in real-world science.

Following the research strategy developed by Dunbar (Dunbar, 1995, 1996), we will investigate the way that scientists design experiments by using data that we have recently collected from an immunology laboratory at a major Canadian university. We have found that one place that scientists design and modify experiments on-line is at the weekly laboratory meeting (Dunbar, 1996). Thus, the data that we will discuss in this paper consists of audio recordings of a laboratory meeting. The advantage of using laboratory meetings as our source of data is that we obtain spontaneous statements about the design of experiments by real-world scientists in a natural way, rather than using verbal protocols, or a microworld, to investigate the experimental design process.

Method

This study is part of an ongoing research project initiated by Dunbar that has investigated various aspects of reasoning and problem solving using data from real-world science laboratories (e.g., Baker & Dunbar, in preparation; Dunbar, 1995, 1996; Dunbar & Baker, 1994; Dunbar, Patel, Baker, & Dama, 1995). The data for this study was drawn from a laboratory meeting of an immunology laboratory (excerpts from the meeting are shown in Table 1). While the laboratory was guaranteed confidentiality, we were given broad access to meetings, papers, grant proposals, and other laboratory records. At meetings of this laboratory, graduate students and other laboratory members take turns presenting recent experimental results and discussing what experiments they plan to do next. Laboratory members who were present at the meeting we analyzed include the principal investigator (PI), a postdoctoral fellow (Victoria[1]), three graduate students (including Ellen and Monica), one undergraduate honors student, and two technicians. The entire meeting was tape recorded and transcribed, and then a segment of this

---

[1]All names and some identifying features of the experiments have been changed.

Ellen: [1] And uh I also plan to do *in situ* with the X probes, [2] and uh with each one I will try a different modification to the initial protocols s uh [3] those modifications would be aimed at increasing the accessibility of the uh probes to the target and reducing the background. [4] So that the overall aim would be to increase the signal over uh the noise ratio. [5] OK, so example of the modica uh modification that I will do is like to use fresh frozen tissues instead of uh perfused tissues . . .

PI: [6] Are you going to be able to do all this in the next two weeks?

Ellen: [7] Well I will try fresh frozen tissues, that's for sure. [8] Perfused tissues, yes. [9] Um maybe I don't know if if I will like to treat with uh chloroform. [10] But RNAase I would like to do that as well. [11] Because in one experiment in one *in situ* we can combine all these things together.

PI: [12] All this is going into one experiment?

Ellen: [13] Yes.

PI: [14] What's the tissue?

Ellen: [15] Um hamster liver and spleen . . .

PI: [16] There's a positive control in this experiment?

Ellen: [17] Positive control would be TRX cells but that [18] I will I would mainly concentrate on tissues first

PI: [19] I think at the very very least and we're really I'm talking about the bottom before we start discussing the experiment properly, [20] there ought to be TRX induced versus uninduced. [21] Which you know already gives you a signal versus no signal. [22] I think that's got to be there minimum [23] and then we can interpret from there . . .

---------------------- *[other aspects of experiments are discussed]* --------------------

PI: [24] And amongst all the treatments that you describe . . . which one corresponds to the industry standard, [25] and how often have you tried that one?

Ellen: [26] Uh, I will I will try it for the first time the the fresh frozen tissues [27] are what they used.

PI: [28] So that's the industry standard? [29] I mean the the likeliest way to make *in situ* hybridization work on tissues?

Ellen: [30] No there are there are people using perfused tissues as well. [31] I think published. [32] Fresh frozen tissues it's harder to get [33] especially when it's spleen. [34] I think uh this treatment and [35] and then if we don't fix before it it's very hard to to get.

PI: [36] How many people are publishing that they can get RPAF signal on fixed tissue? Is it is it more than one lab?

Ellen: [37] Yes, yes, yes . . .

PI: [38] I wonder whether you shouldn't, whether you need to, invest a huge amount of effort on fresh frozen tissue that [39] now that people can tell me this uh what they think . . .

Ellen: [40] I have the tissues.

PI: [41] You have the tissues? [42] Then most of the effort is already taken care of? . . . OK . . .

Monica: [43] But if you were to get the same results from fixed and from fresh frozen [44] probably you would choose to use fixed in the future because fixed is easier for you to work with.

Ellen: [45] OK . . .

PI: [46] The impression I get is that fixed tissue [47] I mean I have my own favorites in the business OK? [48] And it's partly bias [49] and it's partly, I see their papers around. [50] But one of my favorites is the Y lab . . . [51] They work on fixed tissue [52] and they're doing a lot of stuff that interests us [53] and we would like, in fact, to be where they are. [54] So I have this personal bias that if they can do it we can do it, [55] and it looks like easier work than using fresh tissue. [56] So what I'm trying to do is to reduce the amount of work you have to do to get a result, [57] and what's frustrating me, of course, as it always does in *in situ* [58] is the length of time before we know how it's gone. [59] Any experiment most experiments end up getting done a few times before you get a good result, and many there many many failures along the way . . . [60] But I guess what you're telling me is that you're going to do experiments blindly for a while until you start reeling in the data.

Monica: [61] Even from molecular biology though you have to . . . test a couple of different ways [62] and then as soon as you hit on the one that works OK then you know go that way. [63] And that that's what it sounds like Ellen's trying to do . . . [64] Unfortunately it takes five weeks to get the answer [65] but she says that she's gonna do a number of different tests in the in the same experiment [66] and then at the end of that five weeks

PI: [67] Within the same experiment I hadn't pick up on that's where I started asking I I was afraid that we were talking about ten different experiments.

Ellen: [68] It would it would be in into two experiments . . .

Monica: [69] All right. But you could do one one week and one the next . . . And so it would be within six weeks you would you would go, [70] Oh the fixed way...works.

PI: [71] So the comparison is going to be...fresh tissue versus

Ellen: [72] Fixed . . . Yes.

Table 1: Meeting excerpts referring to possible use of fresh frozen tissue.

meeting was selected for analysis because it involved an extended discussion of possible experimental designs. Protocol analysis techniques were used to analyze comments related to the design of future experiments. These comments were analyzed to determine the general structure of the experimental design process and the particular issues researchers took into account in designing experiments.

Analyses

Summary of the Meeting

In the meeting segment analyzed, a graduate student, Ellen, and other laboratory members discussed several possible modifications Ellen might make to a particular experimental approach. We have analyzed the entire segment; however, for explanatory clarity, here and in Table 1 we will present all references to a particular problem, the issue of what type of tissue preparation method Ellen will use.

Ellen's goal at this point in her research is to get an experimental technique called *in situ* hybridization to work. *In situ* hybridization involves placing a "probe" (in this case, a DNA probe for the enzyme RPAF) on a tissue sample and observing where on the tissue the probe adheres. Ellen hypothesizes that RPAF is involved in a particular disease. If specific adherence of the probe is achieved, Ellen will be able to see which, if any, cells in the tissue are binding to RPAF. Up to the time of this meeting, Ellen has failed to get the *in situ* hybridization technique to work.

With respect to the particular issue addressed in these meeting excerpts, Ellen is considering two possible tissue preparation methods. The first, which she has used in the past, involves "fixing" the animal tissue chemically so that experiments can be done on it. The alternate method that Ellen is considering is to freeze the tissue.

At the beginning of the meeting segment analyzed (items [1-5] in Table 1; all subsequent bracketed numerals will refer to items in Table 1), Ellen is discussing experimental manipulations she may do to try to get *in situ* hybridization to work. In particular, she says [5] she may try using "fresh frozen" tissue in her next experiments instead of the fixed, perfused tissue she has used in the past.

After Ellen describes her possible experiments, the PI asks [6] which of the experimental manipulations she intends to do immediately, and Ellen responds [7] that (among other things [8-10]) she will definitely do the fresh frozen tissue manipulation. The PI next asks Ellen [14, 16] to specify other components of her proposed experiment, including what "positive control" she will use. In using the term "positive control," the PI appears to suggest that Ellen should include as a control a type of cell to which she knows binding should occur, so that she will be able to tell whether the *in situ* procedure is working properly. Using only the experimental cells, if there is no binding Ellen will not be able to tell whether her hypothesis is wrong or whether the technique is not working. At this point Ellen says that she plans [17-18] to try only the tissue manipulation with her experimental cells and not to use control cells. However, the PI argues [19-23] that she should use control cells in the experiment.

Later in the meeting, after other aspects of Ellen's experiments have been discussed, the PI tries to evaluate [24] the experiment as a whole with respect to current standards of scientific practice. Ellen claims [27] that fresh frozen tissue preparation is the standard of the field, but under questioning from the PI [28, 36] she then admits [30-31, 37] that some laboratories also use fixed tissue. She says [32-35] that the fresh frozen method is more difficult than the fixed tissue method. Monica then argues [43-44] that Ellen should favor the fixed method because it is easier. The PI also argues [46-56] that Ellen should not try to use fresh frozen tissue, since it is both harder to work with than fixed tissue and not clearly the standard of the laboratories doing this kind of work.

The ensuing discussion [57-70] is part of an effort to coordinate all the experiments Ellen wants to do. Because *in situ* hybridization requires a wait of six weeks to obtain results, she plans to do multiple experiments soon without waiting to find out the results of each one. Because of these time frame issues, Ellen will go ahead [71-72] with the fresh frozen manipulation despite laboratory members' reservations about the fresh frozen preparation method.

Analysis of the Experimental Design Process

The previous section outlined the process scientists went through in one portion of this meeting to develop a piece of an experimental design. Beginning with an experimental approach that was not working (*in situ* hybridization), Ellen and other laboratory members examined and evaluated various alterations in methods and materials that she could implement in order to get the *in situ* technique to work. The excerpts analyzed in the last section focused on one only particular issue: whether Ellen should use fresh frozen rather than fixed perfused tissue. However, a more complete analysis of the entire meeting segment indicated that processes present in this segment occurred throughout the meeting. In this section, we analyze the general experimental design process used in this laboratory. This process is depicted in Figure 1. Figure 1 does not specify a temporal order of events; rather, it portrays an overall structure that controls the experimental design process. Often, events moved temporally from left to right to bottom in Figure 1, but elements from the three different sections were intermixed throughout this meeting segment.

At the time this meeting occurred, Ellen had already chosen to the use the *in situ* hybridization experimental approach or paradigm. Experimental paradigms are rarely constructed from scratch; rather, they may be retrieved from experiments previously done by the particular scientist, in the same laboratory, or in other laboratories (cf. Dunbar, 1996). The choice of a particular experimental paradigm constitutes the creation of a frame with particular slots corresponding to features in the experimental design (cf. Friedland & Iwasaki, 1985; Schunn & Klahr, 1995).

Unpack/specify slots in experimental design. The first part of the experimental design process exhibited by the scientists was "unpacking" the design and specifying component elements of the experiment. That is, at the

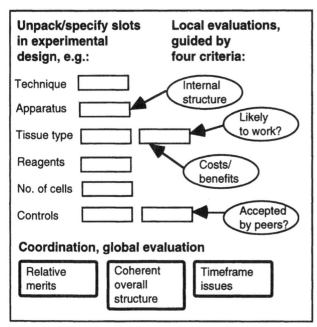

Unpack/specify slots in experimental design, e.g.:

Technique
Apparatus
Tissue type
Reagents
No. of cells
Controls

Local evaluations, guided by four criteria:

Internal structure
Likely to work?
Costs/benefits
Accepted by peers?

Coordination, global evaluation

| Relative merits | Coherent overall structure | Timeframe issues |

Figure 1: Diagram of general experimental design process.

beginning of the meeting Ellen had specified that she would continue to use the *in situ* hybridization technique and that she would attempt the fresh frozen method of tissue preparation. However, there were still many elements of the experimental design that had not been specified, and the PI and other laboratory members prompted Ellen to specify these [14, 16]. The scientists are able to unpack the experimental design in this way because they know the "slots" in the experimental design that need to be filled for any given experimental approach.

Local evaluation of design elements. Subsequent to, or simultaneous with, the unpacking and specification process, the scientists often evaluated specific elements of the proposed design. This type of evaluation, which was constrained to only one or a few elements of the proposed design, may be thought of as "local evaluation." Evaluation is guided by at least four sets of criteria. First, the scientists attempt to design experiments that will be "interpretable;" that is, that have a robust internal structure. This is often achieved through the use of control conditions (e.g., [16-23]) that enable the scientist to interpret the meaning of results on non-control, or experimental, conditions. Second, the scientists try to optimize the chances that the experiment will "work;" that is, that results will not be thrown off by experimental error. In this meeting the scientists tried to make sure the experiment would work by evaluating Ellen's level of expertise with the fresh frozen tissue preparation method [25] and using methods that had a proven track record (i.e., had been used successfully in other laboratories [24, 28, 36, 46-54]). Third, the scientists performed what might be considered a costs/benefits analysis. For instance, they considered how easy or difficult different methods would be to implement [32-35, 40-44, 55-56]. Fourth and finally, the scientists tried to design experiments whose results would be accepted as valid by the larger scientific

community. For instance, elsewhere in this meeting the PI urged Ellen to include a particular probe because it was "an industry standard of something that you ought to find . . . everybody agrees it ought to be there."

Coordination and global evaluation. The final step in the experimental design process is coordination of different possible experiments and a global evaluation of how different approaches fit together and which experiments should be done in what order (e.g., [57-70]). Global evaluations are still guided by the same criteria described in the last paragraph, but they are used to judge the merits of different design elements and approaches relative to each other.

Discussion

The findings reported in the previous section indicate that scientists have well-developed strategies for designing and choosing among possible experiments. The analysis of these strategies suggests interesting theoretical interpretations, some of which are explored in this section.

Experimental Design: Beyond the Hypothesis

As we argued in the introduction, experimental design has most often been portrayed in the cognitive literature as a process of instantiating variables of a hypothesis in the features of an experiment. We do not deny that the scientists' current hypotheses constrain the type of experiments they choose. However, we argue that hypotheses do not *completely* constrain the design of experiments. That is, there are many possible experiments that could be used to test any given hypothesis. Even after the hypothesis is determined, the scientist still has to choose among experimental techniques, protocol steps, control conditions, and many other elements before the experimental design is complete.

In the example analyzed for this case study, Ellen had formed her hypothesis many months before the meeting, and yet she was continuing to struggle with the experimental component of her work. Ellen's hypothesis, in fact, is only obliquely referred to in the entire text of this meeting. In part, this may be because she has already chosen the experimental paradigm she will use (*in situ* hybridization); choice of experimental paradigm is perhaps more likely to involve reference to theory than later steps in the design process (cf. Friedland & Iwasaki, 1985).

Instead of translating hypothesis to experiment, the laboratory members focus on solving a technical problem (getting a new technique to work) and how to design experiments using this technique that will give interpretable results. The four sets of criteria that guide evaluation have little to do with the constraints imposed by the scientist's hypothesis. That is, a good experiment will not only test the scientist's theory, but will also be robust in internal structure (i.e. the results are expected to be interpretable), will involve methodologies at which are likely to work, will be optimal from a costs/benefits standpoint, and will produce results that will be accepted by the larger scientific community. It is particularly interesting to note that there are complex reasoning processes involved in experimental design even after the process of translating from theory to experiment has been completed. Experimental design has its own "internal" heuristics and reasoning processes separate from the task of relating hypothesis to experiment.

There is a limited amount of earlier research that considered elements of the design process independent of theory-experiment coordination. Our results correspond to this earlier work in some ways. The interpretability criteria highlighted in our analysis correspond to the notion of "observability" of experiments developed in Klahr, Dunbar, and Fay (1990). In both cases, the scientists and subjects tried to design experiments whose results could be interpreted unambiguously. The general structure of our model of experimental design, in which slots in a frame are unpacked and specified, is similar to Friedland and Iwasaki's (1985) model of experimental design as refinement of skeletal plans. Therefore, our work is consistent with earlier research that investigated aspects of experimental design other than theory-to-experiment translation. This research may be seen as the beginning of a body of work that goes beyond the hypothesis and investigates the complex processes "internal" to the experimental design task.

Effect of Potential Error on Experimental Design

In most cognitive models of science, including psychology laboratory experiments, artificial intelligence models, and normative philosophical models, the subject/scientist runs one experiment (with one experimental condition and no control conditions) and obtains one outcome, which is presumed to be correct. In other words, experimentation in most cognitive models appears unproblematic compared to the elaborate processes we have uncovered in real-world science, where scientists struggle to choose between alternate methods and materials and design multi-condition experiments with numerous controls. The question we address in this section is: Why is the real-world process so much more complex than that depicted in earlier cognitive models?

We argue that the issue of "potential error" is what underlies many of the criteria real-world scientists take into account when designing experiments. It is a commonplace among practicing biologists that at least as many experiments "don't work" as "do work" (cf. [59]). Techniques that appear straightforward in the biology textbook or the equipment manual are in practice difficult to implement. Among other potential problems, materials may be contaminated, cells may die if not maintained in precise growing conditions, reagents may fail to adhere to or interact with other materials, and/or equipment may not be calibrated properly or may malfunction. Scientists in the laboratories studied often spent weeks or months attempting to "get a system working," and even then degradation of materials or problems implementing protocols could cause some experiments not to work.

The issue of error in experimental results has been addressed before in the psychological literature (e.g. Gorman, 1986). However, potential error has generally been treated as a probabilistic issue in the psychology laboratory; that is, on any given experiment there is some percentage chance that the result will be reported incorrectly, and subjects are expected to take this possibility of error into account when evaluating experimental results. In the real-world biology laboratory, error is not treated as a probabilistic construct. When experiments "don't work," the biologists rarely consider it a chance occurrence. Rather, they believe the failure can be causally attributed to something that went wrong during the running of the experiment. By using the appropriate experimental controls, the scientists hope to tell whether the experiment failed and also what went wrong to cause it to fail. Hence, this need to control for possible error drives the strategies involved in designing experiments with robust internal structure. The second set of criteria, directed toward getting the experiment to "work," explicitly address this issue of possible error. In addition, it may be this possibility of error that is behind the development of scientific community standards for what is accepted as a valid experimental finding: by setting standards, the community ensures that scientists can evaluate the possibility of error in other laboratories' reported results. Thus the possibility of error factors into the fourth set of criteria as well.

In short, what was unproblematic in most cognitive models—trusting the results of experiments—becomes highly problematic in the real-world science laboratory. The criteria scientists take into account when designing and evaluating potential experimental designs can be seen as a well-developed set of heuristics that have arisen to deal with the constraints of this task environment, in particular the potential for error in experimental results.

Toward a General Model of Experimental Design

Researchers building models of human problem solving have long recognized that the task environment severely constrains the types of strategies that the problem-solver will employ (e.g., Newell & Simon, 1972). Experimental design is no exception: Designing an experiment in a science laboratory is a complex problem with multiple constraints. The experimental design process depicted in Figure 1 is in fact a collection of strategies used by scientists in one laboratory to solve a portion of the experimental design problem. To the extent that these strategies have been developed by scientists in response to a task environment, it is probable that similar strategies will be manifested in laboratories confronted with similar task environments. In other words, the process depicted in Figure 1 will likely lead toward a general model of the experimental design process throughout science if laboratories in other science disciplines face similar constraints to those faced in this immunology laboratory.

We argue that the task environment for experimental design in most science domains is more similar than different from discipline to discipline and from laboratory to laboratory. For example, the particular slots scientists must fill in to complete an experimental design will vary dramatically from discipline to discipline, but the strategy of "unpacking" the design so as to make particular components of it available for analysis is likely to be used in science laboratories of many disciplines, because the structure of experiments in modern scientific disciplines is almost always very complex.

Similarly, the criteria used to locally evaluate elements of an experimental design are a response to the general nature of 20th-century scientific practice, and not ad hoc heuristics useful only in a particular laboratory. The standards of experimental science as it currently exists require that scientists ensure a robust internal structure to their experiments. Likewise, the extensive social structure of science today requires that scientists keep in mind the likely community response to their reported results. Particular issues within these categories may vary in different scientific domains, but practitioners in all modern science laboratories must take into account these general criteria. Similarly, cutting edge science in all disciplines requires the use of new, imperfect techniques; indeed, it is the use of these techniques that often defines "cutting edge" science. Thus costs/benefits decisions and concerns about individual expertise are always present, and, more generally, when each experiment represents a large commitment of time, effort, and money, there is a need to prioritize and coordinate different experiments. For these reasons, it is not unlikely that the basic features of the model presented in Figure 1 would be present in any general model of real-world experimental design.

Acknowledgements

This research was supported by a McGill Major Graduate Fellowship to the first author. The second author was funded by grant number OGP0037356 from NSERC and grants from FCAR and SSHRC.

References

Baker, L. M. & Dunbar, K. (in preparation). How scientists deal with unexpected findings: A discovery heuristic.

Dunbar, K. (1995). How scientists really reason: Scientific reasoning in real-world laboratories. In R. J. Sternberg & J. Davidson (Eds.), *Mechanisms of insight*. Cambridge, MA: MIT Press.

Dunbar, K. (1996). How scientists think: Online creativity and conceptual change in science. In T. B. Ward, S. M. Smith, & J. Vaid (Eds.), *Conceptual structures and processes: Emergence, discovery, and change*. Washington, DC: American Psychological Association Press.

Dunbar, K., & Baker, L. (1994). Goals, analogy, and the social constraints of scientific discovery. *Behavioral and Brain Sciences, 17*, 538-39.

Dunbar, K., Patel, V., Baker, L., & Dama, M. (1995, November). *Group reasoning strategies in knowledge-rich domains*. 36th Annual Meeting of the Psychonomic Society, Los Angeles.

Friedland, P. E., & Iwasaki, Y. (1985). The concept and implementation of skeletal plans. *Journal of Automated Reasoning, 1*, 161–208.

Gorman, M. E. (1986). How the possibility of error affects falsification on a task that models scientific problem solving. *British Journal of Psychology, 77*, 85-96.

Klahr, D., & Dunbar, K. (1988). Dual space search during scientific reasoning. *Cognitive Science, 12*, 1-48.

Klahr, D., Dunbar, K., & Fay, A. L. (1990). Designing good experiments to test bad hypotheses. In J. Shrager & P. Langley (Eds.), *Computational models of scientific discovery and theory formation*. San Mateo, CA: Morgan Kaufmann.

Klayman, J., & Ha, Y. (1987). Confirmation, disconfirmation, and information in hypothesis testing. *Psychological Review, 94*, 211–228.

Kulkarni, D., & Simon, H. A. (1988). The processes of scientific discovery: The strategy of experimentation. *Cognitive Science, 12*, 139–175.

Langley, P., Simon, H. A., Bradshaw, G. L., & Zytkow, J. M. (1987). *Scientific discovery: Computational explorations of the creative processes*. Cambridge, MA: MIT Press.

Nersessian, N. (1992). How do scientists think? Capturing the dynamics of conceptual change in science. In R. N. Giere (Ed.), *Minnesota studies in the philosophy of science, Vol. XV: Cognitive models of science*. Minneapolis: University of Minnesota Press.

Newell, A., & Simon, H. A. (1972). *Human Problem Solving*. Englewood Cliffs, NJ: Prentice-Hall, Inc.

Schunn, C. D., & Klahr, D. (1995). A 4-space model of scientific discovery. In *Proceedings of the 17th Annual Conference of the Cognitive Science Society*. Hillsdale, NJ: Erlbaum.

Thagard, P. (1992). *Conceptual Revolutions*. Cambridge, MA: MIT Press.

Teaching/Learning Events in the Workplace: a Comparative Analysis of their Organizational and Interactional Structure

Rogers Hall and **Reed Stevens**
Education, EMST Division
University of California, Berkeley
Berkeley, CA 94720
rhall@garnet.berkeley.edu
reed@garnet.berkeley.edu

Abstract

It is widely acknowledged that teaching and learning are organized quite differently in and out of school settings. This paper describes two strips of interaction, selected from a data corpus that documents naturally-occurring work in adult settings often considered to be targets for science and mathematics education. In the first strip (civil engineering), we follow how engineers with different levels of organizational responsibility use an evaluative term, "brutal," in relation to features of a proposed roadway design. In the second strip (field biology), we follow participants' initially conflicting uses of the register terms, "difference" and "distance," as they collaborate across disciplinary specialties. In both cases, disagreements about the use of terms are detected in ongoing interaction, alternative meanings are actively assembled across different types of media, and disagreements are resolved around pre-existing organizational asymmetries. We raise three general questions about teaching/learning in the workplace: (i) What is accessible to participants as teachers/learners under different organizational conditions; (ii) How are disagreements about shared meaning managed, given asymmetries between participants in these events; and (iii) What do these kinds of studies tell us about the acquisition of word meaning as an unproblematic relation between term and referent?

Introduction

It has been widely acknowledged for several decades that teaching and learning are organized quite differently in and out of school settings (Becker, 1986; Collins, Brown & Newman, 1989; Lave & Wenger, 1991; Resnick, 1987; Rogoff, 1990). In addition, most contemporary theories of learning and development claim that learning, as a process, occurs continuously in people's activity (Case, 1992; Newell, 1990). Despite the fact that instructional practices over the past several decades have proceeded as if teaching, learning, and doing were separate activities, it is not the case that people learn exclusively in school and then use what they have learned in other settings (e.g., at home or in the workplace).

It may be obvious that people learn outside of school settings, but we have relatively few studies of how teaching and learning get organized in the ongoing practical activities of workplaces (Hutchins, 1995; Saxe, 1991; Traweek, 1988; Wenger, 1990). This is particularly true of technical or scientific work settings that comprise the proposed "application" of much mathematics and science in secondary and undergraduate education. This paper presents a comparative case study of teaching and learning events in two such places: a civil engineering firm and a field biological research station. In each setting, we use observation, interviewing, collected documents, and video records of naturally occurring workplace activity as our primary data. Observational notes and interviews are used to identify "typical chunks of work" (a term we use with research participants) for recording, and these records then provide a corpus for more detailed interactional analysis of how people work together . For the purposes of this paper, we have selected what we think are representative teaching and learning events, based on our analysis of the entire recorded corpus and our understanding of the broader organizational structure of work in these settings. We use these cases as one approach to documenting and analyzing how teaching and learning happens between people in specific organizational circumstances. (Hall, 1995).

In the first two sections of this paper, we look closely at strips of interaction in which people work out the meanings of seemingly simple, technical terms. Hilary Putnam (1988) argues that reference, as a social phenomena, involves a "linguistic division of labor" where meanings are differentially distributed across a language community. The implication of this view is that meanings in use can come into conflict. This paper documents two such cases and demonstrates how these conflicts are worked through by interactants. In the civil engineering firm, we follow the contested referential scope of an evaluative term, "brutal," as it is used to describe roadway design alternatives. In the field biology research station, we follow how a coordinated, across-discipline meaning of register terms like "difference" and "distance" is developed to analyze potentially different samples from insect populations.

By following these interactions into surrounding organizational conditions, we show that even these simple negotiations are significant teaching and learning events. These interactions are difficult to recognize from a traditional cognitive science perspective as "teaching" or "learning" events. But they are precisely the kinds of interaction that comprise workplace teaching and learning, at least outside of formal training programs in the workplace settings we have studied. In our view, these kinds of events fill in the theoretical landscape that others have called forms of "legitimate peripheral participation" (Lave & Wenger, 1991) or "guided participation." (Rogoff, 1990) Our analysis of these events works at two, interdependent levels: (1) the routine *organizational structure* of activity in these workplaces, which is available to us through ethnographic observation and interviewing, and (2) the *interactional structure* of participants' work with site- and discipline-specific forms of representation, which is available to us through analysis of video records. Together, these levels of analysis allow us to describe discursive or representational practices in these workplaces, and based on recurrent asymmetries in these practices, the kinds of teaching/learning events through which they are reproduced (i.e., how people learn to participate in practices, and in the process, generate those very practices).

Strip 1: Evaluating Roadway Design Alternatives in a Civil Engineering Firm

There is a strong argument to be made that agreements in judgment are particularly indicative of a sense of shared understanding between people (Bourdieu, 1984; Wittgenstein, 1958). Differing judgments about whether something is "good" or "bad," "too much" or "just right," etc. divide people. In this example, we follow how different uses of a single evaluative term, "brutal," divide two engineers working together to design a network of roadways. Furthermore, we analyze how these different uses occasion a situated teaching and learning event, by which we mean an event that is marked as explicitly pedagogical by neither participant and that occurs in the flow of ongoing practical activity. In this event, we find (i) an initial use of the evaluative term "brutal" by the senior engineer, (ii) its re-use by the junior engineer to evaluate a different design feature, (iii) a challenge by the senior engineer to the junior engineer's usage, and (iv) an account of why, in the current design context, the junior engineer's usage is not appropriate.

Figure 1. A senior engineer evaluates two alternatives for a proposed roadway using a section view

To understand how their joint activity is structured to produce this teaching and learning moment, we first describe relevant organizational details. With respect to the participants' identities, these details include a pair of potentially relevant (Schegloff, 1992), institutionally-organized asymmetries: Jake is the more experienced practitioner, and he maintains a higher status within the firm and within the project. With higher status comes both a

power differential between Jake and Evan and a different responsibility for details of the project's development. These details include a general engineering stricture to "balance the site," which means organizing the removal and replacement of dirt across the entire construction site so that the total amount of dirt "imported" or "exported" is minimized. They also must "meet code" at all governmental levels or develop rationales for code violations that will allow them to argue for "variances" to officials. Finally, with respect to this specific project and its client's needs, Jake and Evan are developing their roadway plan for a hilly and forested site; these features of the land present environmental concerns that require, prior to other considerations, they avoid denuding forested regions of the site.

The ecology of representations (Goodwin, 1995; Hall, 1990; Star, 1995) in these engineers' workspace is densely symbolic and computational. At this meeting, within Jake's partitioned office space, the two engineers gather at a table layered with two-dimensional "paper space" views[1] that model both the site and the proposed design. These views, all partial with respect to the work they must do, are used in coordination to provide for relevant activities, such as, in this example, the production of a design rationale. The paper views are produced from a CAD system, but most of the relevant design is done with and over the paper views; only later are the CAD documents updated. A coordinated reading involves complex temporal and spatial patterns of activity that combine the verbal narration of design features with display and use of deictic, gestural, and graphical spaces (Goodwin, 1994; Hanks, 1990; McNeill, 1992).

After a number of months away from this project, Jake and Evan are refamiliarizing themselves with the design and its overall rationale. Inspecting a set of plans, they notice that Road Four (designed many months prior) has a "grade" that violates city code; the road is about five percent too steep. After Jake coordinates a reading of Road Four's mathematical slope from the vertical and horizontal margin quantities on the profile view, he considers the implications of this slope for the road[2].

Jake: Yeah, (1)this huh road (laughing) is a, is a . . . STRETCH. You know? (6 sec.) It's gonna be brutal

---

[1] For a full description of the variety of representations used by these engineers to "see" the site and to "project" potential design features, see (Hall & Stevens, 1995). Generally, these engineers share a set of "views" that resemble those of other design professionals (topographic maps, plan views, section views, and profiles). These two dimensional, metricized representations are used in coordination to plan and design for three dimensional space.

[2] Transcript conventions include: turns at talk start with named speakers; embodied action descriptions appear in italics below each turn; the onset of embodied action is indexed by numbers in parentheses within the turn; spoken EMPHASIS is shown by upper case; stretch:::ed words are shown with repeated colons; a question mark precedes ?words that were difficult to hear during transcription; and matching left brackets [show the onset of overlapping talk across turns.

man, (2)twenty percent for . . . for ah . . . fifteen
hundred feet. (laughs)
> *1(R hand points below road in profile view)*
> *2(writes 400, 450, 350, 500 at center of profile
> view)*

"Brutal" is a negative evaluation that refers to the road being
excessively steep over a long distance. In this instance, Jake
appears to mean the road will be brutal with respect to some
human activity, probably driving emergency vehicles.
Because this evaluation appears in the natural course of their
ongoing work, we interpret Evan's subsequent turn in the
conversation as a tacit acceptance of this usage of "brutal"
as a negative evaluation.

Evan: Other(1)wise you'd be up here and (2)you'd have
to cut way across [sho::oo
> *1(R hand to upper left of the profile view)*
> *2(R hand sweeps right then left above the
> proposed road)*

Jake: [Ri::ght.

Within the materials jointly at hand, Evan begins to
assemble a rationale for this brutal grade that contrasts their
design choice with an even less desirable alternative
("Otherwise [...] you'd have to cut way across"). Jake's
collaborative completion ("[Ri::ght") indicates they both
judge this design feature to be "brutal." Over the next
several conversational turns, Jake leads a coordinated
narrative and gestural tour through multiple paper views of
the region surrounding Road Four. When he reaches a
particular section view (see Figure 1) in this developing
rationale for an overly steep road, Evan points to the section
and again uses the evaluative term, "brutal." But in this
instance, Evan refers to what he projects as an excessive
amount of dirt needed to fill under this part of the proposed
road.

Evan: (laughs) (1)That's brutal, huh? Well, I don't know.
. . [maybe not.
> *1(L hand points below roadbed in section view)*

Jake: [Yeah . . . well, but . . . look at it THIS way . . .

Evan's use of "brutal" is tentatively offered ("Well, I
don't know"), and as Jake begins to disagree[3] ("Yeah...
well"), Evan retreats even further from the evaluation
("maybe not"). Both participants orient to a contended usage
of the evaluative term: Jake because he challenges Evan's
evaluation, and Evan because he retreats when Jake begins
to disagree. At an interactional level, these are the dynamics
of asymmetry at the organizational level (see Rogoff, 1990,
pp. 204–205), and they are central in determining whose
terms are appropriated and how those terms are used to

---

[3]This form of challenge is described by conversation analysts as
disagreement expressed with a dispreferred form. It is offered with
hesitation and with an affiliative "Yeah... but " rather than a bald
"no" (Goodwin & Heritage, 1990; Pomerantz, 1984).

refer. We understand Evan to be appropriating a term and
improvising its use in participation with a differently-
knowledgeable other; a commonplace type of learning in
practice (Cole, 1985; Lave & Wenger, 1991; Rogoff, 1990).

We take this to be a teaching/learning event that emerges
in the ongoing work of a civil engineering project. As they
continue, Jake does more than simply reject Evan's
evaluation; he again explains, using a coordinated assembly
of narrative, drawing, and deictic pointing why the amount
of fill required in this section is better than the existing
alternatives. By sketching one of these alternatives (Figure
1) he shows that it would save little and require "ripping
down the whole side of the hillside." In this implicit
moment of situated teaching, Jake assembles a broader
rationale of this feature for Evan, but he also strengthens his
own conviction ("it's perfect") that a twenty percent grade
on Road Four is necessary to save a hillside full of trees. As
their project moves towards municipal approval, this
argument may support a request for a variance.

Strip 2: Analyzing Chemical Differences Between Insects in a Field Biology Research Station

Our second strip comes from a regularly scheduled meeting
among an interdisciplinary team of scientists in a field
biology research station . Their work on this project
concerns what they call the "chemical ecology of forest
insects." In this meeting, two entomologists (Mark and
Gary), a chemist (Leah), and a visiting biostatistician (Bill)
discuss how to analyze differences in the chemical makeup
of a waxy residue stripped off of termites' exoskeletons.
They use these chemical differences to classify termite
species and to map the geographic boundaries of termite
colonies (insects in a colony are all of the same species).
This kind of information is helpful for developing and
assessing the effects of new, "environmentally softer"
pesticides, but it is also central to basic research questions
about the distribution and ecological role of a variety of
insects.

Figure 2. A biostatistician illustrates a possible distance
measure using two CGs.

Two organizational features of this setting are important
for our analysis of teaching and learning. First, there are
asymmetries in the hierarchical position of participants
within the project and across disciplines. Mark is a senior

research entomologist and this projects' leader, Gary is also an entomologist (he and Mark hold Ph.D.'s), and Leah is a staff biologist with specialized post-baccalaureate training in chemistry. Bill, on the other hand, attends the meeting as a consulting biostatistician (he also holds a Ph.D.), but he works on a variety of projects across the surrounding field research station. So we find relevant asymmetries both in what people are expected to contribute across disciplinary specialties (e.g., entomology, chemistry, and biostatistics), and because participants in this meeting have quite different responsibilities for different aspects the project's ongoing activities. The second relevant organizational feature concerns the routine structure of work on this project. This meeting is one type of activity within a broader structure which the entomologists call a "biogeographic study." These studies regularly take project participants through distinct types of activity: (i) from field sites where they subdivide the forest floor into rectilinear "plots" and then systematically collect insects from a grid-like structure of "traps," (ii) to a chemistry laboratory in the research station where they extract and identify hydrocarbons from these insects' bodies using a gas-chromatography/mass-spectroscopy (GC/MS) device, and finally (iii) into project meetings like this one, where the resulting chromatograms[4] (CG's, see Figure 2) can be used to identify termite species and to follow the moving boundary of termite colonies.

The strip we examine in this section comes at the end of a biogeographical study of termites, and the consulting biostatistician is helping the project develop a statistical measure that can compare two CG's and support judgments about different species or colonies. The second organizational feature is important because activity and talk in this meeting (e.g., choosing pairs of CG's and announcing a "difference" between them) needs to be held accountable to the broader chain of activities in a biogeographic study. The CG's shown in Figure 1 are the final point in a process that converts bugs into graphs that the entomologists call "hydrocarbon phenotypes." Since there are marked asymmetries between participants in their disciplinary backgrounds, their responsibilities within the project, and their actual work across different aspects of the biogeographical study, each participant can take on the role of a "teacher" or a "learner" during this meeting.

At the outset of the meeting, Gary and Bill (the biostatistician) disagree over whether to use a standardized statistical clustering algorithm to aggregate termite samples, but Mark interrupts, enlisting Leah (the chemist) to help arrange a column of four CG's that they place in front of Bill to demonstrate what Mark calls "a good comparing." Mark shows that two of the CG's are "radically different" and so probably come from different species, another pair "don't look that different" and so may come from the same colony, but a final pair (shown in Figure 2) have the same types of hydrocarbons in slightly different relative proportions and

so probably come from different termite colonies. Each of Mark's pairwise judgments is accomplished using deictic points to specific peaks being compared across CG's, then Gary and Mark collaboratively summarize the final comparison as having "no QUALitative difference between here, just quantitative difference" (i.e. same species but different colony). Across multiple occasions in which we have observed project members using CG's, this is a typical discursive practice: narrative judgments of qualitative and quantitative difference are made as the entomologists use their hands to select specific peaks that, as they put it, "JUMP out at you."

In our analysis, this collaborative summary marks the end of a teaching event staged for the benefit of Bill (the biostatistician), who is a newcomer (i.e., asymmetrically located) both in these entomologists' discursive practices for comparing CG graphs and in the routine organization of their project work. In this sense, he needs to learn enough about their activities to be able to give advice about constructing a statistical measure that will behave sensibly. So as Bill takes the next turn in this conversation, he has been positioned by members of the project team as a learner who needs to display his understanding of "a good comparing" of CG's, but he simultaneously takes the role of a consultant who needs to teach these project members about a statistical approach to their differences. At the first turn boundary of Bill's carefully worded opening, Mark emphatically disagrees with Bill's usage of the term "distance."

Bill: You know the (1)part, part of the thing is, is how you define, again how will we go about defining a distance ?up here. (2)You're trying to use your eyes to, to, to (3)match these two up and see where there are differences and where there aren't?
    1(R point circles over two CG's)
    2(R point traces up vertical, across horizontal of a CG)
    3(open R hand, taps thumb on bottom display, middle finger on top display)

Mark: DIFFERENCES, not distances, differences.

Bill repairs in his next turn, reiterating that what "we're trying to get" is a way to combine all the "differences" used by these entomologists into "one number," something that Mark then says he would "LOVE." Bill goes on to describe various approaches to combining these differences, sweeping his hands over a pair of CG's to show how they would be aggregated, but he continues to use what appears to be a specific, statistical meaning for "distance." As Bill finishes narrating and manually illustrating this set of statistical possibilities, Mark again challenges this use of the term "distance," referring to a drawing of a field sampling plot to show Bill what he means by "distance."

Mark: What I'd like to do is, sort of... (1)get rid of the distance. I don't know what you're talking about. When I'm talking about distance, (2)I'm talking about geography, [j:: ?linear ?measure

[4]Chromatograms are graphs that show GC/MS retention time along the horizontal axis (i.e., hydrocarbons pass through the device at specific times) and relative abundance along the vertical axis (i.e., the height of a peak shows how much of a specific hydrocarbon is present).

1(hands up, pushing away towards Bill)
2(R point to white board, then traces and shifts gaze to Bill)

Bill: [And I'm, but I'm talking about (1)some sort of measure, to say... how di::fferent these, [two... uh:::
1(hands flat over two CG's, then R hand rockers between them)

Mark: [Yeh, ok. And that's what you're calling a distance?

Following this relatively direct disagreement, Bill repeats his offer to produce "one number" that can be used to judge whether CG's are from the same colony. Mark nods in agreement, then begins using Bill's statistical meaning for "distance" as a "statistic" for comparing CG's. As the meeting continues, both of these participants manage a coordinated use, across disciplines, of "differences" (i.e., entomological judgments) and "distance" (i.e., a statistical aggregate over those judgments). As this strip ends, Mark jokingly suggests that this new distance measure might be named after him. We take this to be end of a mutual teaching/learning event, in which Bill and Mark each appropriate aspects of the other's meanings for register terms.

Discussion

This paper gives a close description of two strips of interaction, selected from a data corpus that documents naturally-occurring work in settings often considered to be targets for education in science and mathematics. Our aim has been to give sufficient ethnographic background about the organizational conditions of people's work to support a detailed analysis of the interactional structure of teaching/learning events. The interactional details of how these events emerge and are carried out need to be held accountable (in our analysis, as in their work) to the very conditions that bring the events about. We take a narrow focus on learning, asking how people outside of school or laboratory conditions learn the meaning of terms that are important in their work (i.e., evaluative and register terms). In both cases, disagreements about the use of terms are detected in ongoing interaction, alternative meanings are actively assembled across different types of media, and disagreements are resolved around pre-existing organizational asymmetries.

We close by raising three general questions about teaching/learning in the workplace: (i) What is accessible to participants as teachers/learners under different organizational conditions; (ii) How are disagreements about shared meaning managed, given asymmetries between participants in these events; and (iii) What do these kinds of studies tell us about the acquisition of word meaning as an unproblematic relation between term and referent?

In the events we have analyzed, people learn by participating in the activities that establish meanings for words, so they must have access to these activities. Similar to Hutchins (1995) analysis of observational "horizons" in the work of navigation, we find that access to discursive practices occurs at two levels. First, the organizational

structure of work in large measure determines who will be present when critical activities are undertaken. The civil engineers we studied work together on most phases of a design project, but in the biology research station, the biostatistician (Bill) did not work in field collection sites or the chemistry lab where an articulated chain of activities produce the CG's he is asked to compare. As a result, the project team needs to make parts of this chain of work visible to Bill, and the meaning of register terms within this chain of activity is hotly contested. Second, the types of representational media being used in the context of teaching/learning events (Hutchins calls these "open tools") greatly influences the visibility of meaning, as an accomplishment, within ongoing discursive practices. This is particularly vivid in our analysis of civil engineers, who must work together to "see" specific regions in their ongoing design (i.e., two hands and one pair of eyes cannot manage some aspects of their work in "paper space").

On the issue of differences of meaning and how they are recognized and managed, it may be that teaching/learning events outside of schools and psychological laboratories are densely clustered around breakdowns (de la Rocha, 1986), some of which are marked in conversation as disagreements about otherwise shared meanings. Following disagreements at an interactional level of analysis then provides a window onto potential teaching/learning events. In our comparative analysis, we identify disagreements and then follow their consequences for evidence that someone has "taught" and someone else has "learned" (e.g., Mark's appropriation of Bill's usage of "distance"). Conversational forms (see Engle & Greeno, 1994, on "intellectual conversations") and their entailments for learning will likely change under different conditions of asymmetry (e.g., project hierarchies, levels of schooling, gender, or disciplinary specialization).

Finally, when following people's activities out of school or laboratory situations that 'freeze' the organization and intended meaning of "tasks" (see Newman, Griffin & Cole, 1989 for a similar critique), traditional notions about word meaning as a relation between term and referent need to be reconsidered and empirically grounded in people's situated activities. Here, we find terms (evaluative and register) being deployed in situations where their referents are actively assembled and frequently contested. Having a "meaning" at any given point requires the ability to participate in a coordinated set of representational practices across narration (e.g., "a good comparing"), inscriptions (e.g., an ordered column of CG's), and embodied action (e.g., deictic points selecting CG peaks that "jump out at you"). If, in representing human action, we delete these interactional resources and their coordinated assembly, we likewise delete central phenomena in the creation and circulation of meaning.

Acknowledgements

This work was supported by NSF Grant ESI 94552771 and an NSF Spatial Cognition Traineeship to Reed Stevens.

References

Becker, H. S. (1986). A school is a lousy place to learn anything in, *Doing things together : selected papers* . Evanston, IL: Northwestern University Press.

Bourdieu, P. (1984). *Distinction: a social critique of the judgement of taste.* Cambridge, MA: Harvard University Press.

Case, R. (1992). Neo-Piagetian theories of child development. In R. J. Sternber & C. A. Berg (Eds.), *Intellectual development.* (pp. 161-196). Cambridge: Cambridge University Press.

Cole, M. (1985). The zone of proximal development: where culture and cognition create each other. In J. W. Wertsch (Ed.), *Culture, communication, and cognition: Vygotskian perspectives.* New York: Cambridge University Press.

Collins, A., Brown, J. S., & Newman, S. E. (1989). Cognitive apprenticeship: teaching the crafts of reading, writing, and mathematics. In L. B. Resnick (Ed.), *Knowing, learning, and instruction: essays in honor of Robert Glaser,* (pp. 453-494). Hillsdale, NJ: Lawrence Erlbaum and Associates, Publishers.

de la Rocha, O. L. (1986). *Problems of sense and problems of scale: An ethnographic study of arithmetic in everyday life.* University of California at Irvine.

Engle, R. A., & Greeno, J. G. (1994,). *Managing disagreement in intellectual conversations: coordinating interpersonal and conceptual concerns in the collaborative construction of mathematical explanations.* Paper presented at the Cognitive Science Society, Atlanta, GA.

Goodwin, C. (1994). Professional Vision. *American Anthropologist.* 96(3), 606-633.

Goodwin, C. (1995). Seeing In Depth. *Social Studies Of Scienc.,*25(2), 237-274.

Goodwin, C., & Heritage, J. (1990). Conversation analysis. *Annual Review of Anthropology.*19, 283-307.

Hall, R. (September 1995). Exploring design-oriented mathematical practices in school and work settings. *Communications of the ACM, 62.*

Hall, R., & Stevens, R. (1995). Making space: a comparison of mathematical work in school and professional design practices. In S. L. Star (Ed.), *The cultures of computing,* (pp. 118-145). London: Basil Blackwell.

Hall, R. P. (1990). *Making mathematics on paper: constructing representations of stories about related linear functions.* University of California at Irvine.

Hanks, W. F. (1990). *Referential practice : language and lived space among the Maya.* Chicago, IL: University of Chicago Press.

Hutchins, E. (1995). *Cognition in the Wild.* Cambridge, MA: MIT Press.

Lave, J., & Wenger, E. (1991). *Situated learning: legitimate peripheral participation.* Cambridge: Cambridge University Press.

McNeill, D. (1992). *Hand and mind: what gestures reveal about thought.* Chicago, IL: University of Chicago Press.

Newell, A. (1990). *Unified theories of cognition.* Cambridge, MA: Harvard University Press.

Newman, D., Griffin, P., & Cole, M. (1989). *The construction zone.* Cambridge: Cambridge University Press.

Pomerantz, A. (1984). Agreeing and disagreeing with assessments: some features of preferred/dispreferred turn shapes. In J. M. Atkinson & J. Heritage (Eds.), *Structures of social action: studies in conversation analysis.*(pp. 57-101). Cambridge: Cambridge University Press.

Putnam, H. (1988) *Representation and Reality.* Cambridge, MA: MIT Press.

Resnick, L. B. (1987). Learning in school and out. *Educational Researcher.*16, (13-20).

Rogoff, B. (1990). *Apprenticeship in thinking : cognitive development in social context.* New York: Oxford University Press.

Saxe, G. B. (1991). *Culture and cognitive development: studies in mathematical understanding.* Hillsdale, NJ: Lawrence Erlbaum and Associates, Publishers.

Schegloff, E. A. (1992). On talk and its institutional occasions. In P. Drew & J. Heritage (Eds.), *Talk at work : interaction in institutional settings.* Cambridge: Cambridge University Press.

Star, S. L. (1995). *Ecologies of knowledge: work and politics in science and technology.* Albany, NY: State University of New York Press.

Traweek, S. (1988). *Beamtimes and lifetimes: the world of high energy physicists.* Cambridge, Massachusetts: Harvard University Press.

Wenger, E. (1990). *Toward a theory of cultural transparency: elements of a social discourse of the visible and the invisible.* University of California at Irvine.

Wittgenstein, L. (1958). *Philosophical Investigations.* (2nd ed.). New York: Macmillan.

Distributed Reasoning:
An Analysis of Where Social and Cognitive Worlds Fuse

Mike Dama and **Kevin Dunbar**
Department of Psychology
McGill University
1205 Dr. Penfield Ave. West
Montreal, Quebec H3A 1B1 Canada
dama@ego.psych.mcgill.ca or dunbar@ego.psych.mcgill.ca

Abstract

The goal of this paper was to examine the influence of social and cognitive factors on distributed reasoning within the context of scientific laboratory meetings. We investigated whether a social factor, status, and cognitive factors such as discussion topic and time orientation of the research influenced distributed reasoning. The impact of status on distributed reasoning was examined using 3 lab meetings in which a technician presented (low status) and 3 lab meetings in which a graduate student presented (high status). Two cognitive variables were also examined; focus of discussion topic (theory, method, findings, and conclusions) and the time orientation of the distributed reasoning (past, current and future research). Pooled (cross sectional/time series) analysis, a regression technique, was used to perform the analyses. We found that status of the presenter influenced the structure of distributed reasoning: When the presenter was of high status, the principal investigator was an important influence on distributed reasoning. In contrast, when the presenter was of low status, other lab members were more likely to contribute to distributed reasoning. Our analyses also show that distributed reasoning is not influenced by the discussion topic but appears to focus on the discussion of future research.

Distributed Reasoning:

An Analysis of Where Social and Cognitive Worlds Fuse

Contemporary models of human reasoning have focused on the reasoning processes that individual subjects engage in while they perform a task in a psychological experiment (e.g., Anderson, 1993; Newell & Simon, 1972). While these models have been very successful in accounting for subject's performance in psychology experiments, a number of researchers have turned to understanding the types of reasoning strategies that people use in real-world situations (e.g., Dunbar, 1995, 1996; Hutchins, 1990; Olson et al. 1992). All of these researchers have found that a large amount of reasoning in real-world contexts occurs in groups rather than in individuals. The finding that reasoning occurs

in groups raises a number of important questions concerning the nature of group reasoning. One question that we have been investigating is the way components of reasoning are shared among members of a group. We have found that reasoning in groups is distributed over individuals rather than residing within one individual's head (Dunbar, 1995, 1996). That is, different components of a reasoning process, such as an induction, can be performed by a number of individuals. Up until now, we have not investigated the constraints on cognition imposed by social factors in distributed reasoning. The goal of the research reported in this paper is investigate the influence of social and cognitive factors on distributed reasoning.

For the past 5 years we have been investigating the reasoning processes that scientists use in their day-to-day research and have found that distributed reasoning plays a crucial role (Dunbar 1995, 1996; Dunbar, Patel, Baker & Dama, 1995). One place where distributed reasoning is particularly important is in the weekly laboratory meetings that scientists have. We have found that distributed reasoning helps scientists quickly solve problems, propose hypotheses, and design experiments. Analyses of distributed reasoning episodes reveals that one of the main cognitive events that occurs during distributed reasoning is the parallel generation of multiple representations. Having multiple representations available makes it possible for a scientist to quickly search for a representation that will solve their current problem. In this presentation, we will turn to the social mechanisms involved in distributed reasoning. Much research on groups in social psychology has shown that the status of members in a group, and the composition of a group influences group acceptance and discussion of ideas (e.g., Shaw 1981; Weisband, Schneider, & Connolly, 1995). However, this type of research has not addressed the issue of distributed reasoning. Furthermore, given that distributed reasoning is the place that the cognitive and social worlds fuse, it is important to discover the impact of social variables on distributed reasoning. What we will do is analyze laboratory meetings to discover whether social factors such as status have an effect on distributed reasoning and also what the cognitive components of distributed reasoning are. We will also introduce a new statistical tool

Graduate Student		Technician	
Meeting	N of 2 Minute segments	Meeting	N of 2 Minute segments
1	17	1	12
2	22	2	12
3	28	3	38
Totals	67		62

Table 1: Number of observations for each meeting

into the analysis of distributed reasoning that makes it possible to investigate these issues.

This paper will be divided into four main sections. First we will give background information on the meetings that we analyze. Second, we will provide an overview of the statistical technique that we use to analyze distributed reasoning. Third we will present our analyses of distributed reasoning. Finally we will address the issue of how social and cognitive processes interact to produce distributed reasoning.

Distributed Reasoning in Scientific Laboratories

The analysis of distributed reasoning is a component of a research program that is concerned with understanding the cognitive and social processes underlying science as it is practiced. Over the past five years we have collected data from six biological laboratories at two renowned universities, four in the United States, and two in Canada (see Dunbar 1995, 1996 for overviews of the research program). The actual data that we have been analyzing consists of the weekly laboratory meetings that occur in all the labs. We use lab meetings as our data source as the lab meetings are one of the main sources of problem solving, reasoning, and hypothesis generation in the laboratories. For the purpose of this paper we will focus on distributed reasoning in three molecular biology laboratories. All three laboratories are of similar size and use similar techniques. One laboratory is concerned with understanding how a gene in the HIV virus functions, another lab with understanding how a gene works on a parasite, and the third laboratory investigates the function of a particular gene in causing a certain type of cancer. All three of the labs use similar research methods and questions regarding the functions of their respective genes.

Method

Data

The data consisted of 6 audiotaped laboratory meetings. Three of the meetings were where the presenter was of low status (a technician), and three were where the presenter was of higher status (a graduate student). By having presenters of different status, it is thus possible to investigate the role of presenter status in distributed reasoning. In each meeting, current research was presented by either a graduate student or technician. Each audiotaped meeting was transcribed and divided into consecutive 2 minute time segments. For each two minute segment, the number of statements (regardless

of whether the statement was coded as one of the variables) were counted. Additionally, within each 2 minute segment, the number of statements were counted for each variable. Each of the variables was converted to a percentage by dividing its count for a time segment by the total number of statements for the time segment. For example, if in a particular time segment 3 distributed reasoning statements occurred out of 10 total statements for the time segment, 30 percent of the time segment was scored as distributed reasoning. Table 1 shows the number of 2 minute segments for each of the six meetings.

Coding of Variables

The variables of interest were generated by coding each statement from the transcribed meetings. Statements consisted of sentences and simple yes/no comments by laboratory members. Each statement was coded for the presence of the following.

(I) Distributed Reasoning. A statement in which a person added a new element to the reasoning of another speaker was coded as distributed reasoning. In addition, any one reasoning episode that was part of a distributed reasoning block was coded as distributed reasoning.

(II) Participation of Principal Investigator/ Others. Statements made by the principal investigator were coded as participation of principal investigator. Statements made by all other participants (excluding the presenter) were coded as participation of others.

(III) Discussion Topic. Four discussion topics were coded. Statements involving background information and current understanding were coded as theory. A statement focusing on how an experiment was conducted was coded as method. Statements involving experimental results were coded as findings. Statements in which the speaker gave an opinion about an experimental result were coded as conclusions.

(IV) Time Orientation of Research. Statements focusing on the discussion of research performed in the past were coded as past research. Statements focusing on the discussion of research in progress or recently completed by the presenter were coded as current research. Statements in which the speaker proposed a methodology, result or a conclusion for a study not yet underway were coded as future research.

Status	Presenter	R Square	B	Beta
PI (high)	Grad Student	.31**	1.14	.56**
	Technician	.16*	.65	.42**
Others (lower)	Grad Student	.21**	.93	.50**
	Technician	.50**	.67	.72**

* $p < .05$. ** $p < .01$.

Table 2: Distributed Reasoning
Predicted From High and Lower Status Lab Members

The PCSTS Statistical Technique

Pooled (cross sectional/time series) analysis was used to analyze distributed reasoning. A parametric regression technique used in econometrics and political science (e.g., Stimson, 1985; Kmenta, 1986), pooled (or PCSTS) analysis was developed to examine data that consists of measurement of variables over time (i.e., a time series) for a number of cross sections or units (e.g., lab meetings). The rationale behind PCSTS analysis is that the researcher may not have enough time series data to warrant the use of most time series models. Additionally, the researcher may not have sufficient cross section data to analyze differences between cross sections. For example, assume we have a data set consisting of 10 time measurements for each of 5 units. Ten time measurements are not enough to perform a time series. Additionally, 5 units are not enough to compare units. In comparison, since PCSTS analysis uses both the time measurements and cross section information, a PCSTS analysis would have 50 observations for analysis, (10 time measurements for each of 5 units). Thus, a PCSTS analysis of time series and cross sectional data makes it possible to increase the number of observations in the analyses. This technique therefore allows us to perform statistical analyses on small data sets such as the data that we analyze in this paper.

Results

PCSTS analysis was performed separately on the graduate student and technician data sets to examine if there were differences in the factors predicting distributed reasoning for graduate students and technicians. To address this question, a regression equation with dummy variables was used. In the dummy variables model, N - 1 dummy variables are entered for the unit of interest, to control for dependent variable differences between units (Stimson, 1985). Thus for each regression equation, 2 dummy variables were entered to control for distributed reasoning differences between the 3 meetings. For a particular equation, the calculated percentages for the variables at each time segment were entered as separate observations in the regression equation. For example, in predicting distributed reasoning from principal investigator comments, the 67 distributed reasoning percentages and their corresponding principal investigator percentages were treated as separate observations for the graduate student meetings.

Question I: Does the status of the presenter influence the structure of distributed reasoning?

The purpose of our first set of analyses was to determine whether the structure of distributed reasoning was influenced by the status of the presenter. Specifically, we were interested in whether the status of the presenter interacted with the contribution by high and low status lab members during distributed reasoning. For a high status presenter, (i.e., a graduate student) two regression equations were run. In the first equation, distributed reasoning was predicted from statements by a high status person (i.e., principal investigator), while in the second equation, distributed reasoning was predicted from statements by lower status lab members (i.e., all other lab members). In addition, the same regression equations were run for a low status presenter (i.e., a technician). The R squares and unstandardized (B) and standardized (Beta) regression weights for the regression equations are given in Table 2.

Examination of the beta weights indicates that statements made by both the principal investigator and others are positively related to distributed reasoning for the graduate student and technician presentations. However, examination of the R squares demonstrates differences between the graduate student and technician presentations. Specifically, statements made by the principal investigator account for more distributed reasoning in the graduate student presentations than in the technician presentations. In contrast, statements made by others account for more distributed reasoning in the technician presentations than in the graduate student presentations. Overall these analyses suggest that the status of the presenter does influence the structure of distributed reasoning.

Question II: Are some topics more likely to be discussed during distributed reasoning than others?

We were interested in determining which of 4 topics (i.e., theory, method, findings, and conclusions) were discussed during distributed reasoning. This question was analyzed by predicting distributed reasoning from discussion of the 4 topics (i.e., theory, method, findings, and conclusions) using separate regression equations for each of the topics.

As can be seen from Table 3, the R squares suggest that none of the 4 discussion topics are strong predictors of distributed reasoning; only one regression equation has an R square above .20. While examination of the significant beta weights indicates that discussion of findings are negatively related to distributed reasoning and discussion of

168

Topic	Presenter	R Square	B	Beta
Theory	Grad Student	.03	.70	.17
	Technician	.06	-.54	-.19
Method	Grad Student	.01	.10	.09
	Technician	.06	.18	.20
Findings	Grad Student	.10	-.34	-.32**
	Technician	.13*	-.33	-.34**
Conclusions	Grad Student	.12*	.75	.37**
	Technician	.21**	.81	.44**

* p < .05. ** p < .01.

Table 3: Distributed Reasoning Predicted From Discussion Topics

conclusions are positively related to distributed reasoning, the R squares are fairly low. The reason for the negative relationship between discussion of findings and distributed reasoning is that a number of time segments had high levels of discussion of findings in the absence of distributed reasoning. This resulted in a negative relationship between discussion of findings and distributed reasoning.

Question III: Is distributed reasoning related to the discussion of past, current or future research?

We were interested in determining whether the discussion of past, current or future research was related to distributed reasoning. This question was analyzed by predicting distributed reasoning from discussion of past research, current research and future research, using separate regression equations for each of the 3 time orientations (see Table 4 for the results).

Examination of the R squares indicates that discussion of future research accounts for more distributed reasoning than discussion of current research. An inspection of the beta weights indicates that discussion of current research is negatively related to distributed reasoning, while discussion of future research is positively related to distributed reasoning. The reason for the negative relationship between discussion of current research and distributed reasoning is that a number of time segments had high levels of discussion of current research in the absence of distributed reasoning. This resulted in a negative relationship between discussion of current research and distributed reasoning.

Conclusion

The goal of the analyses performed in this paper was to investigate the interaction of cognitive and social processes in distributed reasoning. We have found that social status does indeed have an effect on when and how distributed reasoning occurs. In contrast, in the technician presentations, the principal investigator making comments does not lead to more distributed reasoning. The presenter status thus influences the flow and structure of distributed reasoning. Currently we are investigating factors which may be responsible for the structure of distributed reasoning. For example, the complexity of the experiments performed by the presenter and presenter expertise may influence the structure of distributed reasoning.

A second finding arising out of our analyses is that that none of the 4 topics (theory, method, findings, and conclusions) were strongly related to distributed reasoning. This result was surprising in that we expected more distributed reasoning to occur when the scientists were discussing the findings of experiments. We are now conducting more detailed analyses where we are examining whether more distributed reasoning occurs during discussion of unexpected findings as compared to expected findings.

Finally, our analysis demonstrated that an important component of distributed reasoning is future research rather than past or current research. Again, this result was surprising. We expected that much of distributed reasoning would focus on current research rather than on research not yet conducted.

On the use of Pooled Cross-Sectional Time series Analysis (PCSTS)

We have introduced PCSTS analysis as a statistical tool in our examination of the laboratory meetings. In particular, we have used an Ordinary Least Squares model with dummy variables to control for distributed reasoning differences between lab meetings. Use of PCSTS analysis allowed us to examine relationships among variables within a limited number of lab meetings.

Time	Presenter	R Square	B	Beta
Past	Grad Student	.01	-.15	-.13
	Technician	.03	-.07	-.06
Current	Grad Student	.18**	-.43	-.51**
	Technician	.32**	-.44	-.58**
Future	Grad Student	.34**	.74	.59**
	Technician	.56**	.71	.73**

* p < .05. ** p < .01.

Table 4: Distributed Reasoning Predicted From Discussion of Past, Current and Future Research

However, PCSTS has the potential to be used to address many different types of questions that are of interest to cognitive scientists. For example, some PCSTS models allow for the use of variables from earlier time intervals (i.e., lagged predictors) and current time intervals, giving the researcher a method of examining how preceding events influence current events (Sayrs, 1989). We plan to use such models to examine how preceding laboratory meeting events impact later occurrences of distributed reasoning.

Acknowledgments

This research was supported by a McGill Major Graduate Fellowship to the first author and the following grants to The second author was funded by grants number OGP0037356 from NSREC and grants from FCAR and SSHRC. We would like to thank Craig Leth-Steensen for his comments on an earlier version of this paper and his assistance on the use of the PCSTS technique. We would also like to thank Rhonda Amsel for her comments on the manuscript and Romana Ahmad and Annie Maude St-Laurent for their assistance in coding the data.

References

Anderson, J.R. (1993). *Rules of the Mind*. Hillsdale, NJ: LEA.

Dunbar, K. (1995). How scientists really reason: Scientific reasoning in real-world laboratories. In R. J. Sternberg & J. Davidson (Eds.), *Mechanisms of insight*. Cambridge, MA: MIT Press.

Dunbar, K. (1996). How scientists think: Online creativity and conceptual change in science. In T. B. Ward, S. M. Smith, & J. Vaid, *Conceptual structures and processes: Emergence, discovery, and change*. Washington, DC: American Psychological Association Press.

Dunbar, K., Patel, V., Baker, L., & Dama, M. (1995, November). *Group reasoning strategies in knowledge-rich domains*. 36th Annual Meeting of the Psychonomic Society, Los Angeles.

Hutchins, E. (1990). The technology of team navigation. In J. Galegher, R.E. Kraut, & C. Edgido (Ed.), *Intellectual teamwork: Social and technological foundations of cooperative work*. Hillsdale, NJ: LEA.

Kmenta, J. (1986). *Elements of Econometrics* (2nd ed.). New York, NY: Macmillan.

Newell, A., & Simon, H. A. (1972). *Human Problem Solving*. Englewood Cliffs, NJ: Prentice-Hall, Inc.

Olson, G.M., Olson, J.S., Carter, M., & Storrsten, M. (1992). Small group design meetings: An analysis of collaboration. *Human Computer Interaction*, 7, 347-374.

Sayrs, L. W. (1989). *Pooled Time Series Analysis*. Beverly Hills, CA: Sage.

Shaw, M. E. (1981). Group Dynamics: The psychology of small group behavior, (3rd ed.). New York, NY: McGraw-Hill.

Stimson, J. (1985). Regression in space and time: A statistical essay. *American Journal of Political Science*, 29, 914-947.

Weisband, S. P, Schneider, S. K, & Connolly, T. (1995). Computer-mediated communication and social information: Status salience and status differences. *Academy of Management Journal*, 38, 1124-1151.

The Impact of Letter Classification Learning on Reading

Gale L. Martin
MCC
3500 Balcones Center Drive
Austin, Texas 78759
galem@mcc.com

Abstract

When people read, they classify a relatively long string of characters in parallel. Machine learning principles predict that classification learning with such high dimensional inputs and outputs will fail unless biases are imposed to reduce input and output variability and/or the number of candidate input/output mapping functions evaluated during learning. The present paper draws insight from observed reading behaviors to propose some potential sources of such biases, and demonstrates, through neural network simulations of letter-sequence classification learning that: (1) Increasing dimensionality does hinder letter classification learning and (2) the proposed sources of bias do reduce dimensionality problems. The result is a model that explains word superiority and word frequency effects, as well as consistencies in eye fixation positions during reading, solely in terms of letter classification learning.

Introduction

Models of word recognition and reading typically focus on processes that occur after letters are classified. They explain reading behaviors in terms of the processes that act on the outputs of letter detectors, rather than in terms of the processes that convert the image of a letter string to the corresponding outputs of the letter detectors. For example, Morton's Logogen model (Morton, 1969) focuses on word-level representations, and explains *word frequency effects* [1] in terms of lowered activation thresholds for word detectors. Similarly, McClelland & Rumelhart's (1981) Interactive Activation model focuses on associations and interactions between letter detectors and word detectors, and explains word frequency and *word superiority effects* [2] by proposing that these associations amplify the activation coming from letter detectors. The present paper departs from this tradition by proposing a model of letter classification learning. The model explains word frequency and word superiority effects, as well as certain regularities in eye fixation positions solely in terms of factors that determine letter classification learning.

The model was suggested by an interesting difference between human reading and machine-based Opti-

cal Character Recognition (OCR) systems (see Figure 1). Whereas OCR systems classify individual letters; human readers classify letter sequences. That is, people classify a sequence of as many as 8-13 characters within a single fixation (Rayner, 1979) and within such a fixation, the classification occurs in parallel (Reicher, 1969; Blanchard, McConkie, Zola & Wolverton, 1984).

One reason why this is an interesting difference is that if people classify a sequence of letters together, within essentially one operation, then we might expect that the familiarity of the letter sequence would impact letter classification operations, as well as subsequently occurring processes. In other words, we might expect general reading behaviors to be determined by letter classification processes, as well as processes that involve higher-level representations.

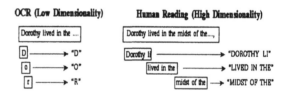

Figure 1: Character classification versus character sequence classification.

A second reason why the difference between OCR systems and human reading is interesting is that OCR systems are designed to classify single characters to minimize the so-called *curse of dimensionality* (Denker, et al, 1987). This machine learning principle predicts that high dimensionality (for example, large, high detail inputs) will cause classification learning to fail. If no constraints are placed on inputs, outputs, and input-output mapping functions, increased dimensionality leads to exponential increases in the number of different inputs, outputs, and mapping functions. Classification learning corresponds to approximating a particular mapping function by sampling from its population of input-output pairs. Learning will fail, with high dimensional inputs and outputs, because: (1) the system can not sample enough pairs to capture the full variability of inputs and outputs; thereby causing low generalization, and/or (2) it has insufficient capacity to describe even the sampled training pairs. Geman, Bienenstock & Doursat (1992) point out that the answer to this dilemma is not to put

---

[1] People identify high frequency words faster than low frequency words

[2] People identify letters within words and pronounceable non-words faster than they identify isolated letters and letters within unpronounceable non-words

one's energies into developing yet another new learning algorithm, because all classification learning algorithms will be subject to the curse. Instead they recommend developing an understanding of how to appropriately bias learning in given domains. Biasing corresponds to implementing *a priori* assumptions that rule out, or render less likely, some portion of the set of all possible inputs, outputs, and/or mapping functions.

This machine learning perspective, combined with the psychological evidence that people do learn to classify high dimensional images of letter sequences, suggests that it might be useful to view reading behaviors in terms of biases that make accurate letter classification possible. The model proposed here assumes that people would fail to learn to classify high dimensional letter sequences unless such learning was biased, and that specifying these biases may help explain a variety of reading behaviors. Three sources of bias, or methods for reducing learning complexity, are proposed here: (1) Limiting mapping functions to those based on position-invariant local feature detectors, and limiting the range of inputs and outputs by limiting the range of, or variability in, (2) eye fixation positions, and (3) allowed character sequences. This paper describes three experiments that support the model. Each consists of a set of backpropagation (Rumelhart, Hinton, & Williams, 1986) neural net simulations of letter classification learning, in which the inputs are images of individual letters or letter strings and the outputs are the corresponding letter categories.

Materials and Network Architectures

Training and testing materials came from the story *The Wonderful Wizard of Oz* by L. Frank Baum. Text line images were created from 120 pages of text (about 160,000 characters, 33,000 total words, or 2,600 different words), divided into 6 sets of 20 pages each. Each set was printed in 1 of 3 fonts, and in either all upper case characters or the original mix of lower and upper case (see Figure 2). Two of the three font types had variable-width characters, and one had constant-width characters. It was important to include variations in character widths because classifying letter sequences involves locating the relative positions of each character identified. Each image was labeled with the categories and horizontal positions of the letters depicted. Text line images were normalized with respect to height, but not width. Training and test sets contained an equal mix of the six font/case conditions. Two generalization sets were used, for test and cross-validation, and each consisted of about 14,000 characters. Training performance was measured by two metrics: (1) Asymptotic accuracy on the training data, and (2) amount of training required to reach asymptote. Generalization performance was measured by accuracy on test set, and on the cross-validation set.

The neural network architectures used here are extensions of the local receptive field, shared weight architectures (see Figure 3) used in some OCR systems (LeCun, et al, 1990; Martin & Pittman, 1991). In this earlier version, the input is the image of a single letter, and the

Dorothy lived in the midst of the great Kansas Prairies.
DOROTHY LIVED IN THE MIDST OF THE GREAT KANSAS PRAIRIES.
Dorothy lived in the midst of the great Kansas Prairies.
DOROTHY LIVED IN THE MIDST OF THE GREAT KANSAS PRAIRIES.
Dorothy lived in the midst of the great Kansas Prairies.
DOROTHY LIVED IN THE MIDST OF THE GREAT KANSAS PRAIRIES.

Figure 2: Samples of type font and case conditions

output a vector representing the letter category. Hidden nodes receive input from a local region (e.g., a 6x6 area) in the layer below. Hidden layers are visualized as cubes, made up of separate planes. Hidden nodes within a plane share weights. Corresponding weights in the nodes' receptive fields are randomly initialized to the same value and updated by the same error, so that different hidden nodes within a plane learn to detect the same feature at different locations. Different feature detectors emerge from hidden nodes within different planes due to different random initializations. Output nodes are connected to all nodes in the previous layer, but not each other.

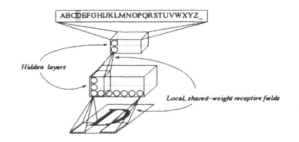

Figure 3: Local, shared weight architecture common in OCR systems.

The extension to an architecture that classifies character sequences is illustrated in Figure 4, for the case in which k, the number of to-be-classified characters, is equal to 4. The input window is expanded horizontally to cover k of the widest characters ("WWWW"). The image of a string of narrower characters will depict additional characters to the right, which the net must learn to ignore. Hidden layers are also expanded horizontally. Network capacity is described by the depth (the number of different feature detectors, or planes) and width of each hidden layer. Each output node represents a character category in one of the kth ordinal positions in the string. Networks were trained until the training set accuracy failed to improve by at least .1% across 5 passes through the training set. Nets were monitored for overfitting using the test set, but such overfitting never occurred.

This architecture biases learning by selectively reducing network capacity relative to that of a comparable globally connected net. The bias seems to be favorable, in that these nets could be trained with at least moderate success; whereas attempts to train globally connected nets on character sequence images failed miserably.

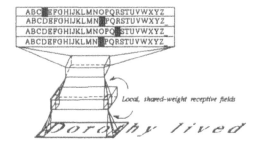

Figure 4: Net architecture for parallel character sequence classification, $k=4$ characters.

A limited claim can also be made that the biases imposed are similar to those imposed by mammalian visual systems. Like the local, shared-weight architecture, mammalian visual systems appear to use spatially local feature detectors that are replicated across the visual array (Hubel & Wiesel, 1979). There is also some very rough similarity between the oriented edge and bar detectors that emerge in both systems (Hubel & Wiesel, 1979; Martin & Pittman, 1991), as illustrated in Figure 5, which depicts some receptive fields that developed in first hidden-layer nodes with the local, shared-weight networks trained on letter images (Martin & Pittman, 1991). These receptive fields indicate that the corresponding feature detecting nodes discriminate on the basis of oriented edges and bars, but beyond this, any similarity to human or mammalian vision systems is unknown.

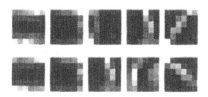

Figure 5: Feature detectors that emerged in OCR neural nets

Curse of Dimensionality Effects

The purpose of Experiment 1 was to test whether high dimensionality is associated with decreased training and generalization accuracy, even when learning is biased through the use of the local, shared-weight architecture. That is, the goal was to determine if classification learning becomes increasingly difficult as we move from the situation in which only single characters are classified, to that in which a letter sequence is classified. Four levels of dimensionality were examined (see Figure 6), ranging from a 20x20 input window, $k=1$; to an 80x20 input window, $k=4$. Input images were generated by starting the window at the left edge of the text line, with the first character centered 10 pixels from the left of the window, and then successively scanning to the right, pausing at each character position. Five different training set sizes

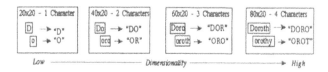

Figure 6: Four levels of input/output dimensionality used in the experiment.

were used (roughly 700 samples to 50,000), as well as a lower and higher capacity version of each network (15 vs 18 different feature detectors in each hidden layer). 40 different networks were trained, one for each combination of dimensionality, training set size and relative network capacity (4x5x2). Some nets required several months to train.

Accuracy is reported as percent of fields in which all characters were correctly classified. The results (see Figure 7) confirm the curse of dimensionality prediction that increasing dimensionality hinders both training and generalization. Increasing dimensionality lowers asymptotic accuracy achieved on the training set ($F(3, 27) = 15.15, p < .01$), and increases the number of training passes required to reach the asymptote ($F(3, 27) = 14.44, p < .01$). It also decreases generalization accuracy rates on both the test set ($F(3, 27) = 33.9, p < .01$) and the validation set ($F(3, 27) = 61.38, p < .001$). These results suggest that, even with the constrained architecture, high dimensionality leads to inadequate classification learning. Since human reading appears to involve even higher dimensionality than that modeled here, these results argue for the need for factors that reduce variance.

Constraints on Fixation Positions

One method for reducing the variance in to-be-classified images is to constrain the variability in fixation positions within a word. The input images in Experiment 1 were generated from fixations at each character position within a word, and thus were highly variable. However, people fixate most often at a *preferred viewing location*– slightly to the left of the middle of a word (Rayner, 1979). The non-randomness of eye fixation positions would have the effect of reducing image variability, and hence should aid classification learning. Accordingly, people do identify a word more quickly when the eyes are fixated near this location (O'Regan & Jacobs, 1992). Besides the benefit of consistency, the location may be optimal in that the average variability in the distance of characters from fixation is minimized when a point toward the middle of a word is fixated.

Experiment 2 used four different conditions to examine whether such consistent and optimal positioning reduces dimensionality problems. The *consistent and optimal positioning* condition used an 80x20 input window positioned with respect to the 3rd character of each word of 3 or more characters (see Figure 8)[3] and the net was trained to classify the first 4 characters in the word. The

---

[3]This is a simplification of the fixation position consisten-

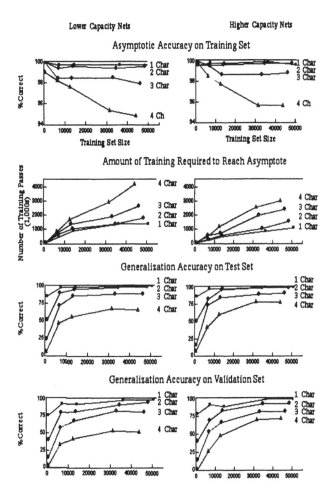

Figure 7: Impact of dimensionality on training and generalization.

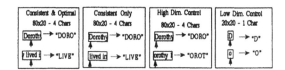

Figure 8: Window positioning and dimensionality manipulations in Experiment 2

$F(3, 32) = 1022.6, p < .001$). Subsequent t-tests revealed that the high dimensional control condition networks did worse than the nets in the other three conditions across all three of the metrics which resulted in significant analysis of variance results. Moreover, the consistent and optimal positioning networks yielded better asymptotic training and generalization accuracies than those in the consistent positioning only condition, and better than or equivalent to those in the low dimensionality control condition. The consistent positioning only condition generally performed better than the high dimensionality control. These results support the value of both consistent positioning and optimal positioning in reducing the negative effects of dimensionality on classification learning.

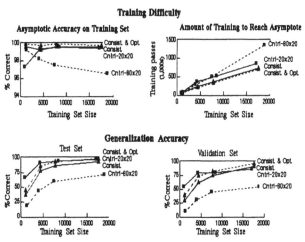

Figure 9: Impact of consistent & optimal window positions.

consistent positioning only condition differed from this only in that positioning was with respect to the first character of a word. The *high dimensionality control* condition used the same input/output dimensionality, but the window was positioned at all character positions during training, and at the first character in a word during testing. The *low dimensionality control* used a 20x20 input window, with $k=1$, and the net trained and tested only on the first 4 characters. Four levels of training set size were used, with three replications of each training set size x window condition, resulting in 4 x 4 x 3 = 48 networks trained and tested. All networks employed 18 different feature detectors for each hidden layers.

The results support the value of both consistent and optimal positioning in reducing dimensionality problems (see Figure 9). The effects of positioning were significant with respect to asymptotic accuracy ($F(3, 32) = 71.83, p < .001$), and generalization in both the test and validation sets ($F(3, 32) = 861.9, p < .001$; and

Character Sequence Regularities

Another factor that may reduce the complexity of classification learning stems from the fact that English words constitute a subset of all possible letter sequences, and of this subset, not all sequences have an equal likelihood of being encountered. People appear to take advantage of such constraints when they read, in that they are better at reading familiar, as compared to unfamiliar, letter sequences. They identify letters within words faster than letters within non-words, and letters within pronounceable non words faster than letters within random character strings (Baron & Thuston, 1973; Reicher, 1969), and they identify high frequency words more quickly than low frequency words (Solomon & Postman, 1952). Note

cies in human reading, which are better described in terms of a probability distribution, the mean of which falls toward the center of a word.

that the reading system could take advantage of the non-randomness of letter sequences at the letter classification learning level, to improve classification accuracy; and/or at subsequent processing levels, to correct letter classification errors. As noted in the introduction, most conceptions of reading and word recognition focus on the latter processing levels. The present focus is on the impact of letter sequence familiarity on letter classification, exclusive of more abstract levels of processing.

It is also important to point out that the feedforward networks used here can not reflect processing times directly, since each forward pass in the net takes the same amount of time. Therefore, in modeling word superiority and word frequency effects, it is assumed that lower accuracy rates translate to slower performance, either because lower accuracy rates would require additional, time-consuming post-processing mechanisms to correct classification errors or because, in an interactive activation network, the reduced activation associated with less certain responses would be reflected in longer times to reach thresholds of activation.

Experiment 3 involved seeing if the three best consistent and optimal positioning nets from Exp. 2 exhibit human-like word superiority and frequency effects in the sense of exhibiting lower accuracy for the less familiar letter sequences. The control condition used the nets trained in the low dimensional control condition to distinguish between effects due to individual letter familiarity and effects due to letter sequence familiarity. New text images were created to produce the following sets or conditions. The *word* set had 30 4-letter words, drawn from the Oz text, of which 15 occurred very frequently in the text (e.g., SAID), and 15 occurred infrequently (e.g., PAID). The *pronounceable non-word* set had 30 4-letter pronounceable non-words (e.g., TOID). The *random non-words* had 30 4-letter random strings (e.g., SDIA). The *alternating case words* used the word set but the letters were printed in AlTeRnAtInG cases. This latter set was created to see if the nets exhibit human-like behavior in being able to read despite such manipulations (McClelland, 1976). Word superiority results were analyzed in terms of a split-plot analysis of variance with letter sequence type and dimensionality as factors, and associated *t*-tests. Word frequency results were analyzed with *t*-tests.

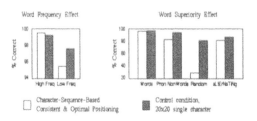

Figure 10: Sensitivity to word frequency and character sequence regularities

As shown in Figure 10, the consistent and optimal positioning nets mimic word frequency and word superiority effects. In the case of word superiority effects, significant main effects were found for letter sequence type ($F(3, 12) = 181.8, p < .001$) and dimensionality ($F(1, 4) = 77.4, p < .001$). The interaction was also significant ($F(3, 12) = 80.2, p < .001$). Paired comparison tests confirmed the advantage for words over the other letter sequence types; and for pronounceable non-words and aLtErNaTiNg case words over random non-words. Letter classification accuracy remains high in spite of the words being printed in alternating cases, which is presumably due to the local, shared-weight architecture biasing the system toward local, rather than word-level, feature detectors. The consistent and optimal positioning nets also showed a tendency to classify high frequency words more accurately than low frequency words ($p = .05$). These results are interesting because they support the notion that word superiority and word frequency effects can be explained without reference to higher levels of processing.

Discussion

More generally, the results presented here support the value of viewing reading behaviors in terms of biases that make it possible to learn to accurately classify letters. Experiment 1 demonstrated that classification accuracy drops dramatically with increases in the size of the to-be-classified image and the number of to-be-classified letters. Experiment 2 demonstrated that these negative effects of dimensionality can be offset, at least to some extent, through the use of a simplified form of the consistent fixation positions used in human reading. Experiment 3 demonstrated that the letter classification learning system exhibited word superiority and word frequency effects similar to those of human readers, even though there were no higher level representations such as words or phonological codes in the system.

The results also raise several issues for discussion. One of these is the question of whether or not additional processing levels also determine word frequency and word superiority effects. It might be argued on the grounds of parsimony that there is no need to model additional processing mechanisms, since the relatively low level, classification mechanism can account for the findings. However, it seems more reasonable to assume that learning acts at multiple levels because letter classification processes are likely to need all the help they can get. Current extensions of the work reported here involve expanding the input window to cover 8 or more letters, as well as requiring the network to learn to classify 8 or more letters. This work indicates that classification accuracy drops considerably with such extensions, and therefore it seems reasonable to propose that word-level or phonological-level coding would still play a critical role in improving letter classification accuracy.

The results also raise the question of whether or not factors that determine letter classification learning also determine reading disabilities and developmental stages of reading. The present work demonstrates the importance of consistencies in eye fixation positions. Some reading problems are associated with reduced input/output dimensionality, as measured by perceptual span (Rayner, 1986; Rayner, et al., 1989) and with irregular eye fixation patterns (Rayner & Pollatsek, 1989). Such irregularities would increase input/output variability, and hence reduce the dimensionality at which high accuracy levels could be maintained. This pattern supports the relevance of letter classification learning factors to reading disabilities and developmental differences. Perceptual and classification processes have sometimes been discounted as causes of reading disabilities on the grounds that reading disabilities and developmental differences become more apparent with more difficult content. Content factors have traditionally been associated with processes beyond letter classification. The present results suggest that this assumption warrants further consideration since a factor that is often associated with content difficulty–word frequency–was shown to impact classification accuracy.

A third issue pertains to the question of why the human reading system doesn't avoid all of these dimensionality problems by taking the same approach chosen by developers of optical character recognition systems–classifying individual letters rather than letter sequences. One possibility is that the brain can't easily separate small (letter sized) individual parts of an image, classify each and retain the original order of the images to infer letter sequence information, and so it is forced into dealing with the high dimensionality. In this case, the human mechanisms would be less optimal than the corresponding machine-based mechanisms. Alternatively, it is possible that incorporating letter sequence familiarity at multiple stages of processing, as is possible in the current system, would lead to higher overall accuracy rates. In this case, the human mechanisms would be superior to the machine-based mechanisms.

The final issue pertains to the direction of future research. As noted earlier, the current focus is on developing a model that can at least partially classify between 8 to 13 letters within a single "fixation." Once this model has reached some degree of stable performance, the focus will shift to incorporating additional aspects of reading. One of these aspects is the control of eye movements. Previous work (Martin, Rashid & Pittman, 1993) indicates that it is possible to train networks to generate ballistic and corrective saccades to navigate along a path of text. Other aspects include integrating the information obtained from successive fixations, and using word-level information to improve classification accuracy.

References

Blanchard, H., McConkie, G., Zola, D., & Wolverton, G. (1984) Time course of visual information utilization during fixations in reading. *Jour. of Exp. Psych.: Human Perc. & Perf., 10,* 75-89.

Denker, J., Schwartz, D., Wittner, B., Solla, S., Howard, R., Jackel, L., & Hopfield, J. (1987) Large automatic learning, rule extraction and generalization, *Complex Systems, 1,* 877-933.

Geman, S., Bienenstock, E., and Doursat, R. (1992) Neural networks and the bias/variance dilemma. *Neural Computation, 4,* 1-58.

Hubel, D. & Wiesel, T. (1979) Brain mechanisms of vision. *Sci. Amer., 241,* 150-162.

LeCun, Y., Boser, B., Denker, J., Henderson, D., Howard, R., Hubbard, W., & Jackel, L. (1990) Handwritten digit recognition with a backpropagation network. In *Adv. in Neural Inf. Proc. Sys. 2,* D. Touretzky (Ed) Morgan Kaufmann.

Martin, G. L. & Pittman, J. A. (1991) Recognizing handprinted letters and digits using backpropagation learning. *Neural Computation, 3,* 258-267.

Martin, G. L., Rashid, M., & Pittman, J. A. (1993) Integrated segmentation and recognition through exhaustive scans or learned saccadic jumps. In *Advances in Pattern Recognition Systems Using Neural Network Technologies,* I. Guyon and P. S. P. Wang (Eds). World Scientific.

McClelland, J. L. (1976) Preliminary letter identification in the perception of words and nonwords. *Jour. of Exp. Psych.: Human Perc. & Perf., 2,* 80-91.

McClelland, J. & Rumelhart, D.(1981) An interactive activation model of context effects in letter perception: Pt. 1 *Psych. Rev., 88,* 375-

Morton, J. (1969) Interaction of information in word recognition. *Psychological Review, 76,* 165-178.

O'Regan, J. & Jacobs, A.(1992) Optimal viewing position effect in word recognition. *Jour. of Exp. Psych.: Human Perc.& Perf., 18,* 185-197.

Rayner, K. (1986) Eye movements and the perceptual span in beginning and skilled readers. *Jour. of Exp. Child Psych., 41,* 211-236.

Rayner, K. (1979) Eye guidance in reading. *Perception, 8,* 21-30.

Rayner, K., Murphy, L., Henderson, J. & Pollatsek, A. (1989) Selective attentional dyslexia. *Cognitive Neuropsych., 6,* 357-378.

Rayner, K. & Pollatsek, A. (1989) *The Psychology of reading.* Prentice Hall

Reicher, G. (1969) Perceptual recognition as a function of meaningfulness of stimulus material. *Jour. of Exp. Psych., 81,* 274-280.

Rumelhart, D., Hinton, G., & Williams, R. (1986) Learning internal representations by error propagation. In D. Rumelhart and J. McClelland, *Parallel. Distributed Processing, 1.* MIT Press.

Solomon, R. & Postman, L. (1952) Frequency of usage as a determinant of recognition thresholds for words. *Jour. of Exp. Psych., 43,* 195-210.

Where Defaults Don't Help: the Case of the German Plural System

Ramin Charles Nakisa and **Ulrike Hahn**

Department of Experimental Psychology, Oxford University

South Parks Road

Oxford, OX1 3UD

{ramin,ulrike}@psy.ox.ac.uk

Abstract

The German plural system has become a focal point for conflicting theories of language, both linguistic and cognitive. We present simulation results with three simple classifiers – an ordinary nearest neighbour algorithm, Nosofsky's 'Generalized Context Model' (GCM) and a standard, three-layer backprop network – predicting the plural class from a phonological representation of the singular in German. Though these are absolutely 'minimal' models, in terms of architecture and input information, they nevertheless do remarkably well. The nearest neighbour predicts the correct plural class with an accuracy of 72% for a set of 24,640 nouns from the CELEX database. With a subset of 8,598 (non-compound) nouns, the nearest neighbour, the GCM and the network score 71.0%, 75.0% and 83.5%, respectively, on novel items. Furthermore, they outperform a hybrid, 'pattern-associator + default rule', model, as proposed by Marcus et al. (1995), on this data set.

Introduction

The German plural system has been the subject of a wide variety of theoretical accounts ranging from traditional 'Item and Process accounts' (Mugdan, 1977) to schema theories (Bybee (1995); Köpcke (1988; 1993)) and recent 'default rule + pattern associator' accounts (Marcus et al., 1995). Furthermore, it has been championed as a crucial test case (Marcus et al., 1995) in the debate on the psychological reality of linguistic rules triggered by Rumelhart and McClelland's (1986) model of the English past tense.

Decision between the various theoretical accounts is, at present, difficult; though they have the virtue of dealing with a wide range of phenomena, they are not explicit enough to allow suitably fine-grained evaluation. Extant computational models, on the other hand, neither deal with the German plural[1] nor attempt to capture the full range of phenomena such as pluralization of truncations, acronyms, quotes etc. compiled by Marcus et al. (1995). What is now required is the development of explicit computational models which allow quantitative assessment against real data. As a starting point, we have implemented and tested three 'minimal models' – simple, off-the-shelf classifiers – which, given phonological information about the singular alone, predict the correct plural class with surprising accuracy. These are not advanced as full-blown cognitive models of the German plu-

ral, but rather as benchmarks against which more complex accounts must be compared. As an example of this, we also pitted these models against three versions of a hybrid, 'associative memory+default rule' model (Marcus et al., 1995), which subsumes them in the associative component.

The Task

The Data Sets Our dataset is drawn from the 30,100 German nouns in the CELEX database.[2] Since the CELEX classification is fraught with error, we automatically classified nouns according to the nature of the transformation from singular to plural phonology. Four general types of transformation occur: identity mappings, suffixation, umlaut (vowel change) and rewriting of the final phoneme(s). The classification yields approximately 60 categories (some of which contain only one member).

We then discard categories with a type frequency of less than 0.1% resulting in a database of 24,640 nouns with 15 different plural categories (see table 1).[3] This step removes primarily latinate and Greek words and a small number of German words with arbitrary plurals (suppletion, or singly occurring transformations). In effect this brings our classification into accord with the plural types described in standard linguistic analysis (Köpcke, 1988). The only further amendment in this direction was that the umlauts (ä, ö, ü) were treated as one as is consensual in the literature.

For computational reasons this set was further reduced to a set of 8,598 "non-compound" nouns. A "non-compound" noun was defined as a noun that did not contain another noun from the database as its rightmost lexeme.[4] This is justified by the fact that, in German, the plural of a noun-compound is determined exclusively by the right-most lexeme, making the remainder of the word redundant. That this reduction does not distort the similarity structure of the German lexicon is borne out by the fact that the performance of the nearest neighbour classifier on the entire data set and the subset were virtually identical (72% and 71% respectively). This dataset of 8,598

---

[1] with the exception of Goebel and Indefrey (1994).

[2] CELEX can be obtained by contacting celex@mpi.nl.

[3] 45 words and 2 duplicates were manually removed because they were obviously incorrect (e.g. incorrectly pluralized proper names and entries with errors in phonological form).

[4] This leaves complex nouns which are not noun-compounds, and noun-compounds for which the right-most lexeme is not listed individually.

nouns was split roughly in half to give a training set (4,273 words) and a testing set (4,325 words). A copy of the training set which had all 282 words that took a +s suffix removed (leaving 3,991 training words) was used to train the hybrid rule-associative models.

Input Representation A phonological representation of the nouns was created by taking the phonetic singular and plural forms of each word as given in the CELEX database and rewriting them as a bundle of 15 phonetic features taken from Wurzel (1981). Sixteen phonetic slots were used, so each word was represented as a vector with 240 elements. Since words vary in length, their representations must be zero-padded. Vectors were right-justified since word endings are most salient for determining the plural type of German nouns.[5]

Output In all cases a model was required to produce the correct plural category for a given input. Two of the models (GCM and the network) produce graded responses (probabilities or activations). The single highest probability/activation was taken to be the output. Only exact matches were scored as correct. In the following simulations the simple pattern classifiers were trained on the training data set of 4,273 non-compound nouns. Performance was then assessed on the test data set of 4,325 words.

Associative Model Performance

Nearest Neighbour Classifier A nearest neighbour classifier simply adopts the classification of the item in memory most similar to the new item. It is the simplest kind of exemplar model. In linguistic terms, it constitutes a 'weak analogy' model in Köpcke's (1988) sense. It could also straightforwardly form the heart of an associative memory system (Pinker, 1993); all that would be required in addition is a component which generates the appropriate phonological form according to the computed plural class. The nearest neighbour algorithm simply states: for a novel exemplar $\vec{e}$, find the most similar (nearest) neighbour $\vec{n}$ and adopt its plural class. As a similarity metric we used Euclidean distance. Tested on the 4,325 word testing set, the nearest neighbour classifier scored 71%. The pattern of errors, which was basically the same for all models, reveals an interaction between type-frequency and class topology. Generally peformance declines with dropping frequency, but particular low frequency classes can nevertheless be classified very accurately.[6] In addition, this classifier was also tested on the entire data set. Here, each noun was individually "removed" from the data set and classified according to the remaining nearest neighbours giving a classification accuracy of 72%.

Nosofsky's Generalized Context Model Nosofsky's well-known 'Generalized Context Model' (Nosofsky, 1990), which accurately fits human performance data on a range of classification tasks, is a more sophisticated exemplar-model, providing a probabilistic response. Here, the strength of making a category J response (R_J) given presentation of stimulus i (S_i) is found by summing the (weighted) similarity of stimulus i to all presented exemplars of category J (C_J) then multiplying by the response bias for category J. The denominator normalises by summing the strengths over all categories.

$$P(R_J|S_i) = \frac{b_J \sum_{j \in C_J} L(j, J)\eta_{ij}}{\sum_k b_K \sum_{k \in C_K} L(k, K)\eta_{ik}} \quad (1)$$

In equation 1 η_{ij} ($\eta_{ij} = \eta_{ji}$, $\eta_{ii} = 1$) gives the similarity between exemplars i and j, b_J ($0 \leq b_J \leq 1$, $\sum b_K = 1$) is the bias associated with category J and $L(j, J)$ is the relative frequency (likelihood) with which exemplar j is presented during training in conjunction with category J. The distance d_{ij} is scaled and converted to a similarity measure using the transformation $\eta_{ij} = \exp -(d_{ij}/s)^p$ where $p = 1$ yields an exponential decay similarity function and $p = 2$ gives a gaussian similarity function.[7] When the scaling parameter s was optimised for the gaussian similarity function ($\eta_{ij} = \exp -(d_{ij}/s)^2$) the performance was 75.0% ($s = 1.46$). When optimised for the exponential ($\eta_{ij} = \exp(-d_{ij}/s)$) accuracy was 74.4% ($s = 0.35$). The gaussian similarity function was used in the following.

Neural Network The neural network most directly resembles the pattern-associator posited as a module necessary for inflectional morphology by Pinker (1993), and Marcus et al. (1995), with one exception; our network classifies the input as belonging to one of the 15 plural types (see table 1) instead of directly producing the plural form, in order to allow comparison with the nearest neighbour and the GCM. For a full model, a component producing this form on the basis of class must be assumed.

The network was a three-layer, feed-forward network with 240 input and 15 output units. Different numbers of hidden units – 10, 20, 30, 40 and 50 – were tried. Training used back-propagation, duration being varied from 5 to 50 epochs in steps of 5 epochs and using 3 different initial random seeds. The best set of weights (defined by generalisation accuracy on the testing set) was used. It was found that for all numbers of hidden units the score was at roughly 80% after 5 epochs and remained above 80% up to 50 epochs. The accuracy of the best network (with 50 hidden units and after 35 training epochs) was 83.5%.

Comparing Associative and Rule-Associative Models

Defining Interaction of Associative and Rule Components

The most recent account of the German plural system by Marcus et al. (1995) argues that +s is the 'regular' plural in Ger-

---

[5] This was determined by comparison of performance on left-justified, centre-justified and right-justified words using ID3 (Quinlan, 1992).

[6] The network deviates slightly from this pattern insofar as the lower frequency classes – from ʊm→ən onward – are highly sensitive to the initial random seed, so that perfomance can vary drastically between networks.

---

[7] Bias terms were omitted to limit the number of free parameters.

| Plural | All Nouns | | Non-Compound Nouns | |
Type	Frequency	% of Total	Frequency	% of Total
+ən	7012	28.109	2646	30.775
+n	4477	17.947	1555	18.086
+ə	4460	17.879	1178	13.701
Identity	4201	16.840	1992	23.168
Umlaut+ə	2017	8.085	239	2.780
+s	978	3.920	571	6.641
Umlaut+ər	692	2.774	54	0.628
+ər	289	1.159	36	0.419
Umlaut	255	1.022	35	0.407
ʊm→ən	135	0.541	95	1.105
a→ən	121	0.485	81	0.942
ʊs→ən	88	0.353	69	0.803
ʊm→a	45	0.180	40	0.465
+tən	27	0.108	1	0.012
+iən	25	0.100	6	0.070

Table 1: Frequencies of different plural types in the complete set of nouns in CELEX and for the non-compound nouns. Suffixation is indicated by +*suffix*, rewrites are indicated as *"phonemes"*→*"phonemes"*.

man; it is produced by a (cognitively real) default rule *'add -s'* which is applied whenever 'memory fails'. This lexical memory is thought to include a phonologically-based, possibly connectionist, pattern-associator as a subcomponent, hence explaining the limited productivity of the 'irregulars'.

The inflection of the 'regulars' on this account, is independent of the lexicon, resulting from the 'rule-route'. This suggests a simple comparison between pattern associators, which treat the 'regulars' like every other group, and a hybrid rule+pattern associator model, in which the 'regulars' are removed from the pattern-associator and inflected via the rule-route if 'memory fails'. As outlined, all three models above can form the heart of an associative memory system, and, thus, can be used for such a comparison. This comparison requires that Marcus et al.'s notion of memory failure must be made computationally explicit. We did this through the definition of a threshold t, as follows:

(1) for *nearest neighbour* 'memory failure' occurs if the nearest neighbour in the phonological space is at a distance greater than t. In this case the default inflection +s is used.

$$\text{if distance}(\vec{e} - \vec{n}) < t \quad \begin{array}{l} \text{inflect as n} \\ \text{otherwise use default inflection} \end{array} \tag{2}$$

This means, that for very low values of t the nearest neighbour memory always fails because there is never a neighbour close enough so that every singular is classified as a +s. For very large values of t there is always a nearest neighbour closer than t so the default rule is never used and the singular is classified using the plural type of its nearest neighbour. In other words, as t increases, the algorithm in equation 2 asymptotically reverts to the nearest neighbour algorithm.

(2) In the *GCM* memory 'fails' if the largest class probability P_J was less than a threshold value.

$$\text{if MAX}(\vec{P_J}) > t \quad \begin{array}{l} \text{inflect as most probable class} \\ \text{otherwise use default inflection} \end{array} \tag{3}$$

P_J is low and memory failure occurs if the noun is surrounded by roughly equal numbers of two or more classes of noun or is in a sparsely populated region of the phonological space.

(3) For the *neural network*, finally, memory 'fails' if the greatest output unit activity $MAX(\vec{o_i})$ was less than a threshold value t.

$$\text{if MAX}(\vec{o_i}) > t \quad \begin{array}{l} \text{inflect as class of most active unit} \\ \text{otherwise use default inflection} \end{array} \tag{4}$$

For testing, we compute values for t throughout the entire interval ($0.0 < t < 1.0$ for GCM and network and $0.0 < t < \infty$ for nearest neighbour) in search of an optimal value, and compare the performance of the hybrid with the simple classifier at each point.

Rule-Associative Model Performance

The hybrid models were assessed on the same test set of 4,325 nouns as the simple classifiers. In these hybrid models, however, the training set had the +s nouns removed, since the hybrid model requires that these are dealt with by the rule alone. Performances are compared with that of the respective simple classifier trained on the set that included +s nouns.

Nearest Neighbour Classifier In order for the addition of a default rule to improve performance the singular forms of the nouns that take +s would have to be far away from other singular forms in sparsely populated areas of the phonological space. However, the results in figure 1 clearly show that this is not the case: the classification accuracy increases monotonically with increasing t. In other words, as the frequency of using the default rule increases from zero, it always deteriorates the performance of the system. At no value of t does the default improve the performance above that of the purely associative nearest neighbour classifier, making the default rule route completely redundant.

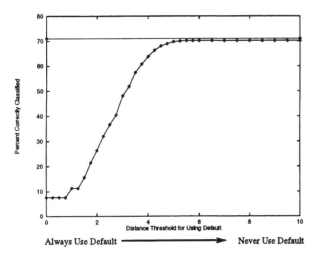

Figure 1: Performance of nearest neighbour classifier on 4,325 German nouns. Horizontal line shows the performance of a nearest neighbour classifier with no default rule and +s plurals included in the training set. Curve shows the performance of a hybrid rule-associative classifier with +s plurals excluded from the training set. Increasing use of the default rule from never being used (threshold = 10) to always being used (threshold = 0) monotonically reduces classification accuracy.

Nosofsky's GCM The removal of the +s singulars from the training set changed the optimal value of s, so the model was re-optimised using the training set without +s plurals. The error surface was sampled in the range $s = 1.4$ to $s = 1.5$ in steps of 0.01 and $t = 0$ to $t = 1.0$ in steps of 0.01. It was found that the optimal value of s was changed slightly to $s = 1.48$ and the optimal value of t was $t = 0.29$ giving a classification accuracy of 74.6%.

Unlike the nearest neighbour, this pattern associator had an optimum value for the threshold.[8] There was a 0.2% increase in performance to 74.6% correct at a probability threshold of 0.29 from 74.4% correct at probability threshold 0.0 (see figure 2). Performance of the rule-associative classifier never reached that of the purely associative classifier.

Network Classifier For the rule-associator classifier, the network was trained on the training set with +s nouns removed

---

[8]Notice that the threshold value is a *probability*. for this model, so the performance drops as the threshold value increases, whereas for the nearest neighbour the threshold was the *distance* of the nearest neighbour so that performance increased with increasing threshold values.

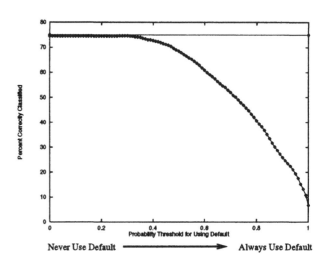

Figure 2: Performance of the GCM on 4,325 German nouns. Horizontal line shows the performance of the similarity based classifier with no default rule and +s plurals included in the training set. Curve shows the performance of a hybrid rule-associative classifier with +s plurals excluded from the training set.

and tested on the standard testing set. Results for this model again showed a decrease in performance on the addition of a rule (see figure 3). There was a 1.2% increase in accuracy to 82.4% correct at an activity threshold of 0.22 from 81.2% correct at an activity threshold 0.0. This remained below the 83.5% accuracy of a purely associative classifier.

Pattern Associator	Simple	Hybrid
Nearest Neighbour	71.0	70.2
Nosofsky GCM	75.0	74.6
Three-layer Perceptron	83.5	81.4

Table 2: Summary of associative and rule-associative model evaluations. The performance of the associative classifier was greater than that of the hybrid rule-associative classifiers for all three types of pattern associator.

Where a Default *Would* Help

The failure of the hybrid models to outperform the simple models reflects an important distributional fact about the language. Performance is never superior because even for the optimum value of t the rule produces false positives. Increasing performance on the regulars *decreases* the systems performance on the irregulars. This is because the distances between the regulars are not sufficiently different from the within-group distances of the irregulars. If they were, then it would be possible to "drive a wedge" between them i.e. select a value of t that correctly classifies regulars whilst leaving the irregulars untouched. These considerations suggest that distributions are possible for which a default *would* help.

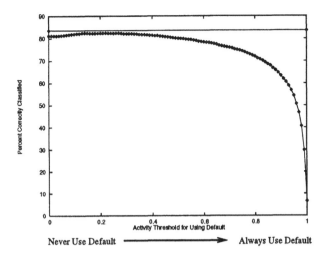

Figure 3: Performance of 3 layer network classifier on 4,325 German nouns. Horizontal line shows the performance of the network classifier with no default rule and +s plurals included in the training set. Curve shows the performance of a hybrid rule-associative classifier with +s plurals excluded from the training set.

We generated two simple artificial languages to illustrate this. Both languages consisted of five plural types distributed in a two-dimensional "phonological" space. Each noun class was generated around a centroid with a gaussian distribution. For the first language, all five plural types had the same variance, whereas for the second, one group, the "default", was exploded to occupy the entire space homogeneously. Both distributions are depicted in figure 4.

For the first language, where the "default" plural type had the same variance as the other types, the simple nearest neighbour classifier outperformed the hybrid classifier. By contrast, in the second language, the hybrid nearest neighbour classifier outperformed the simple nearest-neighbour classifier. For a distribution where the irregulars are relatively compact and the regular is homogeneously distributed, adding a default can be beneficial for generalization.

The default helps by increasing accuracy on a particular subset of the regulars. It is the regulars forming a shell around each of the irregular clusters that are correctly classified by the hybrid model but not by the simple classifier. We call these regulars "interfacial" because they are distributed on the surface of the irregular clusters. Regulars in isolated regions of the space, "isolated regulars", are equally well classified by hybrid and simple models. Thus, increasing the ratio of "interfacial" to "isolated" regulars increases the benefit of the default. This can be achieved both by increasing the number of irregular plural types and (or) by increasing the surface area of irregular plural types.

It is not just the fact that regulars are distributed homogeneously throughout phonological space (Marcus et al., 1995) that matters, but the existence of interfacial regulars that is

crucial. Isolated regulars alone only allow a threshold t at which the hybrid's performance is not worse, they do not enable it to do better. In summary, for particular distributions a default rule can help. Our results suggest that the German plural system is not of this kind.

Discussion

It is hard to estimate the maximal score any model performing prediction could hope to achieve. German has lexical items with conflicting plural entries and the system as a whole is generally not presumed to be completely deterministic, allowing a certain degree of arbitrary exceptions. Whether this means a maximal score should be placed at 85 or 99%, the performance of all three purely associative models seems remarkably high; none are in any way specifically designed or adjusted for the task, and the input information is minimal. Other sources of information which have been advanced as determinants of German plural morphology are semantics (Mugdan, 1977) and gender (Mugdan, 1977; Köpcke, 1988); additionally, syllable structure, stress and token frequency are likely contributors. Future work will seek to determine exactly what additional benefits these sources provide.

For generalisation accuracy on test items drawn from the extant German lexicon, then, a 'default rule' model has no gain whatsoever, and, in fact, slightly decreases performance (see table 2 for summary).[9] Of course, the primary motivation for the 'default rule' account is the fact that it parsimoniously unifies 21 otherwise seemingly heterogeneous phenomena to which the s-plural is exclusively or predominantly applied – such as quotations, acronyms, truncations, proper names – (Marcus et al., 1995), which are not captured in our data set. However, the same threshold t, which best fits the common nouns investigated here must also give the right mixtures between 'regular inflection' and 'irregulars' for each of the remaining phenomena. This may or may not be possible; there is no a priori reason to believe that it is. This can only be resolved by further empirical work. In the meantime, these results warn of the way in which the general, theoretical accounts mentioned in the introduction are prone to taking computationally consequential details for granted.

Acknowledgements

The order of the authors is arbitrary. Thanks go to Paul Cairns with whom this project began, and to Nick Chater who first suggested nearest neighbour and GCM. Thanks also to Todd Bailey, Kim Plunkett and two anonymous reviewers for helpful comments on the manuscript. Ulrike Hahn is supported by ESRC grant No. R004293341442. Ramin Nakisa is supported by a Training Fellowship from the Medical Research Council.

---

[9] In terms of the systems confidence, adding a default has no visible impact on the irregulars. Trivially, confidence on the regulars is increased to certainty. Whether this is desirable, is an open psychological question.

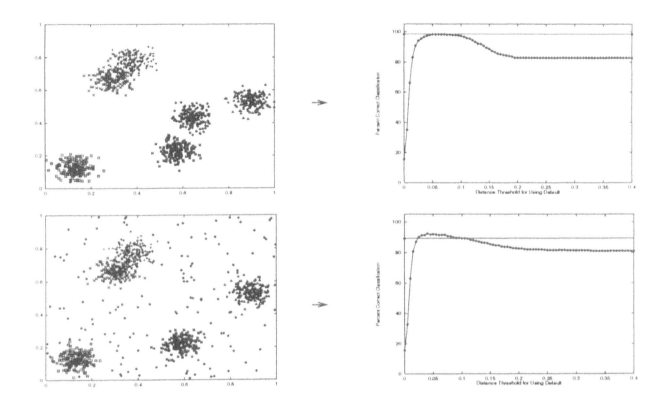

Figure 4: Two pseudolanguages (left) and their corresponding simple and hybrid classifier performances (right). The regular class in both languages is shown as diamonds. The top language (language 1) has equal variances for all plural types, whereas the bottom language (language 2) has the "regular" class exploded to occupy the entire space homogeneously.

References

Bybee, J. 1995. Regular Morphology and the Lexicon. *Language and Cognitive Processes*, **10**, 425–455.

Forrester, N., and Plunkett, K. 1994. The inflectional morphology of the arabic broken plural: a connectionist account. *In: Proc. of the 16th Annual Meeting of the Cognitive Science Society.*

Goebel, R., and Indefrey, P. 1994. The Performance of a recurrent network with short term memory capacity learning the German -s plural. *In: Workshop on Cognitive Models of Language Acquisition. Tilburg, The Netherlands.*

Köpcke, K. 1988. Schemas in German Plural Formation. *Lingua*, **74**, 303–335.

Köpcke, K. 1993. *Schemata bei der Pluralbildung im Deutschen: Versuch einer kognitiven Morphology.* Tübingen: Narr.

Marcus, G., Brinkmann, U., Clahsen, H., Wiese, R., and Pinker, S. 1995. German Inflection: The Exception That Proves the Rule. *Cognitive Psychology*, **29**, 189–256.

Mugdan, J. 1977. *Flexionsmorphologie und Psycholinguistik.* Tübingen: Narr.

Nosofsky, R. M. 1990. Relations between Exemplar-Similarity and Likelihood Models of Classification. *Journal of Mathematical Psychology*, **34**(4), 393–418.

Pinker, S. 1993. Rules of Language. *In:* Bloom, P. (ed), *Language Acquisition: Core Readings.* Harvester Wheatsheaf, New York; London.

Quinlan, R. 1992. *C4.5 Software : Programs for machine learning.* Morgan Kaufmann Publishing.

Rumelhart, D., and McClelland, J. 1986. On learning the past tenses of English verbs. Implicit rules or parallel distributed processing? *In:* McClelland, J., Rumelhart, D., and the PDP Research Group (eds), *Parallel Distributed Processing: Explorations in the microstructure of cognition.* MIT Press: Cambridge, Mass.

Wurzel, W. 1981. *Grundzüge einer deutschen Grammatik.* Berlin: Akademie-Verlag. Chap. Phonologie: Segmentale Struktur, pages 898–990.

Selective attention in the acquisition of the past tense

Dan Jackson
Cognitive Science & Linguistics 0108

University of California, San Diego
La Jolla, CA 92093
jackson@ling.ucsd.edu

Rodger M. Constandse
Computer Science & Engineering 0114
Institute for Neural Computation
University of California, San Diego
La Jolla, CA 92093
rconstan@cs.ucsd.edu

Garrison W. Cottrell
Computer Science & Engineering 0114
Institute for Neural Computation
University of California, San Diego
La Jolla, CA 92093
gary@cs.ucsd.edu

Abstract

It is well known that children generally exhibit a "U-shaped" pattern of development in the process of acquiring the past tense. Plunkett & Marchman (1991) showed that a connectionist network, trained on the past tense, would exhibit U-shaped learning effects. This network did not completely master the past tense mapping, however. Plunkett & Marchman (1993) showed that a network trained with an incrementally expanded training set was able to achieve acceptable levels of mastery, as well as show the desired U-shaped pattern. In this paper, we point out some problems with using an incrementally expanded training set. We propose a model of selective attention that enables our network to completely master the past tense mapping and exhibit U-shaped learning effects without requiring external manipulation of its training set.

Introduction

It is well known that in the process of acquiring the past tense, children generally exhibit a "U-shaped" pattern of development. The first past tense forms produced are generally correct, regardless of whether or not those forms are regular. After this period of correct performance, children go through a period of overgeneralization in which irregular forms are incorrectly inflected (e.g. *goed*). Finally, children seem to identify some forms as exceptions to the general regular pattern, and the overgeneralization errors decrease. Plunkett & Marchman (1991) (P&M hereafter) showed that U-shaped learning effects can emerge in connectionist networks in the absence of any discontinuities in the training regime.[1] P&M showed that such networks go through "micro U-shaped development." This is contrasted with the idealized vision of "macro U-shaped development" that predominates in anecdotal descriptions of children's patterns of acquisition. Macro U-shaped development refers to a rapid and sudden change from the memorization stage, where regular and irregular forms are reproduced with relatively equal levels of error, to a stage where the /-ed/ suffix is applied indiscriminately, resulting in overgeneralization for all irregular verbs. Micro U-shaped

development, on the other hand, is characterized by selective application of the /-ed/ suffix, resulting in a period in which some irregular verbs are regularized, while others are produced correctly. Although most anecdotal descriptions of children's acquisition of the past tense have implied macro U-shaped development, studies of naturalistic past tense production (e.g. Marcus et al. (1992)) and studies using elicitation procedures (e.g. Marchman (1988)) show that micro U-shaped development is a better description of how children learn the past tense.

Although P&M (1991) were successful in showing that connectionist networks go through a micro U-shaped pattern of development, none of the networks they trained achieved mastery of all of the past tense mappings. In particular, the mean performance on the regular (add /-ed/) mapping was 84% (P&M (1991), p. 71), which is well below the percentage of regulars that most adult humans are able to inflect correctly (near 100%).

P&M (1993) demonstrated that networks can achieve acceptable levels of mastery and still show U-shaped learning effects if their training set is expanded incrementally. Unlike Rumelhart & McClelland (1986), they did not introduce a discontinuity in the training regime. Rather, they trained their networks on a small number of verbs at first, and then gradually expanded the training set. Trained in this way, the networks described by P&M (1993) were able to master the given vocabulary (correctly inflecting 97-98% of the regulars) after a period of micro U-shaped development.

This is an interesting result, but the use of an incrementally expanding training set must be justified. P&M (1993) note that "verb acquisition in children is a gradual process which follows an *incremental* learning trajectory (p. 27)," and go on to mention Elman's (1991) application of incremental training to the acquisition of simple and complex syntactic forms. There are, however, some crucial differences between the account of language acquisition implied by Elman's model and that implied by P&M (1993).

Elman's recurrent network was unable to learn adequately if it was trained on the entire set of simple and complex sentences at once. He showed that it could learn if it was trained on an incrementally expanded training set, beginning with the simple sentences, and working up to the complex ones. Nevertheless, he argued explicitly against using an

---

[1] See Pinker and Prince's (1988) critique of Rumelhart & McClelland (1986). They argue that Rumelhart & McClelland's model exhibited U-shaped learning effects because of discontinuities in its training set.

incrementally expanded training set in models of language acquisition, claiming that "children hear exemplars of all aspects of the adult language from the beginning (p. 6)." He then tried expanding his network's memory capacity, rather than incrementally expanding its training set. During the first phase of training, the recurrent feedback was eliminated after every third or fourth word. As training progressed, the network's memory window was gradually increased until the feedback was no longer interfered with at all.

Using this schedule of expanding memory, Elman was able to get the network to learn the entire training set. This is a reasonable account of language acquisition because we know that children have limited memory capacity early in development, and that this capacity increases as development continues. Furthermore, the network is exposed to the entire adult language, which is more realistic than using a subset of the language for training.

P&M's (1993) model did not have a limited memory--it was not a recurrent network, and did not have a memory in the sense that Elman's (1991) model did. P&M had to resort to limiting its training set, which was then gradually expanded. P&M (1993) claim that it is "unlikely that children attempt to learn an entire lexicon all of a piece (p. 27)." Perhaps what they had in mind was that children have access to the entire vocabulary, but only pay attention to a limited number of words. In this case, the way they have modeled attention is questionable. At the outset of training, the network was given 20 verbs, on which it is trained to 100% accuracy before expansion began. In effect, the network was being told which verbs to pay attention to at the outset, and trained on them to perfection before it could start attending to other verbs. By the end of training, the network had the entire vocabulary in its training set--it was paying attention to each element of the vocabulary to the same degree. Clearly, we need a better way to model attention.

In this paper, we examine the effect of selective attention on a network's ability to learn the past tense mappings. We do not specify the examples to which the network should pay attention, and we do not restrict the set of examples to which the network can be exposed. Like Elman, we believe that in order for our model to be realistic, the entire vocabulary must be accessible to the network from the start. We show that networks with this mechanism of selective attention master the past tense mapping and exhibit micro U-shaped learning effects in the absence of any external manipulation of their training set.

Selective Attention Model

Our model of selective attention is based on the method of *active selection* (Plutowski & White (1993)). This method was originally used for incrementally growing a training set by using a partially trained network to guide the selection of new examples. Plutowski et al (1993) introduced the idea of using maximum error as the criterion for selection. In our implementation, this criterion is used for selecting examples for weight adjustment (cf. Baluja & Pomerleau (1994), whose network ignores sections of the input with high prediction error). Instead of using active selection for incrementally growing the training set, we assume a fixed size training queue of size N corresponding to the child's working or perhaps episodic memory. As the child samples the environment, we assume the child computes his error on any verb, and then compares this error with what is currently in the training queue. If the error on the sampled example is worse than what is currently in the queue, the example is inserted in the queue and the best example in the queue is "forgotten." We may view this error as a measure of the novelty or salience of the verb.

To simulate this, at the beginning of an epoch the simulator randomly selects a window of W examples from the vocabulary and tests the network on them. The likelihood of any particular example being chosen for the sample window depends on its frequency in the vocabulary. The above procedure is applied to update the queue. Thus, the entire set of examples may change from one epoch to the next depending on N, W, and the error on the samples.

The network's initial exposure to a form results in its being placed in the sample window. Weight adjustment does not occur until the form has been put into the training queue. Training on a verb is therefore "off-line" in the sense that it occurs some time after the verb is initially encountered.

It is reasonable to suppose that children are not able to cycle through every verb in the language in order to choose the ones they need to pay attention to for the purposes of synaptic adjustment, so it was important to limit the size of the sample window. We might think of the window as the network's short-term memory (for recently heard verbs). It needs to hold a limited number of items in memory so that it can compare them to choose the queue elements when updating the queue.

Methods

Our input-output pairs were taken from the database used by P&M. The interested reader should refer to P&M (1991, 1993) for details about the representations. The network is given a verb stem as input and must produce the inflected verb as its output. The transformations from the stems to the past tense forms are classified into four possible classes: arbitrary, identity, vowel change, and regular. Each of these corresponds to a possible English past tense transformation.

	Arbitrary	Identity	Vowel Change	Regular
Type Frequency	2	20	68	410
Token Frequency	100	2	5	1

Table 1: Type and Token frequencies of the past tense mappings

For the arbitraries, there is no relation between the stem and the past tense form, e.g. 'go→went.' For the identities, the past tense form is identical to the verb stem. This mapping requires that the verb stem end in a dental consonant (/t/ or /d/), e.g. 'hit→hit.' For the vowel changes, a vowel in the stem may be replaced by a different

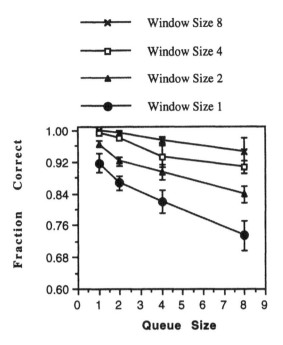

Figure 1: Performance on regular verbs after 120,000 weight updates as a function of queue and window size.

vowel in the inflected form of the verb, depending on the original vowel and the consonant that follows. We had 10 different types of vowel changes in our vocabulary, analogous to 'ring→rang,' 'blow→blew,' etc. Finally, for the regulars, a suffix is appended to the verb stem. The form of the suffix depends upon the final vowel/consonant in the stem. If the stem ends in a dental (/t/ or /d/), then the suffix is /-id/, e.g. 'pat→pat-id.' If the stem ends in a voiced consonant or vowel, then the suffix is voiced /d/, e.g. 'dam→dam-d.' If the stem ending is unvoiced, the suffix is unvoiced /t/, e.g. 'pak→pak-t.'

The type and token frequencies of each of these classes in our vocabulary are shown in Table 1. The type frequencies are identical to those used by P&M (1991), but the token frequencies are somewhat different. For each type of past tense mapping, we took the averages of a small, but representative sample of verb frequencies from Kucera & Francis (1967), and then normalized them by the frequency of the regulars.

Our networks were trained with the back propagation algorithm. The network architecture consisted of 18 input units (each verb stem was formed from 3 phonemes each requiring 6 units to represent), 30 hidden units and 20 output units (2 suffix units were needed in addition to the transformed stem). The choice of 30 hidden units was made to parallel the architecture used by P&M (1993). The learning rate and momentum were also set according to the values used by P&M (1993), namely a learning rate of 0.1 and a momentum of 0.0. To evaluate network performance, the output for each phoneme in the stem was mapped to the closest legal phoneme (using Euclidean distance). Then the output was compared with the target.

We investigated the effects of different sample window and training queue sizes by letting W and N take on the values 1, 2, 4 or 8 and training networks with all sixteen possible combinations. Five sets of networks were trained, with initial weight values the same within each set, but varying between them.

Results

Figure 1 shows the effect of using different training queue and sample window sizes. The average performance for each combination of W and N is plotted in Figure 1, with standard deviation indicated by error bars. The networks that performed best were the ones that had large sample windows and small training queues. The larger the sample window, the more examples the network has to choose from. Once an example is chosen and trained on, however, the network's error will change not only for that verb, but for other verbs as well. If the network trains on a regular verb, for example, we expect its error on other regular verbs to go down slightly, as well. Thus, it is better for the network to "pay attention to one thing at a time," because this allows it to choose its training example based on its error on that example immediately prior to training, rather than using an error value that may have changed due to training on another verb in the queue.

Figure 2 shows the average performance of 5 networks trained using the selective attention mechanism with sample windows of size 8 and training queues of size 1. Because of the method of training we are using, it is more meaningful to analyze the networks according to the number of weight updates they have undergone. This makes it difficult to compare our results with those of P&M, however, because they graph results in terms of epochs, and the size of the training set changes with each epoch. For the purposes of comparison, therefore, we ran 5 networks using the traditional method for selecting training examples (the one used by P&M (1991)) on the same data. The average performance of these networks on regular verbs is shown in figure 3.

The networks with selective attention performed very well. By 125,000 weight updates, all 5 networks had mastered all of the past tense mappings (with a standard deviation of 0.0). When the networks without selective attention had reached 125,000 weight updates, they only inflected an average of 85% of the regulars correctly (with a standard deviation of 0.013). This is the level of performance reached by P&M's (1991) best network at the end of training (p. 71). Even after 500,000 weight updates, these networks only got an average of 95% correct (with a standard deviation of 0.007). In summary, the network with selective attention was better both in final performance and learning speed.

Figure 4 shows the networks' ability to generalize. The first graph shows the average performance of the five networks on novel verbs that did not fall into any of the vowel change classes or end in a dental consonant--the indeterminates. The error bars indicate standard deviation.

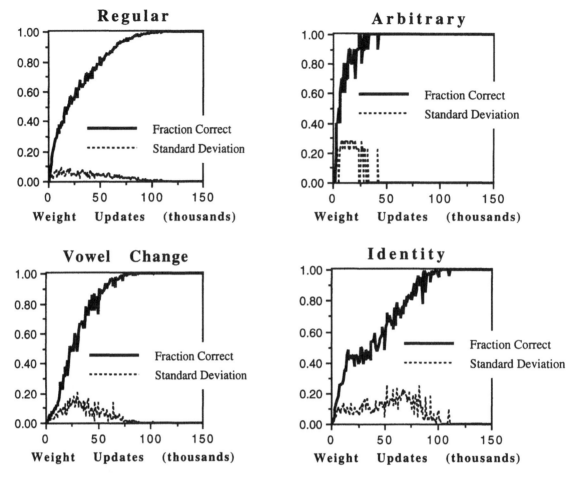

Figure 2: Average fraction correct and standard deviation for the five selective attention networks tested on all of the regular, arbitrary, vowel change and identity verbs in the training set.

As can be seen in the graph, the networks generalize fairly well. The dashed line shows the fraction of indeterminate novel verbs the networks inflected with a suffix (around 90%), irrespective of whether the form of the stem was correct. The dashed line shows the fraction of indeterminate novel verbs the networks inflected as regulars with no changes to the stem (around 70%).

The novel dental and vowel change graphs show that the regular mapping is not applied indiscriminately to novel forms--the fraction of verbs inflected as regulars is lower in these graphs. The networks have learned something about the phonological regularities inherent in the vocabulary. In particular, the novel vowel change graph shows that verbs that are phonologically similar to the vowel change verbs in the training set are as likely to be inflected with a vowel change as they are to be regularized.

Figure 5 shows the number of times each verb token was in the training queue for a particular simulation. Note that some regular verbs never make it into the queue, i.e. are never trained on. Since we happen to know all verbs were sampled, the network must have had low error on these verbs when they were in the window. This is further evidence that the network has learned the regular rule, and shows that our procedure avoids unnecessary computation.

Discussion

We have presented a model of selective attention which chooses training examples from a random sample of the training set. The size of the window from which the training example can be chosen is limited and the training queue itself is limited. Whether only one or both of these should be considered "memory" is a question of interpretation, but here we have suggested that the queue can be considered the memory. One could also break the processing down into two stages, one where samples are put into memory for later processing, and then a stage in which they are organized according to salience, and then practiced.

The idea that children process a significant amount of the linguistic input they receive after the fact is corroborated by data concerning crib speech--monologues and language practice (including grammatical modifications and imitation/repetition) that children engage in when they are alone in their bed before going to sleep (Jespersen (1922), Weir (1962), Kuczaj (1983)). Crib speech is characterized by a freedom (because of the lack of communicative intent) to use free association to generate sequences of sounds and words, the associations being either phonological, syntactic

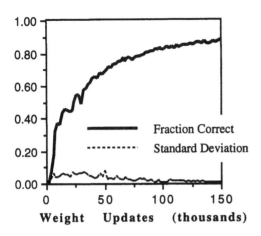

Figure 3: Average fraction correct and standard deviation for five networks without selective attention tested on regular verbs.

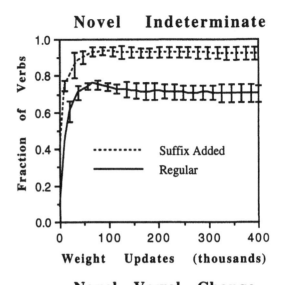

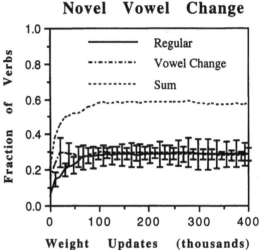

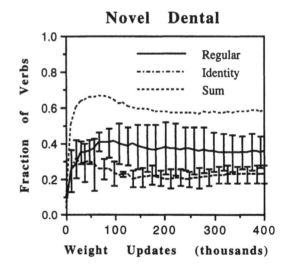

Figure 4: Average generalization on 132 novel indeterminates, 62 novel vowel change verbs and 28 novel dentals.

or semantic (Britton (1970)). Probably because of this freedom, children are more likely to engage in language practice in crib speech than in social-context speech (in terms of relative frequency) (Black (1979), Britton (1970), Kuczaj (1983)).

As Kuczaj writes:

...children process linguistic information at (at least) two levels: (a) the level of initial processing, which occurs in short-term memory shortly after children have been exposed to the input, and (b) the level of post-initial processing, which occurs at some later time when children are attempting to interpret, organize, and consolidate information that they have experienced over some longer period of time...children are most likely to notice discrepancies between their knowledge of language and linguistic input at the level of post-initial processing, and...crib speech is a context in which children may freely engage in overt behaviors that facilitate both post-initial processing and the successful resolution of moderately discrepant events. Although older children and adults may be able to notice discrepancies during the initial processing of linguistic information, it is unlikely that young children are able to do so...Children may initially store new forms and new meanings and later compare these new acquisitions with previous ones in post-initial processing (Kuczaj (1983), pp. 167-168).

The model we have presented is completely compatible with these observations, if one assumes both the queue and the window are part of the memory. The "discrepancies" in this case are the error signals the network generates for each verb in the sample window. The network can generate the form it expects to see in a particular context, and compare this with what it actually heard. In this way, the network supplies itself with indirect negative evidence (Elman (1991)), which is used in the adjustments of its weights. As Kuczaj suggests is true for children, our networks could not

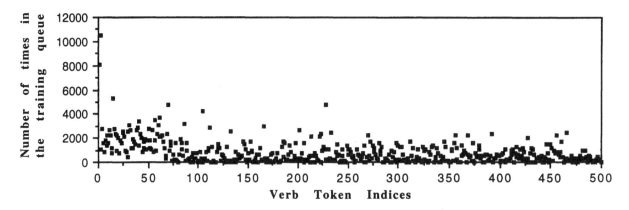

Figure 5: Total number of times each verb token was in the training queue for a single simulation. Verbs with indices 1-2 are arbitrary, 3-70 are vowel change, 71-90 are identity and 91-500 are regular.

"notice" the discrepancies during the initial processing of the linguistic information. The initial processing occurs when the verb is put into the sample window. Later, when the time comes to update a network's weights, the mechanism of selective attention comes into play. At this point, the network generates error signals and chooses the verb with the highest error for the purposes of weight adjustment.

In future work, we may try to develop a connectionist implementation of the training queue. We would also like to investigate other strategies for deciding what the network should pay attention to. Finally, we plan to use our model of selective attention in more primary tasks, such as learning word meaning.

Conclusion

The mechanism of selective attention we introduced allowed the networks to guide their own training. The networks focused on the examples for which they needed the most training. As a result, they performed extremely well. They completely mastered the regular, identity, vowel change and arbitrary past tense mappings and showed the ability to generalize. They also showed micro U-shaped learning effects. Most importantly, our networks achieved their high level of performance without requiring us to externally manipulate their training sets.

Acknowledgments

We would like to thank the GEURU research group for helpful comments. This research was supported in part by NSF grant IRI 92-03532.

References

Baluja, S. & Pomerleau, D.A. (1994) "Using a saliency map for active spatial selective attention: implementation & initial results." In: Advances in Neural Information Processing Systems 7, (Tesauro, Touretsky & Leen, eds.). Cambridge, MA: The MIT Press.

Black, R. (1979) "Crib talk and mother-child interaction: A comparison of form and function. Papers and reports on child language development, 17, 90-97.

Britton, J. (1970) Language and learning. London: Penguin Books.

Elman, J. (1991) "Incremental learning, or the importance of starting small." CRL Technical Report No. 9101. University of California, San Diego.

Jespersen, O. (1922) Language: its nature, development and origin. New York: Allen and Unwin.

Kucera, H. & Francis, W.N. (1967) Computational analysis of present-day American English. Providence, RI: Brown University Press.

Kuczaj, S.A. (1983) Crib speech and language play. New York: Springer-Verlag.

Marchman, V. (1988) "Rules and regularities in the acquisition of the English past tense." Center for Research in Language Newsletter, 2 (4).

Marcus, G.F., Ullman, M., Pinker, S., Hollander, M., Rosen, T.J., & Xu, F. (1992) "Overregularization in language acquisition." Monographs of the Society for Research in Child Development, 57 (4), Serial No. 228.

Plunkett, K., Marchman, V. (1991) "U-shaped learning and frequency effects in a multi-layered perceptron: Implications for child language acquisition." Cognition 38, 43-102.

Plunkett, K., Marchman, V. (1993) " From Rote Learning to System Building: Acquiring Verb Morphology in Children and Connectionist Nets." Cognition 48, 21-69.

Plutowski, M., White, H. (1993) "Selecting concise training sets from clean data" IEEE Transactions on neural networks, 3:1.

Plutowski, M., Cottrell G.W., White, H. (1993) "Learning Mackey-Glass from 25 examples, plus or minus 2." In: Advances in Neural Information Processing Systems 6, (Hanson, Cowan and Giles, eds.). San Mateo, CA: Morgan Kaufmann.

Rumelhart, D. E., McClelland, J.L. (1986) "On Learning the Past Tense of English Verbs", PDP: Explorations in the Microstructure of Cognition, Vol 2.

Weir, R.H. (1962) Language in the crib. The Hague: Mouton.

Word Learning and Verbal Short-Term Memory: A Computational Account

Prahlad Gupta

Beckman Institute for Advanced Science and Technology
University of Illinois at Urbana-Champaign
Urbana, IL 61801
prahlad@uiuc.edu

Abstract

Recent behavioral evidence suggests that human vocabulary acquisition processes and verbal short-term memory abilities may be related (Gathercole & Baddeley, 1993). Investigation of this relationship has considerable significance for understanding of human language, of working memory, and of the relationship between short- and long-term memory systems. This paper presents a computational model of word learning, nonword repetition, and immediate serial recall. By providing an integrated account of these three abilities, the model provides a specification of how the mechanisms of immediate serial recall may be related to mechanisms of language processing more generally. Furthermore, the model provides fresh insight into the observed behavioral correlations between word learning and immediate serial recall. According to the model, these correlations can arise because of the common dependence of these two abilities on core phonological and semantic processing mechanisms. This contrasts with the explanation proposed in the working memory literature, viz., that word learning is dependent on verbal short-term memory (Gathercole et al., 1992). It is discussed how both explanations can be reconciled in terms of the present model.

Introduction

A variety of recent evidence suggests that human vocabulary acquisition processes and aspects of human verbal short-term memory may be related. In children, reliable correlations have been obtained between digit span, nonword repetition ability, and vocabulary achievement, even when other possible factors such as age and general intelligence have been factored out (e.g., Gathercole & Baddeley, 1989; Gathercole et al., 1992). Studies of normal adults suggest that factors known to affect verbal short-term memory also interfere with word learning ability (e.g., Papagno et al., 1991). It also appears that there is a population of neuropsychologically impaired patients in whom language function is largely preserved, but who exhibit selective deficits in verbal short-term memory and in word learning ability (Baddeley et al., 1988). It is not possible to describe these studies in detail here (see Gathercole & Baddeley, 1993, for a review). The point is that there is now a considerable body of evidence to suggest that word learning, verbal short-term memory, and nonword repetition are a related triad of abilities.

The studies mentioned above have been conducted within the framework of the *working memory model* (Baddeley, 1986). In that model, one subsystem of working memory is

verbal short-term memory. This subsystem has been termed the "articulatory loop", and its study has relied on immediate serial recall (ISR) tasks, in which a subject is presented with sequences of unrelated verbal items (such as digits or words), and is required to recall the sequence in correct order, immediately following its presentation. The articulatory loop consists of two parts. One part consists of a *phonological store* for verbal material, within which memory traces decay within 1-2 seconds. The second part consists of mechanisms that enable *rehearsal*, a process that can "refresh" decaying traces in the phonological store (Baddeley, 1986).

Within this paradigm, the relationship between word learning and verbal short-term memory has been interpreted as indicating that the articulatory loop, and in particular, the phonological store, underlies vocabulary learning (e.g., Gathercole et al., 1992). However, this conjecture has not been elaborated in processing terms, and it is unclear what the nature of such shared processing might be. This paper presents a computational model that attempts to specify in detail what the relationship might be between word learning, nonword repetition, and immediate serial recall.

Such investigation of shared mechanisms underlying verbal short-term memory and vocabulary acquisition is important for at least two reasons. First, it offers a new processing-oriented approach to examining vocabulary acquisition. Second, exploration of this connection can illuminate the relations between short- and long-term memory systems.

A Computational Model

Architecture and computational mechanisms. The goal of the model described in this paper is to examine the computational basis of the relationship between word learning, nonword repetition, and immediate serial recall. The tasks for the model, therefore, are to simulate (1) immediate repetition of novel word forms, (2) the learning of novel word forms, and (3) immediate serial recall of lists of known word forms. In attempting this, the model builds on many previous ideas (Burgess & Hitch, 1992; Grossberg, 1978; Hartley & Houghton, in press; Houghton, 1990), each of which addresses certain, but not all, aspects of the target phenomena.

The model is depicted in Figure 1(a). There are three crucial levels of representation. The Phoneme Layer is a level of output phonology at which phonemes are represented. At this

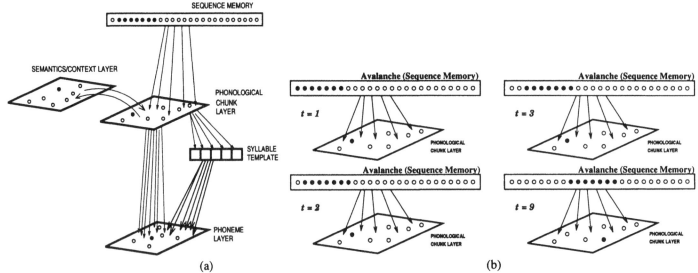

Figure 1: A model of word learning and immediate serial recall. (a) Architecture of the model. (b) Sequencing mechanisms.

level, for example, there are representations of the phonemes /a/, /t/, and so on. Second, there is a level at which word forms are represented (the Phonological Chunk Layer). At this level, there are representations for word forms; these representations are shared by input and output phonology. A third level represents semantic and/or contextual information about word forms, and is designated the Semantics/Context Layer. Information about the meaning of the word form *dog* is represented at this level, as also information about contexts of usage in which the word form *dog* has been encountered. In fact, semantics is viewed loosely as a special case of context.

These levels of representation are related via connection weights. The Semantics/Context Layer is bidirectionally connected to the Phonological Chunk Layer, so that representations at these two levels influence each other interactively. The Phonological Chunk Layer has connection weights to the Phoneme Layer. Production of a word form is a serially ordered process, therefore the representation of a word form at the Phonological Chunk Layer has to be able to produce a specific sequence of phonemes at the Phoneme Layer. Each of these levels of representation is comprised of a pool of units, each of which receives input from other units, summates its input, and produces an output which is a sigmoidal function of its summed input. The model also incorporates a *syllable template* between the Phoneme Layer and Chunk Layer, which functions as a parser, assigning syllable structure to the incoming stream of phonemes, and also imposing syllable structure on the output of word forms from the system (Hartley & Houghton, in press).

There is a general sequencing mechanism (designated as the Sequence Memory) that provides immediate memory for sequences of word forms. The Sequence Memory has connections to the Phonological Chunk Layer, which enable it to replay a sequence of activations that have occurred recently

at the Phonological Chunk Layer. The connection weights from the Sequence Memory are subject to decay, and therefore the memory for specific sequences is short-lived. The Sequence Memory is the present model's version of the *phonological store* postulated by the working memory model (Baddeley, 1986). The basic mechanism I adopt for such sequence memory is the *avalanche* (Grossberg, 1978). A variant of this mechanism has been incorporated in Houghton's (1990) Competitive Queueing (CQ) architecture, and used in its CQ form by Burgess & Hitch (1992), Hartley & Houghton (in press), and others.

An avalanche is composed of an array of units, as shown for the Sequence Memory in Figure 1(a). A crucial property of an avalanche is that a wave of activation propagates along this pool of units, activating them in a specific and replicable sequence. Presentation of a sequence of word forms to the system is modeled as a sequence of activations of the appropriate word form units at the Phonological Chunk Layer. Concurrently with the sequence of activations at the Chunk Layer, the wave of activation propagates along the Sequence Memory avalanche, and at each time step, connection weights from the avalanche units to the Chunk Layer are adjusted by a Hebbian process. This means that each Sequence Memory avalanche unit encodes whatever pattern of activation was present over the Chunk Layer at the time step(s) when that avalanche unit was active. The process of recall requires that the wave of activation must travel along the avalanche once again. When it does, each avalanche unit will recreate its encoded pattern of activations over the Chunk Layer, provided the connections weights from the avalanche to the Chunk Layer have not decayed too much.

Figure 1(b) depicts several time steps of processing during presentation of a sequence of inputs to the Chunk Layer. The figure shows the wave of activation propagating along the Sequence Memory avalanche units over several time steps of

190

presentation. At each time step, Hebbian adjustment occurs on the connection weights from the avalanche to the Chunk Layer. At recall, reinstantiation of the wave of activation over the avalanche units will lead to production of the sequence of Chunk Layer activations.

Thus the Sequence Memory (SM) shown at the top of Figure 1(a) is implemented as an avalanche that encodes sequences of word forms. In addition, each node at the Phonological Chunk Layer also represents an avalanche. Thus phonemes are bound to a Chunk Layer avalanche in much the same way as Chunk Layer nodes are bound to the SM avalanche. This constitutes a second level of sequencing, whereby the Chunk Layer representation of a particular word form can encode and reproduce the serial ordering of its constituent phonemes.

The model assumes the existence of *word recognition* processes, input from which causes activation of one Phoneme Layer node at a time, and one Chunk Layer node at a time, at each time point in processing, during presentation of word forms.

Simulations

Simulation of word learning. As an example of word learning in the model, let us consider how the novel word form /zæt/ is learned (it may be helpful to refer to Figure 1(a) as needed). Learning occurs during presentation of the word form, as follows. Propagation of activation along the Sequence Memory (SM) avalanche units is initiated. At time step 1, the phoneme unit for /z/ is activated (at the Phoneme Layer). The appropriate Syllable Template node is activated. A new node is allocated at the Phonological Chunk Layer. A new node is also allocated at the Semantics/Context Layer. The following automatic processes occur: (1) Hebbian adjustment of Chunk → Phoneme weights, and Chunk → Template weights. (2) Hebbian adjustment of SM → Chunk weights. (3) Hebbian adjustment of Chunk ↔ Semantics/Context weights. (4) Decay of Chunk → Phoneme weights and Chunk → Template weights. (5) Decay of SM → Chunk weights.

At the next time step, the phoneme unit for /z/ is inactivated, and the phoneme unit for /æ/ is activated. The same automatic processes take place. This procedure is repeated at presentation of /t/. These processes provide the basis for word learning. Note that there are two aspects of learning. First, learning increases the Chunk ↔ Semantics/Context weights. For novel words, these weights are developed on the fly during presentation, and will be lower than those that have developed (over multiple exposures) for known words. Second, learning results in the development of Chunk → Phoneme weights and Chunk → Template weights. For novel word forms, these weights are also developed online during presentation. There is no difference in the magnitude of these weights for known and novel word forms. However, for known words, these weights are assumed to have saturated, and neither increase nor decay during presentation. For novel word forms, these weights are subject to decay. Thus known

words have higher Chunk ↔ Semantics/Context than do nonwords; and the Chunk → Phoneme weights and Chunk → Template weights do not change, for known words, whereas they decay for nonwords. These two effects characterize the difference between words and nonwords in the model.

Note also that the automatic processes described above occur irrespective of whether /zæt/ is a known or novel word form. That is, processing during presentation of a *known* word form is identical to that during presentation of a nonword – except that, as noted above, for the already known word, the Chunk → Phoneme weights and Chunk → Template weights will neither increase nor decay.

Simulations of word learning were set up to model a cued-recall task. Ten two-syllable, three-syllable, and four-syllable word forms were used, taken from the Children's Test of Nonword Repetition (Gathercole et al., 1994). 30 simulations were run at each word length. During presentation of each set of word forms (i.e., all the word forms at a particular word length), word learning occurred, as described above. As part of this process, a semantics node was created for each word form. After all the word forms had been presented once, cued recall was tested. The semantics nodes associated with each word in the set were activated, one at a time, representing the cueing of a word with its semantics. Interactive activation then resulted in the activation of chunk nodes. At each time step during recall, activations of the semantics/context units, the chunk units, and the phoneme units were updated. Correct recall of a word would require that the correct sequence of phonemes be produced.

All the words were learned on the first presentation. At all three word lengths, performance was perfect on the very first cued recall trial. Thus the model exhibits word learning performance corresponding to human subjects' abilities to learn words within a very few presentations (Carey, 1978; Dollaghan, 1985).

Simulation of nonword repetition. The automatic processes that occur when a novel word form is presented to the system have already been described as part of the foregoing discussion of word learning. Testing whether that novel word has been *learned* involves testing whether the Semantics/Context → Chunk weights are sufficiently strong to produce the correct Chunk Layer pattern of activation, in the absence of any support from the Sequence Memory, whose weights are assumed to have decayed beyond the point where they can contribute to the chunk retrieval process; and whether the retrieved Chunk Layer pattern can spell out its constituent sequence of phonemes at the Phoneme Layer. Testing *immediate repetition* of the nonword, by contrast, involves testing whether the SM → Chunk weights are still strong enough to allow retrieval of the correct Chunk Layer pattern of activation, and hence activation of the correct sequence of phonemes at the Phoneme Layer.

Simulations were run of immediate repetition of the same 30 nonwords used in the word learning simulations, with 30

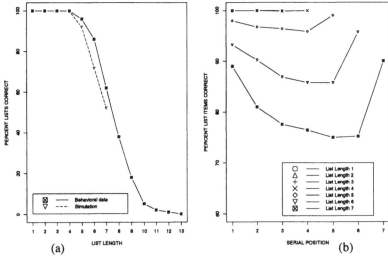

Figure 2: Performance on ISR of lists of known words. (a) Percent lists correctly recalled: simulation, and behavioral data (Guildford & Dallenbach, 1925). (b) Serial position curves (simulation).

attempts to repeat each set of 10 nonwords. Repetition performance was 100% correct at all three syllable lengths. This corresponds to essentially error-free performance in normal adult human subjects. The errors that adults do make in nonword repetition are due to uncertainties in the perception of nonwords, rather than than to any difficulty in being able to repeat them. The model has no analogue of imperfect perception, and so does not make any errors in repetition, even of unfamiliar word forms.

Simulation of immediate serial recall. Immediate serial recall was simulated by presenting sequences of word forms to the model, and then examining recall, when the Sequence Memory avalanche was re-activated immediately following presentation. Figure 2(a) shows the simulated proportion of lists correctly recalled at each list length, as well as the human data (Guildford & Dallenbach, 1925). Figure 2(b) shows simulated serial position curves for ISR of lists of known words, for list lengths 1 through 7. For list lengths 5 and above, the curves show the characteristic primacy and recency effects. Note that the model's performance is perfect for list lengths 1 through 4, as shown in Figure 2(a); therefore in Figure 2(b), the serial position curves for these four list lengths show 100% correct performance at all serial positions, and are superimposed.

It should be noted that what the model simulates is serial recall abilities that are automatic and non-strategic. These are the abilities involved when subjects report "reading out" the recall sequence from memory, as they commonly do for lists of up to 5 digits. Such memory involves no rehearsal. It corresponds to the initial part of the serial recall curve, where performance is almost perfect for up to approximately 5 digits (Guildford & Dallenbach, 1925). As can be seen from Figure 2(a), the model's performance drops below that of human subjects for lists beyond length 4. This reflects the fact that human performance beyond list length 4 or 5 is increas-

ingly dependent on strategies that are not incorporated in the current model.

Word Learning and Serial Recall: The Relationship

We have seen that the model's performance of immediate serial recall (ISR), nonword repetition (NWR), and word learning (WL) is in agreement with human behavioral data. Let us now examine the relationship between these abilities in greater detail. There are four structural components of the model: (1) the Sequence Memory (SM); (2) the Chunk Layer; (3) the Phoneme Layer and Syllable Template (which I classify as one component); and (4) the Semantics/Context Layer. The model's performance in ISR, NWR, and WL depends on the effectiveness of the mappings between these components.

In the model, the effectiveness of these mappings depends on the strengths of connection weights between these components, and the magnitude of the weights in turn depends on the rate of weight change (the learning rate) for each of these sets of connections. These learning rates are parameters of the model that have been set so that the model approximates normal adult human performance, as described in the various simulations so far. The learning rates will be denoted by α for the weights from the Chunk Layer to the Phoneme Layer and Syllable Template, together designated as the Chunk $\rightarrow$ Phoneme weights; θ for the SM $\rightarrow$ Chunk weights; and γ for the Chunk $\leftrightarrow$ Semantics/Context weights.

To understand how NWR, WL, and ISR might be differentially dependent on the various components of the model, the effectiveness of each component was varied, by varying the associated learning rate. In all simulations described earlier, the values of learning rates were $\alpha = 0.43, \theta = 1.06, \gamma = 0.3$. The value of each of these learning rate parameters was now varied, one at a time. For example, Figure 3(a) shows the effect of varying α; the seven combinations of learning rate shown were obtained by combining seven different levels of α with the fixed values $\theta = 1.06, \gamma = 0.3$. The seven learning

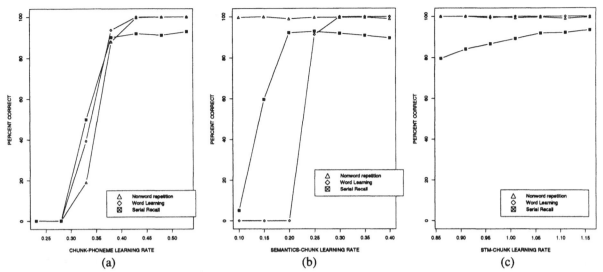

| (a) | (b) | (c) |

Figure 3: Effect of various learning rates on Nonword Repetition, Word Learning, and Immediate Serial Recall. (a) Effect of learning rate α of weights from Chunk Layer to Phoneme Layer and Syllable Template. (b) Effect of learning rate γ of bidirectional weights between Chunk Layer and Semantics/Context Layer. (c) Effect of learning rate θ of weights from SM to Chunk Layer.

rate combinations in Figures 3(b) and (c) were constructed in analogous fashion, varying either γ or θ respectively, in combination with fixed values of the other two parameters.

For NWR, each data point represents the proportion of 4-syllable nonwords repeated correctly, averaged over 30 simulations of NWR at the particular combination of learning rates. For WL, each data point represents the proportion of novel 4-syllable word forms produced correctly in cued recall, averaged over 30 simulations at the particular combination of learning rates. For ISR, each data point represents the proportion of lists of 5 known words correctly recalled, averaged over 30 simulations.

As can be seen from Figure 3, nonword repetition is dependent on the rate of change (α) of weights from the Chunk Layer to the Phoneme Layer and Syllable Template. However, it is unaffected by the other learning rates. Word learning is sensitive to α, and also to the rate of change (γ) of bidirectional weights between the Chunk Layer and the Semantics/Context Layer. However, it is unaffected by the rate of change (θ) of weights from the SM to the Chunk Layer. Immediate Serial Recall is dependent on all three rates of weight change. These dependencies are summarized in Table 1.

To consider what these dependencies indicate, it is worth reiterating what the variations in "learning rates" represent. The Chunk → Phoneme mapping represents long-term phonological knowledge (knowledge about the serial order of phonemes within words). The effectiveness of this knowledge is represented by the strength of connection weights in this component of the model. In the model, the strength of these connection weights depends on the learning rate α. Variation in the learning rate parameter α is thus a shorthand for variation in the strength or effectiveness of long-term phonological knowledge in the system. Similarly, variation of the learning rate parameter γ represents variation in the strength of long-term knowledge about the semantics of

Ability	Ability is affected by:		
	Chunk → Phoneme learning rate (α)	Context ↔ Chunk learning rate (γ)	SM → Chunk learning rate (θ)
Nonword repetition	✓	X	X
Word Learning	✓	✓	X
Immediate Serial recall	✓	✓	✓

Table 1: Analysis of dependencies in the model: Factors influencing Nonword Repetition (NWR), Word Learning (WL), and Immediate Serial Recall (ISR).

words in the system. Variation in the learning rate parameter θ represents variation in the inherent capacity of the *short-term* Sequence Memory.

The dependencies in Table 1 thus indicate that ISR ability is affected by the effectiveness of long-term phonological knowledge, long-term semantic knowledge, and short-term phonological store capacity. Word learning ability is affected by the strength of long-term phonological knowledge and long-term semantic knowledge. Nonword repetition ability is affected by the strength of long-term phonological knowledge.

Conclusions

These results suggest a more precise specification of the relationship between NWR, WL, and ISR. In the model, these abilities are related because they are all dependent on the effectiveness of the Chunk → Phoneme mapping. That is, the model ascribes the relationship between these three abilities to their common reliance on long-term phonological knowledge about phoneme serial ordering.

Thus one of the ways in which word learning and immediate serial recall are related is through their common reliance on this long-term phonological knowledge. In addition (see Table 1), these two abilities are also related through their reliance on the Semantics/Context ↔ Chunk mapping, i.e., on long-term semantic knowledge. Both the Chunk → Phoneme mapping and the Semantics/Context ↔ Chunk mapping represent fundamental aspects of phonological/linguistic processing, and represent long-term knowledge.

It is important to note how this account differs from one that ascribes a causal role to the working memory model's Phonological Store (cf. Gathercole et al., 1992). In the present model, the relationship between ISR and WL arises *not* because of the Sequence Memory/Phonological Store, but because ISR is dependent on core phonological/semantic processes that underlie word learning. As we have seen, word learning is unaffected by the rate of change θ of weights from the SM to the Chunk Layer, whereas ISR is affected by the effectiveness of the Chunk → Phoneme mapping, and by the effectiveness of the Semantics/Context ↔ Chunk mapping.

If the present model were to incorporate connectivity from the Sequence Memory directly to the Phoneme Layer, it is likely that this would aid the effectiveness of NWR, WL, and ISR. All three abilities would then be dependent on a mechanism (the Sequence Memory/Phonological Store) that primarily subserves ISR. Thus the present model does not rule out the possibility of a causal role for the phonological store in word learning. Rather, it suggests that NWR, ISR and WL may be related even in the absence of such a connection.

It is perhaps most likely that these abilities are related in both ways. This would help to explain the findings that, whereas nonword repetition ability is more predictive of vocabulary ability (than vice versa) at earlier ages, vocabulary ability becomes more predictive of nonword repetition ability and ISR ability (than vice versa) by about 8 years of age (Gathercole et al., 1992). This would be explicable in the present model in that word learning might benefit from the support of Sequence Memory → Phoneme Layer connections more when the effectiveness of the Chunk → Phoneme mapping is low than when it is high. A similar explanation has been proposed by Gathercole et al. (1992). The present model provides a computational basis for seeing why this might be so.

Of course, word learning and ISR may *also* be related through their common reliance on rehearsal mechanisms. According to this view, in immediate serial recall, rehearsal can help maintain phonological representations of the recall stimuli in an active state. In vocabulary acquisition, likewise, rehearsal may aid the formation of new phonological representations, by allowing the learner repeated access to the word form so as to consolidate the new memory.

In conclusion, in its present form, the model makes the important demonstration that word learning and immediate serial recall may be related at the level of core phonological processing. Using the model to investigate how these abilities might be related via the phonological store and via rehearsal is a goal for further research.

Acknowledgements

I would like to thank Brian MacWhinney, Jay McClelland, Dave Plaut, and Gary Dell for helpful discussion of this work, and Tom Hartley for generously making available program code for the computer model described in Hartley & Houghton (in press), which formed a starting point in developing the present simulations.

References

Baddeley, A. D. (1986). *Working Memory*. New York, Oxford University Press.

Baddeley, A. D., Papagno, C., & Vallar, G. (1988). When long-term learning depends on short-term storage. *Journal of Memory and Language*, 27, 586–595.

Burgess, N. & Hitch, G. J. (1992). Toward a network model of the articulatory loop. *Journal of Memory and Language*, 31, 429–460.

Carey, S. (1978). The child as word learner. In M. Halle, J. Bresnan, & G. Miller (Eds.), *Linguistic Theory and Psychological Reality*. Cambridge, MA, MIT Press.

Dollaghan, C. (1985). Child meets word: "fast mapping" in preschool children. *Journal of Speech and Hearing Research*, 28, 449–454.

Gathercole, S. E. & Baddeley, A. D. (1989). Evaluation of the role of phonological STM in the development of vocabulary in children: A longitudinal study. *Journal of Memory and Language*, 28, 200–213.

Gathercole, S. E. & Baddeley, A. D. (1993). *Working Memory and Language*. Hillsdale, NJ, Lawrence Erlbaum.

Gathercole, S. E., Willis, C., Emslie, H., & Baddeley, A. D. (1992). Phonological memory and vocabulary development during the early school years: A longitudinal study. *Developmental Psychology*, 28, 887–898.

Gathercole, S. E., Willis, C. S., Baddeley, A. D., & Emslie, H. (1994). The children's test of nonword repetition: A test of phonological working memory. *Memory*, 2, 103–127.

Grossberg, S. (1978). A theory of human memory: Self-organization and performance of sensory-motor codes, maps, and plans. In R. Rosen & F. Snell (Eds.), *Progress in Theoretical Biology*, Volume 5. New York, Academic Press.

Guildford, J. P. & Dallenbach, K. M. (1925). The determination of memory span by the method of constant stimuli. *American Journal of Psychology*, 36, 621–628.

Hartley, T. & Houghton, G. (in press). A linguistically constrained model of short-term memory for nonwords. *Journal of Memory and Language*.

Houghton, G. (1990). The problem of serial order: A neural network model of sequence learning and recall. In R. Dale, C. Mellish, & M. Zock (Eds.), *Current Research in Natural Language Generation*. New York, Academic Press.

Papagno, C., Valentine, T., & Baddeley, A. D. (1991). Phonological short-term memory and foreign-language learning. *Journal of Memory and Language*, 30, 331–347.

Spatial cognition in the mind and in the world
- the case of hypermedia navigation

Nils Dahlbäck
Department of Computer and
Information Science
Linköping University
S-581 83 Linköping, Sweden
nilda@ida.liu.se

Kristina Höök
SICS
Box 1263
S164 28 Kista, Sweden
kia@sics.se

Marie Sjölinder
Department of Computer and
Systems Sciences
Stockholm University/KTH
Electrum 230
S-164 40 Kista, Sweden
hazze@frekvens.se

Abstract

We present the results of a study of spatial cognition and its relationship to hypermedia navigation. The results show that a distinction can be made between two kinds of spatial cognition. One that concerns the concomitant acting in the physical world, and on that is a pure internal mental activity. This conclusion is supported by two kinds of data. First, a factor analysis of the subtests used in this study groups them into these two categories, and second, it is shown that only the internal one of these factors is related to the subjects performance in using a hypertext-based on-line help system. In the final section we point to the theoretical connections between this work and work in areas of situated cognition and on different kinds of mental representations, and discuss various possibilities that the results from this study suggest for the development of interface tools that will help users with low spatial abilities to use hypermedia systems.

Introduction

The present study investigates the relation between spatial ability and the ability to navigate in hypermedia. It has one applied and one theoretical foci. On the applied side, it can be seen as an attempt to diagnose the reasons behind differential difficulties in using hypermedia, with the goal of suggesting improvements in the design of these. On the theoretical side it can be seen as a contribution to the clarification of different aspects of spatial and graphical reasoning, and hence to the clarification of the concepts involved.

The paper is structured as follows. First we discuss some applied motivations for the present work. We then report on an experimental study on the relationship between individual differences in spatial cognition and the ability to use a hypertext based on-line manual. In the final section we discuss the implications of the results obtained for the development of user-friendly hypermedia systems and mention some of the theoretical questions which we suggest emerge from this study.

Navigation in the World and in Computer Systems

Navigation in large hypermedia information structures has long been recognized as a difficult task. The expression 'lost in hyperspace' to describe what happens when users loose track of where they are and where to go next in the hypertext, see for example (Nielsen, 1990). Navigation in hypermedia and large information spaces in general, may be compared to navigation in cities and natural surroundings, although it is not obvious that they are comparable situations. Still, we need to find tools and designs that help users to find their way just as maps, signs and other devices have helped navigation in general. In order to do so, we must find out more about when navigation is difficult, to whom and why?

While there are similarities between navigation in the real world and navigation in the virtual world of hypermedia, there is also at least one important difference. In the former case people live in the world and they can move physically in it, whereas in the latter the *groundedness* is more limited, we cannot move with our bodies and physically manipulate objects in the virtual hypermedia world. The question then arises whether the same tools (maps etc.) can be used to help users navigating in hypermedia systems, as well as whether the same cognitive abilities are used in the two kinds of navigation.

Individual Differences

Individual differences appear to have a big impact on human-computer interaction (Egan 1988). When designing tools for navigation in hypermedia, individual differences can be one crucial factor that a system should accommodate to. Vicente and Williges found that spatial ability could be linked with whether users get lost in a hierarchical file system (1988). Benyon and Murray (1993) found that spatial ability determined how well users performed with different interfaces to a database system. Users with low spatial ability performed better with a aided-navigation interface with a constrained dialogue, while users with high ability made better use of a non-aided navigation interface with a flexible command-based dialogue. In one of our previous studies (Bladh and Höök 1995) on a hypermedia documentation

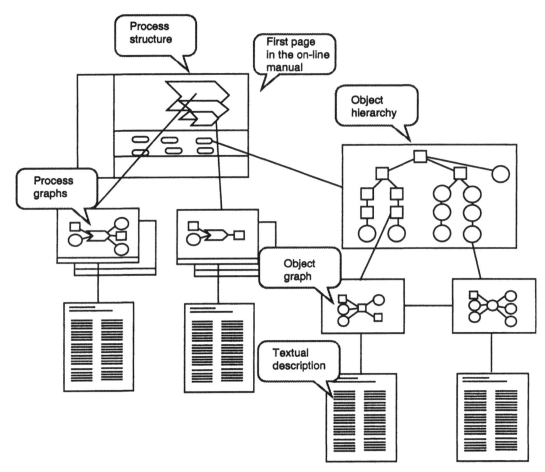

Figure 1 A schematic picture of the on-line manual. The two overview pictures show the process structure and the object hierarchy. From those, each process and object description can be reached.

system (described in section two), we found that the user group could be divided into two sub-groups. One found the graphs provided by the system helpful as tools for navigating to documents. The other group was annoyed by the graphs, and would have preferred other ways to navigate and search for information. We believe that it is important that these kinds of individual preferential differences are catered for in the design of computer systems and their interfaces. While many users today appreciate and find graphical interfaces easy to use, the current 'one size fits all'-approach to interfaces risk leaving a large subset of the user population behind. And we believe that the more complex the systems' domain spaces become, the more important becomes this issue.

The initial aim of the present study was to investigate whether the observed differences in interface preferences can be related to spatial, visual or other cognitive factors.

Characteristics of the Hypermedia Tool Studied

Before presenting the details of the study, we give in this section a short description of the help system and the domain it is used in. The hypermedia tool used as the target domain in this study contains information about a software development method, SDP. The method consists of *pro-*

cesses which are activities done during the project phases, and *objects* which are specifications, codes, etc. produced as a result of the method. Processes and objects are related, objects are related to objects and processes to processes.

The user of the on-line documentation of SDP that we studied has no other means of finding a particular document, but through clicking in several graphs until the document is reached. A schematic picture of the structure of the on-line manual can be found in figure 1. The *process structure* and the *object hierarchy* function as maps to the two main structure in the domain: the process structure and the object structure. From the process structure it is possible to reach descriptions of each process, the *process graphs*. From the process graphs in turn, textual descriptions of each process can be reached. From the object hierarchy the *object graphs* can be reached, and from those the textual descriptions of each object .

So, in order to get to a textual description of a process or object, it is necessary to navigate via a set of graphs until the desired process or object graph is reached. From there, and only from there, is it possible to get to the textual description.

Note that there are two aspects of the domain studied which are spatial in their nature. First, the domain itself is an abstract structure with relations between the domain's concepts of processes and objects (see section 1.4 for a description of the domain). Second, the on-line manual is structured in a set of documents with specified relations between the documents[1]. The structure of the on-line manual is only partly based on the structure of the domain. Hence, it is not sufficient to be knowledgeable in the domain to be able to use the on-line manual. Knowledge of both domains is required, as well as being able to map between these, probably making the use of the system a task requiring high levels of spatial competence.

Method

Subjects

There where 23 subjects in the experiment, 19 male and 4 female, all employed at a telecommunications company in Sweden. The subjects where in a range of 20-55 years old (m=34 years). All had some computer training, but not all had gone through higher academic training (18 with higher academic training and 5 with no higher academic training). All had recently gone through a four day course on the method that was described in the information base that we tested them on, but they had received little or no training on how to use the on-line manual.

Materials and Procedure

The experiment consisted of three parts. The first tested different cognitive abilities, the second was a questionnaire on the subjects' previous knowledge in the domain, and the third was a set of navigation tasks in the hypertext-based on-line manual. The subjects were tested in individual sessions which lasted approximately 3 hours.

Cognitive Abilities. We used 6 tests from the Düremann-Sälde test battery (Psykologiförlaget 1971). This is a widely used Swedish standardized test of cognitive abilities. These cognitive tests took approximately 2 hours per subject and the tested abilities as described in the test manual were:

• *verbal ability* which was tested in a synonym test where the subject should choose one of five words that meant the same as the word in the task.

• *logical-inductive ability* which was tested through classification of images where one of five should be chosen on bases of its differences from the others.

• *perceptual analysis ability* which was tested through drawing imitation of images

•*spatial ability* which was tested with three different tests:

• *rotation of images* where the subject should choose, by turning the images in their head, the images that were identical with the image in the task. The number of correct chosen images differed in each task, but they always came from a group of seven.

• *left or right hand identification* in pictures of hands that were turned in different ways

• a *block test* (Kohs' blocks test) where the subject should make a pattern with blocks, witch should be identical with a pattern on a card that the subjects were shown.

The results from the cognitive tests were transformed into stanine-scores based on the standardization of the tests on a sample of 166 persons balanced for age (between 15 and 64) and sex. In some cases standardization data from a group of subjects with higher education were used.

Questionnaire

In nine questions subjects were asked to estimate their own knowledge, on a scale from 0 to 5, of the SDP method and the on-line manual, of computers in general, of other hypermedia systems, of point and click interfaces and of their own judged spatial ability (if they were good using maps, if they had good sense of direction etc.).

Hypermedia Navigation Task

Finally the subjects were asked to complete a set of six information seeking tasks and after each to evaluate their own performance, as whether they thought they had found the answer and whether they found it in the most efficient way. The six tasks to be solved with the on-line manual and the evaluation of the own performance took approximately 1/2 - 1 hour per subject. To ensure the ecological validity and relevance of the tasks used in the study, we only used questions that we had collected in a previous study from users actually working with the method.

The information seeking tasks were designed to have the following properties: 1. They should force the subjects to navigate between the different graphs, that to see if and how the subjects used a mental model of the information space. 2. Some of the questions solutions were in the object-view and some in the process-view, that to see if there were any differences in the way of seeking information in the different views (see figure 1). (A number of other requirements not relevant to the results presented in the present paper were also considered.) The on-line manual was available on Sun workstations.

The performance on the solving of the six tasks was recorded on video and analyzed. Task completion time was calculated from the first "click" to the last written letters in the answer. Number of "clicks" in the graphs was counted for each task, and a map depicting how a particular user has moved in the on-line manual between graphs and texts was drawn. After each task the subjects were asked a number of questions, i.e. how certain they were that they had found the correct answer, if they had found it using the shortest path etc.

Results and Discussion

The results will be presented in two steps[2]. First we show the analysis of the pattern of different cognitive abilities. We

---

[1] 'Spatial' is here used to denote relations between objects in a space that need not necessarily be visually presented or represented.

[2] We will here only present results relevant to the issue of different kinds of spatial cogniton. For a complete description of this study, see Sjölinder (1996) and Höök, Dahlbäck,

Cognitive test	Factor 1	Factor 2	Factor 3
Synonym test	-.164	*.843*	-.046
Image classification	.284	*.810*	-.041
Figure drawing	*.958*	.071	-.071
Figure rotation	.227	-.393	*.654*
Hand test	.00001	.067	*.940*
Block test	*.792*	-.001	.376

Figure 2: Results from the factor analysis of the cognitive tests

then illustrate the relationship between these identified factors and the performance when using the on-line manual.

Patterns of Cognitive Abilities

An orthogonal factor analysis of the results of the six cognitive tests revealed three underlying factors, with two tests with high loading in each factor (see fig 2). Factor 1 with high loading on figure drawing test and the block test, factor 2 with high loading on the tests of synonyms and the classification of images, and factor 3 with high loading on the tests on rotation of images and of hand identification.

What is especially noteworthy here is that the pattern obtained seem to put in question the test manual's classification of these tests. We find two factors (1 and 3) which both seem to relate to visual-spatial cognition, but with the factor loadings very differently distributed[3]. What seems to be the critical difference here is that the test that have high loadings on factor 1 both concern the active manipulation of physical objects, whereas the tests with high loadings on factor 3 are require a purely mental effort to obtain the correct answer. This could indicate that from a psychological point of view there is a difference between the manipulation of spatial information in the mind and the acting in the world, even if both from a superficial point of view seem to concern the same kind of information processing.

Having shown that it is possible to group the tests into these groups does not of course entail that the distinction is of any theoretical or practical relevance. Following the path set by recent work by Stenning and Oberlander (1995, Stenning, Cox, and Oberlander, 1995), we will instead try to see whether the suggested theoretical distinction can be related to performance in other tasks, in our case hypermedia navigation. If it can be shown that the subjects different abilities is correlated with differential performance in other tasks, the validity of the distinction is given some further credence, something which seems necessary before discussing connections to other theoretical constructs.

Sjölinder (1996). For a description of the PUSH project, see Höök, Karlgren, Waern, Dahlbäck, Jansson, Karlgren, and Lrmaire (*forthcoming*)

[3] Note that while the image classification test uses pictorial material, this is primarily a test of logic-inductive ability.

Cognitive Abilities and Task Performance

To get a simple measure of the factors we added the standardized stanine points for the two tests most strongly associated with each factor. The correlation between the different factors and the task performance as measured by the time to complete the 6 tasks was then computed. These tests showed that the only significant correlation was with the internal spatial ability as measured with the two tests in factor 3. ($r = .56$, $p < .005$). No other correlations achieved or even approached significance. (Factor 1 $r = .04$, factor 2 $r = .13$) The same pattern is revealed when looking at the correlations between the dependent variable and the six different tests taken separately. The strongest correlations were with the two tests of internal spatial cognition, whereas the correlation between the completion time and the blocks test was for instance only $r = .04$.

There are two conclusions that can be drawn from this. First, this analysis supports the validity of the distinction being made here between spatial tasks that also involve some external physical manipulation or transformation of the objects, and where therefore visual feedback is available, and tasks where the entire transformation is done in the mind without any external support.

Second, that there is a correlation between users' spatial abilities and their ability to use the hypertext based system. But this is only true for a subset of the different spatial tests used in this study, namely the ones measuring internal spatial cognition. Another illustration of this connection can be made by first dividing the subjects into two groups, one with high scores on the spatial tests and one with low scores, and then compare the time used for solving the tasks for the two groups. This difference between the groups with high and low internal spatial ability is 16.94 minutes vs. 25.47 minutes. This difference is statistically significant ($F(1,21)=5.53$, $p<0.05$). When dividing the groups on how well they performed on the external spatial tasks, the difference between the groups' task completion time is much smaller (20.18 vs. 22.10 minutes) and not statistically significant.

In our questionnaire, we asked the subjects to estimate their own ability to read and use maps and their "sense of location". This is of course a very indirect measure of this ability. But it has been shown by Streeter and Vitello (1985) that subjects ability to read and use maps was strongly correlated with their actual map-reading ability. It is also the case that those who tend to like maps will use maps more

198

often and thereby improve their performance. So, our subjects own estimate of the map-reading ability can with some caution be taken as a measure of their actual ability.

We found that the subjects map-reading ability was correlated with factor 1 (the "external" spatial ability) in our cognitive tests, r=.42, P<.05, while there was no correlation between map-reading ability and factor 3 (the "internal" spatial ability).

Again, this would indicate that there is a difference between spatial ability for solving problems in the world (where groundedness is possible) and spatial ability for abstract structures in non-grounded domains.

Concluding Remarks

On the theoretical side we have argued that a distinction could, and perhaps should, be made between spatial tasks that are performed as bodily actions in the world and those that take place solely in the mind. The crucial difference between these is probably that in the former but not the latter tasks continuous visual feedback on the results of the transformations (actions) performed is available. Our analysis of the subjects' response pattern on the cognitive abilities test gave some support for that notion. Further support was gained from the fact that the only cognitive abilities tests that correlated with the performance in using the help system was those that seemed to measure internal spatial tasks. We are aware of the fact that it is possible to make connections between the pattern obtained here and recent discussions on situated cognition, and on mental imagery and other aspects of mental representations. A full treatment of the issues involved here would take us beyond the scope (and the space limitations) of the current paper, not the least since both the concepts of 'mental imagery' and 'spatial cognition' for a long time have been subject to intense theoretical discussions. Let us instead just mention one issue which we will consider in our future work in this area; what is the relationship between the 'internal' spatial ability discussed here and the ability to use visual imagery? Do the subjects that perform well on our internal tasks use mental imagery to a larger extent than the low performers? Our current data do not make it possible to answer this question, since we did not ask the subjects how they performed their tasks, nor did we include any test on imaginability.

On the applied side, we found that users differed in their navigation performance, and that this could be related to the ability to perform spatial tasks which did not have any external support, but not to other kinds of spatial or other cognitive abilities. The question then arises whether it is possible to device support for the users who find the navigation tasks difficult. Some work by (Vicente and Williges 1988) suggests that this can be the case. They have shown that users with low spatial ability are helped by system where parts of the previous state of the interface is visible after the user has made an action at the interface. Their explanation for this is by creating what they call a *visual momentum* the interface provides memory support for the users, since it is no longer required that they recall where they are and where they should go next in the hyperspace. Instead they can recognize the structure and the links and

basing their decisions on that recognition. An alternative or complementary hypothesis, based on the results from the present study, would be that the visual information on the screen transforms an internal spatial task to an external one.

It could of course be the case that map reading ability is related to the internal spatial ability described here, in which case it would probably be difficult to help the low performing subjects with some kind of map-like tool for navigation support.

We have no data that can give a definite answer to this question. But since we found that subjects' own judgment on their map reading ability correlated only with their results on Factor 1, i.e. external spatial tasks, and since it has been shown by Streeter and Vitello (1986) that people's own judgment of their ability on this is rather accurate, we at least consider it a hypothesis worth exploring further.

Acknowledgments

This work was supported by grants from NUTEK and Ellemtel. We would also like to thank all the other members of the PUSH project for their support. Stefan Samuelsson assisted with the statistical analysis.

References

Allen, B. Cognitive Differences in End User Searching of a CD-ROM Index, *15th Annual International SIGIR992*, ACM, Denmark, 1992.

Anderson, J. R. Arguments concerning representations for mental imagery. *Psychological Review*, **85**, 249-277.

Benyon, David R., and Murray, Diane (1993) Developing Adaptive Systems to Fit Individual Aptitudes, *Proceedings of IWIUI*, Orlando, 1993.

Bladh, Malin, and Höök, Kristina (1995) Satisfying User Needs Through a Combination of Interface Design Techniques, In: K. Nordby, P.H. Helmersen, D.J. Gilmore and S.A. Arnesen (eds.), *Human-Computer Interaction INTERACT'95*, Chapman & Hall, Oxford, 1995.

Eaglestone, B. and Vertegaal, R. (1994) Intuitive Interfaces for an Audio-database. In *User Interfaces to Databases*. Ambleside, UK: Lancaster University, pp. 315-328.

Hutchins, E. (1994). *Cognition in the wild*, Cambridge, MA.: The MIT Press.

Höök, K. (1991), *An Approach to a Route Guidance Interface*, Licentiate Thesis, Dept. of Computer and Systems Sciences, Stockholm University, ISSN 1101-8526.

Höök, K., Karlgren, J., Waern, A., Dahlbäck, N., Jansson, C., Karlgren, K., and Lemaire (*forthcoming*) A Glass-Box Approach to Adaptive Hypermedia. To appear in *International Journal of User Modeling and User-Adaptive Interaction*.

Höök, K, Sjölinder, M, and Dahlbäck, N (1996) Individual differences and navigation in hypermedia. SICS Research Report, R96:01, SICS, Sweden 1996.

Jennings, F., Benyon, D. and Murray, D. (1990). Adapting systems to differences between individuals. *Acta Psychologica*, vol 76

Kosslyn, S (1980) *Image and Mind*, Cambridge, MA: Harvard University Press.

Palmer, S. E. (1978). Fundamental Aspects of Cognitive Representation. In E. Rosch and B.B. Lloyd (Eds.) *Cognition and Categorization*. Hillsdale, NJ: Erlbaum.

Psykologiförlaget (1971) Manual till DS-batteriet (Manual for the DS-tests), Stockholm: Psykologiförlaget AB. (*In Swedish*).

Pylyshyn, Z. (1981) The Imagery Debate: Analogue Media versus Tacit Knowledge. *Psychological Review*, **88**, 16-45.

Reisner, P. (1977) Use of psychological experimentation as an aid to development of a query language IEEE Transactions on Software Engineering, SE-3 218-229

Sellen, A. and Nicol, A. (1990) *Building User-centred On-line Help*. In B. Laurel (ed.) The Art of Human-Computer Interface Design. Addison-Wesley, 143-153

Stenning, K and Oberlander, J. (1995) A Cognitive Theory of Graphical and Linguistic Reasoning: Logic and Implementation. *Cognitive Science* 19, 97 - 140.

Stenning, K., Cox, R. and Oberlander, J. (1995) Contrasting the Cognitive Effects of Graphical and Sentential Logic Teaching: Reasoning, Representation and Individual Differences.

Streeter, Lynn A. , Diane Vitello, and Susan A. Wonsiewicz (1985) 'How to Tell People Where to Go: Comparing Navigational Aids', *Int. J. Man-Machine Studies*, 22: 549-562.

Streeter, Lynn A and Vitello, Diane (1986) A Profile of Drivers' Map-Reading Abilities. *Human Factors*, **28**(2).

G.C. van der Veer (1989) Individual Differences and the User Interface, *Ergonomics*, 32, 1431- 1449.

Vicente K. J. and Williges, R. C. (1988) *Accommodating individual differences in searching a hierarchical file system* International Journal of man Machine Studies, 29 647 - 668

200

Individual differences in proof structures following multimodal logic teaching

Jon Oberlander and Richard Cox and Padraic Monaghan
Keith Stenning and Richard Tobin
Human Communication Research Centre
University of Edinburgh
2 Buccleuch Place, Edinburgh EH8 9LW, Scotland
{J.Oberlander|R.Cox|P.Monaghan|K.Stenning|R.Tobin}@ed.ac.uk

Abstract

We have been studying how students respond to multimodal logic teaching with Hyperproof. Performance measures have already indicated that students' pre-existing cognitive styles have a significant impact on teaching outcome. Furthermore, a substantial corpus of proofs has been gathered via automatic logging of proof development. We report results from analyses of final proof structure, exploiting (i) 'proofograms', a novel method of proof visualisation, and (ii) corpus-linguistic bigram analysis of rule use. Results suggest that students' cognitive styles do indeed influence the structure of their logical discourse, and that the effect may be attributable to the relative skill with which students manipulate graphical abstractions.

Introduction: multimodal logical discourse

Computer-based multimodal tools are giving people the freedom to express themselves in brand new ways. But what do people actually *do* when given these tools? Does everyone end up generating the same forms of multimodal discourse? Do multimodal systems lead to better performance than monomodal systems?

These questions arise in many areas related to human-computer interaction, but they are particularly important in educational applications, since multimodality is believed to be especially helpful to novices (di Sessa 1979, Schwarz and Dreyfus 1993). Hyperproof is a program created by Barwise and Etchemendy (1994) for teaching first-order logic (see Figure 1). Inspired by a situation-theoretic approach to heterogeneous reasoning, it uses multimodal (graphical and sentential) methods, allowing users to transfer information to and fro, between modalities (see Figure 2).

We have been carrying out a series of experiments on Hyperproof, to help evaluate its effects on students learning logic. The study has established that there are important individual differences in the way students respond to logic taught multimodally (Cox, Stenning and Oberlander 1994; Stenning, Cox and Oberlander 1995). In the course of this larger study, we have built up a substantial corpus of proofs. These 'hyperproofs' are an unusual form of discourse, for two main reasons. Firstly, they are primarily used for *self*-communication: a student arranges proof steps and rules in an external representation as an aid to their individual problem-solving activities. Secondly, hyperproofs are, of course, *multimodal* discourse: they involve both language and graphics, and are therefore in some ways more complex than text or speech.

We believe that the corpus of hyperproofs can provide a detailed insight into the paths which students follow in their

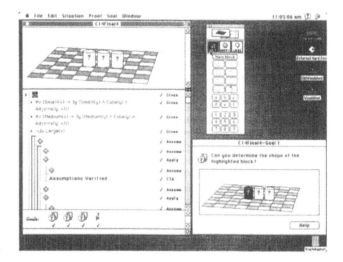

Figure 1: The Hyperproof Interface. The main window (top left) is divided into an upper graphical pane, and a lower calculus pane. The tool palette is floating next to the main window, and other windows can pop up to reveal a set of goals which have been posed.

Apply Extracts information from a set of sentential premises; expresses it graphically

Assume Introduces a new assumption into a proof, either graphically or sententially

Observe Extracts information from the situation; expresses it sententially

Inspect Extracts common information from a set of cases; expresses it sententially

Merge Extracts common information from a set of cases; expresses it graphically

Close Declares that a sentence is inconsistent with either another sentence, or the current graphical situation

CTA (Check truth of assumptions) Declares that all sentential and graphical assumptions are true in the current situation

Exhaust Declares that a part of a proof exhausts all the relevant cases

Figure 2: A set of relevant Hyperproof rules.

pursuit of proof goals. In this paper, we therefore first frame some hypotheses concerning the relation between the individual differences in teaching outcome which we found, and the structures to be found in students' proofs. We then outline the relevant aspects of the design of the main study, indicating how it distinguishes two styles of student. We then describe (i) the way 'proofograms' are used to track the way students deal with abstractions; and (ii) the application of bigram and trigram analyses of rule use patterns in the data corpus, demonstrating that the differing styles of student end up producing multimodal proofs of distinctive types.

Hypotheses

The observation that graphical systems require certain classes of information to be specified goes back at least to Bishop Berkeley. Elsewhere, we have termed this property 'specificity', and argued that it is useful because inference with specific representations can be very simple (Stenning and Oberlander 1991, 1995). We have also urged that actual graphical systems do allow abstractions to be expressed, and it is this that endows them with a usable level of expressive power. Thus, Hyperproof maintains a set of abstraction conventions for objects' spatial or visual attributes. As well as concrete depictions of objects, there are 'graphical abstraction symbols', which leave attributes under-specified: the *cylinder*, for instance, depicts objects of unknown size (see Figure 1). A key step, then, in mastering an actual graphical system is to learn which abstractions can be expressed, and how.

As we describe below, our pre-tests independently allowed us to divide subjects into two cognitive style groups, on the basis of their performance on a certain type of problem item. Loosely, one group is 'good with diagrams', and the other less so. The good diagrammers turned out to benefit more from Hyperproof-based teaching than the others. Our belief is that those who benefit most from Hyperproof do so because they are better able to manipulate the graphical abstractions it offers. Call this view the *abstraction ability hypothesis*.

A secondary issue concerns the relation between our binary distinction in cognitive styles and more traditional dimensions of individual difference—such as the 'visualiser–verbaliser' dimension. One hypothesis is that the good diagrammers are simply those subjects who have a preference for the visual modality. Call this view the *visual preference hypothesis*.

In what follows, we aim to show that the first hypothesis is vindicated by the analysis, but that the second is not, and that a rival view might fit the data better.

Method

In the full study, two groups of subjects were compared; one ($n = 22$ at course end) attended a one-quarter duration course taught using the multimodal Hyperproof. A comparison group ($n = 13$ at course end) were taught for the same period, but in the traditional syntactic manner supplemented with exercises using a graphics-disabled version of Hyperproof.

Distinguishing cognitive styles

Subjects were administered two kinds of pre- and post-course paper and pencil test of reasoning. The first of these is most relevant to the current discussion. It tested 'analytical reasoning' ability, with two kinds of item derived from the GRE

scale of that name (Duran, Powers and Swinton 1987). One subscale consists of verbal reasoning/argument analysis. The other subscale consists of items often best solved by constructing an external representation of some kind (such as a table or a diagram). We label these subscales as 'indeterminate' and 'determinate', respectively. Scores on the latter subscale were used to classify subjects within both Hyperproof and Syntactic groups into DetHi and DetLo sub-groups. The score reflects subjects' facility for solving a type of item that often is best solved using an external representation; DetHi scored well on these items; DetLo less well. For the moment, we may consider DetHi subjects to be more 'diagrammatic', and DetLo to be less so. Obviously, the relation between diagrammatic ability and the visualiser–verbaliser dimension is an issue to which we return below.

Computer-based protocols

Both the Hyperproof and Syntactic groups contained DetHi and DetLo sub-groups. All subjects sat post-course, computer-based exams, although the questions differed for the two groups, since the Syntactic group had not been taught to use Hyperproof's systems of graphical rules. Student-computer interactions were dynamically logged—this approach might be termed 'computer-based protocol taking'. The logs were time stamped and permitted a full, step-by-step, reconstruction of the time course of the subject's reasoning.

Here, we discuss only the data from the 22 Hyperproof subjects, all of whom completed the exams. The four questions that these students were set contained two types of item: determinate and indeterminate. Here, determinate problems were taken to be those whose problem statement did not utilise Hyperproof's abstraction conventions. That is: determinate problems contained only concrete depictions of objects in their initially given graphical situation, whereas indeterminate problems—such as that in Figure 1—could contain graphical abstraction symbols in the initial situation.

Results

A proof log captures both the *process* of proof development, and its *product*—the final proof submitted by the subject. Here we discuss the data extracted from the latter.

Proofograms

What evidence is there for the abstraction ability hypothesis? Among the Hyperproof students, do the two sub-groups—DetHi and DetLo—use graphical abstraction symbols in characteristically different ways? To investigate this, we scored each step of each proof on the basis of number of concrete situations compatible with the graphical depiction. We give each graphical symbol in a situation a score: for each visible attribute (size, shape, and location) a symbol scores 1 if that attribute is specified, and 0 otherwise. By totalling the scores for the individual symbols, we can give each situation in a proof a score. For example, in Figure 3, the total concreteness score for the situation shown would be 9, since each object is fully specified; in Figure 5, the score would be just 6, since one object is specified only for location, and another only for size and location. A low score indicates more abstraction; a higher score indicates more concreteness.

We can explore the way concreteness varies through the course of a proof by graphing it against the hierarchical struc-

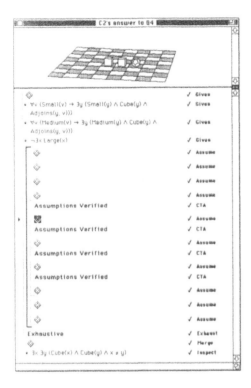

Figure 3: Submitted proof for a DetLo subject (C2) attempting an indeterminate question (Q4). The situation on view is from the 9th step of the proof.

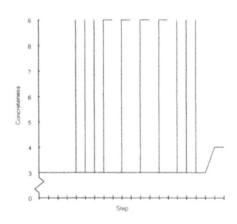

Figure 4: Proofogram for C2 attempting Q4. Proof steps are plotted on the x-axis; the concreteness of the current graphical situation is computed for each step of the proof, and is plotted on the y-axis. Horizontal lines indicate dependency structure; vertical lines indicate uses of Assume; sloping lines indicate uses of Apply or Merge. C2's proofogram is 'spikey', indicating a series of independent, concrete cases.

ture of the proof. We call such graphs 'proofograms'. Figures 3 and 5 show how subjects C2 and C14 tackle an indeterminate exam question; Figures 4 and 6 give their proofograms.

The visual differences between proofograms are quite striking: one group is 'spikey'—as in Figure 4; and the other is 'layered'—as in Figure 6. The differences are most pronounced on the 2 indeterminate exam questions. The visual grouping of proofograms suggests the existence of a 'staging phenomenon': DetHi introduce concreteness *by stages*, whereas DetLo introduce it more immediately. In terms of proof structure, DetHi tend to produce structured sets of cases, with superordinate cases involving graphical abstraction; DetLo tend to produce sets of cases without such overt superordinate structure.

To assess whether this apparent patterning was reliable, the 88 proofograms (4 exam questions for each of the 22 Hyperproof subjects) were printed. The proofograms were randomly ordered, and two prototypes (one spikey, one layered) were selected as category exemplars. Two independent raters then assigned each proofogram to either the 'spikey' or 'layered' category, under a forced choice regime. There was a high degree of inter-rater agreement, with a discrepancy on only 2 of the 88 proofograms. A third observer was employed to resolve the two categorisation disagreements.

To test for existence of the staging phenomenon, the concordance between subject type (DetLo/Hi) and proofogram style was analysed. For each of the 4 exam questions, 2 × 2 tables were produced, showing the number of items in each cell (DetLo/spikey; DetLo/layered; DetHi/spikey;

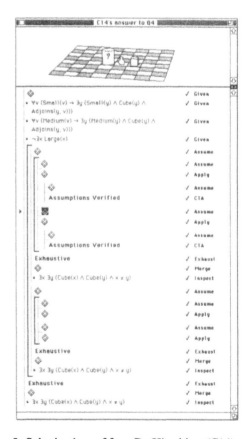

Figure 5: Submitted proof for a DetHi subject (C14) attempting an indeterminate question (Q4). The situation on view is from the 9th step of the proof.

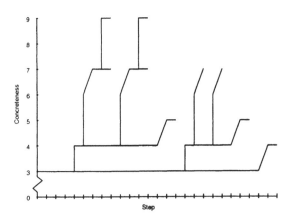

Figure 6: Proofogram for C14 attempting Q4. C14's proofogram is 'layered', indicating parallel sub-case structures with abstract superordinate cases.

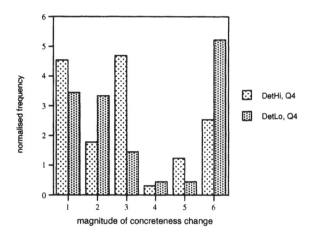

Figure 7: Frequencies with which DetHi and DetLo subject groups employ changes in proof concreteness of varying magnitude, when attempting Question 4. The frequency is normalised to take into account the differing size of the subject groups (DetHi $n = 13$, DetLo $n = 9$).

DetHi/layered). A nonparametric measure of association (ϕ coefficient) was calculated for each table. The results indicated that the hypothesised association only held on indeterminate questions (on question 2, $\phi = .43^*$; on question 4, $\phi = .28$). On questions 1 and 3 (determinate questions), both raters assigned all proofograms to the spikey category.

It seems, then, that on indeterminate questions, DetHi subjects do differ from DetLo subjects, in that they are more prone to develop layered proofs, introducing concreteness by stages. Evidence for the staging phenomenon therefore provides support for the abstraction ability hypothesis: the two groups are certainly using abstractions in different ways.

It would, of course, be convenient to be able to encapsulate the graphical attributes of the proofogram in numerical form. Our first attempts to do so have involved computing mean change in concreteness per proof step per proof. However, the change only exceeds unity on the most indeterminate exam problem—question 4. In fact, we can consider the frequency with which subjects employ changes in concreteness of varying magnitude. Figure 7 graphs the differing behaviour of the subject groups on question 4. This reinforces the idea that DetHi subjects tend to make small changes in concreteness, whereas DetLo subjects make larger changes.

Corpus analysis

Of Hyperproof's rules, only Assume, Apply and Merge increase concreteness. We therefore examined the kind of patterns in which they occur through proof-corpus analysis. The proofogram results already indicate that DetHi and DetLo differ in the way they handle concreteness. Since Assume is by far the most frequent means of adding concreteness (see, for instance, Table 3 below), the corpus analysis distinguishes between uses of the rule which introduce totally concrete graphical situations, and those which leave some abstractness in the graphic. The term Fullassume denotes the former type of use, and assume denotes the latter.

Using techniques developed originally for the analysis of linguistic corpora, we have carried out bigram and trigram analyses of rule use, utilising Dunning's (1993) 'Log-

Likelihood Test', which can be applied to relatively small corpora. The test is designed to "highlight particular A's and B's that are highly associated in text" (p.71). Ranking the bigrams according to this test provides a good *profile* of the individual's, or the group's, rule use in the corpus. We can then compare the profiles for the sub-groups on the two question types, assessing the significance of a given bigram by using the χ^2 test on the log-likelihood value.

Tables 1 and 2 illustrate the nature of the resulting profiles, and show the most important parts of the bigram profiles for DetHi and DetLo on indeterminate and determinate questions, respectively. Taking the profiles for the two groups, we can consider differences both between-groups and within-groups; the former are the most interesting.

On indeterminate questions, we find that the bigrams assume Apply, Merge Inspect, CTA Observe, assume Close, Given assume, and assume Fullassume are significant in DetHi proofs, but not in DetLo ones. Conversely, only the bigram Inspect Merge is significant in DetLo proofs, but not in DetHi ones. The profiles are weakly but significantly correlated ($r = 0.167^*$).[1] When taking into account only those bigrams that are significantly associated in the profiles, the correlation is higher, but not significant ($r = 0.315, ns$).

On determinate questions, the bigrams assume Apply, CTA Observe and Close Fullassume are significant in DetHi proofs, but not in DetLo ones. Conversely, as with the indeterminate questions, the only bigram significant in DetLo proofs, but not in DetHi ones, is Inspect Merge. Here, the two subject group's profiles are significantly correlated ($r = 0.537^{**}$). The correlation between significantly-associated bigrams is even stronger and still highly significant ($r = 0.918^{**}$).

This finding accords with the proofograms' indication that it is indeterminate questions which best discriminate the two subject groups. Recall that these are the questions in which the

---

[1]Correlations reported here are non-parametric (Spearman's ρ). Significance at the $p < .05$ level is denoted by *; significance at the $p < .001$ level by **.

Table 1: Bigram profiles for subjects' indeterminate questions: (a) DetHi; (b) DetLo. The first column indicates Dunning's 'log-likelihood'; the higher the number, the more 'natural' the association. $k(AB)$ is a count of the number of times the bigram AB occurs, $k(A \sim B)$ is a count of the number of times A is followed by a rule other than B, and so on. For reasons of space, we show only those bigrams that are significantly associated ($p < .05$).

DETHI

-2logλ	k(AB)	k(A~B)	k(~AB)	k(~A~B)	A	B
145.43	57	22	29	355	Fullassume	CTA
123.52	26	13	5	419	Exhaust	Merge
78.72	33	85	3	342	assume	Apply
69.47	17	11	12	423	Merge	Inspect
53.63	39	43	40	341	CTA	Fullassume
36.46	2	77	116	268	Fullassume	assume
26.16	14	68	7	374	CTA	Observe
26.01	12	27	17	407	Exhaust	Inspect
25.06	15	103	4	341	assume	Close
19.56	17	9	101	336	Given	assume
19.55	6	112	73	272	assume	Fullassume

DETLO

-2logλ	k(AB)	k(A~B)	k(~AB)	k(~A~B)	A	B
134.90	67	33	15	221	Fullassume	CTA
78.70	19	13	5	299	Exhaust	Inspect
36.75	10	8	11	307	Inspect	Merge
34.48	1	99	54	182	Fullassume	assume
33.09	45	35	55	201	CTA	Fullassume
27.97	11	21	10	294	Exhaust	Merge

Table 2: Bigram profiles for subjects' determinate questions: (a) DetHi; (b) DetLo. For reasons of space, we again show only those bigrams that are significantly associated ($p < .05$).

DETHI

-2logλ	k(AB)	k(A~B)	k(~AB)	k(~A~B)	A	B
112.37	24	11	5	366	Exhaust	Merge
72.82	48	73	14	271	Fullassume	CTA
65.00	15	13	6	372	Merge	Inspect
36.39	35	86	17	268	Fullassume	Close
26.79	10	16	15	365	Given	Apply
26.16	16	36	19	335	Close	Exhaust
23.08	11	27	14	354	assume	Apply
20.19	32	25	89	260	CTA	Fullassume
13.65	10	47	12	337	CTA	Observe
10.78	26	26	95	259	Close	Fullassume

DETLO

-2logλ	k(AB)	k(A~B)	k(~AB)	k(~A~B)	A	B
51.49	13	8	5	207	Exhaust	Merge
50.03	28	47	4	154	Fullassume	CTA
41.35	10	8	4	211	Given	Apply
38.05	9	6	5	213	Merge	Inspect
24.93	23	52	9	149	Fullassume	Close
19.20	11	21	11	190	Close	Exhaust
13.99	4	2	14	213	Inspect	Merge
12.59	18	11	57	147	CTA	Fullassume

initial graphical situation is abstract, so that all concreteness must be introduced explicitly by the subjects.

Discussion

The proofogram and corpus analyses provide evidence that subjects differ in the way that they use the graphical abstraction conventions of Hyperproof. On questions where the subject must construct the concrete graphic, it seems that DetHi subjects exhibit staging behaviour, and build their graphics incrementally, whereas DetLo subjects are prone to construct their concrete graphics in one go. The abstraction ability hypothesis thus seems plausible, since the 'stagers' are exactly those whom our main study showed benefit most from teaching with Hyperproof (Stenning, Cox and Oberlander, 1995).

Snow (1987) and colleagues, in their studies of aptitude-treatment interactions (ATI), characterise such within-person adaptations and flexibilities as an important source of individual differences in complex skill performance. Snow (1987) reports that subjects' ability to 'strategy-shift' is particularly detectable on tests of complex spatial visualization such as the paper-folding test (Test VZ2 in Ekstrom, French and Harmon, 1976). Such tests involve mental manipulations that are very similar to those required for skilled use of a multimodal system such as Hyperproof.

However, to characterise the difference between subjects solely in terms of visuo-spatial ability differences—or in terms of cognitive style differences along a 'visualiser–verbaliser' dimension—may be too hasty. To be sure, the visual preference hypothesis has some initial plausibility: if the DetHi are 'good with diagrams', perhaps they are simply the visualisers, and have a preference for the visual modality. However, the evidence from the corpus goes against the hypothesis.

First, consider the way that use of assume and Fullassume varies between the DetHi and DetLo groups, as shown in Table 3. DetHi make more use of assume than DetLo, while the latter make more use of Fullassume than the former. The bigram assume Fullassume is found to be significant in DetHi indeterminate proofs, but not in DetLo proofs. However, these facts do not support the hypothesis that DetHi prefer visual over verbal. On the contrary, DetLo subjects' favouring of Fullassume over assume confirms that they are not 'stagers': in a sense, it is *they* who exhibit a preference for the graphical modality. By contrast, DetHi subjects' use of assume indicates gradual addition of information to the graphical window pane, either by assumption, or by transfer from the sentential pane (via Apply). The difference seems to be that the DetHi group *operate over* the graphical situations, frequently using a graphic as input to further stages of proof construction. The DetLo, on the other hand, seem just to *output* graphics, without subsequently using them.

Table 3: Occurrences of Assume, Apply, and Observe.

RULE	frequency per group		frequency per subject	
	DetHi	DetLo	DetHi	DetLo
assume	143	62	11	6.9
Fullassume	222	186	17	20.7
Apply	61	24	4.7	2.7
Observe	27	9	2.1	1

In addition, Table 3 indicates that DetHi subjects make more use of rules that transfer information between the modalities. DetHi make the bigram **assume Apply** a significant component of all their proofs, and use it more frequently than DetLo: 44 times to just 7. By contrast, DetLo exhibit a tendency to invoke Apply as the first rule in their proofs (giving rise to the bigram **Given Apply**). Subsequent interaction between the modalities is thereby reduced, with case construction being performed only within the graphical window.

Thus, DetHi subjects do *not* show a simple preference for the visual–graphical modality. Rather, what distinguishes the DetHi subjects is their greater tendency to *translate* between graphical and sentential modalities in *both* directions.

Perhaps, as Monaghan (1995) has suggested, the individual differences between subjects might be better captured by two or more cognitive style dimensions. There may, for example, be an interaction between individuals' *processing* style and the preferences that they may exhibit for information *representation*. One promising candidate for the second factor is the field-dependence and field-independence dimension. Field-independent individuals have been found to prefer more formal methods of instruction, to rely more upon internal frames of reference, and to perform better on tasks that require cognitive re-structuring. They also seem better able than field-dependents to represent concepts analytically rather than taking on ideas as presented (Jonassen and Grabowski, 1993; Witkin and Goodenough, 1981). So, DetHi individuals might well be more field independent—but we should not immediately conclude that the differences are purely representational, as opposed to operational.

Another possibility is that DetHi subjects may just have higher levels of expertise. Research in the physics domain (such as Chi, Feltovich and Glaser, 1981; Larkin, McDermott, Simon and Simon, 1980) has shown that expertise is characterised by greater domain knowledge, with an ability to classify problems according to deep structure and physical principles, whereas novices tend to classify problems on the basis of surface features. Experts also tend to spend more time than novices on analysing and understanding problems, but produce faster solutions. Working forward is typical of experts, whereas novices tend to work backwards.

An account of the differences in terms of expertise seems implausible, however, for at least two reasons. First, subjects in both groups received equal exposure to Hyperproof and it is difficult to see how the DetHi could have acquired more domain knowledge than the DetLo. Secondly, the expertise literature would predict that DetHi produce faster solutions. However, the two groups did not differ significantly in terms of solution times on any of the four Hyperproof exam questions.

Traditional psychometric approaches to the measurement of cognitive and learning styles contribute detailed and useful characterisation of human behaviour, but at the level of description and taxonomy. Micro-analyses of process, of rule usage patterns, is a methodology that promises to extend such accounts and is one that we expect to pursue. The next phase will involve the building of computational models, testing the theoretically important parameter of abstraction ability. This approach should make a useful contribution to the development of a cognitive characterisation of just what it means in computational terms to be a 'verbal' or 'visual' thinker.

Acknowledgements

The support of the Economic and Social Research Council for HCRC is gratefully acknowledged. The work was supported by UK Joint Councils Initiative in Cognitive Science and HCI, through grant G9018050 (Signal); and by NATO Collaborative research grant 910954 (Cognitive Evaluation of Hyperproof). The first author is supported by an EPSRC Advanced Fellowship. Special thanks to John Etchemendy, Tom Burke and Mark Greaves at Stanford, and Chris Brew at Edinburgh; our thanks also to our three anonymous referees, for their helpful comments.

References

Barwise, J. and Etchemendy, J. (1994). *Hyperproof*. CSLI Lecture Notes. Chicago: Chicago University Press.

Chi, M. T. H., Feltovich, P. J. and Glaser, R. (1981). Categorisation and representation of physics problems by experts and novices. *Cognitive Science*, **5**, 121–152.

Cox, R., Stenning, K. and Oberlander, J. (1994). Graphical effects in learning logic: reasoning, representation and individual differences. In *Proceedings of the 16th Annual Meeting of the Cognitive Science Society*, pp237–242, Atlanta, Georgia, August.

Dunning, T. (1993). Accurate methods for the statistics of surprise and coincidence. *Computational Linguistics* **19**, 61–74.

Duran, R., Powers, D. and Swinton, S. (1987). Construct Validity of the GRE Analytical Test: A Resource Document. ETS Research Report 87–11. Princeton, NJ: Educational Testing Service.

Ekstrom, R. B., French, J. W. and Harmon, H. H. (1976). *Manual for Kit of Factor Referenced Cognitive Tests*. Princeton, NJ: Educational Testing Service (ETS).

Jonassen, D. H. and Grabowski, B. L. (1993). *Handbook of individual differences, learning and instruction*. Hillsdale, NJ: Lawrence Erlbaum Associates.

Larkin, J. H., McDermott, J., Simon, D. and Simon, H. A. (1980). Expert and novice performance in solving physics problems. *Science*, **208**, 1335–1342.

Monaghan, P. (1995). A corpus-based analysis of individual differences in proof-style. MSc Thesis, Centre for Cognitive Science, University of Edinburgh.

Schwarz, B. and Dreyfus, T. (1993). Measuring integration of information in multirepresentational software. *Interactive Learning Environments*, **3**, 177–198.

di Sessa, A. A. (1979). On 'learnable' representations of knowledge: A meaning for the computational metaphor. In Lochhead, J. and Clement, J. (Eds.) *Cognitive Process Instruction*. Philadelphia, PA: The Franklin Institute Press.

Snow, R. E. (1987). Aptitude complexes. In Snow, R. E. and Farr, M. J. (Eds.) *Aptitude, learning, and instruction, Volume 3: Conative and affective process analysis*. Hillsdale, NJ: Lawrence Erlbaum Associates.

Stenning, K., Cox, R. and Oberlander, J. (1995). Contrasting the cognitive effects of graphical and sentential logic teaching: reasoning, representation and individual differences. *Language and Cognitive Processes*, **10**, 333–354.

Stenning, K. and Oberlander, J. (1991). Reasoning with Words, Pictures and Calculi: computation versus justification. In Barwise, J., Gawron, J. M., Plotkin, G. and Tutiya, S. (Eds.) *Situation Theory and Its Applications*, Volume 2, pp607–621. Chicago: Chicago University Press.

Stenning, K. and Oberlander, J. (1995). A cognitive theory of graphical and linguistic reasoning: Logic and implementation. *Cognitive Science*, **19**, 97–140.

Witkin, H. A. and Goodenough, D. R. (1981). *Cognitive styles: Essence and origins: Field dependence and field independence*. New York, NY: International Universities Press.

Functional Roles for the Cognitive Analysis of Diagrams in Problem Solving

Peter C-H. Cheng
ESRC Centre for Research in Development, Instruction and Training
Department of Psychology, University of Nottingham
Nottingham, NG7 2RD, U.K.
peter.cheng@nottingham.ac.uk

Abstract

This paper proposes that a novel form of cognitive analysis for diagrammatic representations is in terms of the functional roles that they can play in problem solving. Functional roles are capacities or features that a diagram may possess, which can support particular forms of reasoning or specific problem solving tasks. A person may exploit several functional roles of a single diagram in one problem. A dozen functional roles have been identified, which can be considered as a framework to bridge the gulf between (i) studies of the properties of diagrams in themselves and (ii) investigations of human reasoning and problem solving with diagrammatic representations. The utility of the framework is demonstrated by examining how the functional roles can explain why certain diagrams facilitate problem solving in thermodynamics. The thermodynamics diagrams are interesting, in themselves, as examples of complex cognitive artefacts that support a variety of sophisticated forms of reasoning.

Introduction

Work on the nature and use of diagrammatic representations in cognitive science and related fields can be roughly divided into two quite general approaches. First, there is empirical and computational modelling work that examines cognitive processes involved in reasoning with diagrams. For instance, Larkin & Simon (1987) demonstrated that diagrams can (sometimes) be more effective than informationally equivalent sentential representations for problem solving. Koedinger and Anderson (1990) have shown that expert knowledge in some domains may use diagrams encoded in perceptual chunks, or diagrammatic configuration schema. Cheng (Cheng & Simon, 1995; Cheng, in press) has suggested that diagrams may have had a significant role in some important historical episodes of scientific discoveries. (See Kulpa, 1994, for further examples.) The second approach involves the theoretical and empirical study of the properties of diagrams in themselves, without special regard to the problem solving contexts in which they may be found. For instance, Bertin (1981) provides a taxonomy of graphical objects and their relations. By asking subjects to rank diagrams on a number of dimensions, Lohse *et al.* (1994) have obtained a taxonomy of visual representations. (See Wickens, 1992,

for further examples.)

However, there is a need for work in the middle ground between the two approaches, which attempts to give some understanding of how properties of diagrams are related to the cognitive processes embedded in different diagrammatic representations. Diagrams are not a homogenous class of representations, but have diverse formats and uses. Many studies of diagrams from a cognitive perspective have tended to focus on a particular type of diagram for one kind of problem, as in some of examples mentioned above. As yet, there is no systematic way to judge whether particular findings for one type of diagram are applicable to other diagrammatic formats, without merely repeating the studies with those formats.

For example, Larkin and Simon's (1987) seminal work analysed the computational benefit of diagrammatic versus sentential representations, comparing representations that are informationally equivalent; information in one representation can be directly translated or mapped into the other. However, in real problem domains the available alternative representations are rarely equivalent in this sense. So, an alternative way to analyse aspects of different representations may be useful, serving as a basis for comparisons and to explain differences between diagrams. Given a particular domain and some characterization of diagrams, how can we determine what will be useful and effective diagrams for particular problems? The design of diagrammatic representations is an issue in cognitive science and related fields, such as learning and instruction, program visualization, and human computer interaction.

There are many ways in which complex phenomena or artefacts can be decomposed, with different units of analysis giving insights on different levels. Previous studies of the properties of diagrams have tended to focus on either (i) whole diagrams (e.g., Lohse *et al.*, 1994) or (ii) on diagrammatic elements (lines, angles; e.g., Bertin, 1981). Here, the properties of diagrams will be considered at an intermediate level that is more directly suited to considerations of the forms of information processing that may be done with them.

Functional roles of diagrams will be the units of analysis. They are capacities or features that diagrams may have, which support particular forms of reasoning or specific problem solving tasks, by making relevant information available to reasoners with little symbolic computation and only minor additions or changes (if any) to the diagrams themselves. Different functional roles make different kinds of information readily accessible.

A person may exploit several functional roles of a single diagram in one problem, or may use alternate ones in different problems. The roles are distinct but are naturally dependent on each other. They should have a familiar feel, even though they may not have been explicitly recognised before. A dozen functional roles have been identified and constitute a framework linking properties of diagrams to cognitive processes, which begins to address the problem of how to design effective diagrams for particular problem domains.

The paper has three main sections. In the first section a dozen roles of diagrams are described. In the following section the framework is used to explain the occurrence of particular diagrams in thermodynamics to illustrate the functional roles and to begin to demonstrate the utility of the framework. The final discussion section considers some implications of the framework.

Functional Roles of Diagrams

The following list of functional roles was compiled by examining many diagrams from a variety of domains (engineering, physical science, social science, and medicine). Sources included: collections of diagrams, text books, instruction manuals, published papers, design plans, and laboratory note books. Some diagrams have multiple functional roles. The types of information processing associated with each diagram was studied, and 12 functional roles were identified (although no claim is made about the completeness of this list).

F1 Showing spatial structure and organization. A functional role of some diagrams is to depict the spatial features of objects and the arrangement of their components, with some fidelity. Such diagrams have close spatial mappings from the shape and location of target objects to the shape and position of symbols representing them. Capturing spatial structure is an important function of engineering and architectural drawings or "blue prints". Such drawings show local and global structure of objects symbolically, rather than pictorially. Details hidden by intervening material may be shown by cut-away sections and symbolic conventions used to hide unnecessary detail or provide extra information (e.g., centre lines).

F2 Capturing physical relations. Diagrams can be used to highlight selected physical relations that are of importance in a target domain, without showing the spatial structure of objects and the spatial relations among their

Figure 1: Tower of Hanoi.

components. In schematic diagrams of electrical circuits, for instance, the inter-connectivity and sequence of the components is shown, but the location of symbols in the diagram may bear little relation to the physical location of the components on the circuit board.

F3 Showing physical assembly. A functional role of some diagrams is to show how an object is physically assembled from components; what parts there are and how they go together. This may be achieved by explicitly showing a series of subassemblies or depicting the object as if it had been systematically dismantled. Showing subassemblies is common in engineering "blue prints" and often used in instruction manuals for construction toys (e.g., Lego, Mechano). Where such diagrams provide information about the order of assembly they are also depicting a process (see F8).

F4 Defining and distinguishing variables, terms and components. Some diagrams are used to define or identify components, variables and features pertaining to a target domain. Written labels may be used to name or specify particular components or features. Diagrammatic elements may themselves be special symbols, which have conventional meanings in particular domains, such as the component symbols in electrical circuit diagrams.

F5 Displaying values. A function of some diagrams is to depict values of variables in a manner that facilities qualitative and quantitative reasoning about them, usually in the form of comparisons. Often standard formats or reference systems will be used, such as Cartesian graphs, histograms and pie charts. Problem solvers use their knowledge of the conventions governing the formats when reasoning.

F6 Depicting states. Some diagrams depict the state a system, without special reference to transitions from one state to another. For example, some operating manuals for electronic equipment include schematic diagrams of factory set positions of internal (DIP) switches. By comparing the diagram to the actual switches, we can see whether the equipment is in its default state. Weather charts have the depiction of states as one of their main functions. Figure 1 shows a familiar diagram, a single state of the Tower of Hanoi problem.

F7 Depicting state spaces. A functional role of some diagrams, which logically follows the previous one, is the depiction of state spaces (but not necessarily problem spaces). These diagrams have several components depicting two or more states, with adjacent components normally representing closely related states. The Periodic table of chemical elements is an example. Each element may be considered as an individual state, with its horizontal and vertical position being meaningful in chemical terms. The transition state space for the 3-disc Tower of Hanoi problem is shown in Figure 2. Each node represents one state; at the corners all the discs are on one of the pegs. The lines represent legal transitions between states; one disc moved between pegs.

F8 Encoding temporal sequences and processes.

Diagrams may illustrate the temporal order or flow of a process, by depicting states and the changes to those states. Some of the ways this is done are: (i) placing diagrammatic elements in an ordered sequence; (ii) using arrows to show progress or movement; and, (iii) having contours labelled with time increments.

One purpose of this functional role is to provide some kinesthetic sense of the processes being depicted, perhaps as an aid to generating a mental model. The path of a particular problem solver through the problem space of the Tower of Hanoi can be shown by adding arrows or numbering the links in Figure 2.

F9 Abstracting process flow and control. A functional role of some diagrams is to abstractly represent the flow of complex non-linear processes. Such processes may include cycles, iterative loops, contingent branching and parallel tasks. These diagrams use conventional symbols (icons) to represent process stages without depicting the states themselves.

Traditional computer program data flow diagrams have this as one of their main functions. Different processes are named and those of similar type share the same symbol shape; for example, diamonds to depict decisions. The flow of information is shown, but the state of the information is not usually depicted. Gantt charts perform a similar function by naming stages and showing the order and dependency of processes.

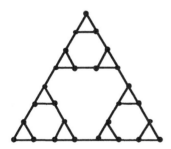

Figure 2 A state space.

F10 Capturing laws. A functional role of some diagrams is to capture a law by the means of its internal structure, such that the diagram does not merely display values of variables, but embodies the law. For example, in physics, the resultant of two forces acting at a point may be found by constructing a parallelogram (two adjacent sides represent the given forces, and the line from the given point to the opposite corner provides the resultant force). Such diagrams capture, and happen to operationalize, vector addition.

Capturing laws is one of the distinguishing characteristics of Law Encoding Diagrams, LEDs, (Cheng, 1994, 1995). LEDs have geometric, spatial or topological constraints that govern their structure, such that the form of the diagram is always consistent with the target laws of a domain.

F11 Doing computations. Computations can to be done directly using the structure of some diagrams. The prime example for numerical calculations are nomograms, which are closely related to slide-rules. Law Encoding Diagrams also allow computations to be made using their structure.

F12 Computation sequencing. Diagrams can help organise, plan and track complex sequences of computations. For example, when doing numerical integration, say by the Simpson's method, a diagram can be used to explain why the calculation takes the form that is does. Tabachneck, Leonardo and Simon (1994) describe how an expert in economics used a graph as a place holder during reasoning and as a summary.

The twelve functional roles have been described and brief examples given. The next section provides a single integrated example covering most of the functional roles.

Diagrams in Thermodynamics

To demonstrate the use of the proposed framework and to further clarify some of the functional roles, this section considers diagrams found in thermodynamics. The domain was chosen because it has complex diagrams that are of interest in their own right, which problem solvers use in sophisticated ways. The diagrams may be considered as cognitive artefacts, which have evolved over the history of the field as effective cognitive tools for problem solving.

Diagrams in thermodynamics texts are mainly of two kinds: (i) component diagrams, which show the structure of particular pieces of equipment or the parts of a plant; and, (ii) property diagrams, which are graphs showing the thermodynamic properties of the fluid in the plant. Figures 3a and 3b are typical examples. An interesting observation regarding these diagrams is their occurrence in complementary pairs when complex heat engine cycles or refrigeration cycles are being considered. In other circumstances they tend to be found alone. Figures 3a and 3b are such a pair for a particular steam power cycle. The diagrams are used to explain the operation of the cycle and to solve problems, such as determining the power output and efficiency of a steam plant, given a few fixed values.

Rogers and Mayhew (1980) is a popular standard

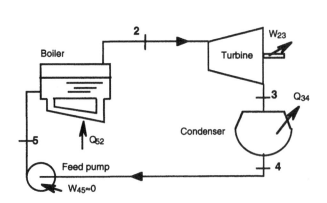

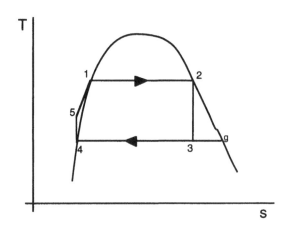

Figure 3a: Steam Plant Component Diagram.

Figure 3b: Steam Cycle Property Diagram.

undergraduate text in thermodynamics (a fourth edition was published in 1992). It has three chapters on complex power and refrigeration cycles, in which 23 of the 56 (41%) diagrams are complementary pairs of component and property diagrams. The rest of the book (24 chapters) contains nearly 200 diagrams, but fewer than 10 (<5%) are complementary pairs. Further, observations of experienced instructors, expert in thermodynamics problem solving, showed that they usually draw complementary pairs of diagrams as the first step when solving problems of this kind. Clearly, some benefit is gained by using the complementary pair of diagrams in problem solving on complex thermodynamic cycles.

Explanations of the benefits that problem solvers gain by using these diagrams can be given in terms of existing theories or hypotheses. For example, Larkin and Simon (1987) have shown how diagrams similar to the component diagram can help in the processes of search and recognition during problem solving. Similarly, it is conceivable that experts may have perceptual schemas for different parts of property diagrams, in the form of diagrammatic configuration schemas (Koedinger and Anderson, 1990). However, these theories are not well suited, nor intended, to explain phenomena like the complementary diagram pairs in thermodynamics.

The functional roles framework provides an analysis of a different kind, which is more suited to explaining the diagram pairs phenomena — the two diagrams have different but complementary sets of functional roles. From informal observations of expert problem solvers in thermodynamics working on a range of different problems, and from the study of worked examples from thermodynamics texts, the functional roles possessed by the two kinds of diagrams were identified. Both the component diagram and the property diagram, Figure 3, identify and define things that are important for problem solving (function F4). The plant diagram uses labels and conventional symbols to indicate what items are part of the plant; e.g., the pump is a circle with lines representing its inlet and outlet. Locations

of properties of interest are indicated by the diagram; for instance W_{23} is the power output of the turbine and Q_{52} is the heat needed to change the water to steam in the boiler.

The property diagram is a Cartesian graph, with temperature (T) and entropy (s) on the ordinate and abscissa, respectively. The "bell" curve shows the boundary between different phases of water and is known as the *saturation curve*. To its left the water is liquid. To its right the water is a vapour. Under the curve the water is a mixture of liquid and vapour. This is basic background knowledge for problem solvers in this domain. The numbers in the diagram indicate points in the cycle corresponding to the numbered locations in the component diagram, which is the only direct means that problem solvers have of interrelating the two diagrams. There is no '1' in the component diagram, because there is no unique location in the boiler that has properties corresponding to that point in the property diagram. The lines between numbered points in the property diagrams are changes that occur within the components of the plant.

The component diagram shows how the parts of the steam plant are physically connected (F2) (but does not show not true spatial locations, F1). An important function of the property diagram is to show the values of the temperature and entropy around the cycle (F5). This defines the thermodynamic character of cycle and allows comparisons to be made; for example $T_1=T_2$ and $s_2=s_3$. The property diagram may also be considered as a depicting one of many possible states (F6), other states being alternative cycles that have different shapes in the T-s space. The component diagram aids visualization of the process (F8), showing the direction of flow of the fluid around the circuit and the exchanges of heat and work to and from the system. The property diagram also supports visualization, but in terms of the thermodynamic properties of the system and with regard to the physical states of the fluid in the cycle (using the saturation curve).

The development of temperature and entropy graphs in

thermodynamics is significant, because they captures some useful laws in diagrammatic form (F10). (Pressure-volume graphs are more easily conceptualized but they are less useful in problem solving.) In T-s graphs, the area directly under any curve (to the s axis) represents a quantity of heat; for example, the area under $line_{34}$ is the heat lost in the condenser; that is Q_{34} in the component diagram. Similarly, the size of the area enclosed by a loop or cycle, such as $loop_{12345}$ in Figure 3b, indicates the net amount of heat received by the system, and hence from the first law of thermodynamics, the area represents the net amount of mechanical energy produced by the system. The direction of cycle is significant; clockwise means the system produces useful power, and anti-clockwise means that it consumes energy (refrigerators). Because the property graph captures these important relations in a simple diagrammatic fashion, the graph is a useful model for problem solving. For example, a problem solver can visualize how to increase the power output of the cycle by increasing the enclosed area, without changing its shape. This may be done by increasing both T_1 and T_2 or reducing both T_3 and T_4, but not by independently increasing s_3 (as it would no longer equal s_2).

Further, it is possible to do calculations with the property graph (F11). When calculating the output conditions of the turbine, point 3, it is necessary to know how much of the fluid is vapour and how much is liquid, the dryness fraction. This can be found from the lengths of $line_{43}$ and $line_{4g}$. The ratio of their respective lengths equals the dryness fraction (because of its definition with respect to changes in entropy). At point 4 the fraction is zero (all liquid) and at 3 the fraction is approximately 0.8 (largely vapour). The property diagram allows perceptual inferences to be made about the equality of many of the variables, because the cycle is represented by several vertical and horizontal lines. For example, given T_2 the value of s_2 can be found from standard steam tables, because point 2 is on the saturation line. Then by inspection we see that s_3 equals s_2. Knowing the dryness fraction, the temperature T_4 can be found by calculation and hence T_3 is known. This sequence of inferences also illustrates how the property diagram can be used to help plan and execute a series of computations (F12).

In this example, the component diagram and property diagram shared few functional roles, and when they did they involved different sets of information. Thus, a possible explanation of why both diagrams are needed for effective problem solving, on complex thermodynamic cycles, is that between them they support a broad range of the kinds of problems solving tasks that are required.

Discussion

The concept of functional roles and the identifying of actual functions shows that there may be a useful level of analysis of the properties of diagrams that falls between general characterisations of whole diagrams and analyses of the properties of elementary diagrammatic components. Different combinations of functional roles will determine the overall character of a diagram, by making different kinds of information more readily accessible; as seen in the two thermodynamic diagrams. This final section of the paper considers issues raised by the functional roles framework, beginning with the more specific questions.

The next stage in this research will be to apply the framework to an interesting class of diagrams, Law Encoding Diagrams, which appear to be effective representations for some forms of problem solving and for learning (Cheng, 1994, 1995, 1996, in press). A possible explanation of their advantage is that they manage to combine many functional roles in a single diagram.

It will be interesting to study whether experts exploit more of the available functional roles of diagrams than novices. Larkin and Simon (1987) consider a pulley system problem, in which the diagram of the physical arrangement of the system provides useful locational information for problem solving. This is appears to be a factor that underpins both the functional roles of depicting physical relations, F2, and sequencing computations, F12. Although Larkin and Simon's computation models do not deal with learning, it is the case that as problem solvers become more experienced on pulley problems, they can solve them by inspecting the diagram without recourse to written calculations. This might be explained by hypothesizing that they have learned that diagrams of pulley sub-assemblies capture a specific version of the lever law, perhaps in the form of a diagrammatic configuration schema (Koedinger & Anderson, 1990). This more expert-like use of the diagram could be seen in terms of exploiting the functional role of capturing laws by means of the structure of the diagram, F10. Detailed study of expert versus novice problem solving in thermodynamics would be a suitable place to begin the examination of this issue.

Wickens (1992) effectively demonstrates the need for compatibility between visual displays of information with problem solvers' mental models; an important issue for human computer interaction. The framework of functional roles may be considered as providing a further compatibility dimension for the design of such displays. A diagram or display has greater compatibility, in terms of the framework, when more of the problem solving tasks are directly supported by functional roles of the diagram(s) being used. In the thermodynamics example, if either diagram were absent, it is likely that the solutions to problems would be harder, because there is less information available to constrain problem solvers mental models of processes that are happening in the plant.

The effectiveness of a diagram for a particular functional role will, in part, depend on the way information is embodied by particular forms and combinations of elementary diagrammatic components. Cleveland and McGill (1985) have studied the perceptual processes involved in qualitative and quantitative judgements using traditional graphical representations. This may be considered as an analysis of the cognitive processes needed to exploit the displaying values functional role, F5. Similar studies could be conducted for the other functional roles; for example, what cognitive processes that are implicated in the use of a diagram that captures a law in its internal structure, (F10)?

The emphasis of the functional roles framework is on the kinds of information are available for reasoning and problem solving tasks, rather than the way in which information is structured and processed. The kinds of questions that this approach aims to address concern the types of problems to which particular diagrams are well suited. This is different, but complementary, to the previous work, described in the introduction, that considers the cognitive processes found in reasoning with diagrams, without special attention to the semantic content of the information being processed. The motivation, in part, for the present approach is to provide a principled method for the selection and design of effective diagrams for particular problems. By focusing on the functional roles of diagrams, which directly relate to the kinds of information that are easily accessible in diagrams, the framework may provide a link between the task requirements of problems and the types of activity supported by different diagrams. Work is progressing on the specification of a methodology for the selection and design of diagrams using the framework.

Investigation of the framework in relation to representations in general is also currently being pursued. The concept of functional roles is applicable to other graphical representations, such as tables, as well as to character string notations, such as algebra and written English. The central issue in this regard is to devise principled ways to identify and differentiate different the kinds of information that may be available in a representation. The work is concentrating on formal approaches to the classification of types of information, with the examination of ontologies of problem solving tasks and methods.

Acknowledgements

This research was supported by the U.K. Economic and Social Research Council. Thanks must go to members of the Centre for Research in Development Instruction and Training for their help in this work, with special thanks to David Wood, Fernand Gorbet and Shaaron Ainsworth.

References

Bertin, J. (1981). *Graphics and Graphic Information Processing*. Berlin: Walter de Gruyter.

Cheng, P. C.-H. (1994). An empirical investigation of law encoding diagrams for instruction. In *Proceedings of the 16th Annual Conference of the Cognitive Science Society*. (pp. 171-176). Hillsdale, NJ: Lawrence Erlbaum Associates.

Cheng, P. C.-H. (1995). Law encoding diagrams for instructional systems. *Journal of Artificial Intelligence in Education*, 7(1).

Cheng, P. C.-H. (1996). Learning Qualitative Relations in Physics with Law Encoding Diagrams. In *Proceeding of the Eighteenth Annual Conference of the Cognitive Science Society* Hillsdale, NJ: Lawrence Erlbaum.

Cheng, P. C.-H. (in press). Scientific discovery with law encoding diagrams. *Creativity Research Journal*.

Cheng, P. C.-H., & Simon, H. A. (1995). Scientific Discovery and Creative Reasoning with Diagrams. In S. Smith, T. Ward, & R. Finke (Eds.), *The Creative Cognition Approach* (pp. 205-228). Cambridge, MA: MIT Press.

Cleveland, W. S., & McGill, R. (1985). Graphical perception and graphical methods for analysing scientific data. *Science*, 229, 828-833.

Koedinger, K. R., & Anderson, J. R. (1990). Abstract planning and perceptual chunks: Elements of expertise in geometry. *Cognitive Science*, 14, 511-550.

Kulpa, Z. (1994). Diagrammatic representations and reasoning. *Machine Graphics and Vision*, 3(1/2), 77-103.

Larkin, J. H., & Simon, H. A. (1987). Why a diagram is (sometimes) worth ten thousand words. *Cognitive Science*, 11, 65-99.

Lohse, G., Biolsi, K., Walker, N., & Rueter, H. (1994). A classification of visual representations. *Communications of the ACM*, 37(12), 36-49.

Rogers, G. F. C., & Mayhew, Y. R. (1980). *Engineering Thermodynamics* (3rd ed.). New York, NY: Longman.

Tabachneck, H. J. M., Leonardo, A. M., & Simon, H. A. (1994). How does an expert use a graph? A model of visual and verbal inferencing in economics. In *Proceedings of the 16th Annual Conference of the Cognitive Science Society*. (pp. 842-847). Hillsdale, NJ: Lawrence Erlbaum Associates.

Wickens, C. D. (1992). *Engineering Psychology and Human Performance* (2nd ed.). New York, NY: Harper Collins.

A Study of Visual Reasoning in Medical Diagnosis

Erika Rogers

Dept. of Computer & Information Science
Clark Atlanta University
Atlanta, GA 30314
erika@pravda.gatech.edu

Abstract

The purpose of this paper is to describe experimental work conducted in the area of diagnostic radiology, with an emphasis on how perception and problem solving interact in this type of task. This work was part of a larger project whose goals included the development of an information-processing model of visual interaction, and the subsequent design of an intelligent cooperative assistant for this domain.

Verbal protocol data was collected from eight radiologists (six residents and two experts) while they examined seven different computer-displayed chest x-rays. A brief overview of the methodology and analysis techniques is presented, together with specific results from one x-ray case. More general results are then discussed in the framework of issues important to the later modeling effort.

Introduction

The current trend towards telemedicine diagnosis has created a need for enhanced software capabilities which not only enable high-speed image transmission, but which can also support the visual reasoning needed both at the local and remote sites. The cognitive load still remains squarely on the human expert's shoulders who must examine these images and make diagnostic evaluations, often without the benefit of any further tools, and with the disadvantage that these images may be both spatially- and contrast-degraded from the original film. The importance of AI tools to support such activities is therefore increasing. However, in order to build these tools, human capabilities in these tasks must be better understood, and this requires extensive cognitive study and engineering.

The study described in this paper was part of a larger project which was conducted in collaboration with the Radiology Department of Emory University Hospital. This project had three major goals: 1) to explore the nature of radiological diagnosis with a view to understanding how perception and problem solving exchange information in this type of visual reasoning task; 2) to incorporate this knowledge into an information-processing type of model of visual interaction; and 3) to utilize this cognitive foundation for the design of an intelligent cooperative assistant. The purpose of this paper is to describe some of the initial experimental work, and to show how it led to insights about visual reasoning activities.

Studies of the radiological process have varied from eye movement studies (Kundel & Nodine, 1975), to task-related hand movements (McNeill et al., 1988), to cognitive modeling studies of expertise involving think-aloud verbal protocols (Lesgold et al., 1981). While the latter provided the strongest

methodological guidelines for the study described in this paper, more emphasis was placed on the range of novice-expert performance rather than on the differences. Also, the main part of this study utilized digitized computer-displayed x-ray images rather than films, since the ultimate goal of the project was to design a computer-based assistant. A preliminary study on the effects of the laboratory environment and the computerized images showed no noticeable impact on the subjects' ability to perform diagnosis (Rogers, 1992), and therefore the next phase proceeded with more extensive think-aloud protocol collection.

Data Collection and Analysis

The goal of the verbal protocol data collection was to obtain in-depth, detailed data from the subjects while they were interpreting and diagnosing a selection of computer-displayed chest x-rays. Eight participants were recruited from the Emory University Hospital radiology program, and included two experts, plus two each from second- to fourth-year residency. Seven cases were selected for display and included one normal chest x-ray as well as the following abnormalities: lung lesion due to bronchogenic carcinoma, hilar adenopathy, tuberculosis, lung mass with appearance of elevated diaphragm, and mitral stenosis. Three of the seven images had a brief case history associated with them, and the images were presented in the Imaging Sciences laboratory at the hospital.

For each case, the subjects viewed the image as long as desired, while concurrently articulating their thoughts. When examination of the image was completed, a formal diagnostic report was produced, and each case was concluded by a set of clarifying questions, subject ratings for image quality, confidence in diagnosis and case difficulty, as well as some retrospective questions for archival purposes. All seven cases were completed in one session, which was videotaped and subsequently transcribed.

In the analysis of this data, the focus was primarily on the functions or characteristic actions that could be attributed to perception, problem solving, and the interaction between the two. Therefore, the first goal was to develop an appropriate encoding scheme which would enable these kinds of concepts to be extracted from the verbal reports.

A preliminary task analysis combined some of the earlier experimental results with Lesgold's task description of radiological diagnosis (Lesgold et al., 1981) and other problem solving concepts in medical diagnosis. A subset of the actual protocols (three of the seven cases) was then used to refine this general concept list into a more comprehensive encoding

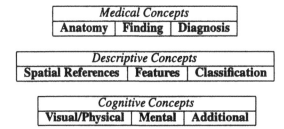

Figure 1: Concept Categories of Encoding Scheme.

	Primary Abnormality	Secondary Abnormality	Other Concepts
↓ ↓ T	LOOK-AT(ANATOMY) LOOK-AT(FINDING1.1) DESCRIBE(SIZE) DESCRIBE(EDGE) DESCRIBE(SHAPE)...		
I M			LOOK-AT(ANATOMY) CLASSIFY(NORMAL)
E ↓ ↓		LOOK-AT(ANATOMY) SEEK(FINDING2.1) NOT-FOUND(SEEK)	

Figure 2: Example of Contextual Encoding of Statements.

scheme, consisting of three major categories and a number of minor categories as shown in Figure 1. This encoding scheme was then applied to all of the remaining thirty-two verbal protocol reports[1]. The fully encoded protocols were then analyzed with respect to task-related and time-related patterns, as shown in Figure 2. (Experience-related differences were not studied at this time.)

It was found that similar clusters of concepts did occur at corresponding times for particular cases, that the groupings within the clusters or patterns showed tendencies towards perceptual or problem solving compositions, and that there appeared to be an ordering of activities in the movement towards a diagnostic solution.

A summary of the bronchogenic carcinoma case is now presented together with the expert's diagnostic report in Figure 3 to illustrate some of the features of the analysis process. This case provided the richest source of information due to the perceptual features of the image as well as the problem solving complexities of the diagnosis itself.

Figure 4 shows the subjects' ratings of this case according to image quality, overall confidence in diagnosis, and case difficulty. The image quality was considered to be adequate or better by the majority of the subjects, and therefore this did not seem to impair the examination of the case. This case was considered to be challenging by five of the subjects, even though the overall average assessment of difficulty fell somewhere between easy and challenging (2.4/5.0). Overall confidence tended to be fairly high (3.8/5.0) with only two subjects registering medium or lower confidence in their diagnoses. (In this case it was interesting to note that the subject with the lowest confidence also had the worst performance

with respect to noticing the critical secondary abnormality and producing a correct diagnosis).

Almost all of the subjects noticed and labelled the abnormality in the lung immediately upon viewing the x-ray image. This abnormality was then described by different descriptive and spatial features including (in order of frequency): size, horizontal localization, edge, vertical localization, shape, texture, out-of-plane localization and configuration. On the average, the subjects mentioned six of the above categories, which made this type of finding the most detailed in description from all of the cases examined.

One particularly noteworthy aspect of this case concerned the use of secondary findings in the diagnostic process. The bone lesion in the left posterior fifth rib was an important piece of evidence, as explained in the expert's report. Of the eight subjects, five saw the bony abnormality, three of these correctly identified it as a bone lesion, and two actually used the correct identification in the formulation of the correct diagnostic hypothesis.

The activity of localizing the primary finding also appeared to be very important, although it was perhaps made somewhat more difficult in the test situation because only one view of the patient was presented. It is more common to have two views (frontal and lateral) available, and this provides more information, particularly for anterior-posterior localization.

Results

The following discussion presents an overview of some of the results of the protocol analysis with respect to the roles of description, levels of abstraction, context, attention and expectation. These were considered to be key issues which would impact the subsequent development of the information-processing model.

---

[1] An independent observer was recruited to participate in a reliability study. Details can be found in (Rogers, 1992)

Report: A frontal film of the chest shows a large, lobulated mass in the upper right hemithorax, abutting on the mediastinum. It does not obliterate the silhouette of the superior vena cava and ascending aorta and probably lies posterior in the chest. No other lesions are seen in the lungs. The right hilum appears normal. There is no hilar or mediastinal adenopathy on the left side. However, there is a destructive lesion of the left 5th rib. There is no evidence of pleural effusion. The heart appears normal.

Impression: Bronchogenic carcinoma with distant metastasis to the left 5th rib.

Comments: The presence of a lobulated mass in a patient of this age should make carcinoma the first diagnosis. However, conceivably another lesion such as a hamartoma could produce a similar appearance. I did not mention that there is no calcification within the lesion although I should have. What makes this diagnosis unequivocal in this case is the destruction of the rib on the left side. This may be difficult to see as the area of destruction is caused by the anterior end of the 2nd rib and unless they look carefully they will not pick it up. The other descriptions are simply pertinent negatives in a patient who is suspected of having carcinoma. Key words - mass, lobulated, rib destruction, hamartoma, carcinoma, adenopathy. Because of the rib lesion not being obvious, this should be considered a median difficult case unless you give it a history pointing to the correct area.

Figure 3: Expert's Report for Case 3 - Bronchogenic Carcinoma.

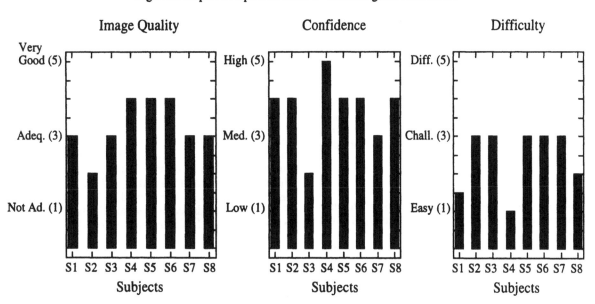

Figure 4: Subject Ratings for Case 3.

Description

For all the cases considered, the characterization of abnormalities in terms of distinct descriptive features was accomplished using a relatively small number of categories. Size, shape, edge, texture, and quantity descriptions were used in varying degrees, depending upon the type of abnormality presented. Sometimes features of the primary finding figured notably in the diagnostic process, while at other times, the findings were described in less detail, and other information such as case history figured more prominently in eliciting accurate diagnostic hypotheses. This suggested that the importance of particular features may vary depending upon the type of abnormality under consideration, and an accurate perceptual characterization of a finding may still not be sufficient to produce a distinct disease diagnosis.

Abnormalities were also described in terms of spatial relations, with references to horizontal and vertical directions most prevalent. The out-of-plane third dimension appeared to be important in cases where there was a mass that appeared to span more than one anatomical landmark. In these cases, shadows on the frontal two-dimensional view could give some clues to location, if the film was of relatively good quality, but often, a lateral view would have served to disambiguate these cases.

Levels of Abstraction

The characterization of findings (i.e., abnormalities in the image) at different levels of abstraction provides an important transition between low-level perceptual detection and higher level problem solving activities. For example, the statement "there is a density" really only means "I have detected a light area", without conveying any further semantic information regarding what this object might represent. On the other hand, a term such as "there is a mass" implies certain associated features such as size, shape and edge, while a statement about a "malignant tumor" suggests not only specific features, but specific diagnostic hypotheses as well.

215

15.	Now...let's see, the heart's normal.
16.	The hilar structures are normal.
17.	The aorta's normal.
18.	The trachea's normal.
19.	The right para...stripe, tracheal wall seems to be normal.
20.	The bony structures are normal.

Figure 5: Landmark Search.

6.	Looking at the rest of the lungs, I don't see any areas of consolidation or evidence of pneumonia there.
7.	I don't see any effusions.
8.	I'm going to look at the remainder of the superior mediastinum
9.	to see if I see any other adenopathy
10.	and sort of in the left heart border I see a kind of a double bulge

Figure 6: Bottom-Up Secondary Finding Search.

7.	but the first thing I saw was the heart,
8.	and I, it's just a little bit big.
9.	Now patients with heart failure can get something like a cough with a little bit of pink frothy sputum.
10.	It's not really sputum, it's just sometimes they can cough up some pink stuff.
11.	So I'm going to think about heart failure,
12.	and look for pulmonary edema,
13.	or signs of heart failure.

Figure 7: Top-Down Secondary Finding Search.

Not only is the type of labeling activity important, but the manner in which the labeled percepts are used can seriously affect the outcome of the diagnostic process. Different levels of oversights occurred in the transition between perception and problem solving. At the perceptual level, a *detection* oversight occurred when the subject did not notice or see the abnormal object or feature at all. On the other hand, at the identification level, a *labeling* error occurred when the subject saw the abnormality in question, but labeled it incorrectly. Finally, at the problem solving level, difficulty with *integration* was encountered when the subject saw and labeled the abnormality correctly, but failed to use this information in the generation of diagnostic hypotheses. An implication of these results is that the design of computerized assistance really should span the visual interaction spectrum between perception and problem solving, and not just address the poles of the problem, for example, through either image enhancements to aid perception or expert systems to aid decision-making.

Context

When the radiologist begins a diagnostic session, the information available prior to viewing any of the images includes the knowledge of the particular anatomical region under consideration and the particular imaging modality used to collect the image data. The anatomical region normally implies a certain set of anatomical objects in a particular configuration (e.g., a chest normally contains two lungs, a heart on the lower left side, etc.), while the imaging modality calls into play knowledge of the kinds of perceptual cues that are to be expected.

This knowledge is typically organized into a kind of checklist that leads to a relatively orderly plan for examination. An example of this is seen in Figure 5, which shows a sequential set of statements by a subject looking at the normal chest case.

Unlike the landmark search, which can be said to always be of a top-down nature, the search for secondary abnormalities may be either bottom-up or top-down. If no diagnostic hypothesis has been invoked, and the subject is still gathering data, then the search for such abnormalities may appear as a subplan within the landmark search. Figure 6 illustrates such a bottom-up search in the sarcoidosis case. On the other hand, top-down reasoning implies that one or more diagnostic hypotheses are currently active, and that particular secondary findings might support these hypotheses. An example of this is seen in Figure 7, which is an excerpt from the mitral stenosis case.

Further suggestions of plan-like activity can be found in the description of a primary finding in terms of its features and location. For some types of findings, a large number of characteristic features are expressed and utilized in the diag-

nostic process. An example is shown in Figure 8, taken from a subject's report on the tuberculosis case. In other cases, features were sought which led to either more specific finding hypotheses, or even diagnostic hypotheses. Thus the data supports the claim that the "direction of reasoning provides the procedural context" (Evans & Gadd, 1989), and that there are different types of plans, and different levels of planning. Furthermore, the direction of reasoning affected the different types of perceptual information used to support the diagnostic stages. Bottom-up or data-driven reasoning was supported by use of secondary *findings* to generate diagnostic hypotheses, use of *features* of primary findings to specialize labeling of primary findings, and use of *features* of primary findings to generate diagnostic hypotheses. On the other hand, top-down or expectation-driven reasoning involved confirmation of expectation of secondary *findings* to support diagnostic hypotheses, use of *features* of primary findings to rule out competing findings and diagnostic hypotheses, and use of *features* of primary findings to match or contradict expectations.

Attention

In the cases reviewed, at least two different types of attention activity were noted. The first, characterized by a relatively

5.	I'm kind of focussing in on the main abnormality, which is in the right upper lobe,
6.	and I see a cavitary lesion in the right upper lobe, with some atelectatic changes.
...	
13.	The lesion is poorly defined, and has a cavitary area in the center, and the wall is probably about 3 to 4 millimeters thick, and it's irregular.
14.	There are some linear densities leading from the hilar region to the mass.

Figure 8: Features of Primary Finding.

> ...It looks like the mass itself is not as dense as you might expect for something that large.
>
> ...I'm thinking in terms of a neurogenic tumor, and you might expect to see...some involvement of the vertebral bodies...
>
> ...Ah, in a young person, you really wouldn't be expecting to see something like that anyway. It would be unlikely.
>
> ...I looked at the ribs. I didn't see anything and I wasn't expecting to see anything there.

Figure 9: Expectations.

fast noticing and labeling of an abnormality as soon as the x-ray image appeared was called "immediate visual capture", and it was often coupled with a brief description of the abnormality in question (for example, size and shape). This type of attentional behavior has also been described by Kundel and Nodine who showed that even under restricted conditions, selective attention was drawn to the area of the chest having the greatest abnormality (Kundel & Nodine, 1975).

In more general experiments on attention, Treisman showed that simple property differences (e.g., color, brightness, or line orientation) would be seized upon by the initial stage of visual processing so that they appear to "pop out" of a scene (Treisman, 1982). Immediate visual capture appears to be consistent with these findings: if an object composed primarily of water (such as a tumor) overlies an object composed primarily of air (such as lung), then the first object will appear brighter. If the same object overlies bone, it will appear darker. Thus certain types of brightness features in the x-ray image may be more conducive to such preattentive visual pop-out.

Treisman also required subjects to find a target distinguished by the *lack* of a feature present in the distractor. She found that pop-out occurred when the target had the feature, and serial search occurred when the target lacked the feature. In our data analysis, attention was focused purposefully and serially in the activities of deliberate landmark search and serial search for secondary abnormalities which might or might not be in the image. Although Treisman's work emphasizes simple objects and features, it is possible that similar behavior may occur if someone has been trained to recognize particular objects and features in a manner that is meaningful to a problem solving task such as diagnostic radiology.

Expectation

Throughout the reports of the subjects, there was evidence that prior experience and medical knowledge were often used in conjunction with current observations to produce anticipation of particular kinds of related information from the image. These anticipations include presence or absence of features related to a finding, findings related to a diagnosis, and findings or diagnoses related to case history. These are called expectations, and Figure 9 shows examples of excerpts from the raw data of a number of subjects that lend support to this idea.

Expectations may be used by the problem solver to optimize plans for the gathering of information that will converge on a solution. For example, if a diagnostic hypothesis is cur-

rently active, it may be more efficient to explore findings and features that are usually expected to be associated with that hypothesis first, rather than just gather unstructured perceptual information in the hope that some of it may be useful. Expectation-driven exploration is the hallmark of top-down processing. When observations match expectations, confidence in the originating hypothesis should increase. On the other hand, when observations fail to meet expectations, a decision must be made as to whether this information can be overlooked, or whether it signals that the hypothesis should be abandoned. In the task of diagnostic radiology, it appears that expectations are largely perceptual in nature, especially in the absence of other information about the patient, such as test results, or physical examination. That is, most expectations have to do with anticipations about what can be seen in the image. In this sense, the expectations generated in this task appear to be dual in nature, in that they can originate with an abstract statement of intent, such as "I'm going to look for pleural effusions", that may be part of a larger plan to distinguish between some hypotheses, but they result in an act of looking: "I don't see any." Thus, expectation may be one of the mechanisms that bridges the gap between perception and problem solving.

Discussion

All of the above issues are closely coupled in the visual reasoning task of chest x-ray diagnosis. Context sets the scene for a particular collection of declarative and procedural knowledge to be retrieved from memory and brought to bear on the problem. This knowledge creates expectations of what the practitioner is likely to see, and plans to explore these expectations emerge, that then guide the attention process in deliberate search. However, there are often unexpected phenomena in the image, which seem to capture attention immediately, and cause currently active plans to be interrupted or abandoned in favor of new exploratory activity[2]. Descriptive features are used to characterize findings, which, in turn, are labelled at different levels of abstraction.

In the interplay between these issues, a pattern of interaction between perception and problem solving begins to emerge. Descriptive features can be said to lie closer to the perceptual side, while context seems to originate with more abstract thought related to problem solving. Expectations appear to lie between these two poles, originating with problem solving, but resulting in the activation of perceptual schemas through focus of attention, which direct acts of looking. These schemas allow perceptual information to be delivered back, and the levels of abstraction mentioned above provide a way to transform the information between expectation and perceptual schema, so that it can be used by the process concerned with achieving a solution to the problem.

These results may also provide a perceptual foundation for the diagnostic strategies employed by the radiologists, and an indication of why such strategies might succeed or fail. For example, in the case presented earlier, one of the subjects exhibited a very typical hypothetico-deductive strategy, where immediate visual capture provided initial data, some search of

---

[2]This is also consistent with Lesgold et al's (1988) contention that expert radiologists are opportunistic planners. However, we saw this kind of activity in less experienced radiologists as well.

the primary finding provided more evidence, and a diagnostic hypothesis was then produced. However, particular evidence was then obtained which contradicted the ensuing expectation, causing the original hypothesis to be abandoned in favor of a new (more accurate) one. Based on this new hypothesis, the subject then looked for supporting evidence, found it in the image, and thereby increased confidence. On the other hand, a second (more experienced) subject examined the same case, but spent most of the diagnostic period gathering perceptual evidence about the primary finding, and never really generated a diagnostic hypothesis at all.

A third example involved a case with an ambiguous primary finding [3]. For this case, some subjects who generated diagnostic hypotheses based on the incorrect finding, never did recover from the original error, while other subjects who appeared to engage in a more deliberate prolonged collection of perceptual information (not specifically related to a diagnostic hypothesis), eventually "saw" a clue, which led to the correct labelling of the finding. This case is interesting from the point of view that there is no really accurate *diagnosis* associated with the x-ray. However, the correct labelling of the finding is the best solution that can be attained, and is important to direct the next step in the patient care. It also suggests that a "not-enough-information" strategy might have been more appropriate in this case, rather than the hypothetico-deductive reasoning which generated early, but inaccurate diagnostic hypotheses.

In the absence of immediate visual capture, deliberate search of landmarks appears to be the common strategy employed. It is often repeated at least once if the patient appears to have a normal chest. It may also be a useful strategy when there is ambiguity in the x-ray image that might be removed by a more thorough investigation of the landmarks. For example, in the previously described ambiguous case, the visual clue concerned a part of the lung which was hard to see, but visible nonetheless. The subjects who looked specifically at that landmark area saw the clue.

Conclusion

The results from this work have been incorporated into a model of visual interaction between perception and problem solving, described in (Rogers, 1995a). This model has been further used as the basis for the design of a blackboard-based computer system called VIA (Visual Interaction Assistant), which incorporates the user, the image display and the program modules into a cooperative, problem solving system. The design has been instantiated into a prototype system for diagnostic radiology called VIA-RAD, and was tested in a small observational study with radiologist subjects (Rogers, 1995b). It is felt that the promising results of this work are due largely to the in-depth study of how practitioners actually perform their task. This approach provides not only further insight into visual diagnostic reasoning but also establishes a firm cognitive foundation for the development of intelligent computerized assistants.

---

[3]The subjects commonly mislabelled the finding as an elevated diaphragm, when it was really a mass inside the lung.

Acknowledgements

This work has been supported by NSF grant IRI-9502289, Army Center of Excellence in Information Science ARO Grant DAAL03-92-G-0377, and the Emory/Georgia Tech Biotechnology Research Center. Special thanks to the members of the Radiology Dept. and the Imaging Sciences Laboratory at Emory University Hospital.

References

Evans, D. A. & Gadd, C. S. (1989). Managing coherence and context in medical problem-solving discourse. In D. A. Evans, & V. L. Patel (Eds.), *Cognitive Science in Medicine* (pp. 211–255). Cambridge, MA: MIT Press.

Kundel, H. & Nodine, C. (1975). Interpreting chest radiographs without visual search. *Radiology*, 116, 527–532.

Lesgold, A., Rubinson, H. R., Feltovich, P. F., Glaser, R., Klopfer, D., & Wang, Y. (1988). Expertise in a complex skill: Diagnosing x-ray pictures. In M. T. H. Chi, R. Glaser, & M. J. Farr (Eds.), *The Nature of Expertise* (pp. 311–342). Hillsdale, NJ: Lawrence Erlbaum Associates.

Lesgold, A., Feltovich, P. F., Glaser, R., & Wang, Y. (1981). The acquisition of perceptual diagnostic skill in radiology. Tech. Rep. PDS-1, LRDC.

McNeill, K. M., Seeley, G. W., Maloney, K., Fajardo, L., & Kozik, M. (1988). Comparison of digital workstations and conventional reading for evaluation of user interfaces in digital radiology. In *SPIE Medical Imaging II*, 914, 872–876.

Rogers, E. (1992). *Visual Interaction: A Link Between Perception and Problem-Solving*. (Tech. Rep. GIT-CC-92/59). Doctoral dissertation. Atlanta: Georgia Institute of Technology, College of Computing.

Rogers, E. (1995a). A cognitive theory of visual interaction. In B. Chandrasekaran, J. Glasgow, & N. H. Narayanan (Eds.), *Diagrammatic Reasoning: Computational and Cognitive Perspectives* (pp. 481–500). Menlo Park, CA: AAAI/MIT Press.

Rogers, E. (1995b). Via-rad: A blackboard-based system for diagnostic radiology. *Artificial Intelligence in Medicine*, 7, 343–360.

Treisman, A. (1982). Perceptual grouping and attention in visual search for features and for objects. *Journal of Experimental Psychology, Human Perceptual Performance*, 8(2), 194–214.

The Interaction of Semantic and Phonological Processing

Lorraine K. Tyler[1]
J. Kate Voice[2]
Centre for Speech and Language
Department of Psychology
Birkbeck College
Malet Street
London WC1E 7HX
Tel: (44) 171 631 6589
fax: (44) 171 631 6312

[1] ubjta39@ccs.bbk.ac.uk
[2] ubjta70@ccs.bbk.ac.uk

&
Helen E. Moss
Department of Psychology
Glasgow University,
Glasgow

helen@psy.gla.ac.uk

Abstract

Models of spoken word recognition vary in the ways in which they capture the relationship between speech input and meaning. Modular accounts prohibit a word's meaning from affecting the computation of its form-based representation, whereas interactive models allow semantic activation to affect phonological processing. To test these competing hypotheses we manipulated word familiarity and imageability, using auditory lexical decision and repetition tasks. Responses to high imageability words were significantly faster than to low imageability words. Response latencies were also analysed as a function of cohort variables; cohort size and frequency of cohort members. High and low imageable words were divided into 2 sets: (a) large cohorts with many high frequency competitors, (b) small cohorts with few high frequency competitors. Analyses showed that there was only a significant imageability effect for the words which were members of large cohorts. These data suggest that when the mapping from phonology to semantics is difficult (when a spoken word activates a large cohort consisting of many high frequency competitors), semantic information can help the discrimination process. Because highly imageable words are "semantically richer" and/or more context-independent, they provide more activation to phonology than do low imageability words. Thus, these data provide strong support for interactive models of spoken word recognition.

Introduction

Models of spoken word recognition vary in the ways in which they capture the relationship between phonology and semantics. Accounts assuming a modular structure, with the speech input passing through a series of stages until the meaning of the word is accessed (e.g. Forster, 1979), share the view that the speech input is initially mapped onto a level of form representation. Only when this process is completed can meaning be accessed; the meaning of a word cannot affect the computation of its form-based representation. In contrast, interactive models of word recognition (e.g. McClelland & Elman, 1986) assume feedback between different levels of processing. Although there is no extant interactive model which captures the entire process of spoken word recognition, from analysing the speech input to accessing meaning, we can extrapolate from existing models which capture part of the word recognition process. In TRACE, for example, the speech input is initially mapped onto a featural level of representation, then onto a phoneme level and finally onto a word level (McClelland & Elman, 1986). Interaction is achieved by feedforward and feedback between levels. If this model was extended beyond the word-form level to semantics, and assuming the same structure, semantic information would feed back to the word-form level. Thus, this kind of model would predict that the computation of a word's form could be affected by its meaning.

Experimental investigations of the relationship between form and meaning have often exploited imageability[1] (see Balota, Ferraro & Connor, 1991 for a review). The imageability of a word is the degree to which its referent can be perceived through the senses; for example, *table* is highly imageable whereas *hope* is low in imageability. The empirical issue is whether a purely semantic variable - imageability - can affect phonological processing. If it does,

---

[1] We use the terms imageability and concreteness interchangeably here

this might result in high imageability words being recognised more easily than low imageability words; this would be evidence that meaning variables affect word identification.

However, testing this claim crucially requires a task which taps into the early stages of word recognition; a task which reflects the automatic activation of phonological and semantic information during the process of recognising a spoken word. There are two primary candidates: word naming and lexical decision (cf Balota et al, 1991). Naming is generally considered to tap early activation processes, whereas lexical decision may include a post-access decision stage, making it less suitable for probing early word recognition processes.

Although few studies have directly explored the relationship between phonology and meaning, a number of experiments have focussed on a related issue - whether meaning has an early influence on word recognition. These experiments typically involve subjects making lexical decisions to written words of varying degrees of imageability. Some, although not all, have reported an advantage for highly imageable words in lexical decision (e.g. Rubenstein, Garfield & Millikan, 1970; de Groot, 1989; Schwanenflugel, Harnishfeger & Stowe, 1988), but it is difficult to argue on the basis of LD data alone for the early influence of semantics, given the possibility that LD latencies may involve post-access phenomena.

A more direct test of the relationship between phonology and meaning involves subjects naming written words. Semantic effects in word naming are even more elusive, with studies showing either very small (deGroot, 1989) or no effects of imageability (Brown & Watson, 1987). Recently, however, Strain, Patterson & Seidenberg (1995) have reported an imageability effect for low frequency exception words with naming, arguing that when the orthographic to phonological mapping is slow, inefficient or error prone, meaning plays a larger role in word naming.

The semantics/phonology interaction is most directly studied by investigating imageability effects in spoken word recognition. This avoids any problems with the orthography-phonology mapping. The question we ask in the studies reported here is whether imageability affects the computation of a phonological representation during the processing of a spoken word. If it does, this is evidence for a highly interactive word recognition system.

Experiments

In this research we manipulate imageability and use two tasks - word repetition and auditory lexical decision - in order to probe the effect of semantics on phonology. Using LD allows a direct comparison with research in the visual domain looking at imageability effects, and repetition is considered to be a more direct reflection of the automatic activation of phonological information without accompanying post-access processes (Balota et al, 1991).

Auditory lexical decision

In this study, subjects heard a mixed list of words and non-words and made a lexical decision to each item. The set was comprised of 46 high imageability words (imageability and concreteness ratings>540) and 46 low imageability words (<400), which were further grouped into 2 equal-sized familiarity bands; high familiarity (familiarity rating >550) and low familiarity (<420). High and low imageability words within the same familiarity band were matched as closely as possible in terms of frequency and familiarity, number of syllables, number of phonemes and phoneme onset (Table 1). Familiarity and imageability ratings were from the MRC database (Coltheart, 1981); frequencies were calculated using the LOB norms (Johansson & Hofland, 1989). We could not perfectly match the frequencies of the two sets of high frequency words, but the higher frequency of the low imageability words is a conservative solution since it should increase the probability of faster responses to low imageability words, thus loading the dice against our pedicted outcome. The words, all of which were 1-2 syllable nouns, were pseudo-randomly mixed with an equal number of non-words.

Familiarity	High		Low	
Imageability	Low	High	Low	High
Mean concreteness	314	600	314	594
Mean imageability	351	600	331	571
Mean familiarity	578	588	353	373
Mean frequency	222	90	6	2
Mean No. syllables	1.5	1.5	1.8	1.6
Mean No. phonemes	4.4	4.2	4.7	4.6

Table 1: Statistics of the high and low imageability words.

The results given below are for 14 subjects, all native speakers of British English. An ANOVA showed a main effect of imageability ($F^1[1,13]$=53.18, p<.001; $F^2[1,84]$=5.49, p<.02), with LD latencies being faster to high (817 ms) compared to low imageability words (854ms). Highly familiar words (798 ms) were also identified significantly faster than low familiarity words (877 ms). Imageability did not interact with familiarity.

Imageability	Familiarity	
	High	Low
Low	829	881
High	769	872
Difference	60	9

Table 2: Lexical decision latencies (ms).

Repetition

The same real words were then run in a repetition study, with subjects repeating each word as rapidly as possible. Repetition latencies for 12 subjects were significantly faster for high imageability (397 ms) compared to low imageability (442 ms) words ($F^1[1,11]$=10.63, p<.001; $F^2[1,84]$=5.43, p<.02). Once again, there was a significant effect of familiarity (high: 396 ms; low:441 ms) and no interactions.

	Familiarity	
Imageability	High	Low
Low	424	456
High	371	428
Difference	53	28

Table 3: Repetition latencies (ms).

Cohort analyses

Because we were dealing with spoken rather than written words, we also analysed repetition and lexical decision latencies as a function of cohort variables which may affect the recognition of spoken words; cohort size and frequency of cohort competitors. Cohorts were defined as those words sharing the initial consonant-vowel or consonant-vowel cluster. We also measured the frequency of the target word in relation to the frequency of its cohort competitors [frequency of target/total frequency of cohort members x 100]. High and low imageable words were divided into 2 sets according to whether they were members of large cohorts with many high frequency competitors or small cohorts with few high frequency competitors. (Table 4).

Imageability	High		Low	
Cohort size	Large	Small	Large	Small
Mean concreteness	587	597	317	311
Mean cohort size	236	22	280	40
Mean % cohort*	3.5	22	6	22

*the smaller the value, the greater the competition

Table 4: Cohort variables.

We included the cohort variable in further ANOVAs and found that there was only a significant imageability effect for the words which were members of large cohorts. These results are shown in Tables 5 & 6.

	Cohort size	
Imageability	Large	Small
Low	898	812
High	794	829
Difference	104*	-17

* F^1 & F^2 significant at the .05 level or beyond

Table 5: Lexical decision latencies (ms).

	Cohort size	
Imageability	Large	Small
Low	438	438
High	367	423
Difference	71*	15

* F^1 & F^2 significant at the .05 level or beyond

Table 6: Repetition latencies (ms).

Discussion

Our results are compatible with interactionist models in which: (a) there is parallel activation of multiple candidates initiated by the speech input, and (b) where phonological and semantic representations interact with each other. This includes hierarchically structured models in which there is continuous feedback and feedforward throughout the system, as well as interactionist models in which there is no hierarchical structure, such as that of Gaskell & Marslen-Wilson, 1995. In their model, phonological and semantic representations reside at the same level in the system, and are simultaneously co-activated by the speech input.

Our data suggest that when a spoken word activates a large cohort consisting of many high frequency competitors the mapping from phonology to semantics becomes more difficult; highly activated words compete with the less highly activated target word. Although there is continuous interaction between phonology and semantics for all words, irrespective of imageability, semantic information has a larger role to play as the discrimination process becomes more difficult. Highly imageable words provide more activation to phonology than do low imageability words. This may be because they are "semantically richer" in that they have more and varied semantic representations, as Plaut & Shallice (1993) have suggested, or because their representations are more context-independent.

Our data, and the account we provide of them, is consistent with the recent findings of Strain et al (1995). In a word naming task in which subjects were asked to name regular and exception words varying in imageability and familiarity, they only found an advantage for high imageability low frequency exception words. Strain et al (1995) argue that semantic representations have their greatest influence when the mapping from orthography to phonology is most difficult. Similarly, we argue that as it becomes more difficult to discriminate between a word and its competitors (when cohort members increase in number and frequency), semantics becomes increasingly influential. In general, these data are incompatible with models which assume a strict separation between phonological and semantic levels, and instead provide strong support for interactive models of spoken word recognition.

References

Balota, D., Ferraro, R., & Connor, L. (1991) On the early influence of meaning in word recognition: A review of the literature. In: P. Schwanenflugel (Ed.) *The Psychology of Word Meanings*. LEA: Hillsdale.

Brown, G.D. & Watson, F. L. (1987) First in, last out: Word learning age and spoken word frequency as predictors of word familiarity and word naming latency. *Memory and Cognition*, 15, 208-216.

Coltheart, M. (1981) The MRC psycholinguistic database. *Quarterly Journal of Experimental Psychology*, 33a, 497-505.

deGroot, A.M.B. (1989) Representational aspects of word imageability and word frequency as assessed through word associations. *Journal of Experimental Psychology: Learning, Memory & Cognition*, 15, 824-845.

McClelland, J. & Elman, J. (1986) The TRACE model of speech perception. In McClelland, J.L. & Rumelhart, D. (Eds) *Parallel distributed processing: Explorations in the microstructure of cognition.* Cambridge, Mass: Bradford Books.

Forster, K. (1979) Levels of processing and the structure of the language processor. In W.E. Cooper & E. Walker (Eds) *Sentence processing: Psychological studies presented to Merrill Garrett*, Hillsdale, NJ: LEA

Gaskell, G. & Marslen-Wilson, W.D. (1995) Modelling the perception of spoken words. *Proceedings of the 17th Annual Cognitive Science Conference*, Hillsdale, NJ: Erlbaum.

Johansson, S. & Hofland, K. (1989) *Frequency analysis of English vocabulary and grammar*. Oxford: Oxford University Press.

Rubenstein, H. Garfield, L. & Millikan, J. (1970) Homographic entries in the internal lexicon. *Journal of Verbal Learning and Verbal Behaviour*, 9, 487-494.

Schwanenflugel, P. Harnishfeger, K. & Stowe, R. (1988) Context availability and lexical decisions for abstract and concrete words. *Journal of Memory and Language*, 27, 499-520.

Strain, E., Patterson, K.E & Seidenberg, M. (1995) Semantic effects in single word naming. *Journal of Experimental Psychology: Learning, Memory & Cognition.*

The combinatorial lexicon: Priming derivational affixes

William D. Marslen-Wilson, Mike Ford, Lianne Older, and Zhou Xiaolin
Centre for Speech and Language
Birkbeck College
London WC1E 7HX England
w.marslen-wilson@psyc.bbk.ac.uk

Abstract

In earlier research we argued for a morphemically decomposed account of the mental representation of semantically transparent derived forms, such as *happiness, rebuild,* and *punishment.* We proposed that such forms were represented as stems linked to derivational affixes, as in {happy} + {-ness} or {re-} + {build}. A major source of evidence for this was the pattern of priming effects, between derived forms and their stems, in a cross-modal repetition priming task. In two new experiments we investigated the prediction of this account that derivational affixes, such as {-ness} or {re-}, should also exist as independent entities in the mental lexicon, and should also be primable. We tested both prefixes and suffixes, split into productive and unproductive groups (where "unproductive" means no longer used to form new words), and found significant priming effects in the same cross-modal task. These effects were strongest for the productive suffixes and prefixes, as in prime-target pairs such as *darkness/toughness* and *rearrange/rethink,* where the overall effects were as strong as those for derived/stem pairs such as *absurdity/absurd,* and where possible phonological effects are ruled out by the absence of priming in phonological control and pseudo-affix conditions. We interpret this as evidence for a combinatorial approach to lexical representation.

Introduction

In previous papers delivered to this society, and elsewhere, we have argued for a morphological approach to the mental lexicon (e.g., Marslen-Wilson, Tyler, Waksler, & Older, 1992; 1994). In particular, we have argued that morphologically complex words in English, such as *happiness, disconnect, breakable,* etc., are mentally represented as two or more morphemes - *happy + ness, dis + connect, break + able* - rather than as single units. The research we report here takes this work a significant step further, showing priming between derivational affixes. This is strong evidence not only for the *combinatorial* nature of the mental computations underlying lexical representation and processing, but also for the truly *morphological* - and not simply semantic - nature of the effects we are dealing with.

We will begin by outlining our basic claims about the properties of lexical representations, summarising the kinds of evidence and the experimental techniques involved in establishing these claims. The first point to make clear is that what we are talking about is the properties of the *lexical entry* - of the modality-independent central representation of a word's semantic, syntactic, and morphological properties. We distinguish this from any modality-specific *access representations* involved in the initial mapping from speech or text onto the lexical entry.

We are concerned, then, with these core structures of the mental lexicon. To ensure that this is the level that we are tapping into experimentally, we have mainly used a *cross-modal repetition priming* task (which we also use in the experiments reported here). This is a task where subjects hear an auditorily presented prime word, and immediately at the offset of this word they see a visual target - a word or nonword to which they have to make a lexical decision.

The advantage of this task is that it allows us to tap directly into the state of representations at the level of the lexical entry. Cross-modal priming reflects repeated access to lexical representations shared by prime and target. The word *happiness,* for example, primes the word *happy* (relative to some control prime), because both prime and target have in common the morpheme {happy}. The activation of this morpheme, as a consequence of hearing the prime, speeds up subsequent recognition (and hence lexical decision) for the same morpheme when presented as a word on its own.

On the basis of several experiments looking at derivationally suffixed and prefixed words in English, we have argued for a morphologically decomposed mental lexicon. Specifically, we propose a model where morphologically complex forms are mentally represented in a {stem + affix} format. Each complex word is made up of a stem and one or more affixes. These stems are always free morphemes - that is, they can stand alone as individual words in English. For example, the morpheme {govern} functions in this framework both as a word on its own, and as a stem in forms like *government, misgovern, ungovernable,* and so on.

Crucially, this decomposed {stem + affix} arrangement only applies to semantically transparent derived forms. A word like *department,* for example, cannot be meaningfully decomposed into the stem *depart* plus the affix *-ment,* and must be represented at the level of the lexical entry as a simple form, without any internal structure, just as if it were a monomorphemic word.

Here we see an important contrast between *stored* lexical representations, which are in some sense *looked up*, because they already exist in the system as complete structures, as opposed to the representation of more transparent words, like *rebuild* or *lateness*. These, we argue, are not stored in the same way. Their meanings, and their grammatical properties, have to be computed as the word is heard or read, by combining the properties of the stem with the properties of the affix.

This is a strongly combinatorial view of lexical representation and processing, and it assigns a crucial role not just to the stem morphemes but also to the *affixes*; the derivational suffixes and prefixes in English which combine with stems to form new words, often with very different syntactic and semantic properties. Combining the affix {-ness} with the stem {dirty}, for example, converts an adjective into an abstract noun (*dirtiness*). Combining the affix {-er} with the stem {build}, converts a verb into a noun (*builder*), and so on.

These are powerful operations, and any morphologically based theory of lexical representation will have to have some way of accommodating them. But although linguistic accounts of morphology have had a lot to say about affixes, there has been very little experimental work on their mental representation. Psycholinguistic work, ours included, has been much more interested in the properties of stems. But until we understand more about affixes, and about how they fulfil their central role in lexical representation and processing, any theory of the mental lexicon will be incomplete; especially any theory arguing for a morphemically decomposed lexicon organised around combinatorial operations.

As a first step in this direction, we address here the question of whether derivational affixes are independent entities in the lexical system. The affixes we are dealing with are all *bound* morphemes. This means that they cannot, unlike free morphemes, stand alone as words in English. There is no word *ness*, corresponding to the -*ness* in *darkness*; there is no word *ment*, corresponding to the -*ment* in *punishment*; there is no word *re*, corresponding to the *re-* in *rebuild* or *reopen*. These are all bound morphemes that can only occur in conjunction with a stem. But does this also mean that they cannot stand alone as cognitive elements, represented separately from the stems to which they apply?

It follows from our decompositional approach to lexical representation that this should be the case; that affixes should be independently represented as morphemic elements. On a strongly combinatorial view, the -*ness* in *happiness* should be the same as the -*ness* in *darkness*; the *re-* in *refill* should be the same as the *re-* in *rebuild*, and so on. This predicts that we should be able to get priming between these forms. *Darkness* should prime *happiness*, in much the same way, and for the same reasons, as two forms sharing the same stem. If we do get priming, this would be a strong confirmation of the approach we have been developing

In contrast, on an approach where morphologically complex words are separately represented, so that *happiness* does not share a morpheme with *happy*, and where the *ness* in *happiness* is not the same processing entity as the *ness* in *darkness*, then there should be no priming between items which share the same affix. We report here two experiments designed to test these questions.

Experiment 1

The first goal of the experiment is to compare affix priming with stem priming. Will we get affix priming at all? Will it be comparable to typical stem priming effects?

In this first experiment we include the two major *affix types* in English: *suffixes* and *prefixes*. Suffixes in English, such as *-ment*, *-ness*, *-ation*, typically have major syntactic and semantic effects on their stems, converting them into quite different linguistic objects. English prefixes, such as *un-*, *re-*, *-dis*, typically have more restricted effects. They normally do not change syntactic class - *rebuild* is still a verb - but introduce notions such as negation or repetition, Where there is no *a priori* reason to expect priming results to vary as a function of affix type, it is still an important variable to keep controlled.

The second important factor is *affix productivity* - whether an affix is still being used in ordinary speech to form new words. This may well interact with possible priming effects. Productive affixes like *-ness* or *re-* are more likely to be independently represented - and therefore primable - than affixes like *en-* (as in *enslave*) or *-th* (as in *depth*) which are no longer productive in the language.

The design of the resulting cross-modal priming experiment (auditory primes, visual targets) is outlined in Table 1. The two variables of affix type and productivity give us 4 sets of 24 affixed prime-target pairs, with a further comparison set of 24 prime-target words sharing the same stems. All stimuli, whether primes or targets, were semantically transparent, as established on the basis of the appropriate pretests. Each related prime was paired with an unrelated control prime, matched in frequency and number of syllables, to provide a baseline for measuring possible priming effects.

Suffixes	**Prime**	**Target**
Productive	darkness	toughness
UnProductive	development	government
Prefixes		
Productive	rearrange	rethink
UnProductive	enslave	encircle
Stems	absurdity	absurd

Table 1. Experiment 1: Design and sample stimuli

The productive suffixes included affixes such as *-ation*, *-able*, and *-ness*, contrasting with nonproductive suffixes such as *-ment*, *-al*, and *-ate*. Productive prefixes included *re-*, *pre-*, and *dis-*, contrasting with unproductive prefixes like *en-*, *in-*, and *mis-*.

The results, listed in Table 2, are straightforward. There is a significant priming for productive suffixes and prefixes, and this is of the same order of magnitude as the effects obtained for the comparison group of stem priming stimuli. In contrast, effects are reduced for the unproductive affixes, with no significant effect for the suffixes, and only marginal effects for the prefixes. There is, however, no overall statistical interaction between productivity and priming effects; just the overall main effect of prime type (F1[1,25] = 30.2, p<.001; F2[1,82] = 23.4, p<.001).

Suffixes	Test	Control	Priming
Productive	569	596	27*
Unproductive	554	566	12
Prefixes			
Productive	566	597	31**
Unproductive	589	612	23(*)
Stems	533	563	30**

** p<.01, * p <.05, (*) p <.10

Table 2. Experiment 1: Lexical decision RTs (ms)

We take this to be strong preliminary evidence for the independent status in the lexical system not just of stems but also of bound morphemes, such as the derivational affixes tested here. This is, however, a result which needs to be replicated, not only to confirm the existence of affix priming, but also to exclude the possibility that the results are due to the phonological overlap between prime and target. Although cross-modal priming is a task where form similarity has generally played little role in determining priming effects, it is important to exclude this possibility for these types of stimulus.

Experiment 2

The second experiment included two new kinds of comparison, both designed to test for the possibility of phonological effects (see Table 3 below). The first was a set of pseudo-affix conditions, where the same primes were used as in the suffix and prefix experiments, but where the targets were now pseudo-affixed words like *dagger*, *carnation*, or *region*. If the reason that *swimmer* primes *gambler* is because of phonological overlap in the last syllable, then the same amount of priming should be found for pairs like *swimmer* and *dagger*, which share exactly the same phonological material.

The second comparison controls directly for phonological overlap, with pairs that overlap either word initially (like *pilgrim/pilfer* or *vintage/vindicate*) or word finally (like *jacket/bucket* or *volcano/casino*), and where no potential morphological relations are involved. Again,

if the priming effects in Experiment 1 can be reduced to, or are contributed to, by form similarities between prime and target, we should also see priming between stimuli of this type.

	Prime	Target
Suffixes		
Productive	darkness	toughness
Unproductive	adjustment	government
Prefixes		
Productive	rearrange	rewrite
Unproductive	misfire	misbehave
Pseudo-Suffixes		
Productive	darkness	harness
Unproductive	adjustment	garment
Pseudo-Prefixes		
Productive	rearrange	recent
Unproductive	misfire	mistress
Phonological Overlap		
Initial Overlap	vintage	vindicate
Final Overlap	puritan	charlatan
Stems	absurdity	absurd

Table 3. Experiment 2: Design and stimuli

Turning to the affixed prime/target pairs, these again were broken down by affix type and productivity, with these divisions mirrored in the design for the pseudo-affix sets (see Table 3). Each test prime was paired with an unrelated control prime, matched for frequency and number of syllables. There were 20 prime-target pairs in each condition (affixed, pseudo-affixed, phonological overlap, stem).

The cross-modal priming results, as summarised in Figures 1 and 2, are clear-cut, and comprehensively rule out any interpretation in terms of phonological relations between primes and targets. First, as shown in Figure 1, there is strong priming for productive suffixes and prefixes, averaging 31 msec, which again parallels the stem priming effects (24 msec). Priming for unproductive suffixes and prefixes, while still significant, is somewhat weaker, averaging 15 msec. This pattern generally replicates the findings for Experiment 1, with similar affix and stem effects.

Turning to the Pseudo-affix and Phonological Overlap conditions, none of these show any significant facilitation. The word-initial overlap condition (*vintage/vindicate*) in fact generates a significant interference effect of -32 msec. In the final overlap (*jacket/bucket*) condition there is a minor overall effect of -5 msec.

More importantly, the comparison between Affixed and Pseudo-affixed conditions not only rules out phonological effects, but also, as illustrated in Figure 2, clarifies the importance of affix productivity. Collapsing over affix type, since prefixes and suffixes behave similarly throughout, it is clear that there is little difference (averaging 8 msec) between Affixed and

225

Pseudo-affixed items when they involve Unproductive affixes. In contrast, there is a highly significant difference of 36 msec for the Productive items (p<.01), where the Affix stimuli show an increase in priming whereas the Pseudo-affix pairs show a tendency to interference, especially in the Pseudo-Suffix condition.

These effects are reflected in the interaction between Productivity, Target Type (Affix/Pseudo-affix), and Prime Type (Test/Control) in the analyses of variance conducted on these data. (F1[1, 43] = 5.36, p = .03; F2[1, 124] = 3.19, p = .07

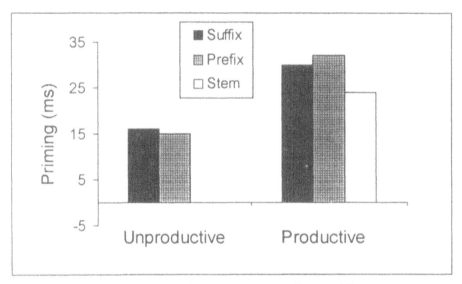

Figure 1: Priming effects for Suffixes, Prefixes, and Stems

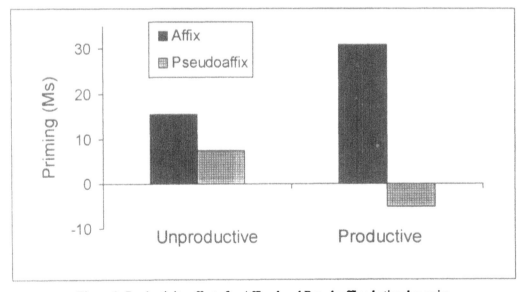

Figure 2: Productivity effects for Affixed and Pseudoaffixed stimulus pairs

Conclusions

The important result is that we have clear evidence that bound morphemes - English derivational affixes - are isolable and independent processing structures in the mental lexicon. We find priming across the board for prefixes and suffixes, under the same conditions and at the same level that we find priming between words sharing the same stem. It is hard to see how this can be explained except in terms of a strongly combinatorial, morphemically decomposed view of the mental lexicon, where the representation and access of morphologically complex forms involves computational processes that combine stems and affixes, and where both partners in these computations - free and bound morphemes - have underlyingly equal status as processing agents.

The picture is strengthened by the effects of productivity. Affix productivity is a gradient phenomenon, but nonetheless priming is consistently stronger for productive affixes like *-ness*, *re-* and *-able*. These are the affixes that are currently in productive use in forming new words in the language, and they could not perform this function, either for the speaker coining a new form or for the listener interpreting it, unless they had an independent cognitive status. As new words come into the language (like *microwaveable* and *downloadable* in the 1980's) their interpretability depends on the availability to the perceiver of the syntactic and semantic properties of the affix, and on the successful combination of these properties with those of the stem morpheme.

These are also results that are hard to explain on any simple semantic story, which seeks to explain priming between morphologically related words as a form of semantic priming, along the lines of the priming found between otherwise unrelated pairs like *cello* and *violin*. The bound morphemes that prime here do not have clearly definable semantic identities. They are fundamentally morphological entities, functioning in productive combinatorial linguistic processes, and it is unlikely that priming relations between them can be accounted for in terms which do not take into account their role as part of a linguistic, morphological system.

This is, finally, the beginning of a story rather than the end of one. Given their evident status as active components of lexical processing, how are these bound morphemes represented and processed in the language system? What is the basis of the priming effects we obtained - re-activation of the same structure, or repetition of the same cluster of processing procedures? And how are we to interpret these results under the assumption that the computational infrastructure for human language processing is distributed and sub-symbolic? How does a system of this type, exposed to the complex pattern of phonological and semantic regularities and irregularities in the language input, convert this into a form of internal representation with the morphological and combinatorial properties apparently exposed by the research here?

References

Marslen-Wilson, W.D., Tyler, L.K., Waksler, R., & Older, L. Abstractness and transparency in the mental lexicon. *Proceedings of the Fourteenth Annual Conference of the Cognitive Science Society*, 1992.

Marslen-Wilson, W.D., Tyler, L.K., Waksler, R., & Older, L. Morphology and meaning in the English mental lexicon. *Psychological Review*, **101**, 3-33, 1994.

Lexical Ambiguity and Context Effects in Spoken Word Recognition: Evidence from Chinese

Ping Li   and   **Michael C. Yip**
Department of Psychology   Department of Psychology
University of Richmond   Chinese University of Hong Kong
Richmond, VA 23173   Shatin, NT, Hong Kong
ping@urvax.urich.edu   michaelyip@cuhk.hk

Abstract

Chinese is a language that is extensively ambiguous on a lexical-morphemic level. In this study, we examined the effects of prior context, frequency, and density of a homophone on spoken word recognition of Chinese homophones in a cross-modal experiment. Results indicate that prior context affects the access of the appropriate meaning from early on, and that context interacts with frequency of the individual meanings of a homophone. These results are consistent with the context-dependency hypothesis which argues that ambiguous meanings of a word may be selectively accessed at an early stage of recognition according to sentential context. However, the results do not support a pre-selection process in which the contextually appropriate meaning can be activated prior to the perception of the relevant acoustic signal.

Introduction

Lexical ambiguity has been the focus for the study of context effects in word recognition in the past 20 years (Onifer & Swinney, 1981; Small, Cottrell, & Tanenhaus, 1988; Simpson & Krueger, 1991; Swinney, 1979; Tabossi, 1988). Results from these studies point to two major hypotheses of lexical access. The exhaustive access hypothesis argues that all meanings of a homophone will be accessed momentarily following the occurrence of the word; semantic context can only help to select the appropriate meaning at a post-access decision/selection stage. This hypothesis assumes a modular account of lexical processing in which context does not penetrate lexical access (Fodor, 1983). In contrast, the context-dependency hypothesis argues that the contextually appropriate meaning of a homophone can be selectively accessed early on, if prior context provides strong bias to one of the meanings. It assumes an interactive process in which lexical and contextual information can mutually influence each other at a very early stage (McClelland, 1987).

Few studies have examined these hypotheses in Chinese, a language that is extensively ambiguous on a lexical-morphemic level. According to the Modern Chinese Dictionary (Institute of Linguistics, 1985), 80% of the monosyllables are ambiguous, and half of them have five or more homophones. For example, the syllable "yi" (with the dipping tone) has up to 90 homophones (e.g., skill, justice, benefit, discuss, intention, translate, hundred-million, etc.), and this number would increase to 171 if identical syllables with different tones were considered as homophones. Should we assume that upon hearing "yi", Chinese listeners activate all 90 or more meanings of the syllable? We should, if we accept the exhaustive access hypothesis in its strict sense: according to this hypothesis lexical access is an autonomous and capacity-free process. However, if we follow the context-dependency hypothesis, only the contextually appropriate meaning will be activated when listeners hear the syllable.

The present study is designed to investigate how context, frequency, and homophone density information constrain the access of lexical meanings, using Chinese homophones as a crucial test case.

Method

Subjects
Sixty native Cantonese speakers (38 females and 22 males, mean age = 19.6) who reported no speech or hearing deficits participated in the experiment. All subjects were students at the Chinese University of Hong Kong. They took part in the experiment as a laboratory requirement for credit in an introductory psychology course.

Materials
Thirty spoken homophones (all nouns, see Appendix) were selected, each with at least two different meanings in the same tone (syllables in different tones are not considered homophones in this study). Each homophone was embedded in two sentences with prior context biasing either of the two selected meanings. A separate group of 20 bilingual speakers was asked to judge the degree of constraint of the prior context on the target homophone. They were given the 60 test sentences with the prior context but without the homophone, and were asked to fill in the word. They were told to think of a Chinese word that would naturally complete the sentence. Their responses were scored on a 1-4 scale, based on the scale proposed by Marslen-Wilson and Welsh (1978): 1 was given for a word identical to the test

word, 2 for a synonym, 3 for a related word, and 4 for an unrelated word. Responses were pooled across the 20 judges, and the mean rating was 1.6. This score was above the high constraint condition in Marslen-Wilson and Welsh (1978). An effort was also made to have prior context of equal length, and the average length of the test sentences (counting the target homophone) was 14 words (ranging from 12 to 17 words).

Four independent variables were manipulated in this experiment:

(1) Probe Type. The visual probe was (a) biased, which was related to the contextually biased meaning of a homophone, or (b) unbiased, which was related to a second meaning not biased by the context, or (c) unrelated control.

(2) Dominance. The prior context biased either the dominant meaning (more frequent) or the subordinate meaning (less frequent) of a homophone. The frequency counts were based on Ho & Jiang (1994).

(3) Homophone Density. A given homophone had either many potential competitors (four or more) or few (two to three). No previous studies have examined this variable to our knowledge.

(4) SOA (stimulus-onset-asynchrony). The visual probe occurred at a given SOA relative to the spoken homophone, either at the onset or at the offset of the homophone.

A homophone example (*zeong*) and the two corresponding test sentences are given below.

(1) Sentence:
Ngo nam hai dungmatjyun leoi-min zeoi daai ge zau hai **zeong**.
I think that the biggest in a zoo is the elephant.
(literally: I think in zoo inside most big 's then is elephant.)
  Probes:
    (a) *syu* "mouse" (biased)
    (b) *gwan* "rod" (unbiased)
    (c) *zat* "quality" (unrelated control)

(2) Sentence:
Popo waa keoi hanglou m fongbin soeng jiu jat-zi **zeong**.
Grandma says that she has trouble walking and wants to have a stick.
(literally: grandma says she walk not convenient think want one stick.)
  Probes:
    (a) *gwan* "rod" (biased)
    (b) *syu* "mouse" (unbiased)
    (c) *zat* "quality" (unrelated control)

All the visual probes were based on a semantic relatedness judgment task with a separate group of 20 native Cantonese speakers. They were asked to think of three nouns that have the same or closely related meaning to each homophone, and their most frequent response was selected as the visual probe for the homophone (see Appendix for a complete list of the probes used in the experiment).

Design
Subjects were divided into two groups of 30 according to two different SOA conditions. Within each SOA condition, the 30 subjects were again randomly assigned to six groups

of five. Each group randomly received an equal number of sentences for each SOA condition in the 2 (Dominance) x 2 (Homophone Density) x 3 (Probe Type) design. This yielded a total of 12 different experimental conditions. The order of presentation for the sentences was pseudorandomly arranged such that the visual probes did not consecutively bias spoken homophones. The order of presentation was counterbalanced across subjects. No subject heard the same target homophone twice.

Experimental Apparatus
The test sentences were read by a native Cantonese speaker at a normal conversation rate, and were tape-recorded and digitized into a PowerMac computer. A sampling rate of 22kHZ with a 16-bit sound format was used for digitizing. The presentation of auditory and visual stimuli was controlled by the PsyScope program (Cohen, MacWhinney, Flatt, & Provost, 1993). Subjects' naming latencies were recorded by the CMU button-box (Cohen et al., 1993). A unidirectional microphone to register listeners' vocal response was connected to the button-box through the box's voice-activated relay.

Procedure
A cross-modal naming technique (e.g., Li, in press; Seidenberg, Tanenhaus, Leiman, & Bienkowski, 1982) was used. Subjects saw a fixation point, and immediately heard on a pair of headphone the sentence in which the homophone was embedded. A visual probe then occurred on the computer screen according to the SOA condition. Their task was to, as accurately and quickly as possible, name the visual probe aloud into a microphone. Subjects were given a maximum of two seconds to respond, counting from the onset of visual probe. This length of time was sufficient for most subjects to give their responses while at the same time putting them under time pressure.

All subjects did the experiment individually. Before the test began, they were given a practice session in which they heard a set of separate but similar sentences. The experiment took about twenty minutes.

Data Analysis
The dependent variable was subjects' response latencies to each visual probe. The latency was measured from the onset of the visual probe to the subject's vocal response.

Results

A 2 x 3 x 2 x 2 (SOA x Probe Type x Dominance x Homophone Density) ANOVA revealed two main effects: SOA ($F_{1,59} = 94.41$, $p < .001$), and Probe Type ($F_{2,58} = 5.13$, $p < .01$). There was also an interaction between SOA and Dominance ($F_{1,119} = 4.78$, $p < .05$). The main effect of Probe Type indicates that the contextually biased meaning affected subjects' naming of the visual probe. It shows that context effects could take place immediately following the occurrence of the homophone, or even within the acoustic boundary of the spoken word. These effects occurred much earlier in our experiment than what has been previously argued for (e.g., about 1.5 seconds following the occurrence of the ambiguous word, see Onifer & Swinney, 1981; Swinney, 1979). The main effect of SOA shows that although context did not pre-select the meaning before any acoustic information of the homophone (in the Onset SOA condition), listeners did show sensitivity to the contextually biased meaning with minimal acoustic information (in the Offset SOA condition). The interaction effect of SOA by Dominance was due to the fact that the frequency of the meanings of a homophone was reflected only in the Onset SOA condition. In order to see more clearly the various main effects and interactions in each SOA condition, we conducted two separate 3 x 2 x 2 (Probe Type x Dominance x Homophone Density) ANOVAs.

Figure 1 presents the results for response latencies as a function of Probe Type, Dominance, and Homophone Density in the Onset SOA condition. ANOVA shows that only the main effect of Dominance ($F_{1,29} = 4.91$, $p < .05$) was significant. Individual comparisons revealed that this effect was due to differences in the unbiased, low density items ($F_{1,29} = 4.89$, $p < .05$). This effect indicates that when there were few competitors within a homophone, frequency was the main factor for determining subjects' response speed in the unbiased condition. However, when context provides a bias, then frequency effect became weaker.

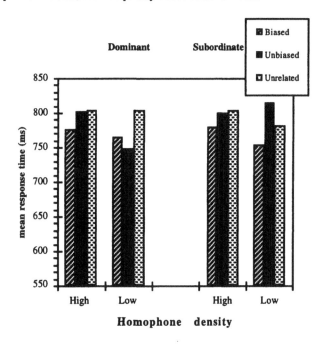

Figure 1: Mean Response Latencies (ms) as a function of Probe Type, Dominance, and Homophone Density in the Onset SOA condition

Figure 2 presents the results for response latencies as a function of Probe Type, Dominance, and Homophone Density in the Offset SOA condition. ANOVA shows that there was a main effect of Probe Type ($F_{2,28} = 8.84$, $p < .001$), indicating that context had an effect in listeners' identification of the contextually biased meaning of a

homophone, which in turn facilitates the naming of the corresponding visual probe. There was also a significant interaction between Probe Type and Dominance ($F_{2,58} = 4.62$, $p < .05$), showing that during recognition context interacted with the frequency of individual meanings of a homophone. In general, dominant meanings were accessed faster than subordinate meanings ($F_{1,59} = 4.83$, $p < .05$). However, when context provided a strong bias, then they did not differ ($F_{1,59} = 2.65$, n.s.).

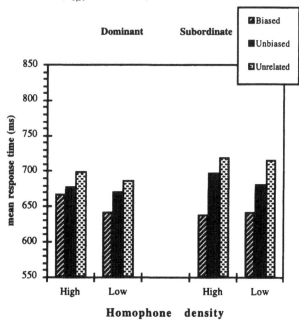

Figure 2: Mean Response Latencies (ms) as a function of Probe Type, Dominance, and Homophone Density in the Offset SOA condition

Note that in both SOA conditions, there was no clear main effect of Homophone Density, nor clear interactions between Dominance and Density. The absence of these effects in our experiment could be due to two confounding factors. First, in this study we used written frequency to approximate the frequency differences for the spoken homophones, due to the unavailability of spoken frequency information for Cantonese. Second, we suspect that the frequency of the visual probes could confound the results. We did not control for the frequency of the visual probes because the visual probes were derived from independent evidence in a semantic relatedness judgment task (see Method), as there have been no semantic associate norms for Cantonese. Our suspicion was confirmed in a separate analysis treating the frequency of the visual probes as an independent variable ($F_{1,59} = 5.97$, $p < .05$).

To summarize, the above results provide a time-course picture of the context effect in spoken word recognition of homophones. In the Onset SOA condition, there is no effect of context as a function of Probe Type, whereas in the Offset SOA condition, contextually appropriate probes are named significantly faster than contextually inappropriate probes. Dominance of the homophone meanings also plays an important role in the recognition process, and it interacts with context in affecting listeners' response speed. In other words, when context provides no clear bias to the individual meanings of a homophone, dominant meanings in general are activated faster; when context provides a clear bias, dominant and subordinate meanings elicit similar naming latencies.

General Discussion

This study attempts to provide new evidence on an old problem. Chinese represents a significantly different language from Indo-European languages, and its lexical properties make the language ideal for testing the lexical ambiguity issue. Our results indicate that given a visual probe at the offset of a spoken homophone, listeners show sensitivity to the contextually biased meaning. These results are consistent with the context-dependency hypothesis which argues that ambiguous meanings of a word may be selectively accessed at an early stage of recognition according to prior sentential context (Simpson, 1981; Simpson & Krueger, 1991; Tabossi, 1988). They point to a much earlier context effect than what has been previously assumed in modular accounts (e.g., Onifer & Swinney, 1981). Recently, Moss and Marslen-Wilson (1993) argue that the offset of an ambiguous word may not be the critical point for tapping into the locus of context effect, because many words in context could be recognized before the word offset. They suggest that the initial access for semantic information about a word could occur much earlier, and that the selection of the contextually appropriate meaning need not occur after the word. Our results are consistent with these accounts, in that context effects can be clearly observed at the offset of a spoken homophone, within the temporal acoustic boundary of the word.

Although our results support the context-dependency hypothesis in general, they do not provide support for a top-down process of pre-selection of the contextually appropriate meaning without any acoustic information. In our experiment when the listener sees a visual probe at the onset of the spoken homophone, the context shows no clear effect. This result is consistent with the "bottom-up priority" principle of the cohort model (Marslen-Wilson, 1987) which argues that in order for lexical access to take place, there has to be limited bottom-up acoustic information. Our results from the Onset SOA condition seem to suggest that there is a very brief moment of lexical access of multiple meanings following the onset of the acoustic signal. However, this moment is short-lived, and other information such as frequency could start to play a role rapidly thereafter.

The current study also indicates the importance of frequency or dominance information in spoken word recognition of homophones. Although the frequency information used in this study is only an approximation because they are based on written norms, the results do suggest an interactive picture in general, in which frequency and context can mutually interact for the identification of the correct meaning. For example, frequency of the

individual meanings of a homophone shows an effect in the low density items in the Onset SOA condition, counter to hypotheses which argue that frequency effects can only occur later on in the selection stage (e.g., Onifer & Swinney, 1981). Ongoing experiments with several paradigms are being designed in our laboratories to examine context, frequency, and homophone density in greater detail so that we may provide a more comprehensive account of context effects in spoken word recognition.

Acknowledgements

This research was supported by a Direct Research Grant from the Chinese University of Hong Kong. We are very grateful to Elizabeth Bates, François Grosjean, and Greg Simpson for their very helpful discussions of the materials presented here.

References

Cohen, J.D., MacWhinney, B., Flatt, M., and Provost, J. (1983). PsyScope: A new graphic interactive environment for designing psychology experiments. *Behavior Research Methods, Instruments, and Computers*, 25, 257-271.

Fodor, J.A. (1983). *The modularity of mind: An essay on faculty psychology*. Cambridge, MA: MIT Press.

Ho, H.-H. & Jiang, Y.-H. (1994). *Word frequency in Hong Kong in the 90's*. Research Institute of Humanities, Chinese University of Hong Kong.

Institute of Linguistics, The Academy of Social Sciences. (1985). *Xianda Hanyu Cidian* (Modern Chinese Dictionary). Beijing: Commercial Press.

Li, P. (in press). Spoken word recognition of code-switched words by Chinese-English bilinguals. *Journal of Memory and Language*.

Marslen-Wilson, W.D. (1987). Functional parallelism in spoken word recognition. *Cognition*, 25, 71-102.

Marslen-Wilson, W.D., & Welsh, A. (1978). Processing interactions and lexical access during word recognition in continuous speech. *Cognitive Psychology*, 10, 29-63.

McClelland, J.L. (1987). The case for interactionism in language processing. In M. Coltheart (Ed.), *Attention and performance XII: The psychology of reading*. Hillsdale, NJ: Lawrence Erlbaum Associates.

Moss, H., & Marslen-Wilson, W. (1993). Access to word meanings during spoken language comprehension: Effects of sentential semantic context. *Journal of Experimental Psychology: Learning, Memory, and Cognition*, 19, 1254-1276.

Onifer, W., & Swinney, D.A. (1981). Accessing lexical ambiguities during sentence comprehension: Effects of frequency of meaning and contextual bias. *Memory & Cognition*, 9, 225-236.

Seidenberg, M.S., Tanenhaus, M.J., Leiman, J.M., & Bienkowski, M. (1982). Automatic access of the meanings of ambiguous words in context: Some limitations of knowledge-based processing. *Cognitive Psychology*, 14, 538-559.

231

Simpson, G. (1981). Meaning dominance and semantic context in the processing of lexical ambiguity. *Journal of Verbal Learning and Verbal Behavior*, 20, 120-136.

Simpson, G.B., & Krueger, M.A.(1991). Selective Access of Homograph Meanings in Sentence Context. *Journal of Memory and Language*, 30, 627-643.

Small, S., Cottrell, G., & Tanenhaus, M. (1988). *Lexical ambiguity resolution: perspectives from psycholinguistics, neuropsychology, and artificial intelligence.* San Mateo: Morgan Kaufmann Publishers.

Swinney, D.A. (1979). Lexical Access during Sentence Comprehension: (Re)Consideration of Context Effects. *Journal of Verbal Learning and Verbal Behavior*, 18, 645-659.

Tabossi, P. (1988). Accessing Lexical Ambiguity in Different Types of Sentential Contexts. *Journal of Memory and Language*, 27, 324-340.

Appendix: Homophones and Probes
Used in the Experiment

Homophone	DOM	Probe	SUB	Probe
baan1	class	zu3	dot	zi4
baan2	board	yi3	edition	yin4
bo1	ball	qiu2	slope	cao3
bou3	cloth	mian2	newspaper	shi4
ci4	pond	he2	prose	zi4
coeng1	gun	dan4	window	men2
coeng4	wall	zhuan1	playground	cheng2
dou2	island	hai3	gamble	shu1
fo3	goods	cang1	lesson	shu1
gau2	dog	mao1	nine	shu4
jyun4	circle	fang1	ape	hou2
kei4	flag	jun1	date	ri4
kwan4	dress	yi1	group	ji2
maa5	horse	niu2	yard	chi3
min6	face	yan3	noodle	fen3
mou6	fog	yu3	tomb	si3
ping4	vase	zun1	plateau	di4
saam1	clothes	wa4	three	si4
sau2	hand	tui3	tanker	chuan2
seoi3	tax	qian2	year	nian2
si1	silk	tiao2	poem	wen2
sin3	thread	you4	fan	liang2
soeng1	container	he2a	frost	xue3
tong4	sugar	tian2	lesson	xue2
waa6	language	shu1	painting	se4
wan4	cloud	tian1	soul	gui3
wo1	nest	bei4	wok	huo4
wu4	lake	shui3	arc	wan1
zoeng3	debit	zhai4	curtain	ying2
zoeng6	elephant	shu3	stick	gun4

Note: DOM -- Dominant meaning; SUB -- Subordinate meaning. The probes are semantically related to the corresponding meanings.

Phonological Reduction, Assimilation, Intra-Word Information Structure, and the Evolution of the Lexicon of English: Why Fast Speech isn't Confusing

Richard Shillcock
Centre for Cognitive Science
University of Edinburgh
2 Buccleuch Place, Edinburgh
EH8 9LW, U.K.
rcs@cogsci.ed.ac.uk

John Hicks
Centre for Cognitive Science
University of Edinburgh
2 Buccleuch Place, Edinburgh
EH8 9LW, U.K.

Paul Cairns
Centre for Cognitive Science
University of Edinburgh
2 Buccleuch Place, Edinburgh
EH8 9LW, U.K.

Nick Chater
Department of Experimental Psychology
University of Oxford
South Parks Road, Oxford OX1 3UD, U.K.
nick@psy.ox.ac.uk

Joseph P. Levy
Department of Psychology
Birkbeck College
Malet Street, London WC1E 7HX, U.K.
joe@cogsci.ed.ac.uk

Abstract

Phonological reduction and assimilation are intrinsic to speech. We report a statistical exploration of an idealised phonological version of the London-Lund Corpus and describe the computational consequences of phonological reduction and assimilation. In terms of intra-word information structure, the overall effect of these processes is to flatten out the redundancy curve calculated over consecutive segment-positions. We suggest that this effect represents a general principle of the presentation of information to the brain: information should be spread as evenly as possible over a representational surface or across time. We also demonstrate that the effect is partially due to the fact that when assimilation introduces phonological ambiguity, as in *fat man* coming to resemble *fap man*, then the ambiguity introduced is always in the direction of a less frequent segment: /p/ is less frequent than /t/. We show that this observation, the "Move to Markedness", is true across the board for changes in segment identity in English. This distribution of segments means that the number of erroneous lexical hypotheses introduced by segment-changing processes such as assimilation is minimised. We suggest that the Move to Markedness within the lexicon is the result of pressure from the requirements of a very efficient word recognition device that is sensitive to changes of individual phonological features.

Production of Fast, Continuous Speech

Normal speech is fast, casual, continuous and situationally located. These features mean that the pronunciation of any one word is likely to differ substantially from the way that it might be produced in "citation form" – the careful, ideal, isolated "dictionary" pronunciation of that word. First, the word may refer to a given in the discourse or the environment of the discourse, in which case even a poorly specified wordform may be sufficient for the listener to recognise the intended word. Second, the word may be a function word like *which*, *is* or *the*, whose identity is in part predictable from the syntactic context. In this case, top-down processing may augment the

perception of the word (Shillcock & Bard, 1993). Third, the articulators must move between the physical positions required to produce consecutive speech segments and, particularly in faster speech, this may mean that the articulators do not reach the optimum position for any one segment before being required to move to new positions appropriate to the production of the next segment. This means that the pronunciation of any segment may be influenced by adjacent and nearby segments, even if those segments are on the other side of a word boundary. In this paper we develop, from an information processing perspective, a general principle concerning the production of fast speech and we reveal a striking generalisation about the distribution of segments in relation to these fast speech processes and the problem of word recognition[1].

The processes we describe, such as assimilation, are determined at least partly by the physical structure of the articulators. The lexicon of current English has developed against the backdrop of these physical constraints. We assume that the vocabulary of English has accommodated these physical constraints in terms of any implications they may have for information processing, intelligibility or ease of production.

Producing speech, at normal rates of perhaps 100–120 words a minute, is the most complex muscular activity in our repertoire. Similarly, listening to speech and deriving message-level interpretations virtually instantaneously, is arguably as complex a computational task as we undertake in such a timescale. In "fast" (that is, normal) speech processes, these pressures on speaker and listener are both present. We might expect the phonological content of speech to have been shaped so as to be readily speeded up with as little lack of intelligibility as possible. Below, we adopt a corpus-based approach to demonstrate the truth of

---

[1]Phoneticians contrast "citation form" pronunciation with "fast speech" pronunciation. The point we emphasise here is that normal, conversational speech is "fast", in these terms.

this claim. We will describe, in information theoretic terms, the results of building fast speech processes into a phonological transcription of a corpus of conversational speech. First, we describe the generation of the corpus and then we present statistical analyses of the implications for word recognition.

Generating a Realistic Speech Corpus

We describe in detail elsewhere the generation of an idealised phonological transcription of the London-Lund Corpus (LLC) (Svartvik & Quirk, 1980; Shillcock, Hicks, Cairns, Levy & Chater, 1995). The LLC is a corpus of orthographically transcribed conversational English speech, containing some 494,000 word tokens. The speech contains the false starts, filled pauses, repetitions and pausing that characterise normal speech. Some 19% of the word boundaries in the LLC are explicitly marked by pauses or speaker changeovers. The rest is continuous speech. We summarise below the procedure by which an idealised phonological transcription of this corpus was generated. The goal was to develop a phonological corpus that retained the psychologically important scale and representativeness of the original orthographic corpus.

First, the corpus was stripped of all annotations pertaining to speaker identity, prosody, pausing, and other paralinguistic information. Second, the orthographic word tokens were replaced by their respective citation forms, derived from the CELEX database[2]. A minority of tokens were transcribed as exceptions, either because they did not occur in CELEX, or they were fragments of words, or they had been given a phonological transcription in the original LLC. Third, phonological reductions and assimilations were introduced, as described below.

It is not possible to recreate the full richness of the phonological reduction of the original speech, which would differ between speakers, between utterances, and between different tokens of the same word. However, it is possible to create a version of the entire corpus that is rather more representative of normal speech than a simple concatenation of citation forms. One indicator of the validity of the transcription is the degree to which the resulting global statistics predict real processing behaviour. In this respect, there is reason to believe that the overall statistics we have extracted from the phonological version of the LLC are psychologically realistic. We have used these statistics successfully to model phoneme restoration and the acquisition of expressive phonology (see, *e.g.*, Chater, Shillcock, Cairns & Levy, 1995; Shillcock, Chater, Levy & Hicks, 1996).

We incorporated phonological reduction into the corpus for the function words only. In real speech, this class of words is disproportionately affected by phonological reduction, reflecting the fact that such words may be perceptually restored by their syntactic context. A single reduced version of each function word was taken from the

reduced forms listed in the CELEX database, and was substituted for the citation-form version in all instances where this was appropriate to the phonological context. For instance, *had* was transcribed as /həd/, and *and* as /ənd/. Elsewhere we list all of the relevant function words and their reduced forms (Shillcock *et. al.*, 1995). These function words accounted for some 53% of the word tokens.

After the function word reductions had been made, we added to our phonological transcription an approximation of the effects of assimilation. These effects were applied across all words in the corpus, function and content. In real speech, consonants may be assimilated to the place of articulation of the following segment; for instance, the /t/ in *fat man* may be assimilated to the labial place of articulation of the following /m/ so that the /t/ acquires some of the characteristics of a /p/. In the extreme case the /t/ may become a /p/, giving *fap man*, but in other cases the /t/ becomes ambiguous between a /t/ and a /p/. In our phonological transcription of the LLC, we have adopted an idealised case in which the /t/ is changed into a /p/. Specifically, /d/ before a labial became /b/, /t/ before a labial became /p/, /d/ before a velar became /g/, /t/ before a velar became /k/. In addition, the six consonants were replaced by their unreleased versions when they occurred before another consonant. All of the rules regarding assimilation and the inclusion of the unreleased versions of the consonants were applied regardless of any word boundary information. Thus, assimilation could occur across the syllable boundaries within a polysyllabic word, and the first consonants in all consonant clusters became unreleased.

The procedure sketched above produced a phonological version of the LLC that is psychologically realistic in terms of the distributional statistics of its segments, in spite of the relative crudeness of such an automated procedure compared with a close transcription made by a trained phonetician.

The Information Structure of Words

We now consider each segment position in all the words of a particular length, and we calculate the predictability of the contents of that segment position. At one extreme is the case in which every possible segment occurs with exactly equal probability in the *n*th position in all words of length *n* or more: this segment position is therefore maximally informative and minimally redundant. At the other extreme is the case in which only one particular segment ever occurs in the *n*th position in words of length *n* or more: this segment position is minimally informative and maximally redundant. In reality, practically all cases fall between these two extremes. In the discussion below, we will be concerned with redundancy, so that the greater the redundancy, the more predictable is the processing of that particular segment position.

Redundancy was calculated as follows (see, *e.g.*, Yannakoudakis & Hutton, 1992):

Let S = Set of allowed phonemes
$$= \{s_1, s_2, s_3, ..., s_n\}$$
$$P_i = \Pr(s_i)/\Sigma\Pr(s_j)$$

---

[2]CELEX Lexical Database of English (Version 2.5). Dutch Centre for Lexical Information, Nijmegen.

$H\text{-max} = \log_2 n$

$H = -\sum_{i-1}^{n} P_i \log_2 P_i$

Entropy $E = H/H\text{-max}$

Redundancy $R = 1 - E$

Redundancy ranges between 0 and 1. Figure 1 shows an example redundancy curve calculated over the four segment positions for all of the four-letter words in the final phonological version of the LLC. This shows that the general shape of the redundancy curves is one which rises over time: the early segments of spoken words are more informative than the later ones. This is in agreement with the upward slope of the curves reported by Yannakoudakis and Hutton for corpora derived from text, and follows their convention of plotting redundancy, rather than entropy, against segment position. Note that the measure of redundancy used here is concerned only with the distribution of segments within a particular segment position, and not with the phonological information accumulated up to that point in a particular word. In this analysis, redundancy at any one segment position is in no way conditional on what has occurred earlier; later segments are not redundant because the identity of a particular word is constrained by what has gone before.

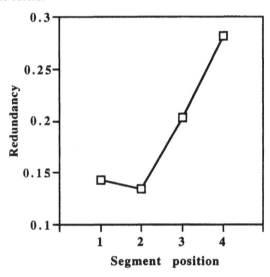

Figure 1: The redundancy curve across the four segment positions for all of the four-letter words in the LLC.

Figure 2 shows the aggregate redundancy curve for all of the words in the LLC of length 1–9 segments. The solid line is the redundancy curve for the words in citation form, before phonological reduction and assimilation. The dotted line is the redundancy curve for the words after the operation of these fast speech processes.

As Figure 2 shows, phonological reduction and assimilation increased the level of redundancy in the early parts of words and decreased it in the later parts of words. The overall effect is of a flattening of the curve, which we explore further, below. We have replicated this result with a different corpus of orthographically transcribed speech,

which we have converted into a phonological transcription using the procedure described above. Figure 3 shows the corresponding data for a comparable amount of speech, the speech addressed to children aged 0–28 months in the CHILDES corpus (MacWhinney, 1991).

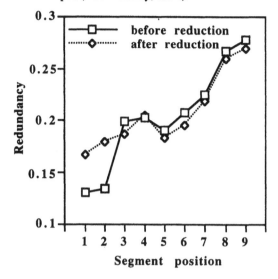

Figure 2: The effects of phonological reduction and assimilation on redundancy, for words of length 1–9 in the LLC.

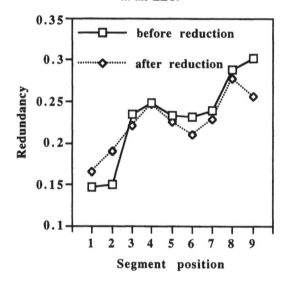

Figure 3: The effects of phonological reduction and assimilation on redundancy, for words of length 1–9 in the CHILDES Corpus.

The increase in redundancy in the earlier part of the curves in Figures 2 and 3 is principally due to the replacement of the closed-class words by their reduced forms. These words are typically short and their phonological reduction involves the replacement of citation form vowels by /ə/, as in *had* and *and*. This causes the distribution of segments in the earlier positions to become more skewed, increasing redundancy. This increase in redundancy is reversed in the later part of the curve in both the LLC and the CHILDES corpora, with redundancy generally lower from the third segment on, following the application of fast speech rules (in Wilcoxon signed ranks tests, $z = -2.197$, $p < .03$; $z = 2.366$, $p < .02$, respectively). This reduction in redundancy is the result of assimilation introducing less frequent segments at the ends of syllables and words, and is discussed below in terms of the implications for word recognition.

The data shown in Figures 2 and 3 are consistent with what may be a general principle of information processing in the brain, that incoming information should be spread as evenly as possible over the relevant representational surface. This is illustrated in topographic mapping, as in Penfield's homunculus, for instance. More somatic stimulation/information at one particular region compared to another leads to more extensive cortical representation of the former. Equal representational space for both would result in an uneconomical use of computational resources. (For further discussion, see, *e.g.*, Smith, 1996.) We propose that the effect demonstrated in Figures 2 and 3 reflects the temporal analogue of this principle: the optimal profile of information over time is flat, the processor should not be subject to fluctuations in the informativeness of the speech signal at the phonological level. In information theoretic terms, the functional motivation for this phenomenon is that the frequency of occurrence of segments is evened out, thus allowing maximum transfer of information in an increasingly noisy channel.

The increasing redundancy curves in Figures 1–3 reflect a broader, communicative pressure on the structure of the lexicon, in that it is desirable for words to be distinguished early in their acoustic lifetimes. (We see this same pressure reflected at the morphological level in terms of a crosslinguistic preference for suffixing over prefixing (Hawkins & Cutler, 1985).) This is an abstract characterisation of the problem, appropriate to central processing in a lexicon of idealised forms. In contrast, the flattened redundancy curves reflect the exigencies of more peripheral processing, in which segment identity must be determined under time pressure in a noisy signal.

Although we only present data concerning across-the-board replacement by phonologically reduced forms for the closed-class words, the effects of reduction of the open-class words may be seen to be in line with the overall flattening of the redundancy curve described above. Open-class words predominantly have metrically strong initial syllables (Cutler & Carter, 1987), containing full vowels and not attracting the degree of phonological reduction that falls to the metrically weak later syllables. The loss of segments, in perception and production, from the later parts of words – as in the second syllable of *station* being replaced by a syllabic /n/, for instance – will remove from the statistics the very frequent, vulnerable segments such as /ə/ and /t/, and contribute to the further lowering of the high-redundancy part of the curve.

Conventionally, phonological reduction in the less informative, later parts of open-class words is seen as reflecting the fact that a particular word may be expected to have been recognised by this point. We present a complementary, alternative analysis here: these segments are more affected because they are more predictable simply on the basis of distance from the beginning of the word. Naturally there are other influences on intelligibility and informativeness, apart from those we have considered above: prosody is one such example. The tendency of fast speech processes to produce flatter redundancy curves is seen here as a general tendency that interacts with other factors.

Implications for Word Recognition

The effects of assimilation are generally taken to be deleterious to word recognition: the identity of a segment is being compromised, either by making it ambiguous with another segment or, as in our idealisation of the effect, by changing its identity completely to that of another segment. Assimilation might be expected to impair word recognition by excluding the intended word from the cohort of lexical candidates and/or by introducing erroneous candidates into the cohort. For instance, in the phrase *street car* the assimilation of the /t/ to the following /k/ appears to introduce the erroneous candidate *streak*. (For further psycholinguistic and modelling explorations of assimilation, see Marslen-Wilson, Nix & Gaskell, 1995; Gaskell, 1993; Gaskell, Hare & Marslen-Wilson, 1995). However, the global statistics derived from the corpus reveal that assimilation can have implications for word recognition that are very different from this pessimistic picture. Figure 4 shows the percentages of words in the LLC that are not uniquely specified in segmental terms before their offsets. These words are like *mar* or *part*, which can go on to become longer words, *mark* and *partner*.

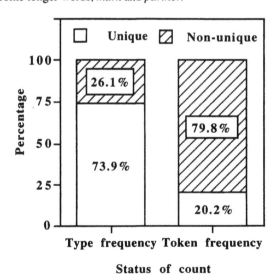

Figure 4: Percentages of uniquely specified words in the LLC, prior to application of the fast speech processes.

The 80% of non-unique tokens is double that reported by Luce (1986) in a similar, but dictionary-based, study, due to the inclusion in the current study of inflected forms, involving pairs such as *their* and *theirs*, and *walk* and *walked*. Compare Figure 4 with Figure 5, which shows the effects of applying phonological reduction and assimilation to the corpus. the result is a considerable reduction in the ambiguity introduced by the non-unique forms. These figures are based on the assumption that assimilated forms of words are lexicalised and count as lexical items, so that *last* expands into three lexical entries, ending with /t/, /k/ and /p/ respectively, the last two resulting from conjunctions like *last call* and *last place*.

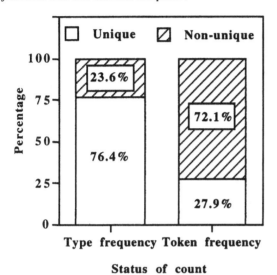

Figure 5: Percentages of uniquely specified words in the LLC, following application of the fast speech processes.

The "lexicalisation solution" of simply storing the assimilated forms as legitimate words is unlikely to be an adequate complete solution to the processing of assimilated forms; indeed, Gaskell *et al.* provide evidence against this solution and in favour of online inferencing to "undo" the assimilation, for certain stimulus materials. However, lexicalisation does not emerge, in the current study, as such a clumsy or expensive option as might have been thought. In this instance, it causes an overall increase from 18,671 word-types to 20,630, an increase of 9.5%, to achieve a 7.7% increase in unique tokens[3]. Lexicalisation of frequently encountered assimilated wordforms and online inferencing as a parallel/back-up process may be an attractive compromise.

The Distribution of Segments

We have seen in Figures 2 and 3 that fast speech processes increase redundancy in early segment positions and decrease it in later segment positions. The phonological reduction of

the, predominantly short, function words is primarily responsible for the early increase in redundancy. Although assimilation was applied across all the words in the corpus irrespective of word boundaries, it has its effect at the ends of syllables and words and is therefore primarily responsible for the decrease in redundancy in the later parts of the curves. We have already briefly alluded to the fact that this effect is due to assimilation replacing frequently occurring segments by less frequently occurring ones. We now elaborate upon this observation concerning segment distribution, which we term the "Move to Markedness", which is true of English and which we predict will hold for other languages:

> "If segment *x* is influenced by the following segment to resemble segment *y*, then *x* will occur more frequently in the language than *y*."

For example, /t/ may be influenced by a following /p/ to resemble /p/ itself, as in *last place*, and statistical analysis of our phonological version of the LLC reveals that /t/ occurs more frequently than /p/. These same overall frequencies (see Shillcock *et al.*, 1995) show that this relation holds for all of the segment changes we list below, which include some assimilations not instantiated in the version of the LLC we have described above, as well as changes involving unreleased consonants: /d/ → /b/, /t/ → /p/, /d/ → /g/, /t/ → /k/, /n/ → /m/, /n/ → /ŋ/, /s/ → /ʃ/, /b/ → /b˺/, /d/ → /d˺/, /k/ → /k˺/, /g/ → /g˺/, /p/ → /p˺/, /t/→ /t˺/. The fact that all 13 of these changes are in the direction of a less frequent segment – towards markedness – is significant by the binomial test, *p* < .001; for the seven assimilations alone, *p* < .008[4].

The functional motivation that we claim for this distributional constraint is that it offsets interference with spoken word recognition from the effects of assimilation. Assimilation causes segments to become more ambiguous or to change their identity. These effects are potentially disruptive to word recognition, given that the processor seems to be sensitive to single changes at the feature level (see, *e.g.*, Marslen-Wilson, 1993): a change from /t/ to /d/ at the end of the word *apricot* is sufficient to switch off priming by that word. The processor needs to prevent a change in segment from causing the activation of a large new cohort of erroneous lexical candidates at the same time as the correct candidate is apparently disqualified. For instance, if the correct candidate is *batman*, it may be excluded from the cohort of active lexical candidates by assimilation producing *bap-*. This candidate can be rescued either by the lexicalisation account discussed above, in

---

[3]Note that there is marginal evidence for the lexicalisation of fast speech forms in those individuals who miswrite *could have* as *could of*, or *handbag* as *hambag*.

[4]Note that this is a conservative test of the observation, in that the judgements were made on a version of the corpus in which the fast speech processes had already been modelled, and in which the numbers of the less frequent segments had therefore been increased. That is, the disparity between the frequencies of /t/ and /p/ is somewhat offset by assimilation, in which the former are turned into the latter. If any aspect of word recognition employs pre-assimilation, citation-form templates, then the observation is true in even more striking form, with greater frequency disparities.

which *bapman* is stored, or by an online process of inference once the following /m/ is encountered. Both of these solutions may exist in human listeners, and may be determined by the frequency of the assimilated wordform. The other aspect of the problem is the possible inclusion of erroneous candidates in the cohort. The Move to Markedness ensures that the number of erroneous candidates is minimised; this is the motivation for the constraint. Its efficacy is ensured by the fact that the new segment identity is lower in frequency than the segment it replaces. This is illustrated by our example: if the /t/ in *batman* becomes a /p/, then *bap*, *baptism*, *baptistery* and *baptise* are erroneously added to the words already activated, but *batch*, *batchy*, *bateau*, *bateleur*, *batik*, *batiste*, *baton*, *batsman*, *battels*, *batten*, *batter*, *battery*, *batting*, *battle*, *battledore*, *battlement*, *battue*, *batty* and *batwoman* will be deactivated (words taken from the Concise Oxford Dictionary). It is impossible to ensure that no erroneous candidates at all are activated, but the fact that the new segment identity is lower in frequency than the segment it replaces reduces the number of new and erroneous candidates. This argument applies even if assimilation only makes the segment ambiguous between two segments as opposed to completely switching its identity; in this case, the Move to Markedness limits the confusion sown rather than actually reducing it.

Finally, the Move to Markedness has implications for speech segmentation. The probability of the transition between consecutive segments is potentially valuable information for deciding that two segments straddle a word boundary (see, *e.g.*, Cairns, Shillcock, Chater & Levy, 1994); more unlikely transitions are better candidates for boundaries. Movements towards markedness make such segmentation decisions more likely, in that they will tend to produce less frequent transitions.

Conclusions

A corpus-based approach can reveal novel aspects of language structure and processing. On the basis of empirical exploration of the London-Lund Corpus, we suggest a general goal of fast speech processes: producing a flatter redundancy curve over segment positions in words. We also report a functional constraint on the distribution of phonological segments, the Move to Markedness. This constraint is motivated by the requirements of the word recognition process, in which there is a virtually instantaneous sensitivity to individual feature changes. We claim that the Move to Markedness is the result of ease of intelligibility selecting for a particular distribution in the lexicon, given the presence of physically determined effects such as assimilation. This analysis reveals the information theoretic consequences of these effects.

Acknowledgements

This research was supported by ESRC (UK) grants R000 23 3649 and R000 22 1435. We would also like to acknowledge valuable discussions with Mark Ellison.

References

Cairns, P., Shillcock, R.C., Chater, N., Levy, J. (1994). Lexical segmentation: the role of sequential statistics in supervised and unsupervised models. In *Proceedings of the Sixteenth Annual Conference of the Cognitive Science Society*, Georgia Institute of Technology.

Chater, N., Shillcock, R., Cairns, P. & Levy, J. (1995). Bottom-up explanation of phoneme restoration: Comment on Elman and McClelland (1988). Submitted to Journal *of Memory and Language*.

Cutler, A. & Carter, D.M. (1987). The predominance of strong initial syllables in the English vocabulary. *Computer Speech and Language*, **2**, 133-142.

Gaskell, G. (1993). *Spoken word recognition: A combined computational and experimental approach*. PhD thesis, Birkbeck College, University of London.

Gaskell, G. Hare, M., & Marslen-Wilson, W.D. (1995). A connectionist model of phonological representation in speech perception. *Cognitive Science*, **19**, 407–439.

Luce, P. (1986). A computational analysis of uniqueness points in auditory word recognition. *Perception and Psychophysics*, **39**, 155–158.

Macwhinney, B. (1991). *The CHILDES project: Tools for analyzing talk*. Hillsdale, NJ, Erlbaum.

Marslen-Wilson, W.D., Nix, A. & Gaskell, G. (1995). Phonological variation in lexical access: Abstractness, inference and English place assimilation. *Language and Cognitive Processes*, **10**, 285–308.

Marslen-Wilson, W.D. (1993). Issues of process and representation in lexical access. In G.T.M. Altmann and R.C. Shillcock (Eds.) *Cognitive Models of Speech Processing: The Second Sperlonga Meeting*, Erlbaum.

Shillcock, R.C. & E.G. Bard. (1993). Modularity and the processing of closed class words. In Altmann, G.T.M. &

Shillcock, R.C. (Eds.) *Cognitive models of speech processing*. The Second Sperlonga Meeting. Erlbaum.

Shillcock, R.C., Chater, N., Levy, J.P., & Hicks, J. (1996). Order of acquisition of expressive phonology in English: the effect of phonotactic range. *Manuscript*.

Shillcock, R.C., Hicks, J., Cairns, P., Levy, J., & Chater, N. (1995). A statistical analysis of an idealised phonological transcription of the London- Lund corpus. *Submitted to Computer Speech and Language*.

Smith, J. (1996). *Neural Networks, Information Theory and Knowledge Representation*. PhD dissertation, University of Edinburgh.

Svartvik, J., & Quirk, R. (eds.) (1980). *A Corpus of English Conversation*. Lund Studies in English 56. Lund: Lund University Press.

Yannakoudakis, E.J. & Hutton, P.J. (1992). An Assessment of *N*-phoneme statistics in phoneme guessing algorithms which aim to incorporate phonotactic constraints. *Speech Communication*, **11**, 581–602.

Color Influences Fast Scene Categorization

Aude Oliva and **Philippe G. Schyns**
Department of Psychology
University of Glasgow, Glasgow
Glasgow, G12 8QQ, UK
{aude,philippe}@psy.gla.ac.uk

Abstract

A critical aspect of early visual processes is to extract shape data for matching against memory representations for recognition. Many theories of recognition assume that this is being done on luminance information. However, studies in psychophysics have revealed that color is being used by many low-level visual modules such as motion, stereopsis, texture, and 2D shapes. Should color really be discarded from theories of recognition? In this paper, we present two studies which seek to understand the role of chromatic information for the recognition of real scene pictures. We used three versions of scene pictures (gray-levels, normally colored and abnormally colored) coming from two broad classes of categories. In the first category, color was diagnostic of the category (e.g., *beach, forest* and *valley*). In the second category color was not diagnostic (e.g., *city, road* and *room*). Results revealed that chromatic information is being registered and facilitates recognition even after a 30 ms exposure to the scene stimuli. Similar results were recorded with exposures of 120 ms. However, influences of color on speeded categorizations were only observed with the color-diagnostic categories. No influence of color was observed with the other categories.

Introduction

There is little doubts that shape is a critical aspect of recognition. In fact, most recognition theories assume that shape serves as the basis of object and scene representations (e.g., Biederman, 1987; Marr & Nishihara, 1978; Tarr & Pinker, 1989). Consequently, a critical aspect of early visual processes is to extract shape data for matching against memory representations. This is accomplished by early visual modules such as edge detection, depth perception, motion and stereo which are often assumed to operate on achromatic information--the luminance, or gray-levels of the image. However, there is a wealth of psychophysical evidence suggesting that early vision operates simultaneously in luminance and chromatic pathways for motion (e.g., Cavanagh & Ramachandran, 1988), simple shapes (Damasio, Yamada, Damasio, Corbett, McKee, 1980), texture (McIlhaga, Hine, Cole & Schneider, 1990) and stereo (Logothetis, Schiller, Charles & Hurlbert, 1990). In light of these evidence, should chromatic information really be discarded from recognition theories?

The influence of chromatic information on object and scene recognition has been little studied, and results are often contradictory. For example, Biederman and Ju (1988) have argued that color had no impact on the identification of an object. Their experiments compared the naming of colored object photographs and line drawings of the same objects. No naming advantage was reported for colored objects (at presentations times of 50 ms and 100 ms), even when the color was characteristic (diagnostic) of the objects. This contrasts with the earlier work of Ostergaard and Davidoff (1985) who reported that objects like fruits and vegetables were named faster when the stimuli were colored slides then when they were gray-level slides (see also Wurm, Legge, Isenberg, & Luebker, 1993). Recently, Tanaka & Bunosky (1996) have shown that color influences objects that have a characteristic color.

Two factors could account for these conflicting data. This first factor is the diagnosticity of chromatic information for a categorization (see Tanaka & Bunoski, 1996). For example, in the *lemon* category, the distribution of color is clustered around only two modes (yellow and green). In contrast, the distribution of color is multi-modal in the *car* category. Thus, an effect of chromatic information on recognition might only be observed when color predicts the categorization, insisting for the requirement to control for color diagnosticity. The second factor is the control of luminance across conditions of stimulation. Too often (e.g., Biederman & Ju, 1988; Ostergaard & Davidoff, 1985), comparisons are made between stimuli whose luminance differs across conditions, making it difficult to know whether the absence of effect of chromaticity in one condition results from an enhanced luminance in the other condition.

While it is probably true that color is not diagnostic of many real world object categories (with the exception of fruits and vegetables), little is known about the possible effects of color on the recognition of real world scenes. Real-world scenes are arguably more diagnosed by their colors than are objects (think for example of beaches, seas, mountains, fields, and so forth. Unfortunately the little research existing on the categorization of real world scene has mostly focused on luminance information (e.g., Oliva & Schyns, 1995; Schyns & Oliva, 1994). However, a recent work of Gegenfurtner, Sharpe, & Wichmann (1995) showed that color entered the way scenes were represented in memory. Their study asked subjects to learn colored and black and white scene pictures to be later tested on their familiarity with these scenes. It was found that subjects performed significantly better for memorized colored images, suggesting that their memory of scenes contained chromatic information.

This paper presents two studies which seek to understand the respective role of luminance and chromatic information in speeded scene categorizations. One could claim that the addition of color has a relatively low-level contribution which facilitates segmentation processes. In this case a beach scene whose sky was painted red, the beach blue, and the sea pink should be categorized faster than its gray-level counterpart. An alternative claim is that color exerts a high-level influence on processing. For example, recognition could operate independently in luminance and color pathways, both of which would provide sources of cues for recognition. In this case, the beach would be recognized faster when the luminance and chromatic cues both represent a beach. However, this should only hold when chromatic information is diagnostic of a category. That is, it should hold only for categories with few dominant colors (e.g., *beach* or *forest*), but not for categories with many variable colors (e.g., *room* or *city*).

Our experiments were designed to get a better understanding of these issues. In a categorization task, all subjects were exposed to three versions of 120 different scene stimuli: normally colored, abnormally colored and gray levels. Precautions were taken to insure that the three versions of a scene had an identical luminance. In Experiment 1, the stimuli were presented for 120 ms and we measured subjects' reaction times of denomination. In Experiment 2, scenes were presented for only 30 ms. Both experiments used the same scene categories. To control for diagnosticity, two classes of categories were used: natural (*beach*, *forest* and *valley*) and artifact (*room*, *road* and *city*). Natural categories have fewer color modes than artifact categories, and color is therefore more diagnostic of the categories. We expected chromatic information to facilitate recognition only when it was diagnostic of a category. Conversely, we expected chromatic information to impair recognition if the colors were abnormal of the category. The difference in presentation times between the two experiments was there to inform about the time course of luminance and chromatic processing.

Experiment 1

Method

Subjects. Twenty Glasgow University students with normal or corrected vision were paid to participate to the experiment.

Stimuli. We chose 120 high quality color scene pictures from the Corel CD Photo Library. These images formed two categories: natural and artifact scenes. Natural and artifact scenes were themselves subdivided into 3

subcategories (*beach, forest, valley* and *city, road, room*) with an equal number of exemplars per category. Our experiments involve transformations of chromatic information. A colored images has two main components: luminance (the gray levels of the image) and chromaticity (the color itself). A standard 3 dimensional encoding of color in Red Green Blue (RGB) space does not separate luminance from chromaticity. Thus, changes of color affect luminance. To control this potential confound we transformed RGB data in a space (L*a*b*) which represents luminance (L*) and color (a*b*) independently. We then obtained three different versions of the same scene. The first version, the Normal Color (NC) scene simply corresponded to the original image. The Incongruent Color (IC) was computed by changing the a* and b* axis in L*a*b*. There are three ways to change color, because the a* and b* axis can be swapped and inverted. To illustrate, if a* represents the red to green spectrum and b* represents the yellow to blue spectrum, a swap of a* and b* (L*b*a*) changes the color of a banana from yellow to red. A swap of the axis plus an inversion of their values would create a blue banana. For each of the 120 scenes, 3 IC images were computed as just explained. A panel of three independent judges was asked to rate how atypical these images appeared of the category. We kept the most atypical color transformation for the IC condition. The final version of a scene (LU) simply discarded all color information, only keeping the L* component of L*a*b* (the LUminance, or gray levels). Stimuli were presented on a computer monitor; images subtended 6.4 x 4.4 degrees of visual angle. As there were 120 original pictures, together, NC, IC and LU composed a set of 360 experimental stimuli.

Procedure. The experiment was composed of 360 trials: 120 NC, 120 IC and 120 LU. Each trial used a different scene picture. A trial consisted of the presentation of a fixation square, followed by a mid-gray image presented for 500 ms, immediately followed by a target image (NC, IC or LU) presented for 120 ms. Subjects were instructed to name the scene as quickly and as accurately as they possibly could. Reaction Times (RTs) were measured with a vocal key. Prior to the experiment, subjects were told that all scene stimuli belonged to one of six possible categories (*beach, city, forest, room, road* and *valley*) and were asked to categorize the pictures with these names. Six practice trials were given to familiarize subjects with the experimental apparatus, and to calibrate the sensitivity of the vocal key. Trials were randomly assigned into 10 blocks of 36 trials. Subjects were allowed a one minute pause between each block.

Results and Discussion

The analysis was only performed on correct categorizations when naming latencies were within 2.5 standard deviations of the means. Figure 1 summarizes the results. A two-way, within-subjects ANOVA with type of scenes (natural vs. artifact) and stimulus conditions (NC, IC and LU) revealed a main effect of scene type, $F(1,19) = 131.71$, $p <$

.0001, a main effect of stimulus condition, $F(2,38) = 24.62$, $p < .0001$, and a significant interaction $F(2,38) = 24.76$, $p <.0001$. Our results demonstrate that chromatic manipulations affect recognition performance. However, the interaction reveals that this influence was different for different categories. We hypothesized that chromatic information would only be useful for recognition when it was diagnostic of a category. That is, categorization times should be significantly faster for a chromatic NC scene than for its gray-level LU equivalent. Indeed, mean RTs were significantly higher when chromatic information was removed from a natural scene, $F(1,38) = 54.755$, $p <.001$, (respectively, LU = 816 ms and NC = 786 ms) but the LU and NC versions of artifact scenes elicited almost identical RTs (742 ms and 738 ms, respectively). Another consequence of processing chromatic information for recognition is that a change of color could in principle impair recognition. However, this should only apply when color is diagnostic of a categorization. To test this hypothesis, we compared categorization latencies of IC and RC stimuli. We found that IC scenes took 46 ms longer to be categorized than NC scenes, $F(1,38) = 124.56$, $p <.0001$, and also that IC were slower to name that LU, $F(1,38) = 14.14$, $p <.001$. No such difference was observed for artifact scenes (see Figure 1).

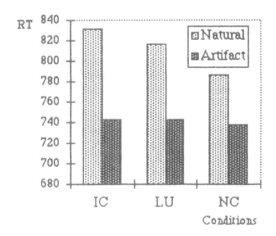

Figure 1: Mean reaction times as a function of type of category (Natural vs. Artefact) and color condition (IC = Incongruent Color, LU = Luminance, NC = Normal Color) for a stimulus presentation of 120 ms.

In sum, in opposition to the general conclusions of Biederman and Ju (1988), color is being used for recognition--at least for the fast identification of scenes. However, in agreement with Ostergaard and Davidoff (1985) this influence is limited to categories which are distinguishable on the basis of their color. Our data suggest that color and luminance are two independent cues available for fast scene recognition. However, we also found that color has no effect when it is not diagnostic of a category.

Experiment 2

The results of Experiment 1 were gathered in conditions of 120 ms presentations of scenes. Other studies have shown that complex scenes may be recognized with very fast accuracy even after shorter presentation times (Schyns & Oliva, 1994). However, these studies did not distinguish between the relative contribution of luminance and chromatic cues for recognition. An argument could be made that the time course of luminance and chromatic pathways are different (Billock, 1995) and that one (e.g., chromaticity) is systematically dependent on processing being initialized in the other (e.g., luminance). Thus, a 120 ms presentation of the stimuli could in fact mask the fact that one source of cues is being registered much later that the other cues. Experiment 2 replicated Experiment 1, using identical stimuli, but we now presented them for 30 ms. Although changes of presentation times do not test time course of processing per se, this experiment could reveal whether a very short presentation time was sufficient to register chromatic information sufficiently well to later speed up recognition.

Method

Subjects. Twenty Glasgow University students with normal or corrected vision were paid to participate to the experiment.

Stimuli. The same 120 color scenes as in Experiment 1, subdivided into natural and artifact scenes, were used in Experiment 2. The experiment was composed of the same 360 trials (120 NC, 120 IC and 120 LU).

Procedure. The procedure was identical to Experiment 1, except that the presentation time of the scenes was now 30 ms. Subject's task was to name the input as fast as they possibly could, using one of the possible category names (*beach, city, forest, room, road and valley*).

Results and Discussion

Subjects' mean RTs were collected for correct categorizations. A two-way within-subjects ANOVA with type of scene (natural vs. artifact) and stimulus condition (NC, IC and LU) revealed a significant of the main effect of scene type, $F(1, 19) = 24.10$, $p < .0001$, stimulus condition $F(2, 38) = 19.30$, $p < .0001$, and a significant interaction, $F(2, 38) = 4.87$, $p <.02$. Figure 2 summarizes the results. Globally, the patterns of results after a 30 ms presentation are similar to those reported for Experiment 1 with a 120 ms presentation: When it is diagnostic, chromatic information exerts a strong influence on scene recognition. This is observed for natural, NC categories which were recognized significantly faster then their LU versions, $F(1,38) = 21.96$, $p <.0001$, but no such effect was observed for artifact scenes (LU = 772 ms and NC = 767 ms). Locally, the categorization times of natural scenes revealed an interesting difference with the results observed in Experiment 1: IC scenes were categorized 36 ms slower than NC scenes, $F(1,38) = 22.21$, $p < .0001$, but not slower than their gray-level counterparts. No such difference existed for artifact scenes.

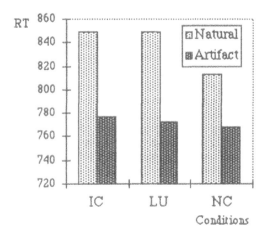

Figure 2: Mean RT as a function of type of category and color condition for a stimulus presentation of 30 ms.

These results confirm that chromatic information is used for speeded scene recognition. Why we did not obtain an interference of incongruent colors when the stimuli were presented very briefly deserves further studies. Clearly, it is not that color registration is impoverished by of a brief presentation, as color facilitates recognition in the NC condition. It could be that very brief presentations did no leave enough time for such an interference to develop.

General Discussion

Experiment 1 and 2 showed that color influences the speeded recognition of scene categories, but only when color is diagnostic. This effect has not been reported before in the scene recognition literature (but see Tanaka & Bunoski, 1996, for object recognition), and doubts have been raised about the control of diagnosticity and luminance in object recognition studies. Our results also suggest that color attributes are stored in memory along with luminance attributes (see Gegenfurtner et al., 1995). Of course, the absence of an effect for artifact scenes does not mean that color is not represented, but that it is less effective in this case as a categorization cue for recognition at a glance.

These results should have a strong impact on computational models of scene recognition which are more traditionally based on luminance (though see Liu & Yang, 1994; Uchiyama & Arbib, 1994). Speeded recognition of natural scenes requires an efficient encoding of different scene aspects. The results suggest that color should now be used as a supplementary categorical cue for complex image recognition. The integration of color and luminance information over time will be the topic of further studies.

References

Biederman, I. (1987). Recognition-by-components : A theory of human image understanding. *Psychological Review*, 94, 115-147.

Biederman, I., & Ju, G. (1988). Surface versus edge-based determinants of visual recognition. *Cognitive Psychology*, 20, 38-64.

Billock, V.A. (1995). Cortical simple cells can extract achromatic information from the multiplexed chromatic and achromatic signals in the parvocellular pathways. *Vision Research*, 35, 2359-2369.

Cavanagh, P. & Ramachandran, V. S. (1988). Structure from motion with equiluminous stimuli. *Annual Meeting CPA, Montreal.*

Damasio, A., Yamada, T., Damasio, H., Corbett, J, & McKee, J. (1980). Central achromatopsia: behavioral, anatomic, and physiological aspects. *Neurology,* 30, 1064-1071.

Gegenfurtner, K.R., Sharpe, L.T., & Wichmann, F.A. (1995). The contribution of color to recognition memory in normal and color-deficient observers. *Perception*, supp. 24, 12.

Liu, J. & Yang, Y. (1995). Multiresolution color image segmentation. *IEEE:PAMI*, 16, 689-700.

Logothetis, N. K., Schiller, P. H., Charles, E. R., & Hurlbert, A. C. (1989). Perceptual deficits and the role of color-opponent and broad-band channels in vision. *Science*, 247, 214-217.

Marr, D., & Nishihara, H.K. (1978). Representation and recognition of the spatial organization of the three-dimensional shapes. *Proceedings of the Royal Society of London*, B200, 269-294.

McIlhaga, W., Hine, T., Cole, G. R., & Snyder, A. W. (1990). Texture segregation with luminance and chromatic contrast. *Vision Research*, 30, 489-498.

Oliva, A., & Schyns, P.G. (1995). Mandatory scale perception promotes flexible scene categorizations. *17th Annual Conference of the Cognitive Science Society*, Pennsylvania, 159-163.

Ostergaard, A.L., & Davidoff, J.B. (1985). Some effects of color on naming and recognition of objects. *Journal of Experimental Psychology : Learning, Memory and Cognition*, 11, 579-587.

Schyns, P.G., & Oliva, A. (1994). From blobs to boundary edges : evidence for time and spatial scale dependant scene recognition. *Psychological Science*, 5, 195-200.

Tanaka, J.W., & Bunoski, L.M. (1996). Is the object recognition system really colorblind? Submitted for publication.

Uchiyama, T., & Arbib, M. A. (1994). Color image segmentation using competitive learning. *IEEE:PAMI*, 16, 1197-1206.

Wurm, L.H., Legge, G.E., Isenberg, L.M., & Luebker, A. (1993). Color improves object recognition in normal and low vision. *Journal of Experimental Psychology : Human Perception and Performance*, 19, 899-911.

Categorical Perception of Novel Dimensions

Robert L. Goldstone, Mark Steyvers, and Kenneth Larimer

Indiana University
Department of Psychology/Program in Cognitive Science
Bloomington, IN. 47405
rgoldsto@indiana.edu, msteyver@indiana.edu, klarimer@indiana.edu

Abstract

Categorical perception is a phenomenon in which people are better able to distinguish between stimuli along a physical continuum when the stimuli come from different categories than when they come from the same category. In a laboratory experiment with human subjects, we find evidence for categorical perception along a novel dimension that is created by interpolating (i.e. morphing) between two randomly selected bezier curves. A neural network qualitatively models the empirical results with the following assumptions: 1) hidden "detector" units become specialized for particular stimulus regions with a topologically structured competitive learning algorithm, 2) simultaneously, associations between detectors and category units are learned, and 3) feedback from the category units to the detectors causes the detectors to become concentrated near category boundaries. The particular feedback used, implemented in an "S.O.S. network," operates by increasing the learning rate of weights connecting inputs to detectors that are neighbors to a detector that produces an improper categorization.

Introduction

Models of category learning typically assume that the stimuli to be categorized can be described in terms of perceptual features or dimensions, and that concept learning involves linking these perceptual descriptions to categories (e.g. Kruschke, 1992). As such, in these "feed-forward" models, processing starts with a perceptual input, and output is in the form of a categorization.

Although categorization is clearly dependent on perceptual input, many researchers have also argued for a reciprocal influence of concept learning on the development of percepts (e.g. Goldstone, 1995). The notion that concepts can influence perception can be traced back at least as far as the Sapir-Whorf hypothesis (Whorf, 1941). The current work explores a version of this hypothesis, and provides a computational mechanism for simultaneous, reciprocal influences between perceptual inputs and acquired concepts. The particular variety of conceptual influence on perception explored here concerns whether specific regions of a novel perceptual dimension can become perceptually sensitized if the region is important for a learned categorization. Our modelling approach for accounting for the observed effects is to develop topologically ordered "detectors" that tend to be densely clustered at the boundary between categories.

Categorical Perception

The most relevant empirical support for categorical influences on perceptual sensitivity comes from work on "categorical perception" (for a review, see Harnad, 1987).

According to this phenomenon, people are better able to distinguish between physically different stimuli when the stimuli come from different categories than when they come from the same category. For example, Liberman, Harris, Hoffman, and Griffith (1957) generated a set of vowel-consonant syllables going from /be/ to /de/ to /ge/ by varying a particular physical value along a dimension. Results showed that when the physical difference between speech sounds was equated, subjects were better able to discriminate between two sounds that belonged to different phonemic categories such as /be/ and /de/ than they were able to discriminate between two sounds that belonged within the /be/ category.

Research in our laboratory has explored the development of categorical perception during an experimental session (Goldstone, 1994). Goldstone first trained subjects in one of several categorization conditions in which one physical dimension (e.g. size or brightness) was relevant and another was irrelevant. Subjects were then transferred to same/different judgments ("Are these two squares physically identical?"). Ability to discriminate between squares in the same/different judgment task, measured by Signal Detection Theory's d', was greater when the squares varied along dimensions that were relevant during categorization training. More relevant to categorical perception effects, regions within a dimension were selectively sensitized if they occurred at the boundary between categories. For example, if objects less than 2.5 cm belonged to Category A and objects greater than 2.5 cm belonged to Category B during training, then transfer results indicated heightened sensitivity to this particular region of the size dimension relative to other size values.

Sensitization versus Construction of Dimensions

The above experiments indicate that laboratory experience can perceptually sensitize dimensions and local regions within a dimension. The experimentally explored dimensions that display categorical perception have been pre-existing dimensions. For example, although laboratory training can sensitize size or regions of the size dimension, nobody doubts that our subjects have a notion of size as a dimension by the time they participate in the experiment. Although Goldstone (1994) found categorization-dependent sensitization within the integral dimensions of color brightness and saturation, categorical perception for truly arbitrary dimensions has not yet been found. Such a demonstration would argue for two levels of perceptual learning. In the first, particular values of existing dimensions are sensitized due to categorization demands. In the second, new dimensions are developed for describing stimuli because of their diagnosticity, or ability to cover the range of stimuli. Some researchers have speculated that this second type of learning has been severely underestimated by the use of laboratory stimuli that are clearly delineated into preexisting dimensions such as orientation, number, and size (e.g. Schyns, Goldstone, & Thibaut, 1995). The current experiment explores whether learned categories can cause sensitization of specific values along novel dimensions.

Experiment in Concept Learning Along an Arbitrary Dimension

In this experiment, a categorization is created that depends on the value of a stimulus along a new dimension. The new dimension is created by selecting two similar, arbitrarily curved objects, and treating these objects as endpoints on a continuum. Intermediate objects are then created by blending these endpoints in varying proportions. Thus, a negative contingency between the proportion of two shapes is formed: the greater the percentage of Shape A in an object, the less Shape B will be present. The arbitrary dimension can be considered as "the proportion of A relative to B" dimension, although subjects may attend to a small region of the shapes during categorization. Subjects learn one of two categorizations based on different cut-off values along this dimension, and then are transferred to a task that measures their perceptual sensitivity at various points along this dimension.

Method

Subjects. One hundred and forty undergraduate students from Indiana University served as participants in order to fulfill a course requirement, not including 12 subjects whose data was excluded for failing to meet a learning criterion of 70% correct categorizations. Forty-nine students were in the left split categorization condition, 45 students were in the right split condition, and 46 students were in the irrelevant categorization condition.

Materials. Stimuli were bezier curves based on 9 control points. Bezier curves are constructed by smoothly passing curves through or near an ordered set of control points. Two random bezier curves were constructed, and 60 intermediate curves were generated by linearly interpolating between the two random endpoints. From these 60 curves, the central 7 curves were selected as the stimuli to be displayed during categorization. An additional set of 7 other curves, to be

used in the control categorization condition, were created in the same manner from two different randomly chosen random curves. In this manner, the 7 curves within a dimension can be considered as intermediate frames from a movie that morphs from one arbitrary shape to another. The 7 stimuli used are shown in Figure 1. By choosing only the central 7 stimuli from the A-to-B continuum, the categorization and perceptual discrimination tasks are set to a reasonably high level of difficulty. Each stimulus was approximately 9 cm wide by 7 cm tall, and was displayed at a distance of 25 cm from the subject.

Procedure. There were two tasks in the hour-long experiment - category learning followed by same-different judgments. There were three categorization conditions: left split, right split, and irrelevant categorization. As shown in Figure 1, for the left split group, the first three curves to the left belonged to Category 1, and the last four curves belonged to Category 2. For the right split group, the first _four_ curves to the left belonged to Category 1, and the remaining curves belonged to Category 2. For the irrelevant categorization group, the first three curves from a dimension with completely different endpoint shapes belonged to Category 1, and the remaining curves belonged to Category 2.

During the categorization training, 40 repetitions of the seven curves were shown in random order. On an individual trial, a curve was shown in a randomly generated location on the screen. The curve remained on the screen until the subject pressed a key corresponding to their guess as to the curve's category. Category responses were made by pressing the keys "1" and "2." After a response was made, feedback was given as to the correctness of the response, and the correct category label was displayed. After 1.5 sec, the screen was erased, and after another 1 sec, the next trial began.

All three categorization training groups received the identical subsequent discrimination experiment, using the seven curves shown in Figure 1. Subjects were shown pairs of adjacent curves as ordered in Figure 1, or the identical curves repeated twice, and responded either "same" or "different." Subjects were instructed to press the "S" key on the keyboard if they believed the two curves to be physically identical, and to press the "D" key if they believed the two curves to differ in any way except location. The interval between trials was 1500 msec. Subjects made 150 same/different judgments in all.

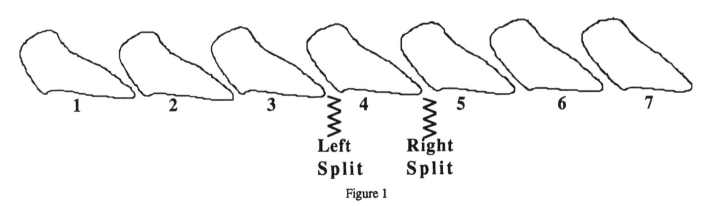

Figure 1

Results

The data of principle interest are subjects' sensitivities at discriminating between various pairs of curves, broken down as a function of their categorization condition. A d' measure of sensitivity was calculated. A d' of 0 indicates a complete lack of sensitivity in distinguishing "Same" from "Different" trials; d' values increase as sensitivity increases.

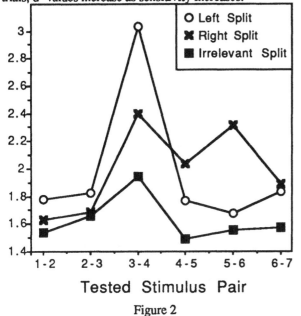

Figure 2

With 7 curves there are 6 pairs of adjacent curves. The d' for each of these 6 pairs in each categorization condition is shown in Figure 2. Overall, there were main effects due to both tested pair, $F(5, 122) = 4.3$, $p < .01$, and categorization condition, $F(2, 122) = 6.5$, $p < .01$. The former effect seems to be attributable to subjects' ability to discriminate between stimuli 3 and 4 (from Figure 1) more easily than other pairs. The latter effect is due to subjects in the left and right split groups having elevated sensitivity relative to the control groups. This effect is consistent with a large literature showing that preexposure to stimuli leads to their heightened discriminability (Hall, 1991).

Most relevant to learned categorical perception, a significant interaction between categorization condition and tested pair was found, $F(10, 122) = 2.9$, $p < .01$. As such, the categorization training in the first stage of the experiment altered the discriminabilities of stimuli in the experiment's second stage. To better visualize the exact effect of this influence, Figure 3 plots the sensitivity (d') obtained from the right split group minus the sensitivity from the left split group, for each of the six pairs of adjacent curves. As such, positive values signify greater sensitivity for the right split group than for the left split group. Although the effects of the splits are not symmetric, the general effect of categorization training seems to be that discriminability is relatively high for stimuli that fall near the category boundary. Even if we restrict our attention just to the 3-4 and 4-5 pairs, significantly higher d's are found when the pair rests on a boundary that was influential for categorization (d' = 2.54) than when it does not (d' =2.08), $F(1,122)=2.5$, $p < .01$.

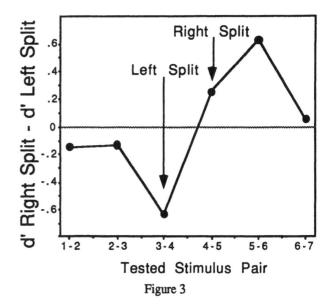

Figure 3

Discussion

The pattern of sensitivity to regions of the continuum formed by interpolating between two randomly selected bezier curves varies across the three categorization groups. This pattern is most accurately described as follows: ability to discriminate between two physically different curves is relatively high when the boundary between laboratory-trained categories falls relatively close to the pair of curves. Although there is only a substantial difference between the categorization groups for three pairs, this generalization applies to all six pairs in Figure 3 - sensitivity is higher for the right split categorization group when, and only when, the tested pair is closer to the right split than the left split.

Modelling Learned Categorical Perception Along a Novel Dimension

One useful property of neural networks for modeling learned categorical perception is that hidden units that intervene between input and output representations are capable of creating internal representations that capture important regularities in the inputted materials. Several models develop hidden units that can be interpreted as learned feature detectors (e.g. Schyns, 1992). Our model will use this technique in order to create topologically ordered feature detectors that tend to respond to specific values along a arbitrary continuum.

Empirical and Theoretical Constraints on Modeling

There are several empirical results, with respect to both categorization and subsequent perceptual sensitivity, that a model of learned categorical perception should show (Harnad, 1987). First, categorization judgments should rapidly change as the boundary between categories is crossed. Second, categorization of "caricatured" items (displaced away from a category's central tendency in the direction opposite to the boundary between the categories) should be at least as good, and often times better, than categorization of the central tendencies of the categories (Goldstone, in press). Third, sensitivity for discriminating physically different stimuli should be higher when the items straddle two categories than when they fall in a single category. Fourth, the current results suggest that elevated sensitivity should also extend to the regions next to the category boundary.

While constrained by the above empirical findings, our model is also constrained by two theoretical motivations. First and foremost, we wanted to supplement the unsupervised learning of feature detectors with feedback regarding categorization. The development of input-to-detector weights is constrained by a competitive learning algorithm (Kohonen, 1982) such that detectors become specialized for particular inputs, but is also influenced by the category units. In essence, if a detector predicts an incorrect categorization for an item, then it sends out an "S.O.S. signal" calling for its neighboring units to quickly move into the same area as the detector. Because detectors that incorrectly categorized will attract other units, the boundary between two categories will be particularly well populated by feature detectors, and consequently the "S. O. S. network" can predict flexible, learned categorical perception effects.

The second theoretical motivation for our model is to develop categorical perception starting from relatively raw, perceptual inputs. As such, the first stage of our network converts gray-scale two-dimensional drawings of curves to Gabor filter representations that describe the inputs in terms of spatially organized line segments. The detectors are trained upon these Gabor filter representations.

Details of the S.O.S. Network

The classification part of the model is a neural network similar to ALCOVE (Kruschke, 1992). The hidden layer of detectors are radial basis exemplar nodes maximally sensitive to stimuli at the position of these exemplar nodes. The output layer consists of nodes that classify the activation pattern of these exemplar nodes. The crucial differences with ALCOVE are that the exemplar nodes are topologically arranged in a one-dimensional lattice, and exemplar nodes can move their position in input space through competitive learning. These features allow the model to self-organize the exemplar nodes along the input dimensions. More importantly, because the learning rate is set proportional to the classification error, greater sensitivity near the category boundary can be predicted.

We used materials of the same type as those used in the experiment. A morphing sequence of 28 bezier curves was created, with each picture having 128x128 pixels. Each stimulus was filtered through Gabor filters (Daugman, 1985) with overlapping receptive fields to extract local features. Gabor filters with orientations of 0, 45, 90 and 135 degrees operated on 6 x 6 overlapping receptive fields that were

regularly spaced over the input picture. In total then, the Gabor filter output vector a, has 144 components. In figure 4a, one bezier curve is shown. Figures 4b, c, d and e, show the filtered activations over the receptive fields in the four orientations for this bezier curve. The transformation from the stimuli in pixel space to the Gabor filter space preserved the local similarity relations of the stimulus sequence; the distance between the Gabor vectors for stimuli k and k+1 was always smaller than the distance of the Gabor vectors for stimuli k and k+2. The inputs to the network are the components a_i of the filter vector a. The hidden, detector node activation, a_j, is determined by the radial basis function:

$$a_j^{hid} = \exp\left[-c\left(\sum_i \left(w_{ji}^{hid} - a_i^{in}\right)^2\right)^{1/2}\right]. \quad (1)$$

The weights, w_{ji} are the positions of the detector nodes in the input space. The drop off in sensitivity for patterns away from w_{ji} is determined by c. For each category k, there is an associated classification node k, with activation, a_k given by:

$$a_k^{out} = f\left(\sum_j w_{kj}^{out} a_j^{hid}\right). \quad (2)$$

The weights w_{kj} connect hidden and output layers and f is the sigmoid discriminant function. The probability of responding with category k is determined by the Luce choice rule,

$$P_{resp}(k) = \frac{a_k^{out}}{\sum_K a_K^{out}}. \quad (3)$$

The sum of squared error,

$$E = \sum_j \left(t_k - a_k^{out}\right)^2, \quad (4)$$

is based on the teacher signal t_k for node k which is 1 if the input stimulus belongs to category k, and 0 otherwise. Gradient descent is used to update the weights. The weights, w_{kj}, from hidden to output nodes are determined by:

$$\Delta w_{kj}^{out} = \lambda a_k^{out}\left(1 - a_k^{out}\right)\left(t_k - a_k^{out}\right)a_j^{hid} \quad (5)$$

where λ is the learning rate. The position weights, w_{ji}, of the hidden nodes are updated with a competitive learning rule,

$$\Delta w_{ji}^{hid} = E\eta \Lambda_{(j,j*)}\left(a_i^{in} - w_{ji}^{hid}\right), \quad (6)$$

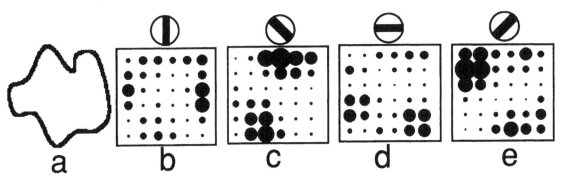

Figure 4

246

where the learning rate is proportional to a constant h and two terms: the neighborhood function $\Lambda_{(j,j^*)}$, and the classification error E. In the function $\Lambda_{(j,j^*)}$, j^* is the hidden detector that has the smallest Euclidian distance to the input pattern. $\Lambda_{(j,j^*)}$ is 1 for $j=j^*$ and falls off as a power function of distance $| j-j^* |$. This learning rule typically leads to a partial or complete topological ordering of the position weights w_{ji} in input space (Kohonen, 1982). The important factor in this model is that the learning rate in the competitive learning rule is also proportional to the classification error E. This leads to a distribution of detector positions that is more dense in regions where classification error is greatest.

Results of Simulation

We performed simulations with 28 input patterns, 14 hidden detectors, and two output nodes. In one simulation, the split between the two categories was placed between patterns 10 and 11 (left split). In another simulation, it was placed between 18 and 19 (right split). In figures 5a and b, the probabilities of responding with either category are shown for the left and right splits, respectively. The classification probabilities are highest between the extremes and the prototypes of the categories; thus, the model exhibits the often observed caricature effect whereby response is maximal not at the prototype of the category (e.g. the stimulus 5.5 for the left category in the left split condition) but at a point displaced from the prototype in the direction opposite to the other category. In figures 5c and d, the responses a_j for each of the 14 detector nodes are shown for each stimulus value. Each curve corresponds to the response profile for one detector. These figures give some insight into the distributions of the position weights w_{ji} of the hidden nodes in input space, because activation a_j is maximal for input at the position weight w_{ji}. The figures show that the hidden nodes are more densely distributed around the

categorization boundary as a result of the feedback of classification error in the learning rule (6). These figures also show that the detector node responses for patterns surrounding the maximally responding detector monotonically decrease with distance from this detector. This reflects the preservation of the local similarity relations by the spatial topology of the detectors.

A sensitivity measure for same/different judgements in the model was constructed by taking the Euclidian distance between the hidden node activation patterns for the two patterns to be judged. In figure 5e and f, sensitivity is shown for comparisons of patterns 1 and 3, 3 and 5, 5 and 7 etc. The peak sensitivity occurs approximately at the category boundary. This occurs because slightly different stimuli that occur near the category boundary will cause substantially different activation patterns on the detector units, given the dense concentration of detectors in this region.

Discussion

The experiment and computer simulation support the possibility that category learning can entail not only the sensitization of regions of a preexisting dimensions, but can also sensitize regions of new dimensions. The dimensions are unlikely to have existed before the experiment because they were created by interpolating between arbitrary curves. The dimension is either interpretable as "Proportion of Shape A relative to Shape B" or in terms of some smaller sub-component that continuously changes from Shape A to B. As with standard categorical perception effects, sensitization relative to the control condition is greatest for stimuli at the boundary between the categories.

The simulation provides insights into the phenomenon of categorical perception along new dimensions. First, Kohonen's self-organizing feature map

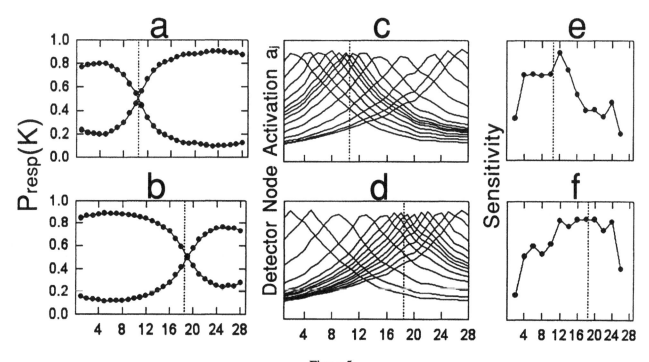

Figure 5

algorithm is typically understood as developing detectors for specific stimuli. Although this is certainly one way to understand our network's behavior, it can also be understood as creating detectors for regions along a dimension. Second, the network shows how the structure implicit in stimuli that fall along a new dimension can be captured by the topological positions of detectors units. The natural similarity relations between adjacent stimuli (in Figure 1) leads, without supervision, to the construction of a locally and globally well-ordered sets of detector units. Once the network has settled, the detectors on the left and right ends will be specialized for the two extreme curves, and the detectors in between will handle the intermediate curves in proper order.

The final major insight of the network's treatment of categorical perception effects, embodied by the S.O.S. principle, is that these effects can be modelled by creating relatively dense representations of items at the border between categories. This treatment of categorical perception differs from other neural network implementations (Anderson, Silverstein, Ritz, & Jones, 1977; Harnad, Hanson, & Lubin, 1994). In these other approaches, each category has its own attractor, and the stimuli that fall into one category will all be propelled toward the category's attractor. Categorical perception occurs because inputs that are very close but fall into different categories will be driven to highly separated attractors. In contrast, in our S.O.S. network, categorical perception emerges because many detectors will congregate at the category boundary, and thus small differences at this boundary will be reflected by different patterns of detector activity. There are two potential advantages of our account. First, categorical perception effects can arise even when there is no demand to categorize the stimuli, once the detectors have moved toward the boundary. This fits the requirements of the same/different task well because physical identity, not category identity, is the basis for these judgments. Second, our account explains how stimuli falling on the same side of a category boundary may also become more discriminable after categorization training, if they are sufficiently close to the category boundary. The results from the human experiment suggest that this is the case for people. In networks that explain categorical perception by creating different attractors for different categories, unique items that are close to the boundary but fall in the same category become more similar with processing, not more distinctive.

In conclusion, category learning can lead to the development of new dimensions. Once developed, regions within these dimensions can be selectively sensitized if they are important for determining category boundaries. The qualitative effect of category learning on perceptual sensitivity can be modeled by a neural network that simultaneously develops detectors for dimension values and associations between detectors and categories. Within this framework, there is a top-down influence of categorization that gives rise to categorical perception - when a detector produces an improper categorization, then learning rates for its neighboring detectors are momentarily increased. In this manner, the difficult-to-categorize regions of a dimension will garner a high density of detectors, thereby permitting sensitive discriminations at the category boundaries.

Acknowledgements

We would like to thank John Kruschke and Philippe Schyns for many helpful comments. This work was funded by National Science Foundation grant SBR-9409232 awarded to Robert Goldstone

References

Anderson, J. A., Silverstein, J. W., Ritz, S. A., & Jones, R. S. (1977). Distinctive features, categorical perception, and probability learning: Some applications of a neural model. Psychological Review, 84, 413-451.

Daugman, J.G. (1985). Uncertainty relation for resolution in space, spatial frequency, and orientation optimized by two-dimensional visual cortical filters. Journal of the Optical Society of America A, 2, 1160-1169.

Garner, W. R. (1974). The processing of information and structure. Hillsdale, NJ: Erlbaum.

Goldstone, R. L. (in press). Isolated and Interrelated Concepts. Memory and Cognition.

Goldstone, R. L. (1994). influences of categorization on perceptual discrimination. Journal of Experimental Psychology: General, 123, 178-200.

Goldstone, R. L. (1995). Effects of categorization on color perception. Psychological Science, 6, 298-304.Hall, G. (1991). Perceptual and associative learning. Clarendon Press: Oxford.

Harnad, S. (1987). Categorical perception. Cambridge University Press: Cambridge.

Harnad, S., Hanson, S. J., & Lubin, J. (1994). Learned categorical perception in neural nets: Implications for symbol grounding. in V. Honavar & L. Uhr (Eds.) Artificial intelligence and neural networks: Steps toward principled integration. Academic Press: Boston

Kohonen, T. (1982). Self-organized formation of topologically correct feature maps. Biological cybernetics, 43, 59-69.

Kruschke, J. K. (1992). ALCOVE: An exemplar-based connectionist model of category learning. Psychological Review, 99, 22-44.

Liberman, A. M., Harris, K. S., Hoffman, H. S., & Griffith, B.C. (1957). The discrimination of speech sounds within and across phoneme boundaries. Journal of Experimental Psychology, 54, 358-368.

Schyns, P. (1992). A modular neural network model of concept acquisition. Cognitive Science, 15, 461-508.

Schyns, P. G., Goldstone, R. L., & Thibaut, J-P (1995). The development of features in object concepts. Indiana University Cognitive Science Technical Report #133. Bloomington, IN.

Whorf, B. L. (1941). Languages and logic. in J. B. Carroll (ed.) Language, Thought, and Reality: Selected papers of Benjamin Lee Whorf. MIT Press (1956), Cambridge, Mass. (pp. 233-245).

Categorical Perception in Facial Emotion Classification

Curtis Padgett and **Garrison W. Cottrell**
Computer Science & Engineering
University of California, San Diego
La Jolla, CA 92093
{cpadgett,gary}@cs.ucsd.edu

Ralph Adolphs
Department of Neurology
University of Iowa, Iowa City
radolphs@blue.weeg.uiowa.edu

Abstract

We present an automated emotion recognition system that is capable of identifying six basic emotions (happy, surprise, sad, angry, fear, disgust) in novel face images. An ensemble of simple feed-forward neural networks are used to rate each of the images. The outputs of these networks are then combined to generate a score for each emotion. The networks were trained on a database of face images that human subjects consistently rated as portraying a single emotion. Such a system achieves 86% generalization on novel face images (individuals the networks were not trained on) drawn from the same database.

The neural network model exhibits categorical perception between some emotion pairs. A linear sequence of morph images is created between two expressions of an individual's face and this sequence is analyzed by the model. Sharp transitions in the output response vector occur in a single step in the sequence for some emotion pairs and not for others. We plan to us the model's response to limit and direct testing in determining if human subjects exhibit categorical perception in morph image sequences.

Introduction

In this paper, we describe a neural network model that classifies static face images based on their emotional content and examine the behavior of the model over a sequence of linearly interpolated images between two differing emotions of the same face. We are specifically looking for emotion pairs where the transition in the output response of the network is abrupt. That is, prior to the transition, the model classifies all the images in the sequence as examples of the first category and all the subsequent images as examples of the second emotion. Such transitions are known as categorical perception and are known to occur in many perceptual tasks [9]. The model's predictions can then be compared with a similar set of tasks performed on human subjects. From this interaction we hope to discern the functional organization of the visual emotion recognition system.

The neural network model consists of an ensemble of two layer, feed-forward networks trained with back propagation. The faces are represented to the network as projections of seven 32x32 pixel blocks from feature regions (both eyes and mouth) onto the principal component space generated from randomly located blocks in the image data set (see Figure 1). This technique is similar to the eigen-face/feature recognition work of Turk and Pentland [14] and Pentland et. al. [13] where projections of faces or features are used to reduce the dimensionality of the image. However, where their work uses fixed locations on the face to generate the eigen-space (result-

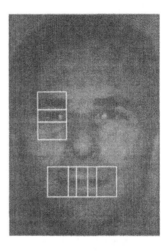

Figure 1: The figure shows the location of the 32x32 pixel blocks in the feature regions (only one eye region is shown, both are used). Each block is projected onto the top 15 eigenvectors, resulting in a 105 dimensional vector for each face.

ing in a face- or feature-like appearance of the templates), we use image areas drawn randomly so that our templates are of a more non-specific nature (see Figure 2).

In previous work we have shown that the generalization obtained with this representation is superior to those obtained using the eigen-face/feature strategy [12]. The expected generalization rate on novel individuals presented to the network making use of the random block representation is 86% while humans do nearly 92% on the same database. These results are comparable with emotion recognition rates obtained by other automated vision systems which require a *neutral to emotion* temporal sequences for training and evaluation [11, 15, 1].

Face Data

In working with emotions in face images, care must be taken to insure that the particular emotion being portrayed is correct. Feigned emotions by untrained individuals exhibit significant differences with the prototypical face expression [7]. These differences often result in disagreement between the observed emotion and the expression the actor is attempting to feign. In previous work, Cottrell and Metcalfe had undergraduates feign emotions. While their network performed well on identity and gender classification, it never did well on emotion. Cottrell and Metcalfe speculated that their results were due to poor portrayal of the emotions by their subjects [5].

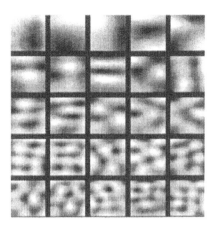

Figure 2: The top 25 eigenvectors from PCA of 32x32 pixel patches drawn randomly over the face database.

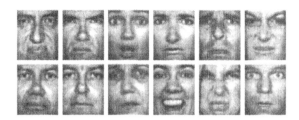

Figure 3: Examples from the Pictures of Facial Affect database normalized and cropped.

To reduce this possibility, we make use of a validated facial emotion database (Pictures of Facial Affect) assembled by Ekman and Friesen [6]. Each of the face images in this set exhibits a substantial agreement between the labeled emotion and the observed response of human subjects. The actors used in this database were trained to reliably produce emotions using FACS [7] and their images were presented to undergraduates for testing. The agreement between the emotion the actor was required to express and the students' observations was at least 70% on all the images incorporated into the database.

Twelve of the fourteen individuals contained in the Pictures of Facial Affect database were used in this study, 6 male and 6 female (the two remaining set of images were inadvertently corrupted during image capture). A total of 97 images each portrays one of 7 emotions– happy, sad, fear, anger, surprise, disgust or neutral. With the exception of the neutral faces, each image in the set is labeled with a response vector of the remaining six emotions indicating the fraction of total respondents classifying the image with a particular emotion.

Although care was taken in collecting the original images, natural variations in lighting, head size and the mouth's expression must be accounted for. The original images exhibited significant variation in the distance between the eyes (2.7 pixels) and in the vertical distance from the eyes to the mouth (5.0 pixels). To achieve scale invariance, each image was scaled so that prominent facial features were located in the same image region. Eye and mouth templates were constructed from a number of images and the most correlated template was used to localize the respective feature. Illumination variances were minimized by individually stretching each of the images to encompass the full grey scale range. Similar techniques have been employed in previous work on faces [3, 4, 14, 13]. Figure 3 shows examples of some of the normalized face images used in the study.

Classifier design and training

The models used to conduct this study consist of ensembles of feed-forward, fully connected neural networks each containing a single hidden layer with 10 nodes. Each network is trained independently using on-line back propagation with the response vectors from the Pictures of Facial Affect database

serving as the target. The input to each network is the projection of the seven locations of the faces shown in Figure 1 onto the top 15 eigenvectors of 900 random 32X32 blocks (the top 3 rows of Figure 2. The projections onto each eigenvector are normalized into Z scores on a per-eigenvalue basis.

Since we had a small dataset of twelve individuals, for each individual, we trained an ensemble of networks on the remaining 11 individuals, and then combined the scores of the ensemble members to get a generalization score on the one individual the ensemble had not seen during training. To minimize the impact of choosing a poor hold out set from the training set, each of the 11 individuals in the training set was in turn used as a hold out. If the error on the hold out set went up over three training epochs, training was stopped. This procedure is illustrated in Figure 4. Thus we end up with 12 independent ensemble network models.

To combine the scores of the 11 networks, a number of different techniques are possible: winner take all, weighted average output, voting, etc. The method that we found to consistently give the highest generalization rate involved using Z scores from the 11 networks for each individual. The average output for each possible emotion across all the networks was calculated along with its deviation over the entire training set. These values were used to normalize the summed output of the 11 networks. The highest output Z score for a particular input was considered to be the emotion found by the ensemble. For any input pattern, we calculate the average of all 11 network outputs for emotion j:

$$a_j = \frac{\sum_{i=1}^{11} o_{ij}}{11}$$

where o_{ij} is the output of net_i on emotion j for that pattern. Then we convert this to a Z score:

$$\hat{a}_j = \frac{a_j - \bar{a}_j}{\sigma_j}$$

where $\bar{a}_j$ and σ_j are the average and deviation for output unit j across all the pattern outputs over the entire 11 networks. The average generalization rate achieved by the classifiers is 86% (± 0.2).

Morph Sequence

A large body of literature in cognitive psychology has demonstrated that certain stimuli, such as phonemes, are perceived categorically by human subjects [10, 9]. Categorical perception is said to occur when stimuli can be discriminated no better than they can be labeled, although in practice somewhat more relaxed criteria are often taken as evidence of categorical

Hold-one-out Cross Validation
Emotion Classifier

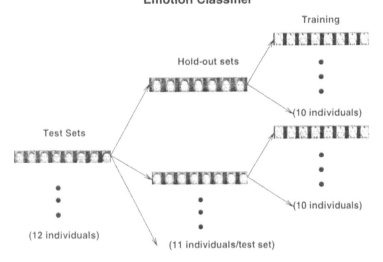

Training

Hold-out sets

(10 individuals)

Test Sets

(10 individuals)

(12 individuals)

(11 individuals/test set)

Figure 4: Structure of training sets used for creating ensemble network.

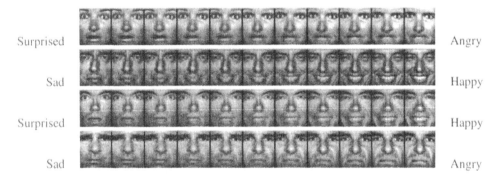

Surprised — Angry

Sad — Happy

Surprised — Happy

Sad — Angry

Figure 5: Typical examples of the morphing process. The original expressions are at the extremes of the sequences while the interior images are linear interpolations of the two images.

perception. Although the evidence for certain "low level" categorical perception is strong (e.g. phonemes, colors), much less is known about how we categorize more complex stimuli. Two recent studies suggest that some of the information signaled by faces, notably their emotional expression [8] and their unique identity [2], is perceived categorically.

The present study concentrates on the perception of emotional facial expressions. We are aware of only a single study that has provided evidence for categorical perception of emotion in facial expressions [8]. That study used line drawings of faces, and morphs of those line drawings, as the stimuli. Transitions between certain emotional expressions appeared to be perceived categorically, while other transitions did not show such an effect. Given these intriguing findings obtained with line drawings of faces, we wanted to approach the issue using images of actual facial expressions of emotion.

To determine the type of transitions that the neural network model exhibits, we linearly transform a face image of an individual expressing one emotion to the same individual expressing another at fixed intervals. The resultant morphed image sequence can then be transformed into the input representation and presented to the classifier in a normal manner.

Figure 5 shows typical image sequences generated by this process.

For the network model, three distinct types of response vectors are generated over the course of the transition sequences. At either end of the morph transition sequence, the network model responds correctly to the original image. When the maximum output response changes from the first to the second emotion, this is termed the *crossover point*.

A *Type 1 transition* is where the network response at the crossover point is high with respect to a threshold response – that is, *both* emotions are above threshold. We set the threshold at 0.5 standard deviations above the average response, which is the maximum value that maintains the 86% generalization rate of the network (in the original work, a correct response was taken as the maximum Z score [12]). For Type 1 transitions, both emotions elicit high responses over a large portion of the sequence indicating similarity between the two emotions in the transition sequence.

A *Type 2 transition* is when both emotion responses are below threshold at the crossover point. This type of transition has a large portion of the morph sequence without any prominent emotions. This indicates that the categories are quite

251

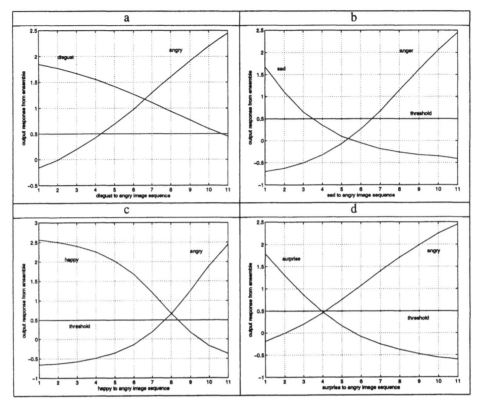

Figure 6: The graphs show the output response of the two emotions of the neural network model for the morph image sequences. Graphs **a** and **b** are examples of Type 1 and 2 transitions respectively, while **c** and **d** illustrate Type 3.

distant in the model space.

A *Type 3 transition* occurs when the crossover point is near the threshold. This indicates a sharp transition in classification of the morph images so that all (or most) images prior to the crossover are classified the same as the original image and those subsequent to it, the same as the morphed–to image. It is this type of transition we associate with categorical perception. Figure 6 presents examples of the output responses of the associated emotions that illustrate the three types of transitions.

Results

To examine the type of transitions between emotion pairs, morph sequences between differing emotions in each of the 12 ensemble network's test set were generated and presented to the appropriate ensemble network for evaluation. A morph sequence of 9 images (plus the 2 originals) was constructed for each distinct emotion pair of the individual (fear to fear morphs for example, were not examined). The total number of morph sequences was 250, approximately 17 sequences for each of the 15 possible emotion combinations.

A simple score was used to evaluate the type of the transition for each of the morph sequences. As the change in the ensemble network's output across the sequence was either monotonically increasing or decreasing, simply counting the number of outputs greater than the threshold of +0.5 standard deviations is sufficient in determining the type of the transition. If we simply add the number of instances where emotion

1 is above the threshold to the number of instances emotion 2 is above the threshold and subtract the length of the sequence from the total, the sign and magnitude of the resultant value provides a simple score indicating the transition type. High positive scores indicate that the ensemble network output was responsive to both emotions over a large number of images (Type 1 transition) while large negative scores indicate that the response vectors of both emotions were below the threshold for a number of images (Type 2 transition). Scores near zero are the Type 3 transitions that indicate categorical perception. Figure 7 presents the experimental results from lowest to highest scores.

The ensemble networks predictions about the type of relationships between the emotion categories that exist in the face image data is presented in Figure 8. The entries in the table are arranged so that the emotion pairs at the top of the columns have the scores most representative of that type. A cut off of ±1.5 steps was used to delimit the range of values associated with Type 3 behavior (i.e. the transition area scores were within 1.5 steps of 0).

The ensemble models' predictions seem reasonable given the nature of the categories. For instance, happy faces, the only positive emotion examined, do not seem particularly close to any of the other five emotions. Happy has no positive scores and the transitions between it and the other emotions consist solely of Types 2 and 3. Type 1 transitions are exhibited by the emotion pairs that are neighbors when the human data from the Pictures of Facial Affects database is subjected

Emotion Pair	Average	Deviation
Fear-Disgust	-4.1	0.4
Surprise-Disgust	-4.0	0.3
Happy-Sad	-3.0	1.3
Fear-Anger	-2.7	0.8
Happy-Anger	-2.5	0.9
Sad-Fear	-2.0	1.0
Happy-Surprise	-2.0	0.5
Sad-Surprise	-1.9	1.8
Happy-Fear	-1.3	0.8
Sad-Anger	-0.4	0.9
Anger-Surprise	-0.1	1.3
Happy-Disgust	-0.1	1.0
Sad-Disgust	2.7	2.3
Anger-Disgust	4.4	1.6
Fear-Surprise	8.9	1.0

Figure 7: Averages and deviations of emotion pair scores of the neural network model.

Type 1	Type 2	Type 3
Fear-Surpr	Fear-Disg	Happy-Disg
Anger-Disg	Surprise-Disg	Anger-Surpr
Sad-Disg	Happy-Sad	Sad-Anger
	Fear-Anger	Happy-Fear
	Happy-Anger	
	Sad-Fear	
	Happy-Surpr	
	Sad-Surpr	

Figure 8: The ensemble network's predictions of the type classifications for the various emotion pairs.

to Multi-Dimensional Scaling (MDS) (data not shown). Type 2 transitions are the most common, indicating significant separation between most emotion pairs (again similar to the circular arrangement found using MDS). Finally, the Type 3 transitions are from emotion pairs that are quite opposite.

Conclusion

We have demonstrated that a relatively simple neural network model is able to recognize emotions and make predictions about how visual categories are related to one another. We intend to use these results to guide us in testing human subjects in order to determine if categorical perception occurs in morph image sequences of actual images. An exhaustive search of all possible morph combinations is difficult (time consuming and costly) when testing humans but the models' predictions should be able to significantly reduce the number and type of combinations tested. We have begun human tests to validate the predictions on the Type 1 and Type 3 transitions. Subjects are randomly shown each image 10 times and make a forced choice between the endpoint emotions. Although our n of 2 is not large enough to be reliable, both subjects showed very sharp (sigmoidal) transitions for Type 3, and very linear trends for Type 1, as predicted by the model. If a comparison of the model and human data is favorable, we can begin to use this type of model to investigate the performance changes encountered in emotion recognition (and other static recognition

tasks) for patients with brain lesions.

Our results provide specific avenues for further research, and make predictions about how human subjects may perceive blends of different emotions signaled by a face. Since it is just such blends of emotion that are most typically encountered in everyday life, this line of research will contribute to human social cognition in general.

Acknowledgements

We wish to thank the GEURU research group at University of California, San Diego and reviewers for helpful comments on this work.

References

[1] M. Bartlett, P. Viola, T. Sejnowski, J. Larsen, J. Hager, and P. Ekman. Classifying facial action. In *Advances in Neural Information Processing Systems 8*, Cambridge, MA, 1996. MIT Press.

[2] J. Beale and F. Keil. Categorical effects in the perception of faces. *Cognition*, 57:217–239, 1992.

[3] D. Beymer. Face recognition under varying pose. Technical Report AI Memo No. 1461, MIT Artificial Intelligence Lab, 1993.

[4] R. Brunelli and T. Poggio. Face recognition: Feature versus templates. *IEEE Trans. Patt. Anal. Machine Intell.*, 15(10), October 1993.

[5] Garrison W. Cottrell and Janet Metcalfe. Empath: Face, gender and emotion recognition using holons. In R.P. Lippman, J. Moody, and D.S. Touretzky, editors, *Advances in Neural Information Processing Systems 3*, pages 564–571, San Mateo, 1991. Morgan Kaufmann.

[6] P. Ekman and W. Friesen. Pictures of facial affect, 1976.

[7] P. Ekman and W. Friesen. *Facial Action Coding System*. Consulting Psychologists, Palo Alto, CA, 1977.

[8] N. Etcoff and J. Magee. Categorical perception of facial expressions. *Cognition*, 44:227–240, 1992.

[9] Stevan R. Harnad. *Categorical perception: the groundwork of cognition*. Cambridge University Press, Cambridge, NY, 1987.

[10] A. Liberman, K. Harris, H. Hoffman, and B. Griffith. The discrimination of speech sounds within and across phoneme boundaries. *Journal of Experimental Psychology*, 54:358–368, 1957.

[11] K. Mase. Recognition of facial expression from optical flow. *IEICE Transactions*, 74(10):3474–3483, 1991.

[12] C. Padgett and G. Cottrell. Identifying emotion in static face images. In *Proceedings of the 2nd Joint Symposium on Neural Computation*, volume 5, pages 91–101, La Jolla, CA, 1995. University of California, San Diego.

[13] A. Pentland, B. Moghaddam, and T. Starner. View-based and modular eigenspaces for face recognition. In *IEEE Conference on Computer Vision & Pattern Recognition*, 1994.

[14] Matthew Turk and Alexander Pentland. Eigenfaces for recognition. *The Journal of Cognitive Neuroscience*, 3:71–86, 1991.

[15] Yacoob and Davis. Recognizing human facial expression. Technical Report CAR-TR-706, University of Maryland Center for Automation Research, 1994.

MetriCat: A Representation for Basic and Subordinate-level Classification

Brian J. Stankiewicz and **John E. Hummel**
Department of Psychology
University of California, Los Angeles
Los Angeles, CA 90095-1563
bstankie@psych.ucla.edu, jhummel@psych.ucla.edu

Abstract

An important function of human visual perception is to permit object classification at multiple levels of specificity. For example, we can recognize an object as a "car," (the basic level) a "Ford Mustang" (subordinate level), and "Joe's Mustang" (instance level). Although this capacity is fundamental to human object perception, most computational models of object recognition either focus exclusively on basic-level classification (e.g., Biederman, 1987; Hummel & Biederman, 1992; Hummel & Stankiewicz, 1996) or exclusively on instance-level classification (e.g., Ullman & Basri, 1991; Edelman & Poggio, 1990). A computational account that naturally integrates both levels of classification remains elusive. We describe a general approach to representing numerical properties (e.g., those that characterize object shape) that simultaneously supports both basic and subordinate/instance-level recognition. The account is based on a general nonlinear coding for numerical quantities describing both featural variables (such as degree of curvature and aspect ratio) and configural variables (such as relative position). Used as the input to a classifier with Gaussian receptive fields, this representation supports recognition at multiple levels of specificity, and suggests an account of the role of attention and time in the classification of objects at different levels of abstraction.

Introduction

One of the most notable properties of human visual perception is our capacity to recognize objects despite variations in the viewing conditions under which the image is presented to the retina (e.g., viewing angle). Numerous models have been proposed in the attempt to account for this property of human object recognition. These models can be divided into two broad classes according to the general strategy they adopt to attack this problem (see Liu, Knill & Kersten, 1995; Tarr, 1995). One class (typically associated with structural description theories of recognition) exploits categorical image properties as the primary basis for object recognition (e.g., Biederman, 1987; Hummel & Biederman, 1992; Hummel & Stankiewicz, 1996). On this account, objects are represented in terms of categorical features (including the categorical relations among those features) that remain unchanged as an object's distance or orientation relative to the viewer varies: Because the features remain the same in many views, recognition is unaffected by many

changes in viewpoint. The other class of models uses alignment (e.g., Ullman, 1989), view interpolation (e.g., Poggio & Edelman, 1990) or other normalizations (see Hummel & Stankiewicz, 1995) to bring new object views into correspondence with stored views: Here, the normalization serves to correct for variations in the locations of an object's features (in the image) that result from variations in viewpoint.

One notable difference between these approaches is that the former emphasizes the role of categorical image properties (such as categorical features and relations), whereas the latter emphasizes the role of holistic metric properties (specifically, the numerical coordinates of object features). In addition to supporting different algorithms for discounting variations due to viewpoint, these differing approaches to object representation also give rise to different "expertise" at different levels of classification (Bülthoff & Edelman, 1992): Categorical models may provide a better account of recognition at the basic level (e.g., recognizing an object as a "car"; Rosch, Mervis, Johnson, & Boyes-Braem, 1976), while metric models may provide a better account of recognition at the subordinate or instance level (e.g., recognizing an object as a "Mustang" or "Joe's Mustang").

The human is expert at both basic- and subordinate-level classification. It is tempting to speculate that this dual expertise reflects the simultaneous operation of both approaches to recognition: Perhaps categorical features or structural descriptions allow us to classify objects at the basic level while metrically-specific holistic representations allow us to classify objects at the subordinate or instance level (Bülthoff & Edelman, 1992; Farah, 1992). While this account is almost certainly correct for some cases of subordinate-level recognition (e.g., face recognition), it is likely inadequate as a complete account of human multi-level classification. One problem with this account is that it predicts that people will classify objects at the subordinate-level faster than they classify objects at the basic-level (holistic representations can be generated much faster than categorical structural descriptions; see Hummel & Stankiewicz, 1996), whereas people are fastest to classify objects at the basic level (e.g., Rosch, et. al, 1976). A second limitation of this account is that it predicts that subordinate level recognition should be more holistic than basic-level classification. While this is true for face recognition (Tanaka & Farah, 1993), it is not true for all subordinate-level classification tasks (e.g., Biederman & Schiffrar, 1987). Given these considerations, it seems likely that the human visual system achieves multi-level classification on the basis of something more sophisticated than a simple hybrid holistic-categorical representation of shape.

This paper presents our progress toward a model of multi-level classification based on a different kind of hybrid metric-categorical representation of object shape. Following the structural approach of Hummel and Biederman (1992; Hummel & Stankiewicz, 1996), we assume that independent attributes are represented on independent units (i.e., rather than representing attributes and their locations holistically as complete "views"). But in contrast to these models, we assume that shape attributes are not coded in a strictly categorical fashion (e.g., "straight vs. curved", "parallel vs. non-parallel," etc.). Rather, we adopt a representation of numerical quantities (such as degree of curvature and degree of parallelism) that captures both the metric and categorical aspects of those quantities. Like a categorical representation, the proposed representation changes fastest across categorical boundaries (such that the representation of curvature 0.1 [slightly curved] differs more from curvature 0 [straight] than it differs from curvature 0.2 [more curved]). But like a metric representation, it also captures differences between numerical values on the same side of a categorical boundary (e.g., between curvature 0.1 and curvature 0.2). In combination with an architecture for classifying objects on the basis of these metric-categorical ("MetriCat") representations, the result is a model that can classify objects at multiple levels of abstraction simultaneously. The model also suggests a natural account of the role of attention and time in classification at different levels of specificity, and the relationship between view specificity and levels of classification.

The MetriCat Representation of Numerical Values

As described here, the model is addressed only to the representation of properties that can be characterized as real values (or differences of real values) along a single dimension. For example, local curvature can be characterized in terms of a real number ranging from $-\infty$ (infinitely curved in one direction) to 0 (straight) to ∞ (infinitely curved in the opposite direction). Similarly, the expansion in the axis between two straight lines can be described by a real number in the range $-\infty \ldots \infty$, where negative values indicate that the axis narrows from end A to end B, positive values indicate that it expands from end A to end B, and zero indicates that the it remains a constant width along its length (i.e., the lines are parallel). A strictly categorical representation of these values might represent curvature = 0 as "straight" and all curvatures $\neq 0$ as "curved"; likewise, the axes might be represented as simply "parallel" (expansion = 0) or "non-parallel" (non-zero expansion). Such codes change rapidly at a single point (the transition point between adjacent values), and do not change at all in between those values. This property is responsible for the utility of categorical codes for class recognition and for discounting variations in viewpoint (see, e.g., Biederman,

1987), but it is a liability as a basis for instance-level recognition: Two shapes that can only be distinguished by, say, the degree of curvature on a given edge will be identical in a strictly categorical code.

MetriCat represents numerical values in an intermediate fashion, in that it emphasizes differences across categorical boundaries (e.g., straight vs. curved.) without completely discarding differences on the same side of a categorical boundary (e.g., different degrees of curvature). Specifically, we represent numerical variables as a logistic function of their raw numerical value (see also Hummel & Stankiewicz, 1995):

$$C = \frac{1}{1 + e^{-R\kappa}},\qquad(1)$$

where C is the represented value, R is the raw numerical value, and κ is a constant. Like a categorical code, C(R) has the property that it changes fastest across categorical boundaries in R. For example, if R is local curvature, then adding a small degree of curvature, say 1, to $R = 0$ (a straight line) has a greater impact on the value of C than adding the same amount of curvature to R = 10 (a curved line) (C(0) - C(1) = 0.5 - 0.731 = -0.231, whereas C(10) - C(11) = 0.99954 - 0.9998 = -0.00044). Thus, like a categorical variable, C changes fastest when the raw value, R, crosses a categorical boundary; but unlike a purely categorical variable, C continues to change even within categorical boundaries of R.

We assume that objects are visually represented in terms of the MetriCat values of each of several numerical quantities (such as the aspect ratio and cross-section curvature of each of their parts; see Biederman, 1987). The value of each variable, C^i, is coded as a vector $\mathbf{c}^i$, where the j th element of $\mathbf{c}^i$ is a unit, c^i_j, with receptive field in C^i that has a specific center, μ^i_j, and a specific width, w^i_j. In the current model, the widths and centers were set to random values in the ranges $0 < w < 0.5$ and $0 \leq \mu \leq 1.0$, respectively.

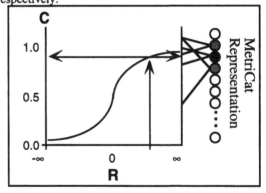

Figure 1: Illustration of the MetriCat representation of a specific value of R. C is a logistic function of R and units (right side) respond to specific values of C.

The bottom-up input to unit c^i_j at time t is:

$$I^i_{j,t} = G(\left| C^i - \mu^i_j \right|, w^i_j),\qquad(2)$$

where G is the Gaussian, C^i is the input real value input on dimension i, μ_j is the center of receptive field j, and w^i_j is the width (standard deviation) of receptive field j. For the purposes of the simulations reported here, we assume that every object is represented by two MetriCat vectors, c^1 and c^2, where each vector encodes the MetriCat representation of one numerical variable. For our current purposes, the precise meanings of these vectors (e.g., "c^1 codes curvature", etc.) is unimportant. Rather, we are interested in the properties of the collection of vectors as a basis for classifying arbitrary objects whose similarity relations are defined to correspond to different basic-level classes (i.e., low similarity, or very different vector representations) and different members of those classes (i.e., high similarity, or similar but non identical vector representations): Will the model treat different members of the same "class" as similar but not identical?

Classification Based on MetriCat Values

To answer this question, it is first necessary to specify an appropriate algorithm to perform classification on the basis of the vectors generated by any given object. For this purpose, the model uses Gaussian radial basis functions (e.g., Poggio & Girosi, 1990; Poggio & Edelman, 1990) in the 50 dimensional space given by the two MetriCat vectors (c^1 and c^2), each with 25 units, c^i_j (j = 1..25). Every object is coded in the model's memory as a collection *classifier units* with Gaussian receptive fields in this 50 dimensional space. The center of a given unit's receptive field corresponds to the "preferred" pattern for the corresponding object. Each object, k, is coded by 3 classifier units with the same center but with different standard deviations, σ (σ take values of 0.02, 0.01 and 0.0066). Small σ allow units to tolerate only small deviations from their preferred patterns; such units thus perform instance-level classification. Larger σ permit larger deviations from the preferred pattern, and permit a unit to perform class recognition (responding to multiple, similar patterns). The input value, I_k, of classifier unit k in response to the vector representation, s, of a given stimulus is given by:

$$I_k = G(\|\mathbf{p}_k - s\|, \sigma_k), \tag{3}$$

where G is the Gaussian, and $\mathbf{p}_k$ is k's preferred vector.

The activation of a given classifier unit k at time t changes as:

$$\Delta A^t_k = 0.9\left(1 - A^t_k\right)I^t_k - 0.25A^t_k. \tag{4}$$

Algorithm

In addition to its bottom-up input (Eq. 1), each MetriCat unit, c^i_j, also receives lateral excitation from other units in c^1. Unit j excites unit i to the extent that its center lies within i's receptive field. The input from j to i is:

$$LE_{ij} = A_j\, G(|\mu_i - \mu_j|, w_i), \tag{5}$$

where G is the Gaussian, and μ_i and μ_j are the centers of receptive fields i and j and A_j is the activation of unit j. Broad units, which will tend to have many other units in their receptive fields, will tend to receive more lateral excitation than narrow units, which will have fewer other units in their receptive fields. As a result, MetriCat units with broad receptive fields tend to become active faster than units with narrow receptive fields: Coarse information about an object's shape becomes available earlier than information about its fine metric details. The utility of this property is that the coarse information is more robust to noise than is fine information. Noise may originate in both the stimulus and the system. Stimulus-induced noise may result from changes in viewpoint (i.e., producing slight deviations from the expected values of an object's metric properties); system-induced noise may result from random variations in the magnitude of neural impulses (or myriad other sources). At the MetriCat level of representation, lateral excitation makes coarse noise-tolerant information available rapidly; at the classifier level, the initial absence of fine metric information has a greater adverse impact on classifier units with narrow receptive fields than it has on units with wide receptive fields. As a result, class recognition precedes instance recognition. This property is apparent in the simulation results.

Simulations

Simulations were run with four one-part objects, A1, A2, B1, and B2. Each object was defined by real values on two dimensions, C^1 and C^2. Objects were created in pairs (A and B) such that members of the same pair were more similar to one another than to either member of the other pair. Object A1 had values [0.25, 0.1] (on C^1 and C^2, respectively), A2 had [0.25, 0.3], B1 had [0.75, 0.1], and B2 had [0.75, 0.3]. Note that members of the same pair have identical values on C1 and, and each member of one pair shares the same value of C2 with one member of the other pair. But overall, objects are more similar within than between pairs. This arrangement permitted us to observe three properties of the model: (1) Can it distinguish highly similar objects? (2) Will classifier units with broad receptive fields respond to both members of a class? and (3) What is the time course of the model's ability to make within- vs. between-class distinctions?

Simulations were run in two phases: 2000 (unsupervised) learning iterations followed by 1000 test iterations. Objects were presented to the model by means of oscillatory gates (Hummel & Stankiewicz, 1996) that controlled the input to the MetriCat units. Each gate was associated with one object (i.e., part), with the result that (a) the properties of one object "fired" (were passed to MetriCat) out of synchrony with the properties of other objects, and (b) there was random noise in inputs to the MetriCat units, especially during transitions between different objects (see Figure 3, lower frame). During learning, new classifier units were recruited whenever (i) the average ΔA_i over all of MetriCat units, i, was less than 0.03, and (ii) the Euclidean distance between the current MetriCat pattern of activation and that of all preferred classifier patterns was greater than 0.1.

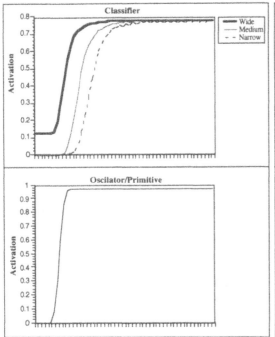

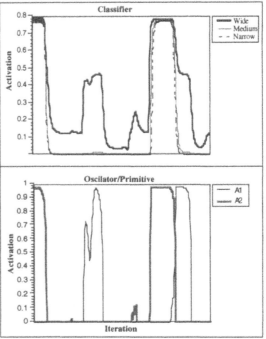

Figure 2: Model responses (over time) on a representative test run. Upper: Activation of three classifier units (one wide, one medium, and one narrow). Lower: Activation of the corresponding oscillator.

Figure 3: Model responses (over time) on a representative test run. Upper: Activation of three classifier units that respond preferentially to A2. Lower: Activation of the A1 and A2 oscillators.

Three different classifier units were recruited in response to each learned MetriCat pattern. The three units for a pattern have the same **p** (preferred pattern) but different σ (receptive field width). Test iterations were run in the same manner as the training iterations except that no learning took place. Figures 2 and 3 show activation as a function of time for three classifier units with the same preferred pattern but different σ (top row) and the corresponding oscillator activations (bottom row). The temporal ordering of classifier responses is apparent in Figure 2. Note that the classifier with the widest receptive field reaches asymptote first, followed by the medium unit and finally the narrow units.

The coarse classification behavior of the wide units is apparent in Figure 3. The wide classifier shown in the figure was recruited to respond primarily to A2. Note that this classifier responds most strongly to A2 but also responds to A1. Although it does not appear in the figure, the wide unit recruited for A1 showed the complementary response pattern. Neither unit responded to B1 or B2. The medium and narrow units responded very little to non-preferred inputs (e.g., the narrow units for A1 did not respond at all to A2). As apparent in Figures 2 and 3, the model classifies its inputs at a coarsest level first and later at finer level: Those units that become active rapidly (Figure 2) are the same as those that respond to patterns that deviate from their preferred patterns (Figure 3).

Discussion

The MetriCat model represents numerical values at multiple levels of specificity and combines the properties of both categorical and metric representations of numerical variables. Coupled with an appropriate classifying routine (e.g., Gaussian basis functions), this approach to the representation of numerical values has a number of desirable properties as a basis for multi-level classification. The preliminary simulations reported here are consistent with this claim. First, information about the general properties of a stimulus are made available faster than specific information. The utility of this property is that coarse information, which becomes available first, is also more robust to noise (e.g., resulting from changes in viewpoint; Biederman, 1987) than is metrically precise information. This property permits rapid recognition that is robust to noise in the input (e.g., as a result of variations in viewpoint) and noise in the system (e.g., as a result of the oscillators). The rapid availability of coarse information also suggests an account of our ability to categorize an object at the basic-level (e.g., "car") faster than we can classify it at the subordinate-level (e.g., "Mustang").

A second important property of this architecture is its ability to capture the hierarchical similarity relations among different stimuli. In some ways this capacity is property of any vector coding of a population of stimuli. However, the architecture here takes this capacity one step further and (by the activity of the classifier at different scales) explicitly tags the level at which to stimuli are similar or different. It is in this respect that the model performs multi-level classification. As visible in Figure 3, the broad classifier responsive to A2 responds to both A1 and A2, but more strongly to A2. Such broad units may be useful for general (e.g., basic level) classification. However, the medium and narrow classifiers responsive to A2 respond only to A2. Such units may be useful for subordinate- and instance-level classification.

In answer to the questions posed above: (1) The model can distinguish highly similar objects on the basis of the classifier units with narrow receptive fields (A1 from A2 and B1 from B2; see Figure 3). (2) Classifier units with broad receptive fields respond to both members of a class. And (3) as illustrated in Figure 2, the model categorizes objects at a general level (via units with wide receptive fields) before it classifies them at the subordinate or instance level (units with medium and narrow receptive fields). Using a unified representation of numerical variables at different levels of specificity (e.g., "categorical" and "metric"), the model suggests an account of why basic-level classification is faster than subordinate- or instance-level classification (Rosch et. al., 1976).

The model's account of this finding relates to the role of noise in the stimulus and in the classifying system. Coarse MetriCat units are both faster to respond and more robust to deviations from their preferred inputs (e.g., as resulting from noise) than are fine units. As a result, coarse (roughly categorical) information becomes available earlier than fine (more metric) information. The classifier units exploit this difference: Because broad classifiers are more robust to deviations from their preferred patterns than narrow classifiers, they are less sensitive to the initial absence of activity in the fine MetriCat units. Broad classifiers therefore respond earlier in processing than narrow classifiers. As processing proceeds, the fine MetriCat units begin to respond, so the resulting pattern better fits any narrow classifier units that are tuned to respond to it. Noise is inevitable under realistic assumptions about the world and neural information processing. The current approach provides a basis for rapid general classification and subsequent detailed classification even in the presence of such noise.

The model also suggests an account of the role of attention in subordinate-level classification. More time is required to activate fine MetriCat units than coarse MetriCat units. Attention may serve in part to devote the necessary processing time to diagnostic elements of an object's shape. Thus rather than generating a holistic representation of an object for the purposes of subordinate-level classification, the current model suggests that attention may instead direct processing to diagnostic elements. Although this idea is intuitive, the current model provides the first computational account of the representations that may serve as the basis for this selective processing, and the classification routines that may exploit it.

The simplified simulations reported here were run with MetriCat as a stand-alone system. However, the utility of the MetriCat approach lies in its properties as a component of a more general object recognition system. In particular, MetriCat can easily be incorporated as a component of a more complete model of object recognition. The problem of object recognition can be broken down into two questions: What general properties does the visual system make explicit an object's image? and How does it represent those properties and match them to memory for the purposes of recognition? The MetriCat model is addressed to the second question. MetriCat differs from other general classification systems (such as Poggio's GRBFs) in that it is addressed not only to the problem of how to classify a stimulus given a particular numerical input (a task for which GRBFs are extremely well suited) but also to the question of how to represent that numerical input.

References

Biederman, I. (1987). Recognition-By-Components: A Theory of Human Image Understanding. *Psychological Review, 94*, 115-147.

Biederman, I. & Shiffrar, M.M. (1987) Sexing day-old chicks: A case study and expert systems analysis of a difficult perceptual-learning task. Journal of Experimental Psychology: *Learning, Memory, & Cognition, 13*, 640-645.

Edelman, S., & Bulthoff, H.H.(1992) Orientation dependence in the recognition of familiar and novel views of three-dimensional objects. *Vision Research, 32*, 2385-2400.

Farah, M. J. (1992). Is an object an object an object? Cognitive and neuropsychological investigations of domain specificity in visual object recognition. *Current Directions in Psychological Science, 1*, 164-169.

Hummel, J. E., & Biederman, I. (1992). Dynamic binding in a neural network for shape recognition. *Psychological Review, 99*, 480-517.

Hummel, J. E., & Stankiewicz, B. J. (1995). Coordinates and spatial relations in object memory. *Technical report 95-01, Shape Perception and Memory Laboratory*, University of California, Los Angeles. Los Angeles, California.

Hummel, J. E., & Stankiewicz, B. J. (1996). An architecture for rapid, hierarchical structural description. T. Inui and J. McClelland (Eds.) In *Attention and Performance XVI*. In Press.

Liu, Z., Knill, D.C. & Kersten, D.(1995) Object classification for human and ideal observers. *Vision Research, 35*, 549-568.

Poggio T., & Edelman S. (1990). A network that learns to recognize 3-Dimensional objects. *Nature, 343*, 263-266.

Poggio, T. & Girosi, F. (1990) Regularization algorithms for learning that are equivalent to multilayer networks. *Science, 247*, 978-982.

Rosch, E., Mervis, C. B., Gray, W. D., Johnson, D. M., & Boyes-Braem, P. (1976). Basic objects in natural categories. *Cognitive Psychology, 8*, 382-439.

Tanaka, J.W. & Farah, M.J. (1993)Parts and wholes in face recognition. *Quarterly Journal of Experimental Psychology: Human Experimental Psychology, 46A*, 225-245.

Tarr, M.J. (1995). Rotating objects to recognize them - a case study on the role of viewpoint dependency in the recognition of three-dimensional objects. *Psychonomic Bulletin & Review, 2*, 55-82.

Ullman, S. (1989) Aligning pictorial descriptions: An approach to object recognition. *Cognition, 32*, 193-254.

Ullman, S., & Basri R. (1991). Recognition by linear combinations of models. *IEEE Transactions on Pattern Analysis and Machine Intelligence, 13*, 992-1006.

Similarity to reference shapes as a basis for shape representation

Shimon Edelman   **Florin Cutzu**   **Sharon Duvdevani-Bar**
Dept. of Applied Mathematics and Computer Science
The Weizmann Institute of Science
Rehovot 76100, Israel
edelman@wisdom.weizmann.ac.il

Abstract

We present a unified approach to visual representation, addressing both the needs of superordinate and basic-level categorization and of identification of specific instances of familiar categories. According to the proposed theory, a shape is represented by its similarity to a number of reference shapes, measured in a high-dimensional space of elementary features. This amounts to embedding the stimulus in a low-dimensional proximal shape space. That space turns out to support representation of distal shape similarities which is veridical in the sense of Shepard's (1968) notion of second-order isomorphism (i.e., correspondence between distal and proximal similarities among shapes, rather than between distal shapes and their proximal representations). Furthermore, a general expression for similarity between two stimuli, based on comparisons to reference shapes, can be used to derive models of perceived similarity ranging from continuous, symmetric, and hierarchical, as in the multidimensional scaling models (Shepard, 1980), to discrete and non-hierarchical, as in the general contrast models (Tversky, 1977; Shepard and Arabie, 1979).

Introduction

All but a few current theoretical treatments of visual representation still adhere to the Aristotelian doctrine of *representation by similarity*, according to which an internal entity represents an external object by virtue of resemblance between the two.[1] Simply put, the original version of that doctrine holds that the representation of a tomato has something of the redness and of the roundness of the real thing. The predominant theories of visual *shape* representation still speak about isomorphism: typically, it is assumed that structural (Biederman, 1987) or metric (Ullman, 1989) information stored in the brain reflects corresponding properties of shapes in the world. In comparison, no student of *color* vision seriously believes that representations of tomatoes are red, or even that the reflectance spectra of tomatoes are explicitly stored; this has been supplanted by the feature detector theory, according to which the response of internal mechanisms tuned to particular sensory stimuli constitute the basic representation for those stimuli. A major goal of the present paper is to show that shape too, over and above color or local orientation, can be encoded in a low-dimensional feature space.

An important step towards that goal has been made by Roger N. Shepard, who pointed out that instead of a first-order isomorphism between the shapes and their representations, it

makes more sense to expect a second-order isomorphism between similarities of shapes and similarities of the internal representations they induce (Shepard, 1968). Essentially, this is a call for representation *of* similarity instead of representation *by* similarity.

A representation of a collection of shapes is veridical in Shepard's sense, if the mapping it implies between (some parameterization of) the distal shape space and the internal, or proximal, representation space preserves similarity ranks. Elsewhere, we show that a distal to proximal mapping realized by a bank of typical connectionist classifiers, each tuned to a particular shape, is likely to satisfy the requirements for similarity rank preservation generically, over appropriately limited regions of the distal space (Edelman, 1995b; Duvdevani-Bar and Edelman, 1995).

Here, we extend this theory of representation in two directions. First, we outline a common framework for treating categorization, recognition and identification as measurements of similarities to subspaces of the image space. Second, we show how similarity can be defined in such a manner as to form a bridge between theories of representation based on continuous feature spaces, and those based on lists of discrete-valued features. We conclude with a brief mention of some of the results supporting the theory, in areas ranging from psychophysics and physiology to computation and philosophy.

Representation = measurement + dimensionality reduction

In any cognitive system, the internal representations are constructed by subjecting the input to a set of measurements, whose aim is to provide an efficient description of the stimuli, e.g., as points in some low-dimensional parameter space. Because such a space is neither directly accessible nor known *a priori*, and because different tasks may call for different aspects of the stimuli to be represented, it is a good strategy to carry out as many measurements as possible, to increase the likelihood of correspondence between some subspace of the measurement space $\mathcal{M}$ and the relevant part of the parameter space. This makes $\mathcal{M}$ high-dimensional, and necessitates subsequent dimensionality reduction, whose aim is to recover the relevant subspace of $\mathcal{M}$. Likewise, the input to an object recognition system – an $n \times n$ image – can be considered as a point in a n^2-dimensional image or *raster* space $\mathcal{R} = R^{n^2}$, which we identify with the measurement space $\mathcal{M}$ (in biological vision, one may think of the space of patterns transmitted by the optic nerve to the brain). The task of recognition is, given $\mathbf{X} \in \mathcal{R}$, to determine whether $\mathbf{X}$ is an image of an

---

[1]"Representation of something is an image, model, or reproduction of that thing," (Suppes, Pavel, and Falmagne, 1994).

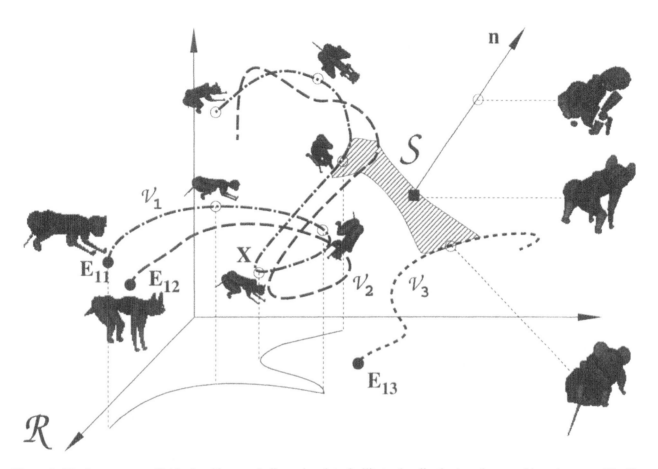

Figure 1: The image space, $\mathcal{R}$ (depicted here as 3-dimensional, to facilitate visualization), and some of its subspaces. The $\mathcal{V}_i$ (shown as dashed lines) are the view spaces for the three exemplars $\mathbf{E}_{1i}$ (marked by filled circles), all of which belong to the same class $\mathcal{C}_1$ (the class of 4-legged animal shapes). Some of the different views of $\mathbf{E}_{11}$ are shown (marked by open circles). The surface patch represents a part of the shape space $\mathcal{S}$, and the vector $\mathbf{n}$ – a normal to it. Movement along this direction in $\mathcal{R}$ corresponds to a reduction in the resemblance between the resulting image and the images of coherently looking objects. Image $\mathbf{X}$ should be classified as belonging to exemplar $\mathbf{E}_{11}$, class $\mathcal{C}_1$, and, of course, to the shape space $\mathcal{S}$.

object (a coherent entity, which, in intuitive terms, looks like something, rather than like random pixel noise), and, if it is, to establish the category to which the object belongs, and, if possible, the object's identity. It is convenient to cast this problem in terms of attributing to $\mathbf{X}$ a proper location, respectively, in the *shape* space $\mathcal{S}$, the *class* space $\mathcal{C}$, and the *exemplar* space $\mathcal{E}$, where $\mathcal{R} \supset \mathcal{S} \supset \mathcal{C}$, and $\mathcal{E} = \mathcal{E}(\mathcal{C})$ (see Figure 1). A complete characterization of an input calls for determining i, j, k, such that $\mathbf{X} \in \mathbf{E}_{jk}$, and $\mathbf{S}_i \subset \mathcal{S}$, $\mathbf{C}_j \subset \mathcal{C}$, $\mathbf{E}_{jk} \subset \mathcal{E}_j$ ($\mathcal{E}_j = \mathcal{E}(\mathbf{C}_j)$).

Basic level. Consider first the basic-level categorization problem: given $\mathbf{X}$, find j such that $\mathbf{X} \in \mathbf{C}_j$. The major obstacle to be overcome here is the dependence of the appearance of $\mathbf{X} \in \mathbf{C}_j$ on factors such as illumination and viewpoint, in addition to the category identity j. If $\mathbf{C}_j$ is taken to correspond to the image of a member of j in some canonical orientation, the viewing conditions can be seen to span a *view* space $\mathcal{V}_j$, which is, to a first approximation, orthogonal to the class space $\mathcal{C}$, and pierces it at $\mathbf{C} = \mathbf{C}_j$. By training a general-purpose function approximation module to perform the mapping $T(j) : \mathcal{V}_j \rightarrow \mathbf{C}_j$, one can largely eliminate the

dependence of categorization on viewing conditions (Poggio and Edelman, 1990). The normalizing transformation $T(j)$ can work even for inputs not previously encountered by the system (that is, for different instances $\mathbf{E}_{jk}$), provided that they belong to the class j (Lando and Edelman, 1995).

Subordinate levels. The central problem in determining the identity k lies in the fine resolution that must be attained within the instance space $\mathcal{E}_j$, in the face of the residual misalignment left over from the action of the normalizing transformation T. This problem can be approached by learning hyperacuity in the instance space, as it is done in other hyperacuity-related tasks (Poggio, Fahle, and Edelman, 1992); experience shows that hyperacuity can be attained despite considerable misalignment of the stimulus as a whole, relative to its "home" or training pose.

Superordinate levels. The most challenging problem arises when the system encounters an unfamiliar shape, belonging to none of the classes for which specially trained categorization modules are available. The key to a solution here lies in considering the *population response* at the basic categorization level (Edelman, 1995b). If the existing modules

261

have sufficiently wide response profiles in the shape space S, a number of modules will respond, effectively representing the similarities between the input and the preferred shape of each module. This highly informative pattern of similarities is lost if the classification decision is made in a winner-take-all manner among the responding modules, rather than based on the ensemble response of several modules (Edelman, Reisfeld, and Yeshurun, 1992).

A Chorus of Prototypes

A collection of modules $\{p_i\}$, each trained to recognize a basic shape category, provides a representational substrate that is suitable for each of the three levels of categorization listed above. We refer to the categories for which such modules are available as *prototypes*; these are defined as $\mathbf{C}_i = \arg\max_{\mathbf{C} \subseteq \mathcal{C}} p_i(\mathbf{C})$. Because a number of modules respond for any given input, the resulting scheme is called a Chorus of Prototypes (Edelman, 1995b). The pattern of responses of the modules to a stimulus $\mathbf{X}$ is the ordered list $\mathbf{p}(\mathbf{X}) = \{p_i(\mathbf{X})\}, i = 1 \ldots k$. Note that $p_i(\mathbf{X})$ depends not on the point-to-point distance between $\mathbf{X}$ and some $\mathbf{X}_i$, but rather on the distance between $\mathbf{X}$ and that member $\mathbf{C}_i$ of the class space $\mathcal{C}$ to which p_i is tuned. In the remainder of this paper, we concentrate on two aspects of the Chorus scheme: (1) the characterization of the shape space S in terms of the prototype response vector $\mathbf{p}$, and (2) the use of $\mathbf{p}$ in tasks that involve judgment of similarity.

Similarities to prototypes and the shape space S

The nature of dimensionality reduction performed by Chorus can be characterized by describing the relationship between the shape space S and the vector of responses of the prototype modules, $\mathbf{p}$. One way to do that is by viewing the action of Chorus as interpolation: intuitively, one would expect the shape space to be a (hyper)surface that passes through the reference classes $\{\mathbf{C}_i\}$ and behaves reasonably in between (see Figure 1). Now, different tasks carry with them different notions of reasonable behavior. Consider first the least specific level in a hierarchy of recognition tasks: deciding whether $\mathbf{X}$ is the image of some (familiar) object. For this purpose, it would suffice to represent S as a scalar field over the image space $S(\mathbf{X}) : \mathcal{R} \to R$, which would express for each $\mathbf{X}$ its degree of membership in S. For example, we may set $S = \max_i\{p_i\}$ (the activity of the strongest-responding prototype module), or shape $= \sum_i p_i$ (the total activity; cf. Nosofsky, 1988). We remark that it should be possible to characterize a superordinate-level category of the input image, and not merely decide whether it is likely to be the image of a familiar object, by determining the identities of the prototype modules that respond above some threshold (i.e., if, say, the cat, the sheep and the cow modules are the only ones that respond, the stimulus is probably a four-legged animal).

At the basic and the subordinate category levels, we are interested in the location of the input *within* S, which, therefore, can no longer be considered a scalar. Note that parametric interpolation is not possible in this case, as the intrinsic dimensionality of S is not given *a priori*.[2] Now, the prototype

response field $\mathbf{p}$ induced by the reference classes $\{\mathbf{C}_i\}$ constitutes a nonparametrically interpolated vector-valued representation of S, in the following sense: (1) changing the shape ("morphing") $\mathbf{C}_i$ into $\mathbf{C}_j$, corresponding to a movement of the point in S, makes the vector $\mathbf{p}$ rotate smoothly between $\mathbf{p}(\mathbf{C}_i)$ and $\mathbf{p}(\mathbf{C}_j)$; the representational value of this property of the Chorus transform is discussed in (Duvdevani-Bar and Edelman, 1995); (2) the interior of the convex hull of the reference classes $\{\mathbf{C}_i\}$ is mapped onto the interior of the convex hull of $\{\mathbf{p}(\mathbf{C}_i)\}$; moreover, the mapping is one-to-one if a minimum-norm (i.e., minimum summed distance to the prototypes) requirement is imposed on its inverse; (3) the Voronoi tessellation induced over $\mathcal{C}$ by $\{\mathbf{C}_i\}$ is preserved by the mapping $\mathbf{p}$.

Similarities to prototypes and similarities between stimuli

In Chorus, each p_i is, in a sense, a feature, whose value for $\mathbf{A} \in \mathcal{R}$ is signified by the activation $p_i(\mathbf{A})$. Consider the similarity structure induced by this feature space over the universe of stimuli. A natural way to measure similarity between two stimuli, $\mathbf{A}$ and $\mathbf{B}$, is by the Euclidean distance between the corresponding feature vectors, $\mathbf{p}(\mathbf{A})$ and $\mathbf{p}(\mathbf{B})$: $s_E(\mathbf{A}, \mathbf{B})^{-1} \sim \sum_{i=1}^{k} \left[p_i(\mathbf{A}) - p_i(\mathbf{B}) \right]^2$. However, a uniform scaling in the responses of all prototype detectors $\mathbf{p} \to c\,\mathbf{p}$ (as in seeing through fog) should not be interpreted as a change in the shape of the stimulus object. To make the similarity insensitive to such scaling, we define similarity by the cosine of the angle between $\mathbf{p}(\mathbf{A})$ and $\mathbf{p}(\mathbf{B})$, in the space spanned by the prototype responses:

$$s_a(\mathbf{A}, \mathbf{B}) \sim \sum_{i=1}^{k} p_i(\mathbf{A}) p_i(\mathbf{B}) \doteq \langle \mathbf{p}(\mathbf{A}), \mathbf{p}(\mathbf{B}) \rangle \quad (1)$$

This definition of similarity must, however, be further modified, for two reasons. First, s_a is independent of context, whereas perceived similarity depends on the "contrast set" against which it is to be judged. Second, s_a is symmetric, whereas human perception of similarity appears to be asymmetric in many cases (Tversky, 1977). To make s_a depend on the context, we introduce a vector of weights, one per prototype, such that $w_i = w_i(\{\mathbf{A}, \mathbf{B}, \mathbf{C}, \ldots\})$. Thus, comparing $\mathbf{A}$ and $\mathbf{B}$ in two contexts, $\{\mathbf{A}, \mathbf{B} \mid \mathbf{C}, \mathbf{D}, \mathbf{E}\}$ and $\{\mathbf{A}, \mathbf{B} \mid \mathbf{F}, \mathbf{G}, \mathbf{H}\}$, may result in different values of similarity between $\mathbf{A}$ and $\mathbf{B}$. To model the asymmetry which frequently arises when subjects are required to estimate the similarity of some stimulus $\mathbf{A}$ to another stimulus $\mathbf{B}$, we observe, following Mumford, that subjects in this case behave as if they take "$\mathbf{A}$ is similar to $\mathbf{B}$" to mean "$\mathbf{B}$ is some kind of prototype in a category which includes $\mathbf{A}$. Thus, the stimulus input $\mathbf{A}$ being analyzed is treated differently from the memory benchmark $\mathbf{B}$" (Mumford, 1991). To give $\mathbf{B}$ the required distinction, each feature $p_i(\mathbf{B})$ can be weighted in proportion to its long-term saliency $\mathrm{sal}(p_i, \mathbf{B})$ in distinguishing between $\mathbf{B}$ and the other stimuli. The resulting expression for similarity, which provides for the effects of context and for asymmetry, is

---

[2]This is unlike the case of the three-dimensional view space, parameterized by the Euler angles. However, it may still be possible to estimate the dimensionality of S by examining the neighbor structure

of the reference points; see, e.g., (Tversky and Hutchinson, 1986).

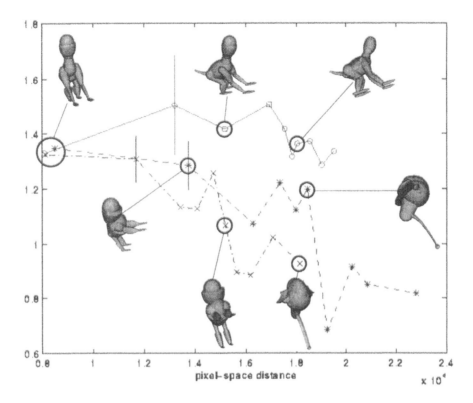

Figure 2: The response of a radial basis function module, trained on 10 random views of a parametrically defined object, to stimuli differing from a reference view of that object (marked by the big circle), in three ways: (1) by progressive view change, marked by o's; (2) by progressive shape change, marked by ×'s; (3) by combined shape and view change, marked by *'s. The points along each curve have been sorted by pixel-space distance between the test and the reference stimuli (shown along the abscissa). Points are means over 10 repetitions with different random view-space and shape-space directions of change; a typical error bar (± standard error of the mean) is shown for each curve. Note the insensitivity of the module's output to view-space changes, relative to shape-space changes. Thus, the output can be interpreted as signalling the proximity of the stimulus to the view space of the reference object.

$$s(\mathbf{A}, \mathbf{B}) \sim \sum_{i=1}^{k} w_i p_i(\mathbf{A}) \left(\frac{p_i(\mathbf{B})}{\mathsf{sal}(p_i, \mathbf{B})} \right) \qquad (2)$$

Note that this definition has the same form as the additive clustering (ADCLUS) similarity measure of (Shepard and Arabie, 1979), which, in turn, instantiates Tversky's (1977) discrete contrast model of feature-based similarity. At the same time, it is built on top of a continuous metric representational substrate – the shape space spanned by proximities to prototypes. The degree of compromise between these two approaches to similarity may depend on the demands of the task at hand, via the parameters of equation 2. At the one extreme, a Chorus-based system may behave as if it maps the stimuli pertaining to a task into a metric space, with the ensuing symmetric similarity and possible interaction among different dimensions; the other extreme may involve discrete all-or-none features, as in the examples surveyed by Tversky (1977).

Similarities to prototypes as a basis for veridical perception

The veridicality of representation of parametrically defined shapes in human subjects has been tested in two recent studies (Edelman, 1995a; Cutzu and Edelman, 1995). In each of a series of experiments, which involved pairwise similarity judgment and delayed matching to sample, subjects were confronted with several classes of computer-rendered 3D animal-like shapes, arranged in a complex pattern in a common parameter space. Response time and error rate data were combined into a measure of subjective shape similarity, and the resulting proximity matrix was submitted to nonmetric multidimensional scaling (MDS; Shepard, 1980). In the resulting solution, the relative geometrical arrangement of the points corresponding to the different objects invariably reflected the complex low-dimensional structure in parameter space that defined the relationships between the stimuli classes (see Figure 3).

Computer simulations showed that the recovery of the low-dimensional structure from *image-space* distances between the stimuli was impossible, as expected. In comparison, the

263

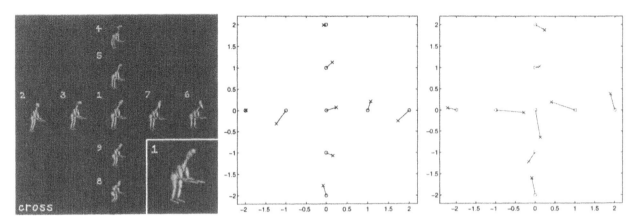

Figure 3: *Left:* the parameter-space configuration used for generating the stimuli in one of the experiments described in (Cutzu and Edelman, 1995). *Middle:* the 2D MDS solution for all subjects. Symbols: o – true configuration; × – configuration derived by MDS from the subject data, then Procrustes-transformed (Borg and Lingoes, 1987) to fit the true one. Lines connect corresponding points. The coefficient of congruence between the MDS-derived configuration and the true one was 0.99. In comparison, the expected random value, estimated by bootstrap (Efron and Tibshirani, 1993) from the data, was 0.86 ± 0.03 (mean and standard deviation); 100 permutations of the point order were used in the bootstrap computation. The Procrustes distance between the MDS-derived configuration and the true one was 0.66 (expected random value: 3.14 ± 0.15). *Right:* the 2D MDS solution for the RBF model; coefficient of congruence: 0.98 (expected random value: 0.86 ± 0.03); Procrustes distance: 1.11 (expected random value: 3.14 ± 0.17).

psychophysical results were fully replicated by a model patterned after a higher stage of object processing, in which nearly viewpoint-invariant representations of individual objects are available; a rough analogy is to the inferotemporal visual area IT; see, e.g., (Tanaka, 1993; Logothetis, Pauls, and Poggio, 1995). Such a representation of a 3D object can be easily formed, if several views of the object are available, by training a radial basis function (RBF) network to interpolate a characteristic function for the object in the space of all views of all objects (Poggio and Edelman, 1990). Following the Chorus approach, we chose a number of reference objects (in Figure 3, the corners of the parameter-space CROSS), and trained an RBF network to recognize each such object (i.e., to output a constant value for any of its views, encoded by the activities of the underlying receptive field layer). At the RBF level, the similarity between two stimuli was defined as the cosine of the angle between the vectors of outputs they evoked in the RBF modules trained on the reference objects (equation 1). The MDS-derived configurations obtained with this model showed significant resemblance to the true parameter-space configurations (see Figure 3, right).

Conclusion

Because the reference shapes can be considered complex features, Chorus effectively extends the notion of representation by feature detection from simple "primary" perceptual qualities such as color to all visual dimensions, including shape. This makes it possible to use multidimensional feature spaces in which different dimensions correspond to radically different qualities, not all of which need even be visual. Moreover, the system can maintain a high degree of plasticity, as new complex features can be learned by memorization, without paying for versatility by the need for dynamic binding, as in structural representation involving generic features.

The ensemble of feature detectors responds (J. J. Gibson would say, resonates) to the environment (while extracting task-specific information), without reconstructing it internally. By merely mirroring proximally the similarity structure of a distal shape space, Chorus embodies the ideas of those philosophers who argued that "meaning ain't in the head" (Putnam, 1988) and that "cognitive systems are largely in the world" (Millikan, 1995), circumvents the severe difficulties encountered by the reconstructionist approaches in computer vision, and may explain the impressive performance of biological visual systems, which, in any case, appear to be too sloppy to do a good job of reconstructing the world (O'Regan, 1992). Thus, in an important sense, Chorus lets the world be its own representation.

Acknowledgments

Thanks to Fiona Newell, Dan Roth, Josh Tenenbaum, Alice O'Toole, and Yair Weiss for useful comments. SE is an incumbent of the Sir Charles Clore Career Development Chair at the Weizmann Institute. FC is now with the Dept. of Cognitive and Linguistic Sciences, Brown University, Providence RI 02192.

References

Biederman, I. 1987. Recognition by components: a theory of human image understanding. *Psychol. Review*, 94:115–147.

Borg, I. and J. Lingoes. 1987. *Multidimensional Similarity Structure Analysis.* Springer, Berlin.

Cutzu, F. and S. Edelman. 1995. Explorations of shape space. CS-TR 95-01, Weizmann Institute of Science.

Duvdevani-Bar, S. and S. Edelman. 1995. On similarity to prototypes in 3D object representation. CS-TR 95-11, Weizmann Institute of Science.

Edelman, S. 1995a. Representation of similarity in 3D object discrimination. *Neural Computation*, 7:407–422.

Edelman, S. 1995b. Representation, Similarity, and the Chorus of Prototypes. *Minds and Machines*, 5:45–68.

Edelman, S., D. Reisfeld, and Y. Yeshurun. 1992. Learning to recognize faces from examples. In G. Sandini, editor, *Proc. 2nd European Conf. on Computer Vision, Lecture Notes in Computer Science*, volume 588, pages 787–791. Springer Verlag.

Efron, B. and R. Tibshirani. 1993. *An introduction to the bootstrap*. Chapman and Hall, London.

Lando, M. and S. Edelman. 1995. Receptive field spaces and class-based generalization from a single view in face recognition. *Network*, 6:551–576.

Logothetis, N. K., J. Pauls, and T. Poggio. 1995. Shape recognition in the inferior temporal cortex of monkeys. *Current Biology*, 5:552–563.

Millikan, R. 1995. *White Queen Psychology and other essays for Alice*. MIT Press, Cambridge, MA.

Mumford, D. 1991. Mathematical theories of shape: do they model perception? In *Geometric methods in computer vision*, volume 1570, pages 2–10, Bellingham, WA. SPIE.

Nosofsky, R. M. 1988. Exemplar-based accounts of relations between classification, recognition, and typicality. *Journal of Experimental Psychology: Learning, Memory and Cognition*, 14:700–708.

O'Regan, J. K. 1992. Solving the real mysteries of visual perception: The world as an outside memory. *Canadian J. of Psychology*, 46:461–488.

Poggio, T. and S. Edelman. 1990. A network that learns to recognize three-dimensional objects. *Nature*, 343:263–266.

Poggio, T., M. Fahle, and S. Edelman. 1992. Fast perceptual learning in visual hyperacuity. *Science*, 256:1018–1021.

Putnam, H. 1988. *Representation and reality*. MIT Press, Cambridge, MA.

Shepard, R. N. 1968. Cognitive psychology: A review of the book by U. Neisser. *Amer. J. Psychol.*, 81:285–289.

Shepard, R. N. 1980. Multidimensional scaling, tree-fitting, and clustering. *Science*, 210:390–397.

Shepard, R. N. and P. Arabie. 1979. Additive clustering: representation of similarities as combinations of discrete overlapping properties. *Psychological Review*, 86:87–123.

Suppes, P., M. Pavel, and J. Falmagne. 1994. Representations and models in psychology. *Ann. Rev. Psychol.*, 45:517–544.

Tanaka, K. 1993. Neuronal mechanisms of object recognition. *Science*, 262:685–688.

Tversky, A. 1977. Features of similarity. *Psychological Review*, 84:327–352.

Tversky, A. and J. W. Hutchinson. 1986. Nearest neighbor analysis of psychological spaces. *Psychological Review*, 93:3–22.

Ullman, S. 1989. Aligning pictorial descriptions: an approach to object recognition. *Cognition*, 32:193–254.

Integrating Discourse and Local Constraints
in Resolving Lexical Thematic Ambiguities

Joy E. Hanna
Dept. of Brain & Cognitive Sciences
University of Rochester
Rochester, NY 14627
hanna@bcs.rochester.edu

Michael J. Spivey-Knowlton
Dept. of Psychology
Cornell University
Ithaca, NY 14583
mjsk@cornell.edu

Michael K. Tanenhaus
Dept. of Brain & Cognitive Sciences
University of Rochester
Rochester, NY 14627
mtan@bcs.rochester.edu

Abstract

We conducted sentence completion and eye-tracking reading experiments to examine the interaction of multiple constraints in the resolution of a lexical thematic ambiguity. The ambiguity was introduced with prepositional "by"-phrases in passive constructions, which can be ambiguous between agentive and locative interpretations (e.g., "built by the contractor" versus "built by the corner"). The temporarily ambiguous sentences were embedded in contexts that created expectations for one or the other interpretation. The constraints involved, including discourse-based expectations, verb biases, and contingent lexical frequencies, were independently quantified with a corpus analysis and a rating experiment. Our results indicate that there was an interaction of contextual and more local factors such that the effectiveness of the contexts was mediated by the local biases. Application of an explicit integration-competition model to the off-line (sentence completion) and on-line (eye-tracking) results suggests that, during the processing of these ambiguous prepositional phrases, there was an immediate and simultaneous integration of the relevant constraints resulting in competition between partially active alternative interpretations.

Introduction

Constraint-based models of sentence processing (MacDonald, Pearlmutter & Seidenberg, 1994; Trueswell & Tanenhaus, 1994) propose that the comprehension system continuously integrates information from a number of sources in order to converge on a consistent interpretation. Within this framework, ambiguity resolution is viewed as a process in which information from contextual and more local sources combines to provide support for competing alternatives.

Recent studies have shown that discourse-based information can rapidly combine with local (within sentence) factors to influence ambiguity resolution (for a recent review, see Tanenhaus & Trueswell, 1995). Moreover, the effectiveness of discourse context is mediated by local constraints, such that context effects are strongest when local biases are relatively weak (MacDonald et al., 1994; Spivey-Knowlton, Trueswell & Tanenhaus, 1993). However, up to this point, constraint-based models of ambiguity resolution have been criticized as vague with regard to the specific constraints involved, their strength, and the exact time-course and nature of their integration. In addition, it is commonly assumed that, while multiple constraints may be integrated in *off-line* processing tasks where there is sufficient time to compute complex contextual biases, the architecture of the language processing system imposes restrictions on the time-course

with which different classes of constraints can be used in *on-line* processing.

In light of these considerations, the research reported here had two primary goals. The first was to further test the claim that discourse context effects are mediated by within-sentence constraints, including contingent lexical frequency and lexical thematic preferences. The second was to independently quantify local and contextual constraints in order to examine their integration in both off-line and on-line comprehension, in particular by applying an explicit integration-competition model to the results (e.g., Spivey-Knowlton, 1994; Spivey-Knowlton & Tanenhaus, submitted).

Much of the research investigating the effects of discourse context has focused on the effects of referential presuppositions in syntactic ambiguity resolution (e.g., Altmann & Steedman, 1988; Britt, 1994). However, the referential manipulations in these experiments may have been confounded with the discourse-based expectations they create (cf. Spivey-Knowlton & Sedivy, 1995). Additionally, the focus on syntactic attachment ambiguities has tended to ignore cases where the indeterminacy hinges on the lexical ambiguity of the preposition itself, including what thematic role is assigned to the object of the preposition.

In order to address the goals stated above, the experiments reported here made use of contextually created expectations which were non-referential in nature, and investigated the resolution of a (non-syntactic) lexical thematic ambiguity. The temporary ambiguity occurred within passive target sentences with the preposition "by." This preposition is lexically ambiguous, introducing a noun phrase that can be assigned the thematic role of an agent (e.g., "built by the contractor") or a location (e.g., "built by the corner") among others. Discourse constraints were manipulated by using embedded questions to establish an expectation for receiving information about an agent or location, without differing in their referential complexity. Example stimuli are shown in (1):

(1) a. **Agent Context/Agent Target Noun:**
The artist decided to go to the gallery. Once he got there he wanted to know *who* had hung his prize painting. He was pleased to discover that his painting had been hung *by the director* earlier in the week.

b. **Location Context/Location Target Noun:**
The artist decided to go to the gallery. Once he got there he wanted to see *where* his prize painting had been hung. He was pleased to discover that his painting had been hung *by the entrance* earlier in the week.

We report a corpus analysis and off-line rating and completion experiments using these materials which quantified the constraints involved in the resolution of this ambiguity and gave a measure of their integration in off-line performance. We also report an eye-tracking reading experiment which demonstrated that discourse-based expectations can affect the resolution of lexical thematic ambiguities. Furthermore, we show that discourse constraints interacted with more local sources of information, including verb preferences and co-occurrence frequencies, in a competitive manner predicted by the off-line ratings and applicable to both off-line and on-line processing.

Rating and Completion Experiments

A rating task was conducted on 24 subjects to obtain ratings for the importance of receiving information about the agent and the location of the relevant event (e.g., "On a scale from 1 to 5, how important is it for you to find out who/where the painting was hung?"). Ratings were elicited for the agent and location biasing contexts alone (the first two sentences of the stimuli), as well as for the target passive sentences alone (e.g., The painting had been hung ...). These importance ratings independently quantified the strength of two constraints: they indicated how strong the discourse expectations were for individual items as well as for agent and location biasing contexts in general; they also quantified the biases for individual passive verbs (in conjunction with their subject nouns).

An analysis of the Treebank Corpus was performed in order to quantify the frequency with which agentive and locative "by"-phrases occur in passive constructions. Out of over 300 passive sentences containing "by"-phrases, not a single one introduced a location, while agents were frequent (Hanna, Barker & Tanenhaus, 1995). This contingent frequency bias indicates that a "by"-phrase following a passive verb provides overwhelming support for the agentive interpretation.

Finally, gated sentence completions were collected in an experiment conducted on a different set of 36 subjects. The percentage of agentive, locative, and other completions were recorded for each of the 24 stimuli in six conditions, crossing the presence of either context or their absence (3) with the presence or absence of the preposition (2). Table 1 shows a summary of the completion results with sentence fragments up to and including "by".

Without the "by", (fragments like "The painting had been hung ..."; the No Context condition without the "by"),

there was in fact a preference for locative over agentive completions; this reflects a general verb preference in the stimulus set for locations over agents as was indicated by the importance ratings. With the addition of the preposition to the fragments, an agentive preference was found (Table 1), as is consistent with the bias revealed by the corpus analysis. Following an Agent Context, agentive completions were even more frequent; following Location Contexts however, agentive and locative completions were equally probable; $F1(2,72)=70.55$, $p<.001$; $F2(2,46)=18.13$, $p<.001$. These results clearly indicate that the discourse context was interacting with the contingent "by" frequency bias to produce the off-line performance. However, the pattern of results over all the verbs in the stimulus set obscures the differential effects of individual verb biases. Using the importance ratings, the stimulus items were divided into the most strongly agent and location biasing verbs (as well as an intermediate group). Agent-biasing verbs strengthened the preference for an agent completion in all conditions, but still showed an effect of context; $F2(2,14)=7.58$, $p<.01$. Likewise, location-biasing verbs strengthened the preference for a location completion in all conditions, and also showed an effect of context; $F2(2,14)=9.01$, $p<.005$

These off-line results were modeled within an integration-competition framework (Spivey-Knowlton & Tanenhaus, submitted) that implements competition between possible alternative interpretations using recurrent feedback and normalization. In the Normalized Recurrence competition algorithm, constraints are defined in terms of their support for the possible alternative interpretations (in this case, an Agentive or Locative interpretation of the "by"-phrase). See Figure 1. Activations of the node pairs for each constraint (C_n) are first normalized: $C_n(norm)=C_n/\Sigma C_n$. Then, activations for the provisional interpretations (I) are calculated as weighted sums of their corresponding constraint nodes (where the weights ω must sum to one): $I=\Sigma \omega_n C_n$. For the final operation within a cycle, the activation of an interpretation node is multiplied by the input that traveled up a particular pathway and added to the corresponding constraint node's current activation: $C_n=C_n(norm)+I\omega_n C_n$. The model cycles through these operations, allowing converging biases among the constraints to cause the interpretation nodes to gradually settle toward one provisional (probabilistic) interpretation of the "by"-phrase.

For simulating the sentence completions (Table 1), with

Completion:	No context Verb+"by"		Agent Context Verb+"by"		Location Context Verb+"by	
	Agentive	Locative	Agentive	Locative	Agentive	Locative
All Verbs	77%	23%	92%	8%	47%	53%
Agent-Biasing Verbs	100%	0%	100%	0%	67%	33%
Location-Biasing Verbs	39%	61%	77%	23%	20%	80%

Table 1: Percentage of Agent and Location Completions

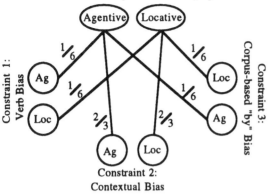

Provisional Interpretation of "by"-phrase

Figure 1: Integration-competition architecture for combining constraints to resolve the "by"-phrase ambiguity. All connections are bidirectional. The heavier weighting of Constraint 2 reflects the strong expectations created by the stimulus contexts.

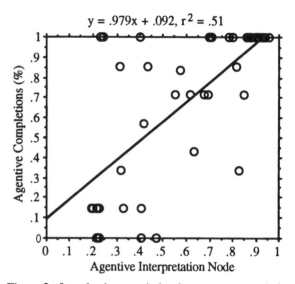

$y = .979x + .092, r^2 = .51$

Figure 2: Item-by-item variation in sentence completion data and simulation results from Normalized Recurrence.

sentence fragments up to and including "by", the quantified constraints from each context and target sentence (provided by ratings and corpus data) were entered into the model, which was allowed to iterate for 10 cycles. After 10 cycles, the activation of the Agentive Interpretation node indicated the percentage (or probability) of Agentive completions for that stimulus item. Weights for the different constraints were varied until a set was found that approximated the sentence completion data. (However, once these weights were set, they were kept constant for the rest of the simulations.)

Item-by-item variation in the data was accounted for by the simulation results. Individual stimulus items that elicited high percentages of Agentive completions tended to have high activation of the Agentive Interpretation node after 10 cycles. Likewise, stimulus items that elicited low percentages of Agentive completions tended to have low activation of the Agentive Interpretation node after 10 cycles. See Figure 2.

This initial simulation demonstrates how the model can account for graded effects in subjects' biases regarding the lexical thematic ambiguity introduced by the "by"-phrase. More importantly, however, this simulation provided a set of weights for the different constraints that we could then use in attempting to simulate on-line reading data, where the duration of competition (number of cycles) should correspond to mean reading times in the various experimental conditions.

Eye-Tracking Reading Experiment

The results of the sentence completions clearly indicate that context, as well as verb bias, plays a strong role in resolving the lexical thematic ambiguity of the "by"-phrase. However, it is frequently argued that multiple constraints from discourse and local sources have a lengthy amount of time to be integrated in an off-line task completion, whereas in an on-line task such as eye-tracking reading, the processing

system imposes restrictions on the sources of information that can be integrated immediately (Rayner, Sereno, Morris, Schmauder, & Clifton, 1989). In order to investigate the time-course of constraint integration in an on-line task, the same materials were used in an eye-tracking reading study in which Agent and Location Contexts were crossed with congruent and incongruent Target Nouns (see, for example, the two congruent conditions in (1)a and b). Eye movements and fixation durations were recorded from 24 subjects reading one version of each stimulus (from the 2 X 2 factorial of Context by Target Noun) amidst 36 filler stimuli. For eye-movement analysis, the target sentences were segmented into four regions: Initial NP / Verb (including the auxiliary) / "by"-phrase / Next two words. The "by"-phrase region is the point of both the ambiguity and its potential resolution given the appropriate interpretation of the target noun.

Figure 3 shows the total reading times for each recording region, including both first pass and regressive fixations. Overall, total reading times at both the "by"-phrase and the next region were slower for Location Targets than Agent Targets; at the "by"-phrase, $F_1(1,20)=14.13$, $p<.01$; $F_2(1,20)=6.76, p<.02$; at the next region, $F_1(1,20)=14.47$, $p<.01$; $F_2(1,20)=12.40, p<.01$. In addition, there was a clear interaction of Context and Target Noun at the "by"-phrase region, such that for Agent Contexts, agentive "by"-phrases were processed much faster than were locative "by"-phrases, while for Location Contexts, both were processed equally quickly at an intermediate rate; $F_1(1,20)=13.23$, $p<.01$; $F_2(1,20)=11.47, p<.01$. This pattern was repeated but only marginally significant at the Next region; $F_1(1,20)=3.65$, $p=.07$; $F_2(1,20)=3.38$, $p=.08$. These results parallel those obtained with the off-line sentence completion task.

This general pattern of results is consistent with accounts that postulate a parsing preference for arguments over adjuncts (assuming agentive "by"-phrases constitute arguments and locative ones adjuncts): locations should be harder to process than agents regardless of context (cf., Liversedge, Pickering & Branigan, 1995). However, the data pattern over all the stimuli conceals differential effects that emerge when verb biases are taken into account. The stimulus items were divided into strongly agent and location biasing verbs and two different patterns emerged, just as in the completion data. Among the eight Agent Biasing Verbs, total reading times at the "by"-phrase were fastest for Agent Targets and slowest for Location Targets, regardless of context; $F2(1,4)=30.10,p<.01$. However, among the eight Location Biasing Verbs, there was a Context by Target interaction such that reading times were slowest for targets that were incongruent with the context, i.e. Agent Context - Location Target and Location Context - Agent Target; $F2(1,4)=18.10,p<.02$. In other words, following Location Contexts and Location Biasing Verbs, subjects actually found it easiest to process Location Targets, a result that argument/adjunct proposals cannot account for.

Although the total reading time results showed a reliable interaction between context and target, it is commonly argued that total reading times, in general, do not provide evidence regarding the initial moments of ambiguity resolution (Rayner et al., 1989). First pass reading times, where fixation durations from regressive eye movements are excluded from the analysis, may provide a more accurate measure of initial processes during ambiguity resolution. Figure 4 shows first pass reading times across critical regions of the target sentence. The results exhibit what looks like an interaction between context and target at the "by"-phrase, but this interaction (where Agent Targets were read slightly faster in Agent Contexts and Location Targets were read slightly faster in Location Contexts) did not achieve statistical significance; $F1(1,20)=1.4$, $p>.1$; $F2(1,20)=1.55$, $p>.1$. Results such as these (first pass reading times failing to show a reliable context effect) are typically interpreted as *clear evidence for a serial application of constraints in which context is not used during initial ambiguity resolution* (e.g., Rayner, Garrod & Perfetti, 1992).

However, in a competition model using Normalized Recurrence (see Figure 1), subtle graded effects of context can be accounted for by conflicting biases arising from the relevant constraints. In this model, ambiguity resolution is not a process of categorically selecting one alternative and possibly having to revise this discrete interpretation at a later time (e.g., Frazier, 1987). Instead, this model allows the alternative interpretations to be simultaneously partially active, and compete against one another over time. Thus, slow reading times are an indication of lengthy competition (due to conflicting constraints), rather than initial misinterpretation followed by revision.

Most importantly, in the model described here, all information sources (context and local constraints) are integrated simultaneously. Therefore, if this parallel model can simulate the first pass reading times at the "by"-phrase

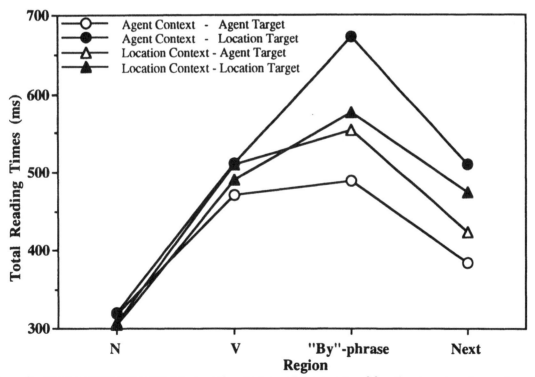

Figure 3: Total reading times for the recording regions of the agent and location target sentences in agent and location biasing contexts. The Location Target Nouns cause more processing difficulty than Agent Target Nouns, but this interacts with Context at the "by"-phrase.

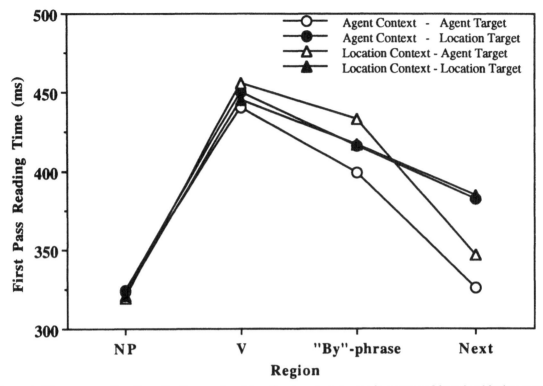

Figure 4: First pass reading times for the agent and location target sentences in agent and location biasing contexts.

(Figure 4), it would pose as an existence proof demonstrating that the data pattern *does not* provide "clear evidence for a serial system in which context is not used during initial ambiguity resolution."

The same computational architecture (with the same inputs and weights) used to simulate the sentence completion data was allowed to iterate until either interpretation node reached a dynamic criterion of activation that decreased over time (1-.01t, where t is the number of cycles that have elapsed). The number of cycles it took for a stimulus item to reach criterion was an indication of how much competition should take place at the "by"-phrase in that stimulus item. Figure 5 shows the mean first pass reading times at the "by"-phrase combined with the mean number of competition cycles for items in those conditions.

In the simulation, the lengthiest competition occurred when a strongly *weighted* constraint (sentence completions were best fit with Context given a weight of $^2/_3$) was pitted against a strongly *biased* constraint (based on the corpus data, "by" is given a .98 bias for Agentive and .02 bias for Locative); this is the Location Context - Agent Target Noun condition. The briefest competition occurred when those two strong constraints both converged on an Agentive interpretation; this is the Agentive Context - Agent Target Noun condition. See Figure 5. Intermediate degrees of conflict between constraints elicited intermediate competition durations, and reading times; these are both Location Target Noun conditions. In particular, readers did not have as much difficulty as might be expected in the

Agent Context - Location Target Noun condition. This could be interpreted as evidence for the delayed use of contextual information. However, the model, which uses all information sources immediately, showed exactly this pattern. In addition, in this condition the model was actually frequently converging relatively quickly (at that point in the sentence) *toward an Agentive interpretation of the "by"-phrase*. Thus, in this condition, the model generally predicts that later on in the sentence, as further information provides

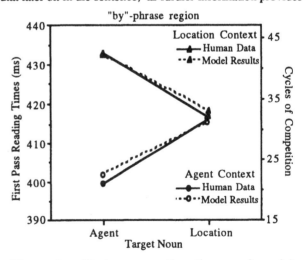

Figure 5: First pass reading times and model predictions at the "by"-phrase region.

support in favor of the Locative interpretation, there would be especially long reading times, and a high probability of regressive eye movements, as the constraints gradually overthrow the supremacy of the Agentive interpretation (or probabilistically "revise" the interpretation). Indeed, this Agent Context - Location Target Noun condition showed the longest total reading times (Figure 3), as well as the kind of regressive eye movements that would accompany a probabilistic "revision" of this sort. Figure 6 shows the probability of a regressive eye-movement from the Next Region (the two words following the "by"-phrase), overlaid with the absolute difference between the activation of the Agentive Interpretation node after competition at "by", and the input from the Target Noun's support for the Agentive interpretation. This metric provides an indication of the degree to which the model's "current" interpretation was incompatible with the new input.

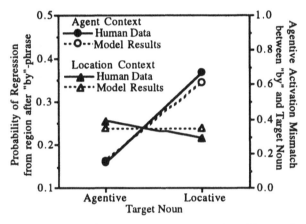

Figure 6: Regressive eye-movements out of the Next region and model simulation of interpretation incompatibility.

General Discussion

The results presented here provide evidence that discourse context effects are mediated by local (within-sentence) constraints. Specifically, contextually created expectations interacted with a contingent lexical frequency bias and verb preferences during the resolution of a lexical thematic ambiguity. This points to the important and immediate role of both discourse and lexical representations during ambiguity resolution (MacDonald et al., 1994; Spivey-Knowlton et al., 1993; Trueswell & Tanenhaus, 1994). Furthermore, by independently quantifying the relevant constraints and examining their interaction within a framework that utilizes an explicit competition algorithm to model processing difficulty, a clearer picture of the time-course and nature of constraint integration and ambiguity resolution emerges. The relevant constraints are immediately and simultaneously integrated, resulting in competition between partially active alternative interpretations. This method of independent constraint quantification and explicit modeling of off-line and on-line data demonstrates that constraint-based modeling can be pursued in a principled fashion. Moreover, this account suggests that patterns of local processing difficulty that have

previously been interpreted as evidence for architecturally imposed delays in the use of certain constraints are in fact a natural consequence of competition among alternatives in a parallel constraint-based system.

Acknowledgments
This work was supported by NIH grant #HD27206 to MKT. We are grateful to Eiling Yee for assistance in data collection.

References
Altmann, G., & Steedman, M. (1988). Interaction with context during human sentence processing. *Cognition, 30,* 191-238.

Britt, M. A. (1994). The interaction of referential ambiguity and argument structure. *Journal of Memory and Language, 33,* 251-283.

Frazier, L. (1987). Theories of syntactic processing. In J. Garfield (Ed.), *Modularity in knowledge representation and natural language processing.* Cambridge: MIT Press.

Hanna, J., Barker, C. & Tanenhaus, M. (1995). Integrating local and discourse constraints in resolving lexical thematic ambiguities. Poster presented at the 8th Annual CUNY Sentence Processing Conference. Tucson, AZ.

Liversedge, S., Pickering, M. & Branigan, H. (1995). The comprehension of sentences that are ambiguous between agentive and locative interpretations. Poster presented at the 8th Annual CUNY Conference on Human Sentence Processing. Tucson, AZ.

MacDonald, M. Pearlmutter N. & Seidenberg, M. (1994). The lexical nature of syntactic ambiguity resolution. *Psychological Review, 101,* 676-703.

Rayner, K., Garrod, S. & Perfetti, C. (1992). Discourse influences in parsing are delayed. *Cognition, 45,* 109-139.

Rayner, K., Sereno, S., Morris, R., Schmauder, R. & Clifton, C. (1989). Eye movements and on-line language comprehension processes. *Language and Cognitive Processes, 4,* 21-50.

Spivey-Knowlton, M. (1994). Quantitative predictions from a constraint-based theory of syntactic ambiguity resolution. *Proceedings of the 1993 connectionist models summer school,* (pp.130-137). Hillsdale, NJ: Erlbaum.

Spivey-Knowlton, M. & Sedivy, J. (1995). Resolving attachment ambiguities with multiple constraints. *Cognition, 55,* 227-267.

Spivey-Knowlton, M. & Tanenhaus, M. (submitted). Syntactic ambiguity resolution in discourse: Modeling the effects of referential context and lexical frequency within an integration-competition framework.

Spivey-Knowlton, M., Trueswell, J. & Tanenhaus, M. (1993). Context effects in syntactic ambiguity resolution. *Canadian Journal of Experimental Psychology*: Special Issue, *47,* 276-309.

Tanenhaus, M. & Trueswell, J. (1995). Sentence comprehension. In J. Miller & P. Eimas (Eds.), *Handbook of cognition and perception.* SD, CA: Academic Press.

Trueswell, J. & Tanenhaus, M. (1994). Toward a lexicalist approach to syntactic ambiguity resolution. In C. Clifton, L. Frazier & K. Rayner (Eds.), *Perspectives on sentence processing.* Hillsdale, NJ: Erlbaum.

Evidence for a Tagging Model of Human Lexical Category Disambiguation.

Steffan Corley and **Matthew W. Crocker**.

Centre for Cognitive Science,
University of Edinburgh,
Edinburgh EH8 9LW, UK.
Steffan.Corley@ed.ac.uk

Abstract.

We investigate the explanatory power of very simple statistical mechanisms within a modular model of the Human Sentence Processing Mechanism. In particular, we borrow the idea of a 'part-of-speech tagger' from the field of Natural Language Processing, and use this to explain a number of existing experimental results in the area of lexical category disambiguation. Not only can each be explained without the need to posit extra mechanisms or constraints, but the exercise also suggests a novel account for some established data.

Introduction.

Much recent research into human sentence processing has concentrated on the use of experience-based statistical knowledge in making initial decisions (Mitchell & Cuetos, 1991; MacDonald, Pearlmutter & Seidenberg, 1994; Tanenhaus & Trueswell, 1994; Corley, Mitchell, Brysbaert, Cuetos & Corley, 1995). We formalise this tendency by introducing the "Statistical Hypothesis":

Statistical mechanisms play a central role in the Human Sentence Processor.

It is worth establishing this as a very broad hypothesis, which avoids making a number of claims that are the subject of debate in the current literature while encompassing a range of models that do. In particular, it does not claim that *all*, or indeed any, initial decisions are made on the basis of statistics, nor that statistics play a role at any particular level of processing. Issues of granularity are also unspecified by the hypothesis.

A number of statistical models have already been proposed and therefore fall within the Statistical Hypothesis. These include Mitchell and Cuetos' (1991) "Tuning", and constraint-based models from MacDonald *et al.* (1994) and Trueswell and Tanenhaus (1994). These models share a common assumption – that all that statistics offer us is an improved heuristic for making decisions in the face of ambiguity and (in the case of the constraint-based models) for discarding parallel analysis. That is, statistics *supplement* a viable, non-statistical architecture.

We argue that statistical mechanisms are most suitable for simple low-level processes that do not form part of traditional models of the human sentence processing mechanism (*HSPM*). We also suggest that a statistical model should differ from traditional approaches in architecture, as well as in decision procedures. Evidence for these views

comes from the A.I. literature, where statistical mechanisms have been used in traditional tasks such as parsing (Magerman & Marcus, 1991), but have been most successful in more constrained, low-level tasks such as lexical category disambiguation and noun phrase boundary detection (Church, 1988).

In this paper, we propose a distinct statistical process performing lexical category disambiguation within a modular *HSPM*. We briefly touch on the mathematics of such a model, and then go on to test the predictions of our model against some established experimental data. The results not only demonstrate the power of such a simple statistical technique, but also cast new light on the experimental data. We conclude with a few wider considerations and lessons learnt.

Lexical Category Disambiguation.

If we are to design a lexical category disambiguation module, the first question must be what statistics should it use?

It seems likely that the *HSPM* could gather statistics relating individual words to their lexical category (e.g. how often "post" appears as a noun or verb). Beyond that, experimental evidence supports the use of limited contextual information (Juliano & Tanenhaus, 1993). The simplest, most coarse-grained, contextual statistics are lexical category co-occurrence statistics (e.g. how often a noun follows a preposition). Given no compelling evidence for finer-grained information, we limit ourselves to these two statistics.

It happens that a simple process using exactly these statistics has been well explored in the A.I. literature. It is called a part-of-speech "tagger". Its job is to determine a preferred set of part-of-speech "tags" for a given set of words. Equation 1 is used to assign a probability to each possible tag set (or "tag path")[1].

$$P(t_0, \ldots t_n, w_0, \ldots w_n) = \prod_{i=1}^{n} P(w_i \mid t_i) P(t_i \mid t_{i-1}) \qquad (1)$$

This equation can be applied incrementally. That is, after each word we may calculate a contingent probability for each tag path terminating at that word; an initial decision may be made as soon as the word is seen. However, this

---

[1] w_i is the word at position i in the sentence, t_i is a possible tag for that word.

decision may be altered by the tagger when later words are encountered (see section 4 for further discussion).

Figure 1 depicts tagging the two words "some men". Supposing we already know the probability of "some" occurring as a determiner, noun or adjective. We can then work out the probability of each tag path in which "men" is a noun by multiplying the relevant probability for "some" by the word-tag ($P(w_i \mid t_i)$, where w_i is "men") and bigram ($P(t_i \mid t_{i-1})$) probabilities. Similar calculations can be performed for tag paths in which the tag for "men" has some other value – for instance adjective or verb. The most likely tag for "men" is the one that occurs in the most probable tag path.

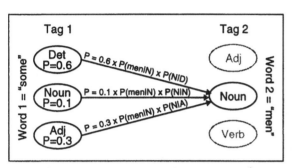

Figure 1: Tagging the words "some men".[2]

As stated, this algorithm is expensive in a real world situation, as it involves remembering all possible tag paths through an arbitrarily long input sentence. However, a large number of clear losers can rapidly be discarded. With this simplification, the algorithm is linear (Viterbi, 1967).

Taggers, in general, are extremely accurate (often 95% – see Charniak, 1993). However, they have distinctive breakdown and repair patterns, which we will argue are similar to those shown by humans.

We propose that a lexical category disambiguation module, functionally equivalent to a tagger, occurs as a distinct process with human lexical access – prior to a modular[3] syntactic component. Its purpose is to make 'quick and dirty' decisions based on limited statistical information. These decisions may then be altered at "higher" levels of processing. In sections 3 and 4 we present existing experimental evidence which supports this claim.

Tagging and Initial Decisions.

Noun-Verb Ambiguities.

Following Frazier and Rayner (1987), MacDonald (1993) investigated processing of sentences where a word is ambiguous between noun and verb readings, following another noun.

1. The union told reporters that the warehouse fires many workers each spring...

[2] The numbers in this figure are invented for the sake of exposition and are not intended to represent real probabilities.
[3] By 'modular', we mean that processes and knowledge are somehow distinct, but we leave for later research the issue of the nature and degree of their communication.

2. The union told reporters that the *corporation fires* many workers each spring...

In 1, the two words form a plausible noun compound ("warehouse fires"). As all her disambiguations favour a verb reading for the ambiguous word[4], MacDonald calls this an "unsupportive bias". In contrast, the potential noun compound in 2 ("corporation fires") is implausible, and so there is a supportive bias.

The experiment also included two unambiguous conditions in which the noun compound was ruled out on syntactic grounds. 3 and 4 are sample materials for the unsupportive and supportive bias versions of this condition.

3. The union told reporters that the *warehouses fire* many workers each spring...

4. The union told reporters that the *corporations fire* many workers each spring...

MacDonald found that bias did appear to influence the initial decision of the *HSPM*. There was a significant increase in reading time for the disambiguating region in unsupportive bias conditions (compared to the analogous unambiguous condition), but almost no difference after a supportive bias. That is, the evidence suggests that 1 is the only case in which the *HSPM* makes an initial decision in favour of the noun compound reading.

MacDonald goes on to correlate "supportive bias" with some fine-grained statistical measures, including word-word co-occurrence frequencies and the head-modifier preference of the first noun ("corporation" or "warehouse" above). The tagger model does not include such fine-grained statistics, and it is therefore clear that our predictions will be substantially different. It so happens that the frequency with which a noun follows another noun is very close to that with which a verb follows a noun in all corpora we have examined. That is, there is unlikely to be any strong contextual bias. The behaviour of the tagger will therefore depend largely on the category bias of the individual ambiguous words used.

Figure 2 represents the noun-verb bias of each of the ambiguous words in MacDonald's experiment[5]. The data was obtained from a corpus count and equation 2 was used to calculate each word's "bias" from the count.

$$bias = \log\left(\frac{noun\ count}{verb\ count}\right) \qquad (2)$$

[4] We refer to MacDonald's second experiment. The first is largely concerned with refuting Frazier and Rayner's (1987) experimental materials, and is therefore of little relevance here.
[5] The mean bias is 3.69 and the standard deviation is 1.97. This data was obtained from the British National Corpus (BNC), which contains over 100 million words of British English. The data only includes the plural ("-s") form of the word (the alternative spelling "programmes" was included in the count for "programs"). However, even if we include both base and plural forms, the results are similar (mean 2.66, standard deviation 1.79). Searching smaller corpora of American English (SUSANNE and part of the TreeBank Corpus) also gives very similar results.

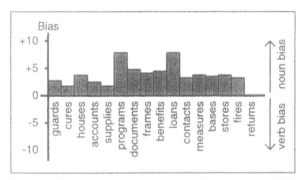

Figure 2: Bias of ambiguous words in MacDonald's (1993) experiment.

It should be clear that the vast majority of MacDonald's experimental materials were strongly biased towards a nominal reading. The initial decision of the tagger depends on two probabilities – $P(t_i | t_{i-1})$, the contextual bias (roughly equal for the noun and verb readings), and $P(w_i | t_i)$, the word bias, represented in figure 2. The tagger model therefore predicts an initial decision in favour of the noun reading for all of MacDonald's experimental items (with the possible exception of those based on the word "returns"). This decision will be rapidly revised following syntactic analysis in 3 and 4, and may be revised following pragmatic analysis in 2. We would expect these revisions to cause processing delays as the word is read.

This partially agrees with MacDonald's reported findings. We predict a similar pattern of results in the disambiguating region. However, we also predict processing delays on the ambiguous word. Fortunately, MacDonald reported the reading times for the ambiguous word (shown in figure 3).

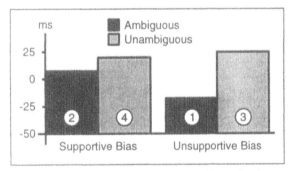

Figure 3: Length-Adjusted Reading Times for the Ambiguous Word from MacDonald (1993).

In conditions 2, 3 and 4, there is a significant processing delay on the ambiguous word compared to condition 1. MacDonald attributes this to the overhead of building the more complex verb phrase structure and calls it a "reverse ambiguity effect" (MacDonald, 1994). However, this processing delay is directly predicted by our model, without introducing complexity measures and using a simpler statistical model.

"That" Ambiguity.

Juliano and Tanenhaus (1993, experiment 1) investigated the initial decisions of the *HSPM* when faced with the ambiguous word "that" in two contexts – sentence initially and following a verb. They forced disambiguation by manipulating the number of the following noun.

5. The lawyer insisted *that experienced diplomat* would be very helpful.
6. The lawyer insisted *that experienced diplomats* would be very helpful.
7. *That experienced diplomat* would be very helpful to the lawyer.
8. *That experienced diplomats* would be very helpful made the lawyer confident.

In 5 and 7, "that" must be a determiner as the following noun is singular. In contrast, the plural noun in 6 and 8 forces the complementiser reading.

Juliano and Tanenhaus found an initial preference for the complementiser reading following a verb (5 and 6), but for the determiner reading sentence initially (7 and 8). This was demonstrated by greater reading times in the disambiguating region in 5 (compared to 6) and in 8 (compared to 7).

It would appear that these results can easily be explained in terms of the tagger architecture. They rely on a regular pattern in the language – that complementisers are more frequent following verbs than sentence initially – which is captured by the lexical category co-occurrence statistics employed by the tagger. Table 1 lists the relevant statistics.

	Prob. of Comp.	Prob. of Det.
Sentence Initial	0.0003	0.0652
Following Verb	0.0234	0.0296

Table 1: Estimated probabilities of complementiser and determiner in two contexts (from BNC).

In both cases the preference is in favour of the determiner reading. However, the tagger also makes use of word-tag statistics, and these are biased the other way ($P(that | comp)$ = 1.0, $P(that | det)$ = 0.171). This bias is strong enough to overcome the comparatively weak contextual bias following a verb, but not the far stronger sentence initial bias. So the predictions for the tagger model match Juliano and Tanenhaus's data – an initial decision in favour of a determiner at the beginning of a sentence, but a complementiser reading is preferred immediately following a verb.

The Tagger's Role in Reanalysis.

The results reported so far demonstrate that the initial decisions made by a tagging model match some established experimental results. However, in the tagging literature there are also good and efficient mechanisms for reassigning tags downstream; that is, reanalysis within the tagger. This section explores whether the tagger's limited reanalysis capabilities may be sufficient to explain some experimental data.

How Tagger Reanalysis Works.

We have already discussed how the tagger assigns a probability to a tag path. Returning to figure 1, suppose that $P(N\,|\,A)$ – the probability of a noun following an adjective – was more than twice $P(N\,|\,D)$ – the probability of a noun following a determiner. The tag path in which "men" is a noun and "some" is an adjective would then have a higher contingent probability than that in which "some" is a determiner. So the tagger would have altered its previous decision about the most likely tag for "some".

Such reanalysis must involve a change in the previous tag (in a bigram model). However, it is possible (though extremely unlikely) that the previous two or more tags will be revised. Figure 4 depicts tagging the two contrasting sentences "without her he was lost" and "without her contributions were lost". We plot the probabilities assigned by the tagger to the two most likely tag paths after each word.

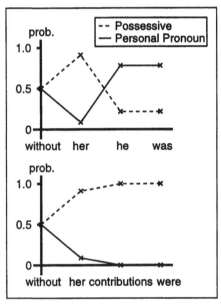

Figure 4: Tagging Two Contrasting Sentences.[6]

The tagger's initial decision when it encounters the word "her" is to favour the possessive reading. However, "he" is unambiguously a personal pronoun and the sequence possessive followed by personal pronoun is extremely unlikely. The tagger's analysis rapidly changes.

In contrast, reanalysis does not occur in the "contributions" case (possessive remains the preferred reading), so we predict a garden path effect on disambiguation. According to Pritchett (1992), this sentence produces a conscious garden path. However, we know of no published experimental evidence to confirm this prediction.

Post-Ambiguity Constraints.

MacDonald (1994) investigated a number of contextual

---

[6] These probabilities, and those in figure 5, have been scaled to add up to 1.

manipulations which can make main verb/reduced relative ambiguities easier to parse. Among these were "post-ambiguity constraints".

9. The sleek greyhound *raced* at the track won four trophies.
10. The sleek greyhound *admired* at the track won four trophies.
11. The sleek greyhound *shown* at the track won four trophies.
12. The sleek greyhound *admired* all day long won four trophies.

MacDonald discovered that sentences such as 9 result in greater reading time for the disambiguating region ("won four trophies") than either 10 or 11 (the unambiguous control). However, the ambiguous region of 10 ("admired at the track") is slower to read than the same region in 9.

MacDonald argues that the difference occurs as "admired" is strongly biased towards a transitive reading. When a transitive verb is not immediately followed by a noun phrase, a strong constraint is violated and an alternative analysis may be sought. In this case, the reduced relative reading becomes the preferred analysis, as the intransitive reading is unlikely. This "post-ambiguity constraint" does not aid in processing 9 as "raced" is more frequently intransitive, and this reading is consistent with a following prepositional phrase.

The constraint MacDonald proposes here is one of lexical category co-occurrence. She also demonstrates that a "poor constraint" – where the constituent following the verb is initially ambiguous between noun phrase and other reading (as in 12) – is less helpful to the reader. These observations appear to match the reanalysis behaviour of a tagger.

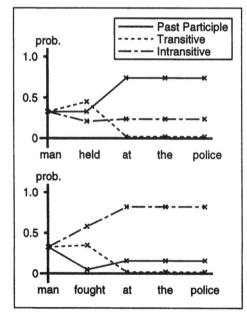

Figure 5: Behaviour of Tagger with Transitive and Intransitive Biased Verbs.

In order to simulate this behaviour, we must train a tagger to assign transitivity information as part of the lexical category. We achieved this by automatically marking all verbs in the SUSANNE corpus for transitivity. Unfortunately, this marking can only be done for this particular corpus, which is rather small. While we obtained reliable tag co-occurrence statistics, we did not have sufficient lexical statistics to tag the same sentences as MacDonald used. We therefore tagged the two sentences "the man held at the police station fainted" and "the man fought at the police station fainted" – which happened, in our corpus, to be biased towards transitive and intransitive respectively. The results are shown in figure 5.

In the "held" case, the tagger initially prefers the transitive reading but rejects this in favour of the reduced relative reading on encountering the following preposition. In this case, we predict increased reading time in the ambiguous region. In contrast, the intransitive reading is preferred and there is no reanalysis in the case of "fought", so we predict increased reading time in the disambiguating region. This agrees with MacDonald's (1994) results, and so the tagger offers a simpler explanation of her "post-ambiguity constraint".

Conclusions.

The primary conclusion of this work is that a tagger model can account for some psychological data. The inclusion of a tagger within a modular model of the *HSPM* provides, at very low cost, a significant aid in ambiguity resolution. This initial study suggests such a model may be psychologically plausible.

Why not a Constraint-Based Model?

We have argued that our "tagger" account may be a plausible model of part of the *HSPM*. However, the experimental results we explain are taken from research into constraint-based models (MacDonald, Pearlmutter & Seidenberg, 1994; Trueswell & Tanenhaus, 1994). Clearly, these can account for the same data. Why should our model be preferred?

Our argument is that a modular model such as the one we are proposing is "simpler". Advocates of constraint-based approaches have argued that their models are structurally simpler (MacDonald, Pearlmutter & Seidenberg, 1994). However, within a probabilistic framework, *structural* simplicity does not seem to be the correct metric.

- In a constraint-based model, a large number of parameters may effect an initial decision during sentence processing. In our model, initial decisions are mitigated by two simple statistical counts, yet we can still account for the same data.

- The range of information types that effect initial decisions in constraint-based models mean that a huge amount of statistical information must be gathered during language learning. Our model is far more "compact".

- Due to the sparsity of some statistical data, it can be difficult to reliably estimate the parameters required by constraint-based models. The interaction of these

parameters also tends to be underspecified, making it difficult to produce concrete predictions. The simpler statistics used by our model mean that it is predictive.

- Constraint-based models allow statistical information to cross levels of representation – for instance, the previous phoneme may be used as a predictor for the next word. We argue that the best predictors tend to occur on the same level of representation. This is built in to our model – again, reducing the number of parameters. Such behaviour may, at best, be emergent from constraint-based models, while it is predicted by ours.

In summary, our model uses simpler statistics, and therefore less parameters, than constraint-based models, and makes no appeal to additional mechanisms, yet still predicts the same data.

Further Conclusions and Lessons Learnt.

We have argued that our model is simpler than a constraint-based model, but can account for the same data. However, the implications are far wider than this.

We are not just using statistics to supplement the decision making process of an existing model. Instead, the use of statistics has informed the architecture of the model. The inclusion of low-level statistical mechanisms could significantly reduce the workload of the structure building component of the *HSPM*. Within a statistical approach, the syntactic module need not be unitary.

We have also learnt two lessons from undertaking this work. The first is that it can be very difficult to intuit the behaviour of a particular statistical system. In order to further the argument, we must build explicit mathematical models as well as argue general principles. The second lesson is that the complexity of behaviour possible with very simple, coarse-grained statistical models can be surprising.

Acknowledgements.

We are thankful to Chris Mellish and the three anonymous reviewers for helpful and supportive comments on earlier drafts of this paper.

The authors also gratefully acknowledge the support of the ESRC (grant R00429334081 to the first author, research fellowship H52427000394 to the second).

References.

Charniak, E. (1993). *Statistical Language Learning*. MIT Press.

Church, K.W. (1988). A Stochastic Parts Program and Noun Phrase Parser for Unrestricted Text. In *Proceedings of the Second Conference on Applied Natural Language Processing* (pp. 136–143). Austin, Texas. ACL.

Corley, M., Mitchell, D.C., Brysbaert, M., Cuetos, F. and Corley, S. (1995). Exploring the Rôle of Statistics in Human Natural Language Processing. In *Proceedings of the 4th International Conference on the Cognitive Science of Natural Language Processing*. Dublin, Ireland.

Frazier, L. and Rayner, K. (1987). Resolution of Syntactic Category Ambiguities: Eye Movements in Parsing Lexically Ambiguous Sentences. *Journal of Memory and Language*, 26, 505–526.

Juliano, C. and Tanenhaus, M.K. (1993). Contingent Frequency Effects in Syntactic Ambiguity Resolution. In *Proceedings of the Fifteenth Annual Conference of the Cognitive Science Society* (pp. 593–598). Lawrence Erblaum Associates.

MacDonald, M.C. (1993). The Interaction of Lexical and Syntactic Ambiguity. *Journal of Memory and Language*, 32, 692–715.

MacDonald, M.C. (1994). Probabilistic Constraints and Syntactic Ambiguity Resolution. *Language and Cognitive Processes*, 9(2), 157–201.

MacDonald, M.C., Pearlmutter, N.J. and Seidenberg, M.S. (1994). Lexical Nature of Syntactic Ambiguity Resolution. *Psychological Review*, 101(4), 676–703.

Magerman, D.M. and Marcus, M.P. (1991). Pearl: A Probabilistic Chart Parser. In *Proceedings: Second International Workshop on Parsing Technologies* (pp. 193–199).

Mitchell, D.C. and Cuetos, F. (1991). The Origins of Parsing Strategies. In C. Smith (Ed.), *Current Issues in Natural Language Processing*. University of Austin, Texas.

Pritchett, B.L. (1992). *Grammatical Competence and Parsing Performance*. University of Chicago Press.

Trueswell, J.C. and Tanenhaus, M.K. (1994). Toward a Lexicalist Framework for Constraint-Based Syntactic Ambiguity Resolution. In C. Clifton, Jr., L. Frazier and K. Rayner (Eds.), *Perspectives on Sentence Processing* (pp. 155–179). Lawrence Erblaum Associates.

Viterbi, A.J. (1967). Error Bounds for Convolution Codes and an Asymptotically Optimal Decoding Algorithm. *IEEE Transactions on Information Theory*, 13, 260–269.

The Importance of Automatic Semantic Relatedness Priming for Distributed Models of Word Meaning

Ken McRae   and   Stephen Boisvert
Department of Psychology
Social Science Centre
University of Western Ontario
London, Ontario, Canada   N6A 5C2
kenm@sunrae.sscl.uwo.ca

Abstract

Recent research on visual word recognition has found that words that are similar in meaning but are not associated do not automatically prime one another (Moss, Ostrin, Tyler, & Marslen-Wilson, 1995; Shelton & Martin, 1992). These results have led to the claim that automatic priming taps word form, but not meaning. Furthermore, they directly contradict predictions of distributed models of semantic memory. In these models, words with similar meaning automatically prime one another, regardless of whether they are associatively related. In Experiment 1, automatic semantic relatedness priming was obtained when prime-target pairs were more similar than those used in previous studies. Single-presentation and short stimulus onset asynchony (SOA) methods were used with both lexical and semantic decision tasks. Experiment 2 ruled out the possibility that these results might have been due to differences in filler items or subject populations by replicating Shelton and Martin's null effect using their stimuli. It was concluded that automatic priming does indeed tap word meaning. Furthermore, as in distributed models, featural similarity is a primary dimension along which semantic memory is organized and an important aspect of semantic relatedness.

Introduction

The semantic priming task and the notion of semantic relatedness have been used in many investigations of language processing (see Neely, 1991, for a recent review), as well as studies of Alzheimer's Dementia (e.g., Nebes et al., 1989), amnesia (e.g., Shimamura & Squire, 1984), and implicit memory (e.g., Schacter, 1992). Although semantic priming has been used to study a number of phenomena, there is no general account of the dimensions of prime-target relatedness that are responsible for the obtained effects. Thus, semantic relatedness has typically been varied on an intuitive basis, making it difficult to draw clear conclusions from these studies. The experiments described in this article were designed to examine semantic memory by focusing on one important aspect of semantic relatedness, featural similarity between lexical concepts. In particular, they were designed to conclusively demonstrate the existence of automatic semantic relatedness priming without association, a prediction that is central to distributed models of semantic memory.

Automatic Semantic Priming

Neely (1977) distinguished between automatic and strategic processes involved in semantic priming. Automatic priming is assumed to tap lexical-internal processing without being influenced by participants' strategies. There are two main strategies, expectancy generation and retrospection. With a long SOA, participants tend to notice that some prime-target pairs are related and then begin to generate potential targets when presented with a prime. An SOA of 250 ms or less has been shown to eliminate this strategy (de Groot, 1984; Neely, 1977, den Heyer et al., 1983). Retrospective processing involves the participant evaluating the relationship between the prime and target subsequent to the target's presentation but prior to responding. For lexical decisions, if a relationship exists, the target must be a word. Three methods have been used to control for retrospective priming. A number of studies have used the naming task because it is believed to be less sensitive to strategic processing in general, and retrospective priming in particular (e.g., Lupker, 1984; Seidenberg et al., 1984). However, it was not used in the present study because the degree to which word meaning influences the computation of phonology from orthography is unclear. The second method is to use a semantic decision task such as "is it a concrete object?" (McRae et al., 1996), which allows for fillers such as LIKE-LOVE to be included. These fillers are related but require a "no" response. The third method, known as single-presentation, avoids overt pairing of prime and target by requiring the participant to respond to every word in the list (Shelton & Martin, 1992). Because participants are less likely to notice relationships among adjacent words, strategic effects are reduced or eliminated. The present research used both short SOA and single-presentation methods.

Lack of Evidence for Featural Overlap Priming

A few studies have worked toward understanding the factors underlying semantic priming by distinguishing between semantic and associative relations. Associative relatedness is typically viewed as temporal contiguity in speech or text (Plaut, 1995), or word co-occurrence within a proposition (McNamara, 1992). Effects of association have been found in a large number of priming experiments (Neely, 1991). In contrast, semantic relatedness is typically viewed as resulting from featural overlap in semantic representations (Shelton & Martin). Only four published studies have used a short SOA or single-presentation paradigm to study semantic relatedness priming without association. Using simultaneous presentation of prime and target, Fischler (1977) found reliable priming effects. However, it is probable that Fischler's double lexical decision task encouraged participants to evaluate prime-target relationships, resulting in large retrospective priming effects. Hodgson (1991) examined the informational bases of semantic priming at short SOAs and found consistent effects using lexical decision. Unfortunately, he informed participants of the related nature of some of the pairs, which likely encouraged strategic processing. Furthermore, Hodgson's effects were small and homogeneous across the types of relationships that he studied (category coordinates, antonyms, synonyms, subordinate-superordinate pairs, conceptual associates, and phrasal associates), prompting him to claim that the effects were due to retrospection.

The remaining two studies, Shelton and Martin (Experiment 4) and Moss et al. (1995, Experiment 3), used single-presentation. However, in both cases, no priming was found in visual lexical decision, prompting Shelton and Martin to claim that "words that are very similar in meaning or sharing many features will not show automatic semantic priming if they are not also associated" (p. 1204). These null results are important for a few reasons. First, they are confusing because they appear to be inconsistent with long SOA studies in which semantic relatedness priming without association has been found (although these long SOA results could be due solely to strategies, Lupker, 1984; Seidenberg et al., 1984). In fact, because of the peculiar nature of these results, they have cast into doubt whether automatic priming taps word meaning at all; Shelton and Martin concluded that automatic priming is due instead to associative relationships at the word form level. In addition, the three main theories of automatic priming, distributed memory (e.g., Masson, 1995; Plaut, 1995), spreading activation (Collins & Loftus, 1975), and compound cue (Ratcliff & McKoon, 1988), predict that automatic semantic relatedness priming should occur, but with differing degrees of conviction. The failures to find priming have not been viewed as damaging to spreading activation nor compound cue theory because it is possible to incorporate the assumption that activation spreads

solely on the basis of associative links, or that the familiarity of a compound cue is influenced solely by associative relationships. In contrast, the existence of automatic semantic relatedness priming is critical to distributed models of semantic memory. A central representational assumption of these models is that similar concepts are encoded as overlapping patterns of activation, typically across microfeature nodes. In simulations of automatic priming, when computing the meaning of a target word, the system begins in the state representing the prime. Thus, priming necessarily results because many of the nodes are already in their appropriate states of activation. In summary, the recent failures to find automatic priming based on similar concepts severely cast doubt upon the primary representational assumption of distributed models.

Experiment 1

Moss et al. and Shelton and Martin chose their prime-target pairs on the basis of their intuition that the concepts possessed sufficient featural overlap to produce a priming effect. This reliance on intuition is particularly problematic given that their conclusions were based on null effects. In order to provide a stronger test, the target items for Experiment 1 were highly similar, as measured over their featural representations from McRae et al. (1996)[1], but were not associated according to free association norms. The greater similarity among our items was demonstrated in a similarity rating study in which participants were asked, "How similar are the things that these words refer to, on a scale of 1 to 9?". The items of Experiment 1 were rated as more similar (6.4) than those of Shelton and Martin (3.6) and Moss et al. (4.5).

Because there are questions about the appropriateness of the different tasks and presentation schemes, both single-presentation and short SOA methods were used with both lexical and semantic decision tasks. The lexical decision task was used because it is the most common task in the literature. The semantic decision task (is it an object?) was included because it unambiguously requires the use of semantic information and it discourages retrospective processing. It was predicted that priming effects would be obtained in both the semantic and lexical decision tasks and in both the single-presentation and short SOA conditions.

Method

Participants. One hundred, sixty-eight native English speaking psychology students at the University of Western Ontario participated for course credit, 42 in each presentation by task condition.

---

[1] In the McRae et al. (1996) study, participants were given the name of an object concept (e.g., truck) and were asked to write down as many of its features as they could. Similarity was computed as the cosine of the resulting feature vectors.

Materials. The 38 prime-target pairs (see Appendix) were chosen from McRae et al. (1996) and were the same for all 4 conditions. All words had concrete referents. Free association was used to rule out prime ⇔ target associations. For all 38 items, 0 of the 20 participants gave the target as a response to the prime. Another 20 participants free associated to the targets. For 23 of the 38 items, the prime was never given. For the other 15, 1 of 20 participants responded with the prime. This item selection procedure was slightly more stringent than those used by Shelton and Martin and Moss et al.

A separate set of 28 participants rated the similarity of the prime-target pairs from Shelton and Martin, Moss et al., and Experiment 1 on a scale from 1 to 9, with 9 being highly similar. The ratings were: Experiment 1, $M = 6.2$, $SE = 0.2$; Shelton and Martin, $M = 3.6$, $SE = 0.2$; and Moss et al., $M = 4.5$, $SE = 0.2$. There was a significant main effect of item source, $F1(2,54) = 256.12$, $p < .0001$, $F2(2,99) = 60.34$, $p < .0001$. Planned comparisons showed that our items were more similar than Shelton and Martin's, $F1(1,54) = 500.44$, $p < .0001$, $F2(1,99) = 117.91$, $p < .0001$, and Moss et al.'s, $F1(1,54) = 200.49$, $p < .0001$, $F2(1,99) = 41.19$, $p < .0001$.

Two lists were created so that subjects saw no prime or target twice. For each list, 19 targets were paired with related primes, and 19 with unrelated primes. For the semantic decision task, 152 filler trials were added to each list in order to have 50% "yes" trials and 25% related trials. These included 38 unrelated nonobject-object pairs (e.g., TREND-CARD), 38 unrelated object-nonobject pairs (e.g., CACTUS-APOLOGY), 19 unrelated nonobject-nonobject pairs (e.g., HASSLE-MIDNIGHT), and 19 related nonobject-nonobject trials (e.g., LIKE-LOVE). For the lexical decision task, the fillers differed only in that the nonobjects were replaced by orthographically legal and pronounceable nonwords. For both tasks, there were 32 practice trials that were constructed to preserve the proportions of each item type used in the experimental trials.

Procedure. Participants were tested individually using PsyScope (Cohen et al., 1993) on a Macintosh LC630. For all conditions, participants were instructed to read "the first word" and respond "only to the second word" by pressing the "yes" or "no" button on a response box positioned in front of them. The index finger of the dominant hand was used for the "yes" response.

A short SOA trial consisted of a fixation point "+" for 250 ms, followed by the prime for 200 ms, a mask (&&&&&&&&) for 50 ms, and the target, which remained on screen until the participant responded. The ITI was 1500 ms. In a single-presentation trial, a prime or target was presented until the participant responded, followed by a 200 ms ISI. Thus, the SOA was the decision latency to the prime plus 200 ms. In the lexical decision task, participants judged whether or not the letter string was an English word. In the semantic decision task, participants judged whether or not the word referred to an object, where an object was defined as something concrete

and touchable. Participants took approximately 20 minutes to complete the task.

Design. The independent variables were relatedness (related vs. unrelated), presentation (single vs. short SOA), and decision (semantic vs. lexical). A list factor (or item rotation group) was included. Relatedness was within participants ($F1$), but presentation and decision were between. All variables were within items ($F2$). The dependent measures were decision latency and accuracy.

Results

Because the error rates were quite low (3% for related targets, 4% for unrelated targets), they were not further analyzed. Decision latencies greater than 3 standard deviations above the mean for that presentation by decision condition were replaced by the cutoff value (2% of the scores). Mean decision latencies are shown in Table 1. Decision latencies for semantically related items were 46 ms faster than for unrelated items, $F1(1,160) = 86.67$, $p < .0001$, $F2(1,37) = 40.76$, $p < .0001$. Critically, the priming effects for related items were significant in all four conditions. There was a 67 ms priming effect in single-presentation semantic decision, $F1(1,160) = 45.30$, $p < .0001$, $F2(1,36) = 66.95$, $p < .0001$; a 41 ms effect in short SOA semantic decision, $F1(1,160) = 17.33$, $p < .0001$, $F2(1,36) = 26.89$, $p < .0001$; a 47 ms effect in single-presentation lexical decision, $F1(1,160) = 22.35$, $p < .0001$, $F2(1,36) = 39.52$, $p < .0001$; and a 29 ms effect in short SOA lexical decision, $F1(1,160) = 8.99$, $p < .004$, $F2(1,36) = 17.75$, $p < .0002$.

Because there was a 57 ms priming effect for the single-presentation condition versus a 35 ms effect for paired-presentation, the interaction between relatedness and presentation was marginal, $F1(1,160) = 4.61$, $p < .04$, $F2(1,36) = 3.54$, $p < .07$. Decision latencies were 102 ms faster for the lexical decision task than for the semantic decision task, $F1(1,160) = 33.90$, $p < .0001$, $F2(1,36) = 201.41$, $p < .0001$. All other effects were nonsignificant.

Discussion

Experiment 1 clearly demonstrates automatic semantic similarity priming with highly similar prime-target pairs and re-establishes that automatic priming taps word meaning. Furthermore, it provides evidence for the central representational assumption of distributed models of semantic memory, namely, that concept similarity (in terms of featural overlap) is a primary organizing principle of semantic memory. The present results are consistent with those of McRae et al. (1996), who used regression analyses to demonstrate that a measure of featural similarity can predict short SOA priming effects.

	Semantic Decision		Lexical Decision	
	Single	Short SOA	Single	Short SOA
Related	695 (21)	699 (24)	592 (12)	613 (13)
Unrelated	762 (21)	740 (22)	639 (14)	642 (15)
Priming Effect	67	41	47	29

Table 1. Mean Decision Latency (and standard error) in ms for Experiment 1

Experiment 2

To ensure that the results were not due to peculiarities in our fillers or subject population, we replicated Shelton and Martin's Experiment 4. The 38 prime-target-pairs from Experiment 1 were replaced by their 36 nonassociated semantically related items. Some of the fillers were also dropped to preserve the ratios of Experiment 1. It was predicted that the priming effect would be non-significant, as they had found.

Method

Participants. Forty-two native English speaking psychology students at the University of Western Ontario participated for course credit.

Materials. The items were the 36 nonassociated related pairs used in Shelton and Martin (Experiments 3 and 4). Two lists were created. For each, 18 targets were paired with related primes and 18 with unrelated primes. The filler items differed from the lexical decision conditions in Experiment 1 only in that 1 or 2 were removed from each cell in order to preserve the proportion of related trials and the probability of a "yes" response. The same practice items were used.

Procedure. The procedure was the same as Shelton and Martin's Experiment 4 and the single-presentation lexical decision in Experiment 1 (200 ms ITI).

Design. The independent variable, relatedness (related vs. unrelated), was within participants and items. List (or item rotation group) was again included.

Results

Because the error rates were quite low (2% for related targets, 3% for unrelated targets), they were not further analyzed. Decision latencies greater than 3 standard deviations above the mean for that presentation by decision condition were replaced by the cutoff value (2% of the scores). Decision latencies were nonsignificantly faster for semantically related items (M =564 ms, SE = 12) than for unrelated items (M = 574 ms, SE = 11), $F1(1,40)$ = 2.73, $p > .1$, $F2(1,34)$ = 1.46, $p > .2$.

General Discussion

The replication of the null effect found by Shelton and Martin indicates that the difference between Experiment 1 and their study is due to differences in the target items. Simply put, the items used by Shelton and Martin (and presumably Moss et al.) did not possess sufficient featural overlap to produce priming.

The existence of automatic semantic similarity priming provides evidence for the assumption that pattern similarity is a central organizational principle of semantic memory. Because this is a primary representational assumption of distributed models of semantic memory, the importance of the current research for them cannot be overstated. All distributed models of semantic memory must predict semantic similarity priming if they use pattern overlap to code similarity. The previous failures of Moss et al. and Shelton and Martin to find this effect were strong indications that the current method of encoding meaning was incorrect, but the present research resolved and explained this inconsistency.

Experiments 1 and 2 are also consistent with the predictions of spreading activation models. For example, Collins and Loftus (1975) explicitly stated that their semantic network is organized by similarity; concepts with numerous shared features are linked through them. The results are also compatible with Ratcliff and McKoon's (1988) compound-cue theory. Items with a number of shared features should provide strong compound cues, thus facilitating the response to the target. It is now no longer necessary for these theories to incorporate the questionable post hoc assumptions that only associated concepts are linked (spreading activation) or only associated concepts form a strong compound cue.

Finally, the null results of Shelton and Martin and Moss et al. had spawned explanations of priming effects in terms of spreading activation in a word form network, implying that automatic priming does not tap semantic memory. However, the present research conclusively demonstrated that word meaning is tapped, thus providing strong support for the utility of automatic semantic priming as a method for revealing the nature of the semantic information that is made available when a word is read or heard. It is now time for further research to take advantage of this, as Hodgson (1991), McRae et al. (1996), and Moss et al. have begun to do.

References

Cohen, J. D., MacWhinney, B., Flatt, M., & Provost, J. (1993). PsyScope: A new graphic interactive environment for designing psychology experiments. *Behavioral Research Methods, Instruments, & Computers, 25*, 257-271.

Collins, A. M., & Loftus, E. F. (1975). A spreading-activation theory of semantic processing. *Psychological Review, 82*, 407-428.

de Groot, A. M. B. (1984). Primed lexical decision: Combined effects of the proportion of related prime-target pairs and the stimulus-onset asynchrony of prime and target. *The Quarterly Journal of Experimental Psychology, 36A*, 253-280.

den Heyer, K., Briand, K., & Dannenbring, G. L. (1983). Strategic factors in a lexical-decision task: Evidence for automatic and attention-driven processes. *Memory & Cognition, 11*, 374-381.

Fischler, I. (1977). Semantic facilitation without association in a lexical decision task. *Memory & Cognition, 5*, 335-339.

Hodgson, J. M. (1991). Informational constraints on pre-lexical priming. *Language and Cognitive Processes, 6*, 169-264.

Lupker, S. J. (1984). Semantic priming without association: A second look. *Journal of Verbal Learning and Verbal Behavior, 23*, 709-733.

Masson, M. E. J. (1995). A distributed memory model of semantic priming. *Journal of Experimental Psychology: Learning, Memory, and Cognition, 21*, 3-23.

McNamara, T. P. (1992). Priming and constraints it places on theories of memory and retrieval. *Psychological Review, 99*, 650-662.

McRae, K., de Sa, V. & Seidenberg, M. S. (1996). *On the nature and scope of featural representations of word meaning.* Manuscript submitted for publication.

Moss, H. E., Ostrin, R. K., Tyler, L. K., & Marslen-Wilson, W. D. (1995). Accessing different types of lexical semantic information: Evidence from priming. *Journal of Experimental Psychology: Learning, Memory, and Cognition, 21*, 863-883.

Nebes, R. N., Brady, C. B., & Huff, F. J. (1989). Automatic and attentional mechanisms of semantic priming in Alzheimer's Disease. *Journal of Clinical and Experimental Neuropsychology, 11*, 219-230.

Neely, J. H. (1977). Semantic priming and retrieval from lexical memory: Roles of inhibitionless spreading activation and limited-capacity attention. *Journal of Experimental Psychology: General, 106*, 226-254.

Neely, J. H. (1991). Semantic priming effects in visual word recognition: A selective review of current findings and theories. In D. Besner & G. W. Humphreys (Eds.), *Basic processes in reading: Visual word recognition* (pp. 264-336). Hillsdale, NJ: Lawrence Erlbaum Associates.

Neely, J. H., & Keefe, D. E. (1989). Semantic context effects of visual word processing: A hybrid prospective-retrospective processing theory. In G. H. Bower (Ed.), *The psychology learning and motivation: Advances in research and theory, Vol. 24* (pp. 207-248). New York: Academic Press.

Plaut, D. C. (1995). Semantic and associative priming in a distributed attractor network. *Proceedings of the Seventeenth Annual Conference of the Cognitive Science Society, 17*, 37-42.

Ratcliff, R., & McKoon, G. (1988). A retrieval theory of priming in memory. *Psychological Review, 95*, 385-408.

Schacter, D. L. (1992). Priming and multiple memory systems: Perceptual mechanisms of implicit memory. *Journal of Cognitive Neuroscience, 4*, 244-256.

Seidenberg, M. S., Waters, G. S., Sanders, M., & Langer, P. (1984). Pre- and postlexical loci of contextual effects on word recognition. *Memory & Cognition, 12*, 315-328.

Shelton, J. R., & Martin, R. C. (1992). How semantic is automatic semantic priming? *Journal of Experimental Psychology: Learning, Memory, and Cognition, 18*, 1191-1210.

Shimamura, A. P., & Squire, L. R. (1984). Paired-associate learning and priming effects in amnesia: A neuropsychological study. *Journal of Experimental Psychology: General, 113*, 556-570.

Acknowledgements

This research was supported by NSERC grant
OGP0155704 to the first author.

Appendix
Prime-target Pairs for Experiment 1

Unrelated Prime	Related Prime	Target
bottle	parakeet	budgie
rifle	whale	dolphin
jeep	finch	canary
lamp	peas	beans
closet	coconut	pineapple
microwave	plum	prune
bus	hoe	shovel
missile	tie	belt
sword	crayon	pencil
crayon	canoe	raft
canoe	sword	spear
tie	missile	bomb
hoe	bus	subway
plum	microwave	toaster
coconut	closet	dresser
peas	lamp	chandelier
finch	jeep	dunebuggy
whale	rifle	pistol
parakeet	bottle	jar
slingshot	eagle	hawk
axe	goose	turkey
motorcycle	duck	chicken
wagon	pumpkin	squash
cannon	radish	beets
cushion	file	sandpaper
yacht	shed	barn
mat	slippers	sandals
shed	bra	camisole
bra	mat	carpet
slippers	yacht	ship
file	cushion	pillow
radish	cannon	bazooka
pumpkin	wagon	cart
duck	motorcycle	scooter
goose	axe	tomahawk
eagle	slingshot	catapult
moose	truck	van
truck	moose	caribou

Parallel Activation of Distributed Concepts: Who put the P in the PDP?

M. Gareth Gaskell

Centre for Speech and Language,
Psychology Department, Birkbeck College,
Malet Street, London WC1E 7HX, England
g.gaskell@psyc.bbk.ac.uk

Abstract

An investigation of the capacity of distributed systems to represent patterns of activation in parallel is presented. Connectionist models of lexical ambiguity have captured this capacity by activating the arithmetic mean of the vectors representing the relevant meanings to form a lexical blend. However, a more extreme test of this system occurs in a distributed model of lexical access in speech perception, which may require a lexical blend to represent transiently the meanings of hundreds of words. I show that there is a strict limit on the number of distributed patterns that can be represented effectively by a lexical blend. This limit is dependent to some extent on the structure and content of the distributed space, which in the case of lexical access corresponds to structure and content of the mental lexicon. This limitation implies that distributed models cannot be simple re-implementations of parallel localist models and offers a valuable opportunity to distinguish experimentally between localist and distributed models of cognitive processes.

Introduction

One of the cornerstones of the connectionist enterprise is the representation of information in a distributed fashion: Each pattern is represented over many processing units and each processing unit forms part of many patterns. This contrasts directly with localist systems, in which each concept is represented by the activation of a single word. Localist models have been valuable in modeling perceptual processes in which the degree of match between sensory input and a set of possible candidates for identification can be represented in terms of a set of activation values; each candidate having a separate activation (e.g., Morton, 1969). The essential point about this type of system is that there is no limit to the number of candidates that can be activated in parallel, since each is independently represented.

Activation of multiple candidates in distributed networks has been achieved by averaging or "blending" the relevant vectors to form a pattern similar to all its constituents. Multiple candidates can be said to be activated to the extent that they are near to the blend in vector space (e.g., Kawamoto, 1993). However, it is not clear whether this approach represents a literal re-implementation of localist

activations or whether it is merely an approximation to the localist systems, with inherent limitations.

In this article, I put the distributed blending approach through its paces, examining a variety of lexical representations. I tackle this problem from an abstract perspective, rejecting actual network simulations in favor of simple mathematical and statistical analyses of vector spaces. This allows a wide range of relevant parameters to be explored without restricting the scope of the analysis to one particular network architecture or learning algorithm.

These analyses are discussed with reference to localist and distributed models of human speech perception. Speech perception provides an important test-bed for questions of parallel activation, partly because the field has been dominated by models in which word candidates are represented in a localist fashion (e.g., Marslen-Wilson, 1987; McClelland & Elman, 1986). More importantly, however, the temporal nature of speech allows us to examine parallel activation during the time-course of perception of words (e.g., Zwitserlood, 1989). This creates the potential for experimentally distinguishing between localist and distributed models of cognitive processing.

A Distributed Model of Speech Perception

Parallel models of speech perception such as Cohort (Marslen-Wilson, 1987) and TRACE (McClelland & Elman, 1986) assume that as a word is heard, many word candidates are assessed simultaneously. The Cohort model goes further, arguing that as these word candidates are evaluated their meanings also become activated. Experimental evidence for this behavior comes from priming studies (e.g., Zwitserlood, 1989), in which an ambiguous word onset (e.g., /kæpt/) facilitates the recognition of targets related in meaning to more than one possible continuation of the stimulus (e.g., *ship* related to *captain*, *prison* related to *captive*). However, the extent to which parallel activation occurs (i.e., whether it extends to large cohorts) remains unknown.

Cohort and TRACE are essentially localist models, in which the goodness of fit between each word candidate and the incoming speech is represented by a separate activation value. Gaskell & Marslen-Wilson (1995) examined the effects of implementing the lexical access process for speech in a distributed learning system. They trained a simple recurrent network to learn the mapping from a stream of phonetic features (segmented into phoneme-like units) onto distributed representations encompassing the meaning and phonological form of words. Lexical access is interpreted in terms of movement through a multi-dimensional space, with word representations being fixed points in this space (see Figure 1). The output of the network plots the course of this movement: As speech information gradually enters the network, the activation of matching words is reflected by constructing a blend of their distributed representations. When the onset of a word is presented at the input, the network outputs a blend of the representations of all the words containing that onset. As more speech comes in, this blend can be refined to represent the reduced set of words that still match the speech input. This refinement continues until the number of words matching the input reduces to 1. At this point (the uniqueness point) the network can isolate the full distributed representation of the remaining word: It has reached an endpoint in the lexical space.

at best output a value half way between the corresponding points in lexical space. When more words are part of a lexical blend, the distance between the blend and the component words is greater (and thus in localist terms, their activations are smaller).

Figure 2 (bold line) illustrates this pattern using a randomly defined lexical space with 200 binary dimensions. Each word is represented by a vector, with each element of the vector having a 50% chance of being on or off. Sets of target patterns were randomly selected and a blend vector was calculated by taking the mean over all target values for each element. The root-mean squared (RMS) distance from this blend vector was then calculated for all the target vectors. Each point in Figure 2 is based on the mean of 64 values. As the number of target patterns increases, their distance from the blend also increases. Thus, word activation as modeled by proximity is highly dependent on the number of candidates remaining active.

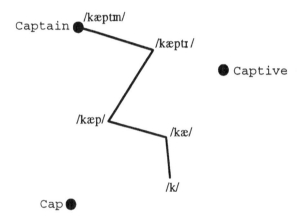

Figure 1. Lexical access as a trajectory through lexical space. The dots mark word representations and the line marks the path of the network output vector as speech is processed.

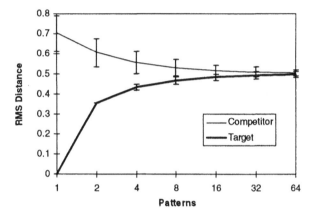

Figure 2. Mean, maximum and minimum distances from blends of targets to target and competitor populations.

Lexical Distance and Activation

Localist models of auditory lexical access use the activation metaphor to indicate the status of recognition process—the degree of match between each word and the incoming speech is reflected in the word's activation value. In the distributed model, this activation is encoded implicitly by the position of the output vector in lexical space—the degree to which any word's lexical representation has been retrieved depends on the proximity of the representation to the output of the network. This proximity value is highly dependent on the number of words that must be activated. If the uniqueness point of a word has been reached, the network merely has to reproduce the lexical representation of that word and so the distance between the output of the network and the representation of that word is likely to be small. This corresponds to a high degree of activation for the word in a localist model. If (as in the *captain/captive* case) the input is temporarily consistent with two words, the network can

It is important to relate the distance of these lexical blends from target representations to the overall population of distances. To be an effective representation of its components a blend should not only be close to the components, it should also be relatively distant from other words. It follows that representational effectiveness can be evaluated in signal detection terms: a blend is an effective representation of its components (the targets) if the target and competitor populations can be separated on the basis of lexical distance alone. Figure 2 also plots the distances from the lexical blends to a set of vectors representing unrelated words in the network's mental lexicon: 3000 randomly chosen vectors with the same properties as the target vectors.

When the number of target patterns is small, lexical blends are much closer to those target vectors than to any of the competitor words. For example, when the lexical blend is based on two target patterns, the RMS distance between those patterns and the blend is 0.36. This is comfortably closer than the nearest competitor, which is 0.53 from the blend. However, as the number of target patterns increases, the signal begins to merge with the noise and the blends become less informative. It soon becomes impossible to work out which of the words the blend is intended to represent on the basis of proximity. It seems that modeling parallel activation in this way imposes a limit on the number of words that can be usefully activated. If too many distributed patterns are blended together, the interference between them becomes large and there is a good chance of some spurious pattern falling closer to the blend than many of the target patterns. Hinton and Shallice (1991) show that a blend of two vectors in this type of system will always be as close to those vectors as any other vector (if not closer). However, for blends of a larger number of words this is not the case: it becomes possible (and even probable) that other vectors will fall closer to the blend than one or more of the target vectors.

It follows that a distributed system cannot implement localist activation models literally. Such models may permit many thousands of candidates to be active early in the processing of a stimulus. Because representations are localist, these candidates can be simultaneously activated without any danger of confusing the active candidates from the inactive ones. The distributed equivalent can reach the same endpoint as a localist model (the correct identification of a perceptual stimulus), but in the early stages of processing its state does not completely distinguish between matching and mismatching candidates. The number of candidates a distributed network can activate effectively in parallel is limited.

This conclusion seems reasonable, but since the assumed lexical system involves a number of arbitrary parameters it should be treated with some caution. In the following sections, I explore the extent to which using different lexical systems alter the properties of a distributed lexical access process.

Dimensionality of Lexical Space

The extent to which multiple lexical representations can be activated simultaneously in a distributed lexicon depends in part on the number of dimensions in that lexical space. In order to discriminate between the components of a lexical blend (the "active" words) and their competitors (all other words in the mental lexicon), the components must match the blend on more features than the competitors. Again, assuming competitors are randomly distributed through the lexical space, this means that each competitor will have a certain chance of matching the blend on each feature. If there is a small number of features and a large number of competitors, then the lexical space becomes crowded and there is a good chance of at least one competitor being sufficiently similar to a lexical blend to cause interference. As the number of dimensions or features rises, this likelihood diminishes and the capability of the lexical system to accommodate multiple representations increases.

This was demonstrated using randomly chosen competitor sets, again with binary dimensions and a 50% chance of each element being set to 1. We defined the separability of target and competitor populations to be the difference between the mean target distance and the minimum competitor distance. This gives a simple measure of the representational effectiveness of the blend. A high separability value implies that the two populations are separable on the basis of distance from the blend vector and indicates that the system is adequately representing the target patterns in parallel.

For each lexical space, consisting of between 50 and 800 dimensions, the separability of the target and competitor sets decreases as the number of patterns in the target increases (see Figure 3). However, as the dimensionality of the space rises, the target representations become easier to separate from the noise. This effect is most obvious in the x-axis zero-crossing points for each space, which can be thought of as a measure of the capacity of the system for simultaneous representation of distributed forms. This capacity rises from about 4 to 32 as the dimensionality of the space rise from 50 to 800. Thus, increasing the number of dimensions in the lexical space improves the capacity for activating multiple representations in parallel. It is difficult to determine where the human system lies along this continuum of dimensionality, but it may be best to think of dimensionality as a measure of richness or degrees of freedom in lexical representations. Each way of distinguishing between two words adds an extra dimension or feature to the representation and more obliquely adds to the capacity of the system to represent multiple lexical entries in parallel.

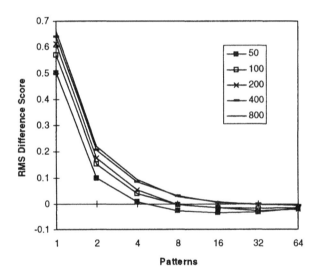

Figure 3. Effect of dimensionality on separability of target and competitor populations. The y-axis plots the minimum competitor distance minus the mean target distance.

Sparseness of Lexical Representations

Many models of cognitive functioning (e.g., Hinton & Shallice, 1991; Plaut & Shallice, 1993) have assumed that distributed lexical representations are sparse, meaning that each word's representation will involve the activation of only a small number of elements. The need for sparse representations is most obvious with binary micro-featural representations of word meaning, where each feature is only relevant to a small minority of words. In less literal representations, sparseness may translate to a high degree of correlation between the distributed vectors representing words. This factor seems bound to affect the capacity for simultaneous activation—after all the localist position, which is ideally suited to parallel activation, occupies one end of the continuum of sparseness. The representations examined so far, in which 50% of all elements were randomly set to 1, lie at the opposite end of this continuum.

Figure 4 shows the effects of manipulating sparseness, using the separability measure defined earlier. Targets and competitor sets in a 200 dimensional space were assigned distributed representations randomly, but the probability of any element being set to 1 (p_{on}) varied from 0.05 to 0.5. Competitor set size was fixed at 3000 words. Also plotted is the same measure for a set of localist representations (local) and for a "near-localist" system of 2 elements on per word (2feat). For the localist representation, the number of competitors is limited by the number of elements in the vector, but since each competitor is equidistant from the blends, this has no effect on the results.

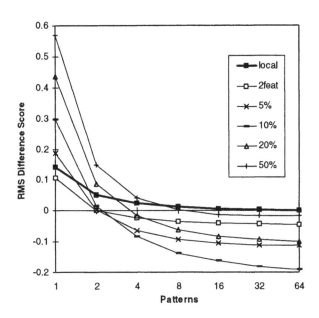

Figure 4. Effect of sparseness of representation on separability. The key gives the mean percentage of elements set to 1 per pattern. The local and 2feat curves are explained in the text.

The pattern that emerges from this manipulation is complex. This is partly because as sparseness decreases the range of possible distances in the lexical space is reduced, which has the effect of flattening the curves for the sparser representations. The most salient feature of each curve is the x-axis zero-crossing point. This marks the point at which the nearest competitor is as close to the blends as the average target and gives an indication of the point at which the signal disappears into the noise. As p_{on} reduces from 0.5

to 0.05, this zero-crossing drops from roughly 8 to 2 patterns. This implies, perhaps surprisingly, that the capacity for multiple representation drops as sparseness increases. The curve for the 2-feature representation fits in with this pattern, crossing the x-axis at roughly 2 patterns. However, the curve for the localist representation is very different: it is still (minimally) above the x-axis for a blend of 64 patterns and in fact should never cross the x-axis.

In summary, increasing sparseness in a distributed representation deepens the problem of representing words simultaneously, despite the fact that the sparser representations seem more similar to a localist representation, which is only limited by the number of elements in the vector. The sparse representations are problematic because they place a restriction on the positions in lexical space that words can occupy. This is similar to reducing the dimensionality of the space, which also reduces the capacity of the system. The localist system is crucially different: it also restricts the lexical space but it guarantees that each word is orthogonal to and equidistant from every other word. This compartmentalizes the space, meaning that a blend of any number of words will always be closer to those words than to all others.

Non-random Distribution in Lexical Space

The lexical systems examined so far have assumed that word representations are randomly distributed through lexical space. This assumption seems implausible if lexical space encodes any kind of similarity between words. Gaskell & Marslen-Wilson (1995) describe lexical access as a mapping onto word representations in a combined phonological and semantic space. Each of these types of knowledge provides structure, which shapes the lexical space and may alter the nature of the blending of representations as speech is perceived.

To address this issue, we need a distributed representation that encodes the similarity structure both of the meanings and the phonological forms of words. Lund, Burgess & Atchley (1995) have argued that similarity in meaning can be captured using co-occurrence statistics drawn from large corpora of language. This method relies on the assumption that words with similar meanings will occur in similar contexts. Although this approach is unlikely to capture the full richness of word meanings, it is a simple and convenient way to capture some aspects of semantic similarity in a distributed system.

Figure 5 compares a random lexical space to two sets of more structured representations taken from Lund et al. (1995). The structured representations are of a set of 2779 word representations (mostly of monosyllabic words). Each one is a 200 element vector with values ranging from 0 to 645. The 200 dimensions were selected from a larger matrix of co-occurrence statistics in order to capture the maximum variance between the vectors for the chosen words. The 64 target words were selected randomly from this set, with all other words acting as competitors. A second analysis used a binary form of these vectors, in which each element was set to either 1 or 0 depending on whether it was above or below the mean value across all words. The random space also had 200 binary dimensions, with each element having a 50% chance of being set to 1.

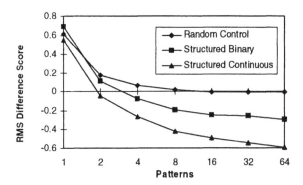

Figure 5. Effect of semantic clustering on separability. The RMS scores for the continuous space are normalized.

The separability curves show that both forms of structured vectors suffer more from the problem of blending than the random vectors. The zero crossing for the random vectors is at roughly 16 patterns, whereas for the binary structured vectors it is between 2 and 4, and for the continuous structured system it is below 2. This implies that for the latter system there is a fair chance of a blend of even 2 vectors falling closer to some other word than to the constituents of the blend.

The more realistic space has more problems distinguishing signal from noise because groups of words form tight clusters in the space. For example, representations of food words may be highly similar to each other but very different to all other representations. This means that when one of these representations is blended with the representation of an unrelated word there is a good chance of one of the other words in the cluster being as close or closer to the blend than the target. The non-binary form of this representation fares even worse because there are no restrictions on the positions word representations can occupy in the space. In particular, words may well occupy positions close to the middle of the space, which is where the blends, being arithmetic means, tend to sit.

In general, therefore, adding more realistic clustering worsens the problem of activating distributed representations simultaneously. However, there is one case in which more realistic clustering lessens this problem. For models of speech perception this is the case where lexical dimensions reflect similarities in the phonological form of words. This is because the phonological representations of words that must be activated in parallel (i.e., cohort members) will be more similar to each other than to unrelated words. Along the dimensions that encode the similarities, the blend will match the target representations exactly, but will mismatch competitors. This gives the targets a head start in terms of their overall distance to the blend in lexical space, and decreases the chances of non-cohort members falling close to the blend vector.

To illustrate this effect, target and competitor word sets were selected using cohort groupings for a word chosen randomly from the 2628 monosyllables in the Lund, Burgess and Atchley (1995) set (the word *bound*). The 223 words with /b/ as initial segment formed the target set for the first blend, with all other words treated as competitor set; the second blend used only the 25 words with onset /ba/ as targets and so on. The lexical space consisted of 52 phonological dimensions, which encoded a modified form of the Plaut, McClelland, Seidenberg & Patterson (1996) monosyllabic representation, and 52 semantic dimensions, which were random, binary and matched the phonological representations on sparseness (p_{on} = 0.08). This space was compared to a control space in which all 104 dimensions were random (see Figure 6). For both lexical spaces, the ability to separate cohort (target) from competitor sets increases further into the word, as the cohort set size decreases. However, the space incorporating phonological structure is more able to separate cohort from competitor sets at all points, reflecting the similarity between cohort members along the phonological dimensions of the lexical space.

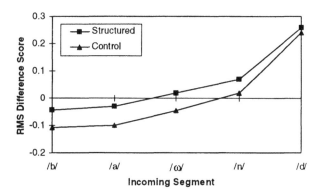

Figure 6. Effect of phonological clustering on separability. The target sets represent the word-initial cohort groups at each point in the word.

Discussion

The previous sections have attempted to quantify the effectiveness of the blending approach to multiple representations in a distributed space. It seems that there is quite a strict limit on the number of distributed patterns that can be usefully combined into a single blend. In general, combining more than a handful of representations results in an unsatisfactory blend, for which simple distance in lexical space does not properly distinguish the components of the blend from their competitors. This means that distributed networks do not simply re-implement localist, activation based systems such as the Cohort (Marslen-Wilson, 1987) or logogen (Morton, 1969) models. This conclusion, although introduced with reference to models of speech perception, may have implications for many domains of cognitive processing, such as short-term memory capacity (e.g., Miller, 1956) or conceptual combination.

Various structural factors affect the capacity for multiple representation. It correlates positively with the number of dimensions or degrees of freedom in the lexical space. Similarly, the sparseness of lexical representations has some effect, with more sparse representations decreasing the capacity to accommodate multiple distributed representations, despite their surface similarity to localist representations. The addition of structure to the distribution of words in lexical space generally increases the problem of multiple distributed representation, because words that are closely packed together in space are difficult to discriminate on the basis of lexical distance alone. This problem becomes more acute when the dimensions of lexical space are continuous rather than binary. The one case in which the addition of structure does help is when the target patterns are all similar along certain dimensions. In the case of speech perception, this occurs when phonology is added to lexical space.

A potential criticism of these findings is that they have all been based on a distance measure. Although this has been the dominant tool for exploring distributed representations, it is possible that some other measure would be more discriminating. In particular, it may be more useful to examine sparse representations by looking at the angle between the relevant vectors. A reanalysis of the sparseness investigation did remove the comparative disadvantage found for the more sparse representations, but if anything it emphasized the gulf between localist and distributed representations in terms of their capacity to represent activation patterns in parallel.

An alternative is that lexical space should not be treated uniformly, so for example, parallel activation of cohort members may reflect only the phonological dimensions, which are more able to distinguish cohort from non-cohort members and are more interpretable when partially activated. Similarly, given the freedom to construct their own distributed space (e.g., in the hidden units), connectionist networks can ensure that words that are frequently coactivated (such as cohort competitors in speech perception) have similar representations. However, the distributed space must also be able to accommodate unlikely or infrequent combinations of items (perhaps, for example, to entertain the notion of a concrete cow). Also, the distributed space may be subject to separate constraints that do not allow such reorganization of representations. Some of the strongest evidence for early multiple activation in speech perception comes from experiments involving semantic priming (Zwitserlood & Schriefers, 1995). If distributed models are to accommodate these data, then the domain of multiple activation must be a distributed semantic space, which by definition does not permit clustering on the basis of phonological form.

At the moment, the experimental data on the extent of parallel activation in speech perception are equivocal. We do not know how many lexical representations can be activated in parallel, nor whether the number of representations activated affects their degree of activation. Maybe the most profitable reaction to this finding is to accept it as a limitation of distributed connectionism and conduct further experiments to see whether it corresponds to a similar property of the human system. Connectionist models are often accused of being too powerful, but here

we have a clear case of something distributed representations find difficult. If this limitation turned out to be one that human systems share, it would be a powerful argument for the validity of modeling cognitive processes using the distributed metaphor.

Acknowledgments

This research was supported by a UK MRC program grant awarded to William Marslen-Wilson and Lorraine Tyler. I am grateful to William Marslen-Wilson, John Bullinaria, Matt Davis, Jeff Elman, Mary Hare and Gary Cottrell for useful discussions of this work.

References

Gaskell, G., & Marslen-Wilson, W. (1995). Modeling the perception of spoken words. In J. D. Moore & J. F. Lehman (Eds.), *Proceedings of the 17th Annual Conference of the Cognitive Science Society* (pp. 19-24). Mahwah, NJ: Erlbaum.

Hinton, G. E., & Shallice, T. (1991). Lesioning an attractor network: Investigations of acquired dyslexia. *Psychological Review*, 98(1), 74-95.

Kawamoto, A. H. (1993). Nonlinear dynamics in the resolution of lexical ambiguity: A parallel distributed processing account. *Journal of Memory and Language*, 32, 474-516.

Lund, K., Burgess, C., & Atchley, R. A. (1995). Semantic and associative priming in high-dimensional semantic space. In J. D. Moore & J. F. Lehman (Eds.), *Proceedings of the 17th Annual Conference of the Cognitive Science Society* (pp. 660-665). Mahwah, NJ: Erlbaum.

Marslen-Wilson, W. D. (1987). Functional parallelism in spoken word recognition. *Cognition*, 25, 71-102.

McClelland, J. L., & Elman, J. L. (1986). The TRACE model of speech perception. *Cognitive Psychology*, 18, 1-86.

Miller, G. A. (1956). The magical number seven, plus or minus two: Some limits on our capacity for processing information. *Psychological Review*, 63, 81-97.

Morton, J. (1969). The interaction of information in word recognition. *Psychological Review*, 76, 165-178.

Plaut, D. C., McClelland, J. L., Seidenberg, M. S., & Patterson, K. E. (1996). Understanding normal and impaired word reading: computational principles in quasi-regular domains. *Psychological Review*, 103, 56-115.

Plaut, D. C., & Shallice, T. (1993). Deep dyslexia: a case study of connectionist neuropsychology. *Cognitive Neuropsychology*, 10, 377-500.

Zwitserlood, P. (1989). The locus of the effects of sentential-semantic context in spoken-word processing. *Cognition*, 32, 25-64.

Zwitserlood, P., & Schriefers, H. (1995). Effects of sensory information and processing time in spoken-word recognition. *Language and Cognitive Processes*, 10, 121-136.

Discrete Multi-Dimensional Scaling

Daniel S. Clouse and **Garrison W. Cottrell**
Computer Science & Engineering 0114
University of California, San Diego
La Jolla, CA 92093
{dclouse,gary}@cs.ucsd.edu

Abstract

In recent years, a number of models of lexical access based on attractor networks have appeared. These models reproduce a number of effects seen in psycholinguistic experiments, but all suffer from unrealistic representations of lexical semantics. In an effort to improve this situation we are looking at techniques developed in the information retrieval literature that use the statistics found in large corpora to automatically produce vector representations for large numbers of words. This paper concentrates on the problem of transforming the real-valued cooccurrence vectors produced by these statistical techniques into the binary- or bipolar-valued vectors required by attractor network models, while maintaining the important inter-vector distance relationships. We describe an algorithm we call *discrete multidimensional scaling* which accomplishes this, and present the results of a set of experiments using this algorithm.

Introduction

Our goal is to develop a connectionist model of lexical access and word sense disambiguation that incorporates a more realistic model of lexical semantics than current models. For the most part, current connectionist models rely either on hand-crafted vector representations of the meanings of words (Kawamoto, 1993; Plaut & Shallice, 1993) or randomly generated vector representations (Cottrell & Plunkett, 1995; Plaut, 1995).

Hand-crafted representations may impose some structure on the fields of the vector (Gallant, 1991; Plaut & Shallice, 1993) in an attempt to provide consistency, or they may be built ad hoc (Kawamoto, 1993). These techniques are motivated by the desire to relate the lexical representations used in the simulation to real words, so that parallels may be drawn to psycholinguistic experiments, and to the intuitions of researchers. There are two main problems with hand-crafted representations. First, they require lots of work to develop, so that the number of words used in a simulation is limited. Second, it is easy to develop a representation without specifying what principles were important in its design.

Randomly-generated representations may be used to avoid both of these problems. The motivation here is usually to generate representations which maintain some interesting set of distance relationships. The parameters can be adjusted to achieve the set of relationships desired. The method is principled and reproducible. Also, the number of vectors which can be generated using this method is essentially unlimited. Unfortunately, using this technique it is not possible to relate the representations to real words, so parallels to specific psycholinguistic stimuli are not possible.

Recently, a third method for generating vector representations of lexical semantics has been gaining acceptance (Schutze, 1993). This method involves gathering word cooccurrence statistics from a large text corpus. Across all occurrences in the corpus of word X, we can count how many times word Y occurs nearby. This number is the cooccurrence count for X and Y. If we gather cooccurrence counts for all pairs of words which occur above a certain frequency, we are left with a large cooccurrence matrix. The row of this matrix corresponding to word X is a vector containing the number of times each other word occurred near word X in the corpus. Insofar as context can be represented by such a "bag of words," this row captures the average context in which word X is seen. Various researchers have proposed methods for refining and reducing the size of the initial cooccurrence vectors. Our method of refinement is to replace each count in the matrix with the mutual information between the row word and column word, then use principal components analysis to shorten the vectors to a reasonable size.

The claim has been made that cooccurrence vectors capture something of the semantics of words. This claim is supported by a number of experiments. Landauer & Dumais (1994), used cooccurrence vectors to pass a portion of the TOEFL (Test of English as a Foreign Language) exam, a test used to evaluate a foreign student's command of English for entry to U.S. colleges and universities. The portion of the test attempted requires the student to choose, from a short list of words, the word which is most similar in meaning to some cue word. To pass the test using cooccurrence vectors, the distance between the cooccurrence vectors for each pair of words was calculated, and the word which was closest to the cue word was chosen. So the distance between the representations of two words serves as a measure of semantic distance.

Schutze (1993) used cooccurrence vectors to tag the senses of ambiguous words in a corpus of text. For each occurrence of an ambiguous word of interest in the text, the cooccurrence vector representations for all nearby words are summed together to produce a context vector. An automatic clustering technique is used to separate these context vectors into groups. All occurrences of the ambiguous word corresponding to context vectors in a single group are tagged with the same sense. This technique works as well as any automatic word disambiguation technique in the literature (89 to 95 percent correct on a short list of words), competing favorably with techniques which start with a more refined source of semantic information such as an on-line thesaurus or dictionary.

Cooccurrence vectors have also been used to model semantic priming. Lund, Burgess & Atchley (1995) present the results of a comparison between a prediction of the size of the semantic priming effect derived using the distances between cooccurrence vectors, and a semantic priming experiment using human subjects. Both the prediction and the experiment used the same set of materials, and show strikingly similar results.

The success of cooccurrence vectors in a variety of semantic tasks suggests them as a good representation in the development of a model of lexical access. The method of generating them is principled and reproducible, the representations can be linked to specific words, and the number of words for which such vectors can be generated is potentially unlimited. So this method appears to combine the best of both the hand-crafted and randomly-generated vector representations.

Unfortunately, there is a problem with the use of cooccurrence vectors for connectionist modeling. A number of recent, successful models of lexical phenomena (Kawamoto, 1993; Plaut & Shallice, 1993; Plaut, 1995) employ attractor networks in their simulations. In these networks, the current output does not rely solely on the input at the current time step, but may be influenced by internal state which has developed over the course of many earlier time steps. The networks are trained to build stable attractors into which activation will settle over time. The time to settle can be measured in different conditions, and compared to reaction time performance of human subjects. This settling performance has been used to account for a number of human priming results: frequency, time course of activation of ambiguous words (Kawamoto, 1993), and semantic versus associative priming (Plaut, 1995). Similar models also exist to explain the effects of neurological damage such as deep dyslexia (Plaut & Shallice, 1993).

Attractor networks tend to work much better when the representations to which they are trained to settle are bit vectors rather than real-valued vectors. We will use the term *bit vector* to refer to a vector whose elements may take on two values. Most often, the two values are either 0 and 1, resulting in a *binary vector*, or -1 and 1, resulting in a *bipolar vector* [1]. When the representations to be stored are bit vectors, the extreme values allowed by the squashing function can be chosen to match those of the bit representation. In the extreme range, a large change in the input to a node has little effect on the output of the node. Thus these extreme ranges make good places to build stable attractors.

So now, we finally get to the main point of this paper! If cooccurrence vectors are to be used as the semantic representation in an attractor network model, we need a way to transform the real-valued cooccurrence vectors into bit vectors. This transformation must be accomplished while maintaining the original distances between vectors in the real space. The remainder of this paper is a report on our attempts to develop an algorithm which performs this transformation, and the performance results of the method which we have found most effective. In the next section we look at possible cost functions to be used by an optimization algorithm. The following section discusses optimization algorithms. Next, we present results of running our algorithm on a number of problems.

---

[1] Similarly, we will use the term *bit space* to refer to the space spanned by a set of either binary or bipolar axes without specifying which.

Finally, we present our conclusions.

Cost Functions

An important constraint on the final representation is that it contain as few bits as possible while still maintaining the original distances between vectors. Thus we share, with the *multidimensional scaling* (MDS) literature (Shepard, 1962; Kruskal, 1964; Borg & Lingoes, 1987) the desire to represent a large amount of data in a smaller space. MDS reproduces a set of proximities (similarities or dissimilarities) defined on some unknown space down to a lower number of dimensions. MDS methods can be divided into metric and non-metric techniques. Metric MDS assumes that the given set of proximities are taken from a metric space. Non-metric MDS makes the weaker assumption that the data was taken from a semi-metric space (i.e. the triangle inequality does not necessarily hold).

The MDS formulation differs from our problem in that, with MDS, the target space is real-valued, and the number of dimensions in the target space is small. In our problem, the target space is a bit space, and the number of bit dimensions required to build an accurate reproduction of the original space may be quite large. Despite the differences, we can easily state our problem in the terms used in this literature.

Let $P = \{(i, j), 1 < i, j < n\}$ be an ordered set of (i, j) pairs that designates the vector pairs for which we have proximities. We will index the elements of P by subscript as p_k. Let $\delta = \{\delta_k : \delta_k = prox(w_i, w_j), p_k = (i, j) \epsilon P\}$ be the set of proximities between items w_i and w_j in the original space, where i and j are designated by P. Then, given a distance metric in s-dimensional bit space, $dist : \mathcal{B}^s \times \mathcal{B}^s \mapsto \mathcal{R}$, $\mathcal{B} = \{0, 1\}$ or $\{-1, 1\}$, our goal is to produce a set of n vectors, V, such that $C(\delta, d)$ is minimized, where $d = \{d_k : d_k = dist(v_i, v_j), p_k = (i, j) \epsilon P\}$ is the set of distances in the new space corresponding to the δs, and C is a cost function which tells how good is the match between the δs and the ds. The cost function, C determines what it means for the original distances to be preserved in bit space. Therefore, our choice of a cost function is very important.

One fairly general specification of an MDS cost function is the following.

$$K(d, \delta) = \frac{\sum_k \left(d_k - \hat{d}_k\right)^2}{\sum_k d_k^2}$$

If the original proximities, δ_k, are sorted so that $\forall k, \delta_k < \delta_{k+1}$, and $\hat{d}_k$ is chosen to be the monotonically increasing function on δ_k which produces the smallest possible value in the numerator of K, then K is the non-metric cost function known as *Kruskal's stress* (Kruskal, 1964). This cost function is one of the best known in the MDS literature, and may serve as a good choice in non-metric applications.

If $\hat{d}_k$ is chosen to be the regression function, which serves as the best sum of squares prediction of d_k given δ_k, then K is a metric cost function (Borg & Lingoes, 1987 p.42), which we will refer to as *metric stress*, or K_m. For our problem, the proximities are derived from a metric space, so it makes sense to use a metric cost function. We have found K_m to be useful when the distance metric in bit space, *dist*, is chosen to be Euclidean distance. This should also work well with

291

other Minkowski metrics (including Hamming or city-block distance), but we have not tried using these.

If, instead of using the regression function, we define $\hat{d}_k = \delta_k$, then K is still a metric cost function, but constrains the final distances to match the original distances as closely as possible. We will refer to this as the *exact match* cost function, or K_x. K_x has proven to be a useful cost function when both the distance metric in the original real space, *prox*, and in bit space, *dist*, are the cosine of the angle between two vectors[2]. This distance metric is used extensively in the information retrieval literature, and works well with our cooccurrence vectors. We have found that K_m only works well with the cosine metric when the number of bits in the final representation is small compared to the number of vectors being reproduced. If the number of bits in the final representation is large, K_m can be minimized by making all the output vectors orthogonal to each other. K_x avoids this problem with the cosine metric by setting the slope of the regression line to a constant 1. This is essentially equivalent to minimizing the sum of squared errors[3]. The results reported in the *Results* section are generated using K_x.

One advantage that K_m and K_x have over Kruskal's stress is that they can easily be computed incrementally. Though the time to calculate any of these cost functions from scratch is $O(n^2 m)$ where n is the number of vectors, and m is the width of a vector, the time to calculate the change in cost when a single bit is changed is $O(n)$ for K_m and K_x. This is a huge advantage for algorithms which search by changing a single bit at a time, such as those presented in the next section. It may be that a similar savings can be achieved with Kruskal's stress, but the implementation is not obvious.

Search Algorithms

The cost functions described in the previous section allow us to evaluate how good a set of bit vectors are in reproducing the distance relationships in the original set of real vectors. In this section we look at two algorithms for searching the space of possible bit vectors for an optimal solution. Both of these are discrete-space algorithms, meaning only points in the final bit-space are considered as candidate solutions. We are also considering continuous-space algorithms, which consider points in real space as intermediate candidate solutions, but we have had little success with these, to date.

The simplest discrete-space search method we have looked at is a Monte-Carlo method we will call `random-walk`. This algorithm maintains a current set of bit vectors, which we will call the current configuration. At all times, the current configuration contains the set of bit vectors which produce the best cost function value so far. From the current configuration,

we search for a better configuration by randomly choosing a single bit of a single vector and seeing what happens to the cost function if that bit is flipped. If flipping the bit results in an improvement in the cost function, then the flipped bit is accepted into the current configuration and the search continues from this new point. If flipping the bit does not result in an improvement, we stay with the current configuration and continue looking at other randomly chosen bits. This kind of iterative improvement continues until there exists no bit which improves the current configuration. At this point the algorithm halts, and the current configuration is returned as the optimal set of bit vectors.

Though you can use a random bit vector as the initial configuration, this algorithm runs faster if the initial configuration is a fairly good one. For bipolar bits, we designate a field of bits to correspond to each real-valued element of the original vectors, and set every bit in the field to the sign of its element. Similarly for binary bits, we set to 1 all bits whose corresponding element is greater than 0.5, and the rest to 0. This, then serves as our initial configuration. There is no constraint in the algorithm to maintain a correspondence between elements in the original vectors and particular fields in the new vectors. Nevertheless, imposing such a correspondence provides a useful method for generating the initial configuration. As an example of how much difference the initial configuration makes, for the 144 bit problem presented in the *Results* section, starting from a random initial configuration required almost twice as much computation as starting using the method presented here, and produced essentially the same cost function value.

A related algorithm is the `optimal-walk` algorithm. In this algorithm, the current configuration is not changed until all possible bit changes have been evaluated. The single bit change which results in the largest improvement in the cost function is accepted into the current configuration, and the search continues from this new point. Like `random-walk`, the algorithm completes when no more improvements can be found. As you might expect, `optimal-walk` requires more time to run than `random-walk`. We had hoped that the the solutions it found might be better than `random-walk`, but this does not appear to be the case. In one trial, we found that `optimal-walk` flipped about 1/3 the number of bits as `random-walk` in the course of finding a solution, but required 50 times as much time overall to run. The final cost function value of the two solutions were almost identical, so `random-walk` appears to perform well compared to `optimal-walk` while requiring much less computation. The results reported in the *Results* section are generated using `random-walk`.

Results

In this section, we present the results of running the `random-walk` algorithm using the cosine K_x cost function on a set of cooccurrence vectors for 233 words which were used as stimuli in Chiarello *et al.* (1990). We started with a 233 by 30000 matrix of cooccurrence counts collected from Internet news groups by Keven Lund and Curt Burgess. We refined this matrix by replacing each cooccurrence count by its mutual information value, then used principal components analysis to reduce each of the 233 vectors to 36 elements. We

---

[2]Instead of $cos(v, w)$, we actually use $\frac{1-cos(v,w)}{2}$. Using this function, large numbers mean the two vectors are far apart, which is an assumption used in the denominator of K.

[3]In the formula for K and K_m, the $\hat{d}$ function is chosen with knowledge of the d_k. If all output vectors are identical, and thus all $d_k = 0$, it is simple to choose a $\hat{d}$ function which minimizes the numerator. The denominator is included to penalize these degenerate solutions. With K_x, the $\hat{d}$ function is fixed, so there is no longer any need for the denominator. Without the denominator, K_x is exactly the sum of squared errors ($\sum_k \left(d_k - \hat{d}_k \right)^2$). The results reported in this paper include the vestigial denominator.

have run the algorithm on other sets of vectors as well with similar results.

Figure 1 (a) plots the minimum value of K_x achieved by a single run of the `random-walk` algorithm at five different bit vector sizes. The x-axis plots the number of bits in each output vector per original real-valued vector element. Since there were 36 real elements in the original vectors, there were 18, 36, 72, 144 and 288 bits respectively in the output vectors portrayed in this graph. Note that by adding more bits to the output representation, we can reduce K_x down to a value somewhat above zero.

Figure 1 (b) plots the number of calculations of the cost function required to generate the stress values in figure 1 (a). This provides a good measure of how the algorithm is affected by the output vector size. Using our incremental technique, the time required for one calculation of the cost function does not depend upon how many bits are included in the output representation, so the dependency on output vector size is simply an indication that that there are more bit combinations to try out with the larger output sizes. On our SparcStation 20, the 18 bit problem required 24 seconds of CPU time to solve. The 288 bit problem required 30 minutes of CPU time.

Figure 2 shows scatter plots of the final configuration for the 36 and 288 bit solutions. Here we plot the distances between every pair of vectors in the original vector space versus the distances between the corresponding vectors in the output space. The horizontal lines in the plots occur because only a limited number of distances are possible between vectors in bit space. Regression lines are also plotted here. Note that as K_x is reduced, the points plotted are pulled in tighter to the regression line. The tightness of the 288 bit solution serves as fairly convincing evidence that we are reproducing the original distances.

We can visualize the success of our algorithm by looking at cluster diagrams. The additive cluster trees (Sattath & Tversky, 1977; Corter, 1982) shown in figure 3 are taken from the original vector space, and the 288 bit vector space. The tree from the original space is on the left. These clusters are extracted from the larger trees which each contain 233 words. Note that the algorithm has maintained the structure of the original trees at two levels. First, these 13 words clustered together in both trees. Second, at a finer level, each tree contains 3 subclusters. Only two words, GOWN and SILK, have changed subclusters between the two trees.

Conclusions

We have demonstrated an algorithm which is capable of transforming real-valued vector representations into bit vector representations while maintaining the intervector distance relationships. This algorithm is capable of generating both binary and bipolar vector representations. It also works with a number of distance metrics, including cosine and Euclidean distance. The algorithm is acceptably fast, and, as we have shown, is capable of finding good solutions. We intend to use this algorithm to help develop realistic semantic representations towards the development of an improved attractor network model of lexical access. One drawback to the current method is that if new words are added, the algorithm must be reapplied. We are currently investigating learning maps between the two spaces that would generalize to novel

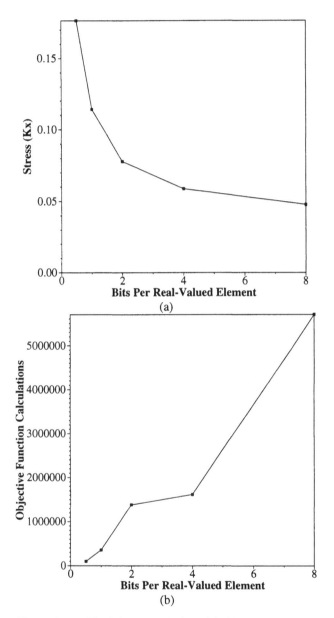

Figure 1: (a) Final Stress at Various Bit Sizes (b) Bit Tests Required

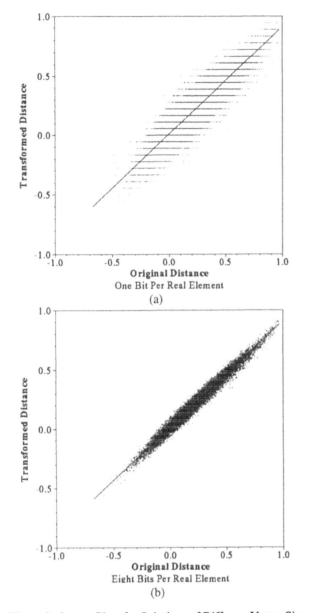

Figure 2: Scatter Plots for Solutions of Different Vector Size

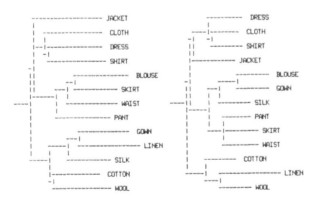

Figure 3: Cluster Trees Before and After Transformation

words.

Acknowledgments

We would like to thank Curt Burgess and Kevin Lund for providing us with the cooccurrence counts we used to develop cooccurrence vectors. Also thanks to the GEURU research group for helpful comments. Daniel Clouse was supported in part by a McDonnell-Pew Predoctoral Fellowship from the San Diego Center for Cognitive Neuroscience, and by a USPHS Predoctoral Traineeship.

References

Borg, I. & Lingoes, J. (1987). *Multidimensional Similarity Structure*. Springer-Verlag, New York.

Cottrell, G.W. & Plunkett, K. (1995). Acquiring the mapping from meaning to sounds. *Connection Science*, 6(4):379–412.

Corter, J.E. (1982). ADDTREE/P: A PASCAL program for fitting additive trees based on Sattath and Tversky's ADDTREE algorithm. *Behavior Research Methods and Instrumentation*, 14(3):353–354.

Gallant, S.I. (1991). A practical approach for representing context and for performing word sense disambiguation using neural networks. *Neural Computation*, 3.

Kawamoto, A.H. (1993). Nonlinear dynamics in the resolution of lexical ambiguity: A parallel distributed processing account. *Journal of Memory and Language*, 32:474–516.

Kruskal, J.B. (1964). Multidimensional scaling by optimizing goodness of fit to a nonmetric hypothesis. *Psychometrika*, 29:1–27.

Landauer, T.K. & Dumais, S. (1994). Memory model reads encyclopedia, passes vocabulary test. Presented at the Psychonomics Society.

Lund, K. & Burgess, C. & Atchley, R.A. (1995). Semantic and associative priming in high-dimensional semantic space. In Moore and Lehman (1995).

Moore, J.D. & Lehman, J.F., editors (1995). *Proceedings of the 17th Annual Conference of the Cognitive Science Society*, July 22 - 25, 1995, University of Pittsburgh, 1995. Lawrence Erlbaum Associates: Hillsdale, NJ.

Plaut, D.C. (1995). Semantic and associative priming in a distributed attractor network. In Moore and Lehman (1995).

Plaut, D.C. & Shallice, T. (1993). Deep dyslexia: A case study of connectionist neuropsychology. *Cognitive Neuropsychology*, 10(5).

Sattath, S. & Tversky, A. (1977). Additive similarity trees. *Psychometrika*, 42(3):319–345.

Schütze, H. (1993). Word space. In S. J. Hanson, J. D. Cowan, and C. L. Giles, editors, *Advances in Neural Information Processing Systems 5*, pages 895–902, Denver, Colorado. Morgan Kaufmann Publishers : San Francisco, CA.

Shepard, R.N. (1962). Multidimensional scaling with an unknown distance function I & II. *Psychometrika*, 27:219–246 & 390–398.

294

Collaboration in Primary Science Classrooms: Learning about Evaporation

Eileen Scanlon, Patricia Murphy, Kim Issroff with Barbara Hodgson and Elizabeth Whitelegg

Open University, Milton Keynes, MK6 7AA

e.scanlon@open.ac.uk

Abstract

We have been studying collaboration in the context of children conducting science investigations in British primary classrooms. The classroom is the site of action where learning occurs and it is the teacher who plays the key role in manipulating the learning environment and selecting and structuring tasks to achieve the best learning effect for all children. In this paper we describe our general approach and focus in particular on the data we collect to explore how children's conceptual understanding of evaporation progresses. The paper highlights some of the messages emerging about how collaboration can sometimes enhance learning, and sometimes thwart it.

Introduction

Collaboration is a key fact of school life for primary children (aged 5 - 12 years old) in the UK. We have been studying how such collaboration mediates the science learning of children of a range of ages working in groups in a variety of classes in a number of primary schools as part of the Collaborative Learning in Primary Science (CLAPS) project. Some other workers (e.g. Howe, 1992) use a laboratory setting and study children's performance on science tasks separate from specific topics being studied by the children in their normal class work. It is very important in our view that our research is based in the classroom. There are two reasons for this- one the influence of context on learning and the other that the complex phenomenon we wish to understand only occurs in the classroom. Artificial contexts only replicate aspects of this phenomenon divorced from the mediating influences of teachers' and childrens' agendas.

The core of this study involves videoing children and teachers at work in the classroom on investigative science tasks. To complement this observation, a range of interviews of teachers and children and probes of cognitive and affective outcomes of the group work were conducted. We have carried out studies in four schools. Children aged from 8 to 12 years have been observed. The situations observed range from a single group in one session, i.e. a snapshot of collaborative learning, to more extended observations of groups lasting a number of weeks. We used radio microphones with target groups of children identified by the teacher as collaborating well and developed and used some questionnaires and interview schedules with children and teachers which focus on their views of science learning, the role of group work and pupil attitudes to it. This paper concentrates on an account of certain features of a part of one case study of year 5 children (8 and 9 -year-olds), studying evaporation. This approach to studying knowledge aquisition in authentic contexts results in rich data and is similar to that advocated by Brown, 1992. Its distinctive feature lies in the approach required to capture the effects of the distinctive investigative curriculum involving children in practical science activities in UK schools.

The focus on investigative learning in science in the UK schools has its roots in the research of the influential Assessment of Performance Unit's science project which identified practical science investigative activity as the synthesis of scientific skills, processes, procedures and concepts (see e.g. Murphy & Scanlon, 1993). Variable-based practical investigations help children develop their scientific knowledge and understanding and engage them in authentic activity (see e.g. Brown et al, 1989) which leads to an understanding of scientific evidence. As children engage in investigative tasks, they use and develop both their conceptual and procedural understanding (Gott & Murphy, 1987), so it is necessary when examining children collaborating on the tasks described below to consider their procedural competency in order to fully understand their conceptual development. So, in what follows we describe both the outcomes in terms of conceptual understanding and the probes used to elicit procedural competency.

Learning about Evaporation

The work on evaporation occupied the middle two weeks of a seven week case study on the topic of water. In our first observations of this class, the teacher had switched the composition of the groups on a week by week basis. For the work on water, two groups were selected by the teacher to work together throughout the period, partly because of his concern that mixed gender groups should develop ways of working together, and partly because, having tried a variety of groupings the teacher felt confident in his knowledge of the individual children's strengths and weaknesses. The target groups were Group 1, a group of three children, two boys and one girl, and Group 2, a group of four children, two boys and girls.

Data Collected. The data collected about the teacher's and the children's views and attitudes is extensive. For this paper, we focus on the specific probes used to ascertain the teacher's approach and the children's conceptual understanding in relation to evaporation and views of group work. In collecting the data about children's understanding we adopt a specific approach. First, we use the teacher's sources of information-in this case children's annotated drawings and accompanying discussions of them - together with the dialogue between children as they plan their investigation of the phenomenon and carry it out, and teacher's and childrens' accounts of the outcomes of the investigations. Secondly, we collect information independently to elaborate the classroom based sources of data. These independent observations include a simple probe prior to the investigation involving a related activity which demonstrates the phenomenon. In this case we used a wet hand print on a paper towel which the children were asked to observe over a period of time as the towel dried (Russell and Watt, 1990). The children's explanations of the phenomenon were recorded and probed to see if they linked their initial understanding of evaporation to this new context. After the children had completed their investigation we probed in recorded interviews what their hypotheses were, what they found out and what they now understood about the process of evaporation. At this point we also returned to the children's annotated diagrams and questioned whether these now represented their thinking and discussed again the 'handprint' phenomenon. The final data collection occured several weeks after the completion of the overall work on water. In this delayed probe, we looked in particular at whether children can apply their understanding of evaporation to new contexts. For these reasons we supplied them with clothes which were wet as they had just been washed and asked for explanations of how clothes dry and and the factors that influence this. Evaporation is not mentioned at this point. After this, we asked children to write and draw about evaporation. Finally, we used a series of photographs of everyday phenomena where evaporation is involved to probe further children's thinking.

The Teacher's View of the Investigations. We interviewed the teacher about his approach to science generally, his approach to specific tasks, his views of what would be achieved by the children and how the work turned out. We also asked about his reasons for grouping children and his views on how the group's work had progressed. His tactic was to group children with similar ideas. When asked about why he did this he said:

because then they will be doing what scientists do really basically which is test their own ideas to see if they are valid rather than, say, give a general question to the whole class where everyone investigates the same thing regardless of their conceptual understanding.

The Investigations. Group 1 investigated what happened when containers were put in hot and cold places. In the words of one girl in the group (1G):

We put a container into an incubator that was hot and one container of water into a fridge ... We thought the one on the fridge would evaporate the quickest but after we done the test and we were half way through it we thought oh no when puddles are out in the road and it's sunny they dry up and they evaporate quicker but we couldn't stop anything then because the test was carrying on ?

The children's accounts of their expectations differ slightly, but all mention the fact that originally they intended to study the effect of moisture on the rate of evaporation. This extract from the conversation between interviewer and the girl quoted above shows the role played by moisture in her thinking about evaporation.

Interviewer:*Can you remember your original ideas then about why the fridge would be quicker*

1G   Em.. because it had less moisture in there and there was more room for it to go up into

Int: *Less moisture in the fridge so more room for the water in*

1G   And then we thought if there wasn't as much moisture in there and there wasn't any moisture going up then nothing was evaporating

This notion of the influence of moisture does reappear in their discussion of results.

In this classroom, a particular focus was made of children deciding for themselves what features to investigate. However the teacher made strong suggestions about the importance of the variable surface area which was taken up by one of the target groups (Group 2). They decided to find out which containers lost the most amount of water, comparing a number of round containers of varying heights and surface areas. As a boy from group 2, 2B describes

We expected that the biggest one would lose the most amount of water... Because it's got a bigger surface area.

However, the experiment hit a snag because the containers were placed in a greenhouse, and another class watered the plants.

The teacher commented later:*I knew this would happen ... so I was going to let them track their result and see if they actually noticed something was wrong ... but the good thing about that was they decided to start again'.*

In fact he had switched his intentions for the activity hoping that these children were learning some useful lessons about scientific procedures. This provides interesting evidence about the potential of an investigation to progress children's conceptual understanding. To understand how surface area affects evaporation is a complex idea beyond most children of this age. At no point do the children in group 2 refer to surface area in their later accounts of evaporation. Furthermore, the teacher switches to a procedural focus which influences his later interactions with them.

Both groups of children planned their investigation and then carried it out over a number of sessions, producing a report of what they found out at a group feedback session.

Group Influences. There were a number of differences in the way that the two groups approached and reacted to the tasks. One key difference was the amount of agreement about what would be the outcome of their investigations. Group 1 shared the hypothesis that heat would alter the rate of evaporation. However, they had differing views about effects of humidity e.g. the boys felt low humidity would enable more water to evaporate, while the girl felt the opposite and they argued this through. In this case, the difference did not alter their ability to design together an investigation to help them explore the issue, they still shared a common task and had developed individual views of it. They did however refer in different ways to their original ideas about the role of moisture. In Group 2, in contrast, all the children shared the hypothesis that water from the wider container would evaporate more quickly but it was a hypothesis provided by the teacher. It is also unclear to what extent the children could understand the surface area as their original ideas and discussion did not take any account of it. In contrast, the 'sun' had featured strongly in most children's prior explanations.

Other differences between the groups was that group 1 in the past had experienced more conflict between group members. In fact, in a prior investigation, the group had experienced enormous difficulty due to differing perceptions of what the task set implied for the design of an activity (see Murphy et al., 1994 for an account). As a consequence they argued through their individual views of the task and were continually attempting to make explicit their thinking.

Outcomes. We used previous research into children's ideas about evaporation to inform our analysis (Russell and Watt, 1990). The categories used to classify children's responses included the vocabulary used (e.g. whether the word evaporated was used, or some other like disappeared,

gone, dissolves, soaked in, pulled, dries up), the location of the water transfer (to air, to sky, to cloth, to clouds, to sun, to ground), the agent of change (e.g. heat, sun, wind, gravity), views about the reversibility of the process (as in rain, as in condensation), the physical state the water is said to have (e.g. whether it has disappeared, or turned into water vapour), and the nature of the transformation involved (e.g. no conservation, change of location, change of location plus physical change). Beveridge (1985) reports that children's prior conceptions of evaporation are resistant to change on instruction. Levins (1992) suggested that it is necessary to study the instructional and developmental sequence further to properly understand how children develop these concepts. We constructed learning trajectories for each child in terms of the information elicited at each stage of the case study. These show what progress each child had made at each stage.

We focus first on the views of one child from group 1 (1B) at each stage of the data collection, and Figure 1 shows his description of evaporation. Before the investigation, when discussing the hand print, he had the idea that the water would have gone both into the air and into the cloth. He then took part in the investigation looking at the influence of heat in the process of evaporation. By the delayed post experiment probe he was able to discuss evaporation in the following terms:*Well first it like gets so hot and it turns into water vapour.. yes it just like ... the sun makes it steam and the steam is like water vapour so then it goes up, rises into the clouds and then you get rain again.*

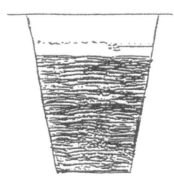

Figure 1 a: Drawings of evaporation made by a boy in group 1 before conducting the investigation (1B)

297

evaporation

If you put some washing out to dry the Sun will evaporate the water by heating the water and turning it in to water vapour then the water vapour will rise and go in to the clouds then when the clouds are full and dark it will rain and it keeps on going like this forever

Figure 1 b: Writing on evaporation by a boy in group 1 after conducting the investigation (1B)

This child was also able to understand that evaporation could occur in a range of circumstances. For example, he was able to say that a person perspiring was a case of evaporation from the skin's surface. He also unprompted began to speculate on the link between evaporation and dissolving.

The construction of learning trajectories for each child made heavy use of data like the extract quoted above. The range of data collected is wide and interpretation of it, as it must always be, is subjective. However, we have the benefit of triangulation from information from more than one source to aid us in the interpretation. In these trajectories, we find some support for the Piagetian picture (1974) of 'the pathway which leads from the child's refusal to accept any 'passage of matter', to an intuitive change of state, and finally to the level in which children described steam as tiny "pieces of water" ' (Levins, 1992, p. 263) By constructing such learning trajectories for all the target pupils we begin to build up a picture of the overall result of the children's investigations of evaporation.

For a child in group 2, however, (2G) investigating surface area progress was limited. For this child the water in the paper hand towel dried up but had *'gone back onto the paper and then its just stayed there ... but its all dried up.'* When asked again about the water after her investigation of evaporation she repeated that *'it [the water] dries up inside the paper.'* This child's initial view of evaporation (shown in Figure 2a) was very similar to her final drawing of the process she provided in the delayed post probe (shown in Figure 2b).

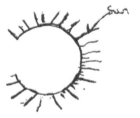

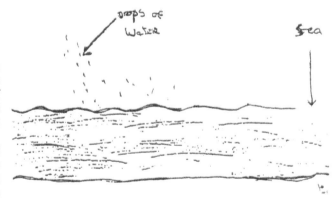

Figure 2 a: Drawings of evaporation made by a girl in group 2 (2G) before conducting the investigation

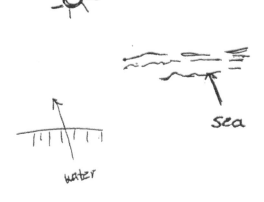

I think evaporation is
something that picks the
water up out of the fabric
and goes to the sun and
then the water falls down
into the sea.

sea

water

Figure 2 b: Drawings of evaporation made by a girl in
group 2 (2G) after conducting the investigation

When asked about washing drying she replied.

Int: *So when the washing dries where do you
think the water goes?*

2G   Em, just think it will evaporate

Int: *You think it will evaporate, so when the
water evaporates where do you think it goes*

2G   It goes up into the sun and then into the
sea

For others in this group, the investigations had
produced more tangible outcomes.

It is not possible to conclude that it was the influence
of the particular investigation performed by an individual
child which changed their views on evaporation, because
they will hear accounts of other children's results of their
investigations and hear and see things outside the
classroom which they try to interpret in terms of their
current conceptual framework. However, our evidence
suggests that most children made some progress (Scanlon

et al., 1995). The most marked progress was for group 1
who explored their own perception of the task. Our initial
analysis suggests that progress is affected by the level of
task engagement which can be influenced by the group
composition. In the case of group 1 the children had
strong views which they argued through. It is also notable
that marked progress was made between the post probe and
the delayed post probe. This is in line with findings by
Howe (1992) and Scanlon et al. (1993) which suggest that
the results of collaborative activity in science often appear
later.

Conclusion and Discussion

By combining observational data from the groups at work,
interview data from children and teachers about their
intentions and actions and probes of conceptual and
procedural understanding we can build up rich pictures of
how group composition influences the group process and
how this in turn influences the learning of individual
children. We have illustrated how data of a variety of types
is necessary to come to an understanding of the way
teacher intentions for the activities are developed and also
the way in which investigations impact on children's
developing ideas. It is our intention to refine such
accounts as these to enable us to better understand the
ways in which classroom conducted science investigations
can aid learning, and the influence of group processes on
this.

A key aspect of those group processes is the effect they
have on the task children agree to pursue and their
individual engagement with it. Our findings suggest that
conflict plays a complex role in children's learning in
groups. We have seen examples of children's behaviour
which suggests that conflict, either between group
members about what outcome is expected, or about how
to plan or conduct an investigation can engender task
engagement. In relation to the work on evaporation, one
group disagreed about their expectations on the influence
of heat because of conflicting views about the role of
humidity in the process. In the post investigation
interviews one child remembered the outcome and her
surprise at it, yet another declared that all that had
happened was what he expected. In this case the conflict in
views seemed to be beneficial, enhancing children's
engagement both with the task and the phenomenon of
evaporation. Sometimes conceptual conflict can be less
beneficial. We have seen occasions in other science
lessons where disagreements in groups have compromised
the conduct of the investigation. Also, perceptions of the
tasks set can vary among members of groups so that
progress is difficult (see Scanlon et al., 1994 and Murphy
et al., 1994 for an account of this.)

Our observations confirm the enormous influence of the
teacher in mediating investigative work in science. The
way in which teachers select and resource tasks, monitor
progress and facilitate children's collaboration is of key
importance. We were interested in the way that the teacher

in the evaporation case study shifted his focus towards procedural matters, and felt the need to import certain variables for the children to study, due to an unease in the the distance needed to travel towards the accepted scientific view. Teachers in general value group work. We are conscious that this is often for the development of social skills rather than the specific science outcomes.

The nature of collaboration on primary science investigations in classrooms is not clearly defined and subject to a number of influences. We have observed three aspects in particular that seem to matter. These are that participants (both pupils and teacher) have a shared task and have developed an explicit individual view of it in relation to their own thinking about the concepts involved; that participants have agreed plans for the investigation and are aware of the consequences of their decisions; and that they develop ways of managing conflict over how to proceed. We have seen in the evaporation case study that conflict can sometimes engender task engagement. Teachers need to be aware of the issue of how to ensure that pupils are engaged in the investigative task they work on. One of the dilemmas is that somehow they need to manage such conflict while protecting task engagement. We have seen examples of pupils themselves managing conflict about the nature of the task, by developing hybrid investigations whose results they cannot understand (Scanlon et al., 1994).

Our intention is to abstract further examples from our collection of rich data in order to explore further the way in which collaboration on investigations in primary science classrooms influences learning.

References

Beveridge, M. (1985). The development of young children's understanding of the process of evaporation. *British Journal of Educational Psychology*, 55, 84-90.

Brown, A. (1992). Design experiments: theoretical and methodological challenges in creating complex interventions in classroom settings. *Journal of the Learning Sciences*, 2(2), 141-178.

Brown, J. S., Collins, A., and Duguid, P. (1989). Situated cognition and the culture of learning. *Educational Researcher*, 18(1), 32-42.

Gott, R. and Murphy, P. (1987). *Assessing investigations*. Assessment of Performance Unit: Science Report for Teachers, No 9 Hatfield, Association for Science Education.

Howe, C. (1992). *Learning through peer interaction*. Presentation to the British Association for the Advancement of Science, Southampton.

Levins, L. (1992). Students' understanding of concepts related to evaporation. *Research in science education*, 22, 263-272.

Murphy, P., Scanlon, E., Issroff, K., Hodgson, B. and Whitelegg, E. (1994). *Developing investigative learning in science- the role of collaboration*. Paper presented at the ECUNET conference, August, Holland.

Murphy, P. and Scanlon, E. (1993). Perceptions of process and content in the science curriculum. In Bourne, J.(ed) *Thinking through primary practice*. London: Routledge Press.

Piaget, J. (1974). *Understanding causality*, New York, Norton.

Russell, T. and Watt, D. (1990).. *Evaporation and condensation*. SPACE project research report, Liverpool University Press.

Scanlon, E. et al. (1993). Promoting conceptual change in children learning mechanics. In *Proceedings of the 15th Cognitive Science Conference*, Boulder, Colorado, June.

Scanlon, E., Murphy, P., Hodgson, B., Whitelegg, E. (1994). A case study approach to studying collaboration in primary science classrooms. In *Proceedings of the International Conference on Group and Collaborative Work*, Glasgow, September, 1994.

Scanlon, E., Murphy, P., and Issroff, K. with Hodgson, B. and Whitelegg, E. (1995). Exploring conceptual development in collaborative work in science. *Paper presented at the Science Education Research Association Conference*, Leeds, April.

Transferring and Modifying Terms in Equations

Richard Catrambone

Georgia Institute of Technology
School of Psychology
Atlanta, GA 30332-0170 USA
rc7@prism.gatech.edu

Abstract

Labeling and elaboration manipulations were used in examples to affect the likelihood of students learning to represent workers' rates and times in algebra word problems dealing with work. Learners studying examples with labels for rates and times were more likely to transfer and correctly modify the representations compared to learners who did not see the labels. An elaborative statement describing the possible representations for the different terms in the work equation did not reliably affect performance. These results extend prior work (Catrambone, 1994, 1995) on subgoal learning by demonstrating that representations, not just sets of steps, can be successfully transferred and modified through a manipulation (labeling) that has been shown to aid subgoal learning.

Introduction

A good deal of research has examined the transfer success people have after studying training materials such as those containing step-by-step instructions (Kieras & Bovair, 1984; Smith & Goodman, 1984), examples (e.g., Ross, 1987, 1989), or both (Fong, Krantz, & Nisbett, 1986). Although there have been some exceptions (e.g., Fong et al., 1986; Zhu & Simon, 1987), the usual finding from such research is that people can carry out new procedures or solve new problems that are quite similar to those on which they were trained, but have difficulty when the novel cases involve more than minor changes from what they had previously studied.

This transfer difficulty seems to stem from a tendency by many learners to memorize a solution procedure from examples that consists of a linear series of steps rather than a more meaningful organization. A linear series of steps provides a learner with little guidance for modifying the solution procedure for problems that can not be solved just like the examples. One potentially useful organization for a solution procedure would be a set of goals and subgoals with methods for achieving them (e.g., Anzai & Simon, 1979; Card, Moran, & Newell, 1983; Catrambone & Holyoak, 1990; Newell & Simon, 1972; Singley & Anderson, 1989).

Problems within a domain typically share the same set of subgoals, although the methods for achieving the subgoals might vary from problem to problem. For instance, in the materials used in the present study, the subgoals to represent each worker's rate and time are in each example and test problem, yet the representations for work and time vary (e.g., a constant, a variable).

Prior work with subgoal learning has demonstrated that if a student learns the subgoal structure for solving problems in a domain, then he or she is more likely to adapt old procedures for novel problems, where novel problems are those involving the same subgoals as the examples but requiring new or modified methods (sets of steps) to achieve the subgoals (Catrambone, 1994, 1995). The present study extends the subgoal-learning work by examining the likelihood of learners transferring and modifying *representations* for conceptual entities in equations as a function of whether they studied training materials emphasizing the subgoals achieved by those representations.

Two manipulations were used to convey subgoals in the present study: 1) the use of examples that contained or did not contain descriptive labels for the terms in the equation, and 2) the use of introductory elaboration prior to the examples that described the possible representations for the different terms in the work equation.

Related Work

The justification for the labeling manipulation is based on a series of studies (Catrambone, 1994, 1995, in press) that develop the subgoal-learning model. In brief, this model proposes that:

1) A label leads learners to group a set of steps;
2) After grouping the steps, learners are likely to try to self-explain why those steps go together;
3) The result of the self-explanation process is the formation of the goal that represents the purpose of that set of steps.

The present study exploits the labeling methodology in order to extend the scope of the model.

Earlier studies involving algebra word problems found that learners were relatively unlikely to successfully modify old representations for terms in equations (Reed, Dempster, & Ettinger, 1985). Rather, they tended to rely on a syntactic approach, that is, learners frequently tried to map old equations from examples to new problems at a symbol by symbol level rather than in terms of the conceptual entities that groups of symbols represented (see also Ross, 1987, 1989). In addition, Reed, and Bolstad

(1991) found that providing learners with rules for solving algebra word problems did not have a large effect on performance.

While some studies have shown that learners can benefit from rule-based instruction for solving problems (e.g., Fong et al., 1986), in general learners seem to prefer and frequently derive more from examples. For instance, Chi, Bassok, Lewis, Reimann, and Glaser (1989) found that after studying a text on mechanics, good and poor students (as defined by a subsequent problem solving test) seemed to possess similar declarative knowledge. However, after studying worked examples, good students were more likely to acquire knowledge about, among other things, the conditions for applying actions/operators and the consequences of those actions. In the framework of the present study, they were better at determining the subgoals being achieved by those actions in the examples.

Overview of Study

The present study has two main purposes. One is to examine whether the benefits of subgoal learning that have been previously found for modifying sets of steps for novel problems (Catrambone, 1994, 1995) will also apply to transferring and modifying the terms used to represent conceptual entities in equations. While some prior work has found that learners can transfer old components into new structures (Elio, 1986), that work focused on reasonably well-practiced procedures rather than transfer after just a small amount of exposure to the training materials. The second purpose is to compare the relative effectiveness of labels (in examples) versus elaborations or rules for representing terms in algebra word problems. Prior work has suggested that examples are more effective than rules in producing knowledge that helps learners to solve novel problems (e.g., Reed & Bolstad, 1991).

Consider the algebra example in Figure 1 in which one has to determine how long it would take someone to do a job given that certain information about their work rate and time and another person's work rate and time are given. This problem involves using an equation for determining work that requires representing each worker's work rate and time: $(Rate_1 \times Time_1) + (Rate_2 \times Time_2) = 1$.

Learners are good at memorizing how to solve problems isomorphic to the one in Figure 1. In this problem, both workers' rates are represented as constants. The time spent working by worker 1 is represented as a variable and worker 2's time is represented as a function of that variable. However, learners may not encode the example solution in terms of determining a representation for each rate and time and then inserting these representations into the equation, but rather have a more superficial understanding of the solution procedure that involves matching the form used in the example, finding similar values in the problem statement, and inserting them into the equation. As a result, if a new problem requires a different representation of the rates and times, these learners might be unable to solve the problem.

For instance, the first problem in Figure 2 requires that worker 2's rate be represented as a variable. In addition, instead of having the workers' times be represented as a variable and a function of that variable (as they were in the example in Figure 1), the times are now represented as a constant and a function of that constant. Nevertheless, the new representations can be inserted into the same equation as the one used for the example in Figure 1. Similarly, the second problem in Figure 2 requires that one worker's rate be represented as a variable and the other worker's rate be represented as a function of that variable. Their times are both represented as constants. These representations are different than those used in the examples.

Mary can rebuild a carburetor in 3 hours and Mike can rebuild one in 4 hours. How long would it take Mary to rebuild a carburetor if she and Mike work together, but Mike works for 1/2 hour more than Mary?

Solution

$\frac{1}{3}$ = Mary's rate

t = time Mary spent rebuilding carburetor

$\frac{1}{4}$ = Mike's rate

$t + \frac{1}{2}$ = time Mike spent rebuilding carburetor

$(\frac{1}{3} * t) + (\frac{1}{4} * (t + \frac{1}{2})) = 1$

$\frac{7}{12} * t = 1 - \frac{1}{8}$

$t = \frac{7}{8} * \frac{12}{7} = \frac{3}{2}$ hours = time Mary spent rebuilding carburetor

Figure 1: Training examples.

1. Mr. Jones can refinish a dresser in 5 hours. After working for 2 hours he is joined by Mrs. Jones. Together they finish the job in 1 hour. How much of the job could Mrs. Jones do in 1 hour when working alone?

Solution (not seen by participants)

$(\frac{1}{5} * (2+1)) + (MrsJ * 1) = 1$

$\frac{3}{5} + MrsJ = 1$

$w = \frac{2}{5} =$ Mrs. Jones' rate; so, in 1 hour Mrs. Jones could do $\frac{2}{5}$ of job

2. Barbara and Connie can finish a job in 6 hours when they work together. Barbara works twice as fast as Connie. How much of the job could Connie do in 1 hour when working alone?

Solution (not seen by participants)

$(2c * 6) + (c * 6) = 1$
$12c + 6c = 1$
$18c = 1$

$c = \frac{1}{18} =$ Connie's rate; so, in 1 hour Connie could do $\frac{1}{18}$ of job

3. Joe can stack a shelf of groceries in 3 hours. Sheila can stack a shelf of groceries twice as fast as Joe. If Joe works for 1 hour alone stacking a shelf and then Sheila starts to help him, how long will Sheila be working with Joe until the shelf is stacked?

Solution (not seen by participants)

$\frac{1}{3} * (t + 1) + (2*\frac{1}{3}) * (t) = 1$

$\frac{1}{3}t + \frac{1}{3} + \frac{2}{3}t = 1$

$t + \frac{1}{3} = 1$

$t = \frac{2}{3}$; so, Sheila will be working with Joe for $\frac{2}{3}$ of an hour

Figure 2: Sample test problems.

The following equation can often be used to solve these problems:
$$(Rate_1 \times Time_1) + (Rate_2 \times Time_2) = Tasks\ Completed$$
where $(Rate_1 \times Time_1)$ is the amount of work completed by the first worker, $(Rate_2 \times Time_2)$ is the amount of work completed by the second worker, and Tasks Completed is the total work completed by both workers. The Rate of a worker can be represented as a constant, a function of a constant, a variable, or a function of a variable. Similarly, the Time a worker works can be represented as a constant, a function of a constant, a variable, or a function of a variable. The particular representation used depends, of course, on the givens in the problem and the question that is being asked by the problem.

Figure 3: Supplemental text seen by elaboration groups.

Learning was assessed by how successfully learners could transfer or modify representations for terms in the work equation. Learners studied examples that used a subset of the possible representations for the terms and then they solved one isomorph and three novel problems. Novel problems were defined as those that required new representations for at least one of the terms from the equation. Two transfer situations for novel problems were examined. The first was the transfer of old representations. The second was how successfully learners could create a new representation for a term. Note that for purposes of the present study, a "new" representation for a term means that the representation had not been used for that term (e.g., rate) in an example even if it had been used for a different term (e.g., time). For instance, even though time was represented as a variable in the training examples (such as the one in Figure 1), if a test problem required rate to be represented as a variable, this would be considered a new representation for rate since rate had been represented only as a constant in the training examples.

The subgoals in the present study involve finding the correct representations for workers' rates and times for algebra word problems. The assumption is that a learner could learn a particular superficial syntax for the work equation without learning the subgoals for representing workers' rates and times. Thus, when faced with a problem that involves new representations for rate and time, the learner might have difficulty. However, if the learner has learned the subgoals to represent each worker's rate and time, then the learner might have a better chance of producing the correct representations in the novel problems. That is, the learner will be more likely to correctly use old representations for rates or times in the context of new representations for rates and times and also that he or she will be able to determine new representations for rates and times. The labeling and elaboration manipulations were used to affect the likelihood of learners acquiring the subgoals to represent workers' rates and times.

Experiment

Method

Participants. Participants were 80 students recruited from several Atlanta-area colleges who received course credit or payment for their participation. In order to participate in the experiment, a student could not have taken a college-level calculus course.

Materials and Procedure. Participants studied three isomorphic example word problems dealing with work, including the example in Figure 1. A cover page included the following statement: "On the next two pages you will find three example algebra problems dealing with work. Work problems typically describe a situation in which two people work together to complete a task."

Two factors were manipulated: labels and elaborations. The Label groups studied examples with descriptions for rates and times of each worker (see the first four lines under the word "Solution" for the example in Figure 1). The No Label groups studied examples that did not contain these descriptions (i.e., lines 1-4 were not present). The Elaboration groups received a supplement to the statement on the cover page that listed the different representations that could be used for rate and time (see Figure 3). The No Elaboration groups did not receive this supplement. The two manipulations were crossed creating four groups with 20 participants per group.

After studying the examples participants received four problems to solve. The first was isomorphic to the training examples. The next three involved both new and old ways of representing rate and/or time for each worker (see Figure 2). Participants could not look back at the examples when working on the test problems.

Results

All participants solved the isomorphic test problem correctly.

Performance on the three novel test problems was scored in the following ways. First, each problem was scored as correct or incorrect. Each participant was then assigned a proportion correct score.

Second, participants were scored on whether they correctly represented the rate and time for each worker for each of the three novel problems. Across the three problems there were a total of four opportunities to use an old representation for rate or time (i.e., RATE: represented as a constant; TIME: represented as a variable or a variable plus a constant). There were a total of eight opportunities to use a new representation for rate or time (i.e., RATE: represented as a variable, a variable multiplied by a constant, or a constant multiplied by a constant; TIME: represented by a constant or the sum of constants). Participants were assigned a proportion correct for old representations and a proportion correct for new representations.

There was a significant effect of label, but not elaboration, on the proportion of novel test problems solved correctly--label: $F(1, 76) = 8.17$, $p = .006$, $MSE = 0.16$; elaboration: $F(1, 76) = 1.44$, $p = .23$ (see Table 1). The interaction was not significant.

| | Elaboration | | No Elaboration | |
	Label ($n = 20$)	No Label ($n = 20$)	Label ($n = 20$)	No Label ($n = 20$)
Proportion of Problems Solved Correctly	.70	.42	.57	.33
Proportion Correct Old Representations	.92	.81	.84	.69
Proportion Correct New Representations	.73	.52	.68	.51

Table 1: Performance on novel test problems.

An analysis of variance was conducted on the proportion of correct representations for rates and times using labels and elaboration as grouping factors and type of representation (old or new) as a within-subjects factor. There was a significant effect of label, $F(1, 76) = 6.40$, $p = .01$, $MSE = 0.16$, but not of elaboration, $F(1, 76) = 1.15$, $p = .29$ (see Table 1). There was also a significant effect of type of representation (old vs new), $F(1, 76) = 43.77$, $p < .0001$, $MSE = 0.04$. There were no significant interactions.

Across the problems, the most common errors that participants made were to inappropriately represent either rate or time in the equation or to write that not enough information was given in the problem.

Discussion

The results from the present experiment are consistent with the hypothesis that students who learned the subgoals of representing workers' rates and times would represent them more successfully on novel problems. This occurred both for old representations in new contexts (i.e., problems that required new representations for at least one term) as well as for new representations. Learners were more successful transferring old representations to novel problems than creating new representations. This is a reasonable finding since the first type of transfer essentially involves the learner recognizing that the old representation is appropriate while the second type of transfer involves the learner creating a representation.

The labeling manipulation affected performance while the elaboration manipulation appeared to be ineffective. This finding is consistent with prior work suggesting that examples play a larger role than explanatory text on the problem solving knowledge students acquire (Chi et al.,1989; LeFevre & Dixon, 1986).

The overall pattern of results is consistent with the claim that when learners are helped to form subgoals for solving problems in a domain, they are more likely to successfully achieve those subgoals in novel problems that require new or modified methods. The twist in the present study is the demonstration that subgoal learning does not benefit just methods that involve a series of steps, but can also benefit a method that is essentially a representation for a conceptual entity in an equation. This finding suggests that the subgoal-learning framework may be applicable to a variety of problem solving situations including those involving changes in representations as well as those involving changes in steps.

Acknowledgements

This research was supported by Office of Naval Research Grant N00014-91-J-1137.

References

Anzai, Y., & Simon, H.A. (1979). The theory of learning by doing. *Psychological Review, 86* (2), 124-140.

Card, S.K., Moran, T.P., & Newell, A. (1983). *The psychology of human-computer interaction.* Hillsdale, NJ: Erlbaum.

Catrambone, R. (1995). Aiding subgoal learning: Effects on transfer. *Journal of Educational Psychology, 87* (1), 5-17.

Catrambone, R. (in press). Generalizing solution procedures learned from examples. *Journal of Experimental Psychology: Learning, Memory, and Cognition.*

Catrambone, R. (1994). Improving examples to improve transfer to novel problems. *Memory & Cognition, 22* (5), 606-615.

Catrambone, R., & Holyoak, K.J. (1990). Learning subgoals and methods for solving probability problems. *Memory & Cognition, 18* (6), 593-603.

Chi, M.T.H., Bassok, M., Lewis, R., Reimann, P., & Glaser, R. (1989). Self-explanations: How students study and use examples in learning to solve problems. *Cognitive Science, 13,* 145-182.

Elio, R. (1986). Representation of similar well-learned cognitive procedures. *Cognitive Science, 10,* 41-73.

Fong, G.T., Krantz, D.H., & Nisbett, R.E. (1986). The effects of statistical training on thinking about everyday problems. *Cognitive Psychology, 18,* 253-292.

Kieras, D.E., & Bovair, S. (1984). The role of a mental model in learning to operate a device. *Cognitive Science, 8,* 255-273.

LeFevre, J., & Dixon, P. (1986). Do written instructions need examples? *Cognition and Instruction, 3,* 1-30.

Newell, A., & Simon, H.A. (1972). *Human problem solving.* Englewood Cliffs, NJ: Prentice-Hall.

Reed, S.K., & Bolstad, C.A. (1991). Use of examples and procedures in problem solving. *Journal of Experimental Psychology: Learning, Memory, and Cognition, 17* (4), 753-766.

Reed, S.K., Dempster, A., & Ettinger, M. (1985). Usefulness of analogous solutions for solving algebra word problems. *Journal of Experimental Psychology: Learning, Memory, and Cognition, 11* (1), 106-125.

Ross, B. (1987). This is like that: The use of earlier problems and the separation of similarity effects. *Journal of Experimental Psychology: Learning, Memory, and Cognition, 13* (4), 629-639.

Ross, B. (1989). Distinguishing types of superficial similarities: Different effects on the access and use of earlier problems. *Journal of Experimental Psychology: Learning, Memory, and Cognition, 15* (3), 456-468.

Singley, M.K., & Anderson, J.R. (1989). *The transfer of cognitive skill.* Cambridge, MA: Harvard University Press.

Smith, E.E., & Goodman, L. (1984). Understanding written instructions: The role of an explanatory schema. *Cognition and Instruction, 1* (4), 359-396.

Zhu, X., & Simon, H.A. (1987). Learning mathematics from examples and by doing. *Cognition and Instruction, 4* (3), 137-166.

305

Understanding Constraint-Based Processes:
A Precursor to Conceptual Change in Physics

James D. Slotta
Graduate School of Education
4611 Tolman Hall
University of California, Berkeley
Berkeley, CA 94720-1670
slotta@violet.berkeley.edu

Michelene T. H. Chi
Learning Research and Development Center
Room 821
University of Pittsburgh
Pittsburgh, PA 15260
chi@vms.cis.pitt.edu

Abstract

Chi (1992; Chi and Slotta, 1993; Slotta, Chi and Joram, 1995) suggests that students experience difficulty in learning certain physics concepts because they inappropriately attribute these concepts with the ontology of *material substances*(MS). According to accepted physics theory, these concepts (e.g., light, heat, electric current) are actually a special type of *process* that Chi (1992) calls *"Constraint-Based Interactions"* (CBI). Students cannot understand the process-like nature of these concepts because of their bias towards substance-like conceptions, and also because they are unfamiliar with the CBI ontology. Thus, conceptual change can be facilitated by providing students with some knowledge of the CBI ontology before they receive the relevant physics instruction. This CBI training was provided by means of a computer-based instructional module in which students manipulated simulations as they read an accompanying text concerning four attributes of the CBI ontology. A control group simply read a (topically similar) text from the computer screen. The two groups then studied a physics textbook concerning concepts of electricity, and performed a post-test which was assessed for evidence of conceptual change. As a result of their training in the CBI ontology, the experimental group showed significant evidence of conceptual change with regards to the CBI concept of electric current.

Introduction

Toward a cognitive theory of instruction

For decades, researchers have studied the science knowledge of novices and experts in a widespread effort to identify and characterize misconceptions of a broad array of science concepts. At the same time, research has also explored different approaches to science instruction which attempt to take these misconceptions into account. Pfund and Duitt (1988) have produced a catalog of nearly 2000 published studies of students' physics misconceptions and instructional attempts at their removal. One important goal of this research (Resnick, 1983) has been to develop a cognitive theory of instruction, which would provide a detailed description of learning in terms of the student's initial knowledge, and how that knowledge interacts with the instructional message. To date, however, there is no instructional theory, nor any methodology which assures that students entering the science classroom will not finish the semester with the same misconceptions they had on the first day of class.

Any instructional theory requires a theory of conceptual change, which provides a cognitive account of students' initial conceptions and the role they play in the learning processes. Chi (1992; Chi, Slotta and deLeeuw, 1993; Slotta and Chi, 1995), has proposed a theory of conceptual change (described below) that is able to account for several important phenomena in the misconceptions literature. A second requirement is a valid means of assessing student conceptions and conceptual change, which is the focus of recent work by Slotta, Chi and Joram (1995). The present study builds on this background by implementing an instructional approach that follows from Chi's theory, and assessing its effectiveness in terms of conceptual change at an ontological level.

Research on student misconceptions

In reviewing research on science misconceptions, Chi (1992) has observed that some misconceptions are easily removed in the course of instruction, while others are characteristically robust, meaning that they survive even when directly confronted by instruction. In one study (McCloskey, 1982), more than half of the university engineering students were still plagued by misconceptions of the basic concept of force. These "robust misconceptions" are typical of certain physics concepts, and may be partly responsible for the difficulty perceived by students and teachers in the physics classroom. In reviewing the literature on physics misconceptions, Reiner, Slotta, Chi and Resnick (in press) found that students often attribute difficult concepts such as force, heat, light, and electricity with materialistic properties. Slotta, Chi and Joram (1995) asked physics novices to solve conceptual problems involving light, heat, and electric current, and observed a clear bias towards materialistic mental models (e.g., reasoning about electric current in a wire as if it were a fluid flowing inside a hose). Any theory of instruction which hopes to account for these robust naive conceptions must be sensitive to this apparent materialistic commitment.

A theory of conceptual change

Chi (1992; Chi, Slotta and deLeeuw, 1993; Slotta and Chi, 1995) has advanced a theory of conceptual change that is able to account for why some physics misconceptions are robust (and others are not), and why there is an apparent preference for materialistic misconceptions. The theory also affords some predictions about how instruction can best proceed in addressing persistent misconceptions. It is upon one such prediction that the present research is founded.

The theory begins with the assumption that people associate all concepts with distinct ontologies (which can be thought of as fundamental categories), such as *processes, ideas,* or *material substances* (throughout the paper, any reference to such ontological categories will be italicized). When a new concept is learned, it is associated with some ontology, which helps the learner understand what kind of concept it is, and what attributes it may possess. Thus, in learning about a new concept such as "osmosis", if person recognizes it (for any reason) as a sort of *process,* then such attributes as "takes some time to occur", and "has a chronological sequence" will become implicitly associated with the concept. Misconceptions arise when a person associates a new concept with the wrong ontology. In learning about the concept of "heat", for example, many children wrongly assume a *material substance* ontology, perhaps because of language conventions such as "close the door, you're letting all the heat out" (Reiner et al., in press). In fact, the concept of heat is more appropriately associated with a *process* ontology, as it is best thought of in terms of the transfer of molecular kinetic energy.

Specifically, Chi has proposed that a particular ontological class of science concepts, which she has called *constraint-based interactions* (a type of *Process*), are characteristically mistaken by novices as possessing the ontology of *material substances*. These are concepts which typically involve constraints such as the equilibration of certain system properties (e.g., inside and outside temperature; voltages; air pressures; etc.) -- properties that are often difficult for a physics novice to perceive. When Slotta et al. (1995) asked physics experts to solve the same conceptual problems that were given to the novices (concerned with topics of light, heat and electricity), their explanations of these problems were consistent with a *constraint-based interaction* ontology, and not a *material substance* one (in contrast with the novices). These observed ontological differences between the conceptions of novices and experts suggests that Chi's account may be accurate: novices may cling to their misconceptions because they are unable to stop thinking of these concepts as material substances.

For example, a student might talk about electric current as "shooting out of the battery", or "leaking out of the wires", even when told explicitly that such descriptions are incorrect. Because of this misconception, the student will experience difficulty in learning about electric current in its scientific sense: as a type of *process* where all of the free electrons in the circuit acquire a uniform velocity component, resulting in a net flow of electric charge through any given point around the circuit. This bias towards the *material substance* ontology may result from a variety of different causes: materialistic biases in language, such as in the heat example above; the dominance of the material substance ontology in our conceptual knowledge, such that it becomes a "default" for novel concepts (i.e., most of our early experience is with material substances and their observed behavior); or the paucity of examples from alternative ontologies (such as that of *constraint-based interactions* ontology). Whatever the origin of this bias, the challenge of teaching certain physics concepts apparently involves convincing students to either relinquish their initial ontological associations, or else gradually forget them.

Methods

Design

The present research applies Chi's theory in a method of instruction whose focus is ontological training. The theory suggests that students may be facilitated in learning *process*-like conceptions if they are first (before any physics instruction) provided with some knowledge of the *Constraint-Based Interactions (CBI)* ontology. We developed a computer-based training module which provides instruction in the *CBI* ontology by means of text and simulations, with no mention of any concepts in electricity. We hypothesize that subjects who receive this *CBI* training will gain some knowledge of the process-like nature of electric current from subsequent instruction in electricity topics. Before receiving the *CBI* training, subjects were pre-tested for misconceptions of electric current, using materials derived from Slotta et al (1995). After the training session, they were provided with instruction in electricity topics, taken directly from a popular conceptual physics text (Hewitt, 1987). Finally, they received the pretest questions a second time, to test for improvement in problem solving, as well as differences in the ontological nature of their explanations. Performance of the experimental subjects was contrasted with that of a control group who did not receive the training module, but instead reviewed a text similar in domain content.

Assessment of conceptual change was performed according to the method developed by Slotta et al (1995), where verbal explanation data is analyzed for its content of a specific set of conceptual attributes that are determined, a priori, to indicate ontologies of *material substance (MS)* or *CBI*, respectively. If a subject talks about electric current in materialistic terms, this is taken to reflect an underlying conception of electric current as a *material substance*[1]. Similarly, the use of verbal predicates which reflect ontological attributes of *constraint-based interactions* are taken to reflect the presence of a *CBI* association. We hypothesize that the experimental group will show a transition from the pretest (where they explain problems in terms of the *MS* ontology), to the post-test (where they will draw upon more *CBI* predicates in their explanations).

---

[1]Note: the use of materialistic words or phrases is not sufficient evidence of a material substance conception. The subject is required to *use* these words or phrases in such a way that s/he predicates the concept with them meaningfully. So the subject's explanation won't necessarily be scored as "materialistic" if she uses the word "moves", whereas if she used the phrase "the electric current moves ___", this would be coded as evidence of a material substance conception.

Apparatus and Materials

***CBI* training module.** This training module consisted of a computer-presented text, which subjects read at their own pace, and which periodically referred to one of several running simulations on the top portion of the screen. Subjects were told that they were learning about "a special type of science concept" called *Equilibration Processes* (which was determined to be a more tenable name than "*constraint-based interactions*"). The training focused on two examples of the *CBI* category - Air Expansion and Liquid Diffusion. The text was organized around four "special qualities" of these *equilibration processes*, which were described as applying to many difficult science concepts.

1. Equilibration Processes have no clear cause-and-effect explanation.
2. Equilibration Processes involve a system of interacting components seeking equilibrium amongst several constraints.
3. In an Equilibration Process, certain constraints behave as they do because they are actually the combined effect of many smaller processes occurring simultaneously and independently within the system.
4. Equilibration Processes have no beginning or ending, even if they arrive at an equilibrium position.

For both topics (Air Expansion and Liquid Diffusion), each of the four attributes was described and illustrated (by means of a simulation). The training text concluded with a summary of all four attributes.

As the reader progressed through the training module, each example (Air Expansion and Liquid Diffusion) was presented in terms of these four attributes, which were illustrated by a running simulation. For the concept of Air Expansion, the simulation consisted of a cylinder-piston system (a rectangle with a moveable "ceiling") with moving air molecules (circles) that collide with the walls of the cylinder and with the piston. When more molecules of air are pumped into the system (by an animated pump which injects more circles into the cylinder), the piston is seen to rise. The first attribute ("no clear cause-and effect explanation") was illustrated by showing students a faulty model that *would* have provided a clear casual account of the piston's rising: marbles (packed circles) were arranged within the cylinder so tightly that they forced against one another; newly added marbles had no room, and thus forced the upper marbles against the piston, which rose. It was pointed out that no such clear chain of cause and effect exists to explain the rising of a piston in a cylinder full of air, and that this special quality is common to all Equilibration Processes (Constraint-Based Interactions). Each of the four attributes was then discussed in turn, defining the *system* (attribute number 2) and its quest for equilibrium, then enumerating the constraints on this process (attribute 3), and stressing the fact that it never arrives at an end-point, but just continuously pursues the equilibrium state (attribute 4).

Pre and post tests. The pre- and post-tests were identical, with eight conceptual problems, each consisting of a simple electric circuit and a question about its behavior. Typically, the subject would be asked whether all the bulbs in a parallel or series circuit would illuminate at exactly the same time when a switch was closed, or whether an illuminated bulb in a circuit would dim or remain the same when a second bulb was added (either in series or parallel with the first) by closing a switch. After choosing an answer for a problem, the subject was asked to explain her response, with frequent prompting to ensure a detailed explanation of what was happening in the problem.

Electricity Text. These materials were seen by both experimental and control groups, and consisted of approximately thirty paragraphs of text drawn from a popular conceptual physics textbook (Hewitt, 1987) and presented in its intended sequence, with the exception that any reference to the famous water analogy for electric circuits was removed.

Subjects
Subjects were 22 university undergraduate students recruited from the University of Pittsburgh and paid for their participation. Male and female students were roughly equal in number, and no subject had any university-level science background, nor any formal training in electricity.

Procedure

Session 1. The study consisted of two sessions, each lasting approximately two hours. In the first session, university students with no science background completed a pre-test consisting of 8 qualitative problems about simple electric circuits. Subjects in the experimental group then received the CBI Ontology Training_Module, which consisted of approximately 25 double-spaced pages of text and two animated simulations, whose purpose was to illustrate elements within the text. As the reader progressed through the training module text, she was occasionally instructed to "click on the simulation button", resulting in some behavior from one of the simulations that was further described and referred to by the text. Subjects in the training module were interrupted periodically by computer-presented explanation prompts, which assured their attention to the content. At the end of the training module, experimental subjects received the training module post-test , which consisted of five broad questions concerning the definition and application of *equilibrium processes (CBI)*. Subjects were aware of this test at the outset of the training module, which provided some motivation for them to attend to the material. Most importantly, it provided a means of assessing the extent to which subjects assimilated the material in the training module.

Control subjects did not receive the CBI Training Module, and spent the first session reading a completely different text from the computer screen (although the same interface was used). This control text was selected from an existing published science text (Hewitt, 1987) so that it was roughly equivalent to the training module text, both in topic (gases and fluids) and level of difficulty. Subjects who receive this control text were also occasionally interrupted by computer-presented explanation prompts. At the end of the session, all control subjects received the control text post-test, which consisted of qualitative questions concerning the definition and properties of the material described in the control text. Subjects were aware of this test at the beginning of the session, so that it provided some motivation for them to attend to the material.

Session 2. All subjects received the same materials and procedure in session 2, which consisted of a physics text concerning electricity and electric circuits. This was a conceptual treatment of electricity, selected from a well-known published physics text (Hewitt, 1987). In the course of reading through this text, subjects (both control and experimental) encountered occasional explanation prompts. After completing the transfer text, all subjects receive the post-test, which was identical to the pre-test. In parting, subjects were asked to complete an exit survey in which they provided information concerning their high school achievement (grade point average and SAT scores), university grade point average, etc.

Analysis of Conceptual Change

Conceptual change was assessed by analyzing subjects' verbal explanations of pre and post test problems according to the presence of attributes from either the *MS* or *CBI* ontology. The attributes were selected based on previous work by Slotta, Chi, and Joram (1995), who measured the patterns of verbal predication in explanations generated by physics novices and experts in response to a set of similar conceptual problems. Slotta et. al interpreted this predicate-use as evidence of ontological commitments. That is, if a subject said, "The current comes down the wire and gets used up by the first bulb, so very little of it makes its way to the second bulb", then these four (underlined) predicates were taken as evidence that she conceptualized current as a substance-like entity which (1) *Moves*, (2) *can be Consumed*, (3) *can be Quantified*, and (4) *Moves*, respectively. Slotta et. al found that experts used predominantly *process* attributes for their descriptions of electric current, whereas novices relied on *substance* attributes almost exclusively.

The six most common attributes of electric current were chosen from the Slotta et al. (1995) novice explanations as a basis set for the *substance* predicates in the present analysis: *Moves* , *is Supplied* , *is Quantified* , *comes to Rest* , *is Absorbed* , and *is Consumed* . Similarly, the six most common attributes of electric current in the explanations of physics experts were chosen as a basis set for the *process* predicates in the present analysis: *System-Wide* , *Movement Process* , *Uniform State* , *Equilibrium State* , *Simultaneity* , and *Independence* . Given a complete coding of all subjects' explanation data (coding each explanation for the presence of all six attributes in each of the two basis sets), we can

quantitatively address such questions as, (1) To what extent do subjects attribute the concept of electric current with substance-like qualities versus process-like qualities? (2) Is a subject's choice of attributes affected by the CBI category training (i.e., is there conceptual change)? and (3) Do subjects who scored highly on the training post-test show more conceptual change than those who did not, as measured by increases in *process* predication or decreases in *substance* predication?

Once all explanations have been coded for the presence of *substance* and *process* attributes, a measure can be derived by simply tabulating the number of predicates from each basis set that were present in an explanation. This sort of "binary" measure loses some frequency information, but avoids many possible distortions, and the need to normalize for protocol length. Thus, if a subject used the *Moves* predicate 15 times in an explanation, it would only be counted once. This results in a maximum score of 6 for both the *Process* and *Substance* attributes (subjects occasionally applied both *process* and *substance* predicates to the concept of electric current in the same explanation). These measures can then be used in quantitative analyses (discussed in Results section: Conceptual Change, below).

Results

Problem Solving Gains

A startling result was that the experimental group showed significant gains in the problem solving task (pre-post test gains), even though this was not a strong goal or prediction of the study. It was not anticipated that a single training session (2 hours) followed by a single session of topic study (2 hours) would have a noticeable impact on students' ability to solve even simple conceptual problems. These test items were intended for use mainly as a means of evoking conceptual discussions and explanations, which are the focus of our analysis of conceptual change. However, experimental subjects showed pre-post test gains of 29% compared to the control group's gain of only 8%. This difference was significant, with $F(1,20) = 6.97$, $p = 0.017$.

Conceptual Change

Both control and experimental groups relied almost entirely on *substance* predicates in explaining their pretest solutions, replicating Slotta et al. (1995). Analysis of post-test explanations revealed the hypothesized conceptual change in the experimental group, who relied greatly on *process* predicates, and very seldom drew upon the *substance* predicates (thus resembling the experts in the Slotta et al. study). Both the increase in *process* predication ($F(1,10) = 39.05$, $p = 0.0002$) and the decrease in *substance* predication ($F(1,10) = 28.5$, $p = 0.0007$) were significant. Control subjects showed no such transition in their preference of conceptual attributes, with no significant differences in level of *process* or *substance* predication. Figure 1 (top of next page) shows a graph of the process and substance predication for the experimental and control groups.

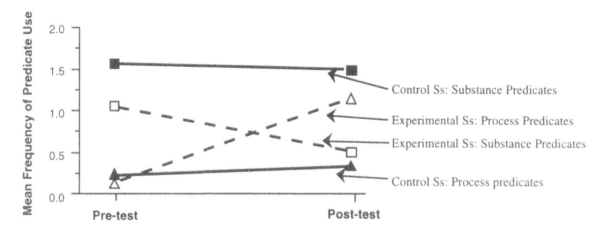

Figure 1. Use of Substance (squares) and Process (triangles) predicates in pre- and post-test explanations.

Because a post-test was administered after the training module (to assess comprehension of, and transferability of the training content), it was possible to split the experimental group into high and low scorers on this test. Figure 2 shows that successful training was indeed a requirement for conceptual change, with the high scoring subjects responsible for nearly all the gains of the experimental group. The interaction suggested by Figure 2 -- between Training Split (high, low, control) and decrease in *substance* predication -- is significant (F(2, 20) = 4.5, p = 0.0200, as is the interaction between Training Split and increase in *process* predication (F2, 20) = 24.7 , p = 0.0001). The low-scoring experimental group did show a reduction in substance predication and an increase in process predication compared to the control group, but significantly less so than the high-scoring training group. In general, all apparent differences between high and low scorers are significant at least to p=0.05.

Discussion

These findings are quite novel to the literature on conceptual change as well as instruction. Many researchers have explored interventions to confront robust physics misconceptions. Yet most have offered interventions which directly target the misconceptions, as if trying to construct the scientific conception from the naive one. Chi's (1992) theory argues that the naive substance-based conceptions should be ignored, and that physics instruction will succeed only to the extent that the student comprehends the novel ontologies involved. We have found that when students are trained in the ontology of *Constraint-Based Interactions*, they show immediate impressive gains in learning the desired conceptions. With only a single focused training session, experimental subjects were able to draw enough new insight from a standard physics text that they substantially revised their responses to conceptual physics problems and (more importantly) offered explanations that were qualitatively distinct from their naive pre-test accounts. Perhaps most important is the fact that the physics training materials were completely unmodified for the purposes of this intervention. Both experimental and control groups received the exact same physics materials, yet control subjects were unable to achieve any substantial progress away from their prior misconceptions.

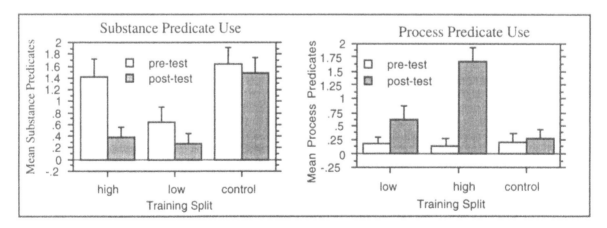

Figure 2. Use of *Substance* (left) and *Process* (right) predicates in pre- and post-test explanations (High vs Low-trained experimental subjects vs controls)

310

The implications of this research for instruction is that there may be certain types of science concepts which are inherently difficult for the novice because they are so completely foreign -- students have never encountered a concept like them before -- and because the students are already possessed of very familiar and comfortable preconceptions which are qualitatively on the wrong track. Conceptual change in these cases may best be served by early training in the *nature* (i.e., ontology) of these concepts, followed by normal physics instruction. Additionally, it is perhaps more clear now that in some (perhaps the most difficult) cases, students cannot make gradual facilitated transition from their preconception to the "scientific" conception, because the two endpoints are separated by a profound ontological barrier.

Acknowledgments

This material is based upon research supported by the Mellon Foundation. Any opinions, findings, and conclusions or recommendations expressed in this publication are those of the authors and do not necessarily reflect the views of the Mellon Foundation. This material was partially prepared while James D. Slotta was a Postdoctoral Researcher at the University of California, Berkeley, and is based on his dissertation research as a student of Dr. Chi.

References

Chi, M. T. H. (1992). Conceptual change within and across ontological categories: Examples from learning and discovery in science. In R. Giere (Ed.), *Cognitive Models of Science: Minnesota Studies in the Philosophy of Science.* (129-160). Minneapolis, MN: Univ. of Minnesota Press.

Chi, M. T. H. , Slotta, J. D., & deLeeuw, N. A. (1992). From things to processes: Toward a theory of conceptual change. In S. Vosniadou (Ed.), special issue of *Learning and Instruction.*

Hewitt, P. G. (1987). Conceptual physics: A high school physics program. (Teacher's ed.). Menlo Park, CA: Addison-Wesley Publishing Company, Inc.

McCloskey, M. (1983). 'Naive Theories of Motion'. In Gentner & Stevens (Eds.) *Mental Models.*

Pfundt, H. & Duit, R. (1988). *Bibliography: Students' Alternative Frameworks and Science Education (2nd ed.).* Kiel, FGR: Institute for Science Education.

Resnick, L. B. (1983). Toward a cognitive theory of instruction. In S. G. Pari, G. M. Olson & H. W. Stevenson (Eds.), *Learning and motivation in the classroom.* Hillsdale, N. J.: Lawrence Erlbaum Associates.

Reiner, M., Slotta, J. D., Chi, M. T. H., and Resnick, L. B. (in press). *Cognition and Instruction.* Naive physics reasoning: A commitment to substance-based conceptions

Slotta, J. D. and Chi, M. T. H. and Joram, E. (1995). *Cognition and Instruction,* 13, (3), 373-400. Assessing students' misclassifications of physics concepts: An ontological basis for conceptual change.

The Role of Generic Models in Conceptual Change[1]

Todd W. Griffith, Nancy J. Nersessian, and **Ashok Goel**
College of Computing
Georgia Institute of Technology
Atlanta, Georgia 30332-0280
(404) 853-9381
{griffith,nancyn,goel}@cc.gatech.edu

Abstract

We hypothesize generic models to be central in conceptual change in science. This hypothesis has its origins in two theoretical sources. The first source, constructive modeling, derives from a philosophical theory that synthesizes analyses of historical conceptual changes in science with investigations of reasoning and representation in cognitive psychology. The theory of constructive modeling posits generic mental models as productive in conceptual change. The second source, adaptive modeling, derives from a computational theory of creative design. The theory of adaptive modeling uses generic mental models to enable analogical transfer. Both theories posit situation independent domain abstractions, i.e. generic models. Using a constructive modeling interpretation of the reasoning exhibited in protocols collected by John Clement (1989) of a problem solving session involving conceptual change, we employ the representational constructs and processing structures of the theory of adaptive modeling to develop a new computational model, ToRQUE. Here we describe a piece of our analysis of the protocol to illustrate how our synthesis of the two theories is being used to develop a system for articulating and testing ToRQUE. The results of our research show how generic modeling plays a central role in conceptual change. They also demonstrate how such an interdisciplinary synthesis can provide significant insights into scientific reasoning.

1. Conceptual Change in Science

In many instances, solving novel or difficult problems leads to conceptual change. Such conceptual change can range from minor changes in existing concepts to the radical kind of change one associates with "scientific revolutions". A significant issue in modeling conceptual change is how existing knowledge can be used in creating genuinely novel understandings. We hypothesize that generic models play a key role in creating these new understandings. These models encompass domain properties, relations, principles, and mechanisms.

To explore this hypothesis we analyze the role of generic models in a problem solving protocol collected by John Clement (1989). Our analysis makes use of the "cognitive-historical" theory of constructive modeling (Section 3) to provide a conceptual interpretation of the problem-solving session (Section 4). We then join this analysis with the computational theory of adaptive modeling (Section 5) that we believe provides the representational constructs and processing structures necessary to model the protocol as so analyzed. Together, the conceptual interpretation and the computational theory enable the development of a new computational theory we call ToRQUE (Theory Revision through Questions, Understanding, and Evaluation) and a system which instantiates this model. (Section 7).

2. The Clement Protocol

The problem posed in the Clement protocol is as follows:

> "... a weight is hung from a spring. The original spring is replaced with a spring made of the same kind of wire; with the same number of coils; but with coils that are twice as wide in diameter. Will the spring stretch form its natural length more, less, or the same amount under the same weight? (Assume the mass of the spring is negligible compared to the mass of the weight.) Why do you think so?" (Figure 1 a & b)

In the study, subjects were asked to assess their confidence in their answer and in their understanding. We focus on one subject, S2, who changed his concept of a spring by incorporating the physical principle of torque into his understanding of how springs function.

Unable to solve the problem directly, S2 began by reasoning that a spring when it is unwound is like a flexible rod (Figure 1c). He then reasoned that a spring of twice the diameter can be unwound into a longer rod, which will bend farther given equal force (Figure 1d). From this he concluded (correctly) that a spring of twice the diameter will stretch farther given equal force. S2, however, unlike most of the participants in the study, was not confident of this answer. He noticed that a significant difference between the stretched spring and the bent rod is that the bent rod has a varying slope, while the spring has a constant slope, i.e., the space between the coils is uniform both before and after the spring is stretched. At this point S2 constructed the models that are the primary focus of our modeling effort (Figure 1e-i). These models were constructed based on salient differences between the spring

---

[1] This research was funded in part by NSF Grant No. IRI-92-10925 and in part by ONR Grant No. N00014-92-J-1234. We thank John Clement for the use of his protocol transcript, James Greeno for his contribution to developing our constructive modeling interpretation of it, and Ryan Tweney for his helpful comments

and the flexible rod, and are designed to resolve what S2 regarded as an anomaly: the nonuniform slope of the bending rod (see Darden 1991 on anomaly resolution). He eventually constructed a model of a hexagonal coil (Figure 1g) that led to the understanding that a spring maintains its constant slope through the twist of the coil wire during stretching. The notion of torque was not present in S2's original model of spring, so we contend that S2's concept of a spring is changed in the problem solving process. Although we are modeling the whole protocol, given space limitations we will focus on just this final piece of reasoning and how we interpret it as employing "generic models".

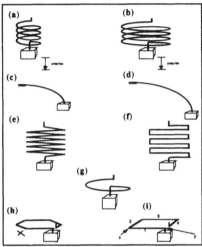

Figure 1: Clement Figures

3. Constructive Modeling

Nersessian (1992, 1995, in press) has argued that general modes of reasoning such as visual reasoning, thought experiment, analogy, and generic abstraction play significant roles in scientific conceptual change. These various modes often are employed together in an iterative reasoning process we call "constructive modeling." Constructive modeling is a semantic process in which the models produced are proposed as interpretations of the target satisfying specific constraints. Figure 2 provides a schematic representation of such a process. Constructing a model starts with properties and relations of a target system that serve as constraints to be satisfied by the initial model. A source domain satisfying some initial target constraints is selected. From this domain an initial analog model is retrieved or is constructed in the case where no direct analogy exists. This initial model - and each constructed model - serves as a source of additional constraints that interact with those provided by the target system to create an enhanced understanding of the target, in particular by making explicit further target constraints. The constraints can be supplied in different informational formats, including equations, texts, kinesthetic, diagrams, pictures, maps, and physical models. The model construction process involves different forms of abstraction (limiting case, idealization, generalization, generic abstraction), constraint satisfaction, adaptation, simulation, and

evaluation. Additional source domains may be called upon throughout the iterations. This cycle is repeated until a satisfactory representation of the target problem is achieved. This representation is a model of the same type as the target problem with respect to the salient target constraints. We interpret S2's reasoning to be a case of constructive modeling .

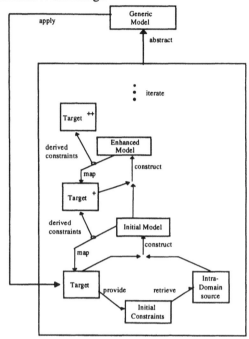

Figure 2: Constructive Modeling

Clearly, to engage in constructive modeling the reasoner needs to know the generative principles and constraints for physical models in one or more domains. This is why analogy plays such a significant role in the constructive modeling process. On our account, the function of analogies is to provide constraints and generative principles for building models. This view is in contrast to the direct transfer view of most computational models (See for example Falkenhainer *et al.*, 1989; Holyoak & Thagard 1989) Thus we view relations between domains in terms of the constraints they share. These constraints and principles may be represented in the different informational formats and knowledge structures that act either as explicit or tacit assumptions employed in constructing and adapting models during problem solving. Since these constraints are domain-specific they need to be understood at a sufficient level of abstraction in order for retrieval, transfer, and integration to be possible. We call this level of abstraction "generic".

What we mean can easily be conveyed by looking at a simple example taken from Polya (1954). Polya considered two cases, abstracting from an equilateral triangle to a triangle-in-general and from it to a polygon-in-general (Figure 3). Loss of specificity is the central aspect of this kind of abstraction process. We call this process "generic abstraction." The generic triangle created in this abstraction process is understood to represent those features that all kinds of triangles have in common. Although the figure entertained by the mind is specific, some of its salient features, the lengths of the sides and the degrees of the angles, must be taken by the reasoner to be unspecified. In contrast to this, a logical generalization from one equilateral triangle to all equilateral triangles maintains the specificity of these salient aspects of "equilateral". In abstracting from the generic triangle to the generic polygon, additional features are left unspecified, viz., the number of sides and the number of angles of the figure. We hypothesize that a reasoner can employ generic abstraction to create a generic mental model during a constructive modeling process or can apply stored models created in previous reasoning.

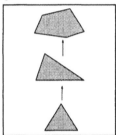

Figure 3: Generic abstraction

Generic models are commonly employed in solving physics problems. For example, in modeling a problem about a pendulum by means of a spring, the scientist understands the spring model as generic, that is, as representing the class of simple harmonic oscillators of which the pendulum is a member. We interpret much of the research in expert physics problem solving as demonstrating this (see for example Chi *et al.*, 1981). Further, we believe generic models facilitate analogical retrieval, mapping, and adaptation in the constructive modeling process. This is exemplified in the psychological literature by Holyoak and collaborators (see for example Gick & Holyoak 1983). Through the mediation of generic models, knowledge from multiple domains can be brought to bear on a problem and can be transformed to such an extent that something truly novel emerges, as is the case in conceptual change.

Goel has developed a theory of generic models in the context of design (see Stroulia & Goel 1992 and Bhatta & Goel 1993). In his work, generic models are learned from specific domain experiences and are used for analogical transfer across design domains (Section 5).

There are several ways in which we interpret generic models as playing a role in S2's constructive modeling process: generic abstraction is employed to create models that incorporate constraints from multiple domains; generic adaptation strategies are employed to make changes to models, and knowledge of generic transformations and principles is used in model construction and adaptation.

4. A Constructive Modeling Interpretation of S2's Reasoning

S2 was a computer scientist with extensive training in topology. In the protocol session, he spent considerable time considering his "physical imagistic intuition" (025)[2] about the slope of the bending rod. We begin here at the point he claimed to have a visual experience that "expressed what [he was] thinking" (049) With the rod one "is always measuring in the vertical -- maybe somehow the way the -- the coiled spring unwinds, makes for a different frame of reference." (049) This insight would lead, though not immediately, to a model of the spring as an open horizontal (3-d) coil (Figure 1g). This part of the session generated a target constraint that was salient in this and the final two models (1e,i) : spring coiling is in the horizontal plane.

At this point S2 was seeking to reconcile the rod (1c) and circular coil (1g) models. He achieved reconciliation by integrating the rod model with target constraints derived during the problem solving process: circularity, lying in the horizontal plane, and uniform distortion during

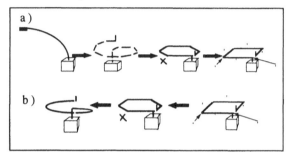

Figure 4: Progression of Models

stretching. S2 recognized that transmitting the force incrementally along the circle in the horizontal plane stretches it bit by bit, as though it had joints, but with even distribution. He now recalled an earlier idea that a "square is sort of like a circle". (117) We interpret him to mean that squares, considered generically are polygons and polygons approximate circles in the limit. He immediately considered bending up the rod into an approximation of the circle to create "a continuous bridge" between the two paradigmatic cases. We take this as his attempt to ascertain if a rod bent in a joint-like fashion in the horizontal plane and a circle bending under a force transmitted incrementally are of the same type with respect to the mechanism of bending. This interaction between the enhanced target (unfolding circle) and the initial source model (flexible rod) led to his constructing a series of generic polygonal models we have represented in Figure 4.

S2 first drew a picture of a horizontal hexagon (Figure 1h) and saw immediately that the hexagonal model is a model of a different type from any considered before for how the constraints would interact in the dynamic case where the spring is stretched. S2's next statement described a simulation that provided a crucial insight: "Just looking at this [1h] it occurs to me that when force is applied here, you not only get a bend on this segment, but because there's a pivot here ['X' in 1h], you get a torsion effect -- around here." (121) He went on, "Aha! -- Maybe the behavior of the spring has something to do with the twist forces ...."

---

[2] These numbers are line numbers from the original protocol.

that might be the key difference between this [flexible rod], which involves no torsion, and this [hexagonal coil]." (122) Finally, S2 constructed the last model, drawing a square coil (1i) in order to exaggerate the torsion effect and considered the possibility that torsion is what "stops the spring from -- from flopping." (126).

We interpret these steps in S2's problem solving as employing generic models of the relational structures and physical properties of the polygonal models. Both the hexagon and the square models incorporate features of the rod because the straight-line segments can bend. However, in this orientation any polygonal model will localize the torsion at the corners, so that the motion in stretching is that of twisting rather than bending at the joints. Thus there is torsion plus bending in this stretching process. The square coil model or the hexagonal coil model or any polygonal model will provide a generic model of the spring coil with respect to the mechanism of torsion. The key difference between the polygonal models (1g-i) and earlier models we have not discussed here (1e,f) is that when the wire is coiled in the horizontal plane the bending segment does not have to change directions, so the bend is in the same relation to each piece and the springiness is distributed evenly, satisfying the target constraints. That the distribution of the twist would be even can be seen by extrapolating the polygon to the limit of a circle, where bending goes to zero. Although these steps are not in the protocol, we interpret generic models as having enabled S2 to grasp immediately the move backwards from the square coil to the hexagon through the intermediate extrapolations to the limit of the circular coil in which the torsion that is localized at the corners spreads itself out in such a way that it becomes a uniform property of the spring (Figure 4b).

5. Adaptive Modeling

Since we view model construction and adaptation as central in conceptual change, we have chosen to start with an AI theory that views design in a similar fashion for identifying representational constructs and processing structures for building computational accounts of constructive modeling in science. In an independent line of research, Goel and collaborators have developed an AI theory of conceptual design of physical devices that views device design as model construction and adaptation . This theory, called "adaptive modeling" , arose from work on the Kritik project (Goel 1991). A designer's comprehension of the functioning of a known device is represented in the form of a structure-behavior-function (SBF) model that provides a functional and causal explanation of how the structure of the device delivers its functions. Figure 5 illustrates the main elements of an SBF model and the interdependencies between them. The computational system designs new devices by constructing SBF models for them, and new device models are constructed by adapting the SBF models of known devices. The SBF models of the new device designs are verified through a form of qualitative simulation, and, if needed, revised.

Recent work along this line of research has led to a theory of creative conceptual design. This theory extends and expands Kritik's theory of adaptive modeling by incorporating analogical transfer as another family of adaptation strategies. It posits generic models for mediating the analogical transfer. In particular, it identifies two kinds of generic models: generic teleological mechanisms (GTMs) and general physical processes (GPPs) (Stroulia & Goel 1992; Bhatta & Goel 1993). A GTM specifies a pattern of functional and causal structure such as feedback while a GPP captures a pattern of behavioral and causal structure such as heat flow. The generic models are abstracted from the SBF device representations of a known design situation, indexed by the functional/behavioral abstractions, and stored in memory. Given a new design situation, the stored generic models are accessed and instantiated to help create SBF representations for the new situation. The IDEAL system (Bhatta & Goel 1993) instantiates this theory of model-based analogy. Depending on the design situation presented to it and its relation to the available knowledge, IDEAL can use different model adaptation strategies ranging from incremental revision of known SBF representations within the problem domain to cross-domain analogical transfer of modeling knowledge in the form of generic models. The SBF theory of device comprehension and the adaptive modeling theory of solving design problems together provide us with the representation and processing structures for beginning to build a computational account of the constructive modeling reasoning process in science.

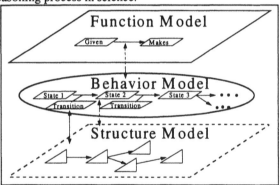

Figure 5: SBF Model

6. Synthesis of Theories

By itself "constructive modeling" provides an outline for a process of scientific reasoning that results in conceptual change. In order to acquire a more specific understanding we have been developing a computational theory based on the principles of adaptive modeling to explore and test our interpretation of the Clement protocol. This collaborative effort engages a problem central to cognitive science as an interdisciplinary research field: How can theories from different disciplines be synthesized to provide a richer understanding of reasoning processes? And how might a synthesis be utilized to develop computational systems for experimentation? In this project we have a cognitive-historical theory of constructive modeling paired with the computational theory of adaptive modeling. The result of this pairing is that we are provided with 2 kinds of constraints for the choices we make in modeling. The first are cognitive constraints draw from a "cognitive-historical" synthesis of philosophical, historical, and psychological studies of human reasoning. These include both interpretive constraints for analyzing data and processing constraints in the form of coarse-grained commitments. The second are computational constraints drawn from computer science and theories of cognition which include tractability, inferencing capability, and representational adequacy. Thus the choices we have made in developing ToRQUE garner support from both theories and the interaction between them. In the next section we explain and justify some of the choices that we have made in the development of ToRQUE with respect to the computational and cognitive constraints of these theories.

7. Computational Analysis

In our computational analysis we have developed a preliminary computational model of S2's reasoning. This analysis models a smaller piece than our constructive modeling interpretation of the protocol i.e. we have not focused on every aspect of S2's reasoning but have focused instead on specific issues such as his use of generic models. Our computational model is described in the SBF language of the theory of adaptive modeling. Thus far in our research the computational model, ToRQUE, has been instantiated in a partial experimental system.

For S2's reasoning the choice of adaptive modeling is particularly apt computationally for two reasons: there is a good match between the SBF formalism and the physical systems in question (i.e. springs, flexible rods, etc.) and, more importantly, SBF representations provide significant benefits with respect to the kinds of inferences available, and the speed with which those inferences are carried out. The structure (S) of S2's initial model of a spring is clearly one of multiple coil components that interact with one another. This interpretation is supported by S2's simplifying the representation by reducing the spring to a single coil: "It occurs to me that a single coil of a spring wrapped once around is the same as a whole spring." (023) The inference is not that a coil is equivalent to a spring, but that it has the same basic function (F) as a spring, because in most respects a coil is not the same as a spring. (e.g. it does not look like a spring or have the same structure as a spring). This inference provides evidence that S2 used separate notions of function (F) and structure (S). A spring and a coil can be "the same" functionally while not being the same structurally or topologically. It also shows that S2 considered the spring as divided into multiple coil components.

The task that S2 completed involves assessing the behavior (B) of a particular physical system with regard to its structure (S). Given a particular property of the spring's structure, e.g. the diameter value, how will the behavior of the spring be affected? S2's attempt to solve this problem requires having a representation of the behavior in question or being able to generate one quickly. One of the advantages of adaptive modeling is that the explicit storage of this behavior provides a significant computational advantage over the generation of the behavior. The kind of inferences that can be made given the stored behavior are also important. For example, when S2 noticed the difference (change in slope in the flexible rod vs. uniform slope in the spring), he did so because the behavior shows this difference to be salient. By separating structure, behavior, and function into separately analyzable units, the SBF formalism prunes away differences that are irrelevant to the task, and makes it easier to target areas of significant difference. Thus once the model is paired with a task it is possible to see the salient differences without being distracted by ontologically distinct kinds of differences.

Once S2 considered a single coil in place of an entire spring we see that he began to focus on the topological feature of circularity. At this point in the protocol he has already considered the behavioral and structural differences, and has made some adaptations with respect to these parts of the model. The difference between the behavior of the flexible rod and the spring provided the initial set of salient differences, and the structural adaptation from many coils to one coil allowed S2 to focus his attention on what turned out to be the most important differences: circularity and orientation.

At this stage in the protocol ToRQUE's SBF model of a coil and the SBF model of a flexible rod each have a single component which has the function of providing a restoring force. Because "Structure" refers to components and the connections of components, the structures of two devices with a single similar component are necessarily the same.

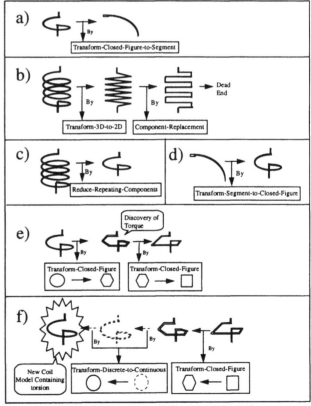

Figure 6: Sequence of Generic Adaptations

316

The topologies of these devices, however, may still be significantly different. That S2 addressed the differences in this order provides further support that SBF structures are a useful ontology for focusing inferences. Problems such as S2's that involve behavioral aspects of the physical system are handled best by focusing on behavioral differences first. Thus S2 is required to make use of the topological differences between the coil and the flexible rod, only after he has pruned away those differences which are presented by the behavior and structure.

Just as IDEAL uses GTMs and GPPs in adapting models, ToRQUE uses generic topological transformations (GTTs) for adapting models. Here we describe the use of these transformations with respect to S2's reasoning in the final insight section interpreted in Section 3. In ToRQUE, the "Reduce-Repeating-Components" transformation is used to reduce the spring to a single coil (Figure 6c). The "Transform-Segment-to-Closed-Figure" and "Transform-Planar-Orientation" bend the rod into a coil (6d). We assume here with S2 that a coil "is a circle with a break in it". Figure 6e shows the progression of closed-figure transformations, which leads to the hexagonal coil, the discovery of torque, and the exaggeration of the effect by the square coil model. By adapting the coil from a circle to a polygon, S2 was able to introduce new components into the model structure. Each side of the square, e.g., could now be treated as a flexible rod component, but with the significant change in orientation that now makes for twisting rather than bending at the joints. Thus a small topological change can result in a fairly large behavioral change, making new knowledge available from which to make inferences.

The most important inference occurs in evaluating the square coil. S2 had recognized the generic physical principle (GPP) of torsion in the hexagonal coil and constructed the square coil to examine it. He was reminded of this principle because of the behavioral and structural similarities between the GPP and the polygonal models. In Section 3 we interpreted S2 as making a final series of inferences only implicit in the protocol that involve the generic abstraction of the square coil with respect to torsion. To be satisfied that he had solved the problem, he needed to hypothesize that if torsion is true of square coils, perhaps it is true of all coils and to make the appropriate extrapolation. ToRQUE incorporates the GPP into the circular coil model through the "Transform-Discrete-to-Continuous" GTT, which depends upon a knowledge of limits which we know S2 possesses: A continuous shape such as a circle can be thought of as containing an infinite number of infinitesimally small segments. Figure 6(f) shows the transformations from the square coil back to an adapted model of the circular coil that capture our interpretation.

Conclusion

Our conceptual analysis provides a plausible interpretation of S2's reasoning as relying significantly on generic models. Our computational analysis shows how generic models such as GPPs (e.g., torque) and GTTs (e.g.,

Transform-Planar-Orientation) can help to achieve conceptual change. Here we highlight two significant conclusions that show the synergy of our interdisciplinary collaboration:

- An important issue in generic modeling is how to make the right inferences at the right times. SBF models enable and constrain these inferences.
- In analyzing protocol and historical data there are places where the reasoning process is not explicit, as in the portion of S2's reasoning we examined here. Interpretations of these gaps gain plausibility through computational models, which like ToRQUE have developed out of an interdisciplinary analysis of creative reasoning.

References

Bhatta, S.R. & Goel, A.K. (1993) Learning Generic Mechanisms from Experiences for Analogical Reasoning. In *Proc. Fifteenth Annual Conference of the Cognitive Science Society*, Boulder, Colorado, July 1993, pp. 237-242, Hillsdale, NJ: Lawrence Erlbaum.

Chi, M.T.H., Feltovich, P.J., & Glaser, R. (1981) Categorization and Representation of Physics Problems by Experts and Novices, *Cognitive Science*, 5, pp. 121-152.

Clement, J. (1989) Learning via Model Construction and Criticism: Protocol Evidence on Sources of Creativity in Science, In *Handbook of Creativity: Assessment, Theory and Research*, Glover, G., Ronning, R., & Reynolds, C. (Eds.), chapter 20, pp. 341-381. New York, NY: Plenum.

Darden, L. (1991) Anomaly Driven Redesign of a Scientific Theory: The TRANSGENE.2 Experiments, Technical Report, Ohio State University.

Falkenhainer, B., Forbus, K.D., and Gentner, D. (1989) The structure-mapping engine: Algorithm and examples. *Artificial Intelligence*, 41, 1-63. (University of Illinois Technical Report UIUCDCS-R-87-1361, July, 1987).

Gick, M.L. & Holyoak, K.J.(1983) Schema induction and analogical transfer. *Cognitive Psychology, 12(3), 306-355*.

Goel, A.K. (1991) Model revision: A theory of incremental model learning. In *Proc. of the Eighth International Conference on Machine Learning,* pages 605-609, Chicago.

Holyoak, K. & Thagard, P. (1989) "Analogical Mapping by Constraint Satisfaction: A Computational Theory." *Cognitive Science,* 13:295-356.

Nersessian, N.J. (1992) How Do Scientists Think? Capturing the Dynamics of Conceptual Change in Science, In *Cognitive Models of Science*, ed. R.N. Giere. pp. 3-44. Minneapolis, MN: University of Minnesota Press.

Nersessian, N.J. (1995) Constructive Modeling in Creating Scientific Understanding, *Science & Education*, 4: 203-226.

Nersessian, N.J. (in press) Abstraction via Generic Modeling in Concept Formation in Science. In *Idealization in Science,* M.R. Jones & N. Cartwright, eds. (Rodophi).

Polya, G. (1954) *Induction and Analogy in Mathematics*, Vol. 1, Princeton University, Princeton.

Stroulia, E. & Goel, A.K. (1992) Generic Teleological Mechanisms and their Use in Case Adaptation, In *Proc. of the Fourteenth Annual Conference of the Cognitive Science Society*, 319-324, Lawrence Erlbaum, Hillsdale, N.J.

Using orthographic neighborhoods of interlexical nonwords to support an interactive-activation model of bilingual memory

Robert M. French
Psychology Department, B32
Université de Liège
4000 Liège, Belgium
french@segi.ulg.ac.be

Clark Ohnesorge
Department of Psychology
Middlebury College,
Middlebury, VT 05753
ohnesorg@midd-unix.middlebury.edu

Abstract

Certain models of bilingual memory based on parallel, activation-driven self-terminating search through independent lexicons can reconcile both interlingual priming data (which seem to support an overlapping organization of bilingual memory) and homograph recognition data (which seem to favor a separate-access dual-lexicon approach). But the dual-lexicon model makes a prediction regarding recognition times for nonwords that is not supported by the data. The nonwords that violate this prediction are produced by changing a single letter of non-cognate interlexical homographs (words like *appoint*, *legs*, and *mince* that are words in both French and English, but have completely different meanings in each language), thereby producing regular nonwords in both languages (e.g., *appaint*, *ligs*, *monce*). These nonwords are then classified according to the comparative sizes of their orthographic neighborhoods in each language. An interactive-activation model, unlike the dual-lexicon model, can account for reaction times to these nonwords in a relatively straightforward manner. For this reason, it is argued that an interactive-activation model is the more appropriate of the two models of bilingual memory.

Introduction

The two opposing camps in the bilingual memory debate are, in essence, comprised of those who adhere to a "separate storage" dual-lexicon view and those who favor a more homogeneous memory organization, rather like monolingual memory, but with twice the number of words. Evidence from bilingual aphasia (Paradis, 1977; Albert & Obler, 1978, ch. 4;), where brain injury will cause the bilingual patient to completely lose one of his or her languages, would also seem to argue for modular language organization. In addition, "separate storage" dual-lexicon models have a certain intuitive appeal, in particular, because proficient bilinguals will report little inter-lexical interference. There have been a number of studies (Grosjean, 1989; Grosjean & Soares, 1986; Macnamara & Kushnir, 1971; Gerard & Scarborough, 1989; etc.) that seem to support a compartmentalized language-specific view of bilingual memory organization.

On the other hand, cross-lingual priming effects have been repeatedly demonstrated in the last twenty years and, in certain cases, interlingual priming effects may be as large as intralingual priming effects (Kolers, 1966; Meyer & Ruddy, 1974; Schwanenflugel & Rey, 1986; Beauvillain & Grainger, 1987; Beauvillain, 1992; Chen & Ng, 1989; De Groot & Nas, 1991; Hernandez, Bates, & Avila, 1995; etc.). Recently, Neumann, McCloskey, and Felio (1994) even claimed to have found conditions under which interlingual excitatory effects disappear but where interlingual inhibitory effects persist.

French & Ohnesorge (1995) proposed a model of bilingual memory based on parallel, self-terminating search through independent lexicons in which the search speed depends on the overall activation of the lexicon. This model did a good job of reconciling both interlingual priming data that would seem to support an overlapping bilingual memory organization (Beauvillain & Grainger, 1987) and homograph-recognition data that would seem to favor a separate-access dual-lexicon approach (specifically, Gerard & Scarborough, 1989).

In this article, however, we will present specific nonword reaction-time data that cannot be readily explained by the parallel-search dual-lexicon model. We will then show that these data are, in fact, compatible with an interactive-activation model. Because an interactive-activation model like those proposed by McClelland and Rumelhart (1981) and, more recently in the context of bilingual memory, by Grainger (1992), are also able to account for the homograph-recognition data in French & Ohnesorge (1995), we conclude that bilingual memory organization may actually turn out to be a lot like distributed, overlapping monolingual memory organization.

318

Interlexical homograph data support both types of bilingual memory models

Non-cognate interlexical homographs are words that have the same spelling but completely different meanings in two separate languages. For example, in French, words such as *fin* (= "end" in French), *pain* (= "bread" in French), *mince* (= "thin" in French), etc. The most interesting set of these words consists of "unbalanced" homographs, i.e., those with a high printed-word frequency in one language and a low frequency in the other (e.g., *fin* is a low-frequency word in English, high frequency in French).

Gerard & Scarborough (1989) made use of unbalanced non-cognate Spanish-English homographs to support the hypothesis that "lexical information is represented in language-specific lexicons and that word recognition requires searching the language-appropriate lexicon." Spanish-English bilinguals were asked to look word/nonword discrimination task in a single target language. Mixed into the single-language list of words were unbalanced English-Spanish non-cognate bilingual homographs. Their results show that word frequency in the currently active language — and not the overall frequency of usage in both languages — predicts homograph recognition time, thus lending support to the language-specific dual-lexicon hypothesis. So, even though *red* (= "net" in Spanish) is a high frequency word in English, Spanish-English bilinguals were no faster in the Spanish-only condition that Spanish monolinguals in recognizing it. The number of times the bilinguals had seen the item in English was of no help in its recognition in the All-Spanish condition. On the other hand, several studies using targets primed by non-cognate interlexical homographs (in particular, Beauvillain & Grainger (1987)) indicate that cross-lingual priming does occur. This would seem to contradict the view of independent language-specific lexicons supported by Gerard & Scarborough.

Parallel, activation-driven search through separate lexicons

French & Ohnesorge (1995) proposed a model that employed parallel search through independent lexicons with the search speed through each lexicon depending on the overall activation of that lexicon. This model seemed to reconcile the apparently contradictory findings of Beauvillain & Grainger and Gerard & Scarborough.

When only a single lexicon was active (for example, when bilinguals saw only words in one language), as in Gerard & Scarborough (1989), this model predicted word recognition reaction times that would correspond to those of a monolingual since the search speed through the inactive lexicon would be extremely slow, slow enough that the version of the bilingual homograph stored in the inactive lexicon would never be reached. The search speed would through the active lexicon would therefore correspond roughly to the monolingual search speed through an equivalent lexicon.

The cross-lingual priming results obtained by Beauvillain & Grainger (1987) can also be accounted for by this type of model. In their experiment all prime words were in French and all target words were in English. The French primes were presented for 100 ms. Since response times to the English words were approximately 600 ms., we can conclude that, on average, the subjects saw English words six times as long as French words. As a result, it is reasonable to conclude that the English lexicon would be considerably more active than the French lexicon. Consequently, when subjects saw the prime word "four" (= "oven" in French), it is quite possible that it was frequently perceived not as a French word, but rather as an English word, due to the fact that the English lexicon was so much more active than the French lexicon. It is therefore not surprising that there would have been some priming of the English target "five," which is what the authors reported.

In short, the dual-lexicon parallel-search model does a remarkably good job at accounting for the apparently contradictory data of Gerard & Scarborough (1989) and Beauvillain & Grainger (1987). French & Ohnesorge (1995) also showed that this model correctly predicted reaction-time shifts for recognition times of interlexical homographs when moving from a monolingual to a mixed-language condition. Unfortunately, this model cannot account for certain *nonword* reaction-time data. For this reason, we introduce interactive-activation models. First, we will claim that these models are functionally equivalent, if intuitively less appealing, to the dual-lexicon parallel-search model for word recognition. We will then go on to present the problematic nonword recognition data and show how an interactive-activation model can handle this data.

The results reported in this paper are based on preveiously unexamined data from French & Ohnesorge (1995). This new study was undertaken because of work reported in Grainger (1992) and Grainger and Dijkstra (1992) on the use of orthographic neighborhoods (Coltheart, 1977) to study bilingual memory organization. Using an orthographic-neighborhood technique similar to the one employed by Grainger & Dijkstra, we examined a set of non-cognate interlexical nonwords (nonwords created from homographs that produced regular nonwords in both languages) contained in our original set of stimuli.

We had anticipated a straightforward confirmation of the prediction our parallel-search dual-lexicon model made with regard to nonwords — namely, that these nonwords would be recognized as not being a word either in French or in English faster in the Mixed Condition (i.e., where both lexicons are active) than in the All-French Condition (i.e., where only the French lexicon is active). This prediction was based on the fact that in order to recognize an item as a nonword (i.e., not a word in either language), both lexicons have to be "exhaustively" searched. This search, even though it is a parallel search of the lexicons, would conclude more quickly — thus allowing the determination that an item is a nonword — when both lexicons were active (Mixed condition), than when only one was (All-French condition).

To our surprise, we found that certain types of nonwords were actually recognized as nonwords *more slowly* in the Mixed Condition than in the All-French Condition. After attempting to fit these results into the framework of a parallel-search, dual-lexicon model, we concluded that:

- distributed interactive-activation models give a better account of this data than the independent-lexicon model;
- interactive-activation models can also account for the homograph-recognition data that the parallel-search dual-lexicon model handled so well.

In what follows we will concentrate on the former point because the nonword reaction time data is the key to distinguishing these two types of models. A parallel-search dual-lexicon model cannot explain nonword reaction time data; an interactive-activation model can. Space limitations do not allow us to explain how interactive-activation models can also account for the homograph reaction-time data presented in French & Ohnesorge (1995).

Experimental design

Participants
The participants were 48 bilingual males and females recruited from the University of Wisconsin (Madison, WI) and the surrounding community. Virtually all were in daily contact with both French and English and judged themselves highly fluent in both French and English. The pool was made up of professors and graduate students in the French department, translators, and native French speakers having lived for many years in the US, etc. Twenty-five of the subjects were native French speakers. The participants were randomly assigned to the two conditions of the experiment.

Stimuli
The critical stimuli consisted of a set of 27 non-cognate interlexical nonwords. These nonwords were produced by changing a single letter of a non-cognate interlexical homograph (i.e., words like *appoint, legs, mince,* etc., all of which have distinct meanings in French and English). This produced regular nonwords in both French and English. For example, starting with the non-cognate interlexical homograph *mince* (= "thin" in French), we produce the non-cognate nonword *monce* by changing the "i" in *mince* to an "o". This gives a regular nonword in both French and English.

Procedure
The experiment consisted of two conditions, an All-French condition in which participants saw only French words/nonwords, and a Mixed condition in which they saw half French and half English words/nonwords. In the condition in which participants saw words only in French, the instructions were also orally explained in French. In the condition in which subjects saw half French and half English items during the test procedure, the instructions were first explained in English. Subsequently, the same instructions in French were then read by the participants on the computer screen.

All-French Condition Participants did the experiment individually in 45-minute sessions in which they responded to 450 experimental trials. The experiment was run on PsyScope (Cohen *et al,* 1993) on a Power Macintosh computer. Participants were seated approximately 20" from the computer monitor. The instructions indicated that they would see letter strings and were to classify them as words (if they were real words in French or in English) or nonwords. Included in the list of lexical items were the critical non-cognate nonwords. Reaction time to these nonwords was the critical dependent variable. Of particular interest were "unbalanced nonwords" that had a large orthographic neighborhood in one language and a small orthographic neighborhood in the other language. After reading the instructions, the participants initiated a block of 40 practice trials. Upon completion of the practice block, they began the experimental trials. On each trial a letter string was presented and remained on the screen until a response was made. After a 500 ms interval the next stimulus was presented. Feedback, in the form of a beep, indicated when a word/nonword had been misclassified. Altogether, participants responded to a total of 450 letter strings: 180 French words, 180 French-based nonwords, 45 regular French/English nonwords and 45 homographs.

Mixed Condition Identical to the All-French condition, except that the "filler" stimuli consisted of an equal mixture of French and English words and nonwords. The word/nonword lexical decision task was the same as in the All-French condition.

Results
French & Ohnesorge (1995) showed that an activation-driven parallel-search dual-lexicon model could account for data reported by Gerard & Scarborough (1989), which seemed to favor a separate-access dual-lexicon model, and Beauvillain & Grainger (1987), which seemed to support an overlapping, distributed model. But a key prediction of their parallel-search dual-lexicon model is that nonwords will be rejected faster in the Mixed Condition than in the All-French Condition. This turned out not to be the case. In what follows we discuss this key prediction and explain how it can be accounted for by an interactive-activation model similar to the Grainger's (1992) Bilingual Interactive Activation (BIA) model, itself based on the

McClelland and Rumelhart's (1981) Interactive-Activation model.

The key prediction for nonword data

The dual-lexicon parallel-search model makes a clear prediction for all nonwords: reaction times will be faster in the Mixed condition than in the All-French condition. This is because in the Mixed condition both lexicons are fully active and are therefore both being searched in parallel at full speed. By contrast, in the All-French condition, the search speed through the English lexicon is less than it would be in the Mixed condition (because the English lexicon is less active than in the Mixed condition since the participant has seen only French words during the experiment). Therefore, it should take less time to recognize a nonword as being neither a real word in French nor in English in the Mixed condition. We will see that this prediction is not supported by the data.

Non-cognate interlexical nonwords

The stimuli that we will examine are nonwords produced by changing a single letter of a non-cognate interlexical homographs, thereby producing regular nonwords in both French and English. For example, starting with the non-cognate interlexical homograph *legs* (= "legacy" in French), the non-cognate nonword *ligs* is produced by changing the "e" in *legs* to an "i". This gives a regular nonword in both French and English.

Non-cognate bilingual nonwords can be classified by means of an orthographic neighborhood technique similar to the one used by Coltheart *et al* (1977) and Grainger & Dijkstra (1992). Words are said to be orthographic neighbors if all of their letters but one match up. (Thus, "mare" is an orthographic neighbor of "more" since the two words match up except at their second position.) The nonwords are classified as High-English-Neighborhood/ Low-French-Neighborhood (HEN/LFN) or Low-English-Neighborhood/High-French-Neighborhood (LEN/HFN), according to the number and word-frequency of their respective orthographic neighbors in the two languages. Thus *ligs* is a High-English-Neighborhood/Low-French-Neighborhood nonword because it has more English neighbors than French neighbors. Its English neighborhood consists of {*digs, figs, jigs, pigs, rigs, wigs, lags, logs, lugs, lugs, lids, lies, lips*} and its French neighborhood is {*lits, lige*}. Incorporating frequency information allows us to classify nonwords such as *appaint* — derived from the interlexical homograph *appoint* (= "additional contribution" in French) — as having a High-English-Neighborhood/Low-French-Neighborhood, even though *appaint* has, strictly speaking, no French-only or English-only neighbors; its only neighbor is the homograph *appoint*. It is classified as HEN/LFN because *appoint* has a considerably higher frequency in English than in French. All nonwords had at least four letters.

(This is certainly not the only way that neighborhoods could have been defined. For example, another technique might have determined neighborhoods on the basis of letter clusters. So for example, all words sharing the ending "tion" or beginning with "st" might have been considered to be part of a neighborhood. We felt, however, that for our purposes the essence of orthographic proximity was adequately captured by Coltheart's (1977) technique.)

An analysis of the HEN/LFN and LEN/HFN non-cognate nonwords produces a striking result (Fig. 1). When going from the All-French to the Mixed Condition, the time required to recognize High-English-Neighborhood/Low-French-Neighborhood (HEN/LFN) nonwords as being nonwords actually *increases* by 62 ms from 805 to 867 ms. (Interaction effect of Neighborhood-Type(HEN/LFN, LEN/HFN) X Language-Condition(All-French, Mixed): over subjects: $F(1,45)=6.3$, $p=0.015$; marginally significant over items: $F(1,24)=3.25$, $p=0.08$. The derivative simple effect of Condition on HEN/LFN nonwords: Tukey HSD(0.01) = 60.2 ms.) For Low-English-Neighborhood/High-French-Neighborhood nonwords there is no significant reaction time difference between the two conditions (853 vs. 850 ms.)

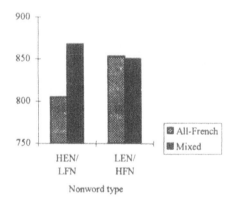

Figure 1. Reaction times to reject non-cognate bilingual nonwords according to the type of neighborhood (HEN/LFN or LEN/HFN) of the nonwords.

Interactive-activation model explanation of non-cognate nonword reaction time data

Even though the dual-lexicon parallel-search model accurately predicts shifts in reaction time from the All-French to the Mixed condition for non-cognate interlexical homographs (French & Ohnesorge, 1995), Figure 1 shows that it gives a highly inaccurate prediction for the shifts that occur for non-cognate interlexical nonwords.

To understand why an interactive-activation model is able to provide a good explanation for the observed shifts in HEN/LFN and LEN/HFN non-cognate nonwords, let us start with the following observation: the more closely a nonword resembles one or many real words, the longer people will take to recognize it as a nonword. This, of course, is why *doned* looks more like a real word than, say, *ptunx*, even though, technically speaking both are regular nonwords in English (even though *pt* and *nx* are rare bigrams in English, they are certainly legal; what child does not know about *pterodactyls* or *sphinxes*?). There are many real words that look a lot like *doned* (e.g., *boned, toned, stoned, cloned, dined,* to say nothing of the fact that the word contains *done*, etc.), while there is almost nothing whatsoever that looks like *ptunx*. In short, to recognize *doned* as a nonword, we must somehow overcome the competition from real words that are similar to it. And this is why it will generally take longer to realize that *doned* is a nonword than *ptunx*. This observation forms the basis of the interactive-activation model explanation of the reaction times to the HEN/LFN and LEN/HFN non-cognate nonwords in Figure 1.

Let us take a closer look at nonword recognition for the particular case of High-English-Neighborhood/Low-French-Neighborhood (HEN/LFN) nonwords. First, consider the All-French condition (Figure 2a). For the purposes of our explanation, we will consider the nonword *ligs*. As indicated above, *ligs* has a large English neighborhood and a small French neighborhood. In the All-French condition, l-i-g-s will send activation to its French-word neighbors *lits* (= "beds") and *lige* (= "liege", a very low frequency word). These words will also receive mutual reinforcement from the activation in the French lexical system (base activation), since this lexicon, and only this lexicon, is active in the All-French condition. At the same time, l-i-g-s will send activation to its English-word neighbors *digs, jigs, lids,* etc. However, these English neighbors, while they will be somewhat active (since subjects are told to reply "Nonword" if the item they see is not a word in either French *or in English*), they will not be

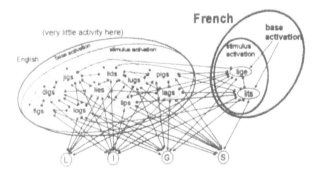

Figure 2a. Non-cognate interlexical nonword recognition in the All-French condition. The words in the English orthographic neighborhood are not as active as in the Mixed Condition.

as active as they would be if the English lexical system were highly active, as in the Mixed condition. The more

numerous and the more highly active the real-word neighbors of a nonword are, the longer it will take to decide — just as in the case of *doned* and *ptunx* — that the item is, in fact, a nonword. In the Mixed condition (Figure 2b), all of the English neighbors will be considerably more active.

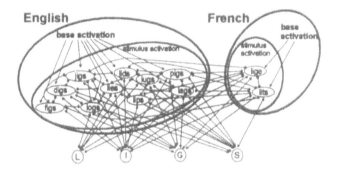

Figure 2b. Non-cognate interlexical nonword recognition in the Mixed condition. The words in the English orthographic neighborhood are considerably more active that in the All-French condition. This additional activation must be overcome before the HEN/LFN nonword "LIGS" can be determined to be a nonword. This results in the longer reaction times in the Mixed Condition.

In other words, in the Mixed condition, a greater number of words will be somewhat nearer perceptual threshold than in the All-French condition, producing a stronger feeling of "knowing" the nonword. Until all of the active real-word "competitors" can be inhibited (or return to baseline activation), one will not judge the item to be a nonword. Since, in the Mixed condition, there are a greater number of active competitors, the interactive-activation model would predict that a nonword decision for High-English-Neighborhood/Low-French-Neighborhood nonwords will take longer in the Mixed condition than in the All-French condition. This corresponds to the data.

A similar argument can be used to explain why reaction times to Low-English-Neighborhood/High-French-Neighborhood nonwords show little change between the two conditions.

Conclusion

French & Ohnesorge (1995) showed how a simple dual-lexicon model using differentially active, parallel search could be used to account for homograph recognition-time data in bilinguals. This model seemed, in addition, to reconcile an apparent conflict between the results of two well known experiments (Gerard & Scarborough, 1989 and Beauvillain & Grainger, 1987). We claim, but for reasons of limited space do not show, that an interactive-activation model can also account for this homograph recognition data. But most importantly, in this paper we uncover what seems to be a major flaw in independent-access dual-lexicon models — namely, they make a clearly inaccurate prediction regarding reaction times for a class of non-cognate interlexical nonwords. We then show how an interactive-activation model could explain the nonword data that the dual-lexicon model could not. In conclusion, it is reasonable to assume, in light of these arguments, that an interactive-activation model is likely to be a better model of bilingual memory than the intuitively more appealing dual-lexicon parallel-search model.

Acknowledgments

This work was supported in part by a grant from the Belgian National Scientific Research Foundation, FNRS Grant No. D.4516.93. The authors would like to thank Annette de Groot, Janet van Hell, Richard Shiffrin, John Theios, and especially, Jim Friedrich and Serge Brédart for their many helpful suggestions concerning this research.

Bibliography

Albert, M. & K. Obler. (1978) "Neuropsychological studies of bilingualism" in *The Bilingual Brain*. New York: Academic Press.

Beauvillain, C. (1992) Orthographic and Lexical Constraints in Bilingual Word Recognition. In *Cognitive Processing in Bilinguals* by R. Harris (ed.) Amsterdam: Elsevier Science Publishers. 221-235.

Beauvillain, C. & J. Grainger. (1987) Accessing Interlexical Homographs: Some Limitations of a Language-selective access. *Journal of Memory and Language, 26*, 658-672.

Chen, H. & Y. Leung. (1989) Semantic facilitation and translation priming effects in Chinese-English bilinguals. *Memory and Cognition, 17*, 454-462.

Cohen, J., B. MacWhinney, M. Flatt, & J. Provost. (1993). PsyScope: A new graphic interactive environment for designing psychology experiments. *Behavioral Research Methods, Instruments & Computers, 25*(2), 257-271.

Coltheart, M., E. Davelaar, J. Jonasson, & D. Besner. (1977) Access to the Internal Lexicon" in *Attention and Performance VI* by S. Dornic (ed.), New York, NY: Academic Press, 535-555.

De Groot, A. & G. Nas. (1991) Lexical representation of cognates and non-cognates in compound bilinguals. *Journal of Memory and Language, 30*, 90-123.

French, R. & C. Ohnesorge. (1995) Using non-cognate interlexical homographs to study bilingual memory organization. In *Proceedings of the 17th Annual Conference of the Cognitive Science Society*. Hillsdale, NJ: Erlbaum. 31–36.

Gerard, L. & D. Scarborough. (1989) Language-specific lexical access of homographs by bilinguals. *Journal of Experimental Psychology: Learning, Memory, and Cognition. 15*(2), 305-315.

Grainger, J. (1992) Visual Word Recognition in Bilinguals. In *The Bilingual Lexicon* (ed.) R. Schreuder, B. Weltens. Amsterdam: John Benjamins Publishing Co.

Grainger, J. & T. Dijkstra. (1992) On the Representation and Use of Language Information in Bilinguals." In *Cognitive Processing in Bilinguals* (ed.) R. J. Harris, 207-220. Amsterdam: North Holland.

Grosjean, F. (1989). Neurolinguists, Beware! The Bilingual is Not Two Monolinguals in One Person. *Brain and Language, 36*, 3-15.

Grosjean, F. & C. Soares, (1986) "Processing Mixed Language: Some Preliminary Findings" In *Language Processing in Bilinguals*. Jyotsna Void (ed.) Hillsdale, NJ: Lawrence Erlbaum, Inc.

Hernandez, A., E. Bates & L. Avila. (1995) Processing across the language boundary: A cross-modal priming study of Spanish-English bilinguals. UCSD Center for Research in Language Technical Report (under review).

Kolers, P. (1966). Interlingual Facilitation of Short-term Memory. *Journal of Verbal Learning and Verbal Behavior. 5*, 314-319.

McClelland, J. & D. Rumelhart. (1981) An Interactive-Activation model of Context Effects in Letter Perception, Part 1: An Account of Basic Findings. *Psychological Review* Vol. 88, 375-405.

Macnamara, J. & S. Kushnir. (1971). Linguistic Independence of Bilinguals: The Input Switch. *Journal of Verbal Learning and Verbal Behavior, 10*, 480-487.

Meyer, D. & M. Ruddy. (1974). Bilingual word-recognition: Organization and retrieval of alternate lexical codes. Paper presented at the meeting of the Eastern Psychological Association, Philadelphia.

Neumann E., M. McCloskey & A. Felio. (1994). Primed lexical decision tasks: Cross-language positive priming disappears, negative priming doesn't. NIMH Laboratory of Socio-Environmental Studies Technical Report presented at the Third Practical Aspects of Memory Confernce, College Park, MD (Aug. 1994).

Paradis, M., (1977). Bilingualism and Aphasia. In Whitaker, H. A. & Whitaker, H. (eds.) *Studies in neurolinguistics, 3*. New York: Academic Press.

Schwanenflugel, P. & M. Rey. (1986) Interlingual semantic facilitation: Evidence for a common representationsl system in the bilingual lexicon. *Journal of Memory and Language, 25*, 605-618.

Conscious and Unconscious Perception: A Computational Theory

Donald W. Mathis and **Michael C. Mozer**
Department of Computer Science & Institute of Cognitive Science
University of Colorado at Boulder
Boulder, CO 80309-0430
mathis@cs.colorado.edu, mozer@cs.colorado.edu

Abstract

We propose a computational theory of consciousness and model data from three experiments in visual perception. The central idea of our theory is that the contents of consciousness correspond to temporally stable states in an interconnected network of specialized computational modules. Each module incorporates a relaxation search that is concerned with achieving semantically well-formed states. We claim that being an attractor of the relaxation search is a necessary condition for awareness. We show that the model provides sensible explanations for the results of three experiments, and makes testable predictions. The first experiment (Marcel, 1980) found that masked, ambiguous prime words facilitate lexical decision for targets related to either prime meaning, whereas consciously perceived primes facilitate only the meaning that is consistent with prior context. The second experiment (Fehrer and Raab, 1962) found that subjects can make detection responses in constant time to simple visual stimuli regardless of whether they are consciously perceived or masked by metacontrast and not consciously perceived. The third experiment (Levy and Pashler, 1996) found that visual word recognition accuracy is lower than baseline when an earlier speeded response was incorrect, and higher than baseline when the early response was correct, consistent with a causal relationship between conscious perception and subsequent processing.

Introduction

In recent years there has been a resurgence of interest in the scientific study of consciousness. Experimental approaches have studied subliminal perception (e.g., Greenwald et. al, 1995), implicit memory and learning (e.g., Hintzman, 1990), neuropsychological dissociations between knowledge and awareness (e.g., Shallice, 1988), and most recently, the problem of finding the *neural correlates* of consciousness (Crick & Koch, 1990). In contrast, we take a computational approach, asking the question: What happens differently in the brain when one is processing information consciously versus unconsciously? We propose a *computational correlate* of consciousness, as part of a cognitive architecture, and evaluate the theory by accounting for experimental data. The theory is motivated by several basic experimental findings, including: (1) conscious percepts are interpretations of stimulus information (Kanizsa, 1979; Kolers & Von Grunau, 1976; Warren, 1970); (2) people are aware of the *results* of higher cognitive processes, not the processes themselves (Nisbett & Wilson, 1977); (3) cortex appears to be function-

ally *modular* (Felleman & Van Essen, 1991), but consciousness appears to be distributed in the brain (e.g., Young & DeHaan, 1991).

The Stability Theory of Consciousness

We propose a *stability theory of consciousness* that is based on a few simple principles. First, the human cognitive architecture consists of a set of functionally specialized, interconnected computational modules. Each module functions as an associative memory in its domain, outputting the best-fitting interpretation of its input, subject to a set of constraints that define reasonable entities in the domain. For example, a visual object-recognition module might output interpretations consistent with constraints governing realizability in three-dimensional space. Second, the operation of a module is a two-stage process. Each module first maps its input to an initial output in a fast *mapping* process. Then a slower, iterative *relaxation search* process transforms this output to one that is *well-formed*—i.e., satisfies the domain constraints. Third, the central hypothesis is that *temporally stable states* enter consciousness. That is, the stable output of the relaxation search process of *any* module enters consciousness. This implies that there is no special "consciousness module"; the contents of consciousness are distributed amongst the modules.

We embody the theory in a connectionist model (Figure 1). The mapping process is implemented by a feedforward network, which has the desired property of producing an output quickly, without iteration. The relaxation search process is implemented by an attractor or constraint-satisfaction network. Attractors of the net are the well-formed states, i.e., interpretations produced by the module. Fully distributed attractor networks have been used for similar purposes (e.g., Hinton & Shallice, 1991), but for simplicity we employ a localist-attractor architecture with a layer of *state* units and a layer of radial basis function (RBF) units, one RBF unit per attractor. The state units receive input from the mapping network and from the RBF units, and are updated with an incremental activation rule

$$s_i(t+1) = h\left(s_i(t) + \alpha e_i(t) - \beta r_0(t) + \gamma \sum_{j \in RBF} r_j(t) a_{ji}\right)$$

where $s_i \in [-1,1]$ is the activity of the ith state unit, e_i is the input to that unit from the mapping net, r_j is the activity of RBF unit j, a_{ji} is the value of component i of the jth attractor state, α, β and γ are small positive constants, and $h(.)$ is a function that simply bounds activity between -1 and $+1$. The zero'th rbf unit, r_0, corresponds to a special *rest state* located at the origin of the state space, in which the system resides at the start of each simulation. The RBF units use the update rule:

$$r_j(t) = exp(-\|s(t) - a_j\|^2/\beta)$$

where β is the *width* of the RBF. We quantify stability as an exponentially-decaying time-average of the reciprocal of the speed of the state vector:

$$stability(T) = \sum_{t=0}^{T} (\lambda^{(T-t)} exp(-\|s(t) - s(t-1)\|))$$

where $0 < \lambda < 1$ is a parameter controlling the window of the time average. When this quantity exceeds a threshold, we say that the state has stabilized.

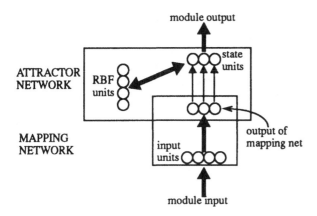

Figure 1: Architecture of a module. Heavy lines denote full connectivity between units in two layers. Thin lines denote copying of activity.

Modeling Experimental Data

Subliminal Semantic Priming & Lexical Ambiguity

Marcel (1980) showed subjects a sequence of three words—the *context*, *prime* and *target*—and instructed them to perform lexical decision on the target. The prime was ambiguous, with two unrelated meanings. There were three experimental conditions relevant to our theory. In the *congruent* condition, the context word was semantically related to one meaning of the prime, and the target word was related to that same meaning. The *incongruent* condition is the same except the target is related to the *other* meaning of the prime. In the *unassociated* condition, the context and target words are unrelated to either meaning of the prime. The prime was

either presented for 500 ms (the *conscious* condition) or for roughly 10 ms and backward-masked to prevent awareness (the *unconscious* condition).

Table 1: Results for simulation of Marcel (1980)

	human data		simulation	
	conscious	unconsc.	conscious	unconsc.
congruent	499 ms	511 ms	44.6 cycles	46.0 cycles
incongruent	547 ms	520 ms	47.9 cycles	46.8 cycles
unassociated	541 ms	548 ms	48.0 cycles	47.9 cycles

When the prime is consciously perceived, Marcel found facilitation for the congruent condition relative to the unassociated condition, but not for the incongruent condition. However, if the prime is not consciously perceived, there is facilitation in both the congruent and incongruent cases. Thus, in the unconscious case, both meanings of the prime are available to facilitate targets, but in the conscious case, only the meaning consistent with the prior context is available. These results show a correlation between the onset of awareness and the selection of one meaning.

Modeling Word Reading, Ambiguity Resolution, Masking, and Priming. Before describing our account of the data, we explain how we model word reading and priming in general. A single module is used to map orthography to meaning (Hinton & Shallice, 1991). Attractor states in this module correspond to meanings of known words, and the rest state is used to represent the state "no meaningful input." The time-course of processing is as follows: With the relaxation net initialized to the rest state, an input is presented, and activity flows through the mapping net, providing input to the state units. This input causes the state units to move into the attractor representing the meaning of the input word. Simple one-word disambiguation occurs as follows: We assume that ambiguous word patterns are associated with multiple attractors, and that the mapping network outputs a semantic pattern that falls between them in semantic space. In the process of settling to one attractor, the relaxation net will effectively *select* one of the meanings.

We model the effect of backward masking by removing input from the word recognition module. If an input is presented briefly, the relaxation net will settle back to the rest state. Since stable (and non-rest) states correspond to conscious perception in our theory, this would correspond to no conscious perception of the input.

To model priming, we adopt a variant of the method used by Becker et al. (1993) of *strengthening* attractors that the system visits during processing. After the network settles, we increase the β (width) parameter of each RBF unit in rough proportion to its activity:

$$\Delta\beta_i = eligibility_i / \sum_{j \in RBF} eligibility_j$$

where

$$eligibility_i = \sum_t exp[-\|s(t) - a_i\|^2].$$

The eligibility of each RBF is normalized to prevent the amount of priming to increase without bound for long exposures.

Simulation. For simplicity, we simulated only the attractor network of the module. Twenty attractor states representing different semantic concepts were randomly chosen. These states were corners of a 50-dimensional hypercube. Semantic relatedness was achieved via overlap in the state vectors. The overlap between semantically unrelated states was 25 bits, and between semantically related states 48 bits. The twenty attractors were grouped into four classes of five patterns. We refer to two patterns in the same class as *neighbors*.

A sequence of three patterns representing the context, prime and target words was presented to the network via external input to the state units. Noise was added by randomly removing inputs with probability 0.03. After each pattern was processed, attractors were strengthened according to the rule above. The network was allowed to settle to an attractor for each input, except in the unconscious prime condition, in which the input was removed after 5 cycles, and with this short stimulus exposure the network always settled back to the rest state.

Table 1 shows the average results obtained from several repetitions of the simulation using different sets of random attractor states. The results qualitatively matched the experimental results: in the conscious condition, statistically significant facilitation was observed only for congruent contexts, whereas in the unconscious condition, significant facilitation was observed for both congruent and incongruent contexts. The reason for this is as follows: When the prime is processed in the conscious condition, the attractor net settles to the attractor representing the meaning of the prime that is related to the context (because the context attractor and related attractors have been strengthened by presentation of the context). This attractor is strengthened much more than the attractor representing the other meaning of the prime (due to the normalization of eligibility), resulting in facilitation of only congruent targets. In contrast, in the unconscious condition, both meanings of the prime are transiently activated before the state vector settles back to the rest state; consequently, both attractors are strengthened, resulting in facilitation of congruent and incongruent targets.

Discussion. The Marcel experiment showed a correlation between the onset of awareness and selection of a word's

meaning. We modeled this correlation, but our theory makes a stronger claim: selection is a necessary precursor to awareness. This is because the state stabilizes only after selection, and awareness requires stability.

One interesting prediction arises from our model. Although both meanings of the prime were facilitated equally in the unconscious condition, this is not absolutely necessary. If the context could be made to strengthen its attractor to a greater degree, the processing of the prime could be biased to the extent that only one meaning would be significantly activated. Consequently, one might observe facilitation of only one meaning even in the unconscious condition. This leads to the as-yet-untested prediction that as context is "strengthened", the amount of priming of noncontextual meanings should decrease.

Metacontrast Masking and Response Time

Alpern (1953) described a metacontrast masking effect in which a square of light is flashed for 50 ms. After a variable stimulus onset asynchrony (SOA), a pair of *flanker* squares appears on either side of the *center* square, also for 50 ms. As the SOA is increased from zero, subjects first report a solid bar of light at short SOAs (~10 ms), the flankers alone at intermediate SOAs (~75 ms), and then the center square *followed* by the flankers at long SOAs (~120 ms). Thus, subjects were unaware of the center square at intermediate SOAs. Fehrer and Raab (1962) performed a variant of this experiment in which subjects were instructed to respond as soon as *any* stimulus was detected. Subjects took the same amount of time to respond at every SOA (~160 ms). There was a dissociation between awareness and reaction time, because if subjects were responding to their *percept*, then at intermediate SOAs they should be substantially slowed since they do not perceive the center square in that case[1].

Simulation. To model these data, we use a simple two-module architecture that captures the essence of the task. The *perceptual module* takes visual patterns as input and produces objects as output. This module has two input units, one for the center square and one for the flanker stimuli. There are three output units, one for each of three competing percepts—the center square alone, the flankers alone, and the center square and flankers together (a solid bar)—and three corresponding RBF units. The output units of the perceptual module feed into the inputs of a *response module* in a 1-1 manner, and this module makes a presence/absence decision about the input. Its mapping network simply sums the activity of the input units and passes this to a single output unit whose well-formed states are 0 and 1.

We do not model the low-level mechanism that give rise

---

1. Kolb & Braun (1995) provide a recent example of a similar dissociation between awareness and ability to respond.

to the masking effect[2]. We simply assume that this mechanism operates inside the mapping network of the perceptual module, and has the effect of suppressing activity stemming from the center square.

We used 5 cycles as the short SOA, 35 as the intermediate SOA, and 60 as the long SOA. The two input units were activated and deactivated appropriately to match the experimental conditions. The degree of stability of the output of the perceptual module was used as a measure of awareness, and the response module's settling time represented the RT for the detection response. The results closely matched those of the experiment: at the short SOA, the perceptual module stabilizes on the bar pattern; this occurs because the center and flanker patterns overlap substantially in time, providing enough activity to the combined "bar" pattern to win the competition. At the intermediate SOA, the perceptual module stabilizes on only the flanker pattern; in this case, the input stimuli do not overlap temporally, but the center square is removed before the perceptual module has time to stabilize on it. At long SOAs, the perceptual module stabilizes first on the center pattern, and then on the flanker pattern; in this case, the perceptual module has time to stabilize before the flanker pattern appears. The detection RTs for the three SOAs were not substantially different: 54, 51, and 51 cycles. The detection response is triggered by the initial flow of activity from the presentation of the center square. The dissociation between awareness and detection RT comes about because the two processes are based on different information—detection on activity and awareness on stability of activity.

Discussion. In the detection task, responses can be accurately initiated based on very coarse information. But if the task required finer detail, e.g., discriminating a center square from a center circle, the evidence that accumulated before the flankers masked the center stimulus might not be sufficient to form a response. In earlier simulations, we found that stability was required to initiate discrimination responses (Mathis and Mozer, 1995). Thus, the dissociation between awareness of a stimulus and ability to respond might not be absolute; it might depend on the response task. This leads to the prediction that the present dissociation should weaken or disappear for more complex discrimination tasks.

The Effect of Conscious States on Cognition

Philosophers raise the issue of whether consciousness is just a "read out" process or whether conscious states affect subsequent processing (Flanagan, 1992)[3]. There is no strong experimental test of this hypothesis yet, but an experiment providing some evidence was conducted by Levy and Pashler (1996), who examined the effects of speeded perceptual decisions on subsequent perceptual processing. Subjects viewed a visually degraded word stimulus, and made either a single unspeeded identification response (verbally reporting the word) or two responses: a speeded response in a 600–900 ms window, followed by an unspeeded response. Levy and Pashler found that in both the single- and dual-response conditions, the probability of a correct unspeeded response was .97. But in the dual-response condition this probability depended on the accuracy of the preceding speeded response. The probability of a correct unspeeded response given a *correct* speeded response was .99. But the probability of a correct unspeeded response given an *incorrect* speeded response was .93. One possible explanation for this is that the process of *making the speeded decision* affects subsequent processing, increasing performance when the speeded decision is correct, and hurting it when incorrect.

Simulation. The simulation consisted of the attractor component of a word-recognition module, as described earlier. Since identifying a visual word requires a fine discrimination, the perceptual module must settle to an attractor before a response can be made. Speeded responses were modeled by forcing the attractor net to settle to the nearest attractor state[4] after a certain number of cycles, chosen such that the probability of a correct speeded response matched that of the experiment (0.61). In the single-response condition, the net was allowed to settle to an attractor, and percent correct was recorded. In the dual-response condition, the net was forced to settle after 20 cycles, and was then allowed to resume processing from that state until settled. The results qualitatively match the data; see Table 2. In the simulation column of the table, all

Table 2: Simulation of Levy & Pashler (1996)

	human data	simulation
Prob(unspeeded correct | dual response)	.967	.962
Prob(unspeeded correct | single response)	.970	.965
Prob(unspeeded correct | speeded correct)	.992	1.000
Prob(unspeeded correct | speeded incorrect)	.925	.901

---

2. There is still no agreement as to an adequate model of metacontrast masking (e.g., see di Lollo et. al., 1993).

3. A stronger version of the issue asks whether qualia can affect cognition, but we address the materialist version.

differences were statistically significant except that

---

4. Computationally, there are several ways this could be done, for example, setting the β parameter to a value close to zero.

between rows one and two. The basic pattern of results is due to a kind of perseverative effect in the network. Forcing the net to settle early may either help or hinder the network. It helps if the network passes through the neighborhood of the correct attractor, and is forced to settle there early, instead of possibly continuing on to an erroneous attractor (due to the noisy input and brief exposure). It hurts if the state vector passes nearby incorrect states on the way to the correct state, and is forced to settle to an incorrect state.

Discussion. In our model there is both a benefit in accuracy and a cost in accuracy of speeded settling, but in this experiment the benefit and cost balance each other. However, this balance may not hold for other measures, such as reaction time, which our model is well-suited to generate. This experiment provides support for our model, but it is consistent with other models as well. It is possible, for example, that the correlation between speeded and unspeeded response accuracy is due to a third factor that both accuracies depend on, and that there is no causal relationship between the two responses. It would be a challenge to experimentalists to devise a way to test the causality issue.

Conclusion

Our aim in this work is to account qualitatively for broad variety of data, rather than to model the full depth of detail in any given experiment. In doing so we hope to contribute ideas that may help constrain the development of more detailed models.

The particular choice of modules used in our simulations and the type of information processed in them depends on the particular domain being modeled. However, our theory proposes that there is one common set of modules that underlie all cognitive behavior, and that each module takes part in many cognitive tasks. It is the subject of future work to attempt to better identify the set of modules, and their specific location and connectivity in the brain.

References

Alpern, M. (1953). Metacontrast. *Journal of the Optical Society of America*, 43, 648-657

Becker, S., Behrmann, M., & Moscovitch, K. (1993), Word priming in attractor networks. *Proceedings of the cognitive science society*, p.231-236.

Crick, F., & Koch, C. (1990). Towards a neurobiological theory of consciousness. *Seminars in the neurosciences*, 2, 263-275

di Lollo, V., Bischof, W., & Dixon, P. (1993). Stimulus-onset asynchrony is not necessary for motion perception or metacontrast masking. *Psychological Science*, 4, 260-263.

Felleman, D. J., & Van Essen, D. C. (1991). Distributed hierarchical processing in the primate cerebral cortex. *Cerebral Cortex*, 1, 1-47

Fehrer, E., & Raab, D. (1962). Reaction time to stimuli masked by metacontrast. *Journal of experimental psychology*, 63, 143-147

Flanagan, O. J. (1992). *Consciousness reconsidered*. Cambridge, Mass. MIT Press.

Greenwald, A. G., Klinger, M. R., & Schuh, E. S. (1995). Activation by marginally perceptible ("subliminal") stimuli: Dissociations of unconscious from conscious cognition. *Journal of experimental psychology: General*, 124, 22-42

Hinton, G. E., & Shallice, T. (1991). Lesioning an attractor network: Investigations of acquired dyslexia. *Psychological Review*, 98(1), 74-95

Hintzman, D. L. (1990). Human learning and memory: Connections and dissociations. *Annual Review of Psychology*, 41, 109-139

Kanizsa, G. (1979). *Organization in vision*. New York: Praeger.

Kolb, F. C., & Braun, J. (1995) Blindsight in normal observers. *Nature*, 377, 336-338

Kolers, P. A., & Von Grunau, M. V. (1976). Shape and color in apparent motion. *Vision Research*, 16, 329-335

Levy, J., & Pashler, H. (1996). Does perceptual analysis continue during selection and production of a speeded response? *Acta Psychologia*

Marcel, T. (1980). Conscious and preconscious recognition of polysemous words: Locating the selective effects of prior verbal context. In R.S. Nickerson (Ed.), *Attention and Performance VIII*, Hillsdale, N.J. Erlbaum.

Mathis, D. W., & Mozer, M. C. (1995). On the computational utility of consciousness. In Tesauro, G., Touretzky, D. S., & Leen, T. K. (Eds.) *Advances in neural information processing systems 7*, 11-18

Nisbett, R.E., & Wilson, T. D. (1977). Telling more than we can know: Verbal reports on mental processes. *Psychological Review*, 84(3), 231-259

Shallice, T. (1988). *From neuropsychology to mental structure*. New York: Cambridge U. Press.

Warren, R. M. (1970). Perceptual restorations of missing speech sounds. Science, 167, 392-393

Young, A.W., & DeHaan, E. H. F. (1990). Impairments of visual awareness. *Mind and language*, 5, 29-48

In Search Of Articulated Attractors

David C. Noelle and **Garrison W. Cottrell**

Computer Science & Engineering 0114
University of California, San Diego
La Jolla, CA 92093-0114
{dnoelle,gary}@cs.ucsd.edu

Abstract

Recurrent attractor networks offer many advantages over feed-forward networks for the modeling of psychological phenomena. Their dynamic nature allows them to capture the time course of cognitive processing, and their learned weights may often be easily interpreted as soft constraints between representational components. Perhaps the most significant feature of such networks, however, is their ability to facilitate generalization by enforcing "well formedness" constraints on intermediate and output representations. Attractor networks which learn the systematic regularities of well formed representations by exposure to a small number of examples are said to possess *articulated attractors*. This paper investigates the conditions under which articulated attractors arise in recurrent networks trained using variants of backpropagation. The results of computational experiments demonstrate that such structured attractors can spontaneously appear in an emergence of systematicity, if an appropriate error signal is presented directly to the recurrent processing elements. We show, however, that distal error signals, backpropagated through intervening weights, pose serious problems for networks of this kind. We present simulation results, discuss the reasons for this difficulty, and suggest some directions for future attempts to surmount it.

Introduction

Recurrent attractor networks have been studied by cognitive modelers since the onset of the recent connectionist renaissance. The hallmark of these networks is the complex evolution of their processing element activity over time. Though dynamic by nature, these networks have been applied to many associational mapping tasks which possess no inherent temporal component. In domains as diverse as content-addressable memory (Hopfield, 1982), schema formation (Rumelhart et al., 1986b), and word naming (Plaut & McClelland, 1993), recurrent networks which settle over time to some stable activation state have displayed some noteworthy advantages over feed-forward models. The attractor networks directly exhibit time-varying processing, allowing them to capture the dynamics of cognition in a manner which may be validated against common psychological measures, such as reaction times. Also, learned connection weights in such recurrent networks often lend themselves to interpretation as soft constraints between representational units, facilitating analysis. Perhaps the most interesting potential advantage of such networks, however, is the manner in which attractor basin formation may aid in generalization to novel inputs.

Attractor networks can encourage generalization by enforcing "well formedness" constraints on the intermediate and output representations produced by an otherwise feed-forward process (Mathis & Mozer, 1995). Such constraints are embodied in these networks as distinct fixed-point attractors for every possible well formed representation. Patterns may be "cleaned up" by such a network via a process of settling over time to one of these meaningful, well formed, and stable activation states. The potentially combinatoric space of valid attractor basins need not be explicitly trained, however, but may arise in the compositional interaction of trained attractors (Plaut & McClelland, 1993). It has long been known that the training of recurrent networks may result in *spurious* attractor basins: fixed-point attractors which are not explicitly trained (Hopfield, 1982). Under appropriate conditions, however, these spurious attractors may actually arise in a systematic manner, producing *serendipitous basins* which encode novel but meaningful patterns of activation. We refer to the dynamics of such networks as containing *articulated attractors* – meaningful attractor basins arising from the compositional interaction of explicitly trained attractors.

This paper provides an empirical analysis of the conditions under which articulated attractors form in recurrent neural networks trained using various versions of backpropagation (Rumelhart et al., 1986a). This work stemmed from our initial attempts to incorporate an attractor network of this kind into our connectionist model of instruction following (Noelle & Cottrell, 1995), a model which develops an internal representation of verbal instructions in the service of a task (St. John, 1992). We discovered that articulated attractors did *not* appear in this model, and this paper sprang from our attempt to explain why. In hopes of acquiring a deep understanding of the learning difficulties experienced by our model, we began with the most simple attractor network architecture possible – a single recurrent layer of processing elements. We incrementally augmented this network with further layers of units, expanding the complexity of the architecture towards the configuration of our instruction following model. This investigation revealed that articulated attractors form readily when the network's recurrent layer is directly provided with a teaching signal, but such systematic dynamics do *not* appear when recurrent weights are shaped by backpropagated error. In addition to demonstrating this finding, this paper also presents some possible explanations for why this is so.

We begin by describing the simple structured memory task which we used to examine attractor formation in a number of recurrent network architectures. We then present simulation results for three successively more complex architectures, and we close with a discussion of these results.

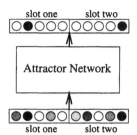

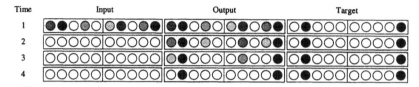

Figure 1: The Slot-Filler Structure Memory Task

A Structured Memory Task

In hopes of facilitating analysis, we selected an extremely simple task for our attractor networks. Each network was presented, for a single time step only, with an encoding of a simple slot-filler structure. The goal of the network was to "clean up" any noise in this representation and to retain the result at the network's output indefinitely, even after the input pattern was removed. Thus, through training, the network needed to acquire a distinct fixed-point attractor for each valid input slot-filler structure. These attractor basins had to be sufficiently wide to capture slightly noisy patterns, and the fixed-points needed to be sufficiently stable to remember the input for an indefinite period.

To be specific, each pattern represented a structure containing two slots, each holding exactly one of five distinct fillers. The contents of the slots were considered independent, with the specific filler in one slot in no way constraining the filler for the other. The whole was encoded as a 10 element binary vector, divided into two groups of five. Since each slot could contain only a single filler, exactly one element in each group of five was turned "on" in each valid pattern. The networks, then, were to learn an attractor for each input pattern involving exactly one of the first five elements "on" and exactly one of the last five elements "on". Thus, with five possibilities for each of two slots, there were only $5^2 = 25$ patterns considered "well formed" out of the $2^{10} = 1024$ possible binary input vectors. This task is depicted schematically in Figure 1. The diagram on the left side of that figure depicts the mapping being performed as the network settles, and the table on the right provides an example of the time course of input activity, expected output activity, and the target output. Note that the input pattern is made available to the network for the first time step *only*, requiring the network to both "clean up" and remember the pattern over time.

Systematic generalization was the focus of these experiments. The goal was to produce a fixed-point attractor for every valid slot-filler structure, given training on only a fraction of these valid patterns. To this end, each network was explicitly trained on some subset of the allowable input patterns, encouraging the formation of attractors for these patterns by the presentation of an error signal on every time step for a fixed settling period. Once trained, each network was then tested on *all* valid slot-filler representations, and the number of fixed-point attractors corresponding to these valid patterns was determined. The dynamic behavior of each trained network was also examined to locate any spurious attractors corresponding to ill formed patterns.

For small training sets, consisting of only a few valid pat-

terns, we expected the networks to simply memorize the training instances – to build attractors only for the presented patterns. We predicted, however, that beyond some threshold in training set size the networks would generalize to *all* valid structures. In order to test this hypothesis, we trained each network architecture on multiple training sets, varying in size. Each trained network was examined to determine the attractor structure resulting from its training. At least five patterns were present in each training set, as this was the minimum number needed to turn each input element "on" at least once over a training set. The largest training set consisted of all 25 well formed patterns. The frequency of each filler in each training set was balanced as much as was possible given the small size of the training sets. Noise was added to input elements during training, but this noise never exceeded 5% of the activation range of the elements (i.e., 0.05 for binary units and 0.10 for bipolar units). Network output targets consisted of the "clean" patterns over the entire time course of network settling, as shown in Figure 1. A settling period of 10 time steps was used during training, and 100 time steps were used during testing.

The Emergence Of Systematicity

The first architecture examined was a single recurrent layer of sigmoidal processing elements. The entire network consisted of ten units which acted as both input and output for the network. This single layer was provided with complete recurrent connections to itself. Each unit also had a bias weight, resulting in a total of 110 adaptable connections. Unlike some single layer networks of this kind, this weight matrix was *not* constrained to be symmetric. The architecture is shown in Figure 2, on the left. The network received an input pattern by clamping the activation state of the processing elements to the input values for a single time step. After this initial time step, the activation state of the network was allowed to freely evolve according to the connection weights. Training was provided by a version of *backpropagation through time* (BPTT) (Rumelhart et al., 1986a) in which error is backpropagated for only a single time step, much as is done for Simple Recurrent Networks (Elman, 1990). An illustration of how this was implemented is also shown in Figure 2. Binary sigmoidal units were used, with a learning rate of 0.01, no momentum term, and a mean squared error objective function. Connection weights were initialized to small random values, normally distributed about 0 with a variance of 0.5. For each training set size, training was conducted for 4000 epochs (i.e., passes through the entire training set) with patterns randomly reordered on each epoch.

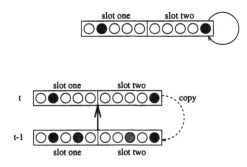

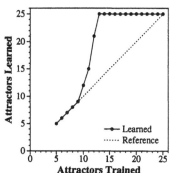

Figure 2: Single Layer Network: The Architecture, Unrolled In Time, And Generalization Performance

A summary of the results over all training set sizes is shown on the right side of Figure 2. That graph displays the number of well formed attractors found in a trained network as a function of the training set size. The plot also includes a reference line which depicts the hypothetical case of *no* generalization outside of the training set. Notice that small training sets resulted in the simple memorization of the trained attractors, but networks that saw at least half of all valid patterns consistently generalized to all 25 allowable structures. Furthermore, none of these networks constructed spurious attractor basins corresponding to ill formed patterns. The weights of these successful networks took the unsurprising form of two uncoupled winner-take-all networks. Each unit had a highly weighted self-connection and inhibited the other four units in its group of five. Weights on connections between units for different slots (i.e., between the two groups of five units) remained close to zero.

Given a sufficiently large training set, these networks consistently exhibited an emergence of systematicity. Generalization was perfect, with a fixed-point attractor formed for every valid pattern.

Input Preprocessing

The next architectural variant we considered involved the inclusion of a matrix of weights between the network input and the recurrent output layer. Instead of providing input patterns by clamping unit activations for the initial time step, noisy inputs were provided at an input layer for the first time step, and activity at this layer was set to zero for all remaining time steps. Activation levels at the recurrent output layer were initialized to zero. This network contained the same recurrent connection architecture as in the single layer case but also included a complete set of connections from the input layer, for a total of 210 adaptable weights. The same learning parameters were used, and training continued, once again, for 4000 epochs. As in the single layer model, weight modification was performed by BPTT, with the network unrolled in time for a single time step. The basic architecture of this network, as well as how it appears when "unrolled", is show in Figure 3. Summarized results are also graphed in that figure. Notice that systematic performance arose from even smaller training sets than in the single layer case. As before, no spurious attractors were found. The recurrent weights, once again, embodied

two separate five-unit winner-take-all networks. Systematic generalization appears to arise spontaneously under this architecture, as well.

It is fairly clear why the inclusion of input weights introduced no additional difficulty for the learning of articulated attractors. The training of the input weights was essentially *decoupled in time* from the training of the recurrent weights. During the initial time step, output activity was at the initialized level of zero, which implied no change to the recurrent weights since this activity plays a multiplicative role in the backpropagation weight update equation. In other words, only the input weights could be updated on the first time step. On the other hand, on every subsequent time step the input layer activity was clamped to zero, directing all weight updates to the recurrent connections. In short, each of the weight matrices was provided with its own direct error signal at regular times during training.

An Indirect Error Signal

The final architecture examined here differed from the previous two in that an error signal was not provided directly to the recurrent layer but was backpropagated through an intervening matrix of weights. The basic architecture is shown in Figure 4. Unlike the last model, activity was propagated forward beyond the recurrent layer to a separate output layer of sigmoidal units. Error was computed at this final output layer and was backpropagated to influence the modification of the recurrent and input weights. This additional layer raised the number of adaptable parameters to 320. The network was trained as a Simple Recurrent Network (SRN) (Elman, 1990), unrolling the recurrent hidden layer for a single time step. As in the previous architecture, noisy input patterns were presented at the input layer for the first time step only, and input activity was set to zero during the rest of the settling period. The same learning parameters were used, but training time was extended to 6000 epochs.

The performance of this configuration, shown in the center of Figure 4, is grim. These networks not only failed to generalize, but they often failed to form attractors for training set patterns. Also, several spurious attractors (as many as 8 for some training set sizes) arose for ill formed patterns. The introduction of an indirect error signal presented a serious obstacle to the formation of articulated attractors.

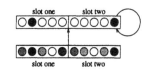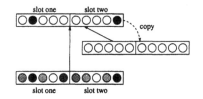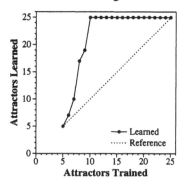

Figure 3: Network With Input Layer: The Architecture, Unrolled In Time, And Generalization Performance

In hopes of remedying this situation, the training procedure for this architecture was modified in a number of substantial ways. The first modification involved the number of time steps experienced by the network during training. An examination of the dynamics associated with well formed patterns revealed that, when presented with a valid pattern, the activation state of the network often drifted away from that well formed configuration, but it did so only very slowly. After 10 time steps of settling (which was the settling period during network training) almost all training set patterns appeared intact at the output layer. This observation suggested that the number of settling time steps experienced by the network during training was sufficient to keep the network from drifting away from the training patterns too quickly but was insufficient to construct the needed stable fixed-point attractors. To correct for this problem, we retrained these networks using incrementally larger settling times during training. In other words, whenever a network successfully retained the training patterns for t time steps during training, the settling time was advanced to $(t + 1)$ for the next training epoch. Unfortunately, this strategy did not work. Invariably, some settling time threshold would be reached, past which the networks would not learn.

Our next modification involved using a more robust estimate of the error gradient by backpropagating error through time all the way to the first time step. Using complete BPTT instead of the SRN training method showed no significant improvement by itself, but when coupled with a switch to a bipolar activation function (units which ranged in activation between -1 and 1) and with a reduced learning rate (0.001), this architecture began to successfully memorize the training set attractors. Systematic generalization remained elusive, however. This performance is shown in Figure 4, on the right.

In the previous two network architectures, the pattern of activation at the recurrent layer was consistently both polarized and sparse. Units tended to be either all the way "on" or all the way "off", and only two of the ten units were "on" for any given valid pattern. These properties of the recurrent layer activation patterns were directly enforced by the error signal provided at the output. In the case of an indirect error signal, however, these properties are no longer directly determined by training. Since the recurrent layer is a hidden layer in these

networks, other patterns of activation are free to arise there. Indeed, the activation patterns at the recurrent hidden layers of these networks were quite distributed, with approximately half of the hidden units being highly positive for any given training pattern. These recurrent layer patterns still tended to be polarized, however, presumably because it is easier to construct stable fixed-point attractors in the corners of activation space.[1] Still, these networks apparently included a sufficient number of free parameters (weights) to associate a fairly arbitrary distributed hidden layer attractor with each training pattern. Unlike the dual winner-take-all structure learned by the previous two architectures, these attractors showed few signs of compositionality.

This problem of hidden layer representation is serious. It is quite possible for a network to learn a hidden layer encoding of input patterns which is consistent with the training items but is inherently incapable of generalizing to other valid patterns. This problem may be illustrated by the simple example show in Figure 5. This diagram displays a small piece of a network, including two hidden units and two output units. Two possible configurations of weights between these processing elements are shown, with the output bias weights always being slightly negative. Both configurations can produce the given training set targets at their outputs, but only the configuration on the left is capable of producing the generalization target. The weights in the right network fragment fail because they collapse too many distinct hidden layer patterns to single output patterns. For generalization to have any hope of occurring, hidden layer activation space must retain distinct correlates to the entire range of valid outputs.

One way to avoid this "collapsing" of hidden layer space is to drive the weight vectors *coming out of* each hidden unit towards mutual orthogonality. This constraint makes the con-

---

[1]Near the corners of the 10 dimensional activation space of the recurrent layer, the derivative of the sigmoidal activation function of each recurrent unit is close to zero. This means that a large weight change is typically needed to change the fixed-point of a corner attractor. By comparison, a fixed-point attractor in the middle of this 10 dimensional space may drift significantly as the result of even a small weight change. In general, with sigmoidal units, fixed-point attractors in the corners of activation space are much less sensitive to small perturbations in weight values than fixed-points in the middle of activation space.

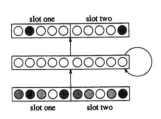
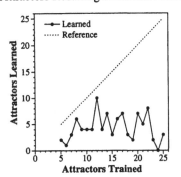
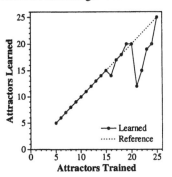

Figure 4: Network With Indirect Error: The Architecture, SRN Results, And BPTT Results

tribution of each hidden unit to the formation of an output pattern orthogonal to the contributions of the other hidden units. Note that the weight set schematically shown on the left in Figure 5, which effectively copies the hidden layer activation pattern to the output layer, is one example of a set of orthogonal outgoing weight vectors which is capable of appropriate generalization. To test this idea of an orthogonality constraint, we added a term to our squared error objective function of the form:

$$E_\perp = \sum_a \sum_b \cos^2 \theta_{ab}$$

...where a and b are hidden unit indices and θ_{ab} is the angle between their outgoing weight vectors. Unfortunately, depending on the proportion with which $E_\perp$ was mixed with squared error, orthogonalization either interfered with the learning of even training set patterns or had little effect at all. We noticed that the orthogonalization term often moved the hidden layer representations away from the corners of activation space, where attractors were typically constructed, so we also added a polarization error term which encouraged bipolar vectors at the hidden layer. This term took the form of:

$$E_p = -\sum_a o_a^2$$

...where o_a is the activation level of hidden unit a. Even when the objective function was augmented with both of these terms, the best networks still did little more than memorize training patterns.

Discussion

These results suggest that systematic generalization may arise easily in recurrent attractor networks when they are presented with a direct error signal. Distal error signals, backpropagated through intervening weights, however, appear to present a profound obstacle to the formation of articulated attractors. This finding is disconcerting since many cognitive models incorporating recurrent attractor networks implicitly assume an error signal conceptually "backpropagated" through some other psychological process while, in actual simulations, they utilize an error signal applied directly to the recurrent layer (Mathis & Mozer, 1995; Plaut & McClelland, 1993). For the theories underlying these models to be valid, there must be

some learning mechanism through which articulated attractors may be shaped by a distal teaching signal.

This problem may be viewed as one of finding a way to bias the learning of a multi-layer network in a way which encourages the general formation of articulated attractors without essentially "hard wiring" the structure of the input patterns. The main question that has yet to be answered is: What is the correct inductive bias for this task? We suggest that this bias should encourage recurrent hidden layer representations which use polarized activation levels and should drive hidden to output weights towards configurations which preserve, as much as possible, accessibility to the whole range of potential output patterns. Polarization is taken as a goal for the sake of the stability of attractor learning. Even with "corner attractors", however, these networks still need to avoid hidden to output mappings which restrict generalization. A technique such as activation sharpening (French, 1991) could potentially produce the kinds of representations needed, but this would require an *a priori* specification of the number of hidden elements "on" for each pattern. Still, an inductive bias of this sort may be the best that is possible under an indirect error signal.

Our future work will focus on solving this indirect error signal problem using two distinct approaches: by modifying the input pattern encoding and by modifying the network architecture. The first of these approaches involves encoding slot fillers in a non-localist fashion. Rather than assigning a single input and output unit to each filler, a more distributed representation could be used for filler values. This might involve a less sparse binary code in which different fillers share "on" elements, or it might involve a real vector encoding which retains the orthogonality of filler representations present in our localist code. Using a more distributed representation would cause weights *from* individual inputs and *to* individual output units to play a significant processing role over multiple filler values. The additional utilization of these weights may facilitate generalization to novel slot-filler patterns.

We will also consider encouraging articulated attractors by constraining the network architecture. In particular, we plan to investigate the possibility of initializing weights at the recurrent layer to a configuration which embodies a collection of winner-take-all networks. These will be implemented using a *softmax* constraint (Bridle, 1990), so backpropagated error can still successfully reach weights feeding into the at-

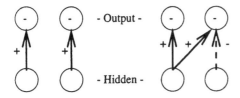

Target	Hidden (Left Net)	Hidden (Right Net)
ON-ON	ON-ON	ON-OFF
ON-OFF	ON-OFF	ON-ON
OFF-OFF	OFF-OFF	OFF-OFF
OFF-ON	OFF-ON	*Impossible!*

Figure 5: Example Of Weight Vector Orthogonality & Its Impact On Generalization

tractor network. Also, restricted receptive fields among the hidden to output connections might be used to approximate an orthogonality constraint on this mapping. Such strong architectural constraints may be necessary to consistently produce articulated attractors from distal error.

If further investigation reveals that the learning of systematic attractor structures from a distal teaching signal requires specific constraints on network architecture, cognitive models which utilize such attractor networks will need to assume some significant innate constraints on learning. This does *not* mean that an architecture specifically tuned to a particular task, such as reading aloud or proper production of verb tense, is necessary. The required innate constraints may simply involve the early presence of lateral inhibition between processing elements grouped into clusters or the existence of map-like structures arising from topologically regular connection patterns. The learning bias introduced by such general connection patterns may be all that is needed. Still, the work presented in this paper suggests that the simple presence of recurrent connections is not enough to produce systematic attractor dynamics. Learning to enforce "well formedness" constraints on internal representations may require somewhat structured network architectures.

Conclusion

Connectionist attractor networks have shown much promise as a mechanism for improving generalization performance by enforcing well formedness constraints on representations. Attractor networks which successfully learn a systematic collection of such constraints given a small training set are said to embody articulated attractors – meaningful attractor basins arising from the compositional interaction of explicitly trained stable fixed-points. We have shown that articulated attractors can readily arise in such networks when an error signal is applied directly to the recurrent processing elements. Distal error signals, however, pose surprisingly profound difficulties for such networks. A strong prior inductive bias, perhaps best seen as genetic in origin, towards compositional structure may be needed to produce articulated attractors at hidden layers in backpropagation networks.

Acknowledgements

The authors extend their thanks to the members of *Gary's & Eric's Unbelievable Research Unit (GEURU)* for their comments and suggestions on this work. Thanks are also due to three anonymous reviewers for their helpful advice concerning the clear presentation of this research.

References

Bridle, J. S. (1990). Training stochastic model recognition algorithms as networks can lead to maximum mutual information estimation of parameters. In Touretzky, D. S. (Ed.), *Advances in Neural Information Processing Systems 2* (pp. 211–217). San Mateo, CA: Morgan Kaufmann Publishers.

Elman, J. L. (1990). Finding structure in time. *Cognitive Science*, 14(2), 179–211.

French, R. M. (1991). Using semi-distributed representations to overcome catastrophic forgetting in connectionist networks. In *Proceedings of the Thirteenth Annual Conference of the Cognitive Science Society* (pp. 173–178). Hillsdale, NJ: Lawrence Erlbaum Associates.

Hopfield, J. J. (1982). Neural networks and physical systems with emergent collective computational abilities. *Proceedings of the National Academy of Sciences*, 79, 2554–2558.

Mathis, D. W. and Mozer, M. C. (1995). On the computational utility of consciousness. In Tesauro, G., Touretzky, D. S., and Leen, T. K. (Eds.), *Advances in Neural Information Processing Systems 7* (pp. 11–18). Cambridge, MA: MIT Press.

Noelle, D. C. and Cottrell, G. W. (1995). A connectionist model of instruction following. In Moore, J. D. and Lehman, J. F. (Eds.), *Proceedings of the Seventeenth Annual Conference of the Cognitive Science Society* (pp. 369–374). Hillsdale, NJ: Lawrence Erlbaum Associates.

Plaut, D. C. and McClelland, J. L. (1993). Generalization with componential attractors: Word and nonword reading in an attractor network. In *Proceedings of the Fifteenth Annual Conference of the Cognitive Science Society* (pp. 824–829). Hillsdale, NJ: Lawrence Erlbaum Associates.

Rumelhart, D. E., Hinton, G. E., and Williams, R. J. (1986a). Learning internal representations by error propagation. In Rumelhart, D. E., McClelland, J. L., and the PDP Research Group (Eds.), *Parallel Distributed Processing: Explorations in the Microstructure of Cognition* (ch. 8). Cambridge, MA: MIT Press.

Rumelhart, D. E., Smolensky, P., McClelland, J. L., and Hinton, G. E. (1986b). Schemata and sequential thought processes in PDP models. In Rumelhart, D. E., McClelland, J. L., and the PDP Research Group (Eds.), *Parallel Distributed Processing: Explorations in the Microstructure of Cognition* (ch. 14). Cambridge, MA: MIT Press.

St. John, M. F. (1992). Leaning language in the service of a task. In *Proceedings of the Fourteenth Annual Conference of the Cognitive Science Society* (pp. 271–276). Hillsdale, NJ: Lawrence Erlbaum Associates.

A Recurrent Network that performs a Context-Sensitive Prediction Task

Mark Steijvers
Department of Psychology
Indiana University
Bloomington IN 47405
msteyver@indiana.edu

Peter Grünwald
Department of Algorithmics
CWI, P.O. Box 4079
1009 AB Amsterdam, The Netherlands
pdg@cwi.nl

Abstract

We address the problem of processing a context-sensitive language with a recurrent neural network (RN). So far, the language processing capabilities of RNs have only been investigated for regular and context-free languages. We present an extremely simple RN with only one parameter z for its two hidden nodes that can perform a prediction task on sequences of symbols from the language $\{(ba^k)^n \mid k \geq 0, n > 0\}$, a language that is context-sensitive but not context-free. The input to the RN consists of any string of the language, one symbol at a time. The network should then, at all times, predict the symbol that should follow. This means that the network must be able to count the number of a's in the first subsequence and to retain this number for future use. We present a value for the parameter z for which our RN can solve the task for $k = 1$ up to $k = 120$. As we do not give any method to find a good value for z, this does not say anything about the *learning* capabilities of our network. It does, however, show that context-sensitive information (the count of a's) can be *represented* by the network; we analyse in detail how this is done. Hence our work shows that, at least from a representational point of view, connectionist architectures can handle more complex formal languages than was previously known.

Introduction

An important issue when modeling grammars and grammatical inference with recurrent neural networks (RNs) is to determine what kind of formal languages a recurrent neural network can process and generate. In this paper we show that a very simple recurrent network of a kind that has often been studied before is able to process a fairly complex language: a language that is neither regular nor context-free.

Regular languages represent the simplest class of formal languages in the Chomsky hierarchy (Hopcroft & Ullman, 1979). Regular languages are generated by regular grammars. Each regular language L has an associated deterministic finite state automaton (DFA) M and vice versa: M accepts all correct sentences of L and rejects all incorrect sentences. A more complex class in the Chomsky hierarchy is that of the context-free languages; the regular languages are a proper subset of this class. For each context-free language there is an associated push-down automaton (and vice versa). An even more complex language class is that of the context sensitive languages with the associated linear bounded automata. This class properly includes all context-free languages.

The theory of these languages and automata from a symbol processing perspective is well established (Hopcroft & Ullman, 1979). It is not clear however, what kind of automata

RNs can implement. So far, only performance on regular and context-free languages has been reported (Cleeremans, Servan-Schreiber & McClelland, 1989; Giles *et al.*, 1992; Sun *et al.*, 1993; Wiles & Elman, 1995). This situation led us to investigate whether it is possible to go beyond these language classes; in this paper, we come up with a RN that performs a prediction task on the symbols of a context-sensitive language that is not context-free. To the best of our knowledge, this has never been attempted before – as RNs already have great difficulties in handling simple context-free languages, we take our task to be quite challenging for RNs. Our work also has repercussions for the role of connectionism in psychology. In our view, in order for connectionism to be a serious paradigm for psychology, it should be clear what its capabilities are when dealing with formal languages which lie at the heart of 'symbol-oriented' models (Wiles & Elman, 1995).

We will consider a type of recurrent neural network that has initially been explored by Jordan (1986) and more recently by Elman (1990) and Pollack (1991). More specifically, we use a second order recurrent network (Giles *et al.*, 1992; Omlin & Giles, 1992) simplified to having only one parameter, and we show by simulation that its nodes can represent the input to the network in a way that captures the essential structure of our context sensitive language.

When RNs are applied to processing languages, the solutions provided by the network are often best understood from a dynamical systems perspective (Omlin & Giles, 1994). This perspective can sometimes offer new insights and provide new mechanisms for solving tasks that are usually dealt with from a more traditional symbolic framework. From this point of view, the problem we will have to face here is to control the non-linear dynamics of the network in such a way that the regions in state space that correspond to the various symbols to be predicted are linearly separable.

The Task

Consider all sequences of the form:

$$b(a)^k b(a)^k \ldots \quad \text{for integers } k \geq 0 \qquad (1)$$

In any such sequence symbol b is followed by k symbols a after which this subsequence repeats itself. Each value of k defines a unique sequence which we will call the k-sequence. For example, here are the initial segments of the 1-,2- and 3-sequences:

$$
\begin{aligned}
bababababa\ldots & \quad (k = 1) \\
baabaabaab\ldots & \quad (k = 2) \\
baaabaaaba\ldots & \quad (k = 3)
\end{aligned}
$$

The task we want our network to perform is the following: for any sequence of the form (1), after having been presented the first n symbols of the sequence, the network should correctly predict the $n + 1$-st symbol of the sequence. The symbols are presented in order: at time $t = 1$ the first symbol is presented, at $t = 2$ the second and so on. Note that before the second b has been presented, the next symbol may turn out to be either a or b as it is not clear yet which sequence the network is dealing with. But after the second b, there is only one possible sequence left, and all future symbols are unambiguously determined. Therefore, if the actual sequence turns out to be $b(a)^k b \ldots$ for some particular k, then we want our network to correctly predict all future symbols at all times $t > k + 2$.

Complexity of the Task

Consider the language $L_{CS} = \{(ba^k)^n \mid k \geq 0, n > 0\}$. Thus for example, *bababababa* and *baaaabaaaa* are correct sentences of the language while *babaaa*, *babab* and *baaba* are not. It is clear that our task can be reinterpreted as follows: after having been presented a few initial symbols (the first 'run' of a's) one must correctly predict what the next symbols in the sequence must be, such that at some point in the future, the part of the sequence seen until then will be a correct sentence of the language L_{CS}.

Now L_{CS} is a context-sensitive language which, moreover, is *not* context-free. This can be proven using standard techniques of formal language theory; an exact proof can be found in the appendix. Intuitively, one can understand why L_{CS} is not context-free if one tries to recognize L_{CS} using a push-down automaton. A push-down automaton is roughly just a non-deterministic finite state automaton with a stack; it is clear that the only way to count the number of a's that have been seen already is to use this stack. After the first b symbol, one can fill the stack with the first k a symbols. Then, after the second b, one can empty the stack again, to produce the next k a symbols, but since the contents of the stack are then empty, the information about k is lost, and further processing of the sequence is impossible. Therefore, a single stack is not sufficient to solve this task. What we really need to do is to implement a counter that counts the number of consecutive a symbols after which it *retains* this value to process the next (more than one!) subsequences of a-symbols.

Just as one cannot use a push-down automaton to *recognize* a language that is not context-free, one cannot use it to *predict* the consecutive symbols of the correct strings of such a language either (Hopcroft & Ullman, 1979). It is in this sense that the power of a recurrent network that would perform well on our prediction task goes beyond the power of context-free grammars or, equivalently, push-down automata.

The Network

We use a second-order recurrent network with two input nodes, I_1 and I_2, two hidden nodes H_1 and H_2 and an output unit O. x_i^t denotes the activation of node X_i at time t. We employ a unary encoding of our symbols: a is encoded as $i_1 = 1$ and $i_2 = 0$, b as $i_1 = 0$ and $i_2 = 1$. The hidden node activations h_1 and h_2 at time t are mapped into those at time

$t + 1$ according to:

$$h_1^{t+1} = f(i_1^t h_1^t w_1 + i_1^t h_2^t w_2 + \qquad (2)$$
$$i_2^t h_1^t w_3 + i_2^t h_2^t w_4 + w_5)$$

$$h_2^{t+1} = f(i_1^t h_1^t w_6 + i_1^t h_2^t w_7 + \qquad (3)$$
$$i_2^t h_1^t w_8 + i_2^t h_2^t w_9 + w_{10})$$

where f is the sigmoid discriminant function: $f(x) = 1/(1 + e^{-x})$. We simplified this network by removing some of the recurrent connections: $w_2 = w_3 = w_4 = w_6 = w_9 = 0$. The substitutions $w_1 = w_7 = w_8 = z$ and $w_5 = w_{10} = -z/2$, simplify the network to:

$$h_1^{t+1} = f(i_1^t h_1^t z - z/2) \qquad (4)$$
$$h_2^{t+1} = f(i_2^t h_1^t z + i_1^t h_2^t z - z/2) \qquad (5)$$

The output O is a linear threshold unit that outputs prediction symbols a and b:

$$O_t = \begin{cases} a & \text{if } w_{O1}h_1^t + w_{O2}h_2^t + \theta_O < 0 \\ b & \text{if } w_{O2}h_1^t + w_{O2}h_2^t + \theta_O \geq 0 \end{cases} \qquad (6)$$

A single parameter, the weight z determines the representation of the input symbols in hidden state space. The weights w_{O1}, w_{O2} and θ_O determine the linear equation[1] that divides the hidden state space in regions where the predicted symbol is a or b.

With computer studies, we wanted to find a z such that there is a combination of w_{O1}, w_{O2} and θ_O such that the predictions of the symbols of the sequences for $k = 1$ up to a maximum of m are correct. Therefore, for these sequences, the hidden node activations corresponding to a processed input sequence where the next symbol is a a or b should be linearly separable.

For $z = 3.9924$, we found that the predictions for the first $m = 120$ sequences of this task are linearly separable. In figure 1, the trajectories in hidden node space are shown for the first 6 sequences. These trajectories go from the left to the right; the successive points of the maps are connected by lines (the return trajectories to the left are omitted). The points indicated by filled circles are the points where k symbols a are received, so at these points, the output symbol should be b. The points indicated by open circles are the points where a symbol a should be predicted. The dashed line shows the linear equation that separates the a and b prediction symbols. Figure 2 shows the trajectories for all 120 sequences.

How the Network Does It

The behavior of the network can best be understood from a dynamical systems viewpoint. As all sequences consist of perpetually self-repeating subsequences, it is clear that for each value of k, the network eventually goes into an associated limit cycle. The real difficulty of our task is to combine

---

[1]Notice that we could just as well have taken the sigmoid discriminant function f again to determine the output activation as $O = f(w_{O1}h_1 + w_{O2}h_2 + \theta_O)$. If we then interpreted $O < 0.5$ as a and $O \geq 0.5$ as b, this would always yield the same predictions as our threshold unit. For recurrent neural networks, usually this latter approach is taken (Omlin & Giles, 1994). We have opted for the equivalent threshold approach in order to clarify the analysis of the hidden node activation space.

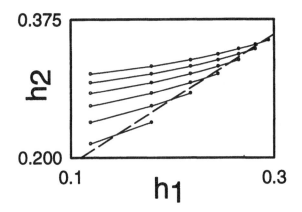

Figure 1: The trajectories of h_1 and h_2 in the network with $z = 3.9924$ are shown for $k = 1$ to 6.

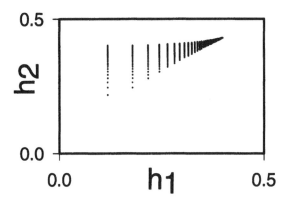

Figure 2: All points of the trajectories in hidden state space for the sequences $k = 1$ to 120.

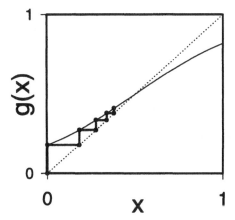

Figure 3: The map $g : x \mapsto 1/(1 + e^{-(z \cdot (x - 1/2))})$ is shown for $z = 3$. This map has only one attractor $x = 1/2$. Five iterations on this map are shown starting on $x = 0$.

the dynamics of every limit cycle in such a way that it is possible to extract useful information from the cycle trajectories in hidden node state space. The non-linear nature of limit cycle trajectories makes it difficult to be combined with the linear nature of the separation functions provided by threshold output units. Our main idea is to simplify the network by introducing a *reset mechanism* for every limit cycle. The endpoints of the trajectories (before reset again) are then linearly separable from all other points of the different trajectories; as will be seen below, this is exactly what is needed for our prediction task. For a more detailed analysis of the network's performance, we need to look at the following function:

$$g(x) = f(z \cdot (x - 1/2)) \qquad (7)$$

Here f is the sigmoid function again. We will write $g^{(0)}(x) = x, g^{(1)}(x) = g(x), g^{(2)}(x) = g(g(x))$ etc. For $0 \leq z < 4$, g has only one fixed point: $g(1/2) = 1/2$ (figure 3). This point is an attractor[2]; as n increases, $g^{(n)}(x)$ converges to $1/2$ for all starting values x. Also shown in figure 3 are the iterations from $g^{(0)}(0)$ to $g^{(5)}(0)$.

Now let us suppose that we feed our network a sequence consisting only of a's (i.e. $i_1^t = 1, i_2^t = 0$). Then, if we start at time t and set x equal to h_1^t, we can see from (4) that updating h_1 becomes identical to iterating g:

$$h_1^{t+i} = g^{(i)}(x) \quad \text{for all } i \geq 0 \qquad (8)$$

Exactly the same applies to H_2: if we had set $x = h_2^t$, then h_2 would have evolved according to g, as can be seen from (5).

But what happens to h_1^t when a symbol b arrives at time t? (i.e. $i_1^t = 0, i_2^t = 1$). We see that

$$
\begin{aligned}
h_1^{t+1} &= f(0 \cdot h_1^t \cdot z - z/2) \\
&= g^{(1)}(0) \qquad (9)
\end{aligned}
$$

Thus each time a b arrives (in particular, at time $t = 1$ when the first one arrives), h_1^t will be 'reset' to $g(0)$. This, together with (8) implies that if, for any t, the previous $i + 1$ symbols were of the form ba^i, then h_1^t will *always* be equal to $g^{(i+1)}(0)$. In what follows, we will write $g^{(i)}(0)$ simply as $g^{(i)}$.

H_2 is influenced in a different manner when a b arrives. If a b arrives in a k-sequence at a time t with $t > 1$ (we will not consider the first b here), then h_2^{t+1} is changed as follows:

$$
\begin{aligned}
h_2^{t+1} &= f(1 \cdot h_1^t \cdot z + 0 \cdot h_2^t \cdot z - z/2) \\
&= g(h_1^t) \\
&= g(g^{(k+1)}(0)) \\
&= g^{(k+2)} \qquad (10)
\end{aligned}
$$

Here h_1^t is equal to $g^{(k+1)}$ because we are in a k-sequence, and thus the b that arrives at time t has been preceded by ba^k.

In other words, whenever a symbol b is processed at time t in a k-sequence, the activation of H_1 is reset to $g^{(1)}$, while H_2 'takes over' from H_1: h_2^{t+1} is set to $g^{(k+2)}$. Returning to figure 2, we can see that in between two b's, node H_1 iterates g starting from $g^{(1)}$ to $g^{(k+1)}$, while H_2 iterates g from $g^{(k+2)}$ to $g^{(2k+2)}$. Thus the points (h_1^t, h_2^t) in hidden node

[2]One can actually prove this; see the work of Omlin & Giles (1994) where the same function is used for a different purpose.

337

activation space will always be of the form $(g^{(1+i)}, g^{(2+k+i)})$ for some $0 \leq i \leq k$. Also, the points $(g^{(1+k)}, g^{(2+2k)})$ coincide exactly with the hidden node activations when all k a's of the k-sequence have been presented, i.e. when a b should be predicted. On the other hand, all points at which an a should be predicted must be of the form $(g^{(1+i)}, g^{(2+k+i)})$ with $i < k$. As $g^{(t)}$ increases with t, this means that it is enough to make sure for all $i > 0$ that $(g^{(i)}, g^{(2i)})$ lies beneath the separating line while $(g^{(i)}, g^{(2i+1)})$ lies above it; see figure 1 and 2 again. As can be seen there, for increasing i, $g^{(i)}$ goes to $1/2$, but (for our choice of z) the points $(g^{(i)}, g^{(2i)})$ are connected through an almost linear function. This partially explains why the points $(g^{(i)}, g^{(2i)})$ and $(g^{(i)}, g^{(2i+1)})$ are linearly separable for such a large range of i.

Related Work

Concerning *regular* languages, Omlin & Giles (1994) provide an algorithm that, given any DFA M as input, outputs (a description of) an equivalent second-order recurrent network R. Here 'equivalent' means that R outputs a 1 if and only if its input is a string of the regular language corresponding to M.

For context-free languages, things get more complicated. Wiles & Elman (1995) studied the behavior of a RN on the language $a^n b^n$ which is context-free but not regular. They trained a small RN to predict the symbols from strings from this language with n ranging from 1 to 12. In one of several training sessions, they found a RN that exhibited generalization to $n = 18$. The similarity to our work consists in the fact that both $a^n b^n$ and L_{CS} can be processed using only a counter rather than a complete stack or tape; however, in Elman & Wiles' work the trained network turned out to count in a completely different manner from ours, namely by combining the dynamics of attractors and repellors that implement counting up and down respectively; like a stack, this mechanism 'forgets' the number of a's after processing the b's.

Sun *et al.* (1993) also studied RNs when trained on context-free languages but their RNs were augmented with a stack. Here, the task for the RN was to accept or reject a string as belonging to the trained language. They achieved very good generalization performance when training their network with short example strings of some context-free languages including $a^n b^n$. The advantage of providing the RN with a real stack is that *different* symbols can be written on the stack and read off again, while it remains to be seen whether that can be achieved with techniques like those used by Wiles & Elman (1995) and us. On the other hand, the stack extension cannot be of any help in representing languages like L_{CS} that are not context-sensitive, and does not show whether RNs by *themselves* are more powerful than DFA's.

Discussion and Conclusion

It is important to realize that we did not use learning algorithms for the network itself to come up with solutions; instead, we 'hard-wired' the weights to solve the task. We felt the need to separate the possibilities of *learning* a language as difficult as a context-sensitive one from the possibility of *representing* it with a RN. It could turn out that there are weights for the RN which make for a good representation of the language, while none of the known learning algorithms for RNs will

ever find these weights. On the other hand, it could be that the representational capability of the RN was not powerful enough to start with. In the words of Minsky & Papert (1988): 'no machine can learn to recognize X unless it possesses, at least potentially, some scheme for representing X'. In this work, we showed that at least some RNs *do* have the representational capabilities to deal with at least some languages that are not context-free. We certainly do not think that RNs will turn out to be capable of handling *any* context-sensitive language; we *do* think however that they can provide a new and interesting manner to process some languages that are rather complex from the point of view of formal language theory.

References

Cleeremans, A., Servan-Schreiber, D., & McClelland, J. (1989). Finite state automata and simple recurrent networks. *Neural Computation*, 1(3),372–381.

Elman, J. (1990). Finding structure in time. *Cognitive Science*, 14,179–211.

Giles, C., Miller, C., Chen, D., Chen, H., Sun, G. & Lee, Y. (1992). Learning and extracting finite state automata with second-order recurrent networks. *Neural Computation*, 2, 331–349.

Hopcroft, J. and Ullman, J. (1979). *Introduction to Automata Theory, Languages and Computation*. Reading, MA: Addison-Wesley.

Jordan, M. (1986). Attractor dynamics and parallelism in a connectionist sequential machine. In *Proceedings of the Ninth Annual conference of the Cognitive Science Society* (pp. 531–546). Hillsdale, NJ: Lawrence Erlbaum Associates.

Minsky, M. & Papert, S. (1988). *Perceptrons*. Cambridge, MA: MIT Press.

Omlin, C. & Giles, C. (1994). Constructing Deterministic Finite-State Automata in recurrent neural networks. Technical report 94-3. Troy, NY: Rensselaer Polytechnic Institute, Department of Computer Science.

Pollack, J. (1991). The induction of dynamical recognizers. *Machine Learning*, 7, 227–252.

Sun, G., Giles, C., Chen, H., & Lee, Y. (1993). The neural network push-down automaton: model, stack and learning simulations. Technical Report UMIACS-TR-93-77 & CS-TR-3118. College Park, MD: UMIACS.

Wiles, J. & Elman, J. (1995). Learning to count without a counter: a case study of dynamics and activation landscapes in recurrent networks. In *Proceedings of the Seventeenth Annual Conference of the Cognitive Science Society*. Cambridge, MA: MIT Press.

Proof that L_{CS} Is Not Context-Free

We want to prove the following:

Theorem 1 *The language L_{CS} defined by $L_{CS} = \{(ba^k)^n \mid k \geq 0, n > 0\}$ is not context-free.*

We will prove this theorem using the pumping lemma for context-free languages, a standard tool for proving certain languages not to be context-free (Hopcroft & Ullman, 1979). Before giving the actual proof, we will first state the pumping lemma and explain the proof technique used. In the following, i, j, k, m and n will be variables taking on non-negative integer values. t, u, v, w, x, y and z will be variables taking on string values. A string is a concatenation of zero or more symbols taken from the alphabet $\Sigma = \{a, b\}$. For any string z, $|z|$ denotes the length of (number of symbols appearing in) string z. xy stands for the concatenation of strings x and y. We are now ready to state the pumping lemma (for a proof of the pumping lemma itself and details about the notation, see for example Hopcroft & Ullman (1979)):

Lemma 1 (Pumping Lemma for Context-Free Languages)
Let L be any context-free language. Then there is a constant n, depending only on L, such that if z is in L and $|z| \geq n$, then we may write $z = uvwxy$ such that

1. $|vx| \geq 1$,
2. $|vwx| \leq n$, and
3. for all $i \geq 0$, uv^iwx^iy is in L.

The general idea behind the proof of theorem 1 is as follows: we first suppose that L_{CS} were context-free. Then the pumping lemma holds, so the constant n mentioned in the pumping lemma exists. The trick is to cleverly pick a string z in L_{CS} with length $|z| \geq n$ such that any choice of u, v, w, x and y with $z = uvwxy$ will violate at least one of the three conditions in the pumping lemma. As the pumping lemma states that the three conditions hold for *any* z in L_{CS} with length $|z| \geq n$, this shows that the pumping lemma does not hold after all. Thus assuming L_{CS} is context-free leads to a contradiction; L_{CS} is therefore not-context free. We now proceed to the actual proof:

Proof of Theorem 1: Suppose that L_{CS} were context-free. Let n be the constant of the pumping lemma. Consider the string $z = ba^nba^nba^n$. It is clear that z is in L_{CS} and that $|z| \geq n$. Write $z = uvwxy$ such that it satisfies the conditions of the pumping lemma. We must now find out where v and x, the strings that can get 'pumped', lie in $ba^nba^nba^n$. Since $|vx| \leq |vwx| \leq n$, vx contains at most one b. We can distinguish two cases: 1) vx contains no b's at all ; 2) vx contains exactly one b.

In case 1), as $|vwx| \leq n$, we must have that $|u| + |v| \geq 2n + 3$. This means that either u can be written as $u = ba^nt$ for some t or y can be written as $y = tba^n$ for some t. Now consider the string uwy (the string uv^iwx^iy with $i = 0$). As $|vx| \geq 1$ and vx contains no b's, the string uwy contains less than $3n$ a's but still three b's. However, either u starts with ba^n or y ends with ba^n. So uwy is of the form $ba^iba^jba^k$, where either i or k must be equal to n and at least one of i, j and k is less than n. This means that uwy is not of the form

$(ba^{k'})^{n'}$, and thus uwy is not in L_{CS}. But by the pumping lemma $uwy = uv^0wx^0y$ must be in L_{CS}; a contradiction.

In case 2), the string uwy contains only 2 b's. Suppose first that the leftmost b is missing in uwy (I.e. u is the empty string and $vx = bt$ for some string t). Then uwy is of the form $a^mba^nba^n$. This string can only be in L_{CS} if $m = 0$. But then $|vx| = |uvwxy| - |uwy| = n + 1$, while $|vx| \leq n$; a contradiction. So suppose that the middle b is missing; then uwy is of the form ba^mba^n. This string can only be in L_{CS} if $m = n$. Again, it follows that $|vx| = n + 1$ so once more, we have arrived at a contradiction. Finally, suppose that the rightmost b is missing. Again, this would lead to $|vx| = n+1$; another contradiction.

We thus see that supposing that L_{CS} is a context-free language inevitably leads to a contradiction. Therefore, L_{CS} is not a context-free language. $\square$

339

Competition in Analogical Transfer:
When Does a Lightbulb Outshine an Army?

Wendy S. Francis and **Thomas D. Wickens**
Department of Psychology
University of California, Los Angeles
Los Angeles, CA 90095
wendy@psych.ucla.edu
twickens@psych.ucla.edu

Abstract

This study investigated competition in analogical transfer to a problem solution. In two experiments, subjects read two stories, then attempted to solve Duncker's (1945) radiation problem, which has both a convergence and an open-passage solution. Stories were constructed that suggested each of these solutions; a third story was irrelevant. Subjects in the competitive conditions read both solution-suggesting stories, and subjects in the two noncompetitive conditions read one of these and the irrelevant story. In Experiment 1, the noncompetitive conditions convergence solutions and open-passage solutions were produced at comparable rates, but in the competitive condition, convergence solutions overwhelmed open-passage solutions. This asymmetry is too large to be explained by unidimensional models of retrieval and reflects the multidimensional nature of retrievability. In Experiment 2, the source stories suggesting each solution type were reversed, and the open-passage solution rate was higher than the convergence solution rate in all three conditions. In both experiments, subjects were able to successfully apply both source stories once cued to do so, indicating that the competition is at the retrieval stage of transfer, not at the mapping stage. Computational models of analogical transfer (e.g., ARCS and MAC/FAC) predict some competition but may have difficulty explaining the extreme nature of these results.

Analogical transfer occurs when a person draws upon knowledge about a familiar situation to make inferences about a new, less familiar, situation. Two situations are analogous when they contain parallel sets of causal relationships. Often, novel solutions to problems are initially generated based on analogies, which makes an understanding of this process critical to a theory of problem solving.

The experimental procedure used to study analogical transfer in problem solving is for subjects to first read a text passage, or *source story* in which a problem is described and solved. Later, subjects are asked to solve a new *target problem*. The basic transfer effect is that subjects are more likely to solve the target problem when the situation in the source story is analogous to the situation in the target problem than when it is not (e.g., Gick & Holyoak, 1980).

The degree of transfer between analogous problem solutions (i.e., problems with identical causal structure) depends on relationships among the analogous problems and conditions of analog presentation. Similarity between source analog and target is a crucial determinant of transfer in several major models of analogical transfer (Gentner, 1983; Holyoak, 1985; Hintzman, 1986; Ross, 1984). The higher the similarity, the more transfer is observed, whether that similarity is on the surface or at a deeper structural level (Holyoak & Koh, 1987; Gentner, 1989). However, different types of similarity play different roles in transfer. *Surface similarity*, similarity in noncausal aspects of story such as related semantic content, appears to have its primary role in analog retrieval, that is, in the identification of the source as a potential analog; *Structural similarity*, similarity in causal structure, appears to have its primary role in analog mapping, that is, in the way that the individual elements of the analogs are linked to each other (Holyoak & Koh, 1987; Gentner, 1989). Some theories of analogy suggest that surface similarity is the first feature used in accessing an appropriate analogy, and structural similarity only comes into the retrieval process when a system chooses among analogies of comparable surface similarity or when no good surface match is found (Gentner, Ratterman, & Forbus, 1993; Reed, Ackinclose, & Voss, 1990).

The number of presented analogs also affects the likelihood of transfer. The rate of transfer is higher when subjects learn several source analogs, each illustrating a common solution to the target problem, than when they learn only one source analog (Catrambone & Holyoak, 1989; Gick & Holyoak, 1980).

Some problems can be solved in more than one way, in which case the approach taken depends on what analogous situation is retrieved from memory. Gick and Holyoak (1980) showed that the type of solution produced in response to a target problem depended on the approach of a previously learned source analog. When a problem solver has learned more than one kind of source analog, it is not clear how the memory system chooses between them.

Numerous studies in the memory literature, going back more than 50 years, have shown that, in general, retrieval of information from memory is competitive (McGeoch, 1932; Melton & Irwin, 1940). One method used to demonstrate this competition has been to show that within-subjects designs or mixed-list presentations yield more dramatic strength effects than between-subjects designs or pure-list presentations. The differences reported are not just in statistical sensitivity (due to reduced within-subject variability); the absolute magnitude of the differences changes substantially. For example, the magnitude of transfer-appropriate processing effects has been shown to be larger for mixed-condition lists than for pure lists (e.g., in picture and word naming, Brown, et al., 1991).

Wharton (1993; Wharton, et al., 1994) investigated competition in analogical reminding. After reading a series of stories, subjects were asked to tell which stories they were reminded of when presented with either related sentences (Experiment 1) or related new stories (Experiment 3). He demonstrated that while effects of structural consistency were minimal in noncompetitive reminding conditions (those in which only one related story had been presented), a marked advantage for consistent over inconsistent analogies was repeatedly observed when those two types of analogies were put in competition with each other.

Analogical transfer differs from other memory tests (and from the analogical reminding paradigm) in two important ways. First, subjects are not specifically cued to recall items from the previously-learned set. Second, the memory is applied to a new situation instead of being reproduced in its original form. A convenient feature of this paradigm is that it allows examination of competition in both spontaneous and directed transfer.

Competition in transfer of source analogs for problem solving is a little-tested prediction of some models of analogical retrieval. For example the ARCS (Analogical Retrieval by Constraint Satisfaction, Thagard, et al., 1990) model uses inhibitory links to pressure one-to-one mapping between analogies. Whichever analogy is most highly activated (i.e., matches the target situation the best) suppresses activation of other candidate analogies. Thus, this model discourages retrieval of multiple analogies and predicts retrieval competition. In MAC/FAC (Many Are Called but Few Are Chosen; Forbus, Gentner, & Law, 1995), the set of potential source analogs with the highest similarity to the target are activated in the first stage, MAC; The second stage, FAC, always retrieves the best structural match out of that set. Thus, this model also predicts retrieval competition, but without inhibitory mechanisms. (In MAC/FAC, the better match outshines its competitors. In ARCS, the better match not only outshines, but obscures its competitors.)

By analogy to the other memory effects, when there are several analogs (items) in memory, any differences between them that tend to make one more salient than another should have greater effects in this competitive situation than when there is only one source analog. The present study investigates what will happen when multiple analogous solution types are simultaneously available in memory. Do they cooperate, or do they compete?

Experiment 1

The first experiment examined competition in transfer of analogous problem solutions using a procedure in which subjects read two stories and then solved a problem. The two stories were either (1) both analogous to the target problem but suggestive of different solution methods or (2) one analogous story and one irrelevant story.

Method

Materials. The target problem in this experiment was Duncker's (1945) Ray problem, in which the subject is asked as a doctor to find a way to use rays to destroy a patient's stomach tumor without harming the surrounding healthy tissue. Two analogies that each suggested a different solution to this problem were selected from previous studies. The first analogy was a version of the Lightbulb story (ultrasound version, Holyoak & Koh, 1987), which suggested a *convergence* solution to the Ray problem (i.e., using several low-intensity rays coming from different directions simultaneously). The second analogy was a version of the General story (open supply-route version, Gick & Holyoak, 1980), which suggested an *open-passage* solution to the Ray problem (i.e., finding an open passage such as the esophagus through which to send high-intensity rays directly to the tumor). A third story that was not analogous to the Ray problem, the Wine Merchants (Gick & Holyoak, 1980), was used as a filler story in the non-competitive conditions.

Procedure. Sixty-eight students from an introductory psychology class at UCLA participated for course credit. Two other subjects were disqualified because they had prior experience with the Ray problem. Participants were tested individually or in small groups. In the first phase of the experiment, two source stories were presented. Subjects had 3 minutes to read and 5 minutes to summarize each of these stories. Between the first and second experimental phases, subjects were given 5 minutes to complete a two-page questionnaire about their language-learning experiences.

In the second phase of the experiment, participants were given four opportunities to write a solution to the target problem. First, subjects were told that they would have 5 minutes to write possible solutions to the problem; no instructions were given to refer back to either source story. Next, a non-specific hint was given by saying that others had found it helpful to consider one of the stories they read earlier. The particular story that might be helpful was left open. They were given 4 more minutes to write a solution. On the third and fourth opportunities, subjects were to write the solutions suggested by the first and second source stories, respectively.

Design. The crucial manipulation was the combination of source stories. There were 3 story combinations. In the two noncompetitive conditions, one of the analogous stories (the Lightbulb or the General) was presented in combination with the nonanalogous story (the Wine Merchants). In the competitive conditions, both of the analogous source stories were presented. Approximately half of the participants were assigned to a competitive condition, and half were assigned to one of the noncompetitive conditions, distributing subjects as evenly as possible across specific forms. The order of source-story presentation was counterbalanced.

Results

Each problem-solving response was coded as a *convergence* solution, an *open passage* solution, or neither of the target solution types, using a lenient coding system. Convergence solutions required aiming low-intensity rays from different directions, but did not require simultaneity. Open-passage solutions required the use of high-intensity rays that did not come into contact with healthy tissue, but the open passage could either be a pre-existing one (e.g., the esophagus) or a newly created one (e.g., an incision or tube). Nontarget solutions were put in an *other* category. Several subjects gave *both* the convergence and open-passage solutions and were so coded. Coding of before-hint and nonspecific-hint solutions was blind to the source story condition. Because specific-hint solutions usually included the title of the corresponding source story, coding was only blind to the identity of the other story presented. Two independent raters coded each response (82% agreement, Cohen's k = .70), and consensus was reached on all discrepancies. Subjects who had given target solutions on the first attempt often gave less complete answers on their second attempt (with the nonspecific hint). Accordingly, categories of solutions given before the hint and after the nonspecific hint were combined to form the coding category for the *total* solution for each participant, as in the analysis of Holyoak & Koh (1987).

No presentation order effects were observed, so data from the two orders of each story combination were pooled. Table 1 shows the solution classifications for the before-hint and nonspecific-hint solutions. As is obvious from the table, the rows are not homogeneous either before the hint $(X^2(6) = 33.77, p < .001)$ or after the nonspecific hint $(X^2(6) = 47.91, p < .001)$. Before the hint, in the noncompetitive conditions, the convergence solution rate (77%, *convergence* and *both* categories, combined) in the Lightbulb story condition only had a slight advantage over the open-passage solution rate (59%, *open-passage* and *both* categories, combined) in the General story condition. However, in the competitive condition, convergence solutions (68%) outnumbered convergence solutions (9%) over 7 to 1. In fact, open-passage solutions were no more frequent in the competitive situation than when the open-passage analogy was not presented. The pattern was similar for the total (before hint + nonspecific hint) solution rates.

The low use of the open-passage solution in the competitive condition is not because subjects were unable to map the General story onto the Ray problem and construct an open-passage solution. When subjects were given a hint specifically identifying the source story suggesting that solution type, the advantage for convergence solutions (85%) over open-passage solutions (68%) in the competitive conditions was similar to that in the noncompetitive conditions (100% and 82% for convergence and open-passage solutions, respectively). The effect is clearly at the retrieval stage rather than the mapping stage of transfer (see Holyoak & Koh, 1987). For the same reason, the low rate of open-passage solutions cannot be attributed to failure to properly encode the General story and its solution.

Discussion

The most striking finding in this study is that the noncompetitive solution rates are fairly balanced for the two analogies, but are strongly asymmetric in the competitive condition. Models of choice that depend on a single strength parameter [e.g., a relative ratio model; more generally, models with simple scalability (Luce & Suppes, 1965)] cannot be used to explain these results. These models cannot explain simultaneously the large asymmetry in convergence and open passage solutions in the competitive condition and the more equivalent use of these solutions in the noncompetitive conditions. Either a multidimensional representation or a staged model [e.g., akin to Tversky's (1972) elimination by attributes model] is needed.

Source Story Condition	Solution Type				n
	Conv.	Both	O.P.	Other	
Before Hint					
Noncompetitive					
Lightbulb - Conv.	.59	.18	.06	.18	17
General - O.P.	.06	.00	.59	.35	17
Competitive	.65	.03	.06	.26	34
After Hint (Total)					
Noncompetitive					
Lightbulb - Conv.	.76	.24	.00	.00	17
General - O.P.	.00	.18	.65	.18	17
Competitive	.62	.26	.00	.12	34

Table 1: Proportions of subjects giving each solution type in Experiment 1
Conv. = convergence; O.P. = open-passage

Experiment 2

The high frequency of convergence solutions in Experiment 1 occurred in conditions in which it was analogous to the Lightbulb story. The effectiveness of this analog could be due to either the presence of the convergence solution per se or to the surface similarity of the Lightbulb story. The second experiment reversed the solution types suggested by each context to disentangle these possibilities. Thus, a convergence version of the General story and an open-passage version of the Lightbulb story were used.

Method

Materials. Two major changes were made from Experiment 1. First, the Lightbulb story was rewritten so as to suggest an open-passage solution (See Appendix A). Second, a convergence version of the General story (Gick & Holyoak, 1980) was used. The target problem was the same as in Experiment 1.

Design and Procedure. The design and procedure were identical to those of Experiment 1. Fifty-one students from an introductory psychology class at UCLA participated for course credit. Three other subjects were disqualified, because they had prior experience with the Ray problem.

Results

The coding criteria were also the same as in Experiment 1. Again, no order effects were observed, so data from the two orders of each story combination were pooled. Table 2 shows the solution classifications for the before-hint and nonspecific-hint solutions. The pattern is very different from that of Experiment 1. No inhomogeneity of the rows can be identified before the hint ($X^2(6) = 4.73$, $p > .50$) but one is present after the nonspecific hint ($X^2(6) = 16.53$, $p < .05$). In contrast to Experiment 1, the before-hint pattern was almost completely dominated by the solution type, with open-passage solutions much more likely in every condition. In the noncompetitive conditions, the open passage solution rate in the Lightbulb condition (53%) had a huge advantage over the convergence solution rate in the General condition (6%) before the hint. In the competitive condition, open-passage solutions (65%) outnumbered convergence solutions (24%) by a smaller margin. The convergent General source analog was unable to attract convergence solutions in the way that the convergent Lightbulb source analog in Experiment 1 did.

After the nonspecific hint, the noncompetitive condition advantage for open-passage over convergence solution rates (82% and 41%, respectively) was still greater than the competitive condition advantage (open-passage and convergence rates of 83% and 65%, respectively). Many subjects can construct a convergence solution after the nonspecific hint, but in this context they do so only after producing the open passage solution. In this respect, the present experiment differs markedly from Experiment 1.

Although open-passage solutions predominate in Table 2, subjects were nevertheless able to map the General story onto the Ray problem by constructing a convergence solution. When subjects in the competitive condition were told to use a specific story, both the percentage of convergence solutions derived from the General story and the percentage of open-passage solutions derived from the Lightbulb story were 88%. Similarly, in the noncompetitive conditions, there was no advantage for open-passage solutions (65% open passage, 76% convergence).

Source Story Condition	Solution Type				n
	Conv.	Both	O.P.	Other	
Before Hint					
Noncompetitive					
Lightbulb - O.P.	.06	.06	.47	.41	17
General - Conv.	.06	.00	.41	.53	17
Competitive	.06	.18	.47	.29	17
After Hint (Total)					
Noncompetitive					
Lightbulb - O.P.	.00	.12	.70	.18	17
General - Conv.	.12	.29	.74	.35	17
Competitive	.06	.59	.24	.12	17

Table 2: Proportions of subjects giving each solution type in Experiment 2
Conv. = convergence; O.P. = open-passage

Discussion

The pattern of results in this study differs from that of Experiment 1. One solution type, the open-passage solution, dominated in both noncompetitive and competitive conditions, even when it was not presented in a source analog. The convergent form of the General story was not able to draw subjects away from the more-dominant open-passage solution. The clearest difference between the two source analogs is that the Lightbulb story, being in a scientific setting, is a better surface match or content match to the medical setting of the Ray problem than is the General story. It appears that to elicit retrieval of a less-dominant solution, it is necessary to have high surface similarity between source and target, such as that between the Lightbulb story and the Ray problem. The dominance of the open-passage solution could not be attributed to either failure to encode or failure to map the convergence solution, because the convergence analogy was successfully retrieved and mapped once a specific hint was given to use its source story.

General Discussion

As is clear from Experiment 2, the open-passage solution has a higher base rate than the convergence solution, consistent with past results (Gick & Holyoak, 1980).

Both experiments demonstrate that the Lightbulb story is more readily retrieved for analogical mapping than the General story, indicating that surface similarity of the source story is important in analogical retrieval. From Experiment 1 to Experiment 2, the solutions suggested by each source story were reversed. In the competitive conditions of both experiments, the solution suggested by the Lightbulb story was more dominant (the convergence solution in Experiment 1, and the open-passage solution in Experiment 2). This solution-type reversal pattern is significant ($X^2(3) = 21.66$, $p < .001$), whereas the pattern of source story used is not ($X^2(3) = 3.76$, $p > .25$). This pattern shows the importance of source-story similarity in retrieval. Specifically, the results could be explained by a multidimensional concept of similarity. Surface similarities and structural similarities play different roles in transfer. Both the Lightbulb story and the General story are good structural matches to the Ray problem.

Both experiments indicate that differences in spontaneous retrieval, not in encoding or mapping, make one source story or solution type dominant. In both experiments, subjects were able to successfully map both of the source stories when given specific instructions to do so. When appropriately cued, they could direct their retrieval toward relevant aspects of the source analog for mapping.

The present study complements the effects of analogical reminding found by Wharton (1993; Wharton et al., 1994). The results of Experiment 1 are similar to his, in that retrieval differences that were undetectable in the noncompetitive conditions were much larger in the competitive conditions. More broadly, the results demonstrate that competition in retrieval from long-term memory extends to situations in which the information is to be retrieved and applied in a new context rather than simply repeated. As it happened, the results of Experiment 2 do not bear on this issue, because the convergent General story was not used at a high rate even in the absence of a competing open-passage source analog.

This study shows that retrieval competition between different source analogies for transfer in problem solving can show an asymmetry that is at odds with the degree of noncompetitive transfer. Although the basic competition effects are consistent with predictions of theories such as ARCS and MAC/FAC, it is not clear how these models would handle the extreme magnitude of the competition that we observed. The pattern of results suggests an active suppression process in which stronger competitors suppress weaker ones, rather than a competition in which stronger competitors merely enjoy a relative advantage. The ARCS model does have active suppression of competitors, which suggests that it may be able to accommodate our findings, although we have not yet attempted to get it to match our particular pattern.

The results of Experiment 1, if reproducible, considerably constrain the class of possible models of analogical retrieval in problem solving. As we noted above, the asymmetry of competitive choice combined with the symmetry of noncompetitive choice is inconsistent with a unidimensional representation (i.e., one with simple scalability). Any model shown to have the property of simple scalability can be ruled out. In particular, these results preclude any model in which spontaneous retrievability of an item is independent of context.

Acknowledgements

The reported experiments form part of the first author's doctoral dissertation. Angelica Garcia, Tianna Pool, and Leo Ramos assisted with data collection and coding. Keith Holyoak and three anonymous reviewers made helpful comments on earlier drafts of this paper.

Appendix A

Lightbulb Story (open-passage version)

In a physics lab at a major university a very expensive lamp which would emit controlled quantities of light was being used in some experiments. The research assistant responsible for operating the sensitive equipment came into the lab one morning and found that the lightbulb no longer worked. The research assistant realized that it was probably because she had accidentally knocked it over the previous night. As a result, the wires connecting the lightbulb to its power source had fused together, but the place where the wires had fused together was inside the lamp casing. The surrounding casing was completely sealed, so there was no way to open it. The lamp could be repaired if a brief, high-intensity ultrasound wave could be used to jar apart the fused parts. Furthermore, the lab had the necessary equipment to do the job.

However, a high-intensity ultrasound wave would also break the fragile casing surrounding the lightbulb and wires. At lower intensities the ultrasound wave would not break the casing, but neither would it jar apart the fused parts. So it seemed that the lamp could not be repaired, and a costly replacement would be required.

The research assistant was about to give up when she had an idea. Although the casing could not be opened, she reasoned that because the lightbulb generated so much heat, the casing must have a vent to let the hot air out. So she took it down off of its stand, and sure enough, there was an opening on top. By carefully inserting a tube through the vent and aligning the ultrasound machine to go through the tube, she was able to send the ultrasound wave directly to the broken wires and jar them apart. Since no spot on the fragile casing was exposed to the wave, the glass was left intact. There was a great relief that the lamp was repaired, and it was possible to successfully complete the experiment.

References

Brown, A. S., Neblett, D. R., Jones, T. C., & Mitchell, D. B. (1991). Transfer of processing in repetition priming: Some inappropriate findings. *Journal of Experimental Psychology: Learning, Memory, and Cognition, 17(3)*, 514-525.

Catrambone, R., & Holyoak, K. J. (1989). Overcoming contextual limitations on problem-solving transfer. *Journal of Experimental Psychology: Learning, Memory, and Cognition, 15(6)*, 1147-1156.

Duncker, K. (1945). On problem solving. *Psychological Monographs, 58*.

Forbus, K. D., Gentner, D., & Law, K. (1995). MAC/FAC: A model of similarity-based retrieval. *Cognitive Science, 19*, 141-205.

Gentner, D. (1989). The mechanisms of analogical reasoning. In S. Vosniadou and A. Ortony (Eds.), *Similarity and analogical reasoning* (pp. 199-241).

Gentner, D. (1983). Structure mapping: A theoretical framework for analogy. *Cognitive Science, 7*, 155-170.

Gentner, D., Ratterman, M. J., & Forbus, K. (1993). The roles of similarity in transfer: Separating retrievability from inferential soundness. *Cognitive Psychology, 25*, 524-575.

Gick, M. L., & Holyoak, K. J. (1980). Analogical problem solving. *Cognitive Psychology, 12*, 306-355.

Hintzman, D. L. (1986). "Schema abstraction" in a multiple-trace memory model. *Psychological Review, 93*, 411-428.

Holyoak, K. J. (1985). The pragmatics of analogical transfer. In G. H. Bower (Ed.), *The psychology of learning and motivation* (Vol. 19). San Diego, CA: Academic Press.

Holyoak, K. J., & Koh, K. (1987). Surface and structural similarity in analogical transfer. *Memory & Cognition, 15*, 332-340.

Luce, R. D., & Suppes, P. (1965). Preference, utility, and subjective probability. In R. D. Luce, R. A. Bush, & E. Galanter (Eds.). *Handbook of mathematical psychology* (Vol. III, Chapter 19). New York, NY: Wiley.

McGeoch, J. A. (1932). Forgetting and the law of disuse. *Psychological Review, 39*, 352-370.

Melton, A. W., & Irwin, J. M. (1940). The influence of degree of interpolated learning on retroactive inhibition and the overt transfer of specific responses. *American Journal of Psychology, 53*, 173-203.

Reed, S. K., Ackinclose, C. C., & Voss, A. A. (1990). Selecting analogous problems: Similarity versus inclusiveness. *Memory & Cognition, 18*, 83-98.

Ross, B. H. (1984). Remindings and their effects in learning a cognitive skill. *Cognitive Psychology, 16*, 371-416.

Thagard, P., Holyoak, K. J., Nelson, G., & Gochfeld, D. (1990). Analog retrieval by constraint satisfaction. *Artificial Intelligence, 46*, 259-310.

Tversky, A. (1972). Elimination by aspects: a theory of choice. *Psychological Bulletin, 79*, 281-299.

Wharton, C. M. (1993). Direct and indirect measures of the roles of thematic and situational knowledge in reminding. Unpublished doctoral dissertation, Department of Psychology, University of California, Los Angeles.

Wharton, C. M., Holyoak, K. J., Downing, P. E., Lange, T. E., Wickens, T. D., Melz, E. R. (1994). Below the surface: Analogical similarity and retrieval competition in reminding. *Cognitive Psychology, 26*, 64-101.

Can a real distinction be made between cognitive theories of analogy and categorisation?

Michael Ramscar[†][††] and **Helen Pain**[†]
[†]Department of Artificial Intelligence
[††]EdCAAD, Department of Architecture
University of Edinburgh
{michael,helen}@aisb.ed.ac.uk

Abstract

Analogy has traditionally been defined by use of a contrast definition: analogies represent associations or connections between things distinct from the 'normal' associations or connections determined by our 'ordinary' concepts and categories. Research into analogy, however, is also distinct from research into concepts and categories in terms of the richness of its process models. A number of detailed, plausible models of the analogical process exist (Forbus, Gentner and Law, 1995; Holyoak and Thagard, 1995): the same cannot be said of categorisation.

In this paper we argue that in the absence of an acceptable account of categorisation, this contrast definition amounts to little more than a convenient fiction which, whilst useful in constraining the scope of cognitive investigations, confuses the relationship between analogy and categorisation, and prevents models of these processes from informing one another. We present a study which addresses directly the question of whether analogy can be distinguished from categorisation by contrasting categorisational and analogical processes, and following from this, whether theories of analogy, notably Gentner's structure mapping theory (Gentner, 1983; Forbus et al, *ibid*.), can also be used to model parts of the categorisation process.

Introduction

Ordinarily one accepts a distinction between category membership and analogy according to realist terms. In categorical judgements, relating a new representation of an object to some kind of stored category representation, objects are felt to be similar to one another in a way in which those objects in judgements of analogical association are not. If two objects are considered to be members of a category, the classification is real; if they are considered to be analogous, it is not. Consider, for example an analogy between a theory and a building (Lakoff and Johnson 1980): we might talk of "the *foundations* of a theory"; "we might wish to *buttress* a theory with more facts"; "theories that we *construct* can also *collapse*". From an everyday, psychologically realist viewpoint, an igloo and a castle and a skyscraper really are similar in a way that similarities between buildings and theories are not.

Research into analogy and metaphor has accepted this tacit realism. Holyoak and Thagard (1995) describe a world in which "we think we see things as they really are", and analogy is used in order to recycle our existing knowledge of the real world to formulate new bits of 'real' knowledge. Similarly, in the case of metaphor, Ortony (1979) makes a distinction between literal and non-literal similarities: 'encyclopaedias are like dictionaries' is true in a literal (real) way, whereas 'encyclopaedias are like goldmines' is only true in a metaphorical (non-real) way. Whether the notion of literal similarity might be problematic or not is barely examined, since the real problem to be addressed is metaphor. Holyoak and Thagard (1995) offer the comment "A metaphor always connects two domains in a way that goes beyond our normal category structure" (pp 217), whilst giving little indication as to what might constitute this 'normal category structure'. Analogies are defined as being distinct from categories, the nature of which are left unexamined, presumed real.

Once the difficulties of giving an account of categorisation are admitted into the picture, distinctions between analogy and metaphor reliant upon a contrast with categorisation cease to distinguish at all. Analogy is consistently defined in contrast to categorisation (Clement and Gentner, 1991; Holyoak and Thagard, 1995); yet in order to make a contrast definition one needs an account of at least one of the contrasting elements. This we don't have. An analogy is defined as an associative judgement between two things that are in different categories, yet an account of what constitutes an association between two things such that they are members of the same category rather than different categories is not available (Medin, Goldstone and Gentner, 1993)[1]. Moreover, on the best accounts of categorisation, the question of whether two things are members of the same category may not be amenable to any straightforward answer (Medin and Ortony, 1989; Ramscar, 1996). Thus analogy

---

[1] Similarly, Glucksberg and Keysar (1990) argue that metaphorical judgements are the *same* as categorisational judgements ("metaphors are understood as they are - as class inclusion statements", pp17). It is hard to see how categorisation is to illuminate metaphor, since they conclude: "The central problem is to understand categorization." (pp 17).

tends to be defined in contrast to what is in itself a largely undefined process. In the light of this, a definition such as:

> "In an analogy, a familiar domain is used to understand a novel domain in order to highlight important similarities between the domains, or to predict new features of the novel domain." *[We interpret domain here to be equivalent to category]* (Clement and Gentner, 1991)

might be more accurately reformulated along the lines of: 'in analogy, a stored representation is used in order to highlight important similarities between it and a new representation of an object or concept, or to predict new features in the new representation of an object or concept'. None of this would be out of place in a definition of categorisation. The distinction between categorisation and analogy is difficult to draw: here we explore the hypothesis that at cognitive levels of description there may no clear distinction to be made at all.

Models of analogy and categorisation

Another factor which favours the abandoning of traditional distinctions between categorisation and analogy are the strong parallels which can be drawn between theories of analogy and the most plausible models of categorisation. It is becoming more widely accepted that structure plays a major role in category formation (Boyd, 1984; Goldstone, 1994; Kiel, 1989; Medin and Ortony, 1989): analogical reasoning research directly addresses a process which reasons amongst structural networks (Falkenhainer, Forbus and Gentner, 1989; Holyoak and Thagard, 1995). Forbus, Gentner and Law (1995; pp 145-6) propose the following theoretical model of analogical reasoning:

- initial selection dependant upon surface similarity
- analogical similarity is determined by deeper structures

this is strikingly similar to Medin and Ortony's (1989; pp 185-6) knowledge representation scheme for categorisation:

- identification procedure based upon surface features
- classification is determined by deeper structures.

Where research into analogy differs from research into categorisation is in the richness of its process models. A number of detailed, plausible models of the analogical process exist (Forbus, Gentner and Law, 1995; Holyoak and Thagard, 1995): the same cannot be said of categorisation. Medin and Ortony offer little detail as to the mechanisms by which surface identification is governed by deeper structures, or indeed the composition of these deeper structures. In the current study we address directly the question discussed above, of whether analogy can be distinguished from categorisation by contrasting categorisational and analogical processes, and following from this, whether theories of analogy can also be used to model parts of the categorisation process.

Gentner's structure mapping theory

Gentner's (1983) Structure Mapping Theory is an attempt to explain how it is that two domains can be considered analogous, and in particular how it is that correspondences between analogues from two domains can be mapped. Structure mapping proposes that the mapping and inference between two domains can be achieved by assigning correspondences between objects and attributes and then mapping predicates with identical names. In order to do this,

Gentner assumes a predicate like representation distinguishing between *objects, object-attributes* and *relations*. Object-attributes are those predicates that have one argument and describe object properties, e.g. RED(lobster). Relations are divided into a hierarchy of orders, with those predicates with two or more arguments which are used to describe relations between objects, for example UPSETS(stomach,lobster) forming the lowest order, and those predicates describing different levels of relationships between relations forming the higher orders e.g.: CAUSE(UPSETS(stomach,lobster),DRINKS(seltzer,diner)).

The theory itself comprises two parts: *mapping rules*, and the *systematicity principle*. Mapping rules state that (a) attributes of objects are not mapped and (b) relations between objects are preserved. The systematicity principle requires that higher order relations (e.g. CAUSE above) are mapped preferentially, followed by the relations that constitute the higher order arguments.

The question of how analogies are accessed, i.e. how representations are selected in order to allow analogical mapping to take place, was addressed experimentally by Gentner, Ratterman and Forbus (1993). Their study showed that analogical access relied primarily upon surface (feature) matches, and they propose that judgements of analogical similarity can be decomposed into two sub-processes:

- *Accessing* a similar (*base*) situation from memory, based primarily on surface similarity
- Creating a *mapping* from base to target using structural commonalities.

Structural systematicity and categorisation

Since the Gentner, Ratterman and Forbus (1993) studies did not directly address categorisation, a tacitly realist position was adopted in respect of the categories amongst which subjects were to analogise (Ramscar, 1996). The most obvious way in which this realist assumption manifests itself is in the classification of match items (the individual stories within the "Karla the hawk" story sets (Gentner, Ratterman and Forbus 1993)). The question of the categorical status of match items is determined in advance, thus story 1 in figure 1 is classified as a base story, whilst story 3 is defined as its analogue. It is tacitly assumed that the two stories are members of distinct and separate categories, and that they share some kind of analogous link. Whilst the study aimed to explore a wider range of determinants of similarity, the particular correspondences determined by structural systematicity were considered to be indicative of analogous similarities (similarities *between* rather than *within* categories). These assumptions determined the predictions that Gentner *et al* made for their experiments, and the evidence they sought with which to test them.

Gentner *et al*'s study explored criteria of similarity, and discovered that the preferred determinant of analogical similarity in subjects was shared structural systematicity. As a consequence of our hypothesis we predicted that if we were to use Gentner et al's methods and materials to explore categorisation rather than analogy, structural systematicity might also serve as a criterion for the determining category membership. Story 3 in figure 1 was assumed by Gentner et al to be an analogue of story 1. Analogues, as posited in traditional accounts of analogy, are defined in contrast to category members. If subjects were to use structural systematicity as a categorisation determinant, then definitions of analogy which rely on shared structure to contrast analogy with categorisation might need some refinement. If both analogy and categorisation produce the same results, then this might imply some shared, structure based mechanism, or that one process is supervenient upon the other. Accordingly, we experimented by presenting subjects with Gentner *et al*'s materials and asking them to categorise them. Given that Gentner *et al* define the analogical mechanism in terms of structure mapping, we accordingly expected structure mapping to determine categorisation: i.e. Gentner *et al* assume that match items with only structural similarities (i.e. analogues) belong to different categories: we predict that they will be categorised together.

The Experiment

Subjects

The subjects were 20 volunteers, a mixture of postgraduate and undergraduate students from the Artificial Intelligence Department at the University of Edinburgh.

Materials

The basic materials used in this study were the 20 sets of "Karla the hawk" stories (Gentner, Ratterman and Forbus, 1993).[2]

Gentner defines the following taxonomy of similarity relationships between the stories:

• *Literal similarity* matches include both common relational structure and common object descriptions;
• *Surface matches*: based upon common object descriptions, plus some first order relations;
• *Structural similarity*, a match based upon a common system of internal relations;
• *First order matches*, where the only common feature is first order relations;
• *Object only matches*, where stories have only object matches in common.

Each set consists of a base (B), a literally similar story (LS), an analogue (TA - with only structural similarities with the base), a mere-appearance story (MA - with surface and first order commonalities with the base), a false analogy (FA - an analogue of MA), and an object only match story (OO - with only surface commonalities with the base). This allowed for a number of potential groupings according to the classification strategy adopted. Our prediction was that subjects would use structural similarity as their categorical similarity determinant, putting analogues and bases into the same categories (i.e. B, LS and TA together), rather than grouping match items at the object level (i.e. grouping B, LS, MA and OO together).

The sets were modified slightly: in Gentner et al's analogy research questions of the asymmetry and direction of comparisons were clearly fixed (all comparisons were in

relation to the base story). Extra features (a varied mix of objects, attributes and relationships) were added to (or removed from) the base story representations (Figure 1, bold face) which did little to affect analogical similarity judgements. In categorisation judgements, aspects such as symmetry and directionality may be more fluid. As we predicted that structure would be an important determinant of categorical similarity judgements, and noting that the directionality of similarity judgements cannot be fixed in

---

Story 1 - Base story

Once there was a teacher named Mrs Jackson who wanted a salary increase. One day, the principal said that he was increasing his own salary by 20 percent. However, he said there was not enough money to give the teachers a salary increase.

When Mrs Jackson heard this she became so angry that she decided to take revenge. The next day, Mrs Jackson used gasoline to set fire to the principal's office.
Then she went to a bar and got drunk.

Story 2 - Literal similarity

Professor Rosie McGhee very much wanted a raise. One day the provost announced that he was giving himself a raise. However, he said that since money was short, no one else would get a raise this year.

After Professor McGhee heard this she became so upset that she decided to get even. One hour later, Professor McGhee blew up the administration building with dynamite.

Story 3 - True Analogy

McGhee was a sailor who wanted a few days of vacation on land. One day, the captain announced that he would be taking a vacation in the mountains. However, he said everyone else would have to remain on the ship.

After McGhee heard this he became so upset that he decided to get revenge. Within an hour McGhee blew up the captain's cabin with dynamite.

Story 4 - Mere appearance: (First order commonalities)

Professor McGhee very much wanted a raise. One day she became so impatient that she used kerosene to burn down the administration building.

After the fire, the provost announced that he was giving himself a raise. However, he said that due to the fire, there was not enough money to give one to anyone else.

Story 5 - False Analogy

McGhee was a sailor who wanted a few days of vacation on land. One day McGhee became so impatient that he tried to blow up the captain's cabin using dynamite.

After this incident, the captain announced that he would be taking a vacation in the mountains. However, he said everyone else would have to remain on board to repair the ship.

Story 6 - Mere appearance: (Object commonalities only)

A teacher once thought that she deserved a pay rise. She asked the principal when her rise was due. She was wearing her best suit. The principal told her that rises were decided by the governors.

Figure 1: Sample stories from Gentner, Ratterman and Forbus (1993) - the text in bold type illustrates extra structure added by Gentner at al to the base stories only.

---

[2] Many thanks to Dedre Gentner for providing the story sets.

categorisation, we accordingly removed Gentner et al's extra features from 65% of the story sets (G- sets: in these, for example, the base / literal similarity relationship were symmetrical), and retained the extra features (and any attendant asymmetries) in 35% of stories (G+ sets).

Procedure

Subjects were given 10 mixed sets of 6 stories[3] and asked to work through them a set at a time. Both sets and stories were presented in randomised order. For each set, they read through each story a number of times in order to familiarise themselves with its content. Subjects were then asked to "Group the stories into the categories that seemed most natural and appropriate to you. These groups can range from putting every member of the story set into the same group, to putting each story into a group on its own." When subjects had made their categorisation decisions, they physically grouped each set of stories by pasting them onto a large sheet of paper and encircling each group in ink. Subjects were then re-presented with their groupings a set at a time, asked to give each group with two or more members

a simple descriptive name, and then to write a few sentences explaining what caused them to classify each named group of stories together[4].

Results

For each story set the groups formed by each subject's classifications were analysed. The pattern of groupings which emerged fell broadly into 5 types (figure 2). Similarities across groupings (i.e. similarity shared by every member of a two or more member group across a categorised story set) according to Gentner et al's taxonomy of similarities could be identified in 96.5% of groupings. Of these, in 5% of cases the stories were grouped according to types 6 and 7. The only similarities across groupings in these types are that the stories in the individual groups had only objects in common. In 4% the stories were classified according to type 3, where the across grouping similarity was shared first order relations. In 79.5% of cases subjects grouped using type 1. Here the only similarity across groupings was a network of systematic causal relations. The full output and incidence of the types is given in Table 1.

Classification Criterion		% of Total
Systematic network of relations in common - Type 1		79.5 %
1 B LS TA	2 FA MA	3 OO
Systematic network of relations in common - Type 2 *(Base classified separately)*		8 %
1 LS TA	2 FA MA	3 B 4 OO
First order relations in common - Type 3		4 %
1 B LS TA FA MA	2 OO	
Only object similarities in common - Types 6 & 7		5 %
1 MA LS B OO	2 FA MA	
1 B OO	2 LS MA	3 TA FA
No classification possible - Types 4, 5, 8 , 9 10		3.5 %
1 B LS MA	2 FA TA	3. OO
1 B TA	2 FA MA	3 LS 4 OO
1 B MA FA	2 LS TA	3 OO
1 B LS TA OO	2 FA MA	
1 FA B TA MA	2 LS	

Figure 2: Output patterns from the categorisation task, showing the groups formed and criteria established. The stories are labelled according to Gentner's taxonomy of similarity (defined above): B = Base; LS = Literal Similarity; TA = True Analogy; FA = False Analogy; MA = Mere Appearance; OO = Object Only match.

	Story Set Type		
Grouping Type	*G+*	*G-*	*% of total*
Type 1	68 %	86.5%	79.5%
Type 2	20 %	0.5%	8%
Other	12%	13%	12.5%

Figure 3: Classification strategies according to set type.

8% of groupings were according to type 2, where the base was put into a category on its own, with the only similarity across other groupings being shared structure. This type was only found once amongst those sets from which Gentner *et al*'s extra features had been removed (0.5% of G- sets; figure 3). The G+ sets, those with added features in the base, were sets 5; 7; 10; 12; 15; 17; and 20. Of these: in set 5 and set 20 the extra features involved higher order relations; in sets 7 10, 15 they involved first order relations; and in sets 12 17 the extra features were objects. 20% of these sets were classified as type 2, with the bulk of these classifications being in the sets with extra higher order relations (figure 4).

	Higher-order relations Sets		Objects only Sets		1st order relations Sets		
	5	**20**	**12**	**17**	**7**	**10**	**15**
Type 1	7	2	7	7	11	9	5
Type 2	9	2	1		2		
Type 3	1	1			1	2	
Types 6 & 7	2						
Types 4, 5, 8, 9 & 10							1
Totals	19	5	8	7	14	11	6

Figure 4: Classification data for the G+ sets.

---

[3]Given the sample size, we concentrated on sets 1 - 10; sets 11 - 20 were used to a more limited extent to check for any marked variations in the data being produced.

---

[4]This data is currently being analysed, and will not be considered here.

349

Story Sets

	1	2	3	4	5+	6	7+	8	9	10+	11	12+	13	14	15+	16	17+	18	19	20+
A					1	1		1	1	1			1	1	1		1	1		
B	3	3	1	1	2	1	1	1	1	1										
C	1	1	1	1	2	1	1	1	1	1										
D	1	1	1	1	2		1				1	2							1	2
E	1	1	1	1	2	1	2	1	1	3										
F	4	1	1	1	2	1	1				1	1					5			
G		8			6	7		1	1				1	6	1		1	1		
H	5	1	1	1	2		1				1	1							1	1
I	1	1	1	1	1		1				1	1							1	2
J	1		1		8	1		1	1		1			1			1	1		
K						1	1	1	1			1	1	1		1	1			1
L	7	1	1	1	2	1	1	1	1	1										
M	1	1	1	1	1	1	1				1	1					1			
N	1	1	1	1	5	2	2				1	1					1			
O						1	1		1	1	1		1	1	1		1		1	
P	6	3	1	1	1		3				7	1							1	3
Q					2	1		1	1	1			2	1	1		1	1		
R	1	10	1	1	1	1	1	1	1	1										
S	1	1	1	1	1	1	1	1	1	1										
T					3	7		9	1	3			7		7	7	1	1		

Subjects

Table 1: Output incidence of subject groupings. Each subject was given 10 story sets (each row represents one subject): the type of grouping is indicated by the type number in the story set column (see also figure 2).
Subject T produced some rather strange results: this was explained by examining the reasons T gave for her groupings, in which she explained that she was exploring a different heuristic for each story set.

Discussion

Our study explored the hypothesis that mechanisms normally considered to be analogical could in fact support categorisation tasks. The most important finding here is the role that shared structure plays in categorisation judgements. 79.5% of the groupings formed by our subjects had only shared systematic structure (traditionally defined as analogy) as a common feature amongst members of the categories formed. In contrast, only 5% of groupings produced had common object descriptions as the common similarity across categories. Traditionally categorisation models have concentrated on object descriptions, making use of very representationally-simple attribute-value lists (Murphy and Medin, 1985), whereas analogy research has examined relationships between highly structured representations (considering the influence of attributes, relations and higher-order relations in judgements of similarity).

The argument for abandoning the current de facto distinction between categorical and analogical associations of objects is twofold: firstly, that the standard distinctions (Clement and Gentner, 1991; Holyoak and Thagard, 1995) between analogy and categorisation actually failed to distinguish between them; and secondly, that by removing the distinction, understanding of the factors which govern mappings between representations that have been gleaned

from analogy research might help illuminate categorisation questions (Ramscar, Lee and Pain, in press). Our results provide evidence that structures, and more pertinently Gentner's structural systematicity, rather than features, are the key to categorical similarity in this instance: this tallies with other evidence, such as Rips (1989) who found that subjects were reluctant to change classifications as a result of feature changes alone.

Our argument is supported not only by the proportion of categorisations that were determined by commonalities between internal structures in the stories, but also by the effects of added structure in the G+ sets where the added structure was a higher-order structure. These might at first appear to present a problem for our attempt to use a structure mapping analysis to model these categorisation judgements. In these cases, Gentner's base stories were put into separate categories from stories to which they were supposed to be literally similar, which were in turn categorised alongside their supposed analogues (both of which were supposed to share structures with the base).

These results can be attributed to the effects of directionality and symmetry upon similarity judgements. Whilst Gentner, Ratterman and Forbus (1993) found that subjects judged literally similar (LS) stories to be very similar to bases, and analogues less so, they did not consider the effect of reversing the directionality and symmetry of the comparisons, for example comparing the base and analogue stories similarity to the LS. Neither did they consider the judging of cumulative similarity, where dissimilarities are also taken into account. During this process, the structural dissimilarities of the base versus the LS and analogue appear from our results to be clearly relevant, whereas the object differences of the analogue versus the LS and base do not. This maximisation of important similarities (i.e. structure matches) relative to lesser dissimilarities (i.e. object matches) amongst groupings appears to play a crucial role in categorisation in this study. Whilst it might be argued that all we have shown here is that subjects will form categories of analogies, such an interpretation (in so far as we can make sense of it) does not affect our argument that it is structure that determines the content of these categories.

All of this strengthens our dubiety with respect to the separation of analogy from categorisation. We should note, however, that asserting that analogy cannot be distinguished from categorisation at a cognitive level is not the same thing as arguing that analogy is the same thing as categorisation. Categorisation is such a central cognitive process that it is hard to see how it can be reduced to a single process (c.f. Goldstone, 1994). It may well be that any given manifest reasoning process - such as rule following or metaphor - might be able to illuminate some aspect of categorisation: i.e. can provide the constraints necessary to determining certain categorical similarities. We argue that the analogical process cannot be distinguished from the 'categorisation process' at a cognitive level. Our hypothesis is that analogy is supervenient upon an important part of the classification process, and that as such analogy research is capable of illuminating[5] some categorisation tasks, for instance, the way in which structural systematicity can determine both analogical and category judgements.

Acknowledgements

Many thanks to Paul Brna, John Lee and Richard White for their contribution to this work, and to Shari Trewin and Robin James for comments on earlier drafts of this paper.

We would also like to acknowledge the helpful and useful comments provided by the anonymous reviewers of this paper.

This work was funded in part by EPSRC Grant GR/J76897.

---

[5]For example, one problem faced by all cognitive theories of categorisation is explaining typicality effects (e.g. Rosch, 1978); how they occur, or even, how the existence of typicality effects can be accommodated by a given model. Gentner et al (1993) have shown how differing aspects of similarity - structural versus surface - affect recall, soundness ratings and judgements of similarity. By showing that judgements of categorical similarity and the recall of category members can be reliant upon different representational features (surface attributes for recall, structural systematicity for similarity and typicality), we might be able to begin to present a model of the categorisation process which can explain and account for at least some typicality effects.

References

Boyd, R. (1984) Natural kinds, homeostasis, and the limits of essentialism. Paper presented at Cornell University

Falkenhainer, B., Forbus, K.D. and Gentner, D. (1989) The structure mapping engine: an algorithm and examples. *Artificial Intelligence*, **41**, 1-63

Clement C.A, and Gentner, D. (1991) Systematicity as a selection constraint in analogical mapping *Cognitive Science*, 15: 89-132.

Gentner, D. (1983) Structure-mapping: a theoretical framework for analogy. *Cognitive Science*, 7: 155-170.

Forbus K, Gentner, D, and Law , K (1995) MAC/FAC: A model of similarity based retrieval *Cognitive Science* 19:2:141-205

Gentner, D Ratterman, M.J. and Forbus, K. (1993) The roles of similarity in transfer. *Cognitive Psychology* 25: 524-575

Goldstone, R.L. (1994) The role of similarity in categorization: providing a groundwork. *Cognition*, 52: 125-157

Glucksberg, S. and Keysar, B. (1990) Understanding metaphorical comparisons: Beyond Similarity. *Psychological Review*, **97**: 1: 3-18

Holyoak, K.J. and Thagard, P. (1995) *Mental Leaps*. MIT Press, Cambridge, Ma.

Kiel, F.C. (1989) *Concepts, kinds and cognitive development*. MIT Press, Cambridge, Mass.

Lakoff, G and Johnson, M (1980) *Metaphors we live by*. University of Chicago Press, Chicago, Ill.

Medin, D and Ortony, A. (1989) What is psychological essentialism? In S. Vosniardou and A. Ortony (Eds) *Similarity and analogical reasoning*. Cambridge University Press.

Medin, D., Goldstone, R. and Gentner, D. (1993) Respects for similarity. *Psychological review*, **100**:2:254-278.

Murphy, G.L. and Medin, D.L. (1985) The role of theories in conceptual coherence. *Psychological review*, **92**, 289 - 316

Ortony, A. (1979) The role of similarity in similes and metaphor. In Ortony, A. (Ed) *Metaphor and thought*. Cambridge University Press.

Ramscar M.J.A. (1996) Judgements of association: connecting cognitive theories of analogy and categorisation - DAI Research Report, Department of Artificial Intelligence, University of Edinburgh, Scotland.

Ramscar, M. J. A, Lee, J. R. and Pain, H (*in press*) A classification-based methodology for the integration of agent views within design systems. To appear in *Design Studies*, Vol. 17, Autumn 1996 .

Rips, L.J. (1989) Similarity, typicality and Categorization. In S. Vosniardou and A. Ortony (Eds) *Similarity and analogical reasoning*. Cambridge University Press.

Rosch, E. (1978) *Cognition and Categorisation*. Lawrence Earlbaum Assoc., New Jersey.

LISA: A Computational Model of Analogical Inference and Schema Induction

John E. Hummel and **Keith J. Holyoak**
Department of Psychology
University of California, Los Angeles
405 Hilgard Ave.
Los Angeles, CA 90095-1563
jhummel@psych.ucla.edu   holyoak@psych.ucla.edu

Abstract

The relationship between analogy and schema induction is widely acknowledged and constitutes an important motivation for developing computational models of analogical mapping. However, most models of analogical mapping provide no clear basis for supporting schema induction. We describe LISA (Hummel & Holyoak, 1996), a recent model of analog retrieval and mapping that is explicitly designed to provide a platform for schema induction and other forms of inference. LISA represents predicates and their arguments (i.e., objects or propositions) as patterns of activation distributed over units representing semantic primitives. These representations are actively (dynamically) bound into propositions by synchronizing oscillations in their activation: Arguments fire in synchrony with the case roles to which they are bound, and out of synchrony with other case roles and arguments. By activating propositions in LTM, these patterns drive analog retrieval and mapping. This approach to analog retrieval and mapping accounts for numerous findings in human analogical reasoning (Hummel & Holyoak, 1996). Augmented with a capacity for intersection discovery and unsupervised learning, the architecture supports analogical inference and schema induction as a natural consequence. We describe LISA's account of schema induction and inference, and present some preliminary simulation results.

Schemas, Induction and Analogy

Cognitive scientists have long appealed to the notion of *schemas* to explain many aspects of human thinking (see Rumelhart, 1980). A schema is a generalized knowledge structure that characterizes the relationships applicable to some class of objects or events. For example, a "permission schema" (Cheng & Holyoak, 1985) might describe the class of situations in which some precondition must be satisfied before permission to perform an act is granted (e.g., one must be over 21 to drink alcohol); a "combustion engine schema" might specify the general relationships among the parts and operation of a combustion engine. Schemas support inferences. For example, a reasoner could use the permission schema to infer that a teenage beer drinker would be in violation of the rule; a reasoner could use the combustion engine schema to anticipate that a Honda 1.6 liter engine will not run after the gas line has been cut (even if that person has never actually cut the gas line of a Honda 1.6 liter engine). An essential property of schemas is that they are *relational structures* rather than simple lists of features or properties. That is,

they explicitly specify how the properties of a class are related to one another: the (legal) drinking of alcohol is *contingent upon* being over 21; the gas line *carries* the gasoline to the carburetor.

An important question regarding schemas concerns their origin: How do we induce a general schema from experience with specific objects and events? As Holland, Holyoak, Nisbett and Thagard (1986) have emphasized, induction cannot proceed by blind search. Rather, it entails discovering systematic correspondences among the elements of specific known instances (objects or events) and using those correspondences to guide the induction of generalized schemas. For example, consider inducing a simple schema describing situations in which a man loves a woman, the woman likes flowers, and the man gives the woman flowers, based on the examples: (1) Jim loves Mary, Mary likes roses, and Jim gives Mary roses, and (2) Bill loves Susan, Susan likes tulips, and Bill gives Susan tulips. To generate the schema from the examples, it is first necessary to appreciate that Jim corresponds to Bill rather than Mary, that loves corresponds to loves rather than gives, and so forth. Knowledge of these correspondences is crucial for knowing which elements to generalize over.

One way to discover the appropriate correspondences is to draw an analogy between the instances. For this reason, it has been argued that analogical reasoning plays an important role in schema induction (Gentner, 1989; Holyoak & Thagard, 1995). Analogical reasoning generally involves using a relatively well-understood *source* analog to guide inferences about a less familiar *target* analog. This process has four major components: (1) using the target to retrieve a potentially useful source from memory; (2) mapping elements of the source onto elements of the target to identify systematic correspondences; (3) using the mapping to draw inferences about the target; and (4) inducing a generalized schema that captures the commonalties between the source and target (e.g., Carbonell, 1983; Gentner, 1989; Gick & Holyoak, 1983).

Numerous models of analogy have been developed that collectively address the stages of analog retrieval, mapping, and inference (e.g., Falkenhainer, Forbus & Gentner, 1989; Forbus, Gentner & Law, 1995; Halford et al., 1994; Hofstadter & Mitchell, 1994; Holyoak & Thagard, 1989; Thagard, Holyoak, Nelson & Gochfeld, 1990). On the face of it, such models provide a basis for modeling schema induction (because they provide a computational account of how to determine the correspondences between elements). However, this apparent connection, while widely recognized, has generally not been computationally realized. In part, this shortcoming reflects the way these models represent analog elements (Hummel & Holyoak, 1996). Most models of analogical mapping represent analogs either as collections of symbols composed into propositions (e.g., Falkenhainer et. al, 1989; Keane, 1995) or as localist units in a connectionist network (e.g., Holyoak & Thagard, 1989; Thagard et. al, 1990). Representations of this type can readily capture structure, making them very attractive as a basis for analogical mapping (an inherently structural problem). But lacking any detailed semantic decomposition, such representations are inadequate for generalization and building abstractions (basic components of schema induction). In general, the twin requirements of structure sensitivity and flexible generalization pose a serious challenge to the design of an architecture that aims to integrate analogical mapping with schema induction.

We have recently developed a computational model of analogy based on very different assumptions about the representation of analog elements and the operations that discover correspondences between them (Hummel & Holyoak, 1996; see Hummel & Holyoak, 1992, and Hummel, Meltz, Thompson, & Holyoak, 1994, for precursors). The heart of the model is an architecture for representing structured information in a distributed fashion, capturing both the structure-sensitivity of a localist or symbolic representation and the flexible generalization provided by a distributed connectionist representation. The model, called *LISA* (*Learning and Inference with Schemas and Analogies*), is designed to provide an integrated account of all four major components of analogy use, from retrieval to schema induction. We have recently shown that LISA accounts for numerous findings concerning human analog retrieval and mapping (Hummel & Holyoak, 1996). This paper describes some preliminary results using LISA for schema induction and inference.

The LISA Model

Analog Representation, Retrieval and Mapping

We will briefly sketch the LISA model and its approach to analog retrieval and mapping. These operations are described in detail (along with simulation results) by Hummel and Holyoak (1996). The core of LISA's architecture is a system for actively (i.e., dynamically) binding roles to their fillers in working memory (WM) and encoding those bindings in LTM. LISA uses synchrony of firing for dynamic binding in WM (Hummel & Holyoak, 1992; Shastri & Ajjenagadde, 1993). Case roles and objects are represented in WM as distributed patterns of activation on a collection of *semantic units* (small circles in Figure 1); case roles and objects fire in synchrony when they are bound together and out of synchrony when they are not.

Every proposition is encoded in LTM by a hierarchy of *structure units* (see Figures 1 and 2). At the bottom of the hierarchy are *predicate* and *object* units. Each predicate unit locally codes one case role of one predicate. For example, *love1* represents the first (agent) role of the predicate "love", and has bidirectional excitatory connections to all the semantic units representing that role (e.g., *emotion1*,

strong1, *positive1*, etc.); *love2* represents the patient role and is connected to the corresponding semantic units (e.g., *emotion2*, *strong2*, *positive2*, etc.). Semantically-related predicates share units in corresponding roles (e.g., *love1* and *like1* share many units), making the semantic similarity of different predicates explicit. Object units are just like predicate units except that they are connected to semantic units describing things rather than roles. For example, the object unit *Mary* might be connected to units for *human*, *adult*, *female*, etc., whereas *rose* might be connected to *plant*, *flower*, and *fragrant*.

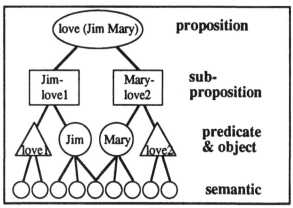

Figure 1: Illustration of the LISA representation of the proposition "love (Jim Mary)".

Sub-proposition units (*SPs*) bind roles to objects in LTM. For example, "love (Jim Mary)" would be represented by two SPs, one binding Jim to the agent of loving, and the other binding Mary to the patient role (Figure 1). The *Jim+agent* SP has bidirectional excitatory connections with *Jim* and *love1*, and the *Mary+patient* SP has connections with *Mary* and *love2*. Proposition (*P*) units reside at the top of the hierarchy and have bidirectional excitatory connections with the corresponding SP units. P units serve a dual role in hierarchical structures (such as "Sam knows that Jim loves Mary"), and behave differently according to whether they are currently serving as the "parent" of their own proposition or the "child" (i.e., argument) of another (see Hummel & Holyoak, 1996). It is important to emphasize that structure units do not encode semantic content in any direct way. Rather, they serve only to store that content in LTM, and to generate (and respond to) the corresponding synchrony patterns on the semantic units.

The final component of LISA's architecture is a set of *mapping connections* between structure units of the same type in different analogs. Every P unit in one analog shares a mapping connection with every P unit in every other analog; likewise, SPs share connections across analogs, as do objects and predicates. For the purposes of mapping and retrieval, analogs are divided into two mutually exclusive sets: a *driver* and one or more *recipients*. Retrieval and mapping are controlled by the driver. (There is no necessary linkage between the driver/recipient distinction and the more familiar source/target distinction.) LISA performs mapping as a form of guided pattern matching. As P units in the driver become active, they generate (via their SP, predicate and object units) patterns on the semantic units (one pattern for each role-argument binding). The semantic units are shared by all propositions, so the patterns generated by one proposition will activate one or more similar propositions in LTM (analogical access) or in WM (analogical mapping). Mapping differs from retrieval solely by the addition of the modifiable mapping connections. During mapping, the weights on the mapping connections grow larger when the units they link are active simultaneously, permitting LISA to learn the correspondences generated during retrieval. These connection weights also serve to constrain subsequent memory access. By the end of a simulation run, corresponding structure units will have large positive weights on their mapping connections, and non-corresponding units will have strongly negative weights.

Inference and Schema Induction

Augmented with intersection discovery and unsupervised learning, LISA's approach to mapping supports inference and schema induction as a natural consequence. Consider the previous "love and flowers" analogs (Figure 2). During mapping, corresponding elements in the two analogs will become active simultaneously. For instance, "love (Jim Mary)" in the driver, will activate "love (Bill Susan)" in the recipient. Corresponding elements (such as *Jim* and *Bill*) will fire in synchrony with one another, and non-corresponding elements (*Jim* and *Susan*) will fire out of synchrony (Figure 3a). *Jim* shares *male* with *Bill*, and *Mary* shares *female* with *Susan*, so a natural proposition to induce from these correspondences is "loves (male, female)" (Figure 3b). To induce this part of the schema, it is necessary to (a) make explicit what corresponding elements have in common, and (b) encode those common elements into LTM as a new proposition.

LISA performs (a) by means of a simple type of intersection discovery. Although we have described the activation of semantic units only from the perspective of the

driver, the recipient analog also feeds activation to the semantic units. The activation of a semantic unit is a linear function of its inputs, so any semantic unit that is common to both the driver and recipient will receive input from both and become roughly twice as active as any semantic unit receiving input from only one analog. Common semantic elements are thus tagged as such by their activation values.

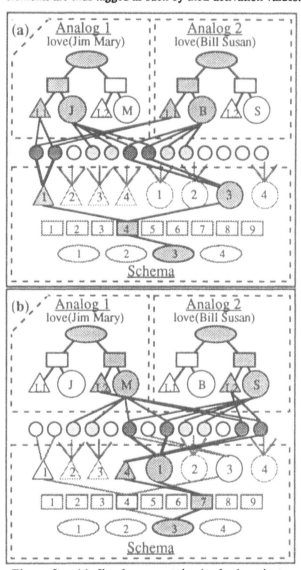

Figure 3: (a) Jim+love-agent in Analog1 activates Bill+love-agent in Analog 2. In the Schema, predicate unit 1 is recruited for love agent, and object unit 3 is recruited for the intersection of Jim and Bill ("human" and "male"). SP 4 is recruited for human male (object 3) bound to love-agent (predicate 1). Proposition unit 3 begins to be recruited. (b) Mary+love-patient in Analog 1 activates Susan+love-patient in Analog 2. Predicate 4 is recruited for love-patient; object 1 is recruited for "human" and "female". SP 7 is recruited for the binding of predicate 4 and object 1. Proposition unit 3 now codes "love(human male, human female)".

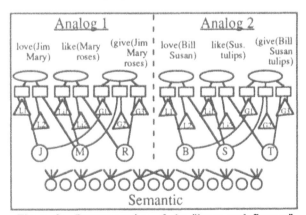

Figure 2: Representation of the "loves and flowers" analogy. Shapes (triangle, rectangle, etc.) correspond to classes of units as in Fig. 1. Not all connections are shown.

These common elements are encoded into LTM by means of an unsupervised learning algorithm. In addition to structure units representing the known source and target analogs, LISA has a collection of *unrecruited* structure units (i.e., units with random connections to one another and to the semantic units) that reside together in a third "schema analog" (Figure 3). Unrecruited predicate and object units have input thresholds that only allow them to receive input from highly active semantic units -- that is, semantic units that are common to both the driver and recipient analogs. Such semantic units are depicted in dark gray in Figure 3. Without the aid of an external teacher, these unrecruited schema units learn to respond to these common elements of the known analogs. Simultaneously, unrecruited SP units learn to respond to specific conjunctions of predicate, object, and (in the case of hierarchical propositions) P units, and unrecruited P units learn to respond to specific combinations of SP units. The result is that propositions describing the common elements of the known analogs are encoded into LTM as a third analog -- a schema. Figure 3 illustrates this process for one proposition in the "love and flowers" analogy.

As we will describe more fully below, LISA accomplishes analogical inference by the same unsupervised learning algorithm as used for schema induction, except that the unrecruited units reside not in a completely separate analog (the to-be-induced schema), but in the target itself.

Simulations

Schema Induction

To simulate the induction of the "love and flowers" schema, we gave LISA the following analogs (schematized in Figures 2 and 3):

Analog 1:	Analog 2:
love (Jim Mary)	love (Bill Susan)
like (Mary roses)	like (Susan tulips)
give (Jim Mary roses)	give (Bill Susan tulips)

Every object (person or flower) was represented by five semantic units. All people shared the features *person*, *Jim* and *Bill* shared *male1* and *male2*, and Mary and Susan shared *female1* and *female2*. Each person also had two unique features, so that no two people were identical. The flowers (*roses* and *tulips*) were each connected to five semantic units, three of which they shared. The predicates were represented by four semantic units each per case role. *Love* shared two units with *like* (*emotion* and *positive*) but only one with *give* (*positive*). There was also a third analog containing only "unrecruited" units -- i.e., units with initially random connections to one another and (in the case of object and predicate units) to the semantic units. This analog served as the schema-learning analog. It had 10 object units, 15 predicate units, 15 SP units, and 10 P units.

Every proposition in Analogs 1 and 2 was selected (activated) twice during the simulation run. As indices of mapping and schema induction, we recorded both the final values of the cross-analog mapping weights and the final values of the (initially random) connections in the third,

schema analog. By the end of the run, there was one object unit in the schema analog that had learned large positive weights (i.e., > 0.7) to the semantic units *person*, *male1* and *male2*, and very small weights (< 0.2) to all other semantic units. This unit had been recruited to represent "male person" and accordingly had developed strong mapping weights to *Jim* and *Bill* and negative weights to all other objects. A different unit had been recruited to represent "female person" and a third to represent "generic flower." These units had strong mapping weights to *Mary* and *Susan* and to *roses* and *tulips*, respectively. The predicates recruited units in an analogous fashion, as did the SP and P units. Although this was only a "toy" example, LISA's performance with it suggests that it can induce a relational schema given specific analogs as examples.

As a more challenging test of LISA's ability to induce schemas from examples, we gave it simplified descriptions of Gick and Holyoak's (1980) "tumor" and "fortress" stories. These stories describe, respectively, situations in which a doctor uses many weak rays (rather than a single powerful one) to destroy a stomach tumor, and a general deploys several small groups of soldiers (rather than one large group) to capture a fortress. Presented with stories of this type and given a task in which they must map them onto one another, people will induce a more general "convergence schema" describing what the stories have in common (Gick & Holyoak, 1983).

We gave LISA these stories in a simplified eight-proposition format and ran them in the same general manner as for the "loves and flowers" analogy. As was the case for the previous example, LISA induced a schema by recruiting one structure unit for each element of the two analogs, abstracting over common elements (e.g., recruiting a single new unit for both "tumor" and "fortress", which play analogous roles in the two stories), and mapping the abstracted (schema) elements to the corresponding original story elements.

Analogical Inference

The same unsupervised learning algorithm that supports schema induction can be used in LISA to perform inductive inference by a form of "copy with substitution and generation" (Falkenhainer et al., 1989; Holyoak, Novick & Melz, 1994). Here, known elements or relations in one analog are used to "fill gaps" in a less familiar analog. Consider, for example, this "uncle" analogy, which we gave LISA:

Analog 1:	Analog 2:
father (Abe Bill)	father (Adam Bob)
brother (Charles Abe)	brother (Cary Adam)
uncle (Charles Bill)	

In Analog 1, Charles is Bill's uncle, a fact that is explicitly stated. In Analog 2, Cary is likewise the uncle of Bob, but this fact is not explicitly stated. We allowed LISA to map the two propositions in Analog 2 onto Analog 1, establishing the correspondences (as mapping connection weights) between Adam and Abe, Bob and Bill, and Cary and Charles.

We then allowed LISA to map Analog 1 back onto Analog 2. When the *father* and *brother* propositions in Analog 1 became active, they simply activated the corresponding propositions in Analog 2, reinforcing the established mappings. But when the *uncle* proposition became active in Analog 1, there was no corresponding proposition in Analog 2. Instead, Analog 2 had a collection of unrecruited units of the type used for schema induction in the previous examples. Because there were no predicate units pre-dedicated for the uncle relation, two unrecruited predicate units learned (without supervision) to respond to the two places of the uncle relation. The unit recruited for *uncle1* (the agent of the uncle relation) fired in synchrony with the *Cary* unit (because *Cary* was being driven by *Charles*, which was firing in synchrony with *uncle1* in Analog 1). As a result, an SP unit was recruited to respond to the conjunction of *Cary* and *uncle1*. Similarly, a predicate unit was recruited for *uncle2* and an SP unit was recruited for the conjunction *Bob-uncle2*. Finally, a P unit was recruited to respond to these two new SPs. Each of these units developed strong mapping connection weights to the corresponding units in Analog 1. The result of these operations was that LISA "inferred" that Cary is the uncle of Bob and stored this inference in LTM as a new proposition in Analog 2.

Conclusion

LISA provides a solution to the problem (forcefully posed by Fodor & Pylyshyn, 1988) of representing knowledge over a distributed set of units while preserving systematic relational structure. Like previous models based on symbolic or localist-connectionist representations, LISA is able to retrieve and map analogs based in large part on structural constraints. But in addition, LISA is able to capitalize on its distributed representations of meaning to integrate analogical mapping with a flexible generalization mechanism. This induction engine can make analogical inferences about a specific target analog; the same basic mechanism can create new schemas by finding and coding the structured intersection between multiple analogs. LISA thus provides an explanation of why people appear to induce generalized schemas as a natural consequence of using analogies (e.g., Novick & Holyoak, 1991; Ross & Kennedy, 1990). Analogical reasoning provides both the input and the trigger for inductive learning.

Achnowledgements

This work was supported by NSF Grant SBR-9511504.

References

Carbonell, J. G. (1983). Learning by analogy: Formulating and generalizing plans from past experience. In R. S. Michalski, J. G. Carbonell, & T. M. Mitchell (Eds.), *Machine learning: An artificial intelligence approach* (pp. 137-161). Palo Alto, CA: Tioga Press.

Cheng, P. W., & Holyoak, K. J. (1985). Pragmatic reasoning schemas. *Cognitive Psychology, 17*, 391-416.

Falkenhainer, B., Forbus, K. D., & Gentner, D. (1989). The structure-mapping engine: Algorithm and examples. *Artificial Intelligence, 41*, 1-63.

Fodor, J. A., & Pylyshyn, Z. W. (1988). Connectionism and cognitive architecture: A critical analysis. In S. Pinker & J. Mehler (Eds.), *Connections and symbols* (pp. 3-71). Cambridge, MA: MIT Press.

Forbus, K. D., Gentner, D., & Law, K. (1995). MAC/FAC: A model of similarity-based retrieval. *Cognitive Science, 19*, 141-205.

Gentner, D. (1989). The mechanisms of analogical learning. In S. Vosniadou & A. Ortony (Eds.), *Similarity and analogical reasoning* (pp. 199-241). New York: Cambridge University Press.

Gick, M. L., & Holyoak, K. J. (1980). Analogical problem solving. *Cognitive Psychology, 12*, 1-38.

Gick, M. L., & Holyoak, K. J. (1983). Schema induction and analogical transfer. *Cognitive Psychology, 15*, 306-355.

Grossberg, S. (1971). Pavlovian pattern learning by nonlinear neural networks. *Proceedings of the National Academy of Science, 68*, 828-831. Washington, D.C.: National Academy of Science.

Halford, G. S., Wilson, W. H., Guo, J., Gayler, R. W., Wiles, J., & Stewart, J. E. M. (1994). Connectionist implications for processing capacity limitations in analogies. In K. J. Holyoak & J. A. Barnden (Eds.), *Advances in connectionist and neural computation theory, Vol. 2: Analogical connections* (pp. 363-415). Norwood, NJ: Ablex.

Hofstadter, D. R., & Mitchell, M. (1994). An overview of the Copycat project. In K. J. Holyoak & J. A. Barnden (Eds.), *Advances in connectionist and neural computation theory, Vol. 2: Analogical connections* (pp. 31-112). Norwood, NJ: Erlbaum.

Holland, J. H., Holyoak, K. J., Nisbett, R. E., & Thagard, P. (1986). *Induction: Processes of inference, learning, and discovery*. Cambridge, MA: MIT Press.

Holyoak, K. J., Novick, L. R., & Melz, E. R. (1994). Component processes in analogical transfer: Mapping, pattern completion, and adaptation. In K. J. Holyoak & J. A. Barnden (Eds.), *Advances in connectionist and neural computation theory, Vol. 2: Analogical connections* (pp. 130-180). Norwood, NJ: Ablex.

Holyoak, K. J., & Thagard, P. (1989). Analogical mapping by constraint satisfaction. *Cognitive Science, 13*, 295-355.

Holyoak, K. J., & Thagard, P. (1995). *Mental leaps: Analogy in creative thought*. Cambridge, MA: MIT Press.

Hummel, J. E., & Holyoak, K. J. (1992). Indirect analogical mapping. In *Proceedings of the Fourteenth Annual Conference of the Cognitive Science Society* (pp. 516-521). Hillsdale, NJ: Erlbaum.

Hummel, J. E., & Holyoak, K. J. (1996). Distributed representations of structure: A theory of analogical access and mapping. Manuscript submitted for publication.

Hummel, J. E., Melz, E. R., Thompson, J., & Holyoak, K. J. (1994). Mapping hierarchical structures with synchrony for binding: Preliminary investigations. In A.

Ram & K. Eiselt (Eds.), *Proceedings of the Sixteenth Annual Conference of the Cognitive Science Society* (pp. 433-438). Hillsdale, NJ: Erlbaum.

Keane, M. T. (1995). On order effects in analogical mapping: Predicting human error using IAM. In J. D. Moore & J. F. Lehman (Eds.), *Proceedings of the Seventeenth Annual Conference of the Cognitive Science Society* (pp. 449-454). Hillsdale, NJ: Erlbaum.

Novick, L. R.., & Holyoak, K. J. (1991). Mathematical problem solving by analogy. *Journal of Experimental Psychology: Learning, Memory, and Cognition, 17,* 398-415.

Ross, B. H., & Kennedy, P. T. (1990). Generalizing from the use of earlier examples in problem solving. *Journal of Experimental Psychology: Learning, Memory, and Cognition, 16,* 42-55.

Rumelhart, D. E. (1980). Schemata: The building blocks of cognition. In R. Spiro, B. Bruce, & W. Brewer (Eds.), *Theoretical issues in reading comprehension* (pp. 33-58). Hillsdale, NJ: Erlbaum.

Shastri, L., & Ajjanagadde, V. (1993). From simple associations to systematic reasoning: A connectionist representation of rules, variables and dynamic bindings using temporal synchrony. *Behavioral and Brain Sciences, 16,* 417-494.

Thagard, P., Holyoak, K. J., Nelson, G., & Gochfeld, D. (1990). Analog retrieval by constraint satisfaction. *Artificial Intelligence, 46,* 259-310.

357

Alignability and Attribute Importance in Choice

Patricia G. Lindemann and **Arthur B. Markman**
Department of Psychology
406 Schermerhorn Hall
Columbia University
New York, NY 10027
pgl@psych.columbia.edu
markman@psych.columbia.edu

Abstract

When people choose between two alternatives, like between two colleges, some of the available information is comparable across the alternatives (alignable) and some is noncomparable (nonalignable). For example, when comparing colleges, the academic reputation of both schools may be known (alignable), while the quality of teaching may only be known for one school (nonalignable). Recent research has shown that people use more alignable than nonalignable information in decision making. In this experiment, we consider whether alignable information is preferred even when nonalignable information is important. In the study, some participants rated the importance and valence of a series of statements about colleges that differed in alignability. Other participants made choices between pairs of colleges whose descriptions incorporated these statements. The results indicate that alignable information is preferred to nonalignable information even when the nonalignable information is important. Results also showed that the interpretation of attribute valence depends on alignability. These observations suggest that alignability is more influential than attribute importance in the processing of choice information and that the use of alignable information may facilitate the interpretation of attribute information.

Imagine that you are a senior in high school beginning the process of applying to college. To help you make the decision, you gather a tremendous amount of information. You read brochures and books. You talk to friends, parents, teachers and counselors. In the end you must evaluate the information you have gathered and make a decision. Your collection of information about the characteristics of colleges contains two types of information. On some topics (e.g., school location and academic reputation) you have corresponding values for all of the schools you are interested in. On other topics (e.g., study abroad programs and availability of extracurricular activities) you have information from some of the schools but not others. Somehow you must combine this information in order to make your final decision.

We suggest that the structural alignment process of comparison is a key element in determining how information is used in choice (Medin, Goldstone & Markman, 1995). Structural alignment has been identified as a critical factor in the psychology of similarity (Gentner, 1983, 1989; Gentner & Markman, 1994; Medin, Goldstone & Gentner, 1993). On this view similarity comparisons involve three types of information - commonalities between the items, differences related to the commonalities (i.e. corresponding or *alignable* differences), and differences unrelated to commonalities (i.e. noncorresponding or *nonalignable* differences). To illustrate, consider the comparison of a dog and a cat. In this comparison, the fact that dogs and cats are both pets is a commonality, the fact that a dog barks and a cat meows is an alignable difference (related to the commonality that both animals make noise) and the fact that the dog fetches and the cat doesn't is a nonalignable difference. In one study, Markman & Gentner (1993) asked subjects to list the commonalities and differences of pairs of items of varying levels of similarity. Overall, participants listed more alignable differences than nonalignable differences. Furthermore, more alignable differences were listed for similar pairs than for dissimilar pairs and more nonalignable differences were listed for dissimilar pairs than for similar pairs. This result demonstrates that alignable differences are the central output of the comparison process. It also suggests that alignable and nonalignable differences are processed differently.

This theory can be applied straightforwardly to decision making. In the college example presented above, the alignable differences are the corresponding properties and the nonalignable differences are the noncorresponding properties. Just as the research in similarity suggests that the alignable differences are more important for comparisons than are nonalignable differences, previous research in choice has demonstrated that decision makers tend to focus more on corresponding pieces of information than on noncorresponding information (Markman & Medin, 1995; Slovic & MacPhillamy, 1974). Similarly, in consumer choice, when deciding between highly different types of products (e.g. a toaster and a smoke alarm) consumers attempt to abstract corresponding qualities (Johnson, 1988), which can be viewed as an attempt to make the properties of dissimilar items more comparable.

The selective use of alignable differences over nonalignable differences raises the possibility that decision makers systematically ignore information they believe to be important simply because it is nonalignable with information from another option. In this study, we examine this possibility directly. In this decision task, we ask subjects to choose which of two universities they prefer after reading short descriptions of the schools. The descriptions are designed so that half of the relevant information is of high importance and half is of low importance. By varying the alignability of these items, we will be able to see whether alignability influences the decision maker's use of both important and unimportant information. We predict that subjects will focus more on important information than on unimportant information, but that they will use more alignable information for both important and unimportant items. In order to assess the information being used by subjects, we will analyze both justifications of choices given by subjects as well as think-aloud protocols from a separate group of subjects. Because we are interested in the impact of alignability on the use of information in choice, we focus on processing measures (e.g., justifications and protocols) rather than outcome measures (e.g., choices).

This study will also look at the way that alignability influences the processing and interpretation of the statements used in the decision task. This question will be addressed with a ratings task. Some subjects will be given corresponding pairs of statements (i.e., alignable statements) to rate, while others will rate the same statements, individually (i.e., nonalignable statements). We will examine these results to see if they can help explain the bias toward using alignable differences in decision making.

Method

Participants

Sixty subjects (20 per group) participated in the ratings task. Fifty-six subjects participated in the decision making task (32 with written task and 24 with verbal protocol task). All subjects were recruited from the Columbia University community and were paid or received course credit for their participation.

Materials

Ratings Task. For the ratings task, stimuli were statements about colleges. The statements were like those in the descriptions of schools in various guidebooks to colleges and universities. There were 16 pairs of statements. Both of the statements in each pair focused on the same topic (e.g., housing options, academic reputation, etc.). In each pair, one of the statements was positive (e.g., "There is a good amount of housing available in a variety of configurations and most of the students who want to live in singles are able to.") and the other was neutral (e.g., "Students are generally housed in double rooms with some single rooms available to seniors who request them."). Half of the pairs focused on topics that we believed Columbia University students would consider to be important college characteristics (e.g., housing options, academic reputation of the school, etc.) and half of the pairs focused on topics that we believed Columbia University students would think of as unimportant (e.g., quality of the gym, attractiveness of the

campus, etc.). Statements were important or unimportant and positive or neutral. Negative statements were not included. Negative statements were omitted because we wanted the descriptions created from the statements to be generally attractive.

There were three groups of subjects. One group of subjects saw all of the statements, presented in pairs (the alignable group). Each of the other two groups saw only half of the statements, one from each pair (the nonalignable groups A and B). Nonalignable group A saw half of the positive statements and half of the neutral statements. Nonalignable group B saw the remaining positive and neutral statements. The materials were presented in booklets with the appropriate ratings scale appearing at the top of each page (i.e., for importance, 1 (not at all important) to 5 (extremely important) and for valence, 1 (extremely negative) to 7 (extremely positive)). The order of the items in each booklet was determined randomly. There were five or six pairs of statements per page for the alignable group and five or six single statements per page for the nonalignable groups. The pages of each booklet were randomly ordered for each subject.

Decision Task. For the decision task, the stimuli were pairs of paragraph descriptions of fictitious colleges and universities. Each description was made up of a cover story (filler sentences) and main sentences. The descriptions were set up so that some properties were directly comparable across the two descriptions in a pair (alignable). For example, both descriptions might talk about available housing options with one school having more options than the other. Other properties were not directly comparable across the two alternatives (nonalignable). For example, only one of the college descriptions might include information about the quality of teaching at the school.

The materials were constructed in the following way. We first wrote four "base pairs" of corresponding descriptions. The base pairs were then used to create the stimulus sets used in the decision task. In a base pair, each sentence in one description had a corresponding sentence in the other description. The descriptions in a base pair consisted of two corresponding cover stories (making up the two initial "filler" sentences and the final "filler" sentence in each description) and four corresponding main sentence slots, as shown in Table 1.

Sentence Type	College A	College B
1 - cover story	filler	filler
2 - cover story	filler	filler
3 - main sentence	positive	neutral
4 - main sentence	neutral	positive
5 - main sentence	positive	neutral
6 - main sentence	neutral	positive
7 - cover story	filler	filler

Table 1 - Listing of all sentences in a base pair

359

Sentence Type	College A	College B	Comparison Type
1 - cover story	filler	filler	commonality
2 - cover story	filler	filler	commonality
3 - main sentence	positive	neutral	nonalignable difference
4 - main sentence	neutral	positive	nonalignable difference
5 - main sentence	positive	neutral	alignable difference
6 - main sentence	neutral	positive	alignable difference
7 - cover story	filler	filler	commonality

Table 2 - Removing 2 noncorresponding positive sentences
leaves 2 alignable and 2 nonalignable differences

In each base pair, the corresponding filler sentences were approximately equivalent in meaning (commonalities). The corresponding main sentence slots were filled at random using the 16 corresponding pairs from the ratings task with the restriction that two positive and two neutral sentences were inserted in each description. Each of the 16 pairs was used once within a set of base pairs. Two different sets of base pairs were created in this way. The written task used stimuli constructed from both sets of base pairs, while the protocol task only used stimuli constructed from the first set.

From each set of base pairs, four different stimulus sets were created by selectively removing individual sentences from each description. To create each stimulus set, two *noncorresponding* sentences of the same valence were removed from each pair of descriptions leaving two alignable differences (the remaining corresponding sentences) and two nonalignable differences (the remaining non-corresponding sentences). This is illustrated in Table 2 where two noncorresponding, positive, main sentences have been removed (sentence 3 from college A and sentence 4 from college B, as indicated by the X's). In this example, two nonalignable differences remain (sentence 3 from college B and sentence 4 from college A - two noncorresponding neutral statements) and two alignable differences remain (sentence 5 from both schools and sentence 6 from both schools).. Different pairs of sentences were removed from the base pairs to create the four different stimulus sets. In this way, each sentence was used as an alignable difference and as a nonalignable difference across the four stimulus sets. This structuring of materials is similar to that used by Markman and Medin (1995) for the descriptions of video games in their second experiment.

Procedure

Ratings Task. Participants in the ratings task were randomly assigned to one of the three conditions - alignable (where all the statements were presented in corresponding pairs) or nonalignable A or B (where half of the statements, one from each pair were presented). Subjects in the alignable condition were told to read both items in a pair before rating them and to consider the items as though they referred to two different universities. The valence ratings task was done first. For this task, subjects considered each statement as though it came from a description of a college and rated its positivity/negativity. After this was completed, they did the importance ratings task. For this task subjects were told to

imagine that they were giving advice to a younger brother or sister applying to college and to rate how important their younger sibling should consider each statement when deciding where to go to school.

Decision Task. Participants in the decision tasks were told to imagine that they were helping a younger sibling to decide where to apply to college. They read a series of pairs of descriptions of colleges and had to choose which school their sibling should apply to. For the written task, subjects read a pair of stories on a computer screen, selected one school and then typed a justification for their selection. For the verbal protocol, subjects first participated in a few warm-up tasks. Then the materials were presented on sheets of paper and subjects read the stories aloud and thought aloud while making their choices. Verbal protocols were recorded on audio tape. For both the written and verbal presentations, the order of presentation of the four pairs of schools was randomly determined and right/left presentation of the descriptions was varied between subjects.

Scoring

The written justification for each choice were scored by counting separately the number of references to the alignable and nonalignable properties from the relevant college descriptions. Only statements that clearly referred to the specific information in the descriptions were counted. When one justification included multiple references to a single alignable or nonalignable property, it was counted as one reference. Any single justification could be counted as mentioning a maximum of two alignable and two non-alignable properties. The verbal protocols were transcribed and then scored in the same way as the written justifications.

Results

First we examine the results from the importance ratings task in order to determine which of the 16 pairs of properties used were considered important and which were unimportant. Next we evaluate the results of the decision tasks to look at the influence of alignability and importance on choice. Finally, we present evidence from the ratings tasks which suggesting that the availability of corresponding (alignable) statements influences the way people evaluate properties of options.

	Properties Mentioned			
Method	Alignable High Importance	Nonalignable High Importance	Alignable Low Importance	Nonalignable Low Importance
Written	1.72	0.91	1.22	0.87
Verbal	3.17	1.58	2.92	2.08

Table 3 - Mean Alignable and Nonalignable Properties used per subject in Written Justifications and Verbal Protocols broken down by importance level.

Importance of Individual Items

Mean importance ratings for the pairs of items were calculated by averaging the importance ratings for both items in each pair in the alignable and nonalignable conditions. The range of mean values for the importance ratings was somewhat restricted (2.72 - 4.40 on a 1 to 5 scale). This reflects the fact that the participants tended not to use the lower end of the scale: 18 of 30 subjects (60%) neglected to use the rating "1" ("not at all important"), even though half of the items were designed to be of little or no importance. The eight items with the lowest mean importance ratings were considered to be the low importance items (Range of means: 2.73 - 3.60) and the eight items with the highest mean importance ratings were considered to be the high importance items (Range of means: 3.75 - 4.40).

Decision Making Tasks

The number of alignable and nonalignable differences mentioned in the justifications and protocols were tabulated using the scoring method outlined above. These tabulations were further broken down for low and high importance items. These results are presented in Table 3 and were analyzed with a 2 X 2 ANOVA.

As predicted, more alignable differences than nonalignable differences were mentioned in both the written justifications (m = 2.94, alignable; m = 1.81 nonalignable; $F (1, 31) = 11.06$, $p < 0.01$) and the protocols (m = 5.96, alignable; m = 3.66, nonalignable; $F (1, 23) = 31.87$, $p < 0.01$). These results confirm the pattern found by Markman & Medin (1995). This pattern was obtained both for the high importance items and for the low importance items in both the written and protocol tasks. This finding is critical because it shows that nonalignable features may receive less attention than alignable features, even when they are considered to be important.

This general trend can also be found at the level of individual subjects and individual items. At the subject level, in the written task, 20 of 32 subjects (63.0%) referred to more alignable differences, there were 6 ties and 6 subjects showing the reverse pattern (18.5% each). For the protocol task, 20 of 24 subjects (83.3%) mentioned more alignable properties, with 2 ties and 2 showing the reverse pattern (8.3% each). At the item level, in the written task 10 of 16 items (62.5%) were listed more often in the alignable condition, there were 5 ties (31.2%) and 1 item showed the reverse pattern (6.3%). In the protocol task, 15 of 16 items (93.7%) were mentioned more often in the alignable condition and there was 1 tie (6.3%).

It is important to note here that the verbal protocols were unplanned, lengthy responses while the written justifications were planned and short, typically only one or two sentences. This difference helps to explain why the participants performing the protocol task mentioned twice as many alignable and nonalignable differences as those performing the written task.

The following example, taken from one of the verbal protocols, illustrates the type of responses given by our subjects. In this example, the subject is choosing between two schools where "faculty accessibility" and "the variety of major programs" were alignable properties and "academic reputation of the school" and "teaching quality" were nonalignable properties. The subject said, "Um . . . well Mountwell University seems to be probably smaller because the teachers are more accessible and more enthusiastic and Hillsdale however has a lot of programs and independent people can make up their own programs which is a good thing . . . some reason I keep picking all the universities on the right hand side . . . but I don't know these are just really similar, but I guess I'd go with Hillsdale because it's not that important to me to have accessible professors."

In this example, the subject mentions both of the alignable properties - faculty accessibility and the variety of majors. Furthermore, the information about faculty accessibility is then used to make an inference about the relative sizes of the universities. The subject does not mention the nonalignable facts that teaching is strongly emphasized at Mountwell and that Hillsdale has an excellent academic reputation, even though these are considered to be among the most important college characteristics to Columbia University students. This subject does not fill-in the missing information and make either of the plausible inferences that Hillsdale's reputation is better or that the teaching at Mountwell is better. In fact the subject seems somewhat at a loss to come up with differences between the schools stating that "they are just really similar". This is illustrative of participants' strong tendency to favor alignable over nonalignable differences.

From this illustration, it is easy to see how this type of data (i.e., protocols and justifications) allows us to examine the way subjects process information relevant to a decision. We can evaluate which information is considered in the decision process and how it is used. We can also evaluate which information does not enter into consideration. Outcome data (i.e., subjects' choices), on the other hand, does not provide this benefit. It is for this reason that we favor analyzing justifications and protocols as a method for learning about the processing of decision information.

Statement Type	Valence Ratings		Importance Ratings	
	Alignable	Nonalignable	Alignable	Nonalignable
Positive	5.86	6.17	3.91	3.77
Neutral	4.04	4.81	3.58	3.55

Table 4 - Valence and Importance ratings of Alignable and Nonalignable Properties
for both positive and neutral statements

Finally there is one surprising result. Contrary to our expectation, the high importance items were not used more often than the low importance items. In the written task, the effect of importance was only marginally significant (m = 2.69, high importance; m = 2.06, low importance; $F(1,31) = 3.54$, $p < 0.07$) and in the protocol task there is was no effect of importance (m = 4.62, high importance; m = 5.00, low importance, $F(1, 23) < 1$). In part, this may be due to some of the materials being insufficiently different in perceived importance. However, this result provides some indication that the importance of information is less crucial to choice than other factors like alignability.

Importance and Valence Ratings

The mean importance and valence ratings are presented in Table 4. There were no significant effects of alignability or item type (positive or neutral) on the importance ratings.

The valence ratings showed a different pattern. As expected, subjects gave higher valence ratings to positive statements (m = 6.02) than to neutral statements (m = 4.43), where 4.0 was the neutral point on the ratings scale, $F(1, 30) = 62.78$, $p < 0.01$. Alignability also influenced valence ratings, with nonalignable statements (m = 5.49) rated higher than alignable statements (m=4.95), $F(1,30) = 11.02$, p<.01. This suggests that statements were perceived more positively when they were presented without a corresponding alternative value.

There is a trend towards an interaction, although it is not significant. The pattern of means suggests that there may be a greater difference between the valence ratings of the positive and neutral items when they are alignable than when they are nonalignable. This pattern can be clearly seen in a post-hoc analysis in which we eliminated from consideration pairs of statements where the positive statement was not rated more positively than the neutral statement by our subjects. We only examined the 12 pairs of statements for which a paired t-test on the alignable valence ratings found the positive items to be of significantly higher valence than the neutral items. For this analysis the main effects that were found in the original analysis were again obtained. The perceived valence of positive statements (m = 6.17) was higher than that of neutral statements (m = 4.51), $F(1, 22) = 60.44$, $p < 0.01$. The perceived valence of nonalignable properties (m = 5.68) was higher than alignable properties (m = 5.01), $F(1, 22) = 37.77$, $p < 0.01$. Finally, the interaction is also significant, $F(1, 22) = 25.71$, $p < 0.01$, reflecting the pattern described above. The difference between the mean perceived valence of positive and neutral properties was greater for the alignable properties (diff. = 2.22) than for the nonalignable (diff. =

1.11) properties. This effect may reflect that it is more difficult to determine the absolute valence of an isolated fact than it is to determine the valence of that same fact relative to an alignable fact.

General Discussion

These results demonstrate that people tend to focus more strongly on alignable differences than on nonalignable differences during choice regardless of the importance of the information. Thus subjects may ignore important information simply because it is nonalignable, and may use unimportant information simply because it is alignable. Surprisingly, we found no evidence that importance influenced the selection of information used to make decisions. This pattern of data was obtained both in an on-line think-aloud protocol task and in a post-hoc written justification task.

The results replicate and extend Markman & Medin's (1995) studies in which more alignable information than nonalignable information appeared in subjects' post-hoc justifications of choices between video games. Further, this study introduced the think-aloud methodology to the study of alignability in decision making. Although this change in methodology increased the amount of information contributed by each subject, it did not alter the pattern of results. Thus the tendency to use alignable information in choice does not seem to be an artifact of the justification method. Further, the think-aloud method is important because it enables us to identify more of the information that subjects use and to look at how it is used. In particular, it will allow for a more detailed analysis of the use of inferences, abstractions and the filling-in of missing values in choice.

The ratings tasks shed light on why people prefer to use alignable information. The valence ratings indicate that people change their interpretations of information depending on whether the information is presented alone or in correspondence with other information. People may prefer to use alignable information when they have difficulty determining the absolute value of an attribute. Alignable information eases interpretation because it provides the decision maker with a point of comparison.

There is some reason to believe that novices and experts may differ in their reliance on alignable information. Experts can fill-in missing values by using their domain knowledge (Gardial & Biehal, 1991). Sanbonmatsu, Kardes & Herr (1992) found that bicycle experts were more likely to take missing information into account than were less knowledgeable subjects. Apparently the less knowledgeable subjects did not know the absolute valence of the missing properties and so they could not incorporate that information into their decisions. This finding suggests that experts may be less dependent on alignable information because they are better able to evaluate attributes. We are currently examining this issue by looking at the decision making processes of students with different levels of expertise about college life.

Acknowledgments

This work was supported by NSF CAREER award SBR-95-10924 given to the second author. The authors wish to thank Tomislov Pavlicic, Yung-Cheng Shen, Saskia Traill and Takashi Yamauchi for their thoughtful comments. We would also like to thank Adalis Sanchez for her help in running subjects.

References

Conover, J. N. (1982). Familiarity and the structure of product knowledge. *Advances in Consumer Research*, 9, 494-498.

Gardial, S., & Biehal, G. (1992). Evaluative and factual ad claims, knowledge level, and making inferences. *Marketing Letters*, 2(4), 349-358.

Gentner, D. (1983). Structure-mapping: A theoretical framework for analogy. *Cognitive Science*, 7, 155-170.

Gentner, D. (1989). The mechanisms of analogical learning. In S. Vosinadou & A. Ortony (Eds.), *Similarity, Analogy and Thought*. New York: Cambridge University Press.

Gentner, D., & Markman, A. B. (1994). Structural alignment in comparison: No difference without similarity. *Psychological Science*, 5(3), 152-158.

Johnson, M. D. (1988). Comparability and hierarchical processing in multialternative choice. *Journal of Consumer Research*, 15, 303-314.

Markman, A. B., & Gentner, D. (1993). Splitting the differences: A structural alignment view of similarity. *Journal of Memory and Language*, 32(4), 517-535.

Markman, A. B., & Medin, D. L. (1995). Similarity and alignment in choice. *Organizational Behavior and Human Decision Processes*, 63(2), 117-130.

Medin, D. L., Goldstone, R. L., & Markman, A. B. (1995). Comparison and Choice: Relations between Similarity Processes and Decision Processes. *Psychonomic Bulletin and Review*, 2(1), 1-19.

Medin, D. L., Goldstone, R. L., & Gentner, D. (1993). Respects for similarity. *Psychological Review*, 100(2), 254-278.

Sanbonmatsu, D. M., Kardes, F. R., & Herr, P. M. (1992). The role of prior knowledge and missing information in multiattribute evaluation. *Organizational Behavior and Human Decision Processes*, 51, 76-91.

Slovic, P., & MacPhillamy, D. (1974). Dimensional commensurability and cue utilization in comparative judgment. *Organizational Behavior and Human Performance*, 11, 172-194.

Computational Bases of Two Types of Developmental Dyslexia

Michael W. Harm and **Mark S. Seidenberg**
University of Southern California
Neuroscience Program
Los Angeles, CA 90089-2520
{mharm,marks}@gizmo.usc.edu

Abstract

The bases of developmental dyslexia were explored using connectionist models. The behavioral literature suggests that there are two dyslexic subtypes: "phonological" dyslexia involves impairments in phonological knowledge whereas in "surface " dyslexia phonological knowledge is apparently intact and the deficit may instead reflect a more general developmental delay. We examined possible computational bases for these impairments within connectionist models of the mapping from spelling to sound. Phonological dyslexia was simulated by reducing the capacity of the models to represent this type of information. The surface pattern was simulated by reducing the number of hidden units. Performance of the models captured the major behavioral phenomena that distinguish the two subtypes. Phonological impairment has a greater impact on generalization (reading nonwords such as NUST); the hidden unit limitation has a greater impact on learning exception words such as PINT. More severe impairments produce mixed cases in which both nonwords and exceptions are impaired. Thus, the simulations capture the effects of different types and degrees of impairment within a major component of the reading system.

1. Introduction

One of the attractions of the connectionist or parallel distributed processing approach is that it can be used to develop unified accounts of normal and disordered behavior. Effects of brain injury or developmental anomaly can be simulated by "damaging" components of a neural network model of normal performance. A prominent example of this approach is provided by research on reading and dyslexia. Becoming a skilled reader involves mastering the correspondences between spelling and pronunciation. Sejnowski and Rosenberg (1987) developed a neural network model of this process, and Seidenberg and McClelland (1989; hereafter SM89) used a similar model to account for detailed aspects of behavior. Dyslexia--failures to acquire age-appropriate reading skills despite normal intelligence and adequate opportunity to learn--is often associated with impairments mapping from spelling to sound (Castles & Coltheart, 1993). Our goal was to see if the behavioral impairments associated with dyslexia could be explained in terms of damage to a model of skilled reading.

There is an emerging consensus that there are two prominent subtypes of developmental dyslexia (Castles & Coltheart, 1993; Murphy & Pollatsek, 1994; Manis et al., 1996). The reading impairment observed in phonological dyslexia is apparently secondary to impaired processing of spoken language. Such children perform poorly on spoken language tasks such as counting the number of syllables in a word or deciding if two words rhyme (see Farmer & Klein, 1995, for review). In reading they are markedly impaired in their ability to use their knowledge of spelling-sound correspondences to pronounce novel letter strings (nonwords such as NUST). These children do not resemble younger children who are learning to read normally. The second subtype has been termed developmental surface dyslexia (Castles & Coltheart, 1993). Such children are also impaired in reading but their phonological processing capacities appear to be intact. They have particular difficulty learning to read words with irregular spelling-sound correspondences, such as GIVE and PINT. These children's performance closely resembles that of much younger normal readers; hence they exhibit a developmental delay.

There are two theoretical accounts of these phenomena, tied to models of normal word recognition. In the dual-route model (Coltheart et al., 1993), there are separate "lexical" and "nonlexical" mechanisms for pronouncing letter strings. The "lexical" mechanism involves knowledge associated with specific words; it provides the only way of pronouncing irregular words such as PINT and cannot be used to pronounce novel strings such as NUST. Surface dyslexia is thought to involve an impairment in acquiring this mechanism. The "nonlexical" mechanism consists of rules governing correspondences between graphemes and phonemes; it can be used to pronounce novel letter strings but not irregular words. Phonological dyslexia is thought to involve an impairment in acquiring the pronunciation rules. Note that Pinker's (1991) theory of the past tense is also a dual-route model, with a rule component distinct from a word-specific component.

A number of behavioral phenomena related to normal performance and effects of brain injury on reading present difficulties for the dual-route theory (Seidenberg, 1995; Plaut et al., 1996). Several aspects of developmental dyslexia present further challenges for this approach. The idea that phonological dyslexia involves an impairment in acquiring grapheme-phoneme correspondence rules misses the fact that these children have broader phonological impairments that are manifested in tasks other than reading. The idea that an impairment in the lexical mechanism underlies the surface pattern fails to explain the fact that such children tend to exhibit a broad developmental delay that affects all aspects of reading (Manis et al., 1996), not just exception words. Finally, it is an embarrassment for the dual-route theory that selective impairments in the two processing subsystems are rarely if ever observed. Most dyslexics are impaired in reading both exception words and nonwords; the dual-route theory can only explain this by assuming that both routes happen to be impaired in most cases, but there is no independent evidence that this is so (Manis et al., 1996).

An alternative to the dual-route account is provided by connectionist models in which there is a single, homogeneous mechanism for mapping between spellings and pronunciations. Such models provide a good account of a broad range of phenomena concerned skilled performance and breakdown following brain injury (SM89; Plaut et al., 1996). The different patterns of developmental dyslexia might be explained within such models in terms of different *types* of damage to a single underlying mechanism, rather than damage to different pronunciation *mechanisms*. For example, Manis et al. (1996) suggest that the phonological subtype could result from impairments in phonological representation in an SM89 style model. Such degraded representations would make it harder to acquire spelling-sound correspondences and also interfere with performance on other tasks involving phonological information. Similarly, the surface form could derive from a limitation on the capacity of the network to encode information--for example, limiting the number of hidden units. This would affect the learning of exception words (see SM89 for details) but a severe enough impairment would affect regular words and generalization as well.

The purpose of the present research was to assess the adequacy of the connectionist account by seeing if we could account for major aspects of the distinct dyslexic subtypes. We implemented a version of an SM89-style model of the mapping from spelling to sound and then ran versions with either phonological or capacity limitations. The models were assessed in terms of their capacities to learn words with regular and irregular pronunciations and to pronounce novel items.

2. Model Architecture

The phonological representation used in the simulations consisted of 6 slots, each slot corresponding to a phoneme in a monosyllabic word, and consisting in turn of 11 phonetic features: sonorant, consonantal, voiced, nasal, degree, labial, palatal, pharyngeal, lower_lip, tongue and radical. These features could take on a continuum of values ranging from between -1 and +1. The slot arrangement was vowel centered, and could encode syllables of CCVVCC format. A word could have at most two consonants before the vowel, and two after. Normal vowels were encoded as a single vowel phoneme and a second empty slot; diphthongs were encoded as pairs of vowel slots. The orthographic representations consisted of 8 slots, representing letter positions. Letters were encoded using a localist representation, with 26 units per position, and were also vowel centered. Up to 3 consonants could be represented before the initial, centered vowel, and up to 4 letters (consonants or vowels) after the vowel.

The 66 phonological units were fully connected to one another with initially random weights ranging from -0.001 to 0.001. An additional set of 20 cleanup units were added, with initially random weights going from each of the phonological units to each cleanup unit, and back from the

cleanup units to the phonological units (see Figure 1). These units are analogous to the cleanup units used in semantic attractor networks (e.g., Plaut & Shallice, 1993). The direct connections between featural units within a phoneme were able to encode intraphonemic constraints; those between slots encoded constraints related to the sequence of phonemes. The cleanup units allowed higher order dependencies among features to be represented.

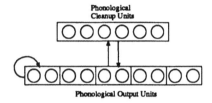

Figure 1: The Phonological Component

The schematic architecture of the "normal" reading model is shown in Figure 2. Orthographic units projected onto a set of 100 hidden units, which in turn projected onto the phonological units of the phonological component. The task of the reading model was to map orthographic representations of words onto the correct phonological units.

We then modified this architecture to examine the effects of phonological impairments on reading acquisition. Two conditions were used which imposed different limitations on the extent to which phonological information could be encoded. The first model was identical to the normal unimpaired model except that the weights in the phonological network were subject to weight decay (see Hinton, 1989). The effect of this decay is to apply pressure to the network to avoid large values on the weights. The network can still encode higher order relationships between the units, but the strength of these encodings is curtailed. A weight decay constant of 0.00005 was used.

In the second, more severely impaired simulation the cleanup units were deleted from the phonological attractor network. By removing the cleanup units, we disabled the network's ability to encode higher order relationships among the phonological units. This impaired phonological component had only direct connections between the phonological units, and hence was limited in the complexity of computations it could perform (see Minsky & Papert, 1969). Both of these simulations had 100 hidden units, the same number as the normal model.

In each condition we first trained the phonological component on a set of phonological word forms. The weights that resulted from this pretraining were used when each phonological component was incorporated in a model that learned to pronounce written words. The goal was to determine how reductions in the capacity to represent phonological information would affect performance on the spelling-sound mapping task.

To assess the effect of reducing the computational resources available to the reading task while preserving phonological knowledge an additional pair of simulations were run. They were identical in architecture to the normal model, except that one models had only 35 hidden units, and a second one had only 20. These models had the same phonological representation as used in the normal condition.

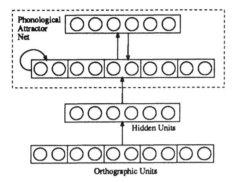

Figure 2: The reading model, with phonological output network in place

3. Training The Models

Phonological Pretraining

The phonological component was trained on a corpus of 3123 monosyllabic words using backpropagation through time (Rumelhart, Hinton & Williams, 1986). The weights from each phonological unit to itself were set to 0.75 and frozen. This gave the phonological units a tendency to hold onto their current value, but decay slowly to zero. Other weights were initially randomized. Each word was given a probability of presentation according to its estimated frequency of occurrence using a sample of 30 million words from the Wall Street Journal. The probability for each word was set to the logarithm of that word's frequency in the WSJ divided by the logarithm of the frequency of the most frequent word ("the"). Training proceeded as follows. A word was probabilistically chosen from the training set. For tick 0, the phonological units were set to the values corresponding to its phonological form. The network was allowed to run for 5 ticks, with all units unclamped for the last 4 ticks. The output of the network during ticks 2 through 4 was compared to the original phonological form of the word. Error was injected into the network based on the difference between output values and the targets, and the weights were adjusted so as to reduce this error. Then another word was chosen randomly and the process repeated. The overall effect of this training regime is to force the weights to encode statistical relationships between the phonological units. Training was halted after 1 million training trials. At the conclusion of training, the baseline network's mean sum squared error was 0.05, the network with weight decay on the phonological weights ended with a mean error of 1.8, and the network with no cleanup connections ended with a mean error of 0.8. These error scores are the average summed error over 66 output units, so the average deviance from unit output to target for the 3 simulations was, respectively, 0.001, 0.027 and 0.012.

To further assess the quality of the phonological representations, a simple pattern completion task was devised. In this task, for each of the words in the training set with an initial consonant cluster, the features of the second consonant slot was left unspecified while the remainder of the word form was clamped to that word's phonological form. The network was then run for 6 ticks, and the value which the unspecified phoneme was drawn into was assessed. The word was scored correct if the segment that was produced (evaluated by the nearest neighbor criterion, described in section 4) was a legal segment for English in that environment. For instance, for the word /b/l/u/, if the net output /b/r/u/ that would also be scored as acceptable. The normal network was able to insert a legal phoneme into the slot 75% of the time. The decay network could only produce a legal phoneme 46% of the time, and the network without cleanup units could only produce a legal output 10% of the time.

This test is not meant to be a full test of the networks' phonological competency, but rather a gross measure of the quality of the phonological attractor basins that the different conditions represent. The network with weight decay is impaired relative to the normal network due to the downward pressure on the magnitude of the weights during training. The network without cleanup units is even more impaired, because this task, like the XOR task, relies on the conjunctive use of other features in the word's environment, and not simply direct relationships between features.

Training on Reading Task

The pretrained phonological components were then used in models that were trained on the reading task. In both the normal model and the reduced resource models the standard phonological component training method was used. The phonologically impaired conditions utilized representations trained with weight decay or cleanup unit deletion, as described above. In each case, weights were initialized to the final values from the relevant pretraining phase. The remaining weights in the network (orthographic to hidden; hidden to phonological) were initialized to small random values. The model was then trained on the same corpus of 3123 words, again using log frequency to determine probabilities of being selected for training. For each word chosen, the orthographic units were clamped with the appropriate values for ticks 0-6. At tick 6, the phonological output was compared with the phonological target, error was injected into the network, and the weights were updated.

Four replications were run for each condition (normal, the 2 reduced resource conditions, and the two phonologically impaired conditions). For each simulation run, a different random number seed was used, resulting in different distributions of initial random weights, and a different ordering of the presentation of words.

4. Results

Two scoring methods were used. In the nearest-neighbor method, the phonological output of each 11 units within a phoneme slot is compared to the representations for each of the phonemes that exist in the training set. The phoneme that is closest in euclidean distance to the output is the one that is taken to be the output. A second, more stringent threshold method was also used, and unless otherwise noted will be the one reported below. For this measure, each feature of a phoneme had to be within a specified distance of the target for the phoneme to be counted as correct. A threshold value of 0.5 was used, covering 25% of the units' activation range of -1 to 1. In both cases, a word was scored as correct only if all of its phonemes were correct. To evaluate the networks' performance on words, we used a set of frequency 93 regular items such as BACK, and 92 exceptions, such as COMB, taken from the "surface list" developed by Patterson & Hodges (1992).[1] For nonwords we constructed a set of 367 items (e.g., GOMB, SOAD, FAIJE) taken from items used by McCann & Besner (1987), Glushko (1979) and Seidenberg et al. (1994). Regular words follow the putative spelling-sound correspondence rules of the language, and exceptions violate them. Nonwords assess the ability to generalize to untrained forms.

All models were evaluated after running for 8.5 million words. In almost all cases, learning had ceased long before this point (see Figures 3-6). Asymptotically, the normal models got an average of 98% of the training set correct when scored with the nearest-neighbor method and 83% of the nonwords[2]. Using the threshold method, the average results were 97% and 75%, respectively. Nonword performance is somewhat lower than levels reported for people, particularly with the threshold method. This measure is quite conservative, however; for example, some small deviations from target values that are scored as incorrect would not be perceivable in humans. Also, we have made no attempt to improve nonword performance using various techniques known to facilitate generalization (e.g., pruning, noise). Plaut et al. (1996) discuss other factors that affect nonword generalization.

Phonological Impairments

Figures 3 and 4 show the developmental curves for the impaired phonological knowledge conditions compared with the normal condition. All plots show the average of four simulation runs. With mild levels of phonological impairment (i.e., weight decay, Figure 3), there are decrements on both the rate of acquisition and asymptotic performance on nonwords. but very little effect on regulars and exceptions (see Figure 7 for a summary of the asymptotic conditions). With the nocleanup net (Figure 4), the exceptions also begin to show a decrement in rate of acquisition relative to the normal network. Acquisition of the capacity to generalize is also being slowed, though less than in the decay condition. Mild phonological impairment has little effect on the rate of acquisition for regular and exception items. With the more extreme impairment, there is slower acquisition of exceptions in addition to poor performance on nonwords throughout development.

These simulations capture the basic characteristic of phonological dyslexia, that nonword generalization is impaired more than performance on vocabulary words. In the

relatively pure cases of phonological dyslexia, subjects' performance on regular and exception words is close to normal, while nonword generalization is poor (Castles & Coltheart, 1993). This result is produced by the decay condition. Many other phonological dyslexics exhibit a "mixed" pattern in which performance on exception words begins to be affected as well. This outcome was observed in the nocleanup condition.

The Reduced Resource Conditions

Figures 5 and 6 summarize the time course of training in the reduced resource conditions relative to the normal baseline model. At the end of training, the reduction to 35 HUs had almost no effect on regular words or on nonword generalization (see Figure 7). However, for exceptions, the 35 HU case shows a drop from 91% to 83% correct in asymptotic performance, relative to the normal network. Decreasing the number of HUs slows learning for all types of items (Figures 4 and 5), but the effect is biggest for the exceptions. With only 20 hidden units, there is a bigger effect on exceptions, and the developmental curves for nonwords and regulars begins to be affected as well.

These simulations capture basic characteristics of the surface dyslexia pattern. In relatively pure cases, reading of regular words and nonwords is intact, but exception words are impaired. With more severe deficits, the regulars and nonwords start to be affected, with exceptions most vulnerable.

5. Discussion

The simulations show that deficits associated with two major patterns of developmental dyslexia can be produced by different types of impairments to a model of normal performance. The phonological pattern derives from impairments in the capacity to represent this type of information. This account can explain why phonological dyslexics are also impaired on spoken language tasks such as rhyme detection. The phonological representations in question are not specific to reading; they are also used in the perception of spoken language. This pattern of correlated reading and spoken language deficits is more difficult to explain within the dual-route model, which attributes phonological dyslexia to an impairment in learning grapheme-phoneme correspondence rules. Why this should also affect spoken language tasks is not clear.

We have derived the surface pattern from a resource limitation, which slows learning across the board. The model retains the capacity to encode the simple and consistent spelling-sound correspondences and eventually masters them with sufficient training; however, its capacity to encode irregular words is limited. This represents an alternative to the standard dual-route account, which holds that the surface pattern results from damage to a "lexical" processing mechanism that encodes the pronunciations of all words. This approach has difficulty accounting for the prevalence of the mixed pattern, in which performance is impaired on both words and nonwords. Thus, on our view the surface pattern represents a kind of general developmental delay that has broad effects on acquisition but especially on

---

[1] Some items from their list were excluded because they cannot be represented in our scheme.

[2] A full listing of the items, with network outputs, is available on a web page at http://maestro.usc.edu:8080/mwharm/cogsci96.html

learning exceptions. Although we have derived the surface pattern by manipulating the number of hidden units, other types of anomalies could be expected to produce similar effects. For example, a visual-perceptual impairment that had the effect of degrading the input orthographic patterns would also cause broad learning delays with the largest impact on the words with unusual spellings or pronunciations.

Why do the different types of anomalies have different effects on network behavior? Degrading the phonological capacity of the network by eliminating the cleanup units and interconnections between featural units forces the network to memorize the training set, yielding poor generalization. With the additional units, the network can encode aspects of the structure of phonological space independently of how this information relates to orthography. An analogous condition exists with the weight decay simulation: the phonological network is prevented from fully developing high quality representations. The normal network, having developed rich attractors in the phonological component, can be more sloppy in its conversion from orthography to phonology, which discourages overfitting of the training set. In effect, it is less likely to become a whole-word reader because it has the phonological safety net in place. Because the hidden units have a higher demand placed on them in the face of phonological impairment, exception words are secondarily impaired: the network has effectively fewer hidden units to learn exception items, because it needs to recruit more to produce an accurate phonological output. In contrast, the reduced resource simulations do not have the capacity to memorize the training set, and focuses instead on the redundant correspondences that characterize the "regular" or "rule-governed" words. At asymptote performance on regulars and nonwords is relatively spared, with an impairment on the exception words. With more severe restrictions on computational resources, the net's capacity to encode even the relatively simple and consistent spelling to sound correspondences would be impaired.

In conclusion, these simulations provide further insight into the nature and causes of the two dissociable forms of developmental dyslexia, while demonstrating the validity of a model of word recognition that employs a single pronunciation mechanism rather than the two "routes" of the dual-route model. There is strong independent evidence concerning the existence of phonological processing impairments in children who exhibit the behavioral profile termed phonological dyslexia (see Farmer & Klein, 1995), and therefore our simulation of this deficit pattern by degrading the phonological component has considerable face validity. The surface pattern is less common and there is no independent evidence whether it arises from a resource limitation, a visual processing deficit, or some other cause. The kinds of computational impairments that could give rise to that behavioral pattern can be seen in the present work, motivating further investigations of their bases in human development.

Acknowledgments

Research support by NIMH grant 47566 and a Research Scientist Development Award to M.S. Seidenberg. We thank Lori Altmann for assistance in developing the phonological representation.

References

Castles, A., & Coltheart, M. (1993). Varieties of developmental dyslexia. *Cognition, 47*(2), 149-180.

Coltheart, M., Curtis, B., Atkins, P., & Haller, M. (1993). Models of reading aloud: Dual-route and parallel-distributed- processing approaches. *Psychological Review, 100*(4), 589-608.

Farmer, M., & Klein, R. (1995). The evidence for a temporal processing deficit linked to dyslexia: A review. *Psychonomic Bulletin & Review, 4*(2), 460-493

Glushko, R. J. (1979). The organization and activation of orthographic knowledge in reading aloud. *Journal of Experimental Psychology: Human Perception and Performance, 5,* 674-691.

Hinton, G.E. (1989). Connectionist learning procedures. *Artificial Intelligence, 40,* 185-234.

Manis, F., Seidenberg, M., Doi, L., McBride-Chang, C., & Peterson, A. (1996). On the basis of two subtypes of developmental dyslexia. *Cognition 58,* 157-195.

McCann, R. S., & Besner, D. (1987). Reading pseudohomophones: Implications for models of pronunciation assembly and the locus of word-frequency effects in naming. *Journal of Experimental Psychology: Human Perception & Performance, 13*(1), 14-24.

Minsky, M., & Papert, S. (1969). *Perceptrons.* Cambridge, MA: MIT Press.

Murphy, L., & Pollatsek, A. (1994). Developmental dyslexia: Heterogeneity without discrete subgroups. *Annals of Dyslexia, 44,* 120-146.

Patterson, K., & Hodges, J. R. (1992). Deterioration of word meaning: Implications for reading. *Neuropsychologia, 30*(12), 1025-1040.

Pinker, S. (1991). Rules of language. *Science 253,* 530-534.

Plaut, D. C., & Shallice, T. (1993). Deep dyslexia: A case study of connectionist neuropsychology. *Cognitive Neuropsychology, 10*(5), 377-500.

Plaut, D. C., McClelland, J. L., Seidenberg, M., & Patterson, K. E. (1996). Understanding normal and impaired word reading: Computational principles in quasi-regular domains. *Psychological Review 103*(1), 56-115.

Rumelhart, D., Hinton, G., & Williams, R. (1986). Learning internal representations by error propagation. In D. Rumelhart & J. McClelland (Eds.), *Parallel distributed processing, vol. 1.,* . Cambridge, MA: MIT Press.

Seidenberg, M.-S., & McClelland, J. L. (1989). A distributed, developmental model of word recognition and naming. *Psychological Review, 96*(4), 523-568.

Seidenberg, M. S., Plaut, D. C., Petersen, A.-S., McClelland, J. L., & et al. (1994). Nonword pronunciation and models of word recognition. *Journal of Experimental Psychology: Human Perception & Performance, 20*(6), 1177-1196.

Seidenberg, M.S., 1995. Visual word recognition: an overview. In J. L. Miller & P. Eimas (Eds), *Speech, Language and Communication*, 1995, Academic Press, Inc.

Sejnowski, T.J., & Rosenberg, C. R. (1987). Parallel networks that learn to pronounce English Text. *Complex Systems, 1*, 145-168.

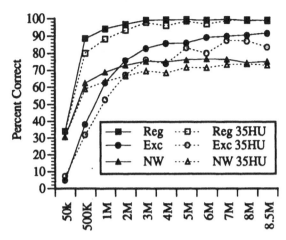

Figure 5: Normal network compared with 35 hidden unit network. Capacity to learn exceptions is impaired.

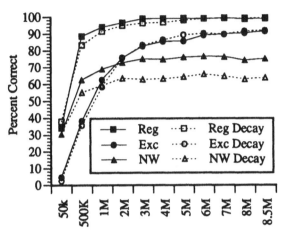

Figure 3: Normal network compared to phonological weight decay network. "Pure pattern" in which only nonwords are affected.

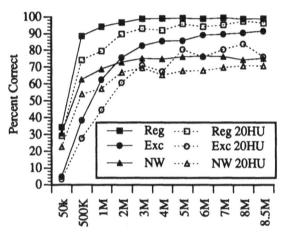

Figure 6: Normal network compared to 20 hidden unit network. Learning of regular correspondences starts to be impaired as well as exceptions.

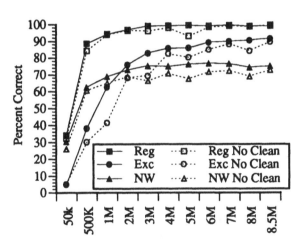

Figure 4: Normal network compared to network without phonological cleanup units. "Mixed" pattern in which exceptions are also affected.

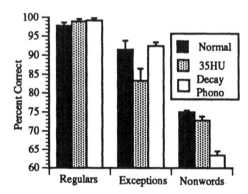

Figure 7: Asymptotic performance for crucial conditions illustrating double dissociation between exception learning and generalization.

Integrating Multiple Cues in Word Segmentation: A Connectionist Model using Hints

Joe Allen and Morten H. Christiansen
Program in Neural, Informational and Behavioral Sciences
University of Southern California
University Park MC-2520
Los Angeles, CA 90089-2520
joeallen@gizmo.usc.edu morten@gizmo.usc.edu

Abstract

Children appear to be sensitive to a variety of partially informative "cues" during language acquisition, but little attention has been paid to how these cues may be integrated to aid learning. Borrowing the notion of learning with "hints" from the engineering literature, we employ neural networks to explore the notion that such cues may serve as hints for each other. A first set of simulations shows that when two equally complex, but related, functions are learned simultaneously rather than individually, they can help bootstrap one another (as hints), resulting in faster and more uniform learning. In a second set of simulations we apply the same principles to the problem of word segmentation, integrating two types of information hypothesized to be relevant to this task. The integration of cues in a single network leads to a sharing of resources that permits those cues to serve as hints for each other. Our simulation results show that such sharing of computational resources allows each of the tasks to facilitate the learning (i.e., bootstrapping) of the other, even when the cues are not sufficient on their own.

Introduction

A theory language of acquisition requires an explanation for how and why children learn the complexities of their native languages so quickly, effortlessly and uniformly. Most traditional answers to this question have taken the form of claims that children are born with language specific constraints, in part because of a gap between the input to which the child is exposed and the competence later exhibited by the adult. The problem, as traditionally characterized, is that the data alone are insufficient to determine the nature of the underlying system, and that therefore additional sources of information are necessary for successful acquisition to occur. Interestingly, a very similar problem has been faced by the engineering oriented branch of the neural network community, in which the problem is construed as learning a function from a limited set of examples. From these investigations have emerged a number of alternative methods for incorporating information not present in the example set into the learning process. These additional sources of information, many based on non-intuitive properties of neural networks, have come to be referred to as "hints". In this paper, we present a novel way of looking at learning with hints within the setting of connectionist modeling of language.

Hints facilitate learning by reducing the number of candidate solutions for a given task (Abu-Mostafa, 1990) and have been shown to result in better generalization (Al-Mashouq & Reed, 1991; Suddarth & Kergosien, 1991) as well as faster learning (Abu-Mostafa, 1990; Al-Mashouq & Reed, 1991; Gällmo & Carlström, 1995; Omlin & Giles, 1992; Suddarth & Kergosien, 1991). The introduction of hints into neural networks has taken various forms, ranging from explicit rule insertion via the pre-setting of weights (Omlin & Giles, 1992), to task specific changes in the learning algorithm (Al-Mashouq & Reed, 1991), to perhaps the most interesting kind of hint: the addition of extra *"catalyst"* output units. Catalyst units are used to represent additional target values expressing a function correlated with, but simpler than, the original target function. The use of catalyst units forces the network to find an internal representation which approximates both the target and the related catalyst function. Suddarth & Kergosien (1991) list a number of simulation experiments in which this approach resulted in faster learning and better generalization. The use of catalyst units has also found its way into engineering applications—e.g., controlling link admissions ATM telecommunication networks (Gällmo & Carlström, 1995).

The idea of inserting information into a network before training has received some attention within cognitive science (albeit not understood in terms of hints). For instance, Harm, Altmann & Seidenberg (1994) demonstrated how pretraining a network on phonology can facilitate the subsequent acquisition of a mapping from orthography to phonology (thus capturing the fact that children normally have acquired the phonology of their native language—that is, they can talk—before they start learning to read). However, catalyst hints have not been explored as a means of improving connectionist models of language. In particular, there is the possibility (not investigated in the engineering hint literature) that such hints could become more than just a catalyst; that is, there may be cases where the learning of two or more functions by the same system may be superior to trying to learn each function individually. Children appear to integrate information from a variety of sources—i.e., from multiple *"cues"*—during language acquisition (Morgan, Shi & Allopenna, 1996), but little attention has been paid to potential mechanisms for such integration. We suggest that cues may serve as "hints" for each other, in that each task constrains the set of solutions available for the other task(s).

In what follows, we show that when two related functions

are learned together each is learned faster and more uniformly. We first provide a simple illustration of the advantage of the integrated learning of two simple functions, XOR and EVEN PARITY, over learning each of them separately. Next, the same idea is applied to a more language-like task: the integrated learning of word boundaries and sequential regularities given a small vocabulary of trisyllabic nonsense words. Finally, in the conclusion, we discuss possible implications for models of language acquisition.

The integrated learning of XOR and EVEN PARITY

In order to provide a simple example of the advantage of allowing two functions to interact during learning, we carried out a series of simulations involving the two simple non-linear functions: XOR and EVEN PARITY. The XOR function has been used before to demonstrate how learning with an extra catalyst unit can decrease convergence time significantly (Gällmo & Carlström, 1995; Suddarth & Kergosien, 1991), but these studies used simpler linear functions (such as, AND) to provide hints about the more complex function. In contrast, we use two functions of equal computational complexity.

input	XOR(1)	EP(1)	XOR-EP	XOR(2)	EP(2)
0 0	0	1	1 0	0 0	1 0
1 1	0	1	1 0	0 0	1 0
1 0	1	0	0 1	0 1	0 0
0 1	1	0	0 1	0 1	0 0

Table 1: The input and required output for the five training conditions.

Given two inputs, i_1 and i_2, XOR is true (i.e., 1) when $(i_1 + i_2) \mod 2 = 1$. EVEN PARITY is the logical negation of XOR and is true when $(i_1 + i_2) \mod 2 = 0$ (in fact, XOR is also known as ODD PARITY). The output of the XOR and EVEN PARITY functions given the four possible binary input combinations is displayed in Table 1 as XOR(1) and EP(1), respectively. These two functions can be learned by a 2-2-1 multi-layer feedforward network. Learning XOR and EVEN PARITY simultaneously requires two output units (i.e., a 2-2-2 net), and the required output is shown as XOR-EP in Table 1. For comparison, two additional 2-2-2 nets were also trained on the individual functions from which the output is labeled XOR(2) and EP(2).

A total of 100 networks (with different initial weight randomizations) were trained for each of the five input/output combinations[1] . Figure 1 illustrates the Root Mean Square (RMS) error history as a function of the number of iterations for nets trained on the XOR-EP, XOR(1), and EP(1) training conditions. Given the assumption that a net has converged

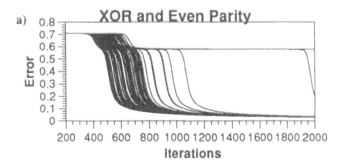

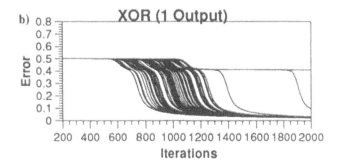

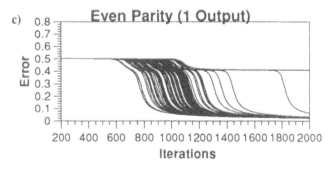

Figure 1: RMS error for 100 sessions of learning a) XOR and EVEN PARITY in a 2-2-2 net, b) XOR in a 2-2-1 net, and c) EVEN PARITY in a 2-2-1 net.

---

[1]Identical learning parameters were applied in all training conditions: learning rate = .1; momentum = .95; initial weight randomization = [-.1;.1]; number of training iterations = 2000.

when the average RMS error for the four input/output combination is .15 or below, we can provide a quantitative analysis of the performance of the nets in the different training conditions. The results in Table 2 clearly show that the networks trained simultaneously on both XOR and EVEN PARITY (see Figure 1a) reach convergence significantly faster than either the 2-2-1 XOR nets (see Figure 1b): $t(184) = 17.589, p < .0001$; or the 2-2-1 EVEN PARITY nets (see Figure 1c): $t(184) = 20.056, p < .0001$. This is also the case in comparison with the 2-2-2 nets trained on XOR alone: $t(189) = 42.797, p < .0001$; and EVEN PARITY alone: $t(189) = 38.876, p < .0001$. Thus, the decrease in convergence time for the XOR-EP trained networks is not a consequence of having additional weights due to the extra output unit. As was to be expected, there was no significant difference between the mean number of iterations to convergence for the single function trained 2-2-1 nets: $t(184) = .610, p = .542$; and between the likewise trained 2-2-2 nets: $t(194) = 1.581, p = .115$. Notice also that the nets trained simultaneously on XOR and EVEN PARITY exhibited a more *uniform* pattern of learning (i.e., less variation) that any of the other training conditions.

Training Condition		Convergence Rate	Mean no. of Iterations	Standard Deviation
XOR + EP		93%	710.96	99.47
XOR	(2-2-1)	93%	1063.87	165.95
EP	(2-2-1)	93%	1077.84	145.69
XOR	(2-2-2)	98%	1519.69	154.32
EP	(2-2-2)	98%	1483.57	165.33

Table 2: Convergence rate, mean number of iterations to convergence, and the standard deviation of this mean for each of the five training conditions (only data from nets converging within 2000 iterations are included in the table).

The results from the above simulation experiments confirm that there are cases where the integrated learning of two functions of equal complexity is better than seeking to learn each of the functions individually. A possible explanation can be found in Suddarth & Kergosien (1991) who analyzed weight changes during the learning of XOR with and without hints. They found that hints allow networks to escape local minima positioned at the origin of weight space. What we have shown here is that a hint need not be a simpler function than the original target function. The results indicate that if two functions are equally complex, but sufficiently correlated, then it may be advantageous to have a single network learn them together. Even though XOR and EVEN PARITY are negations of each other, they are similar in that successful learning of either function requires partitioning the state space in the same way (with the input "1 0" and "0 1" being treated different from "1 1" and "0 0"). The two functions may thus help "bootstrap" each other by forcing their shared resources (in this case the hidden units) toward a common organization of the

input. A mechanism which allows two or more functions to bootstrap each other is of potential relevance to the study of language acquisition since children appear to be sensitive to multiple speech cues which by themselves do not appear to be sufficient to bootstrap language. Of course, learning XOR and EVEN PARITY is a far cry from the task facing children acquiring their native language. We therefore turn to a more language-like application of the idea of bootstrapping via the integrated learning of multiple functions.

Integrating Cues in Word Segmentation

In order to understand an utterance a child must first be able to segment the speech stream into words. While it is likely that adult word level speech segmentation occurs partly as a byproduct of word recognition, infants lack the lexical knowledge which is a pre-requisite to this procedure. A number of proposals regarding bottom up exploitation of sub-lexical cues have been put forward to explain the onset of this capacity (e.g., Jusczyk, 1993). These proposals would require infants to integrate distributional, phonotactic, prosodic and rhythmic information in the segmentation process. In this connection, Brent & Cartwright (in press) have shown that a statistically based algorithm utilizing distributional regularities (including utterance boundary information) is better able to segment words when provided with phonotactic rules. Whereas the process of identifying and verifying the existence and potential of various cues is receiving considerable effort, there has been little attention paid to psychologically plausible mechanisms potentially responsible for integrating these cues. An understanding of possible integrating mechanisms is important for evaluating claims about the potential value of cues. Each of the cues to basic grammatical category measured by Morgan, Shi & Allopenna (1995), for example, had low validity with respect to distinguishing between the categories they considered, but taken together the set of cues was shown to be sufficient in principle to allow a naive learner to assign words to rudimentary grammatical categories with very high accuracy.

Previous connectionist explorations of word segmentation have mainly focused on single cues. Thus, Aslin, Woodward, LaMendola & Bever (1996) demonstrated that utterance final patterns (or boundaries) could be used by a back-propagation network to identify word boundaries with a high degree of accuracy. Cairns, Shillcock, Chater & Levy (1994), on the other hand, showed that sequential phonotactic structure could serve as a cue to the boundaries of words. In contrast, our investigation concentrates on the *integration* of these two cues to word segmentation. The purpose of our simulations is to demonstrate how distributional information reflecting phonotactic regularities in the language may interact with information regarding the ends of utterances to inform the word segmentation task in language acquisition. In particular, we apply the principle of catalyst learning to ask whether learning distributional regularities will assist in the discovery of word boundaries, and whether the learning of word boundaries facilitates the discovery of word internal distributional regularities. As an initial hypothesis, we propose that as a property of the integrating mechanism, the language acquisition system makes use of the efficiency provided by the *sharing of resources* demonstrated in the XOR-EVEN PARITY simulations above to facilitate the task of segmenting the speech stream prior to lexical acquisition.

Saffran, Newport & Aslin (in press) show that adults are capable of acquiring sequential information about syllable combinations in an artificial language such that they can reliably distinguish words that conform to the distributional regularities of such a language from those that do not. For our simulations we constructed a language whose basic constituents were four consonants ("*p*", "*t*", "*b*", "*d*") and three vowels ("*a*", "*i*", "*u*"). These were used to create two vocabulary sets. The first consisted of fifteen trisyllabic words (e.g., "*tibupa*"). Because we hypothesize (like Saffran *et al.*) that variability in the word internal transitional probabilities between syllables[2] serves as an information source regarding the structure of the input language, some syllables occurred in more words, and in more locations within words, than others. Built into this vocabulary were a set of additional restrictions. For example, there are no words that begin with "*b*", and no words ending in "*u*". We will refer to this vocabulary set as "*vtp*" (for variable transitional probability). A "*flat*" vocabulary set, consisting of 12 items, was made up of words with no "peaks" in the word internal syllabic probability distribution; that is, the probability of a given consonant following a vowel was the same for all consonants (and *vice versa* for the vowels)[3]. The flat vocabulary set did not contain any additional restrictions.

Training corpora were created by randomly concatenating 120 instances of each of the words (in a particular vocabulary set) into utterances ranging between two and six words. An additional symbol marking the utterance boundary was added to the end of each utterance, but word boundaries were not marked. The utterances were concatenated into a single large input string. Simple recurrent networks[4] (Elman, 1990) were trained on these corpora by presenting letters one at a time. The task of the networks was to predict the next item in the string. For the testing phase, versions of the input corpora without utterance boundary markers were presented once to

---

[2]The transitional probability between syllables is defined as number of occurrences of syllable X before syllable Y in proportion to the number of occurrences of syllable X; i.e., $\frac{freq.of\,XY}{freq.of\,X}$.

[3]For the vtp vocabulary set, transitional probabilities between syllables word internally ranged from .3 to .7. The transitional probabilities between syllables across word boundaries were lower, ranging between .1 and .3. For the flat vocabulary set, the word internal transitional probabilities between syllables was .667, and did not differ from one another. The transitional probabilities across word boundaries in the full corpus ranged between .007 and .18.

[4]The network architecture consisted of 8 input/output units, (each representing a single letter, plus one representing the boundary marker), 30 hidden units and 30 context units. Identical learning parameters were applied in all training conditions: learning rate .1; momentum .95; initial weight randomization [-.25; .25]; number of training iterations = 7.

a)
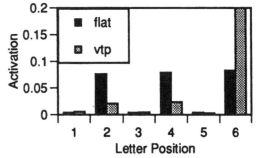

b)
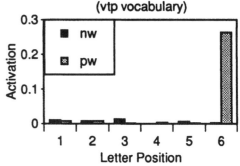

Figure 2: Average activation of the boundary unit from each letter position for a) nets trained, respectively, on the flat and the vtp vocabularies, and b) the net trained on the vtp vocabulary and tested on non-words (nw) and pseudo-words (pw).

the networks.

A comparison between the networks trained respectively on the vtp and flat vocabularies is given in Figure 2(a), which shows the average activation of the boundary unit from each position[5] in a word across the two test corpora. The vtp trained network predicts a boundary with significantly higher confidence at word boundaries than at non word boundaries ($t(12598) = 87.059, p < .0001$). For the vtp trained net, average activation of the boundary unit from the ends of words was .204, while average activation of the boundary unit from positions within words was .04. The network trained on the flat vocabulary, on the other hand, shows almost no discrimination between end-of-word and non-end-of-word positions. Thus the net trained on both the vocabulary with much variation in the syllabic distributional regularities (vtp) and utterance boundary information differentiates ends of words from other parts of words, whereas a network trained only on boundary markers (and the flat vocabulary with little variation

---

[5]Since each network is faced with a prediction task, activation from a position in Figure 2 corresponds to the network's prediction as to the next item in the string; e.g., the network's prediction for letter position 2 is plotted above letter position 1.

in syllabic probability distribution) fails to do so.

In order to assess generalization, we tested the vtp trained network on pseudo-words and non-words. For our pseudo-word trials, we presented the vtp trained network with a set of novel words that were legal in our language (e.g., *"tubipa"*). For our non-word trials, we created a set of words violating the built-in constraints of our language. In this case, we used words ending in *"u"* (e.g., *"tudadu"*). Figure 2(b) shows the average activation level of the boundary unit from each position in the non-word and pseudo-word trials. The activation of the boundary unit stays low for all positions for both types of words except from the final position of the pseudo-words, where the activation level jumps. The average activation of the boundary unit from the end of pseudo-words was .26, whereas it only reached .006 from the end of non-words. Thus, the vtp trained net is able to discriminate between (impossible) non-words and (possible) pseudo-words—as did humans when trained on the similar nonsense language of Saffran *et al.* (in press).

The suggestion that the vtp trained net is treating sequences at the ends of words differently from those at the beginning of words is supported by additional simulations that manipulated the locus of the violation in non-words. When the violation occurred at the beginning of words (e.g., a word starting with *"b"*, which was not a part of the vtp language) the difference in activation patterns between words and non-words was not as readily apparent as when the violation occurred at the ends of words. This result may correspond to the fact that human subjects in the Saffran *et al.* experiments confused legal words with non-words more often when the non-words were made up of the ends of (legal) words than when the non-words were made up of the beginnings of (legal) words.

The results presented above show that if a network learning a simple language with strong variation in the transitional probabilities between syllables has access to the additional information provided by the silences at the ends of utterances, it can use those probabilities to make better hypotheses about the locations of likely word boundaries than a network trained on a language with flat transitional probabilities between syllables. This suggests that the variability in transitional probabilities between syllables may play an important role in allowing learners to identify probable points at which to posit word boundaries. In other words, a network with access to both transitional probabilities and utterance boundary information performs better on a measure of identifying likely word boundaries than a network with access to only utterance boundary information. We can also measure the reverse, i.e., the extent to which utterance boundary information is helpful to learning distributional regularities. In order to do so, we now turn to a simulation that compares the vtp net trained with and without utterance boundary information.

The two nets were tested on a string consisting of the original 15 words in the vocabulary set (with no word or utterance boundaries marked). The test revealed only minor differences between the two networks, in all likelihood because the built-

in distributional regularities are so strong in the small language as to create a ceiling effect. This interpretation is corroborated by a repetition of the experiment using the flat vocabulary: the network trained with boundary markers showed significantly better performance (measured in terms of RMS error) than that trained without boundary markers ($t(142) = 2.012, p < 0.05$). The presence of boundary markers in the input significantly altered the outcome of learning, such that the net trained with boundary markers was better able to learn the sequential regularities which were present in the flat corpus[6]. That is, the integrated learning of two functions again results in better performance. If a network has access to sequential information and utterance markers, it learns the sequential regularities better than a network with access only to sequential information. This result is consistent with the hypothesis that the silences at the ends of utterances may play an important role in the discovery of language specific phonotactic regularities.

Discussion

In the series of simulations reported here we adapted the catalyst hint mechanism previously employed in the engineering literature to the learning of two sufficiently related functions. We demonstrated that the integrated learning of two such functions may result in faster and better learning by combining the well known XOR and EVEN PARITY functions into a single 2-2-2 network. The same idea was then applied to two of the forms of information hypothesized to be relevant to the word segmentation problem by combining strongly constrained distributional information with information about the locations of utterance boundaries in a corpus of utterances generated from an artificial vocabulary of trisyllabic nonsense words. Results suggest that the simultaneous presence of both types of information in the same system may allow them to interact in such a way as to facilitate the acquisition of both phonotactic knowledge and the ability to segment speech into words.

There are several apparent differences between the XOR and EVEN PARITY simulations in section 2 and the simulations presented in section 3. First, the former simulations are of independent functions, both of which can be learned on their own without the presence of the other. The prediction of boundary markers reported in section 3, on the other hand, is not independent of the letter sequences in which they were embedded. That is, although the XOR and EVEN PARITY tasks may be learned separately, learning which of the letter sequences predicts a boundary cannot be learned independently from learning the letter sequences themselves. However, although as observers we can see XOR and EVEN PARITY as independent problems, the network, of course, does not do so. It is treating both (sub)tasks as a part of the larger task to be

---

[6] Although the flat vocabulary did not differ with respect to the transitional probabilities between *syllables*, the transitional probabilities between letters (and sequences longer than the syllable) did differ. We take these to be the source of regularity used by the networks in learning the structure of the flat vocabulary set.

solved. In the XOR-EP simulations, the requirements of each task constrain the solution for the other. A similar claim holds for the simulations presented in section 3. As the simulations themselves verify, these two information sources can be seen as distinct, and can be manipulated independently. But the network is treating both parts of the problem together, and shows an advantage for each task under these conditions.

Although the two sets of simulations differ in important ways, we suggest that the same mechanism is responsible for the results in both section 2 and 3. Just as XOR and EVEN PARITY can be viewed as independent problems, we can see the prediction of word boundaries as a separate task from that of predicting the next letter in the sequence. Because the tasks are learned together, the presence of a secondary task alters the solution applied to the primary task. Specifically, successfully predicting boundaries requires the network to rely on longer sequences than a network required only to predict the next letter. For example, even though consonants can be predicted largely on the basis of the preceeding letter ("*a*" implies "*b*", "*d*", "*t*" and "*p*" roughly equally), the end of an utterance is not predictable unless larger sequences are taken into account (e.g., "*a*" predicts an utterance boundary only when preceeded by "*ub*", etc). The architecture of the network allows it to discover the particular distributional window by which it can perform the entire task optimally. The presence of the word boundary prediction task encourages the net to find an overall solution based on longer letter sequences, just as the presence of the XOR problem encourages the XOR-EP net to find a solution to the EVEN PARITY problem compatible with that which will solve XOR.

Although we have concentrated here on only a few sources of information relevant to the initial word segmentation problem, many additional cues to this task have been proposed (Jusczyk 1993). Our model is not, of course, meant as a complete account of the acquisition of these skills. Admittedly, prior connectionist investigations of the word segmentation problem by Aslin et al. (1996) and Cairns et al. (1994) used more realistic training samples than our artificial language. However, we have concentrated here on the advantages provided by a connectionist integration mechanism, and have successfully extended our approach to a corpus of phonetically transcribed child directed speech (Christiansen, Allen & Seidenberg, in submission). In this connection, a fundamental question for language acquisition theory is why language development is so fast, and so uniform, across children. Although most traditional answers to this question have been based on the idea that children are born with language specific constraints, the speed and uniformity provided by simultaneous learning of related functions may also provide constraints on the development of complex linguistic skills.

References

Abu-Mostafa, Y.S. (1990) Learning from Hints in Neural Networks. *Journal of Complexity*, **6**, 192–198.

Al-Mashouq, K.A. & Reed, I.S. (1991) Including Hints in Training Neural Nets. *Neural Computation*, **3**, 418–427.

Aslin, R. N., Woodward, J. Z., LaMendola, N. P., & Bever, T. G. (1996) Models of Word Segmentation in Fluent Maternal Speech to Infants. In J. L. Morgan & K. Demuth (Eds.), *Signal to Syntax*, pp. 117–134. Mahwah, NJ: LEA.

Brent, M.R. & Cartwright, T.A. (in press) Distributional Regularity and Phonotactic Constraints are Useful for Segmentation. *Cognition*.

Cairns, P., Shillcock, R., Chater, N. & Levy, J. (1994) Lexical Segmentation: The Roles of Sequential Statistics in Supervised and Un-supervised Models. In *Proceedings of the 16th Annual Conference of the Cognitive Science Society*, pp. 136–141. Hillsdale, NJ: LEA.

Christiansen, M., Allen. J. & Seidenberg, M. (in submission) Word Segmentation using Multiple Cues: A Connectionist Model. *Language and Cognitive Processes*.

Elman, J. L. (1990) Finding Structure in Time. *Cognitive Science*, **14**, 179–211.

Gällmo, O. & Carlström, J. (1995) Some Experiments Using Extra Output Learning to Hint Multi Layer Perceptrons. In L.F. Niklasson & M.B. Boden (Eds.), *Current Trends in Connectionism*, pp. 179–190. Hillsdale, NJ: LEA.

Harm, M., Altmann, L., & Seidenberg, M. (1994) Using Connectionist Networks to Examine the Role of Prior Constraints in Human Learning. In *Proceedings of the 16th Annual Conference of the Cognitive Science Society*, pp. 392–396. Hillsdale, NJ: LEA.

Jusczyk, P. W. (1993) From general to language-specific capacities: the WRAPSA Model of how speech perception develops. *Journal of Phonetics*, **21**, 3–28.

Morgan, J., Shi, R., & Allopenna, P. (1996) Perceptual Bases of Rudimentary Grammatical Categories: Toward a Broader Conceptualization of Bootstrapping. In J. Morgan & K. Demuth (Eds.), *From Signal to Syntax*, pp. 263–281. Mahwah, NJ: LEA

Omlin, C.W. & Giles, C.L. (1992) Training Second-Order Recurrent Neural Networks Using Hints. In D. Sleeman & P. Edwards (Eds.), *Proceedings of the Ninth International Conference on Machine Learning*, pp. 363–368. San Mateo, CA: Morgan Kaufmann.

Saffran, J. R., Newport, E. L., & Aslin, R. N. (in press) Word Segmentation: The Role of Distributional Cues. *Journal of Memory and Language*.

Suddarth, S.C. & Kergosien, Y.L. (1991) Rule-injection Hints as a Means of Improving network Performance and Learning Time. In L.B. Almeida & C.J. Wellekens (Eds.), *Neural Networks/EURASIP Workshop 1990*, pp. 120–129. Berlin: Springer-Verlag.

Statistical Cues in Language Acquisition:
Word Segmentation by Infants

Jenny R. Saffran
Department of Brain and
Cognitive Sciences
University of Rochester
Rochester, NY 14627
saffran@bcs.rochester.edu

Richard N. Aslin
Department of Brain and
Cognitive Sciences
University of Rochester
Rochester, NY 14627
aslin@cvs.rochester.edu

Elissa L. Newport
Department of Brain and
Cognitive Sciences
University of Rochester
Rochester, NY 14627
newport@bcs.rochester.edu

Abstract

A critical component of language acquisition is the ability to learn from the information present in the language input. In particular, young language learners would benefit from learning mechanisms capable of utilizing the myriad statistical cues to linguistic structure available in the input. The present study examines eight-month-old infants' use of statistical cues in discovering word boundaries. Computational models suggest that one of the most useful cues in segmenting words out of continuous speech is distributional information: the detection of consistent orderings of sounds. In this paper, we present results suggesting that eight-month-old infants can in fact make use of the order in which sounds occur to discover word-like sequences. The implications of this early ability to detect statistical information in the language input will be discussed with regard to theoretical issues in the field of language acquisition.

Introduction

While it is widely acknowledged that language acquisition is accomplished by an interaction between innate constraints and learning, surprisingly little research has focused on the learning mechanisms which are a critical component of this interaction. Even the richest input imaginable would not allow the child to learn language unless she possessed the mechanisms required to extract pertinent information from this input. Similarly, innate linguistic knowledge would be of no use without mechanisms relating it to linguistic experience. For these reasons, a number of researchers on both sides of the nature/nurture debate have begun to investigate the kinds of learning mechanisms possessed by young language learners.

One class of learning mechanisms which has recently returned to prominence[1] is distributional learning devices, which utilize the statistical properties inherent in linguistic input. The renewed interest in distributional learning in language acquisition results in part from the contributions of recent connectionist models. Importantly, this interest has also been generated by research suggesting that humans extract and remember information about the statistical structure of their native language. Adults possess rich representations of far-flung statistical features of their language, ranging from word-frequency effects to probabilistic prosodic expectancies to frequency-based contingency effects in parsing (e.g., Kelly, 1988; MacDonald, Pearlmutter, & Seidenberg, 1994; Morton, 1969), and can readily learn distributional regularities in laboratory tasks (e.g., Morgan, Meier, & Newport, 1987; Saffran, Newport, & Aslin, in press).

These abilities are not confined to adults. First-grade children, for example, are at least as good as adults at discovering distributional regularities in the lab (Saffran *et al.*, under review). Infants also demonstrate knowledge of some of the statistical regularities of their native language. For example, when nine-month-old infants are presented with phonotactically legal phonetic patterns which are either frequent or infrequent in their native language, they prefer to listen to the frequent patterns (Jusczyk, Luce, & Charles-Luce, 1994). This knowledge must arise through learning from the linguistic environment, suggesting that statistical learning mechanisms exist and, moreover, play a far greater role in language acquisition than most contemporary theories suggest.

The present research seeks to elucidate the nature of the learning mechanisms underlying the acquisition of language. Our strategy in this research is to focus on aspects of language that are undeniably discovered in the language input, rather than potentially an expression of innate knowledge. In particular, we hope to begin to discover how infants' learning mechanisms are structured to make use of the enormous volume of statistical information available in the language input. To do so, we investigated the learning mechanisms underlying word segmentation.

Word Segmentation

One of the earliest and most impressive feats of learning by infants is the discovery of word boundaries. Speech is essentially continuous, without pauses or other consistent acoustic cues present to mark word boundaries. Infants must thus somehow break into the speech stream to discover word boundaries without recourse to silences analogous to the white spaces between printed words. Despite the difficulty of this learning problem (Cole & Jakimik, 1980), experimental evidence indicates that infants can succeed at word segmentation tasks by eight months of age, well before the onset of word production (Jusczyk & Aslin, 1995).

There are many possible cues to word boundaries that might be exploited, including prosodic regularities, as well

---

[1]Once greatly popular among Bloomfieldian linguists (see, e.g., Harris, 1955), distributional analyses of linguistic structure fell into disfavor with the birth of Chomskian generative syntax.

as the occasional occurrence of utterance-final pauses and words spoken in isolation (see, e.g., Christophe *et al.*, 1994; Jusczyk, Cutler, & Redanz, 1993). While all of these types of information are likely to be helpful, none alone is sufficient to solve the word segmentation problem (see Saffran *et al.*, in press, for discussion). However, one important source of potential information lies in the distributional information offered by the sequences of sounds within and between words (Brent & Cartwright, in press; Hayes & Clark, 1970; Harris, 1955; Saffran *et al.*, in press). A word may be defined as a fixed series of sounds. The learner, however, does not have direct access to this information. Rather, what the learner experiences in the input is complex statistical information over a corpus of utterances resulting from the concatenation of subword units. This information will take the form of relatively strong correlations between sounds found within words, contrasted with weaker correlations across word boundaries (Hayes & Clark, 1970; Saffran *et al.*, in press). On this view, one might discover words in linguistic input in much the same way that one discovers objects in the visual environment via motion: the spatial-temporal correlations between the different parts of the moving object will be stronger than those between the moving object and the surrounding visual environment.

Several recent computational models have illustrated the efficacy of distributional cues in word segmentation. One such model demonstrates that distributional information can provide appropriate segmentations when the algorithm used is the minimum description length principle, an evaluation function which minimizes the amount of memory needed to represent a lexicon derived from a previously unsegmented corpus of speech (Brent & Cartwright, in press). Other models indicate that class-based n-gram and feature-based neural network models can segment speech using transitional probabilities (Cairns *et al.*, 1994); similarly, Elman (1990) describes a simple recurrent network able to discover written words in unsegmented text by computing graded co-occurrence statistics (see Wolff, 1975, for similar findings using a non-connectionist architecture). These corpus-based models, along with many others in the machine speech recognition literature, demonstrate that statistical information is sufficient *in principle* for rudimentary word segmentation[2].

Can human learners make use of statistical cues to word boundaries? If not, then this wealth of information would be of little use to humans confronted with continuous speech in an unfamiliar language. Saffran *et al.* (in press) asked whether adult subjects were able to use differences in the

transitional probabilities between sounds to discover word boundaries[3]. Across a language corpus, the transitional probability from one sound to the next will generally be greatest when the two sounds follow one another word-internally; transitional probabilities spanning word boundaries will tend to be relatively low. After only twenty minutes of exposure, adults were able to learn the multisyllabic words of a nonsense language presented as a synthesized speech stream containing no cues to word boundaries except for transitional probabilities (Saffran *et al.*, in press). Moreover, this same result was obtained with first-grade children as well as adults, even when the presentation of the speech stream occurred in the background, while subjects were engaged in another task and neither told to listen nor to learn (Saffran *et al.*, under review). The abilities of human learners to perform such statistical computations implicitly, during mere exposure, are quite impressive. This suggests that this learning mechanism operates automatically, much as one would expect from a learning mechanism hypothesized to underlie learning in children too young to engage in conscious hypothesis testing.

The crucial subjects for such investigations are infants of the age at which rudimentary word segmentation first occurs. Language learning tasks are often seen as too difficult for the limited abilities of infants; indeed, our lack of knowledge regarding infant learning has often led theorists to assume that because a learning task seems difficult, it must be solved innately. However, the sheer volume of information that infants do in fact learn about their native language, much of which could not possibly be encoded innately, suggests that young infants may in fact be far better at extracting statistical regularities from the input than has generally been assumed.

Recent research suggests that infants may in fact be attuned to the kinds of distributional information which serve to cue word boundaries. For example, infants as young as two months of age are able to remember the order of spoken words, as long as the words are spoken with normal sentential prosody (Mandel, Kemler Nelson, & Jusczyk, in press). By eight months of age, infants are able to detect consistently ordered two-syllable units presented in brief repetitive utterances (Goodsitt, Morgan, & Kuhl, 1993). The next step is to determine whether infants are able to keep track of the array of probabilities found in multisyllabic sequences to discover word boundaries, in the absence of any other cues to word boundaries. The present study provides some preliminary indications that infants can in fact use the order of the sounds that they hear to extract word-like units.

Method

This study used a brief familiarization period combined with the headturn preference procedure widely used in infancy research (Jusczyk & Aslin, 1995). In this methodology, infants are first exposed to an auditory stimulus which serves as a potential learning experience. Following this exposure, the infant is presented with two types of auditory stimuli: familiar stimuli, like those presented during the familiarization period, and novel stimuli. The infant's

---

[2]No such algorithm is error-free; neither, however, are young children, who very commonly make segmentation errors (a common undersegmentation error is treating a phrase like "ham'neggs" as a single word). Such errors, however, are not random, but rather reflect the distributional characteristics of the input (e.g., Brown, 1973). Recovery from segmentation errors occurs with more extensive input and the detection of other cues correlated with the correct word boundaries.

[3]The transitional probability of Y/X = $\dfrac{\text{frequency of XY}}{\text{frequency of X}}$

listening preferences are then assessed. Two possible outcomes suggest that learning has occurred. Infants of this age generally prefer to listen to somewhat familiar items; in this case, the infants should prefer to listen to the items similar to those heard during the familiarization period, if learning did in fact occur. However, the opposite effect would also signal learning: if the infants had learned and habituated to the familiarization stimuli, then a novel stimulus would be more engaging. No preference would, of course, fail to indicate that any learning had occurred.

In the present study, infants were familiarized with an artificial speech stream, consisting of four trisyllabic nonsense words repeated in random order by a speech synthesizer. The synthesizer was given no information regarding word boundaries, and thus spoke the speech stream continuously in a monotone, without any acoustic cues to word boundaries. The only cues to word boundaries were statistical; the transitional probabilities between syllables within words were greater than the transitional probabilities between syllables spanning word boundaries. Following a two-minute exposure, the infants' learning was assessed by determining whether they preferred to listen to 'words' from the nonsense language, or 'nonwords', which consisted of the same syllables that the infants had heard during familiarization but now presented in a novel order. A significant preference for either words or nonwords would, as discussed above, signal that the syllable orders heard during familiarization had been learned to the extent that the infants could distinguish them from novel syllable orders.

Subjects. 16 infants (nine male, seven female), approximately eight months of age, participated in the study. Three additional infants were tested but not included in the analysis for the following reasons: experimenter error (2), and crying (1).

Stimuli. Two counterbalanced stimulus conditions were generated. For each condition, 45 tokens of each of four trisyllabic nonsense words (Condition A: *tupiro, golabu, bidaku, padoti*; Condition B: *dapiku, tilado, burobi, pagotu*) were digitized to create two-minute-long speech streams. The words were spoken in random order, with the stipulation that the same word never occurred twice in a row. A speech synthesizer (MacinTalk) generated the speech stream at a rate of 270 syllables/minute with equivalent levels of coarticulation between all syllables; no pauses or any other acoustic or prosodic cues to word boundaries were present. A sample of the speech stream used in Condition A was analogous to the following orthographic representation: *bidakupadotigolabubidakutupiro...* The only cues to word boundaries were the transitional probabilities between syllable pairs over the language corpus, which were higher within words (all 1.0) than across word boundaries (all .33).

To assess learning, each infant was presented with repetitions of four trisyllabic strings (*tupiro, golabu, dapiku, tilado*) during the test phase. For the infants in Condition A, the first two test strings were 'words' which had been played during familiarization, and the last two test strings were 'nonwords', that is, syllables which they had heard during familiarization but now presented in a novel order (the transitional probabilities between the syllables in the nonwords were all zero relative to the familiarization

corpus). For infants in Condition B, the first two test strings were 'nonwords' and the last two test strings were 'words'. This between-subjects counterbalanced design ensured that any observed preferences for words or nonwords across both conditions would not be artifacts of any general preferences for certain syllable strings. A test trial consisted of repetitions of a test string. Each of the four test strings were presented on three different trials, resulting in a total of 12 test trials per infant. Note that the strings used in the test were generated in citation form by the speech synthesizer, and thus had acoustic properties quite different from the same strings presented in the continuous speech stream.

Design. Half of the infants were assigned to each familiarization condition. During the test phase, all infants heard the same 12 test trials, randomized for each subject.

Procedure. During an experimental session, the infant was seated on a parent's lap in a sound attenuated booth. A video camera was placed directly in front of the infant, allowing the experimenter to observe the session via a video monitor outside the booth. Also directly in front of the infant was a blinking red light, used to bring the infant's gaze back to midline between trials. Blinking yellow lights were mounted on the right and left sides of the booth, along with hidden speakers. Both the parent and the experimenter wore headphones playing loud masking music. Because the different test trials were randomly assigned to the right or left speaker, and the experimenter could not hear the stimuli, the experimenter was blind to which stimulus was being presented on any given trial.

During the familiarization phase, the two minute speech stream was played continuously through both speakers. Blinking lights were used to help maintain infants' interest; the lights, but not the speech, were contingent upon the infant's looking behavior. Each trial began with the blinking center light. Once the infant had fixated on the center light, the experimenter signaled the Macintosh Quadra 650 running the study to turn off the center light and blink one of the side lights, whereupon the infant would turn to fixate the now blinking side light. The side light would continue to blink until the infant had looked away from it for two seconds. At that point, the center light would begin flashing, and a new trial would begin.

The test phase was similar, except that the number of repetitions of the test stimuli was contingent upon the infants' listening preferences. When the infant turned to look at the blinking side light, one of the four test strings was repeated from the speaker on that side, until the infant looked away for a preset criterion of two seconds (or until the test string had been repeated 15 times). The lookaway criterion signalled a loss of interest in that particular test string. Each infant thus only heard each test string as long as it remained interesting to him/her. Listening times to each type of test stimulus reflected each infant's listening preferences; these were tabulated on-line by the computer.

Results

We first compared the listening patterns of infants in the two counterbalanced conditions with one another to ensure that there were no overall preferences for any particular test items regardless of familiarization. This was done by computing a difference score between mean listening times for words and nonwords for each infant, and comparing the infants from the two conditions with a t-test. As no differences were found ($t(14) = 1.3$, n.s.), data from the two conditions were combined in the primary analysis.

We then compared listening times to the 'words' versus the 'nonwords'. A matched-pairs t-test revealed that the novel 'nonwords' were listened to significantly longer than the familiar 'words': $t(15) = 2.8$, $p < .02$. Mean listening scores are presented in Figure 1. Twelve of the 16 infants listened longer to the novel stimuli. This novelty preference (or dishabituation effect) indicates that the infants clearly recognized that the novel orderings of test syllables were in fact novel and distinct from the orders that they had learned during the familiarization phase. Moreover, this effect could not have been simply due to memory for the low-level acoustic patterns presented during familiarization, as the acoustic properties of the test 'words' were quite different from the same 'words' present in the speech stream. Rather, the infants appear to have learned and remembered a more abstract representation of the strings of sounds that they heard during familiarization.

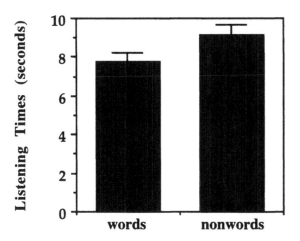

Figure 1: Mean listening times to the familiar (words) and novel (nonwords) stimuli.
Error bars = 1 standard error.

Discussion

Despite the impoverished state of the speech stream used in this study -- a learning stimulus devoid of prosody, pauses, or any other cues to word boundaries save statistical cues -- eight-month-old infants nevertheless succeeded at learning the words of the language to which they were exposed, at least to the extent that they could distinguish them from the same syllables in novel orders. This is by no means a trivial accomplishment. Despite the ubiquity of events which unfold in time, the discovery and representation of serial order is generally considered to be a difficult technical problem (e.g., Elman, 1990). Moreover, infants in this study had no particular incentive to keep track of co-

occurrences. Rather, the discovery of the words within the continuous speech stream appears to be a natural outcome of exposure to patterned input. This process is particularly impressive given the brevity of exposure necessary for learning; the infants in this study were familiarized with the speech for a mere two minutes.

Of course, in actual language learning, other cues are likely to be present and used by infants discovering the word boundaries of their native language. Such cues are likely to be particularly effective when used in tandem with distributional cues. For example, Brent & Cartwright (in press) demonstrated that phonotactic information makes an additive contribution to distributional information in their computational model of word segmentation. Allen and Christiansen (1996) argue that the integration of such cues allows for an interaction which in itself is a powerful catalyst for learning. These modeling results are supported by behavioral data which suggest that 9-month-old infants are sensitive to mismatches of distributional and prosodic regularities (e.g., Morgan & Saffran, 1995).

The results presented here indicate that infants possess at least the minimal computational machinery needed to discover the regularities of their language: the ability to detect and represent serial order information. This in itself is not sufficient for word segmentation, which requires the extraction of relative frequencies of ordered strings to compute transitional probabilities, but it is a necessary prerequisite for this process. In fact, recent research in our laboratory has demonstrated that eight-month-old infants can use the relative frequencies of co-occurrence of sound pairs to detect word boundaries (Saffran, Aslin, & Newport, under review), lending further support to the present results.

More generally, future research must continue to investigate the means by which young learners make use of the wealth of statistical information available to them in the language input. The combination of innately constrained learning mechanisms and statistically rich input is potentially immensely powerful, and it is imperative that we gain a greater understanding of the ways in which this interaction renders young humans such superb language learners. The present experiment is one of a few recent studies which have begun to document the rapidity and extent of infant learning using carefully controlled exposures in the laboratory (see also Goodsitt et al, 1993; Jusczyk & Aslin, 1995; Morgan & Saffran, 1995). It may therefore be premature to assume, as many researchers have, that the prodigious abilities of young infants necessarily reflect innately specified knowledge. Rather, what may be innate is the human capacity to learn and reorganize the regularities which structure our environment, thereby allowing infants to make sense of what may initially be a "blooming, buzzing, confusion".

Acknowledgements

This research was supported by an NSF predoctoral fellowship to J.R.S., NSF grant SBR-9421064 to R.N.A., and NIH grant DC00167 to E.L.N. We thank J. Gallipeau, J. Hooker, P. Jusczyk, A. Jusczyk, K. Ruppert, J. Sawusch, and especially T. Mintz for their help with various aspects of this research.

References

Allen, J., & Christiansen, M. H. (1996). Integrating multiple cues in word segmentation: A connectionist model using hints. In *Proceedings of the Eighteenth Annual Conference of the Cognitive Science Society*. Hillsdale, NJ: Lawrence Earlbaum Associates.

Brent, M. R., & Cartwright, T. A. (in press). Distributional regularity and phonotactic constraints are useful for segmentation. *Cognition*.

Brown, R. (1973). *A first language*. Cambridge, MA: Harvard University Press.

Cairns, P., Shillcock, R., Chater, N., & Levy, J. (1994). Lexical segmentation: The role of sequential statistics in supervised and un-supervised models. *Proceedings of the Sixteenth Annual Conference of the Cognitive Science Society*. Hillsdale, NJ: Lawrence Earlbaum Associates.

Christophe, A., Dupoux, E., Bertoncini, J., & Mehler, J. (1994). Do infants perceive word boundaries? An empirical study of the bootstrapping of lexical acquisition. *Journal of the Acoustical Society of America, 95*, 1570-1580.

Cole, R., & Jakimik, J. (1980). *A model of speech perception*. Hillsdale, NJ: Lawrence Earlbaum Associates.

Elman, J. L. (1990). Finding structure in time. *Cognitive Science, 14*, 179-211.

Goodsitt, J. V., Morgan, J. L., & Kuhl, P. K. (1993). Perceptual strategies in prelingual speech segmentation. *Journal of Child Language, 20*, 229-252.

Harris, Z. S. (1955). From phoneme to morpheme. *Language, 31*, 190-222.

Hayes, J. R., & Clark, H. H. (1970). Experiments in the segmentation of an artificial speech analog. In J. R. Hayes (Ed.), *Cognition and the development of language*. New York: Wiley.

Jusczyk, P. W., & Aslin, R. N. (1995). Infants' detection of the sound patterns of words in fluent speech. *Cognitive Psychology, 29*, 1-23.

Jusczyk, P. W., Cutler, A., & Redanz, L. (1993). Infants' sensitivity to predominant stress patterns in English. *Child Development, 64*, 675-687.

Jusczyk, P. W., Luce, P. A., & Charles-Luce, J. (1994). Infants' sensitivity to phonotactic patterns in the native language. *Journal of Memory and Language, 33*, 630-645.

Kelly, M. H. (1988). Phonological biases in grammatical category shifts. *Journal of Memory and Language, 27*, 343-358.

MacDonald, M. C., Pearlmutter, N. J., & Seidenberg, M. S. (1994). The lexical nature of syntactic ambiguity resolution. *Psychological Review, 101*, 676-703.

Mandel, D., Kemler Nelson, D., & Jusczyk, P. W. (in press). Infants remember the order of words in a spoken sentence. *Cognitive Development*.

Morgan, J. L., Meier, R. P., & Newport, E. L. (1987). Structural packaging in the input to language learning: Contributions of prosodic and morphological marking of phrases to the acquisition of language. *Cognitive Psychology, 19*, 498-550.

Morgan, J. L., & Saffran, J. R. (1995). Emerging integration of sequential and suprasegmental information in preverbal speech segmentation. *Child Development, 66*, 911-936.

Morton, J. (1969). Interaction of information in word recognition. *Psychological Review, 76*, 165-178.

Saffran, J. R., Aslin, R. N., & Newport, E. L. (under review). Learning of sequential statistics by 8-month-old infants.

Saffran, J. R., Newport, E. L., & Aslin, R. N. (in press). Word segmentation: The role of distributional cues. *Journal of Memory and Language*.

Saffran, J. R., Newport, E. L., Aslin, R. N., Tunick, R. A., & Barrueco, S. (under review). Incidental language learning: Listening (and learning) out of the corner of your ear.

Wolff, J. G. (1975). An algorithm for the segmentation of an artificial language analogue. *British Journal of Psychology, 66*, 79-90.

Cognition and the Statistics of Natural Signals

Javier R. Movellan and **George Chadderdon**
Departments of Cognitive Science and Computer Science
University of California, San Diego
La Jolla, CA 92093
movellan@cogsci.ucsd.edu and gchadder@netman.orincon.com

Abstract

This paper illustrates how the statistical structure of natural signals may help understand cognitive phenomena. We focus on a regularity found in audio visual speech perception. Experiments by Massaro and colleagues consistently show that optic and acoustic speech signals have separable influences on perception. From a Bayesian point of view this regularity reflects a perceptual system that treats optic and acoustic speech as if they were conditionally independent signals. In this paper we perform a statistical analysis of a database of audiovisual speech to check whether optic and acoustic speech signals are indeed conditionally independent. If so, the regularities found by Massaro and colleagues could be seen as an optimal processing strategy of the perceptual system. We analyze a small database of audio visual speech using hidden Markov models, the most successful models in automatic speech recognition. The results suggest that acoustic and optic speech signals are indeed conditionally independent and that therefore, the separability found by Massaro and colleagues may be explained in terms of optimal perceptual processing: Independent processing of optic and acoustic speech results in no significant loss of information.

Introduction

This paper illustrates how the analysis of the statistical structure of natural signals may provide a rational basis for understanding human cognition. This approach is not new, and in our case it was inspired on David Marr's ideas about the importance of a functional level of analysis, John Anderson's views on rational analysis, and by David Field's work relating early visual processing to the statistics of natural images (Marr, 1982; Field, 1987; Anderson, 1990). In this paper we analyze a regularity found in a wide variety of experiments on audiovisual speech perception.

Research on audiovisual speech perception shows that visual signals modulate the perception of auditory signals. For example, McGurk and MacDonald (McGurk & MacDonald, 1976), showed that when subjects hear "ba" while seeing "ga", they perceive "da", a percept which is jointly influenced by the optic and the acoustic speech signals. Extensive research has been done to understand how optic and acoustic speech signals combine into a unified percept (Massaro & Cohen, 1983; Massaro, 1987; Braida, 1991). For concreteness, consider the following hypothetical experiment, which illustrates a common design in this area of research. Subjects are repeatedly presented with 9 opto-acoustic speech signals obtained by combining, in a fully factorial design, the acoustic articulations /ba/, /ga/, and /da/ with optic articulations of the same alternatives. Subjects are then presented with these signals and asked to report what they heard. The responses are then organized into a stimulus-response matrix in which each entry indicates the probability of a particular perceptual response when the subject is presented with one of the 9 possible signal combinations. Let $\{\omega_1, \omega_2, \cdots, \omega_n\}$, represent the response alternatives, ξ^o the optic signal and ξ^a the acoustic signals. Massaro and colleagues (Massaro & Cohen, 1983; Massaro, 1987) have repeatedly shown that in a wide variety of experiments of this type, response probability ratios factorize into independent components one controlled by the acoustic signal and one by the optic signal.

$$\frac{p_r(\omega_i|\xi^o\xi^a)}{p_r(\omega_j|\xi^o\xi^a)} = \left(\frac{F_o(\xi^o, \omega_i)}{F_o(\xi^o, \omega_j)}\right)\left(\frac{F_a(\xi^a, \omega_i)}{F_a(\xi^a, \omega_j)}\right) \qquad (1)$$

where $p_r(\omega_i|\xi_k^o\xi_l^a)$ is the probability of subjects choosing response alternative ω_i when presented with the optic signal ξ^o synchronized with the acoustic signal ξ^a. The term

$$\frac{F_o(\xi^o, \omega_i)}{F_o(\xi^o, \omega_j)}, \qquad (2)$$

is interpreted as the relative support of the optic signal ξ^o for the two response alternatives under consideration, and the term

$$\frac{F_a(\xi^a, \omega_i)}{F_a(\xi^a, \omega_j)}, \qquad (3)$$

is interpreted as the relative support of the acoustic signal ξ^a for the two response alternatives under consideration.

The crucial aspect of this result is that response probabilities ratios are separable into independent factors. This type of factorization was first noticed by Morton (Morton, 1969) and thus it is at times recognized as *Morton's law*. Movellan and McClelland (Movellan & McClelland, 1995 submitted for publication) showed that Morton's law is the signature of a perceptual system that processes signals as if they were conditionally independent. If the acoustic and optic speech signals were indeed conditionally independent, Morton's law would reflect an optimal processing strategy of multimodal speech.

To investigate this point, we analyze the statistical structure of a small database of audio-visual speech signals. Our goal is to test whether naturally occurring acoustic and visual speech signals are conditionally independent.

At a formal level, conditional independence is defined as follows,

$$p(\xi^o\xi^a|\omega_j) = p(\xi^o|\omega_j)p(\xi^a|\omega_j) \qquad (4)$$

indicating that the likelihood of each perceptual alternative ω_j, is separable. Intuitively, conditional independence tells us that if we analyze signals belonging to a perceptual category ω_j, we will find that the acoustic and optic signals within that group are statistically independent. From a Bayesian point of view the likelihood is the only source of data-driven information about the perceptual alternatives and thus, conditional independence allows separable processing of the optic and acoustic signals.

Due to the large dimensionality of the opto-acoustic signals we analyze their statistical structure in an indirect manner, by modeling the speech signal using hidden Markov models (HMM), the most successful models for automatic speech recognition. We train HMMs to recognize audiovisual speech. Some of these models are constrained to assume conditional independence some are not. The constrained models are a restricted version of the unconstrained models. We then optimize the entire family of constrained and unconstrained models. If the audio and visual speech signals are conditionally independent, the best constrained model should perform about as well as the best unconstrained model. Otherwise, the best unconstrained models should outperform the best constrained models.

Database

We used Tulips1, a database compiled by Movellan (Movellan, 1995) and consisting of 9 male and 3 female undergraduate students from the Cognitive Science Department at the University of California, San Diego. For each of these, two samples were taken for each of the digits "one" through "four". Thus, the total database consists of 96 digit utterances. The audio sampling rate is 11.1 kHz, and each sample has an 8-bit representation. Each frame in the video track of a movie is an 8-bit grey-scale, 100x75 pixel image, and each movie is sampled at a visual frame rate of 30 frames per second. The subjects were asked to center and align their lips in the camera during the sampling.

Signal processing.

Our signal processing philosophy is to preserve, as much as possible, the information in the original frames. Each frame from the video track is symmetrized along the vertical axis, and a temporal difference frame is then obtained by subtracting the previous symmetrized frame from the current symmetrized frame. The symmetrized and differential symmetrized frames are then low-pass filtered and soft-thresholded (Movellan, 1995), and the left side of the former and the right side of the latter

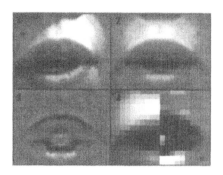

Figure 1: Visual Preprocessing: 1) Raw Image. 2) Symmetrized Image. 3) Difference Image. 4) Final Composite.

are combined to form the final feature frame. Each of these final frames has 300 dimensions (20x15 pixels). No hard feature detection procedures are used to avoid loss of potentially important information. The approach is illustrated in Figure 1.

LPC/cepstral analysis is used for the auditory frontend. This is a fairly standard technique which parameterizes an estimate of the human vocal tract's transfer function. First, the auditory signal is passed through a first-order emphasizer to spectrally flatten it. Then the signal is separated into non-overlapping frames at 30 frames per second. This is done so that there are an equal number of visual and auditory feature vectors for each utterance, and these will be in synch with each other. On each frame we perform the standard LPC/cepstral analysis. Each 30 msec auditory frame is characterized by 26 features: 12 cepstral coefficients, 12 delta-cepstrals, 1 log-power, and 1 delta-log-power. Each of the 26 features is encoded with 8-bit accuracy. The cepstral coefficients are a compact representation of the local power spectrum of the speech signal. The local phase spectrum is lost in this representation. However, loosing local phase does not affect the intelligibility of the acoustic signal.

Statistical modeling of the speech signal.

We model the speech signal using hidden Markov models (HMMs), one per word category, independently trained on signals from the corresponding word categories (see Figure 2). The HMMs were continuous density left-to-right models with a fixed number of states. The probability distribution generated by a state is modeled as a mixture of multivariate Gaussian distributions. A diagonal covariance matrix is used, with the variances of each Gaussian in a particular state tied together. The number of states and number of Gaussian mixtures per state were systematically varied to find the best combination of states and mixtures.

After each model is trained on exemplars from its corresponding word category, classification of an unknown observation proceeds by calculating, for each model, the log-likelihood of the model given the observation. Then the classification corresponding to the model with the highest log-likelihood is chosen as the winner.

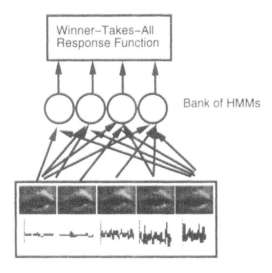

Figure 2: The signal is modeled with a bank of HMMs.

	Acoustic Signal to Noise Ratio				
Model	0 dB	6 dB	12 dB	18 dB	Clean
Unconstrained	94.2	95.2	94.5	93.9	95.5
Constrained	92	95.2	96.4	98.7	98
Auditory Only	75.4	84.6	89.1	92.6	92.3
Visual Only	89.4	89.4	89.4	89.4	89.4

Table 1: Performance at different signal to noise ratios.

the best 2 unconstrained architectures.

Table 1 shows the performance of the best constrained and unconstrained models. For completeness we also show the performance of the best Auditory-only and the best Visual-only models. In most cases the constrained architecture performs marginally better than the unconstrained architecture. Thus, assuming conditional independence does not result in loss of information,

Conclusions

The results of this exploratory study suggest that the optic and acoustic speech signals are indeed conditionally independent. Thus, the emergence of Morton's law in audiovisual speech perception experiments, may reflect an optimal functional organization of the perceptual system.

We need to be cautious about these results since our analysis has important limitations: 1) Our work is based on a small database and it is unclear whether it would generalize to other databases. 2) Since our database is small, it is possible that the potential bias introduced by the assumption of conditional independence may be compensated by the fact that it allows a significant reduction in the number of training parameters. 3) We model the speech signal using HMMs and it is possible, that different approaches would have produced different results. 4) Different results may perhaps be obtained using different signal processing strategies (e.g. feature detectors, Gabor filters ...) 5) Our results do not clarify at which level independence holds. It is possible that the independence obtained when conditioning on words is due to the existence of lower level independence (e.g. when conditioning over sub-word units). Our results can only be used as evidence that independence holds at some level but we cannot specify where this level is located.

We are currently working to overcome these limitations but we believe this exploratory work illustrates how current techniques on artificial pattern recognition may be used to analyze the structure of natural signals and to establish a statistical approach to human cognition.

References

Anderson, J. R. (1990). *The adaptive character of thought.* Hillsdale, NJ: Earlbaum.

Braida, L. (1991). Crossmodal integration and the identification of consonant segments. *Quarterly Journal of Experimental Psychology. A, Human Experimental Psychology, 43(3),* 647–677.

Field, D. (1987). Relations between the statistics of natural images and the response properties of cortical

We use two types of models, which we will refer to as *constrained* and *unconstrained*. The constrained models implement the assumption of conditional independence. Each constrained model consist of two independent sub-models, one auditory and one visual. These are trained on their respective data sets, and during testing, the combined response is obtained by adding the log-likelihood of the auditory and visual models given the observations. This operation enforces the assumption of conditional independence. Classification proceeds by picking the model with the highest combined log-likelihood.

The unconstrained models are trained on the combined opto-acoustic signal. These models are more general than the unconstrained models. If the signals are conditionally independent these models should learn to combine their outputs additively thus performing as well as the previous models. However, if the signals are not conditionally independent these models should perform better.

Results

We tested the two types of models with a variety of signal-to-noise ratios (SNR) in the acoustic signal. Training was done with clean auditory samples, and testing with a variable (SNR). No noise was added to the images either for training or testing. The jack-knife method was used for obtaining each generalization performance estimate. Training was done leaving out the utterances of one of the 12 subjects, and testing was done on the utterances of the excluded subject. This was repeated 12 times, leaving out a different subject each time. Jackknife estimates are based on the average generalization obtained with these 12 samples.

For each of the two types of models (constrained and unconstrained), we systematically tested 45 different architectures by varying the number of states (2,3,4,5,6) and the number of Gaussians per state (2,3,4,5,6,7,8,9,10). We chose the best 2 constrained and cells. *Journal of the Optical Society of America, 4*, 2379–2394.

Marr, D. (1982). *Vision*. New York: Freeman.

Massaro, D. W. (1987). *Speech perception by ear and eye: A paradigm for psychological research*. Hillsdale, NJ: Erlbaum.

Massaro, D. W., & Cohen, M. M. (1983). Integration of visual and auditory information in speech perception. *Journal of Experimental Psychology: Human Perception and Performance, 9*, 753–771.

McGurk, H., & MacDonald, J. (1976). Hearing lips and seeing voices. *Nature, 264*.

Morton, J. (1969). The interaction of information in word recognition. *Psychological Review, 76*, 165–178.

Movellan, J. R. (1995). Visual speech recognition with stochastic neural networks. In G. Tesauro, D. Touretzky, & T. Leen (Eds.), *Advances in neural information processing systems*. Cambridge,Massacusetts: MIT Press.

Movellan, J. R., & McClelland, J. L. (1995, submitted for publication). *Stochastic interactive processing, channel separability and optimal perceptual inference: an examination of morton's law* (Technical Report PDP.CNS.95.4, Available at http://cogsci.ucsd.edu/movellan/publications.html). Carnegie Mellon University.

An Abstract Computational Model of Learning Selective Sensing Skills

Pat Langley[1] (LANGLEY@CS.STANFORD.EDU)
Robotics Laboratory, Computer Science Dept.
Stanford University, Stanford, CA 94305

Abstract

In this paper we review the benefits of abstract computational models of cognition and present one such model of behavior in a flight-control domain. The model's central assumptions are that differences among subjects are due to differences in sensing skills, and that the main form of learning involves updating statistics to distinguish relevant from irrelevant features. We report an implementation of this abstract model of sensory learning, along with a system that searches the space of parameter settings in order to fit the model to observations. We compare the sensory-learning framework to an alternative based on the power law, finding that the latter fits the data slightly better but that it requires many more parameters.

Computational Models of Behavior

Computational models of human cognition date back to the 1950s, soon after researchers realized that computers had general symbol-processing capability. Early computer models like GPS (Newell, Shaw, & Simon, 1960) and EPAM (Feigenbaum, 1963) were implemented in basic list-processing languages like IPL-V and then in LISP. Later models of human behavior were cast in more theory-laden formalisms like production-system and schema languages (Newell, 1973; Norman & Rumelhart, 1975). Ensuing architectures such as ACT (Anderson, 1983) and SOAR (Newell, 1990) incorporated additional knowledge about the human information processor, forcing models stated within those frameworks to satisfy further theoretical constraints.

Many cognitive scientists view this progression as a positive development, leading toward what Newell (1990) has called *unified theories of cognition*. Nevertheless, computational models still require developers to introduce many assumptions, many not central to their theories, before they can produce behaviors and predictions. Moreover, features of models that developers do hold central are often not the source of their models' ability to explain psychological data. One example comes from Richman and Simon (1989), who argue that connectionist and discrimination-network explanations of word-recognition findings are due not to these models' core assumptions of parallel versus sequential processing, but from the way both models structure the task.

These observations suggest that detailed computer models of human behavior, though interesting from an AI perspective, may be misleading or at least unnecessary to explain many interesting phenomena. At first glance, mathematical models seem a natural alternative, in that they describe behavior at a much more abstract level. However, computational models were originally developed in response to perceived limitations of such mathematical methods, which were constrained to simple behaviors and often made restrictive assumptions of their own for the sake of analytical tractability.

Recently, Ohlsson and Jewett (1995; in press) have proposed a promising compromise between these two paradigms, which they refer to as *abstract models*. In this framework, the scientist still implements a running computer program that generates behavior, but the system omits details that are not essential to the phenomena one aims to explain. For example, to model learning in problem-solving domains, they suggest retaining the idea of search through a problem space, but removing details about the states and operators that define the space. Rather, one can describe the structure or connectivity of the space, and model the learning process using mechanisms that add connections or alter the probability of moving toward a goal state.

The idea of abstract computational models is not entirely new. For instance, Shrager, Hogg, and Huberman (1988) present an explanation very similar to Ohlsson and Jewett's for the power law of learning, which they coupled with a mathematical analysis. Rosenbloom and Newell (1987) present a different account of power-law learning, describing both a detailed computer model and an abstract model of this well-known phenomenon. Ohlsson and Jewett's contribution is the realization that neither the mathematical analysis nor the detailed model are necessary, and that researchers may often find it useful to work entirely at the level of abstract models.

However, work on abstract models remains rare, and Ohlsson and Jewett's research program has focused on cognitive tasks. In this paper, we adapt the approach to domains that have a significant sensory-motor component. Below we outline the PHOENIX domain, which involves control of a simulated airplane. After this, we briefly review ICARUS, a theory of the human cognitive architecture, and incorporate its core tenets into an abstract model of behavior on the PHOENIX task. Next we describe a variant model that addresses the influence

---

[1] Also affiliated with the Institute for the Study of Learning and Expertise, 2164 Staunton Court, Palo Alto, CA 94306

of domain knowledge on sensing strategies, along with a simple account of sensory learning. Finally, we consider the model's fit to human behavior and compare its accuracy to that of an alternative account of learning, then discuss some broader issues that our approach raises.

The Sensory-Rich PHOENIX Domain

Goettl (1993, 1994) has described the PHOENIX domain, a simulated training environment that involves flying a simulated airplane through a series of rectangular gates that constitute a three-dimensional slalom course. The aim is to navigate the plane through these gates, preferably following as direct a route as possible. A cockpit window gives subjects information about the size, location, and orientation of the nearest gates as they would appear from an actual plane, along with a horizon line that reflects the plane's pitch and roll. The console display also gives numeric information on the flight speed, thrust, and altitude.

The gates are suspended in air, perpendicular to the ground and parallel to each other. The PHOENIX task begins with the plane facing and heading roughly in the direction of the nearest gate, but the subject must alter the plane's course to accomplish the task of flying through the gates in sequence. A joystick lets the subject affect the plane's pitch and roll, and thus its altitude and heading; additional controls can change thrust and thus flight speed, but this is less central to the basic task.

Goettl (1993) has analyzed the PHOENIX task into 19 separate component skills, which involve subtasks such as changing heading and changing altitude, which in turn break down into even more basic skills like altering the plane's pitch and roll. His experiments revealed a number of regularities in subjects' behavior on this task. For instance, he found that ability on most of the component skills identified during the task analysis were closely associated with ability on the overall slalom task. He also noted major differences in performance, especially between men and women, but also among subjects of the same sex. Determinants of task difficulty included the size of the gates and their distance apart.

Naturally, subjects improve their ability to fly the slalom course with practice. However, Goettl also found that part-task subjects (trained on the component skills) learned more slowly than those in the whole-task group (trained on the overall task), though the former did show positive transfer from practice on the component problems. In studies of a related task that involves shooting stationary targets, Goettl (1994) found that subjects trained on component tasks outperformed those trained on the whole task, provided they get interleaved practice on the components (i.e., one trial on each component per block), but not when they get segregated practice.

We will not attempt to explain all of the above phenomena here; for now we will focus on the basic fact of improvement with experience. However, the variety of results suggests the fertility of this domain for exploring behavior on complex sensory-motor tasks, which recommends it as a testbed for our ideas on abstract models.

A Model of Unskilled Sensing

Our approach to modeling human behavior in the PHOENIX domain builds on the ICARUS architecture (Langley, 1996), in which the basic unit of knowledge is the qualitative state. Each state S specifies a set of conditions that must hold for S to be active, along with optional information about actions to be performed during S, the effects of these actions, and likely successor states. The architecture operates in cycles, checking the conditions of the current state if one is active and selecting a new state from long-term memory otherwise. Constraints on perceptual attention limit the number of sensors updated on each cycle, with the system assuming that the values of unsensed features remain unchanged. When ICARUS detects that the activation conditions for the current state no longer hold, it checks to determine which successor state should become active or, if none hold, which other state seems most appropriate.

For this study, we assume that the agent has already mastered the basic skill of flying through a series of gates, which involves both knowledge of the component skills (states) and the order in which they should occur. Figure 1 shows one possible sequence of states involved in traversing a single gate, and the resulting flight path seen from above the plane. This sequence involves rolling the plane to the left, continuing the roll at the maximum allowed for some period, unrolling the plane right, and taking no action once the plane is aligned with the gate. This sequence assumes the plane is already aligned vertically; if the plane were below the gate, the sequence would also include states for altering the pitch to ascend followed by another state to level out. Alternative locations relative to the gate would produce similar paths based on analogous states, such as decreasing pitch and rolling right. We will not assume this precise decomposition of the slalom task, as other decompositions into states are possible, but we will posit a small number of states for each gate traversal.

Our model of behavior on the slalom task abstracts away from the details of ICARUS and the domain, and focuses on only a few essential parameters. In particular, we suppose that flying through each gate requires a sequence of s states and that each state has $r + i$ activation conditions that involve sensing, but that only r of these conditions actually differ between each state and its successor. This means that, in order to detect that the current state is no longer active, the agent need only sense one of these r relevant features. However, if the agent does not know which features to sense, its detection of state failure may be delayed, and thus it may continue carrying out the current actions longer than appropriate.

Our explanation of errors in this framework revolves around the idea that the agent must reach the final 'Fly Toward' state, in which the plane is aligned with the gate, before passing the gate's location. For a given location of the plane with respect to the gate at the outset of the state sequence, there will be a minimum number of time steps, ignoring time for sensing, for the agent to enter this final state. We will use t to represent the

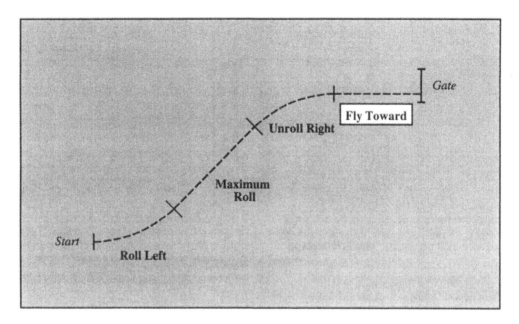

Figure 1: A four-state sequence that takes a plane through a gate when already vertically aligned. Each state continues for a number a time steps, until its activation conditions are no longer satisfied.

number of additional time steps available, beyond this minimum, before the plane passes the gate. Thus, the parameter t corresponds to the amount of 'slack' in a particular slalom task, with smaller values making the problem harder and larger ones making it easier.

According to this account, an agent that knows how to fly through a gate can still make errors because the number of time steps needed to detect a state shift may exceed the slack parameter t, causing the plane to miss the gate. We assume that the agent can sense only one feature on each time step, so that whether it notices a state shift depends on whether it senses relevant or irrelevant features. Lacking any knowledge of which features are relevant, we assume that the true novice has a probability

$$p = \frac{r}{r+i}$$

of selecting a relevant feature on each time step, and thus the same probability of noticing a state shift, once such a change occurs.

This model appears to have four parameters but actually has fewer. Note that the important factor is not the overall slack parameter t, but rather than amount of slack per state, $d = t/s$. Also, the actual number of relevant features r and irrelevant ones i matters less than p, the probability of detecting a state shift when one occurs. However, this quantity is determined not by r and i but by their ratio, $u = i/r$, which gives

$$p = \frac{1}{1+u} \; .$$

Taken together, the parameters d and u specify our abstract model of novice behavior on the PHOENIX slalom task, though it should apply equally well to other sensory-rich domains.

A Model of Skilled Sensing and Learning

The above model posits that the agent samples from among the $r + i$ state activation conditions from a uniform distribution, which produces the probability

$$p = \frac{r}{r+i} = \frac{1}{1+u}$$

of detecting a state shift on each time step after the shift occurs. However, if the agent has additional knowledge about the probability of each condition ceasing to hold, it can use a more selective strategy, based on nonuniform sensing, that produces a higher probability of detecting a state change when one occurs.

In order to model such skilled sensing behavior, we need some additional assumptions. The ICARUS architecture assumes that the agent associates a probability with each activating condition f of a state s, such that, when s is active and f is true, f will still hold on the next time step. Based on these estimates, ICARUS computes the probability that each activation condition (feature) of the current state has changed. Having limited attentional resources, the architecture must choose which features to sense. Here we assume that subjects use a *probability matching strategy*, which samples from among the available features in direct proportion to their estimated probability of changing when a state shift occurs. Probability matching has been implicated in a variety of decision tasks, making it a plausible candidate here.

We can model a subject's knowledge about the relevance of features with one additional parameter, k, that represents the number of times the subject has observed a particular state transition in which the relevant features have changed and the irrelevant ones have not. We can incorporate this information into the probability of

387

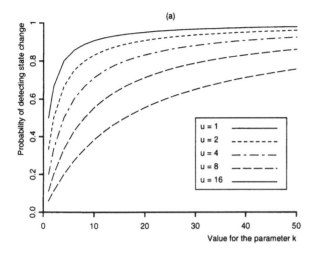
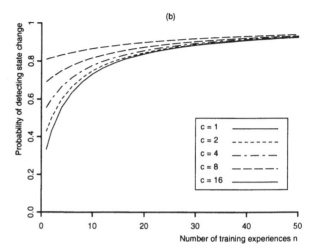

Figure 2: The probability of detecting a state shift as a function of (a) parameters k and u in the novice model and (b) parameters n and c, when $u = 4$, in the skilled model.

selecting a relevant feature, which becomes

$$p = \frac{k \cdot r}{k \cdot r + i} = \frac{k}{k + u} \,.$$

This expression is equivalent to the novice quantity, $1/(1 + u)$, when $k = 1$, but the ratio approaches 1 as k goes to infinity. Figure 2 (a) shows the effect of k on p for different values of $i/r = u$.

Naturally, we do not claim that k remains constant, since subjects learn from their experience in the domain. Here we assume that the subject simply increments the value for k by 1 each time he observes a shift from one state to another, thus increasing the probability p of sensing a relevant feature. This suggests that we let $k = n$, where n is the number of times the subject has encountered the task. However, inspection of data for the slalom task reveals that some subjects start with much higher success rates than others. We can model these differences by introducing another parameter, c, that determines each subject's initial probability of sensing irrelevant features. In this revised model, we have $k = c + n$, so that

$$p = \frac{(c + n) \cdot r}{(c + n) \cdot r + i} = \frac{c + n}{c + n + u} \,,$$

where the value for c partly determines the intercept in each subject's learning curve. Figure 2 (b) shows the effect of n on p for different values of c when $u = 4$.

Let us review the model and its structure. We have one parameter, $d = t/s$, that represents the difficulty of the task. We have a second parameter, $u = i/r$, that indicates the ratio of irrelevant to relevant features. Both d and u take on the same value for all subjects, since they are characteristics of the domain. However, we have a third parameter, c, that is specific to each subject, representing that person's initial bias toward sensing relevant features. The variable n also plays a role in the model, but we assume this represents the number of problems

the subject has solved.[2] Thus, given v subjects with w observations each, we must fit a model with $v + 2$ parameters to $v \cdot w$ data points. For the slalom task, we have 46 subjects and 8 measurements each, giving $46 \cdot 8 = 368$ values to constrain $46 + 2 = 48$ overall parameters.

Fitting the Model to Observations

In principle, we might derive a set of equations that follow from our model and use established statistical methods to determine the best-fitting values for each parameter. However, we have not found any closed-form solutions for the model, which rules out this approach. But it does not preclude us from incorporating the model's assumptions into an abstract computer program, using this program to predict results for given parameter settings, and searching the space of settings to find a good fit to the data.

We implemented the assumptions of the model in such a program, which we embedded in another program designed to search the space of parameter settings. The running model accepted the four variables described earlier – d, u, c, and n – as input and applied the strategy for selective sensing 1000 times to estimate the probability of successfully traversing a gate. The higher-level system computed the squared difference between the predicted and observed probability for each combination of subject and practice level. For the parameter d we told the system to consider only settings between 1 and 3; for u it examined settings from 1 to 20; and for c it considered values from 1 to 10.

The search program involves a number of iterative loops, the outermost devoted to finding the best d value and the next to finding the u setting. The three innermost levels iterate through the set of subjects, through

---

[2]Actually, each subject score is an average over 16 three-minute trials that involved separate passes through the slalom course, but these hold across subjects and thus are constant factors.

Table 1: (a) Sample parameter settings for the abstract sensory-learning model and the variance they explain (r^2) on data from the slalom task, along with (b) the parameters and r^2 for the power-law model. The best fit for the sensory-learning model ($d = 2$, $u = 19$) accounts for less variance than the power law but involves many fewer parameters.

(a) SENSORY-LEARNING MODEL

DIFFICULTY d	RATIO u	INIT. BIAS c	r^2
1	4	[1–8]	0.111
1	12	[1–10]	0.651
2	12	[1–10]	0.580
2	19	[1–10]	0.680
3	12	[1–7]	0.317
3	20	[1–10]	0.652

(b) POWER-LAW MODEL

SLOPE a	INTERCEPT b	r^2
[-1.17–0.07]	[-1.63–0.57]	0.827

values of n, and through settings for c. Inspection of the model's behavior over this parameter space suggested that, when only one parameter varies, the model's fit to the data follows a U-shaped curve. Thus, the system limited search somewhat by starting with a small parameter value and incrementing it only as long as this improved the fit, at which point it halted, having reached a local optimum given the values of other parameters.

Table 1 shows the variance explained (r^2) for a number of parameter settings, including the one that provides the best fit for Goettl's 46-subject data. The table includes a range of values for c, since this parameter varied across different subjects. Note that the best setting for u is 19, accounting for 68 percent of the variance, which implies that subjects considered 19 times as many irrelevant features as relevant ones. The PHOENIX flight simulator does have a complex display, so this value is not impossible, though it is higher than we expected.

One natural issue concerns how well our sensory-learning model compares to alternative explanations of the data. We plan to explore this question at length in future work, but we have already done some initial studies along these lines with a popular model that assumes learning obeys a negatively accelerated power law. Rosenbloom and Newell (1987) and Shrager et al. (1988) have shown that one can derive this law from assumptions about the task environment and learner, but both analyses deal with reaction times rather than error rates.

Here we simply assume that learning follows a power law of the form $E = bN^{-a}$, where E is the percent error after N training experiences, and where a and b are parameters specific to each subject. Taking the log of both sides gives the linear relation $log(E) = log(b) - a \cdot log(N)$, which we can fit to the data using linear regression.

Table 1 also shows the parameter ranges and the r^2 that result from this process. The power law explains somewhat more variance (83 percent) than the sensory-learning model but includes nearly twice as many parameters; thus, we cannot claim that either is superior to the other on these data, and additional studies would appear necessary before we can draw any firm conclusions.

Preliminary analyses of results from another PHOENIX study, involving part-task training, suggest that rapid learners are less affected by the introduction of irrelevant features than slow learners (Goettl, personal communication, 1996). This appears consistent with our sensory-learning theory, but developing a detailed model for this experimental situation, and fitting it to the data, must await future work.

Discussion

Before closing, we should reexamine the theoretical status of our model and its relation to alternative frameworks. We have noted our debt to Ohlsson and Jewett for the notion of an abstract computational model, but our application of this idea differs somewhat from their own. We have used our abstract model, combined with a search engine, to fit data on particular subjects, whereas Ohlsson and Jewett instead explore how alternative models react to variations in parameter values, in order to determine whether their ability to cover phenomena depends on the underlying mechanism or on fortuitous parameter settings. These two approaches are not antithetical, but they do emphasize different issues.

Some readers will detect that our model of sensory learning has features in common with Estes' stimulus sampling theory, the basis for a wide variety of mathematical learning models. The two accounts both assume that subjects' decisions are probabilistic in nature, that they invoke a probability matching strategy, and that learning follows from simple changes to probability distributions. However, the details of the equations for performance and learning differ considerably, as do the underlying accounts that accompany the expressions.

Another issue concerns the degree to which our model, and others like it, explains the data or merely describes it. We hold that the model's processes and associated equations provide explanatory structure, whereas the parameter settings handle description within the structure. A more interesting question concerns the extent to which various model assumptions are necessary or merely sufficient to produce the data. A sufficient assumption can be replaced by another one that, with different parameter values, gives nearly the same results. In contrast, a necessary assumption seems required, in that no alternatives can fit the data, regardless of parameter settings. We have not yet attempted to analyze our account in this fashion, but abstract models seem well suited for such studies, as Ohlsson and Jewett have shown.

A final matter involves the generality of the abstract approach to modeling behavior. Our treatment has ignored many details of the PHOENIX task, such as particular sensory variables and component skills (states), and Ohlsson and Jewett have followed a similar line.

However, we might instead have developed an abstract model that included a separate parameter for each skill, provided data were available (e.g., from part-task studies) to estimate expertise on each. This approach to content-oriented abstract models might even let one distinguish between classes of knowledge, such as functional and structural (e.g., Stroulia & Goel, 1992), given these classes have different implications for subject's behavior.

Concluding Remarks

In this paper we reviewed an approach to cognitive simulation that Ohlsson and Jewett (1995) have called *abstract models*. We considered the advantages of this approach over traditional AI models of human behavior, which force one to specify a complete procedure that operates in the task domain even when the data provide insufficient constraints to justify such detail. We described a domain of this sort, studied by Goettl (1993, 1994), in which subjects must fly a simulated aircraft through a three-dimensional slalom course. Although we have implemented an AI system for this task, cast within the framework of a cognitive architecture, we found this system too complex for useful modeling of available data.

In response, we developed an abstract model of behavior on this task that incorporated parameters for task difficulty, the ratio of irrelevant to relevant features, and initial subject knowledge. The model's central assumptions are that skilled performance on this task involves selective sensing of relevant rather than irrelevant features, and that improvement comes from simple statistical learning about feature relevance. We implemented a program to search the space of parameter settings, and in this way found an instantiated form of the model which approached the fit for a power-law model that had twice as many parameters. These results do not prove that our sensory-learning account is the correct one, but they encourage us to continue exploring this class of models.

In future work, we plan to evaluate our abstract model on more detailed data that Goettl has collected for the PHOENIX domain, as well as compare it to other alternatives besides the power law. We also plan to draw on more sophisticated methods, some available in the statistical literature, for searching the space of parameter settings, and to produce more general tools that can be used with a broad class of abstract models. In the longer term, we hope to use the resulting system to develop and evaluate abstract models for a variety of learning tasks, in an effort to understand the potential of this approach to cognitive simulation.

Acknowledgements

This research was supported by Grant F49620-94-1-0118 from the Computer Science Division of the Air Force Office of Scientific Research. We owe thanks to Barry Goettl for useful discussions about the PHOENIX domain and for making his experimental data available, to Stellan Ohlsson, Wes Regian, and Jeff Shrager for their insights about abstract models, and to Stephanie Sage for fitting the power law to the flight-control data.

References

Anderson, J. R. (1983). *The architecture of cognition*. Cambridge: Harvard University Press.

Feigenbaum, E. A. (1963). The simulation of verbal learning behavior. In E. A. Feigenbaum & J. Feldman (Eds.), *Computers and thought*. New York: McGraw-Hill.

Goettl, B. P. (1993). Analysis of skill on a flight simulator: Implications for training. *Proceedings of the 37th Annual Meeting of the Human Factors and Ergonomics Society* (pp. 1257–1261). Santa Monica, CA: Human Factors and Ergonomics Society.

Goettl, B. P. (1994). Contextual interference effects on acquisition and transfer of a complex motor task. *Proceedings of the 38th Annual Meeting of the Human Factors and Ergonomics Society* (pp. 1220–1224). Nashville: Human Factors and Ergonomics Society.

Langley, P. (1996). *Learning sensory skills for control domains*. Unpublished manuscript, Robotics Laboratory, Computer Science Department, Stanford University, Stanford, CA.

Newell, A. (1973). Production systems: Models of control structures. In W. G. Chase (Ed.), *Visual information processing*. New York: Academic Press.

Newell, A. (1990). *Unified theories of cognition*. Cambridge, MA: Harvard University Press.

Newell, A., Shaw, J. C., & Simon, H. A. (1960). Report on a general problem-solving program for a computer. *Information Processing: Proceedings of the International Conference on Information Processing* (pp. 256–264).

Newell, A., & Simon, H. A. (1972). *Human problem solving*. Englewood Cliffs, NJ: Prentice-Hall.

Norman, D. A., & Rumelhart, D. E. (1975). (Eds.). *Explorations in cognition*. San Francisco: Freeman.

Ohlsson, S., & Jewett, J. J. (1995). Abstract computer models: Towards a new method for theorizing about adaptive agents. *Proceedings of the Eighth European Conference on Machine Learning* (pp. 33–52). Heraclion, Crete: Springer Verlag.

Ohlsson, S., & Jewett, J. J. (in press). Ideal adaptive agents and the learning curve. In J. Brzezinski, T. Maruszewski, & B. Krause (Eds.), *Idealization in psychology*. Amsterdam: Rodopi.

Richman, H. B., & Simon, H. A. (1989). Context effects in letter perception: Comparison of two models. *Psychological Review, 96*, 417–432.

Rosenbloom, P. S., & Newell, A. (1987). Learning by chunking: A production system model of practice. In D. Klahr, P. Langley, & R. Neches (Eds.), *Production system models of learning and development*. Cambridge, MA: MIT Press.

Shrager, J., Hogg, T., & Huberman, B. A. (1988). A graph-dynamic model of the power law of practice and the problem-solving fan effect. *Science, 242*, 414–416.

Stroulia, E., & Goel, A. K. (1992). Generic teleological mechanisms and their use in case adaptation. *Proceedings of the Fourteenth Conference of the Cognitive Science Society* (pp. 319–324). Bloomington, IN: Lawrence Erlbaum.

Epistemic Action Increases With Skill

Paul P. Maglio
IBM Almaden Research Center
650 Harry Road, K54D-B2
San Jose, CA 95120
pmaglio@almaden.ibm.com

David Kirsh
Department of Cognitive Science, 0515
University of California, San Diego
La Jolla, CA 92093
kirsh@cogsci.ucsd.edu

Abstract

On most accounts of expertise, as agents increase their skill, they are assumed to make fewer mistakes and to take fewer redundant or backtracking actions. Contrary to such accounts, in this paper we present data collected from people learning to play the videogame Tetris which show that as skill increases, the proportion of game actions that are later undone by backtracking also increases. Nevertheless, we also found that as game skill increases, players speed up as predicted by the power law of practice. We explain the observed increase in backtracking as the result of an interactive search process in which agent-internal and agent-external actions are interleaved, making the cognitive computation more efficient (i.e., faster). We refer to external actions which simplify an agent's computation as *epistemic actions*.

Introduction

In this paper, we present experimental data which runs counter to an assumption that underlies most theories of skill learning: that more skilled agents take fewer redundant or backtracking actions than less skilled agents (e.g., Anderson, 1982; Logan, 1988; Newell & Rosenbloom, 1981). Intuitively, skilled agents ought to make fewer mistakes than unskilled agents and therefore ought to backtrack less and take fewer redundant actions. However, our studies of how people improve at playing the videogame Tetris reveal that sometimes getting better means backtracking more. Better players use the world better, even in the limited world of a Tetris board. Consequently, we explain the observed increase in backtracking as the result of interactive search in which agents reduce cognitive load by interleaving internal and external actions.

Previously, we introduced the term *epistemic action* to describe external actions that can be used to reduce the memory, time, and probability of error of agent-internal computation (Kirsh & Maglio, 1994). We justified our view by presenting data collected from Tetris players at all skill levels in which many examples of recurring backtracking behaviors could be found. We could not, however, prove that better players performed more epistemic actions. Here we present longitudinal data on the acquisition of Tetris skill which show that: (a) Certain sorts of backtracking increase as skill develops; and (b) despite this increase, Tetris skill resembles other skills in following the power law of practice (Newell & Rosenbloom, 1981). Taken together, these results support our claim that epistemic actions play a substantial role in skilled behavior.

In what follows, we first briefly describe Tetris, and then present analysis and discussion of our behavioral data.

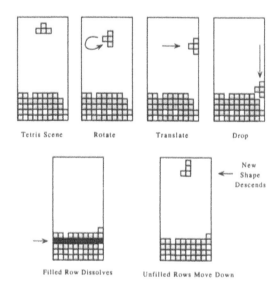

Figure 1: In Tetris, shapes fall one a time from the top of the screen, eventually landing on the bottom or on top of shapes that have already landed. As a shape falls, it can be rotated, and moved to the right or left. The objective is fill rows of squares all the way across the screen. Completely filled rows dissolve and all partially filled rows above move down.

How to Play Tetris

Tetris is a popular videogame in which players maneuver falling shapes into specific arrangements on the computer screen. There are seven shapes (which we call *zoids*): ▯, ⊞, ⊞, ⊞, ⊞, ⊞, ⊞. These fall one at a time from the top of a screen that is 10 squares wide and 30 squares high (see Figure 1). Each zoid freely falls until it lands on the bottom edge of the screen or on top of the squares of a zoid that has already landed. Once a zoid comes to rest, another begins falling from the top, starting the next Tetris *episode*. While a zoid falls, the player can control it, either *rotating* it 90° counterclockwise with a single keystroke, or translating it to the *right* or to the *left* one square with a single keystroke. To gain points, the player must carefully land zoids so that rows fill up with squares all the way across the screen. Filled rows then disappear and all filled squares above it drop down. This process is called *clearing rows*. As more rows are cleared, the game speeds up, and controlling how zoids land becomes more difficult. Filled squares pile up as unfilled, uncleared rows become buried under poorly placed zoids. The game ends when the screen becomes clogged with incomplete rows and new zoids cannot descend. Thus, clearing rows serves the purposes both of scoring points and of delaying the game's end.[1]

We recorded data from two players who practiced Tetris for about 20 hours each, encompassing approximately 40,000 keystroke interactions with the game. Neither participant had played the game before, and both agreed not to play except under computer observation during the course of the study. We now turn to these data.

How Players Improve With Practice

As players practice more, the number of rows they clear— their game score—increases. As Tetris players know, the rate of improvement is misleading, for the game speeds up as rows are cleared. Hence, players encounter different task demands during the course of a single game.

To ensure that we did not compare experts in high speed games with novices in slow speed games in our study, we controlled for the effects of game speed during analysis by separating episodes into three speeds, slow, medium, and fast, a division roughly following skill: everyone plays at slow speeds, better players attain medium speeds, and only the best players achieve fast speeds. Because both participants always played part of their games at slow speeds, we will compare behavior based solely on data gathered from the slow portions of the games.

Speed-ups Follow the Power Law of Practice

Typically, practice improves performane in accordance with a power function of practice time or practice trials (Newell & Rosenbloom, 1981) either by decreasing the time to react to stimuli by taking a single action (Seibel, 1963), or by decreasing the overall time it takes to perform a task that requires a sequence of actions (Crossman, 1959). In Tetris, the time to perform a sequence of actions can be measured within an individual episode as the interval between the time the falling zoid first becomes visible and the time of the last action that the player takes (see Figure 2). The time to take a single action can be measured as the interval between consecutive keypresses in episodes in which more than one action was taken (see Figure 3). In addition, another component of the overall time to place a zoid is the latency of the player's first action, that is, the interval between the time the falling zoid becomes visible in an episode and the time of the player's *first* keypress (see Figure 4).

In all three cases, our data indicate that performance speeds up according to the power law of practice. Figure 5 shows one example: when plotted on a log-log scale, the time between keypresses follows a straight line. To see that all our data are better fit by power curves than by other curves, consider Table 1. Following Newell and Rosenbloom (1981), we compared the correlations of the best-fit regressions for

---

[1]In addition to rotation and translation, the player can *drop* a falling zoid instantly to the bottom, effectively placing it in the position it would eventually land in if no additional keys were pressed. Dropping is an optional maneuver, and not all players use it. Dropping speeds up the pace of the game, creating shorter episodes without affecting the free-fall rate. We will not discuss dropping.

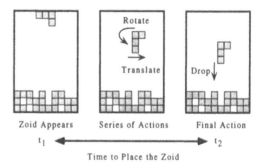

Figure 2: The time to place a zoid is defined as the interval between the time the zoid first appears on the board and the time of the last action that the player takes to maneuver it. In this case, the zoid appears at time t_1 and the last action is taken at time t_2. The overall time, then, is the interval $t_2 - t_1$.

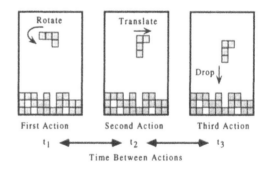

Figure 3: The time between actions is defined as the interval between consecutive keypresses. This figure illustrates two intervals: $t_2 - t_1$ and $t_3 - t_2$.

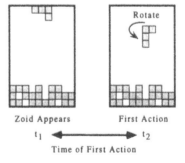

Figure 4: The time of the first action in an episode is measured from when the zoid first appears on the board. In this figure, the zoid first appears at time t_1 and the first action occurs at time t_2. The time of the first action, then, is $t_2 - t_1$.

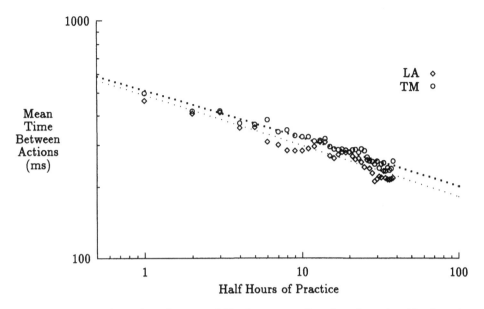

Figure 5: The time between consecutive actions decreases following a power function of practice. The data plotted on this graph are drawn from slow episodes only. The lines are the best-fit linear regressions of the data in log-log space.

	Linear $T = A - BN$			Exponential $T = Be^{-\alpha N}$			Power Law $T = BN^{-\alpha}$		
	A	B	r^2	B	α	r^2	B	α	r^2
Time to Place a Zoid (s)									
LA	4.087	47.78	.7711	5.019	0.012	.8020	6.010	0.149	.8306
TM	5.195	53.82	.6781	5.201	0.012	.7162	6.508	0.171	.8481
Time Between Actions (ms)									
LA	370.2	4.693	.7721	374.2	0.016	.8439	488.1	0.214	.9108
TM	392.6	4.743	.8117	396.6	0.015	.8789	510.0	0.202	.9557
Time of First Action (ms)									
LA	936.8	12.23	.7234	975.2	0.016	.7424	1253	0.210	.7515
TM	1117	12.27	.5332	1106	0.013	.5224	1436	0.189	.6906

Table 1: Power curves fit the data better than lines or exponentials. To determine that the players speed up according to the power law, we followed Newell and Rosenbloom's (1981) method of comparing various regressions—a straight line, an exponential, and a simple power function—on the data. For the equations shown in the table, T is the performance measure (time), N is practice block (30-minute intervals), α is the rate of decrease determined by the regression, and B is a constant also determined by the regression. For both participants and for each measure, a power function fits the data better than a line or an exponential.

lines, exponentials, and simple power functions.[2] As the table shows, in each case, the data are fit best by a power function of practice. This means that *Tetris skill is like most other skills* because power-law improvement is universal (see Newell & Rosenbloom, 1981).

Because players become faster with practice, one might expect that players' actions also become more precise. That is, Tetris experts should not only take action faster than beginners, but they should take only the actions necessary to maneuver the falling zoid to its final position and orientation because experts make fewer mistakes, backtrack less, or simply see the solution sooner than beginners do. As we will show, our data indicate just the opposite: *the number of apparently extraneous actions increases with practice.* This result is surprising because theories that explain power-law improvement, for instance, by accumulating chunks (Newell & Rosenbloom, 1981) or cases (Logan, 1988), assume that behavior becomes more efficient and economical with practice (Crossman, 1959).

Backtracking Increases With Skill

As stated, we found that sometimes more skilled Tetris players actually take more *extra* actions—that is, actions that are later undone by backtracking—than less skilled players. To see that backtracking increases with skill, let us define *backtracking* or *extra* actions in Tetris to be actions that do not lie on the shortest path from the falling zoid's initial location and orientation to its final location and orientation (see Figure 6).

Using this definition of backtracking, we calculated the mean number of extra rotations. For analysis, we grouped the data into three consecutive six-hour intervals. We first calculated the mean number of extra rotations per episode for each game, and then used these averages as the raw scores for analysis. Figure 7 illustrates the results for LA.[3] As shown, the average number of extra rotations per episode is significantly greater in expert games than in intermediate games. Backtracking increases with practice.

Now it may be objected that because the average number of extra rotations for LA is only around 0.2 per epsiode, extra rotations must occur relatively infrequently. Extra rotations occur in 7% of the episodes in which LA was an expert, in 5% of the episodes in which he was an intermediate, and in 4% of the episodes in which he was a beginner. These frequencies differ significantly ($p < .01$), but extra rotations are clearly the exception rather than rule, and therefore it might be illustrative to investigate the contexts in which they occur.

Figure 8 reveals that the percentage of episodes containing extra rotations varies by zoid type, and that the number of

[2]Newell and Rosenbloom (1981) also discuss fitting data to generalized curves by adding an additional parameter to account for prior experience. In particular, they consider fitting exponentials of the form $T = Be^{-\alpha N} + E$, and power functions of the form $T = BN^{-\alpha} + E$, where E is the additional constant used to represent prior experience. By incorporating additional parameters, better fitting regressions can always be found. But because our data contain only 38 points for each participant, there is the danger of overfitting the points. Therefore, we used the *simplest* functions in each case, that is, the functions containing two (rather than three) free parameters.

[3]Because of space limitations, the rest of the discussion will focus on LA's data. See Maglio (1995) for discussion of TM's data.

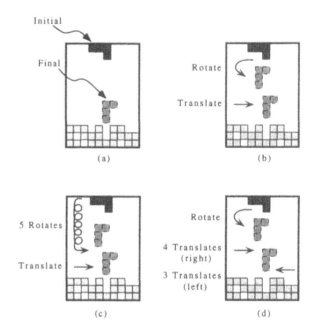

Figure 6: *Backtracking actions* do not lie on the shortest path between a zoid's initial location and orientation and its final position. The trajectory shown in (b) is a shortest path. The trajectories shown in (c) and (d) contain backtracking.

Figure 7: Extra rotations increase with expertise for LA. More precisely, the mean number of extra rotations was greater when LA played at the expert level than when he played at the beginner level.

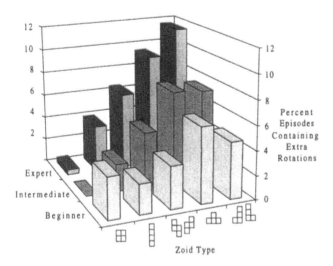

Figure 8: The percentage of episodes containing extra rotations varies both by skill and by zoid type. The data plotted in this graph show that the extra rotations occur more frequently for ⊞ and ⊞ than for other zoids at all skill levels, but especially at the expert level. Although the number of extra rotations increases with skill for all zoid types except ⊞, the number of extra rotations increases most for ⊞ and ⊞.

extra rotations increases most for ⊞ and ⊞. These data suggest that although extra rotations occur infrequently, they cannot be the result of simple motor errors. This follows because motor mistakes ought to affect each type of zoid equally. If extra rotations result from a baseline error in motor control processes (i.e., experts can recover from overshooting the desired orientation but beginners cannot), there is no a priori reason to suppose that the frequency of errors for ⊟ would be less than the the frequency of errors for ⊞. Errors should be distributed randomly. Because the percentage of extra rotations differs among zoid types, the conjecture that extra rotations are the result of recovering from simple motor mistakes must be ruled out.

Perhaps, however, extraneous rotations result from perceptual errors. For example, perceptual confusion might result when the falling zoid is ⊞ but there is a natural place to put ⊞ and not ⊞. More precisely, let us define a *mirror episode* to be a board configuration in which any placement of the falling zoid will create a hole, but in which some placement of the falling zoid's mirror image does not (see Figure 9). Obviously, mirror episodes can only occur for the zoids with mirror images: ⊞⊞ and ⊞⊞. In this case, the percentage of extra rotations in mirror episodes does not differ from the percentage of extra rotations in non-mirror episodes for the relevant types of zoids (see Figure 10). Thus, backtracking rotations are not the result of this type of perceptual error.

Early Rotations Aid Decision Making

We conjecture that rather than being the result of motor or perceptual errors, extra rotations are computationally efficient epistemic actions. For instance, extra rotations might help the player decide where to place the falling zoid. If this is the case,

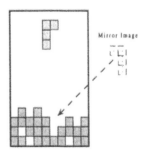

Figure 9: In *mirror episodes*, there is a good place to put the falling zoid's mirror image but no good place to put the falling zoid itself. If players backtrack more because they make perceptual mistakes, extra rotations might be more frequent in mirror episodes.

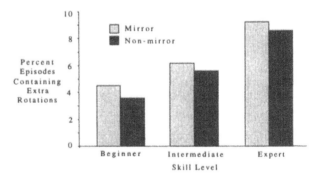

Figure 10: The frequency of extra rotations does not depend on mirror episodes for LA. Within each skill level, the percentage of extra rotations does not differ significantly between the mirror and non-mirror conditions ($\chi^2 < 1$ in all cases).

we would expect extra rotations generally to occur *before* the player has decided where to put the zoid. In particular, if a zoid is rotated into its final orientation before a player has made a final decision about orientation, then the player might continue to rotate the zoid to assist decision making. This implies that extra rotations should occur most often when the zoid is in its final orientation *before* the player is ready to judge whether the orientation is correct. This might happen in two ways: either because the player rotates the zoid very rapidly soon after it appears, or because the zoid appears on the board close to its final orientation. And in fact, the data for LA show that extra rotations do occur primarily when the zoid is in its final orientation early in the decision-making process (see Figure 11). In general, the final decision about orientation is not made much before 1130 milliseconds. For ⊞, the mean time to put the zoid into its final orientation is 1127 ms ($SD = 99$ ms), and for ⊞ and ⊞ the mean is 1122 ms ($SD = 71$ ms). As Figure 11 shows, however, the mean time that these zoids are rotated into their final orientation and then later unnecessarily rotated is 400–500 milliseconds earlier. For ⊞, the mean time is 676 ms ($SD = 149$ ms), and for ⊞ and ⊞ the mean time is 754 ms ($SD = 296$ ms). If extra rotations were the result of motor or perceptual mistakes, however, there is no reason to suppose that they would occur most often early in an episode. Thus, it seems that external

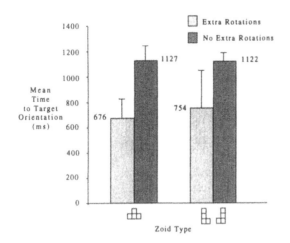

Figure 11: The mean time at which the falling zoid is first rotated into its target orientation is less when there are extra rotations than when there are no extra rotations. The data shown are from slow episodes in which LA was an expert. The mean time with extra rotations differs significantly from the mean time without in both cases: for ⊞, $t(198) = 2.82, p < .005$; for ⊞ ⊞, $t(293) = 2.24, p < .026$.

rotation is being used to help make a placement decision.

To summarize, the number of extraneous rotations performed by LA increased with skill. This finding is counterintuitive because skilled players would be expected to head more precisely toward their goals. Yet because Tetris performance improves according to a power function of practice, Tetris skill must be like most other skills. Taken together, we believe these results support our hypothesis that redundant actions are epistemic actions which both simplify perceptual computation and play a natural role in skilled behavior (Kirsh & Maglio, 1994). We conclude with a brief discussion of some implications of this view.

Epistemic Actions Simplify Perception

It is no surprise, of course, that people offload symbolic computation (e.g., preferring paper and pencil to mental arithmetic; Hitch, 1978), but it is a surprise to discover that people offload perceptual computation as well. In Tetris, we conjecture that extra rotations are used to simplify the search for the best zoid placement by cueing retrieval from an orientation-specific index of zoids and board configurations (Maglio, 1995). In this way, we believe Tetris players set up their external environments to facilitate perceptual processing—much as gin rummy players physically organize the cards they have been dealt (Kirsh, 1995), and much as airline pilots place external markers to help keep track of appropriate speed and flap settings (Hutchins, 1995).

There is empirical evidence that people minimize their use of perceptual computational resources. For example, Ballard, Hayhoe and Pelz (1995) found that people performing a block-arranging task organized their actions and eye movements so as to minimize their working memory load. Rather than using memory of the visual scene to guide their actions, participants tended instead to move their eyes to gain just the information needed for their *next* action. These findings suggest that the

cost of moving the eyes to gather information is low relative to the cost of using short-term memory. It follows that serial processing (i.e., interposing eye movements between internal computations) is more computationally efficient than parallel processing (taking in all the information at once and calculating a plan) because of the high cost of internally holding and using partial results.

But we believe the idea that agents can rely on the world to provide an external memory which substitutes for internal memory (e.g., O'Regan, 1992) is only part of the story. Whereas eye movements are active from the point of view of the visual system—they serve to change the focus, and therefore to act on the agent's perceptual input—they are passsive from the point of view of the task environment. By contrast, skilled Tetris players' extra rotations are *active* in the task environment yet change the perceptual input in much the same way that eye movements do. External rotations do more work than eye movements because rotation is a domain action. Rotating the zoid actually changes the stimulus, whereas moving the eyes does not. Thus, when physically rotating the zoid for its computational effect, the external world functions not as a passive memory buffer, simply holding information to be picked up by looking, but the world in interaction with the agent functions more like a working memory system, that is, like an *interactive visuo-spatial sketchpad*.

Acknowledgements

This research was supported in part by NIA Grant AG11851.

References

Anderson, J. R. (1982). Acquisition of cognitive skill. *Psychological Review, 89*, 369–406.

Ballard, D. H., Hayhoe, M. H., & Pelz, J. B. (1995). Memory representations in natural tasks. *Journal of Cognitive Neuroscience, 7*, 66–80.

Crossman, E. R. (1959). A theory of the acquisition of speed skill. *Ergonomics, 2*, 153–166.

Hitch, G. J. (1978). The role of short-term working memory in mental arithmetic. *Cognitive Psychology, 10*, 302–323.

Hutchins, E. (1995). How a cockpit remembers its speed. *Cognitive Science, 19*.

Kirsh, D. (1995). The intelligent use of space. *Arificial Intelligence, 73*, 31–68.

Kirsh, D. & Maglio, P. (1994). On distinguishing epistemic from pragmatic action. *Cognitive Science, 18*, 513–549.

Logan, G. D. (1988). Toward an instance theory of automatization. *Psychological Review, 9*, 492–527.

Maglio, P. P. (1995). *The computational basis of interactive skill*. Doctoral dissertation, University of California, San Diego.

Newell, A. & Rosenbloom, P. (1981). Mechanisms of skill acquisition and the law of practice. In J. R. Anderson (Ed.), *Cognitive skills and their acquisition*. Hillsdale, NJ: LEA.

O'Regan, J. K. (1992). Solving the "real" mysteries of visual perception: The world as outside memory. *Canadian Journal of Psychology, 46*, 461–488.

Seibel, R. (1963). Discrimination reaction time for a 1,023 alternative task. *Journal of Experimental Psychology, 66*, 215–226.

Perseverative Subgoaling and Production System Models of Problem Solving

Richard Cooper
Department of Psychology
Birkbeck College, University of London
Malet St., London, WC1E 7HX
r.cooper@psyc.bbk.ac.uk

Abstract

Perseverative subgoaling, the repeated successful solution of subgoals, is a common feature of much problem solving, and its pervasive nature suggests that it is an emergent property of a problem solving architecture. This paper presents a set of minimal requirements on a production system architecture for problem solving which will allow perseverative subgoaling whilst guaranteeing the possibility of recovery from such situations. The fundamental claim is that perseverative subgoaling arises during problem solving when the results of subgoals are forgotten before they can be used. This prompts further attempts at the offending subgoals. In order for such attempts to be effective, however, the production system must satisfy three requirements concerning working memory structure, production structure, and memory decay. The minimal requirements are embodied in a model (developed within the COGENT modelling software) which is explored with respect to the task of multicolumn addition. The inter-relationship between memory decay and task difficulty within this task (measured in terms of the number of columns) is discussed.

Introduction

Since the work of Newell & Simon (1972), production system models have been successfully used to account for a number of aspects of human problem solving. Much of this work has been brought together within Soar (Laird, Newell & Rosenbloom, 1987; Newell, 1990), a research programme aimed at modelling all aspects of cognition within a single production system architecture. Central to the Soar production system approach is the *problem space computational model* (Newell, 1990), a model of cognitive processing which embodies a number of findings concerning human problem solving. According to this model, problem solving (and cognition in general) involves the sequential application of operators to a state, successively modifying that state until a goal state is reached or some goal condition is satisfied.

Within the problem space computational model it is assumed that, due to capacity limitations, only a single state can be represented within working memory at a time. This single state principle is held to account for one strategy common in search intensive problem solving: progressive deepening (see, e.g., Newell, 1990). Progressive deepening is characterised by the initial shallow investigation of alternative solution paths, followed by the elimination of some solution paths and the further investigation of those remaining. Critically to the current work, progressive deepening typically involves the repeated solution of the same subgoals as the search space is explored. We refer to the process of solving a subgoal re-

peatedly as *perseverative subgoaling*. Note that, as defined here, perseverative subgoaling is *not* the same as progressive deepening. Perseverative subgoaling is a phenomenon that occurs as a consequence of progressive deepening, but there is more to progressive deepening than perseverative subgoaling, and, crucially, there is no *a priori* reason why perseverative subgoaling should be restricted to situations involving progressive deepening. With this in mind, it is clear that, despite the well established nature of progressive deepening as a cognitive search strategy, it can only account for perseverative subgoaling under conditions which involve some degree of search or look-ahead. Though empirical evidence is scarce, the research reported, and model developed, here are founded on the claim that perseverative subgoaling occurs in situations which do not involve search (but which are nevertheless working memory intensive), and as such, in at least some cases, perseverative subgoaling cannot be explained by an appeal to the single state principle. When perseverative subgoaling occurs in search-free tasks, an alternate explanation is required.

The fact that the Soar research community appeals to the single state principle in order to account for progressive deepening indicates that they are sensitive to the issue of working memory capacity. However, the single state principle operates at the level of the problem space computational model. It does not operate at the level of the production system architecture which is held to implement the problem space computational model. The underlying production system architecture is assumed to have a working memory which is not capacity bound. This assumption of an unlimited working memory within Soar's production system base is one architectural assumption which has been challenged on the grounds that it lacks psychological plausibility (cf. Cooper & Shallice, 1995).

In order to explore the extent to which unlimited working memory is critical to Soar's performance, earlier work (Cooper, Fox, Farringdon & Shallice, in press) explored a number of potential mechanisms for reducing the working memory requirements of the underlying production system. Several soft constraints on working memory capacity (generally forms of memory decay) were implemented and the resulting performance compared within an empirical/computational methodology (cf. Cohen, 1995). It was observed that one such mechanism (probabilistic decay of refractory memory elements) lead to a system which, on occasions, exhibited perseverative subgoaling (independently of progressive deepening). However, unlike human problem solvers, only rarely was the modified Soar system able to recover from this subgoaling and solve the original task. Instead, problem solving would often breakdown irrecoverably, with the system resorting to its default behaviour.

The work reported here further investigates perseverative subgoaling in production system architectures. However, rather than adopting the Soar research strategy of developing, exploring, and possibly extending, a complex production system in order to generalise the domains that it may account for (a strategy which has received substantial criticism: see Cooper & Shallice (1995) and references cited therein), an alternate strategy — that of attempting to determine minimal requirements for the behaviour in question — has been adopted. This strategy is founded on the fact that, given the level at which psychological theorising takes place, any computational model will necessarily include aspects which are not theoretically motivated (i.e., implementation details). It is therefore not sufficient to simply demonstrate that a particular model may simulate interesting behaviour. Rather, it is necessary to know which aspects of that model lead to the interesting behaviour, and which aspects are necessary only for the purposes of implementation. (For more details and justified of this strategy, see Cooper *et al.* (in press).) The aim of this work, then, is to determine minimal requirements on a production system architecture (irrespective of their manifestation in any particular production system) which will allow recoverable perseverative errors without substantially increasing the likelihood of problem solving failure.

The assumption of a production system architecture as an appropriate starting point is justified by the success of such architectures in modelling other aspects of problem solving behaviour (as noted above). Two obvious competitors to this starting point are analogical approaches and connectionist approaches. Connectionist approaches, highly popular in other domains of cognitive science, have offered few insights into problem solving, being limited mainly to the implementation of production systems (e.g., Touretzky & Hinton, 1988) and analogical models (e.g., Holyoak & Thagard, 1989). Analogical approaches to problem solving (e.g., Gentner, 1983; Keane, 1988) offer a more serious alternative. Though they have generally only been applied within problem solving situations where some variant of case-based reasoning is sufficient (i.e., where a sequence of problem solving decisions is not required), perseverative subgoaling should fall within their remit, and future work may explore how perseverative subgoaling might arise in such systems.

Requirements for Perseverative Subgoaling

In order to develop a minimal model of perseverative subgoaling it is necessary to understand why this behaviour occurred when Soar was modified as mentioned above. It is also necessary to understand why perseverative subgoaling was only observed relatively rarely in the modified system. Each of these issues can be understood in the context of a simpler, more standard, production system.

A typical production system (see, for example, Charniak & McDermott, 1985) employs two primary memory components: a production memory (which contains schematic condition/action rules corresponding to problem solving knowledge) and a working memory (which contains a representation of the current problem solving state and which can trigger instances of rules in production memory). Processing is cyclic and consists of repeatedly selecting a rule from production memory whose conditions are satisfied by the contents of working memory, and executing that rule. This typically results in the addition or deletion of elements from working memory, and hence leads to further production rules becoming applicable. Most production systems also employ a third memory component, a refractory memory. This memory contains the set of instances of rule which have already been employed in the current episode of problem solving, and is necessary because it prevents a single set of working memory elements from causing a single production rule to be executed more than once. To accommodate a refractory memory the processing cycle must be modified slightly: selection of an applicable rule from production memory must be limited to instances of rules which have not previously been executed, and when an instance of a production rule is executed, elements should be added to and deleted from working memory as usual, but the instance of the rule must also added to refractory memory.

Within Soar, this picture is somewhat more complicated. Various processes exist which modulate the effects of production firing on working memory (most notably the decision phase). These complications, however, are not germane to the issue of perseverative subgoaling, and are avoided here in the interests of clarity.

Returning then to the issue of perseverative subgoaling, the form of memory decay in Soar under which lead to this phenomenon consisted of a probabilistic decay of refractory memory elements, together with the removal from working memory of any elements that were added by the execution of the decayed refractory memory elements. Thus, on each problem solving cycle, there was a small change (typically of the order of 1 chance in 500) that each refractory memory element would decay (i.e., vanish from refractory memory). If a refractory memory element r did decay, then all those elements which were in working memory at the time of the decay and which had been added by the rule firing corresponding to r were also removed from working memory. This mechanism was designed to enforce some kind of decay on working memory elements (as is often argued for on psychological grounds), but at the same time to allow decayed elements to be replaced if necessary by the repeated firing of the instantiation of the production rule which originally lead to their creation. The constraint is a soft constraint on working memory size. It does not strictly limit the capacity of working memory, but should effectively reduce the cardinality of working memory by implementing the psychologically plausible assumption that working memory is an imperfect storage device.

It should be clear that perseverative subgoaling is a conceivable consequence of refractory memory decay. If, after a subgoal has been solved, the refractory memory element which lead to the subgoal's answer were to decay, then the subgoal's answer would disappear from working memory and it would be necessary to repeat the problem solving necessary to determine that answer. This would be possible because the refractory memory elements which would normally prevent repetition will also be absent. Perseverative subgoaling was not, however, the original intention (or even a prediction) of the introduction of this form of decay. It was observed *post hoc* to arise on a small number of trails. More frequently, refractory memory decay was observed to lead to complete problem solving breakdown. Detailed analysis of the causes of such breakdowns indicates that two additional properties are required of a production system if it is to be subject to recoverable perseverative subgoaling: firstly, production rules must be "fine-grained" (in a sense to be elaborated below), and secondly, memory decay must not result in disconnected subgoals.

The requirement on the granularity of production rules may be stated more formally as the requirement that no production may add more than one element to working memory, and that all productions must explicitly list in their conditions each working memory element which must be present for their application. These restrictions may be rationalised informally by noting that the conditions of all rules must be sensitive to the possibility that working memory may not be complete. Rules can therefore not assume that the presence of one working memory element will guarantee that other working memory elements will necessarily be present. Indeed, the frequent breakdown of problem solving within Soar with refractory memory decay can be traced to such dependencies in Soar's default productions (the productions which control standard problem solving heuristics). This is not intended as a criticism of Soar: the assumptions embodied in the default rules are valid in the normally functioning system, although leaving them implicit does mean that each rule cannot be understood in purely declarative terms.

The prohibition on disconnected subgoals is necessary to prevent problem solving from stalling after successful completion of a disconnected subgoal. Effectively the constraint states that the system cannot forget why it is attempting to solve a subgoal.[1] Without this constraint (and assuming that problem solving is under the service of a goal stack), situations could arise in which no goal would be within the current focus. The system could successfully solve a subgoal, but then be left not knowing what to do next. In Soar, with refractory memory decay, this constraint is satisfied because goal/subgoal relations are not created by production firing. As such, those relations cannot be deleted when refractory memory elements decay. However, in more standard production systems (in which productions can explicitly set subgoals) this constraint could be violated.

A Model of Perseverative Subgoaling
COGENT: The Modelling Environment

The model presented here was developed using the COGENT modelling software. COGENT (previously known as GOOSE: cf. Cooper, 1995) was developed from the Sceptic executable specification language (Hajnal, Fox & Krause, 1989; Cooper & Farringdon, 1993) in work aimed at improving the methodology of computational modelling (cf. Cooper, *et al.*, in press). It provides a set of cognitive "objects" (in the object-oriented sense) and a graphical editor. Together, these allow the specification of executable models in the box/arrow style. This style, it is argued, is more akin to that used by experimental psychologists in outlining their theories of processing than traditional programming languages, and as such allows a more

direct and perspicuous mapping between theory and implementation. In addition, COGENT is a step towards reducing the computer skills required of psychologists who wish to develop their own computational models.

The specification of a model in COGENT involves firstly drawing the appropriate box/arrow diagram (with the aid of the graphical editor) and then specifying properties and other details for the individual boxes employed in the diagram. The provision of a set of basic box classes (represented by different shaped boxes), together with the use of techniques from object-oriented programming, minimises the effort in specifying properties and standardises the definitions of the fundamental box classes employed in a model (cf. Cooper, 1995). Apart from the work reported here, the environment has been employed in the development of models of concept combination (Cooper & Franks, 1996), prospective memory (Ellis, Shallice and Cooper, in submission), the interaction of memory recall and decision making (cf. Fox, 1980), and the creation of long term memory records (cf. Morton, Hammersley & Bekerian, 1985). Details of COGENT availability and system requirements are available from the author.

The Functional Modules

The basic unit of COGENT is the *cognitive object*. This is the software's equivalent of a psychologist's functional module. In the production system model reported here, four major functional modules were employed: *Task Control*, *Working Memory*, *Perceptual Buffer*, and *Memory Decay*. A fifth object, *Transcript*, was used to record the model's behaviour. Figure 1 shows the connectivity of the modules.

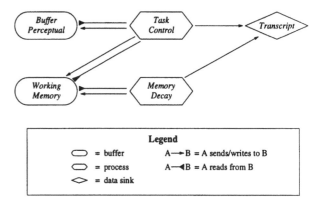

Figure 1: The simplified production system in COGENT

Refractory memory and refractory memory decay were not explicitly modelled. Instead, a simpler alternative was employed in which production rules were not refracted (and so any instantiation of a production rule could fire any number of times), but were modified so as to include in their conditions the logical negation of their actions. Thus a rule which added an element to working memory was modified to include an explicit check that the element in question was not already in working memory. Decay was then imposed on working memory. This scheme, which with the production rules employed in the current model is equivalent to refractory memory decay, leads to a number of simplifications in the basic production system architecture (such as removing the requirement for a refractory memory and an associated test against this memory

---

[1] I am indebted to an anonymous reviewer for this locution.

during the selection of productions to execute), and is consistent with the goal of demonstrating minimal requirements for perseverative subgoaling.

Task Control   Most of the standard production system processing is performed by a single COGENT object: a rule-based process. This object is an instance of a standard object class provided by COGENT, and its behaviour is fully determined by a set of production-like rules which read from and write to other objects in the model (in particular, *Working Memory*). The process operates in a cyclic manner but without any form of conflict resolution. Thus several rules may, in principle, fire on a single cycle.

Task Control contains five declarative rules, each of which is task independent. Together they embody a general approach to tasks with a fixed (and known) goal/subgoal structure. In summary, the functions of the rules are:

1. focus on the first unresolved child of the lowest unresolved goal;

2. directly execute a childless goal (i.e., a primitive operator);

3. merge the results of a goal's subgoals to give the results of the goal;

4. delete intermediate subgoal results if a goal's result is known; and

5. delete intermediate subgoals if a goal's result is known;

All rules modify *Working Memory* by adding or deleting information about goal/subgoal relationships or goal/result relationships. The rules are not refracted, but are fully declarative, so fire only under appropriate conditions (including when their consequent elements decay from working memory).

Three additional pieces of information are required in order to execute a specific task: the task's goal/subgoal structure, the means of effecting all lowest level goals, and the means of assembling the resolution of a goal's subgoals into the resolution of that goal. This additional information is also associated with *Task Control* in the form of Prolog conditions.

Working Memory   Working memory is modelled by an unlimited capacity (symbolic) buffer — another standard class of object provided by COGENT. Elements are added to, and deleted from, this buffer by *Task Control*, which also matches information in the buffer when determining which rules to fire. Note that no explicit constraint is placed on the buffer capacity. A fixed capacity working memory would be no more psychologically plausible than an unlimited capacity working memory. The current work therefore employs a soft constraint derived from working memory decay (explicitly modelled by another process). Assuming that elements can only be added to *Working Memory* at a finite rate, a high decay rate will naturally lead to a low (but variable) capacity.

Memory Decay   Each COGENT object has a set of properties which determine its precise behaviour. Symbolic buffers, such as *Working Memory*, have two properties which govern decay (one specifying a decay function, and one specifying a decay rate). However, this built-in functionality does not take account of structure on the contents of the buffer in question, and so specifying decay from *Working Memory* in this way in the current model could lead to disconnected subgoals. There-

fore, in the model reported here decay of *Working Memory* is explicitly effected by a separate rule-based process, *Memory Decay*. On each production cycle, this process may randomly delete some terminal working memory elements. This behaviour is programmed by a single rule which generates a random number (uniformly distributed between 0 and 1) for each terminal working memory element, and, if that number is less than a preset threshold, deletes the corresponding element from *Working Memory*. The probability of deletion (i.e., the preset threshold) is independent of the working memory element (provided it is a terminal element) and given by a separate parameter of the process.

The use of a separate process governing the decay of working memory is an unsatisfactory aspect of the model, and reflects an inadequacy in the COGENT modelling environment. Ideally, memory decay should be an intrinsic property of the buffer concerned, not the result of some explicit decay process acting on the buffer. Thus, it should be possible to state the appropriate form of decay as a property of the buffer (as discussed in the preceding paragraph). This could be done with COGENT in its current form if 1) refractory memory was explicitly modelled (as in Soar), 2) subgoals were created by some mechanism other than production system firing (as in Soar), and 3) decay was imposed on refractory memory (contrary to Soar).

Perceptual Buffer   In most problem solving situations it is possible to distinguish between two sorts of information: information generated and maintained by internal processes (in this case the contents of *Working Memory*), and perceptual information. Perceptual information is always immediately available to the problem solver. As such there is no clear sense in which it decays. The current model therefore makes use of one further unlimited capacity symbolic buffer, *Perceptual Buffer*, which contains a representation of information available in the external world. The precise contents of this buffer will depend on the external environment of the problem solving agent, but the buffers existence is crucial to the agent's problem solving behaviour.

Transcript   The last functional module employed in the model is *Transcript*, a data sink which is used to record the models behaviour, including the elements which decay from working memory and the models final solution to its problem solving task. This module has no theoretical import.

The Task: Multicolumn Addition

The original work on refractory memory decay in Soar was based on two versions of a standard AI task, the monkey and bananas task. This task has many interesting features, but is more complex than necessary to show recoverable perseverative subgoaling. A different task is therefore considered here. The multicolumn addition task (see, e.g., Anderson, 1993, pp. 4–6) involves adding two "large" integers using the standard algorithm taught in most Western schools: first sum the units column, recording the units digit of the sum and carrying the tens digit (if any) to the next column, then sum the tens column, recording the units digit of the sum and carrying the tens digit (if any) to the next column, and so on. The task has the advantage of having a clear goal/subgoal structure, *viz*:

Goal	Subgoals
multicolumn-add	*process-column(1)*
	process-column(2)
	⋮
	process-remaining-carry
process-column(N)	*get-digits(N)*
	add-digits
	add-previous-carry
	split-answer-units-and-carry

Furthermore, the task can be made to place heavy demands on working memory by requiring that intermediate results (i.e., the sums of individual columns) be remembered during the computation (rather than being written down as the computation progresses), and those demands will increase as the number of columns in the sum increases. As discussed below, this makes the task ideal for empirical investigation.

Multicolumn addition was therefore modelled in COGENT by the inclusion of task specific goal/subgoal information in the *Task Control* object. In addition, the *Perceptual Buffer* was initialised with the stimulus information (a representation of the integers to be summed). As noted above, no decay was specified for this buffer, modelling the fact that this information would always be available throughout the task. Two experimental conditions were examined in the simulations. In the first, intermediate results were not added to the *Perceptual Buffer*, but were instead stored in *Working Memory* for the duration of the task, thus modelling the situation where the subject is required to perform the entire calculation without the aid of an external memory. In this condition, intermediate results are subject to potential decay. In the second condition, the results of summing individual columns were added to the *Perceptual Buffer*, and *Task Control* was able to freely consult this buffer. This condition models the task were the subject is able to record his/her results as problem solving progresses.

An additional rule was added to *Task Control* to detect when the task was complete and print the answer contained in *Working Memory*.

Simulation Results

We consider first the results of the "difficult" condition in which intermediate results are stored in *Working Memory*. Figure 2 shows a trace of the primitive operators invoked by the model on one particular trial when working with a decay rate of 0.03. The model was attempting the sum:

$$895 +$$
$$267$$

Of principal concern is the perseverative subgoaling occurring between cycle 25 and cycle 31. During this period, the model is solving the four subgoals which comprise *process-column(1)*. These subgoals were originally solved during cycles 4–10, after which their results were assembled to produce a result for *process-column(1)*. However, by cycle 25, this result was no longer in *Working Memory* (due to *Working Memory* decay), prompting the model to automatically repeat its prior problem solving. The model recovers after this bout of perseverative subgoaling, and produces the correct answer, although its solution time (measured in number of cycles to completion) is sub-optimal.

Cycle	4	*get-digits(column(1))*
Cycle	6	*add-digits(column(1))*
Cycle	8	*add-previous-carry(column(1))*
Cycle	10	*split-answer(column(1))*
Cycle	15	*get-digits(column(2))*
Cycle	17	*add-digits(column(2))*
Cycle	19	*add-previous-carry(column(2))*
Cycle	22	*split-answer(column(2))*
Cycle	25	*get-digits(column(1))*
Cycle	27	*add-digits(column(1))*
Cycle	29	*add-previous-carry(column(1))*
Cycle	31	*split-answer(column(1))*
Cycle	36	*get-digits(column(3))*
Cycle	38	*add-digits(column(3))*
Cycle	40	*add-previous-carry(column(3))*
Cycle	42	*split-answer(column(3))*
Cycle	47	*process-carry(column(4))*
Cycle	49	STOP: answer = 1162

Figure 2: Perseverative subgoaling in 3-column addition

Figure 2 shows, then, that the model is indeed subject to perseverative subgoaling. Perhaps surprisingly, it is robust against substantially greater decay rates than Soar was in the original experiments. A decay rate of 0.03 (which lead to the transcript in Figure 2) is three times greater than the highest rate for which Soar's behaviour was examined (and found wanting), and yet performance is only moderately impaired, showing slowing but not error.

Extensive experimentation has shown that the model is able to recover from any failure except premature decay of the root of the goal stack. Provided that decay does not occur over the first cycle of problem solving, the model will always solve the task, though the number of cycles required to solve the problem will vary depending on the decay rate and the complexity of the task (which is here determined by the number of columns). However, and in spite of this apparent robustness, the system is prone to error. In particular, the operator *add-previous-carry* assumes that if a carry should be added, it will be in *Working Memory*. Decay of carry information can therefore lead to errors.[2]

Also worthy of note is that the effect of decay on solution time increases super-linearly with the number of columns in the sum. A decay rate of 0.10 working memory elements per cycle led on average to a 1.6 times increase in solution time for two column sums. This grew to 3.2 for three column sums and 13.5 for four column sums. The number of incorrect solutions (due to failure to carry) increases in a similar way with the number of columns in the sum.

With regard to the second experimental condition, where the sums of columns were stored in the *Perceptual Buffer* (and hence not subject to decay), solution times as measured in number of cycles were, as expected, generally shorter than in the first condition, and there was substantially less variance.

---

[2]This source of error, decay of carry information, is not a necessary aspect of the model. The rules could be designed to treat a missing carry as a decayed subgoal result. However, this error appears to be consistent with human performance on the task, and so no attempt was made to avoid it.

Over ten trials of a 4-column task with a decay rate of 0.03, the average number of cycles to solution was 47.1 (s.d. = 2.5). This compares with 59.1 (s.d. = 12.5) for the equivalent task in the difficult condition.

Future Developments

The simulation results suggest that perseverative subgoaling will occur most frequently when working memory capacity is stretched (e.g., in multicolumn addition involving many columns). Future work will empirically explore the nature of perseveration in problem solving with different working memory requirements. Multicolumn addition is an ideal task for this work as the demands on working memory can be easily varied by varying the number of columns in the sum. Alternately, the task can be coupled with some other concurrent, working memory intensive, task in order to investigate the effects of working memory load.

One hypothesis to be addressed by this work is that perseverative subgoaling will be greater when memory resources are in high demand. This hypothesis is motivated by a strengthening of the putative relationship between working memory load and working memory decay — that the rate of decay is dependent on the load, being greater when the load is greater. Should empirical work confirm this hypothesis, the COGENT modelling software will facilitate the exploration of capacity sensitive alternatives to the rules governing working memory decay presented here.

A second area of future work concerns uses of the underlying mechanism which leads to recoverable perseverative subgoaling, i.e., non-refracted fine-grained productions along with refractory memory decay. Together, these produce a mechanism which effectively refreshes working memory when critical elements decay. One clear theoretical domain where such a refreshing mechanism may be appropriate is the articulatory loop (see, e.g., Baddeley, 1986), an area in which network models (notably that of Burgess & Hitch, 1992) have shown some success. The mechanism presented here offers the promise of a symbolic alternative to such network approaches. More generally, the introduction of stochastic elements into symbolic models may allow the development of semantically perspicuous models with sufficient plasticity to rival their connectionist counterparts.

Conclusions

We have isolated three requirements which will lead a production system to exhibit recoverable perseverative subgoaling: refractory memory decay, fine-grained productions, and a decay-free goal stack. None of the three requirements alone is sufficient if the resultant system is to exhibit the effect. The conjunction of the three, however, cannot be claimed to be necessary conditions. With sufficient ingenuity, alternate systems could undoubtably achieve the same effect. The claim here is that no simpler system could do so.

Acknowledgements

I am grateful to Nick Braisby, John Fox, Bradley Franks, and Tim Shallice for advice and discussion on issues related to the work presented here. Part of this work was supported by the Joint Council Initiative in Cognitive Science and Human-Computer Interaction, project grant #G9212530.

References

Anderson, J. R. (1993). *Rules of the Mind*. Lawrence Erlbaum Associates, Hove, UK.

Baddeley, A. D. (1986). *Working Memory*. Oxford University Press, Oxford, UK.

Burgess, N., & Hitch, G. J. (1992). Toward a network model of the articulatory loop. *Journal of Memory and Language*, *31*, 429–460.

Charniak, E., & McDermott, D. (1985). *Introduction to Artificial Intelligence*. Addison–Wesley, Reading, MA.

Cohen, P. R. (1995). *Empirical Methods for Artificial Intelligence*. MIT Press, Cambridge, MA.

Cooper, R. (1995). Towards an object-oriented language for cognitive modeling. In *Proceedings of the 17th Annual Conference of the Cognitive Science Society*, pp. 556–561. Pittsburgh, PA.

Cooper, R., & Farringdon, J. (1993). Sceptic Version 4 User Manual. Tech. rep. UCL-PSY-ADREM-TR6, Department of Psychology, University College London, UK.

Cooper, R., Fox, J., Farringdon, J., & Shallice, T. (In press). A systematic methodology for cognitive modelling. *Artificial Intelligence*, *85*.

Cooper, R., & Franks, B. (1996). The iteration of concept combination in Sense Generation. In *Proceedings of the 18th Annual Conference of the Cognitive Science Society*. This volume. San Diego, CA.

Cooper, R., & Shallice, T. (1995). Soar and the case for Unified Theories of Cognition. *Cognition*, *55*(2), 115–149.

Ellis, J., Shallice, T., & Cooper, R. (1996). Memory for, and the organization of, future intentions. In submission.

Fox, J. (1980). Making decisions under the influence of memory. *Psychological Review*, *87*, 190–211.

Genter, D. (1983). Structure-mapping: A theoretical framework for analogy. *Cognitive Science*, *7*, 155–170.

Hajnal, S., Fox, J., & Krause, P. (1989). *Sceptic User Manual: Version 3.0*. Advanced Computation Laboratory, Imperial Cancer Research Fund, London, UK.

Holyoak, K. J., & Thagard, P. (1989). Analogical mapping by constraint satisfaction. *Cognitive Science*, *13*, 295–355.

Keane, M. T. (1988). *Analogical Problem Solving*. Ellis Horwood, Chichester.

Laird, J. E., Newell, A., & Rosenbloom, P. S. (1987). SOAR: An architecture for general intelligence. *Artificial Intelligence*, *33*, 1–64.

Morton, J., Hammersley, R. H., & Bekerian, D. A. (1985). Headed records: A model for memory and its failures. *Cognition*, *20*, 1–23.

Newell, A. (1990). *Unified Theories of Cognition*. Harvard University Press, Cambridge, MA.

Newell, A., & Simon, H. (1972). *Human Problem Solving*. Prentice–Hall, Englewood Cliffs, NJ.

Touretzky, D. S., & Hinton, G. E. (1988). A distributed connectionist production system. *Cognitive Science*, *12*, 423–466.

Probabilistic Plan Recognition for Cognitive Apprenticeship

Cristina Conati and **Kurt VanLehn**
Intelligent Systems Program
University of Pittsburgh
Pittsburgh, PA, 15260
conati@pogo.isp.pitt.edu, vanlehn+@pitt.edu

Abstract

Interpreting the student's actions and inferring the student's solution plan during problem solving is one of the main challenges of tutoring based on cognitive apprenticeship, especially in domains with large solution spaces. We present a student modeling framework that performs probabilistic plan recognition by integrating in a Bayesian network knowledge about the available plans and their structure and knowledge about the student's actions and mental state. Besides predictions about the most probable plan followed, the Bayesian network provides probabilistic knowledge tracing, that is assessment of the student's domain knowledge. We show how our student model can be used to tailor scaffolding and fading in cognitive apprenticeship. In particular, we describe how the information in the student model and knowledge about the structure of the available plans can be used to devise heuristics to generate effective hinting strategies when the student needs help.

Introduction

The overall goal of our research is to develop a tutoring system that teaches problem solving skills through cognitive apprenticeship [Collins et al., 1989]. In cognitive apprenticeship the tutor *models* for the students how to solve problems, *scaffolds* students as they first try to solve problems on their own, then gradually *fades* the scaffolding. Scaffolding takes many forms. For instance, students can be led to solve the problem by using an optimal solution and by explicitly performing all the steps in the solution. When this kind of scaffolding has faded out, students can solve problems as they please. In addition, scaffolding requires the tutor to provide help and unsolicited hints when the student is lost. Virtually every pedagogical activity involved in scaffolding faces the difficult problem of interpreting the student's actions. For instance, in order to respond to a student's request for help or to provide unsolicited hints, the coach must determine what line of reasoning the student has been following so that it can construct an appropriate hint.

The problem of inferring from an agent's actions the plan or line of reasoning being followed is known in AI as plan recognition [Kautz and Allen, 1986]. Plan recognition usually involves inherent uncertainty [Carberry, 1990, Charniak and Goldman, 1993, Huber et al., 1994] and in cognitive apprenticeship it is an especially hard problem [Self, 1988], since cognitive apprenticeships teach intellectual skills where most of the important activity is hidden from the coaches' view. In this paper we describe an evolving student modeling framework, based on [Conati and Vanlehn, 1996, Martin and VanLehn, 1995], that performs plan recognition by integrating probabilistic reasoning and information on the student's mental state with knowledge of available plans.

Very little research has been devoted to plan recognition in student modeling, none of which includes probabilistic plan recognition. Probabilistic reasoning has been applied in student modeling only to perform *knowledge tracing* [Anderson et al., 1995], that is to assess the student's domain knowledge and possible misconceptions from problem solving performance [Corbett et al., 1995, Martin and VanLehn, 1995, Mislevy, 1995, Petrushin, 1993]. Most of the attempts to apply plan recognition to intelligent tutoring systems rely only on the library of the available plans, without taking into consideration the student's degree of mastery in the target domain assessed by knowledge tracing to help discriminate among alternative interpretations of the students' actions [Genesereth, 1982, Kohen and Greer, 1993, Ross and Lewis, 1988]. The Andersonian tutors [Anderson et al., 1995] perform both knowledge tracing and model tracing, a very simple form of plan recognition, but they do not integrate the two kinds of assessment. Instead, they reduce the complexity of plan recognition by restricting the number of acceptable solutions that the student can follow and by asking the student when there is still ambiguity among two or more solutions.

In the first part of the paper we describe how our student model uses a compact, graph-based representation of plans that encodes the plausible lines of reasoning for solving a problem in the target task domain (Newtonian physics in this application) and how the graph and the student's actions are used to dynamically generate a Bayesian network [Pearl, 1988] that performs plan recognition and knowledge tracing. In the second part of the paper we describe how a tutoring system based on cognitive apprenticeship can use the student model to tailor scaffolding and fading. In particular we describe how we integrate probabilistic plan recognition, knowledge tracing and hint selection rules to generate effective hints when a student needs help.

A graph based model of the problem solving process

In order to decide which line of reasoning underlies a student's action the system must have a set of lines of reasoning that students may pursue. This set represents the solution space of a problem and in domains like physics can be quite large. The data structure that we use to represent the solution space of a problem is the *solution graph*. The solution graph is automatically built from a knowledge base of production

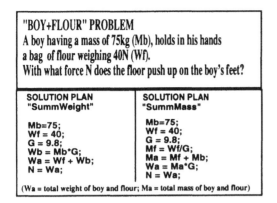

"BOY+FLOUR" PROBLEM
A boy having a mass of 75kg (Mb), holds in his hands
a bag of flour weighing 40N (Wf).
With what force N does the floor push up on the boy's feet?

SOLUTION PLAN "SummWeight"	SOLUTION PLAN "SummMass"
Mb=75; Wf = 40; G = 9.8; Wb = Mb*G; Wa = Wf + Wb; N = Wa;	Mb=75; Wf = 40; G = 9.8; Mf = Wf/G; Ma = Mf + Mb; Wa = Ma*G; N = Wa;

(Wa = total weight of boy and flour; Ma = total mass of boy and flour)

Figure 1: A simple problem and its correct solution plans

rules that contains the physics principles necessary to solve Newtonian physics problems. It can compactly represent the solution space for any given physics problem.

The solution graph contains three types of information, which represent (1) all the plans to solve the problem that can be derived by the rules in the physics knowledge base; (2) all the algebraic solution paths that develop these plans; (3) the reasoning behind each step in a plan. Let's consider, for example, the solution graph for the physics problem in Figure 1. There are two different plans for this problem: either find the weight of the flour and add the weights or find the mass of the boy, add the masses, then convert them to weight. Then equate the total weight of the boy and the flour to the sought normal force. These two plans are represented by the two sets of primitive equations "SummWeight" and "SummMass" in Figure 1. We define as primitive equations those equations that are direct applications of physical laws or mathematical principles, or quantities given in the problem statement.

The primitive equations for a plan can be generated and combined in many different ways, generating a large number of solution paths. Solution paths can be generated, for example, by forward chaining, backward chaining, depth first, breadth first or any combination of these strategies. Existing tutoring systems that provide support during problem solving reduce the number of the acceptable solution paths by forcing the students to follow a particular problem solving strategy [Anderson et al., 1995, Derry and Hawkes, 1993]. Our solution graph, on the other hand, provides a compact representation of all the possible solution paths that develop a given plan and supports tutorial interaction that is more flexible and similar to those generated by human physics tutors.

A simplified solution graph for the problem in Figure 1 is represented in Figure 2A. It contains nodes representing primitive equations and problem variables (ellipses and diamonds respectively in Figure 2A). Primitive equations correspond to the application of rules of the knowledge base that encode quantitative physics principles. When a rule is applied an *application node* representing the corresponding primitive equation is entered in the solution graph, along with its parent nodes representing the known variables and its child node representing the computed variable. Given the solution graph, each equation entered by the user is interpreted by decomposing it into primitive equations and by marking

the corresponding application nodes in the solution graph, as shown in Figure 2A.

Behind each application node stands a dependency network that records the derivation of the corresponding primitive equation. For instance, a simplified dependency network for the equation $N = Wa$ is shown in Figure 3. There is one dependency network for each application node, but the dependency networks of different nodes often share large sub-nets. For simplicity, in the solution graph of Figure 2A the complete dependency networks are represented by single physics rules, the rectangles in the graph. The dependency networks are needed in order to interpret actions that are not equations. For instance, suppose the student initializes a force diagram for the compound object consisting of the boy and the bag. This action corresponds to the darkened node labelled "boy-bag is an object" in Figure 3.

The solution graph allows the tutor to accept the student's actions in any order, as long as they belong to a known plan. In fact any traversal of the graph that connects soughts to givens represents a legal solution path within a specific plan, and vice versa every correct solution path corresponds to a traversal of the solution graph. The solution graph also allows to keep track of the actions that the student's has performed so far.

Bayesian interpretation of student actions

After a student's action has been mapped on the solution graph, the system uses the mapping and the structural information encoded in the solution graph to update a Bayesian network in charge of plan recognition. A Bayesian network [Pearl, 1988] is a directed acyclic graph where nodes represent random variables and arcs represent probabilistic dependencies among the variables. In our Bayesian network, the random variables represent pieces of domain knowledge, possible plans to solve a problem, the student's actions and the possible inferences that might have generated the actions.

Figure 2B shows the state of the Bayesian network after it has been incrementally updated with the two equations $N = Wa$ and $Mf = 40/G$. The nodes at the bottom of the network, called *action nodes*, represent the entered equations. For each action node, there is a *derivation node* for any way found in the graph to derive the equation (nodes *der1* and *der2* in Figure 2B) and an additional derivation node that represents any other way in which the action could have been derived, for example by guessing or by copying from a previous problem (nodes *other1* and *other2* in Figure 2B). The two equations in our example can be derived in only one way, therefore only one derivation node (besides the *other* node) is inserted for each of them. If the student typed the equation $Wa = 775$ the system would find in the graph two ways to generate it, and two derivation nodes would be inserted in the network. Both action and derivation nodes have values TRUE/FALSE representing the probability that the actions or the derivations have (or have not) been performed.

An action node is linked to the corresponding derivation nodes via an OR link matrix, which defines the conditional probability distribution of the action node given the probability distribution of its parents as a logical OR. That is, an action node is TRUE if at least one of its parent derivation nodes is TRUE and FALSE otherwise. Each derivation node is linked through an AND link matrix to its parent nodes, correspond-

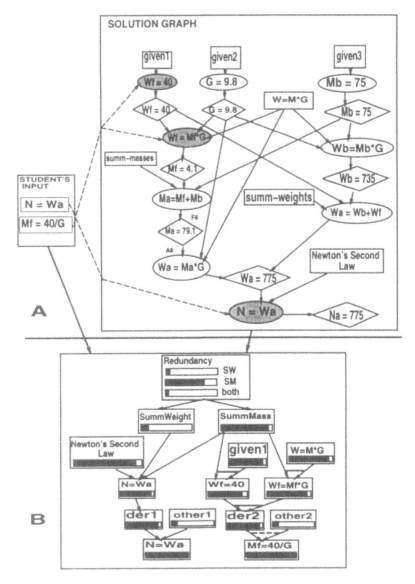

Figure 2: Example of solution graph and Bayesian network for the problem in Figure 1

ing to the application nodes marked in the solution graph as generating the derivation. In Figure 2B, for example, the parent application nodes of the derivation node *der2* are the application nodes labeled $Wf = 40$ and $Wf = Mf * G$. The AND link matrix between derivation and application nodes represent the fact that a derivation occurs if and only if all the necessary rules and givens have been applied.

Each application node is linked to a node that represents the corresponding rule and to a node representing the plan to which the rule application belongs. The solution graph indicates to which plan each application node belongs and the corresponding links are inserted in the Bayesian network. The probability of the TRUE value for a plan node represents the probability that the student is following that plan. The probability of the TRUE value for a rule node represents the probability that the student knows that rule. The link matrix between an application node and its parents is a leaky-AND,

to represent the fact that when a student generates a rule application she almost always knows the parent rule and is following the parent plan, although there is a small probability that she generated the application without actually knowing the rule or without having that plan in mind.

All the plan nodes in the Bayesian network are linked to a common ancestor, the node labeled as *redundancy* in figure figure 2B. The values of this node allows to explicitly represent the probability that the student is following only one of the available plans (values *SW* and *SM* in figure 2B) or more then one plan at a time (value *both* in figure 2B).

The action nodes at the bottom of the network represent evidence coming from the student, therefore their TRUE value is clamped to 1 and that evidence is propagated upward in the network via a Bayesian update algorithm (we use the Lauritzen-Spiegelhalter algorithm [Pearl, 1988]). In Figure 2B the higher probability of the "SummMass" node reflects

405

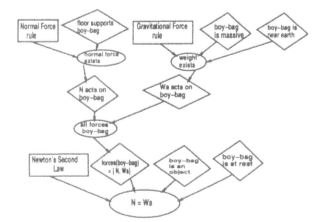

Figure 3: Dependency network for the application node "N=Wa"

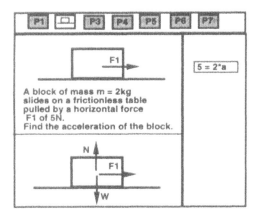

Figure 4: Example of ambiguous student's action

the fact that, although the equation $N = Wa$ belongs to both solutions, the equation $Mf = 40/G$ provides clear evidence for the plan "SummMass". In addition, the propagation of evidence to rule nodes in the network provides assessment on the student's knowledge of the corresponding physics principles. After the student has finished with the problem, the probabilities of the rule nodes and the dependencies between rules are read out of the Bayesian network and become the updated student model [Martin and VanLehn, 1995] that will be used to aid plan recognition in future interactions with the student, as we will see in the next section.

Using the student model to tailor the scaffolding

One form of scaffolding in cognitive apprenticeship consists of forcing the student to explicitly perform all the steps in a solution, for example to draw all the forces involved in a physics problem before entering equations. This kind of scaffolding, called *reification*, is usually applied to novice students and faded when the students become more skilled in the target domain. Fading makes the interpretation of the student's actions more difficult, because more of the student reasoning is hidden from the tutor. Our student model allows the system to handle the increased ambiguity generated by

fading and to make more flexible decisions about when to fade the scaffolding, instead of relying on fixed rules such as "fade reification after the student has solved 5 problems correctly". Let's suppose, for example, that after solving the problem in the previous section with reification turned on our student starts solving the problem in the upper left window in Figure 4. The student types the equation in the right window in Figure 4, without drawing forces in the bottom left window. Should the tutor keep reification turned on and ask the student to draw the forces? The tutor uses the probabilities in the Bayesian network generated after the student's action to make the decision.

The equation that the student typed can be generated either by the correct version of Newton's Second Law, $F = ma$, in which F is the sum of all the three forces acting on the body (shown by the vectors in the bottom left window) or by an incorrect version in which F is any force applied to the body. If this incorrect version of Newton's Second Law is included in the system's knowledge base, a corresponding incorrect plan will be included in the problem's solution graph and the Bayesian network generated after the equation $5 = 2 * a$ will be the one in Figure 5. If the only information available to the system was the entered equation, then propagation of this evidence in the network would assign equal probability to the two possible derivations and to the two possible plans and the only way for the tutor to understand if the student followed the correct or the incorrect plan would be to force the student to draw the forces in the free body diagram. However, since the student model generated by the previous interaction with the student reports a high probability that the student knows all the pieces of knowledge required to correctly apply Newton's Second Law (the rule nodes in Figure 3), then the Bayesian network assigns a high probability to the correct derivation and to the correct plan and the tutor can avoid imposing the reification of forces.

Another fundamental component of scaffolding is the capability to provide help. Providing help during problem solving is a delicate pedagogical problem. A request for help indicates that the student reached an impasse in the problem solving process. The impasse can be turned into a learning episode if the tutor helps the student generate the inferences necessary to fill the knowledge gap that created the impasse. Hinting is one of the strategies often used by human tutors to provide constructive help [Hume et al., 1996]. Of course, the necessary condition to provide useful hints is that the tutor understands why the impasse happened. Sometimes the student can articulate for the tutor what her problem is, but often the student is too confused to be able to tell why she is unable to continue and the tutor must use alternative criteria to decide what is the best way to help the student solving the impasse.

The structural information in the solution graph and the probabilities generated by the Bayesian network can be used to devise strategies for selecting what to hint for (i.e the hint target). The Bayesian network generates predictions about what plan the student is following. Given the plan, a hint generation module determines from the solution graph what steps have already been performed along this plan and what steps are left. The steps left to be performed become the *hinting set* within which the hint generator chooses the target

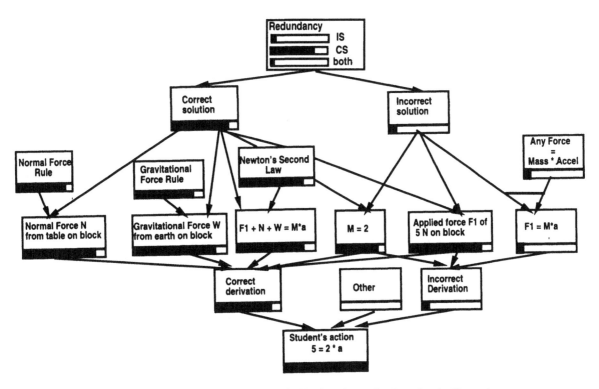

Figure 5: Bayesian network built after the student's action in Figure 3

of the next hint. Let's suppose, for example, that the student asks for help after typing the two equations in Figure 2A. At this point *SummMass* is the most probable plan, as shown in the network in Figure 2B, and the hinting set consists of the following primitive equations:

$\{G = 9.8, Mb = 75, Ma = Mb + Mf, Wa = Ma * G\}$

Several heuristics can be used to select among equations in the hinting set. One heuristic gives minimal priority to hints that simply remind the student of values that are problem givens. In our example this heuristic would rule out using the steps $G = 9.8$ and $Mb = 75$ as hints. Two different heuristics can be based on the probabilistic assessment of the student's knowledge of physics rules. The *reminding* heuristic selects steps related to physics knowledge that has high probability of being mastered. The hints generated by this heuristic are analogous to those categorized in [Hume et al., 1996] as *pointing hints*, that is hints pointing to well-known information that the student doesn't realize is relevant in the current situation. In our example this heuristic would select the step $Wa = Ma * G$, since it is related to the rule $W = M * G$ (see solution graph Figure 2A) which has reached a high probability of being known (see Bayesian network in Figure 2B) after the student typed $Mf = 40/G$.

The second heuristic, the *low knowledge* heuristic, selects for hinting a step related to physics knowledge that is not evidently known by the student. This heuristic generates hints analogous to those classified in [Hume et al., 1996] as *conveying information* hints, that suggest information prompting the student to infer an answer or the next step of a solution. In our example, this heuristic would select for hinting the step $Ma = Mb + Mf$, since there is no direct evidence from the

student's actions that the student knows the related rule "the total mass of a system is the sum of the masses of the system's components".

A third heuristic that can be combined with either of the two above is the *adjacency heuristic*. It selects a step adjacent in the solution graph to the last step performed by the student. In our example, the only step adjacent to the last performed, $Mf = 40/G$, is $Ma = Mb + Mf$. How to combine these heuristics and how to set their priorities when they provide conflicting suggestions is an open research issue, since not many results are available about how human tutors select their hints and how effective they are [Hume et al., 1996]. One of our hypotheses is that the adjacency heuristic should have high priority since it is important that the content of the hint preserves a discernible connection with what the student is trying to do. A second hypothesis is that the *reminding* heuristic should be used with care, to avoid suggesting to the student something that she already knows how to perform. To this regard, a variation of the *reminding heuristic* would be to consider whether the high probability of the target knowledge derives from recent student actions (as in our example) or from actions that the student has performed in previous problems. If the target knowledge has been used recently, it is less likely that the student needs to be reminded of it. For instance, in our example the student has just applied the rule $W = M * G$ to generate $Mf = 40/G$, therefore it is not very plausible that now she is having problems in applying the rule to find Wa. Given this variation the *reminding heuristic* all the three heuristics listed above point to the selection of $Ma = Mf + Mb$ as the hint target. We are planning to test these and additional/alternative hypotheses and heuristics by using them to implement different hint selection strategies and by testing these strategies with real students.

Conclusions

In this paper we have described a student modeling framework that performs knowledge tracing and plan recognition while students solve problems in Newtonian physics. Our approach to plan recognition is innovative in that we use a Bayesian Network to integrate in a principled way knowledge about the student's behavior and mental state with knowledge about the available plans. The available plans are encoded in a graph-based representation that compactly represents all the different orders in which each plan can be implemented and allows maximum flexibility when accepting the students' solutions. We have presented examples of how our student model can be used to tailor cognitive apprenticeship, in particular to generate effective hints when the student needs help.

We have started to evaluate the accuracy of the predictions generated by our model on the solutions generated by three students solving the problem presented in this paper and on the solutions generated by two students solving a more complex problem involving 4 different solution plans and 18 primitive equations. The predictions generated by the model after each step of the 5 solutions have been consistent with the plan that each student actually followed. We plan to perform a more extensive evaluation after we have formalized the hinting rules and reimplemented a more efficient C++ version of the update algorithm for the Bayesian network, currently implemented in Lisp. The results of the evaluation will decide whether we will need to switch to approximate update algorithms[Cousins et al., 1993] to maintain acceptable performances on more complex problems.

Acknowledgements

This research is supported by ONR's Cognitive Science Division under grants N00014-96-1-0260 and N00014-95-1-0950, and by DARPA's Computer Aided Education and Training Initiative under grant N66001-95-C-8367.

References

[Anderson et al., 1995] Anderson, J., Corbett, A., Koedinger, K., and Pelletier, R. (1995). Cognitive tutors: Lessons learned. *The Journal of the Learning Sciences*, 4(2):167–207.

[Carberry, 1990] Carberry, S. (1990). Incorporating default inferences into plan recognition. In *Proceedings of AAAI-90*, pages 471–478.

[Charniak and Goldman, 1993] Charniak, E. and Goldman, R. (1993). A bayesian model of plan recognition. *Artificial Intelligence*, 64(1):53–79.

[Collins et al., 1989] Collins, A., Brown, J. S., and Newman, S. E. (1989). Cognitive apprenticeship: Teaching the craft of reading, writing and mathematics. In Resnick, L. B., editor, *Knowing, learning and instruction: Essays in honor of Robert Glaser*, pages 543–494. LEA, Hillsdale, NJ.

[Conati and Vanlehn, 1996] Conati, C. and Vanlehn, K. (1996). Pola: a student modeling framework for probabilistic on-line assessment of problem solving performance. In *Proc. of UM-96, 5th International Conference on User Modeling*.

[Corbett et al., 1995] Corbett, A. T., Anderson, J. R., and O'Brien, A. T. (1995). Student modeling in the ACT programming tutor. In Nichols, P. D., Chipman, S. F., and Brennan, R. L., editors, *Cognitively Diagnostic Assessment*, pages 19–42. LEA, Hillsdale, NJ.

[Cousins et al., 1993] Cousins, S., Chen, W., and Frisse, M. (1993). A tutorial introduction to stochastic simulation algorithms for belief networks. *Artificial Intelligence in Medicine*, 5:315–340.

[Derry and Hawkes, 1993] Derry, J. S. and Hawkes, L. W. (1993). Local cognitive modeling of problem-solving behavior: An application of fuzzy theory. In Lajoie, S. and Derry, S., editors, *Computers as Cognitive Tools*. Lawrence Erlbaum, Hillsdale, NJ.

[Genesereth, 1982] Genesereth, M. (1982). The role of plans in intelligent teaching systems. In Sleeman, D., editor, *Intelligent tutoring systems*, pages 137–156. Academic Press, New York.

[Huber et al., 1994] Huber, M., Durfee, E., and Wellman, M. (1994). The automated mapping of plans for plan recognition. In *Proceedings of the tenth conference on Uncertainty in Artificial Intelligence*, pages 344–351.

[Hume et al., 1996] Hume, G., Michael, J., and Evens, M. (1996). Hinting as a tactic in one-to-one tutoring. *The Journal of Learning Sciences*, 5(1):23–47.

[Kautz and Allen, 1986] Kautz, H. and Allen, J. (1986). Generalized plan recognition. In *Proceedings of AAAI-86*, pages 32–37.

[Kohen and Greer, 1993] Kohen, G. and Greer, J. (1993). Recognizing plans in instructional systems using granularity. In *Proceedings of the 4th International Conference on User Modeling*, pages 133–138.

[Martin and VanLehn, 1995] Martin, J. and VanLehn, K. (1995). A bayesian approach to cognitive assessment. In Nichols, P., Chipman, S., and Brennan, R. L., editors, *Cognitively diagnostic assessment*. LEA, Hillsdale, NJ.

[Mislevy, 1995] Mislevy, R. J. (1995). Probability-based inference in cognitive diagnosis. In Nichols, P., Chipman, S., and Brennan, R., L., editors, *Cognitively diagnostic assessment*. LEA, Hillsdale, NJ.

[Pearl, 1988] Pearl, J. (1988). *Probabilistic Reasoning in Intelligent Systems: Networks of Plausible inference*. Morgan Kaufmann, Los Altos, CA.

[Petrushin, 1993] Petrushin, V. A. and Sinitsa, K. M. (1993). Using probabilistic reasoning techniques for learner modeling. In *Proceedings of the 1993 World Conference on AI and Education*, pages 426–432.

[Ross and Lewis, 1988] Ross, P. and Lewis, J. (1988). Plan recognition for intelligent tutoring systems. In Ercoli, P. and Lewis, R., editors, *Artificial Intelligence tools in Education*, pages 29–37. Elsevier Science Publishers.

[Self, 1988] Self, J. (1988). Bypassing the intractable problem of student modeling. In *Proc. of ITS-88*, pages 18–24, Montreal, Canada.

Dissociating Performance from Learning:
An Empirical Evaluation of a Computational Model

Alonso H. Vera
Department of Psychology
The University of Hong Kong
Pokfulam Road
Hong Kong
vera@hkucc.hku.hk

Richard L. Lewis
Department of Computer and Information Science
Ohio State University
2015 Neil Avenue Mall
Columbus, OH 43210
rick@cis.ohio-state.edu

Abstract

This paper presents a follow-up to the ATM-Soar models presented at 1993 Meeting of the Cognitive Science Society and the CHI 1994 Research Symposium. The original work described the use of the Soar cognitive architecture to simulate user learning with different ATM interfaces. In particular, it focused on the relative effects of interface instructions (e.g., "Insert card into slot") and perceptual attentional cues (e.g., a flashing area around the card slot) on learning and performance. The study described here involves getting human data on the same tasks to test the predictions of the computational models. The ATM task is simulated on a PC in order to contrast three types of interface conditions: just instructions, instructions plus flashing, and just flashing. Subjects must insert a bank card, check the account balance, and withdraw money. They are asked to repeat the task four times so that the effects of training on performance and learning can be observed. The data suggests that subjects learn to perform the task faster with attentional attractors, as the Soar model predicted. More interestingly, the Soar model also predicted that people would do better *without* instructions when there are attentional attractors. This prediction was supported as well.

In recent years, we have seen the rise of a number of AI cognitive architectures (e.g., Soar (Newell, 1990) and ACT-R (Anderson, 1993)) which attempt to provide unified theories of psychological phenomena. We have also seen the growing use of these architectures in the field of Human-Computer Interaction (HCI). Perhaps the primary scientific motivation for studying HCI is to provide a testing ground for our computational models of cognition, particularly those that describe learning and performance in interactive tasks. This paper reports on a set of studies currently in progress to empirically evaluate the predictions of a Soar model originally presented at the 1993 Meeting of the Cognitive Science Society (Vera, Lewis and Lerch, 1993).

In the 1993 paper, we described a Soar model that simulated a user learning to interact with different ATM interfaces. In particular, we focused on the relative effects

of interface instructions (e.g., "Insert card into slot") and perceptual attentional cues (e.g., flashing area around the card slot) on learning rate for the task. In Soar, the number of memory chunks formed was taken as the measure of ease or difficulty of learning in the different conditions. One of the basic outcomes of the ATM-Soar model was that better interfaces lead to less learning during task performance. This result needs to be evaluated empirically. The follow-up study presented here involves getting human data on these tasks.

The ATM-Soar Models

There were two related goals in building the ATM-Soar model. The first goal was to answer a set of questions about the cognitive processes and representations of the user in the ATM scenario. In particular, we were interested in how the task was mentally represented and accomplished, and how that representation evolved as a function of learning. A good cognitive model should answer the following questions:

- How is behavior initially guided in the task?
- What determines the sequence of actions taken by the user?
- What exactly is learned as a result of performing the task?
- How does the learning affect performance on later trials?
- What constitutes expert or optimal performance on this task?

The second and related goal of the modeling was to understand how aspects of the interface affect performance and learning, and to use that understanding to suggest changes in the interface design. The cognitive model should help answer the following questions:

- What computational, functional, and knowledge demands does the interface and task place on the user?
- How does the interface design affect learning?
- How can the interface be changed to decrease both the time to accomplish the task, and the time required to reach expert performance?

The Soar modeling effort was primarily focused on cognitive skill acquisition and the cognitive demands of the task. We were not concerned with details of motor behavior, or the interleaving of motor execution with cognitive processing. We did not model behavior at the key-stroke level (e.g., John, Vera & Newell, 1994), nor did we present detailed perceptual models (e.g., Wiesmeyer, 1992). All of these approaches are important and useful, and complement the approach we have taken here.

Soar, as an architectural theory, brings with it independently motivated principles of task performance and acquisition (Newell, 1990). A number of other architectures could have also been adopted (e.g., ACT-R); the minimum requirements for our present purposes are that the architecture specifies exactly how goal-directed task behavior unfolds, and how that behavior can change over time as a result of some kind of learning.

Adopting Soar as the underlying theory has a number of important implications for our task that are apparent even before specifying a detailed model. The representation of the task must consist of a set of independent associations in long term memory, cued by the contents of working memory. Task behavior is not fixed in advance by a plan structure or rigid program in memory; rather, behavior is a function of whatever knowledge is immediately cued and assembled at the time of action. Finally, because chunking is an experiential learning mechanism, the task must be learned by doing the task. Although prior preparation (e.g., instructions) may be helpful, there is no substitute for practice.

Cognitive architectures are programmable -- that is their primary functional feature. An architecture without content will not yield behavior. Behavior is a function of the fixed architectural mechanisms, the contents of the memories, and the current situation. This means that to develop a complete model, the theorist must posit the knowledge that a subject brings to the task. (Reducing the degrees of freedom in this step is an important methodological issue for cognitive science; see Newell, 1990; and Lewis, Newell & Polk, 1989, for more discussion).

How do we specify the content of the ATM models? The guiding principle is to make plausible assumptions about the knowledge and skills that a user will bring to the ATM task for the first time. All users bring to the task a set of general cognitive capabilities such as language comprehension and the ability to direct attention to different regions in space. These capabilities are functionally required for the task, but the details of their implementation are not our concern here.

The models developed posited a set of abstract functional capabilities that were realized in the Soar model by a set of operators that served as place holders for the more detailed mechanisms. In particular, the models assume pre-existing operators that comprehended language, shifted attention and intended motor behavior. While this did not permit us to explore the effects of the interface on the internal structure of these operations, it permitted asking critical questions about how these given cognitive functions are deployed to accomplish the task.

In addition to these general capabilities, we must posit some task-specific knowledge as well. Although it would be possible to simply posit expert-level memory structures, we are interested in how these structures arise. Thus, we make fairly minimal assumptions about the knowledge a user brings to the task initially:

1. Knowledge of task objects. The user knows he has an account with a balance, knows he has a plastic card that is required to operate the device, and knows he has a personal identification number (and knows what it is).

2. Knowledge of physical devices. The user knows how to push buttons and insert cards into slots, and furthermore can make some simple associations between aspects of the device and possible task-related actions (for example, the slot may be good for inserting the card, the numeric keypad may be good for specifying dollar amounts or PINs).

3. Minimal task strategy. The user does just what is needed to accomplish the task, and no more. We assume that the basic strategy guiding behavior is simply looking around the device for cues about what to do next, which may take the form of explicit task instructions. The user's goal is not to learn how to use the machine, but to get the account balance (or whatever) and leave.

The basic principles of the ATM-Soar model have already been described in Vera et al., (1993). An extension to that model, presented at a Research Symposium following CHI'94, showed that using perceptual cues in the interface to attract the model's attention to the relevant location greatly reduced the number of chunks built during learning. In other words, much of what the Soar model learned in the original version was a consequence of having to search around the interface in order to find the next relevant information. The second model assumed that attention could be drawn to the relevant part of the interface with perceptual cues.

This second model achieved the same level of performance as the original, but learned much less because it did not have to memorize the sequence of places in the interface to which it needed to attend. The argument presented in this paper is that the same is basically true for human users. To the extent that the interface has to be searched to find the next relevant action to execute, more learning is required in order to improve performance. If, on the other hand, searching is reduced or removed completely by having attention drawn to the relevant part of the interface, then performance improves, but the amount of information the user has to learn should not increase. Here, we present a study that explores these predictions by having subjects perform the ATM task on simulated interfaces with and without perceptual cues.

The ATM Study

The Soar model predicts that attentional-cues should make a big difference in the performance of people using ATMs without instructions. The attentional cues should speed up the process of achieving "expert-level" performance. Moreover, this should be attained without a concomitant increase in learning.

Although it may seem somewhat counterintuitive, what is being suggested is that perceptual cues will lead to a steeper performance improvement curve (i.e., subjects will get better faster) while less actual learning is going on. This is because the cues will guide attention without adding cognitive processing that would increase learning. This raises an important distinction, since learning is often measured in terms of improvements in performance. As the Soar model suggests, the relation between performance and amount learned (number of new chunks in the Soar model) depends strongly on the interface. A user who has learned many new things about one interface may still perform more poorly than a user who has learned little about a different interface. Furthermore, if the Soar model is correct, it leads to another counter-intuitive prediction that, following a number of training trials, performance with the attention cues will actually be faster without the instructions than with the instructions, because the instructions just get in the way at this point. Possible explanations for this are discussed in the Results section.

A flashing border around the relevant interface object was selected as the perceptual cue to be used in these studies although a number of other alternatives were available. Other variables that might have the property of cueing perception in 2-D environments are things like changes in shape and size, appearance/disappearance of objects, movement of objects, and coordinated movement of more than one object. There are also other candidates such as color changes, sound from a particular part of the interface, and so on, but these are not likely to be helpful given the typical physical locations of ATMs in the real world. These latter cues have often been used in interfaces since they tend to be the easiest and most obvious way to attract attention.

The ability of the perceptual cues to attract attention was measured in terms of the time it took to achieve the next task action (i.e., time to the next correct mouse click). Some recent work has treated these sorts of perceptual cues as "affordances", in the Gibsonian (1979) sense that they directly cue action (e.g., Howes & Young, in press). This is not the idea here. The only thing that flashing does is attract the user's attention -- action is generated by independent cognitive processing of task goals and current conditions. The effect of attention cues versus instructions is thus measured in terms of reaction time. This is actually a measure of Attention + Cognition (decide what to do) + Motor (do it). Assuming that the motor behavior itself does not change significantly across the conditions, the difference between the two conditions is due to differences in Attention + Cognition; that is, differences in the time required to decide where and what to initiate next.

Method

Subjects were 96 undergraduate students from The University of Hong Kong. Simulation interfaces were built and run on a 486 PC platform. A high-resolution digitized photograph of an ATM was used to generate the look of the simulation. All of the functional features of the interface worked exactly like those of a real ATM. Subjects interacted with the interface using a mouse. They could drag objects like the bank card, click on buttons, drag money from the dispensing slot, and so on (see Figure 1).

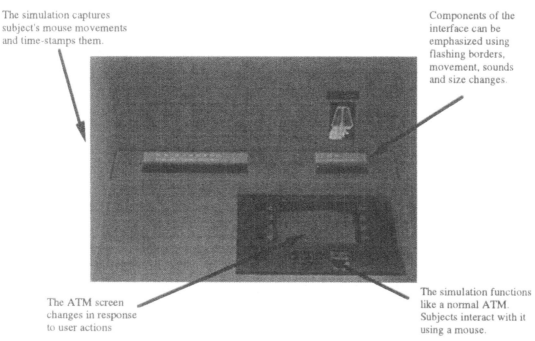

The simulation captures subject's mouse movements and time-stamps them.

Components of the interface can be emphasized using flashing borders, movement, sounds and size changes.

The ATM screen changes in response to user actions

The simulation functions like a normal ATM. Subjects interact with it using a mouse.

Figure 1. Characteristics of the ATM Interface Simulation

411

There were two interface conditions. First, a normal ATM interface was used. All the functions of a common ATM were fully reproduced. Subjects' task was to insert the bank card into the slot, type in their Personal Identification Number (PIN), select a function (get their account balance), select an account to check (from two possibilities: checking and savings), select another function (withdrawal), select an account to debit, enter the amount, and remove the money. They repeated this task four times.

In order to address the fact that subjects had previous experience with ATM machines, the task was also modified in a separate condition so that subjects were not performing an ATM transaction but instead choosing a new telephone card number. The second interface condition was therefore an invented "Phone Machine" which looked just like an ATM except that we replaced the bank logo with a Hong Kong Telecom logo and the ATM card with a phone card. The functional aspects of the interface remained unchanged. The (made-up) functions of the Phone Machine were explained to subjects at the outset. They were told that, among other things, they could settle their accounts with the phone company, check how much they owed, change their personal phone code, and so on. The actual task they performed was to first check how much money they owed the phone company and then change their phone code. The individual steps required them to insert the phone card into the slot, type in their phone code, select a function (get their account balance), select a billing option (from two possibilities: pay by check or charge to credit card), select another function (change secret phone code), select a code to change, enter the new code, and remove a statement. Subjects did this four times.

There were 16 subjects per condition for the ATM task and 16 per condition for the Phone Machine task. Each subject was asked to carry out the same task four times because it was the same number of trials the Soar model required to learn how to perform the task without using the instructions. Each trial was separated by the same distracter task where subjects were asked to count backwards by 17's from 1000 for two minutes. This was done in order to prevent subjects from rehearsing the task once they realized they were doing it repeatedly.

The main manipulation of this study involved varying perceptual aspects of the interface to attract attention to specific areas of the display. The functionally relevant part of the display had a flashing surrounding border. The display objects affected by the flashing were the card slot, the numerical keypad, the information screen, and the buttons around the screen. In one condition subjects saw instructions, but no flashing; in a second condition, they saw both instructions and flashing; and, in the third condition, just flashing with no instructions. There were therefore 6 experimental groups in a 2 task (ATM vs. Phone Machine) X 3 interface (instruction, no flashing vs. instruction and flashing vs. no-instruction, flashing) design. The design was between-subjects design and each subject saw only one task and one interface type.

Results

In order to compare subjects' performance across the three conditions, one component of the task was chosen. The time from the screen change following insertion of the card until the first number of the PIN was clicked was measured. The following comparisons are based on performance on this measure during fourth training trial across subjects. Performance was fastest in the condition with flashing but no instructions, as anticipated. T-tests showed that on the fourth trial, performance was significantly faster in the condition with flashing but no instructions (1.83 sec) than in the condition with flashing as well as instructions (2.25 sec), $t(93)=2.25$, $p<.05$. The performance difference between the condition with flashing but no instructions (1.83 sec) and the condition with instructions but no flashing (2.13 sec) was close to significance at the .1 level. The analyses suggest that people's final performance is faster when there are no instructions present. This follows from the hypothesis that instructions demand cognitive resource even when the user already knows how to perform the task.

The task manipulation (ATM vs. Phone Machine) yielded no significant performance differences across conditions and trials. There are at least two possible explanations for this. The Phone Machine interface may not have been sufficiently dissimilar to the ATM's in terms of its physical and functional characteristics. Alternatively, top-down knowledge from the familiar ATM task may have transferred quite easily to the novel Phone Machine task. If the former is the case, then subjects' performance on the two tasks should have been quite similar from the first trial onward. If the latter is true, then performance should be somewhat better for the ATM condition in the first trial than for the Phone Machine in the first trial, with performance evening out over the subsequent trials. This was not the case however, since there was no significant difference between the performances on each task in the first trial, suggesting that the similarity between the two task conditions was the main factor. This is important because it suggests that tasks variables override top-down knowledge from the beginning. It is clear that if the effects of these manipulations were due largely to top-down knowledge, results regarding interface characteristics would lose some of their meaning.

In summary, subjects perform the task faster with attentional attractors, as the Soar model predicted. More interestingly, the Soar model also predicted that people would do better without instructions when there are attentional attractors. This prediction was also supported. Performance on the fourth trial is slower when instructions are present than when they are not. This is likely due to two independent factors. The first is that instructions draw attention away from the area of the display which is functionally relevant to the next task. For example, ATM user's attention may be drawn toward the instruction screen rather than to the numerical keypad when the PIN needs to be entered. The second reason is that, once attended, the text on the screen is processed automatically (see, e.g.,

412

Fodor (1983) for a discussion of this mandatory quality of input systems, and Newell (1990) and Lewis (1996) for a discussion of how Soar accounts for such modularity effects) and consequently uses additional cognitive resources.

Discussion

Until recently, the consensus in cognitive science was that processes such as memory, problem-solving, categorization, and causal inference were non-optimal because they did not perform maximally in many conditions. This is because these conditions happen to be conditions that do not exist in the real world. Rational analysis (Anderson, 1990) suggests that information in the external world is structured such that our cognitive systems can take maximal advantage of it. Our systems are optimally tuned to information out in the real world because they evolved to predict not just any arbitrary set of external conditions but those that actually hold in this world.

This sort of approach would suggest that structuring the external world (an interface, in the case of HCI) such that users can interact optimally with it is not a matter of turning to concepts such as "affordances" to solve the problem. There is currently no evidence that anything acts like an affordance (in the true Gibsonian sense) in computer interfaces. Although most of today's GUI's use buttons, sliders, and so on, there is little reason to believe that these images are directly cueing action in any way. It is even doubtful whether real world buttons (e.g., in an elevator) *afford* pressing.

The approach of the study here was to enlist low-level perceptual cues to guide attention to relevant parts of the interface. This is based on our computational model's prediction that the critical time bottleneck in this task comes from searching the interface for relevant information. This approach is quite different from attempts to improve performance by redesigning aspects of the interface so that they directly cue or afford the relevant action. While it may be the case that certain object designs are better cues to relevant actions than others, such cues only solve part of the problem. In particular, they do not provide a way to reduce the time spent searching the interface for something relevant because they do not function by explicitly drawing attention. They are important insofar as they facilitate the evaluation of relevancy, and guide action in service of goals once the relevant part of the interface is attended. Indeed, as mentioned earlier, associations from aspects of the interface to possible actions was an important part of the Soar models' initial knowledge.

In short, the two approaches complement each other. The goals of interface design might be best served by working on both problems: guiding attention with low-level perceptual cues, and using object designs that provide good cues for the next set of possible actions. The present Soar models suggest that in certain tasks, guiding attention to reduce search may be the most important factor. Increased search time is detrimental not only to

performance, but also to learning because it forces users to learn more than they have to.

The study presented here looked at the effects of instructions and perceptual cues on *performance*; it did not evaluate the relative effects on *learning*. The next set of studies will attempt to separate the learning components of the task. It seems clear from the results already available that the continued presence of instructions over trials lowers performance. It is also clear that perceptual cues improve it. Furthermore, performance is significantly impaired when instructions are removed. What cannot be determined from the present study is whether performance will deteriorate relatively more when flashing is removed (i.e., when subjects are trained on trials with flashing and then tested on trials without it). The Soar model predicts a greater drop in performance when flashing is removed than when instructions are removed because the flashing condition leads to fewer chunks being built (i.e., less being learned).

The studies presently being conducted present subjects with four training trials, like the study described here, plus three test trials where the instruction / flashing conditions are varied. In particular we are interested in seeing what happens to performance when subjects are trained with flashing but no instructions, and then tested with no flashing or instructions. We expect that performance will deteriorate more in this condition and than in a condition where they go from instructions with no flashing to no instructions and no flashing. This is because, if the model's prediction that flashing leads to better performance but less learning is correct, then performance should fall off steeply when flashing is no longer available since subjects will have learned very little about the task. The goal is therefore to demonstrate that, as predicted by the ATM-Soar model, a better interface is one that requires less learning in order to achieve better performance.

Acknowledgments

Work on the research reported in this paper was supported by CRCG grant 337/014/0021.

References

Anderson, J. R. (1990) *The adaptive character of thought.* Hillsdale, NJ: Lawrence Erlbaum Associates.

Anderson, J. R. (1993). Rules of the mind. Hillsdale, NJ: Lawrence Erlbaum.

Fodor, J. A. (1983) *Modularity of mind.* Cambridge, MA: MIT Press.

Gibson, J. J. (1979) *The ecological approach to visual perception.* Boston, MA: Houghton-Mifflin.

Howes, A. and Young, R. M. (in press). Learning consistent, interactive and meaningful task-action mappings: A computational model. *Cognitive Science.*

John, B. E., Vera, A. H., and Newell, A. (1994). Towards real time GOMS: A model of expert behavior in a highly interactive task. *Behaviour and Information Technology,* **1 3**, 4, pp. 255-267.

Lewis, R. L. (1996). Architecture matters: What Soar has to say about modularity. In Steier, D. and Mitchell, T.,

(Eds.), *Mind Matters: Contributions to Cognitive and Computer Science in Honor of Allen Newell.* Hillsdale, NJ: Erlbaum.

Lewis, R. L., Newell, A. and Polk, T. A. (1989) Toward a Soar theory of taking instructions for immediate reasoning tasks. In P. S. Rosenbloom, J. E. Laird, and A. Newell (Eds.), *The Soar Papers: Research on Integrated Intelligence,* Cambridge, MA: MIT Press.

Newell, A. (1990) *Unified theories of cognition.* Cambridge, MA: Harvard University Press.

Vera, A. H., Lewis, R. L., and Lerch, F. J. (1993). Situated decision-making and recognition-based Learning: Applying symbolic Theories to interactive tasks. In *Proceedings of the Fifteenth Annual Conference of the Cognitive Science Society.* Boulder, CO.

Wiesmeyer, M. D. (1992). An operator-based model of human covert visual attention (Tech Report CSE-TR-123-92). Doctoral Dissertation. Ann Arbor: The University of Michigan, Department of Electrical Engineering and Computer Science.

Rhythmic Commonalities between Hand Gestures and Speech

Fred Cummins and Robert F. Port
Departments of Linguistics and Cognitive Science
Indiana University
Bloomington, IN 47405
fcummins@cs.indiana.edu, port@cs.indiana.edu

Abstract

Studies of coordination in rhythmic limb movement have established that certain phase relationships among cycling limbs are preferred, i.e. patterns such as synchrony and anti-synchrony are produced more often and more reliably than arbitrary relations. A speech experiment in which subjects attempt to place a phrase-medial stress at a range of phases within an overall phrase repetition cycle is presented, and analogous results are found. Certain phase relations occur more frequently and exhibit greater stability than others. To a first approximation, these phases are predicted by a simple harmonic model. The observed commonalities between limb movements and spoken rhythm support Lashley's conjecture that a common control strategy underlies the coordination of all rhythmic activity.

Introduction

In his famous paper on the problem of serial order, Lashley (1951) emphasized the importance of rhythmic coordination in all integrated movement, suggesting that speech and other forms of coordinated action must share common organizational principles. There has been a good deal of research into the rhythmic principles that facilitate and constrain coordination among the limbs and hands (Kelso and Scholz, 1985; Kugler et al., 1980; Bernstein, 1967). Recent work has shown that the relative timing of repeated limb movements can be well modeled by low-dimensional oscillator dynamics. However, there has been little effort to link these findings to the production of speech.

One line of research on finger motion finds that when subjects are asked to wag two fingers, or both hands, cyclically toward and away from the body's midline, subjects have a strong preference for a synchronous phase relation between the fingers or hands, where synchrony means that the limbs move toward and away from the midline simultaneously. The anti-synchrony phase relation, where both move left and then both move right, is less stable but is much more stable (small variance, insensitivity to perturbation) than other arbitrary phase angles between the limbs (Kay et al., 1991; Kelso and Kay, 1987). Furthermore, while both synchrony and anti-synchrony are stable at slower tempos, an increase in tempo eventually leads to a control regime in which

only synchrony is stable. Study of the stability properties of each production mode and of the phase transition between stable modes suggests the existence of an underlying dynamic which is parameterized by rate. The system exhibits two competing attractors at slower rates, a single attractor at fast rates, and hysteresis observed between the two cases. That is, if a subject tries to maintain anti-synchrony between effectors, increasing tempo will eventually lead to a switch to synchrony, and on tempo reduction, synchrony will be maintained beyond the tempo at which the switch previously occurred.

In describing rhythmic coordination in this paper, we will mark the timing of events relative to an overall cycle using phase, with a range of 0 to 1. By arbitrarily taking one of the effectors in the above studies as defining the cycle, the stable patterns observed have relative phases of 0 (synchrony) and 0.5 (anti-synchrony) between the hands.

In the literature on the performance of rhythmic patterns, it is well established that subjects perceive and produce patterns in which the intervals are related as simple integers (1:1, 2:1, 3:1 etc.) with much greater facility than patterns in which the component intervals have arbitrary or complex ratios (e.g. 2.72:1). Fraisse (1982) gives an overview of older work, while Collier and Wright (1995) give a more recent summary. This is true, whether subjects spontaneously tap out groups of, say, 2 to 4 elements, in which case the intergroup intervals tend to relate to the intragroup intervals as 2:1 (Essens and Povel, 1985; Fraisse, 1956) or whether they try to reproduce specific interval ratios (Collier and Wright, 1995; Summers et al., 1989; Tuller and Kelso, 1989), where the intervals produced gravitate towards simple harmonic ratios. Expressed using our phase convention, and taking the largest repeating unit as the cycle, subjects in both these cases are showing strong preferences for events at phases of $\frac{1}{3}$, $\frac{1}{2}$, $\frac{2}{3}$ etc.

The investigation of global speech rhythm has had much less tangible results. Pike (1945) was the first to classify languages as being stress-timed or syllable-timed. Although some data has supported versions of the syllable-timing hypothesis for languages like Japanese (Port et al., 1996; Port et al., 1987), attempts

415

to find evidence for isochrony of stressed syllables for English have been largely fruitless (Dauer, 1983; Lehiste, 1977). A weak tendency towards equally spaced stresses is documented for some English speech (Jassem et al., 1984), but these data do not satisfactorily account for speaker/listener impressions of rhythmicity (Dauer, 1983; Lehiste, 1977). To look just for isochrony, however, is analogous to looking only for 1:1 interval ratios in spontaneous tapping. Little attention has been paid to interstress intervals which might be related as 2:1, 1:2 or other simple ratios. Both Jones (1960, 1st ed. 1918) and Martin (1972) make an explicit connection between the rhythms of music and speech by applying standard Western musical rhythm notation to English phrases. They thus imply that interstress intervals show hierarchical organization, with long and short intervals in speech organized into temporal structures based on harmonic fractions. While neither Jones nor Martin specifically suggest that this hierarchical organization can be identified directly from the speech signal itself, this is certainly implied in these approaches.

In music, events are notated at harmonic phases of the measure cycle. If the description of speech as having a somewhat music-like rhythm is accurate, there should be some events which occur at simple phases within an overall cycle. That is, global speech timing should be harmonically or rhythmically constrained, and should exhibit simple interval ratios, much as are found in the literature on the manual production of rhythmic patterns. We conducted an experiment to see if stress placement within a repeated phrase might act like taps in a repeated tapping task by exhibiting a bias toward the occurrence of stressed syllable onsets at harmonic fractions (eg, $\frac{1}{3}$, $\frac{1}{2}$, $\frac{2}{3}$) of the period of a repeated text. In order to parallel experiments on the manual production of rhythm (Collier and Wright, 1995; Summers et al., 1989, etc.), subjects were instructed to place a phrase-medial stress at specified phase angles.

Stress placement: An experiment

Methods

In our experiment 6 subjects were asked to repeat the simple phrase "Take a pack of cards." The period from the onset of "take" to the next onset of "take" defined the basic phase cycle from 0 to 1. This interval was fixed at 1.5 sec. Auditorily, the subjects were presented with just the words "take" and "cards" with "cards" located at one of 8 phase angles between .3 and .65 relative to the basic cycle.

In a single trial, subjects were asked to continually repeat the phrase "Take a pack of cards" and to align the words "take" and "cards" with those of the stimulus signal, which provided a target phase for the placement of the phrase-medial stress. Each trial contained three sets of phrase repetitions. After speaking along

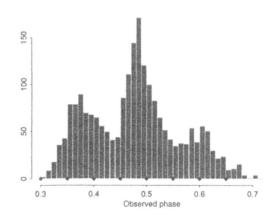

Figure 1: Histogram of all observed phases of the medial stressed syllable "cards" in repetitions of the phrase "Take a pack of cards." Target phases are marked in black on the abscissa. Although there were 8 target phases, the overall distribution is clearly trimodal.

with the stimulus 7 times, the stimulus was turned off, and subjects continued speaking, attempting to maintain the target timing pattern. After another 7 repetitions, they paused for 3 seconds and then performed a third set of 7 repetitions. All 8 target phase angles were tested within a block of 8 trials. There were three blocks, within which the target phase given by the stimulus was either increased from trial to trial within the block, or was decreased, or the order was randomized.

The time of onset of the initial and medial stressed syllables was measured automatically from audio recordings by an onset detector that picks out an increase in the smoothed signal energy envelope, restricted to a frequency range of about 300–2000 Hz. This locates a "beat" very close to the vowel onset of each syllable, and is thus similar to algorithms for locating "P-centers" (Scott, 1993; Marcus, 1981).

Results

The main results pooled across speakers, repetition sets and trial blocks are shown in Figure 1 as a frequency histogram of the measured phase angle of "cards." The first main finding was that subjects could not produce all target phases equally well. Although the target phase angles for the medial stress were equally probable at 8 different phase angles, the produced phase angles exhibit a strong preference for phases close to 0.5, and somewhat weaker preferences for phases near 0.36 and 0.6. These values are close to $\frac{1}{3}$ and $\frac{2}{3}$, predicted by a simple harmonic model for stress location (although the consistent deviation away from actual harmonic predictions merits further attention). Contrary to our expectations, subjects' attempts to reproduce the target phase were no more accurate when speaking simultaneously with the

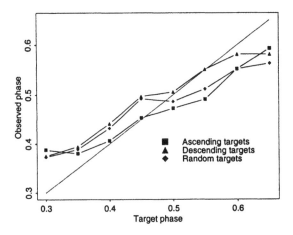

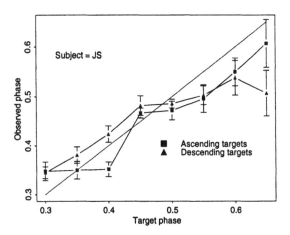

Figure 2: Observed phase of the vowel onset for "cards" as a function of target phase when target phases are increasing, decreasing and randomized across trials. The line $y = x$ is also included for reference. Hysteresis is apparent in that a sequence of trials in which phase increases from trial to trial produces smaller mean phase values than a sequence with decreasing phase.

Figure 3: Sample data for one subject showing the mean and standard deviation for each trial. The two conditions plotted are the phase increasing block and the phase decreasing block.

prompt than they were immediately after its cessation or after the 3 second delay.

A second important result is that the produced phase was influenced by that produced on immediately preceding trials, as shown in Figure 2. For example, the target phases of 0.4 and 0.45 tend to be produced at values close to 0.5 when performed immediately after targets at 0.5 (that is, on descending) yet they tend to stay close to 0.333 when performed after targets at 0.333 (in the ascending condition). Random target ordering yields intermediate values of mean phase. The effect of recent targets on the distribution of observed phases is important information for inferring the symmetry properties of the underlying dynamic.

The data shown so far is averaged across subjects, which obscures considerable intersubject variability. The bias for harmonic fractions can be seen more clearly when individual speakers are examined. By way of example, Figure 3 shows some results for a single subject. Each data point shows the mean observed phase and standard deviation for repetitions within a single trial. As in the previous figure, trials are grouped by block (targets are either ascending or descending across trials). First, essentially the same patterns as in the pooled data are evident: for most target values, the ascending function lies to the right of the descending function, i.e. smaller mean phases are produced. A clear example of bias for targets at harmonic fractions can be seen in the ascending curve for targets at 0.3, 0.35 and 0.4. All were imitated with the same output phase at about 0.35. Then targets of 0.45, 0.5 and 0.55 were all produced very close to 0.5.

As the target changed from 0.4 to 0.45, the subject's productions jumped discretely from $\frac{1}{3}$ to $\frac{1}{2}$. It appears that the actual phases produced by subjects are dependent, not only on the combination of target phase and nearby harmonic attractors, but they are also influenced by context (i.e. productions and targets on previous trials).

Discussion: Speech as harmonically timed

In tapping and limb movement studies, the dependent variable is usually the phase of one limb with respect to a cycle defined by the other. In this study we measured the phase of a phrase-medial stressed syllable with respect to a phase cycle defined by the repetition of the phrase as a whole. Our hypothesis was that harmonic fractions of the larger cycle should serve as attractors for the timing of stressed syllables just as simple harmonic fractions (often expressed as integral interval ratios such as 2:1, 3:1 etc.) are found to be attractors in studies of manually produced rhythmic patterns. The data provide strong support for this.

Our core finding is that subjects produced certain phases much more often than others although target phases are equally distributed. In the finger wagging studies of Kelso, Kay and colleagues, only relative phases of zero and 0.5 were observed to be stable (Kay et al., 1991). We, too, found a phase of 0.5 to be strongly preferred by subjects. Kelso and others have modeled the dynamics of this behavior with oscillatory systems described by second-order differential equations. Yamanishi et al (1980) suggested using two coupled oscillators of identical periods to model the control of two fingers in a bimanual tapping task. Kay et al (1991) likewise consider coupled oscillators as a possible underlying control mechanism. In each case, as the oscillators beat at identical frequencies, the only stable modes of production are at synchrony (relative phase = 0) and anti-synchrony (relative phase = 0.5).

In our speech data, we observed weaker attractors at phases near $\frac{1}{3}$ and $\frac{2}{3}$. This directly parallels the findings of tapping studies in which subjects produce alternating long and short intervals. In each case, the longer interval tends to be very close to twice the length of the smaller interval. This sort of stability can be achieved by allowing the coupling of oscillators of different periods, with one cycling n times for one cycle of the other, where $n = 2$ for the observed relative phase of 0.5, and $n = 3$ for relative phases of $\frac{1}{3}$ and $\frac{2}{3}$ (McAuley, 1995; Treffner and Turvey, 1993). Thus a first pass at modeling these data will refer to two endogenous oscillators of different periods. The slower oscillator is identified with the timing of the repeated phrase as a whole, while the faster corresponds to the control of the metrical foot.

Unpublished data from pilot studies we have conducted suggest that in the absence of a target temporal pattern, subjects will exhibit a very strong tendency to produce approximately harmonic phases. The strong preference for a phase of 0.5 may well figure in a full account of impressions of isochrony. The evidence for "silent beats," in which one inter-stress interval is observed to be twice as long as neighboring intervals, also suggests that harmonic phases are preferred and produced by speakers (Abercrombie, 1967). In the present study, we set task demands which are at odds with these intrinsic tendencies by asking the subjects to produce patterns in which the two oscillators could no longer couple. Their tendency to gravitate towards simple integer ratios was, however, clearly evident in the resulting data.

Conclusions

Together, these results support Lashley's conjecture that there is a common control strategy underlying the global coordination of speech as well other coordinated rhythmic activity. They suggest that 'isochronous timing' for stressed syllables is only one of many temporal relationships that can be supported by a rhythm-based model for speech timing. They also suggest the potential utility for speech researchers of a variety of research methods originally developed for work on limbs. Of course, there remain many issues which need attention, for example, the influence of phonetic content on the observed phases. The stability properties of the stable modes in speech production likewise remain to be investigated. Notwithstanding, the present study appears to be the first to offer direct phonetic timing data in support of music-like rhythms in human speech, and establishes clear links between rhythm in speech and limb movements.

Acknowledgments

We are indebted to Keiichi Tajima, Michael Gasser, Richard Shiffrin and Wendy Goldberg for their contributions to the development of this work and for constructive criticism. This work was supported in part by the Office of Naval Research, Grant number N00001491-J1261 to the second author.

References

Abercrombie, D. (1967). Elements of general phonetics. Aldine Pub. Co., Chicago, IL.

Bernstein, N. (1967). The Coordination and Regulation of Movements. Pergamon Press, London.

Collier, G. L. and Wright, C. E. (1995). Temporal rescaling of simple and complex ratios in rhythmic tapping. Journal of Experimental Psychology: Human Perception and Performance, 21(3):602–627.

Dauer, R. (1983). Stress-timing and syllable-timing reanalyzed. Journal of Phonetics, 11:51–62.

Essens, P. J. and Povel, D. (1985). Metrical and non-metrical representations of temporal patterns. Perception and Psychophysics, 37(1):1–7.

Fraisse, P. (1956). Les Structures Rhythmique. Érasme, Paris.

Fraisse, P. (1982). Rhythm and tempo. In Deutsch, D., editor, The Psychology of Music, pages 149–180. Academic Press, New York.

Jassem, W., Hill, D., and Witten, I. (1984). Isochrony in English speech: its statistical validity and linguistic relevance. In Gibbon, D. and Richter, H., editors, Intonation, Accent and Rhythm, volume 8 of Research in Text Theory, pages 203–225. Walter de Gruyter, Berlin.

Jones, D. (1960). An Outline of English Phonetics. Cambridge University Press, Cambridge, England, 9th edition. 1st edition published 1918.

Kay, B., Saltzman, E., and Kelso, J. A. S. (1991). Steady-state and perturbed rhythmical movements: Dynamical modeling using a variety of analytical tools. Journal of Experimental Psychology: Human Perception and Performance, 17:183–197.

Kelso, J. and Scholz, J. (1985). Cooperative phenomena in biological motion. In Haken, H., editor, Complex Systems: Operational Approaches in Neurobiology, Physics and Computers, pages 124–149. Springer Verlag.

Kelso, J. A. S. and Kay, B. A. (1987). Information and control: a macroscopic analysis of perception-action coupling. In Heuer, H. and Sanders, A. F., editors, Perspectives on Perception and Action, chapter 1, pages 3–32. Lawrence Erlbaum Associates, Hillsdale, NJ.

Kugler, P. N., Kelso, J. S., and Turvey, M. (1980). On the concept of coordinative structures as dissipative structures: I. Theoretical lines of convergence. In Stelmach, G. and Requin, J., editors, Tutorials in Motor Behavior. North-Holland.

Lashley, K. S. (1951). The problem of serial order in behavior. In Jefress, L. A., editor, Cerebral Mechanisms in Behavior, pages 112–136. John Wiley and Sons, New York, NY.

Lehiste, I. (1977). Isochrony reconsidered. Journal of Phonetics, 5:253–263.

Marcus, S. (1981). Acoustic determinants of perceptual center (P-center) location. Perception and Psychophysics, 30:247–256.

Martin, J. G. (1972). Rhythmic (hierarchical) versus serial structure in speech and other behavior. Psychological Review, 79(6):487–509.

McAuley, J. D. (1995). On the Perception of Time as Phase: Toward an Adaptive-Oscillator Model of Rhythm. PhD thesis, Indiana University, Bloomington, IN. Available as Cognitive Science Technical Report No. 151, Cognitive Science Program, Indiana University, Bloomington, IN.

Pike, K. (1945). The Intonation of American English. University of Michigan Press, Ann Arbor, MI.

Port, R., Cummins, F., and Gasser, M. (1996). A dynamic approach to rhythm in language: Toward a temporal phonology. In Luka, B. and Need, B., editors, Proceedings of the Chicago Linguistics Society, pages 375–397. Department of Linguistics, University of Chicago.

Port, R. F., Dalby, J., and O'Dell, M. (1987). Evidence for mora timing in Japanese. Journal of the Acoustical Society of America, 81(5):1574–1585.

Scott, S. K. (1993). P-centers in Speech: An Acoustic Analysis. PhD thesis, University College London.

Summers, J. J., Bell, R., and Burns, B. D. (1989). Perceptual and motor factors in the imitation of simple temporal patterns. Psychological Research, 50:23–27.

Treffner, P. J. and Turvey, M. T. (1993). Resonance constraints on rhythmic movement. Journal of Experimental Psychology: Human Perception and Performance, 19(6):1221–1237.

Tuller, B. and Kelso, J. (1989). Environmentally-specified patterns of movement coordination in normal and split-brain subjects. Experimental Brain Research, 75:306–316.

Yamanishi, J., Kawato, M., and Suzuki, R. (1980). Two coupled oscillators as a model for the coordinated finger tapping by both hands. Biological Cybernetics, 37:219–225.

Modeling Beat Perception with a Nonlinear Oscillator

Edward W. Large

Institute for Research in Cognitive Science
University of Pennsylvania
3401 Walnut St., Suite 400C
Philadelphia, PA 19102
large@grip.cis.upenn.edu

Abstract

The perception of beat and meter is fundamental to the perception of rhythm, yet modeling this phenomenon has proven a formidable problem. This paper outlines a dynamic model of beat perception in complex, metrically structured rhythms that has been described in detail elsewhere (Large, 1994; Large & Kolen, 1994). A study is described in which pianists performed notated melodies and improvised variations on these same melodies. The performances are analyzed in terms of amount of rubato and rhythmic complexity, and the model's ability to simulate beat perception in these melodies is assessed.

Introduction

The ability to perceive beat and meter is, arguably, the most fundamental perceptual capability underlying our experience of musical rhythm. Simply put, *beat perception* refers to the perception of periodicity within a complex rhythm. When one taps one's foot along with a musical performance, for example, one is physically marking beats corresponding to a perceived periodicity. *Meter perception* can be described in similar terms, as the perception of two or more periodicities that coexist on different rhythmic time scales (Lerdahl & Jackendoff, 1983; Yeston, 1976). Relationships among beats of different levels define regular temporal structures that capture relative time relationships. Such *metrical structures* describe patterns of metrical accents that may explain relative prominence: the perception of strong and weak beats that characterizes the experience of musical rhythm. These musical concepts also have close correlates in theories of linguistic rhythm (e.g. Lerdahl & Jackendoff, 1983; Liberman & Prince, 1977).

Researchers in diverse fields have explored the power of such theories to explain various phenomena in the perception of rhythmically structured acoustic signals. As one might expect, this diversity of interest has led to a wide diversity of proposed models, including context-free grammars (e.g. Lerdahl & Jackendoff, 1983; Longuet-Higgins, 1987), symbolic AI algorithms (e.g. Dannenberg & Mont-Reynaud, 1987; Rosenthal, 1992), statistical approaches (e.g. Brown, 1992; Palmer & Krumhansl, 1990; Vercoe & Puckette, 1985), and connectionist models (e.g. Desain & Honing, 1991; Scarborough, Miller, & Jones, 1992). Although each captures certain aspects of beat and meter in idealized rhythms (i.e. rhythms comprised of precise durations as may be found in a musical score), varying levels of difficulty are encountered when models are confronted with the flexible and complex rhythms that humans naturally produce.

The difficulty of modeling the perception of temporal structure in naturally performed rhythms arises from several sources. One source of difficulty is *rubato*. Performers use rubato, or systematic timing deviation, to communicate musical intentions, and such temporal deviation gives rise to nonstationary rhythmic signals. Another source of difficulty is *rhythmic complexity*, which refers to factors such as the number of different duration values present in a rhythm and the use of syncopation. In short, the periodic components of rhythms that correspond to perceived beats are not truly periodic, and even in ideally timed rhythms there are missing events and extraneous events.

In this paper, beat perception is considered as a pattern of coordination that arises between an internally generated periodic process (a self-sustaining oscillator) and a periodicity within a complex external rhythm (Jones, 1976; Large, 1994). A dynamic model of this process, described in detail elsewhere (Large, 1994; Large & Kolen, 1994), is first outlined. Briefly, the coordination of internal and external periodicities is mapped onto the attractor states of a dynamical system comprising an external (driving) rhythm, and an internal (driven) oscillator (cf. Schoner, 1991; Kelso, DeGuzman, & Holroyd, 1990). Further, the intrinsic dynamics of the internal oscillator are assumed to adapt to the external rhythm, accounting for the robustness of beat perception to systematic timing deviations and rhythmic complexities found in naturally produced rhythms. Next, a study is described in which pianists performed notated melodies and then improvised variations on these same melodies. The performances are analyzed in terms of rubato and rhythmic complexity. Finally, the robustness of coordination between a simulated oscillator and a target periodicity within each rhythm is assessed.

A Dynamic Model of Beat Perception

External Rhythms and Internal Rhythms

The current approach relies upon the notion of a (simple) internal rhythm that responds to one periodicity within a (complex) external rhythm. An external rhythm is represented as a sequence of discrete impulses, $s(t)$, each

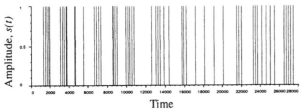

Figure 1: A sequence of discrete impulses, representing the onset of events (notes), drives a nonlinear oscillator.

denoting a single event (e.g. a note onset). Figure 1 shows a such series of impulses, corresponding to note onset times in an improvised melody, collected on a computer-monitored piano. The rhythmic signal serves as a *driver*, and impulses in the signal perturb both the phase and the period of a *driven nonlinear oscillator*, causing changes to the oscillator's behavior.

The internal rhythm is treated as a limit cycle oscillator, a structurally stable dynamical system exhibiting an asymptotically stable limit cycle. The advantage of this approach is that it does not require a great deal of knowledge about the state space or the dynamics of the internal rhythmic process. Rather, the state of the oscillator is reduced to a single variable called *phase*, $\phi(t)$, representing the position of the oscillator around its limit cycle at time t.

Phase is used to model expectations regarding when future events (impulses) are likely to occur. Phase can be defined for $-p/2 \leq t < p/2$ as $\phi(t) = t/p$, where p is *period*, the time required to complete one cycle of the oscillation. According to this definition, phase varies from -0.5 to 0.5. The points $\phi(t_x) = 0$ reflect times at which the oscillator maximally "expects" events to occur. When an event occurs at time $t < t_x$, it is said to be early; when it occurs at time $t > t_x$ is it said to be late. Thus, we have the relation:

$$\phi(t) = \frac{t - t_x}{p}, \qquad t_x - \frac{p}{2} \leq t < t_x + \frac{p}{2}. \qquad \text{(Eqn 1)}$$

The notion of expectation can be further refined by introducing the notion of a pulse function (Large & Kolen, 1994), describing a "soft" expectancy region around $\phi(t_x) = 0$. A pulse function can be defined as:

$$x(t) = 0.5(1 + \tanh\gamma(\cos 2\pi\phi(t) - 1)) \qquad \text{(Eqn 2)}$$

where the *gain* parameter γ describes the width of the pulse (Large & Kolen, 1994). Figure 2 shows this pulse function for $\gamma = 2$. Pulse amplitude is non-zero for a relatively small portion of the oscillator's cycle, defining a *temporal receptive field* for the oscillator. The temporal receptive field corresponds to a sensitive phase for the oscillator; adaptation to external events (below) occurs only when events fall within this region.

Phase Entrainment and Adaptation of Parameters

Coordination of the internal oscillator with an external periodicity is described as phase entrainment (a form of synchronization), supplemented by adaptation of oscillator parameters. Phase entrainment is modeled using a *phase attractive circle map* (cf. Kelso, DeGuzman, & Holroyd, 1990). The circle map predicts the phase, ϕ_{i+1}, at which the next event will occur, as:

$$\phi_{i+1} = \phi_i + \frac{t_{i+1} - t_i}{p_{i+1}} + \eta_\phi f(\phi_i, \gamma_i), \qquad \text{(Eqn 3)}$$

where ϕ_i is the phase of the oscillator at which the ith impulse occurs, $t_{i+1} - t_i$ captures the sequence of inter-onset intervals present in the driving rhythm, and $f(\phi_i, \gamma_i)$, is a nonlinear phase coupling term that describes the alteration of phase brought about by the ith input impulse. The coupling strength, η_ϕ, describes the amount of influence that the driver has upon the attentional oscillator.

The primary advantage to modeling beat perception in this way is temporal stability: the ability of such a system to sustain coordinated patterns in the face of a fluctuating environment, and to reestablish coordination after perturbations (Schoner, 1991). Because of the special complexities of performed musical rhythms, however, adaptation of oscillator parameters is also required. First, because performed musical rhythms are nonstationary (i.e. the period changes in systematic ways), the model oscillator also adapts its intrinsic period:

$$p_{i+1} = p_i + \eta_p h(\phi_i, p_i, \gamma_i). \qquad \text{(Eqn 4)}$$

The coupling function, $h(\phi_i, p_i, \gamma_i)$, describes the adaptations of oscillator period that result from individual input impulses. Adaptation rate η_p (analogous to coupling strength in Equation 3) determines the rate at which oscillator period adapts to changes in the stimulus period.

The model handles rhythmic complexity by defining the functions $f(\phi_i, \gamma_i)$ and $h(\phi_i, p_i, \gamma_i)$ in such a way that phase and period change only when impulses fall within the temporal receptive field. Impulses that fall outside the field do not affect phase and period. This makes the size of the temporal receptive field crucial: if it is too small the oscillator will not robustly handle rubato, yet if it is too large, the oscillator will be led astray by complex rhythms. Thus, γ also adapts to the stimulus, according to the relation:

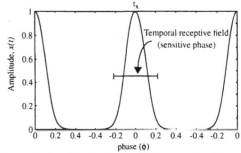

Figure 2: A pulse function and its associated temporal receptive field (sensitive phase).

$$\gamma_{i+1} = (\gamma_i + \eta_\gamma g(\phi_i, \gamma_i))e^{\eta_\gamma r \frac{(t_{i+1} - t_i)}{p_i}} \qquad \text{(Eqn 5)}$$

where $g(\phi_i, \gamma_i)$ describes adaptations of gain that result from individual input impulses. γ also decays each cycle, thus if there is no event in the oscillator's current cycle, γ decreases, widening the temporal receptive field. Finally, confidence, c, a measure derived from gain, varies from zero to one, measuring the overall success of the oscillator in finding a periodicity in the input signal. The functions $f(\phi_i, \gamma_i)$, $h(\phi_i, p_i, \gamma_i)$, and $g(\phi_i, \gamma_i)$ are derived in (Large, 1994).

Performances of Notated Melodies and Improvised Variations

The Test Data Set

To test the robustness of the model in response to musical performances, a test set of sixty melodies was collected as follows (for detailed description of the data collection procedure, see Large, Palmer, & Pollack, 1995). Two pianists performed melodies on a computer-monitored Yamaha Disklavier acoustic upright piano. Three children's melodies were chosen as performance material. For each melody, the pianists performed and recorded the melody, as presented in musical notation, five times. With the musical notation remaining in place, the pianists were then asked to play five improvisations. All performances were of a single-line melody only; pianists were instructed not to play harmonic accompaniment.

Next, skilled musicians transcribed the improvisations in standard musical notation. To assess the amount and distribution of rubato among the performances, a measure of timing deviation was calculated for each performance as a coefficient of variation of performed inter-onset intervals (IOIs), based either on the notation (for performances) or the transcriptions (for improvisations). This measure of deviation was then averaged across the five performances of each melody or improvisation by each pianist. An analysis of variance (ANOVA) on mean rubato by performance type (notated melody vs. improvised variation), subject, and tune was conducted. There was a significant main effect of performance type ($F(1,4) = 33.46$, $p < 0.01$), indicating that, on average, more rubato was used in the improvisation of variations than in the performance of the melodies from notation. Mean rubato was 0.05 for notated melodies, and 0.10 for improvisations. There was also a significant interaction between tune and subject ($F(2, 8) = 13.89$, $p < 0.01$). Pianist 1 performed the melodies and improvisations for the first two tunes with little rubato, but for the third tune with high rubato. Pianist 2 performed tune three with little rubato, and performed tunes one and two with relatively high rubato.

Beat Tracking Performance

Next, the oscillator's ability to model beat perception in these melodies was assessed. The response of the oscillator was intended to model the perception of beats at a particular level in a metrical structure (Lerdahl & Jackendoff, 1983). For each performance, the modal inter-onset interval (IOI) category was determined from the score or transcription, and chosen as the target periodicity. For each performance, the unit was initialized such that $\phi = 0$ at the initial onset, and p was set to the initial IOI of the target periodicity. Thus, the oscillator did not have to cope with finding initial phase or period.

A number of statistical measures of performance were collected. Only mean absolute value of relative phase, $\langle|\phi|\rangle$, is reported here because this measure corresponded most closely to intuitive impressions of successful coordination, gleaned by listening to oscillator output. $\langle|\phi|\rangle$ measures performance as the mean absolute phase of the oscillator on which events marking the beat occurred (as determined by the scores and transcription). $\langle|\phi|\rangle = 0$ means perfect performance, while $\langle|\phi|\rangle = 0.5$ is the poorest performance possible (meaning that the unit was 180° out of phase with the beat throughout the melody), and $\langle|\phi|\rangle < 0.1$ generally corresponded to a subjective impression of good performance. For each melody, oscillator performance was assessed by comparing $\langle|\phi|\rangle$ with the mean rubato score.

Performances of notated melodies and performances of improvised variations differed qualitatively in level of rhythmic complexity, and differed significantly in the magnitude of timing deviations, so results are discussed separately.

Performances of Notated Melodies. First, the oscillator was exposed to the thirty performances of notated melodies. Performances of notated melodies provided a controlled level of rhythmic complexity. Each melody contained three intended duration categories: sixteenth note, eighth note, and quarter note. Statistics were collected, and an analysis of variance (ANOVA) was conducted with factors tune, subject, and analysis type (mean rubato vs. average absolute phase). The ANOVA showed a main effect of analysis type ($F(1, 4) = 27.73$, $p < 0.01$), with mean rubato = 0.05, and average phase = 0.06. Thus, for these performances oscillator performed slightly worse than mean rubato would predict. This value of $\langle|\phi|\rangle$, however, indicates that on average the was able to achieve robust coordination with target periodicities.

To illustrate the nature of oscillator coordination, Figure 3 gives an example of the oscillator's behavior in response to a performance of *Baa baa black sheep*. Panel A provides a notated version of the melody (transcriptions of improvisations do not include grace notes or other ornaments) and a single row of dots from a metrical structure grid (Lerdahl & Jackendoff, 1983) marking the target events. Notes that are not marked by dots correspond to extraneous events; dots that do not correspond to notes mark times when events are "missing" from the target periodicity. Panel B shows both input and output of the oscillator. The dashed lines show impulses in the signal (marking event onset times). Because of the scale, full output pulses are not shown, rather discrete output pulses (shown as solid lines) are displayed at $t = t_x$. These two lines overlap when a target event is performed at precisely the time predicted by the oscillator, that is, at phase zero, $\phi(t) = 0$, of the driven oscillator. Amplitude of the discrete oscillator pulses corresponds to confidence, c. High amplitude of the discrete pulse corresponds to a small temporal receptive field, low amplitude corresponds to a wide receptive field.

Panel C shows a tempo curve for the performance as a solid line. This curve was derived by extracting the target events from the performance and graphing IOIs for these events. This curve gives the IOIs to which the oscillator should respond. Panel C shows actual observed cycle times of the oscillator using a dotted line. Observed cycle time takes into account not only the intrinsic period, p, of the oscillator, but also phase $\phi(t)$ as it is adjusted in each cycle. Beginning at the initial tempo, the unit effectively calculates a local tempo, and follows performance tempo as the performer speeds up and slows down.

Improvisation of Variations. Next, oscillator performance on the thirty improvised variations was examined. The improvisations provided a more difficult situation than the performances of notated melodies for two reasons. The rhythms of the improvisations were more complex than the rhythms of the melodies, making use of syncopation, and containing up to seven different levels of intended durations according to the transcriptions. Also the improvisations showed significantly greater timing deviation than did the performed melodies. The oscillator was exposed to the melo-

dies, statistics were collected, and an analysis of variance (ANOVA) was conducted with factors tune, subject, and analysis type (mean rubato vs. average absolute phase). The ANOVA showed no main effect of analysis type ($F(1, 4) = 0.005$, $p = 0.947$), with mean rubato = 0.10, and average phase = 0.10. This result shows that for these performances, oscillator performance is on par with mean rubato. The ANOVA also indicated a significant interaction of tune and subject ($F(2, 8) = 4.0$, $p < 0.05$), indicating that the oscillator had more trouble with some performances than with others. Case by case examination revealed that in 20 out of the 30 cases, the oscillator coordinated well with its target periodicity ($\langle|\phi|\rangle < 0.10$). In 10 cases the oscillator had some difficulty. The 10 difficult cases were examined; two of the most difficult are discussed here.

Pianist 1's improvisations on *Mary had a little lamb* were performed in a freely timed blues style. The first improvisation had the highest rubato score (rubato = 0.25), and highest mean phase ($\langle|\phi|\rangle = 0.17$). The oscillator's behavior in this case was representative of its performance on this group of melodies, so it was chosen for further study. The time series corresponding to the performance of the oscillator are shown in Figure 4. The tempo curve indicates the presence of large timing deviations at several points in the melody. Points of particular interest are around $t = 3000ms$, $t = 8000ms$, $t = 16000ms$, and $t = 23000ms$. At these points, γ drops (correspondingly, confidence drops) allowing the oscillator to continue to synchronize with the target in spite of the large deviations.

In spite of these difficulties, however, the figure shows that the oscillator did a respectable job of entraining to its target periodicity in this rhythm. Beats are output at approximately the correct times throughout the piece – the oscillator is not lured away by the many distractor events in this rhythmically complex performance. Another way to see this is to note that the value of average absolute phase

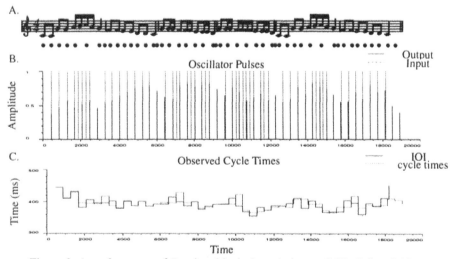

Figure 3: A performance of *Baa baa black sheep* (rubato = 0.05, $\langle|\phi|\rangle = 0.08$).

($\langle|\phi|\rangle$ = 0.17) is lower than mean rubato (0.25). Additionally, oscillator confidence is high for large sections of the piece; by the oscillator's internal measure its performance is good. 9 of the 10 problem cases examined fit the profile of this case. The oscillator had difficulty in certain sections of the performances, but always recovered gracefully, reestablishing coordination after large perturbations.

In 1 of the 10 difficult cases examined, however, the result was poor. Pianist 2's improvisations on *Hush little baby* were the most varied of all the improvisations studied and made heavy use of rubato. The improvisation that proved the most difficult for the model to handle was the third variation. This improvisation made moderately heavy use of rubato and had the highest mean phase, (rubato = 0.16, $\langle|\phi|\rangle$ = 0.30). These numbers suggest extreme difficulty in coordination. Figure 5 shows the actual time series corresponding to the performance of the oscillator. Throughout this improvisation the performer makes use of a sort of "jagged" rubato. The tempo curve, shown in panel C, reveals timing deviations that strictly alternate: slower, faster, slower, faster. Panel C also shows the effect of this pattern on observed cycle times. Cycle times are always one step behind the performed durations because changes to the oscillator's phase and period in the current cycle effect oscillator cycle time for the following cycle.

Because timing deviations zigzagged in this fashion, cycle time decreased when performed duration increased, and vice-versa. This rubato pattern occurred in other performances as well, however in this case the amount of rubato was large enough to pose a serious difficulty for the oscillator. The oscillator responds to the correct events, and outputs pulses at more-or-less the correct locations throughout the piece. However, confidence is low throughout as the oscillator attempts to establish a coordinated pattern. Thus large, alternating rubato patterns represent a limiting case for the single oscillator model.

Discussion

Melodies are perhaps the most difficult cases for beat perception models, because they provide fewer reliable cues than accompanied melodies. Bass lines and harmonic accompaniment tend to be more rhythmically consistent, providing additional information. In this study, performances of notated melodies provided a controlled level of rhythmic complexity, while improvised variations provided syncopation and a great variety of duration categories. Both types of performance contained timing deviations, making the task of coordinating with a single periodicity a challenging one. Yet, in 49 out of 60 cases, the oscillator performed robustly by an objective measure ($\langle|\phi|\rangle$).

In 11 cases, difficulties were encountered ($\langle|\phi|\rangle$ > 0.10). These difficulties were caused by large temporal deviations, stemming from three sources: heavy use of rubato including 'phase-shifts', actual timing errors on the part of performers, and jagged rubato curves resulting from alternating shortened and lengthened durations (Large, 1994). In 10 of the 11 cases, however, the oscillator was well coordinated for large sections of the melodies, having trouble in some areas but reestablishing coordination after large perturbations.

In the most difficult case, an improvisation that coupled heavy rubato with an alternating tempo profile, the oscillator performed poorly $\langle|\phi|\rangle$ = 0.30 . Although it did not lose the beat altogether, it was not able to adequately follow the tempo changes, and its internal measure of performance was consistently low. This case illustrates the limits of a single oscillator model. Note, however, that tempo changes of approximately the same magnitude strictly alternate (Figure 5, Panel C). This means that had the oscillator been operating at the next larger periodicity, it would have found almost no rubato at all. Cases such as this would tend to argue for a multiple oscillator model. In a multiple oscillator model different oscillators operate at different time scales (Large & Kolen, 1994). Internal interactions synchronize internal oscillators, and the perception

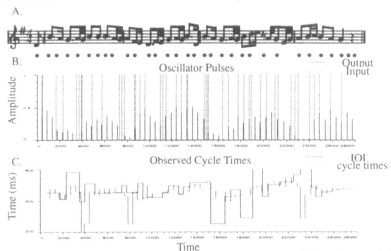

Figure 4: An improvisation on *Mary had a little lamb* (grace notes are not transcribed) (rubato = 0.25, $\langle|\phi|\rangle$ = 0.17).

424

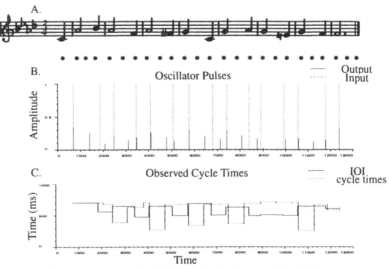

Figure 5: An improvisation on *Hush little baby* (rubato = 0.16, $\langle|\phi|\rangle$ = 0.30).

of metrical structure can emerge from the perception of beat on multiple levels. Building networks of interacting oscillators to model the perception of metrical structure is a focus of current research.

Overall, the single oscillator model coordinated remarkably well with complex rhythms given no information other than event onset times. These analyses suggest that nonlinear oscillators, driven with complex, nonstationary rhythms that arise from musical performance, can adequately model the perception of musical beat, and may ultimately be used to model the perception of musical meter as well.

Acknowledgments

The author wishes to thank Caroline Palmer, Brent Stansfield, and three anonymous reviewers for helpful comments on an earlier version of this paper. This work was supported by The Ohio State University Presidential Fellowship.

References

Brown, J. C. (1992). Determination musical meter using the method of autocorrelation. *Journal of the Acoustical Society of America, 91*, 2374-2375.

Dannenberg, R. B. & Mont-Reynaud, B. (1987). *Following an improvisation in real time*. In Proceedings of the 1987 International Computer Music Conference. Computer Music Association.

Desain, P. & Honing, H. (1991). The quantization of musical time: A connectionist approach. In P. M. Todd and D. G. Loy (Eds) *Music and Connectionism* (pp. 150-160). Cambridge: MIT Press.

Jones, M. R. (1976). Time, our lost dimension: Toward a new theory of perception, attention, and memory. *Psychological Review, 83*, 323 335.

Kelso, J. A. S., deGuzman, G. C., & Holroyd, T. (1990). The self-organized phase attractive dynamics of coordination.

In A. Babloyantz (Ed) *Self Organization, Emerging Properties, and Learning* (pp. 41-62). NATO ASI Series B: Physics, Vol. 260.

Large, E. W. (1994). *Dynamic representation of musical structure*. Unpublished Ph.D. Dissertation. The Ohio State University, Columbus, OH.

Large, E. W. & Kolen, J. F. (1994). Resonance and the perception of musical meter. *Connection Science, 6 (1)*, 177 - 208.

Large, E. W., Palmer, C., & Pollack, J. B. (1995). Reduced memory representations for music. *Cognitive Science, 19*, 53-96.

Lerdahl, F. & Jackendoff, R. (1983). *A generative theory of tonal music*. Cambridge: MIT Press.

Liberman, M. & Prince, A. (1977). An stress and linguistic rhythm. *Linguistic Inquiry, 8*, 249-336.

Longuet-Higgins, H. C. (1987) *Mental Processes*. Cambridge: MIT Press.

Palmer, C., & Krumhansl, C.L. (1990). Mental representations of musical meter. *Journal of Experimental Psychology: Human Perception & Performance, 16*, 728-741.

Rosenthal, D. (1992). Emulation of human rhythm perception. *Computer Music Journal, 16*, 64-76.

Schoner, G. (1991). Dynamic theory of action-perception patterns: The moving room paradigm. *Biological Cybernetics, 64*, 455-462.

Scarborough, D. L., Miller, P., & Jones, J. A. (1992). On the perception of meter. In M. Balaban, K. Ebcioglu, & O. Laske (Eds) *Understanding Music with AI: Perspectives in Music Cognition* (pp. 427-447). Cambridge: MIT Press.

Vercoe, B. & Puckette, M. (1985). *Synthetic rehearsal: Training the synthetic performer*. In Proceedings of the 1985 International Computer Music Conference (pp. 275-278). Computer Music Association.

Emotional Decisions

Allison Barnes and **Paul Thagard**
Philosophy Department
University of Waterloo
Waterloo, Ontario, N2L 3G1, Canada
{albarnes, pthagard}@watarts.uwaterloo.ca

Abstract

Recent research has yielded an explosion of literature that establishes a strong connection between emotional and cognitive processes. Most notably, Antonio Damasio draws an intimate connection between emotion and cognition in practical decision making. Damasio presents a "somatic marker" hypothesis which explains how emotions are biologically indispensable to decisions. His research on patients with frontal lobe damage indicates that feelings normally accompany response options and operate as a biasing device to dictate choice. What Damasio's hypothesis lacks is a theoretical model of decision making which can advance the conceptual connection between emotional and cognitive decision making processes. In this paper we combine Damasio's somatic marker hypothesis with the coherence theory of decision put forward by Thagard and Millgram. The juxtaposition of Damasio's hypothesis with a cognitive theory of decision making leads to a new and better theory of emotional decisions.

Introduction

Emotions are ordinarily conceived as irrational occurrences that cloud judgment and distort reasoning. This view is well entrenched, despite work in both philosophy and psychology that establishes a strong connection between emotion and cognition. During recent years there has been an explosion of research which indicates that rather than being natural adversaries, rational and emotional processes function together. Barnes and Thagard (in press) argue that emotions and inferences are both necessary when we empathize with other people. Social psychologists have explored the function of emotions in social perception and judgment (Forgas, 1991). But the interdependence of emotional and cognitive processes is perhaps most powerfully presented in recent neurobiological studies which establish that emotion is indispensable in rational decision making.

Most notably, in *Descartes' Error: Reason, Emotion and the Human Brain*, neurobiologist Antonio Damasio (1994) provides a "somatic marker hypothesis" which explains how emotions make decision making possible. Damasio's somatic marker hypothesis suggests that the role of emotions in decision making is biologically extensive and complex. What Damasio's somatic marker hypothesis lacks, we maintain, is a theoretical or computational model

of decision making which can advance the conceptual connection between emotional and cognitive decision-making processes. We propose that Damasio's work is best understood and developed by the coherence theory of decision put forward by Thagard and Millgram. Conversely, Damasio's somatic marker hypothesis suggests ways that the coherence theory of decision can be enhanced. After briefly describing Damasio's hypothesis and the coherence theory of decision, we will outline how both projects can merge to form a new and better account of decision making. Our juxtaposition of Damasio's neurobiological hypothesis with a cognitive theory of decision making is preliminary to a possible theory of emotional decision making.

Emotions and the Brain

Damasio re-examines the case of Phineas Gage, the victim of an 1848 mine explosion that hurled an iron rod through his skull and brain. Strangely, Gage recovered except for a severe deficiency in practical and social decision making. According to Damasio, the case of Gage and other patients with similar frontal lobe damage offer convincing evidence that the human brain's regions for making decisions are strongly connected to emotional centers.

Damasio maintains that Gage and other frontal lobe patients with faulty decision making skills have all the information required to make decisions. According to neurological studies by Saver and Damasio (1991), social knowledge in these patients remains intact. Their experimental subject, EVR, could provide response options to social situations, consider the consequences of these options and perform moral reasoning at an advanced level. EVR had normal or better intelligence and memory. Detailed studies by Saver and Damasio suggest that even with all the necessary information, such patients are unable to implement a choice in everyday life.[1] For example, EVR would take hours deciding where to dine by obsessing about each restaurant's seating plan, menu and atmosphere. Even then, he could not reach a final decision.

These neurological studies show that what is damaged in these patients is not memory or intelligence, but the neural connections between the emotional and cognitive centers of the brain. More specifically, the ventromedial frontal region

---

[1] The deficiency is typically confined to practical decision making. Like other patients, EVR had no trouble with hypothetical decision making.

is reported to be responsible for emotional processing and social cognition through connections with the amygdala and hypothalamus. After a series of tests, Saver and Damasio conclude that in the absence of emotional input, EVR's decision making process was overwhelmed by trivial information. With additional studies, the researchers conclude that EVR had no internal goal representation. In order for goals to remain stable for EVR, they had to be represented externally and repeatedly. Otherwise, "...it was as if he forgot to remember short- and intermediate- term goals.... He couldn't keep a problem in perspective in relation to other goals."(1985, p.1737).

The somatic marker hypothesis is presented by Damasio to explain these experimental findings. The hypothesis is that bodily feelings normally accompany our representations of the anticipated outcomes of options. In other words, feelings *mark* response options to real or simulated decisions. Somatic markers serve as an automatic device to speed one to select biologically advantageous options. Those options that are left unmarked are omitted in the decision-making process.[2] Damasio suggests that patients with frontal lobe damage fail to activate these somatic markers which are directly linked to punishment and reward, and originate in previously experienced social situations. EVR's decision making defect is explained by an inability to activate somatic states when ordinary decisions arise; by an inability to mark the implications of a social situation with a signal that would separate good and bad options.[3] EVR was therefore trapped in a never-ending cost-benefit analysis of numerous and conflicting options. In the absence of emotional markers, decision making is virtually impossible.

A Coherence Theory of Decision

Damasio's hypothesis invites a description of how decisions are ordinarily made. According to the coherence theory of decision (Millgram and Thagard, in press; Thagard & Millgram 1995), people make decisions by assessing and ordering various competing actions and goals. For example, someone may want both to get lots of research done and to relax and have fun with his or her friends. Learning how to accomplish both these tasks will take place in the context of goals that cannot be fully realized together. The rational

decision maker chooses complex plans that are *most coherent* with currently held goals. Decisions arise from principles of coherence that govern the relations among actions and goals. In this sense, a decision can be described as an inference to the best plan where the desirability of goals is determined by deliberative coherence. Since goals compete for limited resources, goals that hang together and which produce overlapping plans of action tend to be more easily jointly satisfied. Put simply, actions and plans which best satisfy existing goals are the best options.

Consider Howard, an academic who must decide whether or not to accept a teaching position at another institution. Why are such decisions so difficult? Important life choices such as this one involve many different and sometimes intensely conflicting goals. Perhaps Howard is attracted by the new position because it offers increased salary and prestige, but is concerned that moving would involve considerable dislocation and loss of established relations with colleagues. Moreover, he may have a family with roots in his current community. He thus has to deal with a plethora of interconnected and possibly ill-specified goals that are relevant to what choice he will make.

Thagard and Millgram propose a set of principles designed to specify the kinds of relations that exist among actions and goals and that give rise to coherence estimations that determine not only choices of actions to perform but also adoption of complex plans and revisions of goals. They make no sharp distinction between actions and goals, since what in one context is best described as an action may be best described in another context as a goal. For example, if my main goal is to travel from Waterloo to San Diego, I will set myself the subgoal of getting to Toronto airport, but this subgoal is itself an action to be performed. Actions and goals are referred to as *factors* in decision making. Factors are actions and goals that cohere with each other according to the following six principles.

1. Symmetry. Coherence and incoherence are symmetrical relations: If a factor (action or goal) F_1 coheres with a factor F_2, then F_2 coheres with F_1.

2. Facilitation. Consider actions $A_1 ... A_n$ that together facilitate the accomplishment of goal G. Then

   (a) each A_i coheres with G,

   (b) each A_i coheres with each other A_j, and

   (c) the greater the number of actions required, the less the coherence among actions and goals.

3. Incompatibility.

   (a) If two factors cannot both be performed or achieved, then they are strongly incoherent.

   (b) If two factors are difficult to perform or achieve together, then they are weakly incoherent.

4. Goal priority. Some goals are desirable for intrinsic or other non-coherence reasons.

5. Judgment. Facilitation and competition relations can depend on coherence with judgments about the acceptability of factual beliefs.

6. Decision. Decisions are made on the basis of an assessment of the overall coherence of a set of actions and goals.

DECO is a computer program that incorporates these principles and makes excellent decisions. DECO constructs

---

[2]The somatic marker hypothesis originates with Walle Nauta (1971), 183-184: "The normal individual decides upon a particular course of action by a thought process in which a larger or smaller number of strategic alternatives is compared. It could be suggested- admittedly on introspective grounds- that the comparison in the final analysis is one between the affective responses evoked by each of the various alternatives....If this were indeed the case, it would be readily understandable that loss of the frontal cortex as a major mediator of information exchange between the cerebral cortex and the limbic system is followed not only by an impairment of strategic choice making, but also by a tendency of projected or current action systems to 'fade out' or become over-ridden by interfering influences. "

[3]Damasio, Tranel and Damasio (1990) also speculate that the sociopath's inability to avoid punishment is related to a failure to emotionally anticipate the consequences of behavior.

a connectionist network which represents goals and actions by a network node called a unit. Competing actions are evaluated on the basis of how well they cohere with each other and with goals whose acceptance may be affected both by coherence considerations and intrinsic desirability. When two units cohere, DECO places an excitatory link (with weight greater than 0) between the units that represent them. Whenever two factors incohere, DECO places an inhibitory link (with weight less than 0) between them. Intrinsic desirability of some goals is easily implemented by linking a special unit, which is always active, to each unit representing an intrinsic goal. There can be different weights on the links representing different degrees of coherence and desirability. Finally, with activation spreading from the special unit to the goals and then out to the subgoals and the actions, the network will update activation of the various units in parallel until all units achieve stable activation. The final activation of the units represents either the choice of particular actions or the posterior value of particular goals. Just as some actions are rejected in favor of better ones with which they compete, some goals are rejected or downplayed as part of the overall judgment of deliberative coherence. All links in this system are symmetrical, reflecting their implementation of considerations of coherence and incoherence. But the links from some of the goal units to the always-active special unit introduces an asymmetry of processing: goal units may much more of an effect on action units than vice versa, since activation can flow directly from the special unit to the units representing goals with inherent priority, and only then to units representing actions.[4] DECO provides a means of testing out whether the principles of deliberative coherence can fruitfully be applied to understand real cases of complex decision making. For a more complete description of DECO and a comparison with classical decision theory, see Thagard and Millgram (1995).

Emotional Decisions

We are now in a position to merge Damasio's hypothesis with components of the coherence theory of decision. This junction requires that both Damasio's hypothesis and the coherence theory of decision be modified. These modifications produce a much richer outline of emotional decisions.

The most obvious way to modify Damasio's hypothesis is to link somatic markers to goal priority. Recall that Damasio maintains that somatic states mark *response options*. If decision-making is a matter of evaluating goals, it makes more sense to link somatic states with the representation of *goals*. Under this modified hypothesis, our most important or meaningful goals are accompanied by somatic markers, the most salient having stronger emotional tags. In this way, EVR's deficiency could be redescribed as a failure to deal with numerous and conflicting goals. We can surmise that EVR's goals were not prioritized because they

were not accompanied by emotional states. That is, none of EVR's goals were more important than the others. It was impossible for him to choose where to dine, we suggest, precisely because goals such as saving money and being healthy could not be weighed in the absence of emotional markers.

Damasio claims that un-marked options are not considered by the decision maker. This biasing function of somatic markers is really what makes decision making possible. In the absence of markers, the decision maker has too much information to deal with. The computations involved are so cumbersome that they cannot yield a final decision. In short, emotions dictate and constrain which bits of information are used. Following Damasio, we also propose that un-marked goals are overridden in the decision-making process and do not factor into coherence calculations. This biasing function of emotion has been underlined by various emotion theorists including de Sousa (1990), Frijda (1986) and Oatley (1992).

From the opposite direction, the coherence theory of decision gains much from Damasio's somatic marker hypothesis. Somatic markers explain how goals can be efficiently prioritized by a cognitive system, without having to evaluate the propositional content of existing goals. After somatic markers are incorporated, what is compared by the deliberator is not the goal as such, but its emotional tag. The biasing function of somatic markers explains how irrelevant information can be excluded from coherence considerations. With Damasio's thesis, choice activation can be seen as involving emotion at the most basic computational level. Inferences to the best plan are not only goal- relevant, directed or determined; they are also emotion-relevant, directed or determined.

In conclusion, the combination of somatic markers with DECO provides the following sketch of a possible theory of emotional decisions:
1. Decisions arise when new information is inconsistent with one or more currently held goals. The mismatch yields a negative emotion which produces a rupture in ordinary activity.[5]
2. The decision juncture causes a simulation to occur, in which goals are reevaluated on the basis of new information. This evaluation of goals elicits somatic markers.
3. Once the goals are prioritized by somatic markers, new options are simulated and evaluated.
4. Coherence calculations produce the best option and equilibrium is restored between the present situation and existing goals.
This sketch shows how emotions help to prevent our decision calculations from becoming so complex and cumbersome that decisions would be impossible. Emotions function to reduce and limit our reasoning, and thereby make reasoning possible.

---

[4]For a more complete description of DECO and a comparison with classical decision theory see Thagard & Millgram, "Inference to the Best Plan: A Coherence Theory of Decision" (in press).

[5]This section draws heavily on Frijda's (1986) theory of emotion. Frijda defines an emotion as a change in action readiness. Emotions are always elicited and result from the interaction of an event with our goals or concerns. Emotions are tendencies to establish, maintain or disrupt a relationship with the environment.

Acknowledgments

This research is funded by the Natural Sciences and Engineering Research Council of Canada.

References

Barnes, A., and Thagard, P. (in press). Analogy and empathy. *Dialogue.*

Damasio, A.R. (1994). *Descartes' error: Emotion, reason and the human brain.* New York: Grosset/Putnam Book.

Damasio, A.R. & Tranel, D. & Damasio, H. (1990). Individuals with sociopathic behavior caused by frontal damage fail to respond autonomically to social stimuli". *Behavioural brain research,* 41, 81-94.

de Sousa, R. (1990). *The rationality of emotion..* Cambridge, MA: MIT Press.

Eslinger, P.J. & Damasio, A.R. (1985). Severe Disturbance of Higher Cognition after Bilateral Frontal Lobe Ablation: Patient EVR. *Neurology,* 35, 1731-1741.

Forgas, J.P., ed. (1991). *Emotion and social judgment.* New York: Pergamon Press.

Frijda, N.H. (1986). *The emotions.* Cambridge: Cambridge University Press.

Millgram, E., & Thagard, P. (forthcoming). Deliberative coherence. *Synthese.*

Nauta, W.J.H. (1971). The problem of the frontal lobe: A reinterpretation. *Journal of psychiatric research,* 8, 167-187.

Oatley, K. (1992). *Best laid schemes: The psychology of emotions.* Cambridge: Cambridge University Press.

Pribram, K.H. (1970). Feelings as monitors. In M. B. Arnold (Ed.), *Feelings and Emotions.* New York: Academic Press.

Saver, J.L. & Damasio,A.R. (1991). Preserved access and processing of social knowledge in a patient with acquired sociopathy due to ventromedial frontal damage. *Neuropsychologia,* 29, 1241-1249.

Thagard, P., & Millgram, E. (1995). Inference to the best plan: A coherence theory of decision. In A. Ram & D. B. Leake (Eds.), *Goal-driven learning:* (pp. 439-454). Cambridge, MA: MIT Press.

Thagard, P. *Mind: Introduction to Cognitive Science,* MA: MIT Press, (in press).

Lateral Connections In The Visual Cortex Can Self-Organize Cooperatively With Multisize RFs Just As With Ocular Dominance and Orientation Columns

Joseph Sirosh[1] and **Risto Miikkulainen**
Department of Computer Sciences
The University of Texas at Austin, Austin, TX-78712
sirosh,risto@cs.utexas.edu

Abstract

Cells in the visual cortex are selective not only to ocular dominance and orientation of the input, but also to its size and spatial frequency. The simulations reported in this paper show how size selectivity could develop through Hebbian self-organization, and how receptive fields of different sizes could organize into columns like those for orientation and ocular dominance. The lateral connections in the network self-organize cooperatively and simultaneously with the receptive field sizes, and produce patterns of lateral connectivity that closely follow the receptive field organization. Together with our previous work on ocular dominance and orientation selectivity, these results suggest that a single Hebbian self-organizing process can give rise to all the major receptive field properties in the visual cortex, and also to structured patterns of lateral interactions, some of which have been verified experimentally and others predicted by the model.

Introduction

In their first recordings from the primary visual cortex of the cat, Hubel and Wiesel (1959, 1962) reported that cortical cells were more selective to the width of patterns than were retinal cells. They noted that cortical cells would give no response to a bar covering the whole receptive field (RF), whereas in the retina and the LGN, cells would typically respond to such patterns. Subsequently, detailed studies by Campbell et al. (1969), De Valois et al. (1982) and others showed that cortical cells are narrowly tuned to the spatial frequency of inputs, and had typical bandpass responses, responding only to inputs in a specific frequency range. A continuum of spatial frequencies from low to high were represented in the cortex (Silverman et al. 1989), and cells in each range of spatial frequency were organized into distinct spatial frequency columns (Tootell et al. 1981; Tootell et al. 1988). In essence, cortical cells exhibited an organization of spatial frequency selectivity similar to ocular dominance (OD) and orientation (OR) columns.

Several computational models have been built to demonstrate how other RF properties such as OR preference, OD, and retinotopy can emerge from simple self-organizing processes (e.g. Goodhill 1993; Miller et al.1989; Obermayer et al.

---

[1]Current address: HNC Software Inc., San Diego, CA 92121-3728, and Sloan Center For Theoretical Neurobiology The Salk Institute, La Jolla, CA 92037; sirosh@hnc.com.

1992; von der Malsburg 1973). However, to date, only one computational model has included the development of spatial frequency selectivity (Miller 1994). In Miller's model, OR preference and spatial frequency selectivity develop together, and perhaps because of the interactions between these two domains, does not produce a clear columnar organization of spatial frequency selectivity. Although the above models replicate the self-organization of afferent structures quite well, they are based on the simplification that the neuronal response properties are primarily determined by the organization of afferent synapses. Lateral interactions between neurons are approximated by simple mathematical functions (e.g. Gaussians) and assumed to be uniform throughout the network; the structured lateral connectivity of the cortex is not explicitly taken into account. Such models do not explicitly replicate the activity dynamics of the visual cortex, and therefore can make only limited predictions about interactions between receptive fields and cortical function.

Recent experiments have shown that lateral connection patterns closely follow the neuronal response properties (Gilbert and Wiesel 1989; Malach et al.1993). For example, in the normal visual cortex, long-range lateral connections link areas with similar OR preference (Gilbert and Wiesel 1989). Like neuronal response properties, the connectivity pattern is highly plastic in early development and can be altered by experience (Katz and Callaway 1992). Such patterned lateral connections develop at approximately the same time as the cortical columns (Burkhalter et al. 1993; Katz and Callaway 1992). Together, these observations suggest that the same experience-dependent process drives the development of both neuronal response properties and lateral connectivity.

Previously, we have shown that a single Hebbian self-organizing process can account for the development of patterned lateral connections, afferent receptive fields, topographic maps and OD and OR columns in the cortex (LISSOM, the Laterally Interconnected Synergetically Self-Organizing Map; Sirosh 1995; Sirosh and Miikkulainen 1995a, 1995b, 1996b, 1996a). However, we have not studied the selectivity to different-sized stimuli with LISSOM before, although it is a major component of cortical organization. This article investigates whether the same self-organizing process can give rise to RFs selective to different stimulus sizes. Because size selectivity is closely related to spatial frequency selectivity,

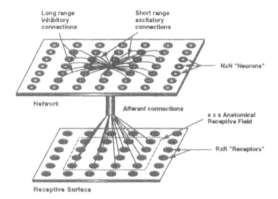

Figure 1: **The Receptive-Field LISSOM architecture.** The afferent and lateral connections of a single neuron in the LISSOM network are shown. The afferents form a local anatomical receptive field on the retina.

such self-organization should account for spatial frequency columns as well.

Several new results are reported in this article. It is shown how afferent RFs of different sizes develop from simple retinal images and organize across the network in a systematic fashion. In addition, lateral connections self-organize cooperatively and simultaneously with the size selectivity properties, producing patterns that follow the receptive field organization. In combination with our previous work, these results suggest that a single unified self-organizing process can give rise to not only all the major receptive field properties in the visual cortex, but also the patterns of lateral interactions.

The Receptive Field LISSOM (RF-LISSOM) model

The LISSOM network is a sheet of interconnected neurons (figure 1). Through afferent connections, each neuron receives input from a "retina". In addition, each neuron has reciprocal excitatory and inhibitory lateral connections with other neurons. Lateral excitatory connections are short-range, connecting only close neighbors. Lateral inhibitory connections link neurons over both short and long distances, and may even implement full connectivity between neurons in the network.

Neurons receive afferent connections from broad overlapping patches on the retina called anatomical RFs. The $N \times N$ network is projected on to the retina of $R \times R$ receptors, and each neuron is connected to receptors in a square area of side s around the projections. Thus, neurons receive afferents from corresponding regions of the retina. Depending on the location of the projection, the number of afferents to a neuron from the retina could vary from $\frac{1}{2}s \times \frac{1}{2}s$ (at the corners) to $s \times s$ (at the center). Typically, R is much less than N and s is large enough to cover many receptors, resulting in large overlap between receptive fields of nearby neurons.

The input to the model consists of gaussian spots of "light" on the retina:

$$\xi_{a,b} = exp(-\frac{(a - x_i)^2 + (b - y_i)^2}{u^2}) \qquad (1)$$

where $\xi_{a,b}$ is the activation of receptor (a, b), u^2 determines the width of the spot, and (x_i, y_i): $0 \leq x_i, y_i < R$ its center. Without normalization, larger-sized spots would produce stronger activation. Therefore, the retinal activity vector is normalized to constant length. The width u is chosen uniformly randomly in a given range, so that inputs of a variety of sizes are presented to the network.

The external and lateral weights are organized through an unsupervised learning process. At each training step, neurons start out with zero activity. The initial response η_{ij} of neuron (i, j) is based on the scalar product

$$\eta_{ij} = \sigma \left(\sum_{a,b} \xi_{ab} \mu_{ij,ab} \right), \qquad (2)$$

where ξ_{ab} is the activation of retinal receptor (a, b) within the anatomical RF of the neuron, $\mu_{ij,ab}$ is the corresponding afferent weight, and σ is a piecewise linear approximation of the familiar sigmoid activation function. The response evolves over time through lateral interaction. At each time step, the neuron combines the above afferent activation $\sum \xi \mu$ with lateral excitation and inhibition:

$$\eta_{ij}(t) = \sigma \left(\sum \xi \mu + \gamma_e \sum_{k,l} E_{ij,kl} \eta_{kl}(t - 1) - \gamma_i \sum_{k,l} I_{ij,kl} \eta_{kl}(t - 1) \right), \qquad (3)$$

where $E_{ij,kl}$ is the excitatory lateral connection weight on the connection from neuron (k, l) to neuron (i, j), $I_{ij,kl}$ is the inhibitory connection weight, and $\eta_{kl}(t - 1)$ is the activity of neuron (k, l) during the previous time step. The constants γ_e and γ_i determine the relative strengths of excitatory and inhibitory lateral interactions. The activity pattern starts out diffuse and spread over a substantial part of the map, and converges iteratively into stable focused patches of activity, or activity bubbles. After the activity has settled, typically in a few iterations of equation 3, the connection weights of each neuron are modified. Both afferent and lateral weights adapt according to the same mechanism: the Hebb rule, normalized so that the sum of the weights is constant:

$$w_{ij,mn}(t + \delta t) = \frac{w_{ij,mn}(t) + \alpha \eta_{ij} X_{mn}}{\sum_{mn} [w_{ij,mn}(t) + \alpha \eta_{ij} X_{mn}]}, \qquad (4)$$

where η_{ij} stands for the activity of neuron (i, j) in the final activity bubble, $w_{ij,mn}$ is the afferent or lateral connection weight (μ, E or I), α is the learning rate for each type of connection (α_a for afferent weights, α_E for excitatory, and α_I for inhibitory) and X_{mn} is the presynaptic activity (ξ for afferent, η for lateral).

Both inhibitory and excitatory lateral connections follow the same Hebbian learning process and strengthen by correlated activity. At long-distances, very few neurons have correlated activity and therefore most long-range connections eventually become weak. Such weak connections are eliminated periodically, and through weight normalization, inhibition concentrates in a closer neighborhood of each neuron.

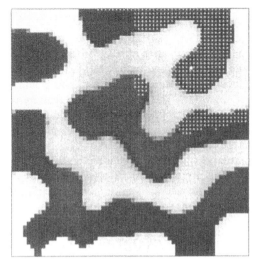

(a) Ocular dominance and lateral connections

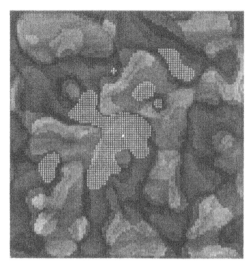

180

0

(b) Orientation columns and lateral connections

Figure 2: **Ocular dominance and orientation columns, and lateral connection patterns.** In figure (a), each neuron in a self-organized LISSOM network is labeled with a grey-scale value (*black → white*) that represents continuously-changing ocular dominance from exlusive left to exclusive right. Small white dots indicate the strongest lateral input connections to the neuron marked with the big white dot, after self-organization. Only the long-range inhibitory connections are shown. The connections of a monocular neuron predominantly link areas of the same ocular dominance. In figure (b), the orientation preference and selectivity of each neuron is represented in grey scale, and the lateral connections of a typical neuron are plotted as in (a). The connections preferentially link similar orientation columns.

The radius of the lateral excitatory interactions starts out large, but as self-organization progresses, it is decreased until it covers only the nearest neighbors (c.f. Self-Organizing Map; Kohonen 1982, 1989). Such pruning of lateral connections produces activity bubbles that are focused and local. As a result, weights change in smaller neighborhoods, and receptive fields become better tuned to local areas of the retina.

Self-Organization of Ocular Dominance and Orientation Columns and Lateral Connections

We have previously used variations of the RF-LISSOM network to model the development of OD and OR columns in the primary visual cortex. Although these phenomena can be modeled with a variety of techniques (Goodhill 1993; Miller et al. 1989; Obermayer et al. 1992; von der Malsburg 1973), RF-LISSOM model is unique in that it also shows how the lateral connections self-organize in the process and what role they play in self-organization and information processing.

In the ocular dominance study (Sirosh and Miikkulainen 1995b; Sirosh and Miikkulainen 1996b), two retinas were connected to the cortical network. Uncorrelated gaussian light spots were used as input, simulating strabismic vision, which is known to result in very pronounced ocular dominance columns (Löwel and Singer 1992). The simulation results are in very good agreement with the biological observations (figure 2a). Sharp and intertwined patterns of ocular dominance form, and neurons are predominantly connected to other neurons with similar selectivity.

In the orientation column experiment (Sirosh and Miik-

kulainen 1995a; Sirosh and Miikkulainen 1996a), elongated gaussians with various orientations and degrees of eccentricity were used as input instead of symmetric gaussians. The cortical network developed a representation of orientation preference and selectivity very similar to those observed in the visual cortex (Blasdel and Salama 1986; Blasdel 1992; figure 2b). Receptive fields of various eccentricity and orientation develop, and neurons are ordered into an orientation map that exhibits linear zones (where orientation preference changes smoothly), pinwheels (singular points around which all orientation preferences appear) and fractures (where preference changes abruptly). The lateral connections again connect neurons that respond to similar inputs. Some of the lateral connection patterns have just recently been discovered, others are predictions of the model.

Self-Organization of Multisize Receptive Fields and Lateral Connections

The hypothesis tested in the present study was whether similar columnar organization and lateral connection patterns would form also when the size of the gaussian light spot was the main dimension of variation in the input. Simulations were carried out on a network of 192×192 neurons, with inputs coming from a 24×24 retina. The anatomical RF size was chosen to be 11×11, so that there is substantial overlap between the RFs. All the connections were initialized to random weights. A total of $25,000$ training steps were used. At each step, a random-size Gaussian spot was presented on the retina as input. The lateral excitatory radius of each neuron started out as

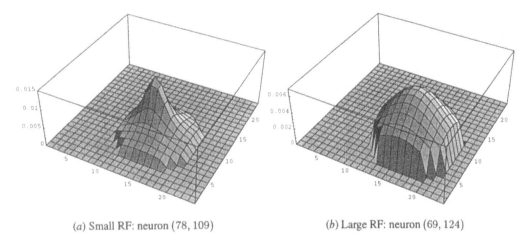

(a) Small RF: neuron (78, 109)   (b) Large RF: neuron (69, 124)

Figure 3: Self-organized receptive fields. The afferent weights of neurons at two different locations in a 192x192 network are shown after self-organization. Initially the weights are completely random, but after self-organization, a smooth hill-shaped weight profile develops. Though the anatomical RFs are the same, the afferent weights are organized into a variety of sizes from narrow, highly peaked receptive fields to large and broad ones.

19, but as training progressed, it was gradually decreased to 1 (as in the Self-Organizing Map algorithm (Kohonen 1989)). The lateral inhibitory connections had a radius of 47, and weak connections were pruned at intervals of 10,000 iterations.

The self-organization of afferents results in smooth, hillshaped RFs. A variety of RFs of different sizes are produced, some narrow and tuned to small stimuli, others large and most responsive to large stimuli (figure 3). Simultaneously with the RFs, each neuron's lateral connections evolve, and by the Hebbian mechanism, are distributed according to how well the neuron's activity correlates with the activities of the other neurons. Let us examine the nature of such activity correlations. The inputs vary in size from $u = 0.75$ to $u = 8.0$, and are normalized. Therefore, the smallest inputs produce very bright activity in a few receptors. They are also smaller than the size of each anatomical receptive field. Therefore, these inputs predominantly stimulate neurons with small receptive fields and having anatomical RFs in the same position as the spot. Such neurons will have strong activity correlations with other small receptive field neurons, but little correlation with neurons having broader receptive fields [2]. The global organization of size preferences and lateral connections can be visualized by labeling each neuron with a color that indicates the width of its RF, and plotting the patterns of lateral connections on top. As figure 4a shows, the RF organization has the form of connected, intertwined patches, similar to OD columns (e.g. see Sirosh and Miikkulainen 1995b), and the lateral connections of neurons connect to regions of the same size preference. The actual strengths of the connections are shown in figure 4b.

Neurons with larger receptive fields have a slightly differ-

ent pattern of activity correlations. The larger spots are not localized within the anatomical RF as are the smaller inputs, and extend beyond it. They produce activity over a wider area in the network than the smaller, localized spots. As a result, the inputs that best stimulate larger RF neurons also cause activity in large parts of the network. Therefore, the activity correlations of such neurons are not as strongly determined by size as that of small RF neurons. Therefore, the lateral connections of neurons with larger RFs often link to smaller RF neurons also. In the cortex, neurobiologists have not yet studied how the patterns of lateral connections relate to either size or spatial frequency preferences.

The columnar organization does not develop in small networks. Simulations show that, for a given variance of the stimuli size, the ratio of neurons in the network to receptors in the retina (the magnification factor) has to be greater than a threshold value for a stable columnar organization to appear. Below the threshold, smooth RFs and an ordered topographic map develop, but all the RFs tend to have the same size, corresponding to the average width of the input stimulus. Above the threshold, symmetry breaking occurs, producing a variety of RF sizes. Such symmetry breaking is similar to that of the Self-Organizing Map (Kohonen 1982, 1989), where an input feature is represented in the network only if its variance is greater than a threshold proportional to the magnification factor (Obermayer et al. 1992).

It is not known whether the long-range lateral connections in the cortex are organized according to size or spatial frequency selectivity. So far, the lateral connection patterns have only been studied in relation to the organization of OD and OR preference (Malach et al. 1993; Löwel and Singer 1992; Gilbert and Wiesel 1989). However, considerable psychophysical and neurobiological evidence indicates selective lateral interactions between neurons tuned to different spatial frequencies (De Valois and Tootell 1983; Bauman and Bonds

---

[2] Note that even small spots produce quite widespread activity in the network, because each retinal receptor connects to a large number of cortical neurons

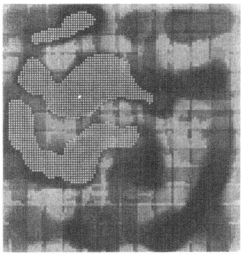

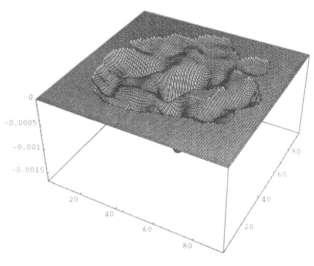

(a) Columns and lateral connections   (b) Lateral inhibitory weights

Figure 4: **Size selective columns, and lateral connection patterns.** In figure (a), each neuron in the network is labeled with a grey-scale value (*black* → *white*) that represents continuously-changing size preference from small values to large values. Small white dots indicate the lateral input connections to the neuron marked with the big white dot. The size preferences are organized systematically across the network into connected, intertwined patches, and the strongest lateral connections predominantly link areas of the same size selectivity. Figure (b) shows the weights of the lateral connections plotted in (a). The connection strengths represent the activity correlations of the neuron with the other neurons in the network. The columnar organization of the RFs is reflected in the weights. The connections also are strongest in the immediate vicinity of the neuron (at center) and become weaker with distance. The large areas of zero weights stand for the connections that have been pruned away during self-organization.

1991). As in the RF-LISSOM model, these interactions are also known to be largely inhibitory (De Valois and Tootell 1983; Vidyasagar and Mueller 1994). The model suggests that the long-range lateral connections could be the anatomical substrate for inhibition between spatial frequency channels. The model further predicts that the patterns of lateral connections in the cortex would be influenced not only by OD and OR preference, but also by selectivity to spatial frequency.

Discussion

Combined with our previous work on OD and OR maps and lateral connections, the new results suggest that a single Hebbian mechanism produces the receptive fields and lateral interactions in the primary visual cortex. It also makes several predictions on the lateral connectivity patterns in the cortex. However, it is important to note that the units and connections in the RF-LISSOM model do not correspond one-to-one to neurons and synapses. Instead, each unit should be seen as a vertical column of neurons, and the connections stand for the interactions between these columns. One important prediction of the model is that long-range lateral interactions are inhibitory: This is computationally necessary for the self-organization of receptive fields to occur. However, it doesn't mean that the synapses on long-range connections necessarily have to be inhibitory, as long as their overall effect on the column is inhibitory.

Perhaps most significantly, the RF-LISSOM model suggests a computational role for self-organized structures in the

primary visual cortex. According to the model, two different computations are performed during sensory processing: First, the inputs are projected onto the principal feature dimensions represented by the afferent receptive field structure. Then, the redundancies are filtered out by the inhibitory lateral interactions. The result is an efficient, redundancy-reduced sparse coding of the visual input which is then passed on to higher processing levels. This prediction can probably be verified experimentally by using information theory to analyze the optical images of cortical activity patterns produced in response to simple retinal images. If confirmed, it would constitue a major step in understanding the function of the observed primary visual cortex structures.

Conclusion

The RF-LISSOM model shows how a columnar organization of multisized receptive fields can develop and how lateral connection patterns follow this organization. Combined with our previous work, these results show how a single local and unsupervised self-organizing process can be responsible for the development of both the afferent and lateral connection structures in the primary visual cortex. The model suggests that afferent receptive fields develop a sparse coding of the visual input, and that recurrent lateral interactions eliminate redundancies in cortical activity patterns.

Acknowledgments

This research was supported in part by National Science Foundation under grant #IRI-9309273. Computer time for the simulations was provided by the Pittsburgh Supercomputing Center under grants IRI930005P and TRA940029P.

References

Bauman, L., and Bonds, A. (1991). Inhibitory refinement of spatial frequency selectivity in single cells of the cat striate cortex. *Vision Research*, 31(6):933–944.

Blasdel, G. G. (1992). Orientation selectivity, preference, and continuity in monkey striate cortex. *The Journal of Neuroscience*, 12:3139–3161.

Blasdel, G. G., and Salama, G. (1986). Voltage-sensitive dyes reveal a modular organization in monkey striate cortex. *Nature*, 321:579–585.

Burkhalter, A., Bernardo, K. L., and Charles, V. (1993). Development of local circuits in human visual cortex. *Journal of Neuroscience*, 13:1916–1931.

Campbell, F., Cooper, G., and Enroth-Cugell, C. (1969). The spatial selectivity of the visual cells of the cat. *Journal of Physiology (London)*, 203:223–235.

De Valois, K. K., and Tootell, R. B. H. (1983). Spatial-frequency-specific inhibition in cat striate cortex cells. *Journal of Physiology (London)*, 336:359–376.

De Valois, R. L., Albrecht, D. G., and Thorell, L. G. (1982). Spatial frequency selectivity of cells in macaque visual cortex. *Vision Research*, 22:545–559.

Gilbert, C. D., and Wiesel, T. N. (1989). Columnar specificity of intrinsic horizontal and corticocortical connections in cat visual cortex. *Journal of Neuroscience*, 9:2432–2442.

Goodhill, G. (1993). Topography and ocular dominance: a model exploring positive correlations. *Biological Cybernetics*, 69:109–118.

Hubel, D. H., and Wiesel, T. N. (1959). Receptive fields of single neurons in the cat's striate cortex. *Journal of Physiology*, 148:574–591.

Hubel, D. H., and Wiesel, T. N. (1962). Receptive fields, binocular interaction and functional architecture in the cat's visual cortex. *Journal of Physiology (London)*, 160:106–154.

Katz, L. C., and Callaway, E. M. (1992). Development of local circuits in mammalian visual cortex. *Annual Review of Neuroscience*, 15:31–56.

Kohonen, T. (1982). Self-organized formation of topologically correct feature maps. *Biological Cybernetics*, 43:59–69.

Kohonen, T. (1989). *Self-Organization and Associative Memory*. Berlin; Heidelberg; New York: Springer. Third edition.

Löwel, S., and Singer, W. (1992). Selection of intrinsic horizontal connections in the visual cortex by correlated neuronal activity. *Science*, 255:209–212.

Malach, R., Amir, Y., Harel, M., and Grinvald, A. (1993). Relationship between intrinsic connections and functional architecture revealed by optical imaging and in vivo targeted biocytin injections in the primate striate cortex. *Proceedings of the National Academy of Sciences, USA*, 90:10469–10473.

Miller, K. D. (1994). A model for the development of simple cell receptive fields and the ordered arrangement of orientation columns through activity-dependent competition between on- and off-center inputs. *Journal of Neuroscience*, 14:409–441.

Miller, K. D., Keller, J. B., and Stryker, M. P. (1989). Ocular dominance column development: Analysis and simulation. *Science*, 245:605–615.

Obermayer, K., Blasdel, G. G., and Schulten, K. J. (1992). Statistical-mechanical analysis of self-organization and pattern formation during the development of visual maps. *Physical Review A*, 45:7568–7589.

Silverman, M. S., Grosof, D. H., De Valois, R. L., and Elfar, S. D. (1989). Spatial frequency organization in primate striate cortex. *Proceedings of the National Academy of Sciences, USA*, 86:711–715.

Sirosh, J. (1995). *A Self-Organizing Neural Network Model of the Primary Visual Cortex*. PhD thesis, Department of Computer Sciences, The University of Texas at Austin, Austin, TX.

Sirosh, J., and Miikkulainen, R. (1995a). Cooperative self-organization of orientation maps and lateral connections in the visual cortex. In *Society for Neuroscience Abstracts*, vol. 21, part 3, page 1751.

Sirosh, J., and Miikkulainen, R. (1995b). Ocular dominance and patterned lateral connections in a self-organizing model of the primary visual cortex. In Tesauro, G., Touretzky, D. S., and Leen, T. K., editors, *Advances in Neural Information Processing Systems 7*. Cambridge, MA: MIT Press.

Sirosh, J., and Miikkulainen, R. (1996a). Self-organization of orientation maps, lateral connections, and dynamic receptive fields in the primary visual cortex. In Sirosh, J., Miikkulainen, R., and Choe, Y., editors, *Lateral interactions in the Cortex: Structure and Function*. Electronic book, http://www.cs.utexas.edu/users/nn/lateral_interactions_book/cover.html. ISBN 0-9647060-0-8.

Sirosh, J., and Miikkulainen, R. (1996b). Topographic receptive fields and patterned lateral interaction in a self-organizing model of the primary visual cortex. *Neural Computation*. In press.

Tootell, R. B., Silverman, M. S., and De Valois, R. L. (1981). Spatial frequency columns in primary visual cortex. *Science*, 214:813–815.

Tootell, R. B., Silverman, M. S., Hamilton, S. L., Switkes, E., and De Valois, R. L. (1988). Functional anatomy of macaque striate cortex. v. spatial frequency. *Journal of Neuroscience*, 8:1610–1624.

Vidyasagar, T. R., and Mueller, A. (1994). Function of GABA inhibition in specifying spatial frequency and orientation selectivities in cat striate cortex. *Experimental Brain Research*, 98(1):31–38.

von der Malsburg, C. (1973). Self-organization of orientation-sensitive cells in the striate cortex. *Kybernetik*, 15:85–100.

Neuronal Homeostasis and REM Sleep

David Horn and **Nir Levy**
School of Physics and Astronomy
Tel-Aviv University Tel Aviv 69978, Israel
and
Eytan Ruppin
Departments of Computer Science & Physiology
Tel-Aviv University Tel Aviv 69978, Israel
horn@vm.tau.ac.il nirlevy@post.tau.ac.il ruppin@math.tau.ac.il

Abstract

We propose a novel mechanism of synaptic maintenance whose goal is to preserve the performance of
an associative memory network undergoing synaptic degradation, and to prevent the development
of pathological attractors. This mechanism is
demonstrated by simulations performed on a low-
activity neural model which implements local neuronal homeostasis. We hypothesize that, whereas
Hebbian synaptic modifications occur as a learning
process during wakefulness and SWS consolidation,
the neural-based regulatory mechanisms proposed
here take place during REM sleep, where they are
driven by bouts of random cortical activity. The
role of REM sleep, in our model, is not to prune
spurious attractor states, as previously proposed by
Crick and Mitchison and by Hopfield Feinstein and
Palmer, but to maintain synaptic integrity in face
of ongoing synaptic turnover. Our model provides
a possible reason for the segmentation of sleep into
repetitive SWS and REM phases.

Introduction

Half a century ago, Hebb (1949) proposed his solution to
the problem of the neural organization of memory. The
concept of Hebbian cell assemblies has since become an
accepted term in the neurosciences, and the idea that
learning takes place through synaptic modifications has
been proved experimentally and has been accepted as
a basic paradigm. There exists however a major problem in this approach: in order to maintain memories
synapses have to stay unchanged when no new learning
occurs. How is that possible in the face of the metabolic
turnover which they undergo all the time? In the present
paper we offer a solution to this problem. Our suggestion is that *synaptic maintenance* occurs via a complementary process to Hebbian learning. We propose that
it is being carried out on the neural level and is driven
by the activity of the single neuron.

Our study is of theoretical nature, based on numerical simulations of a neural network that serves as an
associative memory model, incorporating Hebbian cell
assemblies. The model is described in the next section,
where we introduce synaptic turnover and show that its
effects can be counteracted by a neurally-based synaptic
compensation mechanism. One interesting result which
follows from this process is that it allows, in a natural
way, to obtain a homogeneous distribution of the basins
of attraction of memories. This solves another problem which is inherent in the Hebbian approach: How is
it possible to regulate memories in such a fashion that
pathological situations in which one memory overtakes
all others can be avoided? It turns out that the regulatory mechanism of synaptic maintenance serves this
purpose too.

The regulatory process that we suggest requires a procedure of measuring the activity of a single neuron as a
reaction to stimulation with *random* patterns of activity.
One may wonder which physiological process is responsible for it. REM sleep is a good candidate. Some time
ago Crick and Mitchison (1983) have proposed that the
function of REM sleep is to serve as a 'reverse learning' mechanism whose aim is to remove 'spurious' patterns that are engraved in the brain as a byproduct of
learning. In a companion paper, Hopfield *et al.* (1983)
have examined these ideas in the framework of an associative memory network, and have shown that reverse
learning may indeed allow the network to perform better on subsequent learning and retrieval trials. In our
model there is no problem with spurious states, and no
anti-Hebbian steps are needed to guarantee memory recall. Nonetheless, we can draw on the same physiological
mechanism, associating random activation of the model
with the functional role of REM sleep.

We therefore hypothesize that random activity evoked
in the cortex during REM propels a synaptic buildup
mechanism that takes place during sleep and compen-
sates for synapses that were degraded during the previous day. This proposal complements the recent findings
of Wilson and McNaughton (1994) that support the possibility that memory consolidation, the process of transferring learned information from hippocampal stores to
long-term cortical stores, occurs during slow-wave sleep
(SWS). In accordance, cortical memory storage and cortical synaptic maintenance occur in the SWS and REM
stages of sleep in a segregated manner. In the following,
we shall present a few computational insights as to the
reasons for this segregation, and discuss their implications.

Synaptic Maintenance

Our model is based on previous work in which we
have studied compensatory mechanisms in a model of
Alzheimer's disease, simulated through random synaptic deletion (Horn *et al.*, 1993; Ruppin & Reggia, 1995;

Horn *et al.*, 1996). For our present study we use an excitatory-inhibitory attractor neural network, having M memory patterns that are stored in N excitatory neurons. The coding is sparse, i.e. each Hebbian cell assembly consists of pN active neurons with $p \ll 1$. The synaptic efficacy J_{ij} between the jth (presynaptic) neuron and the ith (postsynaptic) neuron in this network is

$$J_{ij} = \frac{1}{Np} \sum_{\mu=1}^{M} g^\mu \eta^\mu{}_i \eta^\mu{}_j \qquad (1)$$

where $\eta^\mu{}_i$ are the stored memories and allowance is made for different strengths g^μ for embedding different memories. The updating rule for the activity state V_i of the ith binary neuron is given by

$$V_i(t + \Delta t) = P(h_i(t) - T) \qquad (2)$$

where T is the threshold, P is a stochastic function and

$$h_i(t) = c_i \sum_{j \neq i}^{N} w_{ij} J_{ij} V_j(t) - \gamma Q(t) + I_i. \qquad (3)$$

This local field, or input current, includes the Hebbian coupling of all other excitatory neurons, an external input I_i, and inhibition which is proportional to the total activity of the excitatory neurons

$$Q(t) = \frac{1}{Np} \sum_{j}^{N} V_j(t). \qquad (4)$$

As long as its strength obeys $\gamma > Mp^2$ this network performs well.

The factors c_i and w_{ij} are the compensation and degradation terms. To begin with they are assumed to be 1. Degradation, or weakening of synapses, is modeled by imposing a distribution of $w_{ij} < 1$, which serves to represent attenuation of the synapses. Compensation is represented by the factors c_i which correct the values of all synaptic connections of neuron number i. To determine this factor we assume that a measurement period exists, in which the neuron estimates its own activity in response to the stimulation of the whole network by random external inputs. It then changes its compensation strength through

$$\frac{dc_i}{dt} = \kappa c_i \left(1 - \frac{\langle h_i(t) \rangle}{\langle h_i(t=0) \rangle} \right). \qquad (5)$$

From a biological perspective, such computational algorithms may be pre-wired in neuronal regulatory mechanisms. Indeed, several biological mechanisms may take part in neural-level synaptic modifications that self-regulate neuronal activity (see (van Ooyen, 1994) for an extensive review). In other words, there exist feedback mechanisms that act on the neuronal level, possibly via the expression of immediate early genes, to ensure the homeostasis of neuronal activity. This readjustment process is *local* to each neuron, and is done on the *neural*, and not the synaptic, level. Hence the pre-degradation value of each individual synapse is not necessarily reconstructed. This strategy is adopted because in biological

reality each synapse may have a distinct value which should be allowed to change during the learning phase of the system. Thus we have a natural separation between Hebbian synaptic learning and neuronal synaptic regulation.

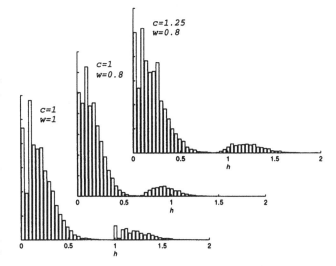

Figure 1: Distribution of the fields h_i in a network with an activity level of $p = 0.1$ in response to the input of an encoded pattern. The three curves display the cases of the original network, of the one with average synaptic attenuation of 0.8, and one where both synaptic weakening and compensation are employed.

To explain why such a compensation mechanism can work we present in Fig. 1 an example of the histogram of the local inputs h_i in such a network. This bimodal distribution accounts for the fact that a fraction p of the neurons (the 'foreground' neurons in the cued pattern) will fire, and a fraction $1 - p$ (the 'background' neurons) will stay quiescent, provided we choose the threshold T to lie in between the two peaks. Once synaptic deterioration occurs, the two parts of the distribution move closer to one another, leading to the source of errors that will eventually cause the demise of the memory system. Compensating with a constant $c = 1/w$, where w is the average of w_{ij}, shifts the two averages to their original locations. Our dynamical compensation algorithm leads to similar results.

In every simulation experiment, a sequence of synaptic degradation and compensation steps is executed. In order to measure the average input field in each compensation step, the system is presented with random inputs and it flows into some of its attractors. After averaging over many inputs one calculates the new c_i. Then the system is presented with its memory repertoire in order to measure its performance, before another degradation step is applied.

Performance of the network is defined by the average recall of all memories. The latter is measured by the *overlap m^μ*, which denotes the similarity between the final state V the network converges to and the memory pattern η^μ that is cued in each trial, defined by

$$m^\mu(t) = \frac{1}{p(1-p)N} \sum_{i=1}^{N} (\eta_i^\mu - p)V_i(t) . \qquad (6)$$

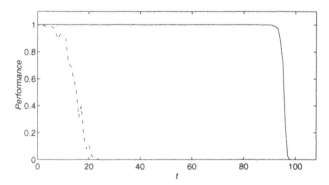

Figure 2: Performance of a network with N=1000 neurons and M=50 memories with activity level of p=0.05 is plotted *vs.* time. The dot-dashed curve represents a case of synaptic turnover without compensation. After a short while the network is unable to perform memory retrieval. When compensation is employed (full curve) the system can continue to serve as an attractor neural network for a long time.

Fig. 2 shows the performance of the network as a function of time. If no compensation is applied, memory retrieval deteriorates fast. With our algorithm performance can be maintained for long times. The factor that determines this time span is the width of the distribution of random synaptic weakening that is employed. For homogeneous weakening compensation is exact. However for random processes, the width of the distribution grows with time, and, at some point the average compensatory factors cannot overcome the distortion which is introduces in the memory system. The latter needs then fresh Hebbian learning to reload its memory.

Homogenization of the Basins of Attraction

Our compensatory process has the characteristics of maintaining the activity of single neurons. As a result it strengthens weakened memories and weakens strong memories. This leads to an interesting regulation process which homogenizes the memories' basins of attraction. Figure 3 shows the results of applying our compensation algorithm, without any synaptic weakening, to a model with 50 memories, of which three have strengths of $g = 4$, 3 and 2, and all the rest have $g = 1$. We see how within a short while the strongest memory, which has dominated in the beginning, looses its big basin of attraction. Afterwards all strong memories continue to decrease together. The shares of the basins of attraction of all memories at the beginning and at the end of the time scale of Fig. 3 are presented in Fig. 4.

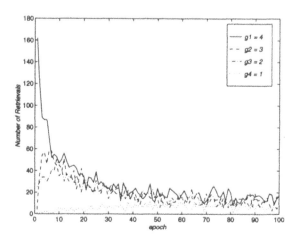

Figure 3: Size of basins of attraction as measured by the number of retrievals of specific memories for 200 random trials at each epoch. No synaptic degradation is performed, but the compensation mechanism is employed. In addition to the 4 memories shown here, this experiment had another 46 memories with strength $g = 1$.

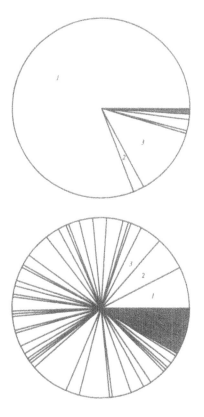

Figure 4: Shares of memory space in the example studied in Fig. 3, for the beginning and the end of the experiment. In the excitatory-inhibitory model that we investigate, random inputs lead either to encoded memories or to the null attractor (gray shading) in which all activity stops.

438

Discussion

The compensation mechanism presented above works also when the network is presented with memory patterns as inputs during the compensation measurement period. However, it works significantly better with random input patterns of activity, since the latter gauge not only the patterns' stability but also their basins of attraction. Much like Crick and Mitchison's theory, this has led us to postulate the existence of random cortical activity during REM sleep, which provides the random patterns of activity needed for synaptic maintenance. This proposal follows the findings that during REM sleep the cortex is periodically stimulated in a diffuse, widespread manner by the brainstem. Hobson and McCarley (1977) have postulated the existence of a 'dream generator' in the pontine reticular formation, which periodically generates ponto-geniculate (PGO) waves. These phasic PGO bursting signals can be viewed as a template of excitatory activity that projects onto cortical networks during REM sleep. Interestingly, the activation of PGO waves depends on withdrawal of noradrenergic inhibition, whose levels are markedly reduced during REM sleep (Jones, 1991). The main functional effects of norepinephrine release are an increase in the signal-to-noise ratio governing neural dynamics, and the facilitation of long-term potentiation (e.g., (Hopkins & Johnston, 1988)). Hence, its low levels during REM result in low signal-to-noise and contribute to the generation of the random activity that is required to homogeneously sample the input space. In addition, its low levels prevent the occurrence of Hebbian cortical LTP changes during PGO phasic burst activity, which otherwise would enhance the formation of pathological attractors.

We are now in a position to address several interesting questions. Why is sleep segregated into distinct SWS and REM phases? The answer to that may be that the tasks of learning new patterns (implemented via Hebbian synaptic changes during SWS) and synaptic maintenance (carried out via neural-based synaptic changes during REM) rely on distinct neurochemical resources. If this is the case, then the segregation of sleep to two repeating phases may provide for the need of periodically replenishing these neurochemical resources, and upregulating the synaptic receptors involved in one pathway while the other one is activated. However, in light of our proposal, the fundamental reasons for REM/SWS separation may be computational. In accordance, while learning involves changes in individual synapses, synaptic maintenance involves concomitant, uniform, changes of all the neuron's synapses. Obviously, these two processes cannot occur together, but need to be segregated. Since synaptic maintenance depends on the activation of random patterns, Hebbian synaptic plasticity must be depressed during that period to prevent the learning of these 'nonsense' patterns. Hence, learning and consolidation are not possible during REM sleep, and must occur in a separate period. On the other hand, synaptic maintenance cannot be performed during the consolidation period (SWS) when only a small set of new patterns is presented to the network, which is insufficient to adequately sample the whole synaptic matrix and achieve a correct evaluation of the neurons' input fields.

Why should the SWS and REM sleep stages appear in a repetitively cyclic manner? Again, there may be several reasons for this sleep pattern which lie outside the computational realm. However, our model offers an interesting computational explanation to this repetitive pattern: efficient synaptic maintenance requires a cyclic, repetitive mode. The reason is that in any given maintenance 'epoch', only the strongest attractors are counteracted, because they overwhelmingly attract random input patterns (see, e.g., (Parisi, 1986; Ruppin et al., 1996)). Hence, the synaptic compensation process must be performed iteratively, each time removing less and less deep attractors. Such a pattern is illustrated in Figure 3. As evident, the basin of attraction of other strong memories begins to shrink only after the initially strongest memory is brought to their strength. Not only should compensation be performed in repeated cycles, but so should learning/consolidation: Associative memory networks are prone to the formation of unbalanced memory storage when Hebbian-like activity-dependent changes are incorporated (Ruppin et al., 1996). Due to an inherent positive feedback loop which exists between the strength of the embedding of a memory pattern and the probability that it will be retrieved, random initial differences in the strength of the synaptic embedding of different memories tend to be magnified. Hence, if left unchecked, a newly learnt memory pattern may bias the learning of other patterns and dominate the retrieval of the network, degrading its performance.

How do our ideas fare when considering REM sleep indices in neurologic and psychiatric disorders? Interestingly, REM sleep time is diminished in Alzheimer's disease (Reynolds et al., 1987). These findings raise the possibility that due to the decrease in REM duration there is less time available for synaptic regulation to occur, resulting in inadequate synaptic compensation. As shown in (Horn et al., 1993; Horn et al., 1996), insufficient synaptic compensation can lead to memory deterioration, a clinical hallmark of Alzheimer's disease. Schizophrenia is apparently not characterized by any notable changes in the duration of either REM or SWS sleep (Benca et al., 1992). Yet, the absence of such overt changes in the length of sleep does not preclude the possibility that sleep is disturbed in a more subtle manner. Increased dopaminergic activity is by far the most notable neurochemical alteration that has been implicated in the pathogenesis of schizophrenia, at least with regard to the formation of positive symptoms. The neuromodulatory action of dopamine, like norepinephrine, is thought to increase the gain of the neuron's activation function, i.e., in terms of our model, decrease its stochastic component (see (Servan-Schreiber et al., 1990) for a review). Thus, the increased dopaminergic activity may severely reduce the fraction of the patterns' space probed during REM sleep, and combined with the enhancement in LTP produced by increased dopaminergic activity (see (Ruppin et al., 1996)), may result in the formation of pathological attractors. Such attractors may contribute to the formation of schizophrenic positive symptoms such as delusions and hallucinations, as they are repetitively activated spontaneously in the absence of an external input trigger (Ruppin et al. , 1996). In summary, our model suggests a link between the specific alterations in REM sleep observed in AD and schizophrenia, and some of their chief clinical symptoms.

Van Ooyen (1994) reviewed a rich body of experimental data supporting the existence of neural-level, activity-dependent mechanisms that regulate neural activity via changes on various levels including synaptic ones. These data testify to the plausibility of our ideas, but obviously do not constitute a direct testimony to their relevance. Our model puts forward, however, a clear prediction which can be tested in a fairly straightforward manner: If one asks subjects to memorize a set of items with different 'embedding strengths' (say different frequencies of presentation), then the retrieval of such freshly learned items should be more homogeneous after REM sleep than before. More elaborate electrophysiological studies in monkeys may be performed (following a paradigm similar to that employed by Miyashita and Chang (1988)) in order to trace the details of the homogenization process on the encoding level.

In this paper we have raised the hypothesis that the function of REM sleep is to serve as a mechanism for maintaining synaptic integrity in cortical associative memory networks. We surveyed the biological data that supports the plausibility of our hypothesis, and demonstrated its viability by using neural networks with a novel, local, synaptic maintenance algorithm. In our view sleep serves two important tasks, at least as far as learning and memory storage are concerned: A. Memory consolidation, which occurs during SWS when the brain is relatively free from the task of processing environmental stimuli. B. Neuronal homeostasis through regulation of synaptic replenishment processes in an activity dependent manner, while the brain is essentially cut-off from the external environment during REM sleep.

References

Benca et al., (1992) R.M. Benca, W.H. Obermeyer, R.A. Thisted, and J.C. Gillin. Sleep and psychiatric disorders. *Archives of General Psychiatry*, 49:651–668, 1992.

Crick and Mitchison, (1983) F. Crick and G. Mitchison. The function of dream sleep. *Nature*, 304:111–114, 1983.

Hebb, (1949) D. O. Hebb. *The Organization of Behavior*. Wiley, 1949.

Hobson and McCarley, (1977) J.A. Hobson and R.W. McCarley. The brain as a dream state generator: an activation-synthesis hypothesis of the dream process. *American journal of Psychiatry*, 134:1335–1368, 1977.

Hopfield et al., (1983) J.J. Hopfield, D.I. Feinstein, and R.G. Palmer. 'unlearning' has a stabilizing effect in collective memories. *Nature*, 304:158–159, 1983.

Hopkins and Johnston, (1988) W.F. Hopkins and D.J. Johnston. Noradrenergic enhancement of long-term potentiation at mossy fiber synapses in the hippocampus. *Journal of Neurophysiology*, 59[2]:667–687, 1988.

Horn et al., (1993) D. Horn, E. Ruppin, M. Usher, and M. Herrmann. Neural network modeling of memory deterioration in alzheimer's disease. *Neural Computation*, 5:736–749, 1993.

Horn et al., (1996) D. Horn, N. Levy, and E. Ruppin. Neuronal-based synaptic compensation: A computational study in alzheimer's disease. *Neural Computation*, 1996. to appear.

Jones, (1991) B.E. Jones. The role of noradrenergic locus coeruleus neurons and neighboring cholinergic neurons of the pontomesencephalic tegmentum in sleep-wake cycles. *Prog. Brain Res.*, 88:533–543, 1991.

Miyashita and Chang, (1988) Y. Miyashita and H.S. Chang. Neuronal correlate of pictorial short-term memory in the primate temporal cortex. *Nature*, 331:68–71, 1988.

Parisi, (1986) G. Parisi. Asymmetric neural networks and the process of learning. *J. Phys. A: Math. Gen.*, 19:L675 – L680, 1986.

Reynolds et al., (1987) C.F. Reynolds, D.J. Kupfer, C.C. Hoch, P.R. Houck, J.A. Stack, S.R. Berman, P.I. Campbell, and B. Zimmer. Sleep deprivation as a probe in the elderly. *Archives of General Psychiatry*, 44:982–990, 1987.

Ruppin and Reggia, (1995) E. Ruppin and J. Reggia. A neural model of memory impairment in diffuse cerebral atrophy. *Br. Jour. of Psychiatry*, 166[1]:19–28, 1995.

Ruppin et al., (1996) E. Ruppin, J. Reggia, and D. Horn. A neural model of positive schizophrenic symptoms. *Schizophrenia Bulletin*, 1996. To appear.

Servan-Schreiber et al., (1990) D. Servan-Schreiber, H. Printz, and J.D. Cohen. A network model of catecholamine effects: gain, signal-to-noise ratio, and behavior. *Science*, 249:892–895, 1990.

van Ooyen, (1994) A. van Ooyen. Activity-dependent neural network development. *Network*, 5:401–423, 1994.

Wilson and McNaughton, (1994) M.A. Wilson and B.L. McNaughton. Reactivation of hippocampal ensemble memories during sleep. *Science*, 265:676–679, 1994.

The perception of causality: Feature binding in interacting objects

John K. Kruschke and **Michael M. Fragassi**
Dept. of Psychology
Indiana University
Bloomington, IN 47405
kruschke@indiana.edu
http://www.indiana.edu/~kruschke/home.html

Abstract

When one billiard ball strikes and launches another, most observers report seeing the first ball *cause* the second ball to move. Michotte (1963) argued that the essence of phenomenal causality is "ampliation" of movement, in which the motion of the first object is perceptually transferred to the second object. Michotte provided only phenomenological evidence, however. We extend the reviewing paradigm of Kahneman, Treisman, and Gibbs (1992) to Michotte-style launching events and report response-time data consistent with Michotte's notion of ampliation. We discuss how contemporary theories of feature binding can extend to the domain of interacting objects and address our results. We also suggest that our treatment of ampliation helps clarify controversies regarding whether perceived causality is direct or interpreted and whether it is innate or learned.

Causality Perceived

Imagine a billiard table. The cue ball rolls across the felt and strikes the 8-ball, launching the 8-ball. Most observers will report seeing the cue ball *cause* the 8-ball to move. The perception of causality has been placed at the foundation of cognition: Kant (1788) argued that causality was an innate and fundamental category of cognition; Piaget (1971) made it an integral part of his theory of development; and, more recently Leyton (1992) has argued that the extraction of causality is at the core of perception and cognition.

The British empiricist philosopher David Hume (1739) argued that impressions of causality are mere fabrications of a sophisticated mind: In the case of the billiard balls, the observer sees the cue ball move, sees the contact of the balls, and sees the subsequent motion of the 8-ball, but does not see causality itself. The impression of causality, Hume argued, is a learned nexus from the first to second ball, based on repeated observations of the conjunction of the two motions, their spatio-temporal contiguity, and the temporal priority of the one motion relative to the other.

Two hundred years later, the Belgian psychologist Albert Michotte impugned Hume, arguing instead that the impression of causality is a spontaneous perceptual gestalt, which is neither learned nor an interpretation via abstract knowledge of physical events (Michotte, 1941, 1963). Michotte claimed that the essence of perceived causality is "ampliation of motion." The neologism, "ampliation," refers to two aspects of the perceived motion. First, the motion of the approaching object is *transferred* to the launched object. Second, for a brief time just after impact (approximately 200ms), the motion is phenomenologically duplicitous: It *belongs* to the first object while the second object *has* it. Thereafter, the motion of the second object becomes autonomous.

Unfortunately, Michotte made only phenomenological observations of perceived causality and gathered no performance data, leaving open the possibility that ampliation of motion is merely an idiosyncratic epiphenomenon (Boyle, 1972; Joynson, 1971). Nevertheless, Michotte's methods and findings are frequently described in textbooks on perception, development, artificial intelligence, etc. (e.g., Boden, 1977; Bower, 1982; Bruce & Green, 1990; Rock, 1975), and a compilation of newly translated articles by Michotte has recently been published (Thinès, Costall, & Butterworth, 1991). In this paper we report a response-time experiment that yielded results consistent with Michotte's theory of ampliation.

We propose that the theory of ampliation can be construed to impact directly on theories of feature integration; i.e., theories of how different visual features of an object, such as shape, color, and movement, are bound into a common identity but distinguished from visual features of other objects in the same field of view (e.g., Treisman, 1986). The key idea is that if the motion is perceptually transferred from one object to the next, then the feature of movement must be unbound from the launching object and bound with the launched object. We discuss how contemporary theories of feature binding can account for Michotte's phenomenology of perceived causality.

Providing a performance measure of ampliation and giving it a theoretical interpretation in terms of feature binding also supplies a new perspective on the relation between ampliation and perceived causality. Rather than debate whether a single process of perceiving causality is either innate or learned, we suggest that the sub-process of ampliation might be perceived directly and developed early in infancy, but the complete perception of causality might be interpreted and learned.

An Empirical Approach to Measuring Ampliation

The Reviewing Paradigm

The performance measure of ampliation that we will describe is an extension of the *reviewing paradigm* invented by Kahneman et al. (1992). In this paradigm, the observer is first shown two objects on a computer screen, such as the triangle

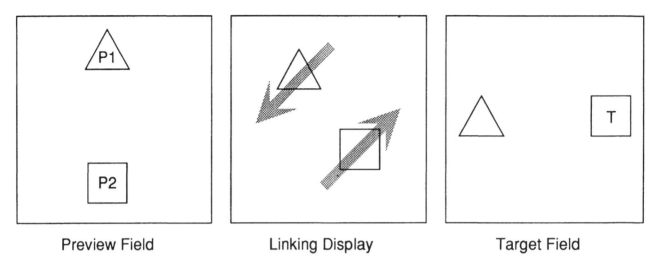

| Preview Field | Linking Display | Target Field |

Figure 1: Example of the reviewing paradigm used by Kahneman et al. (1992).

and square in the left panel of Figure 1. Two letters, labeled "P1" and "P2" in Figure 1, are briefly presented ("previewed") inside each object. After the letters disappear, the empty objects visibly move to new locations, as shown in the middle panel of Figure 1. The motion of the objects links their initial positions to their final positions, and so this motion is called the "linking display." A target letter, labeled "T" in the right panel of Figure 1, then appears in one of the objects. The observer's task is to identify the letter as quickly as possible, by saying the letter's name into a microphone.

The key result is that observers can identify target letters that matched the preview letter from the *same* object faster than they can identify target letters that matched the preview letter from the *other* object. In Figure 1, for example, observers are faster to identify the target, T, when it matches P2 (which was in the same object as the target) than when it matches P1 (which was in the other object). Kahneman et al. (1992) called this effect the *object-specific preview advantage*.

The Reviewing Paradigm Applied to Launching

Kruschke (1987) applied the reviewing paradigm to Michotte-style launching events. Suppose the linking display in the reviewing paradigm did not keep the objects separated, as in Figure 1, but instead showed one object striking and launching the other, as one billiard ball can strike and launch another. Consider what would happen if the target letter appeared in the launched object. Would there still be a strong object-specific preview advantage, or would the preview information from the launching object be transferred, or ampliated, to the launched object? Kruschke (1987) reported that the object-specific preview advantage was significantly reduced in launching, relative to a control event in which the objects did not interact.

We replicated and extended that study in new experiments.

In an event we call *launching*, shown in the left panel of Figure 2, participants saw one circle move toward and contact another, at which time the first circle stopped and the second circle moved away at the same velocity previously had by the first circle. Analogous to the reviewing paradigm of Kahneman et al. (1992), symbols such as "@" or "&" appeared briefly in the initial moments of the event, indicated by P1 and P2 in Figure 2. Then one empty circle launched the other, and a target symbol, indicated by T in Figure 2, appeared in the launched object, at which time the launched object was stationary. Unlike the identification task used in the experiments of Kahneman et al. (1992), the task for our participants was to indicate as quickly as possible whether the target symbol was the same as either of the two preview symbols. Responses were made by pressing a button when the target matched either of the preview symbols, and by pressing a different button when the target did not match either of the preview symbols.

A second event type, called *delayed motion*, began and ended the same way as launching, but had the two circles remain in contact with each other for approximately 890ms. According to Michotte (1963, Experiment 29, p. 91), observers perceive delayed motion as two independent movements without ampliation. The first circle is seen to stop completely, and the second circle then appears to move away with its own motion. Because the two motions are perceived as independent, we would expect to find a robust object-specific preview advantage in delayed motion. In launching, however, we predicted that the object-specific preview advantage would be diminished.

Participants also saw two other events in which the impacted object did not move. The third panel of Figure 2 shows the event we call *target at contact*, and the fourth panel shows *delayed target at contact*. In these events, the target appeared at the moment corresponding to when the first circle contacted the second circle in the launching event. The motivation for

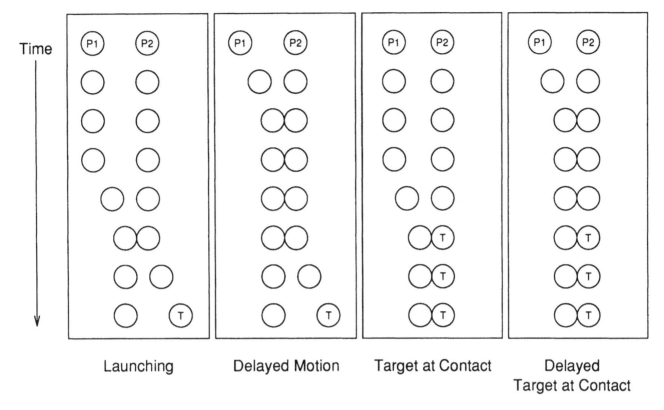

Figure 2: Schematic diagram of the four events in our experiment (not drawn to scale).

these events was to encourage observers to attend to the point of impact (which is where the target appears in these "contact" events). Previous experiments suggested that if observers see only the launching and delay events, they might immediately move their attention after the preview field to the anticipated location of the target, without devoting much attention to the motions of the objects. Attending to the point of impact was deemed important by Michotte for eliciting the best phenomenal ampliation; attending to the point of impact is also important to clearly distinguish launching from delayed motion. We anticipated a strong object-specific preview advantage for delayed target at contact, but a diminished advantage in target at contact.

Method

Participants. Forty-two undergraduates at Indiana University volunteered in partial fulfillment of a psychology course requirement.

Stimuli. Stimuli were presented on a PC-type 13" color monitor in VGA resolution. On every trial, there was a yellow rectangular frame, 256mm wide by 60mm high, which enclosed the relevant region of the the display. The circles had a diameter of approximately 27mm, and were separated center-to-center by approximately 38mm. Every trial began with the circles and their preview symbols in the same posi-

tion, centered laterally on the screen with a small yellow fixation dot centered between them. One circle and symbol were red, the other green. The fixation dot and preview symbols appeared for 500ms. The preview symbols then disappeared, and the empty circles remained stationary for 200ms. For launching (see Figure 2), the circles remained stationary for an additional 890ms and then underwent the launching motion for 230ms. When moving, the speed of the circles was approximately 33cm/s. Then the target letter appeared in the launched object. When the target letter matched a preview letter, the target letter had the same color as the preview letter it matched. The other events had the same total duration, with only the linking display differing between them. For example, in delayed motion, the linking display consisted of approximately 115ms for the motion of the first object, followed by 890ms of contact, following by 115ms for the motion of the second object.

Design and procedure. The design consisted of five crossed factors: (1) type of match between target and preview letters (match same object, match other object, match neither object); (2) direction of motion (left, right); (3) color of the left preview symbol and circle (red, green); (4) time of initial movement (late as in launching and target at contact, early as in the delay events); and (5) time of target appearance (late as in launching, early as in contact). The trials in which

443

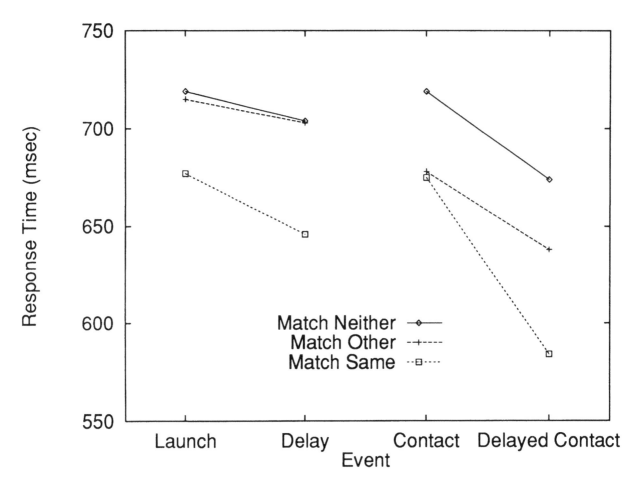

Figure 3: Mean response times for correct responses.

the target did not match a preview letter were doubled in order to equalize the total number of match and no-match trials. Each block consisted of 66 trials: 2 warm-up trials chosen at random from the design, followed by 64 trials that visited each cell of the design once.

After on-screen instructions with several examples of the events, participants had an initial practice block of 35 trials, followed by 8 blocks of 66 trials each, with brief rests between blocks. The experiment lasted about an hour.

Results

Figure 3 shows the mean response times as a function of event and match condition. These factors did not interact with direction of motion or color of symbol. There was indeed a strong object-specific preview advantage for delayed motion and for delayed target at contact, with response times significantly longer for matching the target to the other object than for matching the target to the same object (for delayed motion, RTs for match-other and match-same were 703ms vs. 646ms, respectively, $F(1,41) = 53.71$, $p = .0001$). The magnitude of the object-specific advantage was reduced for launching, al-

though the reduction was statistically of marginal significance (interaction contrast $F(1,41) = 3.78$, $p = .059$). Comparable reductions have been observed in several other experiments conducted in our laboratory, and by Kruschke (1987), so we consider this trend toward reduction to be reliable. The reduction in object-specific preview advantage was quite strong for target at contact, however (interaction contrast $F(1,41) = 13.50$, $p = .0007$). Thus, at the time of impact, there was a complete loss of object-specific preview advantage, but moments later, in the delay events, the object-specific advantage was regained.

These results are intriguing for two reasons. First, regardless of their theoretical interpretation, the results show that the object-specific preview advantage is influenced by the type of interaction between the objects. In particular, mere *contact* of the objects, as in delayed motion, does *not* obliterate the object-specific preview advantage, but contact *with launching* does diminish the advantage. Moreover, the reduction in object-specific preview advantage is temporally localized just after the time of impact, and the object-specific advantage is regained moments later. Second, one interpretation of the re-

444

sults is that information from the launching object is ampliated to the launched object, so that just after impact the previewed symbol from the launching object is as accessible to retrieval as the previewed symbol from the launched object. These results are the first performance measure directly addressing Michotte's (1963) notion of ampliation in perceived causality.

Ampliation as Feature Re-Binding

To explain their results, Kahneman et al. (1992) suggested a "reviewing model," in which the motion of the linking display (middle panel of Figure 1) biases which object will be reviewed first in memory. The model assumes that the motion links the target object with the corresponding preview object, but the model does not incorporate any aspects of the dynamics of the motion. In particular, the model does not suggest why different events would have different biasing effects with different durations, as found in our data. Treisman and Kahneman (Treisman, 1986; Kahneman et al., 1992) have also suggested that visual features are bound together into "object files" that retain each object's immediate history. An object file is tantamount to a tag, or label, on each visual feature, identifying the object to which the feature belongs.

We propose that our results are mediated by binding and unbinding of the visual feature of motion with other features of the objects. One potential (and controversial) mechanism for feature integration is synchronization of neural pulses from different feature detectors. The pulse train acts as an object label for the feature, and synchronization gives the labels from different features a common signature. There is empirical evidence that neurons use this mechanism (for a recent review see Singer & Gray, 1995), and several researchers have applied this binding mechanism in models of visual perception, attention, and memory (e.g. Damasio, 1990; Grossberg & Sommers, 1991; Hummel & Biederman, 1992; Lumer, 1992; Mozer, Zemel, & Behrmann, 1992; Pabst, Reitboeck, & Eckhorn, 1989; Sporns, Tononi, & Edelman, 1991).

Applied to the scenario of launching, these ideas suggest that as the launching object approaches the to-be-launched object, the pulse trains of the motion detectors for the motion of the launching object are synchronized with the pulse trains of the other features of the launching object, all of which are desynchronized from the pulse trains of the features of the to-be-launched object. The question then becomes, What happens to the synchronization of the pulse trains when the objects come into contact?

One answer to this question is suggested by the hypothesis that motion primes other motion detectors along the forward trajectory. Long-range directional priming of motion detectors has been discussed extensively in models of visual motion perception developed by Marshall (1990; Martin & Marshall, 1993), and empirical evidence of long-range directional connections between motion-detecting neurons comes from work by Gabbott, Martin, and Whitteridge (1987) and others cited by Marshall (1990).

Our results might then be explained as follows: In the launching event, the two objects initially have desynchronized pulse trains. At impact, the directional priming of motion detectors causes the new movement of the launched object to have the same synchronization as the launching motion, so that just after impact the motion of the launched object is synchronized with the launching object, but localized with the launched object. This accounts for the duplicity of motion in Michotte's phenomenology: The motion of the launched object is localized with the launched object, but still belongs to (is synchronized with) the launching object. This also accounts for the difficulty and equalization of accessing the history of both objects: The target that appears in the launched object at the moment of impact is not clearly synchronized with either pulse train, and so both preview symbols are retrieved with equal difficulty. After a brief time, the motion of the launched object becomes synchronized with the other features of the launched object, and hence the object-specific preview advantage is resurrected.

This explanation is not committed to pulse train synchronization as the only possible binding mechanism. The explanation merely requires that the process of binding takes some small but non-zero time, and that the object tag of the launching object primes the launched object at the time of impact. Pulse train synchronization is just one possible mechanism for implementing these principles.

Ampliation versus Causality

Michotte (1941, 1963) argued that the perception of causality is not an interpretation based on acquired knowledge of mechanical events, but instead is perceived directly, with ampliation as its essence. Our results do not necessarily support this perspective, in full. It is possible that ampliation, *qua* feature unbinding and rebinding, is a direct perceptual mechanism, but the perception of causality is an additional interpretive process. For example, Weir (1978) described a model that classifies Michotte-style collision events without ever mentioning ampliation, presumably because of the concept's intangibility in Michotte's theories. Reification of ampliation, as suggested by our experiments, calls out for theories to address it, and provides one avenue for distilling which aspects of perceived causality are direct and which are interpreted.

Michotte also argued that the perception of causality is innate. Leslie (1982; Leslie & Keeble, 1987) provided evidence that six-month old infants can distinguish causal from noncausal events, or at least are sensitive to reversals of agency in causal events. Whether the infants perceive such events as causal or not remains an open question. It might be that ampliation develops rapidly, like stereopsis, in response to the visual world, whereas interpretations of causality are learned later in childhood. Perhaps ampliation is used as a perceptual cue for subsequent causal interpretation, and so the two are correlated. Separating ampliation from causality also allows for the possibility of universal sensitivity to ampliation, but individual differences in the perception of causality (Beasley, 1968; Schlottman & Anderson, 1993).

Acknowledgments

This research was supported in part by NIMH FIRST Award 1-R29-MH51572-01 to Kruschke, and by an Indiana University Cognitive Science Program Summer Research Fellowship to Fragassi. Thanks to Michael Erickson, Mark Johansen and Nathaniel Blair for comments on a previous draft, and to Colin Bogan, Amanda Reed, and Eddy Riou for administering experiments. Thanks also to Daniel Kahneman and Anne Treisman for encouragement and access to their lab at U.C. Berkeley in 1986-87.

References

Beasley, N. A. (1968). The extent of individual differences in the perception of causality. *Canadian Journal of Psychology*, *22*, 399–407.

Boden, M. A. (1977). *Artificial intelligence and natural man*. Basic Books, New York.

Bower, T. G. R. (1982). *Development in infancy*. W. H. Freeman, San Francisco.

Boyle, D. G. (1972). Michotte's ideas. *Bulletin of the British Psychological Society*, *25*, 89–91.

Bruce, V., & Green, P. R. (1990). *Visual perception: physiology, psychology & ecology*. Erlbaum, East Sussex, UK.

Damasio, A. R. (1990). Synchronous activation in multiple cortical regions: a mechanism for recall. *Seminars in the Neurosciences*, *2*, 287–296.

Gabbott, P. L. A., Martin, K. A. C., & Whitteridge, D. (1987). Connections between pyramidal neurons in layer 5 of cat visual cortex (area 17). *Journal of Comparative Neurology*, *259*, 364–381.

Grossberg, S., & Sommers, D. (1991). Synchronized oscillations during cooperative feature linking in a cortical model of visual perception. *Neural Networks*, *4*, 453–466.

Hume, D. (1739). *A treatise of human nature*. Oxford, England: Oxford University Press. Republished 1980.

Hummel, J. E., & Biederman, I. (1992). Dynamic binding in a neural network for shape recognition. *Psychological Review*, *99*, 480–517.

Joynson, R. B. (1971). Michotte's experimental methods. *British Journal of Psychology*, *62*, 293–302.

Kahneman, D., Treisman, A., & Gibbs, B. J. (1992). The reviewing of object files: Object-specific integration of information. *Cognitive Psychology*, *24*, 175–219.

Kant, I. (1788). *Critique of pure reason*. St. Martin's Press, New York. Translated by N. K. Smith, 1965.

Kruschke, J. K. (1987). The perception of causality: A performance measure of ampliation.. Paper presented at the Ninth Annual Berkeley-Stanford Conference in Cognitive Psychology. Available from the author.

Leslie, A. (1982). The perception of causality in infants. *Perception*, *11*, 173–186.

Leslie, A., & Keeble, S. (1987). Do six-month-old infants perceive causality?. *Cognition*, *25*, 265–288.

Leyton, M. (1992). *Symmetry, Causality, Mind*. MIT Press, Cambridge, MA.

Lumer, E. D. (1992). Selective attention to perceptual groups: The phase tracking mechanism. *International Journal of Neural Systems*, *3*, 1–17.

Marshall, J. A. (1990). Self-organizing neural networks for perception of visual motion. *Neural Networks*, *3*, 45–74.

Martin, K. E., & Marshall, J. A. (1993). Unsmearing visual motion: Development of long-range horizontal intrinsic connections. In Hanson, S. J., Cowan, J. D., & Giles, C. L. (Eds.), *Advances in Neural Information Processing Systems 5*. Morgan Kaufman.

Michotte, A. (1941). La causalité physique est-elle une donnée phénoménale?. *Tijdschrift voor Philosophie*, *3*, 290–328. Unpublished translation by Krista Hensley, April 30, 1993.

Michotte, A. (1963). *The perception of causality*. New York: Basic Books. Translated from the French by T. R. and E. Miles.

Mozer, M. C., Zemel, R. S., & Behrmann, M. (1992). Learning to segment images using dynamic feature binding. *Neural Computation*, *4*, 650–665.

Pabst, M., Reitboeck, H. J., & Eckhorn, R. (1989). A model of preattentive region definition based on texture analysis. In Cotterill, R. M. J. (Ed.), *Models of Brain Function*, pp. 137–150. Cambridge University Press, Cambridge, England.

Piaget, J. (1971). *Les Explications Causales*. Presses Universitaires de France, Paris. Translation by D. & M. Miles, *Understanding Causality*. New York: Norton. 1974.

Rock, I. (1975). *An introduction to perception*. Macmillan, New York.

Schlottman, A., & Anderson, N. H. (1993). An information integration approach to phenomenal causality. *Memory & Cognition*, *21*, 785–801.

Singer, W., & Gray, C. M. (1995). Visual feature integration and the temporal correlation hypothesis. *Annual Review of Neuroscience*, *18*, 555–586.

Sporns, O., Tononi, G., & Edelman, G. M. (1991). Modeling perceptual grouping and figure-ground segregation by means of active reentrant connections. *Proceedings of the National Academy of Sciences USA*, *88*, 129–133.

Thinès, G., Costall, A., & Butterworth, G. (Eds.). (1991). *Michotte's experimental phenomenology of perception*. Erlbaum, Hillsdale, NJ.

Treisman, A. M. (1986). Features and objects in visual processing. *Scientific American*, *255*(5), 114B–125.

Weir, S. (1978). The perception of motion: Michotte revisited. *Perception*, *7*, 247–260.

Judging the Contingency of a Constant Cue:
Contrasting Predictions from an Associative and a Statistical Model

Frédéric Vallée-Tourangeau,   **Robin A. Murphy**, and **A. G. Baker**
Department of Psychology   Department of Psychology
University of Hertfordshire   McGill University
Hatfield, Hertfordshire   Montréal, Québec
UNITED KINGDOM AL10 9AB   CANADA H3A 1B1
f.vallee-tourangeau
@herts.ac.uk

Abstract

Two contingency judgment experiments are reported where one predictive cue was present on every trial of the task. This constant cue was paired with a second variable cue that was either positively correlated (Experiment 1) or negatively correlated with the outcome event (Experiment 2). Outcome base rate was independently varied in both experiments. Probabilistic contrasts could be calculated for the variable cue but not for the constant cue since the probability of the outcome occurring in the absence of the constant cue was undefined. Cheng & Holyoak's (1995) probabilistic contrast model therefore cannot uniquely specify the way in which the constant cue will be judged. In contrast, judgments of the constant cue were systematically influenced by the variable cue's contingency as well as by the outcome base rate. Specifically, judgments of the constant cue 1) were discounted when the variable cue was a positive predictor of the outcome but were enhanced when the variable cue was a negative predictor of the outcome, and 2) were proportional to the outcome base rate. These effects were anticipated by a connectionist network using the Rescorla-Wagner learning rule.

Introduction

In situations where little is known about the causal structure underlying the occurrence of a predictor event followed by the occurrence of an outcome event, their covariation serves as an important cue that informs a reasoner's judgment of their contingency. A measure of covariation is provided by the difference between the conditional probabilities of the occurrence of the outcome in the presence of the predictor, $p(O \mid P)$, and in its absence, $p(O \mid \text{no P})$, a measure termed ΔP.

Two classes of models, namely statistical and associative, have been developed to explain people's ability to judge inter-event contingency. The probabilistic contrast model (henceforth PCM) is the statistical model that has recently received the most attention (Cheng & Holyoak, 1995). In a judgment task that involves only one predictor event and one outcome, the PCM reduces to ΔP. That is, it postulates that reasoners explicitly consider the difference between the conditional probabilities $p(O \mid P)$ and $p(O \mid \text{no P})$. In situations where two predictors (A and B) signal a common outcome the PCM specifies that the derivation of the conditional probabilities for any given cue must itself be conditional on the presence or absence of another cue. Such a conditionalizing cue may be any cue that covaries with the outcome. Thus, if the outcome is judged to be contingent on B, B may be a conditionalizing cue for A. A's contingency with the outcome is then assessed by calculating a pair of

contrasts, namely its contingency in the presence of B, or $\Delta P_{A|B}$ [i.e., $p(O \mid A \& B) - p(O \mid \text{no A} \& B)$] and its contingency in the absence of B or $\Delta P_{A|\text{no}B}$ [i.e., $p(O \mid A \& \text{no B}) - p(O \mid \text{no A} \& \text{no B})$]. If B is perfectly correlated with the outcome, i.e., the outcome always occurs in B's presence but never in its absence, each contrast for A will equal 0, namely $\{[p(O \mid A \& B) = 1] - [p(O \mid \text{no A} \& B) = 1] = 0\}$ and $\{[p(O \mid A \& \text{no B}) = 0] - [p(O \mid \text{no A} \& \text{no B}) = 0] = 0\}$. In this situation, the conditionalized probabilistic contrasts dictate that A should not be attributed causal importance; it is a redundant cause. And as many have reported (e.g., Baker, Mercier, Vallée-Tourangeau, Frank, & Pan, 1993; Price & Yates, 1993) in judgment tasks where A's contingency is moderately positive but B's contingency is perfectly positive, subjects discount the causal importance of A and rate its contingency near zero.

Associative models do not postulate that reasoners derive conditional probabilities and compute probabilistic contrasts in order to formulate a judgment of contingency. Rather they assume that a reasoner's contingency intuitions reflect the associative strength between a predictor and an outcome that develops on the basis of the *contiguity* between the two events. An associative model commonly discussed is the Rescorla and Wagner (1972; henceforth RW) model of learning which is a single layer localist connectionist network where the input nodes correspond to the predictor events and the output node corresponds to the outcome event. The weights between each predictor and the outcome reflect the strength of the hypothesized association. On any given learning trial, the weight connecting predictor j and the outcome is modified following a delta rule of the form,

$$\Delta w_j = \alpha_j \beta (\lambda - \Sigma w_k)$$

which is the weighted difference between the target activation value of the output node λ (which equals 1 when the outcome is present and 0 when it is absent) and the sum of the weights of the k predictors present on that trial (α_j and β are learning parameters coding for the associability of predictor j and the outcome respectively). This learning rule constrains the nature of the connection weights in two important ways: 1. The connection weight of a given predictor is influenced by the weights of the accompanying predictors and 2. their sum is bounded by λ since when $\Sigma w_k > \lambda$, $(\lambda - \Sigma w_k)$ is negative resulting in a negative adjustment of the weights. The predictions of the RW model are derived by training the network with event frequencies that correspond to the contingencies experienced by human subjects in a given judgment task and comparing the magnitude, order, and polarity of the weights of each predictor with the magnitude, order, and polarity of the judgments of the contingency for these same predictors.

In many judgment tasks the predictions of the PCM and the RW model are identical (Baker, Murphy, & Vallée-Tourangeau, in press; Spellman, in press). For example, in the situation described above where A is a moderate predictor of the outcome but B is a perfect one, the RW model predicts discounting: with training the weight of the perfect predictor B approximates λ, and the moderately correlated cue A develops a connection weight that asymptotes at or near zero.

Judgment tasks that involve a constant cue offer an interesting forum to assess the merit of both models. When a cue is present on every trial of the task, and if the experimental trials make up the set of focal instances over which contrasts are calculated, then probabilistic contrasts cannot be calculated for that cue. There is no conditionalizing cue whose presence or absence identifies a focal set of trials where the conditional probability of the outcome occurring in the absence of a constant cue can be calculated. "Accordingly, subjects will have no positive evidence that any constant cue is causal" (Melz, Cheng, Holyoak, & Waldmann, 1993, p. 1404)[1]. Consequently, the PCM is unable to specify uniquely how people will judge the influence of a cue present on every trial of a judgment task. The power equations in Cheng, Park, Yarlas, and Holyoak (in press; e.g., Eq. 3) suffer the same fate since some of their terms are undefined. In turn, the RW model is able to formulate predictions about how people will judge relationships involving constant cues since the mechanism underlying the predictions is driven by the contiguity between the predictor and the outcome (and not their contingency) as well as by the magnitude of the weights of the accompanying predictors.

The judgment task designed for this study involved two predictor variables and one outcome variable. One of the two predictors (called X) was present on every trial whereas the second (A) was present on some trials and absent on others. In Experiment 1, predictor A was either positively correlated with the outcome, $p(O \mid A) > p(O \mid \text{no } A)$, or was not correlated with the outcome, $p(O \mid A) = p(O \mid \text{no } A)$. In Experiment 2, predictor A was either negatively correlated with the outcome, $p(O \mid A) < p(O \mid \text{no } A)$ or was not correlated. The RW model predicts that judgments of predictor X, the constant cue, will be systematically influenced by the nature of A's contingency. Specifically, in Experiment 1 judgments of X should be lower when A's contingency is positive than when it is zero; in other words, X will have a weaker association with the outcome when A's contingency is positive. In Experiment 2 judgments of X should be greater when A's contingency is negative than when it is zero; that is, X will have a stronger association with the outcome when A's contingency is negative. These predictions hinge on the fact that the weight of predictor A

is proportional to its contingency, and that the weight of the constant cue X is inversely proportional to the weight of A. When A's contingency is greater than zero, Σw_k will be larger than when A's contingency equals zero. Consequently the weight of X will be smaller when A's contingency is positive than when it is zero. In turn, when A's contingency is smaller than zero, Σw_k will be smaller than when A's contingency equals zero. Consequently the weight of X will be larger when A's contingency is negative than when it is zero. Thus while the RW model can formulate predictions about how judgments of X should be influenced by the presence of a variable predictor, the PCM is unable to formulate any prediction about the judgment of a constant cue since the probabilistic contrasts pertaining to X are undefined.

In both experiments, the outcome base rate, namely the proportion of trials where the outcome is present, was manipulated independently of the contingency of the variable predictor. Three different base rates were created: .25, .5, and .75. The RW model predicts that as the outcome base rate increases, judgment of the constant cue X should increase since X's contiguity with the outcome is directly proportional to the outcome base rate. Once again, the PCM is unable to advance predictions on the effect of outcome density on the judgments of a constant cue.

Method for Experiments 1 and 2

Task Scenario and Procedure
Subjects were asked to evaluate the relationships between each of two viruses with a certain disease in six samples of forty fictitious patients. Each sample showed new viruses and a new disease. For each sample the record of each patient was presented on a monitor one at a time informing the subjects of the presence or absence of the two viruses. Subjects were prompted for a diagnosis and then were told whether or not the disease was present. One of the two viruses (X) was present for all patients and the other (A) was sometimes present and sometimes absent. In each sample subjects were asked to rate the relationship between each virus and the disease, using a scale from -100 to 100, after 20 and 40 patients; the analyses reported below were conducted only on the terminal estimates. A virus could be negatively correlated with a disease since, as subject read in the instructions, "some viruses could afford immunity against a disease. The more negative the rating, the greater the immunity."

Design
Each sample of patients corresponded to one of six conditions derived from a 2 by 3 factorial design. The first independent variable was the contingency of the variable virus A and had two values, namely .5 and 0 in Experiment 1, and -.5 and 0 in Experiment 2. The second independent variable was the disease base rate in the sample which could take three values: .25, .5, and .75. The three conditions where A had a zero contingency were designed in both experiments: in the Low Density Zero condition $p(O \mid A) = p(O \mid \text{no } A) = .25$; in the Even Density Zero condition $p(O \mid$

---

[1] In fact, even if such a constant cue is part of a known physical mechanism involving the effect, it is understood to be an "enabling condition" and not a "cause" (Cheng & Novick, 1992).

A) $= p(O|$ no A$) = .5$; and in the High Density Zero condition $p(O \mid A) = p(O \mid$ no A$) = .75$.

In Experiment 1 the remaining three conditions were the three samples where virus A had a contingency of .5. In the Low Density .5 condition $p(O \mid A) = .5$ and $p(O \mid$ no A$) = .0$; in the Even Density .5 condition $p(O \mid A) = .75$ and $p(O \mid$ no A$) = .25$; and in the High Density .5 condition $p(O \mid A) = 1$ and $p(O \mid$ no A$) = .5$. In Experiment 2, the remaining

base rate. A two-factor repeated measures analysis of variance (ANOVA) supported these observations (a .05 rejection criterion was used in all analyses). The main effect of contingency was reliable, $F(1, 22) = 12.6$, as was the main effect of outcome base rate, $F(2, 44) = 11.9$; the interaction was not reliable $[F < 1]$.

The nature of the judgments of the constant predictor seemed clearly determined by the contingency of A as well

Experiment 1						
Trial Type	Low Density Zero	Even Density Zero	High Density Zero	Low Density Positive .5	Even Density Positive .5	High Density Positive .5
AX → O	5	10	15	10	15	20
AX → No O	15	10	5	10	5	0
X → O	5	10	15	0	5	10
X → No O	15	10	5	20	15	10
Experiment 2						
Trial Type	Low Density Zero	Even Density Zero	High Density Zero	Low Density Negative .5	Even Density Negative .5	High Density Negative .5
AX → O	5	10	15	0	5	10
AX → No O	15	10	5	20	15	10
X → O	5	10	15	10	15	20
X → No O	15	10	5	10	5	0
A = Variable Cue; X= Constant Cue; O = Outcome						

Table 1. Event frequencies in the six conditions of Experiments 1 and 2. Frequencies add up to 40 in each condition corresponding to the number of fictitious patients.

conditions were the negative image of these three conditions. Thus, in the Low Density -.5 condition $p(O \mid A) = 0$ and $p(O \mid$ no A$) = .5$; in the Even Density -.5 condition $p(O \mid A) = .25$ and $p(O \mid$ no A$) = .75$; and in the High Density -.5 condition $p(O \mid A) = .5$ and $p(O \mid$ no A$) = 1$. The frequencies of the different kinds of trials in the six conditions of both experiments are shown in Table 1.

The order in which these conditions were presented to the subjects was randomized within each experiment. The labels assigned to the pairs of viruses and the six diseases were counterbalanced.

Subjects

Two different groups of 24 undergraduates from the University of Hertfordshire received course credits for their participation in Experiments 1 and 2. Data from one subject in each experiment were only partially recorded due to a computer malfunction. These subjects were not included in the analyses.

Experiment 1 Results

The mean terminal estimates of the variable predictor (A) and of the constant predictor (X) are plotted in the top left and top right quadrants of Figure 1. The effects of the two independent variables can be clearly observed in both panels. Starting with the judgments of the variable predictor, 1) judgments of A were greater when A's contingency was .5 than when it was zero, and 2) judgments in both contingency conditions were greater the higher the outcome

as the outcome density. Thus, judgments of X were lower when A's contingency was .5 than when it was zero and judgments of X in all conditions were ordered as a function of the outcome base rate. A two factor repeated measures ANOVA confirmed these impressions. The main effect of A's contingency was reliable, $F(1, 22) = 11.9$, as was the main effect of base rate, $F(2, 44) = 39.2$; the interaction was not reliable $[F < 1]$.

Experiment 2 Results

The bottom two quadrants of Figure 1 show the mean terminal estimates for the variable predictor (left) and the constant predictor (right) in Experiment 2. Judgments of the variable predictor were again determined by the actual contingency and the outcome base rate. Judgments of A's contingency were more negative when the contingency was -.5 than when it was 0 and judgments in all conditions were greater the higher the base rate. A two-factor repeated measure ANOVA confirmed these impressions: the main effect of contingency was reliable, $F(1, 22) = 121$, as was the main effect of outcome base rate, $F(2, 44) = 13.4$; the interaction was not reliable $[F < 1]$.

The judgments of the constant predictor in Experiment 2 were the mirror image of the judgments of the constant predictor in Experiment 1. That is, whereas A's positive contingency lowered the judgments of the constant cue in Experiment 1, A's negative contingency increased the judgments of the constant cue in Experiment 2. Again, in all conditions judgments were greater the higher the outcome base rate. Statistical analyses again yielded reliable main effects of A's contingency, $F(1, 22) = 25.5$, and of base rate, $F(2, 44) = 64.1$; the interaction was not reliable [$F(2, 44) = 1.86$].

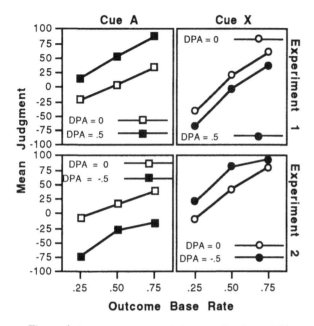

Figure 1. Mean contingency judgments for the variable cue A and the constant cue X in Experiment 1 (top left and top right) and in Experiment 2 (bottom left and bottom right). DPA = Delta P of cue A, or p(O | A) - p(O | no A).

Discussion

In two contingency judgment experiments, a predictor variable was present on every trial. In the first experiment, the constant predictor was paired with a second predictor that had either a positive or a zero correlation with the outcome, and in the second experiment it was paired with a predictor that had either a negative or a zero correlation with the outcome. In spite of the constant cue's identical probability of being paired with the outcome in each outcome base rate condition, judgments of the constant cue were systematically influenced by the nature of the correlation between the second predictor and the outcome. Specifically, judgments of the constant cue were attenuated when the second predictor was positively correlated with the outcome but were enhanced when the second predictor was negatively correlated with the outcome. This is a novel finding and establishes that judgments of constant cues can be discounted or potentiated in the same way as the judgments of variable cues (e.g., Baker et al., 1993). Subjects could have ignored the constant cue and rated its relationship with the outcome as zero, but they did not. Furthermore, in both experiments, judgments of the constant cue were determined by the base rate of the outcome: the more prevalent the outcome, the more positive the judgments of the constant cue. Thus, the participants in these experiments had no difficulty evaluating the nature of a relationship between a constant cue and an outcome even if probabilistic contrasts could not be computed.

Importantly, the dual influences of the contingency of the accompanying cue and of the outcome base rate were anticipated by the RW model.

To account for the judgments of the constant cue the PCM must postulate a focal set of instances whose nature is not constrained by the trials of the task, thereby enabling the derivation of the probability of the outcome in the absence of the constant cue, $p(O \mid no\ X)$. The difficulty, however, is that due to the nature of the judgment task and the fictitious diseases, it is hard to conceive the kinds of life experiences subjects may recruit to define the probability of any of the fictitious diseases in the absence of the constant cues. For example, to use one set of virus-disease labels employed here, what experiences outside the laboratory could subjects use to define the probability of the occurrence of the disease *Ork's Complex* in the absence of *Threbbagia*? Let's assume that for some subjects *Ork's Complex* reminded them of a real world disease (and that these subjects might have assumed also that in those real world cases *Threbbagia* was absent), the probability (*Ork's Complex* | No *Threbbagia*) is no longer undefined. The disease labels used in these experiments (*Ork's Complex*, *Nachmose A*, *Grympox*, *Melastraz*, *Trachtosis*, *Voldusis*) may have reminded different subjects to different degrees of real world diseases, thereby producing focal sets, for some diseases, which defined the probability of the disease in the absence of the constant cue. However, one might predict that subjects would produce highly variable judgments of the constant cue given their variable backgrounds; yet systematic patterns were observed.

More generally, it might be argued that people use an abstract reasoning schema which by default sets the probability of a disease in the absence of a virus to zero. This would correspond to the common understanding of the pathogenic quality of viruses. But subjects would have been ill-served by this reasoning schema since in these experiments some viruses could grant immunity and indeed in the High Density -.5 condition of Experiment 2, the probability of the disease in the absence of virus A equalled 1! Evidently subjects were aware of the different kinds of viruses in this judgment task since they experienced no difficulty rating some virus-disease relationships negatively. It is thus unlikely that they assumed by default that the probability of the disease in the absence of a virus was zero.

Baker, Murphy, and Vallée-Tourangeau (in press) have pointed out that the PCM's difficulties with undefined contrasts may be alleviated by including the inter-trial intervals (ITI) in the calculation of conditional probabilities such as $p(O \mid no\ X)$. For example, the time separating the presentation of each patient's record could be segmented in discrete time intervals where nothing is happening, that is where none of the viruses are present and where the disease is absent as well. When such ITI segments are included in the calculations, the probability of the outcome in the absence of the constant cue is no longer undefined and equals zero. Following this strategy, the probabilistic contrasts for the constant cue in the six conditions of both experiments account partly for the judgment of the constant cue. This can be assessed in Table 2 where the ordering of the mean judgments of X parallels loosely the ordering of

$\Delta P_{X|no\ A}$. This auxiliary assumption, however, is not without problems. One may question of course the plausibility of arguing that subjects consciously considered the inter-trial interval when evaluating the constant cue's effectiveness. More importantly, the medical context in which the task is couched means that the probability of a disease can only be defined with respect to patients that either have it or not, and such patients were absent during the ITI.

While it can be argued that the RW model better accounts for the patterns of judgments of the constant cue, neither model fares well in explaining the strong effect of outcome base rate on judgments of the variable predictor (see the left half of Fig. 1). Probabilistic contrasts are impervious to differences in outcome densities if these densities do not

Experiment 1 and the three -.5 conditions of Experiment 2 were 53.8 and -38.3 respectively. However, the asymmetry was not statistically significant: The absolute magnitude of the overall means did not differ reliably ($t(136) = 1.73$). Furthermore, symmetric judgments of positive and negative contingencies are routinely observed in similar tasks (e.g., Vallée-Tourangeau, Baker, & Mercier, 1994).

Associative models, in turn, usually predict some effect of outcome density on learning as this changes the contiguity between the predictor and the outcome as well as the associative strength of the context in which learning takes place. Specifically, the RW model predicts that for a positively correlated predictor, lower base rates yield larger positive connection weights, and for a negatively correlated predictor, lower base rates yield more negative connection

Experiment 1				
Conditions	$p(O \mid X\ \&\ no\ A)$	$p(O \mid no\ X\ \&\ no\ A)$	$\Delta P_{X|no\ A}$	Mean Judgments
HD 0	0.75	0.00	0.75	60.2
HD .5	0.50	0.00	0.50	36.0
ED 0	0.50	0.00	0.50	21.1
ED .5	0.25	0.00	0.25	-3.3
LD 0	0.25	0.00	0.25	-39.7
LD .5	0.00	0.00	0.00	-64.8
Experiment 2				
Conditions	$p(O \mid X\ \&\ no\ A)$	$p(O \mid no\ X\ \&\ no\ A)$	$\Delta P_{X|no\ A}$	Mean Judgments
HD -.5	1.00	0.00	1.00	92.4
ED -.5	0.75	0.00	0.75	79.2
HD 0	0.75	0.00	0.75	78.7
ED 0	0.50	0.00	0.50	40.7
LD -.5	0.50	0.00	0.50	19.9
LD 0	0.25	0.00	0.25	-10.4
HD = High Density; ED = Even Density; LD = Low Density				

Table 2. Comparisons of the predictions of the PCM given by including the inter-trial interval in the focal set for the constant cue X and the ordering of the mean judgments for X (Experiment 1, top half; Experiment 2 bottom half).

affect the overall contingencies. Again, the PCM can resort to including the ITI in calculating A's contingencies (the conditionalizing cue for A is no longer the constant cue X): counting time segments where nothing happens increases frequency of "no A" observations. The greater the number of ITI observations included in the calculations of $p(O \mid no\ A)$, the smaller $p(O \mid no\ A)$, and the more proportional to $p(O \mid A)$ A's contingency becomes. In this way, the higher $p(O \mid A)$, the higher the judgments. And this is certainly what was observed (assuming that the same number of ITI observations were included in the devaluation of $p(O \mid no\ A)$ in the positive, negative and zero conditions). With this auxiliary assumption however, the PCM is committed to predict an overall positive bias in the estimates of A across both experiments, namely the .5 contingencies in Experiment 1 should be judged more positive than the -.5 contingencies of Experiment 2 should be judged negative. Such an asymmetry was observed: The overall judgment means of the variable cue in the three .5 conditions of

weights (Wasserman, Elek, Chatlosh, & Baker, 1993); for a non-correlated predictor, the weights, at asymptote, should equal zero regardless of the base rates. Ostensibly, the ratings of the varying cue exhibited none of these predicted effects. However, judgments of the varying cue might have been influenced by the associative strength of the constant cue. In an animal conditioning preparation, learning supported by a conditioned stimulus may be better determined on test trials conducted in a test context that is different from the training context. Analogously, subtracting the constant cue ratings from the ratings of the varying cue would yield estimates of the varying cue "freed" of the influence of the constant cue. These adjusted ratings of the varying cue in the two contingency conditions of Experiment 1 and Experiment 2 are shown in Figure 2 (left and right panel respectively). The adjusted ratings of the varying cue in the positive contingency conditions of Experiment 1 show the predicted effect of outcome base rates: they are more positive with smaller base rates.

451

However, this pattern holds for the two zero contingency conditions as well as for the negative contingency condition of Experiment 2. The effects in the noncontingent conditions are in fact preasymptotic predictions of the model, but not in the negative contingency condition. Thus, while the RW model can formulate predictions about the influence of base rates on the judgments of the varying cue, and that these predictions have often been confirmed (e.g., Wasserman et al., 1993, Fig. 5), they were only partially observed in these experiments. Base rate effects on contingency judgments have important implications and future research should aim to elucidate the conditions under which they are and are not observed.

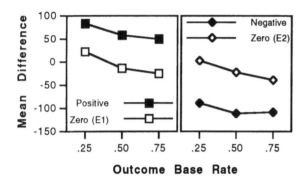

Figure 2. Mean difference between ratings of the varying cue A and the constant cue X for the two contingency conditions in Experiment 1 (left panel) and in Experiment 2 (right panel) as a function of outcome base rate.

In summary, the two experiments reported in this paper showed that discounting and enhancing effects found with variable cues can also occur with constant cues. These experiments raised an important concern about the PCM, namely whether any conceptually acceptable set of focal instances could be derived a priori for constant cues that could predict the dual effect of outcome base rate and the variable cue's contingency on the estimates of the constant cues. Judgments of the constant cue in both experiments were better explained by a mechanism operating on the basis of the contiguity between the constant cue and the outcome, a mechanism that is also constrained by the contiguity of other cues present.

Acknowledgments

This work was supported by grant R000221514 from the Economic & Social Research Council (UK) awarded to FVT. We wish to thank Susan Drew for recruiting and running the participants, and one anonymous reviewer for thoughtful comments.

References

Baker, A. G., Mercier, P., Vallée-Tourangeau, F., Frank, R., & Pan, M. (1993). Selective association and causality judgments: Presence of a strong causal factor may reduce judgments of a weaker one. *Journal of Experimental Psychology: Learning, Memory and Cognition*, 19, 414-432.

Baker, A. G., Murphy, R. A., & Vallée-Tourangeau, F. (In press). Associative and normative models of causal induction: Reacting to versus understanding cause. To appear in D. R. Shanks, K. J. Holyoak, & D. L. Medin (Eds.), *The Psychology of Learning and Motivation*, Vol. 34. San Diego: Academic Press.

Cheng, P. W., & Holyoak, K. J. (1995). Complex adaptive systems as intuitive statisticians: Causality, contingency, and Prediction. In J.-A. Meyer, & H. Roitblat (Eds.), *Comparative approaches to cognitive science* (pp. 271-302). Cambridge, MA: MIT Press.

Cheng, P. W., & Novick, L. R. (1992). Covariation in natural causal induction. *Psychological Review*, 99, 365-382.

Cheng, P. W., Park, J., Yarlas, A. S., & Holyoak, K. J. (In press). A causal-power theory of focal sets. To appear in D. R. Shanks, K. J. Holyoak, & D. L. Medin (Eds.), *The Psychology of Learning and Motivation*, Vol. 34. San Diego: Academic Press.

Melz, E. R., Cheng, P. W., Holyoak, K. J., & Waldmann, M. R. (1993). Cue competition in human categorization: Contingency or the Rescorla-Wagner learning rule? Comment on Shanks (1991). *Journal of Experimental Psychology: Learning, Memory, and Cognition*, 19, 1398-1410.

Price, P. C., & Yates, F. (1993). Judgmental overshadowing: Further evidence of cue interaction in contingency judgment. *Memory & Cognition*, 21, 561-572.

Rescorla, R. A., & Wagner, A. R. (1972). A theory of Pavlovian conditioning: Variations in the effectiveness of reinforcement and non-reinforcement. In A. H. Black, & W. F. Prokasy (Eds.), *Classical conditioning II: Current research and theory* (pp . 64-99). New York: Appleton-Century-Crofts.

Spellman, B. A. (In press). Conditional contingency as an explanation of cue-interaction effects. To appear in D. R. Shanks, K. J. Holyoak, & D. L. Medin (Eds.), *The Psychology of Learning and Motivation*, Vol. 34. San Diego: Academic Press.

Vallée-Tourangeau, F., Baker, A. G., & Mercier, P. (1994). Discounting in causality and covariation judgments. *Quarterly Journal of Experimental Psychology*, 47B, 151-171.

Wasserman, E. A., Elek, S. M., Chatlosh, D. L., & Baker, A. G. (1993). Rating causal relations: Role of probability in judgments of response-outcome contingency. *Journal of Experimental Psychology: Learning, Memory. and Cognition*, 19, 174-188.

What Language Might Tell Us About the Perception of Cause

Phillip Wolff and **Dedre Gentner**
Department of Psychology
Northwestern University
2029 Sheridan Road, Evanston, IL 60208
{wolff, gentner}@aristotle.ils.nwu.edu

Abstract

In English, causation can be expressed with either a lexical or periphrastic causative verb. Lexical causatives include both the notion of CAUSE and the notion of RESULT (frequently change-of-state) (e.g. Mulder *sunk* the boat); Periphrastic causatives encode the notion of CAUSE without the notion of RESULT (e.g. Mulder *made* the boat *sink*). According to many linguists, these two kinds of sentences have different meanings: lexical causatives are used for situations involving *direct causation* while periphrastic causatives are used for situations involving either *direct* or *indirect causation*. This research investigated how this distinction might be cognitively determined. Subjects watched 3D animations of marbles hitting one another and then described the scenes and enumerated the total number of events. When causers were inanimate, lexicalization and enumeration were guided by physical contact. When causers were animate, lexicalization and enumeration were guided by factors other than physical contact, possibly intention or ultimate causation. The results suggest how different kinds of causation and their expression might be related to the perception of events.

Introduction

Languages have multiple ways of expressing causation. Consider a causal happening in which a torpedo moves into a ship causing it to sink. This causal happening can be decomposed into two subevents: a *causing* subevent, the torpedo's movement though the water, and a *caused* subevent, the ship's sinking. In English, there are two major ways of describing a happening of this kind. In one of these ways, the notions of CAUSE and RESULT are encoded in different verbs (see 1a). The verb carrying the notion of CAUSE is refer to as a *periphrastic causative* (e.g. *cause, have, make, get*). A second way is by encoding the notions of CAUSE and RESULT in a single verb (see 1b). Verbs that convey both of these notions are referred to as *lexical causatives* (e.g. *melt, break, kill, sink*).

(1) a. The torpedo *made* the boat *sink*.
   b. The torpedo *sank* the boat.

Although the sentences in (1a) and (1b) are highly similar, they are not paraphrastic: Lexical and periphrastic causatives can refer to different kinds of causal situations. Their differences are revealed by that fact that the two kinds of expressions vary in their acceptability in the context of certain kinds of causers.

(2) a. The cracks made the boat sink.
   b. *The cracks sank the boat.

The periphrastic causative in 2a, but not the lexical causative in 2b, allows *cracks* as a causer. This difference in acceptability is roughly characterized by the assertion that the range of situations referred to by lexical causatives is a subset of the range of situations referred to by periphrastic causatives (See Figure 1). That is, lexical causatives are choosier about what they refer to than are periphrastic causatives.

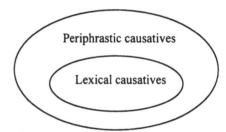

Figure 1. Inclusion relationship holding between many lexical and periphrastic causatives

According to a number of linguists, lexical causatives express *direct causation*, that is, causation that is immediate, strongly coercive or unified, while periphrastic causatives express causation that is either direct or indirect (e.g. Comrie, 1985; Cruse, 1972; Dowty, 1979; Frawley, 1992; Levin & Rappaport Hovav, 1994, Pinker, 1989, Shibatani, 1980; Wierzbicka, 1988, among others). While helpful, this general account of causatives leaves much unsaid. In this research we seek a cognitively motivated account of this distinction by examining how the two ways of expressing causation might be linked to certain properties in the external world, namely *physical contact* and *animacy*.

A related aim of this research is to investigate how these two ways of expressing causation might be associated with the psychological notion of an *event*. It's generally accepted that causatives can be decomposed into two subevents (e.g. Frawley, 1992; Dowty, 1979; Parsons, 1990; Talmy, 1976). The question is whether and when these two subevents can be conceptualized as a single, unified event. According to the *unitization hypothesis,* lexical causatives, unlike periphrastic causatives, refer to happenings that can be conceptualized (unitized) as single events (for similar proposals see Croft, 1990; Delancey, 1991; Frawley, 1992).

One way of motivating the unitization hypothesis is in terms of iconicity. *Iconicity* is the general claim that features or relationships in the world can be reflected in the grammatical structure of a language (Haiman, 1980, 1983; Givón, 1990; see Fisher, in press, for a similar claim). An often cited example is the generalization that concepts that are conceptually close tend to be placed close together in the sentence. Another often cited example is the pattern in which the temporal order of a sequence of events is reflected in the temporal order of clauses. Cases of iconicity deserve notice. Only a handful of conceptual distinctions can be captured in a language's grammatical structure; those that do get captured are likely to be cognitively significant (Slobin, 1995; Talmy, 1983).

Applying these ideas to English, we can ask whether lexical and periphrastic causatives represent another kind of iconicity. The patterns are quite suggestive: Lexical causatives encode happenings within a single clause while periphrastic causatives encoding happenings over two clauses. Language may reserve one-clause expressions, lexical causatives, for happenings that can be conceptualized as single events. Conversely, language may employ multiple clause expressions, periphrastic causatives, for happenings that cannot be conceptualized as single events.

The Contact Criterion. If the distinction between lexical and periphrastic causatives is conceptually important how might it be grounded in the world? In our first experiment, we focused on the role of physical contact. Physical contact has been suggested by a number of linguists as important to the notion of direct causation (Gergely & Bever, 1986; Pinker, 1989; Nedyalkov & Silnitsky, 1973; Shibatani, 1980) and has been studied extensively by psychologists interested in the perception of cause. It is generally acknowledged that although causation does not require physical contact (e.g. Bullock, Gelman, & Baillargeon, 1982; Shultz, 1982; Woodward, Phillips, & Spelke, 1993), contact can make causation easier to perceive (Cohen & Oaks, 1993; Leslie, 1982, Michotte, 1963). It seems reasonable, then, that language might use a property like physical contact to distinguish between different kinds of causality. Specifically, language might reserve lexical causatives for happenings in which the causer and causee make physical contact, using periphrastic

causatives for happenings in which they don't. We will refer to this proposed relationship as the *contact criterion*[1].

The principle is exemplified by the sentences in (3).

(3) a. Scully moved the chair.
    b. Scully caused the chair to move.

The sentence in (3a) strongly suggests physical contact between the causer, Scully, and the causee, the chair, while the sentence in (3b) does not.

There is some empirical evidence for the link between physical contact and the expression of causation. In a study by Ammon (1980), children and adults chose one of three pictures in response to an orally presented sentence which was either a lexical or periphrastic causative. The pictures depicted three kinds of contact: direct contact (e.g. a cartoon character bouncing a ball), indirect contact (e.g. a character pointing a finger at another character bouncing a ball, as if directing her to do so), and no contact (e.g. two characters simply watching a ball bounce). Both children and adults preferred the picture depicting direct contact when the sentence contained a lexical causative. When the sentence contained a periphrastic causative, responses were mixed. Ammon's findings suggest that physical contact may affect how children and adults describe a causal happening. However, certain aspects of her methodology preclude strong conclusions: 1) only three verbs were tested under all sentence types, 2) the sentences used real verbs, so that subject's knowledge may have been specific to these verbs, and 3) the causal happenings were presented as static pictures rather than as actual scenes involving motion and change. (As shown by Kaiser, Proffitt, Whelan, and Hecht (1992), presentation method (either dynamic or static) influences how an event is evaluated.) The first study investigated whether the property of physical contact affects linguistic expression.

Testing the Contact Criterion. The contact criterion makes predictions about how people will chose to describe a causal chain. Imagine a scene where one marble (M1) bumps into a second marble (M2) which then bumps into a third marble (M3) (see Figure 2). If people limit lexical causatives to happenings involving physical contact, they should be willing to use a lexical causative to describe the relationship between M1 and M2, but not M1 and M3.

---

[1] Spelke (1991; Woodward, et. al., 1993) and her colleagues have argued that infants employ a constraint, the *principle of contact* , in their reasoning about the motions of inanimate objects. The constraint is similar to the contact criterion (discussed above), but not the same. The principle of contact states that inanimates will act upon each other if and only if they come into contact. The principle concerns, then, the presence or absence of a causal relationship. The contact criterion, in contrast, concerns whether or not a causal relation is direct or indirect, not present or absent.

Causal relationships between M1 and M3 should only be describable using a periphrastic causative.

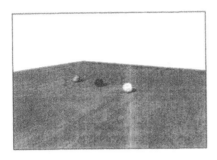

Figure 2. A simple causal chain. Marble 1 bumps into marble 2 which bumps into marble 3.

In Experiment 1, the contact criterion was tested using this logic. Subjects watched causal chains involving three marbles. They then chose between two sentences, a lexical and periphrastic causative. In half of the sentence pairs, the two marbles made physical contact. In the other half of the sentence pairs, the two marbles did not make physical contact. According to the contact criterion, subjects will choose a lexical causative sentence only when the marbles in that sentence make physical contact. In cases where the marbles don't make physical contact, subjects will choose a periphrastic causative sentence, because the lexical causative, which requires contact, is barred.

Testing the Unitization Hypothesis. The unitization hypothesis predicts a strong correlation between happenings that can be described with a lexical causative and those that can be counted as single events. The *chain of marbles* scenario described above can be used to test this prediction. If the unitization hypothesis is correct, subjects will report single events for marbles making physical contact more frequently than for marbles that do not make physical contact.

Experiment 1

Method
Subjects. The subjects were 20 Northwestern University students.

Materials. Sixteen 3D animations were made from an animation package called Autodesk 3D Studio® release 4. Each animation depicted a sequence in which three marbles rolled into one another. The sequences followed one of four possible paths based on whether the second or third marbles hit head on or at an angle. Each path was viewed from four different perspectives. Animation quality was near photorealistic. All colors, except the background, were done with texture mappings. All objects, when appropriate, cast shadows. The marbles were placed on a gray surface against a blue background and were colored either red, yellow, blue, or green. Like real marbles, these colors varied a bit so that their rolling motions could be seen. Each animation was 50 frames in length and was run at approximately 15 frames/second.

Procedure and Design. The animations were presented on DOS-based computers with 17" monitors. The order of the animations was randomized except for the first two which served as practice items. After watching an animation, subjects were asked to "choose the sentence that best describes" the occurrence, based on "what you see in the animations, as well as on your general knowledge of verbs." The choices were a *lexical causative*, a *periphrastic causative*, or *neither of these sentences*. To encourage use of general knowledge we used nonce verbs (e.g. *fendle*, *klop*): Periphrastic sentences were formed using the verb *make* along with the same nonce verb used in the lexical causative sentences. Within a sentence set, the marbles were the same for both sentence types: e.g. "The blue marble fendled the green marble" vs. "The blue marble made the green marble fendle." The sentence sets named three kinds of events: eight in which the marbles made physical contact, eight in which the marbles didn't make physical contact, and four in which the marbles made contact, but did not agree with the sentences. The last four events were drawn systematically from the primary sixteen animations, and served as catch trials, since the correct option, "neither of the above sentence," was unambiguous. After subjects finished the sentence choice task, they watched the animations again and were told to simply count the number of events. The main factor of interest, *contact type*, was within subject and had two levels, contact and gap.

Results
The predictions of the contact criterion and the unitization hypothesis were borne out. As predicted by the contact criterion, lexical causatives were chosen more frequently when the marbles made physical contact (*M*=78%) than when they were gapped (*M*=8%) (Table 1).

| | | Relationship Between Marbles | |
		Contact	Gap
Sentence Type	**Lexical**	**78%**	**8%**
	Periph.	20%	63%
	Total Causal	98%	71%

Table 1: Percentage of sentence types chosen in Experiment 1

This difference was significant across both subjects, t_s (19)=13.86, p < .001, and items, t_i(15)=10.2, p < .001. Subjects were markedly unwilling to use lexical causatives in the gapping condition. (Their 8% response level was significantly less than chance if we assume chance = .5 by sign test, p< .05.) This unwillingness to use lexical causatives in the gapping condition cannot be attributed to their not perceiving a causal relationship. The high level of periphrastic responses in this condition (63%) indicates that the majority of subjects viewed the gapped events as causally connected, but in a sense different from that implied by the lexical causatives.

Relationship Between Marbles

		Contact	Gap
	1 event	24%	3%
Num of events	More than 1 event	76%	97%

Table 2: Percentage choosing one event vs. more than one event in Experiment

Table 2 shows the results with respect to the unitization hypothesis. Single events were reported more frequently when the marbles made physical contact (M=24%) than when they were gapped (M=3%) across both subjects, t_s (19)=2.5, p < .05, and items, t_i(15)=13.73, p < .001. This result is consistent with the hypothesis that the kinds of happenings described by lexical causatives are those that can be conceptualized as single events.

Discussion

The results are consistent with the predictions made by the contact criterion and the unitization hypothesis. However, problems arise when the contact criterion is generalized to a wider range of situations. It is not hard to find sentences that violate the contact criterion, as in (4).

(4) The landlord evicted the tenants.
    Nixon bombed Cambodia.

Both sentences in (4) imply causation in which the causer and causee don't make physical contact. The contact criterion, while useful, must not be the whole story. What, then, might allow people to group objects that don't make physical contact? In terms of the unitization hypothesis, what might allow people to view an extended chain of events as a single event?

The Role of Animacy. The answer might be linked to animacy. Animate causers have properties which may give them special status in causal interactions (Leslie, 1994; Talmy, 1976). One of these properties is *intention*. By means of intention, objects that are spatially distant might be made psychologically close, and as a consequent, causally direct. This hypothesis, in one form or another, has

been linked to the notion of direct causation by a number of linguists (e.g. Brennenstuhl & Wachowicz, 1974; Gergely & Bever, 1986; Kozinsky & Polinsky, 1994). Another property of animates is that they readily act as *ultimate causes*, that is, the very first cause of a causal chain (Delancey, 1991; Croft, 1990). They do this by being able to self-initiate their own actions and generate their own forces (Gelman, Durgin, Kaufman, 1995). Roughly speaking, an ultimate cause might be viewed as a direct cause by being the entity that produces the force that creates an effect. One nice feature of the ultimate cause hypothesis is that it fits nicely with the notion of 'windowing of attention' discussed by Talmy and 'metonymic clipping' by Wilkins and Van Valin (1993), that is, the idea that animate causers can stand in for the entire sequence of events leading to a result. In different ways, then, both hypotheses explain how direct causation might occur by means of animate agents. Linguistic support for this effect has been suggested by Schlesinger (1989). As he notes, "inanimate objects can be agents [of actions involving instruments] only if they act without mediation." The sentences in (5) exemplify this prediction.

(5) a. Two bullets wounded the president.
    b. *The rifle wounded the president with two bullets.
    c. The assassin wounded the president with two bullets.

The sentence in (5a) describes a happening involving physical contact between the agent and patient, allowing, by hypothesis, the agent to be inanimate. The sentences in (5b) and (5c) describe happenings in which the agent and patient do not make physical contact. As predicted, an inanimate agent, (5b), sounds odd while an animate agent, (5c), is acceptable.

Testing the effect of animacy. To test the effect of animacy, we modified the events used in Experiment 1. If animacy allows people to go beyond physical contact, replacing the initiating marble with a hand (indicating an animate agent) should allow people to form lexical causatives between the causer and the last marble, M3 (see Figure 3). If this is true, then the unitization hypothesis makes a further prediction. To the extent that subjects use lexical causatives when agents are animate, they should also tend to conceptualize these happenings as single events.

Experiment 2
Method
Subjects. The subjects were 20 Northwestern University students.

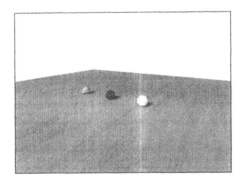

Figure 3. Causal chain initiated by inanimate causer

Causal chain initiated by animate causer

<u>Design and Procedure</u>. As in Experiment 1, the main factor of interest, *contact type*, was within subject and had two levels, contact and gap. The procedures were as those used in Experiment 1.

<u>Materials</u>. The animations were as used in Experiment 1, except that all of the initiating causers were animate, namely, a hand with arm and body attached in the background. In order to increase the number of sequences, the agents performed two kinds of actions. In half of the sequences, a hand flicked a marble to another marble, causing it to move. In the other half, a hand carried a marble to another marble, causing it to move.

Results

The pattern of results changed dramatically from Experiment 1. When given animate agents, subjects were willing to use lexical causatives in the absence of physical contact (42% as compared to 8% in Experiment 1) (Table 3).

Relationship Between Marbles

		Contact	Gap
	Lexical	61%	42%
Sentence Type	Periph.	23%	52%
	Total Causal	83%	94%

Table 3: Percentage of sentence types chosen in Experiment 2

However, even with animate agents, contact still had an effect on lexicalization. As in Experiment 1, lexical causatives were chosen more frequently when the marbles made contact (M=61%) than when they were gapped (M=42%) (significant across items, $t_i(15)$=2.6, p < .02, but not subjects, $t_s(19)$=1.66).

Relationship Between Marbles

		Contact	Gap
	1 event	29%	24%
Num of events	More than 1 event	71%	76%

Table 4: Percentage choosing one event vs. more than one event in Experiment 2

The results provided additional support for the unitization hypothesis. Animacy appeared to have an effect on how the events were enumerated. Subjects were willing to report single events even when the marbles did not make physical contact (see Table 4). In contrast with the pattern in Experiment 1, subjects were equally likely to see the happening as a single event whether the marbles made physical contact (M=29%) or were gapped (M=24%). Taken together, these results support the hypothesis that the kinds of happenings described by lexical causatives are those that can be conceptualized as single events.

Conclusions

Language may tell us something about the perception of cause. Specifically, people may differentiate two different kinds of causality, direct and indirect, and people may use the properties of physical contact and animacy in distinguishing between these two kinds of causality. The role played by these two properties can be summarized by the following conclusions (1) In mechanical causation (i.e. when the causing objects are inanimate), lexicalization is guided by the contact criterion; (2) In agentive causation (i.e. when the causing object objects are animate), lexicalization is guided by further factors, possibly intention or ultimate causation; and (3) lexicalization might be an index of whether a happening can be conceptualized (unitized) as a single event. The results are consistent with the possibility that the properties that determine how a causal event gets expressed are basic to the perception of events. Future research will focus on the nature of the animacy effect, as well as on the question of whether and when these distinctions are available to children.

References

Ammon, M. S. H. (1980). Development in the linguistic expression of causal relations: Comprehension of features of lexical and periphrastic causatives. Ph.D. dissertation, University of California, Berkeley.

Brennenstuhl, W. & Wachowicz, K. (1976). On the pragmatics of control. In H. Thompson & K. Whistler et al. (Eds.), *Proceedings of the Second Annual Meeting of the BLS.*

Bullock, M. & Gelman, R., & Baillargeon, R. (1982). The development of causal reasoning. In W. Friedman (ed.), *The Developmental Psychology of Time*. London: Academic Press.

Cohen L. B. & Oakes, L. M. (1993). How infants perceive a simple causal event. *Developmental psychology*, 29, 421-433.

Comrie, B. (1985). Causative verb formation and other verb-deriving morphology. In T. Shopen (Ed.). *Language typology and syntactic description*, vol 3: Grammatical categories and the lexicon. New York: Cambridge University Press.

Croft, W. A. (1990). Possible verbs and the structure of events. In S. L. Tsohatzidis (Ed.), *Meanings and prototypes: Studies on linguistic categorization*, Routledge, London.

Delancey, S. (1991). Event construal and case role assignment. *Boston Linguistics Society*, 17, 338-353.

Dowty, D. R. (1979). *Word Meaning and Montague Grammar*. Dordrect: Reidel.

Fisher, C. (in press). Structure and meaning in the verb lexicon: Input for a syntax-aided verb learning procedure.

Frawley, W. (1992). *Linguistic Semantics*, Erlbaum, Hillsdale, NJ.

Gelman, R., Durgin, F., Kaufman, L. (1995). Distinguishing between animates and inanimates: Not by motion alone. In D. Sperber, D. Premack, and A. J. Premack (Ed.), *Causal cognition : a multidisciplinary debate*. New York: Oxford University Press.

Gergely, G. & Bever, T. G. (1986). Related intuitions and the mental representation of causative verbs in adults and children. *Cognition*, 23, 211-277.

Givón, T. (1990). *Syntax: A functional typological introduction vol. I*. Philadelphia, PA: John Benjamins Publishing Company.

Haiman, J. (1980). The iconicity of grammar: Isomorphism and motivation. *Language*, 56, 515-540.

Haiman, J. (1983). Iconic and economic motivation. *Language*, 59, 781-819.

Kaiser, M. K., Proffitt, D. R., Whelan, S. M., & Hecht, H. (1992). Influence of animation dynamical judgments. *Journal of Experimental Psychology: Human Perception and Performance*, 18, 669-690.

Levin, B. & Rappaport Hovav, M. (1994). A preliminary analysis of causative verbs in English. *Lingua*, 92, 35-77.

Michotte, A. (1973). *The perception of causality*. London: Methuen.

Nedyalkov, V. P., & Silnitsky, G. G. (1973). The typology of morphological and lexical causatives. In F. Kiefer (Ed.), *Trends in Soviet Theoretical Linguistics*, 1-32. Dordrect-Holland: D. Reidel Publishing Company.

Kozinsky, I. & Polinsky, M. (1993). Causee and patient in the causative of transitive: Coding conflict or doubling of grammatical relations? In B. Comrie and M. Polinsky, *Causative and Transitivity*. Amsterdam: John Benjamins.

Leslie, A. M. (1982). The perception of causality in infants. *Perception*, 11, 173-524.

Parsons, T. (1994). *Events in the semantics of English: A study in subatomic semantics*. Cambridge, MA: The MIT Press.

Pinker, S. (1989). *Learnability and cognition: The acquisition of argument structure*. Cambridge, MA: The MIT Press.

Schlesinger, I. M. (19899). Instruments as agents: On the nature of semantic relations, *Journal of linguistics*, 25, 189-210.

Shibatani, M. (1976). The grammar of causative constructions: A conspectus, In M. Shibatani, (Ed.) *Syntax and Semantics. Vol 6: The grammar of causative constructions*, New York: Academic Press.

Shultz, T. (1982). Rules of causal attribution. *Monographs of the Society for Research in Child Development*, 47 (1).

Slobin, D. I. (in press). Why are grammaticizable notions special? - A reanalysis and a challenge to learning theory. To appear in S.C. Levinson (Ed.), *Language acquisition and conceptual development*, Cambridge Univ. Press.

Spelke, E. S. (1991). Physical knowledge in infancy: Reflections on Piaget's theory. IN S. Carey & R. Gelman (Eds.), *The Epigenesis of Mind: Essays on Biology and Cognition*. Hillsdale, NJ: Erlbaum.

Talmy, L. (1976). Semantic causative types. The grammar of causative constructions: A conspectus, In M. Shibatani, (ed.) *Syntax and Semantics. Vol 6: The grammar of causative constructions*, New York: Academic Press.

Talmy, L. (1983). How language structures space. In H. Pick and L. Acredolo (Eds.), *Spatial orientation: Theory, research, and application* (pp. 225-282). New York: Plenum.

Wierzbicka, A. (1988). Why "kill" does not mean "cause to die": The semantics of action sentences. *Foundations of Language*, 13, 491-528.

Wilkins, D. P., & Van Valin, R. D. (1993 manuscript). The case for case reopened: Agents and agency revisited. Center for Cognitive Science.

Woodward, A. L., Phillips, A. T., & Spelke, E. S. (1993). Infant's expectations about the motion of animate versus inanimate objects. *Proceedings of the 15th annual conference of the Cognitive Science Society*, Hillsdale, NJ: Lawrence Erlbaum Associates.

Mutability, Conceptual Transformation, and Context

Bradley C. Love
Department of Psychology
Northwestern University
2029 Sheridan Road
Evanston, IL 60208
loveb@nwu.edu

Abstract

Features differ in their mutability. For example, a robin could still be a robin even if it lacked a red breast; but it would probably not count as one if it lacked bones. I have hypothesized (Love & Sloman, 1995) that features are immutable to the extent other features depend on them. We can view a feature's mutability as a measure of transformational difficulty. In deriving new concepts, we often transform existing concepts (e.g. we can go from thinking about a robin to thinking about a robin without a red breast). The difficulty of this transformation, as measured by reaction time, increases with the immutability of the feature transformed. Conceptual transformations are strongly affected by context, but in a principled manner, also explained by feature dependency structure. A detailed account of context's effect on mutability is given, as well as corroborating data. I conclude by addressing how mutability-dependency theory can be applied to the study of similarity, categorization, conceptual combination, and metaphor.

1 Introduction: the importance of relations

Cognitive scientists have begun to gain an appreciation that concepts (in the psychological sense) are more than independent sets of features. Any account of concept representation must address the relations that exist among features. Relations help explain why some features are more central to a representation, while others are easily transformable. For instance, relations among features explain why it is difficult to imagine a normal robin without a heart, while imagining a robin without a red breast is more plausible. Having a red breast is a mutable feature of robins, while having a heart is an immutable feature of robins.

There have been varying accounts of why some features are relatively immutable, while others are mutable. On the theory-based view (e.g., Carey, 1985; Keil, 1989), the importance of the heart can be explained by appealing to a biological theory of how a robin functions. Such a theory would deem the heart central to our notion of what it means to be a normal robin, based on the web of relations in which the heart is embedded (e.g. "the heart *pumps* blood", "blood *carries* oxygen", "the brain *needs* oxygen", etc). The relations among features are labeled by the type of relation they represent (e.g. *carries*, *pumps*, *needs*). On this view (Murphy & Medin, 1985; Wellman, 1990), the concept robin coheres by virtue of the explanatory relations that hold between its components (and perhaps those of other concepts).

In contrast, the feature "has a red breast" does not play as critical of a role in the overall explanatory coherence of the concept robin, making the feature more mutable. That is, it is easy to imagine a robin not having a red breast (perhaps the robin has a brown breast). Not having a red breast does not have serious ramifications for a theory of what it means to be a robin.

The story becomes more complex when we consider that the mutability of a feature can vary with context. For instance, in certain contexts, the feature "has a red breast" can become more immutable. If one is reminded or alerted to the mating purposes of having a red breast, the feature will become more immutable. Effectively, the context of mating highlights features with relations in common with the feature "has a red breast", making "has a red breast" more immutable. The effects of context on categorization and similarity ratings are well documented (Medin et. al., 1993). Context can facilitate the interpretation of noun-noun compounds, analogies, and nominative metaphors (Gerrig & Murphy, 1992; Gick & Holyoak, 1980; Gildea and Glucksberg, 1983).

2 The dependency stance: an implemented theory

The theory-based view can explain why certain features are more critical or immutable, but the explanation has an ad hoc flavor and seems overly complex. It is unclear how a theory-based model could be implemented that predicts which features of a concept are mutable and which are immutable. It is difficult to see how qualitative statements like "plays a critical role in the overall explanatory coherence of the concept " can be made formal and yield quantitative predictions. The problem becomes more acute when we allow context to vary.

Since relations among features are labeled by their type, it is not possible to employ a simple algorithm that calculates the importance of a feature, since different types of relations are not directly comparable. One could overcome this difficulty by employing a simpler representational scheme that still captured the basic intuitions of the theory-based view.

I propose (Love & Sloman, 1995) that all types of relations can be collapsed to one primitive type, namely the unidirectional relation of *depends*; for the purposes of calculating feature mutabilities. In such a scheme, the

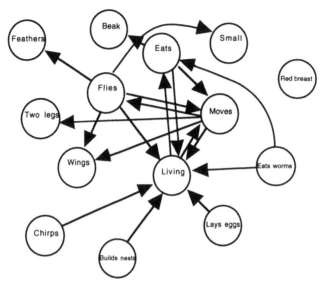

Figure 1: The arrows point from a feature to one that it depends
upon, as rated by subjects (Love & Sloman, 1995).

relations *pumps*, *carries*, and *needs* would all be collapsed to the pairwise relation *depends*. Faced with the challenge of equating different types of relations, people may resort to using only dependency information in certain tasks. Figure 1 illustrates a dependency graph, in which relations among features are only represented as dependencies.

Having many features depending upon a given feature will make it more difficult to transform the given feature since the transformation will disrupt the representation of the concept. Other features that depend upon the immutable feature will also change and this can have ramifications for the entire representation. For example, if you were told that a particular robin did not have wings, you would need to update your default assumption that the robin can fly, since "can fly" depends on "has wings". Performing conceptual transformations across mutable features is relatively easy because other features are unaffected by changes in mutable features. We would expect reaction time to be slower for transformations performed across immutable features. In experiment 1, I test this prediction.

Having one type of relation makes it possible to compare all relations on the basis of magnitude. The mutability of a feature can be calculated by summing the number and strength of the other features that depend on it, which is a straightforward computation, yet accounts for subjects' mutability ratings (Love & Sloman, 1995). Obviously, there are tasks that require people to attend to the labels of relations, such as some reasoning tasks, but interestingly, such tasks require considerably more effort and processing time than tasks that do not demand labeled relations (Ratcilff & Mckoon, 1989).

By positing that people employ a dependency-like representation, an explanation of how context affects perceived mutability is suggested. When forming a concept, one draws upon a huge database of knowledge, only using a fraction of it in forming any particular concept (Barsalou,

1993). An individual can conceive of a category in a number of different ways, depending on context and current goals. Studying these effects is critical to our understanding of concept representation as context can dictate which features are included in forming a concept.

Since a feature is immutable to the extent that other features depend upon it, forming a concept from different sets of features (in different contexts) should affect feature mutability in a principled way. More precisely, if a feature is introduced (or highlighted) that depends upon a given feature, the given feature will become more immutable. Concretely, if I speak extensively of the mating practices of robins, and you know that certain aspects of the mating process depend upon the participants' color, then "has a red breast" should be more immutable in this context than in a context centered around flight.

3 Testing the dependency model

Two studies were conducted to test the following predictions: i. Features rated as mutable should be easier to transform. Subjects should be faster at imagining derivative concepts that vary in a mutable feature than in a immutable feature. ; ii. This transformation is affected by context in a principled way explained by the dependency structure of the representation.

3.1 Experiment 1: Mutability as Transformation

If subjects are performing a transformation of the concept robin to a derivative representation of robin when providing ratings for statements like, "How easily can you imagine a robin that does not have wings?", then one would expect that the ratings for such questions would correspond to the actual difficulty of the transformation. Furthermore, the difficult of a transformation should be measurable through reaction time. Transformations of highly immutable features should take longer than transformations over mutable features. In experiment 1, I tested this prediction.

Method

Subjects. Subjects in the feature mutability rating task were 20 undergraduates from Brown University. They were paid for their participation. Subjects in the reaction time task were 20 undergraduates from Northwestern University. They received course credit in an introductory psychology course for their participation.

Materials and procedure. The stimuli consisted of features from 4 categories (pine tree, robin, cucumber, and apple) taken from Dean and Sloman (1995). Mutability ratings were collected by having subjects answer questions like, "How easily can you imagine a robin without wings?" Subjects responded with a number between 0 and 1 that reflected the ease of the transformation. The number of features per category varied from 17 to 25. The 3 most mutable and immutable features from each category were chosen for the reaction time task, for a total of 24 features. Subjects were shown the name of the category and the feature on a Macintosh computer. They pressed the spacebar when they could imagine a member of the category not having the listed feature, but being normal in every other respect.

To ensure that any difference in reaction time between mutable and immutable features could not be attributed to the goodness, accessibility, salience, or reading times of the features; a feature confirmation task was included as a control. The same stimuli were used with the addition of 24 distractors. Subjects were instructed to press "p" if the category had the given feature, and to press "q" if the category did not possess the feature. Since all the features of interest clearly belonged to their category, 32 distractor features that did not belong to the presented category were included to ensure that subjects would not be biased towards an affirmative response.

Results

All observations more than 3 standard deviations above the mean were discarded (the cutoffs were 14576 msecs for the imagining task, and 3341 msecs for the feature confirmation task). For analysis, reaction times were separated into two groups: mutable and immutable. Subjects took longer to imagine instances of a category varying in an immutable feature (t(539)=4.11, p<.001) with a mean of 5153 msecs for the immutable features and a mean of 4355 msecs for the mutable features. The difference was significant.

There was no statistically significant effect in the control task. Feature's were confirmed with a mean response time of 1373 msecs for the immutable features, compared to 1355 msecs for the mutable features (t(459)=.39, p>.70).

Discussion

As predicted, the time to perform a conceptual transformation varied with the immutability of the feature transformed. The effect cannot be accounted for by any combination of frequency, accessibility, salience, reading

time, etc., since any such effect would be manifest in the feature confirmation control task.

The results suggest that mutability ratings indicate how easy it is to perform a conceptual transformation across a feature's dimension. Such a position is consistent with the finding that immutable features tend to have other features depending on them (Love & Sloman, 1995). Performing a transformation across an immutable feature is more difficult because the other features depending on the immutable feature will be affected by the transformation.

3.2 Experiment 2: Transformation in Context

If the immutability of a feature is determined by the other features that depend upon it, then introducing (or highlighting) features that depend upon a feature should increase the immutability of the feature being depended on. For example, a context of "can fly" should make "has wings" more immutable, but since *depends* is a directional relation, "has wings" should have little effect on the immutability of "can fly". Experiment 2 tested this prediction.

Method

Subjects. Subjects were 20 undergraduates from Northwestern University who received course credit in an introductory psychology course for their participation.

Materials and procedure. The stimuli consisted of a subset of features from 4 categories (apple, chair, guitar, and robin) taken from Rosch, Mervis, Gray, Johnson, and Boyes-Braem (1976). The subset was chosen to allow A-B-C feature triads to be formed from the same category such that feature A depends upon feature B, but feature B does not depend upon feature A, and feature C shares no dependency relations with either features A or B. The dependency ratings were collected from subjects by Love and Sloman (1995). An example of such an A-B-C triad for the category robin is "can fly", "has wings", and "has a red breast".

Subjects rated the mutability of the features in the A and B sets by answering questions on a Macintosh computer such as, "How easily can you imagine the robin without wings?" Responses were made by pressing a number labeled key, with 1 indicating that the modified token was very easy to imagine and 9 indicating that the token was very difficult to imagine. The context was varied by having a feature in the triad precede the rated feature for 3 seconds in a statement like, "The robin can fly." Each subject saw only half of the stimuli to avoid having any subject rate a feature twice.

Results

The results are listed in table 1. When a feature was preceded by another feature that depends on it, the feature was judged more immutable than when it was preceded by a feature it did not share a dependency relation, with a mean of 7.37 compared to 5.52 (t(197)=4.85, p<.001).

This result did not hold for the reversal. When a feature was preceded by another feature that the rated feature depends on, the feature was not judged more immutable than when it was preceded by a feature that it shared no dependency relation: mean of 5.16 compared to 5.06 (t(198)=.25, p>.80).

preceding context	feature rated	mean of rated features
A (------->)	B	7.37
C (no relation)	B	5.52
B (<-------)	A	5.16
C (no relation)	A	5.06

Table 1: Feature A depends upon feature B, but feature B does not depend upon feature A. Features A and B share no dependency relations with feature C. Higher ratings indicate that the feature is more immutable.

Discussion

Experiment 2 supports the prediction that mutability context effects are mediated through dependency relations. Furthermore, it dispels the notion that dependencies are simple associations and that mutability is nothing more than the connectivity of relations, since dependency priming was shown to be asymmetric (e.g. the context of "has wings" did not make "can fly" more immutable, but the context "can fly" did make "has wings" more immutable.).

It may seem strange to some readers to call a feature presented on a computer screen a context. The rationale for this decision is that a richer context would activate the preceding feature. It seems reasonable to assume that a rich context about reproduction and birds would activate the feature "can lay eggs". By presenting the phrase "The robin can lay eggs.", I circumvent the need for a rich context.

4. The Role of Mutability and Dependency in Cognitive Processes

4.1 Categorization and Similarity

Mutability plays a role in determining the relative importance of features in judgments of category membership. A token that matches a category representation in all but a mutable dimension should be a better candidate for category membership than a token that differs in an immutable dimension (Medin & Shoben, 1988). For example, we expect robins without red breasts to be categorized as robins with higher probability than robins that do not eat.

Love and Sloman have unpublished results that support this view. We asked subjects questions like, "Can something be a robin if it does not have a red breast?" The percentage of "yes" responses was highly correlated with mutability judgments in all four categories. I predict that context affects these judgments in the same way that it affects mutability ratings.

Results in a similarity rating task mimic the categorization results. Subjects rate a token lacking a mutable feature as more similar to an ideal category member than a token lacking an immutable feature. This result holds over the entire continuum of feature mutabilities (as in the categorization result). This result suggests that models of similarity should not limit themselves to considering feature matches and mismatches (Tversky, 1977), but should also take into account the mutability of features when calculating similarity. Some features seem to count more than others in determining similarity. Commonalties and differences should be weighted by their immutabilities.

In contrast, Gentner, Markman, and Medin (submitted) propose that similarity comparisons involve an analogy-like process in which representations are aligned based on labeled relations. Distant analogies do require representations that have labeled relations. Calculating the similarity between an atom and a solar system may be an entirely different type of similarity process than calculating the similarity between a baseball and a tennis ball. A baseball and a tennis ball are easily comparable on perceptual properties and do not demand a comparison process that utilizes labeled relations. I would expect that the first similarity task would take longer because it requires the use of labeled relations for comparison. The distinction between using labeled relations and collapsing across relations in favor of dependencies is deeply related to dual processing theories (Sloman, 1996) which pit slow symbolic processes against fast associative processes. Perhaps, instead of proposing two distinct reasoning systems, a theorist only needs to outline the conditions under which relation labels are used instead of being discarded in favor of dependency information.

4.2 Mapping Processes in Metaphor and Conceptual Combination

Mutability may play a key role in the mapping process involved in interpreting nominative metaphors and noun-noun combinations. One can view the interpretation of a nominative metaphor as involving processes that transfer a property from the base noun to the target noun. Mutability theory constrains this mapping process. Immutable features of the target noun will resist conceptual change, while mutable features are more likely to accede to change.

For instance, the metaphor "This desk is a junkyard" can be interpreted as meaning the desk is messy since "is orderly" is a mutable feature of desk. Notice the mapping does not drastically transform or discard an immutable feature of desk, like "has a flat surface". Potential mappings that destroy immutable features of the target are rejected. This application of mutability theory does not suggest mappings, but constrains which mappings can be actualized.

An additional constraint on mapping processes is that the dependency structure of the target must be able to support the feature mapped over from the base. It is much more plausible to interpret the noun-noun combination *frog car*, as a green car, than as a car that hops, because the feature "can hop" has dependencies that are not satisfied in the target. Most cars can't hop. The dependency structure of car cannot support the addition of the feature "can hop". This constraint may also prove useful in searching for possible mappings.

5. Conclusion

I have given an account of how different types of relations can be collapsed to a dependency relation for the purposes of calculating feature mutability. I have also given an account of how context affects the transformation of features.

A question remains: If what is immutable varies with context, then what is the core of a category, if anything? Everything is not as slippery as it seems. Certain features will be present across contexts. Working cars always have engines, people always have brains (even if it doesn't always appear that way), etc. Some features are immutable across contexts. There are also strong constraints on what can be seen as immutable, such as a temporal order constraint (Byrne et. al., 1995; Kahneman & Miller, 1986) which can be viewed as another type of dependency (current events depend on past events). Ahn & Lassaline (1995) have shown that effects are more mutable than causes.

Also, not everything at the core of a category is related to immutability. Some categories have defining properties. For instance, a *red truck* has to be red, but no features of *red truck* depend on the feature "is red". Still, internal structure and dependencies are what scaffolds are understanding of categories.

Acknowledgments

I thank Steven Sloman, Edward Wisniewski, Dedre Gentner, Lance Rips, and the anonymous reviewers for their comments.

References

Ahn, W., & Lassaline, M.E. (1995). Causal Structure in Categorization, *Proceedings of the Seventeenth Annual Conference of the Cognitive Science Society*, 521-526. Pittsburgh, PA.

Barsalou, L.W. (1993). Flexibility, Structure, and Linguistic Vagary in Concepts: Manifestations of a System of Perceptual Symbols. In A.F. Collins, S.E. Gathercole, M.A. Conway, & P.E. Morris (Eds.), *Theories of memory*. Hillsdale, N.J.: Lawrence Erlbaum Associates.

Byrne, R.M., Culhane, R., & Tass, A. (1995). The temporality Effect in Thinking about What Might Have Been, *Proceedings of the Seventeenth Annual Conference of the CognitiveScience Society*, 385-390. Pittsburgh, PA.

Carey, S. (1985). *Conceptual Change in Childhood*. Cambridge: MIT Press.

Collins, A. & Michalski, R. (1989). The logic of plausible reasoning: a core theory. *Cognitive Science, 13*, 1-50.

Dean, W. & Sloman, S. A. work in progress.

Gentner, G., Markman, A. B., & Medin, D. L. (submitted). The Structure of Similarity.

Gerrig, R.J., & Murphy, G.L. (1992). Contextual influences on the comprehension of complex concepts. *Language & Cognitive Processes.*, 7, 205-230.

Gick, M. L., Holyoak, K. J. (1980). Analogical problem solving. *Cognitive Psychology*, 12, 306-355.

Gildea, P., Glucksberg, S. (1983). On understanding metaphor: The role of context. *Journal of Verbal Learning & Verbal Behavior*, 22, 577-590.

Kahneman, D. & Miller, D. T. (1986). Norm Theory: Comparing Reality to Its Alternatives. *Psychological Review, 93*, 136-153.

Keil, F. C. (1989). *Semantic and conceptual development: An ontological perspective*. Cambridge, MA: Harvard University Press.

Love, B.C., & Sloman, S.A. (1995). Mutability and the Determinants of Conceptual Transformability. *Proceedings of the Seventeenth Annual Conference of the CognitiveScience Society*, 654-659. Pittsburgh, PA.

Medin, D. L., Goldstone, R. L., Gentner, D. (1993). Respects for similarity. *Psychological Review*, 100, 254-278.

Medin, D. L. & Shoben, E. J. (1988). Context and structure in conceptual combination. *Cognitive Psychology, 20*, 158-190.

Murphy, G. L. & Medin, D. L. (1985). The role of theories in conceptual coherence. *Psychological Review, 92*, 289-316.

Ratcliff, R. & McKoon, G. (1989). Similarity information versus relational information: Differences in the time course of retrieval. *Cognitive Psychology*, 2, 139-155.

Rosch, E., Mervis, C. B., Gray, W., Johnson, D., & Boyes-Braem, P. (1976). Basic Objects in natural categories. *Cognitive Psychology.*, 8, 382-439.

Sloman, S. A. (1996). The empirical case for two systems of reasoning. *Psychological Bulletin*, 119, 3-22.

Tversky, A. (1977). Features of Similarity. *Psychological Review, 84*, 327-352.

Wellman, H. M. (1990). *The child's theory of mind*. Cambridge: MIT Press.

On putting milk in coffee:
The effect of thematic relations on similarity judgments.

Edward Wisniewski
Department of Psychology
Northwestern University
2029 Sheridan Road
Evanston, IL 60208
(847) 467-1624
edw@nwu.edu

Miriam Bassok
Department of Psychology
University of Chicago
5458 S. University Avenue
Chicago, IL 60637
(312) 702-1962
m-bassok@uchicago.edu

Abstract

All existing accounts of similarity assume that it is a function of matching and mismatching attributes between mental representations. However, Bassok and Medin (1996) found that the judged similarity of sentences does not necessarily reflect the degree of overlap between the properties of paired stimuli. Rather, similarity judgments are often mediated by a process of thematic integration and reflect the degree to which stimuli can be integrated into a common thematic scenario. We present results of a study which extend this surprising finding by showing that it also applies to similarity ratings of objects and occurs whether or not subjects explain their judgments. Also, consistent with the Bassok and Medin findings, the tendency towards thematic integration was more pronounced when the paired stimuli shared few attributes--but was still an important factor in similarity judgments between objects which shared many attributes. We discuss the implications of these findings for models of cognitive processes which use similarity as an explanatory construct.

Introduction

It is taken as self evident that the similarity between two things is a function of their matching and mismatching features. For example, in judging how similar a robin is to a canary a person might identify matching features such as "they are birds," "they have wings," "they fly," "they have beaks, " "they have feathers," and mismatching features such as "one is red and the other is yellow," "one eats worms and the other eats seeds. " This sense of similarity has played an extremely important role in theories of analogy, metaphor, categorization, concept learning, induction, and conceptual combination and is a major component of formal models of these processes. For example, concept learning models compute the likelihood that a novel instance belongs to category based primarily on how well the features of the instance match those in the category's representation. As a second example, in models of induction, a major factor which determines whether a feature associated with one category will be generalized to a second category is the degree of feature overlap between the category representations. Finally, in models of analogy, interpretation and inference are largely determined by the overlap between relational features in the base and target domains.

Much recent work on similarity judgments has investigated how people determine and weight these matching and mismatching features. Inspired by structural-alignment models of analogy (e.g., Gentner, 1983), this research has characterized similarity as a comparison process in which people attempt to align or put into correspondence mental representations (Goldstone, 1994a; Markman, A. & Gentner, 1993; Medin, Goldstone, & Gentner, 1993). This work has identified important constraints on how this alignment is carried out.

This view of similarity notwithstanding, Bassok and Medin (1996) found that similarity judgments do not necessarily reflect the degree of overlap between the properties of the paired stimuli. Rather, contrary to every existing account of similarity, similarity judgments are often mediated by a process of thematic integration and reflect the degree to which paired stimuli can be integrated into a common thematic scenario. Specifically, these researchers asked undergraduate students to rate the degree of similarity between various pairs of simple noun-verb-noun statements and to explain their ratings. When the statements had common verbs (e.g., "The carpenter <u>fixed</u> the chair" and "The electrician <u>fixed</u> the radio") the explanations were consistent with the prevalent definition of similarity (e.g., "Similar because in both statements a professional is doing his job). However, when the statements had common nouns (e.g., "The <u>carpenter</u> fixed the <u>chair</u>" and "The <u>carpenter</u> sat on the <u>chair</u>"), 61% of the explanations generated by the participants were causal or temporal scenarios (e.g., "Similar because the carpenter sat on the chair to see whether he had fixed it well").

Thematic similarity has been previously documented only in young children (see E. Markman, 1989, for a review) and in adults from illiterate cultures (Luria, 1976). In one study, Luria (1976) had illiterate adults compare pairs of objects, asking them what the objects had in common and in what way they were alike. These adults sometimes responded by noting thematic relations between the objects. For example, when one illiterate adult from Uzbekistan was asked by Luria, "what do water and blood have in common?" he responded: "What's alike about them is that water washes off all sorts of dirt, so it can wash off blood too" (p. 82). Given that the undergraduate students in the Bassok and Medin (1995) study were neither young nor illiterate, their results are extremely surprising. That is, such results cannot be simply explained away by lack of knowledge or insufficient understanding of the task at hand. If these results reflect a robust and prevalent tendency to use a process of thematic integration for computing similarity then they should be seriously considered by theoretical accounts of similarity and cognitive processes which rely on similarity as an explanatory construct. Our study follows up on these findings in order to examine their validity and generality. It was designed to answer three interrelated follow-up questions:

(1). Are thematic scenarios unique to comparison of statements ? It is possible that thematic integration mediates similarity judgments only when the stimuli are statements, because statements may induce a tendency for story construction. Our study examined whether thematic integration also mediates similarity judgments for simple pairs of object (e.g., milk-coffee; milk-lemonade). That is, we examined whether and to what extent people consider two things to be more similar if, in addition to having matching attributes (e.g., both are beverages), they are thematically related (e.g., one puts milk into coffee).

(2). Is thematic intergation more likely when it is difficult to align stimuli? It is possible that thematic integration affects similarity judgments only when the paired stimuli cannot be aligned in a satisfactory way. Medin and Bassok (1996) found that thematic scenarios were very rare when the paired statements could be structurally aligned (6% for matching verbs). Extending this logic to similarity between objects predicts a greater tendency for thematic integration when the stimuli can only be poorly aligned (e.g., milk-cow share very few common attributes) than when they can be readily aligned (e.g., milk-coffee share many common attributes). To test this possibility, our study examined the relative effect of thematic integration for object pairs that shared either many or few common attributes.

(3). Does thematic integration affect similarity judgments when people do not explain their ratings? The results of Bassok and Medin (1996) are based on an analysis of explanations that accompanied similarity ratings. However, explanations may change the process by which people arrive at similarity judgments and therefore either over or underestimate the prevalence of thematic scenarios. Alternatively, one could argue that thematic scenarios appear only in post-hoc explanations of judgments but do not affect the process by which people construe similarity (e.g., Nisbett & Wilson, 1977). Our study examined whether thematic integration actually affects similarity ratings, and whether such effects differ when people explain and do not explain their ratings.

Method

Participants. 128 Northwestern University undergraduates participated as part of a course requirement.

Materials. The stimuli were 12 quintuplets of objects, each consisting of a base and four targets. Two targets shared many attributes with the base (M) and the other two shared few attributes with the base (F). The M and T targets in each pair were chosen to be equally similar to the base in terms of their common attributes. However, one of the targets in each pair was thematically related to the base (T) and the other was not. That is, the four targets in each quintuplet had the following structure: MT, M, FT, F. The 12 quintuplets used in our study appear in Table 1.

Four lists of 12 base-target pairs were created by randomly selecting three base-target pairs of each of the four types (MT, M, FT, F), subject to the constraint that only one base-target pair from each quintuplet appeared in a list. The 12 base-target pairs of each list were then typed on sheets of paper, each above a seven-pont similarity rating scale, two per page, in a random order. This procedure yielded one six-page rating booklet per list. In addition, the pages of each form were put in reverse order to yield two alternative booklets per list.

Procedure. Participants read instructions telling them that they would see some pairs of common, everyday things, and that they would have to rate how similar the two things are. If a subject thought a pair of things was very similar, they should circle a 7. If they thought they were not at all similar they should circle a 1. Subjects were instructed to use the other numbers between 1 and 7 to indicate in between degrees of similarity. Participants in the Explanation condition were further instructed to write down an explanation for their rating in the space below the rating scale, i.e., to explain why they thought the two things had the degree of similarity that they did.

Participants were run in groups of 2-4, and each group was randomly assigned to either the Explanation (N = 64) or No Explanation condition (N = 64). Each of the four base-target lists was rated by 16 participants in each condition (8 participants per each order of the rating booklet). The task took about 15 minutes to complete.

Base	MT target	M target	FT target	F target
milk	coffee	lemonade	cow	horse
ship	lifeboat	canoe	sailor	soldier
car	tow truck	pickup truck	mechanic	plumber
chair	table	bed	carpenter	electrician
telephone	ans. machine.	tape recorder	receptionist	waitress
tie	suit	dress	man	woman
chisel	hammer	screwdriver	sculpture	painting
cat	mouse	hamster	veternarian	pediatrician
cup	kettle	pan	tea	wine
fly	spider	beetle	screen	curtain
peanut butter	jelly	cream cheese	knife	fork
apple pie	ice cream	jello	baker	tailor

Table 1: Quintuplets of base and target objects used in the study

Results

Similarity ratings. We performed a 2 X 2 X 2 mixed ANOVA with condition (explanation versus no explanation) as the between-subjects factor and thematic relation (absent versus present) and attribute overlap (many versus few) as the within-subjects factors. Table 2 shows the average similarity ratings in the Explanation and No Explanation conditions for the four types of base-target pairs (MT, M, FT, F).

As one would expect, similarity ratings for targets with many common attributes (M and MT) were significantly higher than for targets with few common attributes (F and FT), $F(1, 127) = 399.34$, MSE = 642.2, $p < .001$. Importantly, consistent with the findings of Bassok and Medin (1996), the existence of a thematic relation between the base and target significantly affected similarity ratings (MT + FT > M + T), $F(1, 127) = 66.63$, MSE = 81.21, $p < .001$.

The interaction between attribute overlap and thematic relation was also highly significant ($F[1, 127] = 75.87$, MSE = 43.41, $p < .001$). That is, the effect of thematic relations on similarity judgments was significantly larger when the targets had few than when they had many attributes in common with the base ([FT-F] > [MT-M]), although even the difference between the ratings for the MT and M pairs was statistically significant ($t[127] = 2.38$, SME =.089, $p < .02$). These results indicate that thematic integration can mediate similarity judgments even when the base and target can be readily aligned in terms of their common attributes.

As can be seen by comparing the two columns of Table 2, there was no reliable difference between the Explanation and No Explanation conditions ($F < 1$) and condition did not interact with either attribute overlap, $F(1, 127) = 1.64$, MSE = 2.64, $p < .21$, or with thematic relations ($F < 1$). Of importance, there was no three way interaction between these variables ($F < 1$). That is, explanations did not affect either the pattern or the magnitude of similarity ratings.

In general, the findings held across the particular items. An ANOVA on the item means revealed the same pattern of significant and nonsignificant findings as in the subject ANOVA. We also compared the rating of each FT pair with its corresponding F pair and each MT pair with its corresponding M pair. Every FT pair had a higher similarity rating than its F pair. However, only half of the MT pairs had higher ratings than their corresponding M pairs. Thus, unlike the subject mean ratings, the difference between the item mean ratings for the MT and M pairs failed to reach statistical significance, ($t[11] = 1.35$, SME = .163, $p < .21$).

Because the presence versus absence of thematic relations was a within-subjects factor, it is possible that the results could be explained by a demand characteristic. In particular, subjects may have noticed obvious thematic relations between some object pairs and not others and assumed that they should give higher ratings to those items which shared the thematic relation. If subjects were using this strategy, then the difference between the ratings of the thematic and non-thematic pairs (e.g., FT vs. F, between subjects) should be relatively higher in the second than in the first half of the rating form. This finding, however, was not obtained: There was no statistically significant interaction between presentation order (first versus second half) and thematic relation (absent versus present).

Justifications. Given that there was no difference between the Explanation and No Explanation conditions, the explanations generated by participants can shed further light on the effect of thematic integration on similarity judgments. Below we report results from a preliminary analysis of the explanations. This preliminary analysis was performed by one of the authors and awaits validation by independent judges.

The explanations were coded into three categories: Thematic, Attributional, and Uninformative. Explanations were coded as Thematic if they explicitly referred to a thematic relation between the base and the target, regardless of whether they also included references to attributional matches and mismatches. Examples included: "some people put milk in their coffee" and "you don't milk a horse." In some cases, thematic justifications also included attributional matches (e.g., "milk is produced from a cow and cows can be whitish like milk is in color"). In the present analysis we do not distinguish between purely thematic explanations and mixtures of thematic and attributional explanations. Explanations were coded as Attributional if they only included references to attributional matches and mismatches. Examples included: "they (milk and coffee) are both liquids that one can consume and digest," "both (milk and lemonade) are refreshing drinks," "both (milk and cow) can be consumed and both can be white," "(milk and horse) are not similar, one is liquid the other solid, one is living the other inanimate." Explanations were coded as Uninformative when they included general statements such as "there are no similarities I can see," "they are related." Blanks (i.e., no explanation) were also coded as Uninformative. Table 3 shows the distribution of these three types of explanations for the four types of base-target pairs (MT, M, FT, F).

Base-Target correspondence	Explanation	No Explanation
MT: Many attr. + Thematic relation	4.88	4.83
M: Many attributes	4.71	4.54
FT: Few attrib. + Thematic relation	3.12	3.29
F: Few attributes	1.79	1.84

Table 2: Average similarity ratings for the four types of base-target correspondence.

466

Base-Target correspondence	Thematic	Attributional	Uninformative
MT: Many attr. + Thematic	29%	69%	2%
M: Many attributes	2%	96%	2%
FT: Few attrib. + Thematic	71%	19%	10%
F: Few attributes	32%	40%	28%

Table 3: Percentage of explanation types generated for the four types of base-target pairs.

As shown in Table 3, the distribution of the explanations is consistent with the pattern of thematic effects documented by the ratings (see Table 2). First, there were higher proportions of thematic explanations for items which shared a thematic relation (50% for MT and FT) compared to those which did not (17% for M and F). In corresponding fashion, the similarity ratings were higher for items which shared a thematic relation. There also was a general tendency towards thematic integration when items shared few (52% for FT and F) versus many attributes (16% for MT and M). Finally, the distribution of thematic explanations for targets with many vs. few attributes mirrored the interaction between attribute overlap and thematic relations observed for the ratings. Specifically, the difference in frequency of thematic explanations between the FT and F targets (39%) was greater than that between the MT and M targets (27%).

Of interest, when the base and target could not be readily aligned in terms of common attributes, participants generated many thematic explanations even for the F targets that did not bear an obvious thematic relation to the base (32%). Participants were sometimes quite creative in thematically relating these items to explain why they were similar (e.g., "a fancy ship could employ a tailor"). These explanations were the closest to those found by Bassok and Medin (1996), because the statements used in their study were not chosen to be thematically related (i.e., did not fit familiar scripts). Other thematic explanations for the F targets seemed to reflect an implicit contrast with familiar thematic relations (e.g., "you don't milk horses," "women do not usually wear ties").

Of importance, note that thematic explanations were not a peculiarity of a few participants. Rather, 89% of the 64 participants in the Explanation condition generated at least one thematic relation in explaining their similarity ratings. The median number of thematic explanations per participant (out of 12 responses in their rating booklets) was 3.5, and the average was 5.1. Moreover, only a handful of these mature and educated participants (about 5%) explicitly pointed out that these thematic relations do not make the paired objects similar to each other.

Discussion

Our findings support and extend Bassok and Medin's (1996) surprising finding that, in addition to comparison of common and distinctive attributes, similarity judgments are mediated by the thematic integration of the paired stimuli into a common scenario. First, the current study shows that the effect of thematic relations on similarity judgments is not unique to ratings of sentences but applies to ratings of objects as well. Moreover, thematic integration is not unique

to situations in which people explain their ratings. In fact, participants who did not explain their judgments gave nearly identical ratings to the same items (see Table 2), indicating that thematic relations affected their judgments as well. The effect of thematic integration on similarity judgments was apparent both in the magnitude of similarity ratings (Table 2) and in the explanations that accompanied these ratings (Table 3).

Also, consistent with the results which Bassok and Medin (1996) found for sentences, thematic integration was much higher when the stimuli could not be readily aligned. Specifically, thematic relations carried more weight in similarity judgments when the paired objects shared few than when they shared many common attributes. Nevertheless, our findings argue against the view that thematic relations only play a role in similarity judgments when there is little attributional similarity. Even among items that shared many attributes, almost one-third of the subjects listed thematic relations, and their ratings were higher for items which shared many attributes and a thematic relation compared to those which only shared many attributes (i.e., the MT versus M pairs). This finding is especially striking when one notes that the MT items (e.g., milk-coffee) shared many attributes but only a single thematic relation. Yet, this single thematic relation influenced similarity ratings and explanations.

One could argue that, despite our efforts to equate the number of common attributes in the paired targets (MT and M, FT and F), those which were thematically related to the base also had more common attributes with the base. We are currently collecting data to test this possibility, but we believe that it is very unlikely. We have divided each explanation into specific reasons given to explain why the pairs were similar or different (excluding uninformative reasons, we coded 1171 such reasons). The average number of attributional matches for the MT targets was actually slightly lower than for the M targets (1.2 vs. 1.5 matches per item, such as "both liquids"). Similarly, the average number of attributional matches for the FT targets was slightly lower than for the F targets (.19 vs. .23 matches per item, such as "both can be white,"). Thus, if there were differences in shared attributes between items, it would appear that they would work against our hypothesis. Obviously, it is difficult to explain why the ratings of the FT items (e.g., milk cow) were approximately 1.75 times higher than those of the F items (e.g., milk-horse) by suggesting that it was only due to differences in the number of common attributes. Recall also that the rating of every FT item was higher than its corresponding F item. It is unlikely that we unintentionally chose every FT item to have more common attributes when we purposely attempted to avoid such discrepancies.

These findings raise two important questions. First, what is the best processing level account of these results? One possibility is that people easily notice the salient, pre-existing thematic relations between our stimuli. These relations then influence judgments (perhaps because the meaning of the word "similarity" is ambiguous). However, Bassok and Medin (1996) showed that in explaining their similarity ratings, subjects actually constructed novel thematic relations between sentences. Similarly, novel thematic integrations were generated for the F targets in our study. Another possibility is that people's responses reflect an interaction between processes that are stimulus-driven and those that are driven by the type of task. That is, properties of the stimuli (e.g., having common attributes, being thematically related) may be difficult to override even though the task instructions are incompatible with those properties. In a recent sudy of ours, subjects who were asked to list the commonalities and differences between pairs of objects sometimes listed thematic relations even though the instructions described an example in which the commonalities and differences only involved attributes.

Second, what are the theoretical implications of these results? Most researchers are interested in factors which influence similarity judgments to the extent that these factors are relevant to cognitive processes which rely on similarity, such as similarity-based learning, categorization, conceptual combination, probabilistic reasoning, etc. Currently, we are examining whether and how thematic integration affects such processes. Previous work suggests that, indeed, probability judgments (Tversky & Kahneman, 1983) and conceptual combination (Wisniewski, in press) are sometimes mediated by thematic associations rather than by feature comparison. Clearly, future work needs to address these questions in order to understand the role that thematic relations play in processes that use similarity and to clarify the extent to which models of these processes must be extended.

References

Bassok, M., & Medin, D. L. (1996). Birds of a feather flock together: Similarity judgments with semantically-rich stimuli. Manuscript submitted for publication.

Gentner, D. (1983). Structure-mapping: A theoretical framework for analogy. Cognitive Science, 7, 155-170.

Goldstone, R.L. (1994). Similarity, interactive activation and mapping. Journal of Experimental Psychology: Learning, Memory, and Cognition, 20(1), 3-28.

Luria, A. R. (1976). Cognitive development: Its cultural and social foundations. Cambridge, MA: Harvard University Press.

Markman, A. B., & Gentner, D. (1993). Structural alignment during similarity comparisons. Cognitive Psychology, 23, 431-467.

Markman, E. M. (1989). Categorization and naming in children. Cambridge, Mass.: MIT Press.

Medin. D. L., Goldstone, R. L., & Gentner, D. (1993). Respects for similarity. Psychological Review, 100, 254-278.

Nisbett, R. E., & Wilson, T.D. (1977). Telling more than what we can know: Verbal reports on mental processes. Psychological Review, 84, 231-259.

Tversky, A., & Kahneman, D. (1983). Extensional versus intuitive reasoning: The conjunction fallacy in probability judgment. Psychological Review, 90, 293-315.

Wisniewski, E. J. (in press) Construal and similarity in conceptual combination. Journal of Memory and Language.

The Role of Situations in Concept Learning

Wenchi Yeh and **Lawrence W. Barsalou**
Department of Psychology
University of Chicago
5848 S. University Ave.
Chicago, IL 60637
yeh1@ccp.uchicago.edu, l-barsalou@uchicago.edu

Abstract

This study examines how situation information is incorporated in concept learning and representation. Unlike most concept learning studies, this study includes situation information during concept learning. Unlike most studies about the influence of situations on episodic memory, this study investigates how situations affects conceptual processing. Experiment 1 demonstrates that people rely on situation information when processing concepts. Subjects verified a concept's property more quickly if the property was learned and tested in the same situation. Experiment 2 shows that in order for a situation to produce priming, the situation must be related to the property in a meaningful manner. Mere cooccurrence between a property and a situation is not sufficient.

Introduction

Though models of concept learning vary considerably, they often assume that concept structure remains the same across contexts. People encounter the same kind of objects in various situations, but they have the ability to extract these objects out of contexts, and represent concepts as isolated entities. The situation information either cancels itself out or is simply not represented together with a concept. Researchers adopting such theories have focused more on the internal structure of the concepts, and have almost always used isolated concepts as stimuli in their experiments, not addressing the effect of situations (e.g., Estes, 1986; Hayes-Roth & Hayes-Roth, 1977; Hintzman, 1986; Homa & Vosburgh, 1976; Katz & Postal, 1964; Kruschke, 1992; Medin & Schaffer, 1978; Nosofsky, 1986; Posner & Keele, 1968; Reed, 1972; Rosch, 1975; Rosch & Mervis, 1975).

In ordinary life, objects almost never occur in isolation, and people seldom learn concepts out of particular contexts, with the possible exception of formal education. Rather, it seems that people encounter objects in typical situations. Flowers usually appear on plants, are bundled as a bouquet, or sit in a vase. Cars are observed running on streets or highways, parked in garages or parking lots, or are being filled with gas at gas stations. Moreover, different aspects of an object seem to be more salient in different situations, and thereby associated with them. For instance, people might be aware of a car's fuel tank and how to fill it at a gas station, but may pay more attention to the car's speed on a highway. It is thus possible that people associate a gas station with a car's fuel tank, while a highway with the car's speed.

Contrary to the orientation of current concept theories, empirical studies outside the concept learning literature suggest that people do incorporate situation information in concept representations. Context effects have been widely demonstrated in episodic memory (see Davies, 1986 for a review). People encode physical environmental context together with the to-be-remembered words, and therefore restating the environment facilitates the recall of the words (Eich, 1985; Godden and Baddeley, 1975; Smith, Glenberg, & Bjork, 1978; Smith, 1979). Furthermore, research on scene processing suggests that people have a schema about the situation in which an object typically occurs, and therefore they expect to see certain objects when given a scene. Subjects recognize objects faster in a typical scene than in an atypical scene or in isolation, and they memorize objects better when they form a meaningful and coherent scene (Biederman, 1972, 1981; Mandler & Parker, 1976; Palmer, 1975). In addition, research using words or sentences as semantic contexts suggests that a concept is not only associated with a typical situation, but also might be associated with more than one typical situation. As the situation varies, people retrieve different information about the same concept. Therefore, when given different sentence contexts for the same concept, subjects activate different properties or different instances of the concept (Barsalou, 1982; Conrad, 1978; Greenspan, 1986; Roth & Shoben, 1983; Tabossi & Johnson-Laird, 1980; Tabossi, 1988; Whitney, McKay, Kellas, and Emerson, 1985; Wisniewski, 1995). Finally, most connectionist's models are based on the idea that if two events cooccur frequently, the link between them will be strengthened (Rumelhart, Smolensky, McClelland, & Hinton, 1986). Therefore, if a property of a concept always occurs in one situation, the link between the property and the situation should be stronger than those between the property and other situations.

The purpose of this study is to examine how situation information is incorporated in concept learning. A situation is defined as a relatively well-bounded region of space that contains a coherent activity. For example, sitting in a living room is a situation in which a chair typically occurs, and parking in a garage is a situation that typically contains a car. Unlike most concept learning studies, this study includes situation information during concept learning. Furthermore, unlike most studies reviewed in the previous section, which examine the influence of situations on episodic memory, this study investigates how situations affects conceptual processing.

Experiment 1

Experiment 1 examines whether retrieving information about a concept is affected by situations. Subjects learned a new concept in two situations, with some of the concept's properties occurring in one situation, and with other properties occurring in the other situation. After learning the novel concept's properties in the two situations, subjects verified the properties in either the same or the alternative situation in which they learned the properties. Subjects also performed a property listing task, in which they were given one of the learning situations and had to list all the concept's properties.

According to a Situation-Independent Hypothesis, people extract what they learn about a concept across situations, and represent the concept in an abstract way, not incorporating any specific situation information. Therefore, priming subjects with a scene of a situation will not help retrieving the properties learned that in situation. Subjects should verify properties learned in the same situation as quickly as those learned in a different situation. Subjects should also list the properties for the two kinds of situations in no particular order.

In contrast, a Situation-Dependent Hypothesis holds that people store, together with a concept, the situations in which they typically encounter it. Therefore a concept is not an isolated entity, but rather, includes the situations in which it typically occurs. Furthermore, since people attend to different properties in different situations, they associate different properties with different situations. Hence, the Situation-Dependent Hypothesis predicts that subjects will verify properties learned in the same situation more quickly than those learned in a different situation, and they will also list properties learned in the test situation earlier than those learned in the other situation.

Method

Materials. Four novel concepts were used in this experiment, two of them being animals, another a plant, and the other an artifact. A cover story was created for each concept to explain how a new concept was discovered and observed, and also to describe the two situations where the concept is normally observed. Each concept had six properties, each being instantiated by four instances. Three of a concept's properties always occurred in one location (usually the plant or animal's natural habitat), and the other three in another location (usually the human context where the animals/plants are studied, see Table 1 for examples of the materials). For example, subjects observed 24 instances of a new kind of animal, a "zod," either 1000 feet under the Pacific Ocean, or in a zoology laboratory where zods were raised. Zods observed in the ocean exhibited the property of *elastic, blind,* or *sticky* (four zods each). Zods observed in

Table 1. Examples of learning materials in Experiment 1.

Concept	Situation	Property
zod (an animal)	the Pacific Ocean	elastic blind sticky
	zoology laboratory	yellow hops carnivorous
foush (a plant)	small village	bluish velvety odorless
	greenhouse	flowering succulent medicinal

the laboratory were *carnivorous, yellow,* or *hops* (four zods each). For each instance and its property, subjects read a sentence instructing them how to imagine the property in the situation. The four instances that shared a common property also shared a common sentence with minor modifications. For example, the sentences describing the four *elastic* zods went like this, "Imagine that a zod *under/beside/between/behind* the rocks is stretching its ELASTIC body..." and the sentences for the four carnivorous zods were "Imagine that the zoologist gives the CARNIVOROUS zod *a fish/a clam/some squid/some shrimp*, and the zod eats it..."

In the property verification test, each concept was tested by six true trials and nine false trials. The six true properties were those learned in the learning phase. The nine false properties were chosen from the other three concepts' properties. Therefore, subjects were equally familiar with the true and false properties, and had to respond by retrieving information from the correct concept. Each concept was tested in only one of the two learning situations (e.g., 1000 feet under the Pacific Ocean), and thus half of the properties were learned and tested in the same situation (e.g., *elastic* was learned and tested in the Pacific Ocean scene), while the other half were tested in a different situation (e.g., *carnivorous* was learned in the zoology laboratory scene, but was tested in the Pacific Ocean scene). The combined set of 60 test properties were presented in a random order to subjects.

In the property listing test, each concept was tested in the learning scene that was not shown in the property verification test. For example, if zods were tested in the Pacific Ocean scene in the property verification test, they were tested in the zoology laboratory scene in the property listing test.

Procedure. In the learning phase of the experiment, subjects first read a cover story about a novel concept, then they saw 24 pictures, each depicting an instance of this concept in a scene. Half of the instances occurred in one scene and the other half in the other. For each instance, subjects read a verbal description of the instance's property in the center of the picture for 2 seconds, and a description about the role of the property in the scene for 7 seconds.

After seeing four such concepts and their properties, subjects performed a property verification task and a property listing task. In the verification task, subjects were primed with one of the two scenes and decided whether a property was true of a concept or not. To verify a property, subjects first saw a picture of a situation on a computer screen for 1.5 seconds. Then, the concept's name appeared in the center of the picture for another 1 second. After a 1 second interval, a fixation point appeared in the center of the picture for 500 msec, followed by a 250 msec interval. Then a possible property appeared, and subjects had to verify as quickly and as accurately as possible whether the property was true of the probed concept by pressing one of the buttons on a button box. Feedback was given if subjects responded incorrectly.

After the property verification test, subjects performed a property listing task, in which they saw, on a page of a booklet, the learning scene that was not shown in the property verification test and the name of a target concept, and they wrote down the properties of the concept. Subjects performed this procedure for all four concepts, presented in a random order.

Subjects. Subjects were 12 University of Chicago undergraduates, who were native speakers of American English. They were paid to participate in the experiment.

Results and Discussion

Property Verification Test. Only correct reaction times on the true trials were included in the analysis. Reaction times longer than 5 seconds (0% of the data) were excluded. On average, subjects responded to properties learned and tested in the same situations at the speed of 1120 msec, which was 177 msec faster than those tested in different situations (average reaction time 1297 msec, $F(1,11)=5.93$, $p<.05$). The result supports the Situation-Dependent Hypothesis. Subjects also made fewer errors in the same situations (error rate 4.17%) than in the different situations (error rate 6.94%), which indicates that the differences of response latencies between the two situations did not result from a trade-off between speed and accuracy.

Property Listing Test. The average positions of the listed properties in the two situations were calculated. Each listed property's absolute position was marked from 0 to 5, with 0 being the first property listed, and 5 the sixth property listed. A property's relative position was then calculated by dividing its absolute position by the total number of properties listed for the concept minus one. Therefore, a property's relative position being 0 means that it was listed first, 1 means that it was listed last, and 0.5 means that it was in the middle of the list. As predicted by the Situation-Dependent Hypothesis, subjects listed the properties learned in the test situations (average relative position 0.38) significantly earlier than those learned in the other situations (average relative position 0.61), $F(1,11) = 20.75$, $p <.001$). The position data again support the

conclusion that people associate a concept's properties with the situations in which they learn the properties, such that they retrieve those properties more quickly when primed with the learning situations.

Experiment 2

Experiment 2 examines how situations become associated with concepts. The results of Experiment 1 suggest that appropriate situations facilitate the retrieval of certain aspects of a concept, but it is not clear how situations become associated with the concept to facilitate retrieval. Situation priming can result from simple cooccurrence relations between situations and properties, or it can result from more meaningful conceptual relations. Two factors may determine such relations: The first is whether the property is predictable from the situation or not. The second is whether the property manifests itself through interacting with the situation, or merely through cooccurring with the situation. Experiment 2 manipulated these two factors, related/neutral and interactive/cooccurring, in a two by two between-subject design.

Based on prior knowledge about a situation, people might expect certain properties to occur in it. For example, *swims* and *scaly* are common properties of underwater animals. Therefore, before actually learning any properties in the learning phase, subjects might expect an underwater animal to be able to swim and to have scales in a scene of the Pacific Ocean. In contrast, a property could be neutral to a situation in the sense that people do not necessarily expect the property to occur in the situation. For example, *swims* and *scaly* are not common properties for jungle animals. To learn that a jungle animal swims, subjects have to rely completely on the information presented in the learning phase. Experiment 1 employed only the latter type of properties. Experiment 2 manipulated both types of situation-property relations. Subjects in the related group learned novel concepts with properties predictable from situations, whereas subjects in the neutral group learned properties unpredictable from situations. If meaningful and conceptual relations are necessary for a situation to influence concept processing, then subjects in the related group should exhibit a stronger situation effect than those in the neutral group. If, on the contrary, simple cooccurrence between a situation and a property is enough to produce a situation effect, subjects in both groups should show the same size of situation effect.

Orthogonal to the related/neutral factor, whether a property interacts with a situation or not could also influence how they associate with each other. A situation may become associated with a concept in the following two ways: One possible mechanism is that a situation cooccurs with a concept's property so many times that when given the situation, subjects can mechanically respond with the property. Such a frequently cooccurring situation might not bear any meaningful relations with a concept, but still facilitate the retrieval of its relevant properties. Alternatively, it could be that a property has to interact in a meaningful way with a situation in order for the situation to prime it. A situation might bias people's attention to certain aspects of a concept, such that a property manifests itself only through interacting with the environment. For example, to associate an underwater animal with *blind*, subjects might imagine a diver swimming around the animal, and shining her spot light on the animal, and not seeing it respond. After repeated presentation of such a scenario, subjects come to associate the *underwater* situation with the property *blind*. Subjects in Experiment 1 received associated properties and situations in an interactive way, because, in the learning phase, they received sentences instructing them how to imagine the properties manifesting themselves in the situations. Experiment 2 examined both interactive and cooccurring associations by manipulating the existence of the sentences.

If a property has to bear a meaningful relation with a situation in order for the situation to prime processing, then the sentences would be crucial, especially when subjects do not expect the property to occur in the situation. Therefore, the situation effect should be stronger in the neutral-interactive condition than in the neutral-cooccurring condition. On the contrary, if simple cooccurrence between a property and a situation is sufficient to produce the situation effect, then it should not matter whether there is a sentence in the learning phase or not.

Method

Subjects and Design. Sixty-four University of Chicago undergraduates were recruited as subjects, all of them being native speakers of American English, and being paid to participate in the experiment. They were randomly assigned to one of the following four groups: related-interactive, related-cooccurring, neutral-interactive, and neutral-cooccurring. For each subject, half of the properties were learned and tested in the same situation, while the other half were tested in a different situation.

Materials. Four novel concepts and eight situations were created. The structure of the stimuli was the same as in Experiment 1, except that two types of materials, related and neutral, were created (see Table 2 for examples of the materials). The properties and situations for the two types

of materials were same, but the situations were matched with the properties in different ways. In the related version, the properties were very likely to occur in the matched situations (e.g., underwater-swims, jungle-poisonous). A separate group of 16 subjects ranked how likely the properties were to occur in those situations, and the average rank for the related situations was 2.45 on a 1 to 10 ranking scale. When rearranging the same set of situations and properties in a different way, the properties were ranked as less likely to occur in the matched situations (e.g., jungle-swims, underwater-poisonous). The average rank for neutral situations was 6.3. As in Experiment 1, each property in the related-interactive and neutral-interactive versions was accompanied by a sentence instructing subjects how to image the property in the situation. In contrast, properties in the related-cooccurring and neutral-cooccurring conditions were not accompanied by any sentences.

Procedure. The procedure of Experiment 2 was similar to that in Experiment 1, except that in the learning phase of the two interactive conditions, the sentences were presented 5 seconds; while for the two cooccurring conditions, the properties simply remained on the screen for 5 seconds. In addition, the presentation time for the name of the concept in the test phase was shortened from 1 second to 0.5 second, and no fixation point was presented in this experiment.

Results and Discussion

Property Verification Test. Reaction times longer than 5 seconds were excluded from the analysis (0.72 % of the data). Figure 1 depicts subjects' mean reaction times to verify true properties in the same and different situations in the four conditions. Subjects in the neutral-interactive condition verified properties tested in the same situation 194 msec faster than those in a different situation (planned comparison $F(1,60)=6.74$, $p<.05$), replicating the pattern in Experiment 1. Subjects in the neutral-cooccurring condition, on the contrary, made no such distinction (planned comparison $F(1,60)=0.60$, n.s.), suggesting that the sentences instructing subjects to imagine the property in

Table 2. Examples of materials in Experiment 2.

Related Condition			Neutral Condition		
Concept	Situation	Property	Concept	Situation	Property
zod (an animal)	underwater	swims slimy scaly	zod (an animal)	rain forest floor	swims slimy scaly
	zoo	apathetic agitated nervous		formal garden	apathetic agitated nervous
foush (a plant)	rain forest floor	lush exotic poisonous	foush (a plant)	desert	lush exotic poisonous
	formal garden	fragrant ornamental perennial		zoo	fragrant ornamental perennial

the situation are crucial to producing the situation effect. Simple cooccurrence between a property name and a situation was not sufficient for the situation to facilitate processing.

Such a difference between interactive and cooccurring conditions, however, was not found in the two related conditions. For both the related-interactive and related-cooccurring conditions, subjects verified properties tested in the same situation faster than those in a different situation. The difference between same and different situations was 238 msec for the related-interactive condition (planned comparison $F(1,60)=10.24$, $p<.01$), and 193 msec for the related-cooccurring condition (planned comparison $F(1,60)=6.70$, $p<.05$), indicating that subjects in the latter condition were able to elaborate relations between situations and properties so that situations affected conceptual processing, even though they were not given the sentences. In other words, based on their pre-existing knowledge about environments, subjects expected to see certain properties in a situation, and thus overcame the lack of the interactive sentences.

As in Experiment 1, subjects in all the four groups made fewer errors in the same situations (average error rate 4.69%) than in the different situations (average error rate 11.33%). This again indicates that the priming effects did not result from a trade-off between speed and accuracy.

Property Listing Test. As illustrated in Figure 2, subjects in all the four groups listed properties learned in the same situation earlier than those learned in the other situation. On average, properties learned in the same situation were listed at the relative position 0.37, and those learned in a different situation were listed at the position

0.60, which was significantly later ($F(1,59) = 67.96$, $p<.0001$). In other words, a situation effect was found in both the property verification test (a recognition task) and the property listing test (a recall task) for the related-interactive, related-cooccurring, and neutral-interactive conditions, suggesting again that meaningful relations between a property and a situation is crucial for the situation to prime conceptual processing of the property. The neutral-cooccurring condition, on the contrary, showed a situation effect only in the property listing test (a recall task), but not in the property verification test (a recognition task). The lack of situation effect in a recognition task is a typical finding in research about environmental context effect on episodic memory (e.g., Godden & Baddeley, 1980; Baddeley, 1982; Smith, Glenberg, & Bjork, 1978), suggesting that subjects in the neutral-cooccurring group did not process the materials conceptually, but rather, they simply remembered the contingency between a scene and a property, without elaborating a meaningful relation between the two.

Conclusion

Experiment 1 demonstrates that subjects verify properties learned and tested in the same situations reliably more quickly than those tested in different situations. In the property listing task, subjects overwhelmingly listed the properties learned in the primed situations earlier than those in the unprimed situations. The results in both tasks support the Situation-Dependent Hypothesis. People not only process a concept but also the situation in which the concept occurs, associating different properties of a concept with different situations.

The results of Experiment 2 suggest that in order for situations to affect conceptual processing, it is crucial that

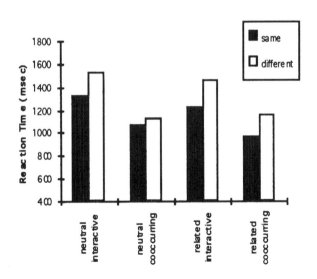

Figure 1. Subjects' mean reaction times to verify properties in the same and different situations as a function of related/neutral and interactive/cooccurring conditions, and whether the property is learned in the same or different situation.

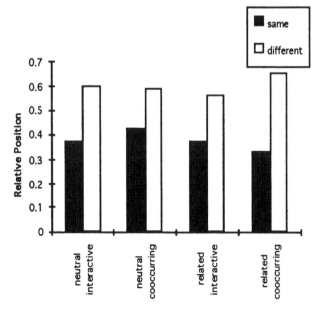

Figure 2. The relative position of properties listed in the property listing task as a function of neutral/related situation and interactive/cooccurring conditions in Experiment 2.

the properties of a concept interact meaningfully with the situations. Subjects could elaborate these relations by reading sentences that specify how a property occurs in a situation, or by using their pre-existing knowledge about the situation. If a property merely occurs contingently with a situation, without any conceptual relation between the two, as in the neutral-cooccurring condition, the situation does not affect how subjects verify properties, but rather, affects only the recall of the properties, as has been frequently found in research on environmental context effects.

Acknowledgments

This research was supported by a National Science Foundation grant to Lawrence Barsalou (SBR-9421326).

References

Baddeley, A. D. (1982). Domains of recollection. *Psychological Review, 89,* 708-729.

Barsalou, L. W. (1982). Context-independent and context-dependent information in concepts. *Memory & Cognition, 10(1),* 82-93.

Biederman, I. (1972). Perceiving real-world scenes. *Science, 177,* 77-80.

Biederman, I. (1981). On the semantics of a glance at a scene In M. Kubovy, & J. R. Pomerantz (Eds), *Perceptual Organization* (pp. 213-253). Hillsdale, NJ: Erlbaum.

Conrad, C. (1978). Some factors involved in the recognition of words. In J. W. Cotton & R. Klatzky (Eds.), *Semantic factors in cognition.* Hillsdale, NJ: Erlbaum.

Davies, G. M. (1986). Context effects in episodic memory: a review. *Cahiers de Psychologie Cognitive, 6,* 157-174.

Eich, E. (1985). Context, memory, and integrated item /context imagery. *Journal of Experimental Psychology: Learning, Memory, & Cognition, 11,* 764-770.

Estes, W. K. (1986). Array models for category learning. *Cognitive Psychology, 18,* 500-549.

Godden, D. R., & Baddeley, A. D. (1975). Context-dependent memory in two natural environments: On land and underwater. *British Journal of Psychology, 66,* 325-331.

Godden, D. R., & Baddeley, A. D. (1980) When does context influence recognition memory? *British journal of Psychology, 71,* 99-104.

Greenspan, S. L. (1986). Semantic flexibility and referential specificity of concrete nouns. *Journal of Memory and Language, 25,* 539-557.

Hayes-Roth, B., & Hayes-Roth, F. (1977). Concept learning and the recognition and classification of exemplars. *Journal of Verbal Learning and Verbal Behavior, 16,* 321-338.

Hintzman, D. L. (1986). "Schema abstraction" in a multiple-trace memory model. *Psychological Review, 93,* 411-428.

Homa, D., & Vosburgh, R. (1976). Category breadth and the abstraction of prototypical information. *Journal of Experimental of Psychology: Human Learning and Memory, 2(3),* 322-330.

Katz, J. J., & Postal, P. M. (1964). *An integrated theory of linguistic descriptions.* Cambridge, MA: MIT Press.

Kruschke, J. K. (1992). ALCOVE: An exemplar-based connectionist model of category learning. *Psychological Review, 99,* 22-44.

Mandler, J. M. & Parker, R. E. (1976). Memory for descriptive and spatial information in complex pictures. *Journal of Experimental Psychology: Human, Learning, and Memory, 2(1),* 38-48.

Medin, D. L. & Schaffer, M. M. (1978). Context theory of classification learning. *Psychological Review, 85(3),* 207-238.

Nosofsky, R. M. (1986). Attention, similarity, and the identification-categorization relationship. *Journal of Experimental Psychology: General, 115,* 39-57.

Palmer, S. (1975). The effects of contextual scenes on the identification of objects. *Memory & cognition, 3,* 519-526.

Posner, M. I. & Keele, S. W. (1968). On the genesis of abstract ideas. *Journal of Experimental Psychology, 77,* 353-363.

Reed, S. K. (1972). Pattern recognition and categorization. *Cognitive Psychology, 3,* 382-407.

Rosch, E. (1975). Cognitive representations of semantic categories. *Journal of Experimental Psychology: General, 104,* 192-233.

Rosch, E., & Mervis, C. B. (1975). Family resemblances: Studies in the internal structure of categories. *Cognitive Psychology, 8,* 382-439.

Roth, E. M., & Shoben, E. J. (1983). The effect of context on the structure of categories. *Cognitive Psychology, 15,* 346-378.

Rumelhart, D. E., Smolensky, P., McClelland, J. L., & Hinton, G. E. (1986). Schemata and sequential thought processes in PDP models. In J.L. McClelland, D.E. Rumelhart, & the PDP Research Group, *Parallel distributed processing: Explorations in the microstructure of cognition: Vol. 2. Psychological and biological models* (pp. 7-57). Cambridge, MA: MIT Press.

Smith, S. M. (1979). Remembering in and out of context. *Journal of Experimental Psychology: Human Learning and Memory, 5,* 460-471.

Smith, S. M., Glenberg, A. M., & Bjork, R. A. (1978). Environmental context and human memory. *Memory & Cognition, 6,* 342-353.

Tabossi, P. (1988). Effects of context on the immediate interpretation of unambiguous nouns. *Journal of Experimental Psychology: Learning, Memory, and Cognition, 14,* 153-162.

Tabossi, P., & Johnson-Laird, P. N. (1980). Linguistic context and the priming of semantic information. *Quarterly Journal of Experimental Psychology, 32,* 595-603.

Whitney, P., McKay, T., Kellas, G., & Emerson, Jr., W. A. (1985). Semantic activation of noun concepts in context. *Journal of Experimental Psychology: Learning, Memory, and Cognition, 11,* 126-135.

Wisniewski, E. J. (1995). Prior knowledge and functionally relevant features in concept learning. *Journal of Experimental Psychology: Learning, Memory, and Cognition, 21(2),* 449-468.

Modeling Interference Effects In Instructed Category Learning

David C. Noelle and **Garrison W. Cottrell**

Computer Science & Engineering 0114
University of California, San Diego
La Jolla, CA 92093-0114
{dnoelle,gary}@cs.ucsd.edu

Abstract

Category learning is often seen as a process of inductive generalization from a set of class-labeled exemplars. Human learners, however, often receive direct instruction concerning the
structure of a category before being presented with examples.
Such explicit knowledge may often be smoothly integrated
with knowledge garnered by exposure to instances, but some
interference effects have been observed. Specifically, errors
in instructed rule following may sometimes arise after the repeated presentation of correctly labeled exemplars. Despite
perfect consistency between instance labels and the provided
rule, such inductive training can drive categorization behavior
away from rule following and towards a more prototype-based
or instance-based pattern. In this paper we present a general
connectionist model of instructed category learning which captures this kind of interference effect. We model instruction as a
sequence of inputs to a network which transforms such advice
into a modulating force on classification behavior. Exemplar-
based learning is modeled in the usual way: as weight modification via backpropagation. The proposed architecture allows
these two sources of information to interact in a psychologically plausible manner. Simulation results are provided on a
simple instructed category learning task, and these results are
compared with human performance on the same task.

Introduction

Investigations into concept formation have often focused on
the learning of category structure solely through exposure to
labeled exemplars. Indeed, much of the success of connectionist learning models may be attributed to their ability to perform exactly this sort of statistical induction. Human learners
often need not rely solely on exemplars, however, to formulate an understanding of a concept. The presence of language
allows us to learn from the direct instruction provided by others. Such explicit advice may simply direct our attention to
relevant features, or it may actually spell out necessary and/or
sufficient conditions for membership in a category. Learning
"by being told" may facilitate an otherwise exemplar-based
learning task, enabling a multistrategy approach integrating
induction and instruction.

Some forms of advice may be seen as explicitly providing
categorization rules to the learner. When viewed in this way,
the integration of exemplar-based induction and direct instruction begins to resemble another form of integration discussed
in the category learning literature. Sometimes human subjects
presented with labeled exemplars appear to induce explicit
classification rules, and sometimes induced category structures are better captured by prototype-based or instance-based

representations. Much evidence has been gathered suggesting
that these two kinds of category representation result from two
dissociable learning mechanisms (Shanks & St. John, 1994),
so a question arises as to how these two processes are integrated in common learning tasks. In terms of instructed
category learning, this question becomes one of how categorization rules provided by direct instruction interact with
exemplar-based knowledge to form a learned category structure.

This work focuses on one particular interference phenomenon which has manifested itself in instructed category
learning studies (Allen & Brooks, 1991; Nosofsky et al.,
1989). Specifically, subjects initially provided with an explicit classification rule may begin to violate that rule after
the presentation of correctly labeled exemplars. While none
of the presented examples contradict the instructed rule in
any way, similarity between instances drives subject behavior
away from rule following and towards a more prototype-based
or instance-based pattern. It appears, in these experiments,
as if an exemplar-based inductive learning process is directly
interfering with an instruction-based rule application process.

The goal of this paper is to demonstrate that our previously
proposed connectionist model of instructed learning (Noelle &
Cottrell, 1995) may capture and account for this interference
effect. To this end, we discuss one psychological experiment
in which this phenomenon has appeared, review our modeling
framework for instructed learning, and present the results of
applying our model to the discussed experimental domain.

An Interference Effect

In the category learning literature a debate has raged over
the internal representation of inductively learned categories.
Some view these as simple sentential rules which are acquired
in response to experience. Others view categories as regions
in some feature space, with region boundaries determined by
some similarity measure and a collection of remembered exemplars or prototypes. In order to test these two competing
views, Nosofsky, Clark, and Shin (1989) designed and conducted a number of elegant experiments. They used a set of
stimuli with two pertinent continuous features – the size of a
circle and the angle of rotation of a radial line. These objects
may be plotted as points in a two dimensional feature space,
as in Figure 1. In that diagram, each letter corresponds to
a potential stimulus object, and the letters enclosed by small
polygons are objects which were presented as labeled training
exemplars. The two enclosing shapes, triangles and squares,
correspond to category labels for two disjoint categories. We

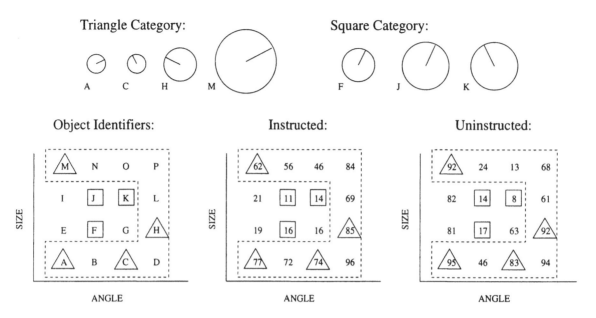

Figure 1: Two Categories: Training Exemplars, Feature Space, And Frequency Of Classification Into The "Triangle" Category For Both Instructed And Uninstructed Subjects

may imagine that distance in this feature space corresponds to perceived "similarity" between objects. How should object "P" be classified? If similarity is used to define categories, object "P" will be placed in the "square" category, due to its close proximity to exemplar "K". If some form of minimum description length sentential rule is used instead (e.g., a rule for the triangle class is "tiny or huge or 155° rotation" – shown as a dotted box), then this object will be labeled as a "triangle". Thus, classification behavior on novel objects can inform explorations into the structure of internal category representations.

In one experiment, Nosofsky and his colleagues compared subjects who were explicitly told a sentential categorization rule before being exposed to the training exemplars with subjects who depended solely on the exemplars to formulate category boundaries. In general, the explicitly instructed subjects exhibited rule governed classification behavior, whereas the uninstructed subjects matched a similarity-based model. However, instructed subjects sometimes *deviated* from their rule-based behavior when classifying objects highly similar to training exemplars from the opposite category.

The situation depicted in Figure 1 produced the most striking results. Subjects were instructed to classify objects as being members of the "triangle" category if and only if they fit the given disjunctive rule. Following this instruction, the subjects received 300 random presentations of the seven training exemplars, and they were asked to classify each of them. After each selection, the subjects were told the true category of the training exemplar, and the next object was presented. Upon completion of this training period, the subjects were tested on the entire collection of 16 objects. The final mean frequencies of classifying objects as members of the "triangle" category are displayed as percentages in Figure 1, along with the same frequencies for subjects who received *no* explicit classification rule before being presented with labeled

exemplars. Of particular note here is object "O", which instructed subjects tended to place in the "square" category more often than not, despite the fact that such classification violated the given rule. Note the low frequency with which *uninstructed* subjects identified this object as a member of the "triangle" category. It would seem that the same inductive process which caused this response in the uninstructed subjects has interfered with the rule processing of the instructed subjects. Our goal is to show that an interference effect of this type may be explained by our connectionist model.

A Connectionist Model

The modeling approach we advocate here is based on our connectionist model of learning "by being told" (Noelle & Cottrell, 1995). This model arises from the recognition that the weight update techniques typically used for inductive learning in artificial neural networks are simply too slow to account for the high speed of behavior change which occurs in response to direct instruction. Activation propagation in such networks, on the other hand, is quite fast. We suggest that instructed learning is properly seen as a process in which presented advice *pushes* the activation state of part of the cognitive system into a novel basin of attraction – a stable region of activation space which encodes the proper operationalization of the given advice. Such novel attractors, corresponding to newly received instructions, come into existence through the componential interaction of basins sculpted via past experience with the instructional language (Plaut & McClelland, 1993). Under this view, advice is seen as a sequence of input activity, presented to a network which transforms such sequences into appropriate behavior.

Our proposed general architecture is shown in Figure 2, on the left. The boxes in that diagram represent layers of sigmoidal processing elements and arrows represent complete interconnections between layers. Categorization rules are en-

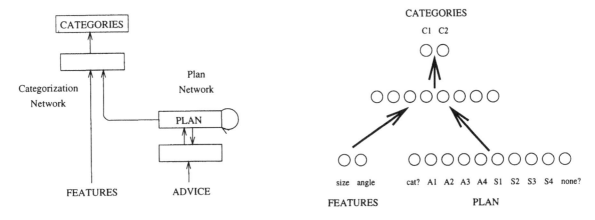

Figure 2: Instructable Network: General Architecture & Isolated Categorization Network

coded as sequences of instruction tokens which are presented, one at a time, at the *advice* input layer. Activation is then propagated through the recurrent "Plan Network" to produce a stable pattern of activation at the *plan* layer. The *plan* is then used to modulate the behavior of a simple feed-forward "Categorization Network", causing the mapping from stimulus *features* to output *categories* to exactly match the rule specified by the input advice.

Initially, this network must be inductively trained to understand the language of instruction. This may be accomplished using a version of *backpropagation through time* (BPTT) (Rumelhart et al., 1986) in which error is backpropagated for only a single time step, much as is done for Simple Recurrent Networks (Elman, 1990). A training regimen similar to that used by the architecturally similar *Sentence Gestalt* network (St. John & McClelland, 1990) may be used, requiring an external error signal only at the final output layer. The output units encode categorization judgements for specific input stimuli in the context of instructions presented at the *advice* layer. By backpropagating error from the final category outputs in this way, the internal representation of instruction sequences, maintained at the *plan* layer, may be learned in the service of the categorization task (St. John, 1992). Once the network has learned to represent advice at the *plan* layer, no further weight modifications are needed to exhibit *immediate* behavior change in response to instruction.

This is the point at which induction and instruction become integrated in this model. While further inductive weight updates are not *needed* in order to exhibit instructed behavior, such inductive learning may commence nonetheless. Indeed, inductive weight modification in the "Categorization Network" provides a means for rule following and exemplar-based induction to interact. Modulating activation from the *plan* layer will bias the network to act in accordance with instructions, but further exemplar-based error feedback may modify weights so as to violate the instructed rule.

While the initial learning of an instructional language is an important component of our general model, the issue of interference effects between exemplar-based induction and instructed rule following is relatively orthogonal to how the instructional language is acquired. In order to focus, then, on interaction effects, we have modeled the instructed cate-

gory learning task using the "Categorization Network" alone. We have fabricated an arbitrary representational format for the *plan* layer, allowing us to replace the "Plan Network" with the direct presentation of encoded categorization rules to the "Categorization Network". Some training in the instructional language is still necessary for the network to discover the "meaning" of our *plan* layer encoding, but this initial preparation is much more rapid than when the recurrent "Plan Network" must be trained simultaneously. Still, we assume that something similar to our *plan* layer representation could be generated by the "Plan Network" from linguistic input, given sufficient training.

The resulting categorization network is shown in Figure 2, on the right. Disjunctive categorization rules were encoded into a ten element *plan* using a bit-vector representation for the set of rule terms. The first *plan* unit was used to indicate if the given disjunctive rule was to describe the members of the "square" category or of the "triangle" category. The next eight units were used to encode the actual rule, with each unit corresponding to one of the four levels of "size" or to one of the four levels of "angle". If a given "size" unit was turned on, this implied that the rule covered all stimuli of that size, and a similar code was used over the "angle" units. Activating multiple units produced disjunctive rules, so the rule in Figure 1 required the activation of the three units: "size = tiny", "size = huge", and "angle = 155°". The last unit in the *plan* vector was used to signal the *absence* of any rule – the uninstructed case. When no rule was available, this last unit was turned on and the activity of the other nine *plan* units was set to a medial value (i.e., 0.5). Unlike the quasi-binary *plan* layer encoding, the two features of observed stimuli, size and angle, were presented to the network in a continuous fashion. One input unit was available for each of the features, and each unit could take on one of four ranked values: 0, $\frac{1}{3}$, $\frac{2}{3}$, or 1. The network possessed two output units – one for each category. The activation levels at these outputs where normalized into conditional class probabilities using Luce ratios (Luce, 1963). The hidden layer consisted of eight processing elements. The result was a network which produced probabilistic categorization judgements from two continuous features and an encoding of an instructed classification rule (or the absence of such a rule).

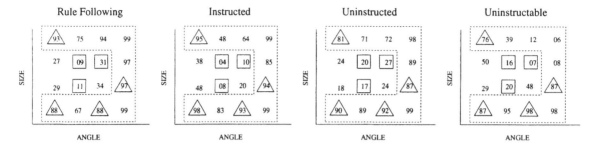

Figure 3: Probability Of Selecting The "Triangle" Category For Various Networks

This network was initially trained on the complete collection of possible disjunctive classification rules, in order to encourage the proper understanding of the rule encoding format. The eight inputs which corresponded to rule terms allowed for $2^8 = 256$ possible disjunctive clauses, and each of these could be used to describe either the "triangle" category or the "square" category, for a total of $256 \times 2 = 512$ possible classification rules. In addition, the network experienced each of these patterns *with the rule removed* (i.e., without instruction) so that it associated the "no rule" input unit with an uninformed 50/50 chance for either category. During this initial training phase all 16 stimulus objects were presented alongside each categorization rule, resulting in a total of $512 \times 2 \times 16 = 16384$ patterns used to train the network in the instructional language. These patterns were presented to the network in random orderings for 200 epochs (i.e., passes through the entire training set). Standard incremental (non-batch) backpropagation of mean squared error was used, with activation levels ranging between 0.0 and 1.0, a learning rate of 0.05, and no momentum. The termination at 200 epochs was arbitrary, being a point at which instruction following behavior was good, but not perfect.[1]

In order to observe interaction effects, this network was then exposed to further inductive training in a *particular classification* of the objects. Specifically, further training of the network involved *only* the seven training exemplars shown in Figure 1. This training was conducted separately under two conditions of instruction: *uninstructed* and *instructed*. In the *uninstructed* case, the input *plan* layer was set to the "no rule" configuration for the duration of this training. In the *instructed* case, the input *plan* layer was set to the disjunctive rule shown in Figure 1 for the duration of this training. In both cases, training on the seven exemplars was conducted using standard incremental (non-batch) backpropagation of mean squared error with a very high learning rate (0.5) for 300 epochs. The high learning rate was needed to produce significant learning over a small number of pattern presentations.

The classification performance was recorded on all 16 stimuli in four distinct network states: *Guessing* (immediately after initial training, given no rule to follow – should be guessing 50/50 category assignments), *Rule Following* (immediately after initial training, given the appropriate rule to follow), *Uninstructed* (trained on the seven exemplars, but

given no explicit rule), and *Instructed* (trained on the seven exemplars with the appropriate rule at the *plan* layer). The basic hypothesis was that the behavior of the *instructed* network would deviate from the behavior of the initial *rule following* network in a manner which brought it closer to that of the *uninstructed* network.

As another baseline, a network of this kind was exposed to the seven training exemplars *without* any initial training in the instructional language. This "uninstructable" network was trained for 600 epochs at a very high learning rate (0.5) with the *plan* layer always set in the "no rule" configuration. This provided a view of how the category partitions would be formed if no knowledge of the instructional language was available at all.

Modeling Results

The results of the network simulations are summarized in Figure 3. That diagram displays the network predicted probabilities, expressed as percentages, of the given stimulus objects being in the "triangle" category. The only condition not appearing in this figure is the "guessing" case, under which the network consistently produced scores between 42% and 46%, showing a slight but consistent bias towards the "square" category.

An examination of the resulting probabilities reveals the phenomenon of interest in the behavior of these networks. The first case of interest is the difference between the "rule following" network and the "instructed" network. Recall that the difference between these is that the "instructed" network received specific training on the 7 exemplars. The classification probabilities for a number of the objects move markedly away from the "rule following" predictions as a result of exemplar-based training. For example, object "O", which showed the greatest change for the human subjects, drops from 94% to only 64% after exposure to the seven training items. A similar change occurs for object "N", which moves from strong "triangle-ness" to uncertainty. Object "L" provides yet another example, and object "I" shows a weaker trend from "square" to "triangle". One thing that is surprising about these probability changes, however, is that they are all *worse* than the probabilities generated by the "uninstructed" network. That is, our "uninstructed" network follows rules too well, compared to the human data. The output of the "uninstructable" network appears, as expected, much less "rule-like". This suggests that the behavior of the "uninstructed" network was overly shaped by its non-specific experience with the instructional language. That is, its representational

---

[1]This termination point is discussed further in our closing discussion.

vocabulary is overly rule-based.

Discussion

This demonstration provides some preliminary support to the notion that interference effects in instructed category learning may be appropriately modeled using connectionist networks. The behavior of the "instructed" network provided a reasonable match to the human data, with 7 of the 9 test exemplars classified in the same way, on average. There are a number of ways, however, in which these simulations could be improved.

While the performance of the "instructed" network displayed the interference effect of interest, the behavior of the "uninstructed" network did not match the human subjects data very well. The pattern of probabilities generated by this network more closely matched that of the "rule following" network than that of the "uninstructable" network. This difference is particularly striking for objects "L", "N", "O", and "P". It appears as if this network preferred categories describable as disjunctive rules.

It is not surprising, in retrospect, that the uninstructed network produced rule-like behavior, since *all* categories presented to the network during initial training in the instructional language possessed the disjunctive rule structure. During this initial training phase, hidden units were recruited to encode portions of the rule-structured categories, and these units were later put to use by the inductive learning process. While this resulted in an "uninstructed" network that produced behavior notably different than that of the uninstructed subjects, it is possible that we are modeling a certain class of subjects. Nosofsky and his colleagues noted that, "...there is support for the idea that some of the category learners did indeed adopt a simple rule-based strategy ...". Indeed, the human data may reflect an average over a bimodal distribution of subjects: those who, like the "uninstructed" network, appeared to induce a rule and others who, like the "uninstructable" network, used a more "similarity based" strategy. Notice that an average of our "uninstructed" and "uninstructable" results provides a somewhat better match to the uninstructed human data than the "uninstructed" network alone.

What is surprising – and this is something for which we have no explanation – is that exposure to the seven exemplars caused the instructed network to deviate from the rule it was given, while the uninstructed network found the correct rule and stuck to it. The difference between these networks rested only in the pattern of activation presented at the *plan* inputs during exemplar training. These inputs were fixed for all seven exemplars, so the inputs acted like a bias during exemplar exposure. In the instructed case, the rule pattern was on, and in the uninstructed case, the "no rule" pattern is on. It could be that this representation actually caused more interference for the network given a rule, because these inputs could be individually combinatorially combined with a *subset* of the possible rules, where the "uninstructed" network had a level playing field from which to select the perfect rule. Our current research is aimed at understanding this puzzle.

In any case, we would like to get something like the effect of combining the "uninstructable" network with the "uninstructed" network in a single network. This might be achieved in two ways. First, initial training on the instructional language could be interspersed with training on random "natural", similarity-based categories over the stimulus space. The network would be equipped with additional output units to represent the category labels for these natural categories. This modified initial training regime would allocate some hidden layer resources to the task of representing the similarity-based categories, and these hidden units could then be redeployed during inductive learning on the seven training exemplars. Alternatively, some hidden units could be architecturally isolated from the instruction inputs, forcing them to encode only similarity information. This would result in a "dual route" mechanism, similar in general configuration to the rule enhanced ALCOVE model (Kruschke & Erickson, 1994). Categorization instructions would be allowed to modulate only "rule-based" hidden units, leaving other hidden units unaffected by the structure of the instructional language. In future work we will examine both of these options, with the goal of producing a network capable of inducing both natural and rule-structured categories.

Another issue for future work involves how the initial instructional language training is controlled. We were required to limit the accuracy of the "rule following" network by limiting the initial training time to 200 epochs. This resulted in a network which followed rules well, but not perfectly. An ideal "rule following" network can be developed by training for 1000 epochs or more, but this is undesirable. The *lack* of perfection in rule following was necessary for this model to work. The reason for this is simple – the network that never makes a mistake has essentially lost plasticity. Interference effects would only arise if actual weight modifications occurred during the exemplar based training phase. Such weight modifications are contingent on a significant error signal. If the network follows rules perfectly, there will be no error signal and, thus, no interference effect from exemplar based training.

This "training to slight imperfection" does not seem very cognitively realistic. It also has unwanted side effects, like the slight "guessing" case bias towards the "square" category which was not corrected by epoch 200. Fortunately, there are a number of other methods that might allow us to learn the instructional language without destroying our error signal. We could introduce normally distributed noise into the network both during training and during regular use. This noise might be localized to the *plan* layer or to the stimuli features, or it might be injected into the net input of every processing element. This noise would generally be averaged out over the course of learning the instructional language, but it would still introduce a non-zero error signal for the exemplar based learning phase.

Conclusion

We have provided some empirical support for the use of our connectionist model of learning "by being told" as a model of instructed category learning. In particular, we have shown that an observed interference effect between instructed rule following and exemplar-based category learning arises naturally in this model. These results also suggest a connectionist mechanism through which both rule governed category structures and "natural" categories may be induced from examples. The observed mismatch between the "uninstructed" network and the uninstructed subjects suggests that we produced a model that is overly biased towards rules. We are currently pursuing modifications to our training procedure to correct this bias.

Acknowledgements

The work of Nosofsky, Clark, & Shin (1989) was suggested to the authors by Mark St. John. Thanks are also due to the members of *Gary's & Eric's Unbelievable Research Unit (GEURU)* for their comments and suggestions on this work. We also extend our thanks to three anonymous reviewers for their helpful advice concerning the clear presentation of this research.

References

Allen, S. W. and Brooks, L. R. (1991). Specializing the operation of an explicit rule. *Journal of Experimental Psychology: General*, 120(1), 3–19.

Elman, J. L. (1990). Finding structure in time. *Cognitive Science*, 14(2), 179–211.

Kruschke, J. K. and Erickson, M. A. (1994). Learning of rules that have high-frequency exceptions: New empirical data and a hybrid connectionist model. In Ram, A. and Eiselt, K. (Eds.), *Proceedings of the Sixteenth Annual Conference of the Cognitive Science Society* (pp. 514–519). Hillsdale, NJ: Lawrence Erlbaum Associates.

Luce, R. D. (1963). Detection and recognition. In Luce, R. D., Bush, R. R., and Galanter, E. (Eds.), *Handbook of Mathematical Psychology*, volume 1 (pp. 103-189). New York, NY: John Wiley & Sons.

Noelle, D. C. and Cottrell, G. W. (1995). A connectionist model of instruction following. In Moore, J. D. and Lehman, J. F. (Eds.), *Proceedings of the Seventeenth Annual Conference of the Cognitive Science Society* (pp. 369–374). Hillsdale, NJ: Lawrence Erlbaum Associates.

Nosofsky, R. M., Clark, S. E., and Shin, H. J. (1989). Rules and exemplars in categorization, identification, and recognition. *Journal of Experimental Psychology: Learning, Memory, and Cognition*, 15(2), 282–304.

Plaut, D. C. and McClelland, J. L. (1993). Generalization with componential attractors: Word and nonword reading in an attractor network. In *Proceedings of the Fifteenth Annual Conference of the Cognitive Science Society* (pp. 824–829). Hillsdale, NJ: Lawrence Erlbaum Associates.

Rumelhart, D. E., Hinton, G. E., and Williams, R. J. (1986a). Learning internal representations by error propagation. In Rumelhart, D. E., McClelland, J. L., and the PDP Research Group (Eds.), *Parallel Distributed Processing: Explorations in the Microstructure of Cognition* (ch. 8). Cambridge, MA: MIT Press.

Shanks, D. R. and St. John, M. F. (1994). Characteristics of dissociable human learning systems. *Behavioral and Brain Sciences*, 17(3), 367–447.

St. John, M. F. (1992). Leaning language in the service of a task. In *Proceedings of the Fourteenth Annual Conference of the Cognitive Science Society* (pp. 271–276). Hillsdale, NJ: Lawrence Erlbaum Associates.

St. John, M. F. and McClelland, J. L. (1990). Learning and applying contextual constraints in sentence comprehension. *Artificial Intelligence*, 46(1–2), 217–257.

Posters

Ethical Reasoning Strategies and Their Relation to Case-Based Instruction: Some Preliminary Results

Kevin D. Ashley and **Matthew Keefer**
University of Pittsburgh
Learning Research and Development Center
3939 O'Hara Street
Pittsburgh, PA 15213
ashley+@pitt.edu, keefer@vms.cis.pitt.edu

Abstract

This paper describes some preliminary results of an experiment to collect, analyze and compare protocols of arguments concerning practical ethical dilemmas prepared by novice and more experienced ethical reasoners. We report the differences we observed between the novice and experienced reasoners' apparent strategies for analyzing ethical dilemmas. We offer an explanation of the differences in terms of specific differences in the difficulty of the strategies' information processing requirements. Finally, we attempt to explain the utility of case-based ethics instruction in terms of the need to inculcate information processing skills required by the experienced reasoners' strategy.

Introduction

In this paper, we report some preliminary findings of an empirical investigation of different strategies for analyzing practical ethical dilemmas employed by novice and more experienced ethical reasoners. We undertook this research in part to identify the relationship between case-based instruction in practical ethics and ethical reasoning strategies. Some recent work has emphasized the use of case-based instruction to acquire case experiences for use in subsequent case-based reasoning. By contrast, our previous work has emphasized the role of case-based instruction in teaching more domain-specific case-based reasoning strategies. Compare Edelson's CREANIMATE program (Edelson, 1996) which teaches young elementary students by having them see and modify case examples of animal adaptations, with the CATO program which teaches first year law students a process of making and responding to case-based legal arguments (Aleven & Ashley, 1995). We sought to investigate what the role of case-based instruction might be concerning practical ethical reasoning, specifically reasoning about dilemmas involving whether to tell the truth or disclose information. In this domain, case-based reasoning is less formalized (and more controversial) than in legal argument, but still more structured than in, say, thinking about animal function and adaptation.

The pedagogical value of focusing ethics instruction on individual cases, on case-based comparison, and on explicit procedures for conducting moral deliberation has been recognized in (Winston, 1990; Arras, 1991). A recent engineering ethics textbook proposes a casuistic (i.e., case-based) model for resolving "line-drawing" problems (Harris,

et al., 1995, pp. 127-135). Medical ethics textbooks and courses of instruction focus on case studies (see, e.g., Beauchamp & McCullough, 1984).

The relationship between case-based ethical instruction and ethical reasoning is more controversial, not least because the nature of ethical reasoning is controversial. Contemporary theorists of moral philosophy have debated the distinction between procedural / principled approaches to ethical reasoning and more agent-oriented approaches (See, e.g., Hampshire, 1983; Taylor, 1989; MacIntyre, 1984). These philosophers have argued that modern moral philosophy represents a "shift away from conceiving the moral life in accordance with the specific contexts and exigencies of the moral actor toward a focus on the acquisition of moral rules, and the use of rules in providing the standard for moral judgment" (Keefer, 1994). The theoretical and empirical work of Piaget (1932/1965) and Kohlberg (see Colby & Kohlberg, 1987) has generally supported this trend, describing moral judgment as passing through a series of stages culminating in the application of high order general principles to practical judgments. Carol Gilligan criticized this view of moral development, showing that many decision makers focus on more practical solution strategies (Gilligan, 1982).

In reaction to the procedural / principled approaches, a number of ethicists have developed "new casuistic" models of practical ethical decision making which involve comparing ethical dilemmas to past or paradigmatic ethical cases (Strong, 1988; Jonsen, 1991; Jonsen and Toulmin, 1988; Brody, 1988; Schaffner, 1994). The casuistic approaches focus on the importance of the moral agents' getting the right description and interpretation of a moral dilemma from which follows the choice of an action. They employ more domain-specific "middle-level" principles and case comparisons to flesh out a more adequate description of the problem and its possible solutions. According to Strong's model, for instance, when faced with a moral problem, one should: first, identify pertinent middle-level principles, role-specific duties, alternative courses of action, and morally relevant ways in which cases of this type can differ from one another (i.e., factors). Then, for each option, one identifies paradigm real or hypothetical cases in which the various options would be justifiable, compares the case at hand with the paradigms and determines which paradigms it is "closest to" (Strong, 1988).

We are interested in understanding the uses of cases in teaching in this domain where even the model of reasoning is debated. There are a number of possibilities. The purpose of case-based instruction in ethics might be to teach students to employ a casuistic model like Strong's and, perhaps, to provide a mental database of paradigmatic cases for purposes of making comparisons. It might be to provide students with practice employing a procedural / principled approach to ethical reasoning and examples of principles and circumstances where they apply. Alternatively, the connection between case-based instruction and ethical reasoning may involve a complex dialectical relationship between principles and cases (Arras, 1991 p. 48f).

Having undertaken an empirical investigation of ethical reasoning strategies among novice and more experienced ethical reasoners, we have identified another plausible hypothesis. We see instruction with cases as a strategy for apprising novices of the importance of description and interpretation in ethical reasoning (Geertz, 1971; Davis, 1991) and teaching them information and methods for meeting the information processing requirements of a particular reasoning strategy we call the RSO (for Role-Specific Obligations) Strategy. As we discuss below, the RSO Strategy is not strictly speaking a case-based strategy, but case-based instruction is uniquely able to inculcate the information processing skills the RSO Strategy requires.

Collecting Ethical Argument Protocols

Recently, we have completed an analysis of protocols generated in an experiment to document and understand the processes by which subjects in two groups reasoned about practical ethical issues. The first group, meant to represent novice ethical reasoners, comprised fourteen high school students in one of the premier suburban public high schools of the Pittsburgh area. The second group, meant to represent more experienced ethical reasoners, comprised six graduate students enrolled in a medical ethics graduate program at the University of Pittsburgh. Our experimental procedure involved presenting the novice group on three different days with twelve ethical dilemmas. We sought to present cases raising issues intrinsically interesting to high school students, but which also fell within the experience and expertise of the graduate students. All of the dilemmas dealt with issues involving whether or not to disclose information. Nine cases dealt with health care worker / client scenarios, while the remaining three dealt with young adult work place scenarios. For the high school students, each day's session lasted for about 1.5 hours. The subjects would begin by reading a set of from three to six of the cases and filling out a questionnaire regarding how they would resolve the cases. Sample questions are:

"In Case A, should the resident tell Jenny's parents about her plans to leave the hospital? Why?" "In Case B, should Jessica tell the insurance agent that her patient was on drugs? Why?" "Should Dr. Lewis report [to Medicare] that his patient has a more serious condition in Case E? Why or why not?" "What is the best way to handle Case A? Why? (i.e., What should Victor do?)"

We then conducted the same experimental procedure on three different days with the experienced ethical reasoner group. The ethics graduate students read the same cases and filled out the same questionnaires as the high school students.

Three Strategies for Analyzing Dilemmas

In this paper, we report the preliminary results of our analysis of the students' answers to the questionnaires. An initial review of the students' responses to the questionnaires suggested that, in analyzing the dilemmas, the subjects employed two primary strategies: (1) a Justification / Principled Strategy (PRINC Strategy) and (2) a Role Specific Obligations Strategy (RSO Strategy).

The key to the PRINC Strategy is the application of a general principle or rule as decisive in determining what ought to be done. Rules deal with cases directly. If the conditions for the application of the rule are judged to be met, the action prescribed by the rule is carried out. Conversely, if the action is carried out, the action may be justified by appeal to the rule. An example of this strategy can be seen in the response of a graduate student to a question whether a physician, who feels that an elderly Medicare patient with hypertension "needs more than three days away from her demanding family to rest and recuperate [three days being the maximum hospital stay reimbursable by Medicare], should "report that his patient has a more serious condition." The student said:

"No. To do so is to cheat all of us who pay for the system. If the old lady has a problem family it is a matter for social services, at worst, or perhaps light personal intervention at best."

We have summarized the PRINC Strategy in the following way. It should be noted that while we express both the PRINC and RSO Strategies as processes for explanatory convenience, we are not, as yet, committed to the claim that their steps are performed serially or in a particular order. Moreover, not all of the steps need be present. In the next section, we define specific classification categories based on subsets of the underlined steps.

PRINC Strategy: Justification/Principled

1. Identify general principles or norms in the dilemma.

1a. The identification process may involve stating hypothetical or assumed conditions necessary for the application of the norm or principle.

2. Determine which norm or principle is decisive.

2a. Identify action(s) in the dilemma which are consistent with the decisive principle or norm.

3. If neither norm or principle is decisive, rewrite the dilemma to accommodate values supported by a norm or principle.

3a. Propose a course of action which is consistent with the norm or principle.

4. When an action is chosen that is consistent with the norm or principle:

4a. Justify action(s) by adducing the norm or principle.

4b. (Counterfactual conditions justification strategy) In order to justify the action chosen, specify hypothetical conditions which would support an alternative action mandating a different action and show that these conditions do not obtain in the present case.

4c. Identify consequences which would ensue or be avoided by performing the action(s) mandated by the norm or principle.

5. Identify an action in the dilemma which is not consistent with a norm or principle and, so, should not be performed. Justify by adducing the norm or principle. Specify alternative action which is consistent with the norm or principle.

Rules and principles have been described by some philosophers as "preformed decisions" or "summaries of the outcomes of conflicts" (cf. Raz, 1990; Nussbaum, 1986) and in their practical role provide subjects' with ready solutions to difficult dilemmas that also carry with them an intermediate level of justification. The graduate student's response quoted above is an example of how, in the exercise of the PRINC Strategy, the determination that one principle is of overriding importance may invoke an "exclusionary" mind-set that can effectively eliminate consideration of conflicting reasons. In this example, the force of the overridden claim (her stress over family problems) is discounted as a medical concern, and viewed rather as a "matter for social services."

By contrast, the RSO Strategy requires recognition of more specific role obligations that can only be derived from knowledge of paradigmatic scenarios or scripts in which they are embedded and from which they acquire their meaning. The RSO Strategy tends to take into account the dilemma's circumstances in the identification of the dilemma as an instance of a paradigm associated with the role specific obligation. For example, consider another graduate student response to the same problem.

"Dr. Lewis should not report a false diagnosis unless there is no other way to provide his patient with adequate care. He should investigate other possibilities ([e.g.,] free care fund at hospital for stay over three days, intermediate options such as independent living type nursing home away from her family, and alternative but correct diagnoses providing longer coverage), and failing other options, if he feels that it is in the medical best interests of his patient to remain hospitalized, he should report a more serious condition. Upon doing so, however, he should attempt to explain to his patient why he is doing this, so as to avoid future confusion about her health status."

In this response, the student clearly states that the protagonist's RSO should be to "provide his patient with adequate medical care." After stating this obligation, the student specifies alternative practical steps that would avoid having to choose between the "horns" of the dilemma and still honor his specification of the RSO. If those options are not possible, the subject argues, the physician should perform the action recommended by the role-specific formulation. Finally, the student also attempts to deal with some of the costs of opting for that "horn" of the dilemma, again in a manner consistent with the RSO. We summarize the RSO Strategy as follows:

RSO Strategy: Role Specific Obligations

1. Identify the relevant role-specific obligations (RSO) and the protagonist's goals the RSO entail which make this dilemma an instance of a particular paradigm.

1a. This process may involve stating hypothetical conditions consistent with the RSO and goals.

2. Determine which action(s) in the dilemma are consistent with the RSO and goals.

2a. Identify the action(s) given in the dilemma which are consistent with the RSO paradigm.

3. If no action given in the dilemma is consistent with the RSO and goals rewrite the dilemma to accommodate values supported by an RSO and goals.

3a. Propose a course of action consistent with the preferred RSO and goals.

4. Having chosen a consistent action:

4a. Justify by explicit reference to middle-level or higher principles associated with the RSO paradigm.

4b. (Counterfactual conditions justification strategy) In order to justify the RSO chosen, specify hypothetical conditions which would support classifying the dilemma as an instance of an alternative RSO paradigm mandating a different action and show that these conditions do not obtain in the present case.

4c. Show the practical consequences of the action that would ensue which are consistent with the RSO and goals.

5. Identify an action in the dilemma which is not consistent with an RSO and goals and, so, should not be performed. Justify by explicit reference to middle-level or higher principles associated with the RSO paradigm. Specify alternative action with is consistent with RSO and goals.

The distinction between the PRINC and RSO strategies maps directly onto the distinction drawn between justification / principled strategies and those which focus on the importance of the moral agents' getting the right description and interpretation of the moral dilemma from which follows the choice of an action (Walzer, 1983; 1994). The RSO Strategy's identifying the duties/obligations of the professional, specifying hypothetical conditions for the dilemma's being an instance of a specific RSO paradigm and specifying practical consequences consistent with the RSO goals are all strategies for adequately describing the dilemma and accounting for its circumstances.

In the course of analyzing the data, another strategy was identified that was judged to be especially prevalent among our high school subjects. The strategy was similar in form to the PRINC strategy, but rather than making appeal to principles or norms (4a) in defense of the solution chosen, these subjects appealed to moral consequences. The strategy was defined using the identical number of components as the RSO and PRINC, and differs mainly in regard to the content of the (4a) justification. An example of a Justification / Consequence or CONSEQ strategy is as follows:

"Yes, the resident should tell Jenny's parents for two reasons. First, Jenny could starve herself to death while at her friends house. Second, if she leaves her parents may sue the hospital and if the resident is found to have known the plot the resident could be reprimanded by the hospital."

Analysis of Questionnaire Protocols

Our protocol analysis applies methods developed in discourse analysis and extends the work of (Keefer, 1995). All protocols were transcribed and segmented for analysis. We only scored the underlined components of the strategies. As we expected, not many of our subjects used all the components of a given strategy. The minimal criteria for scoring a protocol as RSO, PRINC and CONSEQ was the presence of a (2a) or (3a) simple action or interactive plan followed by any (4a) justification - i.e., for the PRINC strategy, a <u>principle or norm</u>, for the CONSEQ strategy, an appeal to <u>consequences</u>, and for an RSO protocol strategy, an appeal to <u>role specific obligations</u>. Of course, many subjects generated more than this minimal criteria for strategy membership. In order to provide a measure of differences in the degree of competence and sophistication in subjects' use of a strategy, each response was further classified as belonging to one of three mutually exclusive levels, A to C. The three levels are hierarchically ordered and defined by rules that specify the (increasingly complex) components of the strategy required for a protocol to be scored at a given level. The rules that define levels A to C are as follows:

A	[Strategy] Min	(2a / 3a and 4a)
B	[Strategy] + 1	(2a / 3a and 4a) + (1a and / or 4c)
C	[Strategy] + 2	(2a / 3a and 4a) + (4b and / or 5) + {optional} (1a and / or 4c)

Results

The relationship between experienced and high school subjects' choice of ethical strategies is shown in Table 1. Of the 63 graduate student responses, 68% evidenced a choice of an RSO strategy (level A, B or C). The 149 high school responses were spread out much more evenly across the different strategies, with 30% evidencing a choice of PRINC, 28% a choice of RSO, 24% CONSEQ, and the rest other. The other category includes protocols classified as nonmoral, unelaborated (i.e., uncodable), and mixed.

Table 2 shows the level of sophistication of the subjects' responses as defined by the levels A to C provided above. For each of the three major strategies, PRINC, RSO or CONSEQ, the Table shows the total percentage of high school and graduate student responses evidencing any of the three strategy levels, A, B or C. Thus, the first column in Table 2 shows that only about 3% of the high school responses reached the C level (the most complex level) of the RSO Strategy. By contrast, the next column shows that nearly 40% of the graduate student responses reached the RSO-C level. The percentage of graduate student RSO responses at each level of complexity decreases monotonically. The high school students use the other strategies and tend not to reach the complex levels of either of them.

It should be noted that these results are preliminary. We have not, as yet, examined inter-rater reliability for coding protocols as either PRINC, RSO or CONSEQ, nor have we tested whether raters can reliably differentiate the components that define each strategy.

Discussion

We interpret the results of Table 1 as indicating that graduate student responses evidenced greater reliance on the RSO Strategy. The high school subjects' choice of strategy was spread more evenly across the three major strategies.

We interpret the results of Table 2 as indicating that the graduate student responses evidenced more complex RSO strategies than those of high school students. This result confirms that while the high school students seemed more willing to recommend simple actions as solutions and to adduce rules, principles or moral consequences in their defense, the graduate students seemed better able to specify conditions under which actions are recommended by RSO's, and to consider those consequences of behavior in light of their normative commitments. Graduate students were also more likely to specify alternative (rewrite) strategies (RSO 5) and to justify solutions using counter-factual case comparisons (RSO 4b).

Since the graduate student responses evidenced greater reliance on the RSO Strategy and more complex strategy levels, we hypothesize that the "information processing requirements" of the RSO Strategy are somewhat more comprehensive and exacting than those of either the PRINC or CONSEQ Strategy. By "information processing requirements" of the strategies, we mean the answers to the following questions: What does one need to know to apply the strategy? How are these information requirements different for each strategy? What are the relative information costs of satisfying the strategies' differing information requirements?

From the examples in the protocols, we have noted that posing hypothetical conditions pursuant to the RSO Strategy requires more expert knowledge in the relevant domain of practice such as medical practice. The high school students lack that knowledge. Is the mere acquisition of knowledge about medical practice sufficient to enable a subject to attain a higher strategy level in analyzing a physician-patient situation? In light of the perceived need to provide medical students with instruction concerning practical ethical decision-making, we believe there is probably more to it than this. Domain-specific knowledge is one prerequisite for greater sensitivity to a dilemmas' circumstances and enables greater specificity and articulation of the relevant RSO's. Even a subject with the requisite technical medical expertise, however, may still need to learn how to pose hypothetical conditions meaningfully and effectively in an ethical analysis and to practice doing so.

We hypothesize that the RSO Strategy is generally more complex than the PRINC or CONSEQ Strategy. Some support for this hypothesis is found in the higher level of sophistication of the graduate students' RSO responses in contrast to the high school subjects' RSO responses.

In the vast majority of examples of the PRINC Strategy, by contrast, the subject simply identifies a rule or principle, an action that is consistent with it and also, perhaps, a justificatory appeal to the more fundamental general values that it supports. The comparative simplicity of these PRINC Strategy examples, we hypothesize, stems from the fact that the rules and principles constitute "exclusionary reasons" which allow decision makers to ignore circumstances of the dilemma that are not consistent with the action recommended by the rule or overriding principle. All that is necessary is knowing which principle or norm is decisive and which actions / interests are consistent with that principle. We also observed this same relatively simple pattern in most examples of the CONSEQ Strategy.

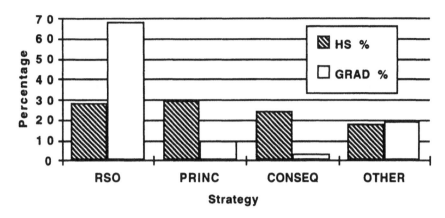

Table 1: Choice of Strategy

Table 2: Level of Strategy

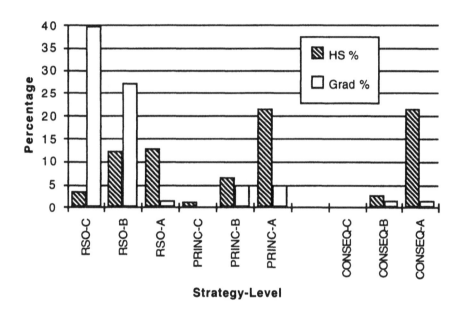

Case-Based Instruction

In designing this experiment, our initial hypothesis had been that more experienced ethical reasoners would adopt a more explicitly "casuistic" reasoning strategy. We expected to see some evidence of explicit comparisons to cases along the lines of Strong's method described above (Strong, 1988). We had, moreover, consciously built into the experiment an opportunity to compare and contrast cases. The dilemmas that were presented to subjects were selected so that they could have drawn analogies from one problem to another, either to show that they presented the same principles and/or role specific obligations, the same conflicts among principles, or an interesting comparison of factual circumstances.

In fact, we observed in the students' responses relatively few explicit cross references to other problems or cases. Our data did not show much case comparison even by the graduate students.

In so far as the RSO Strategy shares some features with Strong's procedure, however, it is more "case-based" than the PRINC or the CONSEQ Strategy: (a) Both the RSO Strategy and Strong's procedure focus on elaborating role-specific duties inherent in the situation. (b) Both involve reasoners in comparing the dilemmas to paradigms. RSO paradigms, however, were considerably more general than a specific case. (c) Both involve elaborating a description of the problem in terms of morally relevant factors or hypothetical conditions.

We hypothesize that case-based instruction assists novices to acquire the information processing knowledge and skills required to perform the RSO Strategy. In other words, practice reasoning with and comparing specific cases selected by a teacher for pedagogical purposes, may apprise novices of the information required by the RSO Strategy and help them learn skills for processing the more complex information requirements. Comparing and contrasting cases can focus attention on the nature of RSO's, their relationship to general norms, morally relevant factors in the ethical domain that can make an RSO paradigm more or less applicable, and the existence of possible alternative actions.

Conclusions

This paper has described some preliminary results of an experiment to collect, analyze and compare protocols of arguments concerning practical ethical dilemmas prepared by novice (high school students) and more experienced ethical reasoners (graduate students in medical ethics). We identified three strategies for ethical reasoning evidenced in the subjects' responses: RSO, PRINC, and CONSEQ, and three levels of complexity of each strategy. The graduate students preferred the RSO Strategy and attained more complex levels of the RSO Strategy than the high school students.

We attempted to explain the differences in terms of specific differences in the difficulty of the strategies' information processing requirements. Finally, we attempted to explain the utility of case-based ethics instruction in terms of the need to inculcate information processing skills required by the experienced reasoners' RSO Strategy.

In related work, we have built a model of case comparison in practical ethics in the TRUTH-TELLER program and will attempt to adapt it to model these different strategies (McLaren & Ashley, 1995). This research will also lead to improved techniques for representing abstract principles and getting interpretive CBR programs (Kolodner, 1993) to integrate reasoning with cases, reasons and underlying principles.

Acknowledgments

We are particularly grateful to Bruce M. McLaren for helping us to decide how best to categorize and present the data.

References

Aleven, V., and K. D. Ashley, 1995. Using a Well-Structured Model to Teach in an Ill-Structured Domain. In CogSci-95: *Proc. 17th Annual Conf. Cognitive Science Soc.*. Mahwah, NJ: Erlbaum.

Arras, J. D. (1991). Getting Down to Cases: The Revival of Casuistry in Bioethics. *J. of Medicine and Philosophy*, 16, 29-51.

Beauchamp, T. and McCullough, L. B. (1984). *Medical Ethics: The Moral Responsibilities of Physicians*. Prentice-Hall, Englewood Cliffs, NJ.

Brody, B. (1988). *Life and Death Decision Making*. New York: Oxford U. Press.

Colby, A., & Kohlberg, L. (1987). *The Measurement of Moral Judgment. Vol. 1: Theoretical Foundations and Research Validation.* and *Vol. 2: Standard Issue Scoring Manual.* New York: Cambridge U. Press.

Davis, D. S. (1991). Rich Cases, The Ethics of Thick Description. Hastings *Center Report* pp. 12-17. Jul.-Aug.

Edelson, D.C. (1996). The Socratic Case-Based Teaching Architecture. To appear in *J. of the Learning Sciences.* Erlbaum: Mahwah, NJ

Geertz, C. (1973). *The Interpretation of Culture.* New York: Basic Books.

Gilligan, C. (1982). *In a Different Voice.* Cambridge, MA: Harvard U. Press.

Hampshire, S. (1983). "Fallacies in moral reasoning". A. MacIntyre, & S. Hauerwas (Eds.), *Changing Perspectives in Moral Philosophy.* Notre Dame: Notre Dame U. Press

Harris, C., Pritchard, M., and Rabins, M. (1995) *Engineering Ethics* Belmont, CA: Wadsworth.

Johnston, D. K. (1988). Adolescents' Solutions to Dilemmas in Fables: Two Moral Orientations--Two Problem Solving Strategies. In Gilligan C. et al (Eds.), *Mapping the Moral Domain* (pp. 49-72). Cambridge, MA: Harvard U. Press.

Jonsen, A. R. (1991). Casuistry as Methodology in Clinical Ethics. *Theoretical Medicine*, 12, 295-307.

Jonsen A. R. and Toulmin S. (1988). *The Abuse of Casuistry: A History of Moral Reasoning.* U. of CA Press, Berkeley.

Keefer, M. W. (1994) *The Moral Orientation Hypothesis: Strategies of Justification and Deliberation.* Ph.D. dissertation: O.I.S.E - U. of Toronto: Toronto, Canada.

Keefer, M.W., Olson, D. (1995) Moral Reasoning and Moral Concern: An Alternative to Gilligan's Gender Based Hypothesis. *Canadian J. of Behavioral Sciences.* pp 420-437

Kolodner, J. (1993) *Case-Based Reasoning* Morgan Kaufmann Publishers, Inc., San Mateo, CA.

MacIntyre, A. (1984) *After Virtue.* (2nd ed.) Notre Dame: U. of Notre Dame Press

McLaren, B. and Ashley, K. D. (1995) Case-Based Comparative Evaluation in TRUTH-TELLER. In *Proc. 17th Annual Conf. Cognitive Science Soc.* pp. 72-77. Erlbaum: Mahwah, NJ. Pittsburgh. July.

Nussbaum, M. (1986) The Fragility of Goodness: Luck and Ethics in Greek Tragedy and Philosophy. Cambridge: Cambridge U. Press.

Piaget, J. (1965) *The Moral Judgment of the Child.* New York: Free Press. (Original work published 1932)

Raz, J. (1990) *Practical Reasoning and Norms.* Princeton: Princeton U. Press.

Schaffner, K. F. (1994) Case-based Reasoning in Bioethics and a Theory of Human Good. To appear in Schaffner, K.F., *Practical Reasoning in Health Care.* In progress.

Strong, C. (1988). Justification in Ethics. In B. A. Brody, (Ed.) *Moral Theory and Moral Judgments in Medical Ethics*, pp. 193-211. Kluwer, Dordrecht.

Taylor, C. (1989). *Sources of the Self.* Cambridge: Harvard U. Press.

Walzer, M (1994) *Thick and Thin: Moral Argument at Home and Abroad.* Notre Dame: Notre Dame U. Press.

Walzer, M. (1983). *Spheres of Justice: A Defense of Pluralism and Equality.* New York: Basic Books.

Winston, M.E. (1990) Ethics Committee Simulations. *Teaching Philosophy* 13:2 June.

Explaining preferred mental models in Allen inferences with a metrical model of imagery

Bettina Berendt

Graduiertenkolleg Kognitionswissenschaft
(Doctoral Programme in Cognitive Science), University of Hamburg
Vogt-Kölln-Str. 30, D-22527 Hamburg, Germany
berendt@informatik.uni-hamburg.de

Abstract

We present a simple metrical representation and algorithm to explain putative imagery processes underlying the empirical mental model preferences found by Knauff, Rauh and Schlieder (1995) for Allen inferences (Allen, 1983). The computational theory is compared with one based on ordinal information only (Schlieder, in preparation). Both provide good fits with the data. They differ psychologically in background theories, visualisation strategies motivated by these, and model construction processes generating models with the properties indicated as desirable by the strategies. They differ computationally in assumptions about knowledge strength (ordinal: weaker) and algorithmic simplicity (metrical: simpler). Our theory and its comparison with the ordinal theory provide the basis for a discussion of issues pertaining to imagery in general: Using the assumption of imagery inexactness, we develop a sketch theory of mental images and motivate a new visualisation strategy ('regularisation'). We demonstrate systematic methods of modelling imagery processes and of analysing such models. We also outline some criteria for comparison (and future integration?) of cognitive modelling approaches.

name	symbol	diagram	point ordering
equals	A = B		$sA{=}sB{<}eB{=}eA$
before	A < B		$sA{<}eA{<}sB{<}eB$
meets	A m B		$sA{<}eA{=}sB{<}eB$
overlaps	A o B		$sA{<}sB{<}eA{<}eB$
starts	A s B		$sA{=}sB{<}eA{<}eB$
finishes	A f B		$sB{<}sA{<}eA{=}eB$
during	A d B		$sB{<}sA{<}eA{<}eB$
during-inverse	A di B		$sA{<}sB{<}eB{<}eA$
starts-inverse	A si B		$sA{=}sB{<}eB{<}eA$
finishes-inverse	A fi B		$sA{<}sB{<}eB{=}eA$
overlaps-inverse	A oi B		$sB{<}sA{<}eB{<}eA$
meets-inverse	A mi B		$sB{<}eB{=}sA{<}eA$
after	A > B		$sB{<}eB{<}sA{<}eA$

Figure 1: The 13 interval relations, adapted from (Schlieder, in preparation). White interval = A, black interval = B; sA, sB, eA, eB = start- and endpoints of A and B.

Allen inferences, preferred mental models, and a computational theory based on ordinal information

Allen relations are the 13 'qualitative' relations which can hold between two intervals, corresponding to relations between the start- and endpoints of the two intervals, between which only the ordinal relations 'is before/smaller than', 'is equal to', and 'is after/larger than' are distinguished, see fig. 1. They have been discussed by Allen (1983) in a logic for reasoning about temporal events and have been used also as a basis for spatial reasoning calculi , e.g. in (Guesgen, 1989; Mukerjee & Joe, 1990). Qualitative relations are of interest to Cognitive Science because they might be employed in programs like Geographical Information Systems (GIS) to model human temporal/spatial reasoning more adequately than models based on numerical specifications. **Allen inferences** are compositions of Allen relations answering the following question: If the Allen relation between intervals A and B is R_1 and that between intervals B and C is R_2, then which Allen relation(s) R_3 can hold between A and C? In some cases, there is only one possible answer (relation R_3); in others, there are several. For example, if A finishes-inverse B and B before C, then A can only be before C. If A finishes-inverse B and B during C, it is possible that A starts C,

overlaps C, or is during C. The second example is shown in fig. 3; the first can easily be reconstructed from this drawing. For full details, see (Allen, 1983).

This composition can be seen as a three-term series in the sense of Johnson-Laird (1972). But how do people reason with Allen relations? Knauff, Rauh and Schlieder (1995) trained subjects in the understanding of Allen relations and then asked them to provide *one* answer to each of 12×12 Allen inference questions (they excluded the trivial compositions with **equals**). In cases where more than one Allen relation is a correct answer ('non-unique cases'), a great majority of subjects chose the same solution. The authors interpret these results as evidence of **preferred mental models**: In the sequential process of constructing the different possible mental models (= the several possibilities of arranging A, B and C such that different Allen relations R_3 hold), a strategy is employed which first leads to the construction of one particular model, the preferred model. Empirically, preferred models (aggregated over subjects) were never non-models; i.e. always yielded correct solutions.

When we try to find a **computational theory** of a strategy like this one, an interesting question concerns the **nature of the knowledge** used (cf., for example, (Huttenlocher, 1968) vs. (Johnson-Laird & Byrne, 1991)). If one assumes imagery

489

in mental models, one needs an 'image' as model, which can be modelled as containing metrical information. The input relations R_1, R_2 and the intervals A, B, C linked by them are given a metrical interpretation, i.e. some placement in the image. This metrical representation is then inspected to obtain the required answer, the Allen relation between A and C. This is based on ordinal relations between A's and C's start- and endpoints. Considering, however, that the whole concept of Allen relations is based on ordinal information, one may want to avoid giving a metrical interpretation to the ordinal Allen relations and try to formulate a theory without imagery, i.e. without metrical representations.

Schlieder (in preparation) develops **a computational theory which operates on ordinal information only.** Development of the theory starts out from the discussion of formal properties of Allen inferences discussed by Ligozat (1990), namely two kinds of symmetries of pairs of inferences. These formal properties were not satisfied empirically: The pairs of inferences identified by Ligozat had asymmetrical empirical model preferences. It is not important to go into the details of the formal argument here; it suffices to note that the observation of formal symmetry and empirical asymmetry implies that in order to explain the data, a model must generate **order effects**: a relation R is sometimes conceptualised differently depending on whether it holds between A and B or between B and C (or B and A or C and B), i.e. the two intervals are placed differently with respect to each other (for an example, see fig. 2; for full details of the formal argument, see (Ligozat, 1990; Schlieder, in preparation)). Schlieder generates order effects by assuming a **focus** in the mental model, a point which, in addition to the start- and endpoints of the intervals already considered, is kept in the representation. Schlieder can explain all but 6 of the 60 non-unique empirical preferences he considers (see fig. 5).[1] He omits compositions of inverses, which are compositions of relations like before and after, i.e. compositions whose results lie in cells along the secondary diagonal of the composition table in fig. 5. A much simpler strategy seems to be applied there: "don't think" – just assume inverses always lead back to the original, i.e. to the Allen relation equals.

However, this model has the **drawback** of being rather **complicated**: There are 6 to 14 (depending on how one counts) 'scanning rules' and rather involved 'insertion schemes' specifying different processes and orders of the insertion of start- and endpoints, and the focus position has to be remembered. These complications were our motivation to devise a **strategy** that requires **stronger information**, namely, metrical knowledge, but is much **simpler** in terms of scanning and insertion.

---

[1]By 'computational theory', we mean that for all compositions, models are generated, i.e. correct Allen inferences. By 'cannot explain', we mean that the computational theory does not generate the empirically preferred mental model for a given composition.

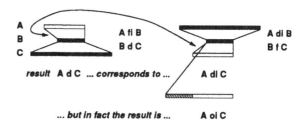

Figure 2: Order effects (example): If the Allen relations are always computed in the same way, and inverse relations are mirror images of each other, i.e. computed by inverting the operations generating the new interval in a composition, the preferred model of A finishes-inverse B and B during C ($AfiB$ and BdC) implies a preferred model for A during-inverse B and B finishes C ($AdiB$ and BfC). However, empirically the first inference has the preferred model A during C (AdC), while the second has A overlaps-inverse C ($AoiC$). An easy explanation is that the transformations linked by the curved line are different: f is *not* the mirror image of fi.

A computational theory based on metrical information

Our main **psychological background assumption** is that **mental images are inexact.** A simple example of empirical evidence for this claim is the finding that discoveries in mental images are common if the patterns to be rotated and the emerging patterns resulting from this transformation are sufficiently robust with respect to slight variations in shape and/or noise, e.g. (Finke & Slayton, 1988). If the given patterns are more complex and emergence is highly dependent on constructing and maintaining an exact representation of the given patterns' shape, however, mental discoveries are not the rule (Reisberg & Chambers, 1991); for discussion, see also (Logie, 1995). We interpret this to mean that imagery cannot represent and/or process fine details which are sensitive to small metrical changes. Image elements are represented metrically, relative to a reference frame specifying scale which is global to the whole image. However, within this frame of reference, they may only be represented inexactly, with noise. Inexactness may arise during construction, maintenance and/or inspection of the image.

For the present task, this **implies** one particular constraint on **what the images of the intervals should look like:** They should be **regular.** To understand this concept, consider the composition of A finishes-inverse B and B during C. One solution is A starts C. However, this result is extremely unstable: Any slight deviation in the lengths or placements of the intervals created by imagery inexactness would lead to A overlaps C or A during C (see fig. 3). As the reader may easily verify, the last two solutions are much more robust with respect to changes in metrical parameters. We call images involving solutions which are 'stable' in this sense (like overlaps and during) *regular*, as opposed to *singular* images involving 'unstable' solutions like starts. The data can be interpreted as showing a preference for regular images: Out of those compositions whose solution includes an unstable relation, this solution is the preferred model only in very few cases. We therefore need a **model construction process** which (a) generates correct Allen inferences, (b) generates order effects, and (c) generates regular images. The easiest metrical process contains

1. **distance parameters** specifying the length of the separation ($<, >$), the overlap (o, oi), or the offset (s, si, f, fi, d, di) of the relations. (m and mi must be 'separated' by a distance of 0.) We use 2 such parameters: Δ_n ("normal") and Δ_l ("large"). They are associated with relations depending on whether these are 'shifts' or 'deformations' and prescribe 'movements' to construct the new interval's start- and endpoints (see fig. 4).

A model containing only distance parameters generates correct Allen inferences, but fails because it cannot generate any order effects (Schlieder, in preparation). We therefore choose the second easiest, which also contains

2. a **correction parameter** ε. This is associated with relations depending on how many relations have been processed before. Using ε leads to slight, **progressive adjustments in the movements' and/or the intervals' lengths.**[2]

These adjustments generate order effects, because Allen relations receive a different metrical interpretation depending on when they are processed, i.e. depending on whether they hold between A and B or between B and C. The adjustments also guarantee regularisation, because newly generated start- and endpoints cannot be equal to existing start- and endpoints 'by coincidence' (of course they must be equal when this is specified by relations s, si, f, fi, m, mi). As an example, consider fig. 3 again: If A finishes-inverse B ($AfiB$) and B during C (BdC), and we moved A's startpoint to the right to construct B and then moved B's startpoint to the left *by the same amount* when we construct C, we would obtain a singular image with A starts C. By moving left a bit more than we have moved right, we obtain the empirically correct A during C.

By considering the changes made to the intervals in fig. 3 as 'shrinking or stretching intervals' instead of 'moving start- and endpoints', we can see that regularisation and (for this composition) the same order effect are generated when interval lengths instead of movement lengths are increased.

It is not clear how to decide on psychological grounds whether movements and/or intervals should be shortened or lengthened. We shall therefore motivate the decision to

[2]When this affects interval length, it corresponds to scaled copying from the pattern activation subsystem into the visual buffer in (Kosslyn, 1994).

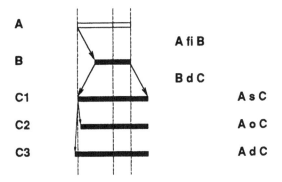

Figure 3: Example of an Allen inference with more than one solution. This shows the instability of singular images containing solutions like starts (s): Slight variations in the lengths or placements of the intervals change the obtained Allen relation.

lengthen them with a computational argument: lengthening leads to an algorithm satisfying the specification given by the data best. Computational reasoning also makes us prefer movement lengthening over interval lengthening (see below).

Δ_n, Δ_l, and ε are defined relative to the standard interval length, i.e. we assume a scale-invariant imagery process.

The following algorithm and fig. 4 summarise how the three parameters control the construction process:[3]

```
X := first interval
insert X into the image at the standard first position
no-of-steps := 0
repeat
    no-of-steps := no-of-steps + 1
    R := next relation
    if R marks a shift (⇔ if R ∈ {<, m, o, oi, mi, >}) then
        Δ := Δₗ else Δ := Δₙ
    adjust and place a copy of X according to R and Δ,
        using ε and no-of-steps
    insert the obtained interval into the image as Y
    X := Y
until no more relations are left
return the Allen relation obtained from reading
    the start- and endpoints of the first and the last interval
```

This theory, despite its great simplicity, fares extremely well when compared either to the data or to the fit of the ordinal theory. Only 9 empirical model preferences out of 60 are not explained when movements are lengthened (see fig. 5). When intervals are lengthened, another 4 preferences are not explained. As in the ordinal model, compositions of inverses were not considered.

We performed a **sensitivity analysis** of the results with respect to variations in the 3 parameters of the algorithm. We defined $errors(\Delta_n, \Delta_l, \varepsilon)$ to be the number of empirical

[3]All LISP program code used to compute the results reported in this paper can be obtained from the author on request.

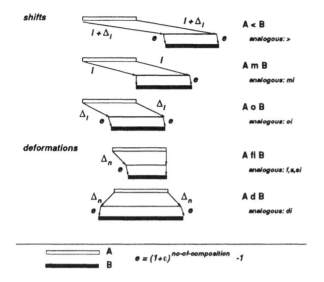

shifts

I + Δ_l   A < B
           analogous: >

I   A m B
           analogous: mi

Δ_l   A o B
           analogous: oi

deformations

Δ_n   A fi B
           analogous: f, s, si

Δ_n   Δ_n A d B
           analogous: di

A
B $e = (1+\varepsilon)^{no\text{-}of\text{-}composition} - 1$

Figure 4: Constructing a new interval: computing start- and endpoints from the previous interval, the Allen relation, and the three parameters, lengthening movement. (Alternative: to lengthen intervals, shift the boundaries of the new interval obtained in the first step *outwards* by e in the second step.)

	<	m	o	fi	s	d	di	si	f	oi	mi	>
<						<,d			o / oi<	o	o	
m						o			o	o		oi / >oi
o				<	< / <o	o	m / o o		o,d		oi	>
fi						d			oi	oi		>
s			o	o			fi / o di			oi		
d			o	o				oi		oi		
di	<	o	o		o			oi	oi	oi	>	
si	<	o	o			d			oi			
f			o				di,oi	oi		oi		
oi	<	o		oi	d / oi oi	oi	mi / oi oi oi oi	mi		>		
mi	< / <o		oi		oi	oi						
>			oi	oi	oi / oi>	>						

Figure 5: Composition table for preferred models in Allen inferences: If AR_1B (R_1 at left end of row i) and BR_2C (R_2 at top of column j), then AR_3C (R_3 in cell ij). Table shows only compositions with non-unique solutions, and no compositions of inverses (see text). Cells containing 1 Allen relation: entry = empirical preference = preference generated by the ordinal theory = preference generated by the metrical theory. Cells containing 3 Allen relations: top entry = empirical preference; bottom left entry = preference generated by the ordinal theory; bottom right entry = preference generated by the metrical theory.

model preferences not explained by the algorithm for a given choice of parameters. *errors* yields "–" if for a given choice of parameters, non-models are produced, i.e. incorrect solutions. We computed *errors* for the relevant ranges, plotted the results, and described the constraints to ensure the best results obtainable geometrically.[4] These **geometrical constraints** turned out to be **qualitative constraints**:

$\varepsilon > 0$: Any value below 0 leads to a marked decrease in fit (up to 12 errors more for movement, 2 for intervals). (A value of exactly 0 leads to singular images, which increases the number of errors dramatically.) In other words, computational reasons suggest that the movements/intervals get progressively 'slightly lenghtened'; it is not just *any* deviation from singular results that happens.

For movement adjustments, there is one constraint to guarantee no non-models: $\Delta_l \leq [1 - (3 + 10\varepsilon)\varepsilon] - \Delta_n$. This could be interpreted to mean that $\Delta_l + \Delta_n$ must not be more than 1 (remember that ε is supposed to be *small*). There are 3 constraints to guarantee not more than 9 errors. $\Delta_n \leq 0.33$ (plus some seemingly unsystematic variation): This could be interpreted as an upper bound of $\frac{1}{3}$ for Δ_n. $\Delta_l \geq 0.51 - 2\varepsilon$: this could be interpreted as a lower bound of $\frac{1}{2}$ for Δ_l. And $\Delta_l \geq -0.05 + 2.5\varepsilon + \Delta_n$: Δ_l should really be a 'larger movement' than Δ_n.

Interval length adjustments produce similar results, but are slightly less robust and produce a worse fit with the data (at least 13 errors). Here too, lengthening is superior to shortening. For reasons of space, we do not give details about constraints and errors here.

The case for preferring movement adjustment (lengthening) over interval adjustment is quite clear on computational grounds: The former produces a better fit.

What can this case study tell us about imagery in general?

As we mentioned above, our psychological background theory is that mental images are inexact. It is likely that people who reason with mental images know about this inexactness. We would therefore want to propose a new approach to inspection processes, which we call **the sketch theory of mental images**: Even though everything in the picture is determined, the picture as a whole is *treated as a sketch*, 'not to be taken literally'.[5] In other words, the meta-knowledge

---

[4] It is straightforward to determine absolute upper and lower bounds for the Δs to ensure that adding/subtracting them from start- and endpoints generates the prescribed Allen relations. ε was only examined systematically in the range (-0.1, 0.1) because first, it is supposed to mark a 'slight adjustment' and second, because larger values showed no interesting change in behaviour.

The constraints should be regarded as approximations, since we only inspected the values at a certain resolution (down to 0.001 for the Δs and ε) and did not perform regression analysis etc. However, the demarcations between levels of goodness-of-fit were quite regular, and only the qualitative relations were of interest.

[5] This idea originally occurred in the context of an exploration of the importance of sketches in interactions between architects and their customers: A recurring problem of preliminary designs pre-

'this is a sketch' induces a different inspection process, which might be: 'only notice which entities are in the picture and take this as an indication of which entities are in the represented scene', 'only notice how entities are ordered in the picture and take this as an indication of how these entities are ordered in the represented scene', or 'don't take metrical relations to be exact'. In terms of spatial knowledge content, this corresponds to: 'extract only containment relations', 'extract only order relations', or 'extract metrical relations, but at a relatively coarse level of granularity'.[6] The third kind of sketch interpretation is important whenever metrical distinctions count. It is important in our example, and constructing regular images aids in this process. For it is essential that the mental images can also depict intended equalities (if A finishes-inverse B, their endpoints *are* the same). So a visualisation strategy must enable the inspection process to distinguish between entities intended to be equal and entities not intended to be equal. There are two principal ways of solving this problem: (1) A model construction strategy generating regular images safeguards against inexactness both during model construction and during model inspection: Entities not intended to be equal are moved far enough apart by choosing a large enough ε. So even if, in construction, placement is inexact (i.e. may deviate from the value computed with the help of ε), the relative placement of entities not intended to be equal will still differ enough from the relative placement of entities intended to be equal to distinguish non-intended from intended equality during inspection: In the image, intended equalities are characterised by no gaps (if construction is exact) or by small gaps (if construction is inexact), other relations (not intended to be equalities) are characterised by large gaps. This can be distinguished both by exact inspection processes (the value read is the value depicted) and by inexact inspection processes (the value read may deviate from the value depicted). (2) The alternative would be to annotate intended equalities. In the image, intended equalities are then characterised by annotations, other relations by no annotations, and gaps can be zero, small or large in both cases. Obviously, (1) is more parsimonious and easily explainable by model construction processes, as we can show in the present case study. We would therefore assume that **regularity is generally a desired property of mental images**. The **image construction process** takes the **easiest** route towards achieving this goal. There is a **preference for copying** metrical prototypes from long-term memory into the image or within the image. If this is recognised as leading to undesired image properties, **movements are lengthened during copying and/or scaled copying is performed**; with the adjustment in length/size of the movements and/or image elements being as small as pos-

sible.

A second visualisation strategy employed in addition to regularisation might be *partitioning*: Relevant portions of the image are of equal size or small integer multiples. This is not directly linked to the argument emanating from mental image inexactness and will therefore be discussed in a separate paper.

Open questions and further research

A very straightforward application and test will be the comparison of the theory's results with the data and the ordinal theory predictions of **Allen four-term series**. These experiments are currently carried out by the authors of the three-term series paper, as are the generations of algorithmic predictions from both theories.

What could be a psychological explanation for construction involving movement or interval lengthening? This distinction reflects a difference either in the way in which temporal aspects of mental model construction are regarded, or the question what can be inspected in an image: image element properties or image element relations. Both construction processes change properties of image elements. Adjusting interval lengths is 'static' in the sense that the information needed to construct the next image element (= the previous interval's length) is 'in the picture', is a property of an image element. Adjusting movements is 'dynamic' in the sense that the information needed to construct the next image element (= the previous movement's length) is 'between the pictures', is a property of a relation between image elements. Only if image element relations can be inspected just like image element properties can this be considered 'static' in the same sense as interval length adjustment. (Of course, both methods also need access to the parameters $\Delta_n, \Delta_l, \varepsilon$, which are not usually 'in the picture'. We assume this does not create a problem.) It would be interesting to investigate further how possible dynamic effects in imagery could be formalised. In our assumption that dynamic effects *exist*, we follow the argument of Logie (1995), who explicitly introduces a spatial component into the visuo-spatial scratch pad of Baddeley and Lieberman (1980). Logie regards movement as the central feature and mechanism of spatial working memory/imagery. It seems plausible to assume that Allen inferences are as good an example of typical *spatial* tasks as is Logie's main example, the Brooks matrix task (Brooks, 1967). However, these thoughts do not answer the question what the **psychological reasons** could be **for preferring** movement or interval **lengthening over shortening**.

We should also address the question of **what criteria could be used to compare cognitive modelling approaches**. We show how our psychological background assumption, that mental images are inexact, motivates our visualisation strategy 'regularise', which in turn motivates our model construction process of movement or interval lengthening. Schliedcr (in preparation) shows how his psychological background assumption, that search processes in mental models should be as simple as possible, motivates his visualisation strategy 'lin-

---

sented as CAD graphics is that they convey the impression of being finished, worked-out designs. Hand-drawn sketches, on the other hand, convey the intended impression of being unfinished, of not having the fixed details that, if the sketch were looked at as a picture, are of course fixed (Strothotte et al., 1994).

[6](Hobbs, 1985); see (Habel, 1991) for an example of a computational treatment of granularity in knowledge about space.

earise and center', which in turn motivates his model construction process of scanning and insertion in a memory structure describing the ordinal positions of interval start- and endpoints and a focus. It seems necessary to **relate the ordinal and the metrical theories**, which raises **psychological** as well as **computational** issues. How do the psychological arguments and their stages relate? In particular: (How) can the theories explain each other's visualisation strategy?[7] By what criteria should the computational tradeoff 'knowledge strength vs. computational simplicity' be judged in the context of cognitive modelling? These issues need further discussion.

Can we hope to be able to generalise these methods and results to other domains of imagery? The advantage of the data underlying the algorithm presented here are that they provide a yardstick that is very easy to employ: The task (Allen inferences) is a sufficiently simple visuo-spatial task, since the entities are abstract entities. Their abstractness also allows us to assume that the entities are conceptualised in 'screen-space'[8] and only there. Direct extension of the results and methods could be possible in the analysis of similar tasks. This could, for example, involve tasks with information learned from books, from programs (screen layout), maybe the layout of machines, control panels and other instruments (although a large tactile component may be involved here) and possibly also some of the tasks designed to test spatial abilities.

Extending the results and methods to an analysis of less abstract and larger spaces requires some more abstraction. This is because the representations are probably 'contaminated' by a lot of other information associated with the entities reasoned about (e.g. aesthetic and functional properties of landmarks along a route), because it is a generally open question what representational and processing assumptions may be transferred between 'spaces' (e.g. from 'screen-space' to 'large-scale space'), and because in large-scale space at least, long-term memory is involved. Nevertheless, some principles appear transferable: We are currently investigating the question of how the methods presented in this paper and, more generally, the sketch theory of mental images can be used in the analysis of distance cognition in large-scale space (Berendt, in preparation). The results of this work will be important for Allen inferences too, if these inferences are to be regarded not as abstract screen tasks, as they are here, but as foundations for entities in the world to be reasoned about, e.g. geographic entities in GIS.

Acknowledgements

I wish to thank Christoph Schlieder, Christian Freksa, and Simone Pribbenow for discussion and comments, two anonymous referees for comments, and the Graduiertenkolleg Kognitionswissenschaft (Doctoral Programme in Cognitive Science) of Hamburg University for financing my work.

References

Allen, J. (1983). Maintaining knowledge about temporal intervals. *Communications of the ACM, 26*, 832–843.

Baddeley, A.D. & Lieberman, K. (1980). Spatial working memory. In R. Nickerson (Ed.), *Attention and Performance VIII* (pp. 521–539). Hillsdale, NJ: Lawrence Erlbaum.

Berendt, B. (in preparation). *Qualitative aspects in cognitive distances.* http://www.informatik.uni-hamburg.de/WSV/hp/bettina-englisch.html

Brooks, L.R. (1967). The suppression of visualisation by reading. *Quarterly Journal of Experimental Psychology, 33A*, 1–15.

Finke, R. & Slayton, K. (1988). Explorations of creative visual synthesis in mental imagery. *Memory & Cognition, 16*, 252–257.

Guesgen, H.W. (1989). *Spatial reasoning based on Allen's temporal logic* (Technical Report ICSI TR-89-049). Berkeley, CA: International Computer Science Institute.

Habel, C. (1991). Hierarchical representations of spatial knowledge: Aspects of embedding and granularity. In *Proceedings of the Second International Colloquium on Cognitive Science (ICCS-91)*. San Sebastian.

Hobbs, J.R. (1985). Granularity. In *Proceedings of the Ninth International Joint Conference on Artificial Intelligence* (pp. 432–435).

Huttenlocher, J. (1968). Constructing spatial images: A strategy in reasoning. *Psychological Review, 75*, 550–560.

Johnson-Laird, P.N. (1972). The three-term series problem. *Cognition, 1*, 58–82.

Johnson-Laird, P.N. & Byrne, R.M.J. (1991). *Deduction*. Hillsdale, NJ: Lawrence Erlbaum.

Knauff, M., Rauh, R. & Schlieder, C. (1995). Preferred mental models in qualitative spatial reasoning: A cognitive assessment of Allen's Calculus. In *Proceedings of the Seventeenth Annual Conference of the Cognitive Science Society*.

Kosslyn, S.M. (1994). *Image and Brain*. Cambridge, MA: MIT Press.

Ligozat, G. (1990). Weak representation of interval algebras. In *Proceedings of the Eighth Conference of the American Association for Artificial Intelligence* (pp. 715–720).

Logie, R.H. (1995). *Visuo-Spatial Working Memory*. Hillsdale, NJ: Lawrence Erlbaum.

Mukerjee, A. & Joe, G. (1990). A qualitative model for space. In *Proceedings of the Eighth Conference of the American Association for Artificial Intelligence* (pp. 721–727).

Reisberg, D. & Chambers, D. (1991). Neither pictures nor propositions: What can we learn from a mental image? *Canadian Journal of Psychology, 45*, 288–302.

Schlieder, C. (in preparation). The construction of preferred mental models in reasoning with Allen's relations. To appear in C. Habel (Ed.) *Mental models in text comprehension and reasoning*.

Strothotte, T., Preim, B., Raab, A., Schumann, J. & Forsey, D.R. (1994). How to render frames and influence people. *Computer Graphics Forum, 13*, 455–466.

---

[7]Thanks to Christoph Schlieder for suggesting this way of parallelising the two theories to me.

[8]analogous to the often-made distinction between such spaces as 'table-top space', 'large-scale space' etc.

Can We Unmask the Phonemic Masking Effect? The Problem of Methodological Divergence

Iris Berent and **Guy C. Van Orden**
Department of Psychology
Arizona State University
Berent@vms.cis.pitt.edu
Guy.Van.Orden@asu.edu

Abstract

In studying cognition, we infer the presence of mental structures in an idealized setting from performance in various experimental settings. Although experimental settings are believed to tap the mental structure of interest, they also always reflect idiosyncratic task-specific properties. Indeed, distinct methods often diverge in their outcomes. How can we assess the presence of the mental structure in the idealized setting given divergent outcomes of distinct methods? We illustrate this problem in a specific example concerning the contribution of phonology in reading. Evidence for the role of phonology in the "idealized" reading setting is assessed by different methods. Methods of masked and unmasked display disagree in their outcomes. The contribution of phonology appears robust under masking, but limited under unmasked display. We outline two alternative explanations for the robustness of phonological effects under masking. On one view, phonemic masking effects are a true reflection of early reading stages (Berent & Perfetti, 1995). Conversely, Verstaen et al. (1995) argue (1) that masking overestimates the contribution of phonology and (2) that phonemic masking effects are eliminated by a manipulation that discourages reliance on phonology. We demonstrate that (2) is incorrect, but (1) cannot be resolved empirically.

In studying cognition, we infer the contents and structure of a cognitive architecture from observed behavior in an experimental setting. Our interest, however, is rarely limited to the specific experimental setting. Instead, we wish to describe the mental structures that pertain to some idealized general setting[1] . Our empirical data, however, provide us with only partial information for making such generalizations. Behavior observed in a given experimental setting is always at least partly due to the idiosyncratic requirements of the experimental task which may be irrelevant to the idealized setting. For instance, our own research attempts to reveal the mental structures underlying performance in an idealized "natural" reading setting. Laboratory tasks all maintain some of the characteristics of this idealized setting, but, in addition, they present some idiosyncratic demands, such as the discrimination of words

from nonwords, speeded naming or identifying words when they can barely be seen due to visual masking. Indeed, distinct methods, believed to tap into a common mental structure, often diverge in their outcomes. Such divergence calls for an interpretation. Given that divergence of outcomes is partly due to methodological differences, how could one assess the generality of an inferred mental structure?

Consider, for instance, a case where two methods, M_1 and M_2 may both reflect the presence of a certain mental structure α at some idealized general setting **M**. Suppose, however, that these methods disagree in their outcomes. Method M_1 yields positive evidence for α whereas no evidence for α is detected by method M_2. One is then left with two related questions. (1) Why do the methods diverge in their outcomes? (2) Which outcome should we trust: Is the mental structure α present in the idealized setting **M**? A reply to these questions might include one of two moves[2]. One may choose to reify the outcome of method M_1 by assuming that M_1's outcome (but not M_2's) is a true marker of the structure α. On this view, structure α generally does underlie performance in the idealized setting **M**. The failure of method M_2 to reflect its presence is due to some task specific factors which reduce its sensitivity. Conversely, one may conclude that method M_1 induces an idiosyncratic bias for detecting the presence of representation α. The detection of α by method M_1 is thus due to some task specific factors that are unrepresentative of the idealized situation. Thus, method M_2's null outcome is the true marker, and structure α generally does not underlie

---

[1] For the present discussion, we disregard the important question of whether such general circumstances exist by referring to an idealized, rather than real, general circumstances.

[2] Two other possible moves are (3) Rejecting the outcomes of both M_1 and M_2 on the grounds that their context-sensitivity as markers of α prevents inference regarding the idealized setting **M** and (4) accepting the outcome of both M_1 and M_2, assuming strategic control over α in the idealized setting. Neither of these moves escapes the induction problem. Practically all known markers of cognitive structures are context sensitive, so move 3 entails the rejection of cognitive psychology as an empirical science. Move 4 equates the study of cognition with the study of context sensitive strategic control--a rather different enterprise than the traditional pursuit of context-free structures (see Van Orden, Aitchison & Podgornik, 1996b). This move, however does not escape theory driven assumptions regarding methods M_1 and M_2 as (true) mirrors of **M**.

performance in the idealized situation **M**. Importantly, each of these moves regarding the presence of α in the idealized setting requires additional assumptions regarding methods M_1 and M_2. If these additional assumptions are derived from the same theory regarding mental structure α, then we face a problem of circularity: Theory-driven assumptions regarding method-properties predetermine the acceptability of evidence pertinent to the same theory (Van Orden, Pennington & Stone, 1996a, Van Orden et al., 1996b). The present research extends the investigation of Van Orden and colleagues to an additional example where theory-driven methodological assumptions determine the interpretation of data in reading experiments. We will not resolve these issues because there does not appear to be a simple correct answer. By reporting this example, we hope to raise specific questions regarding reading research, as well as general questions regarding the larger problem of methodological divergence.

Our example concerns the role of phonology in reading, undoubtedly, one of the most controversial issues in psycholinguistics. It is often assumed that reading a word entails the retrieval of its meaning from a mental lexicon. How is a word's meaning retrieved: Is it achieved solely based on **graphemic** (letter) information, or is it constrained by **phonological** information, assembled by mapping its letters into phonemes? The reading literature includes two contradictory replies to this question. According to the *slow* phonology hypothesis (e.g., Seidenberg, Waters, Barnes & Tanenhaus, 1984), the assembly of phonology is too slow to affect lexical access. Its computation is resource-demanding and subject to strategic control. On this view, words' meanings are retrieved primarily based on graphemic information. In contrast, the *fast* phonology hypothesis (e.g. Van Orden, Pennington & Stone, 1990) assumes that the assembly of phonology is very fast and relatively automatic. Phonology is thus believed to be a general, perhaps mandatory component of reading.

The existing, very large body of evidence pertaining to this question is highly contradictory. In a recent review paper, Berent & Perfetti (1995) suggested that the contradictions regarding the nature of phonology and its contribution to reading are systematically linked to the type of method used. Masking methods, displaying the words for a brief duration (e.g. 15 ms) followed by a masking stimulus, typically portray phonology as a fast and general constraint on reading (e.g., Perfetti & Bell, 1991). In contrast, methods in which words are not masked depict the assembly of phonology as slow, controlled and limited in its effect (e.g., Seidenberg et al., 1984). Berent & Perfetti (1995) explained that divergence within a specific theory of reading, the two cycles model. According to the two cycles model, phonology is assembled in two consecutive stages. The first consonantal cycle is fast and automatic, followed by a second, vowel cycle, which is slow and controlled. The methodological contradictions are thus addressed by assuming temporal changes in the contents of phonological representations which parallel the temporal contrast between experimental methods. Methods using clearly presented, unmasked words portray assembly as slow and controlled

because they tap primarily into the late vowel cycle. In contrast, masking methods tap into the early consonantal cycle, and thus, depict phonology as a fast and general constraint. In essence, this solution to the methodological conflict assumes that both methods provide true reflections of the assembly mechanism.

From the point of view of the slow phonology hypothesis, Berent & Perfetti's (1995) account of results obtained using unmasked words is relatively uncontroversial. The idea that these findings reflect a slow and controlled vowel cycle fits well with the slow phonology hypothesis. It is the robustness of phonological effects found using masking methods that is the subject of debate. Berent and Perfetti assumed that masking procedures provide a faithful reflection of the general contribution of consonant assembly to reading. Conversely, one may question phonological effects found using masking methods by assuming that masking distorts natural reading processes. Such an explanation has been proposed by Verstaen, Humphrey, Olson, & D'Ydewalle (1995). On their view, phonological effects under masking do not reflect an inherent property of reading; they are induced by the masking technique. By contrast, graphemic information is the principal constraint on natural reading. Graphemic information, however, is disrupted by masking (see also Hawkins, 1976; Carr, Davidson & Hawkins, 1978; Carr & Pollatsek, 1985). This forces the reader to rely on phonology, which is otherwise a rather atypical method of deriving a word's meaning.

The previous view of phonology as an optional, weak constraint on reading predicts that phonology effects may be eliminated under conditions discouraging its use. Verstaen et al. (1995) supported this claim using a masking method. In the crux manipulation, homophone words (e.g. sine) were presented briefly followed by a mask composed of letters (e.g. SYNE, SONE). Because the meaning and spelling of a homophone is unpredictable from its phonology, the use of homophones is expected to discourage subjects' reliance on phonology. The contribution of phonology to the identification of these targets was examined by comparing the effects of three masks: A *pseudohomophone*, e.g. SYNE--a nonword whose pronunciation matches the target's; a *graphemic* mask, e.g., SONE-- a nonword matched to the pseudohomophone in graphemic (but not phonological) similarity to the target; and a *control* mask e.g., PRAF-- a nonword that shares neither phonology nor graphemes with the target. The subjects' task is simply to report the spelling of the target. If subjects rely on phonology in this task, then a pseudohomophone mask (SYNE) that reinstates the target's phonology may facilitate identification compared to a graphemic control mask. The differential effect of the pseudohomophone relative to the graphemic mask is referred to as the phonemic masking effect. If subjects may suppress phonology, then the phonemic masking effect may be nullified by the conspicuous presentation of homophone targets. Indeed, Verstaen et al (1995) found that the conspicuous presentation of homophone targets at the beginning of the experiment results in the cancellation of the phonemic masking effect whereas the inconspicuous presentation of homophone targets toward the end of the experiment yields a significant phonemic masking effect.

The results of Verstaen et al (1995) raise questions at several levels. Concerning reading specifically, these results question Berent & Perfetti's (1995) claim that the masking method taps a mandatory component of assembly. Their findings thus challenge both the fast phonology hypothesis and the validity of the masking technique for revealing fast phonology. At a more general theoretical level, these findings illustrate the difficulty of interpreting methodological divergence. Our experiment concerns reading specifically, but we return to the wider implications in the discussion.

The evidence supporting the suppression of phonology always rests on a failure to observe a phonology effect (Van Orden et al., 1990). Obviously, the support of hypotheses by null results is a questionable practice. The specific null effect of Verstaen et al. (1995) further disagrees with existing evidence demonstrating phonological effects under masking despite conditions that discourage reliance on phonology (e.g., Berent, 1995; Van Orden, 1987; Ziegler & Jacobs, 1995; Ziegler, Van Orden & Jacobs, in press). We begin our investigation by revisiting this null effect. We first attempt to replicate the findings of Verstaen et al. using their homophone targets. Following their design, we manipulated subjects' reliance on phonology using two lists consisting of homophone targets and nonhomophone fillers. In the phonology encouraging condition, one group of subjects was presented with the homophone targets after seeing nonhomophone fillers, and they were not informed of the presence of homophones in the list. According to Verstaen et al (1995), these conditions should encourage the reliance on phonology, yielding a significant phonemic masking effect. In contrast, subjects in the phonology discouraging condition were presented with the homophone targets at the beginning of the experiment. Moreover, they were explicitly warned about the presence of homophones and advised to rely on spelling. If phonology may be suppressed under conditions discouraging its use, then this condition should produce a null phonemic masking effect, as found by Verstaen et al. (1995).

Method
Materials
The homophone targets and their masks were 51 of the 54 homophones used by Verstaen et al. (1995)[3]. The nonhomophone fillers were the 48 simple-vowel targets used in Berent & Perfetti, (1995, Experiment 4). Following Verstaen et al., the sets of homophone and nonhomophone targets were arranged in two combinations designed to encourage or discourage the reliance on phonology. In the phonology encouraging condition, the nonhomophone targets were presented first followed by the homophone targets. In the phonology discouraging condition, the homophone targets were presented fist followed by the

---

[3]One target was excluded because its pseudohomophone failed to match the target's pronunciation in American English. Two additional targets were excluded for the purpose of counterbalancing.

nonhomophone targets. Within each condition, the presentation of each target and its nonword masks was counter-balanced. Targets were presented in lower case whereas masks were presented in upper case, and they were each bounded by number signs (#) to the right and left of their outermost letters.

Procedure
At the beginning of the trial, a pattern mask (########) appeared as a fixation at the center of the monitor. Subjects initiated a trial by pressing the space bar. Each trial contained three successive events: A target word, a nonword mask and a pattern mask. The target was followed immediately by the nonword mask and a pattern mask which remained on the screen until the subject responded. The target and mask were each presented for two refresh cycles (28 ms). The order of trials for each subject within each block of trials (homophone vs. nonhomophone) was random. To reduce the visual contrast, all visual stimuli were presented in a blue color on a black background

Subjects were asked to write down the targets and masks they perceived. In the phonology discouraging condition, they were warned about the presence of homophones and advised to attend to spelling disregarding words' pronunciations. These subjects were also warmed up with homophone targets. None of the targets used in the warm up appeared in the experimental session, and they were all followed by a control mask.

Subjects
Subjects were Arizona State University undergraduates who were native English speakers with normal or corrected to normal vision. To eliminate floor and ceiling performances, a cut off procedure was adopted. The level of acceptable performance was set to 10-90% overall accuracy across target types. This cut off yielded 36 subjects per condition and eliminated 6 subjects from the phonology encouraging condition and 4 subjects from the discouraging condition.

Results
Homophone Targets
Correct Identification. The ANOVA on the identification accuracy of homophone targets (2 strategy x 2 mask) revealed a significant interaction of mask by strategy ($F_1(2, 140)=3.419$, MSe=.007, p=.0355; $F_2(2, 100)=3.042$, MSe=.012 p=.0522). In the encouraging condition, the pseudohomophone ($\Delta=7.84\%$, $F_1(1, 140)=15.83$, p=.0001; $F_2(1, 100)=13.256$, p=.0004) and graphemic mask ($\Delta=5.22\%$, $F_1(1, 140)=7.02$, p=.009; $F_2(1, 100)=5.894$, p=.017) each facilitated recognition compared to the control mask. However, the phonemic masking effect was not significant: recognition with the pseudohomophone and graphemic mask did not differ significantly ($\Delta=2.62\%$, $F_1(1, 140)=1.766$, p=.1856; $F_2(1, 100)=1.471$, p=.228). In contrast, the discouraging condition resulted in a significant phonemic masking effect. This effect, however, was inhibitory in nature: Identification accuracy in the presence of the pseudohomophone mask was significantly lower compared to the graphemic mask ($\Delta=4.91\%$, $F_1(1, 140)=6.21$, p=.0138; $F_2(1, 100)=5.155$, p=.0253). In

addition, the graphemic mask (Δ=8.66%, $F_1(1, 140)$=19.32, p=.0000; $F_2(1, 100)$=16.11, p=.0001), but not the pseudohomophone (Δ=3.75%, $F_1(1, 140)$=3.62, p=.059; $F_2(1, 100)$=3.039, p=.0844) improved recognition accuracy compared to the control mask

	Encouraging	Discouraging
Pseudohomophone	26.63	24.50
Graphemic	24.01	29.41
Control	18.79	20.75

Table 1: Target identification accuracy (% correct) as a function of mask type in the phonology encouraging and phonology discouraging condition

Homophone Errors. Of the 1836 trials involving homophone targets, 31 of the responses given in the phonology encouraging condition and 36 of the responses in the phonology discouraging condition were incorrect reports of the target's homophone (e.g., *sign* reported to the target *sine*). The ANOVA on homophone errors (2 strategy x 2 mask) revealed a significant main effect of mask type ($F_1(2, 140)$=5.017, MSe=.001, p=.0079; $F_2(2, 100)$=9.216, MSe=.001, p=.0002). Interestingly, homophone errors reflected a phonology effect. Across strategy conditions, the pseudohomophone mask resulted in a marginally significant increase in homophone errors compared to the graphemic mask (Δ=.0098, $F_1(1, 140)$=2.72, p=.1012; $F_2(1, 100)$=5.005, p=.0275) and the control mask (Δ=.0188, $F_1(1, 140)$=10.028, p=.0019; $F_2(1, 100)$=18.47, p=.0000). The graphemic mask also produced a marginally significant increase in homophone errors compared to the control mask (Δ=.009, $F_1(1, 140)$=2.39, p=.13; $F_2(1, 100)$=4.225, p=.04). An inspection of the cell means, however, revealed that the phonology effect is mainly due to the phonology encouraging condition. In the phonology encouraging condition, the pseudohomophone mask resulted in a significant increase in homophone errors compared to the graphemic mask (Δ=.0147, $F_1(1, 140)$=3.95, p=.049; $F_2(1, 100)$=4.664, p=.0332). In contrast, no such difference in homophone errors was found in the phonology discouraging condition (Δ=.0048, $F_1(1, 140)$<1, $F_2(1, 100)$<1).

	Encouraging	Discouraging	All
Pseudohomophone	.0278	.0278	.0278
Graphemic	.0131	.0229	.0180
Control	.0098	.0082	.0090

Table 2: The mean number of homophone errors produced by a subject per homophone target in the phonology encouraging and phonology discouraging conditions.

Discussion

The present experiment was designed to assess the claim of Verstaen et al (1995) that reliance on phonology may be eliminated by phonology discouraging conditions. In support of their claim, Verstaen and colleagues presented a null effect of phonemic masking obtained when subjects were confronted with homophone targets. The results of the present experiment contradict the attribution of this null effect to the absence of phonology. Although the pseudohomophone mask increased homophone errors compared to the graphemic mask, no phonemic masking effect was obtained in correct target identification. Thus, the strategy manipulation is not *necessary* to produce a null phonemic masking effect. Moreover, the results of the phonology discouraging condition suggest that their strategy manipulation is not *sufficient* to eliminate phonology either[4]. A strong inhibitory phonemic masking effect was obtained under conditions designed to discourage reliance upon phonology. The topology of effects in our data is identical to theirs; A similar nonsignificant inhibitory trend was observed also in each of the studies of Verstaen et al. (1995). Because the pseudohomophone and graphemic mask differ only in their phonological similarity to the target, any difference in their effect must indicate the presence of phonology. What is the reason for this inhibitory effect? Why did it emerge in the discouraging condition?

By definition, the pseudohomophone provides subjects with the target's correct phonology at the price of incorrect spelling. If phonology feeds back activation to spelling (Stone, Vanhoy & Van Orden, in press), then the pseudohomophone phonology may activate the spelling of the target's homophone competitor (e.g. *sign*), introducing additional competition. The activation of multiple spellings may result in a competition which ultimately reduces the activation of the target's correct spelling (Ziegler & Jacobs, 1995; Ziegler et al., in press). Thus, in the presence of homophone targets, the pseudohomophone may not only increase the availability of incorrect spelling information (expressed in homophone errors in the encouraging condition) but also decrease the activation of the target's correct spelling (expressed in failures of target recognition in the discouraging condition). Phonemic masking thus increases the uncertainty regarding targets' spelling. Given the emphasis on correct spelling in the discouraging condition, subjects may adapt to the spelling uncertainty by means of two strategies. They may adopt a cautious report strategy in cases of spelling uncertainty. In addition, subjects may increase their tolerance of incorrect phonemic information associated with non-homophone masks. These two strategies would lead to a decrease in target report with the pseudohomophone and perhaps an increase in the presence of the graphemic mask. The inhibitory phonemic masking effect in the phonology discouraging condition may reflect the combined effect of these two strategies. Interestingly, an inhibitory phonemic masking effect has also been found in the absence of such an explicit strategy manipulation in Hebrew, a language manifesting pervasive homophony (Berent & Frost, in press). An inhibition of inconsistent correspondences between phonemes and graphemes may be necessary to ensure correct spelling in this language. Importantly, however, inhibitory effects of

---

[4]Proponents of the slow phonology hypothesis may still argue that phonology assembly may be eliminated by some other still stronger discouraging manipulation. This pursuit of null phonology effect would seem to carry the burden of proof.

phonemic masking are strong evidence for the contribution of phonology. Thus, in contrast to the conclusion of Verstaen et al. (1995), the present results suggest that reliance on phonology persists under conditions designed to suppress its contribution.

What are the general implications of our findings for the debate regarding the contribution of phonology in reading? We began this discussion with a stalemate. One of the strongest sources evidence supporting the fast phonology hypothesis is the robustness of phonology effects under masking conditions. These findings contrast with outcomes of methods of unmasked display. We outlined two competing accounts for this methodological divergence. Specifically, these accounts concern the phonemic masking effects. Berent & Perfetti (1995) attributed the robustness of phonemic masking effects to the inherent properties of consonant assembly, tapped by the masking procedure. Conversely, Verstaen et al. (1995) argued that masking effects artificially encourage phonology by selectively degrading graphemic information. Our present findings demonstrate that subjects rely on phonology under phonology discouraging masking conditions. Unfortunately, however, these findings do not resolve the stalemate with respect to the role of phonology in reading. The resolution of this stalemate requires a priori, objective knowledge of the masking procedure. The falsification of Verstaen et al.'s (1995) claim that assembly may be suppressed under masking does not discredit their general contention that the masking procedure overestimates the contribution of phonology.

It seems difficult, perhaps impossible, to determine whether evidence for phonology from masking studies reflects the idealized reading setting or artifacts of the masking procedure. Evidence for a mental structure in an experimental setting increases our certainty that this structure is present in the experimental setting, but it does not necessarily increase certainty about its presence in the idealized setting. The tighter the construction of the experimental setting, the greater the difficulty in generalizing its outcomes to the idealized setting. This uncertainty is particularly salient when outcomes of distinct methods diverge. These problems are clearly not limited to any particular experimental method, but they are especially grave with respect to masking. If Berent & Perfetti (1995) are right to claim that the contents of phonology change along the time dimension, then properties of early reading stages are fully confounded with the masking paradigm. Only masking methods may reveal the unique properties of early reading stages. If so, then divergence between the outcomes of masked and unmasked settings is virtually guaranteed.

A methodological divergence invites the labeling of empirical methods as biased mirrors of an idealized setting. Given inherent uncertainty as to how idiosyncratic tasks affect the outcomes of experiments, the resolution of methodological divergence cannot be achieved in a theory-independent fashion. We offer no solution for these problems. However, recognizing the role of theory driven assumptions in such interpretations may reduce the risk of unacknowledged circularity. The illusion that methodological divergence can be resolved based on theory independent inferences is dangerous, since it inevitably licenses theories to ignore conflicting data by stigmatizing methods used in their collection (Van Orden et al., 1996b). Recognizing the role of theory in the evaluation of empirical outcomes could protect against unfounded dismissals of conflicting data. Pluralism may well be our best means for progress.

Acknowledgments
This research was supported by an NIH National Research Science Award (5 F32 DC00186-02) to Iris Berent and an NIH First Award (CMS 5 R29 NS26247-05) to Guy Van Orden.

References

Berent, I. (1995). *Phonological effects in the lexical decision task: Regularity effects are not necessary evidence for assembly*. A manuscript submitted for publication

Berent, I., & Frost, R. (in press). The inhibition of polygraphic consonants in spelling Hebrew: Evidence for a recurrent assembly of spelling and phonology in visual word recognition. To appear in C. Perfetti, M. Fayol, and L. Rieben (Eds.) *Learning to spell.* Hillsdale: Erlbaum.

Berent, I. & Perfetti, C. (1995) . A rose is a REEZ: The two cycles model of phonology assembly in reading English. *Psychological Review, 102,* 146-184.

Carr, T., Davidson, B., & Hawkins, H. (1978). Perceptual flexibility in word recognition: Strategies affect orthographic computation but not lexical access. *Journal of Experimental Psychology: Human Perception and Performance, 4,* 647-690.

Carr, T. & Pollatsek, A. (1985). Recognizing printed words: A look at current models. In D. Besner, T. Walker & G. Mackinnon (Eds.). *Reading research: Advances in theory and practice* (Vol.5, pp. 1-82). Orlando, FL: Academic Press.

Hawkins, H., Reicher, G., & Peterson, L. (1976). Flexible coding in word recognition. *Journal of Experimental Psychology: Human Perception and Performance, 2,* 380-385.

Perfetti, C. & Bell, L. (1991). Phonemic activation during the first 40 ms of word identification: Evidence from backward masking and priming. *Journal of Memory and Language, 30,* 473-485.

Seidenberg, M., Waters, G., Barnes, M. & Tanenhaus, M. (1984). When does irregular spelling or pronunciation influence word recognition? *Journal of Verbal Learning and Verbal Behavior , 23,* 384-404.

Stone, G., Vanhoy, M. & Van Orden, G. (in press). Perception is a two-way street: Feedforward and feedback phonology in visual word recognition. *Journal of Experimental Psychology: Human Perception and Performance.*

Van Orden, G. (1987). A rose is a ROWS: Spelling, sound and reading. *Memory and Cognition, 15,* 181-190.

Van Orden, G., Pennington, B & Stone, G. (1990) Word identification in reading and the promise of subsymbolic psycholinguistics. Psychological Review, 97, 488-522.

Van Orden, G., Pennington, B & Stone, G. (1996a). *What do double dissociations prove? Inductive methods and theory in psychology.* A manuscript submitted for publication.

Van Orden, G., Aitchison, C. & Podgornik, M. (1996b). *When a ROWS is not a ROSE: Null effects and the absence of cognitive structures.* A manuscript submitted for publication.

Verstaen, A., Humphreys, G., Olson, A., & D'Ydewalle, G. (1995). Are phonemic effects in backward masking evidence for automatic prelexical phonemic activation in visual word recognition? *Journal of Memory and Language, 34,* 335-356.

Ziegler, J. & Jacobs, A. (1995). Phonological information provides early source of constraint in the processing of letter strings. *Journal of Memory and Language, 34,* 567-593.

Ziegler, J. C., Van Orden, G. C., & Jacobs, A. M. (in press). Phonology can help or hurt the perception of print. *Journal of Experimental Psychology: Human Perception and Performance.*

The Evaluation of the Communicative Effect

Enrico Blanzieri and **Monica Bucciarelli**
Centro di Scienza Cognitiva, Università di Torino
via Lagrange, 3 - 10123 Torino
{blanzier,monica}@psych.unito.it

Abstract

Aim of our research is an analysis of the inferential processes involved in a speaker's evaluation of the communicative effect achieved on a hearer. We present a computational model where such evaluation process relies on two main factors which may vary according to their strength: 1. the verbal commitment of the hearer to play his role in the behavioral game actually bid by the speaker, 2. the personal beliefs of the speaker concerning hearer's beliefs. The hypothesis was tested as follows. First, we devised a questionnaire in order to collect human subjects' evaluations of communicative effects. Subjects were required to consider some scenarios and to identify themselves with a speaker. Their task was to evaluate, for each scenario, the communicative effect they had reached on the hearer (acceptance to play the game, refusal, or indecision). Then, we implemented our computational model in a connectionist network; we chose a set of input variables whose combination describes all the scenarios, and we used part of the experimental data to train the network. Finally, we compared the outputs of the network with the evaluations performed by the human subjects. The results are satisfactory.

1. Introduction

The reason why a speaker communicates is to reach an effect on a hearer. However, the psychological literature is not much concerned with an analysis of the communicative effect, i.e. perlocutionary effect. Our research is an attempt to analyze the perlocutionary effect from the point of view of the speaker. In particular, we are interested in *what* is relevant to the speaker in order to evaluate the effect reached on the hearer, and *how* the evaluation process is carried on. In what follows, we claim that the speaker takes into account, as pertaining evidence, both the engagement of the hearer to play the game, and hearer's beliefs on the sincerity of the speaker. The evaluation process, we argue, consists in use of the evidence to strengthen or weaken the belief concerning the effect reached on the hearer. The entire process, which in human beings seems to be speedy and effortless, is modeled by a connectionist network.

The paper is organized as follows. Section 2 is devoted to a brief presentation of Cognitive Pragmatics Theory, with special reference to the mental representations involved in the evaluation of the communicative effect. Our model is introduced in section 3, whereas section 4 is concerned with the questionnaire. The network is described in section 5, and the results of the comparison between human subjects' performances and the performances of the network are given in section 6. Finally, conclusions are in section 7.

2. Cognitive Pragmatics Theory

Cognitive Pragmatics Theory is concerned with an analysis of the cognitive processes underlying human communication. The theory, advanced by Airenti, Bara and Colombetti (1993), is presented inside the framework of Speech Acts' Theory and, consistently, claims that communication must be considered part of action (Austin, 1962; Searle, 1969, 1979). Indeed, when actor A communicates, either verbally or not, she aims at reaching an effect on partner P by means of changing his mental states or inducing him to perform an action. Given the assumption that the same analysis holds for both verbal and nonverbal communication, the terms actor and partner are commonly used instead of the terms speaker and hearer. Following the convention, we'll also refer to actor A as a female and to partner P as a male.

One of the major assumption of Cognitive Pragmatics is that, in order to cooperate from the behavioral point of view, the actor and the partner must act on the basis of a plan at least partially shared, that is called *behavior game* between A and P. Consider, for instance, the following example.

[1] (context: a client enters in a shoe-shop)
A: I'm looking for a pair of green shoes.
P: Sorry, but they were all sold out last week.
A: Well, I'll have a look elsewhere. Thanks.

An oversimplification of the behavior game shared by A and P in [1] is the following:

[2] [BUY-SOMETHING]
1. P gives an object x to A
2. A gives an amount of money y to P

A behavior game is a stereotyped pattern of interaction where the moves of A and P are specified and indicate the type of contribute that each of them is expected to provide at a certain point of the game in order to be cooperative. The moves need not be logically necessary as they just describe typical interactions involving the agents. Besides, the game specifies the situation in which the game can be played by the agents, namely its validity conditions. In our example, the game will also specifies that one must ask for an article in the proper shop, e.g. A will not ask for a pair of shoes in a bakery, and will pay the amount required for the article, e.g. A will not pay $5 if the shop assistant declares a price of $60.

The relevance of the notion of behavior game relies on the fact that, according to Cognitive Pragmatics Theory, a speech act realizes a move of a behavior game. Therefore, it is claimed that, in order to deeply understand the communicative intention of an actor, the partner must realize what game she bids by means of the utterance. In particular, Airenti and colleagues analyze the process of comprehension of a communicative act and theoretically decompose it in five phases:

1. *Literal meaning*. The partner reconstructs the mental states literally expressed by the actor.
2. *Speaker's meaning*. The partner reconstructs the communicative intentions of the actor.
3. *Communicative effect*. The partner possibly modifies his own beliefs and intentions.
4. *Reaction*. The intentions for the generation of the response are produced.
5. *Response*. An overt response is constructed.

In phase 2 all the relevant communicative intentions of the actor are reconstructed by the partner; their relevance is established on the fact that they manifest the actor's intention to participate in a behavior game with the partner. Thus, the utterance proffered by A is really understood when it is referred to the behavior game bid by A. For instance, an utterance like :

[3]   A: Can you rise your arm?

may be interpreted by P as a request to rise his arm or as a request about his possibility to rise the arm. If the behavior game suggested by the context is [AT THE TAILOR'S] the intended meaning might be a request. On the other hand, if the game suggested by the context is [MEDICAL EXAMINATION] the actor's meaning might be a request concerning the physical possibility that P rise his arm.

Our research attempts to model part of the communicative process as it is described by Airenti and colleagues, namely A's evaluation of the communicative effect reached on P. In terms of game bidding and acceptance the communicative process can be analyzed as follows :
i. A bids a game to P
ii. P responds
iii. A evaluates if P adheres to the game.
Indeed, A's comprehension of the response produced by P can in turn be theoretically analyzed in the phases outlined by Airenti and colleagues. P's response is a starting point for A's reconstruction of his intention to play the game.

3. The computational model

The evaluation of the perlocutionary effect consists in a reasoning process where, according to Cognitive Pragmatics, two factors play a major role.

First, A has to take into account the engagement of P to play the game. In particular, the engagement to play a move of the game may be considered an acceptance of the game itself. But, obviously, this is not sufficient to account for the evaluation of the perlocutionary effect. It is still possible, for instance, that P lacks of confidence in A. If A believes that this is the case, she may think to have not reached the intended effect, even when P expresses the intention to play the game. Possibilities of this type may account for deceits in communication.

Thus, the second factor involved in evaluating the perlocutionary effect is the set of beliefs concerning the mental states of the partner. In our computational model the beliefs of A concerning P's beliefs play a major role in the evaluation of the communicative effect. Note that the notion of shared knowledge we borrow from Cognitive Pragmatics is a one-sided definition. Since we are concerned with the mental representations of A, it would be the case that:
i. A may take for shared the knowledge that P does not believes to share with her. In particular, A's and P's representations of the behavior game that A is bidding may be different.
ii. A may erroneously attribute certain beliefs to P.

In our computational model the attribution of beliefs to the partner heavily influences the evaluation of the perlocutionary effect, as much as the verbal or nonverbal commitment of the partner to play the game. We refer to the evaluation process as *evidential reasoning*. Indeed, each of the possible evaluations (P accepts the game/P does not accept the game/it is not clear whether or not P accepts the game) is strengthened or weakened on the basis of the evidence. In our model, beliefs concerning partner's beliefs and partner's commitment to play a game are the evidence sought by the actor to evaluate the acceptance of a game. The weight of a given piece of evidence determines how much it should strengthen or weaken the belief that a partner has accepted to play the behavior game.

The cognitive science paradigm dictates three steps for the validation of a computational model. First, the implementation of the model in a program; second, an experiment carried on human subjects and, third, the comparison between the performance of the program and those of the human subjects. As we implement our model into a connectionist network we face the problem of how to use the experimental data. Indeed, in a classical Artificial Intelligence program the computation is completely defined from the beginning, and the experimental data are used just for the comparison with the outputs of the program. On the contrary, a connectionist network is, in principle, general purpose and needs be trained on the experimental data to adapt to a specific task. Thus, we collected human subjects' evaluations of perlocutionary effects both to train the network to evaluate perlocutionary effects, and to observe the fitting of the evaluations of the network with those of the human subjects.

The next section is devoted to the questionnaire we administered to the experimental subjects.

4. The questionnaire

Subjects

Twenty-four undergraduates students of Turin University. They were balanced according to their gender.

Materials and Procedure

Subjects were presented individually with the questionnaire in a quiet room. At the very beginning they were told to read the following instructions:
"Read carefully the story I'll give you, and try to identify yourself with the actor. After reading the story, your task will be to evaluate possible courses of a specific situation. In particular, for each course, you are asked to evaluate whether your partner accepts your proposal to have dinner at home tonight. Possible evaluations are: 'yes' (YES), 'no' (NO) or 'It is not clear' (?). Your evaluations must take into account the story and the information concerning the specific course of the situation."

The story tells about the relationship of the actor A (the experimental subject) with her partner P. In particular, it specifies one of the following relationships: confidence, mistrust and uncertainty about confidence. The questionnaires were balanced according to the three types.

Besides, the story tells about a particular situation of everyday life involving the actor and the partner. For instance, let us consider the story as it is presented to a female experimental subject, where the name of the partner is Paul:
"You and Paul usually have dinner together, sometimes at home, sometimes at a restaurant. When you decide for a home-dinner you are not satisfied with a hot-dog in front of the television; dinner is a rite for you and the table must be laid in the appropriate manner.
Paul is very good at cooking, whereas you are a disaster: you usually attend to buy food.
Now it's 7.00 pm and Paul cannot go out to buy food since he is waiting for a phone call. The table is not laid and you tell him: "I'm going for shopping, but I will not lay the table".
Information concerning possible courses of the situation specify:
i. the engagement of the partner to cook and to lay the table (engagement, no engagement, refusal to engage).

E.g., 'Paul says that he will cook, but he does not intend to lay the table'.
ii. the beliefs of the partner concerning the effective intentions of the actor to buy food and not lay the table (sincerity, uncertainty on sincerity, insincerity).
E.g., 'Paul believes you are sincere when you say that you will buy food and not lay the table.

5. The network

We implemented the model in a Radial Basis Function Network (RBFN). RBFNs are a well-known class of networks that, given a set of samples, approximate an unknown target function. They naturally exhibit symbolic properties (Blanzieri & Giordana, 1995). The RBFN architecture approximates a target function with a weighted sum of receptive field functions (hypergaussians). Such functions are local in that the points of the input space which activate each of them belong to a local area. The weight of each receptive field can be seen as an output value associated to its own local area. The associations between the local areas and the output values can be translated into a production rule of the type:
if <the input is inside the local area of activation>,
then <the output is the one suggested>.
Via this property it is easy to extract symbolic knowledge from the network. The network computes the average of all the activated rules. Thus, the rules are not completely equivalent to the network, rather, they are symbolic representations of the information encoded into it. In our model, the target function is the actor's evaluation of the adherence of the partner to the game. The function depends on the response of the partner and on his beliefs about the sincerity of the actor.

Our network has three layers: five input units, one output unit, and five hidden units, i.e receptive fields. The five input units correspond to the input variables that describe the scenarios presented to the subjects (Figure 1).

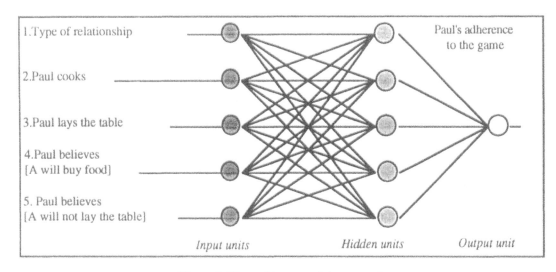

Figure 1. The architecture of the network.

503

The value of input 1 refers to the relationship between A and P: confidence (1), mistrust (0) and uncertainty about confidence (0.5).

The values of inputs 2 and 3 refer to the fact that P has expressed the intention to play a specific move (value 1), not to play the move (value 0), or he is uncertain (value 0.5).

The value of inputs 4 and 5 refer to the attendibility of A's engagement to play his move from P's point of view, as represented by A. Value 1 means that A believes that P believes that A intends to perform the declared move (sincerity). Value 0 means that A believes that P believes that A does not intend to perform the declared move (insincerity). Value 0.5 means that A believes that P believes that A is not reliable, namely A may or not perform the declared move (uncertainty on sincerity).

The output unit represents the actor's evaluation of the degree of adhesion of the partner to the game; he adheres (value 1), he does not adhere (value 0) or his adhesion is uncertain (value 0.5).

The number of units of the hidden layer coincides with the number of production rules. A number of hidden units higher than necessary leads to a poor generalization, i.e. overfitting. If this is the case, the network performs well on the training data set, but has poor performances on the remaining data. On the other hand, a poor number of hidden units prevents the learning. The network with the optimal number of hidden units performs better than the others.

Our experimental data base contains 486 couples scenario/actor's evaluation. The three different types of evaluation occur as follows: adhesion to the game 31.7%, no adhesion 38.5% and uncertain adhesion 29.8%. We adopted the method of randomly select a population of 20 pairs of training and test sets (2/3 and 1/3 of the couples respectively). Then, we verified the generalization performance for each test set on networks containing different number of hidden units (ranging from 4 to 8). The results show that the network with 5 hidden units performs better than the others. The difference is statistically significant (Wilcoxon Test, $p < .05$). Finally, we trained a network with 5 hidden units on the overall data.

6. Comparison between subject's evaluations and network's outputs

The trained RBFN is a functional expression of part of the actor's knowledge of the behavior game.

We presented the network with the 81 scenarios which were presented to the experimental subjects, and we collected 81 different outputs. The output of the network ranges from 0 to 1. We considered as evaluations of adherence to the game the outputs with a value greater than 0.66; as no adhesion the outputs with a value lower than 0.33; as uncertain adhesion the outputs with a value ranging from 0.33 to 0.66.

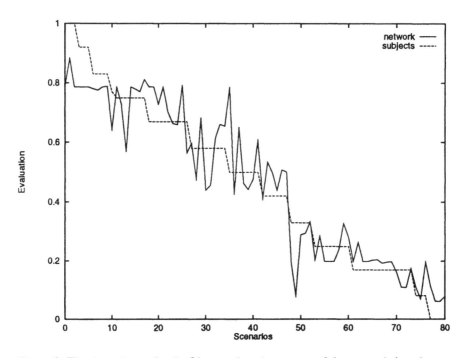

Figure 2. The chart shows, for the 81 scenarios, the outputs of the network (continuous line) and the average values of the subjects' evaluations (dashed line).

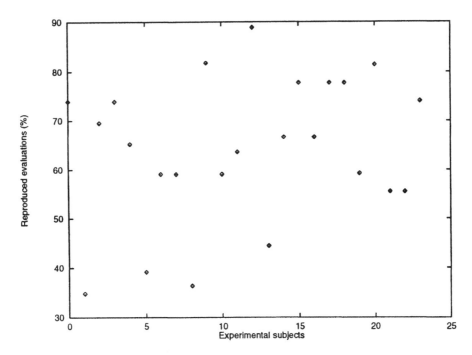

Figure 3. Percentages of evaluations reproduced by the network for each
of the 24 experimental subjects.

First, we present the global results concerning the comparison between overall subjects' evaluations with respect to all the scenarios and the evaluations performed by the network. As each evaluation involves the selection among three alternatives the probability of chance-guessing the evaluation of the experimental subjects is .33. As a matter of fact, the correct prevision rate of the network is 63.7 %. The chart in Figure 2 visualizes the approximation capability of the network.

Second, we compare the evaluations of each subject with those of the network (see Figure 3). Results show that the network reproduces more than 50% of the evaluations of 20 subjects. The network does not predict the evaluations of the remaining 4 subjects.

Finally, the rules extracted from the network are summarized in the Table 1.
As an example, the 5th rule reads as follows:

If   the type of relationship is confidence,
             P says that he will not cook,
             it is uncertain if P will lay the table,
             P believes that A will not buy the food,
therefore P does not accept to play the game.

	Rule 1	Rule 2	Rule 3	Rule 4	Rule 5
1. Relationship	Confidence	Mistrust	About confidence	Mistrust	Confidence
2. P cooks	About yes	Yes	Yes	Irrelevant	No
3. P lays the table	Yes	Irrelevant	No	No/uncertain	Uncertain
4. P believes [A buys food]	No	Uncertain	Irrelevant	Uncertain	No
5. P believs [A lays the table]	Irrelevant	Uncertain	About yes	About no	Irrelevant
Paul's adhesion to the game	About yes	Yes	About no	No	About no

Table 1. The rules extracted from the network. The term 'irrelevant' indicates that
the value of a variable does not affect the activation of the rule.

Note that it is irrelevant whether P believes that A will lay the table or not.

The five rules are psychologically plausible. Besides, as predicted by our model, the third and the fourth rules suggest that the kind of relationship and the beliefs on partner's beliefs do influence the evaluation of the communicative effect, even if the partner declares that he intends to play his role in the game, i.e. to cook.

7. Conclusions

We have presented a model of the cognitive processes involved in the evaluation of the communicative effect. The model is implemented by a connectionist network whose performances are compared with those of human subjects. The results show that the network reproduces most of the experimental subjects' evaluations. Moreover, we argue that the rules extracted from the network shed light on which kind of evidence is relevant in the evaluation of the communicative effect.

Our model is particularly concerned with the notion of thinking about beliefs advanced by Baron (1988). Indeed, the author suggests that thinking is involved in beliefs' formation, namely when people think to decide how strongly to believe something, or which of several competing beliefs is true. In this process, *evidence* consists of any object that helps them to determine the extent to which a possibility achieves some goal. We argue that the concept of evidence is particularly suitable to describe the inferential processes involved in communication, where inferential bounds are built with speedy and effortless. Whereas symbol manipulation seems to account for children and adults ability to draw formal inferences (see, for instance, Bara, Bucciarelli and Johnson-Laird, 1995), it is possible that explicit knowledge is not required in dealing with the evaluation of the perlocutionary effect: the brain may use implicit representations, which are based on a parallel distributed process.

Connectionism postulates distributed representations very different from static symbolic representations, and the dynamics of the system owes more to statistical mechanics than to logic. Nevertheless it may be that these representations and the dynamics which transforms one such representation into another can form the basis of a theory of inference (Levesque, 1988; Oaksford & Chater, 1993). As far as our aims are concerned, a relevant feature of connectionist networks is flexibility: our model deals with flexibility as it claims that the actor's beliefs may vary according to their strength, therefore resulting in possible different evaluations of the communicative effect.

We conclude that a connectionist model may give an account of the cognitive processes involved in the evaluation of the perlocutionary effect. It is plausible that human beings are endowed with mechanisms that allow to weigh evidence collected in the light of specific behavior goals. Such mechanisms would underlay the ability to draw inferences in communicative exchanges.

Acknowledgements

This research was supported by the Italian National Research Council (C.N.R., co-ordinate project, 95.04019. CT11).

The names of the authors are ordered alphabetically.

References

Airenti, G., Bara, B. G. & Colombetti, M. (1993). Conversation and behavior games in the pragmatics of dialogue. *Cognitive Science, 17*, 197-256.

Austin, J. A. (1962). *How to do things with words*. Oxford: Oxford University Press.

Bara, B., Bucciarelli, M. & Johnson-Laird, P. N. (1995). Development of syllogistic reasoning. *American Journal of Psychology, 108, 2*, 157-193.

Baron, J. (1988). *Thinking and Deciding*. Cambridge University Press, Cambridge.

Blanzieri, E. & Giordana, A. (1995). Mapping symbolic knowledge into Locally Receptive Field Networks, in M.Gori & G. Soda *Topics in Artificial Intelligence, Lecture Notes in Artificial Intelligence* vol. 992.

Levesque, H. J. (1988). Logic and complexity of reasoning. *Journal of Philosophical Logic, 17*, 355-389.

Oaksford, M. & Chater, N. (1993). Reasoning theories and bounded rationality. In Manktelow, K. I. & Over, D. E. (ed.), *Rationality: Psychological and Philosophical Perspectives*.

Searle, J. R. (1969). *Speech acts*. Cambridge: Cambridge University Press.

Searle, J.R. (1979). *Expression and meaning*. Cambridge: Cambridge University Press.

Computational Power and Realistic Cognitive Development

David Buckingham and **Thomas R. Shultz**

Department of Psychology
McGill University
1205 Penfield Avenue
Montréal, Québec, Canada H3A 1B1
dave@ego.psych.mcgill.ca
shultz@psych.mcgill.ca

Abstract

We explore the ability of a static connectionist algorithm to model children's acquisition of velocity, time, and distance concepts under architectures of different levels of computational power. Diagnosis of rules learned by networks indicated that static networks were either too powerful or too weak to capture the developmental course of children's concepts. Networks with too much power missed intermediate stages; those with too little power failed to reach terminal stages. These results were robust under a variety of learning parameter values. We argue that a generative connectionist algorithm provides a better model of development of these concepts by gradually increasing representational power.

Introduction

The use of connectionist networks to model cognitive development has placed new emphasis on a fundamental question in cognitive development: How is transition from one stage to another possible (Bates & Elman, 1993)? Although many researchers (e.g., Plunkett & Sinha, 1992; McClelland, 1995) conclude that connection weight adjustment can account for transition, the recent success of models employing a generative algorithm questions this conclusion (Shultz, Schmidt, Buckingham, & Mareschal, 1995). Shultz et al. (1995) argue that, in addition to weight adjustment, transition requires increases in non-linear computational power afforded by the recruitment of hidden units into the network as it learns. To assess the importance of hidden unit recruitment, in this article we explore the ability of a static connectionist algorithm to model children's acquisition of velocity (v), time (t), and distance (d) concepts and compare it to research using a generative connectionist algorithm (Buckingham & Shultz, 1994).

Development of Velocity, Time, and Distance

In classical physics, velocity is defined as $v = d \div t$, time as $t = d \div v$, and distance as $d = v*t$. Wilkening (1981, 1982) designed tasks in which children were asked to infer velocity, time, or distance given information about the other two dimensions. Wilkening found the following regularities: (1) In a distance-inference task, 5-year-olds employed an additive rule, $d = t+v$, whereas adults used the correct multiplication rule, $d = v*t$; (2) in a time-inference task, 10-year-olds and adults employed the correct division rule, $t = d \div v$, whereas 5-year-olds used a subtraction rule, $t = d-v$; and (3) in a velocity-inference task, 10-year-olds and adults used a subtraction rule, $v = d-t$, whereas 5-year-olds used an identity rule, $v = d$.

Simulations Using a Generative Algorithm

Buckingham and Shultz (1994) modeled the acquisition of velocity, time, and distance concepts using cascade-correlation (Fahlman & Lebiere, 1990), a generative connectionist algorithm. Cascade-correlation networks begin with a minimal topology determined by the number of input and output units, without any hidden units. During an output training phase, weights from input units and any installed hidden units are adjusted to minimize the sum of squared error between actual and target outputs. When error can no longer be minimized, an input training phase begins in which weights from input units to a pool of candidate hidden units are adjusted to maximize the correlation between hidden unit activation and output error. The hidden unit that attains the highest correlation is then installed into the network and output training recommences.

Simulation results matched those of Wilkening (1981; 1982) for the most part. For distance inferences, there was a progression from the additive ($d = t+v$) to the multiplicative rule ($d = t*v$). For time and velocity inferences, networks began with identity rules ($t = d$ and $v = d$, respectively), progressed to additive ($t = d-v$ and $v = d-t$, respectively), and finally multiplicative rules ($t = d \div v$ and $v = d \div t$, respectively).[1] Wilkening's participants did the same, except that they showed no identity rule for time inferences and failed to use the multiplicative rule for velocity inferences (Wilkening, 1981, attributed this latter failure to task demands).

Buckingham and Shultz (1994) suggested that the transition from identity stages through intermediate additive stages and finally multiplicative stages was made possible by both weight adjustment and hidden unit recruitment. In order to test this hypothesis, we compare the performance of cascade-correlation networks with that of static networks (i.e., networks in which the architecture is fixed throughout training).

---

[1] Example results are presented in Figure 1a for comparison purposes.

Simulations Using a Static Algorithm

Experiment 1

We used standard back-propagation networks as static networks because these were used by McClelland (1989) in his pioneering work modeling cognitive development on the balance scale task and are the most common connectionist learning networks. To maximize the chances of capturing human performance, we systematically sampled a variety of back-propagation architectures and parameter values. We ran simulations using four differentially powerful architectures: one hidden layer with one, two, or three hidden units; and two hidden layers with two hidden units in each layer. In each architectural condition, 180 networks were run in a crossed experimental design consisting of three levels of learning rate (*eta*) and momentum (*alpha*). The levels of learning rate were 0.025, 0.050 (the default value), and 0.100. The levels of momentum were 0.100, 0.450, and 0.900 (the default value).

The task was the same as in our cascade-correlation simulations. The networks had to predict, as output, the value of one dimension (e.g., velocity) given information about the other dimensions (e.g., distance and time). In order to maximize the ability to compare the performance of static networks with that of generative networks, input and output coding, output unit type, weight updating mode, and training and testing methods were as they had been in the cascade-correlation simulations (Buckingham & Shultz, 1994).

Inference patterns were encoded using *nth* encoding as follows.[2] Two input banks received dimensional values ranging from 1 to 5. The third bank received an input of 0 indicating that it was the dimension to be predicted. Each input bank had five input units for a total of 15 input units. A dimensional value *n* was encoded by assigning an activation of 1 to the *nth* input unit of the bank and 0 to all other units in the bank. Thus, for a given inference pattern, one input bank received activations of 0 on all of its five input units, indicating it was unknown. One unit of each of the other two input banks received an activation of 1. The remaining units in these banks received activations of 0.

As in our work with cascade-correlation, one linear output unit was used. A linear output was used because it is the most natural way of producing a quantitative output similar to the responses made by Wilkening's participants. Target values for the output unit were calculated using the three Newtonian equations ($v = d \div t$, $t = d \div v$, and $d = v*t$), respectively. In addition, distance target values were divided by five so that their range was identical to the ranges of time and velocity target values. Twenty-five instances of each of the three inference problem types were obtained by crossing the five levels of velocity, time, and distance for a total of 75 inference patterns.

At each epoch of training, all 75 inference problems

were presented to the network. Weight updates occurred only after all patterns had been presented to the network. This batch training continued for a maximum of 1500 epochs.

To compare network results with human performance, every fifth epoch of training we diagnosed rules that best captured network performance on each problem type. We computed correlations between the network's responses and those predicted by various plausible rules such as identity ($v = d$, or $v = t$), addition ($v = d+t$, or $v = d-t$), or multiplication ($v = d*t$, $v = t+d$, or $v = d+t$) rules. To be diagnosed as exhibiting stage performance, a rule had to correlate positively with network responses, account for more than 50% of the variance in network responses, and account for more variance than other plausible rules across four consecutive sampled epochs.

Results. A plot of the rules diagnosed as training progressed is shown in Figure 1 (b-e) for one network in each of the architectural conditions. These nets were chosen because they were good exemplars of typical performance across learning rates and momentum values.

For networks with a single hidden unit (Figure 1b), the typical progression involved early onset of time and velocity identity stages, followed by onset of the distance additive stage and, then, oscillation between the additive and multiplicative distance rules. Only 19 of the 180 networks attained a stable multiplicative stage of distance ($d = t*v$). None of the networks attained the multiplicative stages of time and velocity (only four networks progressed beyond the identity stages to the additive stages of time, $t = d-v$, and velocity, $v = d-t$).

In contrast to networks with a single hidden unit, the majority of networks with two hidden units (Figure 1c) progressed beyond the identity stages of time and velocity, attaining the multiplicative stages. However, only 13 of the 180 networks demonstrated the intermediate additive stages of both time and velocity. With respect to distance development, a small majority (94) demonstrated the distance additive stage and, unlike networks with a single hidden unit, a large majority (166) of networks attained a stable distance multiplicative stage.

Performance of networks with three hidden units (Figure 1d) was similar to those with two hidden units although slightly fewer networks demonstrated both time and velocity identity stages (170 vs. 177) and additive stages (4 vs. 13). All 180 networks attained the multiplicative stages of time and velocity. Another difference was that fewer networks (69 vs. 94) demonstrated the distance additive stage. All but one of the 180 networks attained the distance multiplicative stage.

Finally, the majority of networks with two hidden layers (Figure 1e) also failed to demonstrate the time and velocity additive stages. Only six networks attained both intermediate additive stages of time and velocity. The majority of networks (172) attained the multiplicative stages of time and velocity, respectively. Use of a second hidden unit layer increased the number of networks demonstrating the distance additive stage but only slightly (106 vs. 94 networks with one hidden layer of two units). All but six of the 180 networks attained the distance multiplicative stage.

---

[2] In Buckingham (1993), cascade-correlation networks with nth encoding demonstrated the same qualitative stage progression as those with more distributed input encodings. However, networks with nth encoding had a decided advantage in that their solutions were more transparent.

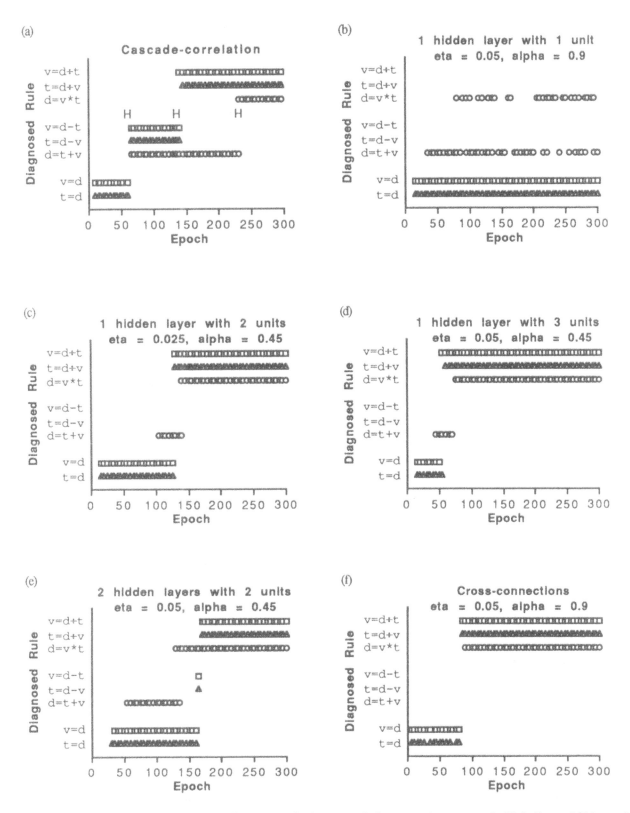

Figure 1: Diagnosed rules of (a) a generative connectionist network from previous research (H indicates hidden unit recruitment); one network in experiment 1 that exemplifies typical performance with one hidden layer of (b) one, (c) two, and (d) three hidden units, and (e) two hidden layers with 2 hidden units in each layer; (f) one network in experiment 2 with one hidden layer containing two hidden units and cross-connections.

In summary, very few static networks demonstrated the entire developmental course: time and velocity identity stages; distance, time, and velocity additive stages; and distance, time, and velocity multiplicative stages. Of the networks with a single hidden unit layer, only five out of 180 networks with two hidden units and three out of 180 networks with three hidden units demonstrated the entire developmental course. None of the networks with a single hidden unit attained the multiplicative stages of time and velocity. Networks with two or three hidden units on one layer typically missed the intermediate additive stages, particularly for time and velocity inferences. Finally, only one of the 180 networks with two hidden layers demonstrated the entire developmental course; these networks also missed the intermediate additive stages for time and velocity inferences.

Experiment 2

Cascade-correlation differs from back-propagation not only in the progressive recruitment of hidden units, but also in the use of cross-connections that bypass hidden unit layers. To assess the possibility that the psychological realism of cascade-correlation simulations might be due to the use of these cross-connections, and not to generative hidden unit creation, we ran 20 static networks with an architecture consisting of cross-connections and one hidden layer with two units. One hidden layer with two units was chosen because it showed the most promise of capturing time and velocity additive stages in Experiment 1. In experiment 2, we used only the default learning rate (0.050) and momentum values (0.900). Everything else was kept constant with Experiment 1.

Results. A plot of the rules diagnosed in one network as training progressed is shown in Figure 1f. This network was chosen because it was a good exemplar of typical performance. Overall the performance of these networks was similar to those in Experiment 1. That is, the majority of networks (14/20) progressed from the identity stages of time and velocity to the multiplicative stages without demonstrating the intermediate additive stages. Of the remaining six networks, three did not exhibit either identity stage and three attained one identity stage but not the other. All 20 networks attained the multiplicative stages of time and velocity. One difference compared to networks in Experiment 1 was that the use of cross-connections resulted in even fewer networks (5/20) first achieving the distance additive stage before the multiplicative stage. All 20 networks attained the distance multiplicative stage.

Discussion

Static networks in both experiments had no difficulty capturing early time and velocity identity stages. The limitation of static networks was their inability to capture both additive and multiplicative stages, regardless of a wide sampling of network architecture and parameter values. Different network architectures could capture one type of stage, but not the other, e.g., additive but not multiplicative, or multiplicative but not additive. Thus,

simple connection weight adjustment is insufficient to capture all stage transitions.

The most general failure of static networks with more than one hidden unit was to miss intermediate additive stages. Although there remains some doubt as to the inter-developmental course of additive stages and whether or not the additive stage of velocity is the terminal stage of velocity development, children clearly pass through these additive stages (Wilkening, 1981; 1982). Static networks with only one hidden layer consisting of one hidden unit often captured additive stages, but failed to reach multiplicative stages. Static networks with the limited computational power provided by one hidden layer with one hidden unit seemed too weak to attain multiplicative stages; static networks with more computational power seemed too powerful because they skipped intermediate stages. There seemed to be no static back-propagation architecture capable of simulating the full range of stages in the domain of velocity-time-distance. In contrast, all generative networks captured identity, additive, and multiplicative stages (Buckingham & Shultz, 1994).

The failure of static networks with cross-connections to successfully capture human performance in Experiment 2 suggests that the use of these cross-connections by cascade-correlation is not sufficient for its success. Rather, progressive recruitment of hidden units appears necessary for capturing correct stage progressions. Cross-connections may prove to be necessary as well, particularly in capturing early linearly separable performance, but this would need to be documented in future simulations.

Other, less direct evidence for the superiority of generative over static connectionist algorithms at simulating human development has been reported. For example, generative networks (Shultz, Mareschal, & Schmidt, 1994) captured the terminal stage of balance scale development more successfully than did static networks (McClelland, 1989; 1995). The present results extend these findings to cases in which static networks, with a sufficiently powerful architecture, successfully capture terminal stages (multiplicative stages) but fail to capture intermediate stages. Simulating the full range of psychologically realistic stages appears to rely on the ability of networks to grow in computational power. A similar point in the realm of grammar learning was made by Elman (1993). To learn an English-like grammar, recursive back-propagation networks had to receive either progressively more complex sentences or grow in working memory capacity.

The fact that realistic connectionist models of development need to grow in computational power suggests that human development involves not only incremental learning but also increases in non-linear representational abilities. What factors cause the emergence of these new representational abilities in children remains an open question.

This research compares only a single exemplar of a static algorithm (back-propagation) to a single exemplar of a generative algorithm (cascade-correlation). Using other exemplars of each class of algorithm could indicate the generality of the conclusions. It might also be interesting to explore the capacity of other generative network techniques to capture cognitive developmental phenomena. For example, must the network grow vertically, as in cascade-correlation, or could it grow horizontally on a single layer (e.g., Ash, 1989)? If cognitive development is characterized by the continual redescription of earlier knowledge representations (Karmiloff-Smith, 1992), then vertical, rather than horizontal, growth would seem to be required. Further, how would network pruning techniques (Hanson & Pratt, 1989; Le Cun, Denker, & Solla, 1990) fare in capturing developmental stages? If cognitive development is characterized by the emergence of qualitatively distinct knowledge representations (Carey, 1991), then recruitment ought to work better than pruning.

Acknowledgments

This research was supported in part by a fellowship from the Fonds pour la Formation de Chercheurs et l'Aide à la Recherche du Québec and an operating grant from the Natural Sciences and Engineering Research Council of Canada.

References

Ash, T. (1989). Dynamic node creation in backpropagation. *Connection Science*, 1, 365-375.

Bates, E. A., & Elman, J. L. (1993). Connectionism and the study of change. In M. H. Johnson (Ed.), *Brain development and cognition* (pp. 623-642). Oxford: Blackwell.

Buckingham, D. (1993). *The developmental course of distance, time, and velocity concepts: A generative connectionist model.* Unpublished Master's thesis, McGill University, Montréal, Québec, Canada.

Buckingham, D., & Shultz, T. R. (1994). A connectionist model of the development of velocity, time, and distance concepts. In *Proceedings of the Sixteenth Annual Conference of the Cognitive Science Society* (pp. 72-77). Hillsdale, NJ: Erlbaum.

Carey, S. (1991). Knowledge acquisition: Enrichment or conceptual change. In S. Carey & R. Gelman (Eds.), *The epigenesis of mind: Essays on biology and cognition* (pp. 257-291). Hillsdale, NJ: Erlbaum.

Elman, J. (1993). Learning and development in neural networks: The importance of starting small. *Cognition.*, 48, 71-99.

Fahlman, S. E., & Lebiere, C. (1990). The cascade-correlation learning architecture. In D. S. Touretzky (Ed.), *Advances in neural information processing systems 2* (pp. 524-532). Los Altos, CA: Morgan Kaufmann.

Hanson, S. J., & Pratt, L. Y. (1989). Comparing biases for minimal network construction with back-propagation. In D. S. Touretzky (Ed.), *Advances in neural information processing systems* (pp. 177-185). Los Altos, CA: Morgan Kaufmann.

Karmiloff-Smith, A. (1992). *Beyond modularity.* Cambridge, MA: MIT Press.

Le Cun, Y., Denker, J. S., & Solla, S. A. (1990). Optimal Brain damage. In D. S. Touretzky (Ed.), *Advances in neural information processing systems 2,* (pp. 598-605). Los Altos, CA: Morgan Kaufmann.

McClelland, J. L. (1989). Parallel distributed processing: Implications for cognition and development. In R. G. M. Morris (Ed.), *Parallel distributed processing: Implications for psychology and neurobiology* (pp. 8-45). Oxford: Oxford University Press.

McClelland, J. L. (1995). A connectionist perspective on knowledge and development. In T. J. Simon, & G. S. Halford (Eds.), *Developing cognitive competence: New approaches to process modeling* (pp. 157-204). Hillsdale, NJ: Erlbaum.

Plunkett, K., & Sinha, C. (1992). Connectionism and developmental theory. *British Journal of Developmental Psychology, 10,* 209-254.

Shultz, T. R., Mareschal, D., & Schmidt, W. C. (1994). Modeling cognitive development on balance scale phenomena. *Machine Learning, 16,* 57-86.

Shultz, T. R., Schmidt, W. C., Buckingham, D., & Mareschal, D. (1995). Modeling cognitive development with a generative connectionist algorithm. In T. Simon & G. Halford (Eds.), *Developing cognitive competence: New approaches to process modeling.* Hillsdale, NJ: Erlbaum.

Wilkening, F. (1981). Integrating velocity, time, and distance information: A developmental study. *Cognitive Psychology, 13,* 231-247.

Wilkening, F. (1982). Children's knowledge about time, distance, and velocity interrelations. In W. J. Friedman (Ed.), *The developmental psychology of time* (pp. 87-112). NY: Academic Press.

Learning Qualitative Relations in Physics with Law Encoding Diagrams

Peter C-H. Cheng
ESRC Centre for Research in Development, Instruction and Training.
Department of Psychology, University of Nottingham,
Nottingham, NG7 2RD, U.K.
`peter.cheng@nottingham.ac.uk`

Abstract

This paper describes a large scale experiment that evaluates the effectiveness of Law Encoding Diagrams (LEDs) for learning qualitative relations in the domain of elastic collisions in physics. A LED is a representation that captures the laws or important relations of a domain in the internal structure of a diagram by means of diagrammatic constraints. The subjects were 88 undergraduate physics students, divided into three learning trial conditions. One group used computer based LEDs, another used conventional computer based representations (tables and formulas), and the third was a non-intervention control group. Only the LED subjects had a significant improvement in their pre-test to post-test qualitative reasoning. The LEDs appear to make it easier for subjects to explore more of the space of different forms of collisions and hence gain a better qualitative understanding of the domain.

Introduction

Law Encoding Diagrams (LEDs) are an interesting class of diagrammatic representations. They capture the law(s) of a domain by means of their internal structure, using geometric, topological or spatial constraints, such that each diagram represents a single instance of the phenomenon or one case of the law. LEDs can be found in the history of science (Cheng, in press) and may have had an significant role in some discoveries, such as finding the law of conservation of momentum (Cheng & Simon, 1992). As LEDs seem to have been useful to original scientists, it is possible that they may help students learn about the same domain. Cheng (1994, 1995) describes a detailed small scale study in which subjects learnt about elastic collisions in physics. The subjects used computer based LEDs in a system called ReMIS-CL. It was found that subjects, physics students, could quickly learn to use LEDs for problem solving with little instruction. In post-tests half the subject used LEDs for problem solving with novel strategies, in contrast to their own ineffective pre-tests solutions. From the detailed analysis of their use of ReMIS-CL, it appears that the successful subjects obtained a better understanding of the diagrammatic constraints of the LEDs, because they comprehensively examined the space of structural forms of the LEDs.

This paper describes a larger scale investigation of computer based LEDs for learning, with 88 undergraduate physics students. The main aim was to evaluate the effectiveness of ReMIS-CL against controls of two kinds: (i)

a group using a similar, but non-diagrammatic, computer based learning environment; and (ii) a non-intervention group. The investigation also provided further evidence to support the hypothesis that successful learning with LED is linked to the extent to which subjects explore the space of different structural forms of LEDs.

The next section of the paper describes the domain of elastic collisions and ReMIS-CL. The method and results are then outlined in the following two sections. The implications of the results are described in the final two sections, which also contrasts the present approach to others in computer based physics learning.

Elastic Collisions and ReMIS-CL

Elastic collisions are important in physics, because both momentum and energy conservation are involved. Here impacts between two bodies (balls) travelling in a straight line are considered. Figures 1 and 2 shows screen displays (minus menu bar) of ReMIS-CL, a computer based discovery learning environment for this domain. At the bottom of the screen, there is an animated simulation of the collision that the user can run at will. The two large areas above have two interactive LEDs: the *one-dimensional property diagram* (1DP diagram) and the *velocity-velocity graph* (VV graph). Figures 1 and 2 show different collisions but LEDs within each represent the same collision. The lines in the diagrams represent magnitudes of velocities and masses: $U1$ and $U2$ are the velocities before impact; and, $V1$ and $V2$ are the velocities after collision. In Figure 1 the bodies approach and depart in different directions but with equal speeds. In the 1DP diagram, mass lines, $m1$ and $m2$, are drawn equidistant between the $U1-U2$ and $V1-V2$ lines. In the V-V graph the masses are represented by the sides of the small triangle. The ratio of the lengths of the mass lines in both LEDs equals the ratio of the masses of the two balls.

Both LEDs can be directly manipulated to change the values of the variables. Figure 2 shows the result of sliding the handle, the small rectangle, at the end of the $U2$ arrow to the right, doubling the initial speed of body-2. The rest of the 1DP diagram's structure is automatically updated to be consistent with its own diagrammatic constraints and thus to satisfy both conservation laws. The LEDs are inter-linked so that the structure of V-V graph is also revised. ReMIS-

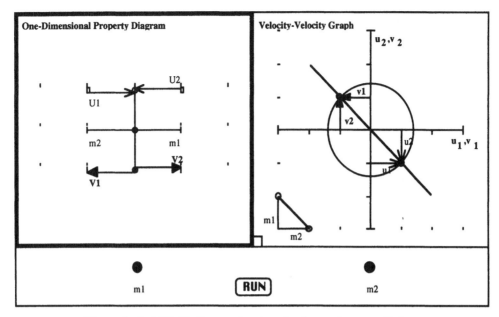

Figure 1: ReMIS-CL Screen showing simple equal mass collision.

CL ensures that the LEDs are always consistent with their diagrammatic constraints.

The three main constraints of the 1DP diagram are: (i) the tail ends of the arrows for the initial velocities and the points of the corresponding final velocity arrows must be in line vertically, making the total length of the *U1—U2* line equal to that of the *V1—V2* line; (ii) the total length of the mass line equals the length of the velocity lines; and, (iii) the ends of the lines not previously fixed in (i) and (ii), indicated by

the small circles, must lie on a straight vertical or diagonal line.

In the V-V graph the straight diagonal line is constant momentum contour and the circle (sometimes an ellipse) is a constant energy contour. There are 3 main constraints. (i) The momentum contour line passes through the points for initial and final velocities, as indicated by the small circles, and is parallel to hypotenuse of the mass triangle. (ii) The centre of the energy circle/ellipse is at the origin of the

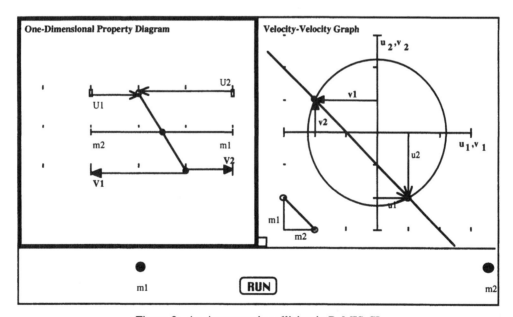

Figure 2: An Asymmetric collision in ReMIS-CL

513

graph and it also passes through the points for initial and final velocities. The intersections of the contours give the solutions to the two conservation laws. (iii) The eccentricity of the ellipse is given by the square-root of the ratio of the masses; $\sqrt{(m1/m2)}$. The law encoding constraints of this LED are more complex than those for the 1DP diagram.

ReMIS-CL logs the actions of the users on the system and stores the values of variables. Different kinds of operations are recorded with time stamps, including: switches between the representations; changes to values of the variables; resets that return the variables to their default values (i.e., Figure 1); and runs of the simulation.

One way to distinguish different collisions is in terms of *configurations*, defined as relations between the pairs of initial (or final) velocities with respect to their signs (directions) and whether they are zero, equal or unequal (Cheng, 1995). There are 7 different configurations for pairs of initial velocities, *U-configurations*. (The same applies for final velocities.) Figures 1 and 2 show different configurations. For different ratios of the masses, alternate final velocity configurations can result from each U-configuration. Combining initial and final velocity configurations, there are 41 possible *complete* configurations. Each corresponds to different structural forms of the LEDs, so this provides a convenient way to record and assess the behaviour of subjects.

Method

Design. There were three experimental learning trial conditions. (1) The LED group used ReMIS-CL with the two LEDs. (2) The Num group used numerical/formula version ReMIS-CL which had the animated simulation but not the LEDs. In their place were: (i) a temporally ordered table of previous sets of values from which particular cases could be simply selected; and, (ii) a structured table of current values of the variables along with values of momentum and energy terms for each body before and after collision. The values of the variables could be changed by selecting a variable and typing a new value. (3) The Con group was a non-intervention control group, so did not use either version of the system.

Subjects. The subjects were first year undergraduate physics students at the University of Nottingham. They participated in the experiment during a weekly computer programming class. Given the constraints on the organization of the class, which was run in six separate groups, it was not possible to randomly assign subjects to the three experimental conditions. Pairs of class groups made up each of the three experimental groups.

Materials and Procedure. The experiment included: a pre-test of the subjects knowledge of the domain; a learning trail on the system (not with the Con group); and, a post-test similar to the pre-test. The trial immediately followed the pre-test and the post-test followed a fortnight later. Pre-test and post-tests lasted 20 minutes and the trial 30 minutes.

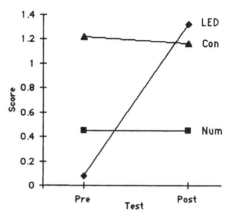

Figure 3: Mean Scores

The pre-test had four sections. The first asked the subjects to state the laws and write the equations governing elastic collisions. The second section had three qualitative questions in which the one or more outcomes of particular collisions had to be given. For example, what are the possible outcomes when the balls have different masses but they approach from opposite directions with the same speed? The third section included two questions about extreme cases, in which outcomes of collisions with large speeds or masses were considered. The final section was a quantitative question in which an exact solution had to be calculated. The questions were written in English and accompanied by a simple diagram depicting the situation (not a LED). Subjects responded by making annotated sketches. Most subjects had insufficient time to complete the last (quantitative) section, so it will not be considered here. The post-test was similar to the pre-test, except the first section was replaced by a general question about what they had thought they had learnt using the system. The LED and Num groups were also given a picture of the ReMIS-CL interface they had used.

During the trials the LED and Num groups worked in pairs. They were given a sheet that described how to use the system. For the LED group this included a brief description of the 1DP diagram and the V-V graph. The subjects were told to use the system to find out as much as they could about elastic collisions and given a log sheet on which to record their discoveries. ReMIS-CL logged the actions performed by the subjects.

For the purposes of analysis, only those subjects who did both the pre-test and post-test are considered. The groups numbers were: LED=25, Num=27 and Con=36.

Results

The subjects had reasonable conceptual understanding of the domain, with 97% and 76% knowing that momentum and energy conservation laws, respectively. There were no apparent differences among the three experimental groups in this respect.

Group	Operations	Proportion of simulations	Ratio of simulation series	Proportion of value changes	Ratio of value change series
LED	132	0.26	0.040	0.56	0.13
Num	52.5	0.44	0.092	0.47	0.093
LED/Num	2.51	0.60	0.44	1.21	1.37
p (*t* test)	<.001	<.001	<.001	<.001	<0.01

Table 1: Numbers and Types of Operations

Figure 3 contrasts the average pre-test and post-tests scores for all three groups on the qualitative problems. The scores were the sum, for all three questions, of the number of correct outcomes less the number of incorrect outcomes. The lowest and highest scores observed were -5 and +5. There was a significant increase in the LED group's score pre-test to post-test ($t= 2.66$, $p=0.014$), but the score for Num group was unchanged and the slight decrease of the Con group was not significant ($t=0.80$, $p>.1$). The difference in the pre-test scores of the LED group and the Con group was significant ($t=2.4$, $p<.05$). In a 3X2 mixed ANOVA of the 3 groups and the 2 tests, there were no significant effects of group or time of test, but there was a significant interaction ($F_{2,85}=3.66$, $p<.05$). There were strong and significant correlations between pre-test and post-test scores of the Num and Con subjects (Pearson; $r=0.75$, $p<.001$, and $r=0.62$, $p<.001$, respectively), but the LED group had a weak (non significant) correlation ($r=0.17$, $p>.05$). The LED group's qualitative reasoning has improved. The Num and Con groups' have not, and it appears that there has been little change in performance at the level of individual subjects.

Table 1 shows various average measures of the behaviour of the LED and Num groups in the trials. The LED group performed 2.5 times more operations than the Num group. Values changes and simulation runs were the most common operations. However, as a proportion of the number of operations of each subject, the LED group did significantly more value changes and ran fewer simulations than the Num group. Num subjects often performed series of two or more consecutive operations of the same kind; e.g., running the simulation three times in a row, with the same values. The ratio of the numbers of such series of operations to the total number of operations, per subject, are also shown in Table 1. For example, on average, 13% of operations by LED subjects were changes to the values followed by a series of at least one more change in the values. The LED group had significantly fewer simulation series and significantly more series of changes of values than the Num group. The LED group had three times the ratio of value change series to simulation series, whereas the Num group had nearly equal ratios. This implies that the two groups may be doing different kinds of reasoning, whilst using the system.

Simple measures of the distribution of U-configurations and complete configurations were devised, such that unity indicates an even distribution in which there are equal numbers of all the different configurations and zero indicates a maximally skewed distribution in which only one configuration is present. Larger values (approaching 1) indicate that a subject has explored more of the space of configurations. Table 2 shows the scores for the two groups, obtained by analysing the logs of subjects on

Group	U	Complete
LED	0.56	0.30
Num	0.47	0.20
LED/Num	1.19	1.5
p (*t* test)	.1>p>.05	<.001

Table 2: Measures of configuration distributions

ReMIS-CL. Both scores for the LED group were higher than those of the Num group, although only the difference in the complete configuration scores was significant. LED subjects are exploring a greater range of the possible configurations of collisions.

Table 3 shows correlations for comparisons of U-configurations with other measures of performance on the systems. The LED group seems to have more thoroughly explored the space of different configurations by concentrating on value changes as opposed to runs of the simulation, shown by the significant positive correlations between the U-configuration distribution and value changes, both proportion and series measures. There are weak negative correlations for simulation measures and U-configurations

	Complete configuration distribution	Proportion of simulations	Ratio of simulation series	Proportion of value changes	Ratio of value changes series
LED	0.86	0.19	-0.06	0.62	0.68
p	<.001	>.05	>.05	<.01	<.001
Num	0.79	-0.33	-0.30	0.23	0.18
p	<.001	>.05	>.05	>.05	>.05

Table 3: Correlations between U-configuration distribution and other trial measures

for the Num group, which implies that running more simulations coincides with less exploration of the space of configurations.

The results for the two extreme problems were similar, with a significant improvement in LED subject's score pre-test to post-test, but no significant improvements in either the Con or the Num groups. However, the details of the results of the extreme case questions are consistent with the qualitative questions results, they add little to the interpretation of the results (in the next section), so are not reported here, due to limited space.

Discussion of Results

The experiment has shown that LEDs implemented as interactive diagrams can be effective for learning about qualitative relations and extreme cases in the domain of elastic collisions. This outcome is noteworthy, because the duration and form of the intervention. The subjects had a short time on the system, 30 minutes. They were not given a carefully designed series of activities, but merely told to look for interesting relations or patterns. As the LED group was the only one to improve, it appears that the gain can be attributed to the role of the LEDs. Alternative explanations will be considered and shown to be implausible.

Comparison of the Num and LED groups shows that the mere use of a computer based system with an animated simulation is not responsible for the gain. The Num group used the simulation more than the LED group. The difference between the pre-test scores of the Con and the LED groups was likely due to the non-random assignment of the subjects to the experimental conditions, which was beyond the control of the experimenter. Thus, it is possible to argue that the effect is due to repeated testing, if two assumptions are made. First, the Con group are experiencing a ceiling effect, so repeated testing will not result in an improvement. Second, the Num group does improve due to repeated testing, but this is matched by an equal degradation due to the use of the numerical/formula version of the system, for some unknown reason. This alternative is less likely than the explanation that the improvement is due to the LEDs, because it is more convoluted and the assumptions are not secure. First, it is unlikely that the Con group is experiencing a ceiling effect, because their average score of 1.2 is much less than the maximum qualitative problem score of 5. The second assumption is also weak, because it requires two independent processes simultaneously working to produced effects that cancel each other out. The strong and highly significant correlation between the Num subjects' pre-test and post-tests scores suggests that no processes are at work, rather than two independent ones.

The improvement in the LED group's score from significantly below to just above the Con group might be explained by contending that the LED group was more highly motivated, because they knew less. This is unlikely given the lack of change in the Num group and the small absolute (though significant) difference between the LED and Num pre-test scores.

Further, there are good reasons to positively attribute the improvement of the LED subjects to the LEDs. Part of the explanation of why the LED group improved, but the Num group did not, may be the sheer numbers of operations that the LED group did compared to the Num group, two and a half times as many. This difference can itself be explained in at least two ways. First, the LED version of the system is easier to use; a human computer interaction factor. The 1DP diagram and the V-V graph can be quickly changed by re-sizing a line. With the numerical/formula system it was necessary to select the variable and then type the required value at the keyboard, a slower process. However, this operational factor is not sufficient to explain the whole difference.

The second explanation, which is itself an explanation of the relative success of the LED group, is in terms of differences in the types of reasoning that the LED and Num subjects were doing. The Num subjects appear to have been spending time relating the values of the variables to the simulations, in the cases they examined. The Num group's greater proportion of simulations and ratio of the simulation series are indications of the load imposed by the need to interpret each set of values. For a particular case, Num subjects were more likely to run the simulation several times, seemingly in an attempt to gain an appreciation of the form of the collision. The LED subjects, on the other hand, can quickly get an appreciation of the form of a collision by looking at the 1DP diagram. The direction of the arrows and their lengths makes the form of the collision available by means of a quick perceptual inferences. Thus, it appears that LEDs subjects may have been comparing successive collisions, rather than individual cases, given their greater proportion of value changes and ratio of value change series.

The explanation of the difference between the LED group and the Num group goes deeper than the fact that the LED subjects could more quickly examine a greater number of collisions. Remember that the measures of value changes and runs of the simulations are relative to the total number of operations executed by each subject; thus the rate at which LED subjects examined different collisions was greater than the Num subjects. This, and the fact that the LED group examined a greater number of different collisions (higher configuration distribution measures), implies that the LEDs seem to make it easier for the subjects to consider different forms of collisions. In the 1DP diagram and the V-V graph, the different collision are distinct patterns or shapes, so considering different forms or configurations requires relatively less cognitive effort than attempting to distinguish different cases from sets of numerical values. Note that the availability of a table of previous values did not appear to help the Num group. To some extent, the LEDs appear to make more of the space of configurations of collision accessible to the system users.

General Discussion

Some general implications for instruction and learning in technical domains follows from the findings of this study.

Providing computer based diagrams that make the underlying relations of a domain more accessible to problem solvers may be an effective way to facilitate the learning of qualitative relations. LEDs make the underlying laws of a domain more accessible by capturing them in the internal structure of diagrams and by having each diagram represent one instance of the phenomenon. This means that the learner is less burdened with the task of interpreting individual cases, so is freer to examine successive cases or to consider extreme and special cases. Such cases usually correspond to distinctive and unexpected patterns in LEDs, which will challenge and help refine the learners understanding of the rules governing the form of the LEDs. Hence, there seems to be a double benefit in making the relations readily accessible.

The findings of this experiment are consistent with the previous small scale experiment on ReMIS-CL (Cheng, 1994, 1995). In that experiment the subjects who successfully used the LEDs in the post-test were the ones who had obtained the most complete understanding of the constraints of the LEDs. They achieved this by exploring more of the space of possible configurations of the LEDs. Both experiments suggest the importance of examining a wide range of cases during learning with LEDs, but this same approach may be effective with other representations. By exploring more of the space of possible configurations of the phenomenon, the learner will see a greater variety of the correct forms of expressions in a representation and thus have greater variety of distinct cases over which to induce the relations underlying the phenomenon. Investigating extreme cases is more likely to provide useful information for establishing the boundary conditions of a law than merely examining normal or typical cases.

The LED approach is now briefly contrasted with some examples of other research on computer based systems for physics learning. Whitelock *et al.* (1993) have also studied learning about collisions and have shown that faulty causal models can be challenged with a computer simulation. This is consistent with White's (1993) findings. Although not in the same domain, White's approach is interesting because it provides learners with correct *intermediate causal models* (ICMs), in addition to animated computer simulations. ICMs act as bridge for the conceptual gulf between abstract general laws and observations of phenomena. Children have successfully learnt about Newtonian dynamics with ICMs, achieving a level of understanding matching students beginning undergraduate science programs.

LEDs may also be considered as representations at an intermediate level of abstraction. However, LEDs capture the formal relations defined by the laws of a domain in a constraint based manner, rather than portraying causation.

Ploetzner *et al.*'s (1990) DiBi system is an intelligent tutoring system for elastic collisions that aims to support and guide students in their construction of sound domain representations. In contrast, ReMIS-CL is a discovery learning environment that has no built in intelligence or student model, but it explicitly provides correct domain representations in the form of LEDs.

The present study has demonstrated the effectiveness of LEDs for learning about some qualitative relations and extreme cases in the domain of elastic collisions. It has also provided a better understanding of some of the processes involved in effective learning with LEDs. However, many issues are raised by this and the research mentioned above. Will LEDs be useful to students attempting to develop conceptual understanding of a domain? Can LEDs be effective for students who have less experience in physics and who are much younger? How important is it to have two complementary LEDs, such as the 1DP diagram and the V-V graph, in a single system? Ongoing research is attempting to address these questions.

Acknowledgements

The research was supported by the U.K. Economic and Social Research Council. I am grateful to the Physics Department at the University of Nottingham, especially John Owens-Bradley and Chris Mellor, for helping me to set up this experiment. Thanks must also go to members of the ESRC Centre for their assistance in my pursuit of this work, and especially to Fernand Gobet for his valuable comments on a draft on this paper.

References

Cheng, P. C.-H. (1994). An empirical investigation of law encoding diagrams for instruction. In *Proceedings of the 16th Annual Conference of the Cognitive Science Society.* (pp. 171-176). Hillsdale, NJ: Lawrence Erlbaum Associates.

Cheng, P. C.-H. (1995). Law encoding diagrams for instructional systems. *Journal of Artificial Intelligence in Education*, 6(4).

Cheng, P. C.-H. (in press). Scientific discovery with law encoding diagrams. *Creativity Research Journal*.

Cheng, P. C.-H., & Simon, H. A. (1992). The right representation for discovery: Finding the conservation of momentum. In D. Sleeman & P. Edwards (Eds.), *Machine Learning: Proceedings of the Ninth International Conference (ML92)* (pp. 62-71). San Mateo, CA: Morgan Kaufmann.

Ploetzner, R., Spada, H., Stumpf, M., & Opwis, K. (1990). Learning qualitative and quantitative reasoning in a microworld for elastic impacts. *European Journal of Psychology of Education*, V(4), 501-516.

White, B. (1993). ThinkerTools: Causal models, conceptual change, and science education. *Cognition and Instruction*, 10(1), 1-100.

Whitelock, D., Taylor, J., O'Shea, T., Scanlon, E., Sellman, R., Clark, P., & O'malley, C. (1993). Challenging models of elastic collisions with a computer simulation. *Computers in Education*, 20(1), 1-9.

517

Building A Baby

Paul R. Cohen, Tim Oates, Marc S. Atkin
Department of Computer Science
Carole R. Beal
Department of Psychology
University of Massachusetts, Amherst, MA 01003
cohen@cs.umass.edu

Abstract

We show how an agent can acquire conceptual knowledge by sensorimotor interaction with its environment. The method has much in common with the notion of image-schemas, which are central to Mandler's theory of conceptual development. We show that Mandler's approach is feasible in an artificial agent.

Introduction

It is a great mystery how adult concepts can develop from infant sensorimotor activity. The title of this paper borrows from two papers by Jean Mandler in which she discusses how this development might work. Central to her theory is *perceptual analysis by image-schemas* (Mandler, 1988; Mandler, 1992; Johnson, 1987; Lakoff and Johnson, 1980; Lakoff, 1984): "I propose that perceptual analysis results in redescriptions of spatial structure in the form of image-schemas. These redescriptions constitute the meanings that infants use to create concepts of objects, such as animate and inanimate things, and relational concepts, such as containment and support." (Mandler, 1992, p. 587). As far as we know, nobody has demonstrated by means of a running computer program that image-schematic redescriptions can produce conceptual structures from sensorimotor interactions. This is the purpose of the research reported here. A second aim of the research is to show that very little prior structure is sufficient to acquire conceptual structures. This result causes us to think that the "models" of the physical world attributed to infants by Spelke, Carey, Baillargeon, and others, might be learned, not innate.

What are image-schemas? Think of them as pattern detectors or filters that map sensory streams onto redescriptions or partial representations. For example, when we see a cat walk across the room, our ANIMATE MOTION image-schema produces a partial representation of the scene; similarly when we see a person walking down the road. But when we see a car zoom past, the ANIMATE MOTION image-schema stays quiet.

As minimalists we are leery of image-schematic theories of conceptual development because they are unconstrained. How many image-schemas are required? Are they all innate or are some learned? Which aspects of sensory experience should image-schemas analyze? One purpose of this paper is to propose a very few, well-motivated image schemas, and show that an artificial agent can use them to learn a lot about the states, objects and processes in its environment.

We have implemented a simulated agent called Neo that learns representations of objects, states and activities, and is poised to learn categories, by a process of perceptual analysis, using several versions of a single learning rule that has many of the properties claimed for image schemas. As it happens, Neo's analysis is of temporal, not spatial, structure. Even so, we present Neo as evidence that Mandler's theory of infant conceptual development is, in its broad outlines, sufficient for an artificial agent to learn concepts.

Baby World

Neo lives in a simulated environment called BabyWorld, which implements Neo's sensations, mental representations, mental and physical activities, and the behavior of objects and other agents that interact with Neo. BabyWorld has two parts: one, Neo, implements everything that Neo does, including learning, moving, mouthing, looking, crying, and so on. The other part, called StreamsWorld, represents Neo's environment, and it implements events that happen around Neo and in response to Neo's actions.

Neo senses its environment through a collection of *streams*, which are divided into discrete time steps. In each time step a stream holds a *token*. Tokens represent *sensations* or processed percepts. For example, one token is **rattle-shape** and it is placed in the appropriate stream whenever Neo's eyes point at an object that is shaped like a rattle. The streams that represent Neo's internal sensations include an affect stream that contains tokens such as happy and sad, a pain stream, a hunger stream, and somatic and haptic streams that are active when Neo moves and grasps.

The Babyworld simulator is simple and probabilistic. For example, Neo gets hungry some time after eating, it cries when it is unhappy or in pain; when Neo cries, Mommy usually visits, unless she is angry at Neo for crying, in which case she stays away. Neo falls asleep intermittently; it can move its arm and head, and grasp several objects, including three rattles, a bottle, a mobile, keys and a knife. The latter causes pain. The rattles make noise when shaken. Currently, Neo is incapable of anything we would call volition. If Neo's eyes alight on a rattle then Neo will grasp the rattle with some probability. However goal-directed this might appear, Neo's mind contains nothing that could be interpreted as a goal.

Redescription of Sensations

When Neo starts to run its experience is "blooming, buzzing confusion," with no apparent structure. (We know this is probably not true of neonates, but we don't want to assume prior mental models of the physical world if these might be acquired through interaction, as we believe they can. Thus we start with very minimal prior structure.) Neo goes through five levels of redescription of its experience: 1) Changes in token values: Tokens in streams are augmented by noticing when they change value. 2) Scopes: Neo finds pairs of correlated streams called scopes. 3) Base fluents: Neo finds common token-value pairs within scopes. 4) Context fluents: Neo finds base fluents that tend to follow each other in time. 5) Chains: These temporal dependencies are combined into temporal chains, which represent activities. Chains are used for activity-based categorization.

Each level of redescription produces an intermediate representation. Representations are interned in Neo's memory when they have accrued sufficient evidence from Neo's experience. The examples in this paper are from a single run of Neo, lasting 30,000 time steps, during which it created thousands of intermediate representations. A single counting mechanism is responsible for deciding when to intern a representation. Neo engages in all five levels of redescription as soon as it is able, but because each instance of intermediate representation requires statistical support, instances of deeper levels of representation are often created before instances of shallower levels.

Noticing When Token Values Change

A stream σ_i is said to change state at time t, denoted $\Delta(i, t)$, when $\sigma_{i,t-1} \neq \sigma_{i,t}$; that is, σ_i changes state at time t when it contains a different token at time t than it did at time $t-1$. Conversely, $\overline{\Delta}(i, t)$ means the stream doesn't change state: $\sigma_{i,t-1} = \sigma_{i,t}$. At this level of redescription, we don't care what the token values actually are, we only care whether they change. As it happens, this reduction in information serves to reduce the combinatorial space of representations at deeper levels (i.e., scopes, base fluents, context fluents and chains) and so is an essential first level of redescription.

Scopes

Neo learns a *scope*, s_{ij}, when streams σ_i and σ_j change together often. Said differently, Neo learns s_{ij} when the joint event $\Delta(i, t)$ & $\Delta(j, t)$ occurs frequently relative to the joint events $\Delta(i, t)$ & $\overline{\Delta}(j, t)$ and $\overline{\Delta}(i, t)$ & $\Delta(j, t)$. To assess the relative frequencies of these events, Neo uses contingency tables like this one:

	Δ(sight-color,t)	$\overline{\Delta}$(sight-color,t)	*total*
Δ(sight-shape,t)	2996	945	3941
$\overline{\Delta}$(sight-shape,t)	826	25232	26058
total	3822	26177	29999

This says that the streams **sight-shape** and **sight-color** changed state simultaneously 2996 times, and one changed when the other didn't $945 + 826 = 1771$ times. To assess the strength of association between **sight-shape** and **sight-color** Neo squares the frequency in the first cell of the contingency table (2996) and divides by the product of the first row and first column margins (3941 and 3822, respectively). The maximum value for this statistic is 1.0, and for the table above it is $2996^2/(3941 \times 3822) = .596$. [1]

---

[1] Neo could use other statistics, such as χ^2 and G, provided the contingency table is scaled to a constant total, preserving the proportions. (Scaling is necessary because χ^2 and G are not independent of sample size.) In practice, Neo learns the same scopes, and ranks them similarly, irrespective of how it measures association in its contingency tables.

Scopes provide a mechanism for cross-modal perception: the same contingency table mechanism will detect cooccurrences in the visual and tactile streams, for example Rose (1990) and Spelke (1987).

Fluents

Fluents represent things that don't change, or that change in highly regular, predictable ways. The sound made by a rattle is a fluent, so is the sensation of holding the rattle, and so are the visual sensations of the shape and color of the rattle. Of course, the concept "rattle" has all these components, so fluents for the color, shape, sound and texture of a rattle must be linked up in a single fluent.

Although the simplest fluents represent sensations, fluents are not identical with sensations. This is an important point, because the distinction between streams and fluents is how we implement the distinction between sensory experience and cognitive experience. Neo can experience the sensations associated with looking at a red rattle without saying, mentally, "Ah, I recognize a red rattle." The sensory experience is implemented as tokens for red and rattle-shaped in the appropriate streams, whereas the cognitive experience of a red rattle involves activating a fluent that represents the red rattle.

Base Fluents

Neo's smallest fluents, called *base fluents*, represent cooccurring tokens within scopes. Suppose stream σ_i contains a at time $t-1$ and b at time t. Then we say token a *stops* in stream i at time $t-1$, denoted $\dashv(i,a,t-1)$, and token b *starts* in stream i at time t, denoted $\vdash(i,b,t)$. Now suppose Neo turns its head and its eyes alight on a red rattle. Neo will detect two simultaneous events, $\vdash$(sight-color,red,t) and $\vdash$(sight-shape,rattle-shape,t). Sometime later, Neo might look somewhere else, which will generate two simultaneous stop events, $\dashv$(sight-color,red,v) and $\dashv$(sight-shape, rattle-shape,v). Simultaneous start events and stop events are evidence that a single object—in this case a red rattle—or a single activity, is making its presence felt in two streams. Of course, two *unrelated* events could occur simultaneously in two streams, but this sort of coincidence is less likely than the coincidence of related events. Contingency tables like the one described earlier count the cooccurrences of start and stop events, and assess whether start and stop events happen simultaneously significantly often. Significant associations create base fluents.

Some of the base fluents discovered by Neo are shown in table 1. They make sense, given what we know about the Neo simulator. The first block of fluents in table 1 deals with mouthing: When Neo is mouthing, its arm is resting ((**mouth mouthing) (arm resting)**) and its voice is quiet ((**mouth mouthing) (voice quiet)**). When it isn't mouthing, Neo can make noises—crying, gurgling and screaming—and its arm can move.

The next block of base fluents in table 1 represents objects in Neo's environment, including the green rattle, the green mobile, the metallic keys, the knife, and so on. Not all the objects have been learned because Neo ran for only 30,000 time steps. The last fluent in this block ((**sight-color dark) (sight-shape none)**) represents what happens when Neo closes its eyes.

It is apparent to us, though not to Neo, that base fluents collectively have structure. Note that the block of ((**sound**

519

```
((mouth mouthing) (arm resting))                 ((mouth mouthing) (voice quiet))
((mouth not-mouthing) (arm move-lf))             ((mouth not-mouthing) (voice cry))
((mouth not-mouthing) (voice gurgle))            ((mouth not-mouthing) (voice scream))

((sight-color green) (sight-shape rattle-like))  ((sight-color green) (sight-shape mobile-like))
((sight-color metallic) (sight-shape blob-like)) ((sight-color metallic) (sight-shape knife-like))
((sight-color orange) (sight-shape blob-like))   ((sight-color orange) (sight-shape rattle-like))
((sight-color red) (sight-shape rattle-like))    ((sight-color white) (sight-shape rattle-like))
((sight-color white) (sight-shape crib-like))    ((sight-color dark) (sight-shape none))

((sound cry) (mouth not-mouthing))               ((sound cry) (tactile-mouth none))
((sound cry) (voice cry))

((sound gurgle) (mouth not-mouthing))            ((sound gurgle) (tactile-mouth none))
((sound gurgle) (voice gurgle))

((sound quiet) (arm resting))                    ((sound quiet) (arm-speed resting))
((sound quiet) (mouth mouthing))                 ((sound quiet) (tactile-mouth skin))
((sound quiet) (tactile-mouth plastic))          ((sound quiet) (voice quiet))

((tactile-hand none) (hand open))                ((tactile-hand plastic) (hand close))
((tactile-hand wood) (hand close))
```

Table 1: **Some of Neo's Base Fluents**

cry) ...) base fluents has exactly the same structure as the block of ((**sound gurgle**) ...) fluents: Neo is not mouthing, it has no tactile sensations in its mouth, and it is doing something with its voice. Regularities like this are the basis for categorization, as we describe below. The ((**tactile hand**) ...) fluents illustrate similar regularities.

Context Fluents

Suppose Neo is holding a rattle, and then it starts to mouth the rattle. While it is holding the rattle, the fluent ((**tactile-hand wood**)(**hand close**)) is active, and when it starts mouthing, the fluent ((**tactile-mouth wood**)(**do-mouth mouth**)) will become active. The latter fluent starts in the context of the former. If this happens significantly often then Neo will form the context fluent,

(CONTEXT   ((tactile-hand wood)(hand close))
            ((tactile-mouth wood)(do-mouth mouth))) .

The contingency table mechanism that learns scopes and base fluents also learns context fluents. Specifically, when fluent F_2 starts at time $t + i$, Neo checks to see whether fluent F_1 is active, and if so, it updates the first cell of the contingency table, ($\vdash F_1, t$ & $\vdash F_2, t + i$). If F_2 starts and F_1 isn't active, then Neo updates the third cell of the table, ($\overline{\vdash F_1, t}$ & $\vdash F_2, t + i$). If F_1 is active but F_2 doesn't start within a window of i time steps, then Neo increments the second cell of the table, ($\vdash F_1, t$ & $\overline{\vdash F_2, t + i}$).

What's missing from this account is what it means for a fluent to be "active." In fact, we finessed this problem earlier, when we described how Neo learns base fluents, implying that every start and stop event within a scope is "active," that is, contributes to the contingency table for some base fluent. A more psychologically plausible mechanism might include some sort of selective attention, so not all scopes are monitored for start and stop events all the time. The

problem of attention is even clearer when we contemplate building context fluents from other fluents, because fluents are representations in memory. The start event $\vdash F_1$ really means, "something happens in the streams, and as a result, the fluent F_1 is retrieved from memory." We haven't explained exactly how the event $\vdash F_1$ is implemented. It is really too simple: When all the token values in a scope change simultaneously, Neo compares the new values to the base fluents it has learned, and if it finds a match, it "activates" the associated base fluent. It activates a context fluent whenever one of its component fluents is activated. As soon as a fluent is activated, its "level of activation" begins to decline, and after a period of time it becomes inactive even if the sensory events that activated it are still present. This is how we implement a crude form of habituation. We are unable to model complex patterns of habituation and dishabituation. Neo's attentional mechanism is the focus of ongoing work.

Some of Neo's context fluents are illustrated in table 2. The first block of fluents begins with the fluent ((**sight-movement resting**) (**arm resting**)). In this context, Neo very often observes the start of the fluents ((**do-hand close**) (**hand close**)), ((**tactile-hand plastic**) (**hand close**)), and ((**tactile-hand wood**) (**hand close**)). That is, Neo has learned three activities that begin when its arm is resting. The first is, "experience the intention to close the hand and the sensation of the closed hand"; the second and third are, "experience the tactile sensation of wood/plastic in the hand and the sensation of the hand closed." The next two context fluents in table 2 have the same endpoints—the hand closing, and tactile sensations in the hand—but they begin with Neo crying and not mouthing. The final two context fluents begin with the tactile sensation in the hand and end with quiet sound and a tactile sensation in the mouth, and with the tactile sensation and mouthing, respectively.

```
(CONTEXT    ((sight-movement resting) (arm resting))
            ((do-hand close) (hand close)))
(CONTEXT    ((sight-movement resting) (arm resting))
            ((tactile-hand plastic) (hand close)))
(CONTEXT    ((sight-movement resting) (arm resting))
            ((tactile-hand wood) (hand close)))

(CONTEXT    ((sound cry) (mouth not-mouthing))
            ((do-hand close) (hand close)))
(CONTEXT    ((sound cry) (mouth not-mouthing))
            ((tactile-hand plastic) (hand close)))

(CONTEXT    ((tactile-hand plastic) (hand close))
            ((sound quiet) (tactile-mouth plastic)))
(CONTEXT    ((tactile-hand plastic) (hand close))
            ((tactile-mouth plastic) (mouth mouthing)))
```

Table 2: **Some of Neo's Context Fluents**

Chains and Classification

Neo aggregates context fluents into *chains*. For example, given the context fluents,

```
(CONTEXT    ((tactile-mouth none) (voice cry))
            ((tactile-hand wood) (hand close)))
(CONTEXT    ((tactile-hand wood)(hand close))
            ((tactile-mouth wood)(do-mouth mouth)))),
```

Neo forms the chain,

```
(CHAIN      ((tactile-mouth none) (voice cry))
            ((tactile-hand wood) (hand close))
            ((tactile-mouth wood)(do-mouth mouth)) ) .
```

Here is another, very similar chain that Neo learned:

```
(CHAIN      ((tactile-mouth none) (voice cry))
            ((tactile-hand plastic) (hand close))
            ((tactile-mouth plastic)(do-mouth mouth)) ) .
```

The only difference between these chains is the object that Neo grabs and mouths: in the first case it is wooden, in the second, plastic. We may form a *class* of things that Neo can grab and mouth. The chains don't say exactly which objects are in the class, but we know they are either wood or plastic, and they are graspable, and mouthable.

GRASPABLE and MOUTHABLE are *interactional* properties (Johnson, 1987) that characterize Neo's activities in its environment. Unlike TEXTURE—wood or plastic—they are in a sense *subjective*: What's graspable by one agent isn't necessarily graspable by another. Whereas TEXTURE is an inherent property of an object, GRASPABLE is a property of the object *and the agent* who may try to grasp it. Interactional properties like GRASPABLE are the basis for categories in Lakoff and Johnson's theory of categorization (Johnson, 1987; Lakoff, 1984; Lakoff and Johnson, 1980) and also in Mandler's theory of conceptual development (Mandler, 1992). However, we believe categories are best defined in terms of *activities*, and the attractiveness of interactional features is due to them describing activities better than objective features such as texture (Cohen, Oates and Atkin, 1996).

In fact, although Neo learns activities, represented as chains, we are responsible for using these chains to identify

features and form classes (Cohen, Oates and Atkin, 1996). The first step is to match up chains that have the same stream names in the same order, creating an *abstract chain* of scopes. For example, the chains above are both described by the abstract chain (**tactile-mouth voice**) → (**tactile-hand hand**) → (**tactile-mouth mouth**). Now when we look at the token values that can instantiate this abstract chain, we find that the **tactile-hand** and **tactile-mouth** streams contains either **none**, **wood** or **plastic**. In other words, the abstract chain identifies an activity in which Neo has nothing in its mouth and is crying, and then has something wood or plastic in its hand and its mouth. We know, because we built the Neo simulator, that the wood or plastic objects include Neo's rattles and bottles, but not the mobile, Mommy, or Neo's own hand. Currently, this class is "implicit." Neo doesn't have an ontology in its head, nor declarative definitions of categories. Still, there is an implicit class of objects that can participate in the abstract chain. (See Cohen, Oates and Atkin, 1996, for further examples.)

Discussion

We have illustrated five levels of redescription of Neo's sensory experience, and suggested how the regularities in these redescriptions can be the basis of classification. Each level of redescription provides the opportunity to learn representations, and one simple mechanism produces all these representations but chains. The mechanism maintains contingency tables for pairs of start (⊢) or stop (⊣) events, and when a measure of association for the table achieves significance, Neo interns a representation. The only thing that changes, from one level of representation to the next, is *what* starts and stops, and whether a lag is allowed between these events.

Each version of this basic contingency-table mechanism can be viewed as an image-schema, in the sense Mandler (1992) intends: It produces a redescription and an intermediate level representation of raw sensory experience. It happens that all Neo's redescription takes place in the temporal domain, but this is appropriate for an agent that is biased to learn a predictive model of events in its environment. Although Mandler presents image-schemas as processors of spatial information, they are equally well described in temporal terms. Mandler cites, for instance, SELF MOTION, ANIMATE MOTION, CAUSED MOTION, and AGENCY as image schemas. We would argue that Neo has learned some of these predicates. For example, the abstract chain (**do-arm arm**) → (**sight-movement arm-speed**) defines a class of actions in which, in the context of an arm movement, Neo sees the arm moving fast. Arguably, this is a SELF MOTION image-schema.

This example raises the question of how many image-schemas is a baby born with, and whether more are learned. Mandler lists many image schemas in her paper; we suggest one for scopes, one for base fluents, and one for context fluents (applied recursively to produce chains). Another mechanism is required to produce abstract chains. Still, we take a distinctly minimalist position: If an image-schema such as SELF MOTION can be learned as described above, we prefer not to assume babies are born with it. We think it is very valuable to implement agents such as Neo to find out how much or little is required in the way of innate structure, especially as image-schemas and the kinds of "models" discussed by Leslie (1988), Spelke (1988), Carey and Spelke (1994), Keil (1994), and others are informal (lacking interpretation as data structures and processes) and their interactions with memory and attention are largely unspecified.

A related question is why particular relationships are image-schemas. We offer two kinds of explanation. Scopes serve to reduce the combinatorial space of potential fluents, so perhaps some image-schemas have evolved for computational reasons. Base fluents are learned when tokens start and stop simultaneously. Simultaneity is rare among independent events, so an image-schema that detects simultaneity is ideal for associating parts of a whole. (Thus it may not be necessary to posit an innate and sophisticated understanding of the physical world, e.g., Spelke, 1988.) Context fluents are learned when one fluent follows another more often than would be expected by chance, which is a necessary though not sufficient condition to infer cause (Suppes, 1970; Cohen, 1995). So Neo has the image-schemas it has because they help Neo identify states, objects and potentially causal sequences.

Conclusion

Let us review what Neo learned: It learned that most of the regularity in its environment takes place in 30 pairs of streams, less than 10% of the $(26 \times 25)/2 = 325$ pairs of streams that it might have focused on. It learned base fluents corresponding to the shape and color of most objects in its environment. It learned the permanent locations of the green mobile (directly overhead) and the crib bars (to the extreme left and right of its field of view). It learned activities, such as grasping an object and mouthing it, or moving its arm and seeing its arm move. It almost learned conditions. For example, it learned a chain that includes ...((**do-hand open**)(**hand open**))((**tactile-mouth skin**)(**mouth mouthing**)), but it has no way to learn that the first fluent is a condition for the second—that the hand *must* be open to be mouthed. It learned chains from which we abstracted classes that make sense in Neo's environment, such as the class of objects that can be grasped and mouthed, and the class of activities that end in seeing the arm moving fast.

Keep in mind that Neo's actions are largely random: when it grabs an object it *can* mouth it, but it's just as likely to drop it, or move its head. The only structure in Neo's actions is provided by conditions (e.g., it cannot mouth an object it hasn't grasped, and it cannot mouth its hand unless the hand is open) and by a handful of simple behavioral dependencies built into the simulator (e.g., it sometimes grabs what it looks at, and it cries if it gets hungry). Keeping in mind also that Neo ran for only 30,000 time steps, it seems to us that it learned quite a lot.

In conclusion, Neo provides preliminary evidence that image-schematic redescription of raw sensations is probably sufficient to form implicit, activity-based categories. Very few image-schemas are required; more may be learned.

References

Susan Carey and Elizabeth Spelke. (1994). Domain-specific knowledge and conceptual change. In Lawrence A. Hirschfeld and Susan A.Gelman, editors, *Mapping the Mind*. Cambridge University Press.

Paul R. Cohen. (1995) *Empirical Methods for Artificial Intelligence*. MIT Press.

Paul R. Cohen, Tim Oates, and Marc S. Atkin. (1996). Preliminary evidence that conceptual structure can be learned by interacting with an environment.

Mark Johnson. (1987). *The Body in the Mind*. University of Chicago Press.

Frank Keil. (1994). The birth and nurturance of concepts by domains. In Lawrence A. Hirschfeld and Susan A.Gelman, editors, *Mapping the Mind*. Cambridge University Press.

George Lakoff. (1984). *Women, Fire, and Dangerous Things*. University of Chicago Press.

George Lakoff and Mark Johnson. (1980). *Metaphors We Live By*. University of Chicago Press.

Alan M. Leslie. (1988). The necessity of illusion: perception and thought in infancy. In L. Weiskrantz, editor, *Thought Without Language*. Oxford University Press (Clarendon).

Jean M. Mandler. (1988). How to build a baby: On the development of an accessible representational system. *Cognitive Development*, 3:113–136.

Jean M. Mandler. (1992). How to build a baby: II. conceptual primitives. *Psychological Review*, 99(4):587–604.

S. A. Rose. (1990). Cross-modal transfer in infants: What is being transferred? In Adele Diamond, editor, *The Development and Neural Bases of Higher Cognitive Functions*. New York Academy of Sciences.

Elizabeth S. Spelke. (1987). The development of intermodal perception. In P. Salapatek and L. Cohen, editors, *The Handbook of Infant Perception*. Academic Press.

Elizabeth S. Spelke. (1988). The origins of physical knowledge. In L. Weiskrantz, editor, *Thought Without Language*. Oxford University Press (Clarendon).

Patrick Suppes. (1970). *A Probabilistic Theory of Causality*. North-Holland Amsterdam.

The Iteration of Concept Combination in Sense Generation

Richard Cooper
Department of Psychology
Birkbeck College, London
Malet Street, London WC1E 7HX
R.Cooper@psyc.bbk.ac.uk

Bradley Franks
Department of Psychology
London School of Economics
Houghton Street, London WC2A 2AE
B.Franks@lse.ac.uk

Abstract

We report work in progress on the computational modelling of a theory of concepts and concept combination. The *sense generation* approach to concepts provides a perspicuous way of treating a range of recalcitrant concept combinations: privative combinations (e.g., *fake gun, stone lion, apparent friend*). We argue that a proper treatment of concept combination must respect important syntactic constraints on the combination process, the simplest being the priority of syntactic modifier over the head in case of conflicts. We present a model of privative concept combinations based on the sense generation approach. The model was developed using COGENT, an object-oriented modelling environment designed to simplify and clarify the implementation process by minimising the 'distance' between the box/arrow 'language' of psychological theorising and the theory's implementation. In addition to simple privatives (i.e., ones with a single modifier, like *fake gun*) the model also handles iterated, or complex, privative combinations (i.e., ones with more than one modifier, like *fake stone lion*), and reflects their associated modification ambiguities. We suggest that the success of this model reflects both the utility of COGENT as a modelling framework and the adequacy of sense generation as a theory of concept combination.

Introduction

Concepts are usually taken to have three basic functions in mental life (see, e.g., Franks, 1992; Rips, 1995): a *representation* function (the representational contents over which thought and inference about the world takes place), a *classification* (or referring) function (the contents employed in determining whether objects fall under the denotation of a term), and a *linguistic* function (the contents accessed in understanding language and concatenated according to linguistically appropriate rules to comprise a mental representation of the meaning of a sentence or utterance). The first two functions have been the primary concern of investigations of concepts in cognitive science.

It is widely accepted that insights about the representation and classification functions of concepts can be obtained from an understanding of the way in which they combine to form complex concepts (e.g., Medin & Shoben, 1988; Smith, Osherson, Rips & Keane, 1988). We suggest that constraints on the process of combination itself should be forthcoming from an understanding of the linguistic function. Hence, accounts of concepts in general can be constrained by ascertaining the extent to which they respect critical factors concerning the linguistic function. In order to begin to make progress on this question, the work reported here focuses on the effects of aspects of the linguistic function on the representational function of concepts (since, arguably, the classification function is parasitic on the representational function).

We present a computational model of concept combination from within the sense generation framework developed elsewhere (e.g., Franks, 1995), employing a computational framework developed in order to clarify the relationship between the specification of theoretical commitments and their implementation (Cooper, Fox, Farringdon & Shallice, in press). This is an essentially symbolic framework for modelling cognitive phenomena: since our focus was on modelling the effect of syntactic relations on concept combination (rather than modelling those syntactic relations per se), the necessary perspicuity and clarity of the sequential ordering in the implementation of the syntax is more directly lent by a symbolic implementation than a connectionist one (such as Miikkulainen, 1993). We present a basic model of concept combinations first (a head noun combining with a single modifier), and then show how this can be extended to handle a simple form of syntactic influence on combination — the iteration of modifiers, with attendant scoping or modification ambiguities that arise for their representation. The model presented is an aspect of work in progress. This work has a goal of locating a model of concept combination within a perspective gained from syntactic constraints on combination and from wider considerations of cognitive modelling.

Sense Generation and Concept Combination

Sense generation is an approach to concepts and concept combination that attempts to respect psychological evidence about classification and representation in the context of pragmatic factors concerning communication. It postulates 'quasi-classical' *lexical concept* representations which express the default content for a concept, comprising attribute-value structures where each attribute takes only one value, and where those values can be overridden by contextual dictates (Franks & Braisby, 1990; Franks, 1995). These representations are quasi-classical in that, although they act as if they were necessary and sufficient conditions for category membership *within* a single context, *across* different contexts their contents are defeasible and so are not classical definitions. A critical distinction between types of attributes is made on the basis of their relationship to category membership: 'central' attributes are ones that reflect deep, theoretical assumptions about the factors that are presumed essential for category membership (see Medin & Ortony, 1989; Braisby, Franks & Hampton, 1994, in press); by contrast, 'diagnostic' attributes are those aspects of the surface appearance of objects that may be used for rough-and-ready identification, but are not infallible guides. Sense generation postulates a generative process that takes bottom-up input from lexical concepts associated with the constituents of a phrase, and outputs a *sense* for the phrase that provides a closer fit to the pragmatic context than would the default content of lexical concepts.

It can be argued (Franks, 1995) that a class of combinations known as 'privatives' constitute a test-case for theories of concept combination, in that they exhibit particularly strong, yet predictable, forms of context-sensitivity. Privative adjectives are analysed by Kamp (1975) as ones for which the following inference is a logical truth: *If x is a privative adjective-noun then x is not a noun*: for example, if *x* is a *fake gun*, then *x* is not a *gun*.

Franks (1995) argues that this analysis should be extended in three ways. First, the characteristic inference should be weakened, to allow for the cognitively plausible classification, if *x* is a *fake gun*, then *x is a gun* in some sense — only with respect to appearance. Second, such an inference is characteristic not only of the effect of a particular set of adjectives on all nouns that they modify, but also of the interaction of the contents of head nouns with modifiers that are not themselves intrinsically privative. Third, 'proper' privatives, in which privative behaviour results from an intrinsic property of the adjective type, in fact come in two kinds — 'negating' privatives (e.g., *fake gun* — where, intuitively, the modifier negates the central attributes of the head), and 'equivocating' privatives (e.g., *apparent friend* — where the modifier casts doubt on the head's central attributes, but does not completely negate them). In both cases, the diagnostic attributes of the head noun concept are not denied in any way — thus preserving the characteristic classification inference based on appearances only, noted above. These types of privative have analogues in which privative behaviour results not from the particular semantic type of the modifier, but from the interaction of the contents of the concepts of head and modifier. Such 'functional' privatives include combinations like *stone lion* or *chocolate teapot* (negating privative analogues of *fake gun*), and *wooden skillet* or *blue orange* (equivocating privative analogues of *apparent friend*). It is clear that, for these cases, there is no intrinsic property of either the head or modifier that produces the privative behaviour (e.g., when *stone* modifies *bridge*, and when *lion* is modified by *brown*, the resulting behaviour is not privative). Hence, privatives embody a particularly strong form of context-sensitivity of concept representations. Producing the sense for a privative combination denies attributes of the head noun, requiring a process that is not rigidly (i.e., monotonically) compositional (for example, as in feature-addition; see Hampton, 1987). This does not preclude a compositional account, however, since the sense produced for a combination is still predictable from the concepts of the parts and their mode of combination.

Despite their constituting a test case for theories of concepts and concept combination, it is not clear that privatives can be handled in, for example, prototype theory (Hampton, 1992), schema theory (Murphy, 1988), or theories that assume that combination operates by a process of either property mapping or slot filling (cf., Wisniewski & Gentner, 1991). Moreover, the requisite marked conflict between attributes of the head

and modifier may also be difficult to express in connectionist terms. By contrast, a unified, compositional account of privatives within the sense generation framework is presented in Franks (1995). The account employs unification-based operations to capture the various aspects of concept combination (e.g., priority unification (Kaplan, 1987), in which the sense for the combination inherits all of the attribute-value pairs of the constituent lexical concept, with the exception that where the two concepts conflict on one of the values of a common attributes, the value of the priority constituent — the modifier — is inherited). The critical difference between negating and equivocating privatives is expressed in terms of different metonymic type coercion operators (cf., Klein & Sag, 1985; Pustejovsky, 1991): for negators, the operator takes as input the head noun's lexical concept (comprising both central and diagnostic attributes), and outputs a coerced representation comprising the head's diagnostic attributes and the negation of its central attributes; for equivocators, the operator outputs the diagnostic attributes of the head and neither the central attributes nor their negation, but rather their being only possibly true of the object being referred to. This corresponds to treating the attribute-value structures as potentially having three truth-values — a value of an attribute may be true of a type of object, false of it, or neither. For functional privatives, the conflict between central attributes for *stone* and *lion* results in those of the latter being negated, whilst the conflict between diagnostic attributes for *wood* and *skillet* results in the central attributes of the latter not being negated but being only possibly true of the type of object described by the phrase.

This treatment captures defining semantic intuitions about objects described by privatives, and hence their characteristic classification inferences. For example, a stone lion possesses central attributes of stone objects, but only diagnostic attributes of real lions. Similarly, fake guns do not possess the central attributes of guns, but only their diagnostic attributes. By contrast, an apparent friend performs diagnostic behaviours of a friend, but this is consistent with only *possibly* possessing central motivational attributes of friendship; similarly, a wooden skillet looks like a real skillet but may or may not be able to support the central function of a skillet. In all cases, the initial, bottom-up combination stage leaves the elaboration and specification of the details of the combination unspecified, producing schematic senses which are consistent with a range of further possible specifications that depend on informational and pragmatic context (e.g., resulting in the addition of the information that the stone lion is a statue, and so has central attributes of a statue, or that an apparent friend really is or is not a friend, with appropriate central attributes).

The model discussed here seeks to test this account in two ways. First of all, to ascertain whether the account of simple privative concept combinations (i.e., ones in which there is a single modifier for the head) is coherent by modelling it. Secondly, to ascertain whether the particular combination operations are adequate for handling iterated or complex concept combinations (in which there is more than one modifier). This also provides a way of beginning to incorporate syntactic constraints into concept combination.

Noun phrases often incorporate multiple modifiers of the head noun. The multiplication of modifiers raises the possibility of ambiguity in the scope of the modification, and this problem is rendered especially complex when the multiplied modifiers are privatives, and hence when a privative combination is itself modified by a privative. For example, *fake stone lion* could have two distinct readings, one in which the first modifier has 'wide' scope over the second modifier and the head (i.e., *fake (stone lion)*: a stone lion that is a fake), and one in which the first modifier has 'narrow' scope over the second modifier only, and they both modify the head (i.e., *(fake stone) lion*: a lion that is made of fake stone).

In essence, in order to arrive at an appropriate representation for such complex combinations, the head-modifier relationships — that is, the scope of the first modifier — must be disambiguated. The disambiguation of such relationships is taken to be provided by a syntax parser that provides input to a conceptual interpreter. This does not imply, of course, that no semantic or thematic lexical information is involved in the process of syntactic disambiguation, merely that detailed conceptual information is not (see, e.g., Trueswell, Tanenhaus & Kello, 1993). The question of interest for our purposes is then, given that the head-modifier relationships have been disambiguated, does the sense generation account of simple privative combinations generalise to complex privatives?

The COGENT Modelling Environment

Our model was constructed in COGENT (Cognitive Objects within a Graphical EnviroNmenT), a developing cognitive modelling tool. This system grew out of independent work aimed at clarifying the relationship between psychological theory and computational implementation within cognitive modelling. In particular, it seeks to make explicit the range of actual architectural commitments made by a psychological theory, as distinct from mere implementation details (cf. Cooper *et al.*, in press; Cooper, 1995).

The COGENT modelling environment provides a set of configurable cognitive "objects" (such as rule-based processes, and buffers with or without capacity limitations and content decay). Central to the environment is a graphical interface which allows the specification of executable models in the box/arrow style. Different shaped boxes correspond to different types of object, and a complete executable model can be developed by specifying appropriate properties and contents for all objects in the model. This minimises the distance between the models traditionally developed by psychologists and their implementations, simplifying the relation between the two. At present, only symbolic objects are provided, but anticipated future developments include extending the environment by incorporating connectionist and network objects. Extant uses include the implementation of production system models (Cooper, 1996), models of decision making (that of Fox, 1980), and models of prospective memory (Ellis, Shallice and Cooper, in submission). Details of COGENT availability and system requirements are available from the authors.

It is important to emphasise that COGENT is an environment, not an architecture. As such the intention is that the system should impose few (if any) constraints on the precise form of a model's implementation. In general, it is the particular theorist's responsibility to provide such constraints. This is not to say that architectures such as Soar (Newell, 1990) have no role in computational work on cognition (though see Cooper & Shallice (1995) for a discussion of some potential short-

comings of architecture-driven modelling), but to provide for theorists who do not subscribe to all of the assumptions embodied in any extant architecture.

In spite of the above intention, one constraint which is imposed by COGENT, and which impacts on the current domain, is the preclusion of recursive procedures (i.e., procedures which call themselves). Most current programming languages allow recursive procedures, and such procedures are of tremendous utility when processing tree-structured data such as natural language. However, true recursion requires a processing stack to maintain the trace of execution throughout recursive calls (in order to recover from the recursion once it bottoms out), and associated dynamic memory allocation for independent copies of local variables used within each recursive call.

While there is no prohibition on a COGENT process triggering itself, there is no processing stack within COGENT so there is no possibility that, on completion, a process could return control to the process that triggered it. (In fact, processing within COGENT is based on a parallel model in which all boxes are constantly potentially active: see Cooper (1995) for more details.) Furthermore, COGENT's assumed correspondence between cognitive objects (i.e., boxes) and functional cognitive structures means that, for example, a process requiring local variables will require an associated buffer in which to store those variables. A truly recursive process would require a separate copy of this buffer for each recursive call. Again, this dynamic memory allocation is not available within COGENT. Notice that the preclusion of recursion in COGENT arises not from any prior prejudice against recursive procedures, but from the directness of the mapping between functional units and COGENT objects, and from the underlying (parallel) processing model.

In light of the above, complex modified noun-phrases cannot be processed in COGENT by recursively processing their parts.

Sense Generation in COGENT

The model consists of a set of interconnected boxes (see Figure 1) of two principal kinds: buffers and rule-based processes. A parsing process breaks input into a set of local trees (i.e., binary branching nodes which disambiguate head/modifier relationships) and adds its output to a temporary storage buffer (*Local Parse Trees*). We are not here concerned with the internal details of this parsing process. A second process, *Conceptual Access*, is triggered by elements in the store, processing them (i.e., accessing the conceptual content associated with their constituents) one at a time. These contents comprise the single-valued attribute value structures (with the major division between central and diagnostic attributes) noted earlier. The order of this processing is constrained by the requirement that the conceptual content of the constituents (i.e., head and modifier) is immediately available (either from the *Mental Lexicon* or from a short term store to which earlier processing may have written its results). As a consequence, processing is bottom-up.

Once the initial content for both the head and modifier has been obtained, the generation of the schematic sense for the phrase proceeds via two further processes. These are also controlled in a bottom-up manner, since they only depend upon the type of operator or upon whether conflicts occur

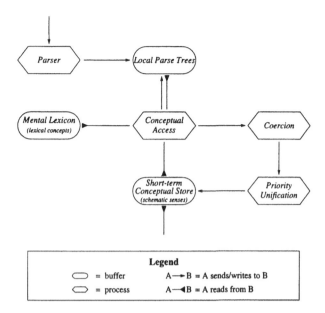

Figure 1: Sense Generation in COGENT

at diagnostic or central levels. The particular detailed contents of lexical concepts are not critical to the generation of a schematic sense. Firstly, the content of the head is coerced in one of two ways (see above): either the head's central attributes are negated (if the modifier is a negating privative adjective, or if the head and modifier conflict on central attributes), or the head's central attributes are undercut or cast into doubt (if the modifier is an equivocating privative adjective, or if the head and modifier conflict on diagnostic attributes). Following this, the coerced central and diagnostic attributes of the head are priority unified with the corresponding attributes of the modifier, with the modifier's attributes taking priority. This produces a schematic sense for the combination, which is temporarily stored in a conceptual store (cf., Potter, 1993). If this sense is associated with a constituent part of a complex noun phrase, then its arrival in the conceptual store will allow processing of its super-ordinate constituent to proceed: generating a sense for the complex noun phrase as a whole will then take inputs both from the *Mental Lexicon* (for lexical sub-constituents) and from the *Short-term Conceptual Store* (for non-lexical sub-constituents). The sense produced in this bottom-up manner *is* only schematic. Any post-combination specification or elaboration of this sense is viewed as involving an interaction between bottom-up and top-down influences and not modelled here.

The full specification of the model in COGENT consists of Figure 1 together with a specification of the configurable properties of each box in that figure. The theoretical differences between the *Mental Lexicon* and the *Short-term Conceptual Store*, for example, are reflected in different configurations of the corresponding boxes. In particular, the *Mental Lexicon* is modelled as a long term store with no decay and no capacity limitations, whereas the *Short-term Conceptual Store* is modelled as a temporary or working store with fixed decay and capacity limitations. Each process is fully specified in

terms of a set of condition/action rules (one rule per process for this model) and some declarative Prolog conditions. The conditions of the rules either match elements from various buffers or perform logical operations (such as priority unification, specified in Prolog) on their data. The rules' actions modify buffer contents or trigger further processes.

The three rules are presented in Figure 2. CH and DH represent the central and diagnostic attributes of the head (respectively). Similarly CM and DM represent the central and diagnostic attributes of the modifier. In Rule 1, the condition conceptual_lookup queries the *Mental Lexicon* and *Short-term Conceptual Store* to determine the content of the phrase's head. The condition conflict_type serves a similar purpose for the modifier, but also takes account of adjectives which serve as operators (and so have no independent conceptual content — e.g., proper privatives like *fake*). If these conditions are met, the rule fires, deleting the local parse tree from its buffer, and triggering *Coercion* with the message coerce(Phrase, Type, CH, CM, DH, DM).

When Rule 2 is triggered, it coerces the type of the central attributes of the head according to that specified by the triggering process, producing CCH (i.e., coerced central head attributes). The process then triggers *Priority Unification* (Rule 3) with the message unify_content(Phrase, CCH, CM, DH, DM).

The triggering of Rule 3 priority unifies the central attributes of the coerced head and modifier, producing the central attributes of the combination (C), and the diagnostic attributes of the head and modifier, producing the diagnostic attributes of the combination (D). The conceptual content of the combination is then added to the *Short-term Conceptual Store*, where it may contribute to the construction of the conceptual content of a larger constituent (via the condition conceptual_lookup called by *Conceptual Access* (Rule 1)).

To illustrate, consider first a simple privative, such as *stone lion*. There is no syntactic ambiguity, and just one local tree. Processing therefore requires just one cycle through the diagram in Figure 1. Once the local tree appears in the *Local Parse Trees* store, *Short-term Conceptual Access* is triggered, thus accessing the lexical concepts for both *stone* and *lion* from the *Mental Lexicon*: both lexical concepts comprise central and diagnostic attributes. *Conceptual Access* also determines the nature of the combination in terms of any conflict of attributes (i.e., negating or equivocating privative for conflicts on central or diagnostic attributes respectively, or affirmative combination for no conflict). In the case of *stone lion*, a conflict of central attributes will be detected, fulfilling the requirements for a negating type coercion. *Conceptual Access* passes this information to the *Coercion* process, which negates the central attributes of the head (*lion*). The output coerced representation then comprises the diagnostic attributes and the negated central attributes from the lexical concept for *lion*. The coerced representation of *lion* and the representation of the lexical concept for *stone* are then input to the *Priority Unification* process, which combines them (giving precedence to *stone*) to yield a representation of a type of object that possesses all of the central and diagnostic attributes of *stone*, and some of the coerced central and diagnostic attributes of *lion*, with the proviso that, where the values of attributes conflict, the values of *stone* take priority. The resulting representation

526

Rule 1: Conceptual Access

IF:	once `local_tree(Phrase, Modifier, Head)` is in *Local Parse Trees*
	`conceptual_lookup(Head, CH, DH)`
	`conflict_type(Modifer, Type, CH, DH, CM, DM)`
THEN:	delete `local_tree(Phrase, Modifier, Head)` from *Local Parse Trees*
	send `coerce(Phrase, Type, CH, CM, DH, DM)` to *Coercion*

Rule 2: Coercion

TRIGGER:	`coerce(Phrase, Type, CH, CM, DH, DM)`
IF:	`type_coerce(Type, CH, CCH)`
THEN:	send `unify_content(Phrase, CCH, CM, DH, DM)` to *Priority Unify*

Rule 3: Priority Unification

TRIGGER:	`unify_content(Phrase, CH, CM, DH, DM)`
IF:	`priority_unify(CM, CH, C)`
	`priority_unify(DM, DH, D)`
THEN:	add `conceptual_content(Phrase, C, D)` to *Short-term Conceptual Store*

Upper-case identifiers correspond to variables which are instantiated when the rule fires.

Figure 2: COGENT rules for Sense Generation

is of a type of object that has central attributes of *stone* (e.g., inorganic) and has negated central attributes of *lion* (e.g., inorganic, genetic structure not of a lion); it also has diagnostic attributes of *stone* (e.g., a grey colour, hard texture), and some, but not all, of *lion* (e.g., it has a lion shape, but not lion colour or lion habitat).

The case of complex noun phrases involving iterated modifiers is analogous, except that alternate possible syntactic structures (reflected in alternate local parse trees) lead to alternate possible senses. For *fake stone lion*, a sense of *stone lion* may be determined as above. The negating privative *fake* may then operate on this sense (temporarily available in the *Short-term Conceptual Store*) to yield a representation for a type of object that does not have the central attributes of *stone lion* (e.g., inorganic) but does have the diagnostic attributes of this combination. The second reading of *fake stone lion* corresponds to the case where the complex nominal *fake stone* modifies *lion* (corresponding to a lion which is made from some kind of fake stone, such as a hard plastic). In this case, the content of *fake stone* will first be determined. The relevant representation will have as central features the negation of the central features of *stone* (but the diagnostic features of *stone*). The result of combining this with the content of *lion* will depend on the precise form of central features of each. If the central features of *fake stone* do not conflict with those of *lion*, then an affirmative combination will be invoked, and all central attributes will be unified. The resulting sense allows that a fake stone lion is actually a real lion (perhaps pretending to be a statue). Equivocating or negating privative readings may also be licensed if there is conflict on diagnostic or central attributes respectively. In this way, the model demonstrates that the sense generation account of simple privatives can generalise to complex, iterated, concept combinations.

Future Developments

Future research will focus on four main areas. Firstly, although this work has shown that sense generation can provide an adequate account of iterated privative combinations, the

model may also be used to assess the generality of the sense generation theory in terms of affirmative (i.e., non-privative) forms of combination (e.g., predicating adjectives like *red* and non-predicating adjectives like *criminal*).

The scoping ambiguities inherent in modifier iteration are, of course, just one of a range of syntactic phenomena that falls within the scope of the sense generation theory. A second strand of further work will therefore involve developing the model itself by addressing further syntactic phenomena. For example, combinations may involve syntactic form-class ambiguities. Thus, when interpreting, say, *stone lion*, a strictly bottom-up parser would initially interpret *stone* as a head noun, only to find that it is in fact a modifier. A fuller treatment of syntax would also incorporate the interaction between conceptual content and more coarse-grained content (such as thematic roles) relevant to resolving ambiguity.

A somewhat different area in which the model is underdeveloped concerns the classification and representational functions of concepts. The current model simply takes concept representations to comprise two different types of attribute. The combination operations are sensitive to these types of attributes but not to the particular attributes themselves. This allows a relatively schematic treatment of representation. However, in order to provide a full model of the representational and classification functions, more detail concerning the post-combination specification of the senses is necessary. This is addressed within the sense generation theory (see Franks (1995) for a full account), according to which any such specification is consistent with the results of the initial (schematic) combination stage. These developments will therefore augment (rather than negate) the current model.

Lastly, it is anticipated that developments in the COGENT software will allow further refinement of the model. More detailed modelling of the classification and representational functions of concepts may, for example, be better handled in a hybrid symbolic + connectionist model in which the *Mental Lexicon* (currently modeled as a static, symbolic, store), and its access, is handled by a connectionist component. Affir-

527

mative combinations in such a model might be handled by a purely connectionist "route", but this route would be interrupted (in the sense of Cooper & Franks, 1993) in the case of privative combinations, where attribute conflicts would trigger type coercion prior to combination.

Conclusions

We have suggested that a plausible account of concept combination must be constrained by an understanding of the linguistic function of concepts, and that this can begin to be handled by modelling complex, iterated combinations. Given that simple privatives are themselves a complex set of combinations that can provide a test case for a theory of concepts, the ability to model complex privatives provides an even stronger criterion for any account's adequacy. We suggest that the findings reported here indicate that sense generation can provide a framework for developing a plausible, generalisable account of concepts and concept combination.

The development of the model within the COGENT modelling environment has also demonstrated the utility of CO-GENT as a general modelling resource. We argue that the diagrammatic representation (Figure 1), together with the three rules which govern the behaviour of the three processes, clarifies the sense generation theory without obscuring essential aspects with implementation detail. In this sense, we aver, both sense generation and COGENT have profited (and will continue to profit) from their interaction in the development of this model

References

Braisby, N. R., Franks, B., & Hampton, J. A. (1994). On the psychological basis for rigid designation. In *Proceedings of the 16th Annual Conference of the Cognitive Science Society*, pp. 56–61. Atlanta, GA.

Braisby, N. R., Franks, B., & Hampton, J. A. (In press). Essentialism, word use, and concepts. *Cognition*.

Cooper, R. (1995). Towards an object-oriented language for cognitive modeling. In *Proceedings of the 17th Annual Conference of the Cognitive Science Society*, pp. 556–561. Pittsburgh, PA.

Cooper, R. (1996). Perseverative subgoaling in a production system model of problem solving. In *Proceedings of the 18th Annual Conference of the Cognitive Science Society*. This volume. San Diego, CA.

Cooper, R., Fox, J., Farringdon, J., & Shallice, T. (In press). A systematic methodology for cognitive modelling. *Artificial Intelligence*, 85.

Cooper, R., & Franks, B. (1993). Interruptibility as a constraint on hybrid systems. *Minds and Machines*, 3, 73–96.

Cooper, R., & Shallice, T. (1995). Soar and the case for Unified Theories of Cognition. *Cognition*, 55(2), 115–149.

Ellis, J., Shallice, T., & Cooper, R. (1996). Memory for, and the organization of, future intentions. In submission.

Fox, J. (1980). Making decisions under the influence of memory. *Psychological Review*, 87, 190–211.

Franks, B. (1992). Folk psychology and the ascription of concepts. *Philosophical Psychology*, 5, 369–390.

Franks, B. (1995). Sense generation: A "Quasi-Classical" approach to concepts and concept combination. *Cognitive Science*, 19, 441–505.

Franks, B., & Braisby, N. R. (1990). Sense generation, or how to make the mental lexicon flexible. In *Proceedings of the 12th Annual Conference of the Cognitive Science Society*. Cambridge, MA.

Hampton, J. A. (1987). Inheritance of attributes in natural concept conjunctions. *Memory & Cognition*, 15, 55–71.

Hampton, J. A. (1992). Prototype models of concepts. In van Mechelen, J., Hampton, J. A., Michalski, R., & Theuns, P. (Eds.), *Categories and Concepts: Theoretical Views and Inductive Data Analysis*. Academic Press, London, UK.

Kamp, H. (1975). Two theories about adjectives. In Keenan, E. L. (Ed.), *Formal Semantics of Natural Language*, pp. 123–155. Cambridge University Press, Cambridge, UK.

Kaplan, R. M. (1987). Three seductions of computational psycholinguistics. In Whitelock, P. J., McGee-Wood, M., Somers, H. L., Johnson, R., & Bennett, P. (Eds.), *Linguistic Theory and Computer Applications*. Academic Press, London, UK.

Klein, E., & Sag, I. (1985). Type-driven translation. *Linguistics and Philosophy*, 8, 163–202.

Medin, D., & Ortony, A. (1989). Psychological essentialism. In Vosniadou, S., & Ortony, A. (Eds.), *Similarity and Analogical Reasoning*. Cambridge University Press, Cambridge, UK.

Medin, D., & Shoben, E. (1988). Context and structure in conceptual combination. *Cognitive Psychology*, 20, 158–190.

Miikkulainen, R. (1993). *Subsymbolic Natural Language Processing*. MIT Press, Cambridge, MA.

Murphy, G. L. (1988). Comprehending complex concepts. *Cognitive Science*, 12, 529–562.

Newell, A. (1990). *Unified Theories of Cognition*. Harvard University Press, Cambridge, MA.

Potter, M. C. (1993). Very short term conceptual memory. *Memory & Cognition*, 21, 156–161.

Pustejovsky, J. (1991). The generative lexicon. *Computational Linguistics*, 17(4), 409–441.

Rips, L. (1995). The current status of research on concept combination. *Mind & Language*, 10, 72–104.

Smith, E. E., Osherson, D., Rips, L. J., & Keane, M. (1988). Combining prototypes: A selective modification model. *Cognitive Science*, 12, 485–527.

Trueswell, J., Tanenhaus, M., & Kello, C. (1993). Verb-specific constraints in sentence processing: Separating effects of lexical preference from garden paths. *Journal of Experimental Psychology*, 19, 528–553.

Wisniewski, E. J., & Gentner, D. (1991). On the combinatorial semantics of noun pairs: Minor and major adjustments to meaning. In Simpson, G. B. (Ed.), *Understanding Word and Sentence*. North-Holland Publ. Comp., Amsterdam.

Sociocultural Approaches to Analyzing Cognitive Development in Interdisciplinary Teams

Lori Adams DuRussel and **Sharon J. Derry**
University of Wisconsin-Madison
Educational Sciences Building, Room 664
1025 W. Johnson St.
Madison, WI 53706
durussel@students.wisc.edu, sderry@macc.wisc.edu

Abstract

This paper considers whether a sociocultural theory of cognition can supply a suitable perspective for analyzing the nature of interdisciplinary collaboration within groups in the National Institute for Science Education (NISE). We discuss the metaphors of apprenticeship and voice in conversation to identify relevant elements of analysis in group discourse. The NISE group shows evidence of cognitive apprenticeship and of multiple voicedness, but the theories do not fully explain the impact of interdisciplinary interaction on group cognitive development. Although both the apprenticeship metaphor and the voice metaphor provide useful tools for analysis, it would be useful to have a metaphor that deals more directly with interaction among members of equal status from mature communities of practice.

Introduction

One activity within the National Institute for Science Education (NISE) is the Cognitive Studies of Interdisciplinary Communications project. The goal of this project is to understand factors affecting interdisciplinary collaboration so as to facilitate more productive communication and better designs for team-based organizations and conferences. This issue is of importance not only to the NISE, but to the scientific and business community at large, as many significant problems and products require contributions from specialists with various backgrounds.

The purpose of this paper is to consider whether a sociocultural theory of cognition can supply a suitable perspective for analyzing the nature and productivity of interdisciplinary conversation that occurs within the NISE. According to Wertsch (1991), sociocultural studies provide an account of human mental processes 'that recognizes the essential relationship between these processes and their cultural, historical, and institutional settings" (Wertsch, 1991, p. 6). From a sociocultural perspective, interdisciplinary interaction is viewed as communication across cultural boundaries, and attending to how such boundaries are revealed and bridged in conversation should lead to important insights about team functioning and growth of team knowledge.

Alternatives to adopting a sociocultural viewpoint include (a) avoiding perspective-based bias altogether, (b) adopting an alternative theory, or (c) using an inductive research method that admits many different theoretical perspectives into the analysis. Based on philosophical arguments that all observations are theory-laden (e.g., Kuhn, 1979; Lakatos, 1978; Popper, 1959), we reject the idea that theoretical bias can be avoided. Concerning option b, we accept the likelihood that alternative suitable analytical perspectives may exist; however, consideration of other theories is outside the boundary of this paper, which seeks only to assess the applicability of sociocultural theories. Regarding option c, we are attracted to the idea of an inductive, interdisciplinary methodology such as Interaction Analysis (IA) (Jordan & Henderson, 1995) that does not privilege one particular theoretical perspective. We are employing IA approaches in some of our work, but the availability of multiple perspectives is limited and we cannot not rely on it entirely. In addition, even for interaction analysis, we need a theory to insure systematicity in our own observations.

Sociocultural Theories of Cognition

The perspective from which we will examine data borrows from several sociocultural theories: Lave and Wenger's situated social cognition theory (e.g., Lave, 1991; Lave & Wenger, 1991; Wenger, 1990), Vygotskian developmental psychology (e.g., Vygotsky, 1978), and Bakhtin's semiotic activity theory (as cited in Wertsch, 1991). These viewpoints are highly compatible and even borrow from one another, though each contributes unique concepts that are useful for our analyses. All lead to the insight that team productivity and growth of team discourse will be highly intertwined.

Knowledge Building

If the purpose of an NISE team is to integrate and create knowledge that can be brought to bear on difficult and important issues, then a team's productivity is largely determined by how well it carries out processes that drive knowledge construction. Sociocultural theories assume that knowledge construction is essentially social in nature. Lave's viewpoint is that knowledge 'lives' within communities of practice where it develops and thrives through social discourse. Individual participation in this discourse requires knowledge of language and other conceptual tools of thought that are shared by other members of the community. Shared community knowledge can change and grow when new language and concepts are assimilated or constructed by the discourse.

The insight that conceptual tools (such as language) and physical tools (such as white boards or flip charts) both shape and comprise the evolving community knowledge base is attributed to Vygotsky (1978). However, physical tools have not yet been a significant factor for the group under observation, which to this point has conducted meetings without the aid of physical props.

Cognitive Apprenticeship

Central to Lave's view is the notion that team survival and growth depend upon a continuing process of apprenticing new members. Intellectual work involves cognitive apprenticeship (e.g., Collins, Brown, and Newman, 1991), whereby experienced community members share problem solving and other conversation with less experienced "novices," supporting their acquisition of community tools, especially language. Lave's view also indicates that team survival and growth depend on a continuing process of apprenticing new members. New members participate in team activities peripherally at first but, through gradually increasing participation can eventually become fully participating members of the discourse.

Multiple Voices

In order to build knowledge as a group, team members need to be able to communicate effectively. This activity may be particularly difficult in new interdisciplinary groups, since members represent different professional communities of practice that vary in terms of value systems, professional languages, and cultural histories. From Wenger's perspective (1990), communication across cultures can be initiated by seeking and using boundary concepts--language subsets that are shared across cultures. An excellent example of a cross-disciplinary boundary language is basic statistics. As new boundary concepts are located and developed through interdisciplinary discourse, a common team language begins to emerge and grow.

Communication can also be initiated by finding common "voice." The Bakhtinian (as cited in Wertsch, 1991) notion of voice refers to the personal perspective that is adopted by a speaker. For example, a chemistry professor may speak as a scientist on one occasion, as a teacher on another occasion, and as a parent on yet another. Use of less technical languages, which are more widely understood, may facilitate interdisciplinary communication. Voices can also be combined in discourse. For example, the chemist can talk to a nonscientist by filtering the voice of the chemist through the voice of a layperson. From the perspective of Lave and Wenger, individuals are capable of multiple voices because they belong to multiple communities of discourse. Shared voices can provide common ground for group cohesion and the beginning of technical exchange.

Group Composition

In this study we consider a sample of conversations from early meetings of one NISE team, asking whether the kinds of analyses suggested by a sociocultural approach provide a useful conceptual fit to the data. The group under observation meets every other month for several hours to examine the issue of how to evaluate systemic educational reform (SER) programs funded by the National Science Foundation. While we plan to continue researching this group throughout its development, our current findings are based on audio recordings and field notes collected during the second and third semimonthly team meetings.

The regularly participating members of the team include four male full professors representing the disciplines of political science, astronomy, chemistry, and mathematics education; two female professors of engineering; one female Ph.D.-level anthropologist who holds a nonteaching academic staff position; and a female representative of the National Center for Improving Science Education with a Ph.D.-level background in chemistry and science education. A male professor of mathematics has participated occasionally. Invitations to join this group were issued by the team's leader and manager, a nonteaching senior scientist. His disciplinary background is primarily mathematics and mathematics education, with a specialty in educational assessment. Approximately 35% of the team leader's full-time research position is devoted to work related to this team's mission.

Applying the Apprenticeship Metaphor

Initially this metaphor seemed inappropriate for the SER team, primarily because this team is a newly formed community, making it impossible for senior mentors to induct novices into team membership. In addition, even new members are full participants from the start, so Lave's concept of peripheral participation does not apply. However, the metaphor can be insightful if we view the team's practice as an extension of an established practicing community of educational researchers and practitioners interested in systemic reform. The rhetoric of SER is indeed present in initial explanatory materials given to members of the newly formed team, as well as in the initial charge presented verbally to the team by its leader. This community-specific rhetoric results in some differentiation between relative newcomers and old-timers; for example, the term "systemic reform" itself was mysterious to some and highly familiar to others.

The apprenticeship metaphor also seems appropriate given that interviews and group discussions reveal evidence of novice-level confusion and deliberate self-apprenticeships of some members not versed in the rhetoric of educational reform. For example, one scientist acknowledged feeling like a relative newcomer:

> I feel like a student in the freshman chemistry course. . . . You sense that you don't really have an appreciation for the significance [of principles being presented] and . . . you don't have the

perspective to allow you to ask the questions that really need to be asked.

Another scientist new to the rhetoric of SER admitted some confusion:

> I haven't the foggiest notion of what you're talking about. . . . This systemic reform is repeated over and over again like a mantra, and I don't know what you think is wrong!

Mentorship on the part of more experienced members was evidenced by the fact that team members involved in the SER community explained terms and concepts that were unfamiliar to other members. At times these explanations were in response to direct questions from relative novices (e.g., "What does system alignment mean?"), while at other times they responded to the overall direction of another team member. For instance, when one scientist indicated that effective SER research should involve isolating variables by looking for reforms changing a single part of the system, a colleague replied with the perspective of someone experienced with SER:

> Let me give you one qualification on that: . . . historically, when people have tried to do one thing, quite often because of other things in the system they just haven't been able to do that [one thing] very well.

We observed that the team leader also monitored the process of educating all members in the rhetoric of systemic reform. In an interview, he described how he tried to ensure that everyone understood the concepts being discussed:

> I'm sure not everybody understands "Chapter One," so let's ask that question, free that up. I really appreciated it when [another member] said, "I don't know what summative/formative evaluation is." I knew that that was a trade term, and that he probably didn't understand that, that it needed to be qualified.

As the above data illustrate, there is evidence that during early development of the SER team, a type of cognitive apprenticeship is occurring as team members unfamiliar with systemic reform are introduced to the community of SER practice. Members experienced in reform serve as mentors in the group, and newcomers recognize that in some ways they are being inducted into a new field, in which they need to acquire knowledge as they contribute their own points of view.

Interaction of Multiple Voices

The Bakhtinian perspective focuses not only on the predominant voice of the community of SER but also on voices from other communities. The NISE group discussions show evidence that multiple voices are shaping the conversation, and that people seem to be aware of the

need to create a common voice in the discourse to facilitate group discussion and team building.

As we discuss use of common or discipline-specific voices, we recognize the difficulty in categorizing individual statements as originating from or belonging to a particular voice. Occasionally, participants explicitly distinguished between voices by associating themselves and their statements with particular disciplines, thus helping to identify the speaking voice. For instance, a comment prefaced by the statement "as a physical scientist" could probably be attributed to the voice of the natural scientists.

The most clearly identified voices in the conversation were those of the natural/applied sciences and the social sciences. Although this classification is useful for analyzing the voices that contribute to the group understanding and group products, it is possible that other classifications may also be appropriate.

Discussion Among Different Voices

As stated above, the group conversation at times seemed to be a dialogue between voices from two disciplines, the natural sciences and the social sciences. A subset of the natural scientists repeatedly called for "calibration control" and separation of influences, suggesting that the group follow a process similar to that used in the natural sciences:

> [The group should identify reforms] that are trying different approaches to the same particular problem and then devise measures for the evaluation, . . . trying to separate it from all myriad other influences. That seems like a natural to me; that's what we would do with a population of twenty-four galaxies.

The voice of the social scientists, however, indicated that social systems differ fundamentally from physical systems, so different types of analyses might be required. One social scientist pointed out a distinction between the natural sciences and education as

> that which you want to know [in physical systems] in order to measure doesn't change in the process of being measured . . . but it changes hugely in social systems.

Later, another social scientist compared control groups in school reform to political changes:

> [In certain cases] the scientific approach is fine. . . . [But] if you pass a law like a gun control law, you don't say this half of the people have to deal with it and these don't, and we'll compare the results. . . . That's not the way a lot of things in politics work, and in school systems [too], ... [In those systems] they all want to be a part of the change.

Another team member who was experienced in educational policy agreed with the difficulty of isolating variables in educational systems, saying,

You can list systemwide indicators, . . . but the *causality* links there, [questions such as], 'Is it a curriculum?", 'Is it a new assessment process?" . . . . "Which component of [the system changes] produces these results?" . . . Those are the things that I find to be very, very difficult to measure. And that's where the strategies really have to be, and that's where the science comes in.

The discourse between these two voices is just beginning. It will be interesting to see how the conversation among conflicting voices will change as the group develops.

Influences of Multivoicedness

There is already evidence that group products are being influenced by voices from several disciplines. Some participants--typically natural scientists--requested a rigorous and specific definition of systemic reform. As one scientist stated,

When I'm called upon to make a measurement, I have to know what I'm measuring. . . . I don't need the same thing to measure the polarization of a galaxy that I do to measure the temperature of the planetary atmosphere.

Another scientist agreed, saying that for

all of us physical scientists . . . the general picture . . . is always anchored in very specific things.

A third team member identified these requests for a systematic approach to analysis as being the voice of natural science.

As the physical scientists are saying, we have to sort of define what we mean, start out from a baseline that we all understand.

This voice was officially recognized when a social scientist experienced in SER suggested that one product for the group could be a paper summarizing current reforms. This paper topic reflected the influence of the voice of the natural sciences.

In addition to multiple voices influencing the group products, there is evidence that the voices also may contribute to how individual participants conceptualize systemic reform, supporting Vygotsky's view that social interaction influences individual cognition. At one point, the team leader mentioned the idea of 'sustainability" as being relevant to the evaluation of a reform effort. Later in the meeting, a natural scientist commented, 'I like that sustainability. . . . That is a good point." The issue of sustainability also was mentioned by several people in subsequent interviews. As one scientist explained,

[One thing] which wasn't something I would have ever thought of on my own is this idea that systemic reform ought to be self-sustaining.

These excerpts show the beginning of the knowledge negotiation process. The interaction of voices of different disciplines has started to influence the direction of the group, define concrete group products such as paper topics, and also help shape the views that group members hold.

Evidence of Common Voices

Although differences between voices shape the group discussion, sociocultural theory predicts the development of commonality in group voices. The existence of communities or voices common to the group members was recognized explicitly by the team leader in an introduction to the second meeting:

We also view each of you as . . . taxpayers, . . . parents possibly, teachers also. You're also consumers of the system in that you are using products [students] that have . . . come from other parts of the system.

Team members also seemed to recognize that they share a common community. During interviews, one scientist explicitly recognized a shared practice of teaching faculty, stating that group members contribute not so much their specific disciplinary expertise but also

their experience as teachers and as consumers of students, and also more specifically just familiarity or awareness with general research methods.

The discussion reveals some common voices that are being used or developed by the NISE participants. One sign of community was reflected by points in meetings where conversation using SER rhetoric was interrupted by comments in a more informal language. We believe that these comments represent an informal social language that is common to university faculty and researchers across disciplines. For instance, at one point in a discussion about funding, one team member likened the amount in question to being equivalent to 'two janitors," and a different amount was later represented as 'half a janitor." This diversion of the discussion from domain-specific rhetoric to terms that are understood immediately by everyone in the room indicates the existence of a common overlapping practice and related 'boundary language" that is used to infuse humor into conversation and serves to create a sense of cohesion and community.

In addition to the team implicitly recognizing and using areas of commonality in the discussion, there was some evidence of team members consciously striving to create links across disciplines by identifying certain ideas or approaches as new boundary concepts. For example, one natural scientist (not an astronomer) compared the problem of evaluating SER to an astronomer's task of interpreting data from distant stars.

> It's kind of like our problem in astronomy, isn't it? Because we are studying [a reform] . . . and we take what few things they [reformers] send out, then look at them and try to dissect all of the information that we get from them. And what they are sending isn't very definitive.

Another scientist tried to draw a link between the natural and social sciences by noting that

> [Natural scientists and educators] can't do experiments. You can't tell them what to do in schools, astronomers can't tweak galaxies.

Sociocultural theories would indicate that, as the group coalesces, these links between communities will strengthen. As shown above, conversation data indicate that common voices are developing in three ways: (a) new members gaining expertise in the dominant rhetoric, (b) the group identifying naturally occurring concepts belonging to communities in which all participants share membership (e.g., teachers, parents, taxpayers), and (c) group members drawing explicit links between concepts that originally belonged to different communities. These processes for expanding social and technical vocabularies can be observed in action and seem important to team functioning.

Conclusions

Sociocultural theories of cognition such as those presented by Lave and Wenger (1991) and Wertsch (1991) provide useful insights on how to examine developing cognition in an interdisciplinary team. Team interaction reveals a type of apprenticeship, and different voices are emerging from the discourse.

However, theories of cognitive apprenticeship do not fully explain interaction among members of mature communities of practice. In the NISE group, established members of different disciplines were invited to the group to contribute knowledge, not merely to be assimilated by the systemic reform community. In this respect the team, lacking the peripheral participation of true novices, does not mesh with Lave's theory. Lave's metaphor does not fully explain the dynamics in a learning environment that expects the dominant community to use knowledge provided by other communities. We seek to develop a metaphor that fully describes how experts in different domains can share information and develop knowledge apart from one dominant community of practice.

Application of sociocultural theories of cognition to these first few meetings of an NISE group also raises the following questions about future team development: As the group gains cohesiveness, how does the emerging common voice incorporate ideas from several disciplines? Will the quality of discourse in the NISE group be dependent on new members continually being introduced into the group, as Lave's theory on communities of practice might suggest? If so, how might activities such as conferences or guest speakers help renew the community?

We will explore these questions in more depth as we continue to observe the group's development. The analytical units of voice, communities of practice and discourse, and boundary objects should help us to better understand the how interdisciplinary collaboration works in order to develop methods to potentially improve it.

Acknowledgments

This research was conducted through the National Institute for Science Education, which is a partnership of the University of Wisconsin-Madison and the National Center for Improving Science Education, Washington, DC, with funding from the National Science Foundation (Cooperative Agreement No. RED-9452971). However, the ideas expressed herein are not endorsed by and may not be representative of positions endorsed by the sponsoring agencies.

We are grateful to members of the ESR working group for their cooperation in our research.

References

Collins, A., Brown, J. S., & Newman, S. E. (1989). Cognitive apprenticeship: Teaching the crafts of reading, writing, and mathematics. In L. B. Resnick (Ed.), *Knowing, learning, and instruction: Essays in honor of Robert Glaser* (pp. 453-494). Hillsdale, NJ: Erlbaum.

Jordan, B. & Henderson, A. (1995). Interaction analysis: Foundations and practice. *The Journal of the Learning Sciences, 4*(1), 39-103.

Kuhn, T. S. (1970). *The structure of scientific revolutions*. Chicago: The University of Chicago Press.

Lakatos, I. (1978). *The methodology of scientific research programmes: Philosophical papers, Vol. 1*. New York: Cambridge University Press.

Lave, J. (1991). Situating learning in communities of practice. In L. Resnick, J. Levine, & S. Teasley (Eds.), *Perspectives on socially shared cognition*. Washington, DC: American Psychological Association.

Lave, J. & Wenger, E. (1991). *Situated learning: Legitimate peripheral participation*. New York: Cambridge University Press.

Popper, K. R. (1959). *The logic of scientific discovery*. New York: Basic Books.

Vygotsky, L. S. (1978). *Mind in society: The development of higher psychological processes*. Cambridge, MA: Harvard University Press.

Wenger, E. (1990). *Toward a theory of cultural transparency*. Unpublished doctoral dissertation. University of California, Irvine.

Wertsch, J. V. (1991). *Voices of the mind: A sociocultural approach to mediated action*. Cambridge, MA: Harvard University Press.

Modeling Qualitative Differences in Symmetry Judgments

Ronald W. Ferguson
Institute for the Learning Sciences
Northwestern University
1890 Maple Avenue
Evanston, IL 60201
ferguson@ils.nwu.edu

Alexander Aminoff
Harvard University
Cambridge, MA 02139
aminoff@wjh.harvard.edu

Dedre Gentner
Department of Psychology
Northwestern University
2029 Sheridan Road
Evanston, IL 60208
gentner@ils.nwu.edu

Abstract

Symmetry perception is an important cognitive process across many areas of cognition. This research explores symmetry as a special case of similarity—self-similarity—and proposes that qualitative relationships play a role in the early perception of symmetry. To support this claim, we present evidence from two psychological studies where subjects performed symmetry judgments for randomly constructed polygons. Subjects were faster and/or more accurate at detecting asymmetry for stimuli with *qualitative* asymmetries than for stimuli with equivalent *quantitative* asymmetries. Aspects of this effect are replicated using the MAGI computational model, which detects symmetry using a method of structural alignment. The results of this study suggest that qualitative information influences early perception of symmetry, and provides further support for the MAGI model.

Introduction

Symmetry serves as an organizing principle in several different areas of perception and cognition, including the Gestalt notion of figural goodness (Garner, 1974; Palmer, 1991), the visual reconstruction of 3D shape (McBeath, Schiano, & Tversky, 1994), and the computation of object-centered reference frames (Palmer, 1989). The breadth of these phenomena suggests that symmetry perception is an important and fundamental cognitive process.

Our research makes two distinctive claims about the perception of symmetry. First, we propose that early symmetry detection is a process of self-comparison that can be modeled as an alignment of maximally similar subsets of perceived structural relations in a figure. This assertion is supported by recent evidence suggesting that perceptual similarity can be modeled using the same kinds of structure-mapping processes that are used to model analogy (Falkenhainer, Forbus & Gentner, 1989; Goldstone, Medin & Gentner, 1991; Markman & Gentner, 1993; Medin, Goldstone & Gentner, 1993). With this in mind, we have implemented a computational model of symmetry detection called MAGI (Ferguson, 1994), which uses structure-mapping to detect symmetry in a way that has many of the characteristics of analogy, including robustness over incomplete or inexact descriptions. MAGI also has the ability to detect multiple axes of symmetry and repetition, and to spontaneously make inferences from one half of a figure to another.

The second claim of this research is that early symmetry processes act over representations that include *qualitative relations*. Qualitative relations have been theorized to provide a foundation for our initial partitioning of the physical world (Forbus, 1984). Qualitative spatial relations have been shown to be important in human processing of spatial scenes (Glenberg & McDaniel, 1992; Palmer, 1989, 1991). Qualitative differences are important in visual similarity comparisons (Goldmeier, 1936/1972).

In this paper, we summarize recent work (Aminoff, Ferguson & Gentner, in preparation) indicating that humans utilize qualitative relationships in symmetry judgments. We then describe a replication of these psychological results using the MAGI computer model. Finally, the implications of this proposal are discussed.

Detecting the Effect of Qualitative Differences in Symmetry Judgments

If we assume that symmetry involves a structural alignment of perceived qualitative relations, we can test this hypothesis by observing how the misalignment of qualitative relations affects symmetry judgment. Qualitative differences—mismatched or misaligned relationships between sides of a

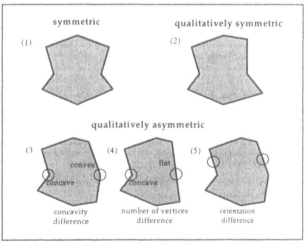

Figure 1: Symmetric, quantitatively asymmetric, and qualitatively asymmetric polygons

figure—should therefore affect symmetry judgment more than would be predicted by of the degree of quantitative difference between the sides of a figure.

Previous research gained insight into how humans process symmetry by examining the conditions under which symmetry is more easily perceived. For example, a large body of research shows that humans detect vertical symmetry more easily (i.e., more quickly or more accurately) than either horizontal or oblique symmetry (Corballis & Roldan, 1975; Palmer & Hemenway, 1978; Rock, 1983). Thus symmetry detection is not orientation-invariant, but depends on a frame of reference.

We are approaching this issue by asking when asymmetry is easy to perceive. Specifically, we hypothesize that figures containing qualitative differences should be easier to judge as asymmetric than figures without such differences, independent of any quantitative metric that we might use to measure asymmetry in a figure.

Although it is difficult to enumerate the full set of perceived qualitative differences, it is straightforward to choose viable candidates, as demonstrated by the polygons in Figure 1. This figure also illustrates a terminological distinction between qualitative and quantitative symmetry. The first polygon is exactly symmetric, with the left and right sides sharing equal dimensions. Thus it is *quantitatively symmetric*. In the second polygon, the left side is structurally similar to the right, but the lengths of corresponding lines differ. Because the sides differ quantitatively but not qualitatively, we call such objects both *quantitatively asymmetric* and *qualitatively symmetric*.

Finally, the bottom three polygons in Figure 1 are *qualitatively asymmetric*, containing three different types of qualitative difference. The first of these polygons contains a *concavity difference*. The polygon's left and right sides align somewhat, but there is a clear difference between the circled vertices—one is concave while the other is convex. The next polygon has a *number-of-vertices difference*, where a concavity on one side is missing on the other. The last of the three polygons has an *orientation difference*, where one line segment leans into the polygon and the other leans away. (Note that while orientation differences often co-occur with concavity differences, they are not equivalent.)

All of these qualitative differences could cause a misalignment or mismatch between opposing sides of the shapes. Just as vertical symmetry is easier to detect than horizontal symmetry, figures containing any of these qualitative differences should be easier to judge asymmetric than figures without them. We now summarize recent experiments that test this assumption.

Psychological Evidence

We tested these predictions in two experiments (Aminoff, Ferguson, & Gentner, in preparation). We presented polygonal stimuli to human subjects, and asked them to quickly judge whether each figure was symmetric. The crucial independent variable was the type of asymmetry—both quantitatively and qualitatively asymmetric objects were included in the stimulus set.

Of course, care must be taken to ensure that if the greater perceived asymmetry is found for qualitative differences that it is not the result of a correlated increase in quantitative difference. In order to control for quantitative differences, the stimuli were selected so that the most important quantitative metric, the sum of squared differences of radii, was equal across conditions. Because some variations in quantitative parameters was unavoidable, we also computed the correlation of our results with 26 other quantitative (and qualitative) measures of asymmetry. Over the two experiments, three types of qualitative difference were used: concavity differences, orientation differences, and number-of-vertices differences. The key measure is subjects' speed and accuracy at detecting asymmetry. (See Aminoff, Ferguson, & Gentner (in preparation) for more details on these experiments.)

Experiment 1

In experiment 1, sixteen subjects were sequentially shown forty 16-sided polygons from a stimulus set of eighty. After a very brief masked presentation (50 ms.) subjects indicated if the polygon was symmetric by pressing one of two computer keys. The stimulus set was evenly divided between symmetric and asymmetric stimuli, with the latter evenly divided between qualitatively and quantitatively asymmetric polygons. Qualitatively asymmetric polygons were further subdivided by qualitative difference type. The forms of qualitative difference used were concavity differences and number-of-vertices differences.

Although experiment 1 showed no significant effect of qualitative difference on reaction time, it did show a significant effect for accuracy (Figure 2). Subjects were much more accurate for polygons that contained either concavity or number-of-vertices differences. This effect was roughly additive: subjects were most accurate at stimuli that had both concavity and number-of-vertices differences. Subjects were also more accurate at correctly classifying

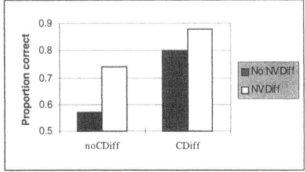

Figure 2: Human accuracy results from experiment 1 (asymmetric figures only).

polygons with number-of-vertices differences than those with concavity differences, and at accurately classifying symmetric polygons than asymmetric polygons.

Experiment 2

Experiment 2 used the same method as Experiment 1 with a slightly easier perceptual task. Simpler 12-sided polygons were displayed at brighter contrast levels in one of two conditions—a fast condition in which the polygon was displayed for 50 ms, and a slow condition in which the stimulus remained on the screen until the subject pressed a key. The number of stimuli was doubled to 160. Of 89 subjects in this study, 54 were assigned to the fast condition and 35 to the slow condition. The qualitative differences used were concavity differences and orientation differences.

Again, subjects were significantly better at stimuli containing qualitative differences. Subjects' accuracy for asymmetric stimuli was uniformly high in the slow condition, but in the fast condition showed a significant effect for the presence of either concavity or orientation differences (Figure 3). Subjects were not significantly more accurate for figures with concavity differences over those with orientation differences, or for symmetric over asymmetric figures.

The reaction time data from experiment 2 showed an effect for figures with concavity differences, but no significant effect for figures with orientations differences. The effect was most significant in the slow condition (Figure 4), but was also marginally significant in the fast condition.

Results

Across two experiments, as predicted by the MAGI model, significant effects were found for qualitative differences in symmetry judgment. For asymmetric objects, subjects were faster and/or more accurate when the asymmetry was manifested in a qualitative difference between the halves of the figure. Subjects responded slower and/or less accurately for asymmetric objects without such qualitative differences. (We have no principled reason to predict whether the early advantage of qualitative asymmetry over quantitative asymmetry should show up in greater accuracy or in faster processing.) Along with supporting the effect of qualitative differences in symmetry detection, these experiments also

suggest that some kinds of differences are more important to symmetry detection than others.

In experiment 1, number-of-vertices differences had a greater effect on accuracy than concavity differences, while experiment 2 in turn showed a greater or equal effect for concavity differences over orientation differences in reaction time measurements. Symmetric figures were classified more accurately and/or more quickly than asymmetric figures in both experiments.

Testing the Results Using the MAGI Model

If MAGI is an accurate model of symmetry detection, it should be able to replicate the results of these experiments, not only in terms of higher accuracy for asymmetrical figures with qualitative differences, but also in terms of which qualitative differences are most important.

The MAGI Model of Symmetry Detection

MAGI (Ferguson, 1994) models symmetry detection as a relational self-similarity mapping that aligns a qualitative representation of a figure with itself. MAGI has been implemented as a computational model using an extension of the Incremental Structure Mapping Engine (I-SME; Falkenhainer, Forbus & Gentner, 1989; Forbus, Ferguson & Gentner, 1994). In essence, MAGI computes a structural alignment between two sides of a figure.

In constructing a mapping, MAGI follows the constraints of I-SME's analogical mapping. Matches must be one-to-one, and arguments of matched expressions must match as well. Only expressions with identical predicates (or non-identical functions that are arguments of other matched expressions) can match. A scoring mechanism encourages relationally deep interconnected systems of matched expressions. In addition, because MAGI maps a description to itself, it blocks expressions from matching to themselves, allowing it only when the self-match is an argument of two different matching parents. MAGI then analyzes the

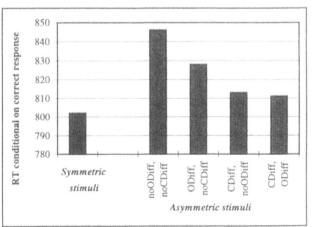

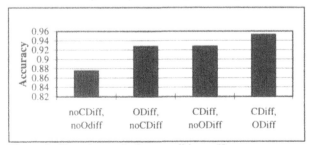

Figure 3: Experiment 2, fast condition. Human accuracy for asymmetric figures

Figure 4: Experiment 2, slow condition. Human reaction time for symmetric and asymmetric stimuli.

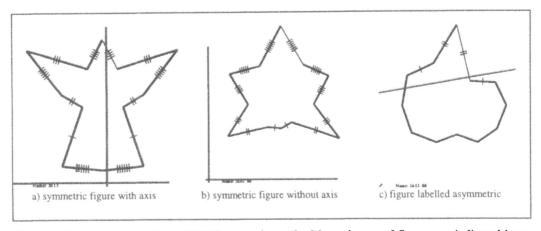

a) symmetric figure with axis   b) symmetric figure without axis   c) figure labelled asymmetric

Figure 5: Representative output MAGI for experiment 2. Mapped parts of figures are indicated by an equal number of hash marks. Gray lines indicate the axis and reference frame suggested by MAGI.

mapping to determine if the mapping merely found a repeated pattern, or found a core of symmetrical matches that makes the whole mapping symmetric.

By mapping qualitative relationships, MAGI can greatly constrain the quantitative calculations and comparisons that it performs. If the mapping is symmetrical, MAGI can compute an axis by using a Hough transform over all the bisecting lines between mapped lines in the figure. Since MAGI's axis-detection only considers a potential axis between symmetrically mapped lines, it is both extremely efficient and robust in the presence of distracters.

To test whether MAGI fits the human results, we ran MAGI on the same stimulus sets used in experiments 1 and 2. The version of MAGI used the same constraints described in Ferguson (1994), but also contained an extension allowing mapping of commutative relationships (such as corner relations and line groups).

Representations Used

Any relational model of perception must make assumptions about types of visual relations that are perceived (Pinker, 1984). The representations given to MAGI are generated using a geometric representation system called GeoRep. GeoRep is not strictly a model of the perception process, but is designed to produce plausible visual representations given simple vector drawings. From the original stimulus data files used in the two experiments, which give each polygon as a set of line segments, GeoRep generates the following polygonal relations: corners, corner concavity or convexity, the presence of perpendicular, obtuse, or acute corners, the presence of protrusions or indentations in the figure (defined, respectively, as adjacent sets of convex or concave corners), and the relative position of protrusions relative to the gravitational reference frame. Relationships are computed only between proximate objects, using a simple proximity metric based on object size and distance. Since some relationships (such as corners or protrusions) can also be the arguments of other geometric relations, the representations tend to be hierarchic.

Figure 6 contains a prototypical subset of an actual representation. Note that although the ABOVE relationships for protrusions in the figure imply a gravitational frame of reference, MAGI does not assume a vertical axis in the figure, although it does encourage vertical over horizontal

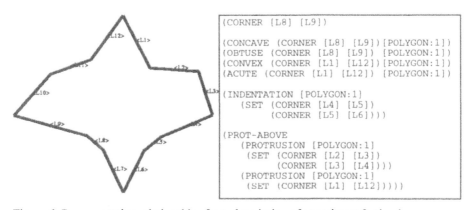

Figure 6: Representative relationships from description of experiment 2 stimulus

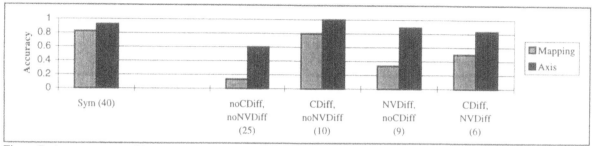

Figure 7: Accuracy rates of MAGI on experiment 1 stimuli, by qualitative difference and criterion type. The number of stimuli in each condition is given in parentheses.

symmetry. However, this is a preference it shares with humans, and so it carries some cognitive validity. However, MAGI can still find horizontal symmetry when a figure has a good intrinsic horizontal axis.

Qualitative differences clearly have an effect upon mapping in representation produced by GeoRep, and so affect the mapping done by MAGI. Number-of-vertices and orientation differences can cause changes in the alignment of the two sides, and affect the perceived protrusions in the figure. Since the representation directly represents concavity, a concavity difference removes an incentive to match corresponding corners from the two sides.

Because MAGI uses a Hough transform to compute an axis, it has a possibly unique characteristic among symmetry-detection algorithms, which is that it can find an object qualitatively symmetric, but then fail to find a straight axis. For this reason, MAGI is equipped with two criteria for judging if a figure is symmetric. A presented stimulus passes the *mapping* criterion for symmetry if more than half the lines in the figure can be mapped symmetrically and if only a small subset of the mapping (less than 20%, in terms of its structural score) is mapped non-symmetrically. A figure can pass the *axis-detection* criterion for symmetry if the corresponding lines actually produce a vertical axis computed using a Hough transform.

Figure 5 shows the output by MAGI for three of the figures from the study. Figure 5(a) maps symmetrically and produces an axis, thus passing both the mapping and axis-detection criteria. In contrast, Figure 5(b) passes only the mapping criteria, because MAGI finds a symmetric alignment of the parts of the figure (as indicated by the hash marks), but cannot find a straight axis based on that

alignment (although it does find a reference orientation, as indicated by the gray lines to the bottom and left in the figure). Figure 5(c) passes neither criterion, and is judged asymmetric by MAGI.

Results

The results for running MAGI on the stimuli sets from experiments 1 and 2 are shown in Figure 7 and Figure 8. For the 80 figures used in experiment 1, the results were suggestive, but not conclusive. MAGI performed extremely well on the symmetric stimuli, classifying over 90% of them correctly. Also, as expected, it performed significantly better on asymmetric figures with qualitative differences (judging them asymmetric in 56% of all instances based on the mapping criterion, and 92% of all instances based on the axis criterion) than on asymmetric figures with only quantitative differences (judging them asymmetric via mapping 13% of the time, and asymmetric via the axis criterion 60% of the time). However, while human subjects clearly were able to use some combinations of qualitative differences better than others, MAGI was unable to replicate that result from experiment 1. We suspect that the lack of strong congruence with the human results might be due to the variance resulting from having a very small number of stimuli. Experiment 2, with a larger number of stimuli, remedies this problem.

On experiment 2's stimuli (Figure 8), MAGI performed in a way that was more congruent with the human data, producing the same ordering among figures' concavity differences and orientation differences that was found in the two psychological experiments. Symmetric figures were classified more accurately than asymmetric figures, and

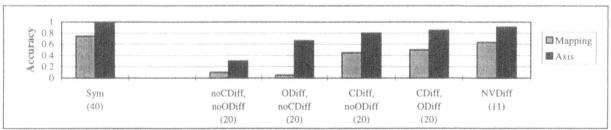

Figure 8: MAGI's accuracy on stimuli sets from experiment 2 for symmetrical figures, and figures with concavity, orientation, and number-of-vertices differences. Number of stimuli in each set is given in parentheses.

concavity differences affected accuracy more than orientation differences did. MAGI was also tested on a subset of experiment 2's stimuli that had marginal number-of-vertices differences, showing that such differences had a more significant effect than either concavity differences or orientation differences, which matches the results from experiment 1.

These results suggest that the human data can be accounted for within the MAGI model. We see these results as a promising lead for future research. For example, the relatively large effect for number-of-vertices differences in MAGI's replication of experiment 2 (Figure 8), leads us to conjecture that figures with number-of-vertices differences may be easier to detect as asymmetric than figures with either concavity or orientation differences.

Conclusion

Qualitative relations are central to human symmetry perception. Just as vertical symmetry is easier to detect, asymmetric figures with qualitative differences are more easily judged asymmetric than figures with quantitative differences. Further, some types of qualitative differences are easier to detect than others.

This preference for qualitative differences in symmetry judgments implies a model that utilizes qualitative perceptual relationships. MAGI currently can model many aspects of this preference, including the distinctions between different kinds of qualitative relations. More research is needed to understand the limitations of the model (which does not yet include perceptual grouping), and to validate GeoRep's assumptions about perceptual representation. MAGI's ability to run on moderately complex line drawings identical to those given human subjects suggest that it is not only a viable psychological model, but also a useful tool for conducting further research into symmetry's fundamental role in cognition.

Acknowledgments

We would like to thank Doug Medin, Ken Forbus, and the analogy and similarity group at Northwestern for many contributions to this research. This research was supported by the Office of Naval Research and a Northwestern University Fellowship to the second author.

References

Aminoff, A., Ferguson, R.W., & Gentner, D. (in preparation). Early detection of qualitative symmetry. Manuscript being prepared for submission.

Corballis, M.C., & Roldan, C.E. (1975). Detection of symmetry as a function of angular orientation. *Journal of Experimental Psychology: Human Perception and Performance, 1*, 221-230.

Falkenhainer, B., Forbus, K.D., & Gentner, D. (1989). The Structure-Mapping Engine: Algorithms and examples. *Artificial Intelligence, 41*(1), 1-63.

Ferguson, R.W. (1994). MAGI: Analogical encoding using symmetry and regularity. In *Proceedings of the Cognitive Science Society*. Atlanta, GA.

Forbus, K.D. (1984). Qualitative Process Theory. *Artificial Intelligence, 24*, 85-168.

Forbus, K.D., Ferguson, R.W., & Gentner, D. (1994). Incremental Structure Mapping. In *Proceedings of the Cognitive Science Society*. Atlanta, GA.

Garner, W.R. (1974). *The processing of information and structure*. Potomac, MD: Erlbaum.

Glenberg, A.M., & McDaniel, M.A. (1992). Mental models, pictures and text: Integration of spatial and verbal information. *Memory and Cognition, 20*(5), 458-460.

Goldmeier, E. (1936/1972). Similarity in visually perceived forms. *Psychological Issues, 8*(1), 14-133.

Goldstone, R.L., Medin, D.L., & Gentner, D. (1991). Relational similarity and the nonindependence of features in similarity judgments. *Cognitive Psychology, 23*, 222-264.

McBeath, M., Schiano, D., & Tversky, B. (1994). Three-dimensional bilateral symmetry assumed in judgments of figural identity and orientation. Paper presented at *The 35th Annual Meeting of the Psychonomic Society*, St. Louis, MO, Nov. 11-13.

Markman, A.B., & Gentner, D. (1993). Structural alignment during similarity comparisons. *Cognitive Psychology, 23*, 431-467.

Medin, D.L., Goldstone, R.L., & Gentner, D. (1993). Respects for similarity. *Psychological Review, 100*(2), 254-278.

Palmer, S.E. (1989). Reference frames in the perception of shape and orientation. In B. E. Shepp & S. Ballesteros (Eds.), *Object perception: Structure and process* (pp. 121-163). Hillsdale: Lawrence Erlbaum Associates.

Palmer, S.E. (1991). Goodness, gestalt, groups, and Garner: local symmetry subgroups as a theory of figural goodness. In Lockhead & Pomerantz (Eds), *The Perception of Structure*.

Palmer, S.E., & Hemenway, K. (1978). Orientation and symmetry: Effects of multiple, rotational, and near symmetries. *Journal of Experimental Psychology: Human Perception and Performance, 4*, 691-702.

Pinker, S. (1984). Visual cognition: An introduction. In Pinker (Ed), *Visual Cognition*. Cambridge, MA: The MIT Press.

Rock, I. (1990). *The Logic of Perception*. Cambridge, MA: The MIT Press.

Unification of Language Understanding, Device Comprehension and Knowledge Acquisition

Ashok Goel, Kavi Mahesh, Justin Peterson, and Kurt Eiselt
College of Computing
Georgia Institute of Technology
Atlanta, GA 30332-0280 USA
Contact: goel@cc.gatech.edu, 404-894-4994

Abstract

Cognitive agents often acquire knowledge of how devices work by reading a book. We describe a computational theory of understanding a natural language description of a device, comprehending how the device works, and acquiring a device model. The theory posits a complex interplay between language, memory, comprehension, problem-solving and learning faculties. Long-term memory contains cases of previously encountered devices and associated structure-behavior-function (SBF) models that explain how the known device works. Language processing is both bottom-up and top-down. Bottom-up processing is done through spreading-activation networks, where the semantics of the nodes and links in the network arises from the SBF ontology. The comprehension process constructs a SBF model for the new device by adapting the known device models - we call this process adaptive modeling. This multi-faculty computational theory is instantiated in an operational computer system called KA that (i) reads and understands English language descriptions of devices from David Macaulay's popular science book *The Way Things Work*, (ii) comprehends how the described device works, and (iii) acquires a SBF model for the device.

1. Motivations and Background

Cognitive agents often acquire knowledge of complex phenomena by reading a book. For example, a naive cognitive agent may acquire knowledge of how air-conditioners work by reading a popular science book such as *The Way Things Work* by David Macaulay [1988]. In general, understanding the natural language description of a device, comprehending how the device works, and acquiring a device model, involves a complex interplay between language, comprehension, memory, problem solving and learning processes. In addition, these processes use many different kinds of knowledge including semantic knowledge of the domain, episodic knowledge from past experiences in the domain, and the information provided in the text.

But most computational models of text interpretation deal with language understanding in vacuum, in more or less complete isolation from other processes. Typically, they either propose a largely bottom-up process in which the interpretation is constructed from the text alone, or a largely top-down process in which a precompiled knowledge structure helps to generate expectations and provides a template for filling in specific details given in the text. In interpreting real texts, however, neither the text always provides sufficient information to enable the construction of a satisfactory interpretation nor does the reader always have a precompiled knowledge

structure that matches the text. Our theory of language understanding for device comprehension and knowledge acquisition not only combines bottom-up and top-down strategies for language processing, but it also integrates the language process with memory, comprehension, problem-solving and learning processes.

In contrast to multi-strategy or multi-task theories, we call our theory *multi-faculty* because it unifies multiple cognitive faculties, not just multiple tasks or strategies within a specific cognitive faculty such as language. The multi-faculty theory is embodied in an operational, but still evolving, computer program called KA.

In [Pittges *et. al.* 1993], we described an early version of the KA system that unified language, memory and comprehension processes in the service of understanding a new design problem stated in English. We also showed how past problem-solving experiences retrieved from long-term memory enable the understanding of new problems. In [Peterson *et. al.* 1994], we described a new version of the KA system that not only integrated language, memory and comprehension processes but also unified them with problem solving . We also showed how problem solving helps to evaluate the output of the language, memory and comprehension processes. The above work grew out of our earlier theory of *adaptive design* in which new design problems are solved and new designs are constructed by adapting past design cases [Goel 1991a, 1991b].

In this article, we describe new work on the KA project that differs from and adds to earlier work in two aspects. Firstly, the input to KA now is not a description of a design problem, but an English language description of a device from the book "The Way Things Work." Secondly, the new version of KA not only unifies language, memory, comprehension, and problem-solving processes but also integrates learning with them. This new work grows out of an evolving theory of *adaptive modeling* in which comprehension of the workings of a system is represented and organized in the form of a structure-behavior-function (SBF) model, and SBF model of a new device is constructed by adapting old models of familiar devices [Goel 1991b, 1996].

Since we already have described the process of language understanding in KA in earlier papers, we will not repeat it here; [Peterson, Mahesh and Goel 1994] provides a detailed account. Instead, we (i) describe our framing of the problem of device comprehension as an abduction task, (ii) present a high-level account of the knowledge and strategies KA uses for addressing this task, and (iii) discuss how KA acquires a

SBF model of new devices from English language description.

2. Case Study: Comprehending the Fire Extinguisher

Let us consider the task of comprehending how a fire extinguisher works from the following description that appears on page 147 of *The Way Things Work*:

> An extinguisher puts out a fire by excluding oxygen so that combustion (see p.154) can no longer continue. The extinguisher must smother the whole fire as quickly as possible, and therefore produces a powerful spray of water, foam, or powder. Some extinguishers produce a jet of carbon dioxide, a heavy gas that prevents burning. A fire extinguisher works in much the same way as a spray can. The extinguishing substance, such as water, is put under high pressure inside the extinguisher, and the pressure forces the substance out of the nozzle.

This text is accompanied with a cutaway diagram of a fire extinguisher revealing its structure, and some brief descriptions of the individual components such as the gas cartridge and the release valve. Figure 1 illustrates this diagram. Note that the annotations on the diagram are more specific to the structure of the extinguisher shown in the diagram than to any part of the text itself. The text describes the behavior of the fire extinguisher, making explicit reference to the descriptions of combustion and spray cans. The reference to the concept of combustion is a forward reference; presumably the reader has not yet read it but may do so for further elaboration and specification. But the spray can is described on the previous page of the book (p. 146), just opposite to the description of the fire extinguisher.

Framing the Comprehension Problem as an Abduction Task

The input to the task of comprehending how a fire extinguisher works in KA is constituted of three elements: the above text, the annotations on the accompanying diagram, and a symbolic representation of the diagram. The symbolic representation of the diagram constitutes a structural model which specifies only the structural elements and the topology of their connections in the fire extinguisher.

But what characterizes acceptable output of the task? We view the task of comprehending how a device works from a natural language description of the device as an instance of the very general abduction task. The abduction task takes a given set of data as input and gives a "best" explanation for the data as output [Josephson and Josephson 1994]. But now the question becomes what characterizes a best explanation?

The explanation of a device must not only specify the structural elements and the functions of the device, but it must also specify how the structure results in the functions. That is, it must specify how the device structure gives rise to the causal processes that result in the device functions. Thus we characterize a device explanation as a functional and causal model of the internal workings of the device. A best explanation of a device must satisfy three properties. First, the explanation must account for as much of the input as possible - ideally, it would cover the whole input. Second, the explanation must be consistent with the input. That is,

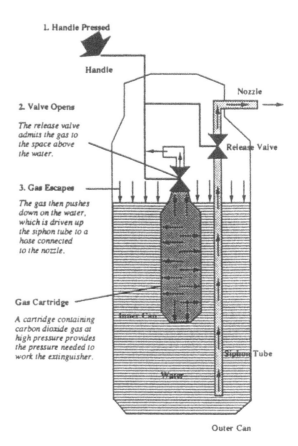

Figure 1: The Fire Extinguisher.

no element of the explanation can be inconsistent with any element in the input. Third, the explanation must be internally consistent. That is, no two elements of the explanation can be mutually inconsistent. In sum, in KA an acceptable output of the task of comprehending how a device works from a natural language description of the device is a functional and causal model of the working of the device that accounts for as much of the description as possible, is consistent with the entire description, and also is internally consistent.

3. KA at Work

Figure 2 illustrates the general functional architecture of KA. Here we only describe the processes linked by bold-faced arrows in the figure.

The long-term memory contains episodic knowledge of previously encountered devices. Each device case has an associated case-specific structure-behavior-function (SBF) model that explains how the device works [Goel 1991a, 1991b]. The SBF model of a device explicitly represents the structural elements and their configuration, the functions, and the internal behaviors of the device. Each behavior specifies a causal process in the device; the causal processes specify how the device structure results in its functions. In particular, they specify how the device functions are composed of the functions of the structural elements of the device. The SBF model for each device case is expressed in a common ontol-

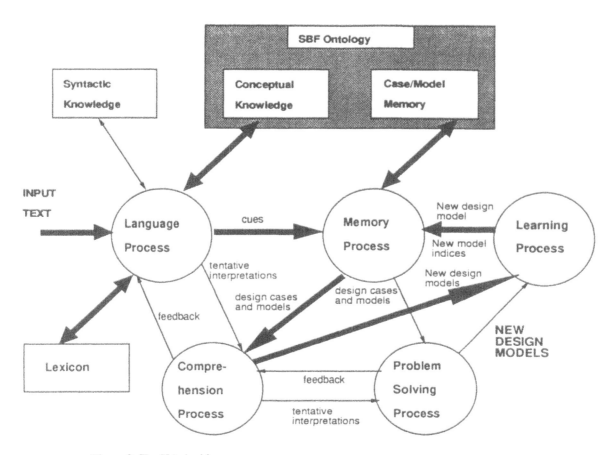

Figure 2: The KA Architecture.

ogy that arises out of earlier work on device representations [Bylander and Chandrasekaran 1985; Sembugamoorthy and Chandrasekaran 1986; Chandrasekaran, Goel and Iwasaki 1993]. The SBF ontology defines the domain concepts and the relations between them, and constitutes the conceptual knowledge of the KA system.

The language process uses lexical and conceptual knowledge to generate cues for the memory process as well as preliminary interpretations for the comprehension process. Conceptual knowledge refers to knowledge of the domain concepts and the relations between them as characterized by the SBF ontology. The language process contains a large semantic network that takes the output of the parser as input and produces conceptual interpretations. The nodes and the links in the network are based on the SBF ontology of domain concepts and the relations between them. The spreading-activation mechanism in the network uses an early-commitment processing strategy with robust error-recovery to resolve word-sense ambiguities [Eiselt, 1987].

The mechanism resolves word-sense ambiguities by considering processing choices in parallel, selecting the alternative that is consistent with the current context, and deactivating but retaining the unchosen alternatives for as long as space and time resources permit. If some later context proves the initial decision to be incorrect, retained alternatives are reactivated without reaccessing the lexicon or reprocessing the text. [Peterson, Mahesh and Goel 1994] provides details of language processing in KA.

The memory process uses cues generated by language process as probes into the long-term memory. It accesses device cases and associated case-specific SBF device models and puts them into a working memory for use by the comprehension and problem-solving processes. The memory process also stores newly learned models in the long-term memory. The device cases are indexed by the functions of the stored devices; the SBF models are indexed by the cases. This indexing scheme is borrowed from our earlier work on adaptive design [Goel 1991a, 1991b].

The comprehension process constructs a SBF model for the new device by adapting the SBF device models accessed by the memory process. It uses generic (abstract, skeletal) modification plans for the task of adapting SBF models of known devices to construct a model of the new device. The selection of relevant modification plans is based on the functional and structural differences between the SBF model of the known device and the description of the new device.

542

KA's method constructing the new SBF model is identical to that of adaptive modeling [Goel 1991b, 1996].

The learning process uses the SBF model of the new device to learn appropriate indices for storing the model in the long-term memory. The new indices depend both on the contents and organization of the memory and the functional and causal explanation provided by the SBF model. Again, KA's method of index learning is identical to that of adaptive modeling [Bhatta and Goel 1995]. (The problem-solving process in Figure 2 plays no direct role in this process of acquiring a SBF model of a new device from an English language description.)

The Case Study

Let us consider the comprehension process in the case study of the fire extinguisher. At this stage of processing, KA's working memory contains three elements: the interpretations of the sentences in the text generated by the language process, the SBF model of the spray can retrieved from the long-term memory, and the symbolically-represented structural model of the fire extinguisher given as part of the input to the system. The current task is to adapt the SBF model of the spray can to construct a model of the fire extinguisher.

The comprehension process notes the sentence interpretations in the working memory and the differences between these interpretations and the SBF model of the spray can. For example, it notes that the fire extinguisher and the spray can contain different substances under pressure. In addition, the comprehension process notes the structural differences between structural models of the fire extinguisher and the spray can. For example, it notes that the two contain different kinds of nozzles. It uses these differences to select generic model-modification plans that help to reduce specific differences and are indexed by the differences they can help to reduce. Examples of model-modification plans include the substance-substitution plan and the component-replacement plan. Given a specific difference between a component in the spray can and a component in the fire extinguisher, instantiating the latter plan in the context of the SBF model of spray can, for example, results in replacing each occurrence of the spray-can component in the SBF model by the corresponding component in the fire extinguisher. The application of this plan also results in the propagation of the causal effects of the new component. The structural models help to establish correspondences between the components in the spray can and the fire extinguisher. The SBF model of the spray can helps to focus the process of plan instantiation and application. The invocation and application of selected model-modification plans, one for each difference between the fire extinguisher and the spray can, results in the generation of a SBF model for the fire extinguisher. This preliminary SBF model provides a functional and causal explanation of the working of the fire extinguisher.

Next, KA evaluates the preliminary model of the fire extinguisher for both internal and external consistency. In reference to internal consistency, the comprehension process makes sure that no new element introduced into the SBF model is inconsistent with any other element. This is done by systematically tracing through the causal behaviors of the new SBF model. If an inconsistent element is detected, then the process retracts the corresponding modification from the SBF model. In reference to external consistency, the comprehension process makes sure that no element in the SBF model is inconsistent with the output of the language process. This is done by cross-checking of the SBF model and the sentence interpretations generated by the language process. Again, if an inconsistent element is detected, then the comprehension process retracts it from the SBF model. The final SBF model is KA's best explanation of the working of the fire extinguisher.

4. Relations

Our work on KA builds on many lines of research in cognitive science including natural language understanding, device comprehension, knowledge acquisition, mental models and model-based reasoning, case-based reasoning and learning, and abductive explanations. Due to limitations of space, however, here we only outline its relationship to earlier work that lies at the intersection of language understanding, device comprehension, and acquisition of device models.

Lebowitz's [1983] RESEARCHER program read natural-language texts in the form of patent abstracts, specifically disk drive patents, and updated its long-term memory with generalizations made from these texts. Its knowledge representation scheme was oriented toward device objects and their structural relationships, which was a departure from most natural language understanding systems of that time which had typically focused on intentional actors and events. The output of the processing was a generalized representation in the form of a structural model of the disk drive which specified its components and the topological relationships among them. The system stored this structural model in its long-term memory and later used this knowledge to aid in the top-down understanding of additional patent texts. However, RESEARCHER's emphasis on components and structural relationships left it unable to build functional and causal models of the mechanisms described. In other words, the system effectively knew how a disk drive was constructed, but it did not know how it worked. In sharp contrast, KA takes a structural model of the new device as part of its input.

Dyer, Hodges, and Flowers [1987] describe EDCA, a conceptual analyzer which serves as a natural language front-end for EDISON, a naive design problem solver. EDCA uses knowledge of the function of physical devices to produce an episodic description of a device's behavior as described by an input text. This episodic description can then be used to generate a new device model to be integrated into long-term memory. The result is a much more comprehensive understanding of the device's functionality than was possible with RESEARCHER, but EDCA's analysis of the device description is not fully integrated with the processes for generating new device models and incorporating them into memory. EDCA, in other words, is but a front end to EDISON.

As Selfridge [1989] notes, separating the process of analyzing the language input from constructing and incorporating the new model is misguided --- the process of understanding a device description *is* the process of constructing a functional and causal model of that device. This is the approach that we have followed in our work on KA. We believe that this approach enables KA to correct the shortcomings of both

RESEARCHER and EDCA.

5. Discussion

KA is a computational theory of a complex cognitive phenomenon. From the viewpoint of cognitive science, one of the major advantages of building complex and elaborate, yet detailed and precise, computational theories such as KA is the identification of interesting interactions among the different processes. At the start of the KA project, we enumerated a set of ten high-level hypotheses about these interactions [Goel and Eiselt 1991]: (i) understanding natural language descriptions of physical devices enables acquisition of device models, (ii) situating language processing in problem solving identifies the meaning of the ''meaning'' of a device description, (iii) past cases and case-specific models, that originally provided the knowledge structures for addressing a class of design problems, also provide the knowledge structures for language processing, (iv) the SBF language for representing device models, originally developed to address design problems, provides the conceptual knowledge needed for text interpretation, (v) the model-based scheme for indexing the stored cases and case-specific models in long-term memory, again originally developed to address design problems, is appropriate for supporting language processing, (vi) the language process generates adequate cues for probing the long-term memory, (vii) the memory process retrieves relevant cases and associated models from the long-term memory into the working memory, (viii) the retrieved case-specific models act as expectation generators, (ix) the model-based expectations guide the language process, and (x) the language process generates adequate cues for guiding the comprehension process in adapting the retrieved models to construct a model for the new device.

Now at the end of this project, we can confidently assert that the KA theory helps to greatly refine these hypotheses, to make them more precise and explicit. We conclude this article with a brief discussion of how the KA theory has helped to refine the last of the ten hypotheses above because this initially surprised us. We found that language processing provides only limited guidance to the comprehension process in adapting the SBF model of a known device (e.g., the spray can) to construct a model of the new device (e.g., the fire extinguisher). The products of the language process do indicate some of the many differences between the two devices. But most of the important differences come from the structural models of the two devices. Also, the text does enable limited verification of the modified model to insure that the new model is consistent with the text. But we were initially surprised to find that language processing does not clearly indicate the precise content and form of the new device model. There are two apparent explanations for this. First, the device descriptions in Macaulay's *The Way Things Work* are coarse-grained while our SBF models, which need to support multiple reasoning processes, are fine-grained. This might be resulting in a mismatch between the text and the model so that text can provide only limited help in adapting the model. Second, the diagram that accompanies the textual description of a device is given to KA in the form of a symbolically represented structural model of the device. This might be resulting in some loss of information. Perhaps more importantly, this may imply that the visual process, and not the language process, might be especially important for model adaptation and construction.

Acknowledgements

Kavi Mahesh now is at the New Mexico State University and Justin Peterson is with CitiBank. This work was done when all four authors were at Georgia Tech, where it was supported by Northern Telecom (research gift), the National Science Foundation (research grant IRI-92-10925), and the Office of Naval Research (research contract N00014-92-J-1234). Jeff Pittges contributed to the programming of an earlier version of the KA system described here.

References

[Bhatta and Goel 1995] S. Bhatta and A. Goel. Model-Based Indexing and Index Learning in Analogical Design. In *Proc. 1995 Seventeenth Annual Conference of the Cognitive Science Society*, Pittsburgh, July 22-25, 1995, NJ, Hillsdale: Erlbaum.

[Bylander and Chandrasekaran 1985] T. Bylander and B. Chandrasekaran. Understanding Behavior Using Consolidation. *Proc. Ninth International Joint Conference on Artificial Intelligence*, pp. 450-454, 1985, Los Altos, CA: Morgan Kauffman.

[Chandrasekaran, Goel and Iwasaki 1993] B. Chandrasekaran, A. Goel, and Y. Iwasaki. Functional Representation as a Basis for Design Rationale. *IEEE Computer*, 26(1):48-56, January 1993.

[Dyer, Hodges and Flowers 1987] M. Dyer, J. Hodges and M. Flowers. Computer Comprehension of Mechanical Device Descriptions. Technical Report UCLA-AI-87-7, University of California, Los Angeles: Artificial Intelligence Laboratory.

[Eiselt 1987] K. Eiselt. Recovering from Erroneous Inferences. In *Proc. Sixth National Conference on Artificial Intelligence*, pages 540-544, Los Altos, CA: Morgan Kauffman.

[Goel 1991a] A. Goel. A Model-Based Approach to Case Adaptation. In *Proc. Thirteenth Annual Conference of the Cognitive Science Society*, Chicago, August 1991, pp. 143-148, Hillsdale, NJ: Lawrence Erlbaum.

[Goel 1991b] A. Goel. Model Revision: A Theory of Incremental Model Learning. In *Proc. Eighth International Conference on Machine Learning*, Chicago, June 1991, pp. 605-609, Los Altos, CA: Morgan Kaufmann.

[Goel 1996] A. Goel. Adaptive Modeling. To appear in *Proc. Tenth International Qualitative Reasoning Workshop*, May 1996, Menlo Park, CA: AAAI Press.

[Goel and Eiselt 1991] A. Goel and K. Eiselt. Mental Models, Natural Language, and Knowledge Acquisition. *ACM SIGART*, Special Issue on Integrated Cognitive Architectures, 2(4): 75:78, August 1991.

[Josephson and Josephson 1994] J. Josephson and S. Josephson (editors). *Abductive Inference: Computation, Technology and Philosophy*. New York: Cambridge University Press.

[Lebowitz 1983] M. Lebowitz. RESEARCHER: An Overview. In *Proc. National Conference on Artificial Intelligence*, pages 232-235, Los Altos: Morgan Kauffman.

[Macaulay 1988] D. Macaulay, *The Way Things Work*, Boston: Houghton Mifflin Company.

[Pittges *et. al.*, 1993] J. Pittges, K. Eiselt, A. Goel, A. Gomez, K. Mahesh, and J. Peterson. KA: Integrating Natural Language Processing and Problem Solving. In *Proc. Fifteenth Annual Conference of the Cognitive Science Society*, Boulder, Colorado, July 1993, pp. 818-823, Hillsdale, NJ: Lawrence Erlbaum.

[Peterson *et. al.* 1994] J. Peterson, K. Mahesh, A. Goel, and K. Eiselt. KA: Situating Natural Language Processing in Design Problem Solving. In *Proc. Sixteenth Annual Conference of the Cognitive Science Society*, August 1994, Atlanta, Georgia, pp. 711-716, Hillsdale, NJ: Lawrence Erlbaum.

[Peterson, Mahesh and Goel 1994] J. Peterson, K. Mahesh and A. Goel. Situating Natural Language Understanding in Experience-Based Design. *International Journal of Human-Computer Studies*, 41: 881-913, 1994.

[Selfridge 1989] M. Selfridge. Toward a natural language-based causal model acquisition system. In *Causal AI Models: Steps Toward Applications*, Werner Horn (editor), pages 107-128, Hemisphere Publishing Corporation.

[Sembugamoorthy and Chandrasekaran 1986] V. Sembugamoorthy and B. Chandrasekaran. Functional Representation of Devices and Compilation of Diagnostic Problem Solving Systems. In *Experience, Memory and Reasoning*, Kolodner and and Riesbeck (editors), Hillsdale, New Jersey: Lawrence Erlbaum Associates, 1986.

Cognitive Modeling of Action Selection Learning

Diana F. Gordon
Naval Research Laboratory, Code 5510
4555 Overlook Avenue, S.W.
Washington, D.C. 20375
gordon@aic.nrl.navy.mil

Devika Subramanian
Department of Computer Science
Rice University
Houston, TX 77005
devika@cs.rice.edu

Abstract

Our goal is to develop a hybrid cognitive model of how humans acquire skills on complex cognitive tasks. We are pursuing this goal by designing hybrid computational architectures for the NRL Navigation task, which requires competent sensorimotor coordination. In this paper, we describe results of directly fitting human execution data on this task. We next present and then empirically compare two methods for modeling control knowledge acquisition (reinforcement learning and a novel variant of action models) with human learning on the task. The paper concludes with an experimental demonstration of the impact of background knowledge on system performance. Our results indicate that the performance of our action models approach more closely approximates the rate of human learning on this task than does reinforcement learning.

Introduction

Our goal is to develop a hybrid cognitive model of how humans acquire skills by explicit instruction and repeated practice on complex cognitive tasks. We are pursuing this goal by designing hybrid computational architectures for the NRL Navigation task, which requires sensorimotor coordination skill. In this paper, we develop a novel method based on parametric action models for actively learning visual-motor coordination. Although similar to previous work on action models, our method is novel because it capitalizes on available background knowledge regarding sensor relevance. We have confirmed the existence and use of such knowledge with extensive verbal protocol data collected from human subjects. In our action models approach, the agent actively interacts with its environment by gathering *execution traces* (time-indexed streams of visual inputs and motor outputs) and by learning a compact representation of an effective policy for action choice guided by the action model.

This paper begins by describing the NRL Navigation task, as well as the types of data collected from human subjects performing the task. We next present the results of fitting the data directly. Then, two learning methods are described: our model-based method and a benchmark reinforcement learning algorithm that does not have an explicit model. Prior results reported in the literature of empirical comparisons of action models versus reinforcement learning are mixed (Lin, 1992; Mahadevan, 1992); they do not clearly indicate that one

method is superior. Here we compare these two methods empirically on the Navigation task using a large collection of execution traces. Our primary goal in this comparison is to determine which performs more like human learning on this task. Both methods include sensor relevance knowledge from the verbal protocols. The results of this empirical comparison indicates that our action models method more closely approximates the time-scales and trends in human learning behavior on this task.

The NRL Navigation and Mine Avoidance Domain

The NRL navigation and mine avoidance domain, developed by Alan Schultz at the Naval Research Laboratory and hereafter abbreviated the "Navigation task," is a simulation that can be run either by humans through a graphical interface, or by an automated agent. The task involves learning to navigate through obstacles in a two-dimensional world. A single agent controls an autonomous underwater vehicle (AUV) that has to avoid mines and rendezvous with a stationary target before exhausting its fuel. The mines may be stationary, drifting, or seeking. Time is divided into episodes. An episode begins with the agent on one side of the mine field, the target placed randomly on the other side of the mine field, and random mine locations within a bounded region. An episode ends with one of three possible outcomes: the agent reaches the goal (success), hits a mine (failure), or exhausts its fuel (failure). Reinforcement, in the form of a binary reward dependent on the outcome, is received at the end of each episode. An episode is further subdivided into decision cycles corresponding to actions (decisions) taken by the agent.

The agent has a limited capacity to observe the world it is in; in particular, it obtains information about its proximal environs through a set of seven consecutive sonar segments that give it a 90 degree forward field of view for a short distance. Obstacles in the field of view cause a reduction in sonar segment length; one mine may appear in multiple segments. The agent also has a range sensor that provides the current distance to the target, a bearing sensor that indicates the direction in which the target lies, and a time sensor that measures the remaining fuel. A human subject performing this task sees visual gauges corresponding to each of these sensors. The turn and speed actions are controlled by joystick motions. The turn and speed chosen on the *previous* decision cycle are additionally available to the agent. Given its delayed reward structure and the fact that the world is presented to the agent via sensors that are inadequate to guarantee correct identification of the current state, the Navigation world is a partially observable Markov decision process (POMDP).

Data from Human Subjects

In the experiments with humans, seven subjects were used, and each ran for two or three 45-minute sessions with the simulations. We instrumented[1] the simulation to gather execution traces for subsequent analysis (Gordon *et al.*, 1994). We also obtained verbal protocols by recording subject utterances during play and by collecting answers to questions posed at the end of the individual sessions.

Fitting the Human Data

Our first task was to directly fit the execution trace data from a human subject who had become an expert at the task. In other words, our goal was to learn a stimulus-response controller that represents the expert policy used by the subject. This control policy can be expressed as the function F, where:

$$F : \text{sensors} \rightarrow \text{actions}$$

The task was configured with a small (5%) amount of sensor noise and 25 stationary mines. We used 312 time-indexed execution trace snapshots collected from an expert subject. Each snapshot had the sensor values plus the corresponding action taken by the subject under these conditions. Four supervised inductive learning paradigms induced controllers from this data: CART (Breiman *et al.*, 1984), C4.5 (Quinlan, 1986), MDL (Rissanen, 1983), and backpropagation in neural networks (Rumelhart & McClelland, 1986). For all of these methods the 12 inputs were the sensor values plus the value of the last turn and last speed, and the output was an action chosen by our subject. One decision tree or neural net was constructed for predicting the subject's next turn. A comparison of the accuracies of the four methods on this prediction task is shown in Table 1. The neural network function fitter had the smallest mean-squared error. We experimented with a wide range of parameters for the neural networks and report the results with the best settings (sweeps = 10^6, 9 hidden units, learning rate $\alpha = 0.1$). Although the mean-squared error of fit for the symbolic learning methods was higher, the structures produced by them (especially C4.5) revealed interesting aspects of the control strategy used by the subject

[1]Note that although human subjects use a joystick for actions, we do not model the joystick but instead model actions at the level of discrete turns and speeds (e.g., turn 32 degrees to the left at speed 20). Human joystick motions are ultimately translated to these turn and speed values before being passed to the simulated task. Likewise, the learning agents we construct do not "see" gauges but instead get the numeric sensor values directly from the simulation (e.g., range is 500).

Method	Accuracy	MSE	Rep. Complexity
CART	85.3	0.25	5 leaves in tree
C4.5	87.8	0.22	10 leaves in tree
MDL	82.05	0.27	17 leaves in tree
NN	92.0	0.11	9 hidden units

Table 1: Results of the construction of stimulus-response controllers from execution trace data collected from human subjects.

that were remarkably consistent with the subject's verbal protocol data. For instance, it demonstrated that the subjects did not give equal importance to all the sonar information. In addition, the last turn action played a crucial role in determining current turn. The insights about the differential relevance of various pieces of information, which was obtained by examining these decision trees inspired us to continue working with C4.5 for modeling action choice (see below).

Methods for Modeling Action Selection Learning

After having fit the data from a human expert at the task, our next goal is to build a model that most closely duplicates the human subject data in *learning* performance, i.e., in transitioning from a novice to an expert. With no sensor noise and only 25 mines, all of our subjects became experts at this task after only a few episodes. Modeling such an extremely rapid learning rate presents a challenge. In developing our learning methods, we have drawn from both the machine learning and cognitive science literature. By far the most widely used machine learning method for tasks like ours is reinforcement learning. Reinforcement learning is mathematically sufficient for learning policies for our task, yet has no explicit world model. More common in the cognitive science literature are action models, e.g., (Arbib, 1972), which require building explicit representations of the dynamics of the world to choose actions.

Reinforcement learning

Reinforcement learning has been studied extensively in the psychological literature, e.g., (Skinner, 1984), and has recently become very popular in the machine learning literature, e.g., (Sutton, 1988; Lin, 1992; Gordon & Subramanian, 1993). Rather than using only the difference between the prediction and the true reward for the error, as in traditional supervised learning, (temporal difference) reinforcement learning methods use the difference between successive predictions for errors to improve the learning. Reinforcement learning provides a method for modeling the acquisition of the function F, described above.

Currently, the most popular type of reinforcement learning is *q-learning*, developed by Watkins, which is based on ideas from temporal difference learning, as well as conventional dynamic programming (Watkins, 1989). It requires estimating the q-value of a sensor configuration s, i.e., $q(s,a)$ is a prediction of the utility of taking action a in a world state represented by s. The q-values are updated during learning based on minimizing a temporal difference error. Action choice is typically stochastic, where a higher q-value implies a higher probability that action will be chosen in that state.

While q-learning with explicit state representations addresses the temporal credit assignment problem, it is standard practice to use input generalization and neural networks to also address the structural credit assignment problem, e.g., (Lin, 1992). The q-value output node of the control neural network corresponding to the chosen action a is given an error that reflects the difference between the current prediction of the utility, $q(s_1, a_i)$, and a better estimate of the utility (using the reward) of what this prediction should be:

$$error_i =$$

$$\begin{cases} (r + \gamma \, max\{q(s_2, k) | k \in A\}) - q(s_1, a_i) & \text{if } a_i = a \\ 0 & \text{otherwise} \end{cases}$$

where r is the reward, A is the set of available actions, a is the chosen action, s_2 is the state achieved by performing action a in state s_1, i indexes the possible actions, and $0 \leq \gamma < 1$ is a discount factor that controls the learning rate. This error is used to update the neural network weights using standard backpropagation. The result is improved q-values at the output nodes.

We selected q-learning as a benchmark algorithm with which to compare because the literature reports a wide range of successes with this algorithm, including on tasks with aspects similar to the NRL Navigation task, e.g., see (Lin, 1992). Our implementation uses standard q-learning with neural networks. One network corresponds to each action (i.e., there are three turn networks corresponding to turn left, turn right, and go straight; speed is fixed at a level frequently found in the human execution traces, i.e., 20/40). Each turn network has one input node for every one of the 12 sensor inputs (e.g., one for bearing, one for each sonar segment, etc.), one hidden layer[2] consisting of 10 hidden units, and a single output node corresponding to the q-value for that action. A Boltzmann distribution is used to stochastically make the final turn choice:

$$probability(a|s) = e^{q(s,a)/T} / \sum_i e^{q(s,a_i)/T} \qquad (1)$$

where s is a state and the temperature T controls the degree of randomness of action choice.

We use a reward r composed of a weighted sum of the sensor values.[3] Our reward models sensor relevance

information derived from the human subjects data we collected. These subjects appeared to learn relevance knowledge and action selection knowledge simultaneously. Here, we assume the relevance is known. Future work will involve methods for acquiring relevance knowledge.

The verbal protocols from human subjects reveal that the sonar and bearing sensors appear to be critical for action selection. Furthermore, the middle three sonar segments (which show what is directly ahead) appear to be the most critical of the sonar segments. This is logical: after all, the middle three sonar segments show a mine straight ahead so you can avoid collisions, and the bearing tells you whether you are navigating toward or away from the target. Based on the verbal protocol data, we have implemented a reward function that weights the bearing equally to the three sonar segments and gives other sensors zero weight. Thus, if the bearing shows the target straight ahead and the middle three sonar segments show no obstacles, then the reward is highest.

The verbal protocols also indicate heuristics for focusing attention on different sensors at different times. This knowledge is implemented in our novel variant of action models, described next. Nevertheless it is not implemented in the q-learner because to do so would require a departure from the standard q-learning architecture reported in the literature, with which we wish to compare as a benchmark.

Learning action models

One of the more striking aspects of the verbal protocols we collected was that subjects exhibited a tendency to build internal models of actions and their consequences, i.e., *forward models* of the world. These expectations produced surprise, disappointment, or positive reinforcement, depending on whether or not the predictions matched the actual results of performing the action. For example, one subject had an expectation of the results of a certain joystick motion: "Why am I turning to the left when I don't feel like I am moving the joystick much to the left?" Another expressed surprise: "It feels strange to hit the target when the bearing is not directly ahead." Yet a third subject developed a specific model of the consequences of his movements: "One small movement right or left seems to jump you over one box to the right or left," where each box refers to a visual depiction of a single sonar segment in the graphical interface.

Action models (i.e., forward models) have appeared in multidisciplinary sources in the literature. Arbib (1972) and Drescher (1991) provide examples in the psychological literature, STRIPS (Nilsson, 1980) is a classic example in the AI literature, and Sutton uses them in DYNA (Sutton, 1988). The *learning* of action models has been studied in the neural networks (Moore, 1992), machine learning (Sutton, 1990; Mahadevan, 1992), and cognitive science (Munro, 1987; Jordan & Rumelhart, 1992) communities.

---

[2]We ran initial experiments to try to optimize the reinforcement learning parameters. For the neural networks, the chosen learning rate is 0.5, momentum 0.1, 10 hidden units, and 10 training iterations for the neural networks and a discount factor of 0.9.

[3]Ron Sun suggested a reward of sensor values for this task (personal communication). Our choice of sensor weights for the reward is 30 for bearing and 10 for each of the three middle sonar segments, and the scale for the reward is between -1.0 and 0.

Our algorithm uses two functions:

$$A : \text{sensors} \times \text{actions} \rightarrow \text{sensors}$$
$$P : \text{sensors} \rightarrow \Re$$

A is an action model, which our method represents as a decision tree. The decision trees are learned using Quinlan's C4.5 system (Quinlan, 1986).[4] P rates the desirability of various sensor configurations. P embodies background (relevance) knowledge about the task. For sonars, high utilities are associated with large values (no or distant mines), and for the bearing sensor high utilities are associated with values closer to the target being straight ahead. Currently, P is supplied by us. At each time step, actions are selected using P and A by performing a 1-step lookahead with model A and rating sensory configurations generated using P. The action models algorithm has the same action set as the q-learning algorithm, i.e., turn right, turn left, or go straight at a fixed speed (20/40).

First, our algorithm goes through a training phase, during which random turns are taken and the execution traces saved as input for C4.5. C4.5 models the learning of the function A. In particular, it constructs two decision trees from the data: one tree to predict (from (s, a)) the *next* composite value of the middle three sonar segments (prediction choices are no-mines, mine-far, mine-mid, mine-fairly-close, or mine-close, where these nominal values are translations from the numeric sonar readings) and one tree to predict the bearing on the next time step. Note that the choice of these two trees employs the same relevance information used in the reinforcement learning reward function, namely, that the middle three sonar segments and bearing are the relevant sensors. The training phase concludes after C4.5 constructs these two decision trees.

During the testing phase, these trees representing the world dynamics (A) are consulted to make predictions and select turns. Given the current state, a tree is chosen. The tree selection heuristic for focus of attention states: if the middle three sonar segments are below a certain empirically determined threshold (150/220), the sonar prediction tree selects the *next* turn. Otherwise, the bearing prediction tree selects the next turn. To make a prediction, the agent feeds the current sensor readings (which include the *last* turn and speed) and a candidate *next* turn to the decision tree and the tree returns the predicted sonar or bearing value. The agent chooses the next turn which maximizes P.[5]

It is unlikely that humans recompute the consequences of actions when the current state is similar to one seen in the past. Therefore, our future work will focus on

memorizing cases of successful action model use so that memory can be invoked, rather than the trees, for some predictions.

Empirical Evaluation of the Methods

To make our comparisons fair, we include a training phase for the reinforcement learner with Boltzmann temperature at 0.5, which results in random actions.[6] A testing phase follows in which the turn with the best q-value is selected deterministically at each time step. In summary, the reinforcement learner takes random actions and learns its q-values during training.[7] It uses these learned q-values for action selection during testing. The action models method takes the same random actions as the q-learner during training (i.e., it experiences exactly the same sensor and action training data as the q-learner), and then from this training data it learns decision tree action models. A heuristic uses the learned trees for action selection during testing. Neither of the two methods learns during testing. Both methods have the same knowledge regarding which sensors are relevant.

We denote the q-learning scheme described above as Q_{rel} and the action model scheme with decision trees described above as A_{rel}. Two schemes in which we have removed sensor relevance knowledge are denoted Q_{remrel} and A_{remrel} respectively and are described below.

We empirically test the following hypotheses:

- *Hypothesis 1:* The slope of A_{rel}'s learning curve is closer than Q_{rel}'s to the slope of the human learning curve, for the Navigation task.

- *Hypothesis 2:* The slope of A_{remrel}'s learning curve (respectively, Q_{remrel}) is lower than that of A_{rel} (respectively, Q_{rel}), for the Navigation task.

The justification for Hypothesis 1 is that our action models method uses an action choice policy specially designed to capitalize on sensor relevance knowledge. The justification for Hypothesis 2 is that removal of relevance knowledge should degrade performance.

In our experimental tests of these hypotheses, the training phase length is varied methodically at 25, 50, 75, and 100 episodes. The testing phase remains fixed at 400 episodes.[8] Each episode can last a maximum of 200 time steps, i.e., decision cycles. In all experiments, the number of mines is fixed at 25, there is a small amount of mine drift, and no sensor noise. These task parameter settings match exactly those used for the human subject whose learning we wish to model.[9] Performance is averaged over 10 experiments because the algorithms

---

[4] We are not claiming humans use decision trees for action models; however, we use this implementation because it appears to have a computational speed that is needed for modeling human learning. We are also investigating connectionist models as in Jordan & Rumelhart (1992). Currently, C4.5 learning is in batch. To more faithfully model human learning, we are planning to use an incremental version of decision tree learning in future implementations.

[5] If the next turn is considered irrelevant by the decision tree, a random action choice is made.

[6] We also tried an annealing schedule but performance did not improve.

[7] Arbib (1972) provides convincing cognitive justification for the role of random exploration of actions in the acquisition of motor skill.

[8] We experimented with the number of episodes and chose a setting where performance improvement leveled off for both algorithms.

[9] Both algorithms go straight (0 turn) for the first three time steps of every episode during training. This not only matches performance we observed in the execution traces

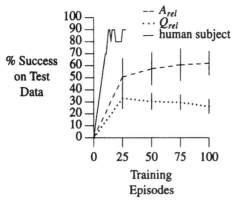

Figure 1: The graph represents the learning curves for A_{rel} and Q_{rel}. Note the learning curve of a human subject superimposed on this graph.

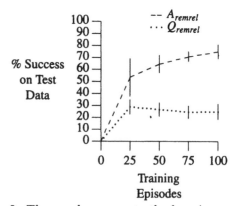

Figure 2: The graph represents the learning curves for A_{remrel} and Q_{remrel}.

are stochastic during training, and testing results depend upon the data seen during training. Graphs show mean performance, and error bars denote the standard deviation.

To test Hypothesis 1, we used data from a typical (the variance between subjects was surprisingly low) subject for a single 45-minute session. Note that we cannot divide the human learning into a training phase and a testing phase during which the human stops learning. Therefore, we have averaged performance over a sliding window of 10 previous episodes. We considered averaging performance over multiple subjects, but that would entail significant information loss.

Figure 1 shows the results of testing Hypothesis 1. The action models method outperforms reinforcement learning at a statistically significant level (using a paired, two-tailed t-test with $\alpha = 0.05$). Thus, Hypothesis 1 is confirmed.[10] Apparently, our novel method for coupling action models with an action choice policy that exploits sensor relevance has tremendous value for this task. We believe that one of the chief reasons for the superior performance of the action models method is the action choice heuristic for deciding when to pay attention to which sensor. Another likely reason for the dominance of action model-based methods is that neural networks with backpropagation tend to learn slowly (Chapman & Kaelbling, 1991).

To test Hypothesis 2, we made all seven, rather than

just the three middle, sonar segments relevant for both algorithms, thereby creating A_{remrel} and Q_{remrel}. Figure 2 shows the results of testing Hypothesis 2. Q_{remrel} performs slightly worse than Q_{rel}. The performance drop is not statistically significant ($\alpha = 0.10$) for training lengths of 25, 50, and 100, but is significant ($\alpha = 0.10$) with a training length of 75. The surprise is that A_{remrel} outperforms A_{rel}. The differences are statistically significant at $\alpha = 0.05$ for training lengths of 75 and 100, but only at $\alpha = 0.20$ for training lengths of 25 and 50. Our results refute Hypothesis 2. Apparently, both methods are knowledge sensitive, though action models is more sensitive. We conjecture that the reason the action models method improves with more sensory information is that the extra sonar segments carry some useful information. The action models heuristic, which separates sonar and bearing information, is able to take advantage of the added sonar information. Because the q-learning method lumps all knowledge into one reward it probably needs longer training to do likewise. Further experiments are needed to test this hypothesis. (Although these results with A_{remrel} and Q_{remrel} refute Hypothesis 2, they provide further confirmation of Hypothesis 1 because the performance improvement of A_{remrel} over that of Q_{remrel} is statistically significant with $\alpha = 0.05$).

Discussion and Future Work

The most immediate pressing question is: why are *both* methods slower learners than the human? We believe humans have more knowledge when they begin this task, perhaps from driving or walking experience. We are presently working to make these forms of knowledge explicit, so we can more closely match human performance using our computational models. Another issue

---

from human subjects, but also aids the learning process by quickly moving the AUV into the mine field.

[10]It is unclear why the performance of the q-learner drops slightly with more training episodes, though perhaps overfitting explains this.

that we are currently investigating is whether the power law of practice holds for human subjects in this task, and whether our models conform to it. Performance levels off rather quickly both for humans and our models, making this determination challenging.

Future work will also focus on studies to determine the source of power of our action models approach over the q-learner for this task. As mentioned above, strong candidate explanations are (1) the focus of attention knowledge in the action models heuristic, (2) the use of an action model *per se*, and (3) the decision tree representation.

Acknowledgements

This research was sponsored by the Office of Naval Research N00014-95-WX30360 and N00014-95-1-0846. Special thanks to Sandy Marshall and William Spears for their helpful comments and suggestions, to Helen Gigley and Susan Chipman for their encouragement and support, to Jim Ballas for the joystick interface, and to Alan Schultz for all the work he did to tailor the simulation to both machine learning and human experimental needs.

References

Arbib, M.A. (1972). *The Metaphorical Brain.* NY: Wiley and Sons Publishers.

Breiman, L., Friedman, J.H. Olshen, R.A.. & Stone, C.J. (1984). *Classification and Regression Trees.* Belmont, CA: Wadsworth International Group Publishers.

Chapman, D. & Kaelbling, L. (1991). Input generalization in delayed reinforcement learning: An algorithm and performance comparisons. In *Proceedings of Twelfth International Joint Conference on Artificial Intelligence* (pp. 726–731). San Mateo, CA: Morgan Kaufmann Publishers.

Drescher, G.L. (1991). *Made-Up Minds.* Canbridge, MA: MIT Press.

Gordon, D., Schultz, A., Grefenstette, J., Ballas, J., & Perez, M. (1994). *User's Guide to the Navigation and Collision Avoidance Task.* Naval Research Laboratory Technical Report AIC-94-013.

Gordon, D. & Subramanian, D. (1993). A Multistrategy Learning Scheme for Agent Knowledge Acquisition. *Informatica*, 17, 331–346.

Jordan, M.I. & Rumelhart, D.E. (1992). Forward models: supervised learning with a distal teacher. *Cognitive Science*, 16, 307–354.

Lin, L. (1992). Self-Improving Reactive Agents Based on Reinforcement Learning, Planning and Teaching. *Machine Learning*, 8, 293–321.

Mahadevan, S. (1992). Enhancing transfer in reinforcement learning by building stochastic models of robot actions. In *Proceedings of the Ninth International Conference on Machine Learning* (pp. 290–299). San Mateo, CA: Morgan Kaufmann Publishers.

Moore, A. (1992). Fast, robust adaptive control by learning only forward models. In *Proceedings of the International Joint Conference on Neural Networks*, 4, (pp. 571–578). San Mateo, CA: Morgan Kaufmann.

Munro, P. (1987). A dual back-propagation scheme for scalar reward learning. In *Proceedings of the Ninth Annual Conference of the Cognitive Science Society* (pp. 165–176). Hillsdale, NJ: Erlbaum.

Nilsson, N. (1980). *Principles of Artificial Intelligence.* Palo Alto, CA: Tioga Publishing Company.

Quinlan, J.R. (1986). Induction of decision trees. *Machine Learning*, 1, 81–107.

Rissanen, J. (1983). *Minimum Description Length Principle.* Report RJ 4131 (45769), IBM Research Laboratory, San Jose.

Rumelhart, D.E. & McClelland, J.L. (1986). *Parallel Distributed Processing : Explorations in the Microstructure of Cognition.* Cambridge, MA: MIT Press.

Skinner, B.F. (1984). Selection by consequences. *The Behavior and Brain Sciences*, 7, 477–510.

Sutton, R. (1988). Learning to Predict by the Methods of Temporal Differences. Machine Learning, 3, 9–44.

Sutton, R. (1990). Integrated architectures for learning, planning, and reacting based on approximating dynamic programming. In *Proceedings of the Seventh International Conference on Machine Learning* (pp. 216-224). San Mateo, CA: Morgan Kaufmann.

Watkins, C. (1989). Learning from Delayed Rewards. Doctoral dissertation. Cambridge, England: Cambridge University.

The Effect of Selection Instructions on Reasoning about Thematic Content Rules in Wason's Card Selection Task

Loranel M. Graham and **Woo-kyoung Ahn**
Department of Psychology
University of Louisville
Louisville, KY 40292
lmgrah01@ulkyvm.louisville.edu
wkahn001@homer.louisville.edu

Abstract

This study examined the effects of selection instruction and thematic content on subjects' reasoning performance on the Wason card selection task. Facilitation has frequently been demonstrated when subjects are instructed to check for violations of a conditional rule that involves thematic content. We noted that the thematic rules previously used are also pragmatic rules that express regulations. We compared reasoning about two kinds of thematic rules: pragmatic and non-pragmatic. Subjects were instructed either to determine if the rule has been violated or to determine if the rule is true or false. The results indicate an interaction between instruction type and thematic rule type. Contrary to previous findings of facilitation on thematic materials with violation instructions, we found facilitation for true/false instructions relative to violation instructions on non-pragmatic content rules. These results stand in contrast to previous descriptions of true/false instructions as more difficult and cognitively demanding than violation instructions. We explain our findings in terms of differences in the inherent status of the two types of thematic rules.

Introduction

This paper is concerned with subjects' performance on Wason's four-card selection task (Wason, 1966). In its original form, the selection task involved presentation of a pack of cards to subjects, each card having a letter on one side and a number on the other side. Subjects were presented four cards, showing E, K, 4, and 7, or the P, Not-P, Q, and Not-Q conditions, respectively. The subjects' task was to select which cards they would need to turn over in order to decide if the following rule was true or false: "If a card has a vowel on one side, then it has an even number on the other side."

Normatively, subjects should select the P and Not-Q cards because these are the only cards that can falsify the rule. That is, if Not-Q lies on the other side of the P card, or P lies on the other side of the Not-Q card, then one can be certain that the rule is false. However, the majority of subjects select either P alone or P and Q.

Since its inception, the task has been investigated with numerous procedural variations. Researchers have examined the effects of thematic versus abstract content, rule explication, selection instructions, and selection justification (Johnson-Laird, Legrenzi, & Legrenzi, 1972; Griggs & Cox, 1982; Hoch & Tschirgi, 1983; Yachanin, 1986). The current study concerns the effects of selection instructions and thematic content.

Wason and Shapiro (1971) reported better performance on a conditional rule involving familiar content. Their subjects showed facilitation when reasoning about the rule, "Every time I go to Manchester, I travel by train." When reasoning about the thematic transport rule, sixty-two percent of subjects chose the correct P and Not-Q combination. Other thematic content rules for which facilitation was subsequently demonstrated include the postal rule (Johnson-Laird, Legrenzi, & Legrenzi, 1972), the drinking age rule (Griggs & Cox, 1982), and the Sears problem (D'Andrade, described by Griggs, 1983).

A number of explanations for superior performance on thematic content rules have been advanced (e.g., Cheng & Holyoak, 1985; Cosmides, 1989; Gigerenzer & Hug, 1992; Griggs & Cox, 1982). For example, Cheng and Holyoak (1985) explained performance on the drinking age, postal, and a number of original rules in terms of pragmatic reasoning schema theory. Pragmatic reasoning schemas concern regulations that involve permission or obligation. These schemas may be triggered by conditional rules that express a precondition and an action (Cheng & Holyoak, 1985). For example, a permission schema may be triggered by a conditional rule specifying that an action may be taken after an initial condition has been met, as is expressed in the rule, "If a person is drinking beer, then the person must be over 19 years of age." Cheng and Holyoak (1985) proposed that facilitation would be found as long as the rule triggered a permission or obligation schema that subsequently maps onto the rule.

Most accounts of facilitation with thematic materials underscore the importance of experience that is related to the rule's content. Of present interest, however, is the contention that the facilitation observed for thematic content rules may be driven in part by the instructions accompanying those rules. Wason (1966) initially presented the task to subjects with instructions to select those cards needed to determine whether the rule is true or false. Although Wason (1968) examined the effects of various selection instructions (e.g., to prove the rule true), selection instructions became a factor of interest when proposed as an explanation for the thematic content effect (Yachanin & Tweney, 1982; Yachanin, 1986). Yachanin (Yachanin, 1986; Yachanin & Tweney, 1982) observed that facilitation with thematic content rules occurs when subjects are instructed to determine if the rule is being *violated*, as opposed to instructions to determine if the rule is *true or false*. Several researchers have suggested that true/false instructions are ambiguous, subject to misinterpretation, and more difficult than violation instructions (Yachanin & Tweney, 1982; Valentine, 1985). Yachanin (1986) argues that the task of checking for violations of a rule is easier than that of determining a rule's truth or falsity. The former involves only the evaluation of a rule given as true, while the latter requires consideration of the rule as true and of the rule as false. Put another way, violation checking involves the testing of a single hypothesis, but a true/false assessment involves the testing of a dual hypothesis. Because of the increased cognitive load for true/false assessments, subjects may adopt "short-circuiting strategies" (Yachanin, 1986, p. 21) resulting in poorer performance for true/false instructions than for violation checking.

Several researchers have investigated performance differences on abstract and thematic versions of the selection task, using true/false or violation checking instructions (Chrostowski & Griggs, 1985; Valentine, 1985; Yachanin, 1986; Kroger, Cheng, & Holyoak, 1993). Although it is clear that violation checking instructions do not by themselves produce facilitation, violation instructions do produce better performance than do true/false instructions for thematic rules. Violation checking instructions have generally not been found to facilitate performance on abstract versions of the task, but do on thematic content versions (Griggs, 1984; Christowski & Griggs, 1985; Yachanin, 1986; Valentine, 1985).

While research has demonstrated a superiority for violation instructions over true/false instructions for thematic content, we observed that the thematic content rules for which reliable facilitation has been demonstrated are primarily regulations (Johnson-Laird, Legrenzi, & Legrenzi, 1972; Griggs & Cox, 1982; D'Andrade, described by Griggs, 1983). These regulations are conventional rules which have been established to hold a certain status in the world. That is, conventional rules are intended to be interpreted as givens. These rules may be followed or may be violated, but their truth or falsity is not reasonably contemplated. By way of example, consider that you have established a rule stating, "If a person enters my office, that person must not smoke." It is clear that you have established this rule to be taken as a regulation by persons wishing to enter your office. The truth or falsity of the rule is not in question. However, the rule may be violated, and checking for violations of the rule is rational and relevant.

Cheng and Holyoak (1985, 1995) assert that facilitation on the selection task will be observed when a violation checking scenario and the rule's content identifies the rule as a regulation, and a pragmatic reasoning schema is applied. For example, the rule, "If a person is drinking beer, then that person must be over 19 years of age," is clearly a conventional regulation, for which a permission schema and violation checking is warranted. We argue that these conventional rules, which are characterized by their pragmatic content, can reasonably be checked for violations, but not truth or falsity. We suggest that the facilitation previously demonstrated for thematic content rules with violation instructions is tied to the pragmatic content of the conventional rules which have been used.

Although pragmatic content rules have been employed as thematic content rules, they comprise only a subset of possible thematic rules. An everyday example of a non-pragmatic, thematic rule could be stated as such: "If it is a stop sign, then it must be red." Although this rule is of thematic content, it should not invoke a pragmatic reasoning schema, as there are no preconditions which would regulate voluntary human action in this rule (Cheng & Holyoak, 1985). Non-pragmatic rules may be stated between categorical relationships (e.g., if it is a dog, it must be an animal), conceptual features (e.g., if it is a stop sign, it must be red), and causal relations (e.g., if it is raining, it must be wet outside). In contrast to pragmatic rules, violation checking is not pertinent to non-pragmatic rules. For example, given our knowledge of categorical relations, it is difficult to imagine what would comprise a violation of the rule, "If it is a dog, it must be an animal." Non-pragmatic rules, however, may be more reasonably considered as either true or false. For example, consider the rule, "If it is a bird, it must fly." It is the case that we can determine whether this non-pragmatic rule is true or false, in other words, whether it represents an actual condition of the world. That is, "If it is a bird, it must fly" represents a *possible* state of the world that may be evaluated for truth or falsity, but which may not reasonably be checked for violations. In contrast, pragmatic rules, such as "If a person enters my office, that person must not smoke," represents a *given* state of the world which may be evaluated for violations, but not truth or falsity.

The present study compared the effects of true/false and violation selection instructions on subjects' performance when reasoning about rules of differing thematic content. Two types of thematic rules were used: pragmatic content rules and non-pragmatic rules. Subjects reasoned about these rules under instructions to either determine whether the rules had been violated or determine whether the rules were true or false. We argue that the facilitation observed for violation instructions is tied to the pragmatic nature of previously used thematic rules. Given our arguments about the relative applicability of violation and true/false instructions to pragmatic and non-pragmatic rules, we predicted that violation instructions would produce superior performance on pragmatic rules, whereas true/false instructions would produce superior performance on non-pragmatic, thematic rules. This prediction stands in contrast to previous views of true/false instructions. If true/false instructions produce more cognitive load or are more ambiguous than violation instructions (Yachanin, 1986; Yachanin & Tweney, 1982), violation instructions would be expected to facilitate reasoning on all thematic rules, regardless of their pragmatic or non-pragmatic content.

Method

Subjects

Subjects were 36 undergraduate students at the University of Louisville, who received credit for their participation toward fulfillment of an introductory psychology course requirement. None of the subjects had previously encountered the Wason card selection task.

Design and Materials

Subjects were tested in one of two instruction conditions: violation or true/false. Each subject was asked to reason about three pragmatic and three non-pragmatic thematic content rules. These factors constitute a 2 X 2 mixed design, with instruction type as a between subjects factor and rule content as a within subjects factor. Subjects randomly received either all three pragmatic rules first or all three non-pragmatic rules first. Ordering of the rules within each rule content type was also randomized.

Selection	True/False Instructions		Violation Instructions	
	Pragmatic rules	Non-pragmatic rules	Pragmatic rules	Non-pragmatic rules
p, not-q	**17**	**28**	**39**	**0**
p, q	11	22	11	29
p	22	11	11	17
q	5	5	0	5
not-p	5	0	0	0
not-q	0	5	0	0
not-p, q	0	0	5	5
not-p, not-q	5	0	0	0
p, not-p	0	0	0	5
q, not-q	0	0	5	5
p, not-p, q	11	5	0	5
p, q, not-q	11	11	0	22
p, not-p, not-q	5	0	0	0
not-p, q, not-q	0	11	0	0
p, q, not-q	0	0	11	0
all	5	0	5	0
none	0	0	11	5

Table 1. Percentage of subjects selecting each combination.

Three pragmatic rules were used. A drinking age rule served as one of these rules, "If a person drinks beer, that person must be over 21 years old." Two other rules were developed for the task. These two rules read as follows: "If you earn income in Kentucky, you must pay federal income tax" and "If a person registers for psychology 322, that person must have taken its prerequisite, psychology 201."

Three non-pragmatic, thematic rules were developed, representing three possible relations: a categorical relation, "If it is a banana, then it must be a fruit"; a conceptual relation, "If it is a bird, then it must have wings"; and a causal relation, "If a person takes cyanide, that person must die."

Procedure

Subjects were tested in small groups of up to six, and were randomly assigned to instruction conditions. The rules were presented to subjects in a booklet with an initial page of instructions, which subjects read themselves. The violation instructions read as follows:

Suppose you are from a different country and you hear about some rules that people follow in the United States. For example, you hear that in this country, "If you want to mail a letter, you must put a stamp on the envelope." Your task in this experiment is to determine if various rules have been violated.

The instructions for the true/false condition were the same, except the last line read, "Your task in this experiment is to determine if various rules are true or false."

Each page of the booklet contained one rule. Following presentation of the rule, subjects saw four "cases" representing the P, Not-P, Q, and Not-Q conditions. For each case, subjects were asked to decide whether they would need to select this case in order to test whether the rule was true or false (or had been violated). Subjects were instructed to circle "yes" if they would definitely need to select that information in order to decide if the rule is true or false, or to circle "no" if they did not need that information. Subjects in the violation condition received the same materials, except that references to true/false were replaced with references to violations.

Results and Discussion

The percentage of subjects selecting the P and Not-Q combination is shown in Table 1. For each rule, selection of the normative P and Not-Q combination was scored as 1 and selection of all other responses was scored as 0. An analysis of variance on these scores revealed no significant main effects for either rule content type or instruction type, but a significant interaction between these two factors, $F(1,34)=5.17$, $p<.03$. This interaction indicates that violation instructions facilitated performance for pragmatic content rules, while true/false instructions produced better performance for non-pragmatic content rules.

Table 1 also shows the percentage of subjects selecting patterns of information other than the normative p and not-q combination. Analyses of variance were also performed on the scores obtained for these non-normative responses. These analyses failed to reveal any significant main effects or interactions of rule content or instruction type.

The results for the P and Not-Q responses are striking, as it appears to be the first time that true/false instructions have produced performance superior to violation instructions on thematic materials. True/false instructions have typically been characterized as being more difficult and cognitively demanding (Yachanin, 1986). If so, violation instructions should produce better performance relative to true/false instructions for all thematic materials. However, we found that true/false instructions produce facilitation relative to violation instructions for some kinds of thematic materials, specifically, non-pragmatic rules. Thus, our findings do not support the interpretation of true/false instructions as inherently more difficult or resulting in the adoption of nonlogical reasoning strategies (Yachanin, 1986). If this were the case, then violation instructions should be expected to facilitate reasoning on all kinds of thematic rules.

We believe our result is due to the intrinsic difference in status of pragmatic and non-pragmatic thematic rules. Pragmatic rules that embody conventional regulations are taken as givens in the world. As such, they are appropriately checked for violations, but are less suited to tests of truth or falsity. Conversely, non-pragmatic rules may be stated that are either true or false and may be evaluated as such. However, these non-pragmatic rules are not subject to violation checking. The results of the present study support our contention, demonstrating differences in thematic content, for which violation checking or true/false instructions may be more or less applicable. Most interestingly, the study revealed conditions under which reasoning in the selection task paradigm may be supported by true/false instructions.

References

Cheng, P. N., & Holyoak, K. J. (1985). Pragmatic reasoning schemas. Cognitive Psychology, 17, 391-416.

Chrostowski, J. J., & Griggs, R. A. (1985). The effects of problem content, instructions, and verbalization procedure on Wason's selection task. Current Psychological Reviews, 4, 99-107.

Griggs, R. A. (1983). The role of problem content in the selection task and THOG problem. In J. St. B. T. Evans (Ed.), Thinking and Reasoning: Psychological Approaches. London: Routledge & Kegan Paul.

Griggs, R. A., & Cox, J. R. (1982). The elusive thematic-material effect on Wason's selection task. British Journal of Psychology, 73, 407-420.

Hoch, S. J., & Tschirgi, J. E. (1983). Cue redundancy and extra-logical inferences in a deductive reasoning task. Memory & Cognition, 11, 200-209.

Johnson-Laird, P. N., Legrenzi, P., & Legrenzi, S. M. (1972). Reasoning and a sense of reality. Journal of British Psychology, 63, 395-400.

Kroger, J. K., Cheng, P. W., & Holyoak, K. J. (1993). Evoking the permission schema: The impact of negation and a violation-checking context. Quarterly Journal of Experimental Psychology, 46A, 615-635.

Wason, P. C. (1966). Reasoning. In B. M. Foss (Ed.), New horizons in psychology. Harmondsworth: Penguin.

Wason, P. C., & Shapiro, D. (1971). Natural and contrived experience in a reasoning problem. Quarterly Journal of Experimental Psychology, 23, 63-71.

Yachanin, S. A. (1986). Facilitation in Wason's selection task: Content and instructions. Current Psychological Research & Reviews, 5, 20-29.

Yachanin, S. A., & Tweney, R. D. (1982). The effect of thematic content on cognitive strategies in the four-card selection task. Bulletin of the Psychonomic Society, 19, 87-90.

Valentine, E. R. (1985). The effect of instructions on performance in the selection task. Current Psychological Research & Reviews, 4, 214-223.

Integration and Shielding of Regular and Irregular Items in MLPs

Brett Gray and **Janet Wiles**
Depts of Computer Science and Psychology
University of Queensland, QLD 4072 Australia
brettg@cs.uq.oz.au janetw@cs.uq.oz.au

Abstract

Multi-layer perceptrons (MLPs) can learn both regular and irregular items given sufficient interleaved training, but not from
sequential presentation of items. McClelland, McNaughton
and O'Reilly (1994) addressed this problem in their proposal
that the hippocampus and neocortex (H/NC) form a two component memory system in which the hippocampus interleaves
training of items to the neocortex so that it can develop structure without interference of later items on earlier ones. We have
been studying such an interleaving system under the constraint
of limiting the capacity of the training batch (analogous to a
finite limit on the hippocampus). In previous simulations (Gray
& Wiles, 1996) we demonstrated that a quasi-regular learning
task trained with a recency rehearsal scheme did not suffer interference to a catastrophic level, but did suffer interference on
irregular and similar regular items. The current study introduces a new rehearsal scheme in which items are retained in a
finite training batch based on how well the MLP has learned
them: Error rehearsal enabled the MLP to learn (1) a high proportion of the domain, (2) retention of both regular and irregular
items from the initial training batch and (3) partial shielding of
both regular and irregular items from later interference. The results demonstrate that although finite training batches can pose
a problem for MLPs, an error rehearsal scheme can reduce interference on both regular and irregular items, even when they
are no longer in the current training batch. Implications for the
role of the hippocampus in interleaving items for the neocortex
are discussed.

Introduction

Memory systems have several functionally different learning
requirements: the primary one is the ability to store events
or items after only one presentation (called one-shot learning or memorisation); a second is a longer term integrative
function that allows a memory system to develop a structure
over the events experienced, and hence generalise to novel
events. When modelling these functions independently, artificial neural network researchers have typically used single
layer networks (s.a. the Matrix Model, Humphreys, Bain &
Pike, 1989, or k-Winner Take All, O'Reilly & McClelland,
1994) to model one-shot learning, and multi-layer perceptrons
(*MLPs*) to model integrative components (Rumelhart, Hinton
& Williams, 1995).

A central problem in modelling human and animal memory is whether the two functions can be produced by a unitary memory system or whether two components are required
(Humphreys, Bain & Pike, 1989; McClelland, McNaughton
& O'Reilly, 1994; O'Reilly & McClelland, 1994): Since
one-shot learning systems need to unambiguously store single events at the time at which they occur, they cannot take
into account information that may be distributed across several events. Attempts to use one-shot learning systems as
integrative systems result in severe restrictions on the types
of generalisation that can occur (e.g., linear combinations in
the Matrix Model; category membership in the k-Winner Take
All). By contrast, integrative systems such as MLPs can utilise
higher-order statistics of events distributed over time, but are
not suitable for unambiguously storing sequentially presented
events. MLPs are traditionally trained by interleaving presentations of all items and attempts to use MLPs as one-shot
memory systems (training without interleaving presentations
of items) display spectacular failures, called "catastrophic interference" (*CI*, McCloskey & Cohen, 1989; Ratcliff, 1990).
In CI, events presented at an early stage in training are completely lost during training on later items.

A key question for two-component models is the relationship between the one-shot and integrative components. Models that seek to combine both these functions have rarely
been explored at a purely computational level, but have been
studied by cognitive neuroscientists with respect to the hip-
pocampus/neocortex (*H/NC*) memory system (McClelland,
McNaughton & O'Reilly, 1994), and the necessity for two
component models has been debated by psychologists studying human memory (see Dennis, 1994, for a history of memory
and learning research) and exception/regular learning (e.g.,
the Dual Route model, Bakker, 1995; Coltheart *et. al.*, 1993).
Our analysis of the computational questions in this project derives from the H/NC research by McClelland and colleagues
(although we see many parallels in related areas of psychological research).

McClelland and colleagues (McClelland, McNaughton &
O'Reilly, 1994; O'Reilly & McClelland, 1994) have proposed
that events are initially stored in the hippocampus (a one-shot
memory which they model as a k-Winner Take All network,
O'Reilly & McClelland, 1994), which then interleaves presentation of all its stored memories to the neocortex (a structured
integrative memory system analogous to an MLP). Such internal interleaving enables multiple presentation of items to
the integrative component (thus providing a mechanism to
mitigate interference and build structure gradually), while requiring events to be presented to the entire "two-component"
system only once.

Our goal in this project is to investigate computational aspects of the interleaving process between the two functional
components of memory systems such as McClelland, Mc-

Naughton and O'Reilly's H/NC model under the constraint of a finite limit on the training batch sizes, analogous to a finite limit on hippocampus (Treves & Rolls, 1994). Following McClelland, McNaughton and O'Reilly's analogy, we used an MLP as an integrative component, and a buffer as the one-shot component.

The focus of this study was the interleaving process (called a rehearsal scheme) and its effect on CI. Several rehearsal schemes have been reported in the neural network literature. Results either showed no significant improvement (s.a., recency rehearsal, Ratcliff, 1990; Robins, 1995) or required the entire domain of previously learned items (s.a., random and sweep rehearsal, Robins, 1995). Note that there are alternative approaches to mitigating CI such as modifying the hidden unit representations (node sharpening, French, 1991, and context biasing, French, 1994, and sparse hidden unit representations, Kruschke, 1992) however, following McClelland, McNaughton and O'Reilly, in light of observed psychological phenomena (s.a., temporally graded retrograde amnesia, see McClelland, McNaughton & O'Reilly, 1994, for a review), we chose to investigate interleaving as the primary method for mitigating CI.

Much of the past work on CI has been performed using domains that lack inherent structure. By contrast most cognitive domains are highly structured (e.g., words are composed of letters, speech of phonemes). Domains comprising events that are represented as multiple components are termed *combinatorial domains*. The regular structure of combinatorial domains is fundamental to the productivity of cognitive systems (e.g., the ability to produce an unlimited number of novel words from a finite set of letters), but, somewhat surprisingly perhaps, purely regular domains are rare, and most cognitive domains contain exceptions to the regular structure (forming "quasi-regular" domains, such as the pronunciation of English words). MLPs trained on combinatorial data have been shown to possess very different properties than those trained on random data (Brousse & Smolensky, 1989; Phillips & Wiles, 1993), in particular demonstrating high levels of generalisation, and some of these findings have been related to a reduction in CI (Brousse & Smolensky, 1989). Due to the cognitive relevance of combinatorial domains and the success of MLPs in learning combinatorial structure, we have studied both regular and quasi-regular combinatorial domains.

Results to date

Previous simulations of the A-B and recency rehearsal tasks[1] (Gray & Wiles, 1996) demonstrated that an MLP can extract the regular structure behind regular and quasi-regular combinatorial domains and that the structure of the data itself mitigates interference to a level that could not be called catastrophic. This result is consistent with expectations from other

studies (Brousse & Smolensky, 1989), however, in our simulations not even large batch sizes eliminated all interference for quasi-regular domains. After irregular items left the current training batch, performance on these items was retained only briefly and then lost permanently. As irregular items were added to the training batch, performance was lost on similar regular items (two letters in common) not present in the training batch.

Aim of Present Work

The current study delved further into the interference effects on MLPs constrained by a limited training batch size. Since our earlier studies showed that CI was not an issue for quasi-regular data, our focus was on the interference that did occur, which we explored by separating the performance of regular and irregular items.

A new rehearsal scheme was designed, similar to recency rehearsal in that after training set A to criterion, new items are added and older items removed from the training batch incrementally. The schemes differ in that in recency rehearsal, the oldest item was removed, whereas in error rehearsal, each item was evaluated with respect to the MLPs performance on the item, and the best learned item (over several trials) was removed.

We hypothesised two ways by which the scheme could improve performance: The first derives directly from the maintenance of less-well-learned items for longer in the training batch, allowing increases in training time and chance of interleaved training with new similar items. The second aspect is more subtle, but directly addresses the critical question of avoiding interference on items that are no longer present in the current training batch (which we call "shielding"): Irregular items entering the training batch would have high error and interfere with the systems performance on similar regular items, increasing their error also. These irregular and similar regular items would then be concentrated in the training batch as the highest error items. Subsequent interleaved presentations would facilitate their separation in HU space, possibly to the extent of shielding the irregulars (after they have left the training batch) from interference by later items.

Method

Simulations were run to compare the new error rehearsal scheme with recency rehearsal. Three measures were of interest: firstly, how well the structure of regular and irregular items is incorporated overall into the HU space (a domain performance measure); secondly, performance on regular and irregular items from the initial batch at the end of training all items in the domain; and thirdly, the degree to which items that are not in the final training batch are maintained (a shielding measure).

For both recency and error rehearsal schemes, changes to the simulations from the previous work (Gray & Wiles, 1996) involved doubling the number of HUs to ensure that capacity was not limiting the performance of the rehearsal schemes, and increasing the maximum number of epochs between training batch updates. All other factors (i.e, data sets and parameters) remained the same (these are reproduced below for completeness).

---

[1]In the A-B task, the MLP is trained on a data set (Set A) until all items are learned, followed by training a second set (Set B) without continuing presentations of Set A. This form of A-B Task is common in catastrophic interference literature - items within each data set are trained using an interleaving process, but no interleaving occurs between the two sets. The Recency Rehearsal Task differs from the A-B Task in that after training the initial Set A to criterion, new items are added and older items removed from the training batch incrementally until all items in the domain have been trained.

Structure of the quasi-regular domain

The data used was from an artificial data set designed by Sally Andrews at the University of New South Wales (personal communication) to reflect effects in mapping three letter syllables to their phonetic pronunciation. The input is formed by combining three letters (the onset, vowel and coda). Each of the three letter positions may adopt one of six letters. For example, the onset is one of the letters B, C, D, G, H or S. The mapping was quasi-regular, in which the outputs for the onsets and codas were identically mapped, but vowels were mapped to one of two possible phonetic representations depending on whether they were long or short. Two of the six vowels were always mapped to their short phonetic representation, with the other four varying depending on the combination of the onset and coda letters. Of the 216 (6x6x6) syllables in the quasi-regular domain, 204 adopted the short phonetic representation, and 12 adopted the long (i.e., giving 5.6% exceptions). The exceptions in the domain were randomly distributed with no underlying structure determining which inputs formed the exceptions.

Structure of the MLPs

To represent the domains for training an MLP, each of the three letter positions of the input was represented by a six-bit local code with one unit active per letter. Combined, the input vector thus contained 18 units, with three units active per syllable. Similarly for the output, each letter's phonetic representation was represented by a local code, resulting in 6 units each for the onset and coda, and 10 units for the vowel. Combined, the output vector thus contained 22 units with three units active for any syllable. 36 hidden units were used, forming an 18-36-22 feedforward MLP.

Training batch sizes

The underlying structure of a domain is revealed through the items in the training batch, and hence the size of the batch is critical to the amount of information available for the network to learn. We tested three batch sizes: a small size of eight (the batch size used by McCloskey & Cohen, 1989), a medium size of 50 (used by Brousse & Smolensky, 1989) and a large batch size of 108 (50% of the entire data set).

Training procedure

The considerations for three batch sizes in both recency and error rehearsal schemes resulted in 6 conditions to test (3 batch sizes x 2 schemes). For each condition, ten replications were run, each with a different training batch and random initial weights. Training was via backpropagation with weights updated after every pattern presentation (parameters were as used by McCloskey and Cohen (1989), i.e., learning rate 0.1, momentum 0.9, targets 0.1 and 0.9 and initial weight range [-0.3, 0.3]) and continued until all output units were within 0.2 of their corresponding targets for all patterns in the batch or the maximum number of epochs between training batch updates exceeded (18, 46 and 76 epochs for the small medium and large training batch sizes respectively). The initial training batch was randomly selected, as were the items incrementally added (using a non-replacing selection scheme).

Results and Discussion
Results for recency rehearsal

The recency rehearsal results were qualitatively similar to our previous study (see Figures 1-3), showing that recency rehearsal allows all of the batch sizes (even the smallest) to learn the underlying regular structure of the domain. This finding replicates the earlier one that interference on regular structure is not a major concern for quasi-regular domains.

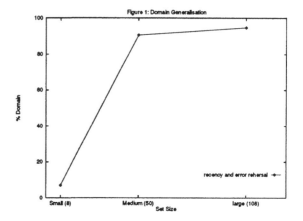

Figure 1: Generalisation to the domain after training the initial batch. This performance characterizes both recency and error rehearsal simulations as the behaviour of the rehearsal schemes is no different at this stage. The small batch size enabled little generalization, indicating that the network had not learned the underlying regular structure behind the domain. Both the medium and large batch sizes enabled the majority of the structure to be learned.

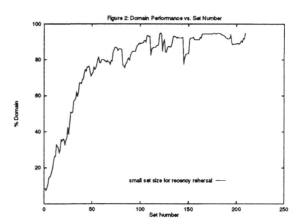

Figure 2: Performance of the domain vs set number for one replication of the small batch size. The graph is qualitatively representative of the behaviour of all replications, showing that immediately after training Set A, the network has learned little of the underlying structure of the domain. As additional items are added to the training batch, performance increases steadily, demonstrating the ability of the MLP to extract structure even from the small batch sizes. This phenomena replicates that observed in earlier simulations using 18 HUs.

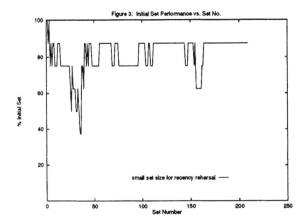

Figure 3: Performance of Set A vs Set Number for the small batch size (same replication as Figure 2). Immediately after training Set A, all items are perfectly learned. Further training results in interference as observed by the drop in performance. The striking aspect of this graph is that as training continues and the MLP learns the underlying structure of the domain, performance on these items returns to a high level. The classic U-shape was observed in all replications.

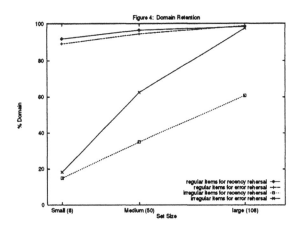

Figure 4: Final performance on the entire domain for both recency and error rehearsal. For both rehearsal schemes, best performance was obtained for the large training batch size (recency - 96.2%; error rehearsal 98.7%). Both schemes show an ability to incorporate irregular items into the regular structure to some degree, however, error rehearsal has incorporated a much higher percentage of the irregular items.

For this simulation, we explored the basis of the performance for the large training batch, as it displayed the best performance: With 36 HUs, recency rehearsal is able to capture the regular structure (98.3% regular items correct), and incorporate some of the irregular structure (60.8% irregular items correct, see Figure 4). We further divided the domain into items present in the training batch, and those that had been dropped. The structure developed in the HUs extended to regular items no longer in the training batch (96.6% correct, see Figure 6) indicating substantial shielding. However, for irregular items that were no longer in the training batch, performance decreased markedly (28.7% correct), showing that recency rehearsal did not shield irregular items from interference after they left the training batch.

With respect to McClelland, McNaughton and O'Reilly's (1994) theory of the H/NC, this result demonstrates that recency rehearsal would not be a suitable model for the interleaving process as it implies that memories that conflict with the majority of the structure in the neocortex would have a low probability of being maintained in the neocortex longer than their duration in the hippocampus.

Comparison of recency and error rehearsal schemes

On all three measures of performance (domain retention, set one retention and shielding - see Figures 4, 5, and 6 respectively) the error rehearsal results were similar to recency rehearsal for regular items, but were markedly improved for irregular items for the medium and large batch sizes. The results indicate two contributing factors - retention of items and shielding:

For the error rehearsal scheme, the domain and set one retention for the large batch size (see Figures 4 and 5) show that regular structure has been maintained with almost all irregular items integrated correctly. These results are understandable given the way in which the error rehearsal scheme retains difficult-to-learn items in the training batch: The error rehearsal scheme concentrated a far higher proportion of irregular items than the initial random distribution, especially for the large training batch (90.0 % of irregular items were retained in the final training batch). Subsequent performance on irregular items is not surprising from a connectionist point of view, but nonetheless may have relevance for cognitive systems as it indicates a method to separate items into functionally regular and irregular, without prior need to define which items are which. It provides one mechanism by which a limited capacity memorisation system could deal with the problems of continually being presented with new items, although retention of items alone is not consistent with the view of the hippocampus as an intermediate term store.

The second contributing factor is due to shielding of items: Figure 6 shows the performance of items that were correct at the end of the simulation but no longer in the training batch (they are the traditional measure in the CI literature). In error rehearsal, a majority of the irregular items were shielded from later interference in the large batch size (58.2% correct compared to 28.7% for recency rehearsal, see Figure 6).

Together the retention of irregular items and shielding provide support for error rehearsal as a suitable model for the interleaving process. Whether such performance is sufficient, or could be further improved is now a feasible question.

There is no direct comparison that can be made with the human data for this type of rehearsal task. Barnes and Underwood (cited by McCloskey & Cohen, 1989) reported retroactive interference of 52% on the AB-AC task, and McCloskey and Cohen (1989) defined CI as substantially lower than this value. At a criterion of 52%, the error rehearsal scheme could be said to be shielding the irregular items no longer in the training batch from CI. Further studies would be required to test the robustness of this result for a variety of quasi-regular domains to have confidence in the numeric value per se, but the results demonstrate a proof of concept.

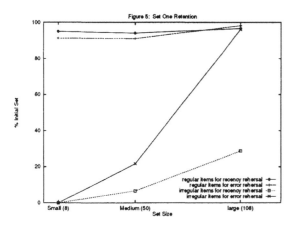

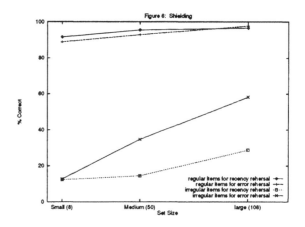

Figure 5: Final retention of the initial batch for both recency and error rehearsal. For both rehearsal schemes, the best performance is achieved for the large batch size (error rehearsal - 98.1%; recency - 92.4%). The results indicate that most of the regular items from set 1 have been retained for all three batch sizes. As in the domain performance (Figure 4), there is a marked difference between the two training schemes for the performance on the irregular items: In particular, for the large batch size on irregular items, error rehearsal gave excellent retention (96.2%) whereas recency rehearsal performance could be considered catastrophic (28.7%).

In conclusion, the simulations have shown that the error rehearsal scheme displays promising ability to not only integrate irregular items into the regular structure of the MLP with a limited training batch size, but also shield items from interference after leaving the current training batch, consistent with theories of the hippocampus as both a finite capacity and an intermediate term memory store.

Acknowledgements

We thank Sally Andrews for use of the data set. This work was partially supported by an ARC grant to the second author.

References

Bakker, P.E (1995). *On the implementation of quasiregular mappings by feedforward connectionist networks*. PhD thesis, Departments of Computer Science and Psychology, The University of Queensland.

Brousse, O. & Smolensky, P. (1989). Virtual memories and massive generalization in connectionist combinatorial learning. In *Proceedings of the 11th Annual Conference of the Cognitive Science Society*, pages 380–387.

Coltheart, M., Curtis, B., Atkins, P., & Haller, M. (1993). Model of reading aloud: Dual route and parallel-distributed-processing approaches. *Psychological Review*, 100(4):589–608.

Dennis, S.J. (1994). *The integration of learning into models of human memory*. PhD thesis, Department of Computer Science, The University of Queensland.

French, R.M. (1991). Using semi-distributed representations to overcome catastrophic forgetting in connectionist networks. Technical Report 51-1991, Center for Research

Figure 6: Shielding of items not present in the final training batch. Regular items are maintained by both schemes. For irregular ones, both schemes are able to maintain some items for the large batch size, but recency rehearsal would be considered catastrophic (28.7%) whereas error rehearsal maintains more than half the irregularities (58.2%).

on Concepts and Cognition, Indiana University, 510 North Fess, Bloomington, Indiana 47408.

French, R.M. (1994). Dynamically constraining connectionist networks to produce distributed, orthogonal representations to reduce catastrophic interference. In *Proceedings of the 16th Annual Conference of the Cognitive Science Society*.

Gray, B. & Wiles, J. (1996). Interference in regular and quasi-regular combinatorial domains: Insights from a two-component memory system. In *Proceedings of the Seventeenth Australian Conference on Neural Networks*. To appear in.

Humphreys, M.S., Bain, J.D. & Pike, R. (1989). Different ways to cue a coherent memory system: A theory for episodic, semantic, and procedural tasks. *Psychological Review*, 96(2):208–233.

Kruschke, J.K. (1992). Alcove: An exemplar-based connectionist model of category learning. *Psychological Review*, 99(1):22–44.

McClelland, J.L., McNaughton, B.L & O'Reilly, R.C. (1994). Why there are complementary learning systems in the hippocampus and neocortex: Insights from the successes and failures of connectionist models of learning and memory. Technical Report PDP.CNS.94.1, Dept. of Psychology, Carnegie Mellon University, ftp://hydra.psy.cmu.edu:/pub/pdp.cns.

McCloskey, M. & Cohen, N.J. (1989) Catastrophic interference in connectionist networks: The sequential learning problem. *The Psychology of Learning and Motivation*, 24:109–165.

O'Reilly, R.C. & McClelland, J.L. (1994). Hippocampal conjunctive encoding, storage and recall: Avoiding a tradeoff. Technical Report PDP.CNS.94.4, Carnegie Mellon University.

Phillips, S. & Wiles, J. (1993). Exponential generalizations from a polynomial number of examples in a combinatorial domain. In *Proceedings, International Joint Conference on Neural Networks, IJCNN'93*, pages 505–508.

Ratcliff, R. (1990). Connectionist models of recognition memory: Constraints imposed by learning and forgetting functions. *Psychological Review*, 97(2):285–308.

Robins, A. (1995). Catastrophic forgetting, rehearsal and pseudorehearsal. *Connection Science*, 7(2):123–146.

Rumelhart, D.E., Hinton, G.E. & Williams, R.J. (1986). Learning internal representations by error propagation. In D. E. Rumelhart and J. L. McClelland, editors, *Parallel distributed processing: Explorations in the microstructure of cognition*, pages 318–362. Bradford Books / MIT Press.

Treves, A. & Rolls, E.T. (1994). Computational analysis of the role of the hippocampus in memory. *Hippocampus*, 4(3):374–391.

Weighting in Similarity Judgements: Investigating the "MAX Hypothesis"

Ulrike Hahn and **Nick Chater** and **Rachel Henley**
Department of Experimental Psychology
University of Oxford
South Parks Rd., Oxford OX1 3UD, England
{ulrike,nick}@psy.ox.ac.uk

Abstract

Most models of similarity assume differential weights for the represented properties. However, comparatively little work has addressed the issue of how the cognitive system assigns these weights. Of particular interest to the modelling of similarity are factors which arise from the comparison process itself. One such factor is defined by Goldstone, Medin & Gentner's (1991) 'MAX Hypothesis'. We present a series of experiments which clarify the main components of 'MAX' and examine its scope.

Introduction

Similarity as an explanatory principle is so ubiquitous in cognition, that stressing its importance borders on banal. Similarity is central to theories of categorization, learning, memory, and problem-solving as virtually any paper on the topic documents (see Goldstone (1994a) for an overview). Its study has two main goals. First is the discovery of the function according to which the various matches and mismatches that the two objects under consideration exhibit are combined into a single similarity judgement. This has been the main focus of similarity research in the past, exemplified by spatial models of similarity or Tversky's contrast model (Shepard, 1962; Tversky, 1977). The second goal, is discovering how the *relevant* properties[1] are determined in the first place: According to what factors are the relevant properties selected from the infinite set of properties any object possesses, and how are they assigned the differential weights most models assume? Given the profound representation-dependence of similarity (Goldstone, Medin & Gentner, 1991; Hahn & Chater, 1996), this latter goal is at least as important as discovering of cognitively plausible similarity functions, but it has remained largely outside the scope of current experimentation and modelling. For theorists, the lack of constraints on which properties are represented gives 'similarity' a flexibility that makes the notion almost vacuous. This has long been at the heart of criticisms of similarity-based explanations in cognition (Goodman, 1972; Medin & Wattenmaker, 1987; Goldstone, Medin & Gentner, 1991).

Though the centrality of selection and weighting to theories of similarity is widely acknowledged, we yet know little about it. In general, two types of influences can be dis-

tinguished: *knowledge-based* and formal, non-knowledge-based factors which we will refer to as *process principles* (see also Goldstone, Medin & Gentner (1991); Hahn & Chater (1996)). As an example of knowledge-based factors, one can think of the impact that 'theories' (scientific or informal) have on what we consider to be important properties of an object (Medin & Wattenmaker, 1987). Process principles, on the other hand, are influences arising from the comparison process itself. A prominent example is Tversky's 'diagnosticity principle' (Tversky, 1977). In assessing the similarity structure of a set of objects we increase the weight of properties which enable further subdivisions of the set, and depress those which are common to all members of the set in question. Hence, for example, the feature 'real' has little diagnostic value in the set of 'mammals' since it is common to all. When the set is extended to include Pegasus, unicorns, and mermaids, however, the diagnostic value, and thus weight, of 'real' is considerably increased, thus indicating a systematic relationship between feature weights and sub-clusters of objects within a set.

Other examples of process principles proposed and experimentally investigated in the psychology literature are the 'focussing hypothesis' (Tversky, 1977) and the role of 'structural alignment' (Goldstone, 1994b). Process principles must be considered central to the study of similarity, not only because they embody constraints on the all-important feature selection and weighting process, but because their general, formal nature makes them candidates for inclusion in future, more explanatory, models of similarity.

It is such a process principle—Goldstone, Medin & Gentner's "MAX-hypothesis" (1991)—that we wish to discuss in this paper. In the following, we will review the MAX hypothesis, present a more explicit version of its various components and present new experimental results. Finally, we discuss implications of these results for the modelling of similarity.

The "MAX-hypothesis"

Goldstone et al. (1991)

The MAX-hypothesis was first put forth and experimentally investigated by Goldstone, Medin & Gentner (1991). It proposes that property weights are, in part, dependent on the particular *type* they belong to as well as the extent to which this type dominates in the stimuli of the similarity comparison.

---

[1] We use 'property' in the widest possible sense to encompass attributes or relations, binary features or continuous dimensions.

The two types in question are *attributes*, i.e. one-place predicates (e.g. 'color(X)'), and *relations*, that is, predicates with an arity of two or more (e.g. 'larger-than(X,Y)'). Specifically, Goldstone et al. claim

"(1) attributional similarities are pooled together, and relational similarities are pooled together, and (2) the weight that a similarity has on the final similarity judgement increases with the size of the pool to which it belongs" (p.228.)

or:

"MAX claims that relations and attributes are psychologically distinct, that similarities are classified as relational or attributional types, and that people attend more to similarities belonging to whichever similarity type is greatest" (p.228.)

This can be illustrated with a brief example. Imagine a group of five stimuli *A,B,C,D,* and *T* as illustrated in Figure 1. Subjects are asked to assess the respective similarities of *A,B,C,* and *D* to the "target stimulus" either through direct judgements (e.g. 'how similar are *A* and *T*?') or a series of forced choices (e.g. 'which is more similar to *T, A* or *B*?').[2]

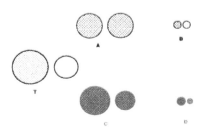

Figure 1: example stimuli

One strategy subjects could adopt is to assign differential weights to the component properties (relations or attributes) *uniformly* for the entire stimulus set; e.g. a match in "size" is twice important as the relation "bigger than". By contrast, the MAX-hypothesis predicts that the weight of relations is differentially boosted in stimuli in which relational matches to the target dominate (here *D*) and are depressed where attribute matches dominate (here *A*). In other words, 'bigger than' is more important in *D* which also shares the target's 'darker than' relation, than it is in *A*. This means that weighting of a property depends not only on its intrinsic salience, but is determined in systematic interaction with the other properties of the stimulus.

The MAX-hypothesis was supported in a series of experiments by Goldstone, Medin & Gentner (1991). Our interest

has been to tease apart various claims implicit in the MAX-hypothesis as stated there, and, on the basis of this, to investigate its generality. We begin with our theoretical considerations.

Spelling out the underlying claims

The MAX-hypothesis involves two claims: first, that relations and attributes are 'pooled' and second, that the largest pool is boosted. Both aspects can be regarded independently. The fact that the largest pool is boosted may be due to a more general principle, which we call the "Closest Dimension Principle" (CD), which can apply to single properties and pools alike. Similarly, pooling may not be restricted to relations and attributes.[3] We address these in turn.

1. The Closest-Dimension Principle.
Part (2) of the MAX-hypothesis as quoted above states that the pool which 'maximizes overall similarity' is selectively boosted in weight. We suspected this was an instance of a more general principle —to be called the "Closest Dimension Principle"—which *generally* states that the dimensions exhibiting the greatest similarity to those of the target are boosted. For example, imagine a set of stimuli differing from the target on two dimensions, size and shade. The Closest Dimension Principle predicts that the importance given to 'shade' as opposed to 'size' will be maximal in the stimulus which is *closest* to the target in shade, whereas 'size' will be maximally weighted in the stimulus closest in size.

Boosting the 'largest pool', then, is merely an instance of this principle: the dimensional value of interest is the size of the particular pool. Through pooling, the pooled properties become a single unit to which the CD-principle is applied.

Experiments 1 and 2, described below, investigated the CD principle in non-pooling (i.e. single dimension) situations, both for (singularly treated) attributes and relations.

2. Pooling.
We suggest that the cognitive system may not adopt a principle which applies uniquely to relations and attributes, but may use a more flexible approach. Perhaps the scope of 'pooling' is both wider and narrower than indicated by the MAX-hypothesis. We expect *pools of other types*, that is pooling along lines other than relation/attribute. We also expect cases were pooling according to relations or attributes fails, because these pools are not suggestive in the particular materials. Pooling, we think, may profitably be viewed as a kind of conceptual 'chunking'.

This suggests a wide field of research into the types of pools subjects form, into pool-size, and into the conditions under which pooling occurs. Experiments 3a, b, and c investigate alternative types of pools, whether relations and attributes are necessarily pooled, and whether alternative pools might be preferred over pooling according relations and attributes.

---

[2]Both forced choice and direct judgements give the same results (Goldstone, Medin & Gentner, 1991).

[3]This possibility is already suggested in Goldstone, Medin & Gentner (1991).

Experimental Results

The CD principle

Principles of Stimulus Design for Experiments 1 and 2
The basic structure of our materials is the same for Experiments 1 and 2 and follows Goldstone, Medin & Gentner's (1991) original experiments. The stimuli come in groups of 5 (as in Fig. 1), one of which is the "target" stimulus which serves as the reference point; subjects are asked to indicate 'which is more similar to T, A or B?'. For reasons of experimental control, total or overall similarity to the target must be equal for each of the four non-target stimuli, or more precisely *would be equal if the CD principle did not apply*. To this end stimuli are constructed according to the following pattern. For each group there are two properties which are varied, such as 'height' and 'degree of tiltedness'. These properties are manifest in five different levels, distributed as follows: The target stimulus has the maximal level for both properties i.e. a 'dimensional value' of 5/5. Next, Stimulus A, has the closest dimensional value for one property and the furthest on the other, i.e. 4/1. Stimuli B and C have the middle values 3/2 and 2/3; D, finally, has 1/4. Hence for all stimuli, the overall "distance" to the target is equal (i.e. five).

The CD principle predicts that 'dimension 1' is selectively boosted in stimulus A and 'dimension 2' selectively boosted in D. This is evidenced as a change in preference of dimension as a criterion for decision. In comparing A and B to T, dimension 1 is viewed as most salient whereas in the judgement C, D dimension 2 becomes more salient. Alternatively, subjects could boost the furthest-dimension or merely stick to one dimensional weighting throughout.

Experiment 1: The CD-Principle and Relations

Materials In Experiment 1, the properties of interest were two single *relations* present in the the stimuli. These relations were 'dimensionalized' to fit the above schema. This is clearest with an example: dimension 1, for instance, could be based on the relation 'distance(x,y)' between two component parts of the stimuli. The distance between x and y in the target stimulus forms the base-line, maximal value. We then construct four stimuli with increasing distance between x and y; the distance closest to that found in the target (i.e. the shortest) forms 'level 1' of the schema above, the next closest 'level 2' and so on. The relations manipulated in this way were spacing, displacement, alignment, overlapping of components, occlusion, symmetry, and relative position. A sample group in which relative distance and occlusion were used is shown in Figure 2.[4]

We used 8 different stimulus sets which involved different kinds of component objects (lines, circles, squares etc.) and different pairs of relations as the two manipulated dimensions. The 32 judgements of interest (4 per group) were presented in booklets, with three trials to the page. Each trial consisted of a target and two comparison stiumuli. The subject was asked to indicate which of the two comparision stimuli was most

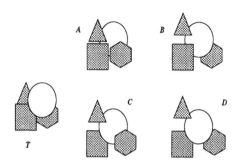

Figure 2: A stimulus group from Exp. 1.

similar to the target by circling it. The order of the comparisons was randomized with the constraint that no two judgements from the same group appear on the same page. The internal order of each comparison pair was randomized and counterblanced between two groups of subjects.

Participants The 14 participants, of which equal numbers were male and female, were members of the departmental subject panel, or students of the university. They represented a wide range of backgrounds and were aged between 18 and 50.

Results The raw data consist of the preferences indicated on the comparisons A,B; A,C; C,D and B,D for each group. These can be classified as following the pattern predicted by the CD principle, as following the opposite of CD, that is boosting the *furthest* dimension (FD), or as using the same weighting throughout. On the null-hypothesis –assumption of a 'same-weighting-throughout' strategy– CD-patterns and FD-patterns are noise and should be expected in equal numbers. Following the logic of Goldstone, Medin & Gentner (1991), subjects are classified as CD or FD subjects depending on which pattern they produced more frequently. This classification yielded 13 CD-subjects and no FD-subjects. 1 subject had equal numbers of CD and FD patterns and so was left out of the analysis. The hypothesis that there would be more CD subjects than FD subjects was tested using a one-tailed binomial test. The null-hypothesis was rejected at level $p < 0.0005$.

Experiment 2: Attributes Experiment 2 differs from Experiment 1 only in that the two manipulated dimensions were attributes, not relations. The main attributes used were shading, size, and orientation. A sample group, manipulating curvature and line-thickness is shown in Figure 3.

The 18 participants were from the departmental subject panel or postgraduate members of the university. Of these, 12 were CD-subjects, and 3 were FD-subjects. 3 subjects had equal numbers of CD and FD patterns and, thus, dropped out of the analysis. There were significantly more CD-subjects than FD-subjects with the null hypothesis rejected at $p < 0.018$, again using a one-tailed binomial test.

In summary, the data in both experiment seem to confirm the Closest-Dimension principle as an important factor

---

[4]Letters, here and in the following, are added to aid the reader; they were not part of the actual stimuli.

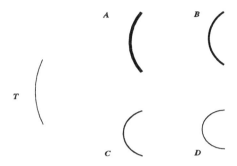

Figure 3: A stimulus group from Exp. 2.

in property weighting.

"Pooling"

Design The point of the remaining three experiments was to investigate the generality of the MAX-hypothesis in two directions: whether other types of properties 'pool' and whether attributes and relations necessarily pool. To address the first issue, we designed objects with properties that could be pooled on the basis of *'theme'*. Themes are groupings such as "colour-related" or "to-do-with-size", which might unite an attribute and a relation in a common pool. For example, the attribute '(actual) size' and the relation 'larger-than' might form the basis of a 'size-related' pool. 'Themes' always involved one attribute and one relation. There were two 'themes' per group, i.e. 2 relations and 2 attributes. Hence, it could be assessed directly whether subjects preferred pooling by theme or by relation/attribute. This can be illustrated with Fig. 1 above. Subjects could pool according to attributes and relations, leading to an increased similarity of stimulus *A* (which matches the target closely on the attributes 'size' and 'shade') and *D* (which matches on the relations 'larger-than' and 'darker-than' between the left and right component) to the target. Alternatively, subjects could form the theme pools 'size-related' and 'colour-related', boosting the similarity of stimulus *B* (matching the target closely in actual shade and the 'darker-than' relation) and *C* (matching closely on actual size and the 'bigger-than' relation). In addition each group had two 'control' stimuli, *E* and *F*, with no (apparent) opportunities for pooling, to allow baseline assessment of whether pooling was occurring at all, and, hence, responsible for any difference in subject's preference between 'theme-pool' objects and 'relation/attribute-pool' objects.

The various properties were distributed across objects according to the scheme in Table 1.

As indicated in the table, the target stimulus for each group has the maximum value for all properties. The overall similarity of the remaining stimuli to the target, disregarding pooling, is held constant. A difficulty is posed by the stimuli which require attribute matches in the absence of relational matches (in particular, object *A*), since two objects cannot completely match attributionally without matching relationally as well. Our strategy was to take middle values or averages in order

to approximate this attributional match. The imperfection of this match was balanced by adding a corresponding decrement to the attributional match in the remaining stimuli even where an exact match would have been possible. A sample group, where this can be seen, is given in Figure 4.

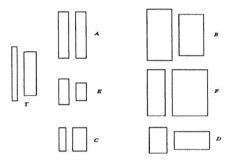

Figure 4: A stimulus group from Exp. 3.

In Figure 4, *A* matches closely in actual size even though it lacks the larger-than relation; [5] The attributional 'match' in actual-size of the theme-stimulus *C* is designed to deviate from the target's values by a corresponding degree, by making both of the component objects slightly larger than in the target.

For maximal experimental control, each subject was asked to give all 12 judgements per group (at 8 groups a total of 96 judgements). In the following, however, we will analyze and present these results as three experiments. All other factors were kept as in Experiment 1 and 2. Participants were 18 members of the university.

Experiment 3a: Pooling According to Themes The first experiment, looks only at the similarity judgements for the 'theme' objects and the two controls, aiming to establish whether pooling according to themes can be found. To this end, the judgements pertaining to the 'theme' stimuli (*B* and *C*) and the two controls are extracted from the 96 judgements. This yields a set which is isomorphic to experiments 1 and 2[6] and which can be analyzed in exactly the same way. What was the single closest dimension in these experiments is now a potential pool. Hence, the MAX-hypothesis applies directly: subjects form pools of properties (here, according to theme) and differentially boost the weight of the properties in the largest pool (hence applying the CD-principle no longer to individual properties but to pools). Following Goldstone, Medin & Gentner (1991), judgements displaying this pattern are classified as MAX. Patterns were the smallest pool is preferred are classified as MIN. Patterns explicable with a single set of weights throughout are classified as "independent". Then subjects are classified as MAX-subjects

[5] Similarly, *A* in Figure 1 closely matches the target in actual colour and actual size, although it lacks the relations darker-than and larger-than.

[6] and now directly corresponds to Goldstone, Medin & Gentner's (1991) experiments except that potential pools are themes instead of relation and attributes.

Possible Combinations of Properties							
	A	B	C	D	E	F	T
relation-*theme1*	-	+	-	+	+	-	+
relation-*theme2*	-	-	+	+	-	+	+
attribute-*theme1*	+	+	-	-	-	+	+
attribute-*theme2*	+	-	+	-	+	-	+

Table 1: The table gives the basic object specification for experiments 3a,3b,3c which allow both relation/attribute and theme pools.

or MIN-subjects, depending on which type of pattern dominates in their results. The MAX-hypothesis predicts more MAX than MIN subjects, while the null-hypothesis (feature independence, i.e. no-pooling) predicts equal numbers. Of the 18 subjects, 14 were MAX-subjects, and only 1 a MIN-subject. 3 subjects had equal numbers of MAX- and MIN-patterns and, hence, were excluded from the analysis. The difference between numbers of MAX- and numbers of MIN-subjects was significant; using a one-tailed binomial test, the null-hypothesis was rejected at $p < 0.0005$.

Experiment 3b: Pooling According to Relations and Attributes The second, Experiment 3b, looks only at the 'relations' and 'attribute' stimuli (A and D in the table above) and the two control objects, to establish whether Goldstone, Medin & Gentner's (1991) pooling of relations and attributes is replicated with our stimuli. The analysis follows directly that of Experiment 3b. This replication failed; in fact, MIN-marginally exceeded MAX subjects. In actual numbers, we found 7 MAX-subjects, 9 MIN-subjects, and 2 subjects with equal numbers of MAX- and MIN- patterns.

Experiment 3c: Pooling-Preferences - Themes vs. Relations/Attributes In the last of the three, Experiment 3c, we directly compared the two theme-stimuli with the 'relations' and the 'attributes' stimulus. Unsurprisingly, given the previous two results, subjects overwhelmingly preferred pooling according to themes (MAX-subjects: 15, MIN-subjects: 2, equal numbers: 1), with the null-hypothesis (independence, i.e. no pooling) rejected by two-tailed binomial test at $p < 0.002$.

Discussion

We identified two seperate factors implicit in the original formulation of the MAX-hypothesis, the Closest Dimension Principle and the existence of pooling. Our results confirm the CD-principle both for single properties (attributes or relations) and for pools. As regards pooling, our results indicate both that pooling can occur along other lines than relations and attributes and that pooling by relations and attributes can fail. This suggests that, contrary to Goldstone, Medin & Gentner's (1991) assumptions, the relations/attributes distinction is not *per se* cognitively salient enough to evoke pooling. Thus, the criteria determining whether or not a particular pool is salient or suggestive remain to be determined. We are threatened with a certain explanatory regress; the task of

determing property weights, i.e. salience, requires determining the salience of potential pools. Only future work can tell whether general principles can be uncovered here.

In the meantime, these results leave the modeller in an awkward position. The Closest Dimension Principle, whether it operates on single dimensions or on pools, has damning consequences for traditional models of similarity such as the contrast model and spatial models of similarity (see Goldstone, Medin & Gentner (1991)). These models omit the feature weighting process, assuming a set of weighted features or dimensions as given. The operation of the CD-principle, however, is *local to the individual comparison*, e.g. target/object1.[7] This means that each individual pairwise comparison requires a different set of weights. There is no single set of weights, even for a group of 5 stimuli as simple as that in Fig. 1. Hence, the contrast model or spatial models of similarity —or any other model which assumes weighted properties as primitives–cannot fit this group of stimuli, but only individual pairwise comparisons. Hence, these models cannot be used to *explain* the similarity structure of even this simple group. They can be extended to include the systematicity in the group only by inclusion of the weighting process itself.

In this respect, however, our results are problematic. They indicate that the conditions under which pooling occurs, may be far more diverse than Goldstone, Medin & Gentner (1991) suggest. Whether they are at all predictable enough to allow inclusion in a formal model remains to be seen.

Acknowledgements

Thanks go to Todd Bailey and three anonymous reviewers who provided helpful comments on earlier versions of this manuscript; remaining errors are, of course, our responsibility. Ulrike Hahn is supported by ESRC grant No. R004293341442.

References

Goldstone, R. (1994a). The Role of Similarity in Categorization: Providing a Groundwork. *Cognition*, 52, 125—157.

---

[7] please note again that the forced choice design of our experiments is extrinsic to the CD-principle as demonstrated by Goldstone, Medin & Gentner (1991).

Goldstone, R. (1994b). Similarity, Interactive Activation, and Mapping. *Journal of Experimental Psychology: Learning, Memory, and Cognition,* 20, 3—28.

Goldstone, R & Medin, D. L. & Gentner, D. (1991) Relational Similarity and the Nonindependance of Features in Similarity Judgements. *Cognitive Psychology,* 23, 222—262.

Goodman, N. (1972). Chapter: Seven Strictures on Similarity. *Problems and Projects.* Indianapolis: Bobbs-Merill Comp.

Hahn, U. and Chater, N. (1996). Concepts and Similarity. *In:* Lamberts, K. & Shanks, D. R. (Eds.), *Knowledge, Concepts, and Categories.* London: UCL Press.

Medin, D. L. & Wattenmaker, W. (1987). Category Cohesiveness, Theories, and Cognitive Archaeology. *In:* Neisser, U. (Ed.), *Concepts and Conceptual Development: Ecological and Intellectual Factors in Categorization.* Cambridge: Cambridge University Press.

Shepard, R. (1962). The analysis of proximities: Multidimensional scaling with an unknown distance function. *Psychometrika,* 125.

Tversky, A. (1977). Features of Similarity. *Psychological Review,* 84, 327—352.

Incremental Centering and Center Ambiguity

Udo Hahn & Michael Strube

(LİF) Computational Linguistics Research Group
Freiburg University
Europaplatz 1
D-79085 Freiburg, Germany
{hahn,strube}@coling.uni-freiburg.de

Abstract

In this paper, we present a model of anaphor resolution within the framework of the centering model. The consideration of an incremental processing mode introduces the need to manage structural ambiguity at the center level. Hence, the centering framework is further refined to account for local and global parsing ambiguities which propagate up to the level of center representations, yielding moderately adapted data structures for the centering algorithm.

Introduction

Psycholinguistic studies have revealed ample evidence for the incrementality of human language comprehension, not only at the phrasal and clausal level but also at the discourse level of anaphora resolution (Just & Carpenter, 1987; Sanford & Garrod, 1989). Correspondingly, incremental processing has also become a major challenge for cognitively plausible, computational models of natural language understanding (Jurafsky, 1992; Sturt, 1995), and text understanding (Granger et al., 1986) in particular. Introducing incrementality into the centering model (Grosz et al., 1995), the methodological framework for our approach to the resolution of (pro)nominal anaphora, however, is not at all straightforward. In particular, incremental processing introduces (local) ambiguities at significant rates, which cannot be properly accounted for at the center level in the original model. Though centering strives for the elimination of *referential* ambiguities, the implications of *structural* ambiguities have been completely ignored so far.

We have gathered some data, summarized in Table 1, to give an empirical assessment of the relevance of the issue under investigation. Altogether 47 texts (product reviews from the information technology domain) were analyzed which consist of 32291 words, with 230 occurrences of (un)ambiguous pronouns.

ambiguous	174	(76 %)		
locally			145	(63 %)
globally			29	(13 %)
unambiguous	56	(24 %)		

Table 1: Ambiguity Distribution Patterns of Pronouns

Given our text corpus, 87% of the sentences could have been processed by the original, non-incremental centering algorithm (only global ambiguities could not). This rate drops dramatically to only 24% when we assume an incremental operation mode. These data reflect the impact of the local ambiguities which are resolved at the sentence level as the parse proceeds and thus are not an issue for the original (non-incremental) centering algorithm. The latter percentage rate, however, gives a realistic picture of the relevance of the problem under scrutiny when one opts for a cognitive adequate, incremental model of text understanding.

Brief Survey of the Centering Model

The framework of our model of anaphora resolution is provided by the well-known *centering* mechanism (Grosz et al., 1995), for which psycholinguistic evidences are provided by Gordon et al. (1993) and Brennan (1995), lacking, however, the consideration of incrementality of language processing. The theory of centering is intended to model the local coherence of discourse, i.e., coherence among the utterances U_i in a particular discourse segment (say, a paragraph of a text). Local coherence is opposed to global coherence, i.e., coherence with other segments in the discourse. Discourse entities serving to link one utterance to other utterances in a particular discourse segment are organized in terms of centers. Each utterance U_i in a discourse segment is assigned a set of *forward-looking centers*, $C_f(U_i)$, and a unique *backward-looking center*, $C_b(U_i)$. The forward-looking centers of U_i depend only on the expressions that constitute that utterance, previous utterances provide no constraints on $C_f(U_i)$. The elements of $C_f(U_i)$ are partially ordered to reflect relative prominence in U_i. The most highly ranked element of $C_f(U_i)$ that is *realized* in U_{i+1} (i.e., is associated with an expression that has a valid interpretation in the underlying semantic/conceptual representation language) is the $C_b(U_{i+1})$. The ranking imposed on the elements of the C_f reflects the assumption that the most highly ranked element of $C_f(U_i)$ is the most preferred antecedent of an anaphoric expression in U_{i+1}, while the remaining elements are (partially) ordered according to decreasing preference for establishing referential links.

The theory of centering, in addition, defines several transition relations across pairs of adjacent utterances (e.g., continuation, retainment, smooth and rough shift), which differ from each other according to the degree by which successive backward-looking centers are confirmed or rejected, and, if they are confirmed, whether they correspond to the most highly ranked element of the current forward-looking centers or not. The theory claims, above all, that to the extent a discourse adheres to all these centering constraints (e.g., realization constraints on pronouns, preferences among types of center transitions), its local coherence will increase and the inference load placed upon the hearer will decrease. Therefore, the tremendous importance of fleshing out the relevant and most restrictive, though still general centering constraints.

Incremental Centering and Ambiguity

In this section, we argue for an extension of the centering model that accounts for ambiguities generated by the incremental operation of the parsing component of a text understanding system. Though we also provide for mechanisms that deal with global structural ambiguities, we here concentrate on local structural ambiguities in the phrase which contains an anaphor. These can be directly attributed to the *incremental* processing mode, where each lexical element is integrated in syntactic structures and semantically interpreted as early as possible. As the anaphora resolution is also executed incrementally, *local* syntactic ambiguities (which cause different referential entities to emerge at the semantic/conceptual level of interpretation) must be accessible through the data structures of the centering algorithm in order to maintain local, alternative center readings.

Consider the text fragment ((1) – (3)) taken from the corpus of product reviews:

(1) In der Leistung konnte *die LPS 105* ebenfalls weitgehend überzeugen.
(As far as performance is concerned, *the LPS 105* also produced rather compelling results.)

(2) Bei der mittleren Zugriffszeit (16,5 ms) erreicht *diese Festplatte die Seagate ST-3144*, womit *sie* in dieser Disziplin den zweiten Platz erzielt.
(Regarding the mean access time (16,5 ms) *this hard disk* compares to the *Seagate ST-3144*, by which *it* scores second-best in this category.)

(3) Auch beim Datendurchsatz erweist *sie* sich als hochkarätiges Produkt.
(Also, considering data throughput *it* turns out to be a high-caliber product.)

Sentence (1) has a unique structural analysis, the *forward-looking centers* (C_f) consist of two semantic/conceptual elements, the LPS-105 hard disk and PERFORMANCE (cf. Table 2). In sentence (2), a nominal anaphor occurs, *"diese Festplatte" (this hard disk)*, which is resolved to LPS-105 from the previous sentence. Unfortunately, the noun phrase *"diese Festplatte"* is nominative as well as accusative and may be alternatively attached to the verb *"erreicht" (compares to)* both in its subject and object role (we assume a dependency grammar framework as briefly described in the following section). In this state, one cannot determine which of the grammatical functions is the correct one, thus a structural ambiguity has been identified. Since the second NP in this sentence *("die Seagate ST-3144")* is ambiguous with respect to both of these

cases, too, the parser produces two structurally and conceptually ambiguous readings (with inverted subject/object instantiations; given appropriate stress marking both readings are equally plausible). As a consequence, two different C_fs[1] have to be created (cf. Table 2), which indicate two different center transitions, *viz.* continuation vs. retention, eligible at the end of the analysis of the second sentence. This choice option becomes crucial for the resolution of the pronoun *"sie" (it)* in sentence (3), as it depends on the appropriate selection of one of the two different C_fs. In the case of the CONTINUE transition (the C_b of the previous utterance is also the highest ranked element of the C_fs of the current utterance) LPS-105 is preferred as the antecedent, while in the case of the RETAIN transition (the C_b of the previous utterance is not the highest ranked element of the C_fs of the current utterance) it is ST-3144. Depending on how the text actually proceeds either one is equally possible. So, for the actual anaphora resolution the transition type preferences (Rule 2 in Grosz et al. (1995)) are of no help at all to decide among any of these variants. We, therefore, conclude that additional representation devices have to be supplied to keep track of these structurally induced ambiguities at the center level.

(1)	Cb: Cf:	LPS-105: LPS 105 [LPS-105: LPS 105, PERFORMANCE: Leistung]	CONTINUE
(2)	Cb1: Cf1:	LPS-105: Festplatte [LPS-105: Festplatte, ST-3144: Seagate ST-3144, ACCESS-TIME: Zugriffszeit, RANK: Platz, CATEGORY: Disziplin]	CONTINUE
	Cb2: Cf2:	LPS-105: Festplatte [ST-3144: Seagate ST-3144, LPS-105: Festplatte, ACCESS-TIME: Zugriffszeit, RANK: Platz, CATEGORY: Disziplin]	RETAIN

Table 2: Centering Data for Sentences (1) and (2)

Grammar Constraints on Anaphora

We now consider several constraints on anaphora which apply both to the sentence-level and text-level of anaphora analysis. These descriptions will later serve as a framework for considering local ambiguity within the centering approach. We here adapt the common binding criteria to the methodological requirements of a fully lexicalized dependency grammar (DG), introducing the central notion of *d-binding*[2] (cf. Strube

---

[1] To simplify the presentation, we will assume the canonical ordering on C_f based on grammatical roles, *viz.* SUBJECT > OBJECT(S) > OTHERS (Grosz et al., 1995, p.214). We have clear evidences, whatsoever, that this is inappropriate, for German and related free word order languages at least, and argue for ordering criteria based on the functional information structure of utterances in terms of topic/comment or theme/rheme patterns in a companion paper (Strube & Hahn, 1996).

[2] The definition of *d-binding* (cf. Table 3) corresponds to the *governing category* in GB terminology, which relies upon the notion of

& Hahn (1995) for an elaborated discussion of *d-binding* criteria). These constraints hold for intra- as well as intersentential anaphora, thus seamlessly incorporating the discourse level of grammatical description (for a comprehensive survey of the grammar formalism, cf. Hahn et al. (1994)).[3]

The possible antecedents that can be reached via anaphoric relations, irrespective of whether they occur within the current sentence or beyond, are described by *isPotentialAnaphoricAntecedentOf* (cf. Table 4), which incorporates *d-binds* (cf. Table 3).

$\mathbf{x}$ **d-binds** y :$\Leftrightarrow$
(x head$^+$ y)
$\wedge \neg \exists$ z: ((x head$^+$ z) $\wedge$ (z head$^+$ y)
$\quad \wedge$ (z $isa_C{}^*$ finiteVerb
$\quad \vee$ (z head u
$\quad\quad \wedge$ ((z spec u $\wedge$ u $isa_C{}^*$ DetPossessive)
$\quad\quad \vee$ (z saxGen u $\wedge$ u $isa_C{}^*$ Noun)
$\quad\quad \vee$ (z ppAtt u $\wedge$ u $isa_C{}^*$ Noun)
$\quad\quad \vee$ (z genAtt u $\wedge$ u $isa_C{}^*$ Noun)))))

Table 3: D-binding Constraint

$\mathbf{x}$ **isPotentialAnaphoricAntecedentOf** y :$\Leftrightarrow$
$\neg\exists$ z: (z d-binds x $\wedge$ z d-binds y)
$\quad \wedge$ ((∃ u: u d-binds y $\wedge$ u head$^+$ x) $\rightarrow$ x left$^+$ y)

Table 4: Constraint on Potential Anaphoric Antecedents

PronAnaphorTest from Table 5 contains the major grammatical agreement constraint (covering gender, number and person) for some anaphoric pronoun and its nominal antecedent, while *NomAnaphorTest* from Table 6 captures the major conceptual subsumption constraint for the nominal antecedent and a corresponding anaphoric definite NP.

---

c-command, while the DG constraint on anaphora (cf. Table 4) relates to the major binding principles of GB (Chomsky, 1981). An approach to the incremental computation of intrasentential coreferences based on Chomsky's binding theory is given by Merlo (1993).

[3] For the definitions of the grammatical predicates below, the following conventions hold: isa_C denotes the subclass relation among lexical classes (parts of speech), $\sqcup$ the unification operation, $\perp$ the inconsistent element. Let u be a complex feature term and l a feature name, then the extraction $u \backslash l$ yields the value of l in u. If l is defined, $u \backslash l$ gives $\perp$ in all other cases. Semantic and conceptual knowledge is represented via a KL-ONE-style classification-based knowledge representation language (MacGregor & Bates, 1987), with isa_F denoting the subclass relation among concepts. Furthermore, *object.attribute* denotes the value of the property *attribute* at *object* and the symbol self refers to the current lexical item. The grammar specification language, in addition, incorporates topological primitives for relations within dependency trees, such as "x occurs left of y" and "x is head of y"; rel$^+$ and rel* denote the transitive and transitive/reflexive closure of a relation rel, respectively. The following dependency relations will be used: specifier-of (spec), Saxon genitive (saxGen), prepositional and genitival attribute (ppAtt, genAtt).

PronAnaphorTest (pro, ante): $\Leftrightarrow$
ante $isa_C{}^*$ Nominal $\wedge$
((pro.features$\backslash$self$\backslash$agr$\backslash$gen)
$\quad\sqcup$ (ante.features$\backslash$self$\backslash$agr$\backslash$gen) $\neq \perp$) $\wedge$
((pro.features $\backslash$self$\backslash$agr$\backslash$num)
$\quad\sqcup$ (ante.features$\backslash$self$\backslash$agr$\backslash$num) $\neq \perp$) $\wedge$
((pro.features$\backslash$self$\backslash$agr$\backslash$pers)
$\quad\sqcup$ (ante.features$\backslash$self$\backslash$agr$\backslash$pers) $\neq \perp$)

Table 5: Constraint on Pronominal Anaphora

NomAnaphorTest (defNP, ante): $\Leftrightarrow$
ante $isa_C{}^*$ Nominal $\wedge$
((defNP.features $\backslash$self$\backslash$agr$\backslash$num)
$\quad\sqcup$ (ante.features$\backslash$self$\backslash$agr$\backslash$num) $\neq \perp$) $\wedge$
ante.concept $isa_F{}^*$ defNP.concept

Table 6: Constraint on Nominal Anaphora

Resolution of Anaphora

The actor computation model (Agha & Hewitt, 1987) provides the background for the procedural interpretation of lexicalized grammar specifications, as those given in the previous section, in terms of so-called word actors. Word actors communicate via asynchronous message passing; an actor can only send messages to other actors it knows about, its so-called acquaintances. The arrival of a message at an actor triggers the execution of a method that is composed of grammatical predicates (for a survey, cf. Neuhaus & Hahn (1996)).

The basic data structures for anaphora resolution are organized as acquaintances of specific actors. Besides word actors for the lexical level of analysis, phrases are encapsulated in *PhraseActors*, and one or more *PhraseActors* which cover the same sequence of words but assign different syntactic interpretations (local ambiguities) to it are encapsulated in *ContainerActors*. For every sentence, its associated unique *ParserActor* is acquainted with a *CenteringActor* which, for reasons of ambiguity handling, is acquainted with one or more *CenterActors*. Each of these *CenterActors* has a preferentially ordered list of *forward-looking centers* (C_f) and a single *backward-looking center* (C_b). The usual criteria for centering apply at this representation level (Grosz et al., 1995). We extend this basic model, however, in that we provide several instances of *CenteringActors* to account for local ambiguities within an utterance, while different *CenterActors* represent global ambiguities of single utterances. Hence, unambiguous centering is a special case, where a single *CenteringActor* is only acquainted with a single *CenterActor*.

Anaphora analysis encompasses the procedural interpretation of the declarative constraints given in the previous section. For *pronominal* anaphors, the *SearchPronAntecedent* message is triggered by the successful syntactic test that the pronoun may be modifier of its head. For *nominal* anaphors, the *SearchNomAntecedent* message is triggered by the attachment of a definite determiner as a modifier to its head noun and a similar syntactic head-modifier compatibility test[4]. We now describe the main threads of the algorithm for local ambiguity management during anaphora resolution (cf. Fig. 1).

Consider, e.g., sentence (2) of the already introduced text fragment. An attachment of the definite NP *"diese Festplatte" (this hard disk)* at its prospective head *"erreicht" (compares to)* is tried. Since the NP is ambiguous with respect to case, a local ambiguity accounting for the subject and object reading is created[5].

1, 1a: Two different *SearchNomAntecedent* messages with the argument *theAttachment* (the dependency relation between the NP and *"erreicht"*, i.e., either subject or object) are sent simultaneously from the *Anaphor* to the *PhraseActor*.

2–4, 2a–4a: Both messages are forwarded from the *PhraseActor* to the *ContainerActor*, the *ParserActor*, and the *CenteringActor* of the preceding sentence.

5, 5a: It is crucial that for every *SearchAntecedent* message which reaches the *CenteringActor*, that actor is copied, leaving the master copy unchanged. This guarantees that each locally ambiguous phrase which contains an anaphor manipulates its own centering data structures.

6, 6a: The messages are distributed to all *CenterActors* where the argument *theAttachment* is copied in order to provide for consistent data in a distributed, concurrent environment (the copy action is of relevance only in those cases where global and local ambiguities are interleaved).

7, 7a: *NomAnaphorTest* succeeds in both cases (the most preferred element of the C_f of sentence (1), viz. LPS-105 fulfills the required conceptual subsumption condition relative to *"Festplatte" (hard disk)*).

8, 8a: Hence two *AntecedentFound* messages are sent to each corresponding anaphor.

9, 9a: The semantic predicate *permit*[6] succeeds with respect to the word actors *LPS 105 (Festplatte)* and *erreicht* for both argument positions, thus the dependency relations *theAttachment*, viz. subject and object, are confirmed.

10, 10a: The resolved anaphors send an *AnaphorSucceed* message to the corresponding *CenterActors*.

11, 11a: At these *CenterActors* the determined antecedents (LPS-105) are removed from the corresponding C_f lists. The removal of the antecedent from the C_f list prevents

---

[4]We strictly separate the search for the proper antecedent and the evaluation of its conceptual compatibility as the modifier of a head.

[5]The bold numbers in the text and the edge numbers in Fig. 1 and 2 refer to the same computation steps. The index *a* indicates parallel distribution of messages. The directed edges in both figures illustrate the basic flow of control caused by the message passing.

[6]*permit* accounts for type and further conceptual admissibility constraints (number restrictions, etc.).

it from being (incorrectly) reused as a possible antecedent for yet another anaphor within the *same* sentence.

As a special case of local ambiguities, consider the second anaphor in sentence (2), the pronoun *"sie" (it)*. Caused by the attachment of *"sie"* to its prospective head *"erzielt" (scores)* in the subordinate clause of sentence (2), and due to the case ambiguity of *"sie"*, viz. nominative and accusative, the corresponding *PhraseActors* are duplicated (as the matrix clause is ambiguous, too, four interpretations must be considered; in the corresponding Fig. 2 only two readings are shown). Four *SearchAntecedent* messages are triggered. Steps **1–8** are performed as described above. As the corresponding C_fs of (1) contain only PERFORMANCE (LPS-105 has already been consumed as a result of previously resolving *"diese Festplatte"*), the predicate *permit* fails with respect to PERFORMANCE and *"erzielt"* (Step 9).

12, 12a: The anaphor sends an *AnaphorReject* message to the *CenterActor*.

13, 13a: The C_f list is exhausted.

14, 14a: Hence, the mechanism for intrasentential anaphora resolution is triggered. The search for an antecedent is performed <u>within</u> the *PhraseActor* which contains both the anaphor and the antecedent (cf. Fig. 2; it differs from Fig. 1 mainly with respect to description of the the dependency structures within each *PhraseActor*, which are depicted in greater detail).

15, 15a: Each *SearchAntecedent* message is forwarded from its initiator *"sie"* to its prospective head *Head1 "erzielt" (scores)* which *d-binds* the initiator.

16, 16a: Next the message is forwarded to *Head2 "erreicht" (compares to)*.

17, 17a: Then the message is forwarded to possible *Antecedents* which are modifiers of *Head2*, where *"diese Festplatte" (this hard disk)* and *"ST-3144"* are reached, respectively.

18, 18a: *PronAnaphorTest* and the semantic predicate *permit* succeed (*"diese Festplatte"*, which is resolved to LPS-105, and *"erzielt"* as well as ST-3144 and *"erzielt"* are both successfully tested by *permit*).

19, 19a: An *AntecedentFound* message is sent to the anaphor. The dependency relation *theAttachment*, viz. subject, is confirmed in both cases between *"erzielt" (scores)* and LPS-105 as well as ST-3144, respectively. Similarly, the object dependency relation ist established, until the accusative phrase *"den zweiten Platz" (second-best in this category)* invalidates this local ambiguity.

Upon completion of the analysis of sentence (2) two *CenterActors* continue to exist with corresponding C_b/C_f data

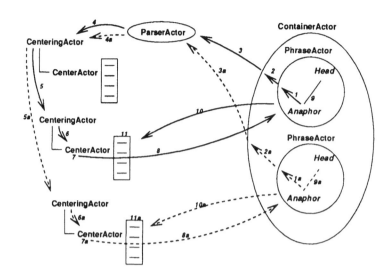

Figure 1: Protocol for the Local Ambiguity Case at the Text Level

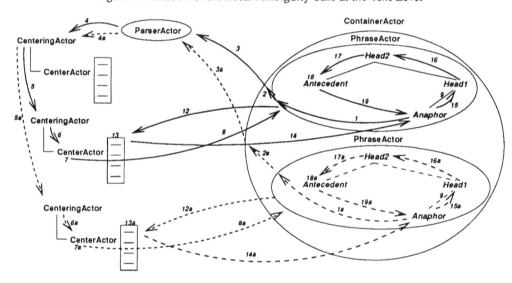

Figure 2: Protocol for the Local Ambiguity Case at the Phrase Level

(cf. Table 2). Hence, the local ambiguity with respect to *"sie"* no longer persists and has been reduced to a global one.

Summarizing, we propose a two-level representation of structural ambiguities for the centering model, one at which local and global structural ambiguities are made explicit. Global ambiguities are represented as sets of forward-looking centers (a so-called *centering set*, in the underlying implementation realized as *CenterActor*), while local ambiguities are represented as a set of such centering sets (in the underlying implementation realized as *CenteringActor*). The creation and management of these sets is under control of the parser, while the management of entities within these centers remains in the realm of the centering theory. The proposal we make does not depend on any choice of the underlying grammar or semantic theory (although binding criteria should be expressable).

Related Work

The centering model, from its inception (Grosz et al., 1983) to its most recent formulation (Grosz et al., 1995), has been considered a methodological framework for anaphora resolution. With the exception of Brennan et al. (1987), whose implementation was interfaced with a concrete HPSG system, the centering approach seems to have been developed as a stand-alone theory vehicle, with almost no attention given to its integration into a larger NLU system framework. This might explain why the issue of *structural* ambiguity handling has been largely ignored in the centering framework. The problem of *referential* ambiguity to which our proposal is equally applicable has recently been discussed by Walker et al. (1994). However, their problem concerns the choice options arising for the assignment of alternative discourse entities from the forward-looking center list to zero-anaphorized arguments of verbs in Japanese, given that the number of candidate antecedents exceeds that of the zero anaphors. Their use of functional notions, viz. topicality and empathy, naturally extend the role preferences of the underlying centering model, but unlike our case, no structural ambiguities are involved. In contrast, our approach applies to the representation of both types of ambiguities.

We motivated the treatment of (structural) ambiguities within the centering framework as a consequence of assuming an *incremental* mode of anaphor resolution, a topic that has not been raised in the centering literature so far. This is surprising insofar as even psycholinguistic studies on centering (Gordon et al., 1993; Brennan, 1995) do not touch upon this issue, though the immediacy of anaphor resolution is a common theme in cognitive text processing studies (Just & Carpenter, 1987; Sanford & Garrod, 1989).

Our proposal, based on a dependency-style grammar model (Hahn et al., 1994), claims to integrate both the sentence-level as well as text-level of anaphora analysis. Furthermore, it is also fully integrated with terminological reasoning facilities as needed for in-depth text understanding, and is based on an incremental, single-pass procedure. Thus, it is superior to the work on binding theory as developed within the GB framework (Chomsky, 1981) that is restricted to the sentence-level of analysis; just recently, however, Merlo (1993) has proposed an incremental procedure for computing intrasentential coreferences based on binding theory constraints. Also Haddock (1987) considers an incremental mode of anaphora resolution which boils down to a variable binding, i.e., a constraint satisfaction problem in the context of a Combinatory Categorial Grammar. Any of these approaches neglects the important aspect of a preference scaling for properly selecting among several candidate discourse units as antecedents. This drawback in the same way applies to the framework of DRT (Kamp & Reyle, 1993), which is also non-incremental.

Conclusions

Our approach to anaphora resolution extends the original centering model by embedding the centering approach into an *incremental*, single-pass processing model, by providing data structures for the centering algorithm which allow for the treatment of local and global (parsing) *ambiguities*, and by homogeneously integrating the resolution of *sentence-level (intrasentential)* as well as *text-level (intersentential)* anaphora based on the strict requirements set up by the *binding criteria* (adapted to a dependency grammar framework).

The anaphora resolution module has been realized as part of a dependency parser for the German language. The parser has been implemented in Actalk (Briot, 1989), an actor language dialect of Smalltalk. The current lexicon contains nearly 3.000 lexical entries and corresponding concept descriptions from two domains (information technology and medicine) available from the LOOM knowledge representation system (MacGregor & Bates, 1987).

Acknowledgments. We would like to thank our colleagues in the *CLIF* group who read earlier versions of this paper. In particular, improvements are due to discussions we had with Peter Neuhaus. This work has been funded by *LGFG Baden-Württemberg* (1.1.4-7631.0; M. Strube) and a grant from *DFG* (Ha 2907/1-3; U. Hahn).

References

Agha, G. & C. Hewitt (1987). Concurrent programming using actors. In A. Yonezawa & M. Tokoro (Eds.), *Object-Oriented Concurrent Programming*, pp. 37–53. Cambridge, Mass.: MIT Press.

Brennan, S. E. (1995). Centering attention in discourse. *Language and Cognitive Processes*, 10(2):137–167.

Brennan, S. E., M. W. Friedman & C. J. Pollard (1987). A centering approach to pronouns. In *Proc. of ACL-87*, pp. 155–162.

Briot, J.-P. (1989). Actalk: A testbed for classifying and designing actor languages in the Smalltalk-80 environment. In *Proc. of ECOOP-89*, pp. 109–129.

Chomsky, N. (1981). *Lectures on Government and Binding*. Dordrecht: Foris.

Gordon, P. C., B. J. Grosz & L. A. Gilliom (1993). Pronouns, names, and the centering of attention in discourse. *Cognitive Science*, 17:311–347.

Granger, R. H., K. P. Eiselt & J. K. Holbrook (1986). Parsing with parallelism: A spreading-activation model of inference processing during text understanding. In J. Kolodner & C. Riesbeck (Eds.), *Experience, Memory, and Reasoning*, pp. 227–246. Hillsdale, N.J.: L. Erlbaum.

Grosz, B. J., A. K. Joshi & S. Weinstein (1983). Providing a unified account of definite noun phrases in discourse. In *Proc. of ACL-83*, pp. 44–50.

Grosz, B. J., A. K. Joshi & S. Weinstein (1995). Centering: A framework for modeling the local coherence of discourse. *Computational Linguistics*, 21(2):203–225.

Haddock, N. (1987). Incremental interpretation and Combinatory Categorial Grammar. In *Proc. of IJCAI-87*, Vol. 2, pp. 661–663.

Hahn, U., S. Schacht & N. Bröker (1994). Concurrent, object-oriented dependency parsing: The *ParseTalk* model. *International Journal of Human-Computer Studies*, 41(1/2):179–222.

Jurafsky, D. (1992). An on-line computational model of human sentence interpretation. In *Proc. of AAAI-92*, pp. 302–308.

Just, M. & P. Carpenter (1987). *The Psychology of Reading and Language Comprehension*. Boston, Mass.: Allyn & Bacon.

Kamp, H. & U. Reyle (1993). *From Discourse to Logic*. Dordrecht: Kluwer.

MacGregor, R. & R. Bates (1987). *The LOOM Knowledge Representation Language*. (ISI/RS-87-18) USC/ISI.

Merlo, P. (1993). For an incremental computation of intrasentential coreference. In *Proc. of IJCAI-93*, Vol. 1, pp. 1216–1221.

Neuhaus, P. & U. Hahn (1996). Restricted parallelism in object-oriented lexical parsing. In *Proc. of COLING-96*.

Sanford, A. & S. Garrod (1989). What, when, and how?: Questions of immediacy in anaphoric reference resolution. *Language and Cognitive Processes*, 4(3/4):235–262.

Strube, M. & U. Hahn (1995). *ParseTalk* about sentence- and text-level anaphora. In *Proc. of EACL-95*, pp. 237–244.

Strube, M. & U. Hahn (1996). Functional centering. In *Proc. of ACL-96*.

Sturt, P. (1995). Incorporating "unconscious reanalysis" into an incremental, monotonic parser. In *Proc. of EACL-95*, pp. 291–296.

Walker, M. A., M. Iida & S. Cote (1994). Japanese discourse and the process of centering. *Computational Linguistics*, 20(2):193–233.

573

A Connectionist Architecture with Inherent Systematicity

James Henderson
Department of Computer Science
University of Exeter
Exeter EX4 4PT
United Kingdom
jamie@dcs.ex.ac.uk

Abstract

For connectionist networks to be adequate for higher level cognitive activities such as natural language interpretation, they have to generalize in a way that is appropriate given the regularities of the domain. Fodor and Pylyshyn (1988) identified an important pattern of regularities in such domains, which they called systematicity. Several attempts have been made to show that connectionist networks can generalize in accordance with these regularities, but not to the satisfaction of the critics. To address this challenge, this paper starts by establishing the implications of systematicity for connectionist solutions to the variable binding problem. Based on the work of Hadley (1994a), we argue that the network must generalize information it learns in one variable binding to other variable bindings. We then show that temporal synchrony variable binding (Shastri and Ajjanagadde, 1993) inherently generalizes in this way. Thereby we show that temporal synchrony variable binding is a connectionist architecture that accounts for systematicity. This is an important step in showing that connectionism can be an adequate architecture for higher level cognition.

Introduction

Connectionist networks have been successfully applied to a wide variety of problems, but they have not had much success with higher level cognitive activities. For example in natural language parsing, connectionist networks have not been able to exhibit the same generalization abilities that statistical approaches based on standard parsing techniques have shown. This inability to generalize in the appropriate way can be attributed to an inadequacy in standard connectionist networks that was first identified by Fodor and Pylyshyn (1988). They pointed out a pattern of regularities in higher level cognitive activities that they called systematicity, and challenged connectionists to show how this pattern could be accounted for within connectionism. In this paper we show that a particular connectionist architecture, called temporal synchrony variable binding (Shastri and Ajjanagadde, 1993), accounts for systematicity through its inherent ability to generalize across entities. In the process, we clarify the notion of systematicity and show its implications for variable binding techniques. This work not only contributes to the continuing debate about systematicity in connectionist networks, it also indicates how connectionist networks' impressive learning abilities for pattern matching tasks can be extended to the more complex domains typical of higher level cognitive activities.

As Fodor and Pylyshyn (1988) describe it, systematicity embodies the kinds of regularities that arise from a compositional generative grammar. Because in such grammars a general-purpose composition operation is used to construct sentences out of their constituents, a given constituent can appear anywhere that its type of constituent is allowed. For example, because "John" and "Mary" are the same type of constituent, a generative grammar would not generate "John loves Mary" without also generating "Mary loves John". Fodor and Pylyshyn (1988) argued that such regularities are an inherent part of human cognitive activity, and thus that connectionism could not be an adequate cognitive architecture until it accounted for this phenomena. Many attempts have been made to meet this challenge (e.g. Smolensky, 1990; Christiansen and Chater, 1994; Niklasson and van Gelder, 1994), but the critics have not been satisfied (Fodor and McLaughlin, 1990; Hadley, 1994a; Hadley, 1994b).[1]

Such difficulties have lead some connectionists investigating higher level cognitive activities to propose extensions to standard connectionist architectures. One such investigation developed a technique called temporal synchrony variable binding for use in fast, common sense reasoning (reflexive reasoning) (Shastri and Ajjanagadde, 1993).[2] This technique can represent multiple features of multiple entities, and it can perform a significant class of computations over this representation. In addition to reflexive reasoning, it has been successfully applied to syntactic natural language parsing (Henderson, 1994b; Henderson, 1994a). This work showed that the kinds of regularities that systematicity embodies could be directly and simply represented in a network that uses temporal synchrony variable binding. In this paper we show that it is not only possible to build a connectionist network that exhibits these regularities, but that these regularities are a consequence of the inherent generalization abilities of temporal synchrony variable binding networks.

Because there has not been general agreement about the exact definition of systematicity, this paper starts with a discussion of this issue based on the work of Hadley (1994a). The resulting definition of systematicity requires a solution to the variable binding problem where learned parameters are independent of variable bindings. Several connectionist approaches to variable binding are then discussed with respect to

---

[1] One proposal (Hadley and Hayward, 1995) has not yet been criticized in the literature. This work will be discussed below in the section on representing variable bindings.

[2] The possibility of using temporal synchrony for encoding feature bindings in the perceptual domain was suggested by von der Malsburg and Schneider (1986), but Shastri and Ajjanagadde were the first to use temporal synchrony to solve complex representational problems in higher level cognitive activities.

this requirement. For most of the proposed methods, there is no apparent way for them to satisfy this requirement. In contrast, temporal synchrony variable binding by its very nature makes learned parameters independent of variable bindings. By showing this we show that temporal synchrony variable binding is a connectionist architecture that can account for systematicity.

The Definition of Systematicity

Although neither (Fodor and Pylyshyn, 1988) nor (Fodor and McLaughlin, 1990) provides a precise definition of systematicity, the concept is meant to embody the pervasive regularities in language (and thought) that are traditionally captured using compositional generative grammars. Such grammars express generalizations about the sentences of a language in terms of their subconstituents. A universal composition operation is then used to combine these constituents to form sentences. Because generalizations are stated in terms of constituents, such an architecture predicts a prevalence of regularities across constituents. This is in fact the case. For example, the pattern of words that can make up a noun phrase is very complex, yet this pattern is virtually identical for subject and object noun phrases. Thus if "John" can be a subject noun phrase and "Mary" can be an object noun phrase (as in "John loves Mary"), then it will also be possible for "Mary" to be a subject noun phrase and "John" to be an object noun phrase (as in "Mary loves John").

Within the connectionist paradigm, the ability to account for regularities is not tested through representing generalizations (as in the classical paradigm), but through learning generalizations. A connectionist architecture accounts for a regularity if it can generalize from a training set to a testing set in accordance with that regularity. Hadley (1994a) uses this criteria to formalize the concept of systematicity. He requires a network to generalize from a set of training sentences to a set of novel testing sentences. He defines three degrees of systematicity, depending on the novelty of the testing sentences. The one which most closely matches Fodor and Pylyshyn's concept is strong systematicity, where the novel testing sentences include words (i.e. simple constituents) in syntactic positions where they did not occur in the training sentences. Going back to our previous example, this means that a network that was trained on sentences in which "Mary" was only in object position would have to handle sentences in which "Mary" appeared in subject position. Unfortunately, as Christiansen and Chater (1994) point out, this definition still has some imprecision in that no definition of "syntactic position" is given. Christiansen and Chater (1994) provide a linguistically motivated definition of syntactic position, but this is not adequate. The network may be using a rather different system of syntactic positions than the one an external observer would find natural.

For the test to guarantee that the network is truly able to generalize to novel pairings of words with syntactic positions, we need to restrict the network's task so that the syntactic position of the word in the training set must be treated as different from the syntactic position of the word in the testing set. Hadley (1994a; 1994b) discusses a fourth type of systematicity which does this. He defines semantic systematicity to be strong systematicity plus the requirement that the system assign appropriate meanings to all words occurring in the novel test sentences (Hadley, 1994b). The task of assigning meaning forces the system to make distinctions between syntactic positions. For example, a network trying to assign meaning to "Mary loves John" must distinguish between the syntactic positions of "Mary" and "John", since neither word can in general be excluded from either the lover or loved roles. This task illustrates how a network can be forced to represent the distinctions between syntactic positions that the experiment presumes. With this restriction on the task, we can be sure that a network that exhibits strong systematicity represents information about syntactic positions and can combine this information with its information about words in novel ways.

Hadley (1994) explicitly excludes from his definition of systematicity a property which Fodor and Pylyshyn (1988) emphasize, namely that the regularities Hadley discusses must be nomic necessities. In other words, these regularities must be inherent to the nature of the connectionist network, not just wired in. Wiring in the regularities constitutes a mere implementation of them, and thus neither explains them nor furthers our understanding of them. This paper argues that connectionist networks which use temporal synchrony variable binding inherently generalize information about words from one syntactic position to another, and thus that strong systematicity is a nomic necessity given the use of temporal synchrony variable binding, as required by Fodor and Pylyshyn (1988). Because we are concerned with demonstrating an inherent property, this paper provides an in-principle argument. Experimental results from an implemented system are neither necessary nor sufficient to demonstrate that a property is inherent to the system.[3]

Learned Parameters versus Variable Bindings

The above definition of systematicity requires that a network make use of information about words, syntactic positions, and the pairings of words with syntactic positions. The pairings are manifested in the sentences that are input to the network, and the task forces these pairings to be manifested in the output of the network. Thus information about these pairings must be communicated from the input to the output, and consequently this information must be represented in some way by the pattern of activation in the network. This is an instance of the variable binding problem. The network must represent the binding between the information about a word and the information about the syntactic position of that word. In classical approaches these bindings are represented using variables. For example, the binding between "Mary" and the subject syntactic position in "Mary loves John" could be represented (simplistically) as $Mary(x) \wedge subject(x)$.

The requirements systematicity places on the representation of variable bindings are rather different from the requirements it places on the representation of words and syntactic positions. In order for a network to generalize from pro-

---

[3]This approach is at odds with standard practise in connectionism, but this divergence is to be expected given that the challenge posed by Fodor and Pylyshyn (1988) is a philosophical one, and not directly empirical. For those who aren't satisfied with an in-principle argument, see the discussion below of (Hadley and Hayward, 1995). Their experimental results can be interpreted as evidence for the generalization ability of temporal synchrony variable binding networks.

cessing one set of sentences to processing another set, the parameters that are determined using the training set (i.e. the link weights) have to represent information that is also true of the testing set. For strong systematicity, both information learned about words and information learned about syntactic positions will be true of the testing set. In contrast, because words and syntactic positions are paired differently in the training and testing sets, any information learned about variable bindings will not be true of the testing set. Since the task requires information about words and syntactic positions to be learned correctly, the parameters that represent this information must not be dependent on variable bindings. In other words, strong systematicity requires that the learned parameters (weights) of a network should be independent of the variable bindings.[4] Classical approaches use quantifiers to express this independence. For example, the learned fact that "Mary" has the interpretation MARY (following a standard notation) could be represented with the rule $\forall y, Mary(y) \Rightarrow MARY(y)$. The truth of this rule is a learned parameter, and it is independent of the variable that the rule is applied to. Applying this rule to x in $Mary(x) \wedge subject(x)$ we get $Mary(x) \wedge subject(x) \wedge MARY(x)$. This state specifies that the subject has the interpretation MARY, despite the fact that the rule is independent of the pairing of "Mary" with the subject.

It should be clear at this point that the requirements of strong systematicity are not specific to the task of natural language interpretation. Information about words and syntactic positions could be replaced with a wide variety of different kinds of information, and we could still find tasks that require these different kinds of information to be independent from their variable bindings. Any such task will display the pattern of regularities that are embodied in the concept of systematicity. For example, grasping a piece of candy that is in ones visual field requires the information that an object is candy, the information about the location of that object, and the binding between these two types of information. Changing the location of the candy does not change its sweetness, and changing the color of the candy does not change the trajectory for grasping. As Fodor and Pylyshyn (1988) argued, such regularities are pervasive in higher level cognitive activities, and thus a proposed cognitive architecture must account for them. In the rest of this paper we will describe a connectionist architecture in which learned parameters are inherently independent of variable bindings, thereby accounting for these regularities.

Representing Variable Bindings

Several researchers have proposed ways in which connectionist networks can represent variable bindings, but most of these methods do not make learned parameters independent of variable bindings, as required by systematicity. The learned parameters of a connectionist network are represented in its link weights. The effect of a link weight on a computation is dependent on which units the link connects and the units' activation levels, but it is not dependent on the time at which the computation takes place.[5] Thus if the time dimension is used to represent variable bindings, then learned parameters will inherently be independent of variable bindings. This is the approach taken in temporal synchrony variable binding. In contrast, if either the space dimension (different units) or activation levels are used to represent variable bindings, then learned parameters will not inherently be independent of variable bindings. It is possible to hardwire the network in such a way as to enforce this independence, but there is no apparent motivation for such hardwired structure other than implementing systematicity, and thus it is not inherent to the network. Perhaps we have missed a method that would address these criticisms, but the existing alternative proposals for connectionist variable binding do not indicate what it would be. Thus currently only temporal synchrony variable binding implies that learned parameters are inherently independent of variable bindings, as required by systematicity.

Tensor product variable binding (Smolensky, 1990) and relative-position encoding (Barnden and Srinivas, 1991) use the space dimension to represent variable bindings. Using such a representation, variable bindings are represented by specifying the units where the computation should take place. The problem with this method is that without additional mechanisms the weights of the links for one set of units will be different from the weights of the links for another set. Thus the learned parameters used in a computation will be different depending on the binding that is manifested in the input, and the network will not exhibit systematicity. If all links are trainable, then the weights for two different sets of units will only be the same if either there is an additional mechanism for enforcing weight equality, or they are trained on equivalent data. Any mechanism for enforcing weight equality across different sets of units is inherently nonlocal, and thus violates one of the basic tenets of connectionism. Thus, while it may be an effective engineering solution, weight sharing does not constitute a connectionist method for capturing systematicity. Given that the training set used in the above test for systematicity is by design biased with respect to the bindings between words and syntactic positions, the data used to train links for different sets of units will not be equivalent without additional, as yet unproposed, mechanisms.

Hadley and Hayward (1995) propose a more plausible way of using tensor product variable binding, but as the system is described they are still hardwiring in the independence between learned parameters and variable bindings. The component of their network which uses tensor product variable binding has no trainable links. This allows the different links in the variable binding component to stay equal throughout training, thus making the effects of the learned parameters independent of which of the variable binding units is used. The resulting network generalizes extremely well on the small grammar they use in their experiments. However, this proposal has at least two problems; no independent motivation is given for this hardwired component, and the hardwired component grows with the size of the systems vocabulary (linearly for units and quadratically for links), which for a real system

---

[4]This requirement does not preclude the use of information that is dependent on the pairings of words with syntactic positions. Such information is simply irrelevant to the issue of systematicity.

[5]Of course a link weight will have a different effect if it changes from one time to another. This is not relevant here because learning is taking place at a much larger time scale than individual computation steps. Therefore if any change did occur it would be negligible.

would be quite large. They justify this use of hardwired structure by saying that their units and links should be interpreted as high-level abstractions which aren't necessarily manifested as collections of neurons and synapses. While all connectionist networks are abstract models, without some plausible connection to the biological substrate it is difficult to see how the network could be anything more than a mere implementation of a classical statistical system. Interestingly, this criticism can be addressed by assuming that Hadley and Hayward's work is not a competing proposal with the one advocated here, but is actually a complementary one. As pointed out by Tesar and Smolensky (1994), temporal synchrony variable binding can be interpreted as an implementation of tensor product variable binding.[6] In addition, there is some evidence that temporal synchrony is used in the brain to do variable binding (see (Shastri and Ajjanagadde, 1993) pages 439–441 for a discussion). Thus if we assume that the variable binding component of Hadley and Hayward's network is an abstract representation of a temporal synchrony variable binding mechanism, then the "mere implementation" criticism is addressed. More arguments against this criticism will be given below. In the other direction, the experiments run by Hadley and Hayward (1995) demonstrate that when systematicity is embodied in a network (as in temporal synchrony variable binding networks), simple connectionist learning techniques can be very effective for grammar induction.

Signatures (Lange and Dyer, 1989), CONSYDERR (Sun, 1992), and pattern-similarity association (Barnden and Srinivas, 1991) use the activation level dimension to represent variable bindings. This complicates the nature of computation in the network, since activation level is also being used to represent what features a variable's entity has. It is conceivable that these two types of information could be folded into individual activation levels, but it isn't at all clear how this could result in different variable bindings being treated the same but the presence or absence of features being treated differently. All the above investigations use the alternative approach, in which these two types of information are represented in the activation levels of two different sets of units. In this approach, coordinating computation between the two sets of units requires representing the bindings between the variables and their entity's features. These bindings do not have to be dynamically instantiated, so fixed spatial relationships can be used. However, systematicity still requires learned parameters to be independent of these bindings. Because these bindings are represented using space, they pose the same problems as using space to represent variable bindings.

Temporal synchrony variable binding (Shastri and Ajjanagadde, 1993) is currently the only proposal for how to use the time dimension to represent variable bindings. In this model, a variable binding is represented by specifying the times during which the computations involving the variable should take place. If two units are representing information about the same variable, then they output activation at the same time

(i.e. synchronously). For our task, if a given word is in a given syntactic position, then the units that represent the word are outputting activation at the same time as the units that represent the syntactic position. Computations are performed when this activation spreads through the network's links. No matter at what time this computation occurs, the same link weights will be used. Thus no matter what variable binding a word or syntactic position participates in, the same learned parameters will apply to it. In other words, learned parameters are independent of variable bindings. Thus the information that the network has learned about a word or syntactic position in one set of word-position pairings will automatically be applied to the same word or syntactic position in different pairings. Therefore the use of temporal synchrony variable binding inherently results in a network which generalizes information about words from one syntactic position to another, and it inherently exhibits strong systematicity.

Temporal Synchrony Variable Binding

Temporal synchrony variable binding is a technique that can be applied to virtually any style of connectionist model. For higher level cognitive activities such as language interpretation recurrent networks are of particular interest. Recurrent networks accept a sequence of inputs over time, and perform a sequence of computations. As with variable binding, the use of time to represent the input sequence allows the learned parameters of a recurrent network to be independent of absolute position in the input sequence. Thereby such networks can generalize what they learn about one position in the input sequence to other positions. This property is imperative for language interpretation, where the absolute position of a word in a sentence carries virtually no information. Thus we need a network that can use the time dimension to represent both input sequence and variable bindings.

All that is needed for a network to represent both input sequence and variable bindings in the time dimension is units that pulse periodically. The periods of the resulting pattern of activation correspond to steps in the computation, and the phases correspond to variable bindings.[7] In effect this method simply time-multiplexes a recurrent network across variables. Such a periodic pattern of activation is illustrated in figure 1, where there are two variables and three computation steps. In the initial computation step the pattern of activation represents the information $Mary(x) \wedge John(y) \wedge subject(x) \wedge object(y) \wedge active$. Then some of the links of the network propagate activation from the "Mary" unit to the "MARY" unit, resulting in the pattern shown in the second and subsequent period. These links implement the rule $\forall z, Mary(z) \Rightarrow MARY(z)$. Information that is not predicated of a variable is represented with units that do not pulse, and thus stay active across phases. Such a unit is shown in figure 1 labeled "active" (for active voice, as opposed to passive voice). These units can be used to represent global context, and to coordinate computation across

---

[6]Tesar and Smolensky (1994) argue that the use of time rather than space to represent variable bindings is purely an implementation issue. This is reasonable when, as they do, one only looks at static representations. However, as argued here, when the issue of learning is taken into consideration the use of time rather than space becomes quite important, even at the architecture level.

[7]While the periodic firing of groups of neurons at the same frequency is overly simplistic, it appears to be an appropriate model at this level of abstraction. The only necessary properties here are that groups of neurons can achieve some form of synchronous firing and maintain that synchrony over some period of time, which they can do (Gray et al., 1991).

variables. In effect they are a subpart of the recurrent network that is not time-multiplexed. Any aspect of a task for which systematicity is not applicable can be handled within this subpart.[8]

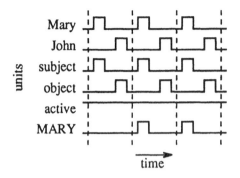

Figure 1: An example of how temporal synchrony can be used to represent variable bindings. Each solid line shows the output of a unit over time. The dashed lines divide this temporal pattern into periods.

The above discussion of temporal synchrony variable binding demonstrates that this technique can be interpreted as an implementation of classical computational architecture. However, it is not a *mere* implementation. The inherent nature of systematicity in temporal synchrony variable binding networks and the biological evidence for this implementation method means that the pervasiveness of systematicity in cognitive activities is explained by this choice of implementation. This is in contrast to the situation in classical approaches, where compositionality is used to capture systematicity. Compositionality has no independent motivations (other than mathematical simplicity), and thus should be considered a description of the phenomena of systematicity, and not an explanation of it. The biological evidence for temporal synchrony variable binding has also been used to explain other cognitive phenomena that were previously described in classical terms, such as Miller's (1956) bound on short term memory of seven plus or minus two things (Shastri and Ajjanagadde, 1993). Furthermore, the less abstract level of description provided by temporal synchrony variable binding has provided insights into cognitive phenomena that have not been achieved at the classical level. For example, some constraints on long distance dependencies in natural language (wh- movement) can be explained by the inability of simple temporal synchrony variable binding networks to generalize over pairs of constituents (Henderson, 1994b). By accounting for these particular phenomena at the implementation level, the classical competence theory of long distance dependencies is greatly simplified. Because temporal synchrony variable binding helps bridge the gap between low level biological evidence and high level cognitive phenomena, more such insights are likely in the future. Even now it is abundantly clear that temporal synchrony variable binding is not *merely* an implementation of a classical computational architecture.

[8]For a more thorough presentation of temporal synchrony variable binding and how it can be used to implement a syntactic parser, see either (Henderson, 1994a) or (Henderson, 1994b).

The parallel between the use of time in recurrent networks and the use of time in temporal synchrony variable binding means that methods for training recurrent networks can be generalized to temporal synchrony variable binding networks. Thus just as a recurrent network can learn that "the" is usually followed by a noun regardless of where it occurs in the sentence, a temporal synchrony variable binding network can learn that "Mary" is usually a noun phrase regardless of what syntactic position it has in the sentence. Some complications arise when it is necessary to learn when to introduce new entities, but these are orthoganal to the issue of systematicity. Methods for effective learning in temporal synchrony variable binding networks is an area of active research by the author and Shastri.

Conclusion

Temporal synchrony variable binding (Shastri and Ajjanagadde, 1993) is a connectionist method for representing multiple entities, each with multiple features. It uses the time dimension to represent the binding between the different features of a given entity (i.e. variable bindings). Because the effect of a link weight on the network's computation is independent of the time at which the computation occurs, the learned parameters of the network are inherently independent of its variable bindings. In other words, learned parameters inherently generalize across entities. In particular, information learned about words and information learned about syntactic positions will both generalize to new pairings of words with syntactic positions. This is the criteria Hadley (1994a) develops in his formalization of Fodor and Pylyshyn's (1988) concept of systematicity. Thus we have succeeded in showing that temporal synchrony variable binding is a connectionist architecture that accounts for systematicity. In the process, we have clarified the notion of systematicity and shown its implications for variable binding techniques.

While this demonstration has been couched in the terms of natural language interpretation, it is clear that the ability to generalize across entities is applicable to a broad range of higher level cognitive activities. Arguably, it is precisely the lack of this generalization ability that has prevented standard connectionist networks from matching the abilities of symbolic systems in these tasks. The work presented in this paper indicates how the impressive learning abilities of connectionist networks for pattern matching tasks can be extended to the more complex domains typical of higher level cognition.

References

Barnden, J. and Srinivas, K. (1991). Encoding techniques for complex information structures in connectionist systems. *Connection Science*, 3(3):269–315.

Christiansen, M.H. and Chater, N. (1994). Generalisation and connectionist language learning. *Mind and Language*, 9(3):273–287.

Fodor, J.A. and McLaughlin, B. (1990). Connectionism and the problem of systematicity: Why smolensky's solution doesn't work. *Cognition*, 35:183–204.

Fodor, J.A. and Pylyshyn, Z.W. (1988). Connectionism and cognitive architecture: A critical analysis. *Cognition*, 28:3–71.

Gray, C.M., Engel, A.K., Koenig, P., and Singer, W. (1991). Properties of synchronous oscillatory neuronal interactions in cat striate cortex. In Schuster, H.G. and Singer, W., editors, *Nonlinear Dynamics and Neural Networks*. Weinheim: VCH Publishers.

Hadley, R.F. (1994a). Systematicity in connectionist language learning. *Mind and Language*, 9(3):247–272.

Hadley, R.F. (1994b). Systematicity revisited: Reply to Christiansen and Chater and Niklasson and van Gelder. *Mind and Language*, 9(4):431–444.

Hadley, R.F. and Hayward, M.B. (1995). Strong semantic systematicity from unsupervised connectionist learning. In *Proceedings of the Seventeenth Conference of the Cognitive Science Society*, pages 358–363, Pittsburgh, PA.

Henderson, J. (1994a). Connectionist syntactic parsing using temporal variable binding. *Journal of Psycholinguistic Research*, 23(5):353–379.

Henderson, J. (1994b). *Description Based Parsing in a Connectionist Network*. PhD thesis, University of Pennsylvania, Philadelphia, PA. Technical Report MS-CIS-94-46.

Lange, T. and Dyer, M. (1989). High-level inferencing in a connectionist network. *Connection Science*, 1(2):181–217.

Miller, G.A. (1956). The magical number seven plus or minus two. *Psychological Review*, 63:81–96.

Niklasson, L.F. and van Gelder, T. (1994). On being systematically connectionist. *Mind and Language*, 9(3):288–302.

Shastri, L. and Ajjanagadde, V. (1993). From simple associations to systematic reasoning: A connectionist representation of rules, variables, and dynamic bindings using temporal synchrony. *Behavioral and Brain Sciences*, 16:417–451.

Smolensky, P. (1990). Tensor product variable binding and the representation of symbolic structures in connectionist systems. *Artificial Intelligence*, 46(1-2):159–216.

Sun, R. (1992). On variable binding in connectionist networks. *Connection Science*, 4(2):93–124.

Tesar, B.B. and Smolensky, P. (1995). Synchronous firing variable binding is a tensor product representation with temporal role vectors. In *Proceedings of the Sixteenth Conference of the Cognitive Science Society*, pages 870–875, Atlanta, Georgia.

von der Malsburg, C. and Schneider, W. (1986). A neural cocktail-party processor. *Biological Cybernetics*, 54:29–40.

Empirical Evidence for Constraint Relaxation in Insight Problem Solving

Guenther Knoblich and **Hilde Haider**
Graduiertenkolleg Kognitionswissenschaft
University of Hamburg
Vogt-Koelln-Str. 30
22527 Hamburg
knoblich@informatik.uni-hamburg.de

Abstract

Using a new developed task environment that allows to control for depth and width of problem space (Match Stick Algebra problems), three experiments were conducted to investigate the role of implicit constraints in insight problem solving. The first experiment showed that constraints caused by prior knowledge of common algebra lead to large differences in solution times, when they were encountered for the first time. No differences were found after the constraints had been relaxed. In the second experiment complimentary moves had to be applied in two different equation structures, one similiar to common algebra, one dissimiliar to common algebra. Consistent with our predictions different problem structures lead to a reversed order of task difficulty for the same moves depending on the activation of prior knowledge from real algebra. In the third experiment it was shown that a re-distribution of activation in a network causes the removing of constraints. Non-detectable priming of the solution lead to significantly more solutions in the experimental group as compared to a control group.

Introduction

Insight can be defined as the act of breaking out of an impasse that has been encountered during problem solving (Ohlsson, 1992). Impasses describe mental states in which no active problem solving occurs. But what is the cause of such impasses and what is their function? One possible cause of impasses are implicit constraints that problem solvers put on the goal state in certain problems. The resolution of impasses (restructuring) then could be caused by constraint relaxation, i.e. a gradual decrease in activation of these constraints.

To avoid the circular definition of insight problems in former studies where insight problems are often defined as problems in which insight occurs (Dominowski & Dallob, 1994), we looked for a task environment where (a) different levels of constraints can be distinguished on the basis of a formal task analysis and b) the depth (i.e., length of solution path) and width (i.e., branching factor) of the problem space can be controlled across individuals.

The domain of Match Stick Algebra (MSA) fulfills these requirements. The goal in MSA problems is always to make an equation true by moving a single stick. For example in IV = III + III or in III = III + III, the solutions are VI = III + III and III = III = III.

The depth of the problem space is constant in these problems because the solution can be obtained in one step (by moving one stick) and no intermediate knowledge state has to be remembered. The width of the problem space is known because the task analysis reveals which moves can be applied to a problem within the given instruction (move one single stick to make the equation true; the resulting equation can only contain Roman numerals between I and XIII and the symbols for +, - and =).

This allows us to vary the number and type of constraints independently from serial problem solving aspects. The obvious source of implicit constraints in this task domain is the subjects' prior knowledge of common algebra. Because the prior knowledge regarding algebra problems is very systematic, clear hypotheses can be formulated to which extent different problems should activate constraints. This fact can be used to select MSA tasks that vary on a dimension from "not activating constraints" to "activating several constraints". The first experiment was carried out to determine the effect of different types of constraints on task difficulty.

Experiment 1: Impasses and Transfer as a Function of Constraints

In Experiment 1, participants solved problems that were more or less likely to activate constraints (see Table 1).

Constraints should not be active in a problem like "VI = VII + I" because this equation can be made true by moving a match from one numeral to another numeral, which is the same as subtracting 1 from one side of the equation and adding 1 to the other side in common algebra.

Table 1: Tasks used in Experiment 1 and the constraints that must be relaxed to solve them. Solutions are shown in parentheses.

Constraint	Block 1	Block 2
NO	VI = VII + I (VII = VI + I)	II = III + I (III = II + I)
OP	I = II + II (I = III - II)	III = V + III (III = VI - III)
EQ	IV = III - I (IV - III = I)	V = III - II (V - III = II)
SEQ	III = III + III (III = III = III)	IV = IV + IV (IV = IV = IV)

In an equation like "I = II + II", a match has to be moved from the plus sign to a numeral, resulting in "I = III - II". This type of operation has no analog in standard algebra and hence requires a relaxation of what we call the OP-constraint i.e., that operators can not be changed in an equation.

An equation like "IV = III - I" requires relaxation of what we call the EQ-constraint i.e., that the equal sign can not be changed in an equation, because it defines an equation. The solution in this case is to move a match from the equal sign to the minus sign, resulting in "IV - III = I".

Finally the SEQ constraint, i.e. that an equation allows only one equal sign, needs to be relaxed in an equation like "III = III + III". Rotating the vertical match of the plus sign results in "III = III = III", which is the solution in this case.

We expected solution times to increase with each type of constraint because the moves that have to be carried out are less and less similiar to moves in common algebra. The constraint relaxation hypothesis predicts that there should be no differences between these problem types, once the constraints have been relaxed. To test this prediction, we presented a second task for each type of move in a transfer condition.

Participants

Twenty undergraduates from the University of Hamburg participated for course credit. They were all assigned to the same condition, because all factors were varied within subjects.

Procedure

The problems were presented on a computer screen. There were two blocks of MSA tasks. In each block 6 tasks (including 1 for each level of constraints, i.e NO, OP, EQ, SEQ, and 2 additional tasks) were presented. Participants were instructed to hit a button as soon as they knew the correct solution and say it out aloud afterwards. Tasks were presented in random order within blocks. If the time participants spent on one task exceeded five minutes, the trial was interrupted and they were told the solution. The time needed for the solution and the number of solution attempts were recorded.

Results

Figure 1 displays the mean solution times for 4 levels of constraints for the first and the second presentation of each task type. The solution times were analyzed by computing a 4 X 2 ANOVA with the levels of constraints (NO vs. OP vs. EQ vs. SEQ, within) and presentation (First vs. Second, within) as the factors.

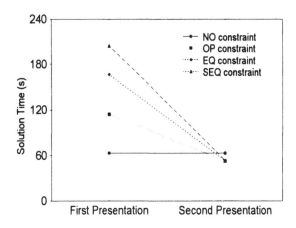

Figure 1: Mean solution times in first and second presentation as a function of constraints (solution times for not solved problems were replaced with maximal solution time = 300 s).

Subjects needed more time for moves that are not allowed in common algebra, resulting in a main effect for levels of constraints, $F(3, 57) = 3.89$, $MS_e = 8636.96$, $p < .05$. There was a large transfer effect between the first and second presentation of a problem type, yielding a significant main effect for presentation, $F(1, 19) = 18.81$, $MS_e = 14094.52$, $p < .001$.

While there were large differences in solution times for different levels of constraints in the first block, there were almost no differences in the second block, resulting in a significant interaction between levels of constraints and presentation, $F(3, 57) = 6.77$, $MS_e = 6308.70$, $p < .001$.

Discussion

Both predictions of the constraint relaxation hypothesis were supported by the results. Problems that require relaxation of more constraints take longer to solve than tasks that require relaxation of fewer constraints. However, once the constraints have been relaxed, these differences disappear.

Experiment 2: Interaction between Structure and Constraints

We conducted Experiment 2 to determine the influence of different task structures on implicit constraints. MSA equations can have three different types of structure:
  (a) Numeral +/- Numeral = Numeral (II + III = V), connection is followed by result (CR);
  (b) Numeral = Numeral +/- Numeral (V = II + III), result is followed by connection (RC);
  (c) Numeral = Numeral = Numeral (VI = VI = VI), a structure with two equal signs (TEQ).

While the CR and the RC structures have a high resemblance to common algebra problems the TEQ structure is very unusual. Therefore prior knowledge of common algebra should receive higher activation from the CR and RC structures than from the TEQ structure. The different amount of activation should affect the ease with which the constraints can be relaxed. We used only the RC and TEQ structures in the experiment.

For two operators that resulted in NO and SEQ constraint in Experiment 1, where only the RC structure was used, there are operators that are complimentary on a feature level in the TEQ structure. A task like VI = VII = V (VI = VI = VI) of the TEQ structure can be solved by moving a stick from one numeral to another numeral as in a task like VI = VII + I of the RC structure. We call this operator "Change of value". It should be easy to apply in both structures, because no implicit constraints are expected to occur.

The situation is quite different for the operator that resulted in the SEQ-constraint in the RC structure (we call it "Change of structure"). As we know from Experiment 1 it was very hard for problem-solvers to obtain the solution to a problem like III = III + III (III = III = III). The complimentary move in the TEQ structure in a task like VI = III = III (VI = III + III) should be much easier to apply because no implicit constraints from common algebra are expected for the TEQ structure. Moreover, changing the equal sign to a plus sign transforms the TEQ structure into the more usual RC structure. Therefore we expect a large difference in task difficulty between RC and TEQ structures for applying that operator.

Table 2: Tasks used in Experiment 2. Complementary moves on the feature level are required to solve problems of the RC and TEQ structures.

Move	RC-Structure	TEQ-Structure
Change of value	VI = VII + I (VII = VI + I)	VI = VII = V (VI = VI = VI)
Change of structure	III = III + III (III = III = III)	VI = III = III (VI = III + III)

Predictions for the transfer between the RC and TEQ structures can also be made from the notion of implicit constraints. While prior experience with problems of the TEQ structure should remove all constraints that normally occur in the RC structure, prior experience with problems of the RC structure should not result in decreased task difficulty for problems of the TEQ structure. This is so because in this structure we do not expect implicit constraints to occur.

Additionally we expect negative effects of prior working on the TEQ structure for Change of value in the RC structure because the prior experience with problems of the TEQ structure should lead to a mental set that favors operators that would normally not be available due to implicit constraints in the RC structure. This should make it harder to carry out the move that is normally the easiest to apply.

Subjects

Twenty-two undergraduates from the university of Hamburg participated for course credit.

Procedure

The procedure was the same as in Experiment 1 except two changes. One group of participants worked on a block of six problems (including one that required Change of value and one that required Change of Structure and four other problems) of the RC structure first and then on a block of six problems (including one that required Change of value and one that required Change of Structure and four other problems) of the TEQ structure. The other group worked on the blocks in reversed order. The time limit was raised to 8 minutes, to allow more solutions to be completed within the time limit.

Results

Figure 2 displays the means for Change of value and Change of structure problems in the RC and TEQ structures for different Order of presentation. The solution times were analyzed by computing a 2 X 2 X 2 ANOVA with the factors Order of presentation (RC-TEQ vs. TEQ-RC, between), Type of structure (RC vs. TEQ, within) and Type of move (Change of value vs. Change of structure, within).

The only significant main effect was for Type of structure, $\underline{F}(1, 20) = 6.44$, $\underline{MS}_e = 10180.46$, $\underline{p} < .05$. The overall difficulty of tasks of the TEQ structure is lower. The significant 2-way interaction between Order of presentation and Type of structure, $\underline{F}(1, 20) = 6.44$, $\underline{MS}_e = 12912.31$, $\underline{p} < .01$, shows that there is transfer from the TEQ structure to the RC structure only. For participants who solved TEQ problems first, Changes of structure were easier to obtain in both structures. For subjects who solved RC problems first, it was easier to Change values in both structures. This is reflected in a significant 2-way-interaction between Order of presentation and Type of move, $\underline{F}(1, 20) = 11.46$, $\underline{MS}_e = 12912.31$, $\underline{p} < .01$.

Further, there is a significant 3-way interaction between Order of presentation, Type of structure and Type of move, $\underline{F}(1, 20) = 7.19$, $\underline{MS}_e = 8726.19$, $\underline{p} < .025$. Long lasting impasses occured only in tasks of the RC structure where problem-solvers had to apply the Change of Structure operator.

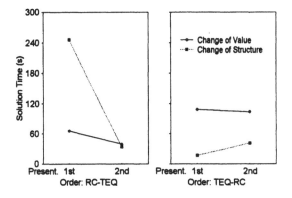

Figure 2: 3-way-interaction between Order of presentation, Type of structure and Type of move

Discussion

The predictions of the constraint relaxation hypothesis were supported by the results. As in Experiment 1 it was very hard for problem-solvers to carry out a move that transformed a common algebraic structure (RC) into an unusual structure (TEQ) because of implicit constraints. The complimentary move that transforms the unusual TEQ-structure into the more common RC-structure was easy to obtain because no implicit constraints occured in this structure. Moreover, prior experience with the TEQ-structure removed all constraints that normally occur in the RC-structure and makes the Change of value move harder to apply.

Experiment 3: Priming the correct solution

Constraint relaxation can be understood as re-distribution of activation over a network. This view implies that adding activation to nodes that are part of the solution should reduce the effect of constraints. An increase of activation of single nodes can be achieved by semantic priming even when the primes are short enough to rule out conscious processing. For the problems that lead to the longest impasses (EQ and SEQ in the Numeral = Numeral +/- Numeral structure) we implemented such a priming procedure. It started after 2 minutes (the time at which least solutions were observed in Experiment 1) if subjects had not solved the problem before. We predicted that such a procedure would prevent or shorten impasses.

Participants:

Thirty-five undergraduates from the university of Hamburg participated for course credit.

Procedure

The procedure was the same as in Experiments 1 and 2 with a time limit of 8 minutes and only one block consisting of 8 different MSA tasks (5 NO constraint tasks, 1 OP-, 1 EQ-, and 1 SEQ-constraint task). In the priming procedure the subjects were instructed to fixate the first position in the task (III in III = III + III) as soon as a sound occurs and to change the fixation to the second position (= in III = III = III) only when the content of the actual position was displayed again after being hidden for 300 msec behind a black mask.

They remained fixated on the second position, until the content of that position was displayed again, after being hidden by a 300 msec black mask. In that manner subjects attended to each part of the equation in succession. In the experimental group at one or two (correct) position(s) the symbol(s) constituting the solution were shown for 17 msec (for example in III = III + III a '=' was shown at the position of the '+'). In the control group only the mask was shown. After having completed this procedure, subjects continued to solve the problem for one minute, then the priming procedure started again. This circle was repeated until subjects solved the problem or the time limit was reached.

Results

Figure 3 shows the cumulative distribution of solution frequencies for the EQ and SEQ problems for different priming intervals in the priming and the control conditions. In the priming condition seven subjects solved one and two subjects solved two of the EQ and SEQ problems after the first and second primes. In the control condition no solutions were observed in this time period.

Using a χ^2-test, we compared the frequency of solutions after the first and second prime with the frequency of solutions that occured after the the third prime (including not solved problems) in both experimental groups. The difference was highly significant, χ^2 (df = 1) = .0004. Subjects in the priming condition solved significantly more problems in the intervals following the first and second primes, although none of the subjects reported having detected the prime during the experiment.

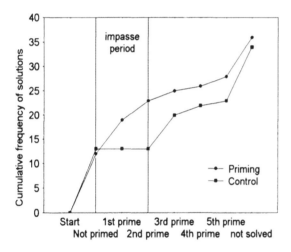

Figure 3: Cumulative frequency of solutions in different priming intervals for the EQ and the SEQ problem in priming and control conditions.

Discussion

The results of experiment 3 provide strong evidence for the notion of re-distribution of activation during insight problem solving. Undetectable semantic primes led to more frequent solutions to insight problems in the impasse phase, where in an control group no subject found a solution to the problem in that phase.

General Discussion

The results of our experiments provide evidence for several facts related to Ohlsson's (1992) framework for insight problem solving, particularly the notion of constraint relaxation. In Experiment 1 it was shown that there are discontinuities in problem solving that can not be attributed to the depth and the width of a problem-solver's problem space (her/his representation of the problem). This can not be explained by theories that hypothesize insight to occur only in problems where a change of problem space becomes necessary, because there are too many possibilities in the original problem space to be tested or certain features of the problem are not included in the problem representation (Kaplan & Simon, 1990). It also rules out any theory that handles insight problem solving from a business-as-usual perspective (Seifert et al., 1994), regarding insight phenomena as an either not important or non-existent cognitive phenomenon (Weisberg, 1981).

Our results support the notion of impasses that describe a mental state in which no problem-solving occurs. They also show that one reason for impasses are implicit constraints that problem-solvers impose on the goal state in insight problems. These constraints are removed as soon as the solution to one problem that activates certain constraints is known. This can be seen from the large transfer to other tasks of the same type.

The results of Experiment 2 show that the structure in which a problem is presented governs the activation of prior knowledge. Different meanings constituted by the structure reversed the pattern of task difficulty. The way in which activation is distributed initially is a function of relations that are established between single parts of a structure, not of every single feature or symbol of that structure. In this sense the actual problem representation is merely one possible interpretation of the task environment.

One restructuring process that leads to the resolution of impasses could be identified in Experiment 3. It was possible to push subjects towards the solution of insight problems by presenting them with undetectable semantic primes. This provides evidence for a continuous process of constraint relaxation, i.e. the decrease of activation in nodes of a semantic network with time, as cause for the subjective experience of sudden restructuring.

584

Acknowledgements

This research was supported by the German Research Foundation and the German Academic Exchange Service (HSPII/AUFE). We thank Stellan Ohlsson, Fredrik Wartenberg, Constanze Clauser, Barbara Kaup, Steffen Egner and Peter Baumann for helpful comments.

References

Dominowski, R. L. & Dallob, P. (1994). Insight and problem solving. In: R. J. Sternberg & J. E. Davidson, *The nature of insight* (33 - 62). Cambridge, MA: MIT press.

Kaplan , C. A. & Simon, H. A. (1990). In search of insight. *Cognitive Psychology*, 22, 374 - 419.

Ohlsson, S. (1992). Information-processing explanations of insight and related phenomena. In: M. Keane & K. J. Gilhooly, *Advances in the psychology of thinking, II* (1 - 44). Hertfordshire: Harvester Wheatsheaf.

Seifert, C. M., Meyer, D. E., Davidson, N., Patalano, A. L. & Yaniv, I. (1994). Demystification of cognitive insight: opportunistic assimilation and the prepared-mind perspective. In: R. J. Sternberg & J. E. Davidson, *The nature of insight* (65 - 124). Cambridge, MA: MIT press.

Weisberg, R. W. & Alba, J. W. (1981). An examination of the alleged role of fixation in the solution of several insight problems. *Journal of Experimental Psychology: General*, 110, 169 - 192.

Context Effects on Problem Solving

Boicho Kokinov[*#]   and   **Marina Yoveva**[*]

* Department of Cognitive Science   # Institute of Mathematics
New Bulgarian University   Bulgarian Academy of Sciences
21, Montevideo Str.   Bl. 8, Acad. G. Bonchev Str.
Sofia 1635, Bulgaria   Sofia 1113, Bulgaria
kokinov@bgearn.acad.bg

Abstract

Context effects on problem solving demonstrated so far in the literature are the result of systematic manipulation of some supposedly irrelevant to the solution *elements of the problem description*. Little attention has been paid to the role of *casual entities in the environment* which are not part of the problem description, but which might influence the problem solving process. The main purpose of the current paper is to avoid this limitation and to study the context effects (if any) caused by such accidental elements from the problem solver's environment and in this way to test the predictions made by the dynamic theory of context and its implementation in the DUAL cognitive architecture. Two experiments have been performed. In Experiment I the entities whose influence is being tested are part of the illustrations accompanying the target problem descriptions and therefore they belong to the core of the context, while in Experiment II the tested entities are part of the illustrations accompanying other problems' descriptions, they are accidental with respect to the target problem and therefore they possibly belong to the periphery of the context (if a context effect could be demonstrated at all). The results demonstrate both near and far context effects on problem solving caused by core (Experiment I) and peripheral elements (Experiment II) of the perception-induced context, respectively.

1. Motivation

Let us recall two famous stories where a particular accidental event or the presence of a particular casual object in the environment has reportedly played a crucial role in human problem solving: (1) Archimedes discovered his law in the bathtub seeing the water overflowing the bathtub when he entered it; (2) seeing an apple falling from a tree gave Newton inspiration for his theory of gravity. Most people will claim they have analogous experience. Surprisingly enough these claims have never been tested in controlled experiments. The current research focuses on exploring whether such accidental objects or events in the problem solvers' environment can influence their reasoning process and on explaining how this could possibly happen.

Although problem solving has always been in the focus of research in Cognitive Science the issues of context influence on problem solving have largely been ignored. Gestalt psychologists initiated the study of context effects on perception and problem solving. However, while in perception they have focused on questions like the figure and background interaction, in problem solving they typically take it as granted that subjects start with a clear problem description (the figure) and the rest of the world is ignored during the problem solving process (the background). Being interested in how the problem representation is being constructed, they have restricted their investigations to cases where all the needed elements are given by the experimenter and the task of the subject is to arrange them in an appropriate way. They have studied some of the obstacles in building correct representations like functional fixedness (Maier, 1931, Dunker, 1945) and set effects (Luchins, 1942), which can be called context effects. Recently Tversky and Kahneman (1981) and Shafir, Simonson and Tversky (1993) have demonstrated context effects on decision making; Johnson-Laird, Legrenzi and Legrenzi (1972), Gick and Holyoak (1980, 1983), McAfee and Proffitt (1991), Cooke and Breedin (1994) have demonstrated context effects on problem solving. However, the context effects demonstrated in the above research are the result of systematic manipulation of some supposedly irrelevant to the solution elements of the problem description. Little attention has been paid to the role of casual entities in the environment which are not part of the problem description, but which might influence the problem solving process.

The main purpose of the current paper is to avoid this limitation and to study the context effects (if any) caused by such accidental elements from the problem solver's environment.

2. A Dynamic Theory of Context

Recently a dynamic theory of context has been proposed (Kokinov, 1995) where context is considered as the set of *all* entities which influence human cognitive behavior on a particular occasion. All these context elements are elements of human working memory. Various entities influence the cognitive process to different degrees, e.g. usually, the goal influences the problem solving process much deeper than a casual object in the problem solver's environment. That is why instead of defining clear-cut boundaries of context it would be better to consider context as a fuzzy set of elements which gradually diminish their influence on human behavior. As a consequence, *context is considered as the dynamic fuzzy set of all associatively relevant memory elements (mental representations or operations) at a particular instant of time.*

There are various sources of context elements: reasoning mechanisms (the set of elements produced and manipulated by them is called *reasoning-induced context*), perceptual mechanisms (the set of elements produced by the perception process and representing entities from the environment is called *perception-induced context*), and memory mechanisms (the set of all elements retrieved/activated by memory processes or being a residue from a previous context is called *memory-induced context*).

The effects of the memory-induced context are usually described as set effects and priming effects while the effects caused by the perception-induced context are usually called simply context effects. There are many experiments on priming effects on perception, categorization, language comprehension, sentence completion, etc. Some experiments performed by the first author have demonstrated priming effects on problem solving (Kokinov, 1990, 1994a) with very clear dynamic properties: the priming effects disappear in the course of time according to an exponential law. Complementary, in the current work we are interested in *context effects* on problem solving.

A cognitive architecture DUAL has been proposed with a special emphasis on the context-sensitive nature of human cognitive processes (Kokinov, 1994b,c). A context-sensitive model of analogical reasoning, AMBR, has been developed on the basis of this architecture (Kokinov, 1994a). The performed simulation experiments with AMBR have replicated the priming effects obtained in the psychological experiments and in addition they made a prediction about context effects on problem solving. Part of the motivation of the current work is to test these predictions.

The DUAL architecture explains context effects in the following way. The perceptual mechanisms build up representations of the objects in the environment and their properties and relations in the Working Memory (WM) or just reactivate existing representations in Long-Term Memory (LTM) and bring them into the WM. During the period of fixation on a particular object its representation becomes a source of activation, i.e. it continuously emits activation to its neighbors for that period. Moreover, depending on the location of the object in the visual field (center/periphery) and the amount of attention devoted to it, the amount of emitted activation will vary. The basic memory process in DUAL is a process of spreading activation where each WM element continuously spreads its activation to its neighbors. The resulting activation levels of the LTM elements determine their availability (accessibility for the declarative elements and speed of running for the procedural elements). The general predictions that this architecture makes are that (1) every element (be it part of the problem description or not) which is being perceived (and therefore activated in WM) can potentially influence the reasoning process if it happens that it is somehow linked (directly or via a chain of links) to a concept which can play a key role in the solution of the problem, (2) the more the element is attended to the higher its potential influence (if the distance between the element and the key concept is the same), i.e. generally the elements of the core of the contexts (e.g. the elements of the problem description) will have greater impact than the elements of the periphery of the context, (3) for a large number of elements that are not intentionally perceived their influence will be at the subconscious level and could not be reported by the subjects.

Two experiments have been performed. In Experiment I the entities whose influence is being tested are part of the illustrations accompanying the target problem descriptions and are supposed to be attended to even if later on they can be considered as irrelevant, therefore they (rather) belong to the core of the context, while in Experiment II the tested entities are part of the illustrations accompanying other problems' descriptions, they are casual with respect to the target problem and might not be attended to at all, therefore they (possibly) belong to the periphery of the context (if a context effect could be demonstrated at all).

3. Experiment I: Near Context Effects

This experiment investigates the influence that some elements of the environment related to the problem description (without being an explicit part of it) can have on the problem solving process. Similar experiments have been performed by Maier (1931) accidentally bumping against a string to get it swinging providing a hint for the solution of the two-string problem and by Cooke and Breedin (1994) studying effects of irrelevant shapes of objects on naive reasoning about motion and trajectories. In this sense this experiment can be considered as a replication of existing experiments in the case of changing the illustrations accompanying some insight problems. However, instead of exploring whether the illustration can play the role of a hint (e.g. it will raise the number of subjects correctly solving the problem) this study focuses on whether the elements of the illustration can change the way in which the problem is being solved.

3.1. Method

3.1.1. Subjects. 257 subjects (high school students and undergraduate students in psychology, law, drama, journalism and economics at NBU) participated in the experiment.

3.1.2. Design. There were two experimental conditions for each target problem – two different contexts in which it was presented and each subject received one of these two versions (i.e. the experiment had a between-subjects design). Subjects were randomly assigned to the two experimental conditions.

For each target problem the variety of solutions was clustered in several categories and each particular solution proposed by a subject was classified as belonging to one of them by two experts. The number of categories differed from problem to problem depending on the richness of the target domain. The measured variable was the type of the solution proposed by the subject.

There were *control* and *context conditions*. In the control condition subjects received just the standard target problem description which does not include a drawing. In the context condition subjects received an additional picture (Figure 1).

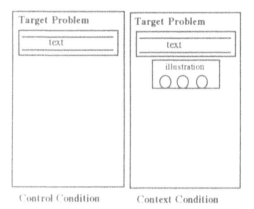

Figure 1. Control and Context Conditions.

3.1.3. Materials. Four target problems were used in the experiment. They can be classified as various insight problems. Because of space limitations only one example target problem will be described.

Target problem (Heating Problem): Imagine you are in a forest by a river and you want to heat up some water. You have only a knife, an axe and a match-box. You have no containers of any kind. You could cut a vessel of wood but it would burn up if placed above the fire. How would you boil your egg using this wooden vessel?

Originally presented in (Kokinov, 1990)

This problem was presented in the following experimental conditions. In the *control condition* subjects received only the textual description of the problem, while in the *context condition* they received a color picture in addition (Figure 2 presents a gray scale copy of it). There are many stones in the picture and the intention was to check whether this would increase the number of subjects using stones in the solution of the problem (as predicted by the simulation experiment).

Figure 2. Picture used as illustration of the target problem in the Context condition.

3.1.4. Procedure. Each subject received sheets of paper each presenting one target problem. They had to solve the problems one by one and for a fixed period of time varying for the different problems (from 1 to 4 minutes). They were not allowed to browse the sheets of papers and look at previous or following problems, or to come later back to previous problems. Subjects were asked to report in case they were familiar with a particular problem and in such cases their results were discarded.

3.2. Results

The solutions produced by the subjects were classified in the corresponding number of categories. Table 1 presents the percentage of generated solutions in each category in each experimental condition for the target problem. The results show that in the presence of the picture significantly more subjects (χ^2=37.89, df=4, p<0.001) produce solutions involving stones (14% produced a solution involving immersing heated stones in the water vs. 5% in the control condition, and 22% produced other solutions involving stones vs. 2% in the control group). This corresponds to the simulation results obtained in (Kokinov, 1994a) and so meets the predictions of the theory.

Similar context effects were demonstrated with the other 3 target problems. Thus our hypothesis about the presence of context effects when manipulating elements of the problem illustration was supported.

	Control	Context
immersing a knife	23	16
immersing an axe	11	10
immersing a stone	5	14
other usage of stones	2	22
other solutions failures	59	37

Table 1. Percentage of answers which fall into the category corresponding to each cell in the Experiment on the Heating Problem.

4. Experiment II: Far Context Effects

This experiment investigates the influence that some marginal elements of the environment (without being part of the description of the problem) can have on the problem solving process. We are not aware of analogous experiments in the literature.

4.1. Method

4.1.1. Subjects. The same subjects who participated in Experiment I participated also in Experiment II.

4.1.2. Design. Experiment II had a similar between-subject design as Experiment I and the same measured variable (type of generated solution). However, on each sheet of paper two problems were presented to the subjects: the first one is the target problem and the second one is the context one.

For each target problem several experimental conditions were designed: a control condition and two or more context conditions differing in the illustration accompanying the second problem on the sheet (Figure 3).

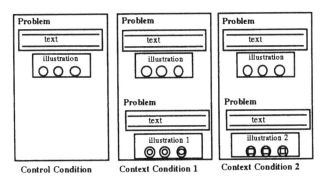

Figure 3. Control and Two Context Conditions.

4.1.3. Materials. Again four insight problems were used in the experiment. The context problems were designed so that the problems themselves and their solutions could not help in the solution of the target problem, but only their illustrations could be found relevant.

Because of space limitations only one such target problem together with the corresponding context problems and their illustrations will be described. Three *different context conditions* were used, i.e. three different context problems were presented in the *different* experimental conditions.

Target Problem 2 (The Spring Problem): Two springs are made of the same steel wire and have the same number of coils. They differ only in the diameters of the coils. Which spring would stretch further down if we hang the same weights on both of them?

Adapted from (Clement, 1988)

Comb Context Problem: From which part of the comb would you produce a higher-pitched sound?

Bent Comb Context Problem: From which part of the comb would you produce a higher-pitched sound?

Beam Context Problem: On a 7 meter long lever two weights are hanging as shown in the picture. If one of the weights is 10 kg, what should the other one be so that the lever remains in balance?

The comb with bent tines in the second illustration (Figure 4) was supposed to activate the concepts of bending and different thickness and consequently the concept of stronger (more robust) material associated with massive (solid) objects and therefore to mislead subjects that the wider spring will stretch less. The lever in the third illustration was supposed to activate the concept of equilibrium and therefore suggests equal stretching of both springs.

The comb in the first illustration was initially designed with the intention to activate bending and different thickness. However, results show that the concept of bending is not activated by this picture (that is why we

designed the second picture) and it seems that the fingers pointing to the thicker tines of the comb are associated with the wider spring which will stretch more (which happened to be the right answer).

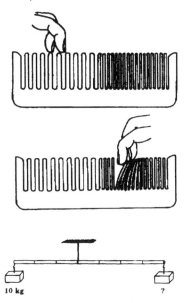

Figure 4. Drawings used for the comb, bent comb and beam context problems.

4.1.4. Procedure. The same procedure as in Experiment I was used, however, the subjects received sheets of paper each containing two problems. There was the following addition to the instruction:

"These sheets of papers were also used in another experiment where the subjects had to solve twice as many problems than in the present experiment. So, when you encounter two problems on the same sheet of paper, please, solve only the first one and skip the second one. In this experiment we are interested only in the first problems."

The reason for instructing subjects to skip the second problem on each sheet (the context one) is that we would like to isolate the context effects from the priming effects, i.e. if the subjects were solving the context problem first or in parallel with the target one then all the concepts used in it would be activated prior to the target problem solving process and would have caused a priming effect, i.e. we would test the influence of the memory-induced context instead of the perception-induced context.

After having finished with the problems the subjects were told the aim of the experiment and its hypothesis and were asked to write down an introspective report on whether they were influenced by the second problems while solving the first ones.

4.2. Results

The solutions produced by the subjects were classified in the corresponding number of categories. Table 2 presents the

589

percentage of generated solutions in each category in each experimental condition.

The results obtained for the spring problem were found to differ significantly in the different context conditions as well as between the control condition and the various context conditions: control condition – comb condition (χ^2=13.07, $p<0.01$), control condition – bent comb condition (χ^2=6.17, $p<0.05$), control condition – beam condition (χ^2=10.63, $p<0.01$), comb condition – beam condition (χ^2=10.83, $p<0.01$), beam condition – bent comb condition (χ^2=15.55, $p<0.001$), comb condition – bent comb condition (χ^2=31.99, $p<0.001$). While in the comb condition 65% of the subjects produced the right answer (in contrast with 46% in the control condition and even fewer in the other context conditions), in the bent comb condition 59% of the subjects gave a preference to the slender spring (in contrast to 45% in the control condition and even less in the other context conditions), and in the lever condition subjects tended to equalize both springs (26% wrote that both springs would stretch equally in contrast to the 9% in the control condition).

condition \ answer	wider spring	slender spring	equally
control	46	45	9
comb	65	21	14
bent comb	29	59	12
beam	42	32	26

Table 2. Percentage of answers which fall into the category corresponding to each cell in the experiment on the target problem.

Many subjects reported in their protocols that they were not aware of any relation between the problems (the target and the context ones) and that (as a result of the instruction and time pressure) they have completely ignored the second problem while solving the first one. (Moreover, some of them (fortunately, not many) have unconsciously covered the second half of the sheet with their hands while solving the target problems). However, the results described above provide evidence that these problems have actually influenced subjects' behavior at the unconscious level.

5. General Discussion

The performed experiments have demonstrated both near and far context effects on problem solving caused by core (Experiment I) and peripheral elements (Experiment II) of the perception-induced context, respectively.

The results obtained from the experiment with the Heating Problem are coherent with the simulation results obtained earlier on the same problem (Kokinov, 1994a).

There are many directions for future work as the current work marks only the beginning of more extensive study of context effects on problem solving. Emphasis will be put on far context effects and an attempt will be made to measure context effect as a function of the physical, conceptual and pragmatic distance between the target and the context problem descriptions.

Acknowledgements

This research has been partially supported by the Bulgarian National Science Fund under contract OHN406/94.

References

Clement, J. (1988). Observed Methods for Generating Analogies in Scientific Problem Solving. *Cognitive Science*, vol. 12, pp. 563-586.

Cooke, N., Breedin, S. (1994). Constructing Naive Theories of Motion on the Fly. *Memory & Cognition*, 22(4), 474-493.

Dunker, K. (1945). On Problem Solving. *Psychological Monographs*, 58:5, (Whole No. 270).

Gick, M., Holyoak, K. (1980). Analogical Problem Solving. *Cognitive Psychology*, 12, 306-355

Gick, M., Holyoak, K. (1983). Schema Induction and Analogical Transfer. *Cognitive Psychology*, 15, 1-38.

Johnson-Laird, P., Legrenzi, P., Legrenzi, M. (1972). Reasoning and a Sense of Reality. British Journal of Psychology, 63, 395-400.

Kokinov, B. (1990). Associative Memory-Based Reasoning: Some Experimental Results. In: *Proceedings of the 12th Annual Conference of the Cognitive Science Society*, Hillsdale, NJ: Lawrence Erlbaum Associates.

Kokinov, B. (1994a) A Hybrid Model of Reasoning by Analogy. Chapter 5. in: K. Holyoak & J. Barnden (eds.) *Analogical Connections, Advances in Connectionist and Neural Computation Theory*, vol.2, Ablex Publ. Corp.

Kokinov, B. (1994b) The DUAL Cognitive Architecture: A Hybrid Multi-Agent Approach. In: A. Cohn (ed.) *Proceedings of ECAI'94*. John Wiley & Sons, Ltd., London.

Kokinov, B. (1994c) The Context-Sensitive Cognitive Architecture DUAL. In: *Proceedings of the 16th Annual Conference of the Cognitive Science Society*. Erlbaum, Hillsdale, NJ.

Kokinov, B. (1995). A Dynamic Approach to Context Modeling. IJCAI Workshop on Context.

Luchins, A. (1942). Mechanization in Problem Solving: The Effect of Einstellung. *Psychological Monographs*, 54:6, (Whole No. 248).

Maier, N. (1931). Reasoning in Humans II: The Solution of a Problem and it Appearance in Consciousness. *Journal of Comparative Psychology*, 12, 181-194.

McAfee, E., Proffitt, D. (1991). Understanding the surface Orientation of Liquids. *Cognitive Psychology*, 23, 483-514.

Shafir, E., Simonson, I., Tversky, A. (1993). Reason-based choice. *Cognition*, 49, 11-36.

Tversky, A., Kahneman, D. (1981). The Framing of Decisions and the Psychology of Choice. *Science*, 211, 453-458.

Linking Adaptation and Similarity Learning

David B. Leake, Andrew Kinley, and David Wilson
Computer Science Department
Lindley Hall 215, Indiana University
Bloomington, IN 47405
{leake,akinley,davwils}@cs.indiana.edu

Abstract

The case-based reasoning (CBR) process solves problems by retrieving prior solutions and adapting them to fit new circumstances. Many studies examine how case-based reasoners learn by storing new cases and refining the indices used to retrieve cases. However, little attention has been given to learning to refine the process for applying retrieved cases. This paper describes research investigating how a case-based reasoner can learn strategies for adapting prior cases to fit new situations, and how its similarity criteria may be refined pragmatically to reflect new capabilities for case adaptation. We begin by highlighting psychological research on the development of similarity criteria and summarizing our model of case adaptation learning. We then discuss initial steps towards pragmatically refining similarity criteria based on experiences with case adaptation.

Introduction

Case-based reasoning (CBR) is a reasoning process that solves new problems by retrieving similar prior problem-solving episodes and adapting their solutions to fit the new situations. Learning by remembering cases is a fundamental part of case-based reasoning: Each problem-solving episode provides a new case for future use. CBR research has also devoted considerable attention to learning by refining the indices used to guide case retrieval. However, little attention has been given to learning how cases should be applied. This paper discusses research modeling how a case-based reasoner can make better use of its prior cases by learning how to adapt them to new circumstances, and by refining the similarity criteria it uses to reflect changes in its adaptation abilities.

Acquisition of case adaptation knowledge is a classic problem for models of case-based reasoning (Kolodner, 1991). CBR systems generally rely on static sets of hand-coded adaptation rules, but developing the needed rules has proven to be a very difficult problem. However, as studies show, human case-based reasoners are adept at applying prior cases (see Kolodner, 1993, for an overview). Consequently, a natural question for CBR as a cognitive model is how the requisite case adaptation knowledge might be acquired.

We are investigating a method for learning specific adaptation knowledge to augment an initial library of very general case adaptation rules (Leake, 1995b). In our approach, a case-based reasoner begins with a small set of abstract rules for transforming cases and for searching memory to find the information needed to make adaptations. This general knowledge is used to perform adaptations from scratch. The system improves its adaptation capabilities by saving traces of the derivations of new adaptations in a library of *adaptation cases* and reusing them for similar adaptation problems. Thus it makes a transition from rule-based to case-based case adaptation (Leake, 1995b; Leake et al., 1996). By saving memory search cases and adaptation cases, a CBR system can acquire specific adaptation knowledge.

Adaptation learning provides the motivation for another type of learning, learning to refine similarity criteria. A central role of similarity judgments in case-based reasoning is to determine which cases to apply to a new situation and how to adapt them to fit new circumstances. Although CBR systems often base similarity judgments on semantic similarity, the real goal of "similarity assessment" in CBR is to determine *adaptability*: how easily an old case can be adapted to fit the requirements of a new situation (Birnbaum et al., 1991; Smyth and Keane, 1995, 1996). If adaptation knowledge is learned, static similarity criteria may not keep pace with new capabilities for performing adaptations. Thus similarity assessment criteria should change as new adaptation knowledge is acquired.

We first discuss the relationship of our approach to psychological results on the development of similarity criteria and pragmatic influences on case adaptation. We then summarize our model's approach to improving case adaptation and some preliminary results on the effects of adaptation learning. Finally, we describe the method we are developing for making similarity assessment reflect adaptation experience and relate our approach to other computer models.

Motivations

Our research investigates how case adaptation strategies for case-based reasoning can be learned, and how the similarity assessment process can be refined as adaptation learning makes particular types of differences between old and new situations easier to overcome.

This approach can be supported directly on functional grounds: The purpose of similarity assessment is to determine the difficulty of adapting cases to new situations, which depends on the reasoner's adaptation knowledge. We are not aware of psychological studies directly examining the connection between adaptability and similarity in case-based reasoning, but psychological studies do provide examples of developmental shift in similarity criteria, of similarity judgments coming to more closely reflect task-relevant features as a task is learned, and of the applicability of an analog to a new problem situation acting as a selection constraint during human analogical reasoning.

Experiments by Gentner & Toupin (1986) demonstrate a developmental shift in the similarity criteria used by children for analogical reasoning, and show that the shift is manifested in how they adapt stories to apply to new characters. Experiments by Suzuki et al. (1992) studying similarity judgments in problem-solving for the Towers of Hanoi problem show that novices' judgments about the similarity of problem states can be characterized by the number of shared surface features, but that experts' judgments are best characterized by the goal-relevant criterion of the number of operators required to transform each problem state to the goal state. Further, Chi et al. (1981) note a dramatic difference between the similarity criteria of novice physics problem-solvers, who rely on surface features, and physics experts, who classify problems according to the underlying methods needed to solve them.

Adaptation factors have also been shown to affect selection of analogues in analogical problem-solving. Experiments by Keane (1994) suggest that when performing analogical problem-solving, subjects favor analogues that are easier to apply to the new problem situation.

Overview of DIAL

We are investigating learning about adaptation and pragmatic similarity in the context of a case-based planner. The planner's task domain is *disaster response planning*, the initial strategic planning used to determine how to assess damage, evacuate victims, etc., in response to natural and man-made disasters (e.g., earthquakes and chemical spills). There are no hard-and-fast rules for disaster response planning; human disaster response planners appear to rely largely on prior cases to guide their decisions (Rosenthal et al., 1989).

Our computer model, DIAL (for **D**isaster response with **I**ntrospective **A**daptation **L**earning), takes as input conceptual representations of news stories describing the initial events in a disaster. It generates candidate response plans by case-based reasoning. The system's case-based planning framework is based in a straightforward way on previous case-based planners such as CHEF (Hammond, 1989).

DIAL's initial knowledge sources are a library of domain cases—disaster response plans from prior disasters—and general (domain-independent) rules about case adaptation and memory search. When a new story is presented to the system, DIAL uses standard indexing techniques to attempt to retrieve cases representing response plans for similar disasters. This process results in a set of candidate response plan cases. A finer-grained analysis selects the candidate expected to be easiest to adapt, based on similarity criteria learned from experience with prior adaptations. The selected case is provided to the system's case adaptation component, along with a list of differences that must be repaired.

Learning and Reusing Adaptations

The foundation of DIAL's adaptation and similarity learning is case-based reasoning about the adaptation process itself. DIAL's adaptation process begins with the system's adaptation component receiving a description of an adaptation task: a disaster response plan case and a list of the problems that prevent it from applying to a new situation. DIAL first attempts case-based adaptation, searching for an adaptation case that applied successfully to a similar adaptation problem. Adaptation cases are indexed in memory by a vocabulary of categories of problems that may require adaptation (see Leake, 1992). If DIAL succeeds in retrieving a relevant adaptation case, the adaptation process traced by that case is re-applied.

Otherwise, DIAL builds up a new adaptation by a combination of rule-based and case-based reasoning. The system first selects a transformation associated with the type of problem that adaptation must repair. (For example, to *substitute* a new plan step for one that does not apply.) Given the transformation, the program generates a *knowledge goal* (Hunter, 1990; Ram, 1987) for the knowledge needed to apply the transformation. (E.g., when performing a substitution, DIAL needs to identify a good substitute: an object that satisfies the relevant constraints on the object being replaced.) The knowledge goal is used to guide a planning process for how to search memory (Leake, 1994; Leake, 1995c). This process builds a memory search plan, using a small set of built-in memory search strategies (e.g., to perform "local search" for similar objects) and *memory search cases* stored after solving previous adaptation problems. When the needed information is found in memory, it enables DIAL to apply the selected transformation to the retrieved response plan.

The adapted response plan is evaluated by a simple evaluator that checks the compatibility of the current plan with explicit constraints from the response plan. A human user performs backup evaluation, detecting more subtle problems. If problems are found, DIAL attempts other adaptations. If the autonomous case adaptation process fails to generate an acceptable solution, an interface allows the user to guide the adaptation process, selecting a transformation and suggesting features to consider. During the adaptation, the system records a trace of the adaptation process. The trace is represented in the same form as the traces of system-generated adaptations and is added to the adaptation case library for future use.

When adaptation is successful, the resulting response plan, adaptation case, and memory search plan are stored for future use.

The Effects of Adaptation Learning

Although our computer model is still under development, we have conducted initial ablation tests studying the benefit of adaptation learning and its relationship to case learning in the initial model. In these tests, starting from an initial memory of 870 concepts and case library of 6 initial cases, DIAL performs a total of 30 adaptations to develop response plans for 5 stories. Stored cases and new stories were based on Clarinet News Service newswire and the *INvironment* newsletter for air quality consultants; stored cases involved an earthquake in Los Angeles, an air quality disaster at a manufacturing plant, a flood in Bainbridge, Georgia, a chemical disaster at a factory, a flood in Izmir, Turkey, and an air quality disaster in a rural elementary school.

In these tests, response plan learning did improve performance, as did adaptation learning. Interestingly, by the measure of memory operations performed, adaptation learning alone was more effective than case learning alone, although both required comparable numbers of memory nodes to be visited. As was also expected, when no adaptation cases are learned, learning additional response plan cases enables the system to solve new problems with less adaptation effort—more similar cases are available. Adding adaptation learning to response plan learning produced insignificant benefits when memory search during adaptations was based on local search. There was much greater benefit when response plan learning was combined with adaptation learning using other memory search strategies. Details on the adaptation learning process and this preliminary test can be found in Leake, Kinley, and Wilson (1996).

We are now "scaling up" the system for additional tests. One particular concern is the potential for a "utility problem" (Francis and Ram, 1995; Minton, 1988) as large numbers of adaptation cases are learned.

Learning Similarity from Adaptability

To realize the full benefits of adaptation learning, similarity learning is needed as well. Learning about how difficult it is to repair particular differences helps to decide which cases are most usefully similar—which will be most easily adapted. For example, initially it might be assumed that the locale of a disaster is comparatively unimportant when deciding similarity. However, adapt-

ing the response for a small town disaster into the response plan for a big city disaster may be quite difficult, because of the added need to work out arrangements for a large-scale evacuation. From experience with this adaptation, a disaster response planner can learn to consider the locale of the disaster when assessing similarity between a new situation and prior disasters.

DIAL improves its similarity assessment process by using learned adaptation cases to provide estimates of the cost of adapting particular types of problems. In order to facilitate later processing, response plans that require less adaptation effort to apply are considered more similar than those requiring expensive adaptation. In DIAL's pragmatic similarity judgment, the "most similar" case is the one expected to be easiest to adapt. This approach to similarity follows the same principle as Leake's (1992) *constructive similarity assessment* and Smyth and Keane's (1995, 1996) *adaptation-guided retrieval* .

If similarity judgments are to be based on adaptability, two questions are how to estimate the cost of adaptation and how to make a reasonable tradeoff between accuracy of adaptation cost estimates and the cost of the estimation process itself. DIAL's retrieval uses two types of similarity assessment in a two-step process. The first step retrieves a rough "first-pass" set of cases based on static semantic similarity criteria applied to the type of disaster (e.g., flood, earthquake, etc.) and its attributes. The second step prioritizes these candidate cases for adaptation according to estimates of their adaptability.

To estimate adaptability, DIAL first identifies inapplicable aspects of the retrieved response plans, using procedures for patten-based anomaly detection, and describes the problems according to a vocabulary of problem types based on Leake (1992). This vocabulary includes, for example, categories to describe the problem when objects specified by the plan are unavailable, or when role-fillers of a schema have been left unspecified and need to be selected. Associated with each category is a frame structure to be filled in with the specifics of the current problem. That frame structure, instantiated with the particulars of the current situation, describes the problem to be repaired by adaptation.

For each problem to be repaired by adaptation, DIAL searches its memory of prior adaptations, and retrieves the adaptation case addressing the most similar prior problem. That previous adaptation case provides information about how to repair the problem. The information is used to estimate the cost of its repair, as follows:

- If the retrieved adaptation case was generated to solve an identical adaptation problem, the solution to that previous adaptation can be reapplied directly, so adaptation cost will be minimal. For example, if a previous adaptation involved adapting the response plan for an American flood to a flood in Turkey, and the Red Cross was involved in the original plan, a new relief agency would have to be found to apply the plan in Turkey, where the Red Cross does not exist. However, replacing the Red Cross by the Red Crescent is a reasonable adaptation. Once that adaptation is learned, the problem of adapting the Red Cross to a relief organization to apply to Turkey is trivial.

- If the retrieved adaptation case dealt with an adaptation problem that was similar but not identical, the cost of adapting the new problem is estimated from the cost of the prior adaptation. How best to perform this estimation is still an open issue, but DIAL's current method is to focus on the cost of performing the memory search needed to find the information to allow the previous adaptation to be performed. To illustrate, if finding a substitution—for example, an appropriate evacuation method—required considerable effort for a previous adaptation, it is assumed that finding a new evacuation route will take considerable effort in the current situation. Consequently, if one of the retrieved plans requires finding an evacuation method, while another avoids evacuation by containing the disaster, it may be reasonable to favor the plan for containing the disaster (if containing the disaster is practical).[1] The rationale for this cost estimation criterion is based on the idea of derivational analogy (Carbonell, 1986; Veloso, 1994): If a previous adaptation for a similar problem had to infer certain features and constraints from the plan, and transform them in certain ways to generate an appropriate adaptation, the process for the current situation is expected to follow analogous steps, even if the specifics of the situation are different.

- If no similar adaptation case is found, DIAL uses an estimate based on the average cost (measured in primitive memory search operations) of adapting problems in each problem category. Kass (1990) proposes a similar method for coarse-grained estimates of adaptation cost.

By basing similarity assessment directly on the current state of its changing adaptation knowledge, DIAL's similarity assessment process reflects information about the actual difficulty of adapting to repair certain types of problems. We are now designing experiments to examine the performance of these simple strategies, to test how they affect the needed adaptation effort and to guide their refinement.

Relationship to Other Computer Models

Some early case-based reasoning systems included components for learning limited forms of adaptation knowl-edge. For example, CHEF (Hammond, 1989) bases its adaptations on both a static library of domain-independent plan repair strategies and a library of special-purpose *ingredient critics* that are learned; PER-SUADER (Sycara, 1988) uses previously-stored adaptation episodes to suggest adaptations. In both examples, the learned adaptations can only be reused in highly similar situations. However, the adaptation cases learned by DIAL can be reused more flexibly. Rather than learning only by storing specific adaptation episodes, DIAL stores both the specific adaptation and its derivational trace. In very similar situations, the adaptation can be reapplied directly; in less similar situations, the steps used to determine the previous adaptation can be replayed, taking into account differing circumstances.

DIAL also differs from previous approaches to adaptation learning in its emphasis on learning about the required memory search. Its characterization of adaptations is inspired by the *adaptation strategies* in SWALE (Kass et al., 1986) and ABE (Kass, 1990), which combine transformations with domain-independent memory search information, and its approach to memory search is inspired by the memory search process of CYRUS (Kolodner, 1984). However, those systems did not learn to improve their search processes. In reasoning about the information needed to carry out the adaptation task, our model also relates closely to Oehlmann's (1995) metacognitive adaptation. It is in a similar spirit both to recent research on applying heuristic search to gathering information for argumentation (Rissland et al., 1994) and to work in information retrieval on strategic reasoning about where to search for needed information (Baudin et al., 1994).

Smyth & Keane (1995, 1996) have developed a CBR system that ties similarity judgments directly to adaptability, using heuristics coded to reflect the difficulty of performing particular types of adaptations. They also demonstrate that their adaptation-guided method produces significant improvements in the cost of performing adaptations. Our approach to similarity judgments is strongly in the spirit of their approach, and their results are encouraging for the potential benefit of adaptation-based criteria compared to traditional semantic similarity criteria. However, in their work, similarity and adaptation knowledge are static.

Learning to refine similarity criteria has been investigated in Prodigy/Analogy (Veloso, 1994). That system's "foot-print" similarity metric focuses consideration on goal-relevant portions of the initial state, in order to retrieve cases that refer to the prior problem situations with the most relevant similarities. Our adaptability-based similarity method focuses on a different issue, estimating the costs of repairing relevant differences that have been found. Finally, two-stage retrieval processes, such as that used in DIAL's initial filtering of retrieval

---

[1]It should be noted that in general, the different plans may each contain useful parts of the solution to a problem (e.g., Ram and Francis, 1996, Redmond, 1992). Extending our model to consider relevant pieces of candidate plans is a topic for future research.

candidates followed by a deeper but more computationally expensive analysis, have been advocated by many previous models (e.g., Bareiss & King, 1989) not only on functional grounds (to restrict processing effort) but on cognitive grounds as well (Gentner and Forbus, 1991). The new contribution of our approach is to tie similarity criteria directly to learning about the relative importance of different types of differences when adapting cases to new situations.

Conclusion

We have described ongoing research on how case-based reasoners can learn to apply cases more effectively, both by learning how to adapt prior cases to new situations and by refining similarity criteria according to experience concerning which types of adaptations are difficult to perform. Our approach to learning case adaptation models the acquisition of specific adaptation knowledge starting from "weak methods" for case adaptation; our approach to learning useful similarity criteria builds on the adaptation learning process, to consider cases "usefully similar" if they are expected to be easy to adapt, given experience with prior adaptations. Preliminary trials of the adaptation learning system are encouraging, but further tests are needed, especially to study how the process "scales up" when large numbers of adaptations are learned. Tests are also needed to examine how well current similarity estimates predict the difficulty of future adaptations. The model is now being refined and extended in preparation for tests of the effects of similarity learning and more extensive tests of the system as a whole.

Acknowledgments

This work was supported in part by the National Science Foundation under Grant No. IRI-9409348.

References

Bareiss, R. and King, J. (1989). Similarity assessment in case-based reasoning. In Hammond, K., editor, *Proceedings of the DARPA Case-Based Reasoning Workshop*, pages 67–71, San Mateo. Morgan Kaufmann.

Baudin, C., Pell, B., and Kedar, S. (1994). Using induction to refine information retrieval strategies. In *Proceedings of the twelfth national conference on artificial intelligence*, pages 553–559, Seattle, WA.

Birnbaum, L., Collins, G., Brand, M., Freed, M., Krulwich, B., and Pryor, L. (1991). A model-based approach to the construction of adaptive case-based planning systems. In Barciss, R., editor, *Proceedings of the DARPA Case-Based Reasoning Workshop*, pages 215–224, San Mateo. DARPA, Morgan Kaufmann.

Carbonell, J. (1986). Derivational analogy: A theory of reconstructive problem solving and expertise acquisition. In Michalski, R., Carbonell, J., and Mitchell, T., editors, *Machine Learning: An Artificial Intelligence Approach*, volume 2, pages 371–392. Morgan Kaufmann, Los Altos, CA.

Chi, M., Feltovich, P., and Glaser, R. (1981). Categorization and representation of physics problems by experts and novices. *Cognitive Science*, 5(2):121–153.

Francis, A. and Ram, A. (1995). A comparative utility analysis of case-based reasoning and control-rule learning systems. In *Eighth European Conference on Machine Learning*, Crete, Greece.

Gentner, D. and Forbus, K. (1991). MAC/FAC: A model of similarity-based retrieval. In *Proceedings of the Thirteenth Annual Conference of the Cognitive Science Society*, pages 504–509, Chicago, IL. Cognitive Science Society.

Gentner, D. and Toupin, C. (1986). Systematicity and surface similarity in the development of analogy. *Cognitive Science*, 10(3):277–300.

Hammond, K. (1989). *Case-Based Planning: Viewing Planning as a Memory Task*. Academic Press, San Diego.

Hunter, L. (1990). Planning to learn. In *Proceedings of the Twelfth Annual Conference of the Cognitive Science Society*, pages 261–268, Cambridge, MA. Cognitive Science Society.

Kass, A. (1990). *Developing Creative Hypotheses by Adapting Explanations*. PhD thesis, Yale University. Northwestern University Institute for the Learning Sciences, Technical Report 6.

Kass, A., Leake, D., and Owens, C. (1986). SWALE: A program that explains. In *Explanation Patterns: Understanding Mechanically and Creatively*, pages 232–254. Lawrence Erlbaum Associates, Hillsdale, NJ.

Keane, M. (1994). Adaptation as a selection constraint on analogical mapping. In *Proceedings of the Sixteenth Annual Conference of the Cognitive Science Society*, pages 490–495, Atlanta, GA.

Kolodner, J. (1984). *Retrieval and Organizational Strategies in Conceptual Memory*. Lawrence Erlbaum Associates, Hillsdale, NJ.

Kolodner, J. (1991). Improving human decision making through case-based decision aiding. *The AI Magazine*, 12(2):52–68.

Kolodner, J. (1993). *Case-Based Reasoning.* Morgan Kaufmann, San Mateo, CA.

Leake, D. (1992a). Constructive similarity assessment: Using stored cases to define new situations. In *Proceedings of the Fourteenth Annual Conference of the Cognitive Science Society*, pages 313–318, Bloomington, IN. Lawrence Erlbaum.

Leake, D. (1992b). *Evaluating Explanations: A Content Theory.* Lawrence Erlbaum Associates, Hillsdale, NJ.

Leake, D. (1994). Towards a computer model of memory search strategy learning. In *Proceedings of the Sixteenth Annual Conference of the Cognitive Science Society*, pages 549–554, Atlanta, GA. Lawrence Erlbaum.

Leake, D. (1995a). Adaptive similarity assessment for case-based explanation. *International Journal of Expert Systems*, 8(2):165–194.

Leake, D. (1995b). Combining rules and cases to learn case adaptation. In *Proceedings of the Seventeenth Annual Conference of the Cognitive Science Society*, pages 84–89, Pittsburgh, PA.

Leake, D. (1995c). Representing self-knowledge for introspection about memory search. In *Proceedings of the 1995 AAAI Spring Symposium on Representing Mental States and Mechanisms*, pages 84–88, Stanford, CA. AAAI Press. Technical Report WS-95-05.

Leake, D., Kinley, A., and Wilson, D. (1996). Acquiring case adaptation knowledge: A hybrid approach. In *Proceedings of the Thirteenth National Conference on Artificial Intelligence*, Menlo Park, CA. AAAI Press. In press.

Minton, S. (1988). *Learning Search Control Knowledge: An Explanation-Based Approach.* Kluwer Academic Publishers, Boston.

Oehlmann, R. (1995). Metacognitive adaptation: Regulating the plan transformation process. In *Proceedings of the Fall Symposium on Adaptation of Knowledge for Reuse.* AAAI.

Ram, A. (1987). AQUA: Asking questions and understanding answers. In *Proceedings of the Sixth Annual National Conference on Artificial Intelligence*, pages 312–316, Seattle, WA. Morgan Kaufmann.

Ram, A. and Francis, A. (1996). Multi-plan retrieval and adaptation in an experience-based agent. In Leake, D., editor, *Case-Based Reasoning: Experiences, Lessons, and Future Directions.* AAAI Press, Menlo Park, CA. In press.

Rissland, E., Skalak, D., and Friedman, M. (1994). Heuristic harvesting of information for case-based argument. In *Proceedings of the Twelfth National Conference on Artificial Intelligence*, pages 36–43, Seattle, WA. AAAI.

Rosenthal, U., Charles, M., and Hart, P., editors (1989). *Coping with crises: The management of disasters, riots, and terrorism.* C.C. Thomas, Springfield, IL.

Smyth, B. and Keane, M. (1995). Experiments on adaptation-guided retrieval in case-based design. In *Proceedings of First International Conference on Case-Based Reasoning*, Sesimbra, Portugal.

Smyth, B. and Keane, M. (1996). Design à la déjà vu: Reducing the adaptation overhead. In Leake, D., editor, *Case-Based Reasoning: Experiences, Lessons, and Future Directions.* AAAI Press, Menlo Park, CA. In press.

Suzuki, H., Ohnishi, H., and Shigermasu, K. (1992). Goal-directed processes in similarity judgment. In *Proceedings of the Fourteenth Annual Conference of the Cognitive Science Society*, pages 343–348, Bloomington, IN. Lawrence Erlbaum.

Sycara, K. (1988). Using case-based reasoning for plan adaptation and repair. In Kolodner, J., editor, *Proceedings of the DARPA Case-Based Reasoning Workshop*, pages 425–434, San Mateo, CA. Morgan Kaufmann.

Veloso, M. (1994). *Planning and Learning by Analogical Reasoning.* Springer Verlag, Berlin.

Lifelong science learning: A longitudinal case study

Marcia C. Linn

Graduate School of Education
4611 Tolman Hall
University of California, Berkeley
Berkeley, CA 94720-1670
mclinn@violet.berkeley.edu

BatSheva Eylon

Weizmann Institute of Science
Department of Science Teaching
76100 Rehovot, Israel
NTEYLON@Weizmann.AC.IL

Abstract

How do students link school and personal experiences to develop a useful account of complex science topics? Can science courses provide a firm foundation for lifelong science learning? To answer these questions we analyze how "Pat" integrates and differentiates ideas and develops models to explain complex, personally-relevant experience with thermal phenomena. We examine Pat's process of conceptual change during an 8th grade science class where a heat flow model of thermal events is introduced as well as after studying biology in ninth grade and after studying chemistry in the 11th grade. Pat regularly links new ideas from science class and personal experience to explain topics like insulation and conduction or thermal equilibrium. Thus Pat links experience with home insulation to experiments using wool as an insulator. This linkage leads Pat to consider "air pockets" as a factor in insulation and to distinguish insulators (with air pockets) from metal conductors that "attract heat." These linkages help Pat construct a heat flow account of thermal events and connect it to the microscopic model introduced in chemistry. Pat's process of conceptual change demonstrates how longitudinal case studies contribute to the understanding of conceptual development. Future work will synthesize the conceptual change process of all 40 students we have studied longitudinally.

Introduction

Theories of scientific conceptual change offer a wide range of conjectures about lifelong learning (e.g., Linn, Songer, & Eylon, in press). Piaget conducted extensive cross-sectional studies to support his view that students develop a formal, abstract reasoning skill during adolescence and use it to advance understanding (e.g., Inhelder & Piaget, 1958; Piaget, 1952). Gagné 1968) studied mathematical problem solving to support the view that learning fits a hierarchical model where students master components before more complex ideas. Ausubel (1963) described how students build on their ideas and reorganize their thoughts. Research showing that students develop intuitive ideas based on observations of the natural world motivated McCloskey (1983) and others to hypothesize that student knowledge development in some sense recapitulates historical advance. Gentner and Stevens (1983) discuss the role of explanatory models in knowledge acquisition. diSessa (1993) among others shows that students entertain a range of ideas as they actively reformulate ideas to develop mature views. White and Frederiksen (1990) demonstrate that students benefit

from learning a series of models of complex phenomena and Thagard (1992) analyzes how coherence influences conceptual change.

In this paper we examine how the student "Pat" develops understanding of thermal equilibrium over a five year period. Pat explains a range of familiar events such as why metal and wood feel different at room temperature. We analyze the contribution of class experiences, illustrating how Pat incorporates instruction about microscopic and macroscopic models of thermal events. During eighth grade Pat's physical science course relies on a heat-flow model. During high school Pat studies biological processes such as diffusion and encounters microscopic models of matter in chemistry.

To characterize conceptual change in these longitudinal interviews we identify explanations and models of thermal events as well as integrations and differentiations of scientific ideas. For this work we define a model as an explanation of scientific observations involving a mechanism. For example Pat accounts for conduction by positing that "metals attract heat." Research suggests that students often develop multiple explanations or models linked to specific contexts rather than seeking abstract principles that transcend context (Linn, diSessa, Pea & Songer, 1994). We describe the repertoire of models Pat uses in varied contexts.

We examine how Pat connects ideas to explanations by identifying differentiations and integrations. We define differentiation as the process of decomposing a scientific idea into two distinguishable scientific ideas each connected to an explanation. Weiser & Carey, (in Gentner & Stevens, 1983), describe the historical process resulting in the differentiation of heat and temperature. Siegler (1976) demonstrated that students struggling to understand the balance beam differentiated cases based on observable features of the situation. Similar differentiations occur as students struggle to understand thermal events. For example, Lewis (1991) reports that many students decompose objects into conductors (objects like aluminum foil that feel cold in a 25 C room) and insulators (objects like styrofoam wrap that feel neutral in a 25 C room) in the context of selecting a material to wrap a cold drink to keep it cold. Often students, based on experience, distinguish heating (adding heat) from cooling (cold flow) rather than seeing these as linked (diSessa, 1993). We define integration as the process of combining two or more scientific ideas into a single concept connected to a single explanation. For example, Pat integrates heating and cooling, saying that heat can flow into or out of an object. The process of integration and differentiation is complex and often varies by context. We seek to describe Pat's conceptual change in terms of models and explanations and in terms of integration and differentiation and to invite discussion of the implications.

Methods

Pat is one of 40 longitudinal participants selected randomly from the more than 300 eighth grade students in a middle school participating in the Computer as Learning Partner (CLP) curriculum during one school year. Pat makes average progress in eighth grade. While taking physical science, eighth grade students were interviewed for 30 minutes every three weeks. In the summer after ninth and 11th grade, students participated in 3 hour interviews in their former middle school classroom. Interviews were tape-recorded and transcribed. Students also responded to classroom tests, surveys, and written assessments. The school, located in a metropolitan area, serves middle income families from diverse cultural and linguistic groups. Following high school graduation, most of the students plan to attend a vocational program, two-year, or four year college; a minority seek jobs immediately.

All students study the CLP curriculum in a one-semester physical science course. CLP emphasizes thermal phenomena, takes advantage of real time data collection, and features an electronic laboratory notebook (Linn, 1992; Linn, in press; Ferguson, in press). The classroom is equipped with 16 networked Macintosh computers donated by Apple Computer, Inc. Classes of 32 students work in groups of two at the computers. Students use the CLP software to design experiments, predict outcomes, collect data in real time, design simulations, display results, record observations, and make reports.

The CLP curriculum introduces a heat flow model to help students make sense of their experiences. For example a principle relevant to thermal equilibrium states, "If two objects that differ only in initial temperature are placed in a cooler surround, heat energy will flow out of the object with the higher initial temperature more quickly." Although the heat flow principles could form the basis for student response to all the interview questions, students draw on a broader base of information. Because the principles are abstract students often find the details of the problems salient and draw on these to form explanations. Thus, Pat reflects on home insulation and develops explanations of explanations based on the fibers, the air between the fibers, or the holes between the fibers.

Lewis (1991) created the interview questions and studied an earlier cohort in her dissertation research. The interviews included questions about thermal phenomena presented in the context of naturally-occurring problems. For example, students were asked, "If you were going to wrap a cold soda to take to school for lunch, what is the best thing to wrap it in?" or "You arrive at a ski cabin during the winter and no heat was left on. The room thermometer reads 5 degrees C. What can you predict about the temperature of the objects in the cabin? Why?" The interviewer then probed, asking about the main reason for the answer, evidence to support the answer, reactions to using materials

such as wool or aluminum foil, and reflections on the character of the answer. The interviewer sought to determine students' views of insulation and conduction, heat flow, thermal equilibrium, as well as heat and temperature. If students contradicted themselves from the perspective of the interviewer, they were asked to explain how their ideas were connected. For example, during the interview after ninth grade Pat responded to the question about the best thing for wrapping a soda as follows:

Pat: Well, we found out last year that it's not aluminum. It would be like plastic wrap or bubble wrap I think was the best...

Interviewer (I):   And why is that? ...

Pat: So whatever is in the little metal particles attract heat and so they would, the heat energy would kind of be sucked on to the can and would go into the soda and warm it.

I: But that a lot of people do wrap sodas in foil. ...But if you wrapped it in you were saying plastic wrap or bubble wrap, what would be different about that?

Pat: Because of the air pocket.

I: What would the air pockets do?

Pat: There's something with how the air is an insulator. If you have like um, let's say the Styrofoam wrap, that's really porous. So then the air kind of holds in the little holes and then it insulates against heat energy coming in.

To analyze Pat's conceptual change the authors each independently identified integrations/differentiations, and explanations/models used by the student. We then jointly reviewed the interviews and constructed the summary in Figures 1 and 2 to report the course of knowledge development in two aspects of thermal equilibrium. In the next section we discuss the models Pat uses to make sense of the topic and show how these models both help and hinder progress in understanding the material.

Results and Discussion

Results fall in three categories. First, we describe Pat's integrations and differentiations. Second, we analyze the models Pat develops to connect experiences both in school and in everyday life. Third, we discuss how Pat's models incorporate eighth grade instruction about thermal events and high school courses that relate to these topics but do not address them directly.

Integrations and differentiations

As shown in Figures 1 and 2 Pat makes a number of integrations and differentiations to sort out aspects of thermal equilibrium. For example, in the area of insulators and conductors, prior to instruction Pat predicted that wood and metal would behave differently in the context of a room and an oven. Salient information about insulators (made up of fibers, have holes like in thermal blankets) lead Pat to emphasize a class of insulators that rely on air pockets to contribute to their effectiveness. Pat contrasts these with metals and develops an explanation for conducting based on metals attracting heat.

To make sense of thermal equilibrium, Pat distinguishes the steady state of equilibrium from the process of temperature change to get to equilibrium. Since conductors change towards equilibrium much faster than insulators Pat initially predicts that conductors come close to equilibrium with their surroundings but that insulators remain closer to their starting temperature or "room temperature" when placed in an oven or refrigerator. Eventually Pat connects room temperature to a view of "rooms" as having any temperature saying, "An oven is like a room." In later interviews Pat connects any environment to the idea of a room and predicts that insulators and conductors will both reach the temperature of any "room." This results in two integrations: one involving conductors and insulators and another involving warm and cold rooms.

Pat struggles to explain why some objects feel colder than others in a room at thermal equilibrium. In early interviews, Pat takes the rate of conduction between the hand and the object as an indicator of the temperature of the object (see Figure 2). In later interviews, Pat integrates conduction with the "feel" of the object, adds the idea that the hand has a temperature of its own, and explains the feel of objects on the basis of temperature difference and rate of conduction.

Thermal equilibrium also involves realizing that heating and cooling are the same process in different directions. Natural scientists describe heat as flowing when there is a temperature difference. Pat generally employs a notion of heat flow starting at about the fourth interview. In the interview just prior to tenth grade, however, Pat also discusses a cold flow model as shown in this segment:

Pat: OK. The metal would kind of, like aluminum foil, would kind of pull the cold out of the soda into the air because um, it moved to the. The cold like, it just moved right out onto the metal because metal is the conductor and then it would be released into the air. I forget if it happened that way or if the heat in the air, like the metal pulled the heat in from the air into the soda. I forget if the cold left or if the heat came in, but it's probably both.

I: Does that make sense that there could be both?

[Reflection question]

Pat: Yeah, it makes sense.

I: So cold could go out and heat could come in.

Pat: But it could also be just one. The heat could come in or the heat would leave depending on whether it was hot or cold.

I: Which sort of makes more sense to you? Or does it?

Pat: I really never kind of understood whether there was both or not.

Pat also differentiates heat flow in solids and gasses (air especially). In later interviews Pat begins to link all these ideas in a heat flow model and to distinguish materials on the basis of how fast heat flows through them.

Models

Pat's thermal models illustrate the course of scientific knowledge development as well as the role of personal and school experience. Pat starts with no model for thermal equilibrium but soon appropriates a model of metals attracting heat to explain why metals cool faster than wood and a separate model for insulation ("air pockets make heat energy not go"). Pat also posits a role for air, expressed as metals "pulling the heat in from the air." Pat describes insulators as porous and able to contain air, saying, "the air kind of flows in the little holes and then it insulates against heat energy coming in." Finally, Pat integrates a view of all things being at room temperature with the process of insulation and conduction, and connects all these ideas to the notion of heat flow emphasized in class instruction.

To explain everyday experiences Pat also employs the heat flow model. For example, to explain why metals and pottery behave differently Pat brings in experience with terra cotta bun warmers, saying, ".....you put them in your bread basket to keep the rolls warm....I think those are pottery and not metal because I think once you take the metal out the heat will just go....It wouldn't feel as hot as the metal but it would hold the heat longer, it wouldn't dissipate as fast."

Models help Pat synthesize material and keep track of complex information but they also direct attention to ideas and topics that might be peripheral or idiosyncratic. For example, the holes in materials model motivates Pat to focus on holes to the exclusion of the material that creates the holes. Pat makes both productive combinations and unproductive linkages.

Lifelong learning

Do Pat's models help or hinder later learning? Pat adopts the heat flow model to explain most situations by the end of eighth grade and finds many connections to the model in high school biology and chemistry as well as in everyday examples. For example, after studying biology Pat integrates the concept of diffusion with heat flow, connecting two macroscopic views that have useful similarities. After chemistry Pat attempts to integrate a microscopic model of heat transfer with the heat flow model and makes some productive connections. For example, Pat says to explain thermal equilibrium, "...these are like heat energy waves transferring and so even so you want an equilibrium and energy, but its different from saying you want your carbon atoms to be balanced." There remain limits to integration, however. Distinguishing mechanisms for insulation and conduction poses problems for the heat flow model. In 10th grade Pat entertains a substance model of heat, saying "I want heat energy to be a particle" but cannot find a way to connect this idea. In 12th grade Pat makes more connections between a microscopic and macroscopic model but eventually concludes, "I guess they are the same but they just seem different." Eventually Pat distinguishes substance of material from constraints on flow.

Conclusions

This case study demonstrates how students integrate and differentiate thermal ideas and illustrates how a qualitative and macroscopic model like heat flow can form a firm foundation for subsequent instruction. Pat takes seriously the challenge to integrate scientific ideas across contexts, attempting to reconcile multiple models and diverse interpretations of everyday events. Pat connects ideas to the heat flow model in middle school and continues to refine these ideas and develop a microscopic model in high school.

This case study of knowledge integration and differentiation is consistent with a view of the learner as constructing understanding by building on and refining existing ideas as suggested by diSessa (1993) , White (1990) , and others. Siegler's (1976) study of student understanding of balance beam problems illustrates the process of differentiation and integration elaborated in this case study. Whereas Siegler postulated that students "muddled through" complex integrations of ideas, this case suggests that integrations usually make sense from the perspective of the learner. The case illustrates the value of asking students to explain their ideas both in class and in interviews compatible with research on self explanations (Chi & Bassok, 1989; Bielaczyc, Pirolli, & Brown, 1995). By attempting to explain complex events Pat often comes up with more powerful models or connects diverse ideas. And, Pat gains insight into science learning, remarking in twelth grade, "memorize *if* you understand science."

This study suggests the benefit of instruction that provides a supportive learning environment as well as opportunities for personal autonomy as suggested by Collins, Brown, and Holum (1991). Students who struggle to make sense of their class and personal experiences develop valuable skills as well as a perspective on the nature of scientific reasoning. Instruction that includes metacognitive information about ways that scientific ideas develop and methods for matching scientific ideas to new problems will help students continue to learn after they finish their classes. Developing the propensity for reflection and self-explanation seems productive given that students are likely to follow idiosyncratic paths. And, selecting models for science courses such as the heat flow model that students can connect to their experiences also will help students become lifelong learners.

Acknowledgments

This material is based upon research supported by the National Science Foundation under grant MDR-9155744. Any opinions, findings, and conclusions or recommendations expressed in this publication are those of the authors and do not necessarily reflect the views of the National Science Foundation. This material was partially prepared while the Marcia C. Linn was a Fellow at the Center for Advanced Study in the Behavioral Sciences with financial support provided by the Spencer Foundation. This work draws on the research of the Computer as Learning Partner project. The authors appreciate the contributions of the other group members including Doug Kirkpatrick, Eileen Lewis, Jacquie Madhock, Mark Thomas, and Judith Stern. Thanks also to Dawn Davidson and Jean Near for help in the production of this manuscript..

References

Ausubel, D. P. (1963). *The psychology of meaningful verbal learning: An introduction to school learning*. New York: Grune & Stratton.

Bielaczyc, K., Pirolli, P. L., & Brown, A. L. (1995). Training in self-explanation and self-regulation strategies: Investigating the effects of knowledge acquisition activities on problem solving. *Cognition and Instruction, 13(*2), 221-252.

Chi, M. T. H., & Bassok, M. (1989). Learning from examples via self-explanations. In L. B. Resnick (Ed.), *Knowing, learning, and instruction: Essays in honor of Robert Glaser,* (pp. 251-282). Hillsdale, NJ: Lawrence Erlbaum Associates.

Collins, A., Brown, J. S., & Holum, A. (1991). Cognitive apprenticeship: Making thinking visible. *American Educator, 15*(3), 6-11, 38-39.

diSessa, A. (1993). Toward an epistemology of physics. *Cognition and Instruction, 10(*2-3), 105-225.

Ferguson, D. L. (Ed.). (in press). *Advanced technologies in the teaching of mathematics and science*. Berlin: Springer-Verlag.

Gagné, R. (1968). Instructional variables and learning outcomes. Los Angeles: University of California Press.

Gentner, D., & Stevens, A. L.

Inhelder, B., & Piaget, J. (1958). *The growth of logical thinking from childhood to adolescence; an essay on the construction of formal operational structures*. New York: Basic Books.

Lewis, E. L. (1991). *The process of scientific knowledge acquisition among middle school students learning thermodynamics.* Unpublished Unpublished doctoral dissertation, University of California, Berkeley, CA.

Linn, M. C. (1992). The computer as learning partner: Can computer tools teach science? In K. Sheingold, L. G. Roberts, & S. M. Malcolm (Eds.), *This year in school science 1991: Technology for teaching and learning,.* Washington, DC: American Association for the Advancement of Science.

Linn, M. C. (in press). From separation to partnership in science education: Students, laboratories, and the curriculum. In R. Tinker & T. Ellermeijer (Eds.), *NATO advanced research workshop on microcomputer based labs: Educational research and standards.* Brussels, Belgium: Springer-Verlag.

Linn, M. C., diSessa, A., Pea, R. D., & Songer, N. B. (1994). Can research on science learning and instruction inform standards for science education? *Journal of Science Education and Technology*. 3(1), 7-15.

Linn, M. C., Songer, N. B., & Eylon, B. S. (in press). Shifts and convergences in science learning and instruction. In R. Calfee & D. Berliner (Eds.), *Handbook of educational psychology,.* Riverside, NJ: Macmillan.

McCloskey, M. (1983). Naive theories of motion. In D. Gentner & A. L. Stevens (Eds.), *Mental Models,* (pp. 299-324). Hillsdale, NJ: Lawrence Erlbaum Associates.

Siegler, R. S. (1976). Three aspects of cognitive development. *Cognitive Psychology*, 8, 481-520.

Thagard, P. (1992). *Conceptual Revolutions*. Princeton, NJ: Princeton University Press.

White, B. Y., & Frederiksen, J. R. (1990). Causal model progressions as a foundation for intelligent learning environments. *Artificial Intelligence*, 24(1), 99-157.

Interview Session	Context	Description*	Explanation/Model	Integration/Differentiation
Eighth Grade—Prior to Instruction	Objects in a room	*All objects come to room temperature* / *Temperature of the room stays the same unless an object is large.*	Go into the air and the temperature would make it room temperature	
	Objects in an oven	*Temperature of the wood would be lower than temperature of the oven* / *Metal would be about oven temperature*	Wood is not a conductor; metal is a conductor	
Eighth Grade—Following Probing Your Surroundings	Cold cabin and hot car trunk	All objects come to room temperature / *Car trunk is like a room*	Go to the temperature of the room or the surroundings	*Integration* of thermal equilibrium for any environment
Eighth Grade—Following Rate of Heating and Cooling	Drying oven and air conditioned hotel	All objects come to room temperature / *Conductors reach equilibrium faster than insulators*	Heat energy goes into conductors faster / Metals attract heat	*Differentiation* of rate of change from thermal equilibrium / *Integration* of rate of change with conduction and insulation / Uses attraction model as mechanism
Eighth Grade—Following Insulation and Conduction	Warming Oven	All objects come to room temperature / Conductors reach equilibrium faster than insulators	Heat energy goes into conductors faster	Persistence of ideas
Eighth Grade—Following Instruction	Objects in a room and objects in an oven	All objects come to room temperature	Heat energy goes into them all the time / Flows in for colder, flows out for hotter so they all get to room temperature / "Like another room in the oven"	*Integration* of rate of change, heat energy, direction of heat flow and thermal equilibrium using heat flow mechanism
Tenth Grade—Following Biology	Cold ski cabin and hot car trunk	All objects come to room temperature / *Larger objects reach thermal equilibrium more slowly*	Diffusion longer for large objects / If heat energy had a brain would want to make everything isotonic / Heat particles would diffuse	*Integration* of heat flow and diffusion / *Differentiation* of insulation and mass / Use of anthropomorphic mechanism
Twelfth Grade—Following Chemistry	Objects in chemistry drying oven and objects in a room	All objects come to room temperature / *Larger objects reach thermal equilibrium more slowly; Conductors reach thermal equilibrium faster*	Would take heat energy longer to reach the center of a large object / Atoms that lack heat energy would *want* to take heat energy away from warmer object	Attempt to *integrate* microscopic model and heat flow

* New ideas in *italics*

Figure 1: One student's integration and differentiation of thermal equilibrium from eighth to twelfth grade

Interview Session	Context	Description*	Explanation/Model	Integration/Differentiation
Eighth Grade—Prior to Instruction	Objects in oven and objects in room	*Conductors and insulators feel different temperatures*	Conductors feel colder than insulators; I don't know if they are different temperatures	
Eighth Grade—Following Probing Your Surroundings	Objects in unheated ski cabin and objects in room	*Hand is warmer than the object* / *Metal heats up when touched* / *Wood remains the same temperature when touched*	Conductor takes heat energy from hand to object / I don't know why wood remains the same / Mentions holes model for wood in another context	*Differentiates* conductor in room from conductor wrapped around an object
Eighth Grade—Following Rate of Heating and Cooling	Warm and cold objects	Hand is warmer/colder than the object / Metal heats up or heats hand when touched / *Heat from hand flows through the wood when cold; flows from wood to hand when hot*	Holes from the wood let heat flow through the wood so there is no change in the temperature of the wood	Confusion about heat leaving the hand and change in temperature / *Differentiates* flow of heat from hand (has own temperature) with flow of heat in thermal equilibrium / *Integrates* insulator as wrap for object with feel of insulators using the holes model
Eighth Grade—Following Insulation and Conduction	Warm and cold objects	Hand is different temperature than object / *Hand heats up metal faster than insulator or metal warms hand faster than insulator* / *Wood becomes warmer or colder*	Metals attract heat / Object gets hotter or colder depending on which is warmer	*Integrates* rate of heating from hand for both insulators and conductors / *Integrates* metal as conductor when touched and when wrapped around warmer or colder object / Indicates that these integrations aided by instruction
Eighth Grade—Following Instruction	Warm and cold objects	Hand is different temperature than object / Hand heats up metal faster than insulator or metal warms hand faster than insulator / *Wood feels warm and stays warm*	Wood traps heat in the air holes and makes heat energy not go	*Integrates* feel of object with insulation and conduction, direction of heat flow, and flow model
Tenth Grade—Following Biology	Warm and cold objects	Metal feels colder than wood	Metal is a conductor / Wood is porous and has air pockets	*Integrates* porousness with air pockets view. / Relies on poor recall; does not construct
Twelfth Grade—Following Chemistry	Warm and cold objects and objects that produce own heat energy	Metal feels colder or warmer than wood	Heat energy flows from the metal to hand faster than it flows from wood / Metal is a conductor so flow is more noticeable / Child is a source of energy in a room	*Integrates* insulation and conduction with feel of object for self and child / *Integrates* instruction about energy sources / Reconstructs ideas rather than relying on recall

* New ideas in italics

Figure 2: One student's integration and differentiation of ideas about why objects feel warm or cold from eighth to twelfth grade.

Dissociating Semantic and Associative Word Relationships Using High-Dimensional Semantic Space

Kevin Lund
Department of Psychology
University of California, Riverside
Riverside, CA 92521
kevin@locutus.ucr.edu

Curt Burgess
Department of Psychology
University of California, Riverside
Riverside, CA 92521
curt@cassandra.ucr.edu

Chad Audet
Department of Psychology
University of California, Riverside
Riverside, CA 92521
chad@buffy.ucr.edu

Abstract

The Hyperspace Analogue to Language (HAL) model is a methodology for capturing semantics from a corpus by analysis of global co-occurrence. A priming experiment from Lund et al. (1995) which did not produce associative priming with humans or in the HAL simulation is repeated with rearranged control trials. Our experiment now finds associative priming with human subjects, while the HAL simulation again does not produce associative priming. Associative word norms are examined in relation to HAL's semantics in an attempt to illuminate the semantic bias of the model. Correlations with association norms are found in the temporal sequence of words within the corpus. When the associative norm data are split according to simulation semantic distances, a minority of the associative pairsthat are close semantic neighbors are found to be responsible for this correlation. This result suggests that most associative information is not carried by temporal word sequence in language. This methodology is found to be useful in separating typical "associative" stimuli into pure-associative and semantic-associative subsets. The notion that associativity can be characterized by temporal association in language receives little or no support from our corpus analysis and priming experiments. The extent that "word associations" can be characterized by temporal association seems to be more a function of semantic neighborhood which is a reflection of semantic similarity in HAL's vector representations.

One of the most robust cognitive phenomena is the lexical/semantic priming effect. The word-recognition literature is replete with extensions of Meyer and Schvaneveldt's (1971) initial finding that a word prime that is semantically related to a word target (CAT-DOG) will lower the recognition threshold for the target as compared to a semantically unrelated word pairing (FLOWER-DOG). In most lexical/semantic theories, the role of association is thought to be an important component to semantic structure (Collins & Quillian, 1969; McClelland & Kawamoto, 1986; Moss et al., 1995; Plaut, 1995). More recently, a number of investigators have presented evidence that the phenomenon known as the semantic priming effect is essentially associative in nature. Lupker (1984) showed that words that were associated, but not categorically related, produced a reliable priming effect using the naming task. However, words that were only categorically related did not show a priming effect. One conclusion that can be drawn

from this research was that semantic relations are accessed later than the more basic associative relations. More recently, Shelton and Martin (1992) proposed that automatic retrieval of word information in priming is associative. They used a lexical-decision methodology, but tried to insure automatic processing by having subjects make a response to every item (rather than having obvious prime-target pairs) and by having the related trials form only a small proportion of the total trials. Their conclusion, similar to that of Lupker, was that only associatively related items resulted in automatic priming and that semantic (categorical) effects required some type of controlled process, perhaps subject expectancy. From a computational viewpoint, Plaut (1995) presented a model of priming showing that priming effects could be easily be demonstrated by temporal association and that semantic characteristics did not seem to contribute to this effect.

We think that it may be premature to conclude, however, that the mechanism underlying the priming effect is associative rather than semantic. There are two issues that have to be tackled prior to making any definitive conclusion. First, in word relationships, aspects of semantic and associative meaning are typically correlated. This confounding of associative and semantic relationships leads to confusion about how this information might be represented in memory (and in memory models) as well as about how stimuli should be selected for experiments. Thus, it is crucial in experiments and simulations dealing with this issue that there be a straightforward way to operationally define semantics and association, and, moreover, that this operational definition likewise have a straightforward correspondence to a range of empirical findings that already exist. The second issue that has to be adequately addressed is how can semantic representations be modeled in such a way that allows for experimentation across the broad range of semantic phenomena beyond just priming effects? Such phenomena could include basic categorization, the prediction of human semantic judgments (Lund & Burgess, in press), semantic effects in sentence comprehension (Burgess & Lund, 1996), semantic neighborhood effects, as well as semantic impairments that are associated with deep dyslexia and other types of brain damage (Buchanan, Burgess, & Lund, 1996; Burgess & Lund, in press).

The Hyperspace Analogue to Language (HAL) model of semantic memory offers such an approach. In previous papers, we have proposed that the representations acquired by HAL are semantic in nature and that these semantic representations are what underlie the basic priming effect (Lund et al., 1995; Lund & Burgess, in press). For example, experiment 2 of Lund et al. suggests that the priming effect obtained by Shelton and Martin (1992) for the associated word pairs was, at least in part, carried by the semantic similarity of the items. In addition, the absence of a priming effect for the items related only by semantic relatedness may have been due to insufficient semantic similarity.

In our first experiment, we present an extension of our earlier semantic and associative priming experiments that further supports our claim that semantic priming occurs as a function of semantic similarity rather than associative strength of prime-target pairs. In addition, these results suggest that the representations generated by HAL are semantic rather than associative in nature. Experiments 2 and 3 utilize word pairs from word association norms and two operational definitions of associativity. We conclude that semantic neighborhoods can be used to dissociate the semantic and associative components in word meaning.

Simulation Methods

Matrix Construction

The basic methodology of the simulation is to develop a matrix of word co-occurrence values for a given vocabulary. This matrix is then divided into co-occurrence vectors for each word, which can be analyzed for semantic content (see Lund and Burgess, in press, for a more complete account of the matrix-construction methodology and validating studies). An analysis of co-occurrence must define a window size, that is, the largest number of words occurring between a pair of words such that the pair may be considered to co-occur. The limiting case of a small (useful) window is a width of one, which would correspond to counting only immediately adjacent words as co-occurrants. At the other end of the spectrum, one may count all words within a logical division of the input text as co-occurring equally (see Landauer & Dumais, 1994; Schvaneveldt, 1990). A very small window may miss constructs spanning several words (such as lengthy noun phrases), while large windows risk introducing large numbers of extraneous co-occurrences. Therefore, we chose a window width of ten words.

Within this ten-word window, co-occurrence values are inversely proportional to the number of words separating a specific pair. A word pair separated by a nine-word gap, for instance, would gain a co-occurrence strength of one, while the same pair appearing adjacent to one another would receive an increment of ten. Cognitive plausibility was a constraint, and a ten-word window with decreasing co-occurrence strength seemed within these bounds (Gernsbacher, 1990). The product of this procedure is an N-by-N matrix, where N is the number of words in the vocabulary being considered.

Text Source. The corpus that was analyzed was approximately 160,000,000 words of English text gathered from Usenet. All newsgroups containing English dialog

were included. This source was chosen both for volume and content. Roughly ten million words per day are available, with conversational content spanning a wide array of topics.

Vocabulary. The vocabulary used for the analysis consisted of the 70,000 most frequently occurring symbols within the corpus. A check against the standard Unix dictionary showed that about one half of these were valid English words. The remaining symbols were common misspellings, slang, proper names, and sequences of punctuation or numbers.

Similarity Measurement. Once the matrix was constructed, word vectors were extracted. Each word in the vocabulary has one row and one column to represent it in the matrix. By combining the data from a word's row and column, a vector of 140,000 elements is formed for that word.

These vectors may then be compared by any appropriate distance metric. The distance metric used in the following experiments is the Euclidean distance measure. As the Euclidean metric is sensitive to vector magnitude, the vectors are normalized to a constant length before being compared.

Conceptually, these vectors represent points in a high-dimensional space. In this case, 140,000 dimensions, although only a small subset of the vector elements are necessary to produce semantic effects. For example, 200 elements (i.e., a 200 dimensional space) were used in Lund and Burgess (in press); the dimensionality was reduced by retaining only the most variant portions of the co-occurrence matrix. Other methods of dimensionality reduction have also been used with success; Landauer and Dumais (1994), for instance, used singular value decomposition. With high-dimensional semantic space models, similarity is conceptualized as corresponding inversely to inter-point distances; i.e., presumably the more similar two words are, the closer their points.

Experiment 1

Lund, Burgess, and Atchley (1995) used stimuli representing three types of word relationships in a series of experiments in an attempt to dissociate semantic from associative sources of priming. Semantically related words (TABLE - BED) are instances of the same category and share a number of features. Associated words (MOLD - BREAD) are those which are associated as determined by human word association norms. The items selected, however, were not instances of the same category and, therefore, share few semantic features. The third type of word relation are pairs that are both semantically and associatively related (UNCLE - AUNT). These different word relations should allow one to distinguish between the associative and semantic components of priming. Lund et al. (1995) argued that the vector representations generated by HAL are semantic in nature and not associative. Their evidence for this was that by using semantic distances, priming (unrelated - related) was obtained for the semantic as well as for the semantic + associated pairs, but not for the pairs that were related only through their association (Exp. 3). Using the same stimuli pairs in a lexical decision experiment with human subjects, the identical pattern of results was found.

While the parallels between the human and simulation results were striking in the Lund et al. (1995) paper, the parallels between the human results and earlier research were not. Specifically, neither the simulation nor the human subjects showed reliable priming on stimuli which were related only by word associativity. This was somewhat troubling in that associative priming has been demonstrated in earlier research (Chiarello, Burgess, Richards, & Pollock, 1990; Fischler, 1977). Closer inspection of the reaction times in Lund et al. (1995, Exp. 4, see Table 1) shows that the reaction times for the related word pairs in the associated-only condition were actually faster than in the semantic-only case. The lack of a priming effect for the associated-only condition may be due to an unreliable, unrelated baseline condition. A similar pattern is seen in the simulation results. In order to clarify these results, a new set of unrelated word pairs was formed by rearranging the related word pairs; if the prior results occurred due to a problematic set of unrelated word pairs, associated priming should be obtained with human subjects. If, as Lund et al. (1995) claim, the representations generated by HAL are not associative, but semantic, the simulation results should still reflect a lack of an associative priming effect.

	HAL simulation			Human subjects		
	Sem.	Assoc.	Both	Sem.	Assoc.	Both
R	347	322	331	643	623	603
U	413	339	391	673	634	631
U-R	66	17	60	30	11	28
Std.	1.00	0.26	0.91	1.00	0.36	0.93

Table 1. Simulation and human results
(from Lund, Burgess, & Atchley, 1995)

Methods

Twenty-two undergraduate students participated in order to earn course credit. The stimuli used in this lexical-decision priming experiment were taken from Chiarello et al. (1990) and consisted of word pairs of three relational types (associative, semantic, and semantic + associative). These related word pairs were rearranged to form unrelated word pairs; additionally, a number of word-nonword trials equal to the combined number of related and unrelated word-word trials were included. Target words were balanced for both word length and printed frequency, yielding a total of 288 word pairs.

An experimental list included all 288 trials and was preceded by four "warm up" trials. Word primes were counterbalanced so that a target would be preceded by a related word in one list and an unrelated word in a second list. This allowed the targets to act as their own controls. Of the related word-word pairs, one third were word pairs that were only semantically related, one third were only associatively related, and the remaining pairs were both semantically and associatively related.

Stimulus presentation and timing was conducted on PC clones. Each trial began with a 500 ms fixation cross, followed by a prime at this location for 300 ms immediately

followed by the target which remained until either the subject made a lexical decision or 2500 ms elapsed. Accuracy feedback was provided, as well as a time-out signal for lack of response within 2500 ms. A set of fifteen practice trials was presented first.

Results and Discussion

Results are shown in Table 2. As desired, the variance of the unrelated condition for human subjects was reduced (from 11 to 6.2). Reaction times were faster for related trials than for unrelated, $F(1, 285) = 17.91$, $p < 0.0001$. There was an effect of associative type ($F(5, 281) = 2.6$, $p = 0.02$) but no type by relatedness interaction ($F < 1$). Planned comparisons were made at each level of word relation in order to determine priming by stimulus type. Priming was found for all three conditions: semantic, $F(1, 93) = 4.19$, $p = 0.04$; associated, $F(1, 94) = 8.11$, $p = 0.005$; and both semantic and associated, $F(1, 94) = 6.64$, $p = 0.011$. These results are consistent with our hypothesis that the earlier lack of associative priming with human subjects was due to a poor selection of unrelated word pairs. However, in both experiments, the standard procedure was followed to obtain unrelated word pairs (manual rearrangement, being careful to include no clearly related word pairs). The resulting sporadic associative priming in these experiments, contrasted with the consistency of semantic priming, leads us to conclude that the role of associative priming in a lexical decision task is not as straightforward as that of semantic similarity.

The HAL simulation results for the newly rearranged word pairs are similar to those obtained previously. There is an overall priming effect, $F(1, 285) = 21.02$, $p < 0.0001$. There was no reliable effect of associative type ($F < 1$), nor a reliable interaction ($F(2, 281) = 1.26$, $p = 0.28$). Priming is present for the semantic condition, $F(1, 93) = 5.92$, $p = 0.017$, and for the semantic plus associated condition, $F(1, 94) = 10.95$, $p < 0.0013$, but once again no priming is found for the associated-only condition, $F < 1$. Standardized scores are computed by dividing all priming amounts by the semantic priming amount, in order to ease comparisons of priming magnitudes between the simulation and the human results (see Table 2).

The simulation was not sensitive to the changes in stimuli which brought about human associative priming. This result provides further that HAL is more sensitive to semantics than to associativity.

	HAL simulation			Human subjects		
	Sem.	Assoc.	Both	Sem.	Assoc.	Both
R	540	469	416	615	583	591
U	513	487	494	652	626	629
U-R	37	18	78	37	43	38
Std.	1.00	0.48	2.11	1.00	1.16	1.02

Table 2. Simulation and human results

Experiment 2

Experiment 1 showed that the HAL simulation does not produce statistically reliable priming with associated-only word pairs. However, there is a consistent, although not reliable, relatedness advantage found for associated-only stimuli, both in the experiment presented here and in other research. Furthermore, the semantic + associated condition in Experiment 1 produced greater priming than did the semantic-only condition.

For these reasons, a blanket declaration of lack of associativity in HAL's representations seems premature. However, it does seems clear that whatever associative information is available in HAL's vectors will not be found though priming simulations. This is important to clarify since we want to claim that semantic similarity makes an important contribution in priming with humans.

Stimuli construction in word priming and other psycholinguistic experiments often employ word association norms. These norms provide a compilation of a set of people's frequency ordered associations to many words. Word relationships that can be found in word association norms can take a variety of forms. It is not unusual to find many types of associative and semantic relationships in these collections of items. These norms, then, provide an important test of the representations that can be generated using the HAL model. In this experiment, word pairs from the Palermo and Jenkins (1964) norms will be compared with two potential associativity indices available from the co-occurrence matrix. Additionally, the Palermo and Jenkins' data will be compared to semantic distances from the HAL simulation.

Methods

The two HAL-derived candidate associativity indices are co-location frequency and co-location separation. Co-location frequency, computable for any two words, is simply a raw count of the number of times that those two words occurred within the ten-word co-occurrence window during construction of the co-occurrence matrix. This corresponds to one intuitive definition of associativity, namely that words are associated to the degree that they tend to occur together in language (Miller, 1969; Spence & Owens, 1990). This measure is not scaled or normalized for word frequency.

The second associativity measure, co-location separation, is a measure of how many words, on average, separated a certain word pair as they occurred within the co-occurrence window. For instance, if the phrase "ladies and gentlemen" was the only context in which the words "ladies" and "gentlemen" ever occurred within the corpus, those two words would have a co-location separation measure of 1.0, as they are always separated by one word, "and." As the co-occurrence window used in these experiments was ten words wide, this measure can range from zero to nine. Co-location frequency and separation values for some example word pairs are give in Table 3.

These potential associativity metrics were compared to Palermo and Jenkins' (1964) word association norms. In their norms, target words were available along with associates produced by human subjects. Each target-associate pair was ranked by how many subjects produced that particular response. For each target word in the human associativity data, the top five associates were used to form five word pairs (e.g., man-boy). Co-location frequency and separation values for these word pairs were then computed,

as well as semantic distances, and these values were examined for correlations.

Word Pair		Col. Sep.	Col. Freq.
black	white	2.9	3846
man	woman	3.4	1497
led	zeppelin	0.4	290
holy	cow	0.0	64
man	tall	5.2	49

Table 3. Example word pairs.

Results and Discussion

Correlations between human associativity ratings and both co-location separation and frequency are shown in Table 4. Consistent with our earlier claim, there was no reliable correlation between semantic distances and associativity ratings. There was a small correlation between co-location separation and associativity ($r = -0.1$, $p = 0.05$), indicating that, to a minor degree, more highly associated word pairs occur closer to each other than do less associated pairs.

By far the largest correlation found was that between co-location frequency (raw count of co-occurrence within a ten-word window) and word pair associativity ($r = 0.25$, $p < 0.0001$). This supports the intuitive and common operational definition of associativity that associated words tend to appear close to each other in language. It is notable, though, that the larger of the significant correlations was that between associativity and co-location frequency rather than between associativity and co-location distance. In other words, associativity for a word pair was not well predicted by how close, on average, the two words were to each other when they were within the ten-word window, but was predicted rather well simply by the number of times which they co-occurred within the window at any distance.

These results can illuminate much about HAL, semantics, and distributed semantic representations. An examination of the word pairs used as associative pairs reveals substantial semantic overlap. For instance, the top two associates of *man* are listed as *woman* and *boy*.

The associativity of the word pairs used in this experiment is not in doubt; clearly, *man* and *woman* are highly associated (all these stimuli were the strongest five associates to each target). However, a great many of the word pairs are both associated and semantically similar. Experiment 3 will examine this phenomenon in greater detail.

	Distance	Col. Sep.	Col. Freq.
Human	-0.06	-0.1	0.25
Associativity	(p = 0.237)	(p = 0.05)	(p < .0001)

Table 4. Correlations for all associative pairs (n = 389).

Experiment 3

Given that there appears to be considerable semantic overlap between many of the associated word pairs used in the word "association" norms using in Experiment 2, it would be desirable to separate the semantic + associated pairs from the associated-only pairs. We approached this task by differentiating between word pairs which were "semantic neighbors" that can be calculated using HAL and those which were not.

To determine if a word is a semantic neighbor of another word, semantic distances are computed between the first word and all other words using HAL's semantic vectors. These distances are then ranked using this semantic distance. We arbitrarily chose to call the fifty words with the smallest distances "neighbors" of the target word, on the assumption that they are the most highly related words in the available vocabulary (which consists of the most common 70,000 tokens found in our corpus); see Table 5 for some examples of semantic neighborhoods.

Of the 389 original word pairs, 67 (~17%) qualified as semantic neighbors, leaving 322 as non-neighbors (although still all highly associated). As in Experiment 2, correlations were computed between the associativity ratings of these two sets of word pairs (neighbors and non-neighbors) and semantic distance, co-location separation, and co-location frequency.

woman	girl, man, child, piece, huge, woman's, cow
gallon	gallons, liter, inch, pound, megs, litre, meg
red	blue, green, white, black, gold, monster, ring
spider	turtle, shark, angel, dragon, storm, slug, giant

Table 5. Example semantic neighborhoods.

Results and Discussion

Correlations are shown in Table 6. Correlations between associativity and both semantic distance and co-location separation are similar, for both sets of words, to those obtained in Experiment 2. However, a striking difference is found in the correlations for co-location frequency. Here, the correlation for the semantic neighbor set has increased, by nearly a factor of two, to 0.48 ($p < 0.0001$), while the correlation for non-neighbors has become negligible and unreliable. This result suggests that the popular view that association is reflected by word proximity is only true for words which are semantically related (though, for these words, co-location frequency is an excellent predictor of associativity).

	N	Distance	Col. Sep.	Col. Freq.
Non-neighbors	322	0.03 (p = 0.552)	-0.08 (p = 0.16)	0.05 (p = 0.412)
Neighbors	67	-0.13 (p = 0.552)	-0.21 (p = 0.08)	0.48 (p < .0001)

Table 6. Correlations with associativity.

General Discussion

Experiments 2 and 3 validate the distinction between associated and associated-semantic pairs which was made in Experiment 1 (see Chiarello et al., 1990). Clearly, among associates produced by human subjects, there are both associates which co-occur in natural language and those which do not; the distinction appears to be quite sharp, with those not co-occurring in language being the substantial majority.

Temporal contiguity has been thought to be a critical component of learning (Deese, 1965). Since there was not a general correlation between associativity and co-location frequency, it seems unlikely that the majority of associations produced by subjects were learned via temporal contiguity in this fashion (at least from natural language); only those associations which also contain a semantic component appear to influence word order.

Experiment 1 demonstrated that, whatever the method is by which these non-temporal associations are expressed, HAL is not sensitive to them. An example in which HAL picks up semantic information which is not directly temporally expressed, is the relationship between *road* and *street*. The collocation frequency for this word pair is only 74 (as compared to 1497 for *man-woman*), yet the vector representations for *road* and *street* are nearly identical (indicating that they share a great deal of meaning).

The methodology and results presented here have practical applications; stimulus set construction, for instance, could benefit from an objective measure of semantic overlap in associative data. More importantly, this research sheds light on the nature of associativity, dispelling some popular ideas about where it originates. There are several important theoretical conclusions to be drawn from this set of experiments and the earlier work on HAL (Burgess & Lund, 1996; Lund & Burgess, in press; Lund et al., 1995). The reliance of our notions about semantic organization on associative structure is virtually axiomatic. George Miller (1969) proposed that "meanings can be characterized in terms of lexical associations. Lexical associations can be measured by word association tests. The results of word association tests can be accounted for in terms of particular types of sentences we can form with the words" (pp. 234-235). These beliefs have been persistent (Plaut, 1995; Shelton & Martin, 1992; Spence & Owens, 1990). The notion that associativity can be characterized by temporal association in language receives little or no support from our corpus analysis. The extent that "word associations" can be characterized by temporal association seems to be more a function of semantic neighborhood which is a reflection of semantic similarity in HAL's vector representations. This may be counterintuitive, given that HAL's methodology requires it to bootstrap its representations from lexical co-occurrence and that lexical co-occurrence is related to temporal association. The relationship between associative (and thus temporal) connections in memory and semantic representations corresponds to how a memory is initially acquired and how it is ultimately transformed into a more generalized piece of knowledge (its semantic vector in the HAL model). The notion that associations provide the antecedents for semantic structure was early posited in cognitive psychology (Mandler, 1962; Osgood, 1971). This is not to say that associative information may not be important in more generalized structures. For example, while there is not much similarity between the concepts *man* and *tall,* they are strongly associated and that men tend to be tall relative to some standard is important knowledge. However, associative information such as this tends to be more relativistic. An outcome of this is that priming effects using associative relationships may be less stable across sets of items or subjects, as we saw in experiment 1. Associative information that has not become generalized, that is, not semantic, would be more predictive of episodic relationships.

In the HAL model, this distinction between associative and semantic information corresponds to the distinction between *local* co-occurrence and *global* co-occurrence. Temporal information is reflected in local co-occurrence. When one examines global *patterns* of co-occurrence, across a vocabulary, one finds not associative, but semantic information. Only a small proportion of the vector elements are required to obtain the cognitive effects that we find. Thus, the functional representation is abstracted from and is more a measure of word contextuality or global co-occurrence than temporal association. This is an important distinction to make as theories of semantics develop (Burgess & Cottrell, 1995; Burgess & Lund, 1996; Landauer & Dumais, 1996; Lund & Burgess, in press).

Acknowledgments

This research was supported by NSF Presidential Faculty Fellow award SBR-9453406 to Curt Burgess. We thank Catherine Decker and three anonymous reviewers for their helpful comments.

References

Buchanan, L., Burgess, C., & Lund, K. (1996). *Over-crowding in Semantic Neighborhoods: Modeling Deep Dyslexia*. Paper submitted to TENNET VII, Seventh Annual Conference on Theoretical and Experimental Neuropsychology, Montreal, Quebec.

Burgess, C., & Cottrell, G. (1995). Using high-dimensional semantic spaces derived from large text corpora. *Proceedings of the Cognitive Science Society* (pp.13-14). Hillsdale, N.J.: Erlbaum Publishers.

Burgess, C., & Lund, K. (1996). *Parsing constraints and high-dimensional semantic space*. Manuscript submitted for publication.

Burgess, C., & Lund, K. (in press). Modeling cerebral asymmetries of semantic memory using high-dimensional semantic space. In Beeman, M., & Chiarello, C. (Eds.), *Getting it right: The cognitive neuroscience of right hemisphere language comprehension*. Hillsdale, N.J.: Erlbaum Press.

Chiarello, C., Burgess, C., Richards, L., & Pollock, A. (1990). Semantic and associative priming in the cerebral hemispheres: Some words do, some words don't... sometimes, some places. *Brain & Language, 38*, 75-104.

Collins, A.M., & Quillian, M.R. (1969). Retrieval time from semantic memory. *Journal of Verbal Learning and Verbal Behavior, 8*, 240-247.

Deese, J. (1965). *The structure of associations in language and thought*. Baltimore: John Hopkins Press.

Fischler, I. (1977). Semantic facilitation without association in a lexical decision task. *Memory & Cognition, 5*, 335-339.

Gernsbacher, M.A. (1990). *Language comprehension as structure building*. Hillsdale, NJ: LEA.

Landauer, T.K., & Dumais, S. (1994). *Memory model reads encyclopedia, passes vocabulary test*. Paper presented at the Psychonomics Society.

Lund, K., & Burgess, C. (in press). Producing high-dimensional semantic spaces from lexical co-occurrence. *Behavior Research Methods, Instruments, & Computers*.

Lund, K., Burgess, C., and Atchley, R.A. (1995). Semantic and associative priming in high-dimensional semantic space. *Cognitive Science Proceedings*, 1995, 660-665

Lupker, S.J. (1984). Semantic priming without association: A second look. *Journal of Verbal Learning & Verbal Behavior, 23*, 709-733.

Mandler, G. (1962). From association to structure. *Psychological Review, 69*, 415-427.

McClelland, J.L., & Kawamoto, A.H. (1986). Mechanisms of sentence processing: assigning roles to constituents of sentences. *Parallel Distributed Processing, Volume 2*. Cambridge, MA.: MIT Press.

Meyer, D.E., & Schvaneveldt, R.W. (1971). Facilitation in recognizing pairs of words: Evidence of a dependence between retrieval operations. *Journal of Experimental Psychology , 90*, 227-234.

Miller, G. (1969). The organization of lexical memory: Are word associations sufficient? In G. A. Talland & N. C. Waugh (Eds.), *The pathology of memory*. New York: Academic Press.

Moss, H.E., Ostrin, R.k., Tyler, L.K., & Marslen-Wilson, W.D. (1995). Accessing different types of lexical semantic information: Evidence from priming. *Journal of Experimental Psychology: Learning, Memory, and Cognition., 21*, 863-883.

Osgood, C. E. (1971). Exploration in semantic space: A personal diary. *Journal of social issues, 27*, 5-64.

Palermo, D.S., & Jenkins, J.J. (1964). *Word association norms grade school through college*. Minneapolis, MN: University of Minnesota Press.

Plaut, D.C. (1995). Semantic and associative priming in a distributed attractor network. *Cognitive Science Proceedings*, 1995, 37-42

Schvaneveldt, R.W. (1990). Pathfinder associative networks: Studies in knowledge organization. Norwood, NJ: Ablex.

Shelton, J.R., & Martin, R.C. (1992). How semantic is automatic semantic priming? *Journal of Experimental Psychology: Learning, Memory, and Cognition, 18*, 1191-1210.

Spence, D.P., & Owens, K.C. (1990). Lexical co-occurrence and association strength. *Journal of Psycholinguistic Research, 19*, 317-330.

Inferential Realization Constraints on Functional Anaphora in the Centering Model

Katja Markert, Michael Strube & Udo Hahn

ⒸⒾⒻ Computational Linguistics Research Group
Freiburg University
Europaplatz 1
D-79085 Freiburg, Germany
{markert,strube,hahn}@coling.uni-freiburg.de

Abstract

We present an inference-based text understanding methodology for the resolution of functional anaphora in the context of the centering model. A set of heuristic realization constraints is proposed, which incorporate language-independent conceptual criteria (based on the well-formedness and conceptual strength of role chains in a terminological knowledge base) and language-dependent information structure constraints (based on topic/comment or theme/rheme orderings). We state text-grammatical predicates for functional anaphora and then turn to the procedural aspects of their evaluation within the framework of an actor-based implementation of a lexically distributed text parser.

Introduction

Textual forms of anaphora are a challenging issue for the design of parsers for text understanding systems, since lacking recognition facilities either result in referentially incohesive or invalid text knowledge representations. At the conceptual level *functional* anaphora relates a quasi-anaphoric expression to its antecedent by conceptual attributes (or roles) associated with that antecedent (see, e.g., the relation between *"Ladezeit" (charge time)* and *"Akku" (accumulator)* in (3) and (2) below). Thus it complements the phenomenon of *nominal* anaphora, where an anaphoric expression is related to its antecedent in terms of conceptual generalization (as, e.g., *"Rechner" (computer)* refers to *"316LT"*, a particular notebook, in (2) and (1) below). The resolution of text-level nominal (and pronominal) anaphora contributes to the construction of referentially valid text knowledge bases, while the resolution of text-level functional anaphora yields referentially cohesive text knowledge bases.

1. Der *316LT* wird mit einem Nickel-Metall-Hydride-Akku bestückt.
   (The *316LT* is – with a nickel-metal-hydride-accumulator – equipped.)

2. Der *Rechner* wird durch diesen neuartigen *Akku* für ca. 4 Stunden mit Strom versorgt.
   (The *computer* is – because of this new type of *accumulator* – for approximately 4 hours – with power – provided.)

3. Darüberhinaus ist *die Ladezeit* mit 1,5 Stunden sehr kurz.
   (Also, – is – the *charge time* of 1.5 hours quite short.)

In the case of functional anaphora, the conceptual entity that relates the topic of the current utterance to discourse elements mentioned in the preceding one is not explicitly mentioned in the surface expression. Hence, the appropriate conceptual link must be inferred to establish the local coherence of the discourse (for an early statement of that idea, cf. Clark (1975)). In sentence (3) the information is missing that *"Ladezeit" (charge time)* is a property of *"Akku" (accumulator)*. This relation can only be established if conceptual knowledge about the domain, viz. the relation *property-of* between the concepts CHARGE-TIME and ACCUMULATOR, is available.

The solution we propose to account for functional anaphora is embedded in the framework of the centering model (Grosz et al., 1995). In this approach, discourse entities serving to link one utterance to other utterances in a particular discourse segment are organized in terms of centers. The crucial notion for establishing local coherence links in discourse is that of realization. Given a center element of the previous utterance, we say this element is *realized* if it is associated with an expression in the following utterance that has a valid interpretation in the underlying semantic/conceptual representation language. Functional anaphora has only been given insufficient treatment within the centering model in terms of rather sketchy realization conditions as opposed to the more elaborated "direct realization" constraints formulated for (pro)nominal anaphora (cf. Grosz et al. (1995)). As these criteria are overly vague, we intend to supply a more precise, formally grounded notion of realization for the analysis of functional anaphora in the centering framework by proposing a set of heuristic realization constraints to guide the underlying inference processes. These include language-independent conceptual criteria (based on the well-formedness and conceptual strength of role chains in a terminological knowledge base) and language-dependent information structure constraints (based on topic/comment or theme/rheme orderings). The criteria we postulate contribute additional restrictions on the search space of possible referents and also direct inference processes required to understand anaphoric utterances in the discourse. Thus, they can be considered a more adequate explanatory model for local coherence than the original centering model in that they further limit the resource demands for proper text understanding.

Conceptual Constraints

We assume a concept hierarchy to consist of a set of concept names $\mathcal{F}$ = {COMPUTER-SYSTEM, ACCUMULATOR,...} and a subclass relation $isa_{\mathcal{F}}$ = {(NOTEBOOK, COMPUTER-SYSTEM), (NIMH-ACCUMULATOR, ACCUMULATOR),...} $\subset \mathcal{F} \times \mathcal{F}$. The set of relation names $\mathcal{R}$ = {has-physical-part, has-accumulator, charge-time-of,...} contains the labels of possible conceptual roles. These are organized into a hierarchy by the relation $isa_{\mathcal{R}}$ = {(has-accumulator, has-physical-part), (charge-time-of, property-of),...} $\subset \mathcal{R} \times \mathcal{R}$. We also assume the common understanding of the terms range, domain and inverse of a relation.

For the identification and evaluation of suitable conceptual links between an antecedent and a functional anaphor, a *path finder* performs an extensive unidirectional search in the domain knowledge base, looking for *well-formed* paths between the two concepts, while a *path evaluator* selects the *strongests* of the ensuing paths. We will not go into the formal details of well-formedness criteria for a conceptual path $(r_1 \ldots r_n)$ $(r_i \in \mathcal{R})$ linking two concepts $x, y \in \mathcal{F}$. Instead, we only briefly mention that we require complete connectivity (compatibility of domains and ranges of the included relations) and non-cyclicity (exclusions of inverses of relations) for a *conceptually well-formed* path. The latter criterion, though entirely formal, achieves the discrimination alluded to by Resnik's (1995) distinction between similar and semantically related concepts. Additionally, a path from x to y will be excluded from the path list iff it *properly includes* another path from x to y and thus is *conceptually longer*.

Our focus in this paper will be on empirical criteria of path evaluation, *viz.* those which mark certain paths as being preferred over others in terms of commonsense plausibility. Based on the analyses of approximately 60 product reviews from the information technology domain and evidences reported from several (psycho)linguistic studies (e.g., Chaffin, 1992) , we stipulate certain predefined *path patterns*. From those general path patterns and by virtue of the hierarchical organization of conceptual relations, concrete conceptual role chains can *automatically* be derived by the knowledge base system based on the operation of a classifier (we assume a terminological reasoning framework). This allows us to distinguish between a subset $\mathcal{P}$ of all types of well-formed paths, which is labeled *"plausible"*, another subset $\mathcal{M}$ which is labeled *"metonymic"*, and all remaining paths which are labeled *"implausible"*.

Plausible Paths. We now turn to the question what kinds of relation chains should be characterized as plausible ones (forming the set $\mathcal{P}$), i.e., which compositions of relation types are likely to create reasonable role chains. All paths of unit length *1* are included in $\mathcal{P}$ as they are explicitly supplied in the domain knowledge base and are therefore "plausible", by definition. Regarding longer role chains we incorporate observations about the transitivity of *(part-whole)* relations made by Chaffin (1992) and Winston et al. (1987). They distinguish several subtypes of *part-whole* rela-

tions, e.g., integral object-component (corresponding to what we call *has-physical-part*), collection-member, mass-portion, process-phase, event-feature, area-place. The major claim they make is that any of these *subrelations* are transitive, while the most general *part-whole* relation usually is not. In other words, a relation chain containing only relations of one of the above-mentioned subtypes induces *a relation of the same subtype*, whereas a relation chain containing different types of *part-whole* relations is, in general, not reasonable any more. Following this argument, we have included the path patterns (*has-physical-part**), (*collection-member**), (*mass-portion**), (*process-phase**), (*event-feature**), (*area-place**) and the corresponding inverses like (*physical-part-of**), (*member-of**), etc. in $\mathcal{P}$. We refer to the first six of these basic patterns as *transitive-part-whole patterns*, in short $\mathcal{T}$, and to the inverse patterns as $\mathcal{T}^{-1}$. Compositionality of relation types other than *part-whole* relations has not received that much attention in the literature (one of the rare exceptions is the study by Huhns & Stephens (1989)). We follow some of their suggestions and also include (*spatial containment**) and (*connection**) in $\mathcal{P}$.

Metonymic Paths. We also incorporate *whole-for-part*, *part-for-whole*, and *producer-for-product* metonymies (cf. Lakoff, 1987; Fass, 1988). To determine path patterns corresponding to these types of metonymies consider the conceptual link between an instance of the concept C_1 and an instance of the concept C_3, which characterizes a metonymy and thus stands for another instance of a concept C_2. A corresponding well-formed conceptual path $p = (r_1 \ldots r_n)$ with $n \in \mathbb{N}$, $n > 1$, and $r_i \in \mathcal{R}$ $(i = 1, \ldots, n)$ must, first, link C_1 to C_2 via $p_1 = (r_1 \ldots r_{j-1})$ for some $j \in \{2, \ldots, n\}$. C_2 is then linked to C_3 via $p_2 = (r_j \ldots r_n)$. We have restricted the first link p_1 to plausible paths to provide reasonable metonymic chains only. The second link p_2 must express one of the metonymic relations $\mathcal{MS}$ = {has-part, part-of, produced-by}, depending on the specific metonymy[1]. For a *producer-for-product* metonymy, e.g., $j = n$ and r_n = *produced-by* must hold. For a *part-for-whole* or *whole-for-part* metonymy, $j < n$ may be possible, as all paths in $\mathcal{T}$ and $\mathcal{T}^{-1}$ (e.g., (*has-physical-part**)) also express a single *has-part* or *part-of* relation (see the explanations of plausible paths above). For notational convenience, we will consider the paths in $\mathcal{T}$ and $\mathcal{T}^{-1}$ as a single relation so that we may write (*has-physical-part**) $isa_{\mathcal{R}}$ has-part or (*physical-part-of**) $\in \mathcal{MS}$. Thus, we may restrict the above cases of well-formed metonymic paths to the pattern in Table 1 from which special path patterns for specific metonymies can be derived.

---

[1] If the direction of search is reversed (searching from C_3 to C_1) the corresponding inverse relations, $\mathcal{MS}^{-1}$ = {part-of, has-part, produces}, must be considered. This list of metonymic relations is by no means complete and can be supplemented, if necessary. We have, as yet, included only the most frequent types of metonymies that occur in our application domain. The incorporation of further metonymic relations does not affect the operation of the algorithm, whatsoever.

$$
\begin{array}{l}
\text{Metonymic-Path } ((r_1 \ldots r_n)) :\Leftrightarrow \\
\quad (r_1 \ldots r_n) \notin \mathcal{P} \\
\quad \wedge ((n > 1 \wedge (r_1, r_2, \ldots, r_{n-1}) \in \mathcal{P} \wedge r_n \in \mathcal{MS}) \\
\quad \vee (n > 1 \wedge (r_2, r_3, \ldots, r_n) \in \mathcal{P} \wedge r_1 \in \mathcal{MS}^{-1}))
\end{array}
$$

Table 1: Metonymic Path Patterns

The computation of paths between an antecedent x and a functional anaphor y may yield several alternative types of well-formed paths, *viz.* "plausible", "metonymic" or "implausible". In order to make a proper selection we define a ranking on those different path markers according to their intrinsic conceptual strength, which we denote by the relation "$>_{str}$" *(conceptually stronger than)* (cf. Table 2). As a consequence of this ordering, metonymic paths will be excluded from a path list iff plausible paths already exist, while implausible paths will be excluded iff plausible or metonymic paths already exist. Hence, only paths of the strongest type are retained in the final path list for a given concept pair x and y.

$$
\text{"plausible"} >_{str} \text{"metonymic"} >_{str} \text{"implausible"}
$$

Table 2: Ordering of Path Markers by Conceptual Strength

To evaluate these conceptual strength criteria we selected 80 concept pairs at random from the underlying domain knowledge base (459 concepts, 334 relations). We submitted them to the path finder/evaluator and compared the automatically generated conceptual paths with introspective judgments about the kinds of relations linking each pair. The overall error rate was below 5%. The average number of connected paths between two concepts (41.8) was reduced by the non-cyclicity criterion to 10.4 well-formed paths, and by the inclusion criterion to 2.4. The criterion in Table 2 achieves a final reduction to merely 1.8 paths. Hence, the criteria achieve the desired discrimination. We plan a broader evaluation of our approach by running the algorithm on larger-sized knowledge bases in order to test the domain-independence and scalability of the above criteria.

All conceptual paths which meet the above linkage criteria for two concepts, x and y, are contained in a list denoted by $CP_{x,y}$. As, in the case of functional anaphora, we have to deal with paths leading from the anaphoric expression to several alternative antecedents, we usually have to compare pairs of path lists $CP_{x,y}$ and $CP_{x,z}$, where x, y, z $\in \mathcal{F}$. We do this by applying the same criteria we used for evaluating paths linking single concepts. As all paths in $CP_{x,y}$ and $CP_{x,z}$ were computed by the path finder, they already fulfill the connectivity and non-cyclicity condition. The inclusion criterion cannot be applied to any paths $p_1 \in CP_{x,y}$ and $p_2 \in CP_{x,z}$, as p_1 and p_2 do not lead to the same concept ($y \neq z$). However, the criterion which ranks conceptual paths according to their associated path markers is applicable as all paths in a single CP list have the same marker. A function, PathMarker($CP_{i,j}$), yields either "plausible", "metonymic" or "implausible" de-

pending on the type of paths the list contains. Hence, the same ordering of path markers as in Table 2 can be applied to compare two CP lists (cf. Table 3).

$$
\begin{array}{l}
\text{StrongerThan } (CP_{x,y}, \ CP_{x,z}) :\Leftrightarrow \\
\quad \text{PathMarker}(CP_{x,y}) >_{str} \text{PathMarker}(CP_{x,z}) \\
\text{asStrongAs } (CP_{x,y}, \ CP_{x,z}) :\Leftrightarrow \\
\quad \text{PathMarker}(CP_{x,y}) = \text{PathMarker}(CP_{x,z})
\end{array}
$$

Table 3: Comparison of Path Lists by Conceptual Strength

Centering Constraints

Conceptual criteria are of tremendous importance, but they are not sufficient for properly resolving functional anaphora. Additional criteria have to be supplied in the case of equal strength of conceptual path lists for several alternative antecedents. We therefore incorporate into our model various information structure criteria in terms of topic/comment or theme/rheme patterns which originate from (dependency) structure analyses of the underlying utterance. The framework for this type of information is provided by the well-known *centering* mechanism (Grosz et al. (1995)), for which psycholinguistic evidences are provided by Gordon et al. (1993) and Brennan (1995).

The theory of centering is intended to model the local coherence of discourse, i.e., coherence among the utterances U_i in a particular discourse segment (say, a paragraph of a text). Local coherence is opposed to global coherence, i.e., coherence with other segments in the discourse. Each utterance U_i in a discourse segment is assigned a set of *forward-looking centers*, $C_f(U_i)$, and a unique *backward-looking center*, $C_b(U_i)$. The forward-looking centers of U_i depend only on the expressions that constitute that utterance; previous utterances provide no constraints on $C_f(U_i)$. The elements of $C_f(U_i)$ are partially ordered to reflect relative prominence in U_i. The most highly ranked element of $C_f(U_i)$ that is *realized* in U_{i+1} (i.e., is associated with an expression that has a valid semantic interpretation) is the $C_b(U_{i+1})$. The ranking imposed on the elements of the C_f reflects the assumption that the most highly ranked element of $C_f(U_i)$ is the most preferred antecedent of an anaphoric expression in U_{i+1}, while the remaining elements are (partially) ordered according to decreasing preference for establishing referential links.

The theory of centering, in addition, defines several transition relations across pairs of adjacent utterances (e.g., continuation, retention, smooth and rough shift), which differ from each other according to the degree by which successive backward-looking centers are confirmed or rejected, and, if they are confirmed, whether they correspond to the most highly ranked element of the current forward-looking centers or not. The theory claims that to the extent a discourse adheres to all these centering constraints (e.g., realization constraints on pronouns, preferences among types of center transitions), its local coherence will increase and the inference load placed upon the hearer will decrease. Therefore, the tremendous importance of fleshing out the relevant and most restrictive, though still general centering constraints.

The main difference between Grosz et al.'s work and our proposal concerns the criteria for ranking the forward-looking centers. While Grosz assume (for the English language) that *grammatical* roles are the major determinant for the ranking on the C_f, we claim that for German and other languages with relatively free word order it is the *functional* information structure of the sentence in terms of topic/comment or theme/rheme patterns (cf. Strube & Hahn (1996) for a more detailed account). In this framework, the *topic* (*theme*) denotes the given information, while the *comment* (*rheme*) denotes the new information. This distinction can be rephrased in terms of the centering mechanism. The *theme* then corresponds to the $C_b(U_n)$, the most highly ranked element of $C_f(U_{n-1})$ which is realized in U_n. The theme/rheme hierarchy of U_n is determined by the $C_f(U_{n-1})$: elements of U_n which are contained in $C_f(U_{n-1})$ (*context-bound* discourse elements) are less rhematic than elements of U_n which are not contained in $C_f(U_{n-1})$ (*unbound* elements). The distinction between context-bound and unbound elements is important for the ranking on the C_f, since bound elements are generally ranked higher than any other nonanaphoric elements.

Grammar Predicates for Functional Anaphora

We build on a grammar model which employs default inheritance for lexical hierarchies. The grammar formalism (for a survey, cf. Hahn et al. (1994)) is based on dependency relations between lexical heads and modifiers. The dependency specifications allow a tight integration of linguistic (grammar) and conceptual knowledge (domain model), thus making powerful terminological reasoning facilities directly available for the parsing process.[2] The resolution of functional anaphora is based on two major criteria, a conceptual and a structural one. The conceptual strength criterion for role chains is already specified in Table 3. The structural condition is embodied in the predicate *isPotentialFuncAntecedent* (cf. Table 4). A functional anaphoric relation between two lexical items is here restricted to pairs of nouns. The anaphoric phrase which occurs in the *n*-th utterance is restricted to be a definite NP and the antecedent must be one of the forward-looking centers of the preceding utterance.

The predicate *PreferredConceptualBridge* (cf. Table 5) combines both criteria. A lexical item *y* is determined as the proper antecedent of the functional anaphoric expression *x* iff it is a potential antecedent and if there exists no alternative antecedent *z* whose conceptual strength relative to *x* ex-

[2]We assume the following conventions: C = {Word, Nominal, Noun, PronPersonal,...} denotes the set of word classes, and isa_C = {(Nominal, Word), (Noun, Nominal), (PronPersonal, Nominal),...} $\subset C \times C$ denotes the subclass relation which yields a hierarchical ordering among these classes. Furthermore, *object.r* refers to the instance in the text knowledge base denoted by the linguistic item *object* and *object.c* refers to the corresponding concept class C. *Head* denotes a structural relation within dependency trees, viz. *x* being the head of *y*.

$$\text{isPotentialFuncAntecedent (y, x, n)} :\Leftrightarrow$$
$$y \ isa_C{}^* \text{ Nominal} \land x \ isa_C{}^* \text{ Noun}$$
$$\land \exists z: (x \ head \ z \land z \ isa_C{}^* \text{ DetDefinite})$$
$$\land x \in U_n \land y.r \in C_f(U_{n-1})$$

Table 4: Potential Functional Antecedent

ceeds that of *y* relative to *x* or, if the conceptual strength is equal, whose strength of preference under the *TC* relation is higher than that of *y*. "$>_{TC}$" defines a partial order on the conceptual/semantic items of C_f reflecting the functional information structure of the utterance U_n in which their linguistic counterparts, *viz. z* and *y*, occur.

$$\text{PreferredConceptualBridge (y, x, n)} :\Leftrightarrow$$
$$\text{isPotentialFuncAntecedent (y, x, n)}$$
$$\land \neg \exists z: \text{isPotentialFuncAntecedent (z, x, n)}$$
$$\land (\text{StrongerThan (CP}_{x.c,z.c}, \text{CP}_{x.c,y.c})$$
$$\lor (\text{asStrongAs (CP}_{x.c,z.c}, \text{CP}_{x.c,y.c}) \land z >_{TC} y))$$

Table 5: Preferred Conceptual Bridge

The Resolution of Functional Anaphora

The actor computation model (Agha & Hewitt, 1987) provides the background for the procedural interpretation of lexicalized grammar specifications, as those given in the previous section, in terms of so-called word actors. Word actors communicate via asynchronous message passing; an actor can only send messages to other actors it knows about, its so-called acquaintances. The arrival of a message at an actor triggers the execution of a method that is composed of grammatical predicates (for a survey, cf. Neuhaus & Hahn (1996)).

The resolution of functional anaphors within texts depends on the results of the preceding resolution of nominal anaphors (Strube & Hahn, 1995) and the termination of the semantic interpretation of the current utterance. It will only be triggered at the occurrence of the definite noun phrase *NP* when *NP* is not a (pro)nominal anaphor and *NP* is only connected via certain types of relations (e.g., *has-property, has-physical-part*)[3] to referents denoted in the current utterance at the conceptual level.

[3]Associated with the set $\mathcal{R}$ is the set of inverse roles $\mathcal{R}^{-1}$. This distinction becomes crucial for already established relations like *has-property* (subsuming *charge-time*, etc.) or *has-physical-part* (subsuming *has-accumulator*, etc.) insofar as they do not block the initialization of the resolution procedure for functional anaphora (e.g., ACCUMULATOR – *charge-time* – CHARGE-TIME), whereas the existence of their inverses, we here refer to as *POF-type relations*, e.g., *property-of* (subsuming *charge-time-of*, etc.) and *physical-part-of* (subsuming *accumulator-of*, etc.), does (e.g., ACCUMULATOR – *accumulator-of* – 316LT). This is simply due to the fact that the semantic interpretation of a phrase like *"the charge time of the accumulator"* already leads to the creation of the *POF*-type relation the resolution mechanism for functional anaphora is supposed to determine. This is opposed to the interpretation of its elliptified counterpart *"the charge time"* in sentence (3), where the genitive object is zeroed.

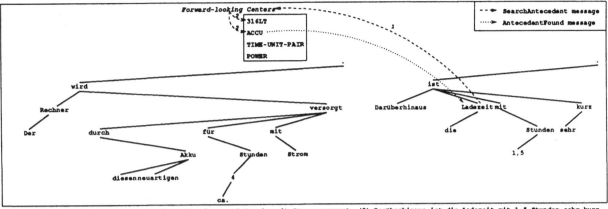

(2) Der Rechner wird durch diesen neuartigen Akku für ca. 4 Stunden mit Strom versorgt. (3) Darüberhinaus ist die Ladezeit mit 1,5 Stunden sehr kurz.

(2) The computer is because of this new type of accumulator for approx. 4 hours with power provided. (3) Also, is the charge time of 1.5 hours quite short.

Figure 1: Sample Parse for the Resolution of a Functional Anaphor

The protocol level of actor-based text analysis encompasses the procedural interpretation of the grammatical predicates mentioned above. Fig. 1 illustrates the protocol for establishing proper conceptual relations, referring to the already introduced text fragment (1) - (3) which is partially repeated at the bottom line of Fig. 1. (3) contains the definite NP *"die Ladezeit"*. Since *"Ladezeit" (charge time)* does not subsume any word at the conceptual level in the preceding utterance, the (pro)nominal anaphora test fails; the definite NP *"die Ladezeit"* has also not been integrated in terms of a functionally relevant conceptual relation as a result of its semantic interpretation. Hence, a *SearchTextFuncAntecedent* message is created by the word actor for *"Ladezeit"*, which consists of two phases:

1. In *phase 1*, the message is forwarded from its initiator *"Ladezeit"* to the *forward-looking centers* of the *previous sentence*, where its state is set to *phase 2*.

2. In *phase 2*, the *forward-looking centers* of the previous sentence are tested for the predicate *PreferredConceptualBridge*, relative to the initiator of the *SearchAntecedent* message, *viz.* $x = $ *"Ladezeit" (charge time)*.

The relevant knowledge base operations are performed on the four concepts associated with the current forward-looking centers, viz. 316LT, ACCUMULATOR, TIME-UNIT-PAIR (the conceptual representation for *"Stunden"*), and POWER[4]. In this case, the instance 316LT (the proper conceptual referent of the nominal anaphor *"der Rechner" (the computer)*) is related to CHARGE-TIME (the concept denoting *"Ladezeit"*) via a *metonymic path*, viz. *(charge-time-of accumulator-of)* indicating a whole-for-part metonymy, while the concept ACCUMULATOR is related to CHARGE-TIME via a *plausible path* (viz. *charge-time-of*). As plausible paths are the

---

[4]Note that only nouns and pronouns are capable of responding to the *SearchTextFuncAntecedent* message and of being tested as to whether they fulfill the required criteria for a functional anaphoric relation.

strongest type of conceptual paths, only an element which is more highly ranked in the centering list *and* is linked via a plausible path to the functional anaphor could be preferred as the functional antecedent of *"die Ladezeit" (the charge time)* over *"Akku" (accumulator)* (according to the constraint from Table 5). As we know already that this is not the case, it is not necessary to test the remaining concepts associated with the current forward-looking centers (namely, TIME-UNIT-PAIR and POWER) and *"Akku"* can be selected as the proper functional antecedent. A *FuncAntecedentFound* message is sent from the word actor *"Akku"* to the initiator of the *SearchAntecedent* message, viz. *"Ladezeit"*. An appropriate update links the corresponding instances via the role *charge-time-of* and, thus, local coherence is established at the conceptual level of the text knowledge base.

Comparison with Related Approaches

Searching links in a taxonomic hierarchy is a common application for spreading activation or marker passing techniques. The paradigm of path finding and evaluating they propose has obvious parallels to our approach. The criteria they employ, however, are mostly based on numerical restrictions, e.g., on weights (Charniak, 1986) or path lengths (Hirst, 1987). This is problematic as the foundation and derivation of these numbers is usually not made explicit (or it is *ad hoc*). We have tried to overcome this problem by stating structural and empirically plausible criteria which do not rely upon numerical restrictions in any way.

A pattern-based approach to inferencing closest in spirit to our approach has been put forward by Norvig (1989). The method he proposes can also be used to resolve (functional) anaphora. The main difference to our work lies in the fact that his path patterns are solely being defined in terms of "formal" link criteria in a knowledge base whose patterns are simply matched against the links being passed, whereas our definitions of path patterns take the semantic hierarchy of relations and their compositional properties into account. This allows

613

for a path-length- and thus granularity-independent and semantically motivated preference ranking of the paths. The principal attraction of Norvig's model is due to its alleged generality permitting to handle various inference classes in a unified framework. But a closer look at his system reveals that quite a number of specific-case rules for coping with individual aspects of inferences have to be introduced, e.g., an antipromiscuity rule which is only applied to some inference classes or recency and focus considerations for the resolution of referential ambiguity. These restrictions and their interdependencies are not expressed clearly, thus detracting from the elegance and generality of the algorithm. Admittedly, this paper addresses only one of Norvig's inferencing problems, but it presents a modular approach with precise and semantically motivated restrictions. Our algorithm combines two equally general, multi-purpose modules, *viz.* a path finder and a path evaluator, which are also used in the parsing process, and a centering mechanism which is applied to other forms of anaphora resolution problems as well. This has the advantage of a specific inference module with lucid triggering conditions.

The original centering model does not provide for methods for the resolution of functional anaphora. Grosz et al. rather sketchily point to the difference between the relations *directly realizes* and *realizes* whose precise definition they suggest depends on the semantic theory one adopts (Grosz et al., 1995, p.209). We have shown, however, that there are a lot of general constraints at the knowledge level which need not be covered by semantic theories at all.

Functional anaphora are also not an issue for standard grammar theories (e.g., HPSG, LFG, GB, CG, TAG). This is not at all surprising, as their advocates pay almost no attention to the text level (with the exception of several forms of pronominal anaphora) and also do not seriously take conceptual criteria as part of grammatical descriptions into account without which true text understanding seems infeasible.

Conclusions

The model of functional anaphora resolution we have outlined considers specific forms of conceptual inferences to be of primary importance. In order to constrain the realization of functional anaphora in the centering framework we propose conceptual well-formedness and strength criteria for role chains in a terminological knowledge base, by which the plausibility of various possible antecedents as proper bridges (Clark, 1975) to functional anaphora can be assessed. Information structure constraints on the underlying utterances in terms of topic/comment patterns contribute further inferential restrictions on proper antecedents for functional anaphora. Altogether, these extensions require a thorough revision of the original centering model. Our proposal has only been tested on moderately sized knowledge bases, with 800 and 500 concept/role specifications for the information technology and medicine domain, respectively, which are implemented in LOOM (MacGregor & Bates, 1987). So the scalability of the model still has to be demonstrated on larger sized

knowledge bases. Also the cognitive (as opposed to merely computational) plausibility of our model extension still needs to be experimentally evaluated in a proper way. The entire anaphora resolution module has been implemented in Actalk (Briot, 1989), an actor language dialect of Smalltalk, as part of a comprehensive text parser for German.

Acknowledgments. We would like to thank our colleagues in the $\mathcal{CLIF}$ group for fruitful discussions. This work has been funded by *LGFG Baden-Württemberg* (1.1.4-7631.0; M. Strube) and a grant from *DFG* (Ha 2907/1-3; U. Hahn). Katja Markert was supported by a DFG graduate research program. We also gratefully acknowledge the provision of the LOOM system from USC/ISI.

References

Agha, G. & C. Hewitt (1987). Actors: A conceptual foundation for concurrent object-oriented programming. In B. Shriver & P. Wegner (Eds.), *Research Directions in Object-Oriented Programming*. Cambridge, Mass: MIT Press, pp.49-74.

Brennan, Susan E. (1995). Centering attention in discourse. *Language and Cognitive Processes*, 10(2):137–167.

Briot, J.-P. (1989). Actalk: A testbed for classifying and designing actor languages in the Smalltalk-80 environment. In *Proc. of ECOOP-89*, pp. 109–129.

Chaffin, R. (1992). The concept of a semantic relation. In A. Lehrer & E.F. Kittay (Eds.), *Frames, Fields and Contrasts*. Hillsdale, NJ: Erlbaum, pp.253-288.

Charniak, E. (1986). A neat theory of marker passing. In *Proc. of AAAI-86*. pp.584-588.

Clark, H. (1975). Bridging. In *Proc. of TINLAP-1*, pp. 169–174.

Fass, D (1988). An account of coherence, semantic relations, metonymy, and lexical ambiguity resolution. In S. Small, G. Cottrell & M. Tanenhaus (Eds.), *Lexical Ambiguity Resolution*. San Mateo, CA: Morgan Kaufmann, pp.151-178.

Gordon, Peter C., Barbara J. Grosz & Laura A. Gilliom (1993). Pronouns, names, and the centering of attention in discourse. *Cognitive Science*, 17:311–347.

Grosz, Barbara J., Aravind K. Joshi & Scott Weinstein (1995). Centering: A framework for modeling the local coherence of discourse. *Computational Linguistics*, 21(2):203–225.

Hahn, U., S. Schacht & N. Bröker (1994). Concurrent, object-oriented natural language parsing: The *ParseTalk* model. *International Journal of Human-Computer Studies*, 41(1/2):179–222.

Hirst, G. (1987). *Semantic Interpretation and the Resolution of Ambiguity*. Cambridge: Cambridge University Press.

Huhns, Michael & Larry Stephens (1989). Plausible inferencing using extended composition. In *Proc. of IJCAI-89*, Vol. 2, pp. 1420–1425.

Lakoff, G. (1987). *Women, Fire and Dangerous Things*. Chicago: Chicago University Press.

MacGregor, R. & R. Bates (1987). *The LOOM Knowledge Representation Language*. USC/ISI.

Neuhaus, P. & U. Hahn (1996). Restricted parallelism in object-oriented lexical parsing. In *Proc. of COLING-96*.

Norvig, P. (1989). Marker passing as a weak method for inferencing. *Cognitive Science*, 13(4):569–620.

Resnik, P. (1995). Using information content to evaluate semantic similarity in a taxonomy. In *Proc. of IJCAI-95*. Vol.1., pp.448-453.

Strube, M. & U. Hahn (1995). *ParseTalk* about sentence- and text-level anaphora. In *Proc. of EACL-95*, pp. 237–244.

Strube, M. & U. Hahn (1996). Functional centering. In *Proc. of ACL-96*.

Winston, M., R. Chaffin & D.J. Herrmann (1987). A taxonomy of part-whole-relations. *Cognitive Science*, 11(1):417–444.

On the Nature of Timing Mechanisms in Cognition

J. Devin McAuley
Department of Psychology
University of Queensland
Brisbane, Queensland 4072
Australia
devin@psy.uq.edu.au

Abstract

The ability to resolve timing differences within and between patterns is critical to the perception of music and speech; similarly, many motor skills such as music performance require fine temporal control of movements. Two important issues concern (1) the nature of the mechanism used for time measurement and (2) whether timing distinctions in perception and motor control are based on the same mechanism. In this paper, clock- and entrainment-based conceptions of time measurement are discussed; and predictions of both classes of model are then evaluated with respect to a tempo-discrimination experiment involving isochronous auditory sequences. The results from this experiment are shown to favor entrainment- over clock-based approaches to timing. The implications of these data are then discussed with respect to the hypothesized role of the cerebellum in timing.

Introduction

The dominant conception of time measurement for both perceptual and motor tasks has been based on a clock timer on a ms scale that records the duration of an event, such as the duration between the onset of two tones, as the number of millisecond "time slices" that occurred during that event. Braitenberg (1967) proposed that such a timer might be implemented in the cerebellum via a series of adjustable delay lines. In order to resolve timing differences that require duration comparisons, it has been commonly assumed that time estimates can be stored in memory, and then later retrieved (Keele et al., 1989). For motor tasks, recorded time measurements retrieved from memory have been assumed to serve as input to a motor program (Keele et al., 1985; Ivry and Keele, 1989).

An alternative view is that time measurement is phase based, involving the entrainment of an oscillatory timer. In contrast to the passive recording of time involved with clock models, entrainment is a dynamic timing process that adapts an oscillator's period to match the target duration; the oscillator's period then provides a direct estimate of duration, and the timing of events can be related to phase. In this paper, the clock and entrainment conceptions of time measurement are discussed in detail, and the predictions of both classes of model are then evaluated with respect to a tempo-discrimination experiment involving isochronous auditory sequences. The results from this experiment are shown to favor entrainment-

over clock-based approaches to timing. The implications of these data are then discussed with respect to the hypothesized role of the cerebellum in timing (Ivry and Keele, 1989).

Clock Models

A wide range of clock models of timing have been proposed, although most share the same basic assumptions of a central timer (or clock), a perceptual store, a reference memory, and a comparator (Church and Broadbent, 1990); they differ mainly in the form of the clock and perceptual store. For many of the models, the clock is a fast neural pacemaker which generates discrete neural pulses at an average rate (λ), and the perceptual store maintains a "count" of the number of pulses that occur during the target interval (T) (Abel, 1972; Creelman, 1962; Treisman, 1963; Divenyi and Danner, 1977). Duration discrimination for two time intervals (T and $T + \Delta T$) is modeled by comparing the number of pulses that occured during the first interval ($\mu = \lambda T$) with the number of pulses that occured during the second interval ($\mu = \lambda[T + \Delta T]$). This approach requires a switch which starts the counting process at the beginning of the target time interval, and clears the counter when the estimate of the target interval is transferred from the perceptual store to the reference memory. Temporal resolving power is modeled by the variance of the pulse generating source, with small inter-pulse-variance corresponding to accurate estimates of duration and high discrimination sensitivity. In modeling duration discrimination across a range of T values, debate has centered on the precise form of the pulse-generating source.

There have been several connectionist approaches to time measurement based on the clock conception (Church and Broadbent, 1990; Miall, 1989). These differ from the "counter" variety in important ways. For Church and Broadbent (1990), the pulse-generating source is replaced by a set of oscillators with periods spanning a wide range of time intervals; the pulse counter is replaced by a binary vector representation of time, according to the +1/-1 phase of each oscillator; and, the reference memory storing the pulse count is replaced by a set of connection weights, permitting more than a single time interval to be stored in the reference memory at once. In connectionist clock models, duration discrimination is based on similarity in the representations of the to-be-compared interval retrieved from memory; if the measure of similarity is less than a pre-specified threshold, the time difference is detected.

A weakness of both the connectionist- and counter-based clock models is that their predictions are usually limited to the perception of isolated intervals (i.e, one interval compared with another in isolation); whereas, important temporal distinctions in music and speech occur within the context of a pattern of intervals. However, in the direction of incorporating pattern context, clock models have recently been proposed to model the effect of isochronous contexts on tempo (rate) discrimination. These models are based on a "multiple-look" hypothesis, in which each interval in an isochronous sequence provides an independent statistical (clock-based) estimate (or "look") (Drake and Botte, 1993; Schulze, 1989). With multiple-observations of the same target interval, the perceiver improves the estimate of the target interval's duration by a process of averaging the multiple-looks, or in the case of tempo discrimination, improves the estimate of the the sequence's tempo, by the same process. An identical suggestion is that the stability of a target interval's memory trace improves with repetitions of the target interval. (Keele et al., 1989; Ivry and Hazeltine, 1995).

Entrainment Models

At the foundation of all entrainment models of timing is the assumption that the timing mechanisms of the nervous system are coupled to the environment. In the development of an entrainment theory, Jones (1976) proposed a central role for rhythm in cognitive processing, suggesting that the temporal organization of perception, attention, and memory is inherently rhythmic. As part of this theory, it is assumed that the rhythms of music and speech entrain periodic attentional "pulses", forming an attentional rhythm. Based on the concept of attentional entrainment, Jones and Boltz (1989) have proposed an expectancy/contrast model of timing. They assume that an isochronous series of tones, marking out identical time intervals (T_i), will entrain an attentional oscillator with a period similar to the T_i's. The pulses of the oscillator provide dynamic "expectancies" for when the next tone (specifying T_{i+1}) will occur. In this way, the adapting period of the oscillator (Ω_i) provides a continuously updated estimate of the time intervals (T_i). Intervals (T_i), which violate the oscillator's period-based expectancies create a temporal contrast $(\Omega_i - T_i)$. As the attentional oscillator is entrained by the sequence, temporal contrast is minimized (i.e., Ω_i approaches T_i).

Temporal resolving power in the Jones and Boltz model is based on the predicted magnitude of temporal contrasts. It is assumed that with small temporal contrasts, listeners will be more sensitive to a timing change than with larger temporal contrasts. Thus, similar to the "multiple-look" model, the expectancy/contrast model predicts that increasing the number of tones in an isochronous sequence should improve listeners' ability to detect a difference in the timing of an interval that continues the sequence, and should also improve listeners' ability to detect changes in the tempo of that

sequence. The expectancy/contrast model also predicts that listeners' temporal resolution should be better with metrical sequences (of which isochronous sequences are an instance) than for irregularly-timed sequences, since attentional entrainment should occur more readily with regularly-timed sequences.

Adaptive Oscillators

A shortcoming of the expectancy/contrast model is that the hypothesized process of attentional entrainment is a descriptive component of the model, and not linked to a specific mathematical model of coupled oscillation. This makes the expectancy/contrast model, and other entrainment models (Schulze, 1978) a relatively easy target for criticism, since many of its predictions are under-specified, and open to multiple interpretations (Keele et al., 1989). As steps toward clarifying its predictions, the entrainment model has been formalized and a timing mechanism proposed that is based on an adaptive oscillator (McAuley, 1994; McAuley, 1995). This work parallels similar recent work by Large (1994).

The adaptive oscillator is a processing unit that has some resting rate at which it periodically "fires", but will adapt that resting rate when it is stimulated at different frequencies, combining both phase coupling and period coupling. In its simplest "phase-resetting" form, the adaptive oscillator resets its phase in response to an input pulse and will use the input's phase to adjusts its natural period (Ω) to be a little closer to the "perceived" periodicity of the input. This process permits adaptive oscillators to track periodic components of rhythmic patterns, despite intrinsic or expressive variability in their timing (see McAuley (1995) for a mathematical description of this process).

Time as Phase

For entrainment models of timing, the oscillator period (Ω) provides an implicit estimate of a duration (T). For those that are based on the phase-resetting adaptive oscillator, a time change (ΔT) in the duration (T) will trigger a phase change $(\Delta \phi)$ in the reset-phase of the oscillator mechanism, where

$$\Delta \phi = \frac{T + \Delta T}{\Omega} \quad (\text{mod } 1). \qquad (1)$$

In essence, this phase difference $(\Delta \phi)$ registers the effect of a time difference (ΔT) on an oscillator tracking a series of equal intervals (T). In an entrainment model, the relationship between phase differences $(\Delta \phi)$ and time differences (ΔT) varies as a function of the ratio between the base interval T and the estimate of duration Ω, expressed as the fraction $\frac{T}{\Omega}$. This fraction provides a measure of the amount of over- or underestimation of duration by the entrainment mechanism; for $\frac{T}{\Omega} > 1$, duration is underestimated, for $\frac{T}{\Omega} < 1$ duration is overestimated, and for $\frac{T}{\Omega} = 1.0$ estimated duration is identical to the actual duration.

To understand how the relationship between time differences and phase differences varies as a function of this ratio ($\frac{T}{\Omega}$), it is useful to rewrite Equation 1 as

$$\Delta\phi = [\frac{T}{\Omega}] + [\frac{\Delta T}{\Omega}] \quad (\text{mod } 1) \qquad (2)$$

and to represent phase on $[-0.5, 0.5]$ instead of on $[0, 1]$; in this representation, positive and negative phase differences indicate positive and negative time differences, respectively. For this reason, the phase differences associated with $+\Delta T$ and $-\Delta T$ will be distinguished as $\Delta\phi_+$ and $\Delta\phi_-$. There are then three cases to consider.

Case 1: $\frac{T}{\Omega} = 1.0$. For Case 1, illustrated in Figure 1, estimated duration is equal to actual duration, Equation 2 reduces to

$$\Delta\phi = \pm\frac{\Delta T}{T}. \qquad (3)$$

In this case, lengthening or shortening T by $X\%$ maintains the magnitude of phase difference regardless of whether the time change ΔT is positive or negative (i.e., $|\Delta\phi_-| = |\Delta\phi_+|$). To provide a concrete example, suppose T is lengthened by 10%, then $\Delta\phi_+ = 0.1$. On the other hand, if T is shortening by 10%, then $\Delta\phi_- = -0.1$. For either an increase or decrease in duration of 10%, the magnitudes of the triggered phase differences are equal ($|\Delta\phi_+| = |\Delta\phi_-| = 0.1$).

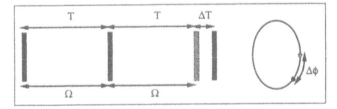

Figure 1: Illustration of Case 1. For an oscillator with a period Ω that is a perfect estimate of T (as shown on the left), lengthening T by ΔT triggers a phase difference $\Delta\phi$ relative to zero phase of the oscillator (as shown on the right).

Case 2: $\frac{T}{\Omega} > 1.0$. For Case 2, illustrated in Figure 2, actual duration is underestimated ($\Omega < T$). As a result, lengthening or shortening T by $X\%$ does not preserve the magnitude of the resulting phase differences. Instead, lengthening T triggers a phase difference that is larger than that for shortening T: $|\Delta\phi_+| > |\Delta\phi_-|$. Another effect of underestimation is that it stretches the mapping between ΔT and $\Delta\phi$; notice that in terms of Equation 2, $\frac{\Delta T}{\Omega}$ is a larger fraction of the base interval T than $\frac{\Delta T}{T}$ is.

Case 3: $\frac{T}{\Omega} < 1.0$. For Case 3, illustrated in Figure 3, actual duration is overestimated ($\Omega > T$). As in case 2, lengthening or shortening T by $X\%$ does not preserve the magnitude of the resulting phase differences. Symmetric with the effect in Case 2, shortening T triggers a phase difference that is larger than lengthening: $|\Delta\phi_-| > |\Delta\phi_+|$. And the additional effect of overestimation is that it compresses the mapping between ΔT

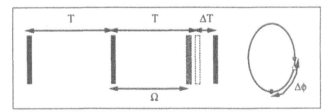

Figure 2: Illustration of Case 2. For an oscillator with a period Ω that is an underestimate of T, lengthening T by ΔT triggers a phase difference $\Delta\phi$ that is larger than that for Case 1.

and $\Delta\phi$; notice that in terms of in Equation 2, $\frac{\Delta T}{\Omega}$ is a smaller fraction of the base interval T than $\frac{\Delta T}{T}$ is.

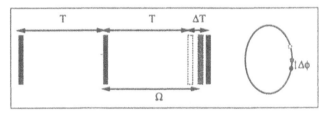

Figure 3: Illustration of Case 3. For an oscillator with a period Ω that is an overestimate of T, lengthening T by ΔT triggers a phase difference $\Delta\phi$ that is smaller than that for Case 1.

The Just-Noticeable Phase Difference

In order to specify the predictions of an entrainment model for tempo discrimination, it was assumed that the detection of tempo differences is linked to the detection of phase differences, triggered by "expectancy violations" in the entrainment process (McAuley, 1995). The suggestion that phase differences are used to detect timing differences pins the predictions of an entrainment model to the dynamics of the underlying oscillatory timer. For the adaptive oscillator mechanism, a just-noticeable phase difference (JND_ϕ) is assumed that specifies the threshold time difference (ΔT) that is detectable in a interval T. Thus, if the magnitude of the phase-difference ($\Delta\phi$) triggered by a time difference (ΔT) is greater than JND_ϕ then the time difference (ΔT) is detected, otherwise it is not. In accordance with the entrainment hypothesis, the just-noticeable phase difference decreases (sensitivity improves) as the tracking adaptive oscillator is entrained by the input (see McAuley (1995) for details).

In evaluating the predictions of the adaptive-oscillator-based model for tempo discrimination, the main focus is the relationship between listeners' sensitivity, measured as the ΔT necessary for unbiased 70% correct performance (the just-noticeable difference or JND) and the model's sensitivity measured as a just-noticeable phase difference. The relationship between JND and JND_ϕ is a dynamic one, depending on the amount of under- or overestimation of the tracking adaptive oscillator and its degree of entrainment by the input. Specific performance predictions are linked to the simulation of the experimental task. However, several general predictions of this entrainment model for tempo discrimination are possible given an understanding of how time differences are mapped onto phase differences, as was examined in the three cases above. In particular, adaptive-oscillator-based predictions regarding differential sensitivity to increases and decreases in tempo will be discussed below, and compared with those derived from clock models.

Tempo Discrimination

In several recent studies, listeners' ability to detect differences in the tempo of isochronous tone sequences has been systematically investigated (Drake and Botte, 1993; Drake and Botte, 1994; McAuley and Kidd, 1994; McAuley and Kidd, 1995). McAuley and Kidd (1994) separately examined sensitivity to increases and decreases in tempo for two- and four-tone sequences for inter-onset-intervals of 100, 400, 700, and 1000 ms. On each trial a standard sequence was followed by two comparison sequences, one of which was faster or slower than the standard. Listeners judged which comparison sequence was different in tempo from the standard. Separate thresholds were obtained for "faster" and "slower" trials using an adaptive tracking procedure (Levitt, 1971). Consistent with Drake and Botte (1993), thresholds were found to be lower with four-tone sequences than with two-tone sequences, especially at the faster tempos. However, at the fastest tempos, listeners showed greater sensitivity to increases in tempo than to decreases in tempo, while the reverse was true at the slower tempos. These data are illustrated in Figure 4.

The results from this experiment confirm the predictions of the entrainment model. If an intrinsic "preferred" period of the system of around 600 ms is assumed, long IOIs (slow tempos) are underestimated and short IOIs (fast tempos) are overestimated, consistent with empirical data (Fraisse, 1982). For entrainment models, under- or overestimation indicates that the phase difference ($\Delta\phi$) corresponding to no time difference ($\Delta T = 0.0$) is skewed from $\Delta\phi = 0$ to a positive or negative value, as described in Cases 2 and 3. With underestimation, a tempo increase of $X\%$ triggers a phase difference that is smaller than that triggered by the same tempo decrease; thus, with underestimation, the model predicts greater sensitivity for tempo decreases (slowing down) than for tempo increases (speeding up). On the other hand, with overestimation, a tempo increase of $X\%$ triggers a phase difference that is larger than that triggered by the same tempo decrease; thus, with overestimation, the model predicts greater sensitivity for tempo increases than for tempo decreases. As described above, this pattern of differential sensitivity is found with listeners (McAuley and Kidd, 1994).

If it is assumed that in the limit (e.g., an isochronous standard sequence with a large number of tones), the adaptive oscillator is perfectly entrained by the tempo of the standard, in which Case 1 applies and $\Omega = T$,

then comparison sequences that are faster or slower by the same percentage will trigger equal phase differences, and the detection thresholds for increases and decreases in tempo will be the same. Thus, in the limit, differential sensitivity should disappear. For the reported data, differential sensitivity did disappear for the four-tone sequences, but only for the fastest tempos. In a simulation of the entrainment model (McAuley, 1995), this same interaction was produced by the dynamic interaction between period-coupling and a period-decay process. At fast rates, the input pulses driving the entrainment process occurred at a fast enough rate to enable the model to achieve perfect entrainment, in spite of the counteracting effects of period-decay. In contrast, at slower rates, the input pulses did not drive entrainment quickly enough to completely counteract the effects of period-decay, and the model did not achieve perfect entrainment; hence, differential sensitivity did not disappear for the slower tempos, as was also found with the listeners.

In contrast, the clock models discussed in this paper do not predict the pattern of differential sensitivity found with listeners, since temporal resolution is based on the variability of the clock process, independent of the stimulus. Consequently, no performance distinctions between faster/slower comparisons are made. In addition, it is not clear how the observed pattern of differential sensitivity could be accounted for by a clock-based model in a parsimonious way; it appears that one would have to at least assume that the distribution of clock variances is skewed, and that this skewness varies as a function of tempo.

Discussion

Wing and Kristofferson (1973) extended the concept of a clock timer to the production of regularly timed intervals (such as finger tapping). They assume that tapping variability arises from two independent processes: the clock component and a motor delay component. By making the independence assumption, they provide an elegant method based on analysis of auto-covariance of inter-tap-intervals, to decompose the tapping variability into the variances of the component processes (see Wing and Kristofferson (1973) for details). They suggest that the negative lag-one covariance often observed in tapping tasks may not be due to a compensatory timing mechanism, but can instead be explained as an implementation delay introduced by an independent motor component.

Based on this decomposition of tapping variability into clock and motor components, Ivry and Keele (1989) propose that the cerebellum acts as a central clock timer for both the perception of duration and the control of movements. They report that for both the perception and production of temporal intervals, larger clock-variability estimates are obtained with neurological patients with cerebellar deficits than are obtained with controls. However, this support for a cerebellar role in timing is linked to the assumptions of the Wing and Kristofferson model, requiring a firm commitment to the nature of the cerebellar timing mechanism, one that is clock-based (see also (Keele et al., 1985)).

618

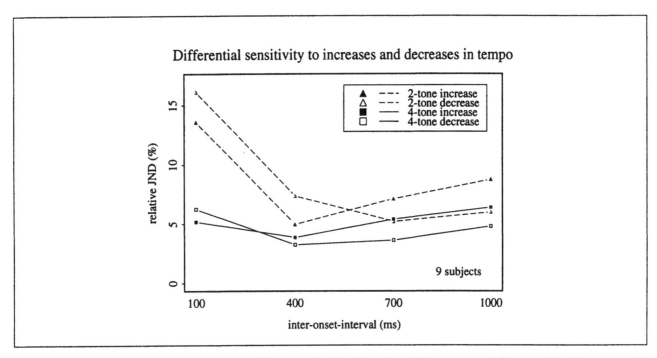

Figure 4: Mean discrimination thresholds of listeners for the detection of increases and decreases in the tempo of two- and four-tone isochronous sequences for base IOIs of 100, 400, 700, and 1000 ms (reproduced from McAuley (1995)).

In this paper, I have argued, based on tempo-discrimination data, that there is sufficient evidence to suggest that the nature of human timing capabilities is entrainment-based and not clock-based, in which case, the assumptions of the Wing and Kristofferson model (1973) are wrong. This calls into question the decomposition of tapping variability into clock and motor components. I do not intend here to argue against a cerebellar role in timing, but rather to suggest that data used to support the cerebellar timing hypothesis should at least be reanalyzed, taking into account *the possibility* that timing is based on entrainment. Braitenberg (1967) proposed that a clock-based timer might be implemented in the cerebellum via a series of adjustable delay lines; it has since been argued that the maximum neural delays in the cerebellum are too short to provide a reasonable clock implementation (Fahle and Braitenberg, 1984). The adaptive-oscillator mechanism discussed in this paper provides an alternative suggestion for a cerebellar timer, one that is entrainment-based.

Acknowledgments

The author thanks Simon Dennis, Gary Kidd and Catherine Rogers for their constructive comments on this research. This research is supported by a University of Queensland Postdoctoral Fellowship.

References

Abel, S. M. (1972). Discrimination of temporal gaps. *Journal of the Acoustical Society of America*, 52(2):519–524.

Braitenberg, V. (1967). Is the cerebellar cortex a biological clock in the millisecond range? *Progress in Brain Research*, 25:334–346.

Church, R. M. and Broadbent, H. A. (1990). Alternative representations of time, number, and rate. *Cognition*, 37:55–81.

Creelman, C. D. (1962). Human discrimination of auditory duration. *Journal of the Acoustical Society of America*, 34(5):582–593.

Divenyi, P. L. and Danner, W. F. (1977). Discrimination of time intervals marked by brief acoustic pulses of various intensities and spectra. *Perception and Psychophysics*, 21(2):125–142.

Drake, C. and Botte, M. C. (1993). Tempo sensitivity in auditory sequences: Evidence for a multiple-look model. *Perception and Psychophysics*, 54(3):277–286.

Drake, C. and Botte, M. C. (1994). The measure and modelization of tempo sensitivity in auditory sequences. *Journal of the Acoustical Society of America*, 95(5):2966.

Fahle, M. and Braitenberg, V. (1984). Some quantitative aspects of cerebellar anatomy as a guide to speculation on cerebellar functions. In *Cerebellar functions*. Spinger-Verlag, Berlin.

Fraisse, P. (1982). Rhythm and tempo. In Deutsch, D., editor, *The Psychology of Music*, pages 149–180. Academic Press, New York.

Ivry, R. I. and Hazeltine, R. E. (1995). Perception and production of temporal intervals across a range of duration: Evidence for a common timing mechanism. *Jour-*

nal of Experimental Psychology: Human Perception and Performance, 21(1):3–18.

Ivry, R. I. and Keele, S. W. (1989). Timing functions of the cerebellum. Cognitive Neuroscience, 1:134–150.

Jones, M. R. (1976). Time, our lost dimension: Toward a new theory of perception, attention, and memory. Psychological Review, 83:323–355.

Jones, M. R. and Boltz, M. (1989). Dynamic attending and response to time. Psychological Review, 96:459–491.

Keele, S. W., Nicoletti, R., Ivry, R. I., and Pokorny, R. A. (1989). Mechanisms of perceptual timing: Beat-based versus interval-based timing. Psychological Research, 50:251–256.

Keele, S. W., Pokorny, R. A., Corcos, D. M., and Ivry, R. I. (1985). Do perception and motor production share common timing mechanisms: a correlational analysis. Acta Psychologica, 60:173–191.

Large, E. W. (1994). Dynamic representation of musical structure. Ph.D. Thesis, The Ohio State University.

Levitt, H. (1971). Transformed up-down methods in psychoacoustics. Journal of the Acoustical Society of America, 49:467–477.

McAuley, J. D. (1994). Time as phase: A dynamic model of time perception. In Proceedings of the Sixteenth Annual Meeting of the Cognitive Science Society, pages 607–612, Hillsdale, New Jersey. Lawrence Erlbaum Associates.

McAuley, J. D. (1995). Perception of Time as Phase: Toward an Adaptive-Oscillator Model of Rhythmic pattern processing. Ph.D. Thesis, Indiana University.

McAuley, J. D. and Kidd, G. R. (1994). Differential sensitivity to increases and decreases in tempo: Evidence for an entrainment model. Journal of the Acoustical Society of America, 96(5):3257.

McAuley, J. D. and Kidd, G. R. (1995). Temporally directed attending in the discrimination of tempo: Further evidence for an entrainment model. Journal of the Acoustical Society of America, 97(5):3278.

Miall, C. (1989). The storage of time intervals using oscillating neurons. Neural Computation, 1(3):359–371.

Schulze, H. H. (1978). The detectability of local and global displacements in regular rhythmic patterns. Psychological Research, 40:173–181.

Schulze, H. H. (1989). The perception of temporal deviations in isochronic patterns. Perception and Psychophysics, 45(4):291–296.

Treisman, M. (1963). Temporal discrimination and the indifference interval: Implications for a model of the internal clock. Psychological Monographs: General and Applied, 77(13).

Wing, A. M. and Kristofferson, A. B. (1973). Response delays and the timing of discrete motor responses. Perception and Psychophysics, 14(1):5–12.

Emergent Letter Perception: Implementing the Role Hypothesis

Gary McGraw[†*] and **Douglas R. Hofstadter**[†]

[†]Center for Research on Concepts and Cognition
510 North Fess Street, Bloomington, IN 47405
http://www.cogsci.indiana.edu

&

[*]Reliable Software Technologies Corporation
21515 Ridgetop Circle, Suite 250, Sterling, VA 20166
http://www.rstcorp.com
gem@rstcorp.com   dughof@cogsci.indiana.edu

Abstract

Empirical psychological experimentation (very briefly reviewed here) has provided evidence of top-down conceptual constraints on letter perception. The role hypothesis suggests that these conceptual constraints take the form of structural subcomponents (roles) and relations between subcomponents (r-roles). In this paper, we present a fully-implemented computer model based on the role hypothesis of letter recognition. The emergent model of letter perception discussed below offers a cogent explanation of human letter-perception data — especially with regard to error-making. The model goes beyond simple categorization by parsing a letterform into its constituent parts. As it runs, the model dynamically builds (and destroys) a context-sensitive internal representation of the letter that it is perceiving. The representation emerges as by-product of a parallel exploration of possible categories. The model is able to successfully recognize (*i.e.*, conceptually parse) many diverse letters at the extremes of their categories.

The role hypothesis

Results from a series of previously reported psychological experiments in human letter recognition provide empirical evidence for the existence of conceptual-level representations of letter-parts that we call *roles* (McGraw et al., 1994; McGraw, 1995). The *role hypothesis* of human letter recognition jibes with other psychological theories of perception that posit higher-level relational structure, including work by Palmer (1977), Treisman and Gelade (1980), Hock et al. (1988), Biederman (1987), and Sanocki (1986). In the role hypothesis, the conceptual components of a letter representation are not explicit shapes *per se* but are ideas about what acceptable bounds for letter-part shapes are, how far such shapes can be stretched before they lose their interpretation, and how they interact with other roles to form a complete object.

Letterforms, or *physical* instances of letters, are made up of parts that correspond to the conceptual roles of the *mental* level. Little work on machine-based letter-recognition systems has considered intermediate-level parts (sometimes called "high-level features" in the literature), let alone collections or groups of such parts (Mori et al., 1984; Gaillat & Berthod, 1979). One important exception to this trend is the work done some two decades ago by Barry Blesser's research group[1] (Blesser

et al., 1973). The Blesser group's approach to machine letter recognition was, like ours, strongly based on the psychology of human letter perception (Naus & Shillman, 1976). The idea was to describe letters not in terms of their physical attributes, but in terms of more general descriptions of their underlying representations. Rich also briefly mentions an idea for a part-based model of letter recognition in her introductory AI text (Rich, 1983). The model she sketches is similar in spirit to the implemented work of Sanocki (1986; 1991).

Letter concepts, roles, and parts

Figure 1: Three common conceptualizations of the letter 'b', featuring two roles apiece.

Figure 1 is a graphical representation of three common ways one can break the abstract concept of letter 'b' into conceptual pieces according to the role hypothesis. Roles (the wiggly outlines) and r-roles that include relationships between roles (the black dots) make up the internal structure of a letter category and together define a particular *conceptualization* of a letter. Category membership at the whole-letter level is partially determined by category membership at the lower level of roles. (We say "partially" because the interaction between roles also matters. For example, a graphic shape might have a strong exemplar of *post* to the left of a strong exemplar of *loop* and yet the way they interact might still make them look more like 'lo' than 'b'.)

Figure 2 shows how actual letterforms (*e.g.*, shapes on a page) are comprised of *parts* that fill a letter-conceptualization's roles. During perception, representations of such parts are formed under top-down pressure from roles and are sensitive to context. As stated by Palmer (1978) [p. 96], "components [or parts] enter into relationships with other components, resulting in larger structural units whose importance supersedes that of [their] constituents." We hold that most of the

---

[1]Blesser's group included Shillman, Cox, Naus, Kuklinski, Ventura, and Eden.

"importance" attributed to the emerging parts stems directly from their role-filling ability. In other words, the way in which a part fills a role directly determines its "goodness". Experimental evidence reported in (McGraw, 1995) supports this claim by showing that human subjects prefer parts that correspond to natural roles over parts that fit the Gestalt criteria described by Palmer (1978).

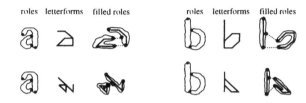

Figure 2: Parsing letterforms into high-level parts occurs under the top-down influence of roles. The top two examples show straightforward parsings (or, *role-fillings*) requiring little plasticity. The bottom two are more complicated, with role-plasticity performing a critical function during recognition.

Roles are "plastic" — their plasticity resulting from the fact that a role can be filled by a whole host of differently shaped parts. Roles are defined in terms of *norms*. Sometimes norms associated with roles must be *violated* in order to accommodate a given letterform's parts. The plasticity of a role is context-sensitive and varies according to conceptual pressures brought to bear by the situation.

Conceptual-level letter recognition

Human letter recognition has many distinct flavors. Letter recognition used while reading sentences in a uniform book-face, for example, is far different than recognition of a style-rich letter in a display face for advertising. The sort of recognition that we strive to model is more closely-related to display-face recognition. Specifically, our research concentrates on recognizing one letter at a time with no word-level context. Particular letters range all the way from very normal to stylistically-loaded. The human results that we use for comparative purposes were collected during just this sort of recognition task — that is, the recognition of single letters with no word-level context. Our model is driven by the need for a flexible and powerful letter-recognizer to be included in an analogy-based model of typeface creation called Letter Spirit.

Our model is based on the tenets of high-level perception, in which concepts dynamically provide top-down influence on the formation of perceptual structures during the process of categorization. The resulting perceptual structures, which emerge from the stochastic activities of a large number of tiny processing agents, are well-suited for further analogical processing (Mitchell, 1993). These perceptual structures include important information about the stylistic attributes of a letterform (as opposed to a mere categorization, like "is an 'a'"). This "conceptual parsing" is critical to the design of stylis-

tically uniform alphabets — the ultimate aim of Letter Spirit.

Why focus on cognitive plausibility of recognition models instead of engineering efficiency? Because human recognition of letterforms (especially highly-stylized ones) is still far superior to that of machines. We believe that a human-like approach will significantly enhance the capacity of computers to correctly recognize a wide variety of non-standard letterforms.

Letter Spirit

The Letter Spirit project is an attempt to model central aspects of human high-level perception and creativity on a computer, focusing on the creative act of artistic letter-design.[2] The aim is to model the process of rendering the 26 lowercase letters of the roman alphabet in many different, artistically coherent styles. Two important and orthogonal aspects of letterforms are basic to the project: the *categorical sameness* possessed by instances of a single letter in various styles (*e.g.*, the letter 'a' in Baskerville, Palatino, and Helvetica) and the *stylistic sameness* possessed by instances of various letters in a single style (*e.g.*, the letters 'a', 'b', and 'c' in Baskerville). Figure 3 shows the relationship of these two ideas. Initial work on the Letter Spirit project has been focused on the "letter" aspect. The model described in this paper is able to successfully recognize hundreds of letters from all 26 categories. We aim to show that the model does this in a similar fashion to the way people do.

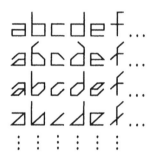

Figure 3: Items in any column have *letter* in common. Items in any row have *spirit* in common.

To avoid the need for modeling low-level vision and to focus attention on the deeper aspects of letter recognition, we developed an idealized micro-domain. Letterforms are restricted to short line segments on a fixed grid of 21 points arranged in a 3 × 7 array. Legal line segments, connect a point to any of its nearest neighbors. There are 56 possible segments, as shown in Figure 4. This restriction allows much of low-level vision to be bypassed and forces concentration on higher-level cognitive processing, particularly the abstract and context-dependent character of concepts.

[2] For information about the on-going Letter Spirit project see (Hofstadter & McGraw, 1993) and (McGraw & Hofstadter, 1993), available on the World Wide Web through URL http://www.cogsci.indiana.edu.

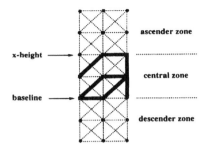

Figure 4: The Letter Spirit grid, with line segments instantiating one of many possible 'a's turned on.

Emergent letter perception

The fully-implemented gridletter recognizer in Letter Spirit is called the role model. All perceptual and creative processes in the role model are emergent, in the sense that they result from the actions of a large number of independent *codelets* — computational micro-agents that create, examine, and modify structures representing parts, roles, letters, stylistic traits, and so forth. Codelets perform these activities in (simulated) parallel. Newly created codelets wait to be run in a structure called the *Coderack*, which can be thought of as a stochastic waiting room. In contrast to a standard operating-systems queue, where processes wait before being deterministically given their slice of CPU time, the Coderack features stochastic selection of actions. To each codelet is attached an *urgency* value — a number that determines its probability of being chosen next. Urgency values are based on how well a codelet's possible effect coheres with structures already built.

Actions of every sort — gluing, labeling, scanning, matching, adjusting, regrouping, destroying, and so on — are carried out by codelets. The effect of each codelet considered by itself is very slight; however, as many codelets run, their independent effects build upon one another into a coherent collective behavior.

Over a long period of time, *processes* are interleaved in a manner reminiscent of time-sharing. (A process consists of many codelets, which *ex post facto* can be seen to have been acting in concert.) One notable difference between this and conventional time-sharing is that the biased nondeterministic selection of codelets amounts to having different processes run at different speeds. The speeds themselves are regulated over time, by varying the urgencies of the codelets involved, in an effort to favor more-promising directions over less-promising ones. Since codelets have very small effects, it is never critical that any particular codelet get selected. What does matter is that certain broad-stroked courses of action as a whole run faster than others. Probabilistic selection based on urgencies allows this to happen.

Many of the ideas behind this model (and its Copycat predecessor (Mitchell, 1993)) were originally inspired by the Hearsay II speech-understanding system (Erman et al., 1980). Hearsay II introduced the idea of simultaneous bottom-up and top-down influences interacting

in the process of perception. A complete comparison of the role model and Hearsay II, including a discussion of many important distinctions and differences can be found in (McGraw, 1995).

Processing in the role model

The role model operates roughly as follows, although this outline may give the impression that processing is more serial and well-ordered than it really is. In reality, processing occurs in a more parallel manner, with various aspects described below often proceeding concurrently. See (McGraw, 1995) for a thorough account of the role model.

- Line segments are probabilistically bonded together (by local perceptual codelets) with different amounts of "glue". (For example, more glue tends to be deposited at straight junctions than at angles.) The gluing codelets agents execute in a completely bottom-up fashion.

- When enough glue has been deposited, the glued shape is metaphorically "shaken". This amounts to probabilistically breaking the glued shape into chunks of segments at weak joints, resulting in a set of parts (usually made up of between two and four line segments).

- Each part is scanned by multiple codelets that probabilistically attach *syntactic labels* to the part. Labels reflect very simple properties of parts like curviness, length, width, location, and so on, and in no way involve the set of categories (either at the level of roles or wholes) into which these stimuli will eventually be channeled. Each syntactic label has a real number associated with it, standing for the strength with which the label applies to its part.

- When a part has accumulated enough syntactic labels (once again, a probabilistically determined event), it is allowed to send activation to one or more *roles*.

- The presence of a particular label on a given part serves as a cue that tends to lightly activate one or more roles with which the label is associated (*i.e.*, roles of which the given label is at least somewhat diagnostic). For instance, the labels "left-side", "straight", "skinny", and "tall" would tend to activate the "left-post" role found in 'b', 'h', 'k', and sometimes 'l'. It is important to understand that even a label such as "straight" is probabilistic, in the sense that a not-totally-straight part *might* get that label, with probability diminishing with its non-straightness. The real number associated with each label reflects this "goodness of fit".

- A part that does not strongly activate any roles will be slated for destruction, with its constituent line segments subjected to the part-forming process all over again.

- The various light activations coming from a given part's labels sum up to a *total* activation-level for each role that the part matches sufficiently. If activated highly enough, roles associate themselves with labeled parts, with the best-matching roles getting the most activation from a part. Each particular role may be filled by one part at any given time, although inter-part competition for the role's attention is ongoing and sometimes fierce.

- As roles and parts attempt to "mate", a given part may need to be slightly altered in order to be a good mate for a given role. A quantum or two may need to be stolen from one or more neighboring parts to make the part in question more attractive to a possible match. Likewise, small pieces that seem to make a part ugly in the eyes of possible role-mates may need to be given away or simply detached. The resulting structures composed of groups of the initial line segments are now results of the combined influence of bottom-up and top-down processing. As such, these parts are no longer totally syntactic entities, and we call them *(semantically) adjusted parts.*

- Roles compete for parts throughout the letter, adjusting the parts as they go. When this adjustment-and-association phase is over, there is a fairly strong match-up between roles and semantically-adjusted parts.

- Each instantiated role has a few tags attached, stating *how well* the given part instantiates the role. This information focuses on how the part deviates from various norms associated with the role.

- Each realized role begins to alert one or more *wholes* (*i.e.*, full role-sets, such as those shown in Figure 1) for which it provides evidence, in the sense of fitting a particular conceptualization of that letter. Role/whole coupling is analogous to part/role coupling, only it occurs at a higher (more semantic) level. Particular letter-conceptualizations are activated according to how strongly their component roles are realized in the actual grid letter.

- The activation level of each hypothesized whole is adjusted according to whether the whole's r-roles (*i.e.*, inter-role relations) approve of the structure discovered so far. When r-roles for a particular whole are checked, activation is taken away from any whole whose roles are not appropriately related or filled. This is a critical inhibitory aspect of the categorization process.

- Different wholes thus become activated to different extents. Each sufficiently-activated whole attempts to match itself up with the shape on the grid.

- If there is a clear leading contender among the wholes, it is deemed the winner. If there is a close race between several, the letterform is deemed ambiguous and therefore unacceptable. In a borderline case between clear-winner and close-race, a probabilistic decision is made that chooses between the two courses of action.

- In the end, the winning whole has been parsed into constituent, non-overlapping parts. These parts fill specific roles in the whole to a greater or lesser extent. The tags attached to roles according to how well they are filled by their associated parts are also available when processing ends. For example, a 't' whose spine is too tall or is bent over at the top, or whose crossbar is too short, too high, or tilted, will have tags stating such things attached to its filled conceptualization. This information can be used in further processing, including checking the style of a letterform and designing related letterforms by analogy.

The entire labeling and role-association process happens in parallel for each of the initial parts created after shaking. In general, processing proceeds from low-level syntactic processing to high-level semantic (or conceptual-level) processing, but is not completely linear in nature. Conflicting perceptual structures compete against each other in the context of current perceptual trends. Weak structures tend to be destroyed and strong ones to be strengthened. A perceptual parsing in terms of role-filling parts emerges as a result of this perceptual "competition".

Emergence, subsymbols, and symbols

It is difficult to pigeonhole the role model as belonging to any particular well-known cognitive-science school, as it is neither fully symbolic nor fully connectionist. Instead, it takes some of the central features of both paradigms and mixes them together, and thus could be said to fall somewhere between symbolic AI and connectionism.

In common with connectionism, the role model has many important subsymbolic characteristics of the sort that Smolensky advocates (Smolensky, 1988). In the subsymbolic paradigm, cognitive representations are built of *subsymbols* that in turn give rise to symbol-like structures. In systems of the subsymbolic vein, symbols are *statistically emergent* entities that are represented by patterns of activation over large numbers of subsymbols. The role model's fine-grained parallelism, local actions, competition for limited computational resources, spreading activation, and emergent concepts are all faithful to the subsymbolic enterprise. Also closely related is the interaction of top-down and bottom-up processing in the model.

The role model's representations also have something in common with more traditional symbolic methods. The emergent representations that the system develops are able to be quickly and easily *referenced* and *explicitly manipulated* since they are cut from symbolic cloth (*i.e.*, they are made up of Scheme structures, albeit with attached and dynamically varying activation values). Furthermore, these symbolic structures are built up in a workspace similar in some respects to a short-term memory — something not often found in connectionist models. The notion of *reference* is a critical one in models of higher-level cognitive activities such as analogy-making (Indurkhya, 1992). By their very nature, symbols — even of the active, emergent variety that we model — provide a natural avenue for such reference.

Performance of the role model

An intuitive way to illustrate the flexibility inherent in and emergent from the role model's architecture is to consider a series of runs on groups of letters. Doing this gives some idea of the sorts of letterforms the model is capable of recognizing and the sorts of letterforms it fails on. Figure 5, below, shows the extent to which the role model can handle cases where stylistic aspects of a letterform begin to overcome its category.

The particular group of letters we discuss here is taken from page 424 of (Hofstadter & FARG, 1995). The dataset consists of 88 lowercase gridfont 'a's. We ran the role model at least ten times on each of the 'a's in the original illustration, in order to discover which ones are easily recognized by the model and which are not. In Figure 5 we have arranged the 'a's of the original chart into a bull's-eye pattern, whose center is made up of 'a's that were correctly recognized 10 times out of 10. Concentric rings surrounding the bull's-eye the remaining 'a's into "recognition bins", the first consisting of 'a's recognized from 5 to 9 times over 10 runs, the second being those recognized from 2 to 4 times. Finally, outside of the outermost closed curve are those 'a's that the role

624

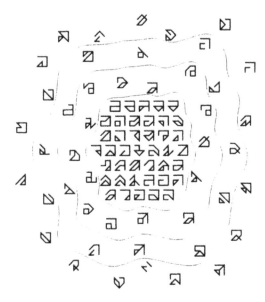

Figure 5: How the role model fares on 88 'a's.

model never categorized correctly. The more poorly a letter is categorized by the role model, the farther from the center of the picture it is placed. It is very interesting to note what the role model *can* do in terms of flexibly stretching its roles, and what the role model *can't* do. A detailed analysis of the model's behavior on this and other datasets may be found in (McGraw, 1995).

Overviews such as this provide a general feel for categorization in the role model. As can be seen from the letterforms in the center, the role model exhibits a remarkable flexibility in its categorization, making its notion of 'a'-ness very rich. Generally speaking, letterforms that are never properly recognized (those shown at the outskirts of the picture) are indeed letterforms at the "fringes of the category **a**", although there are a few exceptions that, by disappointing us, keep life lively.

Comparison with human data

A more objective measure of the role model's performance may be had by comparing its recognition data with human gridfont recognition data over the same dataset. The series of psychology experiments from which our comparative data is drawn can only briefly be described here. However, they are fully explained in (McGraw et al., 1994) and (McGraw, 1995). The idea is very basic: 35 subjects were presented with a series of grid-bound letterforms one at a time on a macintosh monitor and asked to identify the letters as quickly and accurately as possible. The letterforms were presented as darkened line segments on a lighter grid such that the grid provided some degree of noise. The computer tracked both reaction time and accuracy data. Error-making, which often provides insight into the behavior of complex cognitive systems, was carefully tracked. Predictions based on the role hypothesis were confirmed during analysis reported in (McGraw et al., 1994). In addition to this simple experiment, another study (alluded to on the first page) showed that given letterforms as stimuli, people prefer parts that correspond to roles over

parts that are supposedly "better" according to Palmer's rules. The study also included as a control non-letter stimuli made of flipped and inverted letterforms in which the "role-based" parts were not prefered over the Palmer parts.

The entire dataset reported here, called PSYCH, is made up of 544 tokens coming from all 26 letter categories. The full dataset can be split into two subsets: NORMALS (388 relatively strong letters) and FONTS (156 letters ranging from somewhat stylized to completely eccentric). Division of the dataset was initially completed by a human letterform expert. This division was confirmed empirically through *post facto* analysis.

Table 1 shows accuracy values of humans and the role model on the PSYCH dataset. The values were computed by averaging the correct-response percentages of each letter category.

Dataset	Humans	Role model
PSYCH	80.1	76.6
NORMALS	85.0	93.8
FONTS	65.4	51.4

Table 1: Accuracy percentages.

Large 544×26-entry confusion matrices can be built for both the human data and the role model. These matrices differ considerably from others like them in the psychology literature since they include data about a *large variety* of lowercase alphabetic styles instead of just one. Even though the dataset is made up of arguably idiosyncratic gridletters, our stimuli are more realistic than many past datasets, in the sense that they capture more of the natural variability found among letterforms. This leads to a more thorough treatment of errors than has been evident in past work.

Dataset	r-value	points
PSYCH	.8872	10764
NORMALS	.9511	6708
FONTS	.7274	4056

Table 2: Token-level correlation of role model and human error matrices. (All correlations are significant $p > 0.0001$.)

Table 2 shows the correlation values of the *token-level* confusion matrix of the role model against the human confusion matrix over our large and varied dataset.[3] Since error-making tends to highlight the type of processing that a cognitive system is doing, it is important to take errors into account during correlation. Favorable comparisons of these correlation values with those of simple connectionist models and a brute-force symbolic model can be found in (McGraw, 1995). Unfortunately, space constraints do not allow us to introduce those results or comparisons here. In-depth analysis of

---

[3]Category-level correlations are routinely higher (*e.g.*, the category-level correlation over PSYCH is 0.9821), but offer less resolution for inter-model comparison of the sort in (McGraw, 1995).

particular trends in error-making are also analyzed in (McGraw, 1995) and corroborate the general claims regarding the role-model's strength.

Conclusions

Our fully-implemented role model provides one possible implementation of the role hypothesis. It has proven to be a very strong model of letter recognition, as it clearly explains much of human letter-recognition behavior (especially with regard to error-making). Among the critical portions of the recognition process in the role model are these: building preliminary parts in a bottom-up fashion from low-level data, adjusting parts under top-down influence from roles, noting aspects of style — norm violations — that result from filling roles with particular parts, evaluating prospective filled role-sets as matches of different letter categories, tracking the strengths of activation of competing categories, and searching for new perceptual parsings if initial attempts at recognition result in only weak categorization.

Unlike many recognition programs, the role model does not simply perform very well on one style, only to crash and burn on others. It was designed specifically to handle a huge variety of styles. Tests using large datasets show that we have captured at least some of the perceptual fluidity exhibited by people. The role model is able to recognize both standard and stylistically eccentric letterforms.

A distinct advantage that the role model holds over simpler models lies in the nature of its output. The role model returns not only the usual category label, but also a parsing of a letterform in terms of its constituent parts. Part-level parsings correspond to role-level conceptualizations of letters. Further processing — for instance, the extraction of style information, or the analogical design of other letterforms — is possible only with the kind of structural information that the role model provides. The ability to parse a letterform into natural parts corresponding to roles is of critical importance to Letter Spirit's capability to design stylistically-consistent alphabets.

References

Biederman, I. (1987). Recognition by components: A theory of human image understanding. *Psychological Review*, 94(2), 115–147.

Blesser, B., Shillman, R., Cox, C., Kuklinski, T., Ventura, J., and Eden, M. (1973). Character recognition based on phenomenological attributes. *Visible Language*, 7(3), 209–223.

Erman, L., Hayes-Roth, F., Lesser, V., Raj Reddy, D. (1980). The Hearsay II speech-understanding system: Integrating knowledge to resolve uncertainty. *Computing Surveys*, 12(2), 213–253.

Gaillat, G. and Berthod, M. (1979). Panorama des techniques d'extraction de traits caractéristiques en lecture optique des caractères. *Revue Technique Thomson-CSF*, 11(4), 943–959.

Hock, H., Tromley, C., and Polmann, L. (1988). Perceptual units in the acquisition of visual categories.

Journal of Experimental Psychology: Learning, Memory, and Cognition, 14, 75–84.

Hofstadter, D. and FARG (1995). *Fluid Concepts and Creative Analogies: Computer Models of the Fundamental Mechanisms of Thought*. New York: Basic Books. "FARG" is an acronym for the "Fluid Analogies Research Group".

Hofstadter, D. and McGraw, G. (1995). Letter Spirit: Esthetic perception and creative play in the rich microcosm of the alphabet. In Hofstadter, D. and FARG, *Fluid Concepts and Creative Analogies: Computer Models of the Fundamental Mechanisms of Thought* (pp. 407–466). New York: Basic Books.

Indurkhya, B. (1992). *Metaphor and Cognition: An Interactionist Approach*. Norwell, MA: Kluwer.

McGraw, G. (1995). Letter Spirit (part one): Emergent High-Level Perception of Letters Using Fluid Concepts. Doctoral dissertation. Bloomington, IN: Indiana University, CRCC. Available on the web http://www.cogsci.indiana.edu/farg/mcgrawg/thesis.html.

McGraw, G. and Hofstadter, D. (1993). Perception and creation of diverse alphabetic style. *Artificial Intelligence and Simulation of Behaviour Quarterly*, 85, 42–49.

McGraw, G., Rehling, J., and Goldstone, R. (1994). Letter perception: Toward a conceptual approach. In *Proceedings of the Sixteenth Annual Conference of the Cognitive Science Society* (pp. 613–618). Hillsdale, NJ: Lawrence Erlbaum Associates.

Mitchell, M. (1993). *Analogy-making as Perception*. Cambridge, MA: MIT Press/Bradford Books.

Mori, S., Yamamoto, K., and Yasuda, M. (1984). Research on machine recognition of handprinted characters. *IEEE Transactions on Pattern Analysis and Machine Intelligence*, PAMI-6(4), 386–405.

Naus, M. and Shillman, R. (1976). Why a Y is not a V: A new look at the distinctive features of letters. *Journal of Experimental Psychology: Human Perception and Performance*, 2(3), 394–400.

Palmer, S. (1977). Hierarchical structure in perceptual representation. *Cognitive Psychology*, 9, 441–474.

Palmer, S. (1978). Structural aspects of visual similarity. *Memory & Cognition*, 6(2), 91–97.

Rich, E. (1983). *Artificial Intelligence*. New York: McGraw-Hill.

Sanocki, T. (1986). Visual Knowledge Underlying Letter Perception: A Font-Specific Approach. Doctoral dissertation. Madison, WI: University of Wisconsin, Department of Psychology.

Sanocki, T. (1991). Effects of early common features on form perception. *Perception & Psychophysics*, 50(5), 490–497.

Smolensky, P. (1988). On the proper treatment of connectionism. *Behavioural and Brain Sciences*, 11, 1–74.

Treisman, A. and Gelade, G. (1980). A feature-integration theory of attention. *Cognitive Psychology*, 12(12), 97–136.

Deafness Drives Development of Attention to Change in the Visual Field

Teresa V. Mitchell and Linda B. Smith

Department of Psychology
Indiana University
Bloomington, IN 47405
temitche@indiana.edu   smith4@indiana.edu

Abstract

Deaf (n = 37) and hearing (n = 37) subjects ages 6-7, 9-10, and 18 + participated in a visual attention experiment designed to test the hypothesis that vision in the deaf becomes specialized over developmental time to detect change in the visual field. All children, regardless of hearing status, should attend to change in the visual field. However, the differing developmental experiences and sensory "tools" between deaf and hearing create different demands on their visual systems. Hearing individuals may become capable of ignoring many changes in the visual field because they can simultaneously monitor the world auditorially and attend to task-relevant information visually. If so, then deaf individuals may find it difficult to ignore change in the visual field because their visual system must both monitor the world and attend to task-relevant information without simultaneous auditory input. Subjects in this experiment completed two attentional capture tasks in which they searched for a uniquely shaped target in the presence of two irrelevant stimulus manipulations (color or motion). This manipulation was applied to the target on half the task trials and to a distractor on the other half. Attention to the irrelevant manipulations will create differential reaction times (RTs) when the target is manipulated versus when a distractor is manipulated. Results indicated divergent development between the two groups. Both deaf and hearing children produced differential RTs in the two tasks, while only deaf adults attended to the task-irrelevant changes. Further, while hearing subjects were more affected by motion than color, deaf subjects are more equally affected by both. Results are discussed as compensatory changes in visual processing as a result of auditory deprivation.

Introduction

There is a popular notion that unimodal sensory deprivation affects intersensory interaction by leading to the development of compensatory functioning in the other, intact modalities -- that deaf people <u>see</u> better and blind people <u>hear</u> better, for example. The fact, however, is that changes in intact modalities following unimodal sensory deprivation are not global, and can not necessarily be characterized as simply "better" or "worse." Rather, one has to consider the developing individual as a complex, changing system, adapting the configurations of its sensory systems to the specific task at hand. A close inspection of the roles of each modality in an intact system, of the ways each modality informs the others, as well as an analysis of the types of task problems the deprived system must solve are necessary in order to make precise, differential hypotheses about how intact modalities should function. In this research, we sought to understand these developmental processes in one domain: the role of audition in the development of visual attention.

Sensory systems do not develop independently. Research on altered sensory development in laboratory animals shows that manipulating the developmental timing of potentially competing, simultaneous sensory inputs can change the trajectory of development. For example, Turkewitz & Kenny (1985) found that introducing visual input to rat pups prior to its typical onset disrupted homing behavior, which is acquired very early and is dependent on olfactory information. Small (1978) showed that after removal of the olfactory bulb in neonate hamsters, a thermal preference continues to dominate homing behavior through the period when this preference is normally overtaken by olfaction. The manipulation of multimodal input also changes the organization of individual sensory systems at the neural level. For example, Krech, Rosenzweig, and Bennet (1963) reared rats in environments rich in opportunities for tactile and haptic stimulation. Those rats that had been reared in the dark developed heavier somatosensory cortical areas than did light-reared rats and dark-reared rats evidenced greater biochemical activity in nonvisual areas than did light-reared rats. Together, these results illustrate that behavioral and neural organization depends in part on the nature and developmental timing of correlated sensory input from multiple modalities (see also Stein & Meredith, 1993).

There is also evidence from human development in support of these ideas. Neville and her colleagues (Neville & Lawson, 1987a & b) reported enhanced processing of peripheral visual events in deaf subjects relative to hearing subjects. Deaf adults responded faster and more accurately than hearing adults to peripheral targets, while no group differences were found in responses to foveally presented targets (Neville & Lawson, 1987a & b; see also Loke & Song, 1991). Neville also found that deaf subjects' evoked responses to peripheral stimuli had higher amplitude and shorter latency than hearing adults'. Furthermore, deaf subjects produced activity in brain regions that are generally involved in the processing of auditory information in hearing adults (Neville & Lawson, 1987a & b). Additional study revealed that deaf individuals' enhanced sensitivity to peripheral information results somehow from a lack of auditory experience and not from the use of a visual language (Neville & Lawson, 1987c). Specifically, hearing adults who were raised by deaf parents and whose first language was American Sign Language performed like hearing subjects and not like deaf subjects.

While deaf adults show enhanced responding to peripheral visual information, research indicates that deaf children perform poorly in comparison to hearing children on tasks requiring sustained attention to centrally presented visual information (Quittner, Smith, Osberger, Mitchell & Katz, 1994; Mitchell & Quittner, 1996). When asked to respond to a two-digit target sequence in a stream of individually presented stimuli, deaf children attend more to non-target information and produce lower d-prime and higher beta scores than hearing children. Together these results suggest that visual processing develops differently in the absence of audition, leading to enhanced attention to peripheral events and perhaps decreased vigilance to central events.

One way of understanding the differences between deaf and hearing individuals is in terms of a normally multimodal attentional system *adapting to* the lack of auditory input. In the hearing individual, audition provides information from both near and far environmental events. Thus, sound can be used to monitor the world for changing events and to reorient visual attention if necessary while the visual system is free to focus in on task-specific information. For deaf individuals, the absence of audition means that the visual system must become responsible for monitoring the world, both near and far, as well as picking up the relevant information for the task at hand. In brief, we predict that the differences between hearing and deaf individuals' experiences monitoring and orienting to events in the world, with and without the support of audition, leads to the emergence of differences in visual attention over developmental time. To test this idea, we track the development of visual attention in deaf and hearing individuals. This is the first study of this kind.

We tested the hypothesis that vision in deaf individuals become specialized over developmental time to detect change in the visual field. We predicted that development would <u>diverge</u> between deaf and hearing subjects. Young children, regardless of their hearing status, are poor selective attenders and should therefore attend to any change in the visual field. But, as these two groups age, their different sensory experiences should have cumulative effects. Hearing adults should be good at ignoring changes that are not task relevant. Deaf adults, because of the lack of accompanying auditory information, should need to attend to any change in the visual field, regardless of its task specificity. To test the hypothesis, deaf and hearing children and adults were presented with a task in which they searched for a target among distractors. We measured the degree to which performance was disrupted or helped by changes in the visual field.

Method

Subjects

Normally hearing subjects (n=37) were recruited from departmental subject files and from an undergraduate subject pool. Subjects were recruited from three age groups: 6-7, 9-10, adult. These age groups were chosen because of the degree to which attention changes in the early school years, and because we wanted to assess the cumulative effects of differing developmental experience.

Deaf subjects (n=37) were recruited from students and staff of two residential state schools for the deaf. These subjects were all prelingually deaf, were primary users of sign

language, had hearing losses above 90dB (average pure tone threshold in better ear), and had no additional handicapping conditions. Deaf subjects were recruited from the same age groups as hearing subjects.

Task and Procedure

We employed a computerized search task, modeled after the attentional capture paradigm (see Yantis, 1993), in which shape was the relevant stimulus dimension. A uniquely shaped target was embedded among one, three, or five homogeneously shaped distractors. Figure 1 presents the stimuli (1.62 degree visual angle each), which were arranged in a circular fashion (9.11 degree visual angle) in the center of the computer screen. Stimuli were presented with a 13 1/2" RGB color screen. Subjects sat approximately two feet from the screen with one hand on the mouse throughout the task. The experimenter sat behind and to the left of the subject, out of the line of vision, controlling stimulus presentations with the keyboard. All subjects were tested individually in a quiet, dimly lit room.

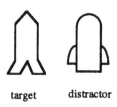

target   distractor

Figure 1. task stimuli

All subjects completed three versions of this task: a training task, a motion task, and a color task. Presentation of the motion and color tasks was counterbalanced across subjects. In the training task, all stimuli were in black outline and subjects were told to search for the oddly shaped target and respond by pressing the mouse button immediately upon detection of the target. They were told to work as quickly as they could without making mistakes. Reaction time was measured. Catch trials in which there was no target were embedded within each task. On these trials, subjects were told simply to indicate to the experimenter by speech, gesture, or sign that no target was present and reaction time (RT) was not measured. The experimenter then forwarded the task to the next trial. These "target absent" trials were included only as catch trials to check for subject compliance.

In the motion task, we introduced apparent motion as an irrelevant stimulus dimension. All stimuli were in black outline and on half of the trials, the target produced apparent motion (target trial), while on the other half of the trials, one of the distractors produced apparent motion (distractor trial). Subjects were told about the motion manipulation prior to the task and to ignore it as they searched for the target. If subjects could not ignore this irrelevant stimulus change, they would be fast on target trials, and slow on distractor trials. Similarly, the overall ratio of distractor trial RT to target trial RT will be large if subjects cannot ignore the stimulus manipulation.

Similarly in the color task, we introduced color as an irrelevant stimulus dimension. All stimuli were in green outline except for one stimulus, which was red. This red stimulus corresponded to the target on half of the trials and corresponded to a distractor on the other half of the trials. Subjects were told about the color manipulation prior to the task and to ignore it as they searched for the target. Again, if subjects could not ignore this irrelevant stimulus change, they would be fast on target trials, slow on distractor trials, and would produce large distractor to target RT ratios.

Results

Hearing subjects

Analyses of RT results included factors for age (3 levels), and trial type (target vs. distractor), while ratios were analyzed according to age. As shown in Table 1, hearing subjects' RT in the motion task decreased with age (F(2) = 30.297, $p < .001$), subjects were slower on distractor trials than target trials (F(1) = 121.893, $p < .001$), and the discrepancy in RT between distractor and target trials decreased with age (F(2) = 6.939, $p < .01$). Significant change in the ratio of distractor trial RT to target trial RT, depicted in Figure 2, occurred between the ages of 9-10 and adult (F(1) = 8.483, $p < .01$).

age group	target trials	distractor trials
6-7	RT = 668	RT = 761
	sd = 178	sd = 186
9-10	RT = 516	RT = 616
	sd = 56	sd = 83
adult	RT = 344	RT = 380
	sd = 40	sd = 53

Table 1: Motion task data, hearing subjects

As shown in Table 2, hearing subjects' RT in the color task decreased with age (F(2) = 24.418, $p < .001$), all subjects were slower on distractor trials than target trials (F(1) = 65.124, $p < .001$), and the discrepancy between target RT and distractor RT decreased with age (F(2) = 7.909, $p < .001$). Both child groups produced similar ratios, which were larger than adults' (9-10 and adult: F(1) = 4.523, $p < .05$), as depicted in Figure 2.

We directly compared hearing subjects' performance in the motion and color tasks to see if there was a qualitative difference in the way hearing subjects searched for the target in the face of dynamic information versus static information. Analysis of RT data indicated no task effects due to greater overall variability in the color task (F(1) = 1.802, $p > .05$). Ratios were marginally larger in the motion task than in the color task (F(1) = 3.067, $p = .08$): task irrelevant motion in the visual field is somewhat more difficult to ignore than color.

age group	target trials	distractor trials
6-7	RT = 699	RT = 804
	sd = 172	sd = 223
9-10	RT = 550	RT = 625
	sd = 58	sd = 92
adult	RT = 388	RT = 412
	sd = 109	sd = 116

Table 2: Color task data, hearing subjects

In summary, the major change with development is that hearing subjects become more able to ignore an irrelevant stimulus dimension as they search for a target, with the largest change occurring between the ages of 9-10 and adulthood. Dynamic change in the visual field affects target search somewhat more than static difference, across all age groups.

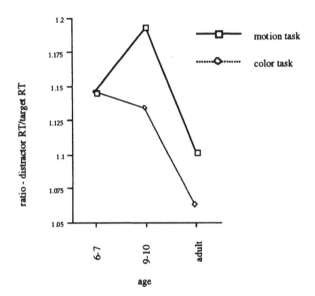

Figure 2. Hearing subjects, ratios - both tasks

Deaf subjects

In the motion task, deaf subjects' RT decreased with age $(F(2) = 9.573, p < .001)$ and all subjects were slower on distractor trials than target trials $(F(1) = 76.459, p < .001)$, as shown in Table 3. However, the discrepancy between target and distractor trials in the motion task decreased only marginally with age as shown by RT data $(F(2) = 3.152, p = .056)$ and ratio data (9-10 and adult: $F(1) = 3.614, p = .06$; see Figure 3).

age group	target trials	distractor trials
6-7	RT = 663 sd = 132	RT = 778 sd = 198
9-10	RT = 573 sd = 163	RT = 678 sd = 195
adult	RT = 411 sd = 66	RT = 463 sd = 87

Table 3: Motion task data, deaf subjects

As shown in Table 4, deaf subjects' RT in the color task decreased with age $(F(2) = 8.481, p < .01)$, subjects were slower on distractor trials than target trials in both tasks $(F(1) = 75.010, p < .001)$, and the discrepancy between target and distractor trials decreased significantly with age $(F(2) = 6.691, p < .01)$. Figure 3 illustrates that 6-7 year olds produced larger ratios than 9-10 year olds in the color task $(F(1) = 7.374, p = .01)$, with 9-10 year olds and adults producing similar ratios $(F(1) = 2.573, p > .05)$.

age group	target trials	distractor trials
6-7	RT = 766 sd = 203	RT = 892 sd = 233
9-10	RT = 675 sd = 263	RT = 730 sd = 295
adult	RT = 428 sd = 91	RT = 481 sd = 100

Table 4: Color task data, deaf subjects

Direct comparison of deaf subjects' RTs in the color and motion tasks showed that subjects were faster in the motion task $(F(1) = 10.253, p < .01)$, and ratio data, shown in Figure 2, indicated that dynamic information was more difficult to ignore than color information $(F(1) = 4.468, p < .05)$, but only for 9-10 year olds.

In summary, deaf subjects also develop the ability to ignore task-irrelevant information, but do so at a faster rate in the face of color information. By adulthood, deaf subjects are equally affected by static and dynamic information.

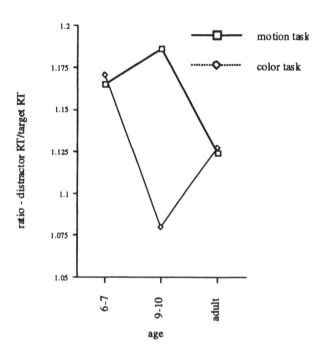

Figure 3. Deaf subjects, ratios - both tasks

Comparison of deaf and hearing performance

Direct comparison of deaf subjects to hearing subjects was done within each of the three age groups because of the high degree of variability between age groups. Analyses of RT results included factors for age (3 levels), group (2 levels), and trial type (target vs. distractor), while ratios were analyzed according to age and group. In the motion task, deaf and hearing 6-7 year olds performed similarly with regard to both RT $(F(1) = .0079, p > .10)$ and ratio measures $(F(1) = .185, p > .05)$, as did 9-10 year olds (RT: $F(1) = 1.167, p > .10$; ratio: $F(1) = .033, p > .10$). Adult hearing subjects were faster than adult deaf subjects $(F(1) = 9.563, p < .01)$, but ratio scores were not different $(F(1) = .620, p > .05)$.

In the color task, 6-7 year olds were again highly similar in RT $(F(1) = .575, p > .10)$ and ratio scores $(F(1) = .192, p > .10)$. Nine to ten year olds produced similar RTs $(F(1) = 2.085, p > .10)$, but hearing subjects produced marginally larger ratios than deaf subjects $(F(1) = 3.519, p = .07)$. Deaf adults were slower than hearing adults to respond, but only on distractor trials $(F(1) = 6.169, p < .001)$, and produced marginally larger ratios than hearing adults $(F(1) = 3.946, p = .051)$.

Thus, the two subject groups diverged in performance on our tasks. Six to seven year old children performed similarly in both tasks, while deaf adults were slower overall and were more affected by color than hearing adults were. Performance of the two groups was most similar in the face of apparent motion.

630

Discussion

The data we have presented support our hypothesis: early onset deafness produces greater attention to change in the visual field over developmental time. Deaf and hearing children performed similarly in both tasks, but by adulthood, deaf subjects were slower overall, and their search time increased when a distractor was manipulated while hearing subjects' search time did not.

The two groups also differed in their attention to dynamic and static information. Hearing subjects were more affected by dynamic information than static information as they searched for the target. This may be due to the correspondence between motion and sound in their normal experience. Deaf subjects, however, were affected strongly by both dynamic and static information. Any change in the visual field may become important for deaf individuals if their normal experience does not include auditory information that would differentiate between environmental events.

While this study revealed no differences in attention to irrelevant stimuli between deaf and hearing children, previous research has (Mitchell & Quittner, 1996; Quittner, Smith, Osberger & Katz, 1994). Differences in the experimental tasks are likely to have elicited different performance. First, stimulus presentation in this study was not speeded as it was in the previous studies. Subjects in this study were instructed to respond as quickly as possible, but stimuli were present until the response was made and natural saccades, blinks, and eye movements were not discouraged by the task. Second, previous research required subjects to attend to a two-digit sequence in a continuous stream of individually presented stimuli, which introduces both short-term and long-term memory constraints. No such constraints were introduced by the task in this study. It is possible, however, that a more sensitive measure than RT may reveal developmental differences earlier than those reported here.

The results of this study suggest that individuals develop a way of attending visually that is based on two things: the equipment they have and the input they receive. Hearing individuals receive multimodal, redundant information from their auditory and visual systems. This information leads to decreased attention to change in the visual field (or greater selectivity), and less responsivity to static information in comparison to dynamic information. Deaf individuals, on the other hand, rely primarily on visual information alone and therefore become more responsive to change in the visual field, regardless of whether it is static or dynamic information.

The finding that unimodal sensory deprivation produces greater attention to change in an intact modality is not unique. Studies using event-related potentials reveal enhanced, automatic processing of deviations in auditory stimulation in blind adults but not sighted adults (Kujala, et al, 1995). This is strong convergent evidence that attention functions like a gating mechanism, letting in information that is needed and selecting out that which is not as defined on-line by the organism, its sensory capabilities, and its developmental tasks. In this manner, the degree of attention to change or deviation shifts with the amount of information available to an organism. An organism that must rely on less information - either in real or developmental time - may become more attentive to changes or deviations in that information than an organism that has more available input. The alternative hypothesis, that a deprived system would become *more* selective and thereby ignore more information, has received no empirical support thus far. All of these results highlight the importance of a developmental analysis of attention and how it emerges over lifetime history to fit the configuration of abilities and task demands.

Recall that our larger hypothesis is that deafness affects visual processing in two ways: it makes vigilance to a restricted area of the visual field quite expensive to the system, and it makes vision specialize in detecting and attending to change. Evidence for each branch of this hypothesis has been reported in separate experiments. The strongest test of the larger hypothesis now will require giving subjects a dual attention task in which they must be vigilant to the center of the visual field, but also detect events in the periphery. We would expect to find, relative to normally hearing individuals, that deaf individuals sacrifice performance in the central task in order to maintain detection of events in the periphery.

The mechanism(s) that produces greater responsiveness to peripheral events in deaf adults, as documented by Neville and her colleagues, is currently unknown. First, deaf individuals might literally scan their visual field more often by moving their eyes or moving their heads. However, we know that individuals are capable of attending to nonfoveal information without moving their eyes: a second possibility is that deaf individuals may develop this capability to a greater extent than normally hearing individuals do. Finally, it is possible that deaf individuals develop a wider scope of attention than normally hearing individuals. These mechanisms, which are not mutually exclusive and are likely to change over development, have yet to be directly investigated and have implications for the development of attention to foveal events as well. A second experiment is currently underway in which we assess deaf and hearing subjects' attention to change using peripheral stimuli.

There is a great deal to be learned about the development of attention, about intersensory interaction, and the mechanisms of development itself by studying individuals with unimodal sensory deprivation. Understanding the manner in which the sensory systems interact under such perturbations will provide important, testable hypotheses regarding the way these systems interact in the intact organism.

References

Krech, D., Rosenzweig, M. R., & Bennett, E. L. (1963). Effects of complex environment and blindness on rat brain. *Archives of Neurology*, 8, 403-412.

Kujala, T., Alho, K., Kekoni, J., Hamalainen, H., Reinikainen, K., Salonen, O., Standertskjold-Nordenstam, C. G., & Naatanen, R. (1995). Auditory and somatosensory event-related brain potentials in early blind humans. *Experimental Brain Research*, 104, 519-526.

Loke, W. H., & Song, S. (1991). Central and peripheral visual processing in hearing and nonhearing individuals. *Bulletin of the Psychonomic Society*, 29(5), 437-440.

Mitchell, T. V., & Quittner, A. L. (1996). A multimethod study of attention and behavior problems in hearing-impaired children. *Journal of Clinical Child Psychology*, 25, 83-96.

Neville, H. J., & Lawson, D. (1987a). Attention to central and peripheral visual space in a movement detection task: an event-related potential and behavioral study. I. Normal hearing adults. *Brain Research*, 405, 253-267.

Neville, H. J., & Lawson, D. (1987b). Attention to central and peripheral visual space in a movement detection task: an event-related potential and behavioral study. II. Congenitally deaf adults. *Brain Research*, 405, 268-283.

Neville, H. J., & Lawson, D. (1987c). Attention to central and peripheral visual space in a movement detection task: an event-related potential and behavioral study. III. Separate effects of auditory deprivation and acquisition of a visual language. *Brain Research*, 405, 284-294.

Quittner, A. L., Smith, L. B., Osberger, M. J., Mitchell, T. V., & Katz, D. B. (1994). The impact of audition on the development of visual attention. *Psychological Science*, 5(6), 347-353.

Small, R. (1978). Functional and anatomical reorganization in developing hamsters after early postnatal lesions of the olfactory system. Unpublished doctoral dissertation. City University of New York.

Stein, B. E., & Meredith, M. A. (1993). *The merging of the senses*. Cambridge, MA: MIT Press.

Turkewitz, G., & Kenny, P. A. (1985). The role of developmental limitations of sensory input on sensory/perceptual organization. *Developmental and Behavioral Pediatrics*, 6(5), 302-306.

Yantis, S. (1993). Stimulus-driven attentional capture. *Current Directions in Psychological Science*, 2(5), 156-161.

632

Backward Masking Reflects the Processing Demand
of the Masking Stimulus

Clark Ohnesorge
Department of Psychology
Middlebury College
Middlebury, VT 05753
ohnesorg@midd-unix.middlebury.edu

John Theios
Department of Psychology
University of Wisconsin-Madison
Madison, WI 53706
theios@macc.wisc.edu

Abstract

Backward masking is often used to limit visual processing in studies of word recognition, semantic priming, and text processing. However, the manner in which the masking stimulus interferes with perception of the target is not well understood. Several explanations of the backward masking effect are considered, a termination hypothesis, an attention capture hypothesis, and a capacity sharing hypothesis. A point of distinction, the effect of manipulating the processing demands of the masking stimulus, is tested in two experiments. Frequency in print of the masking stimulus is manipulated in a first experiment and both frequency and repetition of the masking stimulus are tested in the second. The results disconfirm two of the hypotheses, termination and attention capture, and support the capacity sharing hypothesis.

Introduction

In backward pattern masking a stimulus is presented to the observer and after a brief interval is followed by another stimulus presented in the same location of the visual field. These are called the target and mask respectively. The presentation of the mask interferes with the processing of the target; the extent of this interference is typically indexed by response accuracy. When the interval between the onsets of the target and mask is small, target recognition is poor. As the time between the onsets of target and mask increases, target recognition improves.

Backward masking is a very useful tool in cognitive and perceptual psychology in spite of the fact that it is not clear exactly how or why the masking stimulus interferes with the visual recognition of the target. Many researchers have adopted, at least implicitly, the notion that the presentation of the mask terminates visual processing of the target. This assumption is instantiated in current models of backward masking, for example Lupker & Massaro (1979) and Muise, LeBlanc, Lavoie, & Arsenault, (1991). These models assume that visual information relevant to target identification begins to accrue shortly after target presentation and continues to build until visual processing of the target is terminated by presentation of the mask. Muise et al. (1991) presented their basic model

in terms of the following exponential growth function:

$$d' = \alpha (1 - e^{-\theta t}).$$ Where d' is the measure of performance, "α" represents the total information available in the display, and "e" is the base of the natural log. The critical parameters are "θ" (the growth rate of effective information) and "t" (time between target and mask). The accrual of information effective for target identification ceases at time "t"; in other words, visual processing of the target is terminated by the presentation of the mask. The sole determinant of information accrual is "t", or the amount of time the target has enjoyed uninterrupted access to whatever resources are necessary for recognition. This model does a very good job of predicting performance with single-letter targets and a much larger, brighter, pattern mask. However, backward masking is employed effectively in situations in which the mask and target are much more equivalent in terms of spatial extent and luminance (Perfetti & Bell, 1991; Perfetti, Bell, & Delaney,1988; Naish, 1983; Taylor & Chabot, 1978; Theios & Amrhein, 1989a). Further, research from two distinct areas suggests that the activation resulting from target processing is not necessarily obliterated or terminated by the presentation of the mask.

The first is a class of results grouped under the heading of perception without awareness. The empirical result is that under conditions of masking so severe that observers cannot reliably identify a prime word, facilitation of semantically related targets results (Dietrich & Theios, 1994; Evett & Humphreys, 1981; Greenwald, Klinger & Liu, 1989; Marcel, 1983; Morgan, 1994). Marcel (1983), Coltheart (1980), and Theios & Marmolejo (1991) have all offered similiar theoretical interpretations of the backward masking effect. They argue that the presentation of the masking stimulus "snatches" or captures attention away from the target stimulus, preventing conscious awareness of the target but not destroying all results of perceptual processes.

Another line of evidence against the termination hypothesis is provided by Dember and colleagues: Dember & Purcell (1967), Dember, Schwartz, & Kocak (1978), Briscoe, Dember & Warm (1983). In several experiments these researchers have demonstrated that it is possible to "mask the mask and unmask the target" . This is accomplished by adding a second mask, following the first mask, to the sequence of stimuli.

Like the studies on perception outside of awareness, these results support a conclusion that the mask interferes with attentional processes leading to the conscious perception of the target, but does not obliterate activation resulting from target processing.

How could the process of recognizing the mask interfere with recognition of the target? Coltheart (1980), Marcel (1983), Morgan (1993), Ohnesorge & Theios (1991a) and Theios & Marmolejo (1991) have all suggested that attention is captured away from the target by the presentation of the masking stimulus. A reasonable prediction, based on this notion, is that masking stimuli that are easily or quickly recognized should capture attention quickly, resulting in more or better masking than masks that are difficult to process and capture attention more slowly. However, a different conceptualization of the masking effect leads to a contrasting prediction.

Given that the transfer of information from iconic representation to short term memory is dependent in some sense on capacity (Gegenfurtner & Sperling, 1993; LaBerge & Brown, 1989; Reeves, 1986) it seems plausible that masking might be in part a result of insufficient capacity to concurrently process both target and mask to a level sufficient for conscious awareness. The result of this line of thinking is the capacity sharing hypothesis. Masks that require more processing resource, rather than less, will result in the greatest degree of masking.

With these three hypotheses there is an exhaustive partition of the possibility space. The termination hypothesis predicts no effect of manipulating the processing demands of the mask, the attention capture hypothesis predicts more masking with low demand masks, and the capacity sharing hypothesis predicts more masking with high demand masks.

The Processing Demand of the Mask

The following experiments will hold constant the low-level physical characteristics of masking words and manipulate higher order characteristics of the masking stimuli that can reasonably be associated with processing demands. We assume that the demand for resources can be indexed through response time and accuracy, with longer response times and lower accuracy rates indicating a greater demand for processing resources. Word Frequency and Stimulus Repetition are both good candidates for manipulating the processing demands of lexical stimuli. The word frequency effect (WFE) is ubiquitous, words that are high in printed frequency are responded to more quickly, and with fewer errors than low frequency or less familiar words (Scarborough, Cortese, & Scarborough, 1977). Likewise, stimuli that are repeated within an experimental context yield faster and more accurate recognition scores than non-repeated stimuli (Forster & Davis, 1984; Scarborough, Cortese, & Scarborough, 1977; Theios & Walter 1973; Woltz 1990) Manipulating either the printed word frequency or repetition of stimuli used as masks should affect the amount of processing required for their recognition, and allow a critical test of the termination, attention capture, and capacity sharing hypotheses.

Word frequency and repetition are useful variables to manipulate because explanations of the somewhat vague term "processing resources" can be made with respect to models of word recognition that incorporate processing cycles in simulations of the word recognition process (e.g. the Activation-Verification model of Paap, Newsome, McDonald, & Schvaneveldt, 1982; or the Interactive Activation model of McClelland & Rummelhart, (1981, 1985). A slightly different conceptualization of word frequency and repetition effects is embodied in the activation level account of the Logogen model (Morton, 1969). Our first experiment examines the effect of manipulating the printed frequency of the mask. On the basis of a pilot study we concentrated on levels of SOA up to 53 milliseconds.

Experiment One

Subjects
Twenty-three students with normal or corrected vision at the University of Wisconsin-Madison participated.

Apparatus
The experiment was designed and conducted using the software program PsyScope (Cohen, MacWhinney, Flatt & Provost, 1993). A Power Macintosh 7100 controlled the display sequence and collected the data. **Design** There were two within-subjects variables, Stimulus Onset Asynchrony or SOA, and Mask Frequency. There were four levels of SOA (13.3, 26.6, 40, 53.3 ms.) and two levels of Mask Frequency, (High and Low).

Procedure
Subjects sat 500 millimeters from the computer monitor. Each trial consisted of 300 ms of fixation, a 50 ms blank interval, a 13 ms presentation of the target, one of the four randomly selected levels of SOA, and, following a 300 ms blank interval, the choice alternative pair until response. The computer provided feedback on each trial of the 45 practice and 216 experimental trials.

Stimuli
The stimuli were selected using the third index of the Kucera and Francis (1967) word frequency corpus. The experimental stimuli comprised three sets: a set of 216 low frequency choice alternative pairs, a set of 216 high frequency masks and a set of 216 low frequency masks. All of the words used in the experiment, both masks and targets, were four letters long. The vast majority were single syllable. The target set was constructed by selecting pairs of words that differed by one or two letters. The substituted letter ranged across the four possible positions within words (e.g. "LAVA & JAVA" vary in the first position, "HECK & HICK" in the second). The target for each trial was randomly selected, the other member of the pair became the foil in the identification phase. The printed frequency of all words in the choice alternative pair set was between 1 and 10, with a mean frequency of 3.3. The low frequency masking words ranged from 1 to 10, with a mean frequency of 3.6. The high frequency masking words ranged

from 50 to 500 occurrences, with a mean frequency of 187. Summed Positional Bigram Frequency (SPBF) for the stimulus sets was calculated using the norms published by Massaro, Taylor, Venezky, Jastrzembski, & Lucas, (1980). The masking sets differed greatly in frequency but only slightly in SPBF.

Results

The effect of Mask Frequency was significant, $F(1,22) = 17.3$, $p < .05$. The mean percentage of targets correctly recognized in the High Frequency mask condition was 62%, versus 57% in the Low Frequency mask condition. The effect of SOA was also significant, $F(3,66) = 8.9$, $p < .05$. The interaction of Mask Frequency and SOA did not approach significance $F(3,66) = .18$, $p > .05$. Cohen's epsilon ($\underline{e}$) revealed a strong relationship between Mask Frequency and target recognition performance, $\underline{e} = .64$.

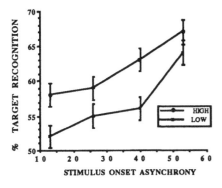

Figure 1: Target recognition under masking by High and Low Frequency masking words.

Discussion

This result provides support for the capacity sharing hypothesis and infirms the termination and attention capture hypotheses. Target recognition is influenced by the demand of the mask. Low frequency (high demand) masks, are more effective than high frequency masks, i.e. result in lower levels of target recognition. The frequency effect produces about 5% difference in recognition accuracy between conditions in this 2AFC design. However, the proportion of variance accounted for, $\underline{e}^2 = .41$, is large enough to show that this difference is not trivial.

Experiment Two

Word frequency is a manipulation of processing difficulty that can be understood within current simulations of word recognition processes. In order to further test the distinctive predictions of the three hypotheses we conducted an experiment that manipulated the demand of the mask using a repetition manipulation. The stimulus repetition effect is quite robust; faster and more accurate processing upon subsequent exposures to a stimulus (Forster & Davis, 1984; Theios & Walter, 1973, Woltz 1990). By inference

masking stimuli that are repeated will require less processing than masks that are presented only once. The predictions for Experiment Two are analogous to those derived for Experiment One. The termination hypothesis predicts no effect of repeating the mask, the attention capture hypothesis predicts <u>more</u> masking when the mask is repeated, and the capacity sharing hypothesis predicts <u>less</u> masking when the mask is repeated.

Subjects Twenty-six students with normal or corrected vision from the University of Wisconsin-Madison participated in the experiment.

Design There were two within-subjects variables, Mask Frequency (High & Low) and Mask Repetition (Single Exposure & Repeated Exposure), with a single SOA of 26 milliseconds.

Stimuli

The stimuli were those used in Experiment 1.

Procedure

There were two significant differences in the procedure used in experiement two. First, only one level of SOA was used to reduce the overall complexity of the task. Second, an additional stimulus was presented for one second immediately prior to the target:mask sequence. This stimulus was either the mask that would appear later in the trial (repeated exposure condition) or a different mask of the appropriate frequency (single exposure condition).

Results

The effect of frequency was again significant, $F(1,25) = 13.1$, $p < .05$, and the strength of asociation was relatively high, $\underline{e} = .56$. The main effect of the Mask Repetition factor was also significant, $F(1,25) = 44.1$. $p < .05$. Observers correctly identified more targets in the Repeated Exposure condition (mean = 70%) than in the Single Exposure condition (mean = 62%). The Repetition factor was also strongly related to performance, $\underline{e} = .79$. The interaction of Frequency and Repetition was not significant $F(1,25) = .021$.

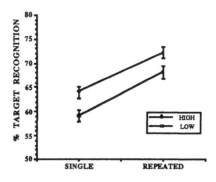

Figure 2: Target recognition under masking by High and Low frequency masking words presented once (single condition) or twice (repeated condition).

Conclusion

The interpretation of these studies is straightforward. Factors that affect the processing demand of a masking stimulus affect the degree of masking that occurs. This finding is sufficient to disconfirm the termination hypothesis. Were the termination hypothesis true the manipulation of masking word frequency and mask repetition should not have affected the extent of masking that occurred. Given our tight stimulus control, only changes in target processing time (the parameter "t" in the model described by Muise et al., 1991) should have affected the accrual of information and thus recognition performance. The attention capture hypothesis is also disconfirmed. The attention capture hypothesis admits a role for higher-level processesing resources in backward masking but makes a prediction in the opposite direction from that which occurred. In contrast, the capacity sharing hypothesis is supported. Masks that are more easily processed interfere less with the processing of the target, allowing better target recognition performance. In hindsight, the capacity sharing hypothesis can be seen to fit neatly into the large body of work on dual-task performance. When the difficulty of one task is increased, performance on a concurrent task falls, to the extent that the two tasks compete for common resources. The results of these studies support the conclusion that the target and mask compete for resources from a common pool that are needed by both for recognition. Given its later arrival, the mask enjoys privileged access to this pool and can demand sufficient resources to support its own recognition, with an attendant reduction in resources available for target recognition.

Acknowledgements

The authors would like to thank Robin Chapman, William Epstein, Robert French, Morton Gernsbacher, Mike Hogan, Bob Kachelski, and Steve Morgan for their contributions to this research. Special thanks go to Virginia Marchman for her many helpful comments on stimulus materials and to Josh Reichman for his help in implementing the studies.

References

Briscoe, G., Dember, W., & Warm, J. (1983). Target recovery in visual backward masking: No clear explanation in sight. Journal of Experimental Psychology, Human Perception and Performance, 9(6), 898-911.

Coltheart, M. (1980). Iconic memory and visible persistence. Perception & Psychophysics, 27, 183-228.

Dember, W. N., & Purcell, D.G. (1967). Recovery of masked visual targets by inhibition of the masking stimulus. Science, 157, 1335-1336.

Dember, W., Schwartz, M., & Kocak, M. (1978). Substantial recovery of a masked visual target and its theoretical interpretation. Bulletin of the Psychonomic Society, 11(5), 285-287.

Dietrich, D. & Theios, J. (1992). Priming outside of awareness and subsequent stimulus identification. Perceptual and Motor Skills, 75, 483-493.

Forster, K., & Davis, C. (1984). Repetition priming and frequency attentuation in lexical access. Journal of Experimental Psychology: Learning, Memory, and Cognition, 10(4), 680-698.

Forster, K., Booker, J., Schacter, D., & Davis, C. (1990). Masked repetition priming: Lexical activation or novel memory trace? Bulletin of the Psychonomic Society, 28(4), 341-345.

Gegenfurtner, K., & Sperling, G. (1993). Information transfer in iconic memory experiments. Journal of Experimental Psychology, Human Perception and Performance, 19(4), 845-866.

Greenwald, A. G., Klinger, M.R., & Liu T.J. (1989). Unconscious processing of dichoptically masked words. Memory & Cognition, 17 35-47.

LaBerge, D., & Brown, V., (1989). Theory of attentional operations in shape identification. Psychological Review, 96(1), 101-124.

Lupker, S., & Massaro, D. (1979). Selective perception without confounding contributions of decision and memory. Perception & Psychophysics, 25(1), 60-69.

Marcel, A. (1983). Conscious and unconscious perception: An approach to the relations between phenomenal experience and perceptual processes. Cognitive Psychology, 15, 238-300.

Massaro, D., Taylor, G., Venezky, R., Jastrzembski, J., & Lucas, P. (1980). Letter and word perception. Amsterdam, The Netherlands: North Holland publishing company.

McClelland, J., L., & Rumelhart, D., E. (1981). An interactive activation model of context effects in letter perception: 1. An account of basic findings. Psychological Review, 88, 375-407.

McClelland, J., L., & Rumelhart, D., E. (1985). Distributed memory and the representation of general and specific information. Journal of Experimental Psychology: General, 114, 159-188.

Morgan, S., T. (1993). Shifts of visual-spatial attention initiated by unconscious symbolic cues. Unpublished doctoral dissertation, University of Wisconsin-Madison

Muise, G., LeBlanc, R., Lavoie, M., & Arsenault, A. (1991). Two-stage model of backward masking: Sensory transmission and accrual of effective information as a function of target intensity and similiarity. Perception & Psychophysics, 50(3), 197 204.

Ohnesorge, C.G. & Theios J. (1991a). The Effect of Extremely Small Intensity Differences in Tachistoscopic Presentations of Picture-Word Pairs. Paper presented at Midwestern Psychological Association, (May), Chicago, Ill.

Ohnesorge, C.G. & Theios J. (1991b). Signal Detection Analysis of Two Extremely Brief Stimuli, Paper presented at Meeting of the Society for Mathematical Psychology, (August), Bloomington, In.

Paap, K., Newsome, S., McDonald, J., & Schvaneveldt, R. (1982). An activation-verification model for letter and word recognition: The word-superiority effect. Psychological Review, 89 (5), 573-594.

Perfetti, C.A., Bell, L.C., & Delaney, S. M. (1988). Automatic (prelexical) phonetic activation in silent word reading: evidence from backward masking. Journal of Memory and Language, 27, 59-70.

Perfetti, C.A., & Bell, L.C. (1991). Phonemic activation during the first 40 ms of word identification: evidence from backward masking and priming. Journal of Memory and Language, 30, 473-485.

Reeves, A. (1986). Attention and the order of items in short term visual memory. Special issue : Visual Attention Psychological Research, 48(4), 239-250.

Scarborough, D., Cortese, C., & Scarborough, H. (1977). Frequency and repetition effects in lexical memory. Journal of Experimental Psychology, Human Perception and Performance, 3(1), 1-17.

Theios, J., & Marmolejo, G. (1991). A backwardly masked stimulus is not subliminal. Paper presented at the 32nd Annual Meeting of the Psychonomic Society, (November), San Francisco, CA.

Theios, J., & Morgan, S., T. (1990). On the evolution of a visual percept. In *Proceedings of the Twelfth Annual Meeting of the Cognitive Science Society.* Hillsdale N.J.: Lawrence Erlbaum Associates, Publishers, 590 597.

Theios, J., & Walter, D., G. (1973). Stimulus and response frequency and sequential effects in memory scanning reaction times. Journal of Experimental Psychology, **102**(6) 1092-1099.

Turvey, M. (1973). On peripheral and central processes in vision: inferences from an information-processing analysis of masking with patterned stimuli. Psychological Review, **80**(1) 1-52.

Woltz, D. (1990). Repetition of semantic comparisons: Temporary and persistent priming effects. Journal of Experimental Psychology: Learning, Memory, and Cognition, **16** (3), 392-403.

The Emergence of Perceptual Category Representations
During Early Development: A Connectionist Analysis

Paul C. Quinn
Department of Psychology
Washington & Jefferson College
Washington, PA 15301, USA
pquinn@vms.cis.pitt.edu

Mark H. Johnson
MRC Cognitive Development Unit
4 Taviton Street
London, WC1H 0BT, UK
mark@cdu.ucl.ac.uk

Abstract

A number of recent studies on early categorization suggest that young infants form category representations for stimuli at both global and basic levels of exclusiveness (i.e., mammal, cat). A set of computational models designed to analyze the factors responsible for the emergence of these representations are presented. The models (1) simulated the formation of global-level and basic-level representations, (2) yielded a global-to-basic order of category emergence and (3) revealed the formation of two distinct global-level representations -- an initial "self-organizing" perceptual global level and a subsequently "trained" arbitrary (i.e., non-perceptual) global level. Information from the models is used to make a number of testable predictions concerning category development in infants.

Introduction

Investigators interested in early cognitive development have been examining the origins and development of complex category representations during the first two years of life (e.g., Mandler, Bauer, & McDonough, 1991; Mervis, 1987; Quinn, Eimas, & Rosenkrantz, 1993). Empirical efforts have been concerned with (1) the age and means by which individuated representations can be formed for basic-level categories (e.g., cats, chairs) from the same global-level structure (e.g., mammal, furniture), and (2) whether these representations begin to cohere to form global-level representations or whether global-level representations precede basic-level representations.

One set of relevant studies has shown that young infants can form perceptually-based category representations at both basic and global levels of exclusiveness (reviewed in Quinn & Eimas, in press-a). At the basic level, 3- to 4-month-olds familiarized with domestic cats will generalize familiarization to novel cats, but dishabituate to birds, horses, dogs, tigers and even female lions. The data provide evidence that the infants can form a representation for cats that includes novel cats, but excludes exemplars from a variety of related basic-level categories. Behl-Chadha (in press) has extended these findings to human-made artifacts by showing that 3- to 4-month-olds can form individuated representations for chairs and couches each of which excludes instances of the other as well as beds and tables.

At the global level, 3- and 4-month-olds familiarized with instances from a number of mammal categories (e.g., cats, dogs, tigers, rabbits, zebras, elephants) generalized familiarization to novel mammal categories (e.g., deer), but dishabituated to instances of birds, fish and furniture (Behl-Chadha, in press), indicating that the infants can form a representation of mammals that includes novel mammal categories, but excludes instances of non-mammalian animals (i.e., birds and fish) and human-made artifacts (e.g., furniture). In the same series of experiments, Behl-Chadha obtained evidence that 3- to 4-month-olds can also form a representation for furniture that includes beds, chairs, couches, dressers, and tables, but excludes the mammals mentioned above. The evidence thus suggests that young infants can form global-level representations for at least some natural (i.e., mammals) and artifactual (i.e., furniture) categories.

Of interest is the information that enables infants to form category representations at the basic and global levels in these studies. The age of the subjects and the nature of the stimuli (i.e., static pictorial instances of the categories) make it improbable that the infants are relying on conceptual knowledge about the "kind of thing" something is to perform successfully in these tasks (cf. Mandler & McDonough, 1993). The studies therefore support the position that both basic and global levels of representation can have a perceptual basis.

Given this state of affairs, at least two important issues remain unresolved. First, is there a sequence to the development of category representations at the two levels in younger infants (i.e., from basic to global or vice versa)? Second, what is the basis of such a sequence? To examine these issues, we have been exploring the emergence of basic-level and global-level category representations in connectionist learning systems. Using as input the dimensions of the stimuli employed in the experiments cited above, we have found that a variety of two layered (i.e., input-output) and three layered (i.e., input-hidden-output) network architectures produce both basic- and global-level category representations and reveal that global-level categories precede basic-level categories in order of appearance. In this paper, we consider the performance of two of these models in detail and examine possible reasons for the observed global-to-basic developmental trajectory.

Simulation 1: Global before Basic

Method

Network Architecture and Training Stimuli. The network had 13 input nodes, 3 hidden nodes and 10 output nodes. Each hidden node received input from all 13 input nodes and in turn sent input to all 10 output nodes. The input nodes encoded 13 attributes of pictorial instances of cats, dogs, elephants, rabbits, chairs, tables, beds and dressers -- stimuli used in the studies described earlier (Behl-Chadha, in press; Quinn & Eimas, in press-a). These stimuli were realistic color photographs, each displaying an individual mammal or furniture item. They were selected to be nearly the same size as possible so that the infant would use cues other than size as bases for categorization. Three instances of each category were randomly selected as training inputs and an additional instance was randomly selected for generalization testing. Stimulus attributes that served as inputs were head length, head width, eye separation, ear separation, ear length, nose length, nose width, mouth length, number of legs, leg length, vertical extent of the stimulus, horizontal extent of the stimulus, and tail length. The attribute values were measured directly from the stimuli in centimeters and then linearly scaled so that the highest value on any given attribute was 1.0. If a stimulus did not possess an attribute, then the value for that attribute was encoded on its respective input node as 0.0.

This manner of parsing input patterns into component attributes, and using the attribute values along with certain assumptions about processing to make predictions about the formation of category representations, has been used in previous infant categorization investigations (e.g., Strauss, 1979; Younger, 1990). The attributes of horizontal and vertical extent were chosen because of their correspondence with the width and height of the furniture and mammal stimuli. The large number and detailed nature of the facial attributes were selected because of evidence that infants are highly attracted to facial configuration information (e.g., Johnson & Morton, 1991). Young infants also appear to use information from the face and head region of cats and dogs to categorically distinguish between them (Quinn & Eimas, in press-b). For example, infants familiarized with cat stimuli in which only the face and head region was visible (the body information had been occluded), preferred novel dog faces over novel cat faces. However, infants familiarized with cat stimuli in which only the body information was visible (the face and head region was occluded), looked equivalently to novel dog and cat bodies. Subsequent control experiments revealed that the dog preference in the "face and head visible" group could not be attributed to a spontaneous preference for dog faces or to an inability to discriminate among cat faces. Facial information would thus seem to provide infants with a necessary and sufficient basis to form a category representation for cats that excludes dogs. Quinn and Eimas also showed that the cues for this category representation of cats resided in the internal facial region (inclusive of the eyes, nose and mouth) and along the external contour of the head.

Ten output nodes were responsible for indicating the basic and global category identity of the stimuli: cat, dog, elephant, rabbit, chair, table, bed, dresser, mammal and furniture. Each stimulus was associated with two of the ten output nodes, one for the basic level, the other for the global level. Given that the range of activation of the units was from 0.0 to 1.0, the system was considered to have correctly recognized the category identity(ies) (i.e., global and basic) for a given stimulus if it activated the output node(s) associated with that stimulus to a value(s) greater than 0.50 and activated the output nodes corresponding to stimuli from other categories to values less than 0.50.

Training and Testing Procedure. Training consisted of presentation of the 24 stimuli in a random order with replacement for 7200 training sweeps (1 sweep = 1 presentation of a single stimulus). Generalization testing consisted of one presentation of a novel exemplar from each category.

Implementation. The simulation was run on the neural network simulator **tlearn** that makes use of a backpropagation learning algorithm (Plunkett & Elman, in press). The network was trained with a random seed of 47, a learning rate of 0.3 and a momentum of 0.7. Comparable results were obtained with two other random seeds. Thus, while we present data from one random seed in detail, the basic results (with only minor variations) are extendable to a variety of starting seeds (and this is true for each of the simulations reported in the paper).

Results and Discussion

Performance of the network is shown in Figure 1 where the Root Mean Square (RMS) Error (reflecting the discrepancy between actual and correct response for a given input) is plotted as a function of training sweeps. Category learning began at 120 sweeps with the global distinction between mammals and furniture. At 960 sweeps, the elephant exemplars were learned. By 3600 sweeps, the beds, cats, dogs, dressers, rabbits and tables were categorized. Learning was completed at 7200 sweeps when chairs were correctly classified.

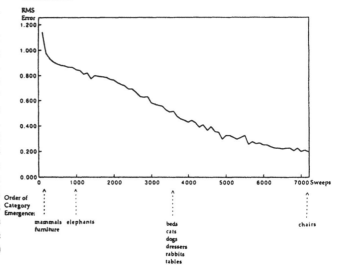

Figure 1. Root mean square error of Simulation 1 as a function of training sweeps. Category labels along the sweep axis are positioned to show the categories that have emerged at 120, 960, 3600 and 7200 sweeps.

It is interesting to consider the representations of the input patterns that emerged on the hidden units during training. Figure 2 presents a 3-dimensional plot of the mean activation values on hidden nodes 1, 2 and 3 (relabeled as X, Y and Z) generated by the 8 categories of stimuli at three points in training. Panel A (left) shows that at 8 sweeps, all 8 categories cluster closely together. Panel B (center) shows

639

that at 480 sweeps, only mammals and furniture were segregated. Finally, Panel C (right) reveals that at 7200 sweeps mammals and furniture were segregated along the z-axis and each basic-level category had its own location

recognized as distinct basic-level categories in this simulation. The results show that the global-to-basic sequence is obtained even without the face and tail information from the mammal stimuli, indicating that it is

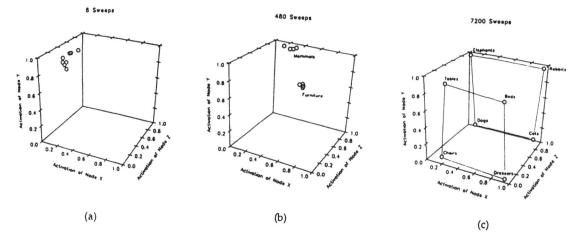

(a)　　　　　　　　　　(b)　　　　　　　　　　(c)

Figure 2. Mean activation values of hidden nodes 1, 2 and 3 (relabeled as X, Y and Z) for each category at (a) 8 sweeps, (b) 480 sweeps and (c) 7200 sweeps.

within the "mammal" and "furniture" planes. Figure 2 thus provides an illustrative example of how category structure emerges over time on the representational units.

The results of the simulation are consistent with the findings that young infants can form perceptually based category representations for mammals and furniture at both global and basic levels (Behl-Chadha, in press; Quinn et al., 1993). The complete learning sequence is also consistent with a developmental progression from global- to basic-level category distinctions, a pattern which corresponds with the developmental course of category acquisition in older infants, but with what were presumed to be conceptually based representations for animals and artifacts (Mandler et al., 1991; see also McClelland, McNaughton & O'Reilly, 1995).

One question that arises is whether the early appearance of the global-level representations occurred because the mammals provided activation on the various input nodes devoted to the processing of face and tail information, whereas the furniture stimuli did not. One way of asking this question is: Will the global-to-basic sequence be observed in a model operating on input that does not include the face and tail information? To provide an answer, we repeated the initial simulation, but in this case with just 4 input nodes (number of legs, leg length, vertical extent and horizontal extent).

By 7200 sweeps, the no face-no tail network differentiated the global-level categories; only the basic-level category of dressers had appeared at this point (and if one looks earlier into the training sequence, one finds that dressers were first responded to as furniture and only subsequently as dressers). Basic-level categorization of rabbits and tables (14,400 sweeps), elephants (21,600 sweeps), chairs (28,800 sweeps) and beds (43,200 sweeps) completed the learning sequence. Dogs and cats were not

not simply a consequence of specialized processing for mammals and that it may be generalizable beyond the mammal-furniture distinction. In addition, the inability of the model to categorically differentiate cats and dogs is consistent with the finding that young infants rely on head and face information to distinguish between them (Quinn & Eimas, in press-b).

A second issue raised by the finding of global-to-basic category development is whether the global level would have emerged before the basic level if the network had not been trained at the global level. To answer this question, we repeated the initial simulation (with 13 inputs), but in this case without the two global-level output nodes. There was thus no teaching signal at the global level. While this manipulation prevents us from determining whether the patterns were responded to as mammals and furniture at the output layer, we can still inspect the representation of the patterns at the hidden layer at different points during training.

What is observed in this simulation is that the global level of representation still emerges before the basic level. At 480 sweeps, the mean activation values for cats, dogs, elephants and rabbits on hidden node 1 were 0.191, 0.160, 0.084 and 0.212, whereas those for chairs, tables, beds and dressers were 0.816, 0.795, 0.833 and 0.831. This global-level separation was maintained throughout the remainder of training. In contrast, hidden nodes 2 and 3 at 480 sweeps did not allow for partitioning of inputs into basic-level categories. Consistent with these observations is the timing of emergence of the basic-level categories as assessed by their corresponding output activation values. Elephants were distinguished at 960 sweeps, followed by dogs, rabbits, chairs and dressers at 3600 sweeps, beds at 7200 sweeps and cats and tables at 10,800 sweeps. The results of this simulation are important because they suggest that the early appearance of global-level categories occurs even when the network is not being trained at the global level. The global level may thus be thought of as a "primary" representation that occurs in the course of mapping a set of structured (but uncategorized) inputs onto basic-level categories.

Simulation 2: Arbitrary Global-level Category Learning

In this section, we examine a possible reason for the global-to-basic developmental sequence. One idea is that global occurs before basic because of the nature of global-level categories. This idea can be tested by orthogonalizing (i.e., crossing) the stimulus dimensions relevant for the global level. That is, one can change the nature of the categories at the global level and determine if the global-to-basic trend still emerges. To this end, we examined the performance of a network taught to assign cats, elephants, chairs and beds to one arbitrary global-level category called A and to respond to dogs, rabbits, tables and dressers as members of a second global-level category called B.

Method

The only change from the first simulation described in the preceding section was that the output node previously coding for mammals was reassigned to code for A stimuli (cats, elephants, chairs and beds) and the output node that earlier coded for furniture now coded for B stimuli (dogs, rabbits, tables and dressers).

and chairs and beds (3600 sweeps) activated the A output node, and concluded with tables recognized as members of the B category (7200 sweeps). Thus, both arbitrary global-level and basic-level categories were learned, but in no particular order.

A more complex picture regarding performance of this simulation emerges when one examines the mean activation values on the 3 hidden nodes for the various categories. Figure 3 presents a 3-dimensional plot of these values at 8, 480 and 7200 sweeps. The 8 sweeps plot (Panel A) reveals no clear partitioning of the categories. However, at 480 sweeps (Panel B), the mammals and furniture have been segregated, indicating that perceptual global-level category structure emerged even when the network was being taught on a different "arbitrary" (i.e., non-perceptual) global-level distinction. At 7200 sweeps (Panel C), the arbitrary global differentiation into categories A and B has appeared. There is also a segregation of mammals and furniture. This figure reveals that the hidden nodes coded for two distinct global levels of representation during the course of training: an initial "perceptually based" global level of mammals and furniture and a subsequent "conceptually based" global level of A and B. Such a finding is consistent with the idea that distinct perceptual and conceptual representations develop for object categories during early development (Mandler & McDonough, 1993).

The major result of this simulation is that manipulating the structure of the global level categories interfered with

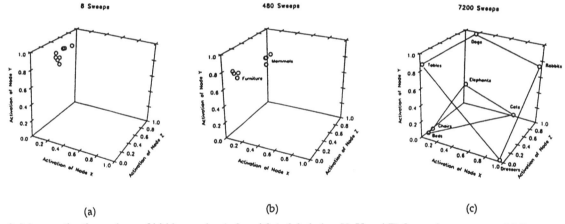

Figure 3. Mean activation values of hidden nodes 1, 2 and 3 (relabeled as X, Y and Z) for each category at (a) 8 sweeps, (b) 480 sweeps and (c) 7200 sweeps. In (c) the connected points indicate members of one arbitrary global-level category. Separation between perceptual global-level categories can also be seen.

Results and Discussion

In this simulation, learning occurred at both basic and arbitrary global levels, without one level clearly preceding the other. At the basic level, the order of classification of the training exemplars was: elephants (960 sweeps), rabbits (1920 sweeps), cats and dressers (2760 sweeps), and dogs, tables and beds (3600 sweeps). Chairs, even at 7200 sweeps, failed to elicit a consistent response from the appropriate output node. Learning at the arbitrary global level also began at 960 sweeps with elephants activating the A output node and dogs, rabbits and dressers activating B. Arbitrary global-level classification continued as cats (1920 sweeps)

the global-to-basic order of category development at least for the arbitrary global-level categories. No clear timing difference was observed in the emergence of representations at the basic and arbitrary global levels. However, the perceptual global level (i.e., mammals distinct from furniture) was the first level of category representation to appear, even though the network was not explicitly taught to make this distinction. The overall pattern of performance thus indicates that the nature of global categories (i.e., perceptual vs. arbitrary) is a critical factor in their early appearance during training.

General Discussion

Connectionist accounts of cognitive development are growing in influence (Elman, Bates, Karmiloff-Smith, Johnson, Parisi & Plunkett, in press; McClelland, 1989) and this paper represents an attempt to apply a connectionist analysis to the issue of how category representations arise at basic and global levels during early development. A set of simple network simulations were found to learn categories at basic and global levels and in a global-to-basic sequence.

A striking result of the simulation with arbitrary global-level category training was that both perceptual and arbitrary global-level categories were formed, despite there being no explicit training for the former. This is reminiscent of the views of Mandler & McDonough (1993) who have argued for distinct perceptual and conceptual levels of category representation in human infants. A key difference between our model and the one proposed by Mandler & McDonough is that in our model a single network forms both types of representations, whereas in their view perceptual and conceptual representations are the products of two complementary processes.

Predictions

Models are often judged by the degree to which they can generate interesting experimental predictions. We therefore offer the following:

1. On the assumptions that our results generalize to other categories and that the early-appearing representations that have emerged for global-level categories are stronger than those coding for the later-appearing basic-level categories (cf. Munakata, McClelland, Johnson, & Siegler, submitted), it should be possible to manipulate task parameters that will make categorization more difficult and observe that basic-level representations are affected to a greater degree than those at the global level. For example, reducing the amount of time a stimulus is exposed to an infant decreases its memorability (Fagan, 1974), so reducing the amount of familiarization time for each of a group of exemplars should make categorization more difficult. The reported simulations suggest that basic-level distinctions would be the first to be affected by a moderate decrease in study time per exemplar.

2. Both global- and basic-level category representations have been observed with 3- to 4-month-old infants (e.g., Quinn & Eimas, in press-a). The global-to-basic sequence observed in the simulations would therefore predict that global-level representations should emerge before basic-level ones sometime prior to 3 months of age.

3. It should be possible to train models with one or more deleted input nodes and examine which, if any, category representations fail to emerge. Such manipulations should be helpful in determining which aspects of the input are critical for certain category distinctions. For example, the no face-no tail model predicts that face and tail information is not necessary for making the category distinction between mammals and furniture, a prediction that can be tested on infants with simple alterations to the mammal stimuli. In addition, it should be possible to remove one or more inputs from the face and head region of cats and dogs to predict which are needed to make this basic-level distinction,

predictions than can be tested by presenting altered cat and dog stimuli to infants (cf. Quinn & Eimas, in press-b).

4. The arbitrary global-level category learning simulation indicates that it may be possible to train subjects, either infants or toddlers, to assign stimuli to arbitrary global-level categories. The simulation also predicts that in the context of such training an initial perceptual global level of category representation will precede formation of both basic- and arbitrary global-level categories.

5. It is of interest to examine the representations that emerge in models with larger numbers of hidden nodes. For example, we have observed that when the number of hidden nodes is 8, 9, 10 or 11, the global-to-basic sequence still emerges. In addition, during the course of training, there is a gradual decrease in the proportion of the overall representation that codes for the global level and a gradual increase in the proportion of the overall representation that codes for the basic level. These findings predict that if infants could be repeatedly familiarized with instances of a given category in successive sessions, then there would be a steady transition from global- to basic-level representation. The results also predict that frequently experienced environmental stimuli may tend to elicit basic-level responding (albeit subsequent to global-level responding).

Concluding Comments

In our view, a strength of the approach we have presented is the correspondence between the experimental work on infant categorization and the network simulations. That is, the input to the models were the dimensions of stimuli presented to infants in a series of studies on the development of perceptual categorization in early infancy (Quinn & Eimas, in press-a). Data from the experimental studies were used in decisions about what inputs to present to the models. There is also evidence that infants use correlated attribute information to perform successfully in various kinds of categorization tasks (e.g., Younger, 1990) -- a manner of information processing that is broadly consistent with the way in which neural networks learn information.

A limitation of the input scheme used in these simulations is that the visual representations infants (or adults) use to recognize objects are still unknown. Moreover, we did not use the object parsing schemes advocated in some contemporary models of object recognition (e.g., Biederman, 1987). It therefore becomes important to examine whether implementations of our models with a range of input descriptions would produce comparable results. However, we believe that our basic observations on perceptual category formation will be robust for the reason that all models of object recognition would encode greater similarity between different mammals than between a mammal and an item of furniture, for example. It is this similarity structure in the input that we believe to be important for the results obtained, rather than the details of what elements of the visual array are encoded.

A second possible limitation is that the networks reported in this paper were trained by a backpropagation learning algorithm -- a teaching signal that drives the gradual reduction of error observed in the networks. One can claim that this manner of learning is questionable in the present context for at least two reasons. First, there are some who maintain that backpropagation is a biologically unrealistic form of learning (e.g., Crick, 1989). Second, there is no external teacher supervising infants in the perceptual kinds of categorization tasks we have attempted to simulate.

We make three observations regarding these points. First, at least one level of category representation, the perceptual global level, was obtained without an explicit teaching signal. Second, backpropagation has not been ruled out as a biologically plausible form of learning. For example, Plunkett (1996) has speculated that backprojecting neurons might be one mechanism by which backpropagation in the nervous system could be accomplished. Third, backpropagation is thought to be one of an equivalence class of learning algorithms with similar computational properties. For example, networks trained with backpropagation in some instances develop the same representations as those produced by more biologically plausible, Hebbian learning algorithms (e.g., Plaut & Shallice, 1993).

In conclusion, we believe that many of the effects we have observed in these simulations would be extendable to other connectionist architectures, input formats, and learning rules (including unsupervised networks). We also believe that the findings of the simulations along with the experimental predictions generated from them represent an important first step toward a research program which combines experimental studies of infant categorization with techniques of connectionist modelling. Such a program may hold promise for developing a formalized account of category formation by young infants.

Acknowledgements

This research was supported by Grant HD 28606 from the National Institute of Child Health and Human Development (PCQ), the UK Medical Research Council (MHJ), the Human Frontier Science Program (MHJ and PCQ) and the British Academy (MHJ and PCQ). We thank Clay Mash for his assistance in preparing Figures 2 and 3. We also thank Peter Eimas, Annette Karmiloff-Smith, Jean Mandler, Denis Mareschal, Frédéric Vallée-Tourangeau, and Steven Young for helpful discussion.

References

Behl-Chadha, G. (in press). Basic-level and superordinate-like categorical representations in early infancy. *Cognition.*

Biederman, I. (1987). Recognition by components: A theory of human image understanding. *Psychological Review*, **94**, 115-147.

Crick, F. H. C. (1989). The real excitement about neural networks. *Nature*, **337**, 129-132.

Elman, J. L., Bates, E. A., Karmiloff-Smith, A., Johnson, M. H., Parisi, D., & Plunkett, K. (in press). *Rethinking innateness: Connectionism in a developmental framework.* Cambridge, MA: MIT Press.

Fagan, J. F. (1974). Infant recognition memory: The effects of length of familiarization and type of discrimination task. *Child Development*, **45**, 351-356.

Johnson, M. H., & Morton, J. (1991). *Biology and cognitive development.* Cambridge, MA: Blackwell.

Mandler, J. M., Bauer, P., & McDonough, L. (1991). Separating the sheep from the goats: Differentiating global categories. *Cognitive Psychology*, **23**, 263-298.

Mandler, J. M., & McDonough, L. (1993). Concept formation in infancy. *Cognitive Development*, **8**, 291-318.

McClelland, J. L. (1989). Parallel distributed processing: Implications for cognition and development. In R. G. M. Morris (Ed.), *Parallel Distributed Processing: Implications for Psychology and Neurobiology* (pp. 8-45). Oxford: Clarendon Press.

McClelland, J. L., McNaughton, B. L., & O'Reilly, R. C. (1995). Why there are complementary learning systems in the hippocampus and neocortex: Insights from the successes and failures of connectionist models of learning and memory. *Psychological Review*, **102**, 419-457.

Mervis, C. B. (1987). Child-basic object categories and early lexical development. In U. Neisser (Ed.), *Concepts and conceptual development: Ecological and intellectual factors in categorization* (pp. 201-233). Cambridge, UK: Cambridge University Press.

Munakata, Y., McClelland, J. L., Johnson, M. H., & Siegler, R. S. (submitted). Rethinking infant knowledge: Toward an adaptive process account of successes and failures in object permanence tasks.

Plaut, D. C., & Shallice, T. (1993). Deep dyslexia: A case study of connectionist neuropsychology. *Cognitive Neuropsychology*, **10**, 377-500.

Plunkett, K. (1996). Development in a connectionist framework: Rethinking the nature-nurture debate. *The Newsletter of the Center for Research in Language (UCSD)*, **10**, 3-14.

Plunkett, K., & Elman, J. L. (in press). *Simulating nature and nurture: A handbook of connectionist exercises.* Cambridge, MA: MIT Press.

Quinn, P. C., & Eimas, P. D. (in press-a). Perceptual organization and categorization in young infants. In C. Rovee-Collier & L. P. Lipsitt (Eds.), *Advances in infancy research, Vol. 10.* Norwood, NJ: Ablex.

Quinn, P. C., & Eimas, P. D. (in press-b). Perceptual cues that permit categorical differentiation of animal species by infants. *Journal of Experimental Child Psychology.*

Quinn, P. C., Eimas, P. D., & Rosenkrantz, S. L. (1993). Evidence for representations of perceptually similar natural categories by 3-month-old and 4-month-old infants. *Perception*, **22**, 463-475.

Strauss, M. S. (1979). Abstraction of prototypical information by adults and 10-month-old infants. *Journal of Experimental Psychology: Human Learning and Memory*, **5**, 618-632.

Younger, B. A. (1990). Infants' detection of correlations among feature categories. *Child Development*, **61**, 614-620.

Improving the Use of Analogies by Learning to Encode Their Causal Structure

Stephen J. Read
Department of Psychology
University of Southern California
Los Angeles, CA 90089-1061.
Read@rcf.usc.edu.

Robyn W. Johnson
2931 Plaza Del Amo, #32
Torrance, CA 90503

Abstract

We investigated whether training in how to encode the causal structure of problems would improve individual's use of analogies to previously encountered cases. Subjects were trained either in how to encode the causal structure of business cases or given a lecture of equal length on a variety of decision making procedures. They were then asked to study several business cases and their successful solution. One week later, when asked to solve new problems, subjects who were trained in causal analysis, compared to the control group, were more likely to use an appropriate analogy from the previously studied cases (positive transfer) and were less likely to use an inappropriate analogy (negative transfer). Further analyses showed that training in causal analysis increased subjects' ability to encode the causal structure of the problem and increased the likelihood of being reminded of the analogy. Thus, the ability to encode causal structure and use analogies appropriately is not responsive only to increasing domain knowledge, but can also be improved by general training in the identification and encoding of the central components of the causal structure of problems.

Introduction

We often solve new problems by using solutions to past problems. Central to such analogical reasoning is the extraction of the relational structure of the past problem and its application to the new problem (Gentner, 1983; Gick & Holyoak, 1983; Holyoak, 1985; Read, 1984).

Unfortunately, people often fail to use analogies appropriately. They do so in at least two ways. First, they may attempt to inappropriately apply a past situation to the present problem. For example, Jervis (1976) and May (1973) have persuasively argued that foreign policy decision makers often rely on inappropriate historical analogies in developing policies, and as a result can make highly questionable decisions. In such cases, the decision maker seems to have been seduced by salient features of the previous case and failed to carefully examine its causal structure.

Second, people may fail to notice or be reminded of relevant past situations. If decision makers have failed to properly encode the causal structure of past problems, they might often fail to notice that the past situation is relevant to the current situation.

This suggests that encoding of the causal structure of situations plays a central role in successful analogical reasoning. Consistent with this, several researchers (e.g., Carbonell, 1983; Gentner, 1983; Holyoak, 1985) have argued that encoding the causal structure is key to both appropriate retrieval and application of analogies. By being able to identify and understand the specific relational or causal features of an analogy, the problem solver can better understand why a particular outcome did or did not occur. As a result, they may be more likely to be reminded of an applicable analogy and, if they have remembered it, be better able to apply it.

This study examines whether people could be trained to use analogical reasoning more effectively by providing them with an explicit technique to analyze and encode the causal structure of problems. The training procedure instructed subjects in the use of Carbonell's (1983) Means-Ends Analysis (MEA) framework for analogical reasoning, based on Newell and Simon's (1973) approach to problem-solving. Although proposed as a framework for retrieval, the present study examined its impact on encoding and application of analogies, as well. This framework involves the identification of four aspects of the causal structure of the past and present problems and the subsequent attempt to match those aspects of the structure of the old problem to the new problem:

1. the existing or current states of the new and previously solved problems.

2. the goal states of the new and solved problems.

3. actions that can be taken to move the system from the existing to the goal state.

4. constraints for the new and solved problems, such as limitations on time and resources, that can affect the ability to carry out the actions.

This should provide people with a mechanism to encode the causal structure of past events and as a result influence the three general phases of analogical reasoning: (a) encoding of the base, (b) reminding of a past situation by the target, and (c) application of the analogy (including both mapping and transfer).

This study is also relevant to the interest in the relative role of surface and structural features in analogical reasoning. Many of the studies that have examined the use of analogies (e.g., Bassok & Holyoak, 1989; Gick & Holyoak, 1980, 1983; Gick, & McGarry, 1992; Holyoak & Koh, 1987; Novick, 1988; Reed, 1987; Ross, 1987, 1989) have focused on the role of surface and structural features of the base analog in its retrieval and application to a new, analogous target. Surface features should not effect the application of a base, as they are not part of its relational or causal structure. Structural features are the relational components that define the causal structure of the base and thus should affect whether it can be correctly mapped to the target.

As expected, retrieval is largely influenced by surface similarity, with structural similarity playing a minor role (for a review see Wharton et al., 1994; for an exception see Read and Cesa (1991)). In contrast, the applicability of analogies is almost entirely affected by structural similarity (Gentner & Landers, 1985; Reed, 1987; and Holyoak & Koh, 1987).

However, under some conditions surface similarities do influence application, particularly when structural mappings are unclear (Ross, 1987; and Johnson, 1988). Apparently, people use corresponding surface features to help identify corresponding structural relations. Unfortunately, when surface features are not correlated with structural relations this may lead to negative transfer of a base to a target that shares only surface similarities (Novick, 1988; Bassok & Holyoak, 1989).

Novick (1988) proposed a framework for conceptualizing the conflicting findings of the role that surface and structural features play in access and use of analogies. When she compared novices and experts, she found that when source and target problems shared structural features, experts exhibited more positive transfer than novices. In contrast, when source and target problems shared surface features, but not structural features, novices were much more likely than experts to show negative transfer, inappropriately applying a non-relevant analogy.

This suggests that surface similarities can influence mapping of an analogy when the causal structure has not been encoded, whereas structural similarities will influence mapping when the structure has been encoded. Both Novick (1988) and Ross (1987) implied that providing experience in analogical mapping should increase positive transfer and decrease negative transfer.

Consistent with this is Brown's (1989) work on the impact of age-related differences in children's knowledge of causal structure. Spontaneous transfer was more likely if children understood the causal structure of problems. However, Brown also argued that when children have not yet differentiated the causal structure, surface features are important in analogical transfer.

This implies that training in a technique for encoding and mapping the causal structure of a problem, such as Carbonell's MEA framework, should improve analogical reasoning. This should be exhibited as an increase in positive transfer, and a decrease in negative transfer.

To examine this possibility, half of the participants in the present study received training in applying MEA to the analysis of the causal structure of analogs, and half did not. Participants were exposed to scenarios that dealt with a variety of marketing and strategic business issues.

The nature of the similarity of base and target was varied so that the effectiveness of training could be assessed on analogies which were and were not appropriate matches for the target. One base was totally non-analogous to the target, sharing neither surface nor structural features. A

second base was primarily similar on surface features to a target, but shared little structural similarity. Subjects who failed to encode its causal structure should inappropriately apply it to the target problem (negative transfer). The third base was similar to a target in underlying causal structure, but not in surface features. Subjects who had encoded its causal structure should be more likely to apply it to the target (positive transfer).

Thus, trained individuals were predicted to be less likely than the untrained to transfer a solution from a base that was similar only on surface features (less negative transfer). In contrast, trained individuals would be more likely than the untrained to transfer a solution from a base that shared all four structural components but no surface features (more positive transfer).

Method

Subjects

One hundred and twenty men and women participated. Fifty-seven were students participating to receive extra credit in introductory psychology at the University of Southern California. The remaining 63 were employees of a health care company in Southern California. Subjects from the two groups were equally distributed across the two training conditions. Trained and untrained subjects were run in separate sessions, with seven to ten subjects in a session.

Design and Procedure

The study was a 2 X 3 mixed design. The between subjects factor was the type of training received, either training in Means-Ends Analysis (MEA) or training in general problem solving. The within subjects factor was the nature of the similarity of a set of three base stories to three targets, either non analogous, surface similarity only, or structural similarity only.

Subjects were randomly assigned in equal numbers to the trained or the untrained group. Both groups received the same stimulus materials. The trained group was trained on Carbonell's MEA framework for problem solving by analogy. The untrained group received an informative presentation on problem-solving and decision making approaches that lasted the same amount of time as the experimental training, approximately one hour. However, no specific framework or tools for problem-solving were provided. The untrained session was designed to show that the impact of MEA training goes beyond simply focusing people on thinking about the problems.

Five sets of business problems were developed, based on "real life" marketing and business scenarios. The base stories presented a problem and a solution, whereas the targets only presented a problem. Two sets of scenarios were used as training examples. The other three sets of base-target pairs were used to manipulate the three within subjects similarity conditions. The three conditions were: (1) **Non-Analogous**. Subjects received a base-target pair in which the two stories were completely unrelated to one another, with neither surface nor structural similarity. (2) **Negative Transfer**. The base story had mainly surface similarities (such as a similar industry) to the target. Structural components such as the operators and constraints were unmatchable, whereas the existing states and goal states, were, for the most part, matchable. (3) **Positive Transfer**. The structure of the base story was directly mappable to the target, such that the existing states and goal states, operators, and constraints of the base were congruent with those of the target. However, surface characteristics (e.g., type of industry) differed between base and target. Thus, there were three possible bases for each target.

Trained Session. The trained subjects were first given two practice base problems, without their solutions, to read and solve. They were then asked to discuss their solutions. Then they received and read the predetermined solutions to the practice problems to see how they compared with their solutions.

Next, subjects received a detailed description of the MEA procedure, including definitions of the four components, instructions on how to recognize them, and how to match them from the base to the target. They then got the targets that were matched to the base problems they had read, and were given instructions, rehearsal, and feedback, as the group analyzed the base-target example using the MEA framework.

The first practice target, the structurally similar base-target pair, was used to exemplify positive transfer, by showing how structural features were conducive to mapping this base solution to the target problem. Subjects were walked through comparisons of each of the four structural components. The same procedure was used with the second practice problem, the surface similar base-target pair. This was used to illustrate how solely mapping surface similarities of the base to the target, without attending to the underlying structural components, may potentially lead to mapping an inappropriate analogy.

Untrained Session. The untrained group was also given the two practice problems to read, solve and discuss. They then received information on how the decision making and problem-solving environment is changing in business. This included a historical perspective beginning with a traditional problem-solving approach and ending with a summary of five different approaches (creative and analytical) and implications about the pros and cons of each. While analogical reasoning was alluded to, a description was not given.

Subjects then received the matched target to the base problems they had read, and were given instructions, rehearsal, and participation feedback as the group analyzed the base-target examples from the perspective of the problem-solving approaches discussed in the previous presentation. This session lasted the same amount of time as that for the trained group.

Encoding Exercise. Upon completion of the training, all subjects received a packet of three base problems and their solutions. One base was non-analogous to a later target, the second similar in surface attributes only (negative transfer condition), and the third had structural similarities (positive transfer condition). All subjects received the same 3 target

stories.

Subjects were instructed to read carefully and remember the problems and their solutions, as they would be asked some questions about them at a later time. To ensure that scenarios were processed, they were also asked to write a brief summary of each problem and solution.

Subjects returned one week later and received a booklet of 3 target problems without solutions. Each was matched to one of the three base stories they received previously. Subjects were instructed to provide a clear and concise solution to the target problems. They were also asked to write down any other solution they could think of.

After suggesting solutions for all targets, subjects were instructed to refer back to the target stories and indicate if each story reminded them of anything they had read the week before. If so, they were to write down briefly which story and its solution they were reminded of.

Results

Scoring: Transfer Task

Subject's proposed solutions were scored from 0 to 2. A 0 indicated no similarity to the base solution (a solution that was completely made up or that included a combination of a negative and positive transfer solution). A 1 indicated a positive transfer solution. A 2 indicated negative transfer, a solution that was inappropriately transferred to the target problem from a base.

All data were coded by the second author. Inter-rater reliability was calculated by having a second person, blind to conditions and hypotheses, code the data from 10% of the subjects. Agreement was .85, using Cohen's Kappa (described in Bakeman & Gottman, 1986).

Impact of Training on Transfer

As expected, in the positive transfer condition, trained subjects were much more likely than untrained subjects to provide an appropriate solution (positive transfer) (see Table 1). Conversely, untrained subjects were more likely than trained to provide a made up solution. In the negative transfer condition, untrained subjects were quite likely to be led astray by the inappropriate analogy and exhibit negative transfer, whereas trained subjects almost never did. In the non-analogous condition, over 90% of the solutions for both trained and untrained subjects were made up.

Thus, these findings demonstrate that training strongly improved people's ability to provide the appropriate analogous solution and ignore an inappropriate one. A significant interaction would therefore be expected between Training (Trained versus Untrained), Analogy condition (Non-analogous, Negative Transfer, or Positive Transfer), and the type of Solution (Non-analogous/Made up, Negative Transfer or Positive Transfer). This was tested using a backwards elimination approach to log-linear modeling. One starts with the full model, including all main effects and interactions, and first removes the highest order interaction to see if it is necessary to account for the pattern of frequencies. If it is not, then one eliminates it and proceeds to systematically remove the lower order interactions.

	Positive Transfer Solution	Negative Transfer Solution	Made-up Solution
Non-analogous Condition			
Trained Group (N=60)	3%	3%	94%
Untrained Group (N=60)	3%	0%	97%
Negative Transfer Condition			
Trained Group	90%	3%	7%
Untrained Group	3%	70%	27%
Positive Transfer Condition			
Trained Group	90%	0%	10%
Untrained Group	58%	2%	40%

Table 1: Frequency of Subjects Giving Each of Three Types of Solution in the Non-analogous, Negative and Positive Transfer Conditions

With the backward elimination approach, the difference in X^2 between the model with all terms, and the model with one term removed, indicates whether that term significantly contributes to the fit of the model. Because the highest order interaction, the three way interaction among Training, Analogy condition, and Solution, was the key prediction of the study, the backward elimination approach was an efficient way to test this prediction. Removing this three way interaction from the full model, resulted in a significant reduction in goodness of fit, $X^2(4)$ diff = 23.6, p < .01. Thus, this interaction was needed and the central prediction of the study was supported, making it unnecessary to test lower order terms.

To better understand this interaction, we did two follow-up comparisons, one comparing the performance of the trained with the untrained groups in the positive transfer condition and the other comparing the performance of the two groups in the negative transfer condition. As predicted, in the positive transfer condition, the trained group was far more likely to give the positive transfer solution than was the untrained group, $X^2(2) = 15.856$, p < .01. And in the negative transfer condition, the trained group was far <u>less</u> likely to give the negative transfer solution than was the untrained group, $X^2(2) = 91.84$, p < .01. Unexpectedly, trained subjects frequently gave the positive transfer solution in the negative transfer condition. In hindsight, the negative transfer problems always presented two different solutions that had been considered. The solution that was actually used was an inappropriate solution for the target. However, the untried alternative was appropriate for the target. In essence, when trained subjects determined that the previous solution was inappropriate for the target, the base provided them with an alternative solution that was appropriate for the new target.

Impact of Training on encoding and reminding

Subjects' summaries of the bases provided further evidence that training increased encoding of the causal structure. In the positive transfer condition all 60 trained subjects encoded the problem, as indicated by giving a clear summary of the key aspects of the problem, whereas only 36 of the 60 untrained subjects did so. In the negative transfer condition, almost all of the trained subjects (58 out of 60) encoded the problem, whereas only 40 out of 60 untrained subjects did.

Further, training increased reminding of previous bases. In the positive transfer condition, 39 out of 60 trained subjects were reminded of the similar base, whereas only 20 out of the 60 untrained were reminded. Results were comparable in the negative transfer condition, with 36 out of 60 trained subjects being reminded, but only 21 out of the 60 untrained.

Discussion and Conclusions

Although the ability to encode the causal structure of a problem has been argued to be key to the retrieval and appropriate application of analogies (Carbonell, 1983; Holyoak, 1985; and Brown, 1989), the present study is the first direct test of whether the ability to do so can be improved by training. This study demonstrates that training in causal analysis can dramatically improve people's ability to encode the causal structure of an analogy and, as a result, increase the likelihood that subjects' use of analogies will be sensitive to the underlying relational structure of the base and target. Thus, subjects who were trained in causal analysis were <u>more</u> likely to apply a potential base to a new situation when the causal structure matched (i.e., exhibit positive transfer), but were <u>less</u> likely to apply a potential base to a new situation when it failed to match on important causal features (i.e., exhibit less negative transfer.) Further, training in causal encoding also increased the likelihood of being reminded of similar situations. Finally, in the absence of such training, surface similarities strongly influenced transfer of inappropriate analogies.

Thus, increases in the ability to encode causal structure and use analogies appropriately are not responsive only to increasing domain knowledge, as the work of Novick (1988) and Brown (1989) might seem to suggest. Analogical reasoning can also be improved by general training in the identification and encoding of the central components of the causal structure of problems.

References

Bakeman, R. & Gottman, J. M. (1986). <u>Observing</u>

interaction-An introduction to sequential analysis. (pp. 70-99). New York: Cambridge University Press.

Bassok, M. & Holyoak, K. J. (1989). Interdomain transfer between isomorphic topics in algebra and physics. Journal of Experimental Psychology: Learning, Memory, and Cognition, 15, 153-166.

Brown, A. L. (1989). Analogical learning and transfer: What develops? In S. Vosniadou & A. Ortony (Eds.), Similarity and analogical reasoning. Cambridge; New York: Cambridge University Press.

Carbonell, J. G. (1983). Learning by analogy: Formulating and generalizing plans from past experience. In R. Michalski, J.G. Carbonell, & T.M. Mitchell (Eds.), Machine learning: An artificial intelligence approach. Palo Alto, CA: Tioga Press.

Gentner, D. (1983). Structure-mapping: A theoretical framework for analogy. Cognitive Science, 7, 155-170.

Gentner, D., & Landers, R. (1985). Analogical Reminding: A good match is hard to find. In Proceedings of the International Conference on Systems, Man and Cybernetics, Tucson, AZ.

Gick, M. L. & Holyoak, K. J. (1980). Analogical problem solving. Cognitive Psychology, 12, 306-355.

Gick, M. L. & Holyoak, K. J. (1983). Schema induction and analogical transfer. Cognitive Psychology, 15, 1-38.

Gick, J. L., & McGarry, S. J. (1992). Learning from mistakes: Inducing analogous solution failures to a source problem produces later successes in analogical transfer. Journal of Experimental Psychology: Learning, Memory, and Cognition, 18, 623-639.

Holyoak, K. J. (1985). The pragmatics of analogical transfer. In G. H. Bower (Ed.), The psychology of learning and motivation (Vol. 19, pp. 59-87). New York: Academic Press, Inc.

Holyoak, K. J. & Koh, K. (1987). Surface and structural similarity in analogical transfer. Memory & Cognition, 15(4), 332-340.

Jervis, R. (1976). How decision-makers learn from history. In R. Jervis (Ed.), Perception and misperception in international politics (pp. 217-287). Princeton, N.J.: Princeton University Press.

Johnson, R. W. (1988). Analogical Reasoning: The effect of surface and structural features in social problem situations. Master's Thesis, University of Southern California.

Novick, L. R. (1988). Analogical transfer, problem similarity, and expertise. Journal of Experimental Psychology: Learning, Memory, and Cognition, 14(3), 510-520.

Read, S. J. (1984). Analogical reasoning in social judgment: The importance of causal theories. Journal of Personality and Social Psychology, 46, 14-25.

Read, S. J., & Cesa, I. L. (1991). This reminds me of the time when...: Expectation failures in reminding and explanation. Journal of Experimental Social Psychology, 27, 1-25.

Reed, S. K. (1987). A structure-mapping model for word problems. Journal of Experimental Psychology: Learning, Memory, and Cognition, 13, 124-139.

Ross, B. H. (1987). This is like that: The use of earlier problems and the separation of similarity effects. Journal of Experimental Psychology: Learning, Memory, and Cognition, 13(4), 629-639.

Wharton, C. M., Holyoak, K. J., Downing, P. E., Lange, T. E., Wickens, T. D., & Melz, E. R. (1994). Below the surface: Analogical similarity and retrieval competition in reminding. Cognitive Psychology, 26, 64-101.

Confidence Judgements, Performance, and Practice, in Artificial Grammar Learning

Martin Redington, Matt Friend and **Nick Chater**
Department of Experimental Psychology
University of Oxford
South Parks Road
Oxford, U.K.
OX1 3UD
{fmr@sable,matt.friend@magd,nick@psy}.ox.ac.uk

Abstract

Artificial grammar learning is noted for the claim that subjects are unaware of their knowledge. Chan (1992) and Dienes *et al.* (in press) have demonstrated that subjects are unaware in the sense that they lack meta-knowledge. Dissociations between subjects' performance and their confidence in their decisions suggest that the learning mechanism may be in some sense encapsulated from the "confidence system". Here we tested the alternative hypothesis that the confidence system is initially poorly calibrated, or does not know which aspects of the learning mechanism to attend to, by training and testing subjects over four weekly sessions. On all four weeks we found a strong, near-perfect association between confidence and performance for trained subjects, but a dissociation for untrained control subjects. We discuss possible explanations for these results, and previously observed dissociations.

Artificial grammar learning is notable for the controversial claim that subjects acquire knowledge which allows them to distinguish strings which follow the same rules as a set of previously memorised strings, from those which do not, but that they are not consciously aware of this knowledge (Reber, 1967, 1989). However, measuring subjects' conscious knowledge is plagued with the problems of finding suitably sensitive, explicit tests, and of ensuring that the knowledge these explicit tests measure is the same as the knowledge subjects use to perform the classification (see Shanks and St. John, 1995, and commentaries).

Chan (1992) and Dienes, Altmann, Kwan and Goode (in press) set issues of consciousness aside and focus instead on behaviour: Subjects' ability to make confidence judgements about their performance. This tests meta-knowledge, or "what subjects know about what they know". Chan (1992) showed that subjects' confidence in their judgements was unrelated to the likelihood that those judgements were correct. Similarly, Dienes *et al.* (in press) showed that even when subjects thought that they were guessing, their performance was above chance (and untrained control) levels.

Chan (1992) and Dienes *et al.* (in press) propose that the dissociation between confidence and accuracy is evidence that subjects lack meta-knowledge. This suggests that the learning mechanism is to a certain extent encapsulated from the "confidence system", so that its inner workings (*e.g.* the strengths of its rules, or connection weights, or its error signals) are inaccessible.

In this paper, we present a study which aimed to test a possible alternative explanation for this dissociation; that meta-knowledge is in principle available, but simply that extraction of this knowledge requires learning or calibration, and is initially inaccurate.

Dienes and Perner's (in press) discussion of the extent and manner in which neural networks possess meta-knowledge should clarify this point. They suggest that if the "confidence system" is able to observe, and knows the significance of, the output activation of the learning mechanism (which in a network might indicate the extent to which the current test string is consistent with the training strings, *e.g.* Dienes, 1992), then confidence and performance should be correlated. However, if the confidence system can only observe whether the learning mechanisms' output is on or off (where the "better" the test string, according to the learning mechanism, the more likely the output is to be activated), then confidence and accuracy will be unrelated.

In these terms, our alternative hypothesis suggests that the confidence judgement mechanism might be initially ignorant or uncertain of the identity and/or significance of the learning mechanism's output, but that with practice, or the opportunity to observe the learning mechanism more closely, the confidence judgement mechanism will be able to accurately identify the learning mechanism's output.

Dienes and Perner also suggest that if the learning mechanism's output was only accessible to the confidence system on a transformed scale, so that the cut-off for responding "grammatical" was unknown, then accurate confidence judgments could be made, but only by comparing the current transformed values to previous values (*e.g.* if the value is low compared to previous ones, respond 'grammatical' with low confidence, or 'non-grammatical' with high confidence). However, initially, when the sample of previous values is small, confidence may be relatively inaccurate. Extensive experience may allow the construction of a sufficiently large sample that accurate confidence judgements can be made.

Previous dissociations between confidence judgements and performance were observed during a single test session. If the learning mechanism is genuinely opaque to the confidence system, then these dissociations should be maintained across multiple test sessions. Alternatively, if the learning mechanism is in principle transparent, then with practice, confidence may come to accurately reflect performance.

We tested these conflicting hypotheses by training and testing subjects over a four-week period. The paradigm used was the guessing game (Redington & Chater, 1994). Here, prior to making a grammaticality, and confidence, judgement about each string, subjects are first required to reconstruct the string, guessing each letter until it is correctly identified, and then proceeding to the next letter. This provides a detailed measure of subjects' knowledge of the possible continuations at each point. There were two conditions: one group of subjects memorised the training strings each week, prior to testing, while an untrained control group never saw the training strings.

Method

Design. This was a $2 \times 4 \times 2$ mixed design. The between-subjects factor was training, with subjects randomly assigned to the trained or untrained condition. The within-subjects factors were Week (1–4), and Non-Grammatical String Violation Type (non-grammatical strings contained either non-permissible pairs and non-permissible triples).

Materials. The stimuli were exactly those used by Gomez and Schvaneveldt (1994). There were 18 training strings, and 51 test strings, of which 17 were grammatical, 17 were non-grammatical because they contained illegal pairs of letters (non-permissible pairs; NPP), and 17 were non-grammatical consisting entirely of legal pairs of letters, but in illegal combinations (non-permissible triples; NPT[1]). All the strings were between 3 and 8 letters long. See Gomez and Schvaneveldt (1994) for details of the grammar and exact strings used. The experiment was run on Apple PowerPC's.

Subjects. The 20 subjects were undergraduate or postgraduate students at Oxford University. A small (£20) payment was made for their participation. One subject (assigned to the control condition) did not attend for the final week's session, due to illness.

Procedure. Subjects performed an identical procedure each week for four weeks. The weekly procedure was closely modelled on that used in Redington and Chater (1994). It was stressed before each session

---

[1] Gomez and Schvaneveldt (1994) refer to this kind of error as "non-permissible location". Here we use the more mnemonic term, following Gomez (1996).

that subjects should pay care and attention to the task. Trained subjects then saw the following instructions;

> This is a simple memory experiment. When you press the button labelled 'Start', you will see 18 strings, constructed from 5 different letters. The items will run from three to eight letters in length. Your task is to learn and remember as much as possible about all 18 items. You have 10 minutes. If you have any questions about the task, please ask the Experimenter now. Press "Start" when you are ready to begin.

The learning strings were displayed for 10 minutes, in three left-justified columns of six strings each. The order of the strings was randomised separately for each S. Trained subjects then saw the following instructions:

> The order of letters in the set you saw was determined by a rather complex set of rules. The rules allow only certain letters to follow other letters. Now you will be presented with a set of test strings. Some of these obey the same rules as the the training strings, and some violate these rules in some way. For each test string, you must guess the letters of the string, one at a time, and then indicate whether it obeys the rules or not. You guess letters by pressing the button corresponding to the letter which you think comes next. If your guess is correct, the letter will appear on the screen, and you can proceed to the next letter. If your guess is incorrect, the button will disappear, and you must take another guess. The button labelled 'End' is for guessing that the string is complete. The strings are all between 3 and 8 letters long.

> Once you have completed the item, two more buttons will appear, labelled 'Correct' and 'Incorrect'. If you think the item that you have just guessed follows the same rules as the original items, then press 'Correct'. If you think it violates those rules then press 'Incorrect'.

Untrained subjects performed only the test phase. Their instructions closely followed this above, except that they commenced:

> You will be presented with a set of test strings. Some of these obey a certain set of rules, which dictate which letters can follow other letters. For each test string...

These instructions were reiterated verbally before the subjects commenced the test phase. Subjects were also told that after each judgement, they would be asked to rate how confident they were that their decision was correct, on a scale from 50% (guessing) to 100% (absolutely certain).

The test display initially showed a (blank) string display, centred on the screen, and below this, a row of five guessing buttons, labelled from left to right with the appropriate letters (in random order) and 'End'. Subjects guessed by clicking on the appropriate button with the mouse. Following a wrong guess (*i.e.* not matching the next letter of the current item), the button disappeared. If their response was correct, then the letter was appended to the string display, and all the guessing buttons reappeared for the next letter to be guessed. The 'End' button acted in an identical manner to the other guessing buttons; an 'End' guess was correct if the item was otherwise complete (all its letters had been guessed), and incorrect otherwise. Following a correct 'End' guess, the guessing buttons disappeared, the string display was centred, and two buttons labelled 'Correct' and 'Incorrect' appeared to the right of the string display. After the subject responded by clicking one of these, a dialog box appeared, asking "How certain are you that your judgement is correct?". A drop-down menu allowed the subjects to indicate 50, 60, 70, 80, 90, or 100%. There was no default value; subjects had to indicate a confidence value before proceeding. Once this was done, the display was reset for the next test string.

The 17 grammatical and 34 non-grammatical test items were each presented twice, resulting in 102 trials.

Results

Grammaticality Judgements

Grammaticality judgement scores were assessed in terms of *violation sensitivity*: The proportion of non-grammatical items correctly classified minus the proportion of grammatical items incorrectly classified (correct rejections − misses, see Gomez & Schvaneveldt, 1994). Violation sensitivity was calculated separately for NPP and NPT type violations. Summary statistics for violation sensitivity are shown in Table 1.

	\multicolumn{4}{c}{Week}			
	One	**Two**	**Three**	**Four**
Trained:				
NPP	.30 (.14)	.77 (.12)	.84 (.13)	.82 (.11)
NPT	.16 (.16)	.24 (.28)	.26 (.23)	.33 (.25)
Control:				
NPP	.23 (.18)	.36 (.19)	.39 (.21)	.38 (.22)
NPT	.10 (.08)	.11 (.10)	.13 (.10)	.18 (.14)

Table 1: Mean Violation sensitivity by Group, Violation Type (NPP and NPT), and Week. Standard deviations are shown in parentheses.

A three-way ANOVA comparing violation sensitivity, with Group (trained or control) as a between-subjects variable, and both Week and Violation Type (NPP or NPT) as within-subjects variables indicated that *all* main effects and interactions were reliable. Trained subjects outperformed controls (F(1, 17) = 19.95, p = 0.0003, MS_e = 0.10); subjects were more sensitive to NPP than to NPT type violations (F(1, 17) = 63.94, p = 0.0001, MS_e = 0.06), but this difference was less marked

in trained subjects (F(1, 17) = 10.06, p > 0.006, MS_e = 0.06); subjects in both groups improved over weeks (F(3, 51) = 28.02, p = 0.0001, MS_e = 0.02); trained subjects improved at a faster rate than controls (F(3, 51) = 7.00, p = 0.0005, MS_e = 0.02); the increased sensitivity to NPP type violations changed over the weeks (F(3, 51) = 12.46, p = 0.0001, MS_e = 0.01); there was a reliable Violation Type × Group × Week interaction (F(3, 51) = 3.59, p > 0.02, MS_e = 0.01).

As in previous guessing game studies (Redington & Chater, 1994) untrained control subjects performed reliably above chance (the lower 95% confidence limit of violation sensitivity was above zero on all four weeks, for both kinds of violation).

For our present purpose, these results serve to confirm that the main experimental manipulations (training, practice, and violation type) have had the expected effect on subjects' grammaticality judgement (performance is improved by training and practice, with more subtle non-grammatical violations being harder to detect). Given this, we can be relatively confident that any effects on meta-knowledge are genuinely due to these manipulations.

The Guessing Game

Subjects' guessing game performance was assessed in terms of $\hat{H}$, the amount of information in their guesses. The less that a subject has learnt during the training phase, the more guesses (and thus feedback) they will take to reconstruct the test items. $\hat{H}$ is a measure of the amount of information in the feedback (via an ingenious argument of Shannon, 1951):

$$\hat{H} = - \sum_{i=1,2,\ldots,n} \hat{p}_i \log_2(\hat{p}_i) \qquad (1)$$

where $\hat{p}_i$, the estimated probability that the subject will require i guesses to identify an element of the sequence, is derived from observed relative frequencies of i guesses being required.

A three-way ANOVA comparing $\hat{H}$, with Group as a between-subjects variable, and both Week and Grammaticality (grammatical, NPP, or NPT) as within-subjects variable revealed effects which predictably paralleled those in the grammaticality judgement data: all subjects needed reliably less feedback to reconstruct grammatical strings (F(2, 34) = 230.37, p = 0.0001, MS_e = 0.01), but this advantage was greatest for the trained subjects (F(2, 34) = 7.46, p = 0.0021, MS_e = 0.01); subjects required less feedback in later weeks (F(3, 51) = 102.34, p = 0.0001, MS_e = 0.01), but the improvements were reliably greater for trained subjects (F(3, 51) = 10.26, p = 0.0001, MS_e = 0.01), and for grammatical strings (F(6, 102) = 9.92, p = 0.0001, MS_e = 0.004). There was no reliable Group × Week × Grammaticality interaction for the guessing data (F(6, 102) = 1.55, p = ns, MS_e = 0.004).

The main effect of Group (trained or control) was reliable on a 1-tailed test ($F(1, 17) = 3.09, p < 0.05, MS_e = 0.21$).

These findings closely mirror those for grammaticality judgements (as in previous studies with the guessing game), and serve as further confirmation that the experimental manipulations of training, practise, and violation type did have the predicted effects.

Meta-Knowledge

Subjects' meta-knowledge was assessed according to the guessing criterion (Cheeseman & Merikle, 1984, Dienes *et al.*, in press), and the extent to which confidence was correlated with accuracy (Chan, 1992; Dienes *et al.*, in press).

The Guessing Criterion. According to Cheeseman and Merikle (1984), if subjects score above chance, when they claim to be guessing, then they lack meta-knowledge. Violation sensitivity was calculated for those trials on which subjects rated their confidence at 50%. This constituted only 5% of all judgements with the untrained group making more than the trained group (7% vs. 3%), and both groups making fewer over the four weeks).

There was no indication that the trained subjects performed above chance when they claimed that they were guessing. Violation sensitivity did not differ reliably from zero on any week, for either NPP or NPT type violations (by 1-group *t*-tests, all *p*'s > 0.05), and 6 of the 8 values were numerically below zero.

There were some indications that control subjects performed above chance when they claimed they were guessing. Violation sensitivity was reliably above zero on Week 4, for NPP type violations ($M = .41, t(8) = 2.17, p < 0.05$), and for NPL type violation, on Weeks 1 and 4 the effect was marginally reliable ($M = .13, t(9) = 1.57, p = 0.075$, and $M = .28, t(8) = 1.77, p = 0.058$). However, in general there was no indication of a consistent, reliable effect.

The Zero-Correlation Criterion. Chan (1992) proposed that if subjects possessed meta-knowledge, then confidence and accuracy should be correlated.

Dienes *et al.* (in press) suggest that instead of testing for a correlation, the difference between subjects' confidence in correct and incorrect judgements can be used as a measure of subjects' meta-knowledge. If this value is reliably greater than zero, then subjects were more confident in correct decisions, and did possess meta-knowledge.

We rejected this approach for the current data, as it doesn't take account of response bias[2]. Instead, we looked at how subjects' violation sensitivity was related to confidence. Table 2 shows the Pearson's correlation coefficient between confidence and mean violation sensi-

tivity by Group, Violation Type, and Week.

	Week			
	One	Two	Three	Four
Trained:				
NPP	.93*	.95*	.96*	.99*
NPT	.75*	.84*	.97*	.56
Control:				
NPP	.21	.29	-.11	.11
NPT	-.87*	-.18	-.17	-.58

Table 2: The correlation coefficient between confidence level and mean violation sensitivity, for trained subjects. The criterion value for a 1-tailed test is 0.73 (see Bruning and Kintz, 1977, p. 174) and values in excess of this are marked *.

These results suggest strongly that as trained subjects' confidence increased, so did their sensitivity to both types of violations. In other words, we found no evidence for a dissociation between confidence and accuracy. There is no indication that the strength of this association increased over the four weeks. The failure to find a reliable correlation on Week 4 for NPT type violations can be reasonably considered as an anomaly, given the strong, highly reliable, positive relationships otherwise observed.

In the results for untrained controls (see Table 2) we see no evidence of an association between confidence and performance (and obviously no indication of an improvement over weeks). Indeed, the only reliable correlation is negative, for NPT type violations on Week 1; the more confident subjects were, the less sensitive they became.

Discussion

By both the guessing and zero-correlation criteria, our results indicate that trained subjects possessed considerable meta-knowledge, on all four weeks of testing. Thus under some conditions, subjects can make accurate confidence judgements about their performance in artificial grammar learning.

How can we reconcile this observation with previously observed dissociations between confidence and performance? One obvious explanation is that the guessing procedure provided a basis for subjects' confidence judgements, which was absent in the standard, "grammaticality judgement only" procedure. Thus subjects might be confident that a string whose letters were relatively easy to guess was grammatical, and confident that

---

[2]For instance, by Dienes *et al.*'s measure, subjects possessed *negative* meta-knowledge of NPT type violations, as they were less confident when responding non-grammatical to these items. However, at high levels of confidence, subjects were less likely to misclassify grammatical items as non-grammatical, so violation sensitivity to NPT violations nevertheless increased with confidence.

a string which was relatively difficult to reconstruct was non-grammatical. This is a plausible explanation, and some replication of this study without the guessing game paradigm is obviously required.

Dienes *et al.* (in press: Experiment 2) demonstrated a similar case, when subjects had to say which of three test items were grammatical, in a forced choice procedure. Dienes *et al.* point out that the learning mechanism might be strongly encapsulated, with a binary output, but that meta-knowledge could still be *inferred*, simply by being more confident in a choice when it was the only "grammatical" string, according to the learning mechanism.

In the present case, we do not find this a completely convincing explanation. Our choice of the guessing game paradigm was intended to maximise both the amount of attention that subjects paid to the test strings, and to encourage the "confidence system" to focus on relevant aspects of the learning mechanism's output. But the situation here is quite different from that of Dienes *et al.* Even in a standard "grammaticality judgement only" situation, one can imagine that subjects might play an "internal" guessing game, assessing strings on the basis of how unexpected each successive letter is. Indeed, this is how some computational models of artificial grammar learning, simple recurrent networks, function (see Berry & Dienes, 1993), and this prediction information is available to subjects, as guessing game performance demonstrates. The guessing game therefore does not appear to provide additional information, that subjects' might not possess similar amounts of meta-knowledge in its' absence.

A second possible explanation for the positive association is that trained subjects engaged in rule-searching behaviour, rather than implicit learning. Chan (1992) found an association between confidence and performance, in subjects given rule-searching instructions during training. However, whilst this possibility may apply to later weeks, where subjects were aware of the rule-governed nature of the strings, in Week one, when the subjects were naive, a strong association was still observed.

A third possibility is that there is some subtle motivational or procedural factor, which differs between those studies where confidence and performance are associated (Manza & Reber, cited in Dienes *et al.*, in press, and the present study), and those where a dissociation has been observed (Chan, 1992; Dienes *et al.*, in press). For instance, it may be that subjects in the Manza and Reber study were somehow encouraged to play an "internal guessing game" as suggested above, whilst those in Chan's and Dienes *et al.*'s studies made their confidence judgements on some much less reliable basis.

This factor might lead subjects to infer meta-knowledge that is not available from the learning mech-

anism directly (as Dienes and Perner suggest), or it may cause the confidence system to focus on the appropriate aspects of the learning mechanism (the alternative hypothesis that the present study was intended to test).

Some support for the effect of motivational factors on confidence judgements comes from our control groups results. These subjects did perform reliably above chance, but showed some tendency towards above chance classification when their confidence was 50%, and a clear dissociation between confidence and performance by the zero-correlation criterion. If the guessing game was responsible for the association observed in trained subjects, then we should observe a similar association in controls.

Of course, the range of guessing performance is lower for controls, and so confidence judgements which were cued by guessing performance might be less strongly associated with grammaticality judgement performance. However, this would not account for the reversal of the relationship between confidence and performance that we find for control subjects with NPT type strings; the more confident they were, the less sensitive to NPT type violations they became. The main motivational difference between the two groups was that having seen no training strings, the control subjects had no good external reason to believe that they could accurately classify the test strings.

To conclude, it appears that under some conditions confidence and performance may be highly associated, whilst in others, a clear dissociation may be observed. Gaining a clear understanding of what influences this relationship may allow us to draw strong inferences about the nature of the learning mechanism, and the extent to which its processing and representations are available to, or encapsulated from, conscious awareness. However, for the present, these influences remain far from clear.

Acknowledgements

This research was supported in part by the U.K. Economic and Social Research Council (ESRC). Grant number R000236214.

References

Berry, D. C. & Dienes, Z. (1993). *Implicit Learning: Theoretical and Empirical Issues*. Hove: Lawrence Erlbaum Associates.

Bruning, J. L. & Kintz, B. L. (1977). *Computational Handbook of Statistics*. Glenview, IL: Scott, Foresman and Company.

Chan, C. (1992). *Implicit cognitive processes: Theoretical issues and applications in computer systems design*. Doctoral Thesis. Oxford, UK: University of Oxford, Department of Experimental Psychology.

Cheeseman, J. & Merikle, P. M. (1984). Priming with and without awareness. *Perception and Psychophysics*, 36, 387–395.

Dienes, Z. (1992). Connectionist and memory-array models of artificial grammar learning. *Cognitive Science* , 16, 41–79.

Dienes, Z., Altmann, G. T. M., Kwan, L. & Goode, A. (in press). Unconscious knowledge of artificial grammars is strategically applied. *Journal of Experimental Psychology: Learning, Memory, and Cognition.*

Dienes, Z. and Perner, J. (in press). Implicit knowledge in people and connectionist networks. In G. Underwood (Ed.), *Implicit Cognition*. Oxford, UK: Oxford University Press.

Gomez, R. L. (1996). *Transfer and Complexity in Artificial Grammar Learning*. Manuscript.

Gomez, R. L. & Schvaneveldt, R. W. (1994). What is learned from artificial grammars? Transfer tests of simple associations. *Journal of Experimental Psychology: Learning, Memory, and Cognition*, 20, 396–410.

Manza, L. & Reber, A. S. (1994). *Representation of tacit knowledge: Transfer across stimulus forms and modalities.* Manuscript submitted for publication.

Reber, A. S. (1967). Implicit learning of artificial grammars. *Journal of Verbal Learning and Verbal Behavior*, 5, 855–863.

Reber, A. S. (1989). Implicit learning and tacit knowledge. *Journal of Experimental Psychology: General*, 118, 219–235.

Redington, M., & Chater, N. (1994). The guessing game: A paradigm for artificial grammar learning. In *Proceedings of the Sixteenth Annual Meeting of the Cognitive Science Society*, 745–749. Hillsdale, NJ: Lawrence Erlbaum Associates.

Shanks, D. R., & St. John, M. F. (1994). Characteristics of dissociable human learning systems. *Behavioral and Brain Sciences*, 17, 367–447.

Shannon, C. E. (1951). Prediction and entropy of printed English. *Bell System Technical Journal*, 30, 50–64.

A Symbolic Model of Cognitive Transition

William C. Schmidt
Department of Psychology, Dalhousie University
Halifax, NS. Canada. B3H 4J1
wcs@or.psychology.dal.ca

Charles X. Ling
Department of Computer Science
Hong Kong University, Hong Kong.
ling@cs.hku.hk

Abstract

Study of cognitive development on the balance scale task has inspired a wide range of human and computational work. The task requires that children predict the outcome of placing a discrete number of weights at various distances on either side of a fulcrum. The current project examined the adequacy of the symbolic learning algorithm C4.5 as a model of cognitive transition on this task. Based on a set of novel assumptions, our C4.5 simulations were able to exhibit regularities found in the human data including orderly stage progression, U-shaped development, and the torque difference effect. Unlike previous successful models of the task, the current model used a single free parameter, is not restricted in the size of the balance scale that it can accommodate, and does not require the assumption of a highly structured output representation or a training environment biased towards weight or distance information. The model makes a number of predictions differing from those of previous computational efforts.

Introduction

The balance scale task consists of showing a child a balance scale supported by blocks so that it stays in the balanced position. Next, a discrete number of weights are placed around one of a number of evenly spaced pegs on either side of the fulcrum (see the left side of Figure 1), and it becomes the child's task to predict which arm will go down, or whether the scale will balance, once the supporting blocks are removed.

The psychological task requires the integration of information from the dimensions of weight and distance through the course of development. Perfect performance on this task can be achieved by computing torques for both the left and right arms by multiplying weight by distance, and the side with the largest torque goes down. If torques are equal, then the scale will balance.

Siegler (1981) has partitioned the set of possible balance scale problems into the six sets of distinct problem types shown in Figure 1. Performance on the different problem types is used to gage the level of expertise that children have acquired and to gain insight into the types of information that children use to solve balance scale problems.

The first three types of problems are referred to as *simple* problems because the dimension of greater magnitude determines which side of the scale will tip. The final three problem types are referred to as *conflict* problems because the cue of weight conflicts with the cue of distance, and

there is no simple way of determining the outcome. The side with the greater weight or distance drops respectively in *conflict-weight* and *conflict-distance* problems, while the scale balances for *conflict-balance* problems.

Siegler (1981) reported that children's performance on the balance scale task progresses through four distinct stages. In stage 1, children use only weight information to determine if the scale will balance. In stage 2, children emphasize weight information but use distance if weights on both sides of the fulcrum are equal. In stage 3 both weight and distance information is utilized for simple problems, but children seem to respond indecisively to conflict problems. By stage 4, there is a correct integration of weight and distance information resulting in the near flawless performance of the task. Figure 1 presents the predicted percentages of correct responses, broken down by problem type, for each of these four stages.

While orderly stage progression constitutes a major regularity of balance scale development, a second regularity can be observed by examining the predicted pattern of errors in Figure 1 for conflict-weight problems. In stages 1 and 2, children answer these problems correctly because of their early reliance on weight information. In stage 3 however, when weight and distance cues are in conflict, children often perform poorly on the same problems they had previously answered correctly. This situation is rectified by stage 4 however, at which point correct answers reoccur. This trend is referred to in the developmental literature as U-shaped development, reflecting the pattern of the longitudinal plot of performance.

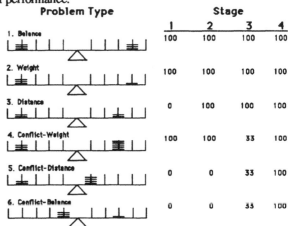

Problem Type	Stage			
	1	2	3	4
1. Balance	100	100	100	100
2. Weight	100	100	100	100
3. Distance	0	100	100	100
4. Conflict-Weight	100	100	33	100
5. Conflict-Distance	0	0	33	100
6. Conflict-Balance	0	0	33	100

Figure 1. Predictions of percent problems correct for children using different rules.

A third major balance scale regularity was reported by Ferretti and Butterfield (1986). These researchers discovered that the rule classifications of many children systematically varied when assessed with different sets of testing problems drawn from the theoretically equivalent problem types. It was discovered that children's judgments about problems with a greater absolute difference in the amount of torque between the two arms (*torque difference*) were more often correct than similar types of problems with smaller torque differences. Therefore, Siegler's rule assessment procedure is systematically sensitive to the magnitudes of problems selected for use in stage diagnosis. This last phenomenon is dubbed the *torque difference effect* (TDE).

A number of computational models of the balance scale task exist. The most successful of these models, in terms of capturing the major developmental regularities, have utilized connectionist learning algorithms as mechanisms of cognitive transition (McClelland,1989; Shultz, Mareschal, & Schmidt, 1994; Shultz, Schmidt, Mareschal, & Buckingham, 1995). The goal of the current project was to investigate whether a popular symbolic learning algorithm could act as a transition mechanism for a successful model, in the hopes that the assumptions and predictions of such a model might provide alternative insight into the origins of the human data.

C4.5 - A Symbolic Classification System
Quinlan's (1993) C4.5 acted as a transition mechanism in our model. Given a set of training examples which vary along a set of attributes, C4.5 extracts rule-like regularity from the examples and builds a decision tree that classifies the examples with some degree of tolerated error. Like its connectionist cousins, C4.5 is a supervised learning algorithm.

C4.5 constructs a decision (sub)tree by computing the *information gain ratio* (IGR) for each of the possible attributes that could potentially be used to partition the data. The IGR is a heuristic method that evaluates an attribute's ability to reduce randomness in unclassified examples. The attribute with the greatest IGR is chosen as the root of a subtree. This method of building subtrees is applied recursively until the resulting tree fully classifies all of the training examples.

C4.5 provides a user specified parameter, m, which during decision tree construction, roughly controls the degree of tolerated error. To implement the transition component of a balance scale model, the number of cases (specified by m) required to merit a subtree branching operation was decreased with time. This manipulation resulted in the gradual emergence of an increasingly discerning decision tree. By assuming that what develops in children is an ability to assimilate more information over time, a series of decision trees can be constructed, each of which builds on its predecessor. Applying C4.5 with a large m yields smaller, less comprehensive decision trees because few attributes qualify to act as decision nodes. As m decreases, more attributes qualify to be split, more regularity in the training set is captured, and deeper and more complex trees are built.

Early in development, children have limited mental abilities. Their poor performance can be modeled with a

large m value in C4.5. Performance and capacity improvement can be modeled by the gradual decrease of the m parameter. The following simulations demonstrate that the order of attributes C4.5 picks up in a series of decision trees with decreasing m coincides with the order of attributes children utilize during development, thereby demonstrating that C4.5 can provide a good model of developmental transition.

Simulation 1 - The Basic Model
Early in development, children rely more heavily on information derived from the weight dimension than the distance dimension, even though equal information from these dimensions is available. Any accurate model, therefore, requires some set of assumptions such that the transition mechanism relies more heavily on information from one dimension over the other. In McClelland's (1989) back-propagation model of this task, separate processing of the weight and distance dimensions were enforced architecturally, and the training environment gave the network more experience with weight information. These assumptions about cognitive architecture and the environment resulted in a realistic progression of the model, with weight information favored over distance information early in development. The Shultz, Mareschal, & Schmidt (1994) cascade-correlation model also required a strong environmental bias favoring weight information, but did not require the architectural assumption. The other successful connectionist model of this task, the Shultz, Schmidt, Mareschal, & Buckingham (1995) cascade-correlation model, removed the requirement for both a biased training environment and a modular separation of weight and distance processing, by biasing initial network weights such that early in development, weight but not distance information was favorably processed.

A further architectural assumption is made by all connectionist models of balance scale development, whereby their output information is encoded in a highly structured manner requiring algorithmic interpretation. Additionally, the models by McClelland (1988) and Shultz et al. (1994) required a further assumption regarding the level of training exemplar variability.

To produce results comparable to the connectionist simulations, we examined a five peg, five weight version of the balance scale task. For purposes of learning with C4.5, the set of 625 possible five peg, five weight problems needs to be represented in terms of a set of values on attributes with an associated classification. The set of attributes that yield a successful model provide at minimum, an existence proof about the types of information sufficient for producing the human data. Hence, attributes that yield a successful model, make predictions about the types of information that humans may use, or may be sensitive to, during development.

Although we experimented with a number of attribute sets, we found that few led to a successful model of the human data. Experimentation led to presenting C4.5 with seven attributes.

The first three attributes presented summary information about each problem that can be immediately derived from the visual input. Siegler's (1981) work suggested that children reason with information about which side of the balance scale has the greatest weight or distance, and whether the sides of the balance scale are equivalent for a given dimension. The first attribute concerned whether the problem presents an equal number of weights at equal distances on either side of the fulcrum, and took values of *yes* or *no*. The inclusion of this attribute was based on the perceptual salience of simple balance problems, the only problems of the set which are wholly symmetrical. The second and third attributes concerned the side of the scale with greater weight or distance respectively, and each took on one of three values: *left arm*, *neither arm*, or *right arm*. Siegler's (1981) rule models directly incorporated such information. Making this information primitively available to the learning algorithm presents it with the opportunity to capitalize on any informational value that such attributes may have for predicting problem outcomes. Because weight and distance information are equally predictive of problem outcomes, one dimension (i.e., weight) can be primarily relied upon by specifying it first. This order effect is equivalent to assuming that childrens' development internally relies on information from one dimension over the other.

The remaining four attributes were the actual number of weights and distances on either balance scale arm, and each of these was declared to be a continuous attribute taking on integer values ranging from 1 to 5. The inclusion of these attributes, again reflected that humans have such information readily accessible to them when confronted with balance scale problems.

Unlike many previous computational attempts, our model did not need to assume an explicit environmental bias favoring one input dimension. It did however, assume that simple balance problems (equal number of weights occur at equal distances on either side of the fulcrum) are particularly salient for the purposes of children's learning. This assumption was reflected in the choice of the first attribute, and by including three times as many simple balance problems as naturally occurs within the problem set, thereby giving C4.5 extra balance experience.

The C4.5 program was run, incrementally decreasing the *m* parameter which systematically resulted in the learning of increasingly complex decision trees. The gradual decrease in *m* corresponded to an assumption that the child's cognitive capacity increases in a gradual fashion yielding a processing structure in which successors build upon predecessors. Structures generated at each level of *m* were taken to represent the processing structures present for a discrete *era* of development.

Each era, the decision tree induced was used to classify the 425 examples which corresponded to the complete set of problems that could be classified into Siegler's six problem types. The responses to 24 problems (four from each of the six problem types), identical to those used to evaluate models by McClelland (1989) and Shultz et al. (1995) were then used in subsequent analyses to assess the model's success.

Results and Discussion

Figure 2 presents the stage classifications for each era of training, as diagnosed by using a procedure identical to that used with human children (Siegler, 1981). From the figure, it is apparent that the C4.5 model has captured the requirement of orderly stage progression.

Figure 3 presents the mean longitudinal performance of the simulation on the entire set of conflict-weight and conflict-distance problems. The model clearly exhibits U-shaped development on conflict-weight problems. By comparing the time of occurrence of this performance with the stage classification of the same simulation from Figure 2, it can be seen that the U-shaped developmental trend corresponds precisely with the period in which the simulation is classified at stage 3 (from approximately era 40 through era 80). The early reliance on weight information by C4.5 was interfered with during this period by the gradual integration and use of distance information on conflict problems. This can be verified by examining the longitudinal performance of the simulation on conflict-distance problems during stage 3 (Figure 3). At precisely the beginning of the decline in conflict-weight performance, distance information began to be assimilated. From Figure 3, it appears that there is a gentle vacillation between the learning algorithm's incorporation of weight and distance information with the inclusion of information from one of these dimensions conflicting with performance on the other. A negative correlation between conflict-weight and conflict-distance performance ($r=-0.86$; $r^2=0.73$) over the first 80 eras, confirms this discovery.

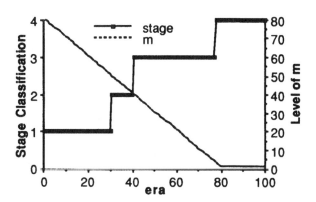

Figure 2. Longitudinal stage progression of Simulation 1 (left scale), and corresponding values of *m* (right scale).

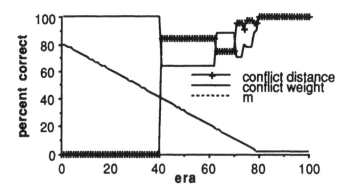

Figure 3. Performance on conflict-weight and conflict distance problems.

The final major effect characteristic of balance scale development, the TDE, was evaluated in the current simulation by classifying the model's performance using four different sets of testing patterns whose problems were drawn from four different ranges of torque difference. The TDE requires that the same set of simulation responses be classified at different stage levels depending upon the torque difference level of the testing problems used for stage evaluation. To correspond with the human data, testing sets with problems from larger torque difference levels should result in classifications at higher stages than testing sets with small torque difference problems.

Each testing set had the same balance and conflict-balance testing problems since the torque difference for these types of problems is always zero. The torque difference level for the other testing sets varied. Torque difference level 1 had problems with a torque difference of 1. Levels 2, 3 and 4 consisted of problems with torque differences in the range of 2-5, 6-9 and 10-20 respectively.

Only at stage 3, did stage classifications vary in accordance with the predictions of the TDE. Hence, the simulation was not capturing the TDE at all points in development.

An examination of the rule sets derived by C4.5 revealed that multiple rule sets mapped onto many of the stages. Stage 1 was achieved as the result of two distinct sets of rules while a single set of rules (identical to those derived by Siegler, 1981) mapped onto stage 2 performance. Stage 3 was accomplished through a set of five distinct rule systems, and two distinct decision trees resulted in stage 4 performance. No explicit computation and comparison of torques occurred. After the initial decision tree, each subsequent tree expanded upon previously derived structures.

Simulation 2 - The Expanded Model

In order to exhibit the TDE, a model must discriminate, and answer differently, problems from Siegler's theoretically equivalent problem types. If contingencies in the training data exist which distinguish problems based on information other than that used by Siegler (1981), then the TDE could arise if the learning algorithm were to pick up on such

contingencies. Siegler's rule models, and our first simulation's stage 1 and 2 rules, all failed to distinguish problems with different input magnitudes. Instead, the induced rules considered only the side of the balance scale with greater weight or distance. Our model's stage 3 rules distinguished problems on the basis of their graded input levels, and its stage classifications did vary with torque difference levels.

It would appear that in order to get the TDE at all stages of development, C4.5 would be required to build rules which discriminated between problems with different levels of inputs. For our second simulation we augmented our model by changing only the representational format of the attribute specifying which side of the balance scale had greater weight or distance. Instead of classifications of left arm, right arm, or neither arm, these attributes took on values in the range of $-4 \leq x \leq 4$ (determined by subtracting the right side value from the left side value for each of the weight and distance dimensions). By doing this, we have prevented C4.5 from being able to consider the side of the balance scale with larger weight or distance information in an all or none fashion, and instead have forced it to consider the attribute in terms of a graded representation. No other conditions of the model were altered, and training and assessment were carried out as before.

Results and Discussion

An examination of the model's performance revealed that as in Simulation 1, every stage was classifiable, and orderly stage progression ensued. Longitudinal conflict-weight performance showed the characteristic U-shaped regression in performance that coincides with stage 3, however conflict-weight performance at the very earliest stage of development was slightly poorer. Nonetheless, the simulation exhibited the first two regularities required by a successful model.

To examine the model for the presence of the TDE, each era was independently assessed with four different sets of testing problems drawn from the four different torque difference intervals outlined earlier. Stage classifications varied on each of the first 77 eras. Beyond era 77, the simulation reached a saturation point, and all of the problem sets were classified at a stage 4 level of performance.

Performance on the entire set of problems in the four torque difference ranges was also examined by calculating the percentage of correct responses at the median era of each stage. This amounted to evaluating the model at eras 3, 25, 43 and 79 for stages 1, 2, 3 and 4 respectively. The mean increase in performance between torque difference levels at each of these points in development was 4%, 8%, 8%, and 4%. As dictated by the TDE, the model demonstrated superior performance on problems from larger torque difference intervals. From the results of these analyses for the TDE, it is clear that the model exhibits all of the regularities of the human data.

General Discussion

The C4.5 symbolic model was successful at capturing the three characteristic developmental findings of the balance scale task: orderly stage progression, U-shaped learning, and the TDE. The model assumed that balance problems are especially salient to children, and that the majority of children are internally biased towards processing the weight dimension over the distance dimension. In addition the model implicitly assumed that children have access to, and reason with, information about which side of the balance scale is larger for a given dimension. By implementing these assumptions and applying the C4.5 learning algorithm, these simulations provide an alternative developmental model, capable of successfully capturing many aspects of the human data.

The success of C4.5 in producing an accurate model of development demonstrates that a symbolic supervised learning algorithm can act as a mechanism for simulating cognitive transition. Like its connectionist cousins, graded representations seem to be a critical feature of the success of C4.5, as does the incrementality of the processing structures that it derives.

In contrast to the fragility of pilot work with the competing connectionist models regarding the size of the balance scale problems undertaken, the model that we report appears to be robust in this regard. The C4.5 model worked as well for smaller (4 peg, 4 weight) and larger (6 peg, 6 weight) balance scale simulations as it did for the five peg, five weight version. It is still an open empirical question whether balance scale data of other sizes can be easily accommodated using connectionist techniques.

C4.5 was also robust with respect to the format of its output encoding. While connectionist models' success hinges on the architectural assumption underlying the inclusion of a distributed encoding of two outputs (McClelland, 1989; Shultz et al, 1994; 1995), with the C4.5 model, alternative methods of representing the response yields identical results. Finally, in contrast to the vast space of possible connectionist implementations, which possess a large number of degrees of freedom and require the setting of a large number of free parameters, the C4.5 model varied only m. The C4.5 model makes a number of predictions that are different than, or opposed to, those made by previous approaches. First, while many connectionist accounts assume an environment strongly biased towards presenting information about the weight dimension (McClelland, 1989; Shultz et al., 1994), the C4.5 model

predicts that the weight and distance dimensions are equally and symmetrically present in the natural world. Like Shultz et al. (1995), the current approach internalizes the early preference for information from a single dimension. If this characterization is correct, then these models suggest that despite sharing a common environment, there will be individual differences in the input dimension that children find most salient. Some support for this notion comes from related tasks requiring the integration of information from two dimensions, in which variability in the favored dimension exists (Siegler, 1981).

A second prediction of the C4.5 model is that simple balance problems are particularly salient and important in childrens' learning. Third, the model predicts that reasoning with primitive information derived from the initial presentation of the balance scale problem being solved is an important component of childrens' cognition. Fourth, the model predicts that stage 3 classifications of human performers masks a vacillation between relying more strongly on one dimension at the expense of integrating information from the other (see Figure 3).

It is our hope that the predictions derived from this alternative account will inspire further study of human development on the balance scale and related tasks, with an aim of determining the reasonableness of the assumptions that various models are based upon.

Acknowledgments

This research was supported by NSERC Canada Post Graduate funding and an Honorary Izaak Walton Killam Scholarship to William C. Schmidt. A more thorough and highly detailed examination of these simulations will appear in *Machine Learning*.

References

Ferretti, R. P., & Butterfield, E. C. (1986). Are children's rule assessment classifications invariant across instances of problem types?, *Child Development*, **57**, 1419-1428.

McClelland, J. L. (1989). Parallel distributed processing: Implications for cognition and development. In R.G.M. Morris (Ed.), *Parallel Distributed Processing: Implications for Psychology and Neurobiology*, pp. 8-45. Oxford: Clarendon Press.

Quinlan, J. R., (1993). *C4.5: Programs for machine learning*. San Mateo, California: Morgan Kaufmann.

Shultz, T. R., Mareschal, D., & Schmidt, W. C. (1994). Modeling cognitive development on balance scale phenomena. *Machine Learning*, , 57-86.

Shultz, T. R., Schmidt, W. C., Buckingham, D., & Mareschal, D. (1995). Modeling cognitive development with a generative connectionist algorithm. In T. Simon & G. Halford (Eds.) *Developing cognitive competence: New approaches to process modeling*, pp. 205-261. Hillsdale, NJ: Erlbaum.

Siegler, R. S. (1981). Developmental sequences between and within concepts. *Monographs of the Society for Research in Child Development*, **46** (Whole No. 189).

Practice Effects and Learner Control on Acquisition, Outcome, and Efficiency

Valerie J. Shute
Armstrong Laboratory/HRTI
1880 Carswell Ave. Bldg 9020
Lackland AFB, TX 78236-5507
(210) 671-2734
vshute@colab.brooks.af.mil

Lisa A. Gawlick
Galaxy Scientific Corporation
1880 Carswell Ave. Bldg 9020
Lackland AFB, TX 78236-5507
(210) 671-2667
lgawlick@colab.brooks.af.mil

Abstract

This paper presents results from a study that attempted to replicate unexpected findings from a previous study (Shute & Gawlick, 1995) which investigated the effects of differential practice opportunities on skill acquisition, outcome, efficiency, and retention. These same variables were examined in a new study ($N = 380$), and the following results were replicated: (1) Learners receiving fewer practice opportunities completed the curriculum significantly faster than the other practice conditions, but at the expense of greater errors; and (2) Despite acquisition differences, all groups performed comparably on the outcome measure. This study also examines the effects of learner control (LC) on these same parameters. We included a condition where students chose their degree of practice, per problem set. Overall, this group completed the curriculum faster, and showed the highest outcome efficiencies, relative to the other conditions. Preliminary results from the retention part of this study ($n = 76$) continue to show an overall LC advantage, as well as a significant condition × gender interaction. That is, the LC condition is optimal for males, while the extended practice condition is best for females. We discuss the implications of these findings in relation to the design of efficacious instruction.

How does practice affect knowledge and skill acquisition, learning outcome, efficiency, and retention? On the one hand, there is a lot of support for the "practice makes perfect" position (e.g., Bryan & Harter, 1899; Schneider & Shiffrin, 1977). More recently, Anderson (1993) has provided compelling evidence for, and concluded that, *"Students achieve at higher levels if they solve more problems, whatever the regimen."* (p. 160). On the other hand, Schmidt and Bjork (1992) presented some interesting studies showing how, relative to a "standard" practice condition, acquisition conditions that slowed the rate of improvement, or decreased performance during practice, still yielded enhanced post-training performance. What is ultimately learned may therefore be obscured during the acquisition process, as relatively permanent effects become confounded with temporary performance effects that may disappear after the practice session is finished, or when the test conditions change.

The literature on learner control is even less definitive. Computerized learning environments can be characterized by the amount of learner control supported during the learning process. This dimension can be viewed as a continuum ranging from minimal (e.g., rote or didactic environments) to almost complete learner control (e.g., discovery environments). Two opposing perspectives address the issue of the best learning environment to build in intelligent instructional software. One approach is to develop an environment which provides the learner freedom to explore and learn (e.g., Collins & Brown, 1988; Shute, Glaser, & Raghavan, 1989). The other approach argues that it is more efficacious to develop directive learning environments (e.g., Corbett and Anderson, 1989; Sleeman, Kelly, Martinak, Ward, & Moore, 1989). Actually, this disparity may be resolved by, instead of looking for main effects of learning environment, additionally considering learner characteristics with the goal of identifying optimal learning environments for specific kinds of persons.

This paper reports the results from a large-scale study ($N = 380$) conducted to replicate previously-obtained (and unexpected) findings that also tested practice effects on skill acquisition, learning outcome, efficiency, and retention. In addition, we examine the role of learner control in relation to these same parameters. We report the results from phase 1 of the study that's been completed, and present preliminary results from a follow-on portion of the experiment where the same learners return, after 6 months, to see how much they remember, and if that differs due to original practice condition.

Our previous learning criterion task (Shute & Gawlick, 1995) was an intelligent tutoring system teaching flight engineering knowledge and skills, divided into two main curriculum sections. Each section had two alternative conditions, differing only in the number of practice opportunities across problem sets: "Abbreviated" (A) and "Extended" (E). Thus, there were four practice conditions: AA, AE, EA, EE. Despite differences in acquisition (i.e., learners in the abbreviated conditions made more errors during problem solution compared to the other groups receiving more practice opportunities), groups performed the same across *all* learning outcome measures (surprise #1). We speculated that practice effects, while not readily apparent, may show up after some period of time had elapsed. In fact, the second experiment showed evidence for practice effects on long-term retention (i.e., after more than *two years*), but not in the predicted direction (surprise #2). That is, learners in the mixed conditions (switched 3/5 of the way through the curriculum from one practice condition to another) showed significantly greater retention compared to those assigned to either of the two homogeneous conditions.

In the current study, we use the same four treatment conditions as in the previous study, but have employed a completely different instructional environment (i.e., Stat Lady, teaching introductory statistics) to test the generalizability of the previous findings in a different domain. Furthermore, we include a fifth treatment condition,

Learner Control (LC), which allows learners to select the number of problems to solve, per problem set, rather than solving a fixed number of problems. By including this new treatment condition, we can test the effects on these same learning parameters when learners are in control of their practice opportunities. Do individuals, in general, have the necessary metacognitive skills to know when additional help is needed, or when they've had enough practice? Are there individual differences in terms of who benefits most by this condition?

Hypotheses

Skill Acquisition. Based on previous findings, and given fewer practice opportunities in which to apply newly-developing knowledge and skills, we expected learners assigned to the more limited practice conditions to exhibit more errors during learning compared to those learning from the more extended conditions. We further expected learners in the LC condition to perform about average during skill acquisition, making a moderate number of errors compared to the other conditions. This was based on the belief that these learners would elect to solve a large range of problems due to individual differences in general aptitude, metacognitive skills, and personality traits. The result was expected to balance out at a middle level of performance.

Learning Outcome. We predicted no differences on the posttest measure among groups, given findings from the previous study. However, if there *were* any differences, we expected learners in the most extended conditions to perform better on the outcome measures compared to learners in the abbreviated conditions given they would have had significantly more practice opportunities (Anderson, 1993). With regard to the LC condition, we speculated that these individuals would show an intermediate level of outcome performance given greater variability in the number of problems they chose to solve.

Learning Efficiency. The time taken to complete the tutor should be a direct function of practice condition. Thus, learners in the most abbreviated conditions would take the least amount of time to complete the curriculum given fewer problems to solve, and learners in the most extended conditions would take the most amount of time. Learners in the LC condition were expected to take an intermediate amount of time as we believed that learners are often not cognizant of their cognitive strengths and weaknesses, nor are many of them sufficiently motivated to continue practicing until a skill is mastered.

Retention. On the basis of our earlier findings (Shute & Gawlick, 1995), we hypothesized that learners in the mixed practice conditions would show greater retention of the material compared to learners in the homogeneous conditions following a 6-month lag between original and retention testing. We also hypothesized that learners originally assigned to the LC condition would show average, to above-average levels of retention based on a fairly typical finding in the learner-control literature which suggests that increased control over one's environment renders the learning experience more enjoyable, particularly

for high-ability learners (e.g., Hannafin & Sullivan, 1996; Shute & Gawlick-Grendell, 1994; Swanson, 1990). Finally, in addition to testing for main effects of condition on retention, we were interested in examining the role of gender; specifically in terms of a possible interaction with condition. While we did not expect to see a main effect of gender, we did posit a gender × condition interaction whereby males were expected to show greater retention having learned in the LC condition (compared to the other conditions), and females to show better retention having learned from more extended practice conditions. This hypothesis was motivated by Shute & Gluck (in press) who reported that males showed significantly more independent/exploratory behaviors than females when learning from an on-line instructional system, and this particular tendency would be well-suited to the LC condition, possibly resulting in increased retention.

Method

Participants

A total of 380 individuals participated in this experiment, obtained from local temporary employment agencies. The age range of the sample was between 18-30 years (Mean = 22), and all had a high school diploma or equivalent. Overall, 66% of the sample was male, and no one had any prior exposure to statistics courses. Participants were paid for taking part in the study and informed that they needed to return in 6 months for phase 2--retention testing. To motivate their return, we offer a monetary bonus. Currently, we have collected data from a total of 76 individuals who have returned for the second part of the study.

Materials

The first module of the Stat Lady Descriptive Statistics series (DS-1, Shute & Gluck, 1994) was used as the complex learning task in the experiments described in this paper (for more on this module, see Shute, 1995). The curriculum was decomposed via a cognitive task analysis into curriculum elements (CEs), representing low-level bits of knowledge and skill (e.g., identify the symbol for summation, sum all frequencies in a given sample). In this study, participants received 77 CEs, arranged from simple to more complex concepts and skills, and spread across five main problem sets or topics: (a) frequency distributions, (b) proportions and percentages, (c) grouped frequency distributions, (d) cumulative frequency distributions, and (e) plotting. Each CE (or small group of related CEs) was instructed by Stat Lady, then individuals were assessed for CE mastery on the basis of their problem solving performances. In this study, the number of problems that learners solved (per problem set) was solely a function of assigned condition. All learners had to solve between 1 to 4 CE-related problems before moving on to the next problem set. If a learner gave an incorrect answer or solution, Stat Lady intervened with progressively more specific feedback related to the particular error. Learners were allowed up to three errors before Stat Lady provided the correct answer.

Because each CE was directly mapped to a specific question/problem (note: some CEs had several associated questions), participants in the extended condition received three more questions per CE than learners in the abbreviated condition (maintaining a 4:1 ratio between extended and abbreviated practice opportunities). At the end of the tutor, the system computed each learner's average number of questions and errors, per CE. The "questions" variable was constant for learners in the fixed practice conditions (but varied for the LC condition) while the "errors" variable differed for all learners, reflecting degree of problem-solving difficulty. Stat Lady's three-level feedback thus allowed learners to make between 0 to 3 errors, per question.

To assess learning outcome, duplicate items were created to assess knowledge/skill related to each of the 77 CEs. This resulted in two parallel forms of a test (A and B) that were administered on-line, before and after the tutor. For more details on the specifics of these tests, see Shute (1995).

Design and Procedure

In the previous study, participants were either switched to a new practice condition (e.g., A→E), or remained in the same one (e.g., E→E) about 3/5 of the way through the tutor. Similarly, in this study, learners (not in the LC condition) were either switched to a new condition or remained in the same one, after the 3rd (of 5) problem sets. Thus, there were a total of 5 practice conditions: (a) AA (*n*=86), (b) AE (*n*=60), (c) EA (*n*=58), (d) EE (*n*=88), and (e) LC (*n*=88).

Participants were tested in groups of about 20, and randomly assigned to a condition. Given the two parts of the tutor and the 4:1 ratio described above, the total number of problems presented, per condition, were: AA (5), AE (11), EA (14), EE (20), and LC (variable, between 5 - 20).

On-line demographic questionnaires and pretests were administered to all participants. After completing both, they proceeded to learn from the tutor which took, on average, about 5 hr to complete. Finally, all participants were administered an on-line posttest assessing the full range of knowledge and skills acquired from the tutor.

Participants in the first phase of this study were asked to return 6 months after learning from Stat Lady to take part in the follow-up portion (phase 2) of the study. Currently, 20% of the original sample has returned (*n*=76). The average lag between original and retention testing = 26.3 weeks (*SD* = 2.7 wk). The distribution of the returning participants, by condition, is: AA (*n*=13), AE (*n*=12), EA (*n*=16), EE (*n*=12), and LC (*n*=23).

Testing for the retention part of the study is being conducted in small groups of about 5 persons, over one day. Prior to taking the first retention test (consisting of items which are isomorphic to those used in phase 1), test administrators brief each group on the importance of trying to remember as much as they can from their original session. After the first test has been completed, participants are given a 30-minute break, followed by the second retention test. At the conclusion of the second test, all returning participants are administered an on-line battery of cognitive ability tests assessing working memory capacity, information processing speed, inductive reasoning skill, and

fact learning ability, in the quantitative domain. This battery requires, on average, about one hour to complete.

Results

Prior to making comparisons between practice conditions, we needed to insure that learners within each condition were demographically comparable. Several one-way ANOVAs were computed on age, gender, number of years of education, and computer experience, by condition. None of these variables showed significant differences across the five practice conditions.

Skill Acquisition

Does practice condition affect acquisition accuracy? We examined this issue first by comparing the *number of errors* made during learning, averaged across all CEs. As mentioned, this value could range from 0 to 3 errors, per CE. Significant differences were found: $F(4, 368) = 7.46$, $p < .001$. By condition, the order of average errors was: LC (1.67) < AA (1.70) < AE (2.41) < EA (2.47) < EE (2.96). However, learners in the Extended condition received four times as many questions per CE compared to learners in the Abbreviated condition, so their "error" values should be considered in relation to the number of problems they solved (note: the average number of questions that LC learners chose to solve fell midway between AA and AE conditions). Thus, to test for differences in *acquisition accuracy*, we computed a new variable--the number of errors divided by the number of questions, averaged across CEs. For this index, values close to 1.0 denote average performance; values *less than* 1.0 denote more accurate performance (fewer mistakes relative to the number of questions) and values *greater than* 1.0 denote more inaccurate performance (more errors relative to questions received).

For our sample, this value ranged from 0.40 to 2.09 and was significantly different among conditions: $F(4, 362) = 20.45$, $p < .01$. The order of this variable by condition was: EE < EA < AE < LC < AA. Thus, as with the previous study, the EE learners' acquisition accuracy was the highest among conditions--they made fewer mistakes relative to their greater number of questions. Learners in the AA condition showed the lowest acquisition accuracy--they tended to commit more mistakes on relatively fewer questions. Learners in the LC condition showed accuracy indices that were about midway between the AA and the EE conditions. See Figure 1.

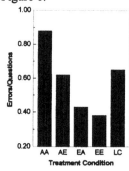

Figure 1: Acquisition accuracy across treatment conditions.

Learning Outcome

We first examined the pretest data to insure the five groups were comparable in prior knowledge and skills related to statistics. We computed an ANOVA on pretest scores, by condition. Although there were no significant differences among conditions, $F(4, 375) = 2.32$, $p = .06$, the F-value was sufficiently large to justify controlling for pretest data in subsequent analyses. Specifically, the EE group (by chance) began with the highest pretest Mean (greatest incoming knowledge), the AA with the lowest, and the LC participants, in between.

An ANOVA was computed on the posttest data (Means adjusted for pretest score) by condition, and there were no significant differences: $F(4, 375) = 2.94$, $p = .06$. However, as predicted, the order of posttest scores was: AA (68.3) < AE (71.4) < LC (71.9) < EA (74.5) ≈ EE (74.6).

Learning Time

We decomposed the total tutor-time variable into two parts--instruction and problem-solving time, representing two distinct parts of the Stat Lady program. Instruction time should vary in relation to one's facility in acquiring and understanding the new material, while problem-solving time should vary in relation to condition.

Table 1: Instruction, problem-solving, and overall tutor time (hrs) by condition.

Condition	Instruction	Prob-Solving	Total
AA (n = 86)	2.05	1.98	*4.03*
AE (n = 60)	1.88	2.96	*4.84*
EA (n = 58)	1.67	3.16	*4.85*
EE (n = 88)	1.52	3.96	*5.47*
LC (n = 88)	1.78	2.13	*3.91*
F (4, 375)	8.78	40.38	*12.74*
p	< 0.001	< 0.001	*< 0.001*

Notes: A = Abbreviated, E = Extended, and LC = Learner Control practice conditions.

Three ANOVAs were computed on instruction time, problem-solving time, and total time required to complete the tutor. All three variables showed significant differences due to condition. The order of total time by condition was unexpected: LC < AA < AE = EA < EE. Contrary to our hypothesis, the LC learners were fastest of all (see Table 1).

The final variable that we examined combined outcome score (i.e., adjusted posttest data) and tutor-completion time to yield an *outcome-efficiency* index (i.e., posttest score divided by time on tutor). The interpretation of this variable is that larger values reflect greater efficiency (i.e., higher learning outcome scores relative to time spent on the tutor). Lower values indicate less efficient learning.

We computed an ANOVA on this ratio by condition and the results were significant: $F(4, 375) = 6.00$, $p < .001$. The ordering of this index, by condition, was: EE < AE ≈ EA < AA < LC. As can be seen in Figure 2, LC learners showed superior learning efficiency relative to the other conditions.

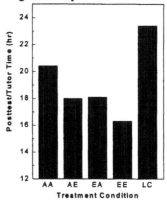

Figure 2: Learning outcome efficiency data by condition.

Retention (Preliminary Results)

Currently, we have data from $n = 76$ of the original $N = 380$ participants for the retention part of the study (i.e., phase 2). This phase will be completed June 1996. The question here is how the practice conditions, in general, affect retention of this material. Because this represents an incomplete study, the following should be viewed as preliminary analyses and tentative conclusions.

Prior to making comparisons among conditions on retention, we needed to insure that the subset of returning learners were comparable to the original sample (phase 1 data overall, and per practice condition). We computed one-way ANOVAs on demographic measures (age, gender, education, computer experience), by phase. None of these measures were significantly different. We also compared returning to original participants' data on phase 1 posttest scores (adjusted for pretest). Scores from the returning sample did not differ significantly from the original sample on this measure, $t(454) = -0.11$, $p = .91$.

Next, we computed a factor analysis (principal components analysis) on the cognitive ability test data (percent correct scores). This resulted in the extraction of a single factor: general aptitude. The percentage of variance accounted for by this factor was 64.0%, with $M = 0$, and $SD = 1$. Factor scores were saved for each person and used as a covariate in subsequent analyses.

We then combined data from individuals originally learning from the AE and EA conditions because: (a) their acquisition, outcome, and efficiency data from phase 1 were not significantly different to warrant their separation, (b) this increases the power of the upcoming analyses, and (c) this same procedure was followed in the original Shute & Gawlick (1995) study. Furthermore, we combined the two retention test scores into an average retention score.

To test our hypotheses concerning condition and gender effects on retention, we computed an ANOVA with *retention* as the within-subjects variable (i.e., the adjusted posttest scores from phase 1 and average retention scores from phase 2 as the repeated measures). *Condition* (AA, AE/EA, EE, LC) and *gender* (male, female) were the between-subjects variables. We included the *aptitude* factor score as a covariate in the equation to control for any differences in aptitude that may mediate any obtained main effects or interactions. Results from the ANOVA showed no main effect on retention due to original practice *condition* ($F < 1$), no main effect of *gender* ($F < 1$), but a significant *condition* × *gender* interaction: $F(3, 67) = 3.79$, $p = .01$. This interaction is depicted in Figure 3.

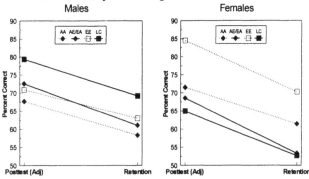

Figure 3. Condition by gender interaction on retention

Finally, we created a *retention-efficiency* index--retention score (with adjusted posttest score from phase 1 partialled out and the retention score residuals saved for each person) divided by original learning time. Again, higher numbers mean greater retention relative to acquisition time. We computed an ANOVA on this index by condition and the results were significant: $F(3, 72) = 3.54$, $p = .02$. By condition, the ordered indices were: EE (13.4), AE/EA (14.2), AA (18.7), and LC (24.6). Comparing just the relative indices related to the LC and EE conditions, the effect size = 1.6, with a strong LC advantage over the EE condition.

Discussion

Is it really the case that more practice opportunities yield better achievement, regardless of regimen; or is the relationship more complicated? The first purpose of this study was to replicate rather unexpected findings from our original study (Shute & Gawlick, 1995) that tested this query. Disregarding the learner control manipulation for a moment, we specifically replicated the following: (a) Reduced practice opportunities result in worse accuracy acquisition, but (b) despite these acquisition differences, outcome performances across all conditions are equivalent (even in this different domain), and (c) learners in the abbreviated condition(s) complete the tutor significantly faster than learners in the more extended conditions. Moreover, when we view tutor-time data separated into its component parts (instruction and problem-solving time), we see, predictably, that problem-solving time increases as a function of practice condition (AA < AE < EA < EE). However, instruction time shows a *reversal* of this ordering: EE < EA < AE < AA. This suggests that abbreviated learners may have been attempting to compensate for their

sparse practice environments by spending relatively more time reviewing the instructional sections of the tutor.

A second goal of phase 1 of this study was to examine the effects of learner control on these same parameters (i.e., acquisition, outcome, and efficiency). While the LC learners did show an intermediate level of acquisition accuracy, surprisingly, they completed the tutor faster than any other condition. And when we computed and tested an outcome-efficiency index by condition, results showed the LC learners greatly surpassed the other groups (see Figure 2).

In the second phase of this study, we are (a) attempting to replicate findings from a previous retention study (Shute & Gawlick, 1995), where greater retention of flight engineering knowledge and skills were exhibited by those who originally learned from mixed-practice conditions (AE and EA), and (b) examining the effects of practice condition and gender on retention.

Following six months between original instruction (phase 1) and retention testing (phase 2) in the present study, using a different domain, we found no significant main effect of original practice condition on retention, thus we failed to replicate the finding of the mixed-practice condition's advantage on retention (although the data are still incomplete). However, we have found a very interesting condition by gender interaction. Figure 3 clearly shows that for males, learning from the LC condition represents the superior learning environment--their outcome and retention scores are much higher compared to males learning in the other practice conditions. The female data reveal a very different story--females learn better and remember more from the consistently extended condition (EE); their poorest performances are associated with the LC condition. This interaction is even more compelling in that it appears even with aptitude being controlled in the equation.

What would account for the obtained gender by condition interaction in relation to differential retention, particularly for the LC condition? First, aptitude-treatment interaction (ATI) research has shown that certain learner characteristics are better suited to specific kinds of environments to achieve optimal outcome performance (see Shute, Glaser, & Raghavan, 1989; Tobias, 1989, 1994). Second, Shute (1993) reported that individuals demonstrating greater exploratory behaviors perform better in more open learning environments (similar to the LC condition, and contrasting with more didactic ones) while the converse was found for less-exploratory individuals. Third, a different study (Shute & Gluck, in press) further examined exploratory behaviors in terms of optional, on-line tool usage, and reported gender effects related to tool use. That is, males tended to more spontaneously employ the on-line tools compared to females, and there was a main effect of tool use on learning outcome (i.e., more was better, overall). Finally, exploratory and independent kinds of behaviors have been linked to endogenous testosterone level, and males have significantly more testosterone than females (e.g., Broverman, Klaiber, Kobayashi, & Vogel, 1968; Kimura, 1992; Newcombe, 1982). Testosterone affects brain functions in a manner similar to an adrenergic stimulant--exerting an influence on precisely those traits that are best suited to a learning environment offering more learner control.

Obviously, more research is needed to test all of these relationships. We are currently completing a series of six studies that examine gender effects across a range of learning environments and domains, assessing testosterone levels, and relating these variables to performance. Many new gender by treatment interactions are emerging that have direct implications for adaptive instructional design.

In conclusion, participants in the LC condition complete the tutor much faster than the other fixed-practice conditions, yet perform no differently on the outcome measure compared to those having the most extensive practice opportunities. Moreover, we continue to see advantages for the LC condition after six months, illustrated by this group's large retention-efficiency index relative to the other conditions. The only downside is that this condition appears to be better for males than females, at least with regard to retention. Overall, these findings suggest that the design of automated instructional systems may be enhanced, and learning efficiency improved, by providing greater student control during learning. Furthermore, females may benefit by receiving pre-training that specifically focuses on ways to improve self-monitoring skills. In fact, we have data that suggests that, within the LC condition, males tend to adjust their requests for problems in relation to perceived need (i.e., asking for additional questions in relation to more difficult CEs, and fewer questions for less problematic CEs). On the other hand, our data show that females, in general, tend to ask for fewer problems. We plan to explore these issues in greater detail once all of the retention data have been collected.

Acknowledgments

We'd like to thank Kevin Gluck, Barry Goettl, Nancy Lefort, Jason Miller, Wayne Crone, Linda Robertson-Schüle, Rickard Robbins, Cathy Gomez and Shirley Snooks for their different (and excellent) contributions to this study.

The research reported in this paper was conducted as part of the Armstrong Laboratory, TRAIN Project, Brooks AFB, TX. Funds for this research were provided by the Air Force Office of Scientific Research. The opinions expressed in this article are those of the authors and do not necessarily reflect those of the Air Force. Correspondence concerning this paper should be addressed to the first author.

References

Anderson, J. R. (1993). *Rules of the mind*. Hillsdale, NJ: Erlbaum.

Broverman, D. M,. Klaiber, E. L., Kobayashi, Y., & Vogel, W. (1968). Roles of activation and inhibition in sex differences in cognitive abilities. *Psychological Review*, 75, 23-50.

Bryan, W. L., & Harter, N. (1899). Studies on the telegraphic language: The acquisition of a hierarchy of habits. *Psychological Review*, 6, 345-375.

Collins, A. & Brown, J. S. (1988). The computer as a tool for learning through reflection. In H. Mandl and A. Lesgold (Eds.), *Learning issues for intelligent tutoring systems* (pp. 1-18). New York, NY: Springer-Verlag.

Corbett, A. T. & Anderson, J. R. (1989). Feedback timing and student control in the Lisp intelligent tutoring system.

In D. Bierman, J. Brueker, & J. Sandberg (Eds.), *Proceedings of the 4th International Conference on Artificial Intelligence and Education* (pp. 64-72). Springfield, VA: IOS.

Hannafin, R. D., & Sullivan, H. J. (1996). Preferences and learner control over amount of instruction. *Journal of Educational Psychology*, 99(1), 162-173.

Kimura, D. (1992). Sex differences in the Brain. *Scientific American*, 119-125.

Newcombe, N. (1982). Sex-related differences in spatial ability. In M. Potegal (Ed.), *Spatial ability: Development and physiological foundations* (pp. 223-250). New York, NY: Academic Press.

Schmidt, R. A., & Bjork, R. A. (1992). New conceptualizations of practice: Common principles in three paradigms suggest new concepts for training. *Psychological Science*, 3(4), 207-217.

Schneider, W., & Shiffrin, R. M. (1977). Controlled and automatic human information processing. Detection, search, and attention. *Psychological Review*, 84, 1-66.

Shute, V. J. (1993). A comparison of learning environments: All that glitters... In S. P. Lajoie & S. J. Derry (Eds.), *Computers as cognitive tools* (pp. 47-74). Hillsdale, NJ: Erlbaum.

Shute, V. J. (1995). SMART: Student Modeling Approach for Responsive Tutoring. *User Modeling and User-Adapted Interaction*, 5, 1-44.

Shute, V. J. & Gawlick, L. A. (1995). Practice effects on skill acquisition, learning outcome, and retention. *Human Factors*, 37(4), 781-803.

Shute, V. J. & Gawlick-Grendell, L. A. (1994). What does the computer contribute to learning? *Computers and Education: An International Journal*, 23(3), 177-186.

Shute, V. J., Glaser, R. & Raghavan, K. (1989). Inference and discovery in an exploratory laboratory. In P. L. Ackerman, R. J. Sternberg, & R. Glaser (Eds.), *Learning and individual differences* (pp. 279-326). New York, NY: W. H. Freeman.

Shute, V. J. & Gluck, K. A. (in press). Patterns of Exploratory Behavior: Causes and Effects. *The Journal of the Learning Sciences*.

Shute, V. J., & Gluck, K. A. (1994). *Stat Lady: Descriptive Statistics Module 1*. [Unpublished computer program]. Brooks Air Force Base, TX: Armstrong Laboratory.

Sleeman, D., Kelly, A. E., Martinak, R., Ward, R. D., & Moore, J. L. (1989). Studies of diagnosis and remediation with high school algebra students. *Cognitive Science*, 13(4), 551-568.

Swanson, J. H. (1990, April). The effectiveness of tutorial strategies: An experimental evaluation. *Paper presented the American Educational Research Association*, Boston, MA.

Tobias, S. (1989). Another look at research on the adaptation of instruction to student characteristics. *Educational Psychologist*, 24(3), 213-227.

Tobias, S. (1994). Interest, prior knowledge, and learning. *Review of Educational Research*, 64(1), 37-54.

A Connectionist Model of Reflective Reasoning Using Temporal Properties of Node Firing

Jacques Sougné

Department Psychology
University of Liège
4000 Liège, Belgium
sougne@vml.ulg.ac.be

Abstract

This paper presents a connectionist model of human reasoning that uses temporal relations between node firing. Temporal synchrony is used for representing variable binding and concepts. Temporal succession serves to represent rules by linking antecedent to consequent parts of the rule. The number of successive synchronies is affected by two well-known neurobiological parameters, the frequency of neural rythmic activity and the precision of neural synchronization. Reasoning is predicted to be constrained by these variables. An experiment manipulating the amount of successive synchronies is presented. Experimental results would seem to confirm the predictions.

Introduction

Shastri & Ajjanagadde (1993) described SHRUTI, a connectionist model of tractable reasoning. They intended to build a neurally plausible model based mainly on temporal properties of observed rythmic neural firing patterns in the brain. Certain neurons tend to oscillate in synchrony at a frequency of 30 to 80 Hz. (i.e. every 33 to 12 ms). The model of Shastri & Ajjanagadde used this property in the attempt to solve the binding problem. Variables and their respective contents fired in synchrony making appropriate bindings between roles and fillers. The use of this temporal property to solve the binding problem was first studied by Clossman (1988).

Their model is able to draw inferences with great efficiency. But reasoning is limited to what Shastri & Ajjanagadde call *reflexive reasoning*. This concept describes the type of reasoning that people do effortlessly, immediately, almost reflexively. It is contrasted with *reflective reasoning*, demanding more effort and attention and taking more time. Deductive reasoning that has been studied extensively in cognitive psychology pertains to the class of reflective reasoning. In this paper I will attempt to extend the properties of Shastri & Ajjanagadde model to allow it to also handle reflective reasoning. From the model, I will derive certain predictions and provide empirical evidence substantiating these predictions.

There is neurobiological evidence for considering synchronization as a binding mechanism (Gray & al. 1989, Singer 1995, Nelson 1995). The interval between two spikes of a neuron (π) is approximately 12 to 33 ms. Inside this interval a number of different synchronies can occur. This number is constrained by π and by ω, the width of a window of synchrony. Nodes that fire within a lag of less than $\omega/2$ are considered to fire in synchrony (figure 1).

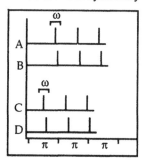

Figure 1: A representation of rhythmic activation and synchrony. Node B fires in synchrony with node A and node D fires in synchrony with node C (since the precision is less than $\omega/2$)

The precision of synchronization between neurons has been reported to be approximately 3 ms. (König & al., 1995). This means that ω should be around 6 ms. These values π and ω limit the number of different possible synchronies to around 10. This corresponds to the well known number 7±2, the span of working memory (Miller, 1956, Lisman & Idiart, 1995). Within a particular window of synchrony, however, numerous concepts can fire at the same time. The relevant constraint is the length of the chain of reasoning. As its length increases, the probability for an error to occur increases.

A good example of reflective reasoning is deduction, which has been widely studied. Typically subjects take approximately 5 sec to draw a single deductive inference (Clark 1969). This delay is far longer than those described by the Shastri & al. model for reflexive inference. There are two ways to extend the Shastri & al. model to allow it to produce these inferences with these delays. Either deductive reasoning tasks require, a succession of different reflexive episodes, or they require learning to initially encode the problem, followed by the building of an appropriate chain of reasoning that will link the data to a more abstract rule that enables inference by appropriate bindings.

The first solution requires an explanation of the nature of the relationship between successive dynamic bindings. The second requires a learning algorithm to build a new chain of reasoning and the presence of abstract knowledge at the end of the chain of reasoning, for example pragmatic reasoning schemas (Cheng & Holyoak 1985).

I choose the second solution, which meant including in the model of Shastri & al. a mechanism for adding windows of synchrony during the reasoning process. In SHRUTI the form of the query must contain all windows of synchrony necessary for a conclusion to be drawn. Deductive reasoning tasks often require adding new windows of synchrony because the variables of the conclusion may be bound to a different content than those of the premises. For example, consider a conditional reasoning task with a rule: "If Tom gives a candy to Gus, then Tom has stolen money from Mary" and a premise: "Tom gives a candy to Gus". In order to generate the correct conclusion ("Tom has stolen money from Mary"), "candy" and "money" cannot fire in synchrony, nor can "Gus" and "Mary". Otherwise there would be confusion about exactly what is stolen or given and to whom it is stolen or given.

Shastri & Ajjanagadde (1993) describe a learning algorithm that enables nodes to fire in synchrony starting with a noisy temporal firing distribution. Learning is not only necessary to synchronize firing of appropriate nodes, but also to link the given rule to a more abstract rule that enables the generation of the conclusion.

Shastri & Grannes (1995) modified SHRUTI to enable it to perform negation and detection of inconsistencies. They added a negative collector node to every predicate. This option was not chosen in the present model since in their extension, the negation of each predicate must be specifically included. This seemed somewhat unrealistic since negation is a general concept and need not be specifically associated with each predicate.

The Shastri & al. model makes use of different kinds of nodes: fact nodes, collector nodes, enabler nodes, etc. According to Ajjanagadde (1994) this set of node types, as well as the distinction between roles and fillers, is unnecessary. He describes a system that uses a set of excitatory and inhibitory links, called a link bundle. These link bundles preserve the qualities of SHRUTI while simplifying the representation. I adapted this solution to the present model.

Description of the Model

Network Structure

The network is composed of a set of nodes which are not fully connected. Each node is either excitatory or inhibitory. Excitatory nodes can send only excitatory messages, and inhibitory nodes only inhibitory messages. While excitatory links bind two nodes, inhibitory links bind a node to a excitatory connection. This enables a temporary blocking of a specific excitatory transmission. (figure 2).

Each connection has a weight which has two functions: determining the probability of transmission of activation, and, in the event of transmission, the amount of activation

transmitted. Connections also have a length which determines the delay for the activation to propagate from the afferent node to the efferent node.

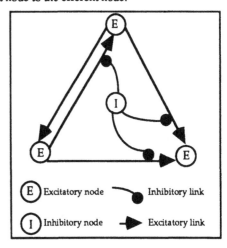

Figure 2: Structure of the net

A node represents a small cluster of neural units (akin to the Hebbian notion of cell assemblies) and a set of nodes firing in synchrony represents a concept or a set of bound concepts. In figure 4 the concept "Consequent" is composed of 4 nodes and is bound to "Lawrence" because they both fire in synchrony (figure 3). In this network architecture, unlike many connectionist architectures, there is no notion of layer.

Activation Propagation

Excitatory activation is stochastically transmitted along connections. Connection weights represent the strength of activation passing and the probability of propagation through the connections. According to their weight, connections are stochastically selected. Once selected, the afferent node receives an activation equal to the value of weight. If the sum of activations arriving at a node reaches a threshold, the node fires. Activation propagation along a connection takes time and the propagation speed is randomly selected from a particular interval which is modified by the learning algorithm. Inhibitory activation follows the same principles, except that activation propagates from nodes to excitatory connections.

Once a node fires, it tends to fire rhythmically with a frequency between 30 and 80 Hz (i.e. between 33 and 12 ms). Following Shastri & Ajjanagadde's (1993) notation, this inter-spike delay is called π. The width of windows of synchrony last 3 to 6 ms and this value is noted ω.

Synchronous firing of nodes either produces variable binding or associates units that participate in a concept representation. The temporal sequence of synchronous firing indicates relations between concepts, enabling the representation of rules. For example, in figure 3, "Antecedent" fires before "Consequent" and stands for the rule: "If *Antecedent* then *Consequent*".

Learning

Learning modifies weights and connection delays on the basis of information from the external world. It is assumed that facts perceived are composed of a series of concepts. The activation of these concepts has a particular temporal order. The task of the learning algorithm is to reproduce this temporal order and to link concepts to the rest of the knowledge base. External activation should therefore be distinguished from internal autonomous activation of the net. Modification of weights and delays depends on the overlap of external and internal activation. In the current model, when activations overlap, the weights of excitatory connections increase, and the delay intervals shift to focus around the most recently selected delay duration. In addition, the weights of connections inhibiting excitatory connections also decrease. When activations do not overlap the process is inverted. Delay learning can rapidly focus on a particular value, enabling nodes to change their partners of synchrony and therefore permitting plasticity in variable binding.

Predictions of the Model

This model predicts that reasoning will take more time and be more difficult as the number of synchronies increases. The number of possible temporal synchronies depends on the frequency of rhythmic pattern or the inter-spike delay (π) and the width of windows of synchrony (ω). When the number of synchronies increases, the frequency must decrease (i.e., π becomes larger) and/or ω must decrease. If this last value decreases too much, the probability of confusion between synchronies increases and the probability of errors increases. In addition, the time for the network to reach a stable state will increase.

Experiment 1

To test the last prediction we ran a reasoning experiment comparing two situations. The first situation requires six windows of synchrony (6ω), the second requires eight windows of synchrony (8ω). Thirty subjects received the following instructions: "A rule written in blue will appear on the screen, you must read it and tell me when you have understood it. Afterward, a statement, written in red will appear on the screen. You should relate it to the rule and tell me what you conclude". Subjects were given a series of similar arithmetic exercises to familiarize them with the procedure. Subjects were randomly assigned to one of the two groups.

In the first group ($6w$), subjects received this rule: "If Tom gives a candy to Gus then Tom has given a candy to Lawrence" and the questions appearing in a random order were: "Tom gives a candy to Gus", "Tom does not give a candy to Gus", "Tom has given a candy to Lawrence" and "Tom has not given a candy to Lawrence". This task of conditional reasoning makes reference to material implication. Subjects' inferences are of four types: Modus Ponens $\frac{p\rightarrow q,\ p}{q}$, Modus Tollens $\frac{p\rightarrow q,\ \neg q}{\neg p}$ (sound inferences) Denying the antecedent $\frac{p\rightarrow q,\ \neg p}{\neg q}$ and Affirming the consequent $\frac{p\rightarrow q,\ q}{p}$ (sound only in material equivalence). Table 1 shows these inferences.

	Modus Ponens	Denying the Antecedent	Affirming the Consequent	Modus Tollens
Group 1 6ω	from *Tom gives a candy to Gus* infer *Tom has given a candy to Lawrence*	from *Tom does not give a candy to Gus* infer *Tom has not given a candy to Lawrence*	from *Tom has given a candy to Lawrence* infer *Tom gives a candy to Gus*	from *Tom has given a candy to Lawrence* infer *Tom does not give a candy to Gus*
Group 2 8ω	from *Tom gives a candy to Gus* infer *Tom has stolen money from Mary*	from *Tom does not give a candy to Gus* infer *Tom has not stolen money from Mary*	from *Tom has stolen money from Mary* infer *Tom gives a candy to Gus*	from *Tom has not stolen money from Mary* infer *Tom does not give a candy to Gus*

Table 1: instantiation of inferences

Starting with the query: "Tom gives a candy to Gus", the model predicts a rhythmic pattern with 6 windows of synchrony that could be represented by figure 3 and a network state enabling sound inferences as in figure 4. With 6 windows of synchrony, if ω is 3 ms., π must be $\geq$ 18 ms. (the frequency must be inferior to 56 Hz.); if ω is 6 ms, π must be $\geq$ 36 ms. (the frequency must be inferior to 28 Hz.). In figure 3, π is equal to 24 ms. (42 Hz.) and ω is equal to 4 ms.

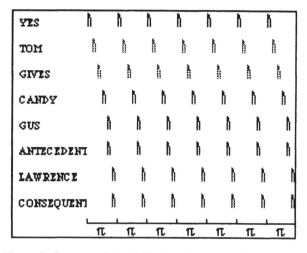

Figure 3: Concepts firing following the query: "Tom gives a candy to Gus" in the situation 1. Gus and Antecedent are firing in synchrony as well as Lawrence and Consequent

Connections represented in figure 4 enable sound material implication inferences. When the premise is "Yes, Tom gives a candy to Gus", activation is propagated from "Gus" to "Antecedent", from "Antecedent" to "Consequent" and from "Consequent" to "Lawrence". When the premise is "No, Tom gives a candy to Gus", "No" inhibits the connection from "Antecedent" to "Consequent" thus prevents any conclusion. When the premise is "Yes, Tom gives a candy to Lawrence", "Lawrence" activates "consequent" but "Yes" inhibits the connection from "Consequent" to "Antecedent" thus prevents any conclusion. When the premise is "No, Tom gives a candy to Lawrence" no inhibition occurs and activation is propagated to enable "Gus" nodes to fire.

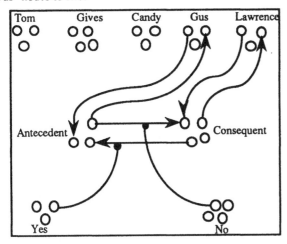

Figure 4: A network configuration that enables sound infe-rences with regard to material implication. Each concept is represented by a set of interconnected nodes although it is not showed. (Note that some nodes could be used by more than one concept, and that only a small number of connections are represented). Affirmation and negation nodes are necessary for sound material implication inference through inhibition mechanism.

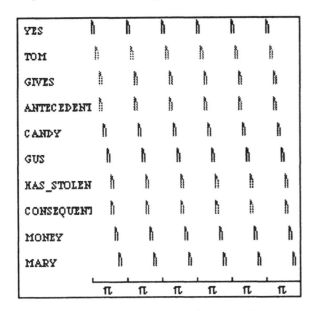

Figure 5: Concepts firing following the query: "Tom gives a candy to Gus" in the situation 2. Gives and Antecedent are firing in synchrony as well as Has_stolen and Consequent

For the second group (8ω), subjects received this rule: "If Tom gives a candy to Gus then Tom has stolen money from Mary" and the questions were: "Tom gives a candy to Gus", "Tom does not give a candy to Gus", "Tom has stolen money from Mary" and "Tom has not stolen money from Mary" appearing in a random order. The required 8 windows

of synchrony can be represented as in figure 5 and the state of the network as in figure 6. With 8 windows of synchrony, if ω is 3 ms, π must be ≥ 24 ms. (the frequency must be inferior to 42 Hz.), if ω is 6 ms, π must be ≥ 48 ms. (the frequency must be inferior to 21 Hz.) which is out of realistic range. In Figure 5, π is equal to 28 ms. (36 Hz.) and ω is equal to 3 ms.

The connections shown in figure 6 enable sound material implication inferences. For each of the four premises, the activation is correctly propagated.

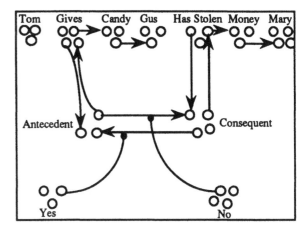

Figure 6: A network configuration that enables sound inferences with regard to material implication. Each concept is represented by a set of interconnected nodes although it is not showed.

Experimentally evaluating the difficulty of the task is not easy. It is well known that subjects often do not follow rules related to material implication. In some situations of everyday life, sound inferences related to material implication are less adequate than these of material equivalence. But we cannot separate these types of people in two groups, those who accept material implication and those who accept material equivalence. A number of biases affect subjects responses (Evans 1989). Content and context also modify the pattern of responses (Cheng & Holyoak, 1985). To compare the performance between groups, we could compare response patterns that are sound for material implication or material equivalence to other types of patterns. The sound inferences for material implication are Modus Ponens $\frac{p \supset q, p}{q}$ and Modus Tollens $\frac{p \supset q, \neg q}{\neg p}$, for material equivalence, Modus ponens $\frac{p \equiv q, p}{q}$, Denying the antecedent $\frac{p \equiv q, \neg p}{\neg q}$, Affirming the consequent $\frac{p \equiv q, q}{p}$ and Modus Tollens $\frac{p \equiv q, \neg q}{\neg p}$. We compare subjects with consistent responses to subjects who contradict themselves from one inference to another.

As the figure 7 shows, the proportion of consistent patterns of responses is significantly higher in the group where the presented rule require six windows of synchrony (χ^2 (1)= 5.129 p < .05).

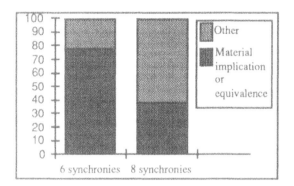

Figure 7: Percentage of consistent and inconsistent patterns of inferences for the two groups.

Even though this criterion measures consistency among successive inferences, it might be criticized as being simply a measure of task difficulty. The time taken by subjects to draw an inference can also be used. The time from the appearance of the question to the response was recorded, giving the averages indicated in Table 2.

Group 1 (6ω)	Group 2 (8ω)
4894 ms	6528 ms

Table 2: Average time in ms. between the question presentation and the response. Student t (103) = -3.046 p < .005

These data show a highly significant difference between the two groups. Subjects doing the task requiring eight windows of synchrony take more time to make an inference than subjects doing the other task. As predicted, when the number of windows of synchrony increases, the likelihood of confusion between synchronies increases, encoding or learning time increases, and the subject's response is delayed.

Psychological data about multiple instantiation tend to show that people deal more efficiently with a problem in which predicates are instantiated more than once. For example, De Soto & al. (1965) showed that subjects make less errors when inferring "A is better than C" from the premises "A is better than B" and "B is better than C" than from the premises "B is better than C" and "B is worse than A". My hypothesis involves an abstraction, a replacement of the multiple premises by a chunked summary that describes the situation. In this example, the predicate extends the number of its possible arguments to combine those of additional instantiated predicates. When it receives the second premise "B is better than C" of the first situation, the system merges the first premise to include C and may transform a representation "Better than: A, B" to "Better than: A, B, C". The second situation requires an additional process, that of using the opposite predicate to transform "B is worse than A" into "A is better than C".

Experiment 2

The above hypothesis concerning multiple instantiations was tested experimentally. However, for the moment, the

present model cannot do multiple instantiation. I used two situations involving the same number of instantiations of the same predicate, but involving a different number of transformations in order to make a summarized conclusion. The first group of subjects received these premises: "Allan is in love with Mary", "Mary is in love with Allan", "Peter is in love with Barbara", "Barbara is in love with Peter". The second group received these premises; "Peter is in love with Mary", "Barbara is in love with Allan", "Allan is in love with Mary" and "Mary is in love with Peter". The four premises were presented in a random order to both groups. After reading these premises, subject had to infer which people were happy (i.e. where their love was reciprocated). A higher proportion of subjects gave the correct answer in the first group where relations are all reciprocal (.92), than in the second group (.66). Response times were also shorter for the first group (mean: 3874 ms) than for the second (mean: 10262 ms) Student t (18) = -3.352 p < .005.

These data show that multiple instantiation can be treated rapidly when only a small number of transformations are required to get a summarized representation. Subjects are far less efficient as the number of required transformations increases. However, there should be a mechanism leading to a summarized representation that maintains a trace of previous instantiations while the current instantiations are active.

Discussion

The present system attempts to model not only certain low-level neurobiological facts about synchrony of neural firing but also higher level psychological data on deductive reasoning. The reader can refer to Shastri & Ajjanagadde (1993) for a discussion of the neurobiological plausibility of this type of model.

We know from Johnson-Laird's work (e.g. Johnson-Laird & Byrne, 1991) that reasoning is highly constrained by working memory capacity and we know from Cheng & Holyoak's work (e.g. Cheng & Holyoak, 1985, Holyoak & Cheng, 1995) that reasoning is also constrained by pragmatic principles which are the result of the acquisition and generalization of knowledge. This model attempts to incorporate both levels in a single system. Working memory is conceived as the synchronous and rhythmic firing of nodes. This process is the consequence of the content of long term memory since working memory is viewed as the current activation of long term memory.

The parallel activation of nodes in this model gives it the theoretical possibility of avoiding problems of combinatorial explosion in a scaled-up version. This is also one of the most interesting feature of the Shastri & al. model (Shastri, 1993). Many of the sequential models of deductive reasoning have been shown to be intractable in scaled-up versions (Oaksford & Chater, 1995).

Among the limitations of this model are the problem of the multiple instantiation and catastrophic forgetting in the learning process. Multiple instantiation has been treated by Mani & Shastri (1993). For n instantiations of a concept, the amount of nodes required in their model is n^2. There is no mechanism in the present model for dealing with multiple instantiation. But experiment 2 could guide our research. The number of simultaneous instantiations seems to be bounded around 2. We could imagine that nodes pertaining to a doubly instantiated predicate would fire at a rythm twice as fast as the others. As rythm is bounded by the refractory period of neurons, multiple instantiation is also bounded. This hypothesis seems reasonable since the frequency of oscillations has been found to be dependent on the amount of activity that a neuron receives.

Catastrophic forgetting is characterized by an interference of the newly learned content on previously learned information making this information lost. In my computational simulation, this limitation means that the problem must be encoded at the same time as the long term knowledge is stored. A separation of the architecture into a "long term memory" component and a "medium term memory" component might be an effective way of dealing with this problem (French, 1994).

Conclusions

A good model of human reasoning should explain the mechanisms by which people solve reasoning problems, the cause of systematic biases, and how the content of a problem affects performance. In this paper, I have focused on a possible low-level mechanism — namely, synchrony — that enables (and perturbs) deductive reasoning. However, I did not focus on systematic biases as described in Evans (1989). It is known that a problem's content affects the reasoning process. The present model attempts to give an emergent explanation for this phenomenon, rather than proposing a specific context-independent mechanism for it, we could incorporate the Pragmatic Reasoning Schemas (Cheng & Holyoak, 1985 Holyoak & Cheng, 1995) or possibly Social Exchange (Cosmides 1989). The model presented here attempts to combine neurobiological and psychological plausibility. In addition, experimental data confirmed a number of predictions of the model.

Acknowledgments

This research was supported by the Belgian FNRS Grant D.4516.93 and by the PAI. Thanks to Robert French for his assistance in the work presented here.

References

Ajjanagadde, V. (1994). Unclear Distinctions lead to Unnecessary Shortcomings: Examining the rule vs fact, role vs filler, and type vs predicate distinctions from a connectionist representation and reasoning perspective. *Proceedings of the AAAI-94.*

Cheng, P. W. & Holyoak, K. J. (1985). Pragmatic Reasoning Schemas. *Cognitive Psychology, 17,* 391-416.

Clark, H. H. (1969). Linguistic processes in deductive reasoning. *Psychological Review, 76,* 387-404.

Clossman, G. (1988). *A Model of Categorization and Learning in a Connectionist Broadcast System.* Unpublished Ph. D. thesis. Indiana University.

Cosmides, L. (1989). The Logic of Social Exchange: Has natural selection shaped how humans reason? Studies with the Wason selection task. *Cognition, 31,* 187-276.

De Soto, C. B., London, M. & Handel, S. (1965). Social reasoning and spatial paralogic. *Journal of Personality an Social Psychology, 2,* 513-521.

Evans, J. St B. T. (1989). *Bias in Human Reasoning: Causes and Consequences..* Hove: Lawrence-Erlbaum Ass.

French, R. M. (1994). Catastrophic Forgetting in Connectionist Networks, can it be prevented? In J. Cowan, G. Tesaro & J. Alspector (Eds.) *Advances in Neuro-Processing Systems 6.* San Francisco Ca.: Morgan-Kaufmann.

Gray, C. M., König, A., Engel, A. K. & Singer, W. (1989). Oscillatory responses in cat visual cortex exhibit inter-columnar synchronization which reflects global stimulus properties. *Nature, 338,* 334-337.

Holyoak, K. J. & Cheng, P. W. (1995). Pragmatic Reasoning With a Point of View. *Thinking and Reasoning, 1,* 289-313.

Johnson-Laird, P. N., & Byrne, M. J. (1991). *Deduction.* London: Lawrence-Erlbaum Ass.

König, P., Engel, A. K., Roelfsema, P. R., & Singer, W. (1995). How Precise is Neuronal Synchronization? *Neural Computation, 7,* 469-485.

Lisman, J. E. & Idiart, M. A. P. (1995). Storage of 7 ± 2 Short-Term Memories in Oscillatory Subcycles. *Science, 267,* 1512-1515.

Mani, D. R. & Shastri, L. (1993). Reflexive Reasoning with Multiple Instanciation in a Connectionist Reasoning System with a Type Hierarchy. *Connection Science, 5,* 205-242.

Miller, G. A. (1956). The Magical Number Seven, Plus or Minus Two. *Psychological Review, 63,* 81-97.

Nelson, J. I. (1995). Binding in the Visual System. In M. A. Arbib (Ed.) *The Handbook of Brain Theory and Neural Networks.* Cambridge Ma.: MIT Press.

Oakford, M. & Chater, N. (1995). Theories of Reasoning and the Computational Explanation of Everyday Inference. *Thinking and Reasoning, 1,* 121-152.

Shastri, L. (1993). A Computational Model of Tractable Reasoning: taking inspiration from cognition. *Proceedings of the Thirteen International Joint Conference on Artificial Intelligence.*

Shastri, L. & Ajjanagadde, V. (1993). From Simple Associations to Systematic Reasoning: A connectionist representation of rules, variables and dynamic bindings using temporal synchrony. *Behavioral and Brain Sciences, 16,* 417-494.

Shastri, L. & Grannes, D. J. (1995). *Dealing with negated knowledge and inconsistency in a neurally motivated model of memory and reflexive reasoning.* International Computer Science Institute TR-95-041.

Singer, W. (1995). Synchronization of Neuronal Response as a Putative Binding Mechanism. In M. A. Arbib (Ed.) *The Handbook of Brain Theory and Neural Networks.* Cambridge Ma.: MIT Press.

Culture Enhances the Evolvability of Cognition

Lee Spector* †

lspector@hampshire.edu

*School of Cognitive Science and Cultural Studies
Hampshire College
Amherst, MA 01002

Sean Luke †

seanl@cs.umd.edu

†Department of Computer Science
University of Maryland
College Park, MD 20742

Abstract

This paper discusses the role of culture in the evolution of cognitive systems. We define "culture" as any information transmitted between individuals and between generations by nongenetic means. Experiments are presented that use genetic programming systems that include special mechanisms for cultural transmission of information. These systems evolve computer programs that perform cognitive tasks including mathematical function mapping and action selection in a virtual world. The data show that the presence of culture-supporting mechanisms can have a clear beneficial impact on the evolvability of correct programs. The implications that these results may have for cognitive science are briefly discussed.

Introduction

Interactions between cultural and evolutionary processes are discussed in the literatures of several fields, including cognitive science (Donald, 1991), ethology (Bonner, 1980), sociobiology (Lumsden and Wilson, 1981), and primatology (Quiatt and Itani, 1994). This paper reports related work in the field of evolutionary computation, in which problems are solved by use of computational mechanisms that have been derived from evolutionary processes. In particular, results are presented for genetic programming systems, in which executable computer programs are automatically produced through processes of recombination and natural selection (Koza, 1992). Genetic programming systems can automatically produce computer programs for a variety of interesting cognitive tasks including circuit design, grammar induction, block stacking, and action selection (Koza, 1992; Spector, 1994, 1996).

The representations and algorithms employed by artificially evolved cognitive systems may bear little resemblance to those of natural cognitive systems. They nonetheless exemplify *possible* cognitive mechanisms, and as such they may be of interest to cognitive science more broadly. For purposes of cognitive modeling one can also constrain the evolutionary process in various ways. For example, one can restrict the set of functions and data structures out of which programs are constructed to a set that has been deemed cognitively plausible. The overall architecture of evolved programs can be similarly constrained.

One can measure the *computational effort* required to evolve systems under different conditions (e.g., when the systems are architecturally constrained in various ways). By use of such measurements one can assess the *evolvability* of cognitive systems of various sorts given the specified conditions. Because all natural cognitive systems presumably

arose through evolutionary processes, this information may be used as evidence for or against hypotheses about cognitive mechanisms in natural systems.

This study examines the effect that *culture* has on the evolvability of cognitive systems. We define "culture" as any information transmitted between individuals and between generations by non-genetic means.[1] Related notions of culture have been explored in other evolutionary computation paradigms (Bankes, 1995; Reynolds, 1994; Hutchins and Hazlehurst, 1993). In this paper experiments are presented in which genetic programming systems evolve programs that perform cognitive tasks (mathematical function mapping and action selection). Special mechanisms are added to support cultural transmission of information, and the resulting impacts on evolvability are observed. The data show that the presence of culture-supporting mechanisms can have a clear beneficial impact on the evolvability of correct programs.

From an engineering perspective, the results show that the efficiency of genetic programming can be improved through the addition of culture-supporting mechanisms; since the mechanisms are also simple and easy to add, practitioners of evolutionary computation should consider their use for other problems. From a cognitive science perspective, the results may shed some light on the relations between evolution and culture more broadly, and they may also suggest new uses of evolutionary computation in cognitive modeling.

The next section describes the experimental method used in this study, with subsections on genetic programming, the measurement of computational effort, indexed memory (the mechanism on which the implementation of culture is based), culture, and two test problems: symbolic regression of $y = x^4 + x^3 + x^2 + x$ and action selection in Wumpus world. Results are then presented in the form of computational effort measurements, and the meaning and generality of the results are discussed.

Method

Genetic Programming

Genetic programming is a technique for the automatic generation of computer programs by means of natural selection (Koza, 1992). The genetic programming process starts by creating a large initial population of programs that are random combinations of elements from problem-specific function and terminal sets. Each program in the initial population is then assessed for fitness, and the fitness values are used in produc-

---

[1] Bonner (1980) provides a similar definition.

ing the next generation of programs by means of a variety of genetic operations including reproduction, crossover, and mutation. After a preestablished number of generations, or after the fitness improves to some preestablished level, the best-of-run individual is designated as the result and is produced as the output from the genetic programming system. Details of program representation and algorithms for all genetic operators, along with full source code for genetic programming systems, can be found in (Koza, 1992) and (Koza, 1994).

Computational Effort

Koza has developed a technique for measuring the computational effort required to solve a problem with genetic programming (Koza, 1994). Because the genetic programming algorithm includes random choices at several steps, data is collected from a large number of independent runs. One first calculates $P(M,i)$, the cumulative probability of success by generation i using a population of size M. For each generation i this is simply the total number of runs that succeeded on or before the ith generation, divided by the total number of runs conducted. One then calculates $I(M,i,z)$, the number of individuals that must be processed to produce a solution by generation i with probability greater than z (where z is usually 99%). $I(M,i,z)$ is calculated using the formula:

$$I(M, i, z) = M * (i + 1) * \left\lceil \frac{\log(1 - z)}{\log(1 - P(M, i))} \right\rceil$$

The minimum of $I(M,i,z)$ over the range of i is defined as the "computational effort" required to solve the problem with the given system (Koza, 1994).

Indexed Memory

Indexed memory is a mechanism that allows programs developed by genetic programming to make use of runtime memory (Teller, 1994). The mechanism consists of a linear array of memory locations and two functions, READ and WRITE, that are added to the set of functions from which programs are created. The memory is initialized at the start of each program execution. READ takes a single argument and returns the contents of the memory location indexed by that argument. WRITE takes two arguments, a memory index and a data item, and stores the data item in the memory at the specified index. WRITE returns the *previous* value of the specified memory location. Teller (1994) showed that indexed memory can help to evolve correct programs for certain problems, and that the combination of indexed memory and iteration allows genetic programming to produce any Turing-computable function. Others have further examined the utility of indexed memory; for example, Andre (1995) has experimented with problems that *require* the use of memory, and has explored the ways in which evolved programs use indexed memory in solving these problems.

Culture

"Culture" can be implemented by modifying Teller's indexed memory mechanism to cause all individuals to share the same memory. The memory should be initialized only at the start of a genetic programming run. Subsequent changes to the memory by any individual will persist and be available to other individuals. This makes it possible for a program to pass information to itself (in later executions in the run), to its contemporaries, to its offspring, and to unrelated members of future generations. The order in which the population is evaluated for fitness can clearly have an effect; the evaluation order within each generation can be randomized to prevent systematic exploitation of this effect.

A culture is the collective product of all individuals throughout evolutionary time. This means that any "good idea" developed by any individual may be preserved for use by all other individuals. Unfortunately, it also means that a single destructive individual can erase a great deal of valuable information. For most of the problems studied so far, the positives outweigh the negatives—the availability of a culture speeds evolution.

A program evolved with culture will generally function correctly only when run in an appropriate cultural context. The cultural context within which a program was evolved is therefore an intrinsic part of the program, and the genetic programming system should report the appropriate cultural context (initial cultural memory state) along with the best-of-run program.

Test Problems

Symbolic Regression   The goal of the symbolic regression problem, as described by Koza (1992), is to produce a function, in symbolic form, that fits a provided set of data points. For each element of a set of (x, y) points, the function should map the x value onto the appropriate y value. This is the sort of problem faced by a scientist who has obtained a set of experimental data points and suspects that a simple formula will suffice to explain the data. The scientist may further suspect that such a formula can be constructed from a particular set of arithmetic and trigonometric operators. In searching for the correct formula the scientist is attempting to solve a symbolic regression problem. Once the correct formula is found the scientist may use it to map new x values onto their y values.

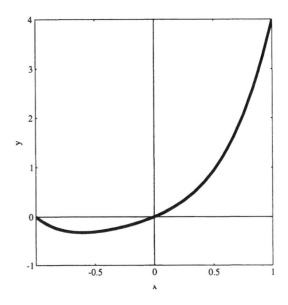

Figure 1: The target function for the symbolic regression problem: $y = x^4 + x^3 + x^2 + x$.

For the described experiments data points were obtained from the equation $y = x^4 + x^3 + x^2 + x$ (see Figure 1), which is a standard example from the literature (Koza, 1992). One can view the task of the genetic programming system as that of "rediscovering" or inducing this formula from the data points used as fitness cases. 20 fitness cases were used for the data presented here, with randomly selected x values between -1 and 1. A program was considered to be successful if it returned a value within 0.01 of the target y value for all 20 cases.

The functions that could be used in evolved programs were the 2-argument addition function +, the 2-argument subtraction function -, the 2-argument multiplication function *, the 2-argument protected division function %, two 1-argument trigonometric functions SIN and COS, the 1-argument exponential function EXP, and the 1-argument protected logarithm function RLOG (as in (Koza, 1992)). Programs could also refer to the independent variable X, and to "ephemeral random constants" between -1 and 1 (also as in (Koza, 1992)). Tournament selection was used (tournament size = 5), along with a 90% crossover rate, a 10% reproduction rate, no mutation, a population size of 1000, and a maximum of 51 generations per run. Detailed descriptions of the meanings of these parameters can be found in (Koza, 1992); it suffices here to note that these values are reasonably standard.

For the runs with indexed-memory and for those with culture a 100-element memory array was added, along with READ and WRITE functions that behave as described above. The "index" arguments of these functions were coerced to the proper range ([0–99]) by multiplying them by 100 and by then taking them modulo 100.

Wumpus World Wumpus world (Russell and Norvig, 1995) is a problem environment within which an agent must select actions to navigate within a dangerous world to achieve goals. The use of genetic programming for the evolution of Wumpus world agents has been described elsewhere (Spector, 1996). This section describes the problem informally; see (Spector, 1996) for a detailed description of the Wumpus world simulator, the function set, and other parameters.

Wumpus world is cave represented as a grid of squares surrounded by walls. A 6-by-6 grid was used for the experiments described here.[2] The agent's task is to start in a particular square, to move through the world to find and to pick up the piece of gold, to return to the start square, and to climb out of the cave. The cave is also inhabited by a "wumpus" — a beast that will eat anyone who enters its square. The wumpus produces a stench that can be perceived by the agent from adjacent (but not diagonal) squares. The agent has a single arrow that can be used to kill the wumpus. When hit by the arrow the wumpus screams; this can be heard anywhere in the cave. The wumpus still produces a stench when dead, but it is harmless. The cave also contains bottomless pits that will trap unwary agents. Pits produce breezes that can be felt in adjacent (but not diagonal) squares. The agent perceives

---

[2] Although the experiments described in (Spector, 1996) also used a 6-by-6 grid, the world's "walls" occupied space in the simulator used for those experiments. The actual playing area for those experiments was therefore 4x4, and the results are therefore not directly comparable to those described here.

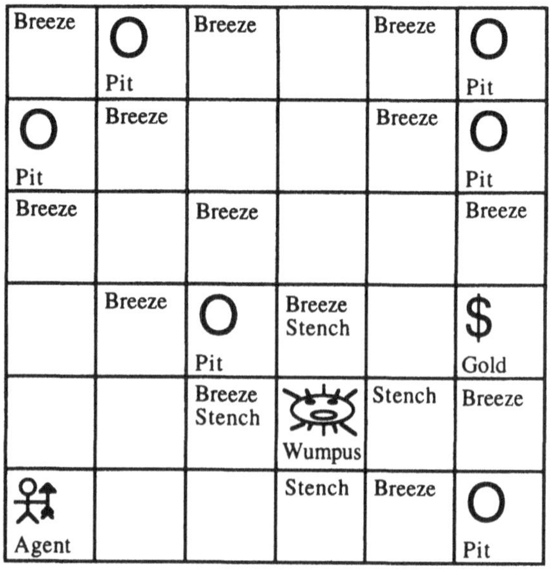

Figure 2: An instance of a 6-by-6 Wumpus world.

a bump when it walks into a wall, and a glitter when it is in the same square as the gold. Figure 2 shows an instance of a 6-by-6 Wumpus world.

The wumpus world agent can perform only the following actions in the world: go forward one square; turn left 90°; turn right 90°; grab an object (e.g., the gold) if it is in the same square as the agent; release a grabbed object; shoot the arrow in the direction in which the agent is facing; climb out of the cave if the agent is in the start square.

The agent's program is invoked to select a single action for each time-step of the simulation. The program returns one of the valid actions and the simulator then causes that action, and any secondary effects, to happen in the world. The agent can maintain information between actions by use of a persistent memory system. The agent's program has a single parameter, a "percept" that encodes all of the sensory information available to the agent. The agent's program can refer to the components of the percept arbitrarily many times during its execution.

Agents are assessed on the basis of performance in four randomly generated worlds (new worlds are generated for each assessment). In each world the agent is allowed to perform a maximum of 50 actions, and the agent's score is determined as follows: 100 points are awarded for obtaining the gold, there is a 1-point penalty for each action taken, and there is a 100-point penalty for each unit of distance between the agent and the gold at the end of the run.[3] "Standardized fitness" values (for which lower values are better (Koza, 1992)) are the average of the scores from the four random worlds, subtracted from 100. Agents are not explicitly rewarded for climbing out of the cave, although less action penalties are accumulated if an agent climbs out and thereby ends the simulation. An agent

---

[3] In the experiments described in (Spector, 1996) agents were also charged an explicit 100-point penalty for dying. In the version used here the only penalty for death is implicit—after one dies one can no longer get closer to the gold or pick it up.

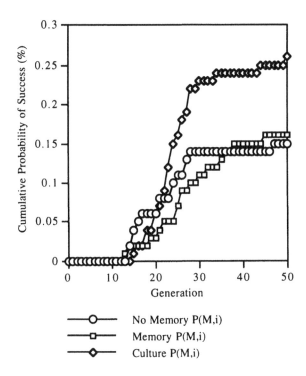

Figure 3: $P(M,i)$ for the symbolic regression problem.

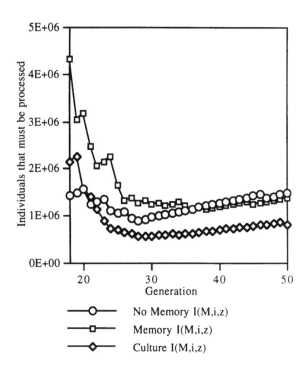

Figure 4: $I(M,i,z)$ for the symbolic regression problem.

is considered to have solved the problem if its average score in four random worlds is greater than zero. To have obtained such a score an agent must have grabbed the gold in at least one and usually two or more of the four random worlds. This is difficult; in many cases it is necessary to risk death in order to navigate to the gold, and in some cases the gold may be unobtainable because it is in a pit or in a square surrounded by pits.

For the experiments described here, a C-language re-implementation of Russell and Norvig's wumpus world simulator was used for fitness evaluation. The world size was 6-by-6, the population size was 1,000 and the maximum number of generations per run was 21. Tournament selection was used with a tournament size of 7.

Results

Symbolic Regression

100 runs were performed with no memory, 100 with indexed memory, and 100 with culture. Figure 3 shows a graph of $P(M,i)$, the cumulative probability of success by generation. Note that the highest probability was obtained in the runs that had access to culture. Figure 4 shows $I(M,i,z)$, the number of individuals that must be processed to produce a solution with probability greater than z=99%. Note that the lowest number of individuals was obtained using culture. $I(M,i,z)$ values are always very high in early generations; early generations are therefore not shown in graphs of $I(M,i,z)$ so that the detail in the later generations can be seen. The computational effort results (the minima of the $I(M,i,z)$ graphs) are summarized in Table 1.

Wumpus World

400 runs were performed with no memory, 509 with ordinary indexed memory, and 800 with culture.[4] Figure 5 shows a graph of $P(M,i)$, the cumulative probability of success by generation. Note that the highest probability was obtained in the runs that had access to culture. Figure 6 shows $I(M,i,z)$, the number of individuals that must be processed to produce a solution with probability greater than z=99%. Note that the lowest number of individuals was obtained using culture. The computational effort results are summarized in Table 2.

Discussion

Conclusions from Computational Effort Results

The symbolic regression results show that the addition of an ordinary indexed memory *increases* the computational effort required to solve the problem. This may be because there are many programs that compute the desired function ($y = x^4 + x^3 + x^2 + x$) without using memory. In addition, the functions READ and WRITE may act as noise in the function set, contributing little to success while filling positions that could instead be filled with useful functions. Nevertheless, when the memory is shared between individuals as culture, the system is able to take advantage of this, and the computational effort is reduced to 61% of that required when no memory is available (49% of that required with ordinary indexed memory).

---

[4]Computational effort comparisons are indeed valid between sets of different numbers of runs. For these computationally expensive runs we started processes on several machines and stopped them when it was clear that we had obtained sufficient data; the exact numbers of runs are therefore arbitrary.

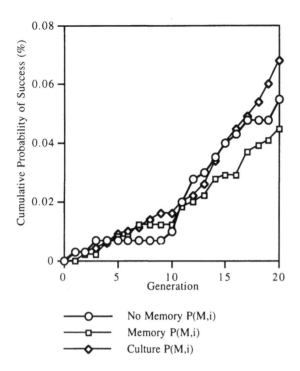

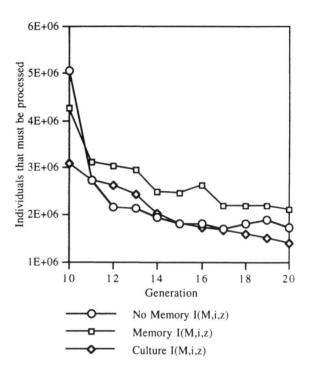

Figure 5: *P(M,i)* for the Wumpus world problem.

Figure 6: *I(M,i,z)* for the Wumpus world problem.

Condition	Computational Effort
No memory	899,000
Memory	1,131,000
Culture	551,000

Table 1: Computational efforts for symbolic regression.

Condition	Computational Effort
No memory	1,710,000
Memory	2,100,000
Culture	1,386,000

Table 2: Computational efforts for Wumpus world.

The Wumpus world results exhibit the same pattern, although the results are noisier and the interpretation is therefore less clear. When culture is used the computational effort required to produce a successful Wumpus world agent is reduced to 81% of that required when no memory is available (66% of that required when ordinary indexed memory is used). Surprisingly, indexed memory once again increases computational effort over the "no memory" condition. It appears that the reactive strategies are at least as useful as knowledge-based strategies for this domain.

The results show that culture-supporting mechanisms may be quite useful within some cognitive system architectures. Their utility is demonstrated by their impact on the computational effort required for evolution; less effort is required to produce successful cognitive systems when the culture-supporting mechanisms are present than is required when they are not. In summary, culture enhances the evolvability of cognition, at least for the tasks and evolutionary mechanisms presented here.

Generality

While culture has been useful in most of the domains to which we have applied it, further work must be conducted to characterize the relationship between domain characteristics and the expected impact of the technique. For example, the Wumpus world environment can be varied in many ways, and the relative utility of memory and culture may differ in each of these variants. We are currently conducting experiments with several variants and it is clear from the preliminary results that culture is *not always* beneficial in Wumpus world. In particular, for a configuration similar to that of (Spector, 1996) it appears that ordinary indexed memory is best, followed by culture. Here we may gain insights from biological examples; not *all* animals use culture, and there are presumably many niches in which culture confers no adaptive advantage. On the other hand, culture appears to be extremely useful in certain situations (e.g., for humans). This suggests that we might expect correspondingly large impacts in certain genetic programming domains.

Although the evolution-enhancing effects of culture were demonstrated only for genetic programming systems, there are reasons to believe that the effects are more general. Bonner (1980) has described a number of ways in which culture can enhance adaptation and alter the course and speed of evolutionary processes. Several features of organisms and of their environments can contribute to the possible utility of culture, and there is no reason to believe that the genetic programming paradigm exploits these features any more effectively than might other evolutionary computation systems or natural biological evolution. The utility of culture is largely driven by the demands and resources of a task environment; if it contains important regularities that can be *taught* and *learned* then it may be advantageous for individuals to transmit such information behaviorally. One reason is that the encoding of the information in behavior (including "writing" and "teaching" behaviors) may be simpler than the encoding of the same information in the organism's genetic code. Another reason is that information can spread through a population much more quickly by behavioral means than it can by genetic means.

Future Work

From an engineering perspective, the present study suggests several directions for additional research. The generality of the observed effects should be further studied through applications to other problem environments. The combined use of ordinary indexed memory and culture should also be examined. Variations of the technique, for example to limit the destructive effects that unfit individuals can have on the culture, should also be explored. All of these studies may further enhance the utility that culture provides in the genetic programming of problem-solving systems.

From a cognitive science perspective, the present study suggests a new research paradigm that could be applied not only to the further study of interactions between evolution and culture, but also to the study of other aspects of cognition. Computational modeling has a long history in cognitive science, but modeling by means of evolutionary computation is relatively new. Within this framework models are automatically generated by evolutionary processes. One immediate benefit is that the development of models may thereby require comparatively little time and effort. The resulting models may in some cases be difficult to analyze, but several sorts of meaningful data may nonetheless be extracted. For example, the models may be run on new inputs, compared to hand-crafted models in various ways, or "lesioned" to assess their fault-tolerance and failure modes. Alternatively, as in the present study, meaningful data may be extracted from the evolutionary process, rather than from the resulting models. Evidence against a set of hypothesized cognitive mechanisms could be produced, for example, by showing that it is difficult or impossible to evolve the appropriate sorts of cognitive systems using the hypothesized mechanisms as primitives. Similar strategies could be employed to provide evidence for or against general cognitive architectures. Existing techniques can be used to measure the computational effort required to evolve systems under various conditions, and the comparisons can be made "fair" by using the same evolutionary mechanisms for each set of conditions. This contrasts to ordinary computational cognitive modeling, in which different models are often produced by different programming teams. In some of these cases it may not be clear which aspects of the performance of the resulting systems are due to the underlying theories, and which are due to the strengths and weaknesses of the programmers.

Acknowledgments

Some of the ideas in this paper were refined in discussions with Jordan Grafman and Daniel Kimberg. The authors also wish to thank the anonymous reviewers for helpful comments. This research was supported in part by grants from ONR (N00014-J-91-1451), AFOSR (F49620-93-1-0065), and ARPA contract DAST-95-C0037.

References

Andre, D. (1995). The Evolution of Agents that Build Mental Models and Create Simple Plans Using Genetic Programming. In *Proceedings of the Sixth International Conference on Genetic Algorithms* (pp. 248–255). San Francisco, CA: Morgan Kaufmann Publishers, Inc.

Bankes, S. (1995). Evolving Social Structure in Communities of Agents Through Meme Evolution. In *Proceedings of the Fourth Annual Conference on Evolutionary Programming*. Cambridge, MA: The MIT Press.

Bonner, J.T. (1980). *The Evolution of Culture in Animals.* Princeton, NJ: Princeton University Press.

Donald, M. (1991). *Origins of the Modern Mind: Three Stages in the Evolution of Culture and Cognition.* Cambridge, MA: Harvard University Press.

Hutchins, E. & Hazlehurst, B. (1993). Learning in the Cultural Process. In C.G. Langton, C. Taylor, J.D. Farmer, & S. Rasmussen (Eds.), *Artificial Life II.* Addison-Wesley Publishing Company.

Koza, J.R. (1992). *Genetic Programming: On the Programming of Computers by Means of Natural Selection.* Cambridge, MA: The MIT Press.

Koza, J.R. (1994). *Genetic Programming II: Automatic Discovery of Reusable Programs.* Cambridge, MA: The MIT Press.

Lumsden, C.J., & Wilson, E.O. (1981). *Genes, Mind, and Culture.* Cambridge, MA: Harvard University Press.

Quiatt, D. & Itani, J. (Eds.). (1994). *Hominid Culture in Primate Perspective.* Niwot, CO: University Press of Colorado.

Reynolds, R.G. (1994). An Introduction to Cultural Algorithms. In *Proceedings of the Third Annual Conference on Evolutionary Programming* (pp. 131–139). River Edge, NJ: World Scientific.

Russell, S.J., & Norvig, P. 1995. *Artificial Intelligence, A Modern Approach.* Englewood Cliffs, NJ: Prentice Hall.

Spector, L. (1994). Genetic Programming and AI Planning Systems. In *Proceedings of the Twelfth National Conference on Artificial Intelligence* (pp. 1329–1334). Cambridge, MA: MIT Press.

Spector, L. (1996). Simultaneous Evolution of Programs and their Control Structures. In P. Angeline & K. Kinnear (Eds.), *Advances in Genetic Programming 2.* Cambridge, MA: MIT Press. In press.

Teller, A. (1994). The Evolution of Mental Models. In K.E. Kinnear Jr. (Ed.), *Advances in Genetic Programming* (pp. 199–219). Cambridge, MA: The MIT Press.

Quantifier Interpretation and Syllogistic Reasoning:
an Individual Differences Account

Keith Stenning, Peter Yule and Richard Cox

Human Communication Research Centre
University of Edinburgh
2-6 Buccleuch Place
Edinburgh, U.K.

{keith,pgy,rcox}@cogsci.ed.ac.uk

Abstract

It is frequently assumed that interpretational errors can explain reasoning errors. However, the evidence for this position has heretofore been less than convincing. Newstead (1995) failed to show expected relations between Gricean implicatures (Grice, 1975) and reasoning errors, and different measures of illicit conversion (Begg & Denny, 1969; Chapman & Chapman, 1959) frequently fail to correlate in the expected fashion (Newstead, 1989; 1990). This paper examines the relation between interpretation and reasoning using the more configurational approach to classifying subjects' interpretation patterns, described in Stenning & Cox (1995). There it is shown that subjects' interpretational errors tend to fall into clusters of properties defined in terms of *rashness, hesitancy* and the subject/predicate structure of inferences. First we show that interpretations classified by illicit conversion errors, though correlated with fallacious reasoning, are equally correlated with errors which cannot be due to conversion of premises. Then we explore how the alternative method of subject profiling in terms of hesitancy, rashness and subject/predicate affects syllogistic reasoning performance, through analysis in terms of both general reasoning accuracy and the Figural Effect (Johnson-Laird & Bara, 1984). We show that subjects assessed as rash on the interpretation tasks show consistent characteristic error patterns on the syllogistic reasoning task, and that hesitancy, and possibly rashness, interact with the Figural Effect.

Introduction

How do subjects' explicitly articulated interpretations of the logical force of statements relate to their behaviour when reasoning with these statements? This question is of some theoretical importance for the psychology of reasoning, and cognition in general. The possibility of a link between interpretation and reasoning errors has been used by authors such as Henle (1962) to rationalise reasoning error. There are extensive literatures on interpretation and on reasoning, and it is of some practical and theoretical importance to have a consistent account of data which might naively be expected to be measuring the same structures and processes. But the question is also of practical importance for formal education. Teaching logic involves bringing implicit knowledge of native language and its pragmatics into the explicit focus of attention. Interpretation tasks can be viewed as demands

on the subject to explicitly externalise logical relations. Some reasoning tasks may be closer than others to engaging implicit modes of problem solving.

Newstead (1989; 1990; 1995) has extensively explored the commonest theories of the relation between interpretation and reasoning tasks. He investigates the theories of Illicit Conversion, of the logically unconvertible 'All' and 'Some... not' premiss types, and Gricean implicature (Grice, 1975), which predicts inference patterns based on the Maxim of Quantity. He asks whether these 'fallacious' inference patterns, both of which are evidenced in interpretation tasks, are also responsible for errors in syllogistic reasoning tasks, as has frequently been assumed. His general conclusions from analysis of existing data and new experiments are that the relation, between Illicit Conversion errors (1989; 1990) and Gricean errors (1995) in interpretation tasks, and the errors predicted by these theories in syllogistic reasoning tasks, is at best not substantiated and at worst non-existent. His explanation of the lack of the expected transparent relation is expressed in terms of Mental Models theory (Johnson-Laird, 1983), and is basically a depth of processing explanation. Syllogistic reasoning, a logically more complex task than the 'immediate inference' task used in interpretation studies, engages the subject in deeper processing, and when this happens the Gricean 'delusions' drop away.

Our purpose here is to try to arrive at a more positive account of the relation between interpretation and reasoning. We do this on the basis of a more general framework for understanding interpretation data, and for the separation of different individual differences in 'styles' of interpretation and reasoning. Stenning & Cox (1995) questioned the logical basis of the standard 'immediate inference' task used in Newstead (1989) and Newstead (1990). They showed that asking questions that allowed the subject to distinguish *logical independence* from the situation where either a proposition or its negation followed from a premiss, revealed several strong, generalised but distinct individual patterns of response. They distinguished *hesitant* reasoners who tended to respond that candidate conclusions were independent of premises, from *rash* reasoners who tended to respond either that the candidate conclusion followed, or that its negation followed. But most strikingly, they showed that it was the relation between the subject/predicate structure in premiss and candidate conclusion that most powerfully affected patterns of response—more powerfully, in fact, than quantifier identity. Thus they could distinguish a few groups of subjects on the basis of whether they were rash or hesitant on questions (where *Q1* and *Q2* are quantifiers and may or may not be the same, and *a* and *b* are the terms) of the form *Q1 ab. Does it follow that Q2 ab?* and the form *Q1 ab. Does it follow that Q2 ba?*. The former questions were called *in-place* and the latter *out-of-place* questions, since in the former, the terms occurred in the putative conclusion in the same order as in the premiss, whereas in the latter, the term order was reversed[1].

There are obvious *descriptive* advantages to looking at whole configurations of interpretation behaviour, and to classifying different kinds of subject by configurations of response. Gricean implicature and illicit conversion are generally diagnosed by looking at a small number of responses which leave out the vast majority of the interpretation data. It is also clear from syllogistic reasoning data that more than one kind of subject should be distinguished by qualitatively different reasoning patterns (Ford, 1994; Polk & Newell, 1988). But the approach also offers *theoretical* advantages. The psychological literature on interpretation and reasoning has overwhelmingly focused on errors of *commission*—patterns of inference invalid by the standard of logic. But a configurational approach to interpretation emphasises that there are also errors of *omission*—failures to make inferences which are logically valid—and that there are direct relations between commission on one question and omission on another.

For example, take the two candidate inference patterns *All A are B, so all B are A* and *Some A are B, so some B are A*. Acceptance of the former pattern is well known as 'illicit conversion' error, but failure to accept the latter, perfectly valid inference is unremarked in the psychological literature. But subjects who are generally hesitant toward out-of-place questions will get the first right and the second wrong, whereas subjects who are generally rash on out-of-place questions will get the first wrong and the second right. In Stenning & Cox's (1995) data, both of these patterns linking commission and omission were common, and were exhibited regardless of the quantifiers, though by different groups of subjects. In fact, what drives this interpretation data is attitudes to subject/predicate structuring (in-place vs. out-of-place) in the questioned inferences.

In this paper we seek to explore the relation between this configurational approach to interpretation data and syllogistic reasoning performance. We present a new set of data collected to relate interpretation data to reasoning data, in order to compare the effects of illicit conversion and rashness/hesitancy on reasoning performance. Illicit conversion errors are necessarily restricted to a subset of problems, so we can compare rates of invalid conclusions in conversion-susceptible and unsusceptible problems, for subjects assessed as converters or non-converters in the interpretation tasks.

The link between interpretation and reasoning accuracy is then explored in terms of the rashness/hesitancy configurations. We aim to demonstrate how groups of subjects identified on the basis of their interpretation configurations display different error patterns in the syllogistic reasoning task. Since rashness is here defined as the tendency to infer *more* than is logically valid, i.e. to gain information, rash reasoners should be more liable to produce invalid conclusions than non-rash reasoners; similarly, since hesitancy is the tendency to infer *less* than is logically valid, or to lose information, hesitant reasoners should be more likely to decide that there is No Valid Conclusion (NVC) than non-hesitant reasoners.

Recent work by Ford (1994) raises the possibility of investigating individual differences in relation not only to error tendencies, but also to response biases such as the Figural Effect (Johnson-Laird & Bara, 1984), a robust association linking subject/predicate structuring in premisses to that evidenced in subjects' conclusions. The typical finding is that problems in the ab/bc figure tend to give rise to ac conclusions, even when the converted form is also valid, whereas ba/cb problems tend to give rise to ca conclusions, and ab/cb and ba/bc show no overall bias. Stenning & Yule (1996) have emphasised the importance of problem semantics in the explanation of such effects, so we are interested in whether the Figural Effect might be sensitive to differences in premiss interpretation.

Method

Subjects

120 psychology undergraduates from Edinburgh University participated in the interpretation tasks during a Cognitive Psychology lecture. None had any previous training in logic. Subsequently, 40 of these, assessed as EC-converters (6), II-converters (16), both-converters (7) and non-converters (11) on the basis of their performance in the interpretation tasks, were paid £7.50 to participate in the syllogistic reasoning part of the experiment.

Materials and Procedure

Interpretation Tasks The interpretation tasks were the same as those described in Stenning & Cox (1995).

---

[1] We stress that this definition of rashness should not be taken to imply the possession of some general personality trait, not least because we can distinguish the in-place and out-of-place varieties.

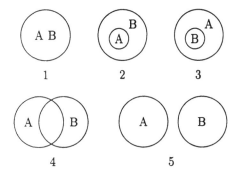

Figure 1: Euler Circle (EC) Task stimuli.

Two questionnaires were used, and their order of presentation was counterbalanced across subjects such that half received the graphical (EC) condition first and half received the sentential (II) condition first.

The Euler Circle (EC) or 'graphical' condition consisted of the five diagrams used by Newstead (1989), and was similar to the EC task presented in that paper (see Figure 1). Diagram 1 was the identity relation (circle 'A' and circle 'B' superimposed); diagram 2 showed a small circle 'A' inside a larger circle 'B'; diagram 3 showed a small circle 'B' inside a larger circle 'A'; diagram 4 showed circles 'A' and 'B' intersecting without either including the other and diagram 5 showed two non-overlapping, disjoint circles 'A' and 'B'. Below the diagrams the 4 premisses were listed in the order ALL, NO, SOME, SOME...NOT. Adjacent to each premiss were the numbers 1 to 5. Subjects were instructed to circle the number(s) of the diagram(s) of which the sentence was true.

The sentential condition was similar to the immediate inference (II) task described by Newstead (1989) with the exception that an additional response option ("Can't tell") was provided. As in Newstead (1989), the questionnaire consisted of four pages. At the top of each page one of the four standard quantified statements was displayed: All A's are B's; No A's are B's; Some A's are B's and Some A's are not B's. These were the premiss statements. Beneath the stimulus statements the four quantified statements were listed (All A's are B's etc.) and the converses of these (All B's are A's etc). These were the response statements. Alongside the eight response statements were response options 'T' (true), 'F' (false) and 'Can't tell'. The order of the four stimulus statement pages was randomised across subjects.

Subjects were instructed to assume the statement at the top of the page was true, and to indicate the truth, falsity or independence of each of the response statements by circling 'T', 'F' or 'can't tell' beside it.

In both EC and II tasks, subjects were instructed to interpret 'some' to mean 'at least one and possibly all'.

Subjects were allowed as much time as they needed to

complete the tasks (approximately 20 minutes).

Syllogistic Reasoning Task The stimulus materials for the syllogistic reasoning task were booklets containing each of the 64 distinct premiss pairs, in random order, one per page. The terms of the problems were 'A's', 'B's' and 'C's', where the end terms, 'A's' and 'C's', appeared in the first and second premisses respectively, and the middle term 'B's' appeared in both premisses. Subjects were instructed to assume the premisses were true, and to determine whether there was any statement, relating the end terms A and C using one of the quantifiers ALL, NONE, SOME and SOME...NOT, which must then be true. If so, they were instructed to write it in the space on the page below the premisses, and otherwise to write 'No valid conclusion'.

Subjects were instructed to assume that some A's, B's and C's existed, and to interpret 'some' to mean 'at least one and possibly all'

Subjects were allowed as much time as they needed to complete the tasks.

Results

Illicit conversion and inference

One way to evaluate claims about illicit conversion in syllogistic reasoning is to divide problems into two groups: those which, all else being equal, are susceptible to conversion errors in the sense that extra conclusions follow if illicit conversion is used, and those which are not. We would expect, on the basis of the illicit conversion hypothesis, that subjects assessed as converters on the interpretation tasks, would produce disproportionately high rates of invalid conclusions on conversion-susceptible problems compared to non-converters. All else being equal, there should be no such differences for conversion-unsusceptible problems. So we expect interactions between problem type and conversion group. Overall differences in invalid conclusion rates between problem types are not of interest, since they have different numbers of problems with and without valid conclusions. Table 1 shows the mean percentages of invalid conclusions to problems which are susceptible to illicit conversion errors, and to those which are not, for each of the four conversion-groups of subjects.

To test these predictions, a mixed-model ANOVA was conducted, using percentage invalid conclusions as the dependent variable, and the independent variables problem type (within-subjects - conversion-susceptible and unsusceptible problems), EC-conversion and II-conversion (both between subjects - converters and non-converters). Both EC-conversion ($F(1, 36) = 9.50$, $p < 0.004$) and II-conversion ($F(1, 36) = 6.14$, $p < 0.02$) significantly affected overall percentages of invalid conclusions. Also, there was a significant difference between unsusceptible and susceptible problem types ($F(1, 36) = 26.25$, $p < 0.0001$), but this does not concern us here.

Problem type	Conversion group			
	Neither	EC	II	Both
Unsusceptible	27.64	51.00	45.94	61.86
Susceptible	42.73	71.33	70.94	77.14
N Ss	11	6	16	7

Table 1: Mean percentages of incorrect conclusions to conversion-susceptible (N=20 problems) and conversion-unsusceptible problems (N=44 problems), for each conversion group.

Notably, there were *no* significant interactions: problem type × EC-conversion ($F(1, 36) = 0.03$, *n.s.*); problem type × II-conversion ($F(1, 36) = 0.04$, *n.s.*); problem type × II-conversion × EC-conversion ($F(1, 36) = 1.25$, *n.s.*).

Therefore, there is no evidence that subjects who illicitly convert premises in the interpretation task make any more illicit conversion errors in the reasoning task, contrary to hypothesis. However, both EC-converters and II-converters produce more invalid conclusions *overall* in the reasoning task.

Subject Profiles

Assignment of subjects to profile groups was conducted in the same manner as reported in Stenning & Cox (1995), using the data from the Immediate Inference task. We label a tendency to respond 'can't tell', where T or F is correct, *hesitancy* (*h*) and a tendency to respond either T or F, where 'can't tell' is correct, *rashness* (*r*). These categories can be defined within Q AB questions and Q BA questions, giving a further subdivision into *in-place* (*i*) and *out-of-place* (*o*), where the conclusion sentence preserves or inverts subject-predicate order respectively. Loglinear modelling permitted cutoff points on each dimension to be iteratively adjusted until residuals were minimized. As in Stenning & Cox (1995), there were no subjects who were hesitant on in-place questions, so the three binary dimensions *ro* (rash out-of-place), *ho* (hesitant out-of-place) and *ri* (rash in-place) were sufficient to fit the data. The resulting assignment of subjects to rashness/hesitancy categories is displayed in Figure 2.

Subject profiles and inference

Reasoning accuracy Table 2 shows the effects of the three rashness/hesitancy variables *ro*, *ho* and *ri* on percentages of each of four response accuracy categories in the syllogistic reasoning task: correct (valid) conclusions, incorrect (invalid) conclusions, correct NVC responses and incorrect NVC responses. The results of unrelated t-tests for each comparison are also shown. For each of the rashness/hesitancy properties, we expect possession of the property to decrease the number of correct conclusions; the differences are all in the predicted direction, but significant for only the rash properties, *ri*

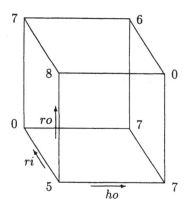

Figure 2: Frequencies of subjects classified as rash or hesitant on out-of-place questions, and rash on in-place questions

	N	Correct Conc.	Incorrect Conc.	Correct NVC	Incorrect NVC
ro−	19	25.08%	40.95%	26.89%	3.95%
ro+	21	20.46%	54.84%	19.05%	3.72%
t (38df)		2.069	-2.112	1.638	0.166
1-tail p		0.025	0.025	0.1	n.s.
ho−	20	23.83%	49.37%	22.19%	2.73%
ho+	20	21.48%	47.11%	23.36%	4.92%
t (38df)		1.009	0.327	-0.237	-1.654
1-tail p		n.s.	n.s.	n.s.	0.1
ri−	20	25.55%	38.98%	28.98%	3.20%
ri+	20	19.77%	57.50%	16.56%	4.45%
t (38df)		2.679	-2.960	2.749	-0.923
1-tail p		0.01	0.005	0.005	n.s.

Table 2: The effects of rashness/hesitancy on percentages of each of four response accuracy categories.

and *ro*. Rash reasoners should produce more conclusions and fewer NVC responses generally; the predicted differences for incorrect conclusions are both significant, but the NVC differences, while in the predicted direction, are mostly insignificant, except that *ri* does significantly reduce numbers of correct NVC conclusions. Hesitant reasoners, on the other hand, should produce fewer incorrect conclusions, and more NVC responses overall; however, although the differences are in the right directions, none of these effects reach significance at the $p < 0.05$ level.

The Figural Effect To a certain extent, the Figural Effect is confounded with the effects of validity, owing to overall differences, between figures, in numbers of valid conclusions with each possible term order. This problem can be overcome by including only *convertible conclusions* in the analysis, defining these as the set of

	N	ab/bc	ba/cb	ab/cb	ba/bc
		figure			
ri− *ho−*	11	82.40	30.39	50.62	56.88
ri− *ho+*	5	85.74	16.62	64.35	58.63
ri+ *ho−*	7	63.16	42.54	48.43	42.82
ri+ *ho+*	12	82.31	25.80	58.48	56.37
Mean		79.00	29.28	54.84	54.15

Table 3: Mean percentages of convertible ac conclusions in each figure, for each combination of levels of *ri* and *ho* (see also Figure 3.)

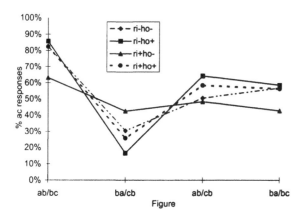

Figure 3: Chart showing effects of *ri* and *ho* on the Figural Effect (data as in Table 3.)

valid conclusions to problems whose strongest conclusions are validly convertible, plus the set of all invalid conclusions. Table 3 shows mean percentages of convertible conclusions with ac term order in each figure, for each combination of *ri* and *ho* (data from 5 subjects were omitted owing to missing values). The same data are plotted on Figure 3, which shows that the most extreme Figural Effect is displayed by *ri − ho+* subjects, whereas *ri + ho−* subjects display the least extreme Figural Effect. Subjects who are both (*ri + ho+*) or neither (*ri − ho−*) display intermediate Figural Effects, so the effects of *ri* and *ho* appear to be in opposition to one another.

A three-way mixed-model ANOVA was conducted to assess the effects, on percentage of convertible ac conclusions, of figure (repeated measures with levels ab/bc, ba/cb, ab/cb, ba/bc) and the between-groups variables *ho* and *ri* (with levels *ho+* and *ho−*, and *ri+* and *ri−* respectively.) Since the data departed from sphericity assumptions ($p < 0.004$), the more conservative Greenhouse-Geisser adjusted tail probabilities were used for the ANOVA. First of all, there were no effects, on overall percentage of ac conclusions, of *ri* ($F(1,31) = 0.37$, *n.s.*) or *ho* ($F(1,31) = 0.54$, *n.s.*),

nor was there an interaction between them ($F(1,31) = 0.25$, *n.s.*). There *was* a main effect of figure ($F(3,93) = 39.79$, *adjusted* $p < 0.0001$), and there was a significant figure × *ho* interaction ($F(3,93) = 4.03$, *adjusted* $p < 0.02$). The figure × *ri* interaction did not reach significance at the 0.05 level ($F(3,93) = 2.29$, *adjusted* $p > 0.10$), and there was no significant three-way interaction between the variables ($F(3,93) = 0.61$, *n.s.*).

Conclusions

Traditional approaches to the explanation of reasoning error by appeal to interpretation errors, based on specific 'fallacies', such as the theories of Gricean implicature (Grice, 1975) and Illicit Conversion (Begg & Denny, 1969; Chapman & Chapman, 1959), have had only limited success. Newstead's (1995) observations that Gricean implicatures are not strongly reflected in reasoning data are here generalised to illicit conversion. Tendency to illicitly convert in interpretation tasks is a general predictor of poor reasoning performance, but does not differentially predict illicit conversion errors during reasoning. This general failure of traditional approaches need not be taken to imply that the entire enterprise is misguided however. These theories are simply too specific, when what is required is a more general and *empirical* approach to the question of (mis)interpretation.

When Stenning & Cox's (1995) configurational approach to single-premiss interpretation is applied to reasoning data, more encouraging results emerge. Our preliminary analysis shows measures of syllogistic reasoning accuracy to be generally affected, in the predicted directions, by well-motivated properties based on the single-premiss interpretation data. In particular, 'rashness', as assessed on the basis of single-premiss interpretation, has a recognisable correlate in more complex reasoning performance, which can be simply summarised as a tendency to draw invalid conclusions.

The finding that the individual difference categories interact with the Figural Effect is also an interesting result. Almost all published experiments are analysed without regard for individual differences, and all show extremely robust Figural Effects (Johnson-Laird & Bara, 1984). However, our results identify a group of subjects (actually the ones who are rash both in-place and out-of-place, but not hesitant) who *fail* to show the effect at all. Hesitancy in exchanging subject and predicate, by contrast, results in a much strengthened Figural Effect. On a moment's reflection, these results are not very surprising—subjects who are unwilling to switch subject and predicate in premisses are 'locked in' to Figural conclusions by the superficial structure of syllogistic premiss pairs, whereas those who switch are not so constrained. Although proponents of Mental Models theory might claim that these results can be accommodated in their account of the Figural Effect, this could only be accomplished at the expense of their theory's explanatory power.

Recent semantic analysis of the syllogism by Stenning & Yule (1996) shows that the Figural Effect may usefully be considered as high-order invariant of a wide range of reasoning strategies. The Figural Effect's robustness, we argue, is not due to a unitary reasoning mechanism in the style of Mental Models, but rather to commonalities between numerous disparate implementations of reasoning which tend to share certain abstract characteristics. This type of account leaves room for individual differences in reasoning style, a topic which has been sadly neglected in the reasoning literature, despite the considerable intuitive plausibility of the idea and the increasing availability of empirical evidence for the existence of such cognitive differences.

References

Begg, I. & Denny, J.P. (1969). Empirical reconciliation of atmospheric and conversion interpretations of syllogistic reasoning errors. *Journal of Experimental Psychology, 81,* 351-354.

Chapman, L.J & Chapman, J.P. (1959). Atmosphere Effect Re-examined. *Journal of Experimental Psychology, 38,* 220-226.

Ford, M. (1994). Two modes of mental representation and problem solution in syllogistic reasoning. *Cognition, 54,* 1-71.

Grice, P. (1975). Logic and conversation. In P. Cole & J.L. Morgan (eds.) *Syntax and Semantics.* Vol. 3: *Speech Acts.* New York: Academic Press.

Henle, M. (1962). On the relation between logic and thinking. *Psychological Review, 4,* 366-378.

Johnson-Laird, P.N. (1983). *Mental Models.* Cambridge: Cambridge University Press.

Johnson-Laird, P.N. & Bara, B. (1984). Syllogistic Inference. *Cognition, 16,* 1-61.

Newstead, S.E. (1989). Interpretational errors in syllogistic reasoning. *Journal of Memory and Language, 28,* 78-91.

Newstead, S.E. (1990). Conversion in Syllogistic Reasoning. In K.J. Gilhooly, M.T.G. Keane, R.H. Logie & G. Erdos (Eds.) *Lines of Thinking: Reflections on the Psychology of Thought, Vol. 1* Wiley: Chichester.

Newstead, S.E. (1995). Gricean Implicatures and Syllogistic Reasoning. *Journal of Memory and Language, 34,* 644-664.

Polk, T.A. & Newell, A. (1988). Modelling human syllogistic reasoning in SOAR. In *Proceedings of the 10th Annual Conference of the Cognitive Science Society.* Hillsdale, New Jersey: Lawrence Erlbaum Associates.

Stenning, K. & Cox, R. (1995). Attitudes to logical independence: traits in quantifier interpretation. In *Proceedings of the 17th Annual Conference of the Cognitive Science Society.* Pittsburgh: Lawrence Erlbaum Associates.

Stenning, K. & Yule, P. (1996). Logic and Implementation in Human Reasoning: A Syllogistic Illustration. HCRC Research Paper RP-75, Human Communication Research Centre, University of Edinburgh. Also submitted to *Cognitive Psychology.*

Bottom-up Skill Learning in Reactive Sequential Decision Tasks

Ron Sun and **Todd Peterson** and **Edward Merrill**
The University of Alabama
Tuscaloosa, AL 35487
rsun@cs.ua.edu

Abstract

This paper introduces a hybrid model that unifies connectionist, symbolic, and reinforcement learning into an integrated architecture for bottom-up skill learning in reactive sequential decision tasks. The model is designed for an agent to learn continuously from on-going experience in the world, without the use of preconceived concepts and knowledge. Both procedural skills and high-level knowledge are acquired through an agent's experience interacting with the world. Computational experiments with the model in two domains are reported.

Introduction

Skill learning (or skill acquisition) is an important area of cognitive science, as skilled performance (and its acquisition) constitutes the majority of human activities. Such skills range from simple motor movements and routine coping in everyday activities all the way to complex intellectual skills such as writing or proving mathematical theorems. There is a hierarchy of skills of varying complexities and cognitive involvement. Most widely studied in cognitive science is cognitive skill acquisition (VanLehn 1995), that is, the abilities to solve problems in more or less intellectual tasks, such as (just to mention a few) arithmetic, elementary geometry, LISP programming, and simulated airtraffic control (e.g., Anderson 1982, 1993, VanLehn 1995, Ackerman 1988). Most of the work assumes a top-down approach; that is, they assume that subjects first acquire a great deal of knowledge in a domain and then practice changes this explicit knowledge into a more usable form, which leads to skilled performance. The explicit knowledge acquired before practice is declarative knowledge while the knowledge directly used in skilled performance is procedural knowledge. It is commonly believed that skills are the result of "proceduralization" of declarative knowledge.

However, there is a substantial literature of work that demonstrates that the opposite may also be true: subjects can learn skilled performance without being provided explicit knowledge prior to practice, such as Berry and Broadbent (1984), Stanley et al (1989), Willingham et al (1992), and Reber (1989). Among them, Berry and Broadbent (1984) and Stanley et al (1989) expressly demonstrate the *dissociation* between prior knowledge and skilled performance, in a variety of tasks. Explicit knowledge is not equivalent to but can arise out of skills.

Reactive sequential decision tasks (Sun and Peterson 1995) is a suitable domain for studying such *bottom-up* skill learning. They generally involve selecting and performing a sequence of actions, in order to accomplish an objective, mostly on the basis of moment-to-moment perceptual information. In such tasks, while skills emerge from repeated practice, declarative knowledge is also formed, on the basis of acquired skilled performance. So the process is the opposite of the commonly assumed top-down approach.

A general specification is as follows: there is an agent that can select, from a finite set of actions, a particular action to perform at each time step. The selection decision is (mainly) based on the current state of the world, presented to the agent through sensory input. The world changes either autonomously or as a result of some action by an agent. Thus, over time, the world is presented to an agent as a sequence of states. At certain points in a sequence, the agent may receive *payoffs* or *reinforcements*. Thus, the agent may need to perform temporal and structural *credit assignment*, to attribute the *payoffs/reinforcements* to various actions at various points in time (that is, the temporal credit assignment problem), in accordance to various aspects of a state (that is, the structural credit assignment problem).

While performing this kind of task, the agent is often under severe time pressure. Often a decision has to be made in a fraction of a second; therefore it cannot do much "information processing", and falls outside of Allen Newell's "rational band". The decision making and learning in the agent thus cannot be too time-consuming. As in humans, the agent may also be severely limited in other resources, such as memory so that memorizing all the previous episodes is considered impossible. The perceptual ability of an agent may also be extremely limited so that only very local information is available. Learning in such a domain is an experiential, trial-and-error process; the agent develops knowledge *tentatively* on an on-going basis, since it cannot wait until the end of an episode. Learning is thus *concurrent* or on-line (Nosofsky et al 1994).

Hybrid Models

In such tasks, with bottom-up learning and without prior knowledge, how can an agent develop a set of coping skills that are highly specific (geared towards particular situations) and thus highly efficient but, at the same time, acquire sufficiently general knowledge that can be readily applied to a variety of different situations? In the current context, one way to learn is through trial-and-error: repeated practice gradually gives rise to a set of procedural skills that deal specifically with the practiced situations and their minor variations. However, such skills may not be transferable to truly novel situations, since they are so embedded in specific contexts and tangled together. The agent needs both procedural and declarative knowledge, or both subconceptual and conceptual knowledge. It is assumed that a balance of the two is essential to the development of complex cognitive agents. Generic declarative knowledge, which can emerge from procedural skills, has the following three advantages: (1) It helps to guide the exploration of novel situations, and reduces the time (i.e., the number of trials) necessary to develop specific skills in new situations. In other words, it helps the transfer of learned skill (as shown through psychological data by Willingham et al 1989). (2) Generic knowledge can help to speed up learning. If properly used, generic knowledge that is extracted on-line during learning can help to facilitate the very learning process itself. (3) Generic knowledge can also help in communicating learned knowledge and skills to other agents.

A two-level hybrid models seem to provide the needed computational framework for representing both types of knowledge (Sun and Bookman 1994). Based on the ideas proposed in Sun (1994, 1995), we developed CLARION. See Figure 1. The bottom level contains specific procedural knowledge (Anderson 1982). The top level contains generic declarative knowledge. An overall pseudo-code algorithm is as follows:

1. Observe the current state x (in a proper representation).
2. Compute in the bottom level the Q-values of x associated with each of all the possible actions: $Q(x, a_1)$, $Q(x, a_2)$, ..., $Q(x, a_n)$.
3. Find out all the possible actions (b_1, b_2, ..., b_m) at the top level, based on the input x and the rules in place.
4. Compare the values of a_i's with those of b_j's, and choose an appropriate action b
5. Perform the action b, and observe the next state y and (possibly) the reinforcement r.
6. Update Q-values in accordance with the Q-learning algorithm
7. Update the rule network in the top level using the RULE-EXTRACTION-GENERALIZATION-REVISION.
8. Go back to Step 1.

In terms of representation in the bottom level, we prefer a subsymbolic distributed representation, such as that provided by a backpropagation network. (Existing evidence indicates that the difference between the two levels lies primarily in their representations; see Reber 1989.) This is because of the implicit nature of procedural skills: there is generally a lack of conceptual-level thinking in performing procedural skills; as a consequence, details of such skills are in general inaccessible (Anderson 1982, Ackerman 1988). A distributed representation naturally captures this property of procedural skills (Sun 1994), with representational units that are capable of accomplishing tasks but are in general uninterpretable and subsymbolic. (Otherwise, a symbolic representation may be used, but then we will have to artificially assume that these representations are not accessible, while some other similar representations are accessible — the distinction is arbitrary and not intrinsic to the media of representations; see Anderson 1993 and also Rosenbloom et al. 1993 regarding accessability of symbolic structures).

In terms of learning, we use reinforcement learning (the temporal difference method). A Q-value is an evaluation of the "quality" of an action in a given state: $Q(x, a)$ indicates how desirable action a is in state x (which consists of some sketchy sensory input). To acquire the Q-

values, we use *Q-learning* (Watkins 1989). In the algorithm, $Q(x, a)$ estimates the maximum discounted cumulative reinforcement that the agent will receive from the current state x on: $\max(\sum_{i=0}^{\infty} \gamma^i r_i)$, where γ is a discount factor that favors reinforcement received sooner relative to that received later, and r_i is the reinforcement received at step i (which may be 0). The updating of $Q(x, a)$ is based on minimizing $r + \gamma e(y) - Q(x, a)$, where γ is a discount factor and $e(y) = \max_a Q(y, a)$. Thus, the updating is based on the *temporal difference* in evaluating the current state and the action chosen. Using Q-learning allows sequential behavior to emerge in an agent. Through successive updates of the Q function, the agent can learn to take into account future steps in longer and longer sequences.

To combine Q-learning with connectionist representation, we use a four-layered network (see Figure 1) in which the first three layers form a backpropagation network for computing Q-values and the fourth layer (with only one node) performs stochastic decision making. The output of the third layer (i.e., the output layer of the backpropagation network) indicates the Q-value of each action (represented by an individual node), and the node in the fourth layer determines probabilistically the action to be performed based on a Boltzmann distribution (Watkins 1989): $p(a|x) = \frac{e^{1/\alpha Q(x, a)}}{\sum_i e^{1/\alpha Q(x, a_i)}}$, where α controls the degree of randomness (temperature) of the decision-making process. The training of the network is based on minimizing the temporal difference as specified before.

Declarative knowledge is handled differently. For declarative knowledge, we prefer a symbolic or localist representation, in which each unit has a clear conceptual meaning or interpretation. This allows declarative knowledge to be highly accessible and inferences to be performed explicitly at a conceptual level (Smolensky 1988, Sun 1994). Because declarative knowledge needed in reactive sequential decision tasks is relatively simple, we will focus on propositional rules. We use a localist connectionist model (see Figure 1) for representing these rules to facilitate correspondence with the bottom level and to encourage uniformity and integration. Basically, we connect the nodes representing conditions of a rule to the node representing the conclusion. However, we need to wire up rules involving conjunctive conditions. For details, see Sun (1992).

Because of the dynamic nature of reactive sequential decision tasks, we need to be able to dynamically acquire a rule representation and to modify it in subsequent encounters if necessary. We thus need a simple and efficient way. We can make use of the bottom level which is trained with reinforcement learning to perform specific procedural skills by extracting information from the network (Towell and Shavlik 1993) and thereby forming and modifying explicit rules. The basic idea for rule learning is as follows: if some action decided by the bottom level is successful the agent extracts a rule that corresponds to the action selected by the bottom level and adds the rule to the top level. Then, in subsequent interactions with the world, the agent tries to verify the extracted rule, by considering the outcome of applying the rule: if the outcome is not successful, then the rule should be made more specific and exclusive of the current case; if the outcome is successful, the agent may try to generalize the rule to make it

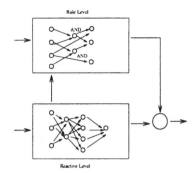

Figure 1: The CLARION Architecture

Figure 2: The initial maze
The starting position is marked by 'S' in which the agent faces
upward to the upper wall. The goal is marked by 'G'.

more universal (Mitchell 1982).

Specifically, three different criteria can be used for extracting rule from the bottom level: (1) direct reinforcement received at a step, (2) temporal difference (as used in updating Q-values), and (3) maximum Q-values in a state. The first criterion is an indication of whether or not an action taken in a given state is *directly* beneficial, but it fails to take into account sequences of actions. The second criterion indicates if further improvement in a Q-value is possible. The third criterion concerns whether the Q-value of a state and an action is close enough to the maximum Q-value in that state, indicating whether that action is close to being optimal in that state. (See Sun and Peterson 1995 for an analysis of these criteria.) We adopt a three-phase approach here, with three criteria being successively applied in different phases. At each step, after an action is selected and performed in a state, a new state is entered and reinforcement is received. Then, one of the three measures above that is applicable to the current phase is compared to a threshold to determine if a rule should be extracted. If so, a rule is formed that relates the state to the action, and the rule is then wired up in the top-level rule network.

After a rule is extracted, generalization and revision operations are used to tune the rule:

- *Expansion:* the value range of a condition is expanded by one interval, when a rule is successfully applied according to the criterion in the current phase.

- *Shrinking:* when a rule leads to unsuccessful results as judged by the criterion in the current phase, we reduce the value ranges of some or all conditions (cf. Michalski et al 1986).

- *Deletion:* remove a rule from the rule network when a counter example to the original case from which the rule was extracted is encountered, according to the current-phase criterion

- *Merge:* when the conditions of two rules are close enough, the two rules may be combined so that a more general rule can be produced.

The necessity of having a two-level architecture can be summed up as follows: (1) Without the bottom level, the agent will not be able to represent procedural skills sufficiently. Such skills may involve graded, uncertain, and inconsistent knowledge and autonomous stochastic exploration (with numeric calculation and probabilistic firing). (2) Without learning in the bottom level, the agent will not be able to learn from experience, and therefore will not be able to dynamically acquire either procedural skill in the bottom level,

or rules in the top level (as in the current model). The bottom level also captures the gradual learning of skills, different from one-shot rule learning. (3) Without the top level, the agent will not be able to represent generic, easily accessible, and crisp knowledge and explicitly access and communicate that knowledge to other agents. When novel situations are encountered and/or when precision, crispness, consistency, and certainty are needed, declarative knowledge is preferred. Explicit access and explanation is also important in facilitating cooperation among agents. (4) Without rule learning, the agent will not be able to acquire *dynamically* and quickly crisp conceptual knowledge for the top level, and therefore has to resort to mostly pre-wired and/or externally given knowledge in the top level.

We try two different methods of combining outcomes from the two levels. One is the percentage method, and the other is the stochastic method. In the percentage method, in (randomly chosen) p percent of the steps, we use the outcome from the rule level, if there is at least one rule indicating an action in the current state; otherwise, we use the outcome of the bottom level (which is always available). In the stochastic method, we combine the corresponding values for each action from the two levels by a weighted sum; that is, if the top level indicates that action a has an activation value v and the bottom level indicates that a has a value q (the Q-value for a), then the weighted sum is $w_1 * v + w_2 * q$. Based on these weighted sums, stochastic decision making (with Boltzmann distribution) is then performed to select an action. The parameters, w_1, w_2, and p, are to be varied.

Experiments

Experiments with Mazes

We carried out some computational experiments in reactive sequential decision domains to show the advantage of the model in learning and transfer as hypothesized earlier. In a simple maze as in Figure 2, the agent has rudimentary sensory inputs regarding its immediate left, front and right side, indicating whether there is a wall, an opening, or the goal; the agent can move forward, turn to the left, or turn to the right. It has no information regarding its location except the simple sensory input described above. Each episode starts with an agent at a fixed starting location and ends when the agent reaches the goal (Figure 2). The reward for an agent reaching the goal is 1, and the punishment for hitting a wall is -0.1.

We first choose (optimize) the structures and parameters of backpropagation and Q-learning through trial-and-error: 8 hidden units are used, the learning rate is 0.1, the momentum parameter is 0.7, network weights are randomly initialized between -0.01 and 0.01; the Q-value discount rate is 0.9, the

	Moves	Rules
Q-learning	15348.48	n/a
Perc.60	4994.52	7.78
Perc.80	5840.14	7.28
Perc.60.gen	5164.36	8.50
Perc.80.gen	5040.84	9.12
Stoc.15.	4602.88	6.62
Stoc.20	4712.70	6.30
Stoc.15.gen	6539.04	6.82
Stoc.20.gen	5574.24	8.14

Figure 3: A Comparison of Learning Speeds

Moves indicate the total numbers of moves during training (averaged over 50 trials). *Rules* indicate the average numbers of rules at the end of training.

		Moves	Q-Moves	R-Moves
Maze 1	Q-learning	149.00	149.00	n/a
	Perc.60	29.76	72.46	94.98
	Perc.80	10.78	36.22	13.48
	Perc.60.gen	42.06	118.24	189.18
	Perc.80.gen	22.02	55.14	106.58
	Stoc.15	28.42	102.70	44.74
	Stoc.20	20.60	81.80	30.54
	Stoc.15.gen	53.90	87.18	108.20
	Stoc.20.gen	36.26	67.18	64.66

Figure 4: Trained Performance

Figure 5: The second maze

randomness parameter for stochastic decision making is set at 0.1. (Note that although these parameters make some differences, performance is not overly sensitive to small variations of their settings.) The lengths of phase 1, 2 and 3 are 3, 20, and 37 episodes, respectively.

Figure 3 shows the differences in learning speed, where learning speed is measured by the total number of moves in the first 60 episodes. *Perc.x* refers to the versions using the percentage combination with rules being applied $p = x\%$ of the times. *Stoc.y* refers to the versions using the stochastic combination with rules being weighted at $y\%$. The symbol *gen* indicates that generalization/revision operations (i.e., *expansion, shrinking*, etc.) on the extracted rules are performed; otherwise, none of these operations is performed. We recorded the results averaged over 50 trials with different random seeds. It is clear from the figure that, when rules are used frequently (e.g., with Perc.80 or Stoc.20), CLARION learns faster than pure Q-learning by large margins. A t test showed the differences were significant with over 99% confidence ($p < 0.01$). The data also indicates that generalization per se did not lead to faster learning.

In Figure 4, we show the average number (averaged over 50 trials) of steps needed to reach the target in one episode, after 60 episodes of training, for different models. The numbers are shown in the *Moves* column. The different versions of CLARION again outperform pure Q-learning by large margins. T tests showed over 99% confidence ($p < 0.01$). Also reported are the average numbers of steps in one episode, after the training, using only the top level (marked as *R-moves*) or using only the bottom level (marked as *Q-moves*). There is a *synergy* between the two levels: Comparing the three values horizontally on each line, the whole CLARION system always performs better than the top level alone or the bottom level alone.

We applied our trained models (after the training of 60 episodes) to a new and larger maze as shown in Figure 5 to access transfer. Transfer occurs because of the similarity of the two mazes. In Figure 6, as indicated by the *Moves* column, the different versions of CLARION transfer much better than Q-learning alone in terms of number of steps to reach the goal in one episode. Furthermore, by comparing the corresponding *Moves*, *Q-moves*, and *R-moves* on each line, we see that often learned rules alone perform better in transfer than the Q-learning network at the bottom level, as well as than the whole CLARION model. The superiority of R-moves

in comparison with Q-moves demonstrates that it is rule induction that facilitates transfer to new and more complicated environments.

We also applied the trained model to an even larger maze as in Figure 7. The result is similar and the same points can be made in this case.

Experiments with Navigation

To further demonstrate CLARION, we tested it on a more complex task: the simulated navigation task. The agent has to navigate an underwater vessel to go through a minefield to reach a target location. The agent receives information only from a number of instruments. The sonar gauge shows how close the mines are in 7 equal areas that range from 45 degrees to the left of the agent to 45 degrees to the right. The fuel gauge shows the agent how much time is left before fuel runs out. The bearing gauge shows the direction of the target from the present direction of the agent. The range gauge shows how far the target is from the current location. Using such limited information, the agent decides on (1) how to turn and (2) how fast to move. The agent, within an allotted time period, can either (a) reach the target (which is a success), (b) hit a mine (a failure), or (c) run out of fuel (a failure again).

		Moves	Q-Moves	R-Moves
Maze 2	Q-learning	1681.48	1681.48	n/a
	Perc.60	770.72	1782.16	559.96
	Perc.80	492.14	1289.78	233.56
	Perc.60.gen	766.38	2049.40	1030.66
	Perc.80.gen	415.52	1581.62	722.48
	Stoc.15	850.70	1481.34	405.94
	Stoc.20	498.40	1586.88	392.08
	Stoc.15.gen	703.80	1690.32	981.94
	Stoc.20.gen	760.70	2028.24	956.50

Figure 6: Transfer to Maze 2

Figure 7: The third maze

	Successful Episodes
Q-learning	38.1
Stoc.10	278.9
Stoc.20	301.5
Stoc.10.gen	301.3
Stoc.20.gen	254.2

Figure 8: Learning

The number of successful episodes during training is included for each case.

In this experiment, each time the minefield is generated anew in a random layout, but it always contains the same number of mines, which in this case is 10. The time alloted to the agent for each episode is 200 steps. Figure 8 shows learning differences, where learning is measured by the total number of successful episodes out of a total 500 training episodes. CLARION again outperforms Q-learning alone.

Discussions

Most of the existing cognitively-motivated models for skill learning that contain both declarative and procedural knowledge explore mainly top-down learning, such as Anderson (1982, 1993), Gelfand et al (1989), and Schneider and Oliver (1991). CLARION explores bottom-up learning, to demonstrate how conceptual/symbolic knowledge can emerge through interacting with the world in the same way as subconceptual procedural knowledge does, and the performance advantage of such emergence.

In addition, while some other hybrid connectionist models try to implement all types of knowledge, symbolic and nonsymbolic, in one kind of network or another (Miikkulainen and Dyer 1991, Barnden 1988, Sun 1992), CLARION takes a different tack and attempts to develop a principled dichotomy of the conceptual vs. the subconceptual in hybrid architectures. CLARION attempts to explore their synergy so that it learns faster and transfers better.

Some existing hybrid models do not, or cannot, perform learning (Sun 1992), while others perform learning in a batch fashion (e.g., Miikkulainen and Dyer 1991) and are thus cognitively implausible in this aspect. In contrast to these hybrid models, CLARION is capable of incremental, on-line (concur-

rent) learning, and *integrative* learning, that is, developing connectionist and symbolic representation along side of each other.

Acknowledgements

This work is supported in part by Office of Naval Research grant N00014-95-1-0440. We wish to thank Susan Chipman, Helen Gigley, Dave Waltz, Devika Subramanian, Diana Gordon, Jim Ballas and Alan Schultz for various helps.

References

P. Ackerman, (1988). Determinants of individual differences during skill acquisition: cognitive abilities and information processing. *Journal of Experimental Psychology: General.* 1117 (3), 288-318.

J. Anderson, (1982). Acquisition of cognitive skill. *Psychological Review.* Vol.89, pp.369-406.

J. Anderson, (1993). *Rules of the Mind.* Lawrence Erlbaum Associates. Hillsdale, NJ.

J. Barnden, (1988). The right of free association. *Proc.10th Conference of Cognitive Science Society*, 503-509, Lawrence Erlbaum Associates, Hillsdale, NJ.

D. Berry and D. Broadbent, (1984). On the relationship between task performance and associated verbalizable knowledge. *Quarterly Journal of Experimental Psychology.* 36A, 209-231.

J. Gelfand, D. Handelman and S. Lane, (1989). Integrating Knowledge-based Systems and Neural Networks for Robotic Skill Acquisition, *Proc.IJCAI*, pp.193-198. Morgan Kaufmann, San Mateo, CA.

J. Kruschke, (1992). ALCOVE: an examples-based connectionist model of category learning. *Psychological Review.* 99, 22-44.

R. Maclin and J. Shavlik, (1994). Incorporating advice into agents that learn from reinforcements. *Proc.of AAAI-94.* Morgan Kaufmann, San Meteo, CA.

R. Michalski et al., (1986). The multi-purpose incremental learning system AQ15. *Proc.of AAAI-86.* 1041-1045. Morgan Kaufmann. San Mateo, CA.

R. Miikkulainen & M. Dyer, (1991). Natural language processing with modular PDP networks and distributed lexicons. *Cognitive Science.* 15(3). pp.343-399.

T. Mitchell, (1982). Generalization as search. *Artificial Intelligence*, 18, 203-226.

R. Nosofsky, T. Palmeri, and S. McKinley, (1994). Rule-plus-exception model of classification learning. *Psychological Review.* 101 (1), 53-79.

A. Reber, (1989). Implicit learning and tacit knowledge. *Journal of Experimental Psychology: General.* 118 (3), 219-235.

P. Rosenbloom, J. Laird, and A. Newell, (1993). *The SOAR papers.* MIT Press.

W. Schneider and W. Oliver (1991), An instructable connectionist/control architecture. In: K. VanLehn (ed.), *Architectures for Intelligence*, Erlbaum, Hillsdale, NJ.

R. Shriffrin and W. Schneider, (1977). Controlled and automatic human information processing II. *Psychological Review.* 84. 127-190.

P. Smolensky, (1988). On the proper treatment of connectionism. *Behavioral and Brain Sciences*, 11(1):1–74.

W. Stanley, et al, (1989). Insight without awareness. *Quarterly Journal of Experimental Psychology*. 41A (3), 553-577.

R. Sun, (1992). On Variable Binding in Connectionist Networks, *Connection Science*, Vol.4, No.2, pp.93-124.

R. Sun, (1994). *Integrating Rules and Connectionism for Robust Commonsense Reasoning*. John Wiley and Sons, New York, NY.

R. Sun, (1995). Robust reasoning: integrating rule-based and similarity-based reasoning. *Artificial Intelligence*. 75, 2. 241-296.

R. Sun and L. Bookman, (eds.) (1994). *Computational Architectures Integrating Neural and Symbolic Processes*. Kluwer Academic Publishers. Norwell, MA.

R. Sun and T. Peterson, (1995). A hybrid learning model of reactive sequential decision making. *The Working Notes of The IJCAI Workshop on Connectionist-Symbolic Integration*.

G. Towell and J. Shavlik, (1993). Extracting Refined Rules from Knowledge-Based Neural Networks, *Machine Learning*.

K. VanLehn, (1995). Cognitive skill acquisition. *Annual review of Psychology*, Vol.47, J. Spence, J. Darly, and D. Foss (eds.) Annual Reviews, Palo Alto, CA.

C. Watkins, (1989). *Learning with Delayed Rewards*. Ph.D Thesis, Cambridge University, UK.

D. Willingham, M. Nissen, P. Bullemer, (1989). On the development of procedural knowledge. *Journal of Experimental Psychology: Learning, Memory, and Cognition*. 15, 1047-1060.

A Dynamical System for Language Processing

Whitney Tabor[1,2] and **Cornell Juliano**[1] and **Michael Tanenhaus**[1]

[1]Department of Brain and Cognitive Sciences
[2]Center for the Sciences of Language
University of Rochester
Rochester, NY 14627
whitney@bcs.rochester.edu

Abstract

A dynamical systems model of language processing suggests a resolution of the debate about the influences of syntactic and lexical constraints on processing. Syntactic hypotheses are modeled as *attractors* which compete for the processor's trajectory. When accumulating evidence puts the processor close to an attractor, processing is quick and lexical differences are hard to detect. When the processor lands between several attractors, multiple hypotheses compete and lexical differences can tip the balance one way or the other. This approach allows us to be more explicit about the *emergent properties* of lexicalist models that are hypothesized to account for syntactic effects (MacDonald, Pearlmutter & Seidenberg, 1994; Trueswell & Tanenhaus, 1994).

Introduction

Readers and listeners have clear preferences for certain syntactic sequences (e.g., NVN as a main clause), as revealed by garden-path effects for temporarily ambiguous sentences that do not conform to these preferences (1).

(1) a. The horse raced past the barn fell.

    b. The patient warned the doctor was incompetent.

However, recent evidence suggests that these garden-path effects can be sharply reduced by strong lexical constraints, as illustrated by the examples in (2), which are structurally similar to those in (1), but do not appear to cause processing difficulty.

(2) a. The land mine buried in the sand exploded.

    b. The patient said the doctor was incompetent.

The interpretation of these lexical effects has been extremely controversial. In the influential class of "structure-first" models, category-based parsing phenomena are accounted for by positing an initial, encapsulated processing stage in which structure is built using syntactic category information and a few, general principles (e.g., Frazier, 1987). Lexically-specific information and other (non-syntactic) constraints apply at a later stage in processing. In contrast, several research groups have argued that many of the phenomena that motivated these category-based principles can be reduced to the effects of interacting lexical constraints (McClelland, St. John, & Taraban, 1989; MacDonald, Pearlmutter, & Seidenberg 1994; Trueswell & Tanenhaus 1994).

The competition between the lexicalist and structuralist claims has focused increased attention on a long-standing, empirical debate about the time-course with which lexical constraints are observed relative to structural constraints during on-line sentence processing (for a recent review see Tanenhaus & Trueswell, 1995). While the results of these experiments have often been equivocal, two generalizations emerge. First, the relative strength of structural and lexical constraints varies across contexts and structures. Second, there are clear circumstances in which local lexical constraints are insufficient to capture important processing generalizations (e.g, island constraints on movement and structural preferences even in the face of strong contrary lexical biases).

Research on automatic parsing has led to a class of models which use corpus-tuned probabilistic grammars to compute *conditional probabilities* of lexical items in contexts (see Charniak, 1993, for review). Recently, models of this type have been used to combine lexical and syntactic information to make reading time predictions (Jurafsky, 1996). These models provide a theoretical basis for incorporating probabilistic lexical information in a model that uses syntactic rules, but they do not provide insight into the variation across contexts of the relative strengths of structural and lexical constraints.

A promising approach to explaining this variation is to treat category-based parsing preferences as generalizations that emerge within a constraint-based learning system because of similarities among "classes" of lexical items (e.g., Juliano & Tanenhaus, 1994). But prior proposals along these lines have been vague. In this paper we show how certain constructs of dynamical systems theory allow us to be more explicit about the nature of the "emergent" representations, their relationship to traditional syntactic categories, and their empirical predictions.

Dynamical Systems Theory

Dynamical systems theory (see Abraham and Shaw 1984 and Strogatz 1994 for introductions) is typically concerned with systems that change continuously with time. Examples of much-studied dynamical systems include: pendulums swinging on rigid arms; stars and planets orbiting one another in space; populations fluctuating in an ecosystem; gases swirling around in the atmosphere. It is useful to consider the trajectories of a dynamical system—i.e., the paths it can follow as time progresses. In the case of a pendulum, some trajectories swing back and forth, others whirl around the circle, and two of them remain at one point indefinitely (hanging down, and, improbably, balanced straight up). If the pendulum is damped, then all trajectories except those leading to the improbable state approach the low point-trajectory in the limit. Such a limiting trajectory is called an *attractor*. Those starting points from which the system gravitates toward a particular attractor *A* are collectively referred to as the *basin of attraction* of *A*. The basin of attraction of the pendulum's low attractor consists of every state except those that lead to the improbable state. In a planetary system, each large mass is surrounded by its own basin of attraction. One particularly interesting property of multiple-attractor systems is that when the system is near an attractor *A* it is dominated by the properties of *A* alone, but when it is further away, it may still be in the basin of *A*, but other attractors can exert an influence on it. Below, we use this *local dominance* property of attractors to model the variable balance of syntactic and lexical influences on processing.

Sentence Processing Data

Some recent experiments by Juliano and Tanenhaus (1993) elucidate the way these dynamical systems notions can help simplify our understanding of the relationship of syntactic and lexical influences on processing. Juliano and Tanenhaus focused on the relationship between verbs that take sentence complements (V[Sbar]'s) and verbs that take noun phrase complements (V[NP]'s or *transitive verbs*). Typically, sentence complements are introduced by the complementizer *that*, although the complementizer can be absent (3).

(3) The grocer insisted/agreed/complained/argued (that) the cheap hotel was pleasant.

When the complementizer is absent and the embedded sentence starts with its subject noun phrase, the beginning of the main sentence has the form NP-V-NP (or "NVN" for short), which makes it abstractly consistent with the transitive pattern. It is well known that, in many ambiguous cases, people prefer to interpret a noun phrase after a verb as a direct object (Frazier, 1987). This preference is part of the evidence that motivates the two-stage model of processing: the preference *could* arise because the processor initially assumes that any NP after a verb is the verb's object. Indeed Juliano and Tanenhaus found high latencies at determiners that immediately followed V[Sbar]'s, in comparison to determiners that immediately followed V[NP]'s (Figure 1; see their "Experiment 3" for details). But the effect was correlated with the context-independent frequency of the verb: verbs low in absolute frequency showed a stronger effect than verbs high in absolute frequency (see also Trueswell, Tanenhaus, and Kello, 1993). The frequency correlation is hard to understand under the two-stage model because that model implies that lexical differences have no effect on initial processing. The results suggest a model in which incorrect hypotheses can exert a marginal influence on correct hypotheses to varying degrees, depending on the frequencies of the items involved. We are thus led to the idea of letting syntactic hypotheses correspond to attractors in a dynamical system.

Another experiment by Juliano and Tanenhaus (1993) (their "Experiment 2"), provides further support for the competing attractors approach. Although the transitive pattern is indeed the most common pattern in English declarative-sentence syntax (if we take the Brown Corpus to be representative), it happens to be the case that when an arbitrary verb is followed by the word *that*, the word *that* is most likely to be a complementizer. Therefore, we might hypothesize that the NVN schema has to compete with another schema of the form V-*that*[Comp]. Following the same line of reasoning as before,

Figure 1: Reading time differences between V[Sbar]-*the* and V[NP]-*the*. (This figure is based on data reported in Juliano and Tanenhaus, 1993, Experiment 3)

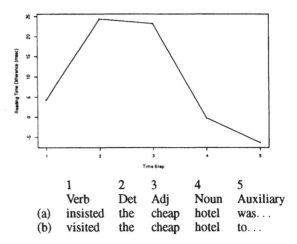

	1	2	3	4	5
	Verb	Det	Adj	Noun	Auxiliary
(a)	insisted	the	cheap	hotel	was...
(b)	visited	the	cheap	hotel	to...

we thus expect people to have difficulty when the direct object of a transitive verb is introduced by the determiner *that*. Juliano and Tanenhaus (1993) find a strong effect in support of this interpretation: when the same transitive verb is followed by *that* and *the*, reading times at *that* are substantially slower. The effect peaks at the adjective following the determiner and diminishes again when the noun is reached. One might be concerned that this result is due either to the high frequency of *the* (there is generally an inverse correlation between the absolute frequency of a word and its processing time), or to the pragmatic strangeness of using determiner *that* without prior mention of its referent (the sentences were presented without a supporting context). However, the same effect is observed when *that* is compared with *those* (Figure 2). *Those* is less frequent than *that* as a determiner (1:3 in the Brown Corpus) and has similar presuppositions to *that*. Thus, the results still seem best explained by positing influence by the V-*that*[Comp] schema on NVN sentences.

Both of these results point in the direction of a dynamical systems treatment. In particular, attractors seem like useful devices for modeling the way in which the correct pattern usually "captures" the processor in the long run while incorrect patterns tend influence its behavior along the way. In the next section we develop a computational model which allows us to explicitly model reading times on this basis.

A Dynamical System for Language Processing

We use a vector space to encode the states of the language processor. Each time the processor encounters a word, it jumps to some location in the vector space. We recapitulate most of the distinctions that a symbolic grammar makes by letting isolated regions correspond to symbolic states. Every time the symbolic processor would be in a state S_i, the vector space processor is in a region, R_i. Additionally, we require that the distances between regions reflect partial similarity properties of the data. For example, since PP-complement

Figure 2: Reading time differences between V[NP]-*that* and V[NP]-*those*

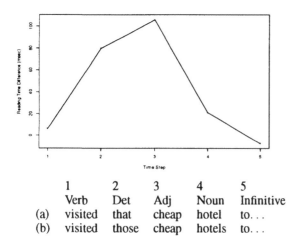

	1	2	3	4	5
	Verb	Det	Adj	Noun	Infinitive
(a)	visited	that	cheap	hotel	to...
(b)	visited	those	cheap	hotels	to...

verbs are relatively similar to transitive verbs in comparison to nouns and prepositions, the region corresponding to the processing of a PP-complement verb is placed relatively near the region corresponding to the processing of a transitive verb. Moreover, within each of the isolated regions, subtle statistical differences between elements are encoded as small within-region contrasts. We refer to the collection of points visited in this representation space during processing of a large sample of language use as a *visitation set*.

Having established the representation space and the visitation set, we assume that processing a word in a corpus involves moving to the appropriate place in the representation space (more on how to do this below) and then migrating to the nearest big cluster, essentially as in a gravitational system. Successful parsing corresponds to arriving at (or getting sufficiently near) a cluster locus. Thus the proposed representation space contains the trajectories of a dynamical system, where the category clusters correspond to attractor basins. Reading time is modeled as the time it takes the processor to gravitate to an attractor. The processor gravitates quickly when it lands near a dense cluster; it gravitates more slowly when it lands near a sparse cluster. Moreover, it reaches the relevant attractor more quickly if it starts near the center of a cluster than if it starts somewhere on the periphery. A verb like, *roll*, positioned on the periphery of the verb cluster because of the competing noun interpretation will take longer to process than an unambiguous verb. Thus the model predicts the general finding that ambiguous elements slow the processor down.

We used a connectionist network for corpus learning to generate the visitation set on which the dynamical model is based. The network had feedforward connections from an input layer through a hidden layer to an output layer and the hidden units were recurrently connected to themselves and one-another (Figure 3). Words were assigned localist representations on the input and output layers and the network was trained using a corpus: each word was presented, in sequence, on the input layer and the weights were adjusted to improve

the network's prediction of the successor word (as in Elman, 1991). Error was propagated using backpropagation through time and the error gradient was approximated by attending to only a few, recent timesteps (see Pearlmutter, 1995's review). The hidden unit space of such a network corresponds to the representation space described in the previous paragraph. The visitation set was thus created by collecting a sample of hidden units visited by the network during the processing of a corpus approximating natural usage.

Figure 3: A recurrent network for word prediction. (The activation of layer HIDDEN$_{t-1}$ was set equal to the activation that layer HIDDEN$_t$ had on the previous time-step. The error signal was backpropagated through 3 time-steps.)

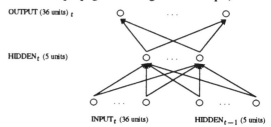

Figure 4: The generating grammar for simulations of Juliano and Tanenhaus's experiments.

1.00	Sroot : S p
1.00	S : NP VP
0.67	VP : VP[NP]
0.33	VP : VP[Sbar]
0.67	VP[NP] : V[NP] NP
0.33	VP[NP] : V[NP]
0.67	VP[Sbar] : V[Sbar] that S
0.33	VP[Sbar] : V[Sbar] S
1.00	NP : Det N
[Zipf]	Det : 0.44 the, 0.22 a, 0.14 which, 0.10 that 0.10 those
[Zipf]	V[NP] : 0.34 called, 0.17 followed, 0.11 pulled, 0.09 caught, 0.07 pushed, 0.06 loved, 0.05 visited, 0.04 studied, 0.04 tossed, 0.03 grabbed
[Zipf]	V[Sbar] : 0.34 thought, 0.17 agreed, 0.11 insisted, 0.09 wished, 0.07 hoped, 0.06 remarked, 0.05 pleaded, 0.04 speculated, 0.04 doubted, 0.03 hinted
[Zipf]	N : 0.34 woman, 0.17 man, 0.11 dog, 0.09 cat, 0.07 blouse, 0.06 hat, 0.05 cake, 0.04 ball, 0.04 watch, 0.03 cypress

To generate a corpus, we used the probabilistic, context free grammar shown in Figure 4. The frequencies of rules in the grammar are set according to a simple rubric called Zipf's Law. Zipf's Law holds that a rank vs. frequency plot of the vocabulary elements drawn from any large corpus forms the cusp of a hyperbola (Zipf, 1943). The law has been confirmed by Zipf and his successors as a fair approximation for numerous corpora in a wide range of languages. We have observed that it also provides a reasonable approximation for several of the major lexical categories in the Brown Corpus (Noun, Verb, Adjective, Adverb, Determiner) and have thus used it to assign frequencies to lexical items in the grammar. Somewhat arbitarily, we have also used it to determine the relative frequencies for the grammar's multi-production syntactic nodes.

After training the network on grammar-generated data until it had learned all of the major distinctions made by the grammar, we formed a visitation set in the following manner. With learning turned off, we let the grammar generate 1000 words in sequence. We presented these to the network in order and formed a visitation set by recording the set of hidden unit locations that the network visited. This visitation set defines the behavior of the dynamical processor. There are a number of slightly different ways of implementing the dynamics. We have experimented with one in which we let each point in the visitation set behave as a point mass and we model the processor as a small test mass which follows a trajectory defined by Newton's Law of Universal Gravitation. The predictions of this model are accurate in the cases we have tried, but it is computationally very expensive. Alternatively, we could let a recurrent neural network form activation-space attractors corresponding to grammatical classifications and treat processing time as relaxation time. Or we could interpret the inverse of density as a potential surface (so that density maxima correspond to valley-bottoms and density minima to hilltops) and model the processor as a ball rolling down this surface. Since we are not yet sure which implementation is best, we take a shortcut here and use an easily computable approximation of attraction time which is most similar to the density-as-potential model but shares the main properties of all the systems mentioned. In particular, for a processing state associated with a juncture, p, between words in a corpus, we let the multiplicative inverse of density provide an estimate of attraction time:

(4) **Def.**

$$Predicted\ Reading\ Time\ at\ p = \frac{1}{1 + Density\ at\ p}$$

For the network trained on the grammar in Figure 4, a two-dimensional projection of part of the visitation set is shown in Figure 5. This projection focuses on cases where a determiner or complementizer occurred after a verb. It was obtained by selecting 1000 cases of determiners/complementizers occurring after verbs and plotting the first two principal components (Jolliffe, 1986) of the corresponding hidden unit locations. The first Principal Component accounts for 97% of the variance, the second for 2%. Thus, the data of Figure 5 are primarily spread out in the x-direction. We show the expanded y-direction for visual clarity.

In this figure, there are two densely populated clusters corresponding to V[Sbar]'s followed by *that* and V[NP]'s followed by an unambiguous determiner. The centers of these two dense clusters are attractors in the dynamical model and they correspond to the two main syntactic patterns involved here: the sentence-complement pattern and the simple transitive (NVN) pattern. There are also two diffuse clusters corresponding to V[NP]'s followed by *that* and S-complement verbs followed by an unambiguous determiner. The locations of these diffuse clusters reflect the attractor influences which give rise to the predictions we are interested in. The V[NP]-*that* cluster corresponds to processor states that are, from the standpoint of the symbolic grammar, equivalent to the states

corresponding to the points in the V[NP]-determiner cluster. Nevertheless, this V[NP]-*that* cluster is drawn over toward the V[Sbar]-*that* cluster because of the strong influence of the V+*that*-as-complementizer attractor. This displacement of the V[NP]-*that* cluster makes the density around its points low compared to the density in the V[NP]-determiner cluster so gravitation times for points in the V[NP]-*that* region are large and we expect high latencies in reading. This is how the model predicts the results of Juliano and Tanenhaus's Experiment 2.

In fact, structural influence effects along the lines of those observed in Experiment 2 were what led researchers to propose the two-stage model. But in this case, it's not clear why processing the word *that* after a transitive verb should be difficult under the standard two-stage model which takes the NVN structure as the first-pass assumption—after all, *that* is a legitimate determiner, and thus does not conflict grammatically with the first-pass hypothesis. Moreover, the full range of data observed in these types of sentences is inconsistent with two-stage model's lack of sensitivity to lexical differences: Juliano and Tanenhaus (1994) showed that replacing the transitive verb with a strong sentence-complement verb like *insisted* makes the difficulty at the word *that* disappear.

These results are also difficult to explain under a model based on conditional probabilities generated by a reasonable linguistic grammar (see Charniak 1993, Jurafsky 1996)[1]. Reading times in such models are most naturally modeled as the uncertainty of probability distributions conditioned on grammatical context. Such models, if they calculate the probabilities accurately, can be thought of as ultra lexically-sensitive. In the present case, a pure transitive verb provides clear information that a complementizer interpretation is out of the question for *that* so the conditional probability models have no reason to predict greater difficulty with *that* than with *those* in such a context.

Turning now to Juliano and Tanenhaus's Experiment 3, similar attractor effects explain the difficulty of processing a unambiguous determiner like *the* after a sentence complement verb. In particular, the attraction of the V[Sbar]-determiner cluster (which is associated with a Sentence-Complement interpretation) over in the direction of the V[NP]-determiner cluster makes the density of points in the V[Sbar]-Determiner cluster low so gravitation times are high and high latencies are expected (Figure 5). Again, the two-stage model has trouble predicting this effect both because the determiner is in keeping with the preferred transitive structure and because of the sensitivity to lexical differences evidenced by the lower reading time at *the* after a transitive verb. The effect may be attributable to a statistical difference in the likelihood of *the*

---

[1]We note that Jurafsky's models and some of the models described by Charniak do not compute exact conditional probabilites but rather approximations. They are forced to do this for lack of sufficient data even in a very large corpus. The approximations they choose may enhance the ability of their models to handle structural influence effects like those described here by weakening the sensitivity to lexical differences. We suspect that under this weakening, their models become similar to the dynamically-interpreted neural network we describe here. We feel the dynamical analysis approach is preferable in light of the current data because it provides an explicit characterization of the structural influences in terms that can be related to known linguistic constructs.

after the two types of verbs, in which case conditional probability models may make the right qualitative prediction, but they have no capability of attributing the influence to adverse structural effects.

As noted above, to make specific reading time predictions, we used density to estimate gravitation times. For each point in the 5-dimensional hidden unit space, we chose a small radius around it[2] and counted the number of visited points within that radius. We measured the predicted reading time using Equation 4. The resulting reading time predictions are shown graphically in Figures 7 and 6. Encouragingly, the model predicts anomalies in essentially the same places as they occur for human subjects.[3]

Figure 5: Hidden unit representations with cluster means labelled. (PC = Principal Component)

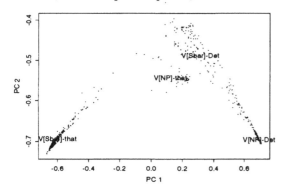

Conclusion

The results of the simulations are encouraging because they suggest theoretical framework for resolving the long-standing dispute in psycholinguistics over whether there is a blind syntactic processing stage. In keeping with the scheme outlined by McClelland, St. John, and Taraban 1989, the answer indicated here is that people commit (to a degree) to syntactic hypotheses as the evidence warrants but the particular commitments made are a function of accumulating lexical indications and do not reflect context-independent defaults. The capability of a wrong hypothesis to pull the processor away from the representation space location corresponding to the correct hypothesis is due to attractor competition and gives rise to the behavior pattern that has led people to posit an

---

[2]0.06 hidden unit units—roughly one third the minimum distance between cluster means in the two-dimensional subspace where determiners and complementizers are distinguished. This seemed like an appropriate region in which to estimate this minimum since some of the subtlest distinctions are made in this region.

[3]The persistence of high predicted latencies at the word *hotel* and the period following *the woman visited that hotel...* in Figure 6 is due to the persisting influence of the V-*that*[Complementizer] attractor as evidenced by the fact that the model shows a nontrivial tendency to predict a verb instead of a period at the 7th timestep. Further training of the model brings this case into line with the human subject data, but tends to diminish the salience of the attractor effects in the plot corresponding to Figure 5 so we decided to use this case as an illustration despite its imperfections.

Figure 6: Comparison of model's predicted reading-time differences ("m") and scaled human subject data ("h") for Juliano and Tanenhaus (1993), Experiment 2. The human subject data are scaled linearly so they fall in the same range as the model's predicted reading times. (Effect is due to the V-*that*[Complementizer] attractor).

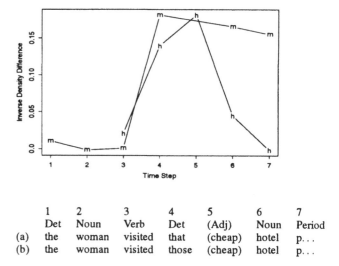

	1	2	3	4	5	6	7
	Det	Noun	Verb	Det	(Adj)	Noun	Period
(a)	the	woman	visited	that	(cheap)	hotel	p...
(b)	the	woman	visited	those	(cheap)	hotel	p...

initial, lexically-blind processing stage. If the incorrect hypothesis/attractor is so strong that all grammatically similar cases get pulled to within a very small radius of the attractor, then no sensitivity to lexical differences is observed. But, in many cases the pulling power is of intermediate strength. In such cases lexical differences can modulate people's propensities to choose the wrong parse. Moreover, adverse attractor influences can result in high processing latencies even when the correct parse is ultimately chosen.

The proposal we make here is very much in keeping with the model of sentence processing proposed by McClelland, St. John, and Taraban (1989). Those authors trained a connectionist network to generate appropriate assignments of constituents to roles as a sentence was being processed. Their model showed some of the same ambivalence in the presence of ambiguous information that our model shows. Although they did not use a dynamical system to probe the representation produced by their network like we do, they are also working with a learning model which is governed by attractor dynamics, so it is likely that the predictions made in both cases have a similar source. The usefulness of introducing dynamical systems analysis to this domain is that it provides a way of identifying the structural entities in connectionist models that are responsible for those abstract constraints on language that are referred to as "syntactic". Without such tools for talking about the nature of synactic organization in connectionist models, it is hard to elucidate the relationship between those models and the standard models which make central reference to syntactic structures.

The attractor-based interpretation makes it clear why neither two-stage models nor conditional probability models based on linguistic grammars can handle all the data. In essence, the two-stage approach attributes too much respon-

Figure 7: Comparison of model's predicted reading-time differences ("m") and scaled human subject data ("h") for Juliano and Tanenhaus (1993), Experiment 3. The human subject data are scaled linearly so they fall in the same range as the model's predicted reading times. (Effect is due to the V-NP[Direct Object] attractor).

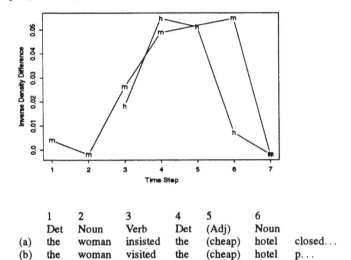

	1 Det	2 Noun	3 Verb	4 Det	5 (Adj)	6 Noun	
(a)	the	woman	insisted	the	(cheap)	hotel	closed...
(b)	the	woman	visited	the	(cheap)	hotel	p...

siblity to structural constraints, while the conditional probability approach is too lexically sensitive.[4] Neither of these approaches allows incompatible structural constraints to interact at a given point in processing. By contrast, the attractor model succeeds by permitting such interaction to occur in a limited way. It holds, in effect, that processing is largely rule-governed, for it is dominated most of the time by single attractors which correspond to absolute interpretations. But it is marginally subject to un-rule-like influences. These occur when competing hypotheses have equal-enough sway that subtler, lexical influences can win the day.

Acknowledgements

We thank Robert Jacobs, Dan Jurafsky, Christopher Duncan and an anonymous reviewer for helpful comments. This research was supported by NICHD grant HD-27206 and NIDCD grant 5T32DC0035. Some of the data from Experiments 1-3 was presented in the 1993 Proceedings of the Cognitive Science Society Meeting.

References

Abraham, R. H. and Shaw, C. D. (1984). *Dynamics—the Geometry of Behavior, Books 0 - 4*. Aerial Press, Inc., P.O. Box 1360, Santa Cruz, CA. Volume 1 of the Visual Mathematics Library.

Charniak, E. (1993). *Statistical Language Learning*. MIT Press, Cambridge, Massachusetts.

Elman, J. L. (1991). Distributed representations, simple recurrent networks, and grammatical structure. *Machine Learning*, 7:195–225.

Frazier, L. (1987). Theories of sentence processing. In Garfield, J. L., editor, *Modularity in knowledge representation and natural-language understanding*, pages 37–62. MIT Press, Cambridge, MA.

Jolliffe, I. T. (1986). *Principal component analysis*. Springer-Verlag, New York.

Juliano, C. and Tanenhaus, M. (1993). Contingent frequency effects in syntactic ambiguity resolution. In *Proceedings of the 15th Annual Cognitive Science Conference*, pages 593–598. Lawrence Erlbaum.

Juliano, C. and Tanenhaus, M. K. (1994). A constraint-based lexicalist account of the subject/object attachment preference. *Journal of Psycholinguistic Research*, 23(6):459–471.

Jurafsky, D. (1996). Conditional probabilities for linguistic access and disambiguation. Paper presented at the 1996 CUNY Sentence Processing Conference, New York, New York.

MacDonald, M. A., Pearlmutter, N. J., and Seidenberg, M. S. (1994a). The lexical nature of syntactic ambiguity resolution. *Psychological Review*, 101:676–703.

MacDonald, M. C., Pearlmutter, N. J., and Seidenberg, M. S. (1994b). Syntactic ambiguity resolution as lexical ambiguity resolution. In C. Clifton, J., Frazier, L., and Rayner, K., editors, *Perspectives on Sentence Processing*, pages 123–154. Lawrence Erlbaum Associates.

McClelland, J., John, M. S., and Taraban, R. (1989). Comprehension: A parallel distribute processing approach. In *Language and Cognitive Processes*, volume 4 (Special Issue), pages 287–335. Lawrence Erlbaum Associates.

Pearlmutter, B. A. (1995). Gradient calculations for dynamic recurrent networks: A survey. *IEEE Transactions on Neural Networks*, 6(5):1212–1228.

Strogatz, S. (1994). *Nonlinear Dynamics and Chaos*. Addison-Wesley, Reading, MA.

Trueswell, J. C. and Tanenhaus, M. K. (1994). Toward a constraint-based lexicalist approach to syntactic ambiguity resolution. In C. Clifton, L. Frazier, . K. R., editor, *Perspectives on sentence processing*. Erlbaum, Hillsdale, NJ.

Trueswell, J. C., Tanenhaus, M. K., and Kello, C. (1993). Verb-specific constraints in sentence processing: Separating effects of lexical preference from garden paths. *Journal of Experimental Psychology*, 19(3):528–553.

Zipf, G. K. (1943). *Human Behavior and the Principle of Least Effort*. Hafner [1965].

---

[4]Again, we note that this lexical sensitivity can be reduced by various smoothing techniques and urge a clarification of the way the structural constraints interact via smoothing.

A Connectionist Model of Metaphor by Pattern Completion.

Michael S.C. Thomas

Psychology Group, King Alfred's College
Sparkford Road, Winchester SO22 4NR, UK.
& Department of Experimental Psychology
University of Oxford, UK.
michael.thomas@psy.ox.ac.uk

Denis Mareschal

Department of Psychology
University of Exeter
Perry Road, Exeter EX4 4QG
UK.
dmaresch@singer.exeter.ac.uk

Abstract

In this paper we present a simple process model (based on connectionist pattern completion) of *A is B* metaphor comprehension. The Metaphor by Pattern Completion (MPC) model capitalizes on an existing semantic memory mechanism. Metaphorical enhancement is produced by presenting a semantic vector representation of the target word (A) to a connectionist network storing the knowledge base (B). Effects found in human data such as meaning enhancement, asymmetric processing, context sensitivity and compound indexing all fall naturally out of the pattern completion mechanism. The MPC model suggests a simple way of separating literal from metaphorical statements. It provides a means of predicting when a metaphor will appear to fail. Moreover, we suggest that the mechanism can form the basis of a comparison procedure that supports analogy. The MPC mechanism avoids the problem of identifying which features of a concept are relevant for similarity matching in analogies, because the prior metaphor stage naturally enhances relevant features and suppresses the irrelevant features. The MPC model is both domain general (in that it does not depend on the structure of the metaphor domain) and parsimonious (in that it does not posit metaphor-specific mechanisms).

1. Introduction

In this paper we describe a simple computational model of the processes involved in comprehending metaphors of the form *A is B* (e.g., "The Apple is a Ball"). These have been referred to as Image Metaphors (Lakoff, 1994) or simply Attribute Mapping (Holyoak and Thagard, 1995). There have been few attempts to build computational models of metaphor because it is assumed that a metaphor is equivalent to an analogy with the comparison made implicit (that is, *A is B* is just *A is like B* with the "like" removed). Although on grounds of parsimony it might be surprising if the processes underlying metaphor and analogy were radically different (Rumelhart, 1979), metaphors are often seen as producing a stronger and subtler effect than similes (Glucksberg and Keysar, 1993). This suggests that important differences may underlie the two processes.

Metaphors can imply a comparison but they are not reducible to comparisons (Black, 1979). It seems reasonable to say "I don't mean Richard is *like* a lion, I mean that Richard *is* a lion." There is a sense in which the metaphorical comparison seems stronger than the analogical comparison. Metaphors can be viewed as an intermediate between literal attribution statements (e.g. Richard is brave) and similes (e.g. Richard is like a lion). By saying that "Richard is a lion", certain properties of a lion (such as bravery) are attributed to Richard. The process by which the features of Richard are modified through the use of a metaphor is still very much an open question.

Because of the confound between metaphors and similes, existing computational models have primarily examined the processes involved in the formation of analogies and in similarity-based retrieval (e.g. ACME: Holyoak and Thagard, 1989; MAC/FAC: Forbus, Gentner, and Law, 1995). These computational models have proposed that analogical comparisons involve either: (a) forming mappings or links between static representations (e.g. ACME), or (b) a kind of "high level perception" in which representations are dynamically configured according to domain specific heuristics (e.g., Copycat: Hofstadter, 1984; Mitchell, 1993; Tabletop: Hofstadter and French, 1994). While most models seem to fall into either the mapping or high level perception camp, Burns and Holyoak (1994) have shown that if enough domain specific information is pre-wired into the systems, then both types of model can behave in a similar fashion.

The comprehension of complex metaphors, requiring the formation of mappings between the elements in two structured representations, may involve task-specific cognitive mechanisms. However, it is questionable how frequently such complex metaphors are understood 'on-line' by the operation of a single cognitive mechanism. Lakoff (e.g., Lakoff, 1994; Lakoff and Johnson, 1980) has proposed that the mappings involved in many "conventional" complex metaphors are derived and agreed in advance of usage, by members of a given linguistic community. Moreover, complex metaphor comprehension is likely to incorporate a range of processes and strategies. The model we present in this paper is intended to capture the 'on-line' comprehension of metaphors occurring at very short time scales (e.g., seconds). We believe that these simple on-line mechanisms may form the basis of (or contribute to) the more complex comprehension strategies occurring at longer time scales (e.g., over minutes).

Simple *A is B* metaphors provide a way of exploring the basic mechanisms which underlie meaning enhancement independently of the need for any prior complex mappings. In particular, we suggest that meaning enhancement can be modeled by a simple domain general processing mechanism. For simple *A is B* metaphors, the Metaphor by Pattern Completion (MPC) model accounts for how the semantic features of a target word (A) are transformed by the semantic properties of a knowledge base (B). The model capitalizes on the properties of existing semantic memory mechanisms and does not posit "metaphor-specific" processes. In this sense it is both domain general (in that it does not depend on the structure of the specific metaphor domain) and parsimonious (in that it does not need to posit new mechanisms).

The heart of the model is based on Black's (1979) interaction theory of *A is B* metaphor genesis. Black's theory contains a number of abstract concepts which attempt to capture the complexity of the process of metaphor. According to Black, *A is B* metaphors gain their effect through an interaction between the target and the source concepts, whereby "associated implications" from the source concept are "projected upon" the target concept. The "associated implications" are derived from the source concept's "implicative complex" which is determined by the "current opinions shared by members of a certain speech-community" (Black, 1979, p. 28). The metaphor involves "a shift in the speaker's meaning - and the corresponding hearer's meaning - what both of them understand by the words as used on the particular occasion." (*ibid.*). The MPC model provides a more tangible expression of these abstract ideas. The model captures four key phenomena of metaphorical comparisons: (1) the semantic effect of the juxtaposition of two concepts; (2) the directional asymmetry of such comparisons (that is, the metaphor *A is B* frequently has a quite different effect from the metaphor *B is A*, even though the similarities between the two concepts are the same in each case); (3) context sensitivity; and (4) compound indexing effects in metaphorical comparisons. Further, the model may provide some clues as to how metaphorical statements can be distinguished from literal statements. Finally it generates a hypothesis of the relation between metaphorical and analogical comparisons and provides an account of when metaphors will fail.

2. The Model.

The MPC model is based on the processing power of three-layered feed-forward connectionist networks. Figure 1 shows the complete network architecture.

Both the inputs and outputs to the network encode semantic features. There are 13 semantic features (though note Balls have 2 extra features, as described in Section 3.4 below).

Input information entering the network is vetted towards separate knowledge bases via a categorization mechanism. This mechanism must be able to separate inputs into appropriate categories as dictated by perceptual or linguistic contextual cues. Hence, the prior ability to categorize inputs is a necessary assumption of this model. The selector mechanism was not actually implemented in a connectionist form since it has no direct impact on the process through which metaphors emerge. However, it could be implemented as a feed-forward network with the same semantic inputs as the knowledge-base network but with a single category output acting as a shunting mechanism for redirecting information flow.

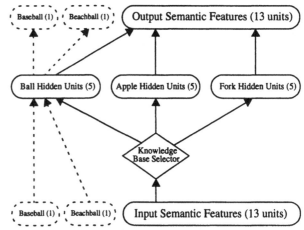

Figure 1. Architecture of the MPC Model.

Table 1: Semantic Features for Concept Prototypes.

	Color				Actions		Shape			Texture		Size		Index	
	Red	Green	Brown	White	Edible	Thrown	Round	Irregular	Pointed	Soft	Hard	Hand Sized	Lap Sized	Baseball	Beachball
Apple	1.0	0.0	0.0	0.0	1.0	0.2	0.8	0.3	0.0	0.3	0.7	1.0	0.0		
	0.0	1.0	0.0	0.0	1.0	0.2	0.8	0.3	0.0	0.3	0.7	1.0	0.0		
(Rotten)	0.0	0.0	1.0	0.0	0.0	0.2	0.8	0.3	0.0	1.0	0.0	1.0	0.0		
Ball Baseball	0.0	0.0	0.0	1.0	0.0	1.0	1.0	0.0	0.0	0.0	1.0	0.9	0.1	1.0	0.0
Beachball	1.0	0.0	0.0	0.0	0.0	1.0	1.0	0.0	0.0	1.0	0.0	0.1	0.9	0.0	1.0
Beachball	0.0	1.0	0.0	0.0	0.0	1.0	1.0	0.0	0.0	1.0	0.0	0.1	0.9	0.0	1.0
Fork	0.0	0.0	0.0	1.0	0.0	0.1	0.0	0.0	1.0	0.0	1.0	0.7	0.3		

In this limited example, we have chosen a small set of features with which to describe the objects. The intention here is to model an 'on-line' mechanism. If this mechanism fails, or the domain is too complex, other strategies can come into play. Because this is a default comprehension mechanism, we suggest that in a scaled up model, all concepts would be represented along a common set of default features (e.g., high frequency or high salience features). These may not represent all concepts sufficiently for all purposes but they should suffice as a default approximation. A concept that is not adequately represented will fail to be understood, both literally and metaphorically (see later), and will trigger a more complex strategy.

In order to generate knowledge bases for separate concepts, the network was trained to autoassociate exemplars of each concept. For simplicity, we restricted the model to the forming of *A is B* metaphors between three concepts: Apples, Balls, and Forks. The concepts were defined by a set of prototypical tokens representing different kinds of apples, balls, and forks that could be encountered in the individual's world (see Table 1). The network was not trained on the prototypes themselves, but on exemplars clustered around these prototypes. Exemplars were generated from each prototype by adding Gaussian noise (variance 0.15) to the original.

The exemplars for each concept formed three training sets used to develop the network's three prior-knowledge bases "about" apples, balls, and forks. The existence of a prior knowledge base is a necessary feature of metaphor comprehension. Prior-knowledge bases are analogous to Black's (1979) "implicative complex" and reflect an individual's personal experience with exemplars of each concept. The apple sub-network was trained to autoassociate patterns from 10 exemplars of each of three apple kinds (e.g., red, green, and rotten) for a total of 30 patterns. Similarly, the ball sub-network was trained to autoassociate 10 exemplars from three different kinds (for a total of 30 patterns). Finally, the fork sub-network was trained to autoassociate 10 exemplars from 1 kind (for a total of 10 patterns). Because there was only 1 kind of fork (as opposed to 3 kinds of both apples and balls), a single blank training pattern (zero input and output) was added to the fork training set to inhibit overlearning of the fork exemplars. All networks were trained with Backpropagation using the following parameter values: learning-rate: 0.1, momentum: 0.0, initial weight range: ±0.5. Each sub-network was trained for 1000 epochs. All reported results are averaged over n=10 replications.

In the MPC model, metaphorical interpretations arise naturally from the pattern completion properties of non-linear connectionist information processing. Pattern completion is often used to "clean up" noisy input patterns. That is, the network transforms the input to make it more consistent with the knowledge stored in the network. In the case of metaphors, however, the input is not a noisy version of a pattern on which the network has previously been trained, but an exemplar of another concept. For example, the sub-network trained on Balls might be presented with an Apple pattern. The resulting output would be an Apple pattern transformed in such a way as to make it more consistent with the prototypical Ball representation stored in the network. The nature of the transformation will depend on the relationship between the Apple and Ball concepts. To cast this in Black's terms, a metaphor is produced when the source concept Ball "projects" its knowledge representation or "associated implications" onto the target concept Apple. The result is a new understanding of Apple in which features are selectively modified according to the Ball prototype.

Metaphors are achieved by the redirection of information flow into one knowledge base or another. The role of the "is" in the A is B metaphor is to trigger that redirection. If the information flow were not redirected, the result would be processing of the input by the knowledge base of which it is an exemplar (e.g., the Apple input would flow through the Apple sub-network). This would "clean-up" the Apple input to make it more apple-like and be akin to "recognizing the input as an apple". This type of semantic representation has been postulated before to account for prototype effects in semantic memory (McClelland and Rumelhart, 1986). Hence the MPC model can be seen as merely capitalizing on existing semantic memory mechanisms.

3. Model Performance.

Figures 2 to 5 show the results of various simulated metaphors. For each *A is B* metaphor, the top bar chart of each pair shows the activation of the semantic feature input representation of the target concept (A). The lower graph shows the semantic feature output representation of the same target (A) once it has been transformed by the source knowledge base (B). The metaphor represented is labeled at the top of the figure. This section reports on four metaphor effects found in humans that fall naturally out of the MPC mechanism.

3.1 Meaning Enhancement

Figure 2 shows the enhancement of the semantic features of an apple concept for the metaphor: "The Apple is a Ball". The input is an exemplar close to its prototype kind. The effect of this metaphor is to reduce the edible label, to suggest that this apple might be suitable for throwing, to increase the hardness and roundness labels, while introducing some ambiguity into the color features. This is the type of enhancement effect outlined by Black (1962, 1979) (see section 1). Note that despite the fact that 20/30 of the Ball exemplars are soft beachballs, the Apple is still made to look harder rather than softer by this metaphor. This is because the apple is closer in size to a hard baseball than it is to a soft beachball. Semantic enhancement is thus not a default imposition of ball features onto those of an apple, but an interaction between stored ball knowledge and the nature of the apple exemplar being presented to the ball sub-network.

3.2 Asymmetric Comparisons.

Real metaphors are rarely symmetrical (i.e., *A is B* is not equivalent to *B is A*), though the similarities between A and B are the same in either case. For example, the metaphors "sermons are slipping pills" and "sleeping pills are sermons" have quite different implications (Glucksberg and Keysar, 1990). Figure 3 shows the result of the metaphor "The Ball is an Apple", the reverse of that shown in Fig.2. The effect of this metaphor is to: reduce the likelihood of being thrown, the size of the ball, and the roundness label, and increase the irregularity label, the softness label and the edibility label. The semantic effect of this metaphor is different from that in the previous case despite the fact that the distance between the sets of prototypes for apples and balls in n-dimensional similarity space remains the same. In fact, the asymmetry only seems problematic if one views the comparison of concepts as involving the measurement of static distances (e.g. Rumelhart and Abrahamson, 1973). In the current model, metaphors are based on dynamic transformations. There is no reason for these transformations to be symmetrical.

3.3 Context sensitivity.

Figure 4 shows the effect of changing the target context on the metaphor process. The effect of the metaphor: "The Ball is an Apple" is similar for both Red and Green balls: roundness and size are reduced, whereas irregularity, softness, and edibility labels are increased. However, a noticeably different enhancement is produced on Brown ball. Here, the softness label is very much increased, and the ball retains a low edibility label. This differential effect

occurs because the Apple knowledge base is constructed around three prototypes (Table 1). Brown/Rotten apples have different properties from other apples. The target and source interact in producing the effect of the metaphor. The context of the target (e.g., brown vs. red) impacts on which aspects of the knowledge base (Apples) are relevant to the metaphor. This is also found in human metaphor interpretations (Black, 1979).

3.4 Compound indexing.

In the apple knowledge base, different kinds are implicitly represented by a distribution of exemplars around three prototypes. It is also possible to index separate kinds explicitly in metaphors (Malgady and Johnson, 1976). In the Ball sub-network, two semantic features were added to the input and output representations in order to code for Baseballs and Beachballs explicitly (Figure 1, dashed outline). Figure 5 shows the effects of the metaphors: "The Apple is a Baseball" and "The Apple is a Beachball". In the Baseball case, the apple is made to look harder and paler and retains its size, while in the Beachball case, the apple remains red and is seen as both softer and larger. Thus a knowledge base can be explicitly distorted to enable a different meaning enhancement.

4. Model Implications and Predictions.

In this section, we describe the implications of interpreting metaphors as arising from pattern completion processes. Each subsection discusses modeling work described in more detail in a forthcoming longer report.

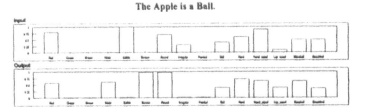

Figure 2. Meaning Enhancement.

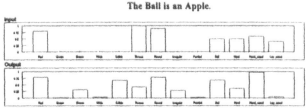

Figure 3. Asymmetric Comparisons.

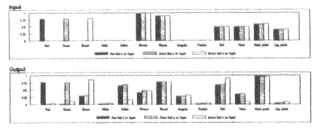

Figure 4. Context Sensitivity.

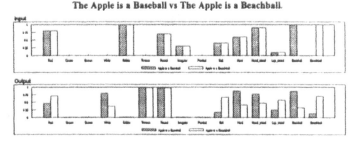

Figure 5. Compound Indexing.

4.1 Distinguishing metaphors & literal statements.

A key issue in metaphor research is how to detect that a statement is metaphorical and not literal (Ortony, 1993). In the MPC model, both types of statements are processed by the same mechanism. A statement is recognized as literal if only small semantic changes occur in the output. For example, in saying "this [apple-like] item is an apple", very little change is produced in the item's output features. However, saying "this [apple-like] item is a ball" results in a large amount of output feature enhancement.

In a given discourse, the listener may be expecting a certain amount of meaning change from a given communication. If the meaning change is greater than that which the listener expects given the context, then he or she may conclude that the communication is metaphorical. Thus the difference between a literal and metaphorical statement of the form A is B may be detected by matching the network error score against a criterion suitable for the current discourse. In our simulations, when testing the metaphors "An Apple is an Apple" and "An Apple is a Ball" using a novel Apple exemplar, the mean error scores were 0.07 and 2.54 respectively (sig. dif., related samples t-test, t=8.04, 9df, p<0.0001). Note that a low error score represents an accurate autoassociation, but also a metaphorically uninteresting juxtaposition: little meaning enhancement has taken place. This corresponds to the inverse relationship between the accuracy of a comparison and its aesthetic impact found in human subjects (Sternberg, Tourangeau, and Nigro; 1979).

4.2 Metaphors and Analogies.

Earlier, we suggested that a metaphor such as "Richard is a lion" can be viewed as intermediate between a literal attribution statement "Richard is brave" and a simile "Richard is like a lion". In the metaphorical case, we know Richard is *not* a lion, and thus must transfer some (relevant) features of the lion to Richard. We have seen how transforming the features for Richard using the knowledge we have about lions might achieve this enhancement. However, the problem of extracting the relevant features also exists for similes. When we are told that Richard is like a lion, how do we know the ways in which he resembles a lion?

One way to address this problem would be to perform the metaphor "Richard is a lion" using the MPC mechanism, as a first step to performing the simile "Richard is like a lion". This would produce an enhanced understanding of Richard, in which his bravery was enhanced, but not his possession of a mane (since Richard has no mane features to be enhanced). If we noted the ways in which Richard's features had been enhanced, we could then take these features to be the relevant similarities between Richard and the lion. These could then be output as the result of the comparison process implied by the simile.

The process of deriving the relevant similarities

would proceed as follows. For an A *is B* metaphor, the similarities between A and B would be computed based on those non-zero features in A that had been enhanced (or at least not suppressed) during the pattern completion process. Conversely, the differences would consist of the semantic features suppressed by the mapping, or previously zero features that had been enhanced. So, in the metaphor "The Apple is a Ball" (Figure 2), the similarities between apples and balls are: Round, Hard, and Red and Soft (to some extent), whereas the differences are Edibility, Thrown, Irregular, White, and Red and Soft (to some extent).

Analogy is then seen as a two stage process. The first stage comprises "seeing A as if it were B", which could be described as a form of high level perception. The second stage involves comparison between static representations to derive similarities. In short, this account of analogy incorporates elements of both the opposing views of the nature of analogy formation outlined in section 1, high level perception and representational mapping.

The MPC model suggests how metaphor and analogy may be related. Instead of being an implicit form of analogy, metaphor is seen as a communicative expression intended to enhance the meaning of a concept by borrowing information from another concept. Analogy on the other hand is a communicative expression intended to focus attention on the similarities between two concepts. Metaphor is the more primary process, highlighting any salient features 'on-line'. Analogy notes the resulting similarities between concepts.

4.3 Predicting when metaphors should fail.

The model suggests two situations under which metaphors will fail. First (and somewhat trivially), a metaphor A *is B* will fail if a subject knows nothing about B (i.e., if the knowledge base is not formed). One must have a representation of apples before apples can be used metaphorically. In other words, one must be able to recognize apples before one can see something else *as if it were an apple*. More interestingly, the process of metaphor will also be fruitless if the target and source have no positive features in common (i.e., if the semantic representation vectors are orthogonal). Pattern completion of target by source would produce no output, and thus no meaning. Figure 6 illustrates this in the case of the metaphor: "The Apple is a Fork". Here, few features show strongly on the output, since apples and forks have very little in common on this default feature set.

Figure 6. When Metaphors Fail.

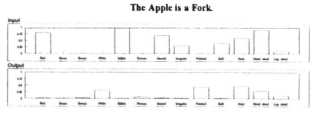

700

5. Conclusion.

The model described in this paper provides a process account of key aspects of metaphor comprehension. It shows how semantic distortion, context sensitivity, and compound indexing fall naturally out of connectionist pattern completion mechanisms. Moreover, it provides a simple explanation of the directional asymmetry effects which have plagued models based on static similarity measures (e.g., Rumelhart and Abrahamson, 1973). The asymmetry effect arises from the fact that network transformations are not normally bi-directional.

All of this is accomplished through a simple and parsimonious mechanism. The MPC model capitalizes on an existing semantic memory mechanism and does not posit domain specific mechanisms. Existing models of analogy posit numerous complex mechanisms. It is worth noting how much can be achieved with so simple a mechanism. However, although compound indexing (Section 3.4) showed this limited case could be extended somewhat, it is not automatically clear how the current model could be extended beyond featural representations to incorporate the structure necessary to account for complex metaphorical comparisons.[1]

We suggested that the pattern completion process could be used as the basis for an 'on-line' analogical comparison procedure which may begin to tackle the problem of determining which features of an object are relevant to a particular comparison. A prior metaphorical stage automatically identifies the relevant features as those that are modified by the metaphor. This account of analogy would incorporate elements of the two opposing views from current research into computational processes underlying analogical processing.

Lastly, we would not want to pretend that this model on its own can explain the full richness (or even mystery!) of metaphor. However, we do believe that it gives us some purchase on a complex and multi-faceted problem, a purchase which is gained at the expense of very few assumptions.

References.

Black, M. (1962). *Models and Metaphors.* Ithaca, NY: Cornell University Press.

Black, M. (1979). More about metaphor. In A. Ortony (Ed.), *Metaphor and Thought* (pp.19-43). Cambridge, England: Cambridge University Press.

Burns, B. D. and Holyoak, K. J. (1994). Competing Models of Analogy: ACME Versus Copycat. *Proceedings of the 16th Annual Meeting of the Cognitive Science Society.* Erlbaum. 100-105.

---

1. However, as outlined in the Introduction, one might question whether the structural mappings necessary in complex metaphors are best described using a single, on-line process model of the type outlined here. For instance a multi-mechanism, iterative process may be more appropriate for stepping through the mappings in complex metaphors.

Forbus, K. D., Gentner, D., and Law, K. (1995). MAC/FAC: A Model of Similarity-based Retrieval. *Cognitive Science, 19, No. 2,* 144-206.

Glucksberg, S. and Keysar, B. (1990) Understanding Metaphorical Comparisons: Beyond Similarity. *Psychological Review, 97, No. 1,* 3-18.

Glucksberg, S. and Keysar, B. (1993). How metaphors work. In A. Ortony (Ed.), *Metaphor and Thought 2nd Ed.* (pp. 401-424). Cambridge, England: Cambridge University Press.

Hofstadter, D. R. (1984). The Copycat project: An experiment in non-deterministic and creative analogies. Cambridge, MA: MIT A.I. Laboratory Memo 755.

Hofstadter, D. R. and French, R. M. (1994). Probing the Emergent Behavior of Tabletop: an Architecture Uniting High-level Perception with Analogy-making. *Proceedings of the 16th Annual Meeting of the Cognitive Science Society.* Erlbaum. 528-533.

Holyoak, K. J. and Thagard, P. (1989). Analogical mapping by constraint satisfaction. *Cognitive Science, 13,* 295-355.

Holyoak, K. J. and Thagard, P. (1995). *Mental Leaps: Analogy in Creative Thought.* Cambridge, MA: MIT Press.

Lakoff, G. (1994) What is Metaphor? In K. J. Holyoak and J. A. Barnden (Eds.), *Advances in connectionist and neural computation theory, Vol.3* (pp. 203-258). Norwood NJ: Ablex.

Lakoff, G. and Johnson, M. (1980). *Metaphors we live by.* Chicago: University of Chicago Press.

Malgady, R. G. and Johnson, M. G. (1976). Modifiers in metaphors: Effects of constituent phrase similarity on the interpretation of figurative sentences. *Journal of Psycholinguistic Research, 5,* 43-52.

McClelland, J. L. and Rumelhart, D. E. (1986). A Distributed Model of Human Learning and Memory. In McClelland, Rumelhart, and The PDP Research Group (1986). *Parallel Distributed Processing: Explorations in the Microstructure of Cognition. Vol. 2: Psychological and Biological Models.* Cambridge, MA: MIT Press. pp. 170-215.

Mitchell, M. (1993). *Analogy-making as perception.* Cambridge, MA: MIT Press.

Ortony, A. (1993). The role of similarity in similes and metaphors. In A. Ortony (Ed.), *Metaphor and Thought 2nd Ed.* (pp. 342-356). Cambridge, England: Cambridge University Press.

Rumelhart, D. E. (1979). Some problems with the notion of literal meanings. In A. Ortony (Ed.), *Metaphor and Thought* (pp. 71-82). Cambridge, England: Cambridge University Press.

Rumelhart, D. E. and Abrahamson, A. A. (1973). A model for analogical reasoning. *Cognitive Psychology, 5,* 1-28.

Sternberg, R. J., Tourangeau, R., and Nigro, G. (1979). Metaphor, induction, and social policy: The convergence of macroscopic and microscopic views. In A. Ortony (Ed.), *Metaphor and Thought* (pp. 277-306). Cambridge, England: Cambridge University Press.

Multi-Level Analysis of Memory Dissociations

Hongbin Wang and **Jiajie Zhang**
Department of Psychology
The Ohio State University
1827 Neil Avenue
Columbus, OH 43210
{wang.190,zhang.52}@osu.edu

Abstract

Dissociations between explicit and implicit memory tests, between recollective and automatic retrieval processes, and between memorial states of awareness of past events all suggest that human memory is not a unitary faculty. Memory dissociations reflect the complex relationship between consciousness and memory. To understand such a complex relationship, any single level of analysis is not enough and may be misleading. A multi-level analysis was proposed. One of the most serious problems with the process-dissociation procedure is its failure to separate process level of analysis and memorial awareness level of analysis. One experiment was reported to support the above arguments.

Introduction

Explicit tests of memory refer to the tests in which subjects are explicitly told the relationship between the prior study and the following test. In this case, in order for subjects to perform the test, intentionally retrieving past events is necessary. In contrast to explicit tests of memory, implicit tests of memory refer to the tests in which subjects are simply told to perform a task as well as possible, without the mentioning of the prior study episode. A large body of data has shown that these two types of tests can be dissociated (for reviews, see Schacter, 1987; Richardson-Klavehn & Bjork, 1988). Dissociations between explicit and implicit tests of memory suggest that (a) human memory is not a unitary faculty and (b) consciousness plays an essential role in dissociable human memory.

A theoretical debate is concerned with whether memory systems or psychological processes are responsible for these task dissociations. Memory systems theories claim that there are distinct memory systems in the human brain and that implicit tests depend on the memory systems that are distinct from those that support explicit tests (e.g., Tulving & Schacter, 1990; Schacter, 1990, 1992). In contrast, processing theories claim that proposing distinct memory systems is neither necessary nor economic, and that dissociations between tests can be and should be understood in terms of the underlying perceptual and conceptual processing operations carried out during study and test phases (e.g., Roediger & McDemott, 1993).

While the theoretical debate remains to be resolved, several researchers have started to challenge the underlying *transparency* (Dunn & Kirsner, 1989) or *process-purity*

(Jacoby, Toth, & Yonelinas, 1993) assumption on which several theoretical approaches are based. For example, they ask why explicit and implicit memory tests must tap distinct memory systems or different retrieval processes, why tests and memory systems must be "transparent", and why tests must be process-pure. These challenges have received some empirical support (e.g., Richardson-Klavehn, Lee, Joubran, & Bjork, 1994), which suggests that different retrieval processes might be involved in a single memory test and memory tests need not be process-pure.

The Process-Dissociation Procedure

The *process-dissociation procedure* (Jacoby, 1991; Jacoby, Toth, & Yonelinas, 1993) has been claimed to provide a general methodological framework for identifying the influences of recollective and automatic retrieval processes in a single memory test. It makes two critical assumptions. The first one is that recollective processes and automatic processes make independent contributions to the overall test performance (see Jacoby, Toth, Yonelinas, & Debner, 1994). The second one is that the difference between recollective and automatic retrieval processes can be considered as an issue of *control*. More specifically, recollective retrieval processes can not only voluntarily activate an action, but also "inhibit an action by opposing influences that would otherwise prevail" (Jacoby, Lindsay, & Toth, 1992, p. 804). In contrast, automatic retrieval processes have no control at all and always occur spontaneously and automatically.

Based on these two assumptions, Jacoby and colleagues claim that by adopting the method of *opposition*, it is possible to oppose the influences of two types of retrieval processes and let the two work in the opposite directions. They call the test in which both types of processes work in the same direction *an inclusion test*, and the test in which both types of processes work in the opposite directions *an exclusion test*. In a word-stem completion task, an inclusion test requires subjects to try to retrieve a previously studied word to complete a stem, while an exclusion test requires subjects to try not to use studied words as the completion (i.e., try to exclude studied words).

They further claim that in an inclusion test, the probability of responding with a studied word is the probability of recollection *(R)* plus the probability of the word automatically coming to mind when there is a failure of recollection [$A(1-R)$]; and in an exclusion test, a studied word will be produced only when it comes to mind automatically and it is not recollected [$A(1-R)$]. That is,

$$I = R + A(1-R). \quad (1)$$
$$E = A(1-R). \quad (2)$$

where I is the inclusion test performance and E is the exclusion test performance. The influences of recollective processes and automatic processes can thus be easily calculated: $R = I - E$, and $A = E/(1-R)$.

Although the process-dissociation procedure has resulted in several empirical findings (e.g., Jacoby, Toth, & Yonelinas, 1993; Toth, Reingold, & Jacoby, 1994), it has also been subject to several criticisms. For example, Joordens and Merikle (1993) argue that the independence assumption underlying the process-dissociation procedure is problematic because a redundancy relationship between the two types of processes is equally plausible. Richardson-Klavehn, Gardiner and Java (in press) even argued that the R and A in equation (1) need not to be equal to the R and A in equation (2). However, as we will show below, perhaps one of the most serious problems with the process-dissociation procedure is its failure to distinguish retrieval processes from memorial states of awareness. This problem is directly reflected in its control assumption.

Where Is Control?

The process-dissociation procedure defines control as the ability to inhibit an action that would otherwise be very likely to occur. It is assumed that recollective retrieval processes have control ability whereas automatic retrieval processes do not have it.

Let us consider how a studied word can be excluded from being used in an exclusion test. No matter how it is produced, whether it will be used as a response depends on how the subject thinks about it. Clearly, while retrieval processes are responsible for producing a word, or bringing a word to mind, it is the subject's memorial awareness about that word that serves as the control criterion for deciding using or excluding. A studied word will be excluded in an exclusion test if and only if subjects judge that it is a studied word. Such a judgment must be based on their subjective experience or memorial awareness of that word but not on the processes which bring that word back to mind.

From this perspective, control is not a function of retrieval processes but a function of memorial states of awareness. Since memorial states of awareness of past events are more likely to be a continuum, control is not an all-or-none but a continuous quantity. On the one hand, conscious recollection experience has absolute control power because once one has recollection experience about a word's earlier presence, this word will definitely be excluded in an exclusion test. On the other hand, different levels of feelings of familiarity may have different degrees of control power. That is, a word that looks more familiar is more likely to be excluded in an exclusion test than a word that looks less familiar.

Summary

Control is not a unique property of recollective retrieval processes. Instead, control is a continuous function of

memorial states of awareness of past events. By using "control" as the key concept, what the process-dissociation procedure really dissociates is the conscious (controlled) and unconscious memorial awareness, but not the underlying recollective and automatic retrieval processes, which the process-dissociation procedure is designed to dissociate. In the next section we presents an experiment supporting the above arguments.

Experimental Study

The main hypothesis of this experiment is that automatic retrieval processes can also be associated with control. In this experiment, subjects performed a cued-recall test. In addition, they were asked to make a confidence judgment about each completion. The basic idea is as follows. If a studied word is produced by recollective retrieval processes, a subject should have absolute control and judge it as an old (studied) word with highest confidence. However, if a studied word comes to mind by automatic retrieval processes instead of recollective retrieval processes, how will a subject behave? Will the subject just make random confidence judgment and show no control, or will the subject show a certain predictable judgment pattern?

The independent variable manipulated in this experiment was the letter order of word-stems given as cues. In the normal-order condition, the letters of each word-stem were presented to subjects in the normal order, e.g., "mem___" for "memory". In the reversed-order condition, the positions of the initial two letters of each word-stem were switched, e.g., "emm___" for "memory". This manipulation was expected to influence automatic retrieval processes but not recollective retrieval processes. This is because automatic retrieval processes are usually based on data-driven processes or *perceptual fluency* (Jacoby, 1983), whereas recollective retrieval processes are usually based on conceptually driven processes. Changing the physical format of a cue might hurt the *fluency* of a studied word's coming to mind but should not hurt recollective retrieval processes.

Method

Subjects. Forty-four native English speakers participated in the experiment in return for credit in an introductory psychology course at The Ohio State University.

Materials. The stimulus set consisted of 120 five or six-letter words with average high frequency. 60 of them were used for study, and all 120 were used for test (thus equating the number of stems at test corresponding to old and new items). Normal-order word-stems consisted of the initial three letters of each word in correct order and 2 or 3 dashes, depending on the word-length. Reversed-order word-stems were created by switching the initial two letters of corresponding normal-order word-stems. Each word-stem could be completed by more than one word. Any two words in the stimulus set have different initial three letters.

Design and Procedure. The word-stem order manipulation is between-subjects design. Subjects were tested individually. The experiment was conducted in two phases, study and test. The study phase was identical for all subjects. Subjects were presented 60 words and were instructed to remember them. Each word was shown for two seconds with an inter-trial interval of one second.

In the test phase, all subjects were presented 120 word-stems. Subjects receiving reversed-order word-stems were told the rule of how to get correct order stems. All subjects were instructed to try to use the studied words to complete each word-stem. If they could not think of a studied word, they were to use the first word that came to mind. If they could not figure out a completion, they could click on the "OK" button to pass the trial. If they got a completion, they were asked to further identify "How likely has this word been studied?" by choosing one of the five confidence levels (see Figure 1). Subjects were explicitly told that the 5th level referred to "conscious recollection" and "remembering", which was qualitatively different from the other 4 levels. If they could not consciously recollect or remember it, they could mark their confidence levels from 4 to 1. The test was self-paced.

Results and Discussion

Stem Completion Data. The test performance was indexed by the proportion of stems completed with studied words at each confidence level. The results are shown in Figure 2.

Statistical analyses show the follows results. First, when words were consciously recollected (the 5th level of confidence), stem order did not have effect. Second, when words were not consciously recollected (from the 1st to 4th level of confidence), stem order had effect (F(1,42)=16.30, $p<0.01$): more studied words were produced with normal-order stems than with reversed-order stems. Third, when words were not consciously recollected, confidence judgment had effect (F(3,126)=40.77, $p<0.01$): more studied words were given higher levels of confidence judgment.

This pattern of data suggests that when there was no conscious recollection, subjects did not randomly make a confidence judgment. Rather, they showed certain control ability and gave more studied words higher levels of confidence judgment.

Process-Dissociation Data. Now, let us consider a hypothetical situation. Suppose subjects were not asked to make confidence judgment. Instead, they were asked to exclude those completions which they thought were old words. It is easy to see that this hypothetical task was essentially identical to the confidence judgment task because subjects usually made their "exclusion or not" decisions based on their confidence about the "old-ness" of a word. Therefore, it was possible to use the stem completion data presented above to predict how subjects would behave in such an hypothetical exclusion test. For example, judging a word to the 5th confidence level would guarantee this word be excluded if the exclusion criterion is "excluding every word which is consciously recollected". Similarly, judging a word to be the 4th confidence level ("probably an old word") would guarantee this world be excluded if the exclusion criterion is "excluding every word which is probably an old world". Thus, a confidence level could be considered as an exclusion criterion; and based on the 5 levels of confidence judgment, 4 different exclusion criteria could be obtained. Thus, by subtracting the proportions excluded from the overall test performance, 4 different exclusion test scores could be predicted. Furthermore, 4 groups of recollective/automatic influences could be estimated by using the equations of the process-dissociation procedure. These estimates are shown in Figure 3.

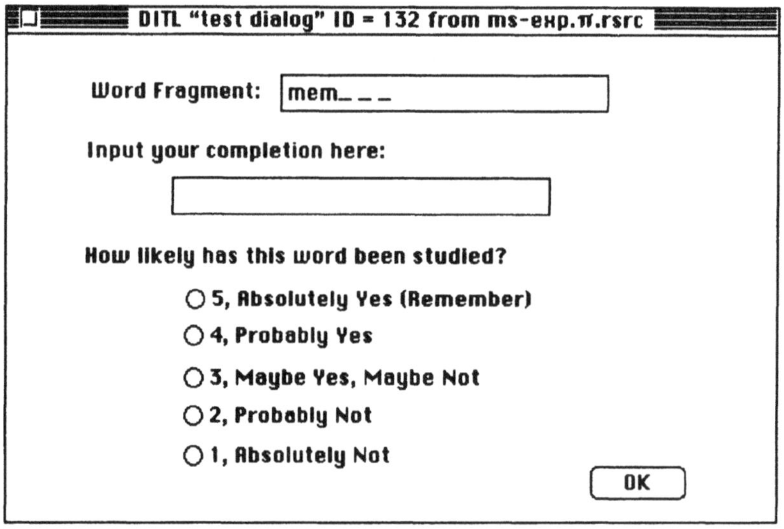

Figure 1: The Macintosh dialog box used in the experiment

704

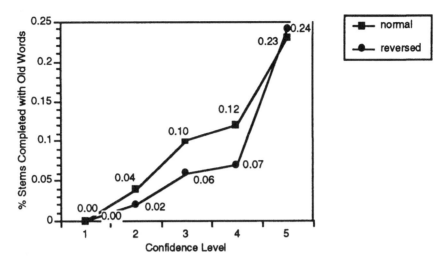

Figure 2: Cued-recall performance as a function of confidence levels for normal-order and reversed-order cues.

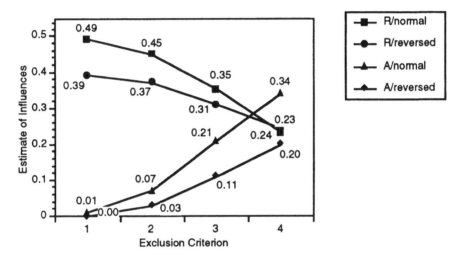

Figure 3: Influence estimates of recollective *(R)* and automatic *(A)* retrieval processes as a function of exclusion criteria for normal-order and reversed-order cues. Exclusion criteria 4, 3, 2, and 1 refer to excluding the performance at confidence levels 5, 5+4, 5+4+3, and 5+4+3+2, respectively.

Statistical analyses show that (a) stem order manipulation affected both recollective processes and automatic processes $(F(1,42)=3.63, p<0.07; F(1,42)=22.18, p<0.01$, respectively); and (b) if different exclusion criteria were adopted, different recollective and automatic influences would be estimated $(F(3,126)=151.81, p<0.01; F(3,126)=180.88, p<0.01$, respectively).

These results were ambiguous because (a) the stem order manipulation is expected to affect only automatic retrieval processes but not recollective retrieval processes, and estimates of recollective and automatic influences are expected to be stable across exclusion criteria; (b) Based on different exclusion criteria, different conclusions were obtained. One reason for these ambiguous results is that the process-dissociation procedure ignores the part of control power that is associated with automatic retrieval processes.

It is this part of control power that produces predictable confidence judgment pattern and results in different exclusion criteria.

General Discussion

Memory dissociations are complex. This complexity may reflect the complex relationship between consciousness and memory. To explain such a complex relationship, any single level of analysis is not sufficient and will inevitably result in oversimplification and misleading conclusions. In order to better understand various memory dissociations, a multi-level analysis is necessary. Figure 4 shows such an attempt.

As shown in Figure 4, memory dissociations can occur at different levels. The first level of dissociations occurs at test level, referring to the dissociations between explicit and implicit tests of memory. Dissociations at this level suggest that the awareness of the study-test relationship plays an important role in human memorial behavior.

The second level of dissociations occurs at process level, referring to the dissociations between recollective (intentional, or voluntary) and automatic (incidental, or involuntary) retrieval processes. Dissociations at this level reflect the operations of retrieval volition, one of the important aspects of consciousness.

The third level of dissociations occurs at memorial awareness level, referring to the dissociations between conscious awareness and unconscious awareness and dissociations between recollection experience and feelings of familiarity. Dissociations at this level reflect the functions of subjective experience in human memorial behavior. It is reasonable to think of memorial states of awareness as a continuum.

Tests and processes can be separated. An single test may involve both recollective and automatic retrieval processes. The fact that a single memory test might involve multiple types of processes suggests that the awareness of study-test relationship and retrieval volition can be separated. Processes and memorial states of awareness can also be separated. Automatic retrieval processes need not be solely associated with unconscious awareness. This separation is especially important for certain memory tests which involve a stage in which subjective experience about an item needs to be assessed. One such an example is the exclusion test introduced by the process-dissociation procedure.

The notion that memory dissociations should be analyzed at multiple levels has significant implications for the studies of implicit cognition in general. Implicit cognition is concerned with the general relationship between consciousness and human cognition. Important issues in implicit cognition include (a) to what extent that there exist unconscious processes; and (b) whether it is conscious or unconscious processes that are more fundamental for human cognition. Debates still remain between different views (for reviews, see Merikle, 1992; Shanks & St. John, 1994). One reason for this situation is that researchers often fail to separate the different roles consciousness plays at levels of tasks, processes, and mental awareness.

References

Dunn, J.C., & Kirsner, K. (1989). Implicit memory: Task or process? In S. Lewandowsky, J.C. Dunn, & K. Kirsner (Eds.), *Implicit Memory: Theoretical Issues*. Hillsdale, New Jersey: Erlbaum.

Jacoby, L.L. (1983). Remembering the data: Analyzing interactive processes in reading. *Journal of Verbal Learning and Verbal Behavior, 22*, 485-508.

Jacoby, L.L. (1991). A process dissociation framework: Separating automatic from intentional uses of memory. *Journal of Memory and Language, 30*, 513-541.

Jacoby, L.L., Lindsay, D.S., & Toth, J.P. (1992). Unconscious influences revealed: Attention, awareness, and control. *American Psychologist, 47(6)*, 802-809.

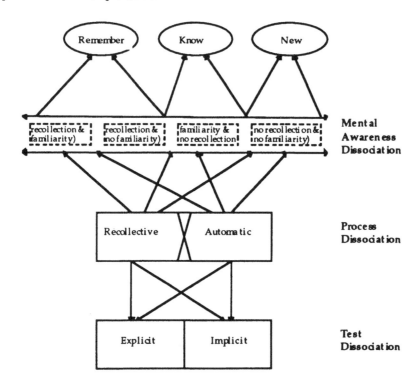

Figure 4: Multi-level analysis of memory dissociations.

Jacoby, L.L., Toth, J.P., & Yonelinas, A.P. (1993). Separating conscious and unconscious influences of memory: Measuring recollection. *Journal of Experimental Psychology: General, 122*, 139-154.

Jacoby, L.L., Toth, J.P., Yonelinas, A.P., & Debner, J.A. (1994). The relationship between conscious and unconscious influences: Independent or redundancy? *Journal of Experimental Psychology: General, 123*, 216-219.

Joordens, S., & Merikle, P.M. (1993). Independence or redundency? Two models of conscious and unconscious influences. *Journal of Experimental Psychology: General, 122*, 462-467.

Merikle, P. M. (1992). Perception without awareness: Critical issues. *American Psychologist, 47*, 792-795.

Richardson-Klavehn, A., & Bjork, R.A. (1988). Measures of memory. *Annual Review of Psychology, 39*, 475-543.

Richardson-Klavehn, A., Lee, M.G., Joubran, R., & Bjork, R.A. (1994). Intention and awareness in perceptual identification priming. *Memory & Cognition, 22*, 293-312.

Richardson-Klavehn, A., Gardiner, J.M., & Java, R.I. (in press). Memory: Task dissociations, process dissociations, and dissociations of consciousness. In G. Underwood (Ed.), *Implicit Cognition*. Oxford: Oxford University Press.

Roediger, H.L.III, & McDermott, K.B. (1993). Implicit memory in normal human subjects. *Handbook of Neuropsychology, 8*, 63-131.

Schacter, D.L. (1987). Implicit memory: History and current status. *Journal of Experimental Psychology: Learning, Memory, and Cognition. 13*, 501-518.

Schacter, D.L. (1990). Perceptual representation systems and implicit memory: Toward a resolution of the multiple memory systems debate. *Annals of the New York Academy of Sciences, 608*, 543-571.

Schacter, D.L. (1992). Understanding implicit memory: A cognitive neuroscience approach. *American Psychologist, 47*, 559-569.

Shanks, D. R., & St. John, M. F. (1994). Characteristics of dissociable human learning systems. *Behavioral and Brain Sciences, 17*, 367-447.

Toth, J.P., Reingold, E.M., & Jacoby, L.L. (1994). Toward a redefinition of implicit memory: process dissociations following elaborative processing and self-generation. *Journal of Experimental Psychology: Learning, Memory, & Cognition, 20*, 290-303.

Tulving, E., & Schacter, D.L. (1990). Priming and human memory systems. *Science, 247*, 301-306.

Order Effects and Frequency Learning in Belief Updating

Jiajie Zhang[1], Todd R. Johnson[2], Hongbin Wang[1]
Department of Psychology[1]
Division of Medical Informatics, Department of Pathology[2]
Center for Cognitive Science[1,2]
The Ohio State University
Columbus, Ohio 43210
zhang.52@osu.edu, johnson.25@osu.edu,
wang.190@osu.edu

Abstract

This paper examines order effects and frequency learning in belief updating. We present an experiment that tests for the existence of order effects for actual decisions during frequency learning and for belief evaluations after frequency learning in a realistic tactical decision making task. The experiment revealed that (a) subjects showed order effects for actual decisions during frequency learning—an effect not reported previously and (b) subjects still showed order effects for belief evaluations even after having correctly learned most of the frequency information. We also present a simulation for the frequency learning behavior and some preliminary results of a simulation for the order effect, and suggest networks for potential combinations of the order effect and frequency learning.

Introduction

A number of experiments indicate that the order in which evidence is presented can affect the strength of a person's belief in hypothesized causes. Different experiments have found that order of evidence can produce no effect, a recency effect, or a primacy effect. Hogarth and Einhorn (1992) proposed an anchoring and adjustment model of belief updating that predicts when these effects will occur based on features of the belief updating task. For example, step-by-step evaluation of beliefs for mixed positive and negative evidence items produces a recency effect: the final evaluation of belief is mainly determined by the last evidence item. However, step-by-step evaluation of beliefs for consistent evidence (all positive or all negative) produces no effect.

A different set of studies and models are concerned with the learning and use of frequency information. When conditional probability and base rates of occurrence are presented explicitly in terms of numeric values, they are very difficult to learn and utilize (see Kahneman, Slovic & Tversky, 1982). However, when they are presented in terms of real events and occurrences, they can often be learned implicitly and used correctly (e.g., Christensen-Szalanski, & Bushyhead, 1981; Medin & Edelson, 1988; for a review, see Hasher & Zacks, 1984). As a result of using real events to present frequency information, many of the well-known biases in human probabilistic reasoning (see Kahneman, Slovic & Tversky, 1982) disappear. However, one important bias that has yet to be studied in this area is the order effect on belief updating described above.

The studies and models of the order effect are usually separated from those on frequency learning and use. As a result, models of belief updating based on frequency acquisition research cannot account for the complete spectrum of order effects. In fact, one of the most well-known examples, the Rescorla-Wagner model (Rescorla & Wagner, 1972), completely ignores the temporal sequence of information. Since many frequency acquisition tasks involve temporal sequences of information, it is important to consider the joint implications of these two research areas. This paper examines order effects and frequency learning in a common task environment. We present an experiment that tests for the existence of order effects during and after the acquisition of frequency information in a natural setting. The experiment revealed that (a) subjects showed order effects for actual decisions during frequency learning—an effect not reported previously and (b) subjects still showed order effects for belief evaluations even after having correctly learned most of the frequency information. We also present a simulation for the frequency learning behavior and some preliminary results of a simulation for the order effect, and suggest networks for potential combinations of the order effect and frequency learning.

Experiment

The experimental task was implemented on the CIC (Combat Information Center) simulator developed by Towne (1995) for the US Navy. Figure 1 shows a simplified radar display of the CIC simulator. It shows an unknown airplane heading toward the Naval ship which is at the center of the radar display. The captain of the ship can check whether the target is on or off a commercial air route by clicking the route button to display all available routes. He can also send a radio verbal warning to request the target to identify itself by clicking the warning button. The target may or may not respond to the warning. In this experiment, when it responds to the warning, it always identifies itself as a commercial airplane. The target can be either friendly or hostile. The task is to use the information about the air route and the information about the identity (ID) obtained from the radio warning to identify whether the target is friendly or hostile. The constraint of the task is that the two evidence items (route and ID) can only be obtained sequentially, one at a time. The order can be either route followed by ID or ID followed by route.

The experiment tests three hypotheses. The first hypothesis is about frequency learning. In a given geopolitical environment, there are certain conditional probabilities about whether the target is friendly or hostile given the two evidence items. When subjects are trained on the task many times with a fixed base rate and conditional probabilities, they can implicitly and accurately acquire most of the frequency information. The second hypothesis is about the order effect for belief evaluations. Previous studies show that when frequency information is accurately and implicitly learned in actual events, certain biases such as the base rate fallacy can be eliminated. We test the hypothesis that even if most of the frequency information is acquired implicitly and accurately, the order effect for belief evaulations, a special type of bias, still exists. That is, when the two evidence items are presented one by one in different temporal orders, the final evaluations of hypotheses about the friendliness of the target are different. The third hypothesis is about the order effect for actual decisions. Previous studies showed order effects only for belief evaluations, not for actual decisions. We test the hypothesis that subjects show order effects for actual decisions during frequency learning.

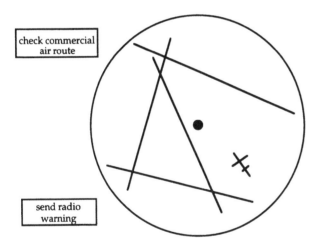

Figure 1. A simplified radar display on the CIC simulator. See text for details.

Method

Subjects. The subjects were 40 undergraduate students in introductory psychology courses at The Ohio State University who participated in the experiment for course credit.

Design & Procedure. There were two evidence items: route and ID. Route indicates whether the target is on or off a commercial air route. ID indicates whether there is any response from the unknown target to a radio warning issued from the ship. The two evidence items were presented in two

different orders: *Route-ID order* in which route information was collected first, followed by ID information; *ID-Route order* in which ID information was collected first, followed by Route information. After having collected both evidence items, subjects made a forced-choice response indicating whether the unknown target was friendly or hostile. After each response, subjects were given feedback indicating whether the response was correct or incorrect. Each subject performed 50 trials. The conditional probabilities of hostility and friendliness for a given set of evident items are shown in Table 1. For half of the 40 subjects, the two evidence items were always presented in the Route-ID order for all 50 trials; for the other half, in the ID-Route order for all 50 trails. The 50 trials for each subject constituted the learning phase for the acquisition of frequency information.

After 50 trials, each subject was given a written questionnaire requesting belief evaluations about the hostility and friendliness of the unknown target after the presentation of a baseline fact and each of the two evidence items. In the questionnaire, Route was always negative (the plane was not on a commercial route) and ID was always positive (the plane indicated that it was a commercial plane). For half of the 20 subjects receiving each of the two training orders (Route-ID and ID-Route) of the 50 trials, the evaluation order of the evidence items was Route-ID; and for the other half, the evaluation order was ID-Route. For example, an evaluation order of Route-ID is shown in Figure 2. The written questionnaire constituted the evaluation phase for belief evaluations.

Thus, this experiment was a 2×2 between-subject design, with the two learning orders as one factor and the two evaluation orders as another factor.

1. *You see a plane which is getting closer to your ship. On a scale from 0 to 100 (with 0 being total disbelief and 100 total belief) please rate your belief in the following hypotheses:*
    1. How likely do you think the plane is hostile?
    2. How likely do you think the plane is friendly?
2. *After consulting commercial air routes, you discover that the plane is not on a commercial air route. Given this new information, please answer the following questions. Again, express your answer on a scale of 0 to 100 with 0 being total disbelief and 100 being total belief.*
    1. How likely do you think the plane is friendly?
    2. How likely do you think the plane is hostile?
3. *When you asked the plane to identify itself, the plane identifies itself as a commercial airplane. Given this new information, please answer the following questions. Again, express your answer on a scale of 0 to 100 with 0 being total disbelief and 100 being total belief.*
    1. How likely do you think the plane is friendly?
    2. How likely do you think the plane is hostile?

Figure 2. The questionnaire for the Route-ID evaluation order.

Table 1. Probability Distribution of Learning Trials

Route	ID	p(Friendly I Route)	p(Friendly I ID)	p(Friendly IRoute, ID)
+	+	0.80	0.80	0.94
+	-	0.80	0.20	0.50
-	+	0.20	0.80	0.50
-	-	0.20	0.20	0.06

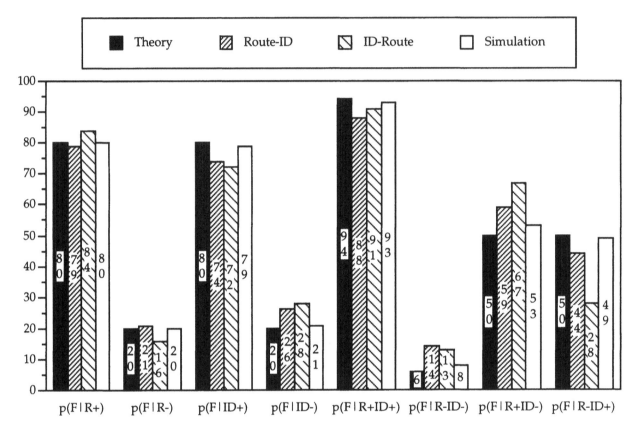

Figure 3. Conditional probabilities from theoretical calculation (Bayes rule), the experiment, and the simulation using the Rescorla-Wagner rule.

Results & Discussion

Frequency Learning. The responses of the 50 trials by each subject were transformed into conditional probabilities, which were then averaged across the 20 subjects for the Route-ID learning order and across the 20 subjects for the ID-Route learning order. The results are shown in Figure 3 under Route-ID and ID-Route.

The conditional probabilities from the experiment were compared with their corresponding theoretical values. For the Route-ID learning order , p(FIID+), p(FIID-), and p(FIR-ID-) were significantly different from the theoretical values (smallest t(19) = 2.82, p < 0.05); p(FIR+), p(FIR-), p(FIR+ID-), p(FIR-ID+), and p(FIR+ID+) were not signifi-

cantly different from the theoretical values (largest t(19) = 2.0, p > 0.05). For the ID-Route order, p(FIID+), p(FIID-), p(FIR-ID-), p(FIR+ID-), and p(FIR-ID+) were significantly different from their theoretical values (smallest t(19) = 2.26, p < 0.05); p(FIR+), p(FIR-), and p(FIR+ID+) were not significantly different from the theoretical values (largest t(19) = 1.31, p > 0.20). These results indicate two findings. First, subjects correctly learned some of the conditional probabilities but not all, and more for the Route-ID order than for the ID-Route order. Second, ID was a less objective evidence item than Route: p(FIID+) was smaller than its theoretical value but p(FIR+) was not different from its theoretical value. This might be because Route was always objectively observed from the radar display whereas ID was obtained from possibly deceptive radio communication.

The conditional probabilities from the two different learning orders were also compared with each other. The only significant difference was p(F|R-ID+) (F(1, 38) = 4.52, p < 0.05). This is clearly a recency order effect: p(F|R-ID+) for the Route-ID order was larger than p(F|R-ID+) for the ID-Route order because the last evidence item in the Route-ID order was positive (ID+) whereas that in the ID-Route order was negative (R-). A similar order effect was also observed for p(F|R+ID-) although the difference between the two learning orders was not statistically significant. This result is an indication that subjects showed order effects for actual decisions during frequency learning.

Belief Evaluation. The results of belief evaluations after the learning phase are shown in Figure 4. For both learning orders, there was a clear order effect: when the two evidence items (positive ID, negative Route) were presented in different temporal orders, the final friendliness evaluations of the unknown target were different. An ANOVA for the final evaluations of friendliness was conducted for the two learning orders and two evaluation orders. The main effect for the two learning orders was significant (F(1, 38) = 4.32, p < 0.05), indicating that the learning order Route-ID produced a more hostile evaluation than the learning order ID-Route. The main effect for the two evaluation orders was also significant (F(1, 38) = 13.41, p < 0.001), indicating that the evaluation order Route-ID produced a more friendly evaluation than the evaluation order ID-Route. This order effect for evaluations was a recency effect, as predicted by Hogarth and Einhorn's model: the final evaluation of friendliness was determined by the last evidence item. For the Route-ID evaluation order, the last evidence ID was positive, producing a more friendly evaluation. In contrast, for the ID-Route evaluation order, the last evidence Route was negative, producing a more hostile evaluation. The interaction between learning order and evaluation was not significant (F(1, 38) = 0.53, p = 0.47).

Simulation: Frequency Learning

The experiment shows that subjects could learn most of the frequency information implicitly and accurately. This section describes a connectionist simulation of frequency learning based on the Rescorla-Wagner rule (Rescorla & Wagner, 1972).

The Rescorla-Wagner rule was initially proposed for classical conditioning in animal associative learning and later extended for human learning (e.g., Gluck & Bower, 1988). It is sensitive to frequencies of observations and conditional probabilities. Let w_{ij} denote the strength of association between observation o_i and hypothesis h_j. If h_j is a correct hypothesis for observation o_i, then the weight change is $\Delta w_{ij} = \eta o_i (max - \sum_{i \in o} w_{ij})$, where η is the learning rate, o_i reflects the reliability of the observation, max is the maximum possible level of associative strength that can be associated with each hypothesis unit h_j and $\sum_{i \in o} w_{ij}$ is the total associative strength for the hypothesis h_j that connects all observations present on that trial. If the hypothesis h_j is an incorrect hypothesis for observation o_i, then the associative strength between o_i and h_j decreases. The weight change is $\Delta w_{ij} = -\eta o_i \sum_{i \in o} w_{ij}$. After a series of trials, w_{ij} will reflect the conditional probability of the hypothesis h_j given the observation o_i.

Figure 5 shows a simple network used to simulate the experimental task described previously. The four observation units represent the four possible outcomes of the two evidence items: Route positive (R+), Route negative (R-), ID positive (ID+), and ID negative (ID-). The two hypothesis units represent the two possible outcomes of the evaluation: Friendly (F) and Hostile (H).

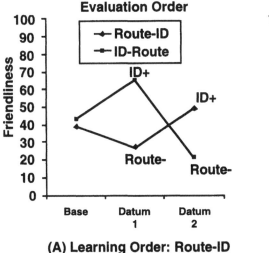

(A) Learning Order: Route-ID

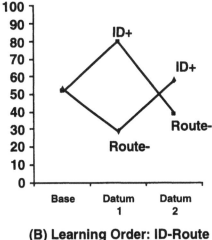

(B) Learning Order: ID-Route

Figure 4. The evaluations of friendliness for the two different evaluation orders under the two different learning orders.

Table 2. The Estimation of Conditional Probabilities for One Evidence Item

input patterns	prob of patterns	output activation		p × output × 100	
R+ R- ID+ ID-	p	o(F)	o(H)	Friendly	Hostile
1 0 1 0	0.34	0.924	0.072	31.42	2.45
1 0 0 1	0.16	0.519	0.467	8.30	7.47
0 1 1 0	0.16	0.487	0.515	7.79	8.24
0 1 0 1	0.34	0.082	0.910	2.79	30.94

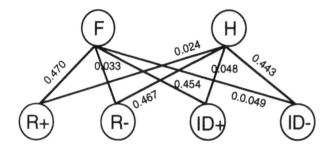

Figure 5. A simple network used to simulate the experimental task. The Rescorla-Wagner learning rule was used. The weights are the average of the weights learned by the network across 20 simulated subjects with 50 trials for each simulated subject.

Method

Subjects. 20 simulated subjects were trained on the network.

Materials. The 50 trials used in the experiment were the 50 trials for the simulated subjects. The presentations of the 50 trials were randomized for each simulated subject. The conditional probabilities of outcomes given conditions of the two evidence items were identical to those in the experiment, which are shown in Table 1.

Design & Procedure. The order effect of the presentation of the evidence items was not considered in this simulation because Rescorla-Wagner rule cannot deal with temporal orders. The two evidence items for each trial were encoded as four observation units (R+, R-, ID+, ID-). For example, positive Route and negative ID were encoded as (1, 0, 0, 1). The outcome for each trial was encoded as two competing hypothesis units (F, H). For example, friendly was encoded as (1, 0).

The parameters of Rescorla-Wagner rule were as follows: $\eta = 0.1$; *max* = 1; initial weights = 0. For each simulated subject, the 50 trials were only presented once, same as in the experiment. The weights were updated after each trial.

Result

The final weights of the 20 simulated subjects were averaged, which are shown in Figure 5. These weights were used to estimate the conditional probabilities of friendliness and hostility for different combinations of the two evidence items.

The calculation of p(F | R, ID) is straightforward. For example, if we use o(F) and o(H) to indicate the activation values of the friendly and hostile units, then

p(F | R+, ID+)
= o(F)/(o(F)+o(H))
= $(w_{FR+}+w_{FID+})/((w_{FR+}+w_{FID+})+(w_{HR+}+w_{HID+}))$
= (0.470+0.454)/((0.470+0.454)+(0.024+0.048))
= 0.93

Similarly, we can get p(F | R+, ID-) = 0.53; p(F | R-, ID+) = 0.49; p(F | R-, ID-) = 0.08. These p values are shown in Figure 3.

To estimate p(F | R) and p(F | ID), we need a different procedure because we cannot use the ratio of activation values or the ratio of weights directly for the following reason. Suppose we have an input vector (R+, R-, ID+, ID-). In an actual input pattern, one of the two Rs is 1 and the other is 0 and one of the two IDs is 1 and the other is 0, e.g., (1, 0, 1, 0). To estimate p(F |R+), for example, we need an input pattern (1, 0, 0, 0), which is a pattern never presented in the training set. Thus, in order to estimate p(F | R) and p(F | ID), we need to consider the distribution of the 50 training patterns, as shown in Table 2. For example, to calculate p(F |R+), we need to consider all the patterns in the 50 training patterns that contain the pattern (1, 0, 0, 0), which are (1, 0, 1, 0) and (1, 0, 0, 1). Given the input (1, 0, 1, 0), the output activation of F is 0.924, which is then weighted by the probability of this pattern (0.34) across the 50 training patterns, producing a product 0.3142. Similarly, we can get the weighted output activation for H (0.0245) for the same pattern and those for F and H for pattern (1, 0, 0, 1): 0.083 and 0.0747. From these values, we get

p(F | R+)
= (31.42+8.30)/((31.42+8.30)+(2.45+7.47))
= 0.80

Similarly, we can get p(F | R-) = 0.20; p(F | ID+) = 0.79; p(F | ID-) = 0.21). These p values are also shown in Figure 3.

From Figure 3 we can see that the conditional probabilities learned by the Rescorla-Wagner rule are identical to the theoretical values. This indicates that the Rescorla-Wagner rule accurately learned conditional probabilities.

Discussion and Conclusion

The experimental results supported our three hypotheses: (a) most of the frequency information was learned implicitly and accurately, (b) there was an order effect for belief evaluation after frequency learning, and (c) there was also an order effect for actual decisions during frequency learning. The first unique contribution of the present experiment is that it shows that the order effect could not be eliminated even if most of the frequency information was learned implicitly and accurately. This is in contrast with previous studies which show that when frequency information is learned implicitly and accurately, certain biases such as the base rate fallacy can be eliminated. The second unique contribution of the present experiment is the demonstration of order effects for actual decisions, which have not been reported previously in the literature.

The simulation results on frequency learning with the Rescorla-Wagner rule were identical to the theoretical values and very close to the values learned by human subjects. It indicates that the Rescorla-Wagner rule can account for both theoretical and empirical data on frequency learning. In addition to the Rescorla-Wagner rule, we also tried a simple recurrent net (Elman, 1993) and a reinforcement net (Sutton, 1988) to simulate the order effect. The simulation results show that both types of networks could produce order effects for the order used for training but they could not be generalized to a new order not present in the training. Other types of networks are being examined for the order effect. The high-level objective of our simulation studies is to find a single architecture that can not only learn frequency information but also produce the full range of order effects.

Acknowledgments

This research was supported by Office of Naval Research Grant No. N00014-95-1-0241 and a summer fellowship from the Center for Cognitive Science at The Ohio State University.

References

Christensen-Szalanski, J. J. J., & Bushyhead, J. B. (1981). Physicians' use of probabilistic information in a real clinical setting. *Journal of Experimental Psychology: Human Perception and Performance, 7* (4), 928-935.

Elman, J. (1990). Finding structures in time. *Cognitive Science, 14,* 179.

Gluck, M. A., & Bower, G. H. (1988). From conditioning to category learning: An adaptive network model. *Journal of Experimental Psychology: General, 117* (3), 227-247.

Hasher, L., & Zacks, R. T. (1984). Automatic processing of fundamental information: The case of frequency of occurrence. *American Psychologist, 39*(12), 1372-1388.

Hogarth, R. M. & Einhorn, H. J. (1992). Order effects in belief updating: The belief-adjustment model. *Cognitive Psychology, 24,* 1-55.

Kahneman, D., Slovic, P., & Tversky, A. (1982). *Judgment under uncertainty: Heuristics and biases.* New York: Cambridge University Press.

Medin, D. L., & Edelson, S. M. (1988). Problem structure and the use of base-rate information form experience. *Journal of Experimental Psychology: General, 117* (1), 68-85.

Rescorla, R. A., & Wagner, A. R. (1972). A theory of Pavlovian conditioning: Variations in the effectiveness of reinforcement and non-reinforcement. In A. H. Black & W. F. Prokasy (Eds.), *Classical Conditioning II: Current Research and Theory.* New York: Appleton-Century-Crofts.

Sutton, R. S. (1988). Learning to predict by the methods of temporal differences. *Machine Learning, 3,* 9-44.

Towne, D. (1995). *CIC: Tactical Decision Making (Version 2.0).* Behavioral Technology Laboratories, University of Southern California.

Direct Visual Access is the only Way to Access the Chinese Mental Lexicon

Xiaolin Zhou and William Marslen-Wilson

Department of Psychology
Birkbeck College
Malet Street, London WC1E 7HX
x.zhou@psychology.bbk.ac.uk

Abstract

We argue for a view that, for written Chinese, direct visual access is the only way to access information stored in the mental lexicon. Phonology plays no role in initial lexical access and has limited effect on access to lexical semantics. Evidence supporting this view is adduced from three sets of experiments that either failed to detect any phonological effect in lexical access, or failed to prove that the phonological effects obtained are pre-lexical in nature, or demonstrate successfully the presence of orthographic effect in lexical access. We conclude that words in the lexicon can be accessed in different ways, depending on the general configurations of the writing systems in different languages.

Introduction

The process of human language understanding begins with mapping of the sensory input onto underlying form representations in the mental lexicon, as the basis for access to stored semantic and syntactic properties. For written language, the traditional dual-route models of reading (e.g., Coltheart, 1978) assume that this mapping process (or initial lexical access) can be conducted in two ways. One is by a direct visual access route, where visual features in the input are projected directly onto underlying orthographic representations, which are in turn related to the activation of stored phonological representations and lexical semantic properties. The other is by a phonologically mediated process, where the orthographic input is first transformed, perhaps through grapheme-phoneme conversion rules, into a phonological code which in turn is used to access lexical phonological representations and semantic and syntactic properties. Connectionist models of reading (e.g., Plaut, McClelland, Seidenberg, & Patterson, 1996), on other hand, discard the localist assumption of lexical entry and the independent, rule-based routes from orthography to phonology. Instead, the lexicon is assumed to be a distributed network in which the knowledge of a word's spellling, pronunciation, meaning etc. is represented as activation patterns over a set of units. The same units are used to encode different words. Lexical processing is just the computation and production of different patterns of activation over sets of units used to represent the information in demand. As far as the activation of semantic properties is concerned, connectionist models share with dual-route models the assumption that the meaning of a word can be activated in two ways, either by direct visual access or via the activation of phonological representations. However, recent years have seen the emergence of a different view. According to this theory (e.g., van Orden, 1987; Lukatela & Turvey, 1994a, 1994b), phonological mediation is the *predominant* process in lexical access, if not the only process. In initial access, phonology is computed from the visual input and mapped onto underlying lexical or semantic representations in the lexicon. Orthographic information is then used to refine the lexical activation begun by phonology. Direct visual access either does not exist, or plays only a minor role in lexical access.

In this paper, we argue for a different view of lexical access, not for English but for Chinese. We will provide experimental evidence which demonstrates that, for written Chinese, direct visual access is the only way for information stored in the lexicon to become available. Phonology plays *no* role in initial lexical access. It is either a consequence or a by-product of the visual access. In other words, there is no such thing as "pre-lexical" phonology or phonological recoding in reading Chinese. Moreover, we argue that access to lexical semantics is predominantly conducted by direct visual mapping from orthography to semantic representations. Although phonological representation may be automatically activated, due to the activation of orthographic representation in initial lexical access, it is normally *not* or *not efficiently* used to mediate the access to meaning. Direct visual access is a psychological consequence of the logographic Chinese writing system which has evolved to represent the meaning rather than the sound of the language (Wang, 1973)[1].

As pointed by van Orden, Pennington, & Stone (1990), unambiguous evidence for direct visual access has been

---

[1] In this language, the basic meaningful units in the writing system are characters. With some exceptions, each character corresponds to one morpheme and has one pronunciation (i.e., a syllable with a specific tone). Because different characters may have the same pronunciation, homophonic morphemes in this language are common rather than exceptional. Most words in the language are either monomorphemic words or disyllabic (two-character) compounds.

scarce or non-existent. One reason for this may be because orthography and phonology are necessarily confounded in alphabetic languages and their effects on lexical access are difficult to separate. Instead, researchers have followed the rationale that if an explicit manipulation of phonology does not produce a detectable effect on word recognition, it is then taken as evidence of visual processes in lexical access. In the present research, we first follow this logic and demonstrate that similar experimental manipulations that produce reliable phonological effects on visual word recognition in alphabetic languages fail to affect the recognition of Chinese words, while semantic or orthographic effects are consistently observed in the same experiments. We further demonstrate that the presence of phonological effects under certain circumstances does not invalidate our claim of direct visual access. Rather, it strengthens our view that phonology in reading Chinese is a by-product of initial lexical access. Furthermore, we present direct evidence of visual effects in lexical access. Such a demonstration of pure orthographic effects is made available through the separation of orthography and phonology in the Chinese writing system. Taken together, the data support our view that direct visual access is the only route into the Chinese mental lexicon in visual word recognition. The issues of access to lexical semantics and the architecture of the Chinese mental lexicon are discussed in the last section.

The Absence of Phonological Effects

Since van Orden (1987), experimental tasks that tap into lexical semantic representations have become some of the major tools for investigating the role of phonology in lexical access. These tasks share the advantage that subjects are not required to attend specifically to the phonological component of visual input and any phonological effect arising from this task is likely to be due to an automatic process in lexical access. In a set of primed naming experiments (Table 1), Lukatela & Turvey (1994a) found that facilitatory effects for words like *frog* can be obtained not only when they are preceded by their semantic associates (e.g., *toad*) but also when they are preceded by words that are homophonic with the associates (e.g., *towed*). This phonologically mediated semantic priming between *towed* and *frog* is taken as strong evidence that, for English, an orthographically deep language, initial lexical access is phonologically constrained. A phonological code is computed from the orthographic input of *towed* and used to access all the corresponding phonological representations (including *toad*) in the lexicon. Lexical activation spreads to other semantically related lexical items (e.g., *frog*) and leads to a facilitatory priming in naming.

We conducted a set of experiments with similar designs (see Table 1) to examine whether phonologically mediated

semantic priming could be obtained in Chinese as well. In Experiments 1 and 2, we used both naming and lexical decision tasks and concentrated on two-character compound words. Words like 卫生 (wei(4) sheng(1)[2], *hygiene*) were preceded by their semantic associates (e.g., 洁净, jie(2) jing(4), *clean*), or by words homophonic with the associates (e.g., 捷径, jie(2) jing(4), *shortcut*), or by unrelated words. There were no orthographic or phonological similarities between primes and targets. As shown in Table 2, there was no phonologically mediated priming effect in either task despite a significant semantic priming effect. Subsequent experiments on single character words with a similar experimental design also failed to find a phonologically mediated semantic priming for words like *towed* and *frog*. If we accept that the presence of a priming effect between *towed* and *frog* in English demonstrates the existence of pre-lexical phonology and phonologically mediated lexical access, the absence of such an effect in Chinese implies that pre-lexical phonology and phonological access process do not exist or do not play a major role in the logographic language.

Semantic	Mediated	Control	Target
TOAD	TOWED	TOLLED	FROG
洁净	捷径	流放	卫生
jie(2)jing(4)	jie(2)jing(4)	liu(2)fang(4)	wei(4)sheng(1)
(clean)	*(shortcut)*	*(banish)*	*(hygiene)*
歌	鸽	锤	舞
ge(1)	ge(1)	chui(2)	wu(3)
(song)	*(pigeon)*	*(hammer)*	*(dance)*

Table 1 Experimental designs of mediated semantic priming

When we turn to more direct manipulation of phonology, we do not see a phonological effect in lexical access either. In a study investigating morphological, orthographic and phonological structures in the Chinese mental lexicon, we examined the priming effects between visually presented two-character compound words which shared one critical

	Semantic	Mediated	Control
Lexical Decision	*581*	*620*	*623*
	(2.7)	*(6.6)*	*(4.9)*
Naming	*609*	*621*	*626*
	(2.1)	*(1.8)*	*(2.7)*

Table 2 Mean response latencies (msec) and error percentages for compound words.

---

[2] The pronunciations of Chinese characters are presented in Pinyin (the Chinese alphabetic system). The numbers in brackets represent tones of syllables.

		Morpheme	Homograph	Homophone	Control
Experiment 1	Visual-Visual	606	648	637	644
		(3.7)	(7.1)	(6.8)	(7.1)
	Masked	563	583	611	609
		(5.1)	(9.1)	(10.1)	(8.1)
Experiment 4	Visual-Visual		676	653	651
			(2.3)	(2.4)	(2.9)
	Masked		653	661	655
			(6.6)	(7.5)	(4.8)

Table 3 Mean response latencies (msec) and error percentages. Homograph constituents were also homophonic in Experiment 1, but not in Experiment 4.

homophonic morpheme (Table 3)[3]. A target word (e.g., 华贵 hua(2) gui(4), *luxurious*) was preceded by either a compound sharing a morpheme with it (e.g., 华丽 hua(2) li(4), *gorgeou*s), or a word having a homographic constituent (e.g., 华侨 hua(2) qiao(2), *overseas Chinese*), or a word (e.g., 滑翔 hua(2) xiang(2), *glide*) whose critical morpheme shared only the pronunciation with the critical morpheme in the target, or a totally unrelated word (e.g., 完整 wen(2) zheng(3), *intact*). In a lexical decision task (SOA=100 msec), no priming effects were observed for words that just had homophonic but non-homographic morphemes, whether primes were masked or not (see Experiments 1 in Table 3). In contrast, the morphological/ semantic priming effects were consistently observed and an orthographic effect was revealed when the primes were masked (SOA=57 msec).

	Semantic	Homophonic	Control
Visual-Visual	604	634	645
	(3.6)	(7.6)	(7.8)
Masked	575	597	597
	(3.2)	(5.7)	(4.7)
Naming	611	599	621
	(2.1)	(2.4)	(2.4)

Table 4 Mean response latencies (mesc) and error percentages. SOA = 57 msec in the masked priming lexical decision experiment. SOA = 100 msec in both visual-visual priming lexical decision and naming experiments.

Experiments conducted on Chinese compound words that have more phonological overlap than just one syllable also failed to reveal any phonological priming effects in masked and unmasked visual priming lexical decision tasks. This held not only for words like 管理 (guan(3) li(3), *manage*) and 惯例 (guan(4) li(4), *usual practice*) that had

the same segmental elements but differed on lexical tones, but also for truly homophonic compounds like 捷径 (jie(2) jing(4), *shortcut*) and 洁净 (jie(2) jing(4), *clean*). In contrast, the semantic priming effect was consistently observed (see Table 4). The fact that semantic effects can be readily obtained but phonological effect are constantly missing while similar tasks for English and French have produced robust priming effects for homophones like *towed* and *toad* (e.g., Grainger & Ferrand, 1994), indicates that logographic and alphabetic words are accessed in different ways. While lexical access for English may be purely phonological, lexical access for Chinese can only be conducted via direct visual access in visual word recognition. Phonology seems play no role in the initial access process.

The Presence of Phonological Effects.

This is not to say that phonological effects in the visual recognition of Chinese words cannot be observed in certain circumstances. However, these effects do not demonstrate a pre-lexical phonology and phonologically mediated access process, although they may imply that phonological information associated with characters is automatically activated as a consequence of visual lexical access. The presence of phonological effects is more likely when the experimental tasks emphasize the use of phonological information or allow subjects more time to make responses.

Thus, although we did not observe any priming effects between compound words having homophonic but non-homographic morphemes (as in the Homophone conditions in Table 3), we did find a phonological effect for compounds having homographic but non-homophonic morphemes (e.g., 重复 chong(2) fu(4), *repeat*; and 重量 zhong(4) liang(4), *weight*). An inhibitory effect was observed for such words in a visual-visual priming lexical decision task and no significant priming was obtained when the primes were masked (see the Homograph condition of Experiment 4 in Table 3). This pattern of homograph priming is in sharp contrast with the homograph priming in Experiment 1, where homographic characters were also homophonic in primes and targets

---

[3] For an auditory-auditory priming version of these experiments, see Zhou & Marslen-Wilson (1995).

716

(e.g., 华侨 hua(2) qiao(2), *overseas Chinese*, and 华贵 hua(2) gui(4), *luxurious*). From this comparison and from the absence of any effects in the Homophonic conditions, it is clear that the effect of phonology on visual recognition of compound words must be based on orthography. Phonology comes into play only when there is sufficient orthographic overlap between primes and targets and when orthographically based lexical access has been started. In other words, no orthography, no phonology.

The phonological effect on Chinese word recognition was also revealed in a naming task. Although we did not find any priming effect between homophonic compound words (e.g., 捷径 jie(2) jing(4), *shortcut* and 洁净 jie(2) jing(4), *clean*) using the lexical decision task, we did observe a facilitatory effect when the naming task was used on the same set of words (see Table 4). Superficially, the facilitatory effect in the naming task replicated what Lukatela and Turvey (1994b) found for English. However, we have a different explanation for the effect in Chinese. While Lukatela and Turvey account for their data in terms of pre-lexical phonology, we specify the effect in Chinese as due to the activation of stored phonological representation in the lexicon and the use of phonological information in the naming task. When target words are presented, the projection of orthographic information onto the lexicon leads to the re-activation of the phonological representations that are shared by primes and targets. The naming of the targets could be more easily executed when primes and targets are homophones than when they are non-homophones. An important moral here is that any phonological priming effect in naming Chinese could be post-lexical and any arguments of pre-lexical phonology based on these data could be fundamentally flawed.

The Presence of Orthographic Effects

Our argument so far for a direct visual access in recognizing Chinese words has come either from the failure of phonological manipulation in producing significant effect or from the failure of demonstrating that the phonological effect obtained is pre-lexical. This null effect evidence is not weak when it is compared with experimental evidence from English in which similar manipulations do produce reliable phonological effect. Nevertheless, we need to demonstrate more directly that the orthographic structure of Chinese words determines lexical access and lexical activation.

Orthographic priming effects can be obtained between compound words having homographic and homophonic morphemes, relative to their phonological control (Table 3). However, this effect might not be pure orthographic because there are phonological relations between primes and targets and hence the appearance of the orthographic effect could be dependent on these phonological relations even though these relations alone do not produce significant priming. In a more stringent experiment in which only structurally simple characters were used, we examined the priming effect between words that are orthographically similar but phonologically and semantically different (e.g., 由 you(2), *because of*; and 申 shen(1), *express*). A significant inhibitory effect was obtained in a primed naming task. This effect can only be visual since no phonology or sublexical phonology is involved. It indicates that, at least for simple characters, lexical access is visual.

Orthographic effects were also obtained for complex characters. A typical complex character is composed of a semantic radical - which, for many characters, indicates the semantic category of the complex character - and a phonetic radical - which itself is a character. Although the phonetic radicals could indicate the pronunciation of the complex characters, in most cases, they do not, creating "irregular" complex characters. In a primed naming study in which we used phonetic radicals (e.g., 也 ye(3), *also*) as primes and "derived" irregular complex characters (e.g., 她 ta(1), *she*) as targets, we varied systematically the frequencies of radicals and complex characters, which were not semantically related and had different pronunciations. In Experiment 1, we manipulated the frequencies of complex targets while keeping the frequencies of their radical primes constant. In Experiment 2, we varied the frequencies of radical primes while keeping the frequencies of the complex targets constant. It is clear from Table 5 that there were strong interactions between the frequency manipulations and the naming latencies of the complex characters. (This pattern of priming effects differed dramatically from that between phonetic radicals and complex characters sharing segmental elements but differing on tones.) Since there were no phonological relations between radicals and complex characters, the pattern of priming effects can only be explained in terms of direct visual access and the competition between lexical representations activated by orthographic input.

Manipulation	Frequency	Test	Control
Target	High	*707*	*617*
		(13.3)	*(4.9)*
	Low	*675*	*653*
		(4.2)	*(5.9)*
Prime	High	*629*	*609*
		(4.4)	*(1.2)*
	Low	*650*	*616*
		(5.9)	*(3.7)*

Table 5 Orthographic Priming between Non-homophonic Phonetic Radicals and Complex Characters. High=high frequency targets (or primes); Low=low frequency targets (or primes). SOA=100 msec.

Almost all existing arguments for pre-lexical phonology in reading Chinese depend on the observation that, for about one third of complex characters in the language, the phonetic radical of a complex character could represent the sound of the whole character. But how and from where does the reader retrieve the phonological information carried by the phonetic radical? The regularity or consistency effects obtained by Seidenberg (1985) and others suggest that there is a decomposition process in lexical access for complex characters in which lexical form representations that correspond to or are related to the phonetic radicals are activated. In a recent study using a semantic priming task we demonstrated more directly that, not only the decompositional access can activate phonological information, the semantic representations of phonetic radicals are also activated when the complex characters are processed. The naming of a character, say 牛 (niu(2), *ox*), was not only facilitated by its semantic associate 马 (ma(3), *horse*), but also by the complex character 冯 (feng(2), a family name) which was not semantically related with 牛 and which had 马 as its phonetic radical. The naming of 冯 (feng(2)) was delayed not only by the previous presence of its radical 马 (ma(3)), but also by the presence of 牛 (niu(2)). However, there is no evidence that this sublexical processing is phonological in nature and the access of the complex characters depends on this sublexical processing. To us, the influence of sublexical processing on naming latencies of complex characters is because both the orthographic input of the complex character as a whole and the phonetic radical part of the input are used to access the corresponding orthographic representations in the lexicon. The phonological and semantic properties of the complex characters and radicals (and perhaps other related items) are consequently activated. The competition or mutual support between the activated phonological representations leads to the regularity or consistency effect in the naming task. Clearly, sublexical processing, just like lexical level processing, is orthographic in nature, having nothing to do with pre-lexical phonology.

Discussion

The data we collected from on-line studies on visual recognition of Chinese words clearly demonstrate that access to the Chinese mental lexicon can only be carried out through the direct visual access. There is no "pre-lexical" phonology in reading Chinese. Moreover, the activation of semantic properties is also orthographically constrained. There is little evidence in our experiments that the meaning of a word is accessed by the activation of its lexical phonological representation alone: *towed* does not prime *frog* in Chinese. The phonological influence on the activation of semantic properties must be coupled with the activation of appropriate orthographic representations. These arguments lead us to a following model of lexical

representation and lexical processing for Chinese, where the solid lines indicate the passing of activation between representations and the broken line between semantic and orthographic representations indicates the weak effect of phonology on the activation of lexical semantics[4].

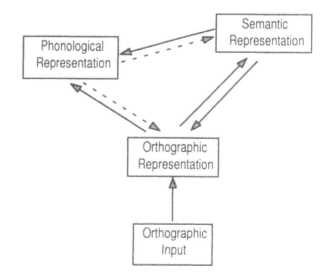

Figure 1 A model of lexical processing in reading Chinese

As it can be seen, this model closely resembles the connectionist structure of lexical representation and processing for alphabetic languages (e.g., Seidenberg & McClelland, 1989). However, we are neutral here about whether the lexical knowledge should be represented distributedly or locally in the Chinese mental lexicon. According to our model, visual input maps directly onto orthographic representations, whose activation automatically leads to the activation of semantic and phonological representations. The relative time course of phonological and semantic activation depends on a number of factors, such as word frequency and the density of semantic features. On the other hand, the phonological activation alone cannot to lead to a significant activation of semantics. One reason for this asymmetry of semantic activation from orthography and from phonology is that while the mapping from orthography to meaning is easy and straightforward, i.e., one-to-one mapping, the mapping from phonology to semantics is usually difficult, since a syllable may represent many homophonic morphemes in the language.

Our model is broadly consistent with most of the data from studies using other experimental tasks (e.g., Perfetti & Zhang, 1991; 1995; Tan, Hoosain, & Peng, 1995). These studies have shown the predominant orthographic effect

---

[4]Of course, the model illustrated here leaves out many details. See Zhou, Marslen-Wilson, Shu, Bi, & Tang (1996).

and the automatic activation of phonology in reading Chinese. They has also shown the earlier activation of phonology than semantics. Although we are not sure about the latter finding because the experiments may have a few design flaws, we can live with it since the earlier activation of phonology does not necessarily mean that access to meaning is phonologically mediated. The activation of semantics and the activation of phonology could be in parallel, having no causal relations.

Our argument for a direct visual access to the Chinese lexicon and the dominant role of orthography in access to meaning contrasts with the claims made by van Orden et al. (1990), Lukatela & Turvey (1994a, 1994b) and others about lexical access in English. However, we see these two views complementary rather than contradictory. The logographic writing system was designed to fit with the integrity[5] of the spoken form (i.e., syllable) of Chinese morphemes and with the cognitive demand of differentiating homophonic morphemes. A character is usually specific, so that it can differentiate homophonic morphemes efficiently. It also corresponds directly with the syllable, rather than with a phonological unit smaller than the syllable. These characteristics leave no room for "pre-lexical" phonology and little room for an inefficient mediated access to meaning. On the other hand, although an alphabetic system may not have such direct differential power and, by design, could not reflect the integrity of the syllable in Chinese, it is efficient in representing complex sound. A small unit in the written form of a word corresponds to a small unit in the spoken form of the word, and this correpondence is systemantically used in other words. The analyses of small units in visual input leads to automatic phonological activation. This property permits the efficient use of phonology in reading and in access to meaning. It is not an accident that lexical access is primarily orthographically constrained in reading logographic Chinese but primarily phonologically constrained in reading alphabetic English. Words in the lexicon can be accessed in different ways, determined by the general configurations of the writing systems in different languages.

References

Coltheart, M. (1978). Lexical access in simple reading tasks. In G. Underwood (Ed.), *Strategies of information processing* (pp. 151-216). San Diego, CA: Academic Press.

Grainger, J. & Ferrand, L. (1994). Phonology and orthography in visual word recognition: Effects of masked homophone primes. *Journal of Memory and Language, 33*, 218-233.

Lukatela, G., & Turvey, M. T. (1994a). Visual lexical access is initially phonological: 1, Evidence from associative priming by words, homophones, and pseudohomophones. *Journal of Experimental Psychology: General, 123*, 107-128.

Lukatela, G., & Turvey, M. T. (1994a). Visual lexical access is initially phonological: 2, Evidence from phonological priming by homophones, and pseudohomophones. *Journal of Experimental Psychology: General, 123*, 331-353.

Perfetti, C. A. & Zhang, S. (1991). Phonological processes in reading Chinese words. *Journal of Experimental Psychology: Learning, Memory, and Cognition, 17*, 633-643.

Perfetti, C. A. & Zhang, S. (1995). Very early phonological activation in Chinese reading. *Journal of Experimental Psychology: Learning, Memory, and Cognition, 21*, 24-33.

Plaut, D C., McClelland, Seidenberg, M. S., & Patterson, K. E. (1996). Understanding Normal and Impaired Word Reading: Computational Principles in Quasi-Regular Domains. *Psychological Review, 103*, 56-115.

Seidenberg, M. S. (1985). The time course of phonological code activation in two writing systems. *Cognition, 19*, 1-30.

Seidenberg, M. S. & McClelland, J. L (1989). A distributed, developmental model of visual word recognition and naming. *Psychological Review, 96*, 523-568.

Tan, L. H., Hoosain, R., & Peng, D-L. (1995). Role of early presemantic phonological code in Chinese character identification. *Journal of Experimental Psychology: Learning, Memory, and Cognition, 21*, 43-54.

Van Orden, G. C. (1987). A ROWS is a ROSE: Spelling, sound, and reading. *Memory & Cognition, 15*, 181-198.

Van Orden, G. C., Pennington, B. F., & Stone, G. O. (1990). Word identification in reading and the promise of subsymbolic psycholinguistics. *Psychological Review, 97*, 488-522.

Wang, W. S. -Y. (1973) The Chinese language. *Scientific American, 228*, 50-56.

Zhou, X. & Marslen-Wilson W. (1995). The morphological structure in the Chinese mental lexicon. *Language and Cognitive Processes, 10*, 545-600.

Zhou, X., Marslen-Wilson, W., Shu, H., Bi, Y., & Tang, Y. (1996). *Phonology in reading Chinese.* Manuscript, Department of Psychology, Birkbeck College, University of London.

---

[5] The integrity of the syllable comes from the fact that a syllable in Chinese has a simple structure with no double consonants and with only two possible syllable-ending consonants (for Mandarin Chinese). The tone, which is used to differentiate lexical items, is carried by the whole syllable rather than by a smaller segment. Moreover, there is no or little interaction between segments of different syllables in continuous speech.

Society Member Abstracts

Watching Spoken Language Perception:
Using Eye-movements to Track Lexical Access

Paul D. Allopenna, James S. Magnuson, and **Michael K. Tanenhaus**
Brain & Cognitive Sciences
University of Rochester
Rochester, NY 14627
{allopen, magnuson, mtan}@bcs.rochester.edu

Introduction

Models of spoken word recognition can be divided into two classes: models such as the Cohort model (Marslen-Wilson, 1987) in which competition among lexical alternatives occurs in a strictly "left-to-right fashion (e.g., "casket" competes with its cohort, "castle," but not with its rhyme, "basket") and activation models – e.g., TRACE (McClelland & Elman, 1986) – which specify that competition can occur throughout words (e.g., "casket" can compete with both "castle" and "basket"). While there is evidence that cohorts compete during on-line processing, evidence for competition between rhymes is less clear.

Tanenhaus et al. (1995) examined the effects of cohort competition in a task with real objects and instructions such as "Pick up the candy." Eye-movements to a target object were closely time-locked to the instruction, i.e., an eye-movement to the candy began shortly after the word ended, indicating that programming began before the end of the word. The presence of a "cohort" competitor (e.g. candle) increased the latency of eye-movements to the target object and induced frequent "false launches" to the competitor. In the present experiment we compare the effects of both cohort and rhyme competitors using a variation of this paradigm.

Method and Results

An Applied Scientific Laboratories free-head eyetracker with an accuracy of approximately 1 degree was used. The stimuli were line drawings of objects presented on a computer screen. At the beginning of each trial, subjects were shown four objects (see Figure 1) and were asked to "pick-up" one of the objects with the mouse and move it to a specified location on a grid. We tracked both eye-movement patterns and latencies starting at the onset of the target word in the instructions.

The objects shown in Figure 1 illustrate a configuration taken from a critical trial. Here, the target (paddle) has both a cohort competitor (padlock) and a rhyme competitor (saddle), as well as a noncompetitive item (castle). Subjects moved targets in four competitor conditions: 1) cohort and rhyme; 2) cohort; 3) rhyme; and 4) no competitors.

A preliminary analysis of the error data shows that both cohorts and rhymes influence initial saccade patterns.

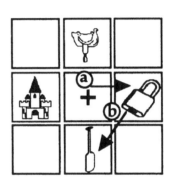

Figure 1: An example of eye-movements when the target is paddle. The first eye-movement (a) is to the cohort competitor, and the subsequent movement (b) is to the appropriate target.

Subjects were more likely to make a "false launch" in the cohort condition than they were in the no competitor condition. This pattern held true for the rhyme condition, although to a lesser degree. The condition with both cohort and rhyme competitors showed both types of effects, with cohort competitors again exhibiting more influence on initial saccades than rhyme competitors. These results support models of lexical access that are based on the spreading activation of lexical competition.

Acknowledgments

Supported by NIH resource grant 1-P41-RR09283; NIH HD27206 to MKT; NIH F32DC00210 to PDA, and an NSF Graduate Research Fellowship to JSM.

References

Marslen-Wilson, W. D. (1987). Functional Parallelism in spoken word-recognition. *Cognition*, 25, 71-102.

McClelland, J. L., & Elman, J. L. (1986). The TRACE model of speech perception. *Cognitive Psychology*, 18, 1-86.

Tanenhaus, M. K., Spivey-Knowlton, M. J., Eberhard, K. M., & Sedivey, J. C. (1995). Integration of visual and linguistic information in spoken language-comprehension. *Science*, 268, 1632-1634.

The Role of Connotation on Interpretation Type

Carine V. Alma
University of Connecticut
Dept. of Psychology, Box U-20
Storrs, CT 06269-1020
alma@uconnvm.uconn.edu

One of the central questions in analogical reasoning concerns the role of surface similarity on access and use of analogies. Ross (1987, 1989) distinguished between story line similarity, which affected access, and object correspondences, which affected use. These findings underscored the complexity of surface similarity. The purpose of this paper is to advance the notion that the same type of surface similarity, negative connotation, affects two types of qualitative retrieval measures in two distinct ways. First, negative connotation leads to the accurate noticing/accessing of the connotation information. However, the same connotation information leads to the inaccurate noticing/accessing of the intended interpretation. The intended interpretation is the most commonly occurring interpretation, found in analogous story pairs (Alma, in progress). Consequently, the prediction for this study is that negative analogies will receive higher measures on connotation and alternate interpretations. Neutral analogies will receive higher measures on intended interpretations.

In the first experiment, individuals read 8 pairs of analogous stories. Four analogies were neutral contexts, and four were negative contexts. An ANOVA indicated that neutral contexts elicited higher measures on intended interpretations (F (1, 23) = 34.2, p = .0001). Conversely, negative contexts elicited higher measures on connotation (F (1, 23) = 16.4, p = .0005) and higher measures on alternate interpretations (F (1, 23) = 5.55, p = .028). The same profile of results occurred for neutral and negative themes. Neutral themes elicited higher measures on intended interpretations (F (1, 23) = 4.02, p = .057). Negative themes elicited higher measures on connotation (F (1, 23) = 8.63, p = .007) and alternate interpretations (F (1, 23) = 10.5, p = .004). Consequently, negative information, which is salient, draws individuals to that information and it appears in the list of retrieved similarities. However, the most commonly occurring interpretation, which incorporates this negative information, is not noticed and accessed. Negative connotation serves as a barrier, which causes individuals to derive alternate (routes) interpretations. Alternate interpretations are potentially useful, because they represent solutions to intractable problems structured around an analogy.

Acknowledgments

This research was supported by pre-doctoral and doctoral dissertation fellowships to the author from the University of Connecticut. The author acknowledges the assistance of Carol Fowler and her speech lab.

References

Alma, C. V. (1996). [Viewing analogy interpretation from a talker-listener perspective]. Unpublished raw data.

Ross, B. H. (1987). This is like that: The use of earlier problems and the separation of similarity effects. Journal of Experimental Psychology: Learning, Memory, and Cognition, 13, 629-639.

Ross, B. H. (1989). Distinguishing types of superficial similarities: Different effects on the access and use of earlier problems. Journal of Experimental Psychology: Learning, Memory, and Cognition, 15, 456-468.

The Contrast-Relation Type Model: An Explanatory Framework for Encoding Status Decisions

Carine V. Alma
University of Connecticut
Dept. of Psychology, Box U-20
Storrs, CT 06269-1020
alma@uconnvm.uconn.edu

Previous research has linked the presence of higher-order relations to judgments of similarity (Gentner, 1989). Other research has drawn distinctions between differences linked to commonalities, termed alignable differences, and differences not connected to commonalities, termed non-alignable differences (Gentner & Markman, 1994). The purpose of this paper is integrate these findings into a model which explains encoding status decisions. An encoding status decision entails categorizing entities as either not analogous (containing few similarities), partially analogous (containing moderate numbers of similarities), or analogous (containing high numbers of similarities).

The Contrast-Relation Type Model makes several predictions: (1) Non-alignable differences serve as a strong difference cue and influence encoding status decisions. The prediction is that partial analogies > analogies, in terms of correct encoding status decisions and "not analogous" decisions. (2) The absence of higher-order relations serves as a weak difference cue. First-order relations (FOR), without higher-order relations, influence "not analogous" decisions. Hence, contexts > themes, in terms of "not analogous" decisions. (3) The presence of higher-order relations serves as a weak "similar" cue. Consequently, themes > contexts, in terms of similarity ratings and "other analogous" decisions.

In this experiment, there were four types of story pairs: context analogies (FOR, similarities), context partial analogies (FOR, similarities, differences), theme analogies (FOR + HOR, similarities) and theme partial analogies (FOR + HOR, similarities, differences). First, partial analogies > analogies on both encoding status (F (1, 19) = 9.22, p = .007) and "not analogous" decisions (F (1, 19) = 5.43, p = .031). Second, contexts > themes on "not analogous" decisions (F (1, 19) = 10.7, p = .004). Third, themes > contexts on similarity ratings (F (1, 19) = 18.7, p = .0004) and "other analogous" decisions (F (1, 19) = 7.04, p = .016). Taken together, the predictions support the notion that contrast and relation type affect encoding status decisions.

Acknowledgments
This research was supported by pre-doctoral and doctoral dissertation fellowships to the author from the University of Connecticut. The author acknowledges the assistance of Carol Fowler and her speech lab.

References
Gentner, D. (1989). The mechanisms of analogical learning. In: S. Vosniadou & A. Ortony (Eds.), Similarity and analogical reasoning (pp. 199-241). New York: Cambridge University Press.

Gentner, D. & Markman, A. B. (1994). Structural alignment in comparison: No difference without similarity. Psychological Science, 5 (3), 152-158.

A Cortical Network Model of
Cognitive Attentional Streams, Rhythmic Expectation, and Auditory Stream Segregation

Bill Baird
Dept Mathematics, U.C.Berkeley,
Berkeley, Ca. 94720. baird@math.berkeley.edu

We have developed a neural network cortical architecture that implements a theory of attention, learning, and communication between cortical areas by adaptive synchronization of 5-15 Hz and 30-80 Hz oscillations (pp 67-75 in "Advances In Neural Information Processing Systems 6", 1994). Here we present a specific model of rhythmic expectancy and the interaction of higher order and primary cortical levels of processing which accounts for the results of psychological experiments of Jones (pp 1059-1073 of the "Journal of Experimental Psychology: Human Perception and Performance", 7, 1981) showing that auditory stream segregation depends on the rhythmic structure of inputs. Further references not cited here may be found in these papers.

Using dynamical systems theory, the architecture is constructed from recurrently interconnected oscillatory associative memory modules that model hypercolumns of associational and higher-order sensory and motor cortical areas. The system learns connection weights between the modules that cause it to evolve under a 10 Hz clocked sensory/motor processing cycle through a sequence of transitions of synchronized 40 Hz oscillatory attractors within the modules. In the brain, we hypothesize these cycles to be adaptively controled by septal and thalamic pacemakers which alter excitability of hippocampal and neocortical tissue through nonspecific biasing currents that appear as the cognitive and sensory evoked potentials of the EEG. The cycles "quantize time" and form the basis of derived rhythms with periods up to 1.5 seconds that entrain to each other in motor coordination and to external rhythms in speech and music perception.

The architecture employs selective "attentional" control of the synchronization of the 30-80 Hz oscillations between modules to direct the flow of communication and computation to recognize and generate sequences. The 30-80 Hz attractor amplitude patterns code the information content of a cortical area, whereas phase and frequency are used to "softwire" the network, since only the synchronized areas communicate by exchanging amplitude information. The system works like a broadcast network where the unavoidable crosstalk to all areas from previous learned connections is overcome by frequency coding to allow attentional communication only between selected areas relevant to the task of the moment. The behavior of the time traces in different modules of the architecture models the temporary appearance and switching

of the synchronization of 5-15 and 30-80 Hz oscillations between cortical areas that is observed during sensory/motor tasks in monkeys and humans.

The "binding" of sequences of attractor transitions between modules of the architecture by synchronization of their activity is similar to the phenomenon of "streaming" in audition. There *successive* perceptual events are bound together into a sequence object or "stream" such that one pays attention to only one source at a time (the "cocktail party" effect). The model illustrates the hypothesis that a thalamically coordinated "cognitive stream" of this synchronized activity loops from primary cortex to associational and higher order sensory and motor areas through hippocampus and back to bind them into an evolving attentional network of intercommunicating cortical areas that directs behavior. The feedback to primary from higher order cortical areas allows top down voluntary control to switch this attentional stream or "searchlight" from one source preattentively bound in primary cortex to another source separately bound at a nearby frequency or phase.

To implement Jones's theory and account for her data, subsets of the oscillatory modules are coupled to form a temporal coordinate frame or rhythmic time base of nested periodicites dividing down the thalamic 10 Hz base clock rate from 10 to .5 Hz. These areas feed their internal 30-80 Hz activity back to primary auditory cortex through fast adapting connections that continually attempt to match incoming patterns. Those patterns which meet these established rhythmic expectancy signals in time are boosted in amplitude and pulled into synchrony with the 30-80 Hz "searchlight signal" to become part of the primary attention stream sending input to higher areas. In accordance with Jones' theory, top down attention can selectively probe input at different hierarchical levels of periodicity by selectively driving a particular cortical patch in the time base set at the particular 30-80 Hz frequency of the attentional stream. This is the temporal analog of the body centered spatial coordinate frame and multiscale covert attention window system in vision. Here the body centered temporal coordinates of the internal time base orient by entrainment to the external rhythm, and the window of covert temporal attention can then select a level of the multiscale temporal coordinate frame.

Neural Networks for Simulating Cognitive Development:
A Case Study in Early Mathematical Abilities

Tracey A. Bale and **Khurshid Ahmad**
Artificial Intelligence Group
Department of Mathematical and Computing Sciences
University of Surrey, Guildford, GU2 5XH, UK
{T.Bale,K.Ahmad}@mcs.surrey.ac.uk

Mathematical development may be investigated through the observation of behaviour, or alternatively, through computer-based modelling. Connectionist models, often referred to as artificial neural networks, can demonstrate aspects of human cognitive development, owing to their capacity to learn. Mathematical abilities have been explored through computer metaphors by developmental psychologists (Wynn, 1995), and through connectionist approaches by cognitive neuropsychologists (McCloskey and Lindemann, 1992) and neuroscientists (Dehaene and Changeux, 1993). We examine how artificial neural networks can be of benefit in the study of mathematical development amongst infants by describing how two specific aspects of this development can be simulated. First, we attempt to simulate a biologically-endowed mechanism for the discrimination and representation of small numerosities of entities: for this model we use a self-organizing neural network in a process of feature extraction. Second, we present arguments as to why and how the so-called recurrent neural networks can be used to model rhythmicity in a simulation of learning the temporal behaviour of counting. The notion of recurrency is examined in this model through a combination of feedback loops with delay elements.

We suggest that three categories of neural network learning procedures appear to describe the component branches of numerical development. Firstly, an unsupervised learning algorithm appears to simulate the acquisition of the earliest, pre-verbal skills: those which appear to spontaneously emerge, such as numerosity discrimination and the acquisition of ordinal concepts. Secondly, the reinforcement learning algorithm appears to simulate conditioned behaviour, and thirdly a supervised learning algorithm may be used to describe aspects of numerical development determined by linguistic knowledge: those later-occurring abilities which are subject to environmental experience, for example, the acquisition of the linguistic counting system and the arithmetic facts.

Furthermore, we propose that a nervous system-level model, a term coined after Kohonen (1990), is an appropriate architecture for a simulation of mathematical development. Such an architecture enables a range of learning strategies to be simulated within a single model. Nervous system-level (organizational) models are composed of a system of interconnected connectionist networks, where the connections themselves are connectionist networks. Each constituent network in a simulation of development is based upon a different, well-grounded architecture and employs an appropriate learning algorithm, in order to mimic an aspect of the development under consideration. Under this approach, the spectrum of pre-verbal and language-dependent mathematical abilities may be modelled within a single architecture.

Acknowlegdement

Tracey Bale would like to acknowledge the support of the Engineering and Physical Sciences Research Council.

References

Dehaene, S. & Changeux, J.-P. (1993). Development of elementary numerical abilities: A neuronal model. *Journal of Cognitive Neuroscience*, 5(4), 390-407.

Kohonen, T. (1990). Notes on Neural Computing and Associative Memory. In J. L. McGaugh, N. M. Weinberger & G. Lynch (Eds.), *Brain Organization and Memory: Cells, Systems and Circuits* (pp. 323-337). New York/Oxford: Oxford University Press.

McCloskey, M. & Lindemann, A. M. (1992). MATHNET: Preliminary results from a distributed model of arithmetic fact retrieval. In J. I. D. Campbell (Ed.), *The Nature and Origins of Mathematical Skills* (pp. 365-409). Elsevier Science Publishers.

Wynn, K. (1995). Origins of numerical knowledge. *Mathematical Cognition*, 1(1), 35-60.

The Decline of Communicative Competence after Closed Head Injury

Bruno G. Bara and **Maurizio Tirassa**
Centro di Scienza Cognitiva
Università di Torino
via Lagrange, 3
10123 Torino (Italy)
{bara,tirassa}@psych.unito.it

Neuropragmatics

Current theories of pragmatics are exclusively interested in the normal adult; most are also underdetermined from a psychological viewpoint, in that they make no attempt at falsification, limiting themselves to analytic considerations and/or formal or computational reformulations.

We aim at the neuropsychological validation of a cognitive theory of human communication (Airenti, Bara & Colombetti, 1993a, 1993b). Our ultimate goal is to sketch the evolution of communicative competence from its acquisition in the child to its decline in the normal and the brain-damaged individual. As a first step we explored some consequences of closed head injury (CHI) (Bara, Tirassa & Zettin 1996).

Experimental Setting

Our experimental subjects were 13 non-aphasic CHI patients. We tested them on five pragmatic phenomena: direct utterances, simple indirect utterances, complex indirect utterances, irony and deceits; each inferential path was explored both in the successful and the failure case.

The whole protocol comprised 21 tasks. Most consisted in the presentation of a brief (10-15 seconds) videotaped scene, showing a simple verbal exchange between two actors. The subject was free to give her own interpretation of the actors' utterances. When she was satisfied, the subsequent scene was shown. A few tasks required simple planning, and a few others were presented *in the wild*, as predefined utterances nonchalantly interwoven in the brief conversation that preceded the formal experimental session.

The tape-records of the sessions were evaluated by two judges, blind with respect to the theoretical approach and to the goal of the research, who marked each task as passed if the subject showed a reasonable (however free) understanding of the dialogue.

Results

We expected a trend of increasing difficulty from successful direct and simple indirect utterances to complex ones, to irony, to deceits; and a parallel, but poorer, trend on the corresponding cases of failure.

These expectations were systematically confirmed to a good or high degree of statistical significance. Since all the tasks were relatively simple, what our data show is that a *simple* irony is easier to CHI patients than a *simple* deceit,

but harder than a *simple* indirect utterance, and so on; but it would be obviously absurd to infer that *any* irony is easier than *any* deceit, and harder than *any* indirect utterance.

The subjects' success on two *theory of mind* tasks ("Maxi" and "Smarties") rules out any incapability to handle the mental states involved in communication. We also administered several standard neuropsychological tests: the main correlation here was with working memory.

The case against direct speech acts

We found a 100% performance on direct and simple indirect utterances (e.g., respectively, "Close the window" and "Could you close the window?"). This contrasts sharply with the previous literature on CHI (see Stemmer [1994] for an overview), but is in perfect agreement with our theoretical framework.

Gricean-Searlean, literality-based models of utterance comprehension would predict an increase in difficulty from direct speech acts to simple indirect ones to complex ones; the performance of inferentially damaged individuals should decrease correspondingly.

In our framework, there are no direct utterances: to understand an utterance *always* requires some inference. Thus, the breaking point is not between direct and indirect utterances, but between simple and complex ones: simple indirect utterances ("Can you close the window?") are as easily understood as direct ones ("Close the window"), whereas complex ones (such as "I don't want to die freezing") are harder. Our data tend to validate this approach.

References

Airenti, G., Bara, B.G. & Colombetti, M. (1993a). Conversation and behavior games in the pragmatics of dialogue. *Cognitive Science*, 17, 197-256.

Airenti, G., Bara, B.G. & Colombetti, M. (1993b). Failures, exploitations and deceits in communication. *Journal of Pragmatics*, 20, 303-326.

Bara, B.G., Tirassa, M. & Zettin, M. (1996). Neuropragmatics: neuropsychological constraints on formal theories of dialogue. *Brain and Language*, in press.

Stemmer, B. (1994). A pragmatic approach to neurolinguistics: requests (re)considered. *Brain and Language*, 46, 565-591.

In Search of Intentional Causation

Steven J. Barrera

Department of Philosophy 0302
University of California, San Diego
La Jolla, CA 92037-0302
sbarrera@ucsd.edu

Introduction

Many approaches to understanding cognition begin with an explanation of how we use intentional states (Cummins, 1989). Intentional states, such as beliefs and desires, supposedly denote just those mental states that an agent takes to meaningfully refer to facts about the world. Agents use these mental states to explain, plan and perform actions. However, reductionist approaches to cognition suggest that behavior can be causally explained in purely neurological/syntactic terms. If a syntactic account of cognition succeeds in explaining behavior, then it would appear that intentional states like 'believing' or 'desiring' are not causally relevant in an explanation of an agent's behavior, since we would have reduced these high-level notions to more basic causal factors. Intentional explanations, on such an account, become 'epiphenomenal' or causally inert.

Allen (1995) argues that intentional states may yet be causally efficacious under such reductionist theories. Allen begins by granting that mental states may be token-identical to brain states. That is, each mental state is constituted by its neurological properties. Allen then claims that standard arguments for such neurological reductions contain an ambiguity. He contends that we must distinguish between the effect a property has on a single token and the effect that possessing that property may have on a group of tokens.

This distinction is illustrated with an analogy to how the property 'genuine' applies to money. Suppose the physical token '20$NOTE' instantiates a twenty-dollar bill. An exact counterfeit of such a token, if it is truly token-identical, will have all the same physical, causal properties of a genuine 20$NOTE. At this point, the property 'genuine' seems causally inefficacious to the value of any particular 20$NOTE. However, Allen claims, if we flood the market with counterfeit 20$NOTEs, we can alter the value of each token 20$NOTE without changing any of their physical characteristics. In this way, potentially having the property 'genuine' or 'counterfeit', though not physically identifiable in the 20$NOTE itself, has a causal effect on the value of such tokens.

Allen's account depends on using the context in which a token is used to supply intentional content. Appropriating Millikan's (1984, 1993) account of action which emphasizes the importance of a token's history in determining its use, Allen argues that the situational elements surrounding the development of a token provide a context which isn't physically expressed in the token itself. That context, however, seems causally efficacious in any explanation of the token's behavior and is necessary for the token's behavior to be successful (for it to actually refer). In the same fashion, intentionality applies only to those tokens with an appropriate history and contextual development. Thus, Allen argues that it isn't that each token must intentionally refer, but that enough tokens must intentionally refer for behaviors to reliably develop. Analagously, most 20$NOTEs must be genuine to have value, though any individual 20$NOTE may be bogus.

I argue against the view that intentionality, so described, is causally efficacious. Counter-examples are presented demonstrating Allen's argument to be inadequate in at least two important ways. First, a serious disanalogy exists between intentionality and genuiness. Allen uses 'genuiness' as a success term, requiring that most tokens possess it for it to be causally efficacious. However, I argue that neurological tokens which 'accidentally' refer to behavioral states do not damage the general use of such tokens. Furthermore, it is possible that *no* physical tokens posses intentionality, whereas Allen begins with a comparison to a property, genuiness, that does exist. By assuming the existence of a meaningful difference between intentional and non-intentional, Allen begs the question at hand. Second, I argue that Allen misconceives where the onus of proof lies in this debate. He relies on a skeptical argument which merely states that intentionality hasn't been disproven. However, as purely physical accounts of behavior become more successful and evidence mounts against the causal role of intentional states, it is incumbent on the defender of intentional causation to show that such states must be included in a causal account.

References

Allen, C. (1995) "It Isn't What You Think: A new idea about intentional causation," *Nous* **29** 1: 115-126.

Cummins, R. (1989) *Meaning and Mental Representation*, Cambridge, MA: MIT Press

Millikan, R. G. (1984) *Language, Thought, and Other Biological Categories*, Cambridge, MA: MIT Press.

Millikan, R. G. (1993) *White Queen Psychology and other essays for Alice*, Cambridge, MA: MIT Press.

Unsupervised Learning of Invariant Visual Representations

Marian Stewart Bartlett[1] and **Terrence J. Sejnowski**[2]

University of California San Diego

[1]Departments of Cognitive Science and Psychology

[2]Department of Biology and Howard Hughes Medical Institute

Computational Neurobiology Lab, The Salk Institute

10010 N. Torrey Pines Road, La Jolla, CA 92037

{marni,terry}@salk.edu

Abstract

The appearance of an object or a face changes continuously as the observer moves through the environment or as a face changes expression or pose. Recognizing an object or a face despite these image changes is a challenging problem for computer vision systems, yet we perform the task quickly and easily. In natural visual experience, different views of an object tend to appear in close temporal proximity. Capturing the temporal relationships among patterns is a way to automatically associate different views of an object without requiring complex geometrical transformations or three dimensional structural descriptions [1].

Temporal association may be an important aspect of invariance learning in the ventral visual stream [2]. There is evidence for temporal association of complex visual patterns by neurons in the inferior temporal lobe [3]. A temporal window for Hebbian learning could be provided by the long open-time of the NMDA channel [4], or by reciprocal connections between cortical regions [5]. Hebbian learning of temporal associations has been explored with idealized input representations [6, 7, 5].

In our first model we used a one layer feedforward network to demonstrate the capability of such mechanisms to acquire invariant representations of complex representations such as gray level images of faces [8; See also 9]. A temporal association (TA) learning rule based on Competitive Learning [10] clusters input patterns by a combination of spatial similarity and temporal proximity. A two layer network presented with sequences of images of faces as subjects gradually change pose learned representations that are invariant to pose (Figure 1)[11].

We next explored the the development of invariances with an attractor state representation. In this framework, representations are sustained pattern of activity across an interconnected assembly of units. Attractor networks with Hebbian learning mechanisms are capable of acquiring temporal associations between randomly generated patterns [12]. We investigate the ability of attractor network dynamics to acquire temporal associations between different views of a face or object. Input to this system consisted of images of faces convolved with Gabor filters of three spatial scales and 4 orientations at 64 locations in the image. Faces are presented to the system in sequence as they rotate from the frontal view. The learn-

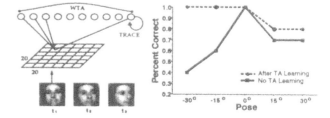

Figure 1: Left: Network architecture. Right: Mean "tuning curve" for pose following competitive learning of frontal views only, and after temporal association (TA) learning. Outputs for non-frontal views were classed as correct if they matched the output for the frontal view of the same face. Data are means for 10 different faces.

ing algorithm [12] caused input patterns that are spatially similar and temporally proximal to be drawn to the same basin of attraction. Corrections in attractor states corresponding to the temporal proximity of the associated input patterns during training revealed the degree to which the network acquired invariant representations.

References

1. Stryker, M. 1991. Temporal Associations. Nature: 354:108-109.
2. Rolls, E. 1995. Learning Mechanisms in the temporal lobe visual cortex. Behav. Brain Res. 66:177-185.
3. Miyashita, Y. 1988. Neuronal correlate of visual associative long-term memory in the primate temporal cortex. Nature: 335(27):817-820.
4. Rhodes, P. 1992. The long open time of the NMDA channel facilitates the self-organization of invariant object responses in cortex. Soc. Neurosci. Abst. 18:740.
5. O'Reilly, R. & Johnson, M. 1994. Object recognition and sensitive periods: A computational analysis of visual imprinting. Neural Comp. 6:357-389.
6. Foldiak, P. 1991. Learning invariance from transformation sequences. Neural Comp. 3:194-200.
7. Weinshall, D.& Edelman, S. 1991. A self-organizing multiple view representation of 3D objects. Bio. Cyber. 64(3):209-219.
8. Bartlett, M. Stewart, and Sejnowski, T., in press. Unsupervised learning of invariant representations of faces through temporal association. In *The Neurobiology of Computation* J.M. Bower, ed. Kluwer Academic Publishers, Boston.
9. Wallis, G. & Rolls, E. 1996. A model of invariant object recognition in the visual system. Technical Report, Oxford University Department of Experimental Psychology.
10. Rumelhart, D. & Zipser, D. 1985. Feature discovery by competitive learning. Cog. Sci. 9:75-112.
11. We thank David Beymer of the MIT Media Lab for the images.
12. Griniasty, M., Tsodyks, M., & Amit, D. (1993). Conversion of temporal correlations between stimuli to spatial correlations between attractors. Neural Comp. 5:1-17.

Multimedia Representations for Science Learning: A Cautionary Tale

Philip Bell

Graduate School of Education
4533 Tolman Hall # 1670
University of California, Berkeley
Berkeley, CA 94720
pbell@violet.berkeley.edu

Introduction

Will Internet access to multimedia resources change science learning in the classroom? What are the cognitive effects of representing information using multimedia technology? Research is beginning to elucidate the role of representation on cognitive processes during problem solving (Larkin & Simon, 1987; Zhang & Norman, 1994) and learning (Kozma, 1991). The empirical research described here further explores these issues by investigating the role of multimedia representations in science learning through a comparison of students' categorical and explanatory responses to a set of text and multimedia isomorphs of scientific evidence.

The Study

The study investigated middle school students working on a science activity within the instructional context of an Internet-focused learning environment called the Knowledge Integration Environment (KIE). As a part of this activity on the nature of light, students developed theoretical accounts of scientific evidence and communicated their findings during a class debate. Students explored and categorized a set of evidence within the conceptual framework of the debate, as well as produced written explanations for the evidence they deemed most relevant. One-half of the students received a mixed set of text and multimedia evidence, while the other half received a complementary set consisting of text and multimedia isomorphs.

Analyses were conducted on students' categorizations of the evidence in order to compare the representational effect of the text and multimedia modalities. Additionally, students' written explanations were coded for subject matter science conceptions like "telescopes look at light which is closer to the light source" (see Guesne, 1985).

Results & Implications

For three-quarters of the evidence pairs, students linked the text and multimedia versions significantly differently to the debate. In other words, the representation of evidence was found to play a strong role in the cognitive behavior of students. This effect was further investigated by comparing the range of conceptions used to describe the evidence in students' explanations. For almost all of the evidence pairs, a trend existed where students associated a broader range of

conceptions (or scientific ideas) to the multimedia evidence than the text isomorph. In spite of these broader connections, students were not found to associate more scientifically normative ideas to the multimedia evidence.

From an instructional perspective, it may be appropriate to incorporate multimedia cautiously given the representational effect described in this research. Multimedia representations may not have the expected effect on learning compared to that of corresponding text representations of similar phenomena. At certain points of instruction, however, it can be beneficial for students to consider a repertoire of ideas to help determine which are more productive, flexible, and more coherent with their prior knowledge (Linn et al., 1994). Results suggest that multimedia instructional materials may be useful in eliciting a broader range of conceptions from a group of students.

Acknowledgments

The research presented in this paper has benefited from the collaborative efforts of the members of the KIE Research Group. Additional information on the KIE project is available at *http://www.kie.berkeley.edu/KIE.html*.

This research was supported by the National Science Foundation under grant No. RED-9453861. Any opinions, findings, and conclusions or recommendations expressed in this publication are those of the author and do not necessarily reflect the view of the National Science Foundation.

References

Guesne, E. (1985). Light. In R. Driver, E. Guesne, & A. Tiberghien (Eds.), *Children's Ideas in Science*, (pp. 11-26). Philadelphia: Open University Press.

Kozma, R. (1991). Learning with media. *Review of Educational Research, 61*(2), 179-211.

Larkin, J. H., & Simon, H. A. (1987). Why a diagram is (sometimes) worth ten thousand words. *Cognitive Science, 11*, 65-99.

Linn, M. C., diSessa, A., Pea, R. D., & Songer, N. B. (1994). Can research on science learning and instruction inform standards for science education? *Journal of Science Education and Technology, 3*(1), 7-15.

Zhang, J., & Norman, D. A. (1994). Representations in distributed cognitive tasks. *Cognitive Science, 18*, 87-122.

Generic Modeling in Analogical Reasoning

Sambasiva R. Bhatta
NYNEX Science & Technology
500 Westchester Ave.
White Plains, NY 10604
bhatta@nynexst.com

Ashok K. Goel
College of Computing
Georgia Institute of Technology
Atlanta, GA 30332-0280
goel@cc.gatech.edu

The use of analogical reasoning in creative problem solving often involves transfer between distant problems. Some cognitively-inspired computational models of analogical reasoning describe "direct transfer" where the knowledge of a source situation is directly transferred to the target situation, e.g., SME (Falkenhainer et al., 1989) and ACME (Holyoak and Thagard, 1989). But some psychological studies, such as Gick and Holyoak's (1983), indicate that sometimes higher-level abstractions may mediate the transfer between the source and the target. Our work on creative device design has led us to a theory, called *model-based analogy* (MBA), that provides a computational account of learning and use of such higher-level abstractions that we call *generic models*. Generic models in device design capture knowledge of functional and causal patterns abstracted from case-specific device models. Since a generic model may be acquired from one design case and instantiated in the context of adapting an entirely different case for solving a target problem, they mediate (cross-domain) analogical transfer.

The Process of Model-Based Analogy

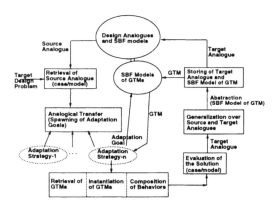

Figure 1: **Part of** IDEAL**'s Process for Analogical Design**

IDEAL is the computer system that implements the MBA theory in the context of device design. IDEAL takes as input a specification of the functional and structural constraints on a desired design (i.e., the target design problem), and gives as output a structure (i.e., the solution) that realizes the specified function and also satisfies the structural constraints. Figure 1 illustrates one part of IDEAL's processing, the part that uses generic models of a specific kind called *generic teleological mechanisms* (GTMs). GTMs specify abstract patterns of re-

lations between output functions and internal behaviors for achieving the functions, for example, feedback. They are "mechanisms" because they specify behaviors (or processes), "teleological" because they are in the service of functions, and "generic" because they pertain to classes of device domains, not just to a specific device or a particular device domain. The case-independent GTMs are abstractions of case-specific *Structure-Behavior-Function* (SBF) models (Goel, 1991) that explain how the structure of a design realizes its function. For details, see (Bhatta, 1995; Bhatta and Goel, 1993).

IDEAL provides a testbed for experimenting with generic modeling in analogical reasoning. We have tested IDEAL in four different domains, namely, the domains of simple electric circuits, heat exchangers, electronic circuits, and mechanical devices (including momentum controllers and velocity controllers) for both learning and use of GTMs. In particular, we tested IDEAL with a dozen design problems from these four different domains that involved learning and use of six different GTMs. IDEAL could not only learn and use the GTMs but it also used the learned GTMs for cross-domain analogical transfer. Our experiments with IDEAL indicate that (1) for analogical device design, useful device abstractions include GTMs that capture patterns of relations between device functions and internal causal behaviors and (2) device abstractions such as GTMs may mediate analogical transfer between different design problems including distant problems in different device domains.

Acknowledgments: This work has been supported by the NSF grant IRI-92-10925 and the ONR contract N00014-92-J-1234.

References

Bhatta, S. (1995). *Model-Based Analogy in Innovative Device Design*. PhD thesis, Georgia Institute of Technology, College of Computing, Atlanta, GA.

Bhatta, S. and Goel, A. (1993). Learning generic mechanisms from experiences for analogical reasoning. In *Procs. of the Fifteenth Annual Conf. of the Cognitive Science Society*, pages 237–242.

Falkenhainer, B., Forbus, K., and Gentner, D. (1989). The structure-mapping engine: Algorithm and examples. *AI*, 41:1–63.

Gick, M. and Holyoak, K. (1983). Schema induction and analogical transfer. *Cognitive Psychology*, 15:1–38.

Goel, A. (1991). A model-based approach to case adaptation. In *Proc. of the Thirteenth Annual Conf. of the Cognitive Science Society*, pages 143–148.

Holyoak, K. and Thagard, P. (1989). Analogical mapping by constraint satisfaction. *Cognitive Science*, 13:295–355.

Behavior-Based Analogy-Making

Douglas S. Blank

Department of Computer Science
Indiana University
Lindley Hall 215
Bloomington, IN 47408
blank@cs.indiana.edu

Most everyone, including the experts, would agree that analogy-making is best defined as a process that creates a mapping between items in one domain (often called the *source*) to "similar" items in another domain (often called the *target*). Based on this definition, many researchers have attempted to model analogy-making by creating a mapping between two sets of data structures that represent the domains (Gentner, 1983; Holyoak and Thagard, 1989).

Defining analogy-making as "making a mapping between domains" creates many assumptions about analogy and how one might model it. For instance, the traditional view assumes that there exist pre-structured representations on which the mapping process operates. It is not at all clear that this assumption is cognitively plausible (Chalmers *et al.*, 1995). This view also suggests that not only can the mapping process be separated from the structure-forming process, but that it is also distinct from more general perceptual processes. This, too, seems unlikely. Although these issues have been partially addressed by Hofstadter and colleagues (1995), one question remains: How could a system *learn* to make analogies?

To create a model capable of learning to make analogies requires re-thinking some basic assumptions. Traditionally, "making an analogy" has meant explicitly producing the entire set of correspondences from one domain to the other. It is difficult to see how a system could learn to do this.

One possible solution, following the general suggestions of Maes (1993), is to frame the task in terms of behavior. One analogy-making task that can be seen entirely in terms of behavior is the "Do this!" task posed by Hofstadter and French (French, 1992). A boiled-down version of this task was defined as follows. Consider Figure 1. Imagine an experimenter pointing to the triangle in the source scene and saying, "Do this!" The subject's task is then to point to the "same" thing in the target scene. If one perceives the triangle as "the object that differs on the dimension of shape," then one might be inclined to choose the square in the target scene, as it, too, differs by shape from the two circles in the target scene. Of course, that is certainly not the only possible answer.

To learn to make this type of analogy, a recurrent backpropagation network was created. A variation on Smolensky's tensor product representation (1990) was developed and used as input to the network. These representations, termed *iconic*, encode an object's location in a scene over a set of local units. A series of these iconic maps, in turn, encodes an object's color and shape, such as *blue* and *square*.

The network was trained to identify the *figure* and *ground* of each scene presented to it. The network was first trained to identify the object being pointed to in the source scene as the figure, and the remaining source objects as the ground. Given the first scene as context, the network was then trained to identify the analogous object from the target as the figure, thereby completing the analogy.

After being successfully trained on many example analogies, the network was shown to generalize by performing well on many novel scenes. Analysis has shown that the network is capable of learning abstract "concepts" such as "differs by shape." Although the current model has some significant limitations, it does suggest a framework for a behavioral approach of analogy-making capable of explaining effects such as "systematicity" (Gentner, 1983) and unifying analogy-making with more general perceptual processes.

References

Chalmers, D., French, R., and Hofstadter, D. (1995). High-level perception, representation, and analogy: a critique of artificial-intelligence methodology. In *Fluid concepts and creative analogies*. Basic Books, New York, NY.

French, R. (1992). *Tabletop: An emergent, stochastic model of analogy-making*. Doctoral dissertation, EECS Department, University of Michigan, Ann Arbor.

Gentner, D. (1983). Structure-mapping: A theoretical framework for analogy. *Cognitive Science*, 7(2).

Hofstadter, D. and the Fluid Analogies Research Group (1995). *Fluid concepts and creative analogies*. Basic Books, New York, NY.

Holyoak, K., and Thagard, P. (1989). Analogical mapping by constraint satisfaction. *Cognitive Science*, 13(3).

Maes, P. (1993). Behavior-based artificial intelligence. In Proceedings of the Fifteenth Annual Conference of the Cognitive Science Society. Boulder, CO.

Smolensky, P. (1990). Tensor product variable binding and the representation of symbolic structures in connectionist systems. *Artificial Intelligence*, 46.

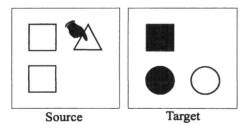

Source   Target

Figure 1. A sample problem adapted from French (1992).

733

A Physical Framework for Explaining Consciousness

C. Franklin Boyle

Advanced Technology Group
Union Switch & Signal Inc.
Pittsburgh, PA 15219
cfboyle@switch.com

David Chalmers (1995) states that "The ultimate goal of a theory of consciousness is a simple and elegant set of fundamental laws, analogous to the fundamental laws of physics." He goes on to suggest that certain psychophysical laws, like higher level principles, are "unlikely to be fundamental . . . analogous to macroscopic principles in physics such as those of thermodynamics or kinematics." and that more fundamental laws "may centrally involve the concept of information." Crick and Koch (Chalmers, 1995) acknowledge that information "may indeed be the key concept, as Chalmers suspects".

If we take information to be fundamental here, then there is a problem: information is, in general, an intuitive notion with little, if any, consensus on just how to scientifically define it (Bunge and Ardila, 1987). Surely we cannot hope to construct an objective theory of consciousness if the foundation on which it rests is abstract and poorly defined. If information is the key to understanding consciousness, then those characteristics of the brain that give rise to it will only be revealed when we have grounded information and information processing.

But how do we go about grounding these? I claim it cannot be done simply by looking at the hardware architectures of systems we consider to be processing information, like digital computers and brains. Rather, it requires a broader and more fundamental physical understanding of information and its processing. To this end I offer a physical framework that classifies object interactions in such a way that different kinds of information processing are identified with different kinds of interactions. This framework is an extension of traditional physical state descriptions used to describe lawfully-determined changes in the values of measured attributes of interacting objects. It could very well be what Chalmers is looking for when he offers "how [information] is physically processed" as the possible explanation for how some information might have an experiential aspect.

The framework is based on the observation that physical objects have two and only two physical aspects: extended structure and measurable properties like mass and velocity. Since everything consists of physical objects, unless information and its processing are non-physical, it must be embodied by one or both of these aspects. We have information about the world because physical objects interact with our sensory systems. Thus objects are informational in that they "inform" us through interactions.

The framework differentiates between physical interactions according to which of the two physical aspects of inter-

acting objects cause the resulting changes. All physical interactions are classified into four types: nomologically-determined change, nomologically-triggered change, pattern matching, and structure-preserving superposition (SPS). The first two result in changes caused by measured attributes and the last two result in changes caused by extended structure.

If we assume that objects are informational through their physical aspects, then we can consider that the different types of physical interactions are the physical basis for different kinds of information processing: nomologically-determined change describes the information processing in analog computers; pattern matching describes the information processing in digital computers; and, I claim, SPS describes the information processing in the brain (Boyle, 1995).

What does this have to do with consciousness? First, information, if it is fundamental, is now grounded in the basic physical interactions that make up all physical processes. Second, one of these basic interaction types, SPS, is so different from the physical interactions that underlie the functioning of all other complex physical systems, that it makes the brain unique, over and above its own enormous complexity. I believe SPS is responsible in part for the brain's remarkable characteristics, such as its intrinsic capacity for reference and, I put forward here, consciousness, and that without SPS there would be no consciousness. Consciousness may require the presence of other physical phenomena, such as electric currents, but SPS is a necessary and fundamental ingredient.

References

Boyle, C.F. (1995) Information as an Intrinsic Property. *Minds and Machines*, 4: 451-467.

Bunge M. and Ardila, R. (1987) *Philosophy of Psychology*. New York, NY: Springer-Verlag.

Chalmers, D.J. (1995) The Puzzle of Conscious Experience. *Scientific American*, 273 (6): 80-86.

Problem-solving in imagery

Matthew Brand

The Media Lab, MIT, Cambridge, MA 02139

brand@media.mit.edu

Mental imagery often plays a role in problem solving, particularly when the problem is complex [2] or the subject must devise a procedure for arriving at a solution [3]. For this reason, imagery use is strongly associated with highly creative problem solving [5]. How are problems transformed into imagery, or solved thereafter? Researchers have pointed out that good problem visualizations capitalize on the imagery machinery's ability to detect and reinforce visual properties such as symmetries, similarities, alignments, relations of size, gestalts (e.g., [4]).

We propose that the transformation to such 'good visualizations' hinges on the discovery of problem invariants: parameters that may be varied or removed without affecting the basic structure of the problem. Invariants indicate ways in which the problem can be decomposed into critical and optional subproblems. In imagery, self-similarities such as repeated patterns, symmetries, and alignments are strongly indicative of invariants. Visual problem solving is a cycle of visualization, discovery of invariants, and reduction to new visualizations that are progressively simpler (reducing cognitive load or increasing alignments or other systematicities that support chunking) and more revealing (with causal structure more salient to the visual system).

To study visualizations in problem solving, we posed four difficult problems in tilings, population dynamics, physics, and mechanical design to seventeen undergraduates, and collected protocols of their reported use of imagery. Although these problems are easily solved when converted to formal representations–logic, geometric series, algebraic equalities, and topological partitions–most subjects reported working through a progression of visualizations. Our analyses found that most successive visualizations were linked via invariants, and that these invariants were 'noticed' as visual properties of the imagery. For example, in solving Wickelgren's [6] checkers-and-dominos problem (figure 1), subjects noted that

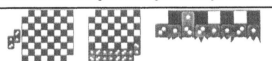

Figure 1: Use of an invariant to simplify the question: Can the mutilated board be tiled with dominos?.

repeated patterns in the checkerboard led them to see how the solution was invariant to the number of pairs of rows, allowing them to reduce the problem to a two-row board.

In one problem, subjects were asked to find a workable connection topology between weights in a kinetic mobile (à la Alexander Calder). Using the invariants discovered by these students, we developed an imagery simulator that robustly designs mobiles with complicated connection topologies and systems of leverages. The simulator models imagery as maps of activity that evolve through simple cell-parallel calculations. Imagery operations such as movement,

alignment, fitting, and grouping are accomplished by field couplings in which activity in one map generates potentials that influence activity in another. Figure 2 shows the fields

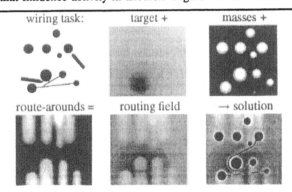

Figure 2: Constructing a routing-field for "wiring" a mobile.

used to route a connecting wire in accordance with an invariant that guarantees mechanically valid mobiles. Figure 3 shows

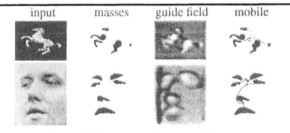

Figure 3: Mobiles derived from images.

some of the finished mobiles that this imagery system has designed. Coupled potential fields can be implemented as neural networks whose organization mimics hypothesized maps in the visual cortex[1]. Thus we can map out and partially automate a full reduction from a high-level design problem to low-level massively parallel computations between maps of neuron-like computing elements.

References

[1] Brand, M. (1996). *Visual problem solving using coupled potential fields*. Technical report, MIT Media Lab.

[2] Denis, M. (1991). Imagery and thinking. In C. Cornoldi and M.A. McDaniel, editors, *Imagery and Cognition*, chapter 3. Springer-Verlag.

[3] Kaufmann, G. (1990). Imagery effects on problem solving. In J.T.E. Richardson, P.J. Hampson, D.F. Marks, editor, *Imagery: Current developments*, chapter 7. Routledge.

[4] Kosslyn, S.M. (1994). *Image and Brain*. MIT Press.

[5] Shepard, R.N. (1978). Externalization of the image and the act of creation. In B.S. Randhawa, editor, *Visual Learning, Thinking, and Communication*. NY: Academic Press.

[6] Wickelgren, W.A. (1974). *How to solve problems*. NY: W.H. Freeman and Company.

Dennett, Phi, and Consciousness

Selmer Bringsjord, Ron Noel, Geoff Ginader and **Elizabeth Bringsjord**
Dept. of Philosophy, Psychology & Cognitive Science
Rensselaer Polytechnic Institute
Troy, NY 12180
{selmer,noelr,ginadg}@rpi.edu • eb9889@csc.albany.edu
http://www.rpi.edu/~brings

Introduction

Perhaps the cornerstone of Daniel Dennett's (1991) case for his "multiple drafts" view of consciousness in his well-known *Consciousness Explained* is a set of inferences he draws from the phi phenomenon. Phi was first introduced by the great gestalt psychologist Max Wertheimer (1912), and a number of fascinating variations have been studied by, among others, Paul Kolers and Michael von Grünau (1976). In the simplest version of phi, two or more small dots are briefly lit in rapid succession, but it seems to the subject that a single spot moves back and forth. In the *color* phi phenomenon (the study of which was prompted by questions from the philosopher Nelson Goodman (1978), the two illuminated spots are different colors (red and green, say). Remarkably, if these two spots are lit for 150msec each (50msec interval)

> the first spot seems to begin moving and then change color abruptly *in the middle of its illusory passage* toward the second location. Goodman wondered: "How are we able ... to fill in the spot at the intervening place-times along a path running from the first to the second flash *before that second flash occurs?*" (Dennett, 1991, p.114, emphasis his)

Dennett holds that the only way to provide an answer to Goodman's question, the only way to explain color phi, is to invoke his (Dennett's) "multiple drafts" theory (MDT) of consciousness, according to which (barbarically encapsulated here) information entering the nervous system is under continuous parallel "editorial revision." MDT is intended by Dennett to supplant traditional accounts of cognition seen, for example, in cognitive psychology—accounts which include subsystems such as long-term memory, short-term memory, etc., as well as the notion of an "executive controller" (cf. Anderson's ACT*; 1983, 1990). Armed with color phi, Dennett also means to overthrow views of the mind which distinguish between some stimulus *s* seeming to be *F* to a subject, and the subject's judging that *s* is in fact *F*. Here Dennett appeals to what is disclosed when subjects introspect about their experience during phi: he claims that such subjects cannot say, in a principled manner, whether they judged the spots to move because of what they seemed to see, or whether they seemed to see movement because they judged there to be movement.

With help from some elementary logic, the situation can be clarified: Denote the color phi experiment by ϕ_c; denote Dennett-targeted traditional theories of cognition by 'TTC.' Dennett's argument, overall, is that ϕ_c is inconsistent with TTC, and that the only other serious contender, MDT, should

therefore be affirmed. However, it is a simple theorem from (modal) logic that in order to show propositions *p* and *q* consistent, it suffices to find an *r* which is consistent with *p* and which entails *q*. Accordingly, our refutation of Dennett will take this form: We will specify an explanation *E* of ϕ_c which is such that

1. *E* is consistent with ϕ_c; and
2. *E* conjoined with ϕ_c entails TTC.

We will include a report on our replication of color phi (and related phenomena) both through Java (you may now experience phi and register your impressions by accessing the relevant part of Bringsjord's web site) and via T-scope in Rensselaer's cognitive science laboratory, and concomitant reports on what subjects say after introspecting in the manner Dennett prescribes. Explanation *E* will be anchored to these reports.

References

Anderson, J.R. (1983) *The Adaptive Character of Thought* (Hillsdale, NJ: Lawrence Erlbaum).

Anderson, J.R. (1983) *The Architecture of Cognition* (Cambridge, MA: Harvard University Press).

Dennett, D. (1991) *Consciousness Explained* (Boston, MA: Little, Brown).

Goodman, N. (1978) *Ways of Worldmaking* (Hassocks, Sussex: Harvester).

Kolers, P.A. & von Grünau, M. (1976) "Shape and Color in Apparent Motion," *Vision Research* 16: 329-335.

Wertheimer, M. (1912) "Experimentelle Studien über das Sehen von Bewegung," *Zeitschrift für Psychologie* 61: 161-265.

Modeling Parsing Constraints in High-Dimensional Semantic Space: On the Use of Proper Names

Curt Burgess, Kay Livesay and **Kevin Lund**
Department of Psychology
University of California, Riverside
Riverside, CA 92521
curt@cassandra.ucr.edu

The Hyperspace Analogue to Language (HAL) semantic model (Lund & Burgess, in press) demonstrates the impoverished semantics of proper names and the richer semantics of famous names. In addition, proper names used as agentive subjects in a parsing experiment fail to show, in our simulation, an effect of semantic information on parsing due to their impoverished semantics.

The role of semantic context in processing syntactic ambiguity raises important issues concerning the function of the language processor. Modular parsers (Frazier, 1978) are insensitive to contextual information. Conversely, constraint-based approaches (MacDonald, Pearlmutter, & Seidenberg, 1994) propose that language subsystems can more freely interact allowing for semantic influence on initial parsing decisions. Using the HAL model (Burgess & Lund, 1996; Lund & Burgess, in press), we present a semantics of proper names followed by a simulation experiment that suggests that proper names do not contain sufficient semantic information to influence syntactic processing.

Experiment 1: Semantics of Names

Proper names carry little semantic information accounting for the difficulty in their retrieval (Cohen and Burke, 1993). However, famous names, such as Reagan, have a richer semantics. Name semantics can be represented using the HAL model as shown by a nearest neighbor analysis. Near neighbors of *Cathy*, are other common proper names. However, famous names, like *Reagan*, has other politicians and political terms. Likewise, *book* has as its neighbors other related objects. In addition, HAL's high-dimensional semantic vectors can distinguish proper names from nouns and verbs.

Experiment 2: Context Effects and Semantic Distances

HAL's high-dimensional semantics can capture the constraints that predict whether semantic context will facilitate syntactic processing (Burgess and Lund, 1996). Shorter semantic distances were found between noun-verb pairs of stimuli that did not result in a gardenpath (1b, *ransom-paid*) than for sentences that did (1a, *man-paid*).

Verbs like that in sentence (2a) rarely take a direct object; while in sentence (2b), the verb can take either a direct object or a sentence complement. Verbs that do not take a direct object could provide considerable guidance to the parser and avoid syntactic misassignment. However, Ferreira and Henderson (1990, FH) found that reading times for sentences like (2a and 2b) were longer than for unambiguous controls with complementizers. FH conclude that biasing verb information did not effect initial parsing decisions.

(1a)   The man paid by the parents was unreasonable.
(1b)   The ransom paid by the parents was unreasonable.
(2a)   Sue hoped Iowa elected better people.
(2b)   Sue wrote Iowa elected better people.
(3)   The student hoped ...

Another potentially rich source of information in this experiment could be the nature of the noun preceding the verb. The mental model that develops with *Sue hoped* can encompass many possibilities and may not be as constraining as the mental model from (3), which offers the verb crucial additional information during comprehension.

We test the stimuli used in two parsing experiments - one that showed an effect of the NP context (Burgess & Tanenhaus, BT) and one, using proper names, that did not (Ferreira & Henderson, FH). Semantic distances were greater for the stimuli (noun-verbs pairs) that did not show the effect of context (FH) than for the stimuli that did (BT).

Discussion

Models of proper-name retrieval emphasize that name retrieval difficulty is due to the lack of meaningful semantic information in a name, and this can be seen with a name's semantic neighbors. Longer semantic distances with the proper name - verb pairs of FH suggests that proper names do not carry compelling semantic information. That HAL's semantic representations can be used to model the outcome of these two parsing experiments extends the generality of this semantic model to parsing phenomena beyond that of just animacy and general plausibility effects.

Acknowledgments

This research was supported by NSF PFF award SBR-9453406 to Curt Burgess.

References

Burgess, C., & Lund, K. (1996). *Parsing constraints and high-dimensional semantic space*. Manuscript submitted for publication.

Burgess, C., & Tanenhaus, M. K. (1992). *Semantic, syntactic and visual factors in syntactic ambiguity resolution*.

Cohen, G., & Burke, D. M. (1993). Memory for proper names: A review. *Memory, 1*, 249-263.

Ferreira, F., & Henderson, J. M. (1990). Use of verb information in syntactic parsing: Evidence from eye-movements and word-by-word self-paced reading. *Journal of Experimental Psychology: Learning, Memory and Cognition, 16*, 555-568.

Frazier, L. (1978). *On comprehending sentences: Syntactic parsing strategies*. Unpublished doctoral dissertation, University of Connecticut.

Lund, K., & Burgess, C. (in press). Producing high-dimensional semantic spaces from lexical co-occurrence. *Behavior Research Methods, Instrumentation, and Computers*.

MacDonald, M. C., Pearlmutter, N., & Seidenberg, M. (1994).The lexical nature of syntactic ambiguity resolution. *Psychology Review, 101*, 676-703.

737

A Pie in the Face for Global FOE Theories

Lawrence Richard Carleton
GDE Systems Inc.
8424 Travis Court
San Diego, CA 92126
(619)592-5297
lrcarleton@aol.com

Focus of optical flow expansion (FOE) detection remains the most intuitively satisfying paradigm for self motion (egomotion) perception theories. Despite evidence that such perception is dominated by information in the periphery of the optical array sample, theories taking the peripheral approach were rejected in favor of theories taking a global approach, because of findings that samples restricted to very small visual angles are sufficient to determine egomotion perception. But global theories fail the looming test: the projection of a looming object, e.g., a pie aproaching one's face, presents an expanding optical region which dominates one's whole sample and exhibits its own FOE. In practice, one perceives a pie about to collide with one's face. But global theories necessarily must determine that the victim will perceive himself as moving toward the pie! Peripheral theories escape this fundamental flaw, and a theory recognizing that the periphery is adjustable is immune to the evidence against the older theories, which assumed a fixed periphery. The optical array region sampled for conscious attention is known to be variable. If the (annular) region for egomotion detection is peripheral to the central attentional area, then it is adjustable as a side effect of central area variation.

Explanatory Coherence as a Model for Belief Revision

Christina Carrick

Computing Science
Simon Fraser University
Burnaby, BC, Canada V5A 1S6
ccarrick@cs.sfu.ca

Introduction

A belief revision system must be able to decide, in the face of contradictory information, which (if any) beliefs should be abandoned. What general principle should be followed to make this decision? In Martins and Shapiro (1988), several specific tasks were described which must be solved in order for a system to successfully revise beliefs in the face of contradictory evidence: inference, dependency recording, nonmonotonicity, and disbelief propagation. A cognitive theory of belief revision should be able to say which beliefs should be retained or abandoned while allowing solutions to the subproblems to be covered by the same theory.

The ECHO Program and Belief Revision

There are two major epistemic theories of belief revision: the *foundational* theory of belief revision and the *coherence* theory. It is desirable for a model of belief revision to have some of the rationality of the foundational theory, but with a behaviour similar to that produced by the coherence model. Explanatory Coherence (EC) makes such an attempt, encompassing aspects of both theories. EC follows the principle of negative uncertainty, given by foundational theory, by requiring some sort of explanatory relationship between two propositions in order for them to be considered coherent. It also conforms to the principle of conservation, however, which is the basis for coherence theory.

Explanatory Coherence is a property of two or more propositions (Thagard, 1989). The greater a proposition coheres with a set of other propositions, the greater its acceptability; a proposition which is incoherent with the set should be rejected. In his paper, Thagard notes the potential for using explanatory coherence for belief revision. Though EC cannot say how to derive new beliefs from old ones, it could be used to decide whether or not a new belief should enter the system on the basis of coherence with the beliefs already maintained.

Based on the principles of explanatory coherence, the ECHO program is described in detail in Thagard (1989). ECHO is an implementation of an associative artificial neural network. Connections in the network are either excitatory, which represents explanatory relations, or inhibitory, which represents contradiction. Each node represents a proposition or an hypothesis, and the connections are, therefore, the relations between them. Since the purpose of ECHO was to determine coherence and not explanatory relationships, all explanatory and contradictory relationships between propositions are entered as input. A "special evidence" unit provides activation to all propositions of observed data, and this ac-

tivation spreads throughout the network via the excitatory (explanation) links and is restricted through the inhibitory (contradiction) links.

Experimentation and Results

The ECHO program was extended only slightly for nonmonotonicity experiments. It was made possible to adjust any or all activations and connection strengths of the network, to simulate a "forgetting" effect or a re-initialization. It was also made possible to disconnect nodes from the special evidence unit, to allow propositions which were once true to become false. Two different original data sets were used for the belief revision experiments, each of which were presented to the network in varying manners (certain subsets of evidence were presented, and then others).

It was found that implementing the nonmonotonic ability is not a straightforward matter. The simple EC processes alone were not enough to cause the shifts in belief that should have occurred. Fading all of the activations provided the network with the capability to re-evaluate the beliefs, which is cognitively plausible given the assumption that there exists a momentary suspension of a person's beliefs when he is confronted with new information.

Future work will involve investigation into the issue of epistemic entrenchment in ECHO. Marker-passing will be explored to facilitate shifts between epistemic states without fading all nodes equally. Experimentation with larger data sets is also necessary, to discover ECHO's ability to scale to more complex data.

References

Gardenfors, P. (1992). The Dynamics of Belief Systems: Foundations versus Coherence Theories. In *Knowledge, Belief, and Strategic Interaction* (pp. 377-396). Cambridge: Cambridge University Press.

Goldman, A. I. (1993). Epistemic Folkways and Scientific Epistemology. In *Readings in Philosophy and Cognitive Science* (pp. 95–114). Cambridge, Massachusettes: MIT Press.

Martins, J. P. & Shapiro, S. C. (1988). A Model for Belief Revision. *Artificial Intelligence*, 35(1), 25–79.

Thagard, P. (1989). Explanatory Coherence. *Behavioural and Brain Sciences*, 12, 435–502.

Towards a Computational Model of Discourse Summarization

Samuel W. K. Chan
School of Computer Science & Engineering
The University of New South Wales
NSW 2052, Australia
swkchan@cse.unsw.edu.au

Abstract

Understanding a discourse is considered to involve a series of specific processing phases which final result is a complete semantic, mental representation (Johnson-Laird, 1983; van Dijk & Kintsch, 1983). This result is not only a representation of the text, but rather of what the text is about. When a reader is asked to summarize a discourse, vast amounts of information within the discourse are selectively ignored in order to produce a distilled version of the original text. This simplification process emphasizes central elements of the discourse while the peripheral details are neglected. It is further demonstrated that discourse can be represented as a skeleton in which the relationships among the clauses could be chunked in a way that replicated the semantic structure of the original discourse (Grosz & Sidner, 1986). Textual continuity, which differentiates a text from a random sequence of sentences, is a prime factor in discourse summarization (Ehrlich & Charolles, 1991).

In this paper, we present a computational model for transforming discourses into Quasi-Mental Clusters (QMCs) through a convergence process. The process is interpreted as a particular transformation of a given set of discourse segments and concepts by examining the textual continuity. Before the process, a cohesion parsing is first conducted in testing the local cohesion amongst the sentences. It is achieved in a constraint net which is formulated as a constraint satisfaction problem over a set of finite elements (Waltz & Pollack, 1985). The elements in the net may represent words, phrases, and more importantly, the buffers which are designated to carry each prior analyzed sentences over into the current processing cycle, in hope that they would serve as common bridging elements between the sentences. An efficient filtering algorithm is employed to reduce the incohesive ones while cohesive links amongst sentences are then defined. In the convergence process, sentences in a discourse are represented as nodes and connected by the links in a modified Brain-State-in-a-Box (BSB) network (Anderson & Murphy, 1986). They are highly interconnected and feedback upon themselves. The BSB network operates by accepting a pattern of activations and amplifying that pattern through the feedback loop. Competing coalitions of the nodes drive the network into a stable equilibration from which the QMCs are extracted. The strongest connection in the QMCs will arise from the pair of nodes that maintain high activations for a prolonged period of time. The model is tested using children's stories and the results attest its validity. The representation of texts in QMCs captures some important aspects of the memory representation of discourses. Thus, the resulting QMCs are the useful data structures in summarization, question answering and knowledge discovery in discourses.

References

Anderson, J.A., & Murphy, G.L. (1986). Psychological concepts in a parallel system. *Physica D*, 22, 318-336.

Ehrlich, M.-F., & Charolles, M. (1991). Aspects of textual continuity: Psycholinguistic approaches. In G. Denhiere & J.-P. Rossi (Eds.), *Text and Text Processing*, North-Holland, 269-285.

Grosz, B.J., & Sidner, C.L. (1986). Attention, intention, and the structure of discourse. *Computational Linguistics*, 12, 175-204.

Johnson-Laird, P.N. (1983). *Mental Models*. Cambridge, MA: Harvard University Press.

van Dijk, T.A., & Kintsch, W. (1983). *Strategies of Discourse Comprehension*. NY: Academic.

Waltz, D.L., & Pollack, J.B. (1985). Massively parallel parsing: a strongly interactive model of natural language interpretation. *Cognitive Science*, 9, 51-74.

Representational Distortion as a Theory of Similarity

Nick Chater and **Ulrike Hahn**
Dept. of Experimental Psychology
University of Oxford, England
{nick,ulrike}@psy.ox.ac.uk

A central drawback of extant psychological theories of similarity is that they are typically defined over very limited classes of representations such as points in a multidimensional space or feature-sets. Our new account, *representational distortion*, can deal with arbitrary representations. Here, similarity between two representations is defined by the amount of distortion required to transform one representation into another.

This theory is based on the *information distance* (Li & Vitanyi, 1993) between representations. Intuitively, the information distance between two representations measures how many instructions must be followed to transform one into the other. The information distance, e.g. between the sequences 1 2 3 4 5 and 2 3 4 5 6 is small, because the simple instruction "add 1 to each digit" transforms one into the other. The information distance between 8 5 7 4 9 and 8 7 9 0 5 is larger, because there is no simple instruction here. This approach is general, because the length of the shortest set of instructions required to transform one representation to another is well-defined for all representations, whether these are feature vectors, a structural description of perceptual input, a parsed sentence, a schema of general knowledge, a pictorial represention or a sequence of motor commands.

Representational distortion can be quantified by applying ideas from a branch of computer science and mathematics known as *Kolmogorov complexity* (Li & Vitanyi, 1993).[1] The fundamental idea of Kolmogorov complexity theory is that the complexity of any mathematical object, x, can be measured by the length of the shortest computer program that is able to generate that object. This length is the Kolmogorov complexity, $K(x)$ of x, a notion which has fruitfully been applied in statistics, inductive inference and machine learning. To quantify representational distortion we use the conditional Kolmogorov complexity, $K(x|y)$, of one object, x, given another object, y. This is the length of the shortest program which produces x as output from y as input—the shorter the program, the simpler the relation between the two objects, and therefore the less representational distortion is required.

This gives a simple account of similarity, with a number of interesting properties (Hahn and Chater, 1996). **Generality**: it applies to representations of all kinds— spatial, feature-based or, crucially, structured representations. **Flexibility**: Similarity is defined over representations of objects, and the goals and knowledge of the subject may affect the representations which are formed, hence, allowing for the great flexibility of human similarity judgements. **Self-similarity**: it is maximal, as no program at all is required to transform an object into itself. **Asymmetry**: Representational distortion allows for asymmetry in similarity judgements: $K(x|y)$ is not in general equal to $K(y|x)$. This asymmetry is particularly apparent when the representations being transformed differ substantially in complexity, as is observed experimentally (Tversky, 1977). Symmetrical judgements are captured by the average of the distances in either direction: $D(x, y) = 1/2(K(x|y) + K(y|x))$. **Background knowledge**: this may radically affect the program length required to transform two objects. 1 5 3 7 2 3 9 0 6 and 3 0 7 4 4 7 8 1, e.g., are very simply related (and, hence, their similarity high) –*if* it is recognized that, as base 10 numbers, the second is double the first. **Shepard's Universal Law of Generalization**: the account provides a derivation of the Universal Law of Generalization (Chater and Hahn, 1996).

References

Chater, N. (in press) Reconciling simplicity and likelihood principles in perceptual organization. *Psychological Review*.

Chater, N. and Hahn, U. (1996). Representational Distortion and the Universal Law of Generalization. *Unpublished manuscript*.

Hahn, U. and Chater, N. (1996). Concepts and Similarity. *In*: Lamberts, K. & Shanks, D. R. (Eds.), *Knowledge, Concepts, and Categories*. London: UCL Press.

Li, M. & Vitanyi, P. (1993). An introduction to Kolmogorov complexity and its applications. New York: Springer-Verlag.

Shepard, R. N. (1987) Toward a universal law of generalization for psychological science. Science, 237, 1317-1323.

Tversky, A. (1977). Features of Similarity. *Psychological Review*, 84, 327—352.

---

[1] This was previously applied in a psychological context as a framework for perceptual organization (Chater, in press).

Using a Multinomial Model to Differentiate Alzheimer's Disease, Vascular Disease, and Elderly Controls Based on an Immediate Recall Task

Jamie Chosak-Reiter[1], William H. Batchelder[1], W. Rodman Shankle[2], and Malcolm B. Dick[3]

[1]Dept. Cognitive Sciences, [2]Dept. Neurology, [3]Dept. Psychobiology
University of California, Irvine
Irvine, CA 92717
jchosak@aris.ss.uci.edu, whbatche@aris.ss.uci.edu, rshankle@uci.edu,
mbdick@uci.edu

Can the ability to freely recall words immediately after reading them from a list differentiate early stages of Alzheimer's Disease (AD), Vascular Dementia (VD), and healthy, elderly controls? Previous studies have suggested that immediate free recall ability does not help to differentiate early AD from controls, while performance on delayed recall can (e.g., Welsh et al., 1991; 1992). However, the methods used typically analyzed only part of the available information, namely, the mean number of items recalled per trial. General Processing Tree (GPT) modeling is a form of multinomial modeling (described in Riefer & Batchelder, 1988) that analyzes more of the available information and may help differentiate these diagnoses. The GPT method provides estimates and confidence intervals for parameters reflecting the probabilities of hypothesized, underlying cognitive processes.

In the present study, we used the GPT approach to analyze AD, VD and control subjects for their pattern of immediate, free recall of each word over the three trials of the CERAD 10-item Word List test. The hypothesized parameters of the model were 1) storing the word into a temporary state, 2) retrieving the word from a partially stored state, and 3) storing and retrieving the word from a more permanent state. In contrast to previously used methods, the GPT model for these data differentiated between early stages of AD, VD, and elderly controls.

Results of the parameter estimates based on the GPT model revealed that early stages of AD affected these parameters in a different way than early stages of VD. As AD and VD progressed, the parameters had a different sequence of changes, which may reflect differences in their pathophysiological mechanisms. Additionally, the results suggested that very mild AD patients stored items into a temporary state better than very mild VD patients, and very mild AD patients had significantly poorer retrieval from the temporary state than healthy elderly controls. However, as the disease progressed, AD patients relied more heavily on temporary storage of the words as their ability to achieve long-term storage diminished. This finding is consistent with neurological evidence of hippocampal damage in AD, which results in a reduced ability for these patients to transfer information to long-term memory for more permanent learning.

References

Riefer, D. M., & Batchelder, W. H. (1988). Multinomial modeling and the measurement of cognitive processes. Psychological Review, 95, 318-339.

Welsh, K., Butters, N., Hughes, J., Mohs, R., & Heyman, A. (1991). Detection of abnormal memory decline in mild cases of Alzheimer's Disease using CERAD neuropsychological measures. Archives of Neurology, 48, 278-281.

Welsh, K. A., Butters, N., Hughes, J. P., Mohs, R. C., & Heyman, A. (1992). Detection and staging of dementia in Alzheimer's Disease. Use of the neuropsychological measures developed for the consortium to establish a registry for Alzheimer's Disease. Archives of Neurology, 49, 448-452.

Individuating Concepts

Ronald L. Chrisley
School of Cognitive & Computing Sciences
University of Sussex
Brighton BN1 9QH, United Kingdom
ronc@cogs.susx.ac.uk

Concept possession vs. concept individuation

Which comes first, an account of concept individuation, or an account of concept possession? The Classical account has it that individuation comes first: concepts are individuated by what they are concepts *of*. But, as has been pointed out [Fodor, 1994], the Classical approach is an infamous and spectacular failure: either the relation between concepts and what they are of is stipulated, making it a mystery how we could possess such things, or it is substantive, yet no account of this relation has been given.

Thus, cognitive science has rejected Classicism. But despite its problems, Fodor claims it is still preferable to anti-Classicism (also called Pragmatism), which denies that concept individuation comes first. I present and reject Fodor's arguments against two anti-Classical positions – Behaviouristic and Definitional Pragmatism – as well as his argument (from compositionality) against Pragmatism in general.

Behaviouristic Pragmatism

Behaviouristic Pragmatism holds that the criteria for concept possession are "expressed in the vocabulary of behavior and/or in the vocabulary of dispositions to behave" [Fodor, 1994, p 101], typically sorting behaviour.

Fodor's main argument against this approach is: given that the two kinds of (broadly-individuated) sorting behaviour "look the same" (e.g., triangle sorting and trilateral sorting), a Behaviourist can use them differentially in giving an account of concept possession (e.g., the concept TRIANGLE vs. the concept TRILATERAL) only if some account is given of the differences between the sorting behaviours themselves. Otherwise, the Behaviouristic reduction has not been completed. Yet such an account can only be given in terms of dispositions to infer, which violates Behaviourism's restriction to non-mentalistic explanations. I argue that a Behaviouristic Pragmatist need not be a reductionist; and furthermore, one need not reduce the difference between sorting behaviours to differences in inferential dispositions; one might reduce them to, e.g., differences in linguistic behaviour.

Definitional Pragmatism

Definitional Pragmatism holds that "Having the concept X *just is* being able to sort Xs and being disposed to draw the inferences that *define X-ness*" [Fodor, 1994, p 104]. Fodor's objection, that most concepts don't have definitions, is based on the undefinability of linguistic concepts, and thus assumes a tight connection between language and thought. Instead, I suggest that we make a distinction between communicative content and cognitive content. Concisely: we don't speak our minds. The essential publicity of linguistic content is the source of its undefinability. Mental concepts, being governed by norms other than inter-subjective use, can be individuated definitionally. Or at least Fodor has not shown that they can't.

If mental concepts are distinct from linguistic ones, as I claim, the standard means of specifying a concept (provide a natural language expression that means that concept) cannot work; some alternative means is necessary. I have proposed some alternatives elsewhere [Chrisley, 1995].

Mere compositionality

A virtue of Definitional Pragmatism is that the concepts it individuates are compositional: "a constituent concept contributes the same content to all complex representations it occurs in" [Fodor, 1994, p 107]. This is a virtue because compositionality (and, if Fodor is right, it alone) can explain the productivity and systematicity of thought. But, Fodor notes, there are inferences which we make about, say, green apples that do not follow just from their being green and from their being apples. Thus Definitional Pragmatism, being merely compositional, cannot explain the possession of the concept GREEN APPLE.

My reply is that a Definitional Pragmatist need not hold that *all* of one's dispositions to infer things concerning green apples are definitional; not all need be explained by the possession of the concept GREEN APPLE. No doubt Fodor believes otherwise because he fails to acknowledge an analytic/synthetic distinction. But to ask the Definitional Pragmatist to reject that distinction would be to beg the question.

References

Chrisley, R. (1995). Taking embodiment seriously: Nonconceptual content and robotics. In K. Ford, C. Glymour, & P. Hayes (Eds.), *Android Epistemology* (pp. 141–166). Cambridge: MIT Press.

Fodor, J. (1994). Concepts: A potboiler. *Cognition, 50*, 95–113.

Does Frequency Determine the Storage of Compounds?
Evidence from Chinese

Timothy C. Clausner
University of Southern California
Hedco Neurosciences Building
Los Angeles, CA 90089-2520
timc@gizmo.usc.edu

Brenda Rapp and **Yi-Ching Su**
Johns Hopkins University
Krieger Hall / 3400 N. Charles Street
Baltimore, Maryland 21218-2685
brenda@mail.cog.jhu.edu
ching@mail.cog.jhu.edu

Abstract

We investigate the role that frequency plays in the storage of morpheme pairs as lexical units. That is, do frequency differences distinguish compounds and phrases? Two hypotheses are considered: 1. Frequency of Co-occurrence (FOC): assumes that a morpheme pair will be stored if the constituents co-occur with sufficient frequency. 2. Idiomaticity (ID): assumes that a morpheme pair will be stored if the combined meaning is sufficiently unpredictable from the meaning of the constituent morphemes. We contrast two sets of morpheme pairs: *Transparent* pairs (i.e. phrases) whose meaning is generally derived from the constituents, e.g. "black coat", and *Idiomatic* pairs (i.e. compounds) whose meaning is not entirely derived from the constituents, e.g. "blackboard". If the two sets are matched for frequency of morpheme co-occurrence <u>and</u> for the frequency of the constituent morphemes, then FOC predicts that the two sets should be comparable on relevant behavioral measures since frequency is held constant. In contrast, ID predicts behavioral consequences based on the differences in idiomaticity even for frequency matched sets.

These hypotheses are not readily tested in English which marks compounds by both phonological stress and the number of orthographic "words". However, Mandarin Chinese does not use phonology or orthography to distinguish between idiomatic and transparent morpheme pairs. The compound "bai tsai" (lit., white vegetable) does not mean any white vegetable, but has the slightly idiomatic meaning, a specific kind of light green cabbage. The phrase "bai qi" (lit., white paint) is transparent in meaning, referring to any paint that is white.

Method. Twenty native speakers of Mandarin Chinese saw compounds, phrases, and nonsense morpheme pairs and were asked to decide whether each pair was meaningful, responding with a key press as quickly and accurately as possible. All pairs were matched for constituent morpheme frequency. Compounds and phrases were also matched for frequency of morpheme co-occurrence.

Results

Analysis 1. The FOC hypothesis predicts that morpheme pairs matched for frequency of co-occurrence should produce similar RTs and error rates, regardless of semantic factors such as idiomaticity. The ID hypothesis predicts that idiomatic morpheme pairs will be stored and transparent pairs will not. Storage should provide an RT and accuracy advantage to lightly idiomatic vs. transparent morpheme pairs. However, results reveal that responses were significantly faster and more accurate for lightly idiomatic vs. transparent pairs. Therefore, FOC is not supported.

Analysis 2. A weaker version of FOC predicts that idiomaticity plays some role but frequency of co-occurrence is nonetheless a sufficient condition for storage of a combined meaning—i.e. high frequency morpheme pairs would be stored regardless of idiomaticity. This predicts no RT or error rate differences between matched high-frequency compounds and phrases. Again, however, RT and error rate differences for the two sets were significant. This indicates that frequency of co-occurrence is not a sufficient condition to establish storage of morpheme pair meaning.

Analysis 3. In order to examine if idiomaticity alone is sufficient for storage we compared results for matched low-frequency co-occurring morpheme pairs. We observed that for low-frequency pairs responses were more accurate for compounds than phrases, although RTs did not differ significantly. Possible explanations for the lack of an RT effect are: (i) idiomaticity and frequency of occurrence may both determine the storage of a compound—i.e. idiomaticity may be a necessary but not a sufficient condition for storage, (ii) we chose problematic low frequency pairs. In fact, the low frequency Verb-Noun pairs differ in RTs and error rates from Adjective-Noun pairs.

Conclusions

From current results we conclude that the frequency of morpheme co-occurence is insufficient for determining a storage difference between idiomatic and transparent morpheme pairs. Idiomaticity is apparently necessary for storage although there is some indication that a certain frequency of co-occurrence may also be required. However, because of possible confounds involving the grammatical category of the stimuli, future work is required to determine if frequency plays any significant role in the lexicalization/storage of morpheme pairs.

A Predictive Perspective on the Cerebellum

Olivier J.M.D. Coenen*   Terrence J. Sejnowski†

Computational Neurobiology Laboratory
Howard Hughes Medical Institute
The Salk Institute for Biological Studies
10010 North Torrey Pines Road
La Jolla, CA 92037, U.S.A.

Departments of †Biology and *†Physics
University of California, San Diego
La Jolla, CA 92093, U.S.A
{olivier,terry}@salk.edu

The cerebellum's role in motor and cognitive functions remains highly controversial. The cerebellum is involved in motor timing, motor coordination, motor learning and sensorimotor integration. For example, cerebellar contributions have been inferred in situations as diverse as timing of the conditioned eyelid response (Perrett and Ruiz, 1993), shifting of attention (Akshoomoff and Courchesne, 1992), adaptation of the vestibulo-ocular reflex (Lisberger et al., 1994) and coordination of eye and hand motor systems (van Donkelaar and Lee, 1994). Some of these studies also suggest that the cerebellum may be involved in some cognitive aspects of information processing. Several theories of cerebellar function have been proposed. The motor learning theories of Marr (1969), and Albus (1971) are often cited; many others have been proposed (Bloedel, 1992; Chapeau,1991; Darlot, 1993; Fujita, 1982; Ito, 1984; Keeler, 1990; Kawato, 1992; Leiner, 1989; Llinas, 1993; Miall et al., 1993; Paulin, 1989; Thach, 1992), yet few of these theories have attempted to give a consistent view of the role of the cerebellum in the diverse tasks in which the cerebellum is involved.

We have developed a new approach based on a predictive function for the cerebellum that provides a consistent explanation for the observed phenomena. We propose that the prediction of sensorimotor neural signals can be used to establish appropriate timing information and can play an important role to construct motor control strategies. In the presentation our approach, we 1) suggest a representation and a role for the climbing fibers of the inferior olive in the process of adaptation in the cerebellum and the deep cerebellar nuclei, 2) determine the representations encoded in the parallel fibers of the cerebellum, 3) propose synaptic learning mechanisms based on the interaction between Purkinje cells, cerebellar parallel fibers and climbing fibers of the inferior olive, as well as between Purkinje cells, climbing fibers and deep cerebellar nuclei neurons, and 4) specify the function of the parasagittal microstructure of Purkinje cells which receives correlated and simultaneous climbing fiber inputs.

The theory provides detailed explanations for a wide range of behaviors. In particular, we present two applications of this theory to the eyelid blink conditioning and the modulation of the vestibulo-ocular reflex.

O.J.M.D.C. was supported by a McDonnell-Pew Graduate Fellowship and T.J.S. by the Howard Hughes Medical Institute.

References

Akshoomoff, N. A. and Courchesne, E. (1992). A new role for the cerebellum in cognitive operations. *Behavioral Neuroscience*, 106(5):731–738.

Darlot, C. (1993). The cerebellum as a predictor of neural messages -I. The stable estimator hypothesis. *Neuroscience*, 56:617–646.

Fujita, M. (1982). Adaptive filter model of the cerebellum. *Biological Cybernetics*, 45:195–206.

Keeler, J. D. (1990). A dynamical system view of cerebellar function. *Physica D*, 42:396–410.

Lisberger, S. G., Pavelko, T. A., Bronte-Stewart, H. M., and Stone, L. S. (1994). Neural basis for motor learning in the vestibuloocular reflex of primates. II. Changes in the responses of horinzontal gaze velocity Purkinje cells in the cerebellar flocculus and ventral paraflocculus. *Journal of Neurophysiology*, 72(2):954–973.

Miall, R. C., Weir, D. J., Wolpert, D. M., and Stein, J. F. (1993). Is the cerebellum a smith predictor ? *Journal of Motor Behavior*, 25(3):203–216.

Paulin, M. G. (1989). A Kalman filter theory of the cerebellum. In Arbib, M. A. and Amari, S.-i., editors, *Dynamic Interactions in Neural Networks: Models and Data*, chapter III, pages 239–259. Springer-Verlag, New York. Research Notes in Neural Computing, Vol. 1.

Perrett, S. P. and Ruiz, B. P. (1993). Cerebellar cortex lesions disrupt learning-dependent timing of conditioned eyelid responses. *Journal of Neuroscience*, 13:1708–1718.

van Donkelaar, P. and Lee, R. G. (1994). Interactions between the eye and hand motor systems: Disruptions due to cerebellar dysfunction. *Journal of Neurophysiology*, 72:1674–1685.

Time Course of Semantic and Phonological Interference Effects in Picture Naming

David P. Corina and **Ty W. Lostutter**
Department of Psychology
University of Washington
Seattle, WA 98105
(corina, tylo)@u.washington.edu

Introduction

Picture naming has become an important experimental paradigm in cognitive psychology. Time course of interference and priming effects observed in these paradigms support a two-stage processing model involved in naming with a semantically driven stage and a phonological driven stage (Kempen and Huijber, 1983). Schriefers, Meyer, and Levelt (1990) used a cross modal word-picture paradigm to illustrate these effects. In this paradigm, subjects are asked to name black and white line drawings under different SOA conditions. In the silent condition, only the line drawing is seen (for example, a picture of a lion). In the interfering stimulus (IS) condition, the picture is accompanied by a auditory stimulus. The (IS) is either a semantically related word or a phonologically related word or an unrelated word. At short SOA's semantic (IS) produces interference while at late SOA's phonological (IS) produce facilitation. This finding has been taken to support for a two-stage processing model involved in naming.

Picture Naming Study

The present study makes use of a cross modal word-picture naming paradigm to explore the time course of lexical activation. The current studies extend previous findings in two important ways. First to more completely document the time course effects we include five SOA's (e.g. -200, -100, 0, +100, +200). Second, to better understand the nature of the interference we compared different types of (IS). We vary phonological (IS) by presenting word initial (IS) (picture:cat, word:cab) (Exp. 1) and word final phonological (IS) (picture:cat, word:mat) (Exp. 2). We vary the nature of the semantic relationships by presenting semantic word associates (picture:cat, word: mouse) (Exp. 1) versus members of semantic categories (picture:cat, word:pig) (Exp. 2).

Discussion

Sixty subjects named simple black and white line drawings (Snodgrass and Vanderwart, 1980). In the (IS) condition, the picture is accompanied by a auditory stimulus. In this experiment the phonological (IS) shared word initial overlap and the semantic (IS) were word associates. Our results are shown in figure 1 below. At -100 msec SOA we find greater semantic interference. At late SOA we observe faster reaction times for picture accompanied by phonological (IS). Our findings are partially consistent with the study of Schriefers et al. (1990). However, the effects at the very early SOA condition (-200 msec) are unexpected. We observe a phonological (IS) effect and lack of a semantic (IS) effect. These findings raise questions concerning whether these stages are discretely ordered or rather reflect independent but simultaneous effects with different time courses. A second study (Exp. 2), currently underway is designed to further explore these effects by varying the nature of the (IS).

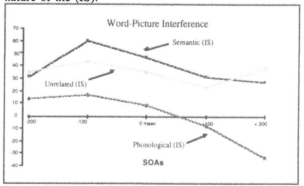

Figure 1: Time course of interference effects.

References

Kempen, G. and Huijbers, P. (1983). The lexicalization process in sentence production and naming: Indirect election of words. *Cognition*, 4(2) 185-209.

Kucera, H. and Francis, W. N. (1967). *Computational Analysis of Present-Day American English.*. Providence, RI: Brown University Press.

Schriefers, H. Meyer, A. S. , Levelt, W. J. (1990). Exploring the time course of lexical access in language production: Picture-word interference studies. *Journal of Memory and Language*, 29(1). 86-102.

Snodgrass, J.G. & Vanderwart, M. (1980). A standard set of 260 pictures: Norms for name agreement, image agreement, familiarity, and visual complexity. *Journal of Experimental Psychology: Human Learning and Memory*, 6(2), 174-215.

Reflexive Sense Generation

Jean-Pierre Corriveau

School of Computer Science, Carleton University
Colonel By Drive, Ottawa, Ontario
CANADA, K1S 5B6
jeanpier@scs.carleton.ca

Concepts are generally viewed as stable representations in long-term memory. As such they are assumed to participate in 'higher' cognitive tasks such as linguistic comprehension. Language understanding is commonly taken to require accessing and combining the concepts associated with linguistic input. Within this framework, a concept typically consists of a set of 'features'. In the most classical (and dominant) interpretation of this last statement, the features of a concept define its boundaries in terms of *necessary* and *sufficient* conditions. In light of the problems entailed by such rigidity, the notion of prototypes has been proposed. In his recent work, Franks (1995) argues that *neither* of these approaches can adequately address the difficulties of assembling concepts. Instead, he puts forth a "quasi-classical" approach to concept combination. In his model, features of a concept each receive one value, but may be defeated or modified through contextual effects. His detailed formal approach focuses in particular on the treatment of "privative" combinations such as *stone lion*, *fake gun*, *apparent friend*, etc. Complex rules and structures are developed to address these problematic examples, which are too often ignored in existing symbolic or connectionist work. More precisely, Franks suggests distinguishing between the "lexical concept" (i.e., the stable information represented in the mental lexicon) and the "sense" of a linguistic unit in context. Most importantly, the sense is *derived* from the lexical concept. A theory of concept combining thus consists in specifying the rules of derivation of sense from lexicon, subject to contextual constraints.

It is our contention that Franks's work on concept combination highlights several facets of linguistic comprehension that existing conceptual theories, *including his own*, do *not* consider.

First, we remark that derivation should not be conflated with generation proper, that is, with the construction of sense. Existing theories generally do not *construct*, they only *derive*, more or less directly from lexicon. Whether through explicit symbolic rules or implicit statistical (e.g., connnectionist) ones, most theories *fail* to acknowledge the *unpredictable* nature of linguistic usage in context, and thus the futility of a quest for an adequate training set or for definitive rules of understanding. In particular, we have explained elsewhere (Corriveau, 1995) that derivation cannot account for two fundamental characteristics of linguistic comprehension, namely, its diachronic nature, and the potential multiplicity of interpretations. Furthermore, derivation appears to preclude the learning of new senses, as well as of new

interpretative strategies. Instead, following Firth (1957), we suggest that every occurrence of a word be viewed a *hapax*. In other words, the interpretation of a linguistic unit is almost always constructed, not derived.

Second, Franks readily admits proposing a "competence-level theory" of concept combining. Doing so, and in particular, locking up concepts in long-term memory, he quickly disposes, like the majority of researchers, of performance issues. Conversely, acknowledging the real-time facet of linguistic comprehension, Shastri (1993) distinguishes between *reflexive* and *reflective* thinking. The former is extremely fast, automatic, unconscious, and pervasive to human cognition. The latter requires conscious deliberation. We emphasize that a theory of concept combining must be reflexive first. From this standpoint, we have developed elsewhere (Corriveau, 1995) a purely mechanistic time-constrained memory-based approach to comprehension. Put simply, we view interpretation as a race for sense.

Finally, any theory at the "competence-level" presents the disadvantage of not being grounded. More specifically, we consider that a "competence-level" theory of concept combining 1) is not rooted in any sort of mechanistic principles, 2) is self-validating, and 3) incorrectly assumes linguistic supervenience. Instead, following Nolan (1994), it is our contentation that the conceptual level must be explained in terms of lower levels and of a learning strategy.

We are currently working on implementing Rastier's theory of semantic 'isotopes' (1991) in order to address these problems.

References

Corriveau, J.-P. (1995). *Time-Constrained Memory*, Lawrence Erlbaum Publishers, Hillsdale, NJ.

Firth, J.R. (1957). A synopsis of linguistic theory: 1930–1950. In: J. R., Firth, (Ed.), Studies in linguistic analysis. Oxford, England: Basil Blackwell.

Franks, B. (1995). Sense Generation: A "quasi-classical" approach to concepts and concept combination, Cognitive Science, 19, 441-505.

Nolan, R. (1994). Cognitive Practices: Human language and human knowledge, Cambridge, MA: Blackwell Publishers.

Rastier, F. (1987). Sémantique Interprétative. Paris: Presses Universitaires de France.

Shastri, L. (1993). A computational model of tractable reasoning: taking inspiration from cognition. IJCAI-93.

Frame-Shifting and Meaning Construction

Seana Coulson and Marta Kutas

Cognitive Science & Neurosciences 0515
University of California, San Diego
La Jolla, CA 92093
coulson@cogsci.ucsd.edu kutas@cogsci.ucsd.edu

Introduction

(1) A thoughtful wife has pork chops ready when her husband comes home from fishing.

Why? Because she knows her husband won't catch any fish. However, the knowledge that the husband is not likely to catch fish comes neither from the meanings of the individual words in the sentence, nor from the output of the parser. Rather, this knowledge results from the interaction of knowledge about fishing and the meaning evoked by the rest of the sentence.

Following Fillmore (1982), we suggest that words have meaning relative to a set of background assumptions known as a *frame* (see Rumelhart & Ortony, 1977 for review). Processing the joke in (1) initially involves the activation of a **good wife** frame – a stereotypical event-frame in which the wife prepares dinner so that it is ready when her husband comes home from work. However, the word *fishing* cues the reader to initiate a process we call *frame-shifting*: semantic reanalysis in which the previously established contextual representation is reorganized into a new frame.

Our proposal that semantic processing relies crucially on the activation of frames from background knowledge motivates distinctions between different categories of contextual facilitation and generates predictions as to context effects. If frame-based activation of background knowledge is a driving factor in semantic processing, scenarios which occasion frame-shifting should present a challenge to the processor which differs from the violation of lexical-level expectancies.

Materials

Sixty one-line jokes were assembled from joke books and normed on an off-line Cloze task (Bloom & Fischler, 1980) to establish their default non-joke interpretations. Stimuli included High Constraint sentence fragments which led readers to expect a particular word, and Low Constraint fragments in which multiple lexical level expectations were possible. Sentence fragments were paired with one of two possible low-Cloze (0% - 5%) Ending Types: Nonjoke Endings congruent with the contextually evoked frame, and Joke Endings which required frame-shifting.

If frame-shifting associated with getting a joke induces a processing cost, Joke Endings should elicit (1) increased reading times relative to Nonjoke Endings on the self-paced reading task; and (2) enhanced N400 am-

plitudes relative to Nonjoke Endings in the event-related brain potential (ERP) measure.

Results

In the self-paced reading study, participants took longer to read Joke than Nonjoke Endings, and longer to read endings of Low than High Constraint fragments. Whereas Nonjoke Endings benefitted from the more constraining contexts, Jokes did not. Faster reading times for Nonjokes, but not Jokes, in High Constraint contexts suggest that commitment to a frame facilitates integration of unexpected words congruent with the evoked frame, but not integration of words which initiate frame-shifting.

A different set of 18 participants read the stimuli for comprehension while ERPs were recorded from 26 scalp sites. A median split separated participants into Good (85%) and Poor (65%) Comprehenders, based on their performance on comprehension probes which followed Jokes. Good Comprehenders' ERPs displayed an enhanced N400 and a Late Positive Component relative to those elicited by Nonjokes. By contrast, Poor Comprehenders ERPs were not modulated by Ending Type. In Good Comprehenders, Joke Endings elicited more N400 activity in both High and Low Constraint contexts. As in the reading time study, the size of the Joke Effect was largest in the High Constraint contexts.

Conclusions

Overall, results show that while both lexical violations and frame-shifting incur a significant processing cost, frame-shifting is more costly and relatively impervious to the effects of contextual constraint. These data highlight the flexibility of the language processor and suggest that frame-based activation of background knowledge is a driving factor in normal comprehension.

References

Bloom, P. & Fischler, I. 1980. Completion norms for 329 sentence contexts. *Memory & Cognition*, 8:6:631-642.

Filmore, C. 1982. Frame semantics. In Linguistic Society of Korea (Ed.) *Linguistics in the morning calm*. Seoul: Hanshin.

Rumelhart, D. & Ortony, A. 1977. The representation of knowledge in memory. In R.C. Anderson, R.J. Spiro, & W.E. Montague (Eds.), *Schooling and the acquisition of knowledge*. Hillsdale, NJ: Lawrence Erlbaum.

A Composite Model of Concept Representation

Paul Davidsson

Department of Computer Science, Lund University, Box 118, S–221 00 Lund, Sweden
`paul.davidsson@dna.lth.se`

Many different approaches to representing concepts has been suggested, e.g., rule- and exemplar-based descriptions and neural networks. This diversity has led to disagreement about which type of representation is the most appropriate. However, the general opinion seems to be that a single one of these is sufficient to capture most relevant aspects of a concept. This state of affairs might be satisfying if we only wanted to use and learn concepts in restricted domains. However, it is not sufficient when dealing with autonomous agents, natural or artificial, acting in the real world, since they need concepts to serve multiple functions. But which are these functions and how do they influence the representation of concepts?

The Functions of Concepts

It is possible to distinguish several functions of concepts, some of them are: (i) *Stability functions*, concepts give our world stability in the sense that we can compare the present situation with similar past experiences. Actually, there are two types of stability functions, *intrapersonal* and *interpersonal*. Intrapersonal stability is the basis for comparisons of cognitive states within an agent, whereas interpersonal stability is the basis for comparisons of cognitive states between agents. (ii) *Cognitive economical functions*, by partitioning the set of objects in the world into categories, in contrast to always treating each individual entity separately, we decrease the amount of information we must perceive, learn, remember, communicate and reason about. (iii) *Linguistic functions*, provides semantics for linguistic entities, so that they can be translated and synonymy relations be revealed. (iv) *Metaphysical functions*, are those that determine what makes an entity an instance of a particular category. (v) *Epistemological functions*, are those that determine how we decide whether the entity is an instance of a particular category (cf. perceptual categorization). (vi) *Inferential functions*, concepts allow us to infer non-perceptual information from the perceptual information we get from perceiving an entity.

A Novel Framework for Composite Concepts

Most present models of concepts concern representations to be used in some categorization task. Thus, they can be said to serve an epistemological function. What we need is a richer composite representation that, in some way, is structured according to the functions of the concept to be represented. My candidate for such a representation contains five components: the *internal* and the *external designator*, the *epistemological*, the *metaphysical*, and the *inferential components*. I argue that this composite structure enables concepts to serve all the functions listed earlier. The last three support the functions indicated by their names, the internal designator supports the intrapersonal stability, and the external designator supports both the interpersonal stability and the linguistic function.[1]

Let us illustrate the composite representation by the category "chair". For the external designator it is natural to choose "chair" (given that the agent communicates in English). The choice of the internal designator, on the other hand, is entirely up to the agent, it should be as convenient and effective as possible for the agent. The epistemological component could for instance be a 3-D model of a prototypical chair, but any representation that can be used by the perceptual system to successfully identify members of the category would be adequate. Since perceptual classification often is dependent of the situation, it might be convenient to have more than one epistemological representation. Similarly, it is useful to have several external designators in domains where many communication languages are used. The metaphysical component defines that something is a chair if it could seat one person. Finally, the inferential component represents the facts that a chair usually has four legs, is often made of wood and so on. There are no sharp distinctions between what types of information is included in these components. They may even contain redundant information, e.g., besides being a part of the epistemological component, the fact that chairs have legs is a natural part of the inferential component. However, the fact is not represented in the same way in these components. For instance, it may be implicitly represented in a 3-D model for the epistemological component and explicitly represented in a logic-based notation for the inferential component.

Depending on the situation, the composite category representation is activated in different ways. External stimuli in the form of direct perception of objects activates the concept via the epistemological component. If the external stimulus is on the linguistic level, as when communicating with other agents, the concept is accessed via the external designator. Finally, if the stimulus is internal, i.e., when the agent is reasoning, the concept is accessed via the internal designator.

To sum up, concepts should not only be used for some limited classification task, they should provide the basis for most of an agent's cognitive tasks.

---

[1] A more detailed description of this model is provided in my PhD thesis "Autonomous Agents and the Concept of Concepts" (1996).

Hierarchical Categorization and the Effects of Contrast Inconsistency in an Unsupervised Learning Task

Jim Davies and **Dorrit Billman**

School of Psychology, Georgia Institute of Technology
Atlanta, GA
psg95jd@prism.gatech.edu and dorrit.billman@cc.gatech.edu

Introduction

Two factors may guide concept learning: catpuring predictive structure in input, and forming groupings which can be categorized by a simple criteria. Experiments from unsupervised learning suggest that there is a strong bias to sort things based on their similarity, similarity being property covariation. These sorts provide maximum predictive utility (Billman & Knutson, 1996; Anderson, 1991). Work on free sorting of examples has found that people frequently sort based on the values of a single dimension (Ahn & Medin, 1992). We find evidence that people will use both biases under different conditions.

Method

The stimuli consisted of drawings of creatures laser printed on cards. There were nine attributes or dimensions (body-shape, mouth, tail, etc.), each of which had six possible values (long, lion-like, snake-like, etc.). Each participant viewed 18 cards. Each deck had two strongly marked *superordinate* categories based on covariation of attributes A, B, and C (since there are only two supers, there were only two values for these attributes). Each of the supers had three *subordinate* categories with three instances each. Subordinate structure was marked by covariation of the values of the remaining six attributes.

Table 1. Stimulus design (Columns are attributes, numbers specify a particular value, x's represent randomly assigned values)

Consistent Condition					Inconsistent Condition			
ABC	DE	FG	HI		ABC	DE	FG	HI
111	11	xx	xx		111	11	xx	xx
111	22	xx	xx		111	xx	11	xx
111	33	xx	xx		111	xx	xx	11
222	xx	11	xx		222	22	xx	xx
222	xx	22	xx		222	xx	22	xx
222	xx	33	xx		222	xx	xx	22

Each row in each condition represents a category with three members. There were two conditions (each with 12 participants): Consistent and inconsistent contrast. Consistent contrast means that within a given superordinate category, the same attributes are predictive of subordinate category membership. If people sort based on predictive utility alone, then there should be no difference in the ability of the two groups to retrieve the intended sort. However, if people sort based on the values of a single dimension, then they will not be able to retreive the intended sort, as there is no global consistency (consistency *across* supers) in either condition. Participants viewed all the cards and then sorted them freely into groups.

Results

Sixty-six percent of participants sorted hierarchically, which is, in general, not predicted by categorization models. In the consistent condition, Forty-one percent of participants in the consistent condition produced the correct (correlation-based) sort, but no one in the inconsistent condition did. Thus people are sensitive to predictive structure when it is organized consistently. The inconsistent condition was very difficult; many pilot participants could not reproduce the correct sort even after seeing it and trying again. Sixty-six percent in the inconsistent condition sorted by a single attribute, compared to the consistent condition, in which only 25% did.

Conclusion

We conclude that participants will sort by correlational structure if it is easy to notice. If stimulus structure or task make it difficult to learn about the structure, subjects will choose the very simple strategy of sorting by a single dimension.. Models which are sensitive to pressures for coherent, compact descriptions and for informative groupings are needed to account for these data.

References

Ahn, W. & Medin, D. L. (1992). A two stage model of category construction. *Cognitive Science.* 16, 81-121.

Anderson, J. R. (1991). The adaptive nature of human categorization. *Psychological Review*, 98, 409-429.

Billman, D. & Knutson, J. (1996). Unsupervised concept learning and value systematicity: a complex whole aids learning the parts. *Journal of Experimental Psychology: Learning, Memory, and Cognition.* 22(2), 458-475.

Representing Regularity: The English Past Tense

Matt Davis and **William Marslen-Wilson**
Centre for Speech and Language
Birkbeck College, University of London
Malet Street, London WC1E 7HX, UK.
m.davis@psyc.bbk.ac.uk   w.marslen-wilson@psyc.bbk.ac.uk

Mary Hare
Center for Research in Language 0256
University of California, San Diego
La Jolla, California 92093, USA.
hare@crl.ucsd.edu

Introduction

For the last ten years, the English past tense has been an important test-case in the debate between rule-based and connectionist accounts of human language processing (Pinker, 1991; Rumelhart and McClelland, 1986). The work we report here focuses on a particular psychological property of regular and irregular past tense verbs; namely the demonstration that regularly inflected verbs prime their stems whereas irregular verbs do not (Marslen-Wilson, Hare and Older 1993; Stanners et al. 1979). This result has been interpreted as supporting a dual mechanism account (Pinker, 1991) in which the past tenses of regular verbs are generated by a rule-based mechanism, whereas irregular past tenses are stored in an associative memory system. Our purpose here is to investigate whether these representational differences between regular and irregular verbs can be accounted for by a single mechanism, connectionist model.

Network and Analysis

We trained a feed-forward network to map from a phonological representation of a stem or inflected verb to an abstract representation of the verb's semantics and tense. This task is analogous to the comprehension of the English inflectional morphology; the reverse of the mapping investigated by Cottrell and Plunkett (1991). The training set consisted of 988 English monosyllabic verbs (11.4% of which were irregular), with the network being trained on both stem and past tense forms. An additional 110 regular verbs were presented in one form only, to allow testing of the network's generalization abilities.

Following training the network generated the appropriate semantic vector and tense for over 97% of the verbs in the training set. The network also identified over 85% of the novel forms of familiar verbs, indicating that it was able to use the regular inflection productively.

To investigate the representations formed by the network, the hidden unit activations produced in response to regular and irregular verbs were recorded. Measuring the RMS difference between the pattern of activation produced

for stems and past tenses shows significant differences in the way that the network represents regular and irregular verbs. The representation of the past tense was more similar to the representation of the stem for regular than for irregular verbs. This difference was greater than would be expected on the basis of phonological similarity between verb stems and past tenses. Since the degree of overlap between two distributed representations correlates with the magnitude of priming observed in a network (Masson 1995), this finding provides a straightforward account of the reduced priming observed for irregular verbs.

The network therefore suggests that behavioral and representational differences between regular and irregular verbs need not imply different processing mechanisms.

References

Cottrell, G. W. & Plunkett, K. (1991). Learning the past tense in a recurrent network: Acquiring the mapping from meanings to sounds. In *Proceedings of the Thirteenth Annual Conference of the Cognitive Science Society*. Hillsdale NJ: Lawrence Erlbaum Associates.

Marslen-Wilson, W., Hare, M., & Older, L. (1993) Inflectional morphology and phonological regularity in the English mental lexicon. In *Proceedings of the Fifteenth Annual Conference of the Cognitive Science Society*. (pp. 693-698). Hillsdale NJ: Lawrence Erlbaum Associates.

Masson, M. E. J. (1995). A distributed memory model of semantic priming. *Journal of Experimental Psychology: Learning, Memory and Cognition.* 2(1), 3-23.

Pinker, S. (1991). Rules of language. *Science*, 253, 530-535.

Rumelhart, D. E., & McClelland, J. L. (1986). On learning the past tense of English verbs. In J. L. McClelland, D. E. Rumelhart and PDP Research Group (Eds), *Parallel distributed processing: Volume 2* (pp. 216-271). Cambridge, MA: MIT Press.

Stanners, R. F., Neiser, J. J., Hernon, W. P., & Hall, R. (1979). Memory representation for morphologically related words. *Journal of Verbal Learning and Verbal Behavior*, 18, 399-412.

The Theoro-centric Bias:
Philosophy of Science and Cognitive Science

Todd N. Davis
Department of Philosophy
Duke University
Durham, NC 27705
davis@hrl.harvard.edu

Epistemology and Scientific Practice

Some important contemporary theories of cognitive and conceptual development have been deeply influenced by philosophy of science. Unfortunately, this influence has been almost completely from philosophy of science that makes scientific theory seem more unified that it is. While Hacking, a critic of this tradition, is sometimes cited, the lessons of his critique of such "theoro-centrism" seem to have either been ignored or missed. It is the task of the work reported here to explore some of the effects the influence of theoro-centrism has had on cognitive science. The focus of this work is on those cognitive theories which hold that there is a strong analogy and continuity between scientific and intuitive theories.

Traditional philosophy of science was dominated by a limited image of scientific theory. This image was the result of construing scientific theory as an epistemological object, that is, making scientific practice fit into a pregiven normative epistemological niche. In order to do this, traditional philosophy of science interpreted scientific theories in abstraction from actual theoretical and experimental practice in science and created the idea of a theory as a relatively autonomous vehicle of inference. By packing into this notion of a theory many importantly different activities and forms of representation, both different senses/levels of "theory" and different theoretical practices, "theoro-centric" philosophy of science interpreted scientific theories as closed, self-contained units and ascribed to them the power of prediction, explanation, description, etc.

Recently, some philosophers of science have begun to explore a different approach to understanding science. Eschewing the traditionalist's idea that scientific practice needed to be reconstructed according to some prior set of epistemological canons and set of epistemic tools, they have focused on scientific practice itself. When such "practice-centered" philosophers examine what are called scientific theories, they find that the ordinary term "theory" in science covers a heterogeneous assortment of practices, from the use of abstract guiding metaphors to particular physical analogies. They also note the ways in which more speculative practices, to borrow Hacking's term, are embedded in other, less narrowly "theoretical" practices such as model-building, idealization, etc. Hacking (1983, 1992) and Cartwright (1995), for example, show that it is this ensemble of practices that allow us to do the things which traditional "theoro-centric" philosophy of science ascribed to a single category or entity, "theory".

Scientific and Intuitive Theories

Gopnik and Wellman (1994) represent well the adoption of theoro-centrism in cognitive science. They explore and defend the "theory theory", i.e., the theory that the development of children's social and psychological competence is best explained by changes in an intuitive theory of mind possessed by children. They argue that such intuitive theories are the same, in crucial respects, as scientific theories as the latter have been understood in (theoro-centric) philosophy of science. Thus the notion of a "theory" is moved from an epistemological role to a hypothetical one. They postulate intuitive theories in order to explain such phenomena as resistance to counterevidence and patterns of explanation and prediction. The problem is that, according to practice-centered philosophy of science, there is no one level of theory or type of theoretical practice that explains all of that in science. I argue that the appeal to a unified notion of "theory" in cognitive science seems no more promising.

My concern is that the use of theoro-centric philosophy of science in cognitive science has produced explanations that cover over phenomena that need better explanations and theoretical options that could provide them. There are other ways to explain how prior conceptualizations affect current and future ones, the psychological aspects of scientific and naive theory use and change, or the sense in which the analogy between children and scientists might be useful.

Acknowledgments

Thanks to Robert Brandon of Duke University and Paul Millman of the Harvard Robotics Lab for comments.

References

Cartwright, N. (1995). The tool-box of science. *Poznan Studies in the Philosophy of the Sciences and the Humanities*, 44, 137-149.

Hacking, I. (1983). *Representing and Intervening*. Cambridge: Cambridge University Press.

Hacking, I. (1992). The self-vindication of the laboratory sciences. In A. Pickering (Ed.), *Science as Practice and Culture*. Chicago: University of Chicago Press.

Gopnik, A. & Wellman, H. (1994). The theory theory. In L. Hirschfeld & S. Gelman (Eds.), *Mapping the Mind* (pp.257-293). Cambridge: Cambridge University Press.

Still Looking for Structural Complexity Effects in Lexical Concepts

Roberto G. de Almeida and **Jerry A. Fodor**
Department of Psychology and Center for Cognitive Science
Psychology Annex, Busch Campus
Rutgers University
New Brunswick, NJ 08903
{almeida,fodor}@ruccs.rutgers.edu

The nature of the representation of concepts is a major issue in the cognitive sciences arena. Most, if not all, linguistic analyses of lexical concepts point to a decompositional view, based on distributional arguments and cross-linguistic data. Lexical-conceptual representations are thus said to be complex structures composed of semantic primitives and to be specified at some cognitively abstract (or linguistically "deep") level of representation (see, e.g., Jackendoff, 1990). Although this has been a pervasive assumption in the history of linguistics, there have been very few attempts to investigate it experimentally; and in all of them, researchers have failed to provide support for the decompositional approach (see Kintsch, 1974; Fodor, Fodor & Garrett, 1975; Fodor et al., 1980; Gergely & Bever, 1986).

In this paper, we present new data and arrive at an old conclusion: Lexical concepts do not show structural complexity effects. The series of experiments reported here show that the representation of causative constructions appears to be no more complex than "simple" transitive constructions. The data were obtained with a new on-line technique --masked priming of a word probe (MPWP)-- which was tested to register other distinctions between structural representations of classes of verbs.

In the experiments that employed the MPWP technique, subjects were presented with a sentence, followed by a forward masked prime word (the uninflected form of the verb) and a target word (the noun object) on which they performed a probe task. Priming effects were taken to reveal the structural distance (relatedness) between subject and direct object in the underlying representation of the sentences. There were two main comparisons between classes of verbs (see Fodor et al., 1980). In the Expect vs. Persuade comparison, reaction times to noun probes were faster in the Expect class than in the Persuade class ($t[184]=3.77$, $p<.001$). In the Causative vs. Transitive comparison, however, there was no significant difference between RT's to probes in the two types of constructions ($t[184]=0.884$, $p=.376$).

In a separate set of experiments, using two variants of the "relatedness intuitions" paradigm (Levelt, 1970), we obtained effects similar to those obtained by Fodor et al. (1980), suggesting that our results are consistent across materials and techniques.

Although the results reported here are preliminary, they suggest the following theses, discussed in the conclusion of the paper: Lexical concepts are not structurally complex mental entities; and the compositionality of mental representations does not imply the decomposition of lexical concepts. Finally, the methodological moral drawn in the paper is that the linguist's distributional arguments and assumptions on mental representations ought to be subject to the same constraints as those imposed in other empirical cognitive sciences. And under the psycholinguistic experimental paraphernalia, lexical concepts do not appear to decompose.

References

Fodor, J. A., Garrett, M. F., Walker, E. C. T., & Parkes, C. H. (1980). Against definitions. *Cognition*, 8, 263-367.

Fodor, J. D., Fodor, J. A., & Garrett, M. F. (1975). The psychological unreality of semantic representations. *Linguistic Inquiry*, 6, 515-531.

Gergely, G. & Bever, T. G. (1986). Related intuitions and the mental representation of causative verbs in adults and children. *Cognition*, 23, 211-277

Jackendoff, R. (1990). *Semantic Structures*. Cambridge, MA: MIT Press.

Kintsch, W. (1974). *The Representation of Meaning in Memory*. New York: Wiley.

Levelt, W. J. M. (1970). A scaling approach to the study of syntactic relations. In G. B. Flores D'Arcais & W. J. M. Levelt (Eds.), *Advances in Psycholinguistics* (pp.109-121). Amsterdam: North-Holland

Cognitive Mapping Theory and the Cognitive Sciences

Carlos Leite de Souza

Group of Cognitive Science, Institute for Advanced Studies
University of Sao Paulo
Sao Paulo SP Brazil
cleite@usp.br

"Cognitive psychology must take the environment more seriosly. Environmental psychology must take the mind more seriously...much of human impact on the environment is influenced by the processes of design and planning."
Kaplan & Kaplan (1989, pp. 1; 119).

Basically, the cognitive mapping theory has been studied by neuroscientists and environmental specialists. The first group has performed laboratorial tests with non-humans in specific spatial situations (as "mazes"), as well as research with humans patients with hippocampal lesions. We know the process in which hippocampus'"place cells" are responsible to acquires, codes, recalls and decodes information about the spatial environment (O'Keefe & Nadel, 1978). These cientists are responsible, recently, for creating artificial (computational) models of cognitive mapping (spatial recognition and place learning): the neural networks (Burgess, Recce & O'Keefe in: Arbib, 1995: pp.468-472; Waxman, Seibert & Bachelder in: Arbib, 1995: pp.1021-1024). The other group, environmental specialists (psychologists, designers and geographers), has been studying the processes of environmental perception and cognition (mental representation of environmental elements) and their relations to the human behavior (Kaplan *et tal.*, 1995; Gärling & Evans, 1991). This group also has been doing research concerning imageability of the built environment, wayfinding process and applied studies on cognitive maps (the influence of some important environmental characteristics which represent something "special" on mental image of the subject, as the seminal studies about *landmarks* and other elements on the imageability of the cities (Lynch, 1960). What we perceive is a gap: there is a relativelly little amount of specific studies concerning cognitive mapping theory on the cognitive science discipline *strictu-sensu*.

If we are trying to discover the brain mechanisms (and, more over, creating artificial models and neural networks), and if we do supose that there is some process occuring on the mind, between these mechanisms and the human behavior concerning the physical environment, we can not neglect the evironmental cognition studies: the cognitive mapping theoretical aspects and research.

Nowadays, the most important researches have been done in a multidisciplinary way, with specialists in different fields working together. In the field of cognitive mapping, we supose there should be three basic areas of studies: the neurosciences, the environmental-design researches and the cognitive psychology. Any researcher in these areas should be able to understand some basic concepts as hippocampal functions; vision pathways of "where system" & "what system"; spatial-memory system processed in hippocampus and adjacent areas; human behavior in spatial environment & some specific protocolar tests in environmental psychology; environmental cognition; spatial perception & gibsonian theories; mental images of built environment (studies in urban image), wayfinding process, egocentric & non-egocentric spaces; the mental imagery debate; artificial/computational models of representation of large-scale space, and so on.

So, we understand that there should be more studies about cognitive mapping made by cognitive scientists with their interdisciplinary approach. After all, we are studying the environmental cognition and the cognitive science is the multidiscipline that appears as the most recent and important field to understand all the processes of internal representations of the human behavior, including environmental representations.

References

Arbib, M. (Ed.). (1995). *The Handbook of Brain Theory & Neural Networks*. Cambridge, MA: MIT Press.

Gärling, T. & Evans, G. (1991). *Environment, Cognition & Action: An Integrated Approach*. New York, NY: Oxford University Press.

Kaplan, S. & Kaplan, R. (1989). *Cognition & Environment*. Ann Arbor, MI: Ulrich's.

Kaplan S.; Chown, E.; Kortenkamp. D. (1995). Prototypes, location & associative networks (PLAN): Towards a unified theory of cognitive mapping. *Cognitive Science*, 19(1), 01-51.

Lynch, K. (1960). *The Image of the City*. Cambridge, MA: MIT Press.

O'Keefe, J. & Nadel, L. (1978). *The Hippocampus as a Cognitive Map*. Oxford: Clarendon Press.

How Human Languages Cohere: Languages Seen as Artificial Life

Karl C. Diller,
Linguistics Program, Hamilton-Smith Hall
University of New Hampshire
Durham, NH 03824, USA
`karl.diller@unh.edu`

This paper takes the conceptual tools of artificial life to examine a question which has been intractable in Chomskian linguistics: the status and characterization of changing and variable natural languages. How do languages cohere across speakers who each have a somewhat different "internalized language"? Because languages are dynamic and variable systems, linguists have been unable to define or characterize in an explicit way the "languages" we commonly refer to, such as 'English' and 'Serbo-Croatian'. "Languages" will not stand still; they keep evolving, and they vary considerably from speaker to speaker, from community to community, from social situation to social situation. A definition or characterization of a language, then, cannot be static.

Chomsky attempted to define languages as static sets of generative rules that would generate all the grammatical sentences of a language and none of the ungrammatical sentences. To do this he needed a "conceptual shift" in linguistics to freeze the language, and study the "internalized language" of an ideal speaker-listener in a homogeneous speech community, where, it was hoped, language could finally be characterized by a coherent, well-defined set of generative rules. He denied that there was any theoretical interest in defining or characterizing the variable "languages" that we talk about in daily life. Chomsky has argued that the very concept of "externalized languages," as he calls them, "appears to play no role in the theory of language" (Chomsky 1986, 26). He maintains that "obscure socio-political and normative factors" are needed to define "the word 'language' as it is used in ordinary discourse" (Chomsky 1988, 36-37), implying that purely linguistic criteria are not adequate.

More recently, under the rubrics of "Cognitive Grammar" (Langacker 1987) or "Cognitive Linguistics" (Lakoff 1987) and "Grammaticalization" (Hopper and Traugott 1993), linguists have been paying attention to the dynamic phenomena of language. Yet even linguists who study the dynamic processes of "grammaticalization" (the self-organization and evolution of grammar in languages),

have a hard time abstracting beyond individual speakers. For example, Hopper and Traugott, in their Cambridge textbook, *Grammaticalization* (Hopper and Traugott 1993, 33), say that "Language does not exist separate from its speakers. It is not an organism with a life of its own."

The conceptual framework of Artificial Life allows us to make a new conceptual shift in linguistics, enabling us to recognize that a language *may be* an organism or system with a life of its own, and that this is not inconsistent with a language's dependence on individual speakers. We will see that the characterization of languages as dynamic systems with permeable boundaries is central to linguistic theory.

The argument revolves around eight propositions:

1. Languages, like artificial life, are man-made systems.

2. Languages are like viruses, requiring hosts.

3. Individual humans are agents of language working in parallel in a shared but variable system.

4. Languages are changed and renewed in the processes of communication.

5. Grammatical change is an inherent result of a decentralized language faculty in individuals in which the modules of language work together in parallel.

6. The characterization of languages as dynamic systems with permeable boundaries is central to linguistic theory.

7. Languages have more of the characteristics of life than computer viruses do, and may be our best example of artificial life.

8. Languages, seen as artificial life, stretch our concept of "life as it *could* be."

Cases or Rules? The Case for Unification

Pedro Domingos
Department of Information and Computer Science
University of California, Irvine
Irvine, California 92717, U.S.A.
pedrod@ics.uci.edu
http://www.ics.uci.edu/~pedrod

Rule induction (either directly or by means of decision trees) and case-based learning (forms of which are also known as instance-based, memory-based and nearest-neighbor learning) arguably constitute the two leading symbolic approaches to concept and classification learning. Rule-based methods discard the individual training examples, and remember only abstractions formed from them. At performance time, rules are applied by logical match (i.e., only rules whose preconditions are satisfied by an example are applied to it). Case-based methods explicitly memorize some or all of the examples; they avoid forming abstractions, and instead invest more effort at performance time in finding the most similar cases to the target one.

There has been much debate over which of these two approaches is preferable. While each one can be extended to fit the results originally presented as evidence for the other, it typically does so at the cost of a more complex, less parsimonious model. In classification applications, each approach has been observed to outperform the other in some, but not all, domains.

In recent years, multistrategy learning has become a major focus of research within machine learning. Its main insight is that a combination of learning paradigms is often preferable to any single one. However, a multistrategy learning system typically operates by calling the individual approaches as subprocedures from a control module of variable sophistication, and again this not completely satisfactory from the point of view of parsimony.

Here we argue that rule induction and case-based learning have much more in common than a superficial examination reveals, and can be unified into a single, simple and coherent model of symbolic learning. The proposed unification rests on two key observations. One is that a case can be regarded as a maximally specific rule (i.e., a rule whose preconditions are satisfied by exactly one case). Therefore, no syntactic distinction need be made between the two. The second observation is that rules can be matched approximately, as cases are in a case-based classifier (i.e., a rule can match an example if it is the closest one to it according to some similarity-computing procedure, even if the example does not logically satisfy all of the rule's preconditions). A rule's extension, like a case's, then becomes the set of examples that it is the most similar rule to, and thus there is also no necessary semantic distinction between a rule and a case.

The RISE algorithm (Domingos, to appear) is a practical, computationally efficient realization of this idea. (Obviously, it is not the only possible approach to unifying the two paradigms.) RISE starts with a rule base that is simply the case base itself, and gradually generalizes each rule to cover neighboring cases, as long as this does not increase the rule base's error rate on the known cases. If no generalizations are performed, RISE acts as a pure case-based learner. If all cases are generalized and the resulting set of rules covers all regions of the instance space that have nonzero probability, it acts as a pure rule inducer. More generally, it will produce rules along a wide spectrum of generality; sometimes a rule that is logically satisfied by the target case will be applied, and in other cases an approximate match will be used. This unified model is more elegant and parsimonious than a subprocedure-style combination. Experiments with a large number of benchmark classification problems have also shown it to consistently outperform either of the component approaches alone, and lesion studies and experiments on artificial domains have confirmed that its power derives from its ability to simultaneously harness the strengths of both components.

Acknowledgements

This work was partly supported by a JNICT/PRAXIS XXI scholarship.

References

Domingos, P. (to appear). Unifying instance-based and rule-based induction. *Machine Learning*.

Playing Go by Search-Embedded Pattern Recognition

Pedro Domingos[1]
Department of Information and Computer Science
University of California, Irvine
Irvine, California 92717, U.S.A.
`pedrod@ics.uci.edu`
`http://www.ics.uci.edu/~pedrod`

Go (Iwamoto, 1976) is one of the hardest known games to play by machine. Its very large branching factor (up to 361) makes search to even a moderate depth problematic, and precludes the use of massive search that has proved successful in games like checkers and chess. As a result, researchers have turned to pure pattern recognition and pattern-based reasoning approaches, which concentrate all their effort in evaluating the current board position, and make no explicit attempt to predict the evolution of the game. However, systems of this type remain far from being able to compete with even a moderately proficient human player. This extended abstract reports on GP, an artificial Go player that combines pattern recognition with limited but flexible search, and won several games against a novice human player.

The basic motivation for GP was the observation that, while humans engage in extensive pattern-based inference when playing Go, they also perform small amounts of look-ahead search. In particular, the latter type of reasoning seems to prevail in situations of immediate attack or defense of groups with few liberties, while the former is prevalent in periods of the game where the players have a greater freedom of choice for the next move. GP recognizes and potentially acts on all variations of seven canonical patterns centered around each enemy stone, but only after it has checked that there are no more immediate tasks, like closing off the few remaining liberties of an enemy group or trying to save a troubled one of its own. If no patterns fire, it plays on handicap points if any are still free, or attempts to consolidate territory bu introducing intermediate stones between separate groups; in the long run this process will lead to the formation of walls.

All these steps are embedded in a conventional minimax search with alpha-beta cutoffs, to which a maximum branching factor is imposed (i.e., not all legal moves are expanded, but only the top few). The search also has a nominal depth limit, which is 2, 4 or 6 plies depending on the playing level chosen, but this limit varies dynamically according to the difficulty of the current situation and the stability of the evaluation. Three different static evaluation heuristics have been implemented, using combinations of points accumulated, liberties and sizes of groups.

In a series of 18 games against a novice human player, on a 9×9 board with a handicap of 3 for the machine, GP on average scored more points than the human opponent with two of the heuristics, at the higher difficulty levels; the average difference was approximately equal to the handicap. Significantly, there was a large improvement from 2-ply to 4-ply maximum depth, showing that there is an advantage to using search, but there was no significant difference between 4-ply and 6-ply, indicating that deeper search is not necessarily productive in Go, even if the available computing power allows it.

References

Iwamoto, Kaoru (1976). *Go for Beginners*. London: Penguin.

---

[1] This abstract describes research conducted at Instituto Superior Técnico, Lisbon, Portugal.

Specific Long- and Short-Term Memory Deficits Producing Dyscalculia in a Physicist: A Single Case Study Carried Out Using the São Paulo MAT Test

Cláudio L.N. Guimarães dos Santos, Angélica N. Nakamura, and
Alexandre T.F. Rosa
Laboratório de Neuropsicolingüística Cognitiva,
Universidade Federal de São Paulo, São Paulo, Brazil
claudiog.morf@epm.br

Introduction

After giving a concise description of the SP-MAT, a test battery developed by our Laboratory in order to study acquired mathematical disabilities, we present the results obtained with its employment in the investigation of AA, a 42-year-old right-handed man, physicist, operated in 1992 in order to remove a left arteriovenous malformation.

Method

The SP-MAT was conceived as a methodological tool sufficiently detailed to yield a precise description of a patient's actual performance during the cognitive processing of mathematical entities both in the elementary and in the advanced level.

It consists of 5 parts designed to assess: (I) deficits related to the perceptual processing of numerical entities, (II) basic arithmetical calculation abilities, (III) abilities required to deal with elementary algebra problems, (IV) abilities involved in solving elementary geometry problems, (V) abilities required to deal with problems of higher mathematics.

Results

AA was examined 43 months after his surgery and only the first two parts of the SP-MAT were given to him.

On the neurological examination, AA presented a right homonymous hemianopia (compensated) with no motor deficits. SPECT showed a dramatic reduction in rCBF values of the left temporal, occipital and inferior parietal regions. Standard neuropsychological assessment showed: (a) a slight impairment of AA's performance during discourse comprehension tasks, (b) a discrete anomia, (c) an important retrograde amnesia mostly affecting the mathematical information the patient normally dealt with before surgery, (d) a below-average reduced memory span, more pronounced for oral than for written stimuli, worse for non-significant syllables than for words and numbers, the span for letters being almost normal, and (e) a mild impairment in AA's arithmetical calculation abilities.

Results showed no deficits related to the perceptual processing of numerical entities.

Results of Part II allowed a precise characterization of AA's calculation impairment, namely: (a) variability of its degree of expression as a function of the type of operation involved: The impairment was more evident during the performance of multiplications and divisions than during the performance of additions and subtractions; (b) presence of an important "row effect": The greater the number of rows involved in AA's processing of a given algorithm, the greater the number of errors detected. Such effect was most evident during the performance of multiplications and additions, but it could also be observed in divisions; (c) presence of a mild "column effect": The greater the number of columns involved in AA's processing of a given algorithm, the greater the number of errors detected. Such effect was most evident during the performance of subtractions and additions, but it could also be observed in divisions; (d) a detailed analysis of the relative frequencies of each type of error revealed a consistent pattern (except in case of subtractions): table value and algorithm errors being much more frequent than any other type of error.

Discussion

We claim that the impairment in AA's calculation abilities can be entirely understood if his specific STM and LTM deficits are taken into account.

Both the "row" and the "column effect" can be understood as being caused by the same set of STM deficits: (a) an increase in the rate of decay of STM traces and (b) a reduction in STM capacity.

Both the variability of the degree of expression of AA's calculation impairment (which is a function of the type of operation involved) and the pattern displayed by the relative frequencies of each type of error can be understood as being produced by the same LTM deficit: an important retrograde amnesia mostly affecting the declarative semantic explicit LTM related to the storage of information concerning the mathematical facts the patient normally dealt with before surgery.

Finally, it is important to point out that AA's lesion affects a set of brain areas which have already been described (e.g., Deloche & Seron, 1987) as possible sites for the group of mechanisms which constitute the cortical network underlying (a) declarative semantic explicit LTM (left temporal area) and (b) STM (left occipital and inferior parietal areas).

Reference

Deloche, G. & Seron, X. (Eds.). (1987). Mathematical disabilities: A cognitive neuropsychological perspective. London: Lawrence Erlbaum Associates.

Perception of Simple Rhythmic Patterns in a Network of Oscillators

Douglas Eck and **Michael Gasser**
Computer Science Department, Cognitive Science Program
Indiana University
Bloomington, IN 47405
`deck@indiana.edu, gasser@indiana.edu`

Introduction

Recently several computational models of the perception of rhythm based on oscillators have been proposed. Oscillator models capture the cognitive predisposition to discover periodicity in auditory patterns, and models in which oscillators exhibit phase and/or period coupling with inputs also tolerate deviations from perfect periodicity.

However, current oscillator models only address tempo and meter perception. In this paper we are concerned with a more complex capacity, the ability to recognize and reproduce rhythmic patterns. While this capacity has not been well investigated, in broad qualitative terms it is clear that people can learn to identify and produce recurring patterns defined in terms of sequences of beats of varying intensity and rests: the rhythms behind waltzes, reels, sambas, etc. Our short-term goal is a model which is "hard-wired" with knowledge of a set of such patterns. Presented with a portion of one of the patterns or a label for a pattern, the model should reproduce the pattern and continue to do so when the input is turned off. Our long-term goal is a model which can learn to adjust the connection strengths which implement particular patterns as it is exposed to input patterns.

Approach

We have developed a connectionist architecture which realizes our short-term goal. The model consists of a single input/output unit and network of coupled oscillators of varying resting periods. These periods are expected to capture the micropulse and harmonic periods characterizing various rhythmic patterns. An identified familiar pattern takes the form of a stable pattern of activation across the network of oscillators.

The network consists of two types of oscillators, pulse oscillators and continuous oscillators.

Pulse oscillators provide an interface between the pulse-like world and internal continuous oscillators. They are activated by the input unit and by other oscillators only when they are near their zero phase angle. They also adjust their phase angle in response to an activated input or oscillator, but again, only near their zero phase angle. Pulse oscillators exhibit a periodic output which activates the network's output unit, as well as other oscillators. At a given period, there is an inhibitory cluster of pulse oscillators which is reponsible for finding a downbeat. Other pulse oscillators at a given period are responsible for beats and rests at points within the measure. Beat pulse oscillators excite and are excited by the input/output unit; rest pulse oscillators inhibit and are inhibited by the input/output unit.

Unlike pulse oscillators, continuous oscillators do not connect directly to the input/output unit. Instead they connect to other continuous and pulse oscillators, responding throughout their phase cycle rather than only near their zero phase angle. Their function is to represent recurring subpatterns of beats and rests which provide the building blocks for complex patterns. Each subpattern is handled by a cluster of continuous oscillators which is stable when the oscillators' phase angles are evenly distributed throughout the phase cycle. Each oscillator in such a cluster is associated with a beat or rest pulse oscillator. For example, the 3/4 pattern consisting of two quarter notes followed by a quarter rest would be handled by three continuous oscillators, each with a period equal to the measure and spaced 1/3 of a phase (one quarter note) away from the others. Two of these oscillators would be connected to a beat pulse oscillator and the other to a rest pulse oscillator. This cluster of six oscillators would take part in turn in more complex 6-beat patterns.

We have tested hard-wired versions of the model on simple 3- and 4-beat patterns, which it is able to distinguish and to continue to reproduce when the input is turned off. It also handles these patterns in the presence of temporal noise.

The model makes numerous predictions about relative pattern difficulty and error types. For example, it predicts errors with complex patterns which result from the substitution of one subpattern for another.

Effects of Irrelevant Symbols in Text on Word Recognition and Saccadic Programming during Reading

Julie Epelboim
Center for the Study of Language and Information
Stanford University
Stanford, CA 94305-4115

James R. Booth
Department of Psychology
Carnegie Mellon University
Pittsburgh, PA 15213

Arash Taleghani   **Rebecca Ashkenazy**   **Robert M. Steinman**

Department of Psychology
University of Maryland at College Park
College Park, MD 20742-4411
`yulya@brissun.umd.edu, jbooth@andrew.cmu.edu,`
`beckya@wam.umd.edu, taly@wam.umd.edu, steinman@brissun.umd.edu`

Introduction

Many experiments have studied the role of spaces between words in text by filling them with irrelevant symbols (*e.g.*, digits, gratings, x's). This practice is based on the assumption that these fillers occlude spaces without disturbing word recognition appreciably. Epelboim, Booth & Steinman (1996) pointed out that there is no empirical evidence to support this assumption and proposed a series of controls that must be performed before the role of spaces and fillers in reading can be evaluated. Recently, we performed these controls and found that texts in all conditions in which words were surrounded by fillers were read slower than normal texts, as long as the fillers shared common features with letters of the text (digits, irrelevant Latin letters and Greek letters). See Epelboim, Booth, Ashkenazi, Taleghani & Steinman (1996) for details. Reading was as slow when words were surrounded by fillers (1like2 8this6), as when fillers replaced spaces (1like2this6). The fact that reading text with fillers, even when spaces were preserved, was slower than reading normal text showed that fillers slowed reading by disturbing word recognition, not simply by occluding spaces. This means that prior experiments that used the filler technique did not provide useful information about the role of spaces in normal text.

We have continued our investigation of fillers and spaces by measuring the reading eye movements in a number of these conditions. Our preliminary findings are reported here.

Method

Eye movements of 3 subjects were recorded, with exceptional precision and accuracy, as they read H. G. Well's "War of the Worlds" aloud. Greek letters were used as fillers. There were 6 text conditions:

1. **Normal:** "This is an example";

2. **Before:** "αThis $\tau$is πan δexample";

3. **After:** "Thisμ isθ isσ andδ exampleϕ;

4. **Surround:** "πThisθ αisσ μanϕ τexampleα";

5. **Filled:** "δThisπisαanσexampleθ";

6. **Unspaced:** "Thisisanexample".

Results and Discussion

Text condition had no effect on % regressions, or on where reading saccades landed within words. However, texts containing fillers were read slower than normal texts and more saccades/line were made in filler conditions than either in **Normal** conditions, or, for 2 of 3 subjects, in **Unspaced** condition. Observed differences in eye movement patterns can be accounted for by a global adjustment to only 1 eye movement parameter, *viz.*, saccade size, made on the basis of the global appearance of the text. No evidence was found that the presence of fillers or the absence of spaces required new strategies for programming individual saccades, suggesting that word recognition and global strategies are more significant in saccadic programming than the the local features of the text.

References

Epelboim, J., Booth, J. R., Ashkenazy, R., Talaghani, A. & Steinman, R. M. (1996). A comparison of fillers and spaces in text: Evidence for the importance of word recognition, *Invest. Ophtal. and Vis. Sci. (suppl.)*, 37.

Epelboim, J., Booth, J. R. & Steinman, R. M. (1996). Much ado about nothing: the place of space in text. *Vision Research*, 36, 465–470.

This research was supported by NIMH 1-F32-MH11282-01; AFOSR F49620-94-1-0333

Learning of Categories Composed of Rules and Exceptions

Michael A. Erickson and **John K. Kruschke**
Department of Psychology and Cognitive Science Program
Indiana University, Bloomington IN 47405
miericks@indiana.edu

Many formal and folk psychological theories conceive of the mind as being composed of quasi-independent modules. From Freud to Fodor the mind has been decomposed into constituent parts. Recently, a number of researchers have proposed modular theories of cognitive phenomena such as categorization (Ashby, Alfonso-Reese, & Turken, 1995; Shanks & St. John, 1994), reasoning (Sloman, 1996), automaticity (Logan, 1988), language (Pinker, 1991), and learning and memory (Squire, 1992). In general, these theories are characterized by descriptions of each module and how each serves in those tasks for which it is best suited. However, these theories do not emphasize how modules *interact* in producing responses and in learning.

We describe two human categorization experiments designed to address the three issues relevant to hybrid rule- and exemplar-based systems: the necessity of rules, the necessity of exemplar memory, and the interaction between these two sub-systems in learning and in classification performance. We account for the participants' classifications using an updated version of the hybrid rule and exemplar model described by Kruschke and Erickson (1994). This hybrid model consists of a rule module, an exemplar module, and a gating mechanism. This gating mechanism controls the influence of each module in decision-making and the extent of learning in each module. We also show that neither of these two sub-systems, acting alone, can adequately account for human behavior. This is significant inasmuch as the exemplar sub-system is a full implementation of ALCOVE (Kruschke, 1992), which has performed well in a variety of categorization tasks.

Human Learning

Three key features of the category structures used in these experiments are: (1) some stimuli could be classified according to a rule whereas other stimuli were exceptions and had to be memorized; (2) different training instances had different relative frequencies; and (3) some stimuli were never used in training and were therefore available to examine generalization.

The stimuli in both experiments varied along two dimensions. In each training trial, a stimulus was presented and participants made a classification, after which the correct label was displayed. During the initial trials, participants' responses were just guesses, but after many trials they began to learn the correct classifications. Most of the training stimuli, the *regular* stimuli, could be classified according to a simple, one-dimensional rule. Two training stimuli were exceptions to the rule, each having its own category label.

During training in Experiment 1, participants never saw the most extreme values of the two dimensions of variation; these were reserved to test generalization. Nevertheless, even when these extreme stimuli were most similar to an exception, they were classified according to the rule. Whereas the hybrid model was able to account for this phenomenon, ALCOVE was not.

Relative instance frequencies were manipulated in Experiment 2, both for rules and exceptions. Higher rule instance frequencies caused more robust generalization. Rule-based explanations that lack exemplar memory cannot account for such behavior. Moreover, ALCOVE failed to account for the S-shape of the exception learning curve shown by participants. The hybrid model did show this same pattern of learning by virtue of its interactive gating of the rule and exemplar modules.

References

Ashby, F. G., Alfonso-Reese, L., & Turken, A. U. (1995). Competition between verbal and implicit rules of category learning. Talk presented at the 36th Annual Meeting of the Psychonomic Society, Los Angeles, CA, 10 November 1995.

Kruschke, J. K. (1992). ALCOVE: An exemplar-based connectionist model of category learning. *Psychological Review, 99*, 22–44.

Kruschke, J. K., & Erickson, M. A. (1994). Learning of rules that have high-frequency exceptions: New empirical data and a hybrid connectionist model. In *The Proceedings of the Sixteenth Annual Conference of the Cognitive Science Society*, pp. 514–519 Hillsdale, NJ. Erlbaum.

Logan, G. D. (1988). Toward an instance theory of automatization. *Psychological Review, 95*, 492–527.

Pinker, S. (1991). Rules of language. *Science, 253*, 530–535.

Shanks, D. R., & St. John, M. F. (1994). Characteristics of dissociable human learning systems. *Behavioral and Brain Sciences, 17*, 367–447.

Sloman, S. A. (1996). The empirical case for two systems of reasoning. *Psychological Bulletin, 119*, 3–22.

Squire, L. R. (1992). Memory and the hippocampus: A synthesis from findings with rats, monkeys, and humans. *Psychological Review, 99*, 195–231.

How do we Scratch an Itch: A Model of Self-Reaching

David Scott Farrar

Department of Cognitive Science
University of California, San Diego
La Jolla, CA 92093-0515
`farrar@cogsci.ucsd.edu`

How do we Scratch an Itch?

Imagine a simple situation: you have an itch on your left arm, and you reach with your right arm to scratch it. Scratching an itch at first seems like a simple, automatic task, but a little more reflection shows that it can actually be quite complicated. We do not need to see; rather, we can accomplish the task knowing only where the itch happens to be on our body, and how far our limbs are flexed or extended: we need only somatosensory information. We move the reaching arm and the itching arm together -- they are coordinated. This bimanual coordination allows us to reach arbitrary parts of our body: we are able to scratch anywhere on either arm. The task cannot always be accomplished just by moving the reaching hand in a straight line; sometimes other parts of our body -- or the itching arm itself -- become obstacles which must be avoided or moved. How are the movements of two arms coordinated to avoid collisions? How is the body-as-a-target represented? How do we reach for a target that may change location in space? How is the brain able to create a motor trajectory that will coordinate the body's limbs, avoid self-collisions, and still achieve the goal of reaching the itch? A framework for this problem is pictured in Figure 1, and some example configurations of the model framework are shown in Figure 2.

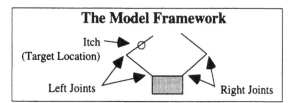

Figure 1: A sketch of the scratch-an-itch problem. The model consists of two arms, each with two joints, which allow both arms to move freely in two dimensions in front of the body. A target can be chosen on either arm. The problem for the model is: given an arbitrary starting position, find a way to move the arms so that the tip of the scratching arm touches the itch (target location), avoiding self-collisions on the way.

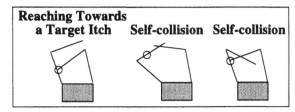

Figure 2: Example configurations of the model.

One way to model the scratch-an-itch task is to break it up into separate elements -- bimanual coordination, somatotopic task specification, and avoidance of self-collisions. We can then build a system or systems that handle each part. These interacting systems provide a framework in which to address high-level questions of coordination and planning.

Bootstrapping a Connectionist Model

We would like to have a "brain-like" solution to this problem, one that might tell us something useful about the brain mechanisms serving bimanual coordination. One way to do this is to train one or more neural networks solve the problem. During training, a neural network's internal structure is altered so that it replicates an input/output mapping which captures the essential character of a solution to the problem. In the process, it develops internal representations appropriate to the problem it is trying to solve. But where do we get the input/output data to train a network? The approach we use is to first build a "traditional" artificial intelligence solution. The problem is viewed as one of planning with goals which are repeatedly decomposed into easily executable subgoals. The AI model of movement planning then executes the task and in so doing can provide input/output data to train a network. While the network is constrained to emulate the input/output behavior of the AI model, its internal representation(s) of the problem need not be the same.

Predictions of the Model

After training, the network's solution to the problem -- its internal structure -- is also a prediction of how the problem may be solved by the brain (Zipser, 1992). This prediction can be tested against neurobiological observations. This verification process involves creating a mapping between units and relations in the model and anatomical or functional substrates in the brain, and using tools to "probe, poke, and push" the model in several ways to compare its behavior to that of the brain and its neurons. For example, the representational behavior of unit activations in the model can be compared with the averaged spiking of single neurons in the motor cortex. The connectivity of the trained network can be compared with the pattern of anatomical projections within the motor cortex. The neural network model provides a framework in which to ask and answer questions about the brain mechanisms serving motor planning and coordination.

References

Zipser, D. (1992) Identification models of the nervous system. *Neuroscience.* 47(4):853-862.

Metacognitive Models and Situation Assessment

Pat-Anthony Federico

Navy Personnel Research and Development Center
53335 Ryne Road
San Diego, CA 92152-7250
federico@nprdc.navy.mil

Schema-driven decision making emphasizes the indispensability of (1) situation assessment in naturalistic settings, and (2) knowledge base, past experience, event sequence, and similarity recognition as cognitive components of situation assessment (Federico, 1995). A theoretically interesting research question is whether subjects' metacognitive models (Metecalfe & Shimamura, 1994) involving these salient elements of an abstract schema-driven decision-making process, are related to their performance on concrete experimental tasks requiring situation assessment. That is, within the metacognitive context of "cognition about cognition," but not on-going monitoring and control, are subjects' higher order cognitions about these crucial cognitive components at an abstract level correlated with their performance on experimental tasks necessitating situation assessment at a concrete level? If subjects are asked to indicate in their metacognitive models the perceived degree of importance of these cognitive components to situation assessment, then is the assigned saliency of each of these elements correlated with their performance on tasks where situation assessment is a prerequisite?

First, assuming subjects were asked to classify tactical situations into two or more discrete clusters, it was hypothesized that the more weight attributed to these metacognitive links by subjects, the more categories they would create, the more time they would use to categorize tactical situations, and the less the number of tactical situations per category derived for them. It was speculated that the more saliency ascribed by subjects to these four metacognitive links, the more they implicitly believe in, and automatically adhere to, the schema-driven decision-making process, where correct classifications or similarity judgments are crucial to proficient performance. Consequently, the more likely these individuals would tacitly discriminate among the tactical situations creating more categories and fewer tactical situations per category, and cognitively process these tactical situations at deeper levels of analysis thus necessitating more time for their classification.

Second, assuming subjects were asked to perform pairwise similarity ratings of tactical situations, it was hypothesized that the attributed metacognitive link weights would be positively related to the derived subjects' weights along each dimension of a multidimensional scaling solution. It was thought that the more importance subjects assigned to these metacognitive link weights, the more they tacitly accept, and unconsciously use, the schema-driven decision-making process. Consequently, the more likely these individuals would weigh indirectly the derived dimensions underlying their perceptions of pairwise similarity among the tactical situations. The perception of similar situations is an important component of schema-driven decision making which is recognition-primed, because schema-driven solutions are invoked by recognizing particular problem types or specific similar situations.

The primary purposes of this research were to experimentally test the above hypotheses, and attempt to shed some light on the raised theoretical issues.

Consequently, seventy-six, volunteer, male, naval officers were asked to (1) represent as graphic weighted networks their metacognitive models of schema-driven tactical decision making, where situation assessment is crucial, and (2) perform experimental tasks requiring categorizing and pairwise similarity ratings of tactical situations. Canonical, regression, and correlation analyses and multidimensional scaling established that two of four metacognitive link weights were significantly associated with (1) three of six measures of sorting performance, and (2) one of two dimensions derived for the scaling solution of pairwise similarity ratings. These results supported what was hypothesized regarding subjects' metacognitive models and sorting and pairwise performance.

References

Federico, P-A. (1995). Expert and novice recognition of similar situations. *Human Factors, 37*, 105-122.

Metcalfe, J., & Shimamura, A. (Eds.). (1994). Metacognition: Knowing about knowing. Cambridge, MA: The MIT Press.

A Computer Simulation Of Emotion Based Development and Processing

Richard D. Ferrante
Gensym Corporation
125 CambridgePark Dr.
Cambridge, Ma. 02134
rdf@gensym.com

This work models the evolution and use of emotional responses by a simulated agent during its development. It investigates the utility of emotions using a realistic script to model an agent's interactions as a child and adult. The roles of emotions that are examined include: goal formation, information processing and emotional development. The purpose of this simulation is to give some insight into the way early experiences are reflected in an individual's selection of partners.

This investigation is a computer based simulation of situations encountered by Philip, the main character in *Of Human Bondage* Somerset Maugham's vintage work of fiction (Maugham, 1915-1992). This research was based upon a novel to minimize the possibility of investigator bias determining the outcome of the investigation (Lenat, 1984). It was also felt this novel having proven itself a classic would represent something resonant with a larger population.This particular novel was also appealing in that the type of events experienced and actions taken are somewhat mundane, little happens that is outside the realm of common human experience.

One of the more controversial aspects of this book is the protagonist's (Philip) attachment to one woman (Mildred) over another (Norah) who seems much more appealing. This simulation was used to investigate this relationship and identify its potential motivation.

In doing this I model the protagonist's emotional development during the events described in the book. The development consists of an evolving set of Idealized Cognitive Models (ICMs) (Lakoff, 1987) which are refined during his interaction with other characters in the book.

Each ICM consists of a model prototype that identifies specific features important to the model. These features are coupled with a model specific neural network to measure the quality of match between individuals and the ICM's idealized representations. All events were entered into the script by hand and represent fragments of important events in *Of Human Bondage*. However both the ICM features and the neural network are derived dynamically by the agent during the simulation.

In this simulation, the agent receives an event and processes it in a manner determined by the type of action and its internal state. The agent's cognitive architecture is framed in terms of previous interactions with other agents over time. An agent's goals and assessments are independent of, albeit influenced by, other agents in the situation.

The result of the simulation indicated that Philip's attachment to Mildred is primarily because she is so unlike another character in the book who had hurt him. This was unexpected as he had been raised by a somewhat aloof couple and it was expected that her similarity to them would be more of a factor.

This result indicates that a simple set of "noticing processes" coupled with the fuzzy matching afforded by neural network-based models can be diagnostic of behavior and goals in simulated agents. This shows the potential of using these mechanisms with a simple set of rules to achieve a good level of discrimination and generalization.

References

Lakoff, G. (1987). Women, Fire, and Dangerous Things;. Chicago, Il.: The University of Chicago Press.

Lenat, D. B. (1984). Why AM and EURISKO appear to work. Artificial Intelligence, 23(3).

Maugham, W. S. (1915-1992). Of Human Bondage. New York, New York: Penguin Books.

Using Simulation to Predict Human Habit-capture Errors

Michael Freed, Roger W.Remington, James C. Johnston
NASA Ames Research Center

We are constructing a system to predict the kinds of errors air traffic controllers are likely to make using given procedures and equipment. The system takes procedure and equipment descriptions as input. Output is produced in two phases. In the simulation phase, the simulated controller carries out tasks in a set of user-defined scenarios. In the subsequent analysis phase, occurrences of operator error are identified in a trace of simulation events; detected errors are then classified as instances of error types, represented as *error-patterns*.

The primary assumptions about human cognitive behavior are defined by a domain-independent cognitive model. Using the current model, the simulation phase can reproduce several classes of human error, including what are sometimes called "habit capture errors." An everyday example of a habit capture error occurs when driving to an unusual destination along a familiar path. For example, a person may drive away from work intending to stop at a convenience store along the way, but inadvertantly arrive at home (the usual destination) instead. Analogous errors can occur in the domain of air traffic control.

A habit capture error can be defined as the selection of habitual (high frequency) action when information that implies that the action is inconsistent with current goals can be recalled from memory or perceived. Habit capture errors are predictable in the sense that certain known factors greatly influence the likelihood of their occurrence. The likelihood of such an error rises when any of the following conditions exist:

- At the moment of decision, no easily perceived feature marked a conflict between a habitual action and current goals
- At some time prior to making a decision, an easily perceived feature marking conflict between habit and goals was insufficiently encoded in memory due to high workload
- During the interval between perceiving conflict information and using that information in a decision, the agent rarely observes reminders of the information
- The agent must cope with high workload at the moment of decision, reducing the time available to recall habit counterindicative information from memory

Our simulated human agent is designed to carry out tasks in complex, dynamic domains, performing competently under normal conditions, but becoming increasingly likely to err when factors such as those listed above are present. The current model approximates human proneness to several different kinds of habit capture error. Future elaborations of the model will produce error suseptibilities of other kinds.

References

Freed, M. and Johnston, J. Simulating Human Cognition in the Domain of Air Traffic Control. Working notes of the 1995 AAAI Spring Symposium on Representing and Reasoning about Mental Behavior. Palo Alto, 1995.

John, B. and Kieras, D.E. The GOMS Family of Analysis Techniques: Tools for Design and Evaluation. Carnegie Mellon University School of Computer ScienceTechnical Report No. CMU-CS-94-181

Reason, J. Human Error. Cambridge University Press, New York, N.Y., 1990.

Realistic Limitations in Natural Language Processing for an Intelligent Tutoring System

Reva Freedman
Department of EECS
Northwestern University
freedman@delta.eecs.nwu.edu

Martha W. Evens
Department of CSAM
Illinois Institute of Technology
mwe@schur.math.nwu.edu

Introduction

Although an intelligent tutoring system (ITS) and a human tutor may have the same goals, they do not have the same skills available for achieving those goals. CIRCSIM-Tutor v. 3 is a natural-language based ITS which tutors students on problem solving in cardiac physiology. We examine a corpus containing over 5000 turns of human-to-human tutoring sessions in order to determine the salient features leading to student success. We determine which of those features can be replicated by an ITS and develop alternatives for the others. To reduce the input processing burden, we substitute mixed-initiative processing (Carbonell, 1970) for true cooperative conversation, short-answer questions for free-text input, and the use of explicit questions for the use of turn-taking rules. To obtain the most "bang for the buck" in text generation, we emphasize precise responses to student input, simulation of the discourse patterns of expert tutors, and the provision of variety in both pedagogy and language as substitutes for complex mental processing. Our goal is to keep the tutoring process as interactive as possible while providing both broader and deeper domain coverage.

Simplifying the Input

True cooperative conversation, where tutor and student are equal partners in choosing and responding to topics, requires the tutor not only to understand free-text input but to track the student's plan as well. Instead, CIRCSIM-Tutor ends each turn with an explicit short-answer question in order to reduce the burden on the input processor without restricting the student's use of language. For example, human tutors might say "First we need to know how HR [heart rate] is controlled," knowing that the student will respond cooperatively, or ask "How is HR controlled?" since they are comfortable with their ability to understand the answer. But people expect a program to give them a clear indication when it is their turn to respond. CIRCSIM-Tutor achieves the communicative intent of questions like those above with short-answer questions such as "By what mechanism is HR controlled?" or "What controls HR?".

Generating the Response

Instead of dividing processing between a pedagogical planner and a text planner, our text planner, TIPS, divides the work between the *tutorial planner*, which makes discourse decisions at the dialogue level, and the *turn planner*, which assembles individual turns.

TIPS uses an expanded form of schemata to simulate discourse patterns of expert tutors. For example, if it notices that the student has given inconsistent values to two variables, it might say, "How can X increase and Y decrease?" Multi-turn schemata are used to simulate more complex patterns, as in the example below.

T: ... What equation determines the value of MAP?
S: MAP = CO * TPR.
T: Correct. And you have predicted CO increases and TPR increases. So how can you say MAP decreases?

To ensure responsiveness to the student, TIPS can replan after every turn. If the student does not understand the point of a multi-turn schema, it can respond to the student's error or drop the schema in favor of a different one. Rather than merely evaluating the student's answers as right or wrong, it can issue acknowledgments, restate answers which are close but not exact, rebut untrue statements, and provide tips for students who are on the path toward a correct answer.

We have tried to provide a variety of ways to teach each topic, including options at the pedagogical, syntactic and lexical levels. Additionally, since the turn planner builds a turn at a time from semantic forms provided by the tutorial planner, we can generate additional variety by combining semantic forms into sentences in different ways.

Acknowledgments

This work was supported by the Cognitive Science Program, Office of Naval Research under Grant No. N00014–94–1–0338, to Illinois Institute of Technology. The content does not reflect the position or policy of the government and no official endorsement should be inferred.

Reference

Carbonell, J. R. (1970). AI in CAI: Artificial intelligence approach to computer assisted instruction. *IEEE Transactions on Man-Machine Systems,* 11(4), 190–202.

Representation of relative velocity in the distal retina is invariant in respect to the illumination of moving object

Boris A. Galitsky
Marketron, Inc., 2929 Campus Dr #400 San Mateo CA 94403
borgal@aol.com

The model

The knowledge on cell physiology of the distal retina gives an ability to represent the functioning of cone - horizontal cell - bipolar neural network as a whole. Six signal operations are combined in the model:

1) phototransduction operation (i.e. signal transformation from light into electrical response in the photoreceptor);
2) chemical synaptic transmission from photoreceptors to second order neurons;
3) electrical coupling between horizontal cells;
4) nonlinear (amplifying) properties of horizontal cell non-synaptic membrane;
5) the feedback from horizontal cells to photoreceptors in triad synapses;
6) dynamics of the bipolar neuron.

The current study develops the distal retina model (*Byzov, Shura-Bura 1986*), allowing the calculation of responses for arbitrary spatial stimuli. Time courses of horizontal cells (achromatic type) membrane potential, obtained experimentally for various temporal and **simple spatial stimuli** for fish and turtle retinas, were reproduced by the diffusion-type equations with the additional temporal constraint (electrical feedback in triad synapse). Experimental work with **complicated** spatial stimuli is hard, so the computational study with a verified model is required to analyze the network responses to movement.

The coding of velocity

The study is mainly focused on the spatial distributions of bipolar potential, which is the base of edge and motion detection. The fact of **weak** linear **dependence of bipolar responses** on stimulus **velocity** is obtained as a basis for the relative velocity representation constancy in respect to stimuli luminosity: $dPotential(Vel)/dVel = const$, though horizontal cells responses have exponential-like dependence.

The system functioning combines the **temporal smoothing** with the **spatial amplification** of area edges with illumination difference. The network estimation of edge intensity increases under the movement along the edge and drops under the transverse movement. For example, front and rear edges of a moving rectangle are smoothed, though the side edges are amplified proportionally to the velocity. The velocity value itself, which is represented by the amplitude, is smoothed under the sharp change.

In general, the optimal velocity for the moving objects detection is low in respect to the system time constant but high enough to be taken into consideration for better perception.

Consistency to noise

The network was analyzed in respect to external noise and deviation of internal parameters under spatial filtering. The network is capable to calculate the spatial derivative and to extract the **illumination difference** much **weaker** than the **variation** of membrane **parameters** from one photoreceptor to another. This feature is provided by the specifics of potential spread through the horizontal cells network and electrical feedback mechanism of the triad synapse.

Relations to psychophysics

Some human visual perception phenomenon can be explained in the bounds of the distal retina, for example, the failure of motion imitation by means of changes in the illumination conditions, while "empty field" specifics (imitation of the absence of relative movement) does not match the system behavior.

Hypothesis

Given the spatial-temporal distribution, it is possible to reconstruct the network functioning of specialized **detectors** (movement of the area edge, stripe, etc.). Hypothetical detectors can correspond to some classes of amacrine and ganglion retinal cells.

There exists the fastest and shortest dynamic link, which provides the high level layers with the information about the object acceleration. It is, probably, necessary, for the instantaneous following of the moving object by means of the pupil motion.

References

Byzov,A.L., Shura-Bura,T.M. (1986) Electrical feedback mechanism in the processing of signal in outer plexiform layer of the retina, *Vision research*, v.26 N1 p.33-44.

McLean J., Palmer L.A. (1994) Organization of simple cell responses in the 3D frequency domain *Visual Neurosci* v.11,N2, pp. 295--306.

Effects of Modality on Subjective Estimates of Frequency of Spoken and Printed Words

Daniel E. Gaygen and **Paul A. Luce**

Language Perception Laboratory and Center for Cognitive Science
State University of New York at Buffalo
dgaygen@acsu.buffalo.edu

The effects of word frequency are ubiquitous in research on visual and spoken word recognition (Forster & Chambers, 1973), and considerable modeling efforts have been devoted to explaining the mechanisms responsible for the findings that higher frequency words are recognized more quickly and accurately than low frequency words. Typically, frequencies of stimuli have been estimated from counts of printed material (e.g., Thorndike & Lorge, 1944, and Kucera & Francis, 1967). Recently, however, subjective ratings of word frequency have provided an alternative measure for investigating effects of frequency on recognition. To obtain subjective ratings, subjects are asked directly how familiar they are with individually presented words. Gernsbacher (1984) has shown that many previous inconsistencies in research on word recognition can be dispelled when objective frequency counts are supplanted by subjective ratings.

Even more recently, researchers have used subjective frequency ratings to examine the degree to which lexical representations that support word recognition are independent of modality of processing (i.e., visual or auditory). If subjective ratings are modality *independent*, ratings should not differ for words presented visually compared to words presented auditorily. On the other hand, modality *dependence* of lexical representations should be revealed by differential judgments of words that are processed in the visual or auditory modalities. If subjects' mental representations of visual and spoken words incorporate possible differences in frequency of processing in the two modalities, subjective frequency ratings should reveal these differences. In short, modality dependence should be reflected in lower correlations between subjective ratings of words processed in the visual and auditory modalities. Conversely, modality independent lexical representations should not produce differentially sensitive ratings.

Early versions of various models of word recognition have made at least implicit claims regarding the modality independence of frequency information. Morton's (1969) logogen model appears consistent with modality independence because logogens accept evidence from both auditory and visual input. Later versions of the model, however, explicitly acknowledge modality dependence by incorporating separate logogen systems for printed and spoken words (Morton, 1979). In addition, Forster's (1973) autonomous search model is consistent with modality dependence because the first stage of the model involves submitting an unanalyzed pattern to peripheral access files made up of bins that contain either frequency-ordered

orthographic entries or frequency-ordered phonetic entries. Thus, in Forster's model, frequency effects should depend directly on modality of processing.

The present research further examined whether frequency is a modality independent, unitary phenomenon. In particular, we attempted to determine if frequency information is coded strictly at an abstract lexical level or if this information is also present at one or more particular, form-based levels of representation, such as phonological and orthographic representations that support perception and production. This research attempted to extend previous findings to determine if form-based, modality dependent representations possess their own frequency indices.

We gathered subjective frequency ratings for 252 words using the following questions: "How often have you read the word ___ in your lifetime?"; "How often have you written the word ___ in your lifetime?"; "How often have you heard the word ___ in your lifetime?"; and "How often have you said the word ___ in your lifetime?". Separate ratings were collected for a list of words presented visually and the same list of words presented auditorily.

We were interested not only in the ratings themselves but also in their implications for processing times. In particular, we were interested in determining the degree to which each of the four types of ratings would correlate with performance in processing tasks. We attempted to determine if subjective ratings of the frequencies of producing words (writing, saying) correlate with performance in experiments with a production component (naming); if subjective ratings of frequencies of perceiving words (reading, hearing) correlate with performance in experiments with perception components (lexical decision); and if ratings of a given input modality correlate with performance within and across modalities. Again, we were interested in determining if frequency differences are coded strictly at an abstract lexical level or if this information is also present at one or more particular, form-based levels of representation.

In experiments 1A and 1B, subjects rated how frequently they read, wrote, heard, and said the stimulus words. Visually presented words and auditorily presented words were rated separately. Experiments 2 through 5 examined processing time and accuracy for the words rated in Experiment 1. These experiments were (1) auditory lexical decision, (2) visual lexical decision, (3) auditory naming, and (4) visual naming. These ratings were then correlated with processing times in auditory and visual lexical decision and naming tasks. Our results suggest modality dependence for some lexical representations, primarily for words that occur fairly rarely in the language.

A Semantic Markov Field Model of Text Recall

Richard M. Golden

Cognition & Neuroscience Program, GR41
School of Human Development
University of Texas at Dallas
Richardson, TX 75083-0688
golden@utdallas.edu

Abstract

A probabilistic model of text recall is proposed which assigns a probability mass to a given recall protocol. Knowledge analyses of semantic relationships among events identified in the text are used to specify the architecture of the probability model. Twelve subjects (the training data group) were then asked to recall twelve texts from memory. The recall protocols generated by the twelve subjects were then used to estimate the strengths of the semantic relationships in the probabilistic model. The Gibbs Sampler algorithm (a connectionist-like algorithm) was then used to sample from the probabilistic model in order to generate synthesized recall protocols. These synthesized recall protocols were then compared with the original set of recall data and recall data collected from an additional group of twelve human subjects (the test data group).

Markov Field Probability Model

In this section, a Markov field probability model which assigns a probability mass to a given recall protocol (i.e., an ordered sequence of complex text propositions or equivalently *text features*) is now explicitly defined. The specific formulas described in this section are discussed in detail and derived elsewhere. The semantic associative links (e.g., causal links) identified by a text knowledge analysis are first used to specify the free parameters of a special d-dimensional matrix which is called the $\mathbf{W}$ matrix. The ijth element of $\mathbf{W}$ indicates the degree to which the activation of the jth text feature, y_j, in the *working memory buffer*, $\mathbf{y} = [y_1, \ldots, y_d]$, influences the probability that the ith text feature will be recalled. Note that only a subset of elements of $\mathbf{W}$ are estimated using quasi-maximum likelihood estimation (i.e., the a priori designated semantic and episodic knowledge links) while the remaining elements of $\mathbf{W}$ are constrained to be equal to zero.

Let $\mathbf{f}_i$ be a d-dimensional vector with a one in position i and zeros in all remaining $d - 1$ positions. The vector $\mathbf{f}_i$ identifies the ith text feature in the text. Let the notation $\mathbf{x}(t) = \mathbf{f}_j$ indicate that the tth item in a human subject's recall protocol was text feature $\mathbf{f}_j$. The working memory buffer of the human subject is assumed to be updated according to the formula $\mathbf{y}(t + 1) = \mathbf{x}(t) + \mu \mathbf{y}(t)$ where the empirically determined $\mu \in [0, 1)$ specifies the working memory node activation *decay rate*.

Let $\mathbf{y}(t) = [y_1(t), \ldots, y_d(t)]$ model the working memory buffer of the human subject after t items have been recalled. Define the *local potential function* $V_{s,i}$ such that:

$$V_{s,i} = \mathbf{f}_i^T [\mathbf{W}\mathbf{y}(s) + \sum_{t=s+1}^{M} [\mathbf{W}\mu^{t-1-s}]^T \mathbf{x}(t)]. \quad (1)$$

Then the conditional probability that the sth item in a recall protocol is the ith text feature recalled given knowledge of all other items in the recall protocol is given by the formula:

$$p_{s,i} = \frac{exp[V_{s,i}]}{\sum_{k=1}^{d} exp[V_{s,k}]}. \quad (2)$$

Probability Model Evaluation

Quasi-maximum likelihood estimates of the strengths of semantic and episodic knowledge links in the $\mathbf{W}$ matrix were computed from recall protocol data collected from twelve human subjects (*training group*) for twelve short 12-15 sentence texts. The Geman and Geman Gibbs Sampler algorithm was then used to sample from the joint probability distribution of recall protocols. An additional (*test group*) of twelve human subjects also recalled the twelve texts from memory. The recall protocols generated from the two groups of human subjects and the recall protocols generated from the Gibbs Sampler algorithm were then compared.

Statement recall probabilities computed from Gibbs Sampler generated recall protocols were *quantitatively* very similar to statement recall probabilities computed from actual human recall protocols. Both human subject recall protocols and Gibbs Sampler generated recall protocols exhibited the well-known finding that statements with more causal connections to other statements in a text are more likely to be included in a recall protocol.

The synthesized recall protocol data may also be directly compared with the human recall protocol data in order to make predictions about the *explicit order* in which items are recalled from memory. For example, the sixth synthesized recall protocol for the *miser* text is the text feature sequence $\mathbf{f}_3, \mathbf{f}_7, \mathbf{f}_{14}, \mathbf{f}_{16}, \mathbf{f}_{17}$ which corresponds to the sequence of English statements:

The miser buried the gold in the ground ($\mathbf{f}_3$). The servant stole the gold ($\mathbf{f}_7$). The neighbor said, "Go and take a stone, and bury it in the hole" ($\mathbf{f}_{14}$). The neighbor said, "The stone will be as useful to you as the gold" ($\mathbf{f}_{16}$). The neighbor said, "When you had the gold, you never used it" ($\mathbf{f}_{17}$).

The Besieged Workplace:
How Cognitive Science Can Respond

Sherrie P. Gott
USAF Armstrong Laboratory
AL/HRMD
7909 Lindbergh Dr.
Brooks AFB, TX 78235
gott@alhrm.brooks.af.mil

Workcenters in the public and private sectors are being invaded by complex, dynamic equipment systems. Global competitiveness and diminished budgets in turn dictate a downsized, but **adaptive** workforce. In this study, innovative data gathering that informed an uncommon instructional system offer a response from cognitive science to the besieged workcenters. Cognitive task analysis methods captured the components of troubleshooting expertise from dozens of Air Force master technicians as they worked on authentic fault scenarios. The codified output and developed scenarios then provided input to an intelligent tutoring system called Sherlock. This tutor targets high-difficulty F15 avionics troubleshooting skills. In a controlled experiment, 41 apprentice and journeyman airmen were pretested on their troubleshooting competence and then randomly assigned to two equivalent groups. The experimental group worked on the tutor 1-1/2 to 2 hours a day over an average of 7 days. The control group continued their standard on-the-job training regimen, working with senior team leaders in the shop during those hours. After the intervention, on both verbal protocol and paper and pencil posttests used to assess troubleshooting performance, the experimental group out-performed the controls ($p = .001$; $p = .009$). Results held up for 6 months after the tutor was removed. (Finding from evaluation of Sherlock prototype.) Also, in the present evaluation, subjects were required to troubleshoot a completely novel equipment system. Again, the experimental group prevailed on both measures ($p = .006$; $p = .025$). The implications of this work are as follows: purposeful learning experiences in systems where knowledge connects with its uses in the world appear to accelerate the development of adaptive, "Information Age" expertise. Innovative communities of practice should not be far behind.

Optical Flow for Visual Speech Recognition

Michael S. Gray[1,3] and **Javier R. Movellan**[1] and **Terrence J. Sejnowski**[2,3]

Departments of Cognitive Science[1] and Biology[2]
University of California, San Diego
La Jolla, CA 92093
and
Howard Hughes Medical Institute[3]
Computational Neurobiology Lab, The Salk Institute
La Jolla, CA 92037
{mgray,jmovellan,tsejnowski}@ucsd.edu

Introduction

Visual speech recognition is a challenging task in sensory integration. Psychophysical work by McGurk and MacDonald (1976) first showed the powerful influence of visual information on speech perception that has led to increased interest in this area. For example, they presented the speech sound /na−na/ with the visible articulation of /pa − pa/. When subjects were asked to identify the sound that they *heard*, many reported /ma − ma/. This sound represents the best compromise of these two conflicting sources of information because /ma−ma/ is similar to /pa−pa/ visually, and /ma−ma/ is similar to /na − na/ acoustically. More generally, the visual signal provides good information about place of articulation, but voicing and nasality are more difficult to determine. The acoustic signal, on the other hand, has good information about voicing, but is ambiguous with respect to place of articulation.

Massaro (1987) used a fuzzy logic model to show that the best explanation of the data was obtained when the visual and acoustic information were treated as independent factors. In other words, human response probabilities for the different combinations of visual and acoustic signals were best described as the result of a process in which each modality makes an independent, multiplicative contribution. This property of the acoustic and visual signals is often referred to as *conditional independence*. Movellan (in press) further tested this conditional independence assumption using hidden Markov models. He compared models that were constrained to utilize visual and acoustic information independently with models that were unconstrained. Because the optimal constrained model did not perform any worse than the optimal unconstrained model, we can assume that the conditional independence assumption holds.

Current Directions

Movellan (1995) recently explored the ability of hidden Markov models to recognize spoken digits using visual information alone. The input representation for the model consisted of smoothed pixel intensity information at each time step, as well as a delta image that showed the pixel by pixel difference between subsequent time steps. Peak performance of this model (89%) closely matched the results of untrained human subjects.

In the current work, an optical flow representation rather than the delta image was used. Cells in area MST of visual cortex selectively respond to specific patterns of optical flow (Duffy & Wurtz, 1991). This flow information has been interpreted as representing egomotion, but may also be valuable for segmenting independently moving objects (Zemel & Sejnowski, 1995) and recognizing different patterns of lip movements. This higher-level visual representation may be more resistant to varying illumination conditions, and other forms of noise, than the pixel-based delta image.

Our optical flow computation was based on the standard *brightness constraint* equation, followed by thresholding. Experimentation with more sophisticated 2nd-order optical flow techniques resulted in extremely noisy output, presumably due to violation of the rigidity constraint. The optical flow representation formed the input to an HMM which was trained on spoken digits from a database of 12 speakers. Peak performance of 61% was obtained with a 9-state model. Adding information about the acceleration of lip features (differences in optical flow) resulted in an additional 10% improvement.

References

Duffy, C.J. & Wurtz, R.H. (1991). The sensitivity of MST neurons to optic flow stimuli. I. A continuum of response selectivity to large field stimuli. *Journal of Neurophysiology*, 65, 1329-1345.

Massaro, D.W. (1987). *Speech Perception by Ear and Eye: A Paradigm for Psychological Inquiry*. Hillsdale, NJ: Lawrence Erlbaum Associates.

McGurk, H. & MacDonald, J. (1976). Hearing lips and seeing voices. *Nature*, 264, 126-130.

Movellan, J.R. (1995). Visual speech recognition with stochastic networks. In G. Tesauro, D.S. Touretzky, & T. Leen (Eds.), *Advances in Neural Information Processing Systems 7* (pp. 851-858). Cambridge, MA: MIT Press.

Movellan, J.R. (in press). Channel separability in the audio visual integration of speech: A Bayesian approach.

Zemel, R.S. & Sejnowski, T.J. (1995). Grouping components of three-dimensional moving objects in area MST of visual cortex. In G. Tesauro, D.S. Touretzky, & T. Leen (Eds.), *Advances in Neural Information Processing Systems 7* (pp. 165-172). Cambridge, MA: MIT Press.

A Sparse Distributed Memory Model of Overregularization

Annemarie Nicols-Grinenko and Martin S. Chodorow
Department of Psychology
Hunter College
New York, N.Y. 10021
mschc@cunyvm.cuny.edu

Introduction

Overregularization (OR) errors and U-shaped learning during past tense acquisition have been used to support the model of a symbolic, two process system of learning requiring both rule use and memorization. Beginning with the work of Rumelhart and McClelland (1986), connectionist networks have attempted to model these phenomena with varying degrees of success. We examine the ability of Kanerva's (1988) sparse distributed memory (SDM) to simulate Palermo and Howe's (1970; hereafter P&H) experimental analogy to past tense acquisition. SDM, like the connectionist networks, does not explicitly encode rules, therefore, if it is able to simulate P&H's behavioral data, the plausibility of a sub-symbolic, one process account will be strengthened.

Sparse Distributed Memory

SDM (Kanerva, 1988) is a content-addressable associative memory system in which only a small, random subset of all possible addresses is realized as "hard" locations. During storage, the probability is small that an exact match will be found for a target address among the hard locations, so the data is stored at hard locations which are "near" the target using a kind of superposition. A similar process occurs during retrieval when the data from the target address's neighboring hard locations are summed. The use of superposition and summation allows SDM to maintain a high level of fidelity despite the many-to-many mappings between addresses and hard locations. For the same reasons SDM is able to exhibit graceful degradation, prototype extraction and noise suppression.

Our implementation of SDM incorporates noise during storage and retrieval, and as such, is a modification of Kanerva's model. Our belief that noise is a critical factor in learning , whose effects diminish as learning proceeds, led to a strategy of decreasing noise during our simulations.

SDM Simulations of Palermo & Howe (1970)

SDM was used to simulate P&H's paired associates learning task in which adult subjects were presented with both regular (rule governed) stimulus-response pairs and more frequent irregular pairs which were exceptions to the rule. Notably, the composition of the training and testing materials did not change through the course of the experiment, i.e., there were no shifts in frequency of presentation over trials. SDM was able to mimic P&H's behavioral data in a number of critical areas: (1) Both P&H's subjects and SDM learned the irregulars much sooner and better than the regular pairs. (2) SDM was able to match the OR rates found among P&H's subjects. (3) SDM replicated the frequency effects exhibited by P&H's subjects: as frequency of presentation increased, both acquisition rates and OR rates decreased. (4) There was no evidence of U-shaped learning either in P&H's subjects or the SDM simulations.

Discussion

OR errors have received much attention in the debate between symbolic and connectionist approaches to cognition. The work presented here does not resolve the debate, but SDM's success at modeling P&H's behavioral data does suggest that a sub-symbolic approach is plausible. We are currently working to determine how well this one process system is able to model other memory phenomena including interference and recognition.

An interesting behavioral question is also raised by this study. While it seems clear that OR errors are not confined to language acquisition, P&H's study provides no evidence that U-shaped learning exists outside this domain. In addition, the child language acquisition data suggest that while U-shaped learning is evident in some children, it may be an exceptional occurrence. So, the question of whether U-shaped learning is a general cognitive phenomenon, or even characteristic of language acquisition, remains to be answered.

References

Kanerva, P. (1988). *Sparse Distributed Memory*. Cambridge, MA: MIT Press.

Palermo, D.S. & Howe, H.E. (1970). An experimental analogy to the learning of past tense inflection rules. *Journal of Verbal Learning and Verbal Behavior*, 9, 410-416.

Rumelhart, D.E. & McClelland, J.L. (1986). On learning the past tenses of English verbs. In J. L. McClelland & D.E. Rumelhart (Eds.), *Parallel Distributed Processing: Explorations in the Microstructure of Cognition* (Vol. 2,. pp. 216-271). Cambridge, MA: MIT Press.

Cognitive Reconstruction in Hindsight: A Model and an Experiment

Ralph Hertwig and **Ulrich Hoffrage**
Center for Adaptive Behavior and Cognition
Max Planck Institute for Psychological Research
Leopoldstrasse 24, 80802 Munich, Germany.
{hertwig,hoffrage}@mpipf-muenchen.mpg.de

Hindsight bias refers to the tendency for people with knowledge and event outcome to recall their original judgment about the event as closer to the outcome than it actually was. No attempt to explain hindsight bias has resulted in a precise model that specifies the cognitive (or motivational) mechanism. Our CRAFT model (Cognitive Reconstruction After Feedback with Take the Best) does.

We apply CRAFT to the typical hindsight bias task in which an <u>original judgment</u> has to be made at time 1, <u>feedback</u> about the correct answer is given at time 2, and the original judgment has to be recalled at time 3.

Time 1: Steps of the Algorithm

We account for the original judgment at time 1 with the basic PMM algorithm (PMM theory; see Gigerenzer, Hoffrage, & Kleinbölting, 1991). A PMM is an inductive device that uses limited knowledge to make fast inferences in tasks in which a choice must be made between two objects a and b (e.g., two food items) on a quantitative target variable (e.g., amount of cholesterol). The knowledge consists of cues (that are correlated with the target variable) as well as the values of a and b (e.g., 2g and 1g saturated fat per ounce, respectively) on each cue.

In a two-alternative choice in which one has to decide which of two food items has more cholesterol, the basic algorithm in the PMM framework, the "Take The Best" (TTB) algorithm, retrieves the items' relation on the most valid cue from memory. The cue is said to <u>discriminate</u> between the two alternatives if its value for a differs from that for b. If the best cue discriminates, the search stops; otherwise, the algorithm repeats the procedure with the next-best cue until a cue that discriminates is found. Finally, the item with the higher cue value on the discriminating cue is chosen.

Time 3: Cognitive Reconstruction

What happens when one's original judgment at time 3 must be recalled after receiving feedback (about a and b's values on the target variable) at time 2? It is assumed that if the original judgment cannot be retrieved at time 3, it will be generated by reconstructing the knowledge on which the judgment at time 1 was based. During this process, the TTB algorithm will be applied again.

Our crucial assumption concerning reconstruction is that it is not completely veridical but rather is shifted toward feedback. The reason is that feedback is a cue strong enough to shift recalled cue relations between objects in the direction consistent with feedback. The impact of feedback is particularly strong when a cue did <u>not</u> <u>discriminate</u> at time 1 because of an unknown cue value.

Aside from <u>systematic</u> (feedback dependent) shifts in cue relations, there also occur <u>random</u> (feedback independent) shifts. Random shifts, which reflect an error component whose importance Erev, Wallsten, and Budescu (1994) and others have demonstrated in modeling human confidence judgments. Random shifts can account for the finding that choices are sometimes reconstructed in a way inconsistent with feedback.

Test of CRAFT: Experiment

A real-world topic with considerable significance for many people is nutrition. The TTB algorithm predicts which of two food items a particular participant will choose as having more cholesterol before and after feedback. The input to the algorithm is participants' knowledge about the values on the saturated fat, calorie, and protein cues for food items which we told them were excellent (80% cue validity), good (70%), and weak (60%) predictors for cholesterol, respectively. To control knowledge, we started the experiment with a <u>learning phase</u> in which participants learned about 50% of the cue values on the saturated fat, calorie, and protein cues for 36 food items. Immediately after the learning phase, participants were given a list of food items and were asked "Which food do you think has the higher amount of cholesterol?

In the second session, the experimental group received feedback for each of the questions they answered previously (the cholesterol values). In addition, they were asked to recall (a) which food they originally chose as having the higher amount of cholesterol and (b) the amounts of saturated fat, calories, and protein that they learned in the learning phase. The control group received no feedback and had to answer the same questions.

By comparing the choices predicted by the TTB algorithm at time 3 with the actual choices (at time 1), CRAFT predicted for each food pair and each participant whether <u>hindsight bias</u> (shift in choice consistent with feedback), <u>reversed hindsight bias</u> (shift inconsistent with feedback), or <u>no hindsight</u> bias would occur.

In the experimental group, CRAFT accurately predicted 82% of the observed outcomes. In the control condition, the algorithm accurately predicted 87% of the observed outcomes.

Towards a Computational Theory of Cognitive Development

Kazuo Hiraki, Steven Phillips and **Akio Sashima**
Presto / Electrotechnical Laboratory
1-1-4 Umezono Tsukuba-shi
Ibaraki, 305 Japan
{khiraki,stevep,sashima}@etl.go.jp

Introduction

This research challenges the traditional approach of theory construction in cognitive development by using the framework of robot learning. Traditionally, researcher in cognitive development (e.g., developmental psychologist) has focused on general and abstract description of experimental data as an explanation for the observations. In contrast to this approach, we propose using autonomous robots as the subject of cognitive development, and constructing computer programs by which robots can behave analogously to infants.

The advantage of using robots is twofold. First, we can utilize a robot's various sensors and actuators as the inputs and outputs of a model. In comparison to standard computer simulation framework this aspect allows us to construct a more realistic model. Second, we can construct a theory absorbing *activeness* in cognitive development. Recently, researchers have emphasized the importance of activeness (i.e., mobility) of infants during development (Thelen and Smith, 1994). However, the theory derived from this stream needs to be tested and refined in more detail. We believe that using robot leads us to a more concrete theory.

Modeling the Process of Spatial Learning

As a first step to constructing an complete computational theory of cognitive development, we are trying to explain the empirical results of Acredelo, Asams & Goodwyn (1984). They conducted experiments to test the role of self-locomotion as opposed to passive transport concerning infant's spatial cognition. Their results suggest the importance of active movement with visual tracking. However it is not clear what information is central in promoting the change from *egocentric representations* to *landmark-based* or *allocentric representations*.

In order to focus on the change, we adopt the idea of *representational redescription* (Karmiloff-Smith, 1992) as a key concept for constructing learning robots. In accordance with this idea we have developed a method called *feature abstraction* (Hiraki,1994). Feature abstraction dynamically defines abstract sensors from primitive sensory information and makes it possible to learn appropriate sensory-motor constraints. This method has been implemented on a real mobile robot as a learning system called ACORN-II.

Even though feature abstraction is a method for changing representation, it has limitations as a general model of developmental change. We are addressing the following issues.

1. **Efficient methods for exploring the feature space (Attention mechanism).** ACORN-II has a small number of sensors/actuators that enable exploration of representational space. On the other hand infants have enormous sensory organs. We need more sophisticated criterion such as attention mechanism.

2. **Mechanism for simulating drastic change(Self-organization).** The change from egocentric behavior to non-egocentric seems to need a drastic change of spatial representation. Though feature abstraction dynamically redefines representation, its basic mechanism is based on the supervised learning framework. In order to simulate infant's representation change, we need a systematic way based on the unsupervised framework.

There are some studies that share some parts of our goal. For instance, Brooks & Lynn (1993) are constructing a humanoid type robot that can simulate part of infant's behavior. They focus on the hardware level instead of developmental changes of representation. However, we believe that the necessity of implementation on real robots provides valuable insights into cognitive mechanisms. As for Acredelo's experiments, we can control the information which is supposed to be perceived by infants during locomotion, and we can verify the hypothesis on self-movement.

References

Thelen, E. & Smith, L. B. (1994). *A Dynamic Systems Approach to the Development of Cognition and Action.* MIT Press.

Acredelo, L.P., Asams, A., & Goodwyn, S.W. (1984). The role of self-produced movement and visual tracking in infant spatial orientation, *Journal of Experimental Child Psychology*, 38, 312-327.

Karmiloff-Smith,A. (1992). *Beyond Modularity*, MIT Press.

Hiraki,K. (1994). Abstraction of Sensory-Motor Features. In *Proceedings of The Sixteenth Annual Conference of the Cognitive Science Society.* (pp. 415–420).

Brooks, R. A., & Lynn, A. S.(1993). Building Brains for Bodies. MIT AI Lab Memo No.1439, August.

A Topological Interpetation of Cognition

William C. Hoffman
2591 W. Cmo. Llano
Tucson, AZ 85742-9074
wilhof@primenet.com

The human brain consists in broad outline of the neocortex, the limbic system, and a midbrain core. The neocortex is connected to the limbic-midbrain system B by many back-and-forth projections, a structure consistent with Pribram's three primary brain systems: the modality-specific posterior intrinsic systems P, the projection systems, and the frontal intrinsic system F. Topologically, such a structure constitutes a fibration, or fibre bundle p: P Æ B, consisting of a base space B and overlying it, a total space P made up of tubular neighborhoods that project down to the base space B. There is also a "lifting map" from the base space to the total space. In the perceptual application, the lifting map consists of afferent nerve signals transmitting sensory stimuli to Short Term Memory, while the projection maps are embodied in efferent and corticortical nerve flows. This structure is consistent with neuroscientists' current general agreement that cortical structure is at the same time "topographic" (e.g., retinotopic), laminar (cytoarchitectural layers), and (micro)columnar. The latter have both a local directional ("orientation") response and an areal one, which together generate visual contours, for example, as "lifts' of retinal stimuli.

The posterior intrinsic systems "mediate invariant properties of specific sensory modalities," e.g., the psychological constancies, shape memory, and the Gestalt "laws." Many researchers in psychology have recognized that cognition requires continuous transformation (Working Memory); some (Berlyne, Cassirer, Culbertson, Dodwell, Hoffman, Palmer, Piaget, Pitts & McCulloch, Rashevsky, Wiener) have further recognized that continuous transformation groups G x P → P ("continuous symmetry") are required for such invariances. In particular the invariances of the psychological constancies: shape, size, color, motion, pitch, loudness, and binaural localization, are structured in this way. In the perceptual case this leads to the LTG/NP ("continuous transformation groups constrained by neuropsychology") theory. The group G's action, which "drags the flow" along the path-curves or "orbits" (e.g., visual contours) of the perceptual field via the local action of the group's Lie derivatives, corresponds to proprioceptor/teleceptor inputs. The result is an "orbifold" made up of visual contours representing such orbits. The Lie derivatives have the proper local morphology to be embodied in the stellate and pyramidal cells of isocortex. Also appearing is a cotangent functor T* generating a local orientation response similar to that of cortical microcolumns.

Cognition consists of two primary entities: percepts and concepts. Percepts represent the outcome of attention (efferent blocking) upon perception. Concepts consist of the semiotic aspects of percepts, procedural and declarative memory, and rational thought, and are colored by emotions imparted by the limbic system. The frontal intrinsic system processes complicated sequences of actions or trains of thought that are consonant with limbic system processing to minimize cognitive dissonance. Such processing has the character of the symmetric difference operation - "one or the other but not both together" - plus its complement, in the familiar paradigm of differences (discriminations and classifications) and similarities (commonalities) and context. This structure is isomorphic to the category of simplicial objects, whose organization is like that of information processing psychology. It then follows that Riegel's dialectical psychology and information processing psychology are, at least for paired comparisons, isomorphic. The fibre bundles of the posterior intrinsic systems constitute a (mathematical) category, which is mapped functorially into fibrations in the sense of Kan in the category of simplicial objects characteristic of the frontal intrinsic systems.

References
W. Hoffman (1985). *Internat. J. Man-Machine Studies* **22**, 613-650.

W. Hoffman (1994). pp. 363-382 in: O. Ying-Lie et al.(Eds.), *Shape in Picture*. Springer-Verlag.

The Guiding of Learning: An Overview, Analysis and Classification of Guides

Robert W. Howard
Department of Education
The University of Newcastle
Callaghan NSW, Australia 2308
edrwh@cc.newcastle.edu.au

Learning needs guidance and a key current issue in cognitive science is what guides exist, how they work and how they interact. Most current cognitive work has examined guides for language learning (e.g. children expect a new word to refer to a category and to a whole object rather than a part) and "theories", which are innate structural principles that guide further knowledge acquisition in a particular domain. For example, children expect objects to be solid and continous and new knowledge must be consistent with this notion. This general problem of guiding learning is studied in several other fields, such as ethology, animal psychology and machine learning. They study the problem from varying viewpoints, however, and with somewhat different assumptions. All the work done on it may usefully be integrated into a single framework, to make some generalizations about the problem and suggest key research issues. I first argue that the problem of how learning is guided is best analysed as part of the more general evolutionary problem of ensuring that an individual has needed information. This general problem has many facets and trade-offs and how it is solved depends on the species, the niche, the learning process and other factors. This paper outlines some general guidelines for solving the problem and some general strategies that nature uses. There are many of these. This paper also outlines a preliminary taxonomy of learning guides. This has three major categories. One type is learning-based, where programming induces organisms to learn specific sorts of thing from specific experiences (e.g. schemas, contingencies) and/or restricts this learning to a limited period. Another type sets or alters motivation or an emotional reaction to a certain stimulus. This may encourage or prevent further learning about that particular stimulus. A third category includes general heurstics, which included responsiveness to stimulus novelty, change, and intensity and being provided with a teacher. These guides operate in various ways. They direct attention to important stimuli and help connect up stimuli that otherwise would not be connected. However, all essentially narrow some number of things down to manageable proportions. Many previously unrelated phenomena may be seen as methods of dealing with the evolutionary problem. Examples are curiosity, posttraumatic stress disorder, the incest taboo, imprinting and bird song learning, and the difficulty of changing some concepts in humans. Some further research issues suggested by the general framework are outlined. I conclude with a suggestion that cognitive scientists to look more at function, at what general problems humans need to solve and how many phenomena may be seen as solutions to these problems.

Learning in Collaborative Electronic Discussion vs. Classroom Discussion in Science

Sherry Hsi

4533 Tolman Hall, Science & Math Education Group
University of California at Berkeley
hsi@garnet.berkeley.edu

Introduction

Can electronic discourse improve scientific discussion among 8th grade students? Classroom discussion can privilege teachers, stifle debate, and silence women. Electronic discussion tools can have several advantages over face-to-face classroom discussion. In this study, electronic discussion and classroom discussion are contrasted, and the role of comment attribute and authority participation is explored.

The Multimedia Forum Kiosk (MFK) is an electronic discussion tool used to research alternative formats for discussion (Hoadley & Hsi, 1993). Two graphical representations of discourse are provided in MFK called the *Opinion Area* and the *Discussion Area* (see URL: http://obelisk.berkeley.edu/kiosk/kiosk.html). Students may browse position statements of other participants in the Opinion Area, or add to an on-going argument in the Discussion Area. The Discussion Area displays discourse as argument trees where all comments are labeled by semantic category. Pilot data suggests that electronic discussion increases student participation, allows students to reflect on a comment before reading another one, and encourages students to link their contributions to existing comments.

Method

Six class periods with a total of 165 students used MFK during an 18-week physical science curriculum as part of the Computers as Learning Partner project (Linn, 1992). Every four weeks, a new topic from the curriculum was posted on MFK and discussed by 11 groups of 15 students each.

The MFK software ran on a pair of Macintosh computers at the side of the classroom; students took turns using the software during breaks between classes, after school, or during free time in class. No time was specifically devoted to using the system other than an in-class demonstration the first time the system was introduced to the classroom.

Equal numbers of boys and girls were randomly assigned into one of three MFK discussion conditions for each topic: anonymous, attributed, or attributed plus authority participation. For the anonymous condition, all participants were assigned unique cartoon identities. For the attributed condition, students' names and photos were displayed, but comments made by researchers or teachers were anonymous. In the authority-participation condition, all comments were attributed to named photos, and the classroom teachers and researchers were prominently identified as science authorities. In the authority-participation condition, an authority entered an opinion in the Opinion Area, was well as participated in the discussion, while the authorities made few comments in the attributed condition. An electronic log recorded all comments and time-stamped all writing and reading interactions. Eight video and field observations of class discussion led by the classroom teacher served as comparison to MFK discussion.

Results

Using MFK, three electronic discussion formats are contrasted: all comments are anonymous, all comments are attributed, and comments are attributed plus authority participation (e.g. the classroom teacher). In all three formats, 78% of the students contributed compared to only 15.3% participation in class discussion. Boys also interrupted more than girls and raised their hands more frequently. In comparison, gender participation in electronic discussion was equitable ($t = .53$, $p = .59$). Girls participated *more* than boys in electronic discussion, and less in classroom discussion compared to boys.

Analyses of comment content indicated all electronic discussions were characterized by high levels of scientific conceptual content, elaborations, and question-asking. While there were no significant differences in quality between electronic discussion formats, the quality of elaborations declined with authority participation.

In summary, electronic discourse can improve science discussion by making discussion more accessible to girls, while improving quality with anonymity and less authority participation. As evidence by their ability to generate multiple scientific conceptions as a group and elaborate their ideas, electronic discussion in MFK supports productive discussions in science.

References

Linn, M. C. (1992). The Computer as Learning partner: Can Computer Tools Teach Science? In K. L. Sheingold, G. Roberts, & S. M. Malcolm (Eds.), This year in school science 1991: Technology for teaching and learning, Washington, DC: AAAS.

Hoadley, C. M., & Hsi, S. (1993). A multimedia interface for knowledge building and collaborative learning. Paper presented at the International Computer Human Interaction Conference (InterCHI) '93., Amsterdam, The Netherlands

Representational Momentum and Boundary Extension: Evidence Suggestive of a More General Displacement Mechanism

Timothy L. Hubbard

Department of Psychology
Texas Christian University
Fort Worth, TX 76129
thubbard@gamma.is.tcu.edu

Introduction

Memory for the position of a moving target is displaced forward from the actual position of the target; this pattern has been called *representational momentum* (for review, see Hubbard, 1995). Memory for the boundaries of a picture is displaced outward from the actual location of the boundaries; this pattern has been called *boundary extension* (see Intraub, Bender, & Mangels, 1992). Both representational momentum and boundary extension involve displacement of memory in the direction beyond the actual stimulus, and both types of displacement have been hypothesized to result from dynamic aspects of memory. Given these similarities, it is possible that representational momentum and boundary extension may reflect the operation of a more general displacement mechanism.

In the experiments reported here, observers were presented with simple square stimuli that were either stationary or portrayed as approaching or receding in depth. The magnitude and direction of displacement in depth (i.e., along the line of sight) was assessed.

Methods and Design

In all experiments, observers viewed targets consisting of computer animated displays that portrayed movement in depth by manipulation of visual angle. In Experiments 1 and 2, targets approached, receded, or maintained a constant distance. In Experiment 3, targets approached, receded, moved toward the left, or moved toward the right. In Experiment 4, one of three different sizes of stationary target was shown, and memory was tested after one of two different retention intervals. In Experiment 5, one of five different sizes of stationary target was shown, and after one of three different retention intervals observers received an auditory cue instructing them to indicate the remembered location of either the top or bottom edge of the target.

Results

In Experiments 1 and 2, faster targets were displaced forward (in the direction of motion) and slower targets were displaced backward. In Experiment 3, motion in the picture plane led to greater forward displacement than motion in depth. In Experiments 1, 2, and 3, greater target velocity led to greater forward (less backward) displacement. In Experiments 1 and 4, memory for stationary targets was displaced away from the observer, and in Experiment 4, the initial displacement away from the observer was followed by a subsequent displacement toward the mean stimulus distance. In Experiment 5, memory for both the top and bottom edges of the target was displaced inward toward the center of the target, a pattern consistent with displacement of the target away from the observer.

Discussion

Displacement in depth consistent with boundary extension or representational momentum was observed in all experiments. The data are consistent with both Freyd and Johnson's (1987) two-component model of the time course of representational momentum and with Intraub et al.'s (1992) two-component model of boundary extension. These data support the hypothesis that representational momentum and boundary extension may be special cases of a deeper and more general extrapolation process that biases spatial memory by distorting memory in directions most consistent with past experience (see also Hubbard, in press).

References

Freyd, J. J., & Johnson, J. Q. (1987). Probing the time course of representational momentum. *Journal of Experimental Psychology: Learning, Memory, and Cognition, 13*, 259-269.

Hubbard, T. L. (1995). Environmental invariants in the representation of motion: Implied dynamics and representational momentum, gravity, friction, and centripetal force. *Psychonomic Bulletin & Review, 2*, 322-338.

Hubbard, T. L. (in press). Displacement in depth: Representational momentum and boundary extension. *Psychological Research/Psychologische Forschung.*

Intraub, H., Bender, R. S., & Mangels, J. A. (1992). Looking at pictures but remembering scenes. *Journal of Experimental Psychology: Learning, Memory, and Cognition, 18*, 180-191.

Approximate Spatial Layout Processing in Early Vision

Michael Hucka[1] **and Stephen Kaplan**[1,2]

[1]Department of Electrical Engineering and Computer Science
[2]Department of Psychology
The University of Michigan
Ann Arbor, MI 48109
{hucka,skap}@umich.edu

Imagine yourself running through rough terrain, perhaps fleeing a predator, or perhaps chasing after prey. Your visual system does not have time to scrutinize the countless trees, rocks, and other objects you pass by. What you need most is enough spatial information to avoid obstacles, to orient yourself, to pick a path. In this situation, even a rough sketch of the spatial layout of the environment can provide crucial information.

Without time or opportunity to perform a more careful analysis, an initial estimate of the layout of visible structures may be all the visual system *can* extract. However, this kind of basic spatial information, while devoid of details about shape and other features useful for object recognition, would often be sufficient to fulfill the requirements above. It could also serve as a stepping-stone to more extensive spatial and object analysis in less constrained situations.

Humans and other natural systems are remarkably adept at extracting spatial organization from vision. Yet the form of this information, and the neural information-processing mechanisms used to obtain it, remain poorly understood. To better understand this capability, it would be useful to know how the visual system can make an initial estimate of the spatial layout of a visual input.

The hypothesis we are exploring is that the system automatically and preattentively extracts the approximate locations, sizes and spatial orientations of major elements in the visual input, thereby obtaining a rough sketch of the spatial layout. We are investigating the mechanisms by which the visual system can extract this from monocular views of natural scenes.

Texture is one well-known source of information that the visual system can exploit (Gibson, 1950). Patterns of texture can be obtained even from brief glimpses, during which a scene will appear static and motion cues are unavailable, and at distances and visual angles at which the effectiveness of stereopsis is limited. Visible texture and texture gradients, arising from markings on surfaces or the spatial arrangements of objects, are useful sources of information both for segregating different regions in a scene and for estimating spatial properties such as surface orientation (Watt, 1995).

Texture and texture gradients can be characterized in terms of the local spatial-frequency content at different points in an image (Bajcsy & Lieberman, 1976). It is widely believed that neurons in the primary visual cortex are responsive to spatial-frequency content. The properties of complex cells in particular would make them highly useful as starting points for texture-based analysis (De Valois & De Valois, 1990). These neurons, together with other neural circuits beyond the pri-

mary visual cortex, could serve as part of the mechanisms for *both* performing a rough segmentation of the scene, *and* estimating the general spatial orientations (slant and tilt) of segmented regions. But the question of how both processes can be combined into a single system has rarely been addressed (Krumm & Shafer, 1994). Most existing models of texture-based segmentation assume that textured regions within the visual input are free of systematic distortions due to surface slant; conversely, most models of texture-based shape estimation assume inputs consisting of a single surface.

For spatial layout analysis, the system should also be able to estimate the locations and sizes of the different regions. There is empirical evidence that the visual system computes the locations of simple figures automatically and preattentively. This location information appears to take the form of the centers-of-mass of the regions (Morgan, Hole & Glennerster, 1990). There is also evidence suggesting that the visual system automatically computes the general sizes of visual stimuli (Findlay, Brogan & Wenban-Smith, 1993).

Taken together, the approximate locations, sizes and spatial orientations of major elements in a scene would provide an agent with a rough, initial sketch of the spatial layout. One of the goals of our research is to develop a biologically reasonable model and simulation of this processing.

References

Bajcsy, R., & Lieberman, L. (1976). Texture Gradient as a Depth Cue. *Computer Graphics and Image Processing*, 5, 52–67.

De Valois, R.L, & De Valois, K.K. (1990). *Spatial Vision*. Oxford University Press.

Findlay, J.M., Brogan, B., & Wenban-Smith, M.G. (1993). The Spatial Signal for Saccadic Eye Movements Emphasizes Visual Boundaries, *Perception & Psychophysics*, 53(6), 633–641.

Gibson, J.J. (1950). The Perception of Visual Surfaces. *The American Journal of Psychology*, 58(3), 367–384.

Krumm, J., & Shafer, S.A. (1994). Segmenting Textured 3D Surfaces Using the Space/Frequency Representation, *Spatial Vision*, 8(2), 281–308.

Morgan, M.J., Hole, G.J., & Glennerster, A. (1990). Biases and Sensitivities in Geometrical Illusions. *Vision Research*, 30(11), 1793–1810.

Watt, R.J. (1995). Some Speculations on the Role of Texture Processing in Visual Perception. In *Early Vision and Beyond* (pp. 59–67). Cambridge, MA: MIT Press.

The Influence of Task Factors on Strategy Use

Lisa F. Huffman and **Norman W. Bray**
Department of Psychology
University of Alabama at Birmingham
415 Campbell Hall
Birmingham, AL 35294
lhuffman.civitan@civmail.circ.uab.edu

Introduction

Task factors such as presentation modality may contribute to observed differences in the use strategies. Studies that have manipulated task variables in order to reduce the amount of verbal processing, such as presenting pictures of to-be-remembered information, have shown increased strategy use (Ornstein, Medlin, Stone, & Naus, 1985). Strategy use may also be related to level of contextual support provided by the task. Gauvain (1993) contends material and symbolic tools may transform thinking. The availability of objects or tools (e.g., manipulatives) provides structure for how an individual attends to and remembers information and may influence the use of a strategy. In addition the effects of memory load or task difficulty may influence strategy use . The present study investigated the three interrelated task factors of presentation modality, availability of tools, and memory load in one task across the entire age range of school-aged children.

Method

Participants were 256 children, 64 7-, 9-, 11-, and 17-year-olds. Participants heard a story about a haunted house and a friendly ghost and were asked to remember where objects where located in an imaginary room. Subjects were randomly assigned to either auditory presentation (heard sentences like "The book is above the ghost") or to visual presentation (saw pictures with the book placed above the ghost). Half of the subjects in each presentation modality either had objects available during presentation of to-be-remembered information or objects were made available only at recall. There were four between subjects conditions, auditory-with-objects (AWO), auditory-no-objects (ANO), visual-with-objects (VWO), and visual-no-objects (VNO). The number of items to-be-remembered (memory load) on each of 18 trials ranged from 1 to 7. Strategy use was scored from videotapes of the session by one of two raters with reliability greater than 90%. If no strategy use was observed on a trial, a brief strategy-use interview followed that trial.

Results

Comparisons of the four conditions revealed a significant difference in the overall frequency of strategy use among the conditions, $F(3, 237) = 6.44$, $p<.001$. The overall frequency of strategy use was greater in both with-objects conditions (AWO 95% and VWO 96%) as compared to both no-objects (ANO 89% and VNO 89%) conditions. There was no significant age effect, with the frequency of strategy use similar across the 7-, 9-, 11-, and 17-year-olds (94%, 92%, 93%, and 90%).

How were specific strategies influenced by task factors? There was a developmental decrease in the use of external strategies without orientation (e.g., pointing to objects or target locations or holding or moving of objects without relation to their final location) $F(3, 120) = 14.52$, $p <.001$. The frequency of external strategies with orientation (e.g., laying objects on a board in the pattern seen in the picture or heard in the sequence) increased with age and with memory load, $F(12, 480) = 5.09$, $p <.001$. There were significant developmental decreases in observed rehearsal [$F(3, 237) = 13.09$, $p<.001$] and in reports of imagery [$F(3, 237) = 6.35$, $p<.001$]. For these strategies there were no condition effects.

However, for reported rehearsal there was a main effect of condition, $F(3, 237) = 5.99$, $p<.001$, with more reported rehearsal in both no-object conditions (44% ANO and 42% VNO) as compared to with-object conditions (31% AWO and 25% VWO). There was also a main effect of condition for accuracy, $F(3, 236) = 61.82$, $p<.001$, with VWO (87%) and VNO (83%) conditions having higher accuracy than AWO (73%) and ANO (63%) conditions.

Conclusions

Interestingly, there were no effects of presentation modality on strategy use. However, the overall frequency of strategy use was higher when tools were available than when they were not available for use lending support to Gauvain's (1993) contention that thinking is influenced by the availability of tools in one's environment. Surprisingly, the overall frequency of strategy use did not increase with age. What did change with age were the types of strategies selected for use.

References

Gauvain, M. (1993). The development of spatial thinking in everyday activity. *Developmental Review*, 13, 92-121.

Ornstein, P. A., Medlin, R. G., Stone, B. A., & Naus, M. J. (1985). Retrieving for rehearsal: An analysis of active rehearsal in children's memory. *Developmental Psychology*, 21, 633-641.

Vertical Foreshortening Effect and the L Illusion

Lumei Hui

Psychology Department
SUNY Potsdam
Potsdam, NY 13676
hui1@potsdam.edu

Abstract

Researchers have found that a perceptual error (an overestimation of the vertical line in comparison to the horizontal) usually occurs with a range of about 11-15% for an inverted letter T (IT) figure and about 3-9% for a letter L(L) figure (Avery & Day, 1969; Brosvic & Cohen, 1988; Collani, 1985; Finger & Spelt, 1947; Kunnapas, 1955, 1957, 1958; McBride, Risser, & Slotnick, 1987; Post & Chaderjian, 1987; Ritter, 1917; Rivers, 1901; Schiffman & Thompson, 1974; Wundt, 1859, 1898). Although these two illusory effects are obviously different, they have been considered as the same illusion, namely the vertical-horizontal illusion. Kunnapas (1955) explicitly hypothesized that a part of the illusory effect of the IT figure is caused by the bisection illusion effect. In other words, the difference between those two figures' illusory effects can be explained by the fact that the horizontal line in the IT is bisected by the vertical line. Therefore, to classify these two illusions as one type of illusion became logically acceptable and it has never been challenged. According to the viewerness-thatness-thereness (VTT) model (Hui, 1996), the L and the IT figures represent two different spatial relationships. Therefore, they are caused by different inferential contents as well as processes. The present paper focuses on the L illusion. According to the VTT model, an L figure would evoke a two-dimensional object representation, in which the vertical line represents its vertical dimension and the horizontal line represents its horizontal dimension, and the two-dimensional object is facing a self-assigned viewer. It resembles a situation, such as a wall which stands in the front of a viewer. Its left edge and the foot line correspond to the two lines of the L figure. Thus, the L illusion might be caused by a vertical foreshortening effect. To support this hypothesis, the present researcher reinterpreted the empirical data from an experiment done by Collani(1985). Then, three figures were designed and named as Trapezoid, Triangle, and Fence-like figures. Although each of these figures contains a vertical line (which bisects the horizontal line, just like in an IT figure), they most likely evoke two-dimensional object representations, such as a trapezoid, a triangle, and a fence. Therefore, a vertical foreshortening process would operate as well, producing about 3-9% of illusory effect as the L figure. In other words, the fact that each of their horizontal lines was bisected would not cause their illusory effects as same as the IT illusion (about 11-15%). The results confirmed the predictions.

Japanese and American Teachers' Implicit Theories of Mathematics Learning and Instruction

Jacobs, J.K., Yoshida, M., Fernandez, C. & Stigler, J.W.
University of California, Los Angeles

Background

While American mathematics teachers are having a difficult time shifting from their traditional approach to instruction to the widely recommended "constructivist" approach, Japanese mathematics teachers consistently and successfully use a constructivist approach in their elementary school classrooms (eg. Stigler, Fernandez & Yoshida, 1990). Research suggests that teachers' beliefs about mathematics and instruction exert a large influence on their classroom behavior (eg. Thompson, 1992).

Our study investigates the nature of American and Japanese teachers' implicit theories regarding mathematics learning and instruction.

Method

Subjects were 4 teachers from Los Angeles and 4 teachers from Kobe, Japan. All of the participants were currently teaching elementary school, and had at least 5 years of experience. The American and Japanese subjects were matched to have roughly comparable teaching experience.

Each teacher participated, individually, in a 2 hour session during which they watched and critiqued a videotaped mathematics lesson, filmed in either Nagano, Japan or Chicago, IL. Half the teachers from each country watched the Japanese lesson, and half from each country watched the American lesson. Both lessons cover the same topic (area of a triangle), but exemplify the different teaching strategies typical of their culture. The foreign tapes were dubbed, and the sessions were held in the teacher's native language. Subjects watched one of the math lessons in its entirety stopping the tape whenever they wanted to make a comment. The teachers were specifically asked to address the strengths and weaknesses in the instruction.

Results

We divided all of the teachers' comments about the lessons into "idea units" -- defined as a distinct shift in focus or change in topic. Interrater agreement in identifying idea units was 86%, and agreement in coding the idea units ranged from 85-95%. We found that the majority of the all the teachers' idea units (82%) could be coded as relevant to one of four issues: what students should do during a lesson, how instructors should use language, how instructors should pace lessons and address ability differences, and how instructional materials should be used.

However the Japanese and American teachers had very different things to say regarding these issues. The Japanese teachers wanted to see: signs of students' intellectual engagement, not too much talking by the teacher, a relatively slow pace with a special concern for slow students, and a blackboard neatly depicting a wide array of student responses. By contrast the American teachers preferred: behavioral indications of student engagement, clear language and explanations by the teacher, a relatively fast pace with a special concern for fast students, and that a blackboard be used by the teacher or fast students.

Conclusions

Four issues - student engagement, teachers' language, pace, and material - are the core features of all of our subjects' theories regarding mathematics learning and instruction. These features fit with both the American and the Japanese teachers, however the parameters are "set" differently. These culturally specified parameters map easily onto existant classroom pratices.

Japanese math teachers typically present an interesting problem for their students to work on, and therefore a main requirement is student intellectual engagement. Teachers use minimal direct instruction, as the students figure out solutions on their own. In a problem-solving lesson, students can search for multiple ways to arrive at the same answer, so there is little need for a rapid pace. Teachers are more concerned with the slower students, and ensuring that each child can find at least one approach to the problem. The blackboard becomes a tool to neatly depict the wide variety of children's solution strategies.

American math lessons are typically teacher-centered. Students' behavioral engagement is critical because the instructor is imparting important information, and the students must remain on-task in order to receive the information. The teachers' role is to clearly transmit knowledge, at a pace rapid enough so that students' do not become bored. Classroom tools are used by the teacher and knowledgeable students, and depict only correct answers.

Implications

Both American and Japanese teachers seem to have coherent implicit theories, which map easily onto their differing classroom instructional approaches. We hypothesize that in order for teachers to reform their classroom practices, they must simultaneously reflect on and question their beliefs about learning and instruction.

References

Stigler, J.W., Fernandez, C. & Yoshida, M. (1992). Traditions of school mathematics in Japanese and American elementary classrooms. In P. Nesher, L.P. Steffe, P. Cobb, G. Goldin, & B. Greer (Eds.), *Theories of Mathematical Learning*. Hillsdale, NJ: Erlbaum.

Thompson, A.G. (1992). Teachers beliefs and conceptions. In D.A. Grouws (Ed.), *Handbook of Research on Mathematics Teaching and Learning*. New York: Macmillan.

A Hybrid Learning Model of Abductive Reasoning

Todd R. Johnson[1], Jiajie Zhang[2] and Hongbin Wang[3]
Division of Medical Informatics, Department of Pathology[1]
Department of Psychology[2,3]
Center for Cognitive Science[1,2]
The Ohio State University
Columbus, Ohio 43210
{johnson.25, zhang.52, wang.190}@osu.edu

Introduction

Abduction is the process of generating a best explanation for a set of observations. Symbolic models of abductive reasoning tend to be far too search-intensive, whereas connectionist models have difficulty explaining higher level abductive reasoning, such as the generation and revision of explanatory hypotheses. In addition, abductive tasks appear to have deliberate and implicit components: people generate and modify explanations using a series of recognizable steps, but these steps appear to be guided by an implicit hypothesis evaluation process.

We propose a hybrid learning model for abduction that tightly integrates a symbolic Soar model for deliberately forming and revising hypotheses with Echo, a connectionist model for implicitly evaluating explanations (Thagard, 1989). In this model, Soar's symbolic knowledge compilation mechanism, chunking, acquires rules for forming and revising hypotheses and for taking actions based on the evaluations of these hypotheses. Thus, chunking models the problem solver's shift from deliberate to automatic reasoning. To complement this, Echo learns to provide better hypothesis evaluations by acquiring explanatory strengths based on the frequencies of events from past experience. Since Echo does not have a learning mechanism, we have extended it by adding the Rescorla-Wagner (1972) learning rule.

Motivation for a Hybrid Model

The hybrid model is motivated by several observations and empirical results concerning the relationship between symbolic and connectionist processes and human abductive reasoning.

To successfully solve abductive problems people must learn to quickly generate possible hypotheses for one or more observations, and then integrate these hypotheses into a coherent explanation for the entire set of observations. Symbolic search based approaches have traditionally performed well at modeling hypothesis generation and modification. Likewise, symbolic knowledge compilation can learn explicit rules based on a single problem solving episode, but it cannot easily learn explanatory strengths from previous experience. In contrast, connectionist learning techniques can easily acquire explanatory strengths, but cannot quickly acquire explicit rules.

Research on implicit acquisition and use of event frequencies supports the hybrid Soar/Echo architecture. When conditional probabilities and base rates of occurrence are presented explicitly in terms of numeric values, they are very difficult to learn and utilize (see Kahneman, Slovic & Tversky, 1982). However, when they are presented in terms of real events and occurrences, they can often be learned implicitly and used correctly (e.g., Christensen-Szalanski, & Bushyhead, 1981). A number of studies indicate that the learning of frequency of occurrence is usually implicit (unconscious) and automatic. The Soar/Echo hybrid architecture is consistent with these results, because Echo appears to Soar as an opaque mechanism that automatically and constantly provides confidence values for hypotheses.

Acknowledgments

This research was supported by Office of Naval Research Grant No. N00014-95-1-0241.

References

Christensen-Szalanski, J. J. J., & Bushyhead, J. B. (1981). Physicians' use of probabilistic information in a real clinical setting. *Journal of Experimental Psychology: Human Perception and Performance, 7* (4), 928-935.

Kahneman, D., Slovic, P., & Tversky, A. (1982). *Judgment under uncertainty: Heuristics and biases.* New York: Cambridge University Press.

Rescorla, R. A., & Wagner, A. R. (1972). A theory of Pavlovian conditioning: The effectiveness of reinforcement and nonreinforcement. In A. H. Black & W. F. Prokasy (Eds.), *Classical Conditioning II: Current Research and Theory* (pp. 64-69). New York: Appleton-Century-Crofts.

Thagard, P. (1989). Explanatory Coherence. *Behavioral and Brain Sciences*, 12, 435-502.

Measuring the Sounds of Silence: Latency and Duration of Word-Initial Plosives

Alan H. Kawamoto, Christopher T. Kello and **Kenneth A. Bame**
Psychology Board of Studies
University of California, Santa Cruz
Santa Cruz, CA 95060
{ahk,kello,kabame}@cats.ucsd.edu

Naming latency, the latency of the onset of acoustic energy arising from a speeded verbal response, is the primary dependent variable in the vast majority of psycholinguistic tasks. Unfortunately, naming latency is not a valid measure of response latency for words beginning with plosive consonants (the obstruents /p/, /t/, /k/, /b/, /d/, and /g/, and the affricates, /ch/ and /j/) because the onset of acoustic energy occurs 50-100 ms after the articulators are in their target position. This delay arises because airflow through the vocal tract must be occluded while pressure is built up prior to the pressure's explosive release that finally generates acoustic energy. Thus, somewhat paradoxically, the onset of acoustic energy marks the end of plosive consonants, not their beginning.

A related problem stemming from the articulatory characteristics of plosives is that naming latency conflates response latency and the duration of the initial phoneme for words beginning with plosive consonants when the standard naming task is used. That is, for pairs of words matched on the initial plosive phoneme, response latency differences cannot be distinguished from initial phoneme duration differences. It is important to distinguish these two dependent variables to determine the locus of on-line processing difficulties: Response latency assesses processing difficulties that arise before the response initiation, whereas duration assesses processing difficulties that arise after a response initiation.

To solve the problem of when the articulation of a plosive begins, we introduce the post-vocalic naming task. Unlike the standard naming task in which the participant is silent immediately preceding the response, the participant says "uuhhh" before the stimulus is presented and continues doing so until producing the response. Thus, response latency corresponds to the offset of the "uuhhh" vocalization (the vocalic offset latency), and the initial phoneme duration corresponds roughly to the duration of the silent gap (the gap duration). The latency for the plosive's release corresponds to naming latency of the standard naming task (the vocalization onset latency).

To determine the locus of processing difficulties, we consider the effect of consistency of pronunciation for words whose vowels have an irregular pronunciation. We compared 16 low frequency words with irregular pronunciations with 16 low frequency words with regular pronunciations matched on initial phoneme, printed frequency, bigram frequency, and number of neighbors.

All words began with a single plosive consonant. The stimuli were presented on a computer, and participants responded as quickly and accurately as possible. The verbal responses were digitized using a 16-bit audio board and stored for off-line analysis. After the experiment, we analyzed the responses to determine whether a word was correctly pronounced. Only correct responses were further analyzed. An algorithm was used to determine the vocalic offset latency and the vocalization onset latency, and the gap duration was simply the difference of these two latencies. Both the vocalic offset latency and gap duration were 14 ms longer for irregular words compared to regular words. The vocalization onset latency was 28 ms longer for irregular words compared to regular words.

Consistent with previous studies, response latencies for irregular words were longer than for regular words. In addition, the longer initial phoneme duration indicated that there was a processing difficulty for irregular words that arose after the response had been initiated. The existence of a duration effect provides evidence that participants begin pronunciation as soon as the initial phoneme of a word is known and do not wait until the entire pronunciation.

Acknowledgements

This work was supported in part by grants from the faculty senate and the Social Sciences Division of UC Santa Cruz.

Divergent Inference in Dynamic Decision Making

Jinwoo Kim and **Hun-Joon Park**
Cognitive Information Engineering Lab
Department of Business Administration
Yonsei University, Seoul, 120-749, Korea
jinwoo@bubble.yonsei.ac.kr

Introduction

People make decisions about various dynamic problems, ranging from very simple to extremely complex ones (Brehmer 1990; Diehl & Sterman 1995). This study proposes a framework of dynamic decision making based on the theory of scientific discovery in dual spaces (Klahr & Dunbar 1988). Two experiments using computer simulated management games were conducted to examine the relationship between the search strategies in the dual spaces and final performances in decision making.

Mental Model and Dynamic Decision Making

Brehmer (1990) views dynamic decision making as the process of achieving control over a system in order to produce a desired outcome. In order to control a system, a decision maker must have a mental model of the dynamic system it seeks to control. Mental models are the mechanisms whereby humans are able to generate descriptions of the system's purpose, explain system functions, and predict future system states (Rouse & Morris, 1986).

Our framework views dynamic decision making as a search process in dual problem spaces. Whereas scientific discovery involves the hypothesis and experimental spaces, dynamic decision making involves the model and decision spaces. In the decision space, people make judgments and choices based on the mental model. In the model space, people search for an appropriate mental model using the INFERENCE operator. The INFERENCE expresses a relation not explicit in the problem descriptions (Johnson-Laird & Byrne, 1991). We hypothesize that generating alternative hypothetical relations by INFERENCE is crucial for avoiding traps in dynamic decision making, because alternative relations produced by divergent inferences aid people to construct more comprehensive mental models, and thereby prevent people from making haphazard and irrational decisions.

Experiment Design and Results

In the first experiment, we use two business simulation games. One is simpler, having two clearly differentiated states, normal and impasse. The other is more complex, because there is no clear beginning of an impasse phase, but rather a gradual worsening as would occur in real life. Subjects were randomly allocated either to a Single (one person) or Pair (group of two people) group, and asked to play either the simple or the complex game. All experimental sessions were videotaped for concurrent verbal protocol analysis.

Results from the first experiment exhibit interesting interaction effects between the complexity of problems and the Single/Pair groups. In the simple problem, the Pair group significantly outperformed the Single group [t(10) = 2.23, P(| t | ≥ T) =0.0156], whereas the variance was not as significant for the complex problem. We can explain this interaction with the diversity of inferences made by subjects. For the complex problem, no significant difference was found between Single and Pair groups in terms of the diversity of inferences. However, for the simple problem, subjects' behavior differed depending on the two phases. In the normal phase, there was no difference between the Single and Pair groups. However, in the impasse phase, Pair groups made significantly more diverse INFERENCES (t(10) = 2.7680, P(| t | ≥ T) = 0.01).

In the second experiment, two different methods for increasing the diversity of inferences were tested with the complex problem. One such method is to force the subjects to infer divergently. For each trial, the experimenter asked subjects to think of at least three different ways in which their decision would affect the other entities. The second method is to provide subjects with a map which shows the possible inferences that can be made. The results indicate that whereas direct enforcement is an effective way of improving performance (F(3,18)=13.22, Pr > 0.002), the map does not have any impact on the final performance of the subjects.

In summary, the diversity of inferences turns out to be a critical factor in dynamic decision making, and only a very strong manipulation, such as direct enforcement, can help to increase the diversity on complex problems.

References

Brehmer, B. (1990) Strategies in real-time dynamic decision making. In R. Horgarth (Ed.), *Insights from decision making*. Chicago: Univ. of Chicago, 262-279.

Diehl, E. & Sterman, J. (1995). Effects of Feedback Complexity on Dynamic Decision Making. *Organizational Behavior and Human Decision Processes*, 52 (2), 198-215.

Johnson-Laird, P. N. & Byrne, R.M.J. (1991). *Deduction*. Hillsdale, NJ: Erbaum.

Klahr, D. & Dunbar, K. (1998). Dual Space Search During Scientific Reasoning. *Cognitive Science*, 12:1-48.

Rouse, W. & Morris, N. (1986). On Looking Into the Black Box: Prospects and Limits in the Search for Mental Models. *Psychological Bulletin*, 100 (3). 349-363.

Working Memory Can Explain Antisaccade Failures Without Inhibition

Daniel Y. Kimberg
Cognitive Neuroscience Section, NINDS, NIH
10 Center Drive MSC 1440
Bethesda, MD 20892-1440
kimberg@helix.nih.gov

Introduction

Claims about inhibitory processes in the prefrontal cortex are generally supported by evidence of inhibitory failures. Such failures are considered to occur when a highly prepotent action – one with a high prior probability of being appropriate – is selected instead of a more contextually appropriate, goal-directed response. Patterns of inhibitory failure are most often reported in human subjects with frontal lobe damage, in human infants and young children, and in normal subjects under cognitive load (or distraction). We argue that in many of these cases, a simpler account of the data would characterize the system at fault as a working memory system, and not as an inhibitory module per se.

Anti-Saccades

In the antisaccade task (Guitton, Buchtel, and Douglas, 1985), subjects are required to respond to a visually presented cue by looking not at the cue itself, but to a location on the opposite side of a fixation point.

Guitton, Buchtel, and Douglas (1985) first reported that frontal-damaged patients have trouble with this task, hypothesizing a frontal lobe role in aborting inappropriate behaviors. Roberts, Hager, and Heron (1994) found that a working memory load caused both slower reaction times and more errors in the antisaccade task, while leaving reflexive pro-saccades unaffected. They described an interaction in which working memory allows one to maintain and use information to be used in inhibiting highly prepotent responses.

Modeling Antisaccade Failures

We propose that working memory and inhibitory processes are not independently necessary to explain this type of data. Since a working memory system should contain all the information necessary to determine the correct response, it is unnecessary to postulate an independent process of inhibiting the prepotent response, except in the implicit sense that the two responses are in competition.

Our model of antisaccade failures is implemented within the framework used by Kimberg and Farah (1993) to simulate other data from patients with prefrontal damage. Within this framework, we characterize the processes that produce behavior in terms of response discrimination. Two

sources of activation (of the four included in the model) are especially important to this task:

Baseline strength reflects the long-term history of a response's use. Responses that have been more useful in the past will generally tend to be activated to a higher level. **Working memory activation** reflects the contribution of relevant declarative representations, such as might be created by giving the subject instructions.

The simulation of the anti-saccade task is extremely simple. Two potential responses compete for activation: **look-towards** and **look-away**. **Look-towards** has a much higher baseline strength. However, a declarative representation of the anti-saccade instructions also provides activation to **look-away**. Normally this representation is only weakly activated. However, when the subject has been given the instructions to perform the anti-saccade task, it is maintained at a higher level of activation.

Since it is only the contribution from working memory that allows the system to override the strong bias in favor of looking towards stimuli, any form of weakening working memory will disproportionately affect the antisaccade task. A memory load (as in Roberts et al., 1994) may be simulated by reducing by a constant factor the activations of all working memory representations. We can also simulate the effect of prefrontal damage, as in our previous model, by weakening associations among working memory elements. Either manipulation has the effect of weakening the effect of instructions in favor of the prepotent response – an apparent disinhibition without damage to an inhibitory module.

References

Kimberg, D.Y. & Farah, M.F. (1993). A unified account of cognitive impairments following frontal lobe damage: The role of working memory in complex, organized behavior. *Journal of Experimental Psychology: General, 122*, 411-428.

Guitton, D., Buchtel, H.A., & Douglas, R.M. (1985). Frontal lobe lesions in man cause difficulties in suppressing reflexive glances and in generating goal-directed saccades. *Experimental Brain Research, 58,* 455-472.

Roberts, R.J., Hager, L.D., & Heron, C. (1994). Prefrontal cognitive processes: Working memory and inhibition in the antisaccade task. *Journal of Experimental Psychology: General, 123*, 374-393.

Cognitive GOMS for Submarine Experts

Susan S. Kirschenbaum
Naval Undersea Warfare Center Division
Newport, RI 02841
Kirsch@c223.npt.nuwc.navy.mil

Wayne D. Gray, and **Brian D. Ehret**
George Mason University
Fairfax, VA
gray@gmu.edu   behret@gmu.edu

Introduction

Decision making is complicated by a dynamically changing, event-driven environment and ambiguous information. Analyzing the cognitive process under these conditions presents challenges to theory and methodology. We report such an analysis for data obtained from a study of submarine Approach Officers (AOs) using a simulated submarine combat system.

Method and Analysis

The subjects were six expert submarine officers. The task they performed was locating an enemy submarine and deciding how to respond to it. Their information gathering and own ship (OS) maneuvers were mediated by a computer operator (called OS-op), just as they are aboard ship. Two hours of data (two to four scenarios) were collected for each AO.

Scenarios were transcribed and each was encoded by two independent coders. Because of the nature of the problem solving task and the interaction mechanics, only *cognitive* operators were encoded.

Results and Discussion

Inter-rater reliabilities on operator encodings for the task scenarios ranged from Kappa = 0.75, Z = 22 to Kappa = 0.64, Z = 16.5, all highly significant (Cohen's Kappa corrects for chance matches).

Operator	Protocol Example
Information	
query	"let's ...see if we can gain our alpha on narrowband"
receive	"we're minus 12.3 SNR"
derive	"the target maneuvered at some point there"
Actions	
maneuverOS	"and let's come up to 12 knots "
setTracker	"Okay,; so I want to track the merchant"
tweakParam	"Can we get down to 15 knots, there we go"
enterSolution	"Why don't you update your solution"

Table 1: Operators and protocol examples

Of the eight encoding operators, 75% were task relevant (Kirschenbaum, Gray, Ehret, & Miller, 1996). These seven relevant operators (see Table 1 for examples) fell into two categories, information-seeking, mean = 90.8%, SD = 3.8 and action-orders (e.g., change course). mean = 9.2%, SD = 3.8.

A shallow goal structure, never more than three deep, accounted for all of the operators. Figure 1 shows levels 1 and 2. The only Level 3 goal, SUPERVISE-OS-op, is not shown.

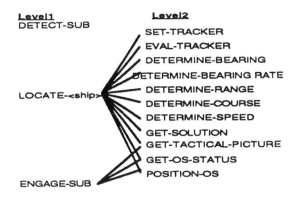

Figure 1: Level 1 and level 2 goals.

We believe that when a goal pops, it returns information to a knowledge schema structure in long-term working memory (Ericsson, & Kintsch, 1995). The schema and/or events determine the next goal.

Acknowledgments

S. Kirschenbaum's work has been jointly sponsored by Office of Naval Research (ONR) (Program element 61153N) and by NUWC's IR Program, as Project A10328. The work at GMU was supported in part by a grant from ONR (#N00014-95-1-0175) to W. Gray. Approved for public release

References

Ericsson, K. A., & Kintsch, W. (1995). Long-term working memory. *Psychological Review, 102*(2), 211-245.

Kirschenbaum, S. S. , Gray, W. D., Ehret, B. D., & Miller, S. L. (1996). When Using The Tool Interferes With Doing The Task. In *CHI'96 Conference Companion.*

An Explication of the Concept of Breakdown in Heidegger, Leontjev, and Dewey

Timothy Koschmann
Dept. of Medical Education
Southern Illinois University
School of Medicine
Springfield, IL 62711
tkoschmann@siumed.edu

Kari Kuutti
Dept. of Information
Processing Science
University of Oulu
Finland
kuutti@rieska.oulu.fi

Larry Hickman
Center for Dewey Studies
Southern Illinois University
Carbondale, IL 62901
lhickman@siu.edu

Heidegger, the German phenomenologist, Leontjev, the Russian psychologist, and Dewey, the American Pragmatist, held surprisingly similar views on the role of breakdown or failure as a means of revealing the nature of the world around us.

For Heidegger, the resources by which we conduct our day-to-day activities do not usually require (nor do they attract) our conscious awareness. Heidegger indicated (1953/1962), however, that when ongoing, non-reflective practice is interrupted, these equipmental aspects of the world become "lit up" or brought "into view". Resources for Heidegger can present themselves in different states or modes of being (e.g., "Available", "Unavailable", "Occurent") with respect to our ongoing activity (Dreyfus, 1991). The status of an entity can, in turn, affect the nature of our activity and our understanding of the object in use. It is the degree of breakdown, however, that determines the status of an entity with respect to our purposes.

Leontjev's (1978) development of breakdown hinges on the analytic distinction he makes among activities, actions, and operations. In this context, to be skilled in using a tool means that one has created a set of tool-using operations. With a large set of well-learnt operations, a tool can really become transparent in the work and all attention can be focused to the object of actions. On the other hand, when the necessary conditions for an operation are absent, the chain of operations becomes transformed ("unfolded") back into an action.

Dewey's notion of breakdown is related to his views on sensory excitation, stimulus and response, and the habit-formation function in the lives of complex organisms. Conflicts can produce a state of disequilibration. Recovery from such an "indeterminate situation" occurs, for Dewey, through the process of "inquiry", which he defined as "the controlled or directed transformation of an indeterminate situation into one that is so determinate in its constituent distinctions and relations as to convert the elements of the original situation into a unified whole" (Boydston, 1986, p. 108).

These three descriptions of breakdown all produce models in which the disruption of ongoing, non-reflective activity results in a shift to a more reflective stance. Though their terminology may vary ("absorbed coping" and "deliberative responding" for Heidegger, transforming "operations" to "actions" for Leontjev, "habits" and "disequilibrium" for Dewey), the process underlying the models they describe appears very similar. The way in which each author describes this process, however, reflects the different philosophical and historical traditions within which each worked. Heidegger's phenomenologic and existential account focuses on how the phenomenon of breakdown is experienced by the individual. His perspective, therefore, is personal and emotive. His treatment of breakdown is also the most elaborate. Leontjev, rooted as he was in dialectical materialism, produced an account that focused on the activity itself and means of production. No less practical is Dewey's analysis, but instead of focusing on the activity *per se*, his focus is on the effects of breakdown on the acting organism, producing a more naturalistic account.

Both Leontjev and Dewey provide implicit learning models within their descriptions of breakdown. The transformation of an action to a series of operations in Leontjev can be considered a mechanism for learning (at least with respect to skill acquisition). Similarly, Dewey provides a mechanism for habit formation. Further, Dewey's notion of inquiry provides a method for learning that he elaborated on several levels.

How might these views on breakdown inform instructional practice? If Heidegger is correct in his claim that breakdown leads to reflection, then the argument can be made that one way of facilitating learning is to induce breakdown on the part of learners. For Dewey, it is the job of the teacher to raise questions and issues that will produce disequilibration or a problematic situation. It is in this way that breakdown becomes a catalyst for both learning and for all productive thought. He makes clear, however, that simply inducing breakdown is not enough—teachers must also support learners in their resulting process of inquiry.

References

Boydston, J.A. (Ed.) (1986). *The collected works of John Dewey: The Later Works, 1925–1953, Vol. 12*. Carbondale, IL: Southern Illinois University Press.

Dreyfus, H. (1991). *Being-in-the-World: A commentary on Heidegger's Being and Time*. Cambridge, MA: MIT Press.

Heidegger, M. (1953). *Sein und Zeit* (8th Ed.). Tübingen, Germany: Max Niemeyer Verlag [translated in 1962 as *Being and time* (J. Macquarrie, & E. Robinson, Trans.). New York: Harper & Row].

Leontjev, A.N. (1978). *Activity, Consciousness, Personality*. Englewood Cliffs, NJ: Prentice Hall.

Order Effects in Abductive Reasoning

Josef F. Krems[1] and **Todd R. Johnson**[2]
Technical University of Chemnitz, Germany[1]
Division of Medical Informatics, Dept. of Pathology, The Ohio State University[2]
krems@phil.tu-chemnitz.de, johnson.25@osu.edu

Abduction is the process of constructing a plausible explanation for a set of observations. It is the fundamental type of reasoning in many complex tasks such as scientific discovery, troubleshooting and diagnosis. Many abductive problems require multicausal explanations in which a conjunction of individual hypotheses together explain the data. In our mental-model theory of multicausal abductive reasoning and skill acquisition, abduction is viewed as the sequential comprehension and integration of data into a single situation model (Johnson & Krems, 1994). Comprehension and integration are accomplished using satisficing search. The model has been implemented in Soar.

One prediction of the model is that order of data (e.g., symptoms in diagnostic reasoning) affects the generation of multicausal explanations. In a first experiment 20 subjects were shown a series of input-output data from a technical device. The order of data presentation was systematically varied. The subjects had to construct a causal explanation for the data using previously acquired causal knowledge that enables subjects to predict the behavior of the device given any input to the device. Results showed that explanations for previously viewed data systematically constrained explanations for new data. Experienced problem solvers were more affected by order of data presentation than novices.

In a second experiment 10 subjects were shown all the data at once, instead of sequentially. The sequence of data interpretation therefore was subject-paced and subject-guided. It could again be shown that the multicausal explanation depended on the sequence, and not just the "causal implications" of the evidence.

The results point to a highly sequential nature of applying causal knowledge. The results are also used to evaluate different types of computational models of abductive reasoning with regard to psychological plausibility. A computational-model implemented in the Soar architecture will be outlined that fits the empirical constraints. It will be compared to "quasi-normative models" like set-covering and the Theory of Explanatory Coherence (Thagard, 1989).

References

Johnson, T. R., Krems, J., & Amra, N. K. (1994). A computational model of human abductive skill and its acquisition. In A. Ram & K. Eiselt (Eds.), *Proceedings of the Sixteenth Annual Conference of the Cognitive Science Society* (pp. 463-468): Lawrence Erlbaum Associates.

Thagard, P. (1989). Explanatory Coherence. *Behavioral and Brain Sciences*, 12, 435-502.

Category-Based Similarity

Kenneth J. Kurtz

Department of Psychology
Jordan Hall, Bldg 420
Stanford University
Stanford, CA 94305-2130
kurtz@psych.stanford.edu

A basic component of human cognition is the ability to comprehend perceived stimuli in terms of stored knowledge. Recent proposals about categorization (eg. Murphy & Medin, 1985) have emphasized the role of theory–like knowledge while questioning the usefulness of similarity as an explanatory construct. It has been suggested that similarity may depend upon rather than determine conceptual structure.

The problem of *respects* for similarity (Medin, Gentner & Goldstone, 1993) is that the similarity of two items is not meaningful without specifying the nature of the comparison. One approach to this problem is to interpret the role of theories in categorization as providing constraints on similarity-based comparison (Medin, 1989). A principled mechanism (ie. a theory) might answer the question: if a concept representation is feature-based, then what features should be used and in what manner?

In order to keep similarity grounded, it is often computed over a feature space of object properties based only on surface perceptual appearance. But in order to account for the range of categorization ability, this notion of similarity must be expanded to include conceptual commonalities (see Goldstone, 1994). The extent to which any two stimuli are alike has a concrete component which is inherent in the perceived structure of the environment *and* an abstract component which is established according to the interaction between people and their environment.

By learning to categorize stimuli in terms of useful abstractions and consequences (such as labels or functions), concept representations develop which capture statistical regularities and which also reflect imposed or category-based similarities that arise from the roles objects take on for the learner in natural experience. Such representations serve as raw material for the appropriate generalization of prior knowledge to novel cases according to a sophisticated, yet constrained similarity mechanism.

Methods

The present research goal is twofold: 1) to assert claims about the flexibility and dependence of similarity, but 2) to explore through behavioral and computational approaches a mechanism of concept formation which produces rich representations and much-needed respects.

This study examines the hypothesis that concept representations are constructed as an integration of perceived structure and learned category-level information. It is predicted that similarity ratings collected from Ss who learn a categorization will systematically diverge from controls. Stimuli from the same learned class should be rated as more similar by those Ss with category knowledge since their learned representations grow closer to reflect the commonality.

Subjects were told they would learn about a set of micro-organisms (realistic line drawings) and then apply their knowledge. In the control condition, the study phase consisted of viewing the stimuli and judging relatedness to the prior stimulus. In the categorization (Cat) condition, Ss also saw three labels and were asked to make a classification judgement. Ss learned with feedback until they could correctly classify the set. After the study phase, Ss in both conditions were shown all pairs and asked to rate similarity.

Results and Discussion

As predicted, Cat Ss rated pairs drawn from the same class as more similar than did the naive Ss. However, there was no evidence of lower similarity ratings by Cat Ss for pairs drawn from different classes. Additional analyses showed that the amount of between group difference was greater when the coherence of the class from which same-category pairs were drawn was lower. The evidence is suggestive of a shift in underlying representation as a function of category learning.

Such a mechanism is naturally instantiated in terms of connectionist models which form internal representations while learning complex input-target mappings. Such simulations were carried out and results suggest that a brain-style mechanism can account for the behavioral findings of category-based similarity.

References

Goldstone, R.L. (1994). The role of similarity in categorization: Providing a groundwork. *Cognition*, 52, 125–157.

Medin, D.L. (1989). Concepts and conceptual strcture. *American Psychologist*, 44, 1469–1481.

Medin, D.L., Goldstone, R.L. & Gentner, D. (1993). Respects for similarity. *Psychological Review*, 100, 254–278.

Murphy, G.L. & Medin, D.L. (1985). The role of theories in conceptual coherence. *Psychological Review*, 92, 289–316.

Image Schema of Emotion in Drawing Task

Takashi Kusumi

Department of Human System Science
Tokyo Institute of Technology
Ohokayama, Meguro-ku, Tokyo 152 JAPAN
kusumi@tp.titech.ac.jp

Introduction

The present study attempts to test experimentally several assumptions raised by cognitive linguists. They assume that the image schematic structures underly the metaphorical expressions on emotions Cognitive linguists analyze emotion concepts such as anger(Lakoff, 1987), happiness(Kovecses, 1991) using linguistic materials. This study introduces a new method: first, direct method to explore image schema by having subjects drawn emotion concepts, second, to compared the image schema of four drawings of emotion concepts.

Method

Subjects

Two hundred and fifteen Japanese university students.

Procedure

The Production Task. Subjects(N=120) drew nonrepresentational each image of two emotions(either anger and happiness or sadness and hope) and verbally described the emotional state.

The Rating Task. Subjects(N=96) rated seven Japanese emotional concepts(anger, sadness, hope, happiness, love, disappear, and anxiety) on seven bipolar scales (e.g. up-down, in-out, balance-unbalance).

Results and Discussions

Figures most frequently drawn by subjects

Two judges classified the image drawings based on configurational similarity. Anger is explosion(35%), jagged forms(32%), and thick lines(15%); sadness is drops(29%), darkness(18%), and fall(12%); happiness is circular forms(57%), radiation(19%), and curving forms(12%); hope is radiation(41%), diffusion(20%), and ascending lines(8%). Fig.1 shows the figures most frequently each emotion concept. The top three drawings covered almost 70 % of the each emotion indicating inter-subjects commonality. Table 1 shows the orientation and the form of the drawings. The results shown in Table 1 indicated that relative frequency of physical characteristics of image drawings correspond to the relative

TABLE 1: Characteristics of Image Drawings(%)

Emotion	Anger[1]	Sadness[2]	Happiness[1]	Hope[2]
Orientation				
up	20.6	2.0	14.3	32.7
horizontal	23.8	4.1	7.9	0.0
down	0.0	44.9	0.0	4.1
divergent	41.3	2.0	19.0	32.7
other	14.3	46.9	58.7	30.6
Shape				
angular	46.0	36.7	11.1	26.5
round	4.8	28.6	71.4	36.7
mixed	47.6	30.6	15.9	36.7
other	1.6	4.1	1.6	0.0

Note [1]N=63 [2]N=49

percentage of word frequency in the verbal descriptions of production task. Result of which the word EXPLOSION(24%) elicited from anger, DOWN(14%), SINKING(10%) and DARK(10%) from sadness; LIGHT(43%) and EXTENSION(18%) from happiness ; LIGHT(21%) from hope.

Major image schema of emotion

Correspondence between image drawings and descriptions could be summarized and expressed as the following image schema, which accord well with the image schema proposed by cognitive linguists(e.g., Kovecses,1991; Lakoff,1987).

(1) ANGER IS EXPLOSION OF CONTAINER. The image of anger is DIFFUSION. It is a HOT FLUID in a PRESSURIZED CONTAINER and the hot fluid pressed out of it. The rating data indicates that anger is energetic(94%) and hot(81%).

(2a)SADNESS IS DOWN. The image of sadness is oriented DOWN(45%) of drops or tear. In the rating data, sadness is DOWN(95%) and DARK(99%).

(2b) SADNESS IS DARK. The image of sadness is DARKNESS(18%) under rain or fog. Some examples of descriptions are " I can't see anything" and "The future seems to be dark".

(3) HAPPY IS UP. The image of happy is jumping or spreading of ROUND shape(71%) and oriented UP(14%). The rating data indicates that happy is UP(89%).

(4) HOPE IS DIFFUSION OF LIGHT. The image of hope is an extension of LIGHT, sunshine, future and possibility. In the rating data, hope is LIGHT(93%).

References

Kovecses, Z. (1991) Happiness: A definitional effort. *Metaphor and Symbolic Activity*, **6 (1)**, 29-46.

Lakoff, G. (1987) *Women, fire, and dangerous things:* University Chicago Press.

Anger [Explosion]   Happiness [Circle]   Sadness [Drop]   Hope [Radiation]

Fig. 1: Figures Most Frequently Drawn by the Subjects

Self-Explanation in Concept Learning

Sylvie Leclerc and **Serge de Maisonneuve**
Département des sciences de l'éducation
Université du Québec à Rimouski
Rimouski, Québec, Canada G5L 3A1
sylvie_leclerc@uqar.uquebec.ca

This abstract reports about a preliminary research relating self-explanation to theory-based categorization. Main question and method are outlined.

Self-explanation is the process of generating an explanation for oneself in the course of learning activities. Many studies showed that this process is associated with problem-solving successes (Chi et al., 1989, 1994; Pirolli and Recker, 1994). These studies considered varied kinds of learning material: worked-out example, expository text. We want to know if similar results would occur within the context of classical concept learning.

This question is put in light with the studies of Wisniewski and Medin (1994) about the interaction of theory and data in concept learning. Since people's intuitive theories have been shown to determine the kind of rules they produce to define a concept and, on the other hand, self-explanation is thought to work by relating material to be studied with pre-existing theory (VanLehn, Jones and Chi, 1992; VanLehn and Jones, 1993), it seems, that in examining the impact of self-explanation in concept learning we could learn more about the constructive process of conceptual category. Moreover, the type of concept learning task using natural-like concept like *drawing made by a creative child* as proposed by Wisniewski and Medin (1994) is more similar to many real-life learning situations than is artificial concept learning and we would benefit to know if the self-explanation effect can be reproduce in those learning situations.

Hypothesis

Wisniewski and Medin (1994) results establish that when subjects can activate intuitive theories in the context of concept learning, they tend to use principles and hypothesis to make sense of the characteristics of the data. Consequently, their rules are loaded with abstract features and can be described as hierarchical since they include abstract properties defined by other properties that are themselves abstract or concrete. As the self-explanation process is thought to amplify the instanciation of intuitive theories, we should observe an augmentation of rules embedding abstract features when induced to self-explanation subjects engage in concept learning task. Our main question is then : does eliciting self-explanation in the context of concept learning within a significant domain modify rules and properties produced? We compare specialization rules that construct target categories by

adding properties to a pre-existing conceptual category and descriptive rules that construct target categories by listing properties associated to. Eliciting self-explanation steer subjects to search for relations between the data and their prior knowledge, consequently they produce more abstract properties, the presence of a significant context enable them to anchor the constructive process in an already made conceptual category producing a specialization rule.

Two hypothesis are considered: H1 : Eliciting self-explanation in the context of concept learning augments rules based on abstract properties. H2 : Eliciting self-explanation in the context of concept learning within a significant domain augments specialization rules.

Method

This study compares performances of subjects exposed to four experimental conditions in a non-incremental rule-learning task in which they produce a classification rule by examining categories of items. Subjects are randomly assigned to a condition where they will be exposed to elicitation to self-explanation or not and where they will have a significant domain for the concept formation task or not in a 2 x 2 factorial design.

References

Chi, M.T.H., Bassok, M., Lewis, M., Reimann, P., & Glaser, R. (1989). Self-explanations: How students study and use examples in learning to solve problems. *Cognitive Science, 13*, 145-182.

Chi, M.T.H., de Leeuw, N., Chiu, M.H., LaVancher, C. (1994). Eliciting self-explanations improves understanding. *Cognitive Science, 18*, 439-477.

Pirolli, P.L. & Recker, M. (1994). Learning strategies and transfer in the domain of programming. *Cognition and Instruction, 12*, 235-275.

VanLehn, K., & Jones, R.M. (1993). What mediates the self-explanation effect. *Journal of the Learning Sciences, 2*, 1-59.

VanLehn, K.A., Jones, R.M. & Chi, M.T.H. (1992). A model of the self-explanation effect. *Journal of the Learning Sciences, 2*, 1-59.

Wisniewski, E.J., & Medin, D.L. (1994). On the interaction of theory and data in concept learning. *Cognitive Science, 18*, 221-283.

Learning together: The effect of materials on individuals and pairs

Adrienne Y. Lee and **Krisela Rivera**

Department of Psychology
New Mexico State University
Las Cruces, New Mexico 80003
alee@nmsu.edu; krivera@crl.nmsu.edu

With the increased availability of computers for schools, educators and researchers have begun to develop tutoring systems and training programs to improve students' learning experiences. However, due to limited resources, students must often share a computer with other students. Although some work has been performed on collaboration when students are doing problem solving, no systematic study of differences due to materials has been performed.

The experiments performed address the hypothesis that different types of materials (topics and not just complexity) may produce different learning results for individuals and pairs. More specifically, as the material to be learned moves from declarative to procedural, more problem solving is required to learn that material. With more problem solving should come more interaction and since pairs provide an opportunity to interact together, an increased amount of learning should be found for pairs as the material becomes more procedural in nature.

Experiment 1 focused on groups versus individual learning from an economics hypertext. Using a hypertext as opposed to a linear text was hypothesized to provide a problem solving context for subjects because they would need to figure out where to go in the text. Students read a hypertext either alone or with a partner. Pairs were tested together or individually for the post-test. (Experiment 1a limited the reading time for subjects whereas Experiment 1b allowed subjects to take as much time as they wanted. Similar results were obtained with higher variance for Experiment 1b.) Results for Experiment 1 showed that individuals improved more between pre-test and post-test than groups (tested alone or together) even though groups read more of the text itself. Reading may be an activity which is not conducive to collaboration. Although pairs were not facilitated for a pure reading task, they may perform better on a task which requires first reading and then problem solving.

Experiment 2 focused on groups versus individual learning from a genetics tutoring system. The tutoring system first presented basic information about genetics and then specific information about how to solve pedigree problems. Subjects solved 4 sets of problems with feedback. Results for Experiment 2 indicated that groups showed more improvement than individuals but this difference may be partially due to the greater improvement of the students taking the test together (for one of the sets of groups). Groups seemed to talk more in Experiment 2; they seemed to talk when problem solving started and did not talk during the initial reading parts of the genetics tutor. Some additional knowledge may be gained by working with another individual, but this is hard to differentiate from the ability to retain information when tested with another person. However, more discussion and interaction does seem to occur in a problem solving situation.

In summary, these results imply that a purely procedural task could be learned most easily by groups as compared with a purely declarative task. This work also indicates that there is not an overwhelming advantage for pairs using computers for learning relatively difficult materials (although these materials were not more difficult than what could be expected from college level students). Text itself may not induce students to discuss the material; whereas, problem solving activities embedded in text may promote students' discussion and better performance. From the work of Chi and colleagues (Chi, et al, 1988), better students often self-explain when material is ambiguous or difficult and the possibility exists that textual material that includes questions may produce better results. We are currently performing experiments to explore both of these issues.

The indication that pair learning may show greater improvement as the type of material becomes more procedural (problem solving) in nature requires some caution. First, although the economics text did not appear to be complicated or difficult, the genetics problem solving material became progressively more challenging as the student progressed through the tutoring system. Thus, the genetics material may have been considered complex by many students. As noted in the introduction, extremely easy and extremely complex materials may be difficult for pairs to handle. While extremely easy material results in floor effects where differences between individuals and pairs may be small, extremely difficult material may cause pairs' performance to be less than optimal depending upon how tenacious the pair of students are at tackling the material. If the students both decide that the material is too difficult, they may both stop working or develop strategies to "outsmart" the computer. On the other hand, if both students decide to tackle the material, incredible performance can be observed. Thus, type and complexity of material may interact. In addition, individual differences may result in very different approaches to the same material.

In conclusion, our study demonstrated that pairs do not outperform individuals in all computer learning tasks. In fact, for purely declarative reading tasks, reading as part of a pair may actually hurt a student's performance. Thus, the type of activity may be a very important factor in determining success of group learning using computer tutors.

Understanding the Theory of Mind

Changsin Lee
PACCS, Department of Philosophy
Binghamton University (SUNY)
Binghamton, NY 13902
chang@turing.paccs.binghamton.edu

Our common understanding of people's actions in terms of mental state concepts has often been referred to as 'the theory of mind', or 'folk-psychology', in cognitive science, psychology and philosophy. Many philosophers and psychologists further argue that such knowledge constitutes a *theory*, not fundamentally different from genuine scientific theories. In this paper, I first analyze two versions of the Theory of Mind hypothesis. On the one hand, we have the *strong* Theory of Mind hypothesis, advocated by Fodor (1987) and Baron-Cohen (1995) who propose the innateness and the modularity thesis. On the other hand, we have the *moderate* Theory of Mind hypothesis by Wellman (1990) and Perner (1991) who endorse the cultural universality and the domain specificity of the Theory of Mind. I argue that both versions of the Theory of Mind hypothesis inadequately try to explain the meaning of mental expressions by reducing it to some internal structures or processes. I propose instead that the meaning of mental expressions is in the tripartite relation between the agent, the linguistic symbols and the environment. I present some evidence for the dynamic interactions of the three elements in the ontogenetic linguistic development of children and in the diachronic changes of a language.

References

Baron-Cohen, S. (1995). *Mindblindness: an essay on autism and theory of mind.* Cambridge, MA: MIT Press.

Fodor, J. (1987). *Psychosemantics: The problem of meaning in the philosophy of mind.* Cambridge, MA: MIT Press.

Perner, J. (1991). *Understanding the Representational Mind.* MA: MIT Press.

Wellman, Henry M. (1990) *The Child's Theory of Mind.* Cambridge, MA: MIT Press.

A Cognitive Approach to the Elicitation of Skills and Specifications

Mihaly Lenart and Ana Pasztor

University of Kassel, Dept. of Architecture
Henschelstr. 2, 34109 Kassel, Germany
School of Computer Science, Florida International University
University Park, Miami, Fl 33199
`michael@architektur.uni-kassel.de; pasztora@scs.fiu.edu`

Introduction

There are two major questions underlying any (human or computer supported) problem solving process: "what" is it the problem solver has to do, and "how" to accomplish this. Answering these questions requires information gathering. In the first case, we look for *specifications*, i.e. the description of constraints, features, and goals of the task at hand. In the second, for procedures or *skills* that are necessary to achieve the goals. Specifications play an important role in design and manufacturing, but also in communication. Skills are the prerequisit for executing or performing tasks. The purpose of the elicitation process is to tranfer or make explicit knowledge of "what" people have in their mind and "how" they perform tasks. Eliciting skills and specifications is fundemantal to human communication and learning. Moreover, knowledge elicitation or acquisition is a major bottleneck in (human or computer supported) problem solving.

Walk-Through

Our first aim is to develop a strategy for eliciting skills and specifications such that the resulting description will be *implementable*. In fact, implementable skills or specifications might lead to computer programs (e.g. knowledge based or expert systems) for solving problems or generating designs. Our second aim is to make the strategy itself implementable and develop tools supporting the elicitation process. Elicitation is done by walking systematically through the process with all the participants and ask questions until a complete, consistent, and implementable description emerges. Although the "walk-through" requires domain knowledge, it is a general purpose, domain-independent strategy. Currently, we are in the process of implementing this strategy i.e. developing an elicitation tool. The "walk-through" is defined recursively (see **LOOP** below). We assume here only two participants, the user and designer. The process starts with the user entering the initial description of the task or skill, say SPEC. SPEC initiates the construction of a specification tree, which becomes the primary description of the skill or specification. After this, the designer defines the operations s/he has to perform to satisfy SPEC. These will be stored in $OP_1, \ldots, OP_n$.

(**begin LOOP**) In general, for each operation OP to be performed by the designer there are three kinds of required information: rules, variables, and suboperations.

Rules: Here the designer lists all rules related to OP in his/her knowledge base. Each rule is of the form $R \rightarrow R'$ and is compared with the current user specification SPEC. If R is a requirement contained in SPEC, then the user is asked whether

R' is consistent with the requirements in SPEC. If the answer is "no", the user changes SPEC to remove the inconsistency, and the "walk-through" backtracks as many steps as needed to accommodate the changed specification.

Variables: Here the designer lists all variables (slots) which need to be given values in order to perform OP. In order to chunk the non-implementable requirements of the current specification SPEC into implementable requirements, the user is asked whether any of the requirements relate to the variables. If the answer is "yes," the user instantiates the relevant variables. Variables which are not instantiated by the user are given default values.

The instantiation of the variables by the user is controlled by the so called Chunking Agents by taking a requirement and checking whether it is common knowledge, quantifiable, or can be calibrated. They recognize common knowledge by looking it up in a domain specific database. A requirement is quantified if it has a *standard* numeric measure assigned to it. Calibration means to match or adjust two value systems to a given scale.

Suboperations: Here the designer lists all suboperations needed to be carried out in order to perform OP. (**end LOOP**)

Now (**begin LOOP**) through (**end LOOP**) is repeated for another operation, until all operations are exhausted and all relevant variables have implementable values. The user is presented with the generated specification tree. If s/he thinks that any of its non-implementable requirements has not been fully redefined using just the variables presented during the "walk-through" process, the Dialogue Agent with the system once again helps find the missing variables and give them values as before. The specification tree is expanded accordingly.

Implementation

For the development and testing of this tool, we analyze and compare four elicitation tasks: with the Department of Biomedical Engineering at the University of Miami the design of a biomedical device for a group of handicapped people, to help them walk with less energy; with the Mechanical Engineering Department at Florida International University, the design of a heart model for testing and teaching purposes; with the Atlantic Meteorology and Oceonagraphic Laboratory/NOAA the design of a database for data collected from drifting buoys; and with the Bascom Palmer Eye Institute of the Universty of Miami the design of an automated system for experimentations on dark-adaptation.

795

In Search of the Hidden Meaning:
Cryptotype and Productivity in Connectionist Language Learning

Ping Li and
Department of Psychology
University of Richmond
Richmond, VA 23173
ping@urvax.urich.edu

Brian MacWhinney
Department of Psychology
Carnegie Mellon University
Pittsburgh, PA 15213
brian+@andrew.cmu.edu

Abstract

Recent debate on the representation of linguistic rules has focused on the role of phonological regularities in governing the mapping process between forms and meanings. The debate has also centered on domains where there is an explicit rule (versus exceptions) on a linguistically descriptive level. In this study, we present a problem where there is no explicit rule even on a descriptive level, and where the mapping is governed primarily by covert semantic structures or "cryptotypes" (see Whorf, 1956). We built a semantically grounded connectionist model to learn the reversive prefixes *un-* and *dis-* in English (Li, 1993; Li & MacWhinney, in press). Simulation results indicate that first, our model captures Whorf's "cryptotypes" in a precise manner. These cryptotypes are traditionally described as "subtle" and "intangible" by symbolic accounts. Second, the model shows how distributed, structured representations of cryptotypes constrain the system's productivity in learning. The simulation results provide insights into the psycholinguistic mechanisms underlying existing empirical data from human children (Bowerman, 1983; Clark, Carpenter, & Deutsch, 1995). Finally, the model displays early plasticity and late rigidity in learning to recover from productive errors, which is consistent with current empirical and computational evidence (see Elman, 1993). Simulations that incorporate both semantic and phonological information show that the model cannot learn the correct mapping by using phonological information alone, attesting to the importance of the semantic basis of the problem (see also Cottrell & Plunkett, 1991). However, the inclusion of phonological information helps the model to recover from errors more effectively and completely.

References

Bowerman, M. (1983). Hidden meanings: the role of covert conceptual structures in children's development of language. In D. Rogers & J. Sloboda (Eds.), *The acquisition of symbolic skills* (pp. 445-470). New York: Plenum.

Clark, E., Carpenter, K., & Deutsch, W. (1995). Reference states and reversals: Undoing actions with verbs. *Journal of Child Language, 22,* 633-662.

Cottrell, G., & Plunkett, K. (1991). Learning the past tense in a recurrent network: Acquiring the mapping from meaning to sound. In *Proceedings of the 13th Annual Conference of the Cognitive Science Society.* Hillsdale, NJ: Lawrence Erlbaum Associates.

Elman, J. (1993). Learning and development in neural networks: the importance of starting small. *Cognition, 48,* 71-99.

Li, P. (1993). Cryptotypes, form-meaning mappings, and overgeneralizations. In E. V. Clark (Ed.), *The Proceedings of the 24th Child Language Research Forum* (pp. 162-178). Center for the Study of Language and Information, Stanford University.

Li, P., & MacWhinney, B. (in press). Cryptotype, overgeneralization, and competition: A connectionist model of the learning of English reversive prefixes. *Connection Science.*

Whorf, B. (1956). Thinking in primitive communities. In J. B. Carroll (Ed.), *Language, thought, and reality.* Cambridge, MA.: The MIT Press.

Emotions and Situated Cognition: A Connectionist Model

Christine L. Lisetti

Psychology Department
Stanford University, Stanford
Stanford, CA 94303
lisetti@psych.stanford.edu

1 Introduction

In Cognitive Science, little research has been done regarding emotions. Yet, Norman (1981), one of the founders of the discipline, had listed the study of emotions as crucial for the success of the new discipline. In this present paper, emotions are considered to range from pre-wired reflex-like responses, to accentuated predispositional tendencies, to recognized interpretations loosening the emotional arousal. In Neuroscience, the autonomic nervous system has been pointed at as offering a key to understanding the arising of emotions (Damasio, 1994).

Emotions are presently modeled as 'stored experience', located along the autonomic nervous system. Usually lying outside of awareness, this portion of the nervous system consists of nerve fibers located along the spinal cord. There are two distinct branches acting as a seesaw: the parasympathetic branch and the sympathetic branch, each stimulated by different neurotransmitters naturally present in the body (Restak, 1994). Each branch of the autonomic nervous system is responsible for the arousal of different emotions, which in turn lead to different behaviors and actions, the result of which feeds back to the cognitive system itself. One portion of the current model provides an illustration of the mutually exclusive effect of the autonomic nervous system branches.

In addition, emotions are presently modeled as 'situated cognition'. From this perspective, cognition is not solely a product of brain functioning but can be considered as a constant coupling between the nervous system and the environment (Varela, 1988). Considering cognition as context-dependent, the situated approach emphasizes the lack of objective representation of a pre-given world by a pre-given mind. Because emotions are strongly context-dependent, the study of emotions best lends itself to the situated approach to understanding cognition. The model therefore accounts for the role of the environment in its coupling with one subset of the nervous system (the autonomic nervous system), in the arising of emotional states: units modeling the nervous system are structurally coupled with units modeling the perceived environment.

Lastly, the modulatory aspect of emotional systems is addressed. Indeed, Zajonc (1994) found that changes of hypothalamic temperature (due to breathing patterns) can facilitate the inhibition or excitation of the release of a variety of neuro-transmitters. The neuro-transmitters are also modulated by the neuro-modulators (Rumelhart, 1994). The presence of a particular neuro-modulator determines the active amount of a specific neuro-transmitter, which in turn activates one branch of the autonomic nervous system. Depending upon which branch is active, different interpretations of the environment are reached. By allowing the network to learn to choose different interpretations of the environment that it is coupled with, the model illustrates how different emotional states can arise from this reinterpretation of the current situation. The *Boltzmann* machine was chosen for its annealing feature which allows to simulate changes of temperature in the network. For implementation details see Lisetti (1995).

2 References

Damasio, A. (1994). *Descartes' Error: Emotion, Reason, and the Human Brain*. New-York, NY: Grosset/Putnam Book.

Lisetti, C. L. (1995). Emotions Around the Wheel of *Karma Via Yoga*: A Connectionist Simulation. Doctoral dissertation. Ann Harbour, MI: University Microfiche, Inc.

Norman, A. (1981). *Perspectives on Cognitive Science*. Norwood, NJ: Ablex.

Restak, R. (1994). *Receptors*. New-York, NY: Bantam Book.

Rumelhart, D. E. (1995). Affect and Neuro-Modulation: A Connectionist Approach. In H. Morowitz, & J. Singer (Eds.), *The Mind, the Brain and Complex Adaptive Systems* (pp. 145–153). Reading, Mass: Addison-Wesley.

Varela, F. (1988). Structural Coupling and the Origin of Meaning in a Simple Cellular Automata. In E. Secarz, F. Celada, N. Mitchinson, & T. Tada (Eds.), *The Semiotics of Cellular Communications in the Immune System*. Springer-Verlag.

Zajonc, R. (1994). Emotional Expression and Temperature Modulation. In S. Van Goozen, N. Van de Poll, & J. Sergeant (Eds.), *Emotions: Essays on Emotion Theory* (pp. 3–27). Hillsdale, NJ: Lawrence Erlbaum Associates.

A Conceptual Framework for Defining Emotion concepts

Changqing Liu and Bo Zhang

Department of Computer Science and Technology,
Tsinghua University,
Beijing, China, 100084
lcq@s1000.dcs.tsinghua.edu.cn

To approach the problem of emotion, physiologists consider some physiological measures, and some AI researchers propose computational processes. Yet the problem remains. We may ask, are these things *emotion* or *emotional*? To determine what emotion is, we must, first of all, clarify what it is meant by "emotion". We argue that actually the concept of emotion and that of desire are one and the same. When we are talking of *thirst*, for instance, we are, by that very token, talking of the *desire to drink*. For illustration, we give some emotions in terms of the notion of desire:

feeling an itch: desiring to scratch;

feeling cold (hot): desiring to warm (cool) oneself;

feeling of fear: desiring to flee, or escape, etc.;

feeling of love: desiring to be with;

hate: desiring to make someone feel pain, die, etc.; desiring to retaliate against someone.

pain (in the general sense of unpleasant feeling): desiring, when P (a fact or a state of affairs) is true, to do something as a result of which P will not hold;

pleasure: desiring to do what is being done.

"Desiring to scratch oneself (feeling an itch) when one is doing so" is an instance of pleasure. "Desiring to lying on a beach in the warm sum when one is doing so", is another instance. Where there is a kind of pleasure, there always exists a pattern of "desire to do... when... is being done". In fact, the concept of pleasure is just constructed out of this behavior pattern. With the definition of pleasure, the accounts for aesthetic feeling of beauty and aesthetic feeling of the sublime are given in this paper. Every emotion can be defined by characterizing what one desires to do when having the emotion.

By abstraction from the cases typically considered as desires, we obtain a type of formalism of desire. What is meant by "desire" can be characterized by $P \xrightarrow{d} a$ reading "whenever P is satisfied by a situation, the action a occurs", P specifying a set of situations that satisfies it. The action part a, which determines what action will be fired if a situation satisfies P, characterizes the desire's quality. The condition part P determines a desire's intensity; if, roughly speaking, Q specifies a stronger condition to be met than R, then $R \xrightarrow{d} a$ is stronger than $Q \xrightarrow{d} a$. As well, this definition for the concept of intensity of desire is obtained by the abstraction of what is meant by "... (desire) is stronger than ...". For illustration, we present an account of the intensity of pleasure yielded when quenching. We demonstrated that the relation "stronger" thus defined satisfies 1) antireflexivity, 2) antisymmetry, 3)transitivity. It is a misconception that emotions have magnitudes in the sense in which physical quantities have. This misconception leads people to view some connected physical parameters as variables modulating or indicating, directly or indirectly, the intensity of emotion. The situation P may include the internal states of the subject. For example, when one feels hungry, one might take no action to eat even if some food is at hand, if one is on a diet; only with the hunger becoming strong enough one would eat the food.

Our paper demonstrates how the referents or semantic elements of mentalistic terms could be dismissed without appealing to neuron science, and quantum mechanics as well. One might agree that emotion causes desire, and desire causes action tendency as defined above, but not agree that they are identical. Behind this position may be the dualism. As Searle points out, it is tempting to think that whenever A causes B there must be two discrete events, one identified as the cause, the other identified as the effect; that all causation functions in the same way as billiard balls hitting each other. This crude model of the causal relationships between the brain and the mind inclines us to accept some kind of dualism. The view underlying our approach to meanings of those so called semantic primitives is that concepts are ultimately constructed out of the regularities of observable behavior, a view which can be traced back to Ryle. Now we shall give brief responses to some possible objections to our theory. One objection might be that for emotion (or desire) is the mental it cannot be defined in non-mental terms. Reply: Intelligence once was thought as the mental. Another objection might be that there are some emotions which are not clearly defined by a particular desire; for example, "excitement". Our answer is: Yes, but aesthetic feeling of beauty, aesthetic feeling of sublime and pleasure are such emotions too. When one experiences excitement, one experiences a pleasure and at the same time senses, say, one's heart pounding, the latter of which, sensing, is no emotion. In fact, our thesis can be stated as that an feeling is called "emotion" if and only it contains desires. We would prefer that our theory is considered as a theory of meaning rather than of emotion, if it is considered extreme.

Does Probability Matching Require Complex Representations?

James S. Magnuson
Brain and Cognitive Sciences
University of Rochester, Meliora Hall
Rochester, NY 14627
magnuson@bcs.rochester.edu

Introduction

Representational approaches to animal behavior (e.g., Gallistel, 1990; Myerson and Miezin, 1980) posit that complex group behavior results from complex representations of events within the central nervous systems of individual animals. For example, ducks feeding from two food sources distribute themselves proportionately to the density of food available at each source. This phenomenon, probability matching, is typically explained by attributing representations of the density of food available at each source within the CNS of each duck.

Are such complex representations necessary to explain probability matching? Drawing on the ecological approach to perception (e.g., Gibson, 1986) and on methods used in artificial life research (e.g., Reynolds, 1987), I propose a simpler model, in which probability matching emerges when each animal follows a simple behavioral rule (go to the nearest morsel of food), and a simple constraint of the environment is assumed (larger morsels take longer to eat than smaller morsels).

Simulations

In order to compare non-representational and representational models, I implemented both in computer simulations. The rates of dispersal and the magnitude of food "morsels" at two food sources on opposite ends of a "pond" could be specified. During a simulation, when a duck made contact with a morsel of food, the duck would remain stationary until it was finished "eating." Eating time, in update cycles, was defined as the magnitude of a morsel of food; given a morsel of magnitude 5, a duck eating that morsel would remain stationary for 5 update cycles. At the beginning of a simulation, a specified number of ducks was randomly distributed throughout the pond. At each time step, or cycle, food was distributed near a source according to that source's dispersal rate. Subsequently, the locations of the ducks were updated in random order, either in accordance with the constraints of the non-representational model, or based on representations of food density at each food source. Fifty simulations were run with both models.

Results and Discussion

Most importantly, the non-representational simulation demonstrated that complex representations are not necessary to explain probability matching, as it can account for data from probability matching experiments. For example, Harper (1982) reported that real ducks matched 1:2 dispersal rate ratios within approximately 90 seconds, and 1:2 morsel magnitude ratios within approximately 300 seconds. In the non-representational simulation, differences in rate were matched within approximately 100 update cycles, and differences in magnitude were matched within approximately 300 update cycles.

Although the representational model (with each individual representing food density at each source) also approximates the results reported with real ducks, it is less stable and less realistic than the non-representational model. It is less stable in that there was much greater variability in the proportions of ducks at each source after the point at which the non-representational simulation had reached a steady state. Various non-realistic behaviors were observed in the simulations of the representational model. For example, since ducks were driven by global rather than local representations of the environment, once a duck had decided to switch food sources, it would ignore new food appearing nearby in order to move to the other source.

The key point is that in implementing a representational model, behaviors for moving about in the world (and for avoiding unrealistic behaviors like the one just described) must be devised. However, the non-representational model demonstrates that extremely simple rules can both provide the behaviors necessary for moving about in the world and account for the complex phenomenon of probability matching.

References

Gallistel, C. R. (1990). *The Organization of Learning.* Boston: MIT.

Gibson, J. J. (1986). *The Ecological Approach to Visual Perception.* Hillsdale, NJ: Erlbaum.

Harper, D. G. C. (1982). Competitive foraging in mallards: Ideal free ducks. *Animal Behaviour,* 30, 575-584.

Myerson, J. and Miezin, F. M. (1980). The kinetics of choice: An operant systems analysis. *Psychological Review,* 87, 160-174.

Reynolds, C. W. (1987). Flocks, herds, and schools. A distributed behavioral model. *Computer Graphics,* 21(4), *(SIGGRAPH '87 Conference Proceedings),* ACM, New York, 25-34.

Modeling the Costs of Ambiguity Resolution and Syntax-Semantics Interaction

Kavi Mahesh
Computing Research Laboratory
Box 30001, Dept. 3CRL
New Mexico State University
Las Cruces, NM 88003-8001, USA
`mahesh@crl.nmsu.edu`

A number of recent cognitive models of human sentence processing have appealed to costs and tradeoffs in resource requirements to support their positions on modularity and interaction effects in resolving syntactic and semantic ambiguities (e.g., Stowe, 1991). However, computational models that analyze the quantitative aspects of sentence processing have only dealt with syntactic parsing (e.g., Abney and Johnson, 1991). Such models have not addressed the tradeoffs in syntactic parsing decisions vis-a-vis local ambiguities and the costs and benefits of making early commitments in semantics. A computational model of the costs and benefits of making both syntactic and semantic decisions at different points in time during sentence processing would provide an excellent formal framework for analyzing the empirical factors involved in sentence processing and for designing cognitive models and experiments. I present such a formal model in this poster.

There have been many previous analyses of parsers as push-down automata that provide measures such as the stack size that enable one to compare and formally evaluate different parsing algorithms. However, one debilitating feature of these models is that their measures, such as the stack size, only take the syntactic complexity of language into account without regard to meaning or the complexity associated with ambiguities in meanings. Worse yet, some analyses do not even consider ambiguities of any kind. In order to perform a meaningful evaluation of a sentence processor, we desire a formal analysis that takes not only such syntactic complexity but also semantic complexity into account in defining a measure to be used as a yardstick to grade different sentence interpreters, not parsers, against each other. By semantic complexity we mean such factors as the costs of lexical semantic ambiguities, of holding on to individual meanings until they are composed with other, and so on.

I propose an abstract model of a sentence interpreter in the form of an enhanced push-down automaton that has a "graph-structured stack" (Mahesh, 1995) in addition to a regular stack. A set of 10 formal operations are defined on this automaton to cover the processes of sentence interpretation. Using this *sentence processing automaton*, I derive a cost metric that takes into account at least the following factors: (i) the cost of keeping around the parts of the syntactic structure of a sentence that must be accessed at a later point, (ii) the cost of syntactic ambiguities, (iii) the cost of holding on to individual word meanings before they are composed with other meanings and the cost of holding on to sentence meanings and the meanings of any embedded clauses, (iv) the difference in cost between holding on to two individual meanings and that of holding on to their composite meaning, (v) the cost of lexical semantic ambiguities, and (vi) the cost of making and holding on to expectations.

Using the above cost metric, I illustrate several tradeoffs in sentence processing with respect to modularity and interactive effects. For example, in the case of a PP-attachment ambiguity, I illustrate the syntactic and semantic tradeoffs in making attachment decisions early (at the preposition), late (at the end of the phrase), or at intermediate points (e.g., at the head noun of the PP).

References

Abney, S. P. and Johnson, M. (1991). Memory requirements and local ambiguities of parsing strategies. *J. Psycholinguistic Research*, 20(3): 233-250.

Mahesh, K. (1995). Syntax-semantics interaction in sentence understanding. PhD Thesis, College of Computing, Georgia Institute of Technology, Atlanta, GA. Technical Report GIT-CC-95/10.

Stowe, L. A. (1991). Ambiguity resolution: Behavioral evidence for a delay. *Proc. 13th Annual Conf. of the Cognitive Science Society*, pp. 257-262.

Fuzzy Logic vs Pre-Logic: Zadeh vs Lévy-Bruhl

Jerald E. Maiers* and Martin J. Maiers **
*Medical Support Services, 1100 Commerce Drive, Racine, WI 53406
**Advanced Biosciences Computing Center, University of Minnesota, St. Paul, MN 55108
(maiers@execpc.com)

Introduction

In 1965 Lofti Zadeh introduced an innovative engineering notion, fuzzy set theory. Zadeh's approach was essentially rejected by the main stream engineering communities of Europe and America. For 25 years, there were only a small set of western fuzzy logic researchers. But in the late 80's fuzzy set theory reached Japan and China where it produced a fury of activity, including heavy government funding of research and a resultant large industry of fuzzy products. There have been "cultural theories" offered for the vivid difference in the response to this mathematical theory, but there is an underlying explanation lies in the work of an early Cognitive Scientist.

Zadeh - Fuzzy Logic

Zadeh's outlined a radical new approach to mathematics and, by extension, to logic. Classical or crisp set theory is based on the concept that an element is either a member of a set or it is not. In classic set theory there might be a set of persons six feet tall or over. Each individual is either in that set or not. Fuzzy set theory is based on the concept that and element has a degree of membership in a set. In this approach an element is a member of a set to some degree; but an element is also not a member of the set to some degree. In fuzzy set theory there might be a set of tall persons. On the 0 to 1 membership scale Zadeh devised a person six feet tall might be a member to a .8 degree.

Since set theory is fundamental to mathematics, a change from crisp sets to fuzzy sets, implied a reformulation of mathematics. In a similar way, fuzzy premises implied a reformulation of logic. The notion of an element having both membership and non-membership leads to a fuzzy logic that does not support a principle of contradiction.

Levy-Bruhl - Pre-logic

In 1910 Lucian Lévy-Bruhl laid the foundation for the field of Cognitive Anthropology in How Natives Think with his description of the pre-logic nature of non-western thought. This book along with his four others on the same topic focused on modelling the mental functions of non-Europeans based on ethnographic studies.

Lévy-Bruhl's set out to present "the most general laws particular to the mentality of primitives. (1985, p14)." The most general law he identified was the "law of participation." which he describes by saying "in the collective representations of primitive mentality, objects, beings, phenomena can be ... both themselves and something other than themselves (1985, p76)." An example Levy-Bruhl offers is that a person can be both a human and a bird at the same time.

Lévy-Bruhl contrasts the abstract nature of categories that are used in western versus non-western thought: "The condition of our abstraction is the logical homogeneity of the concepts which permits of their combinations. Now this homogeneity is closely bound up with the homogeneous representations of space. If the pre-logical mind, on the contrary, imagines the various regions in space as differing in quality, abstractions as we usually conceive of it becomes very difficult to such a mind (1985, p121)."

Lévy-Bruhl describes the absence of the principle of contradiction as a major contrast between pre-logic and western logic. He says, "the opposition between the one and the many, the same and another, and so forth does not impose upon this mentality the necessity of affirming one of the terms if the other be denied or visa versa (1985, p77)" He goes on to say, "It is not antilogical; it is not alogical either. By designating it 'prelogical' I merely wish to state that it does not bind itself down to contradiction (1985, p78)."

Contrast of Fuzzy Logic and Pre-Logic

Lévy-Bruhl contrasted the western " logical homogeneity of the concepts" with the non-western pre-logical concepts based on "the various regions in space as differing in quality." Like Zadeh's fuzzy concepts, Lévy-Bruhl's pre-logic concepts involve some degree of membership and non-membership. And just as there is no principle of contradiction possible in fuzzy logic, Lévy-Bruhl identified the lack of contradiction as one of its most significant characteristics of "native" pre-logic.

The pre-logic which Lévy-Bruhl found characterizing non-western thought, is homologous to Zadeh's fuzzy logic.

This analysis suggests a cognitive science hypothesis for the differential response to fuzzy logic in that the contemporary engineers of the Pacific Rim were more pre-logical than their western counterparts. Empirical research would be required to actually test this notion.

In his conclusion Lévy-Bruhl's insightfully suggested that all humans share a mentality that "is both logical and pre-logical." It would seem, in view of the practical implications of the initial rejection of fuzzy logic by western engineering, that this question could be of general interest to Cognitive Science.

Levy-Bruhl, L, 1985, *How Natives Think*, Princeton University Press, NJ.
Zadeh, L., 1965, "Fuzzy sets," *Information and Control*, 8:338-353.

What (Not Where) are the Sources of the EEG?

Scott Makeig† and Tzyy-Ping Jung††
Dara Ghahremani‡ and Anthony J. Bell‡
Terrence J. Sejnowski‡

† Naval Health Research Center, P.O. Box 85122, San Diego CA 92186-5122
‡ Howard Hughes Medical Institute, The Salk Institute, La Jolla, CA 92037
{scott,jung,dara,tony,terry}@salk.edu

Introduction

The problem of determining brain electrical sources from potential patterns recorded on the scalp surface is mathematically underdetermined. Most efforts to identify EEG sources have focused on performing simultaneous spatial segregation and localization of source activity. Recently, we have applied the ICA algorithm of Bell and Sejnowski [1] to the problem of EEG source identification (*What?*) considered apart from source localization (*Where?*) [2]. By maximizing the joint entropy of a set of output channels derived from input signals by linear filtering without time delays, the ICA algorithm attempts to derive independent source waveforms from highly correlated scalp EEG signals without regard to the physical locations or configurations (focal or diffuse) of the source generators.

In our simulations, we used a prewhitening technique described in [3] and a 'natural gradient' feature introduced in [4] to speed network training. The ICA algorithm performs near ideal source separation when,

(1) the actual sources are independent,

(2) the propagation delays of the mixing medium (here, brain volume conduction) are negligible,

(3) the sources have central probability density functions not too unlike the derivative of the logistic sigmoid, and

(4) the number of independent signal sources is the same as the number of sensors.

Here, we report simulation experiments to determine (1) whether the ICA algorithm can successfully isolate independent components in simulated EEG generated by focal and distributed sources, and (2) whether ICA performance is severely affected by sensor noise and additional low-level brain noise sources.

Methods

A three-shell spherical head model developed by Anders Dale and Martin Sereno [5] was used to test the ability of ICA to separate known signal waveforms projected to six simulated scalp electrodes from five simulated brain source dipole locations. Six nine-second audio signals (man's voice, woman's voice, gong, chorus, synthesizer, drum) were recorded, scaled to different levels, assigned to one or two brain dipoles, and mathematically projected to the six simulated scalp electrodes to produce simulated EEG signals. In some conditions, six additional simulated brain noise sources were introduced (at nearby diffuse-dipole locations) by projecting Gaussian white noise through the scaled and slightly perturbed source signal mixing matrix, and low-level simulated EEG sensor noise, consisting of independent Gaussian white noise, was added to each simulated EEG channel.

Results

Results of the simulations showed: (a) ICA transforms of simulated EEG signals are insensitive to initial weights, (b) In the no-noise condition, ICA separated all six simulated EEG signals with a signal-to-noise ratio (SNR) above 30 dB, (c) In the presence of brain and sensor noise sources, ICA performance degraded smoothly as noise levels were increased relative to those of the sources of interest. Thus, ICA should segregate relatively strong, independent EEG sources into separate output channels with satisfactory SNR. We will show examples of ICA applied to actual EEG and cognitive ERP data [6].

References

[1] A.J. Bell & T.J. Sejnowski (1995). An information-maximization approach to blind separation and blind deconvolution, *Neural Computation* 7:1129-1159.

[2] S. Makeig, A.J. Bell, T-P. Jung, & T.J. Sejnowski (1996). Independent component analysis of electroencephalographic signals. In *Neural Information Processing Systems, 8*, MIT Press.

[3] A.J. Bell & T.J. Sejnowski (1995). Fast blind separation based on information theory, in *Proc. Intern. Symp. on Nonlinear Theory and Applications (NOLTA)*, Las Vegas.

[4] S. Amari, A. Cichocki, & H.H. Yang (1996). A new learning algorithm for blind signal separation. In *Neural Information Processing Systems, 8*, MIT Press.

[5] A.M. Dale & M.I. Sereno (1993) EEG and MEG source localization: a linear approach. *J. Cogn. Neurosci.* 5:162.

[6] S. Makeig, T-P. Jung, D. Ghahremani, A.J. Bell, & T.J. Sejnowski (submitted). Blind separation of event-related brain responses into independent components.

The Notion of 'Dynamic Unit' and its Development in Cognitive Science

Nili Mandelblit
Department of Cognitive Science
University of California, San Diego
La Jolla, CA 92093-0515
mandelbl@cogsci.ucsd.edu

Oron Zachar
Department of Physics
University of California, Los Angeles
Los Angeles, CA 90024-1547
zachar@physics.ucla.edu

Introduction

We suggest a common ground for alternative proposals in different domains of Cognitive Science which have previously seemed to have little in common. The underlying common theme is associated with a redefinition of the basic unit of analysis in each domain of thought. Our paper suggests a dynamic definition of unity which is based not on inherent properties of the elements constituting the unit, but rather on changing patterns of correlation across the elements. We review and examine the evolution of the concept of unit within several Cognitive Science domains in light of our proposed characterization of "dynamic unity". We find that the notion of Dynamic Unit, in each domain of thought, replaces the traditional unit of analysis. The change has been independently dictated in each domain by an increasing body of empirical evidence which challenges the traditional approach.

The following fields of Cognitive Science are discussed: In the domain of Neuroscience, we review alternative solutions to the problem of integration of neural information (Eckhorn et al. 1990, Damasio 1989). Within theories of mental representation, we compare alternative theories of conceptual organization (Fauconnier and Turner 1994, Langacker 1987). In Linguistics, we analyze solutions the problem of 'wordhood' (Ackerman and LeSourd, ms., Mohanan, ms.). And we end with a discussion of collective cognition and the Distributed Cognition framework (Hutchins 1995) as an alternative to traditional approaches. A conceptual (i.e. not physical) connection is made with the conceptual development and identification of elementary units in modern Physics theories (Anderson 1983). The epistemological common-ground that we find across the disciplines of Cognitive Science and Physics suggests that current 'alternative' theories form a collective conceptual revision of basic theoretical principles.

Characteristics of Dynamic Units

We suggest several basic properties that characterize the Dynamic Unit and distinguish it from the 'traditional' unit:

(a) The traditional unit of analysis, in each domain of thought, has been a rigid, locally-integrated unit, whose definition is based on properties inherent to the unit per se. In contrast, the novel unit of analysis is more flexible and dynamic in its construction. Its definition is based on a stable *pattern of correlation* among its elements.

(b) The identification of the Dynamic Unit is inseparable from the context of observation. Under different set-ups, different patterns of correlation may occur, therefore delineating different units. It is in this sense that we regard the characterization of unity as dynamic.

(c) The Dynamic Unit has properties which are not present in the substrate from which the unit is formed. These novel properties emerge from the interaction between the constituents leading to their correlated behavior.

(d) When interacting with the environment, the unit manifests the system's properties as a whole rather than the properties of the individual constituents.

References

Ackerman, F., LeSourd, P. (to appear). Towards a lexical representation of phrasal predicates. In J. Bresnan and P. Sells (Eds.) *Complex Predicates*. CSLI/ University of Chicago Press.

Anderson, P.W. (1983). *Basic Notions of Condensed Matter Physics*. The Benjamin Publishing Company, Inc.

Damasio, A. (1989). The brain binds entities and events by multiregional activation from convergence zones. *Neural Computation*, 1, (pp. 123–132).

Eckhorn, R., Reitboeck, H., Arndt, M., Dicke, P. (1990). Feature linking via synchronization among distributed assemblies: simulation of results from cat visual cortex. *Neural Computation*, 2, (pp. 293–307).

Fauconnier, G., Turner, M. (1994). Conceptual projections and middle spaces. Cognitive Science Technical Report 94401.

Hutchins, E. (1995). *Cognition in the Wild*. Cambridge, MA: MIT Press.

Mohanan, T. (to appear). Wordhood and lexicality: noun-incorporation in Hindi. *Natural Language and Linguistic Theory*.

Why Some Arithmetic Facts Are Harder to Remember

Charlotte F. Manly and **Kathryn T. Spoehr**
Cognitive and Linguistic Sciences
Brown University
Providence, RI 02912
Charlotte_Manly@brown.edu

A continuing puzzle within the study of simple arithmetic fact retrieval is why some facts take longer to retrieve than others. Although reaction times may reflect representational structure or content—and it is the larger arithmetic facts which take longer to retrieve—our results suggest that this *problem size effect* may be due to more general effects of memory underlying cognitive skill.

It has been variously hypothesized that the problem size effect in adults is due to relative fact frequency (large facts are practiced less often; Ashcraft, 1987), order of acquisition (large problems are learned later and suffer intrusions from early problems; Campbell & Graham, 1985), or initial backup strategy (large problems are more error-prone with counting strategies; Siegler, 1988). Two of these hypotheses assume that initial error rates during learning affect later retrieval times, even after extensive practice.

Two experiments used *alphaplication* facts, in which random letters replaced digits in a non-base-10 arithmetic table, to test the above hypotheses. In one experiment, which tested the *relative frequency* and *strategy* hypotheses, subjects were familiarized with counting and addition in the domain; then half were coached to use a repeated addition strategy while the rest used a mnemonic strategy, and all were given extensive practice (40 trials per item for high frequency items) on selected facts. Despite an effect of strategy on initial error rates, there was no significant effect of strategy on retrieval times for well-practiced items. A second experiment, which tested the *order of acquisition* hypothesis and used no strategy coaching, found greater initial error rates for the first fact subset than the second, but no significant differences for test RT after 40 practice trials per item. Thus in neither experiment can differences in initial error rates be considered a predictor of significant differences in RT.

Of these three hypotheses, support was obtained only for the relative frequency hypothesis. However, since relative frequency and total practice trials were confounded, post hoc analyses were performed; these revealed that the frequency effect was due to amount of practice, not to relative frequency during practice. These results are consistent with Logan and Klapp's (1991) findings that the development of automaticity depends on number of trials per item, not total number of trials, set size, or number of sessions.

These results suggest that once direct retrieval has become the primary or only strategy, response time differences indicate differences in retrieval practice, not fact representational structure or content. Moreover, the effect of early errors on later retrieval speed seems to wash out, at least for the production task. It is an open question whether other less-practiced but skill-related tasks, drawing on the same representational content, would be more vulnerable to early errors. Results from additional tasks in these experiments—fact verification and numeric comparison of pairs in the form "a x b" and "c"— support this speculation for the verification task but not numeric comparison. Zbrodoff and Logan (1990) concluded that arithmetic facts are treated as wholes rather than as one-way links from problem to answer; thus answer priming of incorrect trials may be the reason that verification is vulnerable to early errors while production and number comparison are not.

More generally, our results cast doubt on two kinds of memory theories. Semantic memory theories assume that response times reflect semantic memory structure; however, our results indicate that such a simple measure reflects nothing more than practice. Additional data that we have collected test whether RT-based measures of transfer can detect conceptual structure since same-task RT does not. Our results on the effect of relative frequency versus total practice also seem to contradict the prediction of strength theories. Such a theory would scale trials per problem against total trials to yield a strength proportional to relative problem frequency and fairly insensitive (except for proportion of error trials) to absolute number of trials. Our concurrent computer simulation of different memory theories extends these findings into the theoretical domain.

References

Ashcraft, M.H. (1987). Children's knowledge of simple arithmetic: A developmental model and simulation. In J. Bisanz, C.J. Brainerd, & R. Kail (Eds.), *Formal Methods in Developmental Psychology: Progress in Cognitive Development Research* (pp. 302-338). New York: Springer-Verlag.

Campbell, J.I.D., & Graham, D.J. (1985). Mental multiplication skill: Structure, process, and acquisition. *Canadian Journal of Psychology*, 39(2), 338-366.

Logan, G.D., & Klapp, S.T. (1991). Automatizing alphabet arithmetic: I. Is extended practice necessary to produce automaticity? *Journal of Experimental Psychology: Learning, Memory, and Cognition*, 17(2), 179-195.

Siegler, R.S. (1988). Strategy choice procedures and the development of multiplication skill. *Journal of Experimental Psychology: General*, 117(3), 258-275.

Zbrodoff, N.J., & Logan, G.D. (1990). On the relation between production and verification tasks in the psychology of simple arithmetic. *Journal of Experimental Psychology: Learning, Memory, and Cognition*, 16(1), 83-97.

A Multi-Dimensional Scaling Analysis of English Spatial Prepositions

Christina M. Manning, **Herbert L. Pick, Jr.**, and **Maria D. Sera**

University of Minnesota

christie@turtle.psych.umn.edu

People are quite successful at finding their way around in the world by following another person's verbal directions. This is interesting and also somewhat surprising given that a verbal description of a space is limited in the information it provides compared to the information provided by the direct perceptual experience of moving around in an environment. Some previous research has looked at the similarity between perceptual representations and linguistic representations of spatial relations (for example: Hayward & Tarr, 1995), but there has been little empirical examination of the structure of spatial language itself. The main linguistic element by which we talk about spatial location in the English language is the closed-class set of terms called prepositions. In the present study the psychological structure of the meaning of 25 English spatial prepositions was examined. The goal was to determine the most salient dimensions of spatial meaning, and where the various prepositions fall along these dimensions. Different groups of participants rated the similarity in meaning of pairs of prepositions under different context conditions. The first condition was a neutral or no context condition where prepositions were presented alone (for example the words "in" and "on" were presented on a computer screen). Contexts were generated by embedding the prepositions in a carrier sentence containing a figure object and a referent object.

Average similarity ratings for preposition pairs were analyzed using multi-dimensional scaling (MDS). Four spatial dimensions emerged: verticality, containment, front/back, and distance. The dimension of verticality was strongly evident in all contexts, and not much influenced by differences in context. The dimensions of containment, front/back, and distance also emerged consistently across different sentence contexts, but order of individual words within these dimensions changed with different contexts. Additional evidence for the validity of the MDS dimensions was found with a converging measure obtained by presenting a different group of participants with a drawing of each dimension and asking them to place prepositions in order along it.

Thus, the psychological structure of spatial terms is organized around four primary spatial dimensions. These dimensions are very robust across contexts, although the positions of individual prepositions move slightly from one context to another. It would seem that particular prepositions direct attention to the general spatial area being described by indicating a location along each dimension. Context may then modify or constrain the spatial meaning of the preposition. The meaning of each preposition is flexible enough to allow a shift in meaning according to context.

Comparison of Simulated Annealing with Genetic Algorithms in Biological Problems that Use Recurrent Neural Nets

George Marnellos[1,2] and **Eric Mjolsness**[3]

1) Section of Neurobiology, Yale University, New Haven, CT
2) Sloan Center for Theoretical Neurobiology, The Salk Institute, La Jolla, CA
3) Department of Computer Science and Engineering, UCSD, La Jolla, CA
{gmarnell,emj}@cs.ucsd.edu

Abstract

We have used recurrent artificial neural nets (see Mjolsness *et al.*, 1991) to simulate how genes and their interactions in cells determine the phenotypes of animal organs or simple organisms and their development, as well as how such gene interactions evolve under particular (simulated) environmental conditions or constraints: nodes in these neural nets correspond to genes and node activation levels to gene expression levels. We optimize the parameters in these models (node interaction strengths, activation and decay rates, thresholds and so on) in order to either fit experimental data (gene expression patterns) or to impart desired features to the simulated system and make it conform to constraints.

We have examined stochastic optimization techniques for the analytically intractable energy functions of our models; we have compared their performance in terms of convergence speed and quality of solution. Specifically, we have used the techniques of simulated annealing (SA) and genetic algorithms (GA) on the following problems:

- Life history - simulating the development of a simple multicellular organism capable of reproducing and its evolution under various selective environments (see Mjolsness *et al.*, 1995),

- Neurogenesis - fitting gene-expression patterns observed during early neurogenesis in Drosophila, and

- Curve-fitting - fitting multi-dimensional Lissajous curves with the use of a fully-connected neural net (this being an application similar to but simpler than the above two, which incorporate multiple such nets).

The energy functions of the neurogenesis and curve-fitting problems are evaluated directly on node activation patterns, while in the life-history problem node activations are first mapped to phenotype traits of the organism and the energy function is then evaluated on those traits.

Both optimization methods we applied had several parameters that needed tuning. The SA schedule that we used has been described in Lam & Delosme (1988). Our GA is implemented in parallel (one subpopulation per processor); it consists of several constant-size subpopulations evolving in parallel (5 to 9 subpopulations each of 100 to 200 chromosomes) and has mutation, recombination and migration. It is an elitist GA, in that the best chromosome in each subpopulation always survives unchanged to the next generation. The fitness of only a fraction of mutated chromosomes is updated in each generation and this means that at any time there is a number of chromosomes with inaccurate fitness; in combination with low mutation and replacment rates, as we had in our runs, this reduces the number of evaluations of the energy function per generation to only a small fraction of the population size.

Our results indicate that the performance of the two optimization methods varies from problem to problem. In terms of total energy function evaluations, the GA is significantly faster on the life-history problem but SA is faster on the neurogenesis and curve-fitting problems (in terms of real time, the GA is comparable or slightly faster than SA on the curve-fitting problem, since the GA is implemented on several processors in paralel). SA often reaches solutions better by a factor of 2 or more, in terms of energy level, although that may require a very large number of energy function evaluations (and may take several days, in real time, on an SGI Indigo or an IBM PowerPC). It is not clear why the performance of the two optimization methods varies across apparently similar problems. One possible explanation is that energy functions evaluated directly on neural net node activations and energy functions that depend only indirectly on those activations may present different challenges to each of the two methods.

Acknowledgements

This work was partially supported by the Yale Institute for Biospheric Studies (Center for Computational Ecology), the Neuroengineering and Neuroscience Center at Yale and the Yale Center for Parallel Supercomputing. We also thank the GEURU group at the UCSD Computer Science Department for useful discussions.

References

Mjolsness, E., Sharp D.H., & Reinitz, J. (1991). A connectionist model of development. *J.Theor.Biol.*, 152, 429–453.

Mjolsness, E., Garrett, C.D., Reinitz, J. & Sharp, D.H. (1995). Modeling the connection between development and evolution: Preliminary report. In *Evolution and Biocomputation, Computational Models of Evolution* (pp. 103–122), Banzhaf, W. and Eeckman, F.H. (eds.). Springer, Berlin.

Lam, J. & Delosme, J.-M. (1988). An Efficient Simulated Annealing Schedule: Implementation and Evaluation. Technical Report 8817, Engineering Department, Yale University, New Haven, CT.

Beyond Copycat: Toward a Self-Watching Architecture for High-Level Perception and Analogy-Making

James B. Marshall and **Douglas R. Hofstadter**

Center for Research on Concepts & Cognition
Department of Computer Science
Indiana University
510 North Fess Street
Bloomington, IN 47408
{jim,dughof}@cogsci.indiana.edu

This report summarizes recent continuing work on the Copycat project, a stochastic computer model of fluid concepts, high-level perception, and analogy-making developed by Hofstadter and Mitchell (Mitchell, 1993). Copycat perceives analogies between short strings of letters, which can be thought of as representing abstract situations in an idealized microworld. An example of an analogy problem taken from this microworld might be "If **abc** changes to **abd**, how does **srqp** change in an analogous way?" An interesting feature of such problems is that there is no single "right" answer; rather, a range of answers is always possible for each problem. For the previous example, some possible answers might be **srqo**, **trqp**, **srqd**, **drqp**, or even **abd**. Of course, some answers are consistently judged by people to be better than others, for most analogy problems. Furthermore, for some problems, the answers judged to be the "best" are not at all the most "obvious" ones.

Copycat's nondeterministic, stochastic processing mechanisms allow it to find a number of different answers to a given analogy problem, and in its current stage of development, the program is quite good at reproducing the range and frequencies of answers given by people to certain problems, where an answer's frequency corresponds to its "obviousness". The model also incorporates a simple numerical measure of answer quality which agrees well with the relative judgments of answer quality given by people for certain problems.

Unfortunately, such a stark, numerical measure is extremely crude, and reflects a fundamental weakness of the current model: its almost complete lack of any in-depth understanding of the answers it finds. Copycat is unable to explain *why* it considers particular answers to be good or bad. The reason is that Copycat's processing mechanisms focus almost exclusively on perceiving patterns and relationships in the perceptual *data* (the letter strings), while ignoring patterns that occur in its own *processing* when solving an analogy problem. Thus, although it may discover an insightful answer for some problem, it lacks any internal representation or knowledge of the underlying process that led it to discover that answer—knowledge that could provide a basis for explaining the answer's relative strengths or weaknesses, thereby permitting a much richer assessment of its quality. Copycat's lack of any such "self-watching" ability stands in marked contrast to people, who are typically able to give an account of why they consider one answer to be better or worse than another for a particular analogy problem. An interesting related phenomenon, dubbed the *self-explanation effect*, has been studied recently in the context of students learning to solve physics problems from worked-out examples (Chi *et al.*, 1989).

Current work on Copycat is focused on developing mechanisms to allow the program to perceive and remember important processing events that occur as it works on an analogy problem—such as the recognition of key concepts or similarities that arise when the problem is viewed in a particular way—and to create explicit representations of these events. These representations, called *themes*, provide an explicit temporal trace of the program's "train of thought" as it searches for an answer, and can then be stored in memory along with an answer when one is found. In some ways, this approach is similar in flavor to work on derivational analogy (Carbonell, 1986). However, the focus here is not on improving system performance by learning to make *better* analogies, but rather on being able to explain *why* one analogy is judged to be more compelling than another.

Enriching the model's understanding of its answers by incorporating higher-order thematic information gleaned from self-watching should enable Copycat to perceive abstract similarities and differences among the analogies it makes. It should be able to apply the same processing mechanisms that it now uses to perceive relationships in its perceptual input to the more abstract "meta-level" task of perceiving relationships among its answers stored in memory, comparing and contrasting them in a way not currently possible. In short, it should eventually be able to make analogies between analogies. Endowing Copycat with a sophisticated self-watching capability forms the central theme of present efforts to extend and refine the model, and is a logical next step along the road to understanding and capturing the full richness of high-level perception and analogy-making in a compu-tational framework.

References

Carbonell, J. (1986). Derivational analogy. In R. Michalski, J. Carbonell & T. Mitchell, (Eds.), *Machine Learning: An Artificial Intelligence Approach, Volume II* (pp. 371-392). Morgan Kaufmann.

Chi, M., Bassok, M., Lewis, M., Reimann, P. & Glaser, R. (1989). Self-explanations: How students study and use examples in learning to solve problems. *Cognitive Science*, 13, 145-182.

Mitchell, M. (1993). *Analogy-Making as Perception*. Cambridge, MA: MIT Press/Bradford Books.

Meta-Cognitive Attentions: A Case Study of Learning in Game Playing

Yosinob Masatani

NTT Basic Research Laboratories

3-1, Morinosato-Wakamiya, Atsugi-shi, Kanagawa, 243-01, Japan

Yosinob@nuesun.brl.ntt.jp

Introduction

We studied protocols of learning a new problem and observed two kinds of meta-cognitive attentions, i.e. *orientational* attention and *selective* attention. Scopes of these attentions are different in activities. When people confront with a new problem, it is required to regulate weakly coupled activities, such as making better understanding of the problem through experiences and finding immediate solutions using heuristics. Orientational attention is the meta-cognition on this regulation of multiple activities, whereas selective attention is a meta-cognition on reasoning in each activity.

Meta-Cognitive Attentions in Protocols

We request subjects to learn a board game, whose goal is to remove all tiles from the board in the shortest number of moves. Subjects are not informed of rules for legal moves, but they are guided by showing possible moves for each candidate tile selection. Also, partial rules are enough for removing all tiles. Verbal and action protocols are recorded.

The orientational attention appears in usage of move's types. In the case of orientationally attentive type, the usage of specific moves (Figure1: Subject2's striped area between thick lines) remarkably decrease in the middle phase of his self-training process. These moves increase difficulties of game's state although reduce total number of moves. Changes are the result of focusing on immediate solutions rather than well-defined knowledge for optimal solutions.

The selective attention appears in verbal protocols. Verbal protocols are classified into three categories, (1) reactive: simple report of findings and recognition, e.g. "Aha, it turns to red", (2) reasoning: report of plan execution and its evaluation, e.g. "Rightward, here comes disconnection. So, this guy first ...", (3) meta-cognitive: making hypotheses and evaluating reasoning processes, e.g. "Um, the destination must be the same color, sure sure, it can't move." The meta-cognitive verbal protocols come from the selective attention. Table 1. shows the ratio of each categories based on protocols until the first success of each subject.

Conclusion

Two kinds of meta-cognitive attentions are experimentally observable and subject's attentiveness is distinguishable. Although meta-cognitive attentions are different in their scopes for activities, subject's types of attentiveness correlate to each other.

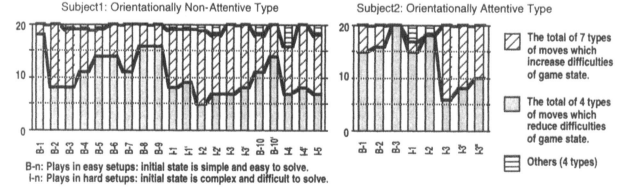

Figure 1: Frequency of move's types used by each subjects during first 20 moves in self-learning

Categories of Verbal Protocols	Subject 1:Selectively Non-Attentive	Subject2:Selectively Attentive
Reactive	4% (114)	11% (409)
Reasoning	71% (2324)	42% (1502)
Meta-cognitive	25% (832)	47% (1691)

Table 1: Categories of verbal protocols (# of characters)

A Situated Approach to Cognitive Interaction Modelling

J. Masthoff

Institute for Perception Research (IPO)
P.O.Box 513, 5600 MB Eindhoven
The Netherlands
masthoff@natlab.research.philips.com

Introduction

From a situated cognition point of view, an agent can not be seen independent of its environment. Hence, interaction should be modelled rather than individual agents. In this paper, four ways are discussed in which a model of an individual agent's behavior can be used to explain the behavior of another agent interacting with it. It is argued that only one of these approaches is reasonable: the one which uses a combination of abstract properties of the other agent's behavior and direct perception. This is illustrated with a case study on task sequencing in a learning task.

An example of teacher-student interaction

Suppose there are two agents. The task of one agent is to learn the translation of a set of words into, say, Japanese. We will call this agent the student. The student does not have a list of the word pairs; only through the other agent the words can be seen. The task of the other agent is to present a word to the student and ask for the translation. When the student has answered, this agent tells the student whether his answer was correct and, if not, what the correct answer is. We will call this agent the teacher. Suppose that the only thing the teacher may vary is the sequence of presentations: she may only determine the next word to present to the student. The rest is independent of the student's performance. The teacher has the assignment to try to let the student learn as efficiently as possible.

Focussing on one individual agent namely the student, this is a traditional paired associates task, and there are numerous models of paired associates learning. The question now is how these kind of models can be used to understand the behavior of the teacher.

Ways to use a model of an agent

There are four ways in which a model of an individual agent can be used to explain the (adaptive) behavior of another agent interacting with it. A first distinction is made between the use of an executable model by an agent to simulate the other agent, and the mere use of functional properties of a model. A second distinction is whether or not perception is regarded as an input to the process of deciding what to do next.

The use of an executable model has several disadvantages. Firstly, if the model is incorrect, then the information on which the choice for the next action is based is incorrect, and the action may turn out to be inappropriate. Secondly, it is difficult to determine the parameters of a model, and it is very likely that errors occur in this estimation process. Lastly, it takes a lot of computing power and time both to run the simulation of a model and to determine the parameters.

Combining an executable model with online-perception has as main advantage that this perception can be used continuously to adjust the parameters, which could reduce the effect of errors in the estimation of the parameters.

The use of only the functional properties of a model that are relevant for the interaction has as advantage that a strategy may be found that is optimal for various models, which diminishes the risk of using an incorrect model. However, the problem of using incorrect properties remains. Because the model does not have to be executed, no parameter estimation has to be done and no extensive computing power is required. However, without the use of online perception no adaptation can take place.

Combining the use of only the functional properties of a model with online-perception produces the only reasonalbe alternative.

A situated task sequencing strategy

We have designed a task sequencing strategy based on perception and simple hypotheses about how a student learns that can be abstracted from the existing learning models (Masthoff & VanHoe, 1996). Several well-controlled experiments have been done to provide experimental evidence that the situated task sequencing strategy gives better results than other strategies because of its adaptivity (Masthoff, 1996).

References

Masthoff, J. (1996). *Design, architecture, and evaluation of an agent-based interactive learning system.* Dissertation in preparation.

Masthoff, J., VanHoe, R. (1996). *The design and evaluation of an agent-based interactive learning system.* Manuscript in preparation.

Apparent Motion on the World Wide Web

Teenie Matlock
Program in Experimental Psychology
University of California, Santa Cruz
Santa Cruz, CA 95064
tmatlock@cats.ucsc.edu

Paul P. Maglio
IBM Almaden Research Center
650 Harry Road, K54D-B2
San Jose, CA 95120
pmaglio@almaden.ibm.com

When people talk about accessing information on the World Wide Web, they use expressions or words that refer to travelling through space. Even though the agent is not actually in motion, the linguistic forms chosen suggest that the agent is moving along a trajectory towards a destination. For instance, people talk about "travelling on the information superhighway", "surfing the net", "going to a web site", and "crashing into a deadend". Such phrases are metaphorical in that they involve a mapping of image-schemata (Lakoff, 1987; Johnson, 1987; Turner, 1987), such as SOURCE-PATH-GOAL, from the source domain of physical travel onto the target domain of information access. This kind of language use is not arbitrary but results from a coherent system of metaphorical thought in which the abstract is expressed in concrete terms.

Our analysis is based on a large corpus of linguistic data relating to the World Wide Web. Some data were gathered from popular press and technical books and articles. Additional data were collected through surveys in which both experienced and naive participants provided written responses to questions about their Web use. One of these surveys appeared on the World Wide Web itself. The remaining data were collected through online verbal protocols obtained while both experienced and naive participants used the web to access specific information.

The data we collected suggest that people conceptualize information as physical objects located at particular points in space. These information objects can be manipulated, moved, and stored; for example, "I picked up that brain from David's web page and moved it over to mine". These objects can be inspected from different directions; for example, "I got here from Yahoo yesterday, but today I found it from the Media Lab." Our data provide substantial evidence to show that even people with little or no exposure to the web understand and respond appropriately to language that reflects metaphorical thought relating to travel in two dimensions. Nevertheless, we also observed a few cases in which people with little prior exposure to the World Wide Web relied on other metaphors to think about and express motion in information space. For instance, two individuals used phrases such as "dial up the web page" or "what is the number I call to see that web page?", which suggests that they were mapping a telephone call onto information access on the web.

Why exactly is it that spatial metaphors are used when talking about accessing information? Lakoff (1987), Gibbs (1994), and others would probably argue that basic conceptual schemas, such as trajectory, motivate such thought and that this is reflected in the language used. Perhaps a more difficult question is why people conceive of themselves as actively moving through information space, when in fact what is actually happening is that information *moves* toward them; more precisely, the data indexed by a particular URL is transmitted from a distal computer to a user's screen at his or her request. We believe the answer lies in people's everyday interactions with objects in the world: ordinarily, when a person wants a distal object, he or she must exert energy and move to obtain it. This accords with Johnson's (1987) view of bodily experience.

Finally, our data suggest that people ordinarily conceive of the Web as a two-dimensional graph that supports mainly local movement. For instance, participants routinely spoke of "going back one" and of "following a chain of links". Yet the Web is multi-dimensional. The very notion of hypertext is of a system of multiply and arbitrarily interconnected nodes. But because people must move through the web in time, its multi-dimensional structure is transformed (both internally and externally) into simpler linear paths. For example, utterances such as "I went to Yahoo, then to entertainment, then to a Smashing Pumpkins web site, and I then I came back to Yahoo" reflect a linear way of thinking about the Web. Thus, even though time is metaphorically conceived as space (Lakoff & Johnson, 1980), in this case, time helps structure spatial concepts as well.

References

Gibbs, R. W. (1994). *The poetics of mind*. New York: Cambridge University Press.

Johnson, M. (1987). *The body in the mind*. Chicago: University of Chicago Press.

Lakoff, G. (1987). *Women, fire, and dangerous things*. Chicago: University of Chicago Press.

Lakoff, G. & Johnson, M. (1980). *Metaphors we live by*. Chicago: University of Chicago Press.

Turner, M. (1987). *Death is the mother of beauty*. Chicago: University of Chicago Press.

Automatic Generation of Test-Cases for Software Testing

Gary McGraw and Christoph Michael

Reliable Software Technologies Corporation
21515 Ridgetop Circle, Suite 250
Sterling, VA 20166
{gem,ccmich}@rstcorp.com   http://www.rstcorp.com

Introduction

In software testing, one is often interested in judging how well a series of test inputs tests a piece of code — the main idea being to uncover as many faults as possible with a potent set of tests. Unfortunately, it is almost impossible to say quantitatively how many "potential faults" are uncovered by a test set, not only because of the diversity of the faults themselves, but because the very concept of a "fault" is only vaguely defined (Friedman & Voas, 1995). This has lead to the development of *test adequacy criteria*, criteria that are believed to distinguish good test sets from bad ones. When a test adequacy criterion has been selected, the question that arises next is how one should go about creating a test set that is "good" with respect to that criterion. That question is the topic of this abstract.

We are specifically concerned with adequacy criteria that require certain features of a program's source code to be exercised. A simple example would be a criterion that says, "Each statement in the program should be executed at least once when the program is tested." Test methodologies that use such criteria are usually called *coverage tests*, because certain features of the source code are to be "covered" by the tests.[1]

The example given above describes *statement coverage*, which is a coverage criterion not in general use. The simplest coverage criterion that *is* used in practice is *branch coverage*. This criterion requires that every conditional branch in the program must be taken at least once. For example, to obtain branch coverage of the code fragment:

```
if (a >= b) { do one thing }
else        { do something else }
```

requires one program input that causes the value of the variable a to be greater than or equal to the value of b, and another that causes the value of a to be less than that of b. One effect of this requirement is to ensure that the "do one thing" and "do another thing" sections of the program are both executed.

There is a hierarchy of increasingly complex coverage criteria having to do with the conditional statements in a program. At the top of the hierarchy is *multiple condition coverage*, which requires the tester to ensure that every permutation of values for the boolean variables in a condition occurs at least once.

With any of these coverage criteria, the question arises of what to do when a test set fails to meet the chosen criterion. Often, the next step is to try to find a test set that *does* satisfy the criterion, but this can be quite difficult because the condition to be covered may be deeply nested in the code, and it is necessary, in essence, to execute the program backwards in order to discover which inputs will cause the criterion to be met. For instance, in the branch coverage example given above, it might be necessary to find a set of inputs that cause a to be less than b. It is easy to demonstrate that finding a set of tests that satisfy multiple condition coverage (as well as most other coverage criteria) is equivalent to solving the halting problem; there is no algorithm that can perform this task successfully in all cases. We suggest that a heuristic approach may hold promise.

In particular, we are investigating the application of case based reasoning (CBR) to the automatic generation of test cases by applying a set of pre-fabricated tweaks to user-defined test-cases (Kolodner, 1993; Turner, 1992). Preliminary work is focused on understanding what strategies human testers resort to when confronted with an initially-poor test set. Research into these methods will guide the creation of a set of tweaks that could in-principle impart a modicum of creativity to a test-set-generation program (Schank & Leake, 1989).

As part of test-case generation, our research effort must by necessity concentrate on tracing backwards through a program. In the example above, for instance, our program is required to automatically devise a way of making sure that a turns out to be less than b in at least one test case. We are also focusing on capturing the inherent "structure" of test cases. CBR should prove especially apropos to this aspect of the task.

References

Friedman, M. and Voas, J. (1995). *Software Assessment: Reliability, Safety, Testability.* New York, NY: John Wiley & Sons.

Kolodner, J. (1994). *Case-Based Reasoning.* San Mateo, CA: Morgan Kaufman Publishers.

Schank, R. and Leake, D. (1989). Creativity and learning in a case-based explainer. *Artificial Intelligence.* 40(1-3).353-385.

Turner, S. (1992). MINSTREL: A Computer Model of Creativity and Storytelling. Doctoral dissertation. Los Angeles: UCLA.

---

[1] There is no reason to believe that the methodology described in this abstract will not work for other kinds of adequacy criteria as well, but certain flavors of coverage testing are of immediate interest because the Federal Aviation Administration requires that safety-critical aviation software be tested with inputs satisfying *multiple condition coverage*, a particular type of coverage test.

Modeling the Role of Phonetic Knowledge in Learning to Read Aloud

Jeanne C. Milostan and **Garrison W. Cottrell**
Computer Science & Engineering 0114
University of California San Diego
La Jolla, CA 92039
jmilosta@cs.ucsd.edu, gary@cs.ucsd.edu

Introduction

When learning to read, a child must develop a mapping from orthography to phonology; that is, from the letters of the word to the correct pronunciation of the word. Although the ultimate goal of reading is comprehension and extraction of the message of the text, to become a fluent reader of English the young child must grasp the alphabetic nature of the language and must develop a fluent and reflexive knowledge of spelling-sound correspondences in order to read with any measure of skill (Adams 1990). Most computational models of reading assume that the phonological form plays a passive role as a static mapping target. However, the child certainly has substantial knowledge of phonological structure before learning to read. Here, we consider what effect that knowledge might have on learning.

Connectionist models of reading (Seidenberg & McClelland 1989; Plaut, McClelland, Seidenberg & Patterson 1994; Plaut & Shallice 1993) have so far addressed many psychological phenomena associated with reading. However, none of these models has addressed how pre-existing knowledge affects the learning process. Recently, Plaut *et al.* (1994) sought to explain the cause of acquired surface dyslexia by training their orthography-to-phonology pathway in the face of an additional "semantics" input. Brain injury is then simulated by removing the additional input; this damaged network produces results consistent with actual dyslexia data. However, the model does not give a realistic account of the process of learning the semantics-to-phonology pathway (nor was it meant to).

Interactions of Learning in Stages

This work concentrates on the effect of learning these aspects of language in stages in a connectionist model of the reading process. We imagine that before learning to read one already has the meaning-to-phonology association, which consists of two components: the semantics-to-phonology mapping and the phonological attractor itself. We investigate the effects of simply having knowledge of the phonological structure of English, modeled through the use of an attractor at the phoneme layer. This phonological attractor is trained with a representative sample of English one-syllable words and is intended to learn regularities which appear in the language and to clean up any noisy or ambiguous input into a valid (American) English pronunciation. The orthography-to-phonology pathway is then trained in the presence of these recurrent phoneme weights; the feedforward portion need only place the network into the appropriate attractor basin and the recurrent links will carry the network activation to a valid pronunciation over subsequent network iterations.

We use these networks to investigate the Phonics method of reading instruction. In the Phonics method, correspondences between printed letters and phonemic sounds are learned in isolation from their context within words. To simulate this, the orthographic feedforward pathway was initialized with random weights and then given some training with a small set of grapheme-phoneme correspondences outside of their context within words. For instance, a typical training example might indicate that the letter t should map onto the phoneme representation for /t/.

Once the orthographic pathway had been exposed to the phonics training set, several simulations were run with these weights. This orthographic net was combined with various configurations of phoneme attractors; these networks and an additional network without any phoneme attractor were then all trained on the full grapheme-to-phoneme training set. Those networks with phoneme attractors did not change the weights of the attractors, although the effects of error propagation through those weights was explored. The networks which combined both the preliminary Phonics training and a phonological attractor were seen to learn fastest. This supports the notion that prior information about the phonetic structure of the language to be learned encourages faster learning of the reading task.

The main goal for the next phase of this project is to incorporate semantic information into training of the feed-forward networks and observe the effect on the learning curve, and to examine the effects of network damage on the network with incorporated semantics and compare the subsequent performance to actual dyslexic subject data.

References

Adams, M. J. (1990). *Beginning to read: Thinking and learning about Print.* Cambridge, MA: MIT Press.

Plaut, D. C., McClelland, J. L., Seidenberg, M. S., & Patterson, K. E. (1994). Understanding Normal and Impaired Word Reading: Computational Principles in Quasi-Regular Domains. *Technical Report* PDP.CNS.94.5, Carnegie Mellon University.

Plaut, D. C. & Shallice, T. (1993). Deep Dyslexia - A case study of connectionist neuropsychology. *Cognitive Neuroscience*, 10(5),377-500.

Seidenberg, M. S. & McClelland, J. L. (1989). A distributed, developmental model of word recognition and naming. *Psychological Review*, 96,523-568.

Development of Skilled Memory for Structured Lists

David E. Mireles
Department of Psychology 1051
Florida State University
Tallahassee, FL 32306
mireles@psy.fsu.edu

Introduction

Contemporary theories of working memory have not been very successful in accounting for basic experimental findings of skilled memory performance. Most theories of working memory are based on the rapid access and storage of information in short-term memory (STM). A growing body of research has demonstrated that experts rely extensively on long-term memory (LTM) for skilled activities. Ericsson and Kintsch's (1995) Long-term Working Memory (LT-WM) theory proposes that skilled memory performance can be accounted for by using LTM to extend working memory limits. Evidence for LT-WM has been demonstrated for specialized skills, such as chess, as well as more common skills such as reading and text comprehension. A preliminary study tested whether subjects can use preexisting schematic knowledge to synthesize a memory skill that uses a LT-WM.

Long-term Working Memory Theory

Evidence suggests that experts rely extensively on the storage capacity of LTM during skilled activities. Experts have been shown to have a much larger working memory capacity than novices for domain activities. Additionally, dual tasks or brief interruptions during a skilled activity lead to little disruptions in an expert's memory retention as compared to novices. These phenomena are difficult to account for if one assumes that experts rely on a transient store to perform skilled activities.

The LT-WM theory proposes that experts use LTM to extend working memory capacity limits with skilled activities. This extension occurs when a large base of domain-relevant knowledge has been acquired and the expert has become familiar enough with an activity that he/she can anticipate future retrieval demands. Selective storage and retrieval from LTM is accomplished by the expert associating new information to appropriate cues in LTM and using the cues to retrieve the new information. A stable set of such cues is referred to as a retrieval structure. Thus, LT-WM can be viewed as the skilled use of LTM to rapidly encode relevant information into retrieval structures and the use of retrieval cues for fast selective access to the encoded information.

Preliminary Experiment

Focused tests of the predictions of LT-WM can be made by examining constraints involved with a simple memory skill. Since most people have extensive knowledge of words and practice at generating coherent mental representations of scenarios, it should be possible to use this knowledge base to assemble LT-WM with very little additional practice.

Eighteen college freshmen were tested for memory retention of 5 lists of 12 words. Each lists was presented as 4 word triplets (5s/triplet). Following each triplet, subjects shadowed digits for 14 seconds. Following each list, subjects were required to recall all 12 words in order. The words for each list were ordered into 12 unique categories. Each list comprised of 4 groups of 3 words. The words were pre-selected to fit into one of 4 scenes. An example of a scene is, "An *Elected Official* was reading a *Type of Reading Material* while riding a *Type of Vehicle*." Example words would be, "chairman, play, taxi." Prior to testing, half of the subjects were informed that the triplets corresponded to 4 scenes and were given practice in using the scenes for encoding. The other half received a comparable practice but were not informed of the scenes.

Subjects learning scenes recalled 9.8 words in correct order and control subjects only 3.7 ($F = 78.84$; $p < .01$). When ordering was not considered, subjects learning scenes recalled 9.9 and control subjects 5.2 ($F = 41.46$; $p < .01$).

Conclusions

Superior performance by subjects who learned the scenes gives evidence that subjects can be quickly trained to use preexisting schematic knowledge to acquire a skill for remembering organized lists of unfamiliar words. Improved performance in spite of a distraction task implicates that those subjects are using a LT-WM. This experiment also highlights the importance of subjects learning to anticipate the type of information that will be retrieved during skill development. Future experiments will explore factors critical for development of retrieval structures by comparing memory performance to other encoding and retrieval techniques, such as the method of loci and cued recall.

References

Ericsson, K. A., & Kintsch, W. (1995). Long-term working memory. *Psychological Review*, 102(2), 211-245.

Incorporating Semantics in a Connectionist Model of Reading Aloud: Surface Dyslexic Behavior with a Single Mechanism

Jay Moody

Department of Cognitive Science, 0515
University of California, San Diego
La Jolla, CA 92093-0515
jmoody@cogsci.ucsd.edu

This study investigates the mechanism by which English words are read aloud. Building on the previous work of Plaut, McClelland, Seidenberg, & Patterson (1996), a semantic representational layer is incorporated into a connectionist model that maps orthographic inputs to phonological outputs. When lesioned, this network exhibits behavior characteristic of surface dyslexics.

Background

In English, the spelling-sound mappings for many but not all words can be described by regular rules. For example, while MINT, TINT, PRINT, and STINT all rhyme, PINT is pronounced differently. The dual mechanism view of word reading (Coltheart, Curtis, Atkins, & Haller, 1993; Pinker 1991) proposes that regular words are read by a rule-based mechanism and that exception words are read by a lexical look-up procedure. Consistency effects (differential processing of words based on "neighboring" words of similar orthography) indicate, however, that neither regular words nor non-words are read by a rule-based procedure that is independent from lexical access. A connectionist model developed by Seidenberg & McClelland (1989) and improved by Plaut, et al. (1996) provides a single-mechanism alternative to the dual mechanism view that not only correctly reads both regular and exception words, but also cleanly accounts for consistency effects.

While consistency effects fall naturally out of the connectionist model, it has been less clear how such a model would account for the behavior of patients with acquired reading disorders. In one disorder, *surface dyslexia*, patients have relatively spared reading of regular words and nonwords, but poor reading of exception words (which are regularized) – as if the rule-based mechanism were intact but the lexical mechanism were damaged. Plaut, et al. (1996) note that surface dyslexia is often accompanied by severe semantic impairments and suggest that this disorder could be explained by a model that incorporates semantic representations, but they do not actually include a semantic layer in their model.

The Model

The current work adds a semantic representational layer to this model and demonstrates, in a network trained on a toy language called *Sheesh*, behavior consistent with surface dyslexia. Sheesh is constructed out of a minimal number of letters and sounds in order to keep the simulation tractable. Words in Sheesh are assigned pronunciations so that the spelling-sound mappings vary from completely regular, to regular but inconsistent (i.e. with a few inconsistent neighbors), to irregular—with proportions of each word type that approximate those found in English. The words are randomly assigned binary semantic representations. The architecture of the model is shown in Figure 1. Because

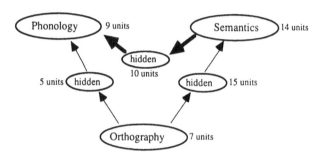

Figure 1: The architecture of the model.

children learn to speak before they learn to read, the weights from semantics to phonology (indicated with bold arrows) are pre-trained and fixed.

Results

With both pathways (orthography to phonology, and orthography to semantics to phonology) trained simultaneously, the network learns to read all of the words of Sheesh. When the semantic pathway is lesioned, but not when the phonological pathway is lesioned, the network shows selective impairment on exception words, as is seen in surface dyslexics. The model thus adds an additional line of support to the single mechanism view of word reading.

References

Coltheart, M., Curtis, B., Atkins, P., & Haller, M. (1993). Models of reading aloud: Dual-route and parallel-distributed-processing approaches. *Psychological Review, 100* (4), 589-608.

Pinker, S. (1991). Rules of Language. *Science, 253*, 530-535.

Plaut, D. C., McClelland, J. L., Seidenberg, M. S., & Patterson, K. E. (1996). Understanding normal and impaired word reading: computational principles in quasi-regular domains. *Psychological Review, 103*(1), 56-115.

Seidenberg, M.S. & McClelland, J. L. (1989). A distributed, developmental model of word recognition and naming. *Psychological Review, 96*, 523-568.

A Lateral Inhibition Account of Release from Proactive Inhibition

C. Craig Morris

Middle Tennessee State University
Psychology Department
Murfreesboro, TN 37132
cmorris@acad1.mtsu.edu

Martindale (1991) suggested a lateral inhibition explanation of buildup and release of proactive inhibition in the Brown-Peterson STM task, but not the neural net architecture and processing details. The present study explains proactive inhibition phenomena as consequences of lateral inhibitory processes in a constraint satisfaction network.

An illustrative network containing hypothetical information about 15 fruits and 15 professions is explored in computer simulations. The category *fruits* is represented by a pool of 15 hidden units corresponding to the fruits (orange, pear, banana, etc.), a pool of 15 units to represent names, a pool of 8 units to represent colors (orange, green, yellow, red, pink, purple, black, brown), a pool of 2 units to represent textures (firm, soft), a pool of 2 units to represent tastes (sweet, sour), and a pool of 2 units to represent shapes (spherical, elllipsoidal). The category *professions* is represented by a pool of 15 hidden units corresponding to the professions (lawyer, teacher, dentist, etc.), a pool of 15 units to represent names, a pool of 3 units to represent status (blue collar, white collar, professional), a pool of 3 units to represent pay (low pay, moderate pay, high pay), a pool of 2 units to indicate complexity (routine, nonroutine), and a pool of 2 units to represent environment (indoor, outdoor). All units within each pool have mutually inhibitory connections. Each hidden unit representing an instance has two-way excitatory connections with all units representing features of the instance. For example, the hidden unit for *lemon* connects to the name *lemon*, the color *yellow*, the taste *sour*, etc. Simulations of the typical release-from-proactive inhibition experiment (Wickens, 1972) were run using the interactive activation subroutine in McClelland and Rumelhart (1988), comparing their activation rule with the Grossberg (1988) activation rule under a variety of parameter values for each rule.

The presentation of a triad of items in the Brown-Peterson STM task results in a brief input to the name units representing those items. Upon removal of the input, the pattern of activation across units in the network evolves during the retention interval. At the end of the retention interval, the three name units with the highest activation among the name units above a resting threshold are recalled. Theoretically, some units coding features of items from prior trials remain partially activated and laterally inhibit other feature nodes in common pools (e.g., *yellow* inhibits *green, red, orange*, etc.). Since some of the inhibited units are needed to code the features of subsequent items in the same category, the encoding and retention of additional items in the same category is impaired - thus producing buildup of proactive inhibition. Switching to a remote category reduces (releases) proactive inhibition, because fewer features of items in the new category are laterally inhibited by activated features of items in the old category. The more remote the new category from the old category in feature space, the more the release from proactive inhibition.

In each condition in the simulations, there were 5 trials, each trial consisting of the brief presentation of 3 items (external inputs to those three item names), then a retention interval in the absence of any external inputs, then the recall of the 3 names highest in activation. To model the Control condition, one set of simulations were run with fruits on all 5 trials, and another set were run with professions on all 5 trials. To model the Switch condition, one set of simulations were run with *fruits* on trials 1-4 then *professions* on trial 5, and another set were run with the *professions* on trials 1-4 then *fruits* on trial 5. On each trial, a recalled item was counted correct if it was one of the presented items on that trial. Recall was averaged over 30 simulated subjects in each condition.

Two models of recall were compared. Under the *Local Recall* model, the three name units highest in activation above resting level within the appropriate pool were recalled. Under the *Global Recall* model, the three name units highest in activation above resting level across both pools were recalled. The *Local Recall* model exhibited buildup and release of proactive inhibition, across various activation rules and parameter values, parallel to the natural phenomena. Although the *Global Recall* model exhibited buildup of proactive inhibition, it often did not show release from proactive inhibition, because items from prior trials remained more highly activated than subsequent items, even when the subsequent items came from a new category. Release from proactive inhibition must therefore involve a gain control mechanism that nonselectively suppresses activation of old items, enhances activation of new items, or both. Grossberg (1988) describes plausible neural net gain control mechanisms that might serve this function.

References

Grossberg, S. (1988). The adaptive self-organization of serial order in behavior: speech, language, and motor control. In S. Grossberg (Ed.), *The Adaptive Brain* (*V. II*), pp. 313-400. New York: Elsevier Science Publishers.

Martindale, C. (1991). *Cognitive psychology: A neural-network approach*. Pacific Grove, CA: Brooks/Cole.

McClelland, J. L., & Rumelhart, D. E. (1988). *Explorations in Parallel Distributed Processing*. Cambridge, MA: MIT Press.

Wickens, D. D. (1972). Characteristics of word encoding. In Melton, A. W., & Martin, E. (Eds.), *Coding processes in human memory*. Washington: W. H. Winston.

Representational Restructuring in Insight Problem Solving

Andrea L. Mosmann and Colleen M. Seifert

Department of Psychology
University of Michigan
525 East University Avenue
Ann Arbor, MI 48109-1109
mosmann@umich.edu

Restructuring (Maier, 1930), or changing from one representation of a problem to another, is often required for successful solution. If solvers do tend to form the "wrong" representation initially, how might one then create an alternative representation that is more amenable to solution? Gestalt psychologists argued that a problem solver often becomes fixated on a single problem representation, and consequently fails to recognize alternative interpretations of the problem's elements (Ohlsson, 1984). Weisberg and Alba (1982) suggest that hints eliminate fixation simply by informing the problem solver that her representation of the problem is flawed.

However, simply knowing a representation is inadequate may not be sufficient to lead to restructuring. While aspects of restructuring have been explored in prior studies, little empirical evidence exists that demonstrates the relationship between differences in problem representations and the likelihood of restructuring.

In the present studies, the initial representations adopted by subjects were manipulated by varying how the problem was initially described. Each "neutral" problem description was modified to include key phrases relevant to specific alternative representations: A *Distractor* version included information consistent with an inappropriate representation (shown in italics), and a *Target* version had information inserted that was consistent with the appropriate representation (shown in boldface). For example, the "Pet Shop" problem was modified as follows:

A pet shop owner decides to put an old parrot on sale. *As a young bird, the parrot had been trained to talk in a household with many children.* He advertises that this bird will repeat anything it hears. It was sold immediately to a little old lady who fell in love with it. A few days later the same lady entered the pet store furious and claimed that the parrot had never repeated anything, although she had spoken to it. **It acted as if it had never heard a word spoken to it.** Yet, the pet shop owner was telling the absolute truth about how any parrot would react. Explain. (Answer: The parrot was deaf)

In a first experiment, undergraduate subjects solved 18 problems in one of three versions, and then were given a second chance to solve the same problems. The results showed that subjects tended to build representations and propose solutions for problems which were consistent with the versions they were given. However, instances of spontaneous restructuring occurred for about a third of the subjects (36%).

In a second experiment, we provided more directive feedback about incorrect solutions to encourage subjects to seek a different representation of the problem. Across all problems, of the trials where subjects report a representation consistent with the distractor version of the problem in task one (35%), they overwhelmingly reject it in favor of the target representation in task 2 (63%). Few subjects persist with an incorrect representation of the problem after getting feedback in task 2. While 14% of trials initially given a distractor version failed to change from a distractor representation between tasks 1 and 2 in Experiment 1, only 2% of Experiment 2 subjects persist with a distractor representation in task 2.

The present experiments support the notion that differences in representations formed may result from differences in the inferences drawn about a problem. The experiments also show that restructuring does not often occur spontaneously. In Experiment 1, the opportunity to reattempt the problems was not conducive to restructuring. In Experiment 2, a hint with *specific* feedback helped subjects to switch to a better representation for solution.

Specific additional information such as hints may be needed to facilitate insight and successful solution. In the absence of additional information, Kaplan and Simon (1990) suggest that repeated, similar failures may be necessary to motivate a change in problem representation. Restructuring may also occur spontaneously at impasses (Van Lehn, 1989), as subjects try to remove obstacles, or explicitly try to find new approaches to solving problems.

References

Kaplan, C. A., & Simon, H. A. (1990). In search of insight. *Cognitive Psychology, 22*, 374-419.

Maier, N.R.F. (1930). Reasoning in Humans: I. On direction. *Journal of Comparative Psychology, 10*, 115-143.

Ohlsson, S. (1984). Restructuring revisited: an information processing theory of restructuring and insight. *Scandinavian Journal of Psychology, 25*, 117-129.

Van Lehn, K. (1989). Problem solving and cognitive skill acquisition. In M. I. Posner (Ed.), *Foundations of Cognitive Science.* Cambridge, MA: MIT, 527-580.

Weisberg, R.W. & Alba, J.W. (1982). Problem solving is not like perception: more on Gestalt theory. *Journal of Experimental Psychology: General, 111(3)*, 326-330.

Gabor Mosaics: A Description of Local Orientation Statistics, with Applications to Machine Perception.

Javier R. Movellan and Ram S. Prayaga

Cognitive Science 0515
University of California, San Diego
La Jolla, CA 92093
{movellan, rprayaga}@cogsci.ucsd.edu

Our goal is to understand the role of natural signal processing by simulating it on machine perception tasks. We use Gabor filters as a first approximation to the operation of primate striate cortex. It has been proposed that besides modeling the receptive fields of simple cells in striate cortex (Jones & Palmer, 1987), Gabor receptive fields provide an efficient and sparse code for natural images (Field, 1994; Daugman, 1989). It has also been proposed that one of the functions of this sparse code may be to facilitate visual pattern recognition (Field, 1994). We test this prediction on a machine vision task: automatic, speaker independent lipreading of the first four digits in English.

Automatic visual speech recognition is being extensively studied in the machine perception and cognitive science communities. Besides its role in improving the intelligibility of acoustic speech, visual information automatically modulates the perception of auditory signals (McGurk & MacDonald, 1976; Massaro & Cohen, 1983). In recent years lipreading has also received attention for its application in the automatic recognition of speech in noisy environments and because it provides a tractable avenue to computational issues on intermodal integration (Yuhas, Goldstein, Sejnowski, & Jenkins, 1990; Bregler, Hild, Manke, & Waibel, 1993; Wolff, Prasad, Stork, & Hennecke, 1994; Movellan, 1995).

In this project, we use a biologically inspired approach to early visual processing. We model striate cortex as a bank of Gabor filter and propose a method to visualize local texture and orientation using these filters. We model later recognition processes as a bank of hidden Markov models, the most successful system for the automatic recognition of visual and acoustic speech(Rabiner & Juang, 1993). The recognition engine was trained and tested using the following database.

Training Sample: The training sample consists of 4504 images (456 movies) of 57 undergraduate students from the Cognitive Science Department at UCSD. Subjects were asked to talk into a video camera and to say the first four digits in English twice. Subjects could see their lips in a monitor and were told to position themselves so that their lips were relatively centered in the monitor. We tried a variety of illumination conditions and allowed the lips not to be entirely centered.

Current Directions: We investigate whether Gabor based representations do indeed create a sparser code in our database. We analyze the resistance of this representation to changes in illumination and present results comparing the performance of a pixel-based approach and the Gabor-based approach.

References

Bregler, C., Hild, H., Manke, S., & Waibel, A. (1993). Improving connected letter recognition by lipreading. *Proc. Int. Conf. on Acoust., Speech, and Signal Processing*, Vol. 1 (pp. 557–560). IEEE, Minneapolis.

Daugman, J. (1989). Entropy reduction and decorrelation in visual coding by oriented neural receptive fields. *IEEE Transactions on Biomedical Engineering*, *36*, 107–114.

Field, D. (1994). What is the goal of sensory coding? *Neural Computation*, *6*, 559–601.

Jones, J. P., & Palmer, L. (1987). An evaluation of the two-dimensional gabor filter model of simple receptive fields in cat striate cortex. *Journal of Neurophysiology*, *58*, 1233–1258.

Massaro, D. W., & Cohen, M. M. (1983). Evaluation and integration of visual and auditory information in speech perception. *Journal of Experimental Psychology: Human Perception and Performance*, *9*, 753–771.

McGurk, H., & MacDonald, J. (1976). Hearing lips and seeing voices. *Nature*, *264*, 746–748.

Movellan, J. R. (1995). Visual speech recognition with stochastic networks. In G. Tesauro, D. Touretzky, & T. Leen (Eds.), *Advances in Neural Information Processing Systems*, Vol. 7. MIT Press.

Rabiner, L. R., & Juang, B.-H. (1993). *Fundamentals of speech recognition*. Englewood Cliffs, NJ: Prentice-Hall.

Wolff, G. J., Prasad, K. V., Stork, D. G., & Hennecke, M. E. (1994). Lipreading by neural networks: Visual preprocessing, learning and sensory integration. In J. D. Cowan, G. Tesauro, & J. Alspector (Eds.), *Advances in Neural Information Processing Systems*, Vol. 6 (pp. 1027–1034). Morgan Kaufmann.

Yuhas, B. P., Goldstein, M. H., Sejnowski, T. J., & Jenkins, R. E. (1990). Neural network models of sensory integration for improved vowel recognition. *Proc. IEEE*, *78*(10), 1658–1668.

Shared Network Resources and Shared Task Properties

Paul W. Munro
Department of Information Science
University of Pittsburgh
Pittsburgh PA 15260
munro@lis.pitt.edu

Introduction

The decomposition of a task as it is processed by the layers in a feed forward network depends on how the network is trained to the task. Analysis of hidden unit representations (using clustering techniques, for example) from networks trained by backpropagation has been used to demonstrate the contribution of individual layers to the full network computation. By training two networks to compute analogous tasks, similar computations might be expected in corresponding layers. This is not necessarily the case; however, if the two networks *share* weights at one of the layers, that shared layer is apt to compute the portion that is common to the tasks. This conjecture is demonstrated using a set of three analogous tasks, A, B, and C. A and B are simultaneously trained on two three-layer nets, where the middle layer of weights is shared. A third network is trained on task C, with the middle layer initialized to the weights learned for the first two tasks. Also, the middle (shared) layer was *not modified* during training on the target task (C) in the cases where A and/or B preceded it. The resulting increase in learning speed supports the conjecture that weights shared by networks computing different (but analogous tasks) come to compute those components of the tasks that are common to both.

Architecture and Tasks

Three networks were trained using backprop (Rumelhart, Hinton, and Williams, 1986) to illustrate the concept put forward in this paper (Figure 1). Networks A and B are trained on analogous tasks, sharing weights at the middle layer (of three layers). The shared layer is then held fixed during training of a third task on Network C. Network A is trained to give the coordinates of the fourth vertex of a square, given the other three, where is square is oriented rectilinearly with respect to the coordinate axes. Note that this task can be accomplished by copying certain input coordinates at the output layer. Network B is trained on the same task, with the squares rotated 45 degrees (in a "diamond" orientation). This task is slightly more complicated, but also easier than Task C which imposes no constraints on the orientation of the square (Figure 2). For the experiments reported here, 4 units were used in each of the hidden layers. The input values were in the range (0,1), both layers of hidden units used sigmoid units (that ranged from -1 to +1), and the output units were linear.

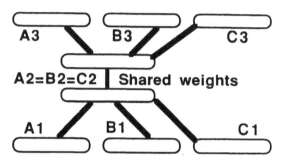

Figure 1. Architecture.

Figure 2. Tasks.

Results

These results, while preliminary, are illustrative. Each represents an average of 5 simulations with different starting weights.

Task C alone:	7200
Using weights from Task A:	3650
Using weights from Task B:	3600
Using weights from Task A and B together:	2950

Discussion

The results are supportive of the paper's conjecture that appropriate weight sharing may extract higher-order structural similarities among tasks. Of course, further work is required to demonstrate the idea convincingly

Reference

Rumelhart, D., Hinton, G. And Williams, R. (1986). Learning internal representations. In: Rumelhart, D., McClelland (Eds.), *Parallel Distributed Processing* Cambridge MA: MIT Press.

A Model of Innately Guided Learning by a Neural Network: The Case of Featural Representation of Speech

Ramin Charles Nakisa

Department of Experimental Psychology, Oxford University
Oxford OX1 3UD
ramin@psy.ox.ac.uk

Introduction

Newly born infants are able to finely discriminate almost all human speech contrasts and their phonemic category boundaries are initially identical, even for phonemes outside their target language. A connectionist model of innately guided learning is described which accounts for this ability. The approach taken has been to develop a model of innately guided learning in which an artificial neural network (ANN) is stored in a "genome" which encodes its architecture and learning rules. The space of possible ANNs is searched with a genetic algorithm for networks that can learn to discriminate human speech sounds. These networks perform equally well having been trained on speech spectra from any human language so far tested (English, Cantonese, Swahili, Farsi, Czech, Hindi, Hungarian, Korean, Polish, Russian, Slovak, Spanish, Ukranian and Urdu). Training the feature detectors requires exposure to just one minute of speech in any of these languages.

Description of the Model

The model builds on previous connectionist models, particularly the broad class of models known as interactive activation models, with three major modifications. Firstly, each network learns using many different, unsupervised learning rules. These use only local information, and so are biologically plausible. Secondly, every network is split into a number of separate subnetworks. This allows exploration of different neuronal architectures, and it becomes possible to use different learning rules to connect subnetworks. Each subnetwork has its own time-constant, and therefore responds to information in a specific range of time-scales. Finally, networks are evolved using a technique called genetic connectionism. Using a genetic algorithm allows great flexibility in the type of neural network that can be used. All the attributes of the neural network can be simultaneously optimised rather than just the connections. In this model the architecture, learning rules and time-constants are all optimised together.

The dynamics of all units in the network are first order and determined by summing activation from all connected units and making a change in activity proportional to the summed input activity, scaled by the time constant. Complex architectures can be represented in the model by using a subnetwork connectivity matrix that determines which learning rule will be used for the connections between any pair of subnetworks.

If an element is zero there are no connections between two subnetworks. A positive integer element indicates that subnetworks are fully connected and the value of the integer specifies which one of the many learning rules to use for that set of connections as shown in figure 1.

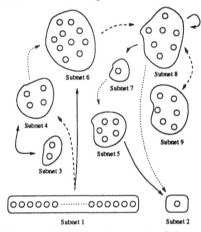

Figure 1: A network with 9 subnetworks. Subnetwork 1 and 2 are the input and output subnetworks, respectively. Arrows represent sets of connections and the type of learning rule employed by those sets of connections. There are three learning rules used; solid arrow (learning rule 1), dashed arrow (learning rule 2) and dotted arrow (learning rule 3).

Results

All of the human languages tested seemed to be equally effective for training the network to represent English speech sounds. To see whether *any* sounds could be used for training, the network was trained on white noise. This resulted in slower learning and a lower fitness. The fitness for a network trained on white noise never reached that of the same network trained on human speech.

The advantages of innately guided learning over conventional self-organising networks are that innate learning is much faster and is *less* dependent on the "correct" environmental statistics. It also offers an account of how infants from different linguistic environments can come up with the same featural representation so soon after birth. The model therefore demonstrates how genes and the environment could interact to ensure rapid development of a featural representation of speech.

An Antidote to Illusory Inferences?

Mary R. Newsome and **P. N. Johnson-Laird**
Department of Psychology
Green Hall
Princeton University
Princeton, NJ 08544
mnewsome@phoenix.princeton.edu

Certain inferences are illusory: they have conclusions that are compelling but wholly wrong. For example, given that only one of the following two assertions is true:

There is a king or an ace in the hand, or both.
There is a queen or an ace in the hand, or both.

subjects judge that the ace is more likely to be in the hand than the king. In fact, it is impossible for an ace to be in the hand. Such illusions were predicted to occur by the mental model theory, which postulates that human reasoners normally represent what is true in their models, but not what is false. If this theory is correct, then a possible antidote to the illusions is to make people more aware of the false instances of premises. We therefore carried out an experiment in which subjects received such an antidote. Twelve illusory and control exclusive disjunctions were presented in two blocks. For each problem in the 'antidote' block, participants were asked first to state what would falsify each of the premises (in inferences such as the one above), then to infer which card was more likely to be in the hand, and at this point they were reminded of their prior falsifications, which they were told were relevant to the task. In the 'no antidote' block, participants solved problems without having first falsified the premises. The 'antidote' block preceded the 'no antidote' block in half of the questionnaires, and this order was reversed in the other half. The antidote was a modest but reliable success. It also unexpectedly improved performance with problems that are not illusory. The results suggest that the tendency to focus on what is true at the expense of what is false is the cause of the illusions, but it is an entrenched attitude that is difficult to overcome.

	Group 1			Group 2			Grand Mean
	No Antidote	Antidote	Overall	Antidote	No Antidote	Overall	
Illusory	14	39	26.5	28	42	35	31
Control	58	75	66.5	64	83	73.5	70
Overall	36	57	46.5	46	62.5	54	50.5

Table 1: Percentages of correct responses

Retrieval from the Social Information Base

Hisao NOJIMA
NTT Basic Research Labs.
3-1 Morinosato Wakamiya, Atsugi-shi, Kanagawa Pref. 243-01 Japan
nojima@ntt-20.ntt.jp

Introduction

Whenever people think and act, they rely on the vast bodies of knowledge that exist in the outside world. Recently there are interests in the roles of other people as information sources, such as help from friends, consultants, and teachers (Bannon, 1986). The purpose of our research is to find out what kind of structure there is in outside knowledge; and how, and from which sources, people select the information in the social context. For the former question, we have found that in some cases there is an emergent structure that members have their own roles in helping others (Goto & Nojima, 1995).

Why users abandon their search?

For the latter question, we have analyzed the process by which people abandon their search in the belief that they cannot find the necessary information. We compared these processes when the searches were conducted on computer database retrieval systems (e.g. DIALOG and CAPTAIN, which is one of Japanese Videotex systems) and in the social information base. The social information base was named after the analogy of computer database. Transactions in the social information base include such activities as people's question asking behavior and helping behavior in daily situations (Nojima, 1995). We are particularly interested in the reasons why they think that they have failed in finding the target information. These reasons from users point of view are important because users decide their further actions to the system (whether to stop using it or to proceed further) based on these reasons.

Results

When people want to find something, they first have to decide whether the search can be achieved at all. First part of Figure 1 indicates that some people abandon the search at this level. This means that they could not have the clear meta-cognition of the system, which might be attributed to the fact that these computer/social-information base failed to give clear system images or self/other images.

Discussion

It is usually believed that information retrieval from computer databases is quite different from that from human networks, but there are some resemblance in the reasons why searches are abandoned. There are several interesting observations in these processes. One is that even though people fail in getting the information they need, they sometimes do not realize their failure. We are building a model of human information retrieval in social settings using the analogy of computer database retrieval.

References

Bannon, L. J. (1986). Helping users help each other. In D. A. Norman & S. W. Draper (Eds.), *User Centered System Design*, (pp. 399–410): Lawrence Erlbaum Associates.

Goto, S. & Nojima, H. (1995). Equilibrium analysis of the distribution of information in human society. In *Artificial Intelligence*, **75**,(pp. 115–130).

Nojima, H. (1995). Society as Database. *Cognitive Studies*, **2**, (pp. 93–101) (in Japanese).

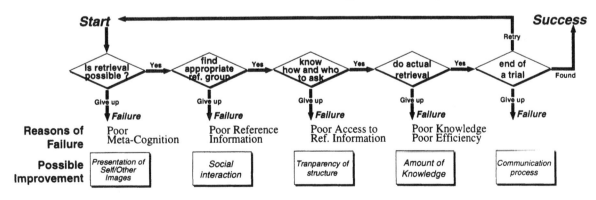

Figure 1: Reasons to abandon search in Social Information Base

A Multi Agent Cognitive Theory

Cyrus F. Nourani*

April 1995

0. Introduction

A multi agent cognitive theory abbreviated by AMAC is being defined . The present cognitive theory proposed the following. Neurons Are Microcomputers Nourani (1991). A neuron might be modeled by a microcomputer composed of thousands of atomic components. Thus a neuron is itself capable of a form of computation. Specialized neurons might compute certain functions in the most efficient manner. Thus the human mind defines a very complex multiagent computing phenomenon. The microcomputers communicate by message passing agents. Each neuron is capable of some form of computation and capable of message communication. The messages could be coded in a form that is not visible to the present day simplistic models of brain. Genetic algorithms are based on hypotheses which indicate the present theories are not far fetched.

1. Multi Agent Active Learning

A Multi Agent Computational Logic is being defined by this author's intelligent tree computing project. A basis for a theory of computing with intelligent languages and an intelligent model theory is presented in Nourani(1994) which might alter the way artificial intelligence logical theories and the computational linguistics logic is viewed. We present intelligent syntax and put forth intelligent tree completion theorems and techniques for defining and generating an intelligent model theory for active learning agents based on tree intelligence. Thus the interplay between syntax and model theory at abstract intelligent syntax trees might be a new area for logic, cognitive science and computational linguistics.

2. Intelligent Trees

By an intelligent language we intend a language with syntactic constructs that allow function symbols and corresponding objects, such that the function symbols are implemented by computing agents in the sense defined by Nourani (1993). A set of function symbols in the language, referred to by Agent Function Set, are function symbols that are modeled in the computing world by AI Agents, see Genesereth and Nilsson (1987), for example. The objects, message passing actions, and implementing agents are defined by syntactic constructs, with agents appearing as functions, expressed by an abstract language capable of specifying modules, agents, and their communications. We have to put this together with syntactic constructs that could run on *Intelligent Tree Computing* theories Nourani (1993,94).

3. Genetic Algorithms And Cognition

The genetic algorithm progress towards problem solving was is another reason to look for an alternative cognitive theory. The biological theories reported in Science by Bloom et.al. (1992) at the Scripps Institute reported brain cells can both secret and and take up RNA and are able to communicate with one another by genetic material exchange. It has been long known that brain cells communicate by neurotransmitters and by electrical impulses. Cellular Automata, put forth by John Holland, the Minsky-Pappert Perceptrons, and the Neural Net computing are example starts. Further biological theories report on brain cells with spontaneous computing behavior by Allman in NY Times (1993) responding to specific shapes like lips, angels, motion or leaves. The Double Vision Computing Paradigm Nourani(1993) is a preliminary theory and a problem solving paradigm for multi agent visual cognition.

*Research Carried out at Project METAAI 73244.377@CompuServe.Com

Acadmic Address USA Also The University of Califonria, Santa Barbara-cyrusfn@cs.ucsb.edu

References

Nourani,C.F.(1991), "The Ultimate Distributed Computer, " METAAI, Inc. A Preliminary memo written to MIT and Stanford AI Labs, August 1991

Genesereth, M. and Nilsson. N.J. (1987). Logical Foundations of Artificial Intelligence, Morgan-Kaufmann, 1987.

Nourani, C.F.(1993)," Double Vision Computing," IAS-4, Intelligent Autonomous Systems, Karlsruhe, Germany, March 1994.

Stratling Scripps Report(1992) , San Diego Union Tribune, by D. Graham Reporter, February 21, 1992.

New York Times(1993), Specialized Brain Cells, Jane Brody, Reporter, Reprinted by the San Diego Union Tribune, May 5, 1993.

Nourani, C.F.(1994) " A Theory For Programming With Intelligent Syntax Trees and Intelligent Decisive Agents,11th ECAI-94, Workshop on Decision Theory for DAI Applications, " August 1994, Amsterdam.

A Preliminary Test of a Theory of the Applicability Conditions for Three Spatial Diagram Representations

Laura R. Novick and **Sean M. Hurley**
Dept. of Psychology & Human Development
Box 512 Peabody
Vanderbilt University
Nashville, TN 37203
{novicklr,hurleysm}@ctrvax.vanderbilt.edu

We are interested in college students' knowledge concerning three types of spatial diagram representations: hierarchies, matrices, and networks (i.e., path diagrams). Abstract diagrams such as these are important tools for thinking (e.g., Barwise & Etchemendy, 1991). For example, using spatial diagrams rather than sentential representations often facilitates learning and problem solving (e.g., Day, 1988; Novick & Hmelo, 1994).

A major goal of the present research was to propose a theory of the applicability conditions for the three aforementioned representations and to provide a preliminary test of that theory. Our study focused on a subset of six properties hypothesized to discriminate among the representations. For example, according to the "representation structure" property, a matrix is most appropriate when the problem specifies a factorial combination of items across two sets; a hierarchy is most appropriate when the items in a single set are organized into distinct levels, with each level identifying a subset of items that have identical status on some dimension; and a network is most appropriate in situations in which there is no formal structure among the items in a set.

To enable a test of our theory, we wrote 18 scenarios describing situations that might arise in a hospital or some other medical context. Each scenario focused on a single property, such as representation structure:

> In the psychiatric ward of a certain hospital, each patient sees only one doctor, who is responsible for diagnosis and treatment. A researcher is interested in determining whether patients would receive different diagnoses from different doctors. Therefore, she selected a group of newly-admitted patients and asked all of the staff psychiatrists to submit a diagnosis for each patient in the group. The department chair would like a diagram showing each doctor's diagnosis for each patient.

The statement that all the psychiatrists submit a diagnosis for each patient should cue the matrix representation, if our analysis is correct, because it describes a factorial combination of patients and psychiatrists. Subjects were given a choice between the type of representation hypothesized to be most appropriate and a contrasting type of representation. They had to choose the one they thought best captured the structure of the scenario and justify their choice. The "accuracy" data provide some information about

subjects' knowledge and about the validity of our theory. More in-depth information will come from coding subjects' verbal justifications for their choices.

We have collected data from 11-12 students in each of three experience categories. Two groups of students are expected to be relatively more knowledgeable about spatial diagram representations and therefore to have more explicit access to the applicability conditions for these representations: (a) Seniors double-majoring in secondary education and mathematics, and (b) junior computer science majors who have completed the three required courses on data structures. The verbal justifications from these students are expected to provide good support for our theoretical analysis. For comparison, we also collected data from a typical group of Vanderbilt juniors and seniors whose most advanced math class was first-year calculus.

Across all scenarios, the 35 subjects chose the type of representation for which we predicted the focused feature to be important an average of 87% of the time (median = 91%). Moreover, many subjects gave quite abstract statements of the hypothesized applicability conditions. For example, for the above-mentioned scenario, one of the more experienced subjects chose the matrix "because you're strictly comparing one group with another group." Another such subject explained that the matrix was superior to the hierarchy because "you're just looking at at all the possibilities of of the of two separate variables, a set of two variables." Preliminary analyses of the protocol data, in combination with the accuracy data, suggest good evidence for many of the hypothesized applicability conditions for the three spatial diagram representations.

References

Barwise, J., & Etchemendy, J. (1991). Visual information and valid reasoning. In W. Zimmermann & S. Cunningham (Eds.), *Visualization in teaching and learning mathematics* (pp. 9-24). Washington, DC: Mathematical Association of America.

Day, R. S. (1988). Alternative representations. In G. H. Bower (Ed.), *The psychology of learning and motivation* (Vol. 22, pp. 261-305). San Diego, CA: Academic Press.

Novick, L. R., & Hmelo, C. E. (1994). Transferring symbolic representations across non-isomorphic problems. *Journal of Experimental Psychology: Learning, Memory, and Cognition, 20,* 1296-1321.

Opportunistic planning: The influence of abstract features on reminding

Andrea L. Patalano, Travis L. Seymour, and Colleen M. Seifert
Department of Psychology
University of Michigan
Ann Arbor, MI 48109-1109
patalano@umich.edu

A pending goal is a goal that has been stored in long term memory for eventual achievement. For example, one might have a pending goal of mailing a letter later in the day, or of buying milk at the grocery store. How do people remember to achieve pending goals? It has been suggested that pending goals are spontaneously associated at encoding with one or more situations under which they might be achieved (Hammond, Converse, Marks, & Seifert, 1993). In this way, opportunities to achieve pending goals are recognized because the opportunities themselves serve as retrieval cues. A number of experiments (Patalano, Hammond, and Seifert, 1993) have shown that recognition of opportunities to achieve pending goals improves when the goals are associated at encoding with concrete descriptions of later opportunities. For example, encoding the goal of mailing a letter (e.g., by thinking of the fact that there is a mailbox on the way to work) increases the likelihood of actually remembering to mail the letter upon passing the mailbox.

No studies to date, however, have provided any suggestion as to whether or not this mechanism extends beyond concrete cue objects, such as mailboxes, to more abstract plan features. For example, does encoding the goal of removing a stuck ring from one's finger by thinking abstractly of using "a lubricant" increase recognition of the opportunity to use a concrete instance of "a stick of butter" to remove the ring? Or must one directly encode the associative link between butter and the goal in order to benefit from elaboration at encoding? Furthermore, there is no evidence regarding whether or not people actually generate these abstract elaborations on their own.

The first of two studies addresses the question of whether or not people generate abstract remindings on their own. In this experiment, during the goal study phase, participants were presented each of a series of goals in the context of a concrete plan for achieving the goal (e.g., Your goal is to remove an elastic band from a high shelf. How could you use a hockey stick in a plan to achieve this goal?). During the reminding phase, participants were presented with objects of each of the following types: identical objects (e.g., hockey stick), same-abstract-plan objects (e.g., yard stick), different-abstract-plan objects (e.g., step ladder), and irrelevant filler objects (e.g., coffee mug).

As a whole, participants recognized the greatest number of opportunities to achieve goals in response to identical objects. This makes sense in that both an elaborative link and a priming effect could play a role in facilitating these remindings. More interestingly, participants also recognized a greater number of opportunities in the context of same-abstract-plan as compared with different-abstract-plan

objects. This suggests that, on the whole, participants did encode the abstract plans implied by the concrete objects presented at encoding. A more in-depth look at individual patterns of responses, however, revealed that only half of the participants showed the above pattern of results. The remainder showed no improvement for same-abstract-plan over different-abstract-plan objects.

In light of the fact that only a subset of participants appeared to spontaneously generate abstract plans, the second experiment explored the more basic question of whether or not people can take advantage of abstract plans if the plans are presented explicitly at the time of encoding. In this experiment, during the goal study phase, participants were presented with goals in the context of abstract plans for achieving each goal (e.g., Your goal is to remove a stuck ring from your finger. If you had a lubricant, you could slide off the ring.). During the reminding phase, participants were presented with: same-abstract-plan objects (e.g., butter), different-abstract-plan objects (e.g., screwdriver), and irrelevant filler objects (e.g., coffee mug).

In this experiment, participants recognized more opportunities to achieve goals in the context of same-abstract-plan as compared with different-abstract-plan objects. Unlike the first experiment, there were no striking individual differences, thus suggesting that people can generally take advantage of abstract plans even when they cannot generate them themselves.

It can thus be concluded from this work that generating abstract plans at encoding is a useful strategy for improving opportunity recognition, but that there may be individual differences in whether or not abstract-plan generation is done spontaneously. This research is important because it suggests that encoding techniques may be developed to help people recognize a wider range of opportunities, thus improving their efficiency and productivity in goal execution. It also suggests that some planning behavior may be accounted for by the same associative memory principles that govern other cognitive tasks.

References

Hammond, K. J., Converse, T. M., Marks, M., & Seifert, C. M. (1993). Opportunism and learning. *Machine Learning, 10 (3)*, 279-310.

Patalano, A. L., Seifert, C. M., & Hammond, K. J. (1993). Predictive encoding: Planning for opportunities. *Proceedings of the Fifteen Annual Cognitive Science Society Conference* (pp. 800-805), Boulder, CO.

Embedding the Process of Science in Cognitive and Representational Processes

Markus F. PESCHL

Dept. for Philosophy of Science, Univ. of Vienna
Sensengasse 8/10
A 1090 WIEN, AUSTRIA/Europe
Tel: +43 1 402-7601/41
Fax: +43 1 408-8838
Email: a6111daa@vm.univie.ac.at

It seems to be an accepted fact that science, scientific theories, and scientific processes are the result of cognitive processes. The question is, however, how are these scientific processes embedded in cognitive/neural processes? Churchland (1995) or Giere (1994) give some hints, how this interaction between these two domains could be realized. This paper will illustrate two links which connect the scientific realm with the cognitive realm: (i) *epistemological link*: the concept of *representation* seems to be the focus of both domains; both are interested in an adequate representation, description, prediction, manipulation, explanation, etc. of the environment. (ii) *Methodological link*: as neural processes are the foundation of any representational process, the approach suggested by computational neuroscience or connectionism seems to offer a method and a conceptual level (of explanation) which is of interest for both the cognitive and the scientific domain.

Structural similarities can be found between cognitive and scientific processes – both are adaptational and constructive feedback processes . These similarities cannot only be found on a structural level, but also on an *epistemological* level: both aim at developing an adequate representation of the environment; the representational relationship between the environment and its (cognitive/neural or theoretical) representation is not a relationship of mapping, but of *functional fitness* (Glasersfeld 1995). Processes of construction, trial-&-error, and adaptation are responsible for acquiring new knowledge and changing existing representations. The claim of this paper is that cognitive science and computational neuroscience can provide interesting insights in these processes.

As is shown in Peschl (1994), the environment is not mapped iso-/homomorphically to the neural substratum. The goal is no longer to map the environment as accurately as possible to the neural substraum, but to incrementally construct and adapt such a neural transformation structure that is capable of generating functionally fitting behavior which ensures the organism's survival. As scientific theories are also developed and represented by the nervous system, a similar representational relationship between an aspect of the environment and its theoretic representation can be found: the latter functionally fits into the structures of the environment. This implies that not only a single theory can account for an environmental phenomenon, but a number of different theories; i.e., all theoretical descriptions which fit into the environmental constraints and which are successful with respect to predicting and manipulating the environmental dynamics are adequate.

In this sense, theories evolve in a "theory space" which is directly embedded in the neural representation space. Developing a theory can be understood as a *search process* in which a point moves around in the theory space until an equilibrium (of functional fitness) between the representation (i.e., the theory) and the environment is found. This euqilibrium is characterized by stable relationship between the predictions and success of the theory and the environmental dynamics. In other words, the theory functionally fits into the environmental constraints like a key fits into a lock. The result is not so much a "positive description", but a strategy how to *successfully cooperate* with the environmental dynamics.

Concepts from computational neuroscience (e.g., learning in the weight space) can be directly applied to this process of developing theories. Evolutionary mechanisms play an important role for paradigmatic shifts (Kuhn 1962) in this view – they are responsible for determining the dimensions of the representational/theory space. I.e., the space of possible theories and possible solutions which has to be searched by learning processes.

References

Churchland, P.M. (1995). *The engine of reason, the seat of the soul. A philosophical journey into the brain*. Cambridge, MA: MIT Press.

Giere, R.N. (1994). The cognitive structure of scientific theories. *Philosophy of Science 61*, 276–296.

Glasersfeld, E.v. (1995). *Radical constructivism: a way of knowing and learning*. London: Falmer Press.

Kuhn, T.S. (1962). *The structure of scientific revolutions*. Chicago: University of Chicago Press.

Peschl, M.F. (1994). Autonomy vs. environmental dependency in neural knowledge representation. In R. Brooks and P. Maes (Eds.), *Artificial Life IV*, Cambridge, MA, pp. 417–423. MIT Press.

Using Models to Stimulate Children's Interactions and Understanding of Science

Cyndi Rader, Page Pulver and **Cathy Brand**

University of Colorado, Boulder
Boulder, CO 80309
crader@cs.colorado.edu

The Science Theater/Teatro de Ciencias (sTc) project is exploring the use of qualitative models to help young students understand science phenomena and gain a broader view of scientific activity. In this particular pilot study, we're using models within a classroom discussion of ethical issues surrounding the science topic of genetics. We would like to know what effect the models have on students' participation, what types of models are most effective in this context, and whether this use of models increases students' understanding of modeling. Ultimately we would like the students to understand that the role of science is to inform but not necessarily make decisions, particularly where value judgments are involved.

The Study

In this study, we are working with a combined 4th/5th-grade class using a visual simulation program from Apple Computer called KidSim©. KidSim uses a programming-by-example approach to creating graphical rules, where the rules specify the "before" and "after" pictures that drive the simulation. During the fall semester, students went through a familiarization phase to learn the KidSim environment. The students then divided into small groups to explore various aspects of genetics, their class science topic. Each group selected one question and built a model that would "answer" that question, often by showing an explanation of the underlying mechanism.

Although the students generally enjoyed creating their own models, we did not think that they had adequate time to reflect on and use their models within the larger framework of scientific inquiry. To provide the opportunity for students to see other ways to utilize models, we created a series of models to use as the focus of a classroom discussion. We chose to discuss ethical issues within genetics because the students can see how these dilemmas are pertinent to their own futures. Problems without simple solutions also encourage a diversity of viewpoints. Drawing on the knowledge acquired during the fall, the students could use the focus models to comprehend and to propose solutions to genuine societal problems.

In our first discussion we used six models, four to provide background information (i.e., how protein is synthesized and causes/effects of mutation) and two that illustrated situations with ethical ramifications (use of DDT and a nuclear power plant). The general format was to present a model, ask for hypotheses about how the model might function, run it, then discuss it and ask for feedback. For the second discussion we added two situation models (a revised DDT model and a DDT in the food chain model) but no new background models. In this discussion we asked more questions to elicit comments on specific issues.

Preliminary Results

Our analysis is based on teacher comments and student responses to a survey completed after the second discussion.

The teacher noted that discussions focused on dynamic models differed substantially from other class activities. The models were presented as tools for examining ideas. Students could ask questions more easily because they could reference explicit objects within the models. Running models in single-step mode allowed students to examine the processes in closer detail and to make predictions about program operation.

The survey responses indicate that students also thought the models made the discussion clearer. Many of their comments indicated that the visual aspect was very important (i.e., "It helped me because instead of just hearing it, I could see it."). Students also rated how much each model helped them understand, with 1 = Didn't Help to 4 = REALLY helpful. The weighted average score for all models was 2.83. The average rank for the more abstract background models was 2.62, while the ranking for the more concrete situational models was 3.16. The teacher also indicated that the concrete models were more accessible to the students.

We have no way to separate the effects of the various activities on students' understanding of how scientists use models. Most of their answers to the question "What do scientists do with models?" displayed an understanding that models have a purpose (i.e., to show ideas or help people understand) and some students even realized that models can be used for experiments or to test ideas. In the discussion, the students understood and took advantage of the dynamic, flexible representations provided by the models and used them as vehicles for reasoning.

Summary

The results of the pilot study are encouraging. Our next step will be to devise a more systematic method for evaluating this activity in light of our goals.

Acknowledgments

We'd like to thank the entire sTc team and Apple Computer. Our grant is funded by the National Science Foundation's Advanced Applications of Technology group.

An Experimental Test of Rule-like Network Performance

Maartje E. J. Raijmakers & P.C.M. Molenaar

Dept. of Psychology, University of Amsterdam, Roetersstr 15, 1018 WB Amsterdam, The Netherlands
op_raijmakers@macmail.psy.uva.nl

Introduction

To what extent can the behavior of a neural network performing a classification task, for example the balance scale, be called rule based? On the one hand, obviously, explicit rules are not available, although the responses of a network might be consistent with rules. On the other hand, networks are not thought to learn fully in accordance with behaviorist theories and are believed to have particular cognitive processing properties such as selective encoding of input patterns. The hidden units should function as mediating concepts. However, it is impossible to study the internal state of the human brain in the same detail as the internal structure of a neural network. We propose a simple empirical test for neural networks that discriminates between the formation of stimulus-driven associations and the formation of cognitive concepts: the discrimination-shift task (Kendler, 1995).

Discrimination-Shift Task

In the discrimination-shift task subjects learn to discriminate on the basis of reinforcement contingencies between four stimuli which are presented in two distinct pairs. The stimuli are distinguishable on two dimensions: for example, shape (round/triangle) and color (white/black). Each stimulus pair appears in two configurations of which only the positions of the stimuli differ. The experiments start with a pre-shift phase during which an initial discrimination of the stimuli is learned. The pre-shift phase continues until the number of correct responses in a sequence of adjacent trials meets a given criterion. The pre-shift is followed by either a reversal shift (RS) or an extradimensional shift (EDS). In both cases, the reinforcement is changed without informing the subject. A RS implies that all stimuli that received positive reinforcement get negative reinforcement, and vice versa. An EDS means that the dimension upon which the reinforcement is based, shape or color, is shifted. According to, for example, Kendler (1995) animals learn a simple discrimination task by forming simple stimulus-driven associations, since they learn an EDS faster than a RS, and humans (older than 6 years) learn the same task by forming mediated concepts, since they learn a RS faster than an EDS.

We applied the test and related tasks to a PDP-model that is previously used to simulate the acquisition of increasingly complex rules on the balance scale task (McClelland & Jenkins, 1991). We varied the number of hidden units and the connection structure between input and hidden units, being constraint, C, or unconstrained, UC. Most tested network architectures learn an EDS faster than a RS. This accords with behaviorist models. The 8-2-2 C networks show no difference between the number of learning cycles in the RS phase and the EDS phase. This gives no clear indication for the learning mode of this network. Therefore, the 8-2-2 C networks are examined by means of a trial-by-trial analy-sis. The result of this analysis agrees fully with predictions from behaviorist theories and results of 4-year-old children.

Optional-Shift Task

A second experimental design is the optional-shift task (Kendler, 1995). The optional shift task starts with the same pre-shift phase as the first described task. During the phase that follows, the shift-discrimination phase, only one of the two stimulus pairs is learned with reversed reinforcement, such that the reinforcement of this stimulus pair agrees with both shifts: a RS and an EDS. During the test series, that is, after the attainment of criterion in the shift-discrimination phase, all stimulus pairs are presented again, but without reinforcement. The responses on these test trials indicate a RS, an EDS, are both right, or are both left. Also in this task, the behavior of networks of all tested configurations respond most of the time with an EDS. Only in a few cases, a RS is performed. If the number of learning trials of the networks is increased, that is, the criterion for an output node being active or inactive is more severe, the responses agree more often with an EDS. These results agree with behavior found in rats but not with children.

Conclusion and Discussion

Simulations show that the learning behavior of all tested network configurations is equivalent to forming stimulus-driven associations, which agrees with behaviorist models and the discrimination-shift behavior of rats. The question now is which alternative architectures will lead to discrimination-shift behavior that coincides with human subjects: children or adults. One aspect of the simulation that could be changed is the representation of the stimuli. Almost no feature extraction takes place, as in the balance scale simulation study. Furthermore, stimuli characteristics of completely different nature, such as color and form, are processed by one module (in the unconstrained networks) or equivalent modules (in the constraint network). A third possible change is adding a sort of attention and bias to a network (see also Kruschke, 1992).

References

Kendler, T.S. (1995). *Levels of Cognitive Development*. Mahwah, New Jersey: Lawr.Erlb.Ass.

Kruschke, J.K. (1992). ALCOVE: An Exemplar-Based Connectionist Model of Category Learning. Psy. Rev., 99(1).

McClelland, J.L., & Jenkins, E. (1991). Nature, nurture, and connections: implications of connectionist models for cognitive development. In (Ed.), *Architectures for intelligence: The twenty-second Carnegie Mellon Symposium on cognition.* (pp. 41-73). Pittsburgh: Lawr. Erlb. Ass.

Raijmakers, M.E.J., van Koten, S., & Molenaar, P.C.M. (1996). On the validity of simulating stagewise development by means of PDP networks: Application of Catastrophe Analysis and an experimental test of rule-like network performance. Cognitive Science, 20 (1).

Total and Partial-Order Planning:
Application of Results from Artificial Intelligence to Children and Lesioned Adults

Mary Jo Rattermann and **Lee Spector**
Cognitive Science and Cultural Studies
Hampshire College
Amherst, MA 01002
{MRattermann, LSpector}@Hampshire.edu

Jordan Grafman
Cognitive Neuroscience Section
NIH/NINDS/MNB
10 Center Drive MSC 1440
Bethesda, Maryland 20892-1440
jgr@box-j.nih.gov

Introduction

This paper examines human planning abilities, using as its inspiration planning techniques developed in artificial intelligence. AI research has shown that in certain problems, which we call 'partial-order/total-order discriminators (or POTODs), *partial-order planners*, which manipulate partial plans while not committing to a particular ordering of subplans, are more efficient than *total-order planners*, which represent all partial plans as totally ordered. This research asks whether total-order planning and/or partial-order planning are accurate descriptions of human planning, and if different populations use different planning techniques.

We examined partial-order and total-order planning in three different populations: children, adults, and adults with damage to the prefrontal cortex. Previous work suggests that young children have difficulty forming flexible plans (Pea & Hawkins, 1987) and will use linear, total-order plans, while adults, capable of using *opportunistic* planning (Hayes-Roth and Hayes-Roth, 1979) will use flexible partial-order plans. Research showing that adults with damage to the prefrontal cortex have planning deficits (Grafman, 1989) suggests that they will exhibit total-order planning.

The Chores Experiments

We presented 17 normal adults, eight 7- to 9-year-old children, eight 10- to 12-year-old children, and five adults with damage to the prefrontal cortex with tasks that could be completed using either total-order or partial-order planning and noted the overall time needed to complete the task. As in AI planning systems, linear growth rates in human performance times in POTODS are suggestive of partial-order planning, while exponential growth rates are suggestive of total-order planning. Using the Chores software (Spector and Grafman, 1994) a Macintosh computer displayed a map of a city with icons representing items to acquire and items already possessed. The task was to perform a series of chores in this city. The relationship between each chore and the items to be acquired was listed on an "Item Info" screen. Because the completion of one chore deleted the item required by the previous chore there was only one correct ordering possible. In the present experiment we varied the number of chores from two to five.

Linear trend analysis revealed that the adults and older children exhibited linear increases in total time as the number of chores increased, while the young children and the adults with damage to the prefrontal cortex exhibited exponential increases. The subjects were also categorized based on their response to ordering violations, with total-order planners completely backtracking and reordering their plan, and partial-order planners backtracking only to the violation, revising and then continuing. Not all of our subjects backtracked, but of those who did all of the younger children (6) and the majority of the adults with damage to the prefrontal cortex (2 out of 3) completely backtracked, while all of the adults (3) and the majority of the older children (4 out of 6) revised and continued their plans.

Conclusions

We have found that the results of analytical work in AI planning can be used to investigate human planning. Specifically, we have evidence that normal human planners use partial-order representations for partial plans, as do most modern AI planning systems. Further evidence suggests that damaged human planning systems use methods akin to those used in less efficient AI systems; specifically, that children with developing frontal lobes and adults with frontal lobe lesions use planning methods similar to those of total-order planners. We believe that the parallels between the human and machine cases are instructive, and that they may lead to further developments in both human and machine studies.

References

Grafman, J. (1989). Plans, actions, and mental sets: Managerial knowledge units in the frontal lobes. In Integrating Theory and Practice in Clinical Neuropsychology, 93-138, Erlbaum.

Hayes-Roth, B., & Hayes-Roth, F. (1979). A cognitive model of planning. Cognitive Science, 3, 275-310.

Pea, R. D., & Hawkins, J. (1987). Planning in a chore-scheduling task. In S. L. Friedman, E. K. Scholnick, & R. R. Cocking (Eds.), Blueprints for Thinking: The Role of Planning in Cognitive Development (pp. 273-302). Cambridge: Cambridge University Press.

Spector, L., & Grafman, J. (1994). Planning, neuropsychology, and artificial intelligence: Cross-fertilization. In R. Johnson, J.C. Baron, J. Grafman, and J. Hendler (Eds.), Handbook of Neuropsychology, Volume 9, Amsterdam: Elsevier Science .

Randomly Changing Transfer in Artificial Grammar Learning

Martin Redington and **Nick Chater**
Department of Experimental Psychology
University of Oxford
South Parks Road
Oxford, U.K.
OX1 3UD
{fmr@sable,nick@psy}.ox.ac.uk

In the artificial grammar learning (AGL) *transfer* paradigm Ss are instructed to memorize a set of strings, which (unbeknownst to them) were generated by a finite state grammar. They are then informed that the strings followed by a set of rules, and asked to categorise novel strings as following or violating those rules. Unlike the standard paradigm (Reber, 1967), the novel strings are composed from a different "alphabet" from the training strings, although the underlying rules are unchanged. Ss are nevertheless able to make the required distinction at above chance (and control) levels.

The transfer phenomenon is the primary evidence for Reber's claim that in AGL Ss acquire representations which are *abstract*, both with respect to individual training items, and also to the surface features (*e.g.* particular letters) of those items.

Whittlesea and Dorken (1993) provide apparently stronger evidence for abstract representations. They changed the test alphabet randomly for every single test item. However, the near-chance performance of their Ss (.53) is not conclusive without comparison against a proper control, such as a group of untrained Ss.

We trained Ss as standard, and tested their performance in a randomly changing transfer test (condition RandTransfer). An untrained group (RandControl) was tested in this condition, to provide an appropriate baseline. We also ran 3 other conditions: Standard (no letter set change), Transfer (a single change of letter set between training and test), and Control (no training, with the same letter set throughout testing).

An additional factor was that the test strings were either composed of the 20 training strings, plus 5 novel strings (the Same condition), or of 20 novel strings, and 5 of the training strings (Different). This tested the effect of similarity to memorised whole exemplars; identical items must be highly similar, and the Same Ss should perform better. Stimuli were taken from the "standard" grammar (see Redington & Chater, 1994).

Prior to making each grammaticality judgement, Ss also performed a guessing game, reconstructing the test item by guessing each letter in turn. The procedure closely followed that used in Redington & Chater, 1994).

Grammaticality judgment results (see Table 1) indicated reliable transfer, in both Transfer and RandTransfer conditions. Same Ss did not perform reliably better than Differ-

Condition	n	Score	Comparison	p
Control	10	.56 (.06)	.5	> .01
Standard	20	.68 (.08)	Control	.0002
Transfer	20	.60 (.06)	Control	.0005
RandControl	10	.53 (.06)	.5	.07
RandTransfer	20	.59 (.09)	RandControl	> .05

Table 1: Mean grammaticality judgment scores (standard deviations in parentheses), and comparisons (1-tailed t-tests) against the appropriate controls

ent (largely novel test strings) Ss, in either the Standard or transfer conditions. Guessing game (prediction) performance generally mirrored the above pattern of results, although there was a marginally reliable overall effect for the Same/Different manipulation, probably due to the similarity between training and test strings at the fragment level.

Above control RandTransfer performance might be taken as strong support for abstract representations. We suggest that transfer generally is equally well explained by the acquisition of surface-based knowledge, and processes of abstraction between old and new surface forms *at test*. Simple models working on this basis can capture the transfer phenomena demonstrated here (Redington & Chater, in press).

Reber (1969) presents the only evidence which unequivocally supports an abstract knowledge account. Ss memorising rule-governed strings maintained a memorisation advantage across letter sets, suggesting that they were encoding the strings' structure independently of surface form. Redington and Chater's simple models cannot capture this effect. Our current research is therefore concerned with replicating, or falsifying, this theoretically crucial phenomenon.

References

Reber, A. S. (1967). Implicit learning of artificial grammars. *Journal of Verbal Learning and Verbal Behavior, 5,* 855–863.

Reber, A. S. (1969). Transfer of syntactic structure in synthetic languages. *Journal of Experimental Psychology,* 81, 115–119.

Redington, M. & Chater, N. (1994). The guessing game: A paradigm for artificial grammar learning. In *Proceedings of the Sixteenth Annual Meeting of the Cognitive Science Society,* 745–749. Hillsdale, NJ: Lawrence Erlbaum Associates.

Redington, M. & Chater, N. (in press). Transfer in artificial grammar learning: A reevaluation. *Journal of Experimental Psychology: General.*

Whittlesea, B. W., & Dorken, M. D. (1993). Incidentally, things in general are particularly determined: An episodic-processing account of implicit learning. *Journal of Experimental Psychology: General,* 122, 227–248.

Managing Complexity: An Organizing Framework for Libraries and Learning in the 21st Century

Wayne Reeves
611 San Conrado Terrace #3
Sunnyvale, CA 94086
elegence@aol.com

"Managing cognitive complexity" can play the role of an organizing framework for a host of 21st century library and learning agendas. These agendas span the design of digital libraries (Marchionini, 1995), resource-based learning, thinking-skill development (Collins & Mangieri, 1992), and information literacy (McClure, 1994). The difference between now and a hundred years ago, or even fifty years ago, is the rise in complexity, in the cognitive load on those attempting to solve problems and make judgments or decisions. Thus, the concept of cognitive complexity, understanding its nature, origins, and developing schemes for addressing it, might very well form the common element, the organizing principle, behind new theory and instructional programs in developing life-long thinking skills. In this century we have had an assault on our view of the world as a simple place, but have been given few means of thinking about it; let alone thriving on it. From the last structured world of Newton we have given way to relativity, quantum probabilities, Heisenberg's uncertainty, Göedel's incompleteness proof, fuzzy logic, analog computing, and chaos theory. Within this zeitgeist the author proposes an operationalized description of cognitive complexity, its five sources, and the necessary capacities and stages of an heuristic, synthesized from a series of advanced problem solving skills, that could be used to manage this complexity under a variety of learning and problem solving modes. This is preliminary research on an heuristic guide for building intelligent systems that are capable of handling real-world complexity.

References

Banathy, B. H. (1991). *Systems design of education.* Englewood Cliffs, NJ: Educational Technologies Publications.

de Bono, E. (1970). *Lateral thinking.* New York: Harper and Row.

Brabek, M. (1983). Critical thinking skills and reflective judgment development: Redefining the aims of higher education. *Journal of Applied Developmental Psychology,* 4, 23-24.

Candy, P. (1991). *Self-direction for lifelong learning.* San Francisco: Jossey-Bass.

Collins, C. & Mangieri, J. (Eds.) (1992). *Teaching thinking.* Hillsdale, NJ: Lawrence Erlbaum.

Cross, K. (1981). *Adults as learners.* San Francisco: Jossey-Bass.

Daloz, L. (1987). *Effective teaching and mentoring.* San Francisco: Jossey-Bass.

Gergen, K. (1991). *The saturated self.* New York: Basic Books.

Kirsch, I. et al (1993). *Adult literacy in America.* Washington D.C.: Office of Educational Research and Improvement, U.S. Dept. of Education.

Knowles, M. (1980). *The modern practice of adult education.* New York: Prentice Hall.

Lipman, M. (1991). *Thinking in education.* New York: Cambridge University Press.

McGrane and Sternberg (1992). Discussion: Fatal vision – the failure of the schools to teaching children to think. In Collins, C. & Mangieri, J. (Eds.), *Teaching thinking.* Hillsdale, NJ: Lawrence Erlbaum.

Majoribanks, K. (1991). *The foundation of students' learning.* Sydney: Pergamon Press.

McClure, C. (1994). Network literacy: A role for libraries? *Information Technology and Libraries*: 13(2):115-125.

Meyers, C. (1988). *Teaching students to think critically.* San Francisco: Jossey-Bass.

Polya, G. (1985). *How to solve it.* Princeton, NJ: Princeton University Press.

Reeves, W. (1996). *Cognition and complexity.* Lanham, MD: Scarecrow Press.

Richardson, J., Eysenck, M. & Piper, D. (Eds.) (1987). *Student learning.* Philadelphia: SRHE and Open University Press.

Runco, M. (1994). *Problem finding, problem solving and creativity.* Norwood, NJ: Ablex.

Schrag, F. (1988). *Thinking in school and society.* London: Routledge.

Stice, J. E. (Ed) (1987). *Developing critical thinking and problem solving abilities.* San Francisco: Jossey-Bass.

Toffler, A. (1970). *Future shock.* New York, NY: Bantam Books.

Wurman, R. S. (1989). *Information anxiety.* New York: Random House.

Young, R. (Ed.) (1980). *New directions for teaching and learning: Fostering critical thinking.* San Francisco: Jossey- Bass.

Resolving Anaphoric Reference: Reading as Enthymemic Reasoning

Russell Revlin and **Mary Hegarty**
Department of Psychology
University of California, Santa Barbara
Santa Barbara, CA 93105
{revlin, hegarty}@psych.ucsd.edu

This study employs reading time and eye-movement paradigms to test a model of how readers understand connected discourse by using signals to textual cohesion. The model (Singer, Revlin & Halldorson, 1990) views the computation of cohesion as a form of enthymemic reasoning in which the reader establishes Goals and Subgoals consistent with a syllogistic structure. In the present study, university students were timed as they read a pair of sentences, half of which were related by a signal to cohesion (e.g., *too*, as in *Juan is a shortstop. Maria is athletic too*). The model claims that in comprehending such sentence pairs, it is necessary for readers to compute bridging inferences (e.g., Singer, Halldorson, Lear, & Andrusiak, 1992) to provide missing information (e.g., "shortstops are athletic" and "Juan is athletic"). To generate such inferences, the sentence relations are represented in an enthymemic format as:

Juan is a shortstop
[missing premise]

----

therefore: Juan is athletic

In contrast, such inferences are not necessary for comprehending non-anaphoric sentence-pairs. Bridging inferences should therefore contribute to reading time only in anaphoric pairs. Consistent with this model, we found that readers require an additional 846 msec to understand anaphoric pairs than non-anaphoric pairs--substantially more time than would be required to read the added adverbial, *too*.

The eye movements of students were tracked as they read the pairs of sentences. Students made significantly more backward gazes while reading anaphoric sentences than when reading unsignaled sentences. These increased gazes were directed primarily at the predicate of the first sentence (e.g., *shortstop*) reflecting a subgoal of drawing an inference linking the contextual information in the first sentence (i.e., *shortstop*) with the new information (e.g., *athletic*) in the second sentence--the hallmark of a bridging inference (Haviland & Clark, 1974).

Following each sentence pair, students answered a question that probed verbatim recall or inferences from the readings. Although these latter sentences are hypothesized to participate in the comprehension of only anaphoric pairs they are available from the reader's long term knowledge independent of the sentence-pair (e.g., *shortstops are athletic*). Verification accuracy was greater and verification latencies shorter when the probe sentences were consistent with proposed bridging inferences.

This pattern of data is consistent with a model of reading which proposes that readers generate bridging inferences to resolve anaphoric reference and that they do so in a manner consistent with solving a logical enthymeme.

References

Haviland, S. E. & Clark, H. H. (1974). What's new? Acquiring new information as a process in comprehension. *Journal of Verbal Learning and Verbal Behavior*, 13, 512--521.

Singer, M., Halldorson, M. Lear, J. C. & Andrusiak, P. (1992). Validation of causal bridging inferences in discourse understanding. *Journal of Memory and Language*, 31, 507--524.

Singer, M., Revlin, R. & Hallsorson, M. (1990). Bridging inferences and Enthymemes. In A. C. Graesser & G. H. Bower (Eds.) *Inferences and Text Comprehension* (pp. 35--51). San Diego, CA: Academic Press.

See It! Draw It! Make It Move!
Dynamic Representations of Causal Models:
The sTc Project

Cecil D. Robinson, Heidi B. Carlone, Cyndi Rader, and **Carlos E. Garcia**

School of Education
University of Colorado, Boulder
Boulder, CO 80309-0249
robinscd@ucsu.Colorado.EDU

The science theater/teatro de ciencias (sTc) project is investigating the use of models to create dynamic representations of scientific concepts with elementary school students. Our research uses the Apple© KidSim application as a tool for students to create their own models. KidSim enables students to represent scientific phenomena through the use of pictorial-based models, by allowing them to apply 'rules' to the 'pieces' of their model. The dynamic interaction that occurs between the student, computer, and resulting model challenges students' existing representations of the phenomena being modeled (Hutchins, 1995) -- as one fifth grader said, the challenge "is getting the model to work." This dynamic distinguishes our approach from other models created through different mediums -- story boards, clay, manipulatives, etc..

Scientific knowledge has been classified into two categories: experimental facts and current conceptual models (Walker, 1963; von Glasersfeld, 1995). Traditional science instruction emphasizes experimental facts, with the resulting view of science as a discrete, arbitrary body of facts and assertions. We, however, think that manipulation of conceptual models in concrete form yields an experience that embodies science: learning through a process of inquiry. Thus, through the use of KidSim, students engage in practicing science instead of just reading about science. The goal is to present science as an evolving process, rather than a rigid discipline that decontextualizes learning with no thought given to how it is used in the scientific community.

Goals

Our curriculum is aimed at developing the following cognitive skills: meaningful question generation, explanation, planning, and problem-solving. The generation of meaningful questions is inherent in successful models; addressing both explanatory and descriptive questions. The task also demands conceptual planning of the model, i.e., what pieces, relationships, appearances, sequencing, and rules will be included in the model. Problem-solving occurs as the students are challenged to accommodate their conceptual understanding to the computer application (Winograd & Flores, 1986).

Results

Our initial work during the past seven months indicates positive student affect and an increased understanding of the utility of models with regards to scientific phenomena.

Examples of student projects include models of genetics, ecosystems, evolution, and etiology of skin cancer. On an open-ended survey completed by 25 fourth and fifth grade students, 24 responded favorably when asked if they liked using computer models. Some of the students' rationale for their responses are as follows: the graphical capabilities of the program, being able to make pieces move, and coming up with a working, polished product. In an interview probing whether students preferred these computer models over traditional school-project models (i.e., posters and clay), a student who did not produce a working model responded, "I would still use the computer, because I can explain things better."

Thus far, the project has been an observational study of individual students creating models. Future instructional approaches will incorporate the scaffolding of the following strategies involved in the process of modeling: social generation of questions, discussion and selection of viable questions for modeling, group planning sessions, observation and manipulation of models, small group model creation, and peer critique.

We believe, when combined with the appropriate curriculum, this technology will aid in the development of cognitive skills requisite for scientific reasoning.

Acknowledgments

The authors would like to thank members of the research team for their input: Dr. Clayton Lewis (project director), Dr. Nancy Butler Songer, Dr. Michael Eisenberg, Teresa Garcia, Linda Hagen, Catherine Crand, and Page Pulver. We would also like to thank Apple Computers Inc. for the use of their software. This project is funded by the Advanced Applications and Technology program of the National Science Foundation.

References

Hutchins, E. (1995). *Cognition In The Wild.* The MIT Press: Cambridge, Massachusetts.

von Glasersfeld, E. (1995). *Radical Constructivism.* The Falmer Press: Washington, D.C.

Walker, M. (1963). *The Nature of Scientific Thought.* Prentice Hall, Inc.: Englewood Cliffs, New Jersey.

Winograd, T., & Flores, F. (1986). *Understanding Computers and Cognition.* Ablex Publishing Corporation: Norwood, New Jersey.

A Protocol Study of Problem Solving in the Game of Go

Yasuki Saito and **Atsushi Yoshikawa**
NTT Basic Research Labs.
3-1 Morinosato Wakamiya, Atsugi-shi, Kanagawa Pref. 243-01 Japan
yaski@ntt-20.brl.ntt.jp

Introduction

We started a series of cognitive studies of Go players, mainly using traditional protocol analyses and eye camera (Yoshikawa, 1996). Go player's protocols in real match situations are gathered and analyzed. Our main purpose is to build a model of Go player's problem solving behaviour.

Following characteristics of Go make it one of the best domain to investigate human complex problem solving: (1) Both pattern knowledge and language level knowledge play an important role in Go. (2) Amount and depth of verbalization seems to increase with expertise in Go. Thus we may be able to unravel the secret of high level expertise. (3) Go is becoming a new challenge to AI, and our effort will benefit AI activity to build a strong Go playing programs.

Go Player's Protocols

We connect two players in separate rooms through a program which enables both players to play Go over the computer network. Each player can talk freely without being heard by the other player. We have done twelve matches in total and obtained 2.8Mbytes of protocol data in total. Most significant part of protocols, namely 'naming', 'candidate move generation', and 'lookahead' are gathered and analyzed in depth.

Results

We started our study using simple two box model as our working hypothesis. This model consists of several iterations of 'Candiate Move Generation' and 'Candidate Move Evaluation'. Main results we obtained concerning this model are:

- Number of candidate moves considered per unit is 1.5 in average. Unit is an interval between consecutive moves.
- Candidate moves are generated very quickly, implying that generation is a pattern based process.
- Evaluation can be divided into two categories: [**Quick evaluation**] Without lookahead. This seems to be pattern based. This is used in 80% of units per game. [**Long evaluation**] Using lookahead. Occurring 20% of units per game.
- Lookahead is almost straight. Progressive deepening search in chess (Newell & Simon 1972) also appears in Go. But very few branching occurs in the lookahead. Thus this is quite different from computer program's search. Lookahead depth ranges from 1 to 11, and average depth is 4 (Scc Figure 1).
- Evaluation at the endpoint of lookahead can also be divided into two cases: [**Pattern based evaluation**] Quick evaluation based on good shape, moyo (large framework of potential territory) etc. [**Language based evaluation**] Many words describing player's own purpose, opponent's purpose, interrelation between multiple purposes all came into play in inferences.

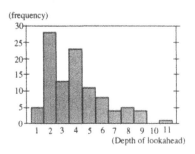

Figure 1: Lookahead depth.

Discussion and Conclusion

Previous work on Chess (Chase, 1973) emphasized the use of pattern knowledge by experts. Go is also full of patterns, but both pattern knowledge AND language level inferences play equally important roles in Go. We found most players use language extensively in their thinking (Saito, 1995). Most important function of language use seems to be search space reduction.

Many findings parallel those of Chess, yet there are significant differences such as the use of language and Go specific terms in Go player's problem solving.

References

Chase, W. G. & Simon, H. A. (1973). Perception in Chess. *Cognitive Psychology*, **4**, pp.55-81.

Newell, A. & Simon, H. A. (1972). *Human Problem Solving.* Prentice-Hall Inc.

Saito, Y. & Yoshikawa, A. (1994). Cognitive study of Go, In *Proc. of the Game Programming Workshop in Japan* (pp.44-55) (In Japanese).

Saito, Y. & Yoshikawa, A. (1995). Do Go Players think in words?, In *Proc. of the 2nd Game Programming Workshop in Japan* (pp.118-127).

Yoshikawa, A. & Saito, Y. (1996). Perception in TsumeGo under 4 Seconds Time Pressure, In *Proc. of the 18th Annual Conference of the Cognitive Science Society.*

The Role of Task and Stimulus Context in Category Development

Larissa K. Samuelson and **Linda B. Smith**
Department of Psychology and the Program in Cognitive Science
Indiana University, Bloomington, IN. 47405 (812/855-8256)
SAMUELSO@Indiana.edu

Traditional theories of categorization, which focus on the stability of cognition, encouraged developmentalists to seek the best task for uncovering represented categories. However the fact that children's categorizations vary across task has caused disputes about whether naming tasks, similarity judgments or property generalizations are the proper task for studying category representation. In contrast, theories of categorization that recognize the flexibility of cognition have encouraged the comparison of children's categorizations across tasks in an effort to understand the processes and information sources that create categories on line. The present research is motivated by this second framework. We report results from three studies of how 3-year-old's category judgments varied as a function of stimulus properties, task, and information about stimulus objects.

Stimulus Properties. Four sets of novel three-dimensional objects were used. Each set consisted of an exemplar and six test objects, two that were the same shape as the exemplar, two that were the same color as the exemplar, and two that were made from the same material as the exemplar. For two the of stimulus sets the exemplar was a made from a rigid material (e.g. wood or hardened clay). For the other two sets the exemplar was made from a non-rigid material (e.g. sponge or plastic).

Tasks. Three tasks were used: similarity judgment, naming and property generalization. In the similarity task subjects were shown an exemplar and asked if each test object was like the exemplar, "see this (exemplar), is this (test object) like this (exemplar)?" In the naming task each exemplar was given a novel name and the child was asked if that name applied to each test object, "see this (exemplar), this is a dax, is this a dax (test object)?". In the property generalization task children were asked to generalize a property of the exemplar object to the test objects, "see this (exemplar), it rolls, can this (test object) roll?"

Information about objects. The properties children were asked to generalize were of two kinds, related and control. In the case of rigid objects, related properties highlighted the object's shape (e.g. rolling or fitting into a puzzle). In the case of non-rigid objects related properties highlighted the material of the exemplar (e.g. squishing or folding). Control properties were not related to the shape, color or material of the objects (e.g. having a sticker on the back). Children either saw a demonstration of what objects could do, or were given a verbal description.

Participants. Twenty-four children participated in experiment 1, twelve each in a similarity and a naming task. Thirty-two children participated in experiment 2, all in a property generalization task. Sixteen children participated in experiment 3, all in a naming task with demonstrations of object properties (i.e., "this is a dax, it rolls, is this a dax?"). The mean age of all subjects was 36 months, 8 days.

Results. Children's categories were measured by the number of times they said yes to each kind of test object. As can be seen in figure 1, variations in task, in the rigidity of objects, and in demonstrations of object properties lead to differences in the categories children form. Specifically, children categorize by shape in naming tasks, but when the task highlights other object properties, such as the materials objects are made of, children's selective attention to shape is decreased.

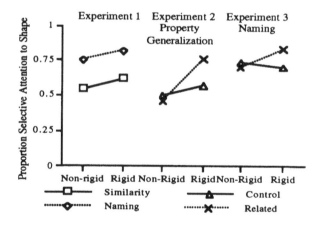

Figure 1. Results of experiments 1-3

Children's ability to smartly make novel categories in various contexts may reflect attentional learning. As children learn the statistical regularities of the world around them, these regularities may tell the child what aspects of the present context to attend to. If in the past every time the child heard "this is a___" was paired with seeing objects that were the same shape, over time the linguistic context of a naming task could come to direct attention to shape. In a similar manner, the contexts of rigid or non-rigid objects and actions on objects could be directing children's attention towards or away from the shape of objects. Consequently, children's categorizations will be the adaptive product of their past experiences and the present context.

Assessing and Supporting Remote Collaborative Problem Solving

Patricia Schank and **Mark Schlager**
SRI International, Center for Technology in Learning
333 Ravenswood Avenue, Menlo Park, CA 94025
schank@unix.sri.com, mark_schlager@qm.sri.com

Introduction

We define cognitive mentoring as joint problem solving involving a more-knowledgeable colleague (mentor) and less-knowledgeable peer (learner) in the context of an authentic task. Schlager, Poirier, and Means (1996) identify several highly iterative mentoring stages (problem definition, problem diagnosis, execution, evaluation, reflection) each involving a number of specific processes (e.g., demonstration, scaffolding) that participants execute. *Distant Mentor* (DM; Schlager, Means, O'day, & Poirier, 1994) was developed to facilitate and examine cognitive mentoring at a distance in the field of engineering. DM allows people in different locations working in a networked UNIX environment to jointly interact with a circuit board manufacturing simulation while maintaining a conversation over the network-based audio channel. DM supports both natural language and point-and-click gestures to query, rewind, and step through the simulation for information needed to diagnose the cause of manufacturing problems, and provides a history of prior queries and answers for easy review. Using the system, we examined questions such as: How does the aid of a mentor improve the speed and quality of subjects' solutions? Does DM afford any advantages over a mode of distant collaboration that is used commonly today—the telephone and FAX machine?

Method

Twelve undergraduates from San Jose State's Industrial and Systems Engineering Department were recruited as subjects, and two department graduates (with related teaching and work experience) were recruited as mentors. Subjects and mentors received training on DM, and mentors worked with at least two pilot subjects prior to the study.

Subjects worked alone or with one of the mentors (located in a separate room) to solve two (increasingly difficult) problems. Three conditions were employed: 1) *Solo*: Subjects used DM to solve problems independently, without the aid of a mentor. 2) *DM*: Subjects solved problems with the help of a mentor, using the full collaborative capability of DM. 3) *FAX*: Subjects had access to the mentor via an audio channel but could only send *snapshots* of the current DM screen to the mentor as needed. In each problem, the simulation was run with one or more parameters changed from the "normal" run, on which all machines were working properly and all boards had the same priority. Hence, the boards finished in a different order, and the subject was asked to diagnose the cause. Complete problem solutions contained 2-4 subparts, and the parameters were varied to ensure that mentors did not know the solution in advance.

Sessions were videotaped, transcribed, and coded into our cognitive mentoring stages. We assessed effects of condition on several measures, including solution time, mentoring time and stages, and solution completeness. See Schlager, Means, and Schank (in prep) for a more detailed discussion of these (and additional) analyses and observations.

Results

Mean solution time was 83 minutes for Solo subjects, while DM and FAX subjects solved the problems significantly faster (36 & 40 minutes, respectively; p<.05). DM subjects solved all problems completely, while FAX subjects solved significantly fewer (only 50%) of the problems completely (p<.05). Solo subjects solved 63% of the problems completely. Overall, problem diagnosis represented the largest percentage of mentor-learner interactions (44%), followed by execution (26%), problem definition (15%), reflection (13%), and evaluation (2%); no effects of condition on these stages were observed.

Discussion

DM appears to afford significant advantages over both individual and collaborative telephone/FAX problem solving. We attribute the reduced problem-solving time for mentored (compared to unmentored) subjects to the help provided by the mentor. Although DM and FAX groups spent a similar amount of time in each mentoring stage, joint interaction with the simulation apparently improves the effectiveness of this time in terms of solution quality. In a post-hoc test of overall problem solving productivity, we summed the mentoring and total solution time and found a significant savings (34%) for DM subjects (only) over the Solo group, demonstrating that the overall time savings more than offset the investment of the mentor's time. These results suggest that investment in network-based cognitive mentoring could significantly improve both productivity and quality of distributed teamwork. Our current (and future) work assesses mentor styles and effects, field implementation issues, and other multi-user collaborative environments.

References

Schlager, M, Poirier, C., & Means, B. (1996). Mentors in the classroom: Bringing the world outside in. In H. McLellan (Ed.), *Situated learning perspectives*. Englewood Cliffs, NJ: Educational Technology Pubs., 243-261.

Schlager, M., Means, B., O'day, V., & Poirier, C. (1994). *Enhancing skills through distant mentoring*. (Technical Report). Menlo Park: SRI International.

Schlager, M., Means, B., & Schank, P. (in prep). *Facilitating collaborative problem solving with Distant Mentor*. (Technical Report). Menlo Park: SRI International.

Some Parallels between Visual and Linguistic Processing

Gabriele Scheler
Institut für Informatik
Technische Universität München
D- 80290 München
scheler@informatik.tu-muenchen.de

The processing of a speech signal may be much more similar to sensory processing, in particular visual processing, than has previously been assumed (Chomsky 1976). In visual perception, certain features are extracted from the retinal (preprocessed) image, and relayed through several centers (Shepherd 1994). Feature extraction utilizes lateral inhibition which serves to enhance the signal-to-noise ratio. Several distinctive pathways for types of information (color perception, motion detection, texture analysis, shape perception) can be anatomically differentiated. 'Relay centers' have an increasing range of input from different centers and turn out features or schemas which are increasingly complex and useful for the organism. They feature interactive sideways and feedback connections (VanEssen & Deyoe 1995).

These concepts may equally be applied to linguistic processing. The processing of a speech signal may be relayed along several distinguishable pathways within a highly interconnected processing scheme.

Parallels in feature extraction, transformation and schema integration can be explored in detail in the area of microfeatures that are extracted from grammatical categories and link to cognitive units. In previous work (Scheler 1995), we have explored a hypothetical pathway for temporal information. The following elements seem to be essential for a biologically realistic model of semantic processing:

- semantic feature extraction as organized using "dimensions" of mutually exclusive features: lateral inhibition creates enhanced recognition

- interactive sideways: by feeding information to other pathways compressed contextual units are created ("wherever useful information arises it is used").

- feature transformation: recognition of affixes, formation of stable grammatical categories, semantic feature recognition, primary schema formation, central schema integration (cf. Fig 1).

- The emergence of a set of cognitive primitives may be seen as an exploration into the cognitive space accessible with language (Scheler & Schumann 1995). They can be interpreted as a set of interrelated primary schemas.

- central schemas as multimodal integration of sensory information may be organized as multiple overlays of the same set of information in various ways ('scripts').

- feedback links as reinforcement connections from logically "higher" levels integrate schema-driven with data-driven analysis. They provide a more flexible scheme than lateral inhibition, allowing for a top-down flow of information. By

activation of lower nodes from higher nodes, decisions can be made faster and schema recognition can be stabilized.

Numeric simulations of a qualitative model may add the essential traits to make empirically testable predictions on the time-course, interference effects, and results of semantic processing.

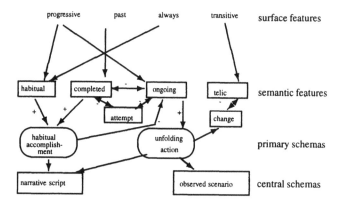

Figure 1: Feedback and Lateral Inhibition in Semantic Analysis of Temporal Meaning. Only a subset of connections and nodes are shown.

Chomsky, N. (1976) *Reflections on Language.* Fontana.

Scheler, G. (1996). Learning the semantics of aspect. In Daniel Jones (ed.) *New Methods in Language Processing.* University College London Press.

Scheler, G. & J. Schumann (1995). A hybrid model of semantic inference. In Alex Monaghan (ed.) *Proceedings of CSNLP, Dublin 1995.*

Shepherd, G.M. (1994). *Neurobiology.* Oxford (3rd ed.)

Van Essen, D. & Edgar A. Deyoe (1995). Concurrent Processing in the Primate Visual Cortex. In Gazzaniga (ed.) *The Cognitive Neurosciences.* MIT Press.

Is Cognitive Science Interdisciplinary?:
Past and Present Perspectives

Christian D. Schunn
Department of Psychology
Carnegie Mellon University
Pittsburgh, PA 15213
schunn@cmu.edu

Kevin Crowley
Department of Psychology
University of California, Santa Cruz
Santa Cruz, CA 95064
crowley@cats.ucsc.edu

Takeshi Okada
Department of Educational Psychology
Nagoya University
Furo-cho, Chikusa-ku, Nagoya, Japan 464-01
j46006a@nucc.cc.nagoya-u.ac.jp

The field of cognitive science is by origin and perhaps by definition an interdisciplinary field. However, it is unclear to what extent truly interdisciplinary work occurs in cognitive science. That is, is cognitive science merely a collection of researchers from different disciplines working separately on common problems? More specifically, does the work presented and published in cognitive science journals and conferences use methods from multiple disciplines? Does the work refer to results and previous work from multiple disciplines? Do researchers from different disciplines work together on projects? Furthermore, does cognitive science really include work from artificial intelligence, linguistics, neuroscience, philosophy, and psychology, as the journal *Cognitive Science*'s subtitle leads one to believe?

To address these questions we focused on three sources of data. First, we gathered data on the backgrounds of participants of the last two Annual Meetings of the Cognitive Science Society (cf., Schunn, Okada & Crowley, 1995). This data suggested that 1) the conference is dominated by cognitive psychology and computer science researchers, but 2) that a majority of the multi-author papers involved interdisciplinary collaborations (i.e., had authors from different disciplines). Further, the interdisciplinary collaborations were more likely to involve equal status working relationships (independent of actual professional status differences) than intradisciplinary collaborations (cf., Okada, Crowley, Schunn & Miwa, 1996; Okada, Schunn, Crowley, Oshima, Miwa, Aoki, & Ishida, 1995).

A second source of data was the content of papers published in the journal *Cognitive Science* and in the *Proceedings of the Annual Meeting of the Cognitive Science Society*. We focused on the prevalence of methods from the two prevailing disciplines in cognitive science: psychology and artificial intelligence. In particular, we analyzed the prevalence of papers reporting experiments, simulations (but not of any particular data), simulations of data, both simulations and experiments, and neither simulations nor experiments. Over the history of the Cognitive Science Society, we found an early rise in the prevalence of papers reporting simulations, and later rise in the prevalence of papers reporting simulations of data and papers reporting both experiments and simulations. However, even in 1995, the papers that were interdisciplinary in content accounted for only a third of all papers.

A third source of data was the references listed in the papers published in the journal *Cognitive Science*. All the references listed in each paper were coded into discipline categories. Preliminary analyses suggest that the patterns of change across time mirrored the results of the content analyses: we find a rise over time in the number of papers with significant referencing of multiple disciplines. However, the great majority of references were to sources from psychology and artificial intelligence, with few linguistics references and very few philosophy and neuroscience references, areas which are supposed to be equal partners in cognitive science.

Overall, these findings suggest that the glass is both half-full and half-empty: cognitive science has a significant interdisciplinary component, yet it is far from entirely interdisciplinary. In particular, work from cognitive psychology and artificial intelligence dominate, and there are still many papers published in cognitive science that do not involve interdisciplinary work.

Acknowledgments

This research was supported by a grant from the Mitsubishi Bank International Foundation to all of the authors. We would like to thank all those who participated in our studies.

References

Okada, T., Schunn, C. D., Crowley, K., Oshima, J., Miwa, K., Aoki, T., & Ishida, Y. (1995). Collaborative scientific research: Analyses of historical and interview data. In the *Proceedings of the 12th Annual Conference of the Japanese Cognitive Science Society*.

Okada, T., Crowley, K., Schunn, C. D., & Miwa, K. (1996). Collaborative scientific research in Japanese cognitive science: Analyses of questionnaire survey data. In the *Proceedings of the 13th Annual Conference of the Japanese Cognitive Science Society*.

Schunn, C. D. , Okada, T., & Crowley, K. (1995). Is cognitive science truly interdisciplinary?: The case of interdisciplinary collaborations. In the *Proceedings of the 17th Annual Conference of the Cognitive Science Society*. Hillsdale, NJ: Erlbaum.

Implicit Learning of Invariants

Carol A. Seger
Department of Psychology
Jordan Hall, Building 420
Stanford University
Stanford, CA 94305
seger@psych.stanford.edu

Implicit learning is learning of complex information, without the use of conscious hypothesis testing strategies, and without resultant consciously accessible knowledge sufficient to account for performance on an indirect test of learning (Seger, 1994). Most research in implicit learning has used tasks in which subjects learn relationships between stimulus elements. For example, in artificial grammar learning, subjects learn letter bigrams and trigrams and rules relating letters to each other (Seger, 1994; Knowlton & Squire 1996). Relatively little work has investigated subjects' ability to implicitly learn about invariant properties of complex stimuli (Frick & Lee, 1995). Learning relationships between items may require different forms of processing than identifying such invariants.

The experiment presented here investigated how well subjects learned two kinds of invariants: an item identity and location invariance, and an item identity and color invariance. In both condition, subjects were presented with displays consisting of 5 differently colored letters. For each subject, there was a particular letter that repeated in each display (the invariant letter). In the location invariant condition, the invariant letter appeared at the same location in each stimulus, whereas in the color invariant condition, it appeared in the same color in each stimulus. Otherwise, the stimuli were constructed randomly. After observing 30 displays and recalling the letters (but not the colors or locations) present in each, subjects were tested two ways. In the single item judgment test (1IJ), subjects were presented with novel patterns, half of which had the invariant and half of which did not. Subjects indicated for each pattern whether it followed the rule present in the studied items or not. The other test was a two alternative forced choice test (2AFC) in which subjects chose which of two patterns presented simultaneously followed the pattern present in the studied items. In both tests, the distractors were of two types: in one type of distractor the invariant letter appeared, but in a different location or color than in the studied exemplars. In other type of distractor the invariant letter was absent.

In order to investigate how much consciously verbalizable knowledge subjects had about the invariant, they were given a questionnaire to complete at the end of testing. Subjects who identified the invariant letter and its location or color on the free response questions, or who guessed the correct letter and indicated a high degree of confidence in their guess, were classified as having explicit knowledge of the invariant and were not included in the analyses. More subjects achieved explicit knowledge of the invariant in the location condition than the color condition, indicating that a letter-location invariance may be more salient than a letter-color invariance.

The 1IJ and 2AFC tests were differentially sensitive to implicit knowledge of the invariant. Subjects performed better on the 2AFC test than on the 1AJ test. The superiority of the 2AFC test could be because in that test subjects can compare the two stimuli and simply select which is more correct, rather than having to compare each stimulus to a mentally held criterion. In other words, relative correctness appears to be easier to determine than absolute correcness.

In addition, there was evidence that subjects did not learn the pairing between the invariant letter and the invariant location or color. Separate scores were calculated for the 2AFC test for pairs in which the distractor lacked the invariant letter altogether, and pairs in which the distractor included the invariant letter but in an incorrect location or color. Subjects performed above chance only on the pairs in which the invariant letter was absent, indicating that they could not reliably differentiate between stimuli solely on the basis of the invariant being in the correct location or color.

Acknowledgement
This research was supported by a NRSA postdoctoral Individual Research Award to the author.

References
Frick, R. W. & Lee, Y.-S. (1995). Implicit learning and concept learning. *Quarterly Journal of Experimental Psychology, 48A,* 762-782.
Knowlton, B. K. & Squire, L. R. (1996). Artificial grammar learning depends on implicit acquisition of both abstract and exemplar-specific information. *Journal of Experimental Psychology: Learning, Memory, and Cognition, 22,* 169-181.
Seger, C. A. (1994a). Implicit learning. *Psychological Bulletin, 115,* 163-196.

Planning Within a Virtual Environment

Travis L. Seymour, Andrea L. Patalano, and **Colleen M. Seifert**
Department of Psychology
University of Michigan
Ann Arbor, MI 48109-1109
{nogard,patalano,seifert}@umich.edu

Pending goals are intentions that are postponed by a planner because they do not fit into the current ongoing goal pursuit. Recognizing later opportunities to achieve pending goals is important because it allows one to defer work on a goal until in a better position to achieve it. Patalano, Seifert and Hammond (1993) show that predictive encoding -- predicting at the time of suspension what resources are needed to solve a pending goal -- serves to facilitate later recognition of opportunities. Moreover, by encoding a functional description of the plan rather than a more specific one, people may maximize the likelihood that they will retrieve a particular goal when a cue relevant to its resolution appears (Patalano & Seifert, 1996). For example, to hang up a poster, one might generate either "stick up with adhesive" or "stick up with glue" as a plan. The former plan may be more likely to induce goal retrieval in the presence of tape, chewing gum, glue, etc., while the latter may miss these opportunities for bringing the goal to mind.

The studies by Patalano & Seifert (1996) used a series of written test cues to examine memory for pending goals, and also presented written descriptions of the goals. To test the effects of predictive encoding on later recognition of opportunities to achieve pending goals in a richer environment, a general-purpose computer-based graphical environment management system (GEMS) was developed. The goal of this project was to allow subjects to navigate around an interactive three dimensional environment in which they might visually encounter problems or situations that encourage them to set up pending goals. More importantly, we wanted an environment whereby subjects could visually notice opportunities to achieve their pending goals and have the capability to try out candidate solutions based on these opportunities. The resulting software is a combination of two programs. The "room editor" allows the specification of the environment (constituent rooms and their appearance), objects within the environment, goals to be completed, potential solutions and their effects, and various output options. A separate program combines these elements into a graphical environment and allows the subject to navigate and interact with objects in the environment.

Each environment is represented by a series of full-screen color photographs. For each potential room or view in the environment, a picture of a corresponding real environment is photographed and digitally scanned into the computer. With the editor, each picture is defined as a "room." Any region within a room's picture (e.g. a door or entryway) can be defined as a "portal" to another room's picture by selecting the appropriate region in the editor. After the relationship has been established between a region on one room's picture and another room's picture, the subjects can

'enter' the target room simple by clicking on the corresponding region with the mouse. For example, clicking on the door to the kitchen from the hallway causes the computer screen to exchange the hallway's picture for the kitchen's picture. Because portals are not limited to between-room navigation, other relationships can be assigned; for example, the designer may allow the subject to click on a distant desktop that is a *portal* to a close-up of the desktop. Also, special symbols may be drawn onto the photograph (e.g. arrows) that allow turning around or returning to a previous room or view. These functions allow the creation of unlimited correspondences between the still photographs for designing virtual environments.

When a collection of pictures has been related in this manner, the subject is able to navigate around the environment by pointing and clicking on the natural portals. Since the pictures can be photographs of real environments, the visual effect lacks the artificiality of computer-generated 3D environments. In the same way that *portals* are defined, regions can be defined as *objects*. Objects can be defined as goal objects (e.g. a poster on the floor) and as solution objects (e.g. a roll of tape). Subjects use one object on another by dragging and dropping with the mouse. When a solution object is used on the appropriate goal object, associated actions can be executed in the environment and appear visually on the image.. This is accomplished by "hiding" and "uncovering" of object regions. For example, if the tape is used on the fallen poster, the designer might specify that the fallen poster then be hidden and that a hung poster is uncovered whenever that action occurs. In this manner, subjects can see their solutions work (or fail) before their eyes wile pursuing suspended goals.

Actions and response times relative to navigation and object manipulation, including which goals were solved and how, are saved to a text file for later analysis. The software was developed with Microsoft Visual Basic 4 for Windows.

The tasks subjects perform in GEMS – navigating around the environment and using objects in service of their goals – are much more realistic than the cued recall paradigm used previously. This more rich environment may help in examining people's ability to notice and respond to opportunities that arise in the course of planning.

References

Patalano, A. L., Seifert, C.M., & Hammond, K.J., (1993). Predictive encoding: Planning for opportunities. *Proceedings of the Fifteen Annual Cognitive Science Society Conference* (pp. 800-805), Boulder, CO.

Patalano, A. L., Seifert, C. M. (1996). *Opportunism in planning: Being reminded of pending goals.* Manuscript under review.

An Analysis of Tutor Response to Student Initiatives in Keyboard-to-Keyboard Tutorial Sessions[1]

Farhana Shah and Martha W. Evens

Computer Science & Applied Math
Illinois Institute of Technology
Chicago, IL 60616
{farhana,csevens}@steve.iit.edu

Introduction

The necessity for building a sophisticated human-machine interface for our intelligent tutoring system, called CIRCSIM-Tutor, has motivated us to explore natural language text understanding and generation. One complex task for the generator is crafting a response to student initiatives. As a basis for our research we studied human tutors' responses to student initiatives. How does a human tutor decide how to respond in real life? Initiative and response can be viewed as a cause and effect relationship where the initiative is the antecedent or cause and the response is the consequent or effect. A student initiative occurs when a student takes control of the tutoring session temporarily by saying something that forces the tutor to change the course of action and respond to the new situation. A question asked by the student in itself is considered to be one kind of initiative. A cooperative and reasonable response is considered as one that addresses the appropriate part of the question. We have analyzed tutor responses to student initiatives and developed twelve classes of tutor response to be used in CIRCSIM-Tutor.

Background

CIRCSIM-Tutor uses natural language dialogue to help students learn to solve problems in qualitative causal reasoning. We set forth to find out how human tutors handle this complex cognitive task. We studied twenty-eight transcripts of human keyboard-to-keyboard tutoring sessions. The tutors are two professors of Physiology at Rush Medical College, Joel Michael and Allen Rovick. They are teaching cardiovascular physiology with the goal of helping students learn solve problems involving the negative feedback system triggered by the baroreceptor reflex. The students are first year medical students who already have some background in the subject matter from attending lectures or reading the text book.

Classes of Initiatives and Responses

Many student initiatives are questions. In other cases the student states a theory and asks for confirmation or shows difficulty in improvement. In order to respond appropriately, the tutor must first understand the initiative and the student plan behind the initiative.

We used the conceptual categories for initiatives developed by (Sanders, 1992), who proposed eight classes containing various categories of the initiatives, viz: 1. The student asks a question about the subject matter or about herself/himself, 2. The student has trouble "seeing" some idea, 3. The student requests repair, 4. The student does repair, 5. The student hedges, 6. The student makes an explicit backward reference, 7. Initiatives specific to the hardware/software environment, 8. Administrative topics.

We analyzed responses to student initiatives in twelve classes based on the goals of the tutors and the tutoring strategies used. They are: 1. Hinting, 2. Directed Line of Reasoning, 3. Acknowledgment, 4. Confirmation, 5. Summary, 6. Instruction in the "Rules of the Game", 7. Teaching the Sublanguage, 8. Teaching the Problem Solving Algorithms, 9. Extending Help, 10. Probing the Student's Inference Process, 11. Brushing Off, 12. Conversational Repair.

The focus of the student initiative can be established by understanding and recognizing the student plan (Carberry, 1990). We have also explored the relationship between the initiative category and the response category and the length of the response.

References

Carberry, S. (1990). *PLan Recognition in Natural Language Dialogue*. Cambridge, MA: MIT Press.

Sanders, G. A., Evens, M. W., Hume, G. D., Rovick,A.A., and Michael, J. A. (1992). An Analysis of How Students Take the Initiative in Keyboard-to-keyboard Tutorial Dialogues in a Fixed Domain. In *Proceedings of the Fourteenth Annual Meeting of the Cognitive Science Society* (pp. 1086--1091). Bloomington, IN: Lawrence Erlbaum Associates.

---

[1]This work was supported by the Cognitive Science Program, Office of Naval Research under Grant No. N00014-94-1-0338, to Illinois Institute of Technology. The content does not reflect the position or policy of the government and no official endorsement should be inferred.

Evidence for Frontal Lobe-based Mechanisms in Prospective Remembering

Lionel R. Shapiro[1], Johnna K. Shapiro[2] and Michael Antholine[2]
Departments of Computer Science[1] and Psychology[2]
Illinois Wesleyan University
Bloomington, IL 61702-2900
lshapiro@sun.iwu.edu

Introduction

Failures of prospective memory are common in everyday life, yet not widely studied in the laboratory. Prospective memory requires the individual to remember to perform a future event. Einstein and McDaniel (1990) have suggested that prospective memory actually involves two components: remembering that something needs to be remembered (the prospective component), and remembering the information itself (the retrospective component). They also make the distinction between event-based prospective memory, which requires some action when an external event takes place, and time-based prospective memory, in which action is required after a specified time interval has passed. Time-based remembering is hypothesized to rely on self-initiated memory processes because no external event acts as a cue for remembering. The individual must continuously shift attentional resources between other tasks and the monitoring of time. This "multi-tasking" aspect of time-based prospective memory may be especially vulnerable to problems with planning and the reallocation of attentional resources, and suggests a possible role in these tasks for the frontal lobes. In Cockburn's (1995) case study of a frontal lobe patient, it was found that the patient could remember to perform actions when they were embedded in an ongoing activity, but had great trouble when the task involved suspension of one activity in order to begin another (contextual shift) (see Kvavilashvili, 1992).

Methods/Discussion

The present study involves participants who have been asked to complete a survey of general knowledge (presented and responses recorded on computer). The participants had two tasks: to inform the researcher of how far they had progressed every five minutes (requiring a contextual shift), and to type their names into the computer upon completion of the survey (an embedded activity). The only time piece available to the participants was on the computer and was accessed by pressing a specified key. Our primary dependent measures were: number of clock checks, timing of clock checks relative to 5 minute epochs, and accuracy on each of the two prospective memory tasks.

We also administered several other cognitive measures to each participant. These included: an intelligence test (Kaufman Brief Intelligence Test), and two measures of executive functioning/cognitive flexibility (Stroop Color Test and Wisconsin Card Sort Test - WISC). The later two measures assess subtly different frontal lobe processes. The Stroop test primarily assesses sensitivity to interference from competing stimuli, while the WISC assesses an individual's tendency to perseverate - a difficulty in shifting from one aspect of a task to another. By correlating these two measures with performance on the prospective memory tasks, we have begun to address which cognitive processes crucial to prospective forms of remembering are carried out by the frontal lobes. Complete results and discussion of implications will be presented.

References

Cockburn, J. (1995). Task interruption in prospective memory: A frontal lobe memory? *Cortex*, 31, 87-97.

Einstein, G. O., and McDaniel, M. A. (1990). Normal aging and prospective memory. *Journal of Experimental Psychology: Learning, Memory and Cognition*, 16, 717-726.

Kvavilashvili, L. (1992). Remembering intentions: A critical view of existing paradigms. *Applied Cognitive Psychology*, 6, 507-524.

The Generation of Creative Inferences

Franz Schmalhofer, Lutz Franken and **Jörg Schwerdtner**
German Research Center for Artificial Intelligence (DFKI)
Erwin-Schrödinger-Str. Bau 57
D 67663 Kaiserslautern, Germany
(schmalho, franken, schwerdt)@dfki.un-kl.de

Two Kinds of Inferences

Inferences are typically generated by applying some inference schemata to a body of knowledge. In deductive reasoning, a schema like the modus ponens (P, P->Q, | Q) may be applied to a rule set and thereby produce some inference (e.g. Q). Inductive inferences are generated by an inference schema which replaces specific by more general terms. The inference of "fruits are eatable" may thus be induced from the assertion "apples are eatable". In a way, such inferences are already implicitly contained in the knowledge base and the inference schemata. In other words, inferencing is often the explication of implicit information. *Creative inferences*, on the other hand, are constructed as novel knowledge units which are not even implicitly contained in the terminology of the knowledge base. Such *creative inferences* may be produced by relating separate terminologies to one another. For example, Boden (1991) has described Kekulé's discovery of the benzene ring as such a creative insight (or inference) where the knowledge about strings of carbon atoms became associated with the knowledge about snakes. A snake which bit its own tail could thus generate the idea of a ring (rather than a string) of carbon atoms. This would be impossible to deduce with the original terminology about carbon atoms. In this paper, we describe a computational model which produces creative inferences.

Model of Creative Inferences

Norvig (1988) has recently described an inferencing method which may also be applied for connecting two separate terminologies or conceptual spaces. By using a marker passing procedure, paths are found which connect concepts from different conceptual spaces. From these paths new hypotheses or assertions are compiled, which are neither implicitly contained in the first nor second conceptual space. Figure 1 shows a schematic diagram of the knowledge construction and inference generation processes which are performed by the computational model. There are six different conceptual spaces. Each one is structured according to a class hierarchy. The conceptual space of THINGS may contain all kinds of physical and living objects. The conceptual space of IDEAS contains abstract concepts like "peace", "justice", "friendships" and other personal relationships. ACTIONS represent goal-oriented changes and EVENTS represent incidental changes of THINGS. Similarly, THOUGHTS represent goal-oriented changes and INSIGHTS represent incidental changes of IDEAS. By

CROSS_LINKS, concepts can be connected between and within different conceptual spaces.

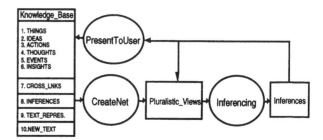

Figure 1: Schematic Diagram of Inference Generation

The computational model is used for simulating creative inferences during text comprehension. A NEW_TEXT is therefore also entered by its conceptual units. The computational model processes a segment of the NEW_TEXT and relates its conceptual units to the appropriate concepts in the respective knowledge bases. A semantic net is thus obtained, which is called Pluralistic_Views. An inference can then be generated by marking two concept nodes of the Pluralistic_Views. A marker passing process will find the connecting paths between these concepts along certain types of links. The marker can be programmed by the user so that its resources for passing different types of links are limited. Furthermore, the order in which different types of links can be traversed may be partially or completely specified. The marker passing process thus implements a spreading activation process which will find specific sequences of links in knowledge bases.

By compilation, an inference can be produced from each path. This inference is then linked to the Pluralistic_Views. The model is intended to simulate knowledge construction processes of Kintsch's (1988) construction-integration theory. It is implemented in C++ and will use EXCEL as a user interface. Simple texts which consist of up to four sentences are applied to demonstrate the capabilities of the model.

Boden, M. A. (1991) The creative mind: Myths and mechanisms. New York: Basic Books Inc. Publishers.

Kintsch, W. (1988). The role of knowledge in discourse comprehension: A construction-integration model. Psychological Review, 95, 163-182.

Norvig, P. (1989). Marker passing as a weak method for text inferencing. Cognitive Science, 13, 569-620.

Cases, Reasoning and Bell's Telephone[1]

Marin D. Simina and **Janet L. Kolodner**
College of Computing
Georgia Institute of Technology
Atlanta, GA 30332–0280
{marin, jlk}@cc.gatech.edu

This poster investigates memory issues that influence long-term creative problem solving and design activity, taking a case-based reasoning (Kolodner & Wills, 1993) perspective. Our exploration is based on a well-documented example: the invention of the telephone by Bell (1908). But to understand this act of creative design, we have to analyze Bell's earlier research goals. We abstract Bell's research method and the reasoning mechanisms he used that appear time and again in long-term creative problem solving. In particular, we identify an understanding mechanism used widely by those processes which rely on previous experience. Finally, we integrate the new mechanisms in a computer model, ALEC, which features creativity elements in case-based design.

Retrospectively, the obvious question related to the invention of the telephone is: what cognitive issues "delayed" the invention of the telephone till 1876? The basic principles of the telephone, electromagnetism and induction, had been known since 1831. Several inventors tried and failed to design the telephone, because they (1) relied too much on prevalent telegraphy practice, (2) ignored the basic principles of electromagnetism, and (3) gave up too soon. It looks like these inventors applied case-based reasoning poorly: they stuck to minor adaptations of telegraphy rather than reassessing the problem and analyzing it from a new perspective. In contrast, Bell reassessed the telephone problem as being acoustical and not electrical. When Bell was stuck in electrical details, he analyzed his telephony experiments using acoustical experiences and expertise.

Bell frequently interpreted and remembered his electrical experiments in terms of acoustics, that he could easily *perceive* without supplementary equipment. Consequently, in some cases he could *recognize opportunities* to solve suspended problems while pursuing other problems (i.e., the "undulatory current" was recognized while working on the multiple telegraph problem, by noticing peculiar acoustical effects). But not all the recognized opportunities fell in the above category. Sometimes, working on several problems *in the same period of time* facilitated knowledge transfer among them without any special perceptual elaboration (i.e., interleaved work on both the telephone and phonautograph inspired the microphone design for the telephone).

Our exploration of creative design (Kolodner & Wills, 1993; Simina & Kolodner, 1995) provides an initial framework (i.e., the IMPROVISER system) for a more enriched and dynamic case-based reasoning able to explain some interesting reasoning issues involved in the invention of the telephone. In this framework a designer evolves concurrently the design specification and a pool of alternatives under consideration, relying on his previous experience. But Bell's *understanding* and interpretation processes, exploring previous experience, seem far more complex than those handled by IMPROVISER. Bell used analogy when simple retrieval failed. When analogy also failed, Bell made new hypotheses by combining attributes of the (partial) design alternatives retrieved. This mechanism led to the famous hypothesis of the "undulatory current", by mixing properties of sound transmission and electrical currents. We realised that understanding is a memory issue that should play a more important role in a framework for creative design. IDeAL (Bhatta & al., 1994) stresses also the role of understanding in design. IDeAL revises its understanding of the problem based on generalizations built from specific experiences.

Based on Bell's case study, we are developing a computer model that integrates understanding and design problem solving to test our hypotheses about the role of case-based reasoning in long-term creative design. In our model the problem solving processes relying on previous experience call an understanding process, adapted from Moorman & Ram's (1994) creative understanding algorithm. The understanding process in turn may call design problem solving processes to achieve a better artifact understanding. We hope that a good understanding of creative design processes will help us build better tools to assist human designers.

References

[Bell, Alexander Graham](1908). *The Bell Telephone: The Deposition of Alexander Graham Bell*, Boston: American Bell Telephone Co.

Kolodner, J. & Wills, L. (1993). Case-based Creative Design. *AAAI Spring Symposium on AI and Creativity*. Stanford, CA. March 1993.

Moorman, K. & Ram, A. (1994). A model of creative understanding. *Proc. Twelfth Annual AAAI Conference.* (pp. 74–79).

Bhatta S., Goel, A. & Prabhakar, S. (1994) Innovation in Analogical Design: A Model-Based Approach. *Proc. Third International Conference on Artificial Intelligence in Design*, Lausanne, Switzerland. (pp. 57–74).

Simina, M., Kolodner, J. (1995). Opportunistic Reasoning: A Design Perspective. *Proc. Seventeenth Conference of the Cognitive Science Society.* (pp. 78–83).

[1]This research was was funded in part by NSF Grant No. IRI-8921256 and in part by ONR Grant No. N00014-92-J-1234.

Does Subitizing Depend on the Magnocellular Visual Pathway?

Tony J. Simon[1], Scott Peterson[1], Gargi Patel[2], and Krish Sathian[2]
[1]School of Psychology
Georgia Institute of Technology
Atlanta GA 30332-0170
tony.simon@psych.gatech.edu

[2]Department of Neurology
Emory University School of Medicine
Atlanta GA 30322
sathian@neuro.emory.edu

Introduction

Visual search of a multi-element display leads, under certain conditions, to "popout" or preattentive perception of a unique or highly salient item in the display (Treisman, 1988). What might be the neural locus of mechanisms underlying such preattentive visual perception? Visual processing occurs along two relatively distinct pathways, termed the magnocellular (M) and parvocellular (P) pathways (Livingstone & Hubel, 1987). Since responding and orienting rapidly to salient features in the environment carries a high survival value, we hypothesized that the phylogenetically older M pathway preferentially mediates the preattentive processing leading to eventual capture of attention by the stimulus of immediate interest.

Due to a number of physiological differences in the response properties of neurons in the two pathways, their relative contributions to visual perception can be psychophysically dissected (Livingstone & Hubel, 1987). For instance, perception of colored stimuli on an isoluminant background depends exclusively on chromatic cues and thus predominantly on the P system, the M system being relatively uninvolved (Livingstone & Hubel, 1987). We predicted that this should selectively impair preattentive, parallel visual processing while leaving later, serial processing relatively unaffected.

The task chosen for this examination was subitizing; the ability to rapidly and accurately enumerate small sets of items (e.g. Trick & Pylyshyn, 1994). Subitizing is a robust phenomenon that has recently been associated with preattentive mechanisms. For example, Trick & Pylyshyn (1994) showed that, when adults were asked to enumerate target letter Os in a field of distractor Xs (a condition where the targets typically "pop out"), the standard subitizing profile was observed. This is a small reaction time slope of around 50ms per item for collections of up to 4 items with a steeper slope in the range of 300ms for larger sets. However, when the Xs were replaced by distractor Qs (thus inducing attentive visual search for targets) reaction time was linearly related to the number of items being enumerated for all set sizes. Since subitizing is apparently possible only when preattentive mechanisms are in operation, we reasoned that it might be affected by manipulations affecting preattentive processing. We therefore adopted a subitizing task to test the hypothesis that preattentive, parallel visual processing depends preferentially on the M system.

Methods and Results

In a within-subjects design, subjects had their isoluminance point individually established and then were presented with 1 to 8 green rectangles which were either isoluminant with (ISO) or considerably greater in luminance (NI) than a red background. Their task was to report as quickly as possible how many rectangles they saw. Presentation time was terminated by subject response. We predicted that enumeration performance would be affected detrimentally by the isoluminant stimuli only and that the effect would occur only in the subitizing range. Our data showed a subitizing span of 3 objects for both ISO and NI stimuli. Within subitizing there was a significant increase in mean reaction time (of about 15 ms) for the ISO stimuli over the NI stimuli ($F(1,29) = 20.70$, $p < .001$). Outside the subitizing range, performance was not significantly different ($F(1,29) = .14$, $p = .713$). Thus, our initial results are as predicted. While further research is needed in order to examine this effect in greater detail, our findings appear to support the suggestion that the magnocellular visual pathway is the preferential processing route for a subitizing task; one that is closely associated with preattentive visual processing.

References

Livingstone, M.S. & Hubel, D.H. (1987). Psychophysical evidence for separate channels for the perception of form, color, movement and depth. *Journal of Neuroscience*, 11, 3416-3468.

Treisman, A. (1988). Features and objects: the fourteenth Bartlett Memorial lecture. *Quarterly Journal of Experimental Psychology* , 40A, 201-237.

Trick, L.M. & Pylyshyn, Z.W. (1994) Why are small and large numbers enumerated differently? A limited-capacity preattentive stage in vision. *Psychological Review*, 101, 80-102.

Mental Content and the Causal History of Neural Substrates

Paul G. Skokowski

McDonnell-Pew Centre for Cognitive Neuroscience
Oxford University
Parks Road
Oxford, OX1 3PT, England,
Paul.Skokowski@psy.ox.ac.uk

Introduction

This paper argues that we can determine the contents of the neural substrates that support implicit beliefs by considering the history of the substrates and their role within the system. Both artificial and biological neural substrates are examined with the goal of showing that structures at the neural level can carry informational content about the types of events which caused them. A brief discussion of the conditions under which states carry information content is given, followed by a sketch of why neural networks carry implicit content, and finally a brief case for implicit content in wetware is made.

Information

I cannot argue the merits of different theories of information content here Therefore I will assume a correlational version of information content in order to see how far it gets us towards determining the content in neural substrates (Dretske, 1981; Dretske, 1988). Say that B carries information about A if the following two conditions are met: (1) A causes B, and (2) B occurs only if A occurs. For example, suppose we train a neural network to recognize chairs. The input layer of the network is say a 100x100 screen of nodes which represent black or white pixels from a digital camera. Then a 2-D pixel image of a chair occurs at the input layer of my network if and only if a chair is in front of the camera. Then the input layer lighting up in this pattern (2-D B/W chair image) carries information that a chair is in front of the camera. So the *input layer* of my network can carry information about its environment. An analogous case is my retina. Retinal rods and cones generally only fire with a chair-like pattern when chairs are present. Though there may be exceptions (e.g. an Ames chair) these are rare, so I will consider the above definition of information to work in most cases.

Both neural networks and people *learn* to recognize chairs. Consider the set of events comprising successful learning of a task over time. Call this set of events a learning history, or **H** for short. We can think of **H** as the cause of an internal change in the cognitive system which results in the learning. For a neural network this history causes a new set of weights **W** to be installed which allows the network to perform the task. The learning history **H** is a sufficient condition for installation of the weights **W**. For example, *if* we take the well-known Gorman and Sejnowski network for distinguishing sonar signals and train it on their training set

for the number of epochs as they've described, *then* it will learn to distinguish submarine from rock sonar signals.

To pass philosophical muster, we should really think of **H** and **W** as types. For example, we could vary the order of the rock and mine signals in the above example and the network would still learn the task equally well. The resulting weight matrix might even have changed in some of its elements, but successful learning will mean the same behavioral result that the network achieves its task to similar accuracy. So a learning history of the type **H** is sufficient to cause a weight matrix of type **W**. It turns out we are already very close to a theory of informational content for the trained weight state **W** in a neural network. We have met condition (1) above, namely, that things of type **H** cause things of type **W**. Now we need to show that **W**'s occur only if **H**'s occur.

Large Numbers, LTP and Content

This is done by using the argument from large numbers, which concludes that the odds against finding a neural network in a certain recognition state are very large. But the human brain is much more complicated than most networks (Churchland, 1989). So finding a structure in the human brain that connects certain perceptual states with certain (non-reflex) motor states is even more likely to have been caused by learning than the analogue state in a simpler neural network.

I next argue that as a result of a causal learning process, with LTP as the current candidate for synaptic modification, a *neural* structure **W** is installed in the brain, becomes a stable, permanent part of the agent, carries content, and allows outputs **M** to be caused whenever the network is presented with an *F*. This may be how we acquire certain implicit beliefs. The states **W** may be installed by learning histories in subtle ways which agents are not explicitly aware of. These histories may be thought of as the environmental *reasons* for states like **W**.

References

Churchland, P.M. (1989). *A Neurocomputational Perspective*. Cambridge, MA: MIT Press.
Dretske, F. (1981). *Knowledge and the Flow of Information*. Cambridge, MA: MIT Press.
Dretske, F. (1988). *Explaining Behavior*. Cambridge, MA: MIT Press.

Individual Differences in Working Memory Capacity and the Duration of Elaborative Inferences

Marie St. George and **Marta Kutas**
Center for Research in Language (0526) and Cognitive Science (0515)
University of California, San Diego
La Jolla, CA 92093
{stgeorge@crl.ucsd.edu,kutas@cogsci.ucsd.edu}

The general consensus among inference researchers is that elaborative inferences are made only under certain circumstances, such as highly predictive contexts, if they are made at all (e.g., Garrod, O'Brien, Morris, & Rayner, 1990; Graesser, Singer, & Trabasso, 1994; McKoon & Ratcliff, 1992; Murray, Klin, & Myers, 1993; Potts, Keenan, & Golding, 1988; van den Broek, 1994). In the present experiment we tested: (1) whether elaborative inferences within *moderately* predictive contexts were made during reading, and (2) whether individual differences in working memory capacity were associated with differences in the length of time the elaborative inferences were maintained. Three and four sentence length paragraphs were designed so that one particular outcome of the story was more likely than other potential outcomes. The outcomes were 70% probable given the context of the paragraphs, based on normative data collected prior to running the study. Typically, outcomes in other studies of elaborative or predictive inferences are between 90% and 100% predictable within the given context. In the present experiment, the final sentence of all of the paragraphs explicitly stated the inference readers may have made. There were four conditions: an Inference condition and a Control condition, with two possible times of test, Immediate or Delayed. Forty-four sets of paragraphs were created, with each set containing a version corresponding to each condition. In the Immediate condition (three sentences in length), the sentence explicitly stating the inference immediately followed the sentence which may have elicited the inference (sentence two). In the Delay condition (four sentences in length), there was a filler sentence related to the story between the eliciting sentence (two) and explicit statement of the inference (sentence four), which neither confirmed nor precluded the inference. A "word-based priming" Control condition was created using the relevant content words from the experimental paragraphs in a slightly different context so that they did not elicit the inference. Immediate and Delay conditions were created for the Control as well as for the Inference condition.

Forty-five subjects (eighteen male; twenty-seven female) participated in the experiment. Their ages ranged from eighteen to twenty-five years.

A moving window reading time paradigm was used, providing a measure of how long readers spent on each word of the paragraphs. The structure of the entire paragraph was on the screen as the subjects read. Dashed lines represented the letters in the words, with spaces between them. When subjects pressed the space bar a new word appeared and the previous word was replaced by dashed lines. Following one-third of the paragraphs subjects answered comprehension questions designed to make sure they were paying attention to the content of the paragraphs.

Overall, the words in the final sentences of the Inference condition were read approximately 25 msec faster than the words in the Control condition. The effect seems to be driven by content words, specifically, the final content word of the sentence, which was read approximately 150 msec faster in the Inference condition compared to the Control. Therefore, it seems a highly predictive context is not necessary for elaborative inferences to be made during reading; elaborative inferences can be made in moderately predictive contexts as well.

In addition, readers with low working memory capacity (as measured by a variation of Daneman & Carpenter's (1980) reading span task) showed faster reading times for the Inference condition relative to the Control <u>only</u> in the Immediate condition; there was no reading time difference between the inference and control in the Delayed condition. Thus the low span readers seem to make the elaborative inference initially, however, they do not seem to have the inference active in memory following the intervening sentence. By contrast, readers with high working memory capacity read the words of the final sentence faster in the Inference condition than in the Control in both the Immediate and Delay conditions.

These data suggest that there is a relationship between working memory capacity and the duration of inferences in working memory. Perhaps one consequence of working memory capacity is how long items are held in working memory when the items (in this case the inference) are not supported explicitly by the context of the sentence. In the Delayed conditions of our paragraphs the intervening sentence neither supported nor contradicted the inference. It may be that the low span group did not have the working memory capacity to "waste" on keeping an inference in working memory when the intervening sentence did not confirm the inference. The high span group, by virtue of their larger working memory capacity, may have had enough to spare to keep the inference in working memory even though the intervening sentence did not confirm the inference.

846

Computational Differences Between
Implicit and Explicit Learning:
Evidence From Learning Crypto-Grammars

Mark F. St. John
Department of Cognitive Science
University of California, San Diego
La Jolla, CA 92093

Abstract

If implicit learning is a form of memorization/prototyping, and explicit learning is a form of hypothesis testing, then they should differ both computationally and behaviorally. Experiments 1 and 2 found that implicit learning in an artificial grammar learning task was unable to learn nonadjacent regularities. Subjects read aloud 60 letter strings containing either adjacent or nonadjacent regularities. In a subsequent categorization task on novel rule-governed vs. rule-violating strings, subjects demonstrated learning of the adjacent rule only. A Simple Recurrent Network (SRN) can simulate subjects' implicit learning behavior whereas previous associative network models (e.g. Dienes, 1992) cannot. Experiment 3 compared implicit and explicit learning: instructions to read strings aloud vs. search for rules. The nonadjacent rule was only learned under explicit learning. A hint making the rule more salient enhanced explicit learning but not implicit learning. Finally, subjects can voluntarily switch strategies. In sum, implicit and explicit learning show different effects and different limitations, supporting the contention that they are indeed different strategies.

Reference

Dienes, Z. (1992). Connectionist and memory-array models of artifical grammar learning. <u>Cognitive Science. 16.</u> 41-80.

Syntactic Comprehension:
Practice Makes Perfect and Frequency Makes Fleet

Mark F. St. John
Department of Cognitive Science
University of California, San Diego
La Jolla, CA 92093

Morton Ann Gernsbacher
Department of Psychology
University of Wisconsin, Madison
Madison, WI 53706

Abstract

Passive and cleft-object constructions are harder to comprehend and breakdown more easily under stress or brain damage than active and cleft-subject constructions. Are they harder because they require special comprehension processes that are localized in brain areas damaged in aphasia, because they require greater central processing capacity that is reduced in aphasia, or because they are simply less frequent and therefore less well practiced and more easily disrupted by brain damage? A PDP model of the word-by-word comprehension process demonstrates that less frequently trained constructions are learned more slowly (though eventually mastered) and break down more easily. The model employed a simple recurrent network architecture similar to St. John and McClelland (1990). The model was trained on 15,912 instances of four sentence constructions (simple active, simple passive, cleft-subject, and cleft-object). The model's task was to determine the agent and patient of a presented sentence. One construction was arbitrarily chosen to be trained 8 times more frequently than the others. The high frequency construction was mastered first, though all were mastered eventually. Generalization to new sentences was high, demonstrating mastery of the syntax rather than memorization of the training instances. Following training, processing breakdown was simulated by adding uniformly distributed noise to the units in the hidden layer of the network. The low frequency constructions were more prone to error than the high frequency construction. Sentence length also increased learning time and the potential for breakdown. Frequency and length are simple but powerful factors throughout cognition; the model demonstrates that they can also be powerful factors in normal and aphasic language comprehension.

Reference

St. John, M. F. & McClelland, J. L. (1990). Learning and applying contextual constraints in sentence comprehension. *Artificial Intelligence, 46,* 217-257.

CONICAL: The Computational Neuroscience Class Library

Joseph J. Strout
University of California, San Diego
3033 Basic Sciences Building
9500 Gilman Drive
La Jolla, CA 92093-0608
jstrout@ucsd.edu

Introduction

Compartmental modeling of biological neurons and neural networks plays an important role in computational neuroscience. Typically, this modeling is accomplished with monolithic Unix-based simulation packages, *e.g.*, *Genesis* (Wilson *et al.*, 1989) or *Neuron* (Hines 1989). These packages are powerful research tools, and well suited for an experienced user with access to an appropriate computer platform. However, such packages suffer several drawbacks for other users: they can be difficult to learn; are not easy to modify, extend, and integrate with other software; and are generally not portable to non-Unix/DOS platforms.

To meet these different requirements, a C++ class library was created. CONICAL, the Computational Neuroscience Class Library, consists of a non-monolithic hierarchy of C++ classes. The library can be used in whole or in part as needed. Each object class is designed to be readily extended or modified through the inheritance mechanism; complex classes are derived from base classes in several steps, allowing behavior to be efficiently overridden at any point. The library has been co-developed and tested with Unix, DOS, and MacOS compilers. C++ constructs which tend to be problematic (e.g., templates and exception handling) have been avoided to ensure maximum portability among various platforms and compilers.

Applications

CONICAL can be used with a very simple main program, in a manner similar to the script-based simulators mentioned above. In direct comparisons, it was found that CONICAL required roughly the same amount of user-written code as the equivalent *Genesis* script. Moreover, since CONICAL is written in C++, learning a new language is not necessary for many users. In this usage, output is sent to the screen or a file for graphing or analysis by other software, and the complete program can be fully cross-platform compatible.

CONICAL can also be embedded in larger software packages, such as graphical simulators, educational packages, or plug-in modules for general-purpose mathematics software. This will allow programmers with little knowledge of compartmental modeling techniques, or physiologists with only modest programming skill, to produce accurate and efficient neural simulations, with a wide range of applications in research and education.

Methods

CONICAL consists of approximately 20 classes. The hierarchy tree has four roots, with the longest branch measuring five classes. Multiple inheritance is applied wherever needed to segregate functionality. Two main branches dominate the hierarchy: one develops compartments, ending in a standard cylindrical compartment; the other contains currents, including voltage- and ligand-gated channels. The library includes a standard Hodgkin-Huxley channel, whose kinetics are set by selecting an equation form and parameters, as well as a standard alpha-function synapse. A more sophisticated Markov-model synapse is also included, as are current injectors and data-recording objects. Numerical integration is done by the exponential Euler method. Documentation is provided in hypertext format via the World-Wide Web.

Conclusion

CONICAL is not intended as a replacement for current simulation packages; rather, it serves a complimentary purpose. It may be the preferred simulation environment in cases where (1) the user prefers C++ to a new script language; (2) considerable modification or extension of the simulator is planned; (3) the user needs to embed a neural model within other software; or (4) simulation is needed on platforms other than Unix or DOS/Windows. The CONICAL library, including source code, may be freely used for non-commercial purposes. It may be obtained via the World-Wide Web[1], or directly from the author.

Acknowledgements

This work was supported in part by an NSF Predoctoral Fellowship.

References

Hines, M. (1989). A program for simulation of nerve equations with branching geometries. *International Journal of Biomedical Computing*, 24, 33-68.

Wilson, M. A., Bhalla, U. S., Uhley, J. D., and Bower, J. M. (1989). GENESIS: A system for simulating neural networks. In D. Touretzky (Ed.), *Advances in Neural Information Processing Systems* (pp. 485-492). San Mateo, CA: Morgan Kaufmann.

---

[1] http://www-acs.ucsd.edu/~jstrout/conical/

Individual Characteristics as Factors in the Navigation Process

Miriam Struchiner
Regina Maria Vieira Ricciardi
Antonia Cinira Melo Diogo
Nilce da Silva Correa
NUTES/UFRJ, Ilha do Fundão, Centro de Ciências da Saúde
bloco A, sala 26, CEP 21949-900 Rio de Janeiro, Brasil
Telephone 011-55-21-270-5847, FAX 011-55-21-270-3944
`mchiner@chagas.biof.ufrj.br`

The navigation process in hyperdocument structures is highly complex. This is due to the vast amount of information, possible pathway options, and richness of visual stimuli. Several studies have reported the effects of different interface approaches and hypertext content structures that produce users misorientation and cognitive overload (Cimino, Elkin & Barnett, 1992). Other studies add information on how these "navigational problems" may be circumstancial due to several users' characteristics. They also approach hypertext research tradition as being much more oriented towards "navigation outcome" rather than "navigation process", and urge research in this field for better understanding users' cognitive processes when interacting with hyperdocuments (Dillon, McKnight & Richardson, 1993).

The present research sought to explore the navigation process beyond the standard treatment of cognitive maps to include the investigation of individual characteristics and previous knowledge schemata that may influence this process. They are: (1) experience with the use of computers and peripherals (hardware schemata); (2) experience with the use of electronic space (software schemata); (3) knowledge of hypertext concepts (hypertext schemata); (4) interest in the content (affective issue); (5) appraisal of the use of the hypertext system (affective issue).

A hyperdocument on the topic of Food Conservation was developed. The design included manipulation facilities and access mechanisms such as keyword index, program menu, content map, along with other artifacts intrinsic to hypertext structures. Following the psychological literature on hypertext (Dillon et al., 1993) these mechanisms would correspond to representations of schemata instantiations (landmarks, routs, and maps) for system users.

Nutrition students (N=30) participated on the study interacting with the hiperdocument. The students were divided into three groups according to their formal previous contact with the content of the program (G1= who have attended the discipline on food conservation before; G2= who were attending the discipline, and G3= who have never attended the discipline). Three basic intruments were used to collect data to study students' navigation processes: (1) recording of the navigation history of each student (dependent variable); (2) observation of students' interaction with the system, and (3) student profile questionnaire and hyperdocument attitude scale.

Observation data on users' interacting with the system, users' appraisal of their experience, and users' general characteristics data (e.g. previous experience with computers, hypertext, content knowledge, etc.) were organized into a "user schemata profile".

Records of each user navigation history were summarized into "navigation maps" (dependent variable) indicating contents (nodes) visited. User pathways (links between nodes) were color coded according to "shemata instantiations" used to access the nodes (e.g. hotwords, index, page browser, content map, and menu). Users'navigation styles divided them into two main categories - browsers and deliberate searchers - compatible with Wright (1993).

Qualitative analyses of users' profiles were compared with their navigation styles. The results indicate that "browsers" differ from "deliberate searchers" in the quantity and quality of some basic schemata. However, affective issues (variables 4 and 5) were indentified as important stimuli for schemata construction during the navigation process.

The results of this study may be useful to guide the design of learning systems which include facilities for developing necessary schemata during the learning process. Furute reserarch would benefit from examining the influence of different navigation styles on content learning through hypermedia.

Acknowledgements

This research is supported by the Brazilian Council for Scientific and Technological Development (CNPq) and by the José Bonifácio Foundation (FUJB).

References

Cimino, J.J., Elkin, P.L., & Barnett, G.O. (1992). As we may think: The Concept Space and Medical Hypertext. Computers and Biomedical Research, 25:238 - 263.

Dillon, Mc.Knight & Richardson (1993). Space - the Final Chapter or Why Physical Representations are not Semantic Intentions. In Mc. Knight, Dillon & Richardson, editors, Hypertext: A Psycological Perspective. London, Ellis Horwood.

Wright, Patricia (1993). To jump or not to jump: strategy selection while reading eletronic texts. In Mc.Knight, Dillon & Richardson, editors, Hypertext: A Psycological Perspective. London, Ellis Horwood.

Computation Matters: An Analog View of Vision

Robert S. Stufflebeam

Philosophy-Neuroscience-Psychology Program
Washington University, Campus Box 1073
One Brookings Dr., St. Louis, MO 63130-4899
rob@twinearth.wustl.edu

Introduction

My purpose for this paper is to show that although the brain *is* a computational device, naturalistic explanations of its processing do *not* require a strong commitment to internal representations. Aside from resolving questions of ontology, the following consideration motivates this project: providing a plausible computational framework from which to mechanisticly explain how the mind/brain works, yet that is consistent with a situated action approach to cognition. The type of cognitive processing of concern here is vision.

Computationalism

Computationalism is the view that a computational framework is essential to explain the workings of intelligent systems. Notwithstanding the widespread notion of synonymy between 'computation' and 'symbolic-digital computation', ignoring hybrids, there are two computational paradigms: symbolic, digital, rule-following, discrete processing [*classicist computation*] and nonsymbolic, analog, rule-governed, continuous processing [*connectionist PDP-style computation*].

A "computational system" is a system/device whose behavior can be interpreted as satisfying some function (Churchland & Sejnowski, 1992). Since every system implements some function, the mind/brain, unsurprisingly, is a computational system.

Since internal representations are said to figure in both types of computational processing, is the status of internal representations in explanations of the mind/brain assured? No. Although symbolic-digital computation requires a medium of internal representations, I provide conceptual and empirical reasons for thinking that brains are not classicist devices. For example, the brain does not [and need not] maintain a 3-D representation that corresponds detail-by-detail to the extra-mental world, for the "world itself is highly stable and conveniently 'out there' to be sampled and resampled" (Churchland, Ramachandran & Sejnowski, 1994, p. 36; Douglas, Mahowald & Mead, 1995; Van Essen & Anderson, 1994). In addition, the nonmodular organization of the brain and the unencapsulated flow of visual information also clash with the symbolic-digital view (Knudsen & Brainard, 1995; Van Essen, Anderson & Olshausen, 1994).

The nonsymbolic-analog view of vision

I argue that brains are *nonsymbolic-analog* computational devices. Drawing upon my analysis in (Stufflebeam, 1995) regarding the individuation of representations and the role and status of 'distributed representations' in explanations of PDP, I argue that distributed patterns of activation are not "internal" representations. Rather, they are extrinsic ones: among other failings, their status as representations depends on the [mere] act of interpretation/description. Though a computational framework demands a "medium" for the input-to-output transformations, I show that computational descriptions neither license nor require a [strong] commitment to internal representations (cf. Fodor, 1975). And if this nonsymbolic-analog approach to vision scales up to a scientific understanding of higher-order cognition, then the need for internal representations in explanations of cognitive processing is minimal.

References

Churchland, P. S., Ramachandran, V. S., & Sejnowski, T. J. (1994). A critique of pure vision. In C. Koch & J. L. Davis (Eds.), *Large-scale neuronal theories of the brain*, (pp. 23-60). Cambridge, MA: MIT Press.

Churchland, P. S., & Sejnowski, T. J. (1992). *The computational brain*. Cambridge, MA: MIT Press.

Douglas, R., Mahowald, M., & Mead, C. (1995). Neuromorphic analogue VLSI. *Annual Review of Neuroscience, 18*, 255-281.

Fodor, J. A. (1975). *The language of thought*. Cambridge, MA: Harvard University Press.

Knudsen, E. I., & Brainard, M. S. (1995). Creating a unified representation of visual and auditory space in the brain. *Annual Review of Neuroscience, 18*, 19-43.

Stufflebeam, R. S. (1995). Representations, explanation, and PDP: Is representation-talk really necessary? *Informatica, 19* (4), 599-613.

Van Essen, D. C., & Anderson, C. H. (1994). Information processing strategies and pathways in the primate visual system, *An introduction to neural and electronic networks*, (pp. 45-76): Academic Press.

Van Essen, D. C., Anderson, C. H., & Olshausen, B. A. (1994). Dynamic routing strategies in sensory, motor, and cognitive processing. In C. Koch & J. L. Davis (Eds.), *Large-scale neuronal theories of the brain*, (pp. 271-299). Cambridge, MA: MIT Press.

An Ecological Approach to the Neural Code

Akaysha C. Tang[1,2] & Terrence J. Sejnowski[1,2]

Howard Hughes Medical Institute[1]
Computational Neurobiology Lab, The Salk Institute
La Jolla, CA 92037
and
Department of Biology[2]
University of California, San Diego
La Jolla, CA 92093
{tang,terry}@salk.edu

Introduction

The primary mode of neural signaling involves the generation, transmission and transformation of spike trains by neurons in the central nervous system. The debate concerning spike timing versus rate coding has received increasing attention among neuroscientists, particularly within computational neuroscience (Shadlen & Newsome, 1994; Softky, 1995; Theunissen & Miller, 1995). It is widely believed that neurons in the nervous system are noisy, and that therefore only the rate or frequency of firing could reliably serve as a neural code. Recently this long held view has been directly challenged by a number of studies. Under tightly controlled input conditions, cortical neurons in the mammalian brain are capable of generating rather precisely timed spike trains, in both rat brain slices and behaving monkeys (Mainen & Sejnowski, 1994; Gallant, 1996). Information theoretic analysis has been successfully applied to this coding problem, and provides answers to the question of how much information is contained in a spike train (Bialek, Rieke, de Ruyter van Stevenick, & Warland, 1991). Although powerful, information theory has not yet answered the crucial question of whether the information measured is relevant to the neural system in the generation of behavioral output.

The specificity hypotheses

From an ecological point of view, the relevance of the information coded in a spike train, be it in a rate code or a spike timing code, depends heavily on the "what" aspect of the information and the survival value of its appropriate processing. Depending on what is to be encoded in the organism's environment, one type of code may serve as a better candidate than another. The onset of a stimulus, *e.g.* the appearance of a tiger, has to be coded with greater temporal precision, and with greater reliability, than the exact pattern of the tiger's fur coat. This proposed dependency of an optimal code on the type of information to be encoded implies at least three classes of testable hypotheses: modality specificity, property specificity, and domain specificity.

First, the optimal coding scheme should depend on the sensory modality under discussion, because different sensory modalities may be of different importance to a given organism in a given environment. Secondly, the optimal coding scheme should show property specificity within a given modality, because different sensory properties, such as color, form, onset/offset, or motion of a stimulus, may be of different predictive values for an organism exploring its environment. Finally, the optimal coding scheme, and in particular whether a spike timing code is required, should depend on whether the physical variables defining the stimulus are rapidly varying in the time domain.

Implications

We investigate these three classes of hypotheses by reviewing and reexamining the single and multicellular recording literature involving multiple sensory modalities and multiple sensory properties within a given modality. The final implication of the specificity hypotheses is that it would be hard, or perhaps even impossible, to find a general coding scheme applicable to all types of information present in the sensory environment. Therefore, conclusions concerning the coding problem without reference to the "what" aspect of the information would be difficult to interpret. Perhaps it is the modality, property, and domain specificity of the neural code that accounts for the heterogeneity of experimental results supporting both rate codes and spike time codes.

References

Bialek, W., Rieke, F., de Ruyter van Stevenick, R. R., & Warland, D. (1991). Reading a neural code. *Science, 252,* 1854–7.

Gallant, J. L. (1996). Neural codes for natural vision. Jackson Hole Workshop on Neural Information and Coding. Invited talk.

Mainen, Z. F., & Sejnowski, T. J. (1994). Reliability of spike timing in neocortical neurons. *Science, 268,* 1503–6.

Shadlen, M. N., & Newsome, W. T. (1994). Noise, neural codes and cortical organization. *Current Opinion in Neurobiology, 4,* 569–579.

Softky, W. R. (1995). Simple codes versus efficient codes. *Current Opinion in Neurobiology,* 239–247.

Theunissen, F., & Miller, J. P. (1995). Temporal encoding in nervous systems: a rigorous definition. *J. Computational. Neurosci., 2,* 149–162.

Processing Effects For Russian Gender

Roman Taraban

Department of Psychology
Texas Tech University
Lubbock, TX 79409-2051
tel: 806 742-1744
email: tirmt@ttacs.ttu.edu

Vera Kempe

Department of Psychology
University of Toledo
Toledo, OH 43606
tel: 419 530-2417
email: vkempe@uoft02.utoledo.edu

The present study investigated the processing of linguistic gender in Russian. For the majority of Russian nouns, gender is marked in a relatively regular manner through the ending of the noun (suffixes for feminine and neuter nouns, the null morpheme for masculine nouns). A subset of Russian nouns ends in palatalized consonants which do not provide reliable gender marking. We will refer to the nouns with end-palatalization as ambiguously marked nouns. A self-paced reading experiment was used to examine how gender-marking and language experience affect speed of processing and accuracy. Twenty-six native speakers of Russian and 18 fluent non-native speakers (typically college professors and graduate students in Russian) read 48 target sentences in which subject-nouns had either regular (e.g. muka) or ambiguous gender marking (e.g. sol') and 60 fillers. The overall sentence structure was *Introductory Phrase--Optional Adjective--Subject Noun--Adverb--Correct vs. Incorrect Verb--Prepositional Phrase*. Half of the subject-nouns were preceded by an adjective and half appeared without an adjective. The adjectives reliably marked the genders of the subject nouns. Participants made a forced-choice between two verb forms -- one that was correctly inflected so as to agree with the gender of the subject-NP and one that did not agree with the gender of the subject-NP. We examined error rates for choosing the correct verb form, reading times for individual words up to the verb, and verb choice times, which included the reading times for the verbs and prepositional phrases. Significance was set at $p < .05$, by subjects and items, in analyses using Group (native vs. non-native), Adjective (present vs. absent), and Ending (regular vs. ambiguous gender marking) as factors. For sentences with regular nouns, native and non-native speakers were highly accurate in the verb choices (error rate < 3%), regardless of whether the subject-noun was preceded by an adjective or not. For sentences with ambiguous subject-nouns, the non-natives made significantly more errors than the natives. Non-natives had extreme difficulty correctly choosing the verb when there was no adjective modifier (error rate = 29%). This condition was significantly different from all the others. The difficulty was significantly reduced when there was an adjective modifier (error rate = 6%). Reading times were generally slower for non-native speakers than for native speakers. As signaled by a significant Group X Adjective interaction at the subject-noun, natives were somewhat slowed down in reading the noun when there was an adjective modifier (666 ms.) than when there was no adjective (613 ms.). The effects for non-natives were in the opposite direction -- 988 ms. with an adjective and 1121 ms. without an adjective. We attribute this interaction to differences in expertise. Natives, who have excellent knowledge of noun genders, may spend time verifying the gender agreement of nouns and adjectives. This tendency may be a consequence of greater sensitivity to the dissociation of referential and grammatical gender occurring in some Russian nouns (e.g. tolstyj muzhchina). Non-natives compensate for their uncertain knowledge of noun gender by strategic use of the adjective gender marking. Moreover, non-natives took significantly longer to read masculine versus feminine gender nouns, which may in part be a consequence of greater variability in the consonant endings of masculine nouns, which non-natives have not yet mastered as completely as the feminine endings. For the adverb following the subject noun, there were no effects for the natives. The non-natives showed significantly slower reading times if an ambiguously marked noun had not been preceded by an adjective. Choice times were significantly slower for non-natives when the subject-NP did not have an adjective (2401 ms.) compared to when it did (1927 ms.) The slowdown was amplified when the subject noun was ambiguously marked for gender (no adjective, regular noun: 2141 ms.; no adjective, ambiguous noun: 2661 ms.). In separate analyses of the native speakers' data (with lower overall variance), we again found that the subject noun was read more slowly when there was an adjective modifier, but reading and choice times in the verb region were significantly faster. These data indicate that gender access in native speakers does not depend on regular marking on the noun, but gender access can be aided by additional cues like gender marking on an earlier adjective. Gender access in non-natives is aided by additional cues too, but also by the regularity of morphological marking. The data suggest that learning grammatical gender is facilitated by regular morphological marking. These data also provide a set of processing effects that constrain possible models of processing Russian gender. We consider how notions of cue validity, competition, and connectionist processing could be useful toward this end.

The Effect of Heuristic Induction on transfer in Mathematical Problem Solving

Atsushi Terao
Department of Systems Science
Tokyo Institute of Technology
Ohokayama Midori-ku Tokyo 152 Japan
terao@tp.titech.ac.jp

Shin'ichi Ichikawa
Department of Education
Tokyo Univercity
Hongo Bunkyo-ku Tokyo 113
ichikawa@tansei.cc.u-tokyo.ac.jp

Takashi Kusumi
Department of Education
Tokyo Institute of Technology
Ohokayama Meguro-ku Tokyo 152
kusumi@tp.titech.ac.jp

The purpose of this study was to explore the effect of Heuristic learning on transfer in mathematical problem solving. Especially, we have focused on following two questions: (1)whether explicit heuristic training is effective, and (2)whether transfer is promoted if students succeed in making good abstraction themselves that referred to the heuristic. The later question is original one. There is few evidence that the appropriate abstraction promotes transfer in high-level mathematical problem solving.

Method

Subjects. Subjects were 51 undergraduates.

Materials. Subjects were given three examples and three test problems. Every problem dealt with straight lines and they can be solved by using the heuristic: represent the straight lines by using parameters. The sample of the problems is presented in the Appendix. All of the subjects were not able to solve Example 1.

Procedure. Subjects were randomly assigned to two conditions, that is, *Instruction* condition and *non-instruction* condition.

In the training session, they were required to solve three example problems. The correct solutions of the examples were shown to subjects after trying to solve each example. In the instruction condition, the explanation about above mentioned heuristic was presented with each correct solution. In the non-instruction condition, the heuristic was not explained at all.

Subjects ware asked to summarize what they had learned from this problem, the solutions, and the mistakes, after each solution was presented. In both condition, subjects were assigned to two groups based on the content of the summary. If a subject referred to the heuristic mentioned above, he or she was assigned to the *good* students group. The subjects who had not referred to the heuristic were treated as *poor* students.

The test session was done one week later. Subjects were required to solve three test problems.

Results and Discussion

Each problem was marked on a scale of 10. In both sessions the scores on the three problems were totaled. Table 1 shows the scores in the test session.

The effect of explicit heuristic training

The percentage of good students was 76 % in the instruction condition and 65 % in the non-instruction condition.

Table 1 The means of subjects' scores in the test session

	instruction		non-instruction	
	poor	good	poor	good
N	6	19	9	17
Mean	2.17	6.11	2.78	9.47
SD	2.56	6.14	4.06	8.68

There was no difference in the percentages between the two conditions. Moreover, the difference of mean scores in test session between two conditions (instruction and non-instruction) was not significant. Thus, we can say that explicit heuristic training was not effective in this experiment.

The effect of Heuristic Induction

Although the explicit heuristic training was not effective, there is an evidence that supports the usefulness of the heuristic. The good students have shown good transfer in the test session. The means of the good students' scores were significantly different from those of the poor students'(t=2.25, df=20.7, p=.04 in the instruction condition; t=2.68, df=23.8, p=.01 in the non-instruction condition). Note that there were no differences between the two students' groups in the training session. The results of this experiment show that transfer in the high-level mathematical problem solving is facilitated if students do good abstraction.

In the non-instruction condition, the good students have induced the heuristic without any instructions about it. The abstraction seemed to be done by self-explanations (Chi *et al*,1989). The results also shows that the good self-explanations facilitates transfer in the high-level mathematics.

We will have to explore why the explicit heuristic training was not effective in contrast to the good performance of the good students.

Appendix

Example 1: A straight line L: $\frac{x+6}{2} = y-2 = \frac{z-6}{-1}$ and a point A(0,-1,-3) is given. Find the coordinate of H: foot of the perpendicular from A to L.

References

Chi, M.T.H., Bassok, M., Lewis, M., Reimann, P., & Glaser, R. (1989). Self-explanations: How students study and use examples in learning to solve problems. *Cognitive Science*, 13, 145–182.

Zombie Killer

Nigel J.T. Thomas

86, S. Sierra Madre Boulevard, #5,

Pasadena, CA 91107

nthomas@calstatela.edu

Zombies are hypothetical beings that are behaviorally and functionally (or perhaps even physically) indistinguishable from humans, but which differ from us in not having conscious (or, at least, qualitatively conscious) mental states. Zombiphiles are those who claim that the existence of zombies is a genuine logical possibility, and that this possibility entails that the mind can never be fully understood in functional (i.e. computational), or perhaps even in physical, terms. The 'zombiphile argument', however, only succeeds if the relevant equivalences are understood quite strictly, which can only be made good by the hypothesis of a 'zombie possible-world', identical to the real world but for the fact that each person's 'zombie twin', despite sharing an identical cognitive constitution, environmental situation, and life history, lacks consciousness.

I argue, however, that maintaining the logical possibility of zombies entails consequences that zombiphiles should find unacceptable. *Ex hypothesi*, a zombie makes the same claims about having conscious states as does a normal human. Such claims must either be true, false, or neither.

If they are construed as *false*, the zombie must be understood as either systematically and undetectably lying or as honestly mistaken. Lying may be ruled out on two grounds: (1) ensuring such systematic, undetectable lying would call for differences between the functional architectures of zombies and humans (which is ruled out *ex hypothesi*); (2) beings without a first-hand understanding of consciousness would be unable reliably to identify all situations where lying would be necessary. Standard examples like *Mary the color scientist* and *the inverted spectrum* can be presented without using any 'red flag' terms like "consciousness", "experience" or "qualia" that would alert the zombie to the need to lie; only terms such as "see", "red" and "know", which the zombie would have to be able to use correctly and truthfully in other contexts, are needed.

Since someone's being mistaken normally implies some sort of less-than-optimal cognitive performance, it is not clear in what sense a zombie, which should be construed as cognitively identical to its conscious human 'twin', could be construed as mistaken where the human would not be. Even without assuming such strict cognitive equivalences, if we allowed that zombies could be genuinely mistaken about being conscious, then we could not legitimately exclude the possibility, that our own claims to consciousness might be mistaken. Some philosophers might welcome this conclusion, but it conflicts not only with powerful and widespread intuitions, but with the polemical aims of zombiphiles.

Zombies might be construed as speaking the truth about their conscious experience if the relevant words in their language have subtly different meanings. It has been suggested that instead of attributing *thoughts* to zombies, we should attribute *thoughts²* to them. However, there seems to be little hope that any sense can be made of a notion of *qualia²*. Qualia are supposed to be precisely those entities for which there is no zombie counterpart, yet at least some zombies (like some humans) will claim to have qualia.

If we allow for zombies that are only loosely cognitively equivalent to we humans, and therefore can be envisaged as living in this world alongside us, then zombies might truthfully *admit* their lack of consciousness: they might be (perhaps a subset of) those people (mostly eliminativist philosophers or behaviorist psychologists) who deny its reality. However, this option does not support the zombiphile argument: at best it suggests a program of research aimed at uncovering the functional (or physical) differences underlying the presence or absence of consciousness in its affirmers and its (sincere, non-confused) deniers.

If zombies are neither lying nor telling the truth when they speak about consciousness, what they say must be *empty of meaning*. However, it would not seem to be possible to confine any such emptiness just to their talk about their consciousness. Statements with non-referring terms do not thereby lack truth value ("I have a jaberwock in my pocket," is *false*), and, conversely, we would want some statements by zombies that involve consciousness related terms (e.g. "I *believe* I have qualia") to come out *true*, not meaningless.

It is only possible to make sense of the claim that *all* zombie speech might be meaningless in the light of something like Searle's notion of original/intrinsic intentionality (henceforth *oii*), and the idea is certainly consistent with (but not actually required by) his "connection principle" and "Chinese Room" arguments. Searle might thus be a consistent zombiphile. However, it is highly counter-intuitive to suppose that zombie speech in general (*ex hypothesi* quite as consistently situationally appropriate as that of a human) could be totally empty of meaning. In order to rule out zombies of this type, we may still accept the concept of *oii*, and its close conceptual linkage with consciousness, but should reject the view that human-like behavior is possible in the absence of *oii*. I also reject Searle's view that *oii* is inexplicable in computational/robotic terms. Scientific efforts to understand consciousness would be better served by an initial focus on original/intrinsic intentionality rather than on qualia.

855

A Framework for Situativity in Dialogue

Maurizio Tirassa
Centro di Scienza Cognitiva
Università di Torino
via Lagrange, 3
10123 Torino (Italy)
tirassa@psych.unito.it

Mind

Minds are the conscious control systems that guide higher biological agents in their interactions with the world (Searle, 1992). Cognitive dynamics may be described as dynamics of mental states. Mental states with contents, i.e., intentional states, are subjective representations of part of the world as it is, was, or could be, entertained by an individual at a certain time. They exist against a nonrepresentational Background (Searle, 1983, 1992) that allows for their semantics and dynamics.

Since the subjective ontology an agent will impose on the world (and, therefore, her cognitive dynamics) is context-dependent, cognitive dynamics cannot be described as knowledge-rich sets of rules: something more abstract is needed. Following in part Pollock (1995), I view an agent as living in a *situation type* (i.e., in a subjective, open interpretation of the world), and striving to make it more to her likings. To act is to modify some characteristic of the situation, with the aim of improving it, at a comparatively reasonable cost.

Thus, an agent's cognitive dynamics may be described as a set of mental states whose contents are situation types with their characteristic, and actions in these situations; and as default chainings of such mental states.

Agency

The mental states needed for deliberative agency are at least the following:

Beliefs encode the knowledge present to the agent's consciousness at a given time; their contents are situations and their characteristics (a characteristic may define a whole situation, since the Background allows to take "the rest" of it for granted).

Situation-likings encode the agent's preferences within represented sets of situations, plans, or actions.

Desires encode the agent's potential goals; their contents are those situations which the agent thinks would be preferable to the current one.

Future-directed intentions encode the agent's actual goals, i.e., among the desired situations, those she commits to;

their contents are partial plans, i.e., possible situations plus activity paths, however ill-defined, which may realize them.

Present-directed intentions encode the agent's behavioral decisions; their contents are basic actions, i.e., actions that the agent may immediately execute in the current situation.

An agent's cognitive dynamics are tightly coupled to the partially unpredictable dynamics of her situation; i.e., changes in the situation (whether caused by the agent herself or not) reverberate on her mental states, so that these keep their adaptedness to the situation.

Social Agency

Social interactions are often conceived of as the joint execution of a multiagent plan, mutually known to the agents involved. The joint plan prescribes, to a variable degree of abstraction, a sequence of actions to be performed by each participant; its execution is initiated by one agent and possibly carried on, upon recognition, by each agent in her turn. Describing a social interaction amounts to describing this plan and its conditions of applicability.

Such script-based accounts of communication suffer from several problems. From a philosophical viewpoint, they fall into a map/territory fallacy (Searle, 1992), whereby behavioral regularities are unwarrantably explained by postulating *ad hoc* rules built in the agents' cognitive machinery. From a psychological viewpoint, they can neither account for situativity in dialogue, nor deal with non-benevolent instances of communication.

A better basis for sociality and communication may be provided by mindreading; i.e., by the agents' capability to understand and reason upon each other's mental states. Indeed, this is a prominent architectural feature of highly social Primates, whose disruption hampers the development of any social interaction but the simplest (Baron-Cohen, 1995; Frith, 1992).

References

Baron-Cohen, S. (1995). *Mindblindness*. Cambridge, MA: MIT Press.

Frith, C.D. (1992). *The cognitive neuropsychology of schizophrenia*. Hove, UK: Lawrence Erlbaum.

Alphabet Arithmetic and ACT–R:
A reply to Rabinowitz and Goldberg

J. Gregory Trafton
Naval Research Laboratory, Code 5513
Washington, DC 20375-5337
`trafton@itd.nrl.navy.mil`

Introduction

How is human knowledge and memory organized? Recently, some researchers have suggested that knowledge is either "active" (e.g., Rabinowitz & Goldberg, in press) or "inert" (e.g., Anderson, 1993a). Theorists who claim that declarative knowledge is active suggest that memory is actively processed, symbol manipulation is not necessary, and that memory is organized in an associative network with inhibitory and excitatory links (Rabinowitz & Goldberg, in press). Theorists who claim that declarative knowledge is inert, or passive, suggest that declarative knowledge is acted upon by productions and gains strength by being accessed (Anderson, Conrad, & Corbett, 1993).

Rabinowitz and Goldberg (in press) have compared and contrasted these two models by running a series of experiments using the "alphabet arithmetic" paradigm. Rabinowitz and Goldberg (in press) presented subjects with a letter and a number. Subjects had to 'add' the number to the letter to generate the second letter. For example, for the problem $C + 3 =?$, subjects should respond F.

Rabinowitz and Goldberg (in press) had two conditions: a retrieval condition and a procedural condition. In the retrieval condition, subjects saw a small set of problems on which they received extended practice. In the procedural condition, subjects saw a large number of problems a few times.

Rabinowitz and Goldberg (in press) found that subjects in the retrieval condition memorized the problems, while subjects in the procedural condition used a "finger counting" procedure to arrive at the correct answer. At the end of the acquisition stage of the experiment, subjects in the retrieval condition were faster than subjects in the procedural condition. On a transfer task, however, subjects in the procedural condition were faster than subjects in the retrieval condition.

Rabinowitz and Goldberg (in press) claimed that this evidence was strong support for a "retrieval" model of knowledge representation where declarative knowledge is active, not inert, as Anderson (1993b) claims.

To examine this hypothesis, a very simple model of alphabet arithmetic was built using ACT–R (Anderson, 1993b).

Results

As Figure 1 shows, the model does a good job of modeling the actual data for both the retrieval and procedural conditions. In addition, the ACT–R model shows the same pattern of results on the posttest that the actual data does. The ACT–R model suggests that subjects are not only learning and strengthening productions, but also strengthening the associations between declarative working memory elements. The model suggests that subjects in the retrieval condition did memorize alphabet arithmetic facts, while the subjects in the procedural condition gained more experience traversing the alphabet itself, thereby strengthening the pertinent associations.

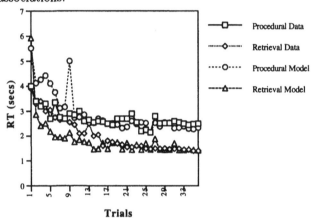

Figure 1: Reaction times (approximated) from Rabinowitz & Goldberg and model data from ACT–R.

In summary, ACT–R can successfully model the data presented by Rabinowitz and Goldberg (in press). This model suggests that the associations between memory elements are critical in this type of task.

References

Anderson, J. R. (1993a). Knowledge representation. In *Rules of the mind*, (pp. 17–44). Hillsdale, NJ: Erlbaum.

Anderson, J. R. (1993b). *Rules of the mind.* Hillsdale, NJ: Erlbaum.

Anderson, J. R., Conrad, F. G., & Corbett, A. T. (1993). The LISP tutor and skill acquisition. In J. R. Anderson (Ed.), *Rules of the mind*, (pp. 143–164). Hillsdale, NJ: Erlbaum.

Rabinowitz, M., & Goldberg, N. (in press). Evaluating the structure-process hypothesis. In F. Weinert, & W. Schneider (Eds.), *Research on memory development: State-of-the-art and future directions.* Hillsdale, NJ: Erlbaum.

Patterns and Effects of Analogies in Scientific Abduction
– A Remarkable Case of Creative Analogy –

Kazuhiro Ueda
Department of Computer & Graphic Sciences
The University of Tokyo
ueda@gould.c.u-tokyo.ac.jp

Introduction

The author investigates how scientists make spontaneous use of analogy in actual scientific abduction using an interview method. The purpose of the study is (1)to classify analogies used not in artificial settings but in actual scientific domains and (2)to report a remarkable case which has not been reported in the previous studies (Dunbar, 1994; Holyoak & Thagard, 1995).

Method

The interviews were designed to explore how scientists used analogy in abduction. The interviewees were 22 leading Japanese researchers in the fields of science and technology whose projects satisfied the following conditions: the research processes were recorded in detail, and the research had been completed or was in progress. The research records were examined by the project leader and the results of analyses were evaluated by other researchers, to verify their reliability.

Results and Discussions

Nineteen cases of analogy were reported. They were analyzed and classified into 3 types according to the similarity used: goal-directed, category-based, and category-formational analogy.

Goal-directed analogy is almost the same as purpose-directed analogy (Kedar-Cabelli, 1985), while category-based one is as regional analogy (Dunbar, 1994). In the latter analogy, there were 2 ways of deciding which knowledge of the source analogue was transferred: one is based on causality and the other is based on some meta-constraints, the latter of which has not been reported in detail.

In category-formational analogy, a source analogue was retrieved on the basis of a category like in category-based analogy, but the category used was the one extended from a pre-existing core category by adding some constraints. This type of analogy is important for creative thinking but has not been reported in detail: a typical but remarkable case is shown as follows.

Theme: To construct a theory which explains the unique behavior of a star cluster.

Situation before Analogy: There was a theory which aimed to explain the unique behavior of a cluster by regarding a cluster as an isothermal gas sphere such as a fixed star (*i.e.* the theory on the inner-structure of a star was the source analogue). However, most researchers in those days recognized this analogy as a fallacy, since a cluster was considered to differ from a star in that the former is a discrete system whereas the latter is a continuous one. The concept of *self-gravitation* is established only in the star domain.

Analogical Reasoning: The researcher assumed that the unique behavior of a cluster was caused by the fact that a cluster is a self-gravitational system. He considered that if the assumption was right, not discreteness of a cluster but self-gravitation itself (*i.e.* the similarity) was the principal factor of the unique behavior. Hence he supposed that the theory on the inner-structure of a star would hold for the cluster domain. In order to take the effects of self-gravitation into account, however, the linear theory (on an isothermal gas sphere) had to be replaced by another theory (on a heterothermal gas sphere). So he introduced both the Prigogine's theory on non-equilibrium thermodynamics and the linearized stability theory, and at last succeeded in formulating the new concept of *selfgravo-thermodynamics*. He found that a cluster is quite similar to a star from the viewpoint, and transferred the theory on the inner-structure of a star to the cluster domain.[1]

This analogy started from the pre-existing fallacious analogy. The new category *selfgravo-thermodynamics* was being formulated by extending the pre-existing core concept *self-gravitation* which had been misused as the similarity in the previous fallacious analogy.

Table 1: Classification of the cases reported (each figure denotes the number of the observed cases).

	causality-based transfer	metaconstraint-based transfer
goal-directed	10	0
category-based	3	4
category-formational	2	0

Summary

All the cases were classified, as shown in Table 1. Of the three types, the goal-directed analogy has the least possibility of mental leaps since it is close to deduction.

---

[1] Then the transferred theory was partially modified based on thematic abstraction (Suzuki, 1994).

Performance of Simple Recurrent Network Indexes Creativity and Predicts Discovery in a Rule Induction Task

Frédéric Vallée-Tourangeau
Department of Psychology
University of Hertfordshire
Hatfield, Hertfordshire
UNITED KINGDOM, AL10 9AB
f.vallee-tourangeau@herts.ac.uk

In the "2:4:6" induction task, participants are told that a rule underlies the generation of number triples of which 2:4:6 is an example. The rule is "any increasing sequence". Subjects are instructed to attempt to discover the rule by producing new triples which the experimenter classifies as conforming or not conforming to the rule. Wason (1960) originally proposed that Popperian falsificationism was the normative hypothesis-testing model against which subjects' behavior should be assessed. This proposal has dictated most of the subsequent research (e.g., Gorman, Stafford, & Gorman, 1987).

This emphasis on *testing* strategies reflects a perspective on discovery that places greater importance on the process by which ideas are justified rather than on the richness of the hypothesis set that underlies the production and interpretation of triples. In an attempt to redress this imbalance Vallée-Tourangeau, Austin, and Rankin (1995) showed that solvers produced a greater variety of positive and negative triples than nonsolvers.

An obvious but important (and neglected) aspect of triple production is that it reflects a sequential process which may exhibit contextual dependencies. Up to now, there has been no analysis of either the local context of the current triple within which a number is generated or the broader context of the preceding set of triples. The proposal outlined in this paper is that successful rule discovery in the *2:4:6* task can be reliably predicted by the extent to which a given number in a sequence departs significantly from its prior context. The challenge, however, is to develop an instrument that is able to measure such departures on the basis of a dynamic charaterization of the prior context. This paper proposes that a simple recurrent connectionist network (Elman, 1990) offers such a tool and reports data that demonstrate that the resulting indices of creativity are among the best predictors of successful rule discovery reported thus far in the literature.

A SRN was used as a statistical exploration tool. The data explored were the triple sequences generated by the participants in Vallée-Tourangeau et al.'s study. These subjects had to produce 15 triples before announcing their guess; they were not asked to formulate a hypothesis at any other moment. The aim of the exploration was to assess whether a SRN could extract regularities in the triples tested that would demarcate solvers from nonsolvers. The input representation encoded features of each number within a triple and its relation to previous numbers along five binary dimensions. Each number was thus translated into a 5-bit input vector and each triple was defined in terms of three consecutive input vectors. The SRN architecture employed consisted of 5 input, 5 output, 2 hidden and 2 context units. The task of the network was to learn to predict the characteristics of the next number within the sequence. The performance of SRNs trained on triples from subjects who announced an incorrect hypothesis was compared to the performance of SRNs trained on triples from correct subjects. According to Vallée-Tourangeau et al., successful subjects show more variable triple production than unsuccessful subjects, and consequently it is expected that the prediction error of a SRN for successful subjects versus unsuccessful subjects will exhibit significant differences

Simulation results showed that the mean output activation values for each number within a triple produced by successful subjects were statistically different from those produced by incorrect subjects. Specifically, the mean output activation values for triples generated by incorrect subjects corresponded more closely to the activation values for the triple given initially, namely *2:4:6*, than the mean values for triples generated by correct subjects. In other words, the profile of the typical triple tested by incorrect subjects resembled the initial triple. In turn, prediction error was statistically greater for triples generated by successful than by unsuccessful subjects. That is the characteristics of the numbers within a triple were more predictable when they were produced by unsuccessful subjects. This suggests that triples produced by successful subjects demonstrated more creativity and were therefore less predictable. Thus, the performance measures of the SRN support the conjecture that discovery in the "2:4:6" task is a function of breaking free from the constraints of the salient features of the initial example. As well they can be interpreted to index the breadth of the exploration of the space of possible triples and successful subjects explored that space more extensively.

References

Elman, J. L. (1990). Finding structure in time. *Cognitive Science*, 14, 179-211.

Gorman, M. E., Stafford, A., & Gorman, M. E. (1987). Disconfirmation and dual hypotheses on a more difficult version of Wason's 2-4-6 task. *Quarterly Journal of Experimental Psychology*, 39A, 1-28.

Vallée-Tourangeau, F. Austin, N. G., & Rankin, S. (1995). Inducing a rule in Wason's 2-4-6 task: A test of the information-quantity and goal-complementarity hypotheses. *Quarterly Journal of Experimental Psychology*, 48A, 895-914.

Wason, P. C. (1960). On the failure to eliminate hypotheses in a conceptual task. *Quarterly Journal of Experimental Psychology*, 12, 129-140.

Building Lexical Neighborhoods

Michael S. Vitevitch and Paul A. Luce

Language Perception Laboratory
Department of Psychology
and Center for Cognitive Science
University at Buffalo
Buffalo, NY 14260
mikev@deuro.fss.buffalo.edu

The neighborhood activation model (NAM) (Goldinger, Luce, and Pisoni, 1989; Luce, 1986; Luce, Pisoni, and Goldinger, 1990) hypothesizes that spoken word recognition is characterized by two successive stages: (1) similarity neighborhood activation, and (2) a frequency-biased decision process. In the first stage, stimulus input (i.e. a spoken word) activates a set of similar sounding representations of words in memory. In the second stage, these multiply activated form-based representations --or neighbors-- are decided among by a decision process that is influenced by the acoustic-phonetic similarity of the neighbors as well as their frequency of occurrence. NAM further posits that the decision process among the competitors in the activated set of representations is influenced by three characteristics of the similarity neighborhoods. These characteristics are: (1) target word frequency, (2) neighborhood density, and (3) neighborhood frequency.

The present research was aimed at elaborating and extending previous work on NAM by directly manipulating the composition of the similarity neighborhoods of nonword targets. We attempted to directly manipulate similarity neighborhoods for two reasons. One reason is that previous experiments used estimates of the neighborhood characteristics for the words used as stimuli. Like all estimates of subjects' knowledge derived from indirect measures, there is some noise associated with the measurement. Consequently, past studies could be considered somewhat correlational, in that the characteristics of the stimuli were not directly manipulated. The control and direct manipulation of neighborhood characteristics would allow us to explicitly test the variables that NAM claims are at work in spoken word recognition and avoid the problems of estimating neighborhood characteristics.

The second reason for directly manipulating similarity neighborhoods was to examine a claim of Bard and Shillcock (1993) that the presence of a single high frequency neighbor --and not density per se-- determines the speed and ease of spoken word recognition. This claim is motivated by the correlation between neighborhood frequency and neighborhood density. Thus, one can not, according to Bard and Shillcock, easily distinguish what is responsible for neighborhood effects: the frequency of the neighbors or the number of neighbors. They suggest that just one high frequency neighbor may be responsible for producing effects similar to those reported earlier. This account proves to be an interesting challenge for the neighborhood activation model.

The present research constitutes an attempt to directly manipulate the composition of similarity neighborhoods of spoken nonwords. In particular, we established a baseline measure of reaction time to a set of nonword target stimuli. Subjects were then exposed to dense and sparse similarity neighborhoods of nonwords that varied in their frequency of presentation in several sessions of a continuous recognition task distributed over four consecutive days. We then examined the effects of target frequency, neighborhood density, and neighborhood frequency on processing times for the target nonwords in an attempt to directly test the predictions of the neighborhood activation model of spoken word recognition.

The results showed a cross-over interaction between target frequency and neighborhood density. This study demonstrates that target frequency and neighborhood density have demonstrable influences on processing. Specifically, high frequency targets with sparse neighborhoods were responded to more quickly with training, while high frequency targets with dense neighborhoods were responded to more slowly after training. Conversely, low frequency targets with sparse neighborhoods were responded to more slowly with training, whereas low frequency targets with dense neighborhoods were responded to more quickly after training. In addition, no effects of neighborhood frequency were found, contrary to the claims made by Bard and Shillcock.

The results for the high frequency targets are consistent with the predictions of NAM. However, the obtained results for low frequency words directly contradict the predicts of NAM. One possible explanation for the inconsistency between the obtained results and the predictions of the model may be the fact the neighborhood activation model may not accurately model the processes and representations used in word recognition.

The Neighborhood Characteristics of Malapropisms

Michael S. Vitevitch

Language Perception Laboratory
Department of Psychology
and Center for Cognitive Science
University at Buffalo
Buffalo, NY 14260
mikev@deuro.fss.buffalo.edu

Fay and Cutler (1977) examined several linguistic factors of malapropisms. They defined a malapropism as a real word that erroneously intrudes on an intended, or target, word. The target and error words are not semantically related but share a close relationship in their pronunciations.

Although Fay and Cutler (1977) found many interesting results regarding the stress pattern, grammatical category, number of syllables, and several other characteristics that malapropisms shared with the intended word, their work provided little information that could predict which words might be likely to be malapropisms. The current analysis was undertaken to examine other characteristics of the intended words that might be useful for predicting which words might be likely to be malapropisms.

Evidence suggests that word frequency affects both word *recognition* and word *production* (Dell, 1990; Stemberger and MacWhinney, 1986) in demonstrable ways. Do other factors that influence speech perception also influence speech production? More specifically, do the characteristics of phonologically similar neighborhoods (Luce, Pisoni, and Goldinger, 1990) --word frequency, neighborhood frequency (the frequency of the words in a neighborhood), and neighborhood density (the number of words in memory that are similar to a target word)--influence word production? To examine this possibility, the current analysis of a malapropism error corpus was conducted.

138 words from Fay and Cutler (1977) were found in an on-line version of the 20,000 word Webster's Pocket Dictionary. The neighborhood characteristics for these 138 words were then calculated. The computations were performed on the phonetic transcriptions contained within the computerized lexicon.

Word frequency was assessed by using the log-frequency of each word. A word was considered to be a low frequency word if the value of its frequency was below the value of log 10. A word with a value above log 10 was considered to be a high frequency word. Neighborhood frequency was assessed in a similar fashion. Neighborhood density was assessed by finding the median value of the data. Values above the median were classified as having dense neighborhoods. Values below the median were classified as having sparse neighborhoods.

The results show that high frequency words from dense neighborhoods tended to be very prevalent in errorful productions. Also, low frequency words from sparse neighborhoods tended to be very prevalent in errorful productions. Additionally, more target words tended to "slip" to words that were of a higher frequency than of a lower frequency compared to the frequency of the target word.

The current results may best be accounted for with a slight modification to an activation based model of speech production (see Dell, 1986, 1988, 1990). A high frequency word that is normally highly activated may be relatively less activated than another word due to the densely populated neighborhood it is found in. A result of a high frequency word being "hidden" by its many neighbors may be the selection, or mis-selection in this case, of an alternate word that is relatively more frequent. The selected word will most likely resemble the intended word due to the organization of the lexicon. These factors may conspire to make a different, more frequent word, even more likely to be selected by the speech production system, resulting in the system producing an error.

Conversely, low-frequency words may not have enough activation on their own to be selected by the speech production system's criteria of "pick the most active candidate." Low-frequency words may need the supportive activation of their neighbors in order to be selected by the speech production system. Thus, low-frequency words in sparse neighborhoods do not receive enough supportive activation from their few neighbors. Consequently, these words may be overlooked by the speech production system, and be involved in more speech errors. These "conspiracy effects" (see Taraban and McClelland, 1987) among words and their neighbors may account for the differential effects of frequency and neighborhood density on the speech production system.

Learning by Observation in Complex Task Environments

Dieter Wallach

Fachrichtung Psychologie
Universität des Saarlandes
66041 Saarbrücken/Germany
dieter@cops.uni-sb.de

In 1986 Donald A. Norman coined the term *Cognitive Engineering*, which denotes a Cognitive Science approach within the Engineering Sciences. The research presented here follows in this tradition and exemplifies applied Cognitive Science by investigating knowledge acquisition processes in naturalistic task domains. While problem-solving research in Psychology formerly concentrated on knowledge-lean tasks like the *Tower of Hanoi*, attention shifted during the eighties to questions of knowledge acquisition, its organization and application in knowledge-rich task domains. A new paradigm, labelled *Complex Problem Solving* (see Frensch & Funke, 1995), deepened Cognitive Psychology by investigating the effects of complexity and uncertainty in dealing with computer-simulated dynamic systems.

When comparing different studies concerning complex problem solving, one central basic assumption can be found: the opportunity of active system control in an initial learning phase is regarded as a necessary precondition for the acquisition of an appropriate *Mental Model* of the system to be controlled. It is an unquestioned assumption that subjects have to be given the possibility of active exploration of a dynamic system in order to cope successfully with it. In contrast, there is a well-established trend in many engineering systems substituting supervisory control for manual control. As a consequence of the still increasing impetus for automatization, operators are removed from the manual operating loops, and their roles are redefined as system monitors.

To investigate the effects of different activity demands on system identification and system control two experiments were conducted. As a scenario for these experiments POWERPLANT, a validated and systems-theoretically well-defined model of a real coal-fired powerstation was constructed and implemented. In both experiments 40 engineering students where assigned to two experimental groups:

- while a *System Control Group* was encouraged in a knowledge acquisition phase to actively explore POWERPLANT, e.g. to freely make interventions, gather data and test hypotheses,
- the interaction of a *Monitoring Group* was restricted to the observation of a corresponding operator from the System Control Group controlling POWERPLANT.

To separate effects of active system exploration from those of pure system observation a yoked control design was used. After the knowledge acquisition phase both groups had to control PowerPlant in a knowledge application phase. To diagnose the students' knowledge about POWERPLANT several knowledge-assessment techniques (e.g. questionnaires, sorting-tasks, thinking aloud) were applied.

In sharp contrast to the prevailing assumption in the area of complex problem solving a significant superiority of the Monitoring Group with respect to system knowledge and control performance in the knowledge application phase was found. Interestingly, while there is a strong association between system knowledge and control performance in the System Control Group ($r > .75$), no correlations were found in the Monitoring Group. Analyzing the think aloud protocols revealed that students from the Monitoring Group generated significant more *self-explanations* (Sandoval, Trafton, & Reiser, 1995) about control strategies and the causal relationship of POWERPLANT'S underlying variables and their dynamics. Students of the System Control Group on the other hand mainly paraphrased the system behavior without tracing it back to physical principles.

Using the data gathered through the knowledge-assessment techniques, a cognitive simulation model on the basis of ACT-R (Anderson, 1993) was implemented and empirically evaluated. ACT-R is a cognitive architecture capable of performing and learning from the same tasks worked on by human subjects. The model not only offers a straightforward explanation of the results and a close fit to the empirical data but can also be seen as a rigorous test of the applicability of the ACT-R framework in naturalistic task domains.

References

Anderson, J.R. (1993). Rules of the Mind. Hillsdale, NJ: Lawrence Erlbaum Associates.

Frensch, P. & Funke, J. (1995). Complex Problem Solving: The European Perspective. Hillsdale, NJ: Lawrence Erlbaum Associates.

Norman, D.A. (1986). Cognitive Engineering. In D. A. Norman & S.W. Draper (Eds.), User centered system design (pp. 31-67). Hillsdale, NJ: Lawrence Erlbaum Associates.

Sandoval, W.A., Trafton, J.G., & Reiser, B.J. (1995). The Effect of Self-Explanation on Studying Examples and Solving Problems. In *Proceedings of the Seventeenth Annual Conference of the Cognitive Science Society* (pp. 259–264). Mahwah, NJ: Lawrence Erlbaum Associates.

The Role of Working Memory in Schema Induction

James A. Waltz and **Keith J. Holyoak**
Department of Psychology
University of California, Los Angeles
405 Hilgard Avenue
Los Angeles, CA 90095-1563
{waltz, holyoak}@psych.ucla.edu

Graeme S. Halford
Department of Psychology
University of Queensland
4072 St. Lucia, Australia
gsh@psych.psy.uq.oz.au

Much progress has been made in the last twenty years both in identifying the mental processes that underlie higher-level cognition and characterizing the cognitive deficits that accompany frontal-lobe damage in patients. As Dunbar and Sussman (1995) note, however, little work has been done to help understand frontal-lobe function by linking cognitive with neuropsychological research. Though our understanding of the role of working memory in cognition has greatly increased, neuropsychologists have only recently begun to discuss the cognitive deficits in frontal-lobe patients in terms of basic processes such as working memory and attention. Thus, while it has been established that patients with frontal-lobe damage often have difficulty in performing problem-solving tasks, until recently little has been known in detail about the role of the frontal lobes in cognition. Recent work, however, has begun to associate functions such as working memory and executive control with specific regions of the frontal cortex. By understanding the roles that working memory and executive control play in higher-level cognition,it should be possible to predict which cognitive deficits should result from injury to which regions. The experiment described here seeks to more precisely characterize the working-memory requirements of one aspect of higher cognitive function, namely induction, by showing the implications that impairment of one particular aspect of working memory can have at the higher cognitive level.

Evidence suggests that the amount of working memory resources devoted to a particular task greatly affects how much is learned. There is reason to believe that working memory also influences the complexity of what is learned We propose that unimpaired executive control is essential to the process of induction through mechanisms such as analogical mapping, whereas it is less vital to simpler cognitive processes such as association learning. We argue that the high working-memory load of analogical problem-solving derives from the fact that in the course of solving problems by analogy, individuals must retain the elements of the source, the elements of the target, and mappings between source and target. In the experiment described here, we used a "dual-task" paradigm (Dunbar & Sussman, 1995) to test the hypothesis that, in situations in which central executive function is impaired, the capacity to form simple associations may remain relatively intact, even when the capacity to form complex associations is severely impaired.

Fifty participants were presented with a series of eight mathematical group problems. Mathematical groups are useful for studying structure mapping because they lend themselves to representation by a relational schema (Halford & Wilson, 1980). In addition, these tasks can be successfully performed through either structure mapping or memory for associations between pairs of stimuli.

We found that, relative to those in the control group, participants who were required to solve the problems while simultaneously performing a distractor task designed to interfere with the central executive showed impairment in the ability to make inferences based on structure mapping, even when they were permitted to learn associations between stimuli to a criterion. We interpret this finding as indicating that impairments in analogical reasoning linked to working memory deficits are at least partially attributable to the fact that analogical problem-solving places more severe demands on executive function than does association learning.

References

Dunbar, K., & Sussman D. (1995). Toward a cognitive account of frontal lobe function: Simulating frontal lobe deficits in normal participants. In J. Grafman, K. J. Holyoak, & F. Boller (Eds.), *Structure and functions of the human prefrontal cortex.* New York: New York Academy of Sciences.

Halford, G. S., & Wilson, W. H. (1980). A category theory approach to cognitive development. *Cognitive Psychology, 12,* 356-411.

On-line Processing of Verbal Agreement in French

Nicole Wicha and Michèle Kail

Laboratoire de Psychologie Expérimentale
URA 316, CNRS, Université de Paris-V
28 rue Serpente; 75006 Paris France
nwicha@cogsci.ucsd.edu,
kail@idf.ext.jussieu.fr

The purpose of this study with native French speaking adults was two-fold: (1) to investigate the factors that affect the detection of verbal agreement violations in the auditory modality, in French sentence processing, and (2) to explore a recent technique of auditory sentence processing, using what we call "cued grammaticality", intended to improve detection times. Though focusing on the French language, this study was designed with a crosslinguistic perspective and follows the Competition Model (CM) in its general hypotheses (MacWhinney, 1987). CM proposes that in processing sentence information, each language assigns differing weights to language cues. Research in French has lead to important changes in the model, revolving around the competition of cues across modalities and across different stages of development in children (Kail, 1989). French adults in the auditory modality tend to rely on verbal agreement more than other sources of information (e.g. word order). Kail and Bassano (1995) in an on-line study of French sentence processing, predicted that verbal agreement violations would be detected significantly faster than word order violations. However, this finding was affected by temporal distance, which can be manipulated by placing a set of words between the noun and verb in the subject-verb (SV) target. Consider the following example:

#1 *Sur la piste, le jongleur, avec prudence, ont*
On the stage, the juggler, with caution, had [*pl.*]

lancé   les couteaux   deux par deux.
thrown the knives   two   by two.

Surprisingly, subjects responded quicker to an agreement violation when a distance was interposed, than when the SV target was contiguous. This was possibly due to a confound between distance and the position of the target word in the sentence. In order to isolate the effect of distance on verbal agreement violation detection, the target word in this study remained in a constant position. We also introduced a new technique, that cues the subject about the point at which a decision must be made, by splicing in a gender change of the speaker's voice (Liu et al., in press). The general hypotheses were as follows: first, it was expected that a temporal distance between a subject and its verb would slow error detection in sentences with verbal agreement violation; second, cued grammaticality judgment was expected to elicit faster detection times than we typically find in error detection studies, maximizing our ability to detect effects of variables. In addition, there were two other variations in the material: SV number mismatch and verb form (*aller/avoir*). The results of this study showed that distance had a significant main effect on violation detection, consistent with the original hypothesis. Other differences in the material had significant main effects as well, but did not interact with distance. Finally, cued grammaticality judgment elicited faster response times than those reported by Kail & Bassano (1995), using a different error detection technique. These results are relevant to current controversies revolving around the effects of timing and short-term memory load, on sentence processing in an inflected language.

References

Kail, M. (1989). Cue validity, cue cost and processing types in sentence comprehension in French and Spanish. In B. MacWhinney & E. Bates (Eds.), *The Crosslinguistic Study of Sentence Processing.* Cambridge: C.U.P.

Kail, M. & Bassano, D. (1995). Word order and verbal agreement in on-line sentence processing in French: Auditory vs. visual modality. (Manuscript submitted for publication).

Liu, H., Bates, E., Powell, T. & Wulfeck, B. (in press) Single-word shadowing and the study of lexical access. *Applied Psycholinguistics.*

MacWhinney, B. (1987). The Competition Model. In B. MacWhinney (Ed.), *Mechanisms of language acquisition.* Hillsdale, NJ: Erlbaum.

The Cognitive Impact and Function of Metaphors Used in Human/Computer Interaction: Why and How Should it be Assessed?

Mary Williamson and **Christine Diehl**
Mathematics, Science and Technology Division
The Graduate School of Education
4533 Tolman Hall
University of California
Berkeley, CA 94720
maryw@cogsci.berkeley.edu   cdiehl@violet.berkeley.edu

Introduction

In our everyday lives, we use metaphors to systematically organize our experiences of the world. These metaphors structure our conceptual understandings and expectations concerning symbols and actions we encounter (Lakoff and Johnson, 1980). User interface designers have commonly drawn on various metaphors for the layout of screen content and for navigation tools (Erickson, 1990). We suggest that for a metaphor to be most useful in the interface it should coincide with user expectations for the metaphor. Additionally, a designer should provide different metaphors to accommodate different user strategies for accomplishing a task (e.g., a user who expects a map in order to navigate an interface should find one, but a user who doesn't want a map shouldn't be forced to use one).

Metaphors in the user interface

Research into the use of metaphors in human/computer interaction is far from complete. In this paper we describe preliminary results from two on-going investigations into the use of metaphors in the interface. One study examines user expectations concerning metaphors in use on the web side Total New York. The second study considers the effects of two different navigation tools, each of which draws on different metaphors, on user strategies in a hypermedia environment. These studies support the notion that users bring expectations to encounters with the user interface, which are based on the metaphors used there, which either facilitate or hinder the human/computer interaction. Additionally, the studies support the more general notion that research into user interfaces that are systematically designed in accordance with a theory of how the information will be cognitively processed will be easier for users to work with and afford greater interaction benefits.

Generative function of metaphors

Metaphors are embedded in several elements of design: the layout of the screen, the manipulatable objects available to a user on the interface (buttons, scroll bars), the icons, tracking mechanisms and navigation tools. In the Total New York study, we hypothesized and found support for the claim that the generative nature of metaphor prototypes would be evident in the user's expectations and reactions, inclining users to expect metaphors to behave consistently with the metaphor prototype and inclining users to look for coherent clusters of metaphors and to tend to overlook and/or be surprised by those metaphors which didn't fit. For example, the subjects expected and found a "home" icon on TNY pages which they anticipated would return them to the initial page of the site. However, the designers of the TNY site provided *different* pictures on the initial page of the site, when a user returned to it a second time. This made subjects feel "unsettled" and "uneasy." One subject described this as "weird." The second study is a follow-up of an earlier study in which undergraduate students were assigned to one of two hypermedia system conditions: a map-like navigation tool or a menu-like navigation tool. It was found that the ability to take advantage of a hypermedia navigation tool was related to the ability to represent the hypermedia environment spatially (Diehl & Ranney, 1996). In the present study, the navigation systems are being examined to determine what type of influence is typical of each navigation method.

References

Diehl, C. and Ranney, M. (1996) Assessing spatial navigation tools in instructional hypermedia. (*Submitted to ICLS conference*, July 1996).

Erickson, T. (1990). Working with interface metaphors. In Laurel, B., ed., *The Art of human/computer interface design*, 65-73. Reading, Mass: Addison Wesley.

Lakoff, G. and Johnson, M. (1980) *Metaphors we live by*. Chicago: The University of Chicago Press.

The use of exemplar information in classification-based and inference-based category learning

Takashi Yamauchi and **Arthur B. Markman**

Psychology Department
Columbia University
New York, NY 10027
takashi@psych.columbia.edu

A prominent aspect of categorization is our ability to extract categories out of a wide range of items. Unlike most experimental situations where a limited set of category instances is presented repeatedly, we are able to learn about a variety of categories in the world even though each exemplar we see may be unique. Two experiments were designed to capture this aspect of categorization. We presented subjects with one of three types of category learning — Classification learning, Inference Learning or Mixed Learning — and examined how these procedures interacted with different types of stimulus depiction in which each feature of a stimulus was depicted by either a single instance or by a large number of distinct instances.

In the two experiments, subjects were randomly assigned to one of three learning conditions — Classification learning, Inference learning and a mixture of the two. Classification learning was a standard category learning procedure, in which subjects saw an entire stimulus and classified it into one of two groups. Subjects learned the categories incrementally via feedback given immediately after each trial. Subjects in the inference learning condition followed a similar procedure except that on each trial they had to fill in the value of a different missing feature given the other features and the category label. The Mixed condition was the mixture of the two learning conditions, on which half of trials were made of classification and half were inference. Subjects conducted one of three learning tasks until they reached a criterion. After learning, subjects made classification and inference transfer of old stimuli as well as new stimuli.

The success of exemplar models suggests that specific exemplar information is processed for classification (Nosofsky, 1986). In contrast, abstract relational information seems to play a crucial role for inference (Lassaline & Murphy, 1996; Markman, Yamauchi & Makin, in press). The current studies tested this hypothesis by contrasting three different learning situations — Inference learning, Classification learning, and the mixture of the two conditions — in two independent experiments. In one experiment, each feature had a single manifestation. For example, the feature "round head" is represented by a single feature instance throughout the experiment. In a second experiment, each stimulus was depicted by different manifestations of features so that no two instances were exactly the same. For example, each feature value (e.g., round head) was depicted by one of four different variations of that feature value.

If classification learning is primarily based on the storage of episodic information of exemplars, it will require many trials to reach a learning criterion when each feature of a stimulus is represented by many distinct instances. In contrast, if inference learning rests more on processing abstract relational information than does classification, the same manipulation may not affect subjects' ability to learn categories.

The results of the two experiments showed that 23 out of 24 subjects given Classification learning were unable to learn the categories in the specified period when a feature of a stimulus was depicted by multiple instances, whereas only 7 out of 24 subjects in the same condition were unable to learn the categories when a feature of a stimulus was shown by a single instance throughout learning. Subjects given Inference learning and subjects given Mixed learning were unaffected by this manipulation: more than 85% of subjects in the two learning conditions could learn categories irrespective of the way each feature was depicted. The results of the experiments suggest that category learning based on classification relies heavily on storing specific exemplar items during learning, whereas category learning based on inference rests on processing some abstract category information. Since classification learning is not suitable to deal with this situation, category formation may be mediated by some other cognitive functions along with classification including inference, comparison, abduction, and reasoning. The results further imply that categorization models based primarily on classification learning are problematic since category learning in natural settings occurs in a situation in which a variety of category instances are experienced.

References

Lassaline, M.E., & Murphy, T. D. (1996). Induction and category coherence. *Psychonomic Bulletin and Review,* 3(1), 95-99.

Markman, A.B., Yamauchi, T., & Makin, V.S. (in press). The creation of new concepts: A multifaceted approach to category learning. To appear in T.B. Ward, S.M. Smith, & J. Vaid (Eds.) *Conceptual Structures and Processes: Emergence, Discovery, and Change.* Washington, DC: American Psychological Association.

Nosofsky, M. R. (1986). Attention, similarity, and the identification -categorization relationship. *Journal of Experimental Psychology: General, 115,* 39-57.

Mental Predicate Logic: An Empirical Examination

Yingrui Yang and **Martin D.S. Braine**
New York University
6 Washington Place, 8th Floor
New York, N.Y. 10003
yang@xp.psych.nyu.edu

Braine's theory of mental predicate logic (unpublished ms.) will be briefly introduced. A preliminary empirical examination for a major subset of 10 schemas proposed by Braine's model will be reported. The methodology is a modified version of that used by Braine, Reiser, & Rumain (1984). We design a large number (64) of reasoning problems of predicate logic sort-most fairly simple-for which the model predicts the reasoning that subjects will use to solve them. In each problem, one or more facts are given-these serve as premises, followed by a conclusion to be evaluated. Subjects must decide whether the proposed conclusion is true or false, given those facts. They are also to rate each problem's subjective difficulty on a 7-point scale right after evaluating the conclusion given. Within this set of problems, the number of reasoning steps is varied. The mental logic must account (among other things) for which reasoning steps are easy and which are difficult, and it is expected that adding additional steps will make a problem more difficult.

There are three major theses: (a) Because the inferences of the model are claimed to be generally available to people, errors made by subjects in judging the truth value of the conclusion given to each problem will be few overall. (b) The difficulty of a problem will be correlated with the number of inference steps required to solve it, as defined by the reasoning routine associated with the inferences. (c) Problem difficulty will be even more closely correlated with the summed difficulties of those inferences. We conducted a study by using three samples (N=20 for each). With respect to Thesis (a), the results found error rates of lower than 3%, i.e., 97% accuracy, confirming the expectation. With respect to Thesis (b), the mean ratings of problem difficulty were very significantly correlated with the number of inferential steps required by the model to solve a problem (r=.8), and the correlations remained significant when extraneous variables, like problem length, were partialed out-again a confirmation of expectation. With respect to Thesis (c), each kind of inference defined in the logic was assigned a difficulty weight estimated from the difficulty ratings of subjects. The difficulty weights are estimated by using the algorithm "Praxis" (Brent, 1973; Gegenfurtner, 1992) to obtain the best least-square fit of predicted problem difficulties to the obtained mean difficulty ratings (taking the predicted difficulty to be the sum of the difficulty weights of inferences involved in solving a problem the model's way). Correlations between predicted and actual difficulties are high (around .93) and remain to .8 when problem length is partialed out. In cross-validation analyses among three samples, the correlations remained at almost the same level.

A certain order of schema difficulty ranks was found consistently among three samples. There are two important applications of this ranking order among schema weights. First, by using this order, we successfully classified the 10 schemas into two groups and made a 2-parameter model. With respect to Theses (b) and (c), by using this 2-parameter model, all the corresponding correlations remained only about .1 lower than that for 10 parameter model. This result offers a simple answer to the question of which inferences are easy and which are more difficult. Second, to form a 2-parameter model by not keeping this ranking order, the results disproved the prediction.

Reference

Braine, M.D.S., (1995). Steps toward a mental predicate logic.

Braine, M.D.S., Reiser, B.J., & Rumain, B. (1984). Some empirical justification for a theory of natural propositional logic. In G.H. Bower (Ed.) *The psychology of learning and motivation: Advances in research and theory* (Vol. 18). New York: Academic Press.

Brent, R.P. (1973). *Algorithms for function minimization without derivatives.* Englewood Cliffs, NJ: Prentic-Hall.

Gegenfurtner, K.R. (1992). PRAXIS: Brent's algorithm for function inimization. *Behavior Resaearch Method Instruments & Computers, 24(4)* 560-564.

Perception in TsumeGo under 4 Seconds Time Pressure

Atsushi Yoshikawa and **Yasuki Saito**

NTT Basic Research Labs.
3-1 Morinosato Wakamiya, Atsugi-shi, Kanagawa Pref. 243-01 Japan
yosikawa@rudolph.brl.ntt.jp

Introduction and Methods

The purpose of our research is to model the perception of Go players. Our previous study shows that with 3 seconds time pressure, Go players will recognize board situations differently according to their skills (Yoshikawa & Saito, 1995). In order to investigate the difference, we used eye camera data.

2 subjects were investigated. One was 6 dan (stronger player), another was 2 kyu (weaker player). They wore NAC EMR-600 eye camera. TsumeGo problems (life and death problems usually near the edge of the board) were displayed on the computer monitor for 4 seconds. They must answer the first move using a mouse within that period of time. They go through 311 problems of various difficulty. Among them, 10 problems appear twice.

Results

Some of the results obtained so far are listed below:

1. **Fixation points:** Eyes fixate on stones themselves and empty points in TsumeGo, while eyes fixate on the boundary of stones and empty points in ordinary Go games (Yoshikawa & Saito, 1993).
2. **Fixation is limited to small area:** Even though there were many stones and empty points on the board, eyes fixated only to a small area in TsumeGo.
3. **Stronger player v.s. Weaker player:** (1) Stronger player has shorter fixation time(200ms) than weaker player (300ms). (2) When a stronger player answered correctly, his eyes fixated at correct point for a long time. But, when his answer was incorrect, his eyes wonder around on several points which were almost irrelevant to the correct answer.
4. **Different eye fixation to the same problems:** (1) Even when the same problems were given, subjects did not fixate at the same points (see Figure 1). But the stronger player's final answer was the same. (2) When fixation time was summed up, the stronger player looked at nearly the same points longer than any other points.
5. **Correct answer:** When the stronger player answered correctly, he usually looked at correct points within 200ms from the problem presentation. A weaker player, regardless to the correctness of his answers, tended to look at several important points, such as Atari (a threat to capture), Kiri (cut), which can be easily identified from the board configuration. When a stronger player was incorrect, his eye movements are similar to weaker player.
6. **Pattern knowledge:** When stronger player points out his answer within 2 seconds by mouse, his eyes fixate on the answer within 300ms. In this case, he seems to use pattern knowledge, because he answered same point to different problems which contain same partial pattern, regardless of his answer's correctness.

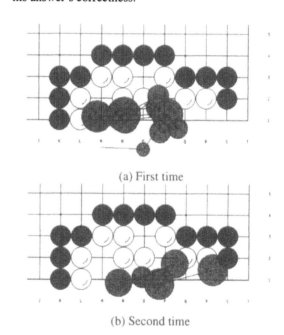

(a) First time

(b) Second time

Figure 1: Stronger Player's Eye movements to the same problem at different occasion.

Conclusions

Through the analysis of TsumeGo solving task under 4 seconds time pressure, we found: (1) stronger player has many pattern knowledge, (2) stronger player's pattern knowledge is not so strict, (3) within 300ms, stronger player can find out the correct answer if he knows the pattern, (4) when stronger player can't use pattern knowledge, the strategy is similar to the weaker player's.

References

Yoshikawa A. & Saito Y. (1993). Cognition of Board Situation in Go. In *Proceedings of SIG-AI of Information Processing Society of Japan* (pp. 41–53).

Yoshikawa A. & Saito Y. (1995). Perception in Tsume-Go under 3 sec. Time Pressure. In *Proceedings of the Game Programming Workshop in Japan '95* (pp.105–112).

The Effect Of Preliminary Sketches
On The Conceptualization Of Design Alternatives

Alex Cuthbert

Education in Mathematics, Science, & Technology (EMST)
Cognitive Science NSF Spatial Cognition Trainee
University of California, Berkeley   Email: alx@violet.berkeley.edu

Abstract

In this study (N=124), eighth graders and professional architects searched the World Wide Web (WWW) for information relevant to a design task involving the storage of heat and the regulation of temperature. One group of students (N=13) did preliminary free-hand sketches of the dwelling before beginning the search and design phases of the activity. The other groups had the option of creating a computer-rendered sketch as part of the final report. Two questions are addressed in this study: (a) What design considerations are typically considered and/or omitted by subjects with well-supported designs vs. those with unsupported designs? and (b) Do preliminary sketches expand the repertoire of models considered by subjects for this particular task? Subjects with certain types of sketches (i.e., aerial views; non-realistic, schematic drawings; and inserts) had significantly better supported designs than those that exclusively used other types of sketches (e.g., perspective, 2D, or realistic sketches). The preliminary sketch group had a higher number of decisions supported by evidence and principled knowledge (as measured by project grades) than the other groups with the effect concentrated in the top performers. Overall, unstructured preliminary sketches appear to hep more advanced students uncover potential design options while having little or no effect on less-advanced students.

KEYWORDS: collaborative design, problem conceptualization, information retrieval, Internet tools, science education.

A New Model for the Stroop Effect
Christopher Koch

Abstract

In general, the Stroop effect demonstrates our inability to ignore meaningful but irrelevant information. Typically, this effect is explained in terms of speed of processing. For instance, in the color-word Stroop task, words are considered to be processed faster than colors, therefore, the word, which is a valid response, either facilitates or interferes with naming the color. In order to examine which dimension (i.e., color or word) is processed faster in the Stroop task, researchers have varied the stimulus onset asynchrony between the color and word dimensions. This research suggests that maximum interference and facilitation occur when the two dimensions are presented within 100 msec of each other. Interestingly, Stroop interference can be found when the word precedes the color and when the color precedes the word. Although these findings do not support the typical explanation of Stroop processing described above, this research was conducted using non-integrated color-word stimuli. A non-integrated color-word stimulus consists of a color word with a color block. An integrated color-word stimulus is a color word printed in a color. The processing of non-integrated stimuli may not be the same as the processing of integrated stimuli. In one experiment, integrated color-word stimuli were presented for varying durations (40 to 1000 msec) and then masked. Stimuli consisted of color congruent, color incongruent, and color neutral words (e.g., BOOK, CHAIR, LADDER, TOP). Results show that color incongruent stimuli produces significantly longer RTs than color congruent words at the shortest durations of 40 and 60 msec. Therefore, the Stroop effect appears to occur only when processing time is limited. A second study attempted to replicate these findings in the parafovea. However, parafoveal presentation of integrated color-word stimuli failed to produce Stroop interference. In order to assess whether the lack of Stroop interference was due to spatially distributing attention over an area which limited attentional resources available to a given stimulus or due to the retinal location of the stimulus (i.e., due to acuity issues, etc.), a third study was conducted in which the location of the color-word stimulus was validly cued on 67% of the trials. The results show Stroop interference for validly cued locations. Therefore, failure to find Stroop interference in the second experiment was due to the spreading of attention. These three experiments suggest that Stroop interference occurs during the initial stages of processing and. is depends upon attention resources. In a fourth study, integrated color-word stimuli were presented in the fovea. Stimuli consisted of color words and nonwords. Subjects were asked to respond either word or nonword instead of responding to the color. Results show that color congruent stimuli were identified as words significantly faster than color incongruent words and nonwords. Therefore, color enhanced word processing. Again, this finding questions the relative speed of processing account of Stroop processing. Finally, a fourth experiment used a color-color version of the Stroop task. Subjects were presented two blocks of color. The two blocks were either the same color (congruent) or different colors (incongruent). Single blocks of color were presented as the neutral condition. The results show that incongruent color blocks produce Stroop interference. This finding demonstrates Stroop interference with information within the same domain (color) instead of two separate domains (color and word). Thus, these findings suggest that the Stroop effect not only occurs during the initial stages of processing and depends on attentional resources but that information within the same domain as the target dimension can cause interference and facilitation. A new model for Stroop processing is presented to accommodate these findings. Implications for neural network accounts of the Stroop effect are also discussed.

870

Visual Speech Information for Face Identification

Deborah A. Yakel
Department of Psychology
University of California, Riverside
Riverside, CA 92521
yakel@citrus.ucr.edu

Lawrence D. Rosenblum
Department of Psychology
University of California, Riverside
Riverside, CA 92521
rosenblu@citrus.ucr.edu

Abstract

Theories of face processing also often consider the recovery of face identity and facial speech information as involving distinct operations (Bruce and Valentine, 1988: Liberman & Mattingly, 1985). This is analogous to traditional theories of auditory speech perception which assume a dissociation between linguistic and voice recovery (Halle, 1985; Liberman & Mattingly, 1985). However, recent observations with auditory speech suggest that these two tasks might not be as separate as once assumed. For example, Remez and his colleagues showed how isolated linguistic (phonetic) information can be informative about speaker identity (Remez, Fellowes, & Rubin, in press). An experiment was conducted to determine if isolated visual speech information can be salient for face recognition. A point-light technique was implemented to isolate visual speech information (Bassili, 1978; Rosenblum & Saldana, in press; Bruce and Valentine, 1988). Speakers were shown on videotape under both full-illumination and point-light conditions, articulating the sentence 'The football game is over'. The same stimuli was also shown under static conditions. A two-alternative forced choice (2AFC) procedure was used to determine if observers could match the correct articulating point-light face to the same articulating fully-illuminated face. Results revealed that dynamic point-light displays afforded high face matching accuracy which was significantly greater than chance and significantly greater face than accuracy with static point-light displays.

References

Bassili, J. N. (1978). Facial motion in the perception of faces and of emotional expression. Journal of Experimental Psychology: Human Perception and Performance, 4(3), 373-379.

Bruce, V., & Valentine, T. (1988). When a nod's as good as a wink: The role of dynamic information in facial recognition. In M. M. Gruneberg, P. E. Morris, & R. N. Sykes (Eds.), Practical aspects of memory: Current research and issues, Vol. 1: Memory in everyday life (pp. 169-174). New York: John Wiley & Sons.

Halle, M. (1985). Speculations about the representation of words in memory. In V. A. Fromkin (Ed.), Phonetic linguistics (pp. 101-104). New York: Academic Press.

Liberman, A. M., & Mattingly, I. G. (1985). The motor theory of speech perception revised. Cognition, 21(1), 1-36.

Remez, R. E., Fellowes, J. M. & Rubin, P. E. (in press). Talker identification based on phonetic information. Journal of Experimental Psychology: Human Perception and Performance.

Rosenblum , L. D., & Saldaña, H. M. (in press). An audiovisual test of kinematic primitives for visual speech perception. Journal of Experimental Psychology: Human Perception and Performance.

Author Index

Author Index